NINTH EDITION

Educational Psychology
Theory and Practice

Robert E. Slavin
Johns Hopkins University
University of York

Upper Saddle River, New Jersey
Columbus, Ohio

Library of Congress Cataloging-in-Publication Data

Slavin, Robert E.
Educational psychology : theory and practice / Robert E. Slavin.—9th ed.
p. cm.
Includes bibliographical references and indexes.
ISBN-13: 978-0-205-59200-5 (pbk.)
ISBN-10: 0-205-59200-7 (pbk.)
1. Educational psychology. I. Title.
LB1051.S615 2009
370.15—dc22

2008001596

Vice President and Editor in Chief: Jeffery W. Johnston
Publisher: Kevin M. Davis
Development Editor: Christien Shangraw
Series Editorial Assistant: Lauren Reinkober
Marketing Manager: Erica DeLuca
Production Editor: Annette Joseph
Editorial Production Service: Omegatype Typography, Inc.
Composition Buyer: Linda Cox
Manufacturing Manager: Megan Cochran
Electronic Composition: Omegatype Typography, Inc.
Interior Designer: Carol Somberg
Photo Researcher: Omegatype Typography, Inc.
Cover Designer: Joel Gendron

This book was set in Bembo by Omegatype Typography, Inc. It was printed and bound by R.R. Donnelley, OH. The cover was printed by Phoenix Color Corp.

Pearson Education Ltd.
Pearson Education Singapore Pte. Ltd.
Pearson Education Canada, Ltd.
Pearson Education–Japan
Pearson Education Australia Pty. Limited
Pearson Education North Asia Ltd.
Pearson Educación de Mexico, S.A. de C.V.
Pearson Education Malaysia Pte. Ltd.

Credits appear on page 570, which constitutes an extension of the copyright page.

Merrill
is an imprint of

www.pearsonhighered.com

10 9 8 7 6 5 4 3 2 1
ISBN-13: 978-0-205-59200-5
ISBN-10: 0-205-59200-7

About the Author

Robert Slavin is director of the Center for Data-Driven Reform in Education, Johns Hopkins University, director of the Institute for Effective Education at the University of York (England), and chairman of the Success for All Foundation. He received his Ph.D. in Social Relations from Johns Hopkins in 1975, and since that time he has authored more than 200 articles and book chapters on such topics as cooperative learning, ability grouping, school and classroom organization, desegregation, mainstreaming, and research review. Dr. Slavin is the author or coauthor of 20 books, including *Cooperative Learning, School and Classroom Organization, Effective Programs for Students at Risk, Preventing Early School Failure, Show Me the Evidence: Proven and Promising Programs for America's Schools, One Million Children: Success for All,* and *Effective Programs for Latino Students.* In 1985 Dr. Slavin received the Raymond Cattell Early Career Award for Programmatic Research from the American Educational Research Association. In 1988 he received the Palmer O. Johnson Award for the best article in an AERA journal. In 1994 he received the Charles A. Dana Award, in 1998 he received the James Bryant Conant Award from the Education Commission of the States, and in 2000 he received the Distinguished Services Award from the Council of Chief State School Officers. Dr. Slavin is pictured here with his daughter Becca.

Brief Contents

Contents

CHAPTER 2
Theories of Development 28

CHAPTER 3
Development during Childhood and Adolescence 62

CHAPTER 4
Student Diversity 90

CHAPTER 5
Behavioral Theories of Learning 126

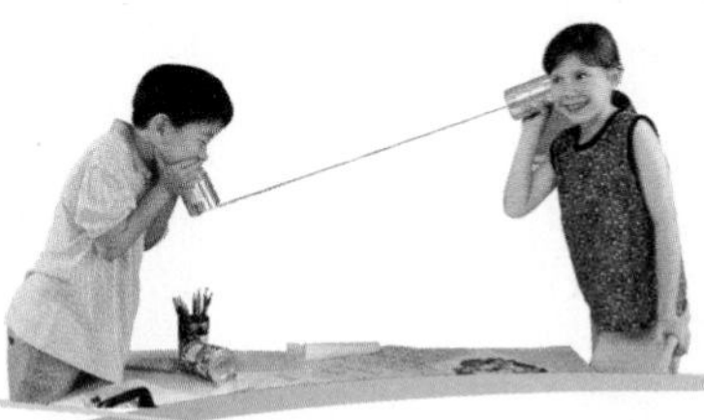

CHAPTER 8
Student-Centered and Constructivist Approaches to Instruction 228

CHAPTER 9
Accommodating Instruction to Meet Individual Needs 260

CHAPTER 10
Motivating Students to Learn 294

CHAPTER 11
Effective Learning Environments 326

CHAPTER 13
Assessing Student Learning 404

List of Features

Personal REFLECTION

THEORY *into* PRACTICE

Teaching Dilemmas: CASES TO CONSIDER

The Intentional TEACHER

Preface

When I first set out to write *Educational Psychology: Theory and Practice,* I had a very clear purpose in mind. I wanted to give tomorrow's teachers the intellectual grounding and practical strategies they will need to be effective instructors. Most of the textbooks published then, I felt, fell into one of two categories: stuffy or lightweight. The stuffy books were full of research but were ponderously written, losing the flavor of the classroom and containing few guides to practice. The lightweight texts were breezy and easy to read but lacked the dilemmas and intellectual issues brought out by research. They contained suggestions of the "Try this!" variety, without considering evidence about the effectiveness of those strategies.

My objective was to write a text that

- presents information that is as complete and up to date as the most research-focused texts but is also readable, practical, and filled with examples and illustrations of key ideas.
- includes suggestions for practice based directly on classroom research (tempered by common sense) so that I can have confidence that when you try what I suggest, it will be likely to work.
- helps you transfer what you learn in educational psychology to your own teaching by making explicit the connection between theory and practice through numerous realistic examples. Even though I have been doing educational research since the mid-1970s, I find that I never really understand theories or concepts in education until someone gives me a compelling classroom example; and I believe that most of my colleagues (and certainly teacher education students) feel the same way. As a result, the words *for example* or similar ones appear hundreds of times in this text.
- appeals to readers; therefore, I have tried to write in such a way that you will almost hear students' voices and smell the lunch cooking in the school cafeteria as you read.

These have been my objectives for the book from the first edition to this, the ninth edition. With every edition, I have made changes throughout the text, adding new examples, refining language, and deleting dated or unessential material. I am meticulous about keeping the text up to date, so this edition has more than 2,000 reference citations, more than half of which are from 2000 or later. Although some readers may not care much about citations, I want you and your professors to know what research supports the statements I've made and where to find additional information.

The field of educational psychology and the practice of education have changed a great deal in recent years, and I have tried to reflect these changes in this edition. Several years ago, direct instruction and related teacher effectiveness research were dominant in educational psychology. Then constructivist methods, portfolio and performance assessments, and other humanistic strategies returned. Now, the emphasis is on accountability, which requires teachers more than ever to plan outcomes and teach purposefully, qualities that I emphasize in this edition as *intentional teaching.* In the first and second editions of this text, I said that we shouldn't entirely discard discovery learning and humanistic methods despite the popularity, then, of direct instruction. In the next editions, I made just the opposite plea: that we shouldn't completely discard direct instruction despite the popularity of active, student-centered teaching and constructivist methods of instruction. I continue to advocate a balanced approach to instruction. No matter what their philosophical orientations, experienced teachers know that they must be proficient in a wide range of methods and must use them thoughtfully.

The ninth edition presents new research and practical applications of many topics. Throughout, this edition reflects the "cognitive revolution" that has transformed educational psychology and teaching. The accompanying figure presents a concept map of the book's organization.

Given the developments in education in recent years, particularly with the introduction of the No Child Left Behind legislature in 2001 and the focus on standards and accountability, no one can deny that teachers matter or that teachers' behaviors have a profound impact on student achievement. To make that impact positive, teachers must have both a deep understanding of the powerful principles of psychology as they apply to education and a clear sense of how these principles can be applied. The intentional teacher is one who constantly reflects on his or her practices and makes instructional decisions based on a clear conception of how these practices affect students. Effective teaching is neither a bag of tricks nor a set of abstract principles; rather, it is intelligent application of well-understood principles to address practical needs. I hope this edition will help you develop the intellectual and practical skills you need to do the most important job in the world—teaching.

HOW THIS BOOK IS ORGANIZED

The chapters in this book address three principal themes: students, teaching, and learning (see the Concept Map). Each chapter discusses important theories and includes many examples of how these theories apply to classroom teaching.

Concept Map
Text Organization in Relation to the Concept of Educational Psychology

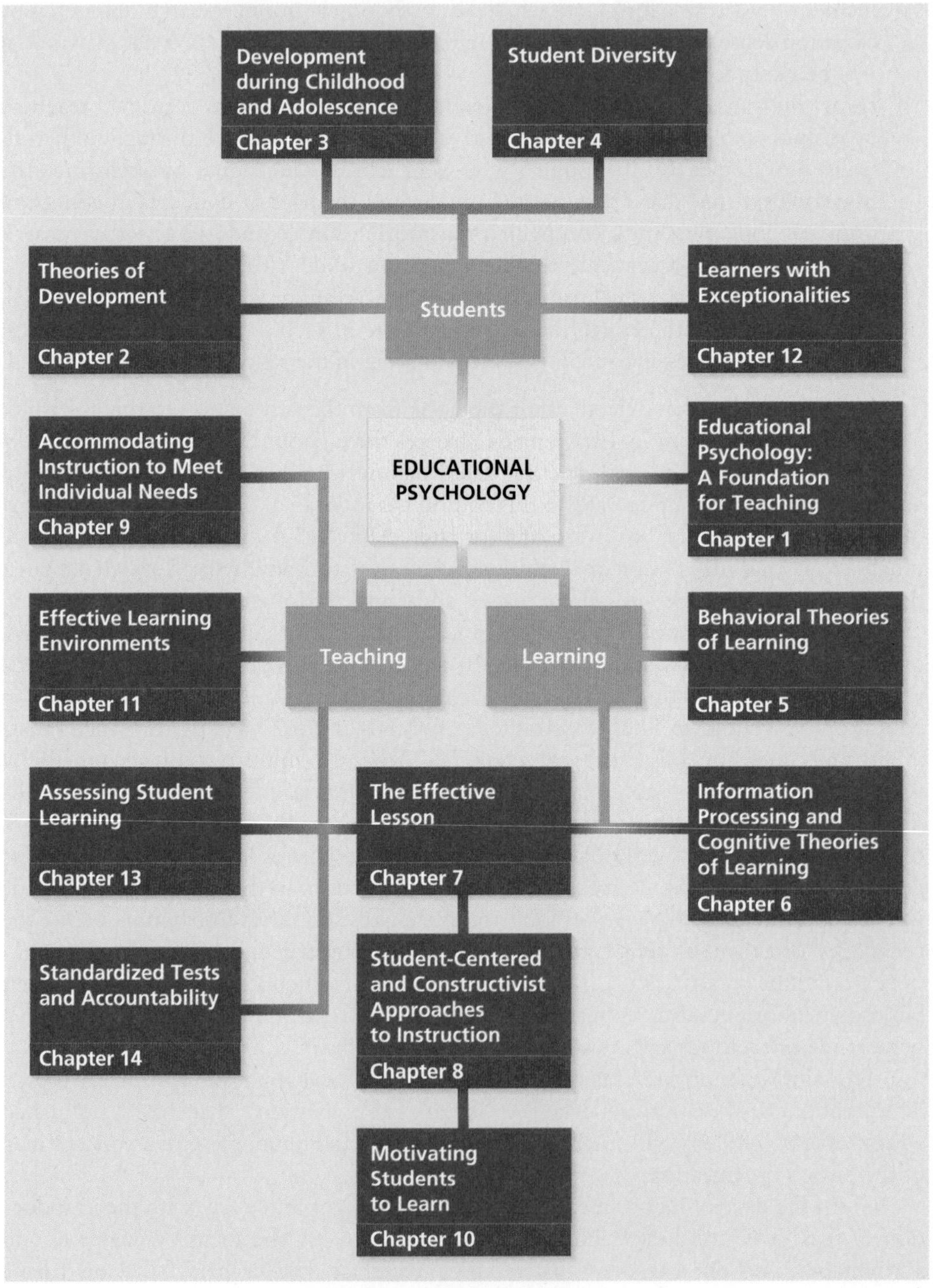

This book emphasizes the intelligent use of theory and research to improve instruction. The chapters on teaching occupy about one-third of the total pages in the book, and the other chapters all relate to the meaning of theories and research practice. Whenever possible, the guides in this book present specific programs and strategies that have been evaluated and found to be effective, not just suggestions of things to try.

NEW AND EXPANDED COVERAGE

Among the many topics that receive new or expanded coverage in this edition are effective programs for English language learners (Chapter 4); the "boy crisis" in education (Chapter 4); multiple intelligences (Chapter 4); nonschool solutions to educational problems (Chapter 4); emerging research in neuroscience (Chapter 6); dual code theory (Chapter 6); assessment for learning (Chapter 7); differentiated instruction (Chapter 9); summer school and after-school programs (Chapter 9); interactive whiteboards (Chapter 9); embedded multimedia (Chapter 9); retention in grade (Chapter 9); IDEA 2004 (Chapter 12); response to intervention (Chapter 12); accountability (Chapter 14); NCLB and criticisms of NCLB (Chapter 14); benchmark assessments and data-driven reform (Chapter 14); and contamination of accountability systems (Chapter 14).

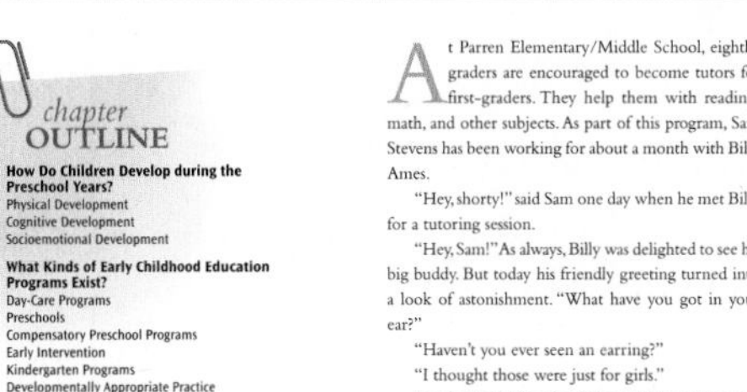

chapter OUTLINE

How Do Children Develop during the Preschool Years?
Physical Development
Cognitive Development
Socioemotional Development

What Kinds of Early Childhood Education Programs Exist?
Day-Care Programs
Preschools
Compensatory Preschool Programs
Early Intervention
Kindergarten Programs
Developmentally Appropriate Practice

How Do Children Develop during the Elementary Years?
Physical Development
Cognitive Development
Socioemotional Development

How Do Children Develop during the Middle School and High School Years?
Physical Development
Cognitive Development
Socioemotional Development

At Parren Elementary/Middle School, eighth-graders are encouraged to become tutors for first-graders. They help them with reading, math, and other subjects. As part of this program, Sam Stevens has been working for about a month with Billy Ames.

"Hey, shorty!" said Sam one day when he met Billy for a tutoring session.

"Hey, Sam!" As always, Billy was delighted to see his big buddy. But today his friendly greeting turned into a look of astonishment. "What have you got in your ear?"

"Haven't you ever seen an earring?"

"I thought those were just for girls."

Sam laughed. "Not like this one! Can you see it?"

Billy squinted at the earring and saw that it was in the shape of a small sword. "Awesome!"

"A lot of guys are wearing them."

"Didn't it hurt to get a hole in your ear?"

"A little, but I'm tough! Boy, was my mom mad though. I have to take my earring off before I go home, but I put it back on while I'm walking to school."

"But didn't your mom . . ."

"Enough of that, squirt! You've got some heavy math to do. Let's get to it!"

The interaction between Sam and Billy illustrates the enormous differences between the world of the adolescent and that of the child. Sam, at 13, is a classic young teen. His idealism and down-deep commitment to the positive are shown in his volunteering to serve as a tutor and in the caring, responsible relationship he has established with Billy. At the same time, Sam is asserting his independence by having his ear pierced and wearing an earring, against his mother's wishes. This independence is strongly supported by his peer group, however, so it is really only a shift of dependence from parents and teachers toward peers. His main purpose in wearing an earring is to demonstrate conformity to the styles and norms of his peers rather than to those of adults. Yet Sam does still depend on his parents and other adults for advice and support when making decisions that he knows have serious consequences for his future, and he does take off his earring at home to avoid a really serious battle with his parents.

Billy lives in a different world. He can admire Sam's audacity, but he would never go so far. Billy's world has simpler rules. For one thing, boys are boys and girls are girls, so he is shocked by Sam's flouting of convention to wear something usually associated with females. He is equally shocked by Sam's willingness to directly disobey his mother. Billy may misbehave, but within much narrower limits. He knows that rules are rules, and he fully expects to be punished if he breaks them.

63

FEATURES

Using Your Experience

Each chapter of the text opens with a vignette depicting a real-life situation that educators encounter. Throughout the chapter narrative, I refer to the issues raised in the vignette. In addition, you have the opportunity to respond to the vignette in several related features, such as the **Using Your Experience** sections that follow each vignette. Each of these sections provides critical and creative thinking questions and cooperative learning activities that allow you to work with the issues brought up in the vignette, activate your prior knowledge, and begin thinking about the ideas the chapter will explore.

water, that matters, they put the same amount of water … the more air space left in the bottle, the lower the sound.

Ms. Logan ends the period with a homework assignment: to read a chapter on sound in a textbook. She tells the students that they will have an opportunity to work in their groups to make certain that every group member understands everything in the sound lesson, and then there will be a quiz in which students will have to show individually that they can apply their new knowledge. She reminds them that their groups can be "superteams" only if everyone knows the material.

The bell rings, and the students pour into the hallway, still talking excitedly about what they have learned. Some groupmates promise to call each other that evening to prepare for the group study the next day. Ms. Logan watches them file out. She's exhausted, but she knows that this group of students will never forget the lessons they've learned about sound, about experiments, and, most important, about their ability to use their minds to figure out difficult concepts.

USING *your* EXPERIENCE

CREATIVE THINKING Write the phrase *Effective Lesson* in the middle of a sheet of paper and circle it. Brainstorm all the types of instructional approaches you can think of that make an effective lesson. Now list the types of instructional approaches that Ms. Logan uses.

CRITICAL THINKING How does Ms. Logan motivate the students? What strategies does she use to encourage retention of the material?

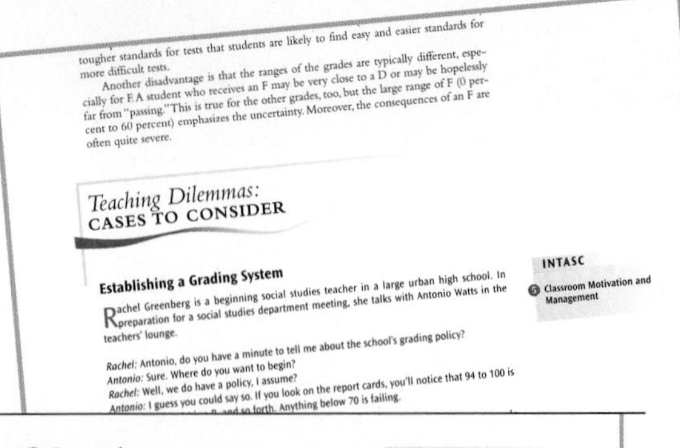

tougher standards for tests that students are likely to find easy and easier standards for more difficult tests.

Another disadvantage is that the ranges of the grades are typically different, especially for F. A student who receives an F may be very close to a D or may be hopelessly far from "passing." This is true for the other grades, too, but the large range of F (0 percent to 60 percent) emphasizes the uncertainty. Moreover, the consequences of an F are often quite severe.

Teaching Dilemmas: CASES TO CONSIDER

Establishing a Grading System

INTASC 5 Classroom Motivation and Management

Rachel Greenberg is a beginning social studies teacher in a large urban high school. In preparation for a social studies department meeting, she talks with Antonio Watts in the teachers' lounge.

Rachel: Antonio, do you have a minute to tell me about the school's grading policy?
Antonio: Sure. Where do you want to begin?
Rachel: Well, we do have a policy, I assume?
Antonio: I guess you could say so. If you look on the report cards, you'll notice that 94 to 100 is ... and so forth. Anything below 70 is failing.

Teaching Dilemmas

To support the focus on intentionality and reflection, this edition introduces new **Teaching Dilemmas: Cases to Consider** throughout the chapters. Each case offers a dialogue or vignette intended to evoke thoughtful discussion and debate on issues educators constantly face: balancing structure and freedom, colorblindness and respect for diversity, high expectations and attainable goals, focusing on tests versus focusing on children, and many more. Each of the Teaching Dilemmas ends with Questions for Reflection that prompt thoughtful consideration about the dilemma, asking students to place themselves in the dilemma and offer possible solutions. No easy answers are readily available, as there are so few in teaching, but there is plenty of room for discussion.

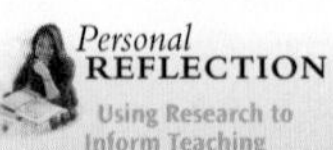

Personal REFLECTION

Using Research to Inform Teaching

INTASC 8 Assessment of Student Learning

As a graduate student, I conducted a study in a residential school for students with emotional and behavioral disorders. The study involved observing the behavior of a group of children who were 9 to 11 years old. The school had a program in which children earned points based on their behavior and could exchange points for various privileges or materials.

Despite my attempts to be as unobtrusive as possible, I was writing notes on a clipboard, and the children were curious about what I was writing. One day, a girl in the class used her points to obtain a clipboard. She put a sheaf of paper on her clipboard and then spent all day walking around writing down all the bad things her classmates were doing. For example, she'd say, "James, I'm giving you another bad mark for not helping clean up."

Of course, the other kids couldn't tolerate this for long, and soon they too used their points to get clipboards. They all then spent every free moment writing each other up for bad behavior, real or imagined. Worst of all, they started writing down bad things about me!

My study was ruined, but I learned firsthand about what is sometimes called Heisenberg's Uncertainty Principle: Studying something may change what you're studying. Research in education always involves people, and people act differently when they're being studied. For this and many other reasons, even research findings with a ton of data should be taken with a grain of salt.

REFLECT ON THIS. Why was my study ruined? What lesson can you learn from this example about using research to be an effective teacher?

Teacher Certification

Before you can become an *intentional* teacher, you have to become a *certified* teacher. Each state, province, and country has its own requirements, but in most places you at least have

Personal Reflections

Also in line with the emphasis on reflective, intentional practice, I've added a feature that is intended to bring a bit of myself from behind the curtain that usually divides author and readers. In sections called **Personal Reflections,** I reflect on my own experiences as a teacher, researcher, and parent to illuminate various aspects of the text. As a reader, it is important for you to know that behind each textbook is an author whose experiences, values, and perspectives shape the text.

How Development Occurs

Recall that Piaget's theory suggests that development precedes learning. In other words, specific cognitive structures need to develop before certain types of learning can take place. Vygotsky's theory suggests that learning precedes development. For Vygotsky, learning involves the acquisition of signs by means of instruction and information from others. Development involves the child's internalizing these signs so as to be able to think and solve problems without the help of others. This ability is called **self-regulation.**

The first step in the development of self-regulation and independent thinking is learning that actions and sounds have a meaning. For example, a baby learns that the process of reaching toward an object is interpreted by others as a signal that the infant wants the object. In the case of language acquisition, children learn to associate certain sounds with meaning. The second step in developing internal structures and self-regulation involves practice. The infant practices gestures that will get attention. The preschooler will enter into conversations with others to master language. The final step involves using signs to think and solve problems without the help of others. At this point, children become self-regulating, and the sign system has become internalized.

"I'm sorry, Miss Scott, but this is outside of my zone of proximal development."

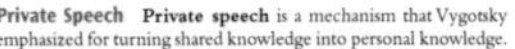

Private Speech **Private speech** is a mechanism that Vygotsky emphasized for turning shared knowledge into personal knowledge. Vygotsky proposed th…

Cartoons

I've added to the text a series of cartoons created just for this book by my colleague James Bravo to illustrate key concepts in educational psychology. These are intended to be humorous but also to make you reflect. I hope you like them!

more likely than other students to respond to failure with helpless behavior (Pintrich & Schunk, 2002). Teachers can prevent or alleviate learned helplessness by giving students (1) opportunities for success in small steps; (2) immediate feedback; and (3) most important, consistent expectations and follow-through (see Alderman, 1990).

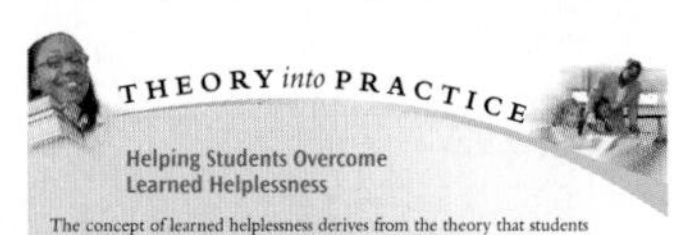

THEORY *into* PRACTICE

Helping Students Overcome Learned Helplessness

The concept of learned helplessness derives from the theory that students might become academic failures through a conditioning process based on negative feedback from teachers, school experiences, peers, and students themselves. Numerous studies show that when students consistently fail, they eventually give up. They become conditioned to helplessness (Seligman, 1975).

Teachers at both the elementary and secondary levels can help to counter this syndrome in a variety of ways, including attribution training, goal restructuring, self-esteem programs, success-guaranteed approaches, and positive feedback systems. The following general principles are helpful for all students, especially students who have shown a tendency to accept failure.

INTASC 7 Instructional Planning Skills

1. ***Accentuate the positive.*** Get to know the student's strengths, then use these as building blocks. Every student has something she or he does well. But be careful that the strength is authentic; don't make up a strength. For example, a student might like to talk a lot but write poorly. Have the student complete assignments by talking rather than writing. As confidence is restored, slowly introduce writing.
2. ***Eliminate the negative.*** Do not play down a student's weaknesses. Deal with them directly but tactfully. In the preceding example, talk to the student about problems with writing. Then have the student develop a plan to improve on the writing. Discuss the plan, and together make up a contract about how the plan will be completed.
3. ***Go from the familiar to the new, using advance organizers or guided discovery.*** Some students have difficulties with concepts, skills, or ideas with which they are not familiar. Also, students relate better to lessons that are linked to their own experiences. For example, a high school math teacher might begin a lesson with a math problem that students might face in the real world, such as calculating the sales tax when purchasing a CD player. Further, the teacher can ask students to bring to class math problems they have encountered outside of school. The whole class can become involved in solving a student's math problem.
4. ***Create challenges in which students actively create problems and solve them using their own knowledge and skills.***

Teacher Expectations and Achievement

On the first day of class, Mr. Erhard called roll. Soon he got to a name that looked familiar. "Wayne Clements?"

"Here!"

"Do you have a brother named Victor?"

"Yes."

"I remember Victor. He was a terror. I'm going to keep my eye on you!"

How can Achievement Motivation be Enhanced 309

Theory into Practice

The **Theory into Practice** sections in each chapter help you acquire and develop the tools you need to be an effective teacher. These sections present specific strategies for applying information to the classroom.

Guided Study

Each chapter offers features to help you regulate your own learning: a **Chapter Outline** to guide your study objectives; glossary and cross-reference **Connections** annotations in the margins; a **Chapter Summary** to help you review your reading; and a list of **Key Terms** with page references at the end of each chapter.

Licensure

This edition has multiple tools to help you apply your learning to licensure and certification. In each chapter you can both identify and practice the appropriate knowledge and skills you have attained.

- To help you assess your own learning and prepare for licensure exams, **Certification Pointers** identify content likely to be on certification tests.
- A special marginal icon identifies content that correlates to **INTASC standards.** These correspond closely to Praxis and many state assessments patterned on Praxis.
- In addition, special **Self-Assessment: Practicing for Licensure** features at the end of each chapter are also designed to resemble the types of questions and content typically encountered on state certification tests.

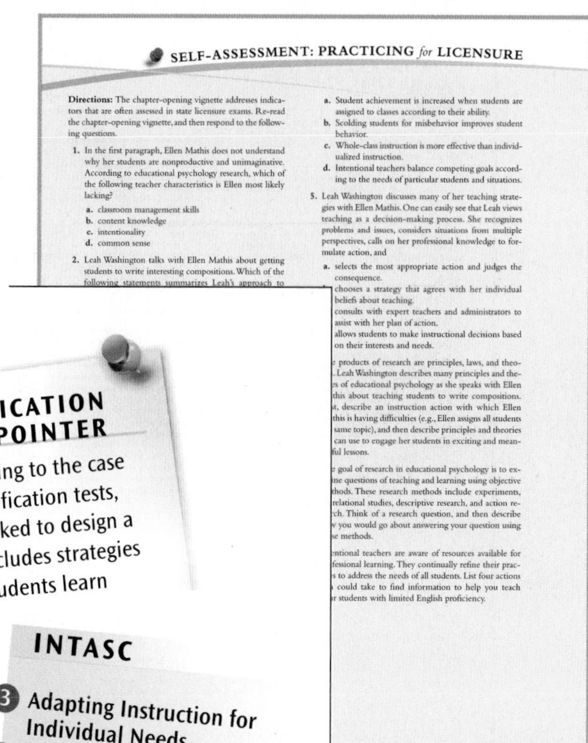

SELF-ASSESSMENT: PRACTICING *for* LICENSURE

Directions: The chapter-opening vignette addresses indicators that are often assessed in state licensure exams. Re-read the chapter-opening vignette, and then respond to the following questions.

1. In the first paragraph, Ellen Mathis does not understand why her students are nonproductive and unimaginative. According to educational psychology research, which of the following teacher characteristics is Ellen most likely lacking?
   a. classroom management skills
   b. content knowledge
   c. intentionality
   d. common sense
2. Leah Washington talks with Ellen Mathis about getting students to write interesting compositions. Which of the following statements summarizes Leah's approach to

a. Student achievement is increased when students are assigned to classes according to their ability.
b. Scolding students for misbehavior improves student behavior.
c. Whole-class instruction is more effective than individualized instruction.
d. Intentional teachers balance competing goals according to the needs of particular students and situations.

5. Leah Washington discusses many of her teaching strategies with Ellen Mathis. One can easily see that Leah views teaching as a decision-making process. She recognizes problems and issues, considers situations from multiple perspectives, calls on her professional knowledge to formulate action, and
   a. selects the most appropriate action and judges the consequence.
   chooses a strategy that agrees with her individual beliefs about teaching.
   consults with expert teachers and administrators to assist with her plan of action.
   allows students to make instructional decisions based on their interests and needs.

e products of research are principles, laws, and theo-. Leah Washington describes many principles and the-es of educational psychology as she speaks with Ellen this about teaching students to write compositions. t, describe an instruction action with which Ellen this is having difficulties (e.g., Ellen assigns all students same topic), and then describe principles and theories can use to engage her students in exciting and mean-ful lessons.

e goal of research in educational psychology is to ex-ine questions of teaching and learning using objective thods. These research methods include experiments, relational studies, descriptive research, and action re-ch. Think of a research question, and then describe v you would go about answering your question using se methods.

entional teachers are aware of resources available for fessional learning. They continually refine their prac-s to address the needs of all students. List four actions could take to find information to help you teach r students with limited English proficiency.

CERTIFICATION POINTER

When responding to the case studies in certification tests, you may be asked to design a lesson that includes strategies for helping students learn

INTASC

3 Adapting Instruction for Individual Needs
4 Multiple Instructional Strategies
6 Communication Skills

On the Web

Educational Psychology: Theory and Practice includes a feature called **On the Web** that appears within the text and lists useful websites providing further information on topics discussed in each chapter. This edition adds many new websites, as the numbers of sites useful to educators is rapidly expanding.

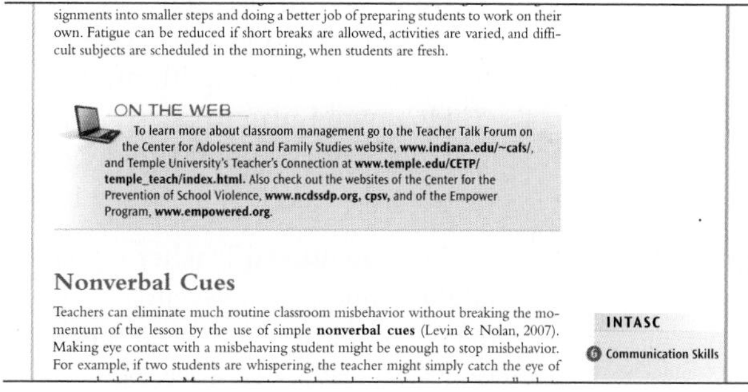

signments into smaller steps and doing a better job of preparing students to work on their own. Fatigue can be reduced if short breaks are allowed, activities are varied, and difficult subjects are scheduled in the morning, when students are fresh.

ON THE WEB

To learn more about classroom management go to the Teacher Talk Forum on the Center for Adolescent and Family Studies website, **www.indiana.edu/~cafs/**, and Temple University's Teacher's Connection at **www.temple.edu/CETP/temple_teach/index.html.** Also check out the websites of the Center for the Prevention of School Violence, **www.ncdssdp.org, cpsv,** and of the Empower Program, **www.empowered.org**.

Nonverbal Cues

Teachers can eliminate much routine classroom misbehavior without breaking the momentum of the lesson by the use of simple **nonverbal cues** (Levin & Nolan, 2007). Making eye contact with a misbehaving student might be enough to stop misbehavior. For example, if two students are whispering, the teacher might simply catch the eye of

INTASC

6 Communication Skills

The Intentional Teacher

One attribute seems to be a characteristic of all outstanding teachers: intentionality, or the ability to do things for a reason, purposefully. Intentional teachers constantly think about the outcomes they want for their students and how each decision they make moves students toward those outcomes. A key feature in each chapter, **The Intentional Teacher** is designed to help you develop and apply a set of strategies to carry out your intentionality. It will help you internalize a set of questions that can aid you in planning, teaching, and revising your practice in intentional ways. In each chapter, you will consider answers to the following questions from a new vantage point grounded in chapter content, and you will find new examples at all grade levels and in all subject areas to illustrate those answers. The Intentional Teacher focuses your attention on these questions:

1. What do I expect my students to know and be able to do at the end of this lesson? How does this contribute to course objectives and to students' needs to become capable individuals?

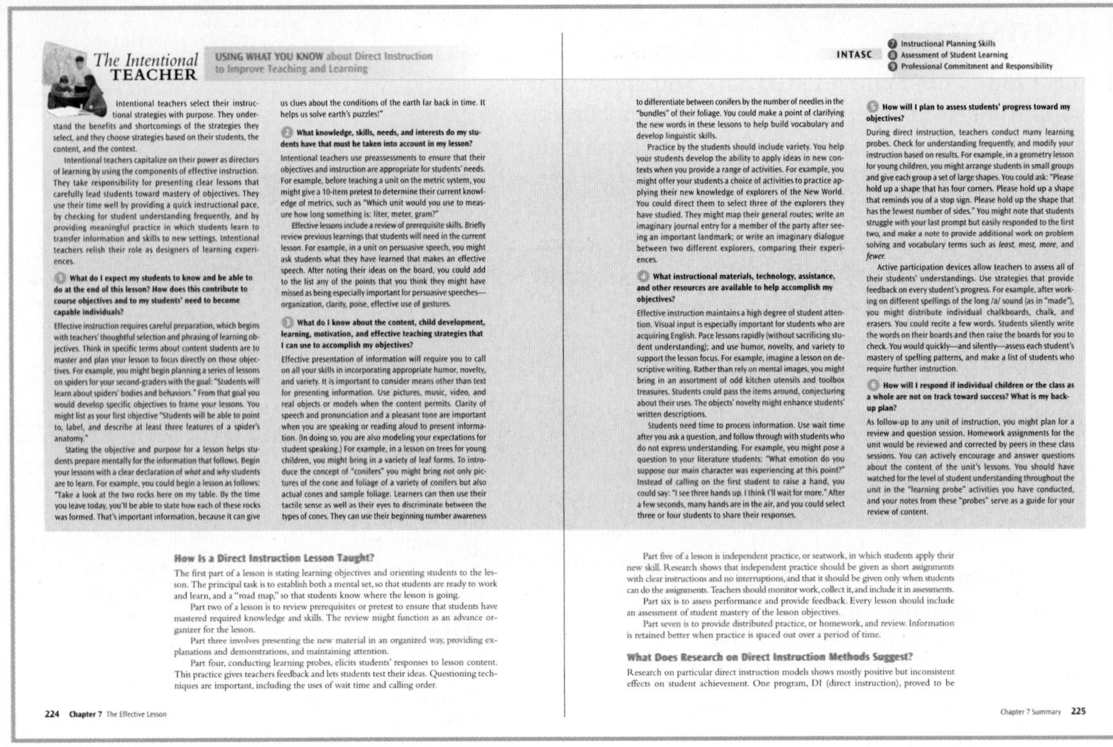

The Intentional TEACHER

USING WHAT YOU KNOW about Direct Instruction to Improve Teaching and Learning

Intentional teachers select their instructional strategies with purpose. They understand the benefits and shortcomings of the strategies they select, and they choose strategies based on their students, the content, and the context.

Intentional teachers capitalize on their power as directors of learning by using the components of effective instruction. They take responsibility for presenting clear lessons that carefully lead students toward mastery of objectives. They use their time well by providing a quick instructional pace, by checking for student understanding frequently, and by providing meaningful practice in which students learn to transfer information and skills to new settings. Intentional teachers relish their role as designers of learning experiences.

1 What do I expect my students to know and be able to do at the end of this lesson? How does this contribute to course objectives and to my students' need to become capable individuals?

Effective instruction requires careful preparation, which begins with teachers' thoughtful selection and phrasing of learning objectives. Think in specific terms about content students are to master and plan your lesson to focus directly on those objectives. For example, you might begin planning a series of lessons on spiders for your second-graders with the goal: "Students will learn about spiders' bodies and behaviors." From that goal you would develop specific objectives to frame your lessons. You might list as your first objective "Students will be able to point to, label, and describe at least three features of a spider's anatomy."

Stating the objective and purpose for a lesson helps students prepare mentally for the information that follows. Begin your lessons with a clear declaration of *what* and *why* students are to learn. For example, you could begin a lesson as follows: "Take a look at the two rocks here on my table. By the time you leave today, you'll be able to state how each of these rocks was formed. That's important information, because it can give us clues about the conditions of the earth far back in time. It helps us solve earth's puzzles!"

2 What knowledge, skills, needs, and interests do my students have that must be taken into account in my lesson?

Intentional teachers use preassessments to ensure that their objectives and instruction are appropriate for students' needs. For example, before teaching a unit on the metric system, you might give a 10-item pretest to determine their current knowledge of metrics, such as "Which unit would you use to measure how long something is: liter, meter, gram?"

Effective lessons include a review of prerequisite skills. Briefly review previous learnings that students will need in the current lesson. For example, in a unit on persuasive speech, you might ask students what they have learned that makes an effective speech. After noting their ideas on the board, you could add to the list any of the points that you think they might have missed as being especially important for persuasive speeches—organization, clarity, poise, effective use of gestures.

3 What do I know about the content, child development, learning, motivation, and effective teaching strategies that I can use to accomplish my objectives?

Effective presentation of information will require you to call on all your skills in incorporating appropriate humor, novelty, and variety. It is important to consider means other than text for presenting information. Use pictures, music, video, and real objects or models when the content permits. Clarity of speech and pronunciation and a pleasant tone are important when you are speaking or reading aloud to present information. (In doing so, you are also modeling your expectations for student speaking.) For example, in a lesson on trees for young children, you might bring in a variety of leaf forms. To introduce the concept of "conifers" you might bring not only pictures of the cone and foliage of a variety of conifers but also actual cones and sample foliage. Learners can then use their tactile sense as well as their eyes to discriminate between the types of cones. They can use their beginning number awareness to differentiate between conifers by the number of needles in the "bundles" of their foliage. You could make a point of clarifying the new words in these lessons to help build vocabulary and develop linguistic skills.

Practice by the students should include variety. You help your students develop the ability to apply ideas in new contexts when you provide a range of activities. For example, you might offer your students a choice of activities to practice applying their new knowledge of explorers of the New World. You could direct them to select three of the explorers they have studied. They might map their general routes; write an imaginary journal entry for a member of the party after seeing an important landmark; or write an imaginary dialogue between two different explorers, comparing their experiences.

4 What instructional materials, technology, assistance, and other resources are available to help accomplish my objectives?

Effective instruction maintains a high degree of student attention. Visual input is especially important for students who are acquiring English. Pace lessons rapidly (without sacrificing student understanding); and use humor, novelty, and variety to support the lesson focus. For example, imagine a lesson on descriptive writing. Rather than rely on mental images, you might bring in an assortment of odd kitchen utensils and toolbox treasures. Students could pass the items around, conjecturing about their uses. The objects' novelty might enhance students' written descriptions.

Students need time to process information. Use wait time after you ask a question, and follow through with students who do not express understanding. For example, you might pose a question to your literature students: "What emotion do you suppose our main character was experiencing at this point?" Instead of calling on the first student to raise a hand, you could say: "I see three hands up. I think I'll wait for more." After a few seconds, many hands are in the air, and you could select three or four students to share their responses.

INTASC
7 Instructional Planning Skills
8 Assessment of Student Learning
9 Professional Commitment and Responsibility

5 How will I plan to assess students' progress toward my objectives?

During direct instruction, teachers conduct many learning probes. Check for understanding frequently, and modify your instruction based on results. For example, in a geometry lesson for young children, you might arrange students in small groups and give each group a set of large shapes. You could ask: "Please hold up a shape that has four corners. Please hold up a shape that reminds you of a stop sign. Please hold up the shape that has the fewest number of sides." You might note that students struggle with your last prompt but easily responded to the first two, and make a note to provide additional work on problem solving and vocabulary terms such as *least, most, more*, and *fewer*.

Active participation devices allow teachers to assess all of their students' understandings. Use strategies that provide feedback on every student's progress. For example, after working on different spellings of the long /a/ sound (as in "made"), you might distribute individual chalkboards, chalk, and erasers. You could recite a few words. Students silently write the words on their boards and then raise the boards for you to check. You would quickly—and silently—assess each student's mastery of spelling patterns, and make a list of students who require further instruction.

6 How will I respond if individual children or the class as a whole are not on track toward success? What is my backup plan?

As follow-up to any unit of instruction, you might plan for a review and question session. Homework assignments for the unit would be reviewed and corrected by peers in these class sessions. You can actively encourage and answer questions about the content of the unit's lessons. You should have watched for the level of student understanding throughout the unit in the "learning probe" activities you have conducted, and your notes from these "probes" serve as a guide for your review of content.

How Is a Direct Instruction Lesson Taught?

The first part of a lesson is stating learning objectives and orienting students to the lesson. The principal task is to establish both a mental set, so that students are ready to work and learn, and a "road map," so that students know where the lesson is going.

Part two of a lesson is to review prerequisites or pretest to ensure that students have mastered required knowledge and skills. The review might function as an advance organizer for the lesson.

Part three involves presenting the new material in an organized way, providing explanations and demonstrations, and maintaining attention.

Part four, conducting learning probes, elicits students' responses to lesson content. This practice gives teachers feedback and lets students test their ideas. Questioning techniques are important, including the uses of wait time and calling order.

Part five of a lesson is independent practice, or seatwork, in which students apply their new skill. Research shows that independent practice should be given as short assignments with clear instructions and no interruptions, and that it should be given only when students can do the assignments. Teachers should monitor work, collect it, and include it in assessments.

Part six is to assess performance and provide feedback. Every lesson should include an assessment of student mastery of the lesson objectives.

Part seven is to provide distributed practice, or homework, and review. Information is retained better when practice is spaced out over a period of time.

What Does Research on Direct Instruction Methods Suggest?

Research on particular direct instruction models shows mostly positive but inconsistent effects on student achievement. One program, DI (direct instruction), proved to be

224 Chapter 7 The Effective Lesson

Chapter 7 Summary 225

2. What knowledge, skills, needs, and interests do my students have that must be taken into account in my lesson?
3. What do I know about the content, child development, learning, motivation, and effective teaching strategies that I can use to accomplish my objectives?
4. What instructional materials, technology, assistance, and other resources are available to help me accomplish my objectives?
5. How will I plan to assess students' progress toward my objectives?
6. How will I respond if individual children or the class as a whole are not on track toward success? What is my backup plan?

The Intentional Teacher will help you combine your increasing knowledge of principles of educational psychology, your growing experience with learners, and your creativity to make intentional instructional decisions that will help students become enthusiastic, effective learners.

"Teacher educators who are developing pedagogies for the analysis of teaching and learning contend that analyzing teaching artifacts has three advantages: it enables new teachers time for reflection while still using the real materials of practice; it provides new teachers with experience thinking about and approaching the complexity of the classroom; and in some cases, it can help new teachers and teacher educators develop a shared understanding and common language about teaching. . . ."[1]

1. Darling-Hammond, L., & Bransford, J., Eds. (2005). *Preparing Teachers for a Changing World.* San Francisco: John Wiley & Sons.

As Linda Darling-Hammond and her colleagues point out, grounding teacher education in real classrooms—among real teachers and students and among actual examples of students' and teachers' work—is an important, and perhaps even an essential, part of training teachers for the complexities of teaching today's students in today's classrooms. For a number of years, we have heard the same message from many of you as we sat in your offices learning about the goals of your courses and the challenges you face in teaching the next generation of educators. Working with a number of our authors and with many of you, we have created a website that provides you and your students with the context of real classrooms and artifacts that research on teacher education tells us is so important. Through authentic in-class video footage, interactive simulations, rich case studies, examples of authentic teacher and student work, and more, **MyEducationLab** offers you and your students a uniquely valuable teacher education tool.

features in print that are significant and can draw attention to patterns of letters, sounds, or phrases.

Socioemotional Development

A young child's social life evolves in relatively predictable ways (see Cummings et al., 2003; McHale et al., 2003). The social network grows from an intimate relationship with parents or other guardians to include other family members, nonrelated adults, and peers. Social interactions extend from home to neighborhood and from preschool or other child-care arrangements to formal school. Erik Erikson's theory of personal and social development suggests that during the preschool years, children must resolve the personality crisis of initiative versus guilt. The child's successful resolution of this stage results in a sense of initiative and ambition tempered by a reasonable understanding of the permissible. Early educators can encourage this resolution by giving children opportunities to take initiative, to be challenged, and to succeed.

Peer Relationships During the preschool years, **peers** (other children who are a child's equal in age) begin to play an increasingly important role in children's social and cognitive development (Hay, Payne, & Chadwick, 2004). Children's relations with their peers differ in several ways from their interactions with adults. Peer play allows children to interact with other individuals whose level of development is similar to their own. When peers have disputes among themselves, they must make concessions and must cooperate in resolving them if the play is to continue; unlike in adult–child disputes, in a peer dispute no one can claim to have ultimate authority. Peer conflicts also let children see that others have thoughts, feelings, and viewpoints that are different from their own. Conflicts also heighten children's sensitivity to the effects of their behavior on others. In this way, peer relationships help young children to overcome the egocentrism that Piaget described as being characteristic of preoperational thinking, and help them see that others have perspectives that are different from their own.

Prosocial Behavior **Prosocial behaviors** are voluntary actions toward others such as caring, sharing, comforting, and cooperation. Research on the roots of prosocial behavior has contributed to our knowledge of children's moral as well as social development. Several factors seem to be associated with the development of prosocial behaviors (Eisenberg, 2001). These include the following:

- Parental disciplinary techniques that stress the consequences of the child's behavior for others and that are applied within a warm, responsive parent–child relationship (Hoffman, 1993).
- Contact with adults who indicate they expect concern for others, who let children know that aggressive solutions to problems are unacceptable, and who provide acceptable alternatives (Konig, 1995).
- Contact with adults who attribute positive characteristics to children when they do well ("What a helpful boy you are!") (Grusec & Goodnow, 1994).

Play Most of a preschooler's interactions with peers occur during play (Hughes, 1995). However, the degree to which play involves other children increases over the preschool years (Howes & Matheson, 1992). In a classic study of preschoolers, Mildred Parten (1932) identified four categories of play that reflect increasing levels of social interaction and sophistication. **Solitary play** is play that occurs alone, often with toys, and is independent of what other children are doing. **Parallel play** involves children engaged in the same activity side by side but with very little interaction or mutual influence. **Associative play** is much like parallel play but with increased levels of interaction in the form of sharing, turn-taking, and general interest in what others are doing. **Cooperative play** occurs when children join together to achieve a common goal, such as building a large castle with each child building a part of the structure. For example, Howes and Matheson (1992) followed a group of children for 3 years, observing their play when they were 1 to 2 years

VIDEO HOMEWORK EXERCISE
Cognitive Development—Early Childhood
Go to **www.myeducationlab.com** and, in the Homework and Exercises section for Chapter 3 of this text, access the video entitled "Cognitive Development—Early Childhood." Watch the video and complete the homework questions that accompany it, saving your work or transmitting it to your professor as required.

CONNECTIONS
For suggested cooperative learning activities, see Chapter 8, pages 243–247.

peers People who are equal in age or status.

prosocial behaviors Actions that show respect and caring for others.

solitary play Play that occurs alone.

parallel play Play in which children engage in the same activity side by side but with very little interaction or mutual influence.

associative play Play that is much like parallel play but with increased levels of interaction in the form of sharing, turn-taking, and general interest in what others are doing.

cooperative play Play in which children join together to achieve a common goal.

How Do Children Develop during the Preschool Years? 69

MyEducationLab is easy to use! Wherever the MyEducationLab logo appears in the margins or elsewhere in the text, you and your students can follow the simple link instructions to access the MyEducationLab resource that corresponds with the chapter content. These include:

- **Video:** Authentic classroom videos show how real teachers handle actual classroom situations.
- **Homework & Exercises:** These assignable activities give students opportunities to understand content more deeply and to practice applying content.
- **Building Teaching Skills:** These assignments help students practice and strengthen skills that are essential to quality teaching. By analyzing and responding to real student and teacher artifacts and/or authentic classroom videos, students practice important teaching skills they will need when they enter real classrooms.
- **Case Studies:** A diverse set of robust cases drawn from some of our best-selling books further expose students to the realities of teaching and offer valuable perspectives on common issues and challenges in education.
- **Simulations:** Created by the IRIS Center at Vanderbilt University, these interactive simulations give hands-on practice at adapting instruction for a full spectrum of learners.
- **Student & Teacher Artifacts:** Authentic student and teacher classroom artifacts are tied to course topics and offer practice in working with the actual types of materials encountered every day by teachers.
- **Individualized Study Plan:** Your students have the opportunity to take pre- and post-tests before and after reading each chapter of the text. Their test results automatically generate a personalized study plan, identifying areas of the chapter they must reread to fully understand chapter concepts. They are also presented with interactive multimedia exercises to help ensure learning. The study plan is designed to help your students perform well on exams and to promote deep understanding of chapter content.
- **Readings:** Specially selected, topically relevant articles from ASCD's renowned *Educational Leadership* journal expand and enrich students' perspectives on key issues and topics.

Other Resources:

- **Lesson & Portfolio Builders:** With this effective and easy-to-use tool, you can create, update, and share standards-based lesson plans and portfolios.

- **News Articles:** Looking for current issues in education? Our collection offers quick access to hundreds of relevant articles from the New York Times Educational News Feed.

MyEducationLab is easy to assign, which is essential to providing the greatest benefit to your student. Visit www.myeducationlab.com for a demonstration of this exciting new online teaching resource.

STUDENT SUPPLEMENTS

- A new **Teaching Dilemma Casebook,** packaged free on instructor request, provides elementary and secondary case studies that demonstrate common dilemmas that arise in today's classrooms. The Casebook includes four detailed cases per chapter that are closely integrated with the content and augmented by guiding questions and sample responses on the text website. Students will read about the ethical, moral, and political conflicts teachers face on a daily basis and reflect on the possible solutions, better preparing them for the split-second decision making required of them as teachers. This supplement can be packaged with the text at no additional charge. Contact your representative for details.
- **Preparing for Licensure Guides** helps students prepare for special state licensure tests, such as Praxis, with exercises closely tied into specific content from the text. Special guides have been prepared for General Certification and Praxis and four state-specific certification tests: Texas, Florida, New York, and California. This supplement can be packaged with the text at no additional charge. Contact your representative for details.

INSTRUCTOR SUPPLEMENTS

- The **Instructor's Resource Manual with Test Items** contains chapter overviews, annotated lecture outlines, suggested readings and media, answers to the textbook Self-Assessment features, handout masters, and a complete offering of assessment items leveled for difficulty.
- The **Computerized Test Bank** contains a variety of testing items. The printed Test Bank is also available electronically through our computerized testing system: TestGen EQ. Instructors can use TestGen EQ to create exams in just minutes by selecting from the existing database of questions, editing questions, or writing original questions. Testing items in the test bank include multiple-choice, true-false, short-answer, conceptual essay, reflective essay, and concept integration questions. Concept integration items ask students to apply a combination of concepts and principles to a written teaching scenario.
- The **Intentional Teacher Video** offers vignettes tied to chapter content that showcase intentional teachers and situations that educators encounter.
- The **PowerPoint™ Presentation** consists of outline slides for use in the classroom and lecture outlines for faculty. (Available for download from Supplement Central at http://suppscentral.ablongman.com.) New enrichment lectures in current areas of interest, such as IDEA 2004 and research on the brain, are also available.
- **Allyn and Bacon Transparencies for Educational Psychology IV** is an updated package that includes over 150 full-color acetates.
- The **"What Every Teacher Should Know About . . ."** series contains short booklets that cover the basic concepts of key topics in Education from Assessment to IDEA and NCLB. (Speak with your Merrill representative.)

- **VideoWorkshop for Educational Psychology** is a new way to bring video into your course for maximized learning! This total teaching and learning system includes quality video footage on an easy-to-use CD-ROM plus a Student Learning Guide and an Instructor's Teaching Guide. The result? A program that brings textbook concepts to life with ease and that helps your students understand, analyze, and apply the objectives of the course. VideoWorkshop is available for your students as a value-pack option with this textbook. (Special package ISBN required from your representative.)

ACKNOWLEDGMENTS

In this edition, I benefited from the skillful assistance of my colleague Bette Chambers, who wrote the Certification Pointers, researched websites, and contributed content throughout the text; as well as from the feedback of special content reviewers Jean Ulman, Ball State University, and Jim Persinger, Emporia State University, on Chapters 12 (Learners with Exceptionalities), 13 (Assessing Student Learning), and 14 (Standardized Tests). I also thank the writers of the supplements: Emilie Johnson (Instructor's Resource Manual), Janet Medina and Christiane DeBauge (Certification Guides), Catherine McCartney and Therese Olejniczak (Assessment Package), Richard Giaquinto (PowerPoint™ Presentation), and Carol A. Scatena (Teaching Dilemma Casebook and Companion Website).

I also wish to thank my many colleagues who served as reviewers and contributors for this edition, as well as those who participated in a special survey. Reviewers' comments provided invaluable information that helped me revise and augment the text. Contributors' work has made the features and supplements to this text first-rate.

Wallace Alexander, Thomas College
Patrick Allen, Graduate College of Union University
Ted Batson, Indiana Wesleyan University
Richard Battaglia, California Lutheran University
Elizabeth Anne Belford Horan, Methodist College
Sandra Billings, Fairfield University
Silas Born, Bethany Lutheran College
Curtis Brant, Baldwin-Wallace College
Camille Branton, Delta State University
Joy Brown, University of North Alabama
Doris Burgert, Wichita State University
Renee Cambiano, Northeastern State University
William Camp, Luzerne County Community College
Ann Caton, Rockford College
Kay Chick, Pennsylvania State University–Altoona
Martha Cook, Malone College
Faye Day, Bethel College
Christiane DeBauge, Indiana University
Donna Duellberg, Wayland Baptist University
Nick Elksnin, The Citadel
Joan Evensen, Towson University
E. Gail Everett, Bob Jones University
R. Joel Farrell, Faulkner University
Susan Frusher, Northeastern State University
Donna Gardner, William Jewell College
Michele Gill, University of Central Florida
Jennifer Gross Lara, Anne Arundel Community College
Raphael Guillory, Eastern Washington University
Jan Hayes, Middle Tennessee State University
James Hedgebeth, Elizabeth City State University
Mark Hopkin, Wiley College
John Hummel, Valdosta State University
Margaret Hurd, Anne Arundel Community College
Daniel Hursh, West Virginia University

Kathryn Hutchinson, St. Thomas Aquinas College
Karen Huxtable-Jester, University of Texas at Dallas
Gretchen Jefferson, Eastern Washington University
Carolyn Jeffries, CSU Northridge
W. Y. Johnson, Wright State University
Jeffrey Kaplan, University of Central Florida
Jack Kaufman, Bluefield State College
Robert Landry, Winston-Salem State University
Dorothea Lerman, Louisiana State University
Jupian J. Leung, University of Wisconsin–Oshkosh
Judith Levine, Farmingdale State University
Judith Luckett, University of Central Florida
Betty Magjuka, Gloucester County College
Laurell Malone, North Carolina Central University
Lloyd McCraney, Towson University
Melanie J. McGill, Stephen F. Austin State University
Lienne Medford, Clemson University
Janet Medina, McDaniel College
DeAnn Miller-Boschert, North Dakota State University
Greg Morris, Grand Rapids Community College
Pamela Nesselrodt, Dickinson College
Joe Nichols, Indiana University-Purdue University Fort Wayne
Kathryn Parr, University of Florida
Jonathan Plucker, Indiana University
Linda Robertello, Iona College
Paul Rufino, Gloucester County College
Lisa Ruiz-Lee, University of Nevada, Las Vegas
Carol Scatena, Lewis University
Tom Scheft, North Carolina Central University
Diane Serafin, Luzerne County Community College–Shamokin
Joshua S. Smith, University of Albany
Donald Snead, Middle Tennessee State University
Louise Soares, University of New Haven
Theresa Sullivan Stewart, University of Illinois at Springfield
Larry Templeton, Ferris State University
Leo Theriot, Central Bible College
Melaine Timko, National University
Diana Treahy, Point Loma Nazarene University
Kathleen Waldron-Soler, Eastern Washington University
George Watson, Marshall University
Roberta Wiener, Pace University
Betty Wood, University of Arkansas at Little Rock
Priscilla Wright, Colorado Christian University
Ronald Zigler, Pennsylvania State University–Abington
Wilkins-O'Riley Zinn, Southern Oregon University

I am also grateful to contributors to previous editions, such as Thomas Andre, Curtis Bonk, Mary Jane Caffey, Sandra Damico, Melissa Dark, Stacie Goffin, Gordon Greenwood, Chuck Greiner, Carole Grove, Andrea Guillaume, Millie Harris, Johanna Keirns, Judy Lewandowski, Elizabeth Sterling, Kathryn Wentzel, and William Zangwill.

I'd also like to thank my Allyn and Bacon Senior Editor, Arnis Burvikovs; Development Editor, Christien Shangraw; and Anne Whittaker, who oversaw the development of all the supplements; as well as Nancy Forsyth, President, and Paul A. Smith, Vice President and Editor in Chief for Education. I am also grateful to the editorial-production team at Omegatype Typography and to the education team at Allyn and Bacon who helped bring this edition to fruition: Annette Joseph, Editorial-Production Administrator; Erica DeLuca, Marketing Manager; Joel Gendron, Cover Administrator; and Anne Whittaker, Editorial Assistant. I am grateful to Sharon Fox and Susan Davis of the Success for All Foundation for work on all aspects of the book—including typing, doing references, proofreading, and lending general good sense—and to James Bravo, the talented artist behind the cartoons.

Finally, it is customary to acknowledge the long-suffering patience of one's spouse and children. In my case, this acknowledgment is especially appropriate. My wife, Nancy Madden, has helped on every edition as well as keeping our research going while I wrote. Our children contributed to this work by providing me with a sense of purpose for writing. I had to keep thinking about the kind of school experience I want for them as a way of making concrete my concern for the school experiences of all children.

This book was written while I was supported in part by grants from the Institute of Education Sciences, U.S. Department of Education (No. R305A040082). However, any opinions I have are mine alone and do not represent IES positions or policy.

R. E. S.

Educational Psychology

Theory and Practice

CHAPTER 1

Educational Psychology: A Foundation for Teaching

chapter OUTLINE

Ellen Mathis was baffled. She was a new teacher who had been trying to teach creative writing to her third-grade class, but things were just not going the way she'd hoped. Her students were not producing much, and what they did write was not very imaginative and was full of errors. For example, she had recently assigned a composition on "My Summer Vacation," and all that one of her students wrote was "On my summer vacation I got a dog and we went swimming and I got stinged by a bee."

Ellen wondered whether her kids were just not ready for writing and needed several months of work on such skills as capitalization, punctuation, and usage before she tried another writing assignment. One day, however, Ellen noticed some compositions in the hall outside of Leah Washington's class. Leah's third-graders were just like Ellen's, but their compositions were fabulous. The students wrote pages of interesting material on an astonishing array of topics. At the end of the day, Ellen caught Leah in the hall. "How do you get your kids to write such great compositions?" she asked.

Leah explained how she first got her children writing on topics they cared about and then gradually introduced "mini-lessons" to help them become better authors. She had the students work in small groups and help one another plan compositions. Then the students critiqued one another's drafts, helped one another with editing, and finally "published" final versions.

"I'll tell you what," Leah offered. "I'll schedule my next writing class during your planning period. Come see what we're doing."

Ellen agreed. When the time came, she walked into Leah's class and was overwhelmed by what she saw. Children were writing everywhere: on the floor, in groups, at tables. Many were talking with partners. Leah was conferencing with individual children. Ellen looked over the children's shoulders and saw one student writing about her pets, another writing a gory story about Ninjas, and another writing about a dream. Marta Delgrado, a Mexican American child, was writing a funny story about her second-grade teacher's attempts to speak Spanish. One student, Melinda Navens, was even writing a very good story about her summer vacation!

After school, Ellen met with Leah. She was full of questions. "How did you get students to do all that writing? How can you manage all that noise and activity? How did you learn to do this?"

"I did go to a series of workshops on teaching writing," Leah said. "But if you think about it, everything I'm doing is basic educational psychology."

Ellen was amazed. "Educational psychology? I got an A in that course in college, but I don't see what it has to do with your writing program."

"Well, let's see," said Leah. "To begin with, I'm using a lot of motivational strategies I learned in ed psych. For instance, when I started my writing instruction this year, I read students some funny and intriguing stories written by other classes, to arouse their curiosity. I got them motivated by letting them write about whatever they wanted, and also by having 'writing celebrations' in which students read their finished compositions to the class for applause and comments. My educational psychology professor was always talking about adapting to students' needs. I do this by conferencing with students and helping them with the specific problems they're having. I first learned about cooperative learning in ed psych, and later on I took some workshops on it. I use cooperative learning groups to let students give each other immediate feedback on their writing, to let them model effective writing for each other, and to get them to encourage each other to write. The groups also solve a lot of my management problems by keeping each other on task and dealing with many classroom routines. I remember that we learned about evaluation in ed psych. I use a flexible form of evaluation. Everybody eventually gets an A on his or her composition, but only when it meets a high standard, which may take many drafts. I apply what we learned about child development just about every day. For example, I adapt to students' developmental levels and cultural styles by encouraging them to write about things that matter to them: If dinosaurs or video games are important right now, or if children are uncomfortable about being Muslim or Jewish at Christmas time, that's what they should write about!"

Ellen was impressed. She and Leah arranged to visit each other's classes a few more times to exchange ideas and observations, and in time, Ellen's writers began to be almost as good as Leah's. But what was particularly important to her was the idea that educational psychology could really be useful in her day-to-day teaching. She dragged out her old textbook and found that concepts that had seemed theoretical and abstract in her ed psych class actually helped her think about teaching problems.

USING *your* EXPERIENCE

CREATIVE THINKING Based on Leah's explanation of her writing instruction, work with one or more partners to brainstorm about what educational psychology is and what you will learn this semester. Guidelines: (1) the more ideas you generate, the better; (2) hitchhike on others' ideas as well as combining them; and (3) make no evaluation of those ideas at this time. Take this list out a few times during the semester and add to it as well as evaluate it.

HOMEWORK EXERCISE
Getting Started

In the margins throughout this text, in notes that look just like this one, you will encounter two kinds of exercises that may be completed online at **www.myeducationlab.com**: Homework Exercises and Building Teaching Skills Exercises. Prepare for the exercises by establishing access to the site now, using the code that came with this text, or purchase it online at the site. For each exercise, you will be able to save your work or transmit it to your professor as required.

educational psychology
The study of learning and teaching.

What is **educational psychology?** An academic definition would perhaps say that educational psychology is the study of learners, learning, and teaching (Reynolds & Miller, 2003). However, for students who are or expect to be teachers, educational psychology is something more. It is the accumulated knowledge, wisdom, and seat-of-the-pants theory that every teacher should possess to intelligently solve the daily problems of teaching. Educational psychology cannot tell teachers what to do, but it can give them the principles to use in making a good decision and a language to discuss their experiences and thinking. Consider the case of Ellen Mathis and Leah Washington. Nothing in this or any other educational psychology text will tell teachers exactly how to teach creative writing to a particular group of third-graders. However, Leah uses concepts of educational psychology to consider how she will teach writing, to interpret and solve problems she runs into, and to explain to Ellen what she is doing. Educational psychologists carry out research on the nature of students, principles of learning, and methods of teaching to give educators the information they need to think critically about their craft and to make teaching decisions that will work for their students (Alexander, 2004).

WHAT MAKES A GOOD TEACHER?

What makes a good teacher? Is it warmth, humor, and the ability to care about people? Is it planning, hard work, and self-discipline? What about leadership, enthusiasm, a contagious love of learning, and speaking ability? Most people would agree that all of these qualities are needed to make someone a good teacher, and they would certainly be correct (see Wayne & Youngs, 2003). But these qualities are not enough.

What characteristics of good teaching might this expert teacher possess? What behaviors does she demonstrate that might make her an effective teacher?

Knowing the Subject Matters (but So Does Teaching Skill)

There is an old joke that goes like this:

Question: What do you need to know to be able to teach a horse?
Answer: More than the horse!

This joke makes the obvious point that the first thing a teacher must have is some knowledge or skills that the learner does not have; teachers must know the subject matter they expect to teach. But if you think about teaching horses (or children), you will soon realize that although subject matter knowledge is necessary, it is not enough. A rancher may have a good idea of how a horse is supposed to act and what a horse is supposed to be able to do, but if he doesn't have the skills to make an untrained, scared, and unfriendly animal into a good saddle horse, he's going to end up with nothing but broken ribs and teeth marks for his troubles. Children are a lot smarter and a little more forgiving than horses, but teaching them has this in common with teaching horses: Knowledge of how to transmit information and skills is at least as important as knowledge of the information and skills themselves. We have all had teachers (most often college professors, unfortunately) who were brilliant and thoroughly knowledgeable in their fields but who could not teach. Ellen Mathis may know as much as Leah Washington about what good writing should be, but she has a lot to learn about how to get third-graders to write well.

For effective teaching, subject matter knowledge is not a question of being a walking encyclopedia. Effective teachers not only know their subjects but also can communicate their knowledge to students. The celebrated high school math teacher Jaime Escalante taught the concept of positive and negative numbers to students in a Los Angeles barrio by explaining that when you dig a hole, you might call the pile of dirt +1, the hole −1. What do you get when you put the dirt back in the hole? Zero. Escalante's ability to relate the abstract concept of positive and negative numbers to his students' experiences is one example of how the ability to communicate knowledge goes far beyond simply knowing the facts.

INTASC

1 Knowledge of Subject Matter

Mastering the Teaching Skills

The link between what the teacher wants students to learn and students' actual learning is called instruction, or **pedagogy.** Effective instruction is not a simple matter of one person with more knowledge transmitting that knowledge to another. If telling were teaching, this book would be unnecessary. Rather, effective instruction demands the use of many strategies.

pedagogy
The study of teaching and learning with applications to the instructional process.

For example, suppose Paula Ray wants to teach a lesson on statistics to a diverse class of fourth-graders. To do this, Paula must accomplish many things. She must make sure that the class is orderly and that students know what behavior is expected of them. She must find out whether students have the prerequisite skills; for example, students need to be able to add and divide to find averages. If any do not, Paula must find a way to teach students those skills. She must engage students in activities that lead them toward an understanding of statistics, such as having students roll dice, play cards, or collect data from experiments; and she must use teaching strategies that help students remember what they have been taught. The lessons should also take into account the intellectual and social characteristics of students in the fourth grade and the intellectual, social, and cultural characteristics of these particular students. Paula must make sure that students are interested in the lesson and are motivated to learn statistics. To see whether students are learning what is being taught, she may ask questions or use quizzes or have students demonstrate their understanding by setting up and interpreting experiments, and she must respond appropriately if these assessments show that students are having problems. After the series of lessons on statistics ends, Paula should review this topic from time to time to ensure that it is remembered.

These tasks—motivating students, managing the classroom, assessing prior knowledge, communicating ideas effectively, taking into account the characteristics of the learners, assessing learning outcomes, and reviewing information—must be attended to at all levels of education, in or out of schools. They apply as much to the training of astronauts as to the teaching of reading. How these tasks are accomplished, however, differs widely according to the ages of the students, the objectives of instruction, and other factors.

CONNECTIONS
For more on effective instruction, see Chapter 7. Pedagogical strategies are also presented in Chapters 8 (p. 249) and 9 (p. 262), as well as throughout the text in features titled The Intentional Teacher.

What makes a good teacher is the ability to carry out all the tasks involved in effective instruction (Burden & Byrd, 2003; Kennedy, 2006). Warmth, enthusiasm, and caring are essential (Cornelius-White, 2007; Eisner, 2006), as is subject matter knowledge and knowledge about how children learn (Wiggins & McTighe, 2006). But it is the successful accomplishment of all the tasks of teaching that makes for instructional effectiveness (Shulman, 2000).

INTASC

5 Classroom Motivation and Management

Can Good Teaching Be Taught?

Some people think that good teachers are born that way. Outstanding teachers sometimes seem to have a magic, a charisma, that mere mortals could never hope to achieve. Yet research has begun to identify the specific behaviors and skills that make up the "magic" teacher (Borman & Kimball, 2005). An outstanding teacher does nothing that any other teacher cannot also do—it is just a question of knowing the principles of effective teaching and how to apply them. Take one small example: In a high school history class, two students in the back of the class are whispering to each other, and they are not discussing the Treaty of Paris! The teacher slowly walks toward them without looking, continuing his lesson as he walks. The students stop whispering and pay attention. If you didn't know what to look for, you might miss this brief but critical interchange and believe that the teacher just has a way with students, a knack for keeping their attention. But the teacher is simply applying principles of classroom management that anyone could learn: Maintain momentum in the lesson, deal with behavior problems by using the mildest intervention that will work, and resolve minor problems before they become major ones. When Jaime Escalante gave the example of digging a hole to illustrate the concept of positive and negative numbers, he was also applying several important principles of educational psychology: Make abstract ideas concrete by using many examples, relate the content of instruction to the students' background, state rules, give examples, and then restate rules.

"If only I could get to my ed psych text . . ."

FIGURE 1.1 **Components of Good Teaching**

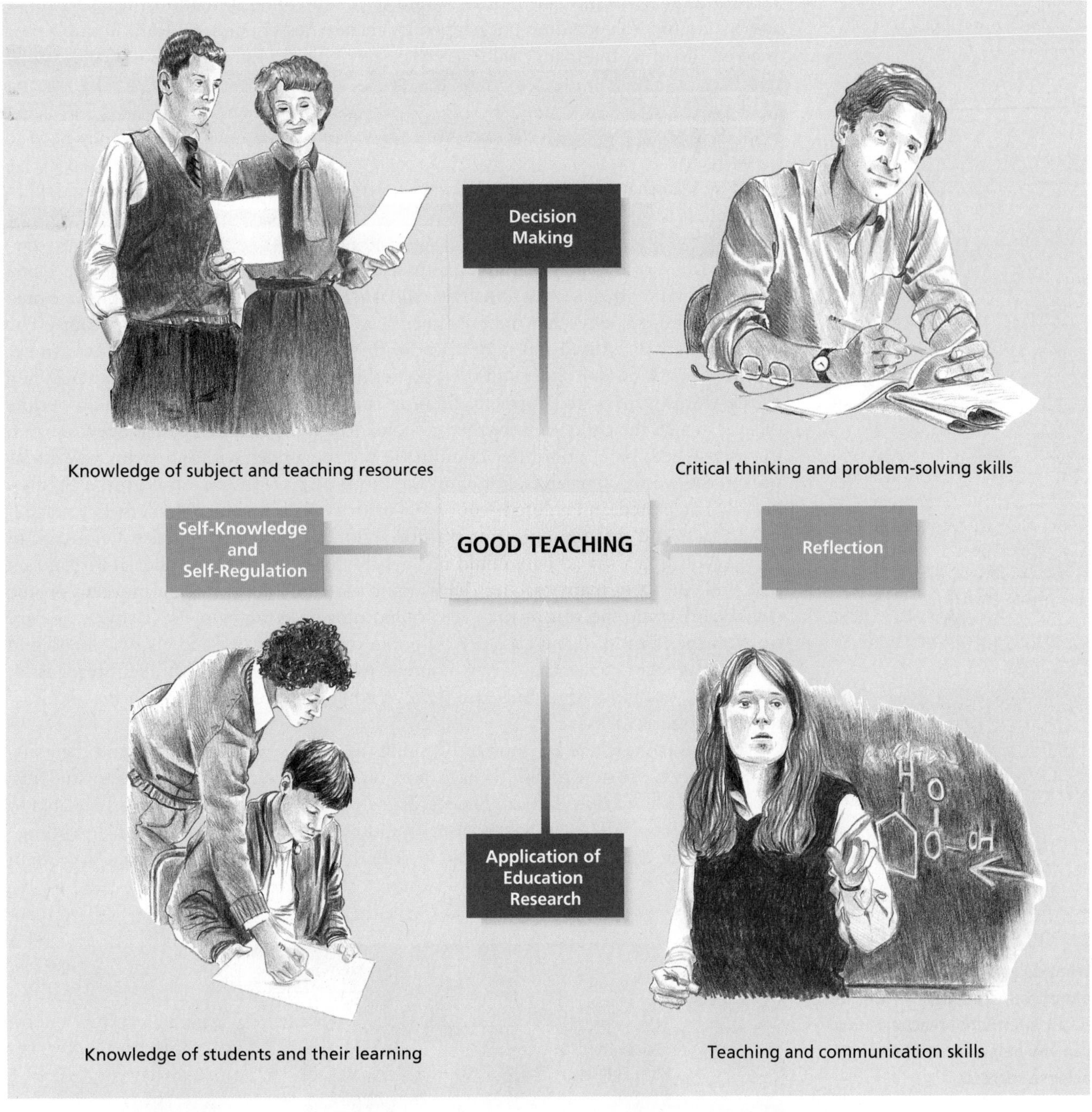

Can good teaching be taught? The answer is definitely yes. Good teaching has to be observed and practiced, but there are principles of good teaching that teachers need to know, which can then be applied in the classroom. The major components of effective instruction are summarized in Figure 1.1.

The Intentional Teacher

intentionality
Doing things for a purpose; teachers who use intentionality plan their actions based on the outcomes they want to achieve.

There is no formula for good teaching, no seven steps to Teacher of the Year. Teaching involves planning and preparation, and then dozens of decisions every hour. Yet one attribute seems to be characteristic of outstanding teachers: **intentionality.** Intentionality means doing things for a reason, on purpose. Intentional teachers are those who are constantly thinking about the outcomes they want for their students and about how each decision they make moves children toward those outcomes. Intentional teachers know that maximum learning does not happen by chance. Yes, children do learn in unplanned ways all the time, and many will learn from even the most chaotic lesson. But to really challenge students, to get their best efforts, to help them make conceptual leaps and organize and retain new knowledge, teachers need to be purposeful, thoughtful, and flexible, without ever losing sight of their goals for every child. In a word, they need to be *intentional.*

The idea that teachers should always do things for a reason seems obvious, and in principle it is. Yet in practice, it is difficult to constantly make certain that all students are engaged in activities that lead to important learning outcomes. Teachers very frequently fall into strategies that they themselves would recognize, on reflection, as being time fillers rather than instructionally essential activities. For example, an otherwise outstanding third-grade teacher once assigned seatwork to one of her reading groups. The children were given two sheets of paper with words in squares. Their task was to cut out the squares on one sheet and then paste them onto synonyms on the other. When all the words were pasted correctly, lines on the pasted squares would form an outline of a cat, which the children were then to color. Once the children pasted a few squares, the puzzle became clear, so they could paste the remainder without paying any attention to the words themselves. For almost an hour of precious class time, these children happily cut, pasted, and colored—not high-priority skills for third-graders. The teacher would have said that the objective was for children to learn or practice synonyms, of course; but in fact the activity could not possibly have moved the children forward on that skill. Similarly, many teachers have one child laboriously work a problem on the chalkboard while the rest of the class has nothing important to do. Many secondary teachers spend most of the class period going over homework and classwork and end up doing very little teaching of new content. Again, these may be excellent teachers in other ways, but they sometimes lose sight of what they are trying to achieve and how they are going to achieve it.

Intentional teachers are constantly asking themselves what goals they and their students are trying to accomplish. Is each portion of their lesson appropriate to students' background knowledge, skills, and needs? Is each activity or assignment clearly related to a valued outcome? Is each instructional minute used wisely and well? An intentional teacher trying to build students' synonym skills during follow-up time might have them

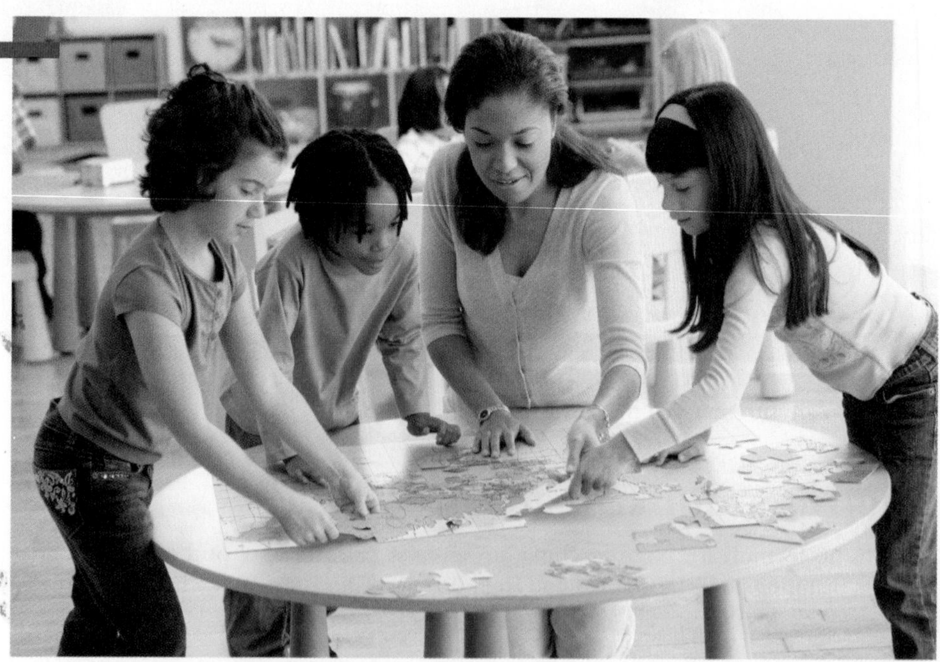

What do you need to know about your students in order to be an intentional teacher? How can you help your students achieve success?

work in pairs to master a set of synonyms in preparation for individual quizzes. An intentional teacher might have all children work a given problem while one works at the board, so that all can compare answers and strategies together. An intentional teacher might quickly give homework answers for students to check themselves, ask for a show of hands for correct answers, and then review and reteach only those exercises missed by many students. An intentional teacher uses a wide variety of instructional methods, experiences, assignments, and materials to be sure that children are achieving all sorts of cognitive objectives, from knowledge to application to creativity, and that at the same time children are learning important affective objectives, such as love of learning, respect for others, and personal responsibility. An intentional teacher constantly reflects on his or her practices and outcomes.

Research finds that one of the most powerful predictors of a teacher's impact on students is the belief that what he or she does makes a difference. This belief, called **teacher efficacy** (Henson, 2002; Tschannen-Moran & Woolfolk Hoy, 2001), is at the heart of what it means to be an intentional teacher. Teachers who believe that success in school is almost entirely due to children's inborn intelligence, home environment, or other factors that teachers cannot influence, are unlikely to teach in the same way as those who believe that their own efforts are the key to children's learning. An intentional teacher, one who has a strong belief in her or his efficacy, is more likely to put forth consistent effort, to persist in the face of obstacles, and to keep trying relentlessly until every student succeeds (Bandura, 1997). Intentional teachers achieve a sense of efficacy by constantly assessing the results of their instruction (Schmoker, 1999); constantly trying new strategies if their initial instruction didn't work; and constantly seeking ideas from colleagues, books, magazines, workshops, and other sources to enrich and solidify their teaching skills (Corbett, Wilson, & Williams, 2005). Groups of teachers, such as all teachers in an elementary school or all teachers in a given academic department, can attain collective efficacy by working together to examine their practices and outcomes, seeking professional development, and helping each other succeed (see Borko, 2004; Sachs, 2000). Collective efficacy can have a particularly strong impact on student achievement (Goddard, Hoy, & Hoy, 2000). The most important purpose of this book is to give tomorrow's teachers the intellectual grounding in research, theory, and practical wisdom they will need in order to become intentional, effective teachers. To plan and carry out effective lessons, discussions, projects, and other learning experiences, teachers need to know a great deal. Besides knowing their subjects, they need to understand the developmental levels and needs of their children. They need to understand how learning, memory, problem-solving skill, and creativity are acquired and how to promote their acquisition. They need to know how to set objectives, organize activities designed to help students attain those objectives, and assess students' progress toward them. They need to know how to motivate children, how to use class time effectively, and how to respond to individual differences among students. Like Leah Washington, the teacher in the vignette that opened this chapter, intentional teachers are constantly combining their knowledge of principles of educational psychology, their experience, and their creativity to make instructional decisions and help children become enthusiastic and effective learners. They are continually experimenting with strategies to solve problems of instruction and then observing the results of their actions to see if they were effective (Duck, 2000). They pay attention to research on effective teaching, and incorporate research findings in their daily teaching (Fleischman, 2006).

This text highlights the ideas that are central to educational psychology and the related research. It also presents many examples of how these ideas apply in practice, emphasizing teaching practices, not only theory or suggestions, that have been evaluated and found to be effective. The text is designed to help you develop **critical-thinking** skills for teaching: a logical and systematic approach to the many dilemmas that are found in practice and research. No text can provide all the right answers for teaching, but this one tries to pose the right questions and to engage you by presenting realistic alternatives and the concepts and research behind them.

Many studies have looked at the differences between expert and novice teachers and between more and less effective teachers. One theme comes through these studies: Expert teachers are critical thinkers (Hogan, Rabinowitz, & Craven, 2003; Mosenthal et al., 2004;

teacher efficacy
The degree to which teachers feel that their own efforts determine the success of their students.

critical thinking
Evaluation of conclusions through logical and systematic examination of the problem, the evidence, and the solution.

Shulman, 2000). Intentional teachers are constantly upgrading and examining their own teaching practices, reading and attending conferences to learn new ideas, and using their own students' responses to guide their instructional decisions. There's an old saying to the effect that there are teachers with 20 years of experience and there are teachers with 1 year of experience 20 times. Teachers who get better each year are the ones who are open to new ideas and who look at their own teaching critically. Perhaps the most important goal of this book is to get you in the habit of using informed reflection to become one of tomorrow's expert teachers.

WHAT IS THE ROLE OF RESEARCH IN EDUCATIONAL PSYCHOLOGY?

Teachers who are intentional, critical thinkers are likely to enter their classrooms equipped with knowledge about research in educational psychology. Every year, educational psychologists discover or refine principles of teaching and learning that are useful for practicing teachers. Some of these principles are just common sense backed up with evidence, but others are more surprising. One problem educational psychologists face is that almost everyone thinks he or she is an expert on the subject of educational psychology. Most adults have spent many years in schools watching what teachers do. Add to that a certain amount of knowledge of human nature, and *voila!* Everyone is an amateur educational psychologist. For this reason, professional educational psychologists are often accused of studying the obvious.

However, as we have painfully learned, the obvious is not always true. For example, most people assume that if students are assigned to classes according to their ability, the resulting narrower range of abilities in a class will let the teacher adapt the instruction to the specific needs of the students and thereby increase student achievement. This assumption turns out to be false. Many teachers believe that scolding students for misbehavior will improve student behavior. Many students will indeed respond to a scolding by behaving better, but for others, scolding may be a reward for misbehavior and will actually increase it. Some "obvious" truths even conflict with one another. For example, most people would agree that students learn better from a teacher's instruction than by working alone. This belief supports teacher-centered direct instructional strategies, in which a teacher actively works with the class as a whole. However, most people would also agree that students often need instruction tailored to their individual needs. This belief, also correct, would demand that teachers divide their time among individuals, or at least among groups of students with differing needs, which would result in some students working independently while others received the teacher's attention. If schools could provide tutors for every student, there would be no conflict; direct instruction and individualization could coexist. In practice, however, classrooms typically have 20 or more students; as a result, more direct instruction (the first goal) almost always means less individualization (the second goal). The intentional teacher's task is to balance these competing goals according to the needs of particular students and situations.

CONNECTIONS
For more on ability grouping, see Chapter 9, pages 265–272.

CONNECTIONS
For more on effectively handling misbehavior, see Chapter 5, page 134.

The Goal of Research in Educational Psychology

The goal of research in educational psychology is to carefully examine obvious as well as less than obvious questions, using objective methods to test ideas about the factors that contribute to learning (Levin, O'Donnell, & Kratochwill, 2003; McComb & Scott-Little,

Personal REFLECTION

INTASC 3 Adapting Instruction for Individual Needs

Adapting

My journey into teaching fits the adage that "life is what happens while you're making other plans." I was certified as a high school social studies teacher; did my student teaching; and was hoping to teach history, geography, and psychology. However, when the time came, I couldn't get a job. There was a huge surplus of teachers that year, and because I couldn't coach a sport other than chess, I didn't have a chance. I did, however, get a job in special education. It so happened that I knew something about special education because I'd had jobs each summer in college working with children with autism and mental retardation.

My first job was in a special school. Originally, I was assigned elementary-aged children, but because I was the only male teacher, I was soon assigned all the older adolescents.

As a young and idealistic teacher, I decided to visit each of my children's homes, to see if I could learn better how to help them. One visit was to the home of a 15-year-old boy I'll call Mark. The other staff members warned me about Mark's mother. "She's crazy," they told me. "She thinks Mark can talk." Mark had been at the school for many years and had never been heard to say a word. In fact, if you asked him to do anything at all, he'd fly into a rage, smash things, tear his clothes, and hit anyone nearby. As a result, the staff had generally left him alone.

When I visited Mark's home, I met his mother. She seemed quite normal to me. I asked her if Mark ever spoke at home. After her experiences with previous teachers, she felt I wouldn't believe her, but she told me that, yes, he did talk. I asked what he talked about, and also asked what he most liked. She gave me a number of words he used and told me that although Mark was indifferent to most things, he was passionate about music.

The next day I got a record player and a few scratched records. I put one on. Mark was enthralled. After a while I picked up the arm, and told Mark I'd put it back if he'd say "record," one of the words his mom had mentioned.

Mark had a huge tantrum. It must have taken an hour to calm him down, but I wouldn't give in. He had to say the word.

At last, in great agitation, he said the magic word, "record," and I put on the record.

Later on I got a tape recorder and played music for Mark if he was behaving appropriately. He developed (or rediscovered) a vocabulary of 200 words, and by the end of the year I was teaching him skills for the sheltered workshop the school district ran—a possibility that would have been unimaginable at the beginning of the year.

Mark taught me more about teaching than any university ever could. I went into teaching thinking that if you knew your subject and you knew your teaching methods, your children were bound to succeed. Mark taught me that that's not enough. You've also got to care enough to challenge them to excel.

REFLECT ON THIS. How is my work with Mark a demonstration of critical thinking? Consider this experience as well as that of Leah Washington in the opening vignette. What can you learn from these experiences that will help you become an intentional teacher?

2003). The products of this research are principles, laws, and theories. A **principle** explains the relationship between factors, such as the effects of alternative grading systems on student motivation. Laws are simply principles that have been thoroughly tested and found to apply in a wide variety of situations. A **theory** is a set of related principles and laws that explains a broad aspect of learning, behavior, or another area of interest. Without theories the facts and principles that are discovered would be like disorganized specks on a canvas. Theories tie together these facts and principles to give us the big picture. However, the same facts and principles may be interpreted in different ways by different theorists. As in any science, progress in educational psychology is slow and uneven. A single study is rarely a breakthrough, but over time evidence accumulates on a subject and allows theorists to refine and extend their theories.

principle
Explanation of the relationship between factors, such as the effects of alternative grading systems on student motivation.

theory
A set of principles that explains and relates certain phenomena.

The Value of Research in Educational Psychology to the Teacher

It is probably true that the most important things teachers learn, they learn on the job—in internships, while student teaching, or during their first years in the classroom (Darling-Hammond, Gendler, & Wise, 1990). However, teachers make hundreds of decisions every day, and each decision has a theory behind it, regardless of whether the teacher is aware of it. The quality, accuracy, and usefulness of those theories are what ultimately determine the teacher's success. For example, one teacher may offer a prize to the student with the best attendance, on the theory that rewarding attendance will increase it. Another may reward the student whose attendance is most improved, on the theory that it is poor attenders who most need incentives to come to class. A third may not reward anyone for attendance but may try to increase attendance by teaching more interesting lessons. Which teacher's plan is most likely to succeed? This depends in large part on the ability of each teacher to understand the unique combination of factors that shape the character of her or his classroom and therefore to apply the most appropriate theory.

Teaching as Decision Making

The aim of research in educational psychology is to test the various theories that guide the actions of teachers and others involved in education. Here is another example of how a teacher might use educational psychology.

Mr. Harris teaches an eighth-grade social studies class. He has a problem with Tom, who frequently misbehaves. Today, Tom makes a paper airplane and flies it across the room when Mr. Harris turns his back, to the delight of the entire class.

What should Mr. Harris do?

As an intentional teacher, Mr. Harris considers a range of options for solving this problem, each of which comes from a theory about why Tom is misbehaving and what will motivate him to behave more appropriately.

Some actions Mr. Harris might take, and the theories on which they are based, are as follows:

Action	Theory
1. Reprimand Tom.	1. A reprimand is a form of punishment. Tom will behave to avoid punishment.
2. Ignore Tom.	2. Attention may be rewarding to Tom. Ignoring him would deprive him of this reward.
3. Send Tom to the office.	3. Being sent to the office is punishing. It also deprives Tom of the (apparent) support of his classmates.
4. Tell the class that it is everyone's responsibility to maintain a good learning environment and that if any student misbehaves, 5 minutes will be subtracted from recess.	4. Tom is misbehaving to get his classmates' attention. If the whole class loses out when he misbehaves, the class will keep him in line.
5. Explain to the class that Tom's behavior is interfering with lessons that all students need to know and that his behavior goes against the rules the class set for itself at the beginning of the year.	5. The class holds standards of behavior that conflict with both Tom's behavior in class and the class's reaction to it. By reminding the class of its own needs (to learn the lesson) and its own rules set at the beginning of the year, the teacher might make Tom see that the class does not really support his behavior.

Each of these actions is a common response to misbehavior. But which theory (and therefore which action) is correct?

Teachers face a number of difficult, and sometimes unexpected, decisions every day and have to be able to respond quickly and appropriately. How can you become an intentional teacher?

The key might be in the fact that his classmates laugh when Tom misbehaves. This response is a clue that Tom is seeking their attention. If Mr. Harris scolds Tom, this might increase Tom's status in the eyes of his peers and may reward his behavior. Ignoring misbehavior might be a good idea if a student were acting up to get the teacher's attention, but in this case it is apparently the class's attention that Tom is seeking. Sending Tom to the office does deprive him of his classmates' attention and therefore may be effective. But what if Tom is looking for a way to get out of class to avoid work? What if he struts out to confront the powers that be, to the obvious approval of his classmates? Making the entire class responsible for each student's behavior is likely to deprive Tom of his classmates' support and to improve his behavior; but some students may think that it is unfair to punish them for another student's misbehavior. Finally, reminding the class (and Tom) of its own interest in learning and its usual standards of behavior might work if the class does, in fact, value academic achievement and good behavior.

Research in education and psychology bears directly on the decision Mr. Harris must make. Developmental research indicates that as students enter adolescence, the peer group becomes all-important to them, and they try to establish their independence from adult control, often by flouting or ignoring rules. Basic research on behavioral learning theories shows that when a behavior is repeated many times, some reward must be encouraging the behavior, and that if the behavior is to be eliminated, the reward must first be identified and removed. This research would also suggest that Mr. Harris consider problems with the use of punishment (such as scolding) to stop undesirable behavior. Research on specific classroom management strategies has identified effective methods to use both to prevent a student like Tom from misbehaving in the first place and to deal with his misbehavior when it does occur. Finally, research on rule setting and classroom standards indicates that student participation in setting rules can help convince each student that the class as a whole values academic achievement and appropriate behavior, and that this belief can help keep individual students in line.

INTASC

9 **Professional Commitment and Responsibility**

Armed with this information, Mr. Harris can choose a response to Tom's behavior that is based on an understanding of why Tom is doing what he is doing and what strategies are available to deal with the situation. He may or may not make the right choice, but because he knows several theories that could explain Tom's behavior, he will be able to observe the outcomes of his strategy and, if it is ineffective, to learn from that and try something else that will work. Research does not give Mr. Harris a specific solution;

that requires his own experience and judgment. But research does give Mr. Harris basic concepts of human behavior to help him understand Tom's motivations and an array of proven methods that might solve the problem. And using research to help him make teaching decisions is one way Mr. Harris can achieve a sense of his own efficacy as a teacher.

THEORY *into* PRACTICE

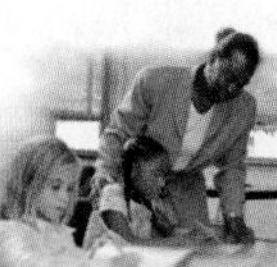

Teaching as Decision Making

If there were no educational problems to solve, there would be no need for teachers to function as professionals. Professionals distinguish themselves from nonprofessionals in part by the fact that they must make decisions that influence the course of their work.

Educators must decide (1) how to recognize problems and issues, (2) how to consider situations from multiple perspectives, (3) how to call up relevant professional knowledge to formulate actions, (4) how to take the most appropriate action, and (5) how to judge the consequences.

Ms. O'Hara has a student named Shanika in her social studies class. Most of the time, Shanika is rather quiet and withdrawn. Her permanent record indicates considerable academic ability, but a casual observer would never know it. Ms. O'Hara asks herself the following questions:

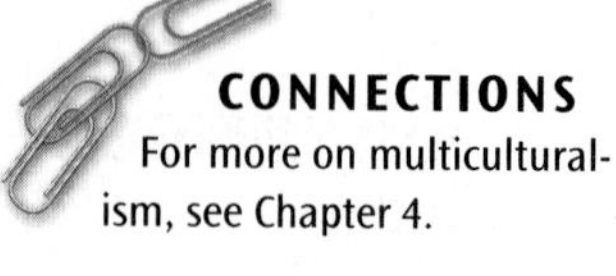

CONNECTIONS
For more on multiculturalism, see Chapter 4.

1. What problems do I perceive in this situation? Is Shanika bored, tired, uninterested, or shy, or might her participation be inhibited by something I or others are doing or not doing? What theories of educational psychology might I consider?
2. I wonder what Shanika thinks about being in this class? Does she feel excluded? Does she care about the subject matter? Is she concerned about what I or others think about her lack of participation? Why or why not? What theories of motivation will help me make a decision?
3. What do I know from theory, research, and/or practice that might guide my actions to involve Shanika more directly in class activities?
4. What might I actually do in this situation to enhance Shanika's involvement?
5. How would I know if I were successful with Shanika?

If Ms. O'Hara asked and tried to answer these questions—not only in the case of Shanika, of course, but at other times as well—she would improve her chances to learn about her work from doing her work. Philosopher John Dewey taught that the problems teachers face are the natural stimuli for reflective inquiry. Intentional teachers accept the problems and think productively about them.

Research + Common Sense = Effective Teaching

As the case of Mr. Harris illustrates, no theory, no research, no book can tell teachers what to do in a given situation. Making the right decisions depends on the context within which the problem arises, the objectives the teacher has in mind, and many other factors, all of which must be assessed in the light of educated common sense. For example, research in mathematics instruction usually finds that a rapid pace of instruction increases achievement (Good, Grouws, & Ebmeier, 1983). Yet a teacher may quite legitimately slow down and spend a lot of time on a concept that is particularly critical or may let students take time to discover a mathematical principle on their own. It is usually much more efficient (that is, it takes less time) to teach students skills or information directly than it is to let them make discoveries for themselves, but if the teacher wants students to gain a deeper understanding of a topic or to know how to find information or to figure things out for themselves, then the research findings about pace can be temporarily shelved.

The point is that although research in educational psychology can sometimes be translated directly to the classroom, it is best to apply the principles with a hefty dose of common sense and a clear view of what is being taught to whom and for what purpose.

Research on Effective Programs

Research in educational psychology not only provides evidence for principles of effective practice but also provides evidence about the effectiveness of particular programs or practices (Fleischman, 2006). For example, in the vignette at the beginning of this chapter, Leah Washington was using a specific approach to creative writing instruction that has been extensively evaluated as a whole (Harris & Graham, 1996a). In other words, there is evidence that, on average, children whose teachers are using such methods learn to write better than those whose teachers use more traditional approaches. There is evidence on the effectiveness of dozens of widely used programs, from methods in particular subjects to strategies for reforming entire schools (see, for example, Ellis, 2001b; Gunter, Estes, & Schwab, 2003; Slavin & Lake, 2006; Slavin, Lake, & Groff, 2007). An intentional teacher should be aware of research on programs for his or her subject and grade level, and should seek out professional development opportunities to learn methods known to make a difference for children.

Impact of Research on Educational Practice

Many researchers and educators have bemoaned the limited impact of research in educational psychology on teachers' practices (see, for example, Hargreaves, 1996; Kennedy, 1997). Indeed, research in education has nowhere near as great an impact on practice as research in medicine (Riehl, 2006). Yet research in education does have a profound indirect impact on educational practice (Hattie & Marsh, 1996), even if teachers are not aware of it. It affects educational policies, professional development programs, and teaching materials. For example, the Tennessee class size study (Finn, Pannozzo, & Achilles, 2003), which found important effects of class size in the early grades on student achievement, had a direct impact on state and federal proposals for class size reduction (Wasley, 2002). Recent research on beginning reading (National Reading Panel, 2000) has begun to dramatically transform curriculum, instruction, and professional development for this subject. Research on the effects of career academies in high schools (Kemple, 1997) has led to a substantial increase in such programs.

It is important for educators to become intelligent consumers of research, not to take every finding or every expert's pronouncement as truth from Mount Olympus (Fleischman, 2006). The following section briefly describes the methods of research that most often produce findings of use to educators.

"In light of research on class size, we're not cutting class, we're helping our classmates get a better education!"

THEORY *into* PRACTICE

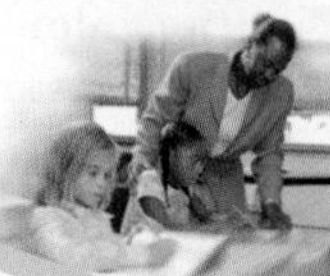

How to Be an Intelligent Consumer of Educational Psychology Research

INTASC

9 Professional Commitment and Responsibility

Let's say you're in the market for a new car. Before laying out your hard-earned money, you'll probably review the findings from various consumer research reports. You may want to know something about how various cars have performed in crash tests, which cars have the best gas mileage, or what trade-in value a particular model has. Before embarking on this major investment, you want to feel as confident as you can about your decision. If you've been in this situation before, you probably remember that all of your research helped you make an informed decision.

Now that you are about to enter the profession of teaching, you will need to apply a similar consumer orientation in your decision making. As a teacher, you will be called on to make hundreds of decisions each day. Your car-buying decision was influenced by a combination of sound research findings and common sense, and your decisions about teaching and learning should follow this same pattern. Teaching and learning are complex concepts subject to a wide variety of influences, so your knowledge of relevant research will serve to guide you into making informed choices.

How can knowing the simple formula *research + common sense = effective teaching* help you to be a more intelligent consumer of educational psychology research? The following recommendations show how you can put this formula into practice:

1. ***Be a consumer of relevant research.*** It's obvious you can't apply what you don't know. As a professional, you have a responsibility to maintain a working knowledge of relevant research. In addition to your course textbooks, which will be excellent resources for you in the future, you should become familiar with the professional journals in your field. You may want to review the following journals, which typically present research that has direct application for classroom practices: *Educational Psychologist, Journal of Educational Psychology,* and *American Educational Research Journal.* In addition, check out *Annual Editions: Educational Psychology,* a yearly publication that reprints articles from various professional journals. Also, don't overlook the value of networking with other teachers, face to face or via the Internet. The example of Ellen Mathis and Leah Washington is an excellent illustration of how collaboration can expand your research base.

2. ***Be an intentional teacher.*** Although there is no recipe for the ingredients that make up a commonsense approach to teaching, the behaviors consistent with being an intentional teacher are about as close as we can get. Intentional teachers are thoughtful. Like Mr. Harris, they consider multiple perspectives on classroom situations. When they take action, they are purposeful and think about why they do what they do. Intentional teachers follow their actions with careful reflection, evaluating their actions to determine whether they have resulted in the desired outcomes. You probably learned about the "scientific method" sometime during high school. Intentional teachers employ such a method in their teaching. That is, they formulate a working hypothesis based on their observations and background knowledge, collect data to test their hypothesis, effectively organize and analyze the data, draw sound conclusions based on the data, and take a course of action based on their conclusions. For many experienced teachers, this cycle becomes automatic and internalized. When applied systematically, these practices can serve to validate research and theory and, as a result, increase a teacher's growing professional knowledge base.

3. ***Share your experiences.*** When you combine your knowledge of research with your professional common sense, you will find yourself engaged in more effective practices. As you and your students experience success, share your findings. Avenues for

CERTIFICATION POINTER

For teacher certification tests, you may need to show that you know how to access the professional literature, professional associations, and professional development activities to improve your teaching.

dissemination are endless. In addition to publishing articles in traditional sources such as professional journals and organizational newsletters, don't overlook the importance of preparing schoolwide in-service presentations, papers for state and national professional conferences, and presentations to school boards. In addition, the Internet offers various newsgroups where teachers engage in ongoing discussions about their work.

WHAT RESEARCH METHODS ARE USED IN EDUCATIONAL PSYCHOLOGY?

How do we know what we know in educational psychology? As in any scientific field, knowledge comes from many sources. Sometimes researchers study schools, teachers, or students as they are, and sometimes they create special programs, or **treatments,** and study their effects on one or more **variables** (anything that can have more than one value, such as age, sex, achievement level, or attitudes). There is no one best or most useful approach to research; any method can be useful when applied to the right set of questions. The principal methods educational researchers use to learn about schools, teachers, students, and instruction are experiments, correlational studies, and descriptive research. The following sections discuss these methods (see Mertler & Charles, 2005; Slavin, 2007).

Experiments

In an **experiment,** researchers can create special treatments and analyze their effects. In one classic study, Lepper, Greene, and Nisbett (1973) set up an experimental situation in which children used felt-tipped markers to draw pictures. Children in the experimental group (the group that received a treatment) were given a prize (a "good player award") for drawing pictures. Children in a control group received no prizes. At the end of the experiment, all students were allowed to choose among various activities, including drawing with felt-tipped markers. The children who had received the prizes chose to continue drawing with felt-tipped markers about half as frequently as did those who had not received prizes. This result was interpreted as showing that rewarding individuals for doing a task they already liked could reduce their interest in doing the task when they were no longer rewarded.

The Lepper study illustrates several important aspects of experiments. First, the children were randomly assigned to receive prizes or not. For example, the children's names might have been put on slips of paper that were dropped into a hat and then drawn at random for assignment to a "prize" or "no-prize" group. **Random assignment** ensured that the two groups were essentially equivalent before the experiment began. This equivalence is critical because if we were not sure that the two groups were equal before the experiment, we would not be able to tell whether it was the prizes that made the difference in their subsequent behavior.

A second feature of this study that is characteristic of experiments is that everything other than the treatment itself (the prizes) was kept the same for the prize and no-prize groups. The children played in the same rooms with the same materials and with the same adults present. The researcher who gave the prize spent the same amount of time watching the no-prize children draw. Only the prize itself was different for the two groups. The goal was to be sure that it was the treatment, not some other factor, that explained the difference between the two groups.

Laboratory Experiments The Lepper et al. (1973) study is an example of a **laboratory experiment.** Even though the experiment took place in a school building, the researchers created a highly artificial, structured setting that existed for a very brief period

treatment
A special program that is the subject of an experiment.

variable
Something that can have more than one value.

experiment
Procedure used to test the effect of a treatment.

random assignment
Selection by chance into different treatment groups; intended to ensure equivalence of the groups.

laboratory experiment
Experiment in which conditions are highly controlled.

of time. The advantage of laboratory experiments is that they permit researchers to exert a very high degree of control over all the factors involved in the study. Such studies are high in **internal validity,** which is to say that we can confidently attribute any differences they find to the treatments themselves (rather than to other factors). The primary limitation of laboratory experiments is that they are typically so artificial and so brief that their results may have little relevance to real-life situations. For example, the Lepper et al. study, which was later repeated several times, was used to support a theory that rewards can diminish individuals' interest in an activity when the rewards are withdrawn. This theory served as the basis for attacks on the use of classroom rewards, such as grades and stars. However, later research in real classrooms using real rewards has generally failed to find such effects (see Cameron & Pierce, 1994). This finding does not discredit the Lepper and colleagues study; it does show that theories based on artificial laboratory experiments cannot be assumed to apply to all situations in real life but must be tested in the real settings.

Randomized Field Experiments Another kind of experiment that is often used in educational research is the **randomized field experiment,** in which instructional programs or other practical treatments are evaluated over relatively long periods in real classes under realistic conditions (Levin, O'Donnell, & Kratochwill, 2003; Mosteller & Boruch, 2002). For example, Pinnell, Lyons, DeFord, Bryk, and Seltzer (1994) compared four approaches to reading instruction for first-graders who were at risk for reading failure. One of these was Reading Recovery, a one-to-one tutoring model for at-risk first-graders that requires extensive training. In each of 10 schools, the 10 lowest-performing students were identified. Four were assigned at random to the **experimental group** using Reading Recovery, and 6 were assigned to a control group. **Control group** students continued to receive the reading program and remedial services they would have received anyway.

After 4 months (in February), all children were tested. Reading Recovery children scored significantly higher than control students on each of four measures. The following October, students were tested again, and Reading Recovery students still performed significantly higher than control students.

Note the similarities and differences between the Pinnell and colleagues (1994) randomized field experiment and the Lepper and colleagues (1973) laboratory experiment. Both used random assignment to make sure that the experimental and control groups were essentially equal at the start of the study. Both tried to make all factors except the treatment equal for the experimental and control groups, but the Pinnell and colleagues study was (by its very nature as a field experiment) less able to do this. For example, experimental and control students were taught by different teachers. Because many teachers were involved, this factor probably balanced out, but the fact remains that in a field setting, control is never as great as in a laboratory situation (see Pressley & Harris, 1994). On the other hand, the fact that the Pinnell and colleagues study took place over a long period of time in real classrooms means that its **external validity** (real-life validity) is far greater than that of the Lepper et al. study. That is, the results of the Pinnell et al. study have direct relevance to reading instruction for at-risk first-graders.

Both laboratory experiments and randomized field experiments make important contributions to the science of educational psychology. Laboratory experiments are primarily important in researchers' efforts to build and test theories, whereas randomized field experiments are the acid test for evaluating practical programs or improvements in instruction. For example, the writing process method that Leah Washington was using has been evaluated many times in comparison to traditional methods and found to be highly effective (Hillocks, 1984). This finding is not a guarantee that this method will work in every situation, but it does give educators a good direction to follow to improve writing.

Recently, the U.S. Department of Education has begun to strongly emphasize research as a basis for practice in education. For example, in the No Child Left Behind Act of 2001, the phrase "based on scientifically-based research" appears 110 times in reference to programs expected to be used under federal funding. What is meant by "scientifically-based research" is primarily studies in which experimental and control groups were assigned at random (see U.S. Department of Education, 2003), although well-designed studies in which matched groups were compared are also valued. These policies, and new funding to support randomized experiments, have greatly increased interest in

internal validity
The degree to which an experiment's results can be attributed to the treatment in question, not to other factors.

randomized field experiment
Experiment conducted under realistic conditions in which individuals are assigned by chance to receive different practical treatments or programs.

experimental group
Group that receives treatment during an experiment.

control group
Group that receives no special treatment during an experiment.

external validity
Degree to which results of an experiment can be applied to real-life situations.

this type of research. You can expect to see many more randomized studies in the coming years, and these studies will matter a great deal for policy and practice (see Mosteller & Boruch, 2002; Slavin, 2003).

Randomized field experiments are very difficult to do in education, as it is rare that teachers are willing to be assigned by chance to one group or another. For this reason, field experiments more often use matching, in which teachers or schools using one method would be matched with those using a different method, or a control group. For example, Calderón, Hertz-Lazarowitz, and Slavin (1998) evaluated a program called Bilingual Cooperative Integrated Reading and Composition (BCIRC) in El Paso, Texas, elementary schools. English language learners in three schools using BCIRC were matched with those in control groups, based on prior achievement levels, socioeconomic status, and other factors. After pretesting, both sets of schools were followed for 2 years. Students in the BCIRC schools scored higher on reading measures than those in the control schools.

Matching is much more practical than random assignment, but its results must be carefully interpreted because there may be reasons that one group of educators took on one method whereas another group did not. Were the teachers in the treatment group more motivated? Did they have greater resources? On the other hand, were they more desperate to try something new? In a matched study, these possibilities need to be considered and ruled out as much as possible (Mertler & Charles, 2005).

Single-Case Experiments One type of experiment that is occasionally used in educational research is the **single-case experiment** (see Franklin, Allison, & Gorman, 1997; Neuman & McCormick, 1995). In one typical form of this type of experiment, a single student's behavior may be observed for several days. Then a special program is begun, and the student's behavior under the new program is observed. Finally, the new program is withdrawn. If the student's behavior improves under the special program but the improvement disappears when the program is withdrawn, the implication is that the program has affected the student's behavior. Sometimes the "single case" can be several students, an entire class, or a school that is given the same treatment.

An example of a single-case experiment is a classic study by Barrish, Saunders, and Wolf (1969). In this study, a fourth-grade class was the single case. Observers recorded the percentage of time that at least one student in the class was talking out (talking without permission) during reading and math periods. After 10 days, a special program was introduced. The class was divided into 2 large teams, and whenever any student on a team misbehaved, the team was given a check mark. At the end of each day, the team with fewer check marks (or both teams if both received fewer than 5 check marks) could take part in a 30-minute free period.

The results of this study are illustrated in Figure 1.2. Before the Good Behavior Game began (baseline), at least one student in the math class was talking out 96 percent of the time, and at least one student was out-of-seat without permission 82 percent of the time. When the game was begun in math, the class's behavior improved dramatically. When the game was withdrawn, the class's behavior got worse again but improved once more when the game was reintroduced. Note that when the game was introduced in reading class, the students' behaviors also improved. The fact that the program made a difference in both math and reading gives us even greater confidence that the Good Behavior Game is effective.

One important limitation of the single-case experiment is that it can be used only to study outcomes that can be measured frequently. For this reason, most single-case studies involve observable behaviors, such as talking out and being out-of-seat, which can be measured every day or many times per day.

single-case experiment
Experiment that studies a treatment's effect on one person or one group by contrasting behavior before, during, and after application of the treatment.

Correlational Studies

Perhaps the most frequently used research method in educational psychology is the **correlational study.** In contrast to an experiment, in which the researcher deliberately changes one variable to see how this change will affect other variables, in correlational

correlational study
Research into the relationships between variables as they naturally occur.

FIGURE 1.2 Results of Successful Single-Case Experiments

The effect of rewarding good behavior in fourth-grade math and reading classes is clear from these graphs. They show that misbehavior was high during the baseline period (before the Good Behavior Game was introduced) but fell during the game. For instance, in reading session 13, before the game was introduced, students were out of their seats during nearly 100 percent of the observed time intervals. In reading session 53, however, when the game was in use, the percentage of time intervals in which students were out-of-seat approached zero. In single-case experiments on treatments affecting behaviors that can be frequently measured, graphs like these can prove a treatment's effectiveness.

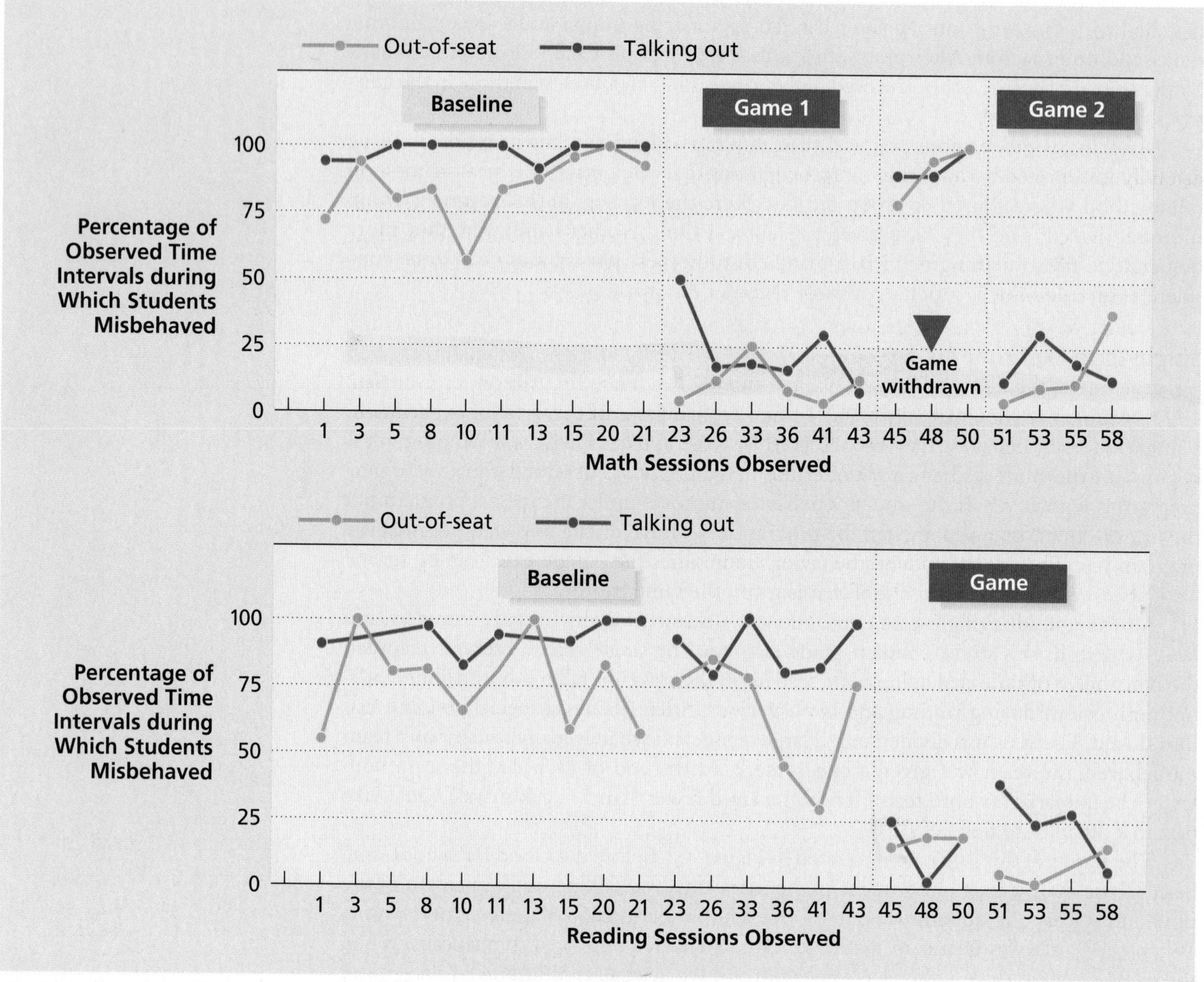

Adapted from H. H. Barrish, M. Saunders, and M. M. Wolf, "Good Behavior Game: Effects of Individual Contingencies for Group Consequences on Disruptive Behavior in a Classroom," *Journal of Applied Behavior Analysis, 2,* 1969, pp. 119–124. Copyright 1969 by the *Journal of Applied Behavior Analysis.* Reprinted by permission.

positive correlation
Relationship in which high levels of one variable correspond to high levels of another.

negative correlation
Relationship in which high levels of one variable correspond to low levels of another.

uncorrelated variables
Variables for which there is no relationship between high/low levels of one and high/low levels of the other.

research the researcher studies variables as they are to see whether they are related. Variables can be positively correlated, negatively correlated, or uncorrelated. An example of a **positive correlation** is the relationship between reading achievement and mathematics achievement. In general, someone who is better than average in reading will also be better than average in math. Of course, some students who are good readers are not good in math, and vice versa; but on the average, skills in one academic area are positively correlated with skills in other academic areas: When one variable is high, the other tends also to be high. An example of a **negative correlation** is days absent and grades. The more days a student is absent, the lower his or her grades are likely to be; when one variable is high, the other tends to be low. With **uncorrelated variables,** in contrast, there is no correspondence between them. For example, student achievement in Poughkeepsie, New York, is probably completely unrelated to the level of student motivation in Portland, Oregon.

One classic example of correlational research is a study by Lahaderne (1968), who investigated the relationship between students' attentiveness in class and their achievements and IQs. She observed 125 students in 4 sixth-grade classes to see how much of the time students were paying attention (e.g., listening to the teacher and doing assigned work). She then correlated attentiveness with achievement in reading, arithmetic, and language and with students' IQs and attitudes toward school. The advantage of correlational studies is that they allow the researcher to study variables as they are, without creating artificial situations. Many important research questions can be studied only in correlational studies. For example, if we wanted to study the relationship between gender and math achievement, we could hardly randomly assign students to be boys or girls! Also, correlational studies let researchers study the interrelationships of many variables at the same time.

The principal disadvantage of correlational methods is that while they may tell us that two variables are related, they do not tell us what causes what. The Lahaderne study of attentiveness, achievement, and IQ raised the question: Does student attentiveness cause high achievement, or are high-ability, high-achieving students simply more attentive than other students? A correlational study cannot answer this question completely. However, correlational researchers do typically use statistical methods to try to determine what causes what. In Lahaderne's study, it would have been possible to find out whether, among students with the same IQ, attentiveness was related to achievement. For example, given two students of average intelligence, will the one who is more attentive tend to achieve more? If not, then we may conclude that the relationship between attentiveness and achievement is simply the result of high-IQ students being more attentive and higher achieving than other students, not the result of any effect of attention on achievement.

Figure 1.3 illustrates two possible explanations for the correlation between attentiveness, achievement, and IQ. In Explanation A, attentiveness causes achievement. In Explanation B, both attentiveness and achievement are assumed to be caused by a third variable, IQ. Which is correct? Evidence from other research on this relationship suggests that both explanations are partially correct—that even when the effect of IQ is removed, student attentiveness is related to achievement.

Another illustration of correlational research is a study by Lubienski and Lubienski (2006). The study used data from the National Assessment of Education Progress (NAEP) to ask whether public or private schools produce better reading and math performance.

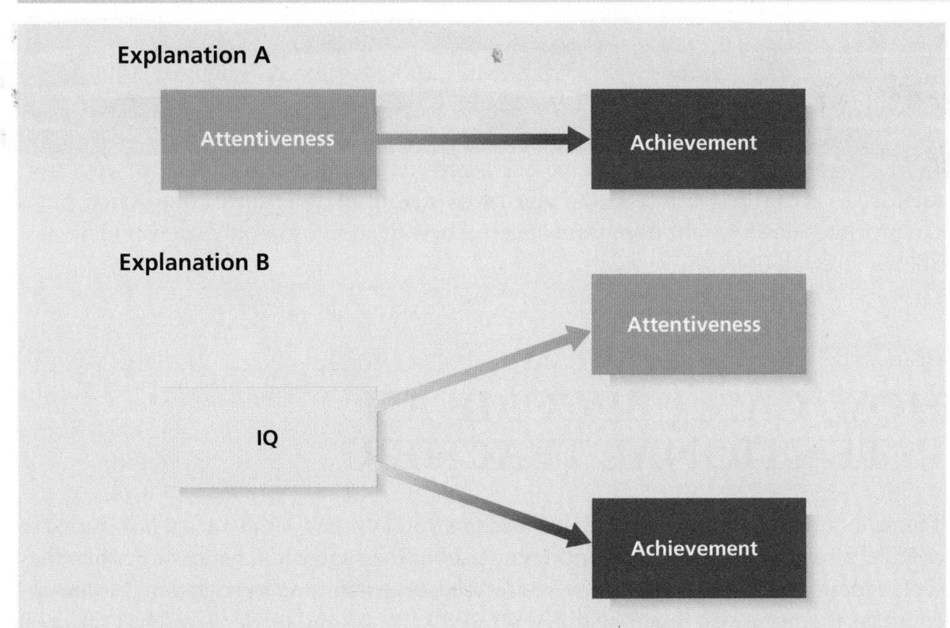

FIGURE 1.3 Possible Explanations for Correlations among Attentiveness, Achievement, and IQ
Correlational studies can show that variables are related, but such studies cannot prove what causes what. In Lahaderne's (1968) study, for example, did the attentiveness of the students cause higher achievement scores (Explanation A), or did a third factor—intelligence—determine both attentiveness and performance on achievement tests (as diagrammed in Explanation B)? Both explanations are partially correct.

Of course, students in private schools have higher achievement scores, but statistically controlling for students' ethnicity, wealth, and other background factors, the researchers found that public school students scored at least as well as similar students in private schools.

Descriptive Research

CONNECTIONS
For more on the use of descriptive research in developmental psychology, see Chapters 2 and 3.

Experimental research and correlational research look for relationships between variables. However, some research in educational psychology simply seeks to describe something of interest. For example, the NICHD Early Child Care Research Network (2005) did a national observational study in 780 third-grade classrooms to describe the wide range of classroom environments children experience. Among other things, the study found that most time in third grade focuses on basic skills, with little time for higher-order skills, but there was enormous variation. In another example, Mosenthal et al. (2004) observed and described six schools in Vermont that consistently had extraordinary reading scores, and found that such schools had particularly focused teachers who constantly evaluated their own teaching. One type of **descriptive research** is a survey or interview. Another, called ethnography, involves observation of a social setting (such as a classroom or school) over an extended period. As an example of ethnography, Anagnostopoulos (2006) spent a year in a Chicago high school observing and interviewing teachers and students to understand their response to a new policy that required students to pass a test to be promoted to the next grade. She found that both students and teachers mentally divided retained students into two categories: "true demotes" and "real students," where the "true demotes" were "bad kids" who deserved to be retained and the "real students" were students who, they thought, did not really deserve to be retained. Descriptive studies provide a much more complete story of what happens in schools and classrooms than could a study that boiled down the findings into cold, hard numbers. Descriptive research usually does not have the scientific objectivity of correlational or experimental research, but it makes up for this lack in richness of detail and interpretation (Creswell, 2002; Northcutt & McCoy, 2004; Rossman & Rallis, 2003).

Developmental psychologists use descriptive research extensively to identify characteristics of children at different ages. The most important research in developmental psychology was done by the Swiss psychologist Jean Piaget (1952b), who began by carefully observing his own children. As a result of his observations, he developed a theory that describes the cognitive development of children from infancy through adolescence (Wadsworth, 2004).

Action Research

Action research is a particular form of descriptive research that is carried out by educators in their own classrooms or schools (Mills, 2000; Reason & Bradbury, 2001). In action research, a teacher or principal might try out a new teaching method or school organization strategy, collect information about how it worked, and communicate this information to others. Because the people involved in the experiment are the educators themselves, action research lacks the objectivity sought in other forms of research, but it can provide deeper insight from front-line teachers or administrators than would be possible in research done by outsiders.

INTASC

9 **Professional Commitment and Responsibility**

HOW CAN I BECOME AN INTENTIONAL TEACHER?

Think about the best, most intentional teachers you ever had—the ones who seemed so confident, so caring, so skilled, so enthusiastic about their subject. Chances are, when they took educational psychology, they were as scared, uncertain, and overwhelmed about becoming a teacher as you might be today. Yet they kept at it and made themselves the great teachers you remember. You can do the same.

descriptive research
Research study aimed at identifying and gathering detailed information about something of interest.

action research
Research carried out by educators in their own classrooms or schools.

Personal REFLECTION

INTASC 8 Assessment of Student Learning

Using Research to Inform Teaching

As a graduate student, I conducted a study in a residential school for students with emotional and behavioral disorders. The study involved observing the behavior of a group of children who were 9 to 11 years old. The school had a program in which children earned points based on their behavior and could exchange points for various privileges or materials.

Despite my attempts to be as unobtrusive as possible, I was writing notes on a clipboard, and the children were curious about what I was writing. One day, a girl in the class used her points to obtain a clipboard. She put a sheaf of paper on her clipboard and then spent all day walking around writing down all the bad things her classmates were doing. For example, she'd say, "James, I'm giving you another bad mark for not helping clean up."

Of course, the other kids couldn't tolerate this for long, and soon they too used their points to get clipboards. They all then spent every free moment writing each other up for bad behavior, real or imagined. Worst of all, they started writing down bad things about me!

My study was ruined, but I learned firsthand about what is sometimes called Heisenberg's Uncertainty Principle: Studying something may change what you're studying. Research in education always involves people, and people act differently when they're being studied. For this and many other reasons, even research findings with a ton of data should be taken with a grain of salt.

REFLECT ON THIS. Why was my study ruined? What lesson can you learn from this example about using research to be an effective teacher?

Teacher Certification

Before you can become an *intentional* teacher, you have to become a *certified* teacher. Each state, province, and country has its own requirements, but in most places you at least have to graduate from a four-year college with a specified distribution of courses. Various alternative certification programs exist as well. You also will need to have a satisfactory student teaching experience. In most states, however, graduation is not enough. You also have to pass a *teacher certification test,* or *licensure test.* Many states base their requirements on the 10 principles of effective teaching developed by the Interstate New Teacher Assessment and Support Consortium (INTASC) shown in Figure 1.4. They form the basis for most teacher certification tests, whether they are tests developed by INTASC, by the Education Testing Service, or by individual state departments of education.

INTASC has developed its own *Test for Teaching Knowledge (TTK).* This is a test that assesses new teachers' knowledge of child development; theories of teaching and learning, assessment, and language acquisition; the role of student background in the learning process; and other basic knowledge and skills important for teaching. Some states are beginning to use this test. To read more about the TTK, visit the Council of Chief State School Officers (CCSSO) website at www.ccsso.org/intasc.

The Praxis Series: Professional Assessments for Beginning Teachers, developed by Educational Testing Service, is the most common test used by states to certify teachers. The Praxis Series includes three categories of assessment that correlate to significant stages in teacher development: Praxis I: Academic Skills Assessment for entering a teacher training program, Praxis II: Subject Assessments for licensure for entering the profession, and Praxis III: Classroom Performance Assessments after the first year of teaching. Praxis II would be the test you would take on completing your teacher preparation program. It offers three principles of learning and teaching (PLT) tests that relate to the content in educational psychology—one for grades K to 6, one for 5 to 9, and one for 7 to 12. These tests cover content in four areas: students as learners, instruction and assessment, communication techniques, and teacher professionalism.

FIGURE 1.4 Interstate New Teacher Assessment and Support Consortium (INTASC) Standards for Beginning Teacher Licensing and Development

From Council of Chief State School Officers, *Model Standards for Beginning Teacher Licensing, Assessment, and Development: A Resource for State Dialogue.* Washington, DC: Author. www.ccsso.org/content/pdfs/corestrd.pdf. The Interstate New Teacher Assessment and Support Consortium (INTASC) standards were developed by the Council of Chief State School Officers and member states. Copies may by downloaded from the council's website at www.ccsso.org.

1. ***Knowledge of Subject Matter:*** The teacher understands the central concepts, tools of inquiry, and structures of the subject being taught and can create learning experiences that make these aspects of subject matter meaningful for students.
2. ***Knowledge of Human Development and Learning:*** The teacher understands how children learn and develop, and can provide learning opportunities that support their intellectual, social, and personal development.
3. ***Adapting Instruction for Individual Needs:*** The teacher understands how students differ in their approaches to learning and creates instructional opportunities that are adapted to diverse learners.
4. ***Multiple Instructional Strategies:*** The teacher uses various instructional strategies to encourage students' development of critical thinking, problem solving, and performance skills.
5. ***Classroom Motivation and Management:*** The teacher uses an understanding of individual and group motivation and behavior to create a learning environment that encourages positive social interaction, active engagement in learning, and self-motivation.
6. ***Communication Skills:*** The teacher uses knowledge of effective verbal, nonverbal, and media communication techniques to foster active inquiry, collaboration, and supportive interaction in the classroom.
7. ***Instructional Planning Skills:*** The teacher plans instruction based upon knowledge of subject matter, students, the community, and curriculum goals.
8. ***Assessment of Student Learning:*** The teacher understands and uses formal and informal assessment strategies to evaluate and ensure the continuous intellectual, social and physical development of the learner.
9. ***Professional Commitment and Responsibility:*** The teacher is a reflective practitioner who continually evaluates the effects of his or her choices and actions on others (students, parents, and other professionals in the learning community) and who actively seeks out opportunities to grow professionally.
10. ***Partnerships:*** The teacher fosters relationships with school colleagues, parents, and agencies in the larger community to support students' learning and well-being.

Each PLT test has four scenarios followed by three short-answer questions related to the scenario. There are also 24 multiple-choice questions, for a total of 36 questions. Detailed information about the Praxis series of tests can be found at www.ets.org/praxis. From this website you can access the tests-at-a-glance page, which includes test outlines, sample questions with explanations for the best answers, and test-taking strategies. There is also a list of state-by-state requirements to determine which Praxis tests each state uses, if any. Note that individual universities may also use Praxis, even if their states do not require it.

Each state, province, or institution that uses the Praxis tests sets its own passing requirements. The passing score for each test for each state is listed on the website and in a booklet you receive with your score report.

Many states, including California, Texas, Florida, and New York, have developed or are developing their own teacher certification tests. These usually include sections much like the Praxis Principles of Learning and Teaching.

Throughout this book you will find tips on topics likely to appear on teacher certification tests. These marginal notes, called *Certification Pointers,* highlight knowledge that is frequently required on state teacher licensure exams, including Praxis Principles of Learning and Teaching.

Beyond Certification

Getting a teaching certificate is necessary but not sufficient to become an intentional teacher. Starting with your student teaching experience and continuing into your first job, you can create or take advantage of opportunities to develop your skills as an intentional teacher in a number of ways.

Seek Mentors Experienced teachers who are themselves intentional teachers are your best resource. Not only are they highly effective, but they also understand and can describe what they're doing (and, hopefully, can help you learn to do those things). Talk with experienced teachers in your school, ask to observe them teaching, and ask them to observe you and share ideas, as Ellen Mathis did in the vignette at the beginning of this chapter. Many school systems provide induction programs for new teachers to help them develop in those crucial first years, but even if yours does not provide such a program, you can create one for yourself by seeking out experienced and helpful mentors.

Seek Professional Development Districts, universities, state departments of education, and other institutions provide all sorts of professional development workshops for teachers on a wide range of topics. Take advantage of every opportunity to participate. The best professional development includes some sort of coaching or follow-up, in which someone who knows a given technique or program comes to your class to observe you trying to use the program and gives you feedback (see Joyce, Calhoun, & Hopkins, 1999; Neufield & Roper, 2003). Workshops in which many teachers from your school participate together, and then have opportunities to discuss successes and challenges, can also be very effective (see Calderón, 1999).

CERTIFICATION POINTER

Teacher certification tests include a section on teacher professionalism. One aspect that is emphasized is being able to read and understand research on current ideas and debates about teaching practices.

Talk Teaching Talk to your colleagues, your former classmates, your friends who teach, even your friends who don't teach. Share your successes, your failures, your questions. Teaching can be an isolating experience if it's just you and the kids. Take every opportunity to share ideas and commiserate with sympathetic colleagues.

ON THE WEB

When your friends and colleagues are worn out from your passion for teaching, try virtual colleagues on the Web. Teacher-oriented websites offer opportunities to share advice, opinions, and observations. A few examples include:

Education World: **www.education-world.com**
The Knowledge Loom: **www.knowledgeloom.org**
K–12 Professional Circle: **www.nces.ed.gov/practitioners/teachers.asp**
The Vent: **www.proteacher.com**

CERTIFICATION POINTER

The teacher professionalism section of Praxis II and other certification tests may ask you to know the titles of several professional journals in your particular field of teaching (e.g., *Journal of Educational Psychology, Educational Leadership, Phi Delta Kappan*).

Keep Up with Professional Publications and Associations Intentional teachers do a lot of reading. Your school may subscribe to teacher-oriented journals, or you might choose to do so. For example, look for *Teacher Magazine, Theory into Practice, Learning, Young Children, Phi Delta Kappan, Educational Leadership,* or subject-specific journals such as the *Reading Teacher* and *Mathematics Teacher.*

In addition, check out professional associations in your subject area or area of interest. The national teachers' unions—the American Federation of Teachers (AFT) and National Education Association (NEA)—have publications, workshops, and other resources from which you can benefit greatly. Your state department of education, regional educational laboratory, or school district office may also have useful resources. A few useful websites include the following:

American Educational Research Association: www.aera.net
American Federation of Teachers: www.aft.org
Canadian Educational Research Association: www.cea-ace.ca
Council for Exceptional Children: www.cec.sped.org
International Reading Association: www.reading.org

CERTIFICATION POINTER

Teaching certification tests might expect you to know what professional associations offer meetings, publications, and dialogue with other teachers (e.g., American Educational Research Association, International Reading Association, American Federation of Teachers, National Education Association).

National Association for Bilingual Education: www.nabe.org
National Association for the Education of Young Children: www.naeyc.org
National Association of Black School Educators: www.nabse.org
National Council for the Social Studies: www.ncss.org
National Council of Teachers of English: www.ncte.org
National Council of Teachers of Mathematics: www.nctm.org
National Education Association: www.nea.org
National Institute for Literacy: www.nifl.gov
National Middle School Association: www.nmsa.org
National Science Teachers Association: www.nsta.org

Teaching Dilemmas: CASES TO CONSIDER

Choosing a New Curriculum

INTASC

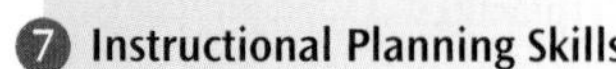

7 Instructional Planning Skills

Jane Spivak and Maurice Brown are both teachers at the elementary level. Susana Rubio teaches in the district's high school. John Hammond coordinates the K–12 math curriculum and teaches at the middle school. Together they serve on a districtwide committee whose job is to evaluate the current math program and choose a new one.

Jane: I like some of the new programs we've looked at. They incorporate problem-solving strategies even in first grade, and they encourage cooperative learning.

John: But do they teach the basic skills? I mean, we're still getting kids in the sixth grade who don't know their basic math facts.

Susana: I agree, but they definitely need more critical thinking about math at earlier ages if they are going to handle some of the expectations at the high school level.

Maurice: I think these would work out great if you started the kids with it in kindergarten, but how about the upper grades? Are you just going to switch them from the relatively traditional program we have now into one that is much more problem-solving oriented and less teacher directed?

John: OK, OK. Another consideration is the expense of these programs, both in time and money to us and the district. I think we all agree that the easiest thing would be to keep what we've got, but the students need more.

Susana: How about a pilot study? You know, purchase materials for one or two classes at selected grade levels and do a careful comparison. We can find out both the difficulties and the benefits, then make our decision. We've certainly done some research already—the workshops we've gone to, visits to other schools using the program. But why don't we do some research of our own?

Jane: OK, but it will have to be well done with a matched control group class using the old program for each one piloting the new. We should compare how each class does at reaching the same set of objectives we've decided on for those grade levels.

Susana: I want some qualitative feedback from teachers too. Maybe some rating scales. We could send a questionnaire home to parents.

QUESTIONS FOR REFLECTION

1. What are the benefits of this type of curriculum evaluation? What might be the drawbacks and limitations?
2. Devise an outline of the proposed research to compare the two curricular approaches.
3. Extend the discussion with the system superintendent. He doesn't want to spend the time or money on research before choosing a curriculum. How will the teachers defend their need for personal research?

ONLINE READING & WRITING EXERCISE
To Blog or Not To Blog, That Is The Question

One of the ways you may want (or your professor may want) you to reflect on your learning in this course is by *blogging* about it. This Online Reading & Writing Exercise will direct you to online material about educational psychology and provide writing prompts to help you respond to the material on a blog you create for this very purpose. You can access this exercise, entitled "To Blog or Not To Blog, That Is The Question," in the Homework and Exercises section for Chapter 1 of this text at **www.mylabschool.com.**

CHAPTER 1 SUMMARY

What Makes a Good Teacher?

Good teachers know their subject matter and have mastered pedagogical skills. They accomplish all the tasks involved in effective instruction with warmth, enthusiasm, and caring. They are intentional teachers, and they use principles of educational psychology in their decision making and teaching. They combine research and common sense.

What Is the Role of Research in Educational Psychology?

Educational psychology is the systematic study of learners, learning, and teaching. Research in educational psychology focuses on the processes by which information, skills, values, and attitudes are communicated between teachers and students in the classroom and on applications of the principles of psychology to instructional practices. Such research shapes educational policies, professional development programs, and teaching materials.

What Research Methods Are Used in Educational Psychology?

Experimental research involves testing particular educational programs or treatments. Random assignment of experimental subjects into groups before the testing helps to ensure that groups are equivalent and findings will be valid. An experimental group receiving the treatment is matched with a control group whose members do not receive treatment. Laboratory experiments are highly structured and short term. All the variables involved are strictly controlled. Randomized field experiments are less structured and take place over a long period of time under realistic conditions in which not all variables can be controlled. A single-case experiment involves observation of one student or group of students over a specified period before and after treatment. Correlational studies examine variables to see whether they are related. Variables can be positively correlated, negatively correlated, or uncorrelated. Correlational studies provide information about variables without manipulating them or creating artificial situations. However, they do not indicate the causes of relationships between variables. Descriptive research uses surveys, interviews, and/or observations to describe behavior in social settings.

KEY TERMS

Review the following key terms from the chapter.

action research 20
control group 16
correlational study 17
critical thinking 7
descriptive research 20
educational psychology 2
experiment 15
experimental group 16
external validity 16
intentionality 5
internal validity 16
laboratory experiment 15
negative correlation 18
pedagogy 3
positive correlation 18
principle 9
random assignment 15
randomized field experiment 16
single-case experiment 17
teacher efficacy 7
theory 9
treatment 15
uncorrelated variables 18
variable 15

SELF-ASSESSMENT: PRACTICING *for* LICENSURE

Directions: The chapter-opening vignette addresses indicators that are often assessed in state licensure exams. Re-read the chapter-opening vignette, and then respond to the following questions.

1. In the first paragraph, Ellen Mathis does not understand why her students are nonproductive and unimaginative. According to educational psychology research, which of the following teacher characteristics is Ellen most likely lacking?
   - **a.** classroom management skills
   - **b.** content knowledge
   - **c.** intentionality
   - **d.** common sense

2. Leah Washington talks with Ellen Mathis about getting students to write interesting compositions. Which of the following statements summarizes Leah's approach to teaching writing?
   - **a.** Select teaching methods, learning activities, and instructional materials that are appropriate and motivating for students.
   - **b.** Have students of similar abilities work together so the teacher can adapt instruction to meet the needs of each group.
   - **c.** When working on writing activities, consider the teacher to be the instruction center.
   - **d.** Individualization is the first goal of instruction; direct instruction is the second goal.

3. According to research on expertise development, what characteristic separates novice teachers from expert teachers?
   - **a.** Novice teachers tend to rely on their pedagogical skills because their content knowledge is less complex than an expert's.
   - **b.** Expert teachers do more short-term memory processing than novices because their thinking is more complex.
   - **c.** Novice teachers have to constantly upgrade and examine their own teaching practices, whereas experts use a "best practices" approach.
   - **d.** Expert teachers are critical thinkers.

4. Educational psychologists are often accused of studying the obvious. However, they have learned that the obvious is not always true. All of the following statements demonstrate this idea except one. Which one is obvious *and* supported by research?
   - **a.** Student achievement is increased when students are assigned to classes according to their ability.
   - **b.** Scolding students for misbehavior improves student behavior.
   - **c.** Whole-class instruction is more effective than individualized instruction.
   - **d.** Intentional teachers balance competing goals according to the needs of particular students and situations.

5. Leah Washington discusses many of her teaching strategies with Ellen Mathis. One can easily see that Leah views teaching as a decision-making process. She recognizes problems and issues, considers situations from multiple perspectives, calls on her professional knowledge to formulate action, and
   - **a.** selects the most appropriate action and judges the consequence.
   - **b.** chooses a strategy that agrees with her individual beliefs about teaching.
   - **c.** consults with expert teachers and administrators to assist with her plan of action.
   - **d.** allows students to make instructional decisions based on their interests and needs.

6. The products of research are principles, laws, and theories. Leah Washington describes many principles and theories of educational psychology as she speaks with Ellen Mathis about teaching students to write compositions. First, describe an instruction action with which Ellen Mathis is having difficulties (e.g., Ellen assigns all students the same topic), and then describe principles and theories she can use to engage her students in exciting and meaningful lessons.

7. The goal of research in educational psychology is to examine questions of teaching and learning using objective methods. These research methods include experiments, correlational studies, descriptive research, and action research. Think of a research question, and then describe how you would go about answering your question using these methods.

8. Intentional teachers are aware of resources available for professional learning. They continually refine their practices to address the needs of all students. List four actions you could take to find information to help you teach your students with limited English proficiency.

Where the Classroom Comes to Life

Now go to **www.myeducationlab.com** to:

- take a Pretest to assess your initial comprehension of the chapter content;
- study chapter content with your individualized Study Plan;
- take a Posttest to assess your understanding of chapter content;
- practice your teaching skills with Building Teaching Skills exercises; and
- build a deeper, more applied understanding of chapter content with Homework and Exercises.

CHAPTER 2

Theories of Development

chapter OUTLINE

Over the course of their first 18 years of life, children go through astounding changes. Most of these changes are obvious—children get bigger, smarter, more socially adept, and so on. However, many aspects of development are not so obvious. Individual children develop in different ways and at different rates, and development is influenced by biology, culture, parenting, education, and other factors. Every teacher needs to understand how children grow and develop to be able to understand how children learn and how best to teach them (Comer, 2005). Consider the following vignettes.

- In the first week of school, Mr. Jones tried to teach his first-graders how to behave in class. He said, "When I ask a question, I want you to raise your right hand, and I'll call on you. Can you all raise your right hands, as I am doing?" Twenty hands went up. All were left hands.
- Because her students were getting careless about handing in their homework, Ms. Lewis decided to lay down the law to her fourth-grade class. "Anyone who does not hand in all his or her homework this week will not be allowed to go on the field trip." It happened that one girl's mother became ill and was taken to the hospital that week. As a result of her family's confusion and concern, the girl failed to hand in one of her homework assignments. Ms. Lewis explained to the class that she would make an exception in this case because of the girl's mother's illness, but the class wouldn't hear of it. "Rules are rules," they said. "She didn't hand in her homework, so she can't go!"
- Ms. Quintera started her eighth-grade English class one day with an excited announcement: "Class, I wanted to tell you all that we have a poet in our midst. Frank wrote such a wonderful poem that I thought I'd read it to you all." Ms. Quintera read Frank's poem, which was indeed very good. However, she noticed that Frank was turning bright red and looking distinctly uncomfortable. A few of the other students in the class snickered. Later, Ms. Quintera asked Frank whether he would like to write another poem for a citywide poetry contest. He said he'd rather not, because he really didn't think he was that good; and besides, he didn't have the time.

USING *your* EXPERIENCE

CRITICAL THINKING Why do you think Frank reacted the way he did? How could Ms. Quintera alter her approach so as to motivate Frank?

CRITICAL THINKING Compare and contrast these three scenarios. Explain which case(s) involved a behavioral, cognitive, social, moral, or physical development dilemma. Specify the dilemma.

WHAT ARE SOME VIEWS OF HUMAN DEVELOPMENT?

INTASC

2 Knowledge of Human Development and Learning

The term **development** refers to how people grow, adapt, and change over the course of their lifetimes, through physical development, personality development, socioemotional development, cognitive development (thinking), and language development. This chapter presents five major theories of human development that are widely accepted: Jean Piaget's theories of cognitive and moral development, Lev Vygotsky's theory of cognitive development, Erik Erikson's theory of personal and social development, and Lawrence Kohlberg's theory of moral development.

Aspects of Development

Children are not miniature adults. They think differently, they see the world differently, and they live by different moral and ethical principles than adults do. The three scenarios just presented illustrate a few of the many aspects of children's thinking that differ from those of adults. When Mr. Jones raised his right hand, his first-graders imitated his action without taking his perspective; they didn't realize that because he was facing them, his right hand would be to their left. The situation in Ms. Lewis's class illustrates a stage in children's moral development at which rules are rules and extenuating circumstances do not count. Ms. Quintera's praise of Frank's poem had an effect opposite to what she intended, but had she paused to consider the situation, she might have realized that highlighting Frank's achievement could cast him in the role of teacher's pet, a role that many students in early adolescence strongly resist.

One of the first requirements of effective teaching is that the teacher understand how students think and how they view the world. Effective teaching strategies must take into account students' ages and stages of development. A bright fourth-grader might appear to be able to learn any kind of mathematics but in fact might not have the cognitive maturity to do the abstract thinking required for algebra. Similarly, Ms. Quintera's public recognition of Frank's poetry might have been quite appropriate if Frank had been 3 years younger or 3 years older.

Issues of Development

Two central issues have been debated for decades among developmental psychologists. One relates to the degree to which development is affected by experience, and the other to the question of whether development proceeds in stages.

development
Orderly and lasting growth, adaptation, and change over the course of a lifetime.

Nature–Nurture Controversy Is development predetermined at birth, by heredity and biological factors, or is it affected by experience and other environmental factors? Today, most developmental psychologists (e.g., Bee & Boyd, 2007; Berk, 2006, Cook &

Cook, 2007; Fabes & Martin, 2000) believe that nature and nurture combine to influence development, with biological factors playing a stronger role in some aspects, such as physical development, and environmental factors playing a stronger role in others, such as moral development.

Continuous and Discontinuous Theories A second issue revolves around the notion of how change occurs. **Continuous theories of development** assume that development occurs in a smooth progression as skills develop and experiences are provided by parents and the environment. Continuous theories emphasize the importance of environment rather than heredity in determining development.

A second perspective assumes that children progress through a set of predictable and invariant stages of development. In this case, change can be fairly abrupt as children advance to a new stage of development. All children are believed to acquire skills in the same sequence, although rates of progress differ from child to child. The abilities that children gain in each subsequent stage are not simply "more of the same"; at each stage, children develop qualitatively different understandings, abilities, and beliefs. Skipping stages is impossible, although at any given point the same child may exhibit behaviors characteristic of more than one stage (Zigler & Gilman, 1998). In contrast to continuous theories, these **discontinuous theories of development** focus on inborn factors rather than environmental influences to explain change over time. Environmental conditions may have some influence on the pace of development, but the sequence of developmental steps is essentially fixed.

Piaget, Vygotsky, Erikson, and Kohlberg focus on different aspects of development. Nevertheless, all are stage theorists, because they share the belief that distinct stages of development can be identified and described. This agreement does not, however, extend to the particulars of their theories, which differ significantly in the numbers of stages and in their details. Also, each theorist focuses on different aspects of development (e.g., cognitive, socioemotional, personality, moral).

Today, most developmentalists acknowledge the role of both inborn factors and experience when explaining children's behavior (see Bronfenbrenner & Morris, 1998; Cook & Cook, 2007). Vygotsky's theories in particular rely on social interactions as well as predictable stages of growth to explain development.

HOW DID PIAGET VIEW COGNITIVE DEVELOPMENT?

Jean Piaget, born in Switzerland in 1896, is the most influential developmental psychologist in the history of psychology (see Flavell, 1996; Wadsworth, 2004). After receiving his doctorate in biology, he became more interested in psychology, basing his earliest theories on careful observation of his own three children. Piaget thought of himself as applying biological principles and methods to the study of human development, and many of the terms he introduced to psychology were drawn directly from biology.

Piaget explored both why and how mental abilities change over time. For Piaget, development depends in large part on the child's manipulation of and active interaction with the environment. In Piaget's view, knowledge comes from action (see Langer & Killen, 1998; Wadsworth, 2004). Piaget's theory of **cognitive development** proposes that a child's intellect, or cognitive abilities, progresses through four distinct stages. Each stage is characterized by the emergence of new abilities and ways of processing information. Many of the specifics of Piaget's theories have been challenged in later research. In particular, many of the changes in cognitive functioning he described are now known to take place earlier, under certain circumstances. Nevertheless, Piaget's work forms an essential basis for understanding child development.

continuous theories of development
Theories based on the belief that human development progresses smoothly and gradually from infancy to adulthood.

discontinuous theories of development
Theories describing human development as occurring through a fixed sequence of distinct, predictable stages governed by inborn factors.

cognitive development
Gradual, orderly changes by which mental processes become more complex and sophisticated.

How Development Occurs

CONNECTIONS

For information on schema theory (a topic related to schemes) in connection with information processing and memory, see Chapter 6, pages 164 and 182.

Schemes Piaget believed that all children are born with an innate tendency to interact with and make sense of their environments. He referred to the basic ways of organizing and processing information as cognitive structures. Young children demonstrate patterns of behavior or thinking, called **schemes,** that older children and adults also use in dealing with objects in the world. We use schemes to find out about and act in the world; each scheme treats all objects and events in the same way. For example, most young infants will discover that one thing you can do with objects is bang them. When they do this, the object makes a noise, and they see the object hitting a surface. Their observations tell them something about the object. Babies also learn about objects by biting them, sucking on them, and throwing them. Each of these approaches to interacting with objects is a scheme. When babies encounter a new object, how are they to know what this object is all about? According to Piaget, they will use the schemes they have developed and will find out whether the object makes a loud or soft sound when banged, what it tastes like, whether it gives milk, and maybe whether it rolls or just goes thud when dropped (see Figure 2.1a).

Assimilation and Accommodation According to Piaget, **adaptation** is the process of adjusting schemes in response to the environment by means of assimilation and accommodation. **Assimilation** is the process of understanding a new object or event in terms of an existing scheme. If you give young infants small objects that they have never seen before but that resemble familiar objects, they are likely to grasp them, bite them, and bang them. In other words, they will try to use existing schemes to learn about these unknown things (see Figure 2.1b). Similarly, a high school student may have a studying scheme that involves putting information on cards and memorizing the cards' contents. She may then try to apply this scheme to learn difficult concepts such as economics, for which this approach may not be effective.

ON THE WEB

For more on Piaget's life and work go to **www.oikos.org/Piagethom.htm.**

Sometimes, when old ways of dealing with the world simply don't work, a child might modify an existing scheme in light of new information or a new experience, a process called **accommodation.** For example, if you give an egg to a baby who has a banging scheme for small objects, what will happen to the egg is obvious (Figure 2.1c). Less obvious, however, is what will happen to the baby's banging scheme. Because of the unexpected consequences of banging the egg, the baby might change the scheme. In the future the baby might bang some objects hard and others softly. The high school student who studies only by means of memorization might learn to use a different strategy to study economics, such as discussing difficult concepts with a friend.

The baby who banged the egg and the student who tried to memorize rather than comprehend had to deal with situations that could not be fully handled by existing schemes. This, in Piaget's theory, creates a state of disequilibrium, or an imbalance between what is understood and what is encountered. People naturally try to reduce such imbalances by focusing on the stimuli that cause the disequilibrium and developing new schemes or adapting old ones until equilibrium is restored. This process of restoring balance is called **equilibration.** According to Piaget, learning depends on this process. When equilibrium is upset, children have the opportunity to grow and develop. Eventually, qualitatively new ways of thinking about the world emerge, and children advance to a new stage of development. Piaget believed that physical experiences and manipulation of the environment are critical for developmental change to occur. However, he also believed that social interaction with peers, especially arguments and discussions, helps to clarify thinking and, eventually, to make it more logical. Research has stressed the importance of confronting students with experiences or data that do not fit into their current

schemes
Mental patterns that guide behavior.

adaptation
The process of adjusting schemes in response to the environment by means of assimilation and accommodation.

assimilation
Understanding new experiences in terms of existing schemes.

accommodation
Modifying existing schemes to fit new situations.

equilibration
The process of restoring balance between present understanding and new experiences.

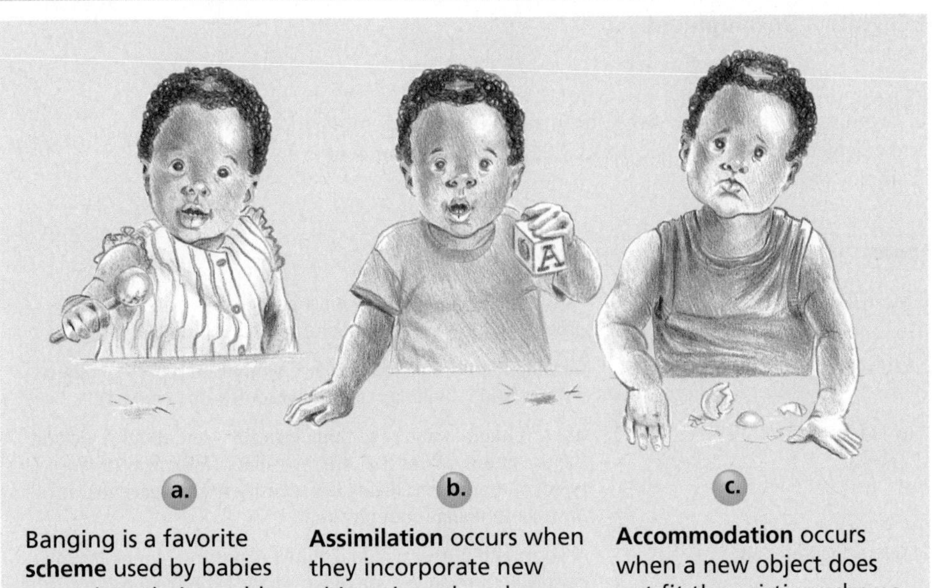

a.
Banging is a favorite **scheme** used by babies to explore their world.
b.
Assimilation occurs when they incorporate new objects into the scheme.
c.
Accommodation occurs when a new object does not fit the existing scheme.

FIGURE 2.1 Schemes
Babies use patterns of behavior called *schemes* to learn about their world.

theories of how the world works as a means of advancing their cognitive development (Chinn & Brewer, 1993).

Piaget's theory of development represents **constructivism,** a view of cognitive development as a process in which children actively build systems of meaning and understandings of reality through their experiences and interactions (Berk, 2006; Cook & Cook, 2007; Wadsworth, 2004). In this view, children actively construct knowledge by continually assimilating and accommodating new information. Applications of constructivist theories to education are discussed in Chapter 8.

CERTIFICATION POINTER

Most teacher certification tests will require you to know that a constructivist approach to learning emphasizes the active role that learners play in building their own understandings.

Piaget's Stages of Development

Piaget divided the cognitive development of children and adolescents into four stages: sensorimotor, preoperational, concrete operational, and formal operational. He believed that all children pass through these stages in this order and that no child can skip a stage, although different children pass through the stages at somewhat different rates (see de Ribaupierre & Rieben, 1995). The same individuals may perform tasks associated with different stages at the same time, particularly at points of transition into a new stage. Table 2.1 summarizes the approximate ages at which children and adolescents pass through Piaget's four stages. It also shows the major accomplishments of each stage.

Sensorimotor Stage (Birth to Age 2) The earliest stage is called **sensorimotor** because during this stage babies and young children explore their world by using their senses and their motor skills.

Piaget believed that all children are born with an innate tendency to interact with and make sense of their environments. Dramatic changes occur as infants progress through the sensorimotor period. Initially, all infants have inborn behaviors called **reflexes.** Touch a newborn's lips, and the baby will begin to suck; place your finger in the palm of an infant's hand, and the infant will grasp it. These and other behaviors are innate and are the building blocks from which the infant's first schemes form.

Infants soon learn to use these reflexes to produce more interesting and intentional patterns of behavior. This learning occurs initially through accident and then through more intentional trial-and-error efforts. According to Piaget, by the end of the sensorimotor stage, children have progressed from their earlier trial-and-error approach to a more planned approach to problem solving. For the first time they can mentally represent objects and events. What most of us would call "thinking" appears now. This is a major advance because it means that the child can think through and plan behavior. For example, suppose a 2-year-old

constructivism
View of cognitive development that emphasizes the active role of learners in building their own understanding of reality.

sensorimotor stage
Stage during which infants learn about their surroundings by using their senses and motor skills.

reflexes
Inborn, automatic responses to stimuli (e.g., eye blinking in response to bright light).

TABLE 2.1 Piaget's Stages of Cognitive Development

People progress through four stages of cognitive development between birth and adulthood, according to Jean Piaget. Each stage is marked by the emergence of new intellectual abilities that allow people to understand the world in increasingly complex ways.

Stage	Approximate Ages	Major Accomplishments
Sensorimotor	Birth to 2 years	Formation of concept of "object permanence" and gradual progression from reflexive behavior to goal-directed behavior.
Preoperational	2 to 7 years	Development of the ability to use symbols to represent objects in the world. Thinking remains egocentric and centered.
Concrete operational	7 to 11 years	Improvement in ability to think logically. New abilities include the use of operations that are reversible. Thinking is decentered, and problem solving is less restricted by egocentrism. Abstract thinking is not possible.
Formal operational	11 years to adulthood	Abstract and purely symbolic thinking possible. Problems can be solved through the use of systematic experimentation.

CERTIFICATION POINTER

When responding to the case studies in certification tests you may be asked to identify appropriateness of instruction according to the students' Piagetian stage of development.

is in the kitchen watching his mother prepare dinner. If the child knows where the step stool is kept, he may ask to have it set up to afford a better view of the counter and a better chance for a nibble. The child did not stumble on to this solution accidentally. Instead, he thought about the problem, figured out a possible solution that used the step stool, tried out the solution mentally, and only then tried the solution in practice.

Another hallmark of the sensorimotor period is the development of a grasp of **object permanence.** Piaget argued that children must learn that objects are physically stable and exist even when the objects are not in the child's physical presence. For example, if you cover an infant's bottle with a towel, the child may not remove it, believing that the bottle is gone. By 2 years of age, children understand that objects exist even if they cannot be seen. When children develop this notion of object permanence, they have taken a step toward more advanced thinking. Once they realize that things exist out of sight, they can start using symbols to represent these things in their minds so that they can think about them (Cohen & Cashon, 2003).

Preoperational Stage (Ages 2 to 7) Whereas infants can learn about and understand the world only by physically manipulating objects, preschoolers have greater ability to think about things and can use symbols to mentally represent objects. During the **preoperational stage,** children's language and concepts develop at an incredible rate. Yet much of their thinking remains surprisingly primitive. One of Piaget's earliest and most important discoveries was that young children lacked an understanding of the principle of **conservation.** For example, if you pour milk from a tall, narrow container into a shallow, wide one in the presence of a preoperational child, the child will firmly believe that the tall glass has more milk (see Figure 2.2). The child focuses on only one aspect (the height of the milk), ignoring all others, and cannot be convinced that the amount of milk is the same. Similarly, a preoperational child is likely to believe that a sandwich cut in four pieces is more sandwich or that a line of blocks that is spread out contains more blocks than a line that is compressed, even after being shown that the number of blocks is identical.

Several aspects of preoperational thinking help to explain the error on conservation tasks. One characteristic is **centration:** paying attention to only one aspect of a situation. In the example illustrated in Figure 2.2, children might have claimed that there was less milk after pouring because they centered on the height of the milk, ignoring its width. In Figure 2.3, children focus on the length of the line of blocks but ignore its density (or the actual number of blocks).

object permanence
The fact that an object exists even if it is out of sight.

preoperational stage
Stage at which children learn to represent things in the mind.

conservation
The concept that certain properties of an object (such as weight) remain the same regardless of changes in other properties (such as length).

centration
Paying attention to only one aspect of an object or situation.

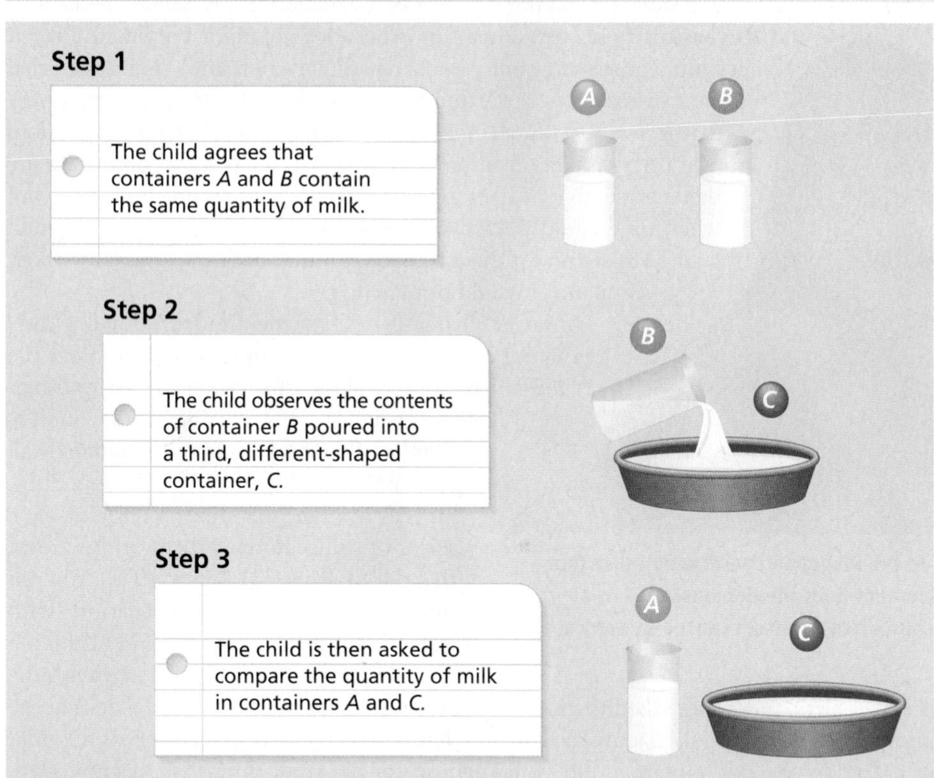

Step 1
The child agrees that containers A and B contain the same quantity of milk.
A
B
Step 2
The child observes the contents of container B poured into a third, different-shaped container, C.
B
C
Step 3
The child is then asked to compare the quantity of milk in containers A and C.
A
C

FIGURE 2.2 The Task of Conservation
This is a typical procedure for studying conservation of liquid quantity.

From Robert V. Kail and Rita Wicks-Nelson, *Developmental Psychology* (5th ed.), p. 190. Copyright © 1993. Reprinted by permission of Prentice Hall, Upper Saddle River, New Jersey.

FIGURE 2.3 Centration
Centration, or focusing on only one aspect of a situation, helps to explain some errors in perception that young children make.

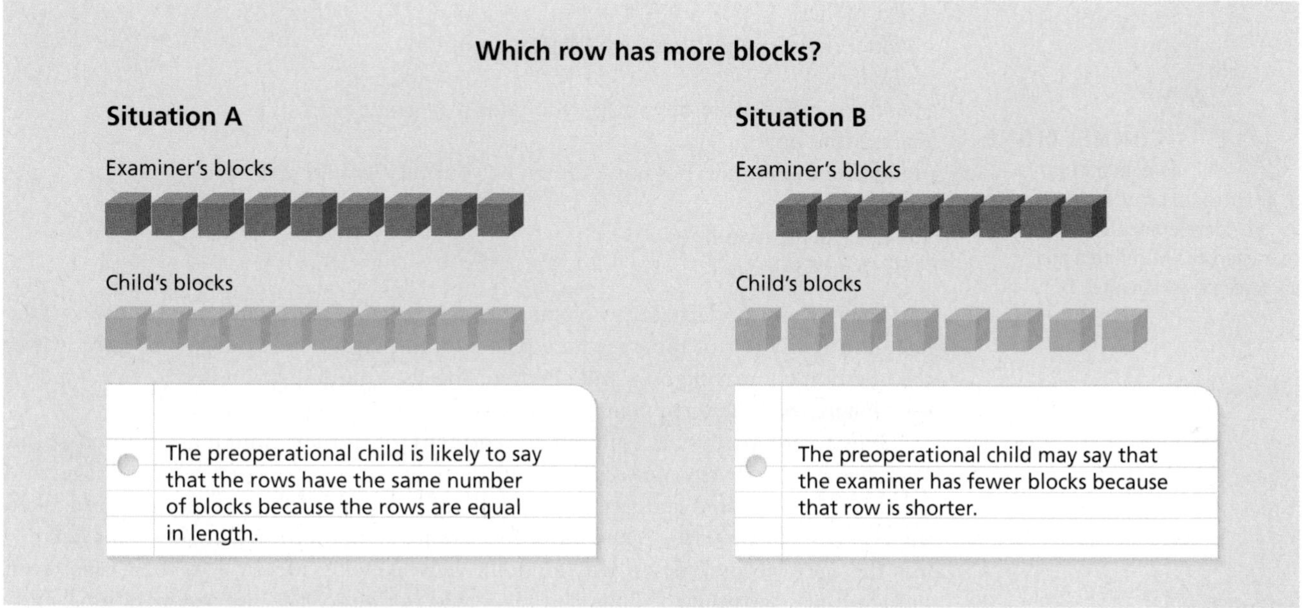

From Barry Wadsworth, *Piaget for the Classroom Teacher,* 1978, p. 225, published by Longman Publishing Group. Adapted by permission of the author.

Preschoolers' thinking can also be characterized as being irreversible. **Reversibility** is a very important aspect of thinking, according to Piaget; it simply means the ability to change direction in one's thinking so that one can return to a starting point. As adults, for example, we know that if 7 + 5 = 12, then 12 − 5 = 7. If we add 5 things to 7 things and then take the 5 things away (reverse what we've done), we are left with 7 things. If preoperational children could think this way, then they could mentally reverse the process of pouring the milk and realize that if the milk were poured back into the tall beaker, its quantity would not change.

How will this child likely respond to the Piagetian conservation task that she is attempting? What stage of development does she demonstrate? As a teacher, how might you help a young child discover errors caused by centration and irreversibility?

Another characteristic of the preoperational child's thinking is its focus on states. In the milk problem the milk was poured from one container to another. Preschoolers ignore this pouring process and focus only on the beginning state (milk in a tall glass) and end state (milk in a shallow dish). "It is as though [the child] were viewing a series of still pictures instead of the movie that the adult sees" (Phillips, 1975). You can understand how a preoccupation with states can interfere with a child's thinking if you imagine yourself presented with the milk problem and being asked to close your eyes while the milk is poured. Lacking the knowledge of what took place, you would be left with only your perception of the milk in the wide, shallow container and your memory of the milk in the tall, narrow glass.

Unlike adults, the young preschooler forms concepts that vary in definition from situation to situation and are not always logical. How else can we explain the 2-year-old's ability to treat a stuffed animal as an inanimate object one minute and an animate object the next? Eventually, though, the child's concepts become more consistent and less private. Children become increasingly concerned that their definitions of things match other people's. But they still lack the ability to coordinate one concept with another. Consider the following conversation:

Adult: Sally, how many boys are in your play group?
Sally: Eight.
Adult: How many girls are in your play group?
Sally: Five.
Adult: Are there more boys or girls in your play group?
Sally: More boys.
Adult: Are there more boys or children in your play group?
Sally: More boys.
Adult: How do you know?
Sally: I just do!

CONNECTIONS

For more on how to accommodate instruction to the developmental characteristics of children and adolescents, see Chapter 3.

Sally clearly understands the concepts of *boy, girl, children,* and *more.* However, she lacks the ability to put these separate pieces of knowledge together to correctly answer the question comparing boys and children. She also cannot explain her answer, which is why Piaget used the term *intuitive* to describe her thinking.

Finally, preoperational children are **egocentric** in their thinking. Children at this stage believe that everyone sees the world exactly as they do. For example, Piaget and Inhelder (1956) seated children on one side of a display of three mountains and asked them to describe how the scene looked to a doll seated on the other side. Children below the age of 6 or 7 described the doll's view as being identical to their own, even though it was apparent to adults that this could not be so. Because preoperational children are unable to take the perspective of others, they often interpret events entirely in reference to themselves. A passage from A. A. Milne's *Winnie-the-Pooh* illustrates the young child's egocentrism. Winnie-the-Pooh is sitting in the forest and hears a buzzing sound.

> That buzzing-noise means something. You don't get a buzzing-noise like that just buzzing and buzzing, without its meaning something. If there is a buzzing-noise, somebody's

reversibility
The ability to perform a mental operation and then reverse one's thinking to return to the starting point.

egocentric
Believing that everyone views the world as you do.

Personal REFLECTION

Egocentrism in Action

Many years ago I was driving with my two sons, ages 4 and 2, through dairy country in Vermont. The boys were admiring the cows. "Why do farmers keep cows?" I asked them. Ben, the 2-year-old, said "So my [I] can look at them!" Jake, his older and wiser brother disagreed. "The farmer likes to play with them."

These different ideas show how egocentrism develops over time. Ben, at 2, thought that everything that happens in the world relates to him. Four-year-old Jake, however, realized that the farmer had his own needs but assumed that those needs were the same as his.

REFLECT ON THIS. How will your understanding of egocentrism help you as a teacher?

> making a buzzing-noise, and the only reason for making a buzzing-noise that I know of is because you're a bee . . . Then he thought for another long time, and said: And the only reason for being a bee that I know of is for making honey . . . And then he got up, and said: And the only reason for making honey is so as I can eat it.

Concrete Operational Stage (Ages 7 to 11) Although the differences between the mental abilities of preoperational preschoolers and concrete operational elementary school students are dramatic, concrete operational children still do not think like adults. They are very much rooted in the world as it is and have difficulty with abstract thought. Flavell describes the concrete operational child as taking "an earthbound, concrete, practical-minded sort of problem-solving approach, one that persistently fixates on the perceptible and inferable reality right there in front of him. A theorist the elementary-school child is not" (1986, p. 103). The term **concrete operational stage** reflects this earthbound approach. Children at this stage can form concepts, see relationships, and solve problems, but only as long as they involve objects and situations that are familiar.

During the elementary school years, children's cognitive abilities undergo dramatic changes. Elementary school children no longer have difficulties with conservation problems because they have acquired the concept of reversibility. For example, they can now see that the amount of milk in the short, wide container must be the same as that in the tall, narrow container, because if the milk were poured back in the tall container, it would be at the same level as before. The child is able to imagine the milk being poured back and can recognize the consequences—abilities that are not evident in the preoperational child.

Another fundamental difference between preoperational and concrete operational children is that the younger child, who is in the preoperational stage, responds to perceived appearances, whereas the older, concrete operational child responds to inferred reality. Flavell (1986) demonstrated this concept by showing children a red car and then, while they were still watching, covering it with a filter that made it appear black. When asked what color the car was, 3-year-olds responded "black," and 6-year-olds responded "red." The older, concrete operational child is able to respond to **inferred reality,** seeing things in the context of other meanings; preschoolers see what they see, with little ability to infer the meaning behind what they see.

One important task that children learn during the concrete operational stage is **seriation,** or arranging things in a logical progression; for example, lining up sticks from

concrete operational stage
Stage at which children develop the capacity for logical reasoning and understanding of conservation but can use these skills only in dealing with familiar situations.

inferred reality
The meaning of stimuli in the context of relevant information.

seriation
Arranging objects in sequential order according to one aspect, such as size, weight, or volume.

smallest to largest. To do this, they must be able to order or classify objects according to some criterion or dimension, in this case length. Once this ability is acquired, children can master a related skill known as **transitivity,** the ability to infer a relationship between two objects on the basis of knowledge of their respective relationships with a third object. For example, if you tell preoperational preschoolers that Tom is taller than Becky and that Becky is taller than Fred, they will not see that Tom is taller than Fred. Logical inferences such as this are not possible until the stage of concrete operations, during which school-age children develop the ability to make two mental transformations that require reversible thinking. The first of these is inversion (+A is reversed by –A), and the second is reciprocity (A < B is reciprocated by B > A). By the end of the concrete operational stage, children have the mental abilities to learn how to add, subtract, multiply, and divide; to place numbers in order by size; and to classify objects by any number of criteria. Children can think about what would happen if . . . , as long as the objects are in view (e.g., "What would happen if I pulled this spring and then let it go?"). Children can understand time and space well enough to draw a map from their home to school and are building an understanding of events in the past.

INTASC

❷ **Knowledge of Human Development and Learning**

Children in the elementary grades also are moving from egocentric thought to decentered or objective thought. Decentered thought allows children to see that others can have different perceptions than they do. For example, children with decentered thought will be able to understand that different children may see different patterns in clouds. Children whose thought processes are decentered are able to learn that events may be governed by physical laws, such as the laws of gravity. A final ability that children acquire during the concrete operational stage is **class inclusion.** Recall the example of Sally, who was in the preoperational stage and believed that there were more boys than children in her play group. What Sally lacked was the ability to think simultaneously about the whole class (children) and the subordinate class (boys, girls). She could make comparisons within a class, as shown by her ability to compare one part (the boys) with another part (the girls). She also knew that boys and girls are both members of the larger class called children. What she could not do was make comparisons between classes. Concrete operational children, by contrast, have no trouble with this type of problem, because they have additional tools of thinking. First, they no longer exhibit irreversibility of thinking and can now re-create a relationship between a part and the whole. Second, concrete operational thought is decentered, so the child can now focus on two classes simultaneously. Third, the concrete operational child's thinking is no longer limited to reasoning about part-to-part relationships. Now part-to-whole relationships can be dealt with too. These changes do not all happen at the same time. Rather, they occur gradually during the concrete operational stage.

Formal Operational Stage (Age 11 to Adulthood) Sometime around the onset of puberty, children's thinking begins to develop into the form that is characteristic of adults. The preadolescent begins to be able to think abstractly and to see possibilities beyond the here and now. These abilities continue to develop into adulthood. With the **formal operational stage** comes the ability to deal with potential or hypothetical situations; the form is now separate from the content.

Inhelder and Piaget (1958) described one task that will be approached differently by elementary school students in the concrete operational stage and by adolescents in the formal operational stage. The children and adolescents were given a pendulum consisting of a string with a weight at the end. They could change the length of the string, the amount of weight, the height from which the pendulum was released, and the force with which the pendulum was pushed. They were asked which of these factors influenced the frequency (the number of times per minute) of the pendulum swinging back and forth. Essentially, the task was to discover a principle of physics, which is that only the length of the string makes any difference in the frequency of the pendulum: The shorter the string, the more swings per minute. This experiment is illustrated in Figure 2.4. The adolescent who has reached the stage of formal operations is likely to proceed quite systematically, varying one factor at a time (e.g., leaving the string the same length and trying different weights). For example, in Inhelder and Piaget's (1958) experiment, one 15-year-old selected 100 grams with a long string and a medium-length string, then

transitivity
A skill learned during the concrete operational stage of cognitive development in which individuals can mentally arrange and compare objects.

class inclusion
A skill learned during the concrete operational stage of cognitive development in which individuals can think simultaneously about a whole class of objects and about relationships among its subordinate classes.

formal operational stage
Stage at which one can deal abstractly with hypothetical situations and can reason logically.

FIGURE 2.4 A Test of Problem-Solving Abilities The pendulum problem uses a string, which can be shortened or lengthened, and a set of weights. When children in the concrete operational stage are asked what determines frequency (the number of times per minute the pendulum swings back and forth), they will tackle the problem less systematically than will adolescents who have entered the stage for formal operations. (The answer is that only the string's length affects the frequency.)

20 grams with a long and a short string, and finally 200 grams with a long and a short string and concluded, "It's the length of the string that makes it go faster and slower; the weight doesn't play any role" (p. 75). In contrast, 10-year-olds (who can be assumed to be in the concrete operational stage) proceeded in a chaotic fashion, varying many factors at the same time and hanging on to preconceptions. One boy varied simultaneously the weight and the impetus (push); then the weight, the impetus, and the length; then the impetus, the weight, and the elevation; and so on. He first concluded, "It's by changing the weight and the push, certainly not the string."

"How do you know that the string has nothing to do with it?"

"Because it's the same string."

He had not varied its length in the last several trials; previously, he had varied it simultaneously with the impetus, thus complicating the account of the experiment (adapted from Inhelder and Piaget, 1958, p. 71).

The transitivity problem also illustrates the advances brought about by formal thought. Recall the concrete operational child who, when told that Tom was taller than Becky and Becky was taller than Fred, understood that Tom was taller than Fred. However, if the problem had been phrased in the following way, only an older child who had entered the formal operational stage would have solved it: "Becky is shorter than Tom, and Becky is taller than Fred. Who is the tallest of the three?" Here the younger concrete operational child might get lost in the combinations of greater-than and less-than relationships. Adolescents in the formal operational stage may also get confused by the differing relationships in this problem, but they can imagine several different relationships among the heights of Becky, Tom, and Fred and can figure out the accuracy of each until they hit on the correct one. This example shows another ability of preadolescents and adolescents who have reached the formal operational stage: They can monitor, or think about, their own thinking.

Generating abstract relationships from available information and then comparing those abstract relationships to each other is a broadly applicable skill underlying many tasks in which adolescents' competence leaps forward. Piaget (1952a) described a task in which students in the concrete operational stage were given a set of 10 proverbs and a set of statements that meant the same thing as the proverbs. They were asked to match each proverb to the equivalent statement. Again, concrete operational children can understand the task and choose answers. However, their answers are often incorrect because they often do not understand that a proverb describes a general principle. For example,

CONNECTIONS
For more on thinking about one's own thinking, or metacognition, see Chapter 6, pages 183–184.

asked to explain the proverb "Don't cry over spilled milk," a child might explain that once milk is spilled, there's nothing to cry about but might not see that the proverb has a broader meaning. The child is likely to respond to the concrete situation of spilled milk rather than understanding that the proverb means "Don't dwell on past events that can't be changed." Adolescents and adults have little difficulty with this type of task.

Hypothetical Conditions Another ability that Piaget and others recognized in the young adolescent is the ability to reason about situations and conditions that have not been experienced. The adolescent can accept, for the sake of argument or discussion, conditions that are arbitrary, that are not known to exist, or even that are known to be contrary to fact. Adolescents are not bound to their own experiences of reality, so they can apply logic to any given set of conditions. One illustration of the ability to reason about hypothetical situations is found in formal debate, in which participants must be prepared to defend either side of an issue, regardless of their personal feelings or experience, and their defense is judged on its documentation and logical consistency. For a dramatic illustration of the difference between children and adolescents in the ability to suspend their own opinions, compare the reactions of fourth- and ninth-graders when you ask them to present an argument in favor of the proposition that schools should be in session 6 days a week, 48 weeks a year. The adolescent is far more likely to be able to set aside her or his own opinions and think of reasons why more days of school might be beneficial. The abilities that make up formal operational thought—thinking abstractly, testing hypotheses, and forming concepts that are independent of physical reality—are critical in the learning of higher-order skills. For example, learning algebra or abstract geometry requires the use of formal operational thought, as does understanding complex concepts in science, social studies, and other subjects.

The thinking characteristic of the formal operations stage usually appears between ages 11 and 15, but there are many individuals who never reach this stage (Niaz, 1997). Individuals tend to use formal operational thinking in some situations and not others, and this remains true into adulthood.

According to Piaget, the formal operational stage brings cognitive development to a close. However, intellectual growth may continue to take place beyond adolescence. According to Piaget, the foundation has been laid, and no new structures need to develop; all that is needed is the addition of knowledge and the development of more complex schemes.

HOW IS PIAGET'S WORK VIEWED TODAY?

Piaget's theory revolutionized, and in many ways still dominates, the study of human development. However, some of his central principles have been questioned in more recent research, and modern descriptions of development have revised many of his views (see Feldman, 2003).

VIDEO HOMEWORK EXERCISE
Cognitive Development

Go to **www.myeducationlab.com** and, in the Homework and Exercises section for Chapter 2 of this text, access the video entitled "Cognitive Development." Watch the video and complete the homework questions that accompany it, saving your work or transmitting it to your professor as required.

Criticisms and Revisions of Piaget's Theory

One important Piagetian principle is that development precedes learning. Piaget held that developmental stages were largely fixed and that such concepts as conservation could not be taught. However, research has established some cases in which Piagetian tasks can be taught to children at earlier developmental stages. For example, several researchers have found that young children can succeed on simpler forms of Piaget's tasks before they reach the stage at which that task is usually achieved (Gelman, 2000; Larivée, Normandeau, & Parent, 2000; Siegler, 1998). Gelman (1979) found that young children could solve the conservation problem involving the number of blocks in a row when the task was presented in a simpler way with simpler language. Boden (1980) found that the same formal operational task produced passing rates from 19 to 98 percent, depending on the complexities of the instructions (see also Nagy & Griffiths, 1982).

Similar kinds of research have also led to a reassessment of children's egocentricity. In simple, practical contexts, children demonstrated their ability to consider the point of view of others (Siegler, 1998). In addition, infants have been shown to demonstrate aspects of object permanence much earlier than Piaget predicted (Baillargeon, Graber, DeVos, & Black, 1990).

The result of this research has been a recognition that children are more competent than Piaget originally thought, especially when their practical knowledge is being assessed. Gelman (1979) suggested that the cognitive abilities of preschoolers are less well established than those of older children and, therefore, are evident only under certain conditions. Piaget (1964) responded to demonstrations of this kind by arguing that the children must have been on the verge of the next developmental stage already—but the fact remains that some of the Piagetian tasks can be taught to children well below the age at which they usually appear without instruction.

Another area in which Piaget's work has been criticized goes to the heart of his "stage" theory. Many researchers now doubt that there are broad stages of development affecting all types of cognitive tasks; instead, they argue that children's skills develop in different ways on different tasks and that their experience (including direct teaching in school or elsewhere) can have a strong influence on the pace of development (see Gelman, 2000; Overton, 1998). The evidence is particularly strong that children can be taught to perform well on the Piagetian tasks assessing formal operations, such as the pendulum problem illustrated in Figure 2.4 (Greenbowe, Herron, Nurrenbern, Staver, & Ward, 1981). Clearly, experience matters. De Lisi and Staudt (1980), for example, found that college students were likely to show formal operational reasoning on tasks related to their majors but not on other tasks. Watch an intelligent adult learning to sail. Initially, he or she is likely to engage in a lot of concrete operational behavior, trying everything in a chaotic order, before systematically beginning to learn how to adjust the tiller and the sail to the wind and direction (as in formal operational thought).

THEORY *into* PRACTICE

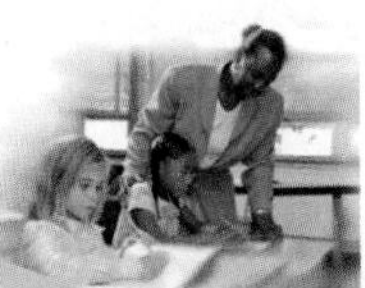

Educational Implications of Piaget's Theory

Piaget's theories have had a major impact on the theory and practice of education (Case, 1998). First, the theories focused attention on the idea of **developmentally appropriate education**—an education with environments, curriculum, materials, and instruction that are suitable for students in terms of their physical and cognitive abilities and their social and emotional needs. Piagetian theory has been influential in constructivist models of learning, which will be described in Chapter 8. Berk (2001) summarizes the main teaching implications drawn from Piaget as follows:

1. ***A focus on the process of children's thinking, not only its products.*** In addition to checking the correctness of children's answers, teachers must understand the processes children use to get to the answer. Appropriate learning experiences build on children's current level of cognitive functioning, and only when teachers appreciate children's methods of arriving at particular conclusions are they in a position to provide such experiences.

2. ***Recognition of the crucial role of children's self-initiated, active involvement in learning activities.*** In a Piagetian classroom the presentation of ready-made knowledge is deemphasized, and children are encouraged to discover for themselves through spontaneous interaction with the environment. Therefore, instead of teaching didactically, teachers provide a rich variety of activities that permit children to act directly on the physical world.

CONNECTIONS
For more on developmentally appropriate practice, see Chapter 3.

INTASC

2 Knowledge of Human Development and Learning

3 Adapting Instruction for Individual Needs

developmentally appropriate education
Instruction felt to be adapted to the current developmental status of children (rather than to their age alone).

3. ***A deemphasis on practices aimed at making children adultlike in their thinking.*** Piaget referred to the question "How can we speed up development?" as "the American question." Among the many countries he visited, psychologists and educators in the United States seemed most interested in what techniques could be used to accelerate children's progress through the stages. Piagetian-based educational programs accept his firm belief that premature teaching could be worse than no teaching at all because it leads to superficial acceptance of adult formulas rather than true cognitive understanding (May & Kundert, 1997).

4. ***Acceptance of individual differences in developmental progress.*** Piaget's theory assumes that all children go through the same developmental sequence but that they do so at different rates. Therefore, teachers must make a special effort to arrange classroom activities for individuals and small groups of children rather than for the total class group. In addition, because individual differences are expected, assessment of children's educational progress should be made in terms of each child's own previous course of development, not in terms of the performances of same-age peers.

Neo-Piagetian and Information-Processing Views of Development

CONNECTIONS
For more on information processing, see Chapter 6, page 158.

Neo-Piagetian theories are modifications of Piaget's theory that attempt to overcome the theory's limitations and address problems its critics have identified. In particular, neo-Piagetians have demonstrated that children's abilities to operate at a particular stage depend a great deal on the specific tasks involved (Gelman & Brenneman, 1994); that training and experience, including social interactions, can accelerate children's development (Birney et al., 2005; Case, 1998; Flavell, 2004; Siegler, 1998); and that culture has an important impact on development (Gelman & Brenneman, 1994; Rogoff & Chavajay, 1995).

HOW DID VYGOTSKY VIEW COGNITIVE DEVELOPMENT?

INTASC

4 Multiple Instructional Strategies

Lev Semionovich Vygotsky was a Russian psychologist who, though a contemporary of Piaget, died in 1934. His work was not widely read in English until the 1970s, however, and only since then have his theories become influential in North America. Vygotskian theory is now a powerful force in developmental psychology, and many of the critiques he made of the Piagetian perspective more than 60 years ago have come to the fore today (see Glassman, 2001; John-Steiner & Mahn, 2003). Vygotsky's theories have also been used as a basis for current theories that he may or may not have supported himself (see, for example, the debates between McVee, Dunsmore, & Gavelek [2005] and Grendler [2004]; and Krasny, Sadowski, & Paivio [2007] and McVee, Gavelek, & Dunsmore [2007]).

Vygotsky's work is based on two key ideas. First, he proposed that intellectual development can be understood only in terms of the historical and cultural contexts children experience. Second, he believed that development depends on the **sign systems** that individuals grow up with: the symbols that cultures create to help people think, communicate, and solve problems—for example, a culture's language, writing system, or counting system.

sign systems
Symbols that cultures create to help people think, communicate, and solve problems.

In contrast to Piaget, Vygotsky proposed that cognitive development is strongly linked to input from others. Like Piaget, however, Vygotsky believed that the acquisition of sign systems occurs in an invariant sequence of steps that is the same for all children.

How Development Occurs

Recall that Piaget's theory suggests that development precedes learning. In other words, specific cognitive structures need to develop before certain types of learning can take place. Vygotsky's theory suggests that learning precedes development. For Vygotsky, learning involves the acquisition of signs by means of instruction and information from others. Development involves the child's internalizing these signs so as to be able to think and solve problems without the help of others. This ability is called **self-regulation.**

The first step in the development of self-regulation and independent thinking is learning that actions and sounds have a meaning. For example, a baby learns that the process of reaching toward an object is interpreted by others as a signal that the infant wants the object. In the case of language acquisition, children learn to associate certain sounds with meaning. The second step in developing internal structures and self-regulation involves practice. The infant practices gestures that will get attention. The preschooler will enter into conversations with others to master language. The final step involves using signs to think and solve problems without the help of others. At this point, children become self-regulating, and the sign system has become internalized.

"I'm sorry, Miss Scott, but this is outside of my zone of proximal development."

Private Speech **Private speech** is a mechanism that Vygotsky emphasized for turning shared knowledge into personal knowledge. Vygotsky proposed that children incorporate the speech of others and then use that speech to help themselves solve problems. Private speech is easy to see in young children, who frequently talk to themselves, especially when faced with difficult tasks (Flavell et al., 1997). Later, private speech becomes silent but is still very important. Studies have found that children who make extensive use of private speech learn complex tasks more effectively than do other children (Al-Namlah et al., 2006; Emerson & Miyake, 2003; Schneider, 2002).

CONNECTIONS
For more on self-regulated learning, see Chapter 8, page 236.

The Zone of Proximal Development Vygotsky's theory implies that cognitive development and the ability to use thought to control our own actions require first mastering cultural communication systems and then learning to use these systems to regulate our own thought processes. The most important contribution of Vygotsky's theory is an emphasis on the sociocultural nature of learning (Karpov & Haywood, 1998; Roth & Lee, 2007; Vygotsky, 1978). He believed that learning takes place when children are working within their **zone of proximal development.** Tasks within the zone of proximal development are ones that a child cannot yet do alone but could do with the assistance of more competent peers or adults. That is, the zone of proximal development describes tasks that a child has not yet learned but is capable of learning at a given time. Some educators refer to a "teachable moment" when a child or group of children is exactly at the point of readiness for a given concept. Vygotsky further believed that higher mental functioning usually exists in conversation and collaboration among individuals before it exists within the individual.

Scaffolding A key idea derived from Vygotsky's notion of social learning is that of **scaffolding** (Wood, Bruner, & Ross, 1976): the assistance provided by more competent peers or adults. Typically, scaffolding means providing a child with a great deal of support during the early stages of learning and then diminishing support and having the child take on increasing responsibility as soon as she or he is able (Rosenshine & Meister, 1992). Parents use scaffolding when they teach their children to play a new game or to tie their shoes (Rogoff, 2003). A related concept is cognitive apprenticeship, which describes the entire process of modeling, coaching, scaffolding, and evaluation that is typically seen

self-regulation
The ability to think and solve problems without the help of others.

private speech
Children's self-talk, which guides their thinking and action; eventually internalized as silent inner speech.

zone of proximal development
Level of development immediately above a person's present level.

scaffolding
Support for learning and problem solving; might include clues, reminders, encouragement, breaking the problem down into steps, providing an example, or anything else that allows the student to grow in independence as a learner.

How is this parent playing an integral role in his child's learning development? How are scaffolding and cognitive apprenticeship similar?

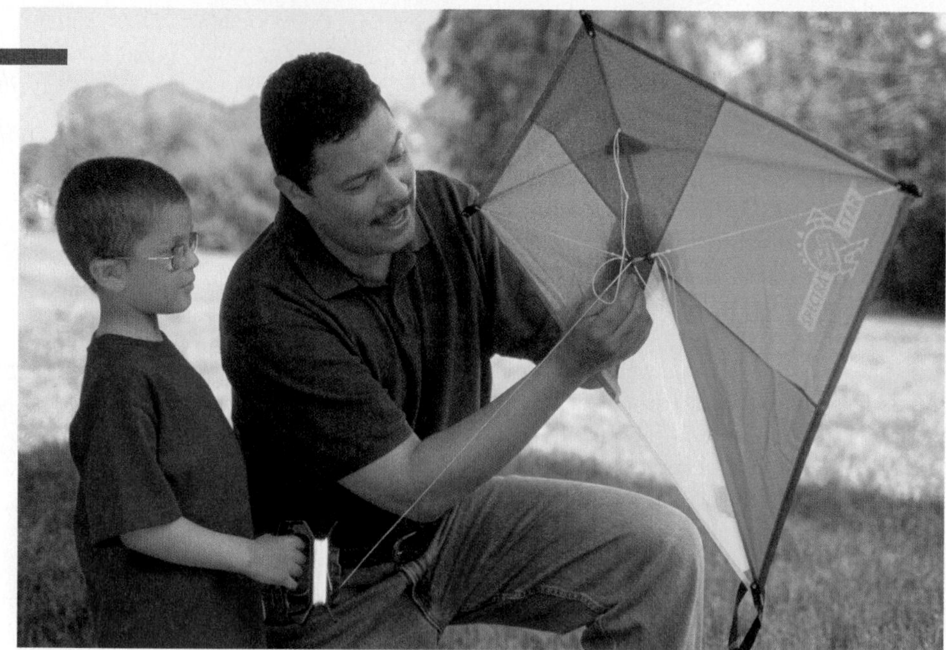

CONNECTIONS
For more on scaffolding, see Chapter 8, pages 236–237.

whenever one-to-one instruction takes place (John-Steiner & Mahn, 2003; Rogoff, 2003). For example, in *Life on the Mississippi,* Mark Twain describes how he was taught to be a steamboat pilot. At first the experienced pilot talked him through every bend in the river, but gradually he was left to figure things out for himself, with the pilot there to intervene only if the boat was about to run aground.

CONNECTIONS
For more on cooperative learning, see Chapter 8, pages 233 and 243–249.

Cooperative Learning Vygotsky's theories support the use of cooperative learning strategies in which children work together to help one another learn (Slavin, Hurley, & Chamberlain, 2003). Because peers are usually operating within each others' zones of proximal development, they often provide models for each other of slightly more advanced thinking. In addition, cooperative learning makes children's inner speech available to others, so they can gain insight into one another's reasoning process. That is, children benefit from hearing each other "thinking out loud," especially when their groupmates talk themselves through a problem (Slavin, in press). Vygotsky (1978) himself recognized the value of peer interaction in moving children forward in their thinking.

BUILDING TEACHING SKILLS SIMULATION EXERCISE
Providing Instructional Supports (Facilitating Mastery of New Skills)

Go to **www.myeducationlab.com** and, in the Building Teaching Skills Exercises section for Chapter 2 of this text, access the Simulation entitled "Providing Instructional Supports (Facilitating Mastery of New Skills)." Execute the Simulation and complete the homework questions that accompany it, saving your work or transmitting it to your professor as required.

Applications of Vygotskian Theory in Teaching

Vygotsky's theories of education have two major implications. One is the desirability of setting up cooperative learning arrangements among groups of students with differing levels of ability. Tutoring by more competent peers can be effective in promoting growth within the zone of proximal development (Das, 1995) as can interactions around complex tasks (Roth & Lee, 2007). Second, a Vygotskian approach to instruction emphasizes scaffolding, with students taking more and more responsibility for their own learning. (See Figure 2.5.) For example, in reciprocal teaching, teachers lead small groups of students in asking questions about material they have read and gradually turn over responsibility for leading the discussion to the students (Palincsar, Brown, & Martin, 1987). Tharp and Gallimore (1988) emphasized scaffolding in an approach they called "assisted discovery," which calls for explicitly teaching students to use private speech to talk themselves through problem solving.

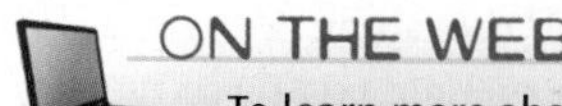

To learn more about applications of Vygotsky's theories to education practice visit **mathforum.org/mathed/vygotsky.html.**

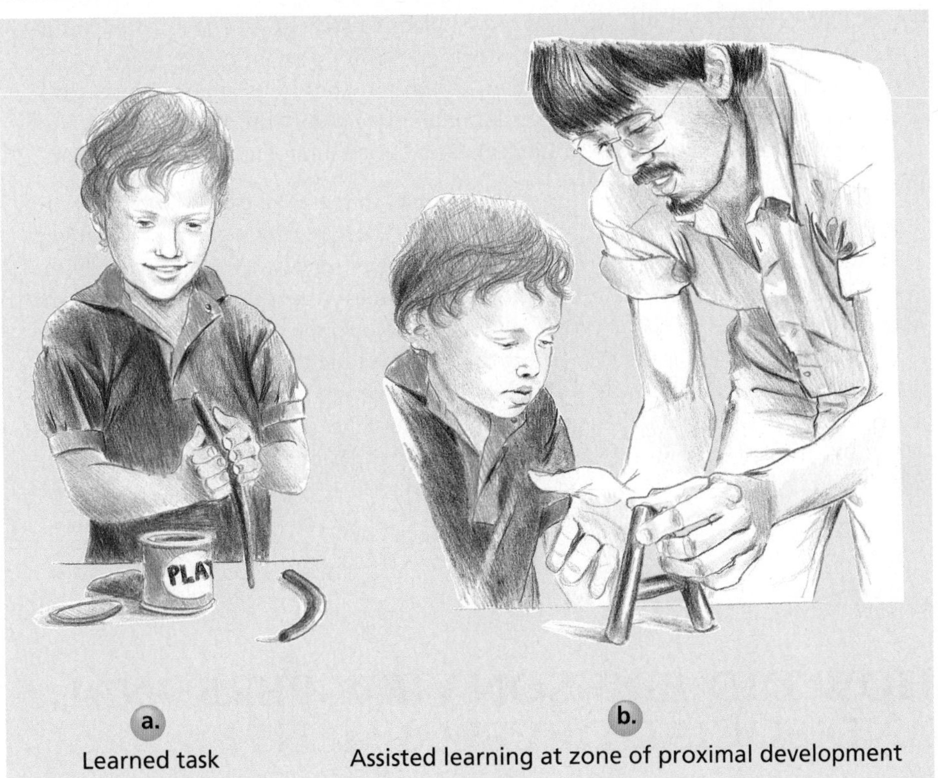

FIGURE 2.5 Teaching Model Based on Vygotsky's Theory

In (a) the child performs a learned task; in (b) the child is assisted by a teacher or peer who interacts with the child to help him move into a new zone of proximal development (unlearned tasks at limits of learner's abilities) with a new learned task.

THEORY *into* PRACTICE

Classroom Applications of Vygotsky's Theory

Vygotsky's concept of the zone of proximal development is based on the idea that development is defined both by what a child can do independently and by what the child can do when assisted by an adult or more competent peer (John-Steiner & Mahn, 2003). The zone of proximal development has several implications for teaching in the classroom.

According to Vygotsky, for the curriculum to be developmentally appropriate, the teacher must plan activities that encompass not only what children are capable of doing on their own but what they can learn with the help of others (Karpov & Haywood, 1998).

Vygotsky's theory does not mean that anything can be taught to any child. Only instruction and activities that fall within the zone of proximal development can be learned. For example, if a child cannot identify the sounds in a word even after many prompts, the child may not benefit immediately from instruction in this skill. Practice of previously known skills and introduction of concepts that are too difficult and complex have little positive impact.

Teachers can use information about Vygotsky's zone of proximal development in organizing classroom activities in the following ways:

- Instruction can be planned to provide practice within the zone of proximal development for individual children or for groups of children. For example, hints and prompts that helped children during a preassessment could form the basis of instructional activities.

CONNECTIONS

For more on reciprocal teaching, see Chapter 8, page 239.

CERTIFICATION POINTER

Lev Vygotsky's work will probably be on your teacher certification test. You may be required to know that the zone of proximal development is the level of development just above where a student is presently functioning and why this is important for both teachers and students.

- Cooperative learning activities can be planned with groups of children at different levels who can help each other learn (Slavin et al., 2003).
- Scaffolding (John-Steiner & Mahn, 2003) provides hints and prompts at different levels. In scaffolding, the adult does not simplify the task, but the role of the learner is simplified "through the graduated intervention of the teacher."

For example, a child might be shown pennies to represent each sound in a word (e.g., three pennies for the three sounds in "man"). To master this word, the child might be asked to place a penny on the table to show each sound in a word, and finally the child might identify the sounds without the pennies. When the adult provides the child with pennies, the adult provides a scaffold to help the child move from assisted to unassisted success at the task (Spector, 1992). In a high school laboratory science class, a teacher might provide scaffolding by first giving students detailed guides to carrying out experiments, then giving them brief outlines that they might use to structure experiments, and finally asking them to set up experiments entirely on their own.

HOW DID ERIKSON VIEW PERSONAL AND SOCIAL DEVELOPMENT?

As children improve their cognitive skills, they are also developing self-concepts, ways of interacting with others, and attitudes toward the world. Understanding of these personal and social developments are critical to the teacher's ability to motivate, teach, and successfully interact with students at various ages. Like cognitive development, personal development and social development are often described in terms of stages. We speak of the "terrible twos," not the "terrible ones" or "terrible threes"; and when someone is reacting in an unreasonable, selfish way, we accuse that person of "behaving like a 2-year-old." The words *adolescent* and *teenager* are associated in Western culture with rebelliousness, identity crises, hero worship, and sexual awakening. These associations reflect stages of development that we believe everyone goes through. This section focuses on a theory of personal and social development proposed by Erik Erikson, which is an adaptation of the developmental theories of the great psychiatrist Sigmund Freud. Erikson's work is often called a **psychosocial theory** because it relates principles of psychological and social development.

Stages of Psychosocial Development

Like Piaget, Erikson had no formal training in psychology, but as a young man he was trained by Freud as a psychoanalyst. Erikson hypothesized that people pass through eight psychosocial stages in their lifetimes. At each stage, there are crises or critical issues to be resolved. Most people resolve each **psychosocial crisis** satisfactorily and put it behind them to take on new challenges, but some people do not completely resolve these crises and must continue to deal with them later in life (Miller, 1993). For example, many adults have yet to resolve the "identity crisis" of adolescence. Table 2.2 summarizes the eight stages of life according to Erikson's theory. Each is identified by the central crisis that must be resolved.

psychosocial theory
A set of principles that relates social environment to psychological development.

psychosocial crisis
According to Erikson, the set of critical issues that individuals must address as they pass through each of the eight life stages.

Stage I: Trust versus Mistrust (Birth to 18 Months) The goal of infancy is to develop a basic trust in the world. Erikson (1968, p. 96) defined basic trust as "an essential trustfulness of others as well as a fundamental sense of one's own trustworthiness." The mother, or maternal figure, is usually the first important person in the child's world. She is the one who must satisfy the infant's need for food and affection. If the mother is inconsistent or rejecting, she becomes a source of frustration for the infant rather than a source of pleasure (Cummings, Braungart-Rieker, & Du Rocher-Schudlich, 2003; Thompson,

TABLE 2.2 Erikson's Stages of Personal and Social Development

As people grow, they face a series of psychosocial crises that shape personality, according to Erik Erikson. Each crisis focuses on a particular aspect of personality and involves the person's relationship with other people.

Stage	Approximate Ages	Psychosocial Crises	Significant Relationships	Psychosocial Emphasis
I	Birth to 18 months	Trust vs. mistrust	Maternal person	To get To give in return
II	18 months to 3 years	Autonomy vs. doubt	Parental persons	To hold on To let go
III	3 to 6 years	Initiative vs. guilt	Basic family	To make (= going after) To "make like" (= playing)
IV	6 to 12 years	Industry vs. inferiority	Neighborhood, school	To make things To make things together
V	12 to 18 years	Identity vs. role confusion	Peer groups and models of leadership	To be oneself (or not to be) To share being oneself
VI	Young adulthood	Intimacy vs. isolation	Partners in friendship, sex, competition, cooperation	To lose and find oneself in another
VII	Middle adulthood	Generativity vs. self-absorption	Divided labor and shared household	To take care of
VIII	Late adulthood	Integrity vs. despair	"Mankind," "My kind"	To be, through having been To face not being

Source: From "Figure of Erikson's Stages of Personality Development," *Childhood and Society* by Erik H. Erikson. Copyright 1950, © 1963 by W. W. Norton & Company, Inc., renewed © 1978, 1991 by Erik H. Erikson. Used by permission of W. W. Norton & Company, Inc.

Easterbrooks, & Padilla-Walker, 2003). The mother's behavior creates in the infant a sense of mistrust for his or her world that may persist throughout childhood and into adulthood.

Stage II: Autonomy versus Doubt (18 Months to 3 Years) By the age of 2, most babies can walk and have learned enough about language to communicate with other people. Children in the "terrible twos" no longer want to depend totally on others. Instead, they strive toward autonomy, the ability to do things for themselves. The child's desires for power and independence often clash with the desires of the parent. Erikson believes that children at this stage have the dual desire to hold on and to let go. Parents who are flexible enough to permit their children to explore freely and do things for themselves, while at the same time providing an ever-present guiding hand, encourage the establishment of a sense of autonomy. Parents who are overly restrictive and harsh give their children a sense of powerlessness and incompetence, which can lead to shame and doubt in one's abilities.

Stage III: Initiative versus Guilt (3 to 6 Years) During this period, children's continually maturing motor and language skills permit them to be increasingly aggressive and vigorous in the exploration of both their social and their physical environment. Three-year-olds have a growing sense of initiative, which can be encouraged by parents, other family members, and other caregivers who permit children to run, jump, play, slide, and throw. "Being firmly convinced that he is a person on his own, the child must now find out what kind of person he may become" (Erikson, 1968, p. 115). Parents who severely punish children's attempts at initiative will make the children feel guilty about their natural urges both during this stage and later in life.

Stage IV: Industry versus Inferiority (6 to 12 Years) Entry into school brings with it a huge expansion in the child's social world. Teachers and peers take on increasing importance for the child, while the influence of parents decreases. Children now want

CERTIFICATION POINTER

For teacher certification tests you will probably be asked about Erik Erikson's stages of personal and social development. You should know that vigorous exploration of their physical and social behavior is a behavior typical of children in Stage III, initiative versus guilt.

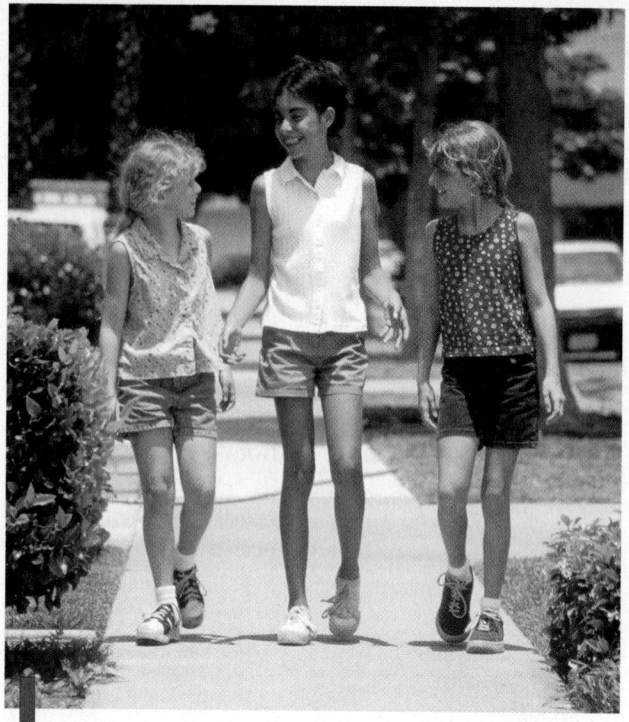

According to Erikson, what is the most important question these young people are trying to answer about themselves at this stage in their development? How might it manifest itself in their behavior? What challenges can this pose for you as a teacher?

to make things. Success brings with it a sense of industry, a good feeling about oneself and one's abilities. Failure creates a negative self-image, a sense of inadequacy that may hinder future learning. And "failure" need not be real; it may be merely an inability to measure up to one's own standards or those of parents, teachers, or brothers and sisters.

Stage V: Identity versus Role Confusion (12 to 18 Years) The question "Who am I?" becomes important during adolescence. To answer it, adolescents increasingly turn away from parents and toward peer groups. Erikson believed that during adolescence the individual's rapidly changing physiology, coupled with pressures to make decisions about future education and career, creates the need to question and redefine the psychosocial identity established during the earlier stages. Adolescence is a time of change. Teenagers experiment with various sexual, occupational, and educational roles as they try to find out who they are and who they can be. This new sense of self, or "ego identity," is not simply the sum of the prior identifications. Rather, it is a reassembly or "an alignment of the individual's basic drives (ego) with his or her endowment (resolutions of the previous crises) and his or her opportunities (needs, skills, goals, and demands of adolescence and approaching adulthood)" (Erikson, 1980, p. 94).

Stage VI: Intimacy versus Isolation (Young Adulthood) Once young people know who they are and where they are going, the stage is set for the sharing of their life with another. The young adult is now ready to form a new relationship of trust and intimacy with another individual, a "partner in friendship, sex, competition, and co-operation." This relationship should enhance the identity of both partners without stifling the growth of either. The young adult who does not seek out such intimacy or whose repeated tries fail may retreat into isolation.

Stage VII: Generativity versus Self-Absorption (Middle Adulthood) Generativity is "the interest in establishing and guiding the next generation" (Erikson, 1980, p. 103). Typically, people attain generativity through raising their own children. However, the crisis of this stage can also be successfully resolved through other forms of productivity and creativity, such as teaching. During this stage, people should continue to grow; if they don't, a sense of "stagnation and interpersonal impoverishment" develops, leading to self-absorption or self-indulgence (Erikson, 1980, p. 103).

Stage VIII: Integrity versus Despair (Late Adulthood) In the final stage of psychosocial development, people look back over their lifetime and resolve their final identity crisis. Acceptance of accomplishments, failures, and ultimate limitations brings with it a sense of integrity, or wholeness; a realization that one's life has been one's own responsibility. The finality of death must also be faced and accepted. Despair can occur in those who regret the way they have led their lives or how their lives have turned out.

> **CLASSROOM ARTIFACT HOMEWORK EXERCISE**
> **Qualities of 11 Year Olds**
>
> Go to **www.myeducationlab.com** and, in the Homework and Exercises section for Chapter 2 of this text, access the Classroom Artifact entitled "Qualities of 11 Year Olds." Examine the artifact and complete the homework questions that accompany it, saving your work or transmitting it to your professor as required.

Implications and Criticisms of Erikson's Theory

As with Piaget's stages, not all people experience Erikson's crises to the same degree or at the same time. The age ranges stated here may represent the best times for a crisis to be resolved, but they are not the only possible times. For example, children who were born into chaotic homes that failed to give them adequate security may develop trust after being adopted or otherwise brought into a more stable environment. People whose negative school experiences gave them a sense of inferiority may find as they enter the work world that they can learn and that they do have valuable skills, a realization that may help them finally to resolve the industry versus inferiority crisis that others resolved in their elementary school years. Erikson's theory emphasizes the role of the environment, both in causing the crises and in determining how they will be resolved. The stages of personal and social development are played out in constant interactions with others and with society as a whole. During the first three stages the interactions are primarily with parents and other family members, but the school plays a central role for most children in Stage IV (industry versus inferiority) and Stage V (identity versus role confusion).

Erikson's theory describes the basic issues that people confront as they go through life. However, his theory has been criticized because it does not explain how or why individuals progress from one stage to another and because it is difficult to confirm through research (Green, 1989; Miller, 1993).

WHAT ARE SOME THEORIES OF MORAL DEVELOPMENT?

INTASC

- 2 Knowledge of Human Development and Learning
- 4 Multiple Instructional Strategies

Society could not function without rules that tell people how to communicate with one another, how to avoid hurting others, and how to get along in life generally. If you are around children much, you may have noticed that they are often rigid about rules. Things are either right or wrong; there is no in-between. If you think back to your own years in middle school or high school, you may recall being shocked to find that people sometimes break rules on purpose and that the rules that apply to some people may not apply to others. These experiences probably changed your concept of rules. Your idea of laws may also have changed when you learned how they are made. People meet and debate and vote; the laws that are made one year can be changed the next. The more complexity you can see, the more you find exists. Just as children differ from adults in cognitive and personal development, they also differ in their moral reasoning. First, we will look at the two stages of moral reasoning described by Piaget, then we will discuss related theories developed by Lawrence Kohlberg. Piaget proposed that there is a relationship between the cognitive stages of development and the ability to reason about moral issues. Kohlberg believed that the development of the logical structures proposed by Piaget is necessary to, although not sufficient for, advances in the area of moral judgment and reasoning.

Piaget's Theory of Moral Development

Piaget's theory of cognitive development also included a theory about the development of moral reasoning. Piaget believed that cognitive structures and abilities develop first. Cognitive abilities then determine children's abilities to reason about social situations. As with cognitive abilities, Piaget proposed that moral development progresses in predictable stages, in this case from a very egocentric type of moral reasoning to one based on a system of justice based on cooperation and reciprocity. Table 2.3 summarizes Piaget's stages of moral development.

To understand children's moral reasoning, Piaget spent a great deal of time watching children play marbles and asking them about the rules of the game. The first thing he discovered was that before about the age of 6, children play by their own idiosyncratic, egocentric rules. Piaget believed that very young children were incapable of interacting in cooperative ways and therefore unable to engage in moral reasoning.

Piaget found that by the age of 6, children acknowledged the existence of rules, though they were inconsistent in following them. Frequently, several children who were supposedly playing the same game were observed to be playing by different sets of rules. Children at this age also had no understanding that game rules are arbitrary and something that a

TABLE 2.3 Piaget's Stages of Moral Development

As people develop their cognitive abilities, their understanding of moral problems also becomes more sophisticated. Young children are more rigid in their views of right and wrong than older children and adults tend to be.

Heteronomous Morality (Younger)	Autonomous Morality (Older)
Based on relations of constraint; for example, the complete acceptance by the child of adult prescriptions.	Based on relations of cooperation and mutual recognition of equality among autonomous individuals, as in relations between people who are equals.
Reflected in attitudes of *moral realism:* Rules are seen as inflexible requirements, external in origin and authority, not open to negotiation; and right is a matter of literal obedience to adults and rules.	Reflected in *rational* moral attitudes: Rules are viewed as products of mutual agreement, open to renegotiation, made legitimate by personal acceptance and common consent, and right is a matter of acting in accordance with the requirements of cooperation and mutual respect.
Badness is judged in terms of the objective form and consequences of actions; fairness is equated with the content of adult decisions; arbitrary and severe punishments are seen as fair.	Badness is viewed as relative to the actor's intentions; fairness is defined as equal treatment or taking account of individual needs; fairness of punishment is defined by appropriateness to the offense.
Punishment is seen as an automatic consequence of the offense, and justice is seen as inherent.	Punishment is seen as affected by human intention.

Source: From *Social and Personality Development,* 1st edition, by Michael E. Lamb, p. 213, © 1978. Reprinted with permission of Wadsworth, a division of Thomson Learning: www.thomsonrights.com. Fax 800-730-2215.

group can decide by itself. Instead, they saw rules as being imposed by some higher authority and unchangeable.

Piaget (1964) labeled the first stage of moral development **heteronomous morality;** it has also been called the stage of "moral realism" or "morality of constraint." *Heteronomous* means being subject to rules imposed by others. During this period, young children are consistently faced with parents and other adults telling them what to do and what not to do. Violations of rules are believed to bring automatic punishment; people who are bad will eventually be punished. Piaget also described children at this stage as judging the morality of behavior on the basis of its consequences. They judge behavior as bad if it results in negative consequences even if the actor's original intentions were good.

Piaget found that children did not conscientiously use and follow rules until the age of 10 or 12 years, when children are capable of formal operations. At this age, every child playing the game followed the same set of rules. Children understood that the rules existed to give the game direction and to minimize disputes between players. They understood that rules were something that everyone agreed on and that therefore, if everyone agreed to change them, they could be changed.

Piaget also observed that children at this age tend to base moral judgments on the intentions of the actor rather than the consequences of the actions. Children often engage in discussions of hypothetical circumstances that might affect rules. This second stage is labeled **autonomous morality** or "morality of cooperation." It arises as the child's social world expands to include more and more peers. By continually interacting and cooperating with other children, the child's ideas about rules and, therefore, morality begin to change. Rules are now what we make them to be. Punishment for transgressions is no longer automatic but must be administered with a consideration of the transgressor's intentions and extenuating circumstances.

According to Piaget, children progress from the stage of heteronomous morality to that of autonomous morality with the development of cognitive structures but also because of interactions with equal-status peers. He believed that resolving conflicts with peers weakened children's reliance on adult authority and heightened their awareness that rules are changeable and should exist only as the result of mutual consent.

heteronomous morality
In Piaget's theory of moral development, the stage at which children think that rules are unchangeable and that breaking them leads automatically to punishment.

autonomous morality
In Piaget's theory of moral development, the stage at which a person understands that people make rules and that punishments are not automatic.

Research on elements of Piaget's theories generally supports his ideas, with one key exception. Piaget is felt to have underestimated the degree to which even very young children consider intentions in judging behavior (see Bussey, 1992). However, the progression from a focus on outcomes to a focus on intentions over the course of development has been documented many times.

CERTIFICATION POINTER

Teacher certification tests are likely to require you to know the theoretical contributions of Lawrence Kohlberg to the understanding of children's development of moral reasoning.

Kohlberg's Stages of Moral Reasoning

Kohlberg's (1963, 1969) stage theory of moral reasoning is an elaboration and refinement of Piaget's. Like Piaget, Kohlberg studied how children (and adults) reason about rules that govern their behavior in certain situations. Kohlberg did not study children's game playing, but rather probed for their responses to a series of structured situations or **moral dilemmas.** His most famous one is the following:

> In Europe a woman was near death from cancer. One drug might save her, a form of radium that a druggist in the same town had recently discovered. The druggist was charging $2,000, ten times what the drug cost him to make. The sick woman's husband, Heinz, went to everyone he knew to borrow the money, but he could only get together about half of what it cost. He told the druggist that his wife was dying and asked him to sell it cheaper or let him pay later. But the druggist said "No." The husband got desperate and broke into the man's store to steal the drug for his wife. Should the husband have done that? Why? (1969, p. 379)

moral dilemmas
In Kohlberg's theory of moral reasoning, hypothetical situations that require a person to consider values of right and wrong.

On the basis of the answers he received, Kohlberg proposed that people pass through a series of six stages of moral judgment or reasoning. Kohlberg's levels and stages are summarized in Table 2.4. He grouped these six stages into three levels: preconventional,

TABLE 2.4 Kohlberg's Stages of Moral Reasoning

When people consider moral dilemmas, it is their reasoning that is important, not their final decision, according to Lawrence Kohlberg. He theorized that people progress through three levels as they develop abilities of moral reasoning.

I. Preconventional Level	II. Conventional Level	III. Postconventional Level
Rules are set down by others. **Stage 1: Punishment and Obedience Orientation.** Physical consequences of action determine its goodness or badness. **Stage 2: Instrumental Relativist Orientation.** What is right is whatever satisfies one's own needs and occasionally the needs of others. Elements of fairness and reciprocity are present, but they are mostly interpreted in a "you scratch my back, I'll scratch yours" fashion.	Individual adopts rules and will sometimes subordinate own needs to those of the group. Expectations of family, group, or nation seen as valuable in own right, regardless of immediate and obvious consequences. **Stage 3: "Good Boy–Good Girl" Orientation.** Good behavior is whatever pleases or helps others and is approved of by them. One earns approval by being "nice." **Stage 4: "Law and Order" Orientation.** Right is doing one's duty, showing respect for authority, and maintaining the given social order for its own sake.	People define own values in terms of ethical principles they have chosen to follow. **Stage 5: Social Contract Orientation.** What is right is defined in terms of general individual rights and in terms of standards that have been agreed on by the whole society. In contrast to Stage 4, laws are not "frozen"—they can be changed for the good of society. **Stage 6: Universal Ethical Principle Orientation.** What is right is defined by decision of conscience according to self-chosen ethical principles. These principles are abstract and ethical (such as the Golden Rule), not specific moral prescriptions (such as the Ten Commandments).

Source: From L. Kohlberg, "Stage and Sequence: The Cognitive–Developmental Approach to Socialization." In David A. Goslin (Ed.), *Handbook of Socialization Theory and Research,* pp. 347–380, 1969, published by Rand McNally, Chicago. Reproduced with permission of David A. Goslin.

conventional, and postconventional. These three levels are distinguished by how the child or adult defines what he or she perceives as correct or moral behavior. As with other stage theories, each stage is more sophisticated and more complex than the preceding one, and most individuals proceed through them in the same order (Colby & Kohlberg, 1984). Like Piaget, Kohlberg was concerned not so much with the child's answer as with the reasoning behind it. The ages at which children and adolescents go through the stages in Table 2.4 may vary considerably; in fact, the same individual may behave according to one stage at some times and according to another at other times. However, most children pass from the preconventional to the conventional level by the age of 9 (Kohlberg, 1969).

ON THE WEB

The Association for Moral Education (AME) provides an interdisciplinary forum for individuals interested in the moral dimensions of educational theory and practice at **www.amenetwork.org.**

Stage 1, which is on the **preconventional level of morality,** is very similar in form and content to Piaget's stage of heteronomous morality. Children simply obey authority figures to avoid being punished. In Stage 2, children's own needs and desires become important, yet they are aware of the interests of other people. In a concrete sense they weigh the interests of all parties when making moral judgments, but they are still "looking out for number one." The **conventional level of morality** begins at Stage 3. Here morality is defined in terms of cooperation with peers, just as it was in Piaget's stage of autonomous morality. This is the stage at which children have an unquestioning belief that one should "do unto others as you would have them do unto you." Because of the decrease in egocentrism that accompanies concrete operations, children are cognitively capable of putting themselves in someone else's shoes. They can consider the feelings of others when making moral decisions. No longer do they simply do what will not get them punished (Stage 1) or what makes them feel good (Stage 2). At Stage 4, society's rules and laws replace those of the peer group. A desire for social approval no longer determines moral judgments. Laws are followed without question, and breaking the law can never be justified. Most adults are probably at this stage. Stage 5 signals entrance into the **postconventional level of morality.** This level of moral reasoning is attained by fewer than 25 percent of adults, according to Kohlberg. Here there is a realization that the laws and values of a society are somewhat arbitrary and particular to that society. Laws are seen as necessary to preserve the social order and to ensure the basic rights of life and liberty. In Stage 6, one's ethical principles are self-chosen and based on abstract concepts such as justice and the equality and value of human rights. Laws that violate these principles can and should be disobeyed because "justice is above the law." Late in life, Kohlberg (1978, 1980) speculated that Stage 6 is not really separate from Stage 5 and suggested that the two be combined.

Kohlberg (1969) believed that moral dilemmas can be used to advance a child's level of moral reasoning, but only one stage at a time. He theorized that the way in which children progress from one stage to the next is by interacting with others whose reasoning is one or, at most, two stages above their own. Teachers can help students progress in moral reasoning by weaving discussions of justice and moral issues into their lessons, particularly in response to events that occur in the classroom or in the broader society (see Nucci, 1987).

Kohlberg found that his stages of moral reasoning ability occurred in the same order and at about the same ages in the United States, Mexico, Taiwan, and Turkey. Other research throughout the world has generally found the same sequence of stages (Eckensberger, 1994), although there are clearly strong influences of culture on moral reasoning as well as moral behavior (Navaez, Getz, Rest, & Thoma, 1999).

preconventional level of morality
Stages 1 and 2 in Kohlberg's model of moral reasoning, in which individuals make moral judgments in their own interests.

conventional level of morality
Stages 3 and 4 in Kohlberg's model of moral reasoning, in which individuals make moral judgments in consideration of others.

postconventional level of morality
Stages 5 and 6 in Kohlberg's model of moral reasoning, in which individuals make moral judgments in relation to abstract principles.

What influence can older children have on the development of moral reasoning in younger children? How can an understanding of moral reasoning help you as a teacher?

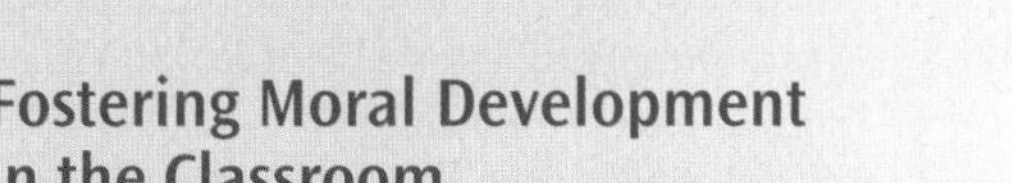

THEORY *into* PRACTICE

Fostering Moral Development in the Classroom

The study of moral development is one of the oldest topics of interest to those curious about human nature, but the implementation of moral education curricula has not taken place without controversy. Educators and families active in these endeavors have grappled with the important distinction that theories deal with moral reasoning rather than with actual moral behavior. Successful programs have incorporated values education at the global, local, and individual levels.

GLOBAL LEVEL—DISTRICTWIDE APPROACH. Many schools have chosen to institutionalize a global, inclusive approach to character building with input from teachers, administrators, parents, and, at the higher grade levels, even students (see Kohlberg, 1980; Lickona, 1992). Here, values education is found across the curriculum, implemented throughout the school building, and connected to the home. Such programs emphasize the individual citizen as a member of the social institution and advocate particular levels of moral behavior. They provide students with a framework of expected behavior; violations of these standards can then be addressed. At the elementary level, students receive guidelines and are invited to discuss violations and their consequences. In middle school and throughout the high school years, students are more involved in the creation and maintenance of guidelines and even play a significant role in the decision making surrounding violations of the guidelines.

LOCAL LEVEL—CLASSROOM INSTRUCTION. At the more local level, the teacher might choose to capitalize on students' natural curiosity and might teach values and decision making through "What if . . . ?" discussions. The classroom is an ideal laboratory in which students can test hypothetical situations and potential consequences. Teachers must recognize the cognitive abilities of those in their class and maximize these abilities through problem-solving activities. Being an effective moral

VIDEO HOMEWORK EXERCISE
Moral Reasoning

Go to **www.myeducationlab.com** and, in the Homework and Exercises section for Chapter 2 of this text, access the video entitled "Moral Reasoning." Watch the video and complete the homework questions that accompany it, saving your work or transmitting it to your professor as required.

educator is no easy task. Teachers must reexamine their teaching role; they must be willing to create cognitive conflict in their classrooms and to stimulate social perspective taking in students.

INDIVIDUAL LEVEL—CONFLICT MANAGEMENT. Families want schools to provide students with the necessary tools to mediate serious conflicts without violence, and teachers and administrators are evaluating or initiating conflict resolution programs in many schools (see Bodine, Crawford, & Schrumpf, 1994).

Criticisms of Kohlberg's Theory

One limitation of Kohlberg's work is that it mostly involved boys. Some research on girls' moral reasoning finds patterns that are somewhat different from those proposed by Kohlberg. Whereas boys' moral reasoning revolves primarily around issues of justice, girls are more concerned about issues of caring and responsibility for others

Personal REFLECTION

Developing Character

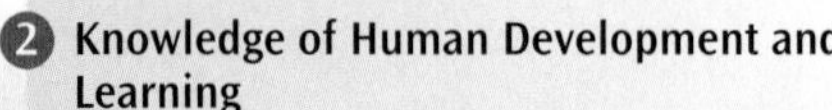

INTASC 2 Knowledge of Human Development and Learning

For a number of years now a "character education" movement has sought solutions to what many in the public perceive as a decline in the moral character of the nation, in general, and of young people specifically. In an article entitled "Moral Teachers, Moral Students" in the March 2003 issue of *Educational Leadership,* author and educator Rick Weissbourd of Harvard argued that "schools can best support students' moral development by helping teachers manage the stresses of their profession and by increasing teachers' capacity for reflection and empathy." The following is an excerpt from his article:

> Once again, the public frets about whether children are becoming good people. Both conservative commentators and researchers decry a steady rise in greed, delinquency, and disrespect. And once again, the public holds schools largely responsible for remedying these troubles.
>
> "Solutions" abound. Many character education efforts in schools now focus on everything from community service to teaching students virtues, building good habits, rewarding positive behavior, and developing students' capacity for moral reasoning (Schaps, Schaeffer, & McDonnell, 2001).
>
> There is value in these solutions. Students surely benefit from performing community service, being reminded of important virtues, and practicing good habits.
>
> But we have been wringing our hands and trying these solutions for decades, in some cases for two centuries, without fundamentally changing students' moral prospects. The moral development of students does not depend primarily on explicit character education efforts but on the maturity and ethical capacities of the adults with whom they interact—especially parents, but also teachers, coaches, and other community adults.
>
> Educators influence students' moral development not simply by being good role models—important as that is—but also by what they bring to their relationships with students day to day: their ability to appreciate students' perspectives and to disentangle them from their own, their ability to admit and learn from moral error, their moral energy and idealism, their generosity, and their ability to help students develop moral thinking without shying away from their own moral authority. That level of influence makes being an adult in a school a profound moral challenge. And it means that we will never greatly improve students' moral development in schools without taking on the complex task of developing adults' maturity and ethical capacities. We need to rethink the nature of moral development itself.

REFLECT ON THIS. Do you agree or disagree with Weissbourd's perspective on moral development? As a student or a teacher, have you had occasion to admit to or learn from moral errors? How could your actions influence your students' moral development? Why are teachers important role models in their students' development?

(Gilligan, 1982; Gilligan & Attanucci, 1988; Haspe & Baddeley, 1991). Carol Gilligan has argued, for example, that males and females use different moral criteria: that male moral reasoning is focused on people's individual rights, whereas female moral reasoning is focused more on individuals' responsibilities for other people. This is why, she argues, females tend to suggest altruism and self-sacrifice rather than rights and rules as solutions to moral dilemmas (Gilligan, 1982). Kohlberg (Levine, Kohlberg, & Hewer, 1985) later revised his theory on the basis of these criticisms. However, most research has failed to find any male–female differences in moral maturity (Bee & Boyd, 2007; Jaffee & Hyde, 2000; Thoma & Rest, 1999); nor is there convincing evidence that women are more caring, cooperative, or helpful than men (Turiel, 1998; Walker, 1991).

CONNECTIONS
For more on gender issues in education, see Chapter 4, pages 112–116.

Another criticism of both Piaget's and Kohlberg's work is that young children can often reason about moral situations in more sophisticated ways than a stage theory would suggest (Rest, Edwards, & Thoma, 1997). For example, although young children often consider consequences to be more important than intentions when evaluating conduct, under certain circumstances, children as young as 3 and 4 years of age use intentions to judge the behavior of others (Bussey, 1992). Six- to 10-year-olds at the stage of heteronomous morality have also been shown to make distinctions between rules that parents are justified in making and enforcing and rules that are under personal or peer jurisdiction (Laupa, 1991; Tisak & Tisak, 1990). Finally, Turiel (1998) has suggested that young children make a distinction between moral rules, such as not lying and stealing, that are based on principles of justice, and social-conventional rules, such as not wearing pajamas to school, that are based on social consensus and etiquette. Research has supported this view, demonstrating that children as young as 2½ to 3 years old make distinctions between moral and social-conventional rules.

Teaching Dilemmas: CASES TO CONSIDER

Using Moral Reasoning

Ms. Jackson administered a unit test to students in her eighth-grade pre-algebra class. As the class began to take the test, however, she was summoned to the office for an urgent call. Rather than interrupt the activity flow, she quickly appointed Nichole, a high-achieving student who always finished tests early, to serve as classroom monitor during her absence. Ms. Jackson expected to be back in class in only a few minutes. She thought the students might not even notice she was gone. Unfortunately, Ms. Jackson was detained. As Nichole watched with growing alarm, Rafael and Martin began to discuss test items and compare answers. Gradually, other students became aware of their behavior.

INTASC

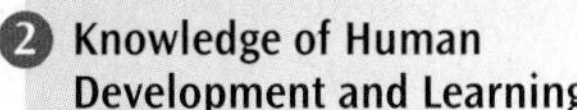

Rafael: What did you get for number two? Mine doesn't look right.
Nichole: Shhhhh.
Martin: I got $x = 4$. But I can't do the first one.
Nichole and Sandy: Shhhhh.
Rafael: I think you have to divide everything by two.
Sandy: They're cheating! That's not fair!
Nichole: If you don't stop right now, I'll have to tell Ms. Jackson you were talking.
Martin: You better not. I'm not the only one. Look around. Marta even has her book open.
Marta: I'm not going to get a bad mark because you guys are cheating.
Rafael: So, if everyone does it then it's fair, right? We could all get good grades.

Dan: That's dumb. If everyone cheated, school would be a total joke. Teachers wouldn't know if we were learning anything. Grades would be worthless.

Carmen: Everybody, shhhh. We shouldn't go against the rules. You're not supposed to cheat. Everybody's going to get into trouble!

Martin: Don't be so self-righteous. The main thing is not getting caught. It's getting caught that's dumb. If nobody's the wiser it doesn't matter, and if you're dumb enough to get caught, then you deserve whatever you get.

Sandy: Cheater!

Marta: Okay, I closed my book. My mother would die if she thought I cheated. You're not going to tell, are you, Nichole?

Nichole: I want to do whatever is best for everyone.

Rafael: Well, I'm not doing detention over this.

Dan: We could all get detention over this, because it's wrong to cheat. Meanwhile, we've lost 10 minutes, so if everyone would just shut up, maybe we'll be able to finish. This is a test!

When Ms. Jackson returned to class, she knew instantly that something had gone wrong. Nichole wore an embarrassed expression and quickly returned to her seat. Martin looked angry and had a paper balled up on his desk. Rafael looked shifty and scared. Marta was gazing sadly out the window, and Sandy seemed to have some secret she desperately wanted to share. Only Dan was able to finish the test by the bell.

The Intentional TEACHER

USING WHAT YOU KNOW about Human Development to Improve Teaching and Learning

Intentional teachers use what they know about predictable patterns of moral, psychosocial, and cognitive development to make instructional decisions. They assess their students' functioning, and they provide instruction that addresses the broad range of stages of development they find in their students. They modify their instruction when they find that particular students need additional challenges or different opportunities. Thinking about student development and watching for it in the classroom helps intentional teachers foster growth for each student.

1 What do I expect my students to know and be able to do at the end of this lesson? How does this contribute to course objectives and to students' needs to become capable individuals?

Teachers need to assess their own students' developmental functioning in light of their understanding of stages of human development. For example, if you were planning a first-grade science program, you might refer to Piaget's theory and recall that 6- and 7-year-olds have to struggle when asked to think about more than one variable at a time (centration). For that reason your science program goals might focus heavily on students' active, open-ended exploration of their world and far less on formal experimentation requiring the control of variables. As a middle school English teacher, you might review your list of semester goals and verify that it includes not only an emphasis on a set of writing conventions but also a focus on students' moral development. You might plan to include activities that challenge students to experience characters' emotional distress or to view good and bad from different characters' perspectives.

2 What knowledge, skills, needs, and interests do my students have that must be taken into account in my lesson?

Every class group has some common, age-appropriate interests, but there is always a range of personal knowledge and interests that you can find out about to address individual needs. You might have discussions about interests, role models, favorite general icons, sports, and so on, and then weave the information you gain into your sessions, heightening motivation and relevance.

3 What do I know about the content, child development, learning, motivation, and effective teaching strategies that I can use to accomplish my objectives?

A broad range of individual differences can be found in each classroom, and individual students exhibit inconsistencies between their thinking and their behavior. Teachers can assess their students' developmental functioning in light of their understanding of general expectations for student development. For example, you might discuss with students problems such as those used by Piaget to assess formal operational thinking, or moral dilemmas such as those used by Kohlberg to assess

QUESTIONS FOR REFLECTION

1. Analyze the differences in moral reasoning evident in the dialogue. How might Piaget have interpreted each speech in relation to stages of moral development? How might Kohlberg classify each speech in relation to stages of moral reasoning? How might Gilligan interpret the dialogue to support her view that males and females reason differently?
2. What should Ms. Jackson do to follow up on her suspicions? Assuming that she learned that cheating had taken place, how should she address cheating as a moral issue in a way that would help her students?

ONLINE READING & WRITING EXERCISE

The Honor Level System: Discipline by Design

Access this exercise, entitled "The Honor Level System: Discipline by Design," in the Homework and Exercises section for Chapter 2 of this text at **www.mylabschool.com.**

The most important limitation of Kohlberg's theory is that it deals with moral reasoning rather than with actual behavior (Arnold, 2000). Many individuals at different stages behave in the same way, and individuals at the same stage often behave in different ways (Walker & Henning, 1997). In addition, the context of moral dilemmas matters. For example, a study by Einerson (1998) found that adolescents used much lower levels of moral reasoning when moral dilemmas involved celebrities than when they involved made-up characters such as Heinz. Similarly, the link between children's moral reasoning and moral behavior may be unclear (Thoma & Rest, 1999). For example, a study by Murdock, Hale, and Weber (2001) found that cheating among middle school students was affected by many factors, including motivation in school, success, and relationships with teachers, which have little to do with stages of moral development.

INTASC

8 Assessment of Student Learning
9 Professional Commitment and Responsibilty

moral development. These will give you insight into the thinking processes of your students.

4 What instructional materials, technology, assistance, and other resources are available to help me accomplish my objectives?

How can you create a rich environment that includes a range of materials and experiences to meet a variety of needs and challenge students at all developmental levels? One solution is to introduce a range of materials likely to appeal to and inform students at a broad range of developmental levels, including magazines, newspapers, children's literature, and almanacs, maps, physical models, and real objects. You might invite students to suggest or bring materials. You might search out CD-ROMs and Internet resources relevant to the subject you teach. These resources can then be incorporated in projects and investigations that enable students of different developmental levels to find and use materials that make sense to them.

5 How will I plan to assess students' progress toward my objectives?

Effective, intentional teachers use a variety of measures to assess student growth. Students will benefit from measures that can assess psychological as well as cognitive growth. For example, you might ask secondary students to write brief analyses of current social issues, and then collect their paragraphs in folders. In spring, for each student, you might pull a sampling of essays from several points in the year to allow students to examine their evolving moral and social perspectives. In an art or shop class, you might collect an early sample of each student's work and ask the students to evaluate their work by writing a paragraph on an index card. Near the end of the term, you might collect another set of samples. Students will be pleased to assess their progress over time and their growing ability to form smooth, sophisticated pieces.

6 How will I respond if individual children or the class as a whole are not on track toward success? What is my back-up plan?

Observe your students carefully to determine whether they are working within their zone of proximal development. Are they experiencing success with the current level of support? More support can be provided for students who are working above their zone of proximal development, and additional challenges might be provided for those working below.

CHAPTER 2 SUMMARY

What Are Some Views of Human Development?

Human development includes physical, cognitive, personal, social, and moral development. Most developmental psychologists believe nature and nurture combine to influence development. Continuous theories of development focus on social experiences that a child goes through, whereas discontinuous theories emphasize inborn factors rather than environmental influence. Development can be significantly affected by heredity, ability, exceptionality, personality, child rearing, culture, and the total environment. Jean Piaget and Lev Vygotsky proposed theories of cognitive development. Erik Erikson's theory of psychosocial development and Piaget's and Lawrence Kohlberg's theories of moral development also describe important aspects of development.

How Did Piaget View Cognitive Development?

Piaget postulated four stages of cognitive development through which people progress between birth and young adulthood. People adjust their schemes for dealing with the world through assimilation and accommodation. Piaget's developmental stages include the sensorimotor stage (birth to 2 years of age), the preoperational stage (2 to 7 years of age), and the concrete operational stage (ages 7 to 11). During the formal operational stage (age 11 to adulthood), young people develop the ability to deal with hypothetical situations and to monitor their own thinking.

How Is Piaget's Work Viewed Today?

Piaget's theory has been criticized for relying exclusively on broad, fixed, sequential stages through which all children progress and for underestimating children's abilities. In contrast, neo-Piagetian theories place greater emphasis on social and environmental influences on cognitive development. Nevertheless, Piaget's theory has important implications for education. Piagetian principles are embedded in the curriculum and in effective teaching practices, and Piaget-influenced concepts such as cognitive constructivism and developmentally appropriate instruction have been important in education reform.

How Did Vygotsky View Cognitive Development?

Vygotsky viewed cognitive development as an outgrowth of social development through interaction with others and the environment. Assisted learning takes place in children's zones of proximal development, where they can do new tasks that are within their capabilities only with a teacher's or peer's assistance. Children internalize learning, develop self-regulation, and solve problems through vocal or silent private speech. Teachers provide interactional contexts, such as cooperative learning groups, and scaffolding.

How Did Erikson View Personal and Social Development?

Erikson proposed eight stages of psychosocial development, each dominated by a particular psychosocial crisis precipitated through interaction with the social environment. In Stage I, trust versus mistrust, the goal is to develop a sense of trust through interaction with caretakers. In Stage II, autonomy versus doubt (18 months to age 3), children have a dual desire to hold on and to let go. In Stage III, initiative versus guilt (3 to 6 years of age), children elaborate their sense of self through exploration of the environment. Children enter school during Stage IV, industry versus inferiority (6 to 12 years of age), when academic success or failure is central. In Stage V, identity versus role confusion (12 to 18 years), adolescents turn increasingly to their peer group and begin their searches for partners and careers. Adulthood brings Stage VI (intimacy versus isolation), Stage VII (generativity versus self-absorption), and Stage VIII (integrity versus despair).

What Are Some Theories of Moral Development?

According to Piaget, children develop heteronomous morality (obedience to authority through moral realism) by around age 6 and later advance to autonomous morality (rational morality based on moral principles). Kohlberg stages of moral reasoning reflect children's responses to moral dilemmas. In Stages 1 and 2 (the preconventional level), children obey rules set down by others while maximizing self-interest. In Stages 3 and 4 (the conventional level), the individual adopts rules, believes in law and order, and seeks the approval of others. In Stages 5 and 6 (the postconventional level), people define their own values in terms of abstract ethical principles they have chosen to follow.

KEY TERMS

Review the following key terms from the chapter.

accommodation 32
adaptation 32
assimilation 32
autonomous morality 50
centration 34
class inclusion 38
cognitive development 31
concrete operational stage 37
conservation 34
constructivism 33
continuous theories of development 31
conventional level of morality 52
development 30
developmentally appropriate education 41
discontinuous theories of development 31
egocentric 36
equilibration 32
formal operational stage 38
heteronomous morality 50
inferred reality 37
moral dilemmas 51
object permanence 34
postconventional level of morality 52
preconventional level of morality 52
preoperational stage 34
private speech 43
psychosocial crisis 46
psychosocial theory 46
reflexes 33
reversibility 36
scaffolding 43
schemes 32
self-regulation 43
sensorimotor stage 33
seriation 37
sign systems 42
transitivity 38
zone of proximal development 43

SELF-ASSESSMENT: PRACTICING *for* LICENSURE

Directions: The chapter-opening vignettes address indicators that are often assessed in state licensure exams. Re-read the chapter-opening vignettes, and then respond to the following questions.

1. Mr. Jones, in the first vignette, is perplexed when he asks his students to follow his example by raising their right hands; instead, they raise their left hands. According to developmental theory, why did this happen?
   - **a.** Kohlberg would say students at the conventional level of moral development cooperate with peers. If one student raises his or her left hand, the others follow.
   - **b.** Vygotsky would say the students are outside their zone of proximal development. They cannot complete the task without assistance.
   - **c.** Piaget would say that students are egocentric, thus unable to consider another person's point of view.
   - **d.** Erikson would say that the students lack the motor skills necessary to complete the task.
2. What simple solution might work to help Mr. Jones to get his students to raise their right hands?
   - **a.** Mr. Jones should have his students draw a diagram of a person raising his or her right hand.
   - **b.** Mr. Jones should position himself in the same direction as his students rather than face them, and then raise his right hand.
   - **c.** Students should write mnemonics to help them remember their right hand from their left hand.
   - **d.** Students should participate in a drill-and-practice activity of "Left is West when Facing North."
3. In the second vignette, why did Ms. Lewis's students refuse to allow the girl with the ill mother to go on the field trip?
   - **a.** According to Erikson's theory, the students were incapable of reversible thought.
   - **b.** Preoperational children are egocentric in their thinking.
   - **c.** The children in Ms. Lewis's class have not yet acquired what Piaget calls "class inclusion."
   - **d.** According to Piaget, children at this age judge the morality of behavior on the basis of its consequence.
4. According to Kohlberg's theory of moral development, how can Ms. Lewis help her students move past their belief that "rules are rules with no exceptions"?
   - **a.** Challenge the student's reasoning with explanations from the next higher stage.
   - **b.** Cancel the field trip for all students.
   - **c.** Bring the mother into the classroom to explain why the girl did not complete the assignment.
   - **d.** Ask each student to write a story about someone who did not follow the rules.
5. According to Erikson's theory of personal development, why did Frank react the way he did to Ms. Quintera's praise of his poetry?
   - **a.** Highlighting Frank's achievement could cast him in the role of teacher's pet, a role that many students in early adolescence strongly resist.
   - **b.** Students in early adolescence prefer to receive praise from teachers of the same gender.
   - **c.** Writing poetry is developmentally inappropriate for students in early adolescence.
   - **d.** Frank didn't think his poetry was good enough to receive praise from his teacher.
6. Write a brief description of a typical (i.e., fits the theories) student at one of the following grade levels: K–6, 5–9, or 7–12. Use the ideas of each theorist from this chapter to guide your description.
7. Make a list of developmentally appropriate teaching strategies for one of the following grade levels: K–5, 5–9, 7–12.

PEARSON

myeducationlab

Where the Classroom Comes to Life

Now go to **www.myeducationlab.com** to:

- take a Pretest to assess your initial comprehension of the chapter content;
- study chapter content with your individualized Study Plan;
- take a Posttest to assess your understanding of chapter content;
- practice your teaching skills with Building Teaching Skills exercises; and
- build a deeper, more applied understanding of chapter content with Homework and Exercises.

CHAPTER 3

Development during Childhood and Adolescence

chapter OUTLINE

At Parren Elementary/Middle School, eighth-graders are encouraged to become tutors for first-graders. They help them with reading, math, and other subjects. As part of this program, Sam Stevens has been working for about a month with Billy Ames.

"Hey, shorty!" said Sam one day when he met Billy for a tutoring session.

"Hey, Sam!" As always, Billy was delighted to see his big buddy. But today his friendly greeting turned into a look of astonishment. "What have you got in your ear?"

"Haven't you ever seen an earring?"

"I thought those were just for girls."

Sam laughed. "Not like this one! Can you see it?"

Billy squinted at the earring and saw that it was in the shape of a small sword. "Awesome!"

"A lot of guys are wearing them."

"Didn't it hurt to get a hole in your ear?"

"A little, but I'm tough! Boy, was my mom mad though. I have to take my earring off before I go home, but I put it back on while I'm walking to school."

"But didn't your mom . . ."

"Enough of that, squirt! You've got some heavy math to do. Let's get to it!"

The interaction between Sam and Billy illustrates the enormous differences between the world of the adolescent and that of the child. Sam, at 13, is a classic young teen. His idealism and down-deep commitment to the positive are shown in his volunteering to serve as a tutor and in the caring, responsible relationship he has established with Billy. At the same time, Sam is asserting his independence by having his ear pierced and wearing an earring, against his mother's wishes. This independence is strongly supported by his peer group, however, so it is really only a shift of dependence from parents and teachers toward peers. His main purpose in wearing an earring is to demonstrate conformity to the styles and norms of his peers rather than to those of adults. Yet Sam does still depend on his parents and other adults for advice and support when making decisions that he knows have serious consequences for his future, and he does take off his earring at home to avoid a really serious battle with his parents.

Billy lives in a different world. He can admire Sam's audacity, but he would never go so far. Billy's world has simpler rules. For one thing, boys are boys and girls are girls, so he is shocked by Sam's flouting of convention to wear something usually associated with females. He is equally shocked by Sam's willingness to directly disobey his mother. Billy may misbehave, but within much narrower limits. He knows that rules are rules, and he fully expects to be punished if he breaks them.

USING *your* EXPERIENCE

CREATIVE THINKING Think of reasons that educators should know about the developmental characteristics of children younger and older than the ones they teach.

Educators must know the principal theories of cognitive, social, and moral development presented in Chapter 2 so that they will understand how young people grow over time in each of these domains (Comer, 2005). However, teachers usually deal with children in a particular age range. A preschool teacher needs to know what preschool children are like. Elementary teachers are concerned with middle childhood. Middle, junior high, and senior high school teachers are concerned with adolescence. This chapter presents the physical, social, and cognitive characteristics of students at each phase of development (see Bee & Boyd, 2007; Berk, 2006; Cook & Cook, 2007). It discusses how the principles of development presented in Chapter 2 apply to children of various ages and adds information on physical development, language development, and self-concept. Figure 3.1 identifies central themes or emphases in development during early childhood, middle childhood, and adolescence.

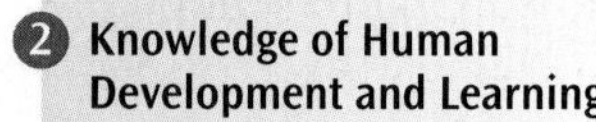

INTASC

2 Knowledge of Human Development and Learning

HOW DO CHILDREN DEVELOP DURING THE PRESCHOOL YEARS?

Children can be termed *preschoolers* when they are between 3 and 5 years of age. This is a time of rapid change in all areas of development. Children master most motor skills by the end of this period and can use their physical skills to achieve a wide range of goals. Cognitively, they start to develop an understanding of classes and relationships and absorb an enormous amount of information about their social and physical worlds. By the age of 6, children use almost completely mature speech, not only to express their wants and needs, but also to share their ideas and experiences. Socially, children learn appropriate behaviors and rules and become increasingly adept at interacting with other children.

As each of these aspects of development is discussed, keep in mind the complexity of development and how all facets of a child's growth are interrelated. Although physical, cognitive, and social development can be put in separate sections in a book, in real life they not only are intertwined but also are affected by the environment within which children grow up.

Physical Development

Physical development describes the changes in the physical appearance of children as well as in their motor skills. During the preschool years, the sequence in which all children develop motor skills is generally the same, though some children gain skills faster than others.

The major physical accomplishment for preschoolers is increased control over the large and small muscles. **Small muscle development,** or fine motor activity, relates to movements requiring precision and dexterity, such as buttoning a shirt or zipping a coat. **Large muscle development,** or gross motor activities, involves such movements as walking and running. Table 3.1 (p. 66) shows the ages at which most children acquire various motor skills.

small muscle development
Development of dexterity of the fine muscles of the hand.

large muscle development
Development of motor skills such as running or throwing, which involve the limbs and large muscles.

By the end of the preschool period, most children can easily perform self-help tasks such as buckling, buttoning, snapping, and zipping. They can go up and down steps with

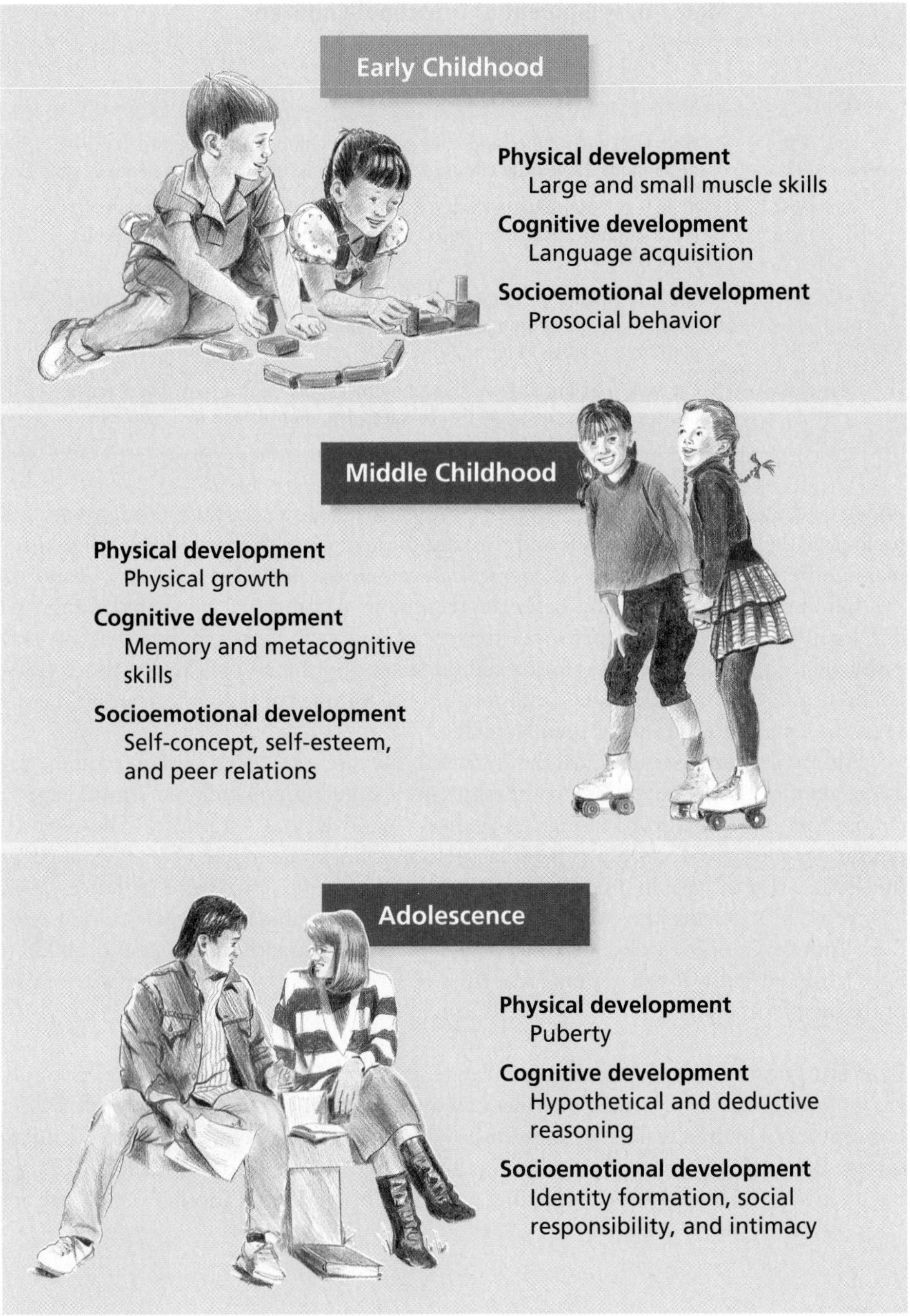

Early Childhood

Physical development
Large and small muscle skills

Cognitive development
Language acquisition

Socioemotional development
Prosocial behavior

Middle Childhood

Physical development
Physical growth

Cognitive development
Memory and metacognitive skills

Socioemotional development
Self-concept, self-esteem, and peer relations

Adolescence

Physical development
Puberty

Cognitive development
Hypothetical and deductive reasoning

Socioemotional development
Identity formation, social responsibility, and intimacy

FIGURE 3.1 Central Issues in Development during Early Childhood, Middle Childhood, and Adolescence These are some developmental concerns that are characteristically (but not exclusively) important during each of the three broad age levels discussed in this chapter.

VIDEO HOMEWORK EXERCISE
Physical Development—Early Childhood

Go to **www.myeducationlab.com** and, in the Homework and Exercises section for Chapter 3 of this text, access the video entitled "Physical Development—Early Childhood." Watch the video and complete the homework questions that accompany it, saving your work or transmitting it to your professor as required.

alternating feet. They can perform fine motor activities such as cutting with scissors and using crayons to color a predefined area. They also begin learning to write letters and words. After 6 or 7 years of age, children gain few completely new basic skills; rather, the quality and complexity of their movements improve (Berk, 2001).

Cognitive Development

Language Acquisition From birth to about 2 years of age, infants understand their world through their senses. Their knowledge is based on physical actions, and their understanding is restricted to events in the present or the immediate past. Only when children make the transition from the sensorimotor stage to the preoperational stage (at about age 2) and begin to talk and to use mental symbols can they use thoughts or concepts to

TABLE 3.1 Motor Development of Preschool Children

Age	Skills
2-year-olds	Walk with wide stance and body sway. Can climb, push, pull, run, hang by both hands. Have little endurance. Reach for objects with two hands.
3-year-olds	Keep legs closer together when walking and running. Can run and move more smoothly. Reach for objects with one hand. Smear and daub paint; stack blocks.
4-year-olds	Can vary rhythm of running. Skip awkwardly; jump. Have greater strength, endurance, and coordination. Draw shapes and simple figures; make paintings; use blocks for buildings.
5-year-olds	Can walk a balance beam. Skip smoothly; stand on one foot. Can manage buttons and zippers; may tie shoelaces. Use utensils and tools correctly.

understand their world. During the preoperational stage, however, their thoughts are still prelogical, tied to physical actions and the way things appear to them. Most children remain in the preoperational stage of cognitive development until they are 7 or 8 years old.

Children normally develop basic language skills before entering school. Language development involves both oral and written communication.Verbal abilities develop very early, and by age 3, children are already skillful talkers. By the end of the preschool years, children can use and understand an almost infinite number of sentences, can hold conversations, and know about written language.

Although there are individual differences in the rates at which children acquire language abilities, the sequence of accomplishments is similar for all children. Around age 1, children produce one-word utterances such as "bye-bye" and "Mommy." These words typically represent objects and events that are important to the child. Over the course of the second year of life, children begin to combine words into two-word sentences (e.g., "More milk"). During the preschool years, children's vocabulary increases, along with their knowledge of the rules of spoken language. By the time they start school, children have mastered most of the grammatical rules of language, and their vocabulary consists of thousands of words.

Oral Language Development of oral language, or spoken language, requires not only learning words but also learning the rules of word and sentence construction (Hoff, 2003). For example, children learn the rules for how to form plurals before they enter kindergarten. Berko (1985) showed preschoolers a picture of a made-up bird, called a "Wug." She then showed them two such pictures and said, "Now there is another one. There are

Personal REFLECTION

Understanding Development

For a reading program we were developing, my colleagues and I developed a set of animations to illustrate letter sounds. As part of the animation process, I supplied the voices for some of the characters. We showed our cartoons to my 4-year-old nephew, Jack, and told him to listen for my voice. He listened intently, but he looked terribly puzzled. He saw a cartoon dinosaur, for example, with my voice! Finally, he asked, "Did you have to wear a dinosaur suit?"

Jack's inability to imagine how my voice could be coming from a cartoon dinosaur is classic preoperational behavior.

REFLECT ON THIS. Why was Jack unable to disconnect my voice from the image of the dinosaur? Why would an understanding of child development be helpful to an early elementary or early childhood teacher?

two of them. There are two _________." The children readily answered "Wugs," showing that they could apply general rules for forming plurals to a new situation. In a similar fashion, children learn to add "-ed" and "-ing" to verbs. As they learn these rules, they initially overgeneralize them, saying "goed" instead of "went," for example, and "mouses" instead of "mice."

Interestingly, children often learn the correct forms of irregular verbs (such as "He broke the chair") and then replace them with incorrect but more rule-based constructions ("He breaked [or broked] the chair"). One 4-year-old said, "I flew my kite." He then thought for a moment and emphatically corrected himself, saying, "I flewed my kite!" These errors are a normal part of language development and should not be corrected (Fenson et al., 1994).

What language acquisition knowledge and skills will these children likely have by the time they enter kindergarten? As a teacher, what general approaches to formal instruction in reading and writing might you use to build on their knowledge and skills?

Just as they learn rules for forming words, children learn rules for sentences. Their first sentences usually contain only two words ("Want milk," "See birdie," "Jessie outside"), but they soon learn to form more complex sentences and to vary their tone of voice to indicate questions ("Where doggie go?") or to indicate emphasis ("Want cookie!"). Three-year-olds can usually express rather complex thoughts, even though their sentences may still lack such words as "a," "the," and "did." Later, children continually expand their ability to express and understand complex sentences. However, they still have difficulty with certain aspects of language throughout the preschool and early elementary school years. For example, Carol Chomsky (1969) showed children a doll that was blindfolded and asked, "Is the doll easy to see or hard to see?" Only 22 percent of 5-year-olds could respond correctly; not until age 9 could all her subjects respond appropriately to the question. Many students confuse such words as "ask" and "tell" and "teach" and "learn" well into the elementary grades.

CERTIFICATION POINTER

For teacher certification tests you may be expected to know that children's overgeneralizations of the rules of grammar are normal for young children and should not be corrected.

Preschoolers often play with language or experiment with its patterns and rules (Garvey, 1990). This experimentation frequently involves changing sounds, patterns, and meanings. One 3-year-old was told by his exasperated parent, "You're impossible!" He replied, "No, I'm impopsicle!" The same child said that his baby brother, Benjamin, was a man because he was a "Benja-man." Children often rearrange word sounds to create new words, rhymes, and funny sentences. The popularity of finger plays, nonsense rhymes, and Dr. Seuss storybooks shows how young children enjoy playing with language.

Oral language development is heavily influenced by the amount and quality of talking parents do with their children. A study by Hart and Risley (1995) found that middle-class parents talked far more to their children than did working-class parents, and that their children had substantially different numbers of words in their vocabularies. The amount of parent speech was as important as socioeconomic status; children of low-income parents who spoke to their children a great deal also had large vocabularies.

INTASC

3 Adapting Instruction for Individual Needs

ON THE WEB

Educators and parents can find links to other websites and resources on communication disorders at **www.familyvillage.wisc.edu/lib_comd.htm.**

Reading Learning to read in the early elementary grades is one of the most important of all developmental tasks, both because other subjects depend on reading and because in our society school success is so often equated with reading success. The process of learning to read can begin quite early if children are read to. Research on **emergent literacy,** or preschoolers' knowledge and skills related to reading (Glazer & Burke, 1994; Pressley, 2003), has shown that children may enter school with a great deal of knowledge about

emergent literacy
Knowledge and skills relating to reading that children usually develop from experience with books and other print media before the beginning of formal reading instruction in school.

reading and that this knowledge contributes to success in formal reading instruction. For example, young children have often learned concepts of print such as that print is arranged from left to right, that spaces between words have meaning, and that books are read from front to back. Many preschoolers can "read" books from beginning to end by interpreting the pictures on each page. They understand about story plots and can often predict what will happen next in a simple story. They can recognize logos on familiar stores and products; for example, very young children often know that *M* is for *McDonald's.* Children have complex language skills that are critical in reading. Children from families in which there are few literacy-related activities can learn concepts of print, plot, and other prereading concepts if they attend preschools or kindergartens that emphasize reading and discussing books in class (Purcell-Gates, McIntyre, & Freppon, 1995; Whitehurst et al., 1994, 1999). Similarly, young children can be taught to hear specific sounds within words (a skill called phonemic awareness), and this contributes to later success in reading (Anthony & Lonigan, 2004; Byrne, Fielding-Barnsley, & Ashley, 2000; Cavanaugh, Kim, Wanzek, & Vaughn, 2004).

Writing Children's writing follows a developmental sequence. It emerges out of early scribbles and at first is spread randomly across a page. This characteristic reflects an incomplete understanding of word boundaries as well as an inability to mentally create a line for placing letters. Children invent spellings by making judgments about sounds and by relating the sounds they hear to the letters they know. In trying to represent what they hear, they typically use letter names rather than letter sounds; short vowels are frequently left out because they are not directly associated with letter names (Snow et al., 1998). For example, one kindergartner labeled a picture of a dinosaur "DNSR."

THEORY *into* PRACTICE

Promoting Literacy Development in Young Children

Many of the educational implications derived from research on children's literacy development transfer findings from two sources: parental and teacher behaviors that encourage oral language development and studies of young children who learn to read without formal classroom instruction. The most frequent recommendations include reading to children; surrounding them with books and other printed materials; making various writing materials available; encouraging reading and writing; and being responsive to children's questions about letters, words, and spellings.

Teachers can use numerous props in the classroom, such as telephone books and office space in a dramatic play area (Neuman & Roskos, 1993). Classrooms can have writing centers with materials such as computers with writing programs, magnetic letters, chalkboards, pencils, crayons, markers, and paper (Wasik, 2001).

Teachers can encourage children's involvement with print by reading in small groups, having tutors read to children individually, and allowing children to choose books to read. Intimate reading experiences allow children to turn pages, pause to look at pictures or ask questions, and read along with an adult.

Predictable books such as *The Three Little Pigs* and *There Was an Old Lady Who Swallowed a Fly* allow beginning readers to rely on what they already know about literacy while learning sound–letter relationships. Stories are predictable if a child can remember what the author is going to say and how it will be stated. Repetitive structures, rhyme and rhythm, and a match between pictures and text increase predictability.

Children's understanding of literacy is enhanced when adults point out the important features of print (Morrow, 1993). Statements such as "We must start at the front, not at the back of the book"; "Move your finger; you're covering the words and I can't see to read them"; and "You have to point to each word as you say it, not to each letter, like this" help to clarify the reading process. Teachers can indicate features in print that are significant and can draw attention to patterns of letters, sounds, or phrases.

Socioemotional Development

A young child's social life evolves in relatively predictable ways (see Cummings et al., 2003; McHale et al., 2003). The social network grows from an intimate relationship with parents or other guardians to include other family members, nonrelated adults, and peers. Social interactions extend from home to neighborhood and from preschool or other child-care arrangements to formal school. Erik Erikson's theory of personal and social development suggests that during the preschool years, children must resolve the personality crisis of initiative versus guilt. The child's successful resolution of this stage results in a sense of initiative and ambition tempered by a reasonable understanding of the permissible. Early educators can encourage this resolution by giving children opportunities to take initiative, to be challenged, and to succeed.

VIDEO HOMEWORK EXERCISE
Cognitive Development—Early Childhood

Go to **www.myeducationlab.com** and, in the Homework and Exercises section for Chapter 3 of this text, access the video entitled "Cognitive Development—Early Childhood." Watch the video and complete the homework questions that accompany it, saving your work or transmitting it to your professor as required.

Peer Relationships During the preschool years, **peers** (other children who are a child's equal in age) begin to play an increasingly important role in children's social and cognitive development (Hay, Payne, & Chadwick, 2004). Children's relations with their peers differ in several ways from their interactions with adults. Peer play allows children to interact with other individuals whose level of development is similar to their own. When peers have disputes among themselves, they must make concessions and must cooperate in resolving them if the play is to continue; unlike in adult–child disputes, in a peer dispute no one can claim to have ultimate authority. Peer conflicts also let children see that others have thoughts, feelings, and viewpoints that are different from their own. Conflicts also heighten children's sensitivity to the effects of their behavior on others. In this way, peer relationships help young children to overcome the egocentrism that Piaget described as being characteristic of preoperational thinking, and help them see that others have perspectives that are different from their own.

Prosocial Behavior **Prosocial behaviors** are voluntary actions toward others such as caring, sharing, comforting, and cooperation. Research on the roots of prosocial behavior has contributed to our knowledge of children's moral as well as social development. Several factors seem to be associated with the development of prosocial behaviors (Eisenberg, 2001). These include the following:

- Parental disciplinary techniques that stress the consequences of the child's behavior for others and that are applied within a warm, responsive parent–child relationship (Hoffman, 1993).
- Contact with adults who indicate they expect concern for others, who let children know that aggressive solutions to problems are unacceptable, and who provide acceptable alternatives (Konig, 1995).
- Contact with adults who attribute positive characteristics to children when they do well ("What a helpful boy you are!") (Grusec & Goodnow, 1994).

CONNECTIONS
For suggested cooperative learning activities, see Chapter 8, pages 243–247.

Play Most of a preschooler's interactions with peers occur during play (Hughes, 1995). However, the degree to which play involves other children increases over the preschool years (Howes & Matheson, 1992). In a classic study of preschoolers, Mildred Parten (1932) identified four categories of play that reflect increasing levels of social interaction and sophistication. **Solitary play** is play that occurs alone, often with toys, and is independent of what other children are doing. **Parallel play** involves children engaged in the same activity side by side but with very little interaction or mutual influence. **Associative play** is much like parallel play but with increased levels of interaction in the form of sharing, turn-taking, and general interest in what others are doing. **Cooperative play** occurs when children join together to achieve a common goal, such as building a large castle with each child building a part of the structure. For example, Howes and Matheson (1992) followed a group of children for 3 years, observing their play when they were 1 to 2 years

peers
People who are equal in age or status.

prosocial behaviors
Actions that show respect and caring for others.

solitary play
Play that occurs alone.

parallel play
Play in which children engage in the same activity side by side but with very little interaction or mutual influence.

associative play
Play that is much like parallel play but with increased levels of interaction in the form of sharing, turn-taking, and general interest in what others are doing.

cooperative play
Play in which children join together to achieve a common goal.

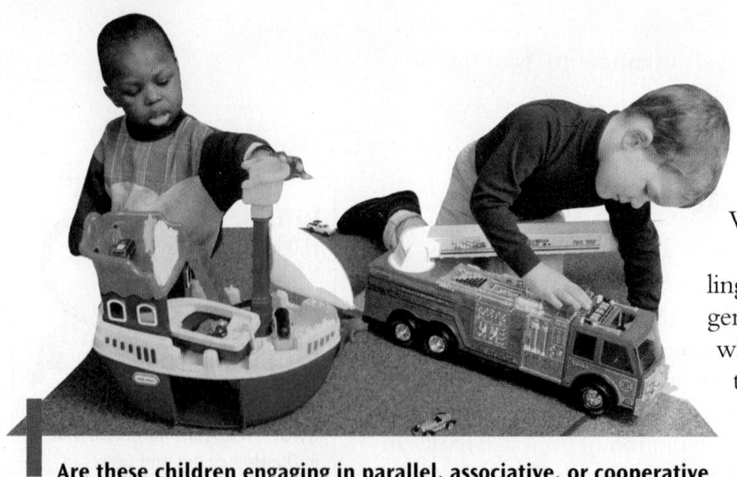

Are these children engaging in parallel, associative, or cooperative play? How might such play sessions benefit their development of pro-social behaviors and peer relations?

old and continuing until they were 3 to 4 years old. They found that children engage in more complex types of play as they grow older, advancing from simple forms of parallel play to complex pretend play in which children cooperate in planning and carrying out activities (Roopnarine et al., 1992; Verba, 1993).

Play is important for children because it exercises their linguistic, cognitive, and social skills and contributes to their general personality development. Children use their minds when playing because they are thinking and acting as if they were another person. When they make such a transformation, they are taking a step toward abstract thinking in that they are freeing their thoughts from a focus on concrete objects. Play is also associated with creativity, especially the ability to be less literal and more flexible in one's thinking. Play has an important role in Vygotsky's theories of development, because it allows children to freely explore ways of thinking and acting that are above their current level of functioning. Vygotsky (1978) wrote, "In play a child is always above his average age, above his daily behavior; in play it is as though he were a head taller than himself" (p. 102).

Preschoolers' play appears to be influenced by a variety of factors. For instance, preschoolers' interactions with peers are related to how they interact with their parents (Ladd & Hart, 1992). Three-year-olds who have warm and nurturing relationships with parents are more likely to engage in social pretend play and resolve conflicts with peers than are children with less secure relationships with their parents (Howes & Rodning, 1992). Children also play better with familiar peers and same-sex peers (Poulin et al., 1997). Providing age-appropriate toys and play activities can also support the development of play and peer interaction skills.

CONNECTIONS

For more on Vygotsky, see Chapter 2, pages 42–46.

WHAT KINDS OF EARLY CHILDHOOD EDUCATION PROGRAMS EXIST?

In almost all the countries of the world, children begin their formal schooling at about 6 years of age, a time when they have typically attained the cognitive and social skills they need for organized learning activities. However, there is much less agreement on what kind of schooling, if any, children younger than the age of 5 need, and there is enormous diversity in the kinds of experiences young children have before entering school (Fitzgerald, Mann, Cabrera, & Wong, 2003; Goelman et al., 2003). Group day-care programs exist for children from infancy on, and organized preschool programs sometimes take children as young as 2. In part because of mothers entering the workforce, preschool attendance has mushroomed; 60 percent of four-year-olds and 40 percent of three-year-olds attend preschool, and half of these are publically funded (Barnett & Ackerman, 2007). As programs for very young children have expanded, the quality of many children's experiences has become higher. Early childhood education has become a major focus of national policy (Barnett & Ackerman, 2007; Carnegie Corporation of New York, 1994, 1996; National Education Goals Panel, 1997; Stipek, 2006).

Day-Care Programs

Day-care programs exist primarily to provide child-care services for working parents. They range from a baby-sitting arrangement in which one adult takes care of several children to organized preschool programs. Research shows that the quality of early child care can have a lasting effect (Carnegie Corporation of New York, 1994; NICHD Early Child

Care Research Network, 2002; Vandell, 2004), especially for children from disadvantaged homes (Scarr, 1998). Unfortunately, research finds that the quality of day-care services provided to disadvantaged children is typically much lower than that provided to middle-class children (Sachs, 2000).

Preschools

The primary difference between day-care and preschool programs is that preschools are more likely to provide a planned program designed to foster the social and cognitive development of young children. Most preschools are half-day programs, with two or three adults supervising a class of 15 to 20 children. A key focus in preschool education is **readiness training:** Students learn skills that are supposed to prepare them for formal instruction later, such as how to follow directions, stick to a task, cooperate with others, and display good manners. Children are also encouraged to grow emotionally and develop a positive self-concept and to improve their large and small muscle skills. The preschool day usually consists of a variety of more and less structured activities, ranging from art projects to group discussion to unstructured indoor and outdoor play. These activities are often organized around themes. For example, a unit on animals might involve making drawings of animals, acting out animal behavior, hearing stories about animals, and taking a trip to the zoo.

Compensatory Preschool Programs

Compensatory preschool programs for children from disadvantaged backgrounds were introduced on a large scale as part of the overall federal Head Start program, begun in 1965. Head Start was part of President Lyndon Johnson's war on poverty, an attempt to break the cycle of poverty. The idea was to give disadvantaged children, who are (as a group) at risk for school failure (McLoyd, 1998; Stipek & Ryan, 1997), a chance to start their formal schooling with the same preacademic and social skills that middle-class children possess. Typically, Head Start includes early childhood education programs that are designed to increase school readiness. However, the program also often includes medical and dental services for children, at least one hot meal per day, and social services for the parents.

Research on Head Start has generally found positive effects on children's readiness skills and on many other outcomes (Bracey & Stellar, 2003). The effects on academic readiness

CONNECTIONS
For more on compensatory programs for students placed at risk, see Chapter 9, pages 286–287.

readiness training
Instruction in the background skills and knowledge that prepare children for formal teaching later.

compensatory preschool programs
Programs that are designed to prepare disadvantaged children for entry into kindergarten and first grade.

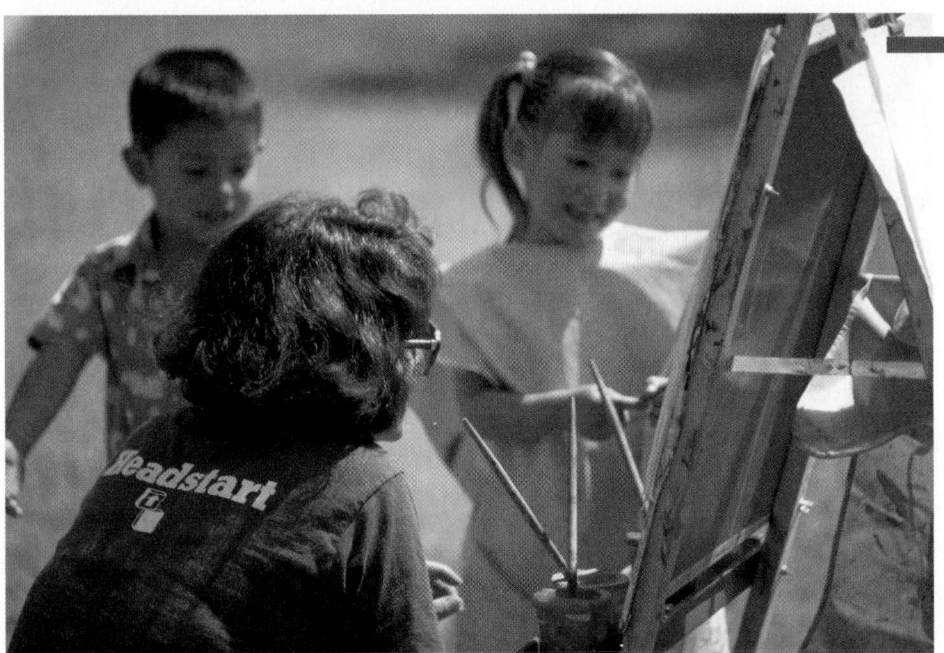

How do compensatory programs, such as Head Start, help level the playing field for children from disadvantaged backgrounds?

CERTIFICATION POINTER

On your teacher certification test, you may be required to know that compensatory education programs are designed to increase the academic success of children who are at high risk of school failure due to poverty.

skills have been greatest for those Head Start programs that stress academic achievement (Abbott-Shim, Lambert, & McCarty, 2003), those that provide a strong family link (Mantzicopoulos, 2003), and those that are higher in quality (Clifford et al., 1999). Research that followed disadvantaged children who participated in several such programs found that these students did better throughout their school years than did similar students who did not participate in the programs. For example, 67 percent of the students in one program, the Perry Preschool, ultimately graduated from high school, compared with 49 percent of students in a control group who did not attend preschool (Schweinhart, Barnes, & Weikart, 1993). Effects of early childhood participation could still be detected at age 27 (Schweinhart & Weikart, 1998) and at age 40 (Nores, Belfield, Barnett, & Schweinhart, 2005). However, preschool programs by themselves are much less effective than are preschool programs followed up by high-quality programs in the early elementary grades (Conyers, Reynolds, & Ou, 2003; Ramey & Ramey, 1998; Reynolds, Temple, Robertson, & Mann, 2002). The research on compensatory early childhood education might seem to indicate that preschool programs are crucial for all students. However, many researchers (e.g., Sachs, 2000) hypothesize that preschool programs are more critical for lower-class children than for middle-class children because many of the experiences that preschools provide are typically present in middle-class homes but may be lacking in homes of lower socioeconomic status.

Despite research supporting the overall effectiveness of Head Start, questions have been raised about the current quality of Head Start programs. Because research finds lasting effects only for high-quality intensive programs (Ramey & Ramey, 1998), improving the quality of Head Start programs is beginning to take precedence over increasing the numbers of children served in Head Start (Neuman, 2003).

Early Intervention

CONNECTIONS

For more on early intervention programs for students placed at risk, see Chapter 9, pages 287–289.

Most compensatory preschool programs, including Head Start, have begun working with children and their parents when the children are 3 or 4 years of age. However, many researchers believe that earlier intervention is needed for children who are at the greatest risk for school failure (Carnegie Corporation of New York, 1994; Powell, 1995). Numerous **early intervention programs** have been developed to start with children as young as 6 months old. One was a program in an inner-city Milwaukee neighborhood for the children of mothers who had mental retardation. An intensive program of infant stimulation, high-quality preschool, and family services made it possible for the children to perform adequately through elementary school; nearly all of the children in a comparison group were assigned to special education programs (Garber, 1988). Several other early intervention programs have also had strong effects on students that have lasted beyond elementary school (Campbell & Ramey, 1995; Ramey & Ramey, 1998; Reynolds, 1998).

Kindergarten Programs

Most students attend kindergarten the year before they enter first grade. However, some states still do not require kindergarten attendance (NCES, 2001). The original purpose of kindergarten was to prepare students for formal instruction by encouraging development of their social skills, but in recent years this function has increasingly been taken on by preschool programs. The kindergarten has focused more and more on academics, emphasizing emergent reading and mathematical skills as well as behaviors that are appropriate in school (such as raising hands, lining up, and taking turns). In some school districts kindergarten programs are becoming similar to what first grades once were (Bodrova & Leong, 2005; deVise, 2007), a trend that most child development experts oppose (Stipek, 2006). Fifty-six percent of kindergarteners attend full-day programs and the rest attend half-day programs (Watson & West, 2004). Research on kindergarten indicates that students of a lower socioeconomic status gain more from well-structured full-day kindergarten programs than from half-day programs (Ackerman, Barnett, & Robin, 2005; Watson & West, 2004). Reading interventions in kindergarten, especially phonemic awareness training designed to help children learn how sounds combine into words, generally have been found to have long-term positive effects (Cavanaugh et al., 2004).

early intervention programs
Compensatory preschool programs that target very young children at the greatest risk of school failure.

Developmentally Appropriate Practice

INTASC

3 Adapting Instruction for Individual Needs

A concept that has become increasingly important in early childhood education is *developmentally appropriate practice.* This is instruction based on students' individual characteristics and needs, not their ages (Bowman, 1993; Elkind, 1989). The National Association for the Education of Young Children (NAEYC) (2004) has described developmentally appropriate practice for students ages 5 through 8 as follows.

Each child is viewed as a unique person with an individual pattern and timing of growth. Curriculum and instruction are responsive to individual differences in ability and interests. Different levels of ability, development, and learning styles are expected, accepted, and used to design curriculum. Children are allowed to move at their own pace in acquiring important skills, including those of writing, reading, spelling, math, social studies, science, art, music, health, and physical activity. For example, it is accepted that not every child will learn how to read at age 6. Most will learn by age 7, but some will need intensive exposure to appropriate literacy experiences to learn to read by age 8 or 9.

The NAEYC and other advocates of developmentally appropriate practice recommend extensive use of projects, play, exploration, groupwork, learning centers, and the like, and a deemphasis on teacher-directed instruction, basal readers, and workbooks (Vandell, 2004). However, a longitudinal study of children who had been in developmentally appropriate or other preschool programs found few differences lasting into the early elementary grades (Van Horn & Ramey, 2003).

HOW DO CHILDREN DEVELOP DURING THE ELEMENTARY YEARS?

Children entering the first grade are in a transitional period from the rapid growth of early childhood to a phase of more gradual development. Shifts in both mental and social development characterize the early school years. Several years later, when children reach the upper elementary grades, they are nearing the end of childhood and entering preadolescence. Children's success in school is particularly important during the early school years because it is in the elementary grades that they largely define themselves as students (Carnegie Corporation of New York, 1996).

Physical Development

As children progress through the primary grades, their physical development slows in comparison with earlier childhood. Children change relatively little in size during the primary years. Girls are typically slightly shorter and lighter than boys until around the age of 9, when height and weight are approximately equal for boys and girls. Muscular development is outdistanced by bone and skeletal development. This may cause the aches that are commonly known as growing pains. Also, the growing muscles need much exercise (Pellegrini & Bohn, 2005), and this need may contribute to the primary-grade child's inability to stay still for long. By the time children enter the primary grades, they have developed many of the basic motor skills they need for balance, running, jumping, and throwing. During the latter part of the fourth grade, many girls begin a major growth spurt that will not be completed until puberty. This spurt begins with the rapid growth of the arms and legs. At this point there is not an accompanying change in trunk size. The result is a gangly or all-arms-and-legs appearance. Because this bone growth occurs before the development of associated muscles and cartilage, children at this growth stage temporarily lose some coordination and strength.

By the start of the fifth grade, almost all girls have begun their growth spurt. In addition, muscle and cartilage growth of the limbs resumes in the earlier maturing females, and they regain their strength and coordination. By the end of the fifth grade, girls are typically taller, heavier, and stronger than boys. Boys are 12 to 18 months behind girls in physical development, so even early maturing boys do not start their growth spurt until age 11. By the start of the sixth grade, therefore, most girls will be near the peak of their growth spurt, and all but the early maturing boys will be continuing the slow, steady growth of late childhood. Girls will usually have started their menstrual period by age 13. For boys the end of preadolescence and the onset of early adolescence is measured by the first ejaculation, which occurs between the ages of 13 and 16.

Cognitive Development

Between the ages of 5 and 7, children's thought processes undergo significant changes (Siegler, 1998). This is a period of transition from the stage of preoperational thought to the stage of concrete operations. As described in Chapter 2, this change allows children to do mentally what was previously done physically. Not all children make this transition at the same age, and no individual child changes from one stage to the next quickly. Children often use cognitive behaviors that are characteristic of two stages of development at the same time. As individuals advance from one stage to the next, the characteristics of the previous stage are maintained as the cognitive behaviors of the higher stage develop.

In addition to entering the concrete operational stage, elementary school-age children are rapidly developing memory and cognitive skills, including metacognitive skills, the ability to think about their own thinking and to learn how to learn.

Socioemotional Development

By the time children enter elementary school, they have developed skills for more complex thought, action, and social influence. Up to this point, children have been basically egocentric, and their world has been that of home, family, and possibly a preschool or day-care center. The early primary grades will normally be spent working through Erikson's (1963) fourth stage, industry versus inferiority. Assuming that a child has developed trust during infancy, autonomy during the early years, and initiative during the preschool years, that child's experiences in the primary grades can contribute to his or her sense of industry and accomplishment. During this stage, children start trying to prove that they are "grown up"; in fact, this is often described as the I-can-do-it-myself stage. Work becomes possible. As children's powers of concentration grow, they can spend more time on chosen tasks, and they often take pleasure in completing projects. This stage also includes the growth of independent action, cooperation with groups, and performing in socially acceptable ways with a concern for fair play (McHale, Dariotis, & Kauh, 2003).

Self-Concept and Self-Esteem Important areas of personal and social development for elementary school children are **self-concept** and **self-esteem** (Swann, Chang-Schneider, & McClarty, 2007). These aspects of children's development will be strongly influenced by experiences at home, at school, and with peers. Self-concept includes the way in which we perceive our strengths, weaknesses, abilities, attitudes, and values. Its development begins at birth and is continually shaped by experience. Self-esteem refers to how we evaluate our skills and abilities.

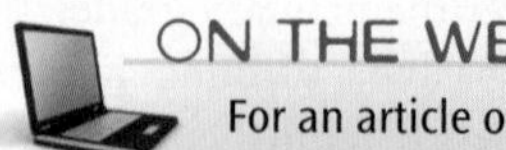

ON THE WEB

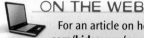

For an article on how to strengthen children's self-esteem go to **www.kidsource.com/kidsource/content2/strengthen_children_self.html.**

self-concept
A person's perception of his or her own strengths, weaknesses, abilities, attitudes, and values.

self-esteem
The value each of us places on our own characteristics, abilities, and behaviors.

As children progress through middle childhood, their ways of thinking become less concrete and more abstract. This trend is also evident in the development of their self-concepts. Preschoolers think about themselves in terms of their physical and material characteristics, including size, gender, and possessions. In contrast, by the early elementary school years, children begin to focus on more abstract, internal qualities such as intelligence and kindness when describing themselves. They can also make a distinction between their private or inner selves and their external, public selves. This becomes especially evident as they depend more on intentions and motives and less on objective behavior in their explanations of their own and others' actions.

During middle childhood, children also begin to evaluate themselves in comparison to others. A preschooler might describe herself by saying, "I like baseball," whereas several years later this same girl is likely to say, "I like baseball more than Sally does." Ruble, Eisenberg, and Higgins (1994) have suggested that younger children use social comparison primarily to learn about social norms and the appropriateness of certain types of conduct. As children get older, they also tend to use **social comparison** to evaluate and judge their own abilities (Borg, 1998).

The trend to use social comparison information to evaluate the self appears to correspond with developmental changes in academic self-esteem. Preschoolers and young children tend to evaluate themselves very positively, in ways that bear no relationship to their school performance or other objective factors (Cole, 1991). By second or third grade, however, children who are having difficulty in school tend to have poorer self-concepts (Chapman, Tunmer, & Prochnow, 2000). This begins a declining spiral. Students who perform poorly in elementary school are at risk for developing poor academic self-concepts and subsequent poor performance in upper elementary and secondary school (Guay, Marsh, & Boivin, 2003; Ma & Kishor, 1997; Marsh & Yeung, 1997).

The primary grades give many children their first chance to compare themselves with others and to work and play under the guidance of adults outside their family. These adults must provide experiences that let children succeed, feel good about themselves, and maintain their enthusiasm and creativity (Canfield & Siccone, 1995; Perry & Weinstein, 1998).

The key word regarding personal and social development is acceptance. The fact is, children do differ in their abilities; and no matter what teachers do, students will have figured out by the end of the elementary years (usually earlier) who is more able and who is less able. However, teachers can have a substantial impact on how students feel about these differences and on the value that low-achieving students place on learning even when they know they will never be class stars.

THEORY *into* PRACTICE

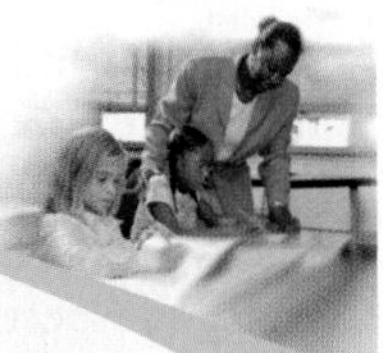

Promoting the Development of Self-Esteem

Our society promotes the idea that people, including students, are of equal worth. That is also the premise in a classroom. But believing students are of equal worth doesn't necessarily mean that they are equally competent. Some students are good in reading, others in math, others in sports, others in art.

Some classroom activities can give certain students the impression that they as individuals are of less value or worth than other students. Research findings indicate that inappropriate competition (Cohen, 1986) or inflexible ability groups within the classroom (MacIver, Reuman, & Main, 1995; Slavin, 1987c) may teach the wrong thing to students.

This kind of research can help teachers avoid practices that may discourage children. However, it is not clear that improving self-esteem results in greater school achievement. In fact, research more strongly suggests that as a student grows more competent in school tasks, his or her self-esteem also improves, rather than the other way around (e.g., Chapman et al., 2000; Ellis, 2001b).

Showing students their success can be an important part of maintaining a positive self-image. Rosenholtz and Simpson (1984) described the multidimensional classroom, in which teachers make it clear that there are many ways to succeed. Such teachers emphasize how much students are learning. For example, many teachers give students pre-tests before they begin an instructional unit and then

social comparison
The process of comparing oneself to others to gather information and to evaluate and judge one's abilities, attitudes, and conduct.

show the class how much everyone gained on a post-test. Multidimensional teachers may stress the idea that different students have different skills. By valuing all these skills, the teacher can communicate the idea that there are many routes to success, rather than a single path (Cohen, 1984).

It is not necessary to lie and say that all students are equally good in reading or math. Teachers can, however, recognize progress rather than level of ability, focusing their praise on the student's effort and growing competence. As the student sees his or her success in school, a feeling of earned self-esteem will also result.

Growing Importance of Peers The influence of the child's family, which was the major force during the early childhood years, continues in importance as parents provide role models in terms of attitudes and behaviors. In addition, relationships with brothers and sisters affect relationships with peers, and routines from home either are reinforced or must be overcome in school. However, the peer group takes on added importance. Speaking of the child's entrance into the world outside the family, Ira Gordon noted the importance of peers:

> If all the world's the stage that Shakespeare claimed, children and adolescents are playing primarily to an audience of their peers. Their peers sit in the front rows and the box seats; parents and teachers are now relegated to the back rows and the balcony. (Gordon, 1957, p. 166)

In the lower elementary grades, peer groups usually consist of same-sex children who are around the same age. This preference may be because of the variety of abilities and interests among young children. By the sixth grade, however, students often form groups that include both boys and girls. Whatever the composition of peer groups, they let children compare their abilities and skills to those of others. Members of peer groups also teach one another about their different worlds. Children learn through this sharing of attitudes and values how to sort out and form their own attitudes and values.

VIDEO HOMEWORK EXERCISE
Friendships

Go to **www.myeducationlab.com** and, in the Homework and Exercises section for Chapter 3 of this text, access the video entitled "Friendships." Watch the video and complete the homework questions that accompany it, saving your work or transmitting it to your professor as required.

Friendships in Middle Childhood During middle childhood, children's conceptions of friendship also mature. Friendship is the central social relationship between peers during childhood, and it undergoes a series of changes before adulthood (Hartup, 1996). Using as a basis Piaget's developmental stages and children's changing abilities to consider the perspective of others, Selman (1981) described how children's understanding of friendship changes over the years. Between the ages of 3 and 7, children usually view friends as momentary playmates. Children of this age might come home from school exclaiming, "I made a new friend today! Jamie shared her doll with me," or "Bill's not my friend anymore 'cause he wouldn't play blocks with me." These comments reveal the child's view of friendship as a temporary relationship based on a certain situation rather than on shared interests or beliefs. As children enter middle childhood, friendships become more stable and reciprocal. At this age, friends are often described in terms of personal traits ("My friend Mary is nice"), and friendships are based on mutual support, caring, loyalty, and mutual give-and-take.

Friendships are important to children for several reasons. During the elementary school years, friends are companions with whom to have fun and do things. They also serve as important emotional resources by providing children with a sense of security in new situations and when family or other problems arise. Friends are also cognitive resources when they teach or model specific intellectual skills. Social norms for conduct, social interaction skills, and how to resolve conflicts successfully are also learned within the context of friendships (McHale et al., 2003).

Peer Acceptance One of the important aspects of peer relations in middle childhood is peer acceptance, or status within the peer group (McCallum & Bracken, 1993). Popular children are those who are named most often by their peers as being someone they like and least often as someone they dislike. In contrast, rejected children are those who are named most often by their peers as being someone they dislike and least often as someone they like. Children are also classified as being neglected; these children are neither frequently named as someone who is liked nor frequently named as someone who is disliked. Controversial children are frequently named as someone who is liked but also frequently named as someone who is disliked. Average children are those who are named as being liked and disliked with moderate frequency.

Children who are not well accepted or are rejected by their peers in elementary school are at high risk (Ladd & Troop-Gordon, 2003; Wentzel, Barry, & Caldwell, 2004). These children are more likely to drop out of school, engage in delinquent behavior, and have emotional and psychological problems in adolescence and adulthood than are their peers who are more accepted (see also Kupersmidt & Coie, 1990; Morrison & Masten, 1991). Some rejected children tend to be highly aggressive; others tend to be very passive and withdrawn, and these children may be victims of bullying (Pellegrini & Bartini, 2000). Children who are rejected, aggressive, and withdrawn seem to be at highest risk for difficulties (Hymel, Bowker, & Woody, 1993).

Many characteristics seem to be related to peer acceptance, including physical attractiveness (Kennedy, 1990) and cognitive abilities (Wentzel et al., 2004). Studies have also linked behavioral styles to peer acceptance (see Coie, Dodge, & Kupersmidt, 1990). Well-accepted and popular children tend to be cooperative, helpful, and caring and are rarely disruptive or aggressive. Children who are disliked by their peers tend to be highly aggressive and to lack prosocial and conflict resolution skills. Neglected and controversial children display less distinct behavioral styles and often change status over short periods of time (Newcomb & Bagwell, 1998).

THEORY *into* PRACTICE

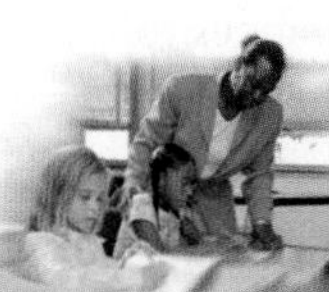

Helping Children Develop Social Skills

Because peer acceptance is such a strong predictor of current and long-term adjustment, many intervention techniques have been designed to improve the social skills and levels of acceptance of unpopular and rejected children. Common approaches involve the following:

1. ***Reinforcing appropriate social behavior.*** Adults can systematically reinforce prosocial skills such as helping and sharing and can ignore antisocial behavior such as fighting and verbal aggression. Reinforcement techniques will be most successful if a teacher or other adult uses them with an entire group of children. This allows the child who lacks skills to observe others being reinforced for positive behavior, and it draws the attention of the peer group to the target child's positive rather than negative actions.
2. ***Modeling.*** Children who observe models learning positive social interaction skills show significant improvement in their own skills.
3. ***Coaching.*** This strategy involves a sequence of steps that include demonstrating positive social skills, explaining why these skills are important, providing opportunities for practice, and giving follow-up feedback.

The effectiveness of any intervention is likely to depend largely on the involvement of the rejected child's peers and classroom teachers. If peers and teachers notice positive changes in behavior, they are more likely to change their opinions of and accept the child than if interventions are conducted in isolation (Olweus, 1994; White & Kistner, 1992).

CONNECTIONS
For more on systematically reinforcing prosocial skills, see Chapter 5, page 132.

HOW DO CHILDREN DEVELOP DURING THE MIDDLE SCHOOL AND HIGH SCHOOL YEARS?

The adolescent period of development begins with puberty. The pubertal period, or early adolescence, is a time of rapid physical and intellectual development. Middle adolescence is a more stable period of adjustment to and integration of the changes of early adolescence. Later adolescence is marked by the transition into the responsibilities, choices, and opportunities of adulthood. In this section we will review the major changes that occur as the child becomes an adolescent, and we will examine how adolescent development affects teaching, curriculum, and school structure.

Physical Development

Puberty is a series of physiological changes that render the immature organism capable of reproduction. Nearly every organ and system of the body is affected by these changes. The prepubertal child and the postpubertal adolescent are different in outward appearance because of changes in stature and proportion and the development of primary and secondary sex features (Susman, Dorn, & Schiefelbein, 2003).

puberty
Developmental stage at which a person becomes capable of reproduction.

Although the sequence of events at puberty is generally the same for each person, the timing and the rate at which they occur vary widely. The average female typically begins pubertal changes 1 to 2 years earlier than the average male. In each sex, however, the range of normal onset ages is approximately 6 years. Like the onset, the rate of changes also varies widely. Some people take only 18 to 24 months to go through the pubertal changes to reproductive maturity; others may require 6 years to pass through the same stage. These differences mean that some individuals may be completely mature before others the same age have even begun puberty. The age of maximum diversity is 13 for males and about 11 for females. The comparisons that children make among themselves, as well as the tendency to hold maturity in high regard, can be a problem for the less mature (Ge, Longer, & Elder, 2001). However, the first to mature are also likely to experience temporary discomfort because they stand out from the less mature majority. Early-maturing girls, for example, are more likely to engage in delinquency and have school problems than other girls (Stice, Presnell, & Bearman, 2001), and early-maturing boys also are more likely to engage in delinquent behavior (Ge et al., 2001).

"No thanks, but I'll call you when I reach puberty!"

Cognitive Development

As the rest of the body changes at puberty, the brain and its functions also change, and the timing of intellectual changes varies widely across individuals. One indication of this is that scores on intelligence tests obtained over several years from the same individual fluctuate most during the period from 12 to 15 years of age. Some researchers refer to an "intellectual growth spurt" at this age (Andrich & Styles, 1994). In Piaget's theory of cognitive development, adolescence is the stage of transition from the use of concrete operations to the application of formal operations in reasoning. Adolescents begin to be aware of the limitations of their thinking. They wrestle with concepts that are removed from their own experience. Inhelder and Piaget (1958) acknowledge that brain changes at puberty may be necessary for the cognitive advances of adolescence. However, they assert that experience with complex problems, the demands of formal instruction, and exchange and contradiction of ideas with peers are also necessary for formal operational reasoning to develop. Adolescents who reach this stage (not all do) have attained an adult level of reasoning. Adolescent cognitive development is characterized more by steady growth in understanding and capabilities (Eccles, Wigfield, & Byrnes, 2003).

CONNECTIONS
For more on Piaget's theories on cognitive development in adolescence, see Chapter 2, pages 38–40.

Hypothetical-Deductive Reasoning One of the characteristics that marks the development of formal operational thinking is hypothetical-deductive reasoning, which emerges by the time children are about 12 years old (Atwater, 1996; Flavell et al., 1993). Before formal operations, thought is concrete operational in nature. Piaget found that the use of formal operations depended on the learner's familiarity with a given subject area. When students were familiar with a subject, they were more likely to use formal operations. When they were unfamiliar with a subject, students proceeded more slowly, tended to use concrete reasoning patterns, and used self-regulation sparingly. Later research has confirmed Piaget's observation that use of formal operational thought differs according to tasks, background knowledge, and individual differences (Cobb, 1995). Not all adolescents develop formal operational thinking, but there is evidence that adolescents who have not reached this level can be taught to solve problems requiring this level of thinking (Vasta & Liben, 1996).

CERTIFICATION POINTER

When responding to case studies in certification tests, you may be asked to design a lesson that would be considered developmentally appropriate for a group of adolescents.

THEORY *into* PRACTICE

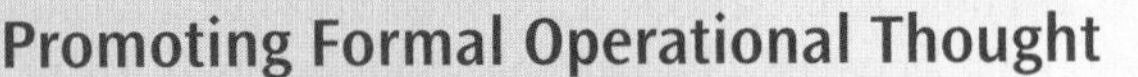

Promoting Formal Operational Thought

Teachers can help adolescents develop and use formal operational thought. Consider the following:

1. When introducing new information, particularly information involving abstract concepts and theories, allow students enough time to absorb the ideas and to use formal thought patterns. Begin with more familiar examples, and encourage students to apply hypothetical-deductive reasoning.
2. Students who have not yet attained formal operational thought may need more support for planning complex tasks. Pairing children who can plan with those who need support is one way of handling the situation.
3. Encourage students to state principles and ideas in their own words and to search for the meaning behind abstract ideas and theories.
4. Incorporate a variety of activities that promote the use of hypothetical-deductive thinking. The following are some examples:

   - Have students write a paper that requires a debate between pro and con arguments and a discussion of the evidence that supports the two perspectives. For younger students you might want to pair children or groups and have one child or group write from one perspective and the other from another perspective.
   - Have students discuss each other's ideas, purposefully picking specific opposing positions. Debates and mock trials are two ways in which this can be done.
   - Develop cooperative activities that require substantial planning and organization. Have students work in groups composed of children with different levels of planning and organizing skills. For children who are still at the concrete operational level, provide an outline of what to think about as the planning process proceeds.

- Develop activities in which facts come from different testimonials that may be contradictory, such as television commercials. For example, use commercials in which Brand X claims to be the best-selling domestic car and to have more features than other cars and Brand Y claims that its cars are the highest rated and have higher levels of owner satisfaction. Have the students discuss and weigh the evidence from these different sources.
- Have students critique their own work. Ask students to generate a list of ways in which one could look for flaws in thinking or other sources that might be used to verify results.

Socioemotional Development

In adolescence, children undergo significant changes in their social and emotional lives as well. Partly as a result of their changing physical and cognitive structures, children in the upper elementary grades seek to be more grown up. They want their parents to treat them differently, even though many parents are unwilling to see them differently. They also report that though they believe that their parents love them, they do not think their parents understand them. For both boys and girls in the upper elementary grades, membership in groups tends to promote feelings of self-worth. Not being accepted can bring serious emotional problems. Herein lies the major cause of the preadolescent's changing relationship with parents. It is not that preadolescents care less about their parents. It is just that their friends are more important than ever. This need for acceptance by peers helps to explain why preadolescents often dress alike (Baumeister & Leary, 1995). The story of Sam Stevens's earring at the beginning of this chapter illustrates how young adolescents express their belongingness with other peer group members through distinctive dress or behavior.

reflectivity
The tendency to analyze oneself and one's own thoughts.

"School uniforms! That'll take away our individuality!"

The middle school years often also bring changes in the relationship between children and their teachers. In primary school, children easily accept and depend on teachers. During the upper elementary years, this relationship becomes more complex (see Roeser, Eccles, & Sameroff, 2000). Sometimes students will tell teachers personal information they would not tell their parents. Some preadolescents even choose teachers as role models. At the same time, however, some preteens talk back to teachers in ways they would never have considered several years earlier, and some openly challenge teachers. Others become deeply alienated from school, starting a pattern that may lead to delinquency and dropout (Murdock, 1999).

Identity Development One of the first signs of early adolescence is the appearance of **reflectivity,** the tendency to think about what is going on in one's own mind and to study oneself. Adolescents begin to look more closely at themselves and to define themselves differently. They start to realize that there are differences between what they think and feel and how they behave. Using the developing intellectual skills that permit them to consider possibilities, adolescents are prone to be dissatisfied with themselves. They critique their personal characteristics, compare themselves to others, and try to change the way they are.

Adolescents may also ponder whether other people see and think about the world in the same way they do (Phelan, Yu, & Davidson, 1994). They become more aware of their separateness from other people and of their uniqueness. They learn that other people cannot fully know what they think and feel. The issue of who and what one "really" is dominates personality development in adolescence. According to Erikson, the stage is set during adolescence for a major concern with one's identity.

Personal REFLECTION

Coping with Change

My oldest son, Jacob, went through a typically stormy adolescence. At one point, when he was about 15, he had little to say to my wife and me that wasn't hostile or dismissive. However, on occasion his old loving self would still shine through. One day he spent all afternoon working with my wife to bake a couple of pies. He didn't say much, but it was heartening just to see him willing to spend time with his mom on such a prosocial activity. He put particular care into making a design on the top crust of each pie, after which he proudly put them in the oven. When the pies were done, we were astonished to see that he'd written a very bad word on each pie!

Jacob's afternoon is a wonderful example of adolescents' conflicted relationships with their parents. He was willing to bake pies with his mom, but he had to do it his way, to show that he was not dependent on his parents, and had to express his independence at every turn. Still, the pies (and the experience, in retrospect) were delicious!

REFLECT ON THIS. Do you remember being conflicted emotionally in middle school or high school as you adjusted to adolescence? How might the internal conflicts have differed for adolescents of different social or ethnic groups? What kind of learning challenges does this time period pose for teachers and students?

James Marcia's Four Identity Statuses On the basis of Erikson's work, James Marcia (1991) identified four identity statuses from in-depth interviews with adolescents. The statuses reflect the degree to which adolescents have made firm commitments to religious and political values as well as to a future occupation. These are as follows:

1. ***Foreclosure:*** Individuals in a state of **foreclosure** have never experienced an identity crisis. Rather, they have prematurely established an identity on the basis of their parents' choices rather than their own. They have made occupational and ideological commitments, but these commitments reflect more an assessment of what their parents or authority figures could do than an autonomous process of self-assessment. Foreclosure indicates a kind of "pseudo-identity" that generally is too fixed and rigid to serve as a foundation for meeting life's future crises.
2. ***Identity diffusion:*** Adolescents experiencing **identity diffusion** have found neither an occupational direction nor an ideological commitment of any kind, and they have made little progress toward these ends. They may have experienced an identity crisis, but if so, they were unable to resolve it.
3. ***Moratorium:*** Adolescents in a state of **moratorium** are those who have begun to experiment with occupational and ideological choices but have not yet made definitive commitments to either. These individuals are directly in the midst of an identity crisis and are currently examining alternate life choices.
4. ***Identity achievement:*** **Identity achievement** signifies a state of identity consolidation in which adolescents have made their own conscious, clear-cut decisions about occupation and ideology. The individual is convinced that these decisions were autonomously and freely made, and that they reflect his or her true nature and deep inner commitments.

By late adolescence (18 to 22 years of age), most individuals have developed a status of identity achievement. However, adolescents' emotional development seems to be linked to their identity status. For instance, levels of anxiety tend to be highest for adolescents in moratorium and lowest for those in foreclosure (Marcia, 1991). Self-esteem also varies, with adolescents in identity achievement and moratorium reporting the highest levels and those in foreclosure and identity diffusion reporting the lowest levels (Marcia, 1991; Wallace-Broscious, Serafica, & Osipow, 1994).

In general, adolescents need to experiment and remain flexible if they are successfully to find their own identity. By trying out ways to be, then testing and modifying them, the adolescent can pick the characteristics that are most comfortable and drop the

foreclosure
An adolescent's premature establishment of an identity based on parental choices, not on his or her own.

identity diffusion
Inability to develop a clear direction or sense of self.

moratorium
Experimentation with occupational and ideological choices without definite commitment.

identity achievement
A state of consolidation reflecting conscious, clear-cut decisions concerning occupation and ideology.

others. To do this, the adolescent must have the self-confidence to experiment and to declare an experiment over; to vary behavior; and to drop characteristics that don't fit, even if the characteristics are supported by others. It helps to have a stable and accepting set of parents, teachers, and peers who will respond positively to one's experimentation.

ON THE WEB

For explorations of many aspects of adolescent development, including identity development and self-esteem, go to the website of Nancy Darling at the University of Pennsylvania—**www.oberlin.edu/faculty/ndarling/lab/ead.htm.**

Self-Concept and Self-Esteem Self-concept and self-esteem also change as children enter and go through adolescence. The shift toward more abstract portrayals that began in middle childhood continues, and adolescents' self-descriptions often include personal traits (friendly, obnoxious), emotions (depressed, psyched), and personal beliefs (liberal, conservative) (Harter, 1998). In addition, the self-concept becomes more differentiated. Susan Harter's work has identified eight distinct aspects of adolescent concept: scholastic competence, job competence, athletic competence, physical appearance, social acceptance, close friendships, romantic appeal, and conduct (Harter, 1998). Marsh (1993) identified five distinct self-concepts: academic verbal, academic mathematical, parent relations, same-sex, and opposite sex.

Self-esteem also undergoes fluctuations and changes during adolescence. Self-esteem is lowest as children enter middle school or junior high school and with the onset of puberty (Jacobs et al., 2002). Early maturing girls tend to suffer the most dramatic and long-lasting decreases in self-esteem. In general, adolescent girls have lower self-esteem than do boys (Jacobs et al., 2002). Global self-esteem or feelings of self-worth appear to be influenced most strongly by physical appearance and then by social acceptance from peers.

Social Relationships As children enter adolescence, changes in the nature of friendships also take place. In general, the amount of time spent with friends increases dramatically; adolescents spend more time with their peers than they do with family members or by themselves (Ambert, 1997). Adolescents who have satisfying and harmonious friendships also report higher levels of self-esteem, are less lonely, have more mature social skills, and do better in school than do adolescents who lack supportive friendships (Kerr, Stattin, Biesecker, & Ferrer-Wreder, 2003).

How do peer relationships affect one's self-concept and self-esteem? What can you as a teacher do to aid your students' emotional development?

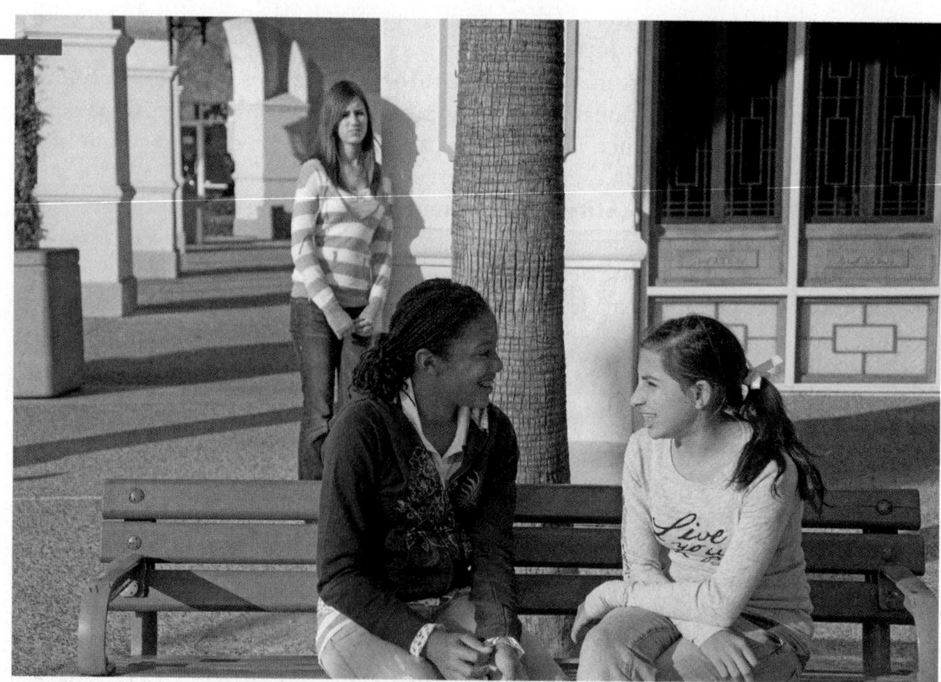

During adolescence, the capacity for mutual understanding and the knowledge that others are unique individuals with feelings of their own also contribute to a dramatic increase in self-disclosure, intimacy, and loyalty among friends. As early adolescents strive to establish personal identities that are independent of those of their parents, they also look increasingly to their peers for security and social support. Whereas elementary school–aged children look to parents for such support, by seventh grade same-sex friends are perceived to be as supportive as parents, and by tenth grade they are perceived to be the primary source of social support (Furman & Buhrmester, 1992).

Relationships with Peers In addition to their close friends, most adolescents also place high value on the larger peer group as a source of ideas and values as well as companionship and entertainment.

The nature of peer relationships in adolescence has been characterized in terms of social status and peer crowds. Social status, or levels of acceptance by peers, is studied with respect to the same status groups that are identified in middle childhood. As with elementary school–aged children, popular and well-accepted adolescents tend to display positive conflict resolution and academic skills, prosocial behavior, and leadership qualities, whereas rejected and low-accepted children tend to display aggressive and antisocial behavior and low levels of academic performance (Parkhurst & Asher, 1992; Wentzel & Erdley, 1993; Zettergren, 2003). These socially rejected children appear to be at great risk for later academic and social problems (Pope & Bierman, 1999). Wentzel and Asher (1995) found, however, that rejected middle school children who were socially submissive did not display the same school-related problems as their rejected aggressive counterparts. These findings suggest that peer rejection and negative behavior together place these children at risk.

CERTIFICATION POINTER

Most teacher certification tests will require you to know how development in one domain, such as physical, may affect a student's performance in another domain, such as social.

Peer relationships in adolescence have also been studied in terms of cliques and crowds with whom adolescents associate (Barber, Eccles, & Stone, 2001). A clique is a fairly small, intimate group that is defined by the common interests, activities, and friends of its members. In contrast, a crowd is a larger group defined by its reputation. Allegiance to a clique or crowd is common during adolescence but not necessarily long term or stable. Although the pressure to conform can be very powerful within these groups, only adolescents who are highly motivated to belong appear to be influenced by these norms in significant ways (Rice, 1996).

Emotional Development Most adolescents experience emotional conflicts at some point. This is hardly surprising because they are going through rapid and dramatic changes in body image, expected roles, and peer relationships. The transitions from elementary to middle school or junior high and then on to high school can also be quite stressful (Harter, Whitesell, & Kowalski, 1992; Midgley, 1993). For most adolescents, emotional distress is temporary and is successfully handled, but for some the stresses lead to delinquency, drug abuse, or suicide attempts (Fisher, 2006; Matheny, Aycock, & McCarthy, 1993).

BUILDING TEACHING SKILLS READING EXERCISE

The Biology of Risk Taking

Go to **www.myeducationlab.com** and, in the Homework and Exercises section for Chapter 3 of this text, access the article entitled "The Biology of Risk Taking." Read the article and complete the homework questions that accompany it, saving your work or transmitting it to your professor as required.

Emotional problems related to the physical, cognitive, and social development of upper elementary school–aged children are common. Though preadolescents are generally happy and optimistic, they also have many fears, such as fear of not being accepted into a peer group, not having a best friend, being punished by their parents, having their parents get a divorce, or not doing well in school.

Other emotions of this age group include anger (and fear of being unable to control it), guilt, frustration, and jealousy. Preadolescents need help in realizing that these emotions and fears are a natural part of growing up. Adults must let them talk about these emotions and fears, even if they seem unrealistic to an adult. Feelings of guilt often arise when there is a conflict between children's actions (based on values of the peer group) and their parents' values. Anger is a common emotion at this age and is displayed with more intensity than many of the other emotions. Just as they often tell their preadolescents that they should not be afraid, parents often tell them that they should not get angry. Unfortunately, this is an unrealistic expectation, even for adults.

Problems of Adolescence Adolescence can be a time of great risk for many, as teenagers are now able, for the first time, to engage in behaviors or make decisions that can have long-term negative consequences (Dryfoos, 1998; National Research Council, 1995).

CONNECTIONS
For more on emotional disorders, see Chapter 12, pages 374–375.

Emotional Disorders Secondary school teachers should be sensitive to the stresses that adolescents face and should realize that emotional disturbances are common (Galambos & Costigan, 2003). They should understand that depressed, hopeless, or unaccountably angry behavior can be a clue that the adolescent needs help, and they should try to put such students in touch with school counselors or other psychologically trained adults (Fisher, 2006).

Bullying Taunting, harassment, and aggression toward weaker or friendless peers occur at all age levels, but can become particularly serious as children enter early adolescence (Juvonen, Nishina, & Graham, 2000; Pellegrini & Bartini, 2000; San Antonio & Salzfass, 2007).

Dropping Out Dropping out of secondary school can put adolescents at considerable risk, as dropouts condemn themselves to low-level occupations, unemployment, and poverty (Bracey, 2006). Of course, the factors that lead to dropping out begin early in students' school careers; school failure, retention (staying back), assignment to special education, and poor attendance all predict dropout (Battin-Pearson et al., 2000; Goldschmidt & Wang, 1999; Pallas, 2002). Dropout rates have generally been declining, especially among African American students, although African Americans are still disproportionately at risk (Balfanz & Legters, 2004; Mishel & Roy, 2006). For Latino students, however, dropout rates remain very high (Secada et al., 1998). Dropout rates among at-risk students can be greatly reduced by programs that give these students individual attention, high-status roles, and assistance with academic deficits (Burt, Resnick, & Novick, 1998; Slavin & Fashola, 1998). Students in smaller and more academically focused high schools tend to drop out less frequently than other students (Lee & Burkam, 2003).

Drug and Alcohol Abuse Substance use continues to be widespread among adolescents (Perkins & Borden, 2003). Eighty percent of high school seniors drink alcohol, and 31 percent have tried marijuana (Johnson et al., 2001). Drug and alcohol abuse are strongly connected to school failure (Bryant & Zimmerman, 2002).

CONNECTIONS
To learn about prevention of delinquency, see Chapter 11, pages 354–358.

Delinquency One of the most dangerous problems of adolescence is the beginning of serious delinquency. The problem is far more common among males than among females. Delinquents are usually low achievers who have been given little reason to believe that they can succeed by following the path laid out for them by the school (Hawkins et al., 2000). Delinquency in adolescence is overwhelmingly a group phenomenon; most delinquent acts are done in groups or with the active support of a delinquent subgroup (Branch, 1998; Farmer et al., 2002; Perkins & Borden, 2003).

Risk of Pregnancy Pregnancy and childbirth are serious problems among all groups of female adolescents but particularly among those from lower-income homes (Coley & Chase-Lansdale, 1998; Susman, Dorn, & Schiefelbein, 2003). Just as adolescent males often engage in delinquent behavior to try to establish their independence from adult control, adolescent females often engage in sex, and in many cases have children, to force the world to see them as adults. Because early childbearing makes it difficult for adolescent females to continue their schooling or get jobs, it is a primary cause of the continuation of the cycle of poverty into which many adolescent mothers were themselves born (Hoffman, Foster, & Furstenberg, 1993). Of course, the other side of teen pregnancy is teen fatherhood. Teen fathers also suffer behavioral and academic problems in school (Hanson, Morrison, & Ginsburg, 1989). Many programs intended to delay intercourse and reduce pregnancy exist. Research on these programs finds that sex education programs that emphasize both abstinence and use of condoms and other birth control methods are more effective than those that emphasize simply abstinence (Kirby, 2000).

Risk of Sexually Transmitted Diseases Compounding the traditional risks of early sexual activity is the rise in AIDS and other sexually transmitted diseases (Kalichman, 1996). AIDS is still very rare during the adolescent years, and rates of infection have been

How can Gay–Straight Alliance groups in a school help to promote tolerance among young people and ease the pressure on gay and lesbian youth? What roles do teachers play in creating a safe environment for young people conflicted over sexual identity?

declining (CDC, 1998). However, because full-blown AIDS can take 10 years to appear, unprotected sex, needle sharing, and other high-risk behavior among teens are what often causes the high rates of AIDS among young adults (Hein, 1993). The appearance of AIDS has made the need for early, explicit sex education critical, potentially a life-or-death matter. However, knowledge alone is not enough (Woodring, 1995); sexually active adolescents must have access to condoms and realistic, psychologically sophisticated inducements to use them (Aronson, 1995).

ONLINE READING & WRITING EXERCISE

Development of Autonomy in Adolescence

Access this exercise, entitled "Development of Autonomy in Adolescence," in the Homework and Exercises section for Chapter 3 of this text at **www.mylabschool.com.**

Sexual Identity It is during adolescence that people begin to explore their sexual identity, including young people who begin to identify with a gay or lesbian orientation. This new awareness can cause great distress for the adolescent and for his or her parents. It also can lead to tension with peer groups, which may have strong norms against homosexuality and may engage in taunting, rejection, or even violent behavior toward gay or lesbian peers. Teachers need to model acceptance of gay and lesbian students and strictly enforce school rules forbidding disrespect toward anyone, gay or straight (Koppelman & Goodhart, 2005).

THEORY *into* PRACTICE

Providing Developmental Assets for Adolescents

G. Stanley Hall, an early American psychologist who studied child development, called adolescence a time of storm and stress. Regardless of whether that is an accurate description of all teenagers, many contemporary writers (e.g., Dryfoos, 1990) believe young people in the United States are at risk because of the choices they make. Such a view of at-risk behaviors can result in a "deficit-thinking" approach to helping teenagers. That is, our society declares "war" on teenage pregnancy, school dropout rates, drug and alcohol abuse, gangs, and violence. As Goleman (1995) noted, however, such programs often come too late and do too little. In a

INTASC

3 Adapting Instruction for Individual Needs

CERTIFICATION POINTER

On your teacher certification test, you may be asked what is the impact on learning of students' physical, social, emotional, moral, and cognitive development.

deficit approach we try to stop adolescents from doing risky things, but adolescents don't always listen.

Instead of trying to deal with problems after they are already serious, many programs have demonstrated success with a wide range of problem behaviors by embedding preventive strategies into the regular curriculum. For example, a number of programs have succeeded in reducing high-risk behaviors by introducing "life skills training," focusing on skills such as making good decisions and resisting peer pressure (Stipek, de la Sota, & Weishaupt, 1999). Another approach is a program of prevention that focuses on building norms of cooperation, altruism, and social responsibility (Battistich et al., 1999). Involving community agencies to engage children in prosocial behaviors is another frequently recommended practice (Kidron & Fleischman, 2006). Comprehensive, whole-school reform models can have an impact on high-risk behaviors, especially truancy and dropping out, in middle school (Balfanz & MacIver, 2000) and high school (Bottoms, 2007; Darling-Hammond, Ancess, & Ort, 2002; Jordan et al., 2000; McPartland et al., 2002).

The Intentional TEACHER

USING WHAT YOU KNOW about Early Childhood, Middle Childhood, and Adolescent Students to Improve Teaching and Learning

Intentional teachers realize that students in their early years, in middle childhood, and in adolescence face different challenges as they develop physically, cognitively, and socially. They will relate student goals to the different levels of development and modify their instruction when they find that particular students need additional—or different—support in their growth toward independence.

1 What do I expect my students to know and be able to do at the end of this lesson? How does this contribute to course objectives and to students' needs to become capable individuals?

Teachers need to build understanding of the issues that typically arise at their students' age levels, and they need to develop understanding of the stress that can be involved as students move from one level to the next. For example, you might build into your long-term plans activities that capitalize on the important influence of the peer culture. Examples include allowing students to study content through connections to topical interests such as fashion, music, and sports.

2 What knowledge, skills, needs, and interests do my students have that must be taken into account in my lesson?

Instruction is most appropriate when it addresses students' current functioning. Both formal and informal measures can provide information about your students' linguistic, physical, and cognitive development. For example, if you were a teacher of young children, you might check for students' concepts about print: Can they identify the front of a book? Do they track from left to right? If you were a middle school teacher, you might use informal conversation and academic materials to assess new students' English language skills. As students work, you might listen for hints that they are becoming increasingly reflective about their inner lives, a sign that marks the adolescent thought process.

As a high school teacher, you might recognize that maturing adolescents are beginning to take a more active role in the learning process, accept responsibility for their own learning, seek for real-life applications of what is being learned, and bring their own experiences into consideration. They are more autonomous, less dependent on others than younger children. You might adapt your instruction to afford more individual choice of research projects and reporting format, encouraging collaborative investigations by groups of students.

3 What do I know about the content, child development, learning, motivation, and effective teaching strategies that I can use to accomplish my objectives?

Students' relationships with peers change over time. Observe students' peer interaction so that you can encourage prosocial behavior. For example, you might observe kindergartners during their free time, taking notes about the different forms of play you observe, or you might listen to older students' lunch

CHAPTER 3 SUMMARY

How Do Children Develop during the Preschool Years?

Physically, young children develop strength and coordination of the large muscles first and then of the small muscles (as in cutting with scissors or writing). Cognitive abilities corresponding to Piaget's sensorimotor and preoperational stages also include the acquisition of language. Oral language is usually acquired by age 3 and includes the development of vocabulary, grammatical rules, and conventions of discourse. The foundations of reading and writing are usually acquired before formal schooling begins.

Socioemotional development in early childhood can be partly described in terms of Erikson's initiative versus guilt stage. Peer relationships help children overcome the egocentrism that Piaget described as characteristic of preoperational thinking. Prosocial behavior includes caring, sharing, comforting, and cooperating. Parten identified four categories of play—solitary, parallel, associative, and cooperative—that reflect increasing levels of social interaction and sophistication. Play exercises children's linguistic, cognitive, social, and creative skills.

INTASC

7 Instructional Planning Skills
8 Assessment of Student Learning
9 Professional Commitment and Responsibility

table conversations, asking yourself: "Do my students compare themselves to their peers in order to evaluate themselves?" You might make a mental note to help them make appropriate comparisons.

4 What instructional materials, technology, assistance, and other resources are available to help accomplish my objectives?

Classroom environments may be most likely to allow for development if they include a rich variety of materials that can foster social, linguistic, physical, and academic development. For example, if you teach young children you might include a puppet center and a storytelling area to encourage oral language development. With all students, you might use classroom meetings, in which students are encouraged to share openly, to help build a sense of community and acceptance that welcomes all students, no matter what their differences.

It is important to check not only your plans and materials but also students' reaction to those plans and materials as well. Do they seem to perceive their activities as moving them forward?

You might review students' portfolios to trace their growth in self-concept, as well as academic mastery. You might watch for patterns that emerge throughout the class and use that information to adjust learning opportunities. If you teach secondary grades, you might review your lesson plans to ensure that they provide opportunities for social interaction and formal problem solving, activities that help adolescents move into Piaget's stage of formal operations, and note student comments about the assignments.

5 How will I plan to assess students' progress toward my objectives?

Assess the information you have gathered from different sources over time. Does it suggest that students are growing in each important area of human development? For example, you might ask elementary students to write in their journals about their friends, and use their entries to help you determine whether students are developing friendships that can provide social and cognitive resources for them.

6 How will I respond if individual children or the class as a whole are not on track toward success? What is my back-up plan?

Proponents of developmentally appropriate practice urge teachers to treat each student as an individual with a unique pattern of growth. For example, you might hold a class discussion, addressing such questions as "What can you do better now than at the beginning of the year?" "What would you still like to improve?" "How can we help each other?" By listening carefully to your students' comments you might identify any areas named as trouble spots by more than one student, determining to address such topics with further instructional activities in future lessons.

What Kinds of Early Childhood Education Programs Exist?

Economic and social factors have led to an increasing demand for early childhood education programs, including day-care centers, preschools, compensatory preschool programs, and kindergartens. Research findings have tended to support trends toward early intervention, school-readiness training, continuation of compensatory programs in the early elementary grades, targeting of students who are at risk, and avoidance of the potential drawbacks of kindergarten retention. Developmentally appropriate practice, instruction based on individuals' characteristics and needs rather than on age, has become increasingly important.

How Do Children Develop during the Elementary Years?

Between the ages of 5 and 7, children have slower growth but greater health and skill. They think in ways described in Piaget's theory as the concrete operational stage. Children in the upper elementary grades move from egocentric thought to more decentered thought. At 9 to 12 years of age, children can use logical, reversible thought, can reason abstractly, and can have insight into causal and interpersonal relationships.

In middle childhood, children may be seen as resolving Erikson's industry versus inferiority psychosocial crisis. School becomes a major influence on development, a place where the child develops a public self, builds social skills, and establishes self-esteem on the basis of academic and nonacademic competencies. In preadolescence, between ages 9 and 12, conformity in peer relations, mixed-sex peer groupings, and challenges to adult authority become more important.

How Do Children Develop during the Middle School and High School Years?

Puberty is a series of major physiological changes leading to the ability to reproduce. Significant differences exist in the age of onset of puberty, and both early maturers and late maturers may experience difficulties. Adolescents develop reflectivity and greater metacognitive skills, such as those described in Piaget's formal operations: combinatorial problem solving and hypothetical reasoning.

Adolescents may be seen as resolving Erikson's identity versus role confusion psychosocial crisis. They pay attention to how other people view them, search the past, experiment with roles, act on feelings and beliefs, and gradually seek greater autonomy and intimacy in peer relations. Foreclosure occurs when the individual chooses a role prematurely, but by late adolescence, most individuals have developed a state of identity achievement. Many factors, such as dropping out, substance abuse, and AIDS, place adolescents at risk.

KEY TERMS

Review the following key terms from the chapter.

SELF-ASSESSMENT: PRACTICING *for* LICENSURE

Directions: The chapter-opening vignette addresses indicators that are often assessed in state licensure exams. Re-read the chapter-opening vignette, and then respond to the following questions.

1. As noted in the interaction between Sam and Billy, there are enormous differences between students of varying ages. According to the information presented in the chapter, which of the following behaviors is more likely to be exhibited by Billy than by Sam?
   - **a.** obey parents
   - **b.** conform to peer demands
   - **c.** assert independence
   - **d.** be idealistic
2. According to the information presented in the chapter, which of the following behaviors is more likely to be exhibited by Sam than by Billy?
   - **a.** follow simple rules
   - **b.** defy convention
   - **c.** expect punishment for disobedience
   - **d.** be dependent on parents
3. Typically, a young child's social life evolves in relatively predictable ways. The social network grows from an intimate relationship with parents or other guardians to
   - **a.** nonrelated adults, peers, and then other family members.
   - **b.** peers, nonrelated adults, and then other family members.
   - **c.** other family members, peers, and then nonrelated adults.
   - **d.** other family members, nonrelated adults, and then peers.
4. For students like Sam Stevens, who is entering what Piaget terms "formal operations," which of the following instructional strategies would be considered developmentally appropriate?
   - **a.** teach Sam to hear specific sounds as he reads (phonemic awareness)
   - **b.** allow Sam to invent spellings by making judgments about sounds and by relating the sounds to the letters he knows
   - **c.** help Sam to resolve the personality crisis of initiative versus guilt
   - **d.** require Sam to write assignments that require debate (argue pro or con on an issue)
5. One of the first signs of early adolescence is the appearance of reflectivity. What is this?
   - **a.** a return to egocentric thought
   - **b.** the development of initiative
   - **c.** the ability to think about one's own mind
   - **d.** joining others in working toward a common goal
6. Design a lesson that would be considered developmentally appropriate for someone Billy's age. Include an explanation as to why you believe it is appropriate.
7. Design a lesson that would be considered developmentally appropriate for someone Sam's age. Include an explanation as to why you believe it is appropriate.
8. One of the most serious problems of adolescence is delinquency. Delinquents are usually
   - **a.** high achievers who turn to delinquency out of boredom.
   - **b.** socially adept at leading others into crime.
   - **c.** low achievers who feel they can't succeed in school.
   - **d.** late-maturing adolescents.

PEARSON

myeducationlab™

Where the Classroom Comes to Life

Now go to **www.myeducationlab.com** to:

- take a Pretest to assess your initial comprehension of the chapter content;
- study chapter content with your individualized Study Plan;
- take a Posttest to assess your understanding of chapter content;
- practice your teaching skills with Building Teaching Skills exercises; and
- build a deeper, more applied understanding of chapter content with Homework and Exercises.

CHAPTER 4

Student Diversity

chapter OUTLINE

Marva Vance and John Rossi are first-year teachers at Emma Lazarus Elementary School. It's November, and Marva and John are meeting over coffee to discuss the event dreaded by many a first-year teacher: the upcoming Thanksgiving pageant.

"This is driving me crazy!" Marva starts. "Our classes are like the United Nations. How are we supposed to cast a Thanksgiving pageant? I have three Navajo children. Should I cast them as Native Americans, or would they be offended? My Vietnamese kids have probably never seen a turkey, and the idea of eating a big bird like that must be revolting to them. I wonder how meaningful this will be to my African Americans. I remember when I was in a Thanksgiving pageant and our teacher had us African American students be stagehands because she said there weren't any African American Pilgrims! Besides, what am I going to do about a narrator? José says he wants to be narrator, but his English isn't too good. Lakesha would be good, but she's often out for debate tournaments and would miss some rehearsals. I've also been worrying about the hunters. Should they all be boys? Wouldn't it be gender stereotyping if the boys were hunters and the girls were cooks? What about Mark? He uses a wheelchair. Should I make him a hunter?"

John sighs and looks into his coffee. "I know what you're talking about. I just let my kids sign up for each part in the pageant. The boys signed up as hunters, the girls as cooks, the Native Americans as such. Maybe it's too late for us to do anything about stereotyping when the kids have already bought into their roles. Where I went to school, everyone was white, and no one questioned the idea that hunters were boys and cooks were girls. How did everything get so complicated?"

USING *your* EXPERIENCE

CRITICAL THINKING Spend 4 or 5 minutes writing a plausible ending to the vignette. What did Marva Vance end up doing, and what were the results?

COOPERATIVE LEARNING In small groups of four students, role-play Marva and John's situation. Then discuss the issues they are raising. After 6 minutes, report your group's conclusions to the class.

Students differ. They differ in performance level, learning rate, and learning style. They differ in ethnicity, culture, social class, and home language. They differ in gender. Some have disabilities, and some are gifted or talented in one or more areas. These and other differences can have important implications for instruction, curriculum, and school policies and practices. Marva and John are concerned with student diversity as it relates to the Thanksgiving pageants they are planning, but diversity and its meaning for education are important issues every day, not only on Thanksgiving. This chapter discusses some of the most important ways in which students differ and some of the ways in which teachers can accept, accommodate, and celebrate student diversity in their daily teaching. However, diversity is such an important theme that almost every chapter in this book touches on this issue. Teachers are more than instructors of students. Together with their students they are builders of tomorrow's society. A critical part of every teacher's role is to ensure that the equal opportunity that we hold to be central to our nationhood is translated into equal opportunity in day-to-day life in the classroom. This chapter was written with this goal in mind.

WHAT IS THE IMPACT OF CULTURE ON TEACHING AND LEARNING?

INTASC

2 Knowledge of Human Development and Learning
3 Adapting Instruction for Individual Needs

If you have ever traveled to a foreign country, you noticed differences in behaviors, attitudes, dress, language, and food. In fact, part of the fun of traveling is in discovering these differences in **culture,** which refers to the shared norms, traditions, behaviors, language, and perceptions of a group (King, 2002). Though we usually think of cultural differences as being mostly national differences, there is probably as much cultural diversity within the United States as between the United States and other industrialized nations. The life of a middle-class family in the United States or Canada is probably more like that of a middle-class family in Italy, Ireland, or Israel than it is like that of a low-income family living a mile away. Yet while we value cultural differences between nations, differences within our own society are often less valued. The tendency is to value the characteristics of mainstream, high-status groups and devalue those of other groups.

By the time children enter school, they have absorbed many aspects of the culture in which they were raised, such as language, beliefs, attitudes, ways of behaving, and food preferences. More accurately, most children are affected by several cultures, in that most are members of many overlapping groups. The cultural background of an individual child is affected by his or her ethnicity, socioeconomic status, religion, home language, gender, and other group identities and experiences (see Figure 4.1). Many of the behaviors that are associated with being brought up in a particular culture have important consequences for classroom instruction. For example, schools expect children to speak standard English. This is easy for students from homes in which standard English is spoken but difficult for those whose families speak other languages or significantly divergent dialects of English. Schools also expect students to be highly verbal, to spend most of their time working

culture
The language, attitudes, ways of behaving, and other aspects of life that characterize a group of people.

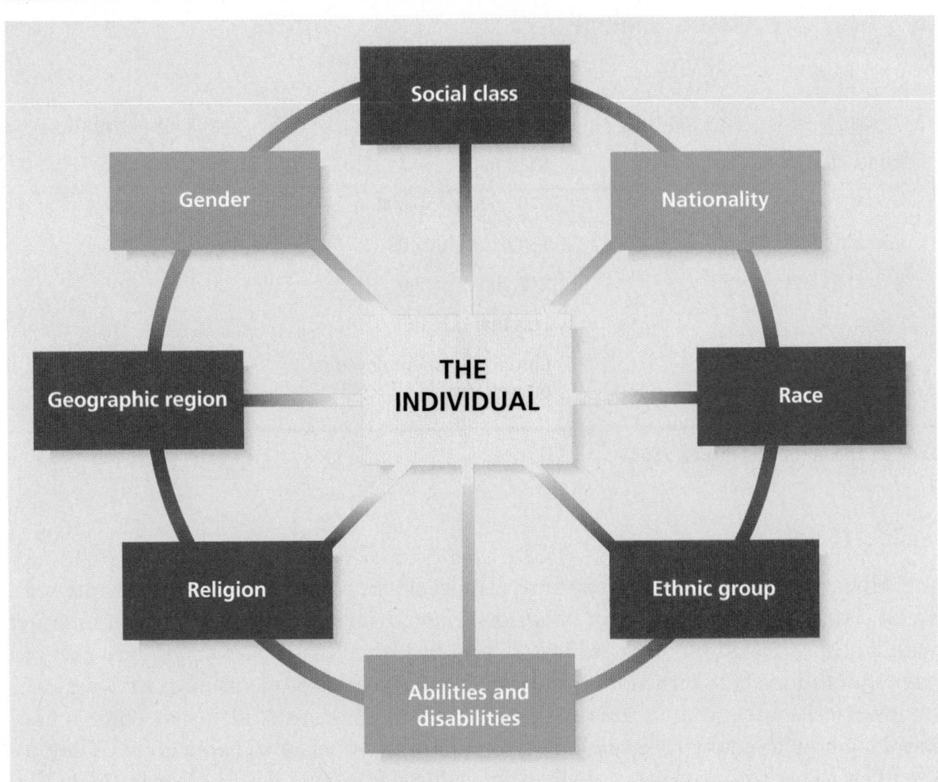

FIGURE 4.1 Cultural Diversity and Individual Identity

Reprinted with permission of the author and publisher from James A. Banks, *Multiethnic Education: Theory and Practice* (3rd ed.), 1993, p. 89. Boston: Allyn & Bacon.

independently, and to compete with other students for grades and recognition. However, many cultures place a higher value on cooperation and peer orientation than on independence and competitiveness (Boykin, 1994a, 1994b). Because the culture of the school reflects mainstream middle-class values (Grossman, 1995), and because most teachers are from middle-class backgrounds, the child from a different culture is often at a disadvantage. Understanding students' backgrounds is critical for effectively teaching both academic material and the behaviors and expectations of the school.

HOW DOES SOCIOECONOMIC STATUS AFFECT STUDENT ACHIEVEMENT?

One important way in which students differ from one another is in social class. Even in small rural towns in which almost everyone is the same in ethnicity and religion, the children of the town's bankers, doctors, and teachers probably have a different upbringing from that experienced by the children of most farmhands or domestic workers.

Sociologists define social class, or **socioeconomic status (SES),** in terms of an individual's income, occupation, education, and prestige in society (Thompson & Hickey, 2008). These factors tend to go together, so SES is most often measured as a combination of the individual's income and years of education because these are most easily quantified. Thompson and Hickey describe six class groupings in the United States as shown in Table 4.1.

In this book the term *middle class* is used to refer to families whose wage earners are in occupations requiring significant education; *working class* to those who have relatively stable occupations not requiring higher education; and *lower class* to those in the urban or rural underclass who are often unemployed and might be living on government assistance.

socioeconomic status (SES)
A measure of prestige within a social group that is most often based on income and education.

TABLE 4.1 Class Groupings

	Income	% of Population
Upper class	$150,000+	5
Upper middle class	$100,000–$150,000	15
Lower middle class	$30,000–$100,000	33
Working class	$16,000–$30,000	30
Lower class	Less than $16,000	14
Poor	Chronically unemployed or on welfare	1

Source: Thompson and Hickey, 2008.

However, social class indicates more than level of income and education. Along with social class goes a pervasive set of behaviors, expectations, and attitudes, which intersect with and are affected by other cultural factors. Students' social-class origins are likely to have a profound effect on attitudes and behaviors in school. Students from working-class or lower-class backgrounds are less likely than middle-class students to enter school knowing how to count, to name letters, to cut with scissors, or to name colors. They are less likely to perform well in school than are children from middle-class homes (Natriello, 2002; Sirin, 2005). Of course, these differences are true only on the average; many working-class and lower-class parents do an outstanding job of supporting their children's success in school, and many working-class and lower-class children achieve at a very high level. Social class cuts across categories of race and ethnicity. Although it is true that Latino and African American families are, on average, lower in social class than are white families, there is substantial overlap; the majority of all low-income families in the United States are white, and there are many middle-class nonwhite families (U.S. Census Bureau, 2001). Definitions of social class are based on such factors as income, occupation, and education, never on race or ethnicity.

What additional challenges do schools and parents in poor communities face with regard to educating the children of the community? What factors make their success more difficult?

TABLE 4.2 NAEP Reading Score (2003) by Parents' Education: Grade 8

Parents' Education	% Scoring at or above Proficient
Graduated college	43
Some education after high school	33
Graduated high school	20
Did not finish high school	13

Source: Based on National Center for Education Statistics, 2003.

Table 4.2 shows the reading performance of eighth-graders on the 2003 National Assessment of Educational Progress (NCES, 2003). Note that children of more educated parents (a key component of social class) consistently scored higher than children of less educated parents. Similarly, among fourth-graders who qualified for free or reduced-price lunches, only 15 percent scored at or above "proficient" on the reading portion of the NAEP, in comparison to 42 percent of fourth-graders who did not qualify (NCES, 2003). The NAEP used qualification for free lunch as an indicator of a child's family income.

The Role of Child-Rearing Practices

Average differences between middle-class and lower-class parents in child-rearing practices are the main reason for differences in school achievement. As one indicator of this, there is much evidence that lower-class children adopted into middle-class homes achieve at much higher levels than their nonadopted brothers and sisters, and at similar levels to their adoptive siblings (van IJzendoorn, Juffer, & Klein Poelhuis, 2005).

Much research has focused on the differences in child-rearing practices between the average middle-class family and the average working-class or lower-class family. Many children from low-income families receive an upbringing that is less consistent with what they will be expected to do in school than that of middle-class children. By the time they enter school, middle-class children are likely to be good at following directions, explaining and understanding reasons, and comprehending and using complex language, whereas working-class or lower-class children may have less experience in all these areas (Parkay, 2006). Children from disadvantaged homes are more likely to have poor access to health care, and to suffer from diseases such as lead poisoning. Their mothers are less likely to have received good prenatal care (McLoyd, 1998). These factors can delay cognitive development, which also affects school readiness. Of course low-income families lack resources of all kinds to help their children succeed. For example, children from disadvantaged families are far more likely to have uncorrected vision, hearing problems, or other health problems that may inhibit their success in school (Natriello, 2002; Rothstein, 2004).

Another important difference between middle-class and lower-class families is in the kinds of activities parents tend to do with their children. Middle-class parents are likely to express high expectations for their children and to reward them for intellectual development. They are likely to provide good models for language use, to talk and read to their children frequently, and to encourage reading and other learning activities. They are particularly apt to provide all sorts of learning materials for children at home, such as books, encyclopedias, records, puzzles, and, increasingly, computers (Yeung, Linver, & Brooks-Gunn, 2002). These parents are also likely to expose their children to learning experiences outside the home, such as museums, concerts, and zoos (Duke, 2000). They are more likely to be able to help their children succeed in school and to be involved in their education (Heymann & Earle, 2000). Middle-class parents are likely to expect and demand high achievement from their children; working-class and lower-class parents are more likely to demand good behavior and obedience (Knapp & Woolverton, 1995;

Trawick-Smith, 1997). Helping poor parents engage in more enriching interactions with their children can have a substantial impact on their children's cognitive performance. For example, the Parent–Child Home Program (PCHP) initiative provides disadvantaged mothers of toddlers with toys and demonstrations of ways to play with and talk with children to enhance their intellectual development. Studies have found strong and lasting effects of this simple intervention on children's cognitive skills and school success, in comparison to children whose parents did not receive PCHP services (Allen & Seth, 2004; Levenstein, Levenstein, & Oliver, 2002).

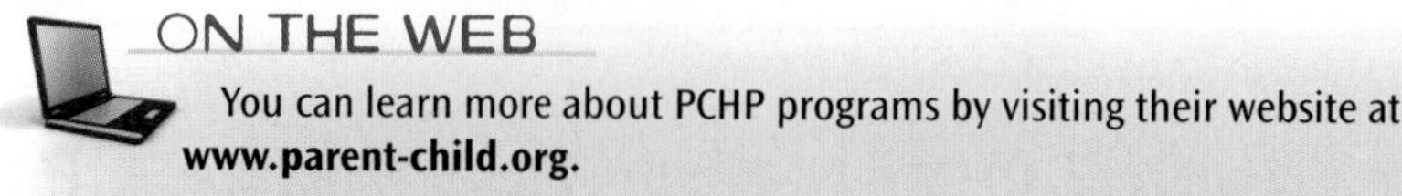

ON THE WEB

You can learn more about PCHP programs by visiting their website at **www.parent-child.org.**

The Link between Income and Summer Learning

Several studies have found that although low-SES and high-SES children make similar progress in academic achievement during the school year, the high-SES children continue to make progress over the summer whereas low-SES children fall behind (Borman, Benson, & Overman, 2005; Cooper, Lindsay, Nye, & Greathouse, 1998; Entwisle, Alexander, & Olson, 2001; Heyns, 2002). These findings suggest that home environment influences not only academic readiness for school but also the level of achievement throughout students' careers in school. Middle-class children are more likely to be engaged in school-like activities during the summer and to have available more school-like materials. Working-class and lower-class children may be receiving less academically relevant stimulation at home and are more likely to be forgetting what they learned in school (Hill, 2001). The "summer slide" phenomenon has led many schools to offer summer school to at-risk students, and research is finding that this can be an effective strategy (Borman & Dowling, 2006).

CONNECTIONS
For more on summer school programs, see Chapter 9.

The Role of Schools as Middle-Class Institutions

CONNECTIONS
For more on cooperative learning strategies, see Chapter 8, pages 243–249.

Students from backgrounds other than the mainstream middle class have difficulties in school in part because their upbringing emphasizes different behaviors from those valued in school. The problem is that the school overwhelmingly represents the values and expectations of the middle class. Two of these values are individuality and future time orientation (see Boykin, 1994a; Jagers & Carroll, 2002). Most U.S. classrooms operate on the assumption that children should do their own work. Helping others is often defined as cheating. Students are expected to compete for grades, for the teacher's attention and praise, and for other rewards. Competition and individual work are values that are instilled early on in most middle-class homes. However, students from lower-class backgrounds (Boykin, 1994a) are less willing to compete and are more interested in cooperating with their peers than are middle-class European Americans. These students have often learned from an early age to rely on their communities, friends, and family and have always also helped and been helped by others. Not surprisingly, students who are most oriented toward cooperation with others learn best in cooperation with others, whereas those who prefer to compete learn best in competition with others (Kagan, Zahn, Widaman, Schwartzwald, & Tyrrell, 1985). Because of the mismatch between the cooperative orientation of many lower-class and minority-group children and the competitive orientation of the school, many researchers (e.g., Boykin, 1994a; Greenfield & Cocking, 1994; Triandis, 1995) have argued that there is a structural bias in traditional classrooms that works against these children. They recommend that teachers use cooperative learning strategies at least part of the time with these students so that they receive instruction that is consistent with their cultural orientations (see Slavin, Hurley, & Chamberlain, 2003).

CERTIFICATION POINTER

Teacher certification tests may require that you identify the factors outside of school that can affect student learning. These include culture, family circumstances, community environments, health, and economic conditions.

School and Community Factors

Often, children from low-income families are placed at risk for school failure by the characteristics of the communities they live in and the schools they attend (Everson & Millsap, 2004). For example, school funding in most areas of the United States is correlated with social class; middle-class children are likely to attend schools with greater resources, better-paid (and therefore better-qualified) teachers, and other advantages (Darling-Hammond, 1995). On top of these differences, schools serving low-income neighborhoods may have to spend much more on security, on services for children having difficulties, and on many other needs, leaving even less for regular education (Persell, 1997). This lack of resources can significantly affect student achievement (Land & Legters, 2002; Rothstein, 2004). In very impoverished neighborhoods, crime, a lack of positive role models, inadequate social and health services, and other factors can create an environment that undermines children's motivation, achievement, and mental health (Behrman, 1997; Black & Krishnakumar, 1998; Vernez, 1998). In addition, teachers often hold low expectations for disadvantaged children, and this can affect their motivation and achievement (Becker & Luthar, 2002; Hauser-Cram, Sirin, & Stipek, 2003). These factors, however, do not automatically doom children to failure. Many at-risk children develop what is called *resilience,* the ability to succeed despite many risk factors (Borman & Overman, 2004; Glantz, Johnson, & Huffman, 2002; Waxman, Gray, & Padron, 2002). But such factors do make success in school much more difficult.

School, Family, and Community Partnerships

INTASC

⑩ Partnerships

If family background is a key factor in explaining differences in student achievement, then it follows that involving families in support of children's school success can be part of the solution. Professional educators can reach out to families and other community members in a variety of ways to improve communication and respect between home and school and to give parents strategies to help their own children succeed. Epstein et al. (2002) describe six types of involvement schools might emphasize in a comprehensive partnership with parents (also see Hoover-Dempsey et al., 2005).

1. ***Parenting.*** Assist families with parenting and child-rearing skills, family support, understanding child and adolescent development, and setting home conditions to support learning at each age and grade level. Obtain information from families to help schools understand families' backgrounds, cultures, and goals for children.
2. ***Communicating.*** Communicate with families about school programs and student progress with school-to-home and home-to-school communications. Create two-way communication channels so that families can easily communicate with teachers and administrators.
3. ***Volunteering.*** Improve recruitment, training, activities, and schedules to

"Mrs. Rogers, I think this is taking the idea of parent involvement a little too far!"

involve families as volunteers and audiences at the school or in other locations to support students and school programs.

4. ***Learning at home.*** Involve families with their children in academic learning activities at home, including homework, goal setting, and other curricular-linked activities and decisions.
5. ***Decision making.*** Include families as participants in school decisions, governance, and advocacy activities through PTA, committees, councils, and other parent organizations. Assist family representatives to obtain information from and give information to those they represent.
6. ***Collaborating with the community.*** Coordinate with community businesses, agencies, cultural and civic organizations, colleges or universities, and other groups. Enable students to contribute service to the community (adapted from Epstein et al., 2002, p. 527).

CERTIFICATION POINTER

Teacher certification tests may require you to outline specific actions that you might take as a teacher to connect the school and students' home environment to benefit your students' learning.

Correlational research on parent involvement has clearly shown that parents who involve themselves in their children's educations have higher-achieving children than other parents (Flouri & Buchanan, 2004; Lee & Bowen, 2006). However, there has been more debate about the impacts of school programs to increase parent involvement. Many studies have shown positive effects of parent and community involvement programs, especially those that emphasize parents' roles as educators for their own children (see Comer, 2005; Epstein et al., 2002; Sanders, Allen-Jones, & Abel, 2002), although there are also many studies that have failed to find such benefits (Mattingly et al., 2002; Schutz, 2006). What the research suggests is that building positive relations with parents and giving parents practical means of helping their children succeed in school are important parts of any intentional educator's plan to improve the achievement and adjustment of all children, but other elements, such as improving instruction and curriculum, are also necessary.

THEORY *into* PRACTICE

Parent Involvement

Parents and other family members have considerable influence over their children's success in school. If you establish positive relationships with parents, you can help them see the importance of supporting the school's educational objectives by doing such things as providing an uncluttered, quiet place for their children to do homework. The more clearly you communicate your expectations for their role in their children's learning in your class, the more likely they will be to play that role. For example, if you expect children to practice reading every evening for homework, having a form for parents to sign each night communicates the importance of the activity. Other strategies for involving parents in their children's learning include

1. ***Home visits.*** At the beginning of the school year, it is useful to arrange for a visit to your students' homes. Seeing where a student is coming from gives you additional understanding for the supports and constraints available to the students for their cognitive and emotional development.
2. ***Frequent newsletters for families.*** Informing families about what their children will be learning and what they can do at home to support that learning can increase student success. If you have English language learners in your class, having the newsletter available in their first language is important both in improving communication and in showing respect.
3. ***Parent workshops.*** Inviting parents to your classroom so you can explain the program of study and what your expectations are can help parents understand how they can support their children's learning.

4. ***Positive calls home.*** Hearing good news about their children's school work or behavior helps set up a productive cycle of positive reinforcement and increases the likelihood of the behavior continuing. This is especially helpful for family members whose own experiences with the school system were less than positive.
5. ***Inviting family members to volunteer.*** Asking parents to help out in your class by sharing their expertise, interests, or hobbies can make family members feel valued. They can demonstrate their occupation, a cultural tradition, or help out with field trips or other special projects. Beyond providing the extra assistance, this communicates to your students that you value the diversity of knowledge and expertise that their families bring to your class.
6. ***Make parents your partners.*** Communicating to parents and other family members that you are a team, working together to promote their children's achievement, makes your job easier and greatly improves parents' attitudes toward school and willingness to work with you in difficult times as well as good ones.

Is the Low Achievement of Children from Low-Income Groups Inevitable?

Schools can do a great deal to enable children from low-income families to succeed in school (Barr & Parrett, 2001; Borman, 2002/03; Cole-Henderson, 2000; Gunter, Estes, & Schwab, 2003; Slavin, 2002). For example, intensive interventions have been designed to help develop children's cognitive skills early in life and to help their parents do a better job of preparing them for school. Studies of these programs have shown long-term positive effects for children growing up in very impoverished families, especially when the programs are continued into the early elementary grades (Conyers et al., 2003; Ramey & Ramey, 1998; Reynolds et al., 2002). Reading Recovery (Lyons, Pinnell, & DeFord, 1993) and other tutoring programs for first-graders have shown substantial effects on the reading achievement of at-risk children (Cox & Hopkins, 2006; Denton, Anthony, Parker, & Hasbrouck, 2004; Morris, Tyner, & Perney, 2000). Success for All (Borman et al., 2007; Slavin & Madden, 2001), which combines effective instructional programs, tutoring, and family support services, has demonstrated substantial and lasting impacts on the achievement of children in high-poverty schools. Significant reductions in class size have been found to be particularly beneficial to children in high-poverty schools (Finn et al., 2003). High-quality summer school programs (Borman & Boulay, 2004) and after-school programs (McComb & Scott-Little, 2003) can provide opportunities to move at-risk students toward success. These and other programs and practices, including health and social interventions that go beyond the school (Jackson, 1999; Rothstein, 2004), demonstrate that low achievement by lower-class children is not inevitable. Achievement can be greatly improved by use of strategies that are readily available to schools.

Nonschool Solutions to Achievement Problems of Disadvantaged Children

In a 2004 book, Richard Rothstein makes an important set of observations about the gaps in achievement between middle-class and disadvantaged children. He notes that major explanations for the gap come from problems not generally under the control of schools, which could be rectified by enlightened policies. Some of the examples he discusses are as follows.

Vision Rothstein notes that poor children have severe vision impairment at twice the normal rate. Surprisingly, juvenile delinquents have extraordinarily high rates of vision problems. Rothstein cites data indicating that more than 50 percent of minority and low-income children have vision problems that interfere with their academic work. Some require eyeglasses, and others need eye-exercise therapies. A study by Harris (2002) found that disadvantaged fourth-graders who received free eyeglasses and therapy gained substantially in achievement relative to a control group. Children in school are usually screened for nearsightedness but not for farsightedness or tracking (Gould & Gould, 2003). Even when low-income children have prescriptions for glasses, they often do not obtain them or do not wear them to school.

Hearing Disadvantaged children have more hearing problems than middle-class children in particular because of the failure to get medical care for ear infections.

Lead Exposure Disadvantaged children are far more likely to live in homes where dust from old lead paint is in the air. Even small amounts of lead can lead to loss of cognitive functioning and hearing loss. Studies have found blood lead levels of poor children to be five times those of middle-class children (Brookes-Gunn & Duncan, 1997).

Asthma Poor, urban children have remarkably high rates of asthma. Studies in New York and Chicago (Whitman, Williams, & Shah, 2004) found that one in four inner-city African American children had asthma, six times the national rate. In turn, asthma is a major cause of chronic school absence, and even in school, untreated asthma interferes with academic performance.

Medical Care Disadvantaged children are much less likely to receive adequate medical care than are middle-class children. This leads to problems with absenteeism; poor motivation because of poor health; and the vision, hearing, and asthma problems mentioned earlier (Starfield, 1997).

Nutrition Although serious malnutrition is rare in the United States, undernutrition is common among poor children, and this affects academic performance. One study (Neisser et al., 1996) found that simply giving children vitamin and mineral supplements improved their test scores.

Rothstein's (2004) argument is that these and other aspects of poverty could be solved, and doing so could have a significant impact on the achievement of low-income children. Even though there are health agencies and social service agencies that are charged with solving these problems, schools have the advantage that they see the children every day. Simple reforms, such as improving school lunches or providing free eyeglasses that stay at school, might be as effective as much more expensive interventions, such as tutoring or special education, which may not be addressing the root causes of children's problems.

Implications for Teachers

Children enter school with varying degrees of preparation for the school behaviors that lead to success. Their behaviors, attitudes, and values also vary. However, the mere fact that some children initially do not know what is expected of them and have fewer entry-level skills than others does not mean that they are destined for academic failure. Although there is a modest positive correlation between social class and achievement, it should not be assumed that this relationship holds for all children from lower-SES families. There are many exceptions. Many working-class and lower-class families can and do provide home environments that are supportive of their children's success in school. Autobiographies of people who have overcome poverty (e.g., Comer, 1990) often refer to the influence of strong parents and role models with high standards who expected nothing less than the best from their children and did what they could to help them achieve. Although educators need to be aware of the problems encountered by many lower-class pupils, they also need to avoid converting this knowledge into stereotypes. In fact, there is evidence that middle-class teachers often have low expectations for working-class and lower-class students (Persell, 1997) and that these low expectations can become a self-fulfilling prophecy, causing students to perform less well than they could have (Becker & Luthar, 2002; Hauser-Cram et al., 2003).

HOW DO ETHNICITY AND RACE AFFECT STUDENTS' SCHOOL EXPERIENCES?

A major determinant of the culture in which students will grow up is their ethnic origin. An **ethnic group** is one in which individuals have a shared sense of identity, usually because of a common place of origin (such as Swedish, Polish, or Greek Americans), religion (such as Jewish or Catholic Americans), or race (such as African or Asian Americans). Note that **ethnicity** is not the same as race; **race** refers only to physical characteristics, such as skin color. Ethnic groups usually share a common culture, which may not be true of all people of a given race. African Americans who are recent immigrants from Nigeria or Jamaica, for example, are from ethnic backgrounds that are quite different from that of African Americans whose families have been in the United States for many generations, even if they are of the same race (King, 2002; Mickelson, 2002). Increasingly, Americans identify with multiple ethnic groups, and this has important consequences for their self-perceptions (Shih & Sanchez, 2005).

Most European Americans identify with one or more European ethnic groups, such as Polish, Italian, Irish, Greek, Latvian, or German. Identification with these groups might affect a family's traditions, holidays, food preferences, and, to some extent, outlook on the world. However, white ethnic groups have been largely absorbed into mainstream U.S. society, so the differences among them have few implications for education (Alba, 1990).

The situation is quite different for other ethnic groups. In particular, African Americans (Loury, 2002), Latinos (Secada et al., 1998), and Native Americans (Deyhle & Swisher, 1995; Lomawaima & McCarty, 2002) have yet to be fully accepted into mainstream U.S. society and have not yet attained the economic success or security that the white and many Asian ethnic groups have achieved (Carter & Goodwin, 1994). Students from these ethnic groups face special problems in school and have been the focus of two of the most emotional issues in U.S. education since the mid-1960s: desegregation and bilingual education. The following sections discuss the situation of students of various ethnic backgrounds in schools today.

VIDEO HOMEWORK EXERCISE
The Importance of Culture

Go to **www.myeducationlab.com** and, in the Homework and Exercises section for Chapter 4 of this text, access the video entitled "The Importance of Culture." Watch the video and complete the homework questions that accompany it, saving your work or transmitting it to your professor as required.

Racial and Ethnic Composition of the United States

The people who make up the United States have always come from many ethnic backgrounds, but every year the proportion of nonwhites and Latinos is increasing. Table 4.3 shows U.S. Census Bureau projections of the percentages of the U.S. population according to ethnicity. Note that the proportion of non-Latino whites is expected to continue to decline; as recently as 1970, 83.3 percent of all Americans were in this category. In contrast, the proportion of Latinos and Asians has grown dramatically since 1990 and is expected to continue to grow at an even more rapid rate from 2000 to 2010. In 2001, the U.S. Census Bureau announced that Latinos had overtaken African Americans as the largest **minority group.** These trends, which are the result of immigration patterns and differences in birth rates, have profound implications for U.S. education. Our nation is becoming far more ethnically diverse (Lapkoff & Li, 2007).

ethnic group
A group within a larger society that sees itself as having a common history, social and cultural heritage, and traditions, often based on race, religion, language, or national identity.

ethnicity
A history, culture, and sense of identity shared by a group of people.

race
Visible genetic characteristics of individuals that cause them to be seen as members of the same broad group (e.g., African, Asian, Caucasian).

minority group
An ethnic or racial group that is a minority within a broader population.

Academic Achievement of Students from Under-Represented Groups

If students from under-represented groups achieved at the same level as European and Asian Americans, there would probably be little concern about ethnic-group differences in U.S. schools. Unfortunately, they don't. On virtually every test of academic achievement,

TABLE 4.3 Percentage of U.S. Population by Race/Ethnicity in 1990, 2000, and 2010 (Projected)

Race/Ethnicity	1990	2000	2010
European American	75.7	71.4	67.4
Hispanic	9.0	11.9	14.6
African American	11.8	12.2	12.5
Asian/Pacific Islander	2.8	3.8	4.8
American Indian	0.7	0.7	0.8

Source: U.S. Census Bureau website, 2001, www.census.gov.

TABLE 4.4 NAEP Reading Scores (2003) by Race/Ethnicity: Grade 4

Race/Ethnicity	% Scoring at or above Proficient
White	41
African American	13
Latino	15
Asian/Pacific Islander	38
American Indian/Alaska Native	16

Source: National Center for Education Statistics, 2003.

African American, Latino, and Native American students score significantly lower than their European and Asian American classmates.

Table 4.4 shows reading scores on the 2003 National Assessment of Educational Progress (NAEP) according to students' race or ethnicity. African American, Latino, and American Indian children scored significantly lower than non-Latino white or Asian American children at all grade levels. These differences correspond closely with differences among the groups in average socioeconomic status, which themselves translate into achievement differences (recall Table 4.2).

The achievement gap between African American, Latino, and white children may be narrowing, but not nearly rapidly enough. During the 1970s there was a substantial reduction, but since the early 1980s the gap has stayed more or less constant in both reading and math on the National Assessment of Educational Progress (NCES, 2003).

Why Have Students from Under-Represented Groups Lagged in Achievement?

INTASC

8 **Assessment of Student Learning**

Why do many students from under-represented groups score so far below European and many Asian Americans on achievement tests? The reasons involve economics, society, families, and culture, as well as inadequate responses by schools (Chatterji, 2006; Gallimore & Goldenberg, 2001; Ladson-Billings, 2006; Okagaki, 2001; Parkay, 2006). The most important reason is that in our society, African Americans, Latinos (particularly Mexican Americans and Puerto Ricans), and Native Americans tend to occupy the lower rungs of the socioeconomic ladder. Consequently, many families in these groups are unable to provide their children with the stimulation and academic preparation that are typical of a middle-class upbringing (Halle, Kurtz-Coster, & Mahoney, 1997). Again, there are many exceptions; nevertheless, these broad patterns largely explain the average differences. Chronic unemployment, underemployment, and employment in very low-wage jobs, which are endemic in many communities of people from under-represented groups, have a negative effect on family life, including contributing to high numbers of single-parent families in these communities (U.S. Census Bureau, 2001).

Another important disadvantage that many students from under-represented groups face is academically inferior, overcrowded schools (Barton, 2003). Middle-class and many working-class families of all ethnicities throughout the United States buy their way out of inner-city schools by moving to the suburbs or sending their children to private or parochial schools, leaving the public schools to serve people who lack the resources to afford alternatives. The remaining children, who are disproportionately members of ethnic minorities, are likely to attend the lowest-quality, worst-funded schools in the country (Biddle & Berliner, 2002; Ferguson & Mehta, 2004; Lee, 2004), where they often have the least qualified and least experienced teachers (Connor, Son, Hindman, & Morrison, 2004; Darling-Hammond, 2006; Haycock, 2001).

Often, minority-group students perform poorly because the instruction they receive is inconsistent with their cultural background (Boykin, 1994b; Jagers & Carroll, 2002; Latham, 1997a; Ogbu, 1999; Ryan & Ryan, 2005). Academic excellence itself may be seen as inconsistent with acceptance in a student's own community; for example, Ogbu (1999), Spencer et al. (2001), Stinson (2006), and others have noted the tendency of many African American students to accuse their peers of "acting white" if they strive to achieve. In contrast, many Asian American parents strongly stress academic excellence as an expectation, and as a result many (though not all) Asian subgroups do very well in school (Ng, Lee, & Park, 2007; Okagaki & Frensch, 1998). African Americans (Boykin, 1994a; Jagers & Carroll, 2002; Lee, 2000), Native Americans (Henry & Pepper, 1990; Lomawaima & McCarty, 2002; Starnes, 2006), and Mexican Americans (Losey, 1995; Padrón, Waxman, & Rivera, 2002) generally prefer to work in collaboration with others and perform better in cooperative settings than in traditional competitive ones. Lack of respect for students' home languages and dialects can also lead to a diminishing of commitment to school (Delpit, 1995). Low expectations for minority-group students can contribute to their low achievement (Nasir & Hand, 2006; Ogbu, 1999; Tenenbaum & Ruck, 2007; Van Laar, 2001). This is especially true if, as often happens, low expectations lead well-meaning teachers or administrators to disproportionately place students from under-represented groups in low-ability groups or tracks (see Braddock, Dawkins, & Wilson, 1995) or in special education (O'Connor & Fernandez, 2006; Reid & Knight, 2006). Interestingly, though African American students often suffer from the low expectations of teachers and others, their expectations for themselves and their academic self-concepts tend to be at least as high as those of their white classmates (Eccles, Wigfield, & Byrnes, 2003; Van Laar, 2001).

CONNECTIONS
To learn about motivational factors that affect some minority-group students and low achievers, including the role of teacher expectations and the phenomenon of learned helplessness, see Chapter 10, pages 307 and 309.

Teaching Dilemmas:
CASES TO CONSIDER

INTASC

- 3 Adapting Instruction for Individual Needs
- 6 Communication Skills
- 10 Partnerships

Meeting Resistance

Fluent in both Spanish and English, Elizabeth Montgomery had changed careers in her mid-thirties to become a bilingual elementary teacher. After earning a Master of Education degree with honors and successfully completing her student-teaching, Elizabeth was hired to teach a fourth-grade Spanish bilingual class at a large elementary school in a working- and lower-class urban community. Of the thirty students in her class, twenty-six are Latino, two are African American, and two are European American.

LaShonda Brown is one of the African American students in Ms. Montgomery's class. After school she is startlingly sweet and often confides pleasant facts about her home life, but she is amazingly recalcitrant during class time. She often comes to school late and usually responds with "I ain't doin' that" to even the smallest request. In class she sits limply during assignments, makes rude noises during reading (which delights her classmates to no end), and refuses to participate in her math group. She seems both angry and dependent. By the fifth week of class, Ms. Montgomery has decided to call LaShonda's mother but plans to describe LaShonda's behavior as depression rather than anger.

Ms. Montgomery: Mrs. Brown, I'm concerned about LaShonda. She doesn't participate in class and seems especially dependent. Could she be depressed about something?

Mrs. Brown: Ms. Montgomery, that girl certainly isn't depressed because even though I'm raising her alone, I work very hard to buy her everything she wants and to make her happy. I'll admit that she's way too dependent, you might even say spoiled, but she isn't depressed.

Ms. Montgomery: Well, perhaps when you come to our class open house next week, we can talk some more about how to help LaShonda participate more in class.

During the open house Ms. Montgomery shows Mrs. Brown and the other parents around the classroom and discusses the bilingual approach she is using. The meeting is pleasant, but there is no opportunity to talk with Mrs. Brown alone about LaShonda, whose behavior is now prompting Ms. Montgomery to send her out of the classroom for small periods so her acting out does not get reinforced by her classmates.

Later that week, Ms. Montgomery receives a letter from Mrs. Brown that says, "It's too bad you can't be bothered to really teach my girl. It seems you prefer the Mexican American children in your class over the black children."

Stunned, Ms. Montgomery shows the letter to the vice principal, an African American woman with whom LaShonda has rapport. Vice Principal Johnson suggests inviting Mrs. Brown to a meeting with her and Ms. Montgomery in her office.

Vice Principal Johnson: Mrs. Brown, I'm so glad you could come in to talk with us about your concerns about LaShonda's class.

Mrs. Brown: Well, I don't mean any disrespect, but I think a white woman from the ritzy suburbs, who calls me up telling me my LaShonda is "depressed" may not be the best teacher for my daughter.

Ms. Montgomery: What would you do, Mrs. Brown, if LaShonda came into the room in the morning and refused to participate or do her work, and then refused to join the group for extra math help?

Mrs. Brown: She does that?

Ms. Montgomery: Every day.

Mrs. Brown: You've never told me this. I can't deal with her if you don't tell me what's going on. I wish you would have told me earlier.

QUESTIONS FOR REFLECTION

1. Discuss how social class, child-rearing practices, and the middle-class values of school may each be a factor in LaShonda's behavior in class.
2. If you were Ms. Montgomery, what would you have done differently with LaShonda and her mother?
3. Role-play the continuing discussion among Vice Principal Johnson, Ms. Montgomery, and Mrs. Brown. What would you say, as one of these three participants, to bring a more positive and cooperative conclusion to the meeting?

Source: Adapted from "What Would You Do, Mrs. Brown?" by June Isaacs Elia, from *Allyn & Bacon's Custom Cases in Education*, edited by Greta Morine-Dershimer, Paul Eggen, and Donald Kauchak (2000).

The low achievement of African American, Latino, and Native American children may well be a temporary problem. Within a few decades, as under-represented groups increasingly achieve economic security and enter the middle class, their children's achievement will probably come to resemble that of other groups. In the 1920s it was widely believed that immigrants from southern and eastern Europe (such as Italians, Greeks, Poles, and Jews) were hopelessly backward and perhaps retarded (Oakes & Lipton, 1994), yet the children and grandchildren of these immigrants now achieve as well as the descendants of the Pilgrims. However, we cannot afford to wait a few decades. The school is one institution that can break the cycle of poverty by giving children from impoverished backgrounds the opportunity to succeed. Most immediately, schools serving many African American, Latino, and Native American children can accelerate the achievement of these children by using comprehensive reform models and other proven practices (Borman et al., 2003; CSRQ, 2006; Lee, 2000; Slavin & Madden, 2001).

Effects of School Desegregation

Before 1954, African American, white, and often Latino and Native American students were legally required to attend separate schools in 20 states and the District of Columbia, and segregated schools were common in the remaining states. Students from under-represented groups were often bused miles away from their nearest public school to separate schools. The doctrine of separate but equal education was upheld in several U.S. Supreme Court decisions. In 1954, however, the Supreme Court struck down this practice in the landmark *Brown v. Board of Education of Topeka* case on the grounds that separate education was inherently unequal (Ancheta, 2006; Cose, 2004; Smith, 2002; Welner, 2006). *Brown v. Board of Education* did away with legal segregation, but it was many years before large numbers of racially different students were attending school together. In the 1970s, a series of Supreme Court decisions found that the continued segregation of many schools throughout the United States was the result of past discriminatory practices, such as deliberately drawing neighborhood boundary lines to separate schools along racial lines. These decisions forced local school districts to desegregate their schools by any means necessary (Bell, 2004; Ogletree, 2004).

Many districts were given specific standards for the proportions of students from under-represented groups who could be assigned to any particular school. For example, a district in which 45 percent of the students were African American might be required to have an enrollment of 35 to 55 percent African Americans in each of its schools. To achieve desegregation, some school districts simply changed school attendance areas; others created special magnet schools (such as schools for the performing arts, for talented and gifted students, or for special vocational preparation) to induce students to attend schools outside their own neighborhoods. However, in many large, urban districts, segregation of neighborhoods is so extensive that districts must bus students to other neighborhoods to achieve racially balanced schools. School desegregation was supposed to increase the academic achievement of low-income students from under-represented groups by giving them opportunities to interact with more middle-class, achievement-oriented peers (Lomotey & Teddlie, 1997). All too often, however, the schools to which students are bused are no better than the segregated schools they left behind, and the outflow of middle-class

Personal REFLECTION

INTASC ③ Adapting Instruction for Individual Needs

Being Sensitive to Race

Long ago I carried out a pilot project in a science class that a friend was teaching in an integrated high school in Portland, Oregon. On the first day, I came to the class and explained to the students that they would be working in groups. I then asked them to divide themselves into groups of four.

The students were delighted and immediately chose their groups: one composed entirely of African American boys, one of African American girls, and one of white boys, one of white girls. I was glad to see that there was one integrated group, but it turned out to be composed of students who rarely came to class!

Another time in the same school I went to visit the classroom of a friend who was teaching English. When I came into his class, the students all came rushing up. "Do you know Mr. ___?" they asked. I said I did. "Is he black or white?" It turned out that my friend, who has a dark complexion, recognized that in this school it might be good not to tell the kids his race to avoid being stereotyped as being on one side or the other.

I've now had three of my own children go through integrated high schools in Baltimore. In most ways their experiences with integration have been wonderful, and they all have friends of all races and backgrounds. Yet more than 50 years after *Brown v. Board of Education,* race is still the critical dividing line in our nation, not only in the obvious boundaries that still exist in economics, housing, and society at large but also most disturbingly in the hearts and minds of young people.

REFLECT ON THIS. What was the racial or ethnic mix of your K–12 experience? What did your school do to ensure full integration among students? Did this reflect the community efforts as a whole? What discussions about diversity have you had in your education classes? How have those discussions influenced your perspectives on classrooms and learning?

families from urban areas (which was well under way before busing began) often means that lower-class African American or Latino students are integrated with similarly lower-class whites (Kahlenberg, 2000; Trent, 1997). Also, it is important to note that because of residential segregation and opposition to busing, most students from under-represented groups still attend schools in which there are few, if any, whites, and in many areas segregation is once again on the increase (Orfield, Frankenberg, & Lee, 2003; Smith, 2002). Support for busing to achieve integration has greatly diminished among African American and Latino parents (Morris, 1999; Wells & Crain, 1997). Recent Supreme Court decisions have eliminated the judicial push for desegregation, and U.S. schools are gradually becoming more segregated (Orfield & Frankenberg, 2007; Orfield & Lee, 2004).

The overall effect of desegregation on the academic achievement of students from under-represented groups has been small, though positive. However, when desegregation begins in elementary school, particularly when it involves busing children from under-represented groups to high-quality schools with substantially middle-class student bodies, desegregation can have a significant positive effect on the achievement of the students from under-represented groups (Trent, 1997; Wells, 1995; Welner, 2006). This effect is thought to result not from sitting next to whites but rather from attending a better school. One important outcome of desegregation is that African American and Latino students who attend desegregated schools are more likely to attend desegregated colleges, to work in integrated settings, and to attain higher incomes than their peers who attend segregated schools (Schofield, 1995; Wells & Crain, 1997).

THEORY *into* PRACTICE

Teaching in a Culturally Diverse School

Following are some recommendations for promoting social harmony and equal opportunity among students in racially and ethnically diverse classrooms and schools (see also Gay, 2004; Howard, 2007; Nieto, 2002/03; Parillo, 2008).

- Use fairness and balance in dealing with students. Students should never have any justification for believing that "people like me [whites, African Americans, Latinos, Vietnamese] don't get a fair chance" (McIntyre, 1992).
- Choose texts and instructional materials that show all ethnic groups in equally positive and nonstereotypical roles (Garcia, 1993). Make sure under-represented groups are not misrepresented. Themes should be nonbiased, and individuals from under-represented groups should appear in nonstereotypical high-status roles (Banks, 2002; Bigler, 1999).
- Supplement textbooks with authentic material from different cultures taken from newspapers, magazines, and other media of the culture.
- Reach out to children's parents and families with information and activities appropriate to their language and culture (Lindeman, 2001). Avoid communicating bias, but discuss racial or ethnic relations with empathy (Stephan & Finlay, 1999) and openly, rather than trying to pretend there are no differences (Polite & Saenger, 2003).
- Avoid stereotyping and emphasize the diversity of individuals, not groups (Aboud & Fenwick, 1999; Levy, 1999).
- Let students know that racial or ethnic bias, including slurs, taunts, and jokes, will not be tolerated in the classroom or in the school. Institute consequences to enforce this standard (Wessler, 2001).
- Help all students to value their own and others' cultural heritages and contributions to history and civilization. At the same time, avoid trivializing or stereotyping cultures merely in terms of ethnic foods and holidays. Because

the United States is becoming a mosaic rather than a melting pot, students need more than ever to value diversity and to acquire a more substantive knowledge and appreciation of other ways of life (Villegas & Lucas, 2007).

- Decorate classrooms, hallways, and the library/media center with murals, bulletin boards, posters, artifacts, and other materials that are representative of the students in the class or school or of the other cultures being studied.
- Avoid resegregation. Tracking, or between-class ability grouping, tends to segregate high and low achievers, and because of historical and economic factors, students from under-represented groups tend to be over-represented in the ranks of low achievers. For this and other reasons, tracking should be avoided (Ferguson & Mehta, 2004; Khmelkov & Hallinan, 1999; Slavin, 1995b).
- Be sure that assignments are not offensive or frustrating to students of diverse cultural groups. For example, asking students to write about their Christmas experiences is inappropriate for non-Christian students.
- Provide structure for intergroup interaction. Proximity alone does not lead to social harmony among racially and ethnically different groups (Parrillo, 2008; Schofield, 1997). Students need opportunities to know one another as individuals and to work together toward common goals (Cooper & Slavin, 2004; Kagan, 2001). For example, students who participate in integrated sports and extracurricular activities are more likely than other students to have friends who are ethnically or racially different from themselves (Braddock, Dawkins, & Wilson, 1995; Slavin, 1995b).
- Use cooperative learning, which has been shown to improve relations across racial and ethnic lines (Cooper & Slavin, 2004; National Research Council, 2000). The positive effects of cooperative learning experiences often outlast the teams or groups themselves and may extend to relationships outside of school. Cooperative learning contributes to both achievement and social harmony (Johnson & Johnson, 1998; Slavin, Hurley, & Chamberlain, 2003) and can increase the participation of children from under-represented groups (Cohen, 2004).

HOW DO LANGUAGE DIFFERENCES AND BILINGUAL PROGRAMS AFFECT STUDENT ACHIEVEMENT?

INTASC

5 Classroom Motivation and Management

As recently as 1979, only 9 percent of Americans ages 5 to 24 were from families in which the primary language spoken was not English. In 1999, this proportion had increased to 17 percent (NCES, 2004), and projections forecast that by 2026, 25 percent of all students will come from homes in which the primary language is not English. Sixty-five percent of these students' families speak Spanish (NCES, 2004). However, many students speak any of dozens of Asian, African, or European languages. The term **language minority** is used for all such students, and **limited English proficient (LEP)** and English language learners (ELL) are terms used for the much smaller number who have not yet attained an adequate level of English to succeed in an English-only program. These students are learning **English as a second language (ESL)** and may attend classes for English language learners in their schools.

Students with limited English proficiency present a dilemma to the educational system (August & Shanahan, 2006a). Clearly, those who have limited proficiency in English need to learn English to function effectively in U.S. society. However, until they are proficient in English, should they be taught math or social studies in their first language or in English? Should they be taught to read in their first language? These questions are not simply pedagogical—they have political and cultural significance that has provoked

language minority
In the United States, native speakers of any language other than English.

limited English proficient (LEP)
Possessing limited mastery of English.

English as a second language (ESL)
Subject taught in English classes and programs for students who are not native speakers of English.

emotional debate. One such issue is that many Latino parents want their children to be instructed in the Spanish language and culture to maintain their group identity and pride (Cline, 1998; Macedo, 2000). Other parents whose language is neither English nor Spanish often feel the same way.

Bilingual Education

The term **bilingual education** refers to programs for students who are acquiring English that teach the students in their first language part of the time while English is being learned. English language learners are typically taught in one of four types of programs. They are as follows.

1. ***English immersion.*** The most common instructional placement for English language learners is some form of English immersion, in which ELL students are taught primarily or entirely in English. Typically, children with the lowest levels of English proficiency are placed in ESL programs to build their oral English to help them succeed in their English-only curriculum. English immersion programs may use carefully designed strategies to build students' vocabularies, simplify instructions, and help ELL students succeed in the content (see, for example, Echevarria, Vogt, & Short, 2004). Such models are often referred to as structured English immersion. Alternatively, ELL students may simply be included in regular English instruction and expected to do the best they can. This "sink or swim" approach is most common when the number of ELL students is small and when ELL students speak languages other than Spanish.

En garde!
En guardia!
J. BRAVO
"Children, this is not what we mean by dual language!"

2. ***Transitional bilingual education.*** A common but declining alternative for ELL students is transitional bilingual education, programs in which children are taught reading or other subjects in their native language (most often, Spanish) for a few years and then transitioned to English, usually in second, third, or fourth grade.

3. ***Paired bilingual education.*** In paired bilingual models, children are taught reading or other subjects in both their native language and in English, usually at different times of the day.

4. ***Two-way bilingual education.*** Two-way, or dual language, models teach all students both in English and in another language, usually Spanish. That is, English proficient students are expected to learn Spanish as Spanish proficient students learn English (Calderón & Minaya-Rowe, 2003; Lessow-Hurley, 2005; Lindholm-Leary, 2005). From the perspective of English language learners, a two-way bilingual program is essentially a paired bilingual program, in that they are taught both in their native language and in English at different times.

CERTIFICATION POINTER

In responding to a case study on a teacher certification test, you may be expected to know that conducting an assessment of students' oral language abilities in both their first language and in English would be a first step in helping English language learners achieve.

Research on bilingual strategies for teaching reading generally supports bilingual approaches, especially paired bilingual methods (Greene, 1997; Slavin & Cheung, 2005). The evidence supporting paired bilingual strategies suggests that English language learners need not spend many years building their oral English, but can learn English reading with a limited level of English speaking skills, and can then build their reading and speaking capabilities together (Slavin & Cheung, 2005). However, the language of instruction is only one factor in effective education for ELL students, and the quality of instruction (whether in English only or in English and another language) is at least as important (August & Shanahan, 2006b).

bilingual education
Instructional program for students who speak little or no English in which some instruction is provided in the native language.

ON THE WEB

The National Association for Bilingual Education provides support for the education of English language learners at **www.nabe.org.**

THEORY *into* PRACTICE

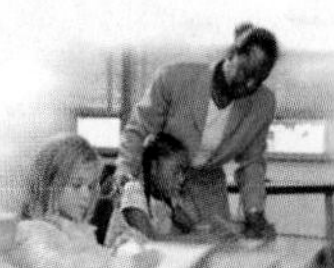

Teaching English Language Learners

Teachers in all parts of the United States and Canada are increasingly likely to have ELLs in their classes. The following are some general principles for helping these students succeed in the English curriculum (see Diaz-Rico, 2004; Echevarria, Vogt, & Short, 2004; Garcia & Jensen, 2007; Gray & Fleischman, 2005; Herrera & Murry, 2005; Short & Echevarria, 2005; Slavin & Calderón, 2001).

1. ***Don't just say it—show it.*** All students benefit from pictures, videos, concrete objects, gestures, and actions to illustrate difficult concepts, but ELLs particularly benefit from teaching that includes visual as well as auditory cues (Calderón, 2001).
2. ***Encourage safe opportunities to use academic English.*** Many ELLs are shy in class, not wanting to use their English for fear of being laughed at. Yet the best way to learn a language is to use it. Structure opportunities for students to use English in academic contexts (Reeves, 2005). For example, when asking questions, first give students an opportunity to discuss answers with a partner, and then call on partner pairs. This and other forms of cooperative learning can be particularly beneficial for ELLs (Calderón et al., 2004; Calderón, Hertz-Lazarowitz, & Slavin, 1998).
3. ***Develop vocabulary.*** All children, but especially ELLs, benefit from explicit teaching of new vocabulary. Give students many opportunities to hear new words in context and to use them themselves in sentences they make up themselves. Learning dictionary definitions is not as useful as having opportunities to ask and answer questions, write new sentences, and discuss new words with partners (Carlo et al., 2004; Fitzgerald & Graves, 2005; Zwiers, 2005).
4. ***Keep instructions clear.*** English language learners (and other students) often know the answers but get confused about what they are supposed to do. Take extra care to see that students understand assignments and instructions, for example, by asking students to restate instructions.
5. ***Point out cognates.*** If you speak the language of your ELLs, point out cases in which a word they know is similar to an English word. For example, in a class with many ELLs, you might help students learn the word *amorous* by noting the similarity to the Spanish and Portuguese word *amor,* the French word *amour,* or the Italian word *amore,* depending on the students' languages (Carlo et al., 2004).
6. ***Never publicly embarrass children by correcting their English.*** Instead, praise their correct answer and restate it correctly. For example, Russian students often omit *a* and *the.* If a student says, "Mark Twain was famous author," you might respond, "Right! Mark Twain was a very famous author," without calling attention to your addition of the word *a.* To encourage students to use their English, establish a classwide norm of never teasing or laughing at English errors.

INTASC

- **4** Multiple Instructional Strategies
- **6** Communication Skills
- **7** Instructional Planning Skills

Increasingly, research on bilingual education is focusing on the identification of effective forms of instruction for language-minority students rather than on the question of which is the best language of instruction (Christian & Genessee, 2001; Lee, 2005; Slavin & Calderón, 2001; U.S. Department of Education, 2000). Cooperative learning programs have been particularly effective both in improving the outcomes of Spanish reading instruction and in helping bilingual students make a successful transition to English-only instruction in the upper elementary grades (August & Shanahan, 2006a; Calderón, 1994; Calderón, Hertz-Lazarowitz, & Slavin, 1998; Cheung & Slavin, 2005). A program called Success for All, which combines cooperative learning with one-to-one tutoring for primary-grade

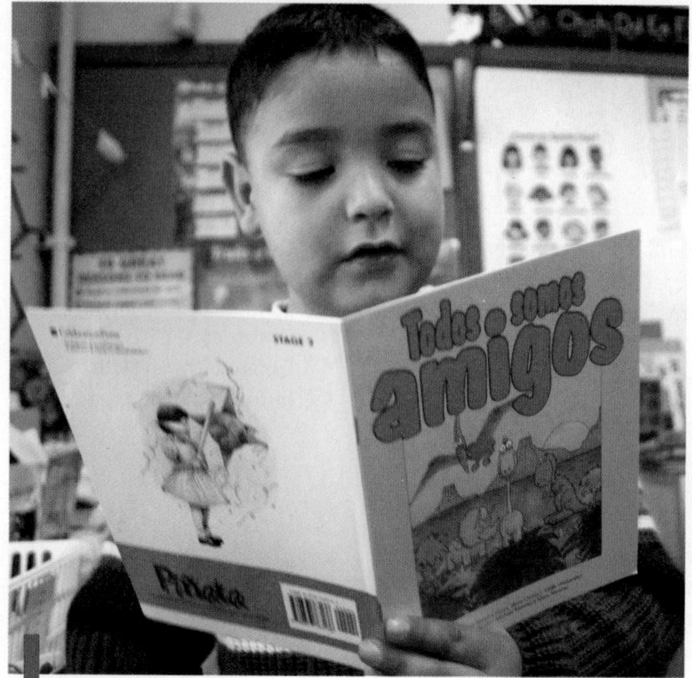

According to research, students in a bilingual program will ultimately achieve in English as well as or better than their peers who are taught only in English. Why do you think this is true?

students, family support services, and other elements, has had positive effects on the Spanish and English reading of children in bilingual programs (Cheung & Slavin, 2005; Slavin & Madden, 1999). Case studies of exceptionally successful schools serving Latino students (e.g., Reyes, Scribner, & Paredes, 1999) also provide practical visions for effective practice.

Recently, there has been a movement to abandon bilingual education in favor of English-only instruction. In California, which has the largest number of language-minority students in the United States, a referendum called Proposition 227 was passed in 1998 (Merickel et al., 2003). It mandates a maximum of 1 year for students with limited English proficiency to receive intensive assistance in learning English. After that, children are expected to be in mainstream English-only classes. This legislation has reduced but not eliminated bilingual education in California, as parents may still apply for waivers to have their children taught in their first language. Massachusetts, Arizona, and other states have also passed legislation limiting bilingual education (Hakuta, Butler, & Witt, 2000). No Child Left Behind (NCLB) requirements for high-stakes testing in English starting in third grade have also caused a reduction in bilingual programs (Zehr, 2007).

Effective Instruction for English Language Learners

A major development in research on English language learners is the recent publication of the report of the National Literacy Panel on Language-Minority Children and Youth (the NLC, for short) (August & Shanahan, 2006a). The NLC was commissioned by the U.S. Department of Education to follow up on the influential National Reading Panel (NRP, 2000), which reviewed research on reading but did not consider issues relating to English language learners in any depth. NLC members, distinguished researchers from many backgrounds, reviewed a broad range of research on English language learners. Some of their major conclusions are as follows.

Language of Instruction The NLC concluded that language-minority students instructed in their native language as well as English perform, on average, better on English reading measures than language-minority students instructed only in English. This is consistent with the conclusions of a review by Slavin and Cheung (2005), which found that Spanish-dominant English language learners taught to read in both Spanish and English (at different times of the day) ended up reading English better than children taught only in English.

VIDEO HOMEWORK EXERCISE
Teaching in a Bilingual Classroom

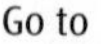

Go to **www.myeducationlab.com** and, in the Homework and Exercises section for Chapter 4 of this text, access the video entitled "Teaching in a Bilingual Classroom." Watch the video and complete the homework questions that accompany it, saving your work or transmitting it to your professor as required.

Effective Programs for English Language Learners Shanahan and Beck (2006) identified several studies that evaluated a variety of approaches to improving the reading performance of English language learners. They concluded that there were positive effects on reading performance of the Success for All comprehensive school reform program (Slavin & Madden, 2001); and they found benefits of cooperative learning, tutoring, and captioned TV (also see Cheung & Slavin, 2005).

Vocabulary Snow (2006) noted that although there was good evidence for the effectiveness of various approaches for many aspects of reading, there was less known about how to improve the English vocabularies of ELLs. Promising practices with Spanish-dominant students include using Spanish words as synonyms in vocabulary instruction and providing extensive opportunities to discuss English vocabulary in cooperative groups (August & Shanahan, 2006b). Also see Hill and Flynn (2006) and Herrera and Murry (2005) for descriptions of approaches to the instruction of English language learners.

WHAT IS MULTICULTURAL EDUCATION?

In recent years, multicultural education has become a much-discussed topic in U.S. education. Definitions of **multicultural education** vary broadly. The simplest definitions emphasize including non-European perspectives in the curriculum; for example, the works of African, Latino, Asian, and Native American authors in English curricula, teaching about Columbus from the point of view of Native Americans, and teaching more about the cultures and contributions of non-Western societies (Banks, 2002; Davidman & Davidman, 2001; Diaz, 2001; Manning & Baruth, 2004). Banks (1993) defines multicultural education as encompassing all policies and practices schools might use to improve educational outcomes not only for students of different ethnic, social class, and religious backgrounds but also for students of different genders and exceptionalities (e.g., children who have mental retardation, hearing loss, or vision loss or who are gifted). Banks (1993) summarizes this definition as follows:

> Multicultural education is an idea stating that all students, regardless of the groups to which they belong, such as those related to gender, ethnicity, race, culture, social class, religion, or exceptionality, should experience educational equality in the schools. (p. 25)

BUILDING TEACHING SKILLS CASE STUDY EXERCISE
Multicultural Education: Parents as (Subversive) Partners

Go to **www.myeducationlab.com** and, in the Homework and Exercises section for Chapter 4 of this text, access the Case Study entitled "Multicultural Education: Parents as (Subversive) Partners." Read the Case Study and complete the homework questions that accompany it, saving your work or transmitting it to your professor as required.

ON THE WEB

For resources and discussions of multicultural education, visit the Multicultural Pavilion at **www.edchange.org/multicultural/mission.html** and the North Central Regional Educational Laboratory at **www.ncrel.org/sdrs/areas/issues/educatrs/presrvce/pe3lk1.htm.**

Dimensions of Multicultural Education

Banks (1999) discusses five key dimensions of multicultural education (see Figure 4.2).

Content integration is teachers' use of examples, data, and information from a variety of cultures. This is what most people think of as multicultural education: teaching about different cultures and about contributions made by individuals from diverse cultures, inclusion in the curriculum of works by members of under-represented groups, including women, and the like (Bettmann & Friedman, 2004; Hicks-Bartlett, 2004).

Knowledge construction refers to teachers helping children "understand how knowledge is created and how it is influenced by the racial, ethnic, and social-class positions of individuals and groups" (Banks, 1995, p. 4). For example, students might be asked to write a history of the early colonization of America from the perspectives of Native Americans or African Americans to learn how the knowledge we take as given is in fact influenced by our own origins and points of view (see Cortés, 1995; Koppelman & Goodhart, 2005).

Prejudice reduction is a critical goal of multicultural education. Prejudice reduction involves both development of positive relationships among students of different ethnic backgrounds (Cooper & Slavin, 2004; Stephan & Vogt, 2004) and development of more democratic and tolerant attitudes toward others (Banks, 1995).

The term **equity pedagogy** refers to the use of teaching techniques that facilitate the academic success of students from different ethnic and social class groups. For example, there is evidence that members of some ethnic and racial groups, especially Mexican Americans and African Americans, learn best with active and cooperative methods (Boykin, 1994a, 1994b; Losey, 1995; Triandis, 1995).

multicultural education
Education that teaches the value of cultural diversity.

content integration
Teachers' use of examples, data, and other information from a variety of cultures.

knowledge construction
Helping students understand how the knowledge we take in is influenced by our origins and points of view.

prejudice reduction
A critical goal of multicultural education; involves development of positive relationships and tolerant attitudes among students of different backgrounds.

equity pedagogy
Teaching techniques that facilitate the academic success of students from different ethnic and social class groups.

FIGURE 4.2 Five Key Dimensions of Multicultural Education

Adapted from James A. Banks, "Historical Development, Dimensions, and Practice," in James A. Banks and Cherry A. Banks (eds.), *Handbook of Research on Multicultural Education,* 1999, New York: Simon & Schuster Macmillan.

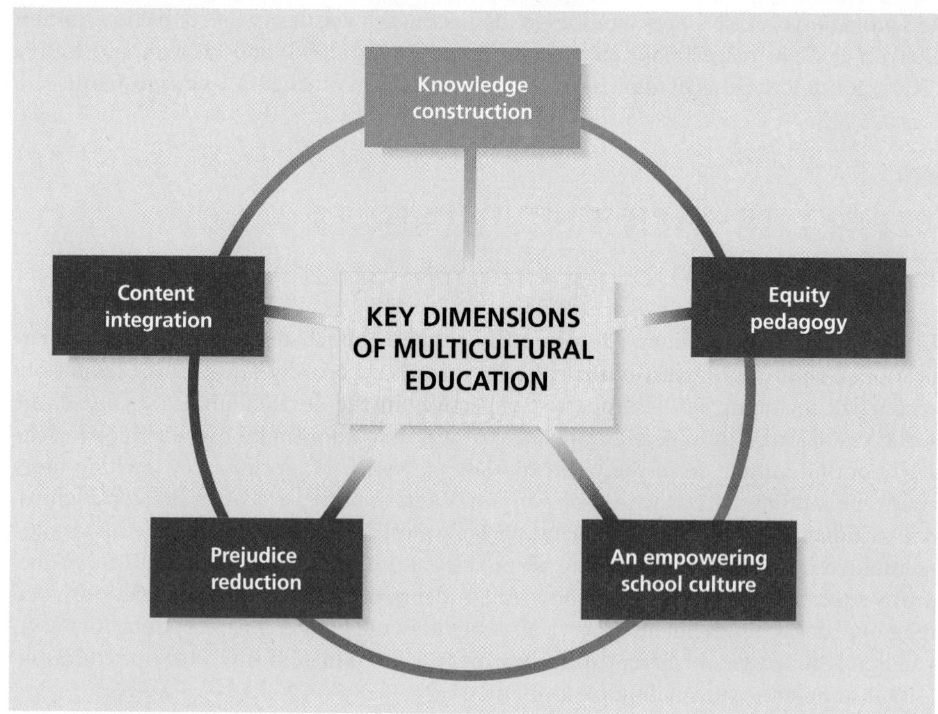

An **empowering school culture** is one in which school organization and practices are conducive to the academic and emotional growth of all students. A school with such a culture might, for example, eliminate tracking or ability grouping, increase inclusion (and reduce labeling) of students with special needs, try to keep all students on a path leading to higher education, and consistently show high expectations. An excellent example of an empowering school culture is the AVID project (Swanson, Mehan, & Hubbard, 1995; Watt, Powell, & Mendiola, 2004), which places at-risk students from under-represented groups in college preparatory classes and provides them with tutors and other assistance to help them succeed in a demanding curriculum.

The first step in multicultural education is for teachers, administrators, and other school staff to learn about the cultures from which their children come and to carefully examine all the policies, practices, and curricula used in the school to identify any areas of possible bias (e.g., teaching only about European and European American culture or history). Books by Banks (2001, 2002), Davidman and Davidman (2001), Diaz (2001), Koppelman and Goodhart (2005), and Manning and Baruth (2004) are good places to start. These and other books identify some of the characteristics of various cultures and teaching strategies and materials that are appropriate to each.

CERTIFICATION POINTER

For your teacher certification test you should recognize the importance of connecting your instruction to your students' cultural experiences.

HOW DO GENDER AND GENDER BIAS AFFECT STUDENTS' SCHOOL EXPERIENCES?

A child's sex is a visible, permanent attribute. Cross-cultural research indicates that gender roles are among the first that individuals learn and that all societies treat males differently from females. Therefore, gender-role or sex-role behavior is learned behavior. However, the range of roles occupied by males and females across cultures is broad. What is considered natural behavior for each gender is based more on cultural belief than on biological

empowering school culture
A school culture in which the institution's organization and practices are conducive to the academic and emotional growth of all students.

necessity. Nevertheless, the extent to which biological differences and gender socialization affect behavioral patterns and achievement is still a much-debated topic. The consensus of a large body of research is that no matter what the inherent biological differences, many of the observed differences between males and females can be clearly linked to differences in early socialization experiences (Feingold, 1992; Grossman & Grossman, 1994).

Do Males and Females Think and Learn Differently?

INTASC

2 Knowledge of Human Development and Learning

Although there is much evidence of differences in temperament and personality between boys and girls (e.g., Else-Quest et al., 2006; Rose & Rudolph, 2006), there is considerable debate about differences in aptitude and achievement. The question of gender differences in intelligence or academic achievement has been debated for centuries, and the issue has taken on particular importance since the early 1970s. The most important thing to keep in mind about this debate is that no responsible researcher has ever claimed that any male–female differences on any measure of intellectual ability are large in comparison to the amount of variability within each sex. In other words, even in areas in which true gender differences are suspected, these differences are so small and so variable that they have few practical consequences (Fennema, Carpenter, Jacobs, Franke, & Levi, 1998; Sadker, Sadker, & Long, 1997). Far more important are differences caused by cultural expectations and norms. For example, twelfth-grade girls score significantly lower than boys on the quantitative section of the Scholastic Assessment Test (SAT) (Gallagher & De Lisi, 1994) and on Advanced Placement tests in mathematics (Stumpf & Stanley, 1996). A summary of 20 major studies by Kim (2001) found that males scored better than females in math, whereas the opposite was true on English tests. Surprisingly, males scored better on multiple-choice tests but not on other formats. There may be a biological basis for such differences, but none has been proven (see Friedman, 1995; Halpern & LaMay, 2000). The most important cause is that females in our society have traditionally been discouraged from studying mathematics and, therefore, take many fewer math courses than males do. In fact, as females have begun to take more math courses over the past 2 decades, the gender gap on the SAT and on other measures has been steadily diminishing (National Center for Education Statistics, 1997).

Bearing these cautions in mind, note that studies generally find that males score higher than females on tests of general knowledge, mechanical reasoning, and mental rotations; females score higher on language measures, including reading and writing assessments (Strand, Deary, & Smith, 2006), and on attention and planning tasks (Warrick & Naglieri, 1993). There are no male–female differences in general verbal ability, arithmetic skills, abstract reasoning, spatial visualization, or memory span (Fennema et al., 1998; Friedman, 1995; Halpern & LaMay, 2000).

In school grades, females start out with an advantage over males and maintain this advantage into high school. Even in math and science, in which females score somewhat lower on tests, females still get better grades in class (Maher & Ward, 2002). Despite this, high school males tend to overestimate their skills in language and math (as measured by standardized tests), whereas females underestimate their skills (Pomerantz, Altermatt, & Saxon, 2002). In elementary school, males are much more likely than females to have reading problems (Ready et al., 2005; Taylor & Lorimer, 2002/03) and are much more likely to have learning disabilities or emotional disorders (Smith, 2001).

Is There a Boy Crisis?

Although there has been a great deal written over the past 30 years about how girls are underserved in schools, in more recent years there has been more concern about the "boy crisis" (Perkins-Gough, 2006; Von Drehle, 2007). It has long been the case that boys are more likely than girls to be assigned to special education, to be held back, to drop out, and to be in trouble with the law (Education Sector, 2006). More recently, girls have become much more likely to go to college and then to graduate, and many co-ed universities and colleges are 60 percent female or more. All of these differences exist despite the advantages boys have on some aptitude tests.

Looking more closely at the data, there is indeed a "boy crisis," but it does not apply across the board. African American and Hispanic boys are significantly more at risk than their sisters, and learning disabilities and ADHD (attention deficit hyperactive disorder; see Chapter 12) are significantly more common (and damaging) among boys. These problems are serious and need to be attended to, but they do not justify panic about the entire gender according to a recent report by Mead (2006). Boys are actually improving on many indicators, such as dropout and college attendance, but girls are improving faster. In fact, our perception of a "boy crisis" may simply be the result of the effects of removing policies and practices that once discouraged girls from excelling in school.

Sex-Role Stereotyping and Gender Bias

If there are so few genetically based differences between males and females, why do so many behavioral differences exist? These behavioral differences originate from different experiences, including reinforcement by adults for different types of behavior.

Male and female babies have traditionally been treated differently from the time they are born. The wrapping of the infant in either a pink or a blue blanket symbolizes the variations in experience that typically greet the child from birth onward. In early studies, adults described boy or girl babies wrapped in blue blankets as being more active than the same babies wrapped in pink. Other masculine traits were also ascribed to those wrapped in blue (Baxter, 1994). Although gender bias awareness has begun to have some impact on child-rearing practices, children do begin to make gender distinctions and have gender preferences by around the age of 3 or 4. Thus, children enter school having been socialized into appropriate gender-role behavior for their age in relation to community expectations (Delamont, 2002). Differences in approved gender roles between boys and girls tend to be much stronger in low-SES families than in high-SES families (Flanagan, 1993).

Socialization into this kind of approved **sex-role behavior** continues throughout life, and schools contribute to it. Though interactions between socialization experiences and achievement are complex and it is difficult to make generalizations, schools differentiate between the sexes in a number of ways. In general, males receive more attention from their teachers than females do (Jones & Dindia, 2004; Koch, 2003). Males receive more disapproval and blame from their teachers than females do, but they also engage in more interactions with their teachers in such areas as approval, instruction giving, and being listened to (Jones & Dindia, 2004; Koch, 2003; Maher & Ward, 2002). Teachers

sex-role behavior
Socially approved behavior associated with one gender as opposed to the other.

What are various examples of how U.S. culture has changed with regard to gender roles? What perceptions have yet to change? What impact might gender bias have on you as a teacher, both personally and professionally?

tend to punish females more promptly and explicitly for aggressive behavior than they do males. Torrance (1986) found that the creative behavior of males was rewarded by teachers three times as often as that of females. Other differentiations are subtle, as when girls are directed to play in the house corner while boys are provided with blocks or when boys are given drums to play in music class and girls are given the triangles.

THEORY *into* PRACTICE

Avoiding Gender Bias in Teaching

"In my science class the teacher never calls on me, and I feel like I don't exist. The other night I had a dream that I vanished" (Sadker & Sadker, 1994). Unfortunately, the girl who complained of being ignored by her teacher is not alone. According to a national study undertaken by the American Association of University Women (1992), schools shortchange female students in a variety of ways, from ignoring instances of sexual harassment to interacting less frequently with females than with males and less frequently with African American females than with white females. Teachers tend to choose boys, boost the self-esteem of their male students, and select literature with male protagonists. The contributions and experiences of girls and women are still often ignored in textbooks, curricula, and standardized tests (Zittleman & Sadker, 2002/03).

INTASC

6 Communication Skills

Teachers, usually without being aware of it, exhibit **gender bias** in classroom teaching in three principal ways: reinforcing gender stereotypes, maintaining sex separation, and treating males and females differently as students (see Koch, 2003; Maher & Ward, 2002). These inequities can have negative consequences for boys as well as girls (Canada, 2000; Weaver-Hightower, 2003).

AVOIDING STEREOTYPES. Teachers should avoid promoting sexual stereotypes. For example, they can assign jobs in the classroom without regard to gender, avoiding automatically appointing males as group leaders and females as secretaries, and can ask both males and females to help in physical activities. Teachers should also refrain from stating stereotypes, such as "Boys don't cry" and "Girls don't fight," and should avoid labeling students with such terms as *tomboy*. Teachers should encourage students who show an interest in activities and careers that do not correspond to cultural stereotypes, such as a female who likes math and science (Sadker, Sadker, & Long, 1997).

PROMOTING INTEGRATION. One factor that leads to gender stereotyping is the tendency for boys and girls (particularly in elementary school) to have few friends of the opposite sex and to engage mostly in activities with members of their own sex. Teachers sometimes encourage this by having boys and girls line up separately, assigning them to sex-segregated tables, and organizing separate sports activities for males and females. As a result, interaction between boys and girls in schools is less frequent than between students of the same sex. However, in classes in which cross-sex collaboration is encouraged, children have less stereotyped views of the abilities of males and females (Klein, 1994).

TREATING FEMALES AND MALES EQUALLY. Too often, teachers do not treat males and females equally. Observational studies of classroom interactions have found that teachers interact more with boys than with girls and ask boys more questions, especially more abstract questions (Sadker et al., 1997). In one study, researchers showed teachers videotapes of classroom scenes and asked them whether boys or girls participated more. Most teachers responded that the girls talked more, even though in fact the boys participated more than the girls by a ratio of 3 to 1 (Sadker et al., 1997).

gender bias
Stereotypical views and differential treatment of males and females, often favoring one gender over the other.

The researchers interpreted this finding as indicating that teachers expect females to participate less and thus see low rates of participation as normal. Teachers must be careful to allow all students equal opportunities to participate in class, to take leadership roles, and to engage in all kinds of activities (Bernard-Powers, 2001; Stein, 2000).

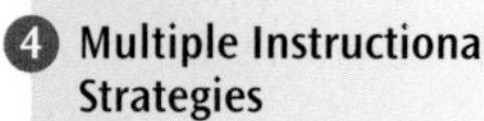

HOW DO STUDENTS DIFFER IN INTELLIGENCE AND LEARNING STYLES?

INTASC

4 Multiple Instructional Strategies

Intelligence is one of those words that all people believe they understand until you ask them to define it. At one level, **intelligence** can be defined as a general aptitude for learning or an ability to acquire and use knowledge or skills. However, even experts on this topic do not agree in their definitions; in a survey of 24 experts by Sternberg and Detterman (1986), definitions varied widely. A consensus definition expressed by Snyderman and Rothman (1987) is that intelligence is the ability to deal with abstractions, to solve problems, and to learn.

The biggest problem comes when we ask whether there is such a thing as general aptitude (Sternberg, 2003). Many people are terrific at calculus but couldn't write a good essay or paint a good picture if their lives depended on it. Some people can walk into a room full of strangers and immediately figure out the relationships and feelings among them; others may never learn this skill. Clearly, individuals vary in their aptitude for learning any specific type of knowledge or skill taught in a specific way. A hundred students attending a lecture on a topic they knew nothing about beforehand will all walk away with different amounts and kinds of learning, and aptitude for that particular content and that particular teaching method is one important factor in explaining these differences. The student who learned the most from the lecture would be likely also to learn very well from other lectures on similar topics. But would this student also learn the most if the lecture were on a different topic or if the same material were presented through hands-on experiences or in small groups?

CONNECTIONS
For more on the measurement of IQ, see Chapter 14, pages 460–462.

The concept of intelligence has been discussed since before the time of the ancient Greeks, but the scientific study of this topic really began with the work of Alfred Binet, who devised the first measure of intelligence in 1904. The French government asked Binet to find a way to identify children who were likely to need special help in their schooling. His measure assessed a broad range of skills and performances but produced a single score, called **intelligence quotient (IQ),** which was set up so that the average French child would have an IQ of 100 (Hurn, 2002).

Definitions of Intelligence

Binet's work greatly advanced the science of intelligence assessment, but it also began to establish the idea that intelligence was a single thing—that there were "smart" people who could be expected to do well in a broad range of learning situations. Ever since Binet, debate has raged about this issue. In 1927 Charles Spearman claimed that although there were, of course, variations in a person's abilities from task to task, there was a general intelligence factor, or "g," that existed across all learning situations. Is there really one intelligence, as Spearman suggested, or are there many distinct intelligences?

intelligence
General aptitude for learning, often measured by the ability to deal with abstractions and to solve problems.

intelligence quotient (IQ)
An intelligence test score that for people of average intelligence should be near 100.

The evidence in favor of "g" is that abilities are correlated with each other. Individuals who are good at learning one thing are likely, on the average, to be good at learning other things. The correlations are consistent enough for us to say that there are not a thousand completely separate intelligences, but they are not nearly consistent enough to allow us to say that there is only one general intelligence (Sternberg, 2003). In recent years, much of the debate about intelligence has focused on deciding how many distinct types of

According to Gardner's theory of multiple intelligences, which of the eight intelligences might these students use to learn? As a teacher, how would you vary your lessons to address student differences in learning style?

intelligence there are and describing each. For example, Sternberg (2002, 2003) describes three types of intellectual abilities: analytical, practical, and creative. Moran, Kornhaber, and Gardner (2006) describe nine **multiple intelligences.** These are listed and defined in Table 4.5.

In recent years, Gardner's (2004) multiple-intelligence (MI) theory has been very popular in education, but it has also been controversial. Waterhouse (2006), for example, notes that there is little evidence to support MI, citing evidence both from brain research

multiple intelligences
In Gardner's theory of intelligence, a person's eight separate abilities: logical/mathematical, linguistic, musical, naturalist, spatial, bodily/kinesthetic, interpersonal, and intrapersonal.

TABLE 4.5 Gardner's Multiple Intelligences

Linguistic. Ability to understand and use spoken and written communication. Ideal vocation: poet.*

Logical-mathematical. Ability to understand and use logic and numerical symbols and operations. Ideal vocation: computer programmer.

Musical. Ability to understand and use such concepts as rhythm, pitch, melody, and harmony. Ideal vocation: composer.

Spatial. Ability to orient and manipulate three-dimensional space. Ideal vocation: architect.

Bodily-kinesthetic. Ability to coordinate physical movement. Ideal vocation: athlete.

Naturalistic. Ability to distinguish and categorize objects or phenomena in nature. Ideal vocation: zoologist.

Interpersonal. Ability to understand and interact well with other people. Ideal vocation: politician; salesperson.

Intrapersonal. Ability to understand and use one's thoughts, feelings, preferences, and interests. Ideal vocation: autobiographer; entrepreneur. (Although high intrapersonal intelligence should help in almost any job because of its role in self-regulation, few paid positions reward a person solely for knowing himself or herself well.)

Existential. Ability to contemplate phenomena or questions beyond sensory data, such as the infinite and infinitesimal. Ideal vocation: cosmologist; philosopher.

*Most vocations involve several intelligences.

Source: Moran, Kornhaber, and Gardner, 2006.

and from research on measurement of IQ to argue that although there are different cognitive strengths and personalities, this does not contradict the idea that there is such a thing as general intelligence (Watkins & Canivez, 2004). Chen (2004) and Gardner and Moran (2006) argue that intelligence is more than what can be measured on an IQ test but admit that the evidence for MI is indirect.

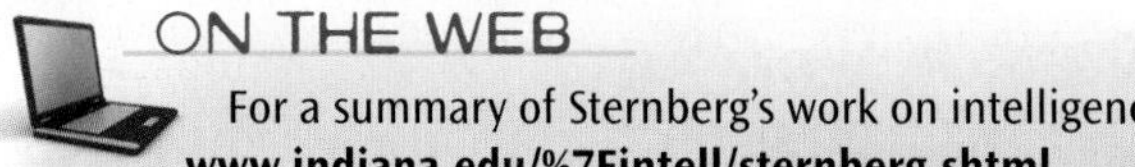

ON THE WEB

For a summary of Sternberg's work on intelligence go to **www.indiana.edu/%7Eintell/sternberg.shtml.**

The precise number of intelligences is not important for educators. What is important is the idea that good or poor performance in one area in no way guarantees similar performance in another. Teachers must avoid thinking about children as smart or not smart because there are many ways to be smart. Unfortunately, schools have traditionally recognized only a narrow set of performances, creating a neat hierarchy of students primarily in terms of what Gardner calls linguistic and logical/mathematical skills (only two of his eight intelligences). If schools want all children to be smart, they must use a broader range of activities and reward a broader range of performances than they have in the past.

THEORY *into* PRACTICE

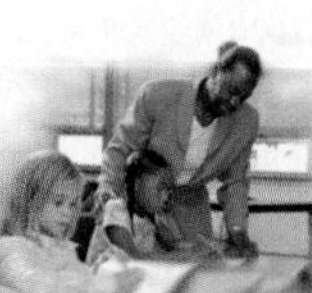

Multiple Intelligences

Gardner's theory of multiple intelligences implies that concepts should be taught in a variety of ways that call on many types of intelligence (Campbell, Campbell, & Dickerson, 2004; Kornhaber, Fierros, & Veenema, 2004; Moran, Kornhaber, & Gardner, 2006). To illustrate this, Armstrong (1994) gives the following examples of different ways to teach Boyle's Law to secondary students.

- Students are provided with a verbal definition of Boyle's Law: "For a fixed mass and temperature of gas, the pressure is inversely proportional to the volume." They discuss the definition. [Linguistic]
- Students are given a formula that describes Boyle's Law: $P \infty V = K$. They solve specific problems connected to it. [Logical/mathematical]
- Students are given a metaphor or visual image for Boyle's Law: "Imagine that you have a boil on your hand that you start to squeeze. As you squeeze it, the pressure builds. The more you squeeze, the higher the pressure, until the boil finally bursts and pus spurts out all over your hand!" [Spatial]
- Students do the following experiment: They breathe air into their mouths so that their cheeks puff up slightly. Then they put all the air into one side of their mouth (less volume) and indicate whether pressure goes up or down (it goes up); then they're asked to release the air in both sides of their mouth (more volume) and asked to indicate whether pressure has gone up or down (it goes down). [Bodily/kinesthetic]
- Students become "molecules" of air in a "container" (a clearly defined corner of the classroom). They move at a constant rate (temperature) and cannot leave the container (constant mass). Gradually, the size of the container is reduced as two volunteers holding a piece of yarn representing one side of the container start moving it in on the "molecules." The smaller the space, the more pressure (i.e., bumping into each other) is observed; the greater the space, the less pressure is observed. [Interpersonal, bodily/kinesthetic]

- Students do lab experiments that measure air pressure in sealed containers and chart pressure against volume. [Logical/mathematical, bodily/kinesthetic]
- Students are asked about times in their lives when they were "under pressure": "Did you feel like you had a lot of space?" (Typical answer: lots of pressure/not much space.) Then students are asked about times when they felt little pressure (little pressure/lots of space). Students' experiences are related to Boyle's Law. [Intrapersonal]

Few lessons will contain parts that correspond to all types of intelligence, but a key recommendation of multiple-intelligence theory for the classroom is that teachers seek to include a variety of presentation modes in each lesson to expand the number of students who are likely to succeed (Campbell, Campbell, & Dickinson, 2004; Gardner, 2003; Kline, 2001).

Origins of Intelligence

The origins of intelligence have been debated for decades. Some psychologists (such as Herrnstein & Murray, 1994; Toga & Thompson, 2005) hold that intelligence is overwhelmingly a product of heredity—that children's intelligence is largely determined by that of their parents and is set the day they are conceived. Others (such as Gordon & Bhattacharyya, 1994; Plomin, 1989; Rifkin, 1998) just as vehemently hold that intelligence is shaped mostly by factors in a person's social environment, such as the amount a child is read to and talked to. Most investigators agree that both heredity and environment play an important part in intelligence (Petrill & Wilkerson, 2000). It is clear that children of high-achieving parents are, on the average, more likely to be high achievers themselves, but this is as much because of the home environment created by high-achieving parents as it is because of genetics (Turkheimer, 1994). French studies of children of low-SES parents adopted into high-SES families find strong positive effects on the children's IQs compared to nonadopted children raised in low-SES families (Capron & Duyme, 1991; Schiff & Lewontin, 1986). One important piece of evidence in favor of the environmental view is that schooling itself clearly affects IQ scores. A review by Ceci (1991) found that the experience of being in school has a strong and systematic impact on IQ. For example, classic studies of Dutch children who entered school late because of World War II showed significant declines in IQ as a result, although their IQs increased when they finally entered school. A study of the children of mothers with mental retardation in inner-city Milwaukee (Garber, 1988) found that a program of infant stimulation and high-quality preschool could raise children's IQs substantially, and these gains were maintained at least through the end of elementary school. Studies of the Abecedarian program, which combined infant stimulation, child enrichment, and parent assistance, also found lasting effects of early instruction on IQ (Ramey & Ramey, 1998). This and other evidence supports the idea that IQ is not a fixed, unchangeable attribute of individuals but can change as individuals respond to changes in their environment (Cardellichio & Field, 1997). Further, some evidence indicates that IQ can be directly changed by programs designed for this purpose (Ellis, 2001a; Feuerstein & Kozulin, 1995).

Intelligence, whether general or specific, is only one of many factors that influence the amount children are likely to learn in a given lesson or course. It is probably much less important than prior knowledge (the amount the student knew about the course beforehand), motivation, and the quality and nature of instruction. Intelligence does become important at the extremes; it is a critical issue in identifying students who have mental retardation or those who are gifted, but in the middle range, where most students fall, other factors are more important. IQ testing has very frequently been misused in education, especially when it has been used to assign students inappropriately to special education or to tracks or ability groups (Hilliard, 1994). Actual performance is far more important than IQ and is more directly susceptible to being influenced by teachers and schools (Sternberg, 2003). Boykin (2000) has argued that schools would do better to focus on developing talents, rather than seeing them as fixed attributes of students.

CONNECTIONS
For a description of studies indicating that IQ can be directly changed by certain programs, see Chapter 8, page 253.

CERTIFICATION POINTER

Teacher certification tests may ask you to design a lesson that would accommodate students' various learning styles, in addition to their developmental needs.

Theories of Learning Styles

Just as students have different personalities, they also have different ways of learning. For example, think about how you learn the names of people you meet. Do you learn a name better if you see it written down? If so, you may be a visual learner, one who learns best by seeing or reading. If you learn a name better by hearing it, you may be an auditory learner. Of course, we all learn in many ways, but some of us learn better in some ways than in others (McCarthy, 1997; Swisher & Schoorman, 2001).

Students may also vary in preferences for different learning environments or conditions. For example, Dunn and Dunn (1993) found that students differ in preferences about such things as the amount of lighting, hard or soft seating, quiet or noisy surroundings, and working alone or with peers. These differences can predict to some extent which learning environments will be most effective for each child.

Aptitude–Treatment Interactions

Given the well-documented differences in learning styles and preferences, it would seem logical that different styles of teaching would have different impacts on different learners; yet this commonsense proposition has been difficult to demonstrate conclusively. Studies that have attempted to match teaching styles to learning styles have only inconsistently found any benefits for learning (Knight, Halpin, & Halpin, 1992; Snow, 1992). However, the search for such **aptitude–treatment interaction** goes on, and a few studies have found positive effects for programs that adapt instruction to an individual's learning style (Dunn, Beaudrey, & Klavas, 1989). The commonsense conclusion from research in this area is that teachers should be alert to detecting and responding to the differences in the ways that children learn (see Ebeling, 2000).

INTASC

3 Adapting Instruction for Individual Needs

4 Multiple Instructional Strategies

THEORY *into* PRACTICE

Understanding Diverse Thinkers

In his article "Celebrating Diverse Minds," author, physician, and educator Mel Levine of the University of North Carolina explores the importance of celebrating "all kinds of minds" as a way of making sure no child is left behind. He asks, "What becomes of students . . . who give up on themselves because they lack the kinds of minds needed to satisfy existing criteria for school success?"

Levine points out that learning differences can

> constitute daunting barriers, especially when they are not recognized and managed. Most important, these breakdowns can mislead us into undervaluing, unfairly accusing, and even undereducating students, thereby stifling their chances for success in school and life.
>
> Many faltering students have specialized minds—brains exquisitely wired to perform certain kinds of tasks masterfully, but decidedly miswired when it comes to meeting other expectations. A student may be brilliant at visualizing, but embarrassingly inept at verbalizing. [A] classmate may reveal a remarkable understanding of people, but exhibit no insight about sentence structure.
>
> . . . Within every student contending with learning differences, an area invariably exists in which her or his mind has been amply equipped to thrive. (Levine, 2003, p. 12)

aptitude–treatment interaction Interaction of individual differences in learning with particular teaching methods.

Levine proposes addressing this problem in three ways:

- ***Broaden student assessment.*** Our understanding of learning differences often focuses on fixing deficits, rather than identifying latent or blatant talents in struggling learners.
- ***Reexamine the curriculum.*** Explore new instructional practices and curricular choices in order to provide educational opportunities for diverse learners and to prepare them for a successful life.
- ***Provide professional development for educators.*** Provide teachers with training on the insights from brain research that will help them understand and support their students' diverse minds.

ONLINE READING & WRITING EXERCISE
Critiquing Ruby Payne

Access this exercise, entitled "Critiquing Ruby Payne," in the Homework and Exercises section for Chapter 4 of this text at **www.mylabschool.com.**

CHAPTER 4 SUMMARY

What Is the Impact of Culture on Teaching and Learning?

Culture profoundly affects teaching and learning. Many aspects of culture contribute to the learner's identity and self-concept and affect the learner's beliefs and values, attitudes and expectations, social relations, language use, and other behaviors.

How Does Socioeconomic Status Affect Student Achievement?

Socioeconomic status—based on income, occupation, education, and social prestige—can profoundly influence the learner's attitudes toward school, background knowledge, school readiness, and academic achievement. Working-class and low-income families experience stress that contributes to child-rearing practices, communication patterns, and lowered expectations that may handicap children when they enter school. Low-SES students often learn a normative culture that is different from the middle-class culture of the school, which demands independence, competitiveness, and goal-setting. However, low achievement is not the inevitable result of low socioeconomic status. Teachers can invite parents to participate in their children's education, and this can improve students' achievement.

How Do Ethnicity and Race Affect Students' School Experiences?

Populations of under-represented groups are growing dramatically as diversity in the United States increases. Students who are members of certain under-represented groups—self-defined by race, religion, ethnicity, origins, history, language, and culture, such as African Americans, Native Americans, and Latinos—tend to have lower scores than those of European and Asian Americans on standardized tests of academic achievement. The lower scores correlate with lower socioeconomic status and reflect in part a legacy of discrimination against under-represented groups and consequent poverty. School desegregation, long intended as a solution to educational inequities as a result of race and social class, has had mixed benefits. Continuing issues include delivering fairness and equal opportunity, fostering racial harmony, and preventing segregation.

How Do Language Differences and Bilingual Programs Affect Student Achievement?

English language learners are typically taught in one of four types of programs: English immersion, transitional bilingual, paired bilingual, and two-way bilingual. Bilingual programs teach students in their native language as well as English. Research suggests that

The Intentional TEACHER

USING WHAT YOU KNOW about Student Diversity to Improve Teaching and Learning

Intentional teachers view student diversity as a rich resource. They learn about their students' home lives, cultures, languages, and strengths, and they value each student as an individual. Intentional teachers examine data from their classrooms and question their own practices, guarding against the possibility that their perspectives may inadvertently limit students' success. Intentional teachers use what they know about their own practices and their particular students to improve the quality of education for all.

1 What do I expect my students to know and be able to do at the end of this lesson? How does this contribute to course objectives and to students' needs to become capable individuals?

Teachers need to examine the influence of their own cultural perspectives on the expectations they hold for students. Ask yourself, "Do my goals reflect only the values of a dominant group?" For example, you might curb your impulse to give stickers to the first five of your third-graders who earn 100 percent on their multiplication facts, deciding that your appreciation of individual competition may not be shared by all. You might decide to give students choices about how they do book reports, so that children with different learning strengths can express themselves in different ways.

Many educators feel that educational goals should reflect, at least to some extent, the community within which children are educated. Ask yourself, "How can we revise our classroom goals to better reflect the needs, values, and interests of all our students and families?" For example, you might begin a class with an informal discussion about what students would like to learn and about students' definitions of success. Students' interests and cultural backgrounds should not entirely determine your goals for a given lesson or course, but they should be taken into account. Algebra is algebra, but there are many paths to proficiency in algebra. Find out the paths your students are most willing and able to travel.

2 What knowledge, skills, needs, and interests do my students have that must be taken into account in my lesson?

Intentional teachers learn about their students and draw on information about their students' home lives and community resources to plan their instruction. What is your understanding of students' cultures and community? Ask yourself, "What experiences and strengths have my students gathered outside of school that can foster their learning?" For example, although you provide instruction in English, you might look for ways to value students' home language, reinforcing the idea that knowing two languages is an asset. You might design a "multilingual dictionary" activity, developing a list of classroom and family words in English, and asking students with different home languages to translate the list into their language. You could print and distribute this short dictionary at a PTA meeting as well as to the class members, who might wish to discuss similarities and differences between the languages represented and the English equivalents. In any class, you could collect colorful expressions, sayings, or slang reflecting the cultural heritages of your students. These "dictionaries" might be exchanged on the Internet or by mail with similar efforts from classes in different regions or parts of town.

bilingual education, especially paired bilingual education, can have benefits for students. Recent legislation in states throughout the country has had a chilling effect on bilingual education.

What Is Multicultural Education?

Multicultural education is calling for the celebration of cultural diversity and the promotion of educational equity and social harmony in the schools. Multicultural education includes content integration, knowledge construction, prejudice reduction, equity pedagogy, and an empowering school culture.

How Do Gender and Gender Bias Affect Students' School Experiences?

Many observed differences between males and females are clearly linked to differences in early socialization, when children learn sex-role behaviors regarded as appropriate. Ongoing research shows very few genetically based gender differences in thinking and abilities. However, gender bias in the classroom, including subtle teacher behaviors

INTASC 7 Instructional Planning Skills
9 Professional Commitment and Responsibility

3 What do I know about the content, child development, learning, motivation, and effective teaching strategies that I can use to accomplish my objectives?

Intentional teachers may provide opportunities for students to choose ways of interacting with subject-matter content that reflect their learning-style preferences. You might vary grouping structures so that students work as a whole class, individually, or in flexible small groups. You might employ principles of sheltered instruction, which makes grade-level content accessible to all, for your English language learners. For example, you could provide graphic organizers of the literature and bring in real examples of the items described in your readings.

4 What instructional materials, technology, assistance, and other resources are available to help accomplish my objectives?

Effective teachers work as part of an educational team. Draw on the strengths that can come from teachers and parents working together. For example, you might survey parents about relevant summer programs. To help students maintain academic gains, you might help them acquire library cards and suggest books for them to read over vacation. You might give them each a journal and invite them—and their parents!—to write to you.

If your class includes a number of bilingual students, you might ask for volunteers to invite an older family member to talk to your art class about the particular art forms of his or her place of origin, and you might explain that the student would be asked to serve as translator and interpreter.

Use children's cultural backgrounds as a springboard to mainstream content and expectations. A Navajo child, for example, has as much need to learn about ancient Greece as any other child, but he or she comes with a rich background that an intentional teacher should evoke to help interpret Greek culture.

5 How will I plan to assess students' progress toward my objectives?

Collect information on your teaching to ensure that your practices are equitable. An observer might gather information, or you might tape your teaching for later analysis. Key questions include:

Do I give equal time to interacting with males and females?

Do I praise and admonish students for the same types of behaviors, no matter what their group?

Are my expectations uniformly high for all students? Do I express this clearly?

To the extent appropriate, do I use the classroom as a forum for students to question mainstream perspectives and existing conditions? To encourage social improvement?

6 How will I respond if individual children or the class as a whole is not on track toward success? What is my backup plan?

You might ask yourself: "How can I confirm my current understanding of my diverse students and how can I learn more about particular groups? Have I made an effort to meet some of the adults that my students speak of as influential in their community or highly regarded by their family? Are the literature selections for class readings representative of a range of authors—by gender, nationality, ethnicity? Is my own personal reading contributing to a better understanding of diversity and individual differences?"

toward male and female students and curriculum materials that contain sex-role stereotypes, has clearly affected student choices and achievement. One outcome is a gender gap in mathematics and science, though this gap has decreased steadily.

How Do Students Differ in Intelligence and Learning Styles?

Students differ in their abilities to deal with abstractions, to solve problems, and to learn. They also differ in any number of specific intelligences, so accurate estimations of intelligence should probably rely on broader performances than traditional IQ tests allow. Therefore teachers should not base their expectations of students on IQ test scores. Binet, Spearman, Sternberg, and Gardner have contributed to theories and measures of intelligence. Both heredity and environment determine intelligence. Research shows that home environments, schooling, and life experiences can profoundly influence IQ.

Students differ in their prior learning and in their cognitive learning styles. Individual preferences in learning environments and conditions also affect student achievement.

KEY TERMS

Review the following key terms from the chapter.

aptitude–treatment interaction 120
bilingual education 108
content integration 111
culture 92
empowering school culture 112
English as a second language (ESL) 107
equity pedagogy 111
ethnic group 101
ethnicity 101
gender bias 115
intelligence 116
intelligence quotient (IQ) 116
knowledge construction 111
language minority 107
limited English proficient (LEP) 107
minority group 101
multicultural education 111
multiple intelligences 117
prejudice reduction 111
race 101
sex-role behavior 114
socioeconomic status (SES) 93

SELF-ASSESSMENT: PRACTICING *for* LICENSURE

Directions: The chapter-opening vignette addresses indicators that are often assessed in state licensure exams. Re-read the chapter-opening vignette, and then respond to the following questions.

1. Marva Vance and John Rossi discuss their students' diverse norms, traditions, behaviors, languages, and perceptions. Which of the following terms best describes the essence of their conversation?
   - **a.** race
   - **b.** socioeconomic status
   - **c.** intelligence
   - **d.** culture
2. Regarding the students of Marva Vance and John Rossi, which of the following statements on socioeconomic status is most likely true?
   - **a.** Students from working-class or lower-class backgrounds perform academically as well as or better than students from middle-class homes.
   - **b.** Students from disadvantaged homes are more likely to have inadequate access to health care.
   - **c.** Students from middle-class and lower-class homes are equally likely to make academic progress over the summer.
   - **d.** Schools overwhelmingly represent the values and expectations of the working class.
3. Marva Vance and John Rossi discuss their students' tendencies to accept the stereotypical roles assigned to them by society. According to research, what should the teachers do about this stereotyping?
   - **a.** Allow students to select their own roles, even if they make stereotypical decisions.
   - **b.** Tell the story of Thanksgiving as realistically as possible: Native American students play Native Americans, girls play cooks, and boys play hunters.
   - **c.** Themes should be nonbiased, and individuals from under-represented groups should appear in non-stereotypical high-status roles.
   - **d.** Write a Thanksgiving play that includes the contributions of all under-represented groups.
4. José, a student in Marva Vance's class, wants to be the narrator of the Thanksgiving pageant, even though he is not proficient in English. According to research on the effectiveness of bilingual programs, which strategy might Ms. Vance use to improve all her students' English speaking and writing skills?
   - **a.** Ms. Vance should avoid bilingual programs because they have been found to be harmful to students in their English development.
   - **b.** Ms. Vance should learn the languages of the students in her class.

c. Ms.Vance should support bilingual education because studies have found that students in bilingual programs ultimately achieve in English as well as or better than students taught only in English.
d. Ms.Vance should speak out about the detrimental effects of bilingual education on a student's self-esteem.

5. Marva Vance and John Rossi discuss stereotypical gender roles in the Thanksgiving pageant. From the research reported in this section, how should the teachers assign male and female students to the roles in the pageant?
   a. The teachers should encourage students to select roles in which they are interested, not roles that society expects them to play.
   b. The teachers should reduce the interactions of males and females in the pageant.
   c. The teachers should assign males and females to authentic roles: males are hunters, females are cooks.
   d. The teachers should assign all students to nontypical racial and gender roles.

6. What is multicultural education? What steps can teachers, administrators, and other school personnel take to reach their students from under-represented groups?

7. Students differ in their prior learning and in their cognitive learning styles. What strategies can teachers use to reach all of their students?

8. List six strategies that a teacher could implement to involve parents or caregivers in helping students meet their potential.

PEARSON
myeducationlab™
Where the Classroom Comes to Life

Now go to **www.myeducationlab.com** to:

- take a Pretest to assess your initial comprehension of the chapter content;
- study chapter content with your individualized Study Plan;
- take a Posttest to assess your understanding of chapter content;
- practice your teaching skills with Building Teaching Skills exercises; and
- build a deeper, more applied understanding of chapter content with Homework and Exercises.

CHAPTER 5

Behavioral Theories of Learning

chapter
OUTLINE

Julia Esteban, first-grade teacher at Tanner Elementary School, was trying to teach her students appropriate classroom behavior.

"Children," she said one day, "we are having a problem in this class that I'd like to discuss with you. Whenever I ask a question, many of you shout out your answers instead of raising your hand and waiting to be called on. Can anyone tell me what you should do when I ask the class a question?" Rebecca's hand shot into the air. "I know, I know!" she said. "Raise your hand and wait quietly!"

Ms. Esteban sighed to herself. She tried to ignore Rebecca, who was doing exactly what she had just been told not to do, but Rebecca was the only student with her hand up, and the longer she delayed, the more frantically Rebecca waved her hand and shouted her answer.

"All right, Rebecca. What are you supposed to do?"

"We're supposed to raise our hands and wait quietly for you to call on us."

"If you know the rule, why were you shouting out your answer before I called on you?"

"I guess I forgot."

"All right. Can anyone remind the class of our rule about talking out of turn?"

Four children raised their hands and shouted together.

"One at a time!"

"Take turns!"

"Don't talk when someone else is talking!"

Ms. Esteban called for order. "You kids are going to drive me crazy!" she said. "Didn't we just talk about how to raise your hands and wait for me to call on you?"

"But Ms. Esteban," said Stephen without even raising his hand. "You called on Rebecca and she wasn't quiet!"

USING *your* EXPERIENCE

CRITICAL AND CREATIVE THINKING Reflect on what Ms. Esteban might do differently in this situation to accomplish her goal.

COOPERATIVE LEARNING Discuss with another student what went wrong here. Also discuss similar ways in which you have seen inappropriate behavior reinforced in the past. Share some of these anecdotes with the class.

Children are excellent learners. What they learn, however, may not always be what we intend to teach. Ms. Esteban is trying to teach students how to behave in class, but by paying attention to Rebecca's outburst, she is actually teaching them the opposite of what she intends. Rebecca craves her teacher's attention, so being called on (even in an exasperated tone of voice) rewards her for calling out her answer. Not only does Ms. Esteban's response increase the chances that Rebecca will call out answers again but also Rebecca now serves as a model for her classmates' own calling out. What Ms. Esteban says is less important than her actual response to her students' behaviors.

The purpose of this chapter is to define learning and then to present behavioral and social learning theories, explanations for learning that emphasize observable behaviors. **Behavioral learning theories** focus on the ways in which pleasurable or unpleasant consequences of behavior change individuals' behavior over time and ways in which individuals model their behavior on that of others. Social learning theories focus on the effects of thought on action and action on thought. Later chapters present **cognitive learning theories,** which emphasize unobservable mental processes that people use to learn and remember new information or skills. Behavioral learning theorists try to discover principles of behavior that apply to all living beings. Cognitive and social learning theorists are concerned exclusively with human learning. Actually, however, the boundaries between behavioral and cognitive learning theories have become increasingly indistinct in recent years as each school of thought has incorporated the findings of the other.

CONNECTIONS
See Chapter 6, Information Processing and Cognitive Theories of Learning.

WHAT IS LEARNING?

What is learning? This seems like a simple question until you begin to think about it. Consider the following four examples. Are they instances of learning?

1. A young child takes her first steps.
2. An adolescent male feels a strong attraction to certain females.
3. A child feels anxious when he sees the doctor coming with a needle.
4. Long after learning how to multiply, a girl realizes on her own that another way to multiply by 5 is to divide by 2 and multiply by 10 (e.g., 428×5 can be figured as follows: $428/2 = 214 \times 10 = 2{,}140$).

Learning is usually defined as a change in an individual caused by experience (Driscoll, 2000; Hill, 2002; Schunk, 2004). Changes caused by development (such as growing taller) are not instances of learning. Neither are characteristics of individuals that are present at birth (such as reflexes and responses to hunger or pain). However, humans do so much learning from the day of their birth (and some say earlier) that learning and development are inseparably linked. Learning to walk (example 1) is mostly a developmental progression but also depends on experience with crawling and other activities. The adolescent sex drive (example 2) is not learned, but learning shapes individuals' choices of desirable partners.

behavioral learning theories
Explanations of learning that emphasize observable changes in behavior.

cognitive learning theories
Explanations of learning that focus on mental processes.

learning
A change in an individual that results from experience.

INTASC

2 Knowledge of Human Development and Learning

A child's anxiety on seeing a doctor with a needle (example 3) is definitely learned behavior. The child has learned to associate the needle with pain, and his body reacts emotionally when he sees the needle. This reaction may be unconscious or involuntary, but it is learned nonetheless.

The fourth example, the girl's insight into the multiplication shortcut, is an instance of internally generated learning, better known as thinking. Some theorists would not call this learning, because it was not caused by the environment. But it might be considered a case of delayed learning, in which deliberate instruction in multiplication plus years of experience with numbers plus mental effort on the part of the girl produced an insight.

Learning takes place in many ways. Sometimes it is intentional, as when students acquire information presented in a classroom or when they look something up on the Internet. Sometimes it is unintentional, as in the case of the child's reaction to the needle. All sorts of learning are going on all the time. As you are reading this chapter, you are learning something about learning. However, you are also learning that educational psychology is interesting or dull, useful or useless. Without knowing it, you are probably learning about where on the page certain pieces of information are to be found. You might be learning to associate the content of this chapter with unimportant aspects of your surroundings as you read it, such as the smell of books in a library or the temperature of the room in which you are reading. The content of this chapter, the placement of words on the page, and the smells, sounds, and temperature of your surroundings are all **stimuli.** Your senses are usually wide open to all sorts of stimuli, or environmental events or conditions, but you are consciously aware of only a fraction of them at any one time.

The problem educators face is not how to get students to learn; students are already engaged in learning every waking moment. Rather, it is how to help students learn particular information, skills, and concepts that will be useful in adult life. How do we present students with the right stimuli on which to focus their attention and mental effort so that they will acquire important skills? That is the central problem of instruction.

VIDEO HOMEWORK EXERCISE
Cooperative Learning

Go to **www.myeducationlab.com** and, in the Homework and Exercises section for Chapter 5 of this text, access the video entitled "Cooperative Learning." Watch the video and complete the homework questions that accompany it, saving your work or transmitting it to your professor as required.

WHAT BEHAVIORAL LEARNING THEORIES HAVE EVOLVED?

The systematic study of learning is relatively new. Not until the late nineteenth century was learning studied in a scientific manner. Using techniques borrowed from the physical sciences, researchers began conducting experiments to understand how people and animals learn. One of the most important early researchers was Ivan Pavlov. Among later researchers, B. F. Skinner was important for his studies of the relationship between behavior and consequences.

Pavlov: Classical Conditioning

In the late 1800s and early 1900s, Russian scientist Ivan Pavlov and his colleagues studied the digestive process in dogs. During the research, the scientists noticed changes in the timing and rate of salivation of these animals. Pavlov observed that if meat powder was placed in or near the mouth of a hungry dog, the dog would salivate. Because the meat powder provoked this response automatically, without any prior training or conditioning, the meat powder is referred to as an **unconditioned stimulus.** Similarly, because salivation occurred automatically in the presence of meat, also without the need for any training or experience, this response of salivating is referred to as an **unconditioned response.**

Whereas the meat will produce salivation without any previous experience or training, other stimuli, such as a bell, will not produce salivation. Because these stimuli have no effect on the response in question, they are referred to as **neutral stimuli.** Pavlov's experiments showed that if a previously neutral stimulus is paired with an unconditioned stimulus, the neutral stimulus becomes a **conditioned stimulus** and gains the power to prompt a response similar to that produced by the unconditioned stimulus. In other words,

stimuli
Environmental conditions that activate the senses; the singular is *stimulus.*

unconditioned stimulus
A stimulus that naturally evokes a particular response.

unconditioned response
A behavior that is prompted automatically by a stimulus.

neutral stimuli
Stimuli that have no effect on a particular response.

conditioned stimulus
A previously neutral stimulus that evokes a particular response after having been paired with an unconditioned stimulus.

CERTIFICATION POINTER

Pavlov's work will probably be on your teacher certification test. Know that a ringing bell was the conditioned stimulus that he used to get dogs to salivate without the presence of meat. The bell became a conditioned stimulus because Pavlov first paired ringing with meat.

after the bell and the meat are presented together, the ringing of the bell alone causes the dog to salivate. This process is referred to as **classical conditioning.** A diagram of Pavlov's theory is shown in Figure 5.1. In experiments such as these, Pavlov and his colleagues showed how learning could affect what were once thought to be involuntary, reflexive behaviors, such as salivating.

Skinner: Operant Conditioning

classical conditioning
The process of repeatedly associating a previously neutral stimulus with an unconditioned stimulus in order to evoke a conditioned response.

Some human behaviors are clearly prompted by specific stimuli. Just like Pavlov's dogs, we salivate when we are hungry and see appetizing food. However, B. F. Skinner proposed that reflexive behavior accounts for only a small proportion of all actions. Skinner

FIGURE 5.1 Classical Conditioning
In classical conditioning, a neutral stimulus (such as a bell) that at first prompts no response becomes paired with an unconditioned stimulus (such as meat) and gains the power of that stimulus to cause a response (such as salivation).

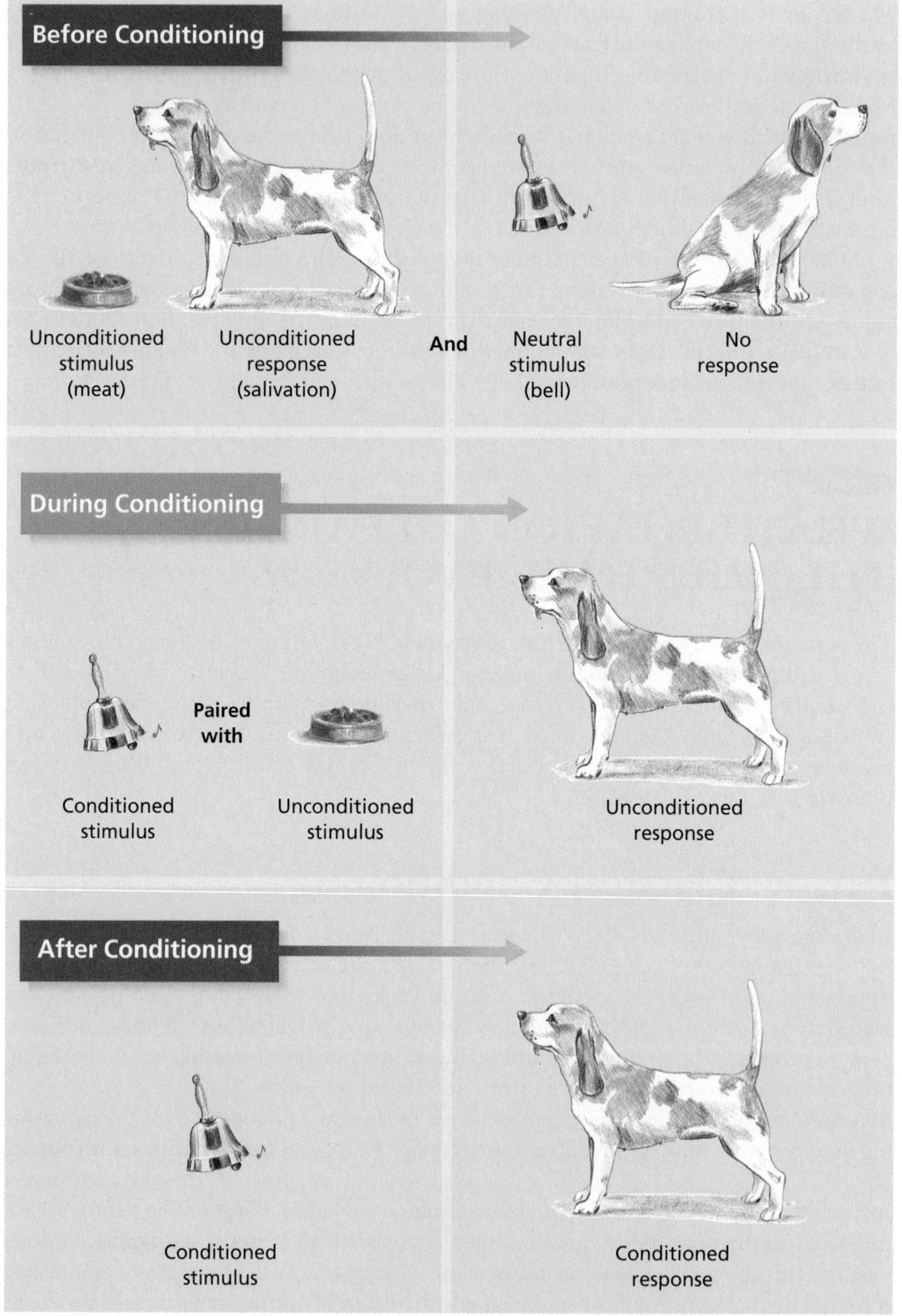

proposed another class of behavior, which he labeled operant behaviors because they operate on the environment in the apparent absence of any unconditioned stimuli, such as food. Skinner's work focused on the relation between behavior and its consequences. For example, if an individual's behavior is immediately followed by pleasurable consequences, the individual will engage in that behavior more frequently. The use of pleasant and unpleasant consequences to change behavior is often referred to as **operant conditioning.**

Skinner's work focused on placing subjects in controlled situations and observing the changes in their behavior produced by systematic changes in the consequences of their behavior (see Bigge & Shermis, 2004; Iversen, 1992). Skinner is famous for his development and use of a device that is commonly referred to as the **Skinner box.** Skinner boxes contain a very simple apparatus for studying the behavior of animals, usually rats and pigeons. A Skinner box for rats consists of a bar that is easy for the rat to press, a food dispenser that can give the rat a pellet of food, and a water dispenser. The rat cannot see or hear anything outside of the box, so all stimuli are controlled by the experimenter.

How does this Skinner box work? What type of conditioning is the rat undergoing? How does that type of conditioning take place, and how is it different from the type of conditioning Pavlov studied?

In some of the earliest experiments involving Skinner boxes, the apparatus was first set up so that if the rat happened to press the bar, it would receive a food pellet. After a few accidental bar presses, the rat would start pressing the bar frequently, receiving a pellet each time. The food reward had conditioned the rat's behavior, strengthening bar pressing and weakening all other behaviors (such as wandering around the box). At this point, the experimenter might do any of several things. The food dispenser might be set up so that several bar presses were now required to obtain food, or so that some bar presses produced food but others did not, or so that bar presses no longer produced food. In each case the rat's behavior would be recorded. One important advantage of the Skinner box is that it allows for careful scientific study of behavior in a controlled environment (Bigge & Shermis, 2004). Anyone with the same equipment can repeat Skinner's experiments.

CERTIFICATION POINTER

Most teacher certification tests will require you to know that when a teacher reinforces a student who raises her hand to speak, she is using operant conditioning.

ON THE WEB

The B. F. Skinner Foundation website at **www.bfskinner.org** aims to improve the understanding of human behavior through the work of B. F. Skinner.

WHAT ARE SOME PRINCIPLES OF BEHAVIORAL LEARNING?

CONNECTIONS

See Chapter 11, Effective Learning Environments, for classroom applications, including applied behavioral analysis.

Principles of behavioral learning include the role of consequences, reinforcers, punishers, immediacy of consequences, shaping, extinction, schedules of reinforcement, maintenance, and the role of antecedents. Each of these principles will be discussed in the sections that follow (also see Alberto & Troutman, 2006; Bigge & Shermis, 2004; Kazdin, 2001; Walker et al., 2004).

operant conditioning
The use of pleasant or unpleasant consequences to control the occurrence of behavior.

Skinner box
An apparatus developed by B. F. Skinner for observing animal behavior in experiments in operant conditioning.

The Role of Consequences

Skinner's pioneering work with rats and pigeons established a set of principles of behavior that have been supported in hundreds of studies involving humans as well as animals. Perhaps the most important principle of behavioral learning theories is that behavior

VIDEO HOMEWORK EXERCISE
Reading Group

Go to **www.myeducationlab.com** and, in the Homework and Exercises section for Chapter 5 of this text, access the video entitled "Reading Group." Watch the video and complete the homework questions that accompany it, saving your work or transmitting it to your professor as required.

changes according to its immediate **consequences.** Pleasurable consequences strengthen behavior; unpleasant consequences weaken it. In other words, pleasurable consequences increase the frequency with which an individual engages in a behavior, whereas unpleasant consequences reduce the frequency of a behavior. If students enjoy reading books, they will probably read more often. If they find stories boring or are unable to concentrate, they may read less often, choosing other activities instead. Pleasurable consequences are called reinforcers; unpleasant consequences are called punishers.

Reinforcers

A **reinforcer** is defined as any consequence that strengthens (that is, increases the frequency of) a behavior. Note that the effectiveness of the reinforcer must be demonstrated. We cannot assume that a particular consequence is a reinforcer until we have evidence that it strengthens behavior for a particular individual. For example, candy might generally be considered a reinforcer for young children, but after a big meal a child might not find candy pleasurable, and some children do not like candy at all. A teacher who says, "I reinforced him with praise for staying in his seat during math time, but it didn't work," may be misusing the term reinforced if there is no evidence that praise is in fact a reinforcer for this particular student. No reward can be assumed to be a reinforcer for everyone under all conditions (Barnhill, 2005).

consequences
Pleasant or unpleasant conditions that follow behaviors and affect the frequency of future behaviors.

reinforcer
A pleasurable consequence that maintains or increases a behavior.

primary reinforcer
Food, water, or other consequence that satisfies a basic need.

secondary reinforcer
A consequence that people learn to value through its association with a primary reinforcer.

Primary and Secondary Reinforcers Reinforcers fall into two broad categories: primary and secondary. **Primary reinforcers** satisfy basic human needs. Some examples are food, water, security, warmth, and sex. **Secondary reinforcers** are reinforcers that acquire their value by being associated with primary reinforcers or other well-established secondary reinforcers. For example, money has no value to a young child until the child learns that money can be used to buy things that are themselves primary or secondary reinforcers. Grades have little value to students unless their parents notice and value good grades, and parents' praise is of value because it is associated with love, warmth, security, and other reinforcers. Money and grades are examples of secondary reinforcers because they have no value in themselves but have been associated with primary reinforcers or with other well-established secondary reinforcers. There are three basic categories of secondary reinforcers. One is social reinforcers, such as praise, smiles, hugs, or attention. When Ms. Esteban recognized Rebecca, she was inadvertently giving Rebecca a social reinforcer: her own attention. Other types of secondary reinforcers are activity reinforcers (such as access to toys, games, or fun activities) and token (or symbolic) reinforcers (such as money, grades, stars, or points that individuals can exchange for other reinforcers).

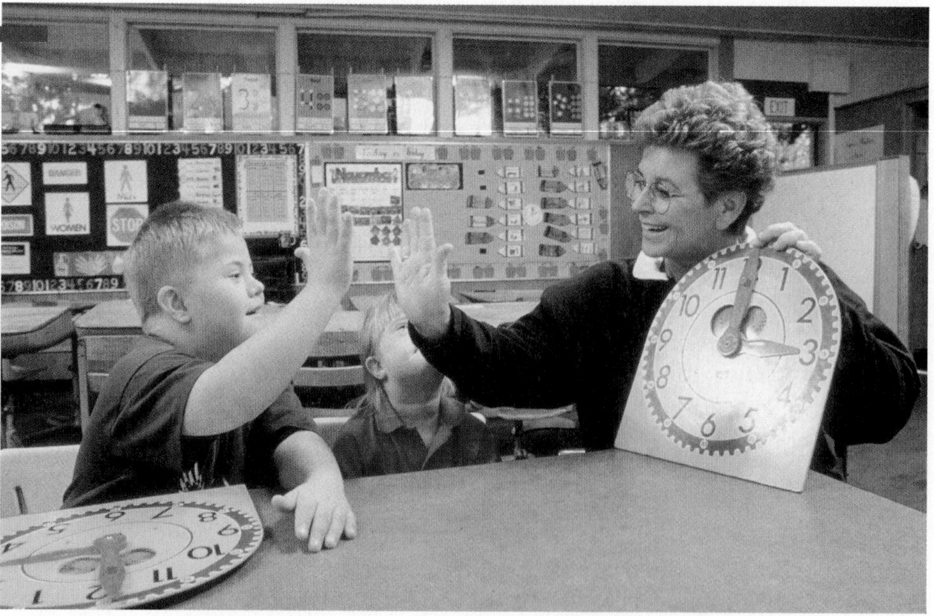

Teachers are a primary source of reinforcement in children's lives. What type of secondary reinforcement is this teacher demonstrating? What are the possible outcomes of this reinforcement?

TABLE 5.1 Consequences in Behavioral Learning

Strengthens Behavior	Discourages Behavior
Positive Reinforcement *Example:* Rewarding or praising	*No Reinforcement* *Example:* Ignoring
Negative Reinforcement *Example:* Excusing from an undesirable task or situation	*Removal Punishment* *Example:* Forbidding a desirable task or situation
	Presentation Punishment *Example:* Imposing an undesirable task or situation

Positive and Negative Reinforcers Most often, reinforcers that are used in schools are things given to students. These are called **positive reinforcers** and include praise, grades, and stars. However, another way to strengthen a behavior is to have the behavior's consequence be an escape from an unpleasant situation or a way of preventing something unpleasant from occurring. For example, a parent might release a student from doing the dishes if the student completes his or her homework. If doing the dishes is seen as an unpleasant task, release from it will be reinforcing. Reinforcers that are escapes from unpleasant situations are called **negative reinforcers.**

This term is often misinterpreted to mean punishment, as in "I negatively reinforced him for being late by having him stay in during recess" (Martella, Nelson, & Marchand-Martella, 2003). One way to avoid this error in terminology is to remember that reinforcers (whether positive or negative) strengthen behavior, whereas punishment is designed to weaken behavior. (See Table 5.1.)

CERTIFICATION POINTER

Teacher certification tests are likely to require you to know that when a teacher says, "If you get an A on tomorrow's test, you won't have to do homework the rest of the week," she's using negative reinforcement (escape from an unpleasant consequence, assuming homework is unpleasant!).

The Premack Principle One important principle of behavior is that we can promote less-desired (low-strength) activities by linking them to more-desired activities. In other words, access to something desirable is made contingent on doing something less desirable. For example, a teacher might say, "As soon as you finish your work, you may go outside" or "Clean up your art project, and then I will read you a story." These are examples of the Premack Principle (Premack, 1965). The **Premack Principle** is sometimes called "Grandma's Rule" from the age-old statement "Eat your vegetables, and then you may play." Teachers can use the Premack Principle by alternating more enjoyable activities with less enjoyable ones and making participation in the enjoyable activities depend on successful completion of the less enjoyable ones. For example, in elementary school it may be a good idea to schedule music, which most students consider an enjoyable activity, after completion of a difficult subject so that students will know that if they fool around in the difficult subject, they will be using up part of their desired music time (Martella et al., 2003).

positive reinforcer
Pleasurable consequence given to strengthen behavior.

negative reinforcer
Release from an unpleasant situation, given to strengthen behavior.

Premack Principle
Rule stating that enjoyable activities can be used to reinforce participation in less enjoyable activities.

THEORY *into* PRACTICE

Classroom Uses of Reinforcement

The behavioral learning principle most useful for classroom practice is also the simplest: Reinforce behaviors you wish to see repeated. This principle may seem obvious, but in practice it is not as easy as it appears. For example, some

INTASC

4 Multiple Instructional Strategies

teachers take the attitude that reinforcement is unnecessary, reasoning, "Why should I reinforce them? They're just doing what they're supposed to do!"

The main guidelines for the use of reinforcement to increase desired behavior in the classroom are as follows (see Jones & Jones, 2004; Kauffman et al., 2002; Marzano, 2003; Miltenberger, 2001).

1. ***Decide what behaviors you want from students, and reinforce these behaviors when they occur.*** For example, praise or reward good work. Do not praise or reward work that is not up to students' capabilities. As students begin a new task, they will need to be reinforced at every step along the way. Close approximations of what you hope to accomplish as a final product must receive positive feedback. Break down new behaviors (classroom assignments) into smaller parts and provide adequate rewards along the way.

2. ***Tell students what behaviors you want; when they exhibit the desired behaviors and you reinforce them, tell them why.*** Present students with a rubric that itemizes the criteria you will use when evaluating their work and include the point value for each criterion. Students then will be able to discriminate their own strengths and weaknesses from the feedback they receive from you.

3. ***Reinforce appropriate behavior as soon as possible after it occurs.*** Delayed reinforcement is less effective than immediate reinforcement. When you are grading an assignment, present feedback to the students as soon as possible. It is important that students know how they are doing in class, so don't delay with their grades. When constructing an assignment, you should always consider the grading scheme that you will use and how long it will take you to provide the intended feedback.

CONNECTIONS
For more on intrinsic and extrinsic motivation, see Chapter 10, page 312.

Intrinsic and Extrinsic Reinforcers

Often, the most important reinforcer that maintains behavior is the pleasure inherent in engaging in the behavior. For example, most people have a hobby that they work on for extended periods without any reward. People like to draw, read, sing, play games, hike, or swim for no reason other than the fun of doing it. Reinforcers of this type are called **intrinsic reinforcers,** and people can be described as being intrinsically motivated to engage in a given activity. Intrinsic reinforcers are contrasted with **extrinsic reinforcers,** praise or rewards given to motivate people to engage in a behavior that they might not engage in without it. There is evidence that reinforcing children for certain behaviors they would have done anyway can undermine long-term intrinsic motivation (Deci & Ryan, 2002). Research on this topic finds that the undermining effect of extrinsic reinforcers occurs only in a limited set of circumstances, in which rewards are provided to children for engaging in an activity without any standard of performance, and only if the activity is one that children would have done on their own without any reward (Cameron & Pierce, 1994, 1996; Eisenberger, Pierce, & Cameron, 1999). Verbal praise and other types of feedback are extrinsic reinforcers that have been found to increase, not decrease, intrinsic interest. What this research suggests for practice is that teachers should be cautious about giving tangible reinforcers to children for activities they would have done on their own. However, for most school tasks, which most students would not have done on their own, there is no basis for concern that use of extrinsic reinforcers will undermine intrinsic motivation, especially if those reinforcers are social and communicate recognition of students' growing mastery and independence.

BUILDING TEACHING SKILLS SIMULATION EXERCISE

You're In Charge! (Developing your own comprehensive Behavior Management Plan)

Go to **www.myeducationlab.com** and, in the Homework and Exercises section for Chapter 5 of this text, access the video entitled "You're In Charge! (Developing your own comprehensive Behavior Management Plan)." Watch the video and complete the homework questions that accompany it, saving your work or transmitting it to your professor as required.

intrinsic reinforcers
Behaviors that a person enjoys engaging in for their own sake, without any other reward.

extrinsic reinforcers
Praise or rewards given to motivate people to engage in behavior that they might not engage in without them.

ON THE WEB
For a debate on the issue of intrinsic versus extrinsic motivation visit the website at **www.restud.com/PDF/intrinsicresfeb4.pdf.**

THEORY *into* PRACTICE

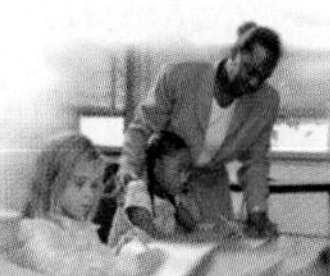

Practical Reinforcers

Anything that children like can be an effective reinforcer, but there are obvious practical limitations on what should be used in classrooms. One general principle of positive reinforcement is that it is best to use the least elaborate or tangible reinforcer that will work. In other words, if praise or self-reinforcement will work, don't use certificates. If certificates will work, don't use small toys. If small toys will work, don't use food. However, do not hesitate to use whatever practical reinforcer is necessary to motivate children to do important things. In particular, try all possible reinforcement strategies before even thinking of punishment (described next). A few categories of reinforcers and examples of each appear here (also see Burden, 2000; Landrum & Kauffman, 2006; Martella et al., 2003). These are arranged from least tangible to most tangible.

1. ***Self-reinforcement.*** Students may be taught to praise themselves, give themselves a mental pat on the back, check off progress on a form, give themselves a short break, or otherwise reinforce themselves for completing a task or staying out of trouble.
2. ***Praise.*** Phrases such as "Good job," "Way to go," "I knew you could do it," and other verbal praise can be effective, but the same message can often be delivered with a smile, a wink, a thumbs-up signal, or a pat on the back. In cooperative learning and peer tutoring, students can be encouraged to praise each other for appropriate behavior (Landrum & Kauffman, 2006).
3. ***Attention.*** The attention of a valued adult or peer can be a very effective reinforcer for many children. Listening, nodding, or moving closer may provide a child with the positive attention she or he is seeking. For outstanding performance or for meeting goals over a longer time period, students might be allowed a special time to visit with the custodian, to help in the office, or to take a walk with the principal (Alber & Heward, 2000).
4. ***Grades and recognition.*** Grades and recognition (e.g., certificates of accomplishment) can be effective both in giving students positive feedback on their efforts and in communicating progress to parents, who are likely to reinforce good reports themselves. Public displays of good work, notes from the principal, and other honors can have the same effect. Quiz scores, behavior ratings, and other feedback given frequently can be more effective than report card grades given for months of work.
5. ***Call home.*** Calling or sending a note to a child's parents to recognize success can be a powerful reinforcer.
6. ***Home-based reinforcement.*** Parents can be effective partners in a reinforcement system. Teachers can work out an arrangement with parents in which parents give their children special privileges at home if the children meet well-specified standards of behavior or performance.
7. ***Privileges.*** Children can earn free time, access to special equipment (e.g., soccer balls), or special roles (such as running errands or distributing papers). Children or groups who behaved well can simply be allowed to line up first for recess or dismissal or to have other small privileges.
8. ***Activity reinforcers.*** On the basis of achieving preestablished standards, students can earn free time, videos, games, or access to other fun activities. Activity reinforcers lend themselves particularly well to group contingencies, in which a whole class can earn free time or special activities if the whole class achieves a standard (Embry, 2002; Theodore et al., 2001).

CONNECTIONS
For more on working with parents to reinforce behavior, see Chapter 11, page 350.

CONNECTIONS
For more on the use of activity reinforcers, see Chapter 11, pages 347–350 and 352–353.

9. ***Tangible reinforcers.*** Children may earn points for achievement or good behavior that they can exchange for small toys, erasers, pencils, marbles, comic books, stickers, and so on. Tangible reinforcers usually work better if children have a choice among several options (Cruz & Cullinan, 2001; Walker et al., 2004).
10. ***Food.*** Raisins, fruit, peanuts, or other healthy snacks can be used as reinforcers.

Punishers

Consequences that weaken behavior are called punishers. Note that there is the same catch in the definition of **punishment** as in the definition of reinforcement: If an apparently unpleasant consequence does not reduce the frequency of the behavior it follows, it is not necessarily a punisher. For example, some students like being sent to the principal's office or out to the hall because it releases them from the classroom, which they see as an unpleasant situation (Driscoll, 2000; Kauffman et al., 2002; Martella et al., 2003). Some students like to be scolded because it gains them the teacher's attention and perhaps enhances their status among their peers. As with reinforcers, the effectiveness of a punisher cannot be assumed but must be demonstrated. Punishment can take two primary forms.

CERTIFICATION POINTER

For teacher certification tests you will probably need to know that unless an unpleasant consequence reduces the frequency of the behavior it follows, it may not be a punisher.

Presentation Punishment **Presentation punishment** is the use of unpleasant consequences, or **aversive stimuli,** as when a student is scolded.

Removal Punishment **Removal punishment** is the withdrawal of a pleasant consequence. Examples include loss of a privilege, having to stay in during recess, or having to stay after school. One frequently used form of removal punishment in classrooms is **time out,** in which a student who misbehaves is required to sit in the corner or in the hall for several minutes (see Nelson & Carr, 2000). Teachers often use time out when they believe that the attention of other students is serving to reinforce misbehavior; time out deprives the miscreant of this reinforcer. The use of time out as a consequence for misbehavior has generally been found to reduce the misbehavior (Alberto & Troutman, 2006).

For example, White and Bailey (1990) evaluated use of a sit-and-watch consequence for physical education classes. Children who misbehaved were told what they had done wrong and were given a 3-minute sand timer and asked to sit and watch until the sand ran out. The program was first tried in an alternative class for fourth- and fifth-graders with serious behavior problems. Figure 5.2 summarizes the findings. After a baseline of up to 343 disruptive behaviors in 10 minutes was observed, a behavioral checklist program was tried, in which teachers rated each child's behavior and sent poorly behaved children to the office or deprived them of a free period. This reduced misbehavior but did not eliminate it. However, when the sit-and-watch procedure was introduced, misbehavior virtually disappeared. The same sit-and-watch method was used in a regular fourth-grade physical education class, and the results were similar.

The issue of if, when, and how to punish has been a source of considerable controversy among behavioral learning theorists. Some have claimed that the effects of punishment, especially presentation (aversive) punishment, are only temporary, that punishment produces aggression, and it causes individuals to avoid settings in which it is used (Kazdin, 2001; Landrum & Kauffman, 2006; Miltenberger, 2001). Even behavioral learning theorists who do support the use of punishment agree that it should be resorted to only when reinforcement for appropriate behavior has been tried and has failed; that when punishment is necessary, it should take the mildest possible form; and that punishment should always be used as part of a careful plan, never inconsistently or out of frustration. Physical punishment in schools (such as spanking) is illegal in most places

punishment
Unpleasant consequences used to weaken behavior.

presentation punishment
An aversive stimulus following a behavior, used to decrease the chances that the behavior will occur again.

aversive stimulus
An unpleasant consequence that a person tries to avoid or escape.

removal punishment
Withdrawal of a pleasant consequence that is reinforcing a behavior, designed to decrease the chances that the behavior will recur.

time out
Procedure of removing a student from a situation in which misbehavior was being reinforced.

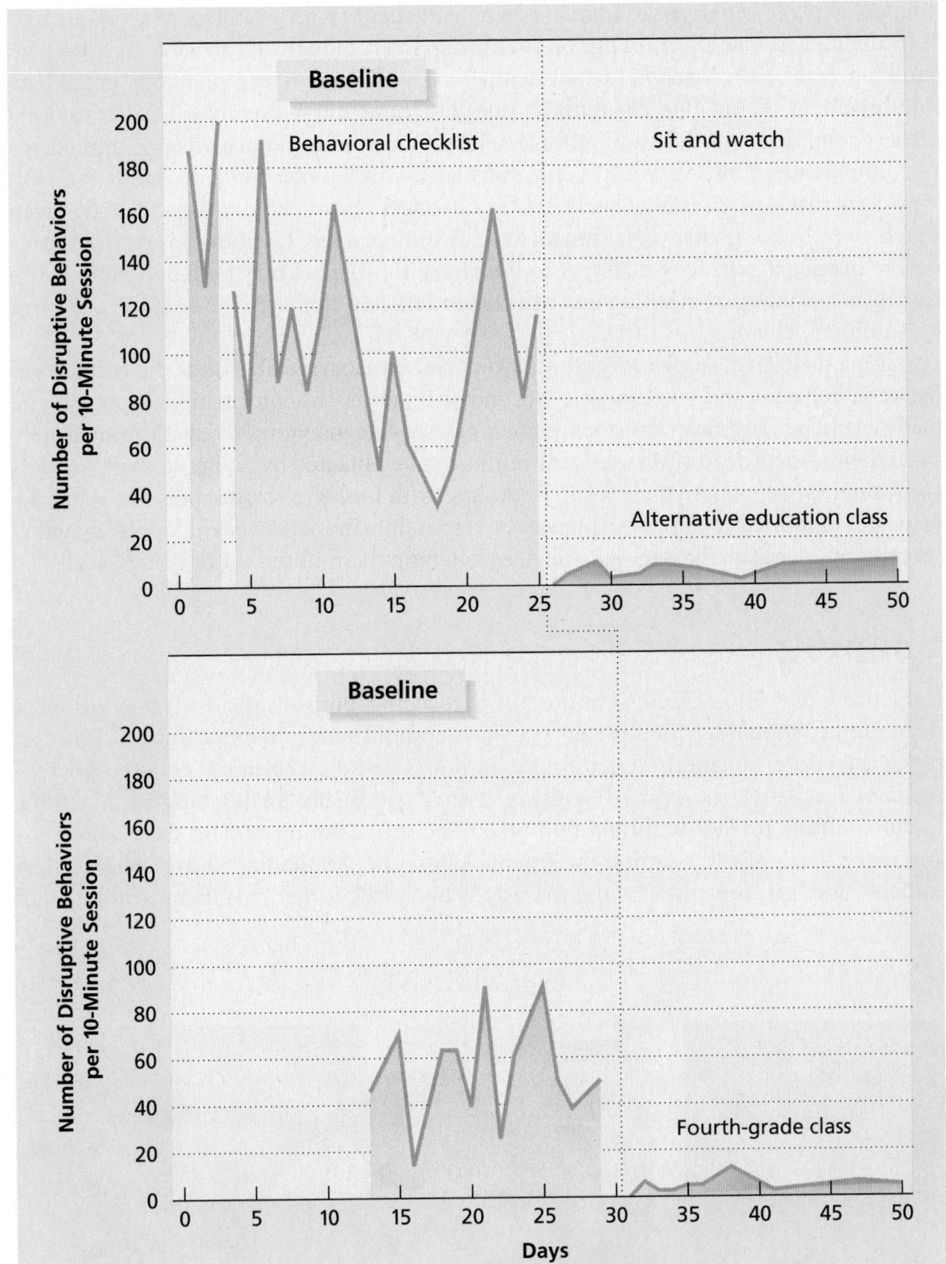

FIGURE 5.2 Reducing Disruptive Behavior with Sit and Watch

The number of disruptive behaviors per 10-minute observation period is shown here.

From A. G. White and J. S. Bailey, "Reducing Disruptive Behaviors of Elementary Physical Education Students with Sit and Watch," *Journal of Applied Behavior Analysis, 3,* 1990, p. 357. Adapted by permission.

(Jones & Jones, 2007; Levin & Nolan, 2007) and is universally opposed by behavioral learning theorists on ethical as well as scientific grounds (see Kazdin, 2001; Malott et al., 2000).

Immediacy of Consequences

One very important principle of behavioral learning theories is that consequences that follow behaviors closely in time affect behavior far more than delayed consequences do. If we waited a few minutes to give a rat in a Skinner box its food pellet after it pressed a bar, the rat would take a long time to learn the connection between bar pressing and food because by the time the food arrived, the rat might be doing something other than bar pressing. A smaller reinforcer that is given immediately generally has a much larger effect than does a large reinforcer that is given later (Alberto & Troutman, 2006). This concept explains much about human behavior. It suggests, for example, why people find it so difficult to give up smoking or overeating. Even though the benefits of giving up smoking or of losing weight are substantial and well known, the small but immediate reinforcement of just one cigarette or one doughnut often overcomes the behavioral effect of the large but delayed reinforcers. In the classroom the principle of immediacy of consequences is also very important. Particularly for younger students, praise for a job well done that is given immediately can be a stronger reinforcer than a good grade given much later. Moving close to a student who is misbehaving, touching his or her shoulder, or making a gesture (e.g., finger to lips to ask for silence) may be much more effective than a scolding or warning given at the end of class (Jones & Jones, 2007; Landrum & Kauffman, 2006).

Immediate feedback serves at least two purposes. First, it makes clear the connection between behavior and consequence. Second, it increases the informational value of the feedback. In practice, few classroom teachers can provide individual feedback immediately to all their students. However, the same results can be obtained by giving students answers right after they complete their work. In dealing with misbehavior, teachers can apply the principle of immediacy of consequences by responding immediately and positively when students are not misbehaving—in effect, by catching them in the act of being good!

Shaping

Immediacy of reinforcement is important to teaching, but so is the decision as to what to reinforce. Should a kindergarten teacher withhold reinforcement until a child can recite the entire alphabet? Certainly not. It would be better to praise children for recognizing one letter, then for recognizing several, and finally for learning all 26 letters. Should a music teacher withhold reinforcement until a young student has played a piano piece flawlessly? Or should the teacher praise the first halting run-through? Most students need reinforcement along the way. When teachers guide students toward goals

Whether teaching children new physical skills or academic skills, teachers and coaches begin with the basics and build from there. What techniques can they use to shape children's behaviors?

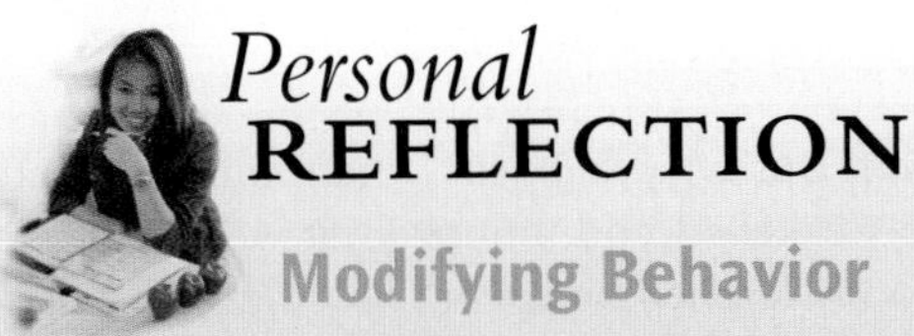

Personal REFLECTION

INTASC 3 Adapting Instruction for Individual Needs

Modifying Behavior

Vanessa was the precocious 8-year-old daughter of a friend. Her mother was trying to teach her to keep her room tidy. Vanessa would leave her toys and clothes littered all over her floor. Her mother would nag her to pick up her things, threaten to give away her toys to less fortunate children, and occasionally deprive Vanessa of her favorite TV show until she cleaned up her room. None of these strategies worked very well or for very long. Then one day, Vanessa's mother learned about behavior modification in her educational psychology class and she decided to try using it to get her daughter to tidy up her room. She created a chart, showed it to Vanessa, and explained that every evening for one week they would record the number of objects on her bedroom floor to establish a baseline. After that, Vanessa would get a sticker on the chart for every day that there were no objects on her bedroom floor. In that first week, which was supposed to be the baseline, there were no objects left on Vanessa's floor! Just the simple fact of charting her behavior with a clear goal was enough feedback to get Vanessa to pick up her clothes and toys. After that, Vanessa's room was the cleanest room in the house.

Children are thinking, feeling beings who do more than simply respond to rewards and punishments, and we need to be prepared as parents and teachers to learn from them what is meaningful to them, not only what is reinforcing.

REFLECT ON THIS. Why do you think the charting strategy was so effective for Vanessa? Describe a time when you used a behavior modification strategy to change something about yourself. Was it successful? How would behavior modification strategies for elementary children differ from strategies used with middle school or high school students?

by reinforcing the many steps that lead to success, they are using a technique called **shaping.**

The term *shaping* is used in behavioral learning theories to refer to the teaching of new skills or behaviors by reinforcing learners for approaching the desired final behavior (Bigge & Shermis, 2004; Driscoll, 2000). For example, in teaching children to tie their shoelaces, we would not simply show them how it is done and then wait to reinforce them until they do the whole job themselves. Rather, we would first reinforce them for tying the first knot, then for making the loops, and so on, until they can do the entire task. In this way we would be shaping the children's behavior by reinforcing all those steps that lead toward the final goal.

Shaping is an important tool in classroom instruction. Let's say we want students to be able to write paragraphs with a topic sentence, three supporting details, and a concluding sentence. This task has many parts: being able to recognize and then produce topic sentences, supporting details, and concluding sentences; being able to write complete sentences using capitalization, punctuation, and grammar correctly; and being able to spell. If a teacher taught a lesson on all these skills, asked students to write paragraphs, and then scored them on content, grammar, punctuation, and spelling, most students would fail and would probably learn little from the exercise.

Instead, the teacher might teach the skills step by step, gradually shaping the final skill. Students might be taught how to write first topic sentences, then supporting details, then concluding sentences. Early on, they might be held responsible only for paragraph content. Later, the requirement for reinforcement might be increased to include grammar and punctuation. Finally, spelling might be added as a criterion for success. At each stage, students would have a good chance to be reinforced because the criterion for reinforcement would be within their grasp. The principle here is that students should be reinforced for behaviors that are within their current capabilities but that also stretch them toward new skills.

shaping
The teaching of a new skill or behavior by means of reinforcement for small steps toward the desired goal.

Extinction

By definition, reinforcers strengthen behavior. But what happens when reinforcers are withdrawn? Eventually, the behavior will be weakened, and ultimately, it will disappear. This process is called **extinction** of a previously learned behavior.

A dinosaur goes through extinction.

Extinction is rarely a smooth process. When reinforcers are withdrawn, individuals often increase their rate of behavior for a while. For example, think of a door that you've used as a shortcut to somewhere on campus you go frequently. Imagine that one day the door will not open. You may push even harder for a while, shake the door, turn the handle both ways, perhaps even kick the door. You are likely to feel frustrated and angry. However, after a short time you will realize that the door is locked and go away. If the door is permanently locked (without your knowing it), you may try it a few times over the next few days, then perhaps once after a month; only eventually will you give up on it.

Your behavior when confronted by the locked door is a classic extinction pattern. Behavior intensifies when the reinforcer is first withdrawn, then rapidly weakens until the behavior disappears. Still, the behavior may return after much time has passed. For example, you could try the door again a year later to see whether it is still locked. If it is, you will probably leave it alone for a longer time, but probably not forever.

The characteristic **extinction burst,** the increase in levels of a behavior in the early stages of extinction, has important consequences for classroom management. For example, imagine that you have decided to extinguish a child's inappropriate calling out of answers (instead of raising his hand to be recognized) by ignoring him until he raises his hand quietly. At first, ignoring the child is likely to increase his calling-out behavior, a classic extinction burst. You might then mistakenly conclude that ignoring isn't working, when in fact continuing to ignore inappropriate call-outs is exactly the right strategy if you keep it up (Landrum & Kauffman, 2006; Martella et al., 2003). Worse, you might finally decide to give in and recognize the child after his third or fourth call-out. This would teach the child the worst possible message: that calling out works eventually if you keep doing it. This would probably result in an increase in the very behavior you were trying to reduce, as children learn that "if at first you don't succeed, try, try again." This was the case in the vignette presented at the beginning of this chapter. Ms. Esteban at first ignored Rebecca's calling out, so Rebecca called out even louder. Then she called on Rebecca, unintentionally communicating to her that only loud and persistent calling out would be reinforced.

Extinction of a previously learned behavior can be hastened when some stimulus or cue informs the individual that behaviors that were once reinforced will no longer be reinforced. In the case of the locked door, a sign saying, "Door permanently locked—use other entrance," would have greatly reduced the number of times you tried the door before giving up on it. Call-outs would be reduced much more quickly if the teacher told the class, "I will no longer respond to anyone unless they are silent and are raising their hand," and then ignored all other attempts to get her attention.

extinction
The weakening and eventual elimination of a learned behavior as reinforcement is withdrawn.

extinction burst
The increase in levels of a behavior in the early stages of extinction.

schedule of reinforcement
The frequency and predictability of reinforcement.

fixed-ratio (FR) schedule
Reinforcement schedule in which desired behavior is rewarded following a fixed number of behaviors.

Schedules of Reinforcement

The effects of reinforcement on behavior depend on many factors, one of the most important of which is the **schedule of reinforcement** (see Alberto & Troutman, 2006; Kazdin, 2001; Miltenberger, 2001). This term refers to the frequency with which reinforcers are given, the amount of time that elapses between opportunities for reinforcement, and the predictability of reinforcement.

Fixed Ratio (FR) One common schedule of reinforcement is the **fixed-ratio (FR) schedule,** in which a reinforcer is given after a fixed number of behaviors. For example, a teacher might say, "As soon as you finish ten problems, you may go outside." Regardless of the amount of time it takes, students are reinforced as soon as they finish

10 problems. This is an example of an FR10 schedule (10 behaviors for one reinforcer). One common form of a fixed-ratio schedule is one in which each behavior is reinforced. This is called continuous reinforcement (CRF), or FR1. Putting money in a soda machine is (usually) an example of continuous reinforcement because one behavior (inserting coins) results in one reinforcer (a soda). Giving correct answers in class is also usually continuously reinforced. The student gives a good answer, and the teacher says, "Right! Good answer!"

One important process in instruction is gradually increasing reinforcement ratios. Early in a sequence of lessons, it may be necessary to reinforce students for every correct answer, such as a single math problem. However, this is inefficient in the long run. As soon as students are answering math problems correctly, it may be possible to reinforce every 5 problems (FR5), every 10 (FR10), and so on. Thinning out the reinforcement schedule in this way makes the student more able to work independently without reinforcement and makes the behavior more resistant to extinction. Ultimately, students might be asked to do entire projects on their own, receiving no reinforcement until the project is completed. As adults, we often take on tasks that take years to complete and years to produce a desired outcome. (Writing an educational psychology text is one such task!)

Fixed-ratio schedules are effective in motivating individuals to do a great deal of work—especially if the fixed ratio starts with continuous reinforcement (FR1) to get the individual going and then moves to high requirements for reinforcement. One reason that high requirements for reinforcement produce higher levels of behavior than low requirements is that reinforcing too frequently can make the value of the reinforcer wear off. Students who were praised for every math problem would soon grow tired of being praised, and the reinforcer might lose its value.

Variable Ratio (VR) A **variable-ratio (VR) schedule** of reinforcement is one in which the number of behaviors required for reinforcement is unpredictable, although it is certain that the behaviors will eventually be reinforced. For example, a slot machine is a variable-ratio reinforcer. It may pay off after 1 pull one time and after 200 the next, and there is no way to predict which pull will win. In the classroom a variable-ratio schedule exists when students raise their hands to answer questions. They never know when they will be reinforced by being able to give the correct answer, but they may expect to be called on about 1 time in 30 in a class of 30. This would be called a VR30 schedule because, on the average, 30 behaviors are required for one reinforcer. Variable-ratio schedules tend to produce high and stable rates of behavior. In fact, almost all gambling games involve VR schedules, and so they can be quite literally addicting. Similarly, use of frequent random checks of student work can help to addict students to steady, careful work.

Variable-ratio schedules are highly resistant to extinction. Even after behaviors are no longer being reinforced, people may not give up working for a long time. Because they have learned that it may take a lot of work to be rewarded, they keep on working in the mistaken belief that the next effort might just pay off.

Fixed Interval (FI) In **fixed-interval schedules,** reinforcement is available only at certain periodic times. The final examination is a classic example of a fixed-interval schedule. Fixed-interval schedules create an interesting pattern of behavior. The individual may do very little until just before reinforcement is available, then put forth a burst of effort as the time for reinforcement approaches. This pattern can be demonstrated with rats and pigeons on fixed-interval schedules, but it is even more apparent in students who cram at the last minute before a test or who write their monthly book reports the night before they are due. These characteristics of fixed-interval schedules suggest that frequent short quizzes may be better than infrequent major exams for encouraging students to give their best effort all the time rather than putting in all-nighters before the exam (Crooks, 1988).

Variable Interval (VI) In a **variable-interval schedule,** reinforcement is available at some times but not at others, and we have no idea when a behavior will be reinforced.

variable-ratio (VR) schedule
Reinforcement schedule in which desired behavior is rewarded following an unpredictable number of behaviors.

fixed-interval schedule
Reinforcement schedule in which desired behavior is rewarded following a constant amount of time.

variable-interval schedule
Reinforcement schedule in which desired behavior is rewarded following an unpredictable amount of time.

An example of this is a teacher making spot checks of students who are doing assignments in class. Students are reinforced if they are working well at the particular moment the teacher comes by. Because they cannot predict when the teacher will check them, students must be doing good work all the time. People may obey traffic laws out of respect for the law and civic responsibility, but it also helps that the police randomly check drivers' compliance with the law. Troopers hide on overpasses or behind hills so that they can get a random sampling of drivers' behavior. If they were always in plain sight, they would be a signal to drive carefully, so the necessity for driving carefully at other times would be reduced.

Teaching Dilemmas: CASES TO CONSIDER

INTASC

2 Knowledge of Human Development and Learning

Dealing with Behavior Problems

Sam, a boy with a talkative and bubbly personality, has just entered Angela Hairston's kindergarten class at Elliott Elementary School. Sam has had a complicated medical history since birth, culminating a year ago in back surgery to correct spinal scoliosis, followed by many months in a full-body cast. Last year, after the surgery, Sam was in Diana Braddock's preschool class at Elliott, where, after a rough start, he made good academic and social progress. Now, however, after 2 weeks of school, Angela is afraid that Sam doesn't have the maturity to be in kindergarten. She meets with Diana Braddock and Sam's mother, Janet, to discuss her concerns.

Angela: Thank you both for taking the time to meet with me this afternoon. I'm concerned because Sam is starting to exhibit some of the same behaviors he showed at the beginning of his preschool year with you, Diana.

Diana: Sam certainly demonstrated separation anxiety when he began preschool. I remember the tantrums he would throw when Janet dropped him off for school. Then he would complain that he felt sick, begin to cry, and even make himself throw up so he could go home.

Janet: Sam became overly dependent on me when he had his back surgery and was in the body cast. But Diana and I worked out a plan that seemed to help Sam get over his problems last year.

Angela: Well, it appears that Sam is having what psychologists call an extinction burst of that behavior now that he's started kindergarten. I was at my wits' end yesterday, Janet, when I had to call you for the second time this week to pick Sam up because he had had a 30-minute tantrum and made himself sick. Diana, tell me again how you helped Sam last year.

Diana: Sure. Janet and I talked about Sam's overdependence on adults and how that could negatively affect his academic progress. We also talked about his need to develop better social skills with his classmates so that he didn't always need to be the center of attention.

Janet: I told Diana how I thought my dad was reinforcing Sam's dependence. Whenever I picked Sam up from preschool because he was "sick," I'd have to take him to work with me. I work for my dad, who has a small business in town. Sam would sit in the reception area while I worked, and the customers would give him their undivided attention because Sam would just turn on the charm.

Diana: Janet and I decided that whenever Sam left school "sick," Janet would ask her father and the customers not to give Sam any attention. Instead, she would tell Sam to rest in a side room until she could take him home and put him to bed.

Janet: Sam got "sick" several more times, but once he realized that Dad, the customers—and I, too—weren't going to give him any attention at the store, he didn't play sick anymore.

Diana: Meanwhile, at school, I had made Sam and one of his classmates the "Attendance Helpers" who took the absence report to the school secretary every day. I rotated Sam's partner often so that he could form one-on-one relationships with several classmates. And

Mrs. Thompson's third-grade class developed a buddy system to help Sam interact with teachers and children in more appropriate ways.

Janet: By winter, Sam had made friends with several children in his class.

Diana: And everyone enjoyed being with him because he didn't demand center stage anymore.

Angela: It's been a big help to hear about all you did for Sam last year. It seems like you did all the right things to help him get over his separation anxiety and to get along better with his peers. I guess I'll just have to try the same techniques again to help him adjust to kindergarten. Janet, I hope you'll support me in this.

Janet: Oh, yes, Mrs. Roberts. I really want Sam to have a good year in kindergarten.

QUESTIONS FOR REFLECTION

1. Do you think that Mrs. Roberts is correct in saying that Sam is showing an extinction burst in the way he is behaving in kindergarten? Why or why not?
2. How effective do you think it will be to repeat in kindergarten the plan Diana used to extinguish Sam's behavior in preschool?
3. If you were Mrs. Roberts, what, if anything, would you do to reinforce Sam's behavior as it improves? What type of schedule of reinforcement would you use?

Source: Adapted from "Kindergarten Is Big Business" by Linda K. Elksnin, Diane Birschbach, and Susan P. Gurganus, from *Allyn & Bacon's Custom Cases in Education,* edited by Greta Morine-Dershimer, Daniel Hallahan, and James Kauffman (2000).

Like variable-ratio schedules, variable-interval schedules are very effective for maintaining a high rate of behavior and are highly resistant to extinction. For example, let's say a teacher has a policy of having students hand in their seatwork every day. Rather than checking every paper, the teacher pulls three papers at random and gives these students extra credit if their seatwork was done well. This variable-interval schedule would probably motivate students to do their seatwork carefully. If the teacher secretly stopped spot-checking halfway through the year, the students might never know it, figuring that their own paper just hadn't been pulled to be checked rather than realizing that reinforcement was no longer available for anyone.

Table 5.2 defines and gives additional examples of schedules of reinforcement.

TABLE 5.2 Schedules of Reinforcement

Specific response patterns during reinforcement and extinction characterize each of the four types of schedules.

Schedule	Definition	Response Patterns	
		During Reinforcement	*During Extinction*
Fixed ratio	Constant number of behaviors required for reinforcement	Steady response rate; pause after reinforcement	Rapid drop in response rate after required number of responses passes without reinforcement
Variable ratio	Variable number of behaviors required for reinforcement	Steady, high response rate	Response rate stays high, then drops off
Fixed interval	Constant amount of time passes before reinforcement is available	Uneven rate, with rapid acceleration at the end of each interval	Rapid drop in response rate after interval passes with no reinforcement
Variable interval	Variable amount of time passes before reinforcement is available	Steady, high response rate	Slow decrease in response rate

Maintenance

The principle of extinction holds that when reinforcement for a previously learned behavior is withdrawn, the behavior fades away. Does this mean that teachers must reinforce students' behaviors indefinitely or they will disappear?

Not necessarily. For rats in a Skinner box, the withdrawal of reinforcement for bar pressing will inevitably lead to extinction of bar pressing. However, humans live in a much more complex world that is full of natural reinforcers for most of the skills and behaviors that we learn in school. For example, students may initially require frequent reinforcement for behaviors that lead to reading. However, once they can read, they have a skill that unlocks the entire world of written language, a world that is highly reinforcing to most students. After a certain point, reinforcement for reading may no longer be necessary because the content of reading material itself maintains the behavior. Similarly, poorly behaved students may need careful, systematic reinforcement for doing schoolwork. After a while, however, they will find out that doing schoolwork pays off in grades, in parental approval, in ability to understand what is going on in class, and in knowledge. These natural reinforcers for doing schoolwork were always available, but the students could not experience them until their schoolwork was improved by more systematic means.

This kind of **maintenance** of behavior also occurs with behaviors that do not need to be reinforced because they are intrinsically reinforcing, which is to say that engaging in these behaviors is pleasurable in itself. For example, many children love to draw, to figure out problems, or to learn about things even if they are never reinforced for doing so. Many of us even complete books of crossword puzzles or other problem-solving activities, even though after we have completed them, no one will ever check our work.

The concept of resistance to extinction, discussed earlier (in the section on schedules of reinforcement), is central to an understanding of maintenance of learned behavior. As was noted, when new behaviors are being introduced, reinforcement for correct responses should be frequent and predictable. However, once the behaviors are established, reinforcement for correct responses should become less frequent and less predictable. The reason for this is that variable schedules of reinforcement and schedules of reinforcement that require many behaviors before reinforcement is given are much more resistant to extinction than are fixed schedules or easy ones. For example, if a teacher praises a student every time the student does a math problem but then stops praising, the student may stop doing math problems. In contrast, if the teacher gradually increases the number of math problems a student must do to be praised and praises the student at random intervals (a variable-ratio schedule), then the student is likely to continue to do math problems for a long time with little or no reinforcement from the teacher.

CERTIFICATION POINTER

Teacher certification tests may require you to know that holding up your hand to get students' attention is cueing, an antecedent stimulus that informs students what behaviors will be reinforced.

The Role of Antecedents

We have seen that the consequences of behavior strongly influence behavior. Yet it is not only what follows a behavior that has influence. The stimuli that precede a behavior also play an important role (Kazdin, 2001).

Cueing **Antecedent stimuli,** events that precede a behavior, are also known as **cues** because they inform us what behavior will be reinforced and/or what behavior will be punished. Cues come in many forms and give us hints as to when we should change our behavior and when we should not. For example, during a math session, most teachers will reinforce students who are working on problems. However, after the teacher has announced that math is over and it is time for lunch, the consequences change. The ability to behave one way in the presence of one stimulus—"It's math time"—and a different way in the presence of another stimulus—"It's time for lunch"—is known as stimulus discrimination.

Discrimination When is the best time to ask your boss for a raise? When the company is doing well, the boss looks happy, and you have just done something especially good? Or when the company has just gotten a poor earnings report, the boss is glowering, and you have just made a costly error? Obviously, the first situation is more likely to lead to success. You know this because you have learned to discriminate between good and bad

maintenance
Continuation (of behavior).

antecedent stimuli
Events that precede behaviors.

cues
Signals as to what behavior(s) will be reinforced or punished.

times to ask your boss to do something for you. **Discrimination** is the use of cues, signals, or information to know when behavior is likely to be reinforced. The company's financial condition, the boss's mood, and your recent performance are discriminative stimuli with regard to the chances that your request for a raise will be successful. For students to learn discrimination, they must have feedback on the correctness or incorrectness of their responses. Studies of discrimination learning have generally found that students need to know when their responses are incorrect as well as correct.

Learning is largely a matter of mastering more and more complex discriminations. For example, all letters, numbers, words, and mathematical symbols are discriminative stimuli. A young child learns to discriminate between the letters *b* and *d*. An older student learns the distinction between the words *effective* and *efficient*. An educational psychology student learns to discriminate negative reinforcement from punishment. A teacher learns to discriminate facial and verbal cues indicating that students are bored or interested by a lecture.

Applying the concept of discriminative stimuli to classroom instruction and management is easy: Teachers should tell students what behaviors will be reinforced. In theory, a teacher could wait until students did something worthwhile and then reinforce it, but this would be incredibly inefficient. Rather, teachers should give students messages that say, in effect, "To be reinforced (e.g., with praise, grades, or stars), these are the things you must do." In this way, teachers can avoid having students spend time and effort on the wrong activities. If students know that what they are doing will pay off, they will usually work hard.

Generalization If students learn to stay in their seats and do careful work in math class, will their behavior also improve in science class? If students can subtract 3 apples from 7 apples, can they also subtract 3 oranges from 7 oranges? If students can interpret symbolism used by Shakespeare, can they also interpret symbolism used in African folk tales? These are all questions of **generalization,** or transfer of behaviors learned under one set of conditions to other situations. Generalization cannot be taken for granted. Usually, when a classroom management program is successfully introduced in one setting, students' behaviors do not automatically improve in other settings. Instead, students learn to discriminate among settings. Even young children readily learn what is encouraged and what is forbidden in kindergarten, at home, and at various friends' houses. Their behavior may be quite different in each setting, according to the different rules and expectations.

For generalization to occur, it usually must be planned for. A successful classroom management program used in social studies class may be transferred to English class to ensure generalization to that setting. Students may need to study the use of symbolism by many authors in many cultures before they acquire the skill to interpret symbolism in general.

Obviously, generalization is most likely to occur across similar settings or across similar concepts. A new behavior is more likely to generalize from reading class to social studies class than to recess or home settings. However, even in the most similar-appearing settings, generalizations may not occur. For example, many students will demonstrate complete mastery of spelling or language mechanics and then fail to apply this knowledge to their own compositions. Teachers should not assume that because students can do something under one set of circumstances, they can also do it under a different set of circumstances.

Techniques for Increasing Generalization There are many techniques for increasing the chances that a behavior learned in one setting, such as a given class, will generalize to other settings, such as other classes or, more importantly, real-life applications (see Alberto & Troutman, 2006; Martella et al., 2003; Walker et al., 2004). Some of these strategies involve teaching in a way that makes generalization easier. For example, arithmetic lessons involving money will probably transfer better to real life if they involve manipulating real or simulated coins and bills than if they involve only problems on paper. Another teaching strategy known to contribute to generalization is using many examples from different contexts. For example, students are more likely to be able to transfer the concept of supply and demand to new areas if they learn examples relating to prices for groceries, prices for natural resources, values of collectibles (such as baseball cards), and wages for common and rare skills than if they learn only about grocery pricing. An obvious strategy for increasing generalization is "on-the-job training": teaching a given skill in the actual environment in which it will be used, or in a simulation of such an environment.

discrimination
Perception of and response to differences in stimuli.

generalization
Carryover of behaviors, skills, or concepts from one setting or task to another.

After initial instruction has taken place, there are many ways to increase generalization. One is to repeat instruction in a variety of settings. For example, after teaching students to use a given test-taking strategy in mathematics, such as "skip difficult problems and go back to them after answering the easy ones," a teacher might give students the opportunity to use this same strategy on a science test, a grammar test, and a health test. Another after-teaching technique is to help students make the link between a new skill and natural reinforcers in the environment so as to maintain that skill. For example, when children are learning to read, they can be given a regular homework assignment to read books or magazines that are of high interest to them, even if those materials are not "good literature." Initially, new reading skills may be better maintained by comic books than by literary classics because for some children the comic books tie their new skill more immediately to the pleasure of reading, making generalization to nonschool settings more likely. Finally, a teacher can increase generalization by directly reinforcing generalization—for example, by praising a student who connects a new idea to a different context or uses a skill in a new application.

HOW HAS SOCIAL LEARNING THEORY CONTRIBUTED TO OUR UNDERSTANDING OF HUMAN LEARNING?

CONNECTIONS
For the relation of social learning theory to social construction of meaning, see Chapter 8, page 231.

Social learning theory is a major outgrowth of the behavioral learning theory tradition. Developed by Albert Bandura, **social learning theory** accepts most of the principles of behavioral theories but focuses to a much greater degree on the effects of cues on behavior and on internal mental processes, emphasizing the effects of thought on action and action on thought (Bandura, 1986).

Bandura: Modeling and Observational Learning

CONNECTIONS
For the relation of social learning theory to Vygotskian and neo-Piagetian views of development, see Chapter 2, page 42.

Bandura noted that the Skinnerian emphasis on the effects of the consequences of behavior largely ignored the phenomena of **modeling**—the imitation of others' behavior—and of vicarious experience—learning from others' successes or failures. He felt that much of human learning is not shaped by its consequences but is more efficiently learned directly from a model (Bandura, 1986; Schunk, 2000). The physical education teacher demonstrates jumping jacks, and students imitate. Bandura calls this no-trial learning because students do not have to go through a shaping process but can reproduce the correct response immediately.

Bandura's (1986) analysis of **observational learning** involves four phases: the attentional, retention, reproduction, and motivational phases.

ON THE WEB

For more on social learning theory go to **http://tip.psychology.org/bandura.html.**

social learning theory
Learning theory that emphasizes not only reinforcement but also the effects of cues on thought and of thought on action.

modeling
Imitation of others' behavior.

observational learning
Learning by observation and imitation of others.

1. ***Attentional phase:*** The first phase in observational learning is paying attention to a model. In general, students pay attention to role models who are attractive, successful, interesting, and popular. This is why so many students copy the dress, hairstyle, and mannerisms of pop culture stars. In the classroom the teacher gains the students' attention by presenting clear and interesting cues, by using novelty or surprise, and by motivating students.

2. ***Retention phase:*** Once teachers have students' attention, it is time to model the behavior they want students to imitate and then give students a chance to practice or rehearse. For example, a teacher might show how to write the letter *A*. Then students would imitate the teacher's model by trying to write *A*'s themselves.

3. ***Reproduction:*** During the reproduction phase, students try to match their behavior to the model's. In the classroom the assessment of student learning takes place during this phase. For example, after seeing the letter *A* modeled and practicing it several times, can the student reproduce the letter so that it looks like the teacher's model?

4. ***Motivational phase:*** The final stage in the observational learning process is motivation. Students will imitate a model because they believe that doing so will increase their own chances to be reinforced. In the classroom the motivational phase of observational learning often entails praise or grades given for matching the teacher's model. Students pay attention to the model, practice it, and reproduce it because they have learned that this is what the teacher likes and they want to please the teacher. When the child makes a recognizable *A*, the teacher says, "Nice work!"

INTASC

2 Knowledge of Human Development and Learning

Vicarious Learning Although most observational learning is motivated by an expectation that correctly imitating the model will lead to reinforcement, it is also important to note that people learn by seeing others reinforced or punished for engaging in certain behaviors (Bandura, 1986; Zimmerman & Schunk, 2003). This is why magazine distributors always include happy winners in their advertisements to induce people to enter promotional contests. We may consciously know that our chances of winning are one in several million, but seeing others so handsomely reinforced makes us want to imitate their contest-entering behavior.

Classroom teachers use the principle of **vicarious learning** all the time. When one student is fooling around, teachers often single out others who are working well and reinforce them for doing a good job. The misbehaving student sees that working is reinforced and (it is hoped) gets back to work. This technique was systematically studied in a classic study by Broden, Hall, Dunlap, and Clark (1970). Two disruptive second-graders, Edwin and Greg, sat next to each other. After a baseline period, the teacher began to notice and praise Edwin whenever he was paying attention and doing his classwork. Edwin's behavior improved markedly under this condition. Of greater interest, however, is that Greg's behavior also improved, even though no specific reinforcement for appropriate behavior was directed toward him. Apparently, Greg learned from Edwin's experience. In the case of Ms. Esteban and Rebecca at the opening of this chapter, other students saw Rebecca get Ms. Esteban's attention by calling out answers, so they modeled their behavior on Rebecca's.

CERTIFICATION POINTER

Teacher certification tests may require you to know that learning vicariously means that you learn from observing or hearing about another's experiences.

One of the classic experiments in social learning theory is a study done by Bandura (1965). Children were shown one of three films. In all three, an adult modeled aggressive behavior. In one film the model was severely punished. In another the model was praised and given treats. In a third the model was given no consequences. After viewing one of the films, the children were observed playing with toys. The children who had seen the model punished engaged in significantly fewer aggressive acts in their own play than did the children who had seen the model rewarded or had viewed the no-consequences film.

vicarious learning Learning based on observation of the consequences of others' behavior.

THEORY *into* PRACTICE

Observational Learning

Have you ever tried to teach someone to tie his or her shoes? Imagine explaining this task to someone without the use of a model or imitation! Such a simple task, and one that many of us take for granted, can be quite a milestone for a kindergartner. Learning to tie our shoes is certainly a prime example of how observational learning works.

Acquiring new skills by observing the behaviors of others is a common part of everyday life. In many situations children watch others talking and acting, and they witness the consequences of those activities as well. Such observations provide models that teach children strategies to use at other times and places.

Although the major focus of research on observational learning has been on specific behaviors, studies have also shown that attitudes, too, may be acquired through observation (Miller, 1993). Teachers and parents alike are concerned with the models emulated by children. The value of these models goes beyond the specific abilities they possess and includes the attitudes they represent. In the classroom the teacher must be certain to exemplify a standard of behavior consistent with the expectations he or she has for the students. For instance, if promptness and politeness are characteristics the teacher wants to foster in the students, then the teacher must be certain to demonstrate those traits.

In cooperative learning groups, the success of the group may depend on the models present in that group. Peers have a strong influence on the behaviors of the individual. For example, when teachers place students in math groups, it may be just as important to include students who possess a high motivation for learning in a group as it is to include students with strong math skills. The attitudes and behaviors that accompany high motivation will be imitated by fellow students.

CONNECTIONS
For more on self-regulated learning, see Chapter 8, page 236.

self-regulation
Rewarding or punishing one's own behavior.

Self-Regulated Learning Another important concept in social learning theory is **self-regulation** (Boekaerts, Pintrich, & Zeidner, 2000; Schunk & Pajares, 2004; Zimmerman, 2000). Bandura (1997) hypothesized that people observe their own behavior, judge it against their own standards, and reinforce or punish themselves. We have all had the experience of knowing we've done a job well and mentally patting ourselves on the back, regardless of what others have said. Similarly, we all know when we've done less than our best. To make these judgments, we have to have expectations for our own performance. One student might be delighted to get 90 percent correct on a test, whereas another might be quite disappointed.

Students can be taught to use self-regulation strategies, and they can be reminded to do so in a variety of contexts so that self-regulation becomes a habit. For example, students might be asked to set goals for the amount of time they expect to study each evening and to record whether they meet their goals. Children who are studying multiplication facts might be asked to time themselves on how quickly and accurately they can complete a 50-item facts test and then to try to beat their own record. Students might be asked to grade their own essays in terms of content, mechanics, and organization, and to see whether they can match the teacher's ratings. Each of these strategies puts students in control of their own learning goals, and each is likely to build a general strategy of setting and meeting personal goals and personal standards (Schunk & Zimmerman, 2003).

As with any skill, self-regulated learning skills are likely to remain limited to one situation or context unless they are applied in many contexts. For example, children who learn to set study goals for themselves when working alone may not transfer these skills to situations in which they are working in groups or in the presence of a teacher (Schunk & Pajares, 2004; Zimmerman, 2000), although they can readily learn to make these generalizations if they are taught or reminded to do so. Similarly, children may not transfer self-regulated learning strategies

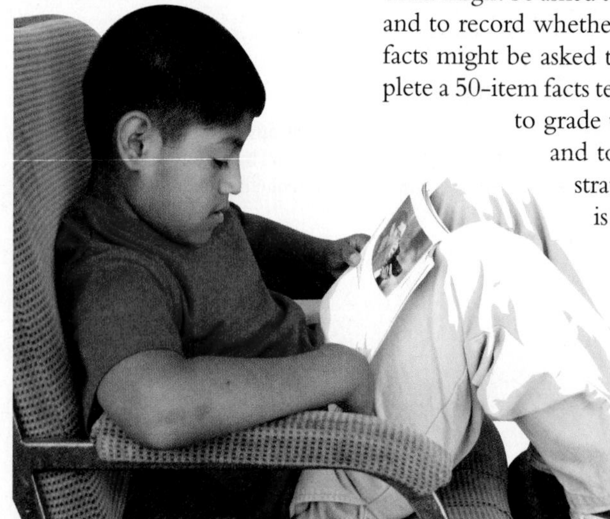

How do community summer reading programs encourage young children to read? How is this a form of self-regulated learning?

from English to math, or even from computations to problem solving (Boekaerts, 1995). For this reason, students need many opportunities to use goal-setting and self-evaluation strategies in a variety of contexts; to monitor and celebrate their progress; and to understand how, when, and why they should self-regulate.

Meichenbaum's Model of Self-Regulated Learning

Students can be taught to monitor and regulate their own behavior. Self-regulated learning strategies of this kind are often called **cognitive behavior modification** (Harris, Graham, & Pressley, 2001; Zimmerman, 2000). For example, Meichenbaum (1977) developed a strategy in which students are trained to say to themselves, "What is my problem? What is my plan? Am I using my plan? How did I do?" This strategy has also been used to reduce disruptive behavior of students at many grade levels (Jones & Jones, 2007; Martella et al., 2003). Manning (1988) taught disruptive third-graders self-statements to help them remember appropriate behavior and to reinforce it for themselves. As one instance, for appropriate hand-raising, students were taught to say to themselves while raising their hands, "If I scream out the answer, others will be disturbed. I will raise my hand and wait my turn. Good for me. See, I can wait!" (Manning, 1988, p. 197). Similar strategies have been successfully applied to help students monitor their own achievement. For example, poor readers have been taught to ask themselves questions as they read and to summarize paragraphs to make sure they comprehend text (Bornstein, 1985).

CONNECTIONS
For the related concept of teaching self-questioning strategies to develop metacognitive skills, see Chapter 6, pages 183–184.

The steps involved in self-instruction are described by Meichenbaum (1977) as follows:

1. An adult model performs a task while talking to self out loud (cognitive modeling).
2. The child performs the same task under the direction of the model's instructions (overt, external guidance).
3. The child performs the task while instructing self aloud (overt self-guidance).
4. The child whispers the instructions to self as he or she goes through the task (faded, overt self-guidance).
5. The child performs the task while guiding his or her performance via private speech (covert self-instruction). (p. 32)

Encouraging self-regulated learning is a means of teaching students to think about their own thinking. Self-regulated learning strategies not only have been found to improve performance on the task students were taught but also have generalized to other tasks (Harris, Graham, & Pressley, 2001; Schunk & Zimmerman, 2003).

One example of a way to help children engage in self-regulated learning is providing students, when assigning a long or complex task, with a form for monitoring their progress. For example, a teacher might assign students to write a report on the life of Martin Luther King Jr. Students might be given the following self-monitoring checklist:

TASK COMPLETION FORM

- ☐ Located material on Martin Luther King Jr. in the library
- ☐ Read and took notes on material
- ☐ Wrote first draft of report
- ☐ Checked draft for sense
- ☐ Checked draft for mechanics:
  - ☐ Spelling
  - ☐ Grammar
  - ☐ Punctuation
- ☐ Composed typed or neatly handwritten final draft

cognitive behavior modification Procedures based on both behavioral and cognitive principles for changing one's own behavior by means of self-talk and self-instruction.

READING HOMEWORK EXERCISE
The Nurturing Potential of Service Learning

Go to **www.myeducationlab.com** and, in the Homework and Exercises section for Chapter 5 of this text, access the article entitled "The Nurturing Potential of Service Learning." Read the article and complete the homework questions that accompany it, saving your work or transmitting it to your professor as required.

The idea behind this form is that breaking down a complex task into smaller pieces encourages students to feel that they are making progress toward their larger goal. Checking off each step allows them to give themselves a mental pat on the back that reinforces their efforts (Manning & Payne, 1996). After seeing many checklists of this kind, students might be asked to make up their own, to learn how to chart their own progress toward a goal. Along similar lines, Trammel, Schloss, and Alper (1994) found that having children with learning disabilities keep records and make graphs of their homework completion significantly increased the amount of homework they did (see also Martella, Marchand-Martella, & Cleanthous, 2001). A review by Robinson, Robinson, and Katayama (1999) found that cognitive behavior modification strategies can have a substantial impact, especially on reducing hyperactive, impulsive, and aggressive behaviors (e.g., Binder, Dixon, & Ghezi, 2000). Several of the studies reviewed found these effects to be long-lasting.

Self-Reinforcement Drabman, Spitalnik, and O'Leary (1973) designed and evaluated a classic procedure to teach students to regulate their own behavior. They asked teachers to rate student behaviors each day and reinforce students when they earned high ratings. Then they changed the program: They asked students to guess what rating the teacher had given them. The students were reinforced for guessing correctly. Finally, the reinforcers were gradually removed. The students' behavior improved under the reinforcement and guessing conditions, and it remained at its improved level long after the program was ended. The authors explained that students who were taught to match the teacher's ratings developed their own standards for appropriate behavior and reinforced themselves for meeting those standards.

CONNECTIONS
For more on self-efficacy beliefs and student success, see Chapter 10, pages 301–302.

Information about one's own behavior has often been found to change behavior (Rosenbaum & Drabman, 1982), even when that information is self-provided. For example, researchers have increased on-task behavior by having children mark down every few minutes whether they have been studying in the last few minutes (Maag, Rutherford, & DiGangi, 1992; Webber et al., 1993). When coupled with self-reinforcement, self-observation often has important effects on student behavior (Jenson et al., 1988). Many of us use this principle in studying, saying to ourselves that we will not take a break for lunch until we have finished reading a certain amount of material.

CERTIFICATION POINTER
The idea that behavioral learning theories apply best to observable behavior (rather than thinking, for example) may appear on teacher certification tests.

Students who feel confident in their ability to use metacognitive and self-motivational behaviors are likely to be high in self-efficacy—the belief that one's own efforts (rather than luck or other people or other external or uncontrollable factors) determine one's success or failure. Self-efficacy beliefs are perhaps the most important factor (after ability) in determining students' success in school (Bandura, 1997; Schunk & Zimmerman, 2003).

Strengths and Limitations of Behavioral Learning Theories

The basic principles of behavioral learning theories are as firmly established as any in psychology and have been demonstrated under many different conditions. These principles are useful for explaining much of human behavior; they are even more useful in changing behavior.

It is important to recognize, however, that behavioral learning theories are limited in scope. With the exception of social learning theorists, behavioral learning theorists focus almost exclusively on observable behavior. This is one reason why so many of the examples presented in this chapter involve the management of behavior (see Driscoll, 2000). Less visible learning processes, such as concept formation, learning from text, problem solving, and thinking, are difficult to observe directly and have, therefore, been studied less often by behavioral learning theorists. These processes fall more into the domain of cognitive learning. Social learning theory, which is a direct outgrowth of behavioral learning theories, helps to bridge the gap between the behavioral and cognitive perspectives.

ONLINE READING & WRITING EXERCISE
What Shamu Taught Me About A Happy Marriage

Access this exercise, entitled "What Shamu Taught Me About A Happy Marriage," in the Homework and Exercises section for Chapter 5 of this text at **www.mylabschool.com.**

Behavioral and cognitive theories of learning are often posed as competing, opposite models. There are indeed specific areas in which these theories take contradictory positions. However, it is more accurate to see them as complementary rather than competitive—that is, as tackling different problems (Kazdin, 2001; Miltenberger, 2001).

CHAPTER 5 SUMMARY

What Is Learning?

Learning involves the acquisition of abilities that are not innate. Learning depends on experience, including feedback from the environment.

What Behavioral Learning Theories Have Evolved?

Early research into learning studied the effects of stimuli on reflexive behaviors. Ivan Pavlov contributed the idea of classical conditioning, in which neutral stimuli can acquire the capacity to evoke behavioral responses through their association with unconditioned stimuli that trigger reflexes. B. F. Skinner continued the study of the relationship between behavior and consequences. He described operant conditioning, in which reinforcers and punishers shape behavior.

What Are Some Principles of Behavioral Learning?

Reinforcers increase the frequency of a behavior, and punishers decrease its frequency. Reinforcement can be primary or secondary, positive or negative. Intrinsic reinforcers are rewards inherent in a behavior itself. Extrinsic reinforcers are praise or rewards. Punishment involves weakening behavior by either introducing aversive consequences or removing reinforcers. The Premack Principle states that a way to increase less-enjoyed activities is to link them to more-enjoyed activities.

Shaping through timely feedback on each step of a task is an effective teaching practice based on behavioral learning theory. Extinction is the weakening and gradual disappearance of behavior as reinforcement is withdrawn.

Schedules of reinforcement are used to increase the probability, frequency, or persistence of desired behavior. Reinforcement schedules may be based on ratios or intervals and may be fixed or variable.

Antecedent stimuli serve as cues indicating which behaviors will be reinforced or punished. Discrimination involves using cues to detect differences between stimulus situations, whereas generalization involves responding to similarities between stimuli. Generalization involves the transfer or carryover of behaviors learned under one set of conditions to other situations.

How Has Social Learning Theory Contributed to Our Understanding of Human Learning?

Social learning theory is based on a recognition of the importance of observational learning and self-regulated learning. Bandura noted that learning through modeling—directly or vicariously—involves four phases: paying attention, retaining the modeled behavior, reproducing the behavior, and being motivated to repeat the behavior. Bandura proposed that students should be taught to have expectations for their own performances and to reinforce themselves. Meichenbaum proposed steps for self-regulated learning that represent a form of cognitive behavior modification.

Behavioral learning theories are central to the application of educational psychology in classroom management, discipline, motivation, instructional models, and other areas. Behavioral learning theories are limited in scope, however, in that they describe only observable behavior that can be directly measured.

The Intentional TEACHER

USING WHAT YOU KNOW about Behavioral and Social Learning Theory to Improve Teaching and Learning

One role of the intentional teacher is functioning as an instructional designer, carefully planning what new abilities learners will acquire. Sometimes called "behavioral" or "performance" objectives, such outcome statements often imply two performance levels. Robert Mager (1997) reminds us to "always state the *main intent*" of an objective. Many important outcomes state performances that *cannot be observed.* You can't see your students adding or composing or comparing or relating, but these "cognitive" actions are often the real goal you intend to help your students achieve. For these "covert," unobservable behaviors, Mager suggests that you, in your role as a designer of instruction, think of "indicator behaviors," observable actions that will show not only you but others, and most important the students themselves, that they can indeed "add," "compose," "compare," "relate," or perform any other meaningful mental behavior aimed at in your lesson.

1 What do I expect my students to know and be able to do at the end of this lesson? How does this contribute to course objectives and to students' needs to become capable individuals?

In considering any plan to improve classroom behavior, remember that we tend to use the term "classroom behavior" in too limited a way, equating "behavior" with "being good" (i.e., sitting still and being quiet). Watch for indications of interest and engagement as students work individually or in groups. For example, as your students work in spirited project groups, you might briefly interrupt their work to ask questions: "Are you on task? Have you said at least one nice thing about someone else's idea?" The questions help students check their own behavior.

Before the school year begins, you should develop a discipline plan that supports appropriate behavior and seeks to extinguish negative behaviors, and then update that plan in light of student behavior. For example, before your noisy sixth period begins, you might rehearse: "I will recognize only those who make an appropriate bid for the floor. *No matter what.* I will ignore attention-seeking behaviors. I will use praise to reinforce on-task behavior."

2 What knowledge, skills, needs, and interests do my students have that must be taken into account in my lesson?

Particular reinforcers vary in their effectiveness for individuals and groups. Determine what kinds of reinforcers are effective for particular students. For example, you might hand out a survey early in the year that asks open-ended questions such as: "If you had time to do any practical fun activity in the classroom, what would you do?" and "When you do a good job in school, what response from teachers makes you the happiest?" and "What message from your teacher to your parents would make you feel most proud?" You would take note of the survey responses to determine useful consequences for various behaviors for this class and particular individuals.

Reinforcers are most effective when they immediately follow the behavior. Provide immediate feedback so that students have knowledge of the results of their actions and learn to link behavior to its consequences.

3 What do I know about the content, child development, learning, motivation, and effective teaching strategies that I can use to accomplish my objectives?

An intentional teacher breaks down complex skills and performances into smaller bits so that students learn gradually by logical steps. For example, you might give students an opportunity to discriminate and to generalize among examples and settings by suggesting the relevant characteristics and information to look for. In teaching second-graders about mammals, you might provide 40 large pictures of animals, pointing out characteristics of mammals. The students could then sort the pictures into mammals and nonmammals, and you might praise them for

KEY TERMS

Review the following key terms from the chapter.

antecedent stimuli 144
aversive stimulus 136
behavioral learning theories 128
classical conditioning 130
cognitive behavior modification 149
cognitive learning theories 128
conditioned stimulus 129
consequences 132
cues 144
discrimination 145
extinction 140
extinction burst 140
extrinsic reinforcers 134
fixed-interval schedule 141
fixed-ratio (FR) schedule 140
generalization 145

their accuracy. In teaching high school students about justice, you might have them sort a set of examples of various forms of civil disobedience into "justifiable" and "not justifiable."

You can increase the likelihood of students' generalizing (transferring) their learning to new situations by using real-life applications and many examples from different contexts. For instance, after studying a variety of graphs with your students, you might prepare a bulletin board and invite students to fill it with examples of graphs from newspapers, advertisements, and other print sources.

4 What instructional materials, technology, assistance, and other resources are available to help accomplish my objectives?

Bandura and Meichenbaum developed these ideas—modeling, observational learning, self-directedness. Some activities that build on the concepts of observational and self-regulated learning follow.

Consider teaching cognitive behavior modification and self-regulation directly. For example, you might plan an art activity for your students designed to create an "illuminated" initial for their name. You model the tasks, describing out loud how you outline the letter, select your favorite color for the letter, and select symbols and designs to decorate the letter, based on your personal interests. You might guide the students through these steps, directing them to "make a big outline of your initial and choose your favorite color to fill it in." "Now choose some designs that represent your own interests—sports, hobbies, et cetera—and decorate the letter." "Now make the initial of your last name and talk yourself through it in a whisper as we just did together." "Finally, put both your initials together, reminding yourself as you work of these steps but not saying anything out loud, just in your mind."

You might sum up the activity by pointing out that this is a process students can use to direct themselves through any task they wish to manage themselves: Think of the steps, say them to themselves in a whisper as they plan the tasks, and then do the steps, talking to themselves silently. You might say, "Talking to yourself can be a great way to get things done!" In other subject areas for this class, you might make use of similar modeling examples.

5 How will I plan to assess students' progress toward my objectives?

In all subject areas and in all grades, you will have developed a number of specific assignments with measurable expected outcomes. You might make a policy of involving students in determining the criteria for grading such assignments, and inform students with each assignment of what the decided-on criteria for performance are.

As an intentional teacher, you should recognize that behavioral learning theories are one set of tools that can help you support positive changes in student behavior and learning. You should develop your observational skills and modify your actions in light of what you perceive of students' reactions to instruction. You should rely on constant observation of your class, developing the "withitness" that is a characteristic of effective teachers.

6 How will I respond if individual children or the class as a whole are not on track toward success? What is my back-up plan?

Gather information on the effects of your instruction by watching students' responses, and change strategies if changes are needed. For example, you might do quick visual sweeps of your class to make note of nonverbal hints from students that they are interested or bored, getting it or lost. Check in with students who are struggling and give them additional explanations, or assign them a peer tutor.

SELF-ASSESSMENT: PRACTICING *for* LICENSURE

Directions: The chapter-opening vignette addresses indicators that are often assessed in state licensure exams. Re-read the chapter-opening vignette, and then respond to the following questions.

1. Julia Esteban, first-grade teacher at Tanner Elementary School, calls on her students when they do not raise their hands, a practice that goes against an established rule in the class. Which of the following types of conditioning can Ms. Esteban use to teach her students about appropriate hand-raising behaviors?
   - **a.** classical conditioning
   - **b.** operant conditioning
   - **c.** modeled conditioning
   - **d.** assisted conditioning
2. Which of the following explanations best summarizes Julia Esteban's problem with her students' failure to raise their hands prior to speaking?
   - **a.** Ms. Esteban is using negative reinforcement rather than positive reinforcement.
   - **b.** Ms. Esteban has failed to apply the Premack Principle when her students break the hand-raising rule.
   - **c.** Ms. Esteban allows her students to make decisions about classroom rules, a practice that research studies have shown to be unsuccessful.
   - **d.** Ms. Esteban should note that pleasurable consequences (rewarding appropriate behaviors) increase a behavior whereas unpleasant consequences weaken the frequency of a behavior.
3. According to research on behavioral learning theories, which strategy might Ms. Esteban use to get her students to raise their hands prior to speaking?
   - **a.** Reward those students who follow the rule.
   - **b.** Punish those students who do not follow the rule.
   - **c.** Ignore those students who follow the rule.
   - **d.** Wait before administering any type of consequence for rule-breakers.
4. Imagine that Ms. Esteban's students have a difficult time breaking their habit of speaking out of turn. Which of the following techniques might she use to reinforce close approximations of the behaviors she wants her students to exhibit?
   - **a.** extinction
   - **b.** maintenance
   - **c.** shaping
   - **d.** discrimination
5. Which type of reinforcement schedule is Ms. Esteban using if she reinforces her students' appropriate behavior after so many behaviors, but the students do not know when the reinforcement will be applied?
   - **a.** continuous
   - **b.** fixed-ratio schedule
   - **c.** fixed-interval schedule
   - **d.** variable-ratio schedule
6. Explain how classical conditioning and operant conditioning are alike and different. Give at least one example of each.
7. Describe Albert Bandura's social learning theory. Bandura's analysis of observational learning involves four phases—describe each phase.

PEARSON

myeducationlab™

Where the Classroom Comes to Life

Now go to **www.myeducationlab.com** to:

- take a Pretest to assess your initial comprehension of the chapter content;
- study chapter content with your individualized Study Plan;
- take a Posttest to assess your understanding of chapter content;
- practice your teaching skills with Building Teaching Skills exercises; and
- build a deeper, more applied understanding of chapter content with Homework and Exercises.

CHAPTER 6

Information Processing and Cognitive Theories of Learning

chapter
OUTLINE

Verona Bishop's biology class was doing a unit on human learning. At the start of one lesson, Ms. Bishop did an experiment with her students. For 3 seconds, using an overhead projector, she flashed a diagram of a model of information processing identical to the one in Figure 6.1. Then she asked students to recall what they noticed. Some mentioned that they saw boxes and arrows. Some saw the words *memory* and *forgotten* and inferred that the figure had something to do with learning. One student even saw the word *learning,* though it wasn't in the figure.

"Come now," said Ms. Bishop. "You noticed a lot more than that! You just may not have noticed what you noticed. For example, what did you smell?"

The whole class laughed. They all recalled smelling the broccoli cooking in the cafeteria. The students caught on to the idea and began to recall all the other details they had noticed that had nothing to do with the diagram: the sounds of a truck going by, details of the classroom and the people in it, and so on.

After this discussion, Ms. Bishop said, "Isn't the brain amazing? In only 3 seconds you received an enormous amount of information. You didn't even know you were noticing the smell of the broccoli until I reminded you about it, but it was in your mind just the same. Also, in only 3 seconds your mind was already starting to make sense of the information in the figure. Cheryl thought she saw the word *learning,* which wasn't there at all. But her mind leaped to that word because she saw words like *memory* that relate to learning.

"Now imagine that you could keep in your mind forever everything that occurred in the 3 seconds you looked at the diagram: the arrows, the boxes, the words, the truck, the broccoli—everything. In fact, imagine that you could keep everything that ever entered your mind. What would that be like?"

"You'd be a genius!" ventured Samphan.

"You'd go crazy!" countered Jamal.

"I think Jamal is closer to the truth," said Ms. Bishop. "If your mind filled up with all this useless junk, you'd be a blithering idiot! One of the most important things we're going to learn about learning is that it is an active process of focusing in on important information, screening out unimportant information, and using what is already in our minds to decide which is which."

Ms. Bishop turned on the overhead projector again.

"When we study this diagram in more detail, you'll use what you already know about learning, memory, forgetting, and diagrams to make sense of it. I hope you'll always remember the main ideas it's trying to show you. You'll soon forget the boxes and arrows, and even the smell of the broccoli will fade from your memory, but the parts of this diagram that make sense to you and answer questions you care about may stay in your memory your whole life!"

USING *your* EXPERIENCE

COOPERATIVE LEARNING Jot down two or three ways in which you try to memorize lists and study new concepts. Share with other students a strategy that you use to learn information better.

COOPERATIVE LEARNING What is your picture of learning, memory, and forgetting? After drafting your own picture, meet with four or five classmates to compose a summary illustration or diagram of human memory and cognition based on your individual ideas. After 10 minutes, share with the class.

INTASC

2 Knowledge of Human Development and Learning

The human mind is a meaning maker. From the first microsecond you see, hear, taste, or feel something, you start a process of deciding what it is, how it relates to what you already know, and whether it is important to keep in your mind or should be discarded. This whole process may take place consciously, unconsciously, or both. This chapter describes how information is received and processed in the mind, how memory and loss of memory work, and how teachers can help students understand and remember critical information, skills, and ideas. This chapter also presents cognitive theories of learning, theories that relate to processes that go on within the minds of learners, and means of helping students use their minds more effectively to learn, remember, and use knowledge.

WHAT IS AN INFORMATION-PROCESSING MODEL?

Information constantly enters our minds through our senses. Most of this information is almost immediately discarded, and we may never even be aware of much of it. Some is held in our memories for a short time and then forgotten. For example, we may remember the seat number on a baseball ticket until we find our seats, at which point we will forget the number. However, some information is retained much longer, perhaps for the rest of our lives. What is the process by which information is absorbed, and how can teachers take advantage of this process to help students retain critical information and skills? These are questions that have been addressed by cognitive learning theorists and that have led to **information-processing theory,** a dominant theory of learning and memory since the mid-1970s.

Research on human memory (see, e.g., Anderson, 2005; Ashcraft, 2006; Bransford, Brown, & Cocking, 1999; Byrnes, 2001; Elias & Saucier, 2006; Solso, 2001; Tulving & Craik, 2000) has helped learning theorists to describe the process by which information is remembered (or forgotten). This process, usually referred to as the Atkinson–Shiffrin model of information processing (Atkinson & Shiffrin, 1968), is illustrated in Figure 6.1.

information-processing theory Cognitive theory of learning that describes the processing, storage, and retrieval of knowledge in the mind.

FIGURE 6.1 The Sequence of Information Processing
Information that is to be remembered must first reach a person's senses, then be attended to and transferred from the sensory register to the working memory, then be processed again for transfer to long-term memory.

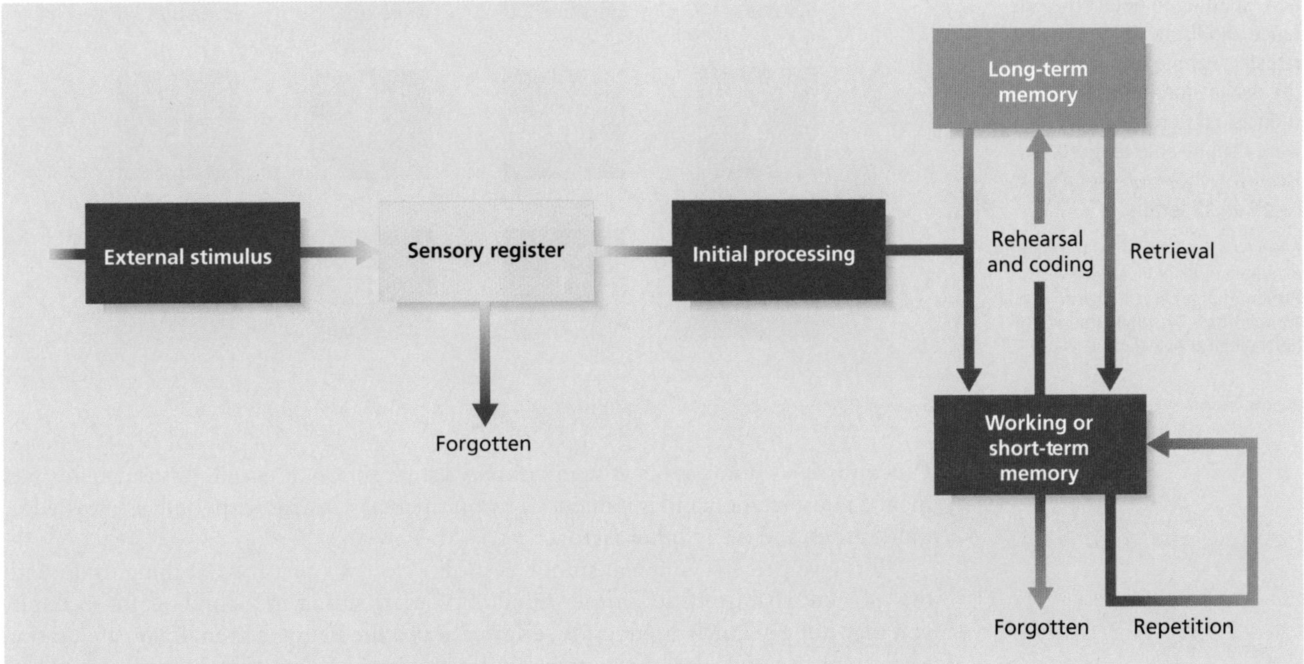

From Charles G. Morris, *Psychology: An Introduction* (8th ed.), p. 233. Copyright © 1993. Adapted by permission of Prentice Hall, Upper Saddle River, New Jersey.

Sensory Register

The first component of the memory system that incoming information meets is the sensory register, shown at the left of Figure 6.1. **Sensory registers** receive large amounts of information from each of the senses (sight, hearing, touch, smell, taste) and hold it for a very short time, no more than a couple of seconds. If nothing happens to information held in a sensory register, it is rapidly lost.

Ingenious experiments have been used to detect sensory registers. A person might be shown a display like that in Figure 6.2 for a very short period of time, say 50 milliseconds. The person is usually able to report seeing 3, 4, or 5 of the letters but not all 12 of them. In a classic early experiment, Sperling (1960) presented a display like Figure 6.2 to people. After the display disappeared, he signaled viewers to try to recall the top, middle, or bottom row. He found that people could recall any one row almost perfectly. Therefore, they must have seen all the letters in the 50 milliseconds and retained them for a short period of time. However, when people tried to recall all 12 letters, the time it took them to do so apparently exceeded the amount of time the letters lasted in their sensory registers, so they lost some of the letters.

The existence of sensory registers has two important educational implications. First, people must pay attention to information if they are to retain it. Second, it takes time to bring all the information seen in a moment into consciousness. For example, if students are bombarded with too much information at once and are not told which aspects of the information they should pay attention to, they may have difficulty learning any of the information at all.

Perception When the senses receive stimuli, the mind immediately begins working on some of them. Therefore, the sensory images of which we are conscious are not exactly the same as what we saw, heard, or felt; they are what our senses perceived.

sensory register
Component of the memory system in which information is received and held for very short periods of time.

FIGURE 6.2 Display Used in Sensory Register Experiments

This is a typical display used by G. A. Sperling to detect the existence and limits of the sensory register. People who were shown the display for an instant and then asked to recall a specific row were usually able to do so. However, they were not able to recall all 12 letters.

From G. A. Sperling, "The Information Available in Brief Visual Presentations," *Psychological Monographs, 74,* 1960, American Psychological Association.

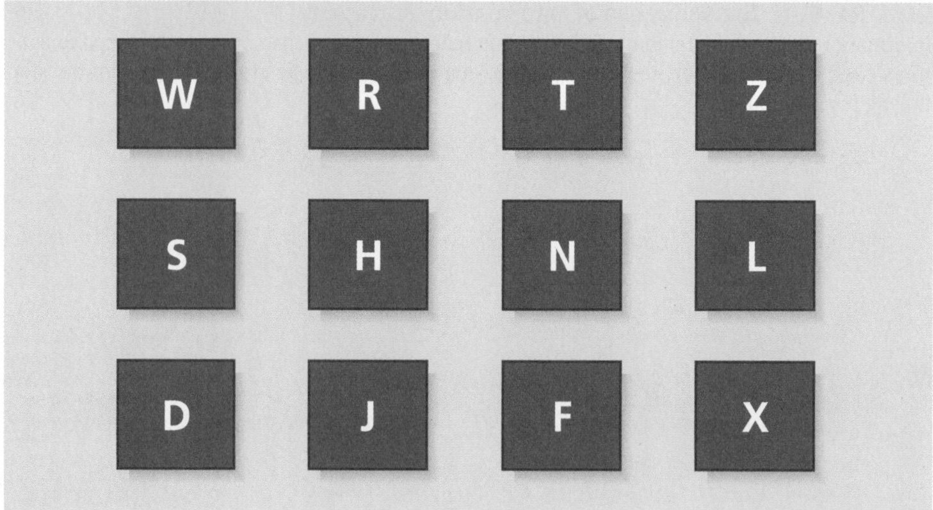

Perception of stimuli is not as straightforward as reception of stimuli. Instead, it involves mental interpretation and is influenced by our mental state, past experience, knowledge, motivations, and many other factors.

First, we perceive different stimuli according to rules that have nothing to do with the inherent characteristics of the stimuli. If you are sitting in a building, for example, you may not pay much attention to, or even hear, a fire engine's siren. If you are driving a car, you pay a great deal more attention. If you are standing outside a burning building waiting for the firefighters to arrive, you pay even more attention. Second, we do not perceive stimuli as we see or sense them but as we know (or assume) they really are. From across a room, a book on a bookshelf looks like a thin strip of paper, but we infer that it is a three-dimensional rectangular form with many pages. You might see just the edge of a table and mentally infer the entire table.

Attention When teachers say to students, "Pay attention" or "Lend me your ears," they are using the words *pay* and *lend* appropriately. Like money, **attention** is a limited resource. When a teacher asks students to spend their limited attention capacity on whatever the teacher is saying, students must give up actively attending to other stimuli, shifting their priorities so that other stimuli are screened out. For example, when people listen intently to an interesting speaker, they are unaware of minor body sensations (such as itches or hunger) and other sounds or sights. An experienced speaker knows that when the audience looks restless, its attention is no longer focused on the lecture but might be turning toward considerations of lunch or other activities; it is time to recapture the listeners' attention.

CERTIFICATION POINTER

For teacher certification tests, you may be expected to detail various strategies for gaining students' attention, such as lowering your voice, using a gesture or surprise, and increasing the emotional content.

Gaining Attention How can teachers focus students' attention on the lesson at hand, and in particular on the most important aspects of what is being taught?

There are several ways to gain students' attention, all of which go under the general heading of arousing student interest. One way is to use cues that indicate "This is important." Some teachers raise or lower their voices to signal that they are about to impart critical information. Others use gestures, repetition, or body position to communicate the same message.

Another way to gain attention is to increase the emotional content of material. Some publications accomplish this by choosing very emotional words. This is probably why newspaper headlines say "Senate Kills Mass Transit Proposal" rather than "Senate Votes Against Mass Transit Proposal."

Unusual, inconsistent, or surprising stimuli also attract attention. For example, science teachers often introduce lessons with a demonstration or magic trick to engage student curiosity.

Finally, informing students that what follows is important to them will catch their attention. For example, teachers can ensure attention by telling students, "This will be

perception
A person's interpretation of stimuli.

attention
Active focus on certain stimuli to the exclusion of others.

on tomorrow's test." Of course, learners make their own decisions about what is important, and they learn more of what they think is important than of other material because they pay more attention to it. Students can be taught to identify what is important in texts and then to devote more attention to those aspects.

Short-Term or Working Memory

Information that a person perceives and pays attention to is transferred to the second component of the memory system: the **short-term memory** (Solso, 2001). Short-term memory is a storage system that can hold a limited amount of information for a few seconds. It is the part of memory in which information that is currently being thought about is stored. The thoughts we are conscious of having at any given moment are being held in our short-term memory. When we stop thinking about something, it disappears from our short-term memory. Another term for short-term memory is **working memory** (Anderson, 2005; Ashcraft, 2006). This term emphasizes that the most important aspect of short-term memory is not its duration but the fact that it is active. Working memory is where the mind operates on information, organizes it for storage or discarding, and connects it to other information. Working memory is so important that many researchers think that working memory capacity is essentially the same as intelligence (Ackerman, Beier, & Boyle, 2005; Colom et al., 2003; Kane et al., 2005).

INTASC

2 Knowledge of Human Development and Learning

As depicted in Figure 6.1, information may enter working memory from sensory registers or from the third basic component of the memory system: long-term memory. Often, both things happen at the same time. When you see a robin, your sensory register transfers the image of the robin to your working memory. Meanwhile, you may (unconsciously) search your long-term memory for information about birds so that you can identify this particular one as a robin. Along with that recognition may come a lot of other information about robins, memories of past experiences with robins, or feelings about robins—all of which were stored in long-term memory but are brought into consciousness (working memory) by your mental processing of the sight of the robin (Gathercole et al., 2004).

"Mrs. Lee, can I be excused? My working memory capacity is full."

One way to hold information in working memory is to think about it or say it over and over. You have probably used this strategy to remember a phone number for a short time. This process of maintaining an item in working memory by repetition is called **rehearsal** (Baddeley, 1999). Rehearsal is important in learning because the longer an item remains in working memory, the greater the chance that it will be transferred to long-term memory. Without rehearsal, items will probably not stay in working memory for more than about 30 seconds. Because working memory has a limited capacity, information can also be lost from it by being forced out by other information. You have probably had the experience of looking up a telephone number, being interrupted briefly, and finding that you had forgotten the number.

Teachers must allocate time for rehearsal during classroom lessons. Teaching too much information too rapidly is likely to be ineffective because, unless students are given time to mentally rehearse each new piece of information, later information is likely to drive it out of their working memories. When teachers stop a lesson to ask students whether they have any questions, they are also giving students a few moments to think over and mentally rehearse what they have just learned. This helps students to process information in working memory and thereby to establish it in long-term memory. This mental work is critical when students are learning new, difficult material.

short-term or working memory
The component of memory in which limited amounts of information can be stored for a few seconds.

rehearsal
Mental repetition of information, which can improve its retention.

Working Memory Capacity Working memory is believed to have a capacity of five to nine bits of information (Miller, 1956). That is, we can think about only five to nine distinct things at a time. However, any particular bit may itself contain a great deal of information. For example, think how difficult it would be to memorize the following shopping list:

flour	orange juice	pepper	mustard
soda pop	parsley	cake	butter
relish	mayonnaise	oregano	canned tomatoes
potatoes	milk	lettuce	syrup
hamburger	hot dogs	eggs	onions
tomato paste	apples	spaghetti	buns

CERTIFICATION POINTER

On a teacher certification test, you may be required to know that organizing material into familiar patterns can help students remember concepts and vocabulary. For example, to help young students remember the names of different animals, you could help students categorize them into pets, zoo animals, and farm animals.

This list has too many bits of information to remember easily. All 24 food items would not fit into working memory in random order. However, you could easily memorize the list by organizing it according to familiar patterns. As shown in Table 6.1, you might mentally create three separate memory files: breakfast, lunch, and dinner. In each, you expect to find food and beverages; in the lunch and dinner files, you expect to find dessert as well. You can then think through the recipes for each item on the menus. In this way, you can recall what you have to buy and you need maintain only a few bits of information in your working memory. When you enter the store, you are thinking, "I need food for breakfast, lunch, and dinner." First, you bring the breakfast file out of your long-term memory. It contains food (pancakes) and a beverage (orange juice). You might think through how you make pancakes step by step and buy each ingredient, plus orange juice as a beverage. When you have done this, you can discard breakfast from your working memory and replace it with the lunch file and then the dinner file, going through the same processes. Note that all you did was to replace 24 little bits of information with 3 big bits that you could then separate into their components.

Working memory can be thought of as a bottleneck through which information from the environment reaches long-term memory. The limited capacity of working memory is one aspect of information processing that has important implications for the design and practice of instruction (Sweller, van Merrienboer, & Paas, 1998). For example, you cannot present students with many ideas at once unless the ideas are so well organized and well connected to information already in the students' long-term memories that their working memories (with assistance from their long-term memories) can accommodate them, as in the case of the shopping list just discussed.

As another illustration of the limited capacity of working memory, Mayer (2001) compared a lesson on lightning storms that included a number of extraneous words, pictures, and music to a lesson without these elements. The simpler lesson produced higher performance on a transfer test. Apparently, the more coherent lesson used working memory capacity more effectively (see Mayer, 2003).

TABLE 6.1 Example of Organization of Information to Facilitate Memory

A 24-item shopping list that would be very hard to remember in a random order can be organized into a smaller number of familiar categories, making the list easier to recall.

Breakfast	Lunch	Dinner
Pancakes: • Flour • Milk • Eggs • Butter • Syrup Beverage: Orange juice	Hot Dogs: • Hot dogs • Buns • Relish • Mustard Potato Salad: • Potatoes • Mayonnaise • Parsley Beverage: Soda pop Dessert: Apple	Spaghetti: • Spaghetti • Onions • Hamburger • Canned tomatoes • Tomato paste • Oregano • Pepper Salad: • Lettuce Beverage: Milk Dessert: Cake

Individual Differences in Working Memory Individuals differ, of course, in the capacity of their working memories to accomplish a given learning task. One of the main factors in enhancing this capacity is background knowledge. The more a person knows about something, the better able the person is to organize and absorb new information (Engle, Nations, & Cantor, 1990; Kuhara-Kojima & Hatano, 1991). However, prior knowledge is not the only factor. Individuals also differ in their abilities to organize information and can be taught to consciously use strategies for making more efficient use of their working memory capacity (Wyra, Lawson, & Hungi, 2007). Strategies of this kind are discussed later in this chapter.

Long-Term Memory

Long-term memory is that part of our memory system where we keep information for long periods of time. Long-term memory is thought to be a very large-capacity, very long-term memory store. In fact, many theorists believe that we may never forget information in long-term memory; rather, we might just lose the ability to find the information within our memory (Tulving & Craik, 2000). We do not live long enough to fill up our long-term memory. The differences among sensory registers, working (short-term) memory, and long-term memory are summarized in Table 6.2.

Ericsson and Kintsch (1995) hypothesize that people store not only information but also learning strategies in long-term memory for easy access. This capacity, which Ericsson and Kintsch call long-term working memory, accounts for the extraordinary skills of experts (such as medical diagnosticians) who must match current information with a vast array of patterns held in their long-term memories.

Theorists divide long-term memory into at least three parts: episodic memory, semantic memory, and procedural memory (Eichenbaum, 2003; Squire et al., 1993). **Episodic memory** is our memory of personal experiences, a mental movie of things we saw or heard. When you remember past events such as what you had for dinner last night or what happened at your high school prom, you are recalling information stored in your long-term episodic memory. Long-term **semantic memory** contains the facts and generalized information that we know; concepts, principles, or rules and how to use them; and our problem-solving skills and learning strategies. Most things that are learned in class lessons are retained in semantic memory.

long-term memory
The components of memory in which large amounts of information can be stored for long periods of time.

episodic memory
A part of long-term memory that stores images of our personal experiences.

semantic memory
A part of long-term memory that stores facts and general knowledge.

TABLE 6.2 Characteristics of Components of Cognitive Storage Systems

Storage Structure	Processes				Cause of Failure to Recall
	*Code**	*Capacity*	*Duration*	*Retrieval*	
Sensory "store"	Sensory features	12–20 items[†] to huge	250 msec.–4 sec.	Complete, given proper cueing	Masking or decay
Short-term memory	Acoustic, visual, semantic, sensory features identified and named	7 ± 2 items	About 12 sec.; longer with rehearsal	Complete, with each item being retrieved every 35 msec.	Displacement, interference, decay
Long-term memory	Semantic, visual knowledge; abstractions; meaningful images	Enormous, virtually unlimited	Indefinite	Specific and general information available, given proper cueing	Interference, organic dysfunctioning, inappropriate cues

*How information is represented
[†]Estimated

Source: From Robert L. Solso, *Cognitive Psychology* (6th ed.), p. 240. Published by Allyn & Bacon, Boston, MA.

Procedural memory refers to "knowing how" in contrast to "knowing that" (Solso, 2001). The abilities to drive, type, and ride a bicycle are examples of skills that are retained in procedural memory.

Episodic, semantic, and procedural memory store and organize information in different ways. Information in episodic memory is stored in the form of images that are organized on the basis of when and where events happened. Information in semantic memory is organized in the form of networks of ideas. Information in procedural memory is stored as a complex of stimulus–response pairings (Anderson, 1995). Recent brain studies (e.g., Bransford, Brown, & Cocking, 1999; Elias & Saucier, 2006; Solso, 2001) have suggested that operations relating to each of these types of long-term memory take place in different parts of the brain. Let's examine in detail what we mean by these three kinds of memory.

Episodic Memory Episodic memory contains images of experiences organized by when and where they happened (Tulving & Craik, 2000). For example, answer this question: In the house in which you lived as a child, when you entered your bedroom, was the head of your bed to the right, left, or away from or pointed toward you? If you are like most people, you answered this question by imagining the bedroom and seeing where the head of the bed was. Now consider this question: What did you do on the night of your senior prom or dance? Most people answer this question by imagining themselves back on that night and describing the events. Finally, suppose you are asked to recall the names of your high school classmates. One psychologist asked graduate students to come to a specific place for 1 hour a day and try to remember the names. Over the course of a month, the students continued to recall new names. Interestingly, they used space and time cues, which are associated with episodic memory, to imagine incidents that allowed them to recall the names. For example, they might recall the day their social studies teacher came to school dressed as an Arctic explorer and then mentally scan the faces of the students who were there.

These demonstrations indicate that images are important in episodic memory and that cues related to space and time help us to retrieve information from this part of memory. You have probably taken an exam and said to yourself, "I should know this answer. I remember reading this section. It was right on the bottom left corner of the page with the diagram in the upper right."

Episodic memories are often difficult to retrieve because most episodes in our lives are repeated so often that later episodes get mixed up in memory with earlier ones, unless something happens during the episode to make it especially memorable. For example, few people remember what they had for lunch a week ago, much less years ago. However, there is a phenomenon called **flashbulb memory** in which the occurrence of an important event fixes mainly visual and auditory memories in a person's mind. For example, people who happened to be eating breakfast at the moment they first heard about the attack on the World Trade Center may well remember that particular meal (and other trivial aspects of the setting) forever. The reason for this is that the unforgettable event of that moment gives us access to the episodic (space and time) memories relating to what would usually be forgotten details.

Martin (1993) has speculated that educators could improve retention of concepts and information by explicitly creating memorable events involving visual or auditory images. For example, uses of projects, plays, simulations, and other forms of active learning could give students vivid images that they could remember and then use to retrieve other information presented at about the same time. In support of this idea, there is much evidence that pictures illustrating text help children to remember the text even when the pictures are no longer presented (Small, Lovett, & Scher, 1993). The pictures presumably tie the semantic information to the child's episodic memory, making the information easier to retrieve. There is also evidence that students often create their own mental pictures, which then help them remember material they have studied (Robinson, Robinson, & Katayama, 1999).

Semantic Memory Semantic (or declarative) memory is organized in a very different way. It is mentally organized in networks of connected ideas or relationships called **schemata** (singular: *schema*) (Anderson, 2005; Bruning et al., 2004). Recall that Piaget introduced the word *scheme* to describe a cognitive framework that individuals use to

procedural memory
A part of long-term memory that stores information about how to do things.

flashbulb memory
Important events that are fixed mainly in visual and auditory memory.

schemata
Mental networks of related concepts that influence understanding of new information; the singular is *schema*.

CONNECTIONS
For more on the concept of schemes, see Chapter 2, page 32.

organize their perceptions and experiences. Cognitive processing theorists similarly use the terms *schema* and *schemata* to describe networks of concepts that individuals have in their memories that enable them to understand and incorporate new information. A schema is like an outline, with different concepts or ideas grouped under larger categories. Various aspects of schemata may be related by series of propositions, or relationships. For example, Figure 6.3 illustrates a simplified schema for the concept "bison," showing how this concept is related to other concepts in memory.

In the figure, the concept "bison" is linked to several other concepts. These may be linked to still more concepts (such as "How did Plains Indians hunt bison?") and to broader categories or concepts (such as "How have conservationists saved many species from extinction?"). Schema theory (Anderson, 2005) holds that we gain access to information held in our semantic long-term memory by mentally following paths like those illustrated in Figure 6.3. For example, you might have deep in your memory the idea that the Spanish introduction of the horse to North America revolutionized how the Plains Indians hunted bison. To get to that bit of information, you might start thinking about characteristics of bison, then think about how Plains Indians hunted bison on horseback, then recall (or imagine) how they hunted bison before they had horses. Many pathways can be used to get at the same bit of information. In fact, the more pathways you have leading to a piece of information and the better established those pathways are, the better access you will have to information in long-term semantic memory (Solso, 2001). Recall that the problem of long-term memory is not that information is lost but that our access to information is lost.

One clear implication of schema theory is that new information that fits into a well-developed schema is retained far more readily than is information that does not fit into a schema. Schema theory will be covered in more detail later in this chapter.

FIGURE 6.3 Schema for the Concept "Bison"
Information in long-term semantic memory is organized in networks of related ideas. The concept "bison," for example, falls under the more general concepts "mammals" and "animals" and is related to many other ideas that help to differentiate it from other concepts in memory.

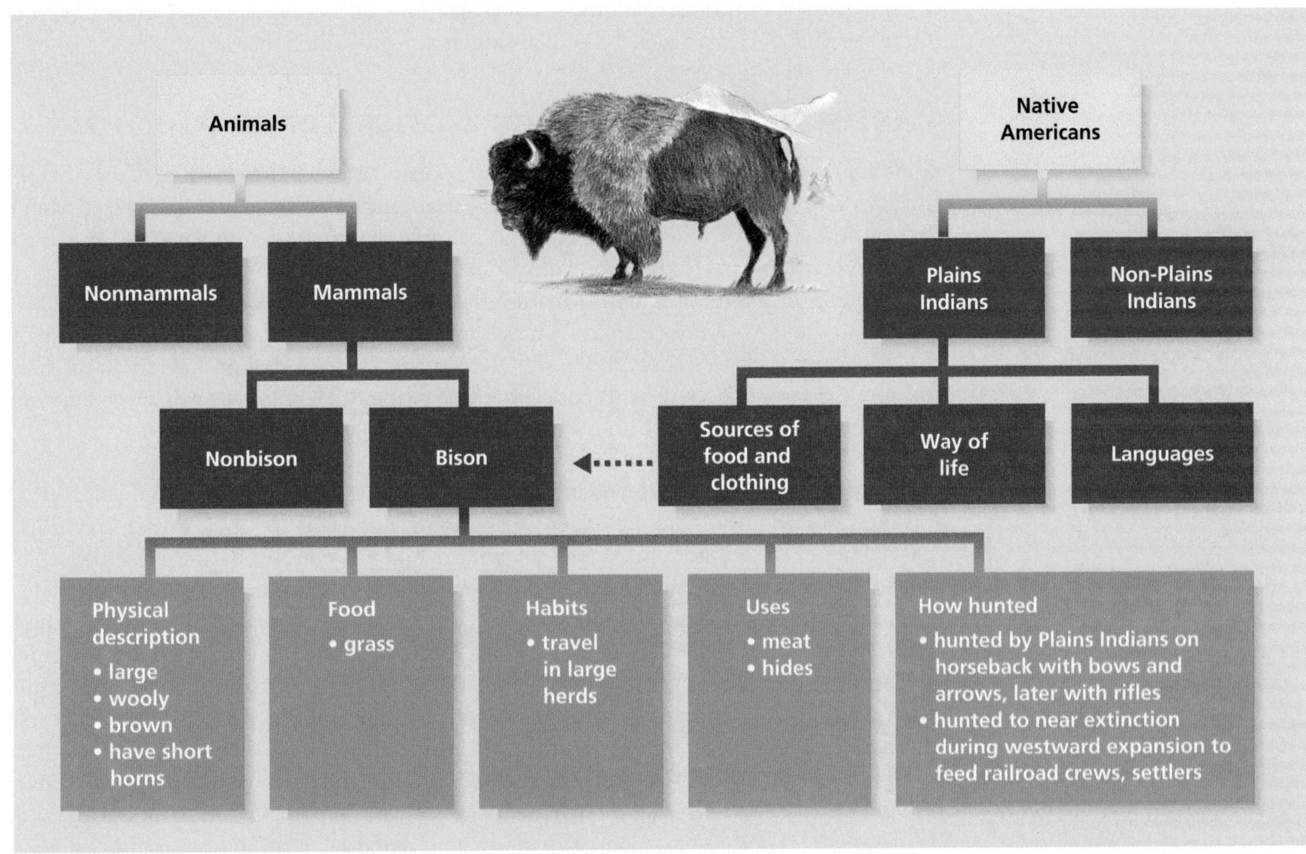

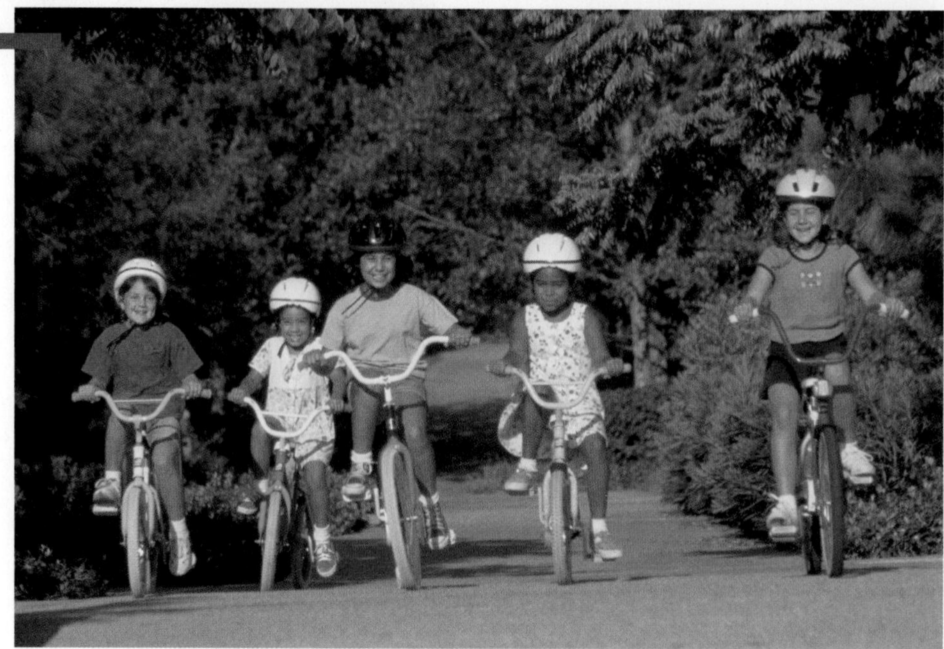

People use procedural memory to recall how to do physical tasks. This type of memory is stored in a different part of the brain from semantic and episodic memories. How can teachers encourage procedural memory in their students?

Procedural Memory Procedural memory is the ability to recall how to do something, especially a physical task. This type of memory is apparently stored in a series of stimulus–response pairings. For example, even if you have not ridden a bicycle for a long time, as soon as you get on one, the stimuli begin to evoke responses. When the bike leans to the left (a stimulus), you "instinctively" shift your weight to the right to maintain balance (a response). Other examples of procedural memory include handwriting, typing, and running skills. Neurological studies show that procedural memories are stored in a different part of the brain than are semantic and episodic memories; procedural memories are stored in the cerebellum, whereas semantic and episodic memories are stored in the cerebral cortex (Black, 2003; Bruning et al., 2004; Eichenbaum, 2003).

Factors That Enhance Long-Term Memory

Contrary to popular belief, people retain a large portion of what they learn in school. Semb and Ellis (1994), in reviewing research on this topic, note that laboratory studies of retention of nonsense words and other artificial material greatly underestimate the degree to which information and skills learned in school can be retained (also see Ellis, Semb, & Cole, 1998). Long-term retention of information that is learned in school varies a great deal according to the type of information. For example, concepts are retained much longer than names (Conway, Cohen, & Stanhope, 1991). In general, retention drops rapidly in the first few weeks after instruction but then levels off (Bahrick & Hall, 1991). Whatever students have retained about 12 to 24 weeks after instruction, they may retain forever.

Several factors contribute to long-term retention. One, not surprisingly, is the degree to which students had learned the material in the first place (Bahrick & Hall, 1991). It is interesting to note that the effects of ability on retention are unclear (Semb & Ellis, 1994). Higher-ability students score better at the end of a course but often lose the same percentage of what they had learned as lower-ability students do.

Instructional strategies that actively involve students in lessons contribute to long-term retention. For example, MacKenzie and White (1982) contrasted students in eighth and ninth grades learning geography under three conditions: traditional classroom instruction, traditional instruction plus fieldwork, and traditional instruction plus fieldwork plus active processing of information involved in fieldwork. Twelve weeks later (after summer vacation), the active processing group had lost only 10 percent of the information, whereas the other two groups had lost more than 40 percent. Similarly, Specht and Sandling (1991) contrasted undergraduates who learned accounting from traditional lectures with others who learned it through role playing. After 6 weeks, the traditionally taught students lost 54 percent of their problem-solving performance, whereas the role-playing group lost only 13 percent.

Other Information-Processing Models

Atkinson and Shiffrin's (1968) model of information processing outlined in Figure 6.1 is not the only one accepted by cognitive psychologists. Several alternative models do not challenge the basic assumptions of the Atkinson–Shiffrin model but elaborate aspects of it, particularly aspects relating to the factors that increase the chances that information will be retained in long-term memory. These alternative theories are as follows.

Levels-of-Processing Theory One widely accepted model of information processing is called **levels-of-processing theory** (Craik, 2000; Tulving & Craik, 2000), which holds that people subject stimuli to different levels of mental processing and retain only the information that has been subjected to the most thorough processing. For example, you might perceive a tree but pay little attention to it. This is the lowest level of processing, and you are unlikely to remember the tree. Second, you might give the tree a name, such as *maple* or *oak*. Once named, the tree is somewhat more likely to be remembered. The highest level of processing, however, is giving meaning to the tree. For example, you might remember having climbed the tree or having commented on the tree's unusual shape, or you might have wondered whether the tree would fall on your house if it were struck by lightning. According to levels-of-processing theory, the more you attend to the details of a stimulus, the more mental processing you must do with a stimulus and the more likely you are to remember it. This was illustrated in a classic study by Bower and Karlin (1974), who had Stanford undergraduates look at yearbook pictures from Yale. Some of the students were told to classify the pictures as "male" or "female," and some were told to classify them as "very honest" or "less honest." The students who had to categorize the faces as "very honest" or "less honest" remembered them far better than did those who merely categorized them as "male" or "female." Presumably, the honesty raters had to do a much higher level of mental processing with the pictures than did the gender raters, and for this reason they remembered the faces better. More recently, Kapur et al. (1994) had students read a series of nouns. One group was asked to identify which words contained the letter "a." Another group had to identify the nouns as "living" or "nonliving." As in the Bower and Karlin study and many others, the students who had to sort the words into "living" and "nonliving" recalled many more words. More interesting, however, was that brain imaging revealed that the "living/nonliving" students were activating a portion of their brains associated with enhanced memory performance, whereas the other students were not. This experiment adds important evidence to the idea that the brain treats "deep processing" and "shallow processing" differently (see Craik, 2000).

Dual Code Theory A concept that is related to levels-of-processing theory is Paivio's **dual code theory of memory,** which hypothesizes that information is retained in long-term memory in two forms: visual and verbal (corresponding to episodic and semantic memory, respectively) (Clark & Paivio, 1991; Mayer & Moreno, 1998; Sadoski, Goetz, & Fritz, 1993). This theory predicts that information represented both visually and verbally is recalled better than information represented only one way. For example, you remember a face better if you also know a name, and you remember a name better if you can connect it to a face (Mayer, 2003).

RESEARCH ON THE BRAIN

In the past, research on learning, memory, and other cognitive functions took place using methods one step away from the brain itself. Scientists used ingenious experiments to learn about brain function from subjects' responses to particular stimuli or tests, examined individuals with unusual brain damage, or made inferences from experiments on

levels-of-processing theory
Explanation of memory that links recall of a stimulus with the amount of mental processing it receives.

dual code theory of memory
Theory suggesting that information coded both visually and verbally is remembered better than information coded in only one of those two ways.

animals. However, in recent years neuroscientists have developed a capacity to actually watch healthy brains in operation, using brain imaging methods such as functional magnetic resonance imaging (fMRI) (Changeux, 2004; Eichenbaum, 2003; Goswami, 2004; Shaywitz, 2003). Scientists can now observe what parts of the brain are activated when an individual hears a symphony, reads a book, speaks a second language, or solves a math problem. This capability has led to an explosion of research on the brain (see, e.g., Bransford, Brown, & Cocking, 1999; Bruer, 1999; Elias & Saucier, 2006; Goswami, 2004; Solso, 2001).

INTASC

2 Knowledge of Human Development and Learning

It has long been known that specific mental functions are carried out in specific locations in the brain. For example, vision is localized in the visual cortex, hearing in the auditory cortex (see Figure 6.4). However, new research is finding that the brain is even more specialized than was thought previously. When you think about a face, you activate a different part of the brain than when you think about a chair, a song, or a feeling. If you are bilingual in, say, Spanish and English, slightly different areas of your brain are activated when you speak each language. The two hemispheres of the brain have somewhat different functions; the left hemisphere is more involved in language, whereas the right is more involved in spatial and nonverbal information. However, despite the specialization within the brain, almost all tasks we perform involve both hemispheres and many parts of the brain working together (Black, 2003; Saffran & Schwartz, 2003).

Many findings from brain research might have importance for education and child development. One has to do with early development, where studies find that the amount of stimulation early in a child's development relates to the number of neural connections, or synapses, which are the basis for higher learning and memory (Black, 2003; Elias & Saucier, 2006). The finding that the brain's capacity is not set at birth, but is influenced by early experience, has had an electrifying impact on the world of early childhood research and education policy. Further, some research is suggesting that extensive training can change brain structures, even into adulthood. For example, a study of London cab-drivers found that their training caused increased activity in a part of the brain that

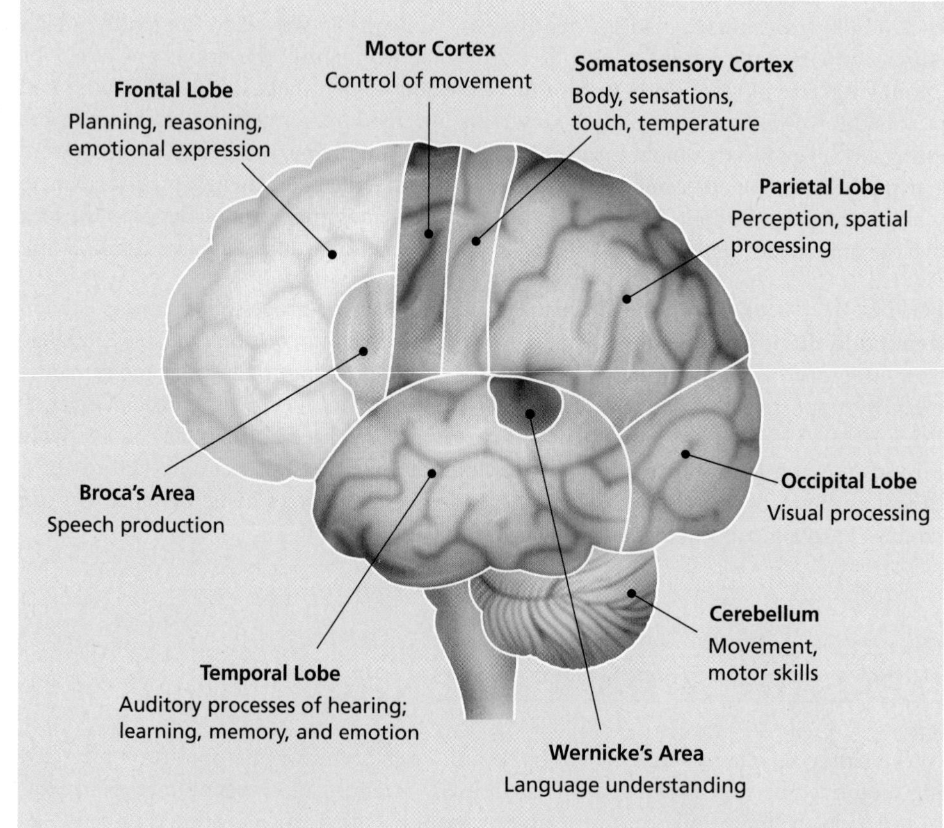

FIGURE 6.4 Brain Physiology and Functions
Each part of the brain specializes in a particular category of functions.

Adapted from Samuel E. Wood, Ellen Green Wood, & Denise Boyd, *The World of Psychology* (6th ed.), p. 53. Published by Allyn & Bacon, Boston, MA. Copyright © 2008 by Pearson Education. Adapted by permission of the publisher.

processes directions (Maguire et al., 2000), and that children who receive intensive tutoring in reading develop brain structures like those of proficient readers (Shaywitz, 2003; Shaywitz & Shaywitz, 2004; Turkeltaub et al., 2003). However, there is considerable debate about what this implies for instruction (Hruby & Hynd, 2006; Shaywitz & Shaywitz, 2007; Willis, 2007).

Another important finding is initially counterintuitive. Up to the age of 18 months, infants generate enormous numbers of neurons and connections between neurons (see Figure 6.5). After that point, they begin to lose them. What is happening is that the brain sloughs off connections that are not being used, so that the remaining connections are efficient and well organized. This process is strongly affected by the environment in which the child lives and continues through early childhood. The plasticity of the brain, or its susceptibility to change by the environment, is highest at the earliest ages and diminishes over time (Elias & Saucier, 2006).

A third important finding of brain research is the discovery that as a person gains in knowledge and skill, his or her brain becomes more efficient. For example, Solso (2001) compared the brain activation of an expert artist to that of novices. On a task familiar to the artist—drawing faces—only a small portion of his brain was active, whereas novices had activity in many parts of their brains (see Figure 6.6). In another series of studies, Eden et al. (1996) compared the brain activation of children with dyslexia with that of normal readers while they were reading. The children with dyslexia activated auditory as well as visual areas of their brains, as though they had to laboriously translate the letters into sounds and then the sounds into meaning. The proficient readers skipped the auditory step entirely. The same difference has been documented between children just learning to read and the same children after they become good readers (Turkeltaub et al., 2003). Research long ago noted the importance of automaticity, or seemingly effortless performance made possible by extensive experience and practice, in the development of expertise. The brain studies show how automaticity can actually allow the brain to skip steps in solving problems.

Recent studies (Shaywitz, 2003) have found that proficient readers primarily activate three regions of the left brain. In contrast, dyslexics overactivate a region in the front of the brain called Broca's area, which controls speaking. In other words, poor readers seem to use an inefficient pathway (print to speech to understanding), whereas good readers use a more efficient pathway (print to understanding). More broadly, individuals with learning disabilities have been found to use less efficient brain processes than other learners (Blair, 2004; Halpern & Schulz, 2006).

CERTIFICATION POINTER

Teacher certification tests will require you to know that as individuals learn more, their brains become more efficient. This leads to automaticity, the effortless performance that comes with the development of expertise.

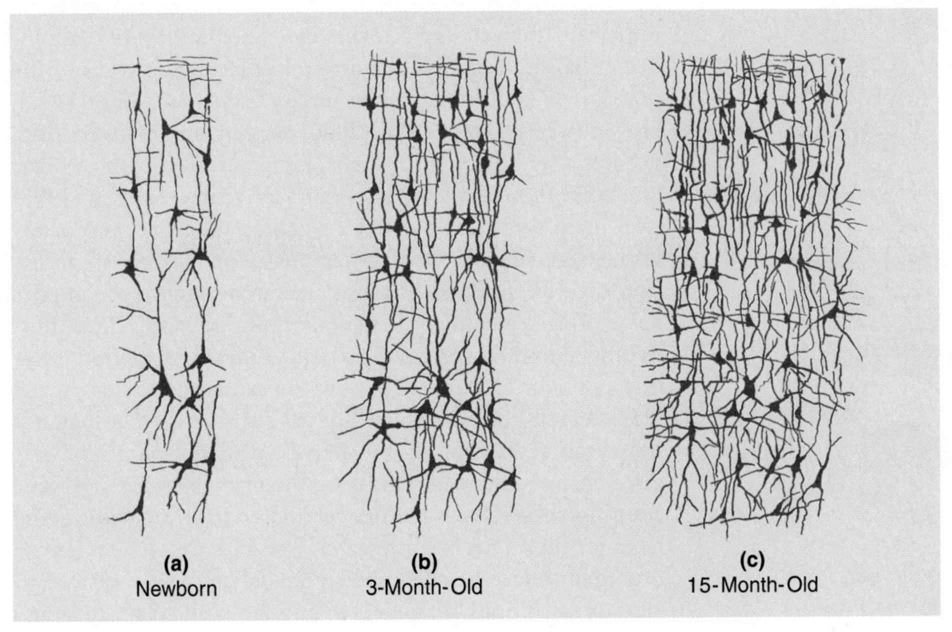

FIGURE 6.5 Development of Neural Connections, from Birth through 15 Months of Age

Neural connections in children's brains develop rapidly from birth through infancy.

From Richard Fabes and Carol Lynn Martin, *Exploring Child Development: Transactions and Transformations* (2nd ed.), p. 116. Published by Allyn & Bacon, Boston, MA. Copyright © 2003 by Pearson Education. Reprinted by permission of the publisher.

FIGURE 6.6 Brain Activity of an Artist and a Nonartist While Drawing
fMRI scans made on an accomplished artist, H.O., and a nonartist control subject showing right parietal activity for both people (see column A). This area is involved in facial perception, but it appears that the nonartist is demanding more energy to process faces than H.O. In columns C and D, there is an increase in blood flow in the right frontal area of the artist, suggesting a higher-order abstraction of information.

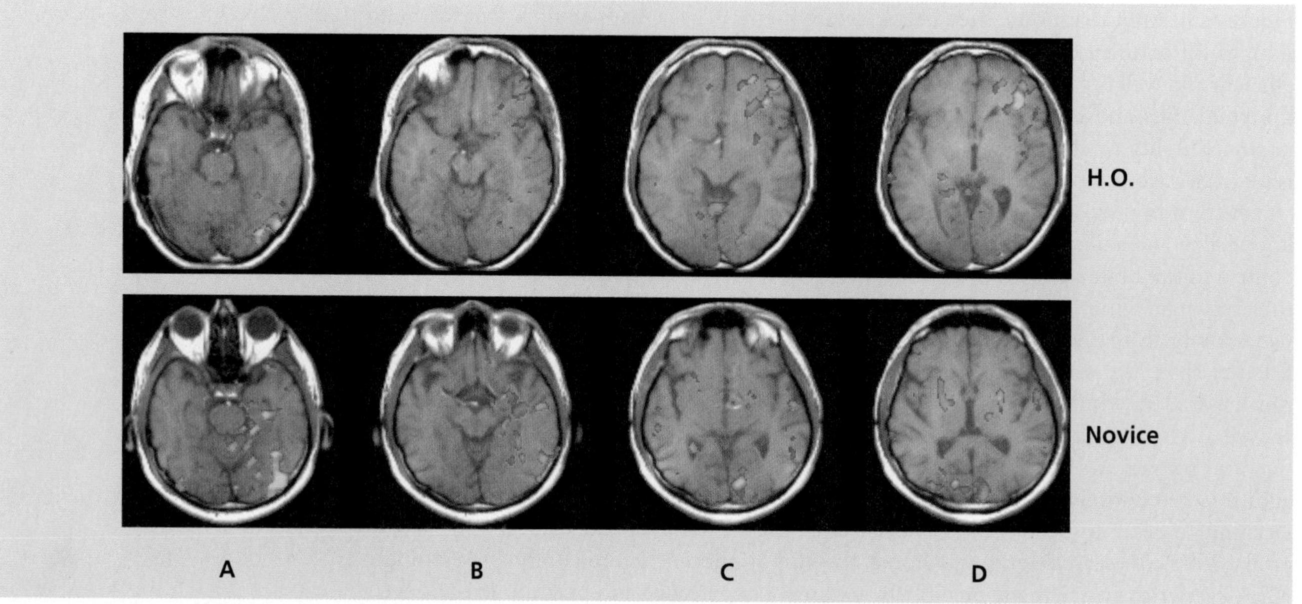

From Robert L. Solso, *Cognitive Psychology* (8th ed.). Published by Allyn & Bacon, Boston, MA. Copyright © 2008 by Pearson Education. Reprinted by permission of the publisher.

"And this is the part of the brain that's responsible for sleep."

These and many other findings of brain research reinforce the conclusion that the brain is not a filing cabinet for facts and skills but is engaged in a process of organizing information to make it efficiently accessible and usable. The process of discarding connections and selectively ignoring or excluding information, as well as the process of making orderly connections among information, is as important, or perhaps more important, than adding information. The progress of brain research has quite naturally led to a call for applications to the practice of education. For example, Caine & Caine (1997), Howard (2000), and Willis (2006) suggest that brain research justifies a shift away from linear, hierarchical teaching toward complex, thematic, and integrated activities. Langer (1997) cites brain research to attack a teaching focus on memorization, suggesting more of an emphasis on flexible thinking. Gardner (2000) claims that brain research supports the importance of early stimulation, of activity in learning, and of music and emotions. All of these and other prescriptions may turn out to be valid, but at present the evidence for them, when it exists at all, comes from traditional cognitive psychology, not from brain research itself. Further, the prescriptions from brain research are remarkably similar to the principles of progressive education described a century ago by John Dewey, without the benefit of modern brain research (see Ellis, 2001c). It may be that brain research will someday vindicate Dewey or lead to clear prescriptions for practice, but the rush to make grand claims for educational methods based on brain research has already led to a substantial body of cautionary literature (e.g., Bruer, 1999; Coles, 2004; Ellis, 2001c; Jensen, 2000). No one denies that the potential of brain research to inform educational practice is vast, but it mainly lies in the future (Katzir & Pare-Blagoev, 2006).

Emerging Research in Neuroscience

Over the past decade, significant new technologies such as magnetic resonance imaging (MRI) have emerged that allow neuroscientists to look directly at brains in live, functioning individuals (Nicholson, 2006). In particular, functional MRIs, or fMRIs, allow us to look at changing pictures of the brain as individuals actually perform tasks, identifying which circuitry is "on line" during a particular activity (Wager, 2006). These methods have their limitations (Dumit, 2004; Uttal, 2001), but they provide a wonderful new tool for neuroscientists. Do they provide new perspectives for educators as well?

The answer is debatable. Willingham (2006) argues that, although neuroscience has been moving forward "in leaps and bounds," significant help for classroom teachers from these advances is still well in the future for most practical purposes. After all, he points out, although fMRI images might tell us which parts of a child's brain are active when she tries to read, that information doesn't really offer anything useful for that child's teacher. According to Willingham (2006), "very exciting research is being conducted. . . . Some of it is of interest to cognitive researchers trying to figure out how the brain works. And virtually all of it is far from being able to guide teachers" (p. 177).

Indeed, Willingham (2006) cautions against trying to apply emerging neuroscientific data directly to the classroom, rather than considering them as pieces of a very large cognitive puzzle. This caution is supported by the way in which such data have gotten into popular culture and into the literature about teaching during the past several decades. He points, for example, to research on left-brain versus right-brain functions that is often used to support a variety of instructional strategies, although brain imaging data now confirm that both brain hemispheres participate in most cognitive tasks. He mentions as well the flurry of activity around providing stimulation for infants and young children, based on misinterpretation of data about stimulus-deprived subjects. Willingham does, however, see an immediate usefulness for neuroscientific findings in identifying children with learning disabilities, particularly dyslexia (see, e.g., the work of Espy, Molfese, Molfese, & Modglin, 2004; Lyytinen et al., 2005).

Despite any reservations about finding direct correlations between neuroscience and classroom teaching, we can, nevertheless, agree that psychological changes, behavioral changes, and changes in cognition as a consequence of learning are all correlated with changes in the operation of the brain. We know something about *how* those changes occur, and we know something about *where* those changes occur. Neuroscience is on the cutting edge of behavioral science; it is supplying additional pieces of the cognitive puzzle all the time. As responsible educators, we should keep ourselves informed about these emerging data, and we should evaluate them thoughtfully and carefully for implications for teaching and learning. We might agree on three conclusions:

1. ***Not all learning is equally likely.*** Some things are easier to learn than other things. For instance, humans acquire language and are attuned to social stimuli. Some learning seems more *intuitive,* or easy: For humans, this kind of learning appears to include language (Pinker, 1995, 1997), understanding about objects and the behavior of objects in space (Rosser, 1994), the geometry of three-dimensional space and the natural number system (Gelman, 2006), and the distinction between living and nonliving things (Inagaki & Hantano, 2006). Other learning can be *counterintuitive,* or hard to learn, and this appears to include mastering fractions, algebra, and Newtonian physics (Rosser, 2003), among other things.

   This is not news, of course, to classroom teachers, who are probably very much aware that language and spatial relationships come more easily to young learners than advanced math concepts.

2. ***Brain development constrains cognitive outcome.*** One cannot alter a brain that is not yet ready for incoming experience to affect it. That is a point made years ago by Jean

Piaget, who studied children's cognition, not their brains, and we now know that there is a correspondence between changes in the brain and cognitive development (Kuhn, 2006). Whereas brain development takes place over a long time, *behavior change through learning cannot exceed the developmental status of the neural structure.*

Developmental research also suggests that cognitive accomplishments in children and adolescents are probably best conceptualized as *domain specific.* Although the left and right hemispheres of the brain appear to participate together in most cognitive tasks, the brain is not entirely a *general problem solver* well adapted to all sorts of different challenges the person might encounter. It may be more accurate to envision the brain as a series of specialized problem solvers with specific regions or circuits well adapted to handling limited kinds of problems, such as finding your way home (a geometric problem solver), figuring out language (a linguistic problem solver), or "reading" social information (a "people" problem solver).

As Willingham (2006) suggests, the classroom applicability of this is not yet clear, but future findings may uncover implications for teachers in stimulating particular domains to achieve particular goals.

3. ***Some regions of the brain may be particularly important for cognitive outcomes, for supporting certain sorts of neural activities related to learning and cognition.*** One region that has become a primary focus of much contemporary research is the prefrontal cortex. This region has been proposed as a mediator of behavioral planning and reasoning (Grafman, 1994); attentional processes (Foster, Eskes, & Stuss, 1994; Panskeep, 1998); impulsivity control (Murji & DeLuca, 1998; Rosser, Stevens, & Ruiz, 2006); and, more recently, planning and executive cognitive functioning (Grafman, Spector, & Ratterman, 2005; Huey, Krueger, & Grafman, 2006), and even the ability to use rules when engaged in cognitive tasks (Bunge & Zelazo, 2006). In short, this appears to be the seat of what we think of as *deliberate cognitive activity,* which is what we try to encourage in the classroom.

Interestingly enough, this region is structurally immature even in adolescence. Gray matter in the frontal cortex peaks at about age 11 in females and at 12.1 years in males (Giedd, 2004; Giedd, Blumenthal, & Jeffries, 1999), whereas white matter volume in this region increases well into adulthood (Casey, Giedd, & Thomas, 2000). This is an area linked to the ability to inhibit impulses, to weigh consequences of decisions, to prioritize and strategize, in short, to act rationally. And it is still being remodeled well into early adulthood.

What does all this mean to the educator facing a classroom full of students? Given what we know about brain development and brain functioning, it means those recipients of instruction are *not* empty, unformed boxes waiting to be "filled up" with information, directions, and skills. It means they are not even finished boxes—that the receptacle itself is still changing and reforming. Learners are, in fact, neural works in progress, altering themselves with every new activity, every engagement, and every new skill acquired and fact learned. That remodeling is ongoing, protracted, and continuous. As neuroscience continues to provide a wealth of new data, and those data are woven together with the data provided by sociologists, behavioral scientists, psychologists, and educators, we may indeed find that brain research provides invaluable insights—and useful strategies—for us as educators.

WHAT CAUSES PEOPLE TO REMEMBER OR FORGET?

Why do we remember some things and forget others? Why can we sometimes remember trivial things that happened years ago but not important things that happened yesterday? Most forgetting occurs because information in working memory was never transferred to long-term memory. However, it can also occur because we have lost our access to information that is in long-term memory.

Forgetting and Remembering

Over the years, researchers have identified several factors that make it easier or harder to remember information (see Schacter, 2001).

According to research on memory and forgetting, what factors determine how well this student remembers the information she learns in class?

Interference One important reason people forget is **interference** (Anderson, 1995; Dempster & Corkill, 1999). Interference happens when information gets mixed up with, or pushed aside by, other information. One form of interference occurs when people are prevented from mentally rehearsing newly learned information. In one classic experiment, Peterson and Peterson (1959) gave subjects a simple task: the memorization of sets of three nonsense letters (such as FQB). The subjects were then immediately asked to count backward by 3s from a three-digit number (e.g., 287, 284, 281, etc.) for up to 18 seconds. At the end of that time the subjects were asked to recall the letters. They had forgotten far more of them than had subjects who had learned the letters and then simply waited for 18 seconds to repeat them. The reason for this is that the subjects who were told to count backward were deprived of the opportunity to rehearse the letters mentally to establish them in their working memories. As was noted earlier in this chapter, teachers must take into account the limited capacity of working memory by allowing students time to absorb or practice (that is, mentally rehearse) new information before giving them additional instruction.

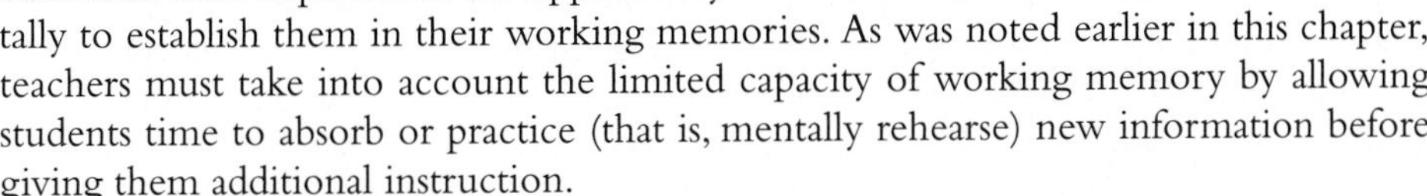

Retroactive Inhibition Another form of interference is called **retroactive inhibition.** This occurs when previously learned information is lost because it is mixed up with new and somewhat similar information. For example, young students may have no trouble recognizing the letter *b* until they are taught the letter *d*. Because these letters are similar, students often confuse them. Learning the letter *d* thus interferes with the previously learned recognition of *b*. In the same way, a traveler might know how to get around in a particular airport but then lose that skill to some extent after visiting many similar airports.

Of all the reasons for forgetting, retroactive inhibition is probably the most important. This phenomenon explains, for example, why we have trouble remembering frequently repeated episodes, such as what we had for dinner a week ago. Last night's dinner will be forgotten because memories of dinners that come after it will interfere, unless something remarkable happens to clearly distinguish last night's dinner from the dinners that will follow.

THEORY *into* PRACTICE

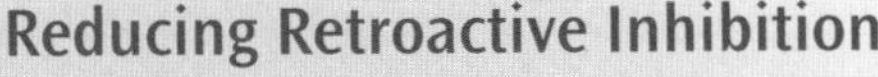

Reducing Retroactive Inhibition

There are two ways to help reduce retroactive inhibition for students. The first is by not teaching similar and confusing concepts too closely in time. The second is to use different methods to teach similar concepts. The first way to reduce retroactive inhibition implies that one of several confusing or similar concepts should be taught thoroughly before the next is introduced. For example, students should be completely able to recognize the letter *b* before the letter *d* is introduced. If these letters are introduced at close to the same time, learning of one may inhibit learning of the other. When the new letter is introduced, the teacher must carefully point out the differences between *b* and *d*, and students must practice discriminating between the two until they can unerringly

interference
Inhibition of recall of certain information by the presence of other information in memory.

retroactive inhibition
Decreased ability to recall previously learned information, caused by learning of new information.

say which is which. As another example, consider the following lists of Spanish and English word pairs:

A	B
llevar—to carry	*perro*—dog
llorar—to cry	*gato*—cat
llamar—to call	*caballo*—horse

List B is much easier to learn. The similarities among the Spanish words in list A (they all are verbs, start with *ll,* end with *ar,* and have the same number of letters and syllables) make them very difficult to tell apart. The English words in list A are also somewhat difficult to discriminate among because all are verbs that start with a *c.* In contrast, the words in list B are easy to discriminate from one another. Because of the problem of retroactive inhibition, presenting all the word pairs in list A in the same lesson would be a poor instructional strategy. Students would be likely to confuse the three Spanish words because of their similar spellings. Rather, students should be completely familiar with one word pair before the next is introduced.

Another way to reduce retroactive inhibition is to use different methods to teach similar concepts or to vary other aspects of instruction for each concept. For example, in social studies a teacher might teach about Spain by using lectures and discussion, about France by using group projects, and about Italy by using films. This would help students avoid confusing information about one country with information about the others.

Most things that are forgotten were never firmly learned in the first place. The best way to ensure long-term retention of material taught in school is to make certain that students have mastered the essential features of the material. This means assessing students' understanding frequently and reteaching if it turns out that students have not achieved adequate levels of understanding.

VIDEO HOMEWORK EXERCISE
Memory

Go to **www.myeducationlab.com** and, in the Homework and Exercises section for Chapter 6 of this text, access the video entitled "Memory." Watch the video and complete the homework questions that accompany it, saving your work or transmitting it to your professor as required.

Proactive Inhibition **Proactive inhibition** occurs when learning one set of information interferes with learning later information. A classic case is that of a North American learning to drive on the left side of the road in England. It may be easier for a North American nondriver to learn to drive in England than for an experienced North American driver because the latter has so thoroughly learned to stay to the right—a potentially fatal error in England.

Individual Differences in Resistance to Interference In a 1999 article, Dempster and Corkill raise the possibility that the ability to focus on key information and screen out interference is at the heart of cognitive performance. Reviewing research from many fields, including brain research, they note strong relationships between measures of resistance to interference and school performance. For example, among children with similar IQs, those with learning disabilities perform much worse on measures of resistance to interference (see Forness & Kavale, 2000). Children with attention deficit hyperactivity disorders (ADHD) are very poor at screening out irrelevant stimuli. If you think about the stereotype of the "absent-minded professor," the ability to focus one's attention on a given problem, to the exclusion of all else, may be a hallmark of extraordinary intellect.

Facilitation It should also be noted that learning one thing can often help a person learn similar information. For example, learning Spanish first may help an English-speaking student later learn Italian, a similar language. This would be a case of **proactive facilitation.** Learning a second language can also help with an already established language. It is often the case, for example, that English-speaking students find that the study of Latin helps them understand their native language better. This would be **retroactive facilitation.**

proactive inhibition
Decreased ability to learn new information, caused by interference from existing knowledge.

proactive facilitation
Increased ability to learn new information based on the presence of previously acquired information.

retroactive facilitation
Increased comprehension of previously learned information because of the acquisition of new information.

For another example, consider teaching. We often have the experience that learning to teach a subject helps us understand the subject better. Because later learning (e.g., learning to teach addition of fractions) increases our understanding of previously learned information (addition of fractions), this is a prime example of retroactive facilitation. Table 6.3 summarizes the relationships among retroactive and proactive inhibition and facilitation.

Primacy and Recency Effects One of the oldest findings in educational psychology is that when people are given a list of words to learn and then tested immediately afterward, they tend to learn the first few and last few items much better than those in the middle of the list. The tendency to learn the first things presented is called the **primacy effect;** the tendency to learn the last things is called the **recency effect.** The most common explanation for the primacy effect is that we pay more attention and devote more mental effort to items presented first. As was noted earlier in this chapter, mental rehearsal is important in establishing new information in long-term memory. Usually, much more mental rehearsal is devoted to the first items presented than to later items (Anderson, 2005). Recency effects, in contrast, are based in large part on the fact that little or no other information intervenes between the final items and the test.

Teachers should consider primacy and recency effects, which imply that information taught at the beginning or the end of the period is more likely to be retained than other information. To take advantage of this, teachers might organize their lessons to put the most essential new concepts early in the lesson and then to summarize at the end. Many teachers take roll, collect lunch money, check homework, and do other noninstructional activities at the beginning of the period. However, it is probably a better idea to postpone these activities, to start the period right away with important concepts and only toward the end of the period deal with necessary administrative tasks.

Automaticity Information or skills may exist in long-term memory, but may take so much time or so much mental effort to retrieve that they are of limited value when speed of access is essential. The classic case of this is reading. A child may be able to sound out every word on a page, but if he or she does so very slowly and laboriously, the child will lose comprehension and will be unlikely to read for pleasure (National Reading Panel, 2000). For reading and for other skills in which speed and limited mental effort are necessary, existence in long-term memory is not enough. **Automaticity** is required; that is, a level of rapidity and ease such that a task or skill involves little or no mental effort. For a proficient reader reading simple material, decoding requires almost no mental effort. Neurological studies show that the brain becomes more efficient as a person becomes a skilled reader (Eden et al., 1996). A beginning reader with serious learning disabilities uses both auditory and visual parts of the brain during reading, trying laboriously to sound out new words. In contrast, a skilled reader uses only a small, well-defined portion of the brain relating to visual processing.

primacy effect
The tendency for items at the beginning of a list to be recalled more easily than other items.

recency effect
The tendency for items at the end of a list to be recalled more easily than other items.

automaticity
A level of rapidity and ease such that tasks can be performed or skills utilized with little mental effort.

TABLE 6.3 Retroactive and Proactive Inhibition and Facilitation

Summary of the effects on memory of retroactive and proactive inhibition and facilitation.

Effect on Learning	Effect on Memory	
	Inhibition (Negative)	*Facilitation (Positive)*
Later learning affects earlier learning	Retroactive inhibition (*Example:* Learning *d* interferes with learning *b*.)	Retroactive facilitation (*Example:* Learning to teach math helps with previously learned math skills.)
Earlier learning affects later learning	Proactive inhibition (*Example:* Learning to drive in the United States interferes with learning to drive in the England.)	Proactive facilitation (*Example:* Learning Spanish helps with later learning of Italian.)

By practicing scales far beyond the amount needed to establish the skills in his long-term memory, this young musician can gain automaticity. How will this benefit him?

Automaticity is primarily gained through practice far beyond the amount needed to establish information or skills in long-term memory (Moors & De Houwer, 2006). A soccer player knows after 10 minutes of instruction how to kick a ball, but the player practices this skill thousands of times until it becomes automatic. A chess player quickly learns the rules of chess but spends a lifetime learning to quickly recognize patterns that suggest winning moves. Bloom (1986), who studied the role of automaticity in the performances of gifted pianists, mathematicians, athletes, and others, called automaticity "the hands and feet of genius."

massed practice
Technique in which facts or skills to be learned are repeated often over a concentrated period of time.

distributed practice
Technique in which items to be learned are repeated at intervals over a period of time.

Practice

The most common method for committing information to memory is also the most mundane: practice. Does practice make perfect?

Practice is important at several stages of learning. As was noted earlier in this chapter, information received in working memory must be mentally rehearsed if it is to be retained for more than a few seconds. The information in working memory must usually be practiced until it is established in long-term memory (Willingham, 2004).

Distributed Practice is better than massed practice for retention
Distributed Practice is better than massed practice for retention
Distributed Practice is better than massed practice for retention
Distributed Practic
J. BRAVO

Massed and Distributed Practice Is it better to practice newly learned information intensively until it is thoroughly learned, a technique called **massed practice?** Or is it more effective to practice a little each day over a period of time—**distributed practice?** Massed practice allows for faster initial learning, but for most kinds of learning, distributed practice is better for retention, even over short time periods (Cepeda et al., 2006). This is especially true of factual learning (Willingham, 2002); cramming factual information the night before a test could get you through that test, but the information probably won't be well integrated into your long-term memory. Long-term retention of all kinds of information and skills is greatly enhanced by distributed practice. This is the primary purpose of homework: to provide practice on newly learned skills over an extended period of time to increase the chances that the skills will be retained.

Enactment Everyone knows that we learn by doing. It turns out that research on **enactment** supports this commonsense conclusion. That is, in learning how to perform tasks of many kinds, individuals learn much better if they are asked to enact the tasks (to physically carry them out) than if they simply read the instructions or watch a teacher enact the task (Cohen, 1989). For example, students learn much more from a lesson on drawing geometric solids (such as cubes and spheres) if they have an opportunity to draw some rather than simply watching the teacher do so.

HOW CAN MEMORY STRATEGIES BE TAUGHT?

Many of the things that students learn in school are facts that must be remembered. These form the framework on which more complex concepts depend. Factual material must be learned as efficiently and effectively as possible to leave time and mental energy for meaningful learning, such as problem-solving, conceptual, and creative activities. If students can memorize the routine things more efficiently, they can free their minds for tasks that involve understanding and reasoning. Some learning involves memorization of facts or of arbitrary associations between terms. For example, *pomme,* the French word for *apple,* is an arbitrary term associated with an object. The capital of Iowa could just as well have been called *Iowapolis* as *Des Moines.* Students often learn things as facts before they understand them as concepts or skills. For instance, students may learn the formula for the volume of a cylinder as an arbitrary fact long before they understand why the formula is what it is.

INTASC

4 Multiple Instructional Strategies

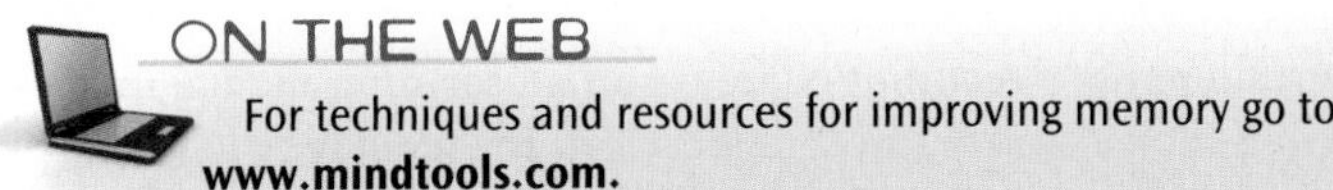

For techniques and resources for improving memory go to **www.mindtools.com.**

Verbal Learning

In many studies psychologists have examined **verbal learning,** or how students learn verbal materials, in laboratory settings (Ashcraft, 2006). For example, students might be asked to learn lists of words or nonsense syllables. Three types of verbal learning tasks that are typically seen in the classroom have been identified and studied extensively: the paired-associate learning task, the serial learning task, and the free-recall learning task.

1. **Paired-associate learning** involves learning to respond with one member of a pair when given the other member of the pair. Usually there is a list of pairs to be memorized. In typical experiments, the pairs are arbitrary. Educational examples of paired-associate tasks include learning the states' capitals, the names and dates of Civil War battles, the addition and multiplication tables, the atomic weights of the elements, and the spelling of words.
2. **Serial learning** involves learning a list of terms in a particular order. Memorization of the notes on the musical staff, the Pledge of Allegiance, the elements in atomic weight order, and poetry and songs are serial learning tasks. Serial learning tasks occur less often in classroom instruction than paired-associate tasks do.
3. **Free-recall learning** tasks also involve memorizing a list, but not in a special order. Recalling the names of the 50 states, types of reinforcements, kinds of poetic feet, and the organ systems in the body are examples of free-recall tasks.

The following sections describe these three verbal learning tasks in more detail.

enactment
A learning process in which individuals physically carry out tasks.

verbal learning
Learning of words (or facts expressed in words).

paired-associate learning
Learning of items in linked pairs so that when one member of a pair is presented, the other can be recalled.

serial learning
Memorization of a series of items in a particular order.

free-recall learning
Learning of a list of items in any order.

FIGURE 6.7 Example of the Use of Images to Aid Recall
An English-speaking student learning French can easily remember that the French word for fencing is *l'escrime* by linking it to the English word *scream* and picturing a fencer screaming.

Paired-Associate Learning

In paired-associate learning, the student must associate a response with each stimulus. For example, the student is given a picture of a bone (the stimulus) and must respond *tibia,* or is given the symbol *Au* and must respond *gold*. One important aspect of the learning of paired associates is the degree of familiarity the student already has with the stimuli and the responses. For example, it would be far easier to learn to associate foreign words with English words, such as *dog—chien* (French) or *dog—perro* (Spanish) than to learn to associate two foreign words, such as *chien—perro.*

Imagery Many powerful memory techniques are based on forming mental images to help remember associations. For example, the French word for fencing is *l'escrime,* pronounced "le scream." It is easy to remember this association (*fencing—l'escrime*) by forming a mental picture of a fencer screaming while being skewered by an opponent, as illustrated in Figure 6.7.

One ancient method of enhancing memory by use of **imagery** is the creation of stories to weave together information (Egan, 1989). For example, images from Greek myths and other sources have long been used to help people recall the constellations.

THEORY *into* PRACTICE

Keyword Mnemonics

One of the most extensively studied methods of using imagery and **mnemonics** (memory devices) to help paired-associate learning is the **keyword method,** which was originally developed for teaching foreign language vocabulary but was later applied to many other areas (Carney & Levin, 2002). The example used earlier of employing vivid imagery to recall the French word *l'escrime* is an illustration of the keyword method. In that case, the keyword was *scream.* It is called a keyword because it evokes the connection between the word *l'escrime* and the mental picture. The Russian word for building, *zdanie,* pronounced "zdan′-yeh,"

imagery
Mental visualization of images to improve memory.

mnemonics
Devices or strategies for aiding the memory.

keyword method
A strategy for improving memory by using images to link pairs of items.

might be recalled by using the keyword *dawn* and imagining the sun coming up behind a building with an onion dome on top. Atkinson and Raugh (1975) used this method to teach students a list of 120 Russian words over a 3-day period. Other students were given English translations of the Russian words and allowed to study as they wished. At the end of the experiment, the students who used the keyword method recalled 72 percent of the words, whereas the other students recalled only 46 percent. This result has been repeated dozens of times, using a wide variety of languages (e.g., Crutcher & Ericsson, 2003; Wyra, Lawson, & Hungi, 2007), with students from preschoolers to adults. However, young children seem to require pictures of the mental images they are meant to form, whereas older children (starting in upper elementary school) learn equally well making their own mental images (Willoughby, Porter, Belsito, & Yearsley, 1999). Furthermore, having students work in pairs or cooperative groups has been found to enhance vocabulary learning using mnemonic strategies (Jones, Levin, Levin, & Beitzel, 2000).

The images that are used in the keyword method work best if they are vivid and active, preferably involving interaction. For example, the German word for *room, zimmer* (pronounced "tsimmer"), might be associated with the keyword *simmer.* The German word would probably be better recalled by using an image of a distressed person in a bed immersed in a huge, steaming cauldron of water in a large bedroom than by using an image of a small pot of water simmering in the corner of a bedroom. The drama, action, and bizarreness of the first image make it memorable; the second is too commonplace to be easily recalled.

Similarly, Rummel, Levin, and Woodward (2002) showed students pictures to help them recall a link between various theorists of intelligence and their contributions. For example, to link Binet and measurement of higher mental processes, Rummel and colleagues showed students a race car driver protecting his *brain* with a *bonnet.* A review of many studies involving various mnemonic strategies found substantial positive effects, on average (Hattie, Bibbs, & Purdie, 1996). However, it should be noted that most of the research done on the use of mnemonic strategies has taken place under rather artificial, laboratory-like conditions, using materials that are thought to be especially appropriate for these strategies. Evaluations of actual classroom applications of these strategies show more mixed results, and there are questions about the long-term retention of material learned by means of keywords (Carney & Levin, 1998; Wang & Thomas, 1995).

Serial and Free-Recall Learning

Serial learning is learning facts in a particular order. Learning the events on a time line, learning the order of operations in long division, and learning the relative hardnesses of minerals are examples of serial learning. Free-recall learning is learning a list of items that need not be remembered in order, such as the names of the Canadian provinces.

Loci Method A mnemonic device for serial learning that was used by the ancient Greeks employs imagery associated with a list of locations (see Anderson, 2005). In the **loci method** the student thinks of a very familiar set of locations, such as rooms in her or his own house, and then imagines each item on the list to be remembered in one specific location. Vivid or bizarre imagery is used to place the item in the location. Once the connections between the item and the room or other location are established, the learner can recall each place and its contents in order. The same locations can be mentally cleared and used to memorize a different list. However, they should always be used in the same order to ensure that all items on the list were remembered.

loci method
A strategy for remembering lists by picturing items in familiar locations.

pegword method
A strategy for memorization in which images are used to link lists of facts to a familiar set of words or numbers.

Pegword Method Another imagery method useful for serial learning is called the **pegword method** (Krinsky & Krinsky, 1996). To use this mnemonic, the student might memorize a list of pegwords that rhyme with the numbers 1 to 10. To use this method, the student creates mental images relating to items on the list to be learned with particular pegwords. For example, in learning the order of the first 10 U.S. presidents, you might picture George Washington eating a bun (1) with his wooden teeth, John Adams tying his shoe (2), Thomas Jefferson hanging by his knees from a branch of a tree (3), and so on.

Initial-Letter Strategies One memory strategy that involves a reorganization of information is taking initial letters of a list to be memorized and making a more easily remembered word or phrase. For example, many trigonometry classes have learned about the imaginary SOHCAHTOA tribe, whose letters help us recall that sine = opposite/hypotenuse; cosine = adjacent/hypotenuse; tangent = opposite/adjacent. Many such **initial-letter strategies** exist for remembering the relative distances of the planets from the sun. The planets, in order, are Mercury, Venus, Earth, Mars, Jupiter, Saturn, Uranus, and Neptune. Students are taught a sentence in which the first letters of the words are the first letters of the planets in order, such as "My very educated monkey just served us nachos."

In a similar fashion, acronyms help people remember the names of organizations. Initial-letter strategies may also help students remember procedural knowledge, such as steps in a process.

WHAT MAKES INFORMATION MEANINGFUL?

Consider the following sentences:

1. Enso flrs hmen matn snoi teha erso iakt siae otin tnes esna nrae.
2. Easier that nonsense information to makes than sense is learn.
3. Information that makes sense is easier to learn than nonsense.

Which sentence is easiest to learn and remember? Obviously, sentence 3. All three sentences have the same letters, and sentences 2 and 3 have the same words. Yet to learn sentence 1, you would have to memorize 52 separate letters, and to learn sentence 2, you would have to learn 10 separate words. Sentence 3 is easiest because to learn it you need only learn one concept, a concept that readily fits your common sense and prior knowledge about how learning takes place. You know the individual words; you know the grammar that connects them; and you already have in your mind a vast store of information, experiences, and thoughts about the same topic. For these reasons, sentence 3 slides smoothly into your understanding.

The message in sentence 3 is what this chapter is all about. Most human learning, particularly school learning, involves making sense out of information, sorting it in our minds until it fits in a neat and orderly way, and using old information to help assimilate new learning. We have limited ability to recall rote information—how many telephone numbers can you remember for a month? However, we can retain meaningful information far more easily. Recall that most of the mnemonic strategies discussed in the previous section involve adding artificial meaning to arbitrary associations in order to take advantage of the much greater ease of learning meaningful information.

The message in sentence 3 has profound implications for instruction. One of the teacher's most important tasks is to make information meaningful to students by presenting it in a clear, organized way; by relating it to information already in students' minds; and by making sure that students have truly understood the concepts being taught and can apply them to new situations.

initial-letter strategies
Strategies for learning in which initial letters of items to be memorized are made into a more easily remembered word or phrase.

rote learning
Memorization of facts or associations that might be essentially arbitrary.

Rote versus Meaningful Learning

Ausubel (1963) discussed the distinction between rote learning and meaningful learning. **Rote learning** refers to the memorization of facts or associations, such as the multiplication tables, the chemical symbols for the elements, words in foreign languages, or the names of bones and muscles in the human body. Much of rote learning involves associations that are essentially arbitrary. For example, the chemical symbol for gold (*Au*) could just as well have been *Go* or *Gd.* In contrast, **meaningful learning** is not arbitrary, and it relates to information or concepts learners already have. For example, if we learn that silver is an excellent conductor of electricity, this information relates to our existing information about silver and about electrical conductivity. Further, the association between "silver" and "electrical conductivity" is not arbitrary. Silver really is an excellent conductor, and although we could state the same principle in many ways or in any language, the meaning of the statement "Silver is an excellent conductor of electricity" could not be arbitrarily changed.

INTASC

4 Multiple Instructional Strategies

Uses of Rote Learning We sometimes get the impression that rote learning is "bad" and meaningful learning is "good." This is not necessarily true. For example, when the doctor tells us we have a fractured *tibia,* we hope that the doctor has mastered the rote association between the word tibia and the leg bone it names. The mastery of foreign language vocabulary is an important case of rote learning. However, rote learning has gotten a bad name in education because it is overused. We can all remember being taught to parrot facts that were supposed to be meaningful but that we were forced to learn as rote, meaningless information. William James, in a book called *Talks to Teachers on Psychology* (1912), gave an excellent example of this kind of false learning:

> A friend of mine, visiting a school, was asked to examine a young class in geography. Glancing at the book, she said: "Suppose you should dig a hole in the ground, hundreds of feet deep, how should you find it at the bottom—warmer or colder than on top?" None of the class replying, the teacher said: "I'm sure they know, but I think you don't ask the question quite rightly. Let me try." So, taking the book, she asked: "In what condition is the interior of the globe?" and received the immediate answer from half the class at once. "The interior of the globe is in a condition of igneous fusion." (p. 150)

Clearly, the students had memorized the information without learning its meaning. The information was useless to them because it did not tie in with other information they had.

Inert Knowledge The "igneous fusion" information that students had memorized in the class James's friend visited is an example of what Bransford, Burns, Delclos, and Vye (1986) call **inert knowledge.** This is knowledge that could and should be applicable to a wide range of situations but is applied only to a restricted set of circumstances. Usually, inert knowledge consists of information or skills learned in school that we cannot apply in life. For example, you may know people who could pass an advanced French test but would be unable to communicate in Paris, or who can solve volume problems in math class but have no idea how much sand to order to fill a sandbox. Many problems in life arise not from a lack of knowledge but from an inability to use the knowledge we already have.

An interesting experiment by Perfetto, Bransford, and Franks (1983) illustrates the concept of inert knowledge. In the experiment, college students were given problems such as the following: "Uriah Fuller, the famous Israeli superpsychic, can tell you the score of any baseball game before the game starts. What is his secret?"

Before seeing the problems, some of the students were given a list of sentences to memorize that were clearly useful in solving the problems; among the sentences was "Before it starts, the score of any game is 0 to 0." Students who were told to use the sentences in their memories as clues performed much better on the problem-solving task than did other students, but students who memorized the clues but were not told to use them did no better than students who never saw the clues. What this experiment tells us is that having information in your memory does not guarantee that you can bring it out and use it when appropriate. Rather, you need to know how and when to use the information you have.

Teachers can help students learn information in a way that will make it useful as well as meaningful to them. Effective teaching requires an understanding of how to make information accessible to students so that they can connect it to other information, think about it, and apply it outside of the classroom (Willingham, 2003).

meaningful learning
Mental processing of new information that relates to previously learned knowledge.

inert knowledge
Learned information that could be applied to a wide range of situations but whose use is limited to restricted, often artificial, applications.

Schema Theory

As was noted earlier, meaningful information is stored in long-term memory in networks of connected facts or concepts called schemata. Recall the representation of the concept "bison" presented in Figure 6.3, showing how this one concept was linked to a wide range of other concepts. The most important principle of **schema theory** (Anderson, 2005; McVee, Dunsmore, & Gavelek, 2005) is that information that fits into an existing schema is more easily understood, learned, and retained than information that does not fit into an existing schema (Anderson & Bower, 1983). The sentence "Bison calves can run soon after they are born" is an example of information that will be easily incorporated into your "bison" schema because you know that (1) bison rely on speed to escape from predators, and (2) more familiar animals (such as horses) that also rely on speed have babies that can run very early. Without all this prior knowledge, "Bison calves can run soon after they are born" would be more difficult to assimilate mentally and more easily forgotten.

Hierarchies of Knowledge It is thought that most well-developed schemata are organized in hierarchies similar to outlines, with specific information grouped under general categories, which are grouped under still more general categories. Recall Figure 6.3. Note that in moving from the top to the bottom of the figure, you are going from general (animals and Native Americans) to specific (how Native Americans hunted bison). The concepts in the figure are well anchored in the schema. Any new information relating to this schema will probably be learned and incorporated into the schema much more readily than would information relating to less established schemata or rote learning that does not attach to any schema.

One important insight of schema theory is that meaningful learning requires the active involvement of the learner, who has a host of prior experiences and knowledge to bring to understanding and incorporating new information (Alexander, 1992). What you learn from any experience depends in large part on the schema you apply to the experience.

The Importance of Background Knowledge One of the most important determinants of how much you can learn about something is how much you already know about it (Alexander, Kulikowich, & Jetton, 1994, 1995; Schneider, 1993). A study in Japan by Kuhara-Kojima and Hatano (1991) illustrates this clearly. College students were taught information about baseball and music. Those who knew a great deal about baseball but not about music learned much more about baseball; the converse was true of those who knew a lot about music and little about baseball. In fact, background knowledge was much more important than general learning ability in predicting how much the students would learn. Learners who know a great deal about a subject have more well-developed schemata for incorporating new knowledge. Not surprisingly, interest in a given subject contributes to background knowledge in it, as well as depth of understanding and willingness to use background knowledge to solve new problems (Tobias, 1994). However, learners often do not spontaneously use their prior knowledge to help them learn new material. Teachers must link new learning to students' existing background knowledge (Bruning et al., 2004; Spires & Donley, 1998).

Teaching Dilemmas: CASES TO CONSIDER

Differing Approaches

Helen Baker and George Kowalski, both eleventh-grade U.S. history teachers, are talking in George's classroom after school. Helen has taught for 7 years and George for 21 years at Garfield High School, home of the current state high school basketball champions. Both teachers are members of the social studies department's curriculum committee, which is in the process of revising the U.S. history course.

schema theory
Theory stating that information is stored in long-term memory in schemata (networks of connected facts and concepts), which provide a structure for making sense of new information.

Helen: I wanted to talk to you about our disagreement about the curriculum revision. I thought that if you and I could work out our differences, maybe the committee would get out of the stalemate we're in.

George: Well, Helen, as I see it, you contend that students first need to master the facts of U.S. history before they can move on to higher-order thinking, like problem solving and working with abstract concepts. My view is just the reverse. For generations we've taught students facts, and they forget them right after the test is over. That's because we don't ask them to use the facts in higher-order thought. To me, that's the only way you can learn to think abstractly and solve problems.

Helen: But, George, trying to think abstractly and solve problems must be based on knowledge. Otherwise, problem solving is a pointless exercise—it amounts to a sharing of ignorance among the uninformed.

George: But I don't think that's as pointless as the other extreme—sticking to lecture and discussion and objective tests on key names, dates, terms, and events!

Helen: I know you use a lot of small-group and independent study work and give essay-type tests. I heard some students talking about how your questions really blew their minds. I think one was "What would the United States be like today if the South had won the Civil War?"

George (chuckling): Yes, that stirred them up a bit!

Helen: But, George, believe it or not, I've asked my students to write on that question from time to time when we're on the Civil War, and their answers were terrible—totally devoid of facts. The kids just wrote their opinions.

George: That's my point, Helen! Students have to learn how to use facts—and practice organizing and incorporating them into answers. Basketball players look terrible the first time they try a slam-dunk. But after they learn the technique, it's easy!

Helen: I think where we really disagree is on strategy. I maintain that learning the facts is the first step and higher-order thinking follows. You begin by posing problems and questions and hope that the kids will learn the facts to answer the questions. That seems like throwing kids into a lake and asking them to swim.

George: Sure, the facts and fundamentals are important, but in my experience, kids simply forget them. But if you compel kids to determine and then use the facts, they'll remember them long after the test. I'll bet some of the things they learn in my course are still with them when they're adults.

Helen: Well, George, I just can't see how we are going to reconcile our two positions. Can you?

INTASC

4 Multiple Instructional Strategies

QUESTIONS FOR REFLECTION

1. How do Helen's and George's positions differ on the nature of information processing, memory, and forgetting? What are the merits and drawbacks of each approach?
2. What does the latest brain-based research tell us that might help settle the argument between Helen and George?
3. Extend the dialogue with a third character who brings a problem-solving approach to the impasse.

HOW DO METACOGNITIVE SKILLS HELP STUDENTS LEARN?

The term **metacognition** means knowledge about one's own learning (McCormick, 2003) or about how to learn. Thinking skills and study skills are examples of **metacognitive skills.** Students can be taught strategies for assessing their own understanding, figuring out how much time they will need to study something, and choosing an effective plan of attack to study or solve problems (McCormick, 2003). For example, in reading this book, you are bound to come across a paragraph that you don't understand on first reading. What do you do? Perhaps you re-read the paragraph more slowly. Perhaps you look

metacognition
Knowledge about one's own learning or about how to learn ("thinking about thinking").

metacognitive skills
Methods for learning, studying, or solving problems.

for other clues, such as pictures, graphs, or glossary terms to help you understand. Perhaps you read further back in the chapter to see whether your difficulty arose because you did not fully understand something that came earlier. These are all examples of metacognitive skills; you have learned how to know when you are not understanding and how to correct yourself (Martinez, 2006; Schunk & Zimmerman, 1997). Another metacognitive strategy is the ability to predict what is likely to happen or to tell what is sensible and what is not. For example, when you first read the word *modeling* in Chapter 5, you knew right away that this did not refer to building models of ships or airplanes because you knew that meaning would not fit in the context of this book.

CONNECTIONS
The term *modeling* is discussed in Chapter 5, page 146, in relation to Bandura's social learning theory.

For an overview of metacognition visit **www.ncrel.org/sdrs/areas/issues/students/learning/lr1metn.htm.**

Although most students gradually do develop adequate metacognitive skills, some do not. Teaching metacognitive strategies to students can lead to a marked improvement in their achievement (Alexander, Graham, & Harris, 1998; Hattie et al., 1996). Students can learn to think about their own thinking processes and apply specific learning strategies to think themselves through difficult tasks (Butler & Winne, 1995; Pressley, Harris, & Marks, 1992; Schunk, 2000). **Self-questioning strategies** are particularly effective (Zimmerman, 1998). In self-questioning, students look for common elements in a given type of task and ask themselves questions about these elements. For example, many researchers (e.g., Dimino, Gersten, Carnine, & Blake, 1990; Stevens, Madden, Slavin, & Farnish, 1987) have taught students to look for characters, settings, problems, and problem solutions in stories. Instructors start with specific questions and then let students find these critical elements on their own. Paris, Cross, and Lipson (1984) and King (1992) found that students comprehended better if they were taught to ask themselves *who, what, where,* and *how* questions as they read. Englert, Raphael, Anderson, Anthony, and Stevens (1991) gave students planning sheets to help them plan creative writing. Among the questions students were taught to ask themselves were: For whom am I writing? What is being explained? What are the steps? Essentially, students are taught to talk themselves through the activities they are engaged in, asking themselves or each other the questions a teacher would ask. Students have been successfully taught to talk themselves through mathematics problem solving (Cardelle-Elawar, 1990), spelling (Block & Peskowitz, 1990), creative writing (Zellermayer, Salomon, Globerson, & Givon, 1991), reading (Chin, 1998; Kucan & Beck, 1997), and many other subjects (see Chan, Burtis, Scardamalia, & Bereiter, 1992; Guthrie, Bennett, & Weber, 1991; McInerney & McInerney, 1998).

VIDEO HOMEWORK EXERCISE
Early and Middle Childhood Early and Late Adolescence and Early and Late Adolescence

Go to **www.myeducationlab.com** and, in the Homework and Exercises section for Chapter 6 of this text, access the videos entitled "Early and Middle Childhood Early and Late Adolescence" and "Early and Late Adolescence." Watch the videos and complete the homework questions that accompany them, saving your work or transmitting it to your professor as required.

WHAT STUDY STRATEGIES HELP STUDENTS LEARN?

INTASC

4 Multiple Instructional Strategies

How are you reading this book? Are you underlining or highlighting key sentences? Are you taking notes or summarizing? Are you discussing the main ideas with a classmate? Are you putting the book under your pillow at night and hoping the information will somehow seep into your mind? Students have used these and many other strategies ever since the invention of reading, and such strategies have been studied almost as long. Even Aristotle wrote on the topic. Yet educational psychologists are still debating which study strategies are most effective (see Mayer, 1996; Pressley, Yokoi, Van Meter, van Etten, & Freebern, 1997).

Research on effective study strategies is confusing at best. Few forms of studying are found to be always effective, and fewer still are never effective. Clearly, the value of study strategies depends on their specifics and on the uses to which they are put (Weinstein &

self-questioning strategies
Learning strategies that call on students to ask themselves who, what, where, and how questions as they read material.

Hume, 1998; Zimmerman, 1998). Research on the most common study strategies is summarized in the following sections.

Note-Taking

A common study strategy that is used both in reading and in learning from lectures is **note-taking.** Note-taking can be effective for certain types of material because it can require mental processing of main ideas as one makes decisions about what to write. However, the effects of note-taking have been found to be inconsistent. Positive effects are most likely when note-taking is used for complex conceptual material in which the critical task is to identify the main ideas (Rickards, Fajen, Sullivan, & Gillespie, 1997). Also, note-taking that requires some mental processing is more effective than simply writing down what was read (Kiewra, 1991; Kiewra et al., 1991; Slotte & Lonka, 1999). For example, Bretzing and Kulhavy (1981) found that writing paraphrase notes (stating the main ideas in different words) and taking notes in preparation to teach others the material were effective note-taking strategies because they required a high degree of mental processing of the information.

One apparently effective means of increasing the value of students' note-taking is for the teacher to provide partial notes before a lecture or reading, giving students categories to direct their own note-taking. Several studies have found that this practice, combined with student note-taking and review, increases student learning (Robinson et al., 2004).

Underlining

Perhaps the most common study strategy is underlining or highlighting. Yet despite the widespread use of this method, research on underlining generally finds few benefits (Anderson & Armbruster, 1984; Gaddy, 1998; Snowman, 1984). The problem is that most students fail to make decisions about what material is most critical and simply underline too much. When students are asked to underline the one sentence in each paragraph that is most important, they do retain more, probably because deciding which is the most important sentence requires a higher level of processing (Snowman, 1984).

Summarizing

Summarizing involves writing brief statements that represent the main ideas of the information being read. The effectiveness of this strategy depends on how it is used (King, 1991; Slotte & Lonka, 1999). One effective way is to have students write one-sentence summaries after reading each paragraph (Wittrock, 1991). Another is to have students prepare summaries that are intended to help others learn the material—partly because this activity forces the summarizer to be brief and to consider seriously what is important and what is not (Brown, Bransford, Ferrara, & Campione, 1983). However, it is important to note that several studies have found no effects of summarization, and the conditions under which this strategy increases comprehension or retention of written material are not well understood (Wittrock, 1991; Wittrock & Alesandrini, 1990).

Writing to Learn

A growing body of evidence supports the idea that having students explain in writing the content they are learning helps them understand and remember it (Klein, 1999). For example, Fellows (1994) had sixth-graders in a 12-week science unit on states of matter write about their understandings of the concepts at several points in the unit. A control group studied the same content without writing. The writing group retained substantially more of the content at post-test. This and other studies find that focused writing assignments help children learn the content about which they are writing. However, evidence is much more mixed regarding the effects of less focused "journal writing," in which students keep logs of their ideas and observations.

note-taking
A study strategy that requires decisions about what to write.

summarizing
Writing brief statements that represent the main idea of the information being read.

Outlining and Mapping

A related family of study strategies requires the student to represent the material studied in skeletal form. These strategies include outlining, networking, and mapping. **Outlining** presents the main points of the material in a hierarchical format, with each detail organized under a higher-level category. In networking and **mapping,** students identify main ideas and then diagram connections between them (Hyerle, 1995; Robinson & Skinner, 1996). For example, the schematic representation of the concept "bison" shown in Figure 6.3 might have been produced by students themselves as a network to summarize factual material about bison and their importance to Plains Indians (see Clark, 1990; Rafoth, Leal, & De Fabo, 1993).

Research on outlining, networking, and mapping is limited and inconsistent but generally finds that these methods are helpful as study aids (Katayama & Robinson, 1998; Robinson & Kiewra, 1995).

CERTIFICATION POINTER

When responding to the case studies in certification tests, you may be asked to design a lesson that includes strategies for helping students learn relationships between ideas using concept mapping.

The PQ4R Method

One of the best-known study techniques for helping students understand and remember what they read is a procedure called the **PQ4R method** (Thomas & Robinson, 1972), which is based on an earlier version known as SQ3R, developed by F. P. Robinson (1961). The acronym stands for *preview, question, read, reflect, recite,* and *review.*

Research has shown the effectiveness of the PQ4R method for older children (Adams, Carnine, & Gersten, 1982), and the reasons seem clear. Following the PQ4R procedure focuses students on the meaningful organization of information and involves them in other effective strategies, such as question generation, elaboration, and distributed practice (opportunities to review information over a period of time) (Anderson, 1990).

CLASSROOM ARTIFACT HOMEWORK EXERCISE
Thank You Note

Go to **www.myeducationlab.com** and, in the Homework and Exercises section for Chapter 6 of this text, access the Classroom Artifact entitled "Thank You Note." Watch the video and complete the homework questions that accompany it, saving your work or transmitting it to your professor as required.

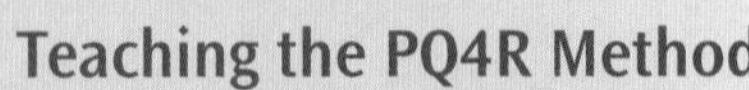

Teaching the PQ4R Method

Explain and model the steps of the PQ4R method for your students, using the following guidelines:

1. ***Preview.*** Survey or scan the material quickly to get an idea of the general organization and major topics and subtopics. Pay attention to headings and subheadings, and identify what you will be reading about and studying.
2. ***Question.*** Ask yourself questions about the material before you read it. Use headings to invent questions using the *wh* words: *who, what, why, where.*
3. ***Read.*** Read the material. Do not take extensive written notes. Try to answer the questions that you posed prior to reading.
4. ***Reflect on the material.*** Try to understand and make meaningful the presented information by (1) relating it to things you already know, (2) relating the subtopics in the text to primary concepts or principles, (3) trying to resolve contradictions within the presented information, and (4) trying to use the material to solve problems suggested by the material.
5. ***Recite.*** Practice remembering the information by stating points out loud and asking and answering questions. You may use headings, highlighted words, and notes on major ideas to generate those questions.
6. ***Review.*** In the final step, actively review the material, focusing on asking yourself questions; re-read the material only when you are not sure of the answers.

outlining
Representing the main points of material in hierarchical format.

mapping
Diagramming main ideas and the connections between them.

PQ4R method
A study strategy that has students preview, question, read, reflect, recite, and review material.

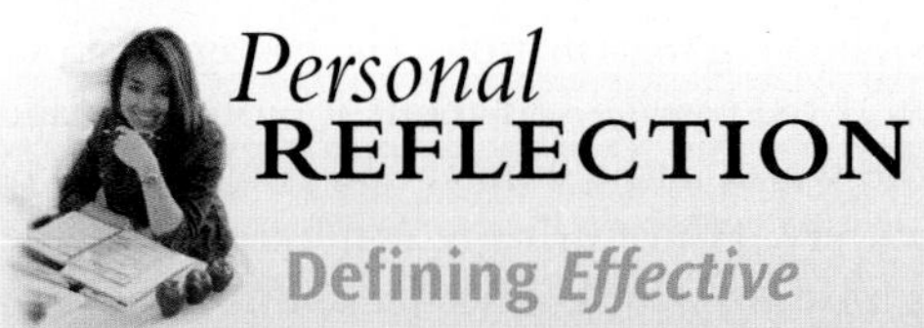

Personal REFLECTION

Defining *Effective*

On a recent trip to China, I visited four schools of education in different parts of the country. In each of these universities, I saw a remarkable phenomenon. Early each morning, students would distribute themselves outside, on benches or on the grass or, often, standing up, and would read their assignments out loud, all by themselves. I heard students at one university reading an English assignment that was a dialogue that happened to explain what they were doing—it stated that to get ahead in life, one must study hard by reading assignments out loud, repeating each section three times.

Is this widespread Chinese study strategy in fact effective? I don't know. It seemed to me that it would have made a lot more sense for the students to read to each other and give each other feedback, rather than simply read to the air. Yet the usual alternative, in North American and European universities I've visited, is silent study, not paired study.

Studying is at the core of the educational experience, so much so that we often take it for granted. We know something about how to help students maximize the effectiveness of their studying, but I think we should know a great deal more. Perhaps three times out loud has real advantages. Wouldn't it be interesting to evaluate?

REFLECT ON THIS. Make a case for why the Chinese method for processing information might be effective. In studying for your classes, do you memorize or do you learn? What have you found to be the best way for you to learn new information and retain it?

HOW DO COGNITIVE TEACHING STRATEGIES HELP STUDENTS LEARN?

INTASC

3. Adapting Instruction for Individual Needs
4. Multiple Instructional Strategies
6. Communication Skills

In *Alice's Adventures in Wonderland* the White Rabbit is unsure how to give his evidence in the trial of the Knave of Hearts. The King of Hearts gives him a bit of advice: "Begin at the beginning . . . and go on until you come to the end: then stop." The "King of Hearts method" is a common means of delivering lectures, especially at the secondary and college levels. However, teachers can do more to help their students understand lessons. They can prepare students to learn new material by reminding them of what they already know, asking questions, and helping students link and recall new information (Carver & Klahr, 2001; McCormick, 2003). Many aspects of effective lesson presentation are covered in Chapter 7; but the following sections discuss practices derived from cognitive psychology that can help students understand, recall, and apply essential information, concepts, and skills.

CONNECTIONS
See, for example, "How Is a Direct Instruction Lesson Taught?" in Chapter 7, page 200.

Making Learning Relevant and Activating Prior Knowledge

Read the following passage:

> With the hocked gems financing him our hero bravely defied all scornful laughter that tried to prevent his scheme. Your eyes deceive he had said. An egg, not a table, correctly typifies this unexplored planet. Now three sturdy sisters sought proof. Forging along, sometimes through calm vastness, yet more often through turbulent peaks and valleys, days became weeks as many doubters spread fearful rumors about the edge. At last, from nowhere, welcome winged creatures appeared signifying momentous success. (Dooling & Lachman, 1971, p. 217)

Now read the paragraph again with the following information: The passage is about Christopher Columbus. Before you knew what the passage was about, it probably made little sense to you. You could understand the words and grammar and could probably infer that the story involved a voyage of discovery. However, once you learned that the story was about Columbus, you could bring all your prior knowledge about Columbus to bear on comprehending the paragraph, so that seemingly obscure references made sense. The "hocked gems" (Queen Isabella's jewelry), the egg (the shape of the earth), the three sturdy sisters (the *Niña, Pinta,* and *Santa Maria*), and the winged creatures (birds) become comprehensible when you know what the story is about.

In terms of schema theory, advance information that the story concerns Columbus activates your schema relating to Columbus. You are ready to receive and incorporate information relating to Columbus, to Isabella and Ferdinand, and to the ships. It is as though you had a filing cabinet with a drawer labeled "Columbus." When you know you are about to hear about Columbus, you mentally open the drawer, which contains files marked "Isabella," "ships," and "scoffers and doubters." You are now ready to file new information in the proper places. If you learned that the *Santa Maria* was wrecked in a storm, you would mentally file that information in the "ships" file. If you learned that most of the educated world agreed with Columbus that the earth was round, you would file that information in the "scoffers and doubters" file. The file drawer analogy is not completely appropriate, however, because the files of a schema are all logically connected with one another. Also, you are actively using the information in your files to interpret and organize the new information.

Advance Organizers David Ausubel (1963) developed a method called **advance organizers** to orient students to material they were about to learn and to help them recall related information that could assist them in incorporating the new information. An advance organizer is an initial statement about a subject to be learned that provides a structure for the new information and relates it to information students already possess (Joyce, Weil, & Calhoun, 2000). For example, in one study (Ausubel & Youssef, 1963), college students were assigned to read a passage on Buddhism. Before reading the passage, some students were given an advance organizer comparing Buddhism to Christianity, whereas others read an unrelated passage. The students who were given the advance organizer retained much more of the material than did the other students. Ausubel and Youssef maintained that the reason for this was that the advance organizer activated most students' knowledge of Christianity, and the students were able to use that knowledge to incorporate information about a less familiar religion.

advance organizers
Activities and techniques that orient students to the material before reading or class presentation.

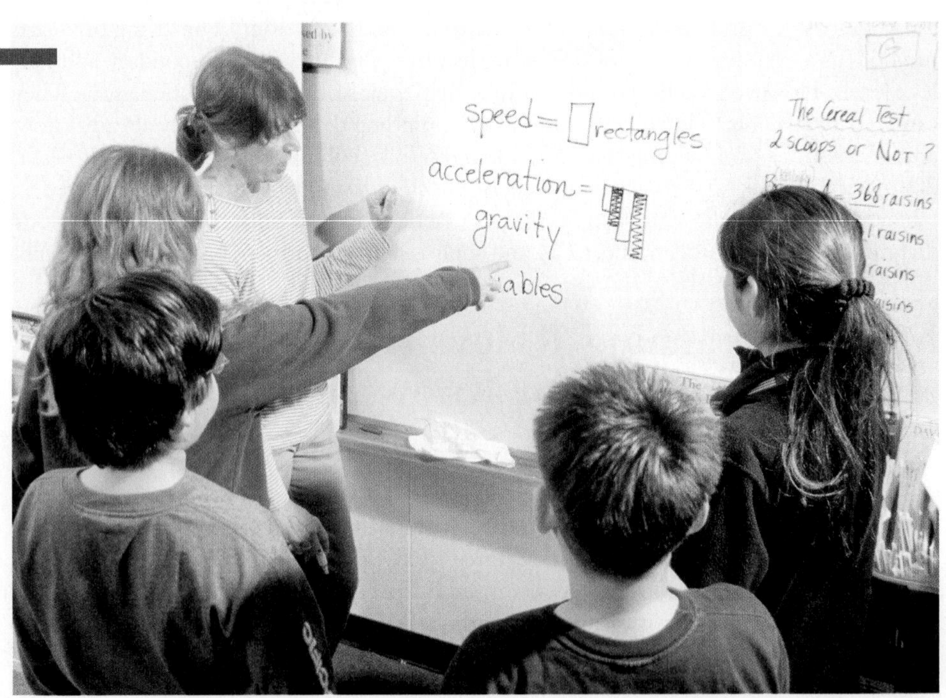

Using advance organizers with students can help activate their prior knowledge before an assignment or lesson. With what types of materials and in what situations do advance organizers work best?

Many studies have established that advance organizers increase students' understanding of certain kinds of material (see Corkill, 1992; Schwartz, Ellsworth, Graham, & Knight, 1998). Advance organizers seem to be most useful for teaching content with a well-organized structure that might not be immediately apparent to students. However, they have not generally been found to help students learn factual information that does not lend itself to a clear organization or subjects that consist of a large number of separate topics (Ausubel, 1978; Corkill, 1992). In addition, methods designed to activate prior knowledge, such as advance organizers, can be counterproductive if the prior knowledge is weak or lacking (Alvermann et al., 1985). If students know little about Christianity, relating Buddhism to Christianity may confuse rather than help them.

The use of advance organizers is a valuable strategy in its own right, but research on advance organizers also illustrates a broader principle that is extremely important: Activating prior knowledge enhances understanding and retention (Pressley et al., 1992). Strategies other than advance organizers draw on this same principle. For example, having students discuss what they already know about a topic before they learn it (Pressley, Tannenbaum, McDaniel, & Wood, 1990) and having them make predictions about material to be learned (Fielding, Anderson, & Pearson, 1990) are additional ways to encourage students to make conscious use of prior knowledge.

CERTIFICATION POINTER

On a teacher certification test, you may be asked to propose a strategy for stimulating the prior knowledge of students described in a particular case.

Analogies Like advance organizers, use of explanatory analogies (comparisons or parallels) can contribute to understanding by linking new information to well-established background knowledge. For example, a teacher could introduce a lesson on the human body's disease-fighting mechanisms by telling students to imagine a battle and to consider it as an analogy for the body's fight against infection. Similarly, a teacher could preface a lesson on termite societies by asking students to think of the hierarchy of citizens within a kingdom, using that as an analogy for such insect societies. **Analogies** can help students learn new information by relating it to concepts they already know (Bulgren, Deshler, Schumaker, & Lenz, 2000; McDaniel & Dannelly, 1996).

One interesting study (Halpern, Hansen, & Riefer, 1990) found that analogies work best when they are most different from the process being explained. For example, college students' learning about the lymph system was aided more by an analogy of the movement of water through a sponge than by one involving the movement of blood through veins. What this probably illustrates is that it is more important that analogies be thoroughly familiar to the learner than that they relate in any direct way to the concepts being taught.

Elaboration Cognitive psychologists use the term **elaboration** to refer to the process of thinking about material to be learned in a way that connects the material to information or ideas that are already in the learner's mind (Ayaduray & Jacobs, 1997). As an example of the importance of elaboration, Stein, Littlefield, Bransford, and Persampieri (1984) conducted a series of experiments in which students were given lists of phrases to learn, such as "The gray-haired man carried the bottle." Some students were given the same phrases embedded in a more elaborate sentence, such as "The gray-haired man carried the bottle of hair dye." These latter students recalled the phrases much better than did those who did not receive the elaboration because the additional words tied the phrase to a well-developed schema that was already in the students' minds. The connection between *gray-haired man* and *bottle* is arbitrary until we give it meaning by linking these words with the *hair dye* idea.

Teachers can apply this principle—that elaborated information is easier to understand and remember—to helping students comprehend lessons. Students may be asked to think of connections between ideas or to relate new concepts to their own lives. For example, it might help students to understand the U.S. annexation of Texas and California if they consider these events from the perspective of Mexicans or if they compare the events to a situation in which a friend borrows a bicycle and then decides not to give it back. In discussing a story or novel, a teacher might ask students from time to time to stop and visualize what is happening or what's about to happen as a means of helping them to elaborate their understanding of the material. Elaboration can be taught as a skill to help students comprehend what they read (Willoughby, Porter, Belsito, & Yearsley, 1999).

analogies
Images, concepts, or narratives that compare new information to information students already understand.

elaboration
The process of connecting new material to information or ideas already in the learner's mind.

Organizing Information

Recall the shopping list discussed earlier in this chapter. When the list was presented in random order, it was very difficult to memorize, partly because it contained too many items to be held in working memory all at once. However, when the list was organized in a logical way, it was meaningful and therefore easy to learn and remember. The specific foods were grouped according to familiar recipes (e.g., flour, eggs, and milk were grouped under "pancakes"); and the recipes and other foods were grouped under "breakfast," "lunch," and "dinner."

Material that is well organized is much easier to learn and remember than material that is poorly organized (Durso & Coggins, 1991). Hierarchical organization, in which specific issues are grouped under more general topics, seems particularly helpful for student understanding. For example, in a classic study by Bower, Clark, Lesgold, and Winzenz (1969), one group of students was taught 112 words relating to minerals in random order. Another group was taught the same words, but in a definite order. Figure 6.8 shows the hierarchy within which the words were organized. The students were taught the words at levels 1 and 2 in the first of four sessions; those at levels 1, 2, and 3 in the second session; and those at levels 1 through 4 in the third and fourth sessions. The students in this second group recalled an average of 100 words, in comparison to only 65 for the group that received the random presentation—demonstrating the effectiveness of a coherent, organized presentation. In teaching complex concepts, not only is it necessary that material be well organized but it is also important that the organizing framework itself be made clear to students (Kallison, 1986). For example, in teaching about the minerals shown in Figure 6.8, the teacher might refer frequently to the framework and mark transitions from one part of it to another, as follows:

"Recall that alloys are combinations of two or more metals."

"Now that we've covered rare and common metals and alloys, let's move on to the second category of minerals: stones."

Using Questioning Techniques One strategy that helps students learn from written texts, lectures, and other sources of information is the insertion of questions requiring

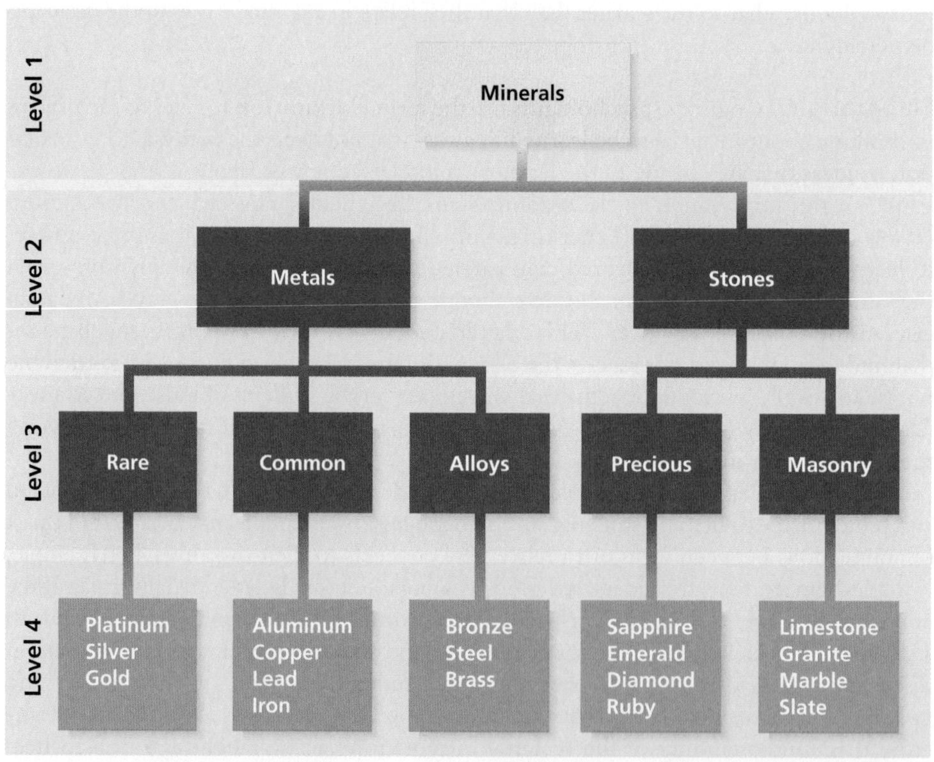

FIGURE 6.8 The Hierarchical Structure for Minerals

From "Hierarchical Retrieval Schemes in Recall of Categorized Word Lists" by G. H. Bower et al., from *Journal of Verbal Learning and Verbal Behavior*, Volume 8, 323–343. Copyright © 1969. Reprinted by permission of Elsevier.

students to stop from time to time to assess their own understanding of what the text or teacher is saying (Pressley et al., 1990). Presenting questions before the introduction of the instructional material can also help students learn material related to the questions, as can having students generate their own questions (Rosenshine, Meister, & Chapman, 1996).

Using Conceptual Models Another means that teachers can use to help students comprehend complex topics is the introduction of conceptual models, or diagrams showing how elements of a process relate to one another. Figure 6.1, which illustrates information processing, is a classic example of a conceptual model. Use of such models organizes and integrates information. Examples of topics that lend themselves to use of conceptual models are electricity, mechanics, computer programming, and the processes by which laws are passed. When models are part of a lesson, not only do students learn more but they also are better able to apply their learning to creatively solve problems (see Hiebert, Wearne, & Taber, 1991; Mayer & Gallini, 1990; Winn, 1991). Knowledge maps, a variation on conceptual models, can be used to teach a wider variety of content. A knowledge map graphically shows the main concepts of a topic of study and the links between them. Giving students knowledge maps after a lesson has been shown to increase their retention of the lesson's content (Nesbit & Adesope, 2006; O'Donnell, Dansereau, & Hall, 2002).

Graphs, charts, tables, matrices, and other means of organizing information into a comprehensible, visual form, have all been found to aid comprehension, memory, and transfer (Carney & Levin, 2002; Shah, Mayer, & Hegarty, 1999). However, these devices lose their effectiveness if they contain too much information that is not quickly communicated by the visuals (Butcher, 2006; Schnotz, 2002; Vekiri, 2002). Atkinson et al. (1999) described a method to confront this problem by combining mnemonics with tables. To teach about the characteristics of various sharks, teachers made tables in which humorous pictures linked the names of the sharks with their characteristics. For example, dogfish sharks live near shore in moderate depth and have sawlike teeth, so the mnemonic showed dogs emerging from a submarine in shallow water holding saws to cut down a "No Dogs Allowed" sign on shore. Fifth-graders retained much more about the characteristics of nine sharks using this method than did students who saw other kinds of displays.

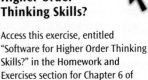

ONLINE READING & WRITING EXERCISE

Software for Higher Order Thinking Skills?

Access this exercise, entitled "Software for Higher Order Thinking Skills?" in the Homework and Exercises section for Chapter 6 of this text at **www.mylabschool.com.**

CHAPTER 6 SUMMARY

What Is an Information-Processing Model?

The three major components of memory are the sensory register, short-term or working memory, and long-term memory. The sensory registers are very short-term memories linked to the senses. Information that is received by the senses but not attended to will be quickly forgotten. Once information is received, it is processed by the mind in accord with our experiences and mental states. This activity is called perception.

Short-term or working memory is a storage system that holds five to nine bits of information at any one time. Information enters working memory from both the sensory register and the long-term memory. Rehearsal is the process of repeating information in order to hold it in working memory.

Long-term memory is the part of the memory system in which a large amount of information is stored for an indefinite time period. Cognitive theories of learning stress the importance of helping students relate information being learned to existing information in long-term memory.

The three parts of long-term memory are episodic memory, which stores our memories of personal experiences; semantic memory, which stores facts and generalized knowledge in the form of schemata; and procedural memory, which stores knowledge of how to do things. Schemata are networks of related ideas that guide our understanding and action. Information that fits into a well-developed schema is easier to learn than

The Intentional TEACHER

USING WHAT YOU KNOW about Cognitive Theories of Learning to Improve Teaching and Learning

Intentional teachers know how information is received, processed, and stored in memory. They demonstrate that teaching is more than telling; they help students connect new information with what they already know, and encourage students to apply information in other contexts. Incorporating research findings about cognition into the classroom allows intentional teachers to help students build lasting and meaningful understandings.

1 What do I expect my students to know and be able to do at the end of this lesson? How does this contribute to course objectives and to students' needs to become capable individuals?

Meaningful information tends to be remembered best. Review your goals and objectives to ensure that you plan for meaningful learning.

For example, if you are teaching about the human body, you might make sure to focus on functions and connections among organs, not only identification. If you are teaching about parts of speech, you might ask students to generate their own examples of sentences using adjectives or adverbs, not only locate adjectives and adverbs in sentences you create.

2 What knowledge, skills, needs, and interests do my students have that must be taken into account in my lesson?

The more students know about a subject, the better they can organize and relate new information. Find out what your students already know about the topics you study.

In your history class, you might begin a unit on the Vietnam War by spending a period charting what students already know about the war. Recognizing that emotion and personal meaning and relevance can help students process information deeply so that they can remember better, you might invite them to share personal stories of family members who might have participated in that combat.

For your science unit on sea life, you might determine in the initial class session that your students are fascinated by whales. You might discuss with them how scientists differentiate among species of whales and help them generate a list of characteristics common to all whales that vary according to the species. You could guide their selection of categories to assure that they list relevant characteristics and give them a reading passage from the text as homework, asking them to write down the questions that come to their minds as they read for discussion in the next session.

3 What do I know about the content, child development, learning, motivation, and effective teaching strategies that I can use to accomplish my objectives?

To make information meaningful and memorable, you should engage students in using new knowledge and skills to create their own new products. In teaching a foreign language, for instance, you might have students make up their own sentences and dialogues using new vocabulary or verb forms. For example, you might ask students in teams to make up gossip about

information that cannot be so accommodated. Levels-of-processing theory suggests that learners will remember only the things that they process. Students are processing information when they manipulate it, look at it from different perspectives, and analyze it. Dual code theory further suggests the importance of using both visual and verbal coding to learn bits of information.

Research on the Brain

Technology that enables scientists to observe the brain in action has led to rapid advances in brain science. Findings have shown how specific parts of the brain process specific types of information in concert with other specific brain sites. As individuals gain expertise, their brain function becomes more efficient. Early brain development is a process of adding neural connections and then sloughing off those that are not used. Neuroscience is discovering much about how the brain operates, but this research does not yet have direct applications to teaching.

What Causes People to Remember or Forget?

Interference theory helps explain why people forget. It suggests that students can forget information when it gets mixed up with, or pushed aside by, other information. Interference theory states that two situations cause forgetting: retroactive inhibition, when learning a second task makes a person forget something that was learned previously, and proactive inhibition, when learning one thing interferes with the retention of things learned later. The primacy and recency effects state that people best remember

INTASC 8 Assessment of Student Learning
9 Professional Commitment and Responsibility

a boy, a girl, a couple, a group of girls, and a school principal, enabling them to use different pronouns, verbs, and adjectives in realistic contexts.

4 What instructional materials, technology, assistance, and other resources are available to help accomplish my objectives?

Schema theory suggests that new information is added to existing networks of connected ideas. With the computer lab teacher, you might explore software for diagramming information and for building data bases. You could plan to demonstrate the use of these programs and then provide follow-up lab time or classroom opportunities for the students to make use of these tools to develop materials for their portfolios in appropriate content areas. Many current software programs allow inclusion of visual as well as verbal material, addressing more than one form of information processing and encouraging students to think about and monitor their learning of the material being manipulated.

5 How will I plan to assess students' progress toward my objectives?

Students need to demonstrate different kinds of understanding: rote learning, meaningful learning, and the ability to use information in new contexts. Give them tasks that allow you to check for different uses of knowledge: Are they forgetting? Are they transferring? Are they applying? Adjust your instruction based on your results. For example, as the teacher of an advanced foreign language class, you could assess students' recall of vocabulary terms, their ability to describe rules and structures of the language, and their ability to communicate in the language you are teaching. You might find that students have good recall of vocabulary but struggle with expressing their own thoughts, so you could plan for opportunities for them to speak in simulated realistic contexts, such as a party, a restaurant, an airport, or a picnic.

6 How will I respond if individual children or the class as a whole are not on track toward success? What is my back-up plan?

Students demonstrate success when they show they can control their own learning. Check to see that students use self-questioning strategies and metacognition to assess their own learning. For example, before you hand your fourth-graders a reading passage on reptiles, you might prompt them to ask themselves questions as they read and suggest they record their findings. After they complete the passage, you could ask them which sections of text were difficult and what they do when they encounter difficult text. Their answers tell you how far they have progressed toward actively monitoring their own learning.

information that is presented first and last in a series. Automaticity is gained by practicing information or skills far beyond the amount needed to establish them in long-term memory so that using such skills requires little or no mental effort. Practice strengthens associations of newly learned information in memory. Distributed practice, which involves practicing parts of a task over a period of time, is usually more effective than massed practice. Enactment also helps students to remember information.

How Can Memory Strategies Be Taught?

Teachers can help students remember facts by presenting lessons in an organized way and by teaching students to use memory strategies called mnemonics. Three types of verbal learning are paired-associate learning, serial learning, and free-recall learning. Paired-associate learning is learning to respond with one member of a pair when given the other member. Students can improve their learning of paired associates by using imagery techniques such as the keyword method. Serial learning involves recalling a list of items in a specified order. Free-recall learning involves recalling the list in any order. Helpful strategies are the loci method, the pegword method, rhyming, and initial-letter strategies.

What Makes Information Meaningful?

Information that makes sense and has significance to students is more meaningful than inert knowledge and information learned by rote. According to schema theory, individuals' meaningful knowledge is constructed of networks and hierarchies of schemata.

How Do Metacognitive Skills Help Students Learn?

Metacognition helps students learn by thinking about, controlling, and effectively using their own thinking processes.

What Study Strategies Help Students Learn?

Note-taking, selective directed underlining, summarizing, writing to learn, outlining, and mapping can effectively promote learning. The PQ4R method is an example of a strategy that focuses on the meaningful organization of information.

How Do Cognitive Teaching Strategies Help Students Learn?

Advance organizers help students process new information by activating background knowledge. Analogies, information elaboration, organizational schemes, questioning techniques, and conceptual models are other examples of teaching strategies that are based on cognitive learning theories.

KEY TERMS

Review the following key terms from the chapter.

advance organizers 188
analogies 189
attention 160
automaticity 175
distributed practice 176
dual code theory of memory 167
elaboration 189
enactment 177
episodic memory 163
flashbulb memory 164
free-recall learning 177
imagery 178
inert knowledge 181
information-processing theory 158
initial-letter strategies 180
interference 173
keyword method 178
levels-of-processing theory 167
loci method 179
long-term memory 163
mapping 186
massed practice 176
meaningful learning 181
metacognition 183
metacognitive skills 183
mnemonics 178
note-taking 185
outlining 186
paired-associate learning 177
pegword method 179
perception 160
PQ4R method 186
primacy effect 175
proactive facilitation 174
proactive inhibition 174
procedural memory 164
recency effect 175
rehearsal 161
retroactive facilitation 174
retroactive inhibition 173
rote learning 180
schemata 164
schema theory 182
self-questioning strategies 184
semantic memory 163
sensory register 159
serial learning 177
short-term memory 161
summarizing 185
verbal learning 177
working memory 161

SELF-ASSESSMENT: PRACTICING *for* LICENSURE

Directions: The chapter-opening vignette addresses indicators that are often assessed in state licensure exams. Re-read the chapter-opening vignette, and then respond to the following questions.

1. According to information-processing theory, which component of the memory system did Verona Bishop's students first use during the 3-second experiment?
   - **a.** sensory register
   - **b.** short-term memory
   - **c.** working memory
   - **d.** long-term memory

2. Verona Bishop asks her students, "[I]magine that you could keep everything that ever entered your mind. What would that be like?" One student responds, "You'd be a genius!" Another responds, "You'd go crazy!" Why does Ms. Bishop side with the second student?
   - **a.** Genius is an inherited trait not associated with memory.
   - **b.** There is no correlation between genius and paying attention to environmental clues.
   - **c.** Being bombarded with too much information at once decreases learning.
   - **d.** People with mental illness absorb more environmental information than do people without mental illness.

3. During the 3-second memory experiment, Verona Bishop asks her students to recall things not associated with the overhead information she presented. What type of memory are students using when they recall smells, sounds, and details of the classroom and the people in it?
   - **a.** semantic memory
   - **b.** procedural memory
   - **c.** dual-code memory
   - **d.** episodic memory

4. Cheryl, one of Verona Bishop's students, recalled seeing the word *learning* on the overhead screen, even though it was not there. How does Ms. Bishop explain this phenomenon?
   - **a.** Ms. Bishop actually said the word during the 3-second experiment, so Cheryl picked it up there.
   - **b.** Humans have a tendency to learn the first and last bits of information presented, so Cheryl thought of the word *learning* after the 3-second experiment.
   - **c.** *Learning* and *memory,* a word that was actually presented, are closely related and most likely stored closely together in memory. When one is recalled, so is the other.
   - **d.** Because the students had only 3 seconds to review the information, Cheryl's report of what she remembered contained guesses.

5. Consider that some of Verona Bishop's students attempted to memorize the information on the overhead screen in a random fashion. Which of the following learning strategies are they using?
   - **a.** free-recall learning
   - **b.** serial learning
   - **c.** paired-associate learning
   - **d.** process learning

6. Verona Bishop summarizes her experiment by telling her students that they will forget some details of the experiment but remember others. Why is this so?
   - **a.** According to levels-of-processing theory, we tend to retain information that has been subject to thorough processing. If the students gave meaning to the information, it is likely to be remembered.
   - **b.** According to dual code theory visual information is more likely to be retained than verbal information. If the students saw the information it is more likely to be remembered than if they heard it.

7. Describe several memory strategies that you can teach your students to help them remember the facts, concepts, and ideas presented to them in a lesson.

PEARSON **myeducationlab**™

Where the Classroom Comes to Life

Now go to **www.myeducationlab.com** to:

- take a Pretest to assess your initial comprehension of chapter content;
- study chapter content with your individualized Study Plan;
- take a Posttest to assess your understanding of chapter content;
- practice your teaching skills with Building Teaching Skills exercises; and
- build a deeper, more applied understanding of chapter content with Homework and Exercises.

CHAPTER 7

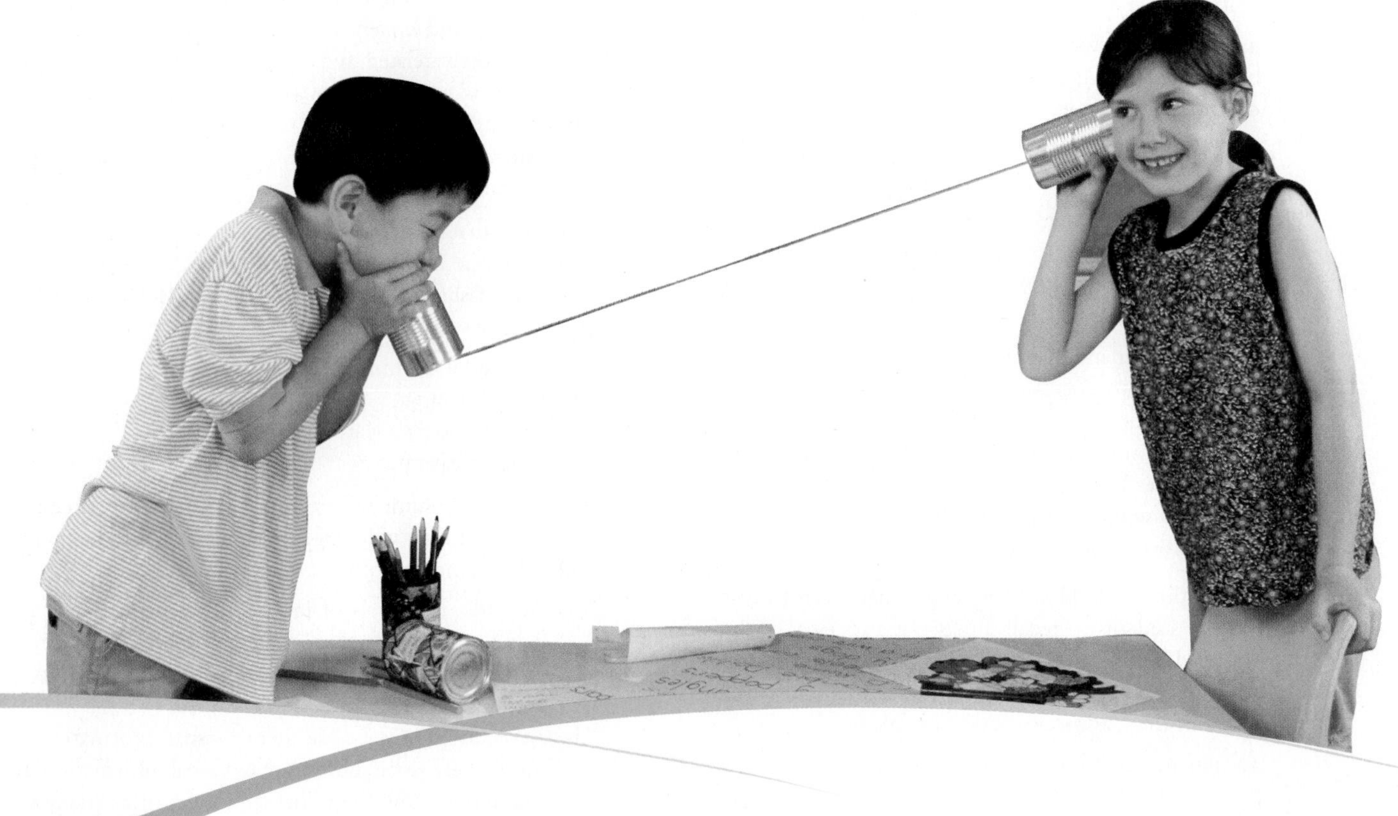

The Effective Lesson

chapter OUTLINE

Jennifer Logan's eighth-grade physical science class is a happy mess. Students are working in small groups at lab stations, filling all sorts of bottles with water and then tapping them to see how various factors affect the sound. One group has set up a line of identical bottles and put different amounts of water in each one so that tapping the bottles in sequence makes a crude musical scale. "The amount of water in the bottle is all that matters," one group member tells Ms. Logan, and her groupmates nod in agreement. Another group has an odd assortment of bottles and has carefully measured the same amount of water into each. "It's the shape and thickness of the bottles that make the difference," says one group member. Other groups are working more chaotically, filling and tapping large and small, narrow and wide, and thick and thin bottles with different amounts of water. Their theories are wild and varied.

After a half hour of experimentation, Ms. Logan calls the class together and asks group members to describe what they did and what they concluded. Students loudly uphold their group's point of view. "It's the amount of water!" "It's the height of the bottles!" "It's the thickness of the bottles!" "No, it's their shape!" "It's how hard you tap the bottles!" Ms. Logan moderates the conversation but lets students confront each other's ideas and give their own arguments.

The next day, Ms. Logan teaches a lesson on sound. She explains how sound causes waves in the air and how the waves cause the eardrum to vibrate, transmitting sound information to the brain. She has two students come to the front of the class with a Slinky and uses the Slinky to illustrate how sound waves travel. She asks many questions of students, both to see whether they are understanding and to get them to take the next mental step. She then explains how sound waves in a tube become lower in pitch the longer the tube is. To illustrate this, she plays a flute and a piccolo. Light bulbs are starting to click on in the students' minds, and Ms. Logan can tell from the responses to her questions that the students are starting to get the idea. At the end of the period, Ms. Logan lets the students get back into their groups to discuss what they have learned and to try to apply their new knowledge to the bottle problem.

When the students come into class on the third day of the sound lesson, they are buzzing with excitement. They rush to their lab stations and start filling and tapping bottles to test out the theories they came up with the day before. Ms. Logan walks among the groups, listening in on their conversations. "It's not the amount of water, it's the amount of air," she hears one student say. "It's not the bottle; it's the air," says a student in another group. She helps one group that is still floundering to get on track. Finally, Ms. Logan calls the class together to discuss their findings and conclusions. Representatives of some of the groups demonstrate the experiments they used to show how it was the amount of air in each bottle that determined the sound.

"How could we make one elegant demonstration to show that it's only the amount of air that controls the sound?" asks Ms. Logan.

The students buzz among themselves and then assemble all their bottles into one experiment. They make one line of identical bottles with different amounts of water. Then to demonstrate that it is the air, not the water, that matters, they put the same amount of water in bottles of different sizes. Sure enough, in each case, the more air space left in the bottle, the lower the sound.

Ms. Logan ends the period with a homework assignment: to read a chapter on sound in a textbook. She tells the students that they will have an opportunity to work in their groups to make certain that every group member understands everything in the sound lesson, and then there will be a quiz in which students will have to show individually that they can apply their new knowledge. She reminds them that their groups can be "superteams" only if everyone knows the material.

The bell rings, and the students pour into the hallway, still talking excitedly about what they have learned. Some groupmates promise to call each other that evening to prepare for the group study the next day. Ms. Logan watches them file out. She's exhausted, but she knows that this group of students will never forget the lessons they've learned about sound, about experiments, and, most important, about their ability to use their minds to figure out difficult concepts.

USING *your* EXPERIENCE

CREATIVE THINKING Write the phrase *Effective Lesson* in the middle of a sheet of paper and circle it. Brainstorm all the types of instructional approaches you can think of that make an effective lesson. Now list the types of instructional approaches that Ms. Logan uses.

CRITICAL THINKING How does Ms. Logan motivate the students? What strategies does she use to encourage retention of the material?

The lesson is where education takes place. All other aspects of schooling, from buildings to buses to administration, are designed to support teachers in delivering effective lessons; they do not educate in themselves. Most teachers spend most of their class time teaching lessons. The typical elementary or secondary school teacher may teach 800 to 1,000 class lessons each year!

Conducting effective lessons is at the heart of the teacher's craft. Some aspects of lesson presentation have to be learned on the job; good teachers get better at it every year. Yet educational psychologists have studied the elements that go into effective lessons, and we know a great deal that is useful in day-to-day teaching at every grade level and in every subject (Arends, 2004; Good & Brophy, 2003; Sternberg & Horvath, 1995). This chapter and the four that follow it present the principal findings of this research and translate them into ways of thinking about the practical demands of everyday teaching.

CERTIFICATION POINTER
You may be asked on your teacher certification test to describe techniques for planning instruction that incorporate learning theory, subject matter, and particular student developmental levels.

As Ms. Logan's lesson illustrates, effective lessons use many teaching methods. In four periods on one topic, she used direct instruction as well as discussion, cooperative learning, and other constructivist techniques. These methods are often posed as different philosophies, and the ideological wars over which is best go on incessantly (see Joyce, Weil, & Calhoun, 2004; Kirschner, Sweller, & Clark, 2006; Pressley et al., 2003). Yet

Personal REFLECTION

INTASC 5 Classroom Motivation and Management 7 Instructional Planning Skills

Balancing Instruction

I once went along with some colleagues from another university to visit a school that was using an exciting discovery science program they'd developed. We watched a teacher present an outstanding lesson, and then the students broke into small groups to work on experiments designed to lead them to discover a key scientific principle. The students got right to work and carried out the experiments with great enthusiasm. Gradually, throughout the class, groups were coming to the same conclusion—which was wrong! I asked the teacher what she did if students "discovered" the wrong answer.

She looked around in a conspiratorial way, and drew me back into a corner out of sight of my friends. "I *teach* them," she whispered.

Discovery learning can be a wonderful part of instruction for topics that lend themselves to it, but discovery needs to be balanced with direct instruction, to make sure that students learn both the joy and excitement of discovery and the basic knowledge and skills needed to be proficient in any subject.

REFLECT ON THIS. What subjects might lend themselves more to discovery learning? As the teacher of this class, how could I turn this lesson around to teach them to arrive at the correct answer?

few experienced teachers would deny that teachers must be able to use all of them and must know when to use each.

This chapter focuses on the strategies that teachers use to transmit information in ways that are most likely to help students understand, incorporate, and use new concepts and skills. Chapter 8 focuses on student-centered methods, in which students play an active role in structuring learning for themselves and for each other. However, the teaching strategies presented in these two chapters should be seen not as representing two sharply conflicting philosophies of education, but as complementary approaches to be used at different times for different purposes.

WHAT IS DIRECT INSTRUCTION?

At times, the most effective and efficient way to teach students is for the teacher to present information, skills, or concepts in a direct fashion (Bligh, 2000; Good & Brophy, 2003; Gunter, Estes, & Schwab, 2003; Kirschner et al., 2006). The term **direct instruction** is used to describe lessons in which the teacher transmits information directly to students, structuring class time to reach a clearly defined set of objectives as efficiently as possible. Direct instruction is particularly appropriate for teaching a well-defined body of information or skills that all students must master (Gunter, Estes, & Schwab, 2003). It is held to be less appropriate when deep conceptual change is an objective or when exploration, discovery, and open-ended objectives are the objects of instruction. However, recent research has supported the idea that direct instruction can be more efficient than discovery in conceptual development as well. Klahr and Nigam (2004) compared third-graders directly taught to do experiments that isolate the effects of one variable to those who carried out their own experiments without direct instruction. Those who received direct instruction performed much better in setting up new experiments.

direct instruction
Approach to teaching in which the teacher transmits information directly to the students; lessons are goal-oriented and structured by the teacher.

A great deal of research was done in the 1970s and 1980s to discover the elements of effective direct instruction lessons. Different authors describe these elements differently (see Evertson, Emmer, Clements, Sanford, & Worsham, 1994; Good et al., 1983; Hunter, 1995; Rosenshine & Stevens, 1986). Researchers and teachers generally agree as to the sequence of events that characterize effective direct instruction lessons. First, the teacher brings students up to date on any skills they might need for today's lesson (e.g., the teacher might briefly review yesterday's lesson if today's is a continuation) and tells students what they are going to learn. Then the teacher devotes most of the lesson time to teaching the skills or information, giving students opportunities to practice the skills or express the information, and questioning or quizzing students to determine whether they are learning the objectives.

VIDEO HOMEWORK EXERCISE
The Direct Instruction Model

Go to **www.myeducationlab.com** and, in the Homework and Exercises section for Chapter 7 of this text, access the video entitled "The Direct Instruction Model." Watch the video and complete the homework questions that accompany it, saving your work or transmitting it to your professor as required.

A brief description of the parts of a direct instruction lesson follows. The next section of this chapter will cover each part in detail.

1. ***State learning objectives and orient students to the lesson:*** Tell students what they will be learning and what performance will be expected of them. Whet students' appetites for the lesson by informing them how interesting, important, or personally relevant it will be to them.
2. ***Review prerequisites:*** Go over any skills or concepts students need in order to understand today's lesson.
3. ***Present new material:*** Teach the lesson, presenting information, giving examples, demonstrating concepts, and so on.
4. ***Conduct learning probes:*** Pose questions to students to assess their level of understanding and correct their misconceptions.
5. ***Provide independent practice:*** Give students an opportunity to practice new skills or use new information on their own.
6. ***Assess performance and provide feedback:*** Review independent practice work or give a quiz. Give feedback on correct answers, and reteach skills if necessary.
7. ***Provide distributed practice and review:*** Assign homework to provide distributed practice on the new material. In later lessons, review material and provide practice opportunities to increase the chances that students will remember what they learned and will be able to apply it in different circumstances.

HOW IS A DIRECT INSTRUCTION LESSON TAUGHT?

INTASC

6 Communication Skills

The general lesson structure takes vastly different forms in different subject areas and at different grade levels. Teachers of older students may take several days for each step of the process, ending with a formal test or quiz. Teachers of younger students may go through the entire cycle in a class period, using informal assessments at the end. Tables 7.1 and 7.2 present two quite different lessons to illustrate how direct instruction would be applied to different subjects and grade levels. The first lesson, "Subtraction with Renaming," is an example of the first of a series of lessons directed at a basic math skill. In contrast, the second lesson, "The Origins of World War II," is an example of a lesson directed at higher-order understanding of critical events in history and their causes and interrelationships. Note that the first lesson (Table 7.1) proceeds step by step and emphasizes frequent learning probes and independent practice to help students thoroughly learn the concepts being taught, whereas the second lesson (Table 7.2, p. 202) is characterized by an alternation between new information, discussion, and questions to assess comprehension of major concepts.

CONNECTIONS
For in-depth coverage of instructional objectives, writing lesson plans, and using taxonomies, see Chapter 13, pages 406–415.

The sequence of activities outlined in these two lessons flows along a logical path, from arousing student interest to presenting new information to allowing students to practice their new knowledge or skills to assessment. This orderly progression is essential to

TABLE 7.1 Sample Lesson for Basic Math: Subtraction with Renaming

Lesson Part	Teacher Presentation
1. State learning objective and orient students to lesson.	"There are 32 students in this class. Let's say we were going to have a party, and I was going to get one cupcake for each student in the class. But 5 of you said you didn't like cupcakes. How many cupcakes would I need to get for the students who do like cupcakes? Let's set up the problem on the chalkboard the way we have before, and mark the tens and ones . . ." tens ones 3 2 Students – 5 Don't like cupcakes "All right, let's subtract: 2 take away 5 is . . . *hey!* We can't do that! Five is more than 2, so how can we take 5 away from 2? We can't! "In this lesson we are going to learn how to subtract when we don't have enough ones. By the end of this lesson, you will be able to show how to rename tens as ones so that you can subtract."
2. Review prerequisites.	"Let's review subtraction when we have enough ones." Put on the chalkboard and have students solve: 47 56 89 – 3 – 23 – 8 How many tens are in 23?____ How many ones are in 30?____ Give answers, discuss all items missed by many students.
3A. Present new material (first subskill).	Have table monitors help hand out 5 bundles of 10 popsicle sticks each and 10 individual sticks to each student. Using an overhead projector, explain how to use sticks to show 13, 27, 30. Have students show each number at their own desks. Walk around to check.
4A. Conduct learning probes (first subskill).	Have students show 23 using their sticks. Check desks. Then have students show 40. Check desks. Continue until all students have the idea.
3B. Present new material (second subskill).	Using an overhead projector, explain how to use sticks to show 6 minus 2 and 8 minus 5. Then show 13 and try to take away 5. Ask for suggestions on how this could be done. Show that by removing the rubber band from the tens bundle, we have a total of 13 ones and can remove 5. Have students show this at their desks. Walk around to check.
4B. Conduct learning probes (second subskill).	Have students show 12 (check) and then take away 4 by breaking apart the ten bundle. Then have students show 17 and take away 9. Continue until all students have the idea.
3C. Present new material (third subskill).	Give students worksheets showing tens bundles and single units. Explain how to show renaming by crossing out a bundle of ten and rewriting it as 10 units and then subtracting by crossing out units.
4C. Conduct learning probes (third subskill).	Have students do the first items on the worksheet one at a time until all students have the idea.
5. Provide independent practice.	Have students continue, completing the worksheet on their own.
6. Assess performance and provide feedback.	Show correct answers to worksheet items on overhead projector. Have students mark their own papers. Ask how many got item 1, item 2, and so on, and discuss all items missed by more than a few students. Have students hand in papers.
7. Provide distributed practice and review.	Hand out homework, and explain how it is to be done. Review lesson content at start of following lesson and in later lessons.

direct instruction lessons at any grade level and in any subject, although the various components and how they are implemented would, of course, look different for different subjects and grades.

CERTIFICATION POINTER

For teacher certification tests, you may be asked to suggest techniques for building bridges between curriculum objectives and students' experiences.

State Learning Objectives

The first step in presenting a lesson is planning it in such a way that the reasons for teaching and learning the lesson are clear. What do you want students to know or be able to

TABLE 7.2 Sample Lesson for History: The Origins of World War II

Lesson Part	Teacher Presentation
1. State learning objective and orient students to lesson.	"Today we will begin to discuss the origins and causes of World War II—perhaps the most important event in the twentieth century. The political situation of the world today—the map of Europe, the political predominance of the United States, the problems of the Eastern European countries formerly under Soviet domination, even the problems of the Middle East—all can be traced to the rise of Hitler and the bloody struggle that followed. I'm sure many of you have relatives who fought in the war or whose lives were deeply affected by it. Raise your hand if a relative or someone you know well fought in World War II." • "Germany today is peaceful and prosperous. How could a man like Hitler have come to power? To understand this, we must first understand what Germany was like in the years following its defeat in World War I and why an unemployed Austrian painter could come to lead one of the largest countries in Europe." • "By the end of this lesson you will understand the conditions in Germany that led up to the rise of Hitler, the reasons he was successful, and the major events of his rise to power."
2. Review prerequisites.	Have students recall from the previous lesson: • The humiliating provisions of the Treaty of Versailles —Reparations —Demilitarization of the Ruhr —Loss of territory and colonies • The lack of experience with democracy in Germany
3. Present new material.	Discuss with students: • Conditions in Germany before the rise of Hitler —Failure of the Weimar Republic —Economic problems, inflation, and severe impact of the U.S. Depression —Belief that Germany lost World War I because of betrayal by politicians —Fear of Communism • Events in Hitler's rise to power —Organization of National Socialist (Nazi) Party —Beer-Hall Putsch and Hitler's imprisonment —*Mein Kampf* —Organization of Brown Shirts (S.A.) —Election and appointment as chancellor
4. Conduct learning probes.	Questions to students throughout lesson should assess student comprehension of the main points.
5. Provide independent practice.	Have students independently write three reasons why the situation in Germany in the 1920s and early 1930s might have been favorable to Hitler's rise, and have students be prepared to defend their answers.
6. Assess performance and provide feedback.	Call on randomly selected students to read and justify their reasons for Hitler's success. Discuss well-justified and poorly justified reasons. Have students hand in papers.
7. Provide distributed practice and review.	Review lesson content at start of next lesson and in later lessons.

do at the end of the lesson? Setting out objectives at the beginning of the lesson is an essential step in providing a framework into which information, instructional materials, and learning activities will fit.

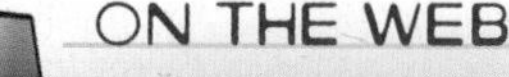

For tips on writing quality learning objectives visit **http://park.edu/cetl/quicktips/writinglearningobj.html.**

THEORY *into* PRACTICE

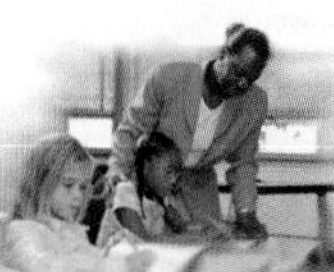

Planning a Lesson

The first step of a lesson, stating learning objectives or outcomes, represents a condensation of much advance **lesson planning** (see Burden & Byrd, 2003; Dick, Carey, & Carey, 2001; Karges-Bone, 2000). As a teacher planning a lesson, you will need, at the least, to answer the following questions:

1. What will students know or be able to do after the lesson? What will be the outcomes of their learning? How will you know when and how well students have achieved these learning outcomes or objectives?
2. What prerequisite skills are needed to learn this content? How will you make sure students have these skills?
3. What information, activities, and experiences will you provide to help students acquire the knowledge and skills they need in order to attain the learning outcomes? How much time will be needed? How will you use in-class and out-of-class time? How will seatwork and homework assignments help students achieve the learning objectives?
4. How will you arouse students' interest in the content? How will you motivate them to learn? How will you give them feedback on their learning?
5. What books and materials will you use to present the lesson? When will you preview or test all the materials and create guidelines for students' responses to them? Are all materials accurate, pedagogically sound, fair to different cultures, and appropriate in content and grade level?
6. What methods of teaching will you incorporate? For example, will you use reading, lecture, role playing, videotape viewing, demonstration, or writing assignments?
7. What participation structures will you use: whole-group or small-group discussions, cooperative learning groups, ability groups, individual assignments? What learning tasks will groups and individuals perform? How will you organize, monitor, and evaluate groups?

Orient Students to the Lesson

At the beginning of a lesson, the teacher needs to establish a positive **mental set,** or attitude of readiness, in students: "I'm ready to get down to work. I'm eager to learn the important information or skills the teacher is about to present, and I have a rough idea of what we will be learning." This mental set can be established in many ways. First, teachers should require students to be on time to class and should start the lesson immediately when the period begins (Evertson et al., 2006). This establishes a sense of seriousness of purpose that is lost in a ragged start. Second, teachers need to arouse students' curiosity or interest in the lesson they are about to learn. The teacher in the first sample lesson (Table 7.1) did this by introducing subtraction with renaming as a skill that would be necessary in connection with counting cupcakes for a class party, a situation of some reality and interest to young students. In the second sample lesson (Table 7.2), the teacher advertised the importance of the lesson on the basis that understanding the origins and events of World War II would help students understand events today, and made the lesson personally relevant to students by having them think of a relative who either fought in World War II or was deeply affected by it. In the chapter-opening vignette, Ms. Logan whetted students' curiosity about sound by giving them an opportunity to experiment with it before the formal lesson.

lesson planning
Procedure that includes stating learning objectives such as what the students should know or be able to do after the lesson; what information, activities, and experiences the teacher will provide; how much time will be needed to reach the objective; what books, materials, and media support the teacher will provide; and what instructional method(s) and participation structures will be used.

mental set
Students' attitude of readiness to begin a lesson.

"Dang. I'm not even ready for fifth period!"

A lesson on genetics might be introduced as follows:

> Did you ever wonder why tall parents have taller-than-average children and red-haired children usually have at least one red-haired parent? Think of your own family. If your father and mother are both taller than average, then you will probably be taller than average. Well, today we are going to have a lesson on the science called genetics, in which we will learn how characteristics of parents are passed on to their children.

This introduction might be expected to grab students' interest because it makes the subject personally relevant.

Humor or drama can also establish a positive mental set. One teacher occasionally used a top hat and a wand to capture student interest by "magically" transforming adjectives into adverbs (e.g., *sad* into *sadly*). Popular and instructionally effective children's television programs, such as *Sesame Street* and *Between the Lions*, use this kind of device constantly to get young children's attention and hold their interest in basic skills. Finally, in starting a lesson teachers must give students a road map of where the lesson is going and what they will know at the end. Stating lesson objectives clearly has generally been found to enhance student achievement of those objectives (Gronlund, 2000). Giving students an outline of the lesson in advance may also help them to incorporate new information (Bligh, 2000).

THEORY *into* PRACTICE

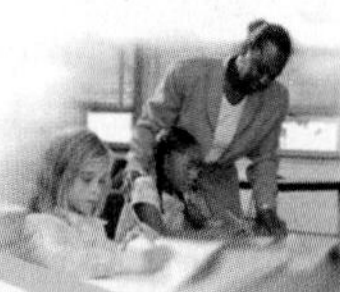

Communicating Objectives to Students

Teacher education programs include training in creating lesson plans, beginning with a consideration of instructional objectives and learning outcomes. Sharing lesson plans with students is a good idea, because research suggests that knowledge of objectives can lead to improvements in student achievement. Practical suggestions follow for sharing lesson objectives with students.

1. The objectives you communicate to students should be broad enough to encompass everything the lesson will teach. Research suggests that giving students too narrow a set of objectives may lead them to devalue or ignore other meaningful aspects of a lesson. In addition, broad objectives provide greater flexibility for adapting instruction as needed once the lesson is under way.
2. The objectives you communicate should be specific enough in content to make clear to students what the outcomes of their learning will be—what they will know and be able to do and how they will use their new knowledge and skills.
3. Consider stating objectives both orally and in writing and repeating them during the lesson to remind students why they are learning. Teachers often use verbal and written outlines or summaries of objectives. Providing demonstrations or models of learning products or outcomes is also effective. For example, an art teacher might show a student's drawing that demonstrates use of perspective to illustrate what students will be able to produce themselves, or a math teacher might show a math problem that students could not do at the beginning of a series of lessons but will be able to do at the end.

4. Consider using questioning techniques to elicit from students their own statements of objectives or outcomes. Their input will likely both reflect and inform your lesson plan. Some teachers ask students to express their ideas for meeting objectives or demonstrating outcomes, because research suggests that students who have a stake in the lesson plan and a sense of control over their learning will be more motivated to learn.

Review Prerequisites

For the next major task in a lesson, teachers need to ensure that students have mastered prerequisite skills and to link information that is already in their minds to the information you are about to present. If today's lesson is a continuation of yesterday's and you are reasonably sure that students understood yesterday's lesson, then the review might simply remind them about the earlier lesson and ask a few quick questions before beginning the new one. For instance, you might say, "Yesterday we learned how to add the suffix *-ed* to a word ending in *y*. Who will tell us how this is done?"

As today's lesson—adding other suffixes to words ending in *y*—is a direct continuation of yesterday's, this brief reminder is adequate. However, if you are introducing a new skill or concept that depends on skills learned much earlier, then more elaborate discussion and assessment of prerequisite skills may be needed.

Sometimes teachers need to assess students on prerequisite skills before starting a lesson. In the first sample lesson (Table 7.1), the teacher briefly quizzed students on subtraction without renaming and numeration skills in preparation for a lesson on subtraction with renaming. If students had shown poor understanding of either prerequisite skill, the teacher would have reviewed those skills before going on to the new lesson.

Another reason teachers should review prerequisites is to provide advance organizers. As defined in Chapter 6, advance organizers are introductory statements by the teacher that remind students of what they already know and give them a framework for understanding the new material to be presented. In the second sample lesson (Table 7.2), the teacher set the stage for the new content (Hitler's rise to power) by reviewing the economic, political, and social conditions in Germany that made Hitler's success possible.

CONNECTIONS
For more about the importance of activating students' prior knowledge, see Chapter 6, page 187.

CONNECTIONS
See page 188 in Chapter 6 for a definition of advance organizers.

Present New Material

Here begins the main body of the lesson, the point at which the teacher presents new information or skills.

Lesson Structure Lessons should be logically organized. Recall from Chapter 6 that information that has a clear, well-organized structure is retained better than less clearly presented information (Fuchs et al., 1997). A lesson on the legislative branch of the U.S. government might be presented as follows:

The Legislative Branch of the Federal Government (First Lesson)

I. Functions and nature of the legislative branch (Congress)
   A. Passes laws
   B. Approves money for executive branch
   C. Has 2 houses—House of Representatives and Senate
II. House of Representatives
   A. Designed to be closest to the people—representatives elected to 2-year terms—proportional representation
   B. Responsible for originating money bills
III. Senate
   A. Designed to give greater continuity to legislative branch—senators elected to 6-year terms—each state has 2 senators
   B. Approves appointments and treaties made by executive branch

CONNECTIONS
See page 190 in Chapter 6 for a discussion of retention of well-organized information.

This would be a beginning lesson; subsequent lessons would present how laws are introduced and passed, checks and balances on legislative power, and so on. The lesson has a clear organization that the teacher should point out to students. For example, you might pause at the beginning of the second topic and say, "Now we are going to learn about the lower house of Congress, the House of Representatives." This helps students form a mental outline that will help them remember the material. Research finds that a clearly laid out structure and transitional statements about the structure of the lesson increase student understanding (Lorch, Lorch, & Inman, 1993).

Lesson Emphasis In addition to making clear the organization of a lesson by noting when the next subtopic is being introduced, instructionally effective teachers give clear indications about the most important elements of the lesson by saying, for example, "It is particularly important to note that . . ." (Alexander & Jetton, 1996). Repeat important points and bring them back into the lesson whenever appropriate. For example, in teaching about the presidential veto in the lesson on the legislative branch of government, a teacher might say:

> Here again, we see the operation of the system of checks and balances we discussed earlier. The executive can veto legislation passed by the Congress, which in turn can withhold funds for actions of the executive. Remember, understanding how this system of checks and balances works is critical to an understanding of how the U.S. government works.

In this way, the teacher emphasizes one of the central concepts of the U.S. government—the system of checks and balances among the executive, legislative, and judicial branches—by bringing it up whenever possible and by labeling it as important.

Lesson Clarity One consistent feature of effective lessons is clarity—the use of direct, simple, and well-organized language to present concepts (Land, 1987; McCaleb & White, 1980; Smith & Land, 1981). Wandering off into digressions or irrelevant topics or otherwise interrupting the flow of the lesson detracts from clarity. Clear presentations avoid the use of vague terms that do not add to the meaning of the lesson, such as the italicized words in the following sentence (from Smith & Land, 1981): "*Maybe* before we get to *probably* the main idea of the lesson, you should review a few prerequisite concepts."

Explanations Research finds that effective teachers also use many explanations and explanatory words (such as *because, in order to,* and *consequently*) and frequently use a pattern of **rule–example–rule** when presenting new concepts (Van Patten et al., 1986). For example:

> Matter may change forms, but it is never destroyed. If I were to burn a piece of paper, it would appear that the paper was gone, but in fact it would have been combined with oxygen atoms from the air and changed to a gas (mostly carbon dioxide) and ash. If I could count the atoms in the paper plus the atoms from the air before and after I burned the paper, we could see that the matter involved did not disappear, but merely changed forms.

Note that the teacher stated the rule ("Matter . . . is never destroyed"), gave an example, and restated the rule in the explanation of how the example illustrates the rule. Also note that a rule–example–rule sequence was used in this textbook to illustrate the rule–example–rule pattern!

Worked Examples Worked examples are an age-old strategy for teaching certain kinds of problem solving, especially in mathematics (Atkinson, Derry, Renkl, & Wortham, 2000). For example, a teacher might pose a problem and then work it out on a chalkboard or overhead, explaining his or her thinking at each step. In this way, the teacher models the strategies an expert would use to solve the problem so that students can use similar strategies on their own. Research on worked examples generally finds that they are effective if they alternate with problems students do on their own (e.g., one worked example

rule–example–rule
Pattern of teaching concepts by presenting a rule or definition, giving examples, and then showing how examples illustrate the rule.

followed by several problems of the same type) (Atkinson et al., 2000; Sweller, van Merrienboer, & Paas, 1998). Teaching students to stop during worked examples to explain to themselves (Renkl, Stark, Gruber, & Mandl, 1998) or to explain to a partner (Renkl, 1998) what is going on in each step enhances the effects of worked examples. Worked examples are particularly effective for students who are new to a given topic or skill (Kalyuga, Chandler, Tuovinen, & Sweller, 2001).

By working through examples with students, a teacher can demonstrate problem solving and decision making. Why is this an important instructional strategy? Why is hands-on experience important for students?

Demonstrations, Models, and Illustrations Cognitive theorists emphasize the importance of students' seeing and, when appropriate, having hands-on experience with concepts and skills. Visual representations are maintained in long-term memory far more readily than is information that is only heard (Hiebert et al., 1991; Sousa, 2001). Showing, rather than simply telling, is particularly essential for children who are acquiring English (August & Shanahan, 2006b). Recall how Ms. Logan gave her students both hands-on experience (filling and tapping bottles) and a visual analogy (the Slinky representing sound waves) to give the students clear and lasting images of the main principles of sound. However, manipulatives (such as counting blocks) can be counterproductive to learning if they do not clearly relate to the concept being taught (Campbell & Mayer, 2004).

Embedded Video Video, television, and DVD have long been used in education. However, a new use is showing particular promise. This is video or DVD material that is embedded in on-screen text or class lessons used to illustrate key concepts. Research on embedded video finds that it helps children learn and retain information to the degree that it is easy to understand and it clearly links to the main content (Mayer & Moreno, 2002). For example, a year-long study by Chambers and colleagues (2006) found that adding brief animations and puppet videos to illustrate letter sounds and sound blending significantly increased first-graders' progress in reading.

Maintaining Attention Straight, dry lectures can be boring, and bored students soon stop paying attention to even the most carefully crafted lesson. For this reason teachers should introduce variety, activity, or humor to enliven the lecture and maintain student attention. For example, the use of humor has been found to increase student achievement (Droz & Ellis, 1996; Ziv, 1988), and illustrating a lecture with easily understood graphics can help to hold students' attention (Mayer, 2001). However, too much variation in mode of presentation can hurt achievement if it distracts students from the lesson content. Several studies have established that students learn more from lessons that are presented with enthusiasm and expressiveness than from dry lectures (Patrick, Hisley, & Kempler, 2000). In one sense, teaching is performing, and it appears that some of the qualities we would look for in a performer are also those that increase teachers' effectiveness (see Timpson & Tobin, 1982).

CONNECTIONS
For more on the importance of attention in learning, see Chapter 6, page 160.

Content Coverage and Pacing One of the most important factors in effective teaching is the amount of content covered. In general, students of teachers who cover more material learn more than other students do (e.g., Barr, 1987; Barr & Dreeben, 1983). This does not necessarily mean that teachers should teach faster; obviously, there is such a thing as going too fast and leaving students behind. Yet research on instructional pace does imply that most teachers could increase their pace of instruction (Good et al., 1983), as long as degree of understanding is not sacrificed. In addition to increasing content coverage, a relatively rapid pace of instruction can help with classroom management.

CONNECTIONS
For more on the impact of time on learning, see Chapter 11, page 329.

Conduct Learning Probes

Imagine an archer who shoots arrows at a target but never finds out how close to the bull's-eye the arrows fall. The archer wouldn't be very accurate to begin with and would certainly never improve in accuracy. Similarly, effective teaching requires that teachers be constantly aware of the effects of their instruction. All too often, teachers mistakenly believe that if they have covered a topic well and students appear to be paying attention, then their instruction has been successful. Students often believe that if they have listened intently to an interesting lecture, they know the material presented. Yet this might not be true. If teachers do not regularly probe students' understanding of the material being presented, students might be left with serious misunderstandings or gaps in knowledge (Hattie & Timperley, 2007; McMillan, 2007; Safer & Fleischman, 2005).

The term **learning probe** refers to a variety of ways of asking for brief student responses to lesson content. Learning probes give the teacher feedback on students' levels of understanding and allow students to try out their understanding of a new idea to find out whether they have it right. Learning probes can take the form of questions to the class, as in the sample lesson on World War II presented in Table 7.2, or brief written or physical demonstrations of understanding, as in the sample subtraction lesson in Table 7.1.

Checks for Understanding Whether the response to the learning probe is written, physical, or oral, the purpose of the probe is checking for understanding (Black, Harrison, Lee, Marshall, & Dylan, 2003; Black, Harrison, Lee, Marshall, & Wiliam, 2004; Reeves, 2007; Stiggins, 2007). That is, teachers use learning probes not so much to teach or to provide practice as to find out whether students have understood what they just heard. Teachers use the probes to set their pace of instruction. If students are having trouble, teachers must slow down and repeat explanations. If all students show understanding, the teacher can move on to new topics. The following interchange shows how a teacher might use learning probes to uncover student strengths and misunderstandings and then adjust instruction accordingly. The teacher, Mr. Swift, has written several sentences containing conversation on an overhead projector transparency, and students are learning the correct use of commas and quotation marks.

Mr. Swift: Now we are ready to punctuate some conversation. Everyone get out a sheet of paper and copy this sentence, adding punctuation where needed: Take the criminal downstairs Tom said condescendingly. Is everyone ready? . . . Carl, how did you punctuate the sentence?

Carl: Quote take the criminal downstairs quote comma Tom said condescendingly period.

Mr. Swift: Close, but you made the most common error people make with quotation marks. Maria, what did you write?

Maria: I think I made the same mistake Carl did, but I understand now. It should be: Quote take the criminal downstairs comma quote Tom said condescendingly period.

Mr. Swift: Good. How many got this right the first time? [Half of class raises hands.] OK, I see we still have some problems with this one. Remember, commas and periods go inside the quotation mark. I know that sometimes this doesn't make much sense, but if English always made sense, a lot of English teachers would be out of work! Think of quotation marks as wrappers for conversation, and the conversation, punctuation and all, goes inside the wrapper. Let's all try another. Drive carefully Tom said recklessly. Samphan?

Samphan: Quote drive carefully comma quote Tom said recklessly period.

Mr. Swift: Great! How many got it? [All but one or two raise hands.] Wonderful, I think you're all with me. The quotation marks "wrap up" the conversation, including its punctuation. Now let's all try one that's a little harder: I wonder Tom said quizzically whether quotation marks will be on the test.

learning probe
A method, such as questioning, that helps teachers find out whether students understand a lesson.

This interchange contains several features worth noting. First, Mr. Swift had all students work out the punctuation, called on individuals for answers, and then asked all students whether they got the right answers. This is preferable to asking only one or two students to work (say, on the chalkboard) while the others watch, thus wasting the time of most of the class. When all students have to figure out the punctuation and no one knows on whom Mr. Swift will call, all students actively participate and test their own knowledge, and Mr. Swift gets a quick reading on the level of understanding of the class as a whole.

Note also that when Mr. Swift found that half the class missed the first item, he took time to reteach the skill students were having trouble with, using a different explanation from the one he had used in his first presentation. By giving students the mental image of quotation marks as wrappers, he helped them to remember the order of punctuation in conversation. When almost all students got the second item, he moved to the next step, because the class had apparently mastered the first one.

Finally, note that Mr. Swift had plenty of sentences prepared on the overhead projector, so he did not have to use class time to write out sentences. Learning probes should always be brief and should not be allowed to destroy the tempo of the lesson. By being prepared with sentences for learning probes, Mr. Swift was able to maintain student involvement and interest. In fact, he might have done even better if he had given students photocopies with unpunctuated sentences on them to reduce the time used in copying the sentences.

Questions Questions to students in the course of the lesson serve many purposes (Dantonio & Beisenherz, 2001). Teachers use questions as Socrates used them, to prompt students to take the next mental step; for example, "Now that we've learned that heating a gas makes it expand, what do you suppose would happen if we cool a gas?" (Tredway, 1995). Teachers also use questions to encourage students to think further about information they learned previously or to get a discussion started; for example, "We've learned that if we boil water, it becomes water vapor. Now, water vapor is a colorless, odorless, invisible gas. In that case, why do you suppose we can see steam coming out of a tea kettle?" With guidance, a class discussion would eventually arrive at the answer, which is that the water vapor recondenses when it hits the relatively cool air and that what is visible in steam is water droplets, not vapor. Teachers often find it helpful to have students generate their own questions, either for themselves or for each other (King, 1992). A great deal of evidence indicates that students gain from generating their own questions (Foos, Mora, & Tkacz, 1994; Rosenshine, Meister, & Chapman, 1996; Wittrock, 1991), especially questions that relate to students' existing background knowledge about a topic they are studying (King, 1994).

Finally, teachers can use questions as learning probes (Airsian, 1994). In fact, any question is to some degree a learning probe, in that the quality of response will indicate to

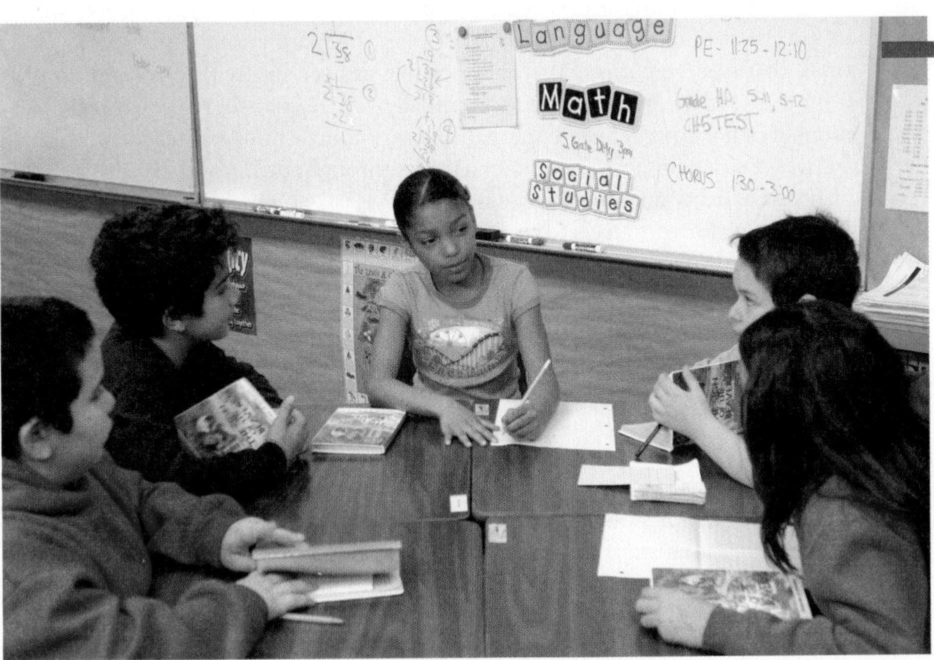

Why are questions valuable learning probes? What value can students gain by learning to ask good questions of each other?

the teacher how well students are learning the lesson. Research on the frequency of questions indicates that teachers who ask more questions related to the lesson at hand are more instructionally effective than are those who ask relatively few questions (Dunkin & Biddle, 1974; Gall et al., 1978; Stallings & Kaskowitz, 1974). At all levels of schooling, factual questions generally help with factual skills (Clark et al., 1979) and questions that encourage students to think about concepts help with conceptual skills (Fagan, Hassler, & Szabo, 1981; Gall, 1984; Redfield & Rousseau, 1981).

THEORY *into* PRACTICE

Assessment for Learning

Formative assessment within class lessons is at the heart of an important movement called Assessment for Learning, begun by two British researchers, Paul Black and Dylan Wiliam (Black, Harrison, Lee, Marshall, & Wiliam, 2003, 2004; Black & Wiliam, 1998). Its authors emphasize the word *for* in the name; there is already too much assessment *of* learning, they argue, but not enough assessment during lessons that can inform teachers and students themselves of students' levels of understanding in ways that are both meaningful enough and timely enough to be useful in improving learning and teaching (Leahy, Lyon, Thompson, & Wiliam, 2005; also see Chappuis, 2005; Popham, 2006). Assessment for Learning suggests dozens of strategies for helping students understand criteria for success, providing feedback, asking peers to provide feedback to each other, and letting students assess and report their own levels of understanding (Leahy et al., 2005; Wiliam, 2007). Examples of these are as follows.

- In any class with a writing component, distribute anonymous writing products (e.g., essays, lab reports, book reports) from the previous year's class, and ask students to judge their quality, before asking students to create their own writing products.
- Ask "big questions" that are at the core of the learning objective and give students time to talk among themselves and then share ideas with the class. For example, a math teacher might ask students to list fractions between one-half and one-fourth, both to understand students' grasp of fractional concepts and to spur their thinking. Students might be off the mark entirely, or they might think that three-eighths is the only possible answer, but with time and hints from the teacher, students might eventually realize that there are an infinite number of fractions between one-half and one-fourth. Similarly, teachers might ask why France supported Napoleon's wars throughout Europe, or why many plants have fruits surrounding seeds.
- Avoid asking for volunteers to respond to questions (because it's always the same students who volunteer). Instead, put students' names on popsicle sticks or cards and call on them at random.
- When appropriate, ask students to respond at once, perhaps by writing an answer on a small chalkboard and holding it up on cue, holding up a card showing A, B, C, or D to answer a multiple-choice question, or giving a choral (unison) response.
- Use "traffic lights": Ask students to assess their own understanding of a lesson and hold up a green card if they are solid, yellow if they are not sure, red if they are not getting it. The teacher can quickly scan the class, and move on if there is a sea of green or stop and reteach if there's a lot of red and yellow. Use cooperative learning strategies to let students work together to help each other, master content, assess each others learning, and lead each other toward productive lines of thinking.

ON THE WEB

For questioning techniques see the Questioning Toolkit at **www.fno.org.**

Wait Time One issue related to questioning that has received much research attention is **wait time,** the length of time the teacher waits for a student to answer a question before giving the answer or going on to another student. Research has found that teachers tend to give up too rapidly on students whom they perceive to be low achievers, a practice that tells those students that the teacher expects little from them (Rowe, 1974; Tobin & Capie, 1982).

Teachers who wait approximately 3 seconds after asking a student a question obtain better learning results than do those who give up more rapidly (Tobin, 1986). Furthermore, following up with students who do not respond has been associated with higher achievement (Anderson, Evertson, & Brophy, 1979; Larrivee, 1985). Waiting for students to respond or staying with them when they do not communicates positive expectations for them. However, there is such a thing as waiting too long. A study by Duell (1994) found that a wait time as long as 6 seconds had a small negative effect on the achievement of university students.

Calling Order In classroom questioning, **calling order** is a concern. Calling on volunteers is perhaps the most common method, but this allows some students to avoid participating in the lesson by keeping their hands down (Brophy & Evertson, 1974).

Common sense would suggest that when the question is a problem to be worked (as in math), all students should work the problem before any individual is called on. When questions are not problems to be worked, it is probably best to pose the question to the class as a whole and then ask a randomly chosen student (not necessarily a volunteer) to answer. Some teachers even carry around a class list on a clipboard and check off the students called on to make sure that all get frequent chances to respond, or put students' names on popsicle sticks and draw them at random from a can (Freiberg, 1999; Weinstein & Mignano, 1997). One teacher put her students' names on cards, shuffled them before class, and randomly selected cards to decide which student to call on. This system worked well until one student found the cards after class and removed his name from the deck!

In conducting learning probes, teachers might find it especially important to ask questions of students who usually perform above, at, and below the class average to be sure that all students understand the lesson.

Choral Response Researchers generally favor the frequent use of **choral responses** when there is only one possible correct answer (Becker & Carnine, 1980; Hunter, 1982; Rosenshine & Stevens, 1986). For example, the teacher might say, "Class, in the words listed on the board [*write, wring, wrong*], what sound does the *wr* make?" To which the class responds together, "Rrrr!" Similarly, when appropriate, teachers can ask all students to use hand signals to indicate true or false, to hold up a certain number of fingers to indicate an answer in math, or to write a short answer on a small chalkboard and hold it up on cue (Hunter, 1982). Research finds this type of all-pupil response has a positive effect on student learning (McKenzie, 1979; McKenzie & Henry, 1979). In the subtraction with renaming example used earlier in this chapter, recall that all students worked with popsicle sticks at their desks, and the teacher walked around to check their work. All-student responses give students many opportunities to respond and give the teacher information on the entire class's level of knowledge and confidence.

Provide Independent Practice

The term **independent practice** refers to work students do in class on their own to practice or express newly learned skills or knowledge. For example, after hearing a lesson on solving equations in algebra, students need an opportunity to work several equations on their own without interruptions, both to crystallize their new knowledge and to help the teacher assess their knowledge. Practice is an essential step in the process of transferring new information in working memory to long-term memory.

wait time
Length of time that a teacher waits for a student to answer a question.

calling order
The order in which students are called on by the teacher to answer questions during the course of a lesson.

choral responses
Responses to questions made by an entire class in unison.

independent practice
Component of instruction in which students work by themselves to demonstrate and rehearse new knowledge.

CONNECTIONS
For more on working memory and long-term memory, see Chapter 6, pages 161 and 163.

Independent practice is most critical when students are learning skills, such as mathematics, reading, grammar, composition, map interpretation, or a foreign language (Topping, Samuels, & Paul, 2007). Students can no more learn arithmetic, writing, or Spanish without practicing than they could learn to ride a bicycle from lectures alone. By contrast, independent practice is less necessary for certain concept lessons, such as the lesson on the origins of World War II outlined in Table 7.2 or a science lesson on the concept of magnetic attraction. In lessons of this kind, teachers can use independent practice to let students rehearse knowledge or concepts on their own, as the teacher did in the World War II lesson, but rehearsal is not as central to this type of lesson as practice of skills is to a subtraction lesson.

Seatwork Classic research on **seatwork,** or in-class independent practice, suggests that it is typically both overused and misused (Anderson, 1985; Brophy & Good, 1986). Several researchers have found that student time spent receiving instruction directly from the teacher is more productive than time spent in seatwork (Brophy & Evertson, 1974; Evertson, Emmer, & Brophy, 1980; Good & Grouws, 1977). For example, Evertson and colleagues (1980) found that the most effective seventh- and eighth-grade math teachers in their study spent about 16 minutes on lecture–demonstration and 19 minutes on seatwork, whereas the least effective teachers spent less than 7 minutes on lecture–demonstration and about 25 minutes on seatwork. Yet studies of elementary mathematics and reading classes found students spending 50 to 70 percent of their class time doing seatwork (Fisher et al., 1978; Rosenshine, 1980). Anderson, Brubaker, Alleman-Brooks, and Duffy (1985) have noted that time spent on seatwork is often wasted for students who lack the motivation, reading skills, or self-organization skills to work well on their own. Many students simply give up when they run into difficulties. Others fill out worksheets with little care for correctness, apparently interpreting the task as finishing the paper rather than learning the material.

VIDEO HOMEWORK EXERCISE
Group Work—Secondary (Parts 1 and 2)

Go to **www.myeducationlab.com** and, in the Homework and Exercises section for Chapter 7 of this text, access the videos entitled "Group Work—Secondary (Parts 1 and 2)." Watch the videos and complete the homework questions that accompany them, saving your work or transmitting it to your professor as required.

Effective Use of Independent Practice Time A set of recommendations for effective use of independent practice time, derived from the work of Anderson (1985), Evertson and colleagues (2000), and Good and colleagues (1983), follows.

1. ***Do not assign independent practice until you are sure students can do it.*** This is probably the most important principle. Independent practice is practice, not instruction, and the students should be able to do most of the items they are assigned to do on their own (Brophy & Good, 1986). In cognitive terms, practice serves as rehearsal for transferring information from working memory to long-term memory. For this to work, the information must first be established in students' working memories.

A high success rate on independent practice work can be accomplished in two ways. First, assignments should be clear and self-explanatory and should cover content on which all students can succeed. Second, students should rarely be given independent practice worksheets until they have indicated in learning probes that they can handle the material. For example, a teacher might use the first items of a worksheet as learning probes, assigning them one at a time and discussing each one after students have attempted it until it is clear that all or almost all students have the right idea.

CERTIFICATION POINTER
Your teacher certification test may require you to choose the *least* effective teaching strategy to achieve a particular curriculum objective. You should know that one of the least effective strategies for having students practice a skill they have just learned is to have them doing long, independent seatwork, on which they do not get feedback.

2. ***Keep independent practice assignments short.*** There is rarely a justification for long independent practice assignments. About 10 minutes of work is adequate for most objectives, but this is far less than what most teachers assign (Rosenshine, 1980). Massed practice (e.g., many items at one sitting) has a limited effect on retention. Students are more likely to profit from relatively brief independent practice in class supplemented by distributed practice such as homework (Dempster, 1989; Krug, Davis, & Glover, 1990).

3. ***Give clear instructions.*** In the lower grades, ask students to read aloud or paraphrase the instructions to be sure that they have understood them.

4. ***Get students started, and then avoid interruptions.*** When students start on their independent practice work, circulate among them to be sure that everyone is under way before attending to the problems of individual students or other tasks. Once students have begun, avoid interrupting them.

seatwork
Work that students are assigned to do independently during class.

5. ***Monitor independent work.*** It is important to monitor independent work (see Medley, 1979), for example, by walking around the class while students are doing their assignment. This helps to keep students working and makes the teacher easily available for questions. Teachers can also look in on students who may be struggling, to give them additional assistance.

6. ***Collect independent work and include it in student grades.*** A major problem with seatwork as it is often used is that students see no reason to do their best on it because it has little or no bearing on their grades. Students should usually know that their seatwork will be collected and will count toward their grade. To this end, it is a good idea to save a few minutes at the end of each class period to briefly read answers to assigned questions and allow students to check their own papers or exchange papers with partners. Then students may pass in their papers for spot checking and recording. This procedure gives students immediate feedback on their seatwork and relieves the teacher of having to check all papers every day. Make this checking time brief to avoid taking time from instruction.

Assess Performance and Provide Feedback

Every lesson should contain an assessment of the degree to which students have mastered the objectives set for the lesson (Reeves, 2007). The teacher might do this assessment informally by questioning students, might use independent work as an assessment, or might give a separate quiz. One way or another, however, teachers should assess the effectiveness of the lesson and should give the results of the assessment to students as soon as possible (Guskey, 2003; Hattie & Timperley, 2007; Safer & Fleischman, 2005; Stiggins, 2007). For example, research has found frequent use of classroom assessment of the content of instruction improves children's reading skills (Taylor, Pearson, Clark, & Walpole, 2000). Students need to know when they are right and when they are wrong if they are to use feedback to improve their performance. In addition to assessing the results of each lesson, teachers need to test students from time to time on their learning of larger units of information. In general, more frequent testing results in greater achievement than does less frequent testing, but any testing is much more effective than none at all (Bangert-Drowns, Kulik, & Kulik, 1986). Feedback to students is important, but feedback to teachers on student performance is probably even more important. If students are learning everything they are taught, it might be possible to pick up the pace of instruction. However, if assessment reveals serious misunderstandings, instructors can re-teach the lesson or take other steps to get students back on track. If some students mastered the lesson and some did not, it might be appropriate to give more instruction only to the students who need it.

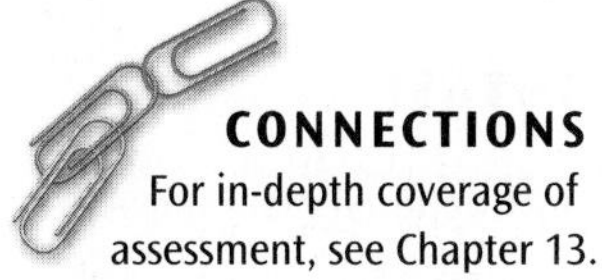

CONNECTIONS
For in-depth coverage of assessment, see Chapter 13.

INTASC

8 Assessment of Student Learning

Provide Distributed Practice and Review

Practice or review spaced out over time increases retention of many kinds of knowledge (Dempster, 1989). This has several implications for teaching. First, it implies that reviewing and recapitulating important information from earlier lessons enhances learning. Students particularly need to review important material at long intervals (e.g., monthly) to maintain previous skills. In addition, teachers should assign homework in most subjects, especially at the secondary level. Homework gives students a chance to practice skills learned in one setting at one time (school) and in another setting at a different time (home). Research on homework finds that it generally does increase achievement, particularly if teachers check it and give comments to students (Cooper et al., 2006; Trautwein, 2007). However, the effects of homework are not as clear in elementary schools as they are at

"My problem is just the opposite. My students want more homework and their parents want less. I'm a sex education teacher!"

the secondary level (Cooper, Robinson, & Patall, 2006; Cooper & Valentine, 2001), and assigning excessively lengthy or boring homework can actually be detrimental to learning and motivation (Corno, 2000). Making homework interesting and worthwhile is critical to its value (Darling-Hammond & Ifill-Lynch, 2006; Marzano & Pickering, 2007). Good and Brophy (2003) recommend 5 to 10 minutes of homework per subject for fourth-graders, increasing to 30 minutes or more per subject for college-bound high school students. Homework can provide a means for parents to become constructively engaged in their children's schooling (Epstein & Van Voorhis, 2001; Xu & Corno, 2003), but it can also become a significant source of conflict in the home, especially for children having difficulty with the content (Walker & Hoover-Dempsey, 2001).

Teaching Dilemmas: CASES TO CONSIDER

Designing Lessons

INTASC

7 Instructional Planning Skills

Mr. Benson has been teaching secondary social studies for several years. When he was a student, he had one remarkable history teacher who made the subject come alive for him and inspired him to become a teacher. When he was hired to teach world history in a high school, he thought that nothing could be better. But over the years he has come to realize that there is simply too much to cover in the course, and he is growing frustrated. Today, he is attending a conference sponsored by the state social studies curriculum adoption committee. In a roundtable discussion with other high school teachers and a professor from a local state university, Mr. Benson learns that he is not alone.

Mr. Benson: My textbook has forty-three chapters, and there are only thirty-six weeks in the school year, so I'm behind before I even start. I teach every lesson in an organized way: On Mondays, we review what we studied last week, and I orient the class to this week's subject matter and learning objectives. On Tuesdays and Wednesdays, I present the new material and question students along the way to be sure they understand the main points. On Thursdays, I have the students work on independent projects, such as papers, debates, or media projects related to the week's material. On Fridays, I give the class a quiz, and we discuss the answers to the quiz, as well as remaining issues from the chapter.

Ms. Rodriguez: And you're trying to pack all of world history into this routine? How do your students handle it?

Mr. Benson: I'm starting to get a lot of remarks like, "I have other classes that I have to read for, too" and "I can't remember all this stuff." And I'm simply not able to make history exciting for them, like it was for me as a student.

Mr. Johnson: We simply can't teach everything. There is too much to learn. Entire college courses are devoted to single units or topics that we are expected to cover within a week or two.

Mr. Benson: But what can we leave out? I know that with state curriculum exams coming up this semester, we'll get the usual criticism afterward that the students simply don't know the facts of history.

Mr. Smith: Is it more important that they know the current and up-to-date historical events than the ancient ones? I know I never get as far as the middle twentieth century, so how many kids really have a good understanding of World War II, the Korean War, or the Vietnam conflict?

Professor Forsyth: At our university, in our social studies methods courses, we're emphasizing "real history"—telling students specific stories that make history come alive. For instance, a lesson can focus on the civil rights movement in one southern community, and students can read some of the legal papers written by Thurgood Marshall about the movement. It's not only coverage of the subject that is important. Real history occurs when one gets a microscope and only looks at one single, small event until it is understood. Then the individual owns it.

Mr. Benson: That's what makes me love history, but if I were to have my students study something in depth and look at historical instances that enrich, I'd have even less time to teach. I have lesson plans to cover, a resource file that's too thick and never gets used, and ideas for cooperative learning activities and critical-thinking questions that I never have time to include. How can I cover it all?

QUESTIONS FOR REFLECTION

1. Evaluate Mr. Benson's use of direct instruction as he describes it. What are the strengths of his approach? What might be its limitations?
2. How can Mr. Benson incorporate Professor Forsyth's "real history" approach into his teaching? What difference do you think this would make in his students' comprehension and appreciation of the subject matter? What difference could it make in their curriculum exam scores?
3. How can Mr. Benson and his colleagues cover it all? Or should they attempt to do so? Discuss your thoughts with your classmates.

Source: Adapted from "Breadth versus Depth: Curricular Conflicts in a Secondary Classroom" by J. Merrell Hansen, from *Allyn & Bacon's Custom Cases in Education,* edited by Greta Morine-Dershimer, Paul Eggen, and Donald Kauchak (2000).

WHAT DOES RESEARCH ON DIRECT INSTRUCTION METHODS SUGGEST?

Most of the principles of direct instruction discussed in this chapter have been derived from **process–product studies,** in which observers recorded the teaching practices of teachers whose students consistently achieved at a high level and compared them to those of teachers whose students made less progress. These principles have been assembled into specific direct instruction programs and evaluated in field experiments; that is, other teachers have been trained in the methods used by successful teachers, and their students' achievement has been compared to that of students whose teachers did not receive the training.

Many studies have found a correlation between student achievement and teachers' use of strategies associated with direct instruction (e.g., Gage & Needels, 1989; Weinert & Helmke, 1995). However, experimental studies that compare the achievement of students whose teachers have been trained in specific direct instruction strategies to that of students whose teachers have not received this training have shown more mixed results. In classic studies of a direct instruction math approach called the Missouri Mathematics Program (MMP), Good and Grouws (1979) and Good et al. (1983) found that fourth-graders whose teachers used the MMP methods learned more than did students whose teachers were not trained in MMP. Evaluations of another direct instruction model, Madeline Hunter's (1982, 1995) Mastery Teaching program, did not generally find that the students of teachers trained in the model learned more than other students (Mandeville, 1992; Mandeville & Rivers, 1991; Slavin, 1986). A more recent study of explicit teaching, a form of direct instruction, found that this method made no difference in reading achievement of low achievers unless the method was supplemented by peer tutoring (Simmons, Fuchs, Fuchs, Mathes, & Hodge, 1995). More successful have been direct instruction models that place a greater emphasis on building teachers' classroom management skills (e.g., Evertson, Weade, Green, & Crawford, 1985) and models that improve teachers' use of reading groups (Anderson et al., 1979).

Studies of Direct Instruction (DI), a direct instruction program built around specific teaching materials and structured methods, have found strong positive effects of this approach in elementary schools, particularly with low achievers and at-risk students (Adams & Engelmann, 1996; Carnine, Grosen, & Silbert, 1995; Ellis, 2001b; Herman, 1999). One study (Meyer, 1984) followed the progress of students from an inner-city Brooklyn, New York, neighborhood who had been in DI classes in first through third grades and found

process–product studies
Research approach in which the teaching practices of effective teachers are recorded through classroom observation.

that these students were considerably more likely to graduate from high school than were students in a similar Brooklyn school who had not been taught with DI.

Although the research on direct instruction models has had mixed conclusions, most researchers agree that the main elements of these models are essential minimum skills that all teachers should have (see Gage & Needels, 1989). In fact, most of the recommendations from direct instruction research are so commonsensical that they seem obvious. A study by Wong (1995), however, found that the opposites of some direct instruction principles also seemed obvious to teachers and university students. When studies find no differences between teachers trained in the models and other teachers, it is often because both groups of teachers already had most of the direct instruction skills before the training took place (see Slavin, 1986).

Advantages and Limitations of Direct Instruction

It is clear that direct instruction methods can improve the teaching of certain basic skills, but it is equally clear that much is yet to be learned about how and for what purposes they should be used. The prescriptions derived from studies of effective teachers cannot be applied uncritically in the classroom and expected to make a substantial difference in student achievement. Structured, systematic instructional programs based on these prescriptions can markedly improve student achievement in basic skills, but it is important to remember that the research on direct instruction has focused mostly on basic reading and mathematics, mostly in the elementary grades. For other subjects and at other grade levels we have less of a basis for believing that direct instruction methods will improve student learning (see Arends, 2004).

HOW DO STUDENTS LEARN AND TRANSFER CONCEPTS?

INTASC

2 Knowledge of Human Development and Learning

4 Multiple Instructional Strategies

A very large proportion of all lessons focus on teaching concepts (see Klausmeier, 1992). A **concept** is an abstract idea that is generalized from specific examples. For example, a red ball, a red pencil, and a red chair all illustrate the simple concept "red." A green book is not an instance of the concept "red." If you were shown the red ball, pencil, and chair and asked to say what they have in common, you would produce the concept "red objects." If the green book were also included, you would have to fall back on the much broader concept "objects."

Of course, many concepts are far more complex and less well defined than the concept "red." For example, the concept "justice" is one that people might spend a lifetime trying to understand. This book is engaged primarily in teaching concepts; in fact, at this very moment you are reading about the concept "concept"!

Concept Learning and Teaching

Concepts are generally learned in one of two ways. Most concepts that we learn outside of school we learn by observation. For example, a child learns the concept "car" by hearing certain vehicles referred to as "cars." Initially, the child might include SUVs or motorcycles under the concept "car"; but as time goes on, the concept is refined until the child can clearly differentiate "car" from "noncar." Similarly, the child learns the more difficult concepts "naughty," "clean," and "fun" by observation and experience.

Other concepts are typically learned by definition. For example, it is very difficult to learn the concepts "aunt" or "uncle" by observation alone. One could observe hundreds of "aunts" and "nonaunts" without deriving a clear concept of "aunt." In this case the concept is best learned by definition: To be an aunt, one must be a female whose

concept
An abstract idea that is generalized from specific examples.

brother or sister (or brother- or sister-in-law) has children. With this definition, instances and noninstances of "aunt" can be readily differentiated.

Definitions Just as children can learn concepts in two ways, instructors can teach them in two ways. Teachers might give students instances and noninstances of a concept and later ask them to derive or infer a definition. Or teachers might give students a definition and then ask them to identify instances and noninstances. Some concepts lend themselves to the example–definition approach. For most concepts that are taught in school, it makes most sense to state a definition, present several instances (and noninstances, if appropriate), and then restate the definition, showing how the instances typify the definition. For example, we might define the concept "learning" as "a change in an individual caused by experience." Instances might include learning of skills, of information, of behaviors, and of emotions. Noninstances might include maturational changes, such as changes in behaviors or emotions caused by the onset of puberty. Finally, we might restate the definition and discuss it in light of the instances and noninstances.

Examples Teaching concepts involves extensive and skillful use of examples. Tennyson and Park (1980, p. 59) suggest that teachers follow three rules when presenting examples of concepts:

1. Order the examples from easy to difficult.
2. Select examples that differ from one another.
3. Compare and contrast examples and nonexamples.

Consider the concept "mammal." Easy examples are dogs, cats, and humans, and nonexamples are insects, reptiles, and fish. No problem so far. But what about dolphins? Bats? Snakes that bear live young? Kangaroos? Each of these is a more difficult example or nonexample of the concept "mammal"; it challenges the simplistic belief, based on experience, that terrestrial animals that bear live young are mammals and that aquatic animals, birds, and other egg-layers are not. The easy examples (dogs versus fish) establish the concept in general, but the more difficult examples (snakes versus whales) test the true boundaries of the concept. Students should thoroughly understand simple examples before tackling the odd cases.

transfer of learning
The application of knowledge acquired in one situation to new situations.

Teaching for Transfer of Learning

Students often get so wrapped up in preparing for tests, and teachers in preparing students to take tests, that both forget the primary purpose of school: to give students the skills and knowledge necessary for them to function effectively as adults. If a student can fill in blanks on a language arts test but cannot write a clear letter to a friend or a prospective employer, or can multiply with decimals and percents on a math test but cannot figure sales tax, then that student's education has been sadly misdirected. Yet all too frequently, students who do very well in school or on tests are unable to transfer their knowledge or skills to real-life situations.

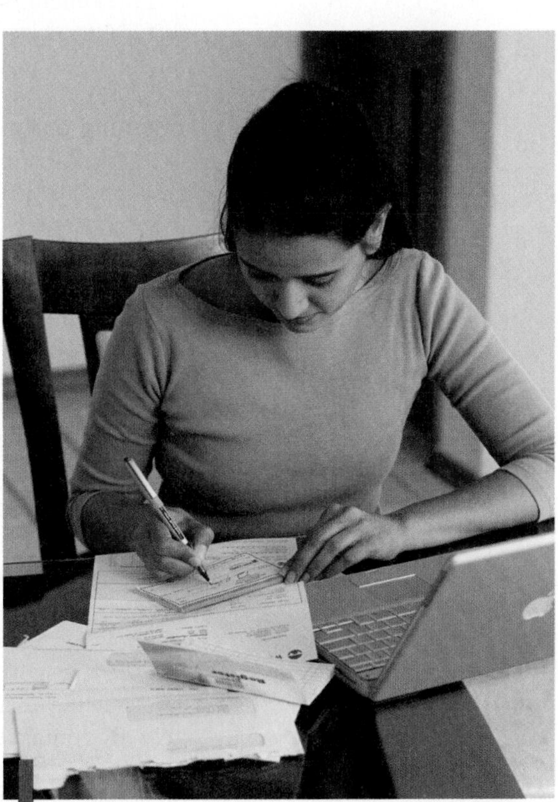

This woman has been able to transfer knowledge about math concepts to help with her personal finances. As a teacher, how will you ensure that your students are able to transfer what they have learned in the classroom to real-life situations?

Real-Life Learning **Transfer of learning** from one situation to another depends on the degree to which the information or skills were learned in the original situation and on the degree of similarity between the situation in which the skill or concept was learned and the situation to which it is to be applied (Bransford, Brown, & Cocking, 1999; Pressley & Yokoi, 1994; Price & Driscoll, 1997; Smagorinsky & Smith, 1992). These principles, known since the beginning of the twentieth century, have important implications for teaching. We cannot simply assume that students will be able to transfer their school learning to practical situations, so we must teach them to use skills in situations like those they are likely to encounter in real life or in other situations to which we expect learning to transfer. Students must receive specific instruction in how to use their skills and information to solve problems and encounter a variety of problem-solving experiences if they are to be able to apply much of what they learned in school.

The most important thing to know about transfer of learning is that it cannot be assumed (Cox, 1997). Just because a student has mastered a skill or concept in one setting or circumstance, there is no guarantee whatsoever that the student will be able to apply this skill or concept to a new setting, even if the setting seems (at least to the teacher) to be very similar (Mayer & Wittrock, 1996). Classic examples are people who score well on tests of grammar and punctuation but cannot apply these skills in their own compositions (Smagorinsky & Smith, 1992) and people who can solve all sorts of math problems in school but do not apply their math knowledge in real life. As an example of this, Lave (1988) describes a man in a weight-loss program who was faced with the problem of measuring out a serving of cottage cheese that was three-quarters of the usual two-thirds cup allowance. The man, who had passed college calculus, measured out two-thirds of a cup of cottage cheese, dumped it out in a circle on a cutting board, marked a cross on it, and scooped away one quadrant. It never occurred to him to multiply $2/3 \times 3/4 = 1/2$, an operation that almost any sixth-grader could do on paper (but few could apply in a practical situation).

Initial Learning and Understanding Not surprisingly, one of the most important factors in transfer of a skill or concept from one situation to another is how well the skill or concept was learned in the first place (Pressley & Yokoi, 1994). However, it matters a great deal how well students understood the material and to what degree it was taught in a meaningful way (Bereiter, 1995; Mayer & Wittrock, 1996). In other words, material that is memorized by rote is unlikely to transfer to new situations no matter how thoroughly it was mastered.

Learning in Context If transfer of learning depends in large part on similarity between the situation in which information is learned and that in which it is applied, then how can we teach in the school setting so that students will be able to apply their knowledge in the very different setting of real life?

One important principle of transfer is that the ability to apply knowledge in new circumstances depends in part on the variety of circumstances in which we have learned or practiced the information or skill (Bereiter, 1995). For example, a few weeks' experience as a parking attendant, driving all sorts of cars, would probably be better than years of experience driving one kind of car for enabling a person to drive a completely new and different car (at least in a parking lot!).

In teaching concepts, one way to increase the chance that students will appropriately apply the concepts to new situations is to give examples from a range of situations. A set of classic experiments by Nitsch (1977) illustrated this principle. Students were given definitions of words and were then presented with examples to illustrate the concepts. Some received several examples in the same context; others received examples from mixed contexts. For example, *minge* is a cowboy word meaning "to gang up on." The examples are shown in Table 7.3.

Students who received only the same-context examples could identify additional examples in the same context but were less successful in applying the concepts to new contexts. By contrast, the students who learned with the varied-context examples had some difficulties in learning the concept at first but, once they did, were able to apply it to new situations. The best strategy was a hybrid in which students received the same-context examples first and then the varied-context examples.

Teachers can use many other ways to increase the probability that information or skills learned in one context will transfer to other contexts, particularly to real-life applications. For example, simulations can approximate real-life conditions, as when secondary students prepare for job interviews by acting out interviews with teachers or peers pretending to

TABLE 7.3 Teaching of Concepts

Research demonstrates that to teach a new concept, teachers should first present examples of the concept used in similar contexts and then offer examples in widely different contexts. This approach promotes the students' abilities to transfer the concept to new situations. The example here comes from a classic study in which students learned new concepts from the traditional culture of cowboys.

Concept to be taught: ***Minge***
Definition: To gang up on a person or thing

Same-Context Examples	Varied-Context Examples
The three riders decided to converge on the cow.	The band of sailors angrily denounced the captain and threatened a mutiny.
Four people took part in branding the horse.	A group in the audience booed the inept magician's act.
They circled the wolf so it would not escape.	The junk dealer was helpless to defend himself from the three thieves.
All six cowboys fought against the rustler.	All six cowboys fought against the rustler.

Source: From John D. Bransford, *Human Cognition*, Wadsworth Publishing, 1979. (Adapted from an unpublished doctoral thesis titled *Structuring Decontextualized Forms of Knowledge* by Nitsch, 1977.) Reprinted by permission of John D. Bransford.

be interviewers. Teachers can also facilitate transfer by introducing skills learned in one setting into a new setting. For example, a history teacher might do well to find out what writing or grammar skills are being taught in English classes and then remind students to use these same skills in history essays (Anderson, Reder, & Simon, 1996; White & Frederiksen, 1998).

Transfer versus Initial Learning What makes transfer tricky is that some of the most effective procedures for enhancing transfer are exactly the opposite of those for initial learning. As the Nitsch (1977) study illustrated, teaching a concept in many different contexts confused students if it was done at the beginning of a sequence of instruction, but it enhanced transfer if it was done after students understood the concept in one setting. This principle holds important implications for teaching. In introducing a new concept, teachers should use similar examples until students understand the concept and use diverse examples that still demonstrate the essential aspects of the concept (Reimann & Schult, 1996).

As one example of this, consider a series of lessons on evolution. In introducing the concept, a teacher should first use clear examples of how animals evolved in ways that increased their chances of survival in their environments, using such examples as the evolution of flippers in seals or the evolution of humps in camels. Then the teacher might present evolution in plants (e.g., evolution of a waxy skin on desert plants), somewhat broadening the concept. Next, the teacher might discuss the evolution of social behaviors (such as cooperation in lions, baboons, and humans); finally, the teacher might explore phenomena that resemble the evolutionary process (such as the modification of businesses in response to selective pressures of free-market economies). In this way, the teacher first establishes the idea of evolution in one clear context (animals) and then gradually broadens the concept until students can see how processes in quite different contexts demonstrate the principles of selective adaptation. If the teacher had begun the lessons with a mixed discussion of animals, plants, societies, and businesses, it would have been too confusing. If the teacher had never moved beyond the evolution of animals, the concept would not have had much chance of transferring to different contexts.

"I wasn't copying. I was transferring knowledge from one context to another!"

After learning about the concept of evolution in many different contexts, students are much more likely to be able to distinguish scientific and metaphorical uses and apply the concept to a completely new context, such as the evolution of art in response to changes in society (Bransford, Brown, & Cocking, 1999).

It is important in teaching for transfer not only to provide many examples but also to point out in each example how the essential features of the concept are reflected (Kosonen & Winne, 1995). In the evolution lessons the teacher might explain the central process as it applied to each particular case. The development of cooperation among lions, for instance, shows how a social trait evolved because groups of lions that cooperated were better able than others to catch game, to survive, and to ensure that their offspring would survive. Pointing out the essential elements in each example helps students apply a concept to new instances they have never encountered (Anderson, Reder, & Simon, 1996). Similarly, comparing cases or situations illustrates a given concept, and pointing out similarities and differences between them can enhance transfer (Bulgren et al., 2002; Gentner, Loewenstein, & Thompson, 2002).

Explicit Teaching for Transfer Students can be explicitly taught to transfer skills to new circumstances. For example, Fuchs and colleagues (2003) evaluated an "explicit transfer" technique in third-grade math classes. Children in the explicit transfer condition were taught what transfer means and were given examples of how the same kind of story problems could be changed using different language, different contexts, and different numbers. They were also taught to look at story problems to see if they resembled problems they had done before. For example, one problem asked how many packages of lemon drops (10 to a package) you'd have to buy to get 32 lemon drops. They then presented the same problem worded differently, with additional questions added, with different contexts, and so on. Teaching students how to look for commonalities among story problems significantly enhanced their success on transfer tasks.

HOW ARE DISCUSSIONS USED IN INSTRUCTION?

INTASC

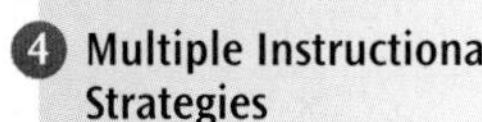

4 Multiple Instructional Strategies

Teachers use discussions as part of instruction for many reasons (see Gall, 1987), as detailed in the sections below.

Subjective and Controversial Topics

Questions in many subjects do not have simple answers. There may be one right answer to an algebra problem or one right way to conjugate a German verb, but is there one right set of factors that explains what caused the Civil War? How were Shakespeare's writings influenced by the politics of his day? Should genetic engineering be banned as a danger to world health? These and many other questions have no clear-cut answers, so it is important for students to discuss and understand these issues instead of simply receiving and rehearsing information or skills. Such subjects as history, government, economics, literature, art, and music include many issues that lend themselves to discussion and multiple and diverse explanations. Research finds that discussing controversial issues increases knowledge about the issues as well as encourages deeper understanding of the various sides of an issue (Johnson & Johnson, 1999).

Difficult and Novel Concepts

In addition to subjective and controversial subjects, discussions can clarify topics that do contain single right answers but which involve difficult concepts that force students to see something in a different way. For example, a science teacher could simply give a lesson on buoyancy and specific gravity. However, because this lesson would challenge a simplistic view of why things float ("Things float because they are light"), students might understand buoyancy and specific gravity better if they had an opportunity to make and defend their own theories about why things float and if they faced such questions as "If things float because they are light, then why does a battleship float?" and "If you threw certain objects in a lake, they would sink part way but not to the bottom. Why would they stop sinking?" In searching together for theories to explain these phenomena, students might gain an appreciation for the meaning of buoyancy and specific gravity that a lecture alone could not provide.

Affective Objectives

Teachers might also use discussions when affective objectives (objectives that are concerned with student attitudes and values) are of particular importance. For example, a course on civics or government contains much information to be taught about how our government works but also involves important values to be transmitted, such as civic duty and patriotism. A teacher could teach "six reasons why it is important to vote," but the real objective here is not to teach reasons for voting, but rather to instill respect for the democratic process and a commitment to register and vote when the time comes. Similarly, a discussion of peer pressure might be directed at giving students the skills and the willingness to say no when classmates pressure them to engage in illegal, unhealthy, or undesirable behaviors. A long tradition of research in social psychology has established that group discussion, particularly when group members must publicly commit themselves, is far more effective at changing individuals' attitudes and behaviors than is even the most persuasive lecture.

Whole-Class Discussions

Discussions take two principal forms. In one, the entire class discusses an issue, with the teacher as moderator (Gunter, Estes, & Schwab, 2003; Tredway, 1995). In the other, students form small groups (usually with four to six students in each group) to discuss a topic, and the teacher moves from group to group, aiding the discussion.

A **whole-class discussion** differs from a usual lesson because the teacher plays a less dominant role. Teachers may guide the discussion and help the class avoid dead ends, but should encourage the students to come up with their own ideas. The following vignette illustrates an inquiry-oriented discussion led (but not dominated) by a teacher, who wants students to explore and develop their own ideas about a topic using information they have recently learned:

Ms. Wilson: In the past few weeks we've been learning about the events leading up to the American Revolution. Of course, because we are all Americans, we tend to take the side of the revolutionaries. We use the term *Patriots* to describe them; King George probably used a less favorable term. Yet many of the colonists were Loyalists, and at times, the Loyalists outnumbered the Patriots. Let's think about how Loyalists would have argued against the idea of independence from Britain.

Beth: I think they'd say King George was a good king.

Vinnie: But what about all the things he did to the colonists?

Ms. Wilson: Give some examples.

Vinnie: Like the Intolerable Acts. The colonists had to put up British soldiers in their own houses, and they closed Boston Harbor.

Tanya: But those were to punish the colonists for the Boston Tea Party. The Loyalists would say that the Patriots caused all the trouble in the first place.

Ms. Wilson: Good point.

Frank: I think the Loyalists would say, "You may not like everything he does, but King George is still our king."

Richard: The Loyalists probably thought the Sons of Liberty were a bunch of thugs.

VIDEO HOMEWORK EXERCISE
Civil War Discussion

Go to **www.myeducationlab.com** and, in the Homework and Exercises section for Chapter 7 of this text, access the video entitled "Civil War Discussion." Watch the video and complete the homework questions that accompany it, saving your work or transmitting it to your professor as required.

whole-class discussion
A discussion among all the students in the class with the teacher as moderator.

ONLINE READING & WRITING EXERCISE

Reflecting on Direct Instruction Models

Access this exercise, entitled "Reflecting on Direct Instruction Models," in the Homework and Exercises section for Chapter 7 of this text at **www.mylabschool.com.**

Ms. Wilson: Well, I wouldn't put it quite that way, but I think you're right. What did they do that makes you think that?

Ramon: They destroyed things and harassed the Loyalists and the British troops. Like they called them names and threw things at them.

Ms. Wilson: How do you think Loyalists would feel about the Boston Massacre?

Beth: They'd say those thugs got what they deserved. They'd think that it was Sam Adams's fault for getting everyone all stirred up.

Ms. Wilson: Let's think about it another way. We live in California. Our nation's capital, Washington, is three thousand miles away. We have to pay all kinds of taxes, and a lot of those taxes go to help people in Boston or Baltimore rather than people here. Many of the things our government does make people in California mad. We've got plenty of food, and we can make just about anything we want to right here. Why don't we have a California Revolution and have our own country?

Sara: But we're part of America!

Tanya: We can't do that! The army would come and put down the revolution!

Ms. Wilson: Don't you think that the Loyalists thought some of the same things?

Vinnie: But we can vote and they couldn't.

Ramon: Right. Taxation without representation!

Beth: I'll bet a lot of Loyalists thought the British would win the war and it would be better to stay on the side of the winners.

In this discussion the teacher was not looking for any particular facts about the American Revolution, but rather was trying to get students to use the information they had learned previously to discuss issues from a different perspective. Ms. Wilson let the students determine the direction of the discussion to a substantial degree. Her main tasks were to keep the discussion rolling, to get students to use specifics to defend their positions, to ensure that many students participated, and to help the students avoid dead ends or unproductive avenues.

ON THE WEB

For an example of how to conduct an effective class discussion go to **www.ncrel.org/sdrs/areas/issues/students/learning/lr1jungl.htm.**

Information before Discussion Before beginning a discussion, teachers must ensure that students have an adequate knowledge base. There is nothing so dreary as a discussion in which the participants don't know much about the topic. The American Revolution discussion depended on students' knowledge of the main events preceding the Revolution. Teachers can sometimes use a discussion before instruction as a means of generating interest in a topic, but at some point they must give students information. In the chapter-opening vignette, for example, Ms. Logan let students discuss and experiment not only before presenting a formal lesson but also after the lesson, when they had more information.

CERTIFICATION POINTER

For your teacher certification test you will need to demonstrate your understanding of the principles and techniques associated with a variety of instructional strategies. For example, you might be asked to identify the curricular goals that whole-class discussion would be appropriate for and how you would structure the discussion so it would be effective.

Small-Group Discussions

In a **small-group discussion,** students work in four- to six-member groups to discuss a particular topic. Because small-group discussions require that students work independently of the teacher most of the time, young or poorly organized students need a great deal of preparation and, in fact, might not be able to benefit from them at all. However, most students at or above the fourth-grade level can profit from small-group discussions.

Like any discussion, most small-group discussions should follow the presentation of information through teacher-directed lessons, books, or videos, or following an opportunity for students to find information for themselves in the library or on the Internet. When students know something about a subject, they might start to work in their groups, pulling desks together if necessary to talk and hear one another more easily.

Each group should have a leader appointed by the teacher. Leaders should be responsible, well-organized students but should not always be the highest-achieving students. Groups may all discuss the same topic, or each may discuss a different subtopic

small-group discussion
A discussion among four to six students in a group working independently of a teacher.

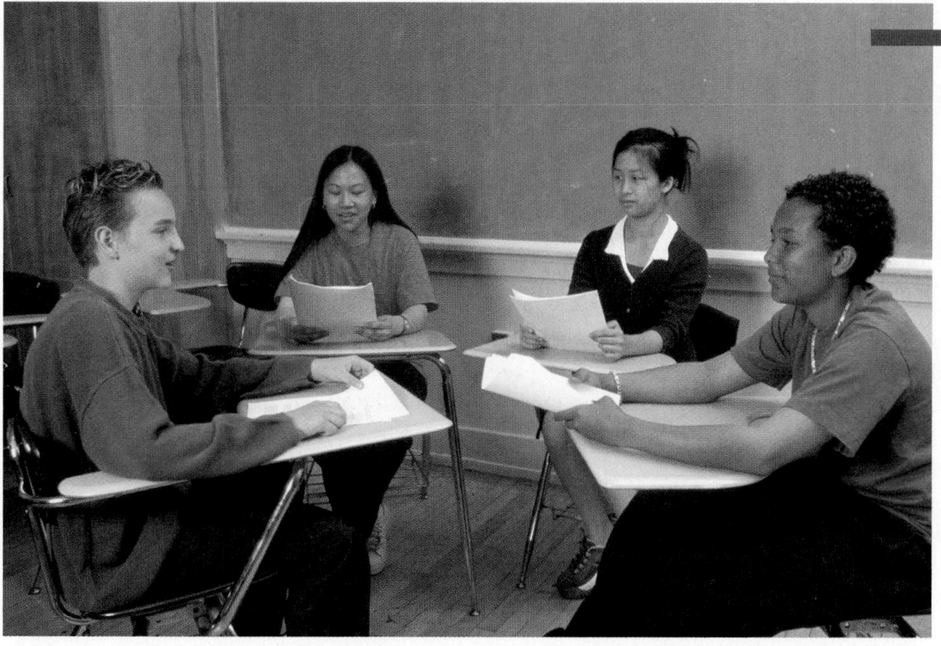

These students are involved in a small-group discussion. What does research tell us about the effectiveness of small-group discussions?

of a larger topic that the whole class is studying. For example, in a unit on the Great Depression, one group might focus on causes of the Depression, another on the collapse of the banking system, a third on the social consequences of the Depression, and a fourth on the New Deal. The teacher should give each group a series of questions to answer on the topic to be discussed. For example, if the topic were the collapse of the banking system, the questions might be the following:

1. What was the connection between the stock market crash of 1929 and the failures of so many banks?
2. What caused savers to lose confidence in the banks?
3. Why did the banks not have enough funds to pay savers who wished to withdraw their money?
4. Why is a widespread run on banks unlikely today?

The leader's role in each discussion group is to make sure that the group stays on the topic and questions assigned to it, and to ensure that all group members participate. A group recorder could be appointed to write down the group's ideas. At the end of the discussion, the group members prepare a report on their activities or conclusions to present to the rest of the class.

Research on small-group discussions indicates that these activities can increase student achievement more than traditional lessons if the students are well prepared to work in small groups and if the group task is well organized (Sharan et al., 1984; Sharan & Shachar, 1988). Also, some research suggests that small-group discussions have greater effects on student achievement if students are encouraged to engage in controversy rather than to seek a consensus (Johnson & Johnson, 1999).

BUILDING TEACHING SKILLS ARTIFACT HOMEWORK EXERCISE

Group Work Instructions

Go to **www.myeducationlab.com** and, in the Homework and Exercises section for Chapter 7 of this text, access the Classroom Artifact entitled "Group Work Instructions." Examine the artifact and complete the homework questions that accompany it, saving your work or transmitting it to your professor as required.

CERTIFICATION POINTER

A certification test question may ask you to respond to a case study by identifying the strengths and weaknesses of the instructional strategies employed in the case.

CHAPTER 7 SUMMARY

What Is Direct Instruction?

Direct instruction is a teaching approach that emphasizes teacher control of most classroom events and the presentation of structured lessons. Direct instruction programs call for active teaching; clear lesson organization; step-by-step progression between subtopics; and the use of many examples, demonstrations, and visual prompts.

The Intentional TEACHER

USING WHAT YOU KNOW about Direct Instruction to Improve Teaching and Learning

Intentional teachers select their instructional strategies with purpose. They understand the benefits and shortcomings of the strategies they select, and they choose strategies based on their students, the content, and the context.

Intentional teachers capitalize on their power as directors of learning by using the components of effective instruction. They take responsibility for presenting clear lessons that carefully lead students toward mastery of objectives. They use their time well by providing a quick instructional pace, by checking for student understanding frequently, and by providing meaningful practice in which students learn to transfer information and skills to new settings. Intentional teachers relish their role as designers of learning experiences.

1 What do I expect my students to know and be able to do at the end of this lesson? How does this contribute to course objectives and to my students' need to become capable individuals?

Effective instruction requires careful preparation, which begins with teachers' thoughtful selection and phrasing of learning objectives. Think in specific terms about content students are to master and plan your lesson to focus directly on those objectives. For example, you might begin planning a series of lessons on spiders for your second-graders with the goal: "Students will learn about spiders' bodies and behaviors." From that goal you would develop specific objectives to frame your lessons. You might list as your first objective "Students will be able to point to, label, and describe at least three features of a spider's anatomy."

Stating the objective and purpose for a lesson helps students prepare mentally for the information that follows. Begin your lessons with a clear declaration of *what* and *why* students are to learn. For example, you could begin a lesson as follows: "Take a look at the two rocks here on my table. By the time you leave today, you'll be able to state how each of these rocks was formed. That's important information, because it can give us clues about the conditions of the earth far back in time. It helps us solve earth's puzzles!"

2 What knowledge, skills, needs, and interests do my students have that must be taken into account in my lesson?

Intentional teachers use preassessments to ensure that their objectives and instruction are appropriate for students' needs. For example, before teaching a unit on the metric system, you might give a 10-item pretest to determine their current knowledge of metrics, such as "Which unit would you use to measure how long something is: liter, meter, gram?"

Effective lessons include a review of prerequisite skills. Briefly review previous learnings that students will need in the current lesson. For example, in a unit on persuasive speech, you might ask students what they have learned that makes an effective speech. After noting their ideas on the board, you could add to the list any of the points that you think they might have missed as being especially important for persuasive speeches—organization, clarity, poise, effective use of gestures.

3 What do I know about the content, child development, learning, motivation, and effective teaching strategies that I can use to accomplish my objectives?

Effective presentation of information will require you to call on all your skills in incorporating appropriate humor, novelty, and variety. It is important to consider means other than text for presenting information. Use pictures, music, video, and real objects or models when the content permits. Clarity of speech and pronunciation and a pleasant tone are important when you are speaking or reading aloud to present information. (In doing so, you are also modeling your expectations for student speaking.) For example, in a lesson on trees for young children, you might bring in a variety of leaf forms. To introduce the concept of "conifers" you might bring not only pictures of the cone and foliage of a variety of conifers but also actual cones and sample foliage. Learners can then use their tactile sense as well as their eyes to discriminate between the types of cones. They can use their beginning number awareness to differentiate

How Is a Direct Instruction Lesson Taught?

The first part of a lesson is stating learning objectives and orienting students to the lesson. The principal task is to establish both a mental set, so that students are ready to work and learn, and a "road map," so that students know where the lesson is going.

Part two of a lesson is to review prerequisites or pretest to ensure that students have mastered required knowledge and skills. The review might function as an advance organizer for the lesson.

Part three involves presenting the new material in an organized way, providing explanations and demonstrations, and maintaining attention.

Part four, conducting learning probes, elicits students' responses to lesson content. This practice gives teachers feedback and lets students test their ideas. Questioning techniques are important, including the uses of wait time and calling order.

between conifers by the number of needles in the "bundles" of their foliage. You could make a point of clarifying the new words in these lessons to help build vocabulary and develop linguistic skills.

Practice by the students should include variety. You help your students develop the ability to apply ideas in new contexts when you provide a range of activities. For example, you might offer your students a choice of activities to practice applying their new knowledge of explorers of the New World. You could direct them to select three of the explorers they have studied. They might map their general routes; write an imaginary journal entry for a member of the party after seeing an important landmark; or write an imaginary dialogue between two different explorers, comparing their experiences.

4 What instructional materials, technology, assistance, and other resources are available to help accomplish my objectives?

Effective instruction maintains a high degree of student attention. Visual input is especially important for students who are acquiring English. Pace lessons rapidly (without sacrificing student understanding); and use humor, novelty, and variety to support the lesson focus. For example, imagine a lesson on descriptive writing. Rather than rely on mental images, you might bring in an assortment of odd kitchen utensils and toolbox treasures. Students could pass the items around, conjecturing about their uses. The objects' novelty might enhance students' written descriptions.

Students need time to process information. Use wait time after you ask a question, and follow through with students who do not express understanding. For example, you might pose a question to your literature students: "What emotion do you suppose our main character was experiencing at this point?" Instead of calling on the first student to raise a hand, you could say: "I see three hands up. I think I'll wait for more." After a few seconds, many hands are in the air, and you could select three or four students to share their responses.

5 How will I plan to assess students' progress toward my objectives?

During direct instruction, teachers conduct many learning probes. Check for understanding frequently, and modify your instruction based on results. For example, in a geometry lesson for young children, you might arrange students in small groups and give each group a set of large shapes. You could ask: "Please hold up a shape that has four corners. Please hold up a shape that reminds you of a stop sign. Please hold up the shape that has the fewest number of sides." You might note that students struggle with your last prompt but easily responded to the first two, and make a note to provide additional work on problem solving and vocabulary terms such as *least, most, more,* and *fewer.*

Active participation devices allow teachers to assess all of their students' understandings. Use strategies that provide feedback on every student's progress. For example, after working on different spellings of the long /a/ sound (as in "made"), you might distribute individual chalkboards, chalk, and erasers. You could recite a few words. Students silently write the words on their boards and then raise the boards for you to check. You would quickly—and silently—assess each student's mastery of spelling patterns, and make a list of students who require further instruction.

6 How will I respond if individual children or the class as a whole are not on track toward success? What is my back-up plan?

As follow-up to any unit of instruction, you might plan for a review and question session. Homework assignments for the unit would be reviewed and corrected by peers in these class sessions. You can actively encourage and answer questions about the content of the unit's lessons. You should have watched for the level of student understanding throughout the unit in the "learning probe" activities you have conducted, and your notes from these "probes" serve as a guide for your review of content.

Part five of a lesson is independent practice, or seatwork, in which students apply their new skill. Research shows that independent practice should be given as short assignments with clear instructions and no interruptions, and that it should be given only when students can do the assignments. Teachers should monitor work, collect it, and include it in assessments.

Part six is to assess performance and provide feedback. Every lesson should include an assessment of student mastery of the lesson objectives.

Part seven is to provide distributed practice, or homework, and review. Information is retained better when practice is spaced out over a period of time.

What Does Research on Direct Instruction Methods Suggest?

Research on particular direct instruction models shows mostly positive but inconsistent effects on student achievement. One program, DI (direct instruction), proved to be particularly successful for teaching reading and mathematics to low achievers and at-risk students.

How Do Students Learn and Transfer Concepts?

Students learn concepts through observation and definition. Concepts are taught through examples and nonexamples and through the rule–example–rule approach, in which teachers first state a definition, then give examples, and finally restate the definition. Unambiguous examples should be given before less obvious ones, and teachers should compare and contrast examples and nonexamples. Students transfer their learning to similar situations and must be taught to transfer concepts to different contexts and real-life situations. Material memorized by rote is unlikely to transfer.

How Are Discussions Used in Instruction?

In whole-group discussion the teacher plays a less dominant role than in a regular lesson. Students need an adequate knowledge base before beginning a discussion. In small-group discussion, each group should have a leader and a specific focus.

KEY TERMS

Review the following key terms from the chapter.

calling order 211
choral responses 211
concept 216
direct instruction 199
independent practice 211
learning probe 208
lesson planning 203
mental set 203
process–product studies 215
rule–example–rule 206
seatwork 212
small-group discussion 222
transfer of learning 217
wait time 211
whole-class discussion 221

SELF-ASSESSMENT: PRACTICING *for* LICENSURE

Directions: The chapter-opening vignette addresses indicators that are often assessed in state licensure exams. Re-read the chapter-opening vignette, and then respond to the following questions.

1. In the chapter-opening vignette, Ms. Logan uses a variety of instructional strategies in the lesson on sound. Which of the following statements from the vignette is an example of Ms. Logan using direct instruction?
   - **a.** Students are working in small groups at lab stations.
   - **b.** After a half hour of experimentation, Ms. Logan calls the class together.
   - **c.** Representatives from some of the groups demonstrate the experiment.
   - **d.** Ms. Logan teaches a lesson on sound.
2. If Ms. Logan were to use a direct instruction approach to a science lesson on gravity, which of the following steps would come first?
   - **a.** conduct learning probes
   - **b.** state the learning objective
   - **c.** present new material
   - **d.** provide independent practice

3. According to research on direct instruction, why should Ms. Logan conduct learning probes during her lesson on sound?

   a. to facilitate in teaching the lesson
   b. to provide students practice with the concepts presented
   c. to give the teacher feedback on the students' level of understanding
   d. to catch students who are not paying attention

4. Ms. Logan plays a flute and a piccolo to demonstrate how sound waves travel through air. She hopes this demonstration will help her students understand the experiment with the bottles of water. What principle of instruction is she using?

   a. reciprocal teaching
   b. distributed practice
   c. transfer of learning
   d. alternative assessment

5. After Ms. Logan's students work in groups to finish the lesson on sound, she tells them they will be tested individually to demonstrate their knowledge; however, their group can only be called "superteam" if everyone knows the material. What instructional strategy is the teacher using?

   a. cooperative learning
   b. small-group discussion
   c. direct instruction
   d. inquiry learning

6. Create a lesson using all of the steps of a direct instruction lesson.

7. What are some advantages and disadvantages of small-group discussions and whole-group discussions?

Now go to **www.myeducationlab.com** to:

- take a Pretest to assess your initial comprehension of chapter content;
- study chapter content with your individualized Study Plan;
- take a Posttest to assess your understanding of chapter content;
- practice your teaching skills with Building Teaching Skills exercises; and
- build a deeper, more applied understanding of chapter content with Homework and Exercises.

CHAPTER 8

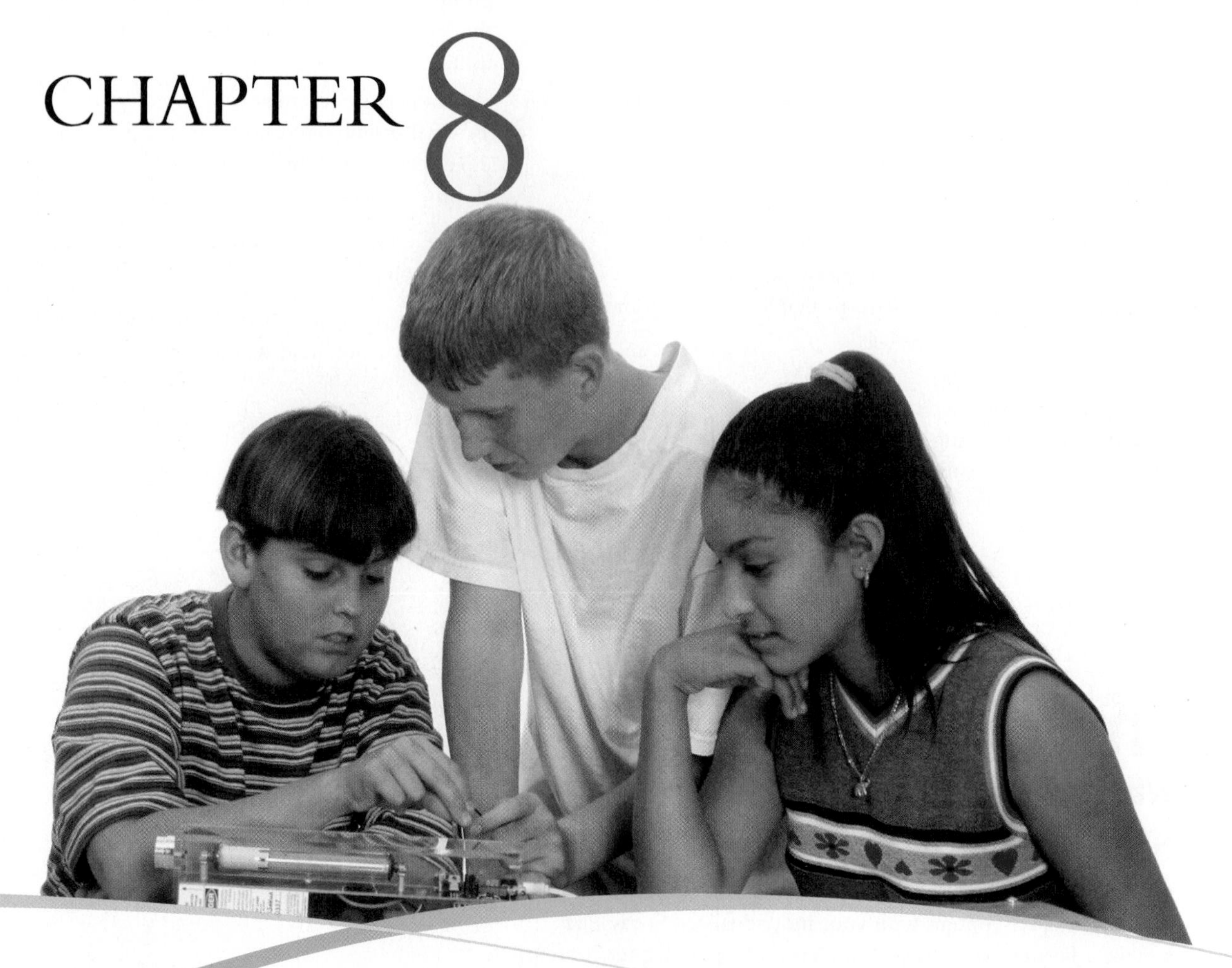

Student-Centered and Constructivist Approaches to Instruction

chapter
OUTLINE

"You'll all recall," began Mr. Dunbar, "how last week we figured out how to compute the area of a circle and the volume of a cube. Today you're going to have a chance to discover how to compute the volume of a cylinder. This time, you're really going to be on your own. At each of your lab stations you have five unmarked cylinders of different sizes. You also have a metric ruler and a calculator, and you may use water from your sink. The most important resources you'll have to use, however, are your minds and your partners. Remember, at the end of this activity, everyone in every group must be able to explain not only the formula for volume of a cylinder but also precisely how you derived it. Any questions? You may begin!"

The students in Mr. Dunbar's middle school math and science class got right to work. They were seated around lab tables in groups of four. One of the groups, the Master Minds, started off by filling all its cylinders with water.

"OK," said Miguel, "we've filled all of our cylinders. What do we do next?"

"Let's measure them," suggested Margarite. She took the ruler and asked Dave to write down her measurements.

"The water in this little one is 36 millimeters high and . . . just a sec . . . 42 millimeters across the bottom."

"So what?" asked Yolanda. "We can't figure out the volume this way. Let's do a little thinking before we start measuring everything."

"Yolanda's right," said Dave. "We'd better work out a plan."

"I know," said Miguel, "let's make a hypo . . . , hypotha . . . , what's it called?"

"Hypothesis," said Yolanda. "Yeah! Let's guess what we think the solution is."

"Remember how Mr. Dunbar reminded us about the area of a circle and the volume of a cube? I'll bet that's an important clue."

"You're right, Miguel," said Mr. Dunbar, who happened to be passing by. "But what are you guys going to do with that information?"

The Master Minds were quiet for a few moments. "Let's try figuring out the area of the bottom of one of these cylinders," ventured Dave. "Remember that Margarite said the bottom of the little one was 42 millimeters? Give me the calculator . . . now how do we get the area?"

Yolanda said, "I think it was pi times the radius squared."

"That sounds right. So 42 squared—"

"Not 42; 21 squared," interrupted Margarite. "If the diameter is 42, the radius is 21."

"OK, OK, I would have remembered. Now, 21 squared is . . . 441, and pi is about 3.14, so my handy-dandy calculator says . . . 13,847."

"Can't be," said Miguel. "Four hundred times three is twelve hundred, so 441 times 3.14 can't be thirteen thousand. I think you did something wrong."

"Let me do it again . . . 441 times 3.14 . . . you're right. Now it's about 1,385."

"So what?" said Yolanda.

"That doesn't tell us how to figure the volume!"

Margarite jumped in excitedly. "Just hang on for a minute, Yolanda. Now, I think we should multiply the area of the bottom by the height of the water."

"But why?" asked Miguel.

"Well," said Margarite, "when we did the volume of a cube, we multiplied length times width times height. Length times width is the area of the bottom. I'll bet we could do the same with a cylinder!"

"The girl's brilliant!" said Miguel. "Sounds good to me. But how could we prove it?"

"I've got an idea," said Yolanda. She emptied the water out of all the cylinders and filled the smallest one to the top. "This is my idea. We don't know what the volume of this cylinder is, but we do know that it's always the same. If we pour the same amounts of water into all four cylinders and use our formula, it should always come out to the same amount!"

"Let's try it!" said Miguel. He poured the water from the small cylinder into a larger one, refilled it, and poured it into another of a different shape.

The Master Minds measured the bases and the heights of the water in their cylinders, wrote down the measurements, and tried out their formula. Sure enough, their formula always gave the same answer for the same volume of water. In great excitement they called Mr. Dunbar to come see what they were doing. Mr. Dunbar asked each of the students to explain what he or she had done.

"Terrific!" he said. "Not only did you figure out a solution, but everyone in the group participated and understood what you did. Now I'd like you to help me out. I've got a couple of groups that are really stumped. Do you suppose you could help them? Don't give them the answer, but help them get on track. How about Yolanda and Miguel helping with the Brainiacs, and Dave and Margarite help with the Dream Team. OK? Thanks!"

USING *your* EXPERIENCE

COOPERATIVE LEARNING AND CRITICAL THINKING After reading this case, randomly select or appoint a four- to eight-member panel of "experts" on constructivism who sit in front of the class to explain why this method of teaching worked so well for Mr. Dunbar in his middle school math and science classroom. (Students might want to volunteer for the panel.) Members of the audience can ask questions once each panelist has spoken.

CRITICAL THINKING Reflect on Mr. Dunbar's teaching style. How would you characterize it (e.g., Piagetian, Vygotskian, discovery, other)? How does he frame the task and interact with students? His addressing of students' prior learning and questioning is critical from a constructivist point of view. Why?

Learning is much more than memory. For students to really understand and be able to apply knowledge, they must work to solve problems, to discover things for themselves, to wrestle with ideas. Mr. Dunbar could have told his students that the formula for the volume of a cylinder is $\pi r^2 h$. With practice the students would have been able to feed numbers into this formula and grind out correct answers. But how much would it have meant to them, and how well could they have applied the ideas behind the formula to other problems? The task of education is not to pour information into students' heads, but to engage students' minds with powerful and useful concepts. The focus of this chapter is to examine ways of doing this.

WHAT IS THE CONSTRUCTIVIST VIEW OF LEARNING?

INTASC

4 Multiple Instructional Strategies

One of the most important principles of educational psychology is that teachers cannot simply give students knowledge. Students must construct knowledge in their own minds. The teacher can facilitate this process by teaching in ways that make information meaningful and relevant to students, by giving students opportunities to discover or apply ideas themselves, and by teaching students to be aware of and consciously use their own strategies for learning. Teachers can give students ladders that lead to higher understanding, yet the students themselves must climb these ladders.

Theories of learning based on these ideas are called **constructivist theories of learning.** The essence of constructivist theory is the idea that learners must individually discover and transform complex information if they are to make it their own (Anderson, Greeno, Reder, & Simon, 2000; Waxman, Padron, & Arnold, 2001). Constructivist theory sees learners as constantly checking new information against old rules and then revising rules when they no longer work. This view has profound implications for teaching because it suggests a far more active role for students in their own learning than is typical in many classrooms. Because of the emphasis on students as active learners, constructivist strategies are often called *student-centered instruction*. In a student-centered classroom the teacher becomes the "guide on the side" instead of the "sage on the stage," helping students to discover their own meaning instead of lecturing and controlling all classroom activities (Weinberger & McCombs, 2001; Windschitl, 1999).

"2 + 2 = 4? What kind of constructivist answer is that?"

Historical Roots of Constructivism

constructivist theories of learning Theories that state that learners must individually discover and transform complex information, checking new information against old rules and revising rules when they no longer work.

The constructivist revolution has deep roots in the history of education. It draws heavily on the work of Piaget and Vygotsky (recall Chapter 2), both of whom emphasized that cognitive change takes place only when previous conceptions go through a process of disequilibration in light of new information. Piaget and Vygotsky also emphasized the social nature of learning, and both suggested the use of mixed-ability learning groups to promote conceptual change.

CONNECTIONS
The work of Piaget and of Vygotsky is discussed on pages 31–46 of Chapter 2.

Social Learning Modern constructivist thought draws most heavily on Vygotsky's theories (see John-Steiner & Mahn, 1996; Karpov & Bransford, 1995), which have been used to support classroom instructional methods that emphasize cooperative learning, project-based learning, and discovery. Four key principles derived from Vygotsky's ideas have played an important role. First is his emphasis on the social nature of learning (Hickey, 1997; O'Connor, 1998; Salomon & Perkins, 1998). Children learn, he proposed, through joint interactions with adults and more capable peers. On cooperative projects, such as the one in Mr. Dunbar's class, children are exposed to their peers' thinking processes; this method not only makes the learning outcome available to all students, but also makes other students' thinking processes available to all. Vygotsky noted that successful problem solvers talk themselves through difficult problems. In cooperative groups, children can hear this inner speech out loud and can learn how successful problem solvers are thinking through their approaches.

CONNECTIONS
For more on the zone of proximal development, see Chapter 2, page 43.

Zone of Proximal Development A second key concept is the idea that children learn best the concepts that are in their zone of proximal development. As discussed in Chapter 2, children are working within their zone of proximal development when they are engaged in tasks that they could not do alone but can do with the assistance of peers or adults. For example, if a child could not find the median of a set of numbers by himself but could do so with some assistance from his teacher, then finding medians is probably in his zone of proximal development. When children are working together, each child is likely to have a peer performing on a given task at a slightly higher cognitive level, exactly within the child's zone of proximal development.

VIDEO HOMEWORK EXERCISE
Discussion of The Scarlet Letter

Go to **www.myeducationlab.com** and, in the Homework and Exercises section for Chapter 8 of this text, access the video entitled "Discussion of The Scarlet Letter." Watch the video and complete the homework questions that accompany it, saving your work or transmitting it to your professor as required.

Cognitive Apprenticeship Another concept derived from Vygotsky that emphasizes both the social nature of learning and the zone of proximal development is **cognitive apprenticeship** (Greeno, Collins, & Resnick, 1996; Harpaz & Lefstein, 2000). This term refers to the process by which a learner gradually acquires expertise through interaction with an expert, either an adult or an older or more advanced peer. In many occupations, new workers learn their jobs through a process of apprenticeship, in which a new worker works closely with an expert, who provides a model, gives feedback to the less experienced worker, and gradually socializes the new worker into the norms and behaviors of the profession. Student teaching is a form of apprenticeship. Constructivist theorists suggest that teachers transfer this long-standing and highly effective model of teaching and learning to day-to-day activities in classrooms, both by engaging students in complex tasks and helping them through these tasks (as a master electrician would help an apprentice rewire a house) (Hamman, Berthelot, Saia, & Crowley, 2000) and by engaging students in heterogeneous, cooperative learning groups in which more advanced students help less advanced ones through complex tasks.

ON THE WEB
For more on cognitive apprenticeship go to **http://mathforum.org/~sarah/Discussion.Sessions/Collins.html**.

Mediated Learning Finally, Vygotsky's emphasis on scaffolding, or mediated learning (Kozulin & Presseisen, 1995), is important in modern constructivist thought. Current interpretations of Vygotsky's ideas emphasize the idea that students should be given complex, difficult, realistic tasks and then be given enough help to achieve these tasks (rather than being taught little bits of knowledge that are expected someday to build up to complex tasks). This principle is used to support the classroom use of projects, simulations, explorations in the community, writing for real audiences, and other authentic tasks (Byerly, 2001; Holt & Willard-Holt, 2000). The term *situated learning* (Anderson, Greeno,

cognitive apprenticeship
The process by which a learner gradually acquires expertise through interaction with an expert, either an adult or an older or more advanced peer.

Reder, & Simon, 2000; Prawat, 1992) is used to describe learning that takes place in real-life, authentic tasks.

Top-Down Processing

Constructivist approaches to teaching emphasize top-down rather than bottom-up instruction. The term *top-down* means that students begin with complex problems to solve and then work out or discover (with the teacher's guidance) the basic skills required. For example, students might be asked to write compositions and only later learn about spelling, grammar, and punctuation. This top-down processing approach is contrasted with the traditional bottom-up strategy, in which basic skills are gradually built into more complex skills. In top-down teaching, the tasks students begin with are complex, complete, and authentic, meaning that they are not parts or simplifications of the tasks that students are ultimately expected to perform but are the actual tasks. As one instance of a constructivist approach to mathematics teaching, consider an example from Lampert (1986). The traditional, bottom-up approach to teaching the multiplication of two-digit numbers by one-digit numbers (e.g., $4 \times 12 = 48$) is to teach students a step-by-step procedure to get the right answer. Only after students have mastered this basic skill are they given simple application problems, such as "Sondra saw some pencils that cost 12 cents each. How much money would she need to buy four of them?"

The constructivist approach works in exactly the opposite order, beginning with problems (often proposed by the students themselves) and then helping students figure out how to do the operations. Lampert's example of this appears in Figure 8.1.

For example, in the chapter-opening vignette, Mr. Dunbar used cooperative groups to help students derive a formula for the volume of a cylinder. Recall how the Master Minds bounced ideas off of each other, tried out and discarded false leads, and ultimately came up with a solution and a way to prove that their solution was correct. None of the students could have solved the problem alone, so the groupwork was helpful in arriving at a solution. More important, the experience of hearing others' ideas, trying out and receiving immediate feedback on proposed solutions, and arguing about different ways to proceed gave the Master Minds the cognitive scaffolding that Vygotsky, Bruner, and other constructivists hold to be essential to higher-order learning (Brooks & Brooks, 1993).

Cooperative Learning

Constructivist approaches to teaching typically make extensive use of cooperative learning, on the theory that students will more easily discover and comprehend difficult concepts if they can talk with each other about the problems. Again, the emphasis on the social nature of learning and the use of groups of peers to model appropriate ways of thinking and expose and challenge each other's misconceptions are key elements of Piaget's and Vygotsky's conceptions of cognitive change (Pontecorvo, 1993). Cooperative learning methods are described in more detail later in this chapter.

INTASC

5 **Classroom Motivation and Management**

Discovery Learning

Discovery learning is an important component of modern constructivist approaches that has a long history in education innovation. In **discovery learning** (Bergstrom & O'Brien, 2001; Wilcox, 1993), students are encouraged to learn largely on their own through active involvement with concepts and principles, and teachers encourage students to have experiences and conduct experiments that permit them to discover principles for themselves. Bruner (1966), an advocate of discovery learning, put it this way: "We teach a subject not to produce little living libraries on that subject, but rather to get a student to think . . . for himself, to consider matters as an historian does, to take part in the process of knowledge-getting. Knowing is a process, not a product" (1966, p. 72).

discovery learning
A constructivist approach to teaching in which students are encouraged to discover principles for themselves.

FIGURE 8.1 Mathematical Stories for Teaching Multiplication

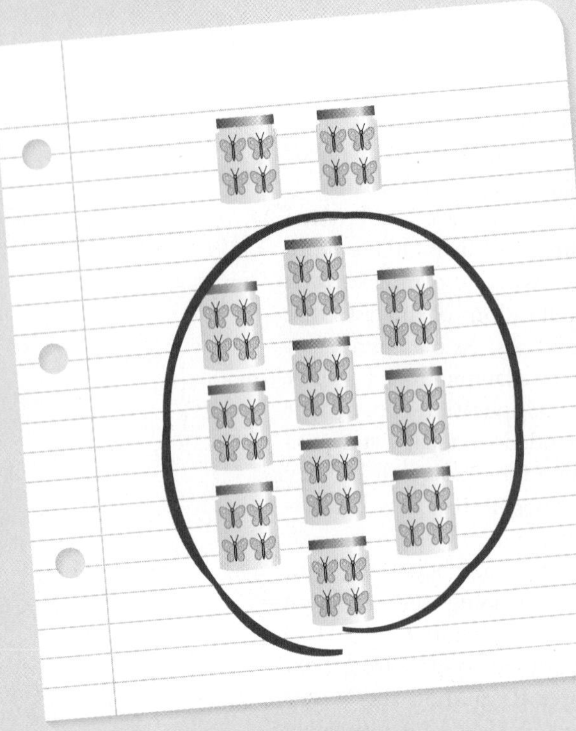

Teacher: Can anyone give me a story that could go with this multiplication . . . 12 × 4?

Student 1: There were 12 jars, and each had 4 butterflies in it.

Teacher: And if I did this multiplication and found the answer, what would I know about those jars and butterflies?

Student 1: You'd know you had that many butterflies altogether.

Teacher: Okay, here are the jars. *[Draws a picture to represent the jars of butterflies—see diagram.]* Now, it will be easier for us to count how many butterflies there are altogether if we think of the jars in groups. And, as usual, the mathematician's favorite number for thinking about groups is?

Student 2: 10

Teacher: Each of these 10 jars has 4 butterflies in it. *[Draws a loop around 10 jars.]*

Teacher: Suppose I erase my circle and go back to looking at the 12 jars again all together: Is there any other way I could group them to make it easier for us to count all the butterflies?

Student 3: You could do 6 and 6.

Teacher: Now, how many do I have in this group?

Student 4: 24

Teacher: How did you figure that out?

Student 4: 8 and 8 and 8. *[He puts the 6 jars together into 3 pairs, intuitively finding a grouping that made the figuring easier for him.]*

Teacher: That's 3 × 8. It's also 6 × 4. Now how many are in this group?

Student 3: 24. It's the same. They both have 6 jars.

Teacher: And how many are there altogether?

Student 5: 24 and 24 is 48.

Teacher: Do we get the same number of butterflies as before? Why?

Student 5: Yeah, because we have the same number of jars and they still have 4 butterflies in each.

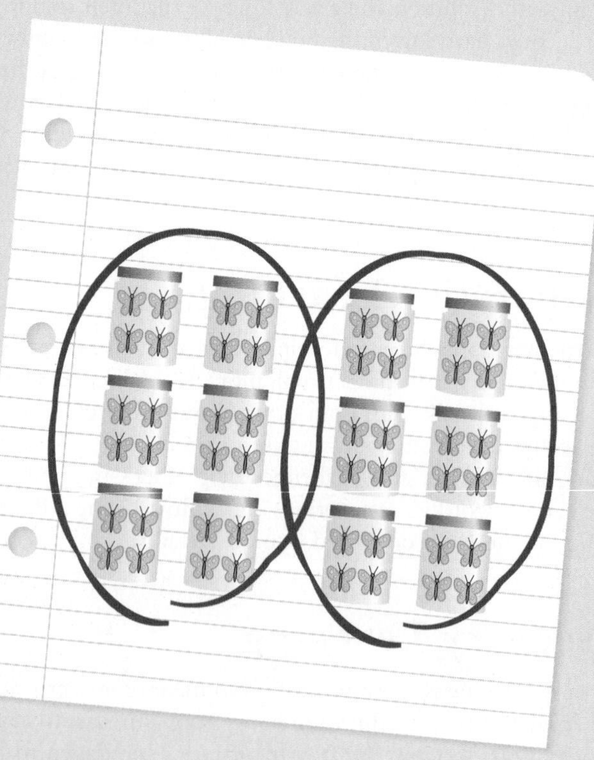

Teaching Dilemmas: CASES TO CONSIDER

Developing Self-Regulating Techniques

Ms. Sanchez has just finished reading *Clifford's Birthday Party* with her first-grade class. This week the students are working on activities related to the story. Ms. Sanchez describes the activities and explains that students should select three activities from the sheet to complete that morning. Activities include writing a story about Clifford, arranging word cards into sentences from the story, and writing a letter to Clifford about his birthday. Students move from center to center working on the activities. Thirty minutes before lunch, Ms. Sanchez asks the students to join her on the rug.

INTASC

3. Adapting Instruction for Individual Needs
5. Classroom Motivation and Management

Ms. Sanchez: We had a lot of different activities this morning, and I wanted to know how you did. Were you successful?

Jessica: I didn't get all three of my activities done.

Ms. Sanchez: Could someone help Jessica by telling her how you planned your activities so that you finished them?

José: I kept working and if my friends talked to me too much, I took my work to another place in the room.

Crystal: I asked my friend to help me spell some of the words so I could write the story about Clifford. I got to use big words!

Ms. Sanchez: I see. José knew that he had to watch out and not get distracted so he could focus on his reading. Crystal knew that she should try to spell the words but that friends can really help us learn new things. Those are good ideas to help us concentrate. Here is another question. Some of you were working with words from the book; you were putting them together so that they were just like the sentences in the story. How did you do that?

Susanna: First, I took out the word that started with a capital letter because I knew it would be the first word.

Ms. Sanchez: You thought about the beginning of the sentence. Did you think about the end, too?

Susanna: Yes, it had a period.

Juwan: I read all the words and kept changing them till they made sense.

Ms. Sanchez: Did you know all the words in the sentence, Tamika?

Tamika: No, I sounded one out. It started with *cl.* I knew *clap,* and I used that to figure out *close.*

Ms. Sanchez: So I hear that some people used the capital letters and punctuation as clues, some kept asking if the words made sense, and some used the letters they already knew to help them sound out new words. Those are all good strategies. You all knew that the sentence was supposed to make sense, just like the story, and you used different ways to do that. Before we go to lunch, I would like to check to see how many students marked off the activities they completed today. [Only half of the students raise their hands.] Do that now. One way you could remember is to make a small mark by each activity you are choosing. Then, before you move on to the next center, mark it off in the box. Any other ideas?

Pasqual: I remember the work I did, and that helps me remember at the end.

Ms. Sanchez: Yes, when you remember the Clifford story you wrote, you can find that on your activity sheet and check it off. Tomorrow, I hope everyone will try some of these good ideas to help them think about how they do their work.

QUESTIONS FOR REFLECTION

1. Some instructional techniques that teachers can use to help students develop self-regulation include modeling, pointing out successful performance, giving feedback for improvement, providing instructions, asking questions, and providing cognitive structures (e.g., identifying the theme of a story as "heroes" or reminding students to use strategies). Find some

examples of these strategies in the dialogue, critique their effectiveness, and change two to be more effective.

2. Could you characterize this instruction as metacognitive? Why or why not?
3. Imagine that Jessica has just announced that she didn't complete her three activities or that she didn't know how to write the letter to Clifford. Rewrite or role-play the dialogue from that point on using different approaches to help her understand and solve her problem.

Discovery learning has applications in many subjects. For example, some science museums have a series of cylinders of different sizes and weights, some hollow and some solid. Students are encouraged to race the cylinders down a ramp. By careful experimentation the students can discover the underlying principles that determine the cylinders' speed. Computer simulations can create environments in which students can discover scientific principles (DeJong & van Joolingen, 1998). After-school enrichment programs (Bergstrom & O'Brien, 2001) and innovative science programs (Singer et al., 2000) are particularly likely to be based on principles of discovery learning.

Discovery learning has several advantages. It arouses students' curiosity, motivating them to continue to work until they find answers. Students also learn independent problem-solving and critical-thinking skills, because they must analyze and manipulate information. However, discovery learning can also lead to errors and wasted time. For this reason, *guided* discovery learning is more common than pure discovery learning (Hmelo-Silver, Duncan, & Chinn, 2007; Pressley et al., 2003). In guided discovery the teacher plays a more active role, giving clues, structuring portions of an activity, or providing outlines.

CONNECTIONS
For more on the motivational aspects of self-regulated learning, see Chapter 10, page 320.

Self-Regulated Learning

A key concept of constructivist theories of learning is a vision of the ideal student as a self-regulated learner (Paris & Paris, 2001). **Self-regulated learners** are ones who have knowledge of effective learning strategies and how and when to use them (Bandura, 1991; Dembo & Eaton, 2000; Schunk & Zimmerman, 1997; Winne, 1997). For example, they know how to break complex problems into simpler steps or to test out alternative solutions (Greeno & Goldman, 1998); they know how and when to skim and how and when to read for deep understanding; and they know how to write to persuade and how to write to inform (Zimmerman & Kitsantas, 1999). Further, self-regulated learners are motivated by learning itself, not only by grades or others' approval (Boekaerts, 1995; Corno, 1992; Schunk, 1995), and they are able to stick to a long-term task until it is done. When students have both effective learning strategies and the motivation and persistence to apply these strategies until a job is done to their satisfaction, then they are likely to be effective learners (Williams, 1995; Zimmerman, 1995) and to have a lifelong motivation to learn (Corno & Kanfer, 1993). Programs that teach children self-regulated learning strategies have been found to increase students' achievement (Fuchs et al., 2003; Mason, 2004; Torrance, Fidalgo, & Garcia, 2007).

CONNECTIONS
For more on scaffolding, see Chapter 2, page 44.

Scaffolding

As was noted in Chapter 2, scaffolding is a practice based on Vygotsky's concept of assisted learning. According to Vygotsky, higher mental functions, including the ability to direct memory and attention in a purposeful way and to think in symbols, are mediated behaviors. Mediated externally by culture, these and other behaviors become internalized in the learner's mind as psychological tools. In assisted learning, or **mediated learning,** the teacher is the cultural agent who guides instruction so that students will master and internalize the skills that permit higher cognitive functioning. The ability to internalize cultural tools relates to the learner's age or stage of cognitive development. Once acquired, however, internal mediators allow greater self-mediated learning.

self-regulated learners
Students who have knowledge of effective learning strategies and how and when to use them.

mediated learning
Assisted learning; an approach in which the teacher guides instruction by means of scaffolding to help students master and internalize the skills that permit higher cognitive functioning.

In practical terms, scaffolding might include giving students more structure at the beginning of a set of lessons and gradually turning responsibility over to them to operate

Early in the scaffolding process, the teacher may provide more structure and then gradually turn responsibility over to the student. What are the possible benefits of this strategy?

on their own (Puntambekar & Hübscher, 2005; Rosenshine & Meister, 1992, 1994; Shepard, 2005). For example, students can be taught to generate their own questions about material they are reading. Early on, the teacher might suggest the questions, modeling the kinds of questions students might ask, but students later take over the question-generating task. For another example of scaffolding, see Figure 8.2.

FIGURE 8.2 Scaffolding

From Laura E. Berk, *Infants, Children, and Adolescents* (2nd ed.), p. 328. Published by Allyn & Bacon, Boston, MA. Copyright © 1996 by Pearson Education. Reprinted by permission of the publisher.

Here is a brief example of an adult scaffolding a young child's efforts to put a difficult puzzle together.

Jason: I can't get this one in. *(Tries to insert a piece in the wrong place)*

Adult: Which piece might go down here? *(Points to the bottom of the puzzle)*

Jason: His shoes. *(Looks for a piece resembling the clown's shoes but tries the wrong one)*

Adult: Well, what piece looks like this shape? *(Points again to the bottom of the puzzle)*

Jason: The brown one. *(Tries it and it fits; then attempts another piece and looks at the adult)*

Adult: There you have it! Now try turning that piece just a little. *(Gestures to show him)*

Jason: There! *(Puts in several more, commenting to himself, "Now a green piece to match," "Turn it [meaning the puzzle piece]," as the adult watches)*

APA's Learner-Centered Psychological Principles

In 1992 the American Psychological Association's Task Force on Psychology in Education published a document called *Learner-Centered Psychological Principles: Guidelines for School Redesign and Reform* (American Psychological Association, 1992, 1997; see also Alexander & Murphy, 1994). Revised in 1997, this publication presents a consensus view of principles of learning and motivation among prominent educational psychologists primarily working within the constructivist tradition. Table 8.1 shows the APA's 14 principles.

The Learner-Centered Psychological Principles paint a picture of the learner as actively seeking knowledge by (1) reinterpreting information and experience for himself or herself, (2) being self-motivated by the quest for knowledge (rather than being motivated by grades or other rewards), (3) working with others to socially construct meaning, and (4) being aware of his or her own learning strategies and capable of applying them to new problems or circumstances.

TABLE 8.1 Learner-Centered Psychological Principles: Cognitive and Metacognitive Factors

Principle	Explanation
Principle 1 Nature of the learning process	The learning of complex subject matter is most effective when it is an intentional process of constructing meaning from information and experience.
Principle 2 Goals of the learning process	The successful learner, over time and with support and instructional guidance, can create meaningful, coherent representations of knowledge.
Principle 3 Construction of knowledge	The successful learner can link new information with existing knowledge in meaningful ways.
Principle 4 Strategic thinking	The successful learner can create and use a repertoire of thinking and reasoning strategies to achieve complex learning goals.
Principle 5 Thinking about thinking	Higher-order strategies for selecting and monitoring mental operations facilitate creative and critical thinking.
Principle 6 Context of learning	Learning is influenced by environmental factors, including culture, technology, and instructional practices.
Principle 7 Motivational and emotional influences on learning	What and how much is learned is influenced by the learner's motivation. Motivation to learn, in turn, is influenced by the individual's emotional states, beliefs, interests and goals, and habits of thinking.
Principle 8 Intrinsic motivation to learn	The learner's creativity, higher-order thinking, and natural curiosity all contribute to motivation to learn. Intrinsic motivation is stimulated by tasks that are of optimal novelty and difficulty, are relevant to personal interests, and provide for personal choice and control.
Principle 9 Effects of motivation on effort	Acquisition of complex knowledge and skills requires extended learner effort and guided practice. Without learners' motivation to learn, the willingness to exert this effort is unlikely without coercion.
Principle 10 Developmental influences on learning	As individuals develop, they encounter different opportunities and experience different constraints for learning. Learning is most effective when differential development within and across physical, intellectual, emotional, and social domains is taken into account.
Principle 11 Social influences on learning	Learning is influenced by social interactions, interpersonal relations, and communication with others.
Principle 12 Individual differences in learning	Learners have different strategies, approaches, and capabilities for learning that are a function of prior experience and heredity.
Principle 13 Learning and diversity	Learning is most effective when differences in learners' linguistic, cultural, and social backgrounds are taken into account.
Principle 14 Standards and assessment	Setting appropriately high and challenging standards and assessing the learner and learning progress—including diagnostic, process, and outcome assessment—are integral parts of the learning process.

Source: This material has been excerpted from "Learner-Centered Psychological Principles: A Framework for School Reform and Redesign." Copyright 1997 by the American Psychological Association. Reproduced with permission. No further reproduction or distribution is permitted without written permission from the American Psychological Association. To view the full document, please go to www.apa.org/ed/cpse/LCPP.pdf. The "Learner-Centered Psychological Principles" is a historical document which was derived from a 1990 APA presidential task force, and was revised in 1997.

Constructivist Methods in the Content Areas

Constructivist and student-centered methods have come to dominate current thinking in all areas of curriculum (see Gabler & Schroeder, 2003; Gagnon & Collay, 2001; Henson, 2004; Mayer, 2001). The following sections describe constructivist approaches in reading, mathematics, and science.

Reciprocal Teaching in Reading One well-researched example of a constructivist approach based on principles of question generation is **reciprocal teaching** (Palincsar & Brown, 1984). This approach, designed primarily to help low achievers in elementary and middle schools learn reading comprehension, involves the teacher working with small groups of students. Initially, the teacher models questions students might ask as they read, but students are soon appointed to act as "teacher" to generate questions for each other. Figure 8.3 presents an example of reciprocal teaching in use. Note in the example how

reciprocal teaching
A small-group teaching method based on principles of question generation; through instruction and modeling, teachers foster metacognitive skills primarily to improve the reading performance of students who have poor comprehension.

FIGURE 8.3 Example of a Reciprocal Teaching Lesson

Teacher: The title of this story is "Genius with Feathers." Let's have some predictions. I will begin by guessing that this story will be about birds that are very smart. Why do I say that?

First student: Because a genius is someone very smart.

Second student: Because they have feathers.

Teacher: That's right. Birds are the only animals that have feathers. Let's predict now the kind of information you might read about very smart birds.

Third student: What kinds of birds?

Teacher: Good question. What kinds would you guess are very smart?

Third student: Parrots or blue jays.

First student: A cockatoo.

Teacher: What other information would you want to know? *[No response from students]*

Teacher: I would like to know what these birds do that is so smart. Any ideas?

Second student: Some birds talk.

Fourth student: They can fly.

Teacher: That's an interesting one. As smart as people are, they can't fly. Well, let's read this first section now and see how many of our predictions were right. I will be the teacher for this section. *[All read the section silently.]*

Teacher: Who is the genius with feathers?

First student: Crows.

Teacher: That's right. We were correct in our prediction that this story would be about birds, but we didn't correctly guess which kind of bird, did we? My summary of the first section would be that it describes the clever things that crows do, which make them seem quite intelligent.

Let's read on. Who will be the teacher for this section? Jim?

Jim: How do crows communicate with one another?

Teacher: Good question! You picked right up on our prediction that this is about the way crows communicate. Whom do you choose to answer your question?

Jim: Barbara.

Barbara: Crows have built-in radar and a relay system.

Jim: That's a good part of it. The answer I wanted was how they relay the messages from one crow to the other crow.

Teacher: Summarize now.

Jim: This is about how crows have developed a system of communication.

Teacher: That's right. The paragraph goes on to give examples of how they use pitch and changes in interval, but these are supporting details. The main idea is that crows communicate through a relay system, Jim?

Jim: It says in this section that crows can use their communication system to play tricks, so I predict the next section will say something about the tricks crows play. I would like Sue to be the next teacher.

Teacher: Excellent prediction. The last sentence of a paragraph often suggests what the next paragraph will be about. Good, Jim.

From Anne Marie Palincsar, "The Role of Dialogue in Providing Scaffolded Instruction," *Educational Psychologist, 21,* 1986, pp. 73–98. Adapted by permission of Lawrence Erlbaum Associates, Inc.

the teacher directs the conversation about crows at first but then turns the responsibility over to Jim (who is about to turn it over to another student as the example ends). The teacher is modeling the behaviors she wants the students to be able to do on their own and then changes her role to that of facilitator and organizer as the students begin to generate the actual questions. Research on reciprocal teaching has generally found this strategy to increase the achievement of low achievers (Alfassi, 1998; Carter, 1997; Lysynchuk, Pressley, & Vye, 1990; Palincsar & Brown, 1984; Rosenshine & Meister, 1994).

THEORY *into* PRACTICE

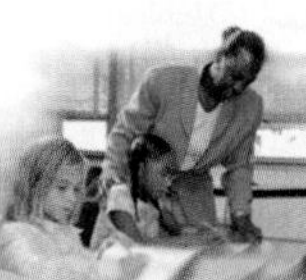

Introducing Reciprocal Teaching

In introducing reciprocal teaching to students, you might begin as follows: "For the coming weeks we will be working together to improve your ability to understand what you read. Sometimes we are so busy figuring out what the words are that we fail to pay much attention to what the words and sentences mean. We will be learning a way to pay more attention to what we are reading. I will teach you to do the following activities as you read:

1. To think of important questions that might be asked about what is being read and to be sure that you can answer those questions
2. To summarize the most important information that you have read
3. To predict what the author might discuss next in the passage
4. To point out when something is unclear in the passage or doesn't make sense and then to see if we can make sense of it

"These activities will help you keep your attention on what you are reading and make sure that you are understanding it.

"The way in which you will learn these four activities is by taking turns in the role of teacher during our reading group sessions. When I am the teacher, I will show you how I read carefully by telling you the questions I made up while reading, by summarizing the most important information I read, and by predicting what I think the author might discuss next. I will also tell you if I found anything I read to be unclear or confusing and how I made sense out of it.

"When you are the teacher, you will first ask the rest of us the questions you made up while reading. You will tell us if our answers are correct. You will summarize the most important information you learned while reading. You will also tell us if you found anything in the passage to be confusing. Several times throughout the story you will also be asked to predict what you think might be discussed next in the passage. When you are the teacher, the rest of us will answer your questions and comment on your summary.

"These are activities that we hope you will learn and use, not only when you are here in reading class but also whenever you want to understand and remember what you are reading—for example, in social studies, science, or history."

DAILY PROCEDURES

1. Pass out the passage for the day.
2. Explain that you will be the teacher for the first segment.
3. Instruct the students to read silently whatever portion of the passage you determine is appropriate. At the beginning, it will probably be easiest to work paragraph by paragraph.
4. When everyone has completed the first segment, model the following:
   - "The question that I thought a teacher might ask is . . ."

- Have the students answer your question. They may refer to the text if necessary. "I would summarize the important information in this paragraph in the following way . . ."
- "From the title of the passage, I would predict that the author will discuss . . ."
- If appropriate, "When I read this part, I found the following to be unclear . . ."

5. Invite the students to make comments regarding your teaching and the passage. For example:

   - "Was there more important information?"
   - "Does anyone have more to add to my prediction?"
   - "Did anyone find something else confusing?"

6. Assign the next segment to be read silently. Choose a student to act as teacher for this segment. Begin with students who are more verbal and who you think will have less difficulty with the activities.
7. Coach the student teacher through the activities as necessary. Encourage the other students to participate in the dialogue, but always give the student teacher for that segment the opportunity to go first and lead the dialogue. Be sure to give the student teacher plenty of feedback and praise for his or her participation.
8. As the training days go by, try to remove yourself more and more from the dialogue so that the student teacher initiates the activities herself or himself with students providing feedback. Your role will continue to be monitoring, keeping students on track, and helping them over obstacles. Throughout the training, however, continue to take your turn as teacher, modeling at least once a session.

Questioning the Author Another constructivist approach for reading is Questioning the Author (Beck & McKeown, 2001; McKeown & Beck, 2004; Salinger & Fleischman, 2005). In this method, children in grades 3–9 are taught to see the authors of factual material as real, fallible people and to then engage in simulated "dialogues" with the authors. As the students are reading a text, the teacher stops them from time to time to ask questions such as "What is the author trying to say, or what does she want us to know?" and then follows up with questions such as "How does that fit in with what she said before?" Ultimately, the students themselves take responsibility for formulating questions of the author's intent and meaning. A study of fifth- and sixth-graders found that students who experienced this technique recalled more from texts than did a comparison group, and were far more likely to describe the purpose of reading as *understanding* rather than simply memorizing the text (McKeown & Beck, 1998). A study of low-achieving kindergartners and first-graders also found positive effects of a similar strategy on vocabulary development (Beck & McKeown, 2007).

Writing Process Models A widely used set of approaches to the teaching of creative writing, writing process models (Calkins, 1983; Graves, 1983) engage students in small peer-response teams in which they work together to help one another plan, draft, revise, edit, and "publish" compositions. That is, children may review each other's drafts and give helpful ideas for improvements in content as well as mechanics (e.g., spelling, punctuation), and ultimately present compositions for some authentic purpose (such as a poetry reading or a literary review). In the process of responding to others' compositions, children gain insight into the process of writing and revision.

Research on writing process methods has found positive effects of these strategies (Harris & Graham, 1996b). Strategies that provide specific scaffolding, such as instruction in graphic organizers to help children use metacognitive strategies for planning and evaluating their own work, have been particularly effective (De La Paz & Graham, 2002; Glasser & Brunstein, 2007; Graham, 2006; Harris, Graham, & Mason, 2006). There is also evidence that teaching writing in various content areas increases content learning in these areas (Bangert-Drowns, Hurley, & Wilkinson, 2004).

Constructivist Approaches to Mathematics Teaching in the Primary Grades Carpenter and colleagues (1994) described four approaches to mathematics instruction for the early elementary grades. In all four, students work together in small groups; teachers pose problems and then circulate among groups to facilitate the discussion of strategies, join students in asking questions about strategies they have proposed, and occasionally offer alternative strategies when students appear to be stuck. In Supporting Ten-Structured Thinking (STST) (Fuson, 1992), children use base-10 blocks to invent procedures for adding and subtracting large numbers. Conceptually Based Instruction (CBI) (Hiebert & Wearne, 1993) makes extensive use of physical, pictorial, verbal, and symbolic presentations of mathematical ideas and gives students opportunities to solve complex problems using these representations and to contrast different representations of the same concepts. Similarly, the Problem Centered Mathematics Project (PCMP) (Murray, Olivier, & Human, 1992) leads children through stages, from modeling with counters to solving more abstract problems without counters. Cognitively Guided Instruction (CGI) (Carpenter & Fennema, 1992; Fennema, Franke, Carpenter, & Carey, 1993), unlike STST and CBI, does not have a specific curriculum or recommended set of activities but provides extensive professional development for teachers of primary mathematics, focusing on principles similar to those used in the other programs. There is good evidence that this program increases student achievement not only on measures related to higher-level thinking in mathematics, which is the program's focus, but also on computational skills (Carpenter & Fennema, 1992; Carpenter, Fennema, Peterson, Chiang, & Loef, 1989).

In these and other constructivist approaches to mathematics, the emphasis is on beginning with real problems for students to solve intuitively and letting students use their existing knowledge of the world to solve problems any way they can (Greeno & Goldman, 1998; Hiebert et al., 1996; Schifter, 1996). The problem and solutions in Figure 8.1 illustrate this approach. Only at the end of the process, when students have achieved a firm conceptual understanding, are they taught formal, abstract representations of the mathematical processes they have been working with (see Clements & Battista, 1990).

Constructivist Approaches in Science Discovery, groupwork, and conceptual change have long been emphasized in science education, so it is not surprising that many elementary and secondary science educators have embraced constructivist ideas (see Greeno & Goldman, 1998). In this subject, constructivism translates into an emphasis on hands-on, investigative laboratory activities (Bainer & Wright, 1998; Pine & Aschbacher, 2006; Singer, Marx, Krajcik, & Chambers, 2000; White & Frederiksen, 1998), identifying misconceptions and using experimental approaches to correct these misconceptions (Hand & Treagust, 1991; Sandoval, 1995), and cooperative learning (Pea, 1993; Wheatley, 1991).

Research on Constructivist Methods

CERTIFICATION POINTER

For teacher certification tests, you may be expected to choose alternative teaching strategies to achieve particular instructional goals.

Research comparing constructivist and traditional approaches to instruction is often difficult to interpret because constructivist methods are themselves very diverse and are usually intended to produce outcomes that are qualitatively different from those of traditional methods. For example, many researchers argue that acquisition of skills and basic information must be balanced against constructivist approaches (Airsian & Walsh, 1997; Harris & Graham, 1996b). But what is the appropriate balance, and for which objectives (Harris & Alexander, 1998; von Glaserfeld, 1996; Waxman, Padrón, & Arnold, 2001)? Also, much of the research on constructivist methods is descriptive rather than comparative. However, there are studies showing positive effects of constructivist approaches on traditional achievement measures in mathematics (e.g., Carpenter & Fennema, 1992), science (e.g., Neale, Smith, & Johnson, 1990), reading (e.g., Duffy & Roehler, 1986), and writing (e.g., De La Paz & Graham, 2002). Furthermore, a study by Knapp (1995) found a correlation between use of more constructivist approaches and achievement gains in high-poverty schools. Weinberger and McCombs (2001) and Cornelius-White (2007) found that students who reported more learner-centered methods used in their classrooms performed at a higher level than other students. Langer (2001) also found that secondary schools that performed better than expected used more constructivist approaches than lower-achieving schools. However, other studies found better results for explicit teaching than for constructivist approaches (Baker, Gersten, & Lee, 2002; Kirschner et al., 2006; Klahr & Nigam, 2004; Kroesbergen, Van Luit & Maas, 2004). Much more research is needed to establish the conditions under which constructivist approaches are effective for enhancing student achievement.

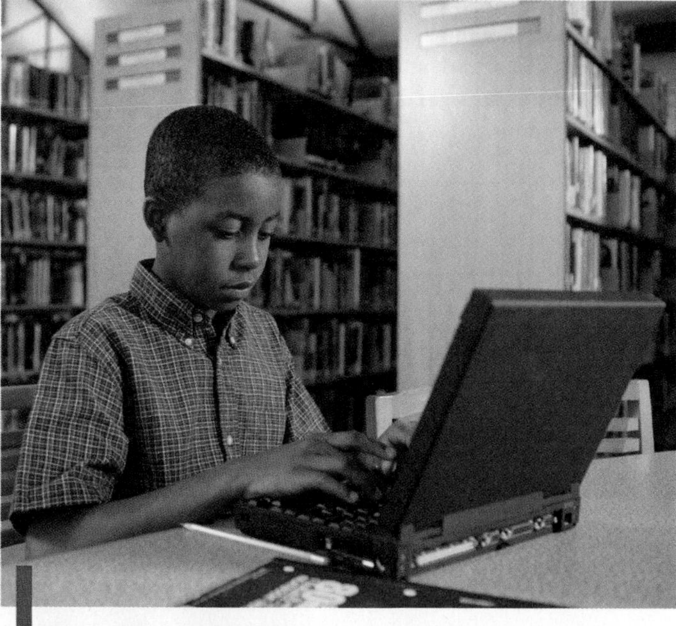

Technology can help a teacher provide students with multiple representations of concepts. How does technology reinforce constructivist learning?

HOW IS COOPERATIVE LEARNING USED IN INSTRUCTION?

In **cooperative learning** instructional methods, or peer-assisted learning (Rohrbeck, Ginsburg-Block, Fantuzzo, & Miller, 2003), students work together in small groups to help each other learn. Many quite different approaches to cooperative learning exist. Most involve students in four-member, mixed-ability groups (e.g., Slavin, 1994a), but some methods use dyads (e.g., Fantuzzo, Polite, & Grayson, 1990; Maheady, Harper, & Mallette, 1991; O'Donnell & Dansereau, 1992), and some use varying group sizes (e.g., Cohen, 1994b; Johnson & Johnson, 1999; Kagan, 1992; Sharan & Sharan, 1992). Typically, students are assigned to cooperative groups and stay together as a group for many weeks or months. They are usually taught specific skills that will help them work well together, such as active listening, giving good explanations, avoiding putdowns, and including other people.

Cooperative learning activities can play many roles in lessons (Webb & Palincsar, 1996). Recall the chapter-opening vignette in Chapter 7: Ms. Logan used cooperative learning for three distinct purposes. At first, students worked as discovery groups, helping each other figure out how water in bottles could tell them about principles of sound. After the formal lesson, students worked as discussion groups. Finally, students had an opportunity to work together to make sure that all group members had learned everything in the lesson in preparation for a quiz, working in a group study format. In the vignette at the beginning of this chapter, Mr. Dunbar used cooperative groups to solve a complex problem.

INTASC

4 Multiple instructional Strategies

5 Classroom Motivation and Management

CERTIFICATION POINTER

On your teacher certification test, you may be required to suggest an appropriate way of assigning students in a case study to cooperative learning groups.

ON THE WEB

For newsletters and resources for cooperative learning, visit the website of the International Association for the Study of Cooperation in Education at **www.iasce.net.**

cooperative learning
Instructional approaches in which students work in small mixed-ability groups.

Cooperative Learning Methods

Many quite different cooperative learning methods have been developed and researched. The most extensively evaluated cooperative learning methods are described in the following sections.

CONNECTIONS

To learn about the benefits of cooperative learning methods in promoting harmony in culturally diverse classrooms, see Chapter 4, page 106.

By working together these students learn from each other. What are some advantages of cooperative learning?

Student Teams–Achievement Divisions (STAD) In **Student Teams–Achievement Divisions (STAD)** (Slavin, 1994a), students are assigned to four-member learning teams that are mixed in performance level, gender, and ethnicity. The teacher presents a lesson, and then students work within their teams to make sure that all team members have mastered the lesson. Finally, all students take individual quizzes on the material, at which time they may not help one another.

Students' quiz scores are compared to their own past averages, and points are awarded on the basis of the degree to which students meet or exceed their own earlier performance. These points are then summed to form team scores, and teams that meet certain criteria may earn certificates or other rewards. In a related method called Teams–Games–Tournaments (TGT), students play games with members of other teams to add points to their team scores.

STAD and TGT have been used in a wide variety of subjects, from mathematics to language arts to social studies, and have been used from second grade through college. The STAD method is most appropriate for teaching well-defined objectives with single right answers, such as mathematical computations and applications, language usage and mechanics, geography and map skills, and science facts and concepts. However, it can easily be adapted for use with less well-defined objectives by incorporating more open-ended assessments, such as essays or performances. STAD is described in more detail in the next Theory into Practice.

THEORY *into* PRACTICE

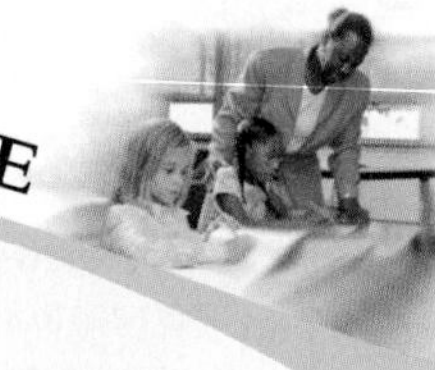

Student Teams–Achievement Divisions (STAD)

An effective cooperative learning method is called Student Teams–Achievement Divisions, or STAD (Slavin, 1994a, 1995a). STAD consists of a regular cycle of teaching, cooperative study in mixed-ability teams, and quizzes, with recognition or other rewards provided to teams whose members excel.

STAD consists of a regular cycle of instructional activities, as follows:

- ***Teach:*** Present the lesson.
- ***Team study:*** Students work on worksheets in their teams to master the material.

Student Teams–Achievement Divisions (STAD)
A cooperative learning method for mixed-ability groupings involving team recognition and group responsibility for individual learning.

- ***Test:*** Students take individual quizzes or other assessments (such as essays or performances).
- ***Team recognition:*** Team scores are computed on the basis of team members' scores, and certificates, a class newsletter, or a bulletin board recognizes high-scoring teams.

The following steps describe how to introduce students to STAD:

1. Assign students to teams of four or five members each. Four are preferable; make five-member teams only if the class is not divisible by four. To assign the students, rank them from top to bottom on some measure of academic performance (e.g., past grades, test scores) and divide the ranked list into quarters, placing any extra students in the middle quarters. Then put one student from each quarter on each team, making sure that the teams are well balanced in gender and ethnicity. Extra (middle) students may become fifth members of teams.
2. Make a worksheet and a short quiz for the lesson you plan to teach. During team study (one or two class periods) the team members' tasks are to master the material you presented in your lesson and to help their teammates master the material. Students have worksheets or other study materials that they can use to practice the skill being taught and to assess themselves and their teammates.
3. When you introduce STAD to your class, read off team assignments.
   - Have teammates move their desks together or move to team tables and allow students about 10 minutes to decide on a team name.
   - Hand out worksheets or other study materials (two of each per team).
   - Suggest that students on each team work in pairs or threes. If they are working problems (as in math), each student in a pair or threesome should work the problem and then check with his or her partner(s). If anyone missed a question, that student's teammates have a responsibility to explain it. If students are working on short-answer questions, they might quiz each other, with partners taking turns holding the answer sheet or attempting to answer the questions.
   - Emphasize to students that they are not finished studying until they are sure that all their teammates will make 100 percent on the quiz.
   - Make sure that students understand that the worksheets are for studying—not for filling out and handing in. That is why it is important for students to have the answer sheets to check themselves and their teammates as they study.
   - Have students explain answers to one another instead of only checking each other against the answer sheet.
   - When students have questions, have them ask a teammate before asking you.
   - While students are working in teams, circulate through the class, praising teams that are working well and sitting in with each team to hear how the members are doing.
4. Distribute the quiz or other assessment, and give students adequate time to complete it. Do not let students work together on the quiz; at this point they must show what they have learned as individuals. Have students move their desks apart if this is possible. Either allow students to exchange papers with members of other teams or collect the quizzes to score after class.
5. Figure individual and team scores. Team scores in STAD are based on team members' improvements over their own past records. As soon as possible after each quiz, you should compute individual team scores, and write a class newsletter (or prepare a class bulletin board) to announce the team scores. If at all possible, the announcement of team scores should be made in the first period after the quiz. This makes the connection between doing well and receiving recognition clear to students, increasing their motivation to do their best. Compute team scores by adding up the improvement points earned by the team

VIDEO HOMEWORK EXERCISE
Cooperative Learning

Go to **www.myeducationlab.com** and, in the Homework and Exercises section for Chapter 8 of this text, access the video entitled "Cooperative Learning." Watch the video and complete the homework questions that accompany it, saving your work or transmitting it to your professor as required.

members and dividing the sum by the number of team members who are present on the day of the quiz.

6. Recognize team accomplishments. As soon as you have calculated points for each student and figured team scores, you should provide some sort of recognition to any teams that averaged 20 improvement points or more. You might give certificates to team members or prepare a bulletin board display. It is important to help students value team success. Your own enthusiasm about team scores will help. If you give more than one quiz in a week, combine the quiz results into a single weekly score. After 5 or 6 weeks of STAD, reassign students to new teams. This allows students to work with other classmates and keeps the program fresh.

Cooperative Integrated Reading and Composition (CIRC) **Cooperative Integrated Reading and Composition (CIRC)** (Stevens & Slavin, 1995a) is a comprehensive program for teaching reading and writing in the upper elementary grades. Students work in four-member cooperative learning teams. They engage in a series of activities with one another, including reading to one another; making predictions about how narrative stories will come out; summarizing stories to one another; writing responses to stories; and practicing spelling, decoding, and vocabulary. They also work together to master main ideas and other comprehension skills. During language arts periods, students engage in writing drafts, revising and editing one another's work, and preparing for publication of team books. Three studies of the CIRC program have found positive effects on students' reading skills, including improved scores on standardized reading and language tests (Slavin, Madden, & Stevens, 1994; Stevens et al., 1987; Stevens & Slavin, 1995a).

Jigsaw In **Jigsaw** (Aronson, Blaney, Stephen, Sikes, & Snapp, 1978), students are assigned to six-member teams to work on academic material that has been broken down into sections. For example, a biography might be divided into early life, first accomplishments, major setbacks, later life, and impact on history. Each team member reads his or her section. Next, members of different teams who have studied the same sections meet in expert groups to discuss their sections. Then the students return to their teams and take turns teaching their teammates about their sections. Because the only way students can learn sections other than their own is to listen carefully to their teammates, they are motivated to support and show interest in one another's work. In a modification of this approach called Jigsaw II (Slavin, 1994a), students work in four- or five-member teams, as in STAD. Instead of each student being assigned a unique section, all students read a common text, such as a book chapter, a short story, or a biography. However, each student receives a topic on which to become an expert. Students with the same topics meet in expert groups to discuss them, after which they return to their teams to teach what they have learned to their teammates. The students take individual quizzes, which result in team scores, as in STAD.

Learning Together **Learning Together,** a model of cooperative learning developed by David Johnson and Roger Johnson (1999), involves students working in four- or five-member heterogeneous groups on assignments. The groups hand in a single completed assignment and receive praise and rewards based on the group product. This method emphasizes team-building activities before students begin working together and regular discussions within groups about how well they are working together.

Group Investigation **Group Investigation** (Sharan & Sharan, 1992) is a general classroom organization plan in which students work in small groups using cooperative inquiry, group discussion, and cooperative planning and projects. In this method, students form their own two- to six-member groups. After choosing subtopics from a unit that the entire class is studying, the groups break their subtopics into individual

Cooperative Integrated Reading and Composition (CIRC)
A comprehensive program for teaching reading and writing in the upper elementary grades; students work in four-member cooperative learning teams.

Jigsaw
A cooperative learning model in which students are assigned to six-member teams to work on academic material that has been broken down into sections for each member.

Learning Together
A cooperative learning model in which students in four- or five-member heterogeneous groups work together on assignments.

Group Investigation
A cooperative learning model in which students work in small groups using cooperative inquiry, group discussion, and cooperative planning and projects, and then make presentations to the whole class on their findings.

tasks and carry out the activities that are necessary to prepare group reports. Each group then makes a presentation or display to communicate its findings to the entire class.

Cooperative Scripting Many students find it helpful to get together with classmates to discuss material they have read or heard in class. A formalization of this age-old practice has been researched by Dansereau (1985) and his colleagues. In it, students work in pairs and take turns summarizing sections of the material for one another. While one student summarizes, the other listens and corrects any errors or omissions. Then the two students switch roles, continuing in this manner until they have covered all the material to be learned. A series of studies of this **cooperative scripting** method has consistently found that students who study this way learn and retain far more than students who summarize on their own or who simply read the material (Newbern, Dansereau, Patterson, & Wallace, 1994). It is interesting that although both participants in the cooperative pairs gain from the activity, the larger gains are seen in the sections that students teach to their partners rather than in those for which they serve as listeners (Spurlin, Dansereau, Larson, & Brooks, 1984). More recent studies of various forms of peer tutoring find similar results (Fuchs & Fuchs, 1997; King, 1997, 1998).

Research on Cooperative Learning

Cooperative learning methods fall into two broad categories (Slavin, Hurley, & Chamberlain, 2003). One category might be called group study methods (Slavin, 1996b), in which students primarily work together to help one another master a relatively well-defined body of information or skills—what Cohen (1994b) calls "well-structured problems." The other category is often called project-based learning or active learning (Stern, 1996). Project-based learning methods involve students working in groups to create a report, experiment, mural, or other product (Webb & Palincsar, 1996). Project-based learning methods such as those described by Blumenfeld, Marx, Soloway, and Krajcik (1996); Cohen (1994a); and Sharan and Sharan (1992) focus on ill-structured problems, which typically have less of a clear expected outcome or instructional objective. Methods of this kind are often referred to as collaborative learning methods (Webb & Palincsar, 1996).

"At least I'm glad to see that you're finally working well as a group."

Most research comparing cooperative learning to traditional teaching methods has evaluated group study methods such as STAD, Jigsaw II, CIRC, and Johnson's methods. More than 100 studies have compared achievement of students in such methods to that of students in traditional classrooms over periods of at least 4 weeks (Slavin, 1995a). The results have consistently favored cooperative learning as long as two essential conditions are met. First, some kind of recognition or small reward must be provided to groups that do well so that group members can see that it is in their interest to help their groupmates learn (O'Donnell, 1996). Second, there must be individual accountability. That is, the success of the group must depend on the individual learning of all group members, not on a single group product. For example, groups might be evaluated on the basis of the average of their members' scores on individual quizzes or essays (as in STAD), or students might be individually responsible for a unique portion of a group task (as in Group Investigation). Without this individual accountability there is a danger that one student

cooperative scripting
A study method in which students work in pairs and take turns orally summarizing sections of material to be learned.

CONNECTIONS
For more on how cooperative learning methods benefit the social integration of students with special education needs in the general education classroom, see Chapter 12, page 399.

might do the work of the others, or that some students might be shut out of group interaction because they are thought to have little to contribute (O'Donnell & O'Kelly, 1994; Slavin, 1995a).

Studies of cooperative learning methods that incorporate group goals and individual accountability show substantial positive effects on the achievement of students in grades 2 through 12 in all subjects and in all types of schools (Ellis, 2001b; Rohrbeck et al., 2003; Slavin, 1995a; Slavin, Hurley, & Chamberlain, 2003). A review of group learning with technology also found positive effects for well-structured methods (Lou, Abrami, & d'Apollonia, 2001). Effects are similar for all grade levels and for all types of content, from basic skills to problem solving (Qin, Johnson, & Johnson, 1995). Cooperative learning methods are usually used for only a portion of a student's school day and school year (Antil, Jenkins, Wayne, & Vadasy, 1998), but one study found that students in schools that used a variety of cooperative learning methods in almost all subjects for a 2-year period achieved significantly better than did students in traditionally organized schools (Stevens & Slavin, 1995b). These effects were particularly positive for the highest achievers (compared to equally high achievers in the control group) and for the special-education students. Other studies have found equal effects of cooperative learning for high, average, and low achievers and for boys and girls (Slavin, 1995a). There is some evidence that these methods are particularly effective for African American and Latino students (Boykin, 1994a; Calderón et al., 1998; Hurley, 2000; Slavin, Hurley, & Chamberlain, 2003). A review of peer assisted learning by Rohrbeck and colleagues (2003) found that effects were strongest on younger, urban, low-income, and minority students. More informal cooperative learning methods, lacking group goals and individual accountability, have not generally had positive effects on student achievement (Chapman, 2001; Klein & Schnackenberg, 2000; Slavin, 1995a; Slavin et al., 2003).

BUILDING TEACHING SKILLS READING EXERCISE
The Many Faces of Constructivism (Perkins)

Go to **www.myeducationlab.com** and, in Building Teaching Skills section for Chapter 8 of this text, access the video entitled "The Many Faces of Constructivism (Perkins)." Read the article and complete the homework questions that accompany it, saving your work or transmitting it to your professor as required.

In addition to group goals and individual accountability, a few classroom practices can contribute to the effectiveness of cooperative learning. For example, students in cooperative groups who are taught communication and helping skills (Fuchs, Fuchs, Kazdan, & Allen, 1999; Prichard, Bizo, & Stratford, 2006; Webb & Mastergeorge, 2003) or are given specific structured ways of working with each other learn more than do students in cooperative groups without these enhancements (Baker, Gersten, & Lee, 2002; Emmer & Gerwels, 2002; Mathes et al., 2003). In addition, students who are taught metacognitive learning strategies (Fantuzzo, King, & Heller, 1992; Friend, 2001; Hoek, Terwel, & van den Eeden, 1997; Jones et al., 2000; Kramarski & Mevarech, 2003) learn more than do students in usual cooperative groups. For example, King (1999) taught students generic question forms to ask each other as they studied, such as "compare and contrast _______ and _______," or "how does _______ affect _______?" Students in classes that used these discourse patterns learned more than students using other forms of cooperative learning. A great deal of research has shown that students who give extensive explanations to others learn more in cooperative groups than do those who give or receive short answers or no answers (Nattiv, 1994; Webb, 1992; Webb, Trooper, & Fall, 1995).

There is less research on the effects of project-based forms of cooperative learning focused on ill-structured problems, but the studies that do exist show equally favorable results of cooperative methods designed for such problems (Blumenfeld et al., 1996; Lazarowitz, 1995; Thousand & Villa, 1994). In particular, a study by Sharan and Shachar (1988) found substantial positive effects of the Group Investigation method on higher-order objectives in language and literature, and studies by Cohen (1994a) have shown that the more consistently teachers implement her Complex Instruction program, the better children achieve.

CERTIFICATION POINTER
On your teacher certification test, you may be asked to determine when you would *not* employ a particular cooperative learning strategy.

In addition to boosting achievement, cooperative learning methods have had positive effects on such outcomes as improved intergroup relations (Slavin, 1995b), self-esteem, attitudes toward school, and acceptance of children with special educational needs (Ginsburg-Block, Rohrbeck, & Fantuzzo, 2006; Shulman, Lotan, & Whitcomb, 1998; Slavin, 1995a; Slavin et al., 2003). Studies find that cooperative learning is very widely used (e.g., Antil et al., 1998; Puma et al., 1997), but the forms of cooperative learning most often used are informal methods lacking group goals and individual accountability.

Personal REFLECTION

INTASC 5 Classroom Motivation and Management

Working Together

I once visited a seventh-grade math class that was using a form of cooperative learning. The students had been taught advanced problem-solving strategies, and the teacher was extraordinarily capable. She posed to the students an exciting question involving a king who decided to release some prisoners according to a mathematical pattern that the students had to discover. The students were asked to work together in groups of four to solve the problem.

The students, in their groups, got right to work, excitedly using their problem-solving strategies to try to find the answer. Everything looked wonderful until I began to listen in on some of the teams. What was happening was that in most teams, one or two students had taken over the task. Other students were simply watching them work. Once a watching student, who happened to be of an ethnic minority, offered a suggestion. "Quiet!" said one of the working students. "We've almost got the answer!"

This experience reinforced for me the importance of group goals and individual accountability in cooperative learning. The teacher's instructions were perfect from a math perspective but disastrous from a cooperative learning perspective. By having the group arrive at a simple solution as quickly as possible, students felt to be less able (or less aggressive) by their peers were sure to be sidelined. Imagine that the goals of the activity were not only to solve the problem but also to ensure that every member of the group could later explain the solution or solve a similar problem working alone. In this case, it would be essential to all students to make sure that everyone was involved and that everyone was learning to solve the problems.

REFLECT ON THIS. **How might the math teacher have structured the cooperative learning to ensure that all students would be involved and all would learn to solve similar problems?**

If this method is to achieve its full potential, educators will need to focus on more research-based strategies.

HOW ARE PROBLEM-SOLVING AND THINKING SKILLS TAUGHT?

INTASC

4 Multiple Instructional Strategies

Students cannot be said to have learned anything useful unless they have the ability to use information and skills to solve problems. For example, a student might be quite good at adding, subtracting, and multiplying but have little idea of how to solve this problem: "Sylvia bought four hamburgers at $1.25 each, two orders of french fries at 65 cents, and three large sodas at 75 cents. How much change did she get from a 10-dollar bill?"

Sylvia's situation is not an unusual one in real life, and the computations involved are not difficult. However, many students (and even some otherwise-competent adults) would have difficulty solving this problem. The difficulty of most applications problems in mathematics lies not in the computations but in knowing how to set the problem up so that it can be solved. **Problem solving** is a skill that can be taught and learned (Fuchs et al., 2006; Martinez, 1998; Mayer & Wittrock, 1996).

The Problem-Solving Process

problem solving
The application of knowledge and skills to achieve certain goals.

General Problem-Solving Strategies Students can be taught several well-researched strategies to use in solving problems (see, for example, Beyer, 1998; Derry, 1991; Tishman,

Perkins, & Jay, 1995). Bransford and Stein (1993) developed and evaluated a five-step strategy called IDEAL:

I Identify problems and opportunities
D Define goals and represent the problem
E Explore possible strategies
A Anticipate outcomes and act
L Look back and learn

IDEAL and similar strategies begin with careful consideration of what problem needs to be solved, what resources and information are available, and how the problem can be represented (e.g., in a drawing, outline, or flowchart) and then broken into steps that lead to a solution. For example, the first step is to identify the goal and figure out how to proceed. Newell and Simon (1972) suggest that the problem solver repeatedly ask, "What is the difference between where I am now and where I want to be? What can I do to reduce that difference?" In solving Sylvia's problem, the goal is to find out how much change she will receive from a 10-dollar bill after buying food and drinks. We might then break the problem into substeps, each with its own subgoal:

1. Figure how much Sylvia spent on hamburgers.
2. Figure how much Sylvia spent on french fries.
3. Figure how much Sylvia spent on sodas.
4. Figure how much Sylvia spent in total.
5. Figure how much change Sylvia gets from $10.00.

Means–Ends Analysis Deciding what the problem is and what needs to be done involves a **means–ends analysis.** Learning to solve problems requires a great deal of practice with different kinds of problems that demand thought. All too often, textbooks in mathematics and other subjects that include many problems fail to present problems that will make students think. For example, they might give students a set of word problems whose solutions require the multiplication of two numbers. Students soon learn that they can solve such problems by looking for any two numbers and multiplying them. In real life, however, problems do not line themselves up neatly in categories. We might hear, "Joe Smith got a 5 percent raise last week, which amounted to $1,200." If we want to figure out how much Joe was making before his raise, the hard part is not doing the calculation, but knowing what calculation is called for. In real life this problem would not be on a page titled "Dividing by Percents." The more different kinds of problems students

means–ends analysis
A problem-solving technique that encourages identifying the goal (ends) to be attained, the current situation, and what needs to be done (means) to reduce the difference between the two conditions.

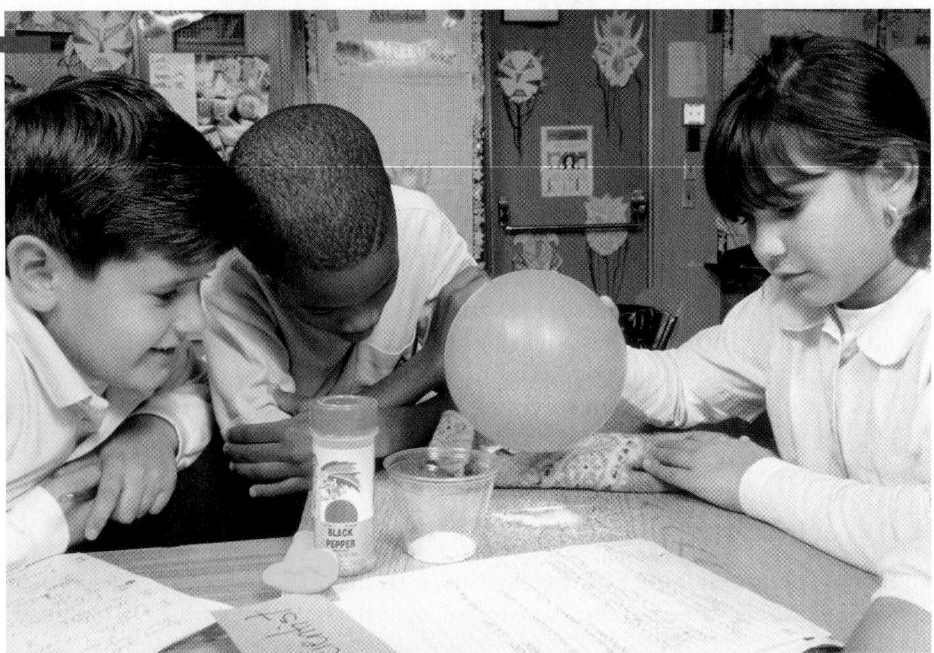

What steps should these students take to successfully solve the problem?

learn to solve, and the more they have to think to solve the problems, the greater the chance that, when faced with real-life problems, students will be able to transfer their skills or knowledge to the new situation.

Extracting Relevant Information Realistic problems are rarely neat and tidy. Imagine that Sylvia's problem was as follows:

> Sylvia walked into the fast-food restaurant at 6:18 with three friends. Between them, they bought four hamburgers at $1.25 each, two orders of french fries at 65 cents, and three large sodas at 75 cents. Onion rings were on sale for 55 cents. Sylvia's mother told her to be in by 9:00, but she was already 25 minutes late by the time she and her friends left the restaurant. Sylvia drove the 3 miles home at an average of 30 miles per hour. How long was Sylvia in the restaurant?

The first part of this task is to clear away all the extraneous information to get to the important facts. The means–ends analysis suggests that only time information is relevant, so all the money transactions and the speed of Sylvia's car can be ignored. Careful reading of the problem reveals that Sylvia left the restaurant at 9:25. This and her arrival time of 6:18 are all that matters for solving the problem. Once we know what is relevant and what is not, the solution is easy.

Representing the Problem For many kinds of problems, graphic representation might be an effective means of finding a solution. Adams (1974) provides a story that illustrates this:

> A Buddhist monk has to make a pilgrimage and stay overnight in a temple that is at the top of a high mountain. The road spirals around and around the mountain. The monk begins walking up the mountain at sunrise. He walks all day long and finally reaches the top at about sunset. He stays all night in the temple and performs his devotions. At sunrise the next day the monk begins walking down the mountain. It takes him much less time than walking up, and he is at the bottom shortly after noon. The question is: Is there a point on the road when he was coming down that he passed at the same time of day when he was coming up the mountain?

This can seem to be a difficult problem because people begin to reason in a variety of ways as they think about the man going up and down. Adams points out one representation that makes the problem easy: Suppose there were two monks, one leaving the top at sunrise and one starting up at sunrise. Would they meet? Of course they would.

In addition to drawings, there are many other ways of representing problems. Students may be taught to make diagrams, flowcharts, outlines, and other means of summarizing and depicting the critical components of a problem (Katayama & Robinson, 1998; Robinson & Kiewra, 1995; van Meter, 2001).

Teaching Creative Problem Solving

Most of the problems students encounter in school might require careful reading and some thought, but little creativity. However, many of the problems we face in life are not so cut-and-dried. Life is full of situations that call for creative problem solving, as in figuring out how to change or end a relationship without hurt feelings or how to repair a machine with a bent paper clip (Plucker, Beghetto, & Dow, 2004).

The following sections describe a strategy for teaching creative problem solving (Beyer, 1998; Fleith, 2000).

Incubation Creative problem solving is quite different from the analytical, step-by-step process that was used to solve Sylvia's problems. In creative problem solving, one important principle is to avoid rushing to a solution; instead, it is useful to pause and reflect on the problem and think through, or incubate, several alternative solutions before choosing a course of action. Consider the following simple problem:

> Roger baked an apple pie in his oven in three quarters of an hour. How long would it take him to bake three apple pies?

Many students would rush to multiply 45 minutes by 3. However, if they took some time to reflect, most would realize that baking three pies in the same oven would actually take about the same amount of time as baking one pie! In teaching this process, teachers must avoid putting time pressures on students. Instead of speed, they should value ingenuity and careful thought.

Suspension of Judgment In creative problem solving, students should be encouraged to suspend judgment, to consider all possibilities before trying out a solution. One specific method based on this principle is called *brainstorming* (Osborn, 1963), in which two or more individuals suggest as many solutions to a problem as they can think of, no matter how seemingly ridiculous. Only after they have thought of as many ideas as possible is any idea evaluated as a possible solution. The point of brainstorming is to avoid focusing on one solution too early and perhaps ignoring better ways to proceed.

Appropriate Climates Creative problem solving is enhanced by a relaxed, even playful environment (Tishman et al., 1995). Perhaps even more important, students who are engaging in creative problem solving must feel that their ideas will be accepted.

People who do well on tests of creative problem solving seem to be less afraid of making mistakes and appearing foolish than do those who do poorly. Successful problem solvers also seem to treat problem-solving situations more playfully (Benjafield, 1992). This implies that a relaxed, fun atmosphere is important in teaching problem solving. Students should certainly be encouraged to try different solutions and not be criticized for taking a wrong turn.

Analysis One method of creative problem solving that is often suggested is to analyze and juxtapose major characteristics or specific elements of a problem (Chen & Daehler, 2000; Lesgold, 1988). For example, careful analysis of the situation might help solve the following problem:

> A tennis tournament was set up with a series of rounds. The winner of each match advanced to the next round. If there were an odd number of players in a round, one player (chosen at random) would advance automatically to the next round. In a tournament with 147 players, how many matches would take place before a single winner would be declared?

We might solve this problem the hard way, making diagrams of the various matches. However, careful analysis of the situation would reveal that each match would produce exactly one loser. Therefore it would take 146 matches to produce 146 losers (and one winner).

CERTIFICATION POINTER

Teacher certification tests will require you to know appropriate strategies for engaging students in active learning to promote the development of creative problem-solving skills.

Engaging Problems One key to the teaching of problem solving is providing problems that intrigue and engage children. The same problem-solving skills could be involved in a context that is either compelling or boring to students, and this matters in the outcomes. For example, Bottge (2001) found that low-achieving secondary students, many with serious learning disabilities, could learn complex problem-solving skills relating to building a cage for a pet or setting up a car racing track. Since John Dewey proposed it a hundred years ago, the motivational value of connecting problem-solving to real life or simulations of real life has been demonstrated many times (Holt & Willard-Holt, 2000; Torp & Sage, 1998; Westwater & Wolfe, 2000).

Feedback Provide practice with feedback (Hattie & Timperley, 2007). Perhaps the most effective way to teach problem solving is to provide students with a great deal of practice on a wide variety of problem types, giving feedback not only on the correctness of their solutions but also on the process by which they arrived at the solutions (Swanson, 1990). The role of practice with feedback in solving complex problems cannot be overemphasized. Mr. Dunbar's students, in the chapter-opening vignette, could not have arrived at the solution to their problem if they had not had months of practice and feedback on simpler problems.

Teaching Thinking Skills

One of the oldest dreams in education is that there might be some way to make students smarter—not only more knowledgeable or skillful but actually better able to learn new information of all kinds (Beyer, 1998). Perhaps someday someone will come up with a "smart pill" that will have this effect; but in the meantime, several groups of researchers have been developing and evaluating instructional programs that are designed to increase students' general thinking skills.

The most widely known and extensively researched of several thinking-skills programs was developed by an Israeli educator, Reuven Feuerstein (1980). In this program, called **Instrumental Enrichment,** students work through a series of paper-and-pencil exercises that are intended to build such intellectual skills as categorization, comparison, orientation in space, and numerical progressions. Figure 8.4 shows one example of an activity designed to increase analytic perception. The Instrumental Enrichment treatment is meant to be administered for 3 to 5 hours per week over a period of at least 2 years, usually to adolescents who are underachievers or learning disabled. Studies of this duration have found that the program has positive effects on tests of aptitude, such as IQ tests, but generally not on achievement (Savell, Twohig, & Rachford, 1986; Sternberg & Bhana, 1986).

Instrumental Enrichment
A thinking skills program in which students work through a series of paper-and-pencil exercises that are designed to develop various intellectual abilities.

Another approach to the teaching of thinking skills is to incorporate them in daily lessons and classroom experiences—to create a "culture of thinking" (Ivey & Fisher,

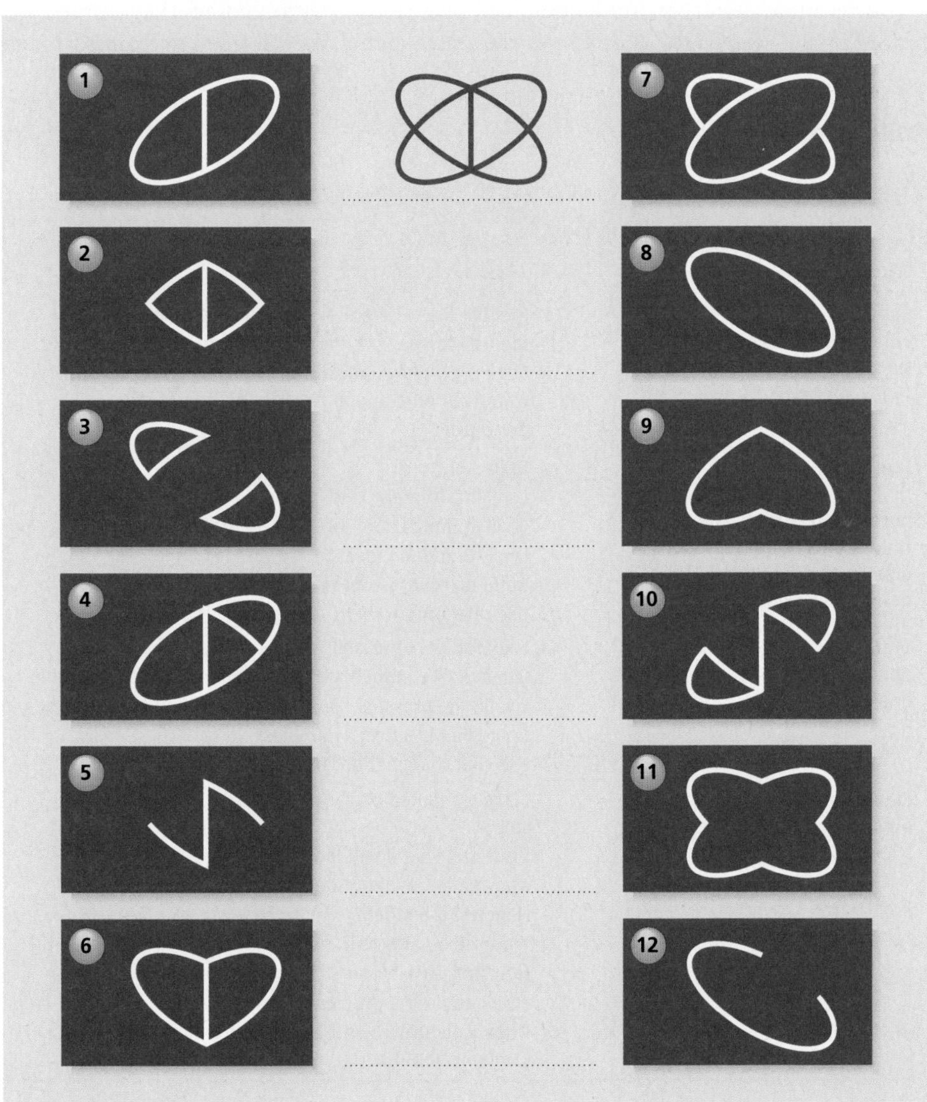

FIGURE 8.4 Examples from Analytic Perception
Look at the three columns at the left. For each drawing in the left column, there is a drawing in the right column that completes it to make the form shown in the middle column. Write the number of the form in the right column needed to complete the form in the first column. The student must select the appropriate drawing from the right to complete the one on the left to obtain a figure identical to the model in the middle column in this figure. The task requires representation, internalization and labeling of the model, definition of the missing parts, systematic work, and comparison to the model for self-criticism.

From Reuven Feuerstein, "Instrumental Enrichment: A Selected Sample of Material for Review Purposes." Jerusalem: The Hadassah-Wizo-Canada Research Institute, May 1973, p. 5. Reprinted by permission of the author.

2006; Sternberg, 2002). As an example of integrating thinking skills into daily lessons, Tishman, Perkins, and Jay (1995) describe an impromptu discussion in a class that has been taught a generic strategy for problem solving. This strategy is built around a four-step process (state, search, evaluate, and elaborate) that is summarized in Table 8.2. In their example, Ms. Mandly's sixth-graders discuss why plants in terrariums the class planted a month earlier are starting to die and what they might do about it. The class learned the steps summarized in Table 8.2 and had a poster identical to the table posted in the classroom. The discussion went as follows:

Ms. Mandly: Let's take a look at the poster. How can we build a strategy to deal with this situation? Which building blocks can we use?

Rory: We should use the search step, to search for a solution to the problem.

Marc: Yeah, but we're not even exactly sure what the problem is. We don't know if the plants in the terrarium are wilted because they have too much water or too little.

Ms. Mandly: Are you suggesting we also need a state step, Marc?

Marc (after a moment of looking at the poster): Yes. In two ways: I think we need to state the problem and we need to state our goal.

Ms. Mandly: That sounds reasonable. Any other building blocks we can use?

Marc: Yeah, that might not be enough. What if you take care of a terrarium, and it still wilts? Other people in your group will want to know what went wrong.

Ms. Mandly: It sounds like we have two goals here. One, decide how to care for the terrarium. And two, make a plan for keeping track of the terrarium's care.

After more discussion, students agreed on exactly what outcomes they wanted and moved to the "search" step. Looking at the search tactics, they decided to brainstorm lots

TABLE 8.2 Thinking Skills: Build a Strategy

Strategy Building Blocks		
When . . .	***Strategy Step***	***Tactics***
When you need to be clear about what you're doing or where you're going . . .	**State** . . . either the problem, the situation, or your goal(s).	Identify the different dimensions of the situation. Identify the parts of the situation you will focus on. State precisely what you want to change or what you want your outcome to be. Be specific!
When you need to think broadly about something . . .	**Search** . . . for ideas, options, possibilities, purposes, features, assumptions, causes, effects, questions, dimensions, hypotheses, facts, or interpretations.	Brainstorm. Look for different kinds of ideas. Look at things from different points of view. Look for hidden ideas. Build on other people's ideas. Use categories to help you search.
When you need to assess, rate, or decide something . . .	**Evaluate** . . . options, plans, ideas, theories, or objects.	Look for lots of reasons. Consider the immediate and long-term consequences. List all the pros and cons, paying attention to both. Try to be objective; avoid bias. Use your imagination: How will it affect others?
When you need to think about the details of something . . .	**Elaborate** . . . possibilities, plans, options, hypotheses, or ideas.	Make a detailed plan: Say what will happen at each step. Visualize what it will look/feel/seem like *in detail.* Ask yourself: What resources will be used? How will it happen? Who will be affected? How long will it take? Think about the different parts. Draw a picture or write a description; imagine *telling* someone about it.

Source: From Shari Tishman, David N. Perkins, and Eileen Jay, *The Thinking Classroom.* Copyright © 1995 by Allyn & Bacon. Reprinted by permission.

of different possible solutions. Ms. Mandly kept track of their ideas on the blackboard and occasionally reminded them to keep in mind some key tactics: to look for hidden ideas and to look for different kinds of ideas. Some of the ideas students came up with are the following:

1. Have a sign-up list.
2. Let the teacher decide who should water.
3. Have one person volunteer to do it all.
4. Make a rotating schedule for each group.
5. Make a rotating schedule, plus have weekly group meetings to discuss progress.

After students reviewed and evaluated their brainstormed list, they unanimously agreed that option 5—rotating schedule plus weekly meetings—was best.

They then went on to step 4: Elaborate, and make a plan. They designed a rotation schedule for each terrarium group, and with Ms. Mandly's help they picked a time for weekly group meetings. Working through the "elaborate step," they invented a detailed checklist for the designated weekly waterer, to help track factors that might contribute to the terrarium's health, such as how much water has been given, the date of watering, the temperature of the classroom, and so on (Tishman et al., 1995).

In the course of discussing the terrarium problem, the students were learning a broadly applicable strategy for approaching and solving complex problems. By calling on this and other strategies frequently as they are appropriate in a classroom context, Ms. Mandly not only gave students useful strategies but also communicated the idea that strategy use is a normal and expected part of daily life.

Critical Thinking

One key objective of schooling is enhancing students' abilities to think critically, to make rational decisions about what to do or what to believe (Marzano, 1995). Examples of **critical thinking** include identifying misleading advertisements, weighing competing evidence, and identifying assumptions or fallacies in arguments. As with any other objective, learning to think critically requires practice; students can be given many dilemmas, logical and illogical arguments, valid and misleading advertisements, and so on (Halpern, 1995). Effective teaching of critical thinking depends on setting a classroom tone that encourages the acceptance of divergent perspectives and free discussion. There should be an emphasis on giving reasons for opinions rather than only giving correct answers. Skills in critical thinking are best acquired in relation to topics with which students

critical thinking
The ability to make rational decisions about what to do or what to believe.

Why is critical thinking particularly important when using the Internet for research or help with homework?

The Intentional TEACHER

USING WHAT YOU KNOW about Student-Centered and Constructivist Approaches to Improve Teaching and Learning

Intentional teachers keep sight of one of the overarching goals of education: to foster students' ability to solve real, complex problems. Intentional teachers work toward this lofty goal by ensuring that schooling provides more than a series of lectures and discrete workbook exercises. Intentional teachers furnish opportunities for students to build their own knowledge, to work with others in discovering important ideas, and to attack challenging real-life issues.

1 What do I expect my students to know and to be able to do at the end of this lesson? How does this contribute to course objectives and to my students' need to become capable individuals?

Intentional teachers build in regular opportunities for students to approach complex, difficult, realistic tasks. Check your goals and curriculum: Where and how often do you encourage students to construct knowledge through student-centered approaches? For example, you might provide regular opportunities for students to study and use mathematics in realistic settings. The class might, for instance, develop, administer, analyze, and act on a schoolwide survey about a current issue, such as the purchase of playground equipment.

Intentional teachers think about the balance between direct, teacher-centered instructional approaches and constructivist, student-centered approaches. Select your teaching strategies based on your goals for students, and realize that a balance of both kinds of approaches might be best for promoting a variety of learning outcomes. For example, imagine that you feel pressed to cover a great deal of information in your government class; as a result, you find yourself lecturing almost daily. Then you recall that your major goal is to help your students become citizens who make informed decisions about complicated issues. Therefore, you review your plan book to ensure that you are using discovery approaches regularly. You begin with a discovery lesson the very next day by distributing nickels and asking students to draw inferences about the culture that created them.

2 What knowledge, skills, needs, and interests do my students have that must be taken into account in my lesson?

Background knowledge affects students' ability to build meaning and solve problems. Gather information about your students' earlier school experiences by conversing with last year's teacher or teachers: Do your learners come with previous experiences in groupwork? What do their records suggest about their preferences and attitudes toward novelty?

Intentional teachers make use of top-down processing by beginning instruction with holistic problems or issues and moving to analysis of their parts. You might begin your lessons with real problems within the context of a supportive atmosphere. For example, you might begin a math class with a question: "If there are five flavors of fruity candies in this bag, how many flavor combinations can I create?" You could note the students' widely varying initial guesses, and then pass out bags of candy and allow them to get to work on the problem. When it becomes evident that they are stymied, you could suggest that they try a charting strategy to work on a single part of the problem: How many combinations of *just two* flavors are there? You and your class could devise the chart below, quickly finding patterns and discovering that there are 10 flavor combinations of two candies. Students should discern that they simply need to make similar charts for 3-, 4-, and 5-flavor combinations to arrive at their answer.

Flavor 1	~~1-1~~ (1-2 1-3 1-4 1-5) (symbols represent flavor 1 with flavors 2, 3, 4, and 5)
Flavor 2	~~2-1~~ ~~2-2~~ (2-3 2-4 2-5)
Flavor 3	~~3-1~~ ~~3-2~~ ~~3-3~~ (3-4 3-5)
Flavor 4	~~4-1~~ ~~4-2~~ ~~4-3~~ ~~4-4~~ (4-5)
Flavor 5	~~5-1~~ ~~5-2~~ ~~5-3~~ ~~5-4~~ ~~5-5~~

CERTIFICATION POINTER

When responding to the case studies in certification tests, you may be asked to design a lesson that includes strategies for teaching critical-thinking skills.

are familiar. For example, students will learn more from a unit evaluating Nazi propaganda if they know a great deal about the history of Nazi Germany and the culture of the 1930s and 1940s. Perhaps most important, the goal of teaching critical thinking is to create a critical spirit, which encourages students to question what they hear and to examine their own thinking for logical inconsistencies or fallacies.

Beyer (1988) identified 10 critical-thinking skills that students might use in judging the validity of claims or arguments, understanding advertisements, and so on:

1. Distinguishing between verifiable facts and value claims
2. Distinguishing relevant from irrelevant information, claims, or reasons
3. Determining the factual accuracy of a statement
4. Determining the credibility of a source

Teach strategies for problem solving: include drawing pictures, acting out situations, and making diagrams. Model a variety of problem-solving strategies, using them as scaffolds to keep students working within their zone of proximal development.

3 What do I know about the content, child development, learning, motivation, and effective teaching strategies that I can use to accomplish my objectives?

As students work on a cooperative project, watch them. What does their nonverbal behavior tell you about how well they are working with peers? How willing are they to take risks? When you see that students are unwilling to accept peers' ideas, you might stop the lesson and provide instruction on working well with others: "When someone gives a new idea, wait before you say no. Think for twenty seconds about how that idea might work. Watch, I'll pretend I'm in your group and you tell me a new idea . . ."

4 What instructional materials, technology, assistance, and other resources are available to help accomplish my objectives?

Emotion, personal meaning, and relevance can help students process information deeply so that they remember better. Begin your lesson in ways that capture student interest, and provide instruction that focuses on developing understanding beyond surface-level features.

You begin a lesson on density by displaying two bottles of soda (one full, one with some air in it) in an aquarium: One sinks, but the other floats! The students' curiosity is piqued and they actively engage themselves in discovering the rule that allows for the cans' behavior. At the lesson's close, you create a powerful visual image of an immense iceberg floating in the chilling sea. You ask students to explain, using their new understanding of density, why the iceberg floats despite its vast size.

Your discussions with colleagues, both in the current setting in which you work, and with former classmates, can serve to help you identify new materials and other resources that will benefit your efforts to become a more intentional, student-centered teacher.

5 How will I plan to assess students' progress toward my objectives?

Students' outputs provide information about success. Examine students' work for evidence of sense-making, of critical thinking, and of creativity. Imagine that you've just collected a stack of essays on students' analysis of a current environmental issue: destruction of the rain forests. You might begin your assessment by listing two questions to help you focus on students' knowledge construction: (a) How well do students marshal factual details to support their position? (b) What evidence is there of creative, inventive thinking?

One of the most challenging aspects of a student-centered orientation to teaching is how to determine whether students have met learning goals and attained intended objectives. Assess your instruction using multiple measures.

Review your plan book and check to see how many realistic opportunities you provided in the past week. Audio or video tape yourself teaching and analyze the kinds of questions and prompts you use. Ask your students for feedback on your teaching, using survey questions like this one: "The teacher _______ [never/sometimes/often/always] gives us opportunities to figure things out on our own."

6 How will I respond if individual children or the class as a whole are not on track toward success? What is my back-up plan?

How can you, as an intentional teacher seeking to incorporate constructivist approaches, help prepare your students for this change from "tell me what I'm supposed to do" to the practices of group learning, inquiry, and open-ended thinking?

To help your students become more self-directed, not only utilize cooperative approaches wherever possible but also provide direct instruction in helping and communication skills at the start of cooperative learning lessons. You can provide instruction on how to give feedback in groupwork, recalling that research has shown that students who give and/or receive extensive explanations learn more in cooperative settings. These techniques will help students to reach group goals.

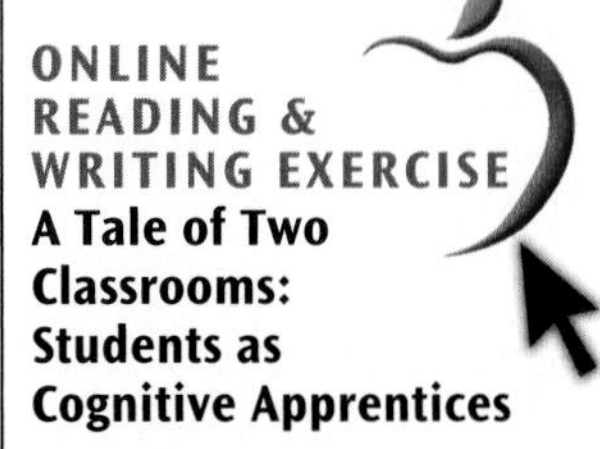

A Tale of Two Classrooms: Students as Cognitive Apprentices

Access this exercise, entitled "A Tale of Two Classrooms: Students as Cognitive Apprentices," in the Homework and Exercises section for Chapter 8 of this text at **www.mylabschool.com.**

5. Identifying ambiguous claims or arguments
6. Identifying unstated assumptions
7. Detecting bias
8. Identifying logical fallacies
9. Recognizing logical inconsistencies in a line of reasoning
10. Determining the strength of an argument or claim. (p. 57)

Beyer notes that this is not a sequence of steps but rather a list of possible ways in which a student might approach information to evaluate whether it is true or sensible. The key task in teaching critical thinking to students is to help them learn not only how to use each of these strategies but also how to tell when each is appropriate.

ON THE WEB

For articles and resources on critical thinking go to **www.criticalthinking.org,** the website of the Foundation for Critical Thinking.

CHAPTER 8 SUMMARY

What Is the Constructivist View of Learning?

Constructivists believe that knowing is a process and that learners must individually and actively discover and transform complex information to make it their own. Constructivist approaches emphasize top-down processing, in which students begin with complex problems or tasks and discover the basic knowledge and skills needed to solve the problems or perform the tasks. Constructivist approaches also emphasize cooperative learning, questioning or inquiry strategies, and other metacognitive skills.

Discovery learning and scaffolding are constructivist learning methods based on cognitive learning theories. Bruner's discovery learning highlights students' active self-learning, curiosity, and creative problem solving. Scaffolding, based on Vygotsky's views, calls for teacher assistance to students at critical points in their learning.

How Is Cooperative Learning Used in Instruction?

In cooperative learning, small groups of students work together to help one another learn. Cooperative learning groups are used in discovery learning, discussion, and study for assessment. Cooperative learning programs such as Student Teams–Achievement Divisions (STAD) are successful because they reward both group and individual effort and improvement, and because groups are responsible for the individual learning of each group member.

How Are Problem-Solving and Thinking Skills Taught?

Problem-solving skills are taught through a series of steps, including, for example, means–ends analysis and problem representation. Creative problem solving requires incubation time, suspension of judgment, conducive climates, problem analysis, the application of thinking skills, and feedback. Thinking skills include, for example, planning, classifying, divergent thinking, identifying assumptions, identifying misleading information, and generating questions. Thinking skills can be taught through programs such as Instrumental Enrichment; creating a culture of thinking in the classroom is another useful technique.

KEY TERMS

Review the following key terms from the chapter.

cognitive apprenticeship 232
constructivist theories of learning 231
Cooperative Integrated Reading and Composition (CIRC) 246
cooperative learning 243
cooperative scripting 247
critical thinking 255
discovery learning 233
Group Investigation 246
Instrumental Enrichment 253
Jigsaw 246
Learning Together 246
means–ends analysis 250
mediated learning 236
problem solving 249
reciprocal teaching 239
self-regulated learners 236
Student Teams–Achievement Divisions (STAD) 244

SELF-ASSESSMENT: PRACTICING *for* LICENSURE

Directions: The chapter-opening vignette addresses indicators that are often assessed in state licensure exams. Re-read the chapter-opening vignette, and then respond to the following questions.

1. Mr. Dunbar, in his lesson on the volume of a cylinder, asks his students to figure out how to measure volume through experimentation. What type of learning strategy is he using?
   a. direct instruction
   b. classical conditioning
   c. discovery learning
   d. teacher-mediated discussion

2. Why didn't Mr. Dunbar just tell his students that the formula for finding the volume of a cylinder is $\pi r^2 h$?
   a. He believes that students will gain deeper understanding if they work it out for themselves.
   b. He thought the lesson would take less time if the students could figure it out.
   c. He knows that discovery learning is superior to direct instruction.
   d. He is applying teaching strategies suggested by B. F. Skinner and other behaviorists.

3. In which of the following examples is Mr. Dunbar demonstrating Vygotsky's "zone of proximal development" concept?
   a. Mr. Dunbar says, "Today we are going to have a chance to discover how to compute the volume of a cylinder."
   b. Mr. Dunbar assigns his students to sit around the lab tables in groups of four.
   c. Mr. Dunbar, as he is passing by the Master Minds group, says, "You're right, Miguel, but what are you going to do with that information?"
   d. Mr. Dunbar praises the Master Minds group for figuring out the answer on its own.

4. Mr. Dunbar effectively uses cooperative learning strategies in his lesson on the volume of cylinders. He does all of the following except
   a. give recognition to the groups when they solve the problem.
   b. assure that each group contains members who have similar abilities.
   c. make certain that each group member learns.
   d. mixes students in terms of race, ethnicity, gender, and special needs.

5. Which of the following cooperative learning strategies is Mr. Dunbar using?
   a. Group Investigation
   b. Learning Together
   c. Jigsaw
   d. STAD

6. Describe an example of discovery learning. What is the teacher's role in a discovery lesson? What strengths and limitations exist with discovery learning?

7. How can teachers improve students' problem-solving abilities?

PEARSON
myeducationlab
Where the Classroom Comes to Life

Now go to **www.myeducationlab.com** to:

- take a Pretest to assess your initial comprehension of chapter content;
- study chapter content with your individualized Study Plan;
- take a Posttest to assess your understanding of chapter content;
- practice your teaching skills with Building Teaching Skills exercises; and
- build a deeper, more applied understanding of chapter content with Homework and Exercises.

CHAPTER 9

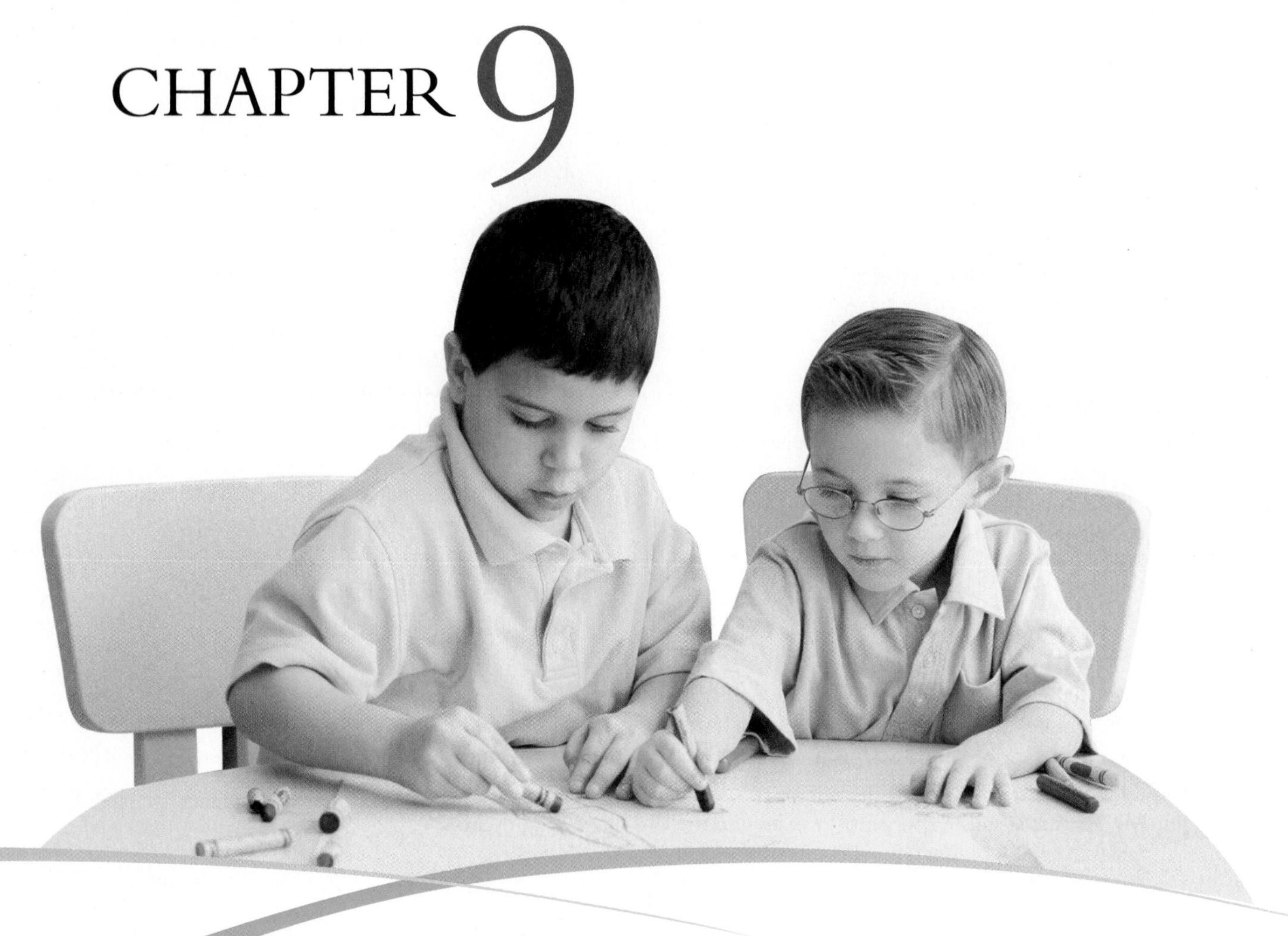

Accommodating Instruction to Meet Individual Needs

chapter OUTLINE

Mr. Arbuthnot is in fine form. He is presenting a lesson on long division to his fourth-grade class and feels that he's never been so clear, so interesting, and so well organized. When he asks questions, several students raise their hands; when he calls on them, they always know the answers. "Arbuthnot, old boy," he says to himself, "I think you're really getting to these kids!"

At the end of the period he passes out a short quiz to see how well his students have learned the long-division lesson. When the papers are scored, he finds to his shock and disappointment that only about a third of the class got every problem right. Another third missed every problem; the remaining students fell somewhere in between. "What went wrong?" he thinks. "Well, no matter, I'll set the situation right in tomorrow's lesson."

The next day, Mr. Arbuthnot is even better prepared, uses vivid examples and diagrams to show how to do long division, and gives an active, exciting lesson. Even more hands than before go up when he asks questions, and the answers are usually correct. However, some of the students are beginning to look bored, particularly those who got perfect papers on the quiz and those who got none right.

Toward the end of the period, he gives another brief quiz. The scores are better this time, but there is still a group of students who got none of the problems correct. He is crestfallen. "I had them in the palm of my hand," he thinks. "How could they fail to learn?"

To try to find out what went wrong, Mr. Arbuthnot goes over the quiz papers of the students who missed all the problems. He immediately sees a pattern. By the second lesson, almost all students were proceeding correctly in setting up the long-division problems. However, some were making consistent errors in subtraction. Others had apparently forgotten their multiplication facts. Their problems were not with division at all; the students simply lacked the prerequisite skills.

"Well," thinks Mr. Arbuthnot, "at least I was doing great with some of the kids." It occurs to him that one of the students who got a perfect paper after the first lesson might be able to give him an idea about how to teach the others better. He asks Teresa how she grasped long division so quickly.

"It was easy," she says. "We learned long division last year!"

USING *your* EXPERIENCE

CRITICAL THINKING List all of the ways in which Mr. Arbuthnot could be more effective in addressing student individual differences. Then list all of the ways in which he is effective in addressing student needs.

COOPERATIVE LEARNING Work with a group of four or five classmates. Pass a sheet of paper around the group, and ask each member to write down an idea to help Mr. Arbuthnot become more effective in addressing students' needs. After one idea is added, the sheet is passed to the next person in the group, who adds an idea and passes the sheet and so on. Share some of these ideas with the class.

WHAT ARE ELEMENTS OF EFFECTIVE INSTRUCTION BEYOND A GOOD LESSON?

INTASC

3. Adapting Instruction for Individual Needs
6. Communication Skills
7. Instructional Planning Skills

As Mr. Arbuthnot learned to his chagrin, effective instruction takes a lot more than effective lectures. He gave a great lesson on long division, yet it was appropriate for only some of his students, those who had the needed prerequisites but had not already learned long division. To make his lesson effective for all of his students, he needed to adapt it to meet their diverse needs. Furthermore, the best lesson in the world won't work if students are not motivated to learn it or if inadequate time is allotted to allow all students to learn.

If the quality of lectures were all that mattered in effective instruction, we could probably find the best lecturers in the world, videotape their lessons, and show the tapes to students. If you think about why videotaped lessons would not work very well by themselves, you will realize how much more is involved in effective instruction than simply giving good lectures. First, the video teacher would have no idea what students already know. A particular lesson might be too advanced or too easy for a particular group of students. Second, some students might be learning the lesson quite well, whereas others would be missing key concepts and falling behind. The video teacher would have no way of knowing which students needed additional help and, in any case, would have no way of providing it. There would be no way to question students to find out whether they were getting the main points and then to reteach any concept they had missed. Third, the video teacher would have no way of motivating students to pay attention to the lesson or to really try to learn it. If students failed to pay attention or misbehaved, the video teacher could not do anything about it. Finally, the video teacher would never know at the end of a lesson whether students had actually learned the main concepts or skills.

This analysis of video teaching illustrates why teachers must be concerned with many elements of instruction in addition to the presentation of information. Teachers must know how to adapt their instruction to the students' levels of knowledge. They must motivate students to learn, manage student behavior, group students for instruction, and assess the students' learning.

To help make sense of all these elements of effective instruction, educational psychologists have proposed models of effective instruction. These models explain the critical features of high-quality lessons and how they relate to one another to enhance learning.

Carroll's Model of School Learning and QAIT

One of the most influential articles ever published in the field of educational psychology was a paper by John Carroll titled "A Model of School Learning" (1963, 1989). In it he describes teaching in terms of the management of time, resources, and activities to ensure student learning. Carroll proposed that learning is a function of (1) time actually spent on learning and (2) time needed to learn. That is, learning is greater the more time students spend on learning in relation to the amount of time they need to learn. Time needed is a product of aptitude and ability to learn; time actually spent depends on clock time available for learning, quality of instruction, and student perseverance.

Slavin (1987d) described a model focusing on the alterable elements of Carroll's model, those that the teacher or school can directly change. It is called the **QAIT model** (quality, appropriateness, incentive, time) of effective instruction.

1. ***Quality of instruction:*** The degree to which presentation of information or skills helps students easily learn the material. Quality of instruction is largely a product of the quality of the curriculum and of the lesson presentation itself.
2. ***Appropriate levels of instruction:*** The degree to which the teacher makes sure that students are ready to learn a new lesson (that is, have the necessary skills and knowledge to learn it) but have not already learned the lesson. In other words, the level of instruction is appropriate when a lesson is neither too difficult nor too easy for students.
3. ***Incentive:*** The degree to which the teacher makes sure that students are motivated to work on instructional tasks and to learn the material being presented.
4. ***Time:*** The degree to which students are given enough time to learn the material being taught.

For instruction to be effective, each of these four elements must be adequate. No matter how high the quality of instruction, students will not learn a lesson if they lack the necessary prior skills or information, if they lack the motivation, or if they lack the time they need to learn the lesson. However, if the quality of instruction is low, then it makes no difference how much students already know, how motivated they are, or how much time they have. Figure 9.1 illustrates the relationship among the elements in the QAIT model.

QAIT model
A model of effective instruction that focuses on elements teachers can directly control: quality, appropriateness, incentive, and time.

FIGURE 9.1 The QAIT Model
Each of the elements of the QAIT model is like a link in a chain, and the chain is only as strong as the weakest link.

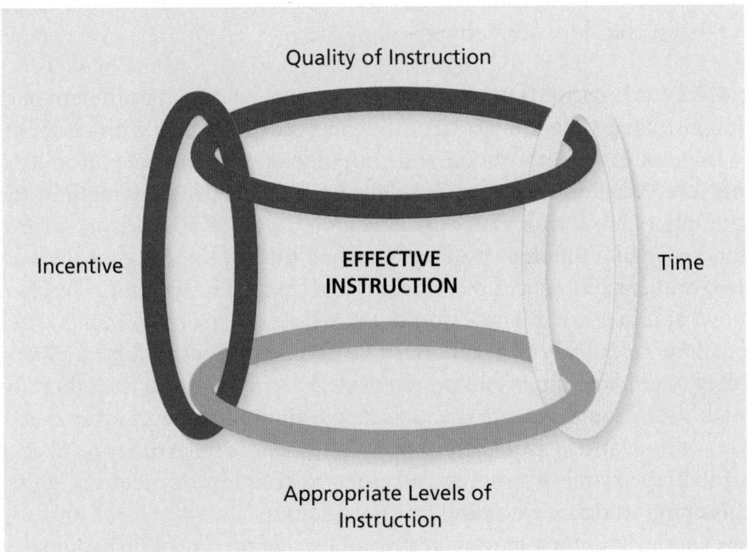

What are some of the challenges to the effectiveness of the QAIT model in a crowded classroom?

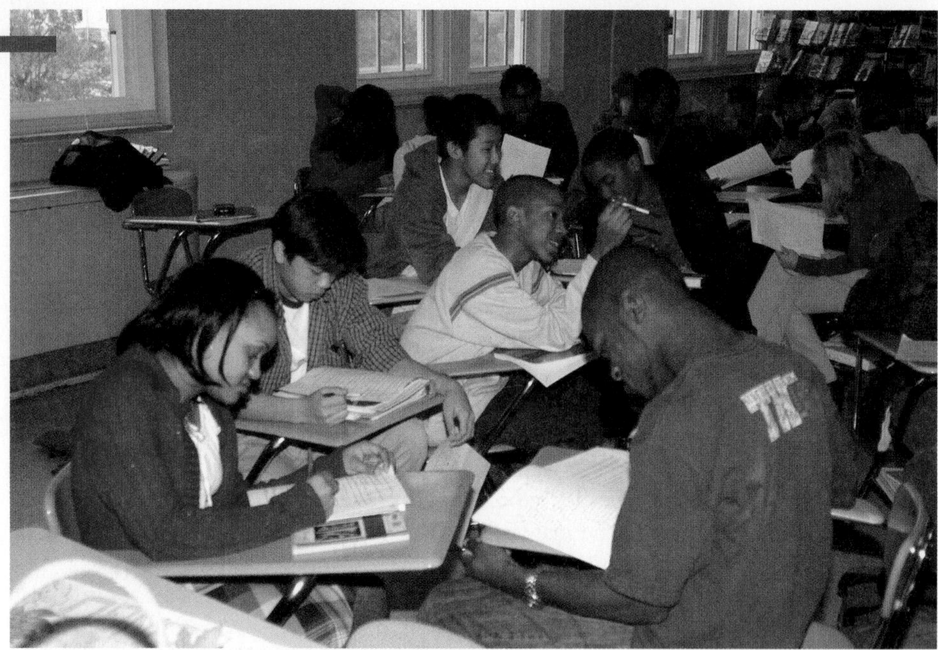

Quality of Instruction Quality of instruction refers to the set of activities most people first think of when they think of teaching: lecturing, calling on students, discussing, helping students with seatwork, and so on. When instruction is high in quality, the information presented makes sense to students, is interesting to them, and is easy to remember and apply.

The most important aspect of quality of instruction is the degree to which the lesson makes sense to students. To ensure that lessons make sense, teachers must present material in an orderly, organized way. They need to relate new information to what students already know. They need to use examples, demonstrations, pictures, and diagrams to make ideas vivid for students. They might use such cognitive strategies as advance organizers and memory strategies. Sometimes a concept will not make sense to students until they discover it or experience it themselves or until they discuss it with others.

Another important aspect of quality of instruction is the degree to which the teacher monitors how well students are learning and adapts the pace of instruction so that it is neither too fast nor too slow. For example, teachers should ask questions frequently to determine how much students have grasped. If the answers show that students are keeping up with the lesson, the teacher might move along a little more rapidly. But if students' answers show that they are having trouble keeping up, the teacher might review parts of the lesson and slow down the pace.

Appropriate Levels of Instruction Perhaps the most difficult problem of classroom organization is dealing with the fact that students come into class with different levels of prior knowledge, skills, and motivation, and with different learning rates (Tomlinson, 2000, 2004). This was Mr. Arbuthnot's main dilemma. Student diversity requires teachers to provide appropriate levels of instruction. Teaching a class of 30 students (or even a class of 10) is fundamentally different from one-to-one tutoring because of the inevitability of student-to-student differences that affect the success of instruction. Teachers can always be sure that if they teach one lesson to the whole class, some students will learn the material much more quickly than others. In fact, some students might not learn the lesson at all; they might lack important prerequisite skills or adequate time (because to give them enough time would waste too much of the time of students who learn rapidly). Recognition of these instructionally important differences leads many teachers to search for ways of individualizing instruction, adapting instruction to meet students' different needs, or grouping students according to their abilities.

However, some of these solutions create problems of their own that could be more serious than the ones they are meant to solve. For example, a teacher might give all students materials that are appropriate to their individual needs and allow students to work at their own rates. This solves the problem of providing appropriate levels of instruction but creates serious new problems of managing the activities of 20 or 30 students doing 20 or 30 different things. A teacher may group students by ability (e.g., Redbirds, Bluebirds, and Yellowbirds) so that each group will have a relatively narrow range of abilities. However, this creates problems, too, because when the teacher is working with the Redbirds, the Bluebirds and Yellowbirds must work without supervision or help. Effective ways of adapting instruction to meet student needs are discussed later in this chapter.

Incentive Thomas Edison once wrote that "genius is one per cent inspiration and ninety-nine per cent perspiration." The same could probably be said of learning. Learning is work. This is not to say that learning isn't or can't be fun or stimulating—far from it. But it is true that students must exert themselves to pay attention, to conscientiously perform the tasks required of them, and to study; and students must somehow be motivated to do these things. This incentive, or motivation, might come from characteristics of the tasks themselves (e.g., the interest value of the material being learned), from characteristics of students (such as their curiosity or positive orientation toward learning), or from rewards provided by the teacher or the school (such as grades and certificates).

INTASC

5 Classroom Motivation and Management

If students want to know something, they will be motivated to exert the necessary effort to learn it. This is why there are students who can rattle off the names, batting averages, number of home runs, and all sorts of other information about every player of the Chicago Cubs but can't name the 50 states or perform basic multiplication. To such students, baseball facts are of great interest, so they are willing to invest a great deal of effort to master them. Some information is naturally interesting to some or all students, but teachers can do much to create interest in a topic by arousing students' curiosity or by showing how knowledge gained in school can be useful outside of school. For example, baseball fans might be much more interested in learning about computing proportions if they are convinced that this information is necessary for computing batting averages.

However, not every subject can be made fascinating to all students at all times. Most students need some kind of recognition or reward if they are to exert maximum effort to learn skills or concepts that might seem unimportant at the moment but will be critical for later learning. For this reason, schools use praise, feedback, grades, certificates, stars, prizes, and other rewards to increase student motivation.

Connections
The rewards and general principles of motivation are discussed throughout Chapter 10.

Time The final element of the QAIT model is time. Instruction takes time. More time spent teaching something does not necessarily mean more learning; but if instructional quality, appropriateness of instruction, and incentive are all high, then more time on instruction will pay off in greater learning. The amount of time that is available for learning depends largely on two factors. The first is the amount of time that the teacher (1) schedules for instruction and (2) actually uses to teach. The other is the amount of time students pay attention to the lesson. Both kinds of time are affected by classroom management and discipline strategies. If students are well behaved, are well motivated, and have a sense of purpose and direction and if teachers are well prepared and well organized, then there is plenty of time for students to learn whatever teachers want to teach. However, many factors, such as interruptions, behavior problems, and poor transitions between activities, eat away at the time available for learning (see Hong, 2001).

Connections
Principles of classroom management and discipline are discussed throughout Chapter 11.

HOW ARE STUDENTS GROUPED TO ACCOMMODATE ACHIEVEMENT DIFFERENCES?

From the day they walk into school, students differ in their knowledge, skills, motivations, and predispositions toward what is about to be taught. Some students are already reading when they enter kindergarten; others need much time and support to learn to read well. A teacher starting a new lesson can usually assume that some students already

Connections
To learn more about student differences in general intelligence, specific aptitudes, and abilities and learning styles, see Chapter 4, page 116.

INTASC

3 **Adapting Instruction for Individual Needs**

know a great deal about the lesson's content, some know less but will master the content early on, and some might not be able to master the content at all within the time provided (see Biemiller, 1993). Some have the prerequisite skills and knowledge they need in order to learn the lesson, whereas others do not. This was Mr. Arbuthnot's problem: Some of his students were not ready to learn long division, whereas others had already learned it before he began. Some of his students lacked basic multiplication and subtraction skills that are crucial for long division. Others already knew long division before he began his lesson, and many probably learned it during the first lesson and did not need the second. If Mr. Arbuthnot stops to review multiplication and division, he will be wasting the time of the better-prepared students. If he sets his pace of instruction according to the needs of his more able students, those with learning problems will never catch up. How can Mr. Arbuthnot teach a lesson that will work for all of his students, who are performing within the normal range but differ in prior knowledge, skills, and learning rates?

Accommodating instruction to student differences is one of the most fundamental problems of education and often leads to politically and emotionally charged policies (Atkins & Ellsesser, 2003; Loveless, 1998). For example, most countries outside of North America attempt to deal with the problem of student differences, or student heterogeneity, by testing children at around 10 to 12 years of age and assigning them to different types of schools, only one of which is meant to prepare students for higher education. These systems have long been under attack and are changing in some countries (such as the United Kingdom) but remain in others (such as Germany). In the United States a similar function is carried out by assignment of students to college preparatory, general, and vocational **tracks.** Tracking, in which students are assigned to a specified curriculum sequence within which they take all their academic courses, has rapidly diminished in the 1980s and 1990s. Today, most secondary schools place students in ability-grouped classes separately by subject area; a student may be in a high-level math class but in a middle- or low-level English class (Loveless, 1998). Many secondary schools allow students, in consultation with counselors, to choose the level of each class, perhaps changing levels if a course turns out to be too difficult or too easy. All of these strategies, which result in students' attending classes that are more or less homogeneous in performance level, are called **between-class ability grouping** (Slavin, 1991). This is the predominant form of ability grouping in middle, junior high, and high schools and is sometimes used in elementary schools. Another common means of accommodating instruction to student differences in elementary schools is **within-class ability grouping,** as in the use of reading groups (Bluebirds, Redbirds, Yellowbirds) that divide students according to their reading performance (Lou et al., 1996). The problem of accommodating student differences is so important that many educators have suggested that instruction be completely individualized so that students can work independently at their own rates. This point of view has led to the creation of individualized instructional programs and computer-based instruction. Others have suggested retaining more children in a grade until they meet grade-level requirements, which reduces the range of skills in each class but also creates its own problems (see Beebe-Frankenberger et al., 2004; Grave & DePerna, 2000; Roderick & Nagaoka, 2005).

Each of the many ways of accommodating students' differences has its own benefits, but each introduces its own problems, which sometimes outweigh the benefits. This chapter discusses the research on various means of accommodating classroom instruction to student differences. Some student differences can be easily accommodated (see Gregory & Chapman, 2001; Tomlinson, 2003). For example, teachers can often accommodate different learning styles by, for example, augmenting oral presentations with visual cues—perhaps writing on the chalkboard or showing pictures and diagrams to emphasize important concepts. A teacher can accommodate other differences in learning styles by varying classroom activities, as in alternating active and quiet tasks or individual and groupwork. Teachers can sometimes work with students on an individual basis and adapt instruction to their learning styles—for example, by reminding impulsive students to take their time or by teaching overly reflective students strategies for skipping over items with which they are having problems so that they can complete tests on time.

Differences in prior knowledge and learning rates are more difficult to deal with. Sometimes the best way to deal with these differences is to ignore them: to teach the

tracks
Curriculum sequences to which students of specified achievement or ability level are assigned.

between-class ability grouping
The practice of grouping students in separate classes according to ability level.

within-class ability grouping
A system of accommodating student differences by dividing a class of students into two or more ability groups for instruction in certain subjects.

whole class at a single pace, perhaps offering additional help to low-achieving students and giving extra extension or enrichment activities to students who tend to finish assignments rapidly (see Meyer & Rose, 2000; Pettig, 2000; Tomlinson, 2000; Tomlinson, Kaplan, & Renzulli, 2001). Appropriate use of cooperative learning methods, in which students of different performance levels can help each other, can be an effective means of helping all children learn (Schniedewind & Davidson, 2000; Slavin, 1995a). Some subjects lend themselves more than others to a single pace of instruction for all (Slavin, 1993a). For example, it is probably less important to accommodate student achievement differences in social studies, science, and English than in mathematics, reading, and foreign languages. This is because in the latter subjects, skills build directly on one another, so teaching at one pace to a heterogeneous class might do a disservice to both low and high achievers; low achievers might fail because they lack prerequisite skills, and high achievers might become bored at what is for them a slow pace of instruction. This was the case in Mr. Arbuthnot's mathematics class.

The following sections discuss strategies for accommodating student achievement differences.

Between-Class Ability Grouping

Probably the most common means of dealing with instructionally important differences is to assign students to classes according to their abilities. This between-class ability grouping can take many forms. In high schools there might be college preparatory and general tracks that divide students on the basis of measured ability. In some junior high and middle schools, students are assigned to one class by general ability, and they then stay with that class, moving from teacher to teacher. For example, the highest-performing seventh-graders might be assigned to class 7–1, middle-performing students to 7–5, and low-performing students to 7–12. In other junior high and middle schools (and in many high schools), students are grouped separately by ability for each subject, so a student might be in a high-performing math class and an average-performing science class (Slavin, 1993b). In high schools this is accomplished by course placements. For example, some ninth-graders take Algebra I, whereas others who do not qualify for Algebra I take general mathematics. Elementary schools use a wide range of strategies for grouping students, including many of the patterns that are used in secondary schools. Often, students in elementary schools will be assigned to a mixed-ability class for homeroom, social studies, and science but regrouped by ability for reading and math. Elementary schools are less likely than secondary schools to use ability grouping between classes but more likely to use ability grouping within classes, especially in reading. At any level, however, provision of separate special-education programs for students with serious learning problems is one form of between-class ability grouping, as is provision of separate programs for academically gifted and talented students.

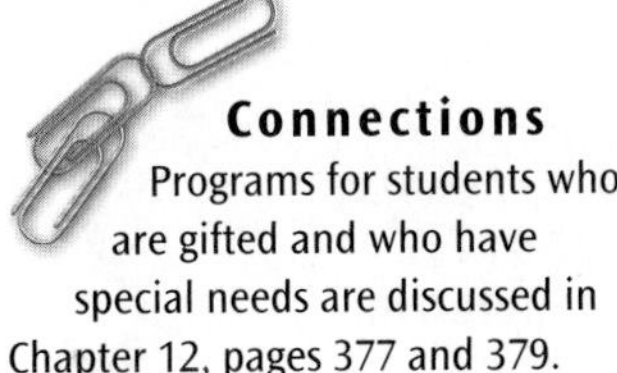

Connections
Programs for students who are gifted and who have special needs are discussed in Chapter 12, pages 377 and 379.

CERTIFICATION POINTER

For teacher certification tests, you may be asked to describe the strengths and weaknesses of between-class ability grouping. You should know that research does not support most forms of between-class ability grouping.

Research on Between-Class Ability Grouping Despite the widespread use of between-class ability grouping, research on this strategy does not support its use. Researchers have found that although ability grouping might have slight benefits for students who are assigned to high-track classes, these benefits are balanced by losses for students who are assigned to low-track classes (Ireson & Hallam, 2001; Oakes & Wells, 1998; Slavin, 1987b, 1990).

ON THE WEB

To read the position of the National Association of School Psychologists on ability grouping see **www.nasponine.org/about_nasp/pospaper_ag.aspx.**

Why is between-class ability grouping so ineffective? Several researchers have explored this question. The primary purpose of ability grouping is to reduce the range of student performance levels that teachers must deal with so that they can adapt instruction to the

Some of these students are reading well above grade level, whereas others are still only learning to read. As a teacher, how might you accommodate instruction to their different abilities? What are the advantages and disadvantages of such strategies as between-class and within-class ability groupings?

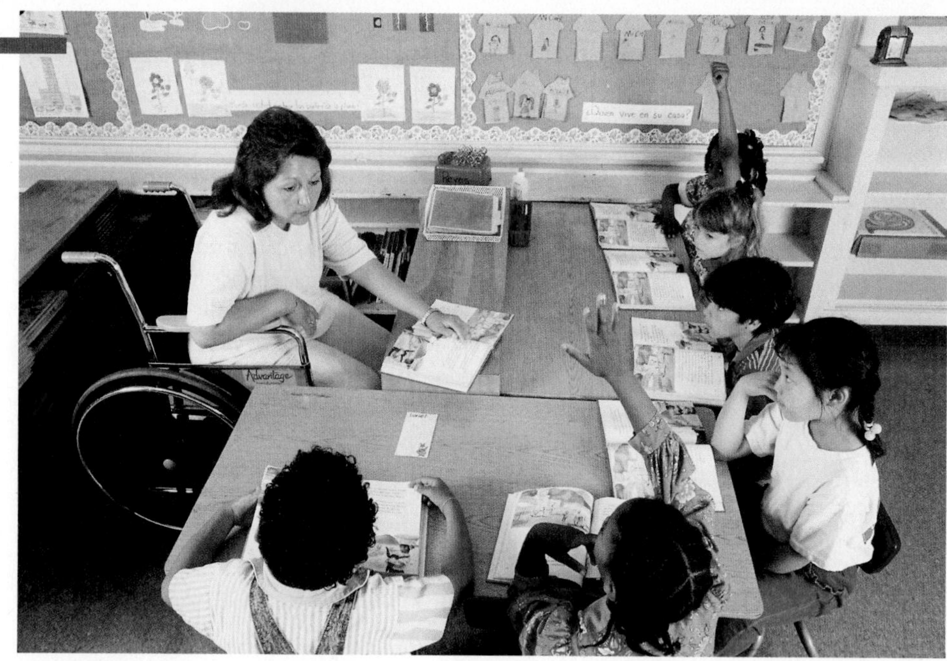

needs of a well-defined group. However, grouping is often done on the basis of standardized test scores or other measures of general ability rather than according to performance in a particular subject. As a result, the reduction in the range of differences that are actually important for a specific class may be too small to make much difference (Oakes, 1995). Furthermore, concentrating low-achieving students in low-track classes seems to be harmful because it exposes them to too few positive role models (Page, 1991). Then, too, many teachers do not like to teach such classes and might subtly (or not so subtly) communicate low expectations for students in them (Weinstein, 1996). Studies find that teachers actually do not make many adaptations to the needs of students in low-ability groups (Ross, Smith, Lohr, & McNelis, 1994). Several studies have found that the quality of instruction is lower in low-track classes than in middle- or high-track classes. For example, teachers of low-track classes are less enthusiastic, are less organized, and teach more facts and fewer concepts than do teachers of high-track classes (Gamoran, Nystrand, Berends, & LePore, 1995; Muskin, 1990; Oakes, 1995; Raudenbush, Rowan, & Cheong, 1993). Instruction in mixed-ability, untracked classes more closely resembles that in high- and middle-track classes than that in low-track classes (Goodlad, 1983; Oakes, 1985). Perhaps the most damaging effect of tracking is its stigmatizing effect on students who are assigned to the low tracks; the message these students get is that academic success is not within their capabilities (Oakes & Guiton, 1995; Page, 1991). Schafer and Olexa (1971) interviewed one noncollege-prep girl who said that she carried her general-track books upside down to avoid being humiliated while walking down the hall. One student described in an interview how he felt when he went to junior high school and found out that he was in the basic track:

VIDEO HOMEWORK EXERCISE
Cooperative Learning

Go to **www.myeducationlab.com** and, in the Homework and Exercises section for Chapter 10 of this text, access the video entitled "Cooperative Learning." Watch the video (you've seen this one before, but the exercise is a new one!) and complete the homework questions that accompany it, saving your work or transmitting it to your professor as required.

> I felt good when I was with my [elementary] class, but when they went and separated us—that changed us. That changed our ideas, our thinking, the way we thought about each other, and turned us to enemies toward each other—because they said I was dumb and they were smart.
>
> When you first go to junior high school you do feel something inside—it's like an ego. You have been from elementary to junior high, you feel great inside . . . you get this shirt that says Brown Junior High . . . and you are proud of that shirt. But then you go up there and the teacher says—"Well, so and so, you're in the basic section, you can't go with the other kids." The devil with the whole thing—you lose—something in you—like it goes out of you. (Schafer and Olexa, 1971, pp. 62–63)

Students in lower-track classes are far more likely than other students to become delinquent and truant and drop out of school (Goodlad, 1983; Oakes, 1985). These problems are certainly in part because students in low-track classes are low in academic performance to begin with. However, this is probably not the whole story. For example, students who are assigned to the low track in junior high school experience a rapid loss of self-esteem (Goodlad, 1983), as the preceding extract illustrates. Slavin and Karweit (1982) found that fifth- and sixth-graders in urban elementary schools were absent about 8 percent of the time. When these same students entered the tracked junior high school, absenteeism rose almost immediately to 26 percent, and the truancy was concentrated among students assigned to the bottom-track classes. The change happened too rapidly to be attributed entirely to characteristics of students. Something about the organization of the junior high school apparently convinced a substantial number of students that school was no longer a rewarding place to be.

One of the most insidious aspects of tracking is that it often creates low-track classes that are composed predominantly of students from lower socioeconomic backgrounds and from minority groups, and upper-track classes that are more often composed of children from higher socioeconomic levels (Braddock & Dawkins, 1993; Cooper, 1998; Dornbusch, 1994). There is evidence that this difference is in part a result of discrimination (intended or not) against African American and Latino students (Hoffer & Nelson, 1993). A study by Yonezawa, Wells, and Serna (2002) found that even in high schools in which students are theoretically given a "free choice" of academic levels, African American and Latino students disproportionately ended up in low-level classes. The creation of groupings that are so often associated with social class and race is impossible to justify in light of the lack of evidence that such groupings are educationally necessary.

Although individual teachers can rarely set policies on between-class ability grouping, it is useful for all educators to know that research does not support this practice at any grade level, and tracking should be avoided whenever possible. This does not mean that all forms of between-class grouping should be abandoned, however. For example, there is probably some justification for acceleration programs, such as offering Algebra I to mathematically talented seventh-graders or offering advanced placement classes in high school (e.g., Swiatek & Benbow, 1991). Also, some between-class grouping is bound to occur in secondary schools, because some students choose to take advanced courses and others do not. However, the idea that having high, middle, and low sections of the same course can help student achievement has not been supported by research. Mixed-ability classes can be successful at all grade levels, particularly if other, more effective means of accommodating student differences are used. These include within-class ability grouping, tutoring for low achievers, and certain individualized instruction programs that are described in this chapter, as well as cooperative learning strategies.

Connections
Cooperative learning strategies are described in Chapter 8, page 243.

Untracking

For many years, educators and researchers have challenged the use of between-class ability grouping at all levels. Influential groups such as the National Governors' Association (1993) and the Carnegie Corporation of New York (1989) recommended moving away from traditional ability grouping practices, and a number of guides to untracking and examples of successful untracking have been published (e.g., Burris, Heubert, & Levin, 2004; Cooper, 1998; Fahey, 2000; Hubbard & Mehan, 1998; Kugler & Albright, 2005; Oakes, Quartz, Ryan, & Lipton, 2000). **Untracking** recommendations focus on having students in mixed-ability groups and holding them to high standards but providing many ways for them to reach those standards, including extra assistance for students who are having difficulties keeping up (Burris, Heubert, & Levin, 2006; Hubbard & Mehan, 1998). Use of appropriate forms of cooperative learning and project-based learning has often been recommended as a means of opening up more avenues to high performance for all children (Cohen, 1992; Hubbard & Mehan, 1998; Pool & Page, 1995). Yet the road to untracking is far from easy, especially in middle schools and high schools (Cooper, 1998; Oakes et al., 2000; Rubin, 2003). In particular, untracking often runs into serious opposition from the parents of high achievers. Oakes and colleagues (2000) and Wells, Hirshberg, Lipton, and Oakes (1995) have pointed out that untracking requires changes in thinking about children's potentials, not only changes in school or classroom practices. Teachers, parents, and students themselves, these researchers claim, must come to see the

Connections
Various forms of cooperative and project-based learning are described in Chapter 8, pages 243–247.

untracking
A focus on having students in mixed-ability groups and holding them to high standards but providing many ways for students to reach those standards.

goal of schooling as success for every child, not as sorting students into categories, if untracking is to take hold (Hubbard & Mehan, 1997; Oakes, Quartz, Ryan, & Lipton, 2000). This change in perception is difficult to bring about; perhaps, as a result, the move toward untracking is going slowly at the secondary level (Hallinan, 2004).

Regrouping for Reading and Mathematics

Another form of ability grouping that is often used in the elementary grades is **regrouping.** In regrouping plans, students are in mixed-ability classes most of the day but are assigned to reading and/or math classes on the basis of their performance in these subjects. For example, at 9:30 A.M. the fourth-graders in a school may move to different teachers so that they can receive reading instruction that is appropriate to their reading levels. One form of regrouping for reading, the **Joplin Plan,** regroups students across grade lines. For example, a reading class at the fourth-grade, first—semester reading level may contain third-, fourth-, and fifth-graders.

One major advantage of regrouping over all-day ability grouping is that in regrouping plans the students spend most of the day in a mixed-ability class. Thus, low achievers are not separated out as a class and stigmatized. Perhaps for these reasons, regrouping plans, especially the Joplin Plan, have generally been found to increase student achievement (Gutiérrez & Slavin, 1992; Slavin, 1987b).

Nongraded (Cross-Age Grouping) Elementary Schools

A form of grouping that was popular in the 1960s and early 1970s that is returning in various forms today is nongraded organization, or cross-age grouping (Fogarty, 1993; Pavan, 1992). **Nongraded programs** (or cross-age grouping programs) combine children of different ages in the same classes. Most often, students aged 5 to 7 or 6 to 8 may be mixed in a nongraded primary program. Students work across age lines but are often flexibly grouped for some instruction according to their needs and performance levels (Kasten & Lolli, 1998). A review of research on the nongraded programs of the 1960s and 1970s found that these programs had a positive effect on achievement when they focused on flexible grouping for instruction but were less effective when they had a strong focus on individualized instruction (Gutiérrez & Slavin, 1992). The nongraded elementary school ultimately became the open classroom, which emphasized individualized learning activities and deemphasized teacher instruction. Research on the open classroom similarly failed to find achievement benefits (Giaconia & Hedges, 1982). There has been little research on today's application of the nongraded primary program (see Pavan, 1992), but one study did find achievement benefits for a nongraded school (Tanner & Decotis, 1994).

Sometimes cross-grade grouping is used out of necessity because there are too few children at a given grade level to make up a whole class. Such combination classes (e.g., grades 3–4 or 5–6) have not been found to enhance student achievement and might even be harmful (Burns & Mason, 2002; Veenman, 1995, 1997).

Within-Class Ability Grouping

Another way to adapt instruction to differences in student performance levels is to group students within classes, as is typical in elementary school reading classes. For example, a third-grade teacher might have the Rockets group using a 3–1 (third-grade, first-semester) text, the Stars group using a 3–2 (third-grade, second-semester) text, and the Planets group using a 4–1 (fourth-grade, first-semester) text.

Within-class ability grouping is far more common in elementary schools than in secondary schools, and it is very common in elementary reading classes (Chorzempa & Graham, 2006). Surveys of principals have found that more than 90 percent of elementary reading teachers use multiple reading groups (Puma et al., 1997), whereas only 15

regrouping
A method of ability grouping in which students in mixed-ability classes are assigned to reading or math classes on the basis of their performance levels.

Joplin Plan
A regrouping method in which students are grouped across grade lines for reading instruction.

nongraded programs
Programs, generally at the primary level, that combine children of different ages in the same class. Also called *cross-age grouping programs.*

to 18 percent of elementary math teachers do so (Good, Mulryan, & McCaslin, 1992; Mason, 1995). Within-class ability grouping is rare in subjects other than reading or mathematics. In reading, teachers typically have each group working at a different point in a series of reading texts and allow each group to proceed at its own pace. Teachers who group in math might use different texts with the different groups or, more often, allow groups to proceed at their own rates in the same book, so the higher-performing group will cover more material than the lower-performing group. In many math classes the teacher teaches one lesson to the whole class and then meets with two or more ability groups during times when students are doing seatwork to reinforce skills or provide enrichment as needed.

CERTIFICATION POINTER

You may be asked on your teacher certification test to describe a technique for grouping students within a reading class to meet a wide range of student reading abilities.

Research on Within-Class Ability Grouping Research on the achievement effects of within-class ability grouping has taken place almost exclusively in elementary mathematics classes. The reason is that researchers want to look at teaching situations in which some teachers use within-class ability grouping and others do not, and this is typically true only in elementary math. Until recently, almost all elementary reading teachers used reading groups, whereas in elementary subjects other than math, and in secondary classes, very few teachers did. Most studies that have evaluated within-class ability grouping methods in math (in which the different groups proceed at different paces on different materials) have found that students in the ability-grouped classes learned more than did students in classes that did not use grouping (Slavin, 1987b). Students of high, average, and low achievement levels seem to benefit equally from within-class ability grouping (Lou et al., 1996). One study by Mason and Good (1993) found that teachers who flexibly grouped and regrouped students according to their needs had better math achievement outcomes than did those who used permanent within-class groups.

The research suggests that small numbers of ability groups are better than large numbers (Slavin & Karweit, 1984). Smaller numbers of groups have the advantage of allowing more direct instruction from the teacher and using less seatwork time and transition time. With three groups this rises to two-thirds of class time. Teachers who try to teach more than three reading or math groups might also have problems with classroom management. Dividing the class into more than three groups does not decrease the magnitude or range of differences within each group enough to offset these problems (see Hiebert, 1983).

It is important to note that the research finding benefits of within-class grouping in elementary mathematics was mostly done many years ago with traditional teaching methods that were intended primarily to teach computation rather than problem solving. As mathematics moves toward the use of constructivist approaches that are more directed at problem solving, discovery, and cooperative learning, within-class grouping might become unnecessary (Good et al., 1992). The main point to be drawn from research on within-class ability grouping is not that it is desirable but that if some form of grouping is thought to be necessary, grouping within the class is preferable to grouping between classes. Beyond its more favorable achievement outcomes, within-class grouping can be more flexible and less stigmatizing and occupies a much smaller portion of the school day than between-class grouping does (Rowan & Miracle, 1983).

Retention

One of the most controversial issues in education is whether low-achieving students should be required to repeat a grade. Primarily as a result of accountability pressures, retention rates have risen dramatically. In recent years, Florida held back 24,000 students, New York City failed 16,000 third-graders, and Miami had 2,000 students in third grade for the third time (McGill-Franzen & Allington, 2006).

Proponents of holding back low-achieving students argue that this gives them a "gift of time" to catch up and sets clear standards that students must strive to achieve. Opponents note that students who are held back lose motivation; in fact, having been retained is one of the strongest predictors of dropping out (Allensworth, 2005; Jimerson, Anderson, & Whipple 2002). Retention is concentrated among students who are male, minority, and disadvantaged (Beebe-Frankenberger et al., 2004).

Is retention beneficial or harmful? In the short term, holding students back increases scores in a given school or district, not because students are learning more but because they are older when they take the test. For this reason, states and districts often report "dramatic gains" on state tests following a new policy of holding students back unless they met a given test standard (Bali, Anagnostopoulos, & Roberts, 2005; McGill-Franzen et al., 2006). In long-term studies, however, students who were retained end up learning less than similar low-achievers of the same age who were not retained (Hong & Raudenbush, 2005; Roderick & Nagaoka, 2005).

The best solutions to the problems of low-achieving students are neither retention nor "social promotion" (promoting students without regard to their levels of achievement). Instead, such children should be given special attention, diagnosis, and intensive interventions, such as tutoring, until their achievement falls within the normal range. An extra year is a very expensive intervention—for that amount of money, students can be given much more effective assistance (Reeves, 2006).

WHAT ARE SOME WAYS OF INDIVIDUALIZING INSTRUCTION?

INTASC

3 Adapting Instruction for Individual Needs

The problem of providing all students with appropriate levels of instruction could be completely solved if schools could simply assign each student his or her own teacher. Not surprisingly, studies of one adult–one student tutoring find substantial positive effects of tutoring on student achievement (Wasik & Slavin, 1993). One major reason for the effectiveness of tutoring is that the tutor can provide **individualized instruction,** tailoring instruction precisely to a student's needs. If the student learns quickly, the tutor can move to other tasks; if not, the tutor can figure out what the problem is, try another explanation, or simply spend more time on the task.

individualized instruction Instruction tailored to particular students' needs, in which each student works at her or his own level and rate.

There are situations in which tutoring by adults is feasible and necessary. Cross-age peer tutors (older students working with younger ones) can also be very effective. In addition, educational innovators have long tried to simulate the one-to-one teaching situation by individualizing instruction. Teachers have long found ways to informally accommodate the needs of different learners in heterogeneous classrooms (Tomlinson,

What type of tutoring is taking place in this picture? What other means of individualizing instruction are available to you as a teacher?

2003, 2004). Individualized instruction, or programmed instruction methods, in which students worked at their own level and pace were popular in the 1960s and 1970s (Fletcher, 1992), but this type of instruction has been replaced by forms of computer-based instruction. These strategies are discussed in the following sections.

Peer Tutoring

Students can help one another learn. In **peer tutoring,** one student teaches another. There are two principal types of peer tutoring: **cross-age tutoring,** in which the tutor is several years older than the student being taught, and same-age peer tutoring, in which a student tutors a classmate. Cross-age tutoring is recommended by researchers more often than same-age tutoring—partly because of the obvious fact that older students are more likely to know the material, and partly because students might accept an older student as a tutor but resent having a classmate appointed to tutor them (Topping & Ehly, 1998). Sometimes peer tutoring is used with students who need special assistance, in which case a few older students might work with a few younger students. Other tutoring schemes have involved, for example, entire fifth-grade classes tutoring entire second-grade classes. In these cases, half of the younger students might be sent to the older students' classroom while half of the older students go to the younger students' classroom. Otherwise, peer tutoring may take place in the cafeteria, the library, or another school facility.

INTASC

6 Communication Skills

Peer tutoring among students of the same age can be easier to arrange and has also been found to be very effective (e.g., King, 1997; Simmons, Fuchs, Fuchs, Mathes, & Hodge, 1995). Among classmates of the same age and performance level, reciprocal peer tutoring, in which students take turns as tutors and tutees, can be both practical and effective (Fantuzzo, King, & Heller, 1992; Greenwood et al., 1993; Mathes, Torgeson, & Allor, 2001).

Connections
For more on reciprocal teaching, see Chapter 8, page 239.

Adequate training and monitoring of tutors are essential (Jenkins & Jenkins, 1987). Tutors who have been taught specific tutoring strategies produce much better results than do those who have not had such training (Fuchs, Fuchs, Bentz, Phillips, & Hamlett, 1994; Merrill, Reiser, Merrill, & Landes, 1995). Also, involving parents in support of a tutoring program enhances its effectiveness (Fantuzzo, Davis, & Ginsburg, 1995).

Research on Peer Tutoring Research evaluating the effects of peer tutoring on student achievement has generally found that this strategy increases the achievement of both tutees and tutors (Fantuzzo et al., 1992; King, Staffieni, & Adelgais, 1998; Simmons et al., 1995; Van Keer, 2004). In fact, some studies have found greater achievement gains for tutors than for tutees (Rekrut, 1992), and peer tutoring is sometimes used as much to improve the achievement of low-achieving older students as to improve that of the students being tutored (Top & Osguthorpe, 1987). As many teachers have noted, the best way to learn something thoroughly is to teach it to someone else. High achievers who tutor other students usually enjoy and value this activity (Thorkildsen, 1993).

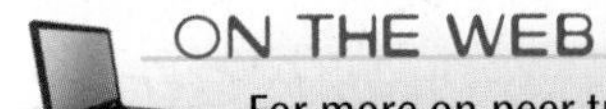

ON THE WEB

For more on peer tutoring see the Northwest Regional Educational Laboratory at **www.nwrel.org.**

Adult Tutoring

One-to-one adult-to-child tutoring is one of the most effective instructional strategies known, and it essentially solves the problem of appropriate levels of instruction. The principal drawback to this method is its cost. However, it is often possible, on a small scale, to provide adult tutors for students who are having problems learning in the regular class setting. For example, adult volunteers such as parents, college students, or senior citizens are often willing to tutor students (Hopkins, 1998; Juel, 1996; Neuman, 1995). Volunteer tutors who are well supervised and who use well-structured materials can have a positive effect on children's reading performance (Baker, Gersten, & Keating, 2000; Tingley, 2001; Wasik, 1997). Tutoring is an excellent use of school aides (Hock, Schumaker, &

peer tutoring
Tutoring of one student by another.

cross-age tutoring
Tutoring of a younger student by an older one.

Deshler, 2001); some school districts hire large numbers of paraprofessional aides precisely for this purpose. In fact, research has found few achievement benefits of classroom aides unless they are doing one-to-one tutoring (see Slavin, 1994b).

There are some circumstances in which the high costs of one-to-one tutoring can be justified. One of these is that of first-graders who are having difficulties learning to read. Failing to learn to read in the lower grades of elementary school is so detrimental to later school achievement that an investment in tutors who can prevent reading failure is worthwhile. A one-to-one tutoring program, Reading Recovery, uses highly trained, certified teachers to work with first-graders who are at risk for failing to learn to read. Research on this strategy has found that students who received tutoring in first grade read significantly better than comparable students (D'Agostino & Murphy, 2004; Pinnell, Lyons, DeFord, Bryk, & Seltzer, 1994). Another effective program, Success for All, makes extensive use of one-to-one tutoring for at-risk first-graders (Slavin and Madden, 2001). Reading Recovery and Success for All are discussed later in this chapter. Other one-to-one tutoring programs for at-risk first-graders have also found substantial positive effects (see Fuchs et al., 2005; Meyer et al., 2002; Morris, 2006: O'Connor et al., 2002; Rabiner et al., 2003; Wasik & Slavin, 1993). In addition, an evaluation of a structured phonetic tutoring program for low-achieving second- and third-graders also found strong and lasting effects on students' reading performance (Blachman et al., 2004; Denton et al., 2004).

THEORY *into* PRACTICE

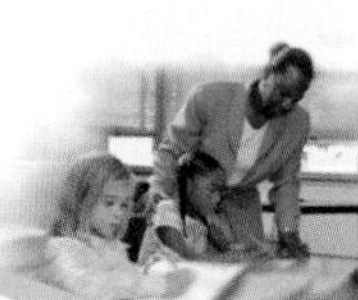

Effectively Using Tutoring Methods to Meet Individual Needs

Peer tutoring is an effective way to improve learning for both the tutee and the tutor, and no one doubts the value of this strategy for meeting individual needs within a classroom. However, it takes more than simply pairing off students to make peer tutoring result in improved learning.

Although you are likely to use informal tutoring practices in your classroom every day (e.g., asking one student to help another student with a problem), establishing a formalized tutoring program requires more involved planning. The following strategies can help you create and sustain an effective program within your classroom. As with most initiatives, if you can work with your building administrator and other teachers to establish a schoolwide tutoring program, you will be able to serve the needs of all students more successfully.

To establish a tutoring program, recognize that specific skills need to be developed in both the tutors and tutees. Whether the tutors are same-age peers, older students, or even adults, use care in selecting tutors. It is always wise to begin with volunteers. Consider not only the knowledge base of the tutors (i.e., their proven proficiency with the subject matter) but also their ability to convey their knowledge clearly.

Typically, training will be minimal and will include basic instruction in modeling, prompting responses from tutees, using corrective feedback and praise/reinforcement, alternating teaching methods and materials (i.e., using multisensory methods), and recording and reporting progress. If this is a schoolwide initiative, classroom teachers or even parents or paraprofessionals can train students who will tutor as part of an extracurricular service activity.

Students receiving tutoring need to be clear about their role in this process. It would be counterproductive to force any student into a tutorial relationship. Therefore, initially select only students who express a willingness to work with a tutor. Steadily make tutoring a part of the natural learning activities within a classroom or an entire school. In this collaborative model, every student at some point

CERTIFICATION POINTER

For your teacher certification test, you will probably need to demonstrate your understanding of appropriate applications of cross-age tutoring. For example, you might be asked to identify the curricular goals that cross-age tutoring would be appropriate for and how you would structure the tutoring so that it would be effective.

in time will have the opportunity to be both tutor and tutee. Even students with less knowledge and skills might be able to find peers or younger students with whom they can work. Many students with special-education needs have gained confidence and improved their own abilities by working with younger students.

During the training process help all students to understand that the tutor represents the teacher and, therefore, should be respected accordingly. In addition, tutees and tutors must understand that the goal of the activity is to have each tutee reach a clear understanding of the concepts, not merely complete an assignment. To make this clear, you might want to use various role-playing activities during the training process. Demonstrate appropriate and inappropriate forms of instruction, feedback, reinforcement, and so on; then allow the participants to practice under supervised conditions. Corrective feedback within this controlled environment will allow you to feel more confident as the tutor–tutee pairs work together without your direct supervision.

Whether you decide to begin this process solely within your own classroom or to develop a schoolwide tutorial program, keep these issues in mind:

1. Tutors need to be trained in specific instructional practices.
2. Tutors and tutees need to have a clear understanding of their roles and expectations.
3. Tutors and tutees need to receive supervision and feedback about their work, particularly during the early stages of the tutoring process.
4. Teachers need to work with the tutors to create effective and efficient ways of recording and reporting the progress of the sessions.

BUILDING TEACHING SKILLS EXERCISE
Lesson Planning

Go to **www.myeducationlab.com** and access the Lesson Planning tool there. Create a lesson plan using the STAD model for teaching a class lesson in small groups. Be sure to highlight or mark each component of STAD in your plan. Save your work or transmit it to your professor as required.

Differentiated Instruction

Differentiated instruction (George, 2005; Tomlinson, 2003, 2004) is an approach to teaching that adapts the content, level, pace, and products of instruction to accommodate the different needs of diverse students in regular classes. The philosophy behind differentiated instruction emphasizes that all children can reach high standards, but some may need tailored assistance to enable them to do so.

For example, a teacher might ask a diverse class to write a biography of Gandhi but provide materials on Gandhi at different reading levels. Another might create a common math test for a heterogeneous class but include a few "challenge questions" for students with stronger preparation in math. During seatwork, teachers might focus on students known to have difficulties with prerequisite skills or provide them preteaching on those skills before class; for example, before a unit on decimals, the teacher might arrange an extra session to review fractions with students who are not solid with fractional concepts central to decimals.

HOW IS TECHNOLOGY USED IN EDUCATION?

INTASC

6 Communication Skills

Watch children of any age playing video games, sending messages to their friends, or looking up information on the Internet. Adults who see this, or experience it themselves, ask themselves why the obvious power of technology, which is transforming every aspect of life, hasn't transformed education. This is not to say that technology is not present in classrooms. Computers, DVDs, interactive whiteboards, and all sorts of other technology are present to one degree or another in every school, and most middle-class children, at least, go home to an array of technology as well (DeBell & Chapman, 2006). Yet only gradually is technology truly changing the core of teaching and learning in America's schools.

differentiated instruction
An approach to teaching that adapts the content, level, pace, and products of instruction to accommodate different needs of diverse students in regular classes.

ON THE WEB

The International Society for Technology in Education (ISTE) has developed standards for technology use in education. It provides guidance for teachers in

- Planning and designing learning environments supported by technology
- Integrating technology-enhanced experiences that address content standards
- Applying technology to assess and track student learning
- Using technology to enhance productivity and professional practice
- Understanding the social, ethical, and legal issues in the use of technology

You can find the complete ISTE National Educational Technology Standards for Teachers (NETS-T) at **iste@iste.org.**

There are three general types of technology applications in education. First, teachers use technology in their classroom teaching, to plan instruction and present content to their classes. Second, students use technology to explore, practice, and prepare papers and presentations. Finally, teachers and administrators use technology to accomplish administrative tasks associated with their profession, such as assessment, record keeping, reporting, and management tasks (see Bitter & Legacy, 2008; Lever-Duffy & McDonald, 2008; Thorsen, 2006). Examples of these three types of technology applications are described next.

Technology for Instruction

Word processors, electronic spreadsheets, and presentation software are the most common electronic technologies that teachers use for instruction. Teachers use word processors for numerous teaching tasks, such as preparing student worksheets, tests, transparencies, classroom signs, and posters. Simple desktop publishing features allow teachers to use simple graphics and art to make texts appealing to students. Word processing makes it easy for teachers to adapt documents to meet specific students' needs. Teachers can make customized presentations of data and create clear summaries for students to use as study guides.

Electronic spreadsheets organize and compute numerical data, producing charts and graphs to illustrate the information. Spreadsheets are particularly helpful for teaching mathematics because they allow teachers to display numeric data visually, such as the impact of changes on variable values.

Presentation software helps teachers make professional presentations with a prearranged group of electronic slides. These presentations can include multimedia elements such as graphics, sound, special effects, animation, and video clips that make the presentations more appealing. These presentations can be printed to provide students with an outline of the presentation. More advanced multimedia and Web authoring systems help teachers create their own multimedia tutorials and Web pages to support their lessons.

Increasingly, technology is being used to combine text and visual content, such as animations or video. This multimedia approach has been found to enhance students' learning as long as the text and visuals directly support each other (Hoeffler & Leutner, 2006; Reed, 2006). For example, adding diagrams or animations to show how lightning works has been found to enhance the text, but adding motivational but nonexplanatory text (such as a picture of an airplane being hit by lightning) adds little to learning (Mayer, 2001). Similarly, a recent study of first-grade reading found that adding video content on letter sounds, sound blending, and vocabulary to teacher-led reading lessons significantly increased students' learning (Chambers et al., 2006).

The many technological tools available make teachers' lessons more dynamic. Initial fears that computers might replace teachers are unfounded. Teachers do make effective use of computer simulations, presentation software, spreadsheets, and other software, but these clearly enhance rather than replace teacher instruction.

Teaching Dilemmas:
CASES TO CONSIDER

Should Computers Be in Labs or Classrooms?

Imagine that your school is writing a grant to the state department of education to obtain funds to purchase computers for your 560 students. You are on the committee that is writing the grant and you need to explain where the computers will be located and how they will be used. The funds available allow only for one computer per class or for one computer lab.

Some benefits of having all the computers in a lab include (1) a whole class is able to work on the same software at the same time, (2) networking the computers is easier and less expensive, and (3) security is easier. However, the lab location requires careful scheduling, reducing flexibility and making integrating computers into the curriculum more difficult.

Having computers distributed among the classrooms means constant availability and easier integration into teachers' lessons. The teachers need to have a greater knowledge of hardware and software and cannot have everyone working on a project together. The cost of supporting the computers in classrooms is higher, and the security is more difficult.

QUESTIONS FOR REFLECTION

1. How would your answer be different if your school were an elementary, middle, or high school?
2. How would you spend the school's technology money? Would you put all of the computers in a computer lab, or would you distribute them among the classrooms?
3. Which uses of computers lend themselves to labs and which to distribution among many classes?

Technology for Learning

In 1998, there were approximately 8.6 million computers in U.S. elementary and secondary schools, or one for every six students, and the number was growing by about 15 percent each year (Becker, 2001). There was an average of 69 computers in each elementary school, 98 in each middle school, and 122 in each high school. The computers were almost evenly divided between classrooms and computer labs (Anderson & Ronnkvist, 1999). Schools serving middle-class and disadvantaged communities have similar numbers of computers, but there are substantial differences in the likelihood that students have computers at home (Azzam, 2006; Children's Partnership, 2006).

Computer use varies considerably across settings. In secondary schools, computers are concentrated in classes on computer use, and in business and vocational courses. When computers are used in traditional academic courses, they are most often used in English classes as word processors. Self-contained elementary classes are much more likely to report extensive computer use than secondary academic subject classes (see Figure 9.2).

The most common use of computers in elementary and secondary schools is for word processing, followed by CD-ROM reference software (see Figure 9.3). Computers have replaced typewriters and encyclopedias, but instructional uses of computers are largely limited to word processing, games, and remediation (Becker, 2001).

Connections
To learn about the use of computers for students with disabilities, see Chapter 12, pages 395–396.

Technology is used for a wide variety of purposes by students in classrooms. The applications of technology use by students fall into the following categories: word processing and publishing, spreadsheets and databases, computer-assisted instruction, the Internet, multimedia, integrated learning systems, and computer programming (see Geisert & Futrell, 2000; Goldman-Segall & Maxwell, 2003; Schwartz & Beichner, 1999; Zhao & Frank, 2003). See Chapter 12 for a discussion of the use of technology in special education and mainstreaming (Blamires, 1999; Woodward & Cuban, 2001).

FIGURE 9.2 Frequent Computer Use by Subject Taught (Percent of Teachers Reporting 20+ Uses by Typical Student in Class during Year)

Source: Adapted from Becker, H. J. (2001). *How are teachers using computers in instruction?* Paper presented at the annual meeting of the American Educational Research Association, Seattle.

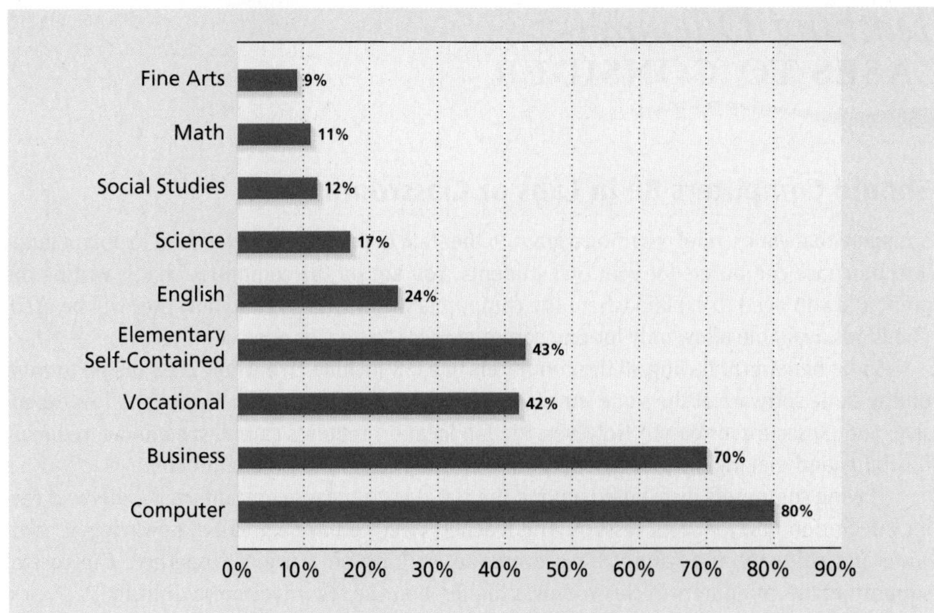

FIGURE 9.3 Software Used by Frequent Computer-Using Teachers (Elementary and Secondary Academic Subjects)

Source: Adapted from Becker, H. J. (2001). *How are teachers using computers in instruction?* Paper presented at the annual meeting of the American Educational Research Association, Seattle.

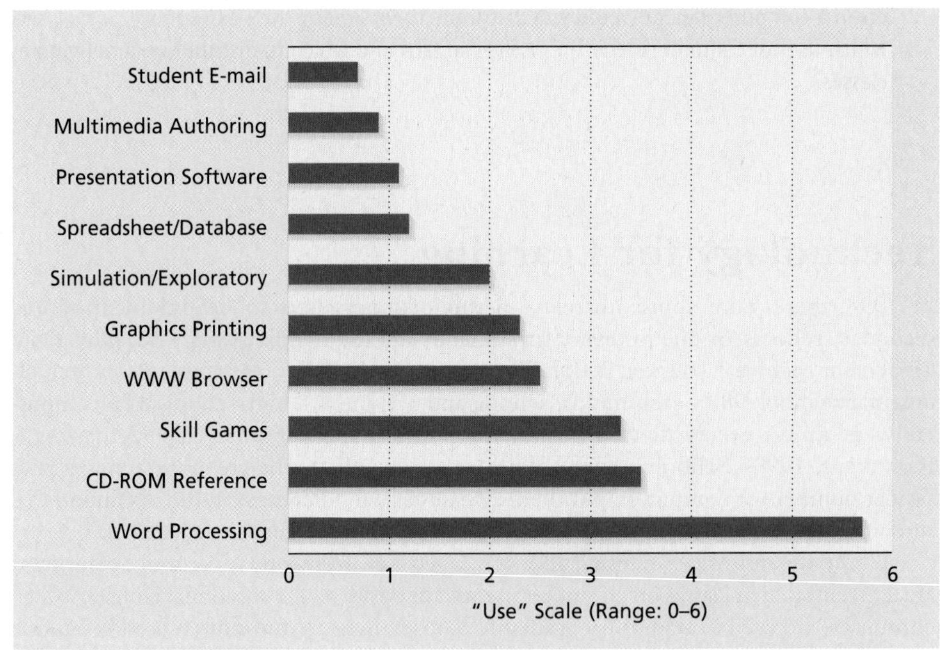

word processing or desktop publishing A computer application for writing compositions that lends itself to revising and editing.

Word Processing and Publishing By far the most common application of computers, especially in grades 4 through 12, is **word processing** or **desktop publishing.** As a result, English teachers are more likely than teachers of other subjects to make frequent use of computers in the secondary grades (Becker, 2001). Increasingly, students are asked to write compositions on classroom computers. A key advantage of word processing over paper-and-pencil composition is that word processing facilitates revision. Spell checkers and other utilities help students to worry less about mechanics and focus on the meaning and organization of their compositions. As writing instruction has moved toward an emphasis on a process of revision and editing, this capability has become very important.

Word processing is probably the best-researched application of computers to instruction. Studies of word processing show that students who use computers write more, revise more, and take greater pride in their writing than do paper-and-pencil writers (Cochran-Smith, 1991). Writing quality tends to be somewhat better when students have access to word processors (Goldberg, Russell, & Cook, 2003; Kamil, Intrator, & Kim, 2000). This writing effect may be enhanced when each student has a laptop, instead of having to share a small number of computers (Lowther, Ross, & Morrison, 2003). Of course, word processing itself has become an essential skill in a vast range of occupations, so teaching students to use word processing programs (e.g., in high school business courses) has obvious value.

Spreadsheets As with word processing, use of **spreadsheets** in education is an extension of software that is widely used by adults. Typically, spreadsheets can convert raw data into graphs, charts, and other data summaries so that students can easily organize information and see the effects of various variables on outcomes. For example, a student could enter data for the number of tadpoles caught in each of five ponds at three times. By assigning a formula to a given column, the student could customize the spreadsheet program to total the numbers for each pond and each time. Changing any number would automatically change row and column totals. The spreadsheet program could then show the data in raw, numeric form or convert the data into a graph. Students are increasingly using spreadsheets to record data from science experiments and to reinforce mathematics skills.

Databases A **database** is a computer program that keeps a lot of information that will be referred to later on and sometimes manipulated. Students can learn to search CD-ROM (ROM stands for read-only memory) databases such as encyclopedias, atlases, road maps, catalogs, and so on to find information for a variety of instructional purposes. Databases of this type can be particularly important in project-based learning because they may put a great deal of information into easy reach for open-ended reports and other projects. Access to CD-ROM technology is growing rapidly; in 1995–1996, 54 percent of schools had this capability (ETS, 1996). After word processing, CD-ROM encyclopedias and related programs are among the most popular applications of computer technology in schools (Becker, 2001).

In many databases, students can use **hypertext** and **hypermedia** to search a database (such as an encyclopedia) by clicking on a word or picture. This leads the student to related or more detailed information on a specific portion of the text. Hypermedia can similarly provide pictures, music, video footage, or other information to illuminate and extend the information on a CD-ROM database (Bortnick, 1995; Dillon & Gabbard, 1998). Hypermedia has exciting possibilities for allowing learners to follow their interests or resolve gaps in understanding more efficiently than with traditional text, but so far, research on use of hypermedia finds limited and inconsistent effects on student learning that depend on both the type of material being studied and the nature of the learners (Dillon & Gabbard, 1998; Kamil, Intrator, & Kim, 2000).

Computer-Assisted Instruction Applications of **computer-assisted instruction (CAI)** range in complexity from simple drill and practice software to complex problem-solving programs.

Drill and Practice. One common application of microcomputers in education is to provide students with **drill and practice** on skills or knowledge. For example, many software programs provide students with practice on math facts or computations, geography, history facts, or science. Computer experts often frown on drill and practice programs, calling them "electronic page turning," and the programs are generally less than exciting. They typically replace independent seatwork and do have several major advantages over seatwork, including immediate feedback; record keeping; and, in many cases, appealing graphics and variations in pace or level of items depending on the student's responses. This can increase students' motivation to do work that might otherwise be boring (Kamil, Intrator, & Kim, 2000; Leu, 2000). Drill and practice programs should not be

spreadsheets
Computer programs that convert data into tables, charts, and graphs.

databases
Computer programs that contain large volumes of information, such as encyclopedias and atlases.

hypertext and hypermedia
Related information that appears when a computer user clicks on a word or picture.

computer-assisted instruction (CAI)
Individualized instruction administered by computer.

drill and practice
Application of computer technology to provide students with practice of skills and knowledge.

These students are using instructional software to learn. What does research say about the advantages and disadvantages of computer-based instruction? Are certain types of computer-assisted instruction more effective?

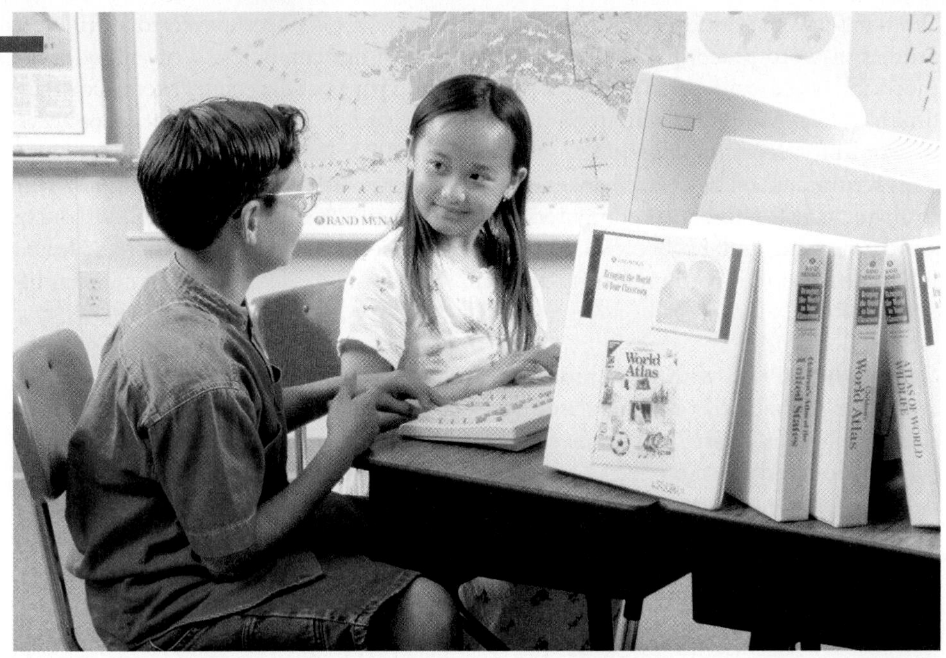

expected to teach by themselves, but they can reinforce skills or knowledge that students have learned elsewhere.

Tutorial Programs. More sophisticated than drill and practice programs, **tutorial programs** are intended to teach new material and present appropriate correction and review based on the student's responses. The best tutorial programs come close to mimicking a patient human tutor. Increasingly, tutorial programs use speech and graphics to engage students' attention and present new information. Students are typically asked many questions, and the program branches in different directions depending on the answers, reexplaining if the student makes mistakes or moving on if a student responds correctly. Very sophisticated computer-managed programs that simulate the behaviors of expert human tutors are being developed and applied in a variety of settings (Lever-Duffy, McDonald, & Mizell, 2003). Computer tutorials have been found to be particularly effective in the natural and social sciences (Kulik, 2003).

Instructional Games. Most children are first introduced to computers through video games, and many educators (and parents) have wondered whether the same intensity, motivation, and perseverance that they see in children playing video games could be brought to the classroom (Shaffer, Squire, Halverson, & Gee, 2005). Many **instructional games** have been designed; most are simple extrapolations of drill and practice designs into a game format, but some are more creative. For example, the popular program "Where in the World Is Carmen Sandiego?" is designed to teach geography by engaging children in tracking a gang of criminals through various countries. Computer games are among the most common applications of computer software in schools (Becker, 2001).

Simulations. **Simulation software** involves students in an interactive model of some sort of reality. Students operate within a simulated environment and, by doing so, learn about that environment from the inside. For example, one of the earliest simulations, "Oregon Trail," gives students limited allocations of food, water, money, horses, and other resources; and students must use these resources wisely to successfully move their wagon trains to the West. Other popular simulations let children build their own civilizations, build new forms of life, and so on. Simulations are engaging, fun, and creative; and recent evidence indicates that they can improve achievement compared to traditional teaching methods, particularly in science (Kulik, 2003).

tutorial programs
Computer programs that teach new material, varying their content and pace according to the student's responses.

instructional games
Drill and practice exercises presented in a game format.

simulation software
Computer programs that model real-life phenomena to promote problem-solving abilities and motivate interest in the areas concerned.

Problem-Solving Programs. The goal of developing students' critical-thinking skills has led to the creation of numerous CAI programs that are designed as problem-solving activities. One innovative **problem-solving program** is the Jasper series, developed and researched at Vanderbilt University (Cognition and Technology Group at Vanderbilt, 1996). In this program, students are shown videos in which a character, Jasper Woodbury, faces a series of challenges that require applications of mathematics and thinking skills. Students must solve the problems Jasper faces before they see his solution. In addition to working with computers, students work in cooperative groups on offline activities that are related to the stories. Evaluations found that in comparison to matched controls, students in classes that used the Jasper program performed similarly in math computations and concepts but better in word problems and planning.

CERTIFICATION POINTER

A teacher certification question may ask you to suggest a strategy for using technology to help students learn various instructional objectives.

Internet

Perhaps the fastest-growing technology applications in U.S. schools involve the **Internet** (Leu, 2000; Lewin, 2001; March, 2006). Internet access for schools is becoming almost universal. In 1998, more than 90 percent of schools had Internet access, and the proportion was rapidly rising (Anderson & Ronnkvist, 1999; Shields & Behrman, 2000). The Internet gives schools access to vast stores of information, including databases on every imaginable subject, libraries throughout the world, and other specialized information (Jukes, Dosaj, & Macdonald, 2000; Linn & Slotta, 2000; Provenzo, 1999). Students can use the Internet to do WebQuests, in which they search the Internet on a given topic or theme. In a project called GLOBE (www.globe.gov), students collect local data on soil and water quality and contribute it to a real national scientific investigation (Means & Coleman, 2000). The Internet can also enable students to communicate with students in other schools, including those far away. Through this capability students can create international projects, carry out cooperative projects with other schools (Lewin, 2001; Means, 2000/2001), and so on. Classes and schools have set up their own Web pages (Havens, 2003) and have created their own virtual museums or encyclopedias by collecting and synthesizing information from many sources. Students can contribute to **wikis** (online encyclopedias), podcasts, and other virtual publications that give them authentic opportunities to communicate their work (Dlott, 2007; Ohler, 2006; Valenza, 2006).

"It's one of those computer viruses. Keep her off the Internet for a week and she'll be fine."

Teachers use Internet-based communications such as e-mail, conferencing, listservs (electronic mailing lists), chat rooms, and video conferencing to connect students to others in other areas of the world. Through these interactions students are exposed to perspectives different from their own (Lever-Duffy, McDonald, & Mizell, 2003).

ON THE WEB

For an example of a website that provides information for WebQuests see **www.edhelper.com.**

There is little research on the achievement outcomes of Internet involvement (Leu, 2000; Wallace, 2004). There are also serious concerns about how to limit children's access to pornography or other inappropriate materials that can be found on the Web (see National Research Council, 2001; Wartella & Jennings, 2000). Yet it seems that the Internet is here to stay, at least as a tool to supplement school libraries with a broad range of information.

problem-solving program Program designed specifically to develop students' critical-thinking skills.

Internet A large and growing telecommunications network of computers around the world that communicate electronically.

wiki A website, such as the Wikipedia, containing content to which the user can add or make modifications.

Multimedia Projects Students can be encouraged to make their own **multimedia** projects—an update of the old-fashioned group report (Simpkins, Cole, Tavalin, & Means, 2002). In project-based multimedia learning, students design, plan, and produce a product or performance, integrating media objects such as graphics, video, animation, and sound. An example is a seventh-grade class that created a social studies and science multimedia presentation about the Black Plague, integrating animations of how the plague virus attacks and the perspectives of fourteenth-century farmers (Simkins, Cole, Tavalin, & Means, 2002).

Students can use a wide array of graphics tools to create their multimedia presentations, including CD-ROMs and videodiscs, digital photos, concept mapping, and graphic organizers. **CD-ROM** databases include clip art, photographs, illustrations, music, and sometimes video. **Videodiscs** make available enormous resources, including videos, films, still pictures, and music. Both CD-ROMs and videodiscs can be valuable in student projects, explorations, and reports. Students can use them to create multimedia reports that combine audio, video, music, and pictures. **Digital photographs** can be used as a stimulus for writing or to illustrate projects. For example, students might take digital photographs of animals on a field trip to the zoo. Back in the classroom, these serve as a reminder to students of what they saw and also are used to illustrate their reports on the trip.

Integrated Learning Systems Early in the microcomputer revolution, schools typically assembled hardware and software from many sources, often with little coordination. Today, schools often purchase **integrated learning systems**—entire packages of hardware and software, including most of the types of software described previously. Integrated learning systems provide many terminals that are linked to each other and to computers that teachers use to monitor individual student work (Lever-Duffy, McDonald, & Mizell, 2003). Research on the effectiveness of commercial integrated learning systems has found modest positive effects on student achievement, mainly in mathematics instruction (Kulik, 2003; Slavin & Lake, 2006; Slavin, Lake, & Groff, 2007).

Instructional Television and Embedded Multimedia

An old technology, educational television, is being used in new ways. Research has long established the learning benefits of watching educational television shows such as *Sesame Street* (Fisch & Truglio, 2000) and *Between the Lions* (Linebarger, Kosanic, Greenwood, & Doku, 2004). Children who watch a lot of educational television become better readers, whereas those who watch a lot of noneducational television become worse-than-average readers (Ennemoser & Schneider, 2007; Wright et al., 2001).

A new application of video in the classroom is called **embedded multimedia** (Chambers, Madden, Slavin, Cheung, & Gifford, 2006). In this approach, brief segments of video content are threaded into teachers' lessons. In two large experiments, Chambers et al. (2006, in press) found that adding to daily reading instruction 5 minutes of animations and puppet skits illustrating letter sounds and sound blending significantly increased children's reading performance.

Interactive Whiteboards

An **interactive whiteboard** is a large touch screen display board that can display to an entire classroom anything that can be shown on a computer screen: print, PowerPoints, pictures, video, or anything from the Internet. Using a finger or a special pen, teachers and students can write on the whiteboard, move words or pictures around, or enter new content; and the computer attached to the whiteboard will record these changes. Connected to the Internet, a whiteboard can bring to the classroom books, art, video content, and more; and teachers can create elaborate, multimedia lessons drawing on content specifically made for the whiteboard or contained on websites or disks.

multimedia
Electronic material such as graphics, video, animation, and sound, which can be integrated into classroom projects.

CD-ROM
A computer database designed for "read-only memory" that provides massive amounts of information, including pictures and audio; it can be of particular importance to students doing projects and research activities.

videodiscs
Interactive computer technology (might include videos, still pictures, and music).

digital photographs
Photographs that can be loaded into a computer and shared electronically.

integrated learning systems
Commercially developed comprehensive, multipurpose packages of interlinked management instructional software, running on a computer network.

embedded multimedia
Video content woven into teachers' lessons.

interactive whiteboard
Large touchscreen that teachers can use to display and modify digital content for an entire class.

An important feature of current interactive whiteboards is **wireless response systems,** or **clickers,** that enable students to enter responses to questions posed by the teacher or on the whiteboard and have them immediately registered on the whiteboard. For example, the teacher might ask a multiple-choice question, and students could answer A, B, C, or D. Their responses could be immediately shown on a graph or chart, telling the teacher (and the students) whether the whole class is keeping up with the lesson content.

Interactive whiteboards exist in about 60 percent of classrooms in Britain and about 15 percent of classrooms in the United States, and are rapidly expanding in use. Research on achievement outcomes of whiteboard use is at an early stage, but a large British study found that whiteboard use correlated with achievement gains (Somekh et al., 2007). Smaller studies have also shown positive effects of whiteboard use (Miller, Glover, Averis, & Door, 2005; Smith, Hardman, & Higgins, 2006; Smith, Higgins, Wall, & Miller, 2005).

VIDEO HOMEWORK EXERCISE
Managing the Use of Technology for Education

Go to **www.myeducationlab.com** and, in the Homework and Exercises section for Chapter 9 of this text, access the video entitled "Managing the Use of Technology for Education." Watch the video and complete the homework questions that accompany it, saving your work or transmitting it to your professor as required.

Technology for Administration

Teachers use a variety of technologies to accomplish the many administrative tasks associated with their work, such as grading, creating reports, writing class newsletters, making invitations, and sending individual notes to parents. E-mail makes it easier for teachers to communicate with teaching assistants, administrators, parents, and others. Part of every teacher's job involves organizing, maintaining, and retrieving different types of data. This ranges from creating student rosters and logging students' contact information, to tracking coverage of the district's language arts objectives. Teachers are beginning to use portfolio assessment software to document student achievement. These programs allow teachers to collect and display the information when it comes time to report to parents (Bitter & Legacy, 2008).

Since the No Child Left Behind Act, schools are being held more accountable for their students' achievement than in the past. School districts are using technology to monitor the progress of individual students, teachers, and schools using database management systems. In addition to tracking students' achievements, these school management systems allow districts to monitor enrollment, attendance, and school expenditures. Data management software makes it easier for teachers to enter, retrieve, and update records and to create accurate, customized, professional reports for administrators or parents. They can track which students are mastering what content areas so that they can better target specific instruction to the students who need it the most.

Research on Computer-Assisted Instruction

Can computers teach? Most large evaluations and reviews of research on the effects of CAI conclude that computer-based instruction has small- to moderate-sized positive effects on achievement (Aviram, 2000; Dynarski et al., 2007; Kulik, 2003; Slavin, Cheung, Groff, & Lake, in press; Slavin & Lake, 2006; Slavin, Lake, & Groff, 2007; Texas Center for Educational Research, 2007). As was noted earlier, there is also evidence favoring specific applications of CAI, especially word processing (Bangert-Drowns, 1993; Goldberg et al., 2003).

INTASC

3 Adapting Instruction for Individual Needs

The potential of computers to improve achievement outcomes remains unclear. Some reviewers have argued that when the content of instruction is carefully controlled, computers are no more effective than other instructional methods (Bebell, O'Dwyer, Russell, & Seeley, 2004; Clark, 2001) or have small and variable effects (Blok, Oostdam, Otter, & Overmaat, 2002). Researchers today generally agree that the computer itself is not magic. What matters is the curriculum, instruction, and social context surrounding the use of the computer (Cognition and Technology Group at Vanderbilt, 1996; Winne, 2006). Asking whether computers enhance learning is like asking whether chalkboards enhance learning. In either case, it depends on how they are used.

A review of research by Lou, Abrami, and d'Apollonia (2001) found that having students work on computers in small groups was, on average, more effective than having them work individually, as long as students used well-specified cooperative learning approaches such as those described in Chapter 8. Simply asking students to work together,

wireless response systems (clickers) Electronic devices on which students enter answers to questions and have them registered on a computer or interactive whiteboard.

VIDEO HOMEWORK EXERCISE
Motivation

Go to **www.myeducationlab.com** and, in the Homework and Exercises section for Chapter 10 of this text, access the video entitled "Motivation." Watch the video and complete the homework questions that accompany it, saving your work or transmitting it to your professor as required.

however, produced no benefit. Outcomes were also enhanced when students worked in pairs rather than in larger groups.

Leaving aside issues of effectiveness, it is clear that students do not all have the same access to computers. Middle-class children are considerably more likely than children of a lower socioeconomic status to have access to computers at home (Becker, 2000; Education Commission of the States, 2000; Holloway, 2000), although the digital divide is rapidly diminishing in schools (Becker, 2001). Within schools, boys tend to spend much more time on computers than do girls (Volman & van Eck, 2001). To the extent that computers become increasingly effective and important in providing state-of-the-art instruction, these inequities must be addressed.

Use of computers and research on CAI are developing so rapidly that it is difficult to anticipate what the future will bring (see McCain & Jukes, 2000; Means et al., 2003). At this time, however, computers are rarely being used to provide basic instruction. In fact, many studies find that even in technology-rich schools, computers are turned off most of the day, and computer use occupies a tiny portion of each student's academic time (e.g., Cuban, Kirkpatrick, & Peck, 2001; Ganesh & Berliner, 2004). In secondary schools, computers are used primarily to teach programming and word processing, and in elementary schools they are used chiefly for enrichment. Many schools that originally bought computers for CAI have ended up using them to teach computer programming

Personal REFLECTION

Computers in Education

I once visited an elementary school in suburban Atlanta that was a special demonstration site for computer use in education. A computer company representative proudly showed me all the cutting-edge technology the school was using, and I spoke with the principal and several teachers, who were excited about what the computers could help them do.

I spent about an hour in a math class. Like all the classes in the school, it had a lot of technology in it, but not enough computers for every child. Therefore, students were rotated from teacher-directed to computer activities.

The computer activity involved using a mouse to manipulate blocks to represent arithmetic. The computer program was clever, appealing, and intuitive, and the students seemed to like it. However, the overall instructional plan was a disaster. The teacher's lessons were constantly being interrupted. When children rotated off of the computers, she had to reteach the portion of the lesson she'd just taught to students who'd been on the computer.

In another math class, I saw similar problems. In that class, children were working on graphs in small groups. In each case, one child had his or her hands on the keyboard, while three children watched. The working children seemed to be having fun. The watching children offered suggestions from time to time but weren't getting the concepts. I took a few watching children aside and asked them to explain the graph the group was creating. They had no idea.

Computers can be powerful tools in the classroom, but they are not magic. Computer activities need to coordinate with noncomputer activities and teacher instruction and should not dominate instructional planning. Even today, after many years of waiting for the "computer revolution," even the most technology-rich schools often have difficulty figuring out the right place for computers and other technology in students' instructional days and fail to reap the great potential technology can offer.

REFLECT ON THIS. How were computers used in your classes when you were in grade school? High school? How do you see technology changing in schools? Do you think access to technology is equal across all social groups? What might be the impact of differences on student learning across social groups?

or computer literacy, giving students hands-on experience with the computer but not depending on it to achieve major instructional objectives (Dugger, 2001; Zhao & Frank, 2003). Of course, as computers become ubiquitous in the world of work, exposure to them becomes important in its own right (Thornburg, 2002; Prensky, 2006); but in helping students learn traditional subjects, computers continue to play a minor role. The majority of teachers still feel uncomfortable with computers and are poorly prepared to use them (Becker, 2001). Several decades into the computer revolution, with billions spent on computer hardware and software (Anderson & Becker, 2001), there is still a long way to go before computers fundamentally change the practice of education (see Becker & Ravitz, 2001; Cuban, 2001; McCain & Jukes, 2000; Salomon, 2002).

WHAT EDUCATIONAL PROGRAMS EXIST FOR STUDENTS PLACED AT RISK?

INTASC

3 Adapting Instruction for Individual Needs

10 Partnerships

Any child can succeed in school. Any child can fail. The difference between success and failure depends primarily on what the school, the parents, community agencies, and the child himself or herself do to create conditions that are favorable for learning (Thomas & Bainbridge, 2001). Before school entry we cannot predict very well which individual children will succeed or fail, but there are factors in a child's background that make success or failure more likely (on the average). For example, students who come from impoverished or single-parent homes, those who have marked developmental delays, or those who exhibit aggressive or withdrawn behavior are more likely to experience problems in school than are other students. These children are often referred to as **students at risk** (Barr & Parrett, 1995; Manning & Baruth, 1995). The term *at risk* is borrowed from medicine, in which it has long been used to describe individuals who do not have a given disease but are more likely than average to develop it. For example, a heavy smoker or a person with a family history of cancer might be at risk for lung cancer, even though not all heavy smokers or people with family histories of cancer actually get the disease. High blood pressure is a known risk factor for heart attacks, even though most people with high blood pressure do not have heart attacks. Similarly, a given child from an impoverished home might do well in school, but 100 such children are likely to perform significantly worse, on the average, than 100 children from middle-class homes (Rossi & Stringfield, 1995).

Connections
For more on factors such as poverty and limited English proficiency that might place students at risk of school failure, see Chapter 4, pages 93 and 107.

Connections
To learn about factors such as problems of childhood and adolescence that might place students at risk of school failure, see Chapter 3, pages 76 and 83.

Recently, the term *at risk* has often been replaced by the term *placed at risk* (Boykin, 2000). This term emphasizes the fact that it is often an inadequate response to a child's needs by school, family, or community that places the child at risk. For example, a child who could have succeeded in reading if he or she had been given appropriate instruction, a reading tutor, or eyeglasses could be said to be placed at risk by lack of these services.

Before children enter school, the most predictive risk factors relate to their socioeconomic status and family structure. After they begin school, however, such risk factors as poor reading performance, grade repetition, and poor behavior become more important predictors of later school problems (such as dropping out) than family background factors (Ensminger & Slusarcick, 1992).

Connections
Special education is discussed in detail in Chapter 12.

Educational programs for students who are at risk fall into three major categories: compensatory education, early intervention programs, and special education. **Compensatory education** is the term used for programs designed to prevent or remediate learning problems among students who are from low-income families or who attend schools in low-income communities. Some intervention programs target at-risk infants and toddlers to prevent possible later need for remediation. Other intervention programs are aimed at keeping children in school. Compensatory and early intervention programs are discussed in the following sections. Special education, discussed in Chapter 12, is designed to serve children who have more serious learning problems as well as children with physical or psychological problems.

students at risk
Students who are subject to school failure because of their own characteristics and/or because of inadequate responses to their needs by school, family, or community.

compensatory education
Programs designed to prevent or remediate learning problems among students from lower socioeconomic status communities.

Compensatory Education Programs

Compensatory education programs are designed to overcome the problems associated with being brought up in low-income communities. Compensatory education supplements the education of students from disadvantaged backgrounds who are experiencing trouble in school or who are thought to be in danger of having school problems. Two such programs, Head Start and Follow Through, are designed to give disadvantaged preschool and primary school children the skills they need for a good start in school. These programs were discussed in Chapter 3. However, the largest compensatory education program, and the one that is most likely to affect regular classroom teachers, is called **Title I** (formerly "Chapter 1"), a federally funded program that gives schools money to provide extra services for students from low-income families who are having trouble in school (see Borman, Stringfield, & Slavin, 2001).

Title I is not merely a transfer of money from the federal government to local school districts. According to the federal guidelines, these funds must be used to "supplement, not supplant" local educational efforts. This means that most school districts cannot use the money to reduce class size for all students or increase teachers' salaries; the funds must go directly toward increasing the academic achievement of low achievers in schools that serve many disadvantaged students. The exception is that schools that serve very disadvantaged neighborhoods—neighborhoods in which at least 40 percent of the students qualify for a free lunch—can use Title I money to improve the school as a whole.

Title I Programs Title I programs can take many forms. Most often, a special Title I teacher provides remedial help to students who are experiencing difficulties in reading and, in many cases, in other subjects as well (Puma, Jones, Rock, & Fernandez, 1993). Programs of this type are called **pull-out programs** because the students are pulled out of their general education classes to take part in the programs.

Pull-out programs have been criticized for many years. One major problem with pull-out programs is that often the regular teacher and the Title I teacher do not coordinate their efforts, so the very students who need the most consistent and structured instruction may have to deal with two completely different approaches (Allington & McGill-Franzen, 1989; Meyers, Gelzheiser, Yelich, & Gallagher, 1990). One study found that half of a group of Title I teachers could not even name the reading text series that their students were using in the general education class; two-thirds could not name the specific book (Johnston et al., 1985). Johnston and colleagues (1985) argue that Title I programs must be directed at ensuring the success of students in the general education classroom and should therefore be closely coordinated with the general education teacher's instructional activities. For example, if a student is having trouble in the general education class with finding the main ideas of paragraphs, the Title I teacher should be working on main ideas, perhaps using the same instructional materials that the classroom teacher is using.

Some school districts are avoiding the problems of pull-out programs by having the Title I teacher or aide work as a team teacher in the general education reading classroom. This way, two teachers can give reading lessons to two groups of students at the same time, a strategy that avoids some of the problems of within-class ability grouping. Team teaching can also increase the levels of communication and collaboration between the general education classroom teacher and the Title I teacher. However, such in-class models of Title I services have not been found to be any more effective than pull-out programs (Anderson & Pellicer, 1990; Borman et al., 1998).

Many other innovative programs have been found to accelerate the achievement gains of disadvantaged students. Among these are tutoring programs; continuous-progress programs, in which students are frequently assessed and regrouped as they proceed through a sequence of skills; and other structured instructional programs that have clear objectives and frequent assessments of students' attainment of these objectives (see Slavin & Madden, 1987; Slavin, Madden, & Karweit, 1989). The most effective approaches, however, are ones that prevent students from ever having academic difficulties in the first place (Hamburg, 1992; Slavin, Karweit, & Wasik, 1994). These include high-quality preschool and kindergarten programs (Berrueta-Clement et al., 1984; Reynolds, 1991), one-to-one tutoring for first-graders who are just beginning to have reading problems (Pinnell, 1990;

Title I
Compensatory programs reauthorized under Title I of the Improving America's Schools Act (IASA) in 1994; formerly known as *Chapter 1.*

pull-out programs
Compensatory education programs in which students are placed in separate classes for remediation.

Wasik & Slavin, 1993), and comprehensive school reform programs that help all children succeed the first time they are taught (Borman, 2002/2003; Borman et al., 2007).

Research on the Effects of Title I Two major nationwide studies of the achievement effects of the programs offered under Title I have been carried out. The first, called the Sustaining Effects Study (Carter, 1984), found that Title I students did achieve better in reading and math than did similar low-achieving students who did not receive Title I services, but that these effects were not large enough to enable Title I students to close the gap with students performing at the national average. The greatest gains were for first-graders, whereas the benefits of Title I participation for students in fourth grade and above were slight.

A major study of the effects of the compensatory services funded under Title I, called *Prospects,* also compared elementary and middle school children receiving compensatory education services both to similar at-risk children not receiving services and to children who were never at risk. Prospects did not find any achievement benefits for children who received Title I services (Puma, Jones, Rock, & Fernandez, 1993). A more detailed analysis by Borman, D'Agostino, Wong, and Hedges (1998) found similarly disappointing outcomes, although there were some positive effects for children who were less disadvantaged and for those who received services during some years but not others. The most disadvantaged, lowest-achieving students were not narrowing their achievement gap with advanced peers.

Although the Prospects data did not find overall positive effects of receiving compensatory services, results were positive in some situations. One particularly influential factor was the degree to which Title I services were closely coordinated with other school services (Borman, 1997; D'Agostino, Borman, Hedges, & Wong, 1998). In other words, schools that closely integrated remedial or instructional Title I services with the school's main instructional program, and especially schools that used Title I dollars to enhance instruction for all students in schoolwide projects, obtained the best outcomes. This kind of integration contrasts with the traditional practice of sending low-achieving students to remedial classes where instruction is poorly coordinated with that in the classes they are leaving.

Although a review of many studies did find positive effects on average (Borman, 2002; Borman & D'Agostino, 2001), no one familiar with the data would argue that Title I impacts are large. This is not a surprising conclusion, given that for most students Title I means no more than a 30-minute daily remedial session (Stringfield et al., 1997).

Research on effective practices in compensatory pull-out classes finds that, in general, practices that are effective in regular classes are also effective in pull-out classes. For example, more instructional time, more time on task, and other indicators of effective classroom management are important predictors of achievement gain in compensatory program classes (Crawford, 1989; Stein, Leinhardt, & Bickel, 1989). A large study of programs for students from high-poverty areas (Knapp, 1995; Knapp, Shields, & Turnbull, 1995) found that students in schools that emphasized instruction for deep understanding and meaning achieved significantly better than did students whose teachers emphasized drill and practice (also see Waxman, Padrón, & Arnold, 2001). Another large study, by Stringfield and colleagues (1997), evaluated a range of programs that are used in high-poverty schools. Two comprehensive school reform programs were particularly effective: Success for All and Comer's School Development Program, both of which are discussed later in this chapter. These and other findings have led Title I policy-makers increasingly to favor schoolwide programs in which Title I funds are used to improve instruction for all children in the school (Wong, Sunderman, & Lee, 1995). In particular, Title I schools are being encouraged to adopt proven, comprehensive reform models for the entire school (see Borman et al., 2001; Slavin & Fashola, 1998).

Early Intervention Programs

Traditionally, Title I and other compensatory education programs have overwhelmingly emphasized remediation. They typically provide services to children only after the children have already fallen behind. Such children might also end up in special education or might be retained. All of the remedial strategies have shown little evidence of effectiveness. In fact, there is evidence that providing such services only after children have failed can be detrimental to student achievement, motivation, and other outcomes (e.g., Roderick,

Reading Recovery is particularly helpful for working with ESL/ELL children. How do such programs differ from traditional compensatory programs?

Connections
For more on prevention and early intervention, see Chapter 12, page 395.

1994; Shepard & Smith, 1989). It makes more sense to focus on prevention and **early intervention** rather than remediation in serving children placed at risk of school failure (see Powell, 1995; Slavin et al., 1994).

Programs that emphasize infant stimulation, parent training, and other services for children from birth to age 5 have been found to have long-term effects on at-risk students' school success. An example is the Carolina Abecedarian program (Campbell & Ramey, 1994), which found long-term achievement effects of an intensive program for children from low-income homes who received services from infancy through school entry. The Perry Preschool program also demonstrates long-term effects of an intensive program for four-year-olds (Schweinhart & Weikart, 1998). Other programs have had similar effects (Garber, 1988; Wasik & Karweit, 1994). In addition to such preventive programs, there is evidence that early intervention can keep children from falling behind in the early grades. For example, Whitehurst et al. (1999) found lasting effects of an early intervention program emphasizing phonemic awareness (knowledge of how sounds blend into words) and other preliteracy strategies. A program called **Reading Recovery** (Lyons, Pinnell, & DeFord, 1993; Pinnell, DeFord, & Lyons, 1988) provides one-to-one tutoring from specially trained teachers to first-graders who are not reading adequately. This program is able to bring nearly all at-risk children to adequate levels of performance and can have long-lasting positive effects. Reading Recovery is used in more than 9,000 U.S. elementary schools. The cost-effectiveness of Reading Recovery and its long-term effects have been somewhat controversial (Hiebert, 1996; Pinnell, Lyons, & Jones, 1996; Shanahan, 1998). Although there is little disagreement that Reading Recovery has a positive effect on the reading success of at-risk first-graders (see Lyons et al., 1993; Pinnell et al., 1994), there are conflicting findings concerning maintenance of these gains beyond first grade and concerning the question of whether positive effects for small numbers of first-graders represent the best use of limited funds for an entire age group of children (see Schachter, 2000).

In addition to Reading Recovery, several other programs have successfully used certified teachers, paraprofessionals, and even well-trained and well-supervised volunteers to improve the reading achievement of first-graders (Morris, Tyner, & Perney, 2000; Wasik, 1997; Wasik & Slavin, 1993). A phonetic tutoring program called Reading Rescue produced substantially better outcomes for first-graders than either a small-group remedial program or no intervention (Ehri, Dreyer, Flugman, & Gross, 2007). An Australian program that used a combination of curricular reform, one-to-one tutoring (Reading Recovery), family support, and other elements showed significant effects on first-graders' reading performance (Crévola & Hill, 1998).

early intervention
Programs that target at-risk infants and toddlers to prevent possible later need for remediation.

Reading Recovery
A program in which specially trained teachers provide one-to-one tutoring to first-graders who are not reading adequately.

Research on Reading Recovery, the Carolina Abecedarian program, and other preventive strategies shows that at-risk children can succeed if we are willing to give them high-quality instruction and intensive services early in their school careers (Slavin, 1997/98). Early intervention also ensures that children who do turn out to need long-term services are identified early—and that those whose problems can be solved early on are not needlessly assigned to special education (see Vellutino et al., 1996).

Comprehensive School Reform Programs

In recent years, a new form of school reform has become widespread, particularly in Title I schools. These *comprehensive school reform (CSR) programs* are schoolwide approaches that introduce research-based strategies into every aspect of school functions: curriculum, instruction, assessment, grouping, accommodations for children having difficulties, parent involvement, and other elements (Borman et al., 2003; CSRQ, 2006a, b; Kilgore, 2005; Slavin, in press). Comprehensive reform models vary widely. Some, such as Success for All (Slavin & Madden, 2001) and Direct Instruction (Adams & Engelmann, 1996) provide specific student materials in each subject and detailed guides to using them, whereas others, such as Accelerated Schools (Hopfenberg & Levin, 1993) and the School Development Program (Comer, Haynes, Joyner, & Ben-Avie, 1996), provide more general guidelines for practice and then help school staffs develop their own approaches. America's Choice (Supovitz, Poglinco, & Snyder, 2001) and Modern Red Schoolhouse (Kilgore, Doyle, & Linkowsky, 1996) focus on infusing standards into school practices, and Co-nect (Goldberg & Richards, 1996) focuses on schoolwide infusion of technology. Collectively, these comprehensive school reform models were used in more than 6,000 U.S. schools in 2001–2002 and are growing rapidly. A federal funding program connected to Title I, called the Comprehensive School Reform Demonstration (CSRD), provides grants to schools to help them adopt "proven, comprehensive reform models," and this funding has contributed significantly to the growth of CSR.

The most widely used and extensively researched of the CSR programs is **Success for All** (Slavin & Madden, 2001), a program that focuses on prevention and early intervention for elementary schools serving disadvantaged programs. Success for All provides research-based reading programs for preschool, kindergarten, and grades 1 through 8; one-to-one tutoring for first-graders who need it; family support services; and other changes in instruction, curriculum, and school organization designed to ensure that students do not fall behind in the early grades. Longitudinal studies of Success for All have shown that students in this program read substantially better than do students in matched control schools throughout the elementary grades and that they are far less likely to be assigned to special education or to fail a grade (see Borman & Hewes, 2001; Borman et al., 2007; Muñoz, Dossett, & Judy-Gullans, 2004; Slavin & Madden, 2000, 2001). In 2004–2005, Success for All was used in more than 1,400 Title I schools.

Another widely researched comprehensive school reform model is James Comer's School Development Program (Comer et al., 1996). Comer's model emphasizes building connections with parents and communities and organizing school staff into collaborative teams to create engaging, effective instruction (Ramirez-Smith, 1995). Two recent randomized experiments evaluating the Comer model had mixed results, but found that schools making the most extensive use of the principles underlying the approach had the greatest achievement gains (Cook et al., 1999; Cook, Murphy, & Hunt, 2000). (For descriptions and reviews of research on these and other comprehensive school reform models, see Borman et al., 2003, 2007; CSRQ, 2006a, b; Kidron & Darwin, 2007; Slavin, in press.)

After-School and Summer School Programs

Increasingly, Title I and other federal, state, and local education agencies are funding programs that extend learning time for students beyond the school day. Both after-school and summer school programs are expanding rapidly.

Success for All
A comprehensive approach to prevention and early intervention for preschool, kindergarten, and grades 1 through 8, with one-to-one tutoring, family support services, and changes in instruction designed to prevent students from falling behind.

The Intentional TEACHER

USING WHAT YOU KNOW about Accommodating Instruction to Meet Individual Needs

Intentional teachers see students' needs, not textbooks, as the starting point for planning and providing instruction. They expect students to have varied areas of strength and struggle, and they plan instruction that meets the needs of individual students. They monitor student progress carefully, and use resources beyond the classroom to meet the needs of students with varying capabilities. Intentional teachers expect to continue learning and mastering strategies that encourage all students to succeed.

1 What do I expect my students to know and be able to do at the end of this lesson? How does this contribute to course objectives and to students' needs to become capable individuals?

Intentional teachers think about instructional quality in terms of many components. As you plan and assess your lessons, analyze the extent to which they focus on providing high-quality, appropriate instruction; student motivation; and appropriate use of classroom time (this chapter's QAIT). For example, imagine that you view a videotape of yourself teaching and are pleased to see that student levels of enthusiasm and engagement are high during most parts of the lesson. However, you note with dismay that you spent nearly 20 minutes of the 50-minute period handling routines and interruptions. You might resolve to try a few management strategies that will allow you and your students to use instructional time to fuller advantage.

2 What knowledge, skills, needs, and interests do my students have that must be taken into account in my lesson?

All students bring a range of experiences and achievements to the classroom. Check students' prerequisite knowledge through strategies such as informal discussion, student drawings, and pre-tests. Then decide whether and how your instruction in specific instances should be modified to reflect differences in students' experiences. For example, you might discover that your math and science students display a wide range of reading achievement. These reading differences have little bearing on your mathematics instruction, but you might modify your science instruction carefully to accommodate students' diverse reading abilities. You might arrange for a variety of print materials and for peer tutoring, and devise skeleton outlines to guide students' reading.

3 What do I know about the content, child development, learning, motivation, and effective teaching strategies that I can use to accomplish my objectives?

Skilled teachers use a variety of approaches and resources to accommodate student differences. When you find relevant student differences, consider a wide variety of strategies that can help you meet needs. Examples include mastery learning, grouping strategies, tutoring, and computer-based instruction. For example, imagine that one-third of your students are working substantially above your grade-level mathematics

After-school programs typically combine some sort of academic activity, such as homework help, with sports, drama, and cultural activities (Friedman 2002/2003). However, studies of after-school programs generally find that for such programs to enhance student achievement, they need to incorporate well-organized coursework, such as individual or small-group tutoring, to extend the academic day (Fashola, 2002; McComb & Scott-Little, 2003).

Summer school sessions are also increasingly seen in schools, particularly as a last chance for students to avoid being retained in their grade. Summer school has long been advocated as a solution to the "summer loss" phenomenon, in which children from families that are low in socioeconomic status tend to lose ground over the summer, whereas middle-class students tend to gain (Entwisle, Alexander, & Olson, 2001). Research on summer school generally finds benefits for children's achievement (Borman & Boulay, 2004). One recent study by Kim (2006) found that simply sending books home with fourth-graders and encouraging them to read with their parents increased their reading performance in the fall.

A recent review by Lauer, Akiba, Wilkerson, Apthorp, Snow, and Martin-Glenn (2006) looked at the research on both types of out-of-school programs, summer school and after school. They found small positive effects of out-of-school programs for reading and math when children who attended these programs were compared to those who did not. When the programs included tutoring, effects were much more positive. Effects were the same for after-school as for summer-school programs. The importance of these findings is that they indicate that struggling children can be helped by extending instructional time for them, especially if the additional time is used for targeted instructional activities.

For more on summer school, see Cooper, Charlton, Valentine, and Muhlenbruck (2000). For more on after-school programs, see McComb and Scott-Little (2003).

ONLINE
READING
& WRITING
EXERCISE
Students Sparking
Each Other?

Access this exercise, entitled "Students Sparking Each Other," in the Homework and Exercises section for Chapter 9 of this text at **www.mylabschool.com.**

INTASC 3 Adapting Instruction for Individual Needs 8 Assessment of Student Learning 7 Instructional Planning Skills 9 Professional Commitment and Responsibility

curriculum, but more than half are wrestling with most concepts and skills. Over coffee, you and an experienced colleague discuss your options. You consider four strategies that might work: (1) combining your students with your colleague's class for peer tutoring; (2) spending a portion of each period in mastery learning, in which you and your colleague would divide students into those who have or have not mastered particular skills; (3) calling in volunteer tutors from a local senior center; (4) arranging for tutorial and drill and practice work in mathematics at your school's computer lab.

4 What instructional materials, technology, assistance, and other resources are available to help accomplish my objectives?

Effective teachers use grouping practices that are supported by research. Think about alternatives to between-class ability grouping. Consider options such as regrouping, within-class grouping, and cross-age grouping. For example, you might ask the principal of your high school to put you on a faculty meeting agenda to discuss alternatives to your school's traditional tracks for college preparatory, basic, and remedial courses. You could share an overview of the research on ability grouping; share some descriptions of schools that have engaged in untracking; and suggest that a committee of teachers, parents, and administrators explore the issue further.

5 How will I plan to assess students' progress toward my objectives?

Effective teachers use a variety of ongoing assessments to monitor how well students are learning, and they use this information to adapt their instruction to accommodate individual needs. Assess student progress frequently and be prepared to modify future lessons based on your findings. For example, you might use semiweekly journal entries and weekly objective quizzes to check student progress in your biology class. To students who demonstrate that they have quickly mastered objectives, you might provide enrichment opportunities to study the content through websites, software packages, readings, and investigations. For students who need additional scaffolding, you provide more intensive instruction.

6 How will I respond if individual children or the class as a whole are not on track toward success? What is my back-up plan?

Assumptions that accommodations are uniformly effective could prove faulty. Gather data to determine the extent to which your accommodations are having the desired effect. Check effects on attitude and self-esteem as well as achievement. For example, you might continually assess children's progress within their reading groups and accelerate students doing well, so that over time students not progressing as fast as others can receive more individual attention.

CHAPTER 9 SUMMARY

What Are Elements of Effective Instruction beyond a Good Lesson?

Teachers must know how to adapt instruction to students' levels of knowledge. According to Carroll's Model of School Learning, effectiveness of instruction depends on time needed (a function of student aptitude and ability to understand instruction) and time actually spent learning (which depends on time available, quality of instruction, and student perseverance).

Slavin's QAIT model of effective instruction identifies four elements that are subject to the teacher's direct control: quality of instruction, appropriate level of instruction, incentive, and amount of time. The model proposes that instruction that is deficient in any of these elements will be ineffective.

How Are Students Grouped to Accommodate Achievement Differences?

Many schools manage student differences in ability and academic achievement through between-class ability grouping, tracking, or regrouping into separate classes for particular subjects during part of a school day. However, research shows that within-class groupings are more effective, especially in reading and math, and are clearly preferable to groupings that segregate or stigmatize low achievers. Untracking recommends students be in mixed-ability groups.The students are held to high standards and are provided with assistance to reach those goals. Nongraded elementary schools combine children of different ages in the same classroom. Students are flexibly grouped according to their needs and performance levels.

What Are Some Ways of Individualizing Instruction?

Peer tutoring, adult tutoring, and differentiated instruction are all methods for individualizing instruction. Research supports all of these solutions.

How Is Technology Used in Education?

Technology in education is used for three general purposes. First, teachers use technology, such as word processors, multimedia, and presentation software, for planning and presenting lessons. Research supports use of presentation technologies such as embedded multimedia, forms of instructional television, and interactive whiteboards. Second, students use technology, such as word processing and CD-ROM reference software, for learning and preparing presentations. Computer-assisted instruction in the form of drill and practice, tutorials, instructional games, simulations, and the Internet are widespread. Third, teachers and administrators use technology for administrative tasks. Research on computer-assisted instruction demonstrates small to moderate positive effects on achievement.

What Educational Programs Exist for Students Placed at Risk?

Students who are at risk are any students who are likely to fail academically for any reason stemming from the student or from the student's environment. Reasons are diverse and might include poverty.

Educational programs for students who are at risk include compensatory education, early intervention programs, and special education. Federally funded compensatory education programs include, for example, Head Start, which aims to help preschool-age children from low-income backgrounds achieve school readiness, and Title I, which mandates extra services to low-achieving students in schools that have many low-income students. Extra services include pull-out programs, tutoring programs, and continuous-progress programs.

Research supports the effectiveness of many prevention and intervention programs such as Reading Recovery, and comprehensive school reform programs such as Success for All, the School Development Program, America's Choice, and Direct Instruction.

After-school and summer school programs are increasingly funded by federal, state, and local education agencies to extend students' learning time. Research is mixed regarding the effectiveness of compensatory education programs.

KEY TERMS

Review the following key terms from the chapter.

between-class ability grouping 266
CD-ROM 282
compensatory education 285
computer-assisted instruction (CAI) 279
cross-age tutoring 273
database 279
desktop publishing 278
differentiated instruction 275
digital photographs 282
drill and practice 279
early intervention 288
embedded multimedia 282
hypermedia 279
hypertext 279
individualized instruction 272
instructional games 280
integrated learning systems 282
interactive whiteboard 282
Internet 281
Joplin Plan 270
multimedia 282
nongraded programs 270
peer tutoring 273
problem-solving program 281
pull-out programs 286
QAIT model 263
Reading Recovery 288
regrouping 270

SELF-ASSESSMENT: PRACTICING *for* LICENSURE

Directions: The chapter-opening vignette addresses indicators that are often assessed in state licensure exams. Re-read the chapter-opening vignette, and then respond to the following questions.

1. How does Mr. Arbuthnot, the fourth-grade teacher in the chapter-opening vignette, incorporate John Carroll's Model of School Learning into his lesson?
   - **a.** Mr. Arbuthnot tries to match the time spent on learning with the time students need to learn.
   - **b.** Mr. Arbuthnot groups students according to their ability level.
   - **c.** Mr. Arbuthnot expects students to learn the concepts of long division through group discussion and inquiry.
   - **d.** Mr. Arbuthnot equates quality of instruction with quantity of instruction.
2. Imagine that Mr. Arbuthnot decides to divide his class into three groups: those who know long division, those who know some long division, and those who do not know long division. What type of ability group would he be using?
   - **a.** tri-grade ability grouping
   - **b.** high–low ability grouping
   - **c.** within-class ability grouping
   - **d.** between-class ability grouping
3. In the opening of the vignette, Mr. Arbuthnot teaches an engaging lesson on long division and then gives students a quiz on the content learned. What type of evaluation is this?
   - **a.** norm-referenced
   - **b.** standardized
   - **c.** minimum competency
   - **d.** formative
4. Mr. Arbuthnot decides that he cannot work individually with all the students who have not yet mastered long division. He decides that some sort of tutoring might solve his problem. If he selects the type of tutoring that is most effective, according to research, which of the following will he use?
   - **a.** cross-age peer tutoring
   - **b.** same-age peer tutoring
   - **c.** tutoring by certified teachers
   - **d.** computer tutoring
5. Explain how Mr. Arbuthnot could integrate technology into his teaching. What does the research on computer-based instruction say?
6. Describe programs that exist for students placed at risk.

CHAPTER 10

Motivating Students to Learn

chapter OUTLINE

The students in Cal Lewis's tenth-grade U.S. history class were all in their seats before the bell rang, eagerly awaiting the start of the period. But Mr. Lewis himself was nowhere to be seen. Two minutes after the bell, in he walked dressed as George Washington, complete with an eighteenth-century costume and powdered wig and carrying a gavel. He gravely took his seat, rapped the gavel, and said, "I now call to order this meeting of the Constitutional Convention."

The students had been preparing for this day for weeks. Each of them represented one of the 13 original states. In groups of two and three, they had been studying all about their states, the colonial era, the American Revolution, and the United States under the Articles of Confederation. Two days earlier, Mr. Lewis had given each group secret instructions from their "governor" on the key interests of their state. For example, the New Jersey and Delaware delegations were to insist that small states be adequately represented in the government, whereas New York and Virginia were to demand strict representation by population.

In preparing for the debate, each delegation had to make certain that any member of the delegation could represent the delegation's views. To ensure this, Mr. Lewis had assigned each student a number from one to three at random. When a delegation asked to be recognized, he would call out a number, and the student with that number would respond for the group.

Mr. Lewis, staying in character as George Washington, gave a speech on the importance of the task they were undertaking and then opened the floor for debate. First, he recognized the delegation from Georgia, represented by Beth Andrews. Beth was a shy girl, but she had been well prepared by her fellow delegates and knew that they were rooting for her.

"The great state of Georgia wishes to raise the question of a Bill of Rights. We have experienced the tyranny of government, and we demand that the people have a guarantee of their liberties!"

Beth went on to propose elements of the Bill of Rights that her delegation had drawn up. While she was talking, Mr. Lewis was rating her presentation on historical accuracy, appropriateness to the real interests of her state, organization, and delivery. He would use these ratings in evaluating each delegation at the end of each class period. The debate went on. The North Carolina delegates argued in favor of the right of states to expand to the West; the New Jersey delegation wanted western territories made into new states. Wealthy Massachusetts wanted taxes to remain in the states where they were collected; poor Delaware wanted national taxes. Between debates, the delegates had an opportunity to do some "horse trading," promising to vote for proposals important to other states in exchange for votes on issues important to them. At the end of the week, the class voted on 10 key issues. After the votes were taken and the bell rang, the students poured into the hall still arguing about issues of taxation, representation, and powers of the executive.

After school, Rikki Ingram, another social studies teacher, dropped into Mr. Lewis's classroom. "I see you're doing your Constitutional Convention again this year. It looks great, but how can you cover all of U.S. history if you spend a month on only the Constitution?"

Cal smiled. "Don't you remember how boring high school social studies was?" he said. "It sure was for me. I know I'm sacrificing some coverage to do this unit, but look how motivated these kids are!" He picked up a huge sheaf of notes and position papers written by the South Carolina delegation. "These kids are working their tails off, and they're learning that history is fun and useful. They'll remember this material for the rest of their lives!"

USING *your* EXPERIENCE

CRITICAL THINKING Rikki Ingram seems concerned that Mr. Lewis's class is not covering the material well enough. What do you think are the advantages, disadvantages, and interesting or unclear aspects of Mr. Lewis's teaching strategy?

COOPERATIVE LEARNING With another student, relate stories of a social studies or other high school teacher who tried methods similar to Mr. Lewis's method of teaching. As a pair, retell your stories to a student from another pair.

INTASC

5 Classroom Motivation and Management

Motivation is one of the most important ingredients of effective instruction. Students who want to learn can learn just about anything. But how can teachers ensure that every student wants to learn and will put in the effort needed to learn complex material?

Mr. Lewis knows the value of motivation, so he has structured a unit that taps many aspects of motivation. By having students work in groups and be evaluated on the basis of presentations made by randomly selected group members, he has created a situation in which students are encouraging each other to excel. Social motivation of this kind is very powerful, especially for adolescents. Mr. Lewis is rating students' presentations according to clear, comprehensive standards and giving them feedback each day. He is tying an important period in history to students' daily lives by having them take an active role in debating and trading votes. All of these strategies are designed not only to make history fun but also to give students many sources of motivation to learn and remember the history they have studied. Mr. Lewis is right. The students will probably never forget their experience in his class and are likely to approach new information about revolutionary history and the Constitution with enthusiasm throughout their lives.

This chapter presents the many ways in which teachers can enhance students' desire to learn academic material and the theories and research behind each method.

WHAT IS MOTIVATION?

One of the most critical components of learning, motivation is also one of the most difficult to measure. What makes a student want to learn? The willingness to put effort into learning is a product of many factors, ranging from the student's personality and abilities to characteristics of particular learning tasks, incentives for learning, settings, and teacher behaviors.

All students are motivated. The question is: Motivated to do what? Some students are motivated more to socialize or watch television than to do schoolwork. The educator's job is not to increase motivation per se but to discover, prompt, and sustain students' motivations to learn the knowledge and skills needed for success in school and in life, and to engage in activities that lead to this learning. Imagine that Cal Lewis had come to class in eighteenth-century costume but had not structured tasks and evaluations to induce students to study U.S. history. The students might have been amused and interested, but we cannot assume that they would have been motivated to do the work necessary to learn the material.

Psychologists define **motivation** as an internal process that activates, guides, and maintains behavior over time (Murphy & Alexander, 2000; Pintrich, 2003; Schunk, 2000; Stipek, 2002). In plain language, motivation is what gets you going, keeps you going, and determines where you're trying to go.

Motivation can vary in both intensity and direction (Ryan & Deci, 2000). Two students might be motivated to play video games, but one of them might be more strongly motivated to do so than the other. Or one student might be strongly motivated to play video games, and the other equally strongly motivated to play football. Actually, though, the intensity and direction of motivations are often difficult to separate. The intensity of a motivation to engage in one activity might depend in large part on the intensity and direction of motivations to engage in alternative activities. If someone has only enough time and money to go to the movies or to play video games, motivation to engage in one of these activities is strongly influenced by the intensity of motivation to engage in the other. Motivation is important not only in getting students to engage in academic activities but also in determining how much students will learn from the activities they perform or from the information to which they are exposed. Students who are motivated to learn something use higher cognitive processes in learning about it and absorb and retain more from it (Driscoll, 2005; Jetton & Alexander, 2001; Pintrich, 2003). They are more likely to transfer their learning to new situations (Pugh & Bergin, 2006).

Motivation to do something can come about in many ways (Stipek, 2002). Motivation can be a personality characteristic; individuals might have lasting, stable interests in participating in such broad categories of activities as academics, sports, or social activities. Motivation can come from intrinsic characteristics of a task: By making U.S. history fun, social, active, and engaging, Cal Lewis made students eager to learn it. Motivation can also come from sources extrinsic to the task, as when Cal Lewis rated students' performances in the Constitutional Convention simulation.

WHAT ARE SOME THEORIES OF MOTIVATION?

The first half of this chapter presents contemporary theories of motivation, which seek to explain why people are motivated to do what they do. The second half discusses the classroom use of incentives for learning and presents strategies for increasing students' motivations to learn and to do schoolwork.

Motivation and Behavioral Learning Theory

motivation
The influence of needs and desires on the intensity and direction of behavior.

The concept of motivation is closely tied to the principle that behaviors that have been reinforced in the past are more likely to be repeated than are behaviors that have not been reinforced or that have been punished. In fact, rather than using the concept of motivation, a behavioral theorist might focus on the degree to which students learn to do schoolwork to obtain desired outcomes (see Bandura, 1986; Bigge & Shermis, 2004; Wielkiewicz, 1995).

CONNECTIONS
For more on reinforcement of behaviors, see Chapter 5, page 132.

Why do some students persist in the face of failure whereas others give up? Why do some students work to please the teacher, others to make good grades, and still others out of interest in the material they are learning? Why do some students achieve far more than would be predicted on the basis of their ability and some achieve far less? Examination of reinforcement histories and schedules of reinforcement might provide answers to such questions, but it is usually easier to speak in terms of motivations to satisfy various needs.

Rewards and Reinforcement One reason that reinforcement history is an inadequate explanation for motivation is that human motivation is highly complex and context-bound. With very hungry animals we can predict that food will be an effective reinforcer. With humans, even hungry ones, we can't be sure what will be a reinforcer and what will not because the reinforcing value of most potential reinforcers is largely determined by personal or situational factors. As an example of this, think about the value of $50 for an hour's light work. Most of us would view $50 as a powerful reinforcer, more than adequate to get us to do an hour of light work. But consider these four situations:

1. Mr. Scrooge offers Bill $60 to paint his fence. Bill thinks this is more than enough for the job, so he does his best work. However, when he is done, Mr. Scrooge says, "I don't think you did sixty dollars' worth of work. Here's fifty."
2. Now consider the same situation, except that Mr. Scrooge originally offers Bill $40 and, when Bill is finished, praises him for an excellent job and gives him $50.
3. Dave and Barbara meet at a party, like each other immediately, and after the party take a long walk in the moonlight. When they get to Barbara's house, Dave says, "Barbara, I enjoyed spending time with you. Here's fifty dollars I'd like you to have."
4. Marta's aunt offers her $50 to teach little Pepa how to play baseball next Saturday. However, if Marta agrees to do so, she will miss her chance to try out for the school baseball team.

In situations 1, 3, and 4, $50 is not a good reinforcer at all. In situation 1, Bill's expectations have been raised and then dashed by Mr. Scrooge. Even though the amount of monetary reward is the same in situation 2, this situation is much more likely to make Bill want to paint Mr. Scrooge's fence again because in this case his reward exceeds his expectation. In situation 3, Dave's offer of $50 is insulting and would certainly not increase Barbara's interest in going out with him in the future. In situation 4, although Marta's aunt's offer would seem generous to Marta under most circumstances, it is insufficient reinforcement this particular Saturday because it interferes with a more highly valued activity.

Determining the Value of an Incentive These situations illustrate an important point: The motivational value of an incentive cannot be assumed because it might depend on many factors. When teachers say, "I want you all to be sure to hand in your book reports on time because they will count toward your grade," the teachers might be assuming that grades are effective incentives for most students. However, some students might not care about grades, perhaps because their parents don't or because they have a history of failure in school and have decided that grades are unimportant. If a teacher says to a student, "Good work! I knew you could do it if you tried!" this might be motivating to a student who had just completed a task he or she thought was difficult, but punishing to one who thought the task was easy (because the teacher's praise implies that he or she had to work especially hard to complete the task). As in the case of Bill and Mr. Scrooge, students' expectations for rewards determine the motivational value of any particular reward. And it is often difficult to determine students' motivations from their behavior because many different motivations can influence behavior. Sometimes, one type of motivation clearly determines behavior; at other times, several motivations are influential.

Motivation and Human Needs

Motivation can be thought of as a drive to satisfy needs, such as needs for food, shelter, love, and maintenance of positive self-esteem. People differ in the degree of importance they attach to each of these needs. Some need constant reaffirmation that they are loved or appreciated; others have a greater need for physical comfort and security. Also, the same person has different needs at different times; a drink of water would be much more appreciated after a 4-mile run than after a 4-course meal.

INTASC

2 Knowledge of Human Development and Learning

CERTIFICATION POINTER

Teacher certification tests will require you to identify which needs Maslow identified as deficiency needs and which he identified as growth needs.

Maslow's Hierarchy of Needs Given that people have many needs, which will they try to satisfy at any given moment? To predict this, Maslow (1954) proposed a hierarchy of needs, which is illustrated in Figure 10.1. In Maslow's theory, needs that are lower in this hierarchy must be at least partially satisfied before a person will try to satisfy higher-level needs. For example, a hungry person or someone who is in physical danger will be less concerned about maintaining a positive self-image than about obtaining food or safety; but once that person is no longer hungry or afraid, self-esteem needs might become paramount. One critical concept that Maslow introduced is the distinction between deficiency needs and growth needs. **Deficiency needs** (physiological, safety, love, and esteem) are those that are critical to physical and psychological well-being; these needs must be satisfied, but once they are, a person's motivation to satisfy them diminishes. In contrast, **growth needs,** such as the need to know and understand things, to appreciate beauty, or to grow and develop in appreciation of others, can never be satisfied completely. In fact, the more people are able to meet their need to know and understand the world around them, the greater their motivation might become to learn still more.

deficiency needs
Basic requirements for physical and psychological well-being as identified by Maslow.

growth needs
Needs for knowing, appreciating, and understanding, which people try to satisfy after their basic needs are met.

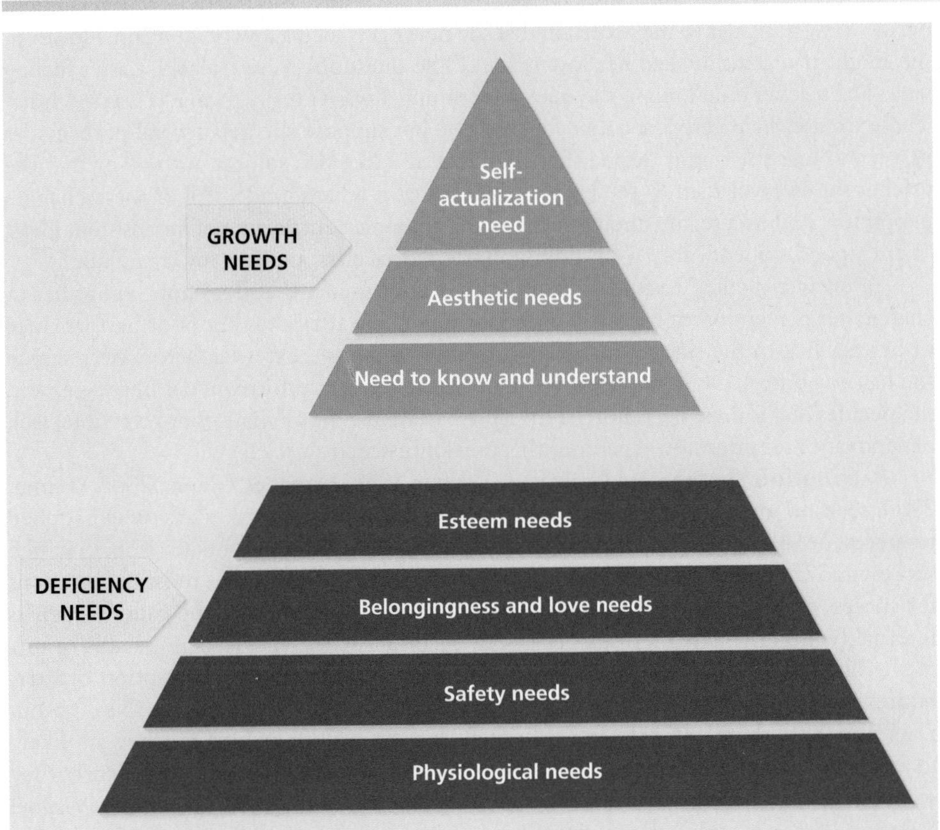

FIGURE 10.1 Maslow's Hierarchy of Needs
Maslow identifies two types of needs: deficiency needs and growth needs. People are motivated to satisfy needs at the bottom of the hierarchy before seeking to satisfy those at the top.

Self-Actualization Maslow's theory includes the concept of the desire for **self-actualization,** which he defines as "the desire to become everything that one is capable of becoming" (Maslow, 1954, p. 92). Self-actualization is characterized by acceptance of self and others, spontaneity, openness, relatively deep but democratic relationships with others, creativity, humor, and independence—in essence, psychological health.

Implications of Maslow's Theory for Education The importance of Maslow's theory for education is in the relationship between deficiency needs and growth needs. Obviously, students who are very hungry or in physical danger will have little psychological energy to put into learning. Schools and government agencies recognize that if students' basic needs are not met, learning will suffer. They have responded by providing free breakfast and lunch programs. The most important deficiency needs, however, are those for love and self-esteem. Students who do not feel that they are loved and that they are capable are unlikely to have a strong motivation to achieve the higher-level growth objectives (Stipek, 2006). A student who is unsure of his or her lovableness or capability will tend to make the safe choice: Go with the crowd, study for the test without interest in learning the ideas, write a predictable but uncreative essay, and so on. A teacher who can put students at ease and make them feel accepted and respected as individuals is more likely (in Maslow's view) to help them become eager to learn for the sake of learning and willing to risk being creative and open to new ideas. If students are to become self-directed learners, they must believe that the teacher will respond fairly and consistently to them and that they will not be ridiculed or punished for honest errors.

CONNECTIONS
Motivational factors affecting the academic performance of students who are at risk of school failure are discussed in Chapter 9, page 287.

Motivation and Attribution Theory

Teresa usually gets good grades but receives a D on a certain quiz. The mark is inconsistent with her self-image and causes her discomfort. To resolve this discomfort, Teresa might decide to work harder to make certain that she never gets such a low grade again. However, she might try to rationalize her low grade: "The questions were tricky. I wasn't feeling well. The teacher didn't tell us the quiz was coming. I wasn't really trying. It was too hot." These excuses help Teresa account for one D—but suppose she gets several poor grades in a row. Now she might decide that she never did like this subject anyway or that the teacher shows favoritism to the boys in the class or is a hard grader. All of these changes in opinions and excuses are directed at avoiding an unpleasant pairing of inconsistent ideas: "I am a good student" and "I am doing poorly in this class, and it is my own fault."

Teresa is struggling to find a reason for her poor grades that does not require her to change her perception of herself as a good student. She attributes her poor performance to her teacher, to the subject matter, or to other students—external factors over which she has no control. Or, if she acknowledges that her poor performance is her own fault, she decides that it must be a short-term lapse based on a momentary (but reversible) lack of motivation or attention regarding this unit of instruction.

Attribution theory (see Graham & Weiner, 1996; Hareli & Weiner, 2002; Weiner, 2000) seeks to understand just such explanations and excuses, particularly when applied to success or failure (wherein lies the theory's greatest importance for education, in which success and failure are recurrent themes). Weiner (2000) suggests that most explanations for success or failure have three characteristics. The first is whether the cause is seen as internal (within the person) or external. The second is whether it is seen as stable or unstable. The third is whether it is perceived as controllable. A central assumption of attribution theory is that people will attempt to maintain a positive self-image (Thompson, Davidson, & Barber, 1995). Therefore, when they do well in an activity, they are likely to attribute their success to their own efforts or abilities; but when they do poorly, they will believe that their failure is based on factors over which they had no control (Vispoel & Austin, 1995). In particular, students who experience failure will try to find an explanation that enables them to save face with their peers (Juvonen, 2000). It has been demonstrated that if groups of people are given a task and then told that they either failed or succeeded (even though all, in fact, were equally successful), those who are told that

self-actualization
A person's ability to develop his or her full potential.

attribution theory
A theory of motivation that focuses on how people explain the causes of their own successes and failures.

they failed will say that their failure was because of bad luck, whereas those who are told that they succeeded will attribute their success to skill and intelligence (Weiner, 2000).

Attributions for others' behavior are also important. For example, students are more likely to respond to a classmate's request for help if they believe that the classmate needs help because of a temporary uncontrollable factor (such as getting hurt in a basketball game) than if they believe that help is needed because of a controllable factor (such as failure to study) (Juvonen & Weiner, 1993).

Attributions for Success and Failure Attribution theory deals primarily with four explanations for success and failure in achievement situations: ability, effort, task difficulty, and luck. Ability and effort attributions are internal to the individual; task difficulty and luck attributions are external. Ability is taken to be a relatively stable, unalterable state; effort can be altered. Similarly, task difficulty is essentially a stable characteristic, whereas luck is unstable and uncontrollable. These four attributions and representative explanations for success and failure are presented in Table 10.1.

Table 10.1 shows how students often seek to explain success and failure differently. When students succeed, they would like to believe that it was because they are smart (an internal, stable attribution) not because they were lucky or because the task was easy or even because they tried hard (because "trying hard" says little about their likelihood of success in the future). In contrast, students who fail would like to believe that they had bad luck (an external, unstable attribution), which allows for the possibility of succeeding next time (Weiner, 2000). Of course, over time, these attributions might be difficult to maintain. As in the case of Teresa, a student who gets one bad grade is likely to blame it on bad luck or some other external, unstable cause. After several bad grades, though, an unstable attribution becomes difficult to maintain; no one can be unlucky on tests week after week. Therefore, a student like Teresa might switch to a stable but still external attribution. For example, she could decide that the course is too difficult or make some other stable, external attribution that lets her avoid making a stable, internal attribution that would shatter her self-esteem: "I failed because I don't have the ability" (Juvonen, 2000). She might even reduce her level of effort so that she can maintain the idea that she could succeed if she really wanted to (Jagacinski & Nicholls, 1990).

CONNECTIONS
Attributions for success or failure that are related to the socioemotional factors of self-esteem and peer relations are discussed in Chapter 3, pages 69, 74–77, and 82–83.

Locus of Control and Self-Efficacy One concept that is central to attribution theory is **locus of control** (Rotter, 1954). The word *locus* means *location*. A person with an internal locus of control is one who believes that success or failure is the result of his or her own efforts or abilities. Someone with an *external locus of control* is more likely to believe

locus of control
A personality trait that determines whether people attribute responsibility for their own failure or success to internal or external factors.

TABLE 10.1 Attributions for Success and Failure

Attribution theory describes and suggests the implications of people's explanations of their successes and failures.

Attribution	**Stability**	
	Stable	***Unstable***
Internal	*Ability*	*Effort*
Success:	"I'm smart."	"I tried hard."
Failure:	"I'm stupid."	"I didn't really try."
External	*Task Difficulty*	*Luck*
Success:	"It was easy."	"I lucked out."
Failure:	"It was too hard."	"I had bad luck."

Source: From Bernard Weiner, "A Theory of Motivation for Some Classroom Experiences," *Journal of Educational Psychology, 71,* pp. 3–25. Copyright © 1979 by the American Psychological Association. Adapted with permission.

Despite being one of the most accomplished female athletes in the world, Mia Hamm often fought off self-doubt. Why is locus of control important to an athlete? How do locus of control and self-efficacy translate to the classroom? As a teacher, how can you influence self-efficacy?

that other factors, such as luck, task difficulty, or other people's actions, cause success or failure. Internal locus of control is often called self-efficacy, the belief that one's behavior makes a difference (Bandura, 1997; Goddard, Hoy, & Hoy, 2004; Schunk & Pajares, 2004; Zimmerman, 1998). Locus of control or self-efficacy can be very important in explaining a student's school performance. For example, several researchers have found that students who are high in internal locus of control have better grades and test scores than do students of the same intelligence who are low in internal locus of control (Capella & Weinstein, 2001; Pajares & Graham, 1999; Zimmerman, 2000). Studies have found locus of control to be the second most important predictor (after ability) of a student's academic achievement (e.g., Bong, 2001; Pajares & Miller, 1994; Pietsch, Walker, & Chapman, 2003; Zimmerman & Bandura, 1994). The reason is easy to comprehend. Students who believe that success in school is because of luck, the teacher's whims, or other external factors are unlikely to work hard. They are likely to procrastinate or avoid difficult tasks (Steel, 2007). In contrast, students who believe that success and failure are primarily because of their own efforts can be expected to work hard (Pressley et al., 2003). In reality, success in a particular class is a product of both students' efforts and abilities (internal factors) and luck, task difficulty, and teacher behaviors (external factors). But the most successful students will tend to overestimate the degree to which their own behavior produces success and failure. Some experiments have shown that even in situations in which success and failure are completely based on luck, students who are high in internal locus of control will believe that it was their efforts that made them succeed or fail (see Weiner, 1992). (See Figure 10.2.)

It is important to note that locus of control can change and depends somewhat on the specific activity or situation. One difficulty in studying the effects of locus of control on achievement is that achievement has a strong effect on locus of control (Bong & Skaalvik, 2003; Weiner, 1992). For example, the same student might have an internal locus of control in academics (because of high academic ability) but an external locus of control in sports (because of low athletic ability). If this student discovered some unsuspected skill in a new sport, he or she might develop an internal locus of control in that sport (but probably still not in other sports).

Implications of Attributions and Self-Efficacy for Education In the classroom, students receive constant information concerning their level of performance on academic tasks, either relative to others or relative to some norm of acceptability. This feedback ultimately influences students' self-perceptions (Bandura, 1997; Schunk, 2004). Attribution theory is important in helping teachers understand how students might interpret and use feedback on their academic performance and in suggesting to teachers how they might give feedback that has the greatest motivational value (see Graham, 1997; Tollefson, 2000).

Motivation and Self-Regulated Learning

Self-regulated learning, discussed in Chapter 6, refers to "learning that results from students' self-generated thoughts and behaviors that are systematically oriented toward their learning goals" (Schunk & Zimmerman, 2003, p. 59). As this definition makes clear, self-regulated learning is closely related to students' goals. Students who are highly motivated to learn something are more likely than other students to consciously plan their learning, carry out a learning plan, and retain the information they obtain (Radosevich et al., 2004; Zimmerman, 2000). For example, students with high reading motivation are more likely to read on their own and to use effective comprehension strategies (Miller, Partelow,

1. If a teacher passes you to the next grade, would it probably be
   a. because she liked you, or
   b. because of the work you did? [*internal*]
2. When you do well on a test at school, is it more likely to be
   a. because you studied for it, or [*internal*]
   b. because the test was especially easy?
3. When you have trouble understanding something in school, is it usually
   a. because the teacher didn't explain it clearly, or
   b. because you didn't listen carefully? [*internal*]
4. Suppose your parents say you are doing well in school. Is it likely to happen
   a. because your school work is good, or [*internal*]
   b. because they are in a good mood?
5. Suppose you don't do as well as usual in a subject in school. Would this probably happen
   a. because you weren't as careful as usual, or [*internal*]
   b. because somebody bothered you and kept you from working?

FIGURE 10.2 Items from the Intellectual Achievement Responsibility Questionnaire

From V. C. Crandall, W. Katkovsky, and V. J. Crandall, "Children's Beliefs in Their Own Control of Reinforcement in Intellectual–Academic Achievement Situations," *Child Development, 36,* 1965, pp. 91–109. © The Society for Research in Child Development, Inc. Reprinted by permission.

& Sen, 2004). This motivation can come from many sources. One is social modeling (Zimmerman & Kitsantas, 2002), such as seeing other students use self-regulated strategies. Another is goal-setting, in which students are encouraged to establish their own learning goals. A third is feedback that shows students that they are making good progress toward their learning goals, especially if the feedback emphasizes students' efforts and abilities. Schunk and Zimmerman (2003) argue that motivation to engage in self-regulated learning is not the same as achievement motivation in general because self-regulated learning requires the learner to take independent responsibility for learning, not to simply comply with the teacher's demands. Fredericks, Blumenfeld, and Paris (2004) use the terms *engagement* and *investment* to describe motivation that leads students to engage in self-regulated learning, rather than simply doing the work and following the rules. Algozzine et al. (2001) use the similar term *self-determination,* and describe a set of successful strategies for building self-determination among individuals with disabilities.

CONNECTIONS
For more on successful strategies for building self-determination, see Chapter 12, page 395.

THEORY *into* PRACTICE

Giving Students Motivating Feedback

Students who believe that their past failures on tasks were because of lack of ability are unlikely to expect to succeed in similar tasks and are, therefore, unlikely to exert much effort (Juvonen, 2000; Weiner, 2000). Obviously, the belief that you will fail can be self-fulfilling. Students who believe that they will fail will be poorly motivated to do academic work, and this might in turn cause them to fail. Therefore, the most damaging idea a teacher can communicate to a student is that the student is "hopelessly stupid."

Few teachers would say such a thing directly to a student, but the idea can be communicated just as effectively in several other ways. One is to use a competitive grading system (e.g., grading on the curve) and to make grades public and relative student rankings important. This practice can make small differences in achievement level seem large, and students who receive the poorest grades might decide that they can never learn.

Alternatively, a teacher who deemphasizes grades and relative rankings but expresses the (almost always correct) expectation that all students in the class can learn is likely to help students see that their chances of success depend on their efforts—an internal but alterable attribution that lets students anticipate success in the future if they do their best.

CONNECTIONS
For more on individualized instruction, see Chapter 9, page 272.

A stable, internal attribution for success ("I succeed because I am smart") is also a poor motivator; able students, too, need to believe that it is their effort, not their ability, that leads to academic success. Teachers who emphasize the amount of effort as the cause of success as well as failure and who reward effort rather than ability are more likely to motivate all their students to do their best than are teachers who emphasize ability alone (Resnick, 1998).

CONNECTIONS
For more on grading student effort, see Chapter 13, page 442.

Some formal means of rewarding students for effort rather than ability are the use of differentiated instruction, in which the basis of success is progress at the student's own level; the inclusion of effort as a component of grading or as a separate grade; and the use of rewards for improvement.

Motivation and Expectancy Theory

Expectancy theory is a theory of motivation based on the belief that people's efforts to achieve depend on their expectations of reward. Atkinson (1964) developed theories of motivation based on the following formula:

Motivation (M) = Perceived probability of success (Ps) × Incentive value of success (Is).

The formula is called an expectancy model, or **expectancy–valence model,** because it largely depends on the person's expectations of reward (see Pintrich, 2003; Stipek, 2002; Wigfield & Eccles, 2000). What this theory implies is that people's motivation to achieve something depends on the product of their estimation of their chance of success (perceived probability of success, Ps) and the value they place on success (incentive value of success, Is). For example, if Mark says, "I think I can make the honor roll if I try, and it is very important to me to make the honor roll," then he will probably work hard to make the honor roll. However, one very important aspect of the $M = Ps \times Is$ formula is that it is multiplicative, meaning that if people believe that their probability of success is zero or if they do not value success, then their motivation will be zero. If Mark would like very much to make the honor roll but believes that he hasn't a prayer of doing so, he will be unmotivated. If his chances are actually good but he doesn't care about making the honor roll, he will also be unmotivated. Wigfield (1995) found that students' beliefs that they were capable and their valuing of academic success were, taken together, more important than their actual ability in predicting their achievement.

expectancy theory
A theory of motivation based on the belief that people's efforts to achieve depend on their expectations of reward.

expectancy–valence model
A theory that relates the probability and the incentive value of success to motivation.

Atkinson (1964) added an important aspect to expectancy theory in pointing out that under certain circumstances an overly high probability of success can be detrimental to motivation. If Mark is very able, it might be so easy for him to make the honor roll that he need not do his best. Atkinson (1958) explained this by arguing that there is a relationship between probability of success and incentive value of success such that success in an easy task is not as valued as is success in a difficult task. Therefore, motivation should be at a maximum at moderate levels of probability of success. For example, two evenly matched tennis players will probably play their hardest. Unevenly matched players will not play as hard; the poor player might want very much to win but will have too low a probability of success to try very hard, and the better player will not value winning enough to exert his or her best effort. Confirming Atkinson's theory, more recent research has shown that a person's motivation increases as task difficulty increases up to a point at which the person decides that success is very unlikely or that the goal isn't worth the effort (DeBacker & Nelson, 1999). This and other research findings indicate that moderate to difficult (but not impossible) tasks are better than easy ones for learning and motivation (Brophy, 1999; Clifford, 1990; Wigfield & Eccles, 2000).

Implications of Expectancy Theory for Education The most important implication of expectancy theory is the commonsense proposition that tasks for students should be neither too easy nor too difficult. If some students believe that they are likely to get an A no matter what they do, then their motivation will not be at a maximum. Similarly, if some students feel certain to fail no matter what they do, their motivation will be minimal. Therefore, grading systems should be set up so that earning an A is difficult (but possible) for as many students as feasible and so that earning a low grade is possible for students who exert little effort. Success must be within the reach, but not the easy reach, of all students.

HOW CAN ACHIEVEMENT MOTIVATION BE ENHANCED?

INTASC

2 Knowledge of Human Development and Learning

One of the most important types of motivation for educational psychology is **achievement motivation** (McClelland & Atkinson, 1948), or the generalized tendency to strive for success and to choose goal-oriented, success/failure activities. For example, French (1956) found that given a choice of work partners for a complex task, achievement-motivated students tend to choose a partner who is good at the task, whereas affiliation-motivated students (who express the need for love and acceptance) are more likely to choose a friendly partner. Even after they experience failure, achievement-motivated students will persist longer at a task than will students who are less high in achievement motivation and will attribute their failures to lack of effort (an internal but alterable condition) rather than to external factors such as task difficulty or luck. In short, achievement-motivated students want and expect to succeed; when they fail, they redouble their efforts until they do succeed (see Weiner, 1992).

Not surprisingly, students who are high in achievement motivation tend to succeed at school tasks (Stipek, 2002). However, it is unclear which causes which: Does high-achievement motivation lead to success in school, or does success in school (based on ability or other factors) lead to high-achievement motivation? Initially, achievement motivation is strongly affected by family experiences (Turner & Johnson, 2003), but after children have been in school for a few years, success and motivation cause each other. Success breeds the desire for more success, which in turn breeds success (Wigfield, Eccles, & Rodriguez, 1998). In contrast, students who do not experience success in achievement settings will tend to lose the motivation to succeed in such settings and will turn their interest elsewhere (perhaps to social activities, sports, or even delinquent activities in which they might succeed). Achievement motivation tends to diminish over the school years, but it is unclear whether this trend is because of the nature of children or the nature of middle and high schools (Hidi & Harackiewicz, 2000; Stipek, 2002).

achievement motivation
The desire to experience success and to participate in activities in which success depends on personal effort and abilities.

learning goals
The goals of students who are motivated primarily by desire for knowledge acquisition and self-improvement. Also called *mastery goals.*

Motivation and Goal Orientations

Some students are motivationally oriented toward **learning goals** (also called task or mastery goals); others are oriented toward **performance goals** (Brophy, 2005; Harackiewicz & Linnenbrink, 2005; Pintrich, 2000). Students with learning goals see the purpose of schooling as gaining competence in the skills being taught, whereas students with performance goals primarily seek to gain positive judgments of their competence (and avoid negative judgments). Students who are striving toward learning goals are likely to take difficult courses and to seek challenges; students with performance goals focus on getting good grades, taking easy courses, and avoiding challenging situations (Urdan & Mestas, 2006).

Learning versus Performance Goals Students with learning goals and those with performance goals do not differ in overall intelligence, but their classroom performances can differ markedly. When they run into obstacles, performance-oriented students tend to become discouraged, and their performance is seriously hampered. In contrast, when learning-oriented students encounter obstacles, they tend to keep trying, and their motivation and performance might actually increase (Pintrich, 2000; Schunk, 2005). Learning-oriented students are more likely to use metacognitive or self-regulated learning strategies (Greene et al., 2004; Pajares, Britner, & Valiante, 2000; Radosevich et al., 2004; Vermetten, Lodewijks, & Vermunt, 2001). They are likely to learn more than performance-oriented students of the same abilities (Shih, 2005). Performance-oriented students who perceive their abilities to be low are likely to fall into a pattern of helplessness, for they believe that they have little chance of earning good grades (Midgley & Urdan, 2001; Pajares, Britner, & Valiante, 2000). There is some evidence that such students

performance goals
The goals of students who are motivated primarily by a desire to gain recognition from others and to earn good grades.

Personal REFLECTION

INTASC ⑤ **Classrom Motivation and Management**

Using Different Styles

A professional acquaintance recently told me of a strong lesson she learned in her childhood that had a major impact on her work as a teacher. As a child growing up in a very athletic family, a lot was expected of Mary both athletically and academically. Her father, a baseball coach, pushed all the kids in the family hard to strive for success; and succeed they did, at the high school and collegiate level. Academically, the pressure came from their mother, although in a much gentler and subtler way than from their father. Mary explained that her father never congratulated her for her achievements or showed any encouragement. Instead, he always focused on the mistakes and areas where she could improve. Eventually, she came to realize that her academic and athletic drive were rooted in a fear of failure and a fear of disappointing her parents, and she often wondered what it would have been like to go into a competition or a test without fearing the possible outcome.

Once out of college and working as a teacher, coach, and youth sports league director, Mary discovered something else about herself. She couldn't criticize her kids. She never yelled in practice, never yelled in class, and didn't push her students or athletes in the same way she had been pushed. She often wondered if she should be more vocal with the kids, but she just couldn't do it.

Mary explained that she knew how much she would have appreciated positive encouragement rather than constantly growing expectations when she was going through school, and she simply was unable to use criticism as a way of changing the behavior of her students and athletes. She certainly had her frustrations working with high school and middle school students, but she found it much more satisfying to use encouragement and reason.

REFLECT ON THIS. Why do you think Mary was unable to use the same strategies with her students and athletes that her parents had used with her? Identify a teacher or coach from your K–12 school days from whom you learned a lot or who brought out the best in you. What methods did this person use? Do you see yourself using some of those same methods as a teacher?

are more prone to cheat (Murdock & Anderman, 2006). Learning-oriented students who perceive their ability to be low are concerned with how much they themselves can learn without regard for the performance of others (Fuchs et al., 1997; Kaplan & Midgley, 1997; Thorkildsen & Nicholls, 1998). Unfortunately, there is evidence that over their years in school, students tend to shift from learning or mastery goals to performance goals (Harackiewicz et al., 2000; Hicks-Anderman & Anderman, 1999; Stipek, 2002).

The most important implication of research on learning goals versus performance goals is that teachers should try to convince students that learning rather than grades is the purpose of academic work (Anderman et al., 2001; Ryan & Patrick, 2001; Wentzel, 2000). This can be done by emphasizing the interest value and practical importance of material students are studying and by deemphasizing grades and other rewards. For example, a teacher might say, "Today we're going to learn about events deep in the earth that cause the fiery eruptions of volcanoes!" rather than "Today we're going to learn about volcanoes. Pay attention so that you can do well on tomorrow's test." In particular, use of highly competitive grading or incentive systems should be avoided. When students perceive that there is only one standard of success in the classroom and that only a few people can achieve it, those who perceive their ability to be low will be likely to give up in advance (Ames, 1992; Summers, 2006). Table 10.2 (from Ames & Archer, 1988) summarizes the differences between the achievement goals of students with mastery (learning) goals and those of students with performance goals. Studies indicate that the types of tasks that are used in classrooms have a strong influence on students' adoption of learning goals. Use of tasks that are challenging, meaningful, and related to real life are more likely to lead to learning goals than are other tasks (Cushman, 2006; Darling-Hammond & Ifill-Lynch, 2006). Table 10.3 (from Maehr & Anderman, 1993) summarizes strategies that teachers can use to promote learning or task goals among students.

CERTIFICATION POINTER

For a case study on your teacher certification test, you may be required to suggest an appropriate strategy for improving student motivation by training students to attribute their successes to controllable causes, especially effort.

Learned Helplessness

An extreme form of the motive to avoid failure is called **learned helplessness,** which is a perception that no matter what one does, one is doomed to failure or ineffectuality: "Nothing I do matters." In academic settings, learned helplessness can be related to an internal, stable explanation for failure: "I fail because I'm stupid, and that means I will always fail" (Diener & Dweck, 1978). Students who experience repeated failures might develop a "defensive pessimism" to protect themselves from negative feedback (Martin, Marsh, & Debus, 2001).

learned helplessness The expectation, based on experience, that one's actions will ultimately lead to failure.

Learned helplessness can arise from inconsistent, unpredictable use of rewards and punishments by parents or teachers—a pattern that can lead students to believe that there is little they can do to be successful. Students with learning disabilities, for example, are

TABLE 10.2 Achievement Goal Analysis of Classroom Climate

Climate Dimensions	Mastery Goal	Performance Goal
Success defined as . . .	Improvement, progress	High grades, high normative performance
Value placed on . . .	Effort/learning	Normatively high ability
Reasons for satisfaction . . .	Working hard, challenge	Doing better than others
Teacher oriented toward . . .	How students are learning	How students are performing
View of errors/mistakes . . .	Part of learning	Anxiety eliciting
Focus of attention . . .	Process of learning	Own performance relative to others'
Reasons for effort . . .	Learning something new	High grades, performing better than others
Evaluation criteria . . .	Absolute progress	Normative

Source: From C. Ames and J. Archer, "Achievement Goals in the Classroom," *Journal of Educational Psychology, 80,* p. 261. Copyright © 1988 by the American Psychological Association. Reprinted with permission.

TABLE 10.3 School and Teacher Policies That Are Likely to Promote Learning or Task Goals

Area	Objectives	Examples of Possible Strategies
Task	Enhance intrinsic attractiveness of learning tasks. Make learning meaningful.	Encourage instruction that relates to students' backgrounds and experience. Avoid payment (monetary or other) for attendance, grades, or achievement. Foster goal setting and self-regulation. Use extra classroom programs that make learning experiences relevant.
Autonomy/ Responsibility	Provide optimal freedom for students to make choices and take responsibility.	Give alternatives in making assignments. Ask for student comments on school life—and take them seriously. Encourage instructional programs that encourage students to take initiatives and evaluate their own learning. Establish leadership opportunities for *all* students.
Recognition	Provide opportunities for *all* students to be recognized for learning. Recognize *progress* in goal attainment. Recognize challenge seeking and innovation.	Foster personal-best awards. Reduce emphasis on honor rolls. Recognize and publicize a wide range of school-related activities of students.
Resources	Encourage the development and maintenance of strategies that enhance task–goal emphases.	Underwrite action taken by staff that is in accord with a task–goal emphasis.
Grouping	Build an environment of acceptance and appreciation of all students. Broaden the range of social interaction, particularly of at-risk students. Enhance social skills development.	Provide opportunities for cooperative learning, problem solving, and decision making. Allow time and opportunity for peer interaction. Foster the development of subgroups (teams, schools within schools, etc.) within which significant interaction can occur. Encourage multiple group membership to increase range of peer interaction. Eliminate ability-grouped classes.
Evaluation	Grading and reporting processes. Practices associated with use of standardized tests. Definition of goals and standards.	Reduce emphasis on social comparisons of achievement by minimizing public reference to normative evaluation standards (e.g., grades, test scores). Establish policies and procedures that give students opportunities to improve their performance (e.g., study skills, classes). Establish grading/reporting practices that portray student progress in learning. Encourage student participation in the evaluation process.
Time	Allow the learning task and student needs to dictate scheduling. Provide opportunities for extended and significant student involvement in learning tasks.	Allow students to *progress at their own rate* whenever possible. Encourage flexibility in the scheduling of learning experiences. Give teachers greater control over time usage through, for example, block scheduling.

Source: From M. L. Maehr and E. M. Anderman, "Reinventing Schools for Early Adolescents," *The Elementary School Journal, 93*(5), 1993, pp. 593–610. Copyright © 1993 by The University of Chicago Press. Adapted by permission.

more likely than other students to respond to failure with helpless behavior (Pintrich & Schunk, 2002). Teachers can prevent or alleviate learned helplessness by giving students (1) opportunities for success in small steps; (2) immediate feedback; and (3) most important, consistent expectations and follow-through (see Alderman, 1990).

THEORY *into* PRACTICE

Helping Students Overcome Learned Helplessness

The concept of learned helplessness derives from the theory that students might become academic failures through a conditioning process based on negative feedback from teachers, school experiences, peers, and students themselves. Numerous studies show that when students consistently fail, they eventually give up. They become conditioned to helplessness (Maier & Seligman, 1976).

Teachers at both the elementary and secondary levels can help to counter this syndrome in a variety of ways, including attribution training, goal restructuring, self-esteem programs, success-guaranteed approaches, and positive feedback systems. The following general principles are helpful for all students, especially students who have shown a tendency to accept failure.

1. ***Accentuate the positive.*** Get to know the student's strengths, then use these as building blocks. Every student has something she or he does well. But be careful that the strength is authentic; don't make up a strength. For example, a student might like to talk a lot but write poorly. Have the student complete assignments by talking rather than writing. As confidence is restored, slowly introduce writing.
2. ***Eliminate the negative.*** Do not play down a student's weaknesses. Deal with them directly but tactfully. In the preceding example, talk to the student about problems with writing. Then have the student develop a plan to improve on the writing. Discuss the plan, and together make up a contract about how the plan will be completed.
3. ***Go from the familiar to the new, using advance organizers or guided discovery.*** Some students have difficulties with concepts, skills, or ideas with which they are not familiar. Also, students relate better to lessons that are linked to their own experiences. For example, a high school math teacher might begin a lesson with a math problem that students might face in the real world, such as calculating the sales tax when purchasing a CD player. Further, the teacher can ask students to bring to class math problems they have encountered outside of school. The whole class can become involved in solving a student's math problem.
4. ***Create challenges in which students actively create problems and solve them using their own knowledge and skills.***

INTASC

7 Instructional Planning Skills

VIDEO HOMEWORK EXERCISE

Motivating Through Problem-Based Learning

Go to **www.myeducationlab.com** and, in the Homework and Exercises section for Chapter 10 of this text, access the video entitled "Motivating Through Problem-Based Learning." Watch the video and complete the homework questions that accompany it, saving your work or transmitting it to your professor as required.

Teacher Expectations and Achievement

On the first day of class, Mr. Erhard called roll. Soon he got to a name that looked familiar. "Wayne Clements?"

"Here!"

"Do you have a brother named Victor?"

"Yes."

"I remember Victor. He was a terror. I'm going to keep my eye on you!"

As he neared the end of the roll, Mr. Erhard saw that several boys were starting to whisper to one another in the back of the room. "Wayne! I asked the class to remain silent while I read the roll. Didn't you hear me? I knew I'd have to watch out for you!"

This dialogue illustrates how teachers can establish expectations for their students and how these expectations can be self-fulfilling. Mr. Erhard doesn't know it, but Wayne is generally a well-behaved, conscientious student, quite unlike his older brother, Victor. However, because of his experience with Victor, Mr. Erhard expects that he will have trouble with Wayne. When he sees several boys whispering, it is Wayne he singles out for blame, confirming for himself that Wayne is a troublemaker. After a few episodes of this treatment, we can expect Wayne to begin playing the role Mr. Erhard has assigned to him.

Research on teachers' expectations for their students has generally found that students live up (or down) to the expectations that their teachers have for them (Jussim & Eccles, 1995; Rubie-Davies, 2007), particularly in the younger grades and when teachers know relatively little about their students' actual achievement levels. Further, there is evidence that students in schools whose teachers have high expectations achieve more than those in other schools (Marks, Doane, & Secada, 1998). Of course, students' expectations for themselves are at least as important as those of their teachers. One study found that students whose self-perceptions exceeded their current performance later tended to increase in grades, whereas those whose self-perceptions were lower than their performance tended to drop in grades (Anderman, Anderman, & Griesinger, 1999).

Communicating Positive Expectations It is important for teachers to communicate to their students the expectation that they can learn (see Babad, 1993). Obviously, it is a bad idea to state the contrary—that a particular student cannot learn—and few teachers would explicitly do so. There are several implicit ways in which teachers can communicate positive expectations of their students (or avoid negative ones).

1. ***Wait for students to respond.*** Rowe (1974) and others have noted that teachers wait longer for answers from students for whom they have high expectations than from other students. Longer wait times may communicate high expectations and increase student achievement (Tobin, 1987).

CONNECTIONS
For more on grouping students, see Chapter 9, page 265.

2. ***Avoid unnecessary achievement distinctions among students.*** Assessment results and grades should be a private matter between students and their teacher, not public information. Students usually know who is good in school and who is not, but teachers can still successfully communicate the expectation that all students, not only the most able ones, are capable of learning (Weinstein, Madison, & Kuklinski, 1995).

3. ***Treat all students equally.*** Call on students at all achievement levels equally often, and spend equal amounts of time with them. In particular, guard against bias.

Teaching Dilemmas: CASES TO CONSIDER

Expectations

Leonard Watkins and Elizabeth Olson are teachers at a diverse high school in a city school district. Elizabeth, a novice English teacher, has come to Leonard, who teaches math, for some advice on one of her students.

INTASC

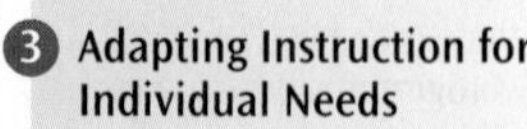

3 Adapting Instruction for Individual Needs

Elizabeth: Leonard, I'm having a problem with one of my students, and I'm hoping you'll help me out.

Leonard: I'm always glad to help. Let me guess. This is about Tyler, right?

Elizabeth: I'm afraid so. He's such a bright child, but he's not working up to his potential. Also, he simply won't listen to me, and he frequently disrupts the class. You have him for math, and I know he does a lot better in your class.

Leonard: What have you tried so far?

Elizabeth: Well, I've asked him to come in after school to talk with me. He's told me about all the problems he has in his family, and how he feels the other kids would make fun of him if he did his best.

Leonard: Do these conversations help?

Elizabeth: A little. But he still comes in late and doesn't always hand in his assignments. He knows I care about him, but I don't think he respects me. I wondered if you had any ideas about ways I could make my teaching more appropriate to his needs.

Leonard: With all due respect, Elizabeth, I think you're already doing too much for that young man. He's getting away with murder!

Elizabeth: But I want to be fair.

Leonard: In my way of thinking, the fairest thing you can do, and the most beneficial for Tyler, is to hold him to the same standards as everyone else. You need to show him you have high expectations for him.

Elizabeth: But what should I do?

Leonard: You said it yourself, Tyler is a bright kid, and he is. But it's worthless to be bright if you don't act bright. If you tell Tyler that you expect excellence from him, he'll rise to your expectations. If you let him slide, he'll slide. In math class, for example, if he doesn't do his best work, I have him come in after school and do it over.

Elizabeth: That sounds right, but . . .

Leonard: Think of your own favorite teachers. I'll bet they were the ones who challenged you, who held you to high standards. Am I right?

Elizabeth: Yes, but . . .

Leonard: It's the same with Tyler. Your job is to help him be the great student you and I both know he can be!

QUESTIONS FOR REFLECTION

1. Reflect on the conversation between Leonard and Elizabeth. Below the surface, what are they really talking about? What are the major issues in their discussion?
2. Do you think Leonard is suggesting that Elizabeth be too tough on Tyler?
3. What specific actions could Elizabeth take to show positive and appropriate expectations for Tyler?
4. Is it possible for expectations to be too high? What if Elizabeth expresses high expectations for Tyler and then he doesn't meet them?
5. Imagine that Tyler is African American. Would that change any of your answers? How would Tyler's cultural background relate to the expectations his teachers have for him?

Anxiety and Achievement

Anxiety is a constant companion of education. Every student feels some anxiety at some time while in school; but for certain students, anxiety seriously inhibits learning or performance, particularly on tests (Cassady & Johnson, 2002; Everson, Smodlaka, & Tobias, 1994).

The main source of anxiety in school is the fear of failure and, with it, loss of self-esteem (Pintrich & Schunk, 2002). Low achievers are particularly likely to feel anxious in school, but they are by no means the only ones. We all know very able, high-achieving students who are also very anxious, maybe even terrified to be less than perfect at any school task.

CONNECTIONS
Programs designed to train test-anxious children in test-taking skills are discussed in Chapter 14, page 481.

Anxiety can block school performance in several ways (Naveh-Benjamin, 1991; Skaalvik, 1997). Anxious students might have difficulty learning in the first place, difficulty using or transferring knowledge they do have, and difficulty demonstrating their

The recent focus on high-stakes testing and achievement leaves students, administrators, and teachers anxious over the outcome of test scores. What can you do to alleviate some of that pressure with your students?

knowledge on tests (Bandalos, Yates, & Thorndike-Christ, 1995). Anxious students are likely to be overly self-conscious in performance settings, a feeling that distracts attention from the task at hand (Tobias, 1992). One particularly common form of debilitating anxiety is math anxiety. Many students (and adults) simply freeze up when given math problems, particularly word problems (Everson, Tobias, Hartman, & Gourgey, 1993).

Teachers can apply many strategies to reduce the negative impact of anxiety on learning and performance. Clearly, creating a classroom climate that is accepting, comfortable, and noncompetitive helps. Giving students opportunities to correct errors or improve their work before handing it in also helps anxious children, as does providing clear, unambiguous instructions (Wigfield & Eccles, 1989). In testing situations, teachers can do many things to help anxious students to do their best. They can avoid time pressure, giving students plenty of time to complete a test and check their work. Tests that begin with easy problems and only gradually introduce more difficult ones are better for anxious students; and tests with standard, simple answer formats help such students. Test-anxious children can be trained in test-taking skills and relaxation techniques, and these can have a positive impact on their test performance (Spielberger & Vagg, 1995).

HOW CAN TEACHERS INCREASE STUDENTS' MOTIVATION TO LEARN?

Learning takes work. Euclid, a Greek mathematician who lived around 300 B.C. and wrote the first geometry textbook, was asked by his king whether there were any shortcuts the king could use to learn geometry, as he was a very busy man. "I'm sorry," Euclid replied, "but there is no royal road to geometry." The same is true of every other subject: Students get out of any course of study only what they put into it.

The remainder of this chapter discusses the means by which students can be motivated to exert the effort learning requires. First, the issue of intrinsic motivation—the motivational value of the content itself—is presented. Extrinsic motivation—the use of praise, feedback, and incentives to motivate students to do their best—is then discussed.

Also in this section are specific strategies for enhancing student motivation and suggestions for solving motivational problems that are common in classrooms, including reward-for-improvement incentive systems.

Intrinsic and Extrinsic Motivation

Sometimes a course of study is so fascinating and useful to students that they are willing to do the work required to learn the material with no incentive other than the interest level of the material itself. For example, many students would gladly take auto mechanics or photography courses and work hard in them, even if the courses offered no credit or grades. For these students the favorite subject itself has enough **intrinsic incentive** value to motivate them to learn. Other students love to learn about particular topics such as insects, dinosaurs, or famous people in history and need little encouragement or reward to do so (Covington, 1999; Gottfried & Fleming, 2001; Schraw, Flowerday, &

intrinsic incentive
An aspect of an activity that people enjoy and, therefore, find motivating.

Lehman, 2001). Students who have a strong "future time perspective" (i.e., are willing to do things today that may benefit them in the future) are often particularly motivated to learn, even without immediate incentives (Husman & Lens, 1999).

However, much of what must be learned in school is not inherently interesting or useful to most students in the short run. Students receive about 900 hours of instruction every year, and intrinsic interest alone will not keep them enthusiastically working day in and day out. In particular, students' intrinsic motivation generally declines from early elementary school through secondary school (Gottfried & Fleming, 2001; Sethi, Drake, Dialdin, & Lepper, 1995). For this reason, schools apply a variety of **extrinsic incentives,** rewards for learning that are not inherent in the material being learned (Brophy, 1998). Extrinsic rewards might range from praise to grades to recognition to prizes or other rewards.

In the vignette at the beginning of this chapter, Cal Lewis tried to enhance both intrinsic and extrinsic motivation. His simulation of the Constitutional Convention was intended to arouse students' intrinsic interest in the subject, and his ratings of students' presentations and his feedback at the end of each period were intended to provide extrinsic motivation.

"The school board decided not to raise teachers' salaries. We didn't want to undermine their intrinsic motivation."

Lepper's Experiment on the Impact of Rewards on Motivation An important question in research on motivation concerns whether the providing of extrinsic rewards diminishes intrinsic interest in an activity. In a classic experiment exploring this topic, Lepper and colleagues (1973) gave preschoolers an opportunity to draw with felt-tip markers, which many of them did quite enthusiastically. Then the researchers randomly divided the children into three groups: One group was told that its members would receive a reward for drawing a picture for a visitor (a Good Player Award), one was given the same reward as a surprise (not dependent on the children's drawing), and one received no reward. Over the next 4 days, observers recorded the children's free-play activities. Children who had received a reward for drawing spent about half as much time drawing with felt-tip markers as did those who had received the surprise reward and those who had gotten no reward. The authors suggested that promising extrinsic rewards for an activity that is intrinsically interesting might undermine intrinsic interest by inducing children to expect a reward for doing what they had previously done for nothing. In a later study (Greene & Lepper, 1974), it was found that simply telling children that they would be watched (through a one-way mirror) had an undermining effect similar to that of a promised reward.

Do Rewards Destroy Intrinsic Motivation? In understanding the results of these studies, it is important to recall the conditions of the research. The students who were chosen for the studies were ones who showed an intrinsic interest in using marking pens; those who did not were excluded from the experiments. Also, drawing with felt-tip pens does not resemble most school tasks. Many children love to draw at home; but few, even those who are most interested in school subjects, would independently study grammar and punctuation, work math problems, or learn the valences of chemical elements. Further, many of our most creative and self-motivated scientists were heavily reinforced as students with grades, science fair prizes, and scholarships for doing science, and virtually all successful artists have been reinforced at some point for engaging in artistic activities. This reinforcement certainly did not undermine the activities' intrinsic interest. Research on older students doing more school-like tasks has generally failed to replicate the results of the Lepper and colleagues (1973) experiment (Cameron & Pierce, 1994, 1996; Eisenberger & Cameron, 1998). In fact, the use of rewards more often increases intrinsic motivation, especially when rewards are contingent on the quality of performance rather than on mere

extrinsic incentive
A reward that is external to the activity, such as recognition or a good grade.

CLASSROOM ARTIFACT HOMEWORK EXERCISE
Count Dracula Story

Go to **www.myeducationlab.com** and, in the Homework and Exercises section for Chapter 10 of this text, access the classroom artifact entitled "Count Dracula Story." Examine the artifact, and complete the homework questions that accompany it, saving your work or transmitting it to your professor as required.

participation in an activity (Cameron, Pierce, Banko, & Gear, 2005; Lepper, 1983; Ryan & Deci, 2000), when the rewards are seen as recognition of competence (Rosenfield, Folger, & Adelman, 1980), when the task in question is not very interesting (Morgan, 1984), or when the rewards are social (e.g., praise) rather than material (Cameron, 2001; Cameron & Pierce, 1994; Chance, 1992; Miller & Hom, 1990; Ryan & Deci, 2000). Cameron (2001) summarizes the situation in which extrinsic rewards undermine intrinsic interest as follows: "A negative effect occurs when a task is of high interest, when the rewards are tangible and offered beforehand, and when the rewards are delivered without regard to success on the task or to any specified level of performance" (p. 40). This is a very narrow set of conditions, characterized by Bandura (1986, p. 246) as "of no great social import because rewards are rarely showered on people regardless of how they behave." However, Deci, Koestner, and Ryan (2001), while acknowledging that there are many forms of extrinsic rewards that have a positive or neutral impact on motivation, nevertheless argue that "the use of rewards as a motivational strategy is clearly a risky proposition, so we continue to argue for thinking about educational practices that will engage students' interest and support the development of their self-regulation" (2001, p. 50).

The research on the effects of extrinsic rewards on intrinsic motivation does counsel caution in the use of material rewards for intrinsically interesting tasks (see Lepper, 1998; Lepper, Keavney, & Drake, 1996; Ryan & Deci, 2000; Sansone & Harackiewicz, 2000). Teachers should attempt to make everything they teach as intrinsically interesting as possible and should avoid handing out material rewards when they are unnecessary, but teachers should not refrain from using extrinsic rewards when they are needed (Ryan & Deci, 2000). Often, extrinsic rewards may be necessary to get students started in a learning activity but may be phased out as students come to enjoy the activity and succeed at it (Stipek, 1993). Also, remember that in any given class, there are students who are intrinsically motivated to do a given activity and those who are not. To ensure that all students learn, strategic use of both intrinsic and extrinsic motivators is likely to be necessary.

How Can Teachers Enhance Intrinsic Motivation?

Classroom instruction should enhance intrinsic motivation as much as possible. Increasing intrinsic motivation is always helpful for learning, regardless of whether extrinsic incentives are also in use (Covington, 1999; Vansteenkiste, Lens, & Deci, 2006). This means that teachers must try to get their students interested in the material they are presenting and then present it in an appealing way that both satisfies and increases students' curiosity about the material itself. A discussion of some means of doing this follows (see also Brophy, 1999; Burden & Byrd, 2003; Covington, 1999; Stipek, 2002).

CERTIFICATION POINTER
On your teacher certification test, you should recognize the value of intrinsic motivation in promoting students' life-long growth and learning.

CONNECTIONS
The importance of student interest in creative problem solving and other constructivist approaches is discussed in Chapter 8, page 251.

INTASC

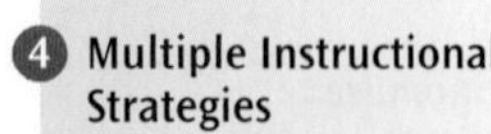

4 Multiple Instructional Strategies

Arousing Interest It is important to convince students of the importance and interest level of the material that is about to be presented to show (if possible) how the knowledge to be gained will be useful to students (Bergin, 1999; Tomlinson, 2002). For example, intrinsic motivation to learn a lesson on percents might be increased by introducing the lesson as follows:

> Today we will begin a lesson on percents. Percents are important in our daily lives. For example, when you buy something at the store and a salesperson figures the sales tax, he or she is using percents. When we leave a tip for a waiter or waitress, we use percents. We often hear in the news things like "Prices rose seven percent last year." In a few years, many of you will have summer jobs, and if they involve handling money, you'll probably be using percents all the time.

Introducing lessons with examples relating the material to students' cultures can be particularly effective. For example, in introducing astronomy to a class with many Latino children, a teacher could say, "Thousands of years ago, people in Mexico and Central America had calendars that accurately predicted the movement of the moon and stars for centuries into the future. How could they do this? Today we will learn about how planets, moons, and stars move in predictable paths." The purpose of these statements is to arouse student curiosity about the lesson to come, thereby enhancing intrinsic motivation to learn the material (Vacca, 2006).

Another way to enhance students' intrinsic interest is to give them some choice about what they will study or how they will study it (Cordova & Lepper, 1996; Stipek, 2002). Choices need not be unlimited to be motivational. For example, students might be given a choice of writing about ancient Athens or Sparta, or a choice of working independently or in pairs.

Maintaining Curiosity A skillful teacher uses a variety of means to further arouse or maintain curiosity in the course of the lesson. Science teachers, for instance, often use demonstrations that surprise or baffle students and induce them to want to understand why. A floating dime makes students curious about the surface tension of liquids. "Burning" a dollar bill covered with an alcohol–water solution (without harming the dollar bill) certainly increases curiosity about the heat of combustion. Guthrie and Cox (2001) found that giving students hands-on experience with science activities greatly increased their learning from books on related topics and provided more motivation.

Less dramatically, surprising or challenging students with a problem they can't solve with their current knowledge can arouse curiosity, and, therefore, intrinsic motivation (see Bottge, 2001). A seventh-grade teacher in England used this principle in a lesson on equivalent fractions. First, he had his students halve and then halve again $\frac{8}{13}$ and $\frac{12}{20}$. Working in pairs they instantly agreed on $\frac{4}{13}$ and $\frac{2}{13}$, $\frac{6}{20}$ and $\frac{3}{20}$. Then he gave them $\frac{13}{20}$. After a moment of hesitation, students came back with 6½/20 and 3¼/20. "Crikey!" he said. "All these fractions inside fractions are making me nervous! Isn't there some other way we can do this?" "Round off?" suggested one student. "Use decimals?" suggested another. Finally, after much discussion and argument, the students realized that they could use their knowledge about equivalent fractions to find the solutions: $\frac{13}{40}$ and $\frac{13}{80}$. Getting the students into a familiar pattern and then breaking that pattern excited and engaged the whole class, making them question *their* question far more effectively than would have been possible by simply teaching the algorithm in the first place. The element of surprise, challenging the students' current understanding, made them intensely curious about an issue they'd never before considered.

Using a Variety of Interesting Presentation Modes The intrinsic motivation to learn something is enhanced by the use of interesting materials, as well as by variety in mode of presentation. For example, teachers can maintain student interest in a subject by alternating use of films, guest speakers, demonstrations, and so on, although the use of each resource must be carefully planned to be sure it focuses on the course objectives and complements the other activities. Use of computers can enhance most students' intrinsic motivation to learn (Lepper, 1985). What makes materials interesting are elements such as the use of emotional material (e.g., danger, sex, money, heartbreak, disaster), concrete rather than abstract examples, cause-and-effect relationships, and clear organization (Bergin, 1999; Jetton & Alexander, 2001; Schraw et al., 2001; Wade, 2001).

CONNECTIONS
The importance of student interest in lesson content and presentation is discussed in Chapter 7, page 203.

One excellent means of increasing interest in a subject is to use games or simulations. A simulation, or role play, is an exercise in which students take on roles and engage in activities appropriate to those roles. Cal Lewis used a simulation to teach students about the Constitutional Convention. Programs exist that simulate many aspects of government; for example, students may take roles as legislators who must negotiate and trade votes to satisfy their constituents' interests or as economic actors (farmers, producers, consumers) who run a minieconomy. Creative teachers have long used simulations that they designed themselves. For example, teachers can have students write their own newspaper; design, manufacture, and market a product; or set up and run a bank.

This student has intrinsic incentive to learn about art projects. As a teacher, how could you maintain or extend his motivation? How could you present the same task to another student for whom the task does not have intrinsic value?

The advantage of simulations is that they allow students to learn about a subject from the inside. Although research on use of simulations (see VanSickle, 1986) finds that they are not usually or are no more effective than traditional instruction for teaching facts and concepts, studies do consistently find that simulations increase students' interest, motivation, and affective learning (Dukes & Seidner, 1978). They certainly impart a different affective knowledge of a subject.

Nonsimulation games can also increase motivation to learn a given subject. The spelling bee is a popular example of a nonsimulation game. Teams–Games–Tournament, or TGT (Slavin, 1995a), uses games that can be adapted to any subject. Team games are usually better than individual games; team games provide an opportunity for teammates to help one another and avoid one problem of individual games—that of more able students consistently winning. If all students are put on mixed-ability teams, all have a good chance of success (see Slavin, 1995a).

Helping Students Set Their Own Goals One fundamental principle of motivation is that people work harder for goals that they themselves set than for goals set for them by others (Ryan & Deci, 2000). For example, a student might set a minimum number of books she expects to read at home or a score she expects to attain on an upcoming quiz. At the next goal-setting conference the teacher would discuss student attainment of (or failure to attain) goals and set new goals for the following week. During these meetings the teacher might help students learn to set ambitious but realistic goals and would praise them for setting and then achieving their goals. Goal-setting strategies of this kind have been found to increase students' academic performance and self-efficacy (Page-Voth & Graham, 1999; Shih & Alexander, 2000).

Principles for Providing Extrinsic Incentives to Learn

Teachers must always try to enhance students' intrinsic motivation to learn academic materials, but they must at the same time be concerned about extrinsic incentives for learning (Brophy, 1998; Hidi & Harackiewicz, 2000). Not every subject is intrinsically interesting to all students, and students must be motivated to do the hard work necessary to master difficult subjects. The following sections discuss a variety of incentives that can help motivate students to learn academic material.

Expressing Clear Expectations Students need to know exactly what they are supposed to do, how they will be evaluated, and what the consequences of success will be. Often, students' failures on particular tasks stem from confusion about what they are being asked to do (see Anderson, Brubaker, Alleman-Brooks, & Duffy, 1985; Brophy, 1998). Communicating clear expectations is important. For example, a teacher might introduce a writing assignment as follows:

> Today, I'd like you all to write a composition about what Thomas Jefferson would think of government in the United States today. I expect your compositions to be about two pages long, and I want them to compare and contrast the plan of government laid out by the nation's founders with the way government actually operates today. Your compositions will be graded on the basis of your ability to describe similarities and differences between the structure and function of the U.S. government in Thomas Jefferson's time and today, as well as on the originality and clarity of your writing. This will be an important part of your 6 weeks' grade, so I expect you to do your best!

Teaching Dilemmas: CASES TO CONSIDER

INTASC

3 Adapting Instruction for Individual Needs
4 Multiple Instructional Strategies

Adapting Strategies

Carlos Suarez, a fourth-grade teacher with 10 years' experience, talks in his classroom after school to Ruth Duncan about Ruth's son Jeremy.

Carlos: I appreciate your taking time to come down today.
Ruth: Oh, I was glad to come. I must say, though, it's tricky. My husband and I run a store, and it's a 24-hour-a-day job. Anyway, how is Jeremy doing?
Carlos: I'm sure you've noticed from his report cards that Jeremy has not been reaching our minimum goals for him in several areas, especially math. He seems to have trouble applying himself in class. His attention wanders. Also, he doesn't always turn in his homework. What happens to the work I send home with him?
Ruth: Well, he certainly doesn't seem to sit down and dig into it on his own. I see some books come home, but when I ask him about what he's supposed to do, he says it's nothing.
Carlos: Hmm. I'd like to see that attitude change. Good work motivation develops early, and Jeremy needs to get a good start.

In math period the next day, the class is working on adding two-digit numbers with renaming. Carlos sets up a store activity with Pete and a reluctant Jeremy.

Carlos: Okay, my desk is the counter, and these empty pencil boxes are new video game cartridges, right? Each one has a price label. And you each have plenty of fake money. *So . . . May I help you, sir?*
Pete: Well, I'll take these two: $17 and $26.
Carlos: Fine. *Now, unfortunately, my cash register is broken, sir, so I need you to add up what you owe me.* Here, use the blackboard.
Pete (working): Seven and six makes thirteen, put down the three . . . *$33?* No, wait. I think I forgot something. We did this yesterday on that worksheet, right? Don't tell me, let me try again. *$43!*
Carlos: Correct. And a good job of sticking with the problem, Pete. *Here you are, sir, enjoy your purchases. Now, sir, what can I do for you?*
Jeremy: Nothing. I don't want to do this.
Carlos: Hey, Jeremy, this isn't hard. You made a good start on these kinds of problems when I worked with you yesterday, remember?
Jeremy: Maybe, but I still don't get it. It's not my fault, Mr. Suarez. I just can't do it. I hate math.
Carlos: Well, let me ask you, what do you like to do at home?
Jeremy: Like? I like riding my bike. I like helping my dad in his store.
Carlos: You help in the store? That's excellent. What do you do to help?
Jeremy: I don't know. Sometimes I just hang around. Or I arrange the displays. Sometimes I tell Dad if we're out of something, or I show people where things are.
Carlos: How about helping out with money? Do you put on price tags or work the cash register?
Jeremy: No, Mr. Suarez! I couldn't do any of that! I can't do math.
Carlos: Well, you just put your finger on the whole point. You need to learn to add and subtract here in school. Then you'll be able to have a lot more responsibility and do a lot of interesting things that you like to do.
Jeremy: I don't care. I'll learn math soon enough, I guess. Anyway, my mom and dad wouldn't ever let me use the cash register. They don't care about me doing math. Anyway, I could do most of those problems if I tried, I bet.
Carlos: You might be right about that. So how about trying?
Jeremy: Yeah, maybe, Mr. Suarez.

QUESTIONS FOR REFLECTION

1. How can Carlos help motivate Jeremy to learn? Is it possible for one person to motivate another, or is motivation something inside a person? How can Carlos encourage intrinsic motivation while using extrinsic motivation?
2. Drawing on what you know about the situation, develop a problem-solving approach for getting Jeremy motivated. How might you involve Jeremy's parents?
3. Is Carlos's approach focused on learning goals or performance goals? How might Carlos change his approach, if at all, depending on Jeremy's orientation toward learning or performance goals?
4. Model your problem-solving approach by extending the dialogue in writing or role play to the next day.

Note that the teacher is clear about what students are to write, how much material is expected, how the work will be evaluated, and how important the work will be for the students' grades. This clarity assures students that efforts directed at writing a good composition will pay off—in this case, in terms of grades. If the teacher had just said, "I'd like you all to write a composition about what Thomas Jefferson would think about government in the United States today," students might write the wrong thing, write too much or too little, or perhaps emphasize the if-Jefferson-were-alive-today aspect of the assignment rather than the comparative-government aspect. They would be unsure how much importance the teacher intended to place on the mechanics of the composition as compared to its content. Finally, they would have no way of knowing how their efforts would pay off, lacking any indication of how much emphasis the teacher would give to the compositions in computing grades.

A study by Graham, MacArthur, and Schwartz (1995) shows the importance of specificity. Low-achieving fifth- and sixth-graders were asked to revise compositions either to "make [your paper] better" or to "add at least three things that will add information to your paper." The students with the more specific instructions wrote higher-quality, longer revisions because they had a clearer idea of exactly what was being asked of them.

CONNECTIONS
Feedback is also discussed in Chapter 7, page 213.

Providing Clear Feedback The word **feedback** means information on the results of one's efforts. The term has been used throughout this book to refer both to information students receive on their performance and to information teachers obtain on the effects of their instruction. Feedback can serve as an incentive. Research on feedback has found that provision of information on the results of one's actions can be an adequate reward in some circumstances (Gibbons, Duffin, Robertson, & Thompson, 1998). However, to be an effective motivator, feedback must be clear and specific and must be given close in time to performance (Hattie & Timperley, 2007). This is important for all students, but especially for young ones. For example, praise for a job well done should specify what the student did well:

- "Good work! I like the way you used the guide words in the dictionary to find the words on your worksheet."
- "I like that answer. It shows you've been thinking about what I've been saying about freedom and responsibility."
- "This is an excellent essay. It started with a statement of the argument you were going to make and then supported the argument with relevant information. I also like the care you took with punctuation and word usage."

Specific feedback is both informative and motivational (Kulhavy & Stock, 1989). It tells students what they did right, so that they will know what to do in the future, and helps give them an effort-based attribution for success ("You succeeded because you worked hard"). In contrast, if students are praised or receive a good grade without any explanation, they are unlikely to learn from the feedback what to do next time to be successful and might form an ability attribution ("I succeeded because I'm smart") or an external

feedback
Information on the results of one's efforts.

attribution ("I must have succeeded because the teacher likes me, the task was easy, or I lucked out"). As was noted earlier in this chapter, effort attributions are most conducive to continuing motivation (Pintrich & Schunk, 2002). Similarly, feedback about mistakes or failures can add to motivation if it focuses only on the performance itself (not on students' general abilities) and if it is alternated with success feedback (see Clifford, 1990).

Providing Immediate Feedback Immediacy of feedback is also very important (Kulik & Kulik, 1988). If students complete a project on Monday and don't receive any feedback on it until Friday, the informational and motivational value of the feedback will be diminished. First, if they made errors, they might continue all week making similar errors on related material that might have been averted by feedback on the performance. Second, a long delay between behavior and consequence confuses the relationship between the two. Young students, especially, might have little idea why they received a particular grade if the performance on which the grade is based occurred several days earlier.

Providing Frequent Feedback Feedback should be delivered frequently to students to maintain their best efforts. For example, it is unrealistic to expect most students to work hard for 6 or 9 weeks in hope of improving their grade unless they receive frequent feedback. Research in the behavioral learning theory tradition has established that no matter how powerful a reward is, it might have little impact on behavior if it is given infrequently; small, frequent rewards are more effective incentives than are large, infrequent ones. Research on frequency of testing has generally found that it is a good idea to give frequent brief quizzes to assess student progress rather than infrequent long tests (Dempster, 1991). Research also indicates the importance of asking many questions in class so that students can gain information about their own level of understanding and can receive reinforcement (praise, recognition) for paying attention to lessons.

Increasing the Value and Availability of Extrinsic Motivators Expectancy theories of motivation, discussed earlier in this chapter, hold that motivation is a product of the value an individual attaches to success and the individual's estimate of the likelihood of success (see Wigfield & Eccles, 2000). One implication of this is that students must value incentives that are used to motivate them. Some students are not particularly interested in teacher praise or grades but might value notes sent home to their parents, a little extra recess time, or a special privilege in the classroom.

CONNECTIONS
For grading methods that recognize progress and effort, see Chapter 13, page 442.

Another implication of expectancy theory is that although all students must have a chance to be rewarded if they do their best, no student should have an easy time achieving the maximum reward. This principle is violated by traditional grading practices, because some students find it easy to earn A's and B's, whereas others believe that they have little chance of academic success no matter what they do. In this circumstance, neither high achievers nor low achievers are likely to exert their best efforts. This is one reason that it is important to reward students for effort, for doing better than they have done in the past, or for making progress, rather than only for getting a high score. For example, students can build a portfolio of compositions, projects, reports, or other work and can then see how their work is improving over time. Not all students are equally capable of achieving high scores; but all are equally capable of exerting effort, exceeding their own past record, or making progress, so these are often better, more equally available criteria for reward.

CONNECTIONS
For more on student portfolios, see Chapter 13, page 436.

Using Praise Effectively

Praise serves many purposes in classroom instruction but is primarily used to reinforce appropriate behaviors and to give feedback to students on what they are doing right. Overall, it is a good idea to use praise frequently, especially with young children and in classrooms with many low-achieving students (Brophy, 1998; Evans, 1996). However, what is more important than the amount of praise given is the way it is given. Praise is effective as a classroom motivator to the extent that it is contingent, specific, and credible

CONNECTIONS
For more on the use of praise as a reinforcer, see Chapter 11, page 343.

Praise is effective as a classroom motivator when it is contingent, specific, and credible. As a teacher, how will you use praise to motivate your students?

CERTIFICATION POINTER
When responding to a case study on your certification test, you should know that providing praise that is contingent, specific, and credible can increase student motivation.

CONNECTIONS
For more on self-regulated learning, see Chapter 5, page 148.

ONLINE READING & WRITING EXERCISE
Punished by Rewards?

Access this exercise, entitled "Punished by Rewards," in the Homework and Exercises section for Chapter 10 of this text at **www.mylabschool.com.**

contingent praise
Praise that is effective because it refers directly to specific task performances.

(Sutherland, Wehby, & Copeland, 2000). **Contingent praise** depends on student performance of well-defined behaviors. For example, if a teacher says, "I'd like you all to open your books to page ninety-two and work problems one to ten," then praise will be given only to the students who follow directions. Praise should be given only for right answers and appropriate behaviors.

Specificity means that the teacher praises students for specific behaviors, not for general "goodness." For example, a teacher might say, "Susan, I'm glad you followed my directions to start work on your composition," rather than, "Susan, you're doing great!"

When praise is *credible,* it is given sincerely for good work. Brophy (1981) notes that when praising low-achieving or disruptive students for good work, teachers often contradict their words with tone, posture, or other nonverbal cues. Brophy's (1981) list of guidelines for effective praise appears in Table 10.4.

In addition to contingency, specificity, and credibility, Brophy's list includes several particularly important principles that reinforce topics discussed earlier in this chapter. For example, guidelines 7 and 8 emphasize that praise should be given for good performance relative to a student's usual level of performance. That is, students who usually do well should not be praised for a merely average performance, but students who usually do less well should be praised when they do better. This relates to the principle of accessibility of reward discussed earlier in this chapter; rewards should be neither too easy nor too difficult for students to obtain.

Teaching Students to Praise Themselves

There is increasing evidence that students can learn to praise themselves and that this increases their academic success. For example, children can learn to mentally give themselves a pat on the back when they finish a task or to stop at regular intervals to notice how much they have done (Corno & Kanfer, 1993; Ross, Rolheiser, & Hogaboam-Gray, 1998). This strategy is a key component of self-regulated learning (see Schunk & Zimmerman, 1997).

ON THE WEB
For more on how teachers can influence student motivation see **www2.selu.edu/Academics/faculty/cehols/selfreg/page4.html.**

TABLE 10.4 Guidelines for Effective Praise

If used properly, praise can be an effective motivator in classroom situations.

Effective Praise

1. Is delivered contingently.
2. Specifies the particulars of the accomplishment.
3. Shows spontaneity, variety, and other signs of credibility; suggests clear attention to the student's accomplishment.
4. Rewards attainment of specified performance criteria (which can include effort criteria, however).
5. Provides information to students about their competence or the value of their accomplishments.
6. Orients students toward better appreciation of their own task-related behavior and thinking about problem solving.
7. Uses students' own prior accomplishments as the context for describing present accomplishments.
8. Is given in recognition of noteworthy effort or success at difficult tasks (for *this* student).
9. Attributes success to effort and ability, implying that similar successes can be expected in the future.
10. Focuses students' attention on their own task-relevant behavior.
11. Fosters appreciation of, and desirable attributions about, task-relevant behavior after the process is completed.

Source: From Jere Brophy, "Teacher Praise: A Functional Analysis," *Review of Educational Research, 51,* p. 26.

ON THE WEB

The Northwest Regional Laboratory has resources for teachers on sparking students' motivation at **www.nwrel.org/request/oct00/.**

CHAPTER 10 SUMMARY

What Is Motivation?

Motivation is an internal process that activates, guides, and maintains behavior over time. There are different kinds, intensities, aims, and directions of motivation. Motivation to learn is critically important to students and teachers.

What Are Some Theories of Motivation?

In behavioral learning theory (Skinner and others), motivation is a consequence of reinforcement. However, the value of a reinforcer depends on many factors, and the strength of motivation may be different in different students.

In Maslow's human needs theory, which is based on a hierarchy of needs, people must satisfy their lower-level (deficiency) needs before they will be motivated to try to satisfy their higher-level (growth) needs. Maslow's concept of the need for self-actualization, the highest need, is defined as the desire to become everything one is capable of becoming.

The Intentional TEACHER

USING WHAT YOU KNOW about Motivation to Improve Teaching and Learning

Intentional teachers know that, although students might be motivated by different things and to varying degrees, every student is motivated. They understand that many elements of motivation can be influenced by the teacher, and they capitalize on their ability to unearth and direct student motivation. They provide instruction that helps students find meaning in learning and in taking pride in their own accomplishments.

1 What do I expect my students to know and be able to do at the end of this lesson? How does this contribute to course objectives and to students' needs to become capable individuals?

Intentional teachers plan how they will support student motivation. Think about how you will discover and sustain your students' drive to participate in learning. Consider principles of motivation in your long- and short-term planning. You might review major findings on motivation and jot down some guiding ideas on an index card that you clip to your plan book.

2 What knowledge, skills, needs, and interests do my students have that must be taken into account in my lesson?

Motivation varies by student, situation, and domain. Determine your students' current motivation. You can gather information about your students' motivation from a variety of sources. For instance, you could observe the students during informal conversations and during instruction, or ask them to write journal entries on such prompts as "What accounts for your score on this test?" You could analyze their answers and your observations to gather information about three areas of motivation: (1) Where do students seem to be functioning in terms of Maslow's hierarchy of needs? (2) Do students seem to be seeking success or avoiding failure? (3) Do students use internal or external causal attributions? Stable or unstable? Controllable or uncontrollable? (4) Are students primarily oriented toward mastery, or learning, or only toward performance, or grades?

3 What do I know about the content, child development, learning, motivation, and effective teaching strategies that I can use to accomplish my objectives?

For motivation to be high, students need to perceive that with effort, success is possible. Provide tasks that require effort but allow students to see that success is within reach. For example, imagine that you check your grade book at the end of the first marking period and find that some of your students have earned D's and F's across the board but that others have a string of apparently easy A's. You could begin your quest to improve instruction by meeting with students individually. You might ask how they earned their grades and what they expect to earn in the future. Based on your conversations, you could develop research projects at the student's correct level of difficulty and devise careful contracts so that students who have yet to achieve see that success is possible.

Attribution theory seeks to understand people's explanations for their success or failure. A central assumption is that people will attempt to maintain a positive self-image; so when good things happen, people attribute them to their own abilities, whereas they tend to attribute negative events to factors beyond their control. Locus of control might be internal (success or failure is based on personal effort or ability) or external (success or failure is the result of luck or task difficulty). Students who are self-regulated learners perform better than those who are externally motivated. Self-regulated learners consciously plan and monitor their learning and thus retain more.

Expectancy theory holds that a person's motivation to achieve something depends on the product of that person's estimation of his or her chance of success and the value he or she places on success. Motivation should be at a maximum at moderate levels of probability of success. An important educational implication is that learning tasks should be neither too easy nor too difficult.

How Can Achievement Motivation Be Enhanced?

Teachers can emphasize learning goals and positive or empowering attributions. Students with learning goals see the purpose of school as gaining knowledge and competence;

Some students display a performance orientation instead of the more useful learning orientation. Help students shift their focus from completion to mastery by emphasizing the practical importance of content. Deemphasize grades and rewards. For example, imagine that your secondary students seem overly concerned with their scores on essays and the grading curve. You might employ portfolio assessments and require students to analyze their growth over time. Students could grade themselves on improvement rather than on how their work compares to that of their peers.

Praise needs to be used effectively. Be certain that your praise is sincere, specific, and contingent on students' behavior. Try to reserve your praise for good performance, to focus on the behavior and not the student, and to be specific about what constitutes good performance: "Jamal, I like the way you blended those two colors. That really adds depth to the painting. It looks real!"

4 What instructional materials, technology, assistance, and other resources are available to help accomplish my objectives?

Always be on the lookout for additional sources of motivation, intrinsic as well as extrinsic. For example, bring in parents or other speakers with life experience relevant to your lesson to excite students about the content. Students will be more interested in trigonometry if they hear a former artilleryman explain how he used trig every day in the army, or they might be more interested in persuasive essays if they hear a volunteer for Amnesty International describe how she writes letters to attempt to gain freedom for prisoners of conscience.

5 How will I plan to assess students' progress toward my objectives?

Students need to develop accurate attributions for their success. Observe your students to note whether they perceive that their efforts contribute to their learning. Intervene when students' attributions are inaccurate. Step up your efforts to help students set goals, take responsibility for their progress, and evaluate their work. Together, you and your students might devise a grading system that rewards performance, effort, and improvement.

6 How will I respond if individual children or the class as a whole are not on track toward success? What is my back-up plan?

Maslow asserted that the goal of psychological health is self-actualization. Review your instruction and your students' learning to determine the extent to which you and the students are meeting the broad span of their needs and reaching their full potential. Consider the following. What evidence is there that (1) the environment is safe and comfortable and encourages students to take risks, (2) instruction is meaningful and lively, and (3) students are active participants in analyzing their growth and setting plans?

these students tend to have higher motivation to learn than do students with the performance goals of positive judgments and good grades. Teachers can use special programs such as attribution training to help students out of learned helplessness, in which students feel that they are doomed to fail despite their actions. Teachers' expectations significantly affect students' motivation and achievement. Teachers can communicate positive expectations that students can learn and can take steps to reduce anxiety.

How Can Teachers Increase Students' Motivation to Learn?

An incentive is a reinforcer that people can expect to receive if they perform a specific behavior. Intrinsic incentives are aspects of certain tasks that in themselves have enough value to motivate students to do the tasks on their own. Extrinsic incentives include grades, gold stars, and other rewards. Teachers can enhance intrinsic motivation by arousing students' interest, maintaining curiosity, using a variety of presentation modes, and letting students set their own goals. Ways to offer extrinsic incentives include stating clear expectations; giving clear, immediate, and frequent feedback; and increasing the value and availability of rewards. Classroom rewards include praise, which is most effective when it is contingent, specific, and credible.

KEY TERMS

Review the following key terms from the chapter.

achievement motivation 305	growth needs 299
attribution theory 300	intrinsic incentive 312
contingent praise 320	learned helplessness 307
deficiency needs 299	learning goals 306
expectancy theory 304	locus of control 301
expectancy–valence model 304	motivation 297
extrinsic incentive 313	performance goals 306
feedback 318	self-actualization 300

SELF-ASSESSMENT: PRACTICING *for* LICENSURE

Directions: The chapter-opening vignette addresses indicators that are often assessed in state licensure exams. Re-read the chapter-opening vignette, and then respond to the following questions.

1. According to behavioral learning theorists, why are Cal Lewis's students motivated to learn about the Constitutional Convention?

a. to obtain reinforcers
b. to satisfy growth needs
c. to eliminate deficiency needs
d. to maximize expectancy effects

2. Mr. Lewis's students see the purpose of lessons about the Constitutional Convention as a way to gain information about the history of the United States. What type of goal orientation is this?

a. performance goal
b. learning goal
c. expectancy goal
d. self-regulated goal

3. Beth Andrews, a shy girl in Mr. Lewis's class, proposes elements of the Bill of Rights to the convention members. If Beth has an internal locus of control, she is most likely to attribute her successful presentation to which of the following factors?

a. the presentation requirements being easy
b. favoritism by the teacher
c. careful preparation
d. good luck

4. Mr. Lewis wants his students to work hard regardless of their ability level or task difficulty. What type of attributions will he attempt to instill in his students?

a. internal-stable
b. internal-unstable
c. external-stable
d. external-unstable

5. Under what circumstances is it most important for Mr. Lewis to avoid the use of external incentives?

a. when students are doing challenging work
b. when the task communicates feedback about students' competence
c. when students are motivated to do the work without extrinsic incentives
d. when students have experienced a great deal of failure

6. Analyze Mr. Lewis's lesson and his students' willingness to participate from the four theories of motivation presented in the chapter: behavioral, human needs, attribution, and expectancy.

7. Describe ways in which a teacher can increase students' motivation to learn.

PEARSON

myeducationlab™

Where the Classroom Comes to Life

Now go to **www.myeducationlab.com** to:

- take a Pretest to assess your initial comprehension of chapter content;
- study chapter content with your individualized Study Plan;
- take a Posttest to assess your understanding of chapter content;
- practice your teaching skills with Building Teaching Skills exercises; and
- build a deeper, more applied understanding of chapter content with Homework and Exercises.

CHAPTER 11

Effective Learning Environments

chapter OUTLINE

The bell rang outside of Julia Cavalho's tenth-grade English class. The sound was still echoing in the hall when Ms. Cavalho started her lesson.

"Today," she began, "you will become thieves. Worse than thieves. Thieves steal only your money or your property. You—" (she looked around the class and paused for emphasis) "—will steal something far more valuable. You will steal an author's style. An author builds his or her style, word by word, sentence by sentence, over many years. Stealing an author's style is like stealing a work of art that someone took years to create. It's despicable, but you're going to do it."

During her speech the students sat in rapt attention. Two students, Mark and Gloria, slunk in late. Mark made a funny "Oops, I'm late" face and did an exaggerated tiptoe to his desk. Ms. Cavalho ignored both of them, as did the class. She continued her lesson.

"To whom are you going to do this dirty deed? Papa Hemingway, of course. Hemingway of the short, punchy sentence. Hemingway of the almost excessive attention to physical detail. You've read *The Old Man and the Sea*. You've read parts of *The Sun Also Rises* and *For Whom the Bell Tolls*."

While Ms. Cavalho talked, Mark made an exaggerated show of getting out his books. He whispered to a neighboring student. Without stopping her lesson, Ms. Cavalho moved near Mark. He stopped whispering and paid attention.

"Today you will become Hemingway. You will steal his words, his pace, his meter, his similes, his metaphors, and put them to work in your own stories."

Ms. Cavalho had students review elements of Hemingway's style, which the class had studied before.

"Everyone think for a moment. How would Hemingway describe an old woman going up the stairs at the end of a long day's work? Mai, what do you think?"

Mai gave her short description of the old woman.

"Sounds great to me. I like your use of very short sentences and physical description. Any other ideas? Kevin?"

Ms. Cavalho let several students give Hemingway-style descriptions, using them as opportunities to reinforce her main points.

"In a moment," she said, "you're going to get your chance to become Ernest Hemingway. As usual, you'll be working in your writing response groups. Before we start, however, let's go over our rules about effective group work. Who can tell me what they are?"

The students volunteered several rules: Respect others, explain your ideas, be sure everyone participates, stand up for your opinion, keep voices low.

"All right," said Ms. Cavalho. "When I say begin, I'd like you to move your desks together and start planning your compositions. Ready? Begin."

The students moved their desks together smoothly and quickly and got right to work. During the transition, Ms. Cavalho called Mark and Gloria to her desk to discuss their lateness. Gloria had a good excuse, but Mark was developing a pattern of lateness and disruptiveness.

"Mark," said Ms. Cavalho, "I'm concerned about your lateness and your behavior in class. I've spoken to some of your other teachers, and they say you're behaving even worse in their classes than you do in mine. Please come here after school, and we'll see if we can come up with a solution to this problem."

Mark returned to his group and got to work. Ms. Cavalho circulated among the groups, giving encouragement to students who were working well. When she saw two girls who were goofing off, she moved close to them and put her hand on one girl's shoulder while looking at the plan for her composition. "Good start," she said. "Let's see how far you can get with this by the end of the period."

The students worked in a controlled but excited way through the end of the period, thoroughly enjoying "stealing" from Hemingway. The classroom sounded like a beehive with busy, involved students sharing ideas, reading drafts to each other, and editing each other's compositions. At the end of the day, Mark returned to Ms. Cavalho's classroom.

"Mark," she said, "we need to do something about your lateness and your clowning in class. How would you suggest that we solve this problem?"

"Gloria was late, too," Mark protested.

"We're not talking about Gloria. We're talking about you. You are responsible for your own behavior."

"OK, OK, I promise I'll be on time."

"That's not good enough. We've had this conversation before. We need a different plan this time. I know you can succeed in this class, but you're making it hard on yourself as well as disrupting your classmates.

"Let's try an experiment," Ms. Cavalho went on. "Each day, I'd like you to rate your own behavior. I'll do the same. If we both agree at the end of each week that you've been on time and appropriately behaved, fine. If not, I'll need to call your parents and see whether we can make another plan. Are you willing to give it a try?"

"OK, I guess so."

"Great. I'm expecting to see a new Mark starting tomorrow. I know you won't let me down!"

USING *your* EXPERIENCE

CRITICAL THINKING What methods of classroom management does Ms. Cavalho use? What potential problems is she preventing?

CREATIVE THINKING Suppose Mark continues to be late for class. Plan a conference with his parents. What are the goals? How will they be implemented?

CRITICAL AND CREATIVE THINKING Analyze two variables, grade level and classroom management strategies, in a matrix. Using Ms. Cavalho's classroom as a starter, create this matrix with grade level on the horizontal (e.g., elementary, middle, and high school), and then brainstorm classroom management strategies down the vertical column. Finally, check off which management strategies are influential at different grade levels.

WHAT IS AN EFFECTIVE LEARNING ENVIRONMENT?

Providing an effective learning environment includes strategies that teachers use to create a positive, productive classroom experience. Often called **classroom management,** strategies for providing effective learning environments include not only preventing and responding to misbehavior but also, more important, using class time well, creating an atmosphere that is conducive to interest and inquiry, and permitting activities that engage students' minds and imaginations. A class with no behavior problems can by no means be assumed to be a well-managed class.

INTASC

5 Classroom Motivation and Management
6 Communication Skills

The most effective approaches to classroom management are those discussed in Chapters 6 through 10. Students who are participating in well-structured activities that engage their interests, who are highly motivated to learn, and who are working on tasks that are challenging yet within their capabilities rarely pose any serious management problems. The vignette involving Ms. Cavalho illustrates this. She has a well-managed class not because she behaves like a drill sergeant, but because she teaches interesting lessons, engages students' imaginations and energies, makes efficient use of time, and communicates a sense of purpose, high expectations, and contagious enthusiasm. However, even a well-managed class is sure to contain individual students who will misbehave. While Ms. Cavalho's focus is on preventing behavior problems, she is also ready to intervene when necessary to see that students' behaviors are within acceptable limits. For some students a glance, physical proximity, or a hand on the shoulder is enough. For others, consequences might be necessary. Even in these cases, Ms. Cavalho does not let behavior issues disrupt her lesson or her students' learning activities.

This chapter focuses on the creation of effective learning environments (also known as classroom management) and on discipline. Creating an effective learning environment involves organizing classroom activities, instruction, and the physical classroom to provide for effective use of time, to create a happy, productive learning environment, and to minimize disruptions. **Discipline** refers to methods used to prevent behavior problems or to respond to existing behavior problems so as to reduce their occurrence in the future (see Charles, 2008; Levin & Nolan, 2007; Marzano, 2003).

There is no magic or charisma that makes a teacher an effective classroom manager. Setting up an effective learning environment is a matter of knowing a set of techniques that any teacher can learn and apply. This chapter takes an approach to classroom management and discipline that emphasizes prevention of misbehavior, on the theory that effective instruction itself is the best means of avoiding discipline problems. In the past, creating an effective learning environment has often been seen as a matter of dealing with individual student misbehaviors (Emmer et al., 2006; Evertson, Emmer, & Worsham, 2006). Teachers who present interesting, well-organized lessons, who use incentives for learning effectively, who accommodate their instruction to students' levels of preparation, and who plan and manage their own time effectively will have few discipline problems to deal with. Still, every teacher, no matter how effective, will encounter discipline problems sometimes, and this chapter also presents means of handling these problems when they arise.

classroom management
Methods used to organize classroom activities, instruction, physical structure, and other features to make effective use of time, to create a happy and productive learning environment, and to minimize behavior problems and other disruptions.

discipline
Methods used to prevent behavior problems from occurring or to respond to behavior problems so as to reduce their occurrence in the future.

WHAT IS THE IMPACT OF TIME ON LEARNING?

Obviously, if no time is spent teaching a subject, students will not learn it. However, within the usual range of time allocated to instruction, how much difference does time make? This has been a focus of considerable research (see Adelman, Haslam, & Pringle, 1996; National Education Commission on Time and Learning, 1994).

INTASC

7 Instructional Planning Skills

Although it is clear that more time spent in instruction has a positive impact on student achievement, the effects of additional time are often modest or inconsistent (Gijselaers & Schmidt, 1995; Karweit, 1989). In particular, the typical differences in lengths of school days and school years among different districts have only a minor impact on student achievement (see Karweit, 1981; Walberg, 1988). What seems to be more important is how time is used in class. **Engaged time,** or **time on-task,** the number of minutes actually spent learning, is the time measure that is most frequently found to contribute to learning (e.g., Marks, 2000; Rowan, Correnti, & Miller, 2002). In other words, the most important aspect of time is the one that is under the direct control of the teacher: the organization and use of time in the classroom (Jones & Jones, 2007; Marzano, 2003).

Using Allocated Time for Instruction

Time is a limited resource in schools. A typical U.S. school is in session about 6 hours a day for 180 days each year. Time for educational activities can be expanded by means of homework assignments or (for some students) participation in after-school activities or summer school, but the total time available for instruction is essentially set. Out of these 6 hours (or so) must come time for teaching a variety of subjects plus time for lunch, recess, and physical education; transitions between classes; announcements; and so on. In a 40- to 60-minute period in a particular subject, many quite different factors reduce the time available for instruction. Figure 11.1 illustrates how time scheduled for mathematics instruction in 12 second- to fifth-grade classes observed by Karweit and Slavin (1981) was whittled away.

The classes that Karweit and Slavin (1981) observed were in schools in and around a rural Maryland town. Overall, the classes were well organized and businesslike, with dedicated and hardworking teachers. Students were generally well behaved and respectful of authority. However, even in these very good schools, the average student spent only 60 percent of the time scheduled for mathematics instruction actually learning mathematics. First of all, about 20 class days were lost to such activities as standardized testing, school events, field trips, and teacher absences. On days when instruction was given, class time was lost because of late starts and noninstructional activities such as discussions of upcoming events, announcements, passing out of materials, and disciplining of students. Finally, even when math was being taught, many students were not actually engaged in

engaged time
Time students spend actually learning; same as *time on-task.*

time on-task
Time students spend actively engaged in learning the task at hand.

FIGURE 11.1 Where Does the Time Go?
Observations of elementary school mathematics classes showed that the time students actually spend learning in class is only about 60 percent of the time allocated for instruction.

Based on data from N. L. Karweit and R. E. Slavin, "Measurement and Modeling Choices in Studies of Time and Learning," *American Educational Research Journal, 18*(2).

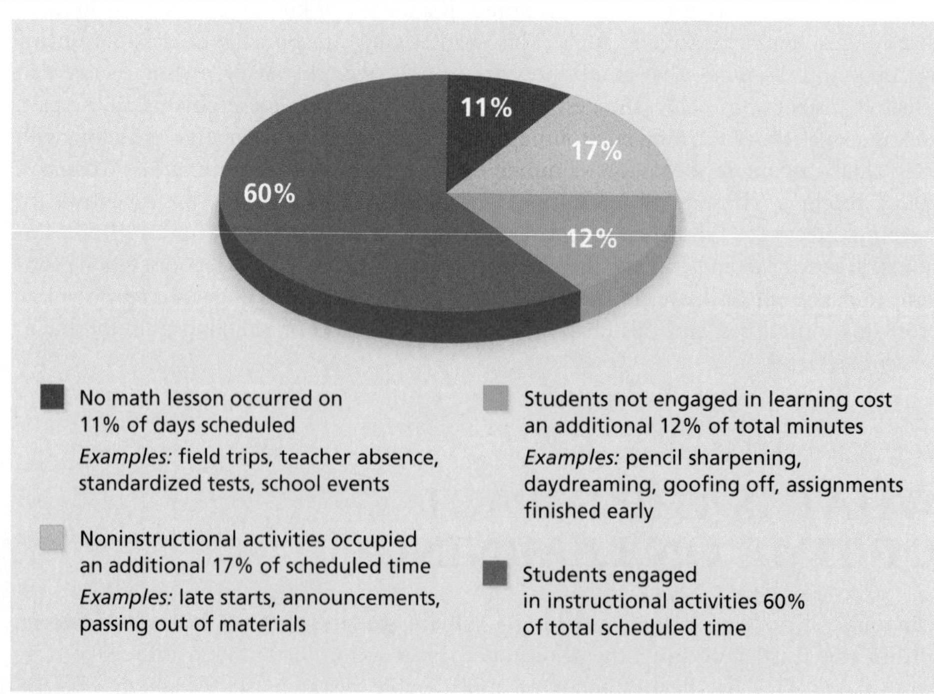

11%
17%
60%
12%
No math lesson occurred on 11% of days scheduled
Examples: field trips, teacher absence, standardized tests, school events
Noninstructional activities occupied an additional 17% of scheduled time
Examples: late starts, announcements, passing out of materials
Students not engaged in learning cost an additional 12% of total minutes
Examples: pencil sharpening, daydreaming, goofing off, assignments finished early
Students engaged in instructional activities 60% of total scheduled time

the instructional activity. Some were daydreaming during lecture or seatwork times, goofing off, or sharpening pencils; others had nothing to do, either because they were finished with their assigned work or because they had not yet been assigned a task. The 60 percent figure estimated by Karweit and Slavin is, if anything, an overestimate. In a much larger study, Weinstein and Mignano (1993) found that elementary school students spent only about one-third of their time engaged in learning tasks (see also Hong, 2001; Meek, 2003).

A term for available instructional time is **allocated time:** the time during which students have an opportunity to learn. When the teacher is lecturing, students can learn by paying attention. When students have written assignments or other tasks, they can learn by doing them. A discussion follows of some common ways in which allocated time can be maximized (see Jones & Jones, 2007).

Preventing Lost Time One way in which much instructional time disappears is through losses of entire days or periods. Many of these losses are inevitable because of such things as standardized testing days and snow days, and we certainly would not want to abolish important field trips or school assemblies simply to get in a few more periods of instruction. However, frequent losses of instructional periods interrupt the flow of instruction and can ultimately deprive students of sufficient time to master the curriculum.

Making good use of all classroom time is less a matter of squeezing out a few more minutes or hours of instruction each year than of communicating to students that learning is an important business that is worth their time and effort. If a teacher finds excuses not to teach, students might learn that learning is not a serious enterprise. In studying an outstandingly effective inner-city Baltimore elementary school, Salganik (1980) described a third-grade teacher who took her class to the school library, which she found locked. She sent a student for the key, and while the class waited, the teacher whispered to her students, "Let's work on our doubles. Nine plus nine? Six plus six?" The class whispered the answers back in unison. Did a couple of minutes working on addition facts increase the students' achievement? Of course not. But it probably did help to develop a perception that school is for learning, not for marking time.

Preventing Late Starts and Early Finishes A surprising amount of allocated instructional time is lost because the teacher does not start teaching at the beginning of the period. This can be a particular problem in self-contained elementary classes, in which there are no bells or fixed schedules to structure the period. It is also a problem in

allocated time
Time during which students have the opportunity to learn.

Teachers' time for instruction is limited by the amount of time used for routine management concerns such as taking attendance. As a teacher, how will you prevent loss of instruction time?

departmentalized secondary schools, where teachers might spend a long time dealing with late students or other problems before starting the lesson. A crisp, on-time start to a lesson is important for setting a purposive tone to instruction. If students know that a teacher does not start on time, they might be lackadaisical about getting to class on time; this attitude makes future on-time starts increasingly difficult. In Ms. Cavalho's class, students know that if they are late, they will miss something interesting, fun, and important. As a result, almost all of them are in class and ready to learn when the bell rings.

Teachers can also shortchange students if they stop teaching before the end of the period. This is less damaging than a ragged or late start but is still worth avoiding by planning more instruction than you think you'll need, in case you finish the lesson early.

Preventing Interruptions One important cause of lost allocated time for instruction is interruptions. Interruptions may be externally imposed, such as announcements or the need to sign forms sent from the principal's office; or they may be caused by teachers or students themselves. Interruptions not only directly cut into the time for instruction but also break the momentum of the lesson, which reduces students' attention to the task at hand.

Avoiding interruptions takes planning. For example, some teachers put a "Do not disturb—learning in progress!" sign on the door to inform would-be interrupters to come back later. One teacher wore a special hat during small-group lessons to remind her other second-graders not to interrupt her during that time. Rather than signing forms or dealing with other "administrivia" at once, some teachers keep a box where students and others can put any forms and then deal with them after the lesson is over.

Anything the teacher can postpone doing until after a lesson should be postponed. For example, if the teacher has started a lesson and a student walks in late, the teacher should go on with the lesson and deal with the tardiness issue later.

Handling Routine Procedures Some teachers spend too much time on simple classroom routines. For example, some elementary teachers spend many minutes getting students ready for lunch or dismissal because they call students by name, one at a time. This is unnecessary. Early in the school year, many teachers establish a routine that only when the entire table (or row) is quiet and ready to go are students called to line up. Lining up for lunch then takes seconds, not minutes.

Other procedures must also become routine for students. They must know, for example, when they may go to the washroom or sharpen a pencil and not ask to do these things at other times. A teacher may collect papers by having students pass them to the front or to the left or by having table monitors collect the table's papers. Distribution of materials must also be planned for. Exactly how these tasks are done is less important than that students know clearly what they are to do. Many teachers assign regular classroom helpers to take care of distribution and collection of papers, taking messages to the office, erasing the blackboard, and other routine tasks that are annoying interruptions for teachers but that students love to do. Teachers should use student power as much as possible.

Minimizing Time Spent on Discipline Methods of disciplining students are discussed at length later in this chapter. However, one aspect of disciplining should be mentioned at this point. Whenever possible—which is almost always—disciplinary statements or actions should not interrupt the flow of the lesson. A sharp glance, silently moving close to an offending student, or a hand signal, such as putting finger to lips to remind a student to be silent, is usually effective for the kind of minor behavior problems that teachers must constantly deal with, and they allow the lesson to proceed without interruption. For example, Ms. Cavalho could have interrupted her lesson to scold Mark and Gloria, but that would have wasted time and disrupted the concentration and focus of the whole class. If students need talking to about discipline problems, the time to do it is after the lesson or after school, not in the middle of a lesson. If Diana and Martin are talking during a quiet reading time instead of working, it would be better to say, "Diana and Martin, see me at three o'clock," than to launch into an on-the-spot speech about the importance of being on-task during seatwork times.

CONNECTIONS
For more information about the importance of time use and time management in effective teaching, see Chapter 9, page 265.

Using Engaged Time Effectively

"When I said you two needed to get engaged, this isn't what I had in mind!"

Engaged time (or time on-task) is the time individual students actually spend doing assigned work. Allocated time and engaged time differ in that allocated time refers to the opportunity for the entire class to engage in learning activities, whereas engaged time may be different for each student, depending on a student's attentiveness and willingness to work. Strategies for maximizing student time on-task are discussed in the following sections. Several studies have found teacher training programs based on principles presented in the following sections to increase student engagement and, in some cases, learning (Good & Brophy, 2003; Jones & Jones, 2007).

Teaching Engaging Lessons The best way to increase students' time on-task is to teach lessons that are so interesting, engaging, and relevant to students' interests that students will pay attention and eagerly do what is asked of them (Weinstein & Mignano, 2003). Part of this strategy calls for the teacher to emphasize active, rapidly paced instruction with varied modes of presentation and frequent opportunities for student participation and to deemphasize independent seatwork, especially unsupervised seatwork (as in follow-up time in elementary reading classes). Research has consistently shown that student engagement is much higher when the teacher is teaching than during individual seatwork (Evertson & Harris, 1992). Giving students many opportunities to participate actively in lessons is also associated with greater learning (Finn & Cox, 1992), and engaged time is much higher in well-structured cooperative learning programs than in independent seatwork (Slavin, 1990).

Maintaining Momentum Maintaining momentum during a lesson is a key to keeping task engagement high. *Momentum* refers to the avoidance of interruptions or slowdowns (Kounin, 1970). In a class that maintains good momentum, students always have something to do and, once started working, are not interrupted. Anyone who has tried to write a term paper only to be interrupted by telephone calls, knocks on the door, and other disturbances knows that these interruptions cause much more damage to concentration and progress than the amount of time they take.

Kounin (1970) gives the following example of teacher-caused slowdowns and interruptions:

> The teacher is just starting a reading group at the reading circle while the rest of the children are engaged in seatwork with workbooks. She sat in front of the reading group and asked, "All right, who can tell me the name of our next chapter?" Before a child was called on to answer, she looked toward the children at seatwork, saying: "Let's wait until the people in Group Two are settled and working." (Actually most were writing in their workbooks.) She then looked at John, who was in the seatwork group, naggingly asking, "Did you find your pencil?" John answered something which was inaudible. The teacher got up from her seat, saying, "I'd like to know what you did with it." Pause for about two seconds. "Did you eat it?" Another pause. "What happened to it? What color was it? You can't do your work without it." The teacher then went to her desk to get a pencil to give to John, saying, "I'll get you a pencil. Make sure the pencil is here tomorrow morning. And don't tell me you lost that one too. And make it a new one, and see that it's sharpened." (p. 104)

This teacher destroyed the momentum of a reading lesson by spending more than a minute dealing with a behavior that could easily have been ignored. Of course, during this interchange, the entire class—both the reading group and the seatwork group—were off-task; but what is worse, they required much more time to get resettled and back to work after the incident.

Kounin found momentum to be strongly related to total time on-task, and Brophy and Evertson (1976) and Anderson, Evertson, and Brophy (1979) found momentum to be related to student achievement.

CONNECTIONS
For more information about arousing student interest and focusing student attention, see Chapter 7, page 207, and Chapter 6, page 160.

CONNECTIONS
For more information about active learning, see Chapter 8, page 247.

INTASC

4 Multiple Instructional Strategies

Maintaining Smoothness of Instruction *Smoothness* is another term Kounin (1970) uses to refer to continued focus on a meaningful sequence of instruction. Smooth instruction avoids jumping without transitions from topic to topic or from the lesson to other activities, which produces "jarring breaks in the activity flow" (Kounin, 1970, p. 97). For example,

> The teacher was conducting a recitation with a subgroup. She was walking toward a child who was reciting when she passed by the fish bowl. She suddenly stopped walking toward the boy, and stopped at the fish bowl, saying: "Oh my, I forgot to feed the fish!" She then got some fish food from a nearby shelf and started to feed the fish, saying: "My, see how hungry it is." She then turned to a girl, saying: "See, Margaret, you forgot to feed the fish. You can see how hungry it is. See how quickly it comes up to eat." (Kounin, 1970, pp. 98–99)

This example illustrates how smoothness and momentum are related. The teacher jumped from her lesson to housekeeping to (unnecessary) disciplining, interrupting one student's recitation and making it impossible for the other students to focus on the lesson. As with momentum, smoothness was found to be strongly associated with student time on-task (Kounin, 1970) and achievement (Anderson et al., 1979; Brophy & Evertson, 1976).

Managing Transitions Transitions are changes from one activity to another; for example, from lecture to seatwork, from subject to subject, or from lesson to lunch. Elementary school classes have been found to have an average of 31 major transitions a day, occupying 15 percent of class time (Burns, 1984). Transitions are the seams of class management at which classroom order is most likely to come apart; Anderson and colleagues (1979) and Evertson, Emmer, and Brophy (1980) found that teachers' efficiency at managing transitions between activities was positively related to their students' achievement.

Following are three rules for the management of transitions:

CERTIFICATION POINTER

You may be asked on your teacher certification test to discuss why it is important for a teacher to plan carefully for transitions and describe what can happen if transitions are not implemented with care.

1. When making a transition, the teacher should give a clear signal to which the students have been taught to respond. For example, in the elementary grades, some teachers use a bell or a hand signal to indicate to students that they should immediately be quiet and listen to instructions.

2. Before the transition is made, students must be certain about what they are to do when the signal is given. For example, a teacher might say, "When I say 'Go,' I want you all to put your books away and get out the compositions you started yesterday. Is everyone ready? All right, go!" When giving instructions to students to begin independent seatwork, the teacher can help them get started with the activity before letting them work independently, as in the following example:

> *Teacher:* Today we are going to find guide words for different pages in the dictionary. Everyone should have an assignment sheet with the words on it and a dictionary. Class, hold up your assignment sheet. [They do.] Now hold up your dictionary. [They do.] Good. Now turn to page eighty-two. [The teacher walks around to see that everyone does so.] Look at the top of the page, and put your finger on the first guide word. [The teacher walks around to check on this.] Class, what is the first guide word?
>
> *Class:* Carrot!
>
> *Teacher:* Good. The first guide word is carrot. Now look to the right on the same page. Class, what word do you see there?
>
> *Class:* Carve!
>
> *Teacher:* Right. The guide words are carrot and carve. Now turn to page five hundred fifty-five and find the guide words. [Students do this.] Class, what is the first guide word on page five hundred fifty-five?
>
> *Class:* Scheme!
>
> *Teacher:* Class, what is the second guide word?
>
> *Class:* Scissors!
>
> *Teacher:* Great! Now do the first problem on your assignment sheet by yourselves, and then check with a partner to see if you agree.

VIDEO HOMEWORK EXERCISE
Making Transitions

Go to **www.myeducationlab.com** and, in the Homework and Exercises section for Chapter 11 of this text, access the video entitled "Making Transitions." Watch the video and complete the homework questions that accompany it, saving your work or transmitting it to your professor as required.

The teacher will then check whether all or almost all students have the first item correct before telling them to complete the worksheet. The idea, of course, is to make sure that students know exactly what they are to do before they start doing it.

3. Make transitions all at once. Students should be trained to make transitions as a group, rather than one student at a time (Charles, 2008). The teacher should usually give directions to the class as a whole or to well-defined groups: "Class, I want you all to put away your laboratory materials and prepare for dismissal as quickly and quietly as you can. . . . I see that Table Three is quiet and ready. Table Three, please line up quietly. Table Six, line up. Table One . . . Table Four. Everyone else may line up quietly. Let's go!"

Maintaining Group Focus during Lessons Maintaining group focus means using classroom organization strategies and questioning techniques that ensure that all students in the class stay involved in the lesson, even when only one student is called on by the teacher. Two principal components of Kounin's concept of maintaining group focus were found to be significantly related to students' on-task behavior: accountability and group alerting.

Kounin (1970) uses the term **accountability** to mean "the degree to which the teacher holds the children accountable and responsible for their task performances during recitation sessions" (p. 119). Examples of tactics for increasing accountability are using choral responses, having all students hold up their work so the teacher can see it, circulating among the students to see what they are doing, and drawing other children into the performance of one child (e.g., "I want you all to watch what Suzanne is doing so you can tell me whether you agree or disagree with her answer"). Ms. Cavalho increased involvement and accountability by having all students prepare a Hemingway-like description and only then asking for a few of them to be read.

The idea behind these tactics is to maintain the involvement of all students in all parts of the lesson. A study of third- and fourth-graders found that students raised their hands an average of once every 6 minutes and gave an answer only once every 15 minutes, with some students hardly ever participating (Potter, 1977). This is not enough participation to ensure student attention. Teachers should be concerned not only about drawing all students into class activities but also about avoiding activities that relegate most students to the role of spectator for long periods. For example, a very common teaching error is to have one or two students work out a lengthy problem on the chalkboard or read an extended passage while the rest of the class has nothing to do. Such methods waste the time of much of the class, break the momentum of the lesson, and leave the door open for misbehavior (Gump, 1982).

Group alerting refers to questioning strategies that are designed to keep all students on their toes during a lecture or discussion. One example of group alerting is creating suspense before calling on a student by saying, "Given triangle ABC, if we know the measures of sides A and B and of angle AB, what else can we find out about the triangle? . . . [Pause] . . . Maria?" Note that this keeps the whole class thinking until Maria's name is called. The opposite effect would have been created by saying, "Maria, given triangle ABC . . . ," because only Maria would have been alerted. Calling on students in a random order is another example of group alerting, as is letting students know that they may be asked questions about the preceding reciter's answers. For example, the teacher might follow up Maria's answer with "What is the name of the postulate that Maria used? . . . Ralph?"

Maintaining Group Focus during Seatwork During times when students are doing seatwork and the teacher is available to work with them, it is important to monitor the seatwork activities and to informally check individual students' work. That is, the teacher should circulate among the students' desks to see how they are doing. This allows the teacher to identify any problems students are having before they waste seatwork time practicing errors or giving up in frustration. If students are engaged in cooperative groupwork, students can check each other's work, but the teacher still needs to check frequently with each group to see that the students are on the right track.

Seatwork times provide excellent opportunities for providing individual help to students who are struggling to keep up with the class, but teachers should resist the temptation to work too long with an individual student. Interactions with students during seatwork

accountability
The degree to which people are held responsible for their task performances or decision outcomes.

group alerting
Questioning strategies that encourage all students to pay attention during lectures and discussions.

should be as brief as possible because if the teacher gets tied down with any one student, the rest of the class may drift off-task or run into problems of their own.

Withitness **Withitness** is another term coined by Kounin (1970). It describes teachers' actions that indicate awareness of students' behavior at all times. Kounin calls this awareness "having eyes in the back of one's head." Teachers who are with-it can respond immediately to student misbehavior and know who started what. Teachers who lack withitness can make the error of scolding the wrong student, as in the following instance:

> Lucy and John, who were sitting at the same table as Jane, started to whisper. Robert watched this, and he too got into the act. Then Jane giggled and said something to John. Then Mary leaned over and whispered to Jane. At this point, the teacher said, "Mary and Jane, stop that!" (adapted from Kounin, 1970, p. 80)

By responding only to Mary and Jane, who were the last to get involved in the whispering and giggling incident, the teacher indicated that she did not know what was going on. A single incident of this kind might make little difference, but after many such incidents, students recognize the teacher's tendency to respond inappropriately to their behavior.

Another example of a lack of withitness is responding too late to a sequence of misbehavior. Lucy and John's whispering could have been easily nipped in the bud, perhaps with simply a glance or a finger to the lips. By the time the whispering had escalated to giggling and spread to several students, a full stop in the lesson was needed to rectify the situation.

A major component of withitness is scanning the class frequently and establishing eye contact with individual students. Several studies have found that more effective classroom managers frequently scan the classroom visually, to monitor the pace of activity as well as individual students' behaviors (Brooks, 1985; Evertson & Emmer, 1982). Effective classroom managers have the ability to interpret and act on the mood of the class as a whole. They notice when students are beginning to fidget or are otherwise showing signs of flagging attention, and they act on this information to change activities to recapture student engagement (Levin & Nolan, 2007).

Overlapping **Overlapping** refers to the teacher's ability to attend to interruptions or behavior problems while continuing a lesson or other instructional activity. For example, one teacher was teaching a lesson on reading comprehension when he saw a student looking at a book that was unrelated to the lesson. Without interrupting his lesson, the teacher walked over to the student, took her book, closed it, and put it on her desk, all while continuing to speak to the class. This took care of the student's misbehavior without slowing the momentum of the lesson; the rest of the class hardly noticed that the event occurred. Similarly, Ms. Cavalho squelched a whispering incident just by moving closer to the whispering students while continuing her lesson.

Another example of a teacher doing a good job of overlapping is as follows:

> The teacher is at the reading circle and Lucy is reading aloud while standing. Johnny, who was doing seatwork at his desk, walks up toward the teacher, holding his workbook. The teacher glances at Johnny, then looks back at Lucy, nodding at Lucy, as Lucy continues to read aloud. The teacher remains seated and takes Johnny's workbook. She turns to Lucy, saying, "That was a hard word, Lucy, and you pronounced it right." She checks about three more answers to Johnny's book saying, "That's fine, you can go ahead and do the next page now," and resumes looking at the reading book as Lucy continues reading. (Kounin, 1970, p. 84)

Johnny's interruption of the reading group might have been avoided altogether by a good classroom manager, who would have assigned enough work to keep all students productively busy during reading circle time and given clear instructions on what they were to do when they finished their seatwork. For example, Johnny's work could have been checked by a partner or teammate. However, interruptions are sometimes unavoidable, and the ability to keep the main activity going while handling them is strongly related to overall classroom order (Copeland, 1983; Kounin, 1970) and to achievement (Anderson et al., 1979; Brophy & Evertson, 1976).

CERTIFICATION POINTER

For your teacher certification test you may be asked to make suggestions for helping students stay on task in a particular case.

withitness
The degree to which the teacher is aware of and responsive to student behavior at all times.

overlapping
A teacher's ability to respond to behavior problems without interrupting a classroom lesson.

Can Time On-Task Be Too High?

A class that is rarely on-task is certainly not a well-managed class. However, it is possible to go too far in the other direction, emphasizing time on-task to the exclusion of all other considerations. For example, in a study of time on-task in elementary mathematics, one teacher's class was found to be engaged essentially 100 percent of the time. The teacher accomplished this by walking up and down the rows of desks looking for the slightest flicker of inattention. This class learned very little math over the course of the year. An overemphasis on engaged time rather than on engaging instruction can produce what Bloome, Puro, and Theodorou (1989) call **mock participation,** in which students appear to be on-task but are not really engaged in learning.

Several studies have found that increasing time on-task in classes in which students were already reasonably well behaved did not increase student achievement (Blackadar & Nachtigal, 1986; Slavin, 1986; Stallings & Krasavage, 1986). An overemphasis on time on-task can be detrimental to learning in several ways. For example, complex tasks involving creativity and uncertainty tend to produce lower levels of time on-task than do simple cut-and-dried tasks (Evertson & Randolph, 1995; Weinstein & Mignano, 2003). Yet it would clearly be a poor instructional strategy to avoid complex or uncertain tasks just to keep time on-task high. Maintaining classroom order is an important goal of teaching, but it is only one of many (see Charles, 2008; Levin & Nolan, 2007).

Classroom Management in the Student-Centered Classroom

It is important to note that most research on classroom management has taken place in traditionally organized classrooms, in which students have few choices as to what they do and few interactions with each other. In more student-centered classrooms, children are likely to be spending much of their time working with each other, doing open-ended projects, writing, and experimenting. Evertson and Randolph (1995) have discussed the shift that must take place in thinking about classroom management for such classrooms. Clearly, classroom management is more participatory in a student-centered classroom, with students

mock participation
Situation in which students appear to be on-task but are not engaged in learning.

Personal REFLECTION

INTASC 6 Communication Skills

Maintaining Control

I was once visiting a fifth-grade class in suburban Baltimore involved in a study we were doing. The teacher was presenting an interesting, well-organized lesson, and most of the students were paying attention. However, one girl had a comic book she was secretly reading, paying no attention to the lesson.

The veteran teacher was aware of everything going on in the class, and he soon noticed that the girl wasn't paying attention. Without interrupting his lesson in the slightest, he strolled sideways toward her desk, took the comic book, closed it, and put it on her desk. This was done so smoothly that few if any of the other students even seemed to notice it. This was a wonderful demonstration, I thought, of Kounin's principles of classroom management. The teacher dealt with the behavior without interrupting the flow of the lesson. Had he stopped and yelled at the girl, he would have broken the lesson, given the whole class an occasion for enjoying either the girl's defiance or her comeuppance, and taken much time to get back on track. The girl may have enjoyed such attention, and other students may have wanted to get in on the act. Instead, the girl received ample feedback (that her behavior was known and not appreciated), but the show went on.

REFLECT ON THIS. Think of examples from your own experience as a student. How did your best teachers create effective learning environments?

centrally involved in setting standards of behavior. Equally clearly, the type of behavior to be expected will be different. It is impossible to imagine a student-centered classroom that is silent, for example. Yet in other respects the requirements for managing student-centered classrooms are not so different from those for managing traditional ones. Rules are still needed and must be consistently communicated to students and consistently enforced (Freiberg, Connell, & Lorentz, 2001). If students in student-centered classrooms are deeply involved and motivated by the variety, activity, and social nature of classroom activities, then disciplinary actions will be less necessary (Weinstein & Mignano, 2003). Inevitably, however, certain students' misbehavior will disrupt others' learning, and the teacher must have strategies to help students live up to norms to which all members of the class have agreed.

The following sections describe strategies for preventing misbehavior in any classroom context and responding effectively to misbehavior when it does occur.

WHAT PRACTICES CONTRIBUTE TO EFFECTIVE CLASSROOM MANAGEMENT?

Research has consistently shown that basic commonsense planning and groundwork go a long way toward preventing discipline problems from ever developing. Simple measures include starting the year properly, arranging the classroom for effective instruction, setting class rules and procedures, and making expectations of conduct clear to students (Marzano, 2003). Further, establishing caring connections between teachers and students helps establish a cooperative tone in the classroom that reduces discipline problems (McNeely et al., 2002; Osher & Fleishman, 2005).

INTASC

7 Instructional Planning Skills

Different grade levels and student groups present different management concerns. For instance, with younger students, teachers need to be concerned about socializing students to the norms and behaviors that are expected in school (Evertson, Emmer, & Worsham, 2006; Weinstein & Mignano, 2003). Programs focusing on establishing consistent, schoolwide behavior expectations and on building positive relationships and school success through the use of cooperative learning have been effective in improving the behavior of elementary school children (Freiberg, Connell, & Lorentz, 2001; O'Donnell, Hawkins, Catalano, Abbott, & Day, 1995).

The relationship you establish with your students will set the tone for learning in your classroom. What do you anticipate being the biggest challenge to establishing a productive classroom?

In middle school and high school, students can grasp the principles that underlie rules and procedures and can rationally agree to observe them (Emmer, Evertson, Clements, & Worsham, 2006; Weinstein, 2003). At the same time, some adolescents resist authority and place greater importance on peer norms. Aggressive behavior, truancy, and delinquency also increase as students enter adolescence. In the upper grades, departmentalization, tracking, and class promotion might become management issues, especially with students who have established patterns of learned helplessness or academic failure. Teachers of older students need to be more concerned with motivating them toward more self-regulation in observing rules and procedures and in learning the course material. Programs that increase the clarity of rules, consistency of rule enforcement, and frequency of communication with the home have been very effective in improving adolescents' behavior (Gottfredson, Gottfredson, & Hybl, 1993).

Starting Out the Year Right

Emmer and colleagues (1980) and Evertson and Emmer (1982) studied teachers' actions at the beginning of the school year and correlated them with students' behaviors later in the year. They found that the first days of school were critical in establishing classroom order. They compared teachers whose classes were mostly on-task over the course of the school year with teachers whose classes were less consistently on-task and found that the better classroom managers engaged in certain activities during the first days of school significantly more often than did the less effective managers (Evertson et al., 2006; see also Wong & Wong, 2004). A list of six characteristics of effective classroom managers follows:

1. More effective managers had a clear, specific plan for introducing students to classroom rules and procedures and spent as many days as necessary carrying out their plan until students knew how to line up, ask for help, and so on.
2. More effective managers worked with the whole class initially (even if they planned to group students later). They were involved with the whole class at all times, rarely leaving any students without something to do or without supervision. For example, more effective managers seldom worked with an individual student unless the rest of the class was productively occupied (Doyle, 1984; Sanford & Evertson, 1981).
3. More effective managers spent extra time during the first days of school introducing procedures and discussing class rules (often encouraging students to suggest rules themselves). These teachers usually reminded students of class rules every day for at least the first week of school (Weinstein & Mignano, 2003).
4. More effective managers taught students specific procedures. For example, some had students practice lining up quickly and quietly; others taught students to respond to a signal, such as a bell, a flick of the light switch, or a call for attention.
5. More effective managers used simple, enjoyable tasks as first activities. Materials for the first lessons were well prepared, clearly presented, and varied. These teachers asked students to get right to work on the first day of school and then gave them instructions on procedures gradually, to avoid overloading them with too much information at a time.
6. More effective managers responded immediately to stop any misbehavior.

Setting Class Rules

One of the first management-related tasks at the start of the year is setting class rules. Three principles govern this process. First, class rules should be few in number. Second, they should make sense and be seen as fair by students. Third, they should be clearly explained and deliberately taught to students (Metzger, 2002). A major purpose of clearly explaining general class rules is to give a moral authority for specific procedures (Kagan, Kyle, & Scott, 2004). For example, all students will understand and support a rule such as "Respect others' property." This simple rule can be invoked to cover such obvious misbehaviors as

VIDEO HOMEWORK EXERCISE
Classroom Rules

Go to **www.myeducationlab.com** and, in the Homework and Exercises section for Chapter 11 of this text, access the video entitled "Classroom Rules." Watch the video and complete the homework questions that accompany it, saving your work or transmitting it to your professor as required.

stealing or destroying materials but also gives a reason for putting materials away, cleaning up litter, and refraining from marking up textbooks. Students may be asked to help set the rules, or they may be given a set of rules and asked to give examples of these rules. Class discussions give students a feeling of participation in setting rational rules that everyone can live by (Gathercoal, 2001; Strout, 2005). When the class as a whole has agreed on a set of rules, offenders know that they are transgressing community norms, not the teacher's arbitrary regulations. One all-purpose set of class rules follows:

1. ***Be courteous to others.*** This rule forbids interrupting others or speaking out of turn, teasing or laughing at others, fighting, and so on.
2. ***Respect others' property.***
3. ***Be on-task.*** This includes listening when the teacher or other students are talking, working on seatwork, continuing to work during any interruptions, staying in one's seat, being at one's seat and ready to work when the bell rings, and following directions.
4. ***Raise hands to be recognized.*** This is a rule against calling out or getting out of one's seat for assistance without permission.

Teaching Dilemmas: CASES TO CONSIDER

Rules of the Room

INTASC

5 Classroom Motivation and Management

Althea Johnson, a third-grade teacher, is standing in front of her new class on the second day of school.

Althea: OK, class. I want to spend a few minutes talking with you about class rules. Let's start by listing some on the board. Please raise your hands if you have a rule you'd like to suggest and wait until I call on you.

In a few minutes Althea has written the following on the board under the heading Rules:

- Do not talk in class.
- Do not run in the hallways.
- Do not put gum under your desk.
- Do not throw spitballs (or paper airplanes).
- Do not draw on your desk.
- Do not fight.
- Do not come late without a note from home.
- Do not yell in class.
- Do raise your hand to be called on.
- Do not bring radios to school.
- Do not pass notes to your friends.
- Do not write in your books.

Althea: Does everyone think these rules are fair? Hands? [Hands go up.] OK, that's a good start. But I see two problems. First, this is a long list to remember. And second, most of them start with *"Do not."* I'd like to try to group these to create a few rules that tell us what we *should* do.

Her students offer ideas, and eventually the board shows the following rules, each with several examples underneath:

1. Respect the rights of others.
2. Respect other people's property.
3. Be courteous to others.
4. Be on-task.
5. Raise your hand to be called on.

Althea: OK, we've all agreed that these rules are fair. But if somebody does forget and breaks a rule, what should happen? What should the consequences be? Clare?

Clare: You go to the principal's office.

Althea: Yes, that could be one consequence. Let's list more.

As before, Althea lists the students' suggestions under the heading Consequences:

- Go to the principal's office.
- Sit in the corner for half an hour.
- Miss recess.
- Stay after school.
- Get a letter sent home to your parents.

Althea: Who has a suggestion for encouraging people to want to keep the rules in the first place, not break them? A kind of reward? Mimi? Clare?

Mimi: Getting gold stars?

Clare: We could all get an extra recess if the whole class was good all day.

Billy (interrupting): We could all just stay home!

Althea: Billy, we've all agreed to raise hands and to be courteous. So are you trying to give the class an example of how not to behave?

Billy: Sorry, Mrs. Johnson.

Althea: OK, now I want everyone to copy our basic rules and think about them. We'll talk a little more about rewards and consequences tomorrow.

QUESTIONS FOR REFLECTION

1. Do you agree with Althea that third-graders should be involved in setting class rules? How might a teacher of kindergarten or high school children approach the same task?
2. For the grade level you plan to teach, develop a problem-prevention plan of action for the first week of school. Model your plan by extending the dialogue in this case with another character; for example, have Althea talk with a novice teacher.

WHAT ARE SOME STRATEGIES FOR MANAGING ROUTINE MISBEHAVIOR?

The preceding sections of this chapter discussed means of organizing classroom activities to maximize time for instruction and minimize time for such minor disturbances as students talking out of turn, getting out of their seats without permission, and not paying attention. Provision of interesting lessons, efficient use of class time, and careful structuring of instructional activities will prevent most such minor behavior problems—and many more serious ones as well (Barr & Parrett, 2001). For example, Kounin (1970) found that teacher behaviors that were associated with high time on-task were also associated with fewer serious behavior problems. Time off-task can lead to more serious problems; many behavior problems arise because students are frustrated or bored in school. Instructional programs that actively involve students and provide all of them with opportunities for success might prevent such problems.

However, effective lessons and good use of class time are not the only means of preventing or dealing with inappropriate behavior. Besides structuring classes to reduce the frequency of behavior problems, teachers must have strategies for dealing with behavior problems when they do occur (Emmer & Stough, 2001).

The great majority of behavior problems with which a teacher must deal are relatively minor disruptions, such as talking out of turn, getting up without permission, failing to follow class rules or procedures, and inattention—nothing really serious, but behaviors that must be minimized for learning to occur. Before considering disciplinary strategies, it is important to reflect on their purpose. Students should learn much more in school than the "Three Rs." They should learn that they are competent learners and that learning is enjoyable and satisfying. A classroom environment that is warm, supportive, and accepting fosters these attitudes (Fay, 2001). Furthermore, there is a strong link between attentive, nondisruptive behavior and student achievement (Finn, Pannozzo, & Voelkl, 1995; Wentzel, 1993).

A healthy classroom environment cannot be created if students do not respect teachers or teachers do not respect students. Though teachers should involve students in setting class rules and take student needs or input into account in organizing the classroom, teachers are ultimately the leaders who establish and enforce rules by which students must live. These class rules and procedures should become second nature to students. Teachers who have not established their authority in the classroom are likely to spend too much time dealing with behavior problems or yelling at students to be instructionally effective. Furthermore, the clearer the structure and routine procedures in the classroom, the more freedom the teacher can allow students (Mackenzie, 1997; Weinstein, 1999). The following sections discuss strategies for dealing with typical discipline problems (Emmer et al., 2006; Evertson et al., 2006; Jones & Jones, 2007; Kyle & Rogien, 2004; Walker & Shea, 1999; Weinstein & Mignano, 2003).

The Principle of Least Intervention

In dealing with routine classroom behavior problems, the most important principle is that a teacher should correct misbehaviors by using the simplest intervention that will work (Gathercoal, 2001; Kyle & Rogien, 2004). Many studies have found that the amount of time spent disciplining students is negatively related to student achievement (Crocker & Brooker, 1986; Evertson et al., 1980). The teacher's main goal in dealing with routine misbehavior is to do so in a way that is both effective and avoids unnecessarily disrupting the lesson (Charles, 2008; Evertson et al., 2006; Jones & Jones, 2007). If at all possible, the lesson must go on while any behavior problems are dealt with. A continuum of strategies for dealing with minor misbehaviors, from least disruptive to most, is listed in Table 11.1 and discussed in the following sections.

Prevention

The easiest behavior problems to deal with are those that never occur in the first place. As was illustrated earlier in this chapter, teachers can prevent behavior problems by presenting interesting and lively lessons, making class rules and procedures clear, keeping

TABLE 11.1 Principle of Least Intervention

Step	Procedure	Example
1	Prevention	Teacher displays enthusiasm, varies activities, keeps students interested.
2	Nonverbal cues	Tanya turns in paper late: teacher frowns.
3	Praise of correct behavior that is incompatible with misbehavior	"Tanya, I hear you completed your science fair project on time for the judging. That's great!"
4	Praise for other students	"I see most of you turned your papers in on time today. I really appreciate that."
5	Verbal reminders	"Tanya, please turn in your next paper on time."
6	Repeated reminders	"Tanya, it's important to turn your paper in on time."
7	Consequences	Tanya spends 10 minutes after class starting on the next paper assignment.

students busy on meaningful tasks, and using other effective techniques of basic classroom management (Colvin, 2004; Fay, 2001; Jones & Jones, 2007; Stipek, de la Sota, & Weishaupt, 1999). Ms. Cavalho's class is an excellent example of this. Her students rarely misbehave because they are interested and engaged.

Varying the content of lessons, using a variety of materials and approaches, displaying humor and enthusiasm, and using cooperative learning or project-based learning can all reduce boredom-caused behavior problems. A teacher can avert frustration caused by material that is too difficult or assignments that are unrealistically long by breaking assignments into smaller steps and doing a better job of preparing students to work on their own. Fatigue can be reduced if short breaks are allowed, activities are varied, and difficult subjects are scheduled in the morning, when students are fresh.

ON THE WEB

To learn more about classroom management go to the Teacher Talk Forum on the Center for Adolescent and Family Studies website, **www.indiana.edu/~cafs/**, and Temple University's Teacher's Connection at **www.temple.edu/CETP/temple_teach/index.html.** Also check out the websites of the Center for the Prevention of School Violence, **www.ncdjjdp.org/cpsv.**

Nonverbal Cues

INTASC

6 Communication Skills

Teachers can eliminate much routine classroom misbehavior without breaking the momentum of the lesson by the use of simple **nonverbal cues** (Levin & Nolan, 2007). Making eye contact with a misbehaving student might be enough to stop misbehavior. For example, if two students are whispering, the teacher might simply catch the eye of one or both of them. Moving close to a student who is misbehaving also usually alerts the student to shape up. If these techniques fail, a light hand on the student's shoulder is likely to be effective (although touch should be used cautiously with adolescents, who may be sensitive about being touched). These nonverbal strategies all clearly convey the same message: "I see what you are doing and don't like it. Please get back to work." The advantage of communicating this message nonverbally is that the lesson need not be interrupted. In contrast, verbal reprimands can cause a ripple effect; many students stop working while one is being reprimanded (Kounin, 1970). Instead of interrupting the flow of concentration for many to deal with the behavior of one, nonverbal cues usually have an effect only on the student who is misbehaving, as was illustrated earlier in this chapter by the example of the teacher who continued his lesson while silently closing and putting away a book one student was reading. That student was the only one in the class who paid much attention to the whole episode.

Praising Behavior That Is Incompatible with Misbehavior

Praise can be a powerful motivator for many students. One strategy for reducing misbehavior in class is to make sure to praise students for behaviors that are incompatible with the misbehavior you want to reduce. That is, catch students in the act of doing right. For example, if students often get out of their seats without permission, praise them on the occasions when they do get to work right away.

Praising Other Students

nonverbal cues
Eye contact, gestures, physical proximity, or touching that a teacher uses to communicate without interrupting verbal discourse.

It is often possible to get one student to behave by praising others for behaving. For example, if Polly is goofing off, the teacher might say, "I'm glad to see so many students working so well—Jake is doing a good job, Carol is doing well, José and Michelle are working nicely. . . ." When Polly finally does get to work, the teacher should praise her, too, without dwelling on her past inattention: "I see James and Walter and Polly doing such good work."

Verbal Reminders

Encouraging Appropriate Behavior

Go to **www.myeducationlab.com** and, in the Homework and Exercises section for Chapter 11 of this text, access the Case Studies entitled "Encouraging Appropriate Behavior." Choose two of the Case Studies in this unit and read them. Do the assignment at the bottom of the page in each Case Study. Follow the guidelines presented in each Case Study for the desired goals or objectives. Incorporate some of the possible strategies identified in each Case Study.

If a nonverbal cue is impossible or ineffective, a simple verbal reminder might help to bring a student into line. The reminder should be given immediately after the student misbehaves; delayed reminders are usually ineffective. If possible, the reminder should state what students are supposed to be doing rather than dwelling on what they are doing wrong. For example, it is better to say, "John, please attend to your own work," than, "John, stop copying off of Alfredo's paper." Stating the reminder positively communicates more positive expectations for future behavior than does a negative statement (Evertson et al., 2006). Also, the reminder should focus on the behavior, not on the student. Although a particular student behavior may be intolerable, the student himself or herself is always accepted and welcome in the classroom.

Repeated Reminders

Most often a nonverbal cue, reinforcement of other students, or a simple reminder will be enough to end minor misbehavior. However, sometimes students test the teacher's resolve by failing to do what has been asked of them or by arguing or giving excuses. This testing will diminish over time if students learn that teachers mean what they say and will use appropriate measures to enforce an orderly, productive classroom environment.

When a student refuses to comply with a simple reminder, one strategy to attempt first is a repetition of the reminder, ignoring any irrelevant excuse or argument. Canter and Canter (2002), in a program called **Assertive Discipline,** call this strategy the *broken record*. Teachers should decide what they want the student to do, state this clearly to the student, and then repeat it until the student complies. An example of the broken record from Canter and Canter (2002) follows:

Teacher: "Craig, I want you to start your project now."
Craig: "I will as soon as I finish my game. Just a few more minutes."
Teacher (firmly): "Craig, I understand, but I want you to start your project now." (Broken record)
Craig: "You never give me enough time with the games."
Teacher (calmly, firmly): "That's not the point. I want you to start your project now."
Craig: "I don't like doing my project."
Teacher (firmly): "I understand, but I want you to start your project."
Craig: "Wow, you really mean it. I'll get to work."

This teacher avoided a lengthy argument with a student by simply repeating the request. When Craig said, "You never give me enough time with the games," and, "I don't like doing my project," he was not inviting a serious discussion but was simply procrastinating and testing the teacher's resolve. Rather than going off on a tangent with him, the teacher calmly restated the request, turning aside his excuses with "That's not the point . . ." and "I understand, but. . . ." Of course, if Craig had had a legitimate issue to discuss or a valid complaint, the teacher would have dealt with it, but all too often students' arguments or excuses are nothing more than a means of drawing out an interaction with the teacher to avoid getting down to work (see Walker, Ramsey, & Gresham, 2003a,b). Recall how Ms. Cavalho refused to be drawn into a discussion of Gloria's lateness when it was Mark's behavior that was at issue.

Applying Consequences

Assertive Discipline
Method of giving a clear, firm, unhostile response to student misbehavior.

When all previous steps have been ineffective in getting the student to comply with a clearly stated and reasonable request, the final step is to pose a choice to the student: Either comply or suffer the consequences (Axelrod & Mathews, 2003; Colvin, 2004). Examples of consequences are sending the student out of class, making the student miss a few minutes of recess or some other privilege, having the student stay after school, and calling the student's parents. A consequence for not complying with the teacher's request should be mildly unpleasant, short in duration, and applied as soon as possible after the behavior occurs. Certainty is far more important than severity; students must know that consequences follow misbehavior as night follows day. One disadvantage of using severe or long-lasting punishment (e.g., no recess for a week) is that it can create resentment in the student and a defiant attitude. Also, it might be difficult to follow through on severe or long-lasting consequences. Mild but certain consequences communicate, "I cannot tolerate that sort of behavior, but I care about you and want you to rejoin the class as soon as you are ready."

Before presenting a student with a consequence for noncompliance, teachers must be absolutely certain that they can and will follow through if necessary. When a teacher says, "You may choose to get to work right away, or you may choose to spend 5 minutes of your recess doing your work here," the teacher must be certain that someone will be available to monitor the student in the classroom during recess. Vague or empty threats ("You stop that or I'll make you wish you had!" or "You get to work or I'll have you suspended for a month!") are worse than useless. If teachers are not prepared to follow through with consequences, students will learn to shrug them off.

After a consequence has been applied, the teacher should avoid referring to the incident. For example, when the student returns from a 10-minute exclusion from class, the teacher should accept her or him back without any sarcasm or recriminations. The student now deserves a fresh start.

HOW IS APPLIED BEHAVIOR ANALYSIS USED TO MANAGE MORE SERIOUS BEHAVIOR PROBLEMS?

The previous section discussed how to deal with behaviors that might be appropriate on the playing field but are out of line in the classroom. There are other behaviors that are not appropriate anywhere. These include fighting, stealing, destruction of property, and gross disrespect for teachers or other school staff. These are far less common than routine classroom misbehavior but far more serious. Behavioral learning theories, described in Chapter 5, have direct application to effective responses to serious misbehavior. Simply put, behavioral learning theories hold that behaviors that are not reinforced or are punished will diminish in frequency. The following sections present **applied behavior analysis,** an analysis of classroom behavior in terms of behavioral concepts, and give specific strategies for preventing and dealing with misbehavior (Alberto & Troutman, 1999; Walker & Shea, 1999).

INTASC

8 Assessment of Student Learning

ON THE WEB

For articles on applied behavior analysis visit the website for the Cambridge Center for Behavioral Studies **www.behavior.org** and click on About Behavior Analysis.

How Student Misbehavior Is Maintained

A basic principle of behavioral learning theories is that if any behavior persists over time, it is being maintained by some reinforcer. To reduce misbehavior in the classroom, we must understand which reinforcers maintain misbehavior in the first place (Chandler & Dahlquist, 2006).

The most common reinforcer for classroom misbehavior is attention—from the teacher, the peer group, or both. Students receiving one-to-one tutoring rarely misbehave,

applied behavior analysis
The application of behavioral learning principles to understanding and changing behavior.

both because they already have the undivided attention of an adult and because no classmates are present to attend to any negative behavior. In the typical classroom, however, students have to go out of their way to get the teacher's personal attention, and they have an audience of peers who might encourage or applaud their misdeeds.

Teacher's Attention Sometimes students misbehave because they want the teacher's attention, even if it is negative. This is a more common reason for misbehavior than many teachers think. A puzzled teacher might say, "I don't know what is wrong with Nathan. I have to stay with him all day to keep him working! Sometimes I get exasperated and yell at him. My words fall off him like water off a duck's back. He even smiles when I'm scolding him!"

When students appear to misbehave to gain the teacher's attention, the solution is relatively easy: Pay attention to these students when they are doing well, and ignore them (as much as possible) when they misbehave. When ignoring their actions is impossible, imposing time out (e.g., sending these students to a quiet corner or to the principal's office) might be effective.

Peers' Attention Another very common reason that students misbehave is to get the attention and approval of their peers. The classic instance of this is the class clown, who is obviously performing for the amusement of his or her classmates. However, many other forms of misbehavior are motivated primarily by peer attention and approval—in fact, few students completely disregard the potential impact of their behavior on their classmates. For example, students who refuse to do what the teacher has asked are consciously or unconsciously weighing the effect of their defiance on their standing among their classmates (Hartup, 2005).

INTASC

4 Multiple Instructional Strategies

Even preschoolers and early elementary school students misbehave to gain peer attention, but beginning around the third grade (and especially during the middle and high school years), it is particularly likely that student misbehavior is linked to peer attention and support. As students enter adolescence, the peer group takes on extreme importance, and peer norms begin to favor independence from authority. When older children and teenagers engage in serious delinquent acts (such as vandalism, theft, and assault), they are usually supported by a delinquent peer group.

CONNECTIONS
For more information about behavioral theory, see Chapter 5, page 131.

Strategies for reducing peer-supported misbehavior are quite different from those for dealing with misbehavior that is meant to capture the teacher's attention. Ignoring misbehavior will be ineffective if the misbehavior is reinforced by peers. For example, if a student is balancing a book on his or her head and the class is laughing, the behavior can hardly be ignored because it will continue as long as the class is interested (and will encourage others to behave likewise). Further, scolding might only attract more attention from classmates or, worse, enhance the student's standing among peers. Similarly, if two students are whispering or talking to each other, they are reinforcing each other for misbehaving, and ignoring their behavior will only encourage more of it.

group contingencies Class rewards that depend on the behavior of all students.

There are two primary responses to peer-supported misbehavior. One is to remove the offender from the classroom to deprive her or him of peer attention. Another is to use **group contingencies,** strategies in which the entire class (or groups of students within the class) is rewarded on the basis of everyone's behavior. Under group contingencies, all students benefit from their classmates' good behavior, so peer support for misbehavior is removed. Group contingencies and other behavior management strategies for peer-supported misbehavior are described in more detail in the following sections.

This student misbehaves to get her peer's attention. Which responses to peer-supported misbehavior will you use in the classroom?

Release from Unpleasant States or Activities A third important reinforcer for misbehavior is release from boredom, frustration, fatigue, or unpleasant activities. As was explained in Chapter 5, escaping from or avoiding an unpleasant stimulus is a reinforcer. Some students see much of what happens in school as unpleasant, boring, frustrating, or tiring. This is particularly true of students who experience repeated failure in school. But even the most able and motivated students feel bored or frustrated at times. Students often misbehave simply to escape from unpleasant activities. This can be clearly seen with students who frequently ask permission to get a drink of water, go to the washroom, or sharpen their pencils. Such students are more likely to make these requests during independent seatwork than during cooperative learning activities or even a lecture because seatwork can be frustrating or anxiety provoking for students who have little confidence in their academic abilities. More serious misbehaviors can also be partially or completely motivated by a desire for release from boredom, frustration, or fatigue. A student might misbehave just to stir things up. Sometimes students misbehave precisely so that they will be sent out of the classroom. Obviously, sending such a student to the hall or the principal's office can be counterproductive.

The best solution for misbehaviors arising from boredom, frustration, or fatigue is prevention. Students rarely misbehave during interesting, varied, engaging lessons. Actively involving students in lessons can head off misbehaviors that are the result of boredom or fatigue. Use of cooperative learning methods or other means of involving students in an active way can be helpful. A teacher can prevent frustration by using materials that ensure a high success rate for all, by making sure that all students are challenged but none is overwhelmed. Changing instruction and assessments to help students succeed can be an effective means of resolving frustration-related behavior problems.

Principles of Applied Behavior Analysis

The behavior management strategies outlined earlier (e.g., nonverbal cues, reminders, mild but certain punishment) might be described as informal applications of behavioral learning theories. These practices, plus the prevention of misbehavior by the use of efficient class management and engaging lessons, will be sufficient to create a good learning environment in most classrooms.

However, more systematic methods are sometimes needed. In classrooms in which most students are well behaved but a few have persistent behavior problems, individual behavior management strategies can be effective. In classrooms in which many students have behavior problems, particularly when there is peer support for misbehavior, whole-class strategies or group contingencies might be needed. Such strategies are most often required when many low-achieving or poorly motivated students are put in one class, as often happens in special-education classes and in schools that use tracking or other between-class ability grouping methods.

CONNECTIONS
For more information about the problems of tracking, see Chapter 9, pages 265–269.

Setting up and using any applied behavior analysis program requires following a series of steps that proceeds from the observation of the behavior through program implementation to program evaluation (see Jones & Jones, 2007; Walker, Colvin, & Ramsey, 2003). The steps listed here are, to a greater or lesser extent, part of all applied behavior analysis programs:

1. Identify target behavior(s) and reinforcer(s).
2. Establish a baseline for the target behavior.
3. Choose a reinforcer and criteria for reinforcement.
4. If necessary, choose a punisher and criteria for punishment.
5. Observe behavior during program implementation, and compare it to baseline.
6. When the behavior management program is working, reduce the frequency of reinforcement.

Individual behavior management strategies are useful for coping with individual students who have persistent behavior problems in school. **Behavior modification** is a systematic application of antecedents and consequences to change behavior (Alberto & Troutman, 1999; Walker & Shea, 1999).

behavior modification
Systematic application of antecedents and consequences to change behavior.

Identify Target Behaviors and Reinforcers The first step in implementing a behavior management program is to observe the misbehaving student to identify one or a small number of behaviors to target first and to see what reinforcers maintain the behavior(s). Another purpose of this observation is to establish a baseline against which to compare improvements. A structured individual behavior management program should aim to change only one behavior or a small set of closely related behaviors. Tackling too many behaviors at a time risks failure with all of them because the student might not clearly see what he or she must do to be reinforced.

The first behavior targeted should be one that is serious; is easy to observe; and, most important, occurs frequently. For example, if a child gets into fights in the playground every few days but gets out of his or her seat without permission several times per hour, you might start with the out-of-seat behavior and deal with the fighting later. Ironically, the more frequent and persistent a behavior, the easier it is to extinguish. This is because positive or negative consequences can be applied frequently, making the connection between behavior and consequence clear to the student.

In observing a student, try to determine what reinforcer(s) are maintaining the target behavior. If a student misbehaves with others (e.g., talks without permission, swears, or teases) or if a student's misbehavior usually attracts the attention of others (e.g., clowning), then you might conclude that the behavior is peer supported. If the behavior does not attract much peer attention but always requires teacher attention (e.g., getting out of seat without permission), then you might conclude that the behavior is supported by your own attention.

Establish Baseline Behavior Observe the student to see how often the target behavior occurs. Before you do this, you will need to clearly define exactly what constitutes the behavior. For example, if the target behavior is "bothering classmates," you will have to decide what specific behaviors constitute "bothering" (perhaps teasing, interrupting, and taking materials).

Select Reinforcers and Criteria for Reinforcement Typical classroom reinforcers include praise, privileges, and tangible rewards. Praise is especially effective for students who misbehave to get the teacher's attention. It is often a good idea to start a behavior management program by using attention and praise for appropriate behavior to see whether this is sufficient. However, be prepared to use stronger reinforcers if praise is not enough (see McDaniel, 1993; Schloss & Smith, 1994). In addition to praise, many teachers find it useful to give students stars, "smilies," or other small rewards when students behave appropriately. Some teachers use a rubber stamp to mark students' papers with a symbol indicating good work. These small rewards make the teacher's praise more concrete and visible and let students take their work home and receive praise from their parents. Figure 11.2 provides suggestions for social reinforcers and preferred activities to encourage positive behavior.

Select Punishers and Criteria for Punishment, If Necessary Behavioral learning theories strongly favor the use of reinforcers for appropriate behavior rather than punishers for inappropriate behavior. The reasons for this are practical as well as ethical. Punishment often creates resentment; so even if it solves one problem, it could create others. Even if punishment would work as well as reinforcement, it should be avoided because it is not conducive to the creation of a happy, healthy classroom environment (Webber & Scheuermann, 1993). Punishment of one kind or another is necessary in some circumstances, and it should be used without qualms when reinforcement strategies are impossible or ineffective. However, a program of punishment for misbehavior (e.g., depriving a student of privileges, never physical punishment) should always be the last option considered, never the first. A punisher is any unpleasant stimulus that an individual will try to avoid. Common punishers used in schools are reprimands, being sent out of class or to the principal's office, and detention or missed recess. Corporal punishment (e.g., spanking) is illegal in some states and districts and highly restricted in others, but regardless of laws or policies, it should never be used in schools. It is neither a necessary nor an effective response to misbehavior in school (Evans & Richardson, 1995; Gregory, 1995).

FIGURE 11.2 Social Reinforcers and Preferred Activities

From Vernon F. Jones and Louise S. Jones, *Comprehensive Classroom Management* (4th ed.), p. 363. Copyright © 1995 by Allyn & Bacon. Adapted by permission.

Social Reinforcers

Praising Words and Phrases

"That's clever."
"Good thinking."
"That shows a great deal of work."
"You really pay attention."
"You should show this to your father."
"That was very kind of you."
"I'm pleased with that."
"Keep up the good work."
"I appreciate your help."
"Now you've got the hang of it."
"That's an interesting point."
"You make it look easy."
"I like the way you got started on your homework."

Nearness

Walking together
Sitting together
Eating lunch together
Playing games with the student
Working after school together

Physical Contact

Touching
Hugging
Shaking hands
Holding hands

Expressions

Smiling
Winking
Nodding up and down
Looking interested
Laughing

Preferred Activities

Going first
Running errands
Getting to sit where he or she wants to
Telling a joke to the class
Having a party
Doing artwork related to studies
Choosing the game for recess
Earning an extra or longer recess
Helping the teacher
Visiting another class
Playing a short game: connect the dots, tic-tac-toe
Taking a class pet home for the weekend
Being team captain
Seeing a movie
Playing with a magnet or other science equipment
Reading with a friend
Getting free time in the library
Being asked what he or she would like to do
Planning a class trip or project

O'Leary and O'Leary (1972) list seven principles for the effective and humane use of punishment:

1. Use punishment sparingly.
2. Make it clear to the child why he or she is being punished.
3. Provide the child with an alternative means of obtaining some positive reinforcement.
4. Reinforce the child for behaviors that are incompatible with those you wish to weaken (e.g., if you punish for being off-task, also reinforce for being on-task).
5. Never use physical punishment.
6. Never punish when you are in a very angry or emotional state.
7. Punish when a behavior starts rather than when it ends.

One effective punisher is called **time out.** The teacher tells a misbehaving student to go to a separate part of the classroom, the hall, the principal's or vice principal's office, or another teacher's class. If possible, the place where the student is sent should be uninteresting and out of view of classmates. One advantage of time-out procedures is that they remove the student from the attention of her or his classmates. Therefore, time out may be especially effective for students whose misbehavior is motivated primarily by peer attention. The sit-and-watch procedure described in Chapter 5 is a good example of the use of time out. Students who misbehaved in a physical education class were given a sand timer and asked to sit and watch for 3 minutes. This consequence, applied immediately and consistently, soon virtually eliminated misbehavior (White & Bailey, 1990).

CONNECTIONS
For more information about sit-and-watch as a punishment for misbehavior, see Chapter 5, page 136 and Figure 5.2.

time out
Removal of a student from a situation in which misbehavior was reinforced.

CERTIFICATION POINTER

For your teacher certification test you will need to demonstrate your understanding of appropriate applications of applied behavioral analysis.

Teachers should assign time outs infrequently. When they do assign them, they should do so calmly and surely. The student is to go straight to the time-out area and stay there until the prescribed time is up. Time-out assignments should be brief, about 5 minutes is usually adequate. However, timing should begin only after the student settles down; if the student yells or argues, that time should not count. During time out, no one should speak to the student. Teachers should not scold the student during time out. Students should be told why they are being given time out but should not otherwise be lectured. If the principal's office is used, the principal should be asked not to speak to the student.

Reduce the Frequency of Reinforcement Once a reinforcement program has been in operation for a while and the student's behavior has improved and stabilized at a new level, the frequency of reinforcement can be reduced. Initially, reinforcers might be applied to every instance of appropriate behavior; as time goes on, every other instance, then every several instances might be reinforced. Reducing the frequency of reinforcement helps to maintain the new behaviors over the long run and aids in extending the behaviors to other settings.

Applied Behavior Analysis Programs

Home-based reinforcement strategies and daily report card programs are examples of applied behavioral analysis involving individual students. A group contingency program is an example of an applied behavioral analysis in which the whole class is involved.

home-based reinforcement strategies
Behavior modification strategies in which a student's school behavior is reported to parents, who supply rewards.

Home-Based Reinforcement Some of the most practical and effective classroom management methods are **home-based reinforcement strategies** (see Barth, 1979). Teachers give students a daily or weekly report card to take home, and parents are instructed to provide special privileges or rewards to students on the basis of these teacher reports. Home-based reinforcement is not a new idea; a museum in Vermont displays weekly report cards from the 1860s.

"Mrs. Jones, I'm just calling to say that Tommy had a great day in school today . . . Mrs. Jones? . . . Mrs. Jones?"

Home-based reinforcement has several advantages over other, equally effective behavior management strategies. First, parents can give much more potent rewards and privileges than schools can. For example, parents control access to such activities as television, trips to the store, and going out with friends. Parents also know what their own children like and, therefore, can provide more individualized privileges than the school can. Second, home-based reinforcement gives parents frequent good news about their children. Parents of disruptive children usually hear from the school only when their child has done something wrong. This is bad for parent–school relations and leads to much blame and finger-pointing. Third, home-based reinforcement is easy to administer. The teacher can involve any adults who deal with the child (other teachers, bus drivers, playground or lunch monitors) in the program by having the student carry a daily report card all day. Finally, over time, daily report cards can be replaced by weekly report cards and then biweekly report cards without loss in effectiveness, until the school's usual 6- or 9-week report cards can be used.

Daily Report Cards Figure 11.3 presents a daily report card for Homer Heath, an elementary school student. His teacher, Ms. Casa, rated his behavior and schoolwork at the end of each academic period, and she arranged to have the lunch monitor and the recess monitor rate his behavior

STUDENT *Homer H.* DAILY REPORT CARD DATE *March 21*

PERIOD	BEHAVIOR	SCHOOLWORK	TEACHER
Reading	1 2 (3) 4	1 (2) 3 4	*Ms. Casa*
Math	1 2 3 (4)	1 2 3 (4)	*Ms. Casa*
Lunch	1 2 (3) 4		*Mr. Mason*
Recess	1 2 (3) 4		*Ms. Hauser*
Language	1 2 3 (4)	1 2 3 (4)	*Ms. Casa*
Science/Soc. Stud.	1 2 (3) 4	1 2 (3) 4	*Ms. Casa*
	1 = Poor 2 = Fair 3 = Good 4 = Excellent	1 = Assignments not completed 2 = Assignments completed poorly 3 = Assignments completed adequately 4 = Assignments completed—excellent!	

Total rating *33* Score needed *30*

FIGURE 11.3 Example of a Daily Report Card

Teachers who use a home-based reinforcement program must set up a daily report card so that a student's work and behavior can be assessed and reported to the student's parents.

From E. Dougherty and A. Dougherty, "The Daily Report Card," *Psychology in the Schools, 14*, pp. 191–195. Copyright © 1977 by the Clinical Psychology Publishing Co., Inc., Brandon, Vermont. Reprinted with permission of John Wiley and Sons, Inc.

when Homer was with them. Homer was responsible for carrying his report card with him at all times and for making sure that it was marked and initialed at the end of each period. Whenever he made at least 30 points, his parents agreed to give him a special privilege: His father was to read him an extra story before bedtime and let him stay up 15 minutes longer than usual. Whenever he forgot to bring home his report card, his parents were to assume that he did not meet the criterion. If Homer had been a middle or high school student or if he had been in a departmentalized elementary school (where he changed classes for each subject), he would have carried his report card to every class, and each teacher would have marked it. Obviously, this approach requires some coordination among teachers, but the effort is certainly worthwhile if the daily report card dramatically reduces a student's misbehaviors and increases his or her academic output, as it has in dozens of studies evaluating this method (Barth, 1979).

THEORY *into* PRACTICE

Using a Daily Report Card System

Steps for setting up and implementing a daily report card system are as follows:

1. ***Decide which behaviors to include in the daily report card.*** Choose a behavior or set of behaviors on which the daily report card is to be based. Devise a rating scheme for each behavior, and construct a standard report card form. Your daily report card might be more or less elaborate than the one in Figure 11.3. For example, you might break behavior down into more precise categories, such as getting along with others, staying on-task, and following class rules.

2. ***Explain the program to parents.*** Home-based reinforcement programs depend on parent participation, so it is critical to inform parents about the program

and to obtain their cooperation. Parents should be told what the daily report card means and should be asked to reward their children whenever they bring home a good report card. In presenting the program to parents, teachers should explain what parents might do to reward their children. Communications with parents should be brief, positive, and informal and should generate a feeling that "we're going to solve this together." The program should focus on rewarding good behavior rather than punishing bad behavior. Examples of rewards parents might use at home (adapted from Walker & Shea, 1999) follow:

- Special activities with a parent (e.g., reading, flying a kite, building a model, shopping, playing a game, going to the zoo)
- Special foods
- Baking cookies or cooking
- Operating equipment that is usually reserved for adults (e.g., the dishwasher or vacuum cleaner)
- Access to special games, toys, or equipment
- Small rewards (such as coloring books, paper, comic books, erasers, or stickers)
- Additional play time, television time, and the like
- Having a friend spend the night
- Later bedtime or curfew

Parents should be encouraged to choose rewards that they can give every day (that is, nothing too expensive or difficult).

The best rewards are ones that build closeness between parent and child, such as doing special activities together. Many children who have behavior problems in school also have them at home and might have less than ideal relationships with their parents. Home-based reinforcement programs provide an opportunity for parents to show their love for their child at a time when the child has something of which to be proud. A special time with Dad can be especially valuable as a reward for good behavior in school and for building the father–son or father–daughter relationship.

3. ***When behavior improves, reduce the frequency of the report.*** When home-based reinforcement works, it often works dramatically. Once the student's behavior has improved and has stabilized, it is time to decrease the frequency of the reports to parents (of course, keep the parents informed about this change). Report cards might then be issued only weekly (for larger but less frequent rewards). As was noted in Chapter 5, the best way to ensure maintenance is to thin out the reinforcement schedule—that is, to increase the interval between reinforcers.

Group Contingency Programs A **group contingency program** is a reinforcement system in which an entire group is rewarded on the basis of the behavior of the group members. Teachers have always used group contingencies, as in "We'll go to lunch as soon as all students have put their work away and are quiet." When the teacher says this, any one student can cause the entire class to be late to lunch. Or the teacher might say, "If the class averages at least ninety on tomorrow's quiz, then you'll all be excused from homework for the rest of the week." This group contingency will depend on the average performance of all group members rather than on any single student's performance.

One important advantage of group contingencies is that they are relatively easy to administer. Most often, the whole class is either rewarded or not rewarded, so the teacher need not do one thing with some students and something else with others. For example, suppose a teacher says, "If the whole class follows the class rules this morning, we will have five extra minutes of recess." If the class does earn the extra recess, they all get it together; the teacher does not have to arrange to have some students stay out longer while others are called inside.

group contingency program
A program in which rewards or punishments are given to a class as a whole for adhering to or violating rules of conduct.

The theory behind group contingencies is that when a group is rewarded on the basis of its members' behavior, the group members will encourage one another to do whatever helps the group gain the reward (Slavin, 1990). Group contingencies can turn the same peer pressure that often supports misbehaviors to pressure opposing misbehavior. When the class can earn extra recess only if all students are well behaved all morning, no one is liable to find it funny when Joan makes silly faces or Quinn speaks disrespectfully to the teacher.

Group contingencies have been used successfully in many forms and for many purposes (Marzano, 2003). Barrish and colleagues (1969) divided a fourth-grade class into two teams during math period. When the teacher saw any member of a team disobeying class rules, the whole team received a check mark on the chalkboard. If a team had five or fewer check marks at the end of the period, all team members would take part in a free-time activity at the end of the day. If both teams got more than five check marks, the one that got fewer would receive the free time. Long-term follow-up studies of first-graders who experienced this approach have found remarkable lasting impacts on children's lives (Kellam et al., 1998; Ialongo et al., 2001).

CERTIFICATION POINTER

Your teacher certification test may require you to describe types of classroom management procedures that would tend to make class discussions more productive.

THEORY *into* PRACTICE

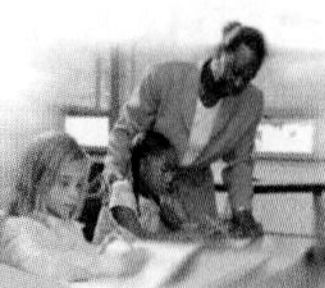

Establishing a Group Contingency Program

As was noted earlier, a group contingency behavior management program can be as simple as the statement "Class, if you are all in your seats, on-task, and quiet this morning, you may have five extra minutes of recess." However, a little more structure than this can increase the effectiveness of the group contingency.

1. ***Decide which behaviors will be reinforced.*** As in any whole-class behavior modification program, the first step in setting up a group contingency is to establish a set of class rules.

2. ***Set up a developmentally appropriate point system.*** There are essentially three ways to implement a group contingency behavior management program. One is simply to rate class behavior each period or during each activity. That is, an elementary school class might receive 0 to 5 points during each individual instructional period such as reading, language arts, and math. A secondary school class might receive one overall rating each period or separate ratings for behavior and completed assignments. The class would then be rewarded each day or week if they exceeded a preestablished number of points.

Another way to set up a group contingency program is to rate the class at various times during the day. For example, you might set a timer to ring on the average of once every 10 minutes (but varying randomly from 1 to 20 minutes). If the whole class is conforming to class rules when the timer rings, then the class earns a point. The same program can be used without the timer if the teacher gives the class a point every 10 minutes or so if all students are conforming to class rules. Canter and Canter (2002) suggest that teachers use a bag of marbles and a jar, putting a marble into the jar from time to time whenever the class is following rules. Each marble would be worth 30 seconds of extra recess. The sound of marbles going into the jar tells the students they are doing well. In secondary schools, where extra recess is not possible, each marble might represent 30 seconds of break time held at the end of the period on Friday.

3. ***Consider deducting points for serious misbehavior.*** The group contingency reward system by itself should help to improve student behavior. However, it might still be necessary to react to occasional serious misbehavior. For example, you might deduct 10 points for any instance of fighting or of serious disrespect for the teacher. When points must be deducted, do not negotiate with students about it. Simply deduct them, explaining why they must be deducted and reminding students that they may earn them back if they follow class rules.

4. ***When behavior improves, reduce the frequency of the points and reinforcers.*** Initially, the group contingency should be applied every day. When the class's behavior improves and stabilizes at a new level for about a week, you may change to giving rewards once a week. Ultimately, the class may graduate from the point-and-reward system entirely, though feedback and praise based on class behavior should continue.

5. ***Combine group and individual contingencies if necessary.*** The use of group contingencies need not rule out individual contingencies for students who need them. For example, students who continue to have problems in a class using a group contingency might still receive daily or weekly report cards to take home to their parents.

Ethics of Behavioral Methods

The behavior analysis strategies described in this chapter can be powerful. Properly applied, they will usually bring the behavior of even the most disruptive students to manageable levels. However, there is a danger that teachers might use such techniques to overcontrol students. They could be so concerned about getting students to sit down, stay quiet, and look productive that they lose sight of the fact that school is for learning, not for social control. Many years ago, Winett and Winkler (1972) wrote an article titled "Current Behavior Modification in the Classroom: Be Still, Be Quiet, Be Docile," in which they warned that behavior modification–based classroom management systems are being misused if teachers mistakenly believe that a quiet class is a learning class. This point parallels the basic premise of the QAIT model of effective instruction presented in Chapter 9. Behavior management systems can increase time for learning; but unless the quality of instruction, appropriate levels of instruction, and incentives for learning are also adequate, the additional time might be wasted (Emmer & Aussiker, 1990).

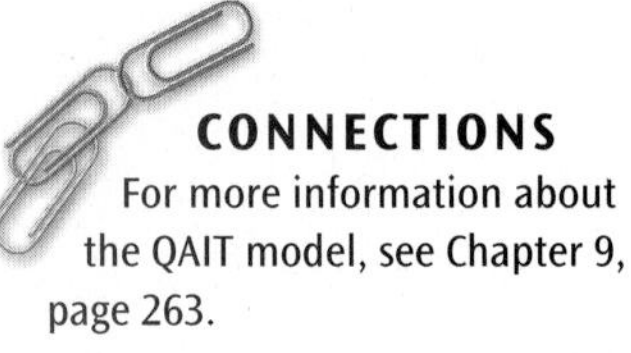

CONNECTIONS
For more information about the QAIT model, see Chapter 9, page 263.

Some people object to applied behavior analysis on the basis that it constitutes bribing students to do what they ought to do anyway. However, all classrooms use rewards and punishers (such as grades, praise, scolding, suspension). Applied behavior analysis strategies simply use these rewards in a more systematic way and avoid punishers as much as possible.

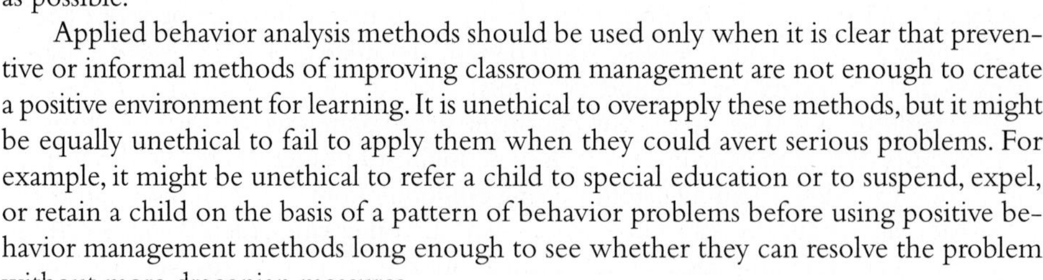

Applied behavior analysis methods should be used only when it is clear that preventive or informal methods of improving classroom management are not enough to create a positive environment for learning. It is unethical to overapply these methods, but it might be equally unethical to fail to apply them when they could avert serious problems. For example, it might be unethical to refer a child to special education or to suspend, expel, or retain a child on the basis of a pattern of behavior problems before using positive behavior management methods long enough to see whether they can resolve the problem without more draconian measures.

HOW CAN SERIOUS BEHAVIOR PROBLEMS BE PREVENTED?

Everyone misbehaves. There is hardly a person on earth who has not at some time done something he or she knew to be wrong or even illegal. However, some people's misbehavior is far more frequent and/or serious than others', and students in this category cause their teachers and school administrators (not to mention their parents and themselves) a disproportionate amount of trouble and concern.

Serious behavior problems are not evenly distributed among students or schools. Most students who are identified as having severe behavior problems are male; from 3 to 8 times as many boys as girls are estimated to have serious conduct problems (Perkins & Borden, 2003). Serious delinquency is far more common among students from impoverished backgrounds, particularly in urban locations. Students with poor family relationships are also much more likely than other students to become involved in serious misbehavior and delinquency, as are students who are low in achievement and those who have attendance problems (see Hawkins et al., 2000; Herrenkohl et al., 2001; Perkins & Borden, 2003).

The school has an important role to play in preventing or managing serious misbehavior and delinquency, but the student and the school are only one part of the story. Delinquent behavior often involves the police, courts, and social service agencies, as well as students' parents and peers. However, there are some guidelines for prevention of delinquency and serious misbehaviors.

Preventive Programs

As noted earlier in this chapter, the easiest behavior problems to deal with are those that never occur. There are many approaches that have promise for preventing serious behavior problems. One is simply creating safe and prosocial classroom environments and openly discussing risky behaviors and ways to avoid them (Learning First Alliance, 2001; Osher, Dwyer, & Jackson, 2004; Stipek, de la Sota, & Weishaupt, 1999). Another is giving students opportunities to play prosocial roles as volunteers, tutors, or leaders in activities that benefit their school and community (Allen, 2003; Rosenberg, McKeon, & Dinero, 1999). Creating democratic, participatory classrooms can give students ways of achieving recognition and control in a positive environment, reducing the need to act out (Hyman & Snook, 2000). Smaller, less impersonal schools have been found to reduce bullying and violence (Pellegrini, 2002). Programs that improve academic achievement also often affect behavior as well (Barr & Parrett, 2001). These kinds of strategies embed preventive activities in the day-to-day lives of students, rather than singling them out for special treatment.

Identifying Causes of Misbehavior

Even though some types of students are more prone to misbehavior than others, these characteristics do not cause misbehavior. Some students misbehave because they perceive that the rewards for misbehavior outweigh the rewards for good behavior. For example, students who do not experience success in school might perceive that the potential rewards for hard work and good behavior are small, so they turn to other sources of rewards. Some, particularly those who are failing in many different domains, find their niche in groups that hold norms that devalue achievement and other prosocial behavior (Wentzel, 2003). The role of the delinquent peer group in maintaining delinquent behavior cannot be overstated. Delinquent acts among adolescents and preadolescents are usually done in groups and are supported by antisocial peer norms (Gardner & Steinberg, 2005; Perkins & Borden, 2003).

Enforcing Rules and Practices

Expectations that students will conform to school rules must be consistently expressed. For example, graffiti or other vandalism must be repaired at once so that other students do not get the idea that misbehavior is common or accepted. However, rules should be enforced firmly but fairly; rigid applications of "zero tolerance" policies have often been found to be counterproductive (Skiba, 2000).

Enforcing School Attendance

Truancy and delinquency are strongly related; when students are out of school, they are often in the community making trouble. There are many effective means of reducing truancy (Haslinger, Kelly, & O'Lara, 1996; Lehr et al., 2003; Minke & Bear, 2000). Brooks (1975) had high school students with serious attendance problems carry cards to be signed by their teachers at the end of each period they attended. Students received a ticket for each period attended, plus bonus tickets for good behavior in class and for going 5 days without missing a class. The tickets were used in a drawing for a variety of prizes. Before the program began, the target students were absent 60 percent of all school days. During the program, absences dropped to 19 percent of school days. Over the same period, truancy among other students with attendance problems who were not in the program increased from 59 percent to 79 percent.

Barber and Kagey (1977) markedly increased attendance in an entire elementary school by making full participation in once-a-month parties depend on student attendance. Several activities were provided during the parties, and students could earn access to some or all of them according to the number of days they attended class.

Fiordaliso, Lordeman, Filipczak, and Friedman (1977) increased attendance among chronically truant junior high school students by having the school call their parents whenever the students were present several days in a row. The number of days before calling depended on how severe the student's truancy had been. Parents of the most truant students, who had been absent 6 or more days per month, were called after the student attended for only 3 consecutive days.

Check and Connect

INTASC

10 Partnerships

Check and Connect is a model that has school-based "monitors" work with students, families, and school personnel to improve the attendance and engagement of students in schools. The program has documented significant gains on attendance in elementary schools (Lehr, Sinclair, & Christenson, 2004), and on dropout and overall school success in middle schools (Sinclair, Christenson, Evelo, & Hurley, 1998). Check and Connect includes the following elements (Lehr et al., 2004, p. 284):

- *Relationship building:* Fostering mutual trust and open communication, nurtured through a long-term commitment that is focused on students' educational success
- *Routine monitoring of alterable indicators:* Systemically checking warning signs of withdrawal (attendance, academic performance, behavior) that are readily available to school personnel and that can be altered through intervention
- *Individualized and timely intervention:* Providing support that is tailored to individual student needs, based on level of engagement with school, associated influences of home and school, and the leveraging of local resources
- *Long-term commitment:* Committing to stay with students and families for at least 2 years, including the ability to follow students during transitions across school levels and follow highly mobile youth from school to school and program to program
- *Persistence plus:* Maintaining a persistent source of academic motivation, a continuity of familiarity with the youth and family, and a consistency in the message that "education is important for your future"
- *Problem solving:* Promoting the acquisition of skills to resolve conflict constructively and to look for solutions rather than a source of blame
- *Affiliation with school and learning:* Facilitating students' access to and active participation in school-related activities and events.

Practicing Intervention

Classroom management strategies should be used to reduce inappropriate behavior before it escalates into delinquency. Improving students' behavior and success in school can prevent delinquency (Gresham, 2005; Walker, Ramsey, & Gresham, 2003a,b). For example, Hawkins et al. (2001) used preventive classroom management methods such as those emphasized in this chapter along with interactive teaching and cooperative learning to help low-achieving seventh-graders. In comparison with control-group students, the students who were involved in the program were suspended and expelled less often, had better attitudes toward school, and were more likely to expect to complete high school. Lapointe and Freiberg (2006) reviewed research on several promising preventive approaches of this kind. Use of applied behavior analysis programs for misbehavior in class can also contribute to the prevention of delinquency (Walker & Gresham, 2003). Group contingencies can be especially effective with predelinquent students because this strategy can deprive students of peer support for misbehavior.

CERTIFICATION POINTER

A teacher certification question may ask you to respond to a case study by suggesting ways of helping students develop the social skills that would help resolve conflicts presented in the case.

Requesting Family Involvement

Involve the student's home in any response to serious misbehavior. When misbehavior occurs, parents should be notified. If misbehavior persists, parents should be involved in establishing a program, such as a home-based reinforcement program, to coordinate home and school responses to misbehavior.

ON THE WEB

For more on how schools can establish a climate that reduces behaviors such as ridicule, bullying, and violence, go to **www.dontlaugh.org.**

Using Peer Mediation

Students can be trained to serve as peer mediators, particularly to resolve conflicts between fellow students. Students who are having problems with other students might be asked to take these problems to peer mediators rather than to adults for resolution, and the peer mediators themselves might actively look for interpersonal problems among their classmates and offer help when they occur. Peer mediators have been found to be effective in resolving a variety of interpersonal problems, from insults and perceptions of unfairness among students to stealing to physical aggression (Johnson & Johnson, 2001; Troop & Asher, 1999). However, peer mediators need to be carefully trained and monitored if they are to be effective (Latham, 1997a). Figure 11.4 shows a guide for peer mediators used in one conflict management program.

These students are demonstrating peer mediation as a way to resolve a conflict. As a teacher, how would you advise student mediators to handle conflicts with a group of students?

1. Introduce yourselves: "Hi, my name is __________. I'm conflict manager and this is my partner __________."
2. Ask the parties: "Do you want to solve the problem with us or with a teacher?" If necessary, move to a quiet place to solve the problem.
3. Explain to the parties: "First you have to agree to four rules":
   a. Agree to solve the problem.
   b. No name-calling.
   c. Do not interrupt.
   d. Tell the truth.
4. Conflict Manager #1 asks Person #1: "What happened? How do you feel?" Conflict Manager #1 repeats what Person #1 said, using active listening: "So, what you're saying is . . ."
5. Conflict Manager #2 asks Person #2: "What happened? How do you feel?" Conflict Manager #2 repeats what Person #2 said, using active listening: "So, what you're saying is . . ."
6. Ask Person #1: "Do you have a solution?" Ask Person #2: "Do you agree with the solution?" If no: "Do you have another solution?" and so on until disputants have reached a solution agreeable to both of them.
7. Have disputants tell each other what they have just agreed to: "So will you tell each other what you've just agreed to?"
8. Congratulate them both: "Thank you for working so hard to solve your problem. Congratulations."
9. Fill out Conflict Manager Report Form.

FIGURE 11.4 Peer Conflict Management

From Classroom Law Project, 6318 S. W. Corbett, Portland, OR 97201. Adapted by permission.

ONLINE READING & WRITING EXERCISE
"You Shoes Is Dusty"

Access this exercise, entitled "You Shoes Is Dusty," in the Homework and Exercises section for Chapter 11 of this text at **www.mylabschool.com.**

Judiciously Applying Consequences

Avoid the use of suspension (or expulsion) as punishment for all but the most serious misbehavior (see Curwin & Mendler, 1999). Suspension often exacerbates truancy problems, both because it makes students fall behind in their work and because it gives them experience in the use of time out of school. In-school suspension, detention, and other penalties are more effective (Axelrod & Mathews, 2003).

When students misbehave, they should be punished; but when punishment is applied, it should be brief. Being sent to a time-out area or detention room is a common punishment and is effective for most students. Loss of privileges may be used. However, whatever punishment is used should not last too long. It is better to make a misbehaving student miss 2 days of football practice than to throw him off the team, in part because once the student is off the team, the school could have little else of value to offer or withhold. Every child has within himself or herself the capacity for good behavior as well as for misbehavior. The school must be the ally of the good in each child at the same time that it is the enemy of misbehavior. Overly harsh penalties or penalties that do not allow the student to reenter the classroom on an equal footing with others risk pushing students into the antisocial, delinquent subculture. When a student has paid her or his debt by losing privileges, experiencing detention, or whatever the punishment might be, he or she must be fully reaccepted as a member of the class.

The Intentional TEACHER

USING WHAT YOU KNOW about Effective Learning Environments to Improve Teaching and Learning

Intentional teachers are leaders in their classrooms who take responsibility for managing time, activities, and behaviors. At the core of their success as classroom managers is high-interest, meaningful instruction. Intentional teachers use instructional time to its fullest by structuring a positive, consistent environment with reasonable rules and time-conscious procedures. They proactively prevent misbehavior and have planned out a range of responses to misbehavior should it occur despite prevention. Intentional teachers' actions reflect their understanding that effective learning environments result from careful planning and vigilant monitoring.

1 What do I expect my students to know and be able to do at the end of this lesson? How does this contribute to course objectives and to students' needs to become capable individuals?

Students learn best when they are productively engaged in instruction. Develop a management plan that aims to prevent misbehavior. Before the school year begins, list some of the strategies that you can employ to help your students make good choices about their behavior. At the top of your list type in bold: **Provide instruction that taps students' curiosity and creativity!** Next, list key terms and brief reminders about actions that can help to prevent misbehavior, such as

Fairness—Show genuine concern for the students and consider their perspectives. Apply consequences consistently and without emotion.

Withitness—remember to monitor all corners of the room.

Research indicates that some teachers lose half—or more—of their instructional time. Make a plan to use your students' time well, and guard your instructional minutes carefully. Commit to teach bell-to-bell, beginning your lessons with an opener—usually a practice exercise or a brain teaser—that is on the overhead projector as students arrive, and closing the lessons with a brief period of independent work during which you can work with students who had difficulties with the lesson.

2 What knowledge, skills, needs, and interests do my students have that must be taken into account in my lesson?

Bored or frustrated students might find greater rewards in avoiding schoolwork than in completing it. Provide instruction that engages students' curiosity and attends to the various preparation levels students bring to the classroom. For example, imagine that a small cluster of students has been unruly during the beginning of your unit on computation with decimals. You could do a task analysis of the concepts and skills required in the unit and find that this small group of students is missing some prerequisite skills: They have not yet committed basic math facts to memory. So that students can succeed with decimal computations, you might allow them to use their fact tables. At the same time, you could plan to introduce math facts games to help your students master basic operations.

3 What do I know about the content, child development, learning, motivation, and effective teaching strategies that I can use to accomplish my objectives?

Different kinds of misbehavior require different levels of intervention. Develop a range of responses to misbehavior,

CHAPTER 11 SUMMARY

What Is an Effective Learning Environment?

Creating effective learning environments involves strategies that teachers use to maintain appropriate behavior and respond to misbehavior in the classroom. Keeping students interested and engaged and showing enthusiasm are important in preventing misbehavior. Creating an effective learning environment is a matter of knowing a set of techniques that teachers can learn and apply.

What Is the Impact of Time on Learning?

Methods of maximizing allocated time include preventing late starts and early finishes, preventing interruptions, handling routine procedures smoothly and quickly, minimizing time spent on discipline, and using engaged time effectively. Engaged time, or time on-task, is the time individual students spend actually doing assigned work. Teachers can maximize engaged time by teaching engaging lessons, maintaining momentum, maintaining smoothness of instruction, managing transitions, maintaining group focus, practicing withitness, and overlapping. In a student-centered classroom, classroom management

INTASC 7 Instructional Planning Skills
9 Professional Commitment and Responsibility

beginning with the lowest level of intensity. When students exhibit serious misbehaviors, consider the motivation for their behavior, and respond in ways that take into account the individual and the problem. You can address most misbehavior through low-level interventions such as nonverbal cues, physical proximity, and hints. A few students, though, demonstrate persistent misbehavior. You might develop home-based reinforcement programs in which students can earn added time at their favorite activities if their school behavior improves.

4 What instructional materials, technology, assistance, and other resources are available to help accomplish my objectives?

Effective managers start the year by teaching and reinforcing classroom rules and procedures. Spend time during the first days of school teaching students your expectations for behavior. Perhaps you could interview a few experienced colleagues about their first-day-of-school plans. From their suggestions, you might develop a plan to (1) devise a set of classroom rules through class discussion; (2) develop consequences for instances when students choose to violate or ignore those rules; and (3) teach the students procedures for submitting homework, collecting work for an absent paper, and working effectively in small groups.

5 How will I plan to assess students' progress toward my objectives?

Collect ongoing information about your use of allocated and engaged time. Ask yourself whether you are devoting enough time to each subject and whether students are engaged during that time in experiences that result in meaningful learning. Review your use of time by, first, examining your schedule to determine whether allocated time is appropriate. Then, for a week, you might track start and end times for each of your lessons to determine where minutes may be lost. Finally, examine students' work to assess the degree to which students demonstrate that their on-task behavior has resulted in significant learning.

Teachers need to review students' responses to their efforts to redirect behavior. Consider changing strategies when misbehavior persists or when you are spending too much time correcting it. For example, when you overhear some of your students bragging about being members of your Three O'Clock Club (after-school detention), you are forced to reconsider its effectiveness as a punishment.

6 How will I respond if individual children or the class as a whole is not on track toward success? What is my back-up plan?

Take frequent "temperature readings" of the motivational climate of your classroom environment. Gather information from several sources to determine that your strategies are productive and that students are happy and learning. For example, ask students to write an anonymous journal entry on their perceptions of how the class is going. You might ask, in particular, whether they feel they have enough say in what happens in the classroom. After searching for patterns in the entries, you might spend a class period on a classroom meeting to set new goals.

is more participatory, with students involved in setting standards of behavior; yet rules are still needed and must be consistently communicated and enforced.

What Practices Contribute to Effective Classroom Management?

Practices that contribute to effective classroom management include starting the year properly and developing rules and procedures. Class rules and procedures should be explicitly presented to students and applied promptly and fairly.

What Are Some Strategies for Managing Routine Misbehavior?

One principle of classroom discipline is good management of routine misbehavior. The principle of least intervention means using the simplest methods that will work. There is a continuum of strategies from least to most disruptive: prevention of misbehavior; nonverbal cues such as eye contact, which can stop a minor misbehavior; praise of incompatible, correct behavior; praise of other students who are behaving; simple verbal reminders given immediately after students misbehave; repetition of verbal reminders; and application of consequences when students refuse to comply. For serious behavior problems, swift and certain consequences must be applied. A call to the student's parents can be effective.

How Is Applied Behavior Analysis Used to Manage More Serious Behavior Problems?

The most common reinforcer for both routine and serious misbehavior is attention from teacher or peers. When the student misbehaves to get the teacher's attention, one effective strategy is to pay attention to correct behavior while ignoring misbehavior as much as possible; scolding often acts as a reinforcer of misbehavior.

Individual behavior management strategies are useful for students with persistent behavior problems in school. After establishing baseline behavior, the teacher selects reinforcers such as verbal praise or small, tangible rewards and punishers such as time outs (removing a child from a situation that reinforces misbehavior). The teacher also establishes criteria for applying reinforcement and punishment.

Home-based reinforcement strategies might involve giving students daily or weekly report cards to take home and instructing parents to provide rewards on the basis of these reports. The steps to setting up such a program include deciding on behaviors to use for the daily report card and explaining the program to parents.

Group contingency programs are those in which an entire group is rewarded on the basis of the behavior of the group members.

One objection to behavior management techniques is that they can be used to overcontrol students. Behavior management strategies should always emphasize praise and reinforcement, reserving punishment as a last resort.

How Can Serious Behavior Problems Be Prevented?

There are few sure methods of preventing delinquency, but some general principles include clearly expressing and consistently enforcing classroom rules, reducing truancy however possible, avoiding the use of between-class ability grouping, using preventive classroom management strategies, involving parents in any response to serious misbehavior, using peer mediation, avoiding the use of suspension, applying only brief punishment, and reintegrating students after punishment. Check and Connect is one program that incorporates many of these principles.

KEY TERMS

Review the following key terms from the chapter.

accountability 335
allocated time 331
applied behavior analysis 345
Assertive Discipline 344
behavior modification 347
classroom management 329

discipline 329
engaged time 330
group alerting 335
group contingencies 346
group contingency program 352
home-based reinforcement strategies 350
mock participation 337
nonverbal cues 343
overlapping 336
time on-task 330
time out 349
withitness 336

SELF-ASSESSMENT: PRACTICING *for* LICENSURE

Directions: The chapter-opening vignette addresses indicators that are often assessed in state licensure exams. Re-read the chapter-opening vignette, and then respond to the following questions.

1. Ms. Cavalho works hard to prevent behavior problems and disruption in her classroom. Which of the following terms refers to her interaction with Mark?

- **a.** management
- **b.** discipline
- **c.** learning environment
- **d.** instruction

2. According to research, how could Ms. Cavalho increase student achievement in her classroom?

- **a.** increase allocated time for instruction by 10 percent above what is normal
- **b.** increase engaged time to 100 percent of the allocated classroom time
- **c.** increase engaged time by 10 percent above what is normal
- **d.** decrease allocated time by starting late and finishing early

3. Ms. Cavalho continues her lesson on writing style even as Mark attempts to interrupt. This is called

- **a.** engaged time.
- **b.** allocated time.
- **c.** momentum.
- **d.** overlapping.

4. Ms. Cavalho uses the principle of least intervention in her classroom. She works to prevent inappropriate behavior first, then if that does not work, she gives nonverbal cues and verbal reminders about how to act. She has used these strategies with Mark. Assume that Mark's behavior does not change after their discussion. What should she do next?

- **a.** apply consequences
- **b.** give praise for appropriate behavior
- **c.** ask students to solve the problem
- **d.** ignore the behavior

5. Daily report cards, group contingency programs, home-based reinforcement programs, and individual behavior management programs are all based on

- **a.** assertive discipline practices.
- **b.** delinquency prevention.
- **c.** behavioral learning theory.
- **d.** the principle of least intervention.

6. Discuss ethical considerations in the use of individual and group behavior management programs.

7. Explain how you would prevent the following misbehaviors: speaking out of turn, teasing, physical fighting.

Where the Classroom Comes to Life

Now go to **www.myeducationlab.com** to:

- take a Pretest to assess your initial comprehension of chapter content;
- study chapter content with your individualized Study Plan;
- take a Posttest to assess your understanding of chapter content;
- practice your teaching skills with Building Teaching Skills exercises; and
- build a deeper, more applied understanding of chapter content with Homework and Exercises.

CHAPTER 12

Learners with Exceptionalities

chapter OUTLINE

Elaine Wagner, assistant principal at Pleasantville Elementary School, came in to work one day and was stopped by the school secretary.

"Good morning," the secretary said. "There's a Helen Ross here to see you. She is interested in enrolling her children. She's waiting in your office. Looks nervous—I gave her some coffee and settled her down."

"Thanks, Beth," said Ms. Wagner. She went into her office and introduced herself to Ms. Ross.

"I appreciate your seeing me," said Ms. Ross. "We're planning to move to Pleasantville next fall, and I wanted to look at the schools before we move. We have one child, Tommy, going into second grade, and Annie is going into kindergarten. I'm really concerned about Tommy. In the school he's in now, he's not doing very well. It's spring, and he's hardly reading at all. His teacher says he might have a learning disability, and the school wants to put him in special education. I don't like that idea. He's a normal, happy kid at home, and it would crush him to find out he's 'different,' but I want to do what's best for him. I guess the main thing I want to see is what you do for kids like Tommy."

"Well," said Ms. Wagner, "the most important thing I can tell you about our school is that our philosophy is that every child can learn, and it is our job to find out how to reach each one. I can't tell you exactly what we'd do with Tommy, of course because I don't know him, but I can assure you of a few things. First, we'll attend to his reading problem right away. We believe in prevention and early intervention. If Tommy is having serious reading problems, we'll probably arrange to give him one-to-one tutoring so that he can catch up quickly with the other second-graders. Second, we'll try to keep him in his regular classroom if we possibly can. If he needs special-education services, he'll get them, but in this school we try everything to solve a child's learning problems before we refer him or her for testing that might lead to special-education placement. Even if Tommy does qualify for special education, we'll structure his program so that he is with his regular class as much as possible. We will develop an individualized education plan for him. Finally, I want to assure you that you will be very much involved in all decisions that have to do with Tommy and that we'll talk with you frequently about his progress and ask for your help at home to make sure that Tommy is doing well."

"Ms. Wagner, that all sounds great. But how can you give Tommy the help he needs and still let him stay in his regular class?"

"Why don't I take you to see some of our classes in operation right now?" said Ms. Wagner. "I think you'll see what I mean."

Ms. Wagner led the way through the brightly lit corridors lined with student projects, artwork, and compositions. She turned in at Mr. Esposito's second-grade class. There, she and Ms. Ross were met by a happy, excited buzz of activity. The children were working in small groups, measuring each other's heights and the lengths of fingers and feet. Some children were trying to figure out how to measure the distance around each other's heads. Another teacher, Ms. Park, was working with some of the groups.

Ms. Wagner and Ms. Ross stepped back into the hall. "What I wanted to show you," said Ms. Wagner, "is how we integrate our students with special needs into the general education classroom. Could you tell which students were special-needs students?"

"No," admitted Ms. Ross.

"That's what we hope to create—a classroom in which children with special needs are so well integrated that you can't pick them out. Ms. Park is the special-education teacher for the younger grades, and she teams with Mr. Esposito during math and reading periods to serve all of the second-graders who need special services. Ms. Park will help any child who is having difficulty, not only students with special needs, because a large part of her job is to prevent students from ever needing special education. Sometimes she'll work with individual kids or small groups that need help. She often teaches skills children will be learning in advance, so they will be better prepared in class. For example, she might have gone over measurement with some of the kids before this lesson so that they'd have a leg up on the concept."

Ms. Wagner led the way to a small room near the library room. She pointed through a window at a teacher working with one child. "What you see there is a tutor working with a first-grader who is having difficulty in reading. If your Tommy were here, this is what we might be doing with him. We try to do anything we can to keep kids from falling behind in the first place so that they can stay out of special education and progress along with their classmates."

Ms. Wagner showed Ms. Ross all over the school. In one class a child with a visual disability was reading text from a computer that had inch-high letters. In another they saw a child with Down syndrome working in a cooperative learning group on a science project. In a third classroom a child using a wheelchair was leading a class discussion.

Ms. Ross was fascinated.

"I had no idea a school could be like this. I'm so excited that we're moving to Pleasantville. This looks like the perfect school for both of my children. I only wish we could have moved here two years ago!"

USING *your* EXPERIENCE

COOPERATIVE LEARNING In groups of five, discuss Tommy Ross and students like him. One person assumes the role of Ms. Wagner; one is his future homeroom teacher, Mr. Esposito; one is Ms. Ross; one is the special-education teacher, Ms. Park; and one is the special-education director for the district. Discuss how Tommy will be screened for a potential learning disability in reading, and list some strategies that his teachers might use if, in fact, he does have a learning disability.

COOPERATIVE LEARNING Divide groups of four classmates into pairs. The pairs interview a partner about what a learning disability in reading might look like (i.e., how a reading disability might be identified) and what a teacher might do to address this situation. The two interviewers share what they have learned within their group. Roles are then reversed. The two new interviewers tell their group what they have learned about reading disabilities.

Pleasantville Elementary School is organized around two key ideas: that all children can learn, and that it is the school's responsibility to find ways to meet each child's needs in the general education classroom to the maximum extent possible.

Pleasantville Elementary is organized to identify children's strengths as well as their problems and to provide the best program it can for each child. Every school has children with exceptionalities who can do well in school when they are given the specific supports they need to learn. This chapter describes children with exceptionalities and programs that are designed to help them achieve their full potential.

INTASC

2 Knowledge of Human Development and Learning

3 Adapting Instruction for Individual Needs

WHO ARE LEARNERS WITH EXCEPTIONALITIES?

In one sense, every child is exceptional. No two children are exactly alike in their ways of learning and behaving, in their activities and preferences, in their skills and motivations. All students would benefit from programs uniquely tailored to their individual needs.

However, schools cannot practically meet the precise needs of every student. For the sake of efficiency, students are grouped into classes and given common instructional experiences designed to provide the greatest benefit to the largest number at a moderate cost. This system works reasonably well for the great majority of students. However, some students do not fit easily into this mold. Some students have physical or sensory disabilities, such as hearing or vision loss or orthopedic disabilities, that restrict their ability to participate in the general education classroom program without special assistance. Other students have mental retardation, emotional or behavioral disorders, or learning disabilities that make it difficult for them to learn in the general education classroom without assistance. Finally, some students have such outstanding talents that the general education classroom teacher is unable to meet their unique needs without help.

To receive special-education services, a student must have one of a small number of categories of disabilities or disorders. These general labels, such as "specific learning disabilities," "mental retardation," and "orthopedic impairments," cover a wide diversity of problems.

Labels tend to stick, making change difficult, and the labels themselves can become handicaps for the student. Education professionals must avoid using labels in a way that unintentionally stigmatizes students, dehumanizes them, segregates them socially from their peers, or encourages discrimination against them in any form (Hehir, 2007). The term **learners with exceptionalities** may be used to describe any individuals whose physical, mental, or behavioral performance is so different from the norm—either higher or lower—that additional services are needed to meet the individuals' needs.

The terms disability and handicap are not interchangeable. A **disability** is a functional limitation a person has that interferes with the person's physical or cognitive abilities. A **handicap** is a condition imposed on a person with disabilities by society, the physical environment, or the person's attitude. For example, a student who uses a wheelchair is handicapped by a lack of access ramps. Handicap, therefore, is not a synonym for disability (Hallahan & Kauffman, 2006).

"People-First" Language

It is important to ensure that our language and choice of vocabulary and terminology in referring to people with disabilities convey the appropriate message of respect. There are two basic principles to keep in mind (Smith, 2001). The first is to *put people first*. An example of this would be to refer to Frankie as a student with a learning disability, not a "learning disabled child." He is a student first; the fact that he has a learning disability is secondary. The second principle is to *avoid making the person equal the disability* (Smith, 2001). There are many characteristics of each student and the disability is only one. To define the child in terms of the disability does him or her an injustice. The following sections discuss characteristics of students with the types of exceptionalities that are most commonly seen in schools.

learners with exceptionalities
Any individuals whose physical, mental, or behavioral performance is so different from the norm—either higher or lower—that additional services are needed to meet the individuals' needs.

disability
The limitation of a function, such as cognitive processing or physical or sensory abilities.

handicap
A condition imposed on a person with disabilities by society, the physical environment, or the person's attitude.

Types of Exceptionalities and the Numbers of Students Served

Some exceptionalities, such as loss of vision and hearing, are relatively easy to define and measure. Others, such as mental retardation, learning disabilities, and emotional disorders, are much harder to define, and their definitions have evolved over time. In fact, recent decades have seen dramatic changes in these categories (Hallahan & Kauffman, 2006). Since the mid-1970s, the numbers of children in categories of disabilities that are most easily defined, such as physical impairments, have remained fairly stable. However, the number of students categorized as learning disabled has steadily increased, and the use of the category "mentally retarded" has diminished.

Figure 12.1 shows the percentages of all students, ages 3 to 21, receiving special-education services in 2001. There are several important pieces of information in this figure. First, notice that the overall percentage of students receiving special education was about 12 percent; that is, 1 out of 8 students, ages 3 to 21, was categorized as exceptional. Of these, the largest proportion was categorized as having specific learning disabilities (6 percent of all students) or speech disabilities (2.3 percent). Figure 12.2 shows the percentages of students ages 6 to 21 receiving special-education services who had various disabilities in 2001 (U.S. Department of Education, 2005). Specific learning disabilities (49.2 percent of all students with disabilities), speech and language impairments (18.6 percent), and mental retardation (10.3 percent) are far more common than physical or sensory disabilities. In a class of 25 a teacher might, on the average, have one or two students with learning disabilities and one with a speech impairment. In contrast, only about 1 class in 40 is likely to have a student who has hearing or vision loss or a physical disability.

Students with Mental Retardation

Just over 1 percent of all students ages 6 to 21 have mental retardation (U.S. Department of Education, 2005). There are several definitions of **mental retardation.** In 2002 the American Association on Mental Retardation (AAMR) defined mental retardation as follows:

> Mental retardation is a disability characterized by significant limitations both in intellectual functioning and in adaptive behavior as expressed in conceptual, social, and practical adaptive skills. This disability originates before age 18. (AAMR, 2002, p. 1)

This definition means that people with mental retardation have low scores on tests of intelligence and also show difficulty in maintaining the standards of personal

FIGURE 12.1 Percentage of Children Ages 3 to 21 Served under IDEA, Part B, by Disability during the 2001 School Year

From U.S. Department of Education, Office of Special Education and Rehabilitative Services, *Annual Report to Congress on the Implementation of the Individuals with Disabilities Education Act,* Washington, DC, 2002.

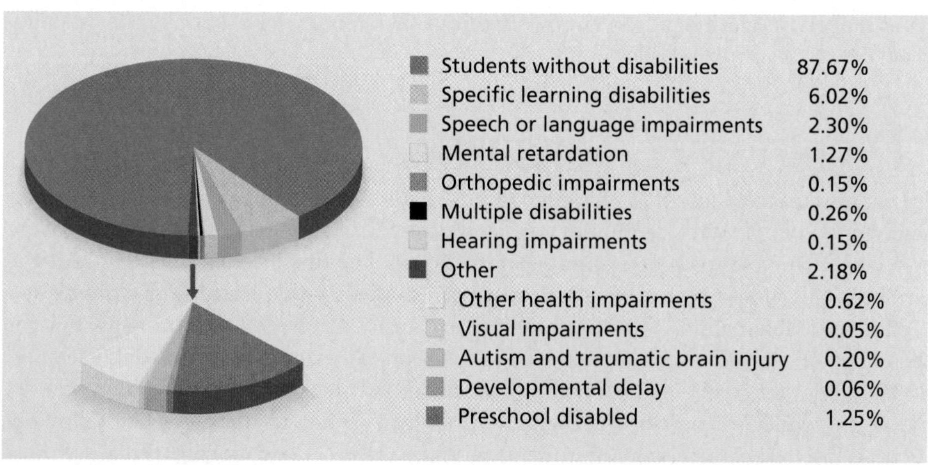

Type of Disability	Percentage of All Students with Disabilities
Specific learning disabilities	49.2
Speech or language impairments	18.6
Mental retardation	10.3
Emotional disturbance	8.1
Multiple disabilities	2.2
Hearing impairments	1.2
Orthopedic impairments	1.3
Other health impairments	5.8
Visual impairments	0.4
Autism	1.7
Deaf blindness	0.0
Traumatic brain injury	0.4
Developmental delay	0.8
All disabilities	**100.0**

FIGURE 12.2 Percentage of Children Ages 6 to 21 Served under IDEA, Part B, by Disability, 2001

From U.S. Department of Education, *Annual Report to Congress on the Implementation of the Individuals with Disabilities Act,* Washington, DC, 2005.

independence and social responsibility that would be expected for their age (Hallihan & Kauffman, 2006; McLean, 1996). In addition, these impairments in intelligence and adaptive behavior become apparent sometime between conception and age 18.

Causes of Mental Retardation Among the many causes of mental retardation are genetic inheritance; chromosomal abnormalities, such as Down syndrome (Turner & Alborz, 2003); diseases passed between mother and fetus in utero, such as rubella (German measles) and syphilis; fetal chemical dependency syndromes caused by a mother's abuse of alcohol or cocaine during pregnancy; birth accidents that result in oxygen deprivation; childhood diseases and accidents, such as encephalitis or traumatic brain injury; and toxic contamination from the environment, such as lead poisoning (McDonnell, Hardman, & McDonnell, 2003).

Intelligence Quotient (IQ) To understand how severity of impairment in children with mental retardation is classified, it is first important to recall the concept of **IQ,** or **intelligence quotient,** derived from scores on standardized tests. Students with IQs above 70 are generally regarded as being in the normal range. Slightly more than 2 percent of students have IQs below this range. However, consistent with AAMR recommendations, education professionals do not use IQs alone to determine the severity of cognitive impairment. They take into account a student's school and home performance, scores on other tests, and cultural background.

CONNECTIONS
For more on IQ, see Chapter 4, page 116.

Classifications of Mental Retardation In the past, individuals with mental retardation were largely categorized according to their IQ scores. For example, the 1983 AAMR manual listed four degrees of severity of mental retardation in terms of ranges of IQ, including mild retardation (IQs 50–55 to 70–75), moderate retardation (IQs 35–40 to 50–55), severe retardation (IQs 20–25 to 35–40), and profound retardation (IQs below 20–25) (Luckasson et al., 1992). This IQ-based classification system has been challenged by some professionals who believe that the emphasis in present-day special education is that all people can learn and that education and training cannot be clearly differentiated (Smith et al., 2008). However, some school districts use this or a similar simplified system of classification.

Current AAMR definitions emphasize the capabilities of individuals with mental retardation in two main areas—intellectual functioning and adaptive skills—and categorize individuals on the basis of the supports they need (Smith, 2001). Table 12.1 defines four categories of services people with mental retardation might need and gives examples of these services.

CONNECTIONS
For more about IQ testing, see Chapter 14, page 460.

mental retardation
A condition, usually present at birth, that results in below-average intellectual skills and poor adaptive behavior.

intelligence quotient (IQ)
An intelligence test score that should be near 100 for people of average intelligence.

TABLE 12.1 Definitions and Examples of Intensities of Supports

Type of Support	Definition and Examples
Intermittent	Supports on an as-needed basis. Characterized by episodic nature, person not always needing the support(s), or short-term supports needed during the life span transitions (e.g., job loss or an acute medical crisis). Intermittent supports may be high or low intensity when provided.
Limited	An intensity of supports characterized by consistency over time, time-limited but not of an intermittent nature, might require fewer staff members and less cost than more intense levels of support (e.g., time-limited employment training or transitional supports during the school to adult period).
Extensive	Supports characterized by regular involvement (e.g., daily) in at least some environments (such as work at home) and not time-limited (e.g., long-term support and long-term home living support).
Pervasive	Supports characterized by their constancy, high intensity; provided across environments; potential life-sustaining nature. Pervasive supports typically involve more staff members and intrusiveness than do extensive or time-limited supports.

Source: From AAMR, *Mental Retardation: Definitions, Classification, and Systems of Supports,* p. 26. Copyright 2002 by American Association on Mental Retardation. Reprinted by permission.

However the categories are defined, children with mild retardation, who need intermittent or limited support, are rarely identified before school entry (Hallahan & Kauffman, 2006). Approximately 89 percent of children with mental retardation have mild mental retardation (U.S. Department of Education, 1994).

There is increasing evidence that as many as 50 percent of all cases of mental retardation could have been prevented by improving prenatal care; ensuring proper nutrition; preventing accidents, diseases, and ingestions of poisons (such as lead paint) among children; and providing children with safe, supportive, and stimulating environments in early childhood (Smith & Luckasson, 1995). Studies of intensive early intervention programs emphasizing infant stimulation, effective preschool programs, parent support programs, and other services have shown lasting impacts on the performance of children who are at risk for mental retardation (Bradley et al., 1994; Campbell & Ramey, 1994; Garber, 1988; Noonan & McCormick, 1993; Ramey & Ramey, 1992). Even children with more pervasive mental retardation benefit substantially from intensive prevention programs in their early childhood years (Casto & Mastropieri, 1986).

The following Theory into Practice section suggests ways in which general education classroom teachers can help students who have mental retardation to acquire adaptive behavior skills. Specific ways of modifying instruction for students with special needs are discussed later in this chapter.

THEORY *into* PRACTICE

Teaching Adaptive Behavior Skills

Instructional objectives for helping students who have mental retardation to acquire adaptive behavior skills are not very different from those that are valuable for all students. Every student needs to cope with the demands of school, develop interpersonal relationships, develop language skills, grow emotionally, and take care of personal needs. Teachers can help students by directly instructing or supporting students in the following areas (see Hardman, Drew, Egan, & Wolf, 1996; Wehmeyer, 2001):

1. ***Coping with the demands of school:*** Attending to learning tasks, organizing work, following directions, managing time, and asking questions.

2. ***Developing interpersonal relationships:*** Learning to work cooperatively with others, responding to social cues in the environment, using socially acceptable language, responding appropriately to teacher directions and cues, and enhancing social awareness.
3. ***Developing language skills:*** Understanding directions, communicating needs and wants, expressing ideas, listening attentively, and using appropriate voice modulation and inflection.
4. ***Socioemotional development:*** Seeking out social participation and interaction (decreasing social withdrawal) and being motivated to work (decreasing work avoidance, tardiness, and idleness).
5. ***Personal care:*** Practicing appropriate personal hygiene, dressing independently, taking care of personal property, and moving successfully from one location to another.

Students with Learning Disabilities

Learning disabilities (LD) are not a single condition but a wide variety of specific disabilities that are presumed to stem from some dysfunction of the brain or central nervous system. The following definition is adapted from the National Joint Committee on Learning Disabilities (1988, p. 1):

> Learning disabilities is a general term for a diverse group of disorders characterized by significant difficulties in the acquisition and use of listening, speaking, reading, writing, reasoning, or computing. These disorders stem from the individual and may occur across the life span. Problems in self-regulatory behaviors, social perception, and social interaction may exist with learning disabilities but do not by themselves constitute a learning disability. Learning disabilities may occur with other handicapping conditions but are not the result of those conditions.

Identifying Students with Learning Disabilities Different interpretations of the many definitions of *learning disability* have led state and local school districts to vary widely in their eligibility requirements and provisions for students with learning disabilities (Bender, 2004). The increasing numbers of students identified as having learning disabilities have contributed to the confusion. In 2000, for example, 45.2 percent of all students ages 3 to 21 with disabilities were identified as having specific learning disabilities (U.S. Department of Education, 2002). However, the growing numbers of students in this category are the result of a shift in its definition, not because of a change in the total number of children at risk.

In some school districts a student who falls more than two grade levels behind expectations and has an IQ in the normal range is likely to be called *learning disabled.* Some characteristics of students with learning disabilities follow:

- Normal intelligence or even giftedness
- Discrepancy between intelligence and performance
- Delays in achievement
- Attention deficit or high distractibility
- Hyperactivity or impulsiveness
- Poor motor coordination and spatial relation ability
- Difficulty solving problems
- Perceptual anomalies, such as reversing letters, words, or numbers
- Difficulty with self-motivated, self-regulated activities
- Overreliance on teacher and peers for assignments
- Specific disorders of memory, thinking, or language
- Immature social skills
- Disorganized approach to learning

learning disabilities (LD)
Disorders that impede academic progress of people who are not mentally retarded or emotionally disturbed.

Definitions of learning disabilities have historically required that there be a serious discrepancy between actual performance and the performance that might have been predicted on the basis of one or more tests of cognitive functioning, such as an IQ test (Meyer, 2000; Siegel, 2003). In practice, many children are identified as having a learning disability as a result of having substantial differences between some subscales of an IQ test and others or between one ability test and another. This emphasis on discrepancies has increasingly come under attack in recent years, however. For example, Fletcher and colleagues (1994) studied children ages 7.5 to 9.5 who were failing in reading. Some of these children had major discrepancies between their IQs and their performance; others had (low) IQ scores consistent with their poor performance. On an extensive battery of assessments, the discrepant and "nondiscrepant" children were nearly identical. In either case, what they lacked were skills that were closely related to reading. A similar pattern has been found for students with mathematics disabilities (Swanson & Jerman, 2006). Many other studies (e.g., Francis, Shaywitz, Shaywitz, Stuebing, & Fletcher, 1996; Metsala, Stanovich, & Brown, 1998; Stanovich, Siegel, & Gottard, 1997) have found similar results. These studies have undermined the idea that there is a sharp-edged definition of learning disabilities as distinct from low achievement (see Hessler, 2001; Stuebing et al., 2002).

Based on this research, the 2004 reauthorization of the main U.S. special-education law, IDEA, eliminated the use of discrepancy as part of the definition of learning disabilities, and asked that states develop new definitions defining learning disabilities as a failure to respond to high-quality instruction based on well-validated principles.

Response to Intervention The emphasis in IDEA 2004 for students with learning disabilities is on **response to intervention,** an approach in which students are identified for special-education services not primarily based on tests, but rather based on their ability to profit from increasingly intensive instruction (Fuchs & Fuchs, 2006; Smith, Polloway, Patton, & Dowdy, 2008; Vaughn, Bos, & Schumm, 2000).

In particular, children who are struggling in reading might be given small-group remediation, one-to-one tutoring, computer-assisted instruction, or other assistance to help them get on track. Only if intensive and long-term interventions have been consistently applied and have not been effective might a child be evaluated for potential learning disabilities, and even at this stage, the child's response to the additional assistance would be as diagnostically important as any test scores.

Response to intervention is intended to replace the long-standing emphasis on IQ-performance discrepancy, which has been found to be a poor predictor of actual performance (Fuchs, Fuchs, & Compton, 2004), with a criterion that focuses directly on the reading problems that cause most referrals in the first place. It also emphasizes immediate, preventive services rather than waiting until children are far behind.

Response to intervention has only been evaluated in small, controlled studies (e.g., Speece, Case, & Molloy, 2003; Vaughn et al., 2007), and outcomes generally appear positive. However, there is a long way to go in establishing what this policy means for classroom practice as well as national policy (Fuchs & Fuchs, 2006; Gersten & Dimino, 2006; Klingner & Edwards, 2006).

Characteristics of Students with Learning Disabilities On the average, students with learning disabilities tend to have lower academic self-esteem than do students who are nondisabled, although in nonacademic arenas their self-esteems are like those of other children (Elbaum & Vaughn, 2001; Kelly & Norwich, 2004; Manning, Bear, & Minke, 2001). On most social dimensions, children with learning disabilities resemble other low achievers (Larrivee & Horne, 1991). Boys are more likely than girls to be labeled as learning disabled. African Americans, Latinos, and children from families in which the head of the household has not attended college tend to be over-represented in special-education classes, whereas female students are under-represented (Harry & Klingner, 2007; O'Connor & Fernandez, 2006). There is a great deal of concern about the overidentification of boys and minority students in special education. The 2004 reauthorization of IDEA requires states and the federal government to monitor racial differences in special-education placements and to change policies that perpetuate them.

response to intervention
Policies in which struggling children are given intensive assistance and are evaluated for possible special-education services only if they fail to respond.

THEORY *into* PRACTICE

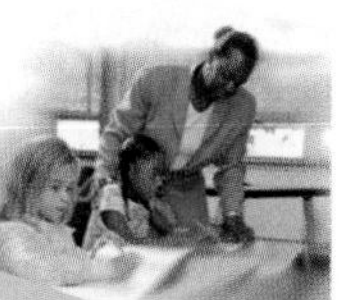

Teaching Students with Learning Disabilities

There are many types of learning disabilities, and issues in teaching students with learning disabilities differ by age level. However, a few broad principles apply across many circumstances. In general, effective teaching for students with learning disabilities uses the same strategies that are effective with other students, except that there might be less margin for error. In other words, a student with learning disabilities is less likely than other students to learn from poor instruction. General concepts of effective teaching for students with learning disabilities include these (see Bender, 2004):

1. ***Emphasize prevention.*** Many of the learning deficits that cause a child to be categorized as having learning disabilities can be prevented. For example, high-quality early childhood programs and primary-grades teaching significantly reduce the number of children identified with learning disabilities (Conyers, Reynolds, & Ou, 2003; Slavin, 1996a; Snow, Burns, & Griffin, 1998). One-to-one tutoring for first-graders struggling with reading can be particularly effective in preventing reading disabilities (Elbaum, Vaughn, Hughes, & Moody, 2000; Lyons et al., 1993; Morris, Tyner, & Perney, 2000; Wasik & Slavin, 1993). Use of early reading strategies emphasizing phonics, beneficial to most children, is essential to a large proportion of children at risk for reading disabilities (Cavanaugh et al., 2004; Schneider, Roth, & Ennemoser, 2000). Clearly, the easiest learning disabilities to deal with are those that never appear in the first place.

Recognizing that the great majority of children labeled as having learning disabilities have problems in reading, the 2004 reauthorization of IDEA encourages schools to provide scientifically validated reading programs to students who are at risk, and it allows schools to spend up to 15 percent of their IDEA funding for prevention and early intervention to help struggling students before they fall far enough behind to require a disability diagnosis.

2. ***Teach learning-to-learn skills.*** Many students with learning disabilities lack good strategies for studying, test-taking, and so on. These skills can be taught. Many studies have shown that students with learning disabilities who are directly taught study strategies and other cognitive strategies perform significantly better in school (Bryant, Ugel, Thompson, & Hampff, 1999; Deshler, Ellis, & Lenz, 1996; Gersten et al., 2001; Harris, Graham, & Pressley, 2001; Jitendra et al., 2004; Swanson, 2001; Swanson & Hoskyn, 1998).

3. ***Give frequent feedback.*** Students with learning disabilities are less likely than other students to be able to work productively for long periods of time with little or no feedback. They do better in situations in which they get frequent feedback on their efforts, particularly feedback about how they have improved or how they have worked hard to achieve something. For example, children with learning disabilities are likely to do better with brief, concrete assignments that are immediately scored than with long-term assignments. If long-term projects or reports are assigned, the students should have many intermediate goals and should get feedback on each (see Deshler et al., 1996).

4. ***Use teaching strategies that engage students actively in lessons.*** Students with learning disabilities are particularly unlikely to learn from long lectures. They tend to do best when they are actively involved. This implies that teachers who have such students in their classes should make extensive use of hands-on projects, cooperative learning, and other active learning methods, although it is important that these activities be well structured and have clear goals and roles (see Putnam, 1998a; Slavin, 1995a; Swanson & Hoskyn, 1998).

INTASC

5 **Classroom Motivation and Management**
7 **Instructional Planning Skills**

5. ***Use effective classroom management methods.*** Because of their difficulties with information processing and language, many students with learning disabilities experience a great deal of frustration in school and respond by engaging in minor (or major) misbehavior. Effective classroom management methods can greatly reduce this misbehavior, especially strategies that emphasize prevention. For example, students with learning disabilities are likely to respond well to a rapid pace of instruction with much variety and many opportunities to participate and respond successfully (Bauer & Shea, 1999; Mather & Goldstein, 2001; Rivera & Smith, 1997).

6. ***Coordinate supplementary services with classroom instruction.*** Many students with learning disabilities will need some sort of supplementary services, such as small-group tutorials, resource teachers, one-to-one tutoring, or computer-assisted instruction. Whatever these services are, they should be closely aligned with the instruction being given in academic classes. For example, if a student is working on *Treasure Island* in class, a tutor should also work on *Treasure Island*. If a student's math class is working on fractions, so should the resource teacher. Of course, there are times when supplementary services cannot be coordinated fully with classroom instruction, as when a student needs work on study strategies or prerequisite skills. However, every effort should be made to create as much linkage as possible so that the student can see an immediate learning payoff for his or her efforts in the supplementary program. The students having the greatest difficulties in learning should not have to balance two completely different kinds of teaching on different topics.

Students with Attention Deficit Hyperactivity Disorder

Students with **attention deficit hyperactivity disorder (ADHD)** have difficulties maintaining attention because of a limited ability to concentrate (Mash & Wolfe, 2003). ADHD includes impulsive actions, attention deficits, and sometimes hyperactive behavior. These characteristics differentiate students with ADHD from students with learning disabilities, who have attention deficits for other unknown reasons (American Psychiatric Association, 1994). Children with ADHD do not qualify for special education unless they also have some other disability condition that is defined in the law (Aleman, 1990). There is much debate about whether ADHD exists as a distinct diagnostic category (Pellegrini & Horvat, 1995; Swanson, Mink, & Bocian, 1999). About 7.8 percent of children ages 4 to 17 have been diagnosed with ADHD (Brown, 2007). Research indicates that males with ADHD outnumber females in ratios varying from 4:1 to 9:1 (American Psychiatric Association, 1994; Parker, 1990). Children with ADHD may be impulsive, acting before they think or without regard for the situation they are in, and often can be inattentive and may find it hard to sit still. Medications for ADHD are widely prescribed, and a variety of drugs have been found to make hyperactive children more manageable and improve their academic performance (Brown, 2007; Evans et al., 2000). They can also have side effects, such as insomnia, weight loss, and blood pressure changes (Wilens, 1998).

attention deficit hyperactivity disorder (ADHD)
A disorder characterized by difficulties maintaining attention because of a limited ability to concentrate; includes impulsive actions and hyperactive behavior.

INTASC

3 Adapting Instruction for Individual Needs
5 Classroom Motivation and Management
7 Instructional Planning Skills

THEORY *into* PRACTICE

Students with ADHD: The Role of the Teacher

Attention deficit hyperactivity disorder (ADHD) is usually associated with inattention, impulsivity, and hyperactivity. Educational implications of ADHD are that students might have significant academic, behavior, and social problems stemming from the inability to pay attention. Specific suggestions for the general education classroom teacher who has students with ADHD include the following (see Brown, 2007; Schlozman & Schlozman, 2000; Smith, 2001; Teeter, 2000):

- Make sure students understand all classroom rules and procedures.
- Consider carefully the seating arrangements of students with ADHD to prevent distractions and to keep these students in proximity to the teacher.
- Adhere to the principles of effective classroom management.
- Understand that certain behaviors, although not desirable, are not meant to be noncompliant—students might not be able to control their behaviors.
- Allow students who are hyperactive to have many opportunities to be active.
- Refrain from implementing a behavior management system that is predicated mostly on the use of punishment or threats.
- Group students with ADHD wisely, taking into consideration the purpose of the group and the other students who will be members of the group.
- Teach students to manage their own behaviors—this includes self-monitoring, self-evaluation, self-reinforcement, and self-instruction (Binder, Dixon, & Ghezi, 2000; Robinson, Smith, Miller, & Brownell, 1999).
- Maintain ongoing communication with the students' homes by using daily report cards or other instruments to convey information (see Chapter 11).
- Collaborate with special-education personnel to develop behavioral and instructional plans for dealing with attention problems.

CERTIFICATION POINTER

For a case study on your teacher certification test, you may be asked to suggest how to help a student with a very limited attention span to focus on a lecture and organize the concepts.

VIDEO HOMEWORK EXERCISE

ADHD

Go to **www.myeducationlab.com** and, in the Homework and Exercises section for Chapter 12 of this text, access the video entitled "ADHD." Watch the video and complete the homework questions that accompany it, saving your work or transmitting it to your professor as required.

Students with Speech or Language Impairments

Some of the most common disabilities are problems with speech and language. About 1 in every 40 students has a communication disorder serious enough to warrant speech therapy or other special-education services.

Although the terms *speech* and *language* are often used interchangeably, they are not the same. Language is the communication of ideas using symbols and includes written language, sign language, gesture, and other modes of communication in addition to oral speech. Speech refers to the formation and sequencing of sounds. It is quite possible to have a speech disorder without a language disorder or to have a language disorder without a speech disorder (Bernstein & Tiegerman-Farber, 2002).

Students with Speech Disorders There are many kinds of **speech disorders.** The most common are articulation (or phonological) disorders, such as omissions, distortions, or substitutions of sounds. For example, some students have difficulty pronouncing *r*'s, saying "sowee" for "sorry." Others have lisps, substituting *th* for *s,* saying "thnake" for "snake."

Misarticulated words are common and developmentally normal for many children in kindergarten and first grade but drop off rapidly through the school years. Moderate and extreme deviations in articulation diminish over the school years, with or without speech therapy. For this reason, speech therapists often decide not to work with a child who has a mild articulation problem. However, speech therapy is called for if a student cannot be understood or if the problem is causing the student psychological or social difficulties (such as being teased).

Speech disorders of all kinds are diagnosed and treated by speech pathologists or speech therapists. The classroom teacher's role is less important here than with other disability areas. However, the classroom teacher does have one crucial role to play: displaying acceptance of students with speech disorders. Most speech disorders will eventually resolve themselves. The lasting damage is more often psychological than phonological; students with speech disorders often are subjected to a great deal of teasing and social rejection. Teachers can model acceptance of the child with speech disorders in several ways. First, teachers should be patient with students who are stuttering or having trouble

speech disorders
Oral articulation problems, occurring most frequently among children in the early elementary school grades.

producing words and never finish a student's sentence or allow others to do so. Second, teachers should avoid putting students who have speech problems into high-pressure situations that require quick verbal responses. Third, teachers should refrain from correcting students' articulation in class.

CONNECTIONS
Problems that result from limited English proficiency are discussed in Chapter 4, page 107.

Students with Language Disorders **Language disorders** are impairments of the ability to understand language or to express ideas in one's native language (Bernstein & Tiegerman-Farber, 2002). Problems that result from limited English-speaking proficiency (LEP) for students whose first language is not English are not considered language disorders.

Difficulties in understanding language (receptive language disorders) or in communicating (expressive language disorders) might result from such physical problems as hearing or speech impairment. If not, they are likely to indicate mental retardation or learning disabilities. Many students come to school with what appear to be receptive or expressive language disorders but that in fact result from a lack of experience with standard English because they speak either a language other than English or a dialect of English (Battle, 1996; Bonner-Tompkins, 2001). Preschool programs that are rich in verbal experience and direct instruction in the fundamentals of standard English have been found to be effective in overcoming language problems that are characteristic of children from disadvantaged homes.

CONNECTIONS
For more on preschool programs that help overcome problems of children from disadvantaged homes, see Chapter 3, page 71.

Students with Emotional and Behavioral Disorders

All students are likely to have emotional problems at some point in their school career; but about 1 percent have such serious, long-lasting, and pervasive emotional or psychiatric disorders that they require special education. As in the case of learning disabilities, students with serious emotional and behavioral disorders are far more likely to be boys than girls, by a ratio of more than 3 to 1 (U.S. Department of Education, 2005).

Students with **emotional and behavioral disorders** have been defined as those whose educational performance is adversely affected over a long period of time to a marked degree by any of the following conditions:

1. An inability to learn that cannot be explained by intellectual, sensory, or health factors
2. An inability to build or maintain satisfactory interpersonal relationships with peers and teachers
3. Inappropriate types of behavior or feelings under normal circumstances
4. A general, pervasive mood of unhappiness or depression
5. A tendency to develop physical symptoms, pains, or fears associated with personal or school problems.

Causes of Emotional and Behavioral Disorders Serious and long-term emotional and behavioral disorders may be the result of numerous potential causal factors in the makeup and development of an individual (Jones, Dohrn, & Dunn, 2004). Neurological functioning, psychological processes, a history of maladaptations, self-concept, and lack of social acceptance all play a role (Smith et al., 2008). Some of the same factors, including family dysfunction and maltreatment (Thompson & Wyatt, 1999), also play a role in disturbances that might temporarily affect a child's school performance.

Many factors that affect families can disrupt a student's sense of security and self-worth for a period of time. Changes in the family structure, for example, might leave a child depressed, angry, insecure, defensive, and lonely, especially in the case of divorce, relocation to a new community, the addition of a younger sibling, the addition of a new stepparent, or the death or serious illness of a family member.

One problem in identifying serious emotional and behavioral disorders is that the term covers a wide range of behaviors, from aggression or hyperactivity to withdrawal or inability to make friends (Epstein & Cullinan, 1992) to anxiety and phobias (King & Ollendick, 1989). Also, children with emotional disorders quite frequently have other disabilities, such as learning disabilities or mental retardation, and it is often hard to tell whether an emotional problem is causing the diminished academic performance or school failure is causing the emotional problem.

language disorders
Impairments in one's ability to understand language or to express ideas in one's native language.

emotional and behavioral disorders
Exceptionalities characterized by problems with learning, interpersonal relationships, and control of feelings and behavior.

Characteristics of Students with Emotional and Behavioral Disorders Scores of characteristics are associated with emotional and behavioral disorders (Rosenberg et al., 2004). The important issue is the degree of the behavior problem. Virtually any behavior that is exhibited excessively over a long period of time might be considered an indication of emotional disturbance. However, most students who have been identified as having emotional and behavioral disorders share some general characteristics. These include poor academic achievement, poor interpersonal relationships, and poor self-esteem (Lewis & Sullivan, 1996). Quay and Werry (1986) noted four general categories: conduct disorder, anxiety–withdrawal, immaturity, and socialized–aggressive disorder. For example, children with **conduct disorders** are frequently characterized as disobedient, distractible, selfish, jealous, destructive, impertinent, resistive, and disruptive. Quay and Werry noted that the first three of these categories represent behaviors that are maladaptive or sources of personal distress. However, socialized–aggressive behavior, which relates to frequent aggression against others, seems to be tied more to poor home conditions that model or reward aggressive behavior and, therefore, might be adaptive (though certainly not healthy or appropriate). The inclusion of conduct disorders in classifications of emotional and behavioral disorders is controversial. By law, students with conduct disorders must also have some other recognized disability or disorder to receive special-education services. IDEA has long protected children who have emotional and behavioral disorders from ordinary punishments (such as suspension) for disruptive behavior. The 2004 reauthorization maintains this protection for behaviors related to the child's disability but not for unrelated behaviors.

VIDEO HOMEWORK EXERCISE
Behavior Disorder

Go to **www.myeducationlab.com** and, in the Homework and Exercises section for Chapter 12 of this text, access the video entitled "Behavior Disorder." Watch the video and complete the homework questions that accompany it, saving your work or transmitting it to your professor as required.

Students Exhibiting Aggressive Behavior Students with conduct disorders and socialized–aggressive behaviors might frequently fight, steal, destroy property, and refuse to obey teachers (Jones, Dohrn, & Dunn, 2004). These students tend to be disliked by their peers, their teachers, and sometimes their parents. They typically do not respond to punishment or threats, though they might be skilled at avoiding punishment. Aggressive children not only pose a threat to the school and to their peers, but also put themselves in grave danger. Aggressive children, particularly boys, often develop serious emotional problems later in life, have difficulty holding jobs, and become involved in criminal behavior (Loeber & Stouthamer-Loeber, 1998; van Goozen et al., 2007). Effective approaches for these children include behavior management strategies like those described in Chapter 11 (see Jones & Jones, 2007)

CONNECTIONS
Behavior management programs for students exhibiting aggressive behavior are described in Chapter 11, page 347.

Students with Withdrawn and Immature Behavior Children who are withdrawn, immature, low in self-esteem, or depressed typically have few friends or play with children much younger than themselves. They often have elaborate fantasies or daydreams and either very poor or grandiose self-images. Some might be overly anxious about their health and feel genuinely ill when under stress. Some students exhibit school phobia by refusing to attend, or by running away from, school.

Unlike children who are aggressive, who can appear quite normal when they are not being aggressive, children who are withdrawn and immature often appear odd or awkward at all times. They almost always suffer from a lack of social skills (see Troop & Asher, 1999).

Students with Autism

In 1990, autism became a formal category of disability. The U.S. Department of Education defined **autism** as a developmental disability that significantly affects social interaction and verbal and nonverbal communication. It is usually evident before the age of 3 and has an adverse affect on educational performance. Children with autism are typically extremely withdrawn and have such severe difficulties with language that they might be entirely mute. They often engage in self-stimulation activities such as rocking, twirling objects, or flapping their hands. However, they might have normal or even outstanding abilities in certain areas. The term *autism spectrum disorder* is now being used to describe a broad range of severity, including a mild form of autism called *Asperger's syndrome* (National Research Council, 2001; Sweeney & Hoffman, 2004). For unknown reasons,

conduct disorders
Socioemotional and behavioral disorders that are indicated in individuals who, for example, are chronically disobedient or disruptive.

autism
A category of disability that significantly affects social interaction, verbal and nonverbal communication, and educational performance.

autism is far more prevalent among boys than among girls (Friend & Bursuck, 1999). It is thought to be caused by brain damage or other brain dysfunction (Volkmar & Pauls, 2003). The National Research Council (2001) reviewed research on autism and suggested that autistic children benefit from education that focuses on building communication skills, social skills, and cognitive skills in a systematic progression.

Students with Sensory, Physical, and Health Impairments

Sensory impairments are problems with the ability to see or hear or otherwise receive information through the body's senses. Physical disorders include conditions such as cerebral palsy, spina bifida, spinal cord injury, and muscular dystrophy. Health disorders include, for example, acquired immune deficiency syndrome (AIDS); seizure disorders; diabetes; cystic fibrosis; sickle-cell anemia (in African American students); and bodily damage from chemical addictions, child abuse, or attempted suicide (Hardman et al., 1996).

Students with Visual Disabilities Most students' visual problems are correctable by glasses or other types of corrective lenses. A **vision loss** is considered a disability only if it is not correctable. It is estimated that approximately 1 out of every 1,000 children has a visual disability. Individuals with such disabilities are usually referred to as *blind* or *visually impaired*. A legally blind child is one whose vision is judged to be 20/200 or worse in the better eye even with correction or whose field of vision is significantly narrower than that of a person with normal vision. Partially sighted persons, according to this classification system, are those whose vision is between 20/70 and 20/200 in the better eye with correction (Rogow, 1988).

It is a misconception to assume that individuals who are legally blind have no sight. More than 80 percent of students who are legally blind can read large- or regular-print books (Levin, 1996). Assistive technology used to enlarge and clarify text has further expanded the numbers of legally blind students who can participate normally in class (Boone & Higgins, 2007). This implies that many students with vision loss can be taught by means of a modification of usual teaching materials. Classroom teachers should be aware of the signs that indicate that a child is having a vision problem. Undoubtedly, children who have difficulty seeing also have difficulty in many areas of learning because classroom lessons typically use a tremendous amount of visual material. Several possible signs of vision loss include the following: (1) child often tilts head; (2) child rubs eyes

sensory impairments
Problems with the ability to receive information through the body's senses.

vision loss
Degree of uncorrectable inability to see well.

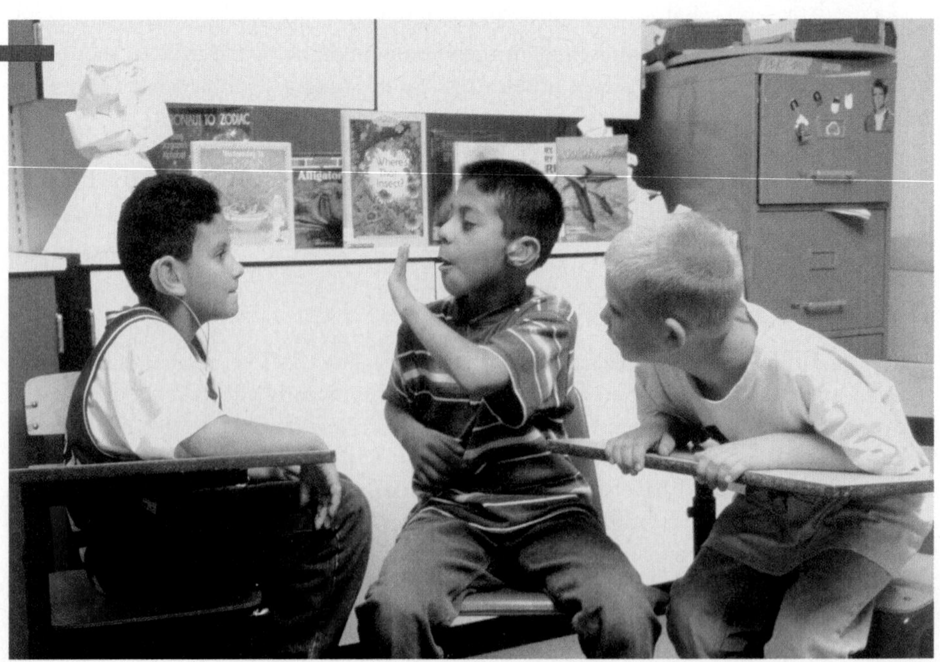

Students with hearing impairments, no matter how slight or severe, can easily fall through the cracks in a busy classroom. As a teacher, what considerations might you need to make in order to fully support the needs of a student who is hearing impaired?

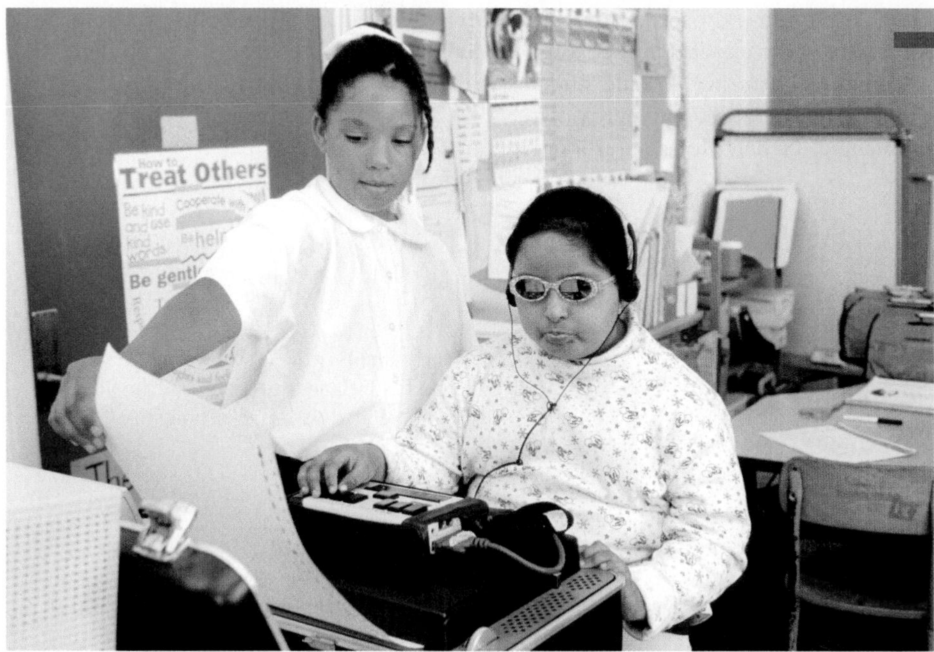

Peers-helping-peers can provide multiple benefits for all parties involved, including the teacher. Describe these benefits.

often; (3) child's eyes are red, inflamed, crusty, or water excessively; (4) child has difficulty reading small print or can't discriminate letters; (5) child complains of dizziness or headaches after a reading assignment (Sornson, 2001). If you notice any of these problems, you should refer the student for appropriate vision screening.

Students Who Are Deaf or Hard of Hearing **Hearing disabilities** can range from complete deafness to problems that can be alleviated with a hearing aid. The appropriate classification of an individual with hearing loss depends on the measures required to compensate for the problem. Simply having a student sit at the front of the classroom might be enough to compensate for a mild hearing loss. Many children can communicate adequately by listening to your voice and watching your lips. Others might need a hearing aid, and those with more severe problems will need to use a nonverbal form of communication such as sign language (see Radziewicz & Antonellis, 2002). Approaches to reading instruction also need to be modified (Schirmer & McGough, 2005). Flexner (2001) argues that a broad range of children can benefit from amplification of the teacher's voice or the use of assistive technology on computers to amplify and clarify speech (Boone & Higgins, 2007). Following are several suggestions to keep in mind:

1. Seat children with hearing problems in the front of the room, slightly off center toward the windows. This will allow them to see your face in the best light.
2. If the hearing problem is predominantly in one ear, students should sit in a front corner seat so that their better ear is toward you.
3. Speak at the student's eye level whenever possible.
4. Give important information and instructions while facing the class. Avoid talking while facing the chalkboard.
5. Do not use exaggerated lip movements when speaking.
6. Learn how to assist a child who has a hearing aid.

Students Who Are Gifted and Talented

Who are the gifted and talented? Almost all children, according to their parents; and in fact many students do have outstanding talents or skills in some area. **Giftedness** was once defined almost entirely in terms of superior IQ or demonstrated ability, such as outstanding performance in mathematics or chess, but the definition now encompasses students with superior abilities in a wide range of activities, including the arts (Olszewski-Kubilius, 2003). High IQ is still considered part of the definition of gifted and talented (Steiner &

hearing disabilities
Degree of deafness; uncorrectable inability to hear well.

giftedness
Exceptional intellectual ability, creativity, or talent.

Carr, 2003), and most students who are so categorized have IQs above 130. However, some groups are underidentified as gifted and talented, including females, students with disabilities, underachievers, and students who are members of racial or ethnic minority groups (Sternberg, 2007). Approximately 3 to 5 percent of students are considered gifted or talented (Heller, Monks, Sternberg, & Subotnik, 2000).

ON THE WEB

Web-Based Resources for Special Needs Educators

Family Friendly Fun with Special Needs:
www.family-friendly-fun.com
This site offers a great collection of resources for use with children with special needs on a variety of topics.

Special Needs Resource:
www.edbydesign.com/specneedsres/links.html
This site showcases international students, assistive technologies, and other resources for special learners.

Internet Resources for Special Children:
www.irsc.org
This organization is dedicated to providing information, activities, and support for learners with special needs.

Special Needs Opportunity Windows:
http://snow.utoronto.ca
Professional development, student activities, and parent resource materials are only a few of the many areas contained on this site.

DREAMMS for Kids, Inc.:
www.dreamms.org
Developmental Research for the Effective Advancement of Memory and Motor Skills is a nonprofit parent and professional service agency that specializes in Assistive Technology (AT)–related research, development, and information dissemination.

CAST (Center for Applied Special Technology):
www.cast.org
CAST is an educational, not-for-profit organization that uses technology to expand opportunities for all people, including those with disabilities.

NCIP (National Center to Improve Practice in Special Education):
www2.edc.org/NCIP
The National Center to Improve Practice in Special Education was federally funded from 1992 to 1998 to improve educational outcomes for students with disabilities by promoting the effective use of assistive and instructional technologies among educators and related personnel serving these students.

Alliance for Technology Access:
www.ataccess.org
The Alliance for Technology Access (ATA) is a network of community-based resource centers, developers and vendors, affiliates, and associates dedicated to providing information and support services to children and adults with disabilities and increasing their use of standard, assistive, and information technologies.

Closing the Gap:
www.closingthegap.com
Closing the Gap is a rich source for information on innovative applications of computer technology for persons with disabilities. This site provides a comprehensive examination of the most current uses of technology by persons with disabilities and the professionals who work with them.

Internet Special Education Resources (ISER):
www.iser.com
ISER is a nationwide directory of professionals who serve the learning disabilities and special-education communities. This site helps parents and caregivers find local special-education professionals to help with learning disabilities and attention deficit hyperactivity disorder assessment, therapy, advocacy, and other special needs.

Adaptive Technologies:
www.washington.edu/doit
The University of Washington has an extensive collection of publications and videos concerning technologies to help people with disabilities.

Characteristics of Gifted and Talented Students Intellectually gifted children typically have strong motivation (Dai, Moon, & Feldhusen, 1998; Gottfried & Gottfried, 2004). They also are academically superior; usually learn to read early; and, in general, do excellent work in most school areas (Gallagher, 1992). One of the most important studies of the gifted, begun by Lewis Terman in 1926, followed 1,528 individuals who had IQs higher than 140 as children. Terman's research exploded the myth that high-IQ individuals were brainy but physically and socially inept. In fact, Terman found that children with outstanding IQs were larger, stronger, and better coordinated than other children and became better adjusted and more emotionally stable adults (Terman & Oden, 1959). Gifted students also have high self-concepts (Hoge & Renzulli, 1993), although they can suffer from perfectionism (Parker, 1997).

Education of Gifted Students How to educate gifted students is a matter of debate (see Karnes & Bean, 2001; Smutny, 2003; Willard-Holt, 2003; Winebrenner, 2000). Some programs for gifted and talented children involve special secondary schools for students who are gifted in science or in the arts. Some programs include special classes for high achievers in regular schools (see Olszewski-Kubilius, 2003). One debate in this area concerns acceleration versus enrichment. Advocates of acceleration (e.g., Pendarvis & Howley, 1996) argue that gifted students should be encouraged to move through the school curriculum rapidly, perhaps skipping grades and going to college at an early age. Others (e.g., Feldhusen, 1996; Gallagher, 1992; Renzulli & Reis, 1997) maintain that rather than merely moving students through school more rapidly, programs for the gifted should engage them in more creative and problem-solving activities.

Research on the gifted provides more support (in terms of student achievement gains) for acceleration than for enrichment (Kulik & Kulik, 1997). However, this could be because the outcomes of enrichment, such as creativity or problem-solving skills, are difficult to measure. **Acceleration programs** for the gifted often involve the teaching of advanced mathematics to students at early ages. A variation on the acceleration theme is a technique called curriculum compacting, in which teachers may skip over portions of the curriculum that the very able students do not need (Willard-Holt, 2003).

Enrichment programs take many forms. Renzulli and Reis (2000) suggest an emphasis on three types of activities: general exploratory activities, such as projects that allow students to find out about topics on their own; group training activities, such as games and simulations to promote creativity and problem-solving skills; and individual and small-group investigations of real problems, such as writing books or newspapers, interviewing elderly people to write oral histories, and conducting geological or archaeological investigations.

One problem with enrichment programs for the gifted and talented is simply stated: Most of the activities that are suggested for gifted and talented students would benefit all students. In recognition of this, many schools are now infusing activities that are characteristic of enrichment programs into the curriculum for all students, thereby meeting the needs of gifted and talented students without physically separating them from their peers (see Feldhusen, 1998; Holloway, 2003; Page, 2000; Renzulli & Reis, 2000; Van Tassel-Baska, 1989). Examples of such activities include increased use of projects, experiments, independent study, and cooperative learning.

WHAT IS SPECIAL EDUCATION?

CERTIFICATION POINTER

Teacher certification tests will require you to identify areas of exceptionality in learning, including learning disabilities, visual and perceptual difficulties, and specific physical challenges.

Special education is any program provided for children with disabilities instead of, or in addition to, the general education classroom program. The practice of special education has changed dramatically in recent years and is still evolving (see Hallahan & Kauffman, 2006; Sorrells, Rieth, & Sindelar, 2004). Federal legislation has been critical in setting standards for special-education services administered by states and local districts.

Public Law 94-142 and IDEA

As recently as the mid-1960s, education of children with exceptionalities was quite different from what it is today. Many "handicapped" students received no special services at all. Those who did get special services usually attended separate schools or institutions for people with mental retardation, emotional disturbances, or vision or hearing loss. In the late 1960s the special-education system came under attack (see Semmel, Gerber, & MacMillan, 1994). Critics argued that people who had serious disabilities were too often shut away in state institutions with inadequate educational services or were left at home with no services at all and that children who are mildly disabled (particularly those with mild mental retardation) were being isolated in special programs that failed to teach them the skills they needed to function in society. Four million of the eight million students of school age who were disabled were not in school.

acceleration programs
Rapid promotion through advanced studies for students who are gifted or talented.

enrichment programs
Programs in which assignments or activities are designed to broaden or deepen the knowledge of students who master classroom lessons quickly.

special education
Programs that address the needs of students with mental, emotional, or physical disabilities.

As a result, in 1975, Congress passed **Public Law 94-142,** the Education for the Handicapped Act. P.L. 94-142, as it is commonly called, profoundly affected both special and general education throughout the United States. It prescribed the services that all disabled children must receive and gave the children and their parents legal rights that they had not previously possessed. A basic tenet of P.L. 94-142 was that every child who is disabled is entitled to special education appropriate to the child's needs at public expense. This means, for example, that school districts or states must provide special education to children who are severely retarded or disabled.

P.L. 94-142 was extended beyond its original focus in two major pieces of legislation. In 1986, Public Law 99-457 extended the entitlement to free, appropriate education to children ages 3 to 5. It also added programs for infants and toddlers who are seriously disabled. Public Law 101-476, which passed in 1990 and changed the name of the special-education law to the **Individuals with Disabilities Education Act (IDEA),** required that schools plan for the transition of adolescents with disabilities into further education or employment starting at age 16, and replaced the term *handicapped children* with the term *children with disabilities.*

In 1997, Public Law 105-17, the Individuals with Disabilities Education Act Amendments of 1997, or IDEA '97, was passed to reauthorize and strengthen the original act (National Information Center for Children and Youth with Disabilities, 1998). Among the goals of this law are raising educational expectations for children with disabilities, increasing the role of parents in the education of their children with disabilities, assuring that regular classroom teachers are involved in planning for and assessment of these children, including students with disabilities in local and state assessments, and supporting professional development for all who educate children with disabilities (U.S. Department of Education, 1998).

IDEA was further updated in 2004 under Public Law 108-446, known as the Individuals with Disabilities Education Improvement Act. This revision emphasized prevention and early intervention, allowing schools to spend special-education funds to prevent children from needing special-education services. It changed the definition of learning disabilities to eliminate the concept of discrepancy between IQ and achievement, asked states to monitor and correct racial disparities in assignment to special education, and coordinated IDEA with other reforms, especially No Child Left Behind. The major provisions of IDEA 2004 are summarized in Table 12.2.

CERTIFICATION POINTER

On your teacher certification test, you should know that the placement of students in the "least restrictive" educational environment developed as a result of efforts to normalize the lives of children with disabilities.

Least Restrictive Environment The provision of IDEA that is of greatest importance to general education classroom teachers is that students with disabilities must be assigned to the **least restrictive environment** that is appropriate to their needs. This provision gives a legal basis for the practice of **mainstreaming,** a term that has now been replaced with the word *inclusion.* This means that general education classroom teachers are likely to have in their classes students with mild disabilities (such as learning disabilities, mild mental retardation, physical disabilities, or speech problems) who might leave class for special instruction part of the day. It also means that classes for students with more serious disabilities are likely to be located in general education school facilities and that these students will probably attend some activities with their nondisabled peers.

Individualized Education Program (IEP) Another important requirement of IDEA is that every student with a disability must have an **Individualized Education Program (IEP)** that guides the services the student receives. The IEP describes a student's problems and delineates a specific course of action to address these problems. Generally, it is prepared by a special services committee composed of school professionals such as special-education teachers, special-education supervisors, school psychologists, the principal, counselors, and/or classroom teachers. Special services teams go by different names in different states; for example, they may be called child study teams or appraisal and review teams. The student's parent must consent to the IEP. The idea behind the use of IEPs is to give everyone concerned with the education of a child with a disability an opportunity to help formulate the child's instructional program. The requirement that a parent sign the IEP is designed to ensure parental awareness of and approval of what the school proposes to do for the child. A parent might hold the school accountable if the child does not receive the promised services.

Public Law 94-142
Federal law enacted in 1975 requiring provision of special-education services to eligible students.

Individuals with Disabilities Education Act (IDEA)
P.L. 101-476, a federal law enacted in 1990 that changed the name of P.L. 94-142 and broadened services to adolescents with disabilities.

least restrictive environment
Provision in IDEA that requires students with disabilities to be educated with nondisabled peers to the maximum extent appropriate.

mainstreaming
The temporal, instructional, and social integration of eligible children with exceptionalities with peers without exceptionalities based on an ongoing, individually determined educational planning and programming process.

Individualized Education Program (IEP)
A program tailored to the needs of a learner with exceptionalities.

TABLE 12.2 Key Components of the Individuals with Disabilities Education Act (IDEA) (2004)

Provisions	Description
Least restrictive environment	Children with disabilities are educated with nondisabled children as much as possible.
Individualized Education Program	All children served in special education must have an Individualized Education Program.
Due-process rights	Children and their parents must be involved in decisions about special education.
Due-process hearing	Parents and schools can request an impartial hearing if there is a conflict over special-education services.
Nondiscriminatory assessment	Students must be given a comprehensive assessment that is nondiscriminatory in nature.
Related services	Schools must provide related services, such as physical therapy, counseling, and transportation, if needed.
Free appropriate public education	The primary requirement of IDEA is the provision of a free appropriate public education to all school-age children with disabilities.
Mediation/Resolution	Parents have a right, if they choose, to mediation or a resolution session to resolve differences with the school. Using mediation should not deny or delay a parent's request for a due-process hearing.
Transfer of rights	When the student reaches the age of majority, as defined by the state, the school shall notify both the parents and the student and transfer all rights of the parents to the child.
Discipline	A child with a disability cannot be expelled or suspended for ten or more cumulative days in a school year without a manifest determination as to whether the child's disability is related to the inappropriate behavior.
State assessments	Children with disabilities must be included in districtwide and statewide assessment programs with appropriate accommodations. Alternative assessment programs must be developed for children who cannot participate in districtwide or statewide assessment programs.
Transition	Transition planning and programming must begin when students with disabilities reach age sixteen.

Source: From Tom E. K. Smith, Edward A. Polloway, James R. Patton, & Carol A. Dowdy, *Teaching Students with Special Needs in Inclusive Settings* (5th ed.), p. 16. Copyright © 2008 by Allyn & Bacon. Reprinted by permission of the publisher.

The law requires that evaluations of students for possible placement in special-education programs be done by qualified professionals. Although general education classroom and special-education teachers will typically be involved in the evaluation process, teachers are not generally allowed to give the psychological tests (such as IQ tests) that are used for placement decisions.

IDEA gives children with disabilities and their parents legal safeguards with regard to special-education placement and programs. For example, if parents believe that a child has been diagnosed incorrectly or assigned to the wrong program or if they are unsatisfied with the services a child is receiving, they may bring a grievance against the school district. Also, the law specifies that parents be notified about all placement decisions, conferences, and changes in program.

For children with special needs who are under the age of 3, a specialized plan focusing on the child and his or her family is typically prepared. This is called an Individualized Family Service Plan (IFSP). At the other end of the education system, an Individualized Transition Plan (ITP) is often written for adolescents with special needs before their 17th birthday (Sax & Thoma, 2002). The ITP anticipates the student's needs as he or she makes the transition from school to work and to adult life.

VIDEO HOMEWORK EXERCISE

Assessment of Special Needs Students

Go to **www.myeducationlab.com** and, in the Homework and Exercises section for Chapter 12 of this text, access the video entitled "Assessment of Special Needs Students." Watch the video and complete the homework questions that accompany it, saving your work or transmitting it to your professor as required.

An Array of Special-Education Services

An important aspect of an IEP is a special-education program that is appropriate to the student's needs. Every school district offers children with special needs an array of services intended to be flexible enough to meet the unique needs of all. In practice, these services are often organized as a continuum going from least to most restrictive, as follows:

1. Direct or indirect consultation and support for general education teacher
2. Special education up to 1 hour per day
3. Special education 1 to 3 hours per day; resource program
4. Special education more than 3 hours per day; self-contained special education
5. Special day school
6. Special residential school
7. Home/hospital

In general, students with more severe disabilities receive more restrictive services than do those with less severe disabilities. For example, a student with severe mental retardation is unlikely to be placed in a general education classroom during academic periods, whereas a student with a speech problem or a mild learning disability is likely to be in a general education classroom for most or all of the school day. However, severity of disability is not the sole criterion for placement; also considered is the appropriateness of the various settings for an individual student's needs. For example, a student in a wheelchair with a severe orthopedic disability but no learning problems could easily attend and profit from general education classes, whereas a student with a hearing deficit might not.

With the exception of students who have physical or sensory disabilities, few students receive special education outside of the school building. The great majority of students who have learning disabilities or speech impairments attend general education classes part or most of the day, usually supplemented by 1 or more hours per day in a special-education resource room. This is also true for the majority of students with physical disabilities and almost half of all students with emotional disorders. Most other students with special needs attend special classes located in their school buildings. The continuum of services available to students with disabilities, from least to most restrictive, is described in the following sections.

General Education Classroom Placement The needs of many students with disabilities can be met in the general education classroom with little or no outside assistance. For example, students who have mild vision or hearing loss may simply be seated near the front of the room. Students with mild to moderate learning disabilities may have their needs met in the general education classroom if the teacher uses strategies for accommodating instruction to student differences. For example, the use of instructional aides, tutors, or parent volunteers can allow exceptional students to remain in the general education classroom. Classroom teachers can often adapt their instruction to make it easier for students to succeed. For example, one teacher noticed that a student with perceptual problems was having difficulties with arithmetic because he could not line up his numbers. She solved the problem by giving him graph paper to work on.

Research generally shows that the most effective strategies for dealing with students who have learning and behavior problems are those used in the general education classroom (Lloyd, Singh, & Repp, 1991). Special-education options should usually be explored only after serious efforts have been made to meet students' needs in the general education classroom (see Smith et al., 2008; Vaughn et al., 2007).

CONNECTIONS
Strategies for accommodating instruction to student differences are discussed in Chapter 9.

Collaboration with Consulting Teachers and Other Professionals In **collaboration,** several professionals work cooperatively to provide educational services. Students with disabilities who are included in the general education classroom benefit from professionals such as the consulting resource room teacher, school psychologist, speech and language specialists, and other professionals who collaborate with the general education teacher to develop and implement appropriate educational experiences for the students. Many school districts provide classroom teachers with consultants to help them adapt

collaboration
Process in which professionals work cooperatively to provide educational services.

their instruction to the needs of students with disabilities. Consulting teachers typically are trained in special education as well as general education. They might come into the classroom to observe the behavior of a student, but most often they suggest solutions to the general education teacher rather than work directly with students (Warger & Pugach, 1996). Research finds that well-designed consulting models can be effective in assisting teachers to maintain students with mild disabilities, particularly those with learning disabilities, in the general education classroom (Rosenfield & Gravois, 1996; Snell & Janney, 2000).

INTASC

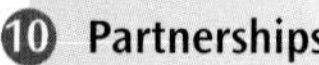

10 Partnerships

For some types of disabilities, itinerant (traveling) teachers provide special services to students a few times a week. This pattern of service is typical of programs for students with speech and language disorders.

Resource Room Placement Many students with disabilities are assigned to general education classes for most of their school day but participate in resource programs at other times. Most often, resource programs focus on teaching reading, language arts, mathematics, and occasionally other subjects. A resource room program usually involves a small number of students working with a special-education teacher. Ideally, the resource teacher meets regularly with the classroom teacher to coordinate programs for students and to suggest ways in which the general education classroom teacher can adapt instruction when the students are in the general education class (Larrivee, Semmel, & Gerber, 1997).

Sometimes resource teachers work in the general education classroom. For example, a resource teacher might work with one reading group while the general education classroom teacher works with another. This arrangement avoids pulling students out of class—which is both inefficient (because of the transition time required) and potentially demeaning because the students are excluded from class for some period of time. Team teaching involving general education and special-education teachers also enhances communication between the teachers (Friend, 2007).

Special-Education Class Placement with Part-Time Inclusion Many students with disabilities are assigned to special classes taught by a special-education teacher but are integrated with nondisabled students part of the school day. These students join other students most often for music, art, and physical education; somewhat less often for social studies, science, and mathematics; and least often for reading. One important difference between this category of special services and the resource room model is that in the resource room, the student's primary placement is in the general education class; the classroom teacher is the homeroom teacher and generally takes responsibility for the student's program, with the resource teacher providing extra support. In the case of a student who is assigned to special education and is integrated part of the day, the situation is reversed. The special-education teacher generally serves as the homeroom teacher and takes primary responsibility.

Self-Contained Special Education A self-contained special-education program is a class located in a school separately from the general education instructional program. Until the mainstreaming movement began in the early 1970s, this (along with separate schools for children with mental retardation) was the typical placement for students with disabilities. Students in self-contained programs are taught by special-education teachers and have relatively few contacts with the general education instructional program.

Some students attend separate, special, day schools. These are typically students with severe disabilities, such as severe retardation or physical disabilities, or students whose presence might be disruptive to the general education school, such as those with serious emotional disturbances. In addition, small numbers of students with disabilities attend special residential schools for students with profound disabilities who require special treatment.

Teaching Dilemmas: CASES TO CONSIDER

Referring a Student

INTASC

2 Knowledge of Human Development and Learning

8 Assessment of Student Learning

Roger Bond is a second-grade teacher at a rural elementary school in the Southwest. He's scheduled an appointment with his principal, Ana Garza, to discuss a child.

Roger: Thanks for meeting with me. I wanted to talk with you about one of my children, Callie Williams. She's really struggling with her reading, and I think she should be in special ed. I know you were a special-ed teacher before you were principal, so I thought you could help.

Ana: I'll do my best. I know Callie, and I know she had some trouble in first grade, too. What do you think the problem is?

Roger: Well, she seems to be able to decode, but she reads very slowly and loses comprehension.

Ana: That's a common problem with second-graders. What makes Callie stand out?

Roger: Well, besides her reading she has a lot of problems with distractibility, and she's always misbehaving in class.

Ana: I see. Have you given her any reading tests to see where her problem is?

Roger: I thought they'd do that when she got referred for special ed. She did get a low score on the state reading test.

Ana: Right, but that doesn't tell you where her problem is.

Roger: Well, if you'll tell me how to start the process, we can get her the testing she needs.

Ana: Not so fast! My philosophy is that you don't start a child toward special education until you've tried everything else.

Roger: But then won't she simply get worse? Also, she's disrupting my class and making it hard for other kids to learn. A special-education teacher would have more expertise in helping students with difficulties, and a smaller class size.

Ana: Assigning a child to special ed is a major step. Let's try some other things first, and we'll watch her carefully. If we've really tried everything, then we'll start the IEP process to see if she qualifies for special ed, but not before!

Roger: Well . . . OK. What should I do?

Ana: First, let's find out what her reading problem is. I'll ask Ms. Jackson, our reading specialist, to give her an individual assessment. If she needs special help with reading fluency, which I suspect, we can assign her to a tutor.

Roger: But what about her behavior?

Ana: Let's look into that, too. The county is doing a series of workshops on behavior management. I'm going to see if I can get you in.

Roger: OK, I'll give it a try. But frankly, I'm surprised. Because you are a former special-ed teacher, I thought you'd back me up.

Ana: If Callie needs special education, I'll see that she gets it. But my experience tells me that special ed isn't magic. Wherever she is, Callie will need good instruction and good classroom management.

Roger: All right. Thanks.

QUESTIONS FOR REFLECTION

1. Is Ana Garza right to deny Roger's request for a special-education evaluation? Is she depriving Callie of services she's entitled to, or is she doing the right thing?
2. What if Callie had been an English language learner? How might the conversation between Roger and Ana have been different?
3. What should Roger do to help Callie? How can Ms. Garza and others in the school help him succeed?

Related Services IDEA 2004 guarantees "related services" for children with disabilites. These are services required by a child with a disability to benefit from general or special education. For example, school psychologists are often involved in the process of diagnosing students with disabilities and sometimes participate in the preparation of IEPs (Reschly, 2003). In addition, they may counsel the student or consult with the teacher about behavioral and learning problems. Speech and language therapists generally work with students on a one-to-one basis, though they may provide some small-group instruction for students with similar problems. These therapists also consult with teachers about ways to address student difficulties. Physical and occupational therapists treat motor difficulties under the direction of a physician.

School social workers and pupil personnel workers serve as a major link between the school and the family and are likely to become involved when problems at home are affecting students' school performance or behavior.

Classroom teachers have important roles in the education of children with disabilities. They are important in referring students to receive special services, in participating in the assessment of students, and in preparing and implementing IEPs. The Theory into Practice section that follows describes the process by which classroom teachers seek special-education services for students (see Hallahan & Kauffman, 1997; Smith, 2001).

THEORY *into* PRACTICE

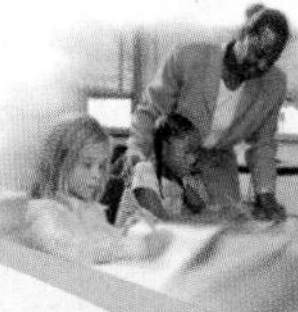

Preparing IEPs

INITIAL REFERRAL. The process of preparing an Individualized Education Program begins when a student is referred for assessment. Referrals for special-education assessment can be made by parents, physicians, principals, or teachers. Classroom teachers most often initiate referrals for children with suspected learning disabilities, mental retardation, speech impairment, or emotional disturbance. Most other disabilities are diagnosed before students enter school. In most schools, initial referrals are made to the building principal, who contacts the relevant school district staff.

INTASC

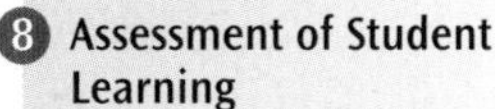

8 Assessment of Student Learning

SCREENING AND ASSESSMENT. As soon as the student is referred for assessment, an initial determination is made to accept or reject the referral. In practice, almost all referrals are accepted. The evaluation and placement team may look at the student's school records and interview classroom teachers and others who know the student. If the team members decide to accept the referral, they must obtain parental permission to do a comprehensive assessment.

Members of the special services team include professionals designated by the school district plus the parents of the referred student and, if appropriate, the referred student. If the referral has to do with learning or emotional problems, a school psychologist or guidance counselor will usually be involved. If the referral has to do with speech or language problems, a speech pathologist or speech teacher will typically serve on the team. The building principal usually chairs the team but may designate a special-education teacher or other professional to do so.

The referred student is then given tests to assess strengths and weaknesses. For learning and emotional problems, these tests are usually given by a school psychologist. Specific achievement tests (such as reading or mathematics assessments) are often given by special-education or reading teachers. Parents must give permission for any specialized assessments. Increasingly, portfolios of student work, teacher evaluations, and other information collected over extended time periods are becoming important parts of the assessment process (Gomez, Grave, & Block, 1991).

If appropriate, the school may try a prereferral intervention before deciding on placement in special education (see Mamlin & Harris, 1998; Rosenfield & Gravois, 1996). For example, a child having serious reading problems might be given a tutor for a period of time before being determined to have a reading disability. For a child with a behavior problem, a home-based reinforcement program or other behavior management program might be set up. If these interventions worked, then the child might not be assigned to special education but could be served within the general education program. Even if a child does need special-education services, the prereferral intervention is likely to provide important information about the kind of services most likely to work.

CONNECTIONS
For more on home-based reinforcement strategies, see Chapter 11, page 350.

WRITING THE IEP. When the comprehensive assessment is complete, the special services team members meet to consider the best placement for the student. If they determine that special education is necessary, they will prepare an IEP. An example of an IEP appears in Figure 12.3. Usually, the special-education teacher and/or the classroom teacher prepares the IEP. The student's parent(s) must sign a consent form regarding the placement decision, and in many school districts a parent must also sign the IEP. This means that parents can (and in some cases do) refuse to have their children placed in special-education programs. At a minimum, the IEP must contain the following information (see Bateman & Linden, 1998).

1. ***Statements indicating the child's present level of performance.*** These typically include the results of specific tests as well as descriptions of classroom functioning. Behavior rating checklists, work samples, or other observation forms may be used to clarify a student's strengths and weaknesses.
2. ***Goals indicating anticipated progress during the year.*** For example, a student might have goals of reading at a fourth-grade level as measured by a standardized test, of improving classroom behavior so that disciplinary referrals are reduced to zero, or of completing a bricklaying course in a vocational education program.
3. ***Intermediate (shorter-term) instructional objectives.*** A student who is having difficulties in reading might be given a short-term objective (STO) of completing a certain number of individualized reading comprehension units per month, or a student with emotional and behavior problems might be expected to get along with peers better and avoid fights.
4. ***A statement of the specific special-education and related services to be provided as well as the extent to which the student will participate in general education programs.*** The IEP might specify, for example, that a student would receive two 30-minute sessions with a speech therapist each week. An IEP for a student with a learning disability might specify 45 minutes per day of instruction from a resource teacher in reading plus consultation between the resource teacher and the classroom teacher on ways to adapt instruction in the general education classroom. A student with mental retardation might be assigned to a self-contained special-education class, but the IEP might specify that the student participate in the general physical education program. The IEP would specify any adaptations necessary to accommodate students in the general education class, such as wheelchair ramps, large-type books, or CDs.
5. ***The projected date for the initiation of services and the anticipated duration of services.*** Once the IEP has been written, the student must receive services within a reasonable time period. Students may not be put on a waiting list; the school district must provide or contract for the indicated services.
6. ***Evaluation criteria and procedures for measuring progress toward goals on at least an annual basis.*** The IEP should specify a strategy for remediating the student's deficits. In particular, the IEP should state what objectives the student is to achieve and how those objectives are to be attained and measured. It is critical to direct special-education services toward a well-specified set of learning or behavior objectives rather than simply deciding that a student falls into some category and, therefore, should receive some service. Ideally, special education for students with mild disabilities should be a short-term, intensive treatment to give students the skills needed in a general education classroom. All too often, a student

BUILDING TEACHING SKILLS VIDEO EXERCISE
IEP Meeting—Meet Star

Go to **www.myeducationlab.com** and, in the Homework and Exercises section for Chapter 12 of this text, access the video entitled "IEP Meeting—Meet Star." Watch the video and complete the homework questions that accompany it, saving your work or transmitting it to your professor as required.

who is assigned to special education remains there indefinitely, even after the problem for which the student was initially referred has been remediated.

IEPs must be updated at least once a year. The updating provides an opportunity for the team to change programs that are not working or to reduce or terminate special-education services when the student no longer needs them.

In Figure 12.3 a flowchart shows how the IEP process operates. Figure 12.4 on pages 388–389 is an example of an IEP.

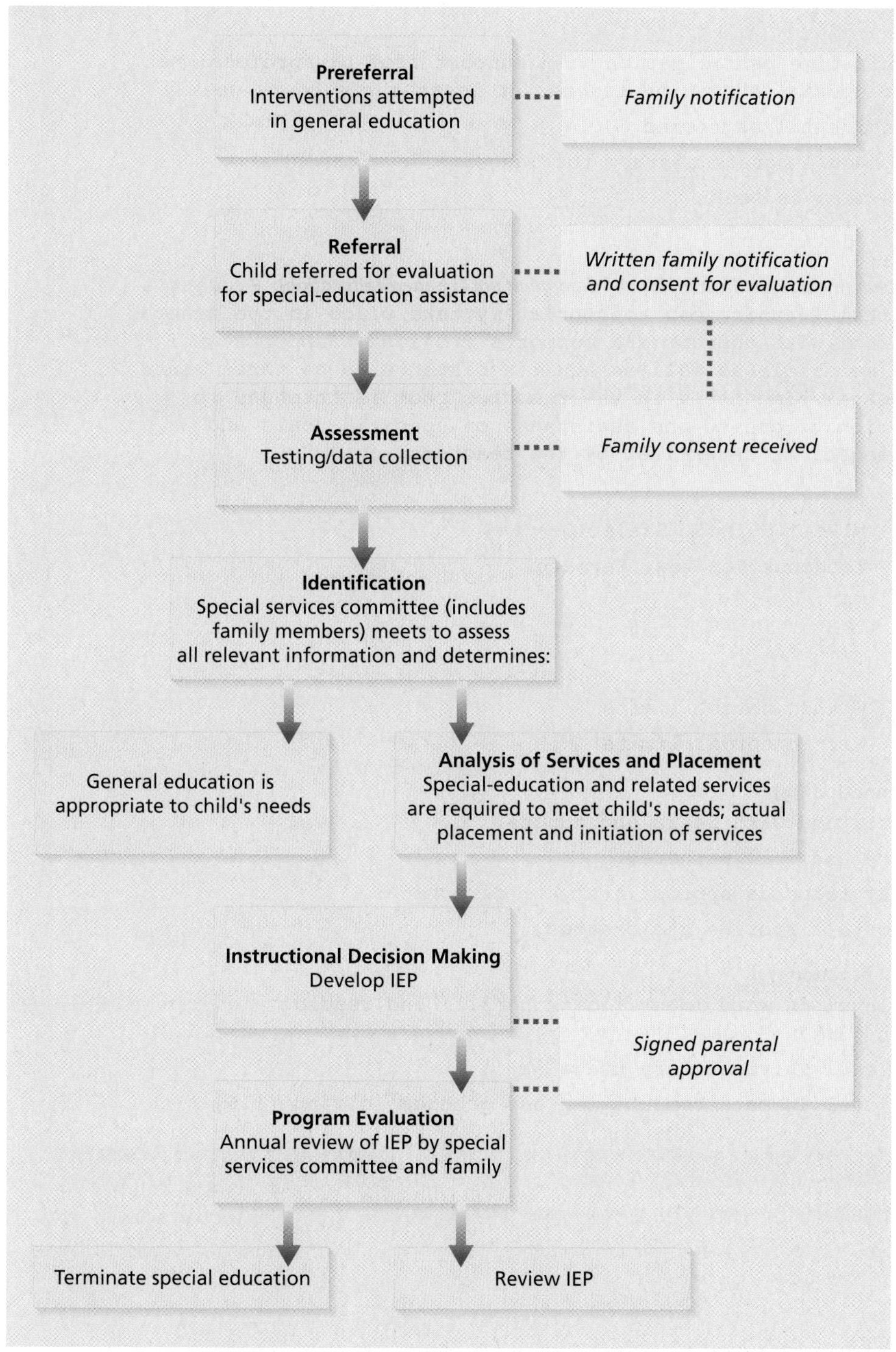

FIGURE 12.3 Flowchart for the Individualized Education Program Process

From Diane Pedrotty Rivera and Deborah Deutsch Smith, *Teaching Students with Learning and Behavior Problems* (3rd ed.), p. 52. Copyright © 1997 by Allyn & Bacon. Reprinted by permission.

FIGURE 12.4 Sample Individualized Education Program

Quentinburg Public Schools—Special-Education Department

Individualized Education Program

Student Name: Jillian Carol
Date of Birth: 4/2/97
School: Jefferson Elementary
Grade: 5
Primary lang.: Home-English Student-English
Date of meeting: 8/28/08
Program start date: 8/28/08
Review date: 8/28/09

Services required

General Education	Full-time participation with support from paraprofessional or special-education teacher at least three hours weekly
Resources	Incidental as needed
Self-Contained	Speech/language therapy for language development
Related Services	40 minutes/week
Other	

Justification for Placement (include justification for any time spent not in general education): Student's needs indicate that learning can appropriately take place in the general education classroom with appropriate supports provided. Supports will include adapted materials as well as adult assistance up to three hours per week. Incidental time noted in the resource room is intended to preserve the option of one-to-one assistance on specific goals and objectives as needed, as determined by the teachers.

Tests Used

Intellectual	WISC-III (Full Scale IQ = 64)
Educational	Woodcock Reading, Keymath
Behavioral	NA
Speech/language	
Other	
Vision	Within normal limits
Hearing	Within normal limits

Strengths (present level of functioning)

Jillian enjoys talking with peers and adults.

Jillian is polite and well mannered.

Jillian generally responds appropriately to directions.

Jillian likes to tell stories she creates.

Weaknesses (present level of functioning)

1. Below grade level in word identification (3.1) and reading comprehension (3.2)
2. Below grade level in vocabulary usage (2.1)
3. Below grade level in math computation and problem solving (1.6)

FIGURE 12.4 Continued

Annual Goal: **Jillian will improve her reading skills to approximately a 3.9 level.**

STO 1: Jillian will read from a 3rd-grade reader at 80 words per minute with fewer than 3 errors per minute.

STO 2: Jillian will answer with 80% accuracy comprehension questions about reading passages at a third-grade level.

Evaluation: Oral performance **Person(s):** Special-education teacher

Annual Goal: **Jillian will use vocabulary at approximately a 3.0 level**

STO 1: Jillian will tell a story using vocabulary from third-grade reading materials.

STO 2: Jillian will use 3rd-grade vocabulary when talking about her out-of-school activities.

STO 3: Jillian will learn at least 40 vocabulary words by using a word bank.

Evaluation: Oral performance, checklist **Person(s):** Special-education teacher
Classroom teacher

Annual Goal: **Jillian will compute and problem solve at approximately a 2.5 level**

STO 1: Jillian will write answers to basic addition and subtraction facts with 100% accuracy.

STO 2: Jillian will accurately compute two-digit addition and subtraction problems without regrouping with 90% accuracy.

STO 3: Jillian will correctly solve word problems written at her reading level and at approximately a 2.5 difficulty level with 90% accuracy.

Evaluation: Written performance **Person(s):** Special-education teacher
Classroom teacher

Team Signatures

LEA Representative	Eva Kim
Parent	Julia Carol
Special-Education Teacher	Vera Delaney
General Education Teacher	
Psychologist	Nadine Showalter
Counselor	
Speech/Language Therapist	Ed Briggs
Other	
Other	

IEP meetings are an outgrowth of IDEA. What is the purpose of such meetings?

WHAT IS INCLUSION?

INTASC

4 Multiple Instructional Strategies

The least restrictive environment clause of P.L. 94-142 revolutionized the practice of special education as well as general education. As has already been noted, it requires that exceptional students be assigned to the least restrictive environment that is appropriate to their needs. Refer to Figure 12.5 for definitions of least restrictive environment and inclusion. This provision has resulted in greatly increased contact between students with disabilities and students without disabilities. In general, students with all types of disabilities have moved one or two notches up the continuum of special-education services. Students who were once placed in special schools are now generally put in separate classrooms in general education schools. Students who were once placed in separate classrooms

FIGURE 12.5 Terminology: Inclusive Education

Mainstreaming means:
"the temporal, instructional, and social integration of eligible exceptional children with normal peers based on an ongoing, individually determined educational planning and programming process" (Kaufman et al., 1975, pp. 40–41).

Least restrictive environment means:
the provision in Public Law 94-142 (renamed the Individuals with Disabilities Education Act, or IDEA) that requires students with disabilities to be educated to the maximum extent appropriate with their nondisabled peers.

Inclusive education means:
"that students attend their home school with their age and grade peers. It requires that the proportion of students labeled for special services is relatively uniform for all of the schools within a particular district. . . . Included students are not isolated into special classes or wings within the school" (National Association of State Boards of Education, 1992, p. 12).

Full inclusion means:
that students who are disabled or at risk receive all their instruction in a general education setting; support services come to the student.

Partial inclusion means:
that students receive most of their instruction in general education settings, but the student may be pulled out to another instructional setting when such a setting is deemed appropriate to the student's individual needs.

in general education schools, particularly students with mild retardation and learning disabilities, are now most often assigned to general education classes for most of their instruction. A growing movement for **full inclusion** calls for including all children in general education classes, with appropriate assistance (see Artiles, Kozleski, Dorn, & Christensen, 2006; Sapon-Shevin, 2001, 2003).

Proponents of full inclusion argue that pull-out programs discourage effective partnerships between general and special educators in implementing IEPs and that students in pull-out programs are stigmatized when they are segregated from other students. These proponents suggest that special-education teachers or paraprofessionals team with classroom teachers and provide services in the general education classroom (Fisher, Sax, & Grove, 2000; Hanline & Daley, 2002; McLeskey & Waldron, 2002; Ruder, 2000; Sapon-Shevin, 2001; Vaughn, Bos, & Schumm, 2007). Opponents of full inclusion argue that general education classroom teachers lack appropriate training and materials and are already overburdened with large class sizes and inadequate support services, and they worry that children with special needs might not receive necessary services (CASE, 1993; Kauffman, Lloyd, Baker, & Riedel, 1995; Shanker, 1994/1995).

Many (perhaps most) classroom teachers have students with disabilities, who are usually receiving some type of special-education services part of the day. Most of these integrated students are categorized as having learning disabilities, speech impairments, mild retardation, or emotional disorders. High-quality inclusion models can improve the achievement and self-confidence of these students. Inclusion also allows students with disabilities to interact with peers and to learn conventional behavior. However, inclusion also creates challenges. When integrated students are performing below the level of the rest of the class, some teachers struggle to adapt instruction to these students' needs—and to cope with the often negative attitudes of the nondisabled students toward their classmates with disabilities (McLeskey & Waldron, 2002; Pearl et al., 1998), which might defeat attempts at social integration. Unfortunately, some classroom teachers are uncomfortable about having students with disabilities in their classes, and many feel poorly prepared to accommodate these students' needs (Vaughn, Bos, & Schumm, 2007). Inclusion provides an opportunity for more effective services but is by no means a guarantee that better services will actually be provided (see Kauffman, McGee, & Brigham, 2004; Riehl, 2000).

VIDEO HOMEWORK EXERCISE
The Inclusive Classroom

Go to **www.myeducationlab.com** and, in the Homework and Exercises section for Chapter 12 of this text, access the video entitled "The Inclusive Classroom." Watch the video and complete the homework questions that accompany it, saving your work or transmitting it to your professor as required.

full inclusion
Arrangement whereby students who have disabilities or are at risk receive all their instruction in a general education setting; support services are brought to the student.

Personal REFLECTION

The Struggle over Inclusion

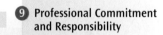

INTASC 9 Professional Commitment and Responsibility

I was once doing a study intended to improve outcomes for children with learning disabilities. The project focused both on integrating children in regular classes and making sure that pull-out special-education teachers were using content and methods closely aligned with those used in the general education classroom.

I remember visiting a special-education teacher who was very resistant to the concept of teaching children the same content they were using in their regular classes. "I think of this (pull-out) class as a club," she said, "a safe place where kids can escape from the pressures they experience the rest of the day."

I was astonished. As part of the research, I'd seen her kids in their general education classes. They were eager to learn what the other kids were learning and were frustrated that they had trouble doing it. The teacher had an opportunity to help them succeed on the content that the kids themselves thought they should learn, much less the school and the state.

Children with learning disabilities want to succeed, and they can do so with additional help. Because they experience a lot of frustration, they need emotional support too, but to my way of thinking, children are happiest when they're succeeding, and they need to have every chance to make it where it matters most to them, in the regular class.

REFLECT ON THIS. What are the possible positive benefits this teacher's children might realize as a result of her belief? What are the potential negative ramifications of her approach? What do you consider to be the best approach to inclusion, and what do you see as your biggest challenge as the classroom teacher?

This student with physical impairments is in a full inclusion program. According to research, how effective are full inclusion and mainstreaming compared to other approaches? As a teacher, how might you foster this boy's social acceptance by peers?

Research on Inclusion

Research on inclusion, often referred to as mainstreaming, has focused on students with learning disabilities, mild retardation, and mild emotional disorders, whose deficits can be termed "mild academic disabilities" (Holloway, 2001; Smith et al., 2008). Several studies have compared students with mild academic disabilities in special-education classes to those in general education classes. When the general education teacher uses an instructional method that is designed to accommodate a wide range of student abilities, students with mild disabilities generally learn much better in the general education classroom than in special-education classes. One classic study on this topic was done by Calhoun and Elliott (1977), who compared students with mild mental retardation and emotional disorders in general education classes with students with the same disabilities in special-education classes. General education classes as well as special-education classes used the same individualized materials, and teachers (trained in special education) were rotated across classes to ensure that the only difference between the general and special programs was the presence of nondisabled classmates. The results of the Calhoun and Elliott (1977) study, depicted in Figure 12.6, suggest the superiority of general education class placement. A study by Roach and Elliott (2006) found that, controlling for many factors, access to the central curriculum was strongly correlated with achievement for students with cognitive disabilities. Other studies (e.g., Gottlieb & Weinberg, 1999; Reynolds & Wolfe, 1999; Saleno & Garrick-Duhaney, 1999) have found more mixed results.

CONNECTIONS Cooperative Integrated Reading and Composition (CIRC) is discussed in Chapter 8, page 246.

Research on programs for general education classrooms that contain students with learning disabilities indicates that one successful strategy is to use individualized instructional programs. For example, the Cooperative Integrated Reading and Composition (CIRC) program described in Chapter 8 has been found to improve the achievement of mainstreamed students with learning disabilities, in comparison to mainstreamed students in traditionally organized classes (Slavin, Madden, & Leavey, 1984a, 1984b; Stevens & Slavin, 1995a).

CONNECTIONS For more on STAD, see Chapter 8, page 244.

Improving the social acceptance of students with academic disabilities is a critical task of inclusion. One consistently effective means of doing this is to involve the students in cooperative learning teams with their nondisabled classmates (Nevin, 1998; Putnam, 1998a). For example, a study of Student Teams–Achievement Divisions (STAD) in classes containing students with learning disabilities found that STAD reduced the social rejection of the students with learning disabilities while significantly increasing their achievement (Madden & Slavin, 1983a). Other cooperative learning programs have found similar effects on the social acceptance of students with mild academic disabilities (Slavin et al., 1984b; Slavin & Stevens, 1991; Stevens & Slavin, 1995a).

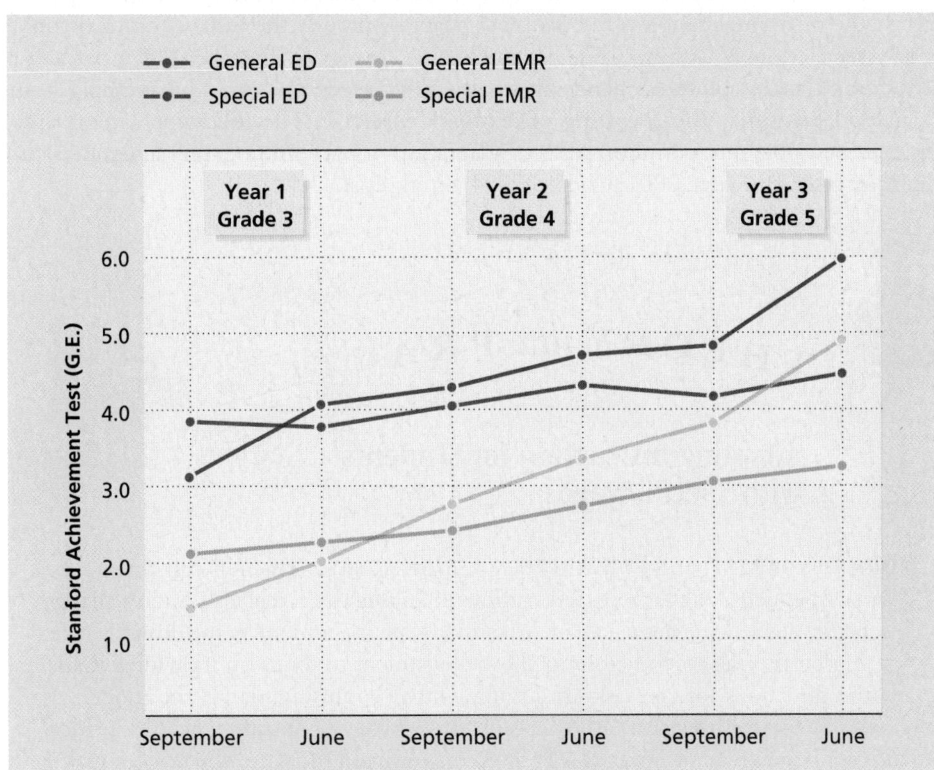

FIGURE 12.6 Achievement of Students in General Education and Special-Education Classes

In a classic study, placement in general education classes rather than special-education classes resulted in higher achievement levels over 3 years for students who are emotionally disturbed (ED) and educable mentally retarded (EMR).

From N. A. Madden and R. E. Slavin, "Mainstreaming Students with Mild Handicaps," *Review of Educational Research, 53*(4), 1983, p. 525. Copyright © 1983 by the American Educational Research Association. Reprinted by permission of the publisher. Based on data from G. Calhoun and R. Elliott, "Self-Concept and Academic Achievement of Educable Retarded and Emotionally Disturbed," *Exceptional Children, 44,* pp. 379–380. Copyright © 1977 by The Council for Exceptional Children. Reprinted with permission.

INTASC

⑩ **Partnerships**

A key element in effective inclusion is maintaining close coordination between classroom and special teachers (Choate, 2004; Friend & Bursuck, 2002; Smith, Polloway, Patton, & Dowdy, 2004). An experiment by Fuchs, Fuchs, and Fernstrom (1993) showed how coordination could improve student performance and accomplish full integration of all students with learning disabilities into general education classes over a period of time. In this study, children in pull-out math programs were given frequent curriculum-based measures assessing their progress relative to the school's math program. Special-education teachers examined the requirements for success in the general education class and prepared children specifically to succeed in that setting. As the children reached a criterion level of skills in math, they were transitioned into the general education class and then followed up to ensure that they were succeeding there. Over the course of a school year, all 21 students involved in the study were successfully transitioned to full-time general education class placement and learned significantly more than matched control students did.

There is very little research on the outcomes of full inclusion programs that integrate children who generally would not have been integrated in traditional mainstreaming models. There are descriptions of outstanding full inclusion programs (e.g., Mahony, 1997; Raison, Hanson, Hall, & Reynolds, 1995; Villa & Thousand, 2003), but there have also been reports of full inclusion disasters (e.g., Baines, Baines, & Masterson, 1994). Research comparing inclusive and special-education programs finds few differences (e.g., Mock & Kauffman, 2005; Zigmond, 2003). However, the goals of including students with even the most profound disabilities in general education classrooms are difficult to measure (see McLeskey & Waldron, 2002). Full inclusion is a goal worth striving toward with care, caution, and flexibility (Capper, Kampschroer, & Keyes, 2000; Downing, 2001).

Adapting Instruction

INTASC

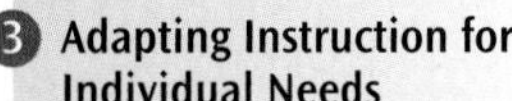

③ **Adapting Instruction for Individual Needs**

Teacher behaviors that are associated with effective teaching for students with disabilities in the general education classroom are essentially the same as those that improve achievement for all students (Swanson & Hoskyn, 1998). Nevertheless, some adaptations in instructional strategies will help teachers to better meet the needs of students with disabilities. When students have difficulty with instruction or materials in learning situations, the recommendation is frequently to adapt or modify the instruction or the materials (see Carolan & Guinn, 2007; Giangreco, 2007; Janney & Snell, 2000). The particular adaptation that is required depends on the student's needs and could be anything from format adaptation to the rewriting of textbook materials. The following Theory into Practice describes four common types of adaptations for accommodating integrated students (also see Browder, 2001; Choate, 2004; Smith et al., 2004).

THEORY *into* PRACTICE

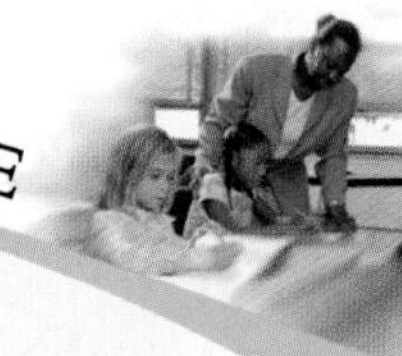

Adapting Instruction for Students with Special Needs

FORMAT ADAPTATIONS FOR WRITTEN ASSIGNMENTS. Teachers can change the format in which a task is presented without changing the actual task. Such a change might be needed for a variety of reasons: (1) an assignment is too long; (2) the spacing on the page is too close to allow the student to focus on individual items; (3) the directions for the task are insufficient or confusing; or (4) the models or examples for the task are either absent, misleading, or insufficient. The critical concept here is that although task and response remain the same, the teacher makes adaptations in the way the material is presented (Kleinert & Kearns, 2001).

Occasionally, the directions for a task or assignment must be simplified. For example, you might substitute in a set of directions the word *circle* for *draw a ring around*. You could also teach students the words that are commonly found in directions (Bender, 2004; Smith et al., 2004). By teaching students how to understand such words, you will help them to be more independent learners. Models or examples presented with a task may also be changed to more closely resemble the task.

CONTENT ADAPTATIONS. In some instances, students might require an adaptation in the content being presented, such as when so much new information is presented that the student cannot process it quickly or when the student lacks a prerequisite skill or concept necessary to complete a task.

One way to adapt the amount of content being presented is to isolate each concept (Bryant, Smith, & Bryant, 2008) and require mastery of each concept as a separate unit before teaching the next concept. Although this type of adaptation involves smaller units of material, the same content will be covered in the end.

Adaptations that are required because students lack essential prerequisites might be as simple as explaining vocabulary or concepts before teaching a lesson. More complex adaptations are required when students lack prerequisite skills or concepts that cannot be explained easily or when students do not have a skill they need to learn the lesson. For example, if the math lesson involves solving word problems that require the division of three-digit numerals and a student has not yet learned how to divide three-digit numerals, this skill will have to be taught before the student can address the word problems.

ADAPTATIONS IN MODES OF COMMUNICATION. Some students require adaptations in either the way in which they receive information or the way in which they demonstrate their knowledge of specific information (Bender, 2004). Many students cannot learn information when their only means of getting it is through reading but can learn if the information is made available in other forms. Be creative in considering the possibilities. You might have students watch a demonstration, filmstrip, film, videotape, television program, computer program, or play. Or you might have them listen to an audiotape, lecture/discussion, or debate.

A different type of adaptation might be required if a student cannot respond as the task directs. If a student has a writing problem, for example, you might ask the student to tell you about the concept in a private conversation and record the student's response on a tape recorder, or ask the student to present an oral report to the class. Or you might let the student represent the knowledge by drawing a picture or diagram or by constructing a model or diorama.

EXTENDING TIME. Extending time for students to complete activities and take tests may be all that is necessary for many students, who may simply be slow workers or anxious in testing circumstances (Sireci, Scarpati, & Li, 2005).

Teaching Learning Strategies and Metacognitive Awareness

Many students do poorly in school because they have failed to learn how to learn. Programs that are directed at helping students learn such strategies as note-taking, summarization, and memorization methods have been very successful with children and adolescents who have learning disabilities (Deshler, 2005; Mastropieri & Scruggs, 1998). Increasingly, research is identifying a variety of strategies for teaching students with learning disabilities to use metacognitive strategies to comprehend what they read (Gersten et al., 2001) and to build "self-determination" skills, such as the ability to work independently (Algozzine et al., 2001).

Prevention and Early Intervention

The debate over inclusion versus special education for children with learning problems revolves around concerns about children whose academic performance is far below that of their agemates. However, many of these children could have succeeded in school in the first place if they had had effective prevention and early intervention programs (Snow, Burns, & Griffin, 1998). Slavin (1996a) proposed a policy of "neverstreaming," which avoids the mainstreaming/special-education dilemma by focusing attention on intensive early intervention that is capable of bringing at-risk learners to performance levels high enough to remove any need for special-education services.

INTASC

4 Multiple Instructional Strategies
6 Communication Skills

There is strong evidence that a substantial portion of students who are now in the special-education system could have been kept out of it if they had had effective early intervention. Studies of high-quality early childhood programs such as the Perry Preschool (Berrueta-Clement et al., 1984), the Abecedarian Project (Ramey & Ramey, 1992), and the Milwaukee Project (Garber, 1988) all showed substantial reductions in special-education placements for students with learning disabilities and mild mental retardation (Siegel, 2003). Programs that provide one-to-one tutoring to first-graders who are struggling in reading have also shown reductions in the need for special-education services for students with learning disabilities (Dev, Doyle, & Valente, 2002; Lyons, 1989; Silver & Hagin, 1990; Slavin, 1996a). Success for All, which combines effective early childhood programs, curriculum reform, and one-to-one tutoring, has reduced special-education placement by more than half (Borman & Hewes, 2003; Slavin, 1996a; Slavin & Madden, 2001) and has substantially increased the reading achievement of children who have already been identified as needing special-education services (Ross, Smith, Casey, & Slavin, 1995; Smith et al., 1994). These and other findings suggest that the number of children who need special-education services could be greatly reduced if prevention and early intervention programs were more widely applied.

CONNECTIONS
For more on the Success for All approach, see Chapter 9, page 289.

Computers and Students with Disabilities

Computers provide opportunities for individualized instruction for students with disabilities. The use of computers to help children with exceptionalities has four major advantages (Curry, 2003; Hasselbring & Williams-Glaser, 2000; Kamil et al., 2000;

CONNECTIONS
For more on computer-based instruction, see Chapter 9, page 275.

Silver-Pacuilla & Fleischman, 2006). First, computers can help to individualize instruction in terms of method of delivery, type and frequency of reinforcement, rate of presentation, and level of instruction (Anderson-Inman & Horney, 2007; McKenna & Walpole, 2007). Second, computers can give immediate corrective feedback and emphasize the active role of the child in learning (Boone & Higgins, 2007). Third, computers can hold the attention of children who are easily distractible. Fourth, computer instruction is motivating and patient. For students with physical disabilities, computers can permit greater ease in learning and communicating information. For example, computers can enlarge text or read text aloud for children with visual disabilities (Kamil et al., 2000; Poel, 2007).

Children in special-education programs seem to like learning from computers. Poorly motivated students have become more enthusiastic about their studies. They feel more in control because they are being taught in a context that is positive, reinforcing, and nonthreatening. However, findings as to the actual learning benefits of computer-assisted instruction for students with disabilities have been inconsistent (MacArthur, Ferretti, Okolo, & Cavalier, 2001; Malouf, Wizer, Pilato, & Grogan, 1990).

CERTIFICATION POINTER
When responding to a case study on your certification test, you should be familiar with adaptive technologies for assisting students with disabilities.

One valuable approach using computers is to provide children who are academically disabled with activities in which they can explore, construct, and communicate. Word processors serve this purpose (Bender, 2004), and other programs have been specifically designed for children with disabilities (Meyer & Rose, 2000; Wagmeister & Shifrin, 2000). Refer to Figure 12.7 for examples of computers and other technology for students with disabilities.

Buddy Systems and Peer Tutoring

One way to help meet the needs of students with disabilities in the general education classroom is to provide these students with assistance from nondisabled classmates, using either a buddy system for noninstructional needs or peer tutoring to help with learning problems (Mastropieri, Scruggs, & Berkeley, 2007).

INTASC
6 Communication Skills

A student who volunteers to be a special-education student's buddy can help that student cope with the routine tasks of classroom life. For example, a buddy can guide a student with vision loss, help a student who is academically disabled to understand directions, or deliver cues or prompts as needed in some classes. In middle school and high school settings, a buddy can take notes for a student with hearing loss or learning disabilities or make photocopies of his or her own notes. The buddy can also ensure that the student with a disability has located the correct textbook page during a lesson and has the materials necessary for a class. The buddy's primary responsibility is to help the student with special needs adjust to the general education classroom, to answer questions, and to provide direction for activities. Use of this resource allows the general education classroom teacher to address more important questions related to instructional activities.

CONNECTIONS
For more on peer tutoring, see Chapter 9, page 273.

Another way of helping students within the general education classroom is to use peer tutoring (Fantuzzo, King, & Heller, 1992). Teachers who use peers to tutor in their classroom should ensure that these tutors are carefully trained. This means that the peer tutor must be taught how to provide assistance by modeling and explaining, how to give specific positive and corrective feedback, and when to allow the student to work alone. Peer tutors and tutees may both benefit: the special-education student by acquiring academic concepts and the tutor by gaining a better acceptance and understanding of students with disabilities. Sometimes, older students with disabilities tutor younger ones; this generally benefits both students (Osguthorpe & Scruggs, 1986; Top & Osguthorpe, 1987).

CERTIFICATION POINTER
For teacher certification tests you may be expected to suggest ways of structuring peer tutoring to help meet the needs of students with disabilities.

Special-Education Teams

When a student with disabilities is integrated into the general education classroom, the classroom teacher often works with one or more special educators to ensure the student's successful integration (Friend, 2007; Friend & Bursuck, 2002; Smith et al., 2004; Snell & Janney, 2000). The classroom teacher might participate in conferences with special-education personnel, the special-education personnel might at times be present in the

FIGURE 12.7 Adaptive Technologies for Students with Disabilities

For Students with Limited Motor Control

- Cursor and mouse enhancements allow students who do not have sufficient fine motor control to use a keyboard. Mouse enhancement utilities can be trained to recognize gestures made with mouse commands. Other features include high visibility, color, and animated cursors.
- Key definition programs allow students to define function keys on their keyboard to complete common tasks with fewer keystrokes.
- Virtual keyboard software displays a picture of a computer keyboard on the screen. Students can "type" on this virtual keyboard using a mouse, trackball, or similar pointing device, instead of pushing keys on a real keyboard.

For Students with Visual Impairments

- Magnification software programs ease reading on a computer monitor by displaying text in large fonts (from 2 to 16 times the normal view) and with foreground and background colors of the user's choice.
- Scanners allow students to scan documents that are then converted into editable word processing and spreadsheet documents. These can be magnified and edited on the screen or read aloud by a speech synthesizer.
- Speech synthesizers read aloud what is displayed on the screen—the contents of the active window, menu options, or text that has been typed. They can save documents in audio format as well. There are speaking calendars and talking calculators that read out every operation, as well as mathematical results.
- Braille readers and writers permit students to access the Internet, send and receive e-mail, and create documents by converting text into Braille.

For Students with Hearing Impairments

- Voice recognition software converts spoken words into written text. It can be programmed to execute particular commands, for example, taking a user to favorite websites with a single voice command.

For Students with Learning Disabilities

- Some word processing programs have a word prediction and abbreviation–expansion program that makes writing faster and easier for those with physical or learning disabilities who use a keyboard to write. Both features help reduce the number of keystrokes needed for typing and can make writing more productive.
- Concept mapping software helps students understand the relationship among concepts by constructing, navigating, sharing, and criticizing knowledge models represented as concept maps.

classroom, or the classroom teacher might consult with a special educator at regular intervals. Whatever the arrangement, the classroom teacher and the special educator(s) must recognize that each has expertise that is crucial to the student's success. The classroom teacher is the expert on classroom organization and operation on a day-to-day basis, the curriculum of the classroom, and the expectations placed on students for performance. The special educator is the expert on the characteristics of a particular group of students with disabilities, the learning and behavioral strengths and deficits of the mainstreamed student, and instructional techniques for a particular kind of disability. All this information is important to the successful integration of students, which is why communication between the general education and special-education teachers is so necessary (Pawlowski, 2001; Tucker, 2001).

INTASC

⑩ **Partnerships**

Communication should begin before students are placed in the general education classroom and should continue throughout the placement. Both teachers must have up-to-date information about the student's performance in each setting to plan and coordinate an effective program. Only then can instruction targeted at improving the student's performance in the general education classroom be designed and presented. In addition, generalization of skills and behaviors from one setting to the other will be enhanced (see Fuchs, Fuchs, Bahr, Fernstrom, & Stecker, 1990).

CONNECTIONS

For more on teaching adaptive skills to help students in their socioemotional development, see Chapter 3, page 77.

Teaching Dilemmas: CASES TO CONSIDER

Finding What Works

INTASC

8 Assessment of Student Learning
10 Partnerships

Arlisa is 2 weeks into her teaching practicum in Ruth Runson's kindergarten class at Central Elementary School. Kwan, a student with special needs who receives help from Amanda, the special-education resource teacher, has surprised Arlisa with an uncharacteristic outburst, screaming at her when she asked him a question and then moving into a corner with his back toward her. Later in the day, Arlisa, Ruth Runson, and Amanda discuss Kwan's situation.

Ruth: Arlisa, don't be disheartened about the way Kwan acted today. This is a common episode for him.

Arlisa: I'm not disheartened, but I don't think I understand the nature of Kwan's special needs, so I don't know what to do in situations like this one.

Amanda: Kwan is very intelligent for his age—he reads very well already—but he has socializing problems.

Ruth: Often, Kwan won't talk to me, either. When he acts like that, just leave him alone until he comes around.

Arlisa: I don't think it's that Kwan won't talk. Earlier this week on the playground, several other kindergarten boys were chasing him and Mary. Kwan was yelling at the boys to leave Mary alone. I stopped the boys and then asked Kwan what had happened. Kwan tried to yell at me, so I took the moment to try to help him with his communication. I encouraged him to calm down and speak to me, rather than yelling, to tell me what was wrong. Eventually, he calmed down enough to shout at me about what had happened, but his shouting seemed more out of frustration with the boys than intentional. I called the boys back, we talked, and the issue was resolved. Kwan and Mary left to play together.

Ruth: I'm surprised, Arlisa, that Kwan listened to you and actually tried to talk! And Kwan hasn't chosen a classmate to play with since the first day of school. Maybe you should capitalize on Kwan's willingness to listen to you.

Amanda: I agree, Arlisa. When we work one-on-one, Kwan has told me that his classmates are too loud on the bus and at circle time. I've scheduled him for a hearing test, but meanwhile I've gotten him a pair of ear plugs to wear on the bus. The driver says this seems to calm him down.

Arlisa: Amanda, what strategies can I use to get Kwan to talk to me, instead of shouting or sulking?

Amanda: Well, he seems to sulk when we ask him to make a decision before he's ready, like when you ask him what he wants to do during choosing time. You should tell him it's OK, and that he should speak to you when he has decided what he wants to do. Then move on to the other children. When he shouts at you, or when he simply points at what he wants, remind him to tell you what he needs or wants. Remind him that it is hard to listen to him when he shouts.

Ruth: He often starts sulking or has an outburst when another child comes to take his or her turn at the computer he has been using. I think that giving him a time limit on the computers will encourage him to play with the other children.

Amanda: That's a good idea, Ruth. And I can work with Kwan and a few other children on additional computer activities during my scheduled time with him to reinforce those ideas.

Arlisa: Isn't there something we can do to build on his strengths, like his reading abilities?

Amanda: That's another good idea. I could start writing responses to him on sticky notes and putting them on his shirt. Then, when he rejoins the entire class, both of you could ask him to read the sticky notes to you. This will reinforce his good reading abilities while also encouraging him to talk.

Arlisa: Do you really think these strategies will help Kwan?

Ruth: We'll try them and see. Amanda and I are still talking with Kwan's parents, diagnosing his needs, and putting together an IEP for him. Then we'll have a better idea of how to help him.

QUESTIONS FOR REFLECTION

1. List the special needs that Kwan seems to demonstrate. What additional instructional adaptations might you suggest to help Kwan succeed in kindergarten?
2. Evaluate the level of collaboration demonstrated among the three teachers. If you were Ruth Runson, the classroom teacher, how would you capitalize on the support offered by Amanda, the special-education teacher? If you were Amanda, how would you propose additional accommodations that Ruth and Arlisa could make for Kwan?
3. Kwan's exceptionalities have not been clearly diagnosed yet, but how has his label as a child with special needs already served as a barrier during the first 2 weeks of kindergarten? How can the three teachers work to remove this barrier?

Source: Adapted from "Student Diversity: Barriers to Getting to Know Our Students" by A. Johnson, from *Allyn & Bacon's Custom Cases in Education,* edited by Greta Morine-Dershimer, Paul Eggen, and Donald Kauchak (2000).

ONLINE READING & WRITING EXERCISE
Things Teachers and Parents Say That Foster Distrust

Access this exercise, entitled "Things Teachers and Parents Say That Foster Distrust," in the Homework and Exercises section for Chapter 12 of this text at **www.mylabschool.com**.

Social Integration of Students with Disabilities

Placement of students in the general education classroom is only one part of their integration into that environment. These students must be integrated socially as well as instructionally (see Wilkins, 2000). The classroom teacher plays a critical role in this process. Much has been written about the effects of teacher expectations on student achievement and behavior. In the case of students with disabilities, the teacher's attitude toward these without disabilities students is important not only for teacher–student interactions but also as a model for the students without disabilities in the classroom. The research on attitudes toward individuals with disabilities provides several strategies that might be useful to the general education classroom teacher who wants to promote successful social integration by influencing the attitudes of nondisabled students. One strategy is to use cooperative learning methods (Nevin, 1998; Slavin & Stevens, 1991; Stevens & Slavin, 1995a). Social skills training has been found to improve the social acceptance of children with disabilities (Troop & Asher, 1999). For practical ways to include secondary students with disabilities in the general education classroom, see Figure 12.8.

INTASC

6 **Communication Skills**

CONNECTIONS

For more on the effects of teacher expectations on student achievement and behavior, see Chapter 10, page 309.

Consider these tips for including secondary students in the general education classroom:

Secondary Students with Learning Disabilities

1. Specifically teach self-recording strategies such as asking, "Was I paying attention?"
2. Relate new material to knowledge that the student with learning disabilities already has, drawing specific implications from familiar information.
3. Teach the use of external memory enhancers (e.g., lists and note-taking).
4. Encourage the use of other devices to improve class performance (e.g., tape recorders).

Secondary Students with Emotional or Behavioral Disorders

1. Create positive relationships within your classroom through the use of cooperative learning teams and group-oriented assignments.
2. Use all students in creating standards for conduct as well as consequences for positive and negative behaviors.
3. Focus your efforts on developing a positive relationship with the student with behavior disorders by greeting him or her regularly, informally talking with him or her at appropriate times, attending to improvement in his or her performance, and becoming aware of his or her interests.
4. Work closely with the members of the teacher assistance team to be aware of teacher behaviors that might adversely or positively affect students' performance.
5. Realize that changes in behavior often occur very gradually, with periods of regression and sometimes tumult.

FIGURE 12.8 Including Secondary Students with Disabilities in the General Education Classroom

From Michael L. Hardman, Clifford J. Drew, and M. Winston Egan, *Human Exceptionality* (5th ed.). Copyright © 1996 by Allyn & Bacon. Adapted by permission.

The Intentional TEACHER

USING WHAT YOU KNOW about Learners with Exceptionalities to Improve Teaching and Learning

Intentional teachers relish their responsibility to reach each of their students. They create inclusive environments and commit to fostering learning for all. Intentional teachers serve as members of professional teams in order to collaborate to meet the needs of students with special needs.

1 What do I expect my students to know and be able to do at the end of this lesson? How does this contribute to course objectives and to students' needs to become capable individuals?

Think about the goals you have established for student learning. Consider the extent to which each of these goals is appropriate for learners with special needs. Work with other professionals to develop formal goal statements, including Individualized Education Programs that shape appropriate goals and instruction for your students with special needs. For example, imagine that Michael and Renee, two students with learning disabilities in reading, struggle with the text for your class, so you consult with the special-education teacher. He reviews the students' IEPs with you, noting that reading comprehension is a goal for both students this year. Together you converse about possible adjustments to your course goals for Michael and Renee, and you discuss appropriate instructional modifications. You chat with the students' parents, who give you additional insights about strategies they have found to be successful.

2 What knowledge, skills, needs, and interests do my students have that must be taken into account in my lesson?

Identification of students' special-educational needs may begin before students enter formal schooling. When students with documented special needs are assigned to your class, talk with students (as appropriate), their parents, and professionals about students' preferences and past successes. Review past records as appropriate. For example, imagine that Angela, a junior who is visually impaired, joins your class. You might set up an informal conference with Angela, her parents, and the resource teacher. They provide you with information about strategies that help Angela, and she talks openly about her likes and her pet peeves. They also refer you to one of your colleagues who was particularly successful last year at providing a supportive environment without dwelling too much on Angela's vision. You might seek assistive technology, such as a computer that greatly enlarges text, to help Angela participate successfully in class.

3 What do I know about the content, child development, learning, motivation, and effective teaching strategies that I can use to accomplish my objectives?

Students might have special needs that have not been identified. Observe carefully for signs that students need extra support. For example, imagine that Sheila, who sits in a back row,

CHAPTER 12 SUMMARY

Who Are Learners with Exceptionalities?

Learners with exceptionalities are students who have special-educational needs in relation to societal or school norms. An inability to perform appropriate academic tasks for any reason inherent in the learner makes that learner exceptional. A handicap is a condition or barrier imposed by the environment or the self; a disability is a functional limitation that interferes with a person's mental, physical, or sensory abilities. Classification systems for learners with exceptionalities are often arbitrary and debated, and the use of labels may lead to inappropriate treatment or damage students' self-concepts.

About 12 percent of students ages 6 to 21 in the United States receive special education. Examples of learners with exceptionalities are students with mental retardation, specific learning disabilities, speech or language disorders, emotional disorders, behavioral disorders, and vision or hearing loss. Students who are gifted and talented are also regarded as exceptional and may be eligible for special accelerated or enrichment programs. Clearly identifying learners with exceptionalities and accommodating instruction to meet their needs are continual challenges.

often looks out the window or looks puzzled during your lessons. Noticing some differences in her enunciation, you suspect a hearing impairment and refer her for testing. In the meantime, you move her to the front row and provide visual input to support your direct instruction.

4 What instructional materials, technology, assistance, and other resources are available to help accomplish my objectives?

Teachers need to create a social environment that fosters acceptance for every student. Think about how you will encourage students to accept and help each other as individuals. For example, imagine that Jarred, a student with cerebral palsy, is placed in your classroom. You and your students might hold a classroom meeting to discuss ways to welcome a new student. You could also talk about areas in which classmates have helped each other this year and the idea that you all have benefited by working with each other because of your varied strengths. You might hand out a "job application" for the position of "buddy" to new students, as several students clamor to be Jarred's buddy.

5 How will I plan to assess students' progress toward my objectives?

Teachers need to use information from a variety of sources to determine success for students with special needs. What evidence do you have that students maintain positive self-concepts? That their classmates' self-concepts are similarly enriched? That students are learning? Collect information that enables you to determine whether students are progressing on an individual basis. For example, imagine that you meet for a midyear review of Patrick's Individualized Education Program. To the review you bring anecdotal notes that you collected as students demonstrated their capacity to care about and help each other. You share vignettes of Patrick's sense of humor and impressive knowledge of dinosaurs. You show his portfolio, which demonstrates marked growth in his letter recognition and drawing. You commit to providing more intensive work in mathematics, though, because he shows less growth in shape and number recognition.

6 How will I respond if individual children or the class as a whole are not on track toward success? What is my back-up plan?

Instruction should meet individual needs. Select from a variety of strategies to modify your instruction when you find that it does not challenge each student. For example, imagine that some of your students are struggling despite your attempts to provide relevant and engaging instruction. You re-read your notes on instructional modifications such as individualized instruction, cooperative learning, computers, and peer tutoring. You might choose peer tutoring to capitalize on your students' social tendencies. You could train peer tutors in learning strategies and work out a schedule so that peer tutors and tutees can meet during class for 20 minutes three times per week.

What Is Special Education?

Special-education programs serve children with disabilities instead of, or in addition to, the general education classroom program.

Public Law 94-142 (1975), which was amended by P.L. 99-457 (1986) to include preschool children and seriously disabled infants, is now called the Individuals with Disabilities Education Act (IDEA). It mandates that every child with a disability is entitled to appropriate special education at public expense. The current version of the law, IDEA 2004, calls for greater involvement of parents and classroom teachers in the education of children with disabilities. The least restrictive environment clause means that students with special needs must be mainstreamed into general education classes as much as possible. A requirement of IDEA is that every student with a disability must have an Individualized Education Program (IEP). The idea behind the use of IEPs is to give everyone concerned with the education of a child with a disability an opportunity to help formulate the child's instruction program. An array of services is available for exceptional students, including support for the general education teacher, special education for part of the day in a resource room, special education for more than 3 hours per day in a special-education classroom, special day schools, special residential schools, and home/hospitals.

What Is Inclusion?

Inclusion means placing students with special needs in general education classrooms for at least part of the time. Full inclusion of all children in general education classes with appropriate assistance is a widely held goal. Research has shown that inclusion is effective in raising many students' performance levels, especially when cooperative learning, buddy systems, peer tutoring, computer instruction, modifications in lesson presentation, and training in social skills are regular parts of classroom learning. Research has also shown that some disabilities, especially reading disabilities, can be prevented through programs of prevention and early intervention.

KEY TERMS

Review the following key terms from the chapter.

acceleration programs 379
attention deficit hyperactivity disorder (ADHD) 372
autism 375
collaboration 382
conduct disorders 375
disability 365
emotional and behavioral disorders 374
enrichment programs 379
full inclusion 391
giftedness 377
handicap 365
hearing disabilities 377
Individualized Education Program (IEP) 380
Individuals with Disabilities Education Act (IDEA) 380
intelligence quotient (IQ) 367
language disorders 374
learners with exceptionalities 365
learning disabilities (LD) 369
least restrictive environment 380
mainstreaming 380
mental retardation 367
Public Law 94-142 380
response to intervention 370
sensory impairments 376
special education 379
speech disorders 373
vision loss 376

SELF-ASSESSMENT: PRACTICING *for* LICENSURE

Directions: The chapter-opening vignette addresses indicators that are often assessed in state licensure exams. Re-read the chapter-opening vignette, and then respond to the following questions.

1. Elaine Wagner, assistant principal at Pleasantville Elementary School, meets with Helen Ross about her son, Tommy, who is having a difficult time in another school. She explains to Ms. Ross that Tommy would need to meet certain criteria to receive special-education services. Which of the following examples is an indication that someone needs special-education services?
   - **a.** The student must have an IQ at or below 120.
   - **b.** The student must have at least one of a small number of categories of disabilities.
   - **c.** The student must be below the 50th percentile in his or her academic work.
   - **d.** All parents who request special-education services for their children must receive them.

2. Suppose you are going to be Tommy's new teacher. If his mother were to ask you about the difference between handicap and disability, what would you say?
   - **a.** A disability is a condition in which a person has difficulty with cognitive functioning, whereas a handicap is a condition in which a person has difficulty with physical functioning.
   - **b.** A disability is a condition in which a person has barriers placed on him or her by society, whereas a handicap is the disabling condition.
   - **c.** A disability is a functional limitation a person has that interferes with her or his physical or cognitive abilities. A handicap is a condition imposed on a person with disabilities by society, the physical environment, or the person's attitude.
   - **d.** The terms *disability* and *handicap* are synonymous.

3. Which of the following public laws gave parents like Helen Ross an increased role in making decisions about the education of their children?
   a. Public Law 94-142, The Education for the Handicapped Act
   b. Public Law 99-457, the amendment to P.L. 94-142
   c. Public Law 101-476, the Individuals with Disabilities Education Act
   d. Public Law 105-17, the Individuals with Disabilities Education Act amendments
4. Assistant Principal Elaine Wagner tells Helen Ross that even if Tommy needs special-education services, he will be placed in the "least restrictive environment." What does this mean for Tommy?
   a. Tommy will be placed in the general education classes as much as possible, and only removed for special-education services if necessary.
   b. Tommy will be placed in a special-education room that does not restrict his movements or academic choices.
   c. Tommy will be eligible for any and all special-education services.
   d. Tommy will receive public funds to pay for his private special-education services.
5. Helen Ross, Tommy's mother, asks Elaine Wagner, "Your school's philosophy on inclusion sounds just right for Tommy. Why don't all schools adopt it? What disadvantages are there?" Ms. Wagner, who is current on her knowledge about inclusion, would most likely make which of the following responses?
   a. Data show that students enrolled in inclusion programs do not do as well academically as those who are enrolled in special-education classrooms.
   b. General education classroom teachers sometimes lack appropriate training and materials and are already overburdened with large class sizes and inadequate support services.
   c. Special-education experts are not convinced that there is such a thing as a learning disability. They believe that all students should be in a general education classroom.
   d. Many parents of general education students do not feel it is fair to adapt instruction to meet the needs of students with disabilities.
6. How would you go about developing an individualized learning plan for Tommy if it is determined that he has a reading disability?
7. Describe the advantages and disadvantages that might occur when students with special needs are enrolled in the general education classroom.

PEARSON

myeducationlab

Where the Classroom Comes to Life

Now go to **www.myeducationlab.com** to:

- take a Pretest to assess your initial comprehension of chapter content;
- study chapter content with your individualized Study Plan;
- take a Posttest to assess your understanding of chapter content;
- practice your teaching skills with Building Teaching Skills exercises; and
- build a deeper, more applied understanding of chapter content with Homework and Exercises.

CHAPTER 13

Assessing Student Learning

chapter
OUTLINE

Mr. Sullivan was having a great time teaching about the Civil War, and his eleventh-grade U.S. history class was having fun, too. Mr. Sullivan was relating all kinds of anecdotes about the war. He described a battle fought in the nude (a group of Confederates was caught fording a river), the time Stonewall Jackson lost a battle because he took a nap in the middle of it, and several stories about women who disguised their gender to fight as soldiers. He told the story of a Confederate raid (from Canada) on a Vermont bank. He passed around real minié balls and grapeshot. In fact, Mr. Sullivan had gone on for weeks about the battles, the songs, and the personalities and foibles of the generals. Finally, after an interesting math activity in which students had to figure out how much Confederate money they would need to buy a loaf of bread, Mr. Sullivan had students put away all their materials to take a test.

The students were shocked. The only question was: What were the main causes, events, and consequences of the Civil War?

Mr. Sullivan's lessons are fun. They are engaging. They use varied presentation modes. They integrate skills from other disciplines. They are clearly accomplishing one important objective of social studies: building enjoyment of the topic. However, as engaging as Mr. Sullivan's lessons are, there is little correspondence between what he is teaching and what he is testing. He and his students are on a happy trip, but where are they going?

USING *your* EXPERIENCE

COOPERATIVE LEARNING In a group of four or five students, draw a value line from 1 to 100, with 1 representing poor teaching and 100 representing great teaching. Take turns marking where you would place Mr. Sullivan on this scale. Let each person explain his or her rating. Now review the ratings and change them as appropriate. Discuss better ways in which Mr. Sullivan might teach and then assess his students.

This chapter discusses an important topic: evaluation. The most important idea in the chapter is that a teacher's lesson objectives are the means by which instruction and evaluation are linked together. The objectives are the teacher's plan for what students should know and be able to do at the end of a course of study; their lessons must be designed to accomplish these objectives; and their evaluation of students must tell them the extent to which each student has actually mastered those objectives by the end of the course (Carr & Harris, 2001; Marzano, Pickering, & Pollock, 2001). Put another way, every teacher should have a clear idea of where the class is going, how it will get there, and how to know whether it has arrived.

WHAT ARE INSTRUCTIONAL OBJECTIVES AND HOW ARE THEY USED?

INTASC

7 Instructional Planning Skills

What do you want your students to know or be able to do at the end of today's lesson? What should they know at the end of a series of lessons on a particular subject? What should they know at the end of the course? Knowing the answers to these questions is one of the most important prerequisites for intentional, high-quality instruction. A teacher is like a wilderness guide with a troop of tenderfeet. If the teacher does not have a map or a plan for getting the group where it needs to go, the whole group will surely be lost. Mr. Sullivan's students are having a lot of fun, but because their teacher has no plan for how his lessons will give them essential concepts relating to the Civil War, they will be unlikely to learn these concepts.

Setting out objectives at the beginning of a course is an essential step in providing a framework into which individual lessons will fit. Without such a framework it is easy to wander off the track, to spend too much time on topics that are not central to the course. One high school biology teacher spent most of the year teaching biochemistry; her students knew all about the chemical makeup of DNA, red blood cells, chlorophyll, and starch but little about zoology, botany, anatomy, or other topics that are usually central to high school biology. Then in late May the teacher panicked because she realized that the class had to do a series of laboratory exercises before the end of the year. On successive days they dissected a frog, an eye, a brain, and a pig fetus! Needless to say, the students learned little from those hurried labs and little about biology in general. This teacher did not have a master plan but was deciding week by week (or perhaps day by day) what to teach, thereby losing sight of the big picture—the scope of knowledge that is generally agreed to be important for a high school student to learn in biology class. Few teachers follow a plan rigidly once they make it, but the process of making it is still very helpful.

instructional objective
A statement of skills or concepts that students should master after a given period of instruction.

An **instructional objective,** sometimes called a behavioral objective, is a statement of skills or concepts that students are expected to know at the end of some period of

TABLE 13.1 Parts of a Behavioral Objectives Statement

	Performance	Conditions	Criterion
Definition	An objective always says what a learner is expected to do.	An objective always describes the conditions under which the performance is to occur.	Whenever possible, an objective describes the criterion of acceptable performance.
Question Answered	What should the learner be able to do?	Under what conditions do you want the learner to be able to do it?	How well must it be done?
Example	Correctly use adjectives and adverbs.	Given 10 sentences with missing modifiers, . . .	. . . the student will correctly choose an adjective or adverb in at least 9 of the 10 sentences.

instruction. Typically, an instructional objective is stated in such a way as to make clear how the objective will be measured (see Mager, 1975). Some examples of instructional objectives are as follows:

- Given 100 division facts (such as 27 divided by 3), students will give correct answers to all 100 in 3 minutes.
- When asked, students will name at least five functions that characterize all living organisms (respiration, reproduction, etc.).
- In an essay, students will be able to compare and contrast the artistic styles of van Gogh and Gauguin.
- Given the statement "Resolved: The United States should not have entered World War I," students will be able to argue persuasively either for or against the proposition.

CONNECTIONS
For more on lesson planning and lesson objectives as components of effective instruction, see Chapter 7, page 201.

Note that even though these objectives vary enormously in the type of learning involved and in the performance levels they address, they have several things in common. Mager (1975), whose work began the behavioral objectives movement, described objectives as having three parts: performance, conditions, and criteria. Explanations and examples are given in Table 13.1.

Planning Lesson Objectives

In practice, the skeleton of a behavioral objective is condition–performance–criterion. First, state the conditions under which learning will be assessed, as in the following:

- Given a 10-item test, students will be able to . . .
- In an essay the student will be able to . . .
- Using a compass and protractor, the student will be able to . . .

The second part of an objective is usually an action verb that indicates what students will be able to do, for example (from Gronlund, 2004):

- Write
- Distinguish between
- Identify
- Match
- Compare and contrast

Finally, a behavioral objective generally states a criterion for success, such as the following:

- . . . all 100 multiplication facts in 3 minutes.
- . . . at least five of the nations that sent explorers to the New World.
- . . . at least three similarities and three differences between U.S. government under the Constitution and the Articles of Confederation.

Sometimes a criterion for success cannot be specified as the number correct. Even so, success should be specified as clearly as possible, as in the following:

- The student will write a two-page essay describing the social situation of women as portrayed in *A Doll's House.*
- The student will think of at least six possible uses for an eggbeater other than beating eggs.

Writing Specific Objectives Instructional objectives must be adapted to the subject matter being taught. When students must learn well-defined skills or information with a single right answer, specific instructional objectives should be written as follows:

- Given 10 problems involving addition of two fractions with like denominators, students will solve at least 9 correctly.
- Given 10 sentences lacking verbs, students will correctly choose verbs that agree in number in at least 8 sentences. Examples: My cat and I [has, have] birthdays in May. Each of us [want, wants] to go to college.
- Given a 4-meter rope attached to the ceiling, students will be able to climb to the top in less than 20 seconds.

Some material, of course, does not lend itself to such specific instructional objectives, and it would be a mistake in such cases to adhere to objectives that have numerical criteria. For example, the following objective could be written:

- The student will list at least five similarities and five differences between the situation of immigrants to the United States in the early 1900s and that of immigrants today.

However, this objective asks for lists, which might not demonstrate any real understanding of the topic. A less specific but more meaningful objective might be the following:

- In an essay the student will compare and contrast the situation of immigrants to the United States in the early 1900s and that of immigrants today.

This general instructional objective would allow students more flexibility in expressing their understanding of the topic and would promote comprehension rather than memorization of lists of similarities and differences.

VIDEO HOMEWORK EXERCISE
Planning for Instruction

Go to **www.myeducationlab.com** and, in the Homework and Exercises section for Chapter 13 of this text, access the video entitled "Planning for Instruction." Watch the video and complete the homework questions that accompany it, saving your work or transmitting it to your professor as required.

Writing Clear Objectives Instructional objectives should be specific enough to be meaningful. For example, an objective concerning immigrants might be written as follows:

- Students will develop a full appreciation for the diversity of peoples who have contributed to the development of U.S. society.

This sounds nice, but what does "full appreciation" mean? Such an objective neither helps the teacher prepare lessons nor helps students understand what is to be taught and how they will be assessed. Mager (1975, p. 20) lists more slippery and less slippery words used to describe instructional objectives:

Words Open to Many Interpretations	Words Open to Fewer Interpretations
to know	to write
to understand	to recite
to appreciate	to identify
to fully appreciate	to sort
to grasp the significance	to solve
to enjoy	to construct

Performing a Task Analysis In planning lessons, it is important to consider the skills required in the tasks to be taught or assigned. For example, a teacher might ask students

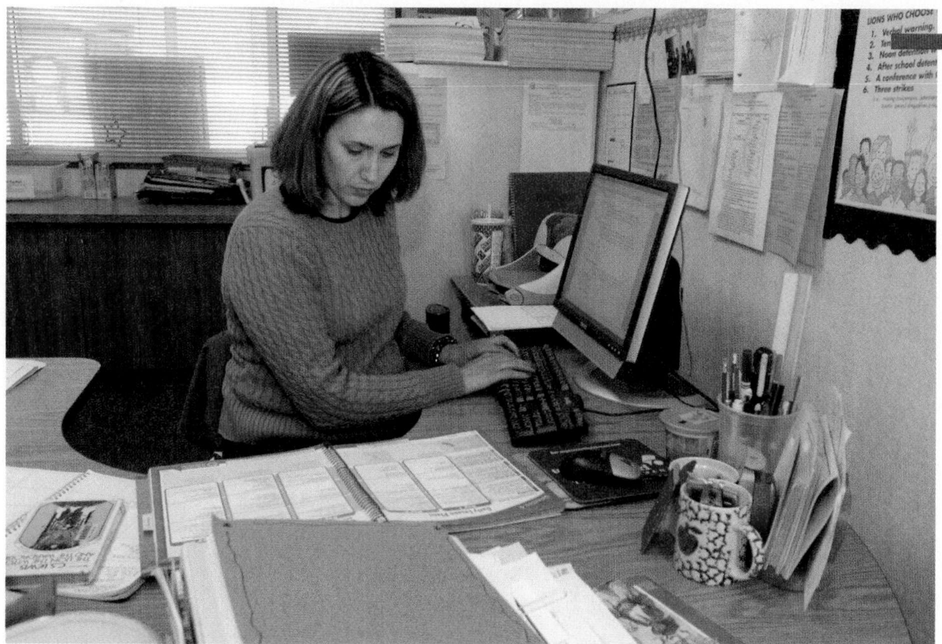

Why is careful planning a critical step in learning and assessing learning? What kinds of ongoing assessment can you build into your lessons that will help you determine if your students are meeting the objectives you establish?

to use the school library to write a brief report on a topic of interest. The task seems straightforward enough, but consider the separate skills involved:

- Knowing alphabetical order
- Using library information resources to find books on a subject
- Knowing how to use the library's information resources and book indexes
- Getting the main idea from expository material
- Planning or outlining a brief report
- Writing expository paragraphs
- Knowing language mechanics skills (such as capitalization, punctuation, and usage)

These skills could themselves be broken down into subskills. The teacher must be aware of the subskills involved in any learning task to be certain that students know what they need to know to succeed. Before assigning the library report task, the teacher would need to be sure that students knew how to use the library's information resources and book indexes, among other things, and could comprehend and write expository material. The teacher might teach or review these skills before sending students to the library.

Similarly, in teaching a new skill, it is important to consider all the subskills that go into it. Think of all the separate steps involved in long division, in writing chemical formulas, or in identifying topic sentences and supporting details. For that matter, consider the skills that go into making a pizza, as illustrated in Figure 13.1.

This process of breaking tasks or objectives down into their simpler components is called **task analysis.** In planning a lesson, a three-step process for task analysis may be used:

1. ***Identify prerequisite skills.*** What should students already know before you teach the lesson? For example, for a lesson on long division, students must know their subtraction, multiplication, and division facts and must be able to subtract and multiply with renaming.

2. ***Identify component skills.*** In the actual lesson, what subskills must students be taught before they can learn to achieve the larger objective? To return to the long-division example, students will need to learn estimating, dividing, multiplying, subtracting, checking, bringing down the next digit, and then repeating the process. Each of these steps must be planned for, taught, and assessed during the lesson.

task analysis
Breaking tasks down into fundamental subskills.

FIGURE 13.1 Example of a Skill Hierarchy
Before students can practice the main skill (making pizza), they must be able to use an oven, make dough, and make sauce. These skills must all be learned before the main skill can be mastered. They are independent of one another and can be learned in any order. Before making dough or making sauce, students must be able to read a recipe and measure ingredients. Finally, to read a recipe the learner first has to learn how to decode abbreviations.

From Robert F. Mager, *Preparing Instructional Objectives* (3rd ed.), p. 38. Copyright © 1997 by The Center for Effective Performance. Adapted by permission.

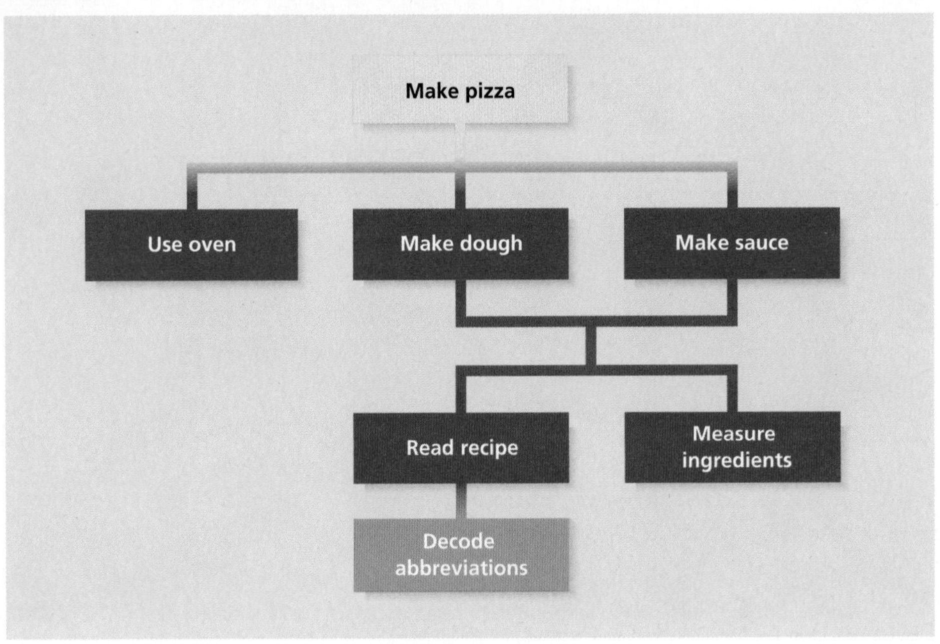

3. ***Plan how component skills will be assembled into the final skill.*** The final step in task analysis is to assemble the subskills back into the complete process being taught. For example, students might be able to estimate, to divide, and to multiply, but this does not necessarily mean that they can do long division. The subskills must be integrated into a complete process that students can understand and practice.

Backward Planning Just as lesson objectives are more than the sum of specific task objectives, the objectives of a course of study are more than the sum of specific lesson objectives. For this reason it makes sense to start by writing broad objectives for the course as a whole, then objectives for large units, and only then specific behavioral objectives (see Gronlund, 2003, 2004). This is known as **backward planning.** For example, Mr. Sullivan would have done well to have identified the objective of his Civil War unit as follows: "Students will understand the major causes, events, and consequences of the Civil War." Then he might have written more detailed objectives relating to causes, events, and consequences, and could have planned units and individual lessons around these objectives. A detailed example of the backward planning process is illustrated in Table 13.2 and described in the next Theory into Practice.

backward planning
Planning instruction by first setting long-range goals, then setting unit objectives, and finally planning daily lessons.

THEORY *into* PRACTICE

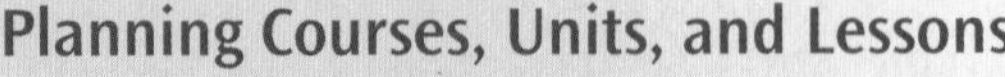

Planning Courses, Units, and Lessons

In planning a course, it is important for a teacher to set long-term, middle-term, and short-term objectives before starting to teach. Before the students arrive for the first day of class, the teacher needs to have a general plan of what will be covered all year, a more specific plan for what will be in the first unit (a connected set of lessons), and a very specific plan for the content of the first lessons (as shown in Table 13.2). Increasingly, states are establishing standards for each subject, and these standards should guide teachers' planning, especially if there are also state assessments based on the standards (see Chapter 14).

TABLE 13.2 Example of Objectives for a Course in Life Science

Teachers can allocate instructional time for a course by (a) deciding what topics to cover during the year or semester, (b) deciding how many weeks to spend on each topic, (c) choosing units within each topic, (d) deciding how many days to spend on each, and (e) deciding what each day's lesson should be.

Course Objectives (Weeks Allocated)		Unit Objectives (Days Allocated)		Lessons
Scientific method	3	Observation and measurement	4	*Lesson 1*
Characteristics of living things	3	Prediction and control	2	Questions
Cells	3	Data	3	Observations
Photosynthesis	3			*Lesson 2*
Respiration	3	Experiments	3	Checking observation with measurement
Human systems	4	Problem solving	3	*Lesson 3*
Reproduction	4			Measurement of length
Environment	3			*Lesson 4*
Adaptation	4			Measurement of mass
Relationships	3			Measurement of volume
Balance	3			

Source: Objectives adapted from Wong, Bernstein, and Shevick, *Life Science* (2nd ed.), 1978.

Table 13.2 implies a backward planning process. First the course objectives are established. Then unit objectives are designated. Finally, specific lessons are planned. The course objectives list all the topics to be covered during the year. The teacher might divide the number of weeks in the school year by the number of major topics to figure what each will require. More or less time could be reserved for any particular topic, as long as adequate time is allowed for the others. A whole semester could be spent on any one of the topics in Table 13.2, but this would be inappropriate in a survey course on life science. The teacher must make hard choices before the first day of class about how much time to spend on each topic to avoid spending too much time on early topics and not having enough time left to do a good job with later ones. Some history teachers always seem to find themselves still on World War I in mid-May and have to compress most of the twentieth century into a couple of weeks!

Table 13.2 shows approximate allocations of weeks to each of the topics to be covered. These are only rough estimates to be modified as time goes on.

UNIT OBJECTIVES AND UNIT TESTS. After course objectives have been laid out, the next task is to establish objectives for the first unit and to estimate the number of class periods to spend on each objective. It is a good idea to write a unit test as part of the planning process. Writing a test in advance helps you to focus on the important issues to be covered. For example, in a 4-week unit on the Civil War you might decide that the most important things students should learn are the causes of the war, a few major points about the military campaigns, the importance of the Emancipation Proclamation, Lincoln's assassination, and the history of the Reconstruction period. These topics would be central to the unit test on the Civil War. Writing this test would put into proper perspective the importance of the various issues that should be covered.

CERTIFICATION POINTER

For your teacher certification test you may be asked to take a goal from a state curriculum standard and write a behavioral objective to meet that standard.

The test that you prepare as part of your course planning might not be exactly the test that you give at the end of the unit. You may decide to change, add, or delete items to reflect the content you actually covered. But this does not diminish the importance of having decided in advance exactly what objectives you wanted to achieve and how you were going to assess them.

Many textbooks provide unit tests and objectives, making your task easier. However, even if you have ready-made objectives and tests, it is still important to review their content and change them as necessary to match what you expect to teach.

If you prepare unit tests from scratch, use the guide to test construction presented later in this chapter. Be sure that the test items cover the various objectives in proportion to their importance to the course as a whole (that is, that the more important objectives are covered by more items), and include items that assess higher-level thinking as well as factual knowledge.

LESSON PLANS AND LESSON ASSESSMENTS. The final step in backward planning is to plan daily lessons. Table 13.2 shows how a given unit objective might be broken down into daily lessons. The next step is to plan the content of each lesson. A lesson plan consists of an objective; a plan for presenting information; a plan for giving students practice (if appropriate); a plan for assessing student understanding; and, if necessary, a plan for reteaching students (or whole classes) if their understanding is inadequate.

Linking Objectives and Assessment

INTASC

8 Assessment of Student Learning

Because instructional objectives are stated in terms of how they will be measured, it is clear that objectives are closely linked to **assessment.** An assessment is any measure of the degree to which students have learned the objectives set out for them. Most assessments in schools are tests or quizzes, or informal verbal assessments such as questions in class. However, students can also show their learning by writing an essay, painting a picture, doing a car tune-up, or baking a pineapple upside-down cake.

One critical principle of assessment is that assessments and objectives must be clearly linked. Students learn some proportion of what they are taught; the greater the overlap between what was taught and what is tested, the better students will score on the test and the more accurately any need for additional instruction can be determined (Carr & Harris, 2001; Marzano, Pickering, & Pollock, 2001). Teaching should be closely linked to instructional objectives, and both should clearly relate to assessment. If any objective is worth teaching, it is worth testing, and vice versa. This idea was illustrated by Mager as follows:

> During class periods of a seventh grade algebra course, a teacher provided a good deal of skillful guidance in the solution of simple equations. . . . When it came time for an examination, however, the test items consisted mainly of word problems, and the students did rather poorly. The teacher's justification for this "sleight of test" was that the students didn't "really understand" algebra if they could not solve word problems. Perhaps the teacher was right. But the skill of solving equations is considerably different from the skill of solving word problems; if he wanted his students to learn how to solve word problems, he should have taught them how to do so. (Mager, 1975, p. 82)

Mager's algebra teacher really had one objective in mind (solving word problems) but taught according to another (solving equations). If he had coordinated his objectives, his teaching, and his assessment, he and his students would have been a lot happier, and the students would have had a much better opportunity to learn to solve algebra word problems.

One way to specify objectives for a course is to actually prepare test questions before the course begins (see Gronlund, 2000). This allows the teacher to write general **teaching objectives** (clear statements of what students are expected to learn through

assessment
A measure of the degree to which instructional objectives have been attained.

teaching objectives
Clear statements of what students are intended to learn through instruction.

instruction) and then to clarify them with very specific **learning objectives** (specific behaviors students are expected to exhibit at the end of a series of lessons), as in the following examples:

Teaching Objective	Specific Learning Objective (Test Questions)
a. Ability to subtract three-digit numbers renaming once or twice	a1. 237 − 184 a2. 412 − 298 a3. 596 − 448
b. Understanding of use of language to set mood in Edgar Allan Poe's "The Raven"	b1. How does Poe reinforce the mood of "The Raven" after setting it in the first stanza?
c. Ability to identify the chemical formulas for common substances	Write the chemical formulas for the following: c1. Water ____ c2. Carbon dioxide ____ c3. Coal ____ c4. Table salt ____

Using Taxonomies of Instructional Objectives

In writing objectives and assessments, it is important to consider different skills and different levels of understanding. For example, in a science lesson on insects for second-graders, you might want to impart both information (the names of various insects) and an attitude (the importance of insects to the ecosystem). In other subjects you might try to convey facts and concepts that differ by type. For example, in teaching a lesson on topic sentences in reading, you might have students first repeat the definition of topic sentences, then identify topic sentences in paragraphs, and finally write their own topic sentences for original paragraphs. Each of these activities demonstrates a different kind of understanding of the concept "topic sentence," and this concept has not been adequately taught if students can do only one of these activities. These various lesson goals can be classified by type and degree of complexity. A taxonomy, or system of classification, helps a teacher to categorize instructional activities.

CONNECTIONS
For information on thinking skills and critical thinking, see Chapter 8, page 255.

Bloom's Taxonomy In 1956, Benjamin Bloom and some fellow researchers published a **taxonomy of educational objectives** that has been influential in the research and practice of education ever since. Bloom and his colleagues categorized objectives from simple to complex or from factual to conceptual. The key elements of what is commonly called Bloom's taxonomy (Bloom, Englehart, Furst, Hill, & Krathwohl, 1956; Marzano, 2001) for the cognitive domain are (from simple to complex):

1. ***Knowledge (recalling information):*** The lowest level of objectives in Bloom's hierarchy, knowledge refers to objectives such as memorizing math facts or formulas, scientific principles, or verb conjugations.

2. ***Comprehension (translating, interpreting, or extrapolating information):*** Comprehension objectives require that students show an understanding of information as well as the ability to use it. Examples include interpreting the meaning of a diagram, graph, or parable; inferring the principle underlying a science experiment; and predicting what might happen next in a story.

3. ***Application (using principles or abstractions to solve novel or real-life problems):*** Application objectives require students to use knowledge or principles to solve practical problems. Examples include using geometric principles to figure out how many gallons of water to put into a swimming pool of given dimensions and using knowledge of the relationship between temperature and pressure to explain why a balloon is larger on a hot day than on a cold day.

learning objectives
Specific behaviors students are expected to exhibit at the end of a series of lessons.

taxonomy of educational objectives
Bloom's ordering of objectives from simple learning tasks to more complex ones.

What stage in Bloom's taxonomy might the students be taking part in here? How could a teacher incorporate all of Bloom's stages into this lesson?

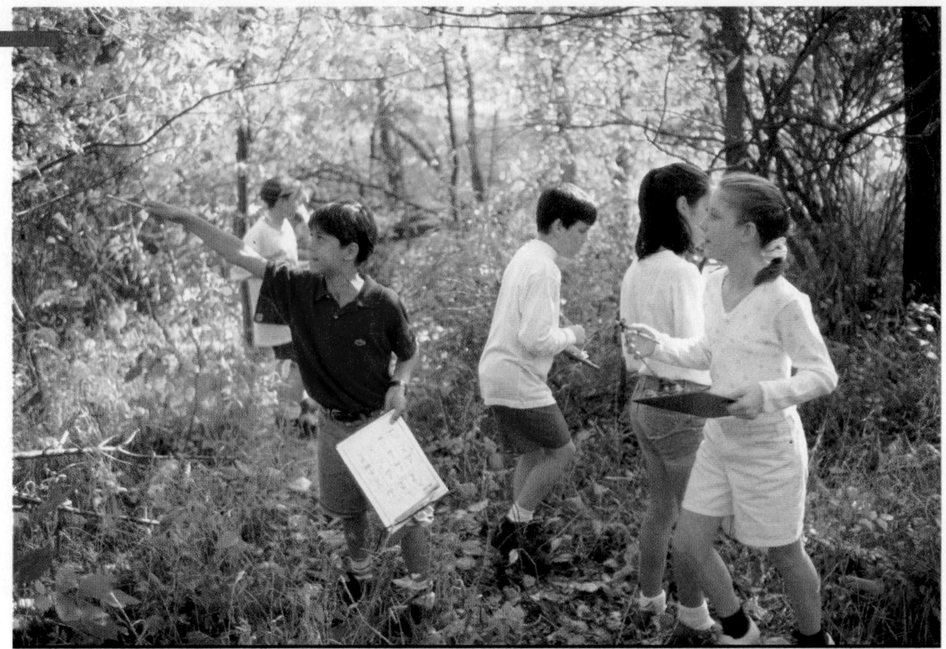

4. ***Analysis (breaking down complex information or ideas into simpler parts to understand how the parts relate or are organized):*** Analysis objectives involve having students see the underlying structure of complex information or ideas. Examples of analysis objectives include contrasting schooling in the United States with education in Japan, understanding how the functions of the carburetor and distributor are related in an automobile engine, and identifying the main idea of a short story.

5. ***Synthesis (creation of something that did not exist before):*** Synthesis objectives involve using skills to create completely new products. Examples include writing a composition, deriving a mathematical rule, designing a science experiment to solve a problem, and making up a new sentence in a foreign language.

6. ***Evaluation (judging something against a given standard):*** Evaluation objectives require making value judgments against some criterion or standard. For example, students might be asked to compare the strengths and weaknesses of two home computers in terms of flexibility, power, and available software.

Because Bloom's taxonomy is organized from simple to complex, some people interpret it as a ranking of objectives from trivial (knowledge) to important (synthesis, evaluation). However, this is not the intent of the taxonomy. Different levels of objectives are appropriate for different purposes and for students at different stages of development.

The primary importance of Bloom's taxonomy is in its reminder that we want students to have many levels of skills. All too often, teachers focus on measurable knowledge and comprehension objectives and forget that students cannot be considered proficient in many skills until they can apply or synthesize those skills (see Iran-Nejad & Stewart, 2007). On the other side of the coin, some teachers fail to make certain that students are well rooted in the basics before heading off into higher-order objectives.

Using a Behavior Content Matrix One way to be sure that your objectives cover many levels is to write a **behavior content matrix.** This is simply a chart that shows how a particular concept or skill will be taught and assessed at different cognitive levels. Examples of objectives in a behavior content matrix appear in Table 13.3. Note that for each topic, objectives are listed for some but not all levels of Bloom's taxonomy. Some topics do not lend themselves to some levels of the taxonomy, and there is no reason that every level should be covered for every topic. However, using a behavior content matrix in setting objectives forces you to consider objectives above the knowledge and comprehension levels.

behavior content matrix
A chart that classifies lesson objectives according to cognitive level.

TABLE 13.3 Examples of Objectives in a Behavior Content Matrix

A behavior content matrix can remind teachers to develop instructional objectives that address skills at various cognitive levels.

Type of Objective	Example 1: The Area of a Circle	Example 2: Main Idea of a Story	Example 3: The Colonization of Africa
Knowledge	Give the formula for area of a circle.	Define *main idea.*	Make a time line showing how Europeans divided Africa into colonies.
Comprehension		Give examples of ways to find the main idea of a story.	Interpret a map of Africa showing its colonization by European nations.
Application	Apply the formula for area of a circle to real-life problems.		
Analysis		Identify the main idea of a story.	Contrast the goals and methods used in colonizing Africa by the different European nations.
Synthesis	Use knowledge about the areas of circles and volumes of cubes to derive a formula for the volume of a cylinder.	Write a new story based on the main idea of the story read.	Write an essay on the European colonization of Africa from the perspective of a Bantu chief.
Evaluation		Evaluate the story.	

Affective Objectives Learning facts and skills is not the only important goal of instruction. Sometimes the feelings that students have about a subject or about their own skills are at least as important as how much information they learn. Instructional goals related to attitudes and values are called **affective objectives.** Many people would argue that a principal purpose of a U.S. history or civics course is to promote values of patriotism and civic responsibility, and one purpose of any mathematics course is to give students confidence in their ability to use mathematics. In planning instruction, it is important to consider affective as well as cognitive objectives. Love of learning, confidence in learning, and development of prosocial, cooperative attitudes are among the most important objectives teachers should have for their students.

Research on Instructional Objectives

Three principal reasons are given for writing instructional objectives. One is that this exercise helps to organize the teacher's planning. As Mager (1975) puts it, if you're not sure where you're going, you're liable to end up someplace else and not even know it. Another is that establishing instructional objectives helps to guide evaluation. Finally, it is hypothesized that development of instructional objectives improves student achievement.

Although it would be a mistake to overplan or to adhere rigidly to an inflexible plan, most experienced teachers create, use, and value objectives and assessments that are planned in advance. Perhaps the most convincing support for the establishment of clear instructional objectives is indirect. Cooley and Leinhardt (1980) found that the strongest single factor predicting student reading and math scores was the degree to which students were actually taught the skills that were tested. This implies that instruction is effective to the degree to which objectives, teaching, and assessment are coordinated with one another. Specification of clear instructional objectives is the first step in ensuring that classroom instruction is directed toward giving students critical skills, those that are important enough to test.

affective objectives
Objectives that have to do with student attitudes and values.

It is important to make sure that instructional objectives that are communicated to students are broad enough to encompass everything the lesson or course is supposed to teach. There is some danger that giving students too narrow a set of objectives might focus them on some information to the exclusion of other facts and concepts.

WHY IS EVALUATION IMPORTANT?

Evaluation, or assessment, refers to all the means used in schools to formally measure student performance (McMillan, 2004; Popham, 2005). These include quizzes and tests, written evaluations, and grades. Student evaluation usually focuses on academic achievement, but many schools also assess behaviors and attitudes. Many elementary schools provide descriptions of students' behavior (such as "follows directions," "listens attentively," "works with others," "uses time wisely"). In upper elementary, middle, and high school the prevalence of behavior reports diminishes successively, but even many high schools rate students on such criteria as "works up to ability," "is prepared," and "is responsible."

Why do teachers use tests and grades? They use them because, one way or another, they must periodically check and communicate about students' learning. Tests and grades tell teachers, students, and parents how students are doing in school. Teachers can use tests to determine whether their instruction was effective and to find out which students need additional help. Students can use tests to find out whether their studying strategies are paying off. Parents need grades to learn how their children are doing in school; grades usually serve as the one consistent form of communication between school and home. Schools sometimes need grades and tests to make student placements. States and school districts need tests to evaluate schools and, in some cases, teachers. Ultimately, colleges use grades and standardized test scores to decide who to admit and employers use grade-based evidence of attainment such as diplomas and other credentials in hiring decisions. Teachers, therefore, must evaluate student learning; few would argue otherwise. Fortunately, research on the use of tests finds that students learn more in courses that use tests than in those that do not (Dempster, 1991).

Student evaluations serve six primary purposes (see Gronlund, 2003):

1. Feedback to students
2. Feedback to teachers
3. Information to parents
4. Information for selection and certification
5. Information for accountability
6. Incentives to increase student effort

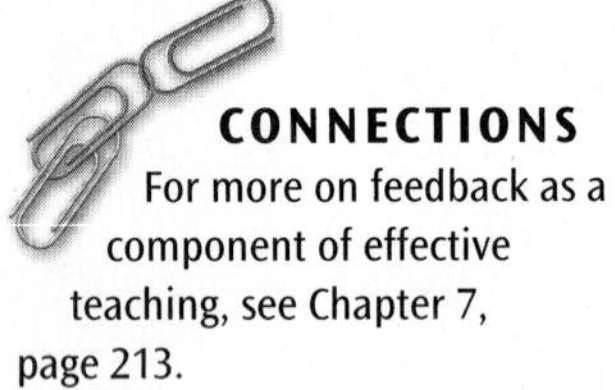

CONNECTIONS
For more on feedback as a component of effective teaching, see Chapter 7, page 213.

Evaluation as Feedback

Imagine that a store owner tried several strategies to increase business—first advertising in the newspaper, then sending fliers to homes near the store, and finally holding a sale. However, suppose that after trying each strategy, the store owner failed to record and compare the store's revenue. Without taking stock this way, the owner would learn little about the effectiveness of any of the strategies and might well be wasting time and money. The same is true of teachers and students. They need to know as soon as possible whether their investments of time and energy in a given activity are paying off in increased learning.

INTASC

8 Assessment of Student Learning

9 Professional Commitment and Responsibility

Feedback for Students Like the store owner, students need to know the results of their efforts (Hattie & Timperley, 2007; Munk & Bursuck, 1998). Regular evaluation gives them feedback on their strengths and weaknesses (Sato & Atkin, 2007). For example, suppose a teacher had students write compositions and then gave back written evaluations. Some students might find out that they needed to work more on content, others on the use of modifiers, still others on language mechanics. This information would help students to improve their writing much more than would a grade with no explanation (Chappuis, 2005; Leahy, Lyon, Thompson, & Wiliam, 2005).

evaluation
Measurement of student performance in academic and, sometimes, other areas; used to determine appropriate teaching strategies.

To be useful as feedback, evaluations should be as specific as possible. For example, Cross and Cross (1980/1981) found that students who received written feedback in addition to letter grades were more likely than other students to believe that their efforts, rather than luck or other external factors, determined their success in school.

Feedback to Teachers One of the most important (and often overlooked) functions of evaluating student learning is to provide feedback to teachers on the effectiveness of their instruction. Teachers cannot expect to be optimally effective if they do not know whether students have grasped the main points of their lessons. Asking questions in class and observing students as they work give the teacher some idea of how well students have learned; but in many subjects brief, frequent quizzes, writing assignments, and other student products are necessary to provide more detailed indications of students' progress. Well-crafted questions can help teachers understand students' thinking and uncover misconceptions (Burns, 2005). Evaluations also give information to the principal and the school as a whole, which can be used to guide overall reform efforts by identifying where schools or subgroups within schools are in need of improvement (Hanna & Dettmer, 2004; Lane & Beebe-Frankenberger, 2004; Trumbull & Farr, 2000).

Evaluation as Information

A report card is called a report card because it reports information on student progress. This reporting function of evaluation is important for several reasons.

CONNECTIONS
For more on information to parents, see Chapter 11, page 350.

Information to Parents First, routine school evaluations of many kinds (test scores, stars, and certificates as well as report card grades) keep parents informed about their children's schoolwork. For example, if a student's grades are dropping, the parents might know why and might be able to help the student get back on track. Second, grades and other evaluations set up informal home-based reinforcement systems. Recall from Chapter 11 that many studies have found that reporting regularly to parents when students do good work and asking parents to reinforce good reports improve student behavior and achievement. Without much prompting, most parents naturally reinforce their children for bringing home good grades, thereby making grades important and effective as incentives.

CONNECTIONS
For more information on ability grouping, see Chapter 4.

Information for Selection Some sociologists see the sorting of students into societal roles as a primary purpose of schools: If schools do not actually determine who will be a butcher, a baker, or a candlestick maker, they do substantially influence who will be a laborer, a skilled worker, a white-collar worker, or a professional. This sorting function takes place gradually over years of schooling. In the early grades, students are sorted into reading groups. Later, for example, some ninth-graders take Algebra I whereas others take prealgebra or general mathematics. In high school, students are often steered toward advanced, basic, or remedial levels of particular courses; and of course a major sorting takes place when students are accepted into various colleges and training programs. Throughout the school years, some students are selected into special-education or gifted programs or into other special programs with limited enrollments.

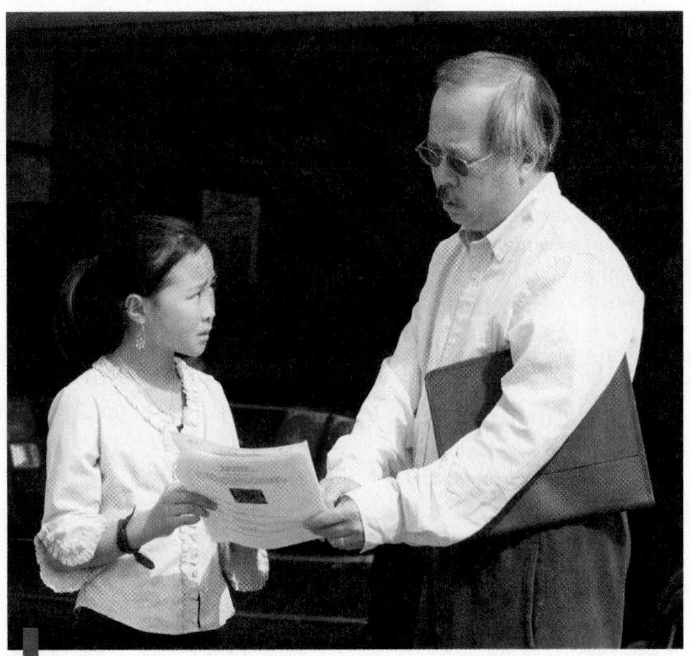

This child discusses her report card with her father. As a teacher, how can you ensure that report cards provide feedback, information, and incentive?

Closely related to selection is certification, a use of tests to qualify students for promotion or for access to various occupations. For example, many states and local districts have minimum competency tests that students must pass to advance from grade to grade or to graduate from high school. Bar exams for lawyers, board examinations for medical students, and tests for teachers such as the National Teachers' Examination are examples of certification tests that control access to professions.

Information for Accountability Often, evaluations of students serve as data for the evaluation of teachers, schools, districts, or even states. Every state has some form of statewide testing program that allows the states to rank every school in terms of student performance (Gandal & Vranek, 2001; Linn, 2000). These test scores are also often used in evaluations of principals, teachers, and superintendents. Consequently, these tests are taken very seriously.

Evaluation as Incentive

One important use of evaluations is to motivate students to give their best efforts. In essence, high grades, stars, and prizes are given as rewards for good work. Students value grades and prizes primarily because their parents value them. Some high school students also value grades because they are important for getting into selective colleges.

HOW IS STUDENT LEARNING EVALUATED?

INTASC

8 Assessment of Student Learning

Evaluation strategies must be appropriate for the uses that are made of them (McMillan, 2004; O'Connor, 2007; Trice, 2000). To understand how assessments can be used most effectively in classroom instruction, it is important to know the differences between formative and summative evaluations and between norm-referenced and criterion-referenced interpretations.

Formative and Summative Evaluations

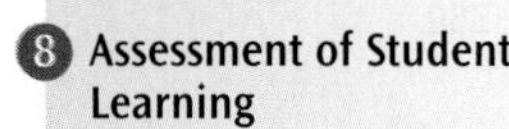

CERTIFICATION POINTER

For your teacher certification test you may be given a case illustrating an evaluation of student performance and you will need to categorize that evaluation as formative or summative.

Assessments can be divided into two categories: *formative* and *summative*. Essentially, a formative evaluation asks, "How well are you doing and how can you be doing better?" A summative evaluation asks, "How well did you do?" A **formative evaluation** is designed to determine whether additional instruction is needed. Formative, or diagnostic, tests are given to discover strengths and weaknesses in learning and to make midcourse corrections in pace or content of instruction. Formative evaluations might even be made "on the fly" during instruction through oral or brief written learning probes (see Chapter 7). Formative evaluation is useful to the degree that it is informative, closely tied to the curriculum being taught, timely, and frequent (McMillan, 2004; Safer & Fleischman, 2005). For example, frequent quizzes that are given and scored immediately after specific lessons might serve as formative evaluations, providing feedback to help both teachers and students improve students' learning.

In contrast, **summative evaluation** refers to tests of student knowledge at the end of instructional units (such as final exams). Summative evaluations may or may not be frequent, but they must be reliable and (in general) should allow for comparisons among students. Summative evaluations should also be closely tied to formative evaluations and to course objectives.

CONNECTIONS

For more on standardized testing, see Chapter 14.

formative evaluations
Evaluations designed to determine whether additional instruction is needed.

summative evaluations
Final evaluations of students' achievement of an objective.

Norm-Referenced and Criterion-Referenced Evaluations

Interpretation in order to attach a degree of value to a student's performance is an important step in an evaluation. The distinction between norm-referencing and criterion-referencing refers to how students' scores are interpreted.

Norm-referenced interpretations focus on comparisons of a student's scores with those of other students. Within a classroom, for example, grades commonly are used to give teachers an idea of how well a student has performed in comparison with classmates. A student might also have a grade-level or school rank; and in standardized testing, student scores might be compared with those of a nationally representative norm group.

Criterion-referenced interpretations focus on assessing students' mastery of specific skills, regardless of how other students did on the same skills. Criterion-referenced evaluations are best if they are closely tied to specific objectives or well-specified domains of the curriculum being taught. Table 13.4 compares the principal features and purposes of criterion-referenced and norm-referenced testing (see also Popham, 2005).

Formative evaluation is almost always criterion-referenced. In formative testing, teachers want to know, for example, who is having trouble with Newton's laws of thermodynamics, not which student is first, fifteenth, or thirtieth in the class in physics knowledge. Summative testing, in contrast, can be either criterion referenced or norm referenced. Even if it is criterion referenced, however, teachers usually want to know on a summative test how each student did in comparison with other students.

norm-referenced interpretations Assessments that compare the performance of one student against the performance of others.

criterion-referenced interpretations Assessments that rate how thoroughly students have mastered specific skills or areas of knowledge.

CERTIFICATION POINTER

Your teacher certification test may require you to evaluate when it would be more appropriate to use a criterion-referenced versus a norm-referenced test.

Matching Evaluation Strategies with Goals

Considering all the factors discussed up to this point, what is the best strategy for evaluating students? The first answer is that there is no one best strategy (Popham, 2005). The best means of accomplishing any one objective of evaluation might be inappropriate for other objectives. Therefore, teachers must choose different types of evaluation for different purposes. At a minimum, two types of evaluation should be used: one directed at providing incentive and feedback and the other directed at ranking individual students relative to the larger group.

TABLE 13.4 Comparison of Two Approaches to Achievement Testing

Norm-referenced tests and criterion-referenced tests serve different purposes and have different features.

Feature	Norm-Referenced Testing	Criterion-Referenced Testing
Principal use	Survey testing	Mastery testing
Major emphasis	Measures individual differences in achievement	Describes tasks students can perform
Interpretation of results	Compares performance to that of other individuals	Compares performance to a clearly specified achievement domain
Content coverage	Typically covers a broad area of achievement	Typically focuses on a limited set of learning tasks
Nature of test plan	Table of specifications is commonly used	Detailed domain specifications are favored
Item selection procedures	Items selected to provide maximum discrimination among individuals (to obtain high score variability); easy items typically eliminated from the test	Includes all items needed to adequately describe performance; no attempt is made to alter item difficulty or to eliminate easy items to increase score variability
Performance standards	Level of performance determined by *relative* position in some known group (e.g., student ranks fifth in a group of 20)	Level of performance commonly determined by *absolute* standards (e.g., student demonstrates mastery by defining 90 percent of the technical terms)

Source: Adapted from Norman E. Gronlund, *How to Make Achievement Tests and Assessments* (5th ed.). Published by Allyn and Bacon, Boston, MA. Reprinted by permission of the publisher.

INTASC

5 Classroom Motivation and Management
6 Communication Skills

Evaluation for Incentive and Feedback Traditional grades are often inadequate as incentives to encourage students to give their best efforts and as feedback to teachers and students. The principal problems are that grades are given too infrequently, are too far removed in time from student performance, and are poorly tied to specific student behaviors. Research has found that achievement is higher in classrooms where students receive immediate feedback on their quizzes than in classrooms where feedback is delayed (Bangert-Drowns, Kulik, Kulik, & Morgan, 1991; Crooks, 1988).

Another reason that grades are less than ideal as incentives is that they are usually based on comparative standards. In effect, it is relatively easy for high-ability students to achieve A's and B's but very difficult for low achievers to do so. As a result, some high achievers do less work than they are capable of doing, and some low achievers give up. As was noted in Chapter 10, a reward that is too easy or too difficult to attain, or that is felt to be a result of ability rather than of effort, is a poor motivator (DeBacker & Nelson, 1999; Wigfield & Eccles, 2000).

CONNECTIONS
Rewards and motivation are discussed in Chapter 5, page 132.

CONNECTIONS
For more on what rewards make poor motivators, see Chapter 10, page 312.

CONNECTIONS
For more on rewards that are too easy to attain, see Chapter 10, page 319.

For these reasons, traditional grades should be supplemented by evaluations that are better designed for incentive and feedback. For example, teachers might give daily quizzes of 5 or 10 items that are scored in class immediately after completion, or they might have students write daily "mini-essays" on a topic the class is studying. These give both students and teachers the information they need to adjust their teaching and learning strategies and to rectify any deficiencies revealed by the evaluations (Shepard, 2005). If teachers make quiz results important by having them count toward course grades or by giving students with perfect papers special recognition or certificates, then quiz scores also serve as effective incentives, rewarding effective studying behavior soon after it occurs. It is important to have a clear and objective set of criteria that student work is compared with so students can see exactly why they scored as they did. If the criteria are illustrated using a rubric that has descriptions of different levels of achievement (scores) as well as examples of student work at the highest levels of achievement (or better yet, that is typical of each possible score students might receive according to the rubric), then students can see exactly how their achievement compares with the criteria (see Stiggins, 2007).

Evaluation for Comparison with Others There are times when teachers need to know and to communicate how well students are doing in comparison to others. This information is important to give parents (and students themselves) a realistic picture of student performance. For example, students who have outstanding skills in science ought to know that they are exceptional, not only in the context of their class or school, but also in a broader state or national context. In general, students need to form accurate perceptions of their strengths and weaknesses to guide their decisions about their futures.

Comparative evaluations are traditionally provided by grades and by standardized tests. Unlike incentive/feedback evaluations, comparative evaluations need not be conducted frequently. Rather, the emphasis in comparative evaluations must be on fair, unbiased, reliable assessment of student performance.

CONNECTIONS
For more on grades and standardized tests, see Chapter 14.

To be fair, comparative evaluations and other summative assessments of student performance must be firmly based on the objectives established at the beginning of the course and must be consistent with the formative incentive/feedback evaluations in format, as well. No teacher wants a situation in which students do well on week-to-week assessments but then fail the summative evaluations because there is a lack of correspondence between the two forms of evaluation. For example, if the summative test uses essay questions, then the formative tests leading up to it should also include essay questions.

There are two keys to reliable summative assessment. First, teachers should use multiple assessment opportunities. No student should receive a grade based on only one test because too much can go wrong with only one assessment. Second, teachers should test learning when it is completed, not as it is developing. It is better to collect summative evaluation information as students complete instructional units as well as to use major unit and final tests.

These students are taking achievement tests. What are the principles for preparing achievement tests?

HOW ARE TESTS CONSTRUCTED?

Once you know the concept domains to be assessed in a test of student learning, it is time to write test items. Writing good achievement tests is a critical skill for effective teaching. This section presents some basic principles of achievement testing and practical tools for test construction (see Carey, 2001; Gronlund, 2003; Trice, 2000). Achievement testing is taken up again in Chapter 14 in relation to standardized tests.

CONNECTIONS
For more on achievement testing in relation to standardized tests, see Chapter 14, page 462.

Principles of Achievement Testing

Gronlund (2003) listed six principles to keep in mind in preparing achievement tests. These are paraphrased as follows:

1. Achievement tests should measure clearly defined learning objectives that are in harmony with instructional objectives. Perhaps the most important principle of achievement testing is that the tests should correspond with the course objectives and with the instruction that is actually provided (Carr & Harris, 2001; Gorin & Blanchard, 2004; Hanna & Dettmer, 2004; Linn, 2000). An achievement test should never be a surprise for students; rather, it should assess the students' grasp of the most important concepts or skills the lesson or course is supposed to teach.

CONNECTIONS
For more on the characteristics and uses of standardized achievement tests, see Chapter 14, page 468.

2. Achievement tests should measure a representative sample of the learning tasks included in the instruction. With rare exceptions (such as multiplication facts), achievement tests do not assess every skill or fact students are supposed to have learned. Rather, they sample from among all the learning objectives. If students do not know in advance what questions will be on a test, then they must study the entire course content to do well. However, the test items must be representative of all the objectives (contents and skills) that were covered. For example, if an English literature course spent 8 weeks on Shakespeare and 2 weeks on other Elizabethan authors, the test should have about 4 times as many items relating to Shakespeare as to the others. Items that are chosen to represent a particular objective must be central to that objective. There is no place in achievement testing for tricky or obscure questions. For example, a unit test on the American

Revolution should ask questions relating to the causes, principal events, and outcomes of that struggle, not who rowed George Washington across the Delaware. (*Answer:* John Glover and his Marblehead Marines.)

3. Achievement tests should include the types of test items that are most appropriate for measuring the desired learning outcomes. Items on achievement tests should correspond as closely as possible to the ultimate instructional objectives (Carr & Harris, 2001; Strong, Silver, & Perini, 2001). For example, in mathematics problem solving, one of the teacher's goals might be to enable students to solve problems like the ones they will encounter outside of school. Matching items or multiple choice might be inappropriate for this kind of exam, because in real life we do not select from a menu of possible solutions to a problem.

4. Achievement tests should fit the particular uses that will be made of the results. Each type of achievement test has its own requirements. For example, a test that is used for diagnosis would focus on particular skills with which students might need help. A diagnostic test of elementary arithmetic might contain items on subtraction involving zeros in the minuend (e.g., 307 minus 127), a skill with which many students have trouble. In contrast, a test that is used to predict future performance might assess a student's general abilities and breadth of knowledge. Formative tests should be very closely tied to material that has recently been presented, whereas summative tests should survey broader areas of knowledge or skills.

For more on the reliability of achievement tests, see Chapter 14, page 475.

5. Achievement tests should be as reliable as possible and should be interpreted with caution. A test is reliable to the degree that students who were tested a second time would fall in the same rank order. In general, writers of achievement tests increase reliability by using relatively large numbers of items and by using few items that almost all students get right or that almost all students miss (Hopkins, 1998). The use of clearly written items that focus directly on the objectives that are actually taught also enhances test reliability. Still, no matter how rigorously reliability is built into a test, there will always be some error of measurement. Students have good and bad days or can be lucky or unlucky guessers. Some students are test-wise and usually test well; others are test-anxious and test far below their actual knowledge or potential. Therefore, no single test score should be viewed with excessive confidence. Any test score is only an approximation of a student's true knowledge or skills and should be interpreted as such.

6. Achievement tests should improve learning. Achievement tests of all kinds, particularly formative tests, provide important information on students' learning progress. Stiggins (2004), for example, urges that assessments *for* learning are more important than assessments *of* learning. Achievement testing should be seen as part of the instructional process and should be used to improve instruction and guide student learning (Black et al., 2004; Trumbull & Farr, 2000). This means that achievement test results should be clearly communicated to students soon after the test is taken; in the case of formative testing, students should be given the results immediately. Teachers should use the results of formative and summative tests to guide instruction, to locate strong and weak points in students' understandings, and to set an appropriate pace of instruction.

THEORY *into* PRACTICE

Making Assessments Fair

INTASC

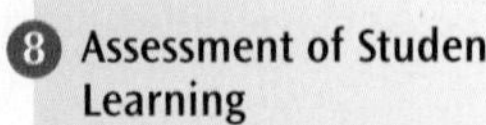
Assessment of Student Learning

Although fairness in assessment is something everyone believes in, defining fairness in assessment is not straightforward. Indeed, the latest edition of the Standards for Educational and Psychological Testing gives four definitions and acknowledges that many more are in the literature (AERA/APA/NCME, 1999). Fairness means being honest, impartial, and free from discrimination.

Besides being ethical, fairness makes good instructional sense. Fair testing encourages students to spend more effort on learning because they will come to see that success depends only on what they know and can do.

Fairness in assessment arises from good practice in four phases of testing: writing, administering, scoring, and interpreting assessments. Practices that lead to fairness in these areas are considered separately below.

WRITING ASSESSMENTS. Base assessments on course objectives. Students expect a test to cover what they have been learning. They also have a right to a test that neither "tricks" them into wrong answers nor rewards them if they can get a high score through guessing or bluffing.

Avoid contexts and expressions that are more familiar and/or intriguing to some students than to others. One challenge in writing tests is to make sure none of your students are advantaged or disadvantaged because of their different backgrounds. For example, music, sports, or celebrity-related examples might be appealing to some students but not others. Language or topics should not be used if they are more well known or interesting to some students than to others. If that proves impossible, then at least make sure the items that favor some students are balanced with others that favor the rest.

GIVING ASSESSMENTS. Make sure students have had equal opportunities to learn the material on the assessment. Regardless of whether students have learned as much as they can, at least they should have had equal chances to do so. If some students are given extra time or materials that are withheld from others, the others likely will not feel they have been treated fairly.

Make sure students are familiar with the formats they will be using to respond. If some students are not comfortable with the types of questions on an assessment, they will not have an equal chance to show what they can do. If that might be the case, some practice with the format beforehand is recommended to help them succeed.

Give plenty of time. Most tests in education do not cover content that will eventually be used under time pressure. Thus, most assessments should reward quality instead of speed. Only by allowing enough time so virtually all students have an opportunity to answer every question will the effects of speed be eliminated as a barrier to performance.

SCORING ASSESSMENTS. Make sure the rubric used to score responses awards full credit to an answer that is responsive to the question asked as opposed to requiring more information than requested for full credit. If the question does not prompt the knowledgeable student to write an answer that receives full credit, then it should be changed. It is unfair to reward some students for doing more than has been requested in the item; not all students will understand the real (and hidden) directions because they have not been told.

INTERPRETING ASSESSMENTS. Base grades on summative, end-of-unit assessments rather than formative assessments that are used to make decisions about learning as it is progressing. The latter are intended as diagnostic and to be used to help accomplish learning. Because grades certify attainment, they should be determined based on assessments made after learning has taken place.

Base grades on several assessment formats. Because students differ in their preferred assessment formats, some are advantaged by selected-response tests, others by essay tests, others by performance assessments, and still others by papers and projects.

Base grades on several assessments over time. As with assessment formats, grades should also depend on multiple assessments taken at different times.

Make sure factors that could have resulted in atypical performance for a student are used to minimize the importance of the student's score on that assessment. If it is known that a student has not done her or his best, then basing a grade or other important decision on that assessment is not only unfair but also inaccurate.

ON THE WEB

DiscoverySchool.com has rubrics for every kind of assessment imaginable, as well as lesson plans and other useful information for educators. Visit their website at **www.discoveryeducation.com/schrockguide/assess.html.**

Using a Table of Specifications

Achievement tests should measure well-specified objectives. The first step in the test development process is to decide which concept domains the test will measure and how many test items will be allocated to each concept. Gronlund (2003) suggests that teachers make up a **table of specifications** for each instructional unit listing the various objectives taught and different levels of understanding to be assessed (also see Guskey, 2005). The levels of understanding might correspond to Bloom's taxonomy of educational objectives (Bloom et al., 1956; Marzano, 2001). Bloom and colleagues (1971) suggest classifying test items for each objective according to six categories, as shown in Table 13.5, a table of specifications for a chemistry unit.

table of specifications
A list of instructional objectives and expected levels of understanding that guides test development.

The table of specifications varies for each type of course and is nearly identical to behavior content matrixes, discussed earlier in this chapter. This is as it should be; a

TABLE 13.5 Table of Specifications for a Chemistry Unit

This table of specifications classifies test items (circled numbers) and objectives according to six categories ranging from knowledge of terms to ability to apply knowledge.

A. Knowledge of Terms		B. Knowledge of Facts		C. Knowledge of Rules and Principles		D. Skill in Using Processes and Procedures		E. Ability to Make Translations		F. Ability to Make Applications	
Atom	①			Boyle's law	⑫						
Molecule	②			Properties of a gas	⑬			Substance into diagram	㉒		
Element	③			Atomic theory	⑯					Writing and solving equations to fit experimental situations	
Compound	④	Diatomic gases	⑪	Chemical formula	⑲			Compound into formula	㉑		㉘
Diatomic	⑤										㉓
Chemical formula	⑥			Avogadro's hypothesis	⑭						㉔
Avogadro's number	⑦			Gay-Lussac's law	⑮						㉕
Mole	⑧			Grams to moles	⑱						㉖
Atomic weight	⑨			Molecular weight	⑰	Molecular weight	⑳				㉗
Molecular weight	⑩										㉙

Source: From *Handbook on Formative and Summative Evaluation of Student Learning* by B. S. Bloom, J. T. Hastings, and G. F. Madaus. Copyright 1971 by McGraw-Hill Companies, Inc. Reproduced with permission of McGraw-Hill Companies, Inc., via Copyright Clearance Center.

behavior content matrix is used to lay out objectives for a course, and the table of specifications tests those objectives.

Once you have written items corresponding to your table of specifications, look over the test in its entirety and evaluate it against the following standards:

1. Do the items emphasize the same things you emphasized in day-to-day instruction? (Recall how Mr. Sullivan, in the chapter-opening vignette, ignored this commonsense rule.)
2. Has an important area of content or any objective been overlooked or underemphasized?
3. Does the test cover all levels of instructional objectives included in the lessons?
4. Does the language of the items correspond to the language and reading level you used in the lessons?
5. Is there a reasonable balance between what the items measure and the amount of time that will be required for students to develop a response?
6. Did you write model answers or essential component outlines for the short essay items? Does the weighting of each item reflect its relative value among all the other items?

Evaluation that is restricted to information acquired from paper-and-pencil tests provides only certain kinds of information about students' progress in school. Other sources and strategies for appraisal of student work must be used, including checklists, interviews, classroom simulations, role-playing activities, and anecdotal records. To do this systematically, you may keep a journal or log to record concise and cogent evaluative information on each student throughout the school year.

Writing Selected-Response Test Items

Test items that can be scored correct or incorrect without the need for interpretation are referred to as **selected-response items.** Multiple-choice, true–false, and matching items are the most common forms. Note that the correct answer appears on the test and the student's task is to select it. There is no ambiguity about whether the student has or has not selected the correct answer. This section discusses these types of test items and their advantages and disadvantages.

Multiple-Choice Items Considered by some educators to be the most useful and flexible of all test forms (Gronlund, 2000; Haladyna, 1997, 1999), **multiple-choice items** can be used in tests for most school subjects. The basic form of the multiple-choice item is a **stem** followed by choices, or alternatives. The stem may be a question or a partial statement that is completed by one of several choices. No truly optimum number of choices exists, but four or five are most common—one correct response and others that are referred to as **distractors.**

Here are two types of multiple-choice items, one with a question stem and the other with a completion stem:

1. What color results from the mixture of equal parts of yellow and blue paint?
   a. black
   b. gray
   c. green [*correct choice*]
   d. red
2. The actual election of the U.S. president to office is done by
   a. all registered voters.
   b. our congressional representatives.
   c. the Electoral College. [*correct choice*]
   d. the Supreme Court.

When writing a multiple-choice item, keep two goals in mind. First, a capable student should be able to choose the correct answer and not be distracted by the wrong alternatives. Second, you should minimize the chance that a student who is ignorant of

selected-response items
Test items in which respondents can select from one or more possible answers, without requiring the scorer to interpret their response.

multiple-choice items
Test items that usually consist of a stem followed by choices or alternatives.

stem
A question or partial statement in a test item that is completed by one of several choices.

distractors
Incorrect responses that are offered as alternative answers to a multiple-choice question.

the subject matter can guess the correct answer. To achieve this, the distractors (the wrong choices; also sometimes called foils) must look plausible to the uninformed; their wording and form must not identify them readily as bad answers. Hence, one of the tasks in writing a good multiple-choice item is to identify two, three, or four plausible, but not tricky, distractors.

THEORY *into* PRACTICE

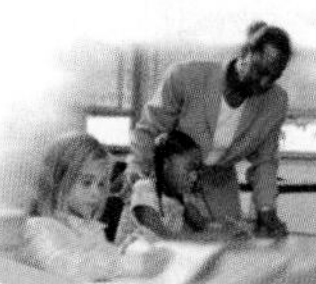

Writing Multiple-Choice Tests (Format Suggestions)

Here are some guidelines for constructing multiple-choice items (see Haladyna, 1997):

1. Make the stem sufficiently specific to stand on its own without qualification. In other words, the stem should contain enough information to set the context for the concepts in it. Here is an example of a stem for which insufficient context has been established:

   Applied behavior analysis can be
   a. classical conditioning.
   b. punishment.
   c. reinforcement contingencies.
   d. self-actualization.

   An improved version of this stem is as follows:

   What is the main emphasis of modern classroom use of applied behavior analysis?
   a. classical conditioning
   b. punishment
   c. reinforcement contingencies [*correct choice*]
   d. self-actualization
2. Avoid long and complicated stems unless the purpose of the item is to measure a student's ability to deal with new information or to interpret a paragraph. The stem should not be too wordy; a test is not the place to incorporate instruction that should have been given in the lessons. Writing the item stems as simple sentences in question form often helps to focus them appropriately.
3. The stem and every choice in the list of potential answers ought to fit grammatically. In addition, phrases or words that would commonly begin each of the alternatives should be part of the stem. It is also a sound idea to have the same grammatical form (say, a verb) at the beginning of each choice. For example:

   The task of statistics is to
   a. *make* the investigation of human beings more precise and rigorous.
   b. *make* the social sciences as respectable as the physical sciences.
   c. *predict* human behavior.
   d. *reduce* large masses of data to an interpretable form. [*correct choice*]
4. Take special care in using no-exception words such as *never, all, none,* and *always.* These words, called specific determiners, are most commonly found in incorrect statements because the admission of no exceptions usually makes statements wrong. In multiple-choice items these words often give clues to the test-wise but concept-ignorant student. Hill (1977) notes also that words allowing

qualification, such as *often, sometimes, seldom, usually, typically, generally,* and *ordinarily,* are most often found in correct statements (or responses that are true) and, along with the no-exception words, this type of specific determiner should be avoided whenever possible, or at least distributed among correct answers and distractors.

5. Avoid making the correct choice the only one that is qualified (e.g., by an "if" clause). Also, it should be neither the longest nor shortest of the alternatives (usually the longest because absolutely correct answers often require qualification and precision). These features make a choice stand out, called **clang.** If the choices vary considerably in length, then having at least two short ones and at least two long ones will reduce clang.
6. Do not allow an item to be answered on the basis of information contained in another item on the same test. This is another form of clang because it allows a student to identify the answer without knowing it beforehand.
7. Avoid overinclusive options that contain other options. For example, the choices "dogs" and "setters" should not be in the same item because a setter is a type of dog. Similarly, be cautious in using "all of the above" as an alternative because it also often reduces the possible correct choices to one or two alternatives. Here is an example illustrating how a student might know very little and get the correct answer. By knowing that only one of the choices is incorrect, a student will reduce the number of plausible choices from four to two:

   What type of research is best for investigating the effects of a new instructional program on mathematics achievement?
   a. correlational
   b. experimental [*correct choice*]
   c. historical
   d. all of the above

   The student who knows that "historical" is not a good choice also knows that *d* must be incorrect, and the answer must be *a* or *b.*
8. After a test, discuss the items with students, and note their interpretations of the wording of the items. Students often interpret certain phrases quite differently from the way the teacher intended. Such feedback will help you revise items for the next test, as well as informing you about students' understandings.
9. Do not include a choice that is transparently absurd. All choices should seem plausible to a student who has not studied or otherwise become familiar with the subject.

Besides these guidelines for writing multiple-choice items, here are some suggestions about format:

- List the choices vertically rather than side by side.
- Use letters rather than numerals to label the choices, especially on scientific and mathematical tests.
- Use word structures that make the stem agree with the choices according to acceptable grammatical practice. For example, a completion-type stem would require that each of the choices begin with a lowercase letter (unless it begins with a proper noun).
- Avoid repeating the same word or phrase in the stem and in only one alternative.
- Avoid overusing one letter position as the correct choice, as well as a pattern in the correct answers. Instead, correct choices should appear in random letter positions.

As an illustration of how test "wiseness" rather than knowledge can help students pass a test, take the brief test in Figure 13.2.

clang
Features that make a choice stand out in multiple-choice questions.

FIGURE 13.2 A Test of "Test Wiseness"

The following test is about a made-up country, Quizzerland. Use your test wiseness to guess the answers to these very bad items.

1. What is the main currency used in Quizzerland?
   a. dollar
   b. peso
   c. quark
   d. pound
2. Describe the pattern of annual rainfall in Quizzerland.
   a. mostly rainy in the highlands, dry in the lowlands
   b. rainy
   c. dry
   d. snowy
3. How many children are there in Quizzerlandian families?
   a. never more than 2
   b. usually 2–3
   c. always at least 3
   d. none
4. What would be the correct response to any question asked here?
   a.
   b.
   c.
   d.

Answers:
1. c (process of elimination)
2. a (longer item with qualifications is usually correct)
3. b ("always" and "never" items are usually wrong)
4. d (this response hasn't been used yet)

True–False Items **True–false items** can be seen as one form of multiple choice. The main drawback of true–false items is that students have a 50 percent chance of guessing correctly. For this reason, they should rarely be used.

Matching Items **Matching items** are commonly presented in the form of two lists, say *A* and *B*. For each item in list *A*, the student has to select one item in list *B*. The basis for choosing must be clearly explained in the directions. Matching items can be used to cover a large amount of content; that is, a large (but not unmanageably so) number of concepts should appear in the two lists. Each list should cover related content (use more than one set of matching items for different types of material). The primary cognitive skill that matching exercises test is *recall*.

Matching items can often be answered by elimination because many teachers maintain a one-to-one correspondence between the two lists. To engage students in the content, not the format, teachers should either include more items in list *B* than in list *A* or allow re-use of the items in list *B*.

true–false items
A form of multiple-choice test items, most useful when a comparison of two alternatives is called for.

matching items
Test items that are presented in two lists, each item in one list matching one or more items in the other list.

Writing Constructed-Response Items

Constructed-response items require the student to supply rather than to select the answer. They also usually require some degree of judgment in scoring.

The simplest form is fill-in-the-blank items, which can often be written to reduce or eliminate ambiguity in scoring. Still, unanticipated responses might lead to ambiguous answers, causing questions in the mind of the instructor on how to score. Constructed-response items also come in short and long essay forms.

Fill-in-the-Blank Items When there is clearly only one possible correct answer, an attractive format is completion, or "fill in the blank," as in the following examples:

1. The largest city in Germany is ________.
2. What is 15 percent of $198.00? ________
3. The measure of electric resistance is the ________.

The advantage of these **completion items** is that they can reduce the element of test-wiseness to near zero. For example, compare the following items:

1. The capital of Maine is ________.
2. The capital of Maine is

   a. Sacramento.
   b. Augusta.
   c. Juneau.
   d. Boston.

A student who has no idea what the capital of Maine is could pick Augusta from the list in item 2 because it is easy to rule out the other three cities. In item 1, however, the student has to know the answer. Completion items are especially useful in arithmetic, in which use of multiple choice may help to give the answer away or reward guessing. For example:

$$\begin{array}{r} 4037 \\ -\ 159 \\ \hline \end{array}$$

a. 4196
b. 4122
c. 3878 [*correct answer*]
d. 3978

If students subtract and get an answer other than any of those listed, they know that they have to keep trying. In some cases they can narrow the alternatives by estimating rather than knowing how to compute the answer.

It is critical to avoid ambiguity in completion items. In some subject areas this can be difficult because two or more answers will reasonably fit a fragment that does not specify the context. Here are two examples:

1. The Battle of Hastings was in ________. [Date or place?]
2. "H_2O" represents ________. [Water or two parts hydrogen and one part oxygen?]

If there is any ambiguity possible, it is probably best to move to a selection type of item such as multiple choice.

Writing and Evaluating Essay Tests

Short essay questions allow students to respond in their own words. The most common form for a **short essay item** includes a question for the student to answer. The answer may range from a sentence or two to a page of, say, 100 to 150 words. A **long essay item** requires more length and more time, allowing greater opportunity for students to demonstrate organization and development of ideas. Although they differ in length, the methods available to write and score them are similar.

The essay form can elicit a wide variety of responses, from giving definitions of terms to comparing and contrasting important concepts or events. These items are especially suited for assessing students' ability to analyze, synthesize, and evaluate. Hence teachers might use them to appraise students' progress in organizing data and applying concepts at the highest levels of instructional objectives. Of course, these items depend heavily on writing skills and the ability to phrase ideas, so exclusive use of essays might cause the teacher to underestimate the knowledge and effort of a student who has learned the material but is a poor writer.

One of the crucial mistakes teachers make in writing essay items is failing to specify clearly the approximate detail required in the response and its expected length. Stating

completion items
Fill-in-the-blank test items.

short essay item
A test question the answer to which may range from a sentence or two to a page of 100 to 150 words.

long essay item
A test question requiring an answer of more than a page.

how much weight an item has relative to the entire test is generally not sufficient to tell students how much detail must be incorporated in a response. Here's an illustration of this point:

Poor Essay Item
Discuss the role of the prime minister in Canadian politics.

Improvement
In five paragraphs or less, identify three ways in which the Canadian prime minister and the U.S. president differ in their obligations to their respective constituencies. For each of the three, explain how the obligations are different.

Note that the improved version expresses a length (five paragraphs or less), the aspect to be treated (differences between the prime minister and the president), the number of points to be covered (three; while some teachers might write "at least three," that would introduce ambiguity into the task), how the points should be selected (differ in their obligations to their respective constituencies), and the direction and degree of elaboration needed (explain how the obligations are different). This item points the student toward the desired response and allows the teacher greater opportunity to explain the criteria by which student responses will be judged.

An essay item should contain specific information that students are to address. Some teachers are reluctant to name the particulars that they wish the student to discuss because they believe that supplying a word or phrase in the instructions is giving away too much information. But if an item is ambiguous, different students will interpret it differently. Consequently, they will be responding to different questions and the test will almost surely not be fair to all of them.

Essay items have a number of advantages in addition to letting students state ideas in their own words. Essay items are not susceptible to correct guesses. They can be used to measure creative abilities, such as writing talent or imagination in constructing hypothetical events. Essay items might require students to combine several concepts in their response. They can assess organization and fluency.

On the negative side is the problem of reliability in scoring essay responses. Some studies demonstrate that independent marking of the same essay response by several teachers results in appraisals ranging from excellent to a failing grade.

A second drawback of essay items is that essay responses take considerable time to evaluate. The time you might have saved by writing one essay item instead of several other kinds of items must be paid back in grading the essays.

Third, essay items in general take considerable response time from students. Consequently, they typically cannot be used to cover broad ranges of content. Nevertheless, essay items allow teachers the opportunity to see how well students can use the material they have been taught. Breadth is sacrificed for depth.

Here are some additional suggestions for writing essay items:

1. As with any item format, match the items with the instructional objectives.
2. Do not use such general directives in an item as "discuss," "give your opinion about . . . ," "tell all you know about. . . ." Rather, carefully choose specific response verbs such as "compare," "contrast," "identify," "list and define," and "explain the difference."
3. Write a response to the item before you give the test to estimate the time students will need to respond. About four times the teacher's time is a fair estimate.
4. Rewrite the item to point students clearly toward the desired response.
5. Require all students to answer all items. Although it seems attractive to allow student choice in which items to answer, that is fundamentally an unfair practice. First, students differ in their ability to make the best selections. Second, the items will not be of equivalent difficulty. And third, some students who know they will have a choice can increase their score by studying very carefully only part of the material.

After writing an essay item—and clearly specifying the content that is to be included in the response—you must have a clear idea of how you will score various elements of a student's response. The first step is to write a model response or a detailed outline of the essential elements students are being directed to include in their responses. You will compare students' responses to this model. If you intend to use evaluative comments but not letter grades, your outline or model will serve as a guide for pointing out to students the omissions and errors in their responses, as well as the good points of their answers. If you are using letter grades to score the essays, you will compare elements of students' responses with the contents of your model and give suitable credit to responses that match the relative weights of elements in the model.

If possible, you should ask a colleague to assess the validity of the elements and their weights in your model response. Going a bit further and having the colleague apply the model criteria to one or more student responses could increase the reliability of your scoring (see Langer & Colton, 2005). Be sure to offer to do the same for them!

One issue relating to essay tests is whether and how much to count grammar, spelling, and other technical features. If you do count these, give students separate grades in content and in mechanics so that they will know the basis on which their work was evaluated.

A powerful use of assessment in instruction is to generate one or more scoring rubrics that can be shared with students well in advance of the test. The rubrics, like the example, should be generic, in that they can be applied to a broad range of essays. Students can see what aspects of their achievement will contribute to a positive evaluation and can practice to make sure their work illustrates those critical elements. You might show students (anonymous) essays from previous years to illustrate the rubric. One rubric for high school math problem solving appears in Figure 13.3.

FIGURE 13.3 Generic Rubric for Brief Constructed-Response Items in High School Mathematics in Maryland

Level 3

The response indicates application of a reasonable strategy that leads to a correct solution in the context of the problem. The representations are essentially correct. The explanation and/or justification is logically sound, clearly presented, fully developed, supports the solution, and does not contain significant mathematical errors. The response demonstrates a complete understanding and analysis of the problem.

Level 2

The response indicates application of a reasonable strategy that may be incomplete or undeveloped. It may or may not lead to a correct solution. The representations are fundamentally correct. The explanation and/or justification supports the solution and is plausible, although it may not be well developed or complete. The response demonstrates a conceptual understanding and analysis of the problem.

Level 1

The response indicates little or no attempt to apply a reasonable stategy or applies an inappropriate strategy. It may or may not have the correct answer. The representations are incomplete or missing. The explanation and/or justification reveals serious flaws in reasoning. The explanation and/or justification may be incomplete or missing. The response demonstrates a minimal understanding and analysis of the problem.

Level 0

The response is completely incorrect or irrelevant. There may be no response, or the response may state, "I don't know."

Explanation refers to the student using the language of mathematics to communicate how the student arrived at the solution.

Justification refers to the student using mathematical principles to support the reasoning used to solve the problem or to demonstrate that the solution is correct. This could include the appropriate definitions, postulates, and theorems.

Essentially correct representations may contain several minor errors such as missing labels, reversed axes, or scales that are not uniform.

Fundamentally correct representations may contain several minor errors such as missing labels, reversed axes, or scales that are not uniform.

From W. D. Schafer, G. Swanson, N. Bené, & G. Newberry, "Effects of Teacher Knowledge of Rubrics on Student Achievement in Four Content Areas," *Applied Measurement in Education, 14,* 2001, pp. 151–170.

THEORY *into* PRACTICE

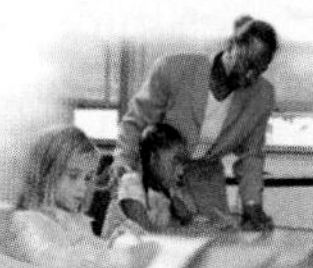

Detecting Bluffing in Students' Essays

Students who are not well prepared for essay tests are likely to try to bluff their way through. Gronlund (2006) suggests that credit should not be given unless the question is specifically answered. Some common types of bluffing are as follows:

1. Student repeats the question in statement form (slightly paraphrased) and tells how important the topic is (e.g., "The role of assessment in teaching is extremely important. It is hard to imagine effective instruction without it.").
2. Student writes on a well-known topic and fits it to the question (e.g., a student who knows testing well but knows little about performance assessment and is asked to compare testing and performance assessment might describe testing in considerable detail and frequently state that performance assessment is much superior for evaluating the type of learning measures by the test).
3. Student liberally sprinkles the answer with basic concepts whether they are understood or not (e.g., asked to write about any assessment technique, the importance of "validity" and "reliability" is mentioned frequently).
4. Student includes the teacher's basic beliefs wherever possible (e.g., "The intended learning outcomes must be stated in performance terms before this type of test is constructed or selected.").

Bluffing is most effective where plans have not been made for careful scoring of the answers.

Writing and Evaluating Problem-Solving Items

CONNECTIONS
For more on problem solving, see Chapter 8, page 249.

In many subjects, such as mathematics and the physical and social sciences, instructional objectives include the development of skills in problem solving, so it is important to assess students' performance in solving problems (Haladyna, 1997). A **problem-solving assessment** requires students to organize, select, and apply complex procedures that have at least several important steps or components. It is important to appraise the students' work in each of these steps or components.

Here are a seventh-grade-level mathematical problem and a seventh-grader's response to it. In the discussion of evaluating problem solving that follows, the essential components are described in specific terms, but they can be applied to all disciplines.

Problem

Suppose two gamblers are playing a game in which the loser must pay an amount equal to what the other gambler has at the time. If Player *A* won the first and third games, and Player *B* won the second game, and they finished the three games with $12 each, with how much money did each begin the first game? How did you get your answer?

A student's response:

After game	*A* had	*B* had
3	$12.00	$12.00
2	6.00	18.00
1	15.00	9.00
In the beginning	$ 7.50	$16.50

When I started with Game 1, I guessed and guessed, but I couldn't make it come out to 12 and 12.

problem-solving assessment Test that calls for organizing, selecting, and applying complex procedures that have at least several important steps or components.

Then I decided to start at Game 3 and work backward. It worked!

How will you objectively evaluate such a response? As in evaluating short essay items, you should begin your preparation for appraising problem-solving responses by writing either a model response or, perhaps more practically, an outline of the essential components or procedures that are involved in problem-solving. As with essays, problem-solving responses may take several different yet valid approaches. The outline must be flexible enough to accommodate all valid possibilities.

THEORY *into* PRACTICE

Peer Evaluations

An evaluation technique often used in cooperative learning, especially in creative writing and (less often) mathematics problem solving, is to have students rate each others' work on a specific set of criteria before the teacher rates them on the same criteria. The peer evaluation does not contribute to a student's score or grade but gives the student feedback that he or she can use to revise the composition or product. Figure 13.4 shows a peer response guide that might be used for a comparison–contrast writing assignment. The partner, and then the teacher, would put a check mark in each space to indicate that the student has done an adequate job in that category. The partner and the teacher would also mark the student's paper to make suggestions for improvement. Peer evaluation provides a formative evaluation for the writer, but it also gives the evaluator an invaluable opportunity to take the teacher's perspective and gain insight into what constitutes good writing.

INTASC

6 Communication Skills

EVALUATING PROBLEM-SOLVING ITEMS. Problem solving involves several important components that fit most disciplines. Those include understanding the problem to be solved, attacking the problem systematically, and arriving at a reasonable answer. Following is a detailed checklist of elements common to most problem solving that can guide your weighting of elements in your evaluation of a student's problem-solving abilities.

Criterion	*Partner*	*Teacher*
Content		
1. Shows how concepts are similar		
2. Shows how concepts are different		
3. Well organized		
4. Good opening sentence		
5. Good concluding sentence		
Mechanics		
1. Spelling correct		
2. Grammar correct		
3. Punctuation correct		
4. At least 2 pages		

FIGURE 13.4 Example of a Partner Response Form for a Comparison–Contrast–Comparison

PROBLEM-SOLVING EVALUATION ELEMENTS

☐ 1. Problem organization

  ☐ a. representation by table, graph, chart, etc.
  ☐ b. representation fits the problem
  ☐ c. global understanding of the problem

☐ 2. Procedures (mathematical: trial and error, working backward, experimental process, empirical induction)

  ☐ a. A viable procedure was attempted.
  ☐ b. The procedure was carried to a final solution.
  ☐ c. Computation (if any) was correct.

☐ 3. Solution (mathematical: a table, number, figure, graph, etc.)

  ☐ a. Answer was reasonable.
  ☐ b. Answer was checked.
  ☐ c. Answer was correct.

☐ 4. Logic specific to the detail or application of the given information was sound.

If you wish to give partial credit for an answer that contains correct elements or want to inform students about the value of their responses, you must devise ways to do this consistently. The following points offer some guidance:

1. Write model responses before giving partial credit for such work as essay writing, mathematical problem solving, laboratory assignments, or any work that you evaluate according to the quality of its various stages.
2. Tell students in sufficient detail the meaning of the grades you give to communicate the value of the work.

The following examples illustrate outlines of exemplary student work from mathematics and social studies or literature.

FROM MATHEMATICS. Students are given the following problem:

> In a single-elimination tennis tournament, 40 players are to play for the singles championship. Determine how many matches must be played.

EVALUATION

☐ a. Evidence that the student understood the problem, demonstrated by depiction of the problem with a graph, table, chart, equation, etc. (*3 points*)

☐ b. Use of a method for solving the problem that had potential for yielding a correct solution—for example, systematic trial and error, empirical induction, elimination, working backward. (*5 points*)

☐ c. Arrival at a correct solution. (*3 points*)

The three components in the evaluation were assigned points according to the weight the teacher judged each to be worth in the context of the course of study and the purpose of the test. Teachers can give full credit for a correct answer even if all the work is not shown in the response, provided that they know that students can do the work in their heads. But it is important to guard against the **halo effect.** This occurs when a teacher knows which student wrote which response and alters the grading of the paper depending on her or his opinion of the student. The same response should receive the same score no matter who wrote it. Use of a detailed rubric, or scoring guide, in evaluation is a way to make scoring more objective and thus to avoid any halo effects.

halo effect
Bias due to carryover of a general attitude about a respondent, as when a teacher knows which student wrote which response and alters the grading depending on his or her opinion of the student.

FROM SOCIAL STUDIES OR LITERATURE. Students are asked to respond with a 100-word essay to the following item:

> Compare and contrast the development of Inuit and Navajo tools on the basis of the climates in which these two peoples live.

EVALUATION

- ☐ a. The response gives evidence of specific and accurate recall of the climates in which the Inuit and Navajos live (*1 point*) and of Inuit and Navajo tools. (*1 point*)
- ☐ b. The essay develops with continuity of thought and logic. (*3 points*)
- ☐ c. An accurate rationale is provided for the use of the various tools in the respective climates. (*3 points*)
- ☐ d. An analysis comparing and contrasting the similarities and differences between the two groups and their tool development is given. (*8 points*)
- ☐ e. The response concludes with a summary and closure. (*1 point*)

These two examples should suggest ways to evaluate items in other subject areas as well. Giving partial credit for much of the work students do certainly results in a more complete evaluation of student progress than does scoring the work as merely right or wrong. The examples show how to organize objective assessments for evaluating work that does not lend itself to the simple forms of multiple-choice, true–false, completion, and matching items. Points do not have to be used to evaluate components of the responses. In many situations, some kind of evaluative descriptors might be more meaningful. **Evaluative descriptors** are statements describing strong and weak features of a response to an item, a question, or a project. In the mathematics example a teacher's evaluative descriptor for item *a* might read, "You have drawn an excellent chart showing that you understand the meaning of the problem, and that is very good, but it seems you were careless when you entered several important numbers in your chart."

Note that each of these examples is much like a rubric and can be generalized to broad ranges of topics. If teachers and students discuss these during instruction, students will have a device that helps them understand what they are working toward and both teachers and students will have a common language that they can use during instruction and in their formative assessments.

WHAT ARE AUTHENTIC, PORTFOLIO, AND PERFORMANCE ASSESSMENTS?

After much criticism of traditional testing (e.g., Rotberg, 2001; Shepard, 2000; Thompson, 2001), critics have developed and implemented alternative assessment systems that are designed to avoid the problems of typical multiple-choice tests. The key idea behind the testing alternatives is that students should be asked to document their learning or demonstrate that they can actually do something real with the information and skills they have learned in school (Campbell, 2000; Carey, 2001; Marzano, Pickering, & Pollock, 2001). For example, students might be asked to keep a portfolio, design a method of measuring wind speed, draw a scale model of a racing car, or write something for a real audience. Such tests are referred to as *authentic assessments* or *performance assessments* (Ellis, 2001a; Stiggins, 2000). One goal of these "alternative assessments" is to demonstrate achievement in realistic contexts. In reading, for example, the authentic assessment movement has led to the development of tests in which students are asked to read and interpret longer sections and show their metacognitive awareness of reading strategies (Roeber & Dutcher, 1989; Valencia, Pearson, Peters, & Wixson, 1989). In science, authentic assessments might involve having students set up and carry out an experiment. In writing, students might be asked to write real letters or newspaper articles. In math, students might solve complex physical problems that require insight and creativity. Authentic tests sometimes require students to integrate knowledge from different domains; for example, to use algebra in the context of reading about and performing a science experiment and to write up the results.

INTASC

8 Assessment of Student Learning

evaluative descriptors
Statements describing strong and weak features of a response to an item, a question, or a project.

Portfolio Assessment

One popular form of alternative assessment is called **portfolio assessment:** the collection and evaluation of samples of student work over an extended period (Carey, 2001; McMillan, 2004; Rolheiser, Bower, & Stevahn, 2000). Teachers may collect student compositions, projects, and other evidence of higher-order functioning and use this evidence to evaluate student progress over time. For example, many teachers have students maintain portfolios of their writings that show the development of a composition from first draft to final product; journal entries, book reports, artwork, computer printouts, or papers showing development in problem solving (Arter & McTighe, 2001; Shaklee, Barbour, Ambrose, & Hansford, 1997). Portfolios are increasingly being maintained in computers to supplement paper files (Diehm, 2004; Niguidula, 2005). Refer to Figure 13.5 for sample criteria for evaluating student writing portfolios.

portfolio assessment
Assessment of a collection of the student's work in an area showing growth, self-reflection, and achievement.

Portfolio assessment has important uses when teachers want to evaluate students for reports to parents or other within-school purposes. When combined with on-demand

FIGURE 13.5 Sample of Criteria for Evaluating Students' Writing Ability through Portfolio Assessment

From Cathy Collins Block, *Teaching the Language Arts: Expanding Thinking through Student Centered Instruction.* Copyright © 1993 by Allyn & Bacon. Reprinted by permission.

Continua of Descriptors

Strong Performance ←	→	Needs Improvement
	Versatility	
Wide variety of reading and writing across genre	Some variety	Little or no variety Collection shows little breadth or depth
	Process	
Samples reveal discoveries or pivotal learning experiences	Process illustrated in inflexible or mechanistic ways	Minimal use of process to reflect on achievements
	Response	
Engaged with story Discusses key issues Evidence of critical questioning	Personal reflection but focus is narrow	Brief retelling of isolated events
	Self-Evaluations	
Multidimensional Wide variety of observations Establishing meaningful goals Notes improvement	Developing insights Some specifics noted Limited goal setting Vague idea of improvement	Single focus, global in nature Goal setting too broad or nonexistent
	Individual Pieces	
Strong control of a variety of elements: organization, cohesion, surface features, etc.	Growing command evidenced; some flaws, but major ideas clear	Needs to improve: sophistication of ideas, text features, and surface features
	Problem Solving	
Wrestles with problems using various resources Enjoys problem solving and learning new ways	Uses limited resources Wants quick fix	Seems helpless Frustrated by problems
	Purposefulness/Uses	
Uses reading and writing to satisfy various goals including sharing with others	Uses reading and writing to meet others' goals	Apathetic, resistant

assessments and used with consistent and public rubrics, portfolios showing improvement over time can provide powerful evidence of change to parents and to students themselves (Cavanna, Olchefske, & Fleischman, 2006).

CERTIFICATION POINTER

A teacher certification question may ask you to respond to a case study by suggesting a way to implement portfolio assessment that would be appropriate for the case.

ON THE WEB

For reports, newsletters, and other publications about assessment, particularly performance and portfolio assessment, visit **www.cresst.org,** the National Center for Research on Evaluation, Standards, and Student Testing (CRESST), located at UCLA.

THEORY *into* PRACTICE

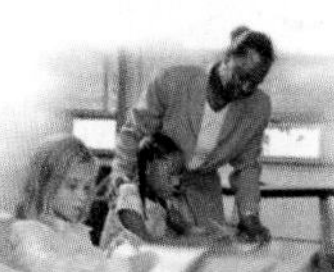

Using Portfolios in the Classroom

PLANNING AND ORGANIZATION

- Develop an overall flexible plan for student portfolios (see Shaklee et al., 1997). What purposes will the portfolios serve? What items will be required? When and how will they be obtained? What criteria will be applied for reflection and evaluation?
- Plan sufficient time for students to prepare and discuss portfolio items. Portfolio assessments take more time and thought than correcting paper-and-pencil tests does.
- Begin with one aspect of student learning and achievement, and gradually include others as you and the students learn about portfolio procedures. The writing process, for instance, is particularly well suited to documentation through portfolios.
- Choose items to be included in portfolios that will show developing proficiency on important goals and objectives. Items that address multiple objectives help to make portfolio assessments more efficient.
- Collect at least two types of items: required indicators (Arter & McTighe, 2001; Murphy & Underwood, 2000) or core items and optional work samples. Required or core indicators are items collected for every child that will show how each child is progressing. Optional work samples show individual student's unique approaches, interests, and strengths.
- Place a list of goals and objectives in the front of each portfolio, along with a list of required indicators and include a place for recording optional items, so that you and the students can keep track of contents.

IMPLEMENTATION

- In order to save time, to ensure that portfolio items are representative of students' work, and to increase authenticity, embed the development of portfolio items into ongoing classroom activities.
- Give students responsibility for preparing, selecting, evaluating, and filing portfolio items and keeping portfolios up to date. Young children will need guidance with this.
- For selected portfolio items, model reflection and self-assessment for students to help them become aware of the processes they used, what they learned and have yet to learn, and what they might need to do differently next time.
- Be selective. A portfolio is not a haphazard collection of work samples, audio or videotapes, pictures, websites, and other products. It is a thoughtful selection of items that exemplify children's learning. Random inclusion of items quickly becomes overwhelming.

- Use information in portfolios to place learners on a sequence of developing skills. For example, Wiggins (1993) presented a developmental spelling sequence that was used in a performance assessment program in a New Jersey district.
- Analyze portfolio items for insight into students' knowledge and skills. As you do this, you will understand more of the students' strengths and needs, thinking processes, preconceptions, misconceptions, error patterns, and developmental benchmarks (Athanases, 1994).
- Use portfolio information to document and celebrate students' learning, to share with parents and other school personnel, and to improve and target classroom instruction. If portfolios are not linked to improving instruction, they are not working. (For guides to portfolio evaluation, see Murphy & Underwood, 2000; Rolheiser, Bower, & Stevahn, 2000; Stiggins, 2000.)

VIDEO HOMEWORK EXERCISE
Performance Assessment

Go to **www.myeducationlab.com** and, in the Homework and Exercises section for Chapter 13 of this text, access the video entitled "Performance Assessment." Watch the video and complete the homework questions that accompany it, saving your work or transmitting it to your professor as required.

Performance Assessment

Tests that involve actual demonstrations of knowledge or skills in real life are called **performance assessments** (Foster & Noyce, 2004; McMillan, 2004; Popham, 2005; Trice, 2000). For example, ninth-graders might be asked to conduct an oral history project, reading about a significant recent event and then interviewing the individuals involved. The quality of the oral histories, done over a period of weeks, would indicate the degree of the students' mastery of the social studies concepts involved. Wiggins (1993) also describes assessments used in the last 2 weeks of school in which students must apply everything they have learned all year to analyze a sludge that mixes a variety of solids and liquids. Some schools are requiring elaborate "exhibitions," such as projects developed over many months, as demonstrations of competence (Sills-Briegel, Fisk, & Dunlop, 1996). More time-limited performance assessments might ask students to set up experiments, respond to extended text, write in various genres, or solve realistic math problems (Egeland, 1996).

A model for performance assessment is the doctoral thesis, an extended project required for Ph.D. candidates that is intended to show not only what students know, but also what they can do (Archibald & Newmann, 1988). Driver's tests, tests for pilots' licenses, and performance tests in medicine are also common examples of performance assessments (Swanson, Norman, & Linn, 1995).

CERTIFICATION POINTER

You may be asked on your teacher certification test to give an example of a performance goal and then to write a behavioral objective, an activity, and an assessment of student learning that would accomplish the goal.

ON THE WEB

To view articles and multimedia related to assessment and other education topics, go to the website of the George Lucas Educational Foundation at **www.edutopia.org.**

How Well Do Performance Assessments Work?

One of the most important criticisms of traditional standardized tests is that they can focus teachers on teaching a narrow range of skills that happen to be on the test (see Popham, 2004). How might performance assessments be better? At least in theory, it should be possible to create tests that would require such a broad understanding of subject matter that the test would be worth teaching to.

For example, consider the performance test in science shown in Figure 13.6. Imagine that you know that your students will have to conduct an experiment to solve a problem

performance assessments
Assessments of students' ability to perform tasks in real-life contexts, not only to show knowledge. Also called *authentic assessments.*

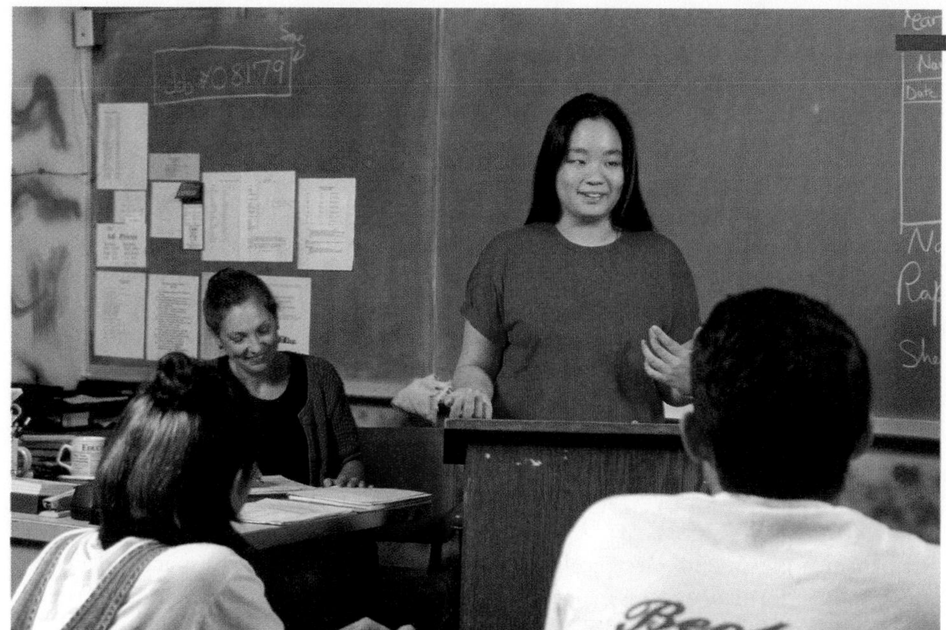

This student's performance is being evaluated by her classmates. What are the advantages and disadvantages of using a performance or group activity as a method for evaluating students?

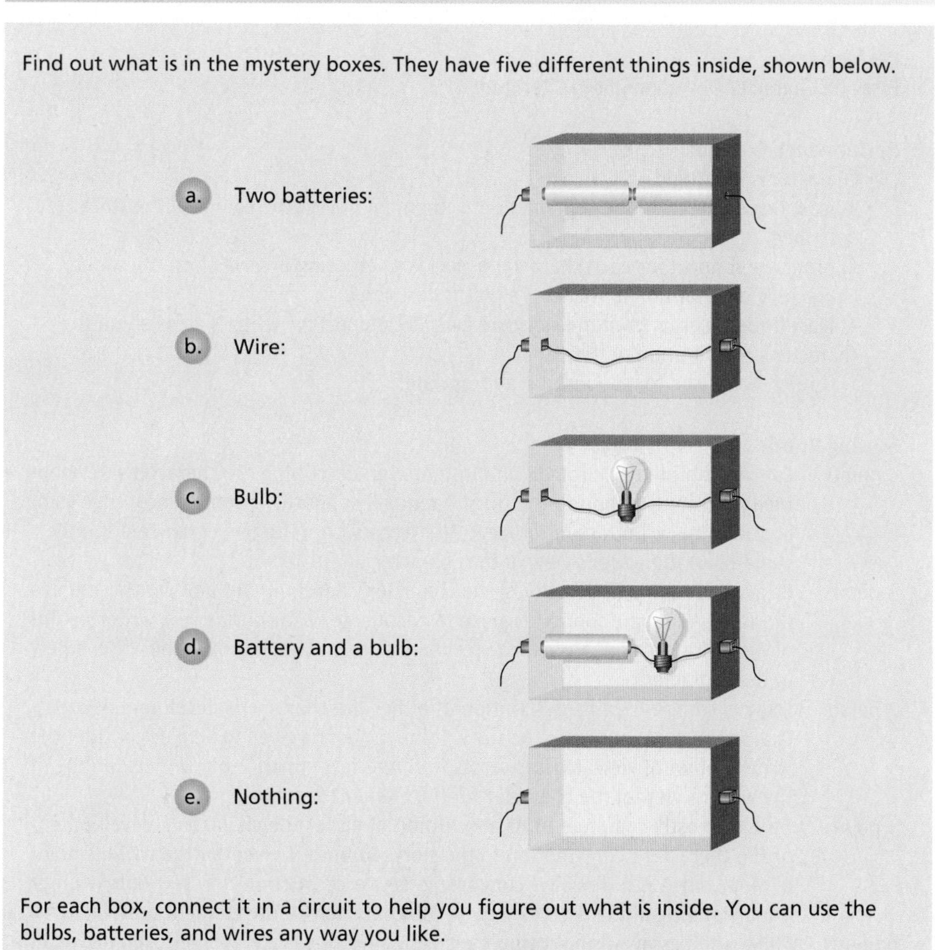

Find out what is in the mystery boxes. They have five different things inside, shown below.
a. Two batteries:
b. Wire:
c. Bulb:
d. Battery and a bulb:
e. Nothing:
For each box, connect it in a circuit to help you figure out what is inside. You can use the bulbs, batteries, and wires any way you like.

FIGURE 13.6 Example of a Performance Assessment Activity

From R. J. Shavelson, G. P. Baxter, and J. Pine, "Performance Assessments: Political Rhetoric and Measurement Reality," *Educational Researcher, 21*(2), p. 23.

like the one posed in the figure (but not that exact problem). The only way to teach such a test will be to expose students to a broad range of information about electricity, experimentation, and problem-solving strategies (see Shepard, 1995).

Beyond all the practical problems and expense of administering and scoring performance tests, it is not yet clear whether performance tests will solve all the problems of standardized testing (Cizek, 1993; Messick, 1994; Moss, 1992; Shepard, 1993b; Worthen & Spandel, 1993). For example, Shavelson, Baxter, and Pine (1992) studied performance assessments in science (Figure 13.6 is taken from their study). They found that student performance on such assessments could be reliably rated, but different performance assessments produced very different patterns of scores, and student scores were still related more closely to student aptitude than to what students were actually taught (see also Educational Testing Service, 1995; Linn, 1994; Supovitz & Brennan, 1997).

Scoring Rubrics for Performance Assessments

Performance assessments are typically scored according to rubrics that specify in advance the type of performance that is expected for each activity (Arter & McTighe, 2001; Lewin & Shoemaker, 1998). Figure 13.7 shows one rubric (from Taylor, 1994) that was developed for an essay on character development in stories students have read.

FIGURE 13.7 Sample Scoring Rubric: Targeted Performance, Performance Criteria, and a Description of Performances at Different Score Points

From Catherine Taylor, "Assessment for Measurement or Standards," *American Educational Research Journal, 31*(2), pp. 231–262.

Performance
Essay on Character Development in Literature

Performance Criteria

- Character is identified.
- At least three aspects of the character's development during the course of the story are described.
- Appropriate support for each character aspect is given using excerpts from the story.
- Character's contribution to the story's plot is described.
- At least three excerpts from the story are given as support for writer's ideas about the character's contribution to the story.
- Text references used for support are appropriate.

Scoring Rubric

4 points	Essay is complete, thorough, and insightful in describing the character's development and contribution to the story. Adequate support is given to encourage us to consider the writer's point of view. All excerpts from the text enhance our understanding of the writer's view of the character.
3 points	Essay is complete in describing the character's development and contribution to the story. Adequate support is given to encourage us to consider the writer's point of view. Most excerpts from the text enhance our understanding of the writer's view of the character.
2 points	Essay is complete in its description of either the character's development *or* the character's contribution to the story. Some support is given to help us consider the writer's point of view. Most excerpts from the text enhance our understanding of the writer's view of the character for the element described.
1 point	Essay is mostly complete in its description of either the character's development or the character's contribution to the story. Support is given for the writer's point of view, but it is not always convincing. Few excerpts from the text enhance our understanding of the writer's view of the character for the element described.
0 points	The written essay was not completed, is significantly lacking in performance of all criteria, or is off-task.

Performance assessment tasks are similar to essay items in that students might approach them in multiple ways. It is, therefore, also important for performance assessments that the criteria for scoring be understood by students. One way to do this is to write a few generic rubrics that are flexible enough to apply to the full range of student performance. Figure 13.3 gave an example of a generic rubric that has been applied to outcomes in high school mathematics. It has been suggested that using rubrics such as this in classroom instruction can enhance student achievement (Schafer, Swanson, Bené, & Newberry, 2001).

Planning for performance assessments takes time, and avoiding the pitfalls of subjectivity in rating performances takes practice (McTighe & O'Connor, 2005; Popham, 2005). However, a few well-thought-out, well-written items for a performance assessment could serve, for example, as a summative evaluation for all or most of your educational objectives for an entire unit. (See Figure 13.8.)

VIDEO HOMEWORK EXERCISE
Forms of Assessment

Go to **www.myeducationlab.com** and, in the Homework and Exercises section for Chapter 13 of this text, access the video entitled "Forms of Assessment." Watch the video and complete the homework questions that accompany it, saving your work or transmitting it to your professor as required.

FIGURE 13.8 Semester-Long Assessment

From Chuck Greiner, high school psychology teacher, James M. Bennett High School, Salisbury, MD.

Psychology Fair Rubric

✓ **Our Psychology Project . . .**

☐ (25 pts) Provides background information—it cites other studies, explains our interest in the topic, and presents a rationale for the topic. [The better the background information, the more detailed, and the more it "fits," the more points you earn.]

Brief example: "We are interested in how dress affects behavior. We always felt better when we were dressed up and also thought that less violence occurs between people who 'dress up.' Cohen and Cohen (1987) found that students who wore uniforms performed 10 percent better on exams and were cited for fewer office referrals. Thus we wanted to look into this topic further."

☐ (25 pts) Gives a description of the study (an abstract—a *general* statement in 100 words or fewer about your project).

Brief example: "This study investigates the relationship between academic performance and the use of uniforms in schools. Three schools in Derry County, Pennsylvania, were surveyed on issues of academic performance and office referrals. The use of uniforms showed an increase in achievement and decreased behavioral problems."

☐ (40 pts) Has a measurable hypothesis with specific variables defined and identified.

☐ (25 pts) Includes at least one graph, chart, or other visual aid which *summarizes the data.* Someone should be able to look at your graph/chart and clearly see what the variables and results were.

☐ (10 pts) Includes a clean copy of any survey or other scale that was used to gather data.

☐ (40 pts) Includes a written procedure that tells the observer *exactly* what we did.

Brief example: "We took 3 days to survey 100 students and 30 teachers."

☐ (30 pts) Includes a section that explains the data and tells whether the hypothesis was accurate.

Brief example: "Our data reflect that our hypothesis was correct: The 30 percent increase in scores reflects the improved achievement of students while . . ." [Again, develop your explanation. If you only say "We were right" or "Our hypothesis is correct/wrong" you will not receive more than half the points.]

☐ (30 pts) Includes a section explaining the significance of the study—why it is important.

Brief example: "This is an important study because it reflects a bias that many people may not be aware of, as well as a way in which students can improve scores and reduce their own behavioral problems. It further . . ."

☐ (50 pts) Is interactive. That is, observers can take the test, view the screen, do the quiz, and so on. [This can be done in a variety of ways. For instance, if the test is long have observers do part of it, or show a video of your procedure.]

Total Points Possible: 275

HOW ARE GRADES DETERMINED?

INTASC

5 Classroom Motivation and Management

One of the most perplexing and often controversial tasks a teacher faces is grading student work (Guskey & Bailey, 2001; Marzano, 2000; O'Connor, 2007; Trumbull & Farr, 2000). Is grading necessary? It is clear that some form of summative student evaluation is necessary, and grading of one kind or another is the predominant form used in most schools.

Establishing Grading Criteria

Many sets of grading criteria exist, but regardless of the level of school that teachers teach in, they generally agree on the need to explain the meaning of grades they give (Guskey & Bailey, 2001; Marzano, 2000). Grades should communicate at least the relative value of a student's work in a class. They should also help students to understand better what is expected of them and how they might improve.

Teachers and schools that use letter grades attach the following general meanings to the letters:

A = superior; exceptional; outstanding attainment
B = very good, but not superior; above average
C = competent, but not remarkable work or performance; average
D = minimum passing, but serious weaknesses are indicated; below average
F = failure to pass; serious weaknesses demonstrated

Assigning Letter Grades

All school districts have a policy or common practice for assigning report card grades. Most use A-B-C-D-F or A-B-C-D-E letter grades, but many (particularly at the elementary school level) use various versions of outstanding-satisfactory-unsatisfactory (Marzano, 2000). Some simply report percentage grades. The criteria on which grades are based vary enormously from district to district. Secondary schools usually give one grade for each subject taken, but most elementary schools and some secondary schools include ratings on effort or behavior as well as on performance.

The criteria for giving letter grades might be specified by a school administration, but grading criteria are most often set by individual teachers using very broad guidelines. In practice, few teachers could get away with giving half their students A's or with failing too many students; but between these two extremes, teachers may have considerable leeway (see Guskey & Bailey, 2001; Marzano, 2000).

Colonial Economics Rubric

Go to **www.myeducationlab.com** and, in the Homework and Exercises section for Chapter 13 of this text, access the Classroom Artifact entitled "Colonial Economics Rubric." Watch the video and complete the homework questions that accompany it, saving your work or transmitting it to your professor as required.

Absolute Grading Standards Grades may be given according to absolute or relative standards. Absolute grading standards might consist of preestablished percentage scores required for a given grade, as in the following example:

Grade	Percentage Correct
A	90–100 percent
B	80–89 percent
C	70–79 percent
D	60–69 percent
F	Less than 60 percent

In another form of absolute standards, called criterion-referenced grading, the teacher decides in advance what performances constitute outstanding (A), above-average (B), average (C), below-average (D), and inadequate (F) mastery of the instructional objective.

Absolute percentage standards have one important disadvantage: Student scores might depend on the difficulty of the tests they are given. For example, a student can pass a true–false test (if a passing grade is 60 percent) by knowing only 20 percent of the answers and guessing on the rest (getting 50 percent of the remaining 80 percent of the items by chance). On a difficult test on which guessing is impossible, however, 60 percent could be a very high score. For this reason, use of absolute percentage criteria should be tempered with criterion-referenced standards. That is, a teacher might use a 60-70-80-90 percent standard in most circumstances but establish (and announce to students) tougher standards for tests that students are likely to find easy and easier standards for more difficult tests.

Another disadvantage is that the ranges of the grades are typically different, especially for F. A student who receives an F may be very close to a D or may be hopelessly far from "passing." This is true for the other grades, too, but the large range of F (0 percent to 60 percent) emphasizes the uncertainty. Moreover, the consequences of an F are often quite severe.

Teaching Dilemmas: CASES TO CONSIDER

Establishing a Grading System

Rachel Greenberg is a beginning social studies teacher in a large urban high school. In preparation for a social studies department meeting, she talks with Antonio Watts in the teachers' lounge.

INTASC

5 Classroom Motivation and Management

Rachel: Antonio, do you have a minute to tell me about the school's grading policy?

Antonio: Sure. Where do you want to begin?

Rachel: Well, we do have a policy, I assume?

Antonio: I guess you could say so. If you look on the report cards, you'll notice that 94 to 100 is an A, 88 to 94 is a B, and so forth. Anything below 70 is failing.

Rachel: What if no one gets in the 94 to 100 range?

Antonio: Then either you don't give any A's, if you think the test was fair, or you adjust the scale by adding on points to every student's score. There's no rigid policy, but if you give too many A's and B's, that could become a problem.

Rachel: How many are too many?

Antonio: Well, certainly there should be more B's than A's and more C's than either A's or B's. You try to approximate the normal bell-shaped curve in a general, flexible way. It all depends on the students' ability level. In an advanced placement history course, I seldom give D's or F's. In the sophomore-level world history course, however, the number of D's and F's fairly closely approximates the number of A's and B's.

Rachel: What if a teacher puts a mastery learning plan into effect, and it works so well that everyone achieves at practically 100 percent? What happens to the bell-shaped curve then?

Antoni: Well, that happened a few years back. One young teacher did give almost all A's and B's. It came to light when the students began comparing grades at report card time. Some other teachers and parents were quite upset. The administration smoothed things over with the parents and other teachers. As for the young teacher, he's at another school now. I hear he's doing a fine job.

Rachel: Oh. Another question: In my history classes I plan to emphasize individual and small-group projects. I am interested in cooperative learning approaches with mixed-ability groups.

Antonio: Group projects are nice, but grading them can be very subjective and hard to defend. I'd go easy on that.

Rachel: So you'd recommend objective tests, not essay tests?

Antonio: Right. Good objective tests are hard to write, but they're worth it because students and parents have a hard time arguing grading bias, favoritism, or subjectivity when you give objective tests. Also, I figure that objective tests help prepare the kids to succeed on standardized achievement tests.

Rachel: I see what you mean, but I try to keep outcomes in mind—overall objectives such as verbal information, intellectual skills, cognitive strategies, and so on. But teaching for those outcomes may not always leave time for teaching to objective tests. What if some of my students get D's and F's? I'm a little afraid of some of the parents.

Antonio: I think communication is the key. If the students—and their parents—think you're fair, you'll have few problems. Spell out very clearly what you expect and what the grading procedures are. After all, our society was founded on competition. Our kids have to learn how to deal with failure as well as success. And parents should understand that too.

Rachel: Thanks, Antonio! I don't know if I altogether agree with you about the value of failure, but I really appreciate your support.

QUESTIONS FOR REFLECTION

1. Do you agree with the advice Rachel received? Why or why not? For the grade level you plan to teach, what departmentwide evaluation strategy would you propose for your subject area?
2. If you were on a committee to evaluate and revise this school's evaluation and grading policies and procedures, what would you recommend and why?
3. Extend the dialogue to express an evaluation approach that would work best for the way Rachel wants to teach.

Relative Grading Standards A **relative grading standard** exists whenever a teacher gives grades according to the students' rank in their class or grade. The classic form of relative grading is specifying what percentage of students will be given A's, B's, and so on. A form of this practice is called *grading on the curve* because students are given grades on the basis of their position on a predetermined distribution of scores.

Relative grading standards have the advantage of placing students' scores in relation to one another without regard to the difficulty of a particular test. However, relative grading standards also have serious drawbacks (see O'Connor, 2007). One is that because they hold the number of A's and B's constant, students in a class of high achievers must get much higher scores to earn an A or B than students in low-achieving classes—a situation that is likely to be widely seen as unfair. Teachers often deal with this problem by giving relatively more A's and B's in high-achieving classes than in others. Another disadvantage of relative grading is that it creates competition among students; when one student earns an A, this diminishes the chances that others may do so. Competition can inhibit students from helping one another and can hurt social relations among classmates (Krumboltz & Yeh, 1996).

Strict grading on the curve and guidelines for numbers of A's and B's have been disappearing in recent years. For one thing, there has been a general grade inflation; more A's and B's are given now than in the past, and C is no longer the expected average grade but often indicates below-average performance. Anderson (1994) summarized a national survey of eighth-graders who were asked to report their English grades since sixth grade. The results were as follows:

Mostly A's: 31 percent
Mostly B's: 38 percent
Mostly C's: 23 percent
Mostly D's: 6 percent
Mostly less than D's: 2 percent

Results were similar in mathematics, and grades were only slightly lower in high-poverty schools than in middle-class schools. It is likely that these self-reported grades are somewhat higher than what students actually received, but it is nevertheless likely that the average grade today is B, not C.

relative grading standard
Grades given according to a student's rank in his or her class or grade.

The most common approach to grading involves teachers looking at student scores on a test, taking into account test difficulty and the overall performance of the class, and assigning grades in such a way that about the "right number" of students earn A's and B's and the "right number" fail. Teachers vary considerably in their estimates of what these right numbers should be, but schools often have unspoken norms about how many students should be given A's and how many should fail.

Performance Grading

One of the most important limitations of traditional grades is that although they might give some indication of how students are doing in comparison to others, they provide no information about what students know and can do. A student who gets a B in English might be disappointed or breathe a sigh of relief, depending on what she expected. However, this grade does not tell her or her parents or teachers what she can do, what she needs to do to progress, or where her strengths or weaknesses are. Furthermore, giving a single grade in each subject can reinforce the idea that students are more able or less able, or perhaps more motivated or less motivated, rather than the idea that all students are growing.

One response to these limitations that is used in some schools is an alternative approach to grading called *performance grading.* In performance grading, teachers determine what children know and can do and then report this in a way that is easy for parents and students to understand (Guskey, 2006).

Figure 13.9 (from Wiggins, 1993) shows one page of a language arts assessment keyed to fifth-grade exit standards, or expectations of what a fifth-grader should know. A parent of a student who receives a form like this could see how the student is progressing toward the kind of performance the school district has defined as essential. Note that the form does provide information on how the student is doing in comparison to other students; the emphasis is on growth over time.

Scoring Rubrics for Performance Grading A key requirement for the use of performance grading is collection of work samples from students that indicate their level of performance on a developmental sequence. Collecting and evaluating work that students are already doing in class (such as compositions, lab reports, or projects) is called portfolio assessment (Herbert, 1998; Shaklee et al., 1997), discussed earlier in this chapter. An alternative is to give students tests in which they can show their abilities to apply and integrate knowledge, skills, and judgment. Most performance grading schemes use some combination of portfolios and on-demand performance tests. In either case the student performance may be evaluated against rubrics, which describe, for example, partially proficient, proficient, and advanced performance, or which indicate a student's position on a developmental sequence.

Other Alternative Grading Systems

Several other approaches to grading are used in conjunction with innovative instructional approaches. In *contract grading,* students negotiate a particular amount of work or level of performance that they will achieve to receive a certain grade. For example, a student might agree to complete five book reports of a given length in a marking period to receive an A. **Mastery grading** involves establishing a standard of mastery, such as 80 or 90 percent correct on a test. All students who achieve that standard receive an A; students who do not achieve it the first time receive corrective instruction and then retake the test to try to achieve the mastery criterion. Finally, many teachers give grades based on improvement or effort usually in combination with traditional grades. In this way a student who is performing at a low level relative to others can nevertheless receive feedback indicating that he or she is on a path leading to higher performance (see Tomlinson, 2001).

mastery grading
Grading requiring an established standard of mastery, such as 80 or 90 percent correct on a test. Students who do not achieve it the first time may receive corrective instruction and then retake the test to try to achieve mastery.

FIGURE 13.9 Sample Performance Grading Criteria

Cherry Creek School District
Polton Community Elementary School Fairplay Progress Report (Language Arts Section)

Student Name ______________________ **Grade 3** _____ **4** _____
Teacher ______________________ **School Year** ______

Performance-based graduation requirements focus on student mastery of the proficiencies. The curriculum and written progress report are geared toward preparing students for this task. A date (for example, 11/02) indicates where a student is performing on a continuum of progress based on the fifth-grade exit standards.

	Basic	Proficient	Advanced
Language Arts Proficiency 1			
Listens, interpreting verbal and nonverbal cues to construct meaning.	Actively listens, demonstrates understanding, and clarifies with questions and paraphrasing.	Actively listens for purpose, demonstrates understanding, and clarifies with questions and paraphrasing.	Actively listens for purpose, demonstrates understanding, clarifies with questions and paraphrasing, classifies, analyzes, and applies information.
Language Arts Proficiency 2			
Conveys meaning clearly and coherently through speech in both formal and informal situations.	Appropriately speaks to inform, explain, demonstrate, or persuade. Organizes a speech and uses vocabulary to convey a message.	Appropriately speaks to inform, explain, demonstrate, or persuade. Organizes a formal speech and uses vocabulary to convey a message.	Appropriately speaks to inform, explain, demonstrate, or persuade. Organizes a formal speech with details and transitions adapting subject and vocabulary. Uses eye contact, gestures, and suitable expression for an audience and topic.
Language Arts Proficiency 3			
Reads to construct meaning by interacting with the text, by recognizing the different requirements of a variety of printed materials, and by using appropriate strategies to increase comprehension.	Reads varied material, comprehends at a literal level. Recalls and builds knowledge through related information. Begins to use strategies to develop fluency, adjusting rate when reading different material.	Reads varied material, comprehends literally and interpretively. Synthesizes and explores information, drawing inferences. Critiques author's intent, analyzes material for meaning and value. Applies strategies to increase fluency, adjusting rate when reading different material.	Reads varied material, comprehends and draws inferences, recalls and builds knowledge through related information. Applies strategies to increase fluency, adjusting rate when reading different material.
Language Arts Proficiency 4			
Produces writing that conveys purpose and meaning, uses effective writing strategies, and incorporates the conventions of written language to communicate clearly.	Appropriately writes on assigned or self-selected topics. Clear main ideas, few details. Weak elements in the beginning, middle, end. Sentence structure lacks variety and contains errors.	Appropriately writes on assigned or self-selected topics. Clear main ideas, interesting details, clear organization, sequencing, varied sentence structure, edits to reduce errors. Appropriate voice and word choice.	Appropriately writes on assigned or self-selected topics. Connects opinions, details, and examples. Effective organization and sequencing, meaningful sentence structure, edits to eliminate most errors. Appropriate voice and word choice.

As compared to the class in the area of Language Arts, your child

Note: The teacher places a check in one box per marking period to indicate child's status in language arts.

1	2	3	Marking Periods
			Displays strong performance
			Demonstrates appropriate development
			Needs practice and support

From Grant Wiggins, "Toward Better Report Cards," *Educational Leadership, 52*(2), 1994, pp. 28–37.

Letting Students Retake Tests Many teachers allow students to retake tests, especially if they failed the first time. This can be a good idea if it gives students an opportunity to do additional studying and master the material the class is studying. For example, a student might be given two days to study the content that was tested and then take an alternative form of the test. (Giving the same test to the student is not recommended because that would allow the student to study only the questions that were asked.) The student might then be given a grade that is one letter grade lower than he or she scored on the second test because the student had an advantage in having an extra opportunity to study. There is some danger that if students know that they can retake tests, they might not study until after attempting the first test; but in general, allowing students a second chance is a good way to allow those who are willing to put in extra effort to improve a poor grade. Some schools give grades of A, B, C, or incomplete, and then provide additional time and support until all students are able to earn at least a C (Kenkel, Hoelscher, & West, 2006).

Assigning Report Card Grades

Most schools give report cards four or six times per year, that is, every 6 or 9 weeks. Report card grades are most often derived from some combination of the following factors (Guskey & Bailey, 2001; Marzano, 2000; O'Connor, 2007):

- Scores on quizzes and tests
- Scores on papers and projects
- Scores on homework
- Scores on seatwork
- Class participation (academic behaviors in class, answers to class questions, and so on)
- Deportment (classroom behavior, tardiness, attitude)
- Effort

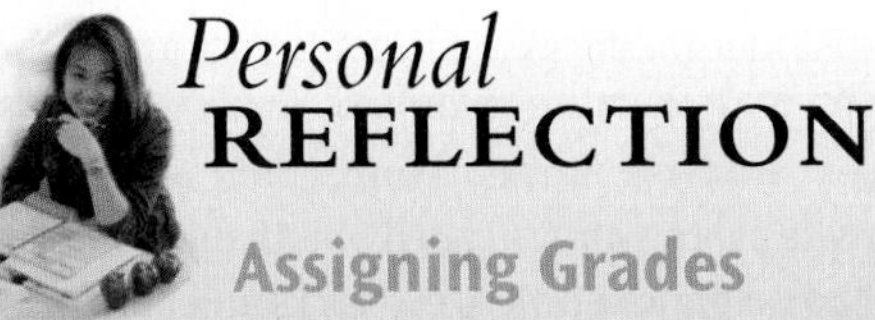

Personal **REFLECTION**

Assigning Grades

INTASC 9 **Professional Commitment and Responsibility**

I think grading is one of the most difficult tasks for any teacher but especially for a beginning teacher. I remember my first grading experience as a student teacher of high school social studies.

My greatest dilemma involved a girl I'll call Jane. She seemed very nice and very bright. Yet she frequently failed to do assignments, skipped class from time to time, and generally did very little. I agonized over Jane. Was there something I was doing wrong? Was there anything I could do? I called her in a few times to tell her that she was headed for trouble, and she always promised to do better, but her resolution never lasted very long.

I spoke with my mentor teacher, who told me I had to give Jane a failing grade. I did so, but not before several sleepless nights. It's terrible to admit, but among all the wonderful students I had that year, Jane's is the only name I still remember.

Of course, with the passage of time and experience, I realized that I didn't fail Jane, she failed herself. I'll never know why, but I'll never forget this hard introduction to one painful reality of teaching.

REFLECT ON THIS. Why do you think a teacher might feel he or she "failed" when a student fails a class? What can you do to make sure you can always justify the grades you give students?

These are listed in order from most formal and reliable measures of achievement to least valid as a learning indicator. The first two are summative assessments and virtually everyone would consider them appropriate for grading. The next two are typically formative and thus indicate how learning is progressing when it is still incomplete. They are less appropriate because they do not convey information about status at the end of instructional units. The final three might contribute to achievement, but they are not achievement. Basing grades on them could miscommunicate information to others about students (see O'Connor, 2007). Teachers often give different weights to various factors, stating (for example) that grades will be based 30 percent on quizzes, 30 percent on a final test, 20 percent on homework, and 20 percent on class participation. This helps communicate to students what is most important to the teacher.

One important issue arises when scores are to be combined for grading—how to treat missing work, such as homework assignments. Some teachers assign a "zero" to missing work. But a zero can be devastating (it is so far from even a passing grade that it is virtually impossible for the student to recover). This practice can only be viewed as punitive.

The Intentional TEACHER

USING WHAT YOU KNOW about Assessing Student Learning to Improve Teaching and Learning

Intentional teachers assess student learning in ways that align with both their goals and their instruction. They use assessment results to adjust their instruction and to provide important feedback to students, families, and communities. Intentional teachers know that no one measure is ideal for every circumstance, and they implement a range of assessments that fits their purposes and circumstances.

1 What do I expect my students to know and be able to do at the end of this lesson? How does this contribute to course objectives and to students' needs to become capable individuals?

One cardinal rule of assessing learning is that tests should be tied directly to learning goals and to instruction. Specify in advance what students are to learn. Design instruction to help students learn those things, and then assess their learning in relation to the specified goals.

The variety and range of objectives to which teachers should teach is large. Write objectives in different domains (for example, cognitive and affective) and at different levels of specificity (for example, long-term goals and lesson objectives, and goals for different levels of understanding according to Bloom's taxonomy). For example, you might begin your year-long planning by examining your state's and district's expected outcomes for the grade and subject you teach. Then you might spread out the teacher's editions of your five texts, flipping each open to the scope and sequence chart that specifies content and learning objectives. This process allows you to examine and evaluate the variety and levels of understanding set by your curricular materials.

2 What knowledge, skills, needs, and interests do my students have that must be taken into account in my lesson?

Formative assessments allow teachers to discover their students' experiences, preferences, and needs. Use frequent formative assessments to gather information about students' attitudes and prior knowledge. For example, to begin a unit on geology, you might conduct interviews with small groups. You could display a variety of rocks and minerals and listen as students converse about the rocks. Your notes document students' enthusiasm about the topic and their extensive out-of-class experiences studying rocks. You could use this information to create a more sophisticated unit than you might have if students had no prior knowledge of rocks and minerals.

3 What do I know about the content, child development, learning, motivation, and effective teaching strategies that I can use to accomplish my objectives?

Students' levels of preparation might affect their performance on tests and other measures. Check to see that your measures truly assess the objective you intended to assess. For example, imagine that a cluster of students who typically are highly successful in solving the challenging word problems you present in mathematics each week scores surprisingly low on the problem-solving items of a school-based achievement test. When you review the items, you wonder whether students' reading ability—and not their problem-solving abilities—accounted for their low scores. To test your hunch, you read similar problems aloud to the students. They solve the problems accurately. This leads you to seek tutorial or other assistance for these students.

A better strategy would be to use a system whereby grades are converted to a reasonable set of numerical grades (e.g., A = 4, B = 3, etc.) and give an F for the missing work. To illustrate the difference in these two strategies, consider a student who misses one assignment out of five. If she is given a zero for the missing work, and her scores for the assignments are 92, 86, 0, 73, and 91; her average score would be 68.4, or a D in a 60-70-80-90 grading scheme. Converting the scores using the letter grades, on the other hand, would give her a mean of 2.6, which would be a solid C.

Sometimes a student's performance on a test or a quiz seems unusually poor for him or her. Such atypical assessments might be because of nonacademic reasons such as a disruption at home or in school. A private conversation with the student about the test or quiz might uncover a problem that should be looked into and the student might be given an opportunity to retake the test. Some teachers drop the lowest score a student receives on quizzes to avoid penalizing the student for one unusual slippage.

One important principle in report card grading is that grades should never be a surprise. Students should always know how their grades will be computed, whether

INTASC

7 Instructional Planning Skills
8 Assessment of Student Learning
9 Professional Commitment and Responsibility

4 What instructional materials, technology, assistance, and other resources are available to help accomplish my objectives?

Assessments should be challenging for all but impossible for none. Use assessments that are fair measures of the objectives and not of general aptitude. Check that your assessments are applied consistently to all students. For example, you might write weekly quizzes with a general format in mind: Put recall-level items first, reasoning that they provide immediate success for all or most students in demonstrating knowledge. Subsequent items test higher levels of understanding and stretch even the best-prepared students to apply content to new situations.

5 How will I plan to assess students' progress toward my objectives?

Assessment equals feedback. Use information from assessments to adjust your instruction and future assessments. Imagine that in reviewing your students' writing portfolios, you discern some trends that offer strong guidance for your instruction. For instance, students' reflections indicate that they seem to find particular meaning in writing autobiographical pieces, and less relevance in other forms of writing. You might build on their interests in autobiography by including prewriting experiences that tap into students' life experiences, no matter what the genre.

Evaluations need to be important to students if they are to serve as incentives for effort. Assure that your students perceive the objectives as important and the assessments as fair, consistent, and driven by clear criteria. For example, if you were assigning a shelf-building project in a woodworking class, you might display a set of samples of varying quality. You could ask the students to brainstorm the qualities of a well-made shelf, and discuss the real-life consequences of poorly constructed shelves, with students laughing at the imagined disasters that accompany shoddy work. You might develop a scoring rubric based on the criteria they have generated and distribute it as students begin their work.

6 How will I respond if individual children or the class as a whole are not on track toward success? What is my back-up plan?

Successful assessments are valid and reliable for the setting. Check the validity and reliability of your measures with the help of students and peers. For example, after writing a summative exam for a given unit, hand the exam to a peer and ask him or her to assess whether the questions appropriately emphasize particular sections of content. When students complete the exam, ask them to turn over their test papers and evaluate the exam for fairness. You might invite them to write the things they know from the unit that were *not* assessed in your test.

ONLINE READING & WRITING EXERCISE
Polski3's Grading Problems

Access this exercise, entitled "Polski3's Grading Problems," in the Homework and Exercises section for Chapter 13 of this text at **www.mylabschool.com.**

classwork and homework are included, and whether class participation and effort are taken into account. Being clear about standards for grading helps a teacher avert many complaints about unexpectedly low grades and, more important, lets students know exactly what they must do to improve their grades (Guskey, 2001).

Many schools give an "interim" grade at the middle of a marking period. These give students an early idea of how they are doing, and a warning if they seem headed for trouble. A variation on this practice is to provide an interim grade only if students are headed for a D or F. Further, adding comments to the grade to explain what the student needs to do to earn a higher grade can be very helpful in maintaining motivation and improving performance (Black et al., 2004).

Another important principle is that grades should be private. There is no need for students to know one another's grades; making grades public only invites invidious comparisons among students. Finally, it is important to restate that grades are only one method of student evaluation. Written evaluations that add information can provide useful information to parents and students (Marzano, 2000). Computerized gradebooks are now widely available and widely used. Guskey (2002), however, warns that teachers should be careful when using this time-saving software and avoid letting the program make decisions that the teacher should make.

CHAPTER 13 SUMMARY

What Are Instructional Objectives and How Are They Used?

Research supports the use of instructional, or behavioral, objectives, which are clear statements about what students should know and be able to do at the end of a lesson, unit, or course. These statements also specify the conditions of performance and the criteria for assessment. In lesson planning, task analysis contributes to the formulation of objectives, and backward planning facilitates the development of specific objectives from general objectives in a course of study. Objectives are closely linked with assessment. Bloom's taxonomy of educational objectives classifies educational objectives from simple to complex, including knowledge, comprehension, application, analysis, synthesis, and evaluation. A behavior content matrix helps to ensure that objectives cover many levels. Formal measures of student performance or learning are important as feedback for students and teachers, as information for parents, as information for selection and certification, as information for assessing school accountability, and as incentives for increasing student effort.

How Is Student Learning Evaluated?

Strategies for evaluation include formative evaluation; summative evaluation; norm-referenced evaluation, in which a student's scores are compared with other students' scores; and criterion-referenced evaluation, in which students' scores are compared to a standard of mastery. Students are evaluated through tests or performances. The appropriate method of evaluation is based on the goal of evaluation. For example, if the goal of testing is to find out whether students have mastered a key concept in a lesson, a criterion-referenced formative quiz or a performance would be the most appropriate.

How Are Tests Constructed?

Tests are constructed to elicit evidence of student learning in relation to the instructional objectives. Achievement tests should be constructed in keeping with six principles: They should (1) measure clearly defined learning objectives, (2) measure a representative sample of the learning tasks included in instruction, (3) include the types of test items most appropriate for measuring the desired learning outcomes, (4) fit the uses that will be made of the results, (5) be as reliable as possible and be interpreted with caution, and (6) improve learning. A table of specifications helps in the planning of tests that correspond to instructional objectives. Types of test items include multiple-choice, true–false, completion, matching, short essay, and problem-solving items. Each type of test item has optimal uses, advantages, and disadvantages. For example, if you want to learn how students think about, analyze, synthesize, or evaluate some aspect of course content, a short essay test might be most appropriate, provided that you have time to administer it and evaluate students' responses.

What Are Authentic, Portfolio, and Performance Assessments?

Portfolio assessment and performance assessment avoid the negative aspects of pencil-and-paper multiple-choice tests by requiring students to demonstrate their learning through work samples or direct real-world applications. Performance assessments are usually scored according to rubrics that specify in advance the type of performance expected.

How Are Grades Determined?

Grading systems differ in elementary and secondary education. For example, informal assessments might be more appropriate at the elementary level, whereas letter grades become increasingly important at the secondary level. Grading standards might be absolute or relative (grading on the curve). Performance grading is a way for teachers to determine what children know and can do. A key requirement for performance grading is judicious collection of work samples from students that indicate level of performance. Another approach is to give students tests in which they can show their abilities. Other systems include contract grading and mastery grading. Report card grades typically average scores on tests, homework, seatwork, class participation, deportment, and effort.

KEY TERMS

Review the following key terms from the chapter.

affective objectives 415
assessment 412
backward planning 410
behavior content matrix 414
clang 427
completion items 429
criterion-referenced interpretations 419
distractors 425
evaluation 416
evaluative descriptors 435
formative evaluations 418
halo effect 434
instructional objective 406
learning objectives 413
long essay item 429
mastery grading 445
matching items 428
multiple-choice items 425
norm-referenced interpretations 419
performance assessments 438
portfolio assessment 436
problem-solving assessment 432
relative grading standard 444
selected-response items 425

short essay item 429
stem 425
summative evaluations 418
table of specifications 424
task analysis 409
taxonomy of educational objectives 413
teaching objectives 412
true–false items 428

SELF-ASSESSMENT: PRACTICING *for* LICENSURE

Directions: The chapter-opening vignette addresses indicators that are often assessed in state licensure exams. Re-read the chapter-opening vignette, and then respond to the following questions.

1. Mr. Sullivan is having a difficult time connecting what he is teaching and what he is testing. Which of the following evaluation tools will most likely help Mr. Sullivan make the connection?
   a. multiple-choice test
   b. instructional objectives
   c. traditional teaching strategies
   d. open-book testing

2. Mr. Sullivan might use a chart showing how a concept or skill will be taught at different cognitive levels in relation to an instructional objective. What is this chart called?
   a. task analysis
   b. backward planning
   c. behavior content matrix
   d. table of specifications

3. Mr. Sullivan might improve the connection between what he teaches and what he tests by following which of the following pieces of advice?
   a. Include all instructional content in the test.
   b. Make a test that includes all item types: true–false, multiple choice, matching, short answer, essay, and problem solving.
   c. Be free from the confines of instructional objectives.
   d. Design a test that fits the particular uses that will be made of the results.

4. Which of the following types of evaluation is Mr. Sullivan using?
   a. summative
   b. aptitude
   c. affective
   d. task analysis

5. Why would Mr. Sullivan construct a table of specifications?
   a. to indicate the type of learning to be assessed for different instructional objectives
   b. to measure a student's performance against a specified standard
   c. to make comparisons among students
   d. to identify conditions of mastery

6. Write a brief essay explaining why evaluation is important.

7. Write instructional objectives, create a table of specifications using Bloom's taxonomy, develop a lesson plan, and write a short test for a topic of study.

Where the Classroom Comes to Life

Now go to **www.myeducationlab.com** to:

- take a Pretest to assess your initial comprehension of chapter content;
- study chapter content with your individualized Study Plan;
- take a Posttest to assess your understanding of chapter content;
- practice your teaching skills with Building Teaching Skills exercises; and
- build a deeper, more applied understanding of chapter content with Homework and Exercises.

CHAPTER 14

Standardized Tests and Accountability

chapter OUTLINE

Jennifer Tranh is a fifth-grade teacher at Lincoln Elementary School. Recently she met with the parents of one of her students, Anita McKay.

"Hello, Mr. and Mrs. McKay," said Ms. Tranh when Anita's parents arrived. "I'm so glad you could come. Please take a seat, and we'll start right in. First, I wanted to tell you what a delight it is to have Anita in my class. She is always so cheerful, so willing to help others. Her work is coming along very well in most subjects, although there are a few areas I'm a bit concerned about. Before I start, though, do you have any questions for me?"

Mr. and Mrs. McKay explained to Ms. Tranh that they thought Anita was having a good year and that they were eager to hear how she was doing.

"All right. First of all, I know you've seen the results of Anita's California Achievement Tests. We call those 'CATs' for short. Most parents don't understand these test scores, so I'll try to explain them to you. First, let's look at math. As you know, Anita has always been a good math student, and her scores and grades reflect this. She got an A on her last report card and a percentile score of 90 on math computations. That means that she scored better than 90 percent of all fifth-graders in the country. She did almost as well on math concepts and applications—her score is in the 85th percentile."

"What does this 'grade equivalent' mean?" asked Mrs. McKay.

"That's a score that's supposed to tell how a child is achieving in relation to his or her grade level. For example, Anita's grade equivalent of 6.9 means that she is scoring more than a year ahead of the fifth-grade level."

"Does this mean she could skip sixth-grade math?" asked Mr. McKay.

Ms. Tranh smiled. "I'm afraid not. It's hard to explain, but a grade equivalent score of 6.9 is supposed to be what a student at the end of sixth grade would score on a fifth-grade test. It doesn't mean that Anita already knows sixth-grade material. Besides, we take any student's testing information with a grain of salt. We rely much more on day-to-day performance and classroom tests to tell how each student is doing. In this case the standardized CAT scores are pretty consistent with what we see Anita doing in class. But let me show you another example that shows less consistency. I'm sure you noticed that even though Anita's reading grades have been pretty good, her scores in reading comprehension were much lower than her scores in most other areas. She got a percentile score of only 30. This is almost a year below grade level. I think Anita is a pretty good reader, so I was surprised. I gave her another test, the Gray Oral Reading Test. This test is given one-on-one, so it gives you a much better indication of how well students are reading. On the Gray, Anita scored at grade level. This score is more indicative of where I see her reading in class, so I'm not concerned about her in this area.

"On the other hand, there is a concern I have about Anita that is not reflected in her standardized tests. She scored near the 70th percentile in both language mechanics and language expression. This might make you think Anita's doing great in language arts, and she is doing well in many ways. However, I'm concerned about Anita's writing. I keep a portfolio of student writing over the course of the year. This is Anita's here. She's showing some development in writing, but I think she could do a lot better. As you can see, her spelling, punctuation, and grammar are excellent, but her stories are very short and factual. As you know, we don't give grades in writing. We use a rating form that shows the student's development toward proficient writing. Based on her portfolio I rated her at proficient, but to go to advanced, I'd like to see her write more and really let her imagination loose. She tells great stories orally, but I think she's so concerned about making a mistake in mechanics that she writes very conservatively. On vacation you might encourage her to write a journal or to do other writing wherever it makes sense."

"But if her standardized test scores are good in language," said Mrs. McKay, "doesn't that mean that she's doing well?"

"Test scores tell us some things, but not everything," said Ms. Tranh. "The CAT is good on simple things such as math computations and language mechanics, but it is not so good at telling us what children can actually do. That's why I keep portfolios of student work in writing, in math problem solving, and in science. I want to see how children are really developing in their ability to apply their skills to doing real things and solving real problems. In fact, now that we've gone over Anita's grades and standardized tests, let's look at her portfolios, and I think you'll get a much better idea of what she's doing here in school."

USING *your* EXPERIENCE

COOPERATIVE LEARNING AND CREATIVE THINKING Act out this parent–teacher conference about test scores. Have volunteers for the roles of Mrs. McKay, Mr. McKay, and Ms. Tranh. One volunteer can act as moderator to clarify any miscommunications and to keep the conference moving.

CRITICAL THINKING What do you know from reading this case? What do you still want to know? And what did you learn here? Has Ms. Tranh told us everything we need to know about Anita's standardized test scores and portfolio assessments in writing, math, and science?

Jennifer Tranh's conversation with the McKays illustrates some of the uses and limitations of grades and standardized tests. The CATs and the Gray Oral Reading Test give Ms. Tranh information that does relate Anita's performance in some areas to national norms, and Anita's grades give Ms. Tranh some idea of how Anita is doing relative to her classmates; but neither standardized tests nor grades provide the detail or comprehensiveness reflected in portfolios of Anita's work and other observations of Anita's performance. Taken together, the cautiously interpreted standardized tests, the grades, the portfolios of Anita's work, and other classroom assessments provide a good picture of Anita's performance. Each has value and all the information should be evaluated in making educational decisions.

WHAT ARE STANDARDIZED TESTS AND HOW ARE THEY USED?

INTASC

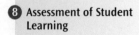

8 Assessment of Student Learning

Do you remember taking SATs, ACTs, or other college entrance examinations? Did you ever wonder how those tests were constructed, what the scores meant, and the degree to which your scores represented what you really knew or could really do? The SATs and other college entrance examinations are examples of **standardized tests.** Unlike the teacher-made tests discussed in Chapter 13, a standardized test is typically given under the same "standardized" conditions to thousands of students who are similar to those for whom the test is designed. This allows the test publisher to establish norms to which any individual score can be compared. For example, if a representative national sample of fourth-graders had an average score of 37 items correct on a 50-item standardized test, then we might say that fourth-graders who score above 37 are "above the national norm" on this test and those who score below 37 are "below the national norm."

VIDEO HOMEWORK EXERCISE
Standardized Tests

Go to **www.myeducationlab.com** and, in the Homework and Exercises section for Chapter 14 of this text, access the video entitled "Standardized Tests." Watch the video and complete the homework questions that accompany it, saving your work or transmitting it to your professor as required.

Traditional standardized tests have been subjected to a great deal of criticism and controversy, and today a wide variety of assessments are used. However, standardized tests of many kinds continue to be used for a wide range of purposes at all levels of education. This chapter discusses how and why standardized tests are used and how scores on these tests can be interpreted and applied to important educational decisions. It discusses the use of standardized tests in holding districts, schools, and teachers accountable for student performance, and No Child Left Behind, a major federal initiative focused primarily on accountability. It also includes information on criticisms of standardized testing and on alternatives that are being developed, debated, and applied.

Standardized tests are usually used to offer a yardstick against which to compare individuals or groups of students that teacher-made tests cannot provide. For example, suppose a child's parents ask a teacher how their daughter is doing in math. The teacher says, "Fine, she got a score of 81 percent on our latest math test." For some purposes this information would be adequate. But for others the parents might want to know much more. How does 81 percent compare to the scores of other students in this class? How about other students in the school, the district, the state, or the whole country? In some contexts the score of 81 percent might help to qualify the girl for a special program for the mathematically gifted; in others it might suggest the need for remedial instruction. Also, suppose the teacher found that the class averaged 85 percent correct on the math test. How is this class doing compared to other math classes or to students nationwide? A teacher-made test cannot yield this information.

Standardized tests are typically carefully constructed to provide accurate information about students' levels of performance. Most often, curriculum experts establish what students at a particular age should know and be able to do in a particular subject. Then questions are written to assess the various skills or information students are expected to possess. The questions are tried out on various groups of students. Items that almost all students get right or almost all miss are usually dropped, as are items that students find unclear or confusing. Patterns of scores are carefully examined. If students who score well on most items do no better than lower-scoring students on a particular item, then that item will probably be dropped.

Eventually, a final test will be developed and given to a large selected group of students from all over the country. Attempts are usually made to ensure that this group resembles the larger population of students who will ultimately use the test. For example, a test of geometry for eleventh-graders might be given to a sampling of eleventh-graders in urban, rural, and suburban locations; in different regions of the country; in private as well as public schools; and to students with different levels of preparation in mathematics. Care will be taken to include students of all ethnic backgrounds. This step establishes the **norms** for the test, which provide an indication of how an average student will score (Popham, 2008). Finally, a testing manual is prepared, explaining how the test is to be given, scored, and interpreted. The test is now ready for general use. The test development process creates tests whose scores have meaning outside of the confines of a particular classroom or school. These scores are used in a variety of ways. Explanations of some of the most important functions of standardized testing follow.

standardized tests
Tests that are usually commercially prepared for nationwide use and designed to provide accurate and meaningful information on students' performance relative to that of others at their age or grade levels.

norms
Standards that are derived from the test scores of a sample of people who are similar to those who will take the test and that can be used to interpret scores of future test takers.

Selection and Placement

Standardized tests are often used to select students for entry or placement in specific programs. For example, the SAT (Scholastic Assessment Test) or ACT (American College Testing Program) that you probably took in high school might have been used to help your college admissions board decide whether to accept you as a student.

CONNECTIONS

For discussions of between- and within-class ability grouping, see Chapter 9, pages 267 and 270.

Similarly, admission to special programs for gifted and talented students might depend on standardized test scores. Standardized tests might also be used, along with other information, to help educators decide whether to place students in special-education programs or to assign students to ability groups. For example, high schools may use standardized tests in deciding which students to place or counsel into college preparatory, general, or vocational programs. Elementary schools may use them to place students in reading groups. Some colleges use them to decide whether entering students have met prerequisites for certain courses. Standardized tests are sometimes used to determine eligibility for grade-to-grade promotion, graduation from high school, or entry into an occupation. For example, most states use standardized tests as part of the teacher certification process.

Diagnosis

Standardized tests are often used to diagnose individual students' learning problems or strengths. For example, a student who is performing poorly in school might be given a battery of tests to determine whether he or she has a learning disability or mental retardation. At the same time the testing might identify specific deficits that need remediation. Teachers frequently employ diagnostic tests of reading skills, such as the Gray Oral Reading Test that Ms. Tranh used, to identify a student's particular reading problem. For example, a diagnostic test might indicate that a student's decoding skills are fine but that his or her reading comprehension is poor; or that a student has good computation skills but lacks problem-solving skills. More fine-grained diagnostic tests might tell a teacher that a physics student is doing well in states of matter but not scientific measurement, or that a foreign language student is doing well in grammar but not so well in expression. Sophisticated assessments can help teachers determine students' cognitive styles and the depth of their understanding of complex concepts.

Evaluation and Accountability

Perhaps the most common use of standardized testing is to evaluate students' progress and teachers' and schools' effectiveness. For example, districts and states use tests to hold educators accountable for the achievement of their students by evaluating the gains that schools make in overall student performance. Parents often want to know how their children are doing in comparison with what is typical of children at their grade level. For individual students, standardized test scores are meaningful as evaluation only if teachers use them along with other information, such as students' actual performance in school and in other contexts, as Ms. Tranh did. Many students who score poorly on standardized tests excel in school, college, or occupations; either they have trouble taking tests or they have important skills that are not measured by such tests. However, some students demonstrate their achievement best on standardized tests. For an extended discussion of accountability and related educational policies, see "How Are Educators Held Accountable for Student Achievement?" later in the chapter.

School Improvement

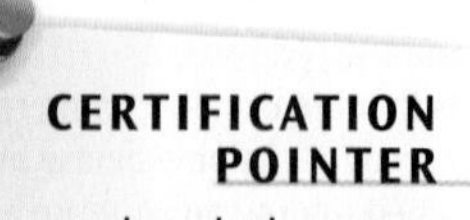

CERTIFICATION POINTER

You may be asked on your teacher certification test to define standardized tests and discuss their purposes.

Standardized tests can contribute to improving the schooling process. The results of some standardized tests provide information about appropriate student placement and diagnostic information that is important in remediation. In addition, achievement tests can guide curriculum development and revision when areas of weakness appear (see Hopkins, 1998; Schmoker, 1999). Standardized tests can play a role in guidance and counseling as well. This is true not only for achievement and aptitude testing but also for more specialized types of measures, such as vocational interest inventories and other psychological scales that are used in the counseling of students.

Schools often turn to academic achievement tests to evaluate the relative success of competing educational programs or strategies. For example, if a teacher or school tries out an innovative teaching strategy, tests can help reveal whether it was more successful than previous methods. Statewide and districtwide test results often serve as a yardstick

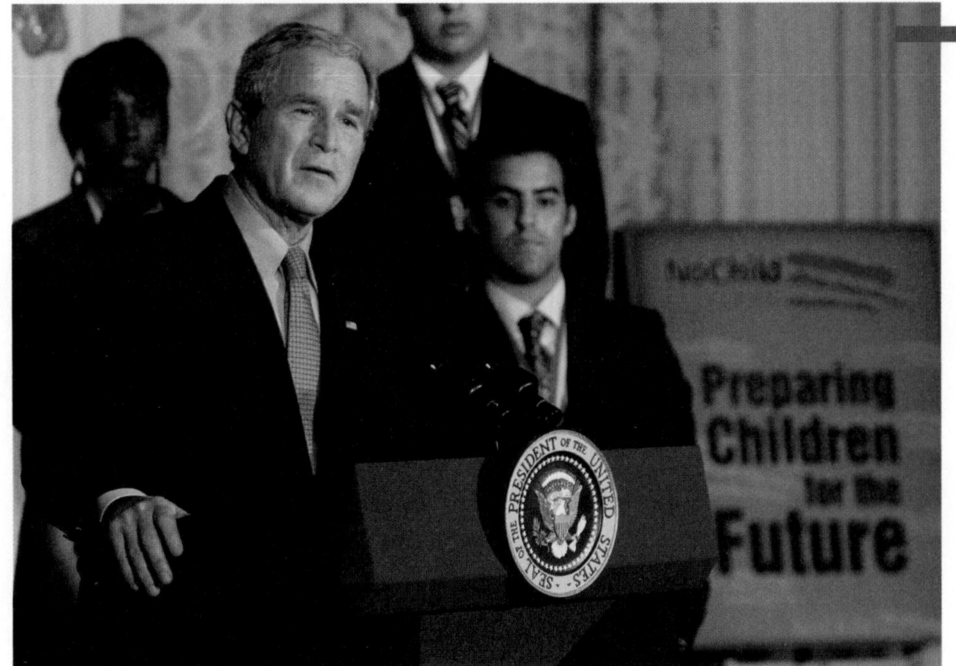

The primary goal of President Bush's No Child Left Behind program has been to level the playing field for students throughout the country, no matter where they attend school. How can high-stakes testing help "level the playing field"?

by which citizens can judge the success of their local schools. Tests are sometimes used to indicate the relative teaching strengths and weaknesses of the school's faculty. However, educating students is a complex process, and standardized tests provide only a small portion of the information that is necessary for evaluating teachers, programs, or schools.

VIDEO HOMEWORK EXERCISE

Assessment Examples Illustrated

Go to **www.myeducationlab.com** and, in the Homework and Exercises section for Chapter 14 of this text, access the video entitled "Assessment Examples Illustrated." Watch the video and complete the homework questions that accompany it, saving your work or transmitting it to your professor as required.

WHAT TYPES OF STANDARDIZED TESTS ARE GIVEN?

Three kinds of standardized tests are commonly used in school settings: aptitude tests, norm-referenced achievement tests, and criterion-referenced achievement tests (Aiken, 2003; Popham, 2008). An **aptitude test** is designed to assess students' abilities. It is meant to predict the ability of students to learn or to perform particular types of tasks rather than to measure how much the students have already learned. The most widely used aptitude tests measure general intellectual aptitude; but many other, more specific tests measure particular aptitudes, such as mechanical or perceptual abilities or reading readiness. The SAT, for example, is meant to predict a student's aptitude for college studies. An aptitude test is successful to the degree that it predicts performance. For example, a reading readiness test given to kindergartners that did not accurately predict how well the students would read when they reached first or second grade would be of little use.

Achievement tests are used to (1) predict students' future performance in a course of study, (2) diagnose students' difficulties, (3) serve as formative tests of students' progress, and (4) serve as summative tests of learning.

Norm-referenced achievement tests are assessments of a student's knowledge of a particular content area, such as mathematics, reading, or Spanish. What makes these tests norm-referenced is that their results can be compared with those of a representative group of students. They are purposely constructed to reveal differences among students. Those differences are expected to be the result of quality of instruction and student learning rather than differences from school to school in curricula. Norm-referenced achievement tests thus assess some but not all of the skills that are taught in any one school. A norm-referenced achievement test cannot range too broadly because it is designed for nationwide use and the curricula for any given subject vary from district to district. For example, if some seventh-graders learn about base-2 arithmetic or Venn

CERTIFICATION POINTER

You may be asked on your teacher certification test to define standardized tests and discuss their purposes.

aptitude test
A test designed to measure general abilities and to predict future performance.

achievement tests
Standardized tests measuring how much students have learned in a given context.

diagrams but others do not, then these topics will be unlikely to appear on a national mathematics test.

A criterion-referenced achievement test also assesses a student's knowledge of subject matter, but rather than comparing the achievement of an individual student against national norms, it is designed to measure the degree to which the student has mastered certain well-specified skills. The information that a criterion-referenced test produces is quite specific: "Thirty-seven percent of Ontario fifth-graders can fill in the names of the major Western European nations on an outline map" or "Ninety-three percent of twelfth-graders at Alexander Hamilton High School know that increasing the temperature of a gas in a closed container increases the gas's pressure." Sometimes criterion-referenced test scores are used in comparisons between schools or between districts, but typically no representative norming group is used. If a group of curriculum experts decides that every fifth-grader in Illinois should be able to fill in an outline map of South America, then the expectation for that item is 100 percent; it is of less interest whether Illinois fifth-graders score better or worse on this item than students in other states. What is more important is that, overall, students improve each year on this item.

intelligence
General aptitude for learning, often measured by ability to deal with abstractions and to solve problems.

mental age
The average test score received by individuals of a given chronological age.

chronological age
The age of an individual in years.

Aptitude Tests

Although aptitude tests, norm-referenced achievement tests, and criterion-referenced tests are distinct from one another in theory, there is in fact considerable overlap among them. For example, aptitudes are usually measured by evaluating achievement over a very broadly defined domain. School learning can thus affect students' aptitude test scores, and a student who scores well on one type of test will usually score well on another (Popham, 2008).

The following subsections discuss the types of aptitude tests most often given in schools.

CONNECTIONS
To learn more about student differences in general intelligence, specific aptitudes, and abilities and learning styles, see Chapter 4, page 116.

General Intelligence Tests The most common kind of aptitude tests given in school are tests of **intelligence,** or general aptitude for school learning. The intelligence quotient, or IQ, is the score that is most often associated with intelligence testing, but other types of scores are also used.

Intelligence tests are designed to provide a general indication of individuals' aptitudes in many areas of intellectual functioning. Intelligence itself is seen as the ability to deal with abstractions, to learn, and to solve problems (Sternberg, 2000), and tests of intelligence focus on these skills. Intelligence tests give students a wide variety of questions to answer and problems to solve.

"According to your vocational aptitude test, you're best suited to a job filling in bubbles with a #2 pencil."

The Measurement of IQ The measurement of the intelligence quotient (IQ) was introduced in the early 1900s by Alfred Binet, a French psychologist, to identify children with such serious learning difficulties that they were unlikely to profit from regular classroom instruction. The scale that Binet developed to measure intelligence assessed a wide range of mental characteristics and skills, such as memory, knowledge, vocabulary, and problem solving. Binet tested a large number of students of various ages to establish norms (expectations) for overall performance on his tests. He then expressed IQ as a ratio of **mental age** (the average test scores received by students of a particular age) to **chronological age,** multiplied by 100. For example, 6-year-olds (chronological age [CA] = 6) who scored at the average for all 6-year-olds (mental age [MA] = 6) would have an IQ of 100 ($6/6 \times 100 = 100$). Six-year-olds who scored at a level typical of 7-year-olds (MA = 7) would have IQs of about 117 ($7/6 \times 100 = 117$).

Over the years the mental age/chronological age comparison has been dropped, and IQ is now defined as having a mean of 100 and a standard deviation of 15 (a *standard deviation* is a measure of how spread out scores are, defined later in this chapter) at any age. Most scores fall near the mean, with small numbers of scores extending well above and below the mean. In theory, about 68 percent of all individuals will have IQs within one standard deviation of the mean; that is, from 85 (one standard deviation below the mean) to 115 (one standard deviation above), and 95 percent will be found in the range up to two standard deviations from the mean (between 70 and 130).

Intelligence tests are designed to provide a general indication of an individual's aptitudes in many areas of intellectual functioning. The most widely used tests contain many different scales. Figure 14.1 shows items like those used on the Wechsler Adult Intelligence Scale (Wechsler, 1955). Each scale measures a different component of intelligence. Most often, a person who scores well on one scale will also do well on others, but this is not always so. The same person might do very well on general comprehension and similarities, less well on arithmetic reasoning, and poorly on block design, for example.

CONNECTIONS
For a discussion of the use of IQ scores in the classification of learners with exceptionalities or for special-education services, see Chapter 12, page 367.

Intelligence tests are administered either to individuals or to groups. Tests that are administered to groups, such as the Otis-Lennon Mental Ability Tests, the Lorge-Thorndike Intelligence Tests, and the California Test of Mental Maturity, are often given to large groups of students as general assessments of intellectual aptitude. These tests are not as accurate or detailed as are intelligence tests administered individually to people by trained psychologists, such as the Wechsler Intelligence Test for Children–Fourth Edition

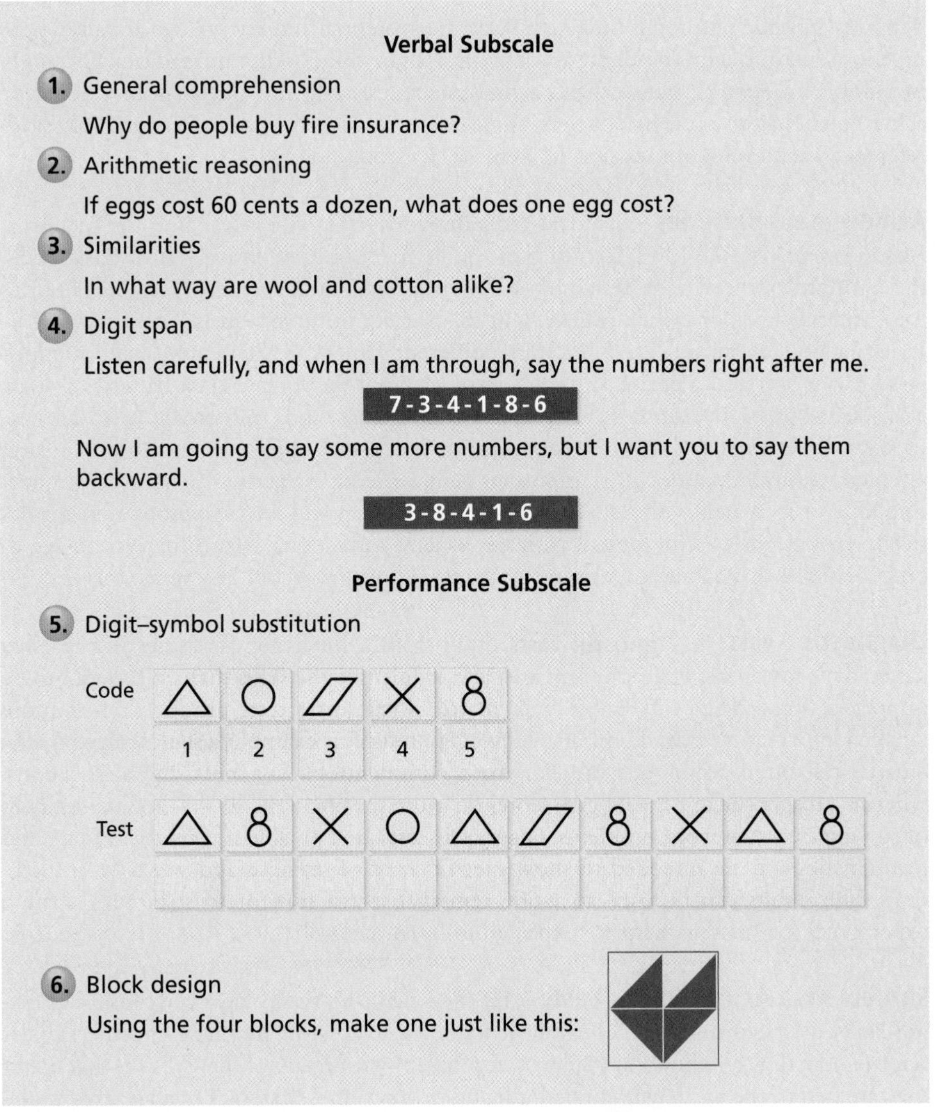

Verbal Subscale
1. General comprehension
Why do people buy fire insurance?
2. Arithmetic reasoning
If eggs cost 60 cents a dozen, what does one egg cost?
3. Similarities
In what way are wool and cotton alike?
4. Digit span
Listen carefully, and when I am through, say the numbers right after me.
7-3-4-1-8-6
Now I am going to say some more numbers, but I want you to say them backward.
3-8-4-1-6
Performance Subscale
5. Digit–symbol substitution
Code
1
2
3
4
5
Test
6. Block design
Using the four blocks, make one just like this:

FIGURE 14.1 Illustrations of Items Used in Intelligence Testing
Intelligence tests focus on skills such as dealing with abstractions and solving problems. This sample of items resembles those used on the Wechsler Adult Intelligence Scale.

From Robert L. Thorndike and Elizabeth P. Hagen, *Measurement and Evaluation in Psychology and Education* (4th ed.), pp. 302–303. Copyright © 1986. Reprinted by permission of Prentice Hall, Upper Saddle River, New Jersey.

(WISC-IV) or the Stanford-Binet test. For example, students who are being assessed for possible placement in special education usually take an individually administered test (most often the WISC-IV), along with other tests.

IQ scores are important because they are correlated with school performance (Ceci, 1992). That is, students who have higher IQs tend, on the average, to get better grades, score higher on achievement tests, and so on. By the time a child is about age 6, IQ estimates tend to become relatively stable, and most people's IQs remain about the same into adulthood. However, some people will experience substantial changes in their estimated IQ, often because of schooling or other environmental influences (Ceci, 1991).

Multifactor Aptitude Tests One other form of aptitude test that provides a breakdown of more specific skills is the **multifactor aptitude battery.** Many such tests are available, with a range of content and emphases. They include scholastic abilities tests such as the SAT; elementary and secondary school tests, such as the Differential Aptitude Test, the Cognitive Abilities Test, and the Test of Cognitive Skills; reading readiness tests, such as the Metropolitan Reading Readiness Test; and various developmental scales for preschool children. At a minimum, most of these tests provide not only overall aptitude scores but also subscores for verbal and nonverbal aptitudes. Often, subscores are even more finely divided to describe more specific abilities.

Norm-Referenced Achievement Tests

Whereas aptitude tests focus on general learning potential and knowledge acquired both in school and out, achievement tests focus on skills or abilities that are traditionally taught in schools. In general, standardized achievement tests fall into one of four categories: achievement batteries, diagnostic tests, single-subject achievement measures, and criterion-referenced achievement measures (Aiken, 2003; Gronlund, 2003).

Achievement Batteries Standardized **achievement batteries,** such as the California Achievement Test, the Iowa Tests of Basic Skills, the Comprehensive Test of Basic Skills, the Stanford Achievement Test, and the Metropolitan Achievement Tests, are used to measure individual or group achievement in a variety of subject areas. These survey batteries include several small tests, each in a different subject area, and are usually administered to a group over a period of several days. Many of the achievement batteries that are available for use in the schools are similar in construction and content. However, because of slight differences among the tests in the instructional objectives and subject matter sampled within the subtests, it is important before selecting a particular test to examine it carefully for its match with a specific school curriculum and for its appropriateness relative to school goals. Achievement batteries usually have several forms for various age or grade levels so that achievement can be monitored over a period of several years.

Diagnostic Tests **Diagnostic tests** differ from achievement batteries in that they generally focus on a specific content area and emphasize the skills that are thought to be important for mastery of that subject matter. Diagnostic tests produce much more detailed information than do other achievement tests. For example, a standardized mathematics test often produces scores for math computations, concepts, and applications, whereas a diagnostic test would give scores on more specific skills, such as adding decimals or solving two-step word problems. Diagnostic tests are available mostly for reading and mathematics and are intended to show specific areas of strength and weakness in these skills. The results can be used to guide remedial instruction or to structure learning experiences for students who are expected to learn the skill.

Subject Area Achievement Tests Teachers make up most classroom tests for assessing skills in specific subjects. However, school districts can purchase specific subject achievement tests for almost any subject. A problem with many of these tests is that unless they are tied to the particular curriculum and instructional strategies that are used in the classroom, they might not adequately represent the content that has been taught. If

multifactor aptitude battery
A test that predicts ability to learn a variety of specific skills and types of knowledge.

achievement batteries
Standardized tests that include several subtests designed to measure knowledge of particular subjects.

diagnostic tests
Tests of specific skills used to identify students' needs and to guide instruction.

standardized achievement tests are considered for evaluating learning in specific areas, the content of the test should be closely examined for its match with the district curriculum, the instruction the students have received, and the district's or state's standards and assessments.

Criterion-Referenced Achievement Tests

Criterion-referenced tests differ from norm-referenced standardized tests in several ways (Aiken, 2003; McMillan, 2007; Popham, 2008). Such tests can take the form of a survey battery, a diagnostic test, or a single-subject test. In contrast to norm-referenced tests, which are designed for use by schools with varying curricula, criterion-referenced tests are most meaningful when constructed around a well-defined set of objectives. For many tests, these objectives can be chosen by the school district, building administrator, or teacher to be applied in a specific situation. The items on the test are selected to match specific instructional objectives, often with three to five items measuring each objective. Therefore, the tests can indicate which objectives individual students or the class as a whole have mastered. Test results can be used to guide future instruction or remedial activities. For this reason these tests are sometimes referred to as objective-referenced tests.

CONNECTIONS
For more on the definitions of norm-referenced and criterion-referenced testing, see Chapter 13, page 418.

Criterion-referenced tests differ from other achievement tests in the way in which they are scored and in how the results are interpreted. On criterion-referenced tests, it is generally the score for each objective that is important. Results could show, for example, how many students can multiply two digits by two digits or how many can write a business letter correctly. Moreover, students' scores on the total test or on specific objectives are interpreted with respect to some criterion of adequate performance independent of group performance. Examples of criterion-referenced tests include tests for drivers and pilots, which were designed to determine who can drive or fly, not who is in the top 20 percent of drivers or pilots. Tests for teachers are also criterion referenced.

CERTIFICATION POINTER
On your teacher certification test you may need to know that a criterion-referenced test would give you better information about how much each student has learned about a particular aspect of the curriculum than a norm-referenced test.

Score reports for criterion-referenced tests are frequently in the form of the number of items that the student got correct on each objective. From these data the teacher can gauge whether the student has mastered the objective.

Standard Setting

When tests are used for making decisions about degree(s) of mastery of a subject or topic, some procedure must be employed to determine the test score cutoff point(s) indicating various proficiency levels (Popham, 2008). Most procedures for the establishment of a **cutoff score** rely on the professional judgment of representative groups of teachers and other educators. Qualified professionals might examine each item in a test and judge the probability that a student with a given level of proficiency would get the item correct. They then base the cutoff score for mastery or proficiency on these probabilities. Standards set using procedures like this are common in licensing exams as well as in many state and district accountability programs.

HOW ARE STANDARDIZED TESTS INTERPRETED?

After students take a standardized test, the tests are usually sent for computer scoring to the central office or the test publisher. The students' raw scores (the number correct on each subtest) are translated into one or more **derived scores,** such as percentiles, grade equivalents, or normal curve equivalents, which relate the students' scores to those of the group on which the test was normed. These statistics are described in the following sections (see Aiken, 2003; McMillan, 2007; Popham, 2008).

cutoff score
The score designated as the minimum necessary to demonstrate mastery of a subject.

derived scores
Values computed from raw scores that relate students' performances to those of a norming group, e.g., percentiles and grade equivalents.

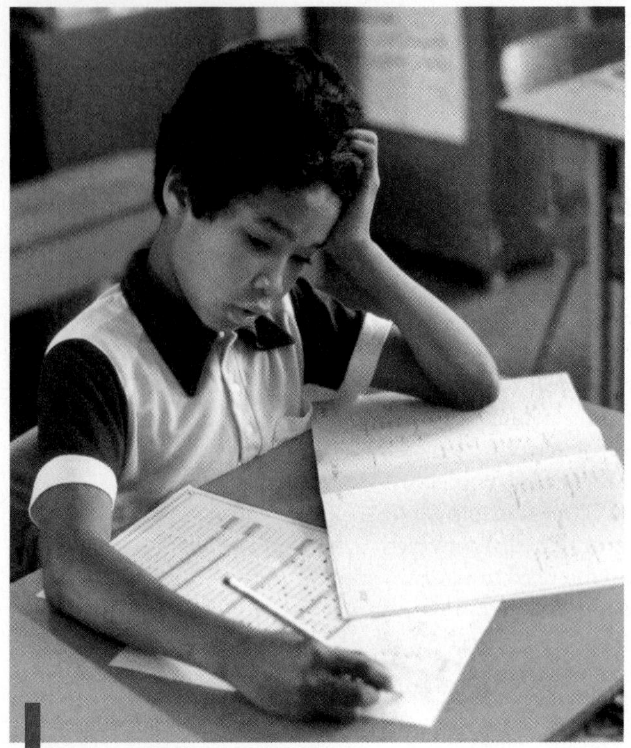

The sight of a child taking a standardized test is a common one these days. What might the results tell us about this child?

Percentile Scores

A **percentile score,** or percentile rank (sometimes abbreviated in test reports as % ILE), indicates the percentage of students in the norming group who scored lower than a particular score. For example, if a student achieved at the median for the norming group (that is, if equal numbers of students scored better and worse than that student), the student would have a percentile rank of 50 because his or her scores exceeded those of 50 percent of the others in the norming group. If you ranked a group of 30 students from bottom to top on test scores, the 25th student from the bottom would score in the 83rd percentile ($25/30 \times 100 = 83.3$).

Grade-Equivalent Scores

Grade-equivalent scores relate students' scores to the average scores obtained by students at a particular grade level. Let's say a norming group achieved an average raw score of 70 on a reading test at the beginning of fifth grade. This score would be established as a grade equivalent of 5.0. If a sixth-grade norming group achieved a test score of 80 in September, this would be established as a grade equivalent of 6.0. Now let's say that a fifth-grader achieved a raw score of 75. This is halfway between the score for 5.0 and that for 6.0, so this student would be assigned a grade equivalent of 5.5. The number after the decimal point is referred to as "months," so a grade equivalent of 5.5 would be read "five years, five months." In theory, a student in the third month of fifth grade should have a score of 5.3 (five years, three months), and so on. Only the 10 months of the regular academic year, September to June, are counted.

CERTIFICATION POINTER

For your teacher certification test you may need to know that a student's grade-equivalent score of 7.3 on a standardized math test would indicate that the student performed as well as an average seventh-grader in the third month of school on that same test, but if students are in a grade level below 7, a grade equivalent of 7.3 does not imply the ability to do seventh-grade work.

The advantage of grade equivalents is that they are easy to interpret and make some intuitive sense. For example, if an average student gains one grade equivalent each year, we call this achieving at expected levels. If we know that a student is performing 2 years below grade level (say, a ninth-grader is scoring at a level typical of seventh-graders), this gives us some understanding of how poorly the student is doing.

However, grade-equivalent scores should be interpreted as only a rough approximation (Gronlund, 2003). For one thing, students do not gain steadily in achievement from month to month. For another, scores that are far from the expected grade level do not mean what they appear to mean. A fourth-grader who scores at, say, the 7.4 grade equivalent is by no means ready for seventh-grade work; this score simply means that the fourth-grader has thoroughly mastered fourth-grade work and has scored as well as a seventh-grader would on the fourth-grade test. Obviously, the average seventh-grader knows a great deal more than what would be on a fourth-grade test, so there is no real comparison between a fourth-grader who scores at a 7.4 grade equivalent and a seventh-grader who does so. The two tests they took would have been very different.

percentile score
A derived score that designates what percentage of the norming group earned raw scores lower than a particular score.

grade-equivalent scores
Standard scores that relate students' raw scores to the average scores obtained by norming groups at different grade levels.

Shifting definitions of grade-level expectations can also confuse the interpretation of scores. For example, New York City school administrators were pleased during the late 1980s to report that 67 percent of students were reading at or above grade level. However, there was a national discussion about what is called the "Lake Wobegon Effect." (In Garrison Keillor's mythical town of Lake Wobegon, "All the children are above average.") Far more than 50 percent of students were scoring "above average" (Cannell, 1987). Test makers renormed their tests, and as a result, administrators in New York City could then claim that only 49 percent of their students were reading at or above grade level (Fiske, 1989). Today, the Lake Wobegon Effect is again in full force, and most standardized tests again produce scores that put many more than 50 percent of students "at grade level" or "above national norms." Because the norms vary from test to test, statements about how many students are at a given level should always be taken with a grain of salt. What is more meaningful is how students are changing over time, or how one district, school, or subgroup compares to another on the same test.

Standard Scores

Several kinds of scores describe test results according to their position on the normal curve. A normal curve describes a distribution of scores in which most fall near the mean, or average, with a symmetrically smaller number of scores appearing the farther we go above or below the mean. A frequency plot of a **normal distribution** produces a bell-shaped curve. For example, Figure 14.2 shows a frequency distribution from a test with a mean score of 50. Each × indicates one student who got a particular score; there are 10 ×'s at 50, so we know that 10 students got this score. Nine students got 49s and nine got 51s, and so on, and very few students made scores above 60 or below 40. Normal distributions like the one shown in Figure 14.2 are common in nature; for example, height and weight are normally distributed throughout the general adult population. Standardized tests are designed so that extremely few students will get every item or no item correct, so scores on them are typically normally distributed.

Standard Deviation One important concept related to normal distributions is the **standard deviation,** a measure of the dispersion of scores. The standard deviation is, roughly speaking, the average amount that scores differ from the mean. For example, consider these two sets of scores:

Set *A*		Set *B*
85		70
70		68
65	< Mean >	65
60		62
45		60
Standard deviation: 14.6		Standard deviation: 4.1

normal distribution
A bell-shaped symmetrical distribution of scores in which most scores fall near the mean, with progressively fewer occurring as the distance from the mean increases.

standard deviation
A statistical measure of the degree of dispersion in a distribution of scores.

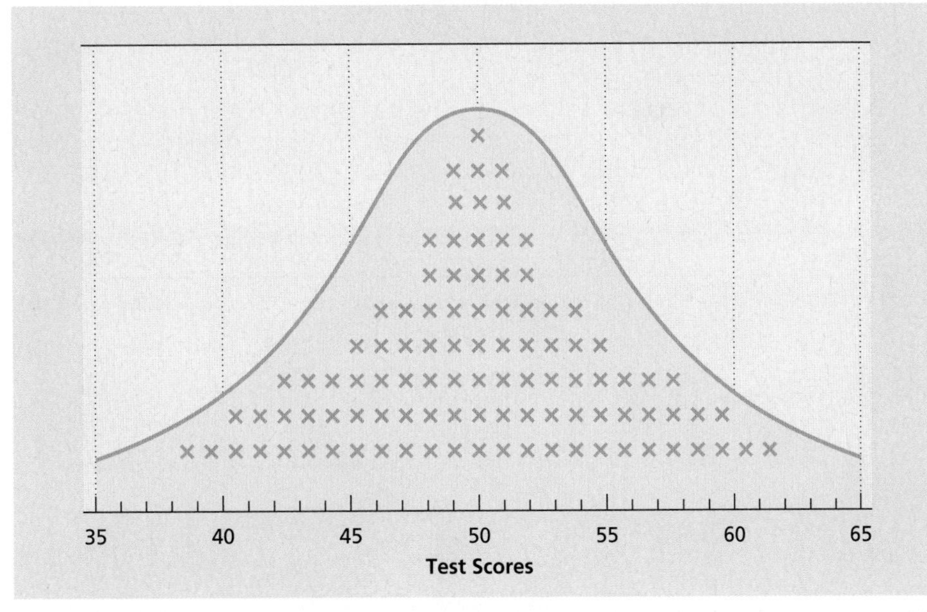

FIGURE 14.2 Frequency of Scores Forming a Normal Curve
If 100 people take a test and the score for each is marked by an x on a graph, the result could suggest a normal curve. In a normal distribution, most scores are at or near the mean (in this case, 50), and the number of scores progressively decreases farther from the mean.

stanine score
A type of standardized score ranging from 1 to 9, having a mean of 5 and a standard deviation of 2.

Note that both sets have the same mean (65) but that otherwise they are quite different, Set *A* being more spread out than Set *B*. This is reflected in the fact that Set *A* has a much larger standard deviation (14.6) than does Set *B* (4.1). The standard deviation of a set of scores indicates how spread out the distribution will be. Furthermore, when scores or other data are normally distributed, we can predict how many scores will fall a given number of standard deviations from the mean. This is illustrated in Figure 14.3, which shows that in any normal distribution, about 34 percent of all scores fall between the mean and one standard deviation above the mean (+1 SD), and a similar number fall between the mean and one standard deviation below the mean (–1 SD). If you go out two standard deviations from the mean, about 95 percent of the scores are included.

"Mr. Rodriguez, I can't make it in today to give the state tests. I'm feeling two standard deviations below the mean!"

Scores on standardized tests are often reported in terms of how far they lie from the mean as measured in standard deviation units. For example, IQ scores are normed so that there is a mean of 100 and a standard deviation of 15. This means that the average person will score 100, someone scoring one standard deviation above the mean will score 115, someone scoring one standard deviation below will score 85, and so on. Therefore, in theory about 68 percent of all IQ scores (that is, a little more than two-thirds) fall between 85 (–1 SD) and 115 (+1 SD). SAT scores are also normed according to standard deviations, with the mean for the Verbal and Quantitative scales set at 500 and a standard deviation of 100. That puts more than two-thirds of all scores between 400 and 600. For IQ, 95 percent will be between 70 (–2 SD) and 130 (+2 SD); for the SAT scale, the comparable range is from 300 to 700.

Stanines A standard score that is sometimes used is the **stanine score** (from the words standard nine). Stanines have a mean of 5 and

FIGURE 14.3 Standard Deviation
When test scores are normally distributed, knowledge of how far a given score lies from the mean in terms of standard deviations indicates what percentage of scores are higher and lower.

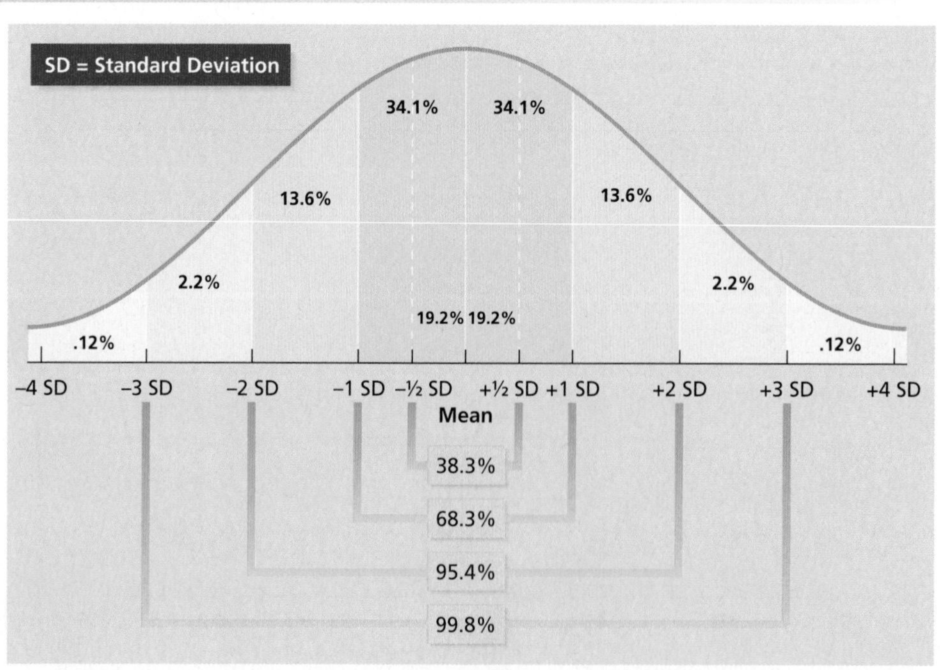

a standard deviation of 2, so each stanine represents 0.5 standard deviation. Stanine scores are reported as whole numbers, so a person who earned a stanine score of 7 (+1 SD) actually fell somewhere between 0.75 SD and 1.25 SD above the mean.

normal curve equivalent
A set of standard scores ranging from 1 to 99, having a mean of 50 and a standard deviation of about 21.

***z*-score**
A standard score having a mean of 0 and a standard deviation of 1.

Normal Curve Equivalents Another form of a standard score that is sometimes used is the **normal curve equivalent** (NCE). A normal curve equivalent can range from 1 to 99, with a mean of 50 and a standard deviation of approximately 21. NCE scores are similar to percentiles, except that intervals between NCE scores are equal (which is not the case with percentile scores). Another standard score, used more often in statistics than in reporting standardized test results, is the ***z*-score,** which sets the mean of a distribution at 0 and the standard deviation at 1. Figure 14.4 shows how a set of normally distributed raw scores with a mean percent correct of 70 percent and a standard deviation of 5 would be represented in *z*-scores, stanines, normal curve equivalents, percentile scores, and equivalent IQ and SAT scores.

Note the difference in the figure between percentile scores and all standard scores (*z*-score, stanine, NCE, IQ, and SAT). Percentile scores are bunched up around the middle of the distribution because most students score near the mean. This means that small changes in raw scores near the mean can produce large changes in percentiles (percentages of students below the score). In contrast, changes in raw scores that are far above or below the mean make a smaller difference in percentiles. For example, an increase of 5 points on the test from 70 to 75 moves a student from the 50th to the 84th percentile, an increase of 34 percentile points; but 5 more points (from 75 to 80) increases the student's percentile rank by only 14 points. At the extreme, the same 5-point increase, from 80 to 85, results in an increase of only 1 percentile point, from 98 to 99.

This characteristic of percentile ranks means that changes in percentiles should be interpreted cautiously. For example, one teacher might brag, "My average kids increased 23 percentile points [from 50 to 73], while your supposedly smart kids gained

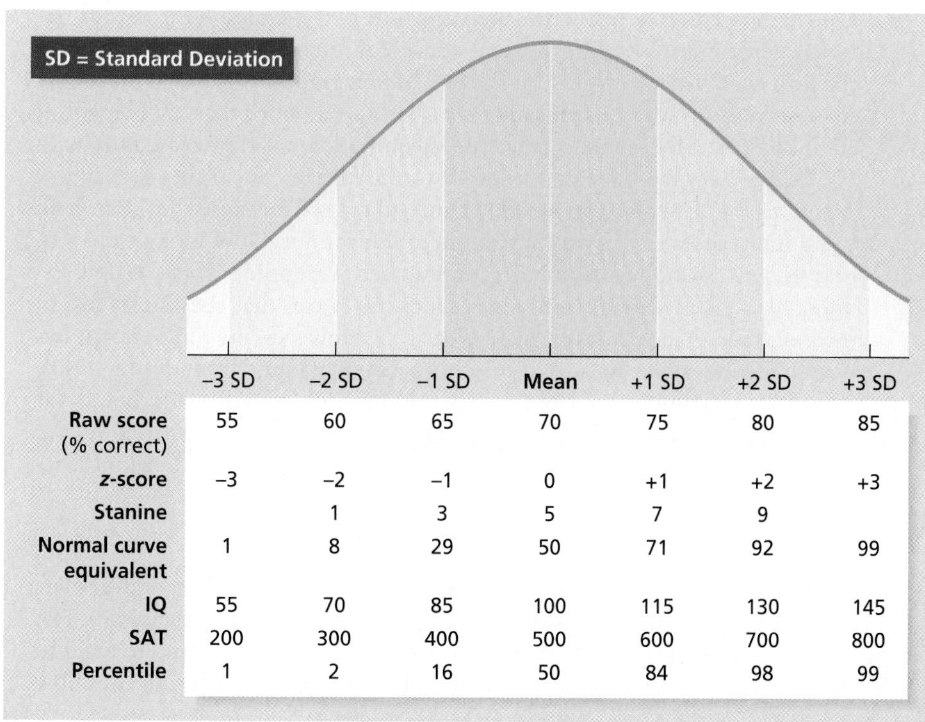

	−3 SD	−2 SD	−1 SD	Mean	+1 SD	+2 SD	+3 SD
Raw score (% correct)	55	60	65	70	75	80	85
z-score	−3	−2	−1	0	+1	+2	+3
Stanine		1	3	5	7	9	
Normal curve equivalent	1	8	29	50	71	92	99
IQ	55	70	85	100	115	130	145
SAT	200	300	400	500	600	700	800
Percentile	1	2	16	50	84	98	99

FIGURE 14.4 Relationships among Various Types of Scores
Raw scores that are normally distributed can be reported in a variety of ways. Each reporting method is characterized by its mean, by the range between high and low scores, and by the standard deviation interval.

only 15 percentile points [from 84 to 99]. I really did a great job with them!" In fact, the bragging teacher's students gained only 3 points in raw score, or 0.6 standard deviations, whereas the other teacher's students gained 10 points in raw score, or 2 standard deviations!

THEORY *into* PRACTICE

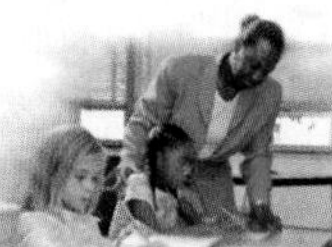

Interpreting Standardized Test Scores

This section presents a guide to interpreting test reports for one widely used standardized test of academic performance, the Terra Nova, published by CTB/McGraw-Hill (1997). Other widely used nationally standardized tests (such as the CAT, the Iowa, and the Stanford) use similar report formats.

CLASS RECORD SHEET. Figure 14.5 on pages 470–471 shows portions of an actual Terra Nova (CTBS/5) pre/post class record sheet for children (whose names have been changed) in a Title I second-grade reading class. The main information on the form is as follows.

Identification Data

Look first at the top of the form. It identifies the tests taken at the end of the previous year (pre) and at the end of the current year (post). The grade (2.7) indicates that at the time of post-testing, students were in month seven of second grade (April; September is month zero). Information at the bottom left shows testing dates, school, district, test norm, and "quarter month" (i.e., weeks since school began).

Scores

Under each column, test scores are shown in two metrics. NP refers to national percentiles; NCE, to normal curve equivalent. For example, look at the fifth child, Marvin Miller. At the end of first grade, his national percentile score in reading was 49, indicating that he scored better than 49 percent of all first-graders. By second grade, his percentile score had increased to 76. In NCEs, however, he increased from 49 to 65. The test form shows a gain of 16 NCEs; NCE scores can be added and subtracted, because they are on an equal interval scale, whereas percentile scores cannot. Now look at the second student, Brittany Duphily. In reading, her percentile scores (and NCEs) dropped from first to second grade. Does this mean that she knows less in second grade than she did in first? Not at all. However, she did perform less well in second grade compared to other second-graders. To understand this, consider a girl who is the third-fastest runner in the fourth grade, but a year later is the twelfth fastest in the fifth grade. The girl has not slowed down, and probably can run faster than before, but other runners are making better progress.

Summary

At the bottom of the form is a summary of the test scores for second-graders in the entire district (a class or school summary would look the same). The scores are presented as median percentiles (the score of the middle child in the district) and the national percentile of the median, which indicates how well the district is doing among all districts. In this district, for example, the middle second-grader is scoring better than 35.3 percent of all second-graders in reading. The last set of numbers shows the mean NCEs for all second-graders and the difference between first-grade NCEs (42.5) and second-grade NCEs (41.6). The difference, a loss of 0.9 NCEs, is very small, essentially indicating that children in this district score at about the same reading level in first and second grades, in comparison to children in other districts.

INDIVIDUAL PROFILE REPORT. Like most standardized tests, the Terra Nova provides a detailed analysis of the test performance of each child. Figure 14.6 (page 472) shows an example for a third-grader, Maria Olthof (a real report, but not her real name). The form gives the following information:

Norm-Referenced Scores

At the top of the report is a list of Maria's scores on 14 scales listed six ways. The first is grade equivalent. In reading, Maria's grade equivalent is 2.0, indicating that her score is like that which would be obtained by an average child just starting second grade. Her NCE of 35 also indicates that she is performing significantly below grade level. (In general, an NCE of 50 is considered "at grade level.") Skip over scale score, which is not interpretable. Maria's local percentile indicates that she is reading extremely poorly in comparison to other children in her class, school, or district (however "local" was defined). A percentile of 1 is the lowest possible score.

Number correct is self-explanatory. In reading, Maria's national percentile indicates that she is scoring better than only 24 percent of all third-graders in the United States. "NP range" indicates the likely range of national percentile scores that Maria might receive if she took the same test many times. That is, there is always a range of scores a student might get, depending on luck, inadvertent errors, testing conditions, motivation, and so on—all factors that could vary each time a student took a test even if his or her level of knowledge or skill stayed the same. The chart on the upper right shows this national percentile range with a diamond indicating the actual percentile score. The shading between the 25th and 75th percentiles indicates the "normal range"; Maria's reading score is below that range, although her own "NP range" suggests that on a very good day she might score within the normal range.

Note that at the bottom of the national percentile chart is a scale indicating stanines. Recall that stanine scores range from 1 to 9, with a score of 5 indicating the national average.

Performance on Objectives

The remainder of the individual profile report breaks Maria's test down into subskills in each area. This breakdown can provide some useful information to explain overall scores. For example, look at Maria's mathematics scores. She scores very well on an "objectives performance index" in every subscale of math but one: problem solving. For Maria, this one low score could be because of her reading problems; or she might need additional work with this skill. However, subscale analyses of this kind should be interpreted very cautiously. The small number of items involved and the lack of a clear connection to the material Maria is studying mean that classroom assessments, perhaps supplemented by more fine-tuned diagnostic tests in mathematics, would be a much better indicator of Maria's strengths, weaknesses, and instructional needs.

CERTIFICATION POINTER

For your teacher certification test you may need to be able to select, construct, and use assessment strategies and instruments appropriate to the learning outcomes being evaluated.

FIGURE 14.5 Sample Class Record Sheet for a Standardized Test

When a class of students takes a standardized test as a pre-test and a post-test, the results may be compared by means of a form similar to the one shown here.

CTB MACMILLAN/MCGRAW-HILL

PRE-POST CLASS RECORD SHEET
CLASS: GRD.2 TCH 3

PRE-TEST: CTBS/5 MA
POST-TEST: CTBS/5 MA

GRADE 2.7

TITLE 1 READING

170508
PAGE 1

STUDENTS	FORM/LEVEL	SCORES	READING			LANGUAGE			MATHEMATICS			TOTAL SCORE		SOCIAL		WORD
			READ	VOCAB	CMPST	LANG	MECH	CMPST	MATH	COMPU	CMPST	++	SCI	STDY	SPELL	ANLYS
BEACHY JULIA M		PRE NP	98			94			76			94				
BIRTH DATE: 5/ 4/90		POST NP	55			81			62			70				
PRE GRADE: 1.7	A-11															
POST GRADE: 2.7	A-12	PRE NCE	94			83			65			82				
CODES/PRE: 3916720000.........		POST NCE	53			69			57			61				
CODES/POST: 391672.......1.....		DIFF	-41			-14			-8			-21				
DUPHILY BRITTN D		PRE NP	79			70			88			82				
BIRTH DATE: 9/25/90		POST NP	53			58			70			62				
PRE GRADE: 1.7	A-11															
POST GRADE: 2.7	A-12	PRE NCE	67			61			74			70				
CODES/PRE: 6613080000.........		POST NCE	52			54			61			57				
CODES/POST: 661308.......1.....		DIFF	-15			-7			-13			-13				
HARRISON ROBERT L		PRE NP	44			30			19			28				
BIRTH DATE: 5/23/90		POST NP	63			34			42			46				
PRE GRADE: 1.7	A-11															
POST GRADE: 2.7	A-12	PRE NCE	47			39			32			37				
CODES/PRE: 4039710000.........		POST NCE	57			41			46			48				
CODES/POST: 403971.......1.....		DIFF	10			2			14			11				
KNOX CARLY M		PRE NP	99			* 99			99			99				
BIRTH DATE: 7/ 9/90		POST NP	84			64			56			71				
PRE GRADE: 1.7	A-11															
POST GRADE: 2.7	A-12	PRE NCE	99			99			99			99				
CODES/PRE: 8441620000.........		POST NCE	71			57			53			62				
CODES/POST: 844162.......1.....		DIFF	-28			-42			-46			-37				
MILLER MARVIN R		PRE NP	49			85			70			73				
BIRTH DATE: 5/11/90		POST NP	76			86			39			71				
PRE GRADE: 1.7	A-11															
POST GRADE: 2.7	A-12	PRE NCE	49			72			61			63				
CODES/PRE: 2905390000.........		POST NCE	65			73			44			62				
CODES/POST: 290539.......1.....		DIFF	16			1			-17			-1				
MOORE RICHAR J		PRE NP	58			66			86			75				
BIRTH DATE: 8/26/90		POST NP	54			76			80			72				
PRE GRADE: 1.7	A-11															
POST GRADE: 2.7	A-12	PRE NCE	54			59			73			64				
CODES/PRE: 352384............		POST NCE	52			65			68			63				
CODES/POST: 352384.......1.....		DIFF	-2			6			-5			-1				

PRE-TEST DATE: 4/14/97
QUARTER MONTH: 31
NORMS: CTBS/5 1996
PATTERN (IRT)
POST-TEST DATE: 4/22/98
QUARTER MONTH: 31
NORMS: CTBS/5 1996
PATTERN (IRT)

SCHOOL: SCHOOL 1
DISTRICT: ANY DISTRICT
CITY: ANY CITY
STATE: CA

++ TOTAL SCORE CONSISTS OF READING, LANGUAGE, MATHEMATICS

*: MAXIMUM OR MINIMUM SCORE

NP: NATIONAL PERCENTILE
NCE: NORMAL CURVE EQUIVALENT
DIFF: DIFFERENCE (POST-SCORE MINUS PRE-SCORE)
DIFFERENCES ARE NOT REPORTED FOR NATIONAL PERCENTILES

CTBID: 98268Q273549001-03-00094-000051

FIGURE 14.5 Continued

CTB MACMILLAN/MCGRAW-HILL

PRE-POST CLASS RECORD SHEET
DISTRICT: ANY DISTRICT

PRE-TEST: CTBS/5 MA
POST-TEST: CTBS/5 MA

GRADE 2

TITLE 1 READING

170508
PAGE 1

DISTRICT SUMMARY	SCORES	READING READ	VOCAB	CMPST	LANGUAGE LANG	MECH	CMPST	MATHEMATICS MATH	COMPU	CMPST	TOTAL SCORE ++	SCI	SOCIAL STDY	SPELL	WORD ANLYS
	PRE MDNP	40.4			39.2			34.3			33.0				
	POST MDNP	35.3			32.5			36.3			34.0				
	PRE NPMN	36			39			36			36				
	POST NPMN	35			35			38			36				
	PRE MNCE	42.5			44.0			42.5			42.5				
	POST MNCE	41.6			42.1			43.4			42.3				
	DIFF	-0.9			-1.9			0.9			-0.2				
** NUMBER OF STUDENTS = 95		91			91			93			90				
PRE-TEST FORM/LEVEL A-11															
POST-TEST FORM/LEVEL A-12															

PRE-TEST DATE: 4/14/97
QUARTER MONTH: 31
NORMS: CTBS/5 1996
PATTERN (IRT)
POST-TEST DATE: 4/22/98
QUARTER MONTH: 31
NORMS: CTBS/5 1996
PATTERN (IRT)
CITY: ANY CITY
STATE: CA

++ TOTAL SCORE CONSISTS OF READING, LANGUAGE, MATHEMATICS

MDNP: MEDIAN NATIONAL PERCENTILE
NPMN: NATIONAL PERCENTILE OF MEAN NORMAL CURVE EQUIVALENT
MNCE: MEAN NORMAL CURVE EQUIVALENT
DIFF: DIFFERENCE (POST-SCORE MINUS PRE-SCORE)
DIFFERENCES ARE NOT REPORTED FOR NATIONAL PERCENTILES

**: SUMMARIES DO NOT INCLUDE STUDENTS WHO WERE RETAINED OR WHO SKIPPED A GRADE

CTBID: 98268Q273549001-03-00078-000002

FIGURE 14.6 Sample Individual Test Record for a Standardized Test

Reports for individuals who take standardized tests may include overall scores and scores on specific content objectives.

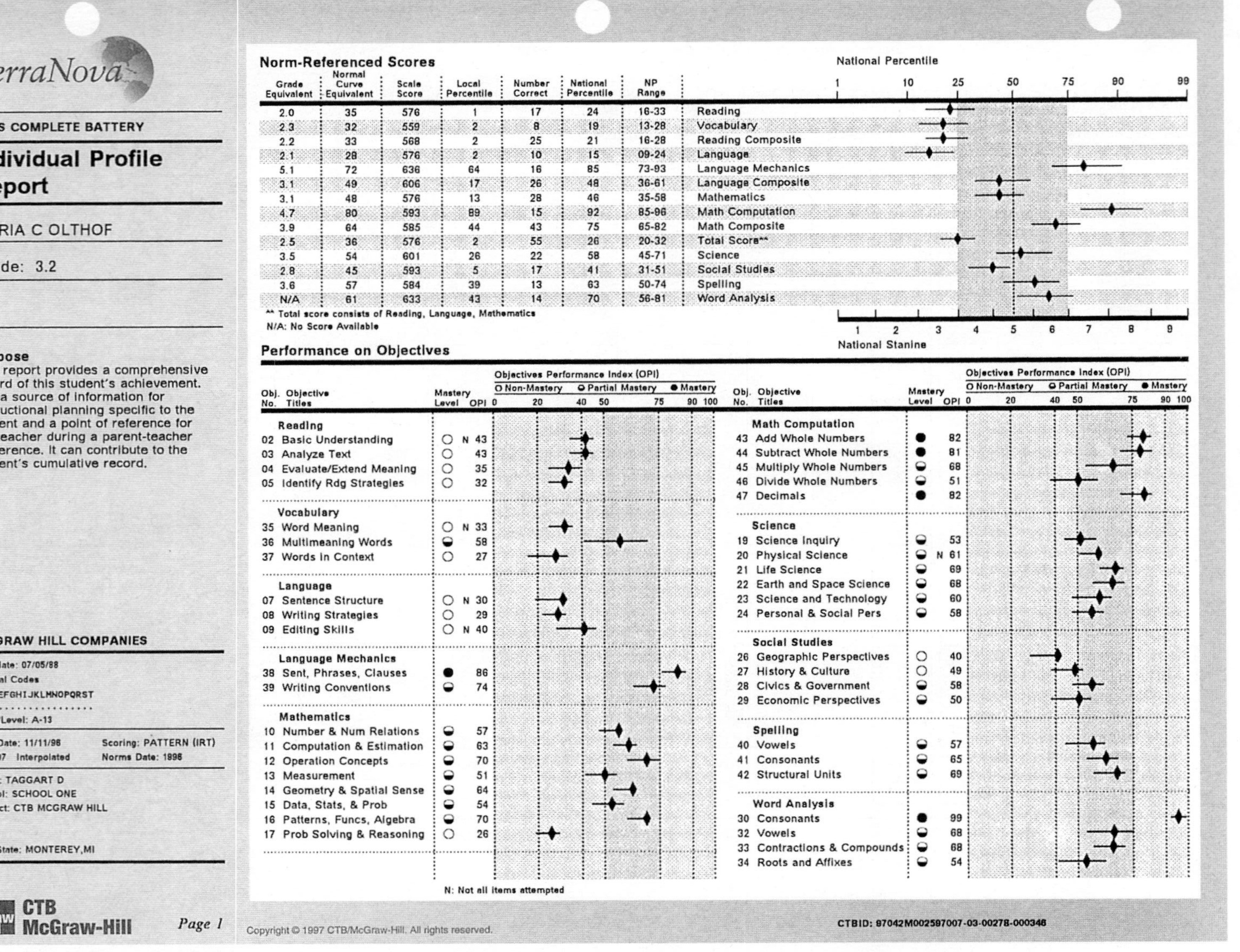

TerraNova

CTBS COMPLETE BATTERY

Individual Profile Report

MARIA C OLTHOF

Grade: 3.2

Purpose

This report provides a comprehensive record of this student's achievement. It is a source of information for instructional planning specific to the student and a point of reference for the teacher during a parent-teacher conference. It can contribute to the student's cumulative record.

MCGRAW HILL COMPANIES

Birthdate: 07/05/88
Special Codes
ABCDEFGHIJKLMNOPQRST
Form/Level: A-13
Test Date: 11/11/96 Scoring: PATTERN (IRT)
QM: 07 Interpolated Norms Date: 1996
Class: TAGGART D
School: SCHOOL ONE
District: CTB MCGRAW HILL
City/State: MONTEREY,MI

CTB McGraw-Hill *Page 1*

Norm-Referenced Scores

Grade Equivalent	Normal Curve Equivalent	Scale Score	Local Percentile	Number Correct	National Percentile	NP Range	
2.0	35	576	1	17	24	16-33	Reading
2.3	32	559	2	8	19	13-28	Vocabulary
2.2	33	568	2	25	21	16-28	Reading Composite
2.1	28	576	2	10	15	09-24	Language
5.1	72	636	64	16	85	73-93	Language Mechanics
3.1	49	606	17	26	48	36-61	Language Composite
3.1	48	576	13	28	46	35-58	Mathematics
4.7	80	593	89	15	92	85-96	Math Computation
3.9	64	585	44	43	75	65-82	Math Composite
2.5	36	576	2	55	26	20-32	Total Score**
3.5	54	601	26	22	58	45-71	Science
2.8	45	593	5	17	41	31-51	Social Studies
3.6	57	584	39	13	63	50-74	Spelling
N/A	61	633	43	14	70	56-81	Word Analysis

** Total score consists of Reading, Language, Mathematics
N/A: No Score Available

Performance on Objectives

Objectives Performance Index (OPI): ○ Non-Mastery ◐ Partial Mastery ● Mastery (0 20 40 50 75 90 100)

Obj. No.	Objective Titles	Mastery Level	OPI
	Reading		
02	Basic Understanding	○	N 43
03	Analyze Text	○	43
04	Evaluate/Extend Meaning	○	35
05	Identify Rdg Strategies	○	32
	Vocabulary		
35	Word Meaning	○	N 33
36	Multimeaning Words	◐	58
37	Words in Context	○	27
	Language		
07	Sentence Structure	○	N 30
08	Writing Strategies	○	29
09	Editing Skills	○	N 40
	Language Mechanics		
38	Sent, Phrases, Clauses	●	86
39	Writing Conventions	◐	74
	Mathematics		
10	Number & Num Relations	◐	57
11	Computation & Estimation	◐	63
12	Operation Concepts	◐	70
13	Measurement	◐	51
14	Geometry & Spatial Sense	◐	64
15	Data, Stats, & Prob	◐	54
16	Patterns, Funcs, Algebra	◐	70
17	Prob Solving & Reasoning	○	26

Obj. No.	Objective Titles	Mastery Level	OPI
	Math Computation		
43	Add Whole Numbers	●	82
44	Subtract Whole Numbers	●	81
45	Multiply Whole Numbers	◐	68
46	Divide Whole Numbers	◐	51
47	Decimals	●	82
	Science		
19	Science Inquiry	◐	53
20	Physical Science	◐	N 61
21	Life Science	◐	69
22	Earth and Space Science	◐	68
23	Science and Technology	◐	60
24	Personal & Social Pers	◐	58
	Social Studies		
26	Geographic Perspectives	○	40
27	History & Culture	○	49
28	Civics & Government	◐	58
29	Economic Perspectives	◐	50
	Spelling		
40	Vowels	◐	57
41	Consonants	◐	65
42	Structural Units	◐	69
	Word Analysis		
30	Consonants	●	99
32	Vowels	◐	68
33	Contractions & Compounds	◐	68
34	Roots and Affixes	◐	54

N: Not all items attempted

CTBID: 97042M002597007-03-00278-000346

WHAT ARE SOME ISSUES CONCERNING STANDARDIZED AND CLASSROOM TESTING?

The use of standardized tests to assess teachers, schools, and districts has increased dramatically in recent years. As noted earlier, all states now have statewide testing programs in which students at selected grade levels take criterion-referenced performance tests and/or standardized achievement tests. State education departments use scores on these tests to evaluate the state's educational program as a whole and to compare the performance of individual school districts, schools, and teachers. These comparisons go under the general heading of accountability programs. Accountability is one of several issues related to uses and abuses of standardized tests. Issues concerning testing, standards, and related topics are among the most hotly debated questions in U.S. education (Chatterji, 2002; Gallagher, 2003). In recent years there have been many developments and proposals for change in testing. These are discussed in the following sections.

Test Validity

We use test scores to make inferences about the students we are measuring. The **validity** of a test is the extent to which those inferences are justified (Aiken, 2003; McMillan, 2007; Moss, Girard, & Haniford, 2006; Popham, 2006). The types of evidence that are used to evaluate the validity of a test vary according to the test's purpose. For example, if a test is being selected to help teachers and administrators determine which students are likely to have some difficulty with one or more aspects of instruction, primary interest will be in how well the test predicts future academic performance. However, if the aim is to describe the current achievement levels of a group of students, primary interest will focus on the accuracy of that description. In short, validity deals with the relevance of a test for its intended purpose (Aiken, 2003).

Because of the various roles that tests are expected to play in schools and in the education process, three classes of evidence of validity are of concern to test users: content, criterion-related, and consequential.

Content Evidence of Validity The most important criterion for the usefulness of a test—especially an achievement test—is whether it assesses what the user wants it to assess (Popham, 2008). This criterion is called **content evidence.** Content evidence in achievement testing is an assessment of the degree of overlap between what is taught (or what should be taught) and what is tested. It is determined by content experts through careful comparison of the content of a test with state or district standards or with the objectives of a course or program. For example, if a test emphasized dates and facts in history but curricula and state or local standards emphasized key ideas of history, the test could not be considered valid.

Criterion-Related Evidence of Validity **Criterion-related evidence** is gathered by looking at relationships between scores on the test and other sets of scores. These are compared with expectations based on understandings about these various assessments. For example, **predictive evidence** of a test's validity might be a measure of its ability to help predict future behavior. If we are using a test to predict students' future school performance, one way to examine the test's validity is to relate the test scores to some measure of students' subsequent performance. If an appropriate level of correspondence exists between the test and later performance, the test can then be used to provide predictive information for students. For example, test scores on SATs and ACTs have been shown to relate to a reasonable degree to performance in college; many college admissions

validity
A measure of the degree to which a test is appropriate for its intended use.

content evidence
A measure of the match between the content of a test and the content of the instruction that preceded it.

criterion-related evidence
A type of evidence of validity that exists when scores on a test are related to scores from another measure of an associated trait.

predictive evidence
A type of criterion-related evidence of validity that exists when scores on a test are related to scores from a measure of a trait that the test could be used to predict.

These students will take nationwide standardized aptitude and achievement tests this year. Will the results be equally fair to them all? Why or why not?

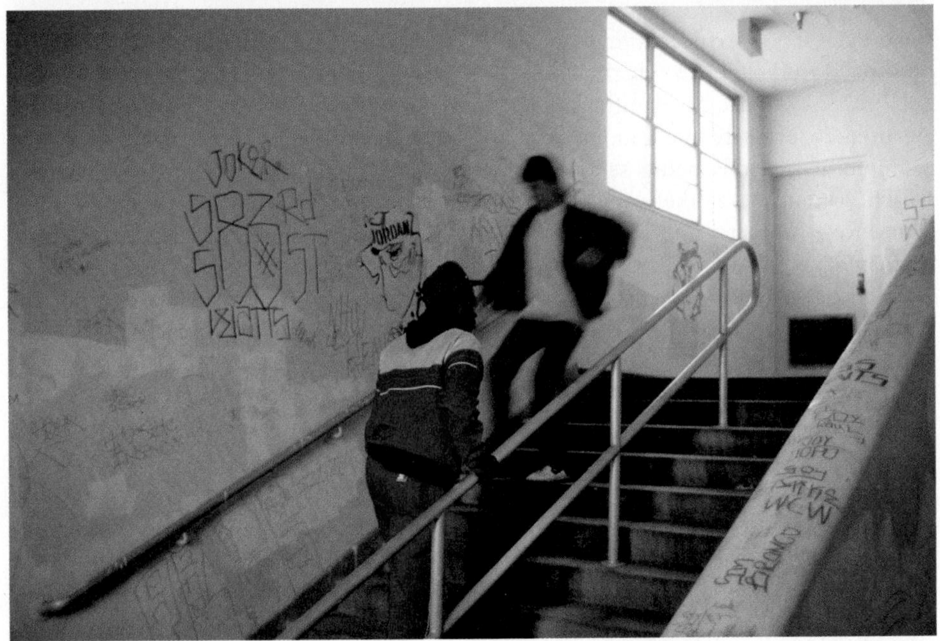

officers therefore use these scores (along with high school grades and other information) in deciding which applicants to accept.

concurrent evidence A type of criterion-related evidence of validity that exists when scores on a test are related to scores from another measure of the same or a very similar trait.

discriminant evidence A type of evidence of validity that exists when scores on a test are unrelated to scores from one or more measures of other traits when educational or psychological theory about these traits predicts they should be unrelated.

Another criterion-related form is called **concurrent evidence** of validity. At issue is whether the test measures the same domain as another test. For example, if a group IQ test were to be substituted for an individual IQ test, one would first want to know whether they yielded comparable scores. By giving the two tests to the same students in a study, the relationship between their scores could be evaluated.

Another form of concurrent evidence is called **discriminant evidence.** Achievement tests, for example, might be expected to show a relative *lack* of relationship with some variables. For example, a test of mechanical aptitude should relate to a test taker's ability to assemble a machine but should *not* correlate too well with verbal aptitude, which is a different skill, or with gender, which has nothing to do with the skill being measured.

Test Reliability

Whereas validity relates to the skills and knowledge measured by a test, the **reliability** of a test relates to the accuracy with which these skills and knowledge are measured (Aiken, 2003; Popham, 2008). Test scores are supposed to result from the knowledge and skill of the students being measured. But when a test is administered, aspects related to both the test itself and the circumstances surrounding its administration could cause the results to be inaccurate. In theory, if a student were to take equivalent tests twice, he or she should obtain the same score both times. The extent to which this would not occur is the subject of reliability. Random features of the assessment such as ambiguous test items, differences in specific item content, lucky or unlucky guessing, inconsistent motivation, and anxiety all affect test scores and could cause results for different administrations of equivalent tests to differ. In addition, on essays or other performance measures, differences between raters reduce reliability. If it could be shown that individuals received similar scores on two administrations of the same test, then some confidence could be placed in the test's reliability. If the scores were greatly inconsistent, it would be difficult to place much faith in a particular test score. Generally, the longer the test and the more similar the items are to each other, the greater is the reliability.

Reliability is commonly measured using a coefficient that has a theoretical range from 0 to 1. The higher the number, the more reliable the test. In general, good standardized achievement tests should have coefficients of .90 or higher. The question of reliability might be thought of as how consistently the test measures something about students. Validity relates to the question of how meaningful a test score is for something we care about. Thus, a test cannot have validity without reliability, but a test can be reliable without being valid. As an example of reliability without validity, consider your reaction if your instructor assigned course grades on the basis of student height. He or she would have a highly reliable assessment (height can be determined quite accurately), but the scores would not be valid indicators of your knowledge or skill. Now, imagine a test of creativity in which students were asked to describe innovative uses for a can opener. If raters could not agree on how to score students' responses, or if scores varied a great deal when students took the same test 6 months later, then the scale would lack reliability and, therefore, could not be considered valid.

Test Bias

Some major criticisms of traditional standardized tests relate to issues of validity and reliability (see Linn, 2000). Critics argue that such tests

- Give false information about the status of learning in the nation's schools (Bracey, 2003)
- Are unfair to (or biased against) some kinds of students (e.g., students from diverse backgrounds, those with limited proficiency in English, females, and students from low-income families) (see Lissitz & Schafer, 2002; Orfield & Kornhaber, 2001; Scheurich et al., 2000; Suzuki et al., 2000)
- Tend to corrupt the processes of teaching and learning, often reducing teaching to mere preparation for testing (Cizek, 1999; Darling-Hammond & Falk, 1997; Rotberg, 2001)
- Focus time, energy, and attention on the simpler skills that are easily tested and away from higher-order thinking skills and creative endeavors (Campbell, 2000; Popham, 2008)

CERTIFICATION POINTER

Your teacher certification test is likely to require you to understand assessment-related issues such as test validity, test reliability, bias, and scoring concerns.

One major issue in the interpretation of standardized test scores is the possibility of **bias** against students from low-income or diverse backgrounds (Lissitz & Schafer, 2002; Suzuki, Ponterotto, & Meller, 2000). In one sense, this is a question of test validity: A test that gave an unfair advantage to one or another category of student could not be considered valid. Of greatest concern is the possibility that tests could be biased because their items assess knowledge or skills that are common to one group or culture but not another. For example, a test that includes a reading comprehension passage about a trip

reliability
A measure of the consistency of test scores obtained from the same students at different times.

bias
An undesirable characteristic of tests in which item content discriminates against certain students.

to the beach could be biased against students who live far from a beach or cannot afford to travel to a beach. A passage about Halloween could be unfair to Jehovah's Witnesses, who do not celebrate Halloween.

Test publishers routinely assess bias in test items (called *item bias*). Items that exhibit lower (or higher) scores for student demographic groups (e.g., gender or race groups) than expected on the basis of the test as a whole are flagged for evaluation. These items are usually referred to a committee with representatives from a broad range of demographic groups, which is likely to exclude the item. A related issue is sensitivity. It should go without saying that test items with any kind of overt cultural or gender stereotyping should be rejected. For example, a test whose items always refer to doctors as "he" or give Hispanic names only to menial workers should not be used.

Teaching Dilemmas: CASES TO CONSIDER

Dealing with High-Stakes Testing

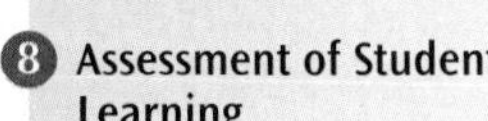

INTASC

8 Assessment of Student Learning

Jerry Natkin is beginning his seventh year of teaching English. Roscoe Carnes is beginning his fourth year as an art teacher. It is early September, and the two friends sit talking in the teachers' lounge of a high school in a medium-sized city.

Roscoe: What's on your agenda in the English department this year, Jerry? Any new plans or projects?

Jerry: Well, it may seem early to be worrying about this, but we're determined to do something about the standardized test results in this school.

Roscoe: What's the matter with them?

Jerry: The scores are still declining. We looked back over 10 years of results. On average, last year's students scored a couple of percentage points below the kids of 5 years ago and even farther below the scores from 10 years ago. I wonder if these kids simply aren't learning.

Roscoe: Did you consider that they might be learning a lot but simply can't show what they know on standardized achievement tests?

Jerry: Maybe. But regardless, the issue is how to get the scores up. I think that in the English department, we should at least make sure that our courses are covering the content of the state standardized test. As I see it, with some changes in course content and classroom testing procedures, we can easily increase the school's overall average score and also our number of state finalists each year.

Roscoe: But, Jerry, that sounds like teaching to the test.

Jerry: It is. What's wrong with that?

Roscoe: Is it ethical? Should tests determine curriculum? Is doing well on standardized tests the reason kids go to school? Is testing fair to all students? Those tests contain cultural and class biases, you know. Anyway, the state exam is practically all multiple choice. If you teach to the exam, you run the risk of lowering your standards—minimums do have a way of becoming maximums. What about higher-order learning like problem solving and creative thinking?

Jerry: Higher-order thinking is always part of English, Roscoe. Don't worry! But I'm convinced we can include higher-order objectives and cover the test better. Also, we need to push the kids more.

Roscoe: How?

Jerry: I'd like to involve the parents. Get them to work with their kids at home, using sample test items and such. You know, kids who score higher on tests make better grades and do better in life. We've got to coach them.

Roscoe: I'd argue with you on that. How would you coach all the kids? Would it be fair to pick only some for special treatment? And what does "doing better in life" mean? Better income? Isn't there more to life than that?

Jerry: Sure, sure. Of course achievement tests aren't everything. And they aren't perfect either. But they're there, and we need them—for feedback! How else can we as teachers know what we've accomplished? We get to see kids make measurable progress.

Roscoe: But I don't think standardized tests are a good measure of students' actual abilities or meaningful knowledge. Maybe your scores tell you something about English proficiency, but I can't measure my kids' progress that way.

Jerry: I bet you could. You could measure creativity.

Roscoe: And then teach to the creativity test? Jerry, do you really think standardized test scores should be guiding your instructional goals as an English teacher?

QUESTIONS FOR REFLECTION

1. Using a problem-solving approach, address Jerry's concerns about declining test scores. How would you evaluate Jerry's plan to improve scores? Is it a good idea? Will it work? What could his department do to increase parents' involvement? How could students be coached?
2. Using a problem-solving approach, address Roscoe's concerns about overrelying on test scores. Do standardized tests lead to lower minimum standards? How could that be avoided? Where should the line be drawn; should achievement tests be used for diagnosis? For prediction? For placement? Why or why not? Can cultural and class biases be removed? How else could student achievement be measured? How else could teachers get feedback?
3. Model your solutions by adding one or more new characters and extending the dialogue in writing or role play.

Computer Test Administration

The use of computers to administer tests is becoming more common. In its simplest form, the same multiple-choice items (in the same order) are administered to students as they would take them if they sat for the typical, paper-and-pencil test. However, the use of a computer makes it possible to tailor the selection of items to the performance of the student. When this is done, the administration is called **computer-adaptive** (Olson, 2005; Wainer, 2000). Typically, a single item is administered first, and depending on whether the student was successful or unsuccessful, a harder or an easier item, respectively, is presented next. As the test progresses, a running estimate of the student's performance over the entire test is continually updated. This can result in real time savings; students can commonly take tests in less than one-third the time for a paper-and-pencil administration with the same degree of accuracy. Also, computer-adaptive testing can zero in on a particular set of skills at the forward edge of what a student knows, giving more accurate information on those skills while avoiding wasting time on items that are very easy or impossible for the student.

ON THE WEB

For more on issues related to the principles of educational assessment go to the website of the National Council on Measurement in Education (NCME) at **www.ncme.org.**

HOW ARE EDUCATORS HELD ACCOUNTABLE FOR STUDENT ACHIEVEMENT?

computer-adaptive
An approach to assessment in which a computer is used to present items and each item presented is chosen to yield the best new information about the examinee based on her or his prior responses to earlier items.

A growing trend in recent years has been the effort to hold teachers, schools, and districts accountable for what students learn. All U.S. states, most Canadian provinces, and England (among other countries) have implemented regular standardized testing programs and publish the results on a school-by-school basis. Many districts supplement these state tests with additional tests, including "benchmark assessments" that are given several times each year to help guide instruction toward meeting state standards. Not surprisingly, principals and other administrators watch these scores the way business owners watch their profit sheets. More and more, standardized tests are becoming "high-stakes" tests, which means that their results have serious consequences for educators and (increasingly) for students themselves. For example, many states and districts now require that students score at a given level on state tests in order to be promoted from grade to grade or to graduate from high school. Many states and districts issue school report cards listing such data as test scores, attendance, retentions, and suspensions; these might be reported in newspapers or otherwise publicized. Test scores are frequently used in decisions about hiring, firing, promotion, and transfer of principals and superintendents, and often teachers.

ON THE WEB

To learn more about accountability and state-level assessment issues, visit the website for the Council of Chief State School Officers (CCSSO) at **www.ccsso.org.** CCSSO is an organization of public officials who lead K–12 education in the 50 states.

The accountability movement stems in part from the public's loss of confidence in education. Legislators (among others), upset by examples of students graduating from high school unable to read or compute, have demanded that schools establish higher standards and that students achieve them (McDermott, 2007).

The accountability movement has many critics, however (Rotberg, 2001; Shepard, 2000; Sirotnik, 2002; Thompson, 2001). Many argue that schools will teach only what is tested, emphasizing reading and mathematics at the expense of, for instance, science and social studies (Marx & Harris, 2006), and emphasizing easily measured objectives (such as punctuation) over more important hard-to-measure objectives (such as composition). Many educators point out that accountability assessments fail to take into account differences in the challenges faced by schools. A school or classroom might test low because the students are from disadvantaged backgrounds or do not yet speak English well rather than because they were given poor instruction. Students in high-poverty schools may have fewer opportunities to learn because their funding is often lower than that of other schools (Orfield & Kornhaber, 2001; Starratt, 2003). High student mobility, especially prevalent in low-SES urban areas, might mean that schools are held accountable for students they have only had for a few weeks or months. School performance year-to-year is unstable, and schools may be rewarded or punished based on minor variations of no statistical importance (Linn & Haug, 2002). High-stakes testing can lead schools and districts to try to adopt policies that artificially inflate scores by removing potentially low-scoring students from the testing pool, such as assigning more children to special education, categorizing more students as limited English proficient, or retaining more students (Booher-Jennings & Beveridge, 2007; Linn, 2000). Many observers have noted that teachers, under extraordinary pressure, sometimes use unethical strategies to increase students' scores (Cizek, 1999; Popham, 2005).

Several researchers (e.g., Amrein & Berliner, 2003; Bracey, 2003; Ellmore & Fuhrman, 2001; Neill, 2003) have questioned whether increased accountability actually leads to higher achievement. Carnoy and Loeb (2002) found only slight differences in NAEP score gains favoring states with strong accountability systems in comparisons with other states, whereas Neill and Gaylor (2001) and Amrein and Berliner (2003) found that states with strong accountability systems had *lower* gains on NAEP than did other states. Chicago studies of grade-to-grade promotion standards found higher student motivation (Roderick & Engel, 2001) and higher achievement (Roderick, Jacob, & Bryk, 2002) than before the standards were implemented.

Regardless of these criticisms, the demand for accountability is here to stay (Gandel & Vranek, 2001; Scherer, 2001). One advantage of accountability is that it does increase the pressure on schools and teachers to pay attention to students who might otherwise fall through the cracks and to help those who need help the most. States are increasingly reporting "disaggregated" scores, meaning that they are separately held accountable for gains of students of each ethnicity, limited English proficient students, and so on. This can focus school leaders on means of ensuring that all groups are making progress (Scheurich, Skrla, & Johnson, 2000). Another advantage is that accountability encourages schools to search out improved instructional methods and guarantees routine evaluation of any innovations schools try (Kennedy, 2003; Streifer, 2002; Gandel & McGiffert, 2003; Lane & Beebe-Frankenberger, 2004).

State accountability tests are based on state standards (Strong, Silver, & Perini, 2001). For a teacher, a principal, or a subject matter specialist, knowing what these standards are is a key to helping students achieve higher test performance (Carr & Harris, 2001). Goals that are understood are more likely to be reached than goals that are unclear.

The standards on which accountability tests are based are usually developed by diverse groups of stakeholders, including teachers, parents, employers, and researchers who express their judgments about what should be taught and learned. Through a consensus-building process, a state or district pools the thinking of educators and noneducators in defining the content domains it demands through its assessments. This process forces education leaders and policymakers to make clear what it is they want children to learn, which can then help them set policies in line with these objectives (Gandel & Vranek, 2001).

No Child Left Behind

The No Child Left Behind (NCLB) legislation is intended to move all children to success on their state standards by 2014. The assessment provisions of NCLB are as follows (see Center on Education Policy, 2003; The Education Trust, 2003; Stecher, Hamilton, & Gonzales, 2003; U.S. Department of Education, 2002).

1. ***Annual testing.*** All states must put in place annual tests of student performance, initially in reading and math, with science to be added eventually. Before NCLB, most states tested children for accountability purposes only in selected grades. Now, states must test in grades 3 through 8, plus one high school grade. Some states develop their own tests, some contract with companies to create customized tests, and some purchase commercial tests such as those described in this chapter.

2. ***Disaggregated reporting of scores.*** Under NCLB, states now must report test scores for each school according to each subgroup in the school: each ethnic group, students in special education, students in poverty, and limited English proficient students. There must be a minimum number of students in a given category for it to be considered a subgroup for NCLB, and this number varies widely from state to state. Schools and districts are held accountable for each subgroup, so it is no longer possible to look successful by succeeding on average if one or more subgroups are failing to make good progress.

3. ***Adequate yearly progress.*** All subgroups in all schools are now expected to make adequate yearly progress (AYP) on all state assessments. This is defined differently in each state, but in essence each subgroup must either be scoring at a high level or have an increasing percentage of students in all subgroups who score at the proficient level each year. Further, subgroups are not considered to be making adequate progress if there are too many missing students (to avoid situations in which schools fail to obtain tests from some low-achieving students). The AYP requirement is, for most schools, the most important aspect of NCLB, as it makes school and district leaders very anxious to ensure that every group is making progress.

"Well now, let's see who made adequate yearly progress this year . . ."

Personal REFLECTION

Mixed Messages

A friend recently told me about a decision by a local school board in her state that had outraged parents in the community, as well as state health education officials. The school district had decided to reduce recess time at all of the elementary schools in the district from 20 minutes each day to 10 minutes. School officials argued that the change was necessary in order to allow more time to help students focus on core academic courses and thereby help raise the district's testing scores.

My friend, a health advocate and former health education specialist, is outraged by the conflicting messages about child health she feels exist today. Daily we hear news reports about the growing concern over the general health of our nation's children, particularly with regard to obesity, asthma, and diabetes. Yet at the same time, each year more and more school districts reduce programs not considered part of the core curriculum, such as physical education and health education, all in the name of improving test scores and meeting the requirements of No Child Left Behind.

My friend worries that the focus on high-stakes testing will affect more than simply children's physical health. She wonders, also, about students' social development. Are we sacrificing important areas of children's development for the sake of test scores?

REFLECT ON THIS. What are some potential negative ramifications of cutbacks to noncore-curricular programs in schools? Who has to pick up the slack in these areas when schools no longer offer such programs? Do you think all communities are affected equally by such cutbacks, regardless of socioeconomic conditions?

4. ***Consequences for not meeting AYP.*** Schools with one or more subgroups not meeting their state's AYP standards may be subject to various consequences, depending on how many years they fail to meet AYP. Schools not meeting AYP for 2 years or more must offer their children supplemental educational services, usually small-group tutorials held after school or over the summer. Also, such schools are supposed to offer parents the opportunity to transfer their children to a more successful school, although in practice very few parents have taken advantage of this. As schools fail to meet AYP for more years, they may be subject to more severe consequences, eventually leading to the possibility of reconstitution (replacing the staff with a new staff), closure, or takeover by the state although these consequences are rarely applied in practice.

"Of course we still make time for art. Right now, for example, we're practicing shading in boxes."

Criticisms of NCLB Although the NCLB Act was supported by Republicans and Democrats (and by both candidates in the 2004 election), its accountability provisions have unleashed a firestorm of criticism from educators. Among the main criticisms:

1. ***Excessive and narrow testing.*** Many educators are concerned that NCLB continues a trend toward excessive testing of children on standardized, mostly multiple-choice tests (Popham, 2003; Sadker & Zittleman, 2004; Wasserman, 2001). In particular, because NCLB focuses on reading, math, and (soon) science, educators are concerned that social studies, art, music, and anything involving creativity or deep understanding will be pushed out (Wasserman, 2001). Elmore and Fuhrman (2001) have expressed concern about NCLB's excessive focus on testing and insufficient focus on building the capacity of teachers.

2. ***State-to-state variations in standards.*** Because NCLB leaves up to the states the testing, passing standards, and other elements that go into determining whether schools have met AYP, there is enormous

variation from state to state. For example, a study by the Northwest Evaluation Association (NWEA, 2003) found that an eighth-grader who performed at the proficient level in Montana would be at the 36th percentile on an NWEA exam, whereas a similar student in Wyoming would score at the 89th percentile on the same test. In addition, states vary in how many students are needed to constitute a subgroup, so states with high requirements (some require fifty students, some as few as five) may not be held accountable for their students in special education or other subgroups, whereas other states with identical test scores may have many schools not meeting AYP because they are accountable for a larger number of subgroups. As a result, some states have the majority of their schools not meeting AYP, whereas others have hardly any schools not meeting AYP. For example in 2004–2005, 28 percent of Florida schools and 97 percent of Oklahoma schools met AYP (Azzam, Parkins-Gough, & Thiers, 2006).

3. ***NCLB is underfunded.*** NCLB brought with it a substantial increase in federal education funding but far less than the amount many of its advocates had hoped (Center on Education Policy, 2004). The problem is that much of the new funding is taken up by the requirements for additional testing, supplemental educational services, and helping parents transfer their children to new schools. Clearly, meeting the ambitious goals of NCLB will require a significant investment (see Orfield & Kornhaber, 2001).

CONNECTIONS
See Chapter 4 for a description of the achievement gap between majority and minority students.

The reasons for this have nothing to do with the levels of achievement in each state but rather with the tests and procedures used. Some state tests are easier than others. Some states require a larger number of students in each subgroup in a school before that group's scores count toward AYP. Some states use "value added" methods that recognize progress toward state standards.

ON THE WEB

For a description of the basics and updated news on No Child Left Behind from the office of the U.S. Secretary of Education visit **www.nclb.gov.**

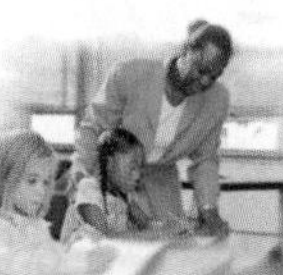

THEORY into PRACTICE

Teaching Test-Taking Skills

As standardized testing has taken on increasing importance in the evaluation of students, teachers, and schools, so too has the preparation of students to take these tests. Of course, the best way to prepare students for tests is to do a good job of teaching them the material. However, schools also need to help many students to become test-wise, to show what they really know on standardized tests, and to get as good a score as possible.

Many ethical issues are involved in helping students do well on standardized tests (Popham, 2008; Smith, 1991). For example, one way to help students score well would be to know the test items in advance and teach students the answers. Clearly, this would be cheating. A much more ethically ambiguous case arises when teachers know what subjects will be on the test and teach only material that they know will be tested. For example, if a standardized test did not assess Roman numerals, a math teacher might skip this topic to spend more time on an objective that would be tested. This practice is criticized as "teaching to the test." It could be argued that it is unfair to test students on material that they have not been taught and that instruction, therefore, should be closely aligned with tests (Popham, 2008). However, a standardized test can assess only a small sample of all objectives that are

CONNECTIONS
For more on teaching test-taking skills in the context of teaching metacognitive awareness and study skills, see Chapter 6, page 183.

taught in school. Gearing instruction toward the objectives that will be on the test, to the exclusion of all others, would produce a very narrow curriculum.

Because of the temptation to limit instruction to the content of upcoming tests, it is important to maintain test security. Specific items on a test should never be shared with teachers in advance of the administration date. Beyond matching instructional content with test objectives, there are many ways to help students learn to do well on tests in general. Research has found that students can be taught to be test-wise and that this increases their standardized test scores (Bangert-Drowns et al., 1991; Scruggs, White, & Bennion, 1986). Students can also be taught coping strategies to deal with their anxiety about testing. These strategies can sometimes help children approach tests with more confidence and less stress (Schutz & Davis, 2000; Zeidner, 1995).

Questions have been raised about the effectiveness of programs that prepare students for the SAT. Because the SAT measures cognitive skills, it is perhaps to be expected that instructional programs can improve scores. The consensus among researchers is that coaching (especially long-term coaching) is effective for the SAT, particularly for minority and low-achieving students (Becker, 1990; Messick, 1982) when it focuses on the skills the SAT measures.

Some ways of helping students to prepare for standardized tests follow (see Hill & Wigfield, 1984):

1. Give students practice with similar item formats. For example, if a test will use multiple-choice formats, give students practice with similar formats in routine classroom quizzes and tests. If a test will use an unusual format such as verbal analogies (e.g., Big:Small::Honest:____), give students practice with this type of item.
2. Suggest that students skip over difficult or time-consuming items and return to them later.
3. If there is no penalty for guessing on a test, suggest to students that they always fill in some answer. If there is a penalty for guessing, students should still be encouraged to guess, especially if they can narrow down the options by eliminating one or more choices.
4. Suggest that students read all options on a multiple-choice test before choosing one. Sometimes more than one answer is correct but only one of them will be the better answer.
5. Suggest to students that they use all available time. If they finish early, they should go back over their answers.

Impacts of NCLB **No Child Left Behind (NCLB)** has significantly changed the landscape of American education. Jennings and Rentner (2006) described 10 "big effects" of NCLB, drawn from their surveys at the Center for Education Policy.

1. ***State and district officials report rising achievement on state tests, but it is not clear if this is meaningful.*** A survey found that three-quarters of state and district officials claimed that their state test scores in reading and math were going up. However, for 20 years state test scores have gone up in most states, whereas the National Assessment of Academic Progress (NAEP) remains unchanged, especially in reading.

2. ***Schools are spending more time on reading and math, sometimes at the expense of subjects not tested.*** Because NCLB accountability focuses only on reading and math, many schools (71 percent, according to Jennings and Rentner, 2006) are reducing time in other subjects, such as social studies and science.

No Child Left Behind (NCLB)
Federal legislation that requires annual testing in grades 3 through 8 plus high school requires schools to make adequate yearly progress, and provides assistance to schools not meeting standards.

3. ***Schools are paying much more attention to test scores and alignment.*** School leaders are learning to watch their test scores carefully and to try to get teachers to

focus their instruction on the objectives and even the test formats most likely to be on the state test.

4. ***Low-performing schools are undergoing makeovers rather than radical restructuring.*** NCLB anticipated that schools that fail to make adequate yearly progress would make major changes, from adopting new schoolwide reform models to complete reconstitution. This has not happened yet. Instead, most schools continue to muddle through, making modest improvements in hopes of better luck next time.

5. ***Teachers have made progress in demonstrating academic qualifications.*** NCLB has also introduced minimum standards for qualifications of teachers and instructional aides. For Title I teachers this means holding at least a bachelor's degree and demonstrating subject area competency (Berry, Hoke, & Hirsch, 2004; Rebell & Hunter, 2004; U.S. Department of Education, 2002). Unavailability of highly qualified teachers, especially in inner-city and rural areas, hinder administrators' attempts to meet this requirement, and a survey by the Center on Education Policy (2007) found that this part of NCLB is not perceived by state officials to be working.

6. ***Students are taking a lot more tests.*** To comply with NCLB, all states must test annually in grades 3 through 8, plus one high school year (usually 11). Previously, most states had only tested in selected grades. In addition, pressure to improve end-of-year test scores has led to the rapidly increasing use of benchmark assessments, tests given three to five times per year to give educators information about how well their students are likely to do on state assessments.

7. ***Schools are paying much more attention to the achievement of particular groups of students.*** Under NCLB, schools are held accountable for the achievement of each of several subgroups of students: African American, Hispanic, and white students; students in special education; and low-income students. Because of this, school leaders report paying a lot more attention to the scores of each of these groups (see Haycock, 2006). This provision of NCLB has also led to a great deal of controversy about assessment of students with disabilities and of English language learners.

8. ***The percentage of schools on state "needs improvement" lists has remained steady; it is not growing.*** About 10 percent of all schools have been designated as being "in need of improvement," which means that they have not met their adequate yearly progress goals for two years in a row. This number of schools has remained constant in most states, with schools being added to and dropping off the list each year. However, states vary widely in the percentages of schools meeting standards because of substantial differences in the difficulty of their tests and their procedures for computing adequate yearly progress.

Under NCLB, students in schools in need of improvement were to be given the opportunity to transfer to more successful schools. This generally is not happening; only 2 percent of eligible students have transferred to new schools. Students in schools in need of improvement are also eligible for "supplemental educational services," usually after-school instruction in small groups. Only 20 percent of eligible students are taking advantage of these services. School leaders are skeptical about the benefits of both of these remedies.

9. ***The federal government is playing a more significant role in education.*** According to the U.S. Constitution, education is a state responsibility, and by tradition it is a local responsibility. NCLB has enormously increased the federal government's involvement in education at all levels, and the U.S. Department of Education is seen to be strictly enforcing the provisions of NCLB.

10. ***Under NCLB, states and districts have expanded roles in the operation of individual schools, but inadequate funds to carry out their new duties.*** State departments of education have increased responsibilities to monitor compliance with NCLB and to help schools and districts in need of improvement. Districts also have an increased role. However, neither states nor districts have received sufficient funding to perform their new roles adequately. Still, NCLB has led to diminished authority and autonomy for principals and school staffs, while increasing district and state authority.

ON THE WEB

For more on the Center for Education Policy's surveys of No Child Left Behind, see **www.cep-dc.org.**

For the official U.S. Department of Education site on NCLB, see **www.ed.gov/nclb/landing.jhtml.**

For criticisms of NCLB, see **http://nochildleft.com; www.educationsector.org.**

The bottom line is that NCLB is greatly increasing accountability pressures on schools, districts, and states. It remains to be seen whether this truly will be beneficial to students. Early indicators suggest that progress on NAEP has not increased since NCLB went into effect (Bracey, 2006; Fuller, Wright, Gesicki, & Kang, 2007), although there have been some gains on state tests (Center on Education Policy, 2007). Overall, *Time* magazine gave NCLB an F in helping schools to improve (Wallis & Steptoe, 2007) but praised its focus on accountability for all students.

Benchmark Assessments

In test-obsessed American schools, you'd think the last thing we'd need is more tests. Yet from coast to coast, the hottest innovation going is just that: **benchmark assessments** that assess children three, five, or even eight times a year, usually in reading and math.

The popularity of benchmark assessments is easy to understand. NCLB has increased the already substantial pressure on schools to improve scores on their state tests. Yet state tests are given too infrequently and the scores arrive too late to be of much use in adjusting instructional policies or practices. For example, most states test in the spring. By the time scores are reported, it is summer or fall. A school might find out in July that its math scores are in trouble. Yet by July, schools have already committed their resources and made their plans for the coming year. Information from fourth-grade test scores, for example, cannot benefit the fourth-graders who took the test and may be too late to be of much value to the next group of fourth-graders as well.

Educators have long understood this problem and have long looked for solutions. In the 1970s, Benjamin Bloom's (1976) mastery learning strategies depended on "formative assessments," low-stakes tests to tell teachers whether their students are headed toward mastery of "summative assessments." Today, a wide array of benchmark assessments designed to give educators useful early information on students' progress are available. Many districts and even individual teachers have designed and used their own benchmark assessments. Benchmark assessments allow educators to identify how each student, class, subgroup, and school is doing on each of the objectives assessed by the state and emphasized in state and district standards, so they can target professional development and reform where they are needed most.

Benchmark assessments can allow schools to take their achievement "pulse," but as in medicine, taking a pulse does not constitute a cure. It's what the doctor and patient do next that matters. Similarly, a benchmark assessment tells schools where they're headed and where they need to focus, but use of benchmark assessments has not yet been shown in itself to increase student achievement.

Benchmark assessments are useful tools in the hands of enlightened educators, but they are nothing more than indicators of children's current achievement. As part of a comprehensive strategy for district and school reform, benchmark assessments can play a key supporting role, but only a supporting role. If we're going to take even more of our children's precious class time for testing, we must use the results intelligently and proactively to improve core teaching and learning.

benchmark assessments
Brief tests given every few months to help educators know whether students are on track toward success on state standards.

data-driven reform
School reform strategies emphasizing careful analysis of data and implementation of proven programs to strengthen areas of need.

Data-Driven Reform

The movement toward the use of benchmark assessments is part of a broader trend toward using data to drive reforms in schools and districts. **Data-driven reform** goes beyond simply looking at scores on state tests. School leaders involved in such reforms organize information from state tests and benchmark assessments by subskill, subgroup, grade level, and other categories; and add information on attendance, dropout programs in use in schools, and so on to find "root causes" for the school's problems. They then carefully consider potential solutions to their problems, ideally programs with strong evidence of effectiveness (see Coalition for Evidence Based Policy, 2003; Slavin, 2002; Towne, Wise, & Winters, 2005), implement those solutions, and then continue to monitor benchmark and test data to see that they are working.

Heritage and Chen (2005) discuss an approach to data-driven reform that uses a Web-based tool called the Quality School Portfolio (QSP) to help school leaders organize and make sense of data. They then describe a process for using data to guide school reform:

1. ***Determine what you want to know.*** Data-based reform should begin with a problem that the educators involved want to solve or a question they want answered. No one pays attention to data that do not tell them something they want to know.

2. ***Collect data.*** Educators involved in data-based reform organize existing data and collect new data to answer the questions they posed. The data could include state and benchmark tests, additional assessments (such as writing or math problem-solving assessments not part of the state test), information on materials and programs being used by teachers, teachers' and students' attitudes, or whatever else might inform decisions about reforms being considered (Bernhardt, 2003, 2005).

3. ***Analyze results.*** The next step is to organize the data, first simply computing averages and then using the data to test ideas about what is causing the problems the school is trying to solve. For example, imagine that a school has lower math scores than it likes. A school committee reviews the state test scores and quarterly benchmark scores, and they all tell the same story: Scores are low, and not improving. Could it be that the teachers are not focusing on all skills tested? The committee looks at scores on portions of the test (e.g., fractions, geometry, word problems) and finds that the scores are low across the board. Could the problem be isolated to certain subgroups? The committee looks at scores for boys and girls, African Americans, Hispanics, and whites. They see one surprising pattern: Girls seem to be doing particularly poorly. The committee arranges to visit classes and see what is happening. When they return to discuss their findings, they have a whole new perspective on the data. Teachers throughout the school are making extensive use of traditional lectures and problem solving, as suggested by their textbooks. In many classes, an aggressive group of boys dominates the discussions, whereas most girls are bored and feel left out of the class activities. They found classes in which most girls never participated and did not say a single thing in a 50-minute lesson. Linking their quantitative data with their observations, the committee decided that the problem might be that teaching methods were not engaging all students.

4. ***Set priorities and goals.*** In data-based reform, it is not enough simply to know the data. The school must take action based on the data. This begins with setting priorities and goals for solutions the school might try. The goals should be measurable, focused on student achievement, realistic, and attainable (Bernhardt, 2005). In the case of the school with the math problem, the committee set a goal of improving the math performance of all students, with a particular focus on the girls, and set up a plan to closely monitor quarterly benchmark data.

5. ***Develop strategies.*** The most important step in data-driven reform is to develop specific strategies to solve identified problems. School leaders need to consider potential solutions for the problems they have observed. For example, to solve an achievement problem, the school might look at the federal What Works Clearinghouse (2007) or the *Best Evidence Encyclopedia* (Center for Data-Driven Reform in Education, 2006), both of which summarize scientific reviews of research on educational programs for grades pre-K to 12.

In the case of the school with the math problem, committee members looked at the *Best Evidence Encyclopedia* (2006) and found that there was good evidence for cooperative learning in elementary math. They reasoned that this could increase the participation of all students. They found a local trainer who trained the teachers to use cooperative learning in math, and over time, they began to see their math benchmark scores improve. Later, when the state test scores came back, the committee was glad to see that math scores had improved for all students, but especially for girls, who were now fully engaged with math in all classrooms.

ON THE WEB

For more on data-driven reform, see

What Works Clearinghouse: **www.whatworks.ed.gov**

Best Evidence Encyclopedia: **www.bestevidence.org**

Center for Data-Driven Reform in Education: **www.cddre.org**

Center for Research on Evaluation, Standards, and Student Testing (CRESST): **www.cse.ucla.edu**

Accommodations for Students with Disabilities

How should students with disabilities participate in standardized testing? This question has taken on greater importance under No Child Left Behind, which requires progress in test scores for students with disabilities as a subgroup for schools to meet their adequate yearly progress standards.

Some kinds of accommodations, such as enlarging text for students with vision problems, are not controversial. Far more controversial are accommodations for students with learning disabilities, such as extending testing time and reading items to students. A review of many studies by Sireci, Scarpati, and Li (2005) examined research on the effects of various accommodations. They found that extending testing time increased scores for all students (not only those with disabilities), although students with disabilities benefitted more than other students. Reading items to students, however, was primarily beneficial to students with disabilities. Given these findings, it is important for policymakers to establish clear guidelines in accountability systems for when accommodations may and may not be used, to avoid biasing scores one way or the other.

Contamination of Accountability Systems

A recent article by McGill-Franzen and Allington (2006) expresses concern that the accountability pressure central to NCLB is causing state accountability tests to be "contaminated." They document several types of contamination (also see Popham, 2005):

1. ***Flunking.*** Retention rates have risen dramatically in recent years. Texas held back 12,000 third-graders recently, Florida held back 24,000, New York City failed 16,000 third-graders, and Miami had 2,000 students in third grade for the third time.

There is considerable debate about whether retention in grade is good or bad for low-achieving students. Most research finds it harmful (e.g., Shepard & Smith, 1989). However, it is clear that increasing retentions changes the meaning of assessment systems. Third-grade norms are based on the assumption that the children taking the tests are 9 years old. Holding students back means that a lot of 10- and 11-year-olds are taking the test. To understand this further, imagine that a Miami student scores 20 percent on a state test in third grade and is retained. The next year, he scores 40 percent, and is retained again. The third time, he scores 60 percent. Has he improved? Of course not. His former classmates are taking the fifth-grade test by now. If the student had passed

ONLINE READING & WRITING EXERCISE

Students Against Testing

Access this exercise, entitled "Students Against Testing," in the Homework and Exercises section for Chapter 14 of this text at **www.mylabschool.com**.

each year, he'd probably be scoring 20 percent in fifth grade, too, but instead, his increases (simply because he is getting older) look like test score gains, which the state and district proudly report in the newspaper.

2. ***Test preparation.*** Accountability pressure causes many schools to spend a lot of time teaching students how to take tests. Up to a point, there is nothing wrong with helping students know how to be strategic test takers, but in some schools "test prep" goes on all the time, pushing out more important learning.

3. ***Inappropriate accommodations for students with disabilities.*** Because students in special education have to make adequate yearly progress gains if their schools are to escape NCLB sanctions, educators are especially concerned about the performance of this group, as noted earlier. NCLB allows for appropriate accommodations for students with disabilities, but there are many documented cases of inappropriate accommodations, such as reading tests to students with reading difficulties.

4. ***Narrowing the curriculum.*** Because reading and math scores are the criteria for adequate yearly progress, many schools worried about their test scores are increasing time for these subjects and reducing time for social studies, science, art, and other subjects (see Cawelti, 2006; Guilfoyle, 2006).

BUILDING TEACHING SKILLS READING EXERCISE

A Guide to Standardized Writing Assessment (Doug Baldwin)

Go to **www.myeducationlab.com** and, in the Homework and Exercises section for Chapter 14 of this text, access the article by Doug Baldwin entitled "A Guide to Standardized Writing Assessment." Read the article and complete the homework questions that accompany it, saving your work or transmitting it to your professor as required.

CHAPTER 14 SUMMARY

What Are Standardized Tests and How Are They Used?

The term *standardized* describes tests that are uniform in content, administration, and scoring and, therefore, allow for the comparison of results across classrooms, schools, and school districts. Standardized tests such as the SAT and CTBS measure individual performance or ability against standards, or norms, that have been established for many other students in the school district, state, or nation for which each test was designed. Standardized test scores are used for selection and placement, such as grade promotion or college admission; for diagnosis and remediation; for evaluation of student proficiency or progress in content areas; and for evaluation of teaching strategies, teachers, and schools.

What Types of Standardized Tests Are Given?

Aptitude tests, such as tests of general intelligence and multifactor batteries, predict students' general abilities and preparation to learn. IQ tests administered to individuals or groups attempt to measure individual aptitude in the cognitive domain. Achievement tests assess student proficiency in various subject areas. Diagnostic tests focus on specific subject matter to discover strengths or weaknesses in mastery. Norm-referenced testing interprets scores in comparison with the scores of other people who took the test, and criterion-referenced testing interprets scores based on fixed performance criteria.

How Are Standardized Tests Interpreted?

Scores that are derived from raw scores include percentiles, the percentage of scores in the norming group that fall below a particular score; grade equivalents, the grade and month at which a particular score is thought to represent typical performance; and standard scores, the students' performance in relation to the normal distribution of scores. Standard scores include stanines (based on the standard deviation of scores), normal curve equivalents (based on a comparison of scores with the normal distribution), and z-scores (the location of scores above or below the mean).

The Intentional TEACHER

USING WHAT YOU KNOW about Standardized Tests to Improve Teaching and Learning

Intentional teachers know that standardized tests can provide some—albeit limited—information about how teachers, schools, and students are performing. They can interpret standardized scores and use results from standardized tests for decision making. Intentional teachers rely on other assessment measures to complete the complicated picture of student learning.

1 What do I expect my students to know and be able to do at the end of this lesson? How does this contribute to course objectives and to students' needs to become capable individuals?

Teachers do well to explore the role of standardized testing in their locale. Talk with experienced colleagues and your administrators to determine the extent to which standardized tests play a role in your professional practice. Ask about district and local expectations for your use of standardized tests. Imagine that after a lunchtime conversation with some experienced peers, you (a first-year teacher in this district) perceive a sense of urgency surrounding standardized testing in this district. Knowing that parents and community members are highly interested in year-end results, you might take some time to reflect on your own position on standardized testing. You might ask yourself, "To what extent do standardized tests measure what we value here? What information do standardized tests provide that can be useful to my school? How do we continue to teach complex thinking and still help our students prepare for tests?" You might call your experienced colleagues and arrange a second lunch date to discuss your answers to tough questions such as these.

2 What knowledge, skills, needs, and interests do my students have that must be taken into account in my lesson?

Teachers can use formal, standardized tests to provide information about their students' needs. Consider the use of diagnostic tests to identify learning problems and cognitive strengths. For example, imagine that Mindy reads at a level that appears to be far above that of her peers. She gives sophisticated analyses of the stories she reads, and although she is a willing learner, she sometimes appears bored with the curriculum. You might call the school psychologist to learn the procedure for obtaining formal testing to determine whether special services for students who are gifted and talented would be appropriate for Mindy.

3 What do I know about the content, child development, learning, motivation, and effective teaching strategies that I can use to accomplish my objectives?

The assessments that teachers use should provide information about each of their students in several domains. Ask yourself about one of your students—pick one at random—and

What Are Some Issues Concerning Standardized and Classroom Testing?

Tests and test items must have validity, the quality of testing what is intended to be tested. Predictive validity means that the test accurately predicts future performance. Reliability means that test results are consistent when the test is administered at different places or times. Test bias in any form compromises validity. Other issues related to standardized testing include ethics in the content of tests, student preparation for testing, the uses of test scores, the relationship of tests to the curriculum, and computer administration of tests.

How Are Educators Held Accountable for Student Achievement?

Educators are increasingly held accountable for student achievement. Test scores are often used in decisions about hiring, firing, and promoting educators. Critics say that holding teachers accountable for student gains is unfair because of different student starting points and may encourage teaching to the test or adopting policies that artificially inflate standardized scores. An advantage of accountability is that it increases pressures on schools to pay attention to students who might otherwise fall through the cracks. Because accountability tests are based on standards about what should be learned, they can help clarify learning objectives.

consider how much you understand about this student's progress. Adjust your use of standardized tests, grades, and other assessment measures to provide more complete information about student learning. Although you might have taken a quick glance at each of your students' standardized scores from the previous year and you have your gradebook filled with letter grades at hand, you might still find yourself unable to give an accurate, trustworthy picture of many students' efforts to date. To round out your understanding of student learning, you could resolve to collect performance-based data through observations and attitudinal data through journal entries and interest inventories.

4 What instructional materials, technology, assistance, and other resources are available to help accomplish my objectives?

The public is increasingly interested in maintaining teachers' and schools' accountability. Check current sources such as your school's annual statement and newspaper reports to determine public perceptions of your success. To what extent do you consider public information a valid measure of schools' (and your!) success? Imagine that a recent newspaper article puts your mean students' districtwide performance at the 48th percentile. The headline of the article is "PLEASANT CITY'S SEVENTH-GRADERS SCORE WELL ON STANDARDIZED TESTS!" How should you interpret this?

5 How will I plan to assess students' progress toward my objectives?

Teachers should be careful consumers when using standardized measures. Check information related to the content, predictive, and construct validity of the tests employed in your district. Ask for information related to test bias. If the information booklet that accompanies the teacher's packet on the statewide test does not provide information about test bias, call the question hot line and ask how the authors have screened for bias against students from minority groups and students acquiring English.

6 How will I respond if individual children or the class as a whole are not on track toward success? What is my back-up plan?

If your students take a standardized test that has consequences for them (such as grade-to-grade promotion), make sure to examine test scores to make sure that they make sense. If a test score seems too low for a student who you see doing well in class, ask if the student can be retested, perhaps using a different test format.

KEY TERMS

Review the following key terms from the chapter.

achievement batteries 462
achievement tests 459
aptitude test 459
benchmark assessments 484
bias 475
chronological age 460
computer-adaptive 477
concurrent evidence 474
content evidence 473
criterion-related evidence 473
cutoff score 463
data-driven reform 484
derived scores 463
diagnostic tests 462
discriminant evidence 474
grade-equivalent scores 464
intelligence 460
mental age 460
multifactor aptitude battery 462
No Child Left Behind (NCLB) 482
normal curve equivalent 467
normal distribution 465

norms 457
percentile score 464
predictive evidence 473
reliability 475
standard deviation 465
standardized tests 457
stanine score 466
validity 473
z-score 467

SELF-ASSESSMENT: PRACTICING *for* LICENSURE

Directions: The chapter-opening vignette addresses indicators that are often assessed in state licensure exams. Re-read the chapter-opening vignette, and then respond to the following questions.

1. Ms. Tranh speaks to Anita's parents about the many measures of achievement she has to assess Anita's academic ability. Which of the following types of assessment would Ms. Tranh use to predict Anita's future performance?
   - **a.** placement test
   - **b.** achievement test
   - **c.** aptitude test
   - **d.** diagnostic test

2. Which of the following interpretations would Ms. Tranh make if Anita were to score at the mean of a standardized test?
   - **a.** percentile = 90, stanine = 0, $z = 20$
   - **b.** NCE = 50, $z = 0$, percentile = 50
   - **c.** GE = 7.2, stanine = 5, NCE = 45
   - **d.** $z = 1$, NCE = 60, percentile = 50

3. Ms. Tranh tells Mr. and Mrs. McKay that Anita's grade equivalent score on the CAT is 6.9. What does this mean?
   - **a.** Anita is almost ready for seventh-grade work.
   - **b.** Anita found the test very easy.
   - **c.** Anita has done as well as an end-of-year sixth-grader.
   - **d.** Anita scored at the 6.9 percentile.

4. Ms. Tranh compares her students' scores on a math test with those of another class. She finds that the students' average score in both classes is 75, but the students in her class have scores that are much more spread out. This means that Ms. Tranh's results will have a larger
   - **a.** mean.
   - **b.** median.
   - **c.** standard deviation.
   - **d.** normal curve.

5. If Anita scored consistently on the CAT over multiple applications, it can be said that the test has
   - **a.** predictive validity.
   - **b.** content validity.
   - **c.** construct validity.
   - **d.** reliability.

6. Write a short essay describing the advantages and major criticisms of standardized tests.

7. What are the advantages and disadvantages of absolute grading and relative grading standards?

PEARSON

myeducationlab™

Where the Classroom Comes to Life

Now go to **www.myeducationlab.com** to:

- take a Pretest to assess your initial comprehension of chapter content;
- study chapter content with your individualized Study Plan;
- take a Posttest to assess your understanding of chapter content;
- practice your teaching skills with Building Teaching Skills exercises; and
- build a deeper, more applied understanding of chapter content with Homework and Exercises.

APPENDIX
Developing Your Portfolio

What Is a Portfolio?

A portfolio is not merely a file of course projects and assignments, nor is it a scrapbook of teaching memorabilia. A portfolio is an organized, goal-driven documentation of your professional growth and achieved competence in the complex act called teaching. Although it is a collection of documents, a portfolio is tangible evidence of the wide range of knowledge, dispositions, and skills that you possess as a growing professional. What's more, documents in the portfolio are self-selected, reflecting your individuality and autonomy.

There are actually two kinds of portfolios that you will be developing: a working portfolio and a presentation portfolio. A working portfolio is characterized by your ongoing systematic collection of selected work in courses and evidence of community activities. This collection would form a framework for self-assessment and goal setting. Later, you would develop a presentation portfolio by winnowing your collection to samples of your work that best reflect your achieved competence, individuality, and creativity as a professional educator.

What Is a Working Portfolio? A working portfolio is always much larger and more complete than a presentation portfolio. It contains unabridged versions of the documents you have carefully selected to portray your professional growth. For example, it might contain entire reflective journals, complete units, unique teacher-made materials, and a collection of videos of your teaching. Working portfolios are often stored in a combination of computer disks, notebooks, and even boxes.

What Is a Presentation Portfolio? A presentation portfolio is compiled for the expressed purpose of giving others an effective and easy-to-read portrait of your professional competence. A presentation portfolio is selective and streamlined because other people usually do not have the time to review all the material in your working portfolio. In making a presentation portfolio, you will find that less is more. For example, since you would be unlikely to take to an interview all your teacher-made learning materials, you might rely on photographs. Most reviewers would not want to assess several videos of your teaching but would be interested in one well-edited and annotated video. Sample pages from a large project would replace an entire project. The two types of portfolios differ in that all documents in a presentation portfolio should be preceded by an explanation of the importance or relevance of the document so that the reviewer understands the context of your work. Because it is important that a presentation portfolio not be cumbersome or unwieldy, we recommend the use of a notebook.

Excerpted from Dorothy M. Campbell et al. (2001). *How to Develop a Professional Portfolio: A Manual for Teachers* (2nd ed.). Boston: Allyn & Bacon.

How Do I Organize My Portfolio?

There is one essential way in which working portfolios and presentation portfolios are alike. From their inception, both need to have a well-established organizational system. There is no one standard way to organize a portfolio, but to be effective it must have a system of organization that is understandable and meaningful to you and other educators. We suggest organizing your portfolio around a set of goals you are trying to achieve. This makes sense when one of your purposes for a portfolio is to demonstrate to others that you are achieving success in meeting standards set for excellence in the teaching profession.

Many professional organizations are setting goals for the teachers of the twenty-first century. These organizations include state departments of education, professional societies such as the National Association for the Education of Young Children or the National Council of Teachers of Mathematics, interagency groups, and university schools of education. The professional goals established by these organizations are called by a variety of names, including standards, principles, performance domains, outcomes, and competencies. They are all attempts to reflect the knowledge, skills, and dispositions that define excellent teachers and therefore are goals for you as a preservice teacher to achieve.

You should become familiar with a number of documents that outline sets of standards for your discipline, your state, and your own university department. As you study these standards, choose or adapt a set of goals that makes sense to you in your particular situation. Regardless of the goals or standards chosen, everything collected for your portfolio should be organized around the chosen goal statements.

What Evidence Should I Include in My Portfolio?

For every standard, you will include artifacts that demonstrate you have met this principle. An artifact is tangible evidence of knowledge that is gained, skills that are mastered, values that are clarified, or dispositions and attitudes that are characteristic of you. Artifacts cannot conclusively prove the attainment of knowledge, skills, or dispositions, but they provide indicators of achieved competence. For example, lesson and unit plans are pieces of evidence that might provide strong indication of your ability to plan curriculum or use a variety of teaching strategies. A video of your teaching might be a convincing indicator of your ability to manage and motivate a group of students. The same artifact may document more than one standard. At first, many artifacts will be collected. Later, artifacts will be selectively placed within each of the standards. Those artifacts that represent your growth and very best professional work should be included as evidence in your professional portfolio. Ask yourself: Would I be proud to have my future employer and peer group see this? Is this an example of what my future professional work might look like? Does this represent what I stand for as a professional educator? If not, what can I do to revise or rearrange so that it represents my best efforts?

Who Is the Audience for My Portfolio?

Information contained in the portfolio will be of interest to individuals who will be assessing your performance and measuring your accountability. While a student, your portfolio will be reviewed by your university faculty and advisors. Moreover, your portfolio will be an excellent way for you to introduce yourself to cooperating teachers and administrators during field experiences and student teaching. During job interviews, your portfolio is likely to be reviewed by superintendents, principals, teachers, and in some cases even school board members. As you begin your teaching career, your portfolio will be a helpful vehicle for mentors, in-service education coordinators, and other colleagues. In some school districts, a portfolio will be relied on by supervisory staff charting ongoing career development or making tenure and promotion decisions. There is also a good possibility that your portfolio will one day be used to facilitate licensing by professional organizations, state agencies, or national consortiums. Most importantly, the portfolio provides you, the author, with an informative and accurate picture of your professional development and growth.

What Are Some Artifact Possibilities?

Article Summaries or Critiques You may have written a summary or evaluation of an article from a professional journal as a class assignment. When including these in your portfolio, choose critiques that address the desired topic very specifically. The title of the article should be reflective of a chosen standard, making an obvious connection. This document is especially helpful if your professor has made positive remarks about your work and these remarks are about the outcome you wish to document.

The article summary or critique may show your ability to analyze any number of teaching skills. For example, suppose you critiqued an article titled "Getting Parents Involved in Their Children's Education." If you discussed your own ideas about parent involvement in your critique, this document may be able to reflect your knowledge of school-home-community cooperation.

Assessments Any forms of assessment you have used or developed to measure child performance would be included in this type of document. Examples of assessments are performance tasks, portfolios, teacher-written tests, informal observations or notes, evaluations from lesson plans, formative assessment notes or charts, and summative charts of student developmental levels. You may want to include the actual assessment instrument you have written, with the children's work on it, if applicable (only one copy is necessary). In addition, you may include notes in a personal journal from observations made during the administration of a standardized test. Your ability to assess children's performance, diagnose progress, and use tests wisely is reflected in this document. In addition, your understanding of child development may be evident.

Awards and Certificates Copies of letters, awards, or certificates that verify your outstanding contribution to the field of education fit in this category. These could include honors conferred, memberships in honorary professional organizations, community recognition, and volunteer recognition. Your professional commitment is reflected in these types of documents.

Bulletin Board Ideas After creating a bulletin board, make a copy of your design or take a photograph of the board. Make sure all spelling, punctuation, and grammar are standard English. This document can be used to show your ability to think creatively, use materials in interesting ways, or motivate students.

Case Studies A case study is a thorough examination of a student's growth over a period of time. When using this as a document, make sure the student is anonymous. Generally, case studies are quite long; therefore, you may want to include a specific part of the paper for documentation of a standard. Your knowledge of child development as well as your observation skills may be evident in this document.

Classroom Management Philosophy This is a written summary of your philosophy of classroom management. Make sure to cite the research and theories that have guided you in the way you influence student behavior and encourage development of self-control. Classroom management skills and knowledge of human development are evident in this document.

Computer Programs This includes examples of various programs you have utilized, developed, or incorporated in your teaching that provide evidence of your ability to use materials in a challenging and appropriate way to encourage active learning.

Also appropriate are programs that demonstrate your ability to conduct online searches and research. Examples include ERIC, Education Index, and Internet programs that link teachers worldwide. You can document your abilities by providing the hard copies of these searches along with an explanation of the reason for your computer searches. These documents reflect your willingness to seek further professional growth.

Cooperative Learning Strategies Have you planned or taught a lesson using a cooperative learning technique? Cooperative learning is a method of teaching in which students work collaboratively in small groups to solve a problem. This type of group work must be obvious in your lesson. You may want to include a copy of the lesson plan and, if the lesson was actually taught, a statement assessing the effectiveness of the cooperative learning technique. This will document your ability to use cooperative learning as a strategy as well as your ability to manage and motivate a class of students.

Curriculum Plans These documents are written plans, or programs, or both designed to organize curriculum. Your curriculum plans can reflect all experiences you have developed for the child while engaged in the process of schooling. Examples may include lesson plans, units, thematic units, learning centers, extracurricular programs, or school–community ventures. These documents portray your instructional planning skills or your ability to use many and varied instructional strategies.

Essays You can use papers from education courses, English composition, or any other class in which you were required to write an essay. Examine the topic you addressed in your paper to be sure its main idea reflects one of the standards you are using.

Goal Statements Professional goals are based on your needs, interests, philosophy of education, and perception of your role as a teacher. Goal statements assist you in determining where you want to be and provide you with information about how to get there.

Think about the important results you should accomplish in your role as a teacher and record these as goal statements. Remember that any short-term goals you establish should be tied to the longer-term goals you have identified in conjunction with your philosophy of education. Periodically review and evaluate your accomplishments in relation to your goal statements. You may wish to list your accomplishments associated with each goal. You will establish new goals as you refine your philosophy of education, your role as a teacher, and your expectations. It is important to keep your list of goal statements current. These statements might appear at the beginning of your portfolio or as documentation of your professional commitment.

Individualized Plans Children with special needs sometimes need tasks to be structured in ways that will allow them to use their strengths and compensate for their specific learning difficulties. Ways in which lesson and unit plans have been adapted for specific students should be documented. Make sure the learning need is defined and clearly addressed. This artifact could document your skills in meeting individual needs, your instructional strategies skills, and your knowledge of child development.

Journals You may have kept journals during field classes or observation assignments. Include them if they address your observations of students as they relate to the desired standard. If necessary, highlight the appropriate sections of the journals. Make sure dates and times are included but not the names of schools or teachers visited.

Lesson Plans Copies of your lesson plans should include all components of a workable plan: objectives, materials, introduction, procedures, closing, and evaluation.

Sometimes plans may be used for more than one standard. In this case, highlight the specific part of the plan that documents the standard. Your ability to execute instructional planning and to use a variety of instructional strategies will be most obviously documented with lesson plans; however, it is possible that knowledge of content, use of environments and materials, communication skills, and knowledge of human development could be documented here.

Media Competencies This type of document includes evidence and descriptions of the various forms of media you are able to incorporate in your instruction. This could include teaching resources such as the slide projector, camcorder and VCR, overhead projector, 16mm projector, computers and printers, interactive video, laser discs, and cable and electronic (educational) television.

You will also want to include evidence of your ability to incorporate technology into the classroom. Examples of how you have used e-mail, remote databases, and distance learning equipment to research and to communicate with students and colleagues regionally, nationally, and internationally should be highlighted. A printout or floppy disk of your Internet address(es), listing of professional online news group and listserv memberships you hold, and examples of printed texts will provide documentation of your ability to share and retrieve information via the Internet.

Projects Projects can include any type of assignment that involves problem solving, group presentations, creating materials, investigating phenomena in classrooms, or researching current information. In a presentation portfolio, include paper copies only and make photographs of anything too large to fit in a notebook. If this is a group project, make that clear but indicate the extent of your input. (Be careful about this one; it is not helpful to brag about doing all the work.)

The documentation possibilities of this artifact depend on the project. Examine the standards to determine whether the project reflects instructional planning skills, professional commitment, the ability to meet individual needs, or knowledge of content.

References References might include statements, evaluations, or both, from your supervisors of your academic work, experiences in the classroom, other work experience with children, or outside employment.

Try to connect the reference with one of your selected standards. For instance, the reference might describe a lesson you taught in a field course or in student teaching. You could use this document to illustrate your competence in the area of instructional strategies. In addition, you may want to place reference letters from your cooperating teachers in a special tabbed section of the portfolio.

Research Papers When selecting a research paper to include in your portfolio, you will need to consider several factors. The content of the research paper might make it appropriate for inclusion under a particular standard. It might, for instance, highlight your knowledge of an academic subject.

Subscriptions If you subscribe to a journal that specifically addresses the standard in its title, include a copy of the cover of the journal, along with the address label showing your name. You might also briefly mention any ideas, instructional techniques, or other helpful information you gathered from reading the journal. Generally, professional commitment is well documented with subscriptions; however, you may find other standards to document with this artifact, depending on the type of journal to which you subscribe.

Teacher-Made Materials These materials may include games, manipulatives, puppets, big books, charts, videotapes, films, photographs, transparencies, teaching aids, costumes, posters, or artwork. Because many of these items are cumbersome, include only paper copies or photographs of the materials. If you do not have copies of the actual materials you have made, you may want to highlight sections of a well-designed lesson plan that show how you would use creative teaching materials. Materials that support learning theory and were designed to suit this purpose are most helpful. Your materials should reflect your ability to encourage active learning and a variety of instructional strategies.

Transcripts A copy of your official transcript can be used in a variety of ways. You may wish to use it to document your knowledge in subject areas such as chemistry, geography, or education courses. Highlight the courses and the grade you wish to document. Include a brief, typewritten explanation of why this transcript is included.

You may even include other information, such as a syllabus from the course that you have highlighted, to show that you have taken essay or other types of tests on the subject.

Unit Plans A unit plan is an integrated plan for instruction on a topic developed over several days or even weeks. Often, units are developed within a discipline, and lessons are organized to build on knowledge acquired in previous lessons. Unit plans generally include purposes, objectives, content outlines, activities, instructional resources, and evaluation methods. Unit plans are particularly good for documenting your ability to use a variety of instructional strategies and instructional planning skills.

Volunteer Experience Descriptions This document might include a list and brief description of volunteer experiences and services provided to the school and community. You should focus on how these activities have enhanced your abilities while providing a contribution to society. You should also emphasize the importance of maintaining positive school–community collaboration through teacher, parent, and student interaction. Depending on what you learned from these experiences, make sure they address the standard under which you have placed this document.

Work Experience Descriptions These are statements you have written to describe work experiences. These might include work with students in both traditional and nontraditional settings and work for which you were compensated or that you performed on a voluntary basis. To be of most interest, these statements should include not only a summary of the setting and your responsibilities but also a reflective statement addressing the intangible aspects of the work experience. In writing these statements, be sure to address how these work experiences relate to the specific standard.

References

AAMR. (2002). Mental Retardation: Definition, classification, and systems of supports (10th ed.). Washington, DC: Author.

Abbott-Shim, M., Lambert, R., & McCarty, F. (2003). A comparison of school readiness outcomes for children randomly assigned to a Head Start program and the program's wait list. *Journal of Education for Students Placed at Risk, 8*(2), 191–214.

Aboud, F., & Fenwick, V. (1999). Exploring and evaluating school-based interventions to reduce prejudice. *Journal of Social Issues, 55*(4), 767–786.

Ackerman, D. J., Barnett, W. S., & Robin, K. (2005). *Making the most of kindergarten: Present trends and future issues and issues in the provision of full-day programs.* New Brunswick, NJ: NIEER.

Ackerman, P., Beier, M., & Boyle, M. (2005). Working memory and intelligence: The same or different constructs? *Psychological Bulletin, 131*(1), 30–60.

Adams, A., Carnine, D., & Gersten, R. (1982). Instructional strategies for studying content area texts in the intermediate grades. *Reading Research Quarterly, 18,* 27–53.

Adams, G. L., & Engelmann, S. (1996). *Research on Direct Instruction: 25 years beyond DISTAR.* Seattle, WA: Educational Achievement Systems.

Adams, J. L. (1974). *Conceptual blockbusting.* San Francisco: Freeman.

Adelman, N. E., Haslam, M. B., & Pringle, B. A. (1996). *The uses of time for teaching and learning.* Washington, DC: U.S. Department of Education.

AERA/APA/NCME. (1999). *Standards for educational and psychological testing.* Washington, DC: American Educational Research Association.

Aiken, L. R. (2003). *Psychological testing and assessment* (11th ed.). Boston: Allyn & Bacon.

Airsian, P. W. (1994). *Classroom assessment* (2nd ed.). New York: McGraw-Hill.

Airsian, P. W., & Walsh, M. E. (1997). Constructivist cautions. *Phi Delta Kappan, 78*(6), 444–449.

Alba, R. D. (1990). *Ethnic identity.* New Haven, CT: Yale University Press.

Alber, S. R., & Heward, W. L. (2000). Teaching students to recruit positive attention: A review and recommendations. *Journal of Behavioral Education, 10,* 177–204.

Alberto, P., & Troutman, A. (1999). *Applied behavior analysis for teachers* (5th ed.). Columbus, OH: Charles E. Merrill.

Alberto, P., & Troutman, A. C. (2006). *Applied behavior analysis for teachers* (7th ed.). Upper Saddle River, NJ: Prentice-Hall/Merrill.

Alderman, M. K. (1990). Motivation for at-risk students. *Educational Leadership, 48*(1), 27–30.

Aleman, S. R. (1990). *Attention deficit disorder.* Washington, DC: Education and Public Welfare Division of the Congressional Research Service.

Alexander, G. A., Graham, S., & Harris, K. R. (1998). A perspective on strategy research: Progress and prospects. *Educational Psychology Review, 10*(2), 129–154.

Alexander, P. (2004). In the year 2020: Envisioning the possibilities for educational psychology. *Educational Psychologist, 39*(3), 149–156.

Alexander, P. A. (1992). Domain knowledge: Evolving themes and emerging concerns. *Educational Psychologist, 27,* 33–51.

Alexander, P. A., & Jetton, T. L. (1996). The role of importance and interest in the processing of text. *Educational Psychology Review, 8*(1), 89–121.

Alexander, P. A., Kulikowich, J. M., & Jetton, T. L. (1994). The role of subject-matter knowledge and interest in the processing of linear and nonlinear texts. *Review of Educational Research, 64,* 201–252.

Alexander, P. A., Kulikowich, J. M., & Jetton, T. L. (1995). Interrelationship of knowledge, interest, and recall: Assessing a model of domain learning. *Journal of Educational Psychology, 87*(4), 559–575.

Alexander, P. A., & Murphy, P. K. (1994, April). *The research base for APA's learning-centered psychological principles.* Paper presented at the annual meeting of the American Educational Research Association, San Francisco, CA.

Alexrod, S., & Mathews, S. (2003). *How to deal with students who challenge and defy authority.* Columbus, OH: Hawthorne Educational Service.

Alfassi, M. (1998). Reading for meaning: The efficacy of reciprocal teaching in fostering reading comprehension in high school students in remedial reading classes. *American Educational Research Journal, 35*(2), 309–332.

Algozzine, B., Browder, D., Karvonen, M., Test, D. W., & Wood, W. M. (2001). Effects of interventions to promote self-determination for individuals with disabilities. *Review of Educational Research, 71*(2), 219–277.

Allen, L., & Seth, A. (2004). Bridging the gap between poor and privileged. *American Educator, 28*(2), 34–42.

Allen, R. (2003). The democratic aims of service learning. *Educational Leadership, 60*(6), 51–54.

Allensworth, E. (2005). Dropout rates after high-stakes testing in elementary school: A study of the contradictory effects of Chicago's efforts to end social promotion. *Evaluation and Policy Analysis, 27*(4), 341–364.

Allington, R. L., & McGill-Franzen, A. (1989). School response to reading failure: Instruction for Chapter 1 and special education students in grades two, four, and eight. *Elementary School Journal, 89*(5), 529–542.

Al-Namlah, A. S., Fernyhough, C., & Meins, E. (2006). Sociocultural influences on the development of verbal mediation: Private speech and phonological decoding in Saudi Arabian and British samples. *Developmental Psychology, 42,* 117–131

Alvermann, D. E., Smith, L., & Readence, J. (1985). Prior knowledge activation and the comprehension of compatible and incompatible text. *Reading Research Quarterly, 20,* 420–436.

Ambert, A. M. (1997). *Parents, children, and adolescents: Interactive relationships and development in context.* New York: Haworth.

American Association of University Women. (1992). *How schools shortchange girls.* Washington, DC: Author.

American Association on Mental Retardation. (2002). *Mental retardation: Definition, classification, and systems of supports* (10th ed.). Washington, DC: American Association on Mental Retardation.

American Psychiatric Association. (1994). *Diagnostic and statistical manual of mental disorders* (4th ed.). Washington, DC: Author.

American Psychological Association. (1992). Working draft report of the APA Presidential Task Force on Psychology in Education.

American Psychological Association. (1997). *Learner-centered psychological principles: A framework for school redesign and reform.* Washington, DC: Author.

Ames, C. (1992). Classrooms: Goals, structures, and student motivation. *Journal of Educational Psychology, 84,* 261–271.

Ames, C., & Archer, J. (1988). Achievement goals in the classroom: Students' learning strategies and motivation processes. *Journal of Educational Psychology, 80,* 260–267.

Amrein, A., & Berliner, D. (2003). The effects of high-stakes testing on student motivation and learning. *Educational Leadership, 60*(5), 32–38.

Anagnostopoulos, D. (2006). "Real Students" and "True Demotes": Ending social promotion and the moral ordering of urban high schools. *American Educational Research Journal, 43*(1), 5–42.

Ancheta, A. (2006). Civil rights, education research, and the courts. *Educational Researcher, 35*(1), 26–29.

Anderman, E. M., Anderman, L. H., & Griesinger, T. (1999). The relation of present and possible academic selves during early adolescence to grade point average and achievement goals. *The Elementary School Journal, 100*(1), 3–18.

Anderman, E. M., Eccles, J. S., Yoon, K. S., Roeser, R., Wigfield, A., & Blumenfeld, P. (2001). Learning to value mathematics and reading: Relations to mastery and performance-oriented instructional practices. *Contemporary Educational Psychology, 26*(1), 76–95.

Anderson, J. (1994). *What do student grades mean? Differences across schools.* Washington, DC: U.S. Department of Education, Office of Educational Research and Improvement.

Anderson, J. R. (1985). *Cognitive psychology and its implications* (2nd ed.). San Francisco: Freeman.

Anderson, J. R. (1990). *Cognitive psychology and its implications* (3rd ed.). New York: Freeman.

Anderson, J. R. (1995). *Learning and memory: An integrated approach.* New York: Wiley.

Anderson, J. R. (2005). *Cognitive psychology and its implications.* (6th ed.). New York: Worth.

Anderson, J. R., & Bower, G. (1983). *Human associative memory.* Washington, DC: Winston.

Anderson, J. R., Greeno, J. G., Reder, L. M., & Simon, H. (2000). Perspectives on learning, thinking, and activity. *Educational Researcher, 29*(4), 11–13.

Anderson, J. R., Reder, L. M., & Simon, H. A. (1996). Situated learning and education. *Educational Researcher, 25*(4), 5–11.

Anderson, L. M., Brubaker, N. L., Alleman-Brooks, J., & Duffy, G. G. (1985). A qualitative study of seatwork in first-grade classrooms. *Elementary School Journal, 86,* 123–140.

Anderson, L. M., Evertson, C. M., & Brophy, J. E. (1979). An experimental study of effective teaching in first-grade reading groups. *Elementary School Journal, 79,* 193–223.

Anderson, L. W., & Pellicer, L. O. (1990). Synthesis of research on compensatory and remedial education. *Educational Leadership, 48*(1), 10–16.

Anderson, R. E., & Becker, H. J. (2001). School investments in instructional technology: Teaching, learning, and computing: 1998 survey (Rep. No. 8). Center for Research on Information Technology and Organizations, University of California, Irvine, and University of Minnesota.

Anderson, R. E., & Ronnkvist, A. (1999). *The presence of computers in American schools.* Irvine, CA: University of California, Center for Research on Information Technology and Organizations.

Anderson, T. H., & Armbruster B. B. (1984). Studying. In P. D. Pearson (Ed.), *Handbook of reading research.* New York: Longman.

Anderson-Inman, L., & Horney, M. (2007). Supported eText: Assistive technology through text transformations. *Reading Research Quarterly, 42*(1), 153–160.

Andrich, D., & Styles, I. (1994). Psychometric evidence of intellectual growth spurts in early adolescence. *Journal of Early Adolescence, 14*(3), 328–344.

Anthony, J. L., & Lonigan, C. J. (2004). The nature of phonological awareness: Converging evidence from four studies of preschool and early grade school children. *Journal of Educational Psychology, 96*(1), 43–55.

Antil, L., Jenkins, J., Wayne, S., & Vadasy, P. (1998). Cooperative learning: Prevalence, conceptualizations, and the relation between research and practice. *American Educational Research Journal, 35*(3), 419–454.

Archibald, D., & Newmann, F. (1988). *Beyond standardized testing: Authentic academic achievement in the secondary school.* Reston, VA: NASSP Publications.

Arends, R. I. (2004). *Learning to teach* (6th ed.). New York: Worth.

Armstrong, T. (1994). *Multiple intelligences in the classroom.* Alexandria, VA: Association for Supervision and Curriculum Development.

Arnold, M. L. (2000). Stage, sequence, and sequels: Changing conceptions of morality, post-Kohlberg. *Educational Psychology Review, 12*(4), 365–383.

Aronson, E. A. (1995). *The social animal.* New York: Freeman.

Aronson, E., Blaney, N., Stephan, C., Sikes, J., & Snapp, M. (1978). *The jigsaw classroom.* Beverly Hills, CA: Sage.

Arter, J., & McTighe, J. (2001). *Scoring rubrics in the classroom.* Thousand Oaks, CA: Corwin.

Artiles, A., Kozleski, E., Dorn, S., & Christensen, C. (2006). Chapter 3: Learning in inclusive education research—Re-mediating theory and methods with a transformative agenda. *Review of Research in Education, 30*(1), 65–108.

Ashcraft, M. H. (2006). *Cognition* (4th ed.). Upper Saddle River, NJ: Prentice-Hall.

Athanases, S. Z. (1994). Teachers' reports of the effects of preparing portfolios of literacy instruction. *The Elementary School Journal, 94*(4), 421–439.

Atkins, J., & Ellsesser, J. (2003). Tracking: The good, the bad, and the questions. *Educational Leadership, 61*(2), 44–47.

Atkinson, J. W. (1958). Towards experimental analysis of human motivation in terms of motive expectancies and incentives.

In J. W. Atkinson (Ed.), *Motives in fantasy, action, and society.* Princeton, NJ:Van Nostrand.

Atkinson, J. W. (1964). *An introduction to motivation.* Princeton, NJ: Van Nostrand.

Atkinson, R. C., & Raugh, M. R. (1975). An application of the mnemonic keyword method to the acquisition of Russian vocabulary. *Journal of Experimental Psychology: Human Learning and Memory, 104,* 126–133.

Atkinson, R. C., & Shiffrin, R. M. (1968). Human memory: A proposed system and its component processes. In K. Spence & J. Spence (Eds.), *The psychology of learning and motivation,* Vol. 2. New York: Academic Press.

Atkinson, R. K., Derry, S. J., Renkl, A., & Wortham, D. (2000). Learning from examples: Instructional principles from the worked examples research. *Review of Educational Research, 70*(2), 181–214.

Atkinson, R., Levin, J., Atkinson, L., Kiewra, K., Meyers, T., Kim, S., Renandya, W., & Hwang, Y. (1999). Matrix and mnemonic text-processing adjuncts: Comparing and combining their components. *Journal of Educational Psychology, 91*(2), 342–357.

Atwater, E. (1996). *Adolescence.* Upper Saddle River, NJ: Prentice-Hall.

August, D., & Shanahan, T. (Eds.). (2006a). *Developing literacy in second-language learners.* Mahwah, NJ: Erlbaum.

August, D., & Shanahan, T. (2006b). Synthesis: Instruction and professional development. In D. August & T. Shanahan (Eds.), *Developing literacy in second-language learners* (pp. 351–364). Mahwah, NJ: Erlbaum.

Ausubel, D. P. (1963). *The psychology of meaningful verbal learning.* New York: Grune and Stratton.

Ausubel, D. P. (1978). In defense of advance organizers: A reply to the critics. *Review of Educational Research, 48,* 251–258.

Ausubel, D. P., & Youssef, M. (1963). Role of discriminability in meaningful parallel learning. *Journal of Educational Psychology, 54,* 331–336.

Aviram, A. (2000). From "computers in the classroom" to mindful radical adaptation by education systems to the emerging cyber culture. *Journal of Educational Change, 1*(4), 331–352.

Axelrod, S., & Matthews, S. (2003). *How to manage behavior.* Austin: Pro-Ed.

Ayaduray, J., & Jacobs, G. M. (1997). Can learner strategy instruction succeed? The case of higher order questions and elaborate responses. *System, 25*(4), 561–570.

Azzam, A. (2005/2006). Digital opportunity. *Educational Leadership, 63*(4), 89–92.

Azzam, A., Perkins-Gough, D., & Theirs, N. (2006). *Educational Leadership, 64*(3), 94–96.

Babad, E. (1993). Pygmalion—25 years after: Interpersonal expectancies in the classroom. In P. D. Blanck (Ed.), *Interpersonal expectations: Theory, research, and application* (pp. 125–152). Cambridge, England: Cambridge University Press.

Baddeley, A. (1999). *Essentials of human memory.* Philadelphia: Psychology Press.

Bahrick, H. P., & Hall, L. K. (1991). Lifetime maintenance of high school mathematics. *Journal of Experimental Psychology, 120,* 20–33.

Baillargeon, R., Graber, M., DeVos, J., & Black, J. (1990). Why do young infants fail to search for hidden objects? *Cognition, 36,* 255–284.

Bainer, D. L., & Wright, D. (1998, April). *Evaluating a constructivist professional development program to improve science teaching.* Paper presented at the annual meeting of the American Educational Research Association, San Diego, CA.

Baines, L., Baines, C., & Masterson, C. (1994). Mainstreaming: One school's reality. *Phi Delta Kappan, 76*(1), 39–40, 57–64.

Baker, S., Gersten, R., & Keating, T. (2000). When less may be more: A two-year longitudinal evaluation of a volunteer tutoring program requiring minimal training. *Reading Research Quarterly, 35*(4), 494–519.

Baker, S., Gersten, R., & Lee, D. S. (2002). A synthesis of empirical research on teaching mathematics to low-achieving students. *The Elementary School Journal, 103*(1), 51–73.

Balfanz, R., & Legters, N. (2004). *Locating the dropout crisis.* Baltimore, MD: Johns Hopkins University, Center for Social Organization of Schools.

Balfanz, R., & MacIver, D. (2000). Transforming high-poverty urban middle schools into strong learning institutions: Lessons from the first five years of the Talent Development Middle School. *Journal of Education for Students Placed at Risk, 5*(1 & 2), 137–158.

Bali, V., Anagnostopoulos, D., & Roberts, R. (2005). Toward a political explanation of grade retention. *Evaluation and Policy Analysis, 27*(3), 133–155.

Bandalos, D. L., Yates, K., & Thorndike-Christ, T. (1995). Effects of math self-concept, perceived self-efficacy, and attributions for failure and success on test anxiety. *Journal of Educational Psychology, 87*(4), 611–623.

Bandura, A. (1965). Influence of models' reinforcement contingencies on the acquisition of imitative responses. *Journal of Personality and Social Psychology, 28*(2), 117–148.

Bandura, A. (1986). *Social foundations of thought and action: A social-cognitive theory.* Englewood Cliffs, NJ: Prentice-Hall.

Bandura, A. (1991). Social cognitive theory of self-regulation. *Organizational Behavior and High Performance, 50,* 248–287.

Bandura, A. (1997). *Self-efficacy: The exercise of control.* New York: Freeman.

Bangert-Drowns, R. L. (1993). The word processor as an instructional tool: A meta-analysis of word processing in writing instruction. *Review of Educational Research, 63*(1), 69–93.

Bangert-Drowns, R. L., Hurley, M., & Wilkinson, B. (2004). The effects of school-based writing-to-learn interventions on academic achievement: A meta-analysis. *Review of Educational Research, 74*(1), 29–58.

Bangert-Drowns, R. L., Kulik, C. C., Kulik, J. A., & Morgan, M. (1991). The instructional effect of feedback in test-like events. *Review of Educational Research, 61*(2), 213–238.

Bangert-Drowns, R. L., Kulik, J. A., & Kulik, C. L. (1986, April). *Effects of frequent classroom testing.* Paper presented at the annual meeting of the American Education Research Association, San Francisco, CA.

Banks, J. A. (1993). *Multiethnic education: Theory and practice* (3rd ed.). Boston: Allyn & Bacon.

Banks, J. A. (1995). Historical development, dimensions, and practice. In J. A. Banks & C. A. M. Banks (Eds.), *Handbook of multicultural education.* New York: Macmillan.

Banks, J. A. (1995c). Multicultural education: Its effects on students' racial and gender role attitudes. In J. A. Banks & C. A. M. Banks (Eds.), *Handbook of multicultural education.* New York: Macmillan.

Banks, J. A. (1999). *An introduction to multicultural education* (2nd ed.). Boston: Allyn & Bacon.

Banks, J. A. (2001). Multicultural education: Goals, possibilities, and challenges. In C. F. Diaz (Ed.), *Multicultural education in the 21st century.* New York: Longman.

Banks, J. A. (2002). *An introduction to multicultural education* (3rd ed.). Boston: Allyn & Bacon

Barber, B., Eccles, J., & Stone, M. (2001). Whatever happened to the jock, the brain, and the princess? Young adult pathways linked to adolescent activity involvement and social identity. *Journal of Adolescent Research, 16,* 429–455.

Barber, R. M., & Kagey, J. R. (1977). Modification of school attendance for an elementary population. *Journal of Applied Behavior Analysis, 10,* 41–48.

Barnett, W., & Ackerman, D. (2007). Boundaries with early childhood education: The significance of the early childhood frontier for elementary and secondary education. In S. Fuhrman, D. Cohen, & F. Mosher (Eds.), *The state of education policy research* (pp. 187–202). Mahwah, NJ: Erlbaum.

Barnhill, G. P. (2005). Functional behavioral assessment in schools. *Intervention in school and clinic, 40,* 131–143.

Barr, R. (1987). Content coverage. In M. J. Dunkin (Ed.), *International encyclopedia of teaching and teacher education.* New York: Pergamon.

Barr, R., & Dreeben, R. (1983). *How schools work.* Chicago: University of Chicago Press.

Barr, R. D., & Parrett, W. H. (1995). *Hope at last for at-risk youth.* Boston: Allyn & Bacon.

Barr, R. D., & Parrett, W. H. (2001). *Hope fulfilled for at-risk and violent youth* (2nd ed.). Boston: Allyn & Bacon.

Barrish, H. H., Saunders, M., & Wolf, M. M. (1969). Good behavior game: Effects of individual contingencies for group consequences on disruptive behavior in a classroom. *Journal of Applied Behavior Analysis, 2,* 119–124.

Barth, R. (1979). Home-based reinforcement of school behavior: A review and analysis. *Review of Educational Research, 49,* 436–458.

Barton, P. (2003). *Parsing the achievement gap: Baselines for tracking progress.* Princeton, NJ: Educational Testing Service.

Bateman, B., & Linden, M. (1998). *Better IEPs* (3rd ed.). Longmont, CO: Sapris West.

Battin-Pearson, S., Newcomb, M., Abbott, R., Hill, K., Catalano, R., & Hawkins, D. (2000). Predictors of early high school dropout: A test of five theories. *Journal of Educational Psychology, 92*(3), 568–582.

Battistich, V., Watson, M., Solomon, D., Lewis, C., & Schaps, E. (1999). Beyond the three R's: A broader agenda for school reform. *The Elementary School Journal, 99*(5), 415–432.

Battle, D. (1996). Language learning and use by African American children. *Topics in Language Disorders, 16,* 22–37.

Bauer, A. M., & Shea, T. M. (1999). *Inclusion 101: How to teach all learners.* Baltimore: Brookes.

Baumeister, R. F., & Leary, M. R. (1995). The need to belong: Desire for interpersonal attachments as a fundamental human motivation. *Psychological Bulletin, 117*(3), 497–529.

Baxter, S. (1994). The last word on gender differences. *Psychology Today, 27*(2), 51–53.

Bear, G. G., Minke, K. M., & Manning, M. A. (2002). Self-concept among students with learning disabilities: A meta-analysis. *School Psychology Review, 31*(3), 405–427.

Bebell, D., O'Dwyer, L., Russell, M., & Seeley, K. (2004). *Estimating the effect of computer use at home and in school on student achievement.* Paper presented at the annual meeting of the American Educational Research Association, San Diego, CA.

Beck, I., & McKeown, M. (2001). Inviting students into the pursuit of meaning. *Educational Psychology Review, 13*(3), 225–242.

Beck, I., & McKeown, M. (2007). Increasing young low-income children's oral vocabulary repertoires through rich and focused instruction. *The Elementary School Journal, 107* (3), 251–272.

Becker, B. E., & Luthar, S. S. (2002). Social-emotional factors affecting achievement outcomes among disadvantaged students: Closing the achievement gap. *Educational Psychologist, 37*(4), 197–214.

Becker, H. J. (1990). Coaching for the scholastic aptitude test: Further synthesis and appraisal. *Review of Educational Research, 60*(3), 373–417.

Becker, H. J. (2000). Who's wired and who's not: Children's access to and use of computer technology. *Children and Computer Technology, 10*(2), 44–75.

Becker, H. J. (2001, April). *How are teachers using computers in instruction?* Paper presented at the annual meeting of the American Educational Research Association, Seattle, WA.

Becker, H. J., & Ravitz, J. L. (2001, April). *Computer use by teachers: Are Cuban's predictions correct?* Paper presented at the annual meeting of the American Educational Research Association, Seattle, WA.

Becker, W., & Carnine, D. (1980). Direct instruction: An effective approach for educational intervention with the disadvantaged and low performers. In B. Lahey & A. Kazdin (Eds.), *Advances in child clinical psychology.* New York: Plenum.

Bee, H., & Boyd, D. (2007). *The developing child.* (11th ed.). Boston: Allyn & Bacon.

Beebe-Frankenberger, M., Bocian, K. L., MacMillan, D. L., & Gresham, F. M. (2004). Sorting second grade students with academic deficiencies: Characteristics differentiating those retained in grade from those promoted to third grade. *Journal of Educational Psychology, 96,* 204–215.

Behrman, R. E. (1997). Children and poverty. *The Future of Children, 7*(2), 4–160.

Bell, D. (2004). *Silent covenants: Brown v. Board or Education and the unfulfilled hopes for racial reform.* New York: Oxford University Press.

Bender, W. N. (2004). *Learning disabilities: Characteristics, identification, and teaching strategies* (5th ed.). Boston: Pearson.

Benjafield, J. G. (1992). *Cognition.* Englewood Cliffs, NJ: Prentice-Hall.

Bereiter, C. (1995). A dispositional view of transfer. In A. McKeough, J. Lupart, & A. Marini (Eds.), *Teaching for transfer: Fostering generalization in learning.* Mahwah, NJ: Erlbaum.

Bergin, D. (1999). Influences on classroom interest. *Educational Psychologist, 34*(2), 87–98.

Bergstrom, J. M., & O'Brien, L. A. (2001). Themes of discovery. *Educational Leadership, 58*(7), 29–33.

Berk, L. E. (2001). *Development through the lifespan* (2nd ed.). Boston: Allyn & Bacon.

Berk, L. E. (2006). *Child Development* (7th ed.). Boston: Allyn & Bacon.

Berko, J. (1985). The child's learning of English morphology. *Word, 14,* 150–177.

Bernard-Powers, J. (2001). Gender effects in schooling. In C. F. Diaz (Ed.), *Multicultural education for the 21st century.* New York: Longman.

Bernhardt, V. (2003). No schools left behind. *Educational Leadership, 60*(5), 26–30.

Bernhardt, V. (2005). Data tools for school improvement. *Educational Leadership, 62*(5), 66–69.

Bernstein, D. K., & Tiegerman-Farber, E. (2002). *Language and communication disorders in children* (5th ed.). Boston: Allyn & Bacon.

Berrueta-Clement, J. R., Schweinhart, L. J., Barnett, W. S., Epstein, A. S., & Weikart, D. P. (1984). *Changed lives.* Ypsilanti, MI: High/Scope.

Berry, B., Hoke, M., & Hirsch, E. (2004). The search for highly qualified teachers. *Phi Delta Kappan, 85*(9), 684–689.

Best Evidence Encyclopedia. (2007). Reviews of research on elementary and secondary reading and mathematics programs. At www.bestevidence.org.

Bettmann, E. H., & Friedman, L. J. (2004). The Anti-Defamation League's A Word of Difference Institute. In W. G. Stephan & W. P. Vogt (Eds.), *Education Programs for Improving Intergroup Relations.* New York: Teachers College Press.

Beyer, B. K. (1988). *Developing a thinking skills program.* Boston: Allyn & Bacon.

Beyer, B. K. (1998). *Improving student thinking: A comprehensive approach.* Boston: Allyn & Bacon.

Biddle, B., & Berliner, D. (2002). Unequal school funding in the United States. *Educational Leadership, 59*(8), 48–59.

Biemiller, A. (1993). Lake Wobegon revisited: On diversity in education. *Educational Researcher, 22*(9), 7–12.

Bigge, M. L., & Shermis, S. S. (2004). *Learning theories for teachers* (6th ed.). Boston: Pearson.

Bigler, R. (1999). The use of multicultural curricula and materials to counter racism in children. *Journal of Social Issues, 55*(4), 687–705.

Binder, L. M., Dixon, M. R., & Ghezi, P. M. (2000). A procedure to teach self-control to children with attention deficit hyperactivity disorder. *Journal of Applied Behavior Analysis, 33,* 233–237.

Birney, D., Citron-Pousiy, J., Lutz, D., & Sternberg, R. (2005). The development of cognitive and intellectual abilities. In M. Borstein & M. Lamb (Eds.), *Developmental science: An advanced textbook* (5th ed., pp. 327–358). Hillsdale, NJ: Erlbaum.

Bitter, G. G., & Legacy, J. M. (2008). *Using technology in the classroom* (7th ed.). Boston: Allyn & Bacon.

Blachman, B., Schatschneider, C., Fletcher, J., Francis, D., Clonan, S., Shaywitz, B., & Shaywitz, C. (2004). Effects of intensive reading remediation for second and third graders and a one year followup. *Journal of Educational Psychology, 96*(3), 444–461.

Black, J. (2003). Environment and development of the nervous system. In M. Gallagher & R. J. Nelson (Eds.), *Handbook of psychology: Vol. 3. Biological psychology* (pp. 655–665). Hoboken, NJ: Wiley.

Black, M. M., & Krishnakumar, A. (1998). Children in low-income, urban settings. Interventions to promote mental health and well-being. *American Psychologist, 53*(6), 635–646.

Black, P., Harrison, C., Lee, C., Marshall, B., & Dylan, W. (2003). Working inside the black box: Assessment for learning in the classroom. *Phi Delta Kappan, 86*(1), 8–21.

Black, P., Harrison, C., Lee, C., Marshall, B., & Wiliam, D. (2004). *Assessment for learning.* New York, NY: Open University Press.

Black, P., & Wiliam, D. (1998). Inside the Black Box: Raising standards through classroom assessment. *Phi Delta Kappan, 80*(2), 139–142.

Blackadar, A. R., & Nachtigal, P. (1986). *Cotapaxi/Westcliffe follow-through project: Final evaluation report.* Denver, CO: Mid-Continental Regional Educational Laboratory.

Blair, C. (2004). Learning disability, intelligence, and fluid cognitive functions of the prefrontal cortex: A developmental neuroscience approach. *Learning Disabilities: A Contemporary Journal, 2*(1), 22–29.

Blamires, M. (Ed.). (1999). *Enabling technology for inclusion.* Thousand Oaks, CA: Corwin.

Blatchford, P., Baines, E., Rubie-Davies, C., Bassett, P., & Chowne, A. (2006). The effect of a new approach to group work on pupil-pupil and teacher-pupil interactions. *Journal of Educational Psychology, 98*(4), 750–765.

Bligh, D. (2000). *What's the use of lectures?* San Francisco: Jossey-Bass.

Block, K. K., & Peskowitz, N. B. (1990). Metacognition in spelling: Using writing and reading to self-check spelling. *Elementary School Journal, 91,* 151–164.

Blok, H., Oostdam, R., Otter, M. E., & Overmaat, M. (2002). Computer-assisted instruction in support of beginning reading instruction: A review. *Review of Educational Research, 721*(1), 101–130.

Bloom, B. S. (1976). *Human characteristics and school learning.* New York: McGraw-Hill.

Bloom, B. S. (1986). Automaticity: The hands and feet of genius. *Educational Leadership, 43,* 70–77.

Bloom, B. S., Englehart, M. B., Furst, E. J., Hill, W. H., & Krathwohl, O. R. (1956). *Taxonomy of educational objectives: The classification of educational goals. Handbook 1: The cognitive domain.* New York: Longman.

Bloom, B. S., Hastings, J. T., & Madaus, G. F. (1971). *Handbook on formative and summative evaluation of student learning.* New York: McGraw-Hill.

Bloome, D., Puro, P., & Theodorou, E. (1989). Procedural displays and classroom lessons. *Curriculum Inquiry, 19*(3), 265–291.

Blumenfeld, P. C., Marx, R. W., Soloway, E., & Krajcik, J. (1996). Learning with peers: From small group cooperation to collaborative communities. *Educational Researcher, 25*(8), 37–40.

Boden, M. A. (1980). *Jean Piaget.* New York: Viking Press.

Bodine, R. J., Crawford, D. K., & Schrumpf, F. (1994). *Creating the peaceable school: A comprehensive program for teaching conflict resolution.* Champaign, IL: Research Press.

Bodrova, E., & Leong, D. (2005). Uniquely preschool. *Educational Leadership, 63*(1), 44–47.

Boekaerts, M. (1995). Self-regulated learning: Bridging the gap between metacognitive and metamotivational theories. *Educational Psychologist, 30*(4), 195–200.

Boekaerts, M., Pintrich, P. R., & Zeidner, M. (Eds.). (2000). *Handbook of self-regulation.* San Diego, CA: Academic Press.

Bong, M. (2001). Between- and within-domain relations of academic motivation among middle and high school students: Self-efficacy, task-value, and achievement goals. *Journal of Educational Psychology, 93*(1), 23–34.

Bong, M., & Skaalvik, E. (2003). Academic self-concept and self-efficacy: How different are they really? *Educational Psychology Review, 15*(1), 1–40.

Bonner-Tompkins, E. (2001, May/June). Effective practices for serving limited English proficient students with disabilities. *Gaining Ground.* Council of Chief State School Officers.

Booher-Jennings, J., & Beveridge, A. (2007). Who counts for accountability? High-stakes test exemptions in a large urban school district. In A. Sadovnik, J. O'Day, G. Bohrnstedt, & K. Borman (Eds.), *No Child Left Behind and the reduction of the achievement gap: Sociological perspectives on federal education policy.* New York: Routledge.

Boone, R., & Higgins, K. (2007). The role of instructional design in assistive technology research and development. *Reading Research Quarterly, 42*(1), 134–160.

Borg, M. (1998). Tests of the internal/external frames of reference model with subject-specific academic self-efficacy and frame-specific academic concepts. *Journal of Educational Psychology, 90*(1), 102–110.

Borko, H. (2004). Professional development and teacher learning: Mapping the terrain. *Educational Researcher, 33*(8), 3–15.

Borman, G. (2002/2003). How can Title I improve achievement? *Educational Leadership, 60*(4), 49–53.

Borman, G., Benson, J., & Overman, L. (2005). Families, schools, and summer learning. *The Elementary School Journal, 106*(2), 131–150.

Borman, G., & Dowling, N. M. (2006). Longitudinal achievement effects of multiyear summer school: Evidence from the Teach Baltimore randomized field trial. *Educational Evaluation and Policy Analysis, 28*(1), 25–48.

Borman, G., & Hewes, G. (2001). *Long-term effects and cost effectiveness of Success for All.* Baltimore: Johns Hopkins University, Center for Research on the Education of Students Placed at Risk.

Borman, G., & Hewes, G. (2003). Long-term effects and cost effectiveness of Success for All. *Educational Evaluation and Policy Analysis, 24*(2), 243–266.

Borman, G., & Kimball, S. (2005). Teacher quality and educational quality: Do teachers with higher standards-based evaluation ratings close student achievement gaps? *The Elementary School Journal, 106*(1), 3–20.

Borman, G., Stringfield, S., & Slavin, R. (Eds.). (2001). *Title I: Compensatory education at the crossroads.* Mahwah, NJ: Erlbaum.

Borman, G. D. (1997). *A holistic model of the organization of categorical program students' total educational opportunities.* Unpublished doctoral dissertation, University of Chicago.

Borman, G. D., & Boulay, M. (2004). *Summer learning: Research, policies, and programs.* Mahwah, NJ: Erlbaum.

Borman, G. D., & D'Agostino, J. V. (2001). Title I and student achievement: A quantitative synthesis. In G. D. Borman, S. C. Stringfield, & R. E. Slavin (Eds.), *Title I: Compensatory education at the crossroads* (pp. 25–57). Mahwah, NJ: Erlbaum.

Borman, G. D., Hewes, G. M., Overman, L. T., & Brown, S. (2003). Comprehensive school reform and achievement: A meta-analysis. *Review of Educational Research, 73*(2), 125–230.

Borman, G. D., D'Agostino, J. V., Wong, K. K., & Hedges, L. V. (1998). The longitudinal achievement of Chapter I students: Preliminary evidence from the Prospects study. *Journal of Education for Students Placed at Risk, 3*(4), 363–399.

Borman, G. D., & Overman, L. T. (2004). Academic resilience in mathematics among poor and minority students. *The Elementary School Journal, 104*(3), 177–195.

Borman, G. D., Slavin, R. E., Cheung, A., Chamberlain, A., Madden, N. A., & Chambers, B. (2007). Final reading outcomes of the national randomized field trial of Success for All. *American Educational Research Journal, 44*(3), 701–731.

Bornstein, P. H. (1985). Self-instructional training: A commentary and state-of-the-art. *Journal of Applied Behavior Analysis, 18,* 69–72.

Bortnick, R. (1995). Interactive learning and hypermedia technology. In J. H. Block, S. T. Everson, & T. R. Guskey (Eds.), *School improvement programs* (pp. 77–90). New York: Scholastic.

Bottge, B. A. (2001). Using intriguing problems to improve math skills. *Educational Leadership, 58*(6), 68–72.

Bottoms, J. E., Feagin, C. H., & Han, L. (2005). *Making high schools and middle grades schools work.* Atlanta, GA: Southern Regional Education Board.

Bower, G. H., Clark, M. C., Lesgold, A. M., & Winzenz, D. (1969). Hierarchical retrieval schemes in recall of categorized word lists. *Journal of Verbal Learning and Verbal Behavior, 8,* 323–343.

Bower, G. H., & Karlin, M. B. (1974). Depth of processing pictures of faces and recognition memory. *Journal of Experimental Psychology, 103,* 751–757.

Bowman, B. (1993). Early childhood education. *Review of Research in Education, 19,* 101–134.

Boykin, A. W. (1994a). Afrocultural expression and its implications for schooling. In E. R. Hollins, J. E. King, & W. C. Hayman (Eds.), *Teaching diverse populations.* Albany: State University of New York Press.

Boykin, A. W. (1994b). Harvesting culture and talent: African American children and educational reform. In R. Rossi (Ed.), *Schools and students at risk* (pp. 116–130). New York: Teachers College Press.

Boykin, A. W. (2000). The talent development model of schooling: Placing students at promise for academic success. *Journal of Education for Students Placed at Risk, 5*(1 & 2), 3–25.

Bracey, G. (2003). The 13th Bracey report on the condition of education. *Phi Delta Kappan, 84*(8), 616–621.

Bracey, G. (2006). Dropping in on dropouts. *Phi Delta Kappan, 87*(10), 798.

Bracey, G., & Stellar, A. (2003). Long-term studies of preschool: Lasting benefits far outweigh costs. *Phi Delta Kappan, 84*(10), 780–783.

Bracey, G. W. (1998). *Put to the test: An educator's and consumer's guide to standardized testing.* Bloomington, IN: Phi Delta Kappan.

Braddock, J. H., & Dawkins, M. P. (1993). Ability grouping, aspirations, and attainments: Evidence from the National Educational Longitudinal Study of 1988. *Journal of Negro Education, 62*(3), 1–13.

Braddock, J. H., Dawkins, M. P., & Wilson, G. (1995). Intercultural contact and race relations among American youth. In W. D. Hawley & A. W. Jackson (Eds.), *Toward a common destiny: Improving race and ethnic relations in America.* San Francisco: Jossey-Bass.

Bradley, R. H., Whiteside, L., Mundfrom, D. J., Casey, P. H., Caldwell, B. M., & Barrett, K. (1994). Impact of the Infant Health and Development Program (IHDP) on the home environments of infants born prematurely and with low birthweight. *Journal of Educational Psychology, 80,* 531–541.

Branch, C. (1998). *Adolescent gangs: Old issues, new approaches.* Philadelphia: Brunner/Mazel.

Bransford, J., Brown, A., & Cocking, R. (Eds.). (1999). *How people learn: Brain, mind, experience, and school.* Washington, DC: National Academy Press.

Bransford, J. D., Burns, M. S., Delclos, V. R., & Vye, N. J. (1986). Teaching thinking: Evaluating evaluations and broadening the data base. *Educational Leadership, 44*(2), 68–70.

Bransford, J. D., & Stein, B. S. (1993). *The ideal problem solver* (2nd ed.). New York: W. H. Freeman.

Bretzing, B. B., & Kulhavy, R. W. (1981). Note taking and passage style. *Journal of Educational Psychology, 73,* 242–250.

Broden, M., Hall, R. V., Dunlap, A., & Clark, R. (1970). Effects of teacher attention and a token reinforcement system in a junior high school special education class. *Exceptional Children, 36,* 341–349.

Bronfenbrenner, U., & Morris, P. A. (1998). The ecology of developmental processes. In Damon, W. (Ed.), *Handbook of child psychology* (vol. 1, pp. 993–1029). New York: Wiley.

Brookes-Gunn, J., & Duncan, G. (1997). The effects of poverty on children. *Children and Poverty,* 7(2) 55–71.

Brooks, B. D. (1975). Contingency management as a means of reducing school truancy. *Education, 95,* 206–211.

Brooks, D. M. (1985). Beginning of the year in junior high: The first day of school. *Educational Leadership, 42,* 76–78.

Brooks, J. G., & Brooks, M. G. (1993). *The case for constructivist classrooms.* Alexandria, VA: Association for Supervision and Curriculum Development.

Brophy, J. (1981). Teacher praise: A functional analysis. *Review of Educational Research, 51,* 5–32.

Brophy, J. (1999). Toward a model of the value aspects of motivation in education: Developing appreciation for particular learning domains and activities. *Educational Psychologist, 34*(2), 75–85.

Brophy, J. (2005). Goal theorists should move on from performance goals. *Educational Psychologist, 40*(3), 167–176.

Brophy, J. E. (1998). *Motivating students to learn.* Boston: McGraw-Hill.

Brophy, J. E., & Evertson, C. M. (1974). Process-product correlations in the Texas teacher effectiveness study: Final report (Research Reports No. 74–4). Austin: Research and Development Center for Teacher Education. University of Texas.

Brophy, J. E., & Evertson, C. M. (1976). *Learning from teaching: A developmental perspective.* Boston: Allyn & Bacon.

Brophy, J. E., & Good, T. L. (1986). Teacher behavior and student achievement. In M. C. Wittrock (Ed.), *Handbook of research on teaching* (3rd ed.). New York: Macmillan.

Browder, D. M. (2001). *Curriculum and assessment for students with moderate and severe disabilities.* New York: Guilford.

Brown, A. L., Bransford, J. D., Ferrara, R. A., & Campione, J. C. (1983). Learning, remembering, and understanding. In J. Flavell & E. M. Markman (Eds.), *Handbook of child psychology* (4th ed., vol. 3, pp. 515–629). New York: Wiley.

Brown, T. (2007). A new approach to attention deficit disorder. *Educational Leadership, 64*(5), 22–28.

Bruer, J. T. (1999). Neural connections: Some you use, some you lose. *Phi Delta Kappan, 81*(4), 264–277.

Bruner, J. S. (1966). *Toward a theory of instruction.* New York: Norton.

Bruning, R. H., Schraw, G. J., Norby, M. M., & Ronning, R. R. (2004). *Cognitive psychology and instruction* (4th ed.). Columbus, OH: Merrill.

Bryant, A. L., & Zimmerman, M. A. (2002). Examining the effects of academic beliefs and behaviors on changes in substance use among urban adolescents. *Journal of Educational Psychology, 94*(3), 621–637.

Bryant, D. P., Smith, D. D., & Bryant, B. R. (2008). *Teaching students with special needs in inclusive classrooms.* Boston: Allyn & Bacon.

Bryant, D. P., Ugel, N., Thompson, S., & Hampff, A. (1999). Instructional strategies for content-area reading instruction. *Intervention in School and Clinic, 34*(5), 293–302.

Bulgren, J. A., Lenz, B. K., Schumaker, J. B., Deshler, D. D., & Marquis, J. G. (2002). The use and effectiveness of a comparison routine in diverse secondary content classrooms. *Journal of Educational Psychology, 94*(2), 356–371.

Bulgren, J., Deshler, D., Schumaker, J., & Lenz, B. (2000). The use and effectiveness of analogical instruction in diverse secondary content classrooms. *Journal of Educational Psychology, 92*(3), 426–441.

Bunge, S. A., & Zelazo, P. D. (2006). A brain-based account of the development of rule use in childhood. *Current Directions in Psychological Science, 15*(3), 118–121.

Burden, P. R. (2000). *Powerful classroom management strategies: Motivating students to learn.* Thousand Oaks, CA: Corwin.

Burden, P. R., & Byrd, D. (2003). *Methods for effective teaching.* Boston: Allyn & Bacon.

Burns, M. (2005/2006). Tools for the mind. *Educational Leadership, 63*(4), 48–53.

Burns, R. B. (1984). How time is used in elementary schools: The activity structure of classrooms. In L. W. Anderson (Ed.), *Time and school learning: Theory, research, and practice.* London: Croom Helm.

Burns, R. B., & Mason, D. A. (2002). Class composition and student achievement in elementary schools. *American Educational Research Journal, 39*(1), 207–233.

Burris, C., Heubert, J., & Levin, H. (2004). Math acceleration for all. *Educational Leadership, 61*(5), 68–71.

Burris, C., Heubert, J., & Levin, H. (2006). Accelerating mathematics achievement using heterogeneous grouping. *American Educational Research Journal, 43*(1), 105–136.

Burt, M. R., Resnick, G., & Novick, E. R. (1998). *Building supportive communities for at-risk adolescents.* Washington, DC: American Psychological Association.

Bussey, K. (1992). Lying and truthfulness: Children's definitions, standards, and evaluative reactions. *Child Development, 63,* 129–137.

Butcher, K. (2006). Learning from text with diagrams: Promoting mental model development and inference generation. *Journal of Educational Psychology, 98*(1), 182–197.

Butler, D. L., & Winne, P. H. (1995). Feedback and self-regulated learning. *Review of Educational Research, 65*(3), 245–281.

Byerly, S. (2001). Linking classroom teaching to the real world through experiential instruction. *Phi Delta Kappan, 82*(9), 697–699.

Byrne, B., Fielding-Barnsley, R., & Ashley, L. (2000). Effects of preschool phoneme identity training after six years: Outcome level distinguished from rate of response. *Journal of Educational Psychology, 92*(4), 659–667.

Byrnes, J. (2001). *Cognitive development and learning* (2nd ed.). Boston: Allyn & Bacon.

Caine, R. M., & Caine, G. (1997). *Education on the edge of possibility.* Alexandria, VA: Association for Supervision and Curriculum Development.

Calderón, M. (1994, April). *Cooperative learning as a powerful staff development tool for school renewal.* Paper presented at the annual meeting of the American Educational Research Association, New Orleans.

Calderón, M. (1999). Teacher learning communities for cooperation in diverse settings. *Theory into Practice, 38*(2), 94–99.

Calderón, M. (2001). Curricula and methodologies used to teach Spanish-speaking limited English proficient students to read English. In R. Slavin and M. Calderón (Eds.), *Effective programs for Latino students.* Mahwah, NJ: Erlbaum.

Calderón, M., August, D., Slavin, R. E., Durán, D., Madden, N. A., & Cheung, A. (2004). *The evaluation of a bilingual transition program for Success for All.* Baltimore, MD: Johns Hopkins University, Center for Research on the Education of Students Placed at Risk.

Calderón, M., Hertz-Lazarowitz, R., & Slavin, R. E. (1998). Effects of bilingual cooperative integrated reading and composition on students making the transition from Spanish to English reading. *Elementary School Journal, 99*(2), 153–165.

Calderón, M. E., & Minaya-Rowe, L. (2003). *Designing and implementing two-way bilingual programs.* Thousand Oaks, CA: Corwin.

Calhoun, G., & Elliott, R. (1977). Self-concept and academic achievement of educable retarded and emotionally disturbed children. *Exceptional Children, 44,* 379–380.

Calkins, L. M. (1983). *Lessons from a child: On the teaching and learning of writing.* Exeter, NH: Heinemann.

Cameron, J. (2001). Negative effects of reward on intrinsic motivation—a limited phenomenon: Comment on Deci, Koestner, and Ryan (2001). *Review of Educational Research, 71*(1), 29–42.

Cameron, J., & Pierce, W. D. (1994). Reinforcement, reward, and intrinsic motivation: A meta-analysis. *Review of Educational Research, 64,* 363–423.

Cameron, J., & Pierce, W. D. (1996). The debate about rewards and intrinsic motivation: Protests and accusations do not alter the results. *Review of Educational Research, 66*(1), 39–51.

Cameron, J., Pierce, W. D., Banko, K., & Gear, A. (2005). Achievement-based rewards and intrinsic motivation: A test of cognitive mediators. *Journal of Educational Psychology, 97*(4), 641–655.

Campbell, D. (2000). Authentic assessment and authentic standards. *Phi Delta Kappan, 81*(5), 405–407.

Campbell, F. A., & Ramey, C. T. (1994). Effects of early intervention on intellectual and academic achievement: A follow-up study of children from low-income families. *Child Development, 65,* 684–698.

Campbell, F. A., & Ramey, C. T. (1995). Cognitive and school outcomes for high-risk African American students at middle adolescence: Positive effects of early intervention. *American Educational Research Journal, 32,* 743–772.

Campbell, J., & Mayer, R. E. (2004, April). *Concrete manipulatives: For whom are they beneficial?* Paper presented at the annual meeting of the American Educational Research Association, San Diego, CA.

Campbell, L., Campbell, B., & Dickerson, D. (2004). *Teaching and learning through multiple intelligences.* Boston: Pearson.

Canada, G. (2000). Raising better boys. *Educational Leadership, 57*(4), 14–17.

Canfield, J., & Siccone, F. (1995). *101 ways to develop students' self-esteem and responsibility.* Boston: Allyn & Bacon.

Cannell, J. J. (1987). *Nationally normed elementary achievement testing in America's public schools: How all fifty states are above the national average.* Daniels, WV: Friends for Education.

Canter, L., & Canter, M. (2002). *Assertive discipline: Positive behavior management for today's schools.* Seal Beach, CA: Lee Canter & Associates.

Cappella, E., & Weinstein, R. (2001). Turning around reading achievement: Predictors of high school students' academic resilience. *Journal of Educational Psychology, 93*(4), 758–771.

Capper, C. A., Kampschroer, E. F., & Keyes, M. W. (2000). *Meeting the needs of students of all abilities: How leaders go beyond inclusion.* Bloomington, IN: Phi Delta Kappan.

Capron, C., & Duyme, M. (1991). Children's IQ's and SES of biological and adoptive parents in a balanced cross-fostering study. *Cahiers de Psychologie Cognitive, II,* 323–348.

Cardelle-Elawar, M. (1990). Effects of feedback tailored to bilingual students' mathematics needs on verbal problem solving. *Elementary School Journal, 91,* 165–175.

Cardellichio, T., & Field, W. (1997). Seven strategies that encourage neural branching. *Educational Leadership, 54*(6), 33–36.

Carey, L. M. (2001). *Measuring and evaluating school learning* (3rd ed.). Boston, MA: Allyn & Bacon.

Carlo, M. S., August, D., McLaughlin, B., Snow, C. E., Dressler, C., Lippman, D., Lively, T., & White, C. (2004). Closing the gap: Addressing the vocabulary needs of English language learners in bilingual and mainstream classrooms. *Reading Research Quarterly, 39*(2), 188–215.

Carnegie Corporation of New York. (1989). *Turning points: Preparing American youth for the 21st century.* New York: Author.

Carnegie Corporation of New York. (1994). *Starting points: Meeting the needs of our youngest children.* New York: Author.

Carnegie Corporation of New York. (1996). *Years of promise: A comprehensive learning strategy for America's children.* New York: Author.

Carney, R. N., & Levin, J. R. (1998). Do mnemonic memories fade as time goes by? Here's looking anew! *Contemporary Educational Psychology, 23*(3), 276–297.

Carney, R. N., & Levin, J. R. (2002). Pictorial illustrations still improve students' learning from text. *Educational Psychology Review, 14*(1), 5–26.

Carnine, D., Grosen, B., & Silbert, J. (1995). Direct instructions to accelerate cognitive growth. In J. H. Block, S. T. Everson, & T. R. Guskey (Eds.), *School improvement programs* (pp. 129–152). New York: Scholastic.

Carnoy, M., & Loeb, S. (2002). Does external accountability affect student outcomes? A cross-state analysis. *Educational Evaluation and Policy Analysis, 24*(4), 305–331.

Carolan, J., & Guinn, A. (2007). Differentiation: Lessons from master teachers. *Educational Leadership, 64*(5), 44–47.

Carpenter, T. P., & Fennema, E. (1992). Cognitively guided instruction: Building on the knowledge of students and teachers. *International Journal of Educational Research, 17,* 457–470.

Carpenter, T. P., Fennema, E., Fuson, K., Hiebert, J., Human, P., Murray, H., Olivier, A., & Wearne, D. (1994, April). *Teaching mathematics for learning with understanding in the primary grades.* Paper presented at the annual meeting of the American Educational Research Association, New Orleans, LA.

Carpenter, T. P., Fennema, E., Peterson, P. L., Chiang, C. P., & Loef, M. (1989). Using knowledge of children's mathematics thinking in classroom teaching: An experimental study. *American Educational Research Journal, 26,* 499–531.

Carr, J. F., & Harris, D. E. (2001). *Succeeding with standards: Linking curriculum, assessment, and action planning.* Alexandria, VA: ASCD.

Carroll, J. B. (1963). A model of school learning. *Teachers College Record, 64,* 723–733.

Carroll, J. B. (1989). The Carroll model: A 25-year retrospective and prospective view. *Educational Researcher, 18,* 26–31.

Carter, C. J. (1997). Why reciprocal teaching? *Educational Leadership, 54*(6), 64–68.

Carter, L. F. (1984). The sustaining effects study of compensatory and elementary education. *Educational Researcher, 13*(7), 4–13.

Carter, R. T., & Goodwin, A. L. (1994). *Racial Identity and Education, 20,* 291–336.

Carver, S. M., & Klahr, D. (2001). *Cognition and instruction: Twenty five years of progress.* Mahwah, NJ: Erlbaum.

Case, R. (1998). The development of conceptual structures. In W. Damon (Ed.), *Handbook of child psychology* (Vol. 2, pp. 851–898). Hoboken, NJ: Wiley.

CASE. (1993). *CASE position paper on delivery of services to students with disabilities.* Washington, DC: Council for Administrators of Special Education.

Casey, B., Giedd, J., & Thomas, K. (2000). Structural and functional brain development and its relation to cognitive development. *Biological Psychology, 54,* 241–257.

Cassady, J. C., & Johnson, R. E. (2002). Cognitive anxiety and academic performance. *Contemporary Educational Psychology, 27,* 270–295.

Casto, G., & Mastropieri, M. A. (1986). The efficacy of early intervention programs: A meta-analysis. *Exceptional Children, 52,* 417–424.

Cavanaugh, C., Kim, A.-H., Wanzek, J., & Vaughn, S. (2004). Kindergarten reading interventions for at-risk students: Twenty years of research. *Learning Disabilities: A Contemporary Journal, 2*(1), 1–8.

Cavanna, A., Olchefske, J., & Fleischman, S. (2006). The potential of the portfolio approach. *Educational Leadership, 63*(8), 89–93.

Cawelti, G. (2006). The side effects of NCLB. *Educational Leadership, 64*(3), 64–68.

Ceci, S. J. (1991). How much does schooling influence general intelligence and its cognitive components? A reassessment of the evidence. *Developmental Psychology, 27,* 703–722.

Ceci, S. J. (1992). The new intelligence theorists: Old liberals in new guises? *Educational Researcher, 21*(6), 25–27.

Center for Data-Driven Reform in Education. (2006). *Best evidence encyclopedia.* Baltimore, MD: Johns Hopkins University. www.bestevidence.org.

Center on Education Policy. (2003). *State and federal efforts to implement the No Child Left Behind Act.* Washington, DC: Author.

Center on Education Policy. (2004). *From the Capitol to the classroom: Year 2 of the No Child Left Behind Act.* Washington, DC: Author.

Center on Education Policy. (2007). *Has student achievement increased since No Child Left Behind?* Washington, DC: Author.

Centers for Disease Control. (1998). *Youth risk behavior surveillance—United States, 1997.* Atlanta, GA: Author.

Cepeda, N. J., Pashler, H., Vul, E., Wixted, J. T., & Rohrer, D. (2006). Distributed practice in verbal recall tasks: A review and quantitative synthesis. *Psychological Bulletin, 132,* 354–380.

Chambers, B., Cheung, A., Madden, N., Slavin, R. E., & Gifford, R. (2006). Achievement effects of embedded multimedia in a Success for All reading program. *Journal of Educational Psychology, 98*(1), 232–237.

Chambers, B., Slavin, R. E., Madden, N. A., Abrami, P. C., Tucker, B. J., Cheung, A., & Gifford, R. (in press). Technology infusion in Success for All: Reading outcomes for first graders. *Elementary School Journal.*

Chan, C. K. K., Burtis, P. J., Scardamalia, M., & Bereiter, C. (1992). Constructive activity in learning from text. *American Educational Research Journal, 29,* 97–118.

Chance, P. (1992). The rewards of learning. *Phi Delta Kappan, 74*(3), 200–207.

Chandler, L., & Dahlquist, C. (2006). *Functional assessment: Strategies to prevent and remediate challenging behavior in school settings.* Upper Saddle River, NJ: Pearson Prentice-Hall.

Changeux, J.-P. (2004). [Review of the book *The physiology of truth: Neuroscience and human knowledge.*] *Educational Leadership, 62*(4), 92.

Chapman, E. (2001, April). *More on moderations in cooperative learning outcomes.* Paper presented at the annual meeting of the American Educational Research Association, Montreal.

Chapman, J., Tunmer, W., & Prochnow, J. (2000). Early reading-related skills and performance, reading self-concept, and the development of academic self-concept: A longitudinal study. *Journal of Educational Psychology, 92*(4), 703–708.

Chappuis, J. (2005). Helping students understand assessment. *Educational Leadership, 63*(3), 39–43.

Charles, C. M. (2008). *Building classroom discipline* (9th ed.). Boston: Allyn & Bacon.

Chatterji, M. (2002). Models and methods for examining standards-based reforms and accountability initiatives: Have the tools of inquiry answered pressing questions on improving schools? *Review of Educational Research, 72*(3), 345–386.

Chatterji, M. (2006). Reading achievement gaps, correlates, and moderators of early reading achievement: Evidence from the Early Childhood Longitudinal Study (ECLS) kindergarten to first grade sample. *Journal of Educational Psychology, 98* (3), 489–507.

Chen, J.-Q. (2004). Theory of multiple intelligences: Is it a scientific theory? *Teachers College Record, 106,* 17–23.

Chen, Z., & Daehler, M. (2000). External and internal instantiation of abstract information facilitates transfer in insight problem solving. *Contemporary Educational Psychology, 25*(4), 423–449.

Cheung, A., & Slavin, R. E. (2005). Effective reading programs for English language learners and other language minority students. *Bilingual Research Journal, 29*(2), 241–267.

Children's Partnership. (2006). *Measuring digital opportunity for America's children.* Available at www.contentbank.org/DOMS.

Chin, C. W. T. (1998, April). *Synthesizing metacognitive interventions: What training characteristics can improve reading performance?* Paper presented at the annual meeting of the American Educational Research Association, San Diego, CA.

Chinn, C. A., & Brewer, W. F. (1993). The role of anomalous data in knowledge acquisition. *Review of Educational Research, 63*(1), 1–49.

Choate, J. (2004). *Successful inclusive teaching* (4th ed.). Boston: Pearson.

Chomsky, C. (1969). *The acquisition of syntax in children from 5 to 10.* M.I.T. Press Research Monogram No. 57. Cambridge, MA: M.I.T. Press.

Chorzempa, B., & Graham, S. (2006). Primary-grade teachers' use of within-class ability grouping in reading. *Journal of Educational Psychology, 98*(3), 529–541.

Christian, D., & Genesee, F. (Eds.). (2001). *Bilingual education.* Alexandria, VA: TESOL.

Cizek, G. J. (1993). Innovation or enervation? Performance assessment in perspective. In K. M. Cauley, F. Linder, & J. H. McMillan (Eds.), *Annual Editions: Educational Psychology 93/94.* Guilford, CT: Dushkin.

Cizek, G. J. (1999). *Cheating on tests: How to do it, detect it, and prevent it.* Mahwah, NJ: Erlbaum.

Clark, C. M., Gage, N. L., Marx, R. W., Peterson, P. L., Stayrook, N. G., & Winne, P. H. (1979). A factorial experiment on teacher structuring, soliciting, and reacting. *Journal of Educational Psychology, 71,* 534–552.

Clark, J. (1990). *Patterns of thinking: Integrating learning skills with content teaching.* Boston: Allyn & Bacon.

Clark, J. M., & Paivio, A. (1991). Dual coding theory and education. *Educational Psychology Review, 3*(3), 149–210.

Clark, R. E. (Ed.). (2001). *Learning from media: Arguments, analysis, and evidence.* Greenwich, CT: Information Age.

Clements, D. H., & Battista, M. T. (1990). Constructivist learning and teaching. *Arithmetic Teacher, 38,* 34–37.

Clifford, M. M. (1990). Students need challenge, not easy success. *Educational Leadership, 48*(1), 22–26.

Clifford, R. M., Early, D. M., & Hills, T. W. (1999). Almost a million children in school before kindergarten: Who is responsible for early childhood services? *Young Children, 12,* 48–51.

Cline, Z. (1998). *Buscando su voz en dos culturas:* Finding your voice in two cultures. *Phi Delta Kappan, 79*(9), 699–705.

Coalition for Evidence Based Policy. (2003). *Identitying and implementing educational practices supported by rigorous evidence: A user friendly guide.* Washington, DC: U.S. Department of Education.

Cobb, N. (1995). *Adolescence.* Mountain View, CA: Mayfield.

Cochran-Smith, M. (1991). Word processing and writing in elementary classrooms: A critical review of related literature. *Review of Educational Research, 61*(1), 107–155.

Cognition and Technology Group at Vanderbilt. (1996). Looking at technology in context: A framework for understanding technology and education research. In D. C. Berliner & R. C. Calfee (Eds.), *Handbook of educational psychology* (pp. 807–840). New York: Macmillan.

Cohen, E. G. (1984). Talking and working together: Status, interaction, and learning. In P. Peterson, L. C. Wilkinson, & M. Hallinan (Eds.), *The social context of instruction: Group organization and group processes.* New York: Academic Press.

Cohen, E. G. (1986). *Designing groupwork: Strategies for the heterogeneous classroom.* New York: Teachers College Press.

Cohen, E. G. (1992, April). *Complex instruction in the middle school.* Paper presented at the annual meeting of the American Educational Research Association, San Francisco, CA.

Cohen, E. G. (1994a). *Designing groupwork: Strategies for the heterogeneous classroom* (2nd ed.). New York: Teachers College Press.

Cohen, E. G. (1994b). Restructuring the classroom: Conditions for productive small groups. *Review of Educational Research, 64*(1), 1–35.

Cohen, E. G. (2004). Producing equal-status interaction amidst classroom diversity. In W. G. Stephan & W. P. Vogt (Eds.), *Education programs for improving intergroup relations.* New York: Teachers College Press.

Cohen, L. B., & Cashon, C. H. (2003). Infant perception and cognition. In R. M. Lerner, M. A. Easterbrooks, & J. Mistry (Eds.), *Handbook of psychology: Vol. 6. Developmental psychology* (pp. 65–89). Hoboken, NJ: Wiley.

Cohen, R. L. (1989). Memory for action events: The power of enactment. *Educational Psychology Review, 1*(1), 57–80.

Coie, J. D., Dodge, K. A., & Kupersmidt, J. (1990). Peer group behavior and social status. In S. R. Asher & J. D. Coie (Eds.), *Peer rejection in children* (pp. 17–59). New York: Cambridge University Press.

Colby, C., & Kohlberg, L. (1984). Invariant sequence and internal consistency in moral judgment stages. In W. Kurtines & J. Gewirts (Eds.), *Morality, moral behavior, and moral development.* New York: Wiley-Interscience.

Cole, D. A. (1991). Change in self-perceived competence as a function of peer and teacher evaluation. *Developmental Psychology, 27,* 682–688.

Cole-Henderson, B. (2000). Organizational characteristics of schools that successfully service low-income African American students. *Journal of Education for Students Placed at Risk, 5*(1–2), 77–91.

Coles, G. (2004). Danger in the classroom: "Brain Glitch" research and learning to read. *Phi Delta Kappan, 85*(5), 344–357.

Coley, R. L., & Chase-Lansdale, P. L. (1998). Adolescent pregnancy and parenthood. *American Psychologist, 53*(2), 152–166.

Colom, R., Flores-Mendoza, C., & Rebello, I. (2003). Working memory and intelligence. *Personality and Individual Differences, 34,* 33–39.

Colvin, G. (2004). *Managing the cycle of acting-out behavior in the classroom.* Longmont, CO: Sopris West.

Comer, J. (2005). Child and adolescent development: The critical missing focus in school reform. *Phi Delta Kappan, 86*(10), 757–763.

Comer, J. (2005). The rewards of parent participation. *Educational Leadership, 62*(6), 38–43.

Comer, J. P. (1990). *Maggie's American dream.* New York: Plume.

Comer, J. P., Haynes, N. M., Joyner, E. T., & Ben-Avie, M. (1996). *Rallying the whole village: The Comer process for reforming education.* New York: Teachers College Press.

Connor, C. M., Son, S. H., Hindman, A. H., & Morrison, F. J. (2004). *Teacher qualifications, classroom practices, and family characteristics: Complex effects on first-graders' vocabulary and early reading outcomes.* Ann Arbor: University of Michigan, Department of Psychology.

Conway, M. A., Cohen, G., & Stanhope, N. (1991). Very long-term memory of knowledge acquired through formal education: Twelve years of cognitive psychology. *Journal of Experimental Psychology: General, 120,* 395–409.

Conyers, L., Reynolds, A., & Ou, S. (2003). The effect of early childhood intervention and subsequent special education services: Findings from the Chicago child–parent centers. *Educational Evaluation and Policy Analysis, 25*(1), 75–95.

Cook, J. L., & Cook, G. (2007). *The world of children.* Boston: Allyn & Bacon.

Cook, T. D., Habib, F., Phillips, M., Settersten, R. A., Shagle, S., & Degirmencioglu, M. (1999). Comer's school development program in Prince George's County, Maryland: A theory-based evaluation. *American Educational Research Journal, 36*(3), 543–597.

Cook, T., Murphy, R. F., & Hunt, H. D. (2000). Comer's school development program in Chicago: A theory-based evaluation. *American Educational Research Journal, 37*(2), 535–597.

Cooley, W. W., & Leinhardt, G. (1980). The instructional dimensions study. *Educational Evaluation and Policy Analysis, 2,* 7–26.

Cooper, H., Charlton, K., Valentine, J. C., & Muhlenbruck, L. (2000). Making the most of summer school: A meta-analytic and narrative review. *Monographs of the Society for Research in Child Development* (Serial No. 260), *65*(1), 1–118.

Cooper, H., Lindsay, J. J., Nye, B., & Greathouse, S. (1998). Relationships among attitudes about homework, amount of homework assigned and completed, and student achievement. *Journal of Educational Psychology, 90*(1), 70–83.

Cooper, H., Robinson, J. C., & Patall, E. (2006). Does homework improve academic achievement? *Review of Educational Research, 76*(1), 1–62.

Cooper, H., & Valentine, J. C. (2001). Using research to answer practical questions about homework. *Educational Psychologist.*

Cooper, R. (1998). Urban school reform: Student responses to detracking in a racially mixed high school. *Journal of Education for Students Placed at Risk, 4*(3), 259–275.

Cooper, R., & Slavin, R. E. (2004). Cooperative learning: An instructional strategy to improve intergroup relations. In W. G. Stephan & W. P. Vogt (Eds.), *Education programs for improving intergroup relations.* New York: Teachers College Press.

Copeland, W. D. (1983, April). *Classroom management and student teachers' cognitive abilities: A relationship.* Paper presented at the annual convention of the American Educational Research Association, Montreal, Canada.

Corbett, D., Wilson, B., & Williams, B. (2005). No choice but success. *Educational Leadership, 62*(6), 8–13.

Cordova, D. I., & Lepper, M. R. (1996). Intrinsic motivation and the process of learning: Beneficial effects of contextualization, personalization, and choice. *Journal of Educational Psychology, 88*(4), 715–730.

Corkill, A. J. (1992). Advance organizers: Facilitators of recall. *Educational Psychology Review, 4,* 33–67.

Cornelius-White, J. (2007). Learner-centered teacher-student relationships are effective: A meta-analysis. *Review of Educational Research, 77*(1), 113–143.

Corno, L. (1992). Encouraging students to take responsibility for learning and performance. *Elementary School Journal, 95,* 69–84.

Corno, L. (2000). Looking at homework differently. *The Elementary School Journal, 100*(5), 529–548.

Corno, L., & Kanfer, R. (1993). The role of volition in learning and performance. *Review of Research in Education, 19,* 301–341.

Cortés, C. E. (1995). Knowledge construction and popular culture: The media as multicultural educator. In J. A. Banks & C. A. M. Banks (Eds.), *Handbook of research on multicultural education.* New York: Macmillan.

Cose, E. (2004). *Beyond Brown v. Board: The final battle for excellence in American education.* A report by Ellis Close to the Rockefeller Foundation.

Covington, M. (1999). Caring about learning: The nature and nurturing of subject-matter appreciation. *Educational Psychologist, 34*(2), 127–136.

Cox, B. D. (1997). The rediscovery of the active learner in adaptive contexts: A developmental-historical analysis of transfer of training. *Educational Psychologist, 32,* 41–55.

Cox, B., & Hopkins, C. (2006). Building on theoretical principles gleaned from Reading Recovery to inform classroom practice. *Reading Research Quarterly, 41*(2), 254–267.

Craik, F. I. M. (2000). Memory: Coding processes. In A. Kazdin (Ed.), *Encyclopedia of psychology.* Washington, DC: American Psychological Association.

Crawford, J. (1989). Instructional activities related to achievement gain in Chapter I classes. In R. E. Slavin, N. L. Karweit, & N. A. Madden (Eds.), *Effective programs for students at risk.* Boston: Allyn & Bacon.

Creswell, J. W. (2002). *Research design: Qualitative, quantitative, and mixed methods approaches* (2nd ed.). Thousand Oaks, CA: Sage.

Crévola, C. A., & Hill, P. W. (1998). Evaluation of a whole-school approach to prevention and intervention in early literacy. *Journal of Education for Students Placed at Risk, 3*(2), 133–157.

Crocker, R. K., & Brooker, G. M. (1986). Classroom control and student outcomes in grades 2 and 5. *American Educational Research, 23,* 1–11.

Crooks, T. J. (1988). The impact of classroom evaluation practices on students. *Review of Educational Research, 58,* 438–481.

Cross, L. H., & Cross, G. M. (1980/1981). Teachers' evaluative comments and pupil perception of control. *Journal of Experimental Education, 49,* 68–71.

Crutcher, R. J., & Ericsson, K. A. (2003). The effects of practice on mnemonic encodings involving prior knowledge and semantic memory. *Journal of Experimental Psychology: Learning Memory and Cognition, 29*(6), 1387–1389.

Cruz, L., & Cullinan, D. (2001). Awarding points, using levels to help children improve behavior. *Teaching Exceptional Children, 33*(3), 16–23.

CSRQ (Comprehensive School Reform Quality Center). (2006a). *CSRQ center report on elementary comprehensive school reform models.* Washington, DC: American Institutes for Research.

CSRQ (Comprehensive School Reform Quality Center). (2006b). *CSRQ center report on middle and high school comprehensive school reform models.* Washington, DC: American Institutes for Research.

Cuban, L., (2001). *Oversold and underused: Reforming schools through technology, 1980–2000.* Cambridge, MA: Harvard University Press.

Cuban, L., Kirkpatrick, H., & Peck, C. (2001). High access and low use of technology in high school classrooms: Explaining an apparent paradox. *American Educational Research Journal, 38*(4), 813–834.

Cummings, E. M., Braungart-Rieker, J. M., & Du Rocher-Schudlich, T. (2003). Emotion and personality development in childhood. In R. M. Lerner, M. A. Easterbrooks, & J. Mistry (Eds.), *Handbook of psychology: Vol. 6. Developmental psychology* (pp. 211–239). Hoboken, NJ: Wiley.

Curry, C. (2003). Universal design accessibility for all learners. *Educational Leadership, 61*(2), 55–60.

Curwin, R. E., & Mendler, A. N. (1999). Zero tolerance for zero tolerance. *Phi Delta Kappan, 81*(2), 119–120.

Cushman, K. (2006). Help us care enough to learn. *Educational Leadership, 63*(5), 34–37.

D'Agostino, J. V., & Murphy, J. A. (2004). Meta-analysis of Reading Recovery in United States schools. *Educational Evaluation and Policy Analysis, 26*(1), 23–28.

Dai, D., Moon, S., & Feldhusen, J. (1998). Achievement motivation and gifted students: A social cognitive perspective. *Educational Psychologist, 33*(1), 45–63.

Dansereau, D. F. (1985). Learning strategy research. In J. Segal, S. Chipman, & R. Glaser (Eds.), *Thinking and learning skills: Relating instruction to basic research, Vol. 1.* Hillsdale, NJ: Erlbaum.

Dantonio, M., & Beisenherz, P. (2001). *Learning to question, questioning to learn.* Boston: Allyn & Bacon.

Darling-Hammond, L. (1995). Inequality and access to knowledge. In J. A. Banks & C. A. M. Banks (Eds.), *Handbook of research on multicultural education* (pp. 465–483). New York: Macmillan.

Darling-Hammond, L. (2006). Securing the right to learn: Policy and practice for powerful teaching and learning. *Educational Researcher, 35*(7), 13–24.

Darling-Hammond, L., Ancess, J., & Ort, S. W. (2002). Reinventing high school: Outcomes of the coalition campus schools project. *American Educational Research Journal, 39*(3), 639–673.

Darling-Hammond, L., & Falk, B. (1997). Using standards and assessments to support student learning. *Phi Delta Kappan, 79*(3), 190–201.

Darling-Hammond, L., Gendler, T., & Wise, A. D. (1990). *The teaching internship: Practical preparation for a licensed profession.* Santa Monica, CA: RAND.

Darling-Hammond, L., & Ifill-Lynch, O. (2006). If they'd only do their work! *Educational Leadership, 63*(5), 8–13.

Das, J. P. (1995). Some thoughts on two aspects of Vygotsky's work. *Educational Psychologist, 30*(2), 993–997.

Davidman, L., & Davidman, P. (Eds.). (2001). *Teaching with a multicultural perspective: A practical guide.* New York: Addison-Wesley.

DeBacker, T., & Nelson, R. M. (1999). Variations on an expectancy-value model of motivation in science. *Contemporary Educational Psychology, 24*(2), 71–94.

DeBell, M., & Chapman, C. (2006). *Computer and internet use by students in 2003.* Washington, DC: National Center for Education Statistics, U.S. Department of Education.

Deci, E., Koestner, R., & Ryan, R. (2001). Extrinsic rewards and intrinsic motivation in education: Reconsidered once again. *Review of Educational Research, 71*(1), 1–27.

Deci, E. L., & Ryan, R. M. (Eds.). (2002). *Handbook of self-determination research.* Rochester: University of Rochester Press.

De Jong, T., & van Joolingen, W. R. (1998). Scientific discovery learning with computer simulations of conceptual domains. *Review of Educational Research, 68*(2), 179–201.

Delamont, S. (2002). Gender and education. In D. L. Levinson, P. W. Cookson, Jr., & A. R. Sadovnik (Eds.), *Education and sociology: An encyclopedia* (pp. 273–279). New York: Routledge Falmer.

de La Paz, S., & Graham, S. (2002). Explicitly teaching strategies, skills, and knowledge: Writing instruction in middle school classrooms. *Journal of Educational Psychology, 94*(2), 687–698.

De Lisi, R., & Staudt, J. (1980). Individual differences in college students' performance on formal operations tasks. *Journal of Applied Developmental Psychology, 1,* 201–208.

Delpit, L. (1995). *Other people's children: Cultural conflict in the classroom.* New York: New Press.

Dembo, M., & Eaton, M. (2000). Self-regulation of academic learning in middle-level schools. *The Elementary School Journal, 100*(5), 472–490.

Dempster, F. N. (1989). Spacing effects and their implications for theory and practice. *Educational Psychology Review, 1,* 309–330.

Dempster, F. N. (1991). Synthesis of research on reviews and tests. *Educational Leadership, 72*(8), 71–76.

Dempster, F. N., & Corkill, A. J. (1999). Interference and inhibition in cognition and behavior: Unifying themes for educational psychology. *Educational Psychology Review, 11*(1), 1–74.

Denton, C. A., Anthony, J. L., Parker, R., & Hasbrouck, J. E. (2004). Effects of two tutoring programs on the English reading development of Spanish-English bilingual students. *The Elementary School Journal, 104*(4), 289–305.

de Ribaupierre, A., & Rieben, L. (1995). Individual and situational variability in cognitive development. *Educational Psychologist, 30*(1), 5–14.

Derry, S. J. (1991). Strategy and expertise in solving word problems. In C. McCormick, G. Miller, & M. Pressley (Eds.), *Cognitive strategies research: From basic research to educational applications.* New York: Springer-Verlag.

Deshler, D. D., Ellis, E. S., & Lenz, B. K. (1996). *Teaching students with learning disabilities: Strategies and methods* (2nd ed.). Denver: Love.

Deshler, D. D. (2005). Adolescents with learning disabilities. *Learning Disabilities Quarterly, 28*(2), 122–123.

Dev, P., Doyle, B. A., & Valente, B. (2002). Labels needn't stick: "At risk" first graders rescued with appropriate intervention. *Journal of Education for Students Placed at Risk,* 7(3), 327–332.

De Vise, D. (2007, May 23). More work, less play in kindergarten. *The Washington Post,* p. A1.

Deyhle, D., & Swisher, K. (1995). Research in American Indian and Alaskan native education: From assimilation to self-determination. In M. W. Apple (Ed.), *Review of research in education, 22* (pp. 113–194). Washington, DC: American Educational Research Association.

Diaz, C. (2001). *Multicultural education for the 21st century.* Boca Raton, FL: Addison-Wesley.

Díaz-Rico, L. T. (2004). *Teaching English learners: Strategies and methods.* Boston: Allyn & Bacon.

Dick, W., Carey, L., & Carey, J. (2001). *The systematic design of instruction* (5th ed.). New York: Longman.

Diehm, C. (2004). From worn-out to web-based: Better student portfolios. *Phi Delta Kappan, 85*(10), 792–795.

Diener, C. I., & Dweck, C. S. (1978). An analysis of learned helplessness: Continuous changes in performance, strategy, and achievement cognitions following failure. *Journal of Personality and Social Psychology, 36,* 451–462.

Dillon, A., & Gabbard, R. (1998). Hypermedia as an educational technology: A review of the quantitative research literature on learner comprehension, control, and style. *Review of Educational Research, 68*(3), 322–349.

Dimino, J., Gersten, R., Carnine, D., & Blake, G. (1990). Story grammar: An approach for promoting at-risk secondary students' comprehension of literature. *Elementary School Journal, 91,* 19–32.

Dlott, A. (2007). A (pod)cast of thousands. *Educational Leadership, 64*(7), 80–82.

Dooling, D. J., & Lachman, R. (1971). Effects of comprehension on retention of prose. *Journal of Experimental Psychology, 8,* 216–222.

Dornbusch, S. (1994). *Off the track.* Paper presented at the annual meeting of the Society for Research on Adolescence, San Diego, CA.

Downing, J. E. (2001). *Including students with severe and multiple disabilities in typical classrooms.* Baltimore: Brookes.

Doyle, W. (1984). How order is achieved in classrooms: An interim report. *Journal of Curriculum Studies, 16,* 259–277.

Drabman, R., Spitalnik, R., & O'Leary, K. (1973). Teaching self-control to disruptive children. *Journal of Abnormal Psychology, 82,* 10–16.

Driscoll, M. P. (2000). *Psychology of learning for instruction* (2nd ed.). Boston: Allyn & Bacon.

Driscoll, M. P. (2005). *Psychology of learning for instruction* (3rd ed.). Boston: Allyn & Bacon.

Droz, M., & Ellis, L. (1996). *Laughing while learning: Using humor in the classroom.* Longmont, CO: Sopris West.

Dryfoos, J. G. (1998). *Safe passage: Making it through adolescence in a risky society.* New York: Oxford University Press.

Dryfoos, J. G. (1990). *Adolescents at risk: Prevalence and prevention.* New York: Oxford University Press.

Duck, L. (2000). The ongoing professional journey. *Educational Leadership, 57*(8), 43–45.

Duell, O. K. (1994). Extended wait time and university student achievement. *American Educational Research Journal, 31*(2), 397–414.

Duffy, G. G., & Roehler, L. R. (1986). The subtleties of instructional mediation. *Educational Leadership, 43*(7), 23–27.

Dugger, W. (2001). Standards for technological literacy. *Phi Delta Kappan, 82*(7), 513–517.

Duke, N. K. (2000). For the rich it's richer: Print experiences and environments offered to children in very low- and very high-socioeconomic status first-grade classrooms. *American Educational Research Journal, 37*(2), 441–478.

Dukes, R., & Seidner, C. (1978). *Learning with simulations and games.* Beverly Hills, CA: Sage.

Dumit, J. (2004). *Picturing personhood: Brain scans and biomedical identity.* Princeton NJ: Princeton University Press.

Dunkin, M. J., & Biddle, B. J. (1974). *A study of teaching.* New York: Holt, Rinehart and Winston.

Dunn, R., Beaudrey, J. S., & Klavas, A. (1989). Survey of research on learning styles. *Educational Leadership, 46*(6), 50–58.

Dunn, R., & Dunn, K. (1993). *Teaching secondary students through their individual learning styles.* Boston: Allyn & Bacon.

Durso, F. T., & Coggins, K. A. (1991). Organized instruction for the improvement of word knowledge skills. *Journal of Educational Psychology, 83,* 108–112.

Dynarski, M., et al. (2007). *Effectiveness of reading and mathematics software products: Findings from the first student cohort.* Washington, DC: Institute of Education Sciences.

Ebeling, D. G. (2000). Adapting your teaching to any learning style. *Phi Delta Kappan, 82*(3), 247–248.

Eccles, J. S., Wigfield, A., & Byrnes, J. (2003). Cognitive development in adolescence. In R. M. Lerner, M. A. Easterbrooks, & J. Mistry (Eds.), *Handbook of psychology: Vol. 6. Developmental psychology* (pp. 325–350). Hoboken, NJ: Wiley.

Echevarria, J., Vogt, M. E., & Short, D. (2004). *Making content comprehensible for English learners: The SIOP model.* Boston: Allyn & Bacon.

Eckensberger, L. H. (1994). Moral development and its measurement across cultures. In W. J. Lonner & R. S. Malpass (Eds.), *Psychology and culture* (pp. 75–79). Boston: Allyn & Bacon.

Eden, G. F., Van Meter, J. W., Rumsey, J. M., Maisog, J. M., Woods, R. P., & Zeffiro, T. A. (1996). Abnormal processing of visual motion in dyslexia revealed by functional brain imaging. *Nature, 382,* 66–69.

Education Commission of the States. (2000). *Technology: Equitable access in schools.* Denver, CO: Author.

Educational Testing Service. (1995). *Performance assessment: Different needs, difficult answers.* Princeton, NJ: Author.

Educational Testing Service. (1996). *Computer classrooms: The status of technology in U.S. schools.* Princeton, NJ: Author.

Egan, K. (1989). Memory, imagination, and learning: Connected by the story. *Phi Delta Kappan, 70,* 455–459.

Egeland, P. (1996). Pulleys, planes, and student performance. *Educational Leadership, 54*(4), 41–45.

Ehri, L. C., Dreyer, L. G., Flugman, B., & Gross, A. (2007). Reading Rescue: An effective tutoring intervention model for language-minority students who are struggling readers in first grade. *American Educational Research Journal, 44,* 414–448.

Eichenbaum, H. (2003). Memory systems. In M. Gallagher & R. J. Nelson (Eds.), *Handbook of psychology: Vol. 3. Biological psychology* (pp. 543–558). Hoboken, NJ: Wiley.

Einerson, M. (1998). Fame, fortune, and failure: Young girls' moral language surrounding popular culture. *Youth and Society, 30,* 241–257.

Eisenberg, N. (2001). The core and correlates of affective social competence. *Social Development, 10,* 120–124.

Eisenberger, R., & Cameron, J. (1998). Reward, intrinsic interest, and creativity: New findings. *American Psychologist, 53*(6), 676–679.

Eisenberger, R., Pierce, W. D., & Cameron, J. (1999). Effects of rewards on intrinsic motivation—negative, neutral, and positive: Comment on Deci, Koestner, and Ryan (1999). *Psychological Bulletin, 125,* 677–691.

Eisner, E. (2006). The satisfactions of teaching. *Educational Leadership, 63*(6), 44–47.

Elbaum, B., & Vaughn, S. (2001). School-based interventions to enhance the self-concept of students with learning disabilities: A meta-analysis. *The Elementary School Journal, 101*(3), 303–330.

Elbaum, B., Vaughn, S., Hughes, M., & Moody, S. (2000). How effective are one-to-one tutoring programs in reading for elementary students at risk for reading failure? A meta-analysis of the intervention research. *Journal of Educational Psychology 92*(4), 605–619.

Elias, L. J., & Saucier, D. M. (2006). *Neuropsychoogy: Clinical and experimental foundations.* Boston: Allyn & Bacon.

Elkind, D. (1989). Developmentally appropriate practice: Philosophical and practical implications. *Phi Delta Kappan, 71*(2), 113–117.

Ellis, A. K. (2001a). Authentic and performance assessment. In A. K. Ellis (Ed.), *Research on educational innovations.* Larchmont, NY: Eye on Education.

Ellis, A. K. (2001b). Cooperative learning. In A. K. Ellis (Ed.), *Research on educational innovations.* Larchmont, NY: Eye on Education.

Ellis, A. K. (2001c). Innovations from brain research. In A. K. Ellis (Ed.), *Research on educational innovations.* Larchmont, NY: Eye on Education.

Ellis, J., Semb, G. B., & Cole, B. (1998). Very long-term memory for information taught in school. *Contemporary Educational Psychology, 23,* 419–433.

Ellmore, R. F., & Fuhrman, S. H. (2001). Holding schools accountable: Is it working? *Phi Delta Kappan, 83*(1), 67–72.

Else-Quest, N., Shibley, J., Goldsmith, H., & Van Hulle, C. (2006). Gender differences in temperament: A meta-analysis. *Psychological Bulletin, 132*(1), 33–72.

Embry, D. D. (2002). The good behavior game: A best practice candidate as universal behavior vaccine. *Clinical Child and Family Psychology Review, 5,* 273–297.

Emerson, M. J., & Miyake, A. (2003). The role of inner speech in task switching: A dual-task investigation. *Journal of Memory and Language, 48,* 148–168.

Emmer, E. T., & Aussiker, A. (1990). School and classroom discipline programs: How well do they work? In O. C. Moles (Ed.), *Student discipline strategies.* Albany, NY: State University of New York Press.

Emmer, E., Evertson, C., Clements, B., & Worsham, M. (2006). *Classroom management for secondary teachers.* Boston: Allyn & Bacon.

Emmer, E. T., Evertson, C. M., & Anderson, L. M. (1980). Effective classroom management at the beginning of the school year. *Elementary School Journal, 80,* 219–231.

Emmer, E. T., & Gerwels, M. C. (2002). Cooperative learning in elementary classrooms: Teaching practices and lesson characteristics. *The Elementary School Journal, 103*(1), 75–91.

Emmer, E. T., & Stough, L. M. (2001). Classroom management: A critical part of educational psychology, with implications for teacher education. *Educational Psychologist, 36*(2), 103–112.

Engle, R. W., Nations, J. K., & Cantor, J. (1990). Is "working memory capacity" just another name for word knowledge? *Journal of Educational Psychology, 82*(4), 799–804.

Englert, C. S., Raphael, T. E., Anderson, L. M., Anthony, H. M., & Stevens, D. D. (1991). Making strategies and self-talk visible: Writing instruction in regular and special education classrooms. *American Educational Research Journal, 28,* 337–372.

Ennemoser, M., & Schneider, W. (2007). Relations of television viewing and reading: Findings from a 4-year longitudinal study. *Journal of Educational Psychology, 99*(2), 349–368.

Ensminger, M. E., & Slusarcick, A. L. (1992). Paths to high school graduation or dropout: A longitudinal study of a first grade cohort. *Sociology of Education, 65,* 95–113.

Entwisle, D., Alexander, L., & Olson, L. S. (2001). Keep the faucet flowing: Summer learning and home environment. *American Educator, 25*(3), 10–15.

Epstein, J. L., Sanders, M. G., Salinas, K., Simon, B., Van Voorhis, F., & Jansorn, N. (2002). *School, family and community partnerships: Your handbook for action* (2nd ed.). Thousand Oaks, CA: Corwin.

Epstein, J. L., & Van Voorhis, F. L. (2001). More than minutes: Teachers' roles in designing homework. *Educational Psychologist, 36*(3), 181–193.

Epstein, M. H., & Cullinan, D. (1992). Emotional/behavioral problems. In M. C. Alkin (Ed.), *Encyclopedia of educational research* (6th ed.) (pp. 430–432). New York: Macmillan.

Ericsson, K. A., & Kintsch, W. (1995). Long-term working memory. *Psychological Review, 102,* 211–245.

Erikson, E. H. (1963). *Childhood and society* (2nd ed.). New York: Norton.

Erikson, E. H. (1968). *Identity, youth and crisis.* New York: Norton.

Erikson, E. H. (1980). *Identity and the life cycle* (2nd ed.). New York: Norton.

Espy, K. A., Molfese, D. L., Molfese, V. J., and Modglin, A. (2004). Development of auditory event-related potentials in young children and relations to word-level reading abilities at age 8 years. *Annals of Dyslexia, 54*(1), 9–38.

Evans, E. D., & Richardson, R. C. (1995). Corporal punishment: What teachers should know. *Teaching Exceptional Children, 27*(2), 33–36.

Evans, S. W., Pelham, W. E., Smith, B. H., Bukstein, O., Gnagy, E. M., Greiner, A. R., Altenderfer, L., & Baron-Myak, C. (2000). Dose-response effect of methylphenidate on ecologically valid measures of academic performance and classroom behavior in adolescents with ADHD. *Experimental and Clinical Psychopharmacology, 9*(2), 163–175.

Evans, T. D. (1996). Encouragement: The key to reforming the classrooms. *Educational Leadership, 54*(1), 81–85.

Everson, H., & Millsap, R. (2004). Beyond individual differences: Exploring school effects on SAT scores. *Educational Psychologist, 39*(3), 157–172.

Everson, H., Smodlaka, I., & Tobias, S. (1994). Exploring the relationship of test anxiety and metacognition on reading test performance: A cognitive analysis. *Anxiety, Stress, and Coping, 7,* 85–96.

Everson, H., Tobias, S., Hartman, H., & Gourgey, A. (1993). Test anxiety and the curriculum: The subject matters. *Anxiety, Stress, and Coping, 6,* 1–8.

Evertson, C., Emmer, E., Clements, B., Sanford, J., & Worsham, M. (1994). *Classroom management for elementary teachers* (3rd ed.). Boston: Allyn & Bacon.

Evertson, C. M., & Emmer, E. T. (1982). Effective management at the beginning of the year in junior high classes. *Journal of Educational Psychology, 74,* 485–498.

Evertson, C. M., Emmer, E. T., & Brophy, J. E. (1980). Predictors of effective teaching in junior high mathematics classrooms. *Journal for Research in Mathematics Education, 11,* 167–178.

Evertson, C. M., Emmer, E. T., & Worsham, M. E. (2000). *Classroom management for elementary teachers* (5th ed.). Boston: Allyn & Bacon.

Evertson, C., Emmer, E., & Worsham, M. E. (2006). *Classroom management for elementary teachers* (7th ed.). Boston: Allyn & Bacon.

Evertson, C. M., & Harris, A. H. (1992). What we know about managing classrooms. *Educational Leadership, 49*(7), 74–78.

Evertson, C. M., & Randolph, C. H. (1995). Classroom management in the learning-centered classroom. In A. C. Ornstein (Ed.), *Teaching: Theory into practice.* Boston: Allyn & Bacon.

Evertson, C. M., Weade, R., Green, J., & Crawford, J. (1985). *Effective classroom management and instruction: An exploration of models.* Nashville, TN: Vanderbilt University.

Fabes, R. A., & Martin, C. L. (2000). *Exploring child development.* Boston: Allyn & Bacon.

Fagan, E. R., Hassler, D. M., & Szabo, M. (1981). Evaluation of questioning strategies in language arts instruction. *Research in the Teaching of English, 15,* 267–273.

Fahey, J. A. (2000). Who wants to differentiate instruction? We did . . . *Educational Leadership, 58*(1), 70–72.

Fantuzzo, J. W., Davis, G. V., & Ginsburg, M. D. (1995). Effects of parent involvement in isolation or in combination with peer tutoring on student self-concept and mathematics achievement. *Journal of Educational Psychology, 87*(2), 272–281.

Fantuzzo, J. W., King, J. A., & Heller, L. R. (1992). Effects of reciprocal peer tutoring on mathematics and school adjustment: A component analysis. *Journal of Educational Psychology, 84,* 33–39.

Fantuzzo, J. W., Polite, K., & Grayson, N. (1990). An evaluation of reciprocal peer tutoring across elementary school settings. *Journal of School Psychology, 28,* 309–323.

Farmer, T., Leung, M.-C., Pearl, R., Rodkin, P., Cadwallader, T., & Van Acker, R. (2002). Deviant or diverse peer groups? The peer affiliations of aggressive elementary students. *Journal of Educational Psychology, 94* (3), 611–620.

Fashola, O. S. (2002). *Building effective after school programs.* Thousand Oaks, CA: Corwin.

Fay, J. (2001). The classroom of your dreams. In B. Sornson (Ed.), *Preventing early learning failure.* Alexandria, VA: ASCD.

Feingold, A. (1992). Sex differences in variability in intellectual abilities: A new look at an old controversy. *Review of Educational Research, 62*(1), 61–84.

Feldhusen, J. F. (1996). How to identify and develop special talents. *Educational Leadership, 53*(5), 66–69.

Feldhusen, J. F. (1998). Programs for the gifted few or talent development for the many? *Phi Delta Kappan, 79*(10), 734–738.

Feldman, D. H. (2003). Cognitive development in childhood. In R. M. Lerner, M. A. Easterbrooks, & J. Mistry (Eds.), *Handbook of psychology: Vol. 6. Developmental psychology* (pp. 195–210). Hoboken, NJ: Wiley.

Fellows, N. J. (1994). A window into thinking: Using student writing to understand conceptual changes in science learning. *Journal of Science Teaching, 31,* 985–1001.

Fennema, E., Carpenter, T. P., Jacobs, V. R., Franke, M. L., & Levi, L. W. (1998). A longitudinal study of gender differences in young children's mathematical thinking. *Educational Researcher, 27*(5), 6–11.

Fennema, E., Franke, M. L., Carpenter, T. P., & Carey, D. A. (1993). Using children's mathematical knowledge in instruction. *American Educational Research Journal, 30*(3), 555–583.

Fenson, L., Dale, P. S., Reznick, J. S., Bates, E., Thal, D. J., & Pethick, S. J. (1994). Variability in early communicative development. *Monographs of the Society for Research in Child Development, 59*(5), 242.

Ferguson, R., & Mehta, J. (2004). An unfinished journey: The legacy of Brown and the narrowing of the achievement gap. *Phi Delta Kappan, 85*(9), 656–669.

Feuerstein, R. (1980). *Instrumental enrichment: An intervention program for cognitive modifiability.* Baltimore: University Park Press.

Feuerstein, R., & Kozulin, A. (1995). The Bell Curve: Getting the facts right. *Educational Leadership, 52*(7), 71–74.

Fielding, L. G., Anderson, R. C., & Pearson, P. D. (1990). *How discussion questions influence children's story understanding* (Tech. Rep. No. 490). Champaign, IL: University of Illinois, Center for the Study of Reading.

Finn, J. D., & Cox, D. (1992). Participation and withdrawal among fourth-grade pupils. *American Educational Research Journal, 29*(1), 141–162.

Finn, J. D., Pannozzo, G. M., & Achilles, C. M. (2003). The "why's" of class size: Student behavior in small classes. *Review of Educational Research, 73*(3), 321–368.

Finn, J. D., Pannozzo, G. M., & Voelkl, K. E. (1995). Disruptive and inattentive-withdrawn behavior and achievement among fourth graders. *The Elementary School Journal, 95*(5), 421–434.

Fiordaliso, R., Lordeman, A., Filipczak, J., & Friedman, R. M. (1977). Effects of feedback on absenteeism in the junior high school. *Journal of Educational Research, 70,* 188–192.

Fisch, S., & Truglio, R. (2000). *G is for Growing: 30 years of research on* Sesame Street. Mahwah, NJ: Erlbaum.

Fisher, C. W., Berliner, D. C., Filby, N. N., Marliave, R., Cahen, L. S., Dishaw, M. M., & Moore, J. E. (1978). *Teaching behaviors, academic learning time, and student achievement: Final report of Phase III-B, beginning teacher evaluation study.* (Tech. Report V-1). San Francisco: Far West Laboratory for Educational Research and Development.

Fisher, D. (2006). Keeping adolescents 'alive and kickin' it: Addressing suicide in schools. *Phi Delta Kappan, 87*(10), 784–786.

Fisher, D., Sax, C., & Grove, K. (2000). The resilience of changes promoting inclusiveness in an urban elementary school. *The Elementary School Journal, 100*(3), 213–228.

Fiske, E. B. (1989, July 12). The misleading concept of "average" on reading tests changes, and more students fall below it. *The New York Times.*

Fitzgerald, H. E., Mann, T., Cabrera, N., & Wong, M. M. (2003). Diversity in caregiving contexts. In R. M. Lerner, M. A. Easterbrooks, & J. Mistry (Eds.), *Handbook of psychology: Vol. 6. Developmental psychology* (pp. 135–167). Hoboken, NJ: Wiley.

Fitzgerald, J., & Graves, M. (2004/2005). Reading supports for all. *Educational Leadership, 62*(4), 68–71.

Flanagan, C. (1993). Gender and social class: Intersecting issues in women's achievement. *Educational Psychologist, 28*(4), 357–378.

Flavell, J. (2004). Theory-of-mind development: Retrospect and prospect. *Merrill-Palmer Quarterly, 50,* 21–45.

Flavell, J. H. (1986, January). Really and truly. *Psychology Today,* 38–44.

Flavell, J. H. (1996). Piaget's legacy. *Psychological Science, 7*(4), 200–203.

Flavell, J. H., Green, F. L., Flavell, E. R., & Grossman, J. B. (1997). The development of children's knowledge about inner speech. *Child Development, 68,* 39–47.

Flavell, J. H., Miller, P. H., & Miller, S. A. (1993). *Cognitive development.* Englewood Cliffs, NJ: Prentice Hall.

Fleischman, S. (2006). Moving to evidence-based professional practice. *Educational Leadership, 63*(6), 87–90.

Fleith, D. (2000). Teacher and student perceptions of creativity in the classroom environment. *Roeper Review, 22,* 148–153.

Fletcher, J. D. (1992). Individualized systems of instruction. In M. C. Alkin (Ed.), *Encyclopedia of educational research* (6th ed.) (pp. 612–620). New York: Macmillan.

Fletcher, J. M., Shaywitz, S. E., Shankweiler, D. P., Katz, L., Liberman, I. Y., Stvebing, K. K., Francis, D. J., Fowler, A. E., & Shaywitz, B. A. (1994). Cognitive profiles of reading disability: Comparisons of discrepancy and low achievement definitions. *Journal of Educational Psychology, 86,* 6–23.

Flexner, C. (2001). Enhancing the listening environment for early learning success. In B. Sornson (Ed.), *Preventing early learning failure.* Alexandria, VA: ASCD.

Flouri, E., & Buchanan, A. (2004). Early father's and mother's involvement and child's later educational outcomes. *British Journal of Educational Psychology, 74*(2), 141–153.

Fogarty, R. (Ed.). (1993). *The multiage classroom.* Palatine, IL: IRI/Skylight.

Foos, P. W., Mora, J. J., & Tkacz, S. (1994). Student study techniques and the generation effect. *Journal of Educational Psychology, 86*(4), 567–576.

Forness, S. R., & Kavale, K. A. (2000). What definitions of disabilities say and don't say: A critical analysis. *Journal of Learning Disabilities, 33*(3), 239–256.

Foster, D., & Noyce, P. (2004). The mathematics assessment collaborative: Performance testing to improve instruction. *Phi Delta Kappan, 85*(5), 367–374.

Foster, J. K., Eskes, G. A., & Stuss, D. T. (1994). The cognitive neuropsychology of attention: A frontal lobe perspective. *Cognitive Neuropsychology,* 11, 133–147.

Francis, D. J., Shaywitz, S. E., Shaywitz, B. A., Stuebing, K. K., & Fletcher, J. M. (1996). Developmental lag versus deficit models of reading disability: A longitudinal, individual growth curves analysis. *Journal of Educational Psychology, 88*(1), 3–17.

Franklin, R. D., Allison, D. B., & Gorman, B. S. (Eds.). (1997). *Design and analysis of single-case research.* Mahwah, NJ: Erlbaum.

Fredricks, J. A., Blumenfeld, P. C., & Paris, A. H. (2004). School engagement: Potential of the concept, state of the evidence. *Review of Educational Research, 74*(1), 59–109.

Freiberg, H. J. (Ed.) (1999). *Beyond behaviorism changing the classroom management paradigm.* Boston: Allyn & Bacon.

Freiberg, H. J., Connell, M. L., & Lorentz, J. (2001). Effects of consistency management on student mathematics achievement on seven Chapter I elementary schools. *Journal of Education for Students Placed at Risk, 6*(3), 249–270.

French, E. G. (1956). Motivation as a variable in work partner selection. *Journal of Abnormal and Social Psychology, 55,* 96–99.

Friedman, L. (1995). The space factor in mathematics: Gender differences. *Review of Educational Research, 65*(1), 22–50.

Friedman, L. (2003). Promoting opportunity after school. *Educational Leadership, 60*(4), 79–82.

Friend, M. (2007). The coteaching partnership. *Educational Leadership, 64*(5), 48–53.

Friend, M., & Bursuck, W. D. (1999). *Including students with special needs: A practical guide for classroom teachers* (2nd ed.). Boston: Allyn & Bacon.

Friend, M., & Bursuck, W. D. (2002). *Including students with special needs* (3rd ed.). Boston: Allyn & Bacon.

Friend, R. (2001). Effects of strategy instruction on summary writing of college students. *Contemporary Educational Psychology, 26*(1), 3–24.

Fuchs, D., & Fuchs, L. S. (1997). Peer-assisted learning strategies: Making classrooms more responsive to diversity. *American Educational Research Journal, 34*(1), 174–206.

Fuchs, D., & Fuchs, L. (2006). Introduction to response to intervention: What, why, and how valid is it? *Reading Research Quarterly, 41*(1), 92–128.

Fuchs, D., Fuchs, L. S., Bahr, M. W., Fernstrom, P., & Stecker, P. M. (1990). Mainstream assistance teams: A scientific basis for the art of consultation. *Exceptional Children, 56,* 493–513.

Fuchs, D., Fuchs, L. S., & Compton, D. L. (2004). Identifying reading disability by responsiveness to instruction: Specifying measures and criteria. *Learning Disability Quarterly, 27,* 216–227.

Fuchs, D., Fuchs, L. S., & Fernstrom, P. (1993). A conservative approach to special education reform: Mainstreaming through transenvironmental programming and curriculum-based measurement. *American Educational Research Journal, 30,* 149–177.

Fuchs, L., Compton, D., Fuchs, D., Palsen, K., Bryant, J., & Hamlett, C. (2005). The prevention, identification, and cognitive determinants of math difficulty. *Journal of Educational Psychology, 97*(3), 493–513.

Fuchs, L., Fuchs, D., Finelli, R., Courey, S., & Hamlett, C. (2003). Expanding schema-based transfer instruction to help third graders solve real-life mathematical problems. *American Educational Research Journal, 41*(2), 419–445.

Fuchs, L., Fuchs, D., Finelli, R., Courey, S., Hamlett, C., Sones, E., & Hope, S. (2006). Teaching third graders about real-life mathematical problem solving: A randomized controlled study. *The Elementary School Journal, 106*(4), 293–312.

Fuchs, L. S., Fuchs, D., Bentz, J., Phillips, N. B., & Hamlett, C. L. (1994). The nature of student interactions during peer tutoring with and without prior training and experience. *American Educational Research Journal, 31*(1), 75–103.

Fuchs, L. S., Fuchs, D., Karns, K., Hamlett, C. L., Katzaroff, M., & Dutka, S. (1997). Effects of task-focused goals on low-achieving students without learning disabilities. *American Educational Research Journal, 34*(3), 513–543.

Fuchs, L. S., Fuchs, D., Kazdan, S., & Allen, S. (1999). Effects of peer-assisted learning strategies in reading with and without training in elaborated help giving. *The Elementary School Journal, 99*(3), 201–221.

Fuller, B., Wright, J., Gesicki, K., & Kang, E. (2007). Gauging growth: How to judge NCLB? *Educational Researcher, 36*(5), 268–278.

Furman, W., & Buhrmester, D. (1992). Age and sex differences in perceptions of networks of personal relationships. *Child Development, 63,* 103–115.

Fuson, K. C. (1992). Research on whole number addition and subtraction. In D. Grouws (Ed.), *Handbook of research on mathematics teaching and learning* (pp. 243–275). New York: Macmillan.

Gabler, I. C., & Schroeder, M. (2003). *Constructivist methods for the secondary classroom*. Boston: Allyn & Bacon.

Gaddy, M. L. (1998, April). *Reading and studying from highlighted text: Memory for information highlighted by others.* Paper presented at the annual meeting of the American Educational Research Association, San Diego, CA.

Gage, N. L. (1991). The obviousness of social and educational research results. *Educational Researcher, 20*(1), 10–16.

Gage, N. L., & Needels, M. C. (1989). Process-product research on teaching: A review of criticism. *Elementary School Journal, 89,* 253–300.

Gagnon, G. W., & Collay, M. (2001). *Designing for learning: Six elements in constructivist classrooms.* Thousand Oaks, CA: Corwin.

Galambos, N. L., & Costigan, C. L. (2003). Emotional and personality development in adolescence. In R. M. Lerner, M. A. Easterbrooks, & J. Mistry (Eds.), *Handbook of psychology: Vol. 6. Developmental psychology* (pp. 351–372). Hoboken, NJ: Wiley.

Gall, M. (1984). Synthesis of research on teachers' questioning. *Educational Leadership, 42,* 40–47.

Gall, M. D. (1987). Discussion methods. In M. J. Dunkin (Ed.), *International encyclopedia of teaching and teacher education.* New York: Pergamon.

Gall, M., Ward, B., Berliner, D., Cahen, L., Winne, P., Glashoff, J., & Stanton, G. (1978). Effects of questioning techniques and recitation on student learning. *American Educational Research Journal, 15,* 175–199.

Gallagher, A. M., & DeLisi, R. (1994). Gender differences in scholastic aptitude test: Mathematics problem solving among high ability students. *Journal of Educational Psychology, 86*(2), 204–211.

Gallagher, C. J. (2003). Reconciling a tradition of testing with a new learning paradigm. *Educational Psychology Review, 15*(1), 83–99.

Gallagher, J. J. (1992). Gifted persons. In M. C. Alkin (Ed.), *Encyclopedia of educational research* (6th ed., pp. 544–549). New York: Macmillan.

Gallimore, R., & Goldenberg, C. (2001). Analyzing cultural models and settings to connect minority achievement and school improvement research. *Educational Psychologist, 36*(1), 45–56.

Gamoran, A., Nystrand, M., Berends, M., & LePore, P. C. (1995). An organizational analysis of the effects of ability grouping. *American Educational Research Journal, 32,* 687–715.

Gandal, M., & McGiffert, L. (2003). The power of testing. *Educational Leadership, 60*(5), 39–42.

Gandal, M., & Vranek, J. (2001). Standards: Here today, here tomorrow. *Educational Leadership, 59*(1), 6–13.

Ganesh, T., & Berliner, D. (2004, April). *Practices of computer use in elementary education: Perceived and missed opportunities.* Paper presented at the annual meeting of the American Educational Research Association, San Diego, CA.

Garber, H. L. (1988). *The Milwaukee Project: Preventing mental retardation in children at risk.* Washington, DC: American Association on Mental Retardation.

Garcia, E., & Jensen, B. (2007). Helping young Hispanic learners. *Educational Leadership, 64* (6), 34–39.

Garcia, J. (1993). The changing image of ethnic groups in textbooks. *Phi Delta Kappan, 75*(1), 29–35.

Gardner, H. (2000). *Intelligence reframed: Multiple intelligences for the 21st century.* New York: Basic Books.

Gardner, H. (2003, April). *Multiple intelligences after twenty years.* Paper presented at the annual meeting of the American Educational Research Association, Chicago, IL.

Gardner, H. (2004). *Multiple intelligences: New horizons, in theory and practice.* New York: Basic Books.

Gardner, H., & Moran, S. (2006). The science of multiple intelligences theory: A response to Lynn Waterhouse. *Educational Psychologist, 41*(4), 227–232.

Gardner, M. & Steinberg, L., (2005). Peer influence on risk taking, risk preference, and risky decision making in adolescence and adulthood: An experimental study. *Developmental Psychology, 41,* 625–635.

Garvey, C. (1990). *Play* (enlarged ed.). Cambridge, MA: Harvard University Press.

Gathercoal, F. (2001). *Judicious Discipline* (5th ed.). San Francisco: Caddo Gap Press.

Gathercole, S. E., Pickering, S. J., Ambridge, B., & Wearing, H. (2004). The structure of working memory from 4 to 15 years of age. *Developmental Psychology, 40,* 177–190.

Gay, G. (2004). The importance of multicultural education. *Educational Leadership, 61*(4), 30–34.

Ge, X., Longer, R. D., & Elder, G. H. (2001). The relation between puberty and psychological distress in adolescent boys. *Journal of Research on Adolescence, 11,* 49–70.

Gee, J. (2005). It's theories all the way down: A response to scientific research in education. *Teachers College Record, 107*(1), 10–18.

Geisert, P. G., & Futrell, M. K. (2000). *Teachers, computers, and curriculum: Microcomputers in the classroom* (3rd ed.). Boston: Allyn & Bacon.

Gelman, R. (1979). Preschool thought. *American Psychologist, 34,* 900–905.

Gelman, R. (2000). Domain specificity and variability in cognitive development. *Child Development, 71,* 854–856.

Gelman, R. (2006). Young natural-number arithmeticians. *Current Directions in Psychological Science.* Vol. 15, No. 4, 193–197.

Gelman, R., & Brenneman, K. (1994). Domain specificity and cultural variation are not inconsistent. In L. A. Hirschfeld & S. Gelman (Eds.), *Mapping the mind: Domain specificity in cognition and culture.* New York: Cambridge University Press.

Gentner, D., Loewenstein, J., & Thompson, L. (2002). Learning and transfer: A general role for analogical encoding. *Journal of Educational Psychology, 94*(2), 393–408.

George, P. S. (2005). A rationale for differentiated instruction in the regular classroom. *Theory into Practice, 44,* 185–193.

Gersten, R., & Dimino, J. (2006). RTI (response to intervention): Rethinking special education for students with reading difficulties (yet again). *Reading Research Quarterly, 41*(1), 99–107.

Gersten, R., Fuchs, L. S., Williams, J. P., & Baker, S. (2001). Teaching reading comprehension strategies to students with learning disabilities: A review of research. *Review of Educational Research, 71*(2), 279–320.

Giaconia, R. M., & Hedges, L. V. (1982). Identifying features of effective open education. *Review of Educational Research, 52,* 579–602.

Giangreco, M. (2007). Extending inclusive opportunities. *Educational Leadership, 64*(5), 34–38.

Gibbons, A. S., Duffin, J. R., Robertson, D. J., & Thompson, B. (1998, April). *Effects of administering feedback following extended problem solving.* Paper presented at the annual meeting of the American Educational Research Association, San Diego, CA.

Giedd, J. N. (2004). Structural magnetic resonance imaging of the adolescent brain. In R. E. Dahl & L. P. Spear (Eds.) *Adolescent brain development. Vulnerabilities and opportunities.* Annals of the New York Academy of Sciences. Vol. 1021. New York: The New York Academy of Science.

Giedd, J. N., Blumenthal, J., & Jeffries, N. O. (1999). Cerebral cortical gray matter changes during childhood and adolescence: A longitudinal MRI study. *Nature Neuroscience, 2*, 861–863.

Gijselaers, W. H., & Schmidt, H. G. (1995). Effects of quantity of instruction on time spent on learning and achievement. *Educational Research and Evaluation, 1*(2), 183–201.

Gilligan, C. (1982). *In a different voice: Sex differences in the expression of moral judgment.* Cambridge, MA: Harvard University Press.

Gilligan, C., & Attanucci, J. (1988). Two moral orientations: Gender differences and similarities. *Merrill-Palmer Quarterly, 34,* 223–237.

Ginsburg-Block, M., Rohrbeck, C., & Fantuzzo, J. (2006). A meta-analytic review of social, self-concept, and behavioral outcomes of peer-assisted learning. *Journal of Educational Psychology, 98*(4), 732–749.

Glantz, M. D., Johnson, J., & Huffman, L. (Eds.). (2002). *Resilience and development: Positive life adaptations.* New York: Kluwer.

Glaser, C., & Brunstein, J. (2007). Improving fourth-grade students' composition skills: Effects of strategy instruction and self-regulation procedures. *Journal of Educational Psychology, 99*(2), 297–310.

Glassman, M. (2001). Dewey and Vygotsky: Society, experience, and inquiry in educational practice. *Educational Researcher, 30*(4), 3–14.

Glazer, S. M., & Burke, E. M. (1994). *An integrated approach to early literacy.* Boston: Allyn & Bacon.

Goddard, R. D., Hoy, W. K., & Hoy, A. W. (2000). Collective teacher efficacy: Its meaning, measure, and impact on student achievement. *American Educational Research Journal, 37*(2), 479–507.

Goddard, R. D., Hoy, W. K., & Woolfolk Hoy, A. (2004). Collective efficacy beliefs: Theoretical developments, empirical evidence, and future directions. *Educational Researcher, 33*(3), 1–13.

Goelman, H., Andersen, C. J., Anderson, J., Gouzouasis, P., Kendrick, M., Kindler, A. M., et al. (2003). In W. M. Reynolds & G. E. Miller (Eds.), *Handbook of psychology: Vol. 7. Educational psychology* (pp. 285–331). Hoboken, NJ: Wiley.

Goldberg, A., Russell, M., & Cook, A. (2003). The effect of computers on student writing: A meta-analysis of studies from 1992 to 2002. *Journal of Technology, Learning, and Assessment, 2*(1), 1–51. Available from www.jtla.org.

Goldberg, B., & Richards, J. (1996). The Co-NECT design for school change. In S. Stringfield, S. Ross, & L. Smith (Eds.), *Bold plans for school restructuring: The new American schools development corporation designs.* Mahwah, NJ: Erlbaum.

Goldman-Segall, R., & Maxwell, J. W. (2003). Computers, the Internet, and new media for learning. In W. M. Reynolds & G. E. Miller (Eds.), *Handbook of psychology: Vol. 7. Educational psychology* (pp. 393–427). Hoboken, NJ: Wiley.

Goldschmidt, P., & Wang, J. (1999). When can schools affect dropout behavior? A longitudinal multilevel analysis. *American Educational Research Journal, 36*(4), 715–738.

Goleman, D. (1995). *Emotional intelligence: Why it can matter more than IQ.* New York: Bantam.

Gomez, M. L., Grave, M. E., & Block, M. N. (1991). Reassessing portfolio assessment rhetoric and reality. *Language Arts, 68,* 620–628.

Good, T., & Brophy, J. (2003). *Looking in classrooms.* Boston: Allyn & Bacon.

Good, T., & Grouws, D. (1977). Teaching effects: A process-product study in fourth grade mathematics classes. *Journal of Teacher Education, 28,* 49–54.

Good, T., & Grouws, D. (1979). The Missouri Mathematics Effectiveness Project: An experimental study in fourth-grade classrooms. *Journal of Educational Psychology, 71,* 355–362.

Good, T., Grouws, D., & Ebmeier, H. (1983). *Active mathematics teaching.* New York: Longman.

Good, T. L., Mulryan, C., & McCaslin, M. (1992). Grouping for instruction in mathematics: A call for programmatic research on small group processes. In D. Grouws (Ed.), *Handbook of research on mathematics teaching and learning* (pp. 165–196). New York: Macmillan.

Goodlad, J. I. (1983). *A place called school.* New York: McGraw-Hill.

Gordon, E. W., & Bhattacharyya, M. (1994). Race and intelligence. In R. J. Sternberg (Ed.), *Encyclopedia of human intelligence.* New York: Macmillan.

Gordon, P. (1957). *The social system of the high school: A study in the sociology of adolescence.* Glencoe, IL: Free Press.

Gorin, J. S., & Blanchard, J. S. (2004, April). *The effect of curriculum alignment on elementary mathematics and reading achievement.* Paper presented at the annual meeting of the American Educational Research Association, San Diego, CA.

Goswami, U. (2004). Neuroscience and education. *British Journal of Educational Psychology, 74*(1), 1–14.

Gottfredson, D. C., Gottfredson, G. D., & Hybl, L. G. (1993). Managing adolescent behavior: A multiyear, multi-school study. *American Educational Research Journal, 30*(1), 179–215.

Gottfried, A. E., & Fleming, J. S. (2001). Continuity of academic intrinsic motivation from childhood through late adolescence: A longitudinal study. *Journal of Educational Psychology, 93*(1), 3–13.

Gottfried, A. E., & Gottfried, A. W. (2004). Toward the development of a conceptualization of gifted motivation. *Gifted Child Quarterly, 48*(2), 121–132.

Gottlieb, J., & Weinberg, S. (1999). Comparison of students referred and not referred for special education. *The Elementary School Journal, 99*(3), 187–200.

Gould, M., & Gould, H. (2003). A clear vision for equity and opportunity. *Phi Delta Kappan, 85*(4), 324–328.

Grafman, J. (1994). Alternative frameworks for the conceptualization of frontal lobe functions. In F. Boller & J. Grafman (Eds.), *Handbook of neuropsychology,* Vol. 9. San Diego: Elsevier.

Grafman, J., Spector, L., & Ratterman, M. (2005). Planning and the brain. In R. Morris & G. Ward (Eds.), *The cognitive psychology of planning.* Hove, England: Psychology Press, 181–198.

Graham, S. (1997). Executive control in the revising of students with learning and writing difficulties. *Journal of Educational Psychology, 89,* 223–234.

Graham, S. (2006). Strategy instruction and the teaching of writing: A meta-analysis. In C. MacArthur, S. Graham, & J. Fitzgerald (Eds.), *Handbook of Writing Research* (pp. 187–207). New York: Guilford Press.

Graham, S., MacArthur, C., & Schwartz, S. (1995). Effects of goal setting and procedural facilitation on the revising behavior and writing performance of students with writing and learning problems. *Journal of Educational Psychology, 87*(2), 230–240.

Graham, S., & Weiner, B. (1996). Theory and principles of motivation. In D. C. Berliner & R. C. Calfee (Eds.), *Handbook of educational psychology* (pp. 63–84). New York: Macmillan.

Grave, M. E., & DePerna, J. (2000). Redshirting and early retention: Who gets the "gift of time" and what are its outcomes? *American Educational Research Journal, 37*(2), 509–534.

Graves, D. (1983). *Writing: Teachers and children at work.* Exeter, NH: Heinemann.

Gray, T., & Fleischman, S. (2004/2005). Successful strategies for English language learners. *Educational Leadership, 62*(4), 84–85.

Green, M. (1989). *Theories of human development.* New York: Prentice-Hall.

Greenbowe, T., Herron, J. D., Nurrenbern, S., Staver, J. R., & Ward, C. R. (1981). Teaching preadolescents to act as scientists: Replication and extension of an earlier study. *Journal of Educational Psychology, 73,* 705–711.

Greene, B. A., Miller, R. B., Crowson, M., Duke, B. L., & Akey, K. L. (2004). Predicting high school students' cognitive engagement and achievement: Contributions of classroom perceptions and motivation. *Contemporary Educational Psychology, 29*(4), 462–482.

Greene, D., & Lepper, M. R. (1974). How to turn play into work. *Psychology Today, 8,* 49–54.

Greene, J. P. (1997). A meta-analysis of the Rossell & Baker review of bilingual education research. *Bilingual Research Journal, 21*(2/3).

Greenfield, P., & Cocking, R. (Eds.). (1994). *Cross-cultural roots of minority child development.* Hillsdale, NJ: Erlbaum.

Greeno, J. G., Collins, A. M., & Resnick, L. R. (1996). Cognition and learning. In D. C. Berliner & R. C. Calfe (Eds.), *Handbook of educational psychology* (pp. 15–46). New York: Macmillan.

Greeno, J., & Goldman, S. (Eds.). (1998). *Thinking practices in mathematics and science learning.* Mahwah, NJ: Erlbaum.

Greenwood, C. R., Terry, B., Utley, C. A., Montagna, D., & Walker, D. (1993). Achievement, placement, and services: Middle school benefits of Classwide Peer Tutoring used at the elementary level. *School Psychology Review, 22*(3), 497–516.

Gregory, G. H., & Chapman, C. (2001). *Differentiated instructional strategies: One size doesn't fit all.* Thousand Oaks, CA: Corwin.

Gregory, J. F. (1995). The crime of punishment: Racial and gender disparities in the use of corporal punishment in U.S. public schools. *Journal of Negro Education, 64*(4), 454–462.

Grendler, M. (2004). *Classroom assessment and learning.* New York: Longman.

Gresham, F. (2005). Methodological issues in evaluating cognitive-behavioral treatments for students with behavioral disorders. *Behavioral Disorders, 30*(3), 213–225.

Gresham, F. M. (2004). Current status and future directions of school-based behavioral interventions. *School Psychology Review, 33,* 326–343.

Gronlund, N. E. (2000). *How to write and use instructional objectives* (6th ed.). Upper Saddle River, NJ: Merrill/Prentice-Hall.

Gronlund, N. E. (2003). *Assessment of student achievement* (7th ed.). Boston: Allyn & Bacon.

Gronlund, N. E. (2004). *Writing instructional objectives for teaching and assessment* (7th ed.). Upper Saddle River, NJ: Prentice-Hall.

Gronlund, N. E. (2006). *Assessment of student achievement.* Boston: Pearson.

Grossman, H. (1995). *Teaching in a diverse society.* Boston: Allyn & Bacon.

Grossman, H., & Grossman, S. H. (1994). *Gender issues in education.* Boston: Allyn & Bacon.

Grusec, J. E., & Goodnow, J. J. (1994). Impact of parental discipline methods on the child's internalization of values. *Developmental Psychology, 30,* 4–19.

Guay, F., Marsh, H. W., & Boivin, M. (2003). Academic self-concept and academic achievement: Developmental perspectives on their causal ordering. *Journal of Educational Psychology, 95*(1), 124–136.

Guilfoyle, C. (2006). NCLB: Is there life beyond testing? *Educational Leadership, 64* (3), 8–13.

Gump, P. V. (1982). School settings and their keeping. In D. L. Duke (Ed.), *Helping teachers manage classrooms* (pp. 98–114). Alexandria, VA: Association for Supervision and Curriculum Development.

Gunter, M. A., Estes, T. H., & Schwab, J. (2003). *Instruction: A models approach* (4th ed.). Boston: Allyn & Bacon.

Guskey, T. (2003). How classroom assessments improve learning. *Educational Leadership, 60*(5), 7–11.

Guskey, T. (2005). Mapping the road to proficiency. *Educational Leadership, 63*(3), 32–37.

Guskey, T. (2006). Making high school grades meaningful. *Phi Delta Kappan, 87*(9), 670–675.

Guskey, T. R. (2001). Helping standards make the grade. *Educational Leadership, 59*(1), 20–27.

Guskey, T. R. (2002). Computerized gradebooks and the myth of objectivity. *Phi Delta Kappan, 83*(10), 775–780.

Guskey, T. R., & Bailey, J. M. (2001). *Developing grading and reporting systems for student learning.* Thousand Oaks, CA: Corwin.

Guthrie, J. T., Bennett, S., & Weber, S. (1991). Processing procedural documents: A cognitive model for following written directions. *Educational Psychology Review, 3,* 249–265.

Guthrie, J. T., & Cox, K. (2001). Classroom conditions for motivation and engagement in reading. *Educational Psychology Review, 13*(3), 283–302.

Gutiérrez, R., & Slavin, R. E. (1992). Achievement effects of the nongraded elementary school: A best evidence synthesis. *Review of Educational Research, 62*(4), 333–376.

Hakuta, K., Butler, Y. G., & Witt, D. (2000). *How long does it take English learners to attain proficiency?* The University of California Linguistic Minority Research Institute, Policy Report 2000/1.

Haladyna, T. M. (1997). *Writing test items to evaluate higher order thinking.* Boston: Allyn & Bacon.

Haladyna, T. M. (1999). *Developing and validating multiple-choice tests.* Mahwah, NJ: Erlbaum.

Hallahan, D. P., & Kauffman, J. M. (1997). *Exceptional learners: Introduction to special education* (7th ed.). Boston: Allyn & Bacon.

Hallahan, D. P., & Kauffman, J. M. (2006). *Exceptional learners: Introduction to special education* (10th ed.). Boston: Allyn & Bacon.

Halle, T. G., Kurtz-Coster, B., & Mahoney, J. L. (1997). Family influence on school achievement in low-income, African-American children. *Journal of Educational Psychology, 89*(3), 527–537.

Hallinan, M. T. (2004). *The detracking movement.* Stanford: The Hoover Institution.

Halperin, J. M., & Schulz, K. P. (2006). Revisiting the role of the prefrontal cortex in the pathophysiology of attention-deficit/hyperactivity disorder. *Psychological Bulletin, 132*(4), 560–581.

Halpern, D. F. (1995). *Thought and knowledge: An introduction to critical thinking* (3rd ed.). Hillsdale, NJ: Erlbaum.

Halpern, D. F., Hansen, C., & Riefer, D. (1990). Analogies as an aid to understanding and memory. *Journal of Educational Psychology, 82,* 298–305.

Halpern, D. F., & LaMay, M. L. (2000). The smarter sex: A critical review of sex differences in intelligence. *Educational Psychology Review, 12*(2), 229–246.

Hamburg, D. A. (1992). *Today's children: Creating a future for a generation in crisis.* New York: Times Books.

Hamman, D., Berthelot, J., Saia, J., & Crowley, E. (2000). Teachers' coaching of learning and its relation to students' strategic learning. *Journal of Educational Psychology, 92*(2), 342–348.

Hand, B., & Treagust, D. F. (1991). Student achievement and science curriculum development using a constructive framework. *Schools, Science, and Mathematics, 91,* 172–176.

Hanline, M. F., & Daley, S. (2002). "Mom, will Haelie always have possibilities?" *Phi Delta Kappan, 84*(1), 73–76.

Hanna, G. S., & Dettmer, P. A. (2004). *Assessment for effective teaching: Using context-adaptive planning.* Boston: Pearson.

Hanson, S. L., Morrison, D. R., & Ginsburg, A. L. (1989). The antecedents of teenage fatherhood. *Demography, 26,* 579–596.

Harackiewicz, J., Barron, K., Tauer, J., & Carter, S. (2000). Short-term and long-term consequences of achievement goals: Predicting interest and performance over time. *Journal of Educational Psychology, 92*(2), 316–330.

Harackiewicz, J., & Linnenbrink, E. (2005). Multiple achievement goals and multiple pathways for learning: The agenda and impact of Paul R. Pintrich. *Educational Psychologist, 40*(2), 75–84.

Hardman, J. L., Drew, C., Egan, M., & Wolf, B. (1996). *Human exceptionality: Society, school, and family* (5th ed.). Boston: Allyn & Bacon.

Hareli, S., & Weiner, B. (2002). Social emotions and personality inferences: A scaffold for a new direction in the study of achievement motivation. *Educational Psychologist, 37*(3), 183–189.

Hargreaves, A. (1996). Transforming knowledge: Blurring the boundaries between research, policy, and practice. *Educational Evaluation and Policy Analysis, 18*(2), 105–122.

Harpaz, Y., & Lefstein, A. (2000). Communities of thinking. *Educational Leadership, 58*(3), 54–57.

Harris, K. R., & Alexander, P. A. (1998). Integrated, constructivist education: Challenge and reality. *Education Psychology Review, 10*(2), 155–127.

Harris, K. R., & Graham, S. (1996a). *Making the writing process work: Strategies for composition and self-regulation.* Cambridge, MA: Brookline.

Harris, K. R., & Graham, S. (1996b). Memo to constructivists: Skills count, too. *Educational Leadership, 53*(5), 26–29.

Harris, K. R., Graham, S., & Mason, L. (2006). Improving the writing, knowledge, and motivation of struggling young writers: Effects of self-regulated strategy development with and without peer support. *American Educational Research Journal, 43*(2), 295–340.

Harris, K. R., Graham, S., & Pressley, M. (2001). Cognitive strategies in reading and written language. In N. N. Singh & I. Beale (Eds.), *Current perspectives in learning disabilities: Nature, theory and treatment.* New York: Springer-Verlag.

Harris, P. (2002). Learning-related visual problems in Baltimore City: A long-term program. *JOVD, 33*(2), 75–115.

Harry, B., & Klingner, J. (2007). Discarding the deficit model. *Educational Leadership, 64*(5), 16–21.

Hart, B., & Risley, T. R. (1995). *Meaningful differences in the everyday experience of young American children.* Baltimore: Brookes.

Harter, S. (1998). The development of self-representations. In W. Damon (Ed.), *Handbook of child psychology* (Vol. 3, pp. 553–618). New York: Wiley.

Harter, S., Whitesell, N. R., & Kowalski, P. (1992). Individual differences in the effects of educational transitions on young adolescents' perceptions of competence and motivational orientation. *American Educational Research Journal, 29,* 777–807.

Hartup, W. W. (1996). The company they keep: Friendships and their developmental significance. *Child Development, 67,* 1–13.

Hartup, W. W. (2005). Peer Intraction: What causes what? *Journal of Abnormal Child Psychology, 33,* 387–394.

Haslinger, J., Kelly, P., & O'Lara, L. (1996). Countering absenteeism, anonymity, and apathy. *Educational Leadership, 54*(1), 47–49.

Haspe, H., & Baddeley, J. (1991). Moral theory and culture: The case of gender. In W. Kurtines & J. L. Gewirtz (Eds.), *Handbook of moral behavior and development* (Vol. 1, pp. 223–250). Mahwah, NJ: Erlbaum.

Hasselbring, T., & Williams-Glaser, C. H. (2000). Use of computer technology to help students with special needs. *Children and Computer Technology, 10*(2), 102–122.

Hattie, J., Bibbs, J., & Purdie, N. (1996). Effects of learning skills interventions on student learning: A meta-analysis. *Review of Educational Research, 66*(2), 99–136.

Hattie, J., & Marsh, H. W. (1996). The relationship between research and teaching: A meta-analysis. *Review of Educational Research, 66*(4), 507–542.

Hattie, J., & Timperley, H. (2007). The power of feedback. *Review of Educational Research, 77*(1), 81–112.

Hauser-Cram, P., Sirin, S. R., & Stipek, D. (2003). When teachers' and parents' values differ: Teachers' ratings of academic competence in children from low-income families. *Journal of Educational Psychology, 95*(4), 813–820.

Havens, J. (2003). Student web pages—a performance assessment they'll love. *Phi Delta Kappan, 84*(9), 710–711.

Hawkins, J. D., Guo, J., Hill, K., Battin-Pearson, S., & Abbott, R. (2001). Long-term effects of the Seattle social development intervention on school bonding trajectories. *Applied Developmental Sciences, 5,* 225–236.

Hawkins, J. D., Herrenkohl, T. I., Farrington, D. P., Brewer, D., Catalano, R. F., Harachi, T. W., & Cothern, L. (2000). *Predictors of youth violence.* Washington, DC: Office of Juvenile Justice and Delinquency Prevention.

Hay, D., Payne, A., & Chadwick, A. (2004). Peer relations in childhood. *Journal of Child Psychology and Psychiatry, 45,* 84–108.

Haycock, K. (2001). Closing the achievement gap. *Educational Leadership, 58*(6), 6–11.

Haycock, K. (2006). No more invisible kids. *Educational Leadership, 64*(3), 38–42.

Hehir, T. (2007). Confronting abelism. *Educational Leadership, 64*(5), 8–15.

Hein, K. (1993). "Getting real" about HIV in adolescents. *American Journal of Public Health, 83,* 492–494.

Heller, K. A., Monks, F. J., Sternberg, R. S., & Subotnik, R. F. (2000). *International handbook of giftedness and talent* (2nd ed.). New York: Pergamon.

Henry, S. L., & Pepper, F. C. (1990). Cognitive, social, and cultural effects on Indian learning style: Classroom implications. *Journal of Educational Issues of Language Minority Students, 7,* 85–97.

Henson, K. T. (2004). *Constructivist teaching strategies for diverse middle-level classrooms.* Boston: Pearson.

Henson, R. K. (2002). From adolescent angst to adulthood: Substantive implications and measurement dilemmas in the development of teacher efficacy research. *Educational Psychologist, 37*(3), 137–150.

Herbert, E. A. (1998). Lessons learned about student portfolios. *Phi Delta Kappan, 79*(8), 583–585.

Heritage, M., & Chen, E. (2005). Why data skills matter in school improvement. *Phi Delta Kappan, 86*(9), 707–710.

Herman, R. (1999). *An educator's guide to schoolwide reform.* Arlington, VA: Educational Research Service.

Herrenkohl, T. I., Maguin, E., Hill, K. G., Hawkins, J. D., & Abbott, R. D. (2001). Developmental risk factors for youth violence. *Journal of Adolescent Health, 26,* 176–186.

Herrera, S. G. & Murry, K. G. (2005). *Mastering ESL and bilingual methods.* Boston: Allyn & Bacon.

Herrnstein, R. J., & Murray, C. (1994). *The bell curve: Intelligence and class structure in American life.* New York: Free Press.

Hessler, G. L. (2001). Who is really learning disabled? In B. Sornson, (Ed.), *Preventing early learning failure.* Alexandria, VA: ASCD.

Heymann, S. J., & Earle, A. (2000). Low-income parents: How do working conditions affect their opportunity to help school-age children at risk? *American Educational Research Journal, 37*(3), 833–848.

Heyns, B. (2002). Summer learning. In D. L. Levinson, P. W. Cookson, Jr., & A. R. Sadovnik (Eds.), *Education and sociology: An encyclopedia* (pp. 645–650). New York: Routledge Falmer.

Hickey, D.T. (1997). Motivational contemporary socio-constructivist instructional perspectives. *Educational Psychologist, 32*(3), 175–193.

Hicks-Anderman, L., & Anderman, E. M. (1999). Social predictors of changes in students' achievement goal orientations. *Contemporary Educational Psychology, 24*(1), 21–37.

Hicks-Bartlett, S. (2004). Forging the chain: "Hands across the campus" in action. In W. G. Stephan & W. P. Vogt (Eds.), *Education Programs for Improving Intergroup Relations.* New York: Teachers College Press.

Hidi, S., & Harackiewicz, J. M. (2000). Motivating the academically unmotivated: A critical issue for the 21st century. *Review of Educational Research, 70*(2), 151–179.

Hiebert, E. (1983). An examination of ability groupings for reading instruction. *Reading Research Quarterly, 18,* 231–255.

Hiebert, E. H. (1996). Revisiting the question: What difference does Reading Recovery make to an age cohort? *Educational Researcher, 25*(7), 26–28.

Hiebert, J., Carpenter, T. P., Fennema, E., Fuson, K., Human, P., Murray, H., Olivier, A., & Wearne, D. (1996). Problem solving as a basis for reform in curriculum and instruction: The case of mathematics. *Educational Researcher, 25*(4), 12–21.

Hiebert, J., & Wearne, D. (1993). Instructional tasks, classroom discourse, and student learning in second grade. *American Educational Research Journal, 30,* 393–425.

Hiebert, J., Wearne, D., & Taber, S. (1991). Fourth graders' gradual construction of decimal fractions during instruction using different physical representations. *Elementary School Journal, 91,* 321–341.

Hill, J. & Flynn, K. (2006). *Classroom instruction that works with English language learners.* ASCD: Alexandria, VA.

Hill, J. R. (1977). *Measurement and evaluation in the classroom.* Columbus, OH: C. E. Merrill.

Hill, K., & Wigfield, A. (1984). Test anxiety: A major educational problem and what can be done about it. *Elementary School Journal, 85,* 105–126.

Hill, N. E. (2001). Parenting and academic socialization as they relate to school readiness: The roles of ethnicity and family income. *Journal of Educational Psychology, 93*(4), 686–697.

Hill, W. F. (2002). *Learning: A survey of psychological interpretations* (7th ed.). Boston: Allyn & Bacon.

Hilliard, A. G. (1994). Misunderstanding and testing intelligence. In J. I. Goodlad & P. Keating (Eds.), *Access to knowledge: The continuing agenda for our nation's schools.* New York: The College Board.

Hillocks, G. (1984). What works in teaching composition: A meta-analysis of experimental treatment studies. *American Journal of Education, 93,* 133–170.

Hmelo-Silver, C., Duncan, R., & Chinn, C. (2007). Scaffolding and achievement in problem-based inquiry learning: A response to Kirschner, Sweller, and Clark (2006). *Educational Psychologist, 42*(2), 99–107.

Hock, M., Schumaker, J., & Deshler, D. D. (2001). The case for strategic tutoring. *Educational Leadership, 58*(7), 50–52.

Hoeffler, T., & Leutner, D. (2006) Instructional animation versus static picture: A meta-analysis. Poster presented at the annual meeting of the *American Educational Research Association,* San Francisco, CA.

Hoek, D., Terwel, J., & van den Eeden, P. (1997). Effects of training in the use of social and cognitive strategies: An intervention study in secondary mathematics in co-operative groups. *Educational Research and Evaluation, 3*(4), 364–389.

Hoff, E. (2003). Language development in childhood. In R. M. Lerner, M. A. Easterbrooks, & J. Mistry (Eds.), *Handbook of psychology: Vol. 6. Developmental psychology* (pp. 171–193). Hoboken, NJ: Wiley.

Hoffer, T., & Nelson, C. (1993, April). *High school effects on coursework in science and mathematics.* Paper presented at the annual meeting of the American Educational Research Association, Chicago, IL.

Hoffman, M. L. (1993). Affective and cognitive processes in moral internalization. In E. T. Higgins, D. Ruble, & W. Hartup (Eds.), *Social cognition and social development* (pp. 236–274). Cambridge, England: Cambridge University Press.

Hoffman, S. D., Foster, E. M., & Furstenberg, F. F. (1993). Reevaluating the costs of teenage childbearing. *Demography, 30,* 1–13.

Hogan, T., Rabinowitz, M., & Craven, J. A., III. (2003). Representation in teaching: Inferences from research of expert and novice teachers. *Educational Psychologist, 38*(4), 235–247.

Hoge, R. D., & Renzulli, J. S. (1993). Exploring the link between giftedness and self-concept. *Review of Educational Research, 63,* 449–465.

Holloway, J. (2003). Grouping gifted students. *Educational Leadership, 61*(2), 89–91.

Holloway, J. H. (2000). The digital divide. *Educational Leadership, 58*(2), 90–91.

Holloway, J. H. (2001). Inclusion and students with learning disabilities. *Educational Leadership, 58*(6), 88–89.

Holt, D. G., & Willard-Holt, C. (2000). Let's get real: Students solving authentic corporate problems. *Phi Delta Kappan, 82*(3), 243–246.

Hong, G., & Raudenbush, S. (2005). Effects of kindergarten retention policy on children's cognitive growth in reading and mathematics. *Evaluation and Policy Analysis, 27*(3), 205–244.

Hong, L. K. (2001). Too many intrusions on instructional time. *Phi Delta Kappan, 82*(9), 712–714.

Hoover-Dempsey, K., Walker, J., Sandler, H., Whetsel, D., Green, C., Wilkins, A., & Closson, K. (2005). Parental involvement: Model revision through scale development. *The Elementary School Journal, 106*(2), 85–104.

Hopfenberg, W. S., & Levin, H. M. (1993). *The accelerated schools resource guide.* San Francisco: Jossey-Bass.

Hopkins, C. J. (1998). "I'm here to help—what do you want me to do?" A primer for literacy tutors. *The Reading Teacher, 52*(3), 310–312.

Howard, G. (2007). As diversity grows, so must we. *Educational Leadership, 64*(6), 16–22.

Howard, P. (2000). *The owner's manual for the brain: Everyday applications from mind-brain research.* Austin, TX: Bard.

Howes, C., & Matheson, C. C. (1992). Sequences in the development of competent play with peers: Social and social pretend play. *Developmental Psychology, 28,* 961–974.

Howes, C., & Rodning, C. (1992). Attachment security and social pretend play negotiations: Illustrative study #5. In C. Howes, O. Unger, & C. C. Matheson (Eds.), *The collaborative construction of pretend: Social pretend play functions* (pp. 89–98). Albany: State University of New York Press.

Hruby, G., & Hynd, G. (2006). Decoding Shaywitz: The modular brain and its discontents. [Review of the book *Overcoming dyslexia: A new and complete science-based program for reading problems at any level.*] *Reading Research Quarterly, 41*(4), 544–566.

Hubbard, L., & Mehan, H. (1997, March). *Scaling up an untracking program: A co-constructivist process.* Paper presented at the annual meeting of the American Educational Research Association, Chicago, IL.

Hubbard, L., & Mehan, H. (1998). Scaling up an untracking program: A co-constructed process. *Journal of Education for Students Placed at Risk, 4*(1), 83–100.

Huey, E. D., Krueger, F., & Grafman, J. (2006). Representations in the human prefrontal cortex. *Current Directions in Psychological Science, 15*(4), 167–171.

Hughes, F. P. (1995). *Children, play and development* (2nd ed.). Boston: Allyn & Bacon.

Hunter, M. (1982). *Mastery teaching.* El Segundo, CA: TIP Publications.

Hunter, M. (1995). Mastery teaching. In J. H. Block, S. T. Everson, & T. R. Guskey (Eds.), *School improvement programs* (pp. 181–204). New York: Scholastic.

Hurley, E. (2000, April). *The interaction of culture with math achievement and group processes among African American and European American children.* Paper presented at the annual meeting of the American Educational Research Association, New Orleans.

Hurn, C. J. (2002). IQ. In D. L. Levinson, P. W. Cookson, Jr., & A. R. Sadovnik (Eds.), *Education and sociology: An encyclopedia* (pp. 399–402). New York: Routledge Falmer.

Husman, J., & Lens, W. (1999). The role of the future in student motivation. *Educational Psychologist, 34*(2), 113–125.

Hyerle, D. (1995). Thinking maps: Seeing is understanding. *Educational Leadership, 53*(4), 85–89.

Hyman, I. A., & Snook, P. A. (2000). Dangerous schools and what you can do about them. *Phi Delta Kappan, 81*(7), 488–501.

Hymel, S., Bowker, A., & Woody, E. (1993). Aggressive versus withdrawn unpopular children: Variations in peer and self-perceptions in multiple domains. *Child Development, 64,* 879–896.

Ialongo, N., Poduska, J., Wethamer, L., & Keller, S. (2001). The digital impact of two first-grade preventive interventions on conduct problems and disorder in early adolescence. *Journal of Emotional and Behavioral Disorders, 9*(3), 146–160.

Inagaki, K., & Hantano, G. (2006). Young children's conception of the biological world. *Current Directions in Psychological Science, 15*(4), 177–181.

Inhelder, B., & Piaget, J. (1958). *The growth of logical thinking from childhood to adolescence.* New York: Basic Books.

Iran-Nejad, A., & Stewart, W. (2007, April). *What's wrong with Bloom's cognitive taxonomy of educational objectives?* Paper presented at the annual meeting of the American Educational Research Association, Chicago, IL.

Ireson, J., & Hallam, S. (2001). *Ability grouping in education.* London: Sage.

Iversen, I. H. (1992). Skinner's early research: From reflexology to operant conditioning. *American Psychologist, 47,* 1318–1328.

Ivey, G., & Fisher, D. (2006). Then thinking skills trump reading skills. *Educational Leadership, 64*(2), 16–21.

Jackson, J. F. (1999). What are the real risk factors for African American children? *Phi Delta Kappan, 81*(4), 308–312.

Jacobs, J., Lanza S., Osgood, D., Eccles, J., & Wigfield, A. (2002). Changes in children's self-competence and values: Gender and domain differences across grades one through twelve. *Child Development, 73,* 509–527.

Jaffee, S., & Hyde, J. S. (2000). Gender differences in moral orientation: A meta-analysis. *Psychological Bulletin, 126,* 703–726.

Jagacinski, C. M., & Nicholls, J. G. (1990). Reducing effort to protect perceived ability: "They'd do it but I wouldn't." *Journal of Educational Psychology, 82,* 15–21.

Jagers, R. J., & Carroll, G. (2002). Issues in educating African American children and youth. In S. Stringfield & D. Land (Eds.), *Educating at-risk students* (pp. 48–65). Chicago: National Society for the Study of Education.

James, W. (1912). *Talks to teachers on psychology: And to students on some of life's ideals.* New York: Holt.

Janney, R., & Snell, M. E. (2000). *Modifying schoolwork.* Baltimore: Brookes.

Jenkins, J. R., & Jenkins, L. M. (1987). Making peer tutoring work. *Educational Leadership, 44*(6), 64–68.

Jennings, J., & Rentner, D. (2006). Ten big effects of the No Child Left Behind Act on public schools. *Phi Delta Kappan, 88*(2), 110–113.

Jensen, E. (2000). Brain-based learning: A reality check. *Educational Leadership, 57*(7), 76–80.

Jenson, W., Sloane, H., & Young, K. (1988). *Applied behavior modification in education.* Englewood Cliffs, NJ: Prentice-Hall.

Jetton, T. L., & Alexander, P. A. (2001). Interest assessment and the content area literacy environment: Challenges for research and practice. *Educational Psychology Review, 13*(3), 303–318.

Jimerson, S. R., Anderson, G. E., & Whipple, A. D. (2002). Winning the battle and losing the war: Examining the relation between grade retention and dropping out of high school. *Psychology in the Schools, 39,* 441–457.

Jitendra, A., Edwards, L., Sacks, G., & Jacobson, L. (2004, April). *What research says about vocabulary instruction for students with learning disabilities.* Paper presented at the annual meeting of the American Educational Research Association, San Diego, CA.

Johnson, D. W., & Johnson, R. T. (1998). Cultural diversity and cooperative learning. In J. W. Putnam (Ed.), *Cooperative learning and strategies for inclusion* (pp. 67–85). Baltimore: Paul H. Brookes.

Johnson, D. W., & Johnson, R. T. (1999). *Learning together and alone: Cooperative, competitive, and individualistic learning.* Boston: Allyn & Bacon.

Johnson, D. W., & Johnson, R. T. (2001). *Teaching students to be peacemakers: A meta-analysis.* Paper presented at the annual convention of the American Educational Researchers Association, Seattle, WA.

Johnson, L. D., O'Malley, P. M., & Bachman, J. G. (2001). *Monitoring the future: National survey results on drug use, 1975–2000: Vol. 1, secondary school students.* Bethesda, MD: National Institute on Drug Abuse.

John-Steiner, V., & Mahn, H. (1996). Sociocultural approaches to learning and development: A Vygotskian framework. *Educational Psychologist, 31*(3 & 4), 191–206.

John-Steiner, V., & Mahn, H. (2003). Sociocultural contexts for teaching and learning. In W. M. Reynolds & G. E. Miller (Eds.), *Handbook of psychology: Vol. 7. Educational psychology* (pp. 125–151). Hoboken, NJ: Wiley.

Johnston, P., Allington, R., & Afflerbach, P. (1985). The congruence of classroom and remedial instruction. *Elementary School Journal, 85,* 465–477.

Jones, M., Levin, M., Levin, J., & Beitzel, B. (2000). Can vocabulary-learning strategies and pair-learning formats be profitably combined? *Journal of Educational Psychology, 92*(2), 256–262.

Jones, S., & Dindia, K. (2004). A meta-analytic perspective on sex equity in the classroom. *Review of Educational Research, 74*(4), 443–472.

Jones, V., Dohrn, E., & Dunn, C. (2004). *Creating effective programs for students with emotional and behavior disorders.* Boston: Pearson.

Jones, V. F., & Jones, L. S. (2004). *Comprehensive classroom management* (7th ed.). Boston: Pearson.

Jones, V. F., & Jones, L. S. (2007). *Comprehensive classroom management* (8th ed.). Boston: Allyn & Bacon.

Jordan, W. J., McPartland, J. M., Legters, N. E., & Balfanz, R. (2000). Creating a comprehensive school reform model: The talent development high school with career academies. *Journal of Education for Students Placed at Risk, 5*(1 & 2), 159–181.

Joyce, B. R., Calhoun, E., & Hopkins, D. (1999). *The new structure of school improvement.* Buckingham, England: Open University Press.

Joyce, B. R., Weil, M., & Calhoun, E. (2000). *Models of teaching* (6th ed.). Boston: Allyn & Bacon.

Joyce, B., Weil, M., & Calhoun, E. (2004). *Models of teaching* (7th ed.). Boston: Pearson.

Juel, C. (1996). What makes literacy tutoring effective? *Reading Research Quarterly, 31,* 268–289.

Jukes, I., Dosaj, A., & Macdonald, B. (2000). *NetSavvy: Bulding information literacy in the classroom* (2nd ed.). ERIC No. ED450685.

Jussim, L., & Eccles, J. (1995). Naturally occurring interpersonal expectancies. In N. Eisenberg (Ed.), *Social development: Review of personality and social psychology, 15* (pp. 74–108). Thousand Oaks, CA: Sage.

Juvonen, J. (2000). The social functions of attributional face-saving tactics among early adolescents. *Educational Psychology Review, 12*(1), 15–32.

Juvonen, J., Nishina, A., & Graham, S. (2000). Peer harassment, psychological adjustment, and school functioning in early adolescence. *Journal of Educational Psychology, 92*(2), 349–359.

Juvonen, J., & Weiner, B. (1993). An attributional analysis of students' interactions: The social consequences of perceived responsibility. *Educational Psychology Review, 5,* 325–345.

Kagan, S. (1992). *Cooperative learning resources for teachers.* San Juan Capistrano, CA: Resources for Teachers.

Kagan, S. (2001). Teaching for character and community. *Educational Leadership, 59*(2), 50–55.

Kagan, S., Kyle, P., & Scott, S. (2004). *Win-win discipline.* San Clemente, CA: Kagan Publishing.

Kagan, S., Zahn, G. L., Widaman, K. F., Schwartzwald, J., & Tyrrell, G. (1985). Classroom structural bias: Impact of cooperative and competitive classroom structures on cooperative and competitive individuals and groups. In R. E. Slavin et al. (Eds.), *Learning to cooperate, cooperating to learn.* New York: Plenum.

Kahlenberg, R. (2006). The new integration. *Educational Leadership, 63*(8), 22–27.

Kahlenberg, R. E. (2000). The new economic school desegregation. *Educational Leadership, 57*(7), 16–19.

Kalichman, S. C. (1996). *Answering questions about AIDS.* Washington, DC: American Psychological Association.

Kallison, J. M. (1986). Effects of lesson organization on achievement. *American Educational Research Journal, 23,* 337–347.

Kalyuga, S., Chandler, P., Tuovinen, J., & Sweller, J. (2001). When problem solving is superior to studying worked examples. *Journal of Educational Psychology, 93*(3), 579–588.

Kamil, M. L., Intrator, S. M., & Kim, H. S. (2000). The effects of other technologies on literacy and literacy learning. In M. L. Kamil, P. B. Mosenthal, P. D. Pearson, & R. Barr (Eds.), *Handbook of Reading Research: Vol. 3.* (pp. 771–788). Mahwah, NJ: Erlbaum.

Kane, M. S., Hambrick, D. Z., & Conway, A. R. A. (2005). Working memory capacity and flud intelligence are strongly related concepts: Comment on Ackerman, Beier, & Boyle (2005). *Psychological Bulletin, 131*(1), 66–71.

Kantor, H., & Lowe, R. (1995). Class, race, and the emergence of federal education policy: From the new deal to the great society. *Educational Researcher, 24*(3), 4–11.

Kaplan, A., & Midgley, C. (1997). The effect of achievement goals: Does level of perceived academic competence make a difference? *Contemporary Educational Psychology, 22*(4), 415–435.

Kapur, S., Craik, F. I. M., Tulving, E., Wilson, A. A., Hoyle, S., & Brown, G. M. (1994). Neuroanatomical correlates of encoding in episodic memory: Levels of processing effect. *Proceedings of the National Academy of Sciences, 91,* 2008–2011.

Karges-Bone, L. (2000). *Lesson planning: Long-range and short-range models for grades K–6.* Boston: Allyn & Bacon.

Karnes, F. A., & Bean, M. (Eds.) (2001). *Methods and materials for teaching the gifted.* Waco, TX: Prufrock Press.

Karpov, Y. V., & Bransford, J. D. (1995). L. S. Vygotsky and the doctrine of empirical and theoretical learning. *Educational Psychologist, 30,* 61–66.

Karpov, Y. V., & Haywood, H. C. (1998). Two ways to elaborate Vygotsky's concept of mediation. *American Psychologist, 53*(1), 27–36.

Karweit, N. (1989). Time and learning: A review. In R. E. Slavin (Ed.), *School and classroom organization.* Hillsdale, NJ: Erlbaum.

Karweit, N. L. (1981). Time in school. *Research in Sociology of Education and Socialization, 2,* 77–110.

Karweit, N. L., & Slavin, R. E. (1981). Measurement and modeling choices in studies of time and learning. *American Educational Research Journal, 18,* 157–171.

Kasten, W. C., & Lolli, E. M. (1998). *Implementing multiage education.* Norwood, MA: Christopher–Gordon.

Katayama, A. D., & Robinson, D. H. (1998, April). *Study effectiveness of outlines and graphic organizers: How much information should be provided for students to be successful on transfer tests?* Paper presented at the annual meeting of the American Educational Research Association, San Diego, CA.

Katzir, T., & Pare-Blagoev, J. (2006). Applying cognitive neuroscience research to education: The case of literacy. *Educational Psychologist, 41*(1), 53–74.

Kauffman, J., McGee, K., & Brigham, M. (2004). Enabling or disabling? Observations on changes in special education. *Phi Delta Kappan, 85*(8), 613–620.

Kauffman, J. M., Lloyd, J. W., Baker, J., & Riedel, T. M. (1995). Inclusion of all students with emotional or behavioral disorder? Let's think again. *Phi Delta Kappan, 76*(7), 542–546.

Kauffman, J. M., Mostert, M. P., Trent, S. C., & Hallahan, D. P. (2002). *Managing classroom behavior: A reflective case-based approach.* Boston: Allyn & Bacon.

Kaufman, M., Gottlieb, J., Agard, J., & Kukic, M. (1975). Mainstreaming: Toward an explication of the construct. *Focus on Exceptional Children,* 7(3), 1–13.

Kazdin, A. E. (2001). *Behavior modification in applied settings* (6th ed.). Belmont, CA: Wadsworth.

Kellam, S. G., Ling, X., Merisca, R., Brown, C. H., & Ialongo, N. (1998). The effect of the level of aggression in the first grade classroom on the course and malleability of aggressive behavior into middle school. *Development and Psychopathology, 10,* 165–185.

Kelly, N., & Norwich, B. (2004). Pupils' perceptions of self and of labels: Moderate learning difficulties in mainstream and special schools. *British Journal of Educational Psychology, 74*(3), 411–435.

Kemple, J. J. (1997). *Career academies: Communities of support for students and teachers: Further findings from a 10-site evaluation.* New York: MDRC.

Kenkel, S., Hoelscher, S., and West, T. (2006). Leading adolescents to mastery. *Educational Leadership, 63*(7), 33–37.

Kennedy, E. (2003). *Raising test scores for all students: An administrator's guide to improving standardized test performance.* Thousand Oaks, CA: Corwin.

Kennedy, J. H. (1990). Determinants of peer social status: Contributions of physical appearance, reputation, and behavior. *Journal of Youth and Adolescence, 19,* 233–244.

Kennedy, M. (2006). From teacher quality to quality teaching. *Educational Leadership, 63*(6), 14–19.

Kennedy, M. M. (1997). The connection between research and practice. *Educational Researcher, 26*(7), 4–12.

Kerr, M., Stattin, H., Biesecker, G., & Ferrer-Wreder, L. (2003). Relationships with parents and peers in adolescence. In R. M. Lerner, M. A. Easterbrooks, & J. Mistry (Eds.), *Handbook of psychology: Vol. 6. Developmental psychology* (pp. 395–419). Hoboken, NJ: Wiley.

Khmelkov, V., & Hallinan, M. (1999). Organizational effects on race relations in schools. *Journal of Social Issues, 55*(4), 627–645.

Kidron, Y., & Darwin, M. (2007). A systematic review of whole-school improvement models. *Journal of Education for Students Placed at Risk, 12*(1), 9–35.

Kidron, Y., & Fleishman, S. (2006). Promoting adolescents' prosocial behavior. *Educational Leadership, 63*(7), 90–91.

Kiewra, K. A. (1991). Aids to lecture learning. *Educational Psychologist, 26,* 37–53.

Kiewra, K. A., DuBois, N. F., Christian, D., McShane, A., Meyerhoffer, M., & Roskelley, D. (1991). Note-taking functions and techniques. *Journal of Educational Psychology, 83,* 240–245.

Kilgore, S. (2005). Comprehensive solutions for urban reform. *Educational Leadership, 62*(6), 44–49.

Kilgore, S., Doyle, D., & Linkowsky, L. (1996). The modern red schoolhouse. In S. Stringfield, S. Ross, & L. Smith (Eds.), *Bold plans for school restructuring: The new American schools development corporation designs.* Mahwah, NJ: Erlbaum.

Kim, J. (2006). Effects of a voluntary summer reading intervention on reading achievement: Results from a randomized field trial. *Educational Evaluation and Policy Analysis, 28*(4), 335–355.

Kim, S. E. (2001, April). *Meta-analysis of gender differences in test performance using HLM.* Paper presented at the annual meeting of the American Educational Research Association, Seattle, WA.

King, A. (1991). Effects of training in strategic questioning on children's problem-solving performance. *Journal of Educational Psychology, 83,* 307–317.

King, A. (1992). Facilitating elaborative learning through guided student-generated questioning. *Educational Psychologist, 27,* 111–126.

King, A. (1994). Guiding knowledge construction in the classroom: Effects of teaching children how to question and how to explain. *American Educational Research Journal, 31*(2), 338–368.

King, A. (1997). Ask to think—tell why: A model of transactive peer tutoring for scaffolding higher level complex learning. *Educational Psychologist, 32*(4), 221–235.

King, A. (1998). Transactive peer tutoring: Distributing cognition and metacognition. *Educational Psychology Review, 10*(1), 57–74.

King, A. (1999). Teaching effective discourse patterns for small-group learning. In R. J. Stevens (Ed.), *Teaching in American schools.* Upper Saddle River, NJ: Merrill/Prentice-Hall.

King, A., Staffieni, A., & Adelgais, A. (1998). Mutual peer tutoring: Effects of structuring tutorial interaction to scaffold peer learning. *Journal of Educational Psychology, 90*(1), 134–152.

King, E. W. (2002). Ethnicity. In D. L. Levinson, P. W. Cookson, Jr., & A. R. Sadovnik (Eds.), *Education and sociology: An encyclopedia* (pp. 247–253). New York: Routledge Falmer.

King, N., & Ollendick, T. (1989). Children's anxiety and phobic disorders in school settings: Classification, assessment, and intervention issues. *Review of Educational Research, 59*(4), 431–470.

Kirby, D. (2000). What does the research say about sexuality education? *Educational Leadership, 58*(2), 72–75.

Kirschner, P., Sweller, J., & Clark, R. (2006). Why minimal guidance during instruction does not work: An analysis of the failure of constructivist, discovery, problem-based, experiential, and inquiry-based teaching. *Educational Psychologist, 41*(2), 75–86.

Klahr, D., & Nigam, M. (2004). The equivalence of learning paths in early science instruction: Effects of direct instruction and discovery learning. *Psychological Science, 15*(10), 661–667.

Klausmeier, H. (1992). Concept learning and concept teaching. *Educational Psychologist, 27,* 267–286.

Klein, J. D., & Schnackenberg, H. L. (2000). Effects of informal cooperative learning and the affiliation motive on achievement, attitude, and student interactions. *Contemporary Educational Psychology, 25*(1), 332–341.

Klein, P. D. (1999). Reopening inquiry into cognitive processes in writing-to-learn. *Educational Psychology Review, 11*(3), 203–270.

Klein, S. F. (1994). Continuing the journey toward gender equity. *Educational Researcher, 23*(8), 13–21.

Kleinert, H. L., & Kearns, J. F. (2001). *Alternate assessment: Measuring outcomes and supports for students with disabilities.* Baltimore: Paul H. Brookes.

Kline, P. (2001). Teaching to all of a child's intelligences. In B. Sornson (Ed.), *Preventing early learning failure.* Alexandria, VA: ASCD.

King, N. J., & Ollendick, T. H. (1989). Children's anxiety and phobic disorders in school settings: Classification, assessment, and intervention issues. *Review of Educational Research, 59*(4), 431–470.

Klingner, J., & Edwards, P. (2006). Cultural considerations with response to intervention models. *Reading Research Quarterly, 41*(1), 108–117.

Knapp, M. S. (1995). *Teaching for meaning in high-poverty classrooms.* New York: Teachers College Press.

Knapp, M. S., Shields, P. M., & Turnbull, B. S. (1995). Academic challenge in high-poverty classrooms. *Phi Delta Kappan, 76*(10), 770–776.

Knapp, M. S., & Woolverton, S. (1995). Social class and schooling. In J. A. Banks & C. A. M. Banks (Eds.), *Handbook of research on multicultural education.* New York: Macmillan.

Knight, C. B., Halpin, G., & Halpin, G. (1992, April). *The effects of learning environment accommodations on the achievement of second graders.* Paper presented at the annual meeting of the American Educational Research Association, San Francisco, CA.

Koch, J. (2003). Gender issues in the classroom. In W. M. Reynolds & G. E. Miller (Eds.), *Handbook of psychology: Vol. 7. Educational psychology* (pp. 259–281). Hoboken, NJ: Wiley.

Kohlberg, L. (1963). The development of children's orientations toward moral order. I: Sequence in the development of human thought. *Vita Humana, 6,* 11–33.

Kohlberg, L. (1969). Stage and sequence: The cognitive–developmental approach to socialization. In D. A. Golsin (Ed.), *Handbook of socialization theory and research* (pp. 347–380). Chicago: Rand McNally.

Kohlberg, L. (1978). Revisions in the theory and practice of moral development. In W. Damon (Ed.), *New directions for child development* (No. 2, pp. 83–87). San Francisco: Jossey-Bass.

Kohlberg, L. (1980). High school democracy and educating for a just society. In M. L. Mosher (Ed.), *Moral education: A first generation of research and development* (pp. 20–57). New York: Praeger.

Konig, A. (1995, March/April). *Maternal discipline and child temperament as contributors to the development of internalization in your children.* Paper presented at the biennial meeting of the Society for Research in Child Development, Indianapolis, IN.

Koppelman, K., & Goodhart, L. (2005). *Understanding human differences: Multicultural education for a diverse America.* Boston: Pearson.

Kornhaber, M., Fierros, E., & Veenema, S. (2004). *Multiple Intelligences: Best Ideas from Research and Practice.* Boston: Allyn & Bacon.

Kosonen, P., & Winne, P. H. (1995). Effects of teaching statistical laws of reasoning about everyday problems. *Journal of Educational Psychology, 87*(1), 33–46.

Kounin, J. (1970). *Discipline and group management in classrooms.* New York: Holt, Rinehart and Winston.

Kozulin, A., & Presseisen, B. Z. (1995). Mediated learning experience and psychological tools: Vygotsky's and Feuerstein's perspectives in a study of student learning. *Educational Psychologist, 30,* 67–75.

Kramarski, B., & Mevarech, Z. R. (2003). Enhancing mathematical reasoning in the classroom: The effects of cooperative learning and metacognitive training. *American Educational Research Journal, 40*(1), 281–310.

Krasny, K., Sadowski, M., & Paivio, A. (2007). A response to McVee, Dunsmore, & Gavelek's "Schema theory revisited," *Review of Educational Research, 77*(2), 239–244.

Krinsky, R., & Krinsky, S. G. (1996). Pegword mnemonic instruction: Retrieval times and long-term memory performance among fifth grade children. *Contemporary Educational Psychology, 21*(2), 193–207.

Kroesbergen, E. H., Van Luit, J. E. H., & Maas, C. J. M. (2004). Effectiveness of explicit and constructivist mathematics instruction for low-achieving students in the Netherlands. *The Elementary School Journal, 104*(3), 233–251.

Krug, D., Davis, T. B., & Glover, J. A. (1990). Massed versus distributed reading: A case of forgetting helping recall? *Journal of Educational Psychology, 82,* 366–371.

Krumboltz, J. D., & Yeh, C. J. (1996). Competitive grading sabotages good teaching. *Phi Delta Kappan, 78*(4), 324–326.

Kucan, L., & Beck, I. L. (1997). Thinking aloud and reading comprehension research: Inquiry, instruction, and social interaction. *Review of Educational Research, 67*(3), 271–299.

Kugler, E., & Albright, E. (2005). Increasing diversity in challenging classes. *Educational Leadership, 62*(5), 42–45.

Kuhara-Kojima, K., & Hatano, G. (1991). Contribution of content knowledge and learning ability to the learning of facts. *Journal of Educational Psychology, 83*(2), 253–263.

Kuhn, D. (2006). Do cognitive changes accompany developments in the adolescent brain? *Perspectives on Psychological Science, 1*(1), 59–67.

Kulhavy, R. W., & Stock, W. A. (1989). Feedback in written instruction: The place of response certitude. *Educational Psychology Review, 1*(4), 279–308.

Kulik, J. A. (2003). *Effects of using instructional technology in elementary and secondary schools: What controlled evaluation studies say. SRI Project Number P10446.001.* Arlington, VA: SRI International.

Kulik, J. A., & Kulik, C.-L. (1988). Timing of feedback and verbal learning. *Review of Educational Research Journal, 21,* 79–97.

Kulik, J. A., & Kulik, C.-L. (1997). Ability grouping. In N. Colangelo & G. A. Davis (Eds.), *Handbook of gifted education* (2nd ed., pp. 230–242). Boston: Allyn & Bacon.

Kupersmidt, J. B., & Coie, J. D. (1990). Preadolescent peer status, aggression, and school adjustment as predictors of externalizing problems in adolescence. *Child Development, 61,* 1350–1362.

Kyle, P., & Rogien, L. (2004). *Opportunities and options in classroom management.* Boston: Pearson.

Ladd, G. W., & Hart, C. H. (1992). Creating informal play opportunities: Are parents' and preschoolers' initiations related to children's competence with peers? *Developmental Psychology, 28,* 1179–1187.

Ladd, G. W., & Troop-Gordon, W. (2003). The role of chronic peer difficulties in the development of children's psychological adjustment problems. *Child Development, 55,* 1958–1965.

Ladson-Billings, G. (2006). From the achievement gap to the education debt: Understanding achievement in U.S. schools. *Educational Researcher, 35*(7), 3–12.

Lahaderne, H. (1968). Attitudinal and intellectual correlates of attention: A study of four sixth-grade classrooms. *Journal of Educational Psychology, 59,* 320–324.

Lampert, M. (1986). Knowing, doing, and teaching multiplication. *Cognition and Instruction, 3,* 305–342.

Land, D., & Legters, N. (2002). The extent and consequences of risk in U.S. education. In S. Stringfield & D. Land (Eds.), *Educating at-risk students* (pp. 1–28). Chicago: National Society for the Study of Education.

Land, M. L. (1987). Vagueness and clarity. In M. J. Dunkin (Ed.), *International encyclopedia of teaching and teacher education.* New York: Pergamon.

Landrum, T. J., & Kauffman, J. M. (2006). Behavioral approaches to classroom management. In C. M. Evertson & C. S. Weinstein (Eds.) *Handbook of classroom management.* Mahwah, NJ: Erlbaum.

Lane, K. L., & Beebe-Frankenberger, M. (2004). *School-based interventions: The tools you need to succeed.* Boston: Pearson.

Langer, E. (1997). *The power of mindful learning.* Reading, MA: Addison-Wesley.

Langer, G., & Colton, A. (2005). Looking at student work. *Educational Leadership, 62*(5), 22–27.

Langer, J. A. (2001). Beating the odds: Teaching middle and high school students to read and write well. *American Educational Research Journal, 38*(4), 837–880.

Langer, J., & Killen, M. (1998). *Piaget, evolution, and development.* Mahwah, NJ: Erlbaum.

Lapkoff, S., & Li, R. (2007). Five trends for schools. *Educational Leadership, 64*(6), 8–17.

LaPointe, J. M., & Freiberg, H. J. (2006, April). *Discipline and classroom management programs: How much research is enough?* Paper presented at the annual meeting of the American Educational Research Association, San Francisco.

Lariveé, S., Normandeau, S., & Parent, S. (2000). The French connection: Some contributions of French-language research in the post-Piagetian era. *Child Development, 71,* 823–839.

Larrivee, B. (1985). *Effective teaching behaviors for successful mainstreaming.* New York: Longman.

Larrivee, B., & Horne, M. D. (1991). Social status: A comparison of mainstreamed students with peers of different ability levels. *Journal of Special Education, 25,* 90–101.

Larrivee, B., Semmel, M. I., & Gerber, M. M. (1997). Case studies of six schools varying in effectiveness for students with learning disabilities. *Elementary School Journal, 98*(1), 27–50.

Latham, A. S. (1997a). Peer counseling: Proceed with caution. *Educational Leadership, 55*(2), 77–78.

Latham, A. S. (1997b). Technology and LD students: What is best practice? *Educational Leadership, 55*(3), 88.

Lauer, P. A., Akiba, M., Wilkerson, S., Apthorp, H., Snow, D., & Martin-Glenn, M. L. (2006). Out-of-school-time programs: A meta-analysis of effects for at-risk students. *Review of Educational Research, 76*(2), 275–313.

Laupa, M. (1991). Children's reasoning about three authority attributes: Adult status, knowledge, and social position. *Developmental Psychology, 27,* 321–329.

Lave, J. (1988). *Cognition in practice.* Boston: Cambridge Press.

Lazarowitz, R. (1995). Learning science in cooperative modes in junior and senior high schools: Cognitive and affective outcomes. In J. E. Pedersen & A. D. Digby (Eds.), *Secondary schools and cooperative learning* (pp. 185–227). New York: Garland.

Leahy, S., Lyon, C., Thompson, M., & Wiliam, D. (2005). Looking at how students reason. *Educational Leadership, 63*(3), 26–31.

Learning First Alliance. (2001). *Every child learning: Safe and supportive schools.* Washington, DC: Author.

Lee, C. D. (2000, April). *The state of knowledge about the education of African Americans.* Paper presented at the annual meeting of the American Educational Research Association, New Orleans, LA.

Lee, J. (2004). Multiple facets of inequity in racial and ethnic achievement gaps. *Peabody Journal of Education, 79*(2), 51–73.

Lee, J., & Bowen, N. (2006). Parent involvement, cultural capital, and the achievement gap among elementary school children. *American Educational Research Journal, 43*(2), 193–218.

Lee, O. (2005). Science education with English language learners: Synthesis and research agenda. *Review of Educational Research, 75*(4), 491–530.

Lee, V. E., & Burkam, D. T. (2003). Dropping out of high school: The role of school organization and structure. *American Educational Research Journal, 40*(2), 353–393.

Lehr, C. A., Hansen, A., Sinclair, M. F., & Christenson, S. L. (2003). Moving beyond dropout prevention to school completion: An integrative review of data based interventions. *School Psychology Review, 32,* 342–364.

Lehr, C. A., Sinclair, M. F., & Christenson, S. L. (2004). Addressing student engagement and truancy prevention during the elementary school years: A replication study of the Check & Connect model. *Journal of Education for Students Placed at Risk, 9*(3), 279–301.

Lepper, M. R. (1983). Extrinsic reward and intrinsic motivation: Implications for the classroom. In J. M. Levine & M. C. Wang (Eds.), *Teacher and student perceptions: Implications for learning* (pp. 281–317). Hillsdale, NJ: Erlbaum.

Lepper, M. R. (1985). Microcomputers in education. Motivational and social issues. *American Psychologist, 40,* 1–18.

Lepper, M. R. (1998). A whole much less than the sum of its parts. *American Psychologist, 53*(6), 675–676.

Lepper, M. R., Greene, D., & Nisbett, R. E. (1973). Undermining children's intrinsic interest with extrinsic rewards: A test of the overjustification hypothesis. *Journal of Personality and Social Psychology, 28,* 129–137.

Lepper, M. R., Keavney, M., & Drake, M. (1996). Intrinsic motivation and extrinsic rewards: A commentary on Cameron & Pierce's meta-analysis. *Review of Educational Research, 66*(1), 5–32.

Lesgold, A. (1988). Problem solving. In R. J. Sternberg & E. E. Smith (Eds.), *The psychology of human thought* (pp. 188–213). New York: Cambridge University Press.

Lessow-Hurley, J. (2005). *The foundations of dual language instruction.* Boston: Pearson.

Leu, D. J., Jr. (2000). Literacy and technology: Deictic consequences for literacy education in an information age. In M. L. Kamil, P. B. Mosenthal, P. D. Pearson, & R. Barr (Eds.), *Handbook of reading research: Vol. 3* (pp. 743–770). Mahwah, NJ: Erlbaum.

Levenstein, P., Levenstein, S., & Oliver, D. (2002). First grade school readiness of former participants in a South Carolina replication of the Parent-Child Home Program. *Journal of Applied Developmental Psychology, 23,* 331–353.

Lever-Duffy, J., & McDonald, J. B. (2008). *Teaching and learning with technology* (3rd ed.). Boston: Allyn & Bacon.

Lever-Duffy, J., McDonald, J., & Mizell, A. (2003). *Teaching and learning with technology.* Boston: Pearson.

Levin, A. V. (1996). Common visual problems in the classroom. In R. H. A. Haslam & P. J. Valletutti (Eds.), *Medical problems in the classroom: The teacher's role in diagnosis and management* (pp. 161–180). Austin, TX: Pro-Ed.

Levin, J. & Nolan, J. F. (2007). *Principles of classroom management* (5th ed.). Boston: Allyn & Bacon.

Levin, J. R., O'Donnell, A. M., & Kratochwill, T. R. (2003). Educational/psychological intervention research. In W. M. Reynolds & G. E. Miller (Eds.), *Handbook of psychology: Vol. 7. Educational psychology* (pp. 557–581). Hoboken, NJ: Wiley.

Levine, C., Kohlberg, L., & Hewer, A. (1985). The current formulation of Kohlberg's theory and a response to critics. *Human Development, 28,* 94–100.

Levy, S. (1999). Reducing prejudice: Lessons from social–cognitive factors underlying perceiver differences in prejudice. *Journal of Social Issues, 55*(4), 745–765.

Lewin, L. (2001). *Using the Internet to strengthen curriculum.* Alexandria, VA: ASCD.

Lewin, L., & Shoemaker, B. J. (1998). *Great performances: Creating classroom-based assessment tasks.* Alexandria, VA: ASCD.

Lewis, M., & Sullivan, M. W. (Eds.). (1996). *Emotional development in atypical children.* Mahwah, NJ: Erlbaum.

Lickona, T. (1992). *Educating for character.* New York: Bantam.

Lindeman, B. (2001). Reaching out to immigrant parents. *Educational Leadership, 58*(6), 62–66.

Lindholm-Leary, K. (2004/2005). The rich promise of two-way immersion. *Educational Leadership, 62*(4), 56–59.

Linebarger, D., Kosniac, A., Greenwood, C., & Doku, N. (2004). Effects of viewing the television program *Between the Lions* on the emergent literacy skills of young children. *Journal of Educational Psychology, 96,* 297–308.

Linn, M. C., & Slotta, J. D. (2000). WISE science. *Educational Leadership, 58*(2), 29–32.

Linn, R. L. (1994). Performance assessment: Policy promises and technical measurement standards. *Educational Researcher, 23*(9), 4–14.

Linn, R. L. (2000). Assessments and accountability. *Educational Researcher, 29*(2), 4–15.

Linn, R. L., & Haug, C. (2002). Stability of school-building accountability scores and gains. *Educational Evaluation and Policy Analysis, 24*(1), 29–36.

Lissitz, R., & Schafer, W. (2002). *Assessment in educational reform: Both means and ends.* Boston: Allyn & Bacon.

Lloyd, J. W., Singh, N. N., & Repp, A. C. (Eds.). (1991). *The Regular Education Initiative: Alternative perspectives on concepts, issues, and models.* DeKalb, IL: Sycamore.

Loeber, R., & Stouthamer-Loeber, M. (1998). Development of juvenile aggression and violence. *American Psychologist, 53*(2), 242–259.

Lomawaima, K. T., & McCarty, T. L. (2002). When tribal sovereignty challenges democracy: American Indian education and the democratic ideal. *American Educational Research Journal, 39*(2), 279–305.

Lomotey, K., & Teddlie, C. (Eds.). (1997). *Forty years after the Brown decision: Social and cultural effects of school desegregation, vol. 14.* New York: AMS Press.

Lorch, R. F., Lorch, E. P., & Inman, W. E. (1993). Effects of signaling topic structure on text recall. *Journal of Educational Psychology, 85,* 281–290.

Losey, K. M. (1995). Mexican American students and classroom interaction: An overview and critique. *Review of Educational Research, 65,* 283–318.

Lou, Y., Abrami, P. C., & D'Apollonia, S. (2001). Small group and individual learning with technology: A meta-analysis. *Review of Educational Research, 71*(3), 449–521.

Lou, Y., Abrami, P. C., Spence, J. C., Poulsen, C., Chambers, B., & D'Apollonia, S. (1996). Within-class grouping: A meta-analysis. *Review of Educational Research, 66*(4), 423–458.

Loury, G. C. (2002). *The anatomy of racial inequality.* Cambridge, MA: Harvard University Press.

Loveless, T. (1998). The tracking and ability grouping debate. *Fordham Report, 2*(8), 1–27.

Lowther, D., Ross, S., & Morrison, G. (2003). *When each one has one: The influences on teaching strategies and student achievement of using laptops in the classroom.* Paper presented at the annual meeting of the American Educational Research Association, Seattle, WA.

Lubienski, S. & Lubienski, T. (2006). School sector and academic achievement: A multilevel analysis of NAEP mathematics data. *American Educational Research Journal, 43*(4), 651–698.

Luckasson, R., Coulter, D., Polloway, E., Reiss, S., Schalock, R., Snell, M., Spitalnik, D., & Stark, J. (1992). *Mental retardation: Definitions, classification, and systems of supports* (9th ed.). Washington, DC: American Association on Mental Retardation.

Lyons, C. (1989). Reading Recovery: A preventative for mislabeling young "at-risk" learners. *Urban Education, 24,* 125–139.

Lyons, C. A., Pinnell, G. S., & DeFord, D. E. (1993). *Partners in learning: Teachers and children in reading recovery.* New York: Teachers College Press.

Lysynchuk, L. M., Pressley, M., & Vye, N. J. (1990). Reciprocal teaching improves standardized reading-comprehension performance in poor comprehenders. *Elementary School Journal, 90,* 469–484.

Lyytinen, H., Guttorm, T. K., Huttunen, T., Hamalainen, J., Leppanen, P. H. T., and Vesterinen, M. (2005). Psychophysiology of developmental dyslexic: A review of findings including studies of children at risk for dyslexia. *Journal of Neurolinguistics, 18,* 167–195.

Ma, X., & Kishor, N. (1997). Attitude toward self, social factors, and achievement in mathematics: A meta-analytic review. *Educational Psychology Review, 9*(2), 89–120.

Maag, J. W., Rutherford, R. B., & DiGangi, S. A. (1992). Effects of self-monitoring and contingency reinforcement on on-task behavior and academic productivity of learning disabled students: A social validation study. *Psychology in the Schools, 29,* 157–172.

MacArthur, C., Ferretti, R., Okolo, C., & Cavalier, A. (2001). Technology applications for students with literacy problems: A critical review. *The Elementary School Journal, 101*(3), 273–302.

Macedo, D. (2000). The illiteracy of English-only literacy. *Educational Leadership, 57*(4), 63–67.

MacIver, D. J., Reuman, D. A., & Main, S. R. (1995). Social structuring of the school: Studying what is, illuminating what could be. *Annual Review of Psychology, 46,* 375–400.

MacKenzie, A. A., & White, R. T. (1982). Fieldwork in geography and long-term memory. *American Educational Research Journal, 19,* 623–632.

Mackenzie, R. J. (1997). Setting limits in the classroom. *American Educator, 21*(3), 32–43.

MacLean, W. E. (1996). *Ellis' handbook of mental deficiency, psychological theory, and research.* Mahwah, NJ: Erlbaum.

Madden, N. A., & Slavin, R. E. (1983a). Effects of cooperative learning on the social acceptance of mainstreamed academically handicapped students. *Journal of Special Education, 17,* 171–182.

Maehr, M. L., & Anderman, E. M. (1993). Reinventing schools for early adolescents: Emphasizing task goals. *The Elementary School Journal, 93*(5), 593–610.

Mager, R. F. (1975). *Preparing instructional objectives.* Belmont, CA: Fearon.

Mager, R. (1997). *Preparing instructional objectives: A critical tool in the development of effective instruction.* Atlanta, GA: The Center for Effective Performance.

Maguire, E. A., Gadian, D. G., Johnsrude, I. S., Good, C. D., Ashburner, J., Frackowiak, R. S. J., & Frith, C. D. (2000). Navigation-related structural change in the hippocampi of taxi drivers. *Proceedings of the National Academy of Sciences, 97*(8) 4398–4403.

Maheady, L., Harper, G. F., & Mallette, B. (1991). Peer-mediated instruction: Review of potential applications for special education. *Reading, Writing, and Learning Disabilities, 7,* 75–102.

Maher, F. A., & Ward, J. V. (2002). *Gender and teaching.* Mahwah, NJ: Erlbaum.

Mahony, M. (1997). Small victories in an inclusive classroom. *Educational Leadership, 54*(7), 59–62.

Maier, S. F., & Seligman, M. E. P. (1976). Learned helplessness: Theory and evidence. *Journal of Experimental Psychology: General, 105,* 3–46.

Malott, R., Malott, M., & Trojan, E. (2000). *Elementary principles of behavior* (4th ed.). Upper Saddle River, NJ: Prentice-Hall.

Malouf, D. B., Wizer, D. R., Pilato, V. H., & Grogan, M. M. (1990). Computer-assisted instruction with small groups of mildly handicapped students. *Journal of Special Education, 24,* 51–68.

Mamlin, N., & Harris, K. R. (1998). Elementary teachers' referral to special education in light of inclusion and prereferral: "Every child is here to learn . . . but some of these children are in real trouble." *Journal of Educational Psychology, 90*(3), 385–396.

Mandeville, G. K. (1992). Does achievement increase over time? Another look at the South Carolina PET program. *The Elementary School Journal, 93*(2), 117–129.

Mandeville, G. K., & Rivers, J. L. (1991). The South Carolina PET study: Teachers' perceptions and student achievement. *Elementary School Journal, 91,* 377–407.

Manning, B. H. (1988). Application of cognitive behavior modification: First and third graders' self-management of classroom behaviors. *American Educational Research Journal, 25,* 193–212.

Manning, B. H., & Payne, B. D. (1996). *Self-talk for teachers and students: Metacognitive strategies for personal and classroom use.* Boston: Allyn & Bacon.

Manning, M. A., Bear, G. G., & Minke, K. M. (2001, April). *The self-concept of students with learning disabilities: Does educational placement matter?* Paper presented at the annual meeting of the American Educational Research Association, Seattle, WA.

Manning, M. L., & Baruth, L. G. (1995). *Students at risk.* Boston: Allyn & Bacon.

Manning, M. L., & Baruth, L. G. (2004). *Multicultural education of children and adolescents* (4th ed.). Boston: Pearson.

Mantzicopoulos, P. (2003). Flunking kindergarten after Head Start: An inquiry into the contribution of contextual and individual variables. *Journal of Educational Psychology, 95,* 268–278.

March, T. (2005/2006). The new www: whatever, whenever, wherever. *Educational Leadership, 63*(4), 14–19.

Marcia, J. E. (1991). Identity and self-development. In R. M. Lerner, A. C. Petersen, & E. J. Brooks-Gunn (Eds.), *Encyclopedia of adolescence* (Vol. 1, pp. 527–531). New York: Garland.

Marks, H., Doane, K., & Secada, W. (1998). Support for student achievement. In F. Newmann et al. (Eds.), *Restructuring for student achievement: The impact of structure and culture in 24 schools.* San Francisco: Jossey-Bass.

Marks, H. M. (2000). Student engagement in instructional activity: Patterns in the elementary, middle, and high school years. *American Educational Research Journal, 37*(1), 153–184.

Marsh, H.W. (1993). The multidimensional structure of academic self-concept: Invariance over gender and age. *American Educational Research Journal, 30,* 841–860.

Marsh, H.W., & Yeung, A. S. (1997). Causal effects of academic self-concept on academic achievement: Structural equation models of longitudinal data. *Journal of Educational Psychology, 89*(1), 41–54.

Martella, R. C., Marchand-Martella, N. E., & Cleanthous, C. (2001). *ADHD: A comprehensive approach.* Dubuque, IA: Rendall/Hunt.

Martella, R. C., Nelson, J. R., & Marchand-Martella, N. E. (2003). *Managing disruptive behaviors in the schools.* Boston: Pearson.

Martin, A. J., Marsh, H. W., & Debus, R. L. (2001). Self-handicapping and defensive pessimism: Exploring a model of predictors and outcomes from a self-protection perspective. *Journal of Educational Psychology, 93*(1), 87–102.

Martin, J. (1993). Episodic memory: A neglected phenomenon in the psychology of education. *Educational Psychologist, 28*(2), 169–183.

Martinez, M. (2006). What is metacognition? *Phi Delta Kappan, 87*(9), 696–699.

Martinez, M. E. (1998). What is problem solving? *Phi Delta Kappan, 70*(8), 605–609.

Marx, R., & Harris, C. (2006). No Child Left Behind and science education: Opportunities, challenges, and risks. *The Elementary School Journal, 106*(5), 467–478.

Marzano, R. (2003). Using data: Two wrongs and a right. *Educational Leadership, 60*(5), 56–60.

Marzano, R. J. (1995). Critical thinking. In J. H. Block, S. T. Everson, & T. R. Guskey (Eds.), *School improvement programs* (pp. 57–76). New York: Scholastic.

Marzano, R. J. (2000). *Transforming classroom grading.* Alexandria: ASCD.

Marzano, R. J. (2001). *Designing a new taxonomy of educational objectives.* Thousand Oaks, CA: Corwin.

Marzano, R. J., Pickering, D. J., & Pollock, J. E. (2001). *Classroom instruction that works: Research-based strategies for increasing student achievement.* Alexandria: ASCD.

Marzano, R., & Pickering, D. (2007). The case for and against homework. *Educational Leadership, 64*(6), 74–79.

Mash, E. J., & Wolfe, D. A. (2003). Disorders of childhood and adolescence. In G. Stricker & T. A. Widigner (Eds.), *Handbook of psychology: Vol. 8. Clinical psychology,* (pp. 27–64). Hoboken, NJ: Wiley.

Maslow, A. H. (1954). *Motivation and personality.* New York: Harper & Row.

Mason, D. A. (1995). Grouping students for elementary school mathematics: A survey of principals in 12 states. *Educational Research and Evaluation, 1*(4), 318–346.

Mason, D. A., & Good, T. L. (1993). Effects of two-group and whole-class teaching on regrouped elementary students' mathematics achievement. *American Educational Research Journal, 30*(2), 328–360.

Mason, L. H. (2004). Explicit self-regulated strategy development versus reciprocal questioning: Effects on expository reading comprehension among struggling readers. *Journal of Educational Psychology, 96*(2), 283–296.

Mastropieri, M. A., & Scruggs, T. E. (1998). Enhancing school success with mnemonic strategies. *Intervention in School and Clinic, 33*(4), 201–208.

Mastropieri, M. A., Scruggs, T. E., & Berkeley, S. (2007). *Educational Leadership, 64*(5), 54–60.

Matheny, K. B., Aycock, D. W., & McCarthy, C. J. (1993). Stress in school-aged children and youth. *Educational Psychology Review, 5*(2), 109–134.

Mather, N., & Goldstein, S. (2001). *Learning disabilities and challenging behaviors.* Baltimore: Brookes.

Mathes, P. G., Torgeson, J. K., & Allor, J. H. (2001). The effects of peer-assisted literacy strategies for first-grade readers with and without additional computer-assisted instruction in phonological awareness. *American Educational Research Journal, 38*(2), 371–410.

Mathes, P. G., Torgesen, J. K., Clancy-Menchetti, J., Santi, K., Nicholas, K., Robinson, C., & Grek, M. (2003). A comparison of teacher-directed versus peer-assisted instruction to struggling first-grade readers. *The Elementary School Journal, 103*(5), 461–479.

Mattingly, D. J., Prisllin, R., McKenzie, T. L., Rodriguez, J. L., & Kayzar, B. (2002). Evaluating evaluations: The case of parent involvement programs. *Review of Educational Research, 72*(4), 549–576.

May, D. C., & Kundert, D. K. (1997). School readiness practices and children at risk. *Psychology in the Schools, 34,* 73–84.

Mayer, R. E. (1996). Learning strategies for making sense out of expository text: The SOI model for guiding three cognitive processes in knowledge construction. *Educational Psychology Review, 8*(4), 357–371.

Mayer, R. E. (2001). *Multimedia learning.* New York: Cambridge University Press.

Mayer, R. E. (2003). Memory and information processes. In W. M. Reynolds & G. E. Miller (Eds.), *Handbook of psychology: Vol. 7. Educational psychology* (pp. 47–57). Hoboken, NJ: Wiley.

Mayer, R. E., & Gallini, J. K. (1990). When is an illustration worth ten thousand words? *Journal of Educational Psychology, 82,* 715–726.

Mayer, R. E., & Moreno, R. (1998). A split-attention effect in multi- media learning: Evidence for dual processing systems in working memory. *Journal of Educational Psychology, 90*(2), 312–320.

Mayer, R. E., & Moreno, R. (2002). Animation as an aid to multimedia learning. *Educational Psychology Review, 14*(1), 87–100.

Mayer, R. E., & Wittrock, M. C. (1996). Problem-solving transfer. In D. C. Berliner & R. C. Calfee (Eds.), *Handbook of educational psychology* (pp. 47–62). New York: Macmillan.

McCain, T., & Jukes, I. (2000). *Windows on the future: Education in the age of technology.* Thousand Oaks, CA: Corwin.

McCaleb, J., & White, J. (1980). Critical dimensions in evaluating teacher clarity. *Journal of Classroom Interaction, 15,* 27–30.

McCallum, R. S., & Bracken, B. A. (1993). Interpersonal relations between school children and their peers, parents, and teachers. *Educational Psychology Review, 5*(2), 155–176.

McCarthy, B. (1997). A tale of four learners: 4 MAT's learning styles. *Educational Leadership, 54*(6), 46–51.

McClelland, D. C., & Atkinson, J. W. (1948). The projective expression of needs: II. The effect of different intensities of the hunger drive on thematic apperception. *Journal of Experimental Psychology, 38,* 643–658.

McComb, E. M., & Scott-Little, C. (2003). *After-school programs: Evaluations and outcomes.* Greensboro, NC: SERVE.

McCormick, C. B. (2003). Metacognition and learning. In W. M. Reynolds & G. E. Miller (Eds.), *Handbook of psychology: Vol. 7. Educational psychology* (pp. 79–102). Hoboken, NJ: Wiley.

McDaniel, M. A., & Dannelly, C. M. (1996). Learning with analogy and elaborative interrogation. *Journal of Educational Psychology, 88*(3), 508–519.

McDaniel, T. R. (1993). Practicing positive reinforcement: Ten behavior management techniques. In K. M. Cauley, F. Linder, &

J. H. McMillan (Eds.), *Annual editions: Educational psychology 93/94.* Guilford, CT: Dushkin.

McDermott, K. (2007). "Expanding the moral community" or "Blaming the victim"? The politics of state education accountability policy. *American Educational Research Journal, 44*(1), 77–111.

McDonnell, J., Hardman, M., & McDonnell, A. (2003). *An introduction to persons with moderate and severe disabilities.* Boston: Allyn & Bacon.

McGill-Franzen, A., & Allington, R. (2006). Contamination of current accountability systems. *Phi Delta Kappan, 87*(10), 762–766.

McHale, S. M., Dariotis, J. K., & Kauh, T. J. (2003). Social development and social relationships in middle childhood. In R. M. Lerner, M. A. Easterbrooks, & J. Mistry (Eds.), *Handbook of psychology: Vol. 6. Developmental psychology* (pp. 241–265). Hoboken, NJ: Wiley.

McInerney, V., & McInerney, D. M. (1998, April). *Metacognitive strategy training in self-questioning: The strengths of multimedia investigations of the comparative effects of two instructional approaches on self-efficacy and achievement.* Paper presented at the annual meeting of the American Educational Research Association, San Diego, CA.

McIntyre, T. (1992). The culturally sensitive disciplinarian. *Severe Behavior Disorders Monograph, 3,* 107–115.

McKenna, M., & Walpole, S. (2007). Assistive technology in the reading clinic: Its emerging potential. *Reading Research Quarterly, 42*(1), 140–145.

McKenzie, G. (1979). Effects of questions and testlike events on achievement and on-task behavior in a classroom concept learning presentation. *Journal of Educational Research, 72,* 348–350.

McKenzie, G. R., & Henry, M. (1979). Effects of testlike events on on-task behavior, test anxiety, and achievement in a classroom rule-learning task. *Journal of Educational Psychology, 71,* 370–374.

McKeown, M. G., & Beck, I. L. (1998). Talking to an author: Readers taking charge of the reading process. In R. Calfoe & N. Nelson (Eds.), *The Reading–Writing Connection* (pp. 112–130). Chicago: National Society for the Study of Education.

McKeown, M. G., & Beck, I. L. (2004). Transforming knowledge into professional development resources: Six teachers implement a model of teaching for understanding text. *The Elementary School Journal, 104*(5), 391–408.

McLeskey, J., & Waldron, N. L. (2002). School change and inclusive schools: Lessons learned from practice. *Phi Delta Kappan, 84*(1), 65–72.

McLoyd, V. C. (1998). Economic disadvantage and child-development. *American Psychologist, 53*(2), 185–204.

McMillan, J. H. (2004). *Classroom assessment: Principles and practice for effective instruction.* Boston: Pearson.

McMillan, J. H. (2007). *Classroom assessment* (4th ed.). Boston: Allyn & Bacon.

McNeely, C. A., Nonnemaker, J. M., & Blum, R. W. (2002). Promoting school connectedness. *Journal of School Health, 72*(4), 138–146.

McPartland, J. M., Balfanz, R., Jordan, W. J., & Legters, N. (2002). Promising solutions for the least productive American high schools. In S. Stringfield & D. Land (Eds.), *Educating at-risk students* (pp. 148–170). Chicago: National Society for the Study of Education.

McTighe, J., & O'Connor, K. (2005). Seven practices for effective learning. *Educational Leadership, 63*(3), 10–17.

McVee, M., Dunsmore, K., & Gavelek, J. (2005). Schema theory revisited. *Review of Educational Research, 75*(4), 531–566.

Mead, S. (2006). *The truth about boys and girls.* Washington, DC: Education Sector.

Means, B. (2001). Technology use in tomorrow's schools. *Educational Leadership, 58*(4), 57–61.

Means, B., & Coleman, E. (2000). Technology supports for student participation in science investigations. In M. J. Jacobson & R. B. Kozma (Eds.), *Innovations in science and mathematics* (pp. 287–319). Mahwah, NJ: Erlbaum.

Means, B., Roschelle, J., & Penuel, W. (2003). Technology's contribution to teaching and policy: Efficiency, standardization, or transformation? *Review of Education in Research, 27,* 159–182.

Medley, D. M. (1979). The effectiveness of teachers. In P. L. Peterson & H. Walberg (Eds.), *Research on teaching: Concepts, findings, and implications* (pp. 11–27). Berkeley: McCutchan.

Meek, C. (2003). Classroom crisis: It's about time. *Phi Delta Kappan, 84*(8), 592–595.

Meichenbaum, D. (1977). *Cognitive behavior modification: An integrative approach.* New York: Plenum.

Merickel, A., Linquanti, R., Parrish, T. B., Pérez, M., Eaton, M., & Esra, P. (2003). *Effects of the implementation of Proposition 227 on the education of English language learners, K-12: Year 3 report.* San Francisco: WestEd.

Merrill, D. C., Reiser, B. J., Merrill, S. K., & Landes, S. (1995). Tutoring: Guided learning by doing. *Cognition and Instruction, 13*(3), 315–372.

Mertler, C. A., & Charles, C. M. (2005). *Introduction to education research* (5th ed.). Boston: Pearson.

Messick, S. (1982). Issues of effectiveness and equity in the coaching controversy: Implications for educational and testing practice. *Educational Psychologist, 17,* 67–91.

Messick, S. (1994). The interplay of evidence and consequences in the validation of performance assessments. *Educational Researcher, 23*(2), 13–23.

Metsala, J. L., Stanovich, K. E., & Brown, G. D. A. (1998). Regularity effects and the phonological deficit model of reading disabilities: A meta-analytic review. *Journal of Educational Psychology, 90*(2), 279–293.

Metzger, M. (2002). Learning to discipline. *Phi Delta Kappan, 84*(1), 77–84.

Meyer, A., & Rose, D. H. (2000). Universal design for individual differences. *Educational Leadership, 58*(3), 39–43.

Meyer, B., Middlemiss, W., Theodorou, E., Brezinski, K., McDougall, J., & Bartlett, B. (2002). Effects of structure strategy instruction delivered to fifth-grade children using the internet with and without the aid of older adult tutors. *Journal of Educational Psychology, 94*(3), 486–519.

Meyer, L. A. (1984). Long-term academic effects of the Direct Instruction Project follow through. *The Elementary School Journal, 84*(4), 380–394.

Meyer, M. (2000). The ability-achievement discrepancy: Does it contribute to an understanding of learning disabilites? *Educational Psychology Review, 12*(3), 315–338.

Meyers, J., Gelzheiser, L., Yelich, G., & Gallagher, M. (1990). Classroom, remedial and resource teachers' views of pullout programs. *Elementary School Journal, 90*(5), 531–545.

Mickelson, R. A. (2002). Race and education. In D. L. Levinson, P. W. Cookson, Jr., & A. R. Sadovnik (Eds.), *Education and sociology: An encyclopedia* (pp. 485–494). New York: Routledge Falmer.

Midgley, C. M. (1993). Motivation and middle level schools. In M. L. Maehr & P. R. Pintrick (Eds.), *Advances in motivation and achievement* (Vol. 8, pp. 217–274). Greenwich, CT: JAI Press.

Midgley, C., & Urdan, T. (2001). Academic self-handicapping and achievement goals: A further examination. *Contemporary Educational Psychology, 26*(1), 61–75.

Miller, A., & Hom, H. L., Jr. (1990). Influence of extrinsic and ego incentive value on persistence after failure and continuing motivation. *Journal of Educational Psychology, 82*(3), 539–545.

Miller, D. J., Glover, D., Averis, D., & Door, V. (2005). The interactive whiteboard—a literature survey. *Technology, Pedagogy, and Education, 14*(2).

Miller, D., Partelow, L., Sen, A. (2004, April). *Self-regulatory reading processes in relation to fourth-graders' reading literacy.* Paper presented at the annual meeting of the American Educational Research Association, San Diego, CA.

Miller, G. A. (1956). The magical number seven, plus or minus two: Some limits on our capacity for processing information. *Psychological Review, 63,* 81–97.

Miller, P. H. (1993). *Theories of developmental psychology* (3rd ed.). New York: Freeman.

Mills, G. E. (2000). *Action research: A guide for the teacher-researcher.* Columbus, OH: Merrill.

Miltenberger, R. G. (2001). *Behavior modification: Principles and procedures* (2nd ed.). Belmont, CA: Wadsworth.

Minke, K. M., & Bear, G. C. (Eds.). (2000). *Preventing school problems—promoting school success.* Bethesda, MD: National Association of School Psychologists.

Mishel, L., & Roy, J. (2006). Accurately assessing high school graduation rates. *Phi Delta Kappan, 88*(4), 287–292.

Mock, D. R., Kauffman, J. M. (2005). The delusion of full inclusion. In J. W. Jacobson, J. A. Mulick, & R. M. Foxx (Eds.) *Fads: Dubious and improbable treatments for developmental disabilities* (pp. 113–128). Mahwah, NJ: Erlbaum.

Moors, A., & De Houwer, J. (2006). Automaticity: A theoretical and conceptual analysis. *Psychological Bulletin, 132*(2), 297–326.

Moran, S., Kornhaber, M., & Gardner, H. (2006). Orchestrating multiple intelligences. *Educational Leadership, 64*(1), 22–29.

Morgan, M. (1984). Reward-induced decrements and increments in intrinsic motivation. *Review of Educational Research, 54,* 5–30.

Morris, D. (2006). Using noncertified tutors to work with at-risk readers: An evidence-based model. *The Elementary School Journal, 106*(4), 351–362.

Morris, D., Tyner, B., & Perney, J. (2000). Early Steps: Replicating the effects of a first-grade reading intervention program. *Journal of Educational Psychology, 92,* 681–693.

Morris, J. E. (1999). What is the future of predominantly black urban schools? The politics of race in urban education policy. *Phi Delta Kappan, 81*(4), 316–319.

Morrison, P., & Masten, A. S. (1991). Peer reputation in middle childhood as a predictor of adaptation in adolescence: A seven-year follow-up. *Child Development, 62,* 991–1007.

Morrow, L. M. (1993). *Literacy development in the early years.* Boston: Allyn & Bacon.

Mosenthal, J., Lipson, M., Torncello, S., Russ, B., & Mekkelsen, J. (2004). Contexts and practices of six schools successful in obtaining reading achievement. *The Elementary School Journal, 104*(5), 343–368.

Moss, P. A. (1992). Shifting conceptions of validity in educational measurement: Implications for performance assessment. *Review of Educational Research, 62*(3), 229–258.

Moss, P., Girard, B., & Haniford, L. (2006). Validity in educational assessment. *Review of Research in Education, 30,* 109–162.

Mosteller, F., & Boruch, R. (Eds.). (2002). *Evidence matters: Randomized trials in educational research.* Washington, DC: Brookings.

Munk, D. D., & Bursuck, W. D. (1998). Can grades be helpful and fair? *Educational Leadership, 55*(4), 44–47.

Muñoz, M. A., Dossett, D., & Judy-Gullans, K. (2004). Educating students placed at risk: Evaluating the impact of Success for All in urban settings. *Journal of Education for Students Placed at Risk, 9*(3), 261–277.

Murdock, T. B. (1999). The social context of risk: Status and motivational predictors of alienation in middle school. *Journal of Educational Psychology, 91*(1), 62–75.

Murdock, T. B., & Anderman, E. (2006). Motivational perspectives on student cheating: Toward an integrated model of academic dishonesty. *Educational Psychologist, 41*(3), 129–145.

Murdock, T. B., Hale, N. M., & Weber, M. J. (2001). Predictors of cheating among early adolescents: Academic and social motivations. *Contemporary Educational Psychology, 26*(1), 96–115.

Murji, S., & DeLuca, J. W. (1998). Preliminary validity of the cognitive function checklist: Prediction of tower of London performance. *Clinical Neuropsychologist, 12,* 358–364.

Murphy, K. P., & Alexander, P. A. (2000). A motivated exploration of motivation technology. *Contemporary Educational Psychology, 25*(1), 3–53.

Murphy, S., & Underwood, T. (2000). *Portfolio practices: Lessons from schools, districts, and states.* Norwood, MA: Christopher-Gordon.

Murray, H., Olivier, A., & Human, P. (1992). The development of young students' division strategies. In W. Geeslin & K. Graham (Eds.), *Proceedings of the sixteenth international conference for the psychology of mathematics instruction* (Vol. 2, pp. 152–159). Durham, NH.

Muskin, C. (1990, April). *Equity and opportunity to learn in high school U.S. history classes: Comparisons between schools and ability groups.* Paper presented at the annual meeting of the American Educational Research Association, Boston, MA.

Nagy, P., & Griffiths, A. K. (1982). Limitations of recent research relating Piaget's theory to adolescent thought. *Review of Educational Research, 52,* 513–556.

Nasir, N., & Hand, V. (2006). Exploring sociocultural perspectives on race, culture, and learning. *Review of Educational Research, 76*(4), 449–476.

National Association for the Education of Young Children (2004). *NAEYC accreditation criteria.* www.naeyc.org/accreditation/criteria98.asp.

National Association of State Boards of Education. (1992). *Winners all: A call for inclusive schools.* Alexandria, VA: Author.

National Center for Education Statistics. (1997). *The condition of education, 1997.* Washington, DC: U.S. Department of Education, NCES.

National Center for Education Statistics (2001). *The condition of education, 2001.* Washington, DC: U.S. Department of Education, NCES.

National Center for Education Statistics. (2003). *The condition of education.* Washington, DC: U.S. Department of Education.

National Center for Education Statistics. (2004). *Language minorities and their educational and labor market indicators—recent trends.* Washington, DC: U.S. Department of Education.

National Center for Education Statistics. (2006). *National household education survey of 2005: Public use data file user's manual, volume 1.* Washington, DC: U.S. Department of Education.

National Education Commission on Time and Learning. (1994). *Prisoners of time: Schools and programs making time work for students and teachers.* Washington, DC: Author.

National Education Goals Panel. (1997). *Special early childhood report 1997.* Washington, DC: Author.

National Governors' Association. (1993). *Ability grouping and tracking: Current issues and concerns.* Washington, DC: Author.

National Information Center for Children and Youth with Disabilities. (1998). *Office of Special Education Programs' IDEA amendments of 1997 curriculum* [Internet]. Retrieved from: www.nichcy.org/Trainpkg/trainpkg.htm.

National Institute of Child Health and Human Development. (2000). *Report of the National Reading Panel. Teaching children to read: an evidence-based assessment of the scientific research literature on reading and its implications for reading instruction: Reports of the subgroups* (NIH Publication No. 00–4754). Washington, DC: U.S. Government Printing Office.

National Joint Committee on Learning Disabilities. (1988). (Letter to NJCLD member organization). Washington, DC: Author.

National Reading Panel. (2000). *Teaching children to read: An evidence-based assessment of the scientific research literature on reading and its implications for reading instruction.* Rockville, MD: National Institute of Child Health and Human Development.

National Research Council. (1995). *Losing generations: Adolescents in high-risk settings.* Hyattsville, MD: American Psychological Association.

National Research Council. (2000). *Improving intergroup relations among youth.* Washington, DC: NRC.

National Research Council. (2001). *Non-technical strategies to reduce children's exposure to inappropriate material on the Internet.* Washington, DC: National Academy Press.

Natriello, G. (2002). At-risk students. In D. L. Levinson, P. W. Cookson, Jr., & A. R. Sadovnik (Eds.), *Education and sociology: An encyclopedia* (pp. 49–54). New York: Routledge Falmer.

Nattiv, A. (1994). Helping behaviors and math achievement gain of students using cooperative learning. *The Elementary School Journal, 94*(3), 285–297.

Navaez, D., Getz, I., Rest, J. R., & Thoma, S. J. (1999). Individual moral judgment and cultural ideologies. *Developmental Psychology, 35,* 478–488.

Naveh-Benjamin, M. (1991). A comparison of training programs intended for different types of test-anxious students: Further support for an information-processing model. *Journal of Educational Psychology, 83,* 134–139.

Neale, D. C., Smith, D., & Johnson, V. G. (1990). Implementing conceptual change teaching in primary science. *Elementary School Journal, 91,* 109–131.

Neill, M. (2003). Leaving children behind: How No Child Left Behind will fail our children. *Phi Delta Kappan, 85*(3), 225–228.

Neill, M. (2003). The dangers of testing. *Educational Leadership, 60*(5), 43–46.

Neill, M., & Gaylor, K. (2001). Do high-stakes graduation tests improve learning outcomes? Using state-level NAEP data to evaluate the effects of mandatory graduation tests. In G. Orfield & M. L. Kornhaber (Eds.), *Raising standards or raising barriers? Inequality and high-stakes testing in public education* (pp. 107–126). New York: Century Foundation Press.

Neisser, U., Boodoo, G., Bouchard, T. J., Boykin, A. W., Brody, N., Ceci, S. J., Halpern, D. F., Loehlin, J. C., Perloff, R., Sternberg, R. J., & Urbina, S. (1996). Intelligence: Knowns and unknowns. *American Psychologist, 51,* 77–101.

Nelson, J. R., & Carr, B. A. (2000). *The Think Time Strategy for schools.* Denver, CO: Sopris West.

Nesbit, J., & Adesope, O. (2006). Learning with concept and knowledge maps: A meta-analysis. *Review of Educational Research, 76*(3), 413–448.

Neufield, B., & Roper, D. (2003). *Coaching: A strategy for developing instructional capacity.* Providence, RI: Annenberg Institute.

Neuman, S. B. (1995). Reading together: A community-based parent tutoring program. *The Reading Teacher, 49*(2), 120–129.

Neuman, S. B. (2003). From rhetoric to reality: The case for high-quality compensatory prekindergarten programs. *Phi Delta Kappan, 85*(4), 286–291.

Neuman, S. B., & McCormick, S. (1995). *Single-subject experimental research.* Newark, DE: International Reading Association.

Neuman, S. B., & Roskos, K. (1993). Access to print for children of poverty: Differential effects of adult mediation and literacy enriched play settings on environmental and functional print tasks. *American Educational Research Journal, 30,* 95–122.

Nevin, A. (1998). Curriculum and instructional adaptations for including students with disabilities in cooperative groups. In J. W. Putnam (Ed.), *Cooperative learning and strategies for inclusion* (pp. 49–66). Baltimore: Paul H. Brookes.

Newbern, D., Dansereau, D. F., Patterson, M. E., & Wallace, D. S. (1994, April). *Toward a science of cooperation.* Paper presented at the annual meeting of the American Educational Research Association, New Orleans, LA.

Newcomb, A. F., & Bagwell, C. L. (1998). The developmental significance of children's friendship relations. In W. M. Bukowski, A. F. Newcomb, & W. W. Hartup (Eds.), *The company they keep: Friendships in childhood and adolescence* (pp. 289–312). New York: Cambridge University Press.

Newell, A., & Simon, H. (1972). *Human problem solving.* Englewood Cliffs, NJ: Prentice-Hall.

Ng, J., Lee, S., & Park, Y. (2007). Contesting the model minority and perpetual foreigner stereotypes: A critical review of literature on Asian Americans in education. *Review of Research in Education, 31,* 95–130.

Niaz, M. (1997). How early can children understand some form of "scientific reasoning"? *Perceptual and motor skills, 85,* 1272–1274.

NICHD Early Child Care Research Network. (2002). Early child care and children's development prior to school entry: Results from the NICHD study of early child care. *American Educational Research Journal, 39*(1), 133–164.

NICHD Early Child Care Research Network. (2005). A day in third grade: A large-scale study of classroom quality and teacher and student behavior. *The Elementary School Journal, 105,* 305–323.

Nicholson, C. (2006). Thinking it over: fMRI and psychological science. *Observer, 19*(9), 20–25.

Nieto, S. M. (2003). Profoundly multicultural questions. *Educational Leadership, 60*(4), 6–10.

Nieto, S. M. (2004). *Affirming diversity: The sociopolitical context of multicultural education* (4th ed.). Boston: Allyn & Bacon.

Niguidula, D. (2005). Documenting learning with digital portfolios. *Educational Leadership, 63*(3), 44–47.

Nitsch, K. E. (1977). *Structuring decontextualized forms of knowledge.* Unpublished doctoral dissertation, Vanderbilt University.

Noonan, M. J., & McCormick, L. (1993). *Early intervention in natural environments.* Pacific Grove, CA: Brooks/Cole.

Nores, M., Belfield, C., Barnett, W., & Schweinhart, L. (2005). Updating the economic impacts of the High/Scope Perry Preschool Program. *Evaluation and Policy Analysis, 27*(3), 245–261.

Northcutt, N., & McCoy, D. (2004). *Interactive qualitative analysis.* Thousand Oaks, CA: Sage.

Nucci, L. (1987). Synthesis of research on moral development. *Educational Leadership, 44,* 86–92.

NWEA (Northwest Evaluation Association). (2003). *The state of state standards: Research investigating proficiency levels in fourteen states.* Seattle, WA: Author.

Oakes, J. (1985). *Keeping track: How schools structure inequality.* New Haven, CT: Yale University Press.

Oakes, J. (1995). Two cities: Tracking and within-school segregation. In L. Miller (Ed.), *Brown plus forty: The promise.* New York: Teachers College Press.

Oakes, J., & Guiton, G. (1995). Matchmaking: The dynamics of high school tracking decisions. *American Educational Research Journal, 32*(1), 3–33.

Oakes, J., & Lipton, M. (1994). Tracking and ability grouping: A structural barrier to access and achievement. In J. I. Goodlad & P. Keating (Eds.), *Access to knowledge: The continuing agenda for our nation's schools.* New York: The College Board.

Oakes, J., Quartz, K., Ryan, S., & Lipton, M. (2000). *Becoming good American schools: The struggle for civic virtue in school reform.* San Francisco: Jossey-Bass.

Oakes, J., & Wells, A. S. (1998). Detracking for high student achievement. *Educational Leadership, 55*(6), 38–41.

O'Connor, C., & Fernandez, S. D. (2006). Race, class, and disproportionality: Reevaluating the relationship between poverty and special education placement. *Educational Researcher, 35*(6), 6–11.

O'Connor, K. (2007). *A repair kit for grading: 15 fixes for broken grades.* Princeton, NJ: Educational Testing Services.

O'Connor, M. C. (1998). Can we trace the "efficacy of social constructivism"? In P. D. Pearson & A. Iran-Nejad (Eds.), *Review of research in education* (pp. 25–72). Washington, DC: American Educational Research Association.

O'Connor, R. E., Bell, K. M., Harty, K. R., Larkin, L. K., Sackor, S. M., & Zigmond, N. (2002). Teaching reading to poor readers in the intermediate grades: A comparison of text difficulty. *Journal of Educational Psychology, 94*(3), 474–485.

O'Donnell, A. M. (1996). Effects of explicit incentives on scripted and unscripted cooperation. *Journal of Educational Psychology, 88*(1), 74–86.

O'Donnell, A. M., & Dansereau, D. F. (1992). Scripted cooperation in student dyads: A method for analyzing and enhancing academic learning and performance. In R. Hertz-Lazarowitz & N. Miller (Eds.), *Interaction in cooperative groups: The theoretical anatomy of group learning* (pp. 120–144). New York: Cambridge University Press.

O'Donnell, A. M., Dansereau, D. F., & Hall, R. H. (2002). Knowledge maps as scaffolds for cognitive processing. *Educational Psychology Review, 14*(1), 71–86.

O'Donnell, A. M., & O'Kelly, J. (1994). Learning from peers: Beyond the rhetoric of positive results. *Educational Psychology Review, 6,* 321–349.

O'Donnell, J., Hawkins, J. D., Catalano, R. F., Abbott, R. D., & Day, L. E. (1995). Preventing school failure, drug use, and delinquency among low-income children: Long-term intervention in elementary schools. *American Journal of Orthopsychiatry, 65*(1), 87–100.

Ogbu, J. (1999, April). *The significance of minority status.* Paper presented at the annual meeting of the American Educational Research Association, Montreal.

Ogletree, C. J. (2004). *All deliberate speed: Reflections on the first half-century of Brown v. Board of Education.* New York: Norton.

Ohler, J. (2006). The world of digital storytelling. *Educational Leadership, 63*(4), 44–47.

Okagaki, L. (2001). Triarchic model of minority children's school achievement. *Educational Psychologist, 36*(1), 9–20.

Okagaki, L., & Frensch, P. A. (1998). Parenting and children's school achievement: A multiethnic perspective. *American Educational Research Journal, 35*(1), 123–144.

O'Leary, K. D., & O'Leary, S. G. (1972). *Classroom management: The successful use of behavior modification.* New York: Pergamon.

Olson, A. (2005). Improving schools one student at a time. *Educational Leadership, 62*(5), 37–41.

Olszewski-Kubilius, P. (2003). Gifted education programs and procedures. In W. M. Reynolds & G. E. Miller (Eds.), *Handbook of psychology: Vol. 7. Educational psychology* (pp. 487–510). Hoboken, NJ: Wiley.

Olweus, D. (1994). Bullying at school: Basic facts and effects of a school-based intervention program. *Journal of Child Psychology and Psychiatry, 35,* 1171–1190.

Orfield, G., & Frankenberg, E. (2007). The integration decision. *Education Week, 26*(43), 44, 34.

Orfield, G., Frankenberg, E., & Lee, C. (2003). The resurgence of school segregation. *Educational Leadership, 60*(4), 16–21.

Orfield, G., & Kornhaber, M. L. (Eds.). (2001). *Raising standards or raising barriers? Inequality and high-stakes testing in public education.* New York: Century Foundation Press.

Orfield, G., & Lee, C. (2004). *Brown at 50: King's dream or Plessy's nightmare?* Cambridge, MA: The Civil Rights Project, Harvard University.

Osborn, A. F. (1963). *Applied imagination* (3rd ed.). New York: Scribner's.

Osguthorpe, R. T., & Scruggs, T. E. (1986). Special education students as tutors: A review and analysis. *Remedial and Special Education, 7*(4), 15–25.

Osher, D., Dwyer, K., & Jackson, S. (2004). *Safe, supportive and successful schools step by step.* Longmont, CO: Sopris West.

Osher, D., & Fleischman, S. (2005). Positive culture in urban schools. *Educational Leadership, 62*(6), 84–86.

Overton, W. F. (1998). Developmental psychology: Philosophy, concepts, and methodology. In W. Damon (Ed.), *Handbook of child psychology,* (Vol. 1, pp. 107–188). New York: Wiley.

Padrón, Y. N., Waxman, H. C., & Rivera, H. H. (2002). Issues in educating Hispanic students. In S. Stringfield & D. Land (Eds.), *Educating at-risk students* (pp. 66–88). Chicago: National Society for the Study of Education.

Page, R. N. (1991). *Lower track classrooms: A curricular and cultural perspective.* New York: Teachers College Press.

Page, S. W. (2000). When changes for the gifted spur differentiation for all. *Educational Leadership, 58*(1), 62–65.

Page-Voth, V., & Graham, S. (1999). Effects of goal setting and strategy use on the writing performance and self-efficacy of students with writing and learning problems. *Journal of Educational Psychology, 91*(2), 230–240.

Pajares, F., Britner, S. L., & Valiante, G. (2000). Relation between achievement goals and self-beliefs of middle school students in writing and science. *Contemporary Educational Psychology, 25*(4), 406–422.

Pajares, R., & Graham, L. (1999). Self-efficacy, motivation constructs, and mathematics performance of entering middle school students. *Contemporary Educational Psychology, 24*(2), 124–139.

Pajares, F., & Miller, M. D. (1994). Role of self-efficacy and self-concept beliefs in mathematical problem solving: A path analysis. *Journal of Educational Psychology, 86*(2), 193–203.

Palincsar, A. S., & Brown, A. L. (1984). Reciprocal teaching of comprehension fostering and comprehension monitoring activities. *Cognition and Instruction, 2,* 117–175.

Palincsar, A. S., Brown, A. L., & Martin, S. M. (1987). Peer interaction in reading comprehension instruction. *Educational Psychologist, 22,* 231–253.

Pallas, A. M. (2002). High school dropouts. In D. L. Levinson, P. W. Cookson, Jr., & A. R. Sadovnik (Eds.), *Education and sociology: An encyclopedia* (pp. 315–320). New York: Routledge Falmer.

Panskeep, J. (1998). Attention deficit hyperactivity disorders, psychostimulants, and intolerance of childhood playfulness: A tragedy in the making? *Current Directions in Psychological Science, 7*(3), 91–97.

Parillo, V. N. (2008). *Understanding race and ethnic relations* (3rd ed.). Boston: Allyn & Bacon.

Paris, S., Cross, D., & Lipson, M. (1984). Informal strategies for learning: A program to improve children's reading awareness and comprehension. *Journal of Educational Psychology, 76,* 1239–1252.

Paris, S. G., & Paris, A. H. (2001). Classroom applications of research on self-regulated learning. *Educational Psychologist, 36*(2), 89–101.

Parkay, F. W. (2006). *Social foundations for becoming a teacher.* Boston: Allyn & Bacon.

Parker, H. C. (1990). *C.H.A.D.D.: Children with attention deficit disorders: Parents supporting parents.* Education position paper, Plantation, FL.

Parker, W. D. (1997). An empirical typology of perfectionism in academically talented children. *American Educational Research Journal, 34*(3), 545–562.

Parkhurst, J. T., & Asher, S. R. (1992). Peer rejection in middle school: Subgroup differences in behavior, loneliness, and interpersonal concerns. *Developmental Psychology, 28,* 231–241.

Parten, M. (1932). Social participation among preschool children. *Journal of Abnormal and Social Psychology, 27,* 243–269.

Patrick, B., Hisley, J., & Kempler, T. (2000). "What's everybody so excited about?": The effects of teacher enthusiasm on student intrinsic motivation and vitality. *Journal of Experimental Education, 68,* 217–236.

Pavan, B. N. (1992). The benefits of nongraded schools. *Educational Leadership, 50*(2), 22–25.

Pawlowski, K. F. (2001). The instructional support team concept in action. In B. Sornson (Ed.), *Preventing early learning failure.* Alexandria, VA: ASCD.

Pea, R. D. (1993). Learning scientific concepts through material and social activities: Conversational analysis meets conceptual change. *Educational Psychologist, 28*(3), 265–277.

Pearl, R., Farmer, T. W., Van Acker, R., Rodkin, P. C., Bost, K. K., Coe, M., & Henley, W. (1998). The social integration of students with mild disabilities in general education classrooms: Peer group membership and peer-assessed social behavior. *The Elementary School Journal, 99*(2), 167–185.

Pellegrini, A. D. (2002). Bullying, victimization, and sexual harassment during the transition to middle school. *Educational Psychologist, 37*(3), 151–163.

Pellegrini, A. D., & Bartini, M. (2000). A longitudinal study of bullying, victimization, and peer affiliation during the transition from primary school to middle school. *American Educational Research Journal, 37*(3), 699–725.

Pellegrini, A. D., & Bohn, C. M. (2005). The role of recess in children's cognitive performance and school adjustment. *Educational Researcher, 34*(1), 13–19.

Pellegrini, A. D., & Horvat, M. (1995). A developmental contextualist critique of attention deficit hyperactivity disorder. *Educational Researcher, 24*(1), 13–18.

Pendarvis, E., & Howley, A. (1996). Playing fair: The possibilities of gifted education. *Journal for the Education of the Gifted, 19,* 215–233.

Perfetto, G. A., Bransford, J. D., & Franks, J. J. (1983). Constraints on access in a problem solving context. *Memory and Cognition, 11,* 24–31.

Perkins, D. F., & Borden, L. M. (2003). Positive behaviors, problem behaviors, and resiliency in adolescence. In R. M. Lerner, M. A. Easterbrooks, & J. Mistry (Eds.), *Handbook of psychology: Vol. 6. Developmental psychology* (pp. 373–394). Hoboken, NJ: Wiley.

Perkins-Gough, D. (2006). Do we really have a "boy crisis"? *Educational Leadership, 64*(1), 93–94.

Perry, K., & Weinstein, R. (1998). The social context of early schooling and children's school adjustment. *Educational Psychologist, 33*(4), 177–194.

Persell, C. H. (1997). Social class and educational equality. In J. A. Banks & C. A. M. Banks (Eds.), *Multicultural education: Issues and perspectives* (pp. 87–107). Boston: Allyn & Bacon.

Peterson, L. R., & Peterson, M. J. (1959). Short-term retention of individual verbal items. *Journal of Experimental Psychology, 58,* 193–198.

Petrill, S. A., & Wilkerson, B. (2000). Intelligence and achievement: A behavioral genetic perspective. *Educational Psychology Review, 12*(2), 185–199.

Pettig, K. L. (2000). On the road to differentiated practice. *Educational Leadership, 58*(1), 14–18.

Phelan, P., Yu, H. C., & Davidson, A. L. (1994). Navigating the psychosocial pressures of adolescence: The voices and experiences of high school youth. *American Educational Research Journal, 31,* 415–447.

Phillips, J. L. (1975). *The origins of intellect: Piaget's theory* (2nd ed.). San Francisco: Freeman.

Piaget, J. (1952a). *The language and thought of the child.* London: Routledge and Kegan-Paul.

Piaget, J. (1952b). *The origins of intelligence in children.* New York: Basic Books.

Piaget, J. (1964). *The moral judgment of the child.* New York: Free Press.

Piaget, J., & Inhelder, B. (1956). *The child's conception of space.* Boston: Routledge and Kegan-Paul.

Pietsch, J., Walker, R., & Chapman, E. (2003). The relationship among self-concept, self-efficacy, and performance in mathematics during secondary school. *Journal of Educational Psychology, 95*(3), 589–603.

Pine, J., & Aschbacher, P. (2006). Students' learning of inquiry in "inquiry" curricula. *Phi Delta Kappan, 88*(4), 308–313.

Pinker, S. (1995). *The language instinct: How the mind creates language.* New York: HarperCollins.

Pinker, S. (1997). *How the mind works.* New York: Norton.

Pinnell, G. S. (1990). Success for low achievers through Reading Recovery. *Educational Leadership, 48*(1), 17–21.

Pinnell, G. S., DeFord, D. E., & Lyons, C. A. (1988). *Reading Recovery: Early intervention for at-risk first graders.* Arlington, VA: Educational Research Service.

Pinnell, G. S., Lyons, C. A., DeFord, D. E., Bryk, A. S., & Seltzer, M. (1994). Comparing instructional models for the literacy education of high risk first graders. *Reading Research Quarterly, 29,* 8–38.

Pinnell, G. S., Lyons, C., & Jones, N. (1996). Response to Hiebert: What difference does Reading Recovery make? *Educational Researcher, 25*(7), 23–25.

Pintrich, P. (2000). Multiple goals, multiple pathways: The role of goal orientation in learning and achievement. *Journal of Educational Psychology, 92*(3), 544–555.

Pintrich, P. R. (2003). A motivational science perspective on the role of student motivation in learning and teaching contexts. *Journal of Educational Psychology, 95*(4), 667–686.

Pintrich, P. R., & Schunk, D. H. (2002). *Motivation in Education: Theory, research, and applications* (2nd ed.). Upper Saddle River, NJ: Merrill/Prentice-Hall.

Plomin, R. (1989). Environment and genes: Determinants of behavior. *American Psychologist, 44*(2), 105–111.

Plucker, J. A., Beghetto, R. A., & Dow, G. T. (2004). Why isn't creativity more important to educational psychologists? Potential, pitfalls, and future directions in creativity research. *Educational Psychologist, 39*(2), 83–96.

Poel, E. (2007). Enhancing what students can do. *Educational Leadership, 64*(5), 64–67.

Polite, L., & Saenger, E. B. (2003). A pernicious silence: Confronting race in the elementary classroom. *Phi Delta Kappan, 85*(4), 274–278.

Pomerantz, E. M., Altermatt, E. R., & Saxon, J. L. (2002). Making the grade but feeling distressed: Gender differences in academic performance and internal distress. *Journal of Educational Psychology, 94*(2), 396–404.

Pontecorvo, C. (1993). Social interaction in the acquisition of knowledge. *Educational Psychology Review, 5*(3), 293–310.

Pool, H., & Page, J. A. (Eds.). (1995). *Beyond tracking: Finding success in inclusive schools.* Bloomington, IN: Phi Delta Kappan Educational Foundation.

Pope, A. W., & Bierman, K. L. (1999). Predicting adolescent peer problems and antisocial activities: The relative roles of aggression and dysregulation. *Developmental psychology, 35,* 335–346.

Popham, J. (2005). How to use PAP to make AYP under NCLB. *Phi Delta Kappan, 86*(10), 787–791.

Popham, W. J. (2003). *Teach better, test better: The instructional role of assessment.* Alexandria, VA: ASCD.

Popham, W. J. (2004). "Teaching to the test": An expression to eliminate. *Educational Leadership, 62*(3), 82–83.

Popham, W. J. (2008). *Classroom assessment: What teachers need to know* (5th ed.). Boston: Pearson.

Popham, W. J. (2006). Diagnostic assessment: A measurement mirage? *Educational Leadership, 64*(2), 90–93.

Popham, W. J. (2007). The lowdown on learning progressions. *Educational Leadership, 64*(7), 83–84.

Potter, E. F. (1977, April). *Children's expectancy of criticism for classroom achievement efforts.* Paper presented at the annual convention of the American Educational Research Association, New York.

Poulin, F., Cillessen, A. H. N., & Coie, J. D. (1997). Children's friends and behavioral similarity in the social contexts. *Social Development, 6,* 224–236.

Powell, D. R. (1995). *Enabling young children to succeed in school.* Washington, DC: American Educational Research Association.

Prawat, R. S. (1992). Teachers' beliefs about teaching and learning: A constructivist perspective. *American Journal of Education, 100*(3), 354–395.

Premack, D. (1965). Reinforcement theory. In D. Levine (Ed.), *Nebraska symposium on motivation.* Lincoln: University of Nebraska Press.

Prensky, M. (2005/2006). Listen to the natives. *Educational Leadership, 63*(4), 8–13.

Pressley, M. (2003). Psychology of literacy and literacy instruction. In W. M. Reynolds & G. E. Miller (Eds.), *Handbook of psychology: Vol. 7. Educational psychology* (pp. 333–355). Hoboken, NJ: Wiley.

Pressley, M., & Harris, K. R. (1994). Increasing the quality of educational intervention research. *Educational Psychology Review, 6*(3), 191–208.

Pressley, M., Harris, K. R., & Marks, M. B. (1992). But good strategy instructors are constructivists! *Educational Psychology Review, 4,* 3–31.

Pressley, M., Roehrig, A. D., Raphael, L., Dolezal, S., Bohn, C., Mohan, L., Wharton-McDonald, R., Bogner, K., & Hogan, K. (2003). Teaching processes in elementary and secondary education. In W. M. Reynolds & G. E. Miller (Eds.), *Handbook of psychology: Vol. 7. Educational psychology* (pp. 153–175). Hoboken, NJ: Wiley.

Pressley, M., Tannenbaum, R., McDaniel, M. A., & Wood, E. (1990). What happens when university students try to answer prequestions that accompany textbook material? *Contemporary Educational Psychology, 15,* 27–35.

Pressley, M., & Yokoi, L. (1994). Motion for a new trial on transfer. *Educational Researcher, 23*(5), 36–38.

Pressley, M., Yokoi, L., Van Meter, P., van Etten, S., & Freebern, G. (1997). Some of the reasons why preparing for exams is so hard: What can be done to make it easier? *Educational Psychology Review, 9*(1), 1–38.

Price, E. A., & Driscoll, M. P. (1997). An inquiry into the spontaneous transfer of problem-solving skill. *Contemporary Educational Psychology, 22*(4), 472–494.

Prichard, J., Bizo, L., & Stratford, R. (2006). The educational impact of team skills training: Preparing students to work in groups. *British Journal of Educational Psychology, 76,* 119–148.

Provenzo, E. F. (1999). *The Internet and the World Wide Web for preservice teachers.* Boston: Allyn & Bacon.

Pugh, K., & Bergin, D. (2006). Motivational influences on transfer. *Educational Psychologist, 41*(3), 147–160.

Puma, M. J., Jones, C. C., Rock, D., & Fernandez, R. (1993). *Prospects: The congressionally mandated study of educational growth and opportunity.* Interim Report. Bethesda, MD: Abt Associates.

Puma, M. J., Karweit, N., Price, C., Ricciuti, A., Thompson, W., & Vaden-Kiernan, M. (1997). *Prospects: Final report on student outcomes.* Cambridge, MA: Abt Associates.

Puntambekar, S., & Hübscher, R. (2005). Tools for scaffolding students in a complex learning environment: What have we gained and what have we missed? *Educational Psychologist, 40*(1), 1–12.

Purcell-Gates, V., McIntyre, E., & Freppon, P. A. (1995). Learning written storybook language in school: A comparison of low-SES children in skills-based and whole language classrooms. *American Educational Research Journal, 32,* 659–685.

Putnam, J. W. (Ed.). (1998a). *Cooperative learning and strategies for inclusion* (2nd ed.). Baltimore: Paul H. Brookes.

Qin, Z., Johnson, D. W., & Johnson, R. T. (1995). Cooperative versus competitive efforts and problem solving. *Review of Educational Research, 65,* 129–143.

Quay, H. C., & Werry, J. S. (Eds.). (1986). *Psychopathological disorders of childhood* (3rd ed.). New York: Wiley.

Rabiner, D. L., Malone, P., & the Conduct Problems Prevention Research Group (2003, February). *The impact of tutoring on early reading achievement for children with and without attention problems.* Paper presented at the annual meeting of the Society for Research on Child Development, Tampa, FL.

Radosevich, D., Vaidyanathan, V., Yeo, S., & Radosevich, D. (2004). Relating goal orientation to self-regulatory processes: A longitudinal field test. *Contemporary Educational Psychology, 29*(3), 207–229.

Radziewicz, C., & Antonellis, S. (2002). Considerations and implications for habilitation of hearing-impaired children. In D. K. Bernstein & E. Tiegerman-Farber (Eds.), *Language and communication disorders in children* (5th ed.). Boston: Allyn & Bacon.

Rafoth, M. A., Leal, L., & De Fabo, L. (1993). *Strategies for learning and remembering: Study skills across the curriculum.* Washington, DC: National Education Association Professional Library.

Raison, J., Hanson, L. A., Hall, C., & Reynolds, M. C. (1995). Another school's reality. *Phi Delta Kappan, 76*(6), 480–484.

Ramey, C. T., & Ramey, S. L. (1992). *At risk does not mean doomed.* Birmingham: Civitan International Research Center, University of Alabama.

Ramey, C. T., & Ramey, S. L. (1998). Early intervention and early experience. *American Psychologist, 53*(2), 109–120.

Ramirez-Smith, C. (1995). Stopping the cycle of failure: The Comer model. *Educational Leadership, 52*(5), 14–19.

Raudenbush, S. W., Rowan, B., & Cheong, Y. F. (1993). Higher order instructional goals in secondary schools: Class, teacher, and school influences. *American Educational Research Journal, 30*(3), 523–553.

Ready, D., LoGerfo, L., Burkam, D., & Lee, V. (2005). Explaining girls' advantage in kindergarten literacy learning: Do classroom behaviors make a difference? *The Elementary School Journal, 106*(1), 21–38.

Reason, P., & Bradbury, H. (Eds.). (2001). *Handbook of action research.* Thousand Oaks, CA: Sage.

Rebell, M., & Hunter, M. (2004). "Highly qualified" teachers: Pretense or legal requirement? *Phi Delta Kappan, 85*(9), 690–696.

Redfield, D. L., & Rousseau, E. W. (1981). A meta-analysis of experimental research on teacher questioning behavior. *Review of Educational Research, 51,* 237–245.

Reed, S. (2006). Cognitive architectures for multimedia learning. *Educational Psychologist, 41* (2), 87–98.

Reeves, D. (2005). "If I said something wrong I was afraid." *Educational Leadership, 62*(4), 72–75.

Reeves, D. (2006). Preventing 1,000 failures. *Educational Leadership, 64* (3), 88–89.

Reeves, D. (2006). Pull the weeds before you plant the flowers. *Educational Leadership, 64* (1), 89–90.

Reeves, D. B. (Ed.) (2007). *Ahead of the curve: The power of assessment to transform teaching and learning.* Bloomington, IN: Solution Tree.

Reid, D., & Knight, M. (2006). Disability justifies exclusion of minority students: A critical history grounded in disability studies. *Educational Researcher, 35*(6), 18–23.

Reimann, P., & Schult, T. J. (1996). Turning examples into cases: Acquiring knowledge structures for analogical problem solving. *Educational Psychologist, 31,* 123–132.

Rekrut, M. D. (1992, April). *Teaching to learn: Cross-age tutoring to enhance strategy acquisition.* Paper presented at the annual meeting of the American Educational Research Association, San Francisco, CA.

Renkl, A. (1998, April). *Learning by explaining in cooperative arrangements: What if questions were asked?* Paper presented at the annual meeting of the American Educational Research Association, San Diego, CA.

Renkl, A., Stark, R., Gruber, H., & Mandl, H. (1998). Learning from worked-out examples: The effects of example variability and elicited self-explanations. *Contemporary Educational Psychology, 23,* 90–108.

Renzulli, J. S., & Reis, S. M. (1997). The schoolwide enrichment model: New directions for developing high-end learning. In N. Colangelo & G. A. Davis (Eds.), *Handbook of gifted education* (2nd ed.) (pp. 136–154). Boston: Allyn & Bacon.

Renzulli, J. S., & Reis, S. M. (2000). The schoolwide enrichment model. In K. A. Heller, F. J. Mönks, R. Subotnik, & R. J. Sternberg (Eds.), *International Handbook of Giftedness and Talent* (2nd ed., pp. 367–382). New York: Pergamon.

Reschly, D. J. (2003). School psychology. In W. M. Reynolds & G. E. Miller (Eds.), *Handbook of psychology: Vol. 7. Educational psychology* (pp. 431–453). Hoboken, NJ: Wiley.

Resnick, L. (1998, April). *From aptitude to effort: A new foundation for our schools.* Paper presented at the annual meeting of the American Educational Research Association, San Diego, CA.

Rest, J., Edwards, L., & Thoma, S. (1997). Designing and validating a measure of moral judgment: Stage preference and stage consistency approaches. *Journal of Educational Psychology, 89*(1), 5–28.

Reyes, P., Scribner, J. D., & Paredes, A. (Eds.). (1999). *Lessons from high-performing Hispanic schools: Creating learning communities.* New York: Teachers College Press.

Reynolds, A., Temple, J., Robertson, D., & Mann, E. (2002). Age 21 cost-benefit analysis of the Title I Chicago child–parent centers. *Educational Evaluation and Policy Analysis, 24*(4), 267–303.

Reynolds, A., & Wolfe, B. (1999). Special education and school achievement: An exploratory analysis with a central-city sample. *Educational Evaluation and Policy Analysis, 21*(3), 249–269.

Reynolds, A. J. (1991). Early schooling of children at risk. *American Educational Research Journal, 28*(2), 392–422.

Reynolds, A. J. (1998). The Chicago child-parent center and expansion program: A study of extended early childhood intervention. In J. Crane (Ed.), *Social Programs that Work* (pp. 110–147). New York: Russell Sage Foundation.

Reynolds, W. M., & Miller, G. E. (2003). Current perspectives in educational psychology. In W. M. Reynolds & G. E. Miller (Eds.), *Handbook of psychology: Vol. 7. Educational psychology* (pp. 3–20). Hoboken, NJ: Wiley.

Rice, E. P. (1996). *The adolescent: Development, relationships, and culture.* Boston: Allyn & Bacon.

Rickards, J. P., Fajen, B. R., Sullivan, J. F., & Gillespie, G. (1997). Signaling, notetaking, and field independence—dependence in text comprehension and recall. *Journal of Educational Psychology, 89*(3), 508–517.

Riehl, C. (2006). Feeling better: A comparison of medical research and education research. *Educational Researcher, 35*(5), 24–29.

Riehl, C. J. (2000). The principal's role in creating inclusive schools for diverse students: A review of normative, empirical, and critical literature on the practice of educational administration. *Review of Educational Research, 70*(1), 55–81.

Rifkin, J. (1998). The sociology of the gene. *Phi Delta Kappan, 79*(9), 649–657.

Rivera, D. P., & Smith, D. D. (1997). *Teaching students with learning and behavior problems.* Boston: Allyn & Bacon.

Roach, A., & Elliott, S. (2006). The influence of access to general education curriculum on alternate assessment performance of students with significant cognitive disabilities. *Educational Evaluation and Policy Analysis, 28*(2), 181–194.

Robinson, D. H., Katayama, A. D., Beth, A., Odom, S., & Hsieh, Y. P. (2004). *Training students to take more graphic notes: A partial approach.* Austin, TX: University of Texas at Austin.

Robinson, D. H., & Kiewra, K. A. (1995). Visual argument: Graphic organizers are superior to outlines in improving learning from text. *Journal of Educational Psychology, 87,* 455–467.

Robinson, D. H., & Skinner, C. H. (1996). Why graphic organizers facilitate search processes: Fewer words or computationally efficient indexing. *Contemporary Educational Psychology, 21*(2), 166–180.

Robinson, D. H., Robinson, S. L., & Katayama, A. D. (1999). When words are represented in memory like pictures: Evidence for spatial encoding of study materials. *Contemporary Educational Psychology, 24*(1), 38–54.

Robinson, F. P. (1961). *Effective study.* New York: Harper & Row.

Robinson, T., Smith, S., Miller, M., & Brownell, M. (1999). Cognitive behavior modification of hyperactivity-impulsivity and aggression: A meta-analysis of school-based studies. *Journal of Educational Psychology, 91*(2), 195–203.

Roderick, M. (1994). Grade retention and school dropout: Investigating the association. *American Educational Research Journal, 31*(4), 729–759.

Roderick, M., & Engel, M. (2001). The grasshopper and the ant: Motivational responses of low-achieving students to high-stakes testing. *Educational Evaluation and Policy Analysis, 23*(3), 197–227.

Roderick, M., Jacob, B., & Bryk, A. (2002). The impact of high-stakes testing in Chicago on student achievement in promotional gate grades. *Educational Evaluation and Policy Analysis, 24*(4), 333–357.

Roderick, M., & Nagaoka, J. (2005). Retention under Chicago's high-stakes testing program: Helpful, harmful, or harmless? *Evaluation and Policy Analysis, 27*(4), 309–340.

Roeber, E., & Dutcher, P. (1989). Michigan's innovative assessment of reading. *Educational Leadership 46*(7), 64–69.

Roeser, R., Eccles, J., & Sameroff, A. (2000). School as a context of early adolescents' academic and social-emotional development: A summary of research findings. *The Elementary School Journal, 100*(5), 443–472.

Rogoff, B. (2003). *The cultural nature of human development*. London: Oxford University Press.

Rogoff, B., & Chavajay, P. (1995). What's become of research on the cultural basis of cognitive development? *American Psychologist, 50,* 859–877.

Rogow, S. M. (1988). *Helping the visually impaired child with developmental problems: Effective practice in home, school, and community.* New York: Teachers College Press.

Rohrbeck, C. A., Ginsburg-Block, M. D., Fantuzzo, J. W., & Miller, T. R. (2003). Peer-assisted learning interventions with elementary school students: A meta-analytic review. *Journal of Educational Psychology, 94*(2), 240–257.

Rolheiser, C., Bower, B., & Stevahn, L. (2000). *The portfolio organizer: Succeeding with portfolios in your classroom.* Alexandria, VA: ASCD.

Roopnarine, J. L., Ahmeduzzaman, M., Donnely, S., Gill, P., Mennis, A., Arry, L., Dingler, K., McLaughlin, M., & Talukder, E. (1992). Social-cognitive play behaviors and playmate references in same-age and mixed-aged classrooms over a 6-month period. *American Educational Research Journal, 29,* 757–776.

Rose, A., & Rudolph, K. (2006). A review of sex differences in peer relationship processes: Potential tradeoffs for the emotional and behavioral development of girls and boys. *Psychological Bulletin, 132*(1), 98–131.

Rosenbaum, M. S., & Drabman, R. S. (1982). Self-control training in the classroom: A review and critique. *Journal of Applied Behavior Analysis, 12,* 264, 266, 467–485.

Rosenberg, M., Wilson, R., Maheady, L., & Sindelar, P. (2004). *Educating students with behavioral disorders.* Boston: Pearson.

Rosenberg, S. L., McKeon, L. M., & Dinero, T. E. (1999). Positive peer solutions: One answer for the rejected student. *Phi Delta Kappan, 81*(2), 114–118.

Rosenfield, D., Folger, R., & Adelman, H. F. (1980). When rewards reflect competence: A qualification of the overjustification effect. *Journal of Personality and Social Psychology, 39,* 368–376.

Rosenfield, S. A., & Gravois, T. A. (1996). *Instructional consultation teams: Collaborating for change.* New York: Guilford.

Rosenholtz, S. J., & Simpson, C. (1984). The formation of ability conceptions: Developmental trend or social construction? *Review of Educational Research, 54,* 31–63.

Rosenshine, B., & Meister, C. (1992). The use of scaffolds for teaching higher-level cognitive strategies. *Educational Leadership, 49*(7), 26–33.

Rosenshine, B., & Meister, C. (1994). Reciprocal teaching: A review of research. *Review of Educational Research, 64,* 479–530.

Rosenshine, B., Meister, C., & Chapman, S. (1996). Teaching students to generate questions: A review of the intervention studies. *Review of Educational Research, 66*(2), 181–221.

Rosenshine, B. V. (1980). How time is spent in elementary classrooms. In C. Denham & A. Lieberman (Eds.), *Time to learn.* Washington, DC: National Institute of Education.

Rosenshine, B. V., & Stevens, R. J. (1986). Teaching functions. In M. C. Wittrock (Ed.), *Third handbook of research on teaching.* Chicago: Rand McNally.

Ross, J. A., Rolheiser, C., & Hogaboam-Gray, A. (1998, April). *Impact of self-evaluation training on mathematics achievement in a cooperative learning environment.* Paper presented at the annual meeting of the American Educational Research Association, San Diego, CA.

Ross, S. M., Smith, L. J., Casey, J., & Slavin, R. E. (1995). Increasing the academic success of disadvantaged children: An examination of alternative early intervention programs. *American Educational Research Journal, 32,* 773–800.

Ross, S. M., Smith, L. J., Lohr, L., & McNelis, M. (1994). Math and reading instruction in tracked first grade classes. *The Elementary School Journal, 95*(2), 105–119.

Rosser, R. A. (1994). *Cognitive development: Psychological and biological perspectives.* Boston: Allyn & Bacon.

Rosser, R. A. (2003). Scientific Reasoning. *Encyclopedia of Cognitive Science.* London: Nature Publishing Group.

Rosser, R. A. Stevens, S. & Ruiz, B. (2006). Cognitive markers of adolescent risk taking: A correlate of drug abuse in at-risk individuals. *The Prison Journal,* 85, 83–96.

Rossi, R. J., & Stringfield, S. C. (1995). What we must do for students placed at risk. *Phi Delta Kappan, 71*(1), 73–76.

Rossman, G. B., & Rallis, S. F. (2003). *Learning in the field: An introduction to qualitative research* (2nd ed.). Thousand Oaks, CA: Sage.

Rotberg, I. C. (2001). A self-fulfilling prophecy. *Phi Delta Kappan, 83*(2), 170–171.

Roth, W.-M., & Lee, Y.-J. (2007). "Vygotsky's neglected legacy": Cultural-historical activity theory. *Review of Educational Research,* 77(2), 186–232.

Rothstein, R. (Ed.). 2004. *Class and schools: Using social, economic, and educational reform to close the black-white achievement gap.* Washington, DC: Economic Policy Institute.

Rotter, J. (1954). *Social learning and clinical psychology.* Englewood Cliffs, NJ: Prentice-Hall.

Rowan, B., Correnti, R., & Miller, R. (2002). *What large-scale, survey research tells us about teacher effects on student achievement: Insights from the Prospects study of elementary schools.* Philadelphia, PA: Consortium for Policy Research in Education, University of Pennsylvania.

Rowan, B., & Miracle, A. (1983). Systems of ability grouping and the stratification of achievement in elementary schools. *Sociology of Education, 56,* 133–144.

Rowe, M. B. (1974). Wait time and rewards as instructional variables, their influence on language, logic, and fate control. I: Wait time. *Journal of Research in Science Teaching, 11,* 81–94.

Rubie-Davies, C. M. (2007, September). *Teacher expectations, student achievement, and perceptions of student attitudes.* Paper presented at the Biennial Conference of the Educational Association for Research in Learning and Instruction, Budapest, Hungary.

Rubin, B. C. (2003). Unpacking detracking: When progressive pedagogy meets students' social worlds. *American Educational Research Journal, 40*(2), 539–573.

Ruble, D. N., Eisenberg, R., & Higgins, E. T. (1994). Developmental changes in achievement evaluation: Motivational implications of self-other differences. *Child Development, 65,* 1095–1110.

Ruder, S. (2000). We teach all. *Educational Leadership, 58*(1), 49–51.

Rummel, N., Levin, J. R., & Woodward, M. M. (2002). Do pictorial mnemonic text-learning aids give students something worth writing about? *Journal of Educational Psychology, 94*(2), 327–334.

Ryan, A. M., & Patrick, H. (2001). The classroom social environment and changes in adolescents' motivation and engagement during middle school. *American Educational Research Journal, 38*(2), 437–460.

Ryan, K., & Ryan, A. (2005). Psychological processes underlying stereotype threat and standardized math test performance. *Educational Psychologist, 40*(1), 53–63.

Ryan, R. M., & Deci, E. L. (2000). Intrinsic and extrinsic motivations: Classic definitions and new directions. *Contemporary Educational Psychology, 25*(1), 54–67.

Sachs, J. (2000). The activist professional. *Journal of Educational Change, 1*(1), 77–95.

Sadker, M., & Sadker, D. (1994). *Failing at fairness: How America's schools cheat girls.* New York: Charles Scribner's Sons.

Sadker, M., Sadker, D., & Long, L. (1997). Gender and educational equality. In J. A. Banks & C. A. M. Banks (Eds.), *Multicultural education: Issues and perspectives* (pp. 131–149). Boston: Allyn & Bacon.

Sadker, M., & Zittleman, L. (2004). Test anxiety: Are students failing tests or are tests failing students? *Phi Delta Kappan, 85*(10), 740–744.

Sadoski, M., Goetz, E. T., & Fritz, J. B. (1993). Impact of concreteness on comprehensibility, interest, and memory of text: Implications for dual coding theory and text design. *Journal of Educational Psychology, 85*(2), 291–304.

Safer, N., & Fleischman, S. (2005). How student progress monitoring improves instruction. *Educational Leadership, 62*(5), 81–83.

Saffran, E. M., & Schwartz, M. F. (2003). Language. In M. Gallagher & R. J. Nelson (Eds.), *Handbook of psychology: Vol. 3. Biological psychology* (pp. 595–627). Hoboken, NJ: Wiley.

Saleno, S., & Garrick-Duhaney, L. (1999). The impact of inclusion on students with and without disabilities and their educators. *Remedial and Special Education, 20*(2), 114–126.

Salganik, M. W. (1980, January 27). Teachers busy teaching make city's 16 "best" schools stand out. *Baltimore Sun,* p. A4.

Salinger, T., & Fleischman, S. (2005). Teaching students to interact with text. *Educational Leadership, 64*(1), 90–93.

Salomon, G. (2002). Technology and pedagogy: Why don't we see the promised revolution? *Educational Technology, 42*(2), 71–75.

Salomon, G., & Perkins, D. N. (1998). Individual and social aspects of learning. In P. D. Pearson & A. Iran-Nejad (Eds.), *Review of research in education* (pp. 1–24). Washington, DC: American Educational Research Association.

San Antonio, D., & Salzfass, E. (2007). How we treat one another in school. *Educational Leadership, 64*(8), 32–39.

Sanders, M. G., Allen-Jones, G. L., & Abel, Y. (2002). Involving families and communities in the education of children and youth placed at-risk. In S. Stringfield & D. Land (Eds.), *Educating at-risk students* (pp. 171–188). Chicago: National Society for the Study of Education.

Sandoval, J. (1995). Teaching in subject matter areas: Science. *Annual Review of Psychology, 46,* 355–374.

Sanford, J. P., & Evertson, C. M. (1981). Classroom management in a low SES junior high: Three case studies. *Journal of Teacher Education, 32,* 34–38.

Sansone, C., & Harackiewicz, J. M. (Eds.). (2000). *Intrinsic and extrinsic motivation.* Orlando, FL: Academic Press.

Sapon-Shevin, M. (2001). Schools fit for all. *Educational Leadership, 58*(4), 34–39.

Sapon-Shevin, M. (2003). Inclusion: A matter of social justice. *Educational Leadership, 61*(2).

Sato, M., & Atkin, J. (2006/2007). Supporting change in classroom assessment. *Educational Leadership, 64*(4), 76–79.

Savell, J. M., Twohig, P. T., & Rachford, D. L. (1986). Empirical status of Feuerstein's "Instrumental Enrichment" (FIE) technique as a method of teaching thinking skills. *Review of Educational Research, 56,* 381–409.

Sax, C. L., & Thoma, C. A. (2002). *Transition assessment: Wise practices for quality lives.* Baltimore: Brookes.

Scarr, S. (1998). American childcare today. *American Psychologist, 53*(2), 95–108.

Schacter, D. L. (2001). *The seven sins of memory: How the mind forgets and remembers.* Boston: Houghton Mifflin.

Schacter, J. (2000). Does individual tutoring produce optimal learning? *American Educational Research Journal, 37*(3), 801–829.

Schafer, W. D., Swanson, G., Bené, N., & Newberry, G. (2001). Effects of teacher knowledge of rubrics on student achievement in four content areas. *Applied Measurement in Education, 14,* 151–170.

Schafer, W. E., & Olexa, C. (1971). *Tracking and opportunity.* Scranton, PA: Chandler.

Schaps, E., Schaeffer, E., & McDonnell, S. (2001, September 12). What's right and what's wrong in character education today. *Education Week,* 40–41.

Scherer, M. (2001). How and why standards can improve student achievement: A conversation with Robert J. Marzano. *Educational Leadership, 59*(1), 14–19.

Scherer, M. (2006). Celebrate strengths, nurture affinities: A conversation with Mel Levine. *Educational Leadership, 64*(1), 8–15.

Scheurich, J., Skrla, L., & Johnson, J. (2000). Thinking carefully about equity and accountability. *Phi Delta Kappan, 82*(4), 293–299.

Schiff, M., & Lewontin, R. (1986). *Education and class: The irrelevance of IQ genetic studies.* Oxford: Clarendon Press.

Schifter, D. (1996). A constructivist perspective on teaching and learning mathematics. *Phi Delta Kappan, 77*(7), 492–499.

Schirmer, B., & McGough, S. (2005). Teaching reading to children who are deaf: Do the conclusions of the National Reading Panel apply? *Review of Educational Research, 75*(1), 84–117.

Schloss, P. J., & Smith, M. A. (1994). *Applied behavior analysis in the classroom.* Boston: Allyn & Bacon.

Schlozman, S. C., & Schlozman, V. R. (2000). Chaos in the classroom: Looking at ADHD. *Educational Leadership, 58*(3), 28–33.

Schmoker, M. (1999). *Results: The key to continuous school improvement.* Alexandria, VA: ASCD.

Schneider, B. (2002). Social capital: A ubiquitous emerging conception. In D. L. Levinson, P. W. Cookson, Jr., & A. R. Sadovnik (Eds.), *Education and sociology: An encyclopedia* (pp. 545–550). New York: Routledge Falmer.

Schneider, W. (1993). Domain-specific knowledge and memory performance in children. *Educational Psychology Review, 5,* 257–273.

Schneider, W., Roth, E., & Ennemoser, M. (2000). Training phonological skills and letter knowledge in children at risk for dyslexia: A comparison of three kindergarten intervention programs. *Journal of Educational Psychology, 92*(2), 284–295.

Schniedewind, N., & Davidson, E. (2000). Differentiating cooperative learning. *Educational Leadership, 58*(1), 24–27.

Schnotz, W. (2002). Towards an integrated view of learning from text and visual displays. *Educational Psychology Review, 14*(1), 101–120.

Schofield, J. W. (1995). Review of research on school desegregation's impact on elementary and secondary school students. In J. A. Banks & C. A. M. Banks (Eds.), *Handbook of research on multicultural education.* New York: Macmillan.

Schofield, J. W. (1997). Causes and consequences of the colorblind perspective. In J. A. Banks & C. A. M. Banks (Eds.), *Multicultural education: Issues and perspectives* (pp. 251–271). Boston: Allyn & Bacon.

Schraw, G., Flowerday, T., & Lehman, S. (2001). Increasing situational interest in the classroom. *Educational Psychology Review, 13*(3), 211–224.

Schunk, D. (2000). *Learning theories* (3rd ed.). Upper Saddle River, NJ: Merrill/Prentice-Hall.

Schunk, D. (2005). Self-regulated learning: The education legacy of Paul R. Pintrich. *Educational Psychologist, 40*(2), 85–94.

Schunk, D. H. (1995). Inherent details of self-regulated learning include student perceptions. *Educational Psychologist, 30,* 213–216.

Schunk, D. H. (2004). *Learning Theories: An educational perspective* (4th ed.). Columbus, OH: Merrill/Prentice-Hall.

Schunk, D. H., & Pajares, F. (2004, April). *Self-Efficacy in Education: Issues and future directions.* Paper presented at the annual meeting of the American Educational Research Association, San Diego, CA.

Schunk, D. H., & Zimmerman, B. J. (1997). Social origins of self-regulatory competence. *Educational Psychologist, 32*(4), 195–208.

Schunk, D. H., & Zimmerman, B. J. (2003). Self-regulation and learning. In W. M. Reynolds & G. E. Miller (Eds.), *Handbook of psychology: Vol. 7. Educational psychology* (pp. 59–78). Hoboken, NJ: Wiley.

Schutz, A. (2006). Home is a prison in a global city: The tragic failure of school-based community engagement strategies. *Review of Educational Research, 76*(4), 691–744.

Schutz, P. A., & Davis, H. A. (2000). Emotions and self-regulation during test taking. *Educational Psychologist, 35*(4), 243–246.

Schwartz, J. E., & Beichner, R. J. (1999). *Essentials of educational technology.* Boston: Allyn & Bacon.

Schwartz, N. H., Ellsworth, L. S., Graham, L., & Knight, B. (1998). Assessing prior knowledge to remember text: A comparison of advance organizers and maps. *Contemporary Educational Psychology, 23*(1), 65–89.

Schweinhart, L. J., Barnes, H. V., & Weikart, D. P. (1993). *Significant benefits: The High/Scope Perry Preschool study through age 27.* Ypsilanti, MI: High/Scope.

Schweinhart, L. J., & Weikart, D. P. (1998). High/Scope Perry Preschool Program effects at age twenty-seven. In J. Crane (Ed.), *Social programs that work* (pp. 148–162). New York: Russell Sage Foundation.

Scruggs, T. E., White, K. R., & Bennion, K. (1986). Teaching test-taking skills to elementary-grade students: A meta-analysis. *Elementary School Journal, 87,* 69–82.

Secada, W. G., Chavez-Chavez, R., Garcia, E., Munoz, C., Oakes, J., Santiago-Santiago, I., & Slavin, R. (1998). *No more excuses: The final report of the Hispanic dropout project.* Washington, DC: U.S. Department of Education.

Selman, R. L. (1981). The child as a friendship philosopher. In S. R. Asher & J. M. Gottman (Eds.), *The development of children's friendships* (pp. 242–272). Cambridge: Cambridge University Press.

Semb, G. B., & Ellis, J. A. (1994). Knowledge taught in school: What is remembered? *Review of Educational Research, 24,* 253–286.

Semmel, M. I., Gerber, M. M., & MacMillan, D. L. (1994). Twenty-five years after Dunn's article: A legacy of policy analysis research in special education. *Journal of Special Education, 27,* 481–495.

Sethi, S., Drake, M., Dialdin, D. A., & Lepper, M. R. (1995, April). *Developmental patterns of intrinsic and extrinsic motivation: A new look.* Paper presented at the annual meeting of the American Educational Research Association, San Francisco, CA.

Shaffer, D., Squire, K., Halverson, R., & Gee, J. (2005). Video games and the future of learning. *Phi Delta Kappan, 87*(2), 104–111.

Shah, P., Mayer, R., & Hegarty, M. (1999). Graphs as aids to knowledge construction: Signaling techniques for guiding the process of graph comprehension. *Journal of Educational Psychology, 91*(4), 690–702.

Shaklee, B. D., Barbour, N. E., Ambrose, R., & Hansford, S. J. (1997). *Designing and using portfolios.* Boston: Allyn & Bacon.

Shanahan, T. (1998). On the effectiveness and limitations of tutoring reading. In P. D. Pearson & A. Iran-Nejad (Eds.), *Review of research in education* (pp. 217–234). Washington, DC: American Educational Research Association.

Shanahan, T., & Beck, I. (2006). Effective literacy teaching for English language learners. In D. August and T. Shanahan (Eds.), *Developing literacy in a second language: Report of the National Literacy Panel.* Mahwah, NJ: Erlbaum.

Shanker, A. (1994/95). Full inclusion is neither free nor appropriate. *Educational Leadership, 52*(4), 18–21.

Sharan, S., Kussell, P., Hertz-Lazarowitz, R., Bejarano, Y., Raviv, S., & Sharan, Y. (1984). *Cooperative learning in the classroom: Research in desegregated schools.* Hillsdale, NJ: Erlbaum.

Sharan, S., & Shachar, C. (1988). *Language and learning in the cooperative classroom.* New York: Springer.

Sharan, Y., & Sharan, S. (1992). *Expanding cooperative learning through group investigation.* New York: Teachers College Press.

Shavelson, R. J., Baxter, G. P., & Pine, J. (1992). Performance assessments: Political rhetoric and measurement reality. *Educational Researcher, 21*(4), 22–27.

Shaywitz, S. (2003). *Overcoming dyslexia: A new and complete science-based program for reading problems at any level.* New York: Knopf.

Shaywitz, S., & Shaywitz, B. (2004). Reading disability and the brain. *Educational Leadership, 61*(3), 7–11.

Shaywitz, S., & Shaywitz, B. (2007). What neuroscience really tells us about reading instruction: A response to Judy Willis. *Educational Leadership, 64*(5), 74–78.

Shepard, L. (2005). Linking formative assessment to scaffolding. *Educational Leadership, 63*(3), 66–71.

Shepard, L. A. (1993b). The place of testing reform in educational reform: A reply to Cizek. *Educational Researcher, 22*(4), 10–13.

Shepard, L. A. (1995). Using assessment to improve learning. *Phi Delta Kappan, 52*(5), 38–43.

Shepard, L. A. (2000). The role of assessment in a learning culture. *Educational Researcher, 29*(7), 4–14.

Shepard, L. A., & Smith, M. T. (Eds.) (1989). *Flunking grades: Research and policies on retention.* Philadelphia: Falmer.

Shields, M., & Behrman, R. (2000). Children and computer technology: Analysis and recommendations. *Children and Computer Technology, 10*(2), 4–30.

Shih, M., & Sanchez, D. (2005). Perspectives and research on the positive and negative implications of having multiple racial identities. *Psychological Bulletin, 131*(4), 569–591.

Shih, S. (2005). Taiwanese sixth graders' achievement goals and their motivation, strategy use, and grades: An examination of the multiple goal perspective. *The Elementary School Journal, 106*(1), 39–58.

Shih, S., & Alexander, J. (2000). Interacting effects of goal setting and self- or other-referenced feedback on children's development of self-efficacy and cognitive skill within the Taiwanese classroom. *Journal of Educational Psychology, 92*(3), 536–543.

Short, D., & Echevarria, J. (2004/2005). Teacher skills to support English language learners. *Educational Leadership, 62*(4), 8–13.

Shulman, J., Lotan, R. A., & Whitcomb, J. A. (1998). *Groupwork in diverse classrooms: A cookbook for educators.* New York: Teachers College Press.

Shulman, L. S. (2000). Teacher development: Roles of domain expertise and pedagogical development. *Journal of Applied Developmental Psychology, 21,* 129–135.

Siegel, L. S. (2003). Learning disabilities. In W. M. Reynolds & G. E. Miller (Eds.), *Handbook of psychology: Vol. 7. Educational psychology* (pp. 455–486). Hoboken, NJ: Wiley.

Siegler, R. S. (1998). *Children's thinking* (3rd ed.). Upper Saddle River, NJ: Prentice Hall.

Sills-Briegel, T., Fisk, C., & Dunlop, V. (1996). Graduation by exhibition. *Educational Leadership, 54*(4), 66–71.

Silver, A., & Hagin, R. (1990). *Disorders of learning in childhood.* New York: Wiley.

Silver-Pacuilla, H., & Fleischman, S. (2006). Technology to help struggling students. *Educational Leadership, 63*(5), 84–85.

Simmons, D. C., Fuchs, L. S., Fuchs, P., Mathes, P., & Hodge, J. P. (1995). Effects of explicit teaching and peer tutoring on the reading achievement of learning-disabled and low-performing students in regular classrooms. *The Elementary School Journal, 95*(5), 387–408.

Simpkins, M., Cole, K., Tavalin, F., & Means, B. (2002). *Increasing student learning through multimedia projects.* Alexandria, VA: ASCD.

Sinclair, M. F., Christenson, S. L., Evelo, D. L., & Hurley, C. (1998). Dropout prevention for high-risk youth with disabilities: Efficacy of a sustained school engagement procedure. *Exceptional Children, 65*(1), 7–21.

Singer, J., Marx, R. W., Krajcik, J., & Chambers, J. C. (2000). Constructing extended inquiry projects: Curriculum materials for science education reform. *Educational Psychologist, 35*(4), 165–178.

Sireci, S., Scarpati, S., & Li, S. (2005). Test accommodations for students with disabilities: An analysis of the interaction hypothesis. *Review of Educational Research, 75*(4), 457–490.

Sirin, S. (2005). Socioeconomic status and academic achievement: A meta-analytic review of research. *Review of Educational Research, 75*(3), 417–453.

Sirotnik, K. A. (2002). Promoting responsible accountability in schools and education. *Phi Delta Kappan, 83*(9), 662–973.

Skaalvik, E. M. (1997). Self-enhancing and self-defeating ego orientation: Relations with task and avoidance orientation, achievement, self-perceptions, and anxiety. *Journal of Educational Psychology, 89*(1), 71–81.

Skiba, R. (2000). *Zero tolerance, zero evidence: An analysis of school disciplinary practice.* Bloomington, IN: Indiana Education Policy Center.

Slavin, R., Cheung, A., Groff, C., & Lake, C. (2007). *Effective reading programs for middle and high schools: A best-evidence synthesis.* Baltimore, MD: Center for Data Driven Reform in Education, Johns Hopkins University.

Slavin, R. E. (1986). The Napa evaluation of Madeline Hunter's ITIP: Lessons learned. *Elementary School Journal, 87,* 165–171.

Slavin, R. E. (1987b). Grouping for instruction in the elementary school. *Educational Psychologist, 22,* 109–127.

Slavin, R. E. (1987c). Ability grouping and student achievement in elementary schools: A best-evidence synthesis. *Review of Educational Research, 57,* 293–336.

Slavin, R. E. (1987d). Mastery learning reconsidered. *Review of Educational Research, 57,* 175–213.

Slavin, R. E. (1990). Ability grouping and student achievement in secondary schools: A best-evidence synthesis. *Review of Educational Research, 60,* 471–499.

Slavin, R. E. (1991). Cooperative learning and group contingencies. *Journal of Behavioral Education, 1,* 105–115.

Slavin, R. E. (1993a). Students differ: So what? *Educational Researcher, 22*(9), 13–14.

Slavin, R. E. (1993b). Ability grouping in the middle grades: Achievement effects and alternatives. *The Elementary School Journal, 93*(5), 535–552.

Slavin, R. E. (1994a). *Using student team learning* (4th ed.). Baltimore: Johns Hopkins University, Center for Research on Elementary and Middle Schools.

Slavin, R. E. (1994b). School and classroom organization in beginning reading: Class size, aides, and instructional grouping. In R. E. Slavin, N. L. Karweit, B. A. Wasik, & N. A. Madden (Eds.), *Preventing early school failure: Research on effective strategies.* Boston: Allyn & Bacon.

Slavin, R. E. (1995a). *Cooperative learning: Theory, research, and practice* (2nd ed.). Boston: Allyn & Bacon.

Slavin, R. E. (1995b). Cooperative learning and intergroup relations. In J. Banks (Ed.), *Handbook of research on multicultural education.* New York: Macmillan.

Slavin, R. E. (1996a). Neverstreaming: Preventing learning disabilities. *Educational Leadership, 53*(5), 4–7.

Slavin, R. E. (1996b). Research on cooperative learning achievement: What we know, what we need to know. *Contemporary Educational Psychology, 21,* 43–69.

Slavin, R. E. (1997/98). Can education reduce social inequality? *Educational Leadership, 55*(4), 6–10.

Slavin, R. E. (2002). The intentional school: Effective elementary education for all children. In S. Stringfield & D. Land (Eds.), *Educating at-risk students* (pp. 111–127). Chicago: National Society for the Study of Education.

Slavin, R. E. (2003). A reader's guide to scientifically based research. *Educational Leadership, 60*(5), 12–16.

Slavin, R. E. (2007). *What works? Issues in synthesizing educational program evaluations.* Manuscript submitted for publication.

Slavin, R. E. (in press). Comprehensive school reform. In T. Good (Ed.), *21st century education: A reference handbook.* Thousand Oaks, CA: Sage.

Slavin, R. E., & Calderón, M. (Eds.). (2001). *Effective Programs for Latino Students.* Mahwah, NJ: Erlbaum.

Slavin, R. E., & Cheung, A. (2005). A synthesis of research on language of reading instruction. *Review of Educational Research, 75*(2), 247–284.

Slavin, R. E., Cheung, A., Groff, C., & Lake, C. (in press). Effective reading programs for middle and high schools: A best-evidence synthesis. *Reading Research Quarterly.*

Slavin, R. E., & Fashola, O. S. (1998). *Show me the evidence: Proven and promising programs for America's schools.* Thousand Oaks, CA: Corwin.

Slavin, R. E., Hurley, E. A., & Chamberlain, A. M. (2003). Cooperative learning and achievement: Theory and research. In W. M. Reynolds & G. E. Miller (Eds.), *Handbook of Psychology, Volume 7* (pp. 177–198). Hoboken, NJ: Wiley.

Slavin, R. E., & Karweit, N. L. (1982, August). *School organizational vs. developmental effects on attendance among young adolescents.* Paper presented at the annual convention of the American Psychological Association, Washington, DC.

Slavin, R. E., & Karweit, N. L. (1984, April). *Within-class ability groupings and student achievement: Two field experiments.* Paper presented at the annual convention of the American Educational Research Association, New Orleans, LA.

Slavin, R. E., Karweit, N. L., & Wasik, B. A. (1994). *Preventing early school failure: Research on effective strategies.* Boston: Allyn & Bacon.

Slavin, R. E., & Lake, C. (2006). *Effective programs in elementary math: A best evidence synthesis.* Manuscript submitted for publication.

Slavin, R. E., Lake, C., & Groff, C. (2007). *Effective programs in middle and high school math: A best evidence synthesis.* Manuscript submitted for publication.

Slavin, R. E., & Madden, N. A. (1987, April). *Effective classroom programs for students at risk.* Paper presented at the annual convention of the American Educational Research Association, Washington, DC.

Slavin, R. E., & Madden, N. A. (1999). Effects of bilingual and English as a second language adaptations of Success for All on the reading achievement of students acquiring English. *Journal of Education for Students Placed at Risk, 4*(4), 393–416.

Slavin, R. E., & Madden, N. A. (2000). Roots & Wings: Effects of whole-school reform on student achievement. *Journal of Education for Students Placed at Risk, 5*(1 & 2), 109–136.

Slavin, R. E., & Madden, N. A. (Eds.) (2001). *One million children: Success for All.* Thousand Oaks, CA: Corwin.

Slavin, R. E., Madden, N. A., & Karweit, N. L. (Eds.). (1989). *Effective programs for students at risk.* Boston: Allyn & Bacon.

Slavin, R. E., Madden, N. A., & Leavey, M. (1984a). Effects of team assisted individualization on the mathematics achievement of academically handicapped and nonhandicapped students. *Journal of Educational Psychology, 76,* 813–819.

Slavin, R. E., Madden, N. A., & Leavey, M. B. (1984b). Effects of cooperative learning and individualized instruction on mainstreamed students. *Exceptional Children, 84,* 409–422.

Slavin, R. E., Madden, N. A., & Stevens, R. J. (1994). Cooperative integrated reading and composition: Applications for the language arts classroom. In R. J. Stahl (Ed.), *Cooperative learning in language arts: A handbook for teachers.* Boston: Addison-Wesley.

Slavin, R. E., & Stevens, R. J. (1991). Cooperative learning and mainstreaming. In J. W. Lloyd, N. N. Singh, & A. C. Repp (Eds.). *The regular education initiative: Alternative perspectives on concepts, issues, and models* (pp. 177–191). Sycamore, IL: Sycamore.

Slotte, V., & Lonka, K. (1999). Review and process effects of spontaneous note-taking on text comprehension. *Contemporary Educational Psychology, 24*(1), 1–20.

Smagorinsky, P., & Smith, M. W. (1992). The nature of knowledge in composition and literary understanding: The question of specificity. *Review of Educational Research, 62*(3), 279–305.

Small, M. Y., Lovett, S. B., & Scher, M. S. (1993). Pictures facilitate children's recall of unillustrated expository prose. *Journal of Educational Psychology, 85,* 520–528.

Smith, D. D. (2001). *Introduction to special education: Teaching in an age of opportunity.* Boston: Allyn & Bacon.

Smith, D. D., & Luckasson, R. (1995). *Introduction to special education* (2nd ed.). Boston: Allyn & Bacon.

Smith, F., Hardman, F., & Higgins, S. (2006). The impact of interactive whiteboards on teacher/pupil interaction in the National Literacy and Numeracy Strategies. *British Educational Research Journal, 32*(3), 437–457.

Smith, H., Higgins, S., Wall, K., & Miller, J. (2005). Interactive whiteboards: Boon or bandwagon? A critical review of the literature. *Journal of Computer-Assisted Learning, 21,* 91–101.

Smith, L. J., Ross, S. M., & Casey, J. P. (1994). *Special education analyses for Success for All in four cities.* Memphis, TN: University of Memphis, Center for Research in Educational Policy.

Smith, L., & Land, M. (1981). Low-interference verbal behaviors related to teacher clarity. *Journal of Classroom Interaction, 17,* 37–42.

Smith, M. L. (1991). Meanings of test preparation. *American Educational Research Journal, 28*(3), 521–542.

Smith, S. S. (2002). Desegregation. In D. L. Levinson, P. W. Cookson, Jr., & A. R. Sadovnik (Eds.), *Education and sociology: An encyclopedia* (pp. 141–149). New York: Routledge Falmer.

Smith, T. E. C., Polloway, E. A., Patton, J. R., & Dowdy, C. A. (2008). *Teaching students with special needs in inclusive settings.* (5th ed.). Boston: Allyn & Bacon.

Smith, T., Polloway, E., Patton, J., & Dowdy, C. (2004). *Teaching students with special needs in inclusive settings* (4th ed.). Boston: Pearson.

Smutny, J. (2003). *Gifted education: Promising practices.* Bloomington, IN: Phi Delta Kappan.

Snell, M. E., & Janney, R. (2000). *Collaborative teaming.* Baltimore: Brookes.

Snow, C. (2006). Cross-cutting themes and future research directions. In D. August and T. Shanahan (Eds.), *Developing literacy in second-language learners* (pp. 631–652). Mahwah, NJ: Erlbaum.

Snow, C. E., Burns, S. M., & Griffin, P. (Eds.). (1998). *Preventing reading difficulties in young children.* Washington, DC: National Academy Press.

Snow, R. E. (1992). Aptitude theory: Yesterday, today, and tomorrow. *Educational Psychologist, 27*(1), 5–32.

Snowman, J. (1984). Learning tactics and strategies. In G. Phye & T. Andre (Eds.), *Cognitive instructional psychology.* New York: Academic Press.

Snyderman, M., & Rothman, S. (1987). Survey of expert opinion on intelligence and aptitude testing. *American Psychologist, 42,* 137–144.

Solso, R. L. (2001). *Cognitive psychology* (6th ed.). Boston: Allyn & Bacon.

Somekh, B., et al. (2007). *Evaluation of the primary schools whiteboards expansion project: Report to the Department for Education and Skills.* Manchester, UK: Manchester Metropolitan University.

Sornson, N. (2001). Vision and learning. In B. Sornson (Ed.), *Preventing early learning failure.* Alexandria, VA: ASCD.

Sorrells, A. M., Rieth, H., & Sindelar, P. (2004). *Critical issues in special education: Access, diversity, and accountability.* Boston: Pearson.

Sousa, D. (2001). *How the brain learns* (2nd ed.). Boston: Allyn & Bacon.

Specht, L. B., & Sandling, P. K. (1991). The differential effects of experiential learning activities and traditional lecture classes in accounting. *Simulation and Games, 2,* 196–210.

Spector, J. E. (1992). Predicting progress in beginning reading: Dynamic assessment of phonemic awareness. *Journal of Educational Psychology, 84*(3), 353–363.

Speece, D., Case, L., & Molloy, D. (2003). Responsiveness to general education as the first gate to learning disabilities identification. *Learning Disabilities: Research and Practice, 18*(3), 147–156.

Spencer, M. B., Noll, E., Stoltzfus, J., & Harpalani, V. (2001). Identify and school adjustment: Revisiting the "acting White" assumption. *Educational Psychologist, 36*(1), 21–30.

Sperling, G. A. (1960). The information available in brief visual presentations. *Psychological Monographs, 74,* No. 498.

Spielberger, C., & Vagg, P. (Eds.). (1995). *Test anxiety: Theory, assessment, and treatment.* Washington, DC: Taylor & Francis.

Spires, H. A., & Donley, J. (1998). Prior knowledge activation: Inducing engagement with informational texts. *Journal of Educational Psychology, 90*(2), 249–260.

Spurlin, J. E., Dansereau, D. F., Larson, C. O., & Brooks, L. W. (1984). Cooperative learning strategies in processing descriptive text: Effects of role and activity level of the learner. *Cognition and Instruction, 1,* 451–463.

Squire, L. R., Knowlton, B., & Musen, G. (1993). The structure and organization of memory. *Annual Review of Psychology, 44,* 453–495.

Stallings, J. A., & Kaskowitz, D. (1974). *Follow-through classroom observation evaluation 1972–73.* Menlo Park, CA: Standard Research Institute.

Stallings, J., & Krasavage, E. M. (1986). Program implementation and student achievement in a four-year Madeline Hunter follow-through project. *Elementary School Journal, 87,* 117–138.

Stanovich, K. E., Siegel, L. S., & Gottard, A. (1997). Converging evidence for phonological and surface subtypes of reading disability. *Journal of Educational Psychology, 89*(10), 114–127.

Starfield, B. (1997). *Quality of primary care: A services perspective.* Primary Care Center Policy White Paper.

Starnes, B. A. (2006). Montana's Indian education for all: Toward an education worthy of American ideals. *Phi Delta Kappan, 88*(3), 184–189.

Starratt, R. (2003). Opportunity to learn and the accountability agenda. *Phi Delta Kappan, 85*(4), 298–303.

Stecher, B., Hamilton, L., & Gonzalez, G. (2003). *Working smarter to leave no child behind.* Santa Monica, CA: RAND.

Steel, P. (2007). The nature of procrastination: A meta-analytic and theoretical review of quintessential self-regulatory failure. *Psychological Bulletin, 133*(1), 65–94.

Stein, B. S., Littlefield, J., Bransford, J. D., & Persampieri, M. (1984). Elaboration and knowledge acquisition. *Memory and Cognition, 12,* 522–529.

Stein, M. K., Leinhardt, G., & Bickel, W. (1989). Instructional issues for teaching students at risk. In R. E. Slavin, N. L. Karweit, & N. A. Madden (Eds.), *Effective programs for students at risk.* Boston: Allyn & Bacon.

Stein, N. (2000). Listening to—and learning from—girls. *Educational Leadership, 57*(4), 18–20.

Steiner, H. H., & Carr, M. (2003). Cognitive development in gifted children: Toward a more precise understanding of emerging differences in intelligence. *Educational Psychology Review, 15*(3), 215–246.

Stephan, W. G., & Finlay, K. (1999). The role of empathy in improving intergroup relations. *Journal of Social Issues, 55*(4), 729–743.

Stephan, W. G., & Vogt, W. P. (Eds.). (2004). *Education programs for improving intergroup relations.* New York: Teachers College.

Stern, D. (1996). *Active learning in students and teachers.* Paris: Organization for Economic Cooperation and Development.

Sternberg, R. J. (2002). Raising the achievement of all students: Teaching for successful intelligence. *Educational Psychology Review, 14*(4), 383–393.

Sternberg, R. J. (2003). Contemporary theories of intelligence. In W. M. Reynolds & G. E. Miller (Eds.), *Handbook of psychology: Vol. 7. Educational psychology* (pp. 23–45). Hoboken, NJ: Wiley.

Sternberg, R. J. (Ed.). (2000). *Handbook of intelligence.* New York: Cambridge University Press.

Sternberg, R. J. (2007). Who are the bright children? The cultural context of being and acting intelligent. *Educational Researcher, 36*(3), 148–155.

Sternberg, R. J., & Bhana, K. (1986). Synthesis of research on the effectiveness of intellectual skills programs: Snake-oil remedies or miracle cures? *Educational Leadership, 44*(2), 60–67.

Sternberg, R. J., & Detterman, D. K. (Eds.). (1986). *What is intelligence?* Norwood, NJ: Ablex.

Sternberg, R. J., & Horvath, J. A. (1995). A prototype view of expert teaching. *Educational Researcher, 24*(6), 9–17.

Stevens, R. J., Madden, N. A., Slavin, R. E., & Farnish, A. M. (1987). Cooperative Integrated Reading and Composition: Two field experiments. *Reading Research Quarterly, 22,* 433–454.

Stevens, R. J., & Slavin, R. E. (1995a). The effects of Cooperative Integrated Reading and Composition (CIRC) on academically handicapped and non-handicapped students' achievement, attitudes, and metacognition in reading and writing. *Elementary School Journal, 95*(3), 241–262.

Stevens, R. J., & Slavin, R. E. (1995b). The cooperative elementary school: Effects on students' achievement, attitudes, and social relations. *American Educational Research Journal, 32,* 321–351.

Stice, E., Presnell, K., & Bearman, S. K. (2001). Relation of early menarche to depression, eating disorders, substance abuse, and comorbid psychopathology among adolescent girls. *Developmental Psychology, 37*(5), 608–619.

Stiggins, R. (2004). New assessment beliefs for a new school mission. *Phi Delta Kappan, 86*(1), 22–27.

Stiggins, R. J. (2000). *Student-involved classroom assessment* (3rd ed.). Bloomington, IN: Phi Delta Kappan.

Stiggins, R. (2007). Assessment through the student's eyes. *Educational Leadership, 64*(8), 22–26.

Stinson, D. (2006). African American male adolescents, school (and mathematics): Deficiency, rejection, and achievement. *Review of Educational Research, 76*(4), 477–506.

Stipek, D. (2002). *Motivation to learn: Integrating theory and practice* (4th ed.). Boston: Allyn & Bacon.

Stipek, D. (2006). No Child Left Behind comes to preschool. *The Elementary School Journal, 106*(5), 455–466.

Stipek, D., de la Sota, A., & Weishaupt, L. (1999). Life lessons: An embedded classroom approach to preventing high-risk behaviors among preadolescents. *The Elementary School Journal, 99*(5), 433–452.

Stipek, D. J. (1993). *Motivation to learn: From theory to practice* (2nd ed.). Boston: Allyn & Bacon.

Stipek, D. J., & Ryan, R. H. (1997). Economically disadvantaged preschoolers: Ready to learn but further to go. *Developmental Psychology, 33*(4), 711–723.

Strand, S., Deary, I. J., & Smith, P. (2006). Sex differences in cognitive abilities test scores: A UK national picture. *British Journal of Educational Psychology, 76,* 463–480.

Streifer, P. (2002). *Using data to make better educational decisions.* Lanham, MD: Scarecrow Education & American Association of School Administrators.

Stringfield, S., Millsap, M. A., Herman, R., Yoder, N., Brigham, N., Nesselrodt, P., Schaffer, E., Karweit, N., Levin, M., & Stevens, R. J. (1997). *Special strategies studies final report.* Washington, DC: U.S. Department of Education.

Strong, R. W., Silver, H. F., & Perini, M. J. (2001). *Teaching what matters most.* Alexandria, VA: ASCD.

Strout, M. (2005). Positive behavioral support on the classroom level: Considerations and strategies. *Beyond Behavior, 14,* 3–8.

Stuebing, K. K., Fletcher, J. M., LeDoux, J. M., Lyon, G. R., Shaywitz, S. E., & Shaywitz, B. A. (2002). *American Educational Research Journal, 39*(2), 469–518.

Stumpf, H., & Stanley, J. C. (1996). Gender-related differences on the College Board's advanced placement achievement tests 1982–1992. *Journal of Educational Psychology, 88*(2), 353–364.

Summers, J. (2006). Effects of collaborative learning in math on sixth graders' individual goal orientations from a socioconstructivist perspective. *The Elementary School Journal, 106*(3), 273–290.

Supovitz, J. A., & Brennan, R. T. (1997). Mirror, mirror on the wall, which is the fairest test of all? An examination of the equitability of portfolio assessment relative to standardized tests. *Harvard Educational Review, 67*(3), 474–505.

Supovitz, J. A., Poglinco, S. M., & Snyder, B. A. (2001). *Moving mountains: Successes and challenges of the America's Choice comprehensive school reform design.* Philadelphia: University of Pennsylvania, Consortium for Policy Research in Education.

Susman, E. J., Dorn, L. D., & Schiefelbein, V. L. (2003). Puberty, sexuality, and health. In R. M. Lerner, M. A. Easterbrooks, & J. Mistry (Eds.), *Handbook of psychology: Vol. 6. Developmental psychology* (pp. 295–324). Hoboken, NJ: Wiley.

Sutherland, K., Wehby, J., & Copeland, S. (2000). Effect of rates of varying behavior-specific praise on the on-task behavior of students with EBD. *Journal of Emotional and Behavioral Disorders, 8,* 2–8, 26.

Suzuki, L. A., Ponterotto, J. G., & Meller, P. J. (Eds.). (2000). *Handbook of multicultural assessment* (2nd ed.). San Francisco: Jossey-Bass.

Swann, W., Chang-Schneider, C., & McClarty, K. (2007). Do people's self-views matter? *American Psychologist, 62*(2), 84–94.

Swanson, D. B., Norman, G. R., & Linn, R. L. (1995). Performance-based assessment: Lessons from the health professions. *Educational Researcher, 24*(5), 5–11, 35.

Swanson, H. (2001). Research on interventions for adolescents with learning disabilities: A meta-analysis of outcomes related to higher-order processing. *The Elementary School Journal, 101*(3), 331–348.

Swanson, H., & Jerman, O. (2006). Math disabilities: A selective meta-analysis of the literature. *Review of Educational Research, 76*(2), 249–274.

Swanson, H. L. (1990). Influence of metacognitive knowledge and aptitude on problem solving. *Journal of Educational Psychology, 82,* 306–314.

Swanson, H. L., & Hoskyn, M. (1998). Experimental intervention research on students with learning disabilities: A meta-analysis of treatment outcomes. *Review of Educational Research, 68*(3), 277–321.

Swanson, H. L., Mink, J., & Bocian, K. (1999). Cognitive processing deficits in poor readers with symptoms of reading disabilities and ADHD: More alike than different? *Journal of Educational Psychology, 91*(2), 321–333.

Swanson, M. C., Mehan, H., & Hubbard, L. (1995). The AVID classroom: Academic and social support for low-achieving students. In J. Oakes & K. H. Quartz (Eds.), *Creating new educational communities.* Chicago: University of Chicago Press.

Sweeney, D., & Hoffman, L. (2004). Research issues in autism spectrum disorders. In R. Rutherford, M. Quinn, & S. Mathur (Eds.), *Handbook of research on emotional and behavioral disorders* (pp. 302–317). New York: Guilford.

Sweller, J., van Merrienboer, J. J. G., & Paas, F. G. W. C. (1998). Cognitive architecture and instructional design. *Educational Psychology Review, 10*(3), 251–296.

Swiatek, M. A., & Benbow, C. P. (1991). Ten-year longitudinal follow-up of ability-matched accelerated and unaccelerated gifted students. *Journal of Educational Psychology, 83*(4), 528–538.

Swisher, K., & Schoorman, D. (2001). Learning styles: Implications for teachers. In C. F. Diaz (Ed.), *Multicultural education in the 21st century.* New York: Longman.

Tanner, C. K., & Decotis, J. D. (1994). The effects of a continuous-progress, non-graded program on primary school students. *ERS Spectrum, 12*(3), 41–47.

Taylor, B., Pearson, P., Clark, K., & Walpole, S. (2000). Effective schools and accomplished teachers: Lessons about primary-grade reading instruction in low-income schools. *The Elementary School Journal, 101*(2), 121–166.

Taylor, C. (1994). Assessment for measurement or standards: The peril and promise of large-scale assessment reform. *American Educational Research Journal, 31*(2), 231–262.

Taylor, D., & Lorimer, M. (2003). Helping boys succeed. *Educational Leadership, 60*(4), 68–70.

Teeter, P. A. (2000). *Interventions for ADHD.* New York: Guilford.

Tenenbaum, H., & Ruck, M. (2007). Are teachers' expectations different for racial minority than for European American students? A meta-analysis. *Journal of Educational Psychology, 99*(2), 253–273.

Tennyson, R. D., & Park, O. (1980). The teaching of concepts: A review of instructional design literature. *Review of Educational Research, 50,* 55–70.

Terman, L. M., & Oden, M. H. (1959). The gifted group in mid-life. In *Genetic studies of genius,* Vol. 5. Stanford, CA: Stanford University Press.

Texas Center for Educational Research, (2007). *Evaluation of the Texas technology immersion pilot: Findings from the second year.* Austin, TX: Author.

Tharp, R. G., & Gallimore, R. (1988). *Rousing minds to life.* New York: Cambridge University Press.

The Education Trust. (2003). *ESEA: Myths versus realities. Answers to questions about the No Child Left Behind Act.* Washington, DC: Author.

Theodore, L., Bray, M., Kehle, T., & Jenson, W. (2001). Randomization of group contingencies and reinforcers for reducing classroom disruptive behavior. *Journal of School Psychology, 39,* 267–277.

Thoma, S. J., & Rest, J. R. (1999). The relationship between moral decision making and patterns of consolidation and transition in moral judgment development. *Developmental Psychology, 35*(2), 323–334.

Thomas, E. L., & Robinson, H. A. (1972). *Improving reading in every class: A sourcebook for teachers.* Boston: Allyn & Bacon.

Thomas, M. D., & Bainbridge, W. L. (2001). "All children can learn": Facts and fallacies. *Phi Delta Kappan, 82*(9), 660–662.

Thompson, R. A., Easterbrooks, M. A., & Padilla-Walker, L. M. (2003). Social and emotional development in infancy. In R. M. Lerner, M. A. Easterbrooks, & J. Mistry (Eds.), *Handbook of psychology: Vol. 6. Developmental psychology* (pp. 91–112). Hoboken, NJ: Wiley.

Thompson, R. A., & Wyatt, J. M. (1999). Current research on child maltreatment: Implications for educators. *Educational Psychology Review, 11*(3), 173–202.

Thompson, S. (2001). The authentic standards movement and its evil twin. *Phi Delta Kappan, 82*(5), 358–362.

Thompson, T., Davidson, J. A., & Barber, J. G. (1995). Self-worth protection in achievement motivation: Performance effects and attributional behavior. *Journal of Educational Psychology, 87*(4), 598–610.

Thompson, W., & Hickey, J. (2008). *Society in focus.* Boston: Pearson.

Thorkildsen, T. A. (1993). Those who can, tutor: High-ability students' conceptions of fair ways to organize learning. *Journal of Educational Psychology, 85*(1), 182–190.

Thorkildsen, T. A., & Nicholls, J. G. (1998). Fifth graders' achievement orientations and beliefs: Individual and classroom differences. *Journal of Educational Psychology, 90*(2), 179–201.

Thornburg, D. (2002). *The new basics: Education and the future of work in the telematic age.* Alexandria, VA: ASCD.

Thorsen, C. (2006). *TechTactics: Technology for Teachers* (2nd ed.). Boston: Allyn & Bacon.

Thousand, J. S., & Villa, R. A. (1994). *Creativity and collaborative learning: A practical guide to empowering students and teachers.* Baltimore: Paul H. Brookes.

Timpson, W. M., & Tobin, D. N. (1982). *Teaching as performing: A guide to energizing your public presentation.* Englewood Cliffs, NJ: Prentice-Hall.

Tingley, J. (2001). Volunteer programs: When good intentions are not enough. *Educational Leadership, 68*(7), 53–55.

Tisak, M. S., & Tisak, J. (1990). Children's conceptions of parental authority, friendship, and sibling relationships. *Merrill-Palmer Quarterly, 36,* 347–368.

Tishman, S., Perkins, D. N., & Jay, E. (1995). *The thinking classroom.* Boston: Allyn & Bacon.

Tobias, S. (1992). The impact of test anxiety cognition in school learning. In K. A. Hagtvet & T. B. Johnsen (Eds.), *Advances in test anxiety research* (Vol. 7, pp. 18–31). Amsterdam: Swets & Zeitlinger.

Tobias, S. (1994). Interest, prior knowledge, and learning. *Review of Educational Research, 63,* 37–54.

Tobin, K. (1986). Effects of teacher wait time on discourse characteristics in mathematics and language arts classes. *American Educational Research Journal, 23,* 191–200.

Tobin, K. (1987). The role of wait time in higher cognitive level learning. *Review of Educational Research, 57,* 69–95.

Tobin, K. G., & Capie, W. (1982). Relationships between classroom process variables and middle-school science achievement. *Journal of Educational Psychology, 74,* 441–454.

Toga, A. W., & Thompson, P. M. (2005). Genetics of brain structure and intelligence. *Annual Review of Neuroscience, 28,* 1–23.

Tollefson, N. (2000). Classroom applications of cognitive theories of motivation. *Educational Psychology Review, 12*(1), 63–84.

Tomlinson, C. (2002). Invitation to learn. *Educational Leadership, 60*(1), 6–11.

Tomlinson, C. (2003). Deciding to teach them all. *Educational Leadership, 61*(2), 6–11.

Tomlinson, C. A. (2000). Reconcilable differences? Standards-based teaching and differentiation. *Educational Leadership, 58*(1), 6–11.

Tomlinson, C. A. (2001) Grading for success. *Educational Leadership 58*(6), 12–16.

Tomlinson, C. A. (2004). Differentiating instruction: A synthesis of key research and guidelines. In T. L. Jetton & J. A. Dole (Eds.), *Adolescent literacy, research and practice* (pp. 228–250). New York: The Guilford Press.

Tomlinson, C. A., Kaplan, S. N., & Renzulli, J. S. (2001). *The parallel curriculum: A model for planning curriculum for gifted students and whole classrooms.* Thousand Oaks, CA: Corwin.

Top, B. L., & Osguthorpe, R. T. (1987). Reverse-role tutoring: The effects of handicapped students tutoring regular class students. *Elementary School Journal, 87,* 413–423.

Topping, K., & Ehly, S. (Eds.). (1998). *Peer-assisted learning.* Mahwah, NJ: Erlbaum.

Topping, K., Samuels, J., & Paul, T. (2007). Does practice make perfect? Independent reading quantity, quality, and student achievement. *Learning and Instruction, 17*(3), 253–264.

Torp, L., & Sage, S. (1998). *Problems as possibilities: Problem-based learning for K–12 education.* Alexandria, VA: Association for Supervision and Curriculum Development.

Torrance, E. P. (1986). Teaching creative and gifted learners. In M. C. Wittrock (Ed.), *Handbook of research on teaching* (3rd ed.). New York: Macmillan.

Torrance, M., Fidalgo, R., & Garcia, J.-N. (2007). The teachability and effectiveness of cognitive self-regulation in sixth-grade writers. *Learning and Instruction, 17*(3), 265–285.

Towne, L., Wise, L., & Winters, T. (2005). *Advancing scientific research in education.* Washington, DC: National Academies Press.

Trammel, D. L., Schloss, P. J., & Alper, S. (1994). Using self-recording evaluation and graphing to increase completion of homework assignments. *Journal of Learning Disabilities, 27,* 75–81.

Trautwein, U. (2007). The homework-achievement relation reconsidered: Differentiating homework time, homework frequency, and homework effort. *Learning and Instruction, 17*(3), 372–388.

Trawick-Smith, J. (1997). *Early childhood development: A multicultural perspective.* Upper Saddle River, NJ: Merrill/Prentice-Hall.

Tredway, L. (1995). Socratic seminars: Engaging students in intellectual discourse. *Educational Leadership, 53*(1), 26–29.

Trent, W. T. (1997). Outcomes of school desegregation: Findings from longitudinal research. *Journal of Negro Education, 66*(3), 255–257.

Triandis, H. (1995). *Individualism and collectivism.* Boulder, CO: Westview.

Trice, A. D. (2000). *A handbook of classroom assessment.* New York: Longman.

Troop, W. R., & Asher, S. R. (1999). Teaching peer relationship competence in schools. In R. J. Stevens (Ed.), *Teaching in American schools.* Upper Saddle River, NJ: Merrill/Prentice-Hall.

Trumbull, E., & Farr, B. (2000). *Grading and reporting student progress in an age of standards.* Norwood, MA: Christopher-Gordon.

Tschannen-Moran, M., & Woolfolk Hoy, A. (2001). Teacher efficacy: Capturing an elusive construct. *Teaching and teacher education, 17,* 783–805.

Tucker, J. A. (2001). Instructional support teams: It's a group thing. In B. Sornson (Ed.), *Preventing early learning failure.* Alexandria, VA: ASCD.

Tulving, E., & Craik, F. I. M. (Eds.) (2000). *The Oxford handbook of memory.* New York: Oxford University Press.

Turiel, E. (1998). The development of morality. In W. Damon (Ed.), *Handbook of child psychology: Vol. 3. Social, emotional, and personality development* (pp. 863–932). Hoboken, NJ: Wiley.

Turkeltaub, P. E., Gareau, L., Flowers, D. L., Zeffiro, T. A., & Eden, G. F. (2003). Development of neural mechanisms for reading. *Nature Neuroscience, 6,* 767–773.

Turkheimer, E. (1994). Socioeconomic status and intelligence. In R. J. Sternberg (Ed.), *Encyclopedia of human intelligence.* New York: Macmillan.

Turner, L. A., & Johnson, B. (2003). A model of mastery motivation for at-risk preschoolers. *Journal of Educational Psychology, 95*(3), 495–505.

Turner, S., & Alborz, A. (2003). Academic attainments of children with Down's syndrome: A longitudinal study. *British Journal of Educational Psychology, 73*(4), 563–583.

U.S. Census Bureau. (2001). Web site (www.census.gov). *Population projections.*

U.S. Department of Education (2005). *Annual Report to Congress on the implementation of the Individuals with Disabilities Act.* Washington, DC: Author.

U.S. Department of Education, Office of Special Education and Rehabilitation Services. (1998, September). *IDEA '97 general information* [Internet]. Retrieved from: www.ed.gov/offices/OSERS/IDEA/overview.html.

U.S. Department of Education. (1994). *Sixteenth annual report to Congress on the implementation of the Individuals with Disabilities Education Act.* Washington, DC: Author.

U.S. Department of Education. (2000). *The 22nd annual report to Congress on the implementation of the Individuals with Disabilities Education Act.* Washington, DC: U.S. Government Printing Office.

U.S. Department of Education. (2002). *No Child Left Behind: A desktop reference.* Washington, DC: Author. (available at www.ed.gov/offices/OESE/reference).

U.S. Department of Education. (2003). *Identifying and implementing educational practices supported by rigorous evidence: A user-friendly guide.* Washington, DC: Author.

Urdan, T., & Mestas, M. (2006). The goals behind performance goals. *Journal of Educational Psychology, 98*(2), 354–365.

Uttal, W. (2001). *The new phrenology: The limits of localizing cognitive processes in the brain.* Cambridge, MA: MIT Press/Bradford Books.

Vacca, R. (2006). They can because they think they can. *Educational Leadership, 63*(5), 56–59.

Valencia, S. W., Pearson, P. D., Peters, C. W., & Wixson, K. K. (1989). Theory and practice in statewide reading assessment: Closing the gap. *Educational Leadership, 46*(7), 57–63.

Valenza, J. (2005/2006). The virtual library. *Educational Leadership, 63*(4), 54–59.

Vandell, D. L. (2004). Early child care: The known and unknown. *Merrill-Palmer Quarterly, 50,* 387–413.

van Goozen, S., Fairchild, G., Snoek, H., & Harold, G. (2007). The evidence for a neurobiological model of childhood antisocial behavior. *Psychological Bulletin, 133*(1), 149–182.

Van Horn, M. L., & Ramey, S. L. (2003). The effects of developmentally appropriate practices on academic outcomes among former Head Start students and classmates, grades 1–3. *American Educational Research Journal, 40*(4), 961–990.

Van IJzendoorn, M. H., Juffer, F., & Klein Poelhuis, C. W. (2005). Adoption and cognitive development: A meta-analytic comparison of adopted and nonadopted children's IQ and school performance. *Pyschological Bulletin, 131*(2), 301–316.

Van Keer, H. (2004). Fostering reading comprehension in fifth grade by explicit instruction in reading strategies and peer tutoring. *British Journal of Educational Psychology, 74*(1), 37–70.

Van Laar, C. (2001). Understanding the impact of disadvantage on academic achievement. In F. Salili & R. Hoosain (Eds.), *Multicultural education: Issues, policies, and practices.* Greenwich, CT: Information Age Publishing.

Van Meter, P. (2001). Drawing construction as a strategy for learning from text. *Journal of Educational Psychology, 93*(1), 129–140.

Van Patten, J., Chao, C. I., & Reigeluth, C. M. (1986). A review of strategies for sequencing and synthesizing instruction. *Review of Educational Research, 56,* 437–471.

Van Sickle, R. L. (1986, April). *A quantitative review of research on instructional simulation gaming: A twenty-year perspective.* Paper presented at the annual convention of the American Educational Research Association, San Francisco, CA.

Vansteenkiste, M., Lens, W., & Deci, E. (2006). Intrinsic vs. extrinsic goal contents in self-determination theory: Another look at the quality of academic motivation. *Educational Psychologist, 41*(1), 19–31.

Van Tassel-Baska, F. S. (1989). Appropriate curriculum for gifted learners. *Educational Leadership 46*(6), 13–15.

Vasta, R., & Liben, L. S. (1996). The water-level task: An intriguing puzzle. *Current Directions in Psychological Science, 5*(6), 171–177.

Vaughn, S., Bos, C. S., & Schumm, J. S. (2000). *Teaching exceptional, diverse, and at-risk students in the general education classroom* (2nd ed.). Boston: Allyn & Bacon.

Vaughn, S., Bos, C. S., & Schumm, J. S. (2007). *Teaching students who are exceptional, diverse, and at risk* (4th ed.). Boston: Pearson.

Vaughn, S., Cirino, P., Linan-Thompson, S., Mathes, P., Carlson, C., Hagan, E., Pollard-Durodola, S., Fletcher, J., & Francis, D. (2006). Effectiveness of a Spanish intervention and an English intervention for English-language learners at risk for reading problems. *American Educational Research Journal, 43*(3), 449–487.

Veenman, S. (1995). Cognitive and noncognitive effects of multigrade and multi-age classes: A best evidence synthesis. *Review of Educational Research, 65*(4), 319–381.

Veenman, S. (1997). Combination classrooms revisited. *Educational Research and Evaluation, 3*(3), 262–276.

Vekiri, I. (2002). What is the value of graphical displays in learning? *Educational Psychology Review, 14*(3), 261–312.

Vellutino, F. R., Scanlon, D. M., Sipay, E. R., Small, S. G., Chen, R., Pratt, A., & Denckla, M. B. (1996). Cognitive profiles of difficult-to-remediate and readily remediated poor readers: Early intervention as a vehicle for distinguishing between cognitive and experimental deficits as basic causes of specific reading disability. *Journal of Educational Psychology, 88*(4), 601–638.

Verba, M. (1993). Cooperative formats in pretend play among young children. *Cognition and Instruction, 11*(3 & 4), 265–280.

Vermetten, Y. J., Lodewijks, H. G., & Vermunt, J. D. (2001). The role of personality traits and goal orientations in strategy use. *Contemporary Educational Psychology, 26*(2), 149–170.

Vernez, G. (1998). *Projected social context for education of children.* Washington, DC: RAND.

Villa, R., & Thousand, J. (2003). Making inclusive education work. *Educational Leadership, 61*(2), 19–23.

Villegas, A., & Lucas, T. (2007). The culturally responsive teacher. *Educational Leadership, 64*(6), 28–33.

Vispoel, W. P., & Austin, J. R. (1995). Success and failure in junior high school: A critical incident approach to understanding students' attributional beliefs. *American Educational Research Journal, 32,* 277–412.

Volkmar, F., & Pauls, D. (2003). Autism. *Lancet, 362,* 1133–1141.

Volman, M., & van Eck, E. (2001). Gender equity and information technology in education: The second decade. *Review of Educational Research, 71*(4), 613–634.

Von Drehle, D. (2007, July 26). The myth about boys. *Time.*

von Glaserfeld, E. (1996). Footnotes to the "many faces of constructivism." *Educational Researcher, 25*(6), 19.

Vygotsky, L. S. (1978). *Mind in society.* M. Cole, V. John-Steiner, S. Scribner, & E. Souberman (Eds.). Cambridge, MA: Harvard University Press.

Wade, S. E. (2001). Research on importance and interest: Implications for curriculum development and future research. *Educational Psychology Review, 13*(3), 243–261.

Wadsworth, B. (2004). *Piaget's theory of cognitive and affective development* (5th ed.). Boston: Pearson.

Wager, T. D. (2006). Do we need to study the brain to understand the mind? *Observer, 19*(9), 24–27.

Wagmeister, J., & Shifrin, B. (2000). Thinking differently, learning differently. *Educational Leadership, 58*(3), 45–48.

Wainer, H. (2000). *Computerized adaptive testing: A primer* (2nd ed.). Mahwah, NJ: Erlbaum.

Walberg, H. (1988). Synthesis of research on time and learning. *Educational Leadership, 45*(6), 76–80.

Walker, H., Colvin, G., & Ramsey, E. (2003). *Antisocial behavior in school: Evidence-based practice.* Pacific Grove, CA: Brooks-Cole.

Walker, H., Ramsey, E., & Gresham, F. (2003a). Heading off disruptive behavior. *American Educator, 27*(4), 6–21.

Walker, H., Ramsey, E., & Gresham, F. (2003b). How disruptive students escalate hostility and disorder—and how teachers can avoid it. *American Educator, 27*(4), 22–27.

Walker, H. M., & Gresham, F. M. (2003). School-related behavior disorders. In W. M. Reynolds & G. E. Miller (Eds.), *Handbook of psychology: Vol. 7. Educational psychology* (pp. 511–530). Hoboken, NJ: Wiley.

Walker, J. E., & Shea, T. M. (1999). *Behavior management: A practical approach for educators* (7th ed.). Upper Saddle River, NJ: Merrill.

Walker, J. E., Shea, T. M., & Bauer, A. M. (2004). *Behavior management: A practical approach for educators* (5th ed.). Upper Saddle River, NJ: Merrill.

Walker, J. M. T., & Hoover-Dempsey, K.V. (2001, April). *Age-related patterns in student invitations to parental involvement in homework.* Paper presented at the annual meeting of the American Educational Research Association, Seattle, WA.

Walker, L. J. (1991). Sex differences in moral reasoning. In W. Kurtines & J. L. Gewirtz (Eds.), *Handbook of moral behavior and development* (Vol. 2, pp. 333–364). Mahwah, NJ: Erlbaum.

Walker, L. J., & Henning, K. H. (1997). Moral development in the broader context of personality. In S. Hala (Ed.), *The development of social cognition* (pp. 297–327). Hove, England: Psychology Press.

Wallace, R. (2004). A framework for understanding teaching with the internet. *American Educational Research Journal, 41*(2), 447–448.

Wallace-Broscious, A., Serafica, F. C., & Osipow, S. H. (1994). Adolescent career development: Relationships to self-concept and identity status. *Journal of Research on Adolescence, 4*(1), 122–149.

Wallis, C., & Steptoe, S. (2007, June 4). How to fix No Child Left Behind. *Time, 169*(3), 34–41.

Wang, A.Y., & Thomas, M. H. (1995). Effect of keywords on long-term retention: Help or hindrance? *Journal of Educational Psychology, 87,* 468–475.

Warger, C. L., & Pugach, M. C. (1996). Forming partnerships around curriculum. *Educational Leadership, 53*(5), 62–65.

Warrick, P. D., & Naglieri, J. A. (1993). Gender differences in planning, attention, simultaneous, and successive (PASS) cognitive processes. *Journal of Educational Psychology, 85*(4), 693–701.

Wartella, E., & Jennings, N. (2000). Children and computers: New technology—old concerns. *Children and Computer Technology, 10*(2), 31–43.

Wasik, B. A. (1997). Volunteer tutoring programs: Do we know what works? *Phi Delta Kappan, 79*(4), 283–287.

Wasik, B. A. (2001). Teaching the alphabet to young children. *Young Children, 56,* 34–45.

Wasik, B. A., & Karweit, N. L. (1994). Off to a good start: Effects of birth-to-three interventions on early school success. In R. E. Slavin, N. L. Karweit, & B. A. Wasik (Eds.), *Preventing early school failure.* Boston: Allyn & Bacon.

Wasik, B. A., & Slavin, R. E. (1993). Preventing early reading failure with one-to-one tutoring: A review of five programs. *Reading Research Quarterly, 28*(2), 178–200.

Wasley, P. A. (2002). Small classes, small schools: The time is now. *Educational Leadership, 59*(3), 6–10.

Wasserman, D. (2001, April). Moving targets: Student mobility and student and school achievement. Paper presented at the annual meeting of the American Educational Research Association, Seattle, WA.

Waterhouse, L. (2006). Multiple intelligences, the Mozart Effect, and emotional intelligence: A critical review. *Educational Psychologist, 4*(4), 207–225.

Watkins, M., & Canivez, G. (2004). Temporal stability of WISC-III composite strengths and weaknesses. *Psychological Assessment, 16,* 6–16.

Watson, J., & West, J. (2004). *Full-day and half-day kindergarten in the United States: Findings from the Early Childhood Longitudinal Study, kindergarten class of 1998–1999.* NCES 2004-078. Washington, DC: U.S. Department of Education, National Center for Education Statistics.

Watt, K. M., Powell, C. A., & Mendiola, I. D. (2004). Implications of one comprehensive school reform model for secondary school students underrepresented in higher education. *Journal of Education for Students Placed at Risk, 9*(3), 241–259.

Waxman, H. C., Gray, J. P., & Padron, N. (2002). Resiliency among students at risk of academic failure. In S. Stringfield & D. Land (Eds.), *Educating at-risk students* (pp. 29–48). Chicago: National Society for the Study of Education.

Waxman, H., Padrón, Y., & Arnold, K. (2001). Effective instructional practices for students placed at risk of academic failure. In G. Borman, S. Stringfield, & R. Slavin (Eds.), *Title I: Compensatory education at the crossroads.* Mahwah, NJ: Erlbaum.

Wayne, A. J., & Youngs, P. (2003). Teacher characteristics and student achievement gains: A review. *Review of Educational Research, 73*(1), 89–122.

Weaver-Hightower, M. (2003). The "boy turn" in research on gender education. *Review of Educational Research, 73*(4), 471–498.

Webb, N., & Mastergeorge, A. (2003). Promoting effective helping behavior in peer-directed groups. *International Journal of Educational Research, 39,* 73–97.

Webb, N. M. (1992). Testing a theoretical model of student interaction and learning in small groups. In R. Hertz-Lazarowitz & N. Miller (Eds.), *Interaction in cooperative groups: The theoretical anatomy of group learning* (pp. 102–119). New York: Cambridge University Press.

Webb, N. M., Trooper, J. D., & Fall, R. (1995). Constructive activity and learning in collaborative small groups. *Journal of Educational Psychology, 87,* 406–423.

Webb, N. M., & Palincsar, A. S. (1996). Group processes in the classroom. In D. C. Berliner & R. C. Calfee (Eds.), *Handbook of Educational Psychology.* New York: Simon & Schuster Macmillan.

Webber, J., & Scheuermann, B. (1993). Managing behavior problems: Accentuate the positive . . . eliminate the negative! In K. M. Cauley, F. Linder, & J. H. McMillan (Eds.), *Annual editions: Educational psychology 93/94.* Guilford, CT: Dushkin.

Webber, J., Scheuermann, B., McCall, C., & Coleman, M. (1993). Research on self-monitoring as a behavior management technique in special education classrooms: A descriptive review. *Remedial and Special Education, 14*(2), 38–56.

Wechsler, D. (1955). *Wechsler Adult Intelligence Scale.* New York: Psychological Corporation.

Wehmeyer, M. L. (2001). *Teaching students with mental retardation: Providing access to the general curriculum.* Baltimore: Brookes.

Weinberger, E., & McCombs, B. L. (2001, April). *The impact of learner-centered practices on the academic and non-academic outcomes of upper elementary and middle school students.* Paper presented at the annual convention of the American Educational Research Association, Seattle, WA.

Weiner, B. (1992). *Human motivation: Metaphors, theories, and research.* Newbury Park, CA: Sage.

Weiner, B. (2000). Intrapersonal and interpersonal theories of motivation from an attributional perspective. *Educational Psychology Review, 12*(1), 1–14.

Weinert, F. E., & Helmke, A. (1995). Interclassroom differences in instructional quality and interindividual differences in cognitive development. *Educational Psychologist, 30*(1), 15–20.

Weinstein, C., & Mignano, A. (1993). *Organizing the elementary school classroom: Lessons from research and practice.* New York: McGraw-Hill.

Weinstein, C. E., & Hume, L. M. (1998). *Study strategies for lifelong learning.* Washington, DC: American Psychological Association.

Weinstein, C. S. (1999). Reflections on best practices and promising programs: Beyond assertive discipline. In H. J. Freiberg (Ed.),

Beyond behaviorism: Changing the classroom management paradigm (pp. 147–163). Boston: Allyn & Bacon.

Weinstein, C. S. (2003). *Secondary classroom management: Lessons from research and practice.* (2nd ed.). New York: McGraw Hill.

Weinstein, C. S., & Mignano, A. J. (1997). *Elementary classroom management: Lessons from research and practice* (2nd ed.). New York: McGraw-Hill.

Weinstein, C. S., & Mignano, A. (2003). *Elementary classroom management: Lessons from research and practice* (3rd. ed.). New York: McGraw Hill.

Weinstein, R. S. (1996). High standards in a tracked system of schooling: For which students and with what educational supports? *Educational Researcher, 25*(8), 16–19.

Weinstein, R. S., Madison, S. M., & Kuklinski, M. R. (1995). Raising expectations in schooling: Obstacles and opportunities for change. *American Educational Research Journal, 32,* 121–159.

Weissbourd, R. (2003). Moral teachers, moral students. *Educational Leadership, 60*(6), 6–12.

Wells, A. S. (1995). Reexamining social science research on school desegregation. *Teachers College Record, 96*(4), 681–690.

Wells, A. S., & Crain, R. L. (1997). *Stepping over the color line.* New Haven, CT: Yale University Press.

Wells, A. S., Hirshberg, D., Lipton, M., & Oakes, J. (1995). Bounding the case within its context: A constructivist approach to studying detracking reform. *Educational Researcher, 24*(5), 18–24.

Welner, K. (2006). K–12 race-conscious student assignment policies: Law, social science, and diversity. *Review of Educational Research, 76*(3), 349–382.

Wentzel, K. R. (1993). Does being good make the grade? Social behavior and academic competence in middle school. *Journal of Educational Psychology, 85*(2), 357–364.

Wentzel, K. R. (2000). What is it that I'm trying to achieve? Classroom goals from a content perspective. *Contemporary Educational Psychology, 25*(1), 105–115.

Wentzel, K. R. (2003). School adjustment. In W. M. Reynolds & G. E. Miller (Eds.), *Handbook of psychology: Vol. 7. Educational psychology* (pp. 235–258). Hoboken, NJ: Wiley.

Wentzel, K. R., & Asher, S. R. (1995). The academic lives of neglected, rejected, popular, and controversial children. *Child Development, 66,* 754–763.

Wentzel, K. R., Barry, C. M., & Caldwell, K. A. (2004). Friendships in middle school: Influences on motivation and school adjustment. *Journal of Educational Psychology, 96*(2), 195–203.

Wentzel, K. R., & Erdley, C. A. (1993). Strategies for making friends: Relations to social behavior and peer acceptance in early adolescence. *Developmental Psychology, 29,* 819–826.

Wessler, S. L. (2001). Sticks and stones. *Educational Leadership, 58*(4), 28–33.

Westwater, A., & Wolfe, P. (2000). The brain-compatible curriculum. *Educational Leadership, 58*(3), 49–52.

What Works Clearinghouse. (2007). Reviews of research on educational programs. At www.whatworks.gov.

Wheatley, G. H. (1991). Constructivist perspectives on science and mathematics learning. *Science Education, 75,* 9–21.

White, A. G., & Bailey, J. S. (1990). Reducing disruptive behaviors of elementary physical education students with sit and watch. *Journal of Applied Behavior Analysis, 3,* 353–359.

White, B. Y., & Frederiksen, J. R. (1998). Inquiry, modeling, and meta-cognition: Making science accessible to all students. *Cognition and Instruction, 16*(1), 3–118.

White, K. J., & Kistner, J. (1992). The influence of teacher feedback on young children's peer preferences and perceptions. *Developmental Psychology, 28,* 933–940.

Whitehurst, G. J., Epstein, J. N., Angell, A. L., Payne, A. C., Crone, D. A., & Fischel, J. E. (1994). Outcomes of an emergent literacy intervention in Head Start. *Journal of Educational Psychology, 86*(4), 542–555.

Whitehurst, G., Crone, D., Zevenbergen, A., Schultz, M., Velting, O., & Fischel, J. (1999). Outcomes of an emergent literacy intervention from Head Start through second grade. *Journal of Educational Psychology, 91*(2), 261–272.

Whitman, S., Williams, C., & Shah, A. (2004). *Sinai Health System's community health survey: Report 1.* Chicago: Sinai Health System.

Wielkiewicz, R. M. (1995). *Behavior management in the schools: Principles and procedures* (2nd ed.). Boston: Allyn & Bacon.

Wigfield, A., & Eccles, J. (1989). Test anxiety in elementary and secondary students. *Educational Psychologist, 24,* 159–183.

Wigfield, A., & Eccles, J. (2000). Expectancy-value theory of achievement motivation. *Contemporary Educational Psychology, 25*(1), 68–81.

Wigfield, A., Eccles, J. S., & Rodriguez, D. (1998). The development of children's motivation in school contexts. In P. D. Pearson & A. Iran-Nejad (Eds.), *Review of research in education* (pp. 73–118). Washington, DC: American Educational Research Association.

Wigfield, A. L. (1995, April). *Relationship of children's competence beliefs and achievement values to their performance and choice of different activities.* Paper presented at the annual meeting of the American Educational Research Association, San Francisco, CA.

Wiggins, G. (1993). Assessment: Authenticity, context, and validity. *Phi Delta Kappan, 75*(3), 200–214.

Wiggins, G., & McTighe, J. (2006). Examining the teaching life. *Educational Leadership, 63*(6), 26–30.

Wilcox, R. T. (1993). Rediscovering discovery learning. In K. M. Cauley, F. Linder, & J. H. McMillan (Eds.), *Annual Editions: Educational Psychology 93/94.* Guilford, CT: Dushkin.

Wilens, T. E. (1998). *Straight talk about psychiatric medications for kids.* New York: Guilford.

Wiliam, D. (2007). Content then process: Teacher learning communities in the service of formative assessment. In D. B. Reeves (Ed.), *Ahead of the curve: The power of assessment to transform teaching and learning.* Bloomington, IN: Solution Tree.

Wilkins, J. (2000). *Group activities to include students with special needs.* Thousand Oaks, CA: Corwin.

Willard-Holt, C. (2003). Raising expectations for the gifted. *Educational Leadership, 61*(2), 72–75.

Williams, J. E. (1995, April). *Use of learning and study skills among students differing in self-regulated learning efficacy.* Paper presented at the annual meeting of the American Educational Research Association, San Francisco, CA.

Willingham, D. (2002). Allocating student study time. *American Educator, 26*(2), 37–39.

Willingham, D. (2003). Students remember what they think about. *American Educator, 27*(2), 37–41.

Willingham, D. T. (2004). Practice makes perfect—but only if you practice beyond the point of perfection. *American Educator, 28*(1), 31–33.

Willingham, D. T. (2006). Brain-based learning: More fiction than fact. *American Educator.* Fall 2006.

Willis, J. (2007). *Research-based strategies to ignite student learning: Insights from a neurologist and classroom teacher.* City, State: ASCD.

Willis, J. A. (2006). Research-based teaching strategies for improving learning success. California Association of Independent Schools (CAIS) *Faculty Newsletter.*

Willoughby, T., Porter, L., Belsito, L., & Yearsley, T. (1999). Use of elaboration strategies by students in grades, two, four, and six. *The Elementary School Journal, 99*(3), 221–232.

Windschitl, M. (1999). The challenges of sustaining a constructivist classroom culture. *Phi Delta Kappan, 80*(10), 751–755.

Winebrenner, S. (2000). Gifted students need an education, too. *Educational Leadership, 58*(1), 52–56.

Winett, R. A., & Winkler, R. C. (1972). Current behavior modification in the classroom: Be still, be quiet, be docile. *Journal of Applied Behavior Analysis, 5,* 499–504.

Winn, W. (1991). Learning from maps and diagrams. *Educational Psychology Review, 3,* 211–247.

Winne, P. (2006). How software technologies can improve research on learning and bolster school reform. *Educational Psychologist, 41*(1), 5–17.

Winne, P. H. (1997). Experimenting to bootstrap self-regulated learning. *Journal of Educational Psychology, 89*(3), 397–410.

Wittrock, M. C. (1991). Generative teaching of comprehension. *Elementary School Journal, 92,* 169–184.

Wittrock, M. C., & Alesandrini, K. (1990). Generation of summaries and analogies and analytic and holistic abilities. *American Educational Research Journal, 27,* 489–502.

Wong, H., & Wong, R. (2004). *The first days of school: How to be an effective teacher.* Mountain View, CA: Harry K. Wong Publications.

Wong, H. K., Bernstein, L., & Shevick, E. (1978). *Life science: Ideas and investigations in science* (2nd ed.). Englewood Cliffs, NJ: Prentice Hall.

Wong, K. K., Sunderman, G. L., & Lee, J. (1995). *When federal Title I works to improve student learning in inner-city schools: Final report on the implementation of schoolwide projects in Minneapolis and Houston.* Chicago: University of Chicago Press.

Wong, L. Y. S. (1995). Research on teaching: Process-product research findings and the feeling of obviousness. *Journal of Educational Psychology, 87,* 504–511.

Wood, D. J., Bruner, J. S., & Ross, G. (1976). The role of tutoring in problem solving. *Journal of Child Psychology and Psychiatry, 17,* 89–100.

Woodring, T. (1995). *Effects of peer education programs on sexual behavior, AIDS knowledge, and attitudes.* Paper presented at the annual meeting of the Eastern Psychological Association, Boston, MA.

Woodward, J., & Cuban, L. (Eds.). (2001). *Technology, curriculum, and professional development: Adapting schools to meet the needs of students with disabilities.* Thousand Oaks, CA: Corwin.

Worthen, B. R., & Spandel, V. (1993). Putting the standardized test debate in perspective. In K. M. Cauley, F. Linder, & J. H. McMillan (Eds.), *Annual Editions: Educational Psychology 93/94.* Guilford, CT: Dushkin.

Wright, J. C., Huston, A. C., Murphy, C., St. Peters, M., Pinon, M., Scantlin, R. M., & Kotler, J. A. (2001). The relations of early television viewing to school readiness and vocabulary of children from low-income families: The early window projects. *Child Development, 72,* 1347–1366.

Wyra, M., Lawson, M., & Hungi, N. (2007). The mnemonic keyword method: The effects of bidirectional retrieval training and of ability to image on foreign language vocabulary recall. *Learning and Instruction, 17*(3), 360–371.

Xu, J., & Corno, L. (2003). Family help and homework management reported by middle school students. *The Elementary School Journal, 103*(5), 503–517.

Yeung, J., Linver, M., & Brooks-Gunn, J. (2002). How money matters for young children's development: Human capital and family process. *Child Development, 73,* 1861–1879.

Yonezawa, S., Wells, A. S., & Serna, I. (2002). Choosing tracks: "Freedom of choice" in detracking schools. *American Educational Research Journal, 39*(1), 37–67.

Zehr, M. (2007, May 8). NCLB seen as a damper on bilingual education programs. Retrieved February 19, 2008 from www.edweek.org/ew/articles/2007/05/09/36biling.h26.html.

Zeidner, M. (1995). Adaptive coping with test situations: A review of the literature. *Educational Psychologist, 30*(3), 123–133.

Zellermayer, M., Salomon, G., Globerson, T., & Givon, H. (1991). Enhancing writing-related metacognitions through a computerized writing partner. *American Educational Research Journal, 28,* 373–391.

Zettergren, P. (2003). School adjustment in adolescence for previously rejected, average and popular children. *British Journal of Educational Psychology, 72*(3), 207–221.

Zhao, Y., & Frank, K. A. (2003). Factors affecting technology uses in schools: An ecological perspective. *American Educational Research Journal, 40*(4), 807–840.

Zigler, E., & Gilman, E. (1998). *The legacy of Jean Piaget.* Mahwah, NJ: Erlbaum.

Zigmond, M. (2003). Where should students with disabilities receive special education services? Is one place better than another? *The Journal of Special Education, 37*(3), 193–199.

Zimmerman, B. (2000). Self-efficacy: An essential motive to learn. *Contemporary Educational Psychology, 25*(1), 82–91.

Zimmerman, B., & Kitsantas, A. (1999). Acquiring writing revision skill: Shifting from process to outcome self-regulatory goals. *Journal of Educational Psychology, 91*(2), 241–250.

Zimmerman, B. J. (1995). Self-regulation involves more than metacognition: A social cognitive perspective. *Educational Psychologist, 30,* 217–221.

Zimmerman, B. J. (1998, April). *Achieving academic excellence: The role of perceived efficacy and self-regulatory skill.* Paper presented at the annual meeting of the American Educational Research Association, San Diego, CA.

Zimmerman, B. J. (2000). Attaining self-regulation: A social cognitive perspective. In M. Boekaerts, P. R. Pintrich, & M. Zeidner (Eds.). *Handbook of self-regulation* (pp. 13–39). San Diego, CA: Academic Press.

Zimmerman, B. J., & Bandura, A. (1994). Impact of self-regulatory influences on writing course attainment. *American Educational Research Journal, 31,* 845–862.

Zimmerman, B. J., & Kitsantas, A. (2002). Acquiring writing revision and self-regulatory skill through observation and emulation. *Journal of Educational Psychology, 94*(4), 660–668.

Zimmerman, B. J., & Schunk, D. H. (Eds.) (2003). *Educational psychology: A century of contributions.* Mahwah, NJ: Erlbaum.

Zittleman, K., & Sadker, D. (2003). The unfinished gender revolution. *Educational Leadership, 60*(4), 59–62.

Ziv, A. (1988). Teaching and learning with humor: Experiment and replication. *Journal of Experimental Education, 57,* 5–18.

Zwiers, J. (2005). The third language of academic English. *Educational Leadership, 62*(4), 60–63.

Name Index

Credits

Text Credit

pp. 36–37, from *Winnie-the-Pooh* by A. A. Milne, illustrated by E. H. Shepard, copyright 1926 by E. P. Dutton, renewed 1954 by A. A. Milne. Used by permission of the Pooh Properties Trust and by permission of Dutton Children's Books, a division of Penguin Young Readers Group, a member of Penguin Group (USA) Inc., 345 Hudson Street, New York, NY 10014. All rights reserved.

Photo Credits

p. xxxviii, GeoStock/Getty; p. 3, Will Hart; p. 6, JLP/Jose L. Pelaez/Corbis; p. 11, Bill Aron/PhotoEdit; p. 28, John Terence Turner/Getty; p. 36, Laura Dwight/Corbis; p. 44, Frank Sherman/PhotoEdit; p. 48, Tony Freeman/PhotoEdit; p. 53, Tony Freeman/PhotoEdit; p. 62, SW Productions/Getty; p. 67, David Young-Wolff/PhotoEdit; p. 70, Will Faller; p. 71, Mark Richards/PhotoEdit; p. 82, Myrleen Ferguson Cate/PhotoEdit; p. 85, Ed Quinn/Corbis; p. 90, Richard Hutchings/PhotoEdit; p. 94, Alan Weiner/Getty; p. 110, Christina Kennedy/PhotoEdit; p. 114, Ezra Shaw/Getty; p. 114, Alik Keplicz/AP; p. 117, Will Hart; p. 126, Ariel Skelley/Corbis; p. 131, Nina Leen/Stringer/Getty; p. 132, Will Hart; p. 138, Corbis; p. 138, Jim Cummins Studio, Inc./Corbis; p. 148, Bill Aron/PhotoEdit; p. 156, Robin Sachs/PhotoEdit; p. 166, Myrleen Ferguson Cate/PhotoEdit; p. 173, Will Hart; p. 176, Myrleen Ferguson Cate/PhotoEdit; p. 188, Bill Aron/PhotoEdit; p. 196, Peter M. Fisher/Corbis; p. 207, Syracuse Newspapers/Image Works; p. 209, Bob Daemmrich/Bob Daemmrich Photography, Inc.; p. 217, Steve Craft/Masterfile; p. 223, Michael Newman/PhotoEdit; p. 228, Robin Sachs/PhotoEdit; p. 237, Michael Newman/PhotoEdit; p. 243, Corbis; p. 244, Gary Conner/PhotoEdit; p. 250, Will Hart; p. 255, Bob Daemmrich/Bob Daemmrich Photography, Inc.; p. 260, JLP/Jose L. Pelaez/Corbis; p. 264, Cleve Bryant/PhotoEdit; p. 268, Michael Newman/PhotoEdit; p. 272, Mary Kate Denny/Getty; p. 280, Jonathan Nourok/PhotoEdit; p. 288, Michael Newman/PhotoEdit; p. 294, Lawrence Migdale; p. 302, STR/Stringer/Getty; p. 312, Will Hart; p. 316, Will Hart; p. 320, Jose Luis Pelaez, Inc./Corbis; p. 326, Jim Craigmyle/Corbis; p. 331, Frank Siteman; p. 338, Will Hart; p. 346, Will Faller; p. 357, Bill Aron/PhotoEdit; p. 362, Robin Sachs/PhotoEdit; p. 377, Robin Sachs/PhotoEdit; p. 376, Michael Newman/PhotoEdit; p. 390, Michael Newman/PhotoEdit; p. 392, Bill Bachmann/PhotoEdit; p. 404, Bob Daemmrich Photography/Image Works; p. 409, Bob Daemmrich/Bob Daemmrich Photography, Inc.; p. 414, Will Faller; p. 417, Cindy Charles/PhotoEdit; p. 421, Tony Freeman/PhotoEdit; p. 439, Dana White/PhotoEdit; p. 454, Jose Luis Pelaez, Inc./Corbis/Bettmann; p. 459, Alex Wong/Staff/Getty; p. 464, Elizabeth Crews; p. 474, Frank Siteman/PhotoEdit; p. 474, Mark Richards/PhotoEdit.

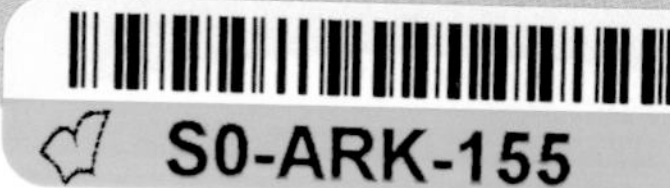

Organizational Behavior

Emerging Realities for the Workplace Revolution

Organizational Behavior

Steven L. McShane
The University of Western Australia

Mary Ann Von Glinow
Florida International University

4th Edition

Boston Burr Ridge, IL Dubuque, IA Madison, WI New York San Francisco St. Louis
Bangkok Bogotá Caracas Kuala Lumpur Lisbon London Madrid Mexico City
Milan Montreal New Delhi Santiago Seoul Singapore Sydney Taipei Toronto

ORGANIZATIONAL BEHAVIOR:
EMERGING REALITIES FOR THE WORKPLACE REVOLUTION
Published by McGraw-Hill/Irwin, a business unit of The McGraw-Hill Companies, Inc., 1221 Avenue of the Americas, New York, NY, 10020.
Some ancillaries, including electronic and print components, may not be available to customers outside the United States.

This book is printed on acid-free paper.
Printed in China

5 6 7 8 9 0 CTP/CTP 0 9 8 7

ISBN 978-0-07-110104-2
MHID 0-07-110104-7

www.mhhe.com

about the authors

Steven L. McShane

Steven L. McShane is Professor of Management in the Graduate School of Management at the University of Western Australia, where he receives high teaching ratings from students in Perth, Singapore, and other cities in Asia where UWA offers its programs. He is also an Honorary Professor at Universiti Tunku Abdul Rahman (UTAR) in Malaysia and previously taught in the business faculties at Simon Fraser University and Queen's University in Canada. Steve has conducted executive seminars with Nokia, Wesfarmers Group, ALCOA World Alumina Australia, and many other organiztions. He is also a popular visiting speaker, having given four-dozen talks to faculty and students in almost a dozen countries over the past three years.

Steve earned his Ph.D. from Michigan State University in organizational behavior, human resource management, and labor relations. He also holds a Master of Industrial Relations from the University of Toronto, and an undergraduate degree from Queen's University in Canada. Steve has served as President of the Administrative Sciences Association of Canada (the Canadian equivalent of the Academy of Management) and Director of Graduate Programs in the business faculty at Simon Fraser University.

Along with co-authoring *Organizational Behavior*, 4e, Steve is the author of *Canadian Organizational Behaviour* 6th ed. (2006) and co-author (with Tony Travaglione) of *Organisational Behaviour on the Pacific Rim*, 2e (2007) and co-author (with Mary Ann von Glinow) of *Organizational Behavior: Essentials* (2007). He has also published several dozen articles, book chapters, and conference papers on diverse topics, including managerial decision making, organizational learning, socialization of new employees, gender bias in job evaluation, wrongful dismissal, media bias in business magazines, and labor union participation.

Steve enjoys spending his leisure time swimming, body board surfing, canoeing, skiing, and traveling with his wife and two daughters.

Mary Ann Von Glinow

Dr. Von Glinow is Director of the Center for International Business Education and Research (CIBER) and is Research Professor of Management and International Business at Florida International University. She also is the 2006 Vice President of the Academy of International Business (AIB) and an editor of JIBS. Previously on the Marshall School faculty of the University of Southern California, she has an MBA and Ph. D in Management Science from The Ohio State University. Dr. Von Glinow was the 1994-95 President of the Academy of Management, the world's largest association of academicians in management and is a Fellow of the Academy, and the Pan Pacific Business Association. She sits on eleven editorial review boards and numerous international panels. She teaches in executive programs in Latin America, Central America, the Caribbean region, Asia and the U.S.

Dr. Von Glinow has authored over 100 journal articles and eleven books. Her most recent include *Managing Multinational Teams*, by Elsevier 2005; *Organizational Learning Capability* by Oxford University Press, 1999 (in Chinese and Spanish translation) which won a Gold Book Award from the Ministry of Economic Affairs in Taiwan in 2002. She also has a popular textbook: *Organizational Behavior*, 2007, McGraw-Hill/Irwin and a recently published *OB Essentials* (2007). She heads an international consortium of researchers delving into "Best International Human Resource Management Practices," and her research in this arena won an award from the American Society for Competitiveness' Board of Trustees. She also received an NSF grant to study globally-distributed work. Dr. Von Glinow is the 2005 Academy of Management recipient of the Distinguished Service Award, one of the Academy's 3 highest honors bestowed.

Mary Ann consults to a number of domestic and multinational enterprises, and serves as a mayoral appointee to the Shanghai Institute of Human Resources in China. Since 1989, she has been a consultant in General Electric's "Work-out" and "Change Acceleration Program" including "Coaching to Management." Her clients have included Asia Development Bank, American Express, Diageo, Knight-Ridder, Burger King, Pillsbury, Westinghouse, Southern California Edison, The Aetna, State of Florida, Kaiser Permanente, TRW, Rockwell Int'l, Motorola, N.Y. Life, Amoco, Lucent, and Joe's Stone Crabs, to name a few. She is on the Board of Friends of WLRN, Fielding University, Friends of Bay Oaks, Pan-Pacific Business Association and Animal Alliance in Los Angeles. She is actively involved in several animal welfare organizations and received the 1996 Humanitarian Award of the Year from Miami's Adopt-a-Pet.

Dedicated with love and devotion to Donna, and to our wonderful daughters, Bryton and Madison

—S.L.M.

To my family and my virtual, globally-distributed family!

—M.A.V.G.

brief contents

contents

preface

Welcome to a new era of organizational behavior! Virtual teams are replacing committees. Values and self-leadership are replacing command-and-control supervision. Knowledge is replacing infrastructure. Companies are looking for employees with emotional intelligence, not just technical smarts. Globalization has become the mantra of corporate survival. Co-workers aren't down the hall; they're at the other end of an Internet connection located somewhere else on the planet.

Organizational Behavior, Fourth Edition, is written in the context of these emerging workplace realities. This edition explains how emotions guide employee motivation, attitudes, and decisions; how values have become the new resource to shape workplace behavior; how companies rely on creativity and a learning orientation as their source of competitive advantage in the knowledge economy; and how appreciative inquiry has become one of the emerging strategies for organizational change. This book also presents the new reality that organizational behavior is not just for managers; it is relevant and useful to anyone who works in and around organizations.

Linking Theory with Reality

Every chapter of *Organizational Behavior,* Fourth Edition, is filled with real-life examples to make OB concepts more meaningful and reflect the relevance and excitement of this field. For example, you will read how Whole Foods Market applies a "yoghurt culture" model to maintain and strengthen its organizational culture as it expands; how W. L. Gore & Associates remains nimble through an organizational structure that has no bosses; how Dubai's Department of Economic Development is becoming a values-based organization; how DaimlerChysler is racing to improve productivity and quality through self-directed work teams in Mexico and the United States; and how Sun Microsystems and IBM are improving internal and external communication through blogs and wikis.

These real-life stories appear in many forms. Every chapter of *Organizational Behavior,* Fourth Edition, offers several detailed photo captions and many more in-text anecdotes. Lengthier stories are distinguished in a feature we call *Connections,* because it "connects" OB concepts with real organizational incidents. Case studies in each chapter and video case studies in each part also connect OB concepts to the emerging workplace realities. These stories provide representation across the United States and around the planet. They also cover a wide range of industries–from software to government, and from small businesses to the Fortune 500.

Global Orientation

One of the first things you might notice about this book is its strong global orientation. This goes beyond the traditional practice of describing how U.S. companies operate in other parts of the world. Instead, this book takes a truly global approach by continually illustrating how organizational behavior concepts and practices are relevant to companies in every part of the world. For example, you will read how Nitro, the Shanghai-based boutique advertising agency, is taking the world by storm with its organic structure; how Panafric Hotel in Nairobi, Kenya, motivates its employees with good old-fashioned recognition; how John Fletcher, CEO of Australian retailer Coles Myer Group, is maintaining the momentum for change after the company's significant improvements to date; and how Infosys, one of India's leading information technology services companies, is developing a better understanding of organizational leadership.

This global orientation is also apparent in our discussion of many organizational behavior topics. The first chapter of *Organizational Behavior,* Fourth Edition, introduces the concept of globalization. Global issues are then highlighted throughout this book, such as cross-cultural values and ethics, job satisfaction and displaying emotions in different societies, employee stress from overwork in China and Japan, cross-cultural issues in the success of self-directed work teams, problems with cross-cultural communication, cultural values and expectations as a factor in the preferred influence tactics, cross-cultural conflict, and preferred leadership styles across cultures.

Active Learning and Critical Thinking Support

We teach organizational behavior, so we understand how important it is to use a textbook that offers deep support for active learning and critical thinking. The fact that business school accreditation associations also emphasize the importance of the learning experience further reinforces our attention on classroom activities. *Organizational Behavior,* Fourth Edition, includes more than two-dozen case studies, many written by instructors from the United States, Mexico, Canada, Malaysia, and Australia. It offers three-dozen self-assessments, including scales that measure emerging concepts such as Guanxi orientation and resilience. This book is also a rich resource for in-class activities, some of which are not available in other organizational behavior textbooks, such as Where in the World are We? and the Cross-Cultural Communication Game.

Contemporary Theory Foundation

Organizational Behavior, Fourth Edition, has a solid foundation of contemporary and classic scholarship. You can see this in the references. Each chapter is based on dozens of articles, books, and other sources. The most recent literature receives thorough coverage, resulting in what we believe is the most up-to-date organizational behavior textbook available. These references also reveal that we reach out to information systems, marketing, and other disciplines for new ideas. At the same time, this textbook is written for students, not the scholars whose work is cited. So, while this book provides new knowledge and its practical implications, you won't find detailed summaries of specific research studies. Also, this textbook rarely names specific researchers and their university affiliations; it focuses on organizational behavior knowledge rather than "who's-who" in the field.

Organizational Behavior was the first textbook in this field to discuss workplace emotions, affective events theory (but without the jargon), somatic marker theory (also without the jargon), social identity theory, appreciative inquiry, bicultural audits, future search events, Schwartz's values model, the effects of job satisfaction on customer service, learning orientation, workaholism, and several other groundbreaking topics. Along with documenting numerous ongoing developments in OB knowledge, this edition continues to lead the way with the latest knowledge on four-drive theory, resilience, employee engagement, communication blogs and wikis, separating socio-emotional conflict from constructive conflict, exceptions to media richness theory, employer branding, problems in identifying opportunities, Goleman's emotional intelligence model, and the automaticity and emotionality of the perceptual process.

Organizational Behavior Knowledge for Everyone

Another distinctive feature of *Organizational Behavior*, Fourth Edition, is that it is written for everyone in organizations, not just "managers". The new reality is that people throughout the organization–systems analysts, production employees, accounting professionals–are assuming more responsibilities as companies remove layers of bureaucracy and give non-management staff more autonomy over their work. Consequently, the philosophy of this book is that everyone who works in and around organizations needs to understand and make use of organizational behavior knowledge.

Changes to the Fourth Edition

Organizational Behavior, Fourth Edition, is the result of reviews over the past three years by more than 100 organizational behavior scholars and teachers in several countries. Chapter structure changes in the previous (3rd) edition proved very popular with instructors, so this 4th edition largely keeps the previous organization of chapters. In addition to substantially updated examples throughout the book, most of the improvements to this edition are in the new and updated topics summarized below:

- *Chapter 1: Introduction to the Field of Organizational Behavior.* This chapter offers more details about work-life balance and reorganizes the organizational behavior trends to include virtual work as a theme. This chapter also updates discussion of globalization effects, such as offshoring and work intensity, and introduces surface and deep level diversity concepts in the section on workforce diversity.
- *Chapter 2: Individual Behavior, Values, and Personality.* This chapter introduces students to the emerging concept of employee engagement, and links this concept to the MARS model of individual behaviour and performance. It also introduces employer branding and guerrilla recruitment to attract job applicants. The section on personal values is also updated with more details about different forms of values congruence.
- *Chapter 3: Perception and Learning in Organizations.* This chapter reflects current thinking about selective attention, organization, and interpretation as automatic unconscious emotional (rather than logical/mechanical) processes. It also writes about categorical thinking as part of the perceptual process, introduces "thin slices" research on perceptions, updates the highly popular concept of social identity theory, provides new details about when self-fulfilling prophecy is more (or less) likely to occur, adds new cross-cultural information about fundamental attribution error, introduces the concept of positive organizational behavior, and further highlights the importance of the learning orientation concept in experiential learning.
- *Chapter 4: Workplace Emotions and Attitudes.* This edition describes the emotions-attitudes-behavior model more clearly in two parts (cognitive vs emotional) and includes discussion of situations where cognitions and emotions conflict with each other. It also describes the important marketing concept about how people "listen in" on their emotions when forming attitudes. This chapter also updates discussion of emotional display norms across cultures, and includes shared values as a predictor of organizational commitment.
- *Chapter 5: Motivation in the Workplace.* Recognizing that needs hierarchy models lack research support, *Organizational Behavior* was the first OB textbook to introduce four-drive theory as an alternative model to understand the dynamics of needs and drives in organizational settings. This edition further explains how that model works, and identifies its implications for practice in the workplace. This chapter also explains the ongoing relevance of Maslow's ideas, and further emphasizes the role of procedural justice in organizational justice.
- *Chapter 6: Applied Performance Practices.* This chapter has relatively minor changes. The chapter is somewhat shorter in this edition by condensing the section on the meaning of money and types of rewards. The chapter also refines some of the

details about scientific management and updates details about how self-leadership is applied in the workplace.

- *Chapter 7: Work-Related Stress and Stress Management.* This edition introduces the important emerging concept of resilience as an individual difference in the reaction to stress. Psychological harassment has been added to this edition, integrating previous edition writing on workplace bullying. The chapter also cites three explanations for the increasing incidence of work overload, and offers a little more detail on how companies monitor or audit stress in the workplace.
- *Chapter 8: Decision Making and Creativity.* The chapter offers a brief history of the origins of the rational choice paradigm. It provides a clearer overview of the reasons why decision makers have difficulty identifying problems, and identifies three ways that emotions affect the evaluation of alternatives. This edition also introduces new evidence about escalation of commitment, intuition in decision making, and how people evaluate opportunities.
- *Chapter 9: Foundations of Team Dynamics.* This edition more explicitly explains why organizations rely on teams. It also lists several types of formal teams in organizations, adds new information about faultlines in team diversity, and provides more details about Brooks's law (mythical man-month).
- *Chapter 10: Developing High Performance Teams.* This chapter further refines our knowledge of self-directed work teams and sociotechnical systems theory. It also updates the section on team trust, including propensity to trust as an individual difference. This chapter also incorporates new research on team decision making, including new knowledge about constructive conflict, groupthink, and brainstorming
- *Chapter 11: Communicating in Teams and Organizations.* Along with updating information about e-mail and instant messaging, this edition discusses the role of blogs and wikis in corporate communication. This chapter also provides new information about the exceptions to media richness, as well as employee attitudes toward the organizational grapevine.
- *Chapter 12: Power and Influence in the Workplace.* This chapter updates our knowledge of power and influence derived from social networks. It organizes influence tactics more clearly around hard and soft tactics, and introduces three contingencies to consider when applying various influence tactics.
- *Chapter 13: Conflict and Negotiation in the Workplace.* This edition offers new information about the relationship between constructive (task-related) conflict and socioemotional conflict, and identifies ways to minimize the latter while engaging in the former. It also summarizes current thinking about how to minimize conflict through communication and understanding. including the role of talking circles.
- *Chapter 14: Leadership in Organizational Settings.* This chapter further elaborates the concept of shared leadership. It also updates information about leadership substitutes, the implicit leadership perspective, and gender differences in leadership. In addition, it provides further evidence separating charismatic from transformational leadership.
- *Chapter 15: Organizational Structure.* This edition updates information about coordination mechanisms, the optimal level of decentralization, and problems with matrix structures. It revises and updates writing on the divisionalized structure, including challenges in choosing the preferred divisionalized structure. The section on contingencies of organizational design has been re-organized to emphasize the external environment as a central contingency.

- *Chapter 16: Organizational Culture.* This chapter revises the organizational culture model to reflect emerging views on its elements. It sharpens the focus on the advantages and limitations of strong organizational cultures. The section on changing and strengthening organizational culture has been revised to reflect key issues and more detailed discussion of these practices.
- *Chapter 17: Organizational Change.* This chapter provides additional information about creating an urgency to change and diffusing change from a pilot project. It also updates information on contingencies of appreciative inquiry.

Supporting the Learning Process

The changes described above refer only to the text material. *Organizational Behavior*, Fourth Edition, also has improved technology supplements, cases, videos, team exercises, and self-assessments. The detailed Walkthrough on the following pages highlights the many learning features available to students and instructors who adopt *Organizational Behavior*, Fourth Edition.

Student-Focused Learning Features

With its core philosophy being "OB is for everyone," every chapter of **Organizational Behavior** is filled with innovative features and exercises to help students learn and apply the knowledge they've gained from chapter material.

What does a swarm of robot bees sound like? Cory Hawthorne tried to figure that out by listening to dozens of sounds and loops. Suddenly the sound effects specialist at Radical Entertainment found the right combination when he mixed his humming through a kazoo with the noise of operating an electric beard trimmer across the surface of his bathtub. The robot bees now had a menacing audio effect in the electronic game that Hawthorne was working on: *The Simpsons: Hit and Run.*

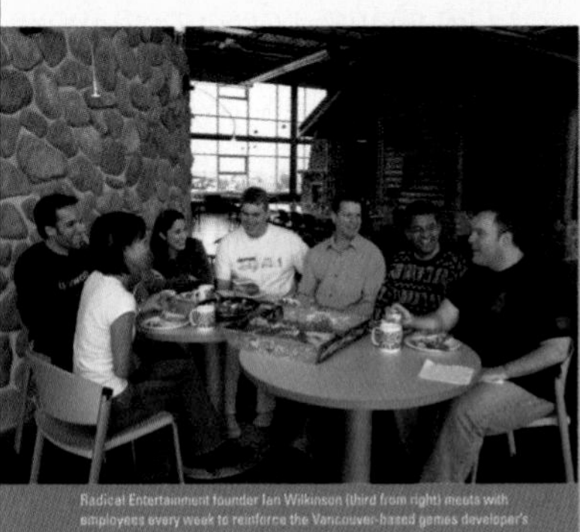
Radical Entertainment founder Ian Wilkinson (third from right) meets with employees every week to reinforce the Vancouver-based games developer's emphasis on creative decision making and employee involvement.

Radical depends on Cory Hawthorne and its other 230 employees to have plenty of such discovery moments to succeed in the competitive video game marketplace. "Hit games are made by people who have the freedom and support to put unconventional ideas in motion," explains Ian Wilkinson, founder and CEO of the Vancouver, Canada, company (now a division of Los Angeles–based Vivendi Universal Games). "So we give our employees the autonomy to drive real change, whatever their role in the company. No other game developer offers this level of creative freedom."

Danielle Michael, Radical's vice president of business development, echoes Wilkinson's view that the best decisions in this fast-paced industry come from employee involvement and autonomy: "People are hugely empowered to be creative, to go beyond the call of duty to come up with great ideas and to actually implement them," says Michael.

To help guide employee decision making, posters hung throughout Radical's headquarters state the company's succinct values, including this one: "Take risks, always learn." Wilkinson takes these values seriously. He lunches with a half dozen employees each week (as shown in this photo—Wilkinson is third from the right), encouraging them to apply the company's values in their everyday decisions.

Creative ideas are also cross-pollinated through Radical's monthly "game fair" day, in which teams show off their products and make presentations to other teams in the organization. "I don't want to be hearing what other companies are doing," Wilkinson advises staff. "I want to do innovative stuff and have some people say we're crazy."[1]

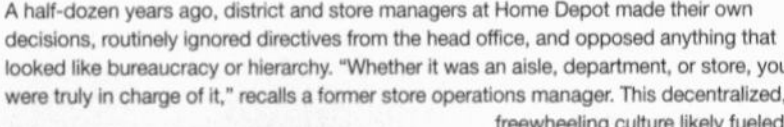

A half-dozen years ago, district and store managers at Home Depot made their own decisions, routinely ignored directives from the head office, and opposed anything that looked like bureaucracy or hierarchy. "Whether it was an aisle, department, or store, you were truly in charge of it," recalls a former store operations manager. This decentralized, freewheeling culture likely fueled Home Depot's phenomenal growth, but it turned into a liability when Lowe's and Wal-Mart brought more intense competition to the marketplace. Home Depot needed more structure and efficiency, so the board of directors plucked Robert Nardelli from General Electric (GE) to become the new CEO and chief architect for change. His objective, not surprisingly, was to "GE-ize" Home Depot, turning it into a much more regimented, centralized, and measurement-focused organization.

Home Depot CEO Robert Nardelli has dramatically changed the big box retailer's culture by introducing systems that reinforce the new values.

Nardelli took a structural approach to change by introducing precise measures of corporate performance and drilling managers with weekly performance objectives around those metrics. The previous hodge-podge of subjective performance reviews was replaced with one centralized fact-based system to evaluate store managers and weed out poor performers. Nardelli instituted quarterly business review meetings in which objective measures of revenue, margins, inventory turns, cash flow, and other key indicators were analyzed across stores and regions. A two-hour weekly conference call became a ritual in which Home Depot's top executives were held accountable for the previous week's goals.

These changes occurred with lightning speed. "The rate of change internally has to be greater than the rate of change externally or else you're pedaling backward," advises Nardelli. For example, Dennis Donovan, one of several GE alumni Nardelli hired into key management posts, was given 90 days to develop a centralized purchasing system that would leverage more buying power than the existing decentralized process. "In the game of change, velocity is your friend," says Donovan, adding that Nardelli works by a stopwatch, not a time clock.

These rapid structural change interventions have helped Home Depot increase operating efficiency and double sales and profits over Nardelli's first five years. Employee engagement scores initially suffered, but they have now risen above the industry average. However, critics point out that these changes resulted in the departure of almost all of Home Depot's top management as well as ongoing turnover rates well above those at Lowe's. "[Nardelli's] lost so much good talent out of that place," observes one former executive. "The guys I still talk to there say they're waiting for the next shoe to drop."

Equally troubling is that Home Depot's customer service levels have sunk to new lows (one survey ranks Home Depot dead last among major U.S. retailers). "[Nardelli's] made Home Depot much more profitable and more streamlined, but messed up everything that has to do with serving the customer," complains one retail consultant. Wall Street isn't impressed, either; Home Depot's share price hasn't budged since Nardelli arrived.[1]

OPENING VIGNETTE

Each chapter begins with an engaging **opening vignette** that sets the stage for the chapter. These brief but interesting case studies introduce students to critical issues, challenge their preconceptions, and highlight some of today's hottest companies.

Foundations of Team Dynamics

LEARNING OBJECTIVES

After reading this chapter you should be able to

1. Define *teams* and distinguish them from informal groups.
2. Discuss the potential benefits of teams in organizations.
3. Outline the model of team effectiveness.
4. Identify six organizational and team environmental elements that influence team effectiveness.
5. Explain how a team's task, size, and composition influence its effectiveness.
6. Summarize the team development process.
7. Discuss how team norms develop and are maintained and how they may be altered.
8. List six factors that influence team cohesiveness.
9. Discuss the limitations of teams.
10. Explain how companies minimize social loafing.

LEARNING OBJECTIVES

A topical guide for the student, a list of Learning Objectives not only can be found at the beginning of each chapter, but correspondingly throughout chapter.

Chapter 9 *Foundations of Team Dynamics* 261

any special circumstances or ulterior motives. A second explanation is provided by social identity theory, which states that individuals define themselves by their group affiliations. Thus we join informal groups–particularly groups viewed favorably by others and that are similar to our existing values–because they shape and reinforce our self-images.[9]

A third reason why people join informal groups is to accomplish tasks that cannot be achieved by individuals working alone. For example, employees will sometimes form a group to oppose organizational changes because the group collectively has more power than individuals complaining alone. A fourth explanation for informal groups is that in stressful situations we are comforted by the mere presence of other people and are therefore motivated to be near them. When in danger, people congregate near each other even though it serves no apparent purpose. Similarly, employees tend to mingle more often when hearing rumors that the company might be sold.[10]

Learning Objectives

After reading the next three sections you should be able to

3. **Outline the model of team effectiveness.**
4. **Identify six organizational and team environmental elements that influence team effectiveness.**
5. **Explain how a team's task, size, and composition influence its effectiveness.**

CAPTIONS BEYOND CURSORY

Going beyond the simple caption, richly detailed photos are accompanied by more in-depth narrative.

Chapter 5 Motivation in the Workplace 137

Belongingness Needs Top the Hierarchy for Some Employees These UBS Warburg employees in Chicago seem to be enjoying each other's company, suggesting that they are experiencing some fulfillment of their belongingness needs. But do they all have the same needs hierarchy? Not according to emerging research and writing on this subject. Contrary to Maslow's well-known theory, needs are not hardwired into a universal hierarchy. Instead a person's needs hierarchy seems to be strongly influenced by his or her value system, so needs hierarchies vary from one person to the next and possibly from one culture to the next. The UBS Warburg staff in this photo probably have somewhat different value systems, so their needs hierarchies would be different.

motivation experts had splintered needs and drives into dozens of categories, each studied in isolation using nontypical subjects (usually animals or people with severe

Connections 4.1

Serious Fun

Walk into the offices of CXtec in Syracuse, New York, and you might think employees are in the middle of a birthday party. Around the cubicles are colorful clusters of helium-filled balloons, each representing a small token of the company's appreciation for performing their work effectively. Employees at the computer networking equipment company also enjoy a break room with billiards, foosball, and air hockey. And if staff want a little more enjoyment, the company also sponsors miniature golf tournaments in the office, tricycle races around the building, and "CXtec Idol" competitions. Of course all of this fits in with what the company stands for: "Part of our core values is that work is fun," explains Paula Miller, CXtec's director of employee and community relations.

Fun at work? It sounds like an oxymoron. But to attract and motivate valuable talent, companies are finding creative ways to generate positive emotions in the workplace. About six times each year, credit department staff at Zebra Technologies in Vernon Hills, Illinois, head off to the Whirlyball center, a large rink where employees grab and toss a ball using handheld scoops and electric bumper cars. The Malaysian operations of Scope International, a division of British bank Standard Chartered, won an award for bringing fun into the workplace—such as color coordination days, in which employees wear the same color clothing on a particular day. Along with enjoying office nerf gun fights, robot combat tournaments, movie nights, and wine tours, employees at Nuvation in San Jose, California, showcase a life-size fiberglass blue and orange moose. "We like to take the moose out to our parties," says Nuvation cofounder Geoff White.

These fun and games may seem silly, but some corporate leaders are serious about their value. "It's pretty simple," explains an executive at Quebecor. "If you want to make the most money, you must attract the best people. To get the best people, you must be the most fun."

CXtec employees in Syracuse, New York, like to live up to their company values, which include having fun at work.

Sources: J. Elliott, "All Work and No Play Can Chase Workers Away," *Edmonton Journal*, 28 February 2000; M.A. Tan, "Management: Having Fun at Work," *The Edge Malaysia*, 10 February 2003; R. Deruyter, "Firm's Goals Are Business Success and Having Fun," *Kitchener-Waterloo Record*, 30 October 2004, p. F1; S.K. Wong, "How Do Some Big companies Spell Teamwork? Whirlyball," *The Columbian* (Vancouver, WA), 19 March 2006, p. E1; T. Knauss, "Small Company Is a Happy Place to Work," *Post Standard/Herald-Journal* (Syracuse, New York), 21 March 2006, p. A1.

CONNECTIONS

Connections boxes connect OB concepts with real organizational incidents.

End-of-Chapter Material Geared Toward Application

SELF-ASSESSMENTS

Experiential exercises and **self-assessments** represent an important part of the active learning process. *Organizational Behavior*, Fourth Edition, offers one or two **team exercises** in every chapter. Many of these learning activities are not available in other organizational behavior textbooks, such as "Where in the World are We?" (Chapter 8) and "A Cross-Cultural Communication Game" (Chapter 11). This edition has **three-dozen self-assessments** in the book or part of the premium content offered with the Online Learning Center or Enhanced Cartridges for course management systems. The self-assessments feature personalize the meaning of several organizational behavior concepts, such as workaholism, corporate culture preferences, self-leadership, empathy, stress, creative disposition, and tolerance of change.

Self-Assessment 12.5
GUANXI ORIENTATION SCALE (STUDENT OLC)

Guanxi, which is translated as interpersonal connections, is an important element of doing business in China and some other Asian countries with strong Confucian cultural values. Guanxi is based on traditional Confucian values of helping others without expecting future repayment. This instrument estimates your guanxi orientation–that is, the extent to which you accept and apply guanxi values. This self-assessment is completed alone so you can rate yourself honestly without concerns of social comparison. However, class discussion will focus on the meaning of guanxi and its relevance for organizational power and influence.

Self-Assessment 12.6
MACHIAVELLIANISM SCALE (STUDENT OLC)

Machiavellianism is named after Niccolò Machiavelli, the 16th-century Italian philosopher who wrote *The Prince*, a famous treatise about political behavior. Out of Machiavelli's work emerged this instrument that estimates the degree to which you have a Machiavellian personality. Indicate the extent to which you agree or disagree that each statement in this instrument describes you. Complete each item honestly to get the best estimate of your level of Machiavellianism.

Self-Assessment 12.7
PERCEPTIONS OF POLITICS SCALE (POPS) (STUDENT OLC)

Organizations have been called "political arenas"– environments where political tactics are common because decisions are ambiguous and resources are scarce. This instrument estimates the degree to which you believe the school where you attend classes has a politicized culture. This scale consists of several statements that might or might not describe the school where you are attending classes. These statements refer to the administration of the school, not the classroom. Please indicate the extent to which you agree or disagree with each statement.

After reading this chapter, if you need additional information, see www.mhhe.com/mcshane4e for more in-depth interactivities that correspond with this material.

TEAM EXERCISES

Team Exercise 8.4 WHERE IN THE WORLD ARE WE?

PURPOSE This exercise is designed to help you understand the potential advantages of involving others in decisions rather than making decisions alone.

MATERIALS Students require an unmarked copy of the map of the United States with grid marks (Exhibit 2). Students are not allowed to look at any other maps or use any other materials. The instructor will provide a list of communities located somewhere on Exhibit 2. The instructor will also provide copies of the answer sheet after students have individually and in teams estimated the locations of communities.

INSTRUCTIONS

1. Write in Exhibit 1 the list of communities identified by your instructor. Then, working alone, estimate the location in Exhibit 2 of these communities, all of which are in the United States. For example, mark a small "1" in Exhibit 2 on the spot where you believe the first community is located. Mark a small "2" where you think the second community is located, and so on. Please be sure to number each location clearly and with numbers small enough to fit within one grid space.
2. The instructor will organize students into roughly equal teams (typically five or six people per team). Working with your team members, reach a consensus on the location of each community listed in Exhibit 1. The instructor might provide teams with a separate copy of the map, or members can identify the team's numbers using a different color pen on the individual maps. The team's decision for each location should occur by consensus, not voting or averaging.
3. The instructor will provide an answer sheet showing the correct locations of the communities. Using this answer sheet, count the minimum number of grid squares between the location you individually marked and the true location of each community. Write the number of grid squares in the third column of Exhibit 1, then add up the total. Next, count the minimum number of grid squares between the location the team marked and the true location of each community. Write the number of grid squares in the fourth column of Exhibit 1, then add up the total.
4. The instructor will ask for information about the totals, and the class will discuss the implications of these results for employee involvement and decision making.

Exhibit 1
List of Selected Communicaties in the United States

Number	Communities	Individual distance in grid units from the true location	Team distance in grid units from the true location
1			
2			
3			
4			
5			
6			
7			
8			
		Total:	Total:

249

CRITICAL THINKING QUESTIONS

Critical Thinking Questions

1. This chapter begins by suggesting that motivating employees has become more challenging in recent years, partly because younger employees (Generation-X and Generation-Y) have different expectations than baby boomers. How do you think these younger and older generation groups differ in their expectations? Generally speaking, what would motivate a typical Generation-Y worker (under 25 years old) more than a typical baby boomer worker (over 45 years old)?
2. Four-drive theory is conceptually different from Maslow's needs hierarchy (as well as ERG theory) in several ways. Describe these differences. At the same time, needs are typically based on drives, so the four drives should parallel the seven needs that Maslow identified (five in the hierarchy and two additional needs). Map Maslow's needs to the four drives in four-drive theory.
3. Use all three components of expectancy theory to explain why some employees are motivated to show up for work during a severe storm whereas others make no effort to leave their homes.
4. What are the limitations of expectancy theory in predicting an individual's work effort and behavior?
5. Using your knowledge of the characteristics of effective goals, establish two meaningful goals related to your performance in this class.
6. When do employees prefer feedback from nonsocial rather than social sources? Explain why nonsocial sources are preferred under these conditions.
7. Several service representatives are upset that a newly hired representative with no previous experience will be paid $3,000 a year above the usual starting salary in the pay range. The department manager explained that the new hire would not accept the entry-level rate, so the company raised the offer by $3,000. All five reps currently earn salaries near the top of the scale ($15,000 higher than the new recruit), although they all started at the minimum starting salary a few years earlier. Use equity theory to explain why the five service representatives feel inequity in this situation.
8. Organizational injustice can occur in the classroom as well as in the workplace. Identify classroom situations in which you experienced feelings of injustice. What can instructors do to maintain an environment that fosters both distributive and procedural justice?

BUSINESS WEEK CASE STUDIES

Found at the end of each chapter, ***BusinessWeek* case studies** introduce the online full-text article and provide critical thinking questions for class discussion or assignments. These cases encourage students to understand and diagnose real-world issues using organizational behavior knowledge. For example, one case study challenges students to analyze how team dynamics supported development of Motorola's highly successful cell phone, the Razr. Another case study asks students to explain who Boeing experienced several serious incidents of ethical misconduct, and to evaluate the likely success of Boeing's actions to improve ethical conduct at the aerospace company.

Case Study 9.2 MOSH PITS OF CREATIVITY

BusinessWeek

The Razr, Motorola's highly successful ultralight cell phone, was designed through a process that differed from the electronics company's traditional research and development center. Much of the critical work on the phone was done in an innovation lab where cross-functional teams of engineers, marketers, and others work together in funky open-space offices that foster information sharing. Mattel, Steelcase, Boeing, Wrigley, Procter & Gamble, and many other firms are also turning to cross-functional teams to creatively and efficiently design new products or solve perplexing problems. Some companies have also designed their workplace to improve informal group dynamics that support the creative process.

This *BusinessWeek* case study examines this trend toward collaborative cross-functional teamwork in product development. It describes the characteristics of these "mosh pits," including their separation from the normal corporate bureaucracy and how employees are rotated through these special centers for inspiration. Read the full text of this *BusinessWeek* article at www.mhhe.com/mcshane4e and prepare for the discussion questions below.

Discussion Questions

1. What elements of the team dynamics model are Motorola, Procter & Gamble, and other companies applying to make these product development teams successful?
2. Identify the potential team dynamics challenges these product development teams might face in the situations described in this case study.
3. How are these companies supporting informal groups, and how might these groups aid the creative process?

Source: J. Weber, "'Mosh Pits' of Creativity," *BusinessWeek*, 7 November 2005, 98.

281

CHAPTER CASES AND ADDITIONAL END-OF-TEXT CASES

Every chapter includes at least one short **case study** that challenges students to diagnose issues and apply ideas from that chapter. Additional comprehensive cases appear at the end of the book. Several cases are new to this book and are written by instructors around the United States and from other countries. Other cases, such as Arctic Mining Consultants, are classics that have withstood the test of time.

Case Study 5.1 BUDDY'S SNACK COMPANY

Russell Casey, Clayton State University, and Gloria Thompson, University of Phoenix

Buddy's Snack Company is a family-owned company located in the Rocky Mountains. Buddy Forest started the business in 1951 by selling homemade potato chips out of the back of his pickup truck. Nowadays Buddy's is a $36 million snack food company that is struggling to regain market share lost to Frito-Lay and other fierce competitors. In the early eighties Buddy passed the business to his son, Buddy Jr., who is currently grooming his son, Mark, to succeed himself as head of the company.

Six months ago Mark joined Buddy's Snacks as a salesperson, and after four months he was quickly promoted to sales manager. Mark recently graduated from a local university with an MBA in marketing, and Buddy Jr. was hoping that Mark would be able to implement strategies that could help turn the company around. One of Mark's initial strategies was to introduce a new sales performance management system. As part of this approach, any salesperson who receives a below-average performance rating would be required to attend a mandatory coaching session with his or her supervisor. Mark Forest is hoping that these coaching sessions will motivate employees to increase their sales. This case describes the reaction of three salespeople who have been required to attend a coaching session because of their low performance over the previous quarter.

Lynda Lewis

Lynda is a hard worker who takes pride in her work ethic. She has spent a lot of time reading the training material and learning selling techniques, viewing training videos on her own time, and accompanying top salespeople on their calls. Lynda has no problem asking for advice and doing whatever needs to be done to learn the business. Everyone agrees that Lynda has a cheery attitude and is a real "team player," giving the company 150 percent at all times. It has been a tough quarter for Lynda due to the downturn in the economy, but she is doing her best to make sales for the company. Lynda feels that failure to make quota during this past quarter is due not to lack of effort, but just bad luck in the economy. She is hopeful that things will turn around in the next quarter.

160

Lynda is upset with Mark about having to attend the coaching session because this is the first time in three years that her sales quota has not been met. Although Lynda is willing to do whatever it takes to be successful, she is concerned that the coaching sessions will be held on a Saturday. Doesn't Mark realize that Lynda has to raise three boys by herself and that weekends are an important time for her family? Because Lynda is a dedicated employee, she will somehow manage to rearrange the family's schedule.

Lynda is now very concerned about how her efforts are being perceived by Mark. After all, she exceeded the sales quota for the previous quarter, yet she did not receive thanks or congratulations for those efforts. The entire experience has left Lynda unmotivated and questioning her future with the company.

Michael Benjamin

Michael is happy to have his job at Buddy's Snack Company, although he really doesn't like sales work that much. Michael accepted this position because he felt that he wouldn't have to work hard and would have a lot of free time during the day. Michael was sent to coaching mainly because his customer satisfaction reports were low; in fact, they were the lowest in the company. Michael tends to give canned presentations and does not listen closely to the customer's needs. Consequently, Michael makes numerous errors in new sales orders, which delay shipments and lose business and goodwill for Buddy's Snack Company. Michael doesn't really care because most of his customers do not spend much money, and he doesn't think it is worth his while.

There has been a recent change in the company commission structure. Instead of selling to the warehouse stores and possibly earning a high commission, Michael is now forced to sell to lower-volume convenience stores. In other words, he will have to sell twice

Chapter Summary

Motivation refers to the forces within a person that affect his or her direction, intensity, and persistence of voluntary behavior in the workplace. Motivation has become more challenging because of an increasingly turbulent work environment, the removal of direct supervision as a motivational instrument, and the lack of understanding about what motivates the new generations of people entering the workforce.

Maslow's needs hierarchy groups needs into a hierarchy of five levels and states that the lowest needs are initially most important, but higher needs become more important as the lower ones are satisfied. Although very popular, the theory lacks research support–as does ERG theory, which attempted to overcome some of the limitations in Maslow's needs hierarchy. Both models assume that everyone has the same hierarchy, whereas emerging evidence suggests that needs hierarchies vary from one person to the next based on their personal values.

Four-drive theory states that everyone has four innate drives–the drives to acquire, bond, learn, and defend. These drives create emotional markers that motivate us. The drives generate competing emotions, however, so we consciously reconcile these competing impulses through a skill set that considers social norms, past experience, and personal values. Four-drive theory offers considerable potential for understanding employee motivation, but it still requires clarification and research to understand how people translate competing emotions into motivated behavior.

McClelland's learned needs theory argues that needs can be strengthened through learning. The three needs studied in this respect have been need for achievement, need for power, and need for affiliation.

The practical implication of needs/drives-based motivation theories is that corporate leaders must provide opportunities for everyone in the workplace to regularly fulfill all four drives; that organizations should avoid too much or too little opportunity to fulfill each drive; and that employees should be offered a choice of rewards rather than given the same reward as everyone else.

Expectancy theory states that work effort is determined by the perception that effort will result in a particular level of performance (E-to-P expectancy); the perception that a specific behavior or performance level will lead to specific outcomes (P-to-O expectancy); and the valences that the person feels for those outcomes. The E-to-P expectancy increases by improving the employee's ability and confidence to perform the job. The P-to-O expectancy increases by measuring performance accurately, distributing higher rewards to better performers, and showing employees that rewards are performance-based. Outcome valences increase by finding out what employees want and using these resources as rewards.

Goal setting is the process of motivating employees and clarifying their role perceptions by establishing performance objectives. Goals are more effective when they are specific, relevant, and challenging; have employee commitment; and are accompanied by meaningful feedback. Participative goal setting is important in some situations. Effective feedback is specific, relevant, timely, credible, and sufficiently frequent (which depends on the length of the task cycle and the employee's knowledge and experience with the task). Two increasingly popular forms of feedback are multisource (360-degree) assessment and executive coaching. Feedback from nonsocial sources is also beneficial

Organization
(perceived fairn
our contribution
others) and proc
used to decide t
ory, which cons

Key Terms

distributive justice, p. 152
drives, p. 135
equity sensitivity, p. 154
equity theory, p. 152
ERG theory, p. 138
executive coaching, p. 150
expectancy theory, p. 143
feedback, p. 148
four-drive theory, p. 138
goal setting, p. 146
Maslow's needs hierarchy, p. 135
motivation, p. 134
multisource (360-degree) feedback, p. 149
need for achievement (nAch), p. 141
need for affiliation (nAff), p. 141
need for power (nPow), p. 141
needs, p. 135
positive organizational behavior, p. 137
procedural justice, p. 162
self-actualization, p. 135
valence, p. 144

Supplementary Choices

Organizational Behavior, Fourth Edition, includes a variety of **supplemental materials** to help instructors prepare and present the material in this textbook more effectively.

INSTRUCTOR'S CD-ROM

The **Instructor's CD-Rom** contains the **Instructor's Manual,** the **Computerized Test Bank, PowerPoint presentation,** and additional downloads of **art from the text.** Written by Steve McShane, the IM includes the learning objectives, glossary of key terms, a chapter synopsis, and complete lecture outline with thumbnail images of corresponding PowerPoint slides, suggested solutions to the end-of-chapter discussion questions. It also includes teaching notes for the chapter case(s), team exercises, and self-assessments and transparency masters. The Test Bank, written with assistance from Amit Shah, Frostburg State University, includes more than 2,400 multiple-choice, true/false, and essay questions, the majority of which have been tested in class examinations. We've also aligned our Testbank with new AACSB guidelines, tagging each question according to its knowledge and skills areas. Categories include Global, Ethics and Social Responsibility, Legal and other External Environment, Communication, Diversity, Group Dynamics, Individual Dynamics, Production, and IT. Previous designations aligning questions with Learning Objectives and features still exist as well.

POWERPOINT

Organizational Behavior includes a complete set of **PowerPoint Presentation** files, with at least 18 slides relating to each chapter. These slides have received high praise for their clean design, use of graphics, and inclusion of some photos from the textbook.

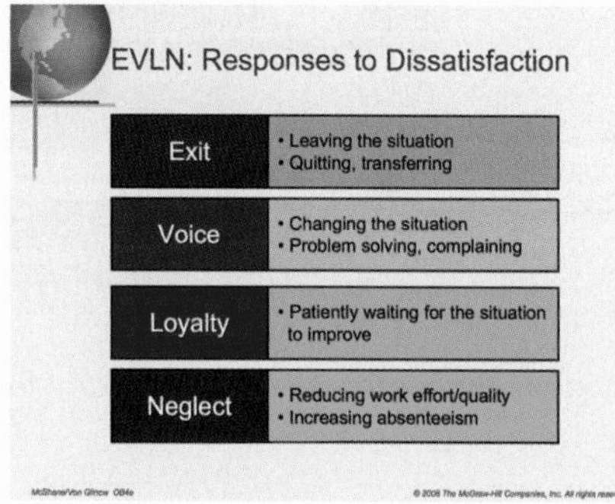

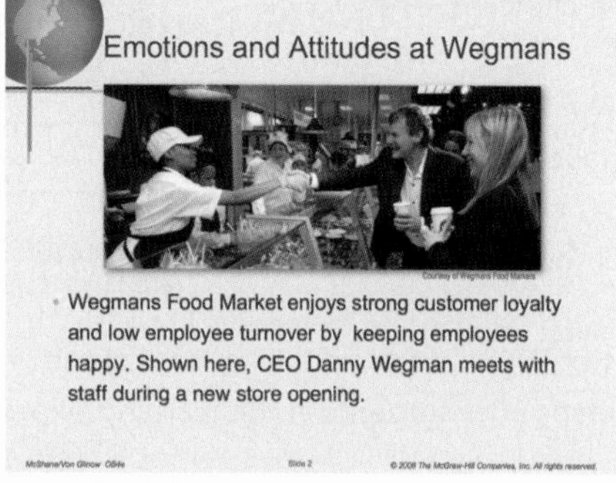

GROUP AND VIDEO RESOURCE MANUAL: An Instructor's Guide to an Active Classroom (in print 0073044342 or online at www.mhhe.com/mobmanual)

Management: Group and Video Guide Manual Matrix (Topics 6-10) - Microsoft Internet Explorer

http://www.mhhe.com/business/management/buildyourmanagementskills/resourcemanual/matrix_by_topic_06_10.htm

Management: Group and Video Guide Resource Manual

An Instructor's Guide to an Active Classroom

Topics 1-5 | Topics 6-10 | Topics 11-15 | Topics 16-20 | Topics 21-25

#.	Topic	Test Your Knowledge	Self-Assessment Exercises	Group Exercises	Hot Seat DVD Applications
6.	MENTORING	Mentoring Exercise | Notes			
7.	MOTIVATION AND GOAL SETTING	Reinforcement Theory Exercise | Notes Reinforcing Performance Exercise | Notes		What Motivates You? Notes | PowerPoint What Rewards Motivate Student Achievement? Notes | PowerPoint	
8.	FEEDBACK		Assessing Your Empathy Skills Exercise | Notes | PowerPoint		
9.	GROUPS AND TEAMS		Team Roles Preference Scale Exercise | Notes | PowerPoint	Identifying Task and Maintenance Roles within Groups Notes | PowerPoint	Project Management: Steering the Committee Notes | PowerPoint Working in Teams: Cross-Functional Dysfunction Notes | PowerPoint
10.	DECISION-MAKING	The Vroom/Yetton/Jago Decision Model Exercise | Notes	Your Preferred Decision-Making Style Exercise | Notes | PowerPoint Assessing Your Ethical Decision Making Skills Exercise | Notes | PowerPoint	Stranded in the Desert: An Exercise in Decision-Making Notes | PowerPoint Applying the Ethical Decision-Making Tree Notes | PowerPoint	Office Romance: Groping for Answers Notes | PowerPoint

McGraw-Hill Irwin

©2006 McGraw-Hill Online Learning. Any use is subject to the Terms of Use and Privacy Policy.

This manual created for instructors contains everything needed to successfully integrate activities into the classroom. It includes a menu of items to use as teaching tools in class. All of our self-assessment exercises, Test Your Knowledge quizzes, group exercises, and Manager's HotSeat exercises are located in this one manual along with teaching notes and PowerPoint slides to use in class. Group exercises include everything you would need to use the exercise in class — handouts, figures, etc.

This manual is organized into 25 topics like ethics, decision-making, change and leadership for easy inclusion in your lecture. A matrix is included at the front of the manual that references each resource by topic. Students access all of the exercises and self-assessments on their textbook's website. The Manager's Hot Seat exercises are located online at www.mhhe.com/MHS

MANAGER'S HOTSEAT ONLINE: www.mhhe.com/MHS

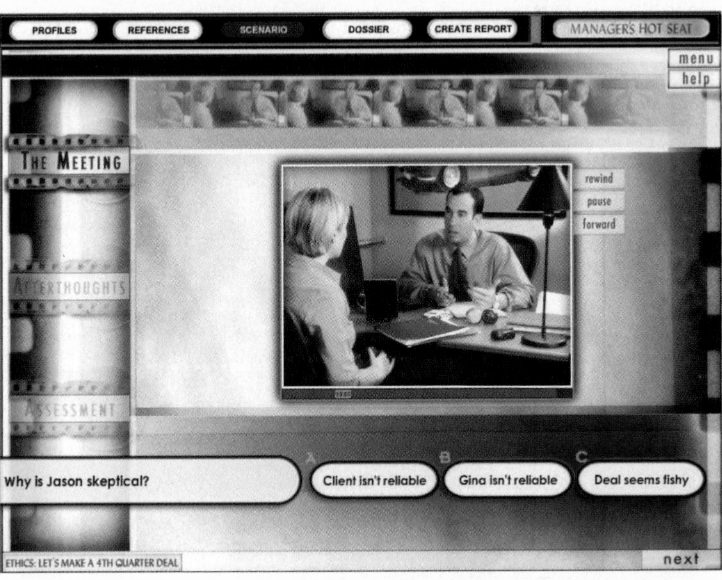

In today's workplace, managers are confronted daily with issues such as **ethics, diversity, working in teams**, and the **virtual workplace**. The Manager's HotSeat is interactive software that allows students to watch video of 15 real managers as they apply their years of experience to confront these issues.

Students assume the role of the manager as they watch the video and answer multiple choice questions that pop up forcing them to make decisions on the spot. They learn from the manager's mistakes and successes, and then do a report critiquing the manager's approach by defending their reasoning.

Reports can be e-mailed or printed out for credit. These video segments are a powerful tool for your course that truly immerses your students in the learning experience.

VIDEO DVD

The new video collection features PBS, NBC, and *BusinessWeek* footage, and original business documentaries that relate to examples and cases in the text. With segments like:

Troubles at General Motors
Good Business Deeds
Workplace Bias
America: An Overworked Nation (Working Smart)

ONLINE LEARNING CENTER

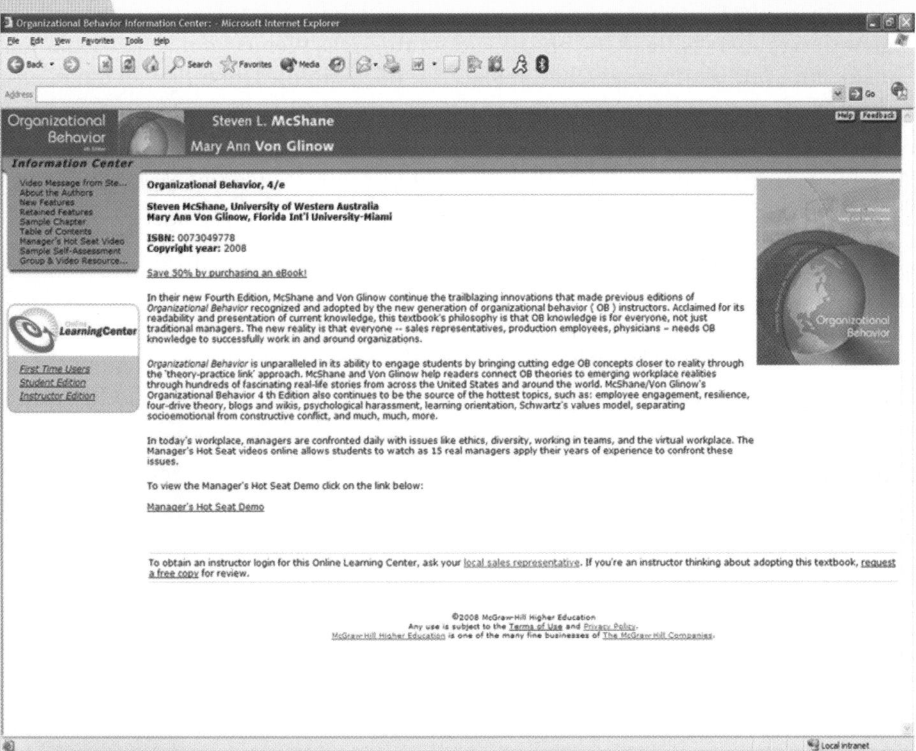

www.mhhe.com/mcshane4e

The Online Learning Center (OLC) is a one-stop shopping Web site with additional course materials, supplements, links, and exercises found chapter by chapter. As students read the book, they can go online to take self-grading quizzes, review material, or work through interactive exercises. OLCs can be delivered in multiple ways—professors and students can access them directly through the textbook Web site, or within a course management system (e.g., WebCT, Blackboard, or eCollege).

acknowledgments

Have you ever worked on a high-performance team where everything just seems to "click"? We have–on this edition! Sure, we spend plenty of time alone writing and researching for this book, and of course there are challenges along the way. But is amazing how teamwork *really does* make a difference. Several people provided valued expertise to smooth out the rough spots of writing, search out the most challenging photos, create a fantastic design, develop the various forms of student and instructor support, and pull together these many pieces into a comprehensive textbook. This teamwork is even more amazing when you consider that the team members live throughout the United States and around the world.

Sponsoring editor Ryan Blankenship led the way with enthusiasm and foresight, while clearing the way of any challenges. Christine Scheid (Senior Development Editor) demonstrated amazingly cool coordination skills as we pushed deadline limits so students have the latest OB knowledge. The keen copy editing skills of Meg McDonald made Organizational Behavior, Fourth Edition, incredibly error-free. Mary Conzachi, our Lead Project Manager, was a true professional as she guided the project through a tight production schedule. Kami Carter delivered an elegant design that captures the global and future-focus themes of this textbook. Jen Blankenship, our photo researcher, makes Sherlock Holmes look like an amateur–she can track down photos from the most obscure sources. Jodi Dowling and the Techbooks team composited the book to high standards. Meg Beamer, our marketing manager, kept everyone focused on customer needs. Thanks to you all. This has been an exceptional team effort!

As was mentioned earlier, more than 100 instructors around the world reviewed parts or all of *Organizational Behavior*, Fourth Edition, or its regional editions over the past three years. Thank you for sharing your thoughts and ideas about what an organizational behavior textbook should look like. Your compliments were energizing, and your suggestions significantly improved the final product. We also want to thank reviewers of previous editions for helping us develop this textbook. The following people from American colleges and universities provided feedback specifically for *Organizational Behavior,* Fourth Edition:

Dr. Gibb Dyer
Brigham Young University

Eleanor H. (Holly) Buttner
UNC-Greensboro

Sandra Deacon Carr
Boston University

Floyd Ormsbee
Clarkson University

George Redmond
Franklin University

B. Kay Snavely
Miami University

Carole Barnett
University of New Hampshire

Joy Benson
University of Illinois–Springfield

Greg Bier
Stephens College

Weldon Blake
Bethune Cookman College

Antonia Bos
Tusculum College

James Breaugh
University of Missouri–St. Louis

Holly Buttner
University of North Carolina–Greensboro

Michael Camarata
Marywood University

Sandra Deacon Carr
Boston University

Beth Chung
San Diego State University

Roger Dean
Washington & Lee University

George Dodge
Clearwater Christian College

Sally Dresdow
University of Wisconsin–Green Bay

Richard Feltman
San Diego State University

Marilyn Fox
Minnesota State University–Mankato

Janice Gates
Western Illinois University

Ronald Humphrey
Virginia Commonwealth University

Rusty Juban
Dallas Baptist University

Dong Jung
San Diego State University

Tom Kolenko
Kennesaw State University

Susan Manring
Elon College

Jennifer Martin
York College of Pennsylvania

Linda Morable
Richland College

Emile Pilafidis
University of La Verne

Liz Ravlin
University of South Carolina

Pete Richardson
Southwest Missouri State University

Jill Roberts
Campbellsville University

Lena Rodriguez
San Diego State University

Michael Shaner
St. Louis University

Jason Shaw
University of Kentucky–Lexington

Tracy Sigler
Northern Kentucky University

Vikki Sitter
Milligan College

Randall Sleeth
Virginia Commonwealth University

Maryalice Smith
Tarrant County College–NE

Gary Stark
University of Minnesota–Duluth

Pat Stubblebine
Miami University–Oxford

Bill Turnley
Kansas State University

Matthew Valle
Elon College

Andrew Ward
Emory University

The authors also extend their sincerest thanks to Amit Shah for assisting Steve with the test Bank. They are also very grateful to the many instructors in the United States and other countries who contributed cases and exercises to this edition of *Organizational Behavior*:

- Marc Bacon, Fabgroups Technologies Inc
- Alicia Boisnier, SUNY at Buffalo
- Martha Burkle, Monterrey Institute of Technology
- Gerard A. Callanan, West Chester University Of Pennsylvania
- Sharon Card, (formerly at) Saskatchewan Institute of Applied Science & Technology
- Russell Casey, Clayton State University
- Jeewon Cho, SUNY at Buffalo
- Mary Gander, Winona State University
- Swee C. Goh, University of Ottawa
- Cheryl Harvey, Wilfrid Laurier University
- Arif Hassan, International Islamic University Malaysia

- Christine Ho, University of Adelaide
- Lisa Ho, Prada, Singapore
- Joseph Kavanaugh, Sam Houston State University
- Theresa Kline, University of Calgary
- Henry S. Maddux III, Sam Houston State University
- Rosemary Maellaro, University of Dallas
- Fiona McQuarrie, University College of the Fraser Valley
- Kim Morouney, Wilfrid Laurier University
- David F. Perri, West Chester University Of Pennsylvania
- Harry Gene Redden, Sam Houston State University
- Joseph C. Santora, Essex County College & TST, Inc.
- Christina Stamper, Western Michigan University
- Gloria Thompson, University of Phoenix
- William Todorovic, Purdue University
- Lisa V. Williams, SUNY at Buffalo
- Thivagar Velayutham, International Islamic University Malaysia

The authors would also like to extend our sincerest thanks to the many instructors in the United States and other countries who contributed cases and exercises to previous editions of *Organizational Behavior:*

- Jeffrey Bagraim, *University of Cape Town, South Africa*
- Hazel Bothma, *University of Cape Town, South Africa*
- Sharon Card, *Saskatchewan Institute of Applied Science & Technology*
- Cynthia Larson-Daugherty, *National University*
- Carolynn Larson-Garcia, *Assesso*
- Aneil Mishra, *Wake Forest University*
- Karen Mishra, *Wake Forest University*
- Joseph C. Santora, *Essex County College and TSTDCG, Inc.*
- James C. Sarros, *Monash University*

Steve would also like to extend special thanks to his students in Perth, Singapore, and Manila for sharing their learning experiences and assisting with the development of the three organizational behavior textbooks in the United States, Canada, and the Pacific Rim, as well as their adaptations in Asia, India, and elsewhere. Steve is also very grateful to his colleagues at the Graduate School of Management, The University of Western Australia, for patiently listening to his ideas, diplomatically redirecting his wayward thoughts, and sharing their experiences using the American and Pacific Rim editions of this book in several locations around Asia and Oceania. But more than anything else, Steve is forever indebted to his wife Donna McClement and to their wonderful daughters, Bryton and Madison. Their love and support give special meaning to Steve's life.

Mary Ann would like to thank the many, many students who have used and hopefully enjoyed this book. I've been stopped on my campus and at occasional meetings by students who tell me that they recognize my picture and wanted to thank me! There are a few that have actually asked for my autograph! (Note, that didn't happen when I was President of the Academy of Management!) Thus it is to the students that I acknowledge many thanks, particularly for making this learning venture fun and exciting. Also, I would like to thank the faculty and staff at Florida International University, who have been very supportive of this effort. By far and away, my coauthor Steve McShane is the penultimate scholar. He has boundless energy and a mind that doesn't seem to quit, particularly with those late night or early morning e-mails! Steve is also the techno-wizard behind this edition. Finally I would like to thank my family–John, Rhoda, Lauren, Lindsay, and Christy–as well as some very special people in my life–Janet, Peter, Bill, Karen, Jerry, Barbara, Kate, Joanne, Mary, Linda, and Steve. I know I never get a chance to thank them enough, so thank you my friends! I also thank Emma, Zack, Molly, and Googun, my babies! A final note of thanks goes to my CIBER family: Tita, Sonia, Juan, Elsa, and KK–you are simply the best! Thank you all, for being there for me!

Steven L. McShane
Mary Ann Von Glinow

Organizational Behavior

Part One

Introduction

Friends were puzzled when Rob Pike decided a few years ago to leave his 20-year career at the prestigious Bell Labs in New Jersey to join a Web search start-up in California with a name that sounded like baby talk. The respected computer scientist's move had nothing to do with money. "I took a huge pay cut to come here," says Pike about his decision to join Google. "The reason is, it's an exciting place to work."

Google has leveraged the power of organizational behavior to attract talented employees who want to make a difference in the Internet world.

Google, the company behind the ubiquitous search engine, has a freewheeling, geeky culture that attracts Rob Pike and other creative thinkers who want to make a difference in the Internet world. Employees are expected to devote a quarter of their time to new ideas of their choosing and to get those ideas into practice as quickly as possible. "Here, you can have an idea on Monday and have it on the Web site by the end of the week," says Pike, citing Google Maps and Gmail as examples of the company's rapid innovation.

Google's culture has clashed to some extent with its meteoric global growth to more than 6,000 employees over the past eight years. In response, the company's chaotic style has been reined in with a more stable structure around teams assigned to projects and functions. "It has scaled [up] pretty well," says Google CEO Eric Schmidt. Google's unofficial ethical philosophy—Don't be evil—is the guideline by which it refuses to favor paid advertisers in its search results (unlike some other search engines) or to allow Web sites that speak against anyone. However, Google has also faced global ethical challenges, such as when it agreed to support China's censorship of democracy and opposition against government policy.

Along with its culture and ethics, Google attracts talent with the Googleplex, the company's campuslike headquarters where high-density team clusters, playful décor, and a legendary cafeteria make everyone feel as though they haven't yet left school. Meetings even start a few minutes after the hour, just like class schedules in a lot of colleges. "That (campus) model is familiar to our programmers," explains Schmidt. "We know it's a very productive environment."

Google chief financial officer George Reyes sums up the main reason for the company's phenomenal success. "We want Google to be the very place to work for the very best computer scientists in the world," says Reyes. "Google is truly a learning organization."[1]

1

Introduction to the Field of Organizational Behavior

LEARNING OBJECTIVES

After reading this chapter, you should be able to

1. Define organizational behavior and give three reasons for studying this field of inquiry.
2. Describe five organizational behavior trends and discuss their effects on the workplace.
3. Debate the advantages and disadvantages of workforce diversity.
4. Summarize the benefits and challenges of telecommuting.
5. Define values and explain why they have become more important in recent years.
6. Define corporate social responsibility and argue for or against its practice in organizations.
7. Identify the five anchors on which organizational behavior is based.
8. Diagram an organization from an open systems view.
9. Define knowledge management and intellectual capital.
10. Identify specific ways in which organizations acquire, share, and preserve knowledge.

Google has become a powerhouse on the Internet, but its real power comes from applying organizational behavior theories and practices. More than ever, organizations are relying on organizational behavior knowledge to remain competitive. For example, Google has an engaged workforce because of its exciting work opportunities, supportive team dynamics, and "cool" workplace. It attracts talented people through its strong culture and ethical values and an environment that supports creativity and a learning organization. These and many other organizational behavior concepts and practices make a difference in the organization's success and employee well-being.

This book is about people working in organizations. Its main objective is to help you understand behavior in organizations and to work more effectively in organizational settings. Although organizational behavior knowledge is often presented for "managers," this book takes a broader and more realistic view that organizational behavior ideas are relevant and useful to anyone who works in and around organizations. In this chapter we introduce you to the field of organizational behavior, outline the main reasons why you should know more about it, highlight some of the trends influencing the study of organizational behavior, describe the anchors supporting the study of organizations, and introduce the concept that organizations are knowledge and learning systems.

Learning Objectives

After reading this section you should be able to

1. Define organizational behavior and organizations and give three reasons for studying this field of inquiry.

The Field of Organizational Behavior

organizational behavior (OB)
The study of what people think, feel, and do in and around organizations.

Organizational behavior (OB) is the study of what people think, feel, and do in and around organizations. OB researchers systematically study individual, team, and organizational-level characteristics that influence behavior within work settings. By saying that organizational behavior is a field of study, we mean that OB experts have been accumulating a distinct knowledge about behavior within organizations–a knowledge base that is the foundation of this book.

By most estimates, OB emerged as a distinct field around the 1940s.[2] However, its origins can be traced much further back in time. The Greek philosopher Plato wrote about the essence of leadership. The writings of Chinese philosopher Confucius in 500 BC are beginning to influence contemporary thinking about ethics and leadership. In 1776 Adam Smith advocated a new form of organizational structure based on the division of labor. One hundred years later German sociologist Max Weber wrote about rational organizations and initiated discussion of charismatic leadership. Soon after, Frederick Winslow Taylor introduced the systematic use of goal setting and rewards to motivate employees. In the 1920s Elton Mayo and his colleagues discovered the importance of formal and informal group dynamics in the workplace, resulting in a dramatic shift towards the "human relations" school of thought. As you can see, OB has been around for a long time; it just wasn't organized into a unified discipline until after World War II.

What Are Organizations?

Organizations have existed for as long as people have worked together. Massive temples dating back to 3500 BC were constructed through the organized actions of many people. Craftspeople and merchants in ancient Rome formed guilds, complete with elected managers. And more than 1,000 years ago, Chinese factories were producing 125,000 tons of iron a year.[3] We have equally impressive examples of contemporary organizations, ranging from Wal-Mart, the world's largest and most successful retailer, to Google, the world's leading search engine. "A company is one of humanity's most amazing inventions," says Steven Jobs, CEO of Apple Computer and Pixar Animation Studios. "It's totally abstract. Sure, you have to build something with bricks and mortar to put the people in, but basically a company is this abstract construct we've invented, and it's incredibly powerful."[4]

organizations
Groups of people who work interdependently toward some purpose.

So what are **organizations?** They are groups of people who work interdependently toward some purpose.[5] Organizations are not buildings or government-registered entities. Rather, they consist of people who interact with each other to achieve a common purpose. "A business is just a registered name on a piece of paper," explains Grahame Maher, who leads Vodafone's operations in the Czech Republic. "It's nothing more than that unless there's a group of people who care about a common purpose for why they are, where they are going, how they are going to be when they are there."[6]

Some OB experts are skeptical about the relevance of goals in a definition of organizations.[7] They argue that an organization's mission statement may be different from its true goals. Also, they question the assumption that all organizational members believe in the same goals. These points may be true, but imagine an organization without goals: It would consist of a mass of people wandering around aimlessly without any sense of direction. Overall, as Vodafone's Grahame Maher stated, organizations consist of people with a collective sense of purpose. This purpose might not be fully understood or agreed upon, but it helps employees to engage in structured patterns of interaction. In other words, they expect each other to complete various tasks in a coordinated way–in an *organized* way.

Why Study Organizational Behavior?

Organizational behavior seems to get more respect from people who have been in the workforce a while than from students who are just beginning their careers. Many of us specialize in accounting, marketing, information systems, and other fields with corresponding job titles, so it's understandable that students focus on these career paths. After all, who ever heard of a career path leading to a "vice president of OB" or a "chief OB officer"? Even if organizational behavior doesn't have its own job title, most people eventually come to realize that this field is a potential gold mine of valuable knowledge. The fact is, everyone in the workforce needs to understand, predict, and influence behavior (both our own and that of others) in organizational settings (see Exhibit 1.1). Marketing students learn marketing concepts, and computer science students learn about circuitry and software code. But everyone benefits from organizational behavior knowledge to address the people issues when trying to apply marketing, computer science, and other fields of knowledge.

Understanding, Predicting, and Influencing Each of us has an inherent need to understand and predict the world in which we live.[8] Because much of our time is spent working in or around organizations, OB theories are particularly helpful in satisfying this innate drive to make sense of the workplace. OB theories also give you the opportunity to question and rebuild your personal mental models that have developed through observation and experience.

Exhibit 1.1
Reasons for Studying Organizational Behavior

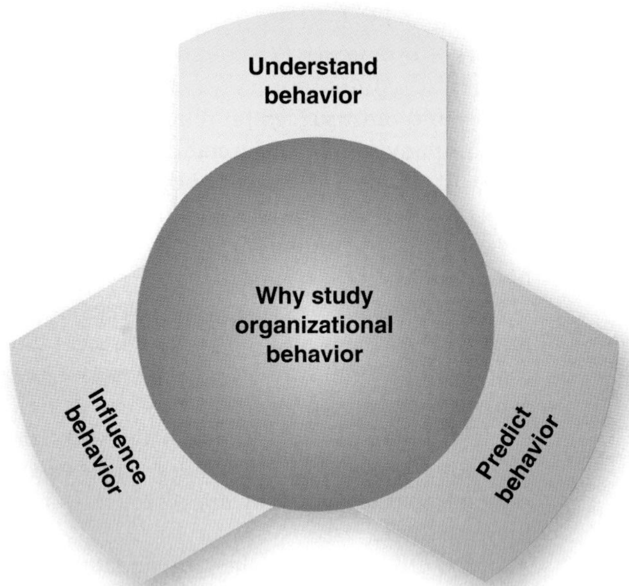

Understanding and predicting are important, but most of us also need to influence the organization in various ways. Whether you are trying to introduce a new marketing strategy, encourage staff to adopt new information technology, or negotiate more flexible work arrangements with your boss, you'll find that OB concepts play an important role in performing your job and working more effectively within organizations. This practical side of organizational behavior is, according to some experts, a critical feature of the best OB theories.[9]

Organizational Behavior Is for Everyone This book takes the view that organizational behavior knowledge is for everyone–not just managers. We all need to understand organizational behavior and to master the practices that influence organizational events. That's why you won't find very much emphasis in this book on "management." Yes, organizations will continue to have managers, but their roles have changed. More important, the rest of us are now expected to manage ourselves, particularly as companies remove layers of management and delegate more responsibilities. In the words of one forward-thinking organizational behavior writer many years ago: Everyone is a manager.[10]

OB and the Bottom Line So far our answer to the question "Why study OB?" has focused on how OB knowledge benefits you as an individual. But organizational behavior knowledge is just as important for the organization's financial health. According to one estimate, firms that apply performance-based rewards, employee communication, work–life balance, and other OB practices have three times the level of financial success as companies where these practices are absent. Another study concluded that companies that earn "the best place to work" awards have significantly higher financial and long-term stock market performance. Essentially these firms leverage the power of OB practices, which translate into more favorable employee attitudes, decisions, and performance. The benefits of OB are well known to Warren Buffett and other financial gurus; they consider the organization's leadership and quality of employees as two of the best predictors of the firm's financial potential.[11]

Learning Objectives

After reading this section you should be able to

2. **Describe five organizational behavior trends and discuss their effects on the workplace.**
3. **Debate the advantages and disadvantages of workforce diversity.**
4. **Summarize the benefits and challenges of telecommuting.**
5. **Define values and explain why they have become more important in recent years.**
6. **Define corporate social responsibility and argue for or against its practice in organizations.**

Organizational Behavior Trends

There has never been a better time to learn about organizational behavior. The pace of change is accelerating, and most of the transformation is occurring in the workplace. Let's take a brief tour through five trends in the workplace: globalization, workforce diversity, evolving employment relationships, virtual work, and workplace values and ethics.

Globalization

Google didn't exist a decade ago, yet today it is one of the best-known names on the Internet around the planet. The Mountain View, California, company offers Web search services in over 100 languages, and over half of its search engine queries come from outside the United States. One-third of Google's revenue is from other countries, and it is already facing sensitive issues in China, France, and other countries that want o censor search results. So far Google has not outsourced work to contractors in low-wage countries, but it has opened its own research centers in India and Japan.[12]

globalization
Economic, social, and cultural connectivity (and interdependence) with poeple in other parts of the world.

Google is a rich example of the globalization of business over the past few decades. **Globalization** refers to economic, social, and cultural connectivity with people in other parts of the world. Google and other organizations globalize when they actively participate in other countries and cultures. Although businesses have traded goods

Whirlpool's Journey to Globalization In the late 1980s 95 percent of Whirlpool's revenue and most of its manufacturing occurred in the United States. Yet executives at the Benton Harbor, Michigan, company knew from excursions to other countries that globalization would soon transform the industry. "We came to the conclusion that the industry would become a global one and that someone had to shape it," recalls David Whitwam, Whirlpool's recently retired CEO. Today Whirlpool is the global leader in the appliance industry, with microwave ovens engineered in Sweden and assembled in China, refrigerators made in Brazil for European consumers, top-loading washers made in Ohio, and front-loading washers made in Germany (shown in photo). This journey toward globalization has required tremendous organizational change. "We need a diverse workforce with diverse leadership," says Whitwam, as well as "strong regional leadership that lives in the culture." Whitwam also believes a global company requires broad-based involvement and an organizational structure that encourages the flow of knowledge.[13]

across borders for centuries, the degree of globalization today is unprecedented because information technology and transportation systems allow a much more intense level of connectivity and interdependence around the planet.[14]

Globalization has given Google and other firms new markets and resources as well as a broader net to attract valuable knowledge and skills. Some experts also argue that globalization potentially improves the financial and social development of poorer nations, although other experts dispute that claim.[15] Against its potential benefits, globalization is criticized for increasing competitive pressures and market volatility. It is also linked to "offshoring"–outsourcing work to lower-wage countries. Collectively these events potentially reduce job security, increase work intensification, and demand more work flexibility from employees. Thus globalization might partly explain why many of us now work longer hours, have heavier workloads, and experience more work–family conflict than at any time in recent decades.[16]

Globalization is now well entrenched, so rather than debate its advantages and disadvantages, the real issue is how corporate leaders and employees alike can lead and work effectively in this emerging reality.[17] OB researchers are turning their attention to this topic, such as determining how well OB theories and practices work across cultures. In the Best Practices Project, for instance, over three dozen scholars are discovering human resource management practices based on companies around the globe. Another consortium, called Project GLOBE, is studying leadership and organizational practices across dozens of countries.[18] Globalization also has important implications for how we learn about organizational behavior. The best-performing companies may be in Helsinki, Singapore, or São Paulo, not just in New York or Miami. That's why this book presents numerous examples from around the planet. We want you to learn from the best, no matter where their headquarters are located.

Workforce Diversity

Walk into the offices of Verizon Communications around the United States and you can quickly see that the communications service giant reflects the communities it serves. Minorities make up 30 percent of Verizon's workforce of 200,000 and 18 percent of top management positions. Women represent 43 percent of its workforce and 32 percent of top management. Verizon's inclusive culture has won awards from numerous organizations representing Hispanics, African Americans, gays and lesbians, people with disabilities, and other groups. You can also see this diversity at Google. Its California headquarters employs people from most countries, which creates a challenge for the company's restaurant staff. "It's a global community here, and you can't just go with one kind of cuisine," says Charlie Ayers, the chef who created Google's kitchens. Even Google's smaller European operations in Dublin, Ireland, employ people from more than 40 nationalities.[19]

Verizon Communications and Google are model employers that reflect the increasing diversity of people living in the United States and in many other countries. Workforce diversity takes many forms. The primary categories in Exhibit 1.2 represent **surface-level diversity,** which include observable demographic or physiological differences in people, such as their race, ethnicity, gender, age, and physical disabilities. This most obvious form of diversity has changed considerably in the United States over the past few decades.

surface-level diversity
Observable demographic or physiological differences in people, such as their race, ethnicity, gender, age, and physical disabilities.

People with nonwhite or Hispanic origin represent one-third of the American population, and this fraction is projected to increase substantially over the next few decades. The Hispanic population recently replaced African Americans as the second largest ethnic group. Within the next 50 years one in four Americans will be

Exhibit 1.2
Primary and Secondary Dimensions of Workforce Diversity

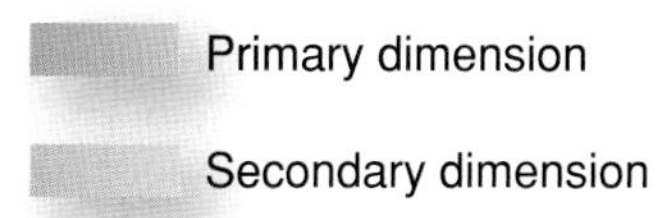

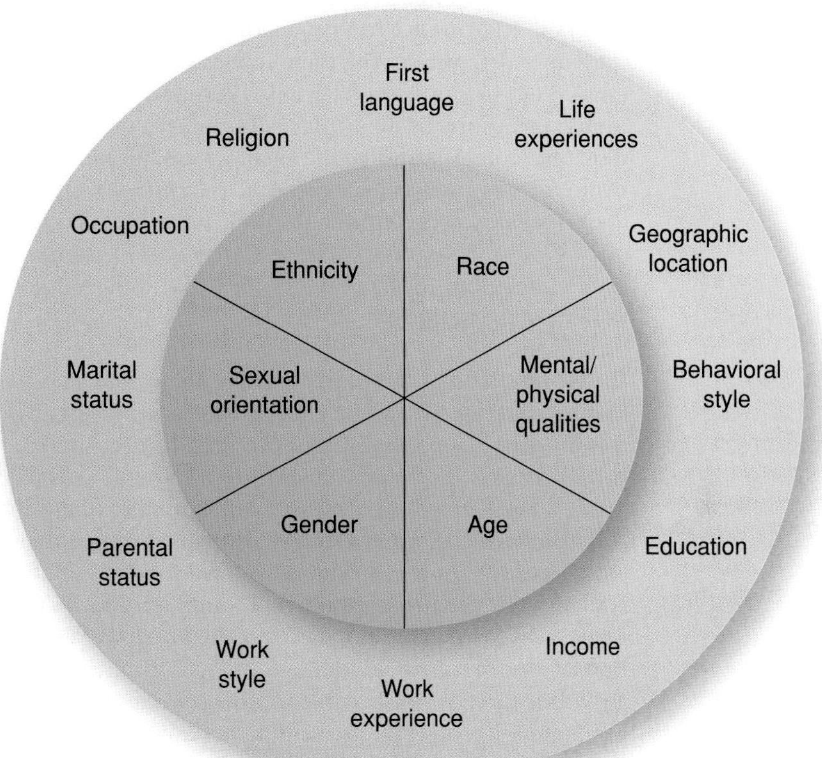

Sources: Adapted from M. Loden, *Implementing Diversity* (Chicago: Irwin, 1996); S. Bradford, "Fourteen Dimensions of Diversity: Understanding and Appreciating Differences in the Workplace," in J. W. Pfeiffer (Ed.), *1996 Annual: Volume 2 Consulting* (San Diego: Pfeiffer and Associates, 1996), pp. 9–17.

Hispanic, 14 percent will be African American, and 8 percent will be of Asian descent. By 2060 non-Hispanic whites will be a minority.[20] Many other countries are also experiencing increasing levels of racial and ethnic diversification. Meanwhile women now account for nearly half of the paid workforce in the United States–more than double the participation rate a few decades ago. Gender-based shifts continue to occur within many occupations. For example, women represent 59 percent of accountants in the United States, compared to just 17 percent in 1960. Similarly, the percentage of women enrolled in medical schools has jumped from 9 percent in 1970 to almost 50 percent today.[21]

deep-level diversity The differences in the psychological characteristics of employees, including personalities, beliefs, values, and attitudes.

Deep-Level Diversity Surface-level diversity is the most obvious and easiest-to-measure form of diversity. In contrast, **deep-level diversity** represents differences in the psychological characteristics of employees, including personalities, beliefs, values, and attitudes.[22] We can't directly see deep-level diversity, but it is evident in a person's decisions, statements, and actions. The secondary dimensions of diversity shown in Exhibit 1.2 don't represent psychological differences, but they and the primary dimensions influence deep-level diversity. Religion and geographic location, for example, influence a person's personal values. Education and work experience shape a person's beliefs and attitudes on a variety of issues. An individual's personal wealth (income), parental status, and other factors influence personal needs and preferences.

One illustration of deep-level diversity is the different attitudes and expectations held by employees across generational cohorts.[23] *Baby boomers*–people born between 1946 and 1964–seem to expect and desire more job security and are more intent on improving their economic and social status. In contrast, *Generation-X* employees–those born between 1965 and 1979–expect less job security and are motivated more by workplace flexibility, the opportunity to learn (particularly new technology), and working in an egalitarian and "fun" organization. Meanwhile, some observers suggest that *Generation-Y* employees (those born after 1979) are noticeably self-confident, optimistic, multitasking, and more independent than even Gen-X coworkers. These statements certainly don't apply to everyone in each cohort, but they reflect the fact that different generations have different values and expectations.

Consequences of Diversity Diversity presents both opportunities and challenges in organizations.[24] In some circumstances and to some degree, diversity can become a competitive advantage by improving decision making and team performance on complex tasks. For many businesses a diverse workforce also provides better customer service in a diverse society. For example, many Vietnamese customers insisted that Southern California Gas Co. field staff remove their steel-toed work boots when entering their homes, yet doing so would violate safety regulations. Some of the gas company's Vietnamese employees found a solution: Customers would be satisfied if employees wore paper booties over the boots. PepsiCo offers a more precise calculation of the diversity advantage. It recently estimated that one-eighth of revenue growth is directly attributable to new products inspired by diversity efforts, such as guacamole-flavored Doritos chips that appeal to Hispanic customers and a wasabi-flavored snack for Asian Americans.[25]

Against the evidence that workforce diversity is a sound business proposition, several experts suggest that the benefits are more subtle and contingent on a number of factors. In fact, the general conclusion is that most forms of diversity offer both advantages and disadvantages.[26] As we will discuss more fully in Chapter 9, diverse employees usually take longer to become a high-performing team. Chapter 11 looks into communication problems that exist between people from different backgrounds. Chapter 13 will explain how diversity is a source of conflict, which can lead to lack of information sharing and, in extreme cases, morale problems and higher turnover.

Whether or not workforce diversity is a business advantage, companies need to make it a priority because surface-level diversity is a moral and legal imperative. Ethically, companies that offer an inclusive workplace are, in essence, making fair and just decisions regarding employment, promotions, rewards, and so on. Fairness is a well-established influence on employee loyalty and satisfaction. "Diversity is about fairness; we use the term *inclusive meritocracy*," says Ann M. Limberg, president of Bank of America New Jersey. "What it does for our workforce is build trust and ensures that individual differences are valued."[27] In contrast, firms that fail to represent the diversity of people in the relevant labor force are unfairly discriminating against those who are significantly underrepresented. Altogether, diversity can make a difference to the organization's reputation and bottom line, but we still need to untangle what types of diversity make a difference and under what circumstances the benefits overtake the problems.

Connections 1.1

Attracting Talent through Work–Life Balance

Five years ago partners at Gray Plant Mooty made the tough decision to reduce the minimum number of billable hours (time paid through client fees) rather than raise the salaries of associates at the Minneapolis law firm. The partners might have expected a backlash when they announced that pay would not increase. Instead the law firm's associates gave the partners a standing ovation. By reducing billable hours, staff could now work fewer hours and have better work–life balance.

Work–life balance has become an important issue for staff at Gray Plant Mooty in Minneapolis as well as in most other companies. In its recent survey of more than 9,000 American university students, Universum Communications reported that more flexible work hours had become the top-ranked attribute that students are looking for in a prospective employer. When 1,000 Canadians were asked to identify the "top indicators of success in your own career," work–life balance ranked first, far ahead of salary level, challenging job, level of responsibility, and other alternatives. Another recent study reporting that work–life balance is the top priority for Canadians considering a new job offer. When 10,000 members of the New Zealand Institute of Chartered Accountants were asked to identify the prime motivation for them to choose and stay in their current jobs, one-third indicated work–life balance, beating out career advancement and money.

Work–life balance isn't always the top priority in employment. American university students placed it lower a few years ago when job prospects were limited. And university students in Europe and Asia place this factor below career advancement and challenging work or international assignments.

But even in these countries where it isn't the top priority, work–life balance is now well established as a business issue. Fuji Xerox's business in Singapore is an example. Not long ago the local managing director would arrive at work around 7:30 in the morning and stay until 10 at night. He would then continue working at home for a few more hours, sending employees e-mail messages with tasks he wanted completed "first thing in the morning." Fuji Xerox staff dutifully followed their boss's schedule, arriving at work much earlier in time to complete the assignments that had been e-mailed overnight. Eventually the managing director realized this unrelenting pace was wearing out both the staff and himself. Now he is out of the office by 6:30 p.m. and shoos his staff out at the same time. Fuji Xerox also gives employees the opportunity to work from home as well as flexibility regarding when they want to begin and end their workdays.[28]

Sources: Ipsos-Reid, "What Are Canadians' Top Indicators of Career Success?" Ipsos-Reid News release (Toronto: 7 May 2003); S.-A. Chia and E. Toh, "Give Employees a Break," *Straits Times (Singapore)*, 23 July 2005; S. Shellenbarger, "Forget Vacation Time, New Grads Want Stability and a Good Retirement Plan," *The Wall Street Journal*, 16 February 2006, p. D1; D. Healey, "Families Come First," *Hamilton Spectator (Canada)*, 16 March 2006, p. A16; S. Hsieh, "Minneapolis Law Firm Promotes Core Values," *Minnesota Lawyer*, 10 April 2006; M. Perry, "Stable Companions?" *Accountancy Age*, 13 April 2006, p. 18; "Money Comes Distant Third on Accountants' Wish List," *Scoop.co.nz*, 6 April 2006.

Evolving Employment Relationships

Globalization and increasing workforce diversity have produced two contrasting changes in relationships between employers and employees: (1) aligning the workplace with emerging workforce expectations and (2) increasing workforce flexibility to increase organizational competitiveness.

work–life balance Minimizing conflict between work and nonwork demands.

Aligning the Workplace with Emerging Workforce Expectations

Work–life balance–minimizing conflict between work and nonwork demands–was seldom mentioned a couple of decades ago. Most employees assumed that they would put in long hours to rise up through the corporate ladder. Asking the boss to accommodate nonwork responsibilities and interests was almost a sign of betrayal.[29] But as Connections 1.1 describes, work–life balance has become one of the most important factors in the employment relationship. Probably the main reason is that technology has turned many former 9-to-5 jobs into 24/7 employment, so people are pushing back with demands for more work–life balance. A second reason is that two-income families put more demands on both partners to provide time for household duties. Gen-X/Gen-Y expectations represent a third factor. Young people today are less willing to completely wrap themselves in their jobs, possibly because they witnessed the problems with this workaholic style in their baby boomer parents.

Along with providing more work–life balance, companies are adjusting to emerging workforce expectations of a more egalitarian workplace by reducing hierarchy and replacing command-and-control management with facilitating and teaching-oriented leaders. Gen-X/Gen-Y employees also want to work in companies that make a difference, which may explain why employers are paying more attention to serving the community rather than just shareholders–a trend we'll discuss in more detail later in this chapter.

Younger employees tend to view the workplace as a community where they spend a large part of their lives (even with work–life balance), so many expect opportunities for more social fulfillment and fun. Again, several companies are making this shift in the employment relationship. Google is a sparkling example. The company's Googleplex (headquarters) in Mountain View, California, "resembles a glimmering playground for 20-somethings," says one observer. The building is outfitted with lava lamps, exercise balls, casual sofas, foosballs, pool tables, workout rooms, video games, a restaurant with free gourmet meals, and a small pool where swimmers exercise against an artificial current. Beach volleyball matches are held in the courtyard, and roller hockey games are in the parking lot. Google executives had to remind some employees that making the Googleplex their permanent residence was against building code regulations.[30]

employability
An employment relationship in which people perform a variety of work activities rather than hold specific jobs, and are expected to continuously learn skills that will keep them employed.

Increasing Workforce Flexibility As some companies are aligning employment practices with emerging workforce expectations, they are also demanding more flexibility from employees to remain responsive to globalization and other sources of turbulence. This increased flexibility occurs partly through **employability,** in which employees are expected to manage their own careers by anticipating future organizational needs and developing new competencies that match those needs.[31] From this perspective, organizations are customers, and employees keep their jobs by continuously developing new competencies for the future and performing a variety of work activities over time. Furthermore, employability shifts the burden of this adaptability to employees rather than employers, although the latter are expected to offer the resources and opportunities to assist in the process. "I think people are starting to understand the concept of lifetime employability rather than lifetime employment," says Rich Hartnett, global staffing director at aerospace manufacturer Boeing. "It's a good idea to stay current with what's out there and take personal responsibility for our own employability."[32]

contingent work
Any job in which the individual does not have an explicit or implicit contract for long-term employment, or one in which the minimum hours of work can vary in a nonsystematic way.

Contingent Work Along with employability, companies are making more use of **contingent work** to increase workforce flexibility. Contingent work includes any job in which the individual does not have an explicit or implicit contract for long-term employment, or one in which the minimum hours of work can vary in a nonsystematic way. This employment relationship includes anyone with temporary or seasonal employment, freelance contractors (sometimes called "free agents"), and temporary staffing agency workers.[33] By some estimates more than 15 percent of the U.S. workforce is employed in some sort of contingent work arrangement. Some experts predict that this trend will continue.

Why has contingent work increased? One reason is that it allows companies to reduce costs by more closely matching employment levels and competencies with product or service demands. This is particularly apparent in service industries, where casual work is most common. It is also the preferred employment relationship for "free agents" with high-demand skills who enjoy a variety of interesting assignments. At the same time, research suggests that contingent workers potentially have higher accident rates as well as lower performance and loyalty. However, these outcomes depend on the type of contingent workers (for example, "free agent" contractors versus new hires on temporary status) as well as whether contingent workers are separated from, or interact regularly with, permanent staff. Another concern is that permanent employees may feel injustice against their employers if contingent workers are treated as second-class citizens.[34]

Virtual Work

Rush hour isn't much of a rush for Tan Swee Hoong. She enjoys breakfast with her three children, heads them off to school, then walks from the kitchen to her study. There the relocation manager at Hewlett-Packard's offices in Singapore checks e-mail and uses the telephone to connect with teammates on her work projects.[35] Tan Swee Hoong's daily routine is an example of **virtual work,** whereby employees use information technology to perform their jobs away from the traditional physical workplace. Tan's variation of virtual work, called *telecommuting* or *teleworking,* involves working at home rather than commuting to the office. Virtual work also includes employees connected to the office while on the road or at clients' offices.

virtual work
Work practices whereby employees use information technology to perform their jobs away from the traditional physical workplace.

Telecommuting is still rare in most Asian countries, making Tan Swee Hoong more of a pioneer than a typical employee in that region. It is somewhat more common in Japan, where 6 percent of employees telecommute. To ease traffic congestion and air pollution, the Japanese government wants to increase that figure to 20 percent by 2010. Various surveys estimate that around 20 percent of Americans work at home at least one day each month. In some firms telecommuting and other forms of virtual work are the norm rather than the exception. For instance, nearly 50 percent of employees at Sun Microsystems complete some of their work from home, cafés, drop-in centers, or clients' offices. More than two-thirds of the employees at Agilent Technologies engage in virtual work some or all of the time.[36]

Some research suggests that virtual work, particularly telecommuting, potentially reduces employee stress by offering better work–life balance and dramatically reducing time lost through commuting to the office. AT&T estimates that by avoiding daily travel, telecommuters reduce pollution and are about 10 percent more productive than before they started working from home. Nortel Networks reports that 71 percent of its U.K. staff feels more empowered through virtual work arrangements. Others point out that virtual work reduces the cost of office space and reduces traffic congestion.[37]

Against these potential benefits, virtual workers face a number of real or potential challenges.[38] Although telecommuting is usually introduced to improve work–life balance, family relations may suffer rather than improve if employees lack sufficient space and resources for a home office. Some virtual workers complain of lack of recognition, although virtual work does not seem to undermine career progression or performance ratings. Social isolation is another common complaint, particularly among virtual workers who rarely visit the office. Virtual work is clearly better suited to people who are self-motivated, organized, can work effectively with broadband and other technology, and have sufficient fulfillment of social needs elsewhere in their life. Virtual work also functions better in organizations that evaluate employees by their performance outcomes rather than by "face time."

virtual teams
Teams whose members operate across space, time, and organizational boundaries, and who are linked through information technologies to achieve organizational goals.

Virtual Teams Another variation of virtual work occurs in **virtual teams:** cross-functional groups that operate across space, time, and organizational boundaries with members who communicate mainly through information technology.[39] Virtual teams exist when some members telecommute, but also when team members are located on company premises at different sites around the country or world. Teams have varying degrees of virtualness, depending on how often and how many team members interact face-to-face or at a distance. Currently a flurry of research activity is studying the types of work best suited to virtual teams and the conditions that facilitate and hinder their effectiveness. As with telecommuting, some people are also better suited than others to virtual team dynamics. Chapter 10 will examine these virtual team issues in detail.

Workplace Values and Ethics

Search through most annual reports and you'll soon discover that corporate leaders view values as the sine qua non of organizational excellence. For example, as described in the opening story to this chapter, Google places paramount importance on the motto "Don't be evil." Vodafone, Xerox, Dell Computer, and a host of other organizations around the world have also reexamined the values that direct employee decisions and behavior. Xerox chief executive Anne Mulcahy claims that reaffirming the company's values "helped save Xerox during the worst crisis in our history."[40]

values
Stable, long-lasting beliefs about what is important in a variety of situations, that guide our decisions and actions.

Values represent stable, long-lasting beliefs about what is important in a variety of situations that guide our decisions and actions. They are evaluative standards that help define what is right or wrong, or good or bad, in the world. Values dictate our priorities, our preferences, and our desires. They influence our motivation and decisions.[41] Although leaders refer to the core values of their companies, values really exist only within individuals as *personal values.* However, groups of people might hold the same or similar values, so we tend to ascribe these *shared values* to the team, department, organization, profession, or entire society.

Importance of Values in the Workplace Values are not new to organizational behavior, but they have become the subject of several popular books, the mantra of corporate leaders, and the foundation of many corporate transformations in recent years.[42] One reason for this attention is that as today's workforce rejects command-and-control supervision, leaders are turning to values as a more satisfactory approach to aligning employees' decisions and actions with corporate goals. Values represent the unseen magnet that pulls employees in the same direction.[43] A second reason is

Values-Based Leadership at Dubai's Department of Economic Development The senior management team at the Department of Economic Development (DED) in the Emirate of Dubai recently devoted several months to identifying the agency's core values: accountability, teamwork, and continuous improvement. Each of these three values is anchored with specific behavior descriptions to ensure that employees and other stakeholders understand their meaning. DED also organized a series of workshops (shown in photo) in which employees participated in a "Values Mystery" exercise to help them recognize values-consistent behaviors. To develop a values-based organization, DED will also use these three values to evaluate employee performance, assess employee competencies, and identify management potential.[44]

that globalization has raised our awareness of and sensitivity to cultural differences in values and beliefs. Increasing cultural diversity also presents new challenges as organizations try to discover shared values acceptable to all employees.

The third reason why values have gained prominence is that organizations are under increasing pressure to engage in ethical practices and corporate social responsibility. **Ethics** refers to the study of moral principles or values that determine whether actions are right or wrong and outcomes are good or bad. We rely on our ethical values to determine "the right thing to do." Ethical behavior is driven by the moral principles we use to make decisions. These moral principles represent fundamental values. Unfortunately executives are receiving low grades on their ethics report cards these days, so ethics and values will continue to be an important topic in OB teaching.

ethics
The study of moral principles or values that determine whether actions are right or wrong and outcomes are good or bad.

Corporate Social Responsibility Over 30 years ago economist Milton Friedman pronounced that "there is one and only one social responsibility of business–to use its resources and engage in activities designed to increase its profits." Friedman is a respected scholar, but this argument was not one of his more popular–or accurate–statements. Today any business that follows Friedman's advice will face considerable trouble in the marketplace. Four out of five Americans say that a company's commitment to a social issue is an important factor in deciding whether to work there and whether to buy the company's products or services. Another poll reported that 97 percent of American and European MBA students would relinquish significant financial benefits to work for an organization with a better reputation for ethics and corporate social responsibility. Almost 80 percent of Canadians say a company's record of corporate social responsibility has either a moderate or a great deal of influence on their decision where to work.[45]

Corporate social responsibility (CSR) refers to an organization's moral obligation toward all of its **stakeholders.** Stakeholders are the shareholders, customers, suppliers, governments, and any other groups with a vested interest in the organization.[46] As part of corporate social responsibility, many companies have adopted the *triple bottom line* philosophy. This means that they try to support or "earn positive returns" in the economic, social, and environmental spheres of sustainability. Firms that adopt the triple bottom line aim to survive and be profitable in the marketplace (economic), but they also intend to maintain or improve conditions for society as well as the physical environment. For instance, Stratham, New Hampshire–based Timberland Co. pays employees to work on community projects and engage in more environmentally friendly behaviors. At The Warehouse, New Zealand's largest retailer, stores are evaluated monthly not just on their sales and profits, but also on how little landfill waste they produced to generate those financial returns.[47]

corporate social responsibility (CSR)
An organization's moral obligation toward its stakeholders.

stakeholders
Shareholders, customers, suppliers, governments, and any other groups with a vested interest in the organization.

Corporate leaders seem to agree that corporate social responsibility is an important part of the organization's obligations, yet many have difficulty translating their good intentions into corresponding behavior. Wal-Mart, the world's largest retailer, claims that it monitors suppliers with one of the toughest codes of conduct in the industry; yet an undercover camera crew recently revealed child labor openly practiced in some overseas factories that manufacture Wal-Mart products. For more than a decade Interface, the world's largest floor covering company, has tried to transform itself into an ecologically friendly manufacturer. The LaGrange, Georgia, firm has made better progress than others in the industry; but critics point out that Interface has fallen short of its original well-publicized goals for sustainability and may have exaggerated a few of its achievements.[48] The point here is that CSR is receiving a lot of attention, but in many organizations the rhetoric runs well ahead of actions.

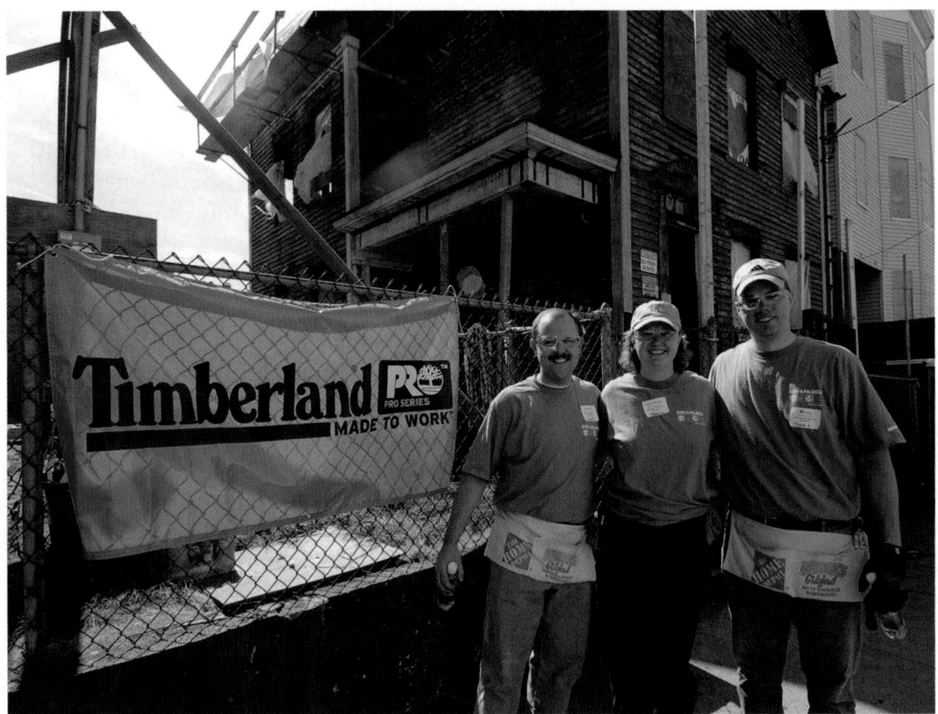

Selling Outdoor Gear and CSR at Timberland Anyone who thinks companies must choose between profits and corporate social responsibility (CSR) should have a conversation with Jeffrey Swartz. The CEO of Timberland Co. doesn't see the dilemma and, in fact, will enthusiastically point out how they can potentially complement each other. The U.S. designer and retailer of outdoor-themed clothing, shoes, and accessories seems to be a good example. Timberland has both growth and profitability, yet it stands out further than most firms in supporting the community and environment. Employees get 40 hours of paid leave every year to work on community projects. The company also closes operations for one day each year so staff can work together to help the community, such as cleaning up or rebuilding playgrounds and homeless shelters. To help the environment, Timberland pays employees $3,000 rebates and gives them preferred parking spots if they buy environmentally friendly hybrid cars. The company is also switching to solar energy in some of its operations.[49]

Learning Objectives

After reading this section you should be able to

7. **Identify the five anchors on which organizational behavior is based.**
8. **Diagram an organization from an open systems view.**

The Five Anchors of Organizational Behavior

Globalization, workforce diversity, evolving employment relationships, virtual work, and workplace values and ethics are just a few of the trends that we will explore in this textbook. To understand these and other topics, the field of organizational behavior relies on a set of basic beliefs or knowledge structures (see Exhibit 1.3). These conceptual anchors represent the way that OB researchers think about organizations and how they should be studied. Let's look at each of these five beliefs that anchor the study of organizational behavior.

Exhibit 1.3
Five Philosophical Anchors of Organizational Behavior

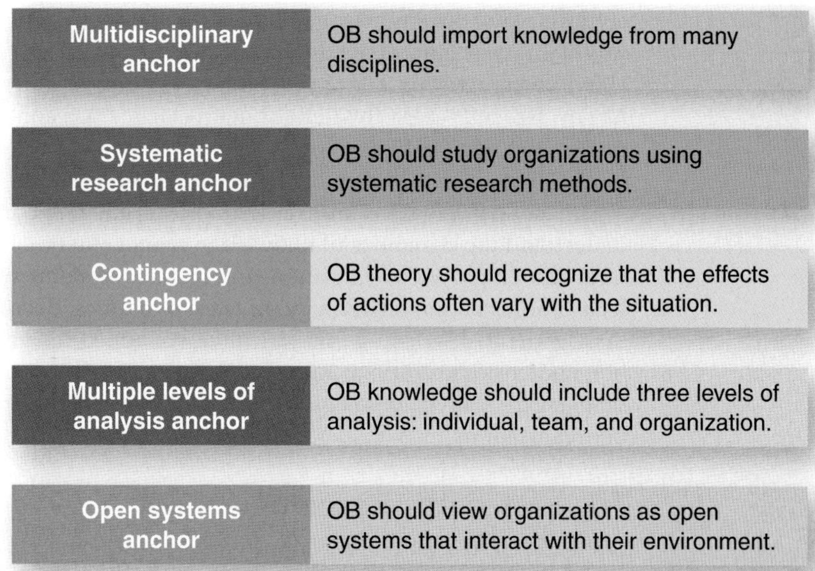

Multidisciplinary anchor
OB should import knowledge from many disciplines.
Systematic research anchor
OB should study organizations using systematic research methods.
Contingency anchor
OB theory should recognize that the effects of actions often vary with the situation.
Multiple levels of analysis anchor
OB knowledge should include three levels of analysis: individual, team, and organization.
Open systems anchor
OB should view organizations as open systems that interact with their environment.

The Multidisciplinary Anchor

Organizational behavior is anchored around the idea that the field should develop from knowledge in other disciplines, not just from its own isolated research base. Some OB experts have recently argued that the field suffers from a "trade deficit"–importing far more knowledge from other disciplines than is exported to other disciplines. Although this is a possible concern, organizational behavior has thrived through its diversity of knowledge from other fields of study.[50]

The upper part of Exhibit 1.4 identifies the traditional disciplines from which organizational behavior knowledge has developed. For instance, sociologists have

Exhibit 1.4
Multidisciplinary Anchor of Organizational Behavior

Discipline	Relevant OB topics
Traditional disciplines	
Psychology	Drives, perception, attitudes, personality, job stress, emotions, leadership
Sociology	Team dynamics, roles, socialization, communication patterns, organizational power, organizational structure
Anthropology	Corporate culture, organizational rituals, cross-cultural dynamics, organizational adaptation
Political science	Intergroup conflict, coalition formation, organizational power and politics, decision making, organizational environments
Economics	Decision making, negotiation, organizational power
Industrial engineering	Job design, productivity, work measurement
Emerging disciplines	
Communications	Knowledge management, electronic mail, corporate culture, employee socialization
Information systems	Team dynamics, decision making, knowledge management
Marketing	Knowledge management, creativity, decision making
Women's studies	Organizational power, perceptions

contributed to our knowledge of team dynamics, organizational socialization, organizational power, and other aspects of the social system. The field of psychology has aided our understanding of most issues relating to individual and interpersonal behavior. Recently even the field of neuroscience has contributed new ideas about human drives and behavior.[51]

The bottom part of Exhibit 1.4 identifies some of the emerging fields from which organizational behavior knowledge is acquired. The communications field helps us understand the dynamics of knowledge management, electronic mail, corporate culture, and employee socialization. Information systems scholars are exploring the effects of information technology on team dynamics, decision making, and knowledge management. Marketing scholars have enhanced our understanding of job satisfaction and customer service, knowledge management, and creativity. Women's studies scholars are studying perceptual biases and power relations between men and women in organizations.

The Systematic Research Anchor

A second anchor for organizational behavior researchers is their belief in the value of studying organizations through systematic research methods. Traditionally scholars have relied on the **scientific method** by forming research questions, systematically collecting data, and testing hypotheses against those data. This approach relies mainly on quantitative data (numeric information) and statistical procedures to test hypotheses. The idea behind the scientific method is to minimize personal biases and distortions about organizational events.

scientific method
A set principles and procedures that help researchers to systematically understand previously unexplained events and conditions.

More recently OB scholars have also adopted qualitative methods and, in particular, **grounded theory** to understand the workplace. Grounded theory is a process of developing a theory through the constant interplay between data gathering and the development of theoretical concepts. Through observation, interviews, and other forms of data collection, researchers form concepts and theories. But as they return to gather more information each time, they also test the concepts and theory created up to that point in the research study.[52] Appendix A at the end of this book provides an overview of research design and methods commonly found in organizational behavior studies.

grounded theory
A process of developing theory through the constant interplay between data gathering and the development of theoretical concepts.

The Contingency Anchor

"It depends" is a phrase that OB scholars often use to answer a question about the best solution to an organizational problem. The statement may seem evasive, yet it reflects an important way of understanding and predicting organizational events, called the **contingency approach.** This anchor states that a particular action may have different consequences in different situations. In other words, no single solution is best in all circumstances.[53]

contingency approach
The idea that a particular action may have different consequences in different situations.

The contingency anchor explains why OB experts tend to be skeptical about surefire recommendations that are so common in the media and consulting literature. Although the ideal situation might be to identify universal theories–where the concepts and practices have equal success in every situation–in reality there are usually too many exceptions to make these "one best way" theories useful. Even when a theory seems to work everywhere, OB scholars remain doubtful: An exception is somewhere around the corner. For example, in Chapter 14 we will learn that leaders should use one style (such as participation) in some situations and another style (perhaps direction) in other situations. Thus when faced with a particular problem or opportunity, we need to understand and diagnose the situation and select the strategy most appropriate *under those conditions.*[54]

Although contingency-oriented theories are necessary in most areas of organizational behavior, we should also be wary about carrying this anchor to an extreme. Some contingency models add more confusion than value over universal ones. Consequently, we need to balance the sensitivity of contingency factors with the simplicity of universal theories.

The Multiple Levels of Analysis Anchor

This textbook divides organizational behavior topics into three levels of analysis: individual, team, and organization. The individual level includes the characteristics and behaviors of employees as well as the thought processes that are attributed to them, such as motivation, perceptions, personalities, attitudes, and values. The team level of analysis looks at how people interact. This includes team dynamics, decisions, power, organizational politics, conflict, and leadership. At the organizational level we focus on how people structure their working relationships and on how organizations interact with their environments.

Although an OB topic is typically pegged into one level of analysis, it usually relates to multiple levels.[55] For instance, communication is located in this book as a team (interpersonal) process, but we also recognize that it includes individual and organizational processes. Therefore, you should try to think about each OB topic at the individual, team, and organizational levels–not just at one of these levels.

The Open Systems Anchor

Northwestern Mutual may have several buildings and financial investments, but CEO Ed Zore says that the insurance company is a living system with several interconnected subsystems. "Together, we're a living organism," suggests Zore in a recent annual meeting. "Every part is integrated, every part is interdependent, and every part is important."[56]

open systems
Organizations that take their sustenance from the environment and, in turn, affect that environment through their output.

Ed Zore is depicting Northwestern Mutual in terms of the fifth anchor of organizational behavior–the view that organizations are **open systems.** The open systems anchor of organizational behavior refers to the notion that organizations are organic systems that need to interact effectively with the external environment. Organizations take their sustenance from the environment and, in turn, affect that environment through their output. Thus a company's survival and success depend on how well employees sense environmental changes and alter their patterns of behavior to fit those emerging conditions.[57] In contrast, a closed system has all the resources needed to survive without dependence on the external environment. Organizations are never completely closed systems, but monopolies come close because they operate in very stable environments and can ignore stakeholders for a fairly long time without adverse consequences.

As Exhibit 1.5 illustrates, organizations acquire resources from the external environment, including raw materials, employees, financial resources, information, and equipment. Inside the organization are numerous subsystems, such as processes (communication and reward systems), task activities (production, marketing), and social dynamics (informal groups, power dynamics). With the aid of technology (such as equipment, work methods, and information), these subsystems transform inputs into various outputs. Some outputs (products and services) may be valued by the external environment, whereas other outputs (employee layoffs, pollution) have adverse effects. The organization receives feedback from the external environment regarding the value of its outputs and the availability of future inputs. This process is cyclical and, ideally, self-sustaining so that the organization may continue to survive and prosper.

Exhibit 1.5
Open Systems View of Organizations

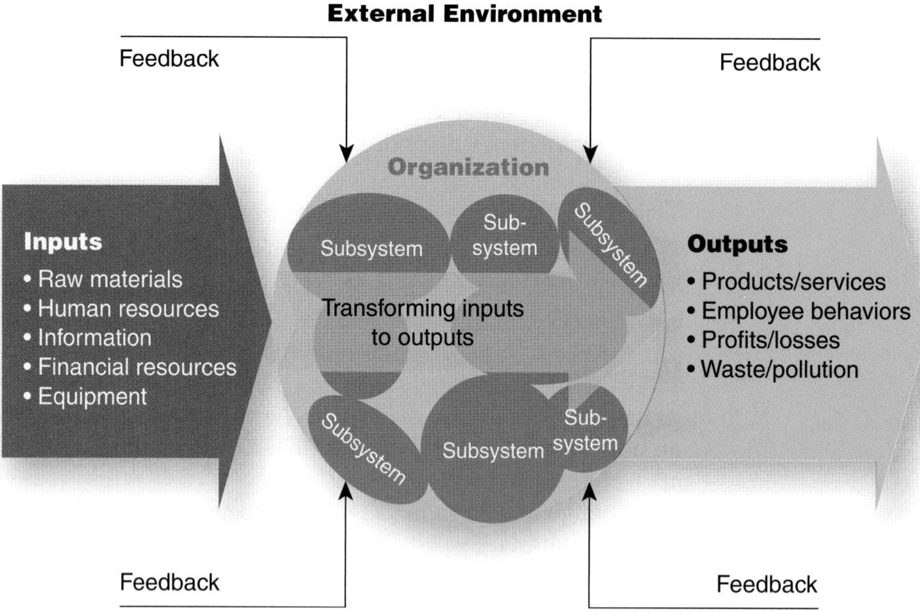

External Environment and Stakeholders As open systems, successful organizations monitor their environments and are able to maintain a close fit with those changing conditions.[58] They do so by reconfiguring their outputs (new products and services, reducing waste) and transforming their processes. At the same time this dynamic capability must not be accelerated to the point where it depletes the organization's resources or gets too far ahead of market demand. The point here is that organizations need to adapt to changing environments–but not so much that they overspend their resources or overshoot stakeholder needs.

Stakeholders represent a central part of the internal and external environment. As mentioned earlier, these include any person or entity with a vested interest in the organization. Stakeholders influence the firm's access to inputs and ability to discharge outputs. And unless they pay attention to the needs of all stakeholders, organizational leaders may find their business in trouble. For instance, leaders may put their organization at risk if they pay attention only to shareholders and ignore the broader corporate social responsibility.[59] We see this stakeholder misalignment when job applicants avoid companies that ignore corporate social responsibility and when organizations fail to treat their employees and suppliers with respect.

Systems as Interdependent Parts The open systems anchor states that organizations consist of many internal subsystems that need to be continuously aligned with each other. As companies grow, they develop more and more complex subsystems that must coordinate with each other in the process of transforming inputs to outputs.[60] These interdependencies can easily become so complex that a minor event in one subsystem may amplify into serious unintended consequences elsewhere in the organization.

The open systems anchor is an important way of viewing organizations. However, it has traditionally focused on physical resources that enter the organization and are processed into physical goods (outputs). This was representative of the industrial economy but not of the "new economy," where the most valued input is knowledge.

Learning Objectives

After reading this section you should be able to

9. Define knowledge management and intellectual capital.

10. Identify specific ways in which organizations acquire, share, and preserve knowledge.

Knowledge Management

knowledge management Any structured activity that improves an organization's capacity to acquire, share, and use knowledge in ways that improve its survival and success.

intellectual capital The sum of an organization's human capital, and relationship capital.

In the opening story to this chapter, Google's chief financial officer George Reyes said that his company "is truly a learning organization." This perspective of organizations, called **knowledge management,** includes any structured activity that improves an organization's capacity to acquire, share, and use knowledge in ways that improve its survival and success.[61] Knowledge management is an offshoot of the open systems view because it presumes that organizations need to interact with their environment.

For instance, Google is a learning organization–it actively applies knowledge management–because it actively seeks out knowledgeable people (such as Rob Pike), supports knowledge sharing and creativity, and encourages employees to quickly transform that knowledge into valuable services such as Google's search engine, Google Desktop, Gmail, Google News, and Google Translate. Even after services have been created, the organization learns from feedback about how the public uses those services.

The stock of knowledge that resides in an organization is called its **intellectual capital,** which is the sum of everything known in an organization that gives it competitive advantage–including its human capital, structural capital, and relationship capital:[62]

- *Human capital.* This is the knowledge that employees possess and generate, including their skills, experience, and creativity.
- *Structural capital.* This is the knowledge captured and retained in an organization's systems and structures. It is the knowledge that remains after all the human capital has gone home.
- *Relationship capital.* This is the value derived from an organization's relationships with customers, suppliers, and other external stakeholders who provide added mutual value for the organization. For example, this includes customer loyalty as well as trust between the organization and its suppliers.

Knowledge Management Processes

To maintain a valuable *stock* of knowledge (intellectual capital), organizations depend on their capacity to acquire, share, and use knowledge more effectively. This *process* is often called *organizational learning* because companies must continuously learn about their various environments to survive and succeed through adaptation.[63] The "capacity" to acquire, share, and use knowledge means that companies have established systems, structures, and organizational values that support the knowledge management process. Let's look more closely at some of the strategies companies use to acquire, share, and use knowledge.

Knowledge Acquisition Knowledge acquisition includes the process of extracting information and ideas from the external environment as well as through insight. One of the fastest and most powerful ways to acquire knowledge is by hiring individuals or acquiring entire companies. Knowledge also enters the organization when employees learn from external sources, such as discovering new resources from suppliers or becoming aware of new trends from clients. For instance, a team of employees at Amcor, one of the world's largest packaging companies, continuously searches around the world for intellectual property and patent licensing opportunities. This knowledge acquisition process recently helped the company develop plastic packaging that prevented table grapes from falling off their stems. A third knowledge acquisition strategy is through experimentation. Companies receive knowledge through insight as a result of research and other creative processes.[64]

absorptive capacity
The ability to recognize the value of new information, assimilate it, and apply it to commercial ends.

An important contingency with knowledge acquisition is that organizations must have enough absorptive capacity to acquire the knowledge. **Absorptive capacity** refers to the ability to recognize the value of new information, assimilate it, and apply it to commercial ends. The absorptive capacity to acquire new knowledge depends on the company's existing store of knowledge. Without basic knowledge of plastics and package manufacturing processes, Amcor engineers could not have effectively applied outside knowledge to improve packaging for table grapes. Thus acquiring new knowledge from the environment requires absorptive capacity, which depends on the organization's existing foundation of knowledge. This absorptive capacity also applies to the ability of entire societies to develop.[65]

Knowledge Sharing Many organizations are reasonably good at acquiring knowledge, but they waste this resource by not effectively spreading it around. As several executives have lamented, "I wish we knew what we know."[66] Valuable ideas sit idly—rather like unused inventory—or remain hidden as "silos of knowledge" throughout the organization. Many organizations improve knowledge sharing by creating digital repositories of knowledge: computer intranets in which employees document and store new knowledge as it becomes available. Although somewhat useful, these electronic storage systems can be expensive to maintain; they also overlook the fact that a lot of knowledge is difficult to document.[67]

communities of practice
Informal groups bound together by shared expertise and passion for a particular activity or interest.

An alternative strategy for knowledge sharing is to give employees more opportunities for informal online or face-to-face communication. One such approach is through **communities of practice:** groups bound together by shared expertise and passion for a particular activity or interest.[68] One pioneer in communities of practice is Clarica Life Insurance Company. Realizing that its agents possess valuable knowledge that is often isolated from other agents, the company created an online forum where knowledge among sales agents can be actively shared with others.[69]

Knowledge Use Acquiring and sharing knowledge are wasted exercises unless knowledge is effectively put to use. To do this, employees must realize that the knowledge is available and that they have enough freedom to apply it. This requires a culture that supports experiential learning, which we will describe in Chapter 3.

Organizational Memory

The Olympic Games are mammoth projects requiring deep knowledge about managing sports events; yet until recently little knowledge was documented and passed on to the next Olympic organizing committee. "You had a situation where every two years, a $2–4 billion Olympic event would be staged somewhere, and every time the organizers would start all over again—no historical data, no corporate knowledge," explains Craig McLatchey, former secretary general of the Australian Olympic Committee and board member of the Sydney Organizing Committee for the Olympic Games (SOCOG). "You would see SOCOG staff literally sitting in front of a blank sheet of paper, trying to work things out."[70]

SOCOG's experience is a reminder that corporate leaders are the keepers of an organizational memory.[71] This unusual metaphor refers to the storage and preservation of intellectual capital. It includes information that employees possess as well as

Evercare's Hard Lesson in Organizational Memory A few years ago Evercare (formerly Helmac) decided to move its headquarters and manufacturing from Flint, Michigan, to Georgia. The move nearly killed the manufacturer of Lint Pic-up products because none of Evercare's production employees wanted to leave Flint. So when the company's executives arrived in Georgia to set up production, they struggled to rebuild the company's manufacturing and distribution systems from scratch. "Nothing was documented," recalls manufacturing vice president John Moore, shown here with vice president of distribution Barbara Tomaszewski. "All of the knowledge, all of the practices were built in people's heads." The good news was that the rebuilt company seems stronger because employees did not learn some of the past practices that didn't work.[72]

knowledge embedded in the organization's systems and structures. It includes documents, objects, and anything else that provides meaningful information about how the organization should operate. One way to maintain an organizational memory is to keep good employees. Progressive companies attract and retain high-quality staff by adopting employment practices compatible with emerging workforce expectations, including work–life balance, egalitarian hierarchy, and a workplace that generates more fun.

A second organizational memory strategy is to systematically transfer knowledge before employees leave. This occurs when new recruits apprentice with skilled employees, thereby acquiring knowledge that is not documented. A third approach is to transfer knowledge into structural capital. This includes bringing out hidden knowledge, organizing it, and putting it in a form that can be available to others. SOCOG applied this strategy by asking every division and functional area to complete an extensive "how to" template based on their experiences in the Sydney Olympics. After the event, SOCOG had produced 90 manuals documenting each area's mission and objectives, key risks, key stakeholders, key interactions, operations plans, budget, organizational charts, multiyear staffing, key considerations, and key lessons and recommendations. This documented memory of the Sydney Olympics became a major resource for Athens and other Olympics.

Before leaving the topic of organizational memory and knowledge management, you should know that successful companies also unlearn. Sometimes it is appropriate for organizations to selectively forget certain knowledge.[73] This means that they should cast off routines and patterns of behavior that are no longer appropriate. Employees need to rethink their perceptions, such as how they should interact with customers and which is the "best way" to perform a task. As we will discover in Chapter 17, unlearning is essential for organizational change.

The Journey Begins

This chapter has given you some background about the field of organizational behavior. But it's only the beginning of our journey. Throughout this book we will challenge you to learn new ways of thinking about how people work in and around organizations. We begin this process in Chapter 2 by presenting a basic model of individual behavior, then introducing over the next six chapters various stable and mercurial characteristics of individuals that relate to elements of the individual behavior model. Next this book moves to the team level of analysis. We examine a model of team effectiveness and specific features of high-performance teams. We also look at decision making and creativity, communication, power and influence, conflict and negotiation, and leadership. Finally we shift our focus to the organizational level of analysis, where the topics of organizational structure, organizational culture, and organizational change are examined in detail.

Chapter Summary

Organizational behavior is the study of what people think, feel, and do in and around organizations. Organizations are groups of people who work interdependently toward some purpose. OB concepts help us to predict and understand organizational events, adopt more accurate theories of reality, and influence organizational events. This field of knowledge also improves the organization's financial health.

There are several trends in organizational behavior. Globalization requires corporate decision makers to be sensitive to cultural differences. Another trend is increasing workforce diversity. Employment relations are also evolving as companies adapt workplace practices to support emerging workforce expectations while also demanding more flexibility through employability and contingent work.

Virtual work, a fourth trend, occurs when employees use information technology to perform their jobs away from the traditional physical workplace. Virtual work includes telecommuting as well as virtual teams–cross-functional groups that operate across space, time, and organizational boundaries with members who communicate mainly through information technology. Values and ethics represent the fifth trend. In particular, companies are learning to apply values in a global environment, and they are under pressure to abide by ethical values and higher standards of corporate social responsibility.

Organizational behavior scholars rely on a set of basic beliefs to study organizations. These anchors include beliefs that OB knowledge should be multidisciplinary and based on systematic research; that organizational events usually have contingencies; that organizational behavior can be viewed from three levels of analysis (individual, team, and organization); and that organizations are open systems.

The open systems anchor suggests that organizations have interdependent parts that work together to continually monitor and transact with the external environment. They acquire resources from the environment, transform them through technology, and return outputs to the environment. The external environment consists of the natural and social conditions outside the organization. External environments are generally highly turbulent today, so organizations must become adaptable and responsive.

Knowledge management develops an organization's capacity to acquire, share, and use knowledge in ways that improve its survival and success. Intellectual capital is knowledge that resides in an organization, including its human capital, structural capital, and relationship capital. Organizations acquire knowledge through various practices, including individual learning and experimentation. Knowledge sharing occurs mainly through various forms of communication, including communities of practice. Knowledge use occurs when employees realize that the knowledge is available and that they have enough freedom to apply it. Organizational memory refers to the storage and preservation of intellectual capital.

Key Terms

absorptive capacity, p. 22
communities of practice, p. 22
contingency approach, p. 18
contingent work, p. 12
corporate social responsibility (CSR), p. 15
deep-level diversity, p. 9
employability, p. 12
ethics, p. 15
globalization, p. 7
grounded theory, p. 18
intellectual capital, p. 21
knowledge management, p. 21
open systems, p. 19
organizational behavior (OB), p. 4
organizations, p. 5
scientific method, p. 18
stakeholders, p. 15
surface-level diversity, p. 8
values, p. 14
virtual teams, p. 14
virtual work, p. 13
work–life balance, p. 11

Critical Thinking Questions

1. A friend suggests that organizational behavior courses are useful only to people who will enter management careers. Discuss the accuracy of your friend's statement.
2. Look through the list of chapters in this textbook and discuss how globalization could influence each organizational behavior topic.
3. Corporate social responsibility is one of the hottest issues in corporate boardrooms these days, partly because it is becoming increasingly important to employees and other stakeholders. In your opinion, why have stakeholders given CSR more attention recently? Does abiding by CSR standards potentially cause companies to have conflicting objectives with some stakeholders in some situations?
4. "Organizational theories should follow the contingency approach." Comment on the accuracy of this statement.
5. A number of years ago, employees in a city water distribution department were put into teams and encouraged to find ways to improve efficiency. The teams boldly crossed departmental boundaries and areas of management discretion in search of problems. Employees working in other parts of the city began to complain about these intrusions. Moreover, when some team ideas were implemented, the city managers discovered that a dollar saved in the water distribution unit may have cost the organization two dollars in higher costs elsewhere. Use the open systems anchor to explain what happened here.
6. After hearing a seminar on knowledge management, a mining company executive argues that this perspective ignores the fact that mining companies could not rely on knowledge alone to stay in business. They also need physical capital (such as digging and ore processing equipment) and land (where the minerals are located). In fact, these two may be more important than what employees carry around in their heads. Discuss the merits of the mining executive's comments.
7. At a recent seminar on information technology, you heard a consultant say that over 30 percent of U.S. companies use software to manage documents and exchange information, whereas firms in Europe are just beginning to adopt this technology. Based on this, the consultant concluded that "knowledge management in Europe is at its beginning stages." In other words, few firms in Europe practice knowledge management. Comment on this consultant's statement.
8. BusNews Corp. is the leading stock market and business news service. Over the past two years BusNews has experienced increased competition from other news providers. These competitors have brought in Internet and other emerging computer technologies to link customers with information more quickly. There is little knowledge within BusNews about howto use these computer technologies. Based on the knowledge acquisition processes for knowledge management, explain how BusNews might gain the intellectual capital necessary to become more competitive in this respect.

Case Study 1.1 INTRODUCING WORK–LIFE BALANCE AT OXFORD MANUFACTURING

Fiona McQuarrie, University College of the Fraser Valley

Oxford Manufacturing is a company with 350 employees in a large Midwestern city. It specializes in producing custom plastic products, although it also manufactures a range of small plastic items (such as storage boxes and water bottles) that it sells to wholesale distributors. Because of the variety of products the firm produces, its workers have a wide range of skill levels and qualifications: engineers with university degrees work on design and production specifications for customized products, and assembly line workers, some of whom did not finish high school, operate machines in the production facility. The company's plant operates 12 hours a day, seven days a week–although if a large order cannot be produced during regular hours, operating hours may be added to meet that demand.

Over the last few years, where Oxford is located, the demand for workers has begun to exceed the supply. Oxford's owners have realized that the company can no longer afford to sit back and let potential employees find them, as was the case in the past. They also realize that the company is now increasingly competing for employees, especially skilled ones, with other manufacturing firms in the same area. These realities have led Oxford's owners to decide that Oxford needs to be seen as a "preferred employer" if it is going to attract and retain the best employees. They have decided to make Oxford a preferred employer by emphasizing how much the company cares about employees' work–life balance. The message communicated to potential and current employees is that Oxford wants to help them achieve a lifestyle in which work and nonwork commitments are equally important. The company has adopted a policy giving each employee five "free days" off per year to use for whatever purpose the employee desires, in addition to generous vacation and sick leave benefits. The company also has encouraged department managers to schedule workers' shifts to accommodate the workers' outside commitments as much as possible. The company managers feel that offering such benefits will not only attract good workers to Oxford but also help retain the ones already working there.

Peter MacNee is a manager of one of the production areas. He has received requests from two of his employees to accommodate their work schedules to their nonwork commitments.

- John Mason is an engineer whose marriage has recently ended. He is now a single parent to a daughter, age 9, and a son, age 6. His parents are helping him with child care, but they are not always available to take care of the children during the day when John is at work. In addition, John's daughter was badly affected by her parents' divorce; occasionally she has temper tantrums and refuses to go to school or stay with her grandparents, insisting that only her father can take care of her. These situations have occasionally resulted in John having to miss work on short notice. Peter has allowed John to use three of his five annual free days to cover these situations, even though company policy states that employees wishing to take free days must notify their supervisor two weeks before the date of the absence. John is asking to work only in the evenings because his parents are regularly available to supervise his children then. He is also offering to work unpaid overtime in exchange for formally being allowed to take his two remaining free days as needed without the required period of notification. He is willing to continue to be available for unpaid overtime if the company gives him a yearly allocation of five additional free days.
- Jane Collier is a supervisor on the production line. She also participates in curling at the local recreation center. When a friend encouraged her to take up curling for fun a few years ago, she was having problems with her health and was also somewhat shy. Because she has been curling regularly, her fitness level has increased, and her health problems are no longer affecting her attendance at work. In addition, because success in curling requires working effectively as part of a team, her social and supervisory skills at work have noticeably improved. Jane's curling team has an opportunity to join a new curling league that is more competitive than the one they currently belong to, but this will allow them to compete at regional, national, and possibly even international levels. Jane's team has decided not only to join this league but also to start working with a coach to improve their technique. Jane is asking to be scheduled for day shifts only because of the time demands of this new level of participation and because most of her curling-related activities will take place in the evenings. She is also asking for two weeklong unpaid leaves per year to attend curling bonspiels (competitions) out of town.

Peter is not sure what to do with these requests. He knows that the company encourages employee work–life balance and expects its managers to support employees trying to manage both work and nonwork activities. He realizes that John and Jane would not have made their requests unless they felt the requested accommodations were the only way they could successfully balance their work lives with their nonwork commitments. However, there is no way he can grant both requests: The products John helps design are manufactured by the production line Jane supervises, and both of them need to be at work at the same time at least twice a week to share information about the products they are working on. He is also aware that John and Jane are talented and experienced employees, and if he turns down these requests, they will have no trouble finding comparable jobs with any of Oxford's competitors.

As Peter is considering this dilemma, he shuffles through the pile of mail that arrived on his desk that morning. An interoffice memo catches his eye, and he pulls it out of the pile and opens it. The memo is from the three office administrators in his area. The administrators complain that they are becoming increasingly upset with their co-workers, most of whom are married and have families, "dumping" work on them because of family crises. The memo describes several recent incidents in which co-workers received phone calls about family problems and then left for the rest of the day, asking the office administrators to cover for them and complete their work. After dealing with their co-workers' unfinished tasks, the administrators often had to stay beyond the end of their scheduled shifts to finish their own work. The last paragraph of the memo states, "We don't mind helping out once in a while, but not having kids or elderly parents to take care of doesn't mean we don't have anything to do besides work. If we have to stay late on short notice, we often have to cancel activities that are important to us. This is unfair; and if other people can't manage their family responsibilities, they should be the ones making the adjustments, not us. We want you to address this problem immediately because it is occurring more and more frequently."

Discussion Questions

1. How should Peter deal with John's and Jane's requests and the complaint from the administrators?
2. What can the organization as a whole do to address problems like these?
3. What organizational behavior issues can you identify in this case?

Case Study 1.2 WAL-MART REACHES FOR THE WHITE HAT

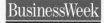

Wal-Mart Stores, Inc., has weathered unpaid hours and sex discrimination lawsuits, claims of supporting sweat-shop factories in Asia, union busting, and other public relations nightmares over the past few years. Now, the world's largest retailer is trying to fight back by more actively embracing corporate social responsibility, and by hiring some of the top guns in the public relations industry to get that message out to the public. Wal-Mart responded quickly with help to victims of Hurricane Katrina. It is working with anit-sweatshop groups to improve monitoring of factories where it purchases products. The retailer is even working with environmental groups to open eco-friendly stores and generally find ways to reduce the amount of packaging.

This *BusinessWeek* case study describes Wal-Mart's responses to criticism that it has failed the corporate social responsibility test. Read the full text of this *BusinessWeek* article at www.mhhe.com/mcshane4e and prepare for the discussion questions below.

Discussion Questions

1. Evaluate Wal-Mart's corporate social responsibility initiatives in the context of the triple bottom line. What else could it do to fulfil the triple bottom line mandate?
2. In addition to introducing new corporate social responsibility initiatives, Wal-Mart is actively communicating its practices through public relations experts. Is this action necessary and appropriate, in your opinion? What are the risks of Wal-Mart's public relations activities?

Source: R. Berner, "Can Wal-Mart Fit Into a White Hat?" *BusinessWeek,* 3 October, 2005, p. 94.

Team Exercise 1.3 HUMAN CHECKERS

PURPOSE This exercise is designed to help you understand the importance and application of organizational behavior concepts.

MATERIALS None, but the instructor has more information about the team's task.

INSTRUCTIONS

1. Form teams with six students. If possible, each team should have a private location where team members can plan and practice the required task without being observed or heard by other teams.
2. All teams will receive special instructions in class about the team's assigned task. All teams have the same task and will have the same amount of time to plan and practice the task. At the end of this planning and practice, each team will be timed while completing the task in class. The team that completes the task in the least time wins.
3. No special materials are required or allowed (see the following rules) for this exercise. Although the task is not described here, you should learn the following rules for planning and implementing the task:
   a. You cannot use any written form of communication or any props to assist in the planning or implementation of this task.
   b. You may speak to other students in your team at any time during the planning and implementation of this task.
   c. When performing the task, you must move only in the direction of your assigned destination. In other words, you can move only forward, not backward.
   d. When performing the task, you can move forward to the next space, but only if it is vacant (see Exhibit 1).
   e. When performing the task, you can move forward two spaces if that space is vacant. In other words, you can move around a student who is one space in front of you to the next space if that space is vacant (see Exhibit 2).

Exhibit 1

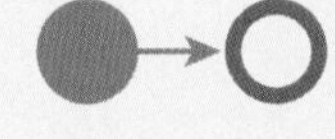

Exhibit 2

4. When all teams have completed their task, the class will discuss the implications of this exercise for organizational behavior.

DISCUSSION QUESTIONS

1. Identify the organizational behavior concepts that the teams applied to complete this task.
2. What personal theories of people and work teams were applied to complete this task?
3. What organizational behavior problems occurred? What actions were (or should have been) taken to solve them?

Web Exercise 1.4 DIAGNOSING ORGANIZATIONAL STAKEHOLDERS

PURPOSE This exercise is designed to help you understand how stakeholders influence organizations as part of the open systems anchor.

MATERIALS You need to select a company and, prior to class, retrieve and analyze information publicly available over the past year or two about that company. This may include annual reports, which are usually found on the Web sites of publicly traded companies. Where possible, you should also scan full-text newspaper and magazine databases for articles published over the previous year about the company.

INSTRUCTIONS The instructor may have you work alone or in groups for this activity. Select a company and investigate the relevance and influence of various stakeholder groups on the organization. Stakeholders can be identified from annual reports, newspaper articles, Web site statements, and other available sources. Stakeholders should be rank ordered in terms of their perceived importance to the organization.

Be prepared to present or discuss your rank ordering of the organization's stakeholders, including the evidence you used.

DISCUSSION QUESTIONS

1. What are the main reasons why certain stakeholders are more important than others for this organization?
2. Based on your knowledge of the organization's environmental situation, is this rank ordering of stakeholders in the organization's best interest, or should specific other stakeholders be given higher priority?
3. What societal groups, if any, are not mentioned as stakeholders by the organization? Does this lack of reference to these unmentioned groups make sense?

Self-Assessment 1.5

IT ALL MAKES SENSE?

PURPOSE This exercise is designed to help you understand how organizational behavior knowledge can help you understand life in organizations.

INSTRUCTIONS (*Note:* This activity may be done as a self-assessment or as a team activity.) Read each of the following statements and circle whether each statement is true or false, in your opinion. The class will consider the answers to each question and discuss the implications for studying organizational behavior.

Due to the nature of this activity, the instructor will provide the answers to these questions. There is no scoring key in Appendix B.

1.	True	False	A happy worker is a productive worker.
2.	True	False	Decision makers tend to continue supporting a course of action even though information suggests that the decision is ineffective.
3.	True	False	Organizations are more effective when they prevent conflict among employees.
4.	True	False	It is better to negotiate alone than as a team.
5.	True	False	Companies are more effective when they have a strong corporate culture.
6.	True	False	Employees perform better without stress.
7.	True	False	Effective organizational change always begins by pinpointing the source of current organizational problems.
8.	True	False	Female leaders involve employees in decisions to a greater degree than do male leaders.
9.	True	False	People in Japan value group harmony and duty to the group (high collectivism) more than Americans do (low collectivism).
10.	True	False	The best decisions are made without emotion.
11.	True	False	If employees feel they are paid unfairly, then nothing other than changing their pay will reduce their feelings of injustice.

Self-Assessment 1.6

TELEWORK DISPOSITION ASSESSMENT (STUDENT OLC)

Some employees adapt better than others do to telework (also called telecommuting) and other forms of virtual work. This self-assessment measures personal characteristics that seem to relate to telecommuting, and therefore provides a rough indication of how well you might adapt to telework. The instrument asks you to indicate how much you agree or disagree with each of the statements provided. You need to be honest with yourself to get a reasonable estimate of your telework disposition. Please keep in mind that this scale considers only your personal characteristics. Other factors, such as organizational, family, and technological systems support, must also be taken into account.

After reading this chapter, if you need additional information, see www.mhhe.com/mcshane4e for more in-depth interactivities that correspond with this material.

Part Two

Individual Behavior and Processes

Shutting down two production furnaces for major repairs effectively idled half of the production employees at Owens Corning's plant in Jackson, Tennessee. But rather than invoke a massive layoff, the company rotated everyone through a one-week quality management training program at full pay. This decision had an immediate and powerful effect. "As our employees returned from training, they were more engaged and more aware of waste," says Owen Corning's plant operations leader. This observation was supported a few months later when the plant's employee engagement scores jumped by 12 points from the previous survey.

Owens Corning is making employee engagement a cornerstone of its business strategy to become a world-class organization.

Employee engagement has become the watchword at Owens Corning and many other organizations. It refers to how much employees identify with and are emotionally committed to their work, are cognitively focused on that work, and possess the ability and resources to do the work. Royal Bank of Scotland calculated that when their employee engagement scores increase, productivity rises and staff turnover falls.

Two separate consultant reports estimate that only about a quarter of American employees are highly engaged, fewer than 60 percent are somewhat engaged, and approximately one-fifth have low engagement or are actively disengaged. Actively disengaged employees tend to be disruptive at work, not just dissatisfied. One recent report estimated that employees in Mexico and Brazil have the highest levels of engagement, whereas several Asian countries (notably Japan, China, and South Korea) and a few European countries (notably Italy, Netherlands, and France) have the lowest levels. Surveys by other consulting firms reveal similar employee engagement scores across countries.

ASB Bank scored well above average in its first employee engagement survey, but that wasn't good enough for the New Zealand financial institution. "We were absolutely shattered," recalls an ASB Bank executive, expecting to be in the top quartile. To boost its employee engagement levels, ASB Bank produced videos showing how managers with the most engaged subordinates perform their jobs. Managers also meet with staff each month, and the bank's chief executive personally teaches new employees about the company's customer service vision. The company also provides opportunities for employees to socialize after work. Today, ASB Bank's employee engagement scores are in the top 10 percent globally, and the company receives some of the highest ratings in New Zealand for customer service.[1]

2

Individual Behavior, Values, and Personality

LEARNING OBJECTIVES

After reading this chapter you should be able to

1. Identify the four drivers of individual behavior and results.
2. Describe three ways to match individual competencies to job requirements.
3. Identify five types of individual behavior in organizations.
4. Define *values* and explain why values congruence is important.
5. Define five values commonly studied across cultures.
6. List three ethical principles.
7. Explain how moral intensity, ethical sensitivity, and the situation influence ethical behavior.
8. Identify the "Big Five" personality dimensions.
9. Summarize the personality concepts behind the Myers-Briggs Type Indicator.
10. Explain how personality relates to Holland's model of vocational choice.

employee engagement Employees' emotional and cognitive (rational) motivation, their ability to perform their jobs, their possessing a clear understanding of the organization's vision and their specific roles in that vision, and a belief that they have been given the resources to get their jobs done.

The groundswell of interest in **employee engagement** makes a great deal of sense because this concept includes most of the drivers of individual behavior and performance results. It refers to employees' emotional and cognitive (rational) motivation, their ability to perform their jobs, their possessing a clear understanding of the organization's vision and their specific roles in that vision, and a belief that they have been given the resources to get their jobs done. This chapter begins by presenting the MARS model, which outlines the four drivers of individual behavior and results. Next this chapter briefly describes the five main types of individual behavior in the workplace.

The latter half of this chapter looks at values and personality–two deeply held characteristics of people that influence their attitudes, motivation, and behavior in the workplace. The section about values describes Schwartz's model of personal values, issues relating to values congruence, the dynamics of cross-cultural values, and key features of ethical values in the workplace. The section about personality introduces the five-factor model of personality, the Myers-Briggs Type Indicator, and other personality characteristics that are often discussed in organizational behavior research.

Learning Objectives

After reading the next two sections you should be able to

1. **Identify the four drivers of individual behavior and results.**
2. **Describe three ways to match individual competencies to job requirements.**
3. **Identify five types of individual behavior in organizations.**

MARS Model of Individual Behavior and Results

Why do individuals behave the way they do and perform well or poorly in the workplace? This question has been the center of much research in organizational behavior, and it is the focus of this chapter and the next five chapters in this book. We begin to answer this question by presenting a basic model of individual behavior and results (called the MARS model) and outlining the main types of behavior in organizational settings. Then we set out to examine the main individual difference topics underlying the MARS model, beginning with two of the most stable influences: values and personality.

The MARS model, illustrated in Exhibit 2.1, is a useful starting point to understanding the drivers of individual behavior and results. The model highlights the four factors that directly influence an employee's voluntary behavior and resulting performance–motivation, ability, role perceptions, and situational factors. These four factors are represented by the acronym "MARS" in the model's name.[2] The MARS model shows that these four factors have a combined effect on individual performance. If any factor weakens, employee performance will decrease. For example, enthusiastic salespeople (motivation) who understand their job duties (role perceptions) and have sufficient resources (situational factors) will not perform their jobs as well if they lack sufficient knowledge and sales skill (ability). Look back at the opening story, and you will see that employee engagement captures all four MARS drivers of individual behavior and results. No wonder employee engagement has become such a popular concept among executives and consultants!

Exhibit 2.1 also shows that the four factors in the MARS model are influenced by several other individual variables that we will discuss over the next few chapters. Personality and values are the most stable characteristics,[3] so we look at them later in this chapter. Emotions, attitudes, and stress are much more fluid characteristics,

Exhibit 2.1 **MARS Model of Individual Behavior and Results**

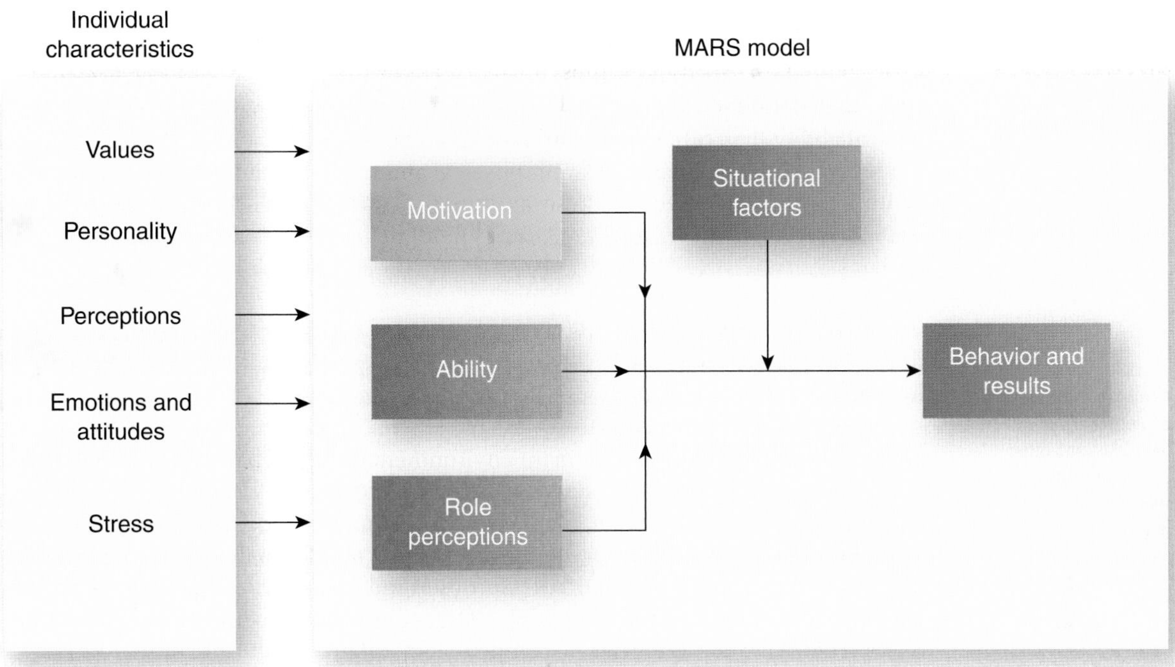

whereas individual perceptions and learning usually lie somewhere between. Each of these factors relates to the MARS model in various ways. For example, personal values affect an employee's motivation through emotions and tend to shape role perceptions through the perceptual process. Learning influences ability, role perceptions, and motivation, as we will learn in Chapter 3. Before examining these individual characteristics, let's briefly introduce the four elements of the MARS model, followed by an overview of the different types of individual behavior in the workplace.

Employee Motivation

motivation
The forces within a person that affect his or her direction, intensity, and persistence of voluntary behavior.

Motivation represents the forces within a person that affect his or her direction, intensity, and persistence of voluntary behavior.[4] *Direction* refers to the path along which people engage their effort. This sense of direction of effort reflects the fact that people have choices about where they put their effort. In other words, motivation is goal-directed, not random. People are motivated to arrive at work on time, finish a project a few hours early, or aim for many other targets. The second element of motivation, called *intensity,* is the amount of effort allocated to the goal. For example, two employees might be motivated to finish their projects a few hours early (direction), but only one of them puts forth enough effort (intensity) to achieve this goal. In other words, intensity is how much you push yourself to complete a task.

Finally, motivation involves varying levels of *persistence*–that is, continuing the effort for a certain amount of time. Employees sustain their efforts until they reach their goals or give up beforehand. To help remember these three elements of motivation, consider the metaphor of driving a car in which the thrust of the engine is your effort. Direction refers to where you steer the car; intensity is how strongly you put your foot down on the gas pedal; and persistence is how long you drive toward that destination.

Ability

ability
Both the natural aptitudes and learned capabilities required to successfully complete a task.

Employee abilities also make a difference in behavior and task performance. **Ability** includes both the natural aptitudes and learned capabilities required to successfully complete a task. *Aptitudes* are the natural talents that help employees learn specific tasks more quickly and perform them better. For example, some people have more natural ability than others to manipulate small objects with their fingers (called finger dexterity). There are many different physical and mental aptitudes, and our ability to acquire skills is affected by these aptitudes. *Learned capabilities* are the skills and knowledge you have actually acquired. These include the physical and mental skills you possess as well as the knowledge you acquire and store for later use.

competencies
Skills, knowledge, aptitudes, and other characteristics of people that lead to superior performance.

Employee Competencies Skills, knowledge, aptitudes, values, drives, and other underlying personal characteristics that lead to superior performance are typically bunched together into the concept of **competencies.** Competencies are relevant to an entire job group rather than just to specific jobs. For instance, American Express recently determined that to thrive in an environment of rapid change and globalization, it would require leaders who have strong competencies in commercial excellence, driving innovation and change, focus on customer and client, and demonstrating personal excellence.[5] Most large organizations spend a lot of money identifying key competencies, but some competencies are described so broadly that they offer little guidance for hiring and training people. Also, companies wrongly assume that everyone should have the same set of competencies, whereas the truth seems to be that people with another combination of competencies may be equally effective.[6]

Person–Job Matching There are three approaches to matching individual competencies with job requirements. One strategy is to select applicants whose existing competencies best fit the required tasks. This includes comparing each applicant's competencies with the requirements of the job or work unit. A second approach is to provide training so employees develop required skills and knowledge.

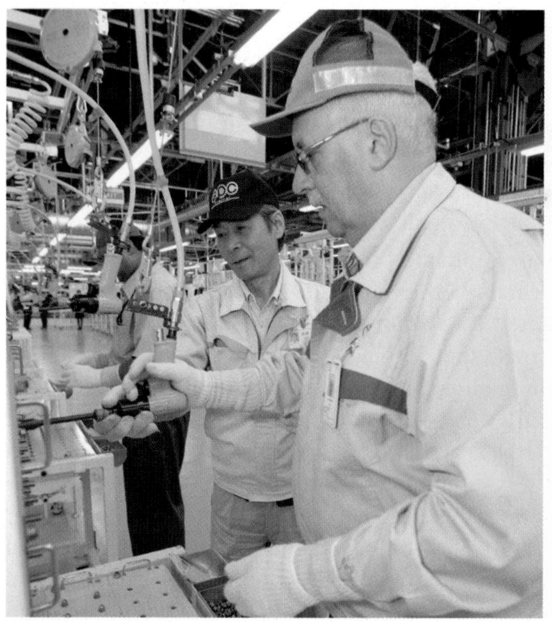

Training the Toyota Way Poised to become the world's largest automaker, Toyota Motor Company is ramping up its training programs around the world to maintain the company's quality standards. Toyota's training methods make extensive use of visual and cognitive aptitudes that require considerable practice and coaching. For example, trainees learn how to spot defects on metal sheet panels where most of us would see none. They also develop visual gap measuring, such as determining how well the edge of the engine hood lines up with the adjacent part of the front grill. This photo shows Toyota production employee Ray Howley (right) from South Africa learning from master trainer Kazuo Hyodo how to tighten bolts so they are snug without being too tight.[7]

The third way to match people with job requirements is to redesign jobs so employees are given only tasks within their capabilities. AT&T's customer service operations in Dallas took this approach when they realized that many employees were overwhelmed by the increasing variety of products (cable, Internet, HDTV, home theater, and so on). "Our employees just said, 'Help! This is way too complex, we're trained on three things and we need help!'" recalls an executive at the American telecommunications giant. AT&T's solution was to redesign jobs so employees could begin with one area of product knowledge, such as video cable, and then progress to a second knowledge area when the first product was mastered.[8]

Role Perceptions

Florida Power & Light (FPL) crew members scrambled to restore power after Hurricane Wilma, the most intense hurricane ever recorded in the Atlantic basin, devastated parts of South Florida. In Boynton Beach alone, 750 FPL staff and electrical workers from other states worked tirelessly from dawn to past dusk to put the area's power grid back together. Dave Bromley, FPL's logistics site manager for the Boynton Beach staging location, admits that it was a challenge to provide accommodation, food, transportation, supplies, laundry services, and other resources to so many people so quickly under such harsh conditions. Yet FPL employees and staff at other organizations that provided logistics support were so dedicated and focused on their tasks that the process soon worked smoothly. "After two or three days, it's a well-oiled machine," says Bromley proudly.[9]

Employees at Florida Power & Light and its service organizations acted like a "well-oiled machine" not just because they knew how to perform their jobs; they had also developed accurate *role perceptions*. Employees have clear role perceptions in three ways. First, they understand the specific tasks assigned to them: They know the specific duties or consequences for which they are accountable. Second, they understand the relative importance of those tasks; in other words, they know the priorities of their various responsibilities, such as the relative importance of quality versus quantity. Third, they understand the preferred behaviors to accomplish those tasks. This refers to situations where more than one method could be applied to a task. Employees know which of these methods is preferred by the organization.

Employees with clear role perceptions feel more engaged in their work because they know where to direct their effort. The most basic way to improve role perceptions is for staff to receive clear job descriptions and ongoing coaching. For instance, the opening vignette to this chapter described how ASB Bank clarified perceptions about the importance of customer service, while managers watched video programs of colleagues to discover the best way to engage employees. Employees also clarify their role perceptions as they work together over time and receive frequent and meaningful performance feedback.

Situational Factors

Even with clear role perceptions and high levels of motivation and ability, employees won't perform their jobs well unless situational factors also support their task goals. Situational factors include conditions beyond the employees' immediate control that constrain or facilitate their behavior and performance.[10] Some situational characteristics–such as consumer preferences and economic conditions–originate from the external environment and, consequently, are beyond the employees' and organization's control. However, other situational factors–such as time, people, budget, and physical work facilities–are controlled by people in the organization. Corporate leaders need to carefully arrange these conditions so employees can achieve their performance potential.

Motivation, ability, role perceptions, and situational factors affect all conscious workplace behaviors and their performance outcomes. The next section outlines the five categories of behavior in organizational settings.

Types of Individual Behavior in Organizations

People engage in many different types of behavior in organizational settings. Exhibit 2.2 highlights the five types of behavior discussed most often in the organizational behavior literature: task performance, organizational citizenship, counterproductive work behaviors, joining and staying with the organization, and work attendance.

Task Performance

Task performance refers to goal-directed behaviors under the individual's control that support organizational objectives. Task performance behaviors transform raw materials into goods and services or support and maintain technical activities.[11] For example, foreign exchange traders at Wachovia make decisions and take actions to exchange currencies. Employees in most jobs have more than one performance dimension. Foreign exchange traders must be able to identify profitable trades, work cooperatively with clients and co-workers in a stressful environment, assist in training new staff, and work on special telecommunications equipment without error. Some of these performance dimensions are more important than others, but only by considering all of them can we fully evaluate an employee's contribution to the organization.

Exhibiting Organizational Citizenship

One of the defining characteristics of engaged employees is that they perform beyond task performance standards or expectations. "When employees become engaged, they develop a stronger conscientiousness about what they can do," explains Bill Erikson, vice chairman of consulting firm Kenexa. "They will go the extra step, or maybe even the extra mile, to support the interest of the organization." In short,

Exhibit 2.2
Types of Work-Related Behavior

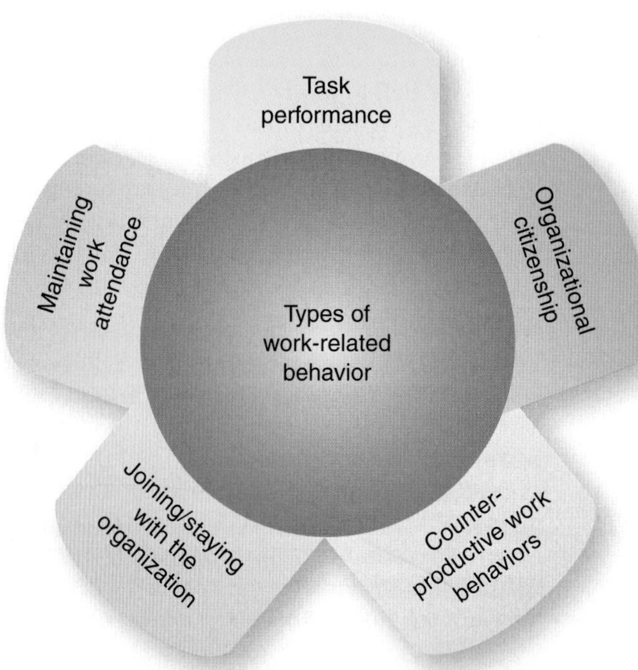

organizational citizenship
Behaviors that extend beyond the employee's normal job duties.

engaged employees practice **organizational citizenship.** They help others without selfish intent, are actively involved in organizational activities, avoid unnecessary conflicts, perform tasks beyond normal role requirements, and gracefully tolerate impositions. Several factors described throughout this book explain why some employees are good organizational citizens and others are not. Later in this chapter, for example, we learn that people with a conscientiousness personality trait have higher organizational citizenship.[12]

Counterproductive Work Behaviors

counterproductive work behaviors (CWBs)
Voluntary behaviors that are potentially harmful to the organization's effectiveness.

Although organizations benefit from task performance and organizational citizenship, we also need to recognize that employees sometimes succumb to **counterproductive work behaviors (CWBs)**—voluntary behaviors that have the potential to directly or indirectly harm the organization. Organizational behavior experts have organized CWBs into five categories: abuse of others (insults and nasty comments), threats (threatening harm), work avoidance (tardiness), work sabotage (doing work incorrectly), and overt acts (theft). CWBs are not minor concerns. One recent study found that units of a fast-food restaurant chain with higher CWBs had a significantly worse performance, whereas organizational citizenship had a relatively minor benefit. Throughout this book we'll identify several ways to minimize counterproductive work behaviors, including better organizational justice (Chapter 5) and less workplace stress (Chapter 7), as well as the propensity of people with a political personality trait known as Machiavellianism to engage in CWBs (Chapter 12).[13]

Joining and Staying with the Organization

Task performance, organizational citizenship, and the lack of counterproductive work behaviors are obviously important; but if qualified people don't join and stay with the organization, none of these performance-related behaviors will occur. Attracting and retaining talented people is particularly important as worries about skills shortages heat up. For instance, a shortage of qualified truck drivers is the main factor restricting growth at Contract Freighters in Joplin, Missouri. "We have plenty of freight; we have plenty of trucks," says company president Herb Schmidt, but the "severe shortage" of qualified drivers is making it impossible to satisfy the growing customer base. Hotels in many parts of the United States are also struggling to find enough staff to keep up with demand. "We're woefully understaffed," says the owner of a St. Petersburg, Florida, resort that employs 265 people and still has 40 unfilled vacancies. "It's horrible."[14] Even Google, which is one of the most widely recognized employer "brands," is feeling the challenge in the war for talent. However, as Connections 2.1 describes, the California-based Internet search engine company has reduced some of its skills shortage through various guerilla recruiting tactics.

A reputable employer brand may attract qualified applicants, but the war for talent also includes ensuring that they stay with the company. Chapter 1 described how much of an organization's intellectual capital is the knowledge carried around in employees' heads. Organizations may try to document information about work processes, corporate values, and customer needs; but much of it remains in employees' heads. Consequently, retaining valued employees is a critical knowledge management strategy. The problem is that many employees don't plan on staying with their current employer very long. A few surveys report that between one-third and one-half of employees say they would change companies if offered a comparable job.[15]

job satisfaction
A person's evaluation of his or her job and work context.

Why do people quit their jobs? Traditionally, OB experts have identified low job satisfaction as the main cause of turnover. **Job satisfaction** is a person's evaluation of his or her job and work context (see Chapter 4). Employees become dissatisfied with

Connections 2.1

Google Goes Guerrilla in the War for Talent

Google relies on guerrilla recruiting, including this innovative ad, to win the war for talent.

To keep up with its blistering growth, Google needs to hire thousands of people in the United States each year. The California-based company that created the world's most popular Internet search engine is also expanding rapidly in India and many other countries. The problem is that Google can't find enough talent to keep up with its growth plans. "Can we hire the quality and quantity of people we want to? No," cofounder Sergey Brin admitted to several hundred investment analysts. "We're under-investing in our business because of the limitations of hiring."

Fortunately Google has also become a master of guerrilla recruiting. Rather than passively waiting for applicants to reply to recruitment ads, Google actively and creatively seeks out talent. One successful tactic has been to host competitions such as "Code Jam," in which contestants around the world are challenged to write code to solve specific problems, then find ways to "break" the code that others have written. Winners in the final round of 100 contestants (out of thousands in the first round) receive up to $10,000, a trip to the Googleplex (Google headquarters), and a job offer.

A related form of guerrilla recruiting is to host internships. Google recently funded a "Summer of Code" event in which 410 college-level students (out of thousands who submitted proposals) received mentoring support from several partner organizations while writing open-source software code. Google paid a small stipend to mentors at the other organizations and $4,500 to students who completed their projects. Summer of Code gave Google (and the other mentoring firms) an inside track on high-quality applicants. "It was a way to start a dialogue with people around the world who might not necessarily be looking for a job—but might become a future employee," says Judy Gilbert, Google's staffing program director.

Even Google's recruitment ads take on a creative guerrilla twist. One example is the billboard (shown in the accompanying photo) and subway banners Google has created, luring curious commuters to follow a series of Web sites with math problems. Only those with top-notch math skills could decipher each puzzle, which eventually led to Google's Web site with an invitation to submit a résumé. "One thing we learned while building Google is that it's easier to find what you're looking for if it comes looking for you," said the Google Web page. "What we're looking for are the best engineers in the world. And here you are!"

Sources: "Google Entices Job Searchers with Math Puzzle," *NPR*, 14 September 2004; S. Olsen, "Google Recruits Eggheads with Mystery Billboard," *CNET News.com*, 9 July 2004; "Google Expansion Is Being Held Back by Hiring Process," *The Wall Street Journal*, 10 February 2005, p. B5; C. Hymowitz, "Busy Executives Fail to Give Recruiting Attention It Deserves," *The Wall Street Journal*, 21 November 2005, p. B1; V. Kopytoff, "How Google Woos the Best and Brightest," *San Francisco Chronicle*, 18 December 2005, p. A1; J. Puliyenthuruthel, "How Google Searches—for Talent," *BusinessWeek*, 11 April 2005; P.-W. Tam and K.J. Delaney, "Talent Search: Google's Growth Helps Ignite Silicon Valley Hiring Frenzy," *The Wall Street Journal*, 23 November 2005, p. A1; "Google Code Jam 2005" (Mountain View, California, 2005), http://www.google.com/codejam/ (accessed 1 March 2006).

their employment relationship, which motivates them to search for and join another organization with better conditions. Although job dissatisfaction builds over time and eventually affects turnover, the most recent opinion is that specific "shock events" need to be considered.[16] These shock events, such as a boss's unfair decision or a conflict episode with a co-worker, create strong emotions that trigger employees to think about and search for alternative employment.

Maintaining Work Attendance

Along with attracting and retaining employees, organizations need everyone to show up for work at scheduled times. Absenteeism occurs for a variety of reasons. One factor is conditions largely beyond employees' control, such as a major storm, car breakdowns, or sick kids with no one else to care for them. Motivation is another factor. Employees who experience job dissatisfaction or work-related stress are more likely to be absent or late for work because taking time off is a way to temporarily withdraw from stressful or dissatisfying conditions. Absenteeism is also higher in organizations with generous sick leave because this benefit limits the negative financial impact of taking time away from work. Yet another factor is team norms. Studies have found that absenteeism is higher in teams with strong absence norms, meaning that team members tolerate and even expect co-workers to take time off.[17]

The MARS model and the five types of individual behavior and results provide a foundation for the ideas presented over the next few chapters. For the remainder of this chapter we will look at two of the most stable individual differences: values and personality.

Learning Objectives

After reading the next two sections you should be able to

4. Define values and explain why values congruence is important.

5. Define five values commonly studied across cultures.

Values in the Workplace

Tom's of Maine encourages its employees to pay attention to their values, not just corporate goals. "It's management by values and objectives, not just management by objectives," says Tom Chappell, who cofounded the personal care products with his wife, Kate Chappell. Chappell explains that objectives are the domain of the mind, whereas values are the domain of the heart. "Values bring the whole person to work," he explains. "We employ the whole person, the mind and the soul." Values are so important that Tom Chappell contributed to the establishment of The Saltwater Institute, a foundation that helps CEOs and entrepreneurs integrate their personal values with their workplace decisions.[18]

Several best-selling management books conclude that Tom's of Maine and other successful companies have a deeply entrenched and long-lasting set of core values.[19] To emulate this success, executives have been keen to identify, communicate, and align a set of core values in their own firms. **Values** are stable, evaluative beliefs that guide our preferences for outcomes or courses of action in a variety of situations.[20] They are perceptions about what is good or bad, right or wrong. Values tell us what we "ought" to do. They serve as a moral compass that directs our motivation and, potentially, our decisions and actions. Values partly define who we are as individuals and as members of groups with similar values.

values
Stable, long-lasting beliefs about what is important in a variety of situations, that guide our decisions and actions.

People arrange values into a hierarchy of preferences, called a *value system*. Some individuals value new challenges more than they value conformity. Others value generosity more than frugality. Each person's unique value system is developed and reinforced through socialization from parents, religious institutions, friends, personal experiences, and the society in which he or she lives. As such, a person's hierarchy of values is stable and long-lasting. For example, one study found that value systems of a sample of adolescents were remarkably similar 20 years later as adults.[21]

Notice that our description of values has focused on individuals, whereas executives often describe values as though they belong to the organization. In reality, values exist only within individuals, which we call *personal values*. However, groups of people might hold the same or similar values, so we tend to ascribe these *shared values* to the team, department, organization, profession, or entire society. The values shared by people throughout an organization (*organizational values*) will receive fuller discussion in Chapter 16 because they are a key part of corporate culture. The values shared across a society (*cultural values*) will receive attention later in this chapter.

Before discussing workplace values in more detail, we need to distinguish between espoused and enacted values.[22] *Espoused values* represent the values that we say we use and, in many cases, think we use. Corporate leaders might say they value environmentalism, creativity, and politeness, whether or not they really do value these things in practice. Values are socially desirable, so people create a positive public image by claiming to believe in values that others expect them to embrace. Also, corporate values are usually considered espoused values because, although leaders might abide by them, we don't know whether lower-level employees share this commitment. *Enacted values,* on the other hand, represent the values we actually rely on to guide our decisions and actions. These values-in-use are apparent by watching people in action. Just as we judge an individual's personality by behavioral tendencies, so too do we judge enacted values by behavioral tendencies.

Types of Values

Values come in many forms, and experts on this topic have devoted considerable attention to organizing them into coherent groups. The model in Exhibit 2.3, developed and tested by social psychologist Shalom Schwartz, has become the most widely

Exhibit 2.3 Schwartz's Values Circumplex

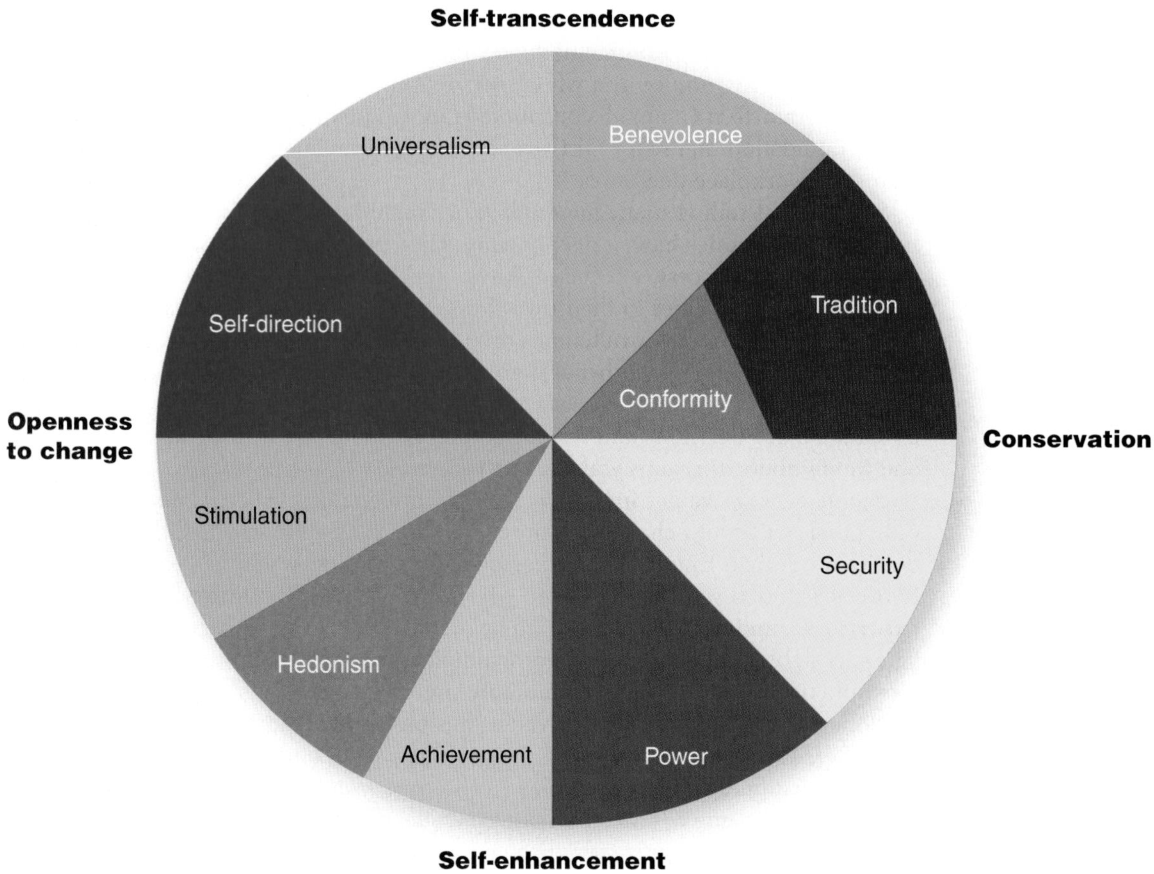

Self-transcendence
Universalism
Benevolence
Self-direction
Tradition
Conformity
Openness to change
Conservation
Stimulation
Security
Hedonism
Achievement
Power
Self-enhancement

Sources: S.H. Schwartz, "Universals in the Content and Structure of Values: Theoretical Advances and Empirical Tests in 20 Countries," *Advances in Experimental Social Psychology* 25 (1992), pp. 1–65; S.H. Schwartz and G. Sagie, "Value Consensus and Importance: A Cross-National Study," *Journal of Cross-Cultural Psychology* 31 (July 2000), pp. 465–97.

studied and generally accepted model today.[23] Schwartz reduced dozens of personal values into these 10 broader domains of values and further organized these domains around two bipolar dimensions.

Along the left side of the horizontal dimension in Schwartz's model is *openness to change,* which represents the extent to which a person is motivated to pursue innovative ways. Openness to change includes the value domains of self-direction (independent thought and action) and stimulation (excitement and challenge). *Conservation,* the opposite end of Schwartz's horizontal dimension, is the extent to which a person is motivated to preserve the status quo. Conservation includes the value clusters of conformity (adherence to social norms and expectations), security (safety and stability), and tradition (moderation and preservation of the status quo).

The vertical dimension in Schwartz's model ranges from self-enhancement to self-transcendence. *Self-enhancement*–how much a person is motivated by self-interest–includes the values of achievement (pursuit of personal success) and power (dominance over others). The opposite of self-enhancement is *self-transcendence,* which refers to the motivation to promote the welfare of others and nature. Self-transcendence includes the values of benevolence (concern for others in one's life) and universalism (concern for the welfare of all people and nature).

Values and Individual Behavior

Values have gained a lot of respect in recent years because they are viewed as anchors that stabilize behavior and keep employees moving collectively in the same direction. They are also considered beacons that keep managers on course under turbulent conditions. "I've always thought that values are a core part of leadership," says Richard Brajer, CEO of LipoScience, a diagnostic testing and analytical company headquartered in Raleigh, North Carolina. "Why? . . . Because, quite frankly, the stresses of a leadership role are very strong. You need to have a solid foundation."[24]

Personal values guide our decisions and actions to some extent, but this connection isn't always as strong as some would like to believe. Habitual behavior tends to be consistent with our values, but our everyday conscious decisions and actions apply our values much less consistently. The main reason for the "disconnect" between personal values and individual behavior is that values are abstract concepts that sound good in theory but are less easily followed in practice. A lot of people say that benevolence is an important value to them, yet they don't think about being benevolent in a lot of situations. Benevolence becomes a truism that gets lost in translation in everyday life.

Benevolence and other values do influence decisions and behavior if three conditions are met.[25] First, a specific value affects our behavior when something makes us mindful (consciously aware) of that value. Co-workers tend to treat each other with much more respect and consideration immediately after a senior executive gives a speech on the virtues of benevolence in the workplace. The speech makes employees temporarily mindful of this value, so they think about it in their behavior toward others. Second, even if a particular value is important and we are mindful of it, we still need to have logical reasons in our head for applying that value. In other words, we tend to apply our values only when we can think of specific reasons for doing so. For example, you will be more motivated to switch your vacation time with a co-worker who needs that time off if you are mindful of your value of benevolence *and* you can think of reasons why it's good to be benevolent.

The third condition that improves the linkage between our values and behavior is the situation. Work environments shape our behavior, at least in the short term–so they necessarily encourage or discourage values-consistent behavior. The fact is that our jobs sometimes require us to act in ways that are inconsistent with our personal values. This incongruence between our personal values and work requirements can also have a powerful effect on employee attitudes and other behaviors, as we'll see next.

Values Congruence

Earlier in this section we noted that Tom's of Maine asks its employees to pay attention to their values. Bill Hetzel is one such employee. As head of purchasing and supply chain management, Hetzel applies Tom's environmental values every day. "Every decision I make is laced with business, technological, environmental, and social factors," explains the MIT chemical engineer and MBA graduate. Equally important, Hetzel is comfortable working within this values framework because it is congruent with his own environmentally conscious values. "It makes a huge difference every day at work that I share the values of my colleagues and my company," he says.[26]

values congruence
A situation wherein two or more entities have similar value systems.

Bill Hetzel experiences a high degree of **values congruence** in his job at Tom's of Maine because his personal values are very similar to the organization's value system. This particular form of values congruence, called *person–organization values congruence,* seems to be elusive in many organizations. Three out of four managers surveyed in one study said their company's values conflict to some extent with their own personal values. Another study reported that managers saw significant differences between their personal values and organizational practices.[27]

Person–organization values incongruence has a number of undesirable consequences, including higher stress and turnover as well as lower organizational citizenship, loyalty, and job satisfaction. Values are guideposts, so incongruence also reduces the chance that employees will make decisions compatible with the organization's values.[28] Does this mean that the most successful organizations perfectly align employee values with the organization's values? Not at all! Although a comfortable degree of values congruence is necessary for the reasons just noted, organizations also benefit from some level of values incongruence. Employees with diverse values offer different perspectives, which often leads to better decision making (see Chapter 8). Furthermore, too much congruence can create a "corporate cult" that potentially undermines creativity, organizational flexibility, and business ethics (see Chapter 16).[29]

Creating Congruent Values at Coles Myer Coles Myer staff indicated through employee surveys that they wanted a coherent set of values to help bind the company together. Chief executive John Fletcher and his executive team felt that these values should come from the employees themselves so that personal and organizational values would be highly congruent. To accomplish this, more than 2,300 employees across all levels at Australia's second largest retailer participated in 203 focus groups around the country. Several dozen employees later met for two days to condense 153 pages of focus group feedback into four values: integrity, respect and recognition, a passion for excellence, and working together. Next, thousands of Coles Myer managers attended one-day workshops where they developed a better understanding of the four values and what behaviors are associated with those values. The company also revised its performance appraisal system to tie 20 percent of managers' bonuses to how well they perform against those values.[30]

Other Types of Values Congruence A second type of values congruence refers to how closely the values apparent in our actions (enacted values) are consistent with what we say we believe in (espoused values). This *espoused–enacted values congruence* is especially important for people in leadership positions because any obvious gap between espoused and enacted values undermines their perceived integrity, a critical feature of effective leaders (see Chapter 14). For instance, Albuquerque, New Mexico, accounting firm Meyners & Co. surveys each manager's subordinates and peers each year to determine how consistent their decisions and actions are with the company's espoused values. Even for nonmanagement staff, espoused–enacted values congruence affects how much co-workers can trust them, which has implications for team dynamics.[31]

A third type of values congruence refers to the compatibility of an organization's dominant values with the prevailing values of the community or society in which it conducts business.[32] For example, an organization headquartered in one country that tries to impose its value system on stakeholders located in another culture may experience higher employee turnover and have more difficult relations with the communities in which the company operates. This creates a delicate balancing act: Companies depend on shared values to maintain consistent standards and behaviors. Airbus, which employs 55,000 people from 80 nationalities, recognizes cross-cultural differences, but it also believes that a few of its values must be applied everywhere. "There are some values that must be retained wherever Airbus components are manufactured," explains Gustav Humbert, CEO of the world's largest commercial aircraft manufacturer. "So as we spread our industrial network [to other countries], the values of quality, safety, and customer care will remain key to making a successful integrated industrial network."[33] Let's look more closely at how values vary across cultures.

Values across Cultures

Anyone who has worked long enough in other countries will know that values differ across cultures. Some cultures value group decisions, whereas others think that the leader should take charge. Meetings in Germany usually start on time, whereas they might be half an hour late in Brazil without much concern. We need to be sensitive to the fact that cultural differences exist and, although often subtle, can influence decisions, behavior, and relations among employees.

Individualism and Collectivism

Let's start by looking at the two most commonly mentioned cross-cultural values: individualism and collectivism. **Individualism** is the extent to which we value independence and personal uniqueness. Highly individualist people value personal freedom, self-sufficiency, control over their own lives, and appreciation of the unique qualities that distinguish them from others. This value relates most closely to the self-direction dimension shown earlier in Exhibit 2.3. **Collectivism** is the extent to which we value our duty to groups to which we belong, as well as group harmony. Highly collectivist people define themselves by their group membership and value harmonious relationships within those groups.[34] Collectivism is located within the conservation range of values (security, tradition, conformity) in Exhibit 2.3.

individualism
The extent to which a person values independence and personal uniqueness.

collectivism
The extent to which people value duty to groups to which they belong, and to group harmony.

You might think from these definitions that high individualism is the same as low collectivism and vice versa. Until recently many scholars thought so, too. However, research indicates that the two concepts are actually unrelated.[35] Some people and cultures might have both high individualism and high collectivism, for example. Someone who highly values duty to his or her group does not necessarily give a low priority to personal freedom and self-sufficiency.

Exhibit 2.4
Individualism and Collectivism in Selected Countries

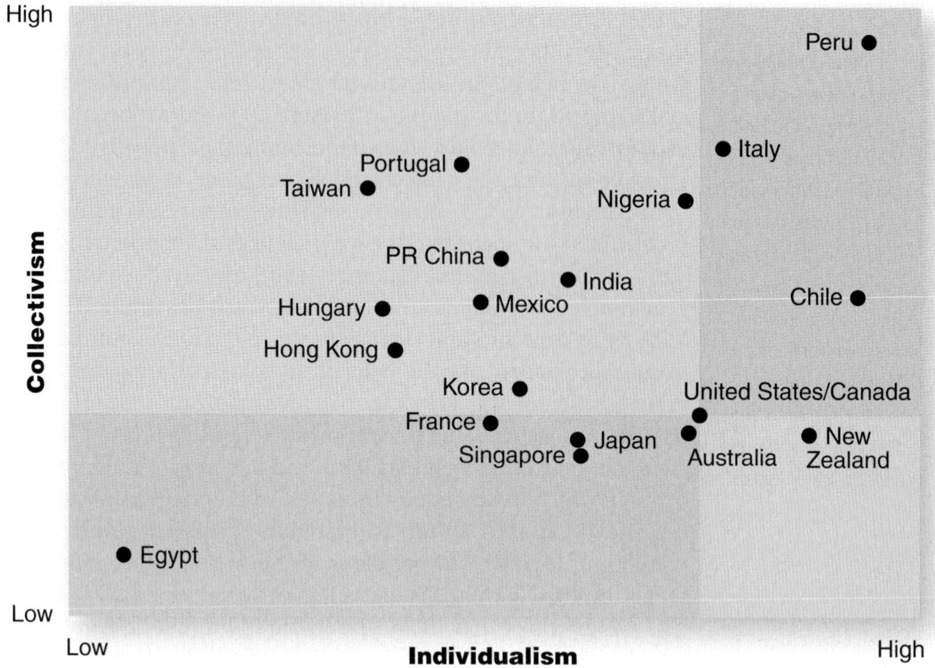

Source: Based on information in D. Oyserman, H.M. Coon, and M. Kemmelmeier, "Rethinking Individualism and Collectivism: Evaluation of Theoretical Assumptions and Meta-Analyses," *Psychological Bulletin* 128 (2002), pp. 3–72. The countries shown here represent only a sample of those in Oyserman's meta-analysis.
Note: The United States/Canada data refer only to people with European heritage in those countries.

How individualistic and collectivistic are people in various countries? Exhibit 2.4 provides the best available answer because it is based on dozens of previous studies combined into a massive single analysis. These findings indicate that Americans with European heritage are more individualistic than people in many other countries. Only people in some South American countries (such as Chile and Peru) apparently score higher on individualism. In contrast, people from Taiwan, Hong Kong, Hungary, and Portugal are among those with much lower individualism. Exhibit 2.4 also shows that Americans, Canadians, and Australians have relatively low collectivism, whereas people in Italy, Taiwan, Peru, Nigeria, and most other countries have higher collectivism.

One notable observation in Exhibit 2.4 is that people in Japan have lower levels of collectivism than people in most other cultures. This is a stark contrast to statements in many cross-cultural books that Japan is one of the most collectivist countries on the planet! The problem was that a major study more than 20 years ago identified Japan as collectivist, but it measured collectivism in a way that bears little resemblance to how the concept is usually defined.[36] Subsequent studies have reported that Japan is relatively low on the collectivist scale (as Exhibit 2.4 reveals), but these persistent results have been slow to replace the old views on this matter.

Power Distance

Stephen Roberts was born in Australia, but experienced a cultural shock after returning to that country following nearly a decade as a manager in Asia. "Managing in Asia was a relatively easy process because no one pushed back," says Roberts,

Anticipating Cross-Cultural Differences at Lenovo A few years ago several Chinese-born managers living in Silicon Valley were recruited to work in Beijing for Lenovo Group, China's giant computer manufacturer. Many of them quit a year later because after living in the United States for several years, they had difficulty with China's high power distance culture. Every morning Lenovo employees had to sing the company song. Their whereabouts in and out of the office was closely monitored throughout the day. Those late for meetings had to stand behind their chairs for a minute in humiliation to discourage future tardiness. "It's very militaristic," recalls one former Lenovo employee recruited from the United States. "You just have to do what you're told." Now, as Lenovo takes control of IBM's personal computer business, cross-cultural differences will likely be apparent again for IBM staff in the United States. "We regard cultural integration as the key factor of our eventual success," says Lenovo CEO Yang Yuanqing. Although Yang points out the good product fit, he acknowledges that there "will be big cultural conflicts and challenges" in bringing together employees from two diverse cultures.[37]

who is currently chief executive of Citigroup Australia/New Zealand. "I remember arriving in Australia and I was asked to present to an executive committee of our equities team, and it felt like a medical examination. I walked out battered and bruised."[38]

power distance
The extent to which people accept unequal distribution of power in a society.

Stephen Roberts experienced the difference between Australia and every Asian country on the value called **power distance:** the extent to which people accept unequal distribution of power in a society.[39] People in Asian countries (with Malaysia and Philippines among the highest) tend to have high power distance scores. They accept and value unequal power, value obedience to authority, and are comfortable receiving commands from their superiors without consultation or debate. High power distance individuals also prefer resolving differences or contradicting their boss indirectly through formal procedures rather than directly.

In contrast, people in Israel, Austria, Denmark, Australia, and other countries with low power distance expect relatively equal power sharing. They view the relationship with their boss as one of interdependence, not dependence; that is, they believe their boss is also dependent on them, so they expect power sharing and consultation before decisions affecting them are made. As Stephen Roberts discovered soon after returning to Australia, employees with low power distance are very comfortable approaching and contradicting their boss.

Other Cross-Cultural Values

uncertainty avoidance
The degree to which people tolerate ambiguity or feel threatened by ambiguity and uncertainty.

Cross-cultural researchers have investigated many other values, but the only two that we will mention here are uncertainty avoidance and achievement–nurturing orientation. **Uncertainty avoidance** is the degree to which people tolerate ambiguity (low uncertainty avoidance) or feel threatened by ambiguity and uncertainty (high uncertainty avoidance). Employees with high uncertainty avoidance value structured situations where rules of conduct and decision making are clearly documented. They usually prefer direct rather than indirect or ambiguous communications. Uncertainty avoidance scores tend to be high among people living in Greece, Portugal, Japan, and South Korea. Studies report low uncertainty avoidance scores in Singapore and Jamaica, and moderately low scores in Malaysia, Hong Kong, and China. Americans score around the middle of the range.

achievement–nurturing orientation
A competitive versus cooperative view of relations with other people.

Achievement–nurturing orientation reflects a competitive versus cooperative view of relations with other people.[40] People with a high achievement orientation value assertiveness, competitiveness, and materialism. They appreciate people who are tough and favor the acquisition of money and material goods. In contrast, people in nurturing-oriented cultures emphasize relationships and the well-being of others. They focus on human interaction and caring rather than competition and personal success. People in Sweden, Norway, and Denmark score very low on achievement orientation (that is, they have a high nurturing orientation). In contrast, high achievement orientation scores have been reported in Japan and Hungary. The United States and United Kingdom score near the middle, slightly toward the achievement orientation.

Before leaving this topic, we need to point out two concerns about the cross-cultural values information provided here.[41] First, the statements about how high or low people in various countries score on power distance, uncertainty avoidance, and achievement–nurturing orientation are based on a survey of IBM employees worldwide more than a quarter century ago. Over 100,000 IBM staff in dozens of countries completed that survey, but it is possible that these IBM employees do not represent the general population. There is also evidence that values have changed quite a bit in some countries since then. A second concern is the assumption that everyone in a society has similar cultural values. This may be true in a few countries, but multiculturalism–where several microcultures coexist in the same country–is becoming more common. On this point, one study reported significantly different values among Javanese, Batik, and Chinese Indonesians. By attributing specific values to an entire society, we are engaging in a form of stereotyping that limits our ability to understand the more complex reality of that society.

Learning Objectives

After reading this section you should be able to

6. **List three ethical principles.**
7. **Explain how moral intensity, ethical sensitivity, and the situation influence ethical behavior.**

Ethical Values and Behavior

When employees are asked to list the most important characteristic they look for in a leader, the top factor isn't intelligence, courage, or even being inspirational. Although these characteristics are important, the most important factor in most surveys is honesty/ethics.[42] **Ethics** refers to the study of moral principles or values that determine whether actions are right or wrong and outcomes are good or bad. People rely on their ethical values to determine "the right thing to do."

ethics
The study of moral principles or values that determine whether actions are right or wrong and outcomes are good or bad.

Unfortunately an ongoing stream of incidents involving corporate wrongdoing continues to raise serious questions about the ethical values of many corporate leaders. Scandals at Enron, Worldcom, Tyco, and other companies led to the Sarbanes-Oxley Act in 2002, which put more controls on U.S. companies and auditing firms to minimize conflict of interest and disclose companies' financial pictures more fully. This legislation might reduce some unethical conduct, but wrongdoing is unlikely to disappear completely. For instance, the founder and former CEO of Gemstar-TV Guide International Inc. was fined for significantly overstating the company's revenue. Ethical problems also continue outside the United States. Several Hong Kong–listed companies have recently suffered heavy losses due to embezzlement by their own executives. And a United Nations report accused the Australian Wheat Board (AWB) of transferring more than $300 million to former Iraq president Saddam Hussein through an intricate system of kickbacks.[43]

Three Ethical Principles

To better understand the ethical dilemmas facing organizations, we need to consider three distinct types of ethical principles: utilitarianism, individual rights, and distributive justice.[44] Although you might prefer one principle more than the others based on your personal values, all three should be actively considered to put important ethical issues to the test.

- *Utilitarianism.* This principle advises us to seek the greatest good for the greatest number of people. In other words, we should choose the option providing the highest degree of satisfaction to those affected. This is sometimes known as a consequential principle because it focuses on the consequences of our actions, not on how we achieve those consequences. One problem with utilitarianism is that it is almost impossible to evaluate the benefits or costs of many decisions, particularly when many stakeholders have wide-ranging needs and values. Another problem is that most of us are uncomfortable engaging in behaviors that seem, well, unethical, to attain results that are ethical.
- *Individual rights.* This principle reflects the belief that everyone has entitlements that let them act in a certain way. Some of the most widely cited rights are freedom of movement, physical security, freedom of speech, fair trial, and freedom from torture. The individual rights principle includes more than legal rights; it also includes human rights that everyone is granted as a moral norm of society. For example, access to education and knowledge isn't a legal requirement everywhere, but most of us believe that it is a human right. One problem with individual rights is that certain individual rights may conflict with others. The shareholders' right to be informed about corporate activities may ultimately conflict with an executive's right to privacy, for example.
- *Distributive justice.* This principle suggests that people who are similar in relevant ways should receive similar benefits and burdens; those who are dissimilar should receive different benefits and burdens in proportion to their dissimilarity. For example, we expect that two employees who contribute equally in their work should receive similar rewards, whereas those who make a lesser contribution should receive less. A variation of the distributive justice principle says that inequalities are acceptable where they benefit the least well off in society. Thus employees in risky jobs should be paid more if this benefits others who are less well off. One problem with the distributive justice principle is that it is difficult to agree on who is "similar" and what factors are "relevant." Most of us agree that race and gender should not be relevant when paychecks are distributed. But should rewards be determined purely by an employee's performance? Or should effort, seniority, and other factors also be taken into account?

Moral Intensity, Ethical Sensitivity, and Situational Influences

Along with ethical principles and their underlying values, we need to consider three other factors that influence ethical conduct in the workplace: the moral intensity of the issue, the individual's ethical sensitivity, and situational factors.

moral intensity
The degree to which an issue demands the application of ethical principles.

Moral intensity is the degree to which an issue demands the application of ethical principles. Decisions with high moral intensity are more important, so the decision maker needs to more carefully apply ethical principles to resolve it. Stealing from your employer is usually considered high on moral intensity, whereas borrowing a company pen for personal use is much lower on the scale. Several factors influence the moral intensity of an issue, such as the extent to which

- The issue clearly produces good or bad consequences.
- Others in the society think it is good or evil.
- The issue quickly affects people.
- The decision maker feels close to the issue.
- How much control the person has over the issue.[45]

ethical sensitivity
A personal characteristic that enables people to recognize the presence and determine the relative importance of an ethical issue.

Even if an issue has high moral intensity, some employees might not recognize its ethical importance because they have low ethical sensitivity. **Ethical sensitivity** is a personal characteristic that enables people to recognize the presence and determine the relative importance of an ethical issue.[46] Ethically sensitive people are not necessarily more ethical. Rather, they are more likely to recognize whether an issue requires ethical consideration; that is, they can more accurately estimate the moral intensity of the issue. Ethically sensitive people tend to have higher empathy. They also have more information about the specific situation. For example, accountants would be more ethically sensitive regarding the appropriateness of specific accounting procedures than would someone who has not received training in this profession.

The third important factor explaining why good people do bad things is the situation in which the unethical conduct occurs. A few recent surveys have reported that employees regularly experience corporate pressure that leads to selling beyond customers' needs, lying to clients, or making unrealistic promises. In one academic study nearly two-thirds of the managers stated that pressure from top management causes people further down in the hierarchy to compromise their beliefs, whereas 90 percent of top management disagreed with this statement.[47] The point here is not to justify unethical conduct. Rather, we need to recognize the situational factors that influence wrongdoing so that organizations can correct these problems in the future.

Supporting Ethical Behavior

Most large and medium-sized organizations in the United States, United Kingdom, and several other countries apply one or more strategies to improve ethical conduct. Ethical codes of conduct are the most common. Ninety-five percent of the *Fortune* 500 companies in the United States and 57 percent of the 500 largest United Kingdom

Long before the scandals at Enron, Worldcom, and Tyco, Adolph Coors Co. put together a variety of ethical practices that today makes it one of the best workplaces in the United States. A cross-functional team rewrote the Golden, Colorado, brewer's ethics code so it would be clearer and user-friendly. Performance evaluations explicitly consider how well employees model this ethics code. An online training program guides employees through real-world scenarios where they see how the company's ethics principles apply to everyday work situations. The activity is set up as an expedition in which employees progress down a mountain to several "camps," where they must resolve ethics violations. The problems begin with clear violations of the company's ethics code, but later camps have much fuzzier dilemmas requiring more careful thought about underlying values. "The goal of the program is to step beyond rules and guidelines and teach employees how to think, clarify, and analyze situations," says Warren Malmquist, shown here with another Coors ethics leader, Caroline McMichen.[48]

companies now have codes of ethics.[49] Critics point out that ethics codes alone do little to reduce unethical conduct. After all, Enron had a well-developed code of ethical conduct, but that document didn't prevent senior executives from engaging in wholesale accounting fraud, resulting in the energy company's bankruptcy. Still, ethics codes lay the foundation for other strategies to support ethical behavior.

Many firms bolster the effectiveness of their ethics codes through training. For instance, Sun Microsystems puts each of its 35,000 employees worldwide through a basic online ethics training program, while its top 1,200 executives participate in a two-day ethics boot camp. Food manufacturer H. J. Heinz Co. is one of many companies that rely on an ethics hotline that employees can use to raise ethical issues or concerns about ethical conduct. At Heinz the hotline operates around the clock and in 150 languages for its global workforce. "They know how to use the hot line in China," comments Jack W. Radke, Heinz's director of ethics. Radke adds that the hotline "has provided an early warning signal of problems we were not aware of."[50]

These programs seem to have some influence on ethical conduct, but the most powerful foundation is a set of shared values–in other words, a strong organizational culture–that supports ethical decisions and behavior. "If you don't have a culture of ethical decision making to begin with, all the controls and compliance regulations you care to deploy won't necessarily prevent ethical misconduct," warns Devin Brougham, director of Vodafone, the British communications giant. This culture is supported by the ethical conduct and vigilance of corporate leaders. By acting with the highest standards of moral conduct, leaders not only gain support and trust from followers; they role-model the ethical standards that employees are more likely to follow.[51]

Learning Objectives

After reading this section you should be able to

8. **Identify the "Big Five" personality dimensions.**
9. **Summarize the personality concepts behind the Myers-Briggs Type Indicator.**
10. **Explain how personality relates to Holland's model of vocational choice.**

Personality in Organizations

Ethical, cultural, and personal values are relatively stable characteristics, so they are an important influence on individual behavior. Another individual characteristic that has long-term stability is personality. In fact, there is considerable evidence that values and personality traits are interrelated and reinforce each other.[52] **Personality** refers to the relatively stable pattern of behaviors and consistent internal states that explain a person's behavioral tendencies. Personality has both internal and external elements. External traits are the observable behaviors that we rely on to identify someone's personality. For example, we can see that a person is extroverted by the way he or she interacts with other people. The internal states represent the thoughts, values, and genetic characteristics that we infer from the observable behaviors. Experts continue to debate the extent to which personality is genetically coded through evolution or shaped from childhood and other early life experiences.[53]

personality
The relatively stable pattern of behaviors and consistent internal states that explain a person's behavioral tendencies.

We say that personality explains behavioral tendencies because individuals' actions are not perfectly consistent with their personality profiles in every situation. Personality traits are less evident in situations where social norms, reward systems, and other conditions constrain our behavior.[54] For example, talkative people remain relatively quiet in a library where "no talking" rules are explicit and strictly enforced.

Personality and Organizational Behavior

Brigitte Catellier's final hurdle to become vice president of legal affairs at Astral Media Inc. wasn't quite what she might have anticipated. For seven hours Catellier sat through eight aptitude, preferences, and personality tests, some of which asked unusual questions such as whether she would prefer to be an astronaut or an acrobat. "I was told very directly there are two candidates and you are both doing the same tests," says Catellier, who was later offered the job at the Montreal-based media giant. Astral decided a few years ago to include psychological tests in the hiring process, including instruments that measure personality traits such as dominance and tolerance. "This helps us to avoid mistakes, and we have made mistakes from time to time in the past," says Astral's vice president of human resources, referring to people hired in the past whose personality didn't fit the company or job requirements.[55]

Astral Media is among the growing number of firms around North America that have introduced psychological testing in the hiring process. Although aptitude tests have been used regularly for decades, personality tests have had a rocky experience in choosing job applicants. At one time scholars commonly explained employee behavior in terms of personality traits, and companies regularly administered personality tests to job applicants. This changed in the 1960s when researchers reported that the relationship between personality and job performance is very weak.[56] They cited problems with measuring personality traits and explained that the connection between personality and performance exists only under narrowly defined conditions. Companies stopped using personality tests due to concerns that these tests might unfairly discriminate against visible minorities and other identifiable groups.

Over the past decade personality has regained some of its credibility in organizational settings.[57] Recent studies have reported that specific personality traits predict specific work-related behaviors, stress reactions, and emotions fairly well under specific conditions. Research indicates that effective leaders have identifiable traits and that personality explains some of a person's positive attitudes and life happiness. Personality traits also seem to help people find the jobs that best suit their needs.[58] Personality is a remote concept, so it isn't the best predictor of most jobs; but it is increasingly clear that some personality traits are relevant. Some of the most relevant personality traits for job performance and well-being are found in the Big Five personality dimensions.

The Big Five Personality Dimensions

Since the days of Plato scholars have been trying to develop lists of personality traits. About 100 years ago a few personality experts tried to catalog and condense the many personality traits that had been described over the years. They found thousands of words in Roget's thesaurus and Webster's dictionary that represented personality traits. They aggregated these words into 171 clusters, then further shrank them down to five abstract personality dimensions. Using more sophisticated techniques, recent investigations identified the same five dimensions–known as the **Big Five personality dimensions.**[59] These five dimensions, represented by the handy acronym CANOE, are outlined in Exhibit 2.5 and described here:

"Big Five" personality dimensions
The five abstract dimensions representing most personality traits: conscientiousness, agreeableness, neuroticism, openness to experience, and extroversion (CANOE).

- *Conscientiousness.* Conscientiousness refers to people who are careful, dependable, and self-disciplined. Some scholars argue that this dimension also includes the will to achieve. People with low conscientiousness tend to be careless, less thorough, more disorganized, and irresponsible.
- *Agreeableness.* This includes the traits of being courteous, good-natured, empathic, and caring. Some scholars prefer the label of "friendly compliance" for

Exhibit 2.5
Big Five Personality Dimensions

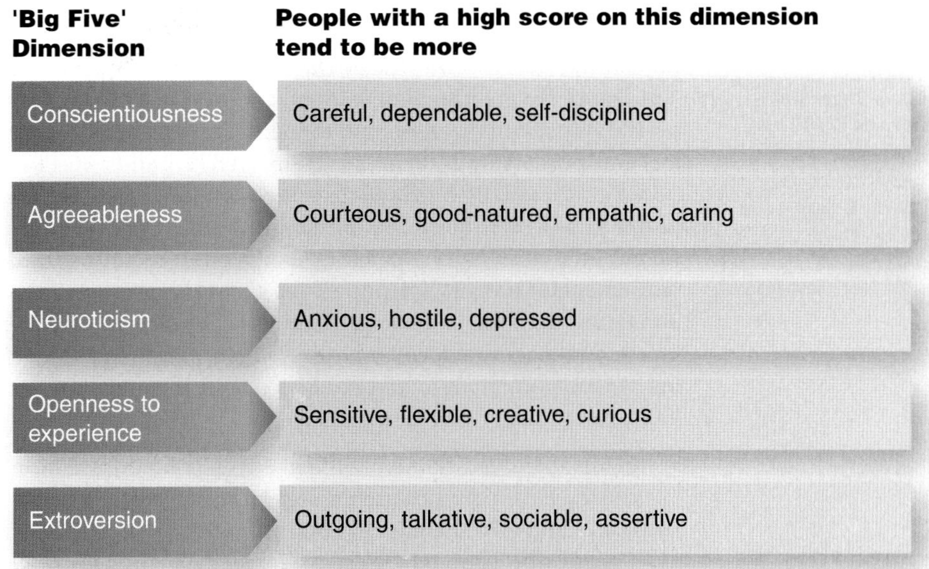

this dimension, with its opposite being "hostile noncompliance." People with low agreeableness tend to be uncooperative, short-tempered, and irritable.

- *Neuroticism.* Neuroticism characterizes people with high levels of anxiety, hostility, depression, and self-consciousness. In contrast, people with low neuroticism (high emotional stability) are poised, secure, and calm.
- *Openness to experience.* This dimension is the most complex and has the least agreement among scholars. It generally refers to the extent to which people are sensitive, flexible, creative, and curious. Those who score low on this dimension tend to be more resistant to change, less open to new ideas, and more fixed in their ways.
- *Extroversion.* **Extroversion** characterizes people who are outgoing, talkative, sociable, and assertive. The opposite is **introversion,** which refers to those who are quiet, shy, and cautious. Introverts do not necessarily lack social skills. Rather, they are more inclined to direct their interests to ideas than to social events. Introverts feel quite comfortable being alone, whereas extroverts do not.

extroversion
A "Big Five" personality dimension that characterizes people who are outgoing, talkative, sociable, and assertive.

introversion
A "Big Five" personality dimension that characterizes people who are quiet, shy, and cautious.

These five personality dimensions affect work-related behavior and job performance to varying degrees.[60] People with high emotional stability tend to work better than others in high-stress situations. Those with high agreeableness tend to handle customer relations and conflict-based situations more effectively. However, conscientiousness has taken center stage as the most valuable personality trait for predicting job performance in almost every job group. Conscientious employees set higher personal goals for themselves, are more motivated, and have higher performance expectations than do employees with low levels of conscientiousness. High-conscientiousness employees tend to have higher levels of organizational citizenship and work better in workplaces that give employees more freedom than in traditional command-and-control workplaces. Employees with high conscientiousness, as well as agreeableness and emotional stability, also tend to provide better customer service.

Myers-Briggs Type Indicator

Myers-Briggs Type Indicator (MBTI)
A personality inventory designed to identify individuals' basic preferences for perceiving and processing information.

More than half a century ago the mother-and-daughter team of Katherine Briggs and Isabel Briggs-Myers developed the **Myers-Briggs Type Indicator (MBTI),** a personality inventory designed to identify individuals' basic preferences for perceiving and processing information. The MBTI builds on the personality theory proposed in the 1920s by Swiss psychiatrist Carl Jung that identifies the way people prefer to perceive their environment as well as obtain and process information. Jung suggested that everyone is either extroverted or introverted in orientation and has particular preferences for perceiving (sensing or intuition) and judging or deciding on action (thinking or feeling). The MBTI is designed to measure these as well as a fourth dimension relating to how people orient themselves to the outer world (judging versus perceiving).[61] Extroversion and introversion were discussed earlier, so let's examine the other dimensions:

- *Sensing/intuition.* Some people like collecting information through their five senses. Sensing types use an organized structure to acquire factual and preferably quantitative details. In contrast, intuitive people collect information nonsystematically. They rely more on subjective evidence as well as their intuition and sheer inspiration. Sensers are capable of synthesizing large amounts of seemingly random information to form quick conclusions.
- *Thinking/feeling.* Thinking types rely on rational cause–effect logic and systematic data collection to make decisions. They weigh the evidence objectively and unemotionally. Feeling types, on the other hand, consider how their choices affect others. They weigh the options against their personal values more than rational logic.
- *Judging/perceiving*–Some people prefer order and structure in their relationship with the outer world. These judging types enjoy the control of decision making and want to resolve problems quickly. In contrast, perceiving types are more flexible. They like to spontaneously adapt to events as they unfold and want to keep their options open.

The MBTI questionnaire combines the four pairs of traits into 16 distinct types. For example, ESTJ is one of the most common types for managers, meaning that they are extroverted, sensing, thinking, and judging types. Each of the 16 types has its strengths and weaknesses. ENTJs are considered natural leaders, ISFJs have a high sense of duty, and so on. These types indicate people's preferences, not the way they necessarily behave all of the time.

Effectiveness of the MBTI Is the MBTI useful in organizations? The city council in Portsmouth, Virginia, thinks so; every council member completed the MBTI prior to recent budget deliberations so they could better understand each other's preferences. Dell founder Michael Dell and company president Kevin Rollins also completed the MBTI to figure out their similarities and differences. In fact, the MBTI is one of the most widely used personality tests in work settings and is equally popular for career counseling and executive coaching.[62] Still, evidence regarding the effectiveness of the MBTI and Jung's psychological types is mixed.[63] The MBTI does a reasonably good job of measuring Jung's psychological types. The MBTI predicts preferences for information processing in decision making and preferences for particular occupations. However, other evidence is less supportive regarding the MBTI's ability to predict job performance. Overall, the MBTI seems to improve self-awareness for career development and mutual understanding, but it probably should not be used in selecting job applicants.

Finding a Career That Fits the Personality While working as a navy diver, Dan Porzio prepared for his next career in financial planning. But he was far from happy in his new field, so he took a job selling cellular telephones. Still unhappy, Porzio moved into the investment industry, where he worked for three years. During that time he visited a career counselor and discovered why he lacked interest in his work. "I thought those other jobs were ones that I wanted to do, but I found out I was doing things that didn't jive with my character," Porzio explains. With that knowledge in hand, Porzio found a job that fit his personality as captain of the Annabelle Lee Riverboat in Richmond, Virginia (where Porzio is shown in photo).[64]

Other Personality Traits

The Big Five personality dimensions represent a broad categorization of personality traits, but organizational behavior also considers traits that are more specific or fall outside the five clusters. Two other personality traits that help to explain individual behavior in the workplace are locus of control and self-monitoring.

locus of control
A personality trait referring to the extent to which people believe events are within their control.

Locus of Control

Locus of control refers to a generalized belief about the amount of control people have over their own lives. Individuals who feel that they are very much in charge of their own destiny have an internal locus of control; those who think that events in their life are due mainly to fate, luck, or powerful others have an external locus of control. Locus of control is a generalized belief, so people with an external locus can feel in control in familiar situations (such as opening a door or serving a customer). However, their underlying locus of control would be apparent in new situations in which control over events is uncertain. Compared to people with an external locus of control, people with a moderately strong internal locus of control tend to perform better in most employment situations, are more successful in their careers, earn more money, and are better suited for leadership positions. Internals are also more satisfied with their jobs, cope better in stressful situations, and are more motivated by performance-based reward systems.[65]

self-monitoring
A personality trait referring to an individual's level of sensitivity to the expressive behavior of others and the ability to adapt appropriately to these situational cues.

Self-Monitoring

Self-monitoring refers to an individual's level of sensitivity to the expressive behavior of others and the ability to adapt appropriately to these situational cues. High self-monitors can adjust their behavior quite easily, whereas low self-monitors are more likely to reveal their emotions, so predicting their behavior from one situation to the next is relatively easy.[66] The self-monitoring personality trait has been identified as a significant factor in many organizational activities. Employees who are high self-monitors tend to be better at social networking, interpersonal conversations, and leading people. They are also more likely than low self-monitors to be promoted within the organization and to receive better jobs elsewhere.[67]

Personality and Vocational Choice

Self-monitoring, locus of control, conscientiousness, and the many other personality traits help to explain individual behavior in organizations. One fairly successful application of personality is in the area of vocational choice. Vocational choice is not just about matching your skills with job requirements. It is a complex alignment of personality, values, and competencies with the requirements of work and characteristics of the work environment. You might be very talented at a particular job, but your personality and values must also be aligned with what the job offers.

John Holland, a career development scholar, was an early proponent of this notion that career success depends on the degree of congruence between the person and his or her work environment.[68] Holland argued that people can be classified into different types relating to their personality and that they seek out and are more satisfied in work environments that are congruent with their particular profiles. Thus *congruence* refers to the extent that someone has the same or similar personality type as the environment in which he or she is working. Some research has found that high congruence leads to better performance, satisfaction, and length of time in that career; but other studies are less supportive of the model.[69]

Holland's Six Types Holland's theory classifies both individual personalities and work environments into six categories: realistic, investigative, artistic, social, enterprising, and conventional. Exhibit 2.6 defines these types of people and work environments and suggests sample occupations representing those environments. Few people fall squarely into only one of Holland's classifications. Instead Holland refers to a person's degree of *differentiation*–that is, the extent to which the individual fits into one or several types. A highly differentiated person is aligned with a single category, whereas most people fit into two or more categories.

Because most individuals fit into more than one personality type, Holland developed a model shaped like a hexagon with each personality type around the points of the model. Consistency refers to the extent that a person is aligned with similar types,

Exhibit 2.6
Holland's Six Types of Personalities and Work Environments

Holland type	Personality traits	Work environment characteristics	Sample occupations
Realistic	Practical, shy, materialistic, stable.	Work with hands, machines, or tools; focus on tangible results.	Assembly worker; dry cleaner, mechanical engineer.
Investigative	Analytic, introverted, reserved, curious, precise, independent.	Work involves discovering, collecting, and analyzing; solving problems.	Biologist, dentist, systems analyst.
Artistic	Creative, impulsive, idealistic, intuitive, emotional.	Work involves creation of new products or ideas, typically in an unstructured setting.	Journalist, architect, advertising executive.
Social	Sociable, outgoing, conscientious, need for affiliation.	Work involves serving or helping others; working in teams.	Social worker, nurse, teacher, counselor.
Enterprising	Confident, assertive, energetic, need for power.	Work involves leading others; achieving goals through others in a results-oriented setting.	Salesperson, stockbroker, politician.
Conventional	Dependable, disciplined, orderly, practical, efficient.	Work involves systematic manipulation of data or information.	Accountant, banker, administrator.

Sources: Based on information in D.H. Montross, Z.B. Leibowitz, and C.J. Shinkman, *Real People, Real Jobs* (Palo Alto, CA: Davies-Black, 1995); and J.H. Greenhaus, *Career Management* (Chicago: Dryden, 1987).

which are next to each other in the hexagon, whereas dissimilar types are opposite. For instance, the enterprising and social types are next to each other in Holland's model, so individuals with both enterprising and social personalities have high consistency.

Practical Implications of Holland's Theory Holland's vocational fit model is the basis of much career counseling today. Still, some aspects of the model don't seem to work. Holland's personality types represent only some of the Big Five personality dimensions, even though other dimensions should be relevant to vocational fit.[70] Also, research has found that some "opposing" categories in Holland's hexagon are not really opposite to each other. There are also doubts about whether Holland's model can be generalized to other cultures. Aside from these concerns, Holland's model seems to explain individual attitudes and behavior to some extent, and it is the dominant model of career testing today.[71]

Personality and values lay some of the foundation for our understanding of individual behavior in organizations. However, people are, of course, also influenced by the environments in which they live and work. These environments are perceived and learned, the two topics presented in the next chapter.

Chapter Summary

Employee engagement refers to how much employees identify with and are emotionally committed to their work, are cognitively focused on that work, and possess the ability and resources to do the work. This concept refers to the four elements of the MARS model–motivation, ability, role perceptions, and situational factors–which identify the four direct predictors of all voluntary behavior and performance. Motivation consists of internal forces that affect the direction, intensity, and persistence of a person's voluntary choice of behavior. Ability includes both the natural aptitudes and learned capabilities required to successfully complete a task. Role perceptions are a person's beliefs about what behaviors are appropriate or necessary in a particular situation. Situational factors are environmental conditions that constrain or facilitate employee behavior and performance. Collectively, these four factors are included in the concept of employee engagement.

The five main types of workplace behavior are task performance, organizational citizenship, counterproductive work behaviors, joining and staying with the organization, and work attendance.

Values are stable, evaluative beliefs that guide our preferences for outcomes or courses of action in a variety of situations. They influence our decisions and interpretation of what is ethical. People arrange values into a hierarchy of preferences called a value system. Espoused values–what we say and think we use as values–are different from enacted values, which are values evident from our actions. Shalom Schwartz grouped the dozens of individual values described by scholars over the years into 10 broader domains, which are further reduced to four quadrants of a circle.

Values are abstract concepts that are not easily followed in practice. A personal value influences our decisions and actions when (1) something makes us mindful of that value, (2) we can think of specific reasons for applying the value in that situation, and (3) the work environment supports behaviors consistent with the value. Values congruence refers to the similarity of value systems between two entities. Person–organization values incongruence has a number of undesirable consequences, but some incongruence is also desirable. Espoused–enacted values congruence is contrary to effective leadership and undermines trust.

Five values that differ across cultures are individualism, collectivism, power distance, uncertainty avoidance, and achievement–nurturing orientation. Three values that guide ethical conduct are utilitarianism, individual rights, and distributive justice. Three factors that influence ethical conduct are the extent that an issue demands ethical principles (moral intensity), the person's ethical sensitivity to the presence and importance of an ethical dilemma, and situational factors that cause people to deviate from their moral values. Companies can improve ethical conduct through a code of ethics, ethics training, ethics hot lines, and the conduct of corporate leaders.

Personality refers to the relatively stable pattern of behaviors and consistent internal states that explain a person's behavioral tendencies. Personality is shaped by both heredity and environmental factors. Most personality traits are represented within the Big Five personality dimensions (CANOE): conscientiousness, agreeableness, neuroticism, openness to experience, and extroversion. Conscientiousness is a relatively strong predictor of job performance.

The Myers-Briggs Type Indicator measures how people prefer to focus their attention, collect information, process and evaluate information, and orient themselves to the outer world. Another popular personality trait in organizational behavior is locus of control, which is a generalized belief about the amount of control people have over their own lives. Another trait, called self-monitoring, refers to an individual's level of sensitivity and ability to adapt to situational cues. Holland's model of vocational choice defines six personalities and their corresponding work environments.

Key Terms

ability, p. 36
achievement–nurturing orientation, p. 47
Big Five personality dimensions, p. 52
collectivism, p. 45
competencies, p. 36
counterproductive work behaviors (CWBs), p. 39
employee engagement, p. 34
ethical sensitivity, p. 50
ethics, p. 48
extroversion, p. 53
individualism, p. 45
introversion, p. 53
job satisfaction, p. 39
locus of control, p. 55
moral intensity, p. 49
motivation, p. 35
Myers-Briggs Type Indicator (MBTI), p. 54
organizational citizenship, p. 38
personality, p. 51
power distance, p. 47
self-monitoring, p. 55
uncertainty avoidance, p. 47
values, p. 41
values congruence, p. 44

Critical Thinking Questions

1. This chapter begins by identifying employee engagement as a combination of the four factors in the MARS model. In your opinion, why would all four factors be important? Also, is it possible for employees to have high levels of engagement and be unethical or unproductive?
2. An insurance company has high levels of absenteeism among the office staff. The head of office administration argues that employees are misusing the company's sick leave benefits. However, some of the mostly female staff members have explained that family responsibilities interfere with work. Using the MARS model, as well as your knowledge of absenteeism behavior, discuss some of the possible reasons for absenteeism here and how it might be reduced.
3. Most large organizations spend a lot of money identifying the key competencies for superior work performance. What are the potential benefits and pitfalls associated with identifying competencies? Are there other useful ways to select employees?
4. Executives at a major consumer products company devoted several days to a values identification seminar in which they developed a list of six core values to drive the company forward. All employees attended sessions in which they learned about these values. In spite of this effort and ongoing communication regarding the six values, the executive team concluded two years later that employees were often making decisions and engaging in behaviors that were inconsistent with these values. Provide three possible explanations why employees have not enacted the values espoused by top management at this company.
5. This chapter discussed the concept of values congruence in the context of an employee's personal values with the organization's values. But values congruence also relates to the juxtaposition of other pairs of value systems. Explain how values congruence is relevant to organizational versus professional values.
6. People in a particular South American country have high power distance and high collectivism. What does this mean, and what are the implications of this information when you (a senior executive) visit employees working for your company in that country?
7. "All decisions are ethical decisions." Comment on this statement, particularly by referring to the concepts of moral intensity and ethical sensitivity.
8. Look over the four pairs of psychological types in the Myers-Briggs Type Indicator and identify the personality type (the four letters) that would be best for a student in this course. Would this type be appropriate for students in other fields of study (such as biology or fine arts)?

Case Study 2.1 COX-2 INHIBITOR DRUGS

Christine Stamper, University of Western Michigan

Treating chronic pain conditions associated with growing older, such as arthritis, has become more important (and more profitable) with the aging of the baby boomers, the largest generation in U.S. society. Pain medications produced by pharmaceutical companies take many forms, including both over-the-counter (aspirin, Tylenol, Motrin, Aleve, and the like) and prescription types of medicine. Investment in the research and development of new drugs costs pharmaceutical companies billions of dollars each year, with approximately 4–6 percent of all researched drugs actually receiving the approval of the Food and Drug Administration (FDA), the watchdog government agency tasked with maintaining public safety pertaining to medicines. Given this low "to-market" rate, top managers in pharmaceutical companies try to protect the drugs that are on the market at all costs.

The last few years have witnessed much concern over a class of drugs called Cox-2 inhibitors, such as Vioxx (manufactured by Merck) and Celebrex and Bextra (both produced by Pfizer). Despite the fact that all of these drugs were approved by the FDA (Celebrex in 1998, Vioxx in 1999, and Bextra in 2001), recent independently conducted research has shown significant negative health effects in people who have taken these medicines long-term (for more than three months). Specifically, all three drugs have been found to increase the risk of heart attack and stroke in patients, and Bextra also may cause fatal skin reactions. Subsequently, Vioxx was taken off the market by Merck in September 2004, and Pfizer stopped selling Bextra in April 2005 at the request of the FDA. However, Celebrex remains on the market.

When first introduced, Cox-2 inhibitors were hailed as a type of "super-aspirin," alleviating the suffering of the patient while causing little risk. They were also viewed as a preferred alternative to existing NSAIDs, which are nonsteroidal anti-inflammatory drugs like aspirin, naproxen (sold as Aleve and Naprosyn), and ibuprofen (sold as Advil and Motrin). When taken for three months or longer, these NSAIDs pose a risk of internal bleeding in the stomach and small intestine areas (approximately 16,000 people die from these effects each year). Vioxx, Celebrex, and Bextra were produced to provide pain relief while protecting the lining of the gastrointestinal tract.

Even knowing that Cox-2 inhibitors carry a potentially large cardiovascular health risk, there are chronic pain sufferers who would voluntarily (and happily) continue to take these drugs. For example, it was reported that one man who suffers from chronic knee, hip, and shoulder pain thought, ". . . whom do I know who has some but isn't taking it? How can I get as much of it as possible before it disappears from the shelves?" He, and many others, would willingly tolerate the health risks of these medicines instead of living with chronic pain. The acting director of the FDA's Center for Drug Evaluation and Research has recognized, in light of the new information about health risks, that it is important to balance these risks with the potential benefits of the medicines before deciding whether to remove them from the market. However, the associate director for science and medicine at the FDA's Office of Drug Safety has argued strongly that the health risks associated with Cox-2 drugs vastly outweigh any potential benefits.

In December 2004 (prior to its request to pull Bextra off the market) the FDA recommended that doctors limit their prescriptions of all Cox-2 inhibitors, including Celebrex, to only those patients at risk for gastrointestinal bleeding. Researchers at Stanford and the University of Chicago argued that millions of patients who did not face this risk were prescribed either Vioxx or Celebrex by their doctors. Each of these drugs can cost 10–15 times as much as the NSAIDs available to treat the same pain symptoms, and critics of big pharmaceutical companies argue that the Cox-2 inhibitors were marketed too aggressively and deceptively to potential patients. It is not clear whether the increase in prescriptions for the Cox-2 inhibitors in lieu of NSAIDs was due to patients asking their doctors specifically for either Vioxx or Celebrex, or to recommendations by physicians that the patients change their medications.

Both Pfizer and Merck still assert the relative safeness of the Cox-2 inhibitors. In February 2005 an FDA advisory panel recommended that Vioxx, Celebrex, and Bextra should continue to be sold despite their health risks because the potential benefits of the drugs outweigh the risks for some patients. The doctors on the panel stated that they felt Vioxx posed the greatest risk to consumers and that Celebrex had the fewest side effects. Research estimates show that

Celebrex increases the risk for heart problems by 1 percent, but only for individuals who routinely take double the normal dosage of 200 milligrams. Also, another recent study indicated that Celebrex may suppress the typical immune function of the body, which may benefit some arthritis sufferers.

The FDA does not always follow the recommendations of its advisory groups, and it subsequently decided to request that Pfizer pull Bextra from the market. A statement released by Pfizer said the company ". . . respectfully disagreed with the FDA's decision on Bextra and that it would work with the agency on Celebrex's label." The FDA has requested that a "black box" warning label be placed on Celebrex, which is the strongest warning procedure available in product labeling. However, the FDA also requested "black box" warnings on NSAIDs like Motrin, Advil, and Aleve. Pfizer has also stopped public advertising of Celebrex, but still argues that it should be available to patients who need it, according to a doctor's recommendation. Two additional Cox-2 drugs are now waiting for the FDA's approval, one of which (Arcoxia) is produced by Merck. Arcoxia has been approved for use in 51 countries worldwide.

As this case was written, Pfizer had just finished a widely publicized strategic planning meeting addressing the future of the company. In the press releases from this meeting, and prior to the FDA asking Pfizer to remove Bextra from the market, corporate representatives expressed their desire to revitalize the sales of both Celebrex and Bextra in the coming months. With the removal of Bextra from the market, financial analysts predicted that Pfizer's earnings would continue to decline for 2005, and the recent predictions for double-digit earnings growth for 2006 and 2007 would have to be revised. In 2004 sales associated with Bextra were $1.3 billion, and Celebrex's sales were estimated at $3.3 billion. Together Bextra, Celebrex, and Vioxx totaled more than 50 million prescriptions in the United States in 2004 (Bextra = 13 million, Vioxx = 14 million, and Celebrex = 24 million).

Discussion Questions

1. Should Pfizer voluntarily pull Celebrex off the market, given that the other two drugs in its class have been withdrawn? What factors are the most important in making this decision? What should the FDA do about Arcoxia?
2. What are the responsibilities (if any) of Merck, Pfizer, and the FDA for the deaths of individuals who took the Cox-2 inhibitors? Who holds primary responsibility?
3. How many deaths per 100,000 people pose an acceptable risk for a drug to be viewed as marketable? Should individual patients have the right to determine if the risk is too great for them? What roles do organizations and consumers play in maintaining consumer safety?

Sources: T. Agovino, "Pfizer's Outlook Darkens with Bextra Ban," Associated Press, as printed in the *Kalamazoo Gazette,* 10 April 2005; Associated Press, "All Drugs Like Vioxx May Cause Problems, Says Merck Official," MSNBC.com, 16 February 2005; Associated Press, "Painkiller Bextra Pulled from Market," MSNBC.com, 7 April 2005; B.J. Feder, "More Lawsuits over Pfizer's Bextra Expected," *The New York Times,* as printed in the *Kalamazoo Gazette,* 10 April 2005; A. Goodnough, "Consumers Weigh Risks of Painkillers, Life without Them," *The New York Times,* as printed in the *Kalamazoo Gazette,* 10 April 2005; Reuters, "Cox-2 Drugs May Suppress Immune Function," MSNBC.com, 7 April 2005; Reuters, "FDA Rules in Favor of Painkillers," MSNBC.com, 19 February 2005; Reuters, "FDA Should Pull Pain Drugs, Says Group," MSNBC.com, 24 January 2005; Reuters, "FDA Tells Doctors to Limit Painkiller Use," MSNBC.com, 31 December 2004; Reuters, "Painkillers May Damage Small Intestines," MSNBC.com, 3 January 2005; Reuters, "Researcher Says 139,000 Harmed by Vioxx," MSNBC.com, 3 January 2005; Reuters, "Scientist: No Need for Arthritis Drugs," MSNBC.com, 17 February 2005; Reuters, "U.S. May Pull Painkillers, Researchers Say," MSNBC.com, 15 February 2005; Reuters, "Vioxx, Celebrex May Be Overprescribed," MSNBC.com, 24 January 2005.

Case Study 2.2 PUSHING PAPER CAN BE FUN

A large city government was putting on a number of seminars for managers of various departments throughout the city. At one of these sessions the topic discussed was motivation–how to motivate public servants to do a good job. The plight of a police captain became the central focus of the discussion:

> I've got a real problem with my officers. They come on the force as young, inexperienced rookies, and we send them out on the street, either in cars or on a beat. They seem to like the contact they have with the public, the

action involved in crime prevention, and the apprehension of criminals. They also like helping people out at fires, accidents, and other emergencies.

The problem occurs when they get back to the station. They hate to do the paperwork, and because they dislike it, the job is frequently put off or done inadequately. This lack of attention hurts us later on when we get to court. We need clear, factual reports. They must be highly detailed and unambiguous. As soon as one part of a report is shown to be inadequate or incorrect, the rest of the report is suspect. Poor reporting probably causes us to lose more cases than any other factor.

I just don't know how to motivate them to do a better job. We're in a budget crunch, and I have absolutely no financial rewards at my disposal. In fact, we'll probably have to lay some people off in the near future. It's hard for me to make the job interesting and challenging because it isn't–it's boring, routine paperwork, and there isn't much you can do about it.

Finally, I can't say to them that their promotions will hinge on the excellence of their paperwork. First of all, they know it's not true. If their performance is adequate, most are more likely to get promoted just by staying on the force a certain number of years than for some specific outstanding act. Second, they were trained to do the job they do out in the streets, not to fill out forms. All through their careers the arrests and interventions are what get noticed.

Some people have suggested a number of things, like using conviction records as a performance criterion. However, we know that's not fair–too many other things are involved. Bad paperwork increases the chance that you lose in court, but good paperwork doesn't necessarily mean you'll win. We tried setting up team competitions based on the excellence of the reports, but the officers caught on to that pretty quickly. No one was getting any type of reward for winning the competition, and they figured why should they bust a gut when there was no payoff.

I just don't know what to do.

Discussion Questions

1. What performance problems is the captain trying to correct?
2. Use the MARS model of individual behavior and performance to diagnose the possible causes of the unacceptable behavior.
3. Has the captain considered all possible solutions to the problem? If not, what else might be done?

Source: T.R. Mitchell and J.R. Larson Jr., *People in Organizations,* 3r ed. (New York: McGraw-Hill, 1987), p. 184. Used with permission.

Case Study 2.3 CLEANING UP BOEING

BusinessWeek

W. James McNerney Jr. didn't mince words when he took the helm of troubled Boeing. At the giant aerospace company's annual meeting held after his arrival, McNerney bluntly warned attendees that "management had gotten carried away with itself," that too many executives had become used to "hiding in the bureaucracy," that the company had failed to "develop the best leadership." McNerney wasn't exaggerating. Boeing had been battered by several ethical scandals ranging from embarrassing to costly. Boeing's former chief financial officer was jailed for holding illegal job negotiations with a senior Pentagon official. A Boeing manager allegedly stole some 25,000 pages of proprietary documents from his former employer, Lockheed Martin Corp. Boeing was accused to pay discrimination against women, and one judicial review concluded that the company helped cover up internal studies supporting those sex discrimination complaints.

This *BusinessWeek* case study looks at the actions that McNerney and his executive team are invoking to improve Boeing's ethical conduct. Read the full text of this *BusinessWeek* article at www.mhhe.com/mcshane4e and prepare for the discussion questions below.

Discussion Questions

1. List the reasons that McNerney and the author of this article identify why Boeing experienced these and possibly other unethical behaviors. Are these explanations reasonably accurate, in your opinion? Are there any other causes that come to mind?
2. What steps is McNerney taking to improve Boeing's ethical conduct? In your opinion, will these actions be effective? What other steps would you take, if in McNerney's situation, to improve the company's ethical conduct?

Source: S. Holmes, "Cleaning Up Boeing," *BusinessWeek,* 13 March 2006, 62.

Team Exercise 2.4 COMPARING CULTURAL VALUES

PURPOSE This exercise is designed to help you determine the extent to which you hold similar assumptions about the values that dominate in other countries.

INSTRUCTIONS The names in the left column represent labels that a major consulting project identified with businesspeople in a particular country, based on its national culture and values. These names appear in alphabetical order. In the right column are the names of countries, also in alphabetical order, corresponding to the labels in the left column.

1. Working alone, connect the labels with the countries by relying on your perceptions of these countries. Each label is associated with only one country, so each label will be connected to only one country, and vice versa. Draw a line to connect the pairs, or put the label number beside the country name.
2. The instructor will form teams of four or five students. Members of each team will compare their results and try to reach consensus on a common set of connecting pairs.
3. Teams or the instructor will post the results for all to see the extent that students hold common opinions about businesspeople in other cultures. Class discussion can then consider the reasons why the results are so similar or different, as well as the implications of these results for working in a global work environment.

Values Labels and Country Names

Country label (alphabetical)	Country name (alphabetical)
1. Affable humanists	Australia
2. Ancient modernizers	Brazil
3. Commercial catalysts	Canada
4. Conceptual strategists	China
5. Efficient manufacturers	France
6. Ethical statesmen	Germany
7. Informal Egalitarians	India
8. Modernizing traditionalists	Netherlands
9. Optimistic entrepreneurs	New Zealand
10. Quality perfectionists	Singapore
11. Rugged individualists	Taiwan
12. Serving merchants	United Kingdom
13. Tolerant traders	United States

Source: Based on R. Rosen, P. Digh, M. Singer, and C. Phillips, *Global Literacies* (New York: Simon & Schuster, 2000).

Team Exercise 2.5 ETHICS DILEMMA VIGNETTES

PURPOSE This exercise is designed to make you aware of the ethical dilemmas people face in various business situations, as well as the competing principles and values that operate in these situations.

INSTRUCTIONS The instructor will form teams of four or five students. Team members will read each of the following cases and discuss the extent to which the company's action in each case was ethical. Be prepared to justify your evaluation using ethics principles and the perceived moral intensity of each incident.

CASE ONE An employee at a major food retailer wrote a Weblog (blog) and, in one of his writings, complained that his boss wouldn't let him go home when he felt sick and that his district manager refused to promote him because of his dreadlocks. His blog named the employer, but the employee didn't use his real name. Although all blogs are on the Internet, the employee claims that his was low-profile and that it didn't show up when doing a Google search of his name or the company. Still, the employer somehow discovered the blog, figured out the employee's real name, and fired him for "speaking ill of the company in a public domain."

CASE TWO Computer printer manufacturers usually sell printers at a low margin over cost and generate much more income from subsequent sales of the high-margin ink cartridges required for each printer. One global printer manufacturer now designs its printers so they work only with ink cartridges made in the same region. Ink cartridges purchased in the United States will not work for the same printer model sold in Europe, for example. This "region coding" of ink cartridges does not improve performance. Rather, this action prevents consumers and gray marketers from buying the product at a lower price in another region. The company says this action allows it to maintain stable prices within a region rather than continually changing prices due to currency fluctuations.

CASE THREE For the past few years the design department of a small (40-employee) company has been using a particular software program, but the three employees who use the software have been complaining for more than a year that the software is out of date and is slowing down their performance. The department agreed to switch to a competing software program costing several thousand dollars. However, the next version won't be released for six months, and buying the current version will not allow much discount toward the next version. The company has put in advance orders for the next version. Meanwhile, one employee was able to get a copy of the current version of the software from a friend in the industry. The company has allowed the three employees to use this current version of the software even though they did not pay for it.

Self-Assessment 2.6

IDENTIFYING YOUR SELF-MONITORING PERSONALITY

PURPOSE This self-assessment is designed to help you to estimate your level of self-monitoring personality.

INSTRUCTIONS The statements in this scale refer to personal characteristics that might or might not be characteristic of you. Mark the box indicating the extent to which the statement describes you. This exercise should be completed alone so you assess yourself honestly without concerns of social comparison. However, class discussion will focus on the relevance of self-monitoring personality in organizations.

Self-Monitoring Scale

Indicate the degree to which you think the following statements are true or false:	Very false	Somewhat false	Slightly more false than true	Slightly more true than false	Somewhat true	Very true
1. In social situations, I have the ability to alter my behavior if I feel that something else is called for.	☐	☐	☐	☐	☐	☐
2. I am often able to read people's true emotions correctly through their eyes.	☐	☐	☐	☐	☐	☐
3. I have the ability to control the way I come across to people, depending on the impression I wish to give them.	☐	☐	☐	☐	☐	☐
4. In conversations, I am sensitive to even the slightest change in the facial expression of the person I'm conversing with.	☐	☐	☐	☐	☐	☐
5. My powers of intuition are quite good when it comes to understanding others' emotions and motives.	☐	☐	☐	☐	☐	☐
6. I can usually tell when others consider a joke in bad taste, even though they may laugh convincingly.	☐	☐	☐	☐	☐	☐
7. When I feel that the image I am portraying isn't working, I can readily change it to something that does.	☐	☐	☐	☐	☐	☐
8. I can usually tell when I've said something inappropriate by reading the listener's eyes.	☐	☐	☐	☐	☐	☐
9. I have trouble changing my behavior to suit different people and different situations.	☐	☐	☐	☐	☐	☐
10. I have found that I can adjust my behavior to meet the requirements of any situation I find myself in.	☐	☐	☐	☐	☐	☐
11. If someone is lying to me, I usually know it at once from that person's manner of expression.	☐	☐	☐	☐	☐	☐
12. Even when it might be to my advantage, I have difficulty putting up a good front.	☐	☐	☐	☐	☐	☐
13. Once I know what the situation calls for, it's easy for me to regulate my actions accordingly.	☐	☐	☐	☐	☐	☐

Source: R.D. Lennox and R.N. Wolfe, "Revision of the Self-Monitoring Scale," *Journal of Personality and Social Psychology* 46 (June 1984), pp. 1348–64. The response categories in this scale have been altered slightly due to limitations with the original scale responses.

Self-Assessment 2.7

IDENTIFYING YOUR DOMINANT VALUES (STUDENT OLC)

Values have taken center stage in organizational behavior. Increasingly, OB experts are realizing that our personal values influence our motivation, decisions, and attitudes. This self-assessment is designed to help you estimate your personal values and value system. The instrument consists of several words and phrases, and you are asked to indicate whether each word or phrase is highly opposed or highly similar to your personal values, or some point in between these two extremes. As with all self-assessments, you need to be honest with yourself when completing this activity to get the most accurate results.

Self-Assessment 2.8

INDIVIDUALISM–COLLECTIVISM SCALE (STUDENT OLC)

Two of the most important concepts in cross-cultural organizational behavior are individualism and collectivism. This self-assessment measures your levels of individualism and collectivism with one of the most widely adopted measures. This scale consists of several statements, and you are asked to indicate how well each statement describes you. You need to be honest with yourself to receive a reasonable estimate of your levels of individualism and collectivism.

Self-Assessment 2.9

IDENTIFYING YOUR LOCUS OF CONTROL (STUDENT OLC)

This self-assessment is designed to help you estimate the extent to which you have an internal or external locus of control personality. The instrument asks you to indicate the degree to which you agree or disagree with each of the statements provided. As with all self-assessments, you need to be honest with yourself when completing this activity to get the most accurate results. The results show your relative position in the internal–external locus continuum and the general meaning of this score.

Self-Assessment 2.10

MATCHING HOLLAND'S CAREER TYPES (STUDENT OLC)

This self-assessment is designed to help you understand Holland's career types. Holland's theory identifies six different types of work environments and occupations in which people work. Few jobs fit purely in one category, but all have a dominant type. Your task is to identify the Holland type that you believe best fits each of the occupations presented in the instrument. While completing this self-assessment, you can open your book to the exhibit describing Holland's six types.

After reading this chapter, if you feel that you need additional information, see www.mhhe.com/mcshane4e for more in-depth interactivities that correspond to this material.

Don't try looking for Grahame Maher in his office; he doesn't have one. Instead the Vodafone executive (currently head of the British telecommunication's company's Czech operations) uses temporary workspace near employees in various departments. Every few months he packs up his cell phone, laptop, personal organizer, and a few files and moves to another department to sharpen his perceptions about the organization. "I haven't had an office for years," says Maher. "[Working among employees] is where I learn most about the business."

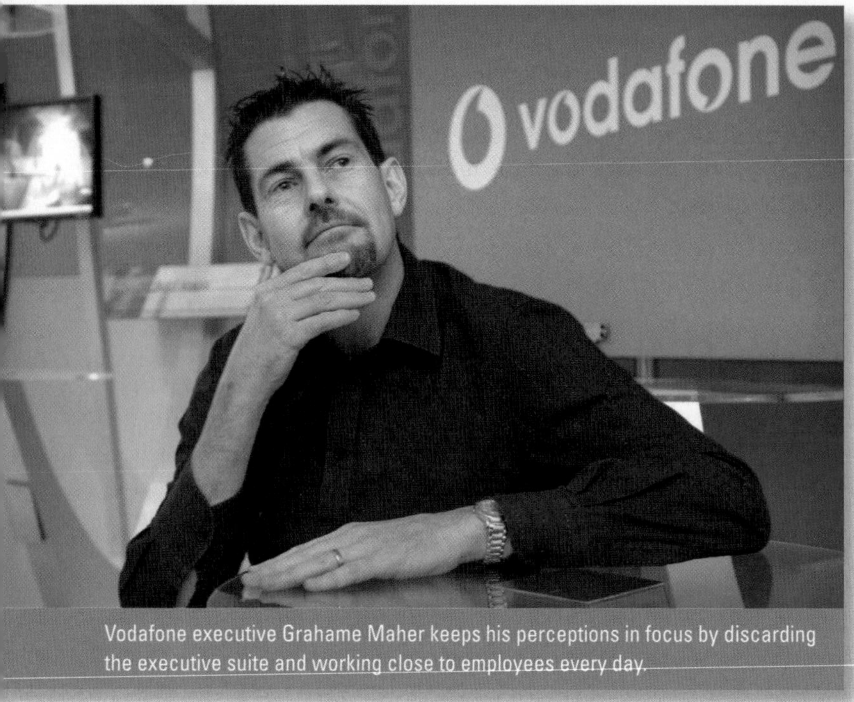

Vodafone executive Grahame Maher keeps his perceptions in focus by discarding the executive suite and working close to employees every day.

Few executives follow Maher's lead by permanently working near frontline staff, but an increasing number improve their understanding of their businesses by occasionally working in or around frontline jobs. David Neeleman, the founder of New York–based discount airline JetBlue, works in the trenches each month with his baggage handlers and ticket takers. Ikea executives work on the shop floor or tend the cash registers during the Swedish retailer's annual Anti-bureaucracy Week. Indianapolis Power & Light (IPL) CEO Ann Murtlow regularly visits line crews in the field, sits in on line crew safety schools, and finds other opportunities to interact with employees throughout the organization. "The plant guys [are] not surprised to see her in a manhole," says Murtlow's executive assistant. "She wants to know what everybody is doing and how it works."

Some companies have extended this practice so nonmanagement staff also understand each other better. Everyone at the head office of British department store Debenhams adopts a store for a year and works on the floor of that store once or twice each month. Newly hired information technology staff at Marriott International spend a week working in one of the company's hotels, shadowing people in sales, front desk, engineering, food services, housekeeping, and other business functions. Every new hire at 1-800-GOT-JUNK?, North America's largest rubbish removal company, spends an entire week on a junk removal truck to better understand how the business works. "How can you possibly empathize with someone out in the field unless you've been on the truck yourself?" asks CEO and founder Brian Scudamore.[1]

3

Perception and Learning in Organizations

LEARNING OBJECTIVES

After reading this chapter you should be able to

1. Outline the perceptual process.
2. Explain how we perceive ourselves and others through social identity.
3. Outline the reasons why stereotyping occurs and describe ways to minimize its adverse effects.
4. Describe the attribution process and two attribution errors.
5. Summarize the self-fulfilling prophecy process.
6. Explain how empathy and the Johari Window can improve a person's perceptions.
7. Define *learning* and explain how it affects individual behavior.
8. Describe the A-B-C model of behavior modification and the four contingencies of reinforcement.
9. Describe the three features of social learning theory.
10. Describe Kolb's experiential learning model and the action learning process.

Grahame Maher, David Neeleman, Ann Murtlow, and other executives work in frontline jobs or otherwise keep in close contact with staff and customers in order to improve their perceptions of the world around them and to learn about the consequences of their actions. **Perception** is the process of receiving information about and making sense of the world around us. It entails deciding which information to notice, how to categorize this information, and how to interpret it within the framework of our existing knowledge. This chapter begins by describing the perceptual process: the dynamics of selecting, organizing, and interpreting external stimuli. Social identity theory, which has become a leading perceptual theory in organizational behavior, is then introduced, followed by a description of stereotyping, including ways of minimizing stereotype biases in the workplace. Next we look at attribution, self-fulfilling prophecies, and other perceptual issues, followed by an overview of empathy and Johari Window as general strategies to minimize perceptual problems.

perception
The process of receiving information about and making sense of the world around us.

The opening vignette also refers to the topic of learning because executives working on the front lines learn about what employees and customers experience every day. Indeed, it is difficult to discuss perceptions without also referring to the knowledge and skills learned from those perceptions. That's why perceptions and learning are combined in this chapter. The latter part of this chapter introduces the concept of learning as well as the related concepts of tacit and explicit knowledge. We then look at three perspectives of learning: behavior modification, social learning theory, and experiential learning.

Learning Objectives

After reading the next two sections you should be able to

1. **Outline the perceptual process.**
2. **Explain how we perceive ourselves and others through social identity.**

The Perceptual Process

The Greek philosopher Plato wrote long ago that we see reality only as shadows reflected on the rough wall of a cave.[2] In other words, reality is filtered through an imperfect perceptual process. This imperfect process, which is illustrated in Exhibit 3.1,

Exhibit 3.1
Model of the Perceptual Process

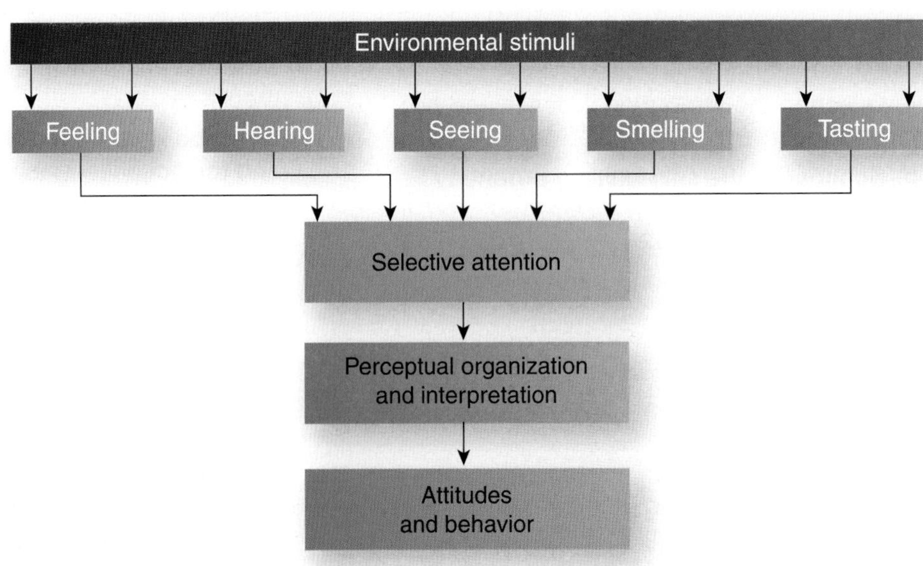

begins when environmental stimuli are received through our senses. Most stimuli are screened out; the rest are organized and interpreted. The resulting perceptions influence our conscious emotions and behavior toward those objects, people, and events.[3]

Selective Attention

Our five senses are constantly bombarded with stimuli. Some things are noticed, but most are screened out. A nurse working in postoperative care might ignore the smell of recently disinfected instruments or the sound of co-workers talking nearby. Yet a small flashing red light on the nurse station console is immediately noticed because it signals that a patient's vital signs are failing. This process of attending to some information received by our senses and ignoring other information is called **selective attention.** Selective attention is influenced by two sets of factors: (1) characteristics of the person or object being perceived and (2) characteristics of the individual doing the perceiving.[4]

selective attention
The process of filtering information received by our senses.

Characteristics of the Object Some things stand out more than others because of their size, intensity, motion, repetition, and novelty. The red light on the nurse station console receives attention because it is bright (intensity), flashing (motion), and a rare event (novelty). As for people, we would notice two employees having a heated debate if co-workers normally don't raise their voices (novelty and intensity). Notice that selective attention is also influenced by the context in which the target is perceived. You might be aware that a client had a German accent if the meeting took place in Houston, but not if the conversation took place in Germany–particularly if you had been living there for some time. On the contrary, your accent would be noticed!

Characteristics of the Perceiver Characteristics of the perceiver play an important role in selection attention, much of it without our awareness.[5] When information is received through the senses, our brain quickly and unconsciously assesses whether it is relevant or irrelevant to us. Emotional markers (worry, happiness, anger) are attached to the relevant information based on this rapid evaluation, and these emotionally tagged bits of stimuli compete for our conscious attention. In extreme cases our emotions almost completely take over. For example, a number of armed off-duty police officers or plainclothes detectives have been killed by "friendly fire" when colleagues thought they were suspects. Strong emotions cause officers to instinctively react to the sight of the handgun, screening out other information suggesting the victim is also an officer.[6]

Although largely unconscious, selective attention is also consciously influenced through our anticipation of future events.[7] If you expect a co-worker to send you some important information by e-mail today, then that e-mail is more likely to get noticed despite the daily bombardment of messages. Unfortunately, expectations also delay our awareness of unexpected information. If we form a theory too early regarding a particular customer trend, we might not notice information indicating a different trend. In other words, our expectations and cognitive attention toward one issue tend to reduce our sensitivity to information about other issues. The solution here is to keep an open mind and take in as much information as possible without forming theories too early.

categorical thinking
The mostly unconscious process of organizing people and objects into preconceived categories that are stored in our long-term memory.

Perceptual Organization and Interpretation

People make sense of information even before they become aware of it. This sense making partly includes **categorical thinking**–the mostly unconscious process of organizing people and objects into preconceived categories that are stored in our

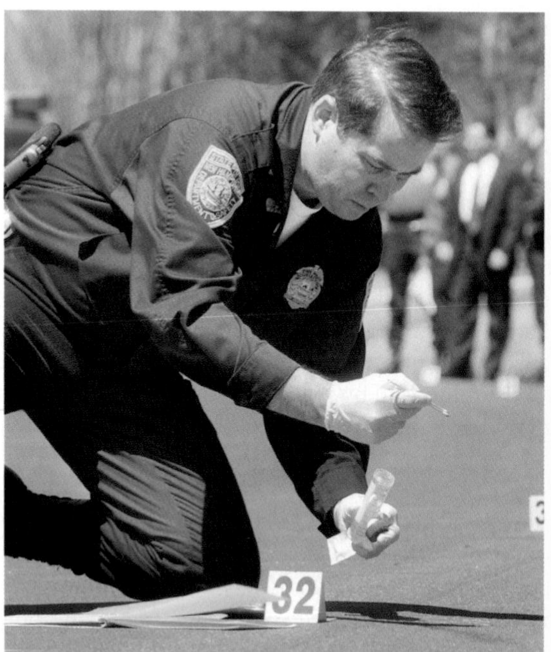

Detectives Avoid Tunnel Vision with Art Appreciation Good detective work involves more than forming a good theory about the crime. It also involves *not* forming a theory too early in the investigation. Keith Findley, codirector of the Wisconsin Innocence Project, warns that becoming preoccupied with a single theory causes police to "focus on a suspect, select and filter the evidence that will build a case for conviction, while ignoring or suppressing evidence that points away from guilt." To minimize this selective attention problem, officers in the New York Police Department are attending art classes, where they learn observation skills and how to develop multiple perspectives. "[The class] reminded me to stop and take in the whole scene and not just have tunnel vision," says NYPD captain David Grossi, who credits the class for helping him to discover evidence outside the area he otherwise would have investigated.[8]

long-term memory.[9] Categorical thinking relies on a variety of automatic perceptual grouping principles. Things are often grouped together based on their similarity or proximity to others. If you notice that a group of similar-looking people includes several professors, for instance, you will likely assume that the others in that group are also professors. Another form of perceptual grouping is based on the need for cognitive closure, such as filling in missing information about what happened at a meeting that you didn't attend (who was there, where it was held). A third form of grouping occurs when we think we see trends in otherwise ambiguous information. Several research studies have found that people have a natural tendency to see patterns in what really are random events, such as presumed winning streaks among sports stars or in gambling.[10]

Making sense also involves interpreting incoming information, and this happens just as quickly as the brain selects and organizes that information. The brain attaches emotional markers to incoming stimuli, which are essentially quick judgments about whether those stimuli are good or bad for us. To give you an idea about how quickly and systematically this unconscious perceptual process occurs, consider the following study:[11] Eight observers were shown video clips of university instructors teaching an undergraduate class, then rated the instructors on several personal characteristics (optimistic, likable, anxious, active, and the like). The observers did not know the instructors and completed their ratings independently, yet they agreed with each other on many characteristics. Equally important, these ratings matched the ratings completed by students who actually attended the entire classes.

These results may be interesting, but the extraordinary discovery is that the observers formed their perceptions based on as little as *six seconds* of video—three segments of two seconds each selected randomly across the one-hour class! Furthermore, the video didn't have any sound. In spite of these very thin slices of information, the observers developed similar perceptions of the instructors, and those perceptions were comparable to the perceptions formed by students attending the entire classes. Other studies have reported parallel results using two 15-second video segments of high school teachers, courtroom judges, and physicians. Collectively these "thin slice" studies reveal that selective attention as well as perceptual organization and interpretation operate very quickly and to a large extent without our awareness.

mental models
The broad worldviews or "theories in-use" that people rely on to guide their perceptions and behaviors.

Mental Models To achieve our goals with some degree of predictability and sanity, we need road maps of the environments in which we live. These road maps, called **mental models,** are internal representations of the external world.[12] They consist of broad worldviews or templates of the mind that provide enough stability and predictability to guide our preferences and behaviors. For example, most of us have a mental model about attending a class lecture or seminar. We have a set of assumptions and expectations about how people arrive, arrange themselves in the room, ask and answer questions, and so forth. We can create a mental image of what a class would look like in progress.

We rely on mental models to make sense of our environment through perceptual grouping; they fill in the missing pieces, including the causal connection among events. Yet mental models may also blind us from seeing that world in different ways. For example, accounting professionals tend to see corporate problems in terms of accounting solutions, whereas marketing professionals see the same problems from a marketing perspective. Mental models also block our recognition of new opportunities. How do we change mental models? It's a tough challenge. After all, we developed models from years of experience and reinforcement. The most important way to minimize the perceptual problems with mental models is to constantly question them. We need to ask ourselves about the assumptions we make. Working with people from diverse backgrounds is another way to break out of existing mental models. Colleagues from different cultures and areas of expertise tend to have different mental models, so working with them makes our own assumptions more obvious.

Social Identity Theory

social identity theory
A conceptual framework based on the idea that how we perceive the world depends on how we define ourselves in terms of our membership in various social groups.

The perceptual process is an interesting combination of our self-perceptions and perceptions of others. Increasingly, experts around the world are discovering that how we perceive the world depends on how we define ourselves. This connection between self-perception and perception of others is explained through **social identity theory.**[13] According to social identity theory, people maintain a *social identity* by defining themselves in terms of the groups to which they belong and have an emotional attachment. For instance, someone might have a social identity as an American, a graduate of the University of Massachusetts, and an employee at Oracle Corporation (see Exhibit 3.2). Everyone engages in this social categorization process because it helps to make sense of where we fit within the social world.

Along with a social identity, people have a *personal identity*–characteristics that make them unique and distinct from people in any particular group. For instance, an unusual achievement that distinguishes you from other people typically becomes a personal identity characteristic. Personal identity refers to something about you as an individual without reference to a larger group. Social identity, on the other hand, defines you in terms of characteristics of the group. By perceiving yourself as an employee at Oracle Corporation, you are assigning characteristics to yourself that you believe are also characteristics of Oracle employees in general.

Social identity is a complex combination of many memberships arranged in a hierarchy of importance. One factor determining this importance is how obvious our membership is in the group. We define ourselves by our gender, race, age, and other observable characteristics because other people can easily identify our membership

Exhibit 3.2
Self-Perception and Social Perception through Social Identity

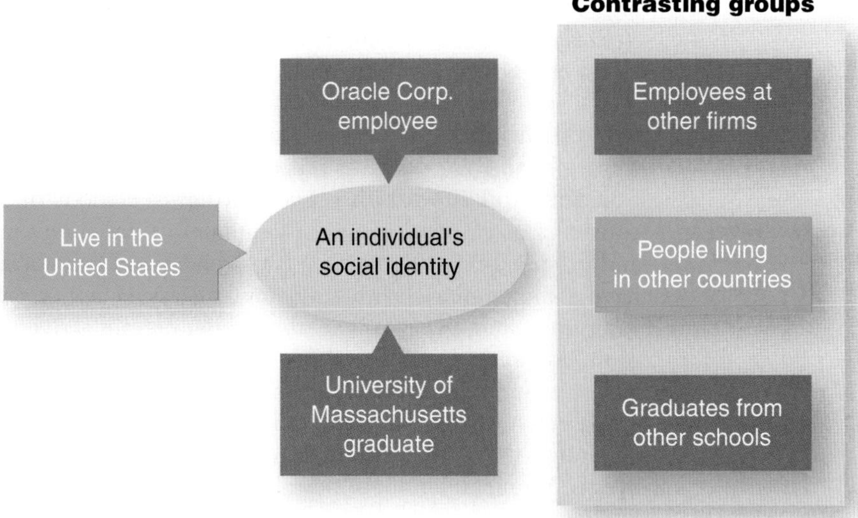

in those groups. It is difficult to ignore your gender in a class where most other students are the opposite gender, for example. In that context gender tends to become a stronger defining feature of your social identity than in social settings where there are many people of the same gender.

Along with our demographic characteristics, group status is typically an important influence on our social identity. Most of us want to have a positive self-image, so we identify with groups that have higher status or respect. Medical doctors usually define themselves in terms of their profession because of its high status, whereas people in low-status jobs tend to define themselves in terms of nonjob groups. Some people define themselves in terms of where they work because their employer has a favorable reputation in the community; other people never mention where they work if the firm has a poor reputation in the community.[14]

Perceiving Others through Social Identity

Social identity theory explains more than just how we develop self-perceptions. It also explains the dynamics of *social perception*–how we perceive others.[15] This social perception is influenced by three activities in the process of forming and maintaining our social identity: categorization, homogenization, and differentiation.

- *Categorization.* Social identity is a comparative process, and that comparison begins by categorizing people into distinct groups. By viewing someone (including yourself) as a Texan, for example, you remove that person's individuality and instead see him or her as a prototypical representative of the group called Texans. This categorization allows you to distinguish Texans from people who live in, say, California or elsewhere.
- *Homogenization.* To simplify the comparison process, we tend to think that people within each group are very similar to each other. For instance, we think Texans collectively have similar attitudes and characteristics, whereas Californians collectively have their own set of characteristics. Of course every individual is unique, but we tend to lose sight of this fact when thinking about our social identity and how we compare to people in other social groups.

- *Differentiation.* Social identity fulfills our inherent need to have a distinct and positive identity–in other words, to feel unique and good about ourselves. To achieve this, we do more than categorize people and homogenize them; we also differentiate groups by assigning more favorable characteristics to people in our groups than to people in other groups. This differentiation is often subtle. Even by constructing favorable images of our own social identity groups, we implicitly form less favorable images of people belonging to other social categories. However, when other groups compete or conflict with our groups, the "good guy–bad guy" contrast becomes much stronger. Under these conditions, the negative image of opponents preserves our self-image against the threatening outsiders.[16]

To summarize, the social identity process explains how we perceive ourselves and other people. We identify ourselves partly in terms of our membership in social groups. This comparison process includes categorizing people into groups, forming a homogeneous image of people within those groups, and differentiating groups by assigning more favorable features to our own groups than to other groups. This perceptual process makes our social world easier to understand and fulfills an innate need to feel unique and positive about ourselves. This social identity process is also the basis for stereotyping people in organizational settings, which we discuss next.

Learning Objectives

After reading the next three sections you should be able to

3. **Outline the reasons why stereotyping occurs and describe ways to minimize its adverse effects.**
4. **Describe the attribution process and two attribution errors.**
5. **Summarize the self-fulfilling prophecy process.**

Stereotyping in Organizational Settings

stereotyping
The process of assigning traits to people based on their membership in a social category.

Stereotyping is an extension of social identity theory and a product of our natural process of organizing information.[17] The first step in stereotyping occurs when we develop social categories and assign traits that are difficult to observe. For instance, students might form a stereotype that professors are both intelligent and absentminded. Personal experiences shape stereotypes to some extent, but stereotypes are provided to us mainly through cultural upbringing and media images (such as movie characters).

The second step in stereotyping involves assigning people to one or more social categories based on easily observable information about them, such as their gender, appearance, or physical location. Observable features allow us to assign people to a social group quickly and without much investigation. The third step consists of assigning the stereotyped group's cluster of traits to people identified as members of that group. For example, we tend to think that professors are absentminded because people often include this trait in their stereotype of professors.

Why Stereotyping Occurs

Stereotyping occurs for three reasons.[18] First, stereotyping relies on categorical thinking which, as we learned earlier, is a natural process to simplify our understanding of the world. We depend on categorical thinking and stereotyping because it is impossible to recall all the unique characteristics of every person we meet. Second, we have an innate need to understand and anticipate how others will behave. We don't have much information when first meeting someone, so we rely heavily on stereotypes to fill in the missing pieces. As you might expect, people with a stronger need for this cognitive closure have a higher tendency to stereotype others.

The third reason why stereotyping occurs is that it enhances our self-perception and social identity. Recall from social identity theory that we tend to emphasize the positive aspects of the groups to which we belong, which implicitly or explicitly generates less favorable views of people in contrasting groups. This explains why we are particularly motivated to use negative stereotypes toward people who hurt our self-esteem.[19] Stereotypes of aloof, greedy executives often fill employees' minds during layoffs, for instance.

Problems with Stereotyping

Stereotypes tend to have some inaccuracies, some overestimation or underestimation of real differences, and some degree of accuracy.[20] Still, they cause numerous problems in the workplace that need to be minimized. One concern is that stereotypes do not accurately describe every person in a social category. For instance, the widespread "bean counter" stereotype of accountants collectively views people in this profession as "single-mindedly preoccupied with precision and form, methodical and conservative, and a boring joyless character."[21] Although this may be true of some accountants, it is certainly not characteristic of all–or even most–people in this profession.

One unfortunate consequence of these negative stereotypes is that they discourage some social groups from entering various professions. As Connections 3.1 describes, the "geek" or "nerd" stereotype of people in engineering and computer science is partly responsible for the low percentage of women in these occupations. Notice how the individual's social identity also plays an important role in deciding whether to enter these professions.

Another problem with stereotyping is that it lays the foundation for discriminatory behavior. Most people experience *unintentional (systemic) discrimination* (also called *disparate impact*), which sometimes occurs when decision makers rely on stereotypes to establish notions of the "ideal" person in specific roles. A person who doesn't fit the ideal is likely to receive a less favorable evaluation. This subtle discrimination often shows up in age discrimination claims, where employers say they are looking for "new blood" or "young dynamic" individuals. Ryanair recently lost an age discrimination case after the Irish discount airline used the latter phrase in its recruitment advertising. The tribunal learned that none of the 28 applicants who applied for Ryanair's job opening was over 40 years old.[22] Recruiters say they aren't biased against older job applicants; yet older workers have a much more difficult time gaining employment even though research indicates they are well qualified.

prejudice
The unfounded negative emotions and attitudes toward people belonging to a particular stereotyped group.

A more overt form of discrimination is **prejudice,** which refers to unfounded negative emotions and attitudes toward people belonging to a particular stereotyped group.[23] Overt prejudice is less apparent today than a few decades ago, but it still exists. In one recent incident a hotel clerk told two Wisconsin investigators of Hispanic and southeast Asian descent, respectively, that there were no vacancies; yet a female colleague who telephoned soon afterward was told the hotel had plenty of rooms available. The Australian army has taken a hammering recently for several examples of overt racism, including one incident where soldiers dressed as Ku Klux Klan members to taunt nonwhite soldiers in the unit. A tribunal in Quebec was recently shocked to discover that one of Canada's largest vegetable farms prevented black employees from eating in the regular cafeteria. Instead they were relegated to a "blacks only" eating area that lacked heat, running water, proper toilets, and refrigeration. Claude

Connections 3.1

Stereotyping and Social Identity Discourage Women from Entering Engineering

Women represent 57 percent of university graduates in the United States but only 19 percent of engineering graduates. One reason for this gap is that the stereotype of engineers and computer scientists doesn't fit the social identities that most women want for themselves. "If you ask a woman to characterize a typical IT professional, she is likely to describe a young man with excess facial hair, sitting behind a computer all day munching pizza and guzzling Coke," quips Ann Swain, chief executive of the Association of Technology Staffing Companies in the United Kingdom. Jo-Ann Cohen, associate dean at North Carolina State University, says the same image problem exists for engineering and science. "I think women have a hard time envisioning themselves as scientists," she says. "There's a lack of role models."

Even if women are not put off by social identity problems, family and friends offer them stereotypical advice. Edna Lee grew up with aspirations of becoming a chemical engineer, but her parents had other ideas. "My parents said that a woman would not be able to get very far as an engineer," recalls Edna, who has since become an accountant. "They thought that engineering was more a 'male' job." Kirsty Last, a third-year mechanical engineering student at the University of Wollongong in Australia, says that this stereotyping exists in subtle ways. "People still gasp when I tell them I'm doing engineering," says Last.

To correct these perceptions, many universities have established summer camps where high school girls meet successful female engineers and discover through hands-on activities that science and math can be fun and fit their self-image. CalTech went one step further five years ago by revising its chemical engineering curriculum to include topics that seem more relevant and appealing, particularly for women (biochemistry, environmental engineering). Today nearly half of the Pasadena college's chemical engineering class consists of women, including (from left in this photo) Shannon Lewis, Michelle Giron, and Haluna Gunterman.[24]

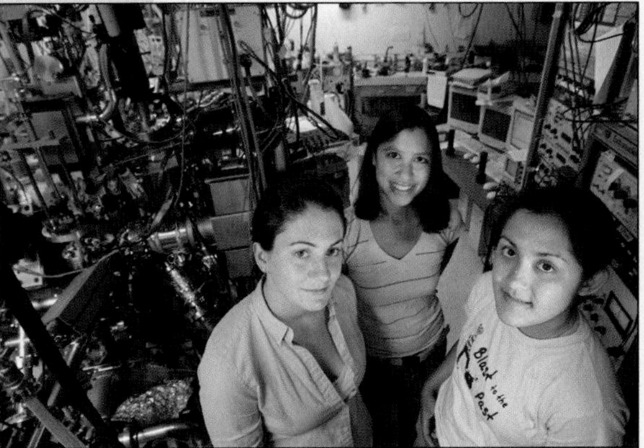

CalTech and other universities are trying to attract more women to engineering and computer science by altering stereotypes and revising programs.

Sources: A. Swain, "Easing a Skills' Shortage—Women in IT," *Guardian (London)*, 13 March 2003, p. 6; P. Shih, "Breaking Down Barriers," *Jasmine Magazine*, Premiere Issue (2003); L. Giovanelli, "Gender Divide," *Winston-Salem Journal*, 3 July 2005, p. 1; V. Reitman, "Caltech to Harvard: Redo the Math," *Los Angeles Times*, 20 June 2005; C. Trenwith, "Engineering a Gender Balance," *Illawarra Mercury (Australia)*, 13 September 2005, p. 22.

Bebear, CEO of French insurance giant AXA, has called for anonymous résumés because he believes that many employers in France routinely "throw away the résumés of people who are from bad parts of town which are supposed to have Arabs or blacks."[25]

Minimizing Stereotyping Bias

If stereotyping is such a problem, shouldn't we try to avoid this process altogether? Unfortunately it's not that simple. Most experts agree that categorical thinking (including stereotyping) is an automatic and unconscious process. Intensive training can minimize stereotype activation to some extent, but for the most part the process is hardwired in our brain cells.[26] Also remember that stereotyping helps us in several valuable (although fallible) ways described earlier: minimizing mental effort, filling in missing information, and supporting our social identity. The good news is that although it is very difficult to prevent the *activation* of stereotypes, we can minimize the *application* of stereotypical information. In other words, we can avoid using our stereotypes in our decisions and actions toward other people. Three strategies for minimizing the application of stereotyping are diversity awareness training, meaningful interaction, and decision-making accountability.

Diversity Awareness Training and Assessment Diversity awareness training tries to minimize discrimination by dispelling myths about people from various cultural and demographic groups and by identifying the organizational benefits of diversity and the problems with stereotyping. Some sessions rely on role-playing and other exercises to help employees discover the subtle yet pervasive effects of stereotyping in their decision making and behavior. Another approach is to complete self-assessments, such as the Implicit Association Test (IAT), which detect subtle race, age, and gender bias in people.[27]

Diversity training and assessment do not correct deep-rooted prejudice; they probably don't even change stereotypes in tolerant people. What they can potentially do, however, is to increase our sensitivity to equality and motivate us to block inaccurate perceptions arising from ingrained stereotypes. Consider Jennifer Smith-Holladay, who recently completed the IAT. Smith-Holladay was surprised to learn that she is biased in favor of white people, a group to which she belongs, and in favor of heterosexuals, a group to which she does not belong. "I discovered that I not only have some ingroup favoritism lurking in my subconscious, but also possess some internalized oppression in terms of my sexuality." Smith-Holladay suggests that this revelation will make her more aware of personal biases and help her minimize their application in decision making. "In the case of my own subconscious ingroup favoritism for white people, for example, my charge is to be color-conscious, not color-blind, and to always explicitly consider how race may affect behaviors and decisions," she says.[28]

Meaningful Interaction The more meaningful interaction we have with someone, the less we rely on stereotypes to understand that person.[29] This statement, which describes the **contact hypothesis,** sounds simple enough; but in reality it works only under specific conditions. Participants must have close and frequent interaction working toward a shared goal where they need to rely on each other (that is, cooperate rather than compete with each other). Everyone should have equal status in that context and should be engaged in a meaningful task. An hour-long social gathering between executives and frontline employees does not satisfy these conditions. On the other hand, having executives work in frontline jobs, which we described at the beginning of this chapter, does seem to represent meaningful interaction. By working in frontline jobs these executives reduce their status differences with other staff, cooperate toward a common goal, and have close and frequent interaction with frontline employees.

contact hypothesis
A theory stating that the more we interact with someone, the less we rely on stereotypes to understand that person.

Decision-Making Accountability A third way to minimize the biasing effects of stereotyping is to hold employees accountable for their decisions.[30] This accountability encourages more active information processing and, consequently, motivates decision makers to suppress stereotypical perceptions in favor of more precise and logical information. In contrast, less concern about accountability allows decision makers to engage in more passive information processing, which includes more reliance on discriminatory stereotypes.

Overall, social identity theory and stereotyping are central activities in the perceptual process, most of which occurs automatically and unconsciously. Without our awareness, our brain identifies and organizes the incoming information around preconceived categories and assigns emotional markers representing an initial reaction

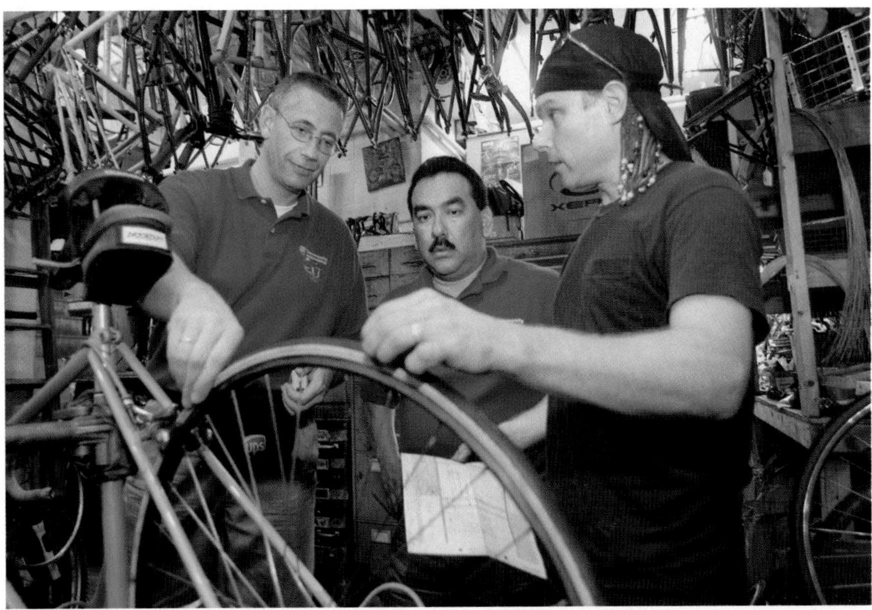

UPS Managers Gain Meaningful Interaction Every year since 1968, the UPS Community Internship Program (CIP) has transported up to 50 UPS managers out of their busy world of package delivery for four weeks and into communities that need their help and are far removed from their own lives. CIP interns help in drug abuse centers, homeless shelters, job training programs, and other community services in Texas, Tennessee, and New York. For example, this photo shows UPS managers (from left) Dirk Fricke and Dan Sotello assisting bike repairer Ed Matthiack at a bicycle recycling shop and job training center in Brooklyn. UPS senior vice president Cal Darden explains that CIP is an important part of leadership development at UPS because it creates meaningful interaction that "develops sensitivity to issues that our employees and communities face every day." "CIP brings you back down to earth," says Michael Michelak, who recently completed the program by assisting the needy in Chattanooga, Tennessee. The UPS manager from Indiana explains further, "When an issue arises, I am more empathetic in dealing with employees."[31]

to whether the information is good, bad, or irrelevant. It may be difficult to prevent this categorization and activation of stereotypes, but we can consciously control the application of stereotypes in decision making and behavior. Now let's look at another perceptual activity: attribution.

Attribution Theory

attribution process
The perceptual process of deciding whether an observed behavior or event is caused largely by internal or by external factors.

The **attribution process** is the process of deciding whether an observed behavior or event is caused largely by the person (internal factors) or the environment (external factors).[32] Internal factors include the individual's ability or motivation, such as believing that an employee performs a job poorly because he or she lacks the necessary competencies or motivation. External factors include lack of resources, other people, or just luck. An external attribution would occur if we believe that the employee performs a job poorly because he or she doesn't receive sufficient resources to do the task.

People rely on the three attribution rules shown in Exhibit 3.3 to determine whether someone's behavior has mainly an internal or external attribution. Internal attributions are made when the observed individual behaved this way in the past (high consistency) and behaves like this toward other people or in different situations

Exhibit 3.3
Rules of Attribution

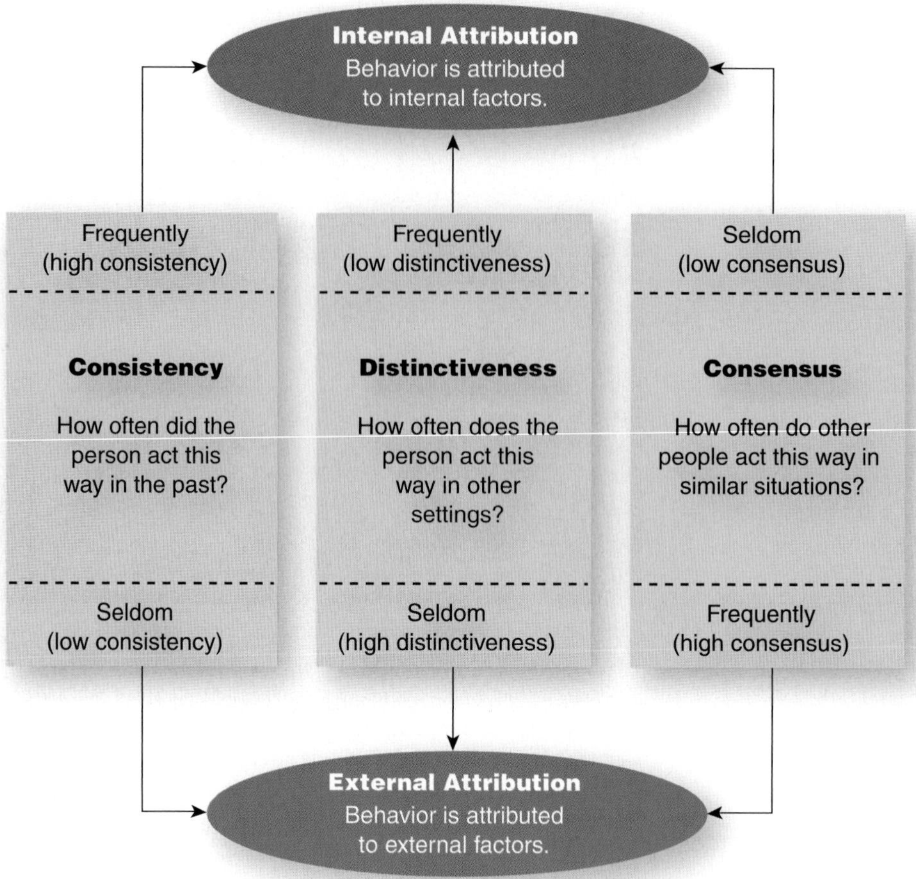

(low distinctiveness), and other people do not behave this way in similar situations (low consensus). On the other hand, an external attribution is made when there is low consistency, high distinctiveness, and high consensus.

Here's an example that will help to clarify the three attribution rules. Suppose an employee is making poor-quality products one day on a particular machine. We would probably conclude that there is something wrong with the machine (an external attribution) if the employee has made good-quality products on this machine in the past (low consistency), the employee makes good-quality products on other machines (high distinctiveness), and other employees have recently had quality problems on this machine (high consensus). We would make an internal attribution, on the other hand, if the employee usually makes poor-quality products on this machine (high consistency), other employees produce good-quality products on this machine (low consensus), and the employee also makes poor-quality products on other machines (low distinctiveness).[33]

Attributions are an essential part of our perceptual world because they link together the various pieces of that world in cause–effect relationships. As a result, our decisions and actions are influenced by our prior attributions.[34] Students who make internal attributions about their poor performance are more likely to drop out of their programs. Our satisfaction with work accomplishments is influenced to a large degree by whether we take credit for those accomplishments or attribute the success to external causes. Whether employees support or resist organizational change initiatives depends on whether they believe management introduced those changes due to external pressures or their personal motives.

Attribution Errors

fundamental attribution errors
The tendency to attribute the behavior of other people more to internal than to external factors.

People are far from perfect when making attributions. One bias, called **fundamental attribution error,** refers to our tendency to see the person rather than the situation as the main cause of that person's behavior.[35] If an employee is late for work, observers are more likely to conclude that the person is lazy than to realize that external factors may have caused this behavior. One reason why fundamental attribution error occurs is that observers can't easily see the external factors that constrain the person's behavior. We didn't see the traffic jam that caused the person to be late, for instance. Another reason is that we tend to believe in the power of the person; we assume that individuals can overcome situational constraints more than they really can.

Although it is fairly common in the United States and other Western countries, fundamental attribution error is less common in Asian cultures.[36] The reason for this East–West difference is that Asians are taught from an early age to pay attention to the context in interpersonal relations and to see everything connected in a holistic way. Westerners, on the other hand, learn about the importance and independence of the individual; the person and situation are separate from each other, not seamlessly connected.

self-serving bias
A perceptual error whereby people tend to attribute their favorable outcomes to internal factors and their failures to external factors.

Another attribution error, known as **self-serving bias,** is the tendency to attribute our favorable outcomes to internal factors and our failures to external factors. Simply put, we take credit for our successes and blame others or the situation for our mistakes. Self-serving bias protects our self-esteem, but it can have the opposite effect for people in leadership positions. We expect leaders to take ownership of their failures, so we have less respect for executives who blame the situation rather than take personal responsibility. Still, self-serving bias is consistently found in annual reports; executives mainly refer to their personal qualities as reasons for the company's gains and to external factors as reasons for the company's losses.[37]

Self-Fulfilling Prophecy

self-fulfilling prophecy
Occurs when our expectations about another person cause that person to act in a way that is consistent with those expectations.

Another important perception–and perceptual error–in organizations is **self-fulfilling prophecy.** Self-fulfilling prophecy occurs when our expectations about another person cause that person to act in a way that is consistent with those expectations. In other words, our perceptions can influence reality. Exhibit 3.4 illustrates the four

Exhibit 3.4
The Self-Fulfilling Prophecy Cycle

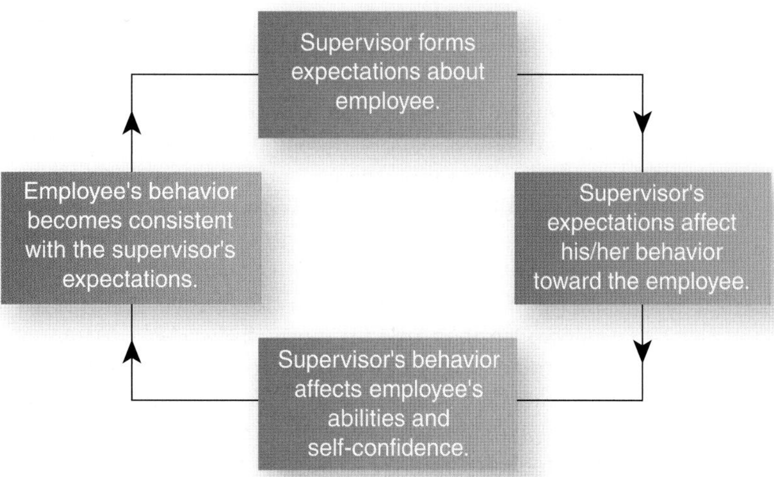

steps in the self-fulfilling prophecy process using the example of a supervisor and subordinate:[38]

1. *Expectations formed.* The supervisor forms expectations about the employee's future behavior and performance. These expectations are sometimes inaccurate because first impressions are usually formed from limited information.
2. *Behavior toward the employee.* The supervisor's expectations influence his or her treatment of employees. Specifically, high-expectancy employees (those expected to do well) receive more emotional support through nonverbal cues (such as more smiling and eye contact), more frequent and valuable feedback and reinforcement, more challenging goals, better training, and more opportunities to demonstrate their performance.
3. *Effects on the employee.* The supervisor's behaviors have two effects on the employee. First, through better training and more practice opportunities, a high-expectancy employee learns more skills and knowledge than a low-expectancy employee. Second, the employee becomes more self-confident, which results in higher motivation and willingness to set more challenging goals.[39]
4. *Employee behavior and performance.* With higher motivation and better skills, high-expectancy employees are more likely to demonstrate desired behaviors and better performance. The supervisor notices this, which supports his or her original perception.

There are plenty of examples of self-fulfilling prophecies in work and school settings.[40] Research has found that women score lower on math tests when people around them convey a negative stereotype of women regarding their perceived ability to do math. Women perform better on these tests when they are not exposed to this negative self-fulfilling prophecy. Another study reported that the performance of Israeli Defense Force trainees was influenced by their instructor's expectations regarding the trainee's potential in the program. Self-fulfilling prophecy was at work here because the instructors' expectations were based on a list provided by researchers showing which recruits had high and low potential, even though the researchers had actually listed these trainees randomly.

Contingencies of Self-Fulfilling Prophecy

Self-fulfilling prophecies are more powerful under some conditions than others.[41] Manager expectations have a stronger effect on employee behavior at the beginning of the relationship (when employees are first hired) than after they have known each other for some time. Self-fulfilling prophecy is also more powerful when several people have these expectations toward an individual than when the expectations are perceived by just one person. In other words, we might be able to ignore one person's doubts about our potential, but not the collective doubts of several people.

A third factor is the individual's past achievements. Both positive and negative self-fulfilling prophecies have a stronger effect on people with a history of low achievement than of those with high achievement. High achievers are less affected by negative expectations because they can draw on the strength of their successful past experiences. Low achievers don't have these past successes to support their self-esteem, so they give up more easily when they sense their boss's low expectations. Fortunately, the opposite is also true: Low achievers respond more favorably than high achievers to positive self-fulfilling prophecy. Low achievers don't receive this positive encouragement very often, so it probably has a strong effect on their motivation to excel.[42]

Positive Self-Fulfilling Prophecies Strengthen Cocoplans After only a dozen years in business, Cocoplans is recognized throughout the Philippines as a top-performing pre-needs (pension and education) insurance company with excellent customer service. This success is partly due to the way Cocoplans executives perceive their sales staff. "At Cocoplans, we treat salespeople as our internal customers, while plan holders are our external customers," explains Cocoplans president Caesar T. Michelena. Michelena believes that by treating employees as customers, Cocoplans managers have positive expectations of those employees, which then results in higher performance results. "It's a self-fulfilling prophecy. If you believe that [employees] will not last, your behavior toward them will show it. . . . You get what you expect."[43]

The main lesson from the self-fulfilling prophecy literature is that leaders need to develop and maintain a positive, yet realistic, expectation toward all employees.[44] This recommendation is consistent with the emerging philosophy of **positive organizational behavior** (a variation of *positive psychology*), which focuses on building positive qualities and traits within individuals or institutions as opposed to focusing on just trying to fix what might be wrong with them. Perceiving and communicating hope are so important that they are identified as critical successful factors for physicians and surgeons. Unfortunately, training programs that make leaders aware of the power of positive expectations seem to have minimal effect. Instead, generating positive expectations and hope depends on a corporate culture of support and learning. Hiring supervisors who are inherently optimistic toward their staff is another way of increasing the incidence of positive self-fulfilling prophecies.

positive organizational behavior
An emerging philosophy that focuses on building positive qualities and traits within individuals or institutions as opposed to focusing on just trying to fix what might be wrong with them.

Other Perceptual Errors

Self-fulfilling prophecy, attribution, and stereotyping are processes that both assist and interfere with the perceptual process. Four other well-known perceptual biases in organizational settings are primacy effect, recency effect, halo effect, and projection bias.

Primacy Effect

primacy effect
A perceptual error in which we quickly form an opinion of people based on the first information we receive about them.

First impressions are lasting impressions. This well-known saying isn't a cliché; it's a well-researched observation known as the **primacy effect.** The primacy effect refers to our tendency to quickly form an opinion of people based on the first information we receive about them.[45] This rapid perceptual organization and interpretation occurs because we need to make sense of the world around us. The problem is that first impressions–particularly negative first impressions–are difficult to change. After categorizing someone, we tend to select subsequent information that supports our first impression and screen out information that opposes that impression. Negative impressions tend to "stick" more than positive impressions because negative characteristics are more easily attributed to the person, whereas positive characteristics are often attributed to the situation.

Recency Effect

recency effect
A perceptual error in which the most recent information dominates one's perception of others.

The **recency effect** occurs when the most recent information dominates our perceptions.[46] This effect is most common when people (especially those with limited experience) make an evaluation involving complex information. For instance, auditors must digest large volumes of information in their judgments about financial documents, and the most recent information received prior to the decision tends to get weighted more heavily than information received at the beginning of the audit. Similarly, when supervisors evaluate the performance of employees over the previous year, the most recent performance information dominates the evaluation because it is the most easily recalled. Some employees, aware of the recency effect, use it to their advantage by getting their best work on the manager's desk just before the performance appraisal is conducted.

Halo Effect

halo effect
A perceptual error whereby our general impression of a person, usually based on one prominent characteristic, colors the perception of other characteristics of that person.

Halo effect occurs when our general impression of a person, usually based on one prominent characteristic, colors our perception of other characteristics of that person.[47] If a supervisor who values punctuality notices that an employee is sometimes late for work, the supervisor might form a negative image of the employee and evaluate that person's other traits unfavorably as well. Generally one trait important to the perceiver forms a general impression, and this impression becomes the basis for judgments about other traits. Halo effect is most likely to occur when concrete information about the perceived target is missing or we are not sufficiently motivated to search for it. Instead we use our general impression of the person to fill in the missing information.

Projection Bias

projection bias
A perceptual error in which an individual believes that other people have the same beliefs and behaviors that we do.

Projection bias occurs when we believe other people have the same beliefs and behaviors that we do.[48] If you are eager for a promotion, you might think that others in your position are similarly motivated. If you are thinking of quitting your job, you start to believe that other people are also thinking of quitting. Projection bias is also a defense mechanism to protect our self-esteem. If we break a work rule, projection bias justifies this infraction by claiming "everyone does it." We feel more comfortable with the thought that our negative traits exist in others, so we believe that others also have these traits.

Learning Objectives

After reading this section you should be able to

6. Explain how empathy and the Johari Window can improve a person's perceptions.

Improving Perceptions

We can't bypass the perceptual process, but we should make every attempt to minimize perceptual biases and distortions. Earlier we learned about diversity awareness, meaningful interaction, and accountability practices to minimize the adverse effects of biased stereotypes. Two other broad practices to improve perceptions are developing empathy and improving self-awareness.

Improving Perceptions through Empathy

empathy
A person's understanding and sensitivity to the feelings, thoughts, and situation of others.

Empathy refers to a person's understanding of and sensitivity to the feelings, thoughts, and situations of others. Empathy has both a cognitive (thinking) and emotional component.[49] The cognitive component, which is sometimes called *perspective taking,* represents a cognitive awareness of another person's situational and individual circumstances. The emotional component of empathy refers to experiencing the feelings of the other person. You have empathy when actively visualizing the other person's situation (perspective taking) and feeling that person's emotions in that situation. Empathizing with others improves a person's sensitivity to external causes of another person's performance and behavior, thereby reducing fundamental attribution error. A supervisor who imagines what it's like to be a single mother, for example, would become more sensitive to the external causes of lateness and other events among these employees.

Our empathy toward others improves through feedback, such as from a supervisor, co-worker, or coach. Executive coaches–consultants who help executives develop their competencies–also provide empathy-related feedback by attending meetings and later debriefing executives regarding how well they demonstrated empathy toward others in the meeting.[50] Another way to improve empathy is to literally walk in the other person's shoes. The opening story to this chapter described how several executives are following this practice by working in frontline jobs once in a while. The more you personally experience the environment in which other people live and work, the better you will understand and be sensitive to their needs and expectations.

Know Yourself: Applying the Johari Window

Johari Window
The model of personal and interpersonal understanding that encourages disclosure and feedback to increase the open area and reduce the blind, hidden, and unknown areas of oneself.

Knowing yourself–becoming more aware of your values, beliefs, and prejudices–is a powerful way to improve your perceptions.[51] Let's say that you had an unpleasant experience with lawyers and developed negative emotions toward people in this profession. Being sensitive to these emotions should enable you to regulate your behavior more effectively when working with legal professionals. Furthermore, if co-workers are aware of your antipathy to lawyers, they are more likely to understand your actions and help you to be objective in the future.

The **Johari Window** is a popular model for understanding how co-workers can increase their mutual understanding.[52] Developed by Joseph Luft and Harry Ingram (hence the name *Johari*), this model divides information about you into four

Exhibit 3.5
Johari Window

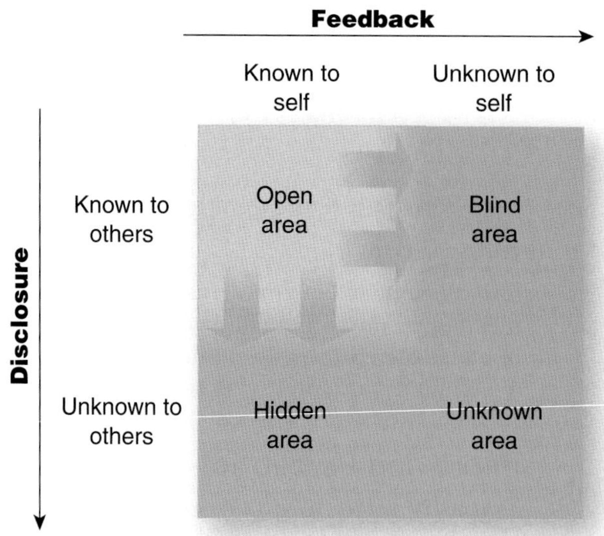

Source: Based on J. Luft, *Group Processes* (Palo Alto, CA: Mayfield, 1984).

"windows"–open, blind, hidden, and unknown–based on whether your own values, beliefs, and experiences are known to you and to others (see Exhibit 3.5). The *open area* includes information about you that is known both to you and to others. For example, both you and your co-workers may be aware that you don't like to be near people who smoke cigarettes. The *blind area* refers to information that is known to others but not to you. For example, your colleagues might notice that you are self-conscious and awkward when meeting the company chief executive, but you are unaware of this fact. Information known to you but unknown to others is found in the *hidden area.* We all have personal secrets about our likes, dislikes, and personal experiences. Finally, the *unknown area* includes your values, beliefs, and experiences that aren't known to you or others.

The main objective of the Johari Window is to increase the size of the open area so that both you and colleagues are aware of your perceptual limitations. This is partly accomplished by reducing the hidden area through *disclosure*–informing others of your beliefs, feelings, and experiences that may influence the work relationship.[53] The open area also increases through *feedback* from others about your behaviors. This information helps you to reduce your blind area because co-workers often see things in you that you do not see. Finally, the combination of disclosure and feedback occasionally produces revelations about information in the unknown area.

The Johari Window applies to some diversity awareness and meaningful contact activities that we described earlier. By learning about cultural differences and communicating more with people from different backgrounds, we gain a better understanding of their behavior. Engaging in open dialogue with co-workers also applies the Johari Window. As we communicate with others, we naturally tend to disclose more information about ourselves and eventually feel comfortable providing candid feedback to them.

The perceptual process represents the filter through which information passes from the external environment to our brain. As such, it is really the beginning of the learning process, which we discuss next.

Learning Objectives

After reading the next four sections you should be able to

7. **Define *learning* and explain how it affects individual behavior.**
8. **Describe the A-B-C model of behavior modification and the four contingencies of reinforcement.**
9. **Describe the three features of social learning theory.**
10. **Describe Kolb's experiential learning model and the action learning process.**

Learning in Organizations

What do employees at Wipro Technologies appreciate most about working at the Indian software giant? Financial rewards and challenging work are certainly on the list, but one of the top benefits is learning. "Wipro provides great learning opportunities," says CEO Vivek Paul. "The core of how employees think about us and value us revolves around training. It simply isn't something we can back off from."[54]

learning
A relatively permanent change in behavior (or behavior tendency) that occurs as a result of a person's interaction with the environment.

Learning is a relatively permanent change in behavior (or behavior tendency) that occurs as a result of a person's interaction with the environment. Learning occurs when the learner behaves differently. For example, we can see that you have "learned" computer skills when you operate the keyboard and software more quickly than before. Learning occurs when interaction with the environment leads to behavior change. This means that we learn through our senses, such as through study, observation, and experience.

Learning influences individual behavior and performance through three elements of the MARS model (see Chapter 2). First, people acquire skills and knowledge through learning opportunities, which gives them the competencies to perform tasks more effectively. Second, learning clarifies role perceptions. Employees develop a better understanding of their tasks and relative importance of work activities. Third, learning occurs through feedback, which motivates employees when they see that they are accomplishing their tasks.

Learning Explicit and Tacit Knowledge

When employees learn, they acquire both explicit and tacit knowledge. Explicit knowledge is organized and can be communicated from one person to another. The information you receive in a lecture is mainly explicit knowledge because the instructor packages and consciously transfers it to you. Explicit knowledge can be written down and given to others.

tacit knowledge
Knowledge embedded in our actions and ways of thinking, and transmitted only through observation and experience.

However, explicit knowledge is really only the tip of the knowledge iceberg. Most of what we know is **tacit knowledge.**[55] You have probably said to someone, "I can't tell you how to do this, but I can show you." Tacit knowledge is not documented; rather, it is action-oriented and known below the level of consciousness. Some writers suggest that tacit knowledge also includes the organization's culture and a team's implicit norms. People know these values and rules exist, but they are difficult to describe and document. Tacit knowledge is acquired through observation and direct experience. For example, airline pilots learn to operate commercial jets more by watching experts and practicing on flight simulators than through lectures. They acquire tacit knowledge by directly experiencing the complex interaction of behavior with the machine's response.

The rest of this chapter introduces three perspectives on learning tacit and explicit knowledge: reinforcement, social learning, and direct experience. Each perspective offers a different angle for understanding the dynamics of learning.

Behavior Modification: Learning through Reinforcement

behavior modification
A theory that explains learning in terms of the antecedents and consequences of behavior.

One of the oldest perspectives on learning, called **behavior modification** (also known as *operant conditioning* and *reinforcement theory*), takes the rather extreme view that learning is completely dependent on the environment. Behavior modification does not question the notion that thinking is part of the learning process, but it views human thoughts as unimportant intermediate stages between behavior and the environment. The environment teaches us to alter our behaviors so that we maximize positive consequences and minimize adverse consequences.[56]

A–B–Cs of Behavior Modification

The central objective of behavior modification is to change behavior (B) by managing its antecedents (A) and consequences (C). This process is nicely illustrated in the A–B–C model of behavior modification, shown in Exhibit 3.6.[57]

Antecedents are events preceding the behavior, informing employees that certain behaviors will have particular consequences. An antecedent may be a sound from your computer signaling that an e-mail message has arrived or a request from your supervisor to complete a specific task by tomorrow. These antecedents let employees know that a particular action will produce specific consequences. Notice that antecedents do not cause behaviors. The computer sound doesn't cause us to read our e-mail. Rather, the sound is a cue telling us that particular consequences are likely to occur if we engage in particular behaviors.

Although antecedents are important, behavior modification focuses mainly on the *consequences* of behavior. Consequences are events following a particular behavior that influence its future occurrence. Generally speaking, people tend to repeat behaviors that are followed by pleasant consequences and are less likely to repeat behaviors that are followed by unpleasant consequences or no consequences at all.

Contingencies of Reinforcement

Behavior modification identifies four types of consequences that strengthen, maintain, or weaken behavior. These consequences, collectively known as the *contingencies*

Exhibit 3.6 **A–B–Cs of Behavior Modification**

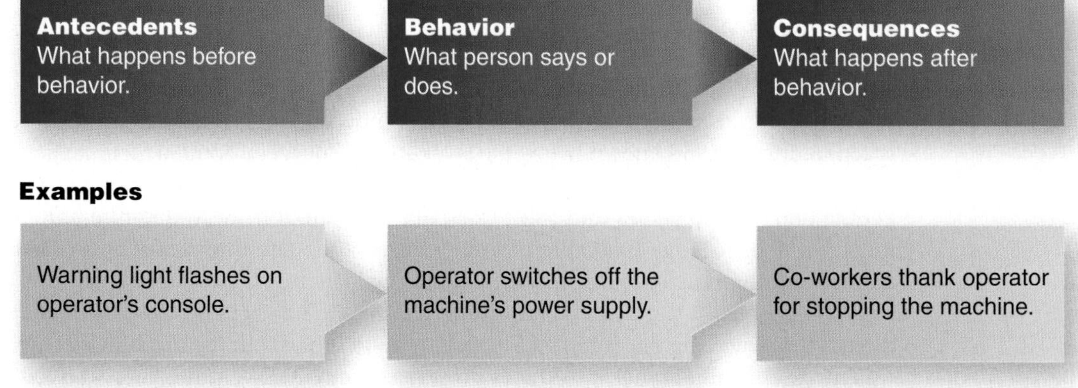

Sources: Adapted from T.K. Connellan, *How to Improve Human Performance* (New York: Harper & Row, 1978), p. 50; F. Luthans and R. Kreitner, *Organizational Behavior Modification and Beyond* (Glenview, IL: Scott, Foresman, 1985), pp. 85–88.

of reinforcement, include positive reinforcement, punishment, negative reinforcement, and extinction:[58]

positive reinforcement Occurs when the introduction of a consequence increases or maintains the frequency or future probability of a behavior.

punishment Occurs when a consequence decreases the frequency or future probability of a behavior.

negative reinforcement Occurs when the removal or avoidance of a consequence increases or maintains the frequency or future probability of a behavior.

extinction Occurs when the target behavior decreases because no consequence follows it.

- *Positive reinforcement.* **Positive reinforcement** occurs when the *introduction* of a consequence *increases or maintains* the frequency or future probability of a specific behavior. Receiving a bonus after successfully completing an important project is considered positive reinforcement because it typically increases the probability that you will use those behaviors in the future.
- *Punishment.* **Punishment** occurs when a consequence decreases the frequency or future probability of a behavior. This consequence typically involves introducing something that employees try to avoid. For instance, most of us would consider a demotion or being ostracized by our co-workers as forms of punishment.[59]
- *Negative reinforcement.* **Negative reinforcement** occurs when the removal or avoidance of a consequence increases or maintains the frequency or future probability of a specific behavior. Supervisors apply negative reinforcement when they *stop* criticizing employees whose substandard performance has improved. When the criticism is withheld, employees are more likely to repeat behaviors that improved their performance. Notice that negative reinforcement is not punishment. It actually reinforces behavior by removing punishment.
- *Extinction.* **Extinction** occurs when the target behavior decreases because no consequence follows it. In this respect, extinction is a do-nothing strategy. Generally, behavior that is no longer reinforced tends to disappear; it becomes extinct. For instance, research suggests that when managers stop congratulating employees for their good performance, that performance tends to decline.[60]

Which contingency of reinforcement should we use in the learning process? In most situations positive reinforcement should follow desired behaviors, and extinction (do nothing) should follow undesirable behaviors. This approach is preferred because punishment and negative reinforcement generate negative emotions and attitudes toward the punisher (supervisor) and organization. However, some form of punishment (dismissal, suspension, demotion) may be necessary for extreme behaviors, such as deliberately hurting a co-worker or stealing inventory. Indeed, research suggests that, under certain conditions, punishment maintains a sense of equity among co-workers.[61]

Schedules of Reinforcement

Along with the types of reinforcement, the frequency and timing of those reinforcers also influence employee behaviors.[62] These reinforcement schedules can be continuous or intermittent. The most effective reinforcement schedule for learning new tasks is *continuous reinforcement*–providing positive reinforcement after every occurrence of the desired behavior. Employees learn desired behaviors quickly and, when the reinforcer is removed, extinction also occurs very quickly.

The other schedules of reinforcement are intermittent and are distinguished by whether they are based on a period of time (interval) or number of behavioral events (ratio), and whether that interval or ratio is fixed or variable. Most people get paid with a *fixed interval schedule* because they receive their reinforcement (paycheck) after a fixed period. A *variable interval schedule* is common for promotions: Employees are promoted after a variable amount of time. If you are given the rest of the day off after completing a fixed amount of work (for example, serving a specific number of customers), then you have experienced a *fixed ratio schedule*–reinforcement after a fixed number of behaviors or accomplishments.

Finally, companies often use a *variable ratio schedule* in which employee behavior is reinforced after a variable number of times. Salespeople experience variable ratio reinforcement because they make a successful sale (the reinforcer) after a varying number of client calls. They might make four unsuccessful calls before receiving an order on the fifth one, then make 10 more calls before receiving the next order, and so on. The variable ratio schedule is a low-cost way to reinforce behavior because employees are rewarded infrequently. It is also highly resistant to extinction. Suppose your boss walks into your office at varying times of the day. Chances are that you would work consistently better throughout the day than if your boss visits at exactly 11 a.m. every day. If your boss doesn't walk into your office at all on a particular day, you might still expect a visit right up to the end of the day if previous visits were random.

Behavior Modification in Practice

Everyone practices behavior modification in one form or another. We thank people for a job well done, are silent when displeased, and sometimes try to punish those who go against our wishes. Behavior modification also occurs in various formal programs to reduce absenteeism, encourage safe work behaviors, and improve task performance. In Arkansas, for example, the North Little Rock School Board introduced an absenteeism reduction plan in which teachers can earn $300 after every six months with perfect attendance. Those with no more than one day of absence receive $100. The Dallas Area Rapid Transit (DART) introduced a behavior modification program in which employees earn points for wellness activities, including getting an annual physical examination, engaging in fitness workouts, and attending wellness lectures. Every point is equivalent to one dollar, which can be used to buy gifts at DART's wellness store and, at the end of each year, a cash payout.[63]

Although behavior modification can be effective, it has several limitations.[64] One problem is "reward inflation," in which the reinforcer is eventually considered an entitlement. For this reason most behavior modification programs must run infrequently and for short durations. A second problem is that some people revolt against the lottery-style variable ratio schedule because they consider gambling unethical. Third, behavior modification's radical "behaviorist" philosophy (that human thinking processes are unimportant) has lost favor because it is now evident that people can learn through mental processes, such as observing others and thinking logically about possible consequences.[65] Thus without throwing away the principles of behavior modification, most learning experts today also embrace the concepts of social learning theory.

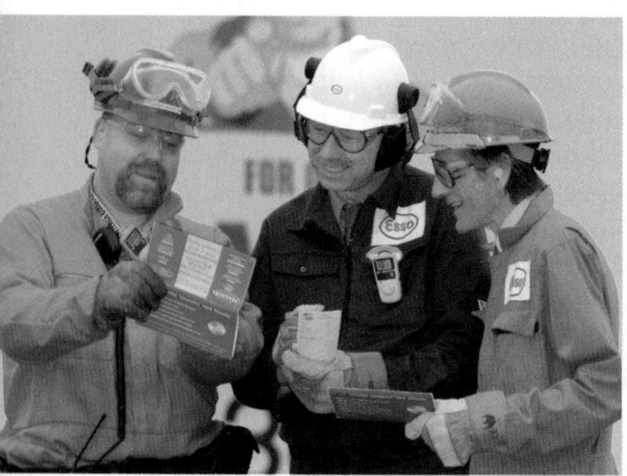

ExxonMobil Reinforces Safety with Leading Indicators
ExxonMobil seems to win as many safety awards as it produces barrels of oil. The Houston-based energy company relies on extensive safety training and leadership, but it also uses classic behavior modification practices to reinforce safe work behaviors. To some extent ExxonMobil rewards employees and work units for accident-free milestones and similar "lagging indicators." In Malaysia, for instance, the company distributes awards to worksites and contractors with zero lost time injuries. However, ExxonMobil mainly reinforces "leading indicators"—work behaviors that prevent accidents. ExxonMobil's U.K. Fawley refinery (shown in the photo) introduced a "Behave Safely Challenge" program in which supervisors rewarded employees and contractors on the spot when they exhibited good safety behavior or intervened to improve the safe behavior of co-workers. The company also introduced a system in which co-workers observe each other's safety behaviors.[66]

Social Learning Theory: Learning by Observing

social learning theory
A theory stating that much learning occurs by observing others and then modeling the behaviors that lead to favorable outcomes and avoiding the behaviors that lead to punishing consequences.

Social learning theory states that much learning occurs as we observe others and then model the behaviors that lead to favorable outcomes and avoid behaviors that lead to punishing consequences.[67] Three related features of social learning theory are behavior modeling, learning behavior consequences, and self-reinforcement.

Behavior Modeling

People learn by observing the behaviors of a role model on a critical task, remembering the important elements of the observed behaviors, and then practicing those behaviors.[68] Behavior modeling works best when the model is respected and the model's actions are followed by favorable consequences. For instance, recently hired college graduates learn better by watching a previously hired college graduate who successfully performs a task.

Behavior modeling is a valuable form of learning for two reasons. First, tacit knowledge and skills are acquired from others mainly through observation. The adage that a picture is worth a thousand words applies here. It is difficult to document or verbally explain every detail of how a master baker kneads dough. Instead this information is more effectively learned by observing the baker's actions and the consequences of those actions. Second, employees have a stronger belief that they can perform work after seeing someone else perform the task. This effect is particularly strong when observers identify with the model, such as someone who is similar with respect to age, experience, and gender. For instance, students are more confident about taking a challenging course when they are mentored by students similar to them who have just completed that course.

Learning Behavior Consequences

A second element of social learning theory says that we learn the consequences of behavior through logic and observation, not just through direct experience. People logically anticipate desirable consequences after completing a task well and undesirable consequences (punishment or extinction) after performing the job poorly. It just makes sense to expect these outcomes until we learn otherwise. We also learn behavioral consequences by observing the experiences of other people. This process, known as *vicarious learning,* occurs all the time in organizational settings. You might notice how co-workers mock another employee who dresses formally at work. By observing this incident, you learn about the group's preference for wearing casual attire. You might see how another worker serves customers better by keeping a list of their names, which teaches you to do the same. In each case you have learned vicariously, not through your own experience.[69]

Self-Reinforcement

self-reinforcement
Occurs whenever someone has control over a reinforcer but delays it until a self-set goal has been completed.

Self-reinforcement, the third element of social learning theory, occurs whenever an employee has control over a reinforcer but doesn't "take" it until completing a self-set goal.[70] For example, you might be thinking about having a snack after you finish reading the rest of this chapter. You could take a break right now, but you don't use this privilege until you have achieved your goal of reading the chapter. Raiding the refrigerator is a form of self-induced positive reinforcement. Self-reinforcement can take many forms, such as taking a short walk, watching a movie, or simply congratulating yourself for completing the task. Self-reinforcement has become increasingly important because employees are given more control over their working lives and are less dependent on supervisors to dole out positive reinforcement and punishment.

Learning through Experience

Mandy Chooi is about to attend a meeting with a lower-level manager who has botched a new assignment. She is also supposed to make a strategy presentation to her boss in three hours, but the telephone won't stop ringing and she is deluged with e-mail. It's a stressful situation. Fortunately the challenges facing the Motorola human resources executive from Beijing on this particular day are not real. Chooi is sitting in a simulation to develop and test her leadership skills. "It was hard. A lot harder than I had expected," she says. "It's surprising how realistic and demanding it is."[71]

Many organizations are shifting their learning strategy away from the classroom and toward a more experiential approach. Classrooms transfer explicit knowledge that has been documented; but most tacit knowledge and skills are acquired through experience as well as observation. Experiential learning has been conceptualized in many ways, but one of the most enduring perspectives is Kolb's experiential learning model, shown in Exhibit 3.7. This model illustrates experiential learning as a cyclical four-stage process.[72]

Concrete experience involves sensory and emotional engagement in some activity. It is followed by *reflective observation,* which involves listening, watching, recording, and elaborating on the experience. The next stage in the learning cycle is *abstract conceptualization.* This is the stage in which we develop concepts and integrate our observations into logically sound theories. The fourth stage, *active experimentation,* occurs when we test our previous experience, reflection, and conceptualization in a particular context. People tend to prefer and operate better in some stages than in others due to their unique competencies and personality. Still, experiential learning requires all four stages in proper balance.

learning orientation
The extent that an organization or individual supports knowledge management, particularly opportunities to acquire knowledge through experience and experimentation.

Experiential Learning in Practice

Learning through experience works best in organizations with a strong **learning orientation**–they value learning opportunities and, in particular, the generation of new knowledge while employees perform their jobs. If an employee initially fails to perform a task, then the experience might still be a valuable learning opportunity. In other words, such organizations encourage employees to appreciate the process of individual and team learning, not just the performance results.

Exhibit 3.7
Kolb's Experiential Learning Model

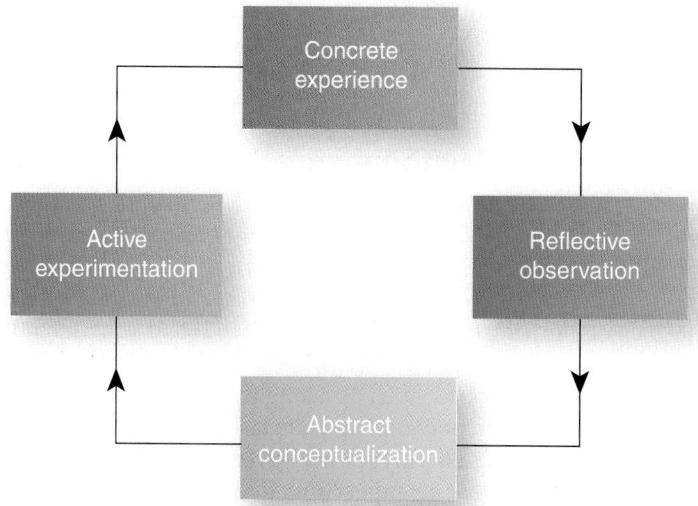

Organizations achieve a learning orientation culture by rewarding experimentation and recognizing mistakes as a natural part of the learning process. They encourage employees to take reasonable risks to ultimately discover new and better ways of doing things. Without a learning orientation, mistakes are hidden and problems are more likely to escalate or reemerge later. It's not surprising, then, that one of the most frequently mentioned lessons from the best-performing manufacturers is to expect mistakes. "[Mistakes] are a source of learning and will improve operations in the long run," explains an executive at Lockheed Martin in Bethesda, Maryland. "[They] foster the concept that no question is dumb, no idea is too wild, and no task or activity is irrelevant."[73]

action learning
A variety of experiential learning activities in which employees are involved in a "real, complex, and stressful problem," usually in teams, with immediate relevance to the company.

Action Learning One application of workplace experiential learning that has received considerable interest, particularly in Europe, is **action learning.** Action learning occurs when employees, usually in teams, investigate and apply solutions to a situation that is both real and complex, with immediate relevance to the company.[74] In other words, the task becomes the source of learning. Kolb's experiential learning

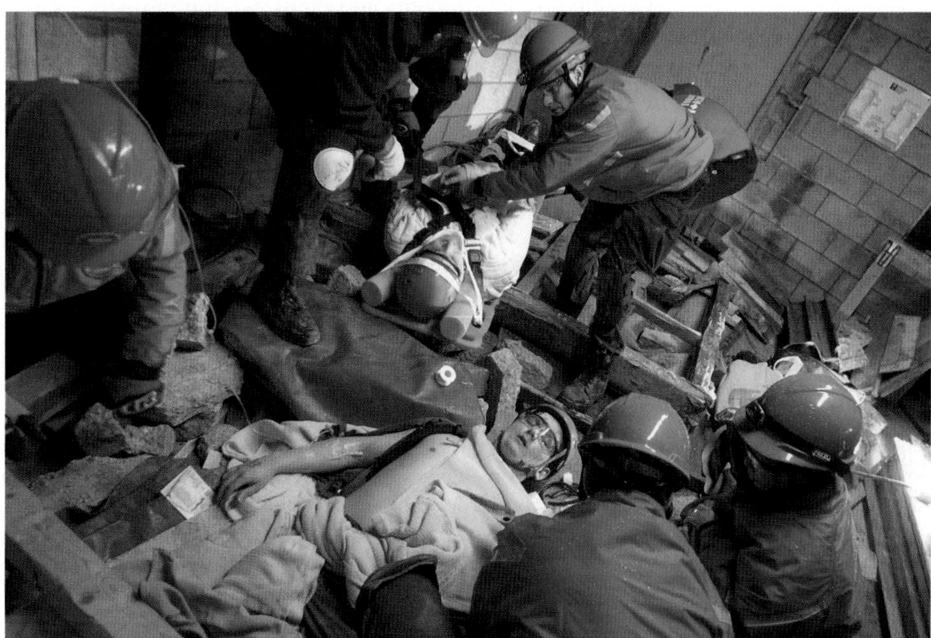

Emergency Response Teams Learn through Simulations Physicians Jonathan Sherbino and Ivy Chong (far right) prepare to amputate the leg of Wesley Bagshaw, who is pinned by a fallen beam in this collapsed building. "If we don't do this, you're going to die," says Sherbino in response to Bagshaw's anguished protests. Fortunately for Bagshaw, the bone saw cuts through a pig's leg rather than his own. The entire incident was a mock disaster to help train the Heavy Urban Search and Rescue (HUSAR) team in Toronto, Canada. For four hours HUSAR crews located the victims with dogs and search equipment at this special operations training center site, secured the structure, treated Bagshaw and 15 other "victims," and extricated them to a mock hospital at a nearby community college. In all over 300 HUSAR and medical professionals were involved. "People from the hospitals love these exercises because they get to try out all the ideas they have and no one is (adversely) affected," explains one of the event's organizers. "It was definitely a lot more realistic than anything we've done in the past."[75]

model presented earlier is usually identified as the main template for action learning. Action learning requires concrete experience with a real organizational problem or opportunity, followed by "learning meetings" in which participants reflect on their observations about that problem or opportunity. Then they develop and test a strategy to solve the problem or realize the opportunity. The process also encourages plenty of reflection so the experience becomes a learning process.

Action learning is considered one of the best ways to develop leadership competencies because it combines conceptual knowledge with real-world issues and reflective learning. Although slowly gaining popularity in North American firms (such as GE and Boeing), action learning is well established in Europe, where companies such as Heineken appreciate how this learning process can add value to the organization. "Action learning has become the primary vehicle for generating creative ideas and building business success at Heineken," says the chairman of the executive board at Europe's largest brewer. MTR Corporation, which operates Hong Kong's commuter train system, recently introduced action learning projects as part of its executive development program. One action learning team discovered a cost savings measure that would fund executive development at MTR for several years.[76]

This chapter has introduced you to two fundamental activities in human behavior in the workplace: perceptions and learning. These activities involve receiving information from the environment, organizing it, and acting on it as a learning process. Our knowledge about perceptions and learning in the workplace lays the foundation for the next chapter, which looks at workplace emotions and attitudes.

Chapter Summary

Perception involves selecting, organizing, and interpreting information to make sense of the world around us. Selective attention is influenced by characteristics of the person or object being perceived (size, intensity, motion, repetition, and novelty) and characteristics of the person doing the perceiving. Perceptual organization engages categorical thinking–the mostly unconscious process of organizing people and objects into preconceived categories that are stored in our long-term memory. To a large extent, our perceptual interpretation of incoming information occurs before we are consciously aware of it. Mental models–broad worldviews or templates of the mind–also help us make sense of incoming stimuli.

The social identity process explains how we perceive ourselves and other people. We identify ourselves partly in terms of our membership in social groups. This comparison process includes categorizing people into groups, forming a homogeneous image of people within those groups, and differentiating groups by assigning more favorable features to our own groups than to other groups.

Stereotyping is a derivative of social identity theory, in which people assign traits to others based on their membership in a social category. Stereotyping economizes mental effort, fills in missing information, and enhances our self-perception and social identity. However, it also lays the foundation for prejudice and systemic discrimination. It is very difficult to prevent the activation of stereotyping, but we can minimize the application of stereotypical information in our decisions and actions. Three strategies to minimize the influence of stereotypes are diversity awareness training, meaningful interaction, and decision-making accountability.

The attribution process involves deciding whether a behavior or event is due largely to the situation (external attributions) or personal characteristics (internal attributions). Attributions are decided by perceptions of the consistency, distinctiveness, and consensus of the behavior. This process links together the various pieces of our world in cause–effect relationships, but it is also subject to attribution errors, including fundamental attribution error and self-serving bias.

Self-fulfilling prophecy occurs when our expectations about another person cause that person to act in a way that is consistent with those expectations. Essentially, our expectations affect our behavior toward the target person, which then affects the target person's opportunities and attitudes, which then influences his or her behavior. Self-fulfilling prophecies tend to be stronger at the beginning of relationships (such as when employees first join a department), when several people hold similar expectations of the employee, and when the employee has a history of low achievement.

Four other perceptual errors commonly noted in organizations are primacy effect, recency effect, halo effect, and projection bias. We can minimize these and other perceptual problems through empathy and becoming more aware of our values, beliefs, and prejudices (the Johari Window).

Learning is a relatively permanent change in behavior (or behavior tendency) that occurs as a result of a person's interaction with the environment. Learning influences individual behavior and performance through ability, role perceptions, and motivation. Some learning results in explicit knowledge, which can be verbally transferred between people. But much of what we learn is tacit knowledge, which is embedded in our actions without conscious awareness.

The behavior modification perspective of learning states that behavior change occurs by altering its antecedents and consequences. Antecedents are environmental stimuli that provoke (not necessarily cause) behavior. Consequences are events following behavior that influence its future occurrence. Consequences include positive reinforcement, punishment, negative reinforcement, and extinction. The schedules of reinforcement also influence behavior.

Social learning theory states that much learning occurs as we observe others and then model behaviors that seem to lead to favorable outcomes and avoid behaviors that lead to punishing consequences. It also recognizes that we often engage in self-reinforcement. Behavior modeling is effective because it transfers tacit knowledge and enhances the observer's confidence in performing the task.

Many companies now use experiential learning because employees do not acquire tacit knowledge through formal classroom instruction. Kolb's experiential learning model is a cyclical four-stage process that includes concrete experience, reflective observation, abstract conceptualization, and active experimentation. Action learning is experiential learning in which employees investigate and act on significant organizational issues.

Key Terms

action learning, p. 91
attribution process, p. 77
behavior modification, p. 86
categorical thinking, p. 69
contact hypothesis, p. 76
empathy, p. 83
extinction, p. 87
fundamental attribution error, p. 79
halo effect, p. 82
Johari Window, p. 83
learning, p. 85
learning orientation, p. 90
mental models, p. 70
negative reinforcement, p. 87
perception, p. 68
positive organizational behavior, p. 81
positive reinforcement, p. 87
prejudice, p. 75
primacy effect, p. 82
projection bias, p. 82
punishment, p. 87
recency effect, p. 82
selective attention, p. 69
self-fulfilling prophecy, p. 79
self-reinforcement, p. 89
self-serving bias, p. 79
social identity theory, p. 71
social learning theory, p. 89
stereotyping, p. 73
tacit knowledge, p. 85

Critical Thinking Questions

1. You are part of a task force to increase worker responsiveness to emergencies on the production floor. Identify four factors that should be considered when installing a device that will get every employee's attention when there is an emergency.
2. What mental models do you have about attending a college or university lecture? Are these mental models helpful? Could any of these mental models hold you back from achieving the full benefit of the lecture?
3. Contrast "personal" and "social" identity. Do you define yourself in terms of the university or college you attend? Why or why not? What are the implications of your answer for your university of college?
4. During a diversity management session, a manager suggests that stereotypes are a necessary part of working with others. "I have to make assumptions about what's in the other person's head, and stereotypes help me do that," she explains. "It's better to rely on stereotypes than to enter a working relationship with someone from another culture without any idea of what they believe in!" Discuss the merits of and problems with the manager's statement.

5. Several studies have reported that self-serving bias occurs in corporate annual reports. What does this mean, and how would it be apparent in these reports? Provide hypothetical examples of self-serving bias in these documents.
6. Describe how a manager or coach could use the process of self-fulfilling prophecy to enhance an individual's performance.
7. Describe a situation in which you used behavior modification to influence someone's behavior. What specifically did you do? What was the result?
8. Why are organizations moving toward the use of experiential approaches to learning? What conditions are required for success?

Case Study 3.1 FROM LIPPERT-JOHANSON INCORPORATED TO FENWAY WASTE MANAGEMENT

Lisa V. Williams, Jeewon Cho, and Alicia Boisnier, SUNY at Buffalo

Part One

Catherine O'Neill was very excited to finally be graduating from Flagship University at the end of the semester. She had always been interested in accounting, following from her father's lifelong occupation, and she very much enjoyed the challenging major. She was involved in many highly regarded student clubs in the business school and worked diligently to earn good grades. Now her commitment to the profession would pay off, she hoped, as she turned her attention to her job search. In late fall she had on-campus interviews with several firms, but her interview with the prestigious Lippert-Johanson Incorporated (LJI) stood out in her mind as the most attractive opportunity. That's why Catherine was thrilled to learn she made it to the next level of interviews, to be held at the firm's main office later that month.

When Catherine entered the elegant lobby of LJI's New York City offices, she was immediately impressed by all there was to take in. Catherine had always been one to pay attention to detail, and her acute observations of her environment had always been an asset. She was able to see how social and environmental cues told her what was expected of her, and she always set out to meet and exceed those expectations. On a tour of the office, she had already begun to size up her prospective workplace. She appreciated the quiet, focused work atmosphere. She liked how everyone was dressed: Most people wore suits, and their conservative apparel supported the professional attitudes that seemed to be omnipresent. People spoke to her in a formal but friendly manner and seemed enthusiastic. Some of them even took the time to greet her as she was guided to the conference room for her individual interviews. "I like the way this place feels, and I would love to come to work here every day," Catherine thought. "I hope I do well in my interview!"

Before she knew it, Catherine was sitting in a nicely appointed office with one of the eight managers in the firm. Sandra Jacobs was the picture of a professional woman, and Catherine naturally took her cue from her about how to conduct herself in the interview. It seemed to go very quickly, although the interview lasted an hour. As soon as Catherine left the office, she could not wait to phone her father about the interview. "I loved it there, and I just know I'm a good fit!" she told her proud father. "Like them, I believe it is important to have the highest ethical standards and quality of work. Ms. Jacobs really emphasized the mission of the firm, as well as its policies. She did say that all the candidates have an excellent skill set and are well qualified for the job, so mostly they are going to base their hiring decision on how well they think each of us will fit into the firm. Reputation is everything to an accounting firm. I learned that from you, Dad!"

After six weeks of apprehensive waiting, Catherine's efforts were rewarded when LJI and another firm contacted her with job offers. Catherine knew she would accept the offer from LJI. She saw the firm as very ethical, with the highest standards for work quality and an excellent reputation. Catherine was grateful to have been selected from such a competitive hiring process. "There couldn't be a better choice for me! I'm so proud to become a member of this company!"

Catherine's first few days at LJI were a whirlwind of a newcomer's experiences. She had meetings with her supervisor to discuss the firm's mission statement, her role in the firm, and what was expected of her. She was also told to spend some time looking at the employee handbook, which covered many important policies of the firm, such as dress code, sick time, grievances, the chain of command and job descriptions, and professional ethics. Everyone relied on the handbook to provide clear guidance about what was expected of each employee. Also, Catherine was informed that she would soon begin participating in continuing professional education, which would allow her to update her skills and knowledge in her field. "This is great," thought Catherine, "I'm so glad to know the firm doesn't just talk about its high standards–it actually follows through with action."

What Catherine enjoyed most about her new job were her warm and welcoming colleagues, who invited her to their group lunches beginning with her first day. They talked about work and home; they seemed close, both professionally and personally. She could see that everyone had a similar attitude about work: They cared about their work and the firm; they took responsibility for their own tasks, and they helped one another out. Catherine also got involved in LJI activities outside work–like baseball and soccer teams, happy hours, picnics, and parties–and she enjoyed the chance to mingle with her co-workers. In what seemed like no time at all, Catherine started to see herself as a fully integrated member of LJI.

Before tax season started, Catherine attended some meetings of the AICPA and other professional accounting societies. There she met many accountants from other firms who all seemed impressed when she told them where she worked. Catherine's pride and appreciation of being a member of LJI grew as she realized how highly regarded the firm was among others in the accounting industry.

Part Two

Over the past seven years Catherine's career in New York had flourished. Her reputation as one of the top tax accountants in her company was well established and was recognized by colleagues outside the firm as well. However, Catherine entered a new chapter of her life when she married Ted Lewis, an oncology intern, who could not turn down an offer of residency at a top cancer center in upstate New York. Wanting to support Ted's once-in-a-lifetime career opportunity, Catherine decided it was time to follow the path of many of her colleagues and leave public accounting for a position that would be more conducive to starting a family. Still, her heart was in the profession, so she took an available position as a controller of a small recycling company located a few miles from Catherine and Ted's new upstate home. She knew that with this position she could both have children and maintain her career.

Fenway Waste Management was small–about 35 employees. There were about 25 people who worked in the warehouse, three administrative assistants, two supervisors, and five people in management. Catherine found that she had to adjust to her new position and surroundings. Often she found herself doing work that formally belonged to someone else; because it was a smaller company managers seemed to "wear many hats." This was quite different from what she had experienced at LJI. In addition, the warehouse workers often had to handle greasy materials, and sometimes they tracked the grease into the offices. Catherine both laughed and worried when she saw a piece of paper pinned to the wall that said, "Clean Up After Yourself!" She supposed that the nature of the business was why the offices were functional but furnished with old pieces. She couldn't imagine having a business meeting there. Also, for most of the employees, the casual dress matched the casual attitudes. But Catherine continued to wear a dressed-down version of her formal LJI attire, even though her new co-workers considered her overdressed.

With all the changes Catherine had experienced, she maintained one familiar piece of her past. Although it was not required for her new position, Catherine still attended AICPA meetings and made a point of continually updating her knowledge of current tax laws. At this year's conference, she told a former colleague, "Being here, I feel so much more like myself–I am so much more connected to these people and this environment than to those at my new job. It's too bad I don't feel this way at Fenway. I guess I'm just more comfortable with professionals who are similar to me."

Discussion Questions

1. Discuss the social identity issues present in this case.
2. What indicated Catherine's positive evaluation of the groups described in Part 1? How did her evaluations foster her social identity?
3. What theory helps us understand how Catherine learned about appropriate behaviors at LJI?
4. Compare and contrast LJI and Fenway.
5. What was Catherine's reaction after joining Fenway Waste Management, and why was her level of social identification different from that at LJI?
6. Is there evidence that Catherine experienced the categorization–homogenization–differentiation process? What details support your conclusion?

Case Study 3.2 HOW FAILURE BREEDS SUCCESS

BusinessWeek Coca-Cola Chairman and CEO E. Neville Isdell knows that the best companies embrace their mistakes and learn from them. That's why Isdell doesn't mind rhyming off the list of Coke's failures over the years. In fact, he is keen to convince employees and shareholders that he will tolerate the failures that will inevitably result from the bigger risks that he wants Coke to take. At the same time, say analysts, balancing a learning culture with a performance culture is a perennial challenge. Intuit, the tax software company, thinks it has a solution. When one of its marketing strategies recently flopped, the company celebrated the failure and spent a lot of time dissecting it.

This *BusinessWeek* case study describes several ways that companies learn from their mistakes while still maintaining a strong focus on performance and the bottom line. Read the full text of this *BusinessWeek* article at www.mhhe.com/mcshane4e and prepare for the discussion questions below.

Discussion Questions

1. Use Kolb's experiential learning model to describe the process that Intuit and other companies follow to learn from their mistakes and failures.
2. What perceptual problems do managers need to overcome with failures? How can these perceptual problems be minimized?

Source: J. McGregor, "How Failure Breeds Success," *BusinessWeek*, 10 July 2006, 42.

Class Exercise 3.3 THE LEARNING EXERCISE

PURPOSE This exercise is designed to help you understand how the contingencies of reinforcement in behavior modification affect learning.

MATERIALS Any objects normally available in a classroom will be acceptable for this activity.

INSTRUCTIONS The instructor will ask for three volunteers, who will be briefed outside the classroom. The instructor will spend a few minutes telling the remaining students in the class about their duties. Then one of the three volunteers will enter the room to participate in the exercise. When the first volunteer has finished, the second volunteer will enter the room and participate in the exercise. Finally the third volunteer will enter the class and participate in the exercise.

For you to gain the full benefit of this exercise, no other information will be provided here. However, your instructor will have more details at the beginning of this fun activity.

Team Exercise 3.4 WHO AM I?

PURPOSE This exercise is designed to help you understand the elements and implications of social identity theory.

MATERIALS None.

INSTRUCTIONS

1. Working alone (no discussion with other students), use the space provided here or a piece of paper to write down 12 words or phrases that answer the question "Who am I?" Write your words or phrases describing you as they come to mind; don't worry about their logical order. Please be sure to fill in all 12 spaces.

Phrases that describe you	Circle S or P	
1. I am ______	S	P
2. I am ______	S	P
3. I am ______	S	P
4. I am ______	S	P
5. I am ______	S	P
6. I am ______	S	P
7. I am ______	S	P
8. I am ______	S	P
9. I am ______	S	P
10. I am ______	S	P
11. I am ______	S	P
12. I am ______	S	P

2. Circle the "S" beside the items that define you in terms of your social identity, such as your demographics and formal or informal membership in a social group or institution (school, company, religious group). Circle the "P" beside the items that define you in terms of your personal identity–that is, unique personality traits, values, or experiences that are not connected to any particular social group. Next underline one or more items that you believe will still be a strong characteristic of you 10 years from now.
3. Form small groups. If you have a team project for this course, your project team would work well for this exercise. Compare your list with those that others in your group wrote about themselves. Discuss the following questions in your group, and prepare notes for class discussion and possible presentation of these questions:
   a. Among members of this team, what was the typical percentage of items representing social versus personal identity? Did some team members have many more or fewer social identity items compared to other team members? Why do you think these large or small differences in emphasis on social or personal identity occurred?
   b. What characteristics did people in your group underline as being the most stable (remaining the same 10 years from now)? Were these underlined items mostly social or personal identity features? How similar or different were the underlined items among team members?
   c. What do these lists say about the dynamics of your group as a team (whether or not your group for this activity is actually involved in a class project for this course)?

Sources: M.H. Kuhn and T.S. McPartland, "An Empirical Investigation of Self-Attitudes," *American Sociological Review* 19 (February 1954), pp. 68–76; C. Lay and M. Verkuyten, "Ethnic Identity and Its Relation to Personal Self-Esteem: A Comparison of Canadian-Born and Foreign-Born Chinese Adolescents," *Journal of Social Psychology* 139 (1999), pp. 288–99; S.L. Grace and K.L. Cramer, "The Elusive Nature of Self-Measurement: The Self-Construal scale versus the Twenty Statements Test," *Journal of Social Psychology* 143 (2003), pp. 649–68.

Web Exercise 3.5 ANALYZING CORPORATE ANNUAL REPORTS

PURPOSE This exercise is designed to help you diagnose evidence of stereotyping and corporate role models that minimize stereotyping in corporate annual reports.

MATERIALS You need to complete your research for this activity prior to class, including selecting a publicly traded company and downloading the past four or more years of its fully illustrated annual reports.

INSTRUCTIONS The instructor may have you work alone or in groups for this activity. Select a company that is publicly traded and makes its annual reports available on the company Web site. Ideally annual reports for at least the past four years should be available, and these reports should be presented in the final illustrated format (typically PDF replicas of the original hard copy report).

Examine closely the images in your selected company's recent annual reports in terms of how women, visible minorities, and older employees and clients are presented. Specifically, be prepared to discuss and provide details in class regarding the following:

1. The percentage of images showing women, visible minorities, and older workers and clients. Be sensitive to the size and placement of these images on the page and throughout the annual report.
2. The roles in which women, visible minorities, and older workers and clients are depicted. For example, are women shown more in traditional or nontraditional occupations and nonwork roles in these annual reports?
3. If several years of annual reports are available, pick one that is at least a decade old and compare its visual representation of and role depictions of women, visible minorities, and older employees and clients.

If possible, pick one of the most blatantly stereotypical illustrations you can find in these annual report to show in class, either as a printout or as a computer projection.

Self-Assessment 3.6

ASSESSING YOUR PERSONAL NEED FOR STRUCTURE

PURPOSE This self-assessment is designed to help you estimate your personal need for perceptual structure.

INSTRUCTIONS Read each of the following statements and decide how much you agree with each according to your attitudes, beliefs, and experiences. Then use the scoring key in Appendix B of this book to calculate your results. There are no right or wrong answers to these questions. This self-assessment should be completed alone so that you can rate yourself honestly without concerns of social comparison. However, class discussion will focus on the meaning of need for structure in terms of how we engage differently in the perceptual process at work and in other settings.

Personal Need for Structure Scale

To what extent do you agree or disagree with each of these statements about yourself?	Strongly agree	Moderately agree	Slightly agree	Slightly disagree	Moderately disagree	Strongly disagree
1. It upsets me to go into a situation without knowing what I can expect from it.	☐	☐	☐	☐	☐	☐
2. I'm not bothered by things that interrupt my daily routine.	☐	☐	☐	☐	☐	☐
3. I enjoy being spontaneous.	☐	☐	☐	☐	☐	☐
4. I find that a well-ordered life with regular hours makes my life tedious.	☐	☐	☐	☐	☐	☐
5. I find that a consistent routine enables me to enjoy life more.	☐	☐	☐	☐	☐	☐
6. I enjoy having a clear and structured mode of life.	☐	☐	☐	☐	☐	☐
7. I like to have a place for everything and everything in its place.	☐	☐	☐	☐	☐	☐
8. I don't like situations that are uncertain.	☐	☐	☐	☐	☐	☐
9. I hate to change my plans at the last minute.	☐	☐	☐	☐	☐	☐
10. I hate to be with people who are unpredictable.	☐	☐	☐	☐	☐	☐
11. I enjoy the exhilaration of being in unpredictable situations.	☐	☐	☐	☐	☐	☐
12. I become uncomfortable when the rules in a situation are not clear.	☐	☐	☐	☐	☐	☐

Source: M.M. Thompson, M.E. Naccarato, and K.E. Parker, "Assessing Cognitive Need: The Development of the Personal Need for Structure and the Personal Fear of Invalidity Scales." Paper presented at the annual meeting of the Canadian Psychological Association, Halifax, Nova Scotia (1989).

Self-Assessment 3.7

ASSESSING YOUR PERSPECTIVE TAKING (COGNITIVE EMPATHY) (STUDENT OLC)

Empathy is an important perceptual ability in social relations, but the degree to which people empathize varies considerably. This self-assessment provides an estimate of one form of empathy, known as *cognitive empathy* or *perspective taking*. This means that it measures the level of cognitive awareness of another person's situational and individual circumstances. To complete this scale, indicate the degree to which each of the statements presented does or does not describe you well. You need to be honest with yourself to get a reasonable estimate of your level of perspective taking. The results show your relative position along the perspective-taking continuum and the general meaning of this score.

Self-Assessment 3.8

ASSESSING YOUR EMOTIONAL EMPATHY (STUDENT OLC)

Empathy is an important perceptual ability in social relations, but the degree to which people empathize varies considerably. This self-assessment provides an estimate of one form of empathy, known as *emotional empathy*. This refers to the extent to which you are able to experience the emotions or feelings of another person. To complete this scale, indicate the degree to which each of the statements presented does or does not describe you well. You need to be honest with yourself to get a reasonable estimate of your level of emotional empathy. The results show your relative position along the emotional empathy continuum and the general meaning of this score.

After reading this chapter, if you feel that you need additional information, see **www.mhhe.com/mcshane4e** for more in-depth interactivities that correspond to this material.

Employees seem to be as genuinely happy as the customers at Wegmans Food Market. That's probably because the company, which is consistently rated as one of the best places to work in America (and number one in two recent years), bends over backward to make sure its employees get plenty of positive emotions at work. In fact, Wegmans motto is "Employees first, customers second." The Wegmans family believes that happy employees provide the best customer service.

Wegmans Food Market enjoys strong customer loyalty and low employee turnover by keeping employees happy.

Wegmans' 33,000 staff members in New York and four nearby states enjoy above-average pay, health benefits, and other perks, resulting in labor costs of about 16 percent of sales compared to 12 percent at most supermarkets. But it's the everyday "family" feeling that seems to make the biggest difference. "The best way to describe it is a family atmosphere," says Mark Fursman, a bakery manager in Buffalo who has worked at Wegmans for 17 years. Katie Southard echoes this view. "It's more you're not part of a company, you're part of a family," says Southard, who works in customer service at a Wegmans' store in Rochester, New York. "You're treated as an individual, not just one of the 350 persons in the store."

Wegmans also invests in its employees, then gives them the freedom to do their jobs. The company sent cheese manager Terri Zodarecky on a 10-day trip to cheesemakers in London, Paris, and Italy. Steve O'Malley has also received "a lot of education," including sojourns to California and advanced training at the Culinary Institute of America. Armed with this knowledge, employees are given the freedom to serve customers as best they see fit. "They let me do whatever comes into my head, which is kind of scary sometimes," says part-time meat department worker Bill Gamer. Wegmans operations chief Jack DePeters agrees, half-jokingly suggesting that "We're a $3 billion company run by 16-year-old cashiers."

The financial rewards, family culture, investment in employees, and employee autonomy seem to have the desired effect. While many grocery chains are shrinking or pulling out, Wegmans continues to expand. With happy employees, Wegmans enjoys one of the highest levels of customer loyalty and lowest levels of employee turnover in the industry. Brenda Hidalgo, who works at Wegmans in Buffalo, sums up the positive experience: "I've worked at other places where you wake up and you say 'Ech, I have to go to work,'" she recalls. "Now I love to go to work."[1]

4

Workplace Emotions and Attitudes

LEARNING OBJECTIVES

After reading this chapter, you should be able to

1. Define *emotions* and identify the two dimensions around which emotions are organized.
2. Explain how cognitions and emotions influence attitudes and behavior.
3. Identify the conditions that require and the problems associated with emotional labor.
4. Describe the four dimensions of emotional intelligence.
5. Summarize the effects of job dissatisfaction in terms of the exit–voice–loyalty–neglect model.
6. Discuss the relationships between job satisfaction and performance as well as between job satisfaction and customer satisfaction.
7. Distinguish affective and continuance commitment, and discuss their influences on employee behavior.
8. Describe five strategies to increase organizational commitment.
9. Contrast transactional and relational psychological contracts, and explain how they vary across cultures and generational cohorts.

Wegmans is a role model for giving employees positive emotional experiences at work. That's because emotions and attitudes can make a huge difference in individual behavior and well-being, as well as in the organization's performance and customer satisfaction. Over the past decade the field of organizational behavior has experienced a dramatic change in thinking about workplace emotions, so this chapter begins by introducing the concept and explaining why researchers are so eager to discover how emotions influence attitudes and behavior.

Next we consider the dynamics of emotional labor, including the conditions requiring emotional labor. This is followed by the popular topic of emotional intelligence, in which we examine the components of emotional intelligence and ways of improving this ability. The specific work attitudes of job satisfaction and organizational commitment are then discussed, including their association with various employee behaviors and work performance. Organizational commitment is strongly influenced by the psychological contract, so the final section of this chapter looks briefly at this topic.

Learning Objectives

After reading this section you should be able to

1. **Define *emotions* and identify the two dimensions around which emotions are organized.**
2. **Explain how cognitions and emotions influence attitudes and behavior.**

Emotions in the Workplace

emotions
Psychological, behavioral, and physiological episodes experienced toward an object, person, or event that create a state of readiness.

Emotions have a profound effect on almost everything we do in the workplace. This is a strong statement–and one that you would rarely find a decade ago in organizational behavior research or textbooks. For most of its history the field of OB assumed that a person's thoughts and actions are governed primarily by conscious reasoning (called *cognitions*). Yet groundbreaking neuroscience discoveries have revealed that our perceptions, attitudes, decisions, and behavior are influenced by both cognition and emotion, and that the latter often has the greater influence. By ignoring emotionality, many theories have overlooked a large piece of the puzzle about human behavior in the workplace. Today OB researchers and their colleagues in marketing, economics, and many other social sciences are catching up by making emotions a key part of their research and theories.[2]

"Biosensors. The whole company knows instantly when I'm displeased."

So what are emotions? **Emotions** are physiological, behavioral, and psychological episodes experienced toward an object, person, or event that create a state of readiness.[3] There are four key elements of this definition. First, emotions are brief events or *episodes.* Your irritation with a customer, for instance, would typically subside within a few minutes. Second, emotions are directed toward someone or something. We experience joy, fear, anger, and other emotional episodes toward tasks, customers, public speeches we present, a software program we are using, and so on. This contrasts with *moods,* which are less intense emotional states that are not directed toward anything in particular.[4]

Third, emotions are experiences. They represent changes in a person's physiological conditions, such as blood pressure, heart rate, and perspiration, as well as changes in behavior, such as facial expression, voice tone, and eye movement. These emotional reactions are involuntary and often occur without our awareness. When aware of these responses, we also develop feelings (worry, fear, boredom) that further mark the emotional experience. The experience of emotion also relates to the fourth element–namely, that emotions put people in a state of readiness. When we get worried, for example, our heart rate and blood pressure increase to better prepare our body to engage in fight or flight. Emotions are also communications to our conscious selves. Some emotions (such as anger, surprise, and fear) are particularly strong "triggers" that interrupt our train of thought, demand our attention, and generate the motivation to take action. They make us aware of events that may affect our survival and well-being.[5]

Types of Emotions

Emotions come in many forms, and experts have generally organized them around two or three dimensions. The most widely recognized arrangement is the circumplex model of emotions shown in Exhibit 4.1, which organizes emotions on the basis of their pleasantness and activation (the extent that the emotion produces alertness and motivation to act).[6] Fear, for example, is an unpleasant experience (we try to avoid conditions that generate fear) and has high activation (it motivates us to act).

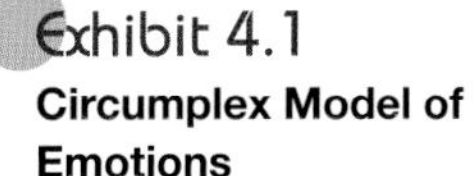

Exhibit 4.1
Circumplex Model of Emotions

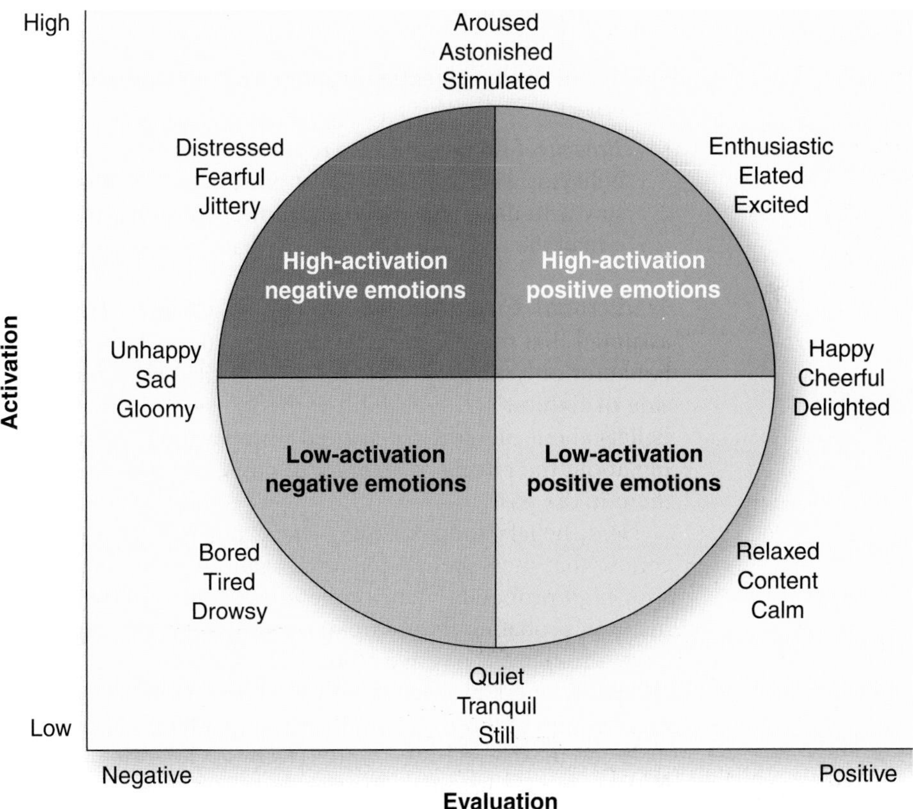

Source: Adapted from J. Larson, E. Diener, and R.E. Lucas, "Emotion: Models, Measures, and Differences," in *Emotions in the Workplace,* ed. R.G. Lord, R.J. Klimoski, and R. Kanfer (San Francisco: Jossey-Bass, 2002), pp. 64–113; J.A. Russell, "Core Affect and the Psychological Construction of Emotion," *Psychological Review* 110, no. 1 (2003), pp. 145–72.

Emotions on the opposite side of the circle have the opposite effect. As we see in Exhibit 4.1, calm is the opposite of fear; it is a pleasant experience that produces little activation in us.

Emotions, Attitudes, and Behavior

attitudes
The cluster of beliefs, assessed feelings, and behavioral intentions toward an object.

Emotions influence our thoughts and behavior, but to explain this effect we first need to know about attitudes. **Attitudes** represent the cluster of beliefs, assessed feelings, and behavioral intentions toward a person, object, or event (called an *attitude object*).[7] Attitudes are *judgments,* whereas emotions are *experiences.* In other words, attitudes involve conscious logical reasoning, whereas emotions operate as events, often without our awareness. We also experience most emotions briefly, whereas our attitude toward someone or something is more stable over time.

Attitudes include three components–beliefs, feelings, and behavioral intentions–and we'll look at each of them using attitude toward mergers as an illustration:

- *Beliefs.* These are your established perceptions about the attitude object–what you believe to be true. For example, you might believe that mergers reduce job security for employees in the merged firms. Or you might believe that mergers increase a company's competitiveness in this era of globalization. These beliefs are perceived facts that you acquire from past experience and other forms of learning.
- *Feelings.* Feelings represent your positive or negative evaluations of the attitude object. Some people think mergers are good; others think they are bad. Your like or dislike of mergers represents your assessed feelings toward the attitude object.
- *Behavioral intentions.* These represent your motivation to engage in a particular behavior with respect to the attitude object. You might plan to quit rather than stay with the company during a merger. Alternatively, you might intend to e-mail the company CEO to say that this merger was a good decision.

Traditional Cognitive Model of Attitudes Until recently, attitude experts assumed that these three attitude components are connected to each other and to behavior only through the cognitive (logical reasoning) process shown on the left side of Exhibit 4.2. Let's look at the left side of the model more closely. First, our beliefs about mergers are formed from various learning experiences, such as reading about the effects of mergers in other organizations or personally experiencing them in the past.

Next, beliefs about mergers shape our feelings toward them. Suppose you are certain that mergers improve the organization's competitiveness (positive outcome with high probability) and sometimes reduce job security (negative outcome with medium probability) for employees in the merged organization. Overall you might have a somewhat positive attitude toward mergers if your feelings about corporate competitiveness are stronger than your feelings about reduced job security. The probabilities of those outcomes also weight their effect on your feelings.

In the third step of the model, feelings directly influence behavioral intentions.[8] However, two people with the same feelings might have different behavioral intentions based on their past experience and personality. Some employees with negative feelings toward mergers may intend to quit, whereas others might want to complain about the decision. People choose the behavioral intention that they think will work best or make them feel most comfortable.

Exhibit 4.2
Model of Emotions, Attitudes, and Behavior

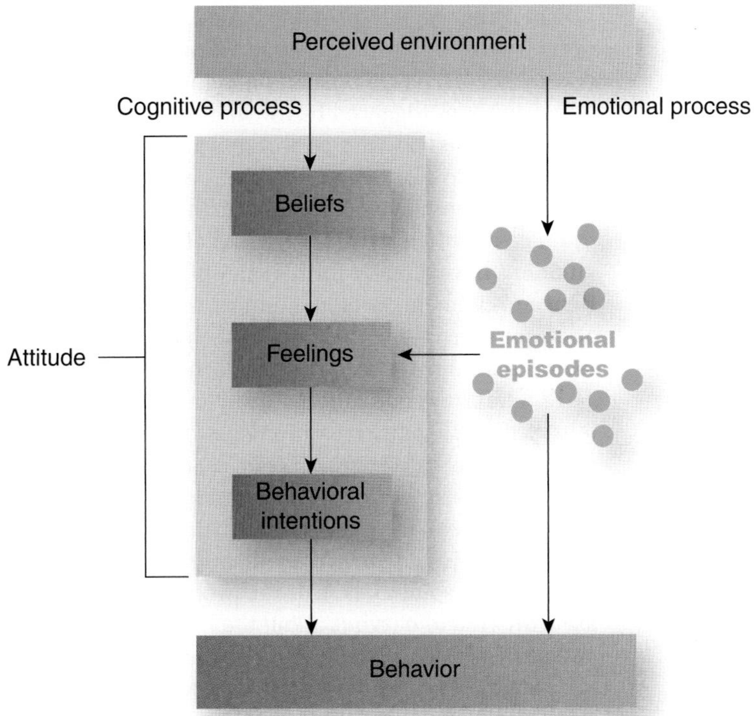

In the final step, behavioral intentions are better than feelings or beliefs at predicting a person's behavior because they are specific to that behavior. Even so, behavioral intentions might not predict behavior very well because intentions represent only the motivation to act, whereas behavior is also caused by the other three factors in the MARS model–ability, role perceptions, and situational factors. You might plan to send an e-mail to management complaining about the announced merger, but perhaps you never get around to this task due to a heavy workload and family obligations.

How Emotions Influence Attitudes and Behavior The cognitive model has dominated attitude research for decades, yet we now know that it describes only partially what really happens.[9] According to neuroscience research, incoming information from our senses is routed to the emotional center as well as the cognitive (logical reasoning) center of our brain.[10] We have already described the logical reasoning process, depicted on the left side of Exhibit 4.2. The right side of Exhibit 4.2 offers a simple depiction of how emotions influence our attitudes and behavior.

The emotional side of attitude formation begins with the dynamics of the perceptual process, particularly perceptual interpretation, described in Chapter 3. When receiving incoming sensory information, we automatically form emotions regarding that information before consciously thinking about it.[11] More specifically, the emotional center quickly and imprecisely evaluates whether the incoming sensory information supports or threatens our innate drives, then attaches emotional markers to the information. These are not calculated feelings; they are automatic and unconscious emotional responses based on very thin slices of sensory information.

Returning to our previous example, you might experience excitement, worry, nervousness, or happiness upon learning that your company intends to merge with a competitor. The large dots on the right side of Exhibit 4.2 illustrate these multiple emotional episodes triggered by the merger announcement, subsequent thinking about the merger, discussion with co-workers about the merger, and so on. These emotions are transmitted to the logical reasoning process, where they swirl around and ultimately shape our conscious feelings toward the attitude object.[12] Thus while you consciously evaluate the merger–that is, logically figure out whether it is a good or bad thing–your emotions have already formed an opinion that then sways your thoughts. If you experience excitement, delight, comfort, and other positive emotions whenever you think about or discuss the merger, then these positive emotional episodes will lean your logical reasoning toward positive feelings regarding the merger.[13]

Emotions operate automatically and unconsciously most of the time, but research tells us that the logical reasoning process actually "listens in" on the person's emotions and uses this information when translating beliefs into feelings.[14] When thinking about whether the announced merger is good or bad, we try to understand our emotional reactions to the event, then use this emotional awareness as factual information in our logical evaluation. In some cases the perceived emotions change the values of some beliefs or the probabilities that they are true. If you sense that you are worried and nervous about the merger, then your logical analysis might pay more attention to your belief about job insecurity and put less weight on your belief that mergers increase the organization's competitiveness.

You can see how emotions affect workplace attitudes. When performing our jobs or interacting with co-workers, we experience a variety of emotions that shape our longer-term feelings toward the company, our boss, the job itself, and so on. The more we experience positive emotions, the more we form positive attitudes toward the targets of those emotions.

The opening story to this chapter described how Wegmans strategically tries to ensure that employees experience plenty of positive emotional episodes each day. Many firms specifically teach employees four principles developed at Pike Place Fish Market in Seattle, Washington. These Fish! principles–play, make their day, be there, and choose your attitude–help staff to be more upbeat at work and contribute to positive emotions in others. The Fish! principles emerged when Pike Place fishmongers turned a money-losing, morale-draining business into a world-famous attraction by deciding to have fun at work. Connections 4.1 looks at other means by which organizations have created positive emotions.

When Cognitions and Emotions Conflict The influence of both logical reasoning and emotions on attitudes is most apparent when they disagree with each other. Everyone occasionally experiences this mental tug-of-war, sensing that something isn't right even though they can't think of any logical reason to be concerned. This conflicting experience indicates that our logical analysis of the situation (left side of Exhibit 4.2) can't identify reasons to support the automatic emotional reaction (right side of Exhibit 4.2).[15] Should we pay attention to our emotional response or our logical analysis? This question is not easy to answer because, as we just learned, the emotional and rational processes interact with each other so closely. However, some studies indicate that while executives tend to make quick decisions based on their gut feelings (emotional response), the best decisions tend to occur when executives spend time logically evaluating the situation.[16] Thus we should pay attention to both the cognitive and emotional sides of the attitude model, and hope they agree with each other most of the time!

Connections 4.1

Serious Fun

CXtec employees in Syracuse, New York, like to live up to their company values, which include having fun at work.

Walk into the offices of CXtec in Syracuse, New York, and you might think employees are in the middle of a birthday party. Around the cubicles are colorful clusters of helium-filled balloons, each representing a small token of the company's appreciation for performing their work effectively. Employees at the computer networking equipment company also enjoy a break room with billiards, foosball, and air hockey. And if staff want a little more enjoyment, the company also sponsors miniature golf tournaments in the office, tricycle races around the building, and "CXtec Idol" competitions. Of course all of this fits in with what the company stands for: "Part of our core values is that work is fun," explains Paula Miller, CXtec's director of employee and community relations.

Fun at work? It sounds like an oxymoron. But to attract and motivate valuable talent, companies are finding creative ways to generate positive emotions in the workplace. About six times each year, credit department staff at Zebra Technologies in Vernon Hills, Illinois, head off to the Whirlyball center, a large rink where employees grab and toss a ball using handheld scoops and electric bumper cars. The Malaysian operations of Scope International, a division of British bank Standard Chartered, won an award for bringing fun into the workplace—such as color coordination days, in which employees wear the same color clothing on a particular day. Along with enjoying office nerf gun fights, robot combat tournaments, movie nights, and wine tours, employees at Nuvation in San Jose, California, showcase a life-size fiberglass blue and orange moose. "We like to take the moose out to our parties," says Nuvation cofounder Geoff White.

These fun and games may seem silly, but some corporate leaders are serious about their value. "It's pretty simple," explains an executive at Quebecor. "If you want to make the most money, you must attract the best people. To get the best people, you must be the most fun."

Sources: J. Elliott, "All Work and No Play Can Chase Workers Away," *Edmonton Journal,* 28 February 2000; M.A. Tan, "Management: Having Fun at Work," *The Edge Malaysia,* 10 February 2003; R. Deruyter, "Firm's Goals Are Business Success and Having Fun," *Kitchener-Waterloo Record,* 30 October 2004, p. F1; S.K. Wong, "How Do Some Big companies Spell Teamwork? Whirlyball," *The Columbian* (Vancouver, WA), 19 March 2006, p. E1; T. Knauss, "Small Company Is a Happy Place to Work," *Post Standard/Herald-Journal* (Syracuse, New York), 21 March 2006, p. A1.

One last observation about the attitude model in Exhibit 4.2 relates to the arrow directly from the emotional episodes to behavior. This indicates that people have direct behavioral reactions to their emotions. Even low-intensity emotions automatically change your facial expressions. High-intensity emotions can have a more powerful effect, which is apparent when an upset employee bangs a fist on a desk or an overjoyed colleague embraces someone nearby. These actions are not carefully thought out. They are fairly automatic emotional responses that serve as coping mechanisms in that situation.[17]

Cognitive Dissonance Emotions and attitudes usually lead to behavior, but the opposite sometimes occurs.[18] Suppose you volunteered to take a foreign assignment. You weren't particularly interested in the posting, but thought that it might be necessary for promotion into senior management. However, you later learn that most people become senior managers in this firm without spending any time in foreign

cognitive dissonance
A psychological tension that occurs when people perceive an inconsistency between their beliefs, feelings, and behavior.

assignment. This inconsistency between a person's beliefs, feelings, and behavior situation creates an uncomfortable tension called **cognitive dissonance.** In this example your behavior (taking a foreign assignment) is inconsistent with your beliefs and feelings toward foreign postings.

Behavior is usually the most difficult element to change, particularly when that behavior has been observed by others (it can't be denied), was done voluntarily, and can't be undone. Thus people usually change their beliefs and feelings to reduce the inconsistency. In our example you might convince yourself that the foreign posting is not so bad after all because it will develop your management skills. Alternatively, you might downplay the features that previously made the foreign posting less desirable. Suddenly a somewhat negative attitude toward foreign assignments has changed to a more favorable one.

Emotions and Personality Coverage of the dynamics of workplace emotions wouldn't be complete unless the role of personality was also mentioned. The extent to which people experience positive or negative emotions at work is partly determined by their personalities, not just workplace experiences.[19] Some people experience positive emotions as a natural trait. These people are generally extroverted–outgoing, talkative, sociable, and assertive (see Chapter 2). In contrast, some people have a tendency to experience more negative emotions. Positive and negative emotional traits affect a person's attendance, turnover, and long-term work attitudes. For example, several studies have found that people with a negative emotional trait have lower levels of job satisfaction. Also, employees with a natural tendency to experience negative emotions tend to have higher levels of job burnout.[20] Although these positive and negative personality traits have some effect, other research concludes that the actual situation in which people work has a noticeably stronger influence on their attitudes and behavior.[21]

Learning Objectives

After reading the next two sections you should be able to

3. **Identify the conditions that require and the problems associated with emotional labor.**
4. **Describe the four dimensions of emotional intelligence.**

Managing Emotions at Work

The Elbow Room Café is packed and noisy on this Saturday morning. A customer at the restaurant in Vancouver, Canada, half-shouts across the room for more coffee. A passing waiter scoffs, "You want more coffee, get it yourself!" The customer only laughs. Another diner complains loudly that he and his party are running late and need their food. This time restaurant manager Patrick Savoie speaks up: "If you're in a hurry, you should have gone to McDonald's." The diner and his companions chuckle.

To the uninitiated, the Elbow Room Café is an emotional basket case, full of irate guests and the rudest staff on Canada's West Coast. But it's all a performance–a place where guests can enjoy good food and play out their emotions about dreadful customer service. "It's almost like coming to a theater," says Savoie, who spends much of his time inventing new ways to insult the clientele.[22]

emotional labor
The effort, planning, and control needed to express organizationally desired emotions during interpersonal transactions.

Whether it's the most insulting service at Elbow Room Café in Vancouver or the friendliest service at Wegmans in Rochester or Albany, New York, employees are usually expected to manage their emotions in the workplace. **Emotional labor** refers to the effort, planning, and control needed to express organizationally desired emotions during interpersonal transactions.[23] When interacting with co-workers, suppliers, and others, employees are expected to abide by *display rules*. These rules are norms requiring employees to display certain emotions and withhold others.

Conditions Requiring Emotional Labor

Don't be surprised if you hear a cheerful voice when calling the Golden Inn. The Atlantic City hotel sent 175 of its employees to a special customer service training program sponsored by New Jersey's Casino Reinvestment Development Authority (CRDA). CRDA arranged the training program for area businesses to correct one of the biggest complaints mentioned by tourists to the Jersey Shore–rude staff. Guest ratings of employee friendliness and courtesy shot up 5 percent after employees completed the program, prompting general manager John Ellison to award staff a 50-cent-per-hour bonus. "We look for smiles," says Ellison, who now carefully considers a person's positive attitude during job interviews. "You can never have too many smiles at the Shore."[24]

Golden Inn and just about every other organization expect employees to engage in some level of emotional labor, and many provide training so staff know exactly what emotions to display and when to display them. For instance, the Ritz-Carlton Hotel Company's motto is "Smile–we are on stage." To ensure that this standard is maintained at the 60 properties it manages around the world, the Ritz developed a detailed training program that teaches staff how to look pleasant in front of guests. Its orientation manual even includes two pages on phrases to use and to avoid saying, such as "My pleasure" rather than "OK, sure." Emotional labor is higher in jobs requiring a variety of emotions (such as anger as well as joy) and more intense emotions (showing delight rather than smiling weakly), as well as where interaction with clients is frequent and for longer durations. Emotional labor also increases when employees must precisely rather than casually abide by the display rules.[25]

Emotional Display Norms across Cultures How much we are expected to hide or reveal our true emotions in public depends to some extent on the culture in which we live. Cultural values in some countries–particularly Ethiopia, Korea, Japan, and Austria–expect people to display a neutral emotional demeanor. In the workplace and other public settings, employees try to subdue their emotional expression and minimize physical contact with others. Even voice intonation tends to be monotonic. In other countries–notably Kuwait, Egypt, Spain, and Russia–cultural values allow or encourage open display of one's true emotions. People are expected to be transparent in revealing their thoughts and feelings, dramatic in their conversational tones, and animated in their use of nonverbal behaviors to get their messages across. These cultural variations in emotional display can be quite noticeable. One survey reported that 83 percent of Japanese believe it is inappropriate to get emotional in a business context, compared with 40 percent of Americans, 34 percent of French, and only 29 percent of Italians. In other words, Italians are more likely to accept or tolerate people who display their true emotions at work, whereas this would be considered rude or embarrassing in Japan.[26]

Emotional Dissonance

Emotional labor can be challenging for most of us because it is difficult to conceal true emotions and to display the emotions required by the job. The main problem is that joy, sadness, worry, and other emotions automatically activate a complex set of facial muscles that are difficult to restrain and equally difficult to fake. Our true emotions tend to reveal themselves as subtle gestures, usually without our awareness. Meanwhile,

Localizing Emotional Display Rules at Four Seasons Hotels As one of the world's leading operators of luxury hotels, Four Seasons Hotels and Resorts trains employees and audits hotel performance to ensure that guests consistently experience the highest standards of service quality. Yet Four Seasons also adapts its legendary service to the local culture. "McDonald's is the same all over. We do not want to be that way; we are not a cookie-cutter company," says Four Seasons executive David Crowl. One of the most obvious forms of localization is in the way Four Seasons staff are allowed to display emotions that reflect their own culture. "What changes [from one country to the next] is that people do it with their own style, grace, and personality," explains Antoine Corinthios, president of Four Seasons' operations in Europe, Middle East, and Africa. "In some cultures you add the strong local temperament. For example, an Italian concierge has his own style and flair. In Turkey or Egypt you experience different hospitality."[27]

pretending to be cheerful or concerned is difficult because several specific facial muscles and body positions must be coordinated. More often than not, observers see when we are faking and sense that we feel a different emotion.[28]

emotional dissonance
A conflict between a person's required and true emotions.

Emotional labor also tends to create a conflict between required and true emotions, called **emotional dissonance.** The larger the gap between the required and true emotions, the more employees tend to experience stress, job burnout, and psychological separation from self.[29] One way to minimize emotional dissonance is by hiring people with a natural tendency to display the emotions required for the job. For example, when CiCi's Pizza opens new stores, it looks for job applicants with a "happy, cheery" attitude. The restaurant franchise believes that it is easier to teach new skills than attitudes. "We hire for attitude and train for skill," says one of CiCi's franchisees.[30]

But even with a good fit between the person's natural disposition and the required emotions for the job, some acting is required to perform the job. The problem is that most of us engage in *surface acting;* we modify our behavior to be consistent with required emotions but continue to hold different internal feelings. For instance, we force a smile while greeting a customer whom we consider rude. The solution is to follow the practice of great actors–namely, engage in *deep acting.* Deep acting involves changing true emotions to match the required emotions. Rather than feeling irritated by a rude customer, you might view your next interaction with that person as an opportunity to test your sales skills. This change in perspective can potentially generate more positive emotions next time you meet that difficult customer, which produces friendlier displays of emotion.[31] However, it also requires considerable emotional intelligence, which we discuss next.

Emotional Intelligence

GM Holden's new production facility at Port Melbourne was General Motors' largest investment in Australia in decades, so executives carefully selected the plant's design team, managers, and production staff. Still, it wasn't long before the project unraveled due to infighting and interpersonal tensions. Consultants called in to analyze the problems offered the following solution: Employees need to improve their emotional intelligence. With this advice, the 30 plant design team members and over 300 other employees from production through management completed an emotional intelligence assessment and attended training modules on effective self-expression, understanding others, controlling emotions, and related topics.

To overcome skepticism about its touchy-feely nature, the emotional intelligence and leadership development program was evaluated to see whether employee scores improved and behavior changed. The results found an average 50 percent increase on EI scores, while behavior became much more cooperative and diplomatic. "It has greatly improved communication within the team and with other teams outside the plant," says GM Holden quality systems engineer Vesselka Vassileva. Some employees also note that it has improved their interpersonal behavior outside the workplace. "I'm not so aggressive or assertive," says manufacturing engineer Alf Moore. "I feel better, and it's helped me at home."[32]

emotional intelligence (EI)
The ability to perceive and express emotion, assimilate emotion in thought, understand and reason with emotion, and regulate emotion in oneself and others.

GM Holden's new production facility started up more smoothly than might have occurred because the company paid attention to **emotional intelligence (EI).** EI is the ability to perceive and express emotion, assimilate emotion in thought, understand and reason with emotion, and regulate emotion in oneself and others.[33] In other words, EI represents a set of *competencies* that allow us to perceive, understand, and regulate emotions in ourselves and in others. Exhibit 4.3 illustrates the most recent EI model. According to this model, EI can be organized into four dimensions representing the recognition of emotions in ourselves and in others, as well as the regulation of emotions in ourselves and in others. Each dimension consists of a set of emotional competencies that people must possess to fulfill that dimension of emotional intelligence.[34]

Exhibit 4.3
Dimensions of Emotional Intelligence

	Self (personal competence)	Other (social competence)
Recognition of emotions	**Self-Awareness** • Emotional self-awareness • Accurate self-assessment • Self-confidence	**Social Awareness** • Empathy • Organizational awareness • Service
Regulation of emotions	**Self-Management** • Emotional self-control • Transparency • Adaptability • Achievement • Initiative • Optimism	**Relationship Management** • Inspirational leadership • Influence • Developing others • Change catalyst • Conflict management • Building bonds • Teamwork and collaboration

Sources: D. Goleman, R. Boyatzis, and A. McKee, *Primal Leadership* (Boston: Harvard Business School Press, 2002), Chapter 3; D. Goleman, "An EI-Based Theory of Performance," in *The Emotionally Intelligent Workplace, ed.* C. Cherniss and D. Goleman (San Francisco: Jossey-Bass, 2001), p. 28.

- *Self-awareness.* Self-awareness refers to having a deep understanding of one's own emotions as well as strengths, weaknesses, values, and motives. Self-aware people are better able to listen to their emotional responses to specific situations and to use this awareness as conscious information.[35]
- *Self-management.* This represents how well we control or redirect our internal states, impulses, and resources. It includes keeping disruptive impulses in check, displaying honesty and integrity, being flexible in times of change, maintaining the drive to perform well and seize opportunities, and remaining optimistic even after failure. Self-management involves an inner conversation that guides our behavior.
- *Social awareness.* Social awareness is mainly about *empathy*–having understanding and sensitivity to the feelings, thoughts, and situations of others (see Chapter 3). This includes understanding another person's situation, experiencing the other person's emotions, and knowing their needs even though unstated. Social awareness extends beyond empathy to include being organizationally aware, such as sensing office politics and understanding social networks.
- *Relationship management.* This dimension of EI refers to managing other people's emotions. It is linked to a wide variety of practices, such as inspiring others,-influencing people's beliefs and feelings, developing others' capabilities, managing change, resolving conflict, cultivating relationships, and supporting teamwork and collaboration. These activities also require effective emotional expression–intentionally communicating emotions to others, usually to influence their emotions and behavior.

These four dimensions of emotional intelligence form a hierarchy.[36] Self-awareness is the lowest level of EI because it does not require the other dimensions; instead it is a prerequisite for the other three dimensions. Self-management and social awareness are necessarily above self-awareness in the EI hierarchy. You can't manage your own emotions (self-management) if you aren't good at knowing your own emotions (self-awareness). Relationship management is the highest level of EI because it requires all three other dimensions. In other words, we require a high degree of emotional intelligence to master relationship management because this set of competencies requires sufficiently high levels of self-awareness, self-management, and social awareness.

EI has its roots in the social intelligence literature introduced more than 80 years ago, but scholars since then focused mainly on cognitive intelligence (IQ). Now leaders at GM Holden and other companies are realizing that EI is an important set of competencies in the performance of most jobs. Recall from Chapter 2 that people perform better when their aptitudes–including general intelligence–match the job requirements. But most jobs also involve social interaction, so employees also need emotional intelligence to work effectively in social settings. The evidence so far indicates that people with high EI are better at interpersonal relations, perform better in jobs requiring emotional labor, and are more successful in many aspects of job interviews. Teams whose members have high emotional intelligence initially perform better than teams with low EI.[37]

Improving Emotional Intelligence

Emotional intelligence is associated with conscientiousness and other personality traits. However, EI can also be learned to some extent, so GM Holden and other companies put employees through EI training programs. "We've developed a seven-hour training program on emotional intelligence," says an executive at BB&T Corp., a large financial services company based in Winston-Salem, North Carolina. "We believe it really helps people grow as employees." In support of the training approach, a recent study reported that business students scored higher on emotional intelligence after taking an undergraduate interpersonal skills course.[38] Although training helps, a more effective way to improve EI is through personal coaching, plenty of practice, and frequent feedback. EI also increases with age; it is part of the process called maturity. Overall, emotional intelligence offers considerable potential, but we also have a lot to learn about its measurement and effects on people in the workplace.

So far this chapter has laid out the model of emotions and attitudes, but we also need to understand specific workplace attitudes. The next two sections of this chapter look at two of the most widely studied attitudes: job satisfaction and organizational commitment.

Learning Objectives

After reading this section you should be able to

5. **Summarize the effects of job dissatisfaction in terms of the exit–voice–loyalty–neglect model.**
6. **Discuss the relationships between job satisfaction and performance as well as job satisfaction and customer satisfaction.**

Job Satisfaction

job satisfaction
A person's evaluation of his or her job and work context.

Job satisfaction, a person's evaluation of his or her job and work context, is probably the most studied attitude in organizational behavior.[39] It is an *appraisal* of the perceived job characteristics, work environment, and emotional experiences at work. Satisfied employees have a favorable evaluation of their jobs, based on their observations and emotional experiences. Job satisfaction is really a collection of attitudes about different aspects of the job and work context. You might like your co-workers but be less satisfied with the workload, for instance.

How satisfied are employees at work? In the most recent surveys, more than 85 percent of Americans are somewhat or very satisfied with their jobs–a level that has been consistent for more than a decade. Exhibit 4.4 shows that Americans also have high levels of job satisfaction compared with people in most other countries. Only employees in Denmark, India, and Norway say they are happier at work. Another survey found that Americans had the third highest job satisfaction, after Brazilians and Canadians, among the 10 largest economies in the world. In contrast, employees in most Asian countries report lower job satisfaction. One study of 115,000 Asian employees reported that 63 percent are satisfied overall with their jobs.[40]

It's probably fair to conclude that employees in India and the United States are more satisfied than in some other parts of the world, but we also need to be somewhat cautious about these and other job satisfaction surveys. One problem is that surveys often use a single direct question, such as "How satisfied are you with your job?" Many dissatisfied employees are reluctant to reveal their feelings in a direct question because this is tantamount to admitting that they made a poor job choice and are not enjoying life. For instance, three recent surveys in the United States, Canada, and Malaysia found that although most employees in those countries say they are satisfied with their job and work environment, more than half would abandon their employers if offered comparable jobs elsewhere![41]

A second problem is that cultural values make it difficult to compare job satisfaction across countries. People in China, South Korea, and Japan tend to subdue their emotions in public, so they probably avoid extreme survey ratings such as "very satisfied." A third problem is that job satisfaction changes with economic conditions.

Exhibit 4.4 **Job Satisfaction across Cultures**

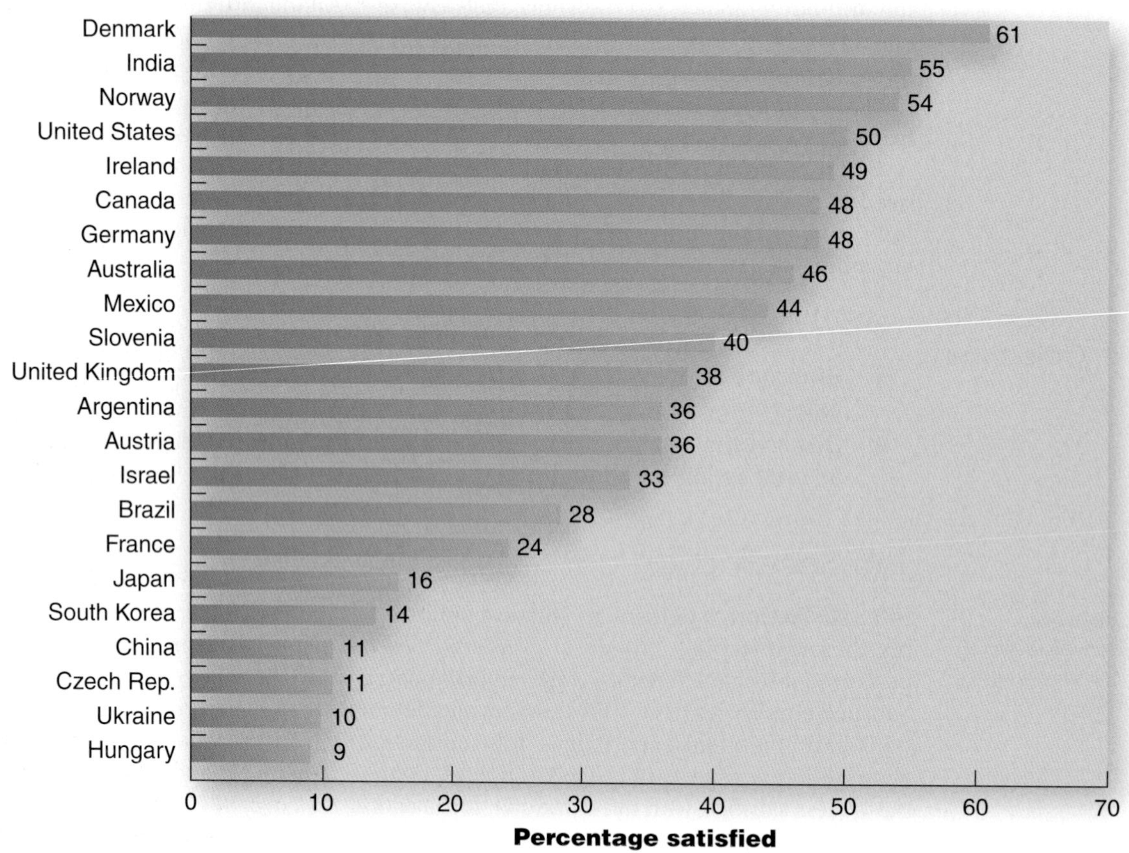

Source: Based on Ipsos-Reid survey of 9,300 employees in 39 countries in mid-2000. See "Ipsos-Reid Global Poll Finds Major Differences in Employee Satisfaction around the World," Ipsos-Reid News Release, 8 January 2001. A sample of 22 countries across the range is shown here, including all of the top-scoring countries.

Employees with the highest job satisfaction tend to be in countries where the economies are booming at the time of the survey.[42]

Job Satisfaction and Work Behavior

exit-voice-loyalty-neglect (EVLN) model The four ways, as indicated in the name, employees respond to job dissatisfaction.

Job satisfaction affects many of the individual behaviors mentioned in Chapter 2. A useful template to organize and understand the consequences of job dissatisfaction is the **exit–voice–loyalty–neglect (EVLN) model.** As the name suggests, the EVLN model identifies four ways in which employees respond to dissatisfaction:[43]

- *Exit.* Exit refers to leaving the organization, transferring to another work unit, or at least trying to make these exits. Employee turnover is a well-established outcome of job dissatisfaction, particularly for employees with better job opportunities elsewhere. Exit usually follows specific "shock events," such as when your boss treats you unfairly.[44] These shock events generate strong emotions that energize employees to think about and search for alternative employment.
- *Voice.* Voice refers to any attempt to change, rather than escape from, a dissatisfying situation. Voice can be a constructive response, such as recommending ways for management to improve the situation; or it can be more confronta-

tional, such as filing formal grievances.[45] In the extreme, some employees might engage in counterproductive behaviors to get attention and force changes in the organization.

- *Loyalty.* Loyalty has been described in different ways, but the most widely held view is that "loyalists" are employees who respond to dissatisfaction by patiently waiting–some say they "suffer in silence"–for a problem to work itself out or get resolved by others.[46]
- *Neglect.* Neglect includes reducing work effort, paying less attention to quality, and increasing absenteeism and lateness. It is generally considered a passive activity that has negative consequences for the organization.

Which of the four EVLN alternatives do employees use? It depends on the person and situation. One determining factor is the availability of alternative employment. With poor job prospects, employees are less likely to use the exit option. Those who identify with the organization are also more likely to use voice rather than exit. Highly conscientious people are less likely to engage in neglect and more likely to engage in voice. Some experts suggest that employees differ in their EVLN behavior depending on whether they have high or low collectivism. Finally, past experience influences our choice of action. Employees who were unsuccessful with voice in the past are more likely to engage in exit or neglect when experiencing job dissatisfaction in the future.[47]

Job Satisfaction and Performance

One of the oldest beliefs in the business world is that "a happy worker is a productive worker." Is this statement true? Over several decades, organizational behavior scholars have flip-flopped on their answers on this question. Long ago they were reasonably confident that the statement was true. Later, doubts emerged as studies found a weak or negligible association between job satisfaction and task performance.[48] Now the evidence suggests that the popular saying may be correct after all. Citing problems with the earlier studies, a recent meta-analysis (which combines results from the previous studies) concluded that there is a *moderate* relationship between job satisfaction and job performance. In other words, happy workers really are more productive workers *to some extent*.[49]

Even with a moderate association between job satisfaction and performance, there are a few underlying reasons why the relationship isn't even stronger.[50] One argument is that general attitudes (such as job satisfaction) don't predict specific behaviors very well. As we learned with the EVLN model, job dissatisfaction can lead to a variety of outcomes rather than lower job performance (neglect). Some employees continue to work productively while they complain (voice), look for another job (exit), or patiently wait for the problem to be fixed (loyalty).

A second explanation is that job performance leads to job satisfaction (rather than vice versa), but only when performance is linked to valued rewards. Higher performers receive more rewards and, consequently, are more satisfied than low-performing employees who receive fewer rewards. The connection between job satisfaction and performance isn't stronger because many organizations do not reward good performance. The third explanation is that job satisfaction might influence employee motivation, but this has little influence on performance in jobs where employees have little control over their job output (such as assembly line work). This point explains why the job satisfaction–performance relationship is strongest in complex jobs, where employees have more freedom to perform their work or to slack off.

Job Satisfaction and Customer Satisfaction

The opening story to this chapter revealed that Wegmans Food Markets has an unusual motto: Employees first, customers second. The grocery chain definitely puts employees on top of the stakeholder list, but why not customers first? Wegmans' rationale is that customer satisfaction follows from employee satisfaction. In other words, it is difficult to keep customers happy if employee morale is low. Virgin Group founder Sir Richard Branson agrees with that theory. "It just seems common sense to me that if you start with a happy, well-motivated workforce, you're much more likely to have happy customers," says Branson.[51]

Fortunately, research generally agrees that job satisfaction has a positive effect on customer satisfaction.[52] There are two main reasons for this relationship. First, employees are usually in a more positive mood when they feel satisfied with their jobs and working conditions. Employees in a good mood display friendliness and positive emotions more naturally and frequently, and this creates positive emotions for customers. Second, satisfied employees are less likely to quit their jobs, so they have better knowledge and skills to serve clients. Lower turnover also gives customers the same employees to serve them, so there is more consistent service. There is some evidence that customers build their loyalty to specific employees, not to the organization, so keeping employee turnover low tends to build customer loyalty.[53]

Before leaving this topic, it's worth mentioning that job satisfaction does more than improve work behaviors and customer satisfaction. Job satisfaction is also an ethical issue that influences the organization's reputation in the community. People spend a large portion of their time working in organizations, and many societies now expect companies to provide work environments that are safe and enjoyable. Indeed, employees in several countries closely monitor ratings of the best companies to work for–an indication that employee satisfaction is a virtue worth considerable goodwill to employers. This virtue is apparent when an organization has low job satisfaction. The company tries to hide this fact, and when morale problems become public, corporate leaders are usually quick to improve the situation.

Happy Staff Means Happy Guests at Outback Restaurants Outback Steakhouse, Inc., has become a phenomenal success story in America's competitive restaurant industry. In 1988 Outback's four partners each opened a restaurant in Tampa, Florida, based on popular images of casual lifestyle and tucker in the land Down Under. Today Outback's 65,000 employees work in 1,100 restaurants around the United States and Canada. Although the Australian theme launched the company's success, Outback founder and CEO says staff quality deserves as much credit. Long before scholars pointed out that satisfied employees provide better customer service, Outback was applying this principle. "Outback's theory of success is that you hire the right people and take care of them," explained founder Chris Sullivan and three colleagues in a recent journal article. The company hires and creates a culture that supports energized employees who stay with the company and provide excellent service. This service makes customers happy, which brings them back and encourages them to recommend Outback to friends. The result of such customer satisfaction is higher sales, which improve company profits.[54]

Learning Objectives

After reading the next two sections you should be able to

7. **Distinguish affective and continuance commitment, and discuss their influences on employee behavior.**
8. **Describe five strategies to increase organizational commitment.**
9. **Contrast transactional and relational psychological contracts, and explain how they vary across cultures and generational cohorts.**

Organizational Commitment

organizational commitment The employee's emotional attachment to, identification with, and involvement in a particular organization.

continuance commitment A calculative decision to remain with an organization because quitting would be costly.

Along with job satisfaction, OB researchers have been intently interested in an attitude called organizational commitment. **Organizational commitment** refers to the employee's emotional attachment to, identification with, and involvement in a particular organization.[55] This definition refers specifically to *affective commitment* because it is an emotional attachment–our feelings of loyalty–to the organization.

Another form of commitment, called **continuance commitment,** occurs when employees believe it is in their own personal interest to remain with the organization. It is a calculated rather than emotional attachment to the organization.[56] Employees have high continuance commitment when they do not particularly identify with the organization where they work but feel bound to remain there because it would be too costly to quit. This reluctance to quit may be due to the risk of losing a large bonus by leaving early or because they are well established in the community where they work.[57]

Consequences of Organizational Commitment

Corporate leaders have good reason to pay close attention to employee loyalty because it can be a significant competitive advantage. Employees with high levels of affective commitment are less likely to quit their jobs and be absent from work. Organizational commitment also improves customer satisfaction because long-tenure employees have better knowledge of work practices, and clients like to do business with the same employees. Employees with high affective commitment also have higher work motivation and organizational citizenship, as well as somewhat higher job performance.[58]

Employees can also have too much affective commitment. One concern is that organizational loyalty reduces turnover, which may limit the organization's opportunity to hire new employees with different knowledge and fresh perspectives. Another concern is that loyalty results in conformity, which can undermine creativity and ethical conduct. For instance, a former executive at Arthur Andersen claims that one reason for the accounting firm's downfall was that it created a cultlike level of employee loyalty where no one questioned or second-guessed top management's decisions.[59]

Consequences of Continuance Commitment Creating too much affective commitment is probably much less of a problem compared with concerns about company practices that increase continuance commitment. Many firms tie employees financially to the organization through low-cost loans, stock options, deferred bonuses, and other "golden handcuffs." Brokerage firms on Wall Street apparently suppress employee turnover through a deferred compensation scheme in which brokers agree to receive up to 25 percent of their pay (often in the form of discounted company stock) two years later, but only if they stay until then.[60]

These financial incentives (or penalties) to remain with the organization tend to reduce turnover, but they also increase continuance commitment, not affective commitment. Research suggests that employees with high levels of continuance commitment have *lower* performance ratings and are *less* likely to engage in organizational citizenship behaviors! Furthermore, unionized employees with high continuance commitment are more likely to use formal grievances, whereas employees with high affective commitment engage in more constructive problem solving when employee–employer relations sour.[61] Although some level of financial connection may be necessary, employers should not confuse continuance commitment with employee loyalty. Employers still need to win employees' hearts (affective commitment) beyond tying them financially to the organization (continuance commitment).

Building Organizational Commitment

There are almost as many ways to build organizational loyalty as topics in this textbook, but the following list is most prominent in the literature:

- *Justice and support.* Affective commitment is higher in organizations that fulfill their obligations to employees and abide by humanitarian values, such as fairness, courtesy, forgiveness, and moral integrity. These values relate to the concept of organizational justice that we discuss in the next chapter. Similarly, organizations that support employee well-being tend to cultivate higher levels of loyalty in return.[62]
- *Shared values.* The definition of affective commitment refers to a person's identification with the organization, and that identification is highest when employees believe their values are congruent with the organization's dominant values. Also, employees experience more comfort and predictability when they agree with the values underlying corporate decisions. This comfort increases their motivation to stay with the organization.[63]
- *Trust.* **Trust** refers to positive expectations one person has toward another person in situations involving risk.[64] Trust means putting faith in the other person or group. It is also a reciprocal activity: To receive trust, you must demonstrate trust. Employees identify with and feel obliged to work for an organization only when they trust its leaders. This explains why layoffs are one of the greatest blows to employee loyalty–by reducing job security, companies reduce the trust employees have in their employers and the employment relationship.[65]

trust
A person's positive expectations toward another person in situations involving risk.

- *Organizational comprehension.* Affective commitment is a person's identification with the company, so it makes sense that this attitude is strengthened when employees understand the company, including its past, present, and future. Thus loyalty tends to increase with open and rapid communication to and from corporate leaders, as well as with opportunities to interact with co-workers across the organization.[66]
- *Employee involvement.* Employee involvement increases affective commitment by strengthening the employees' social identity with the organization. Employees feel that they are part of the organization when they take part in decisions that guide the organization's future. Employee involvement also builds loyalty because giving this power is a demonstration of a company's trust in its employees.

Look closely at some of these recommendations: You will see that one of the key influences on organizational commitment is the employment relationship. In particular, affective commitment is sensitive to how well the organization fulfills the psychological contract, which we look at in the last section of this chapter.

Psychological Contracts

When Katherine Certain joined an ad agency not long ago, her expectations included a wide range of job duties, such as calling potential clients and evaluating marketing plans. The recent college graduate did get those responsibilities, along with a few that weren't on her list–such as watering the plants and walking the owner's dogs each day. After the initial shock that she had been given these tasks, Certain began to feel degraded and confused. Less than a year later Certain jumped to a larger ad agency, where so far she hasn't experienced any surprises.[67]

Katherine Certain experienced the shock of having her psychological contract violated. This isn't unusual. According to one university study, 24 percent of employees are "chronically" angry at work, mostly because they feel their employer violated basic promises and didn't fulfill the psychological contract.[68] The **psychological contract** refers to the individual's beliefs about the terms and conditions of a reciprocal exchange agreement between that person and another party. This is inherently perceptual, so one person's understanding of the psychological contract may differ from the other party's understanding. In employment relationships, psychological contracts consist of beliefs about what the employee is entitled to receive and is obliged to offer the employer in return.[69] For example, Katherine Certain believed that her employer would give her responsibilities related to her career interests. Being assigned the duties of watering plants and walking the boss's dogs clearly violated her expectations.

psychological contract The individual's beliefs about the terms and conditions of a reciprocal exchange agreement between that person and another party.

Types of Psychological Contracts

Psychological contracts vary in many ways.[70] One of the most fundamental differences is the extent to which they are transactional or relational. As Exhibit 4.5 indicates, *transactional contracts* are primarily short-term economic exchanges. Responsibilities are well defined around a fairly narrow set of obligations that do not change over the life of the contract. People hired in temporary positions and as consultants tend to have transactional contracts. To some extent, new employees also form transactional contracts until they develop a sense of continuity with the organization.

Exhibit 4.5 Types of Psychological Contracts in Employment

Contract Characteristics	Contract Type: Transactional	Balanced	Relational
Focus	Economic		Economic and socioemotional
Time frame	Closed-ended and short-term		Open-ended and indefinite
Stability	Static		Dynamic
Scope	Narrow		Pervasive
Tangibility	Well-defined		More subjective

Source: Based on information in D.M. Rousseau and J.M. Parks, "The Contracts of Individuals and Organizations," *Research in Organizational Behavior* 15 (1993), pp. 1–43; D.M. Rousseau, *Psychological Contracts in Organizations* (Thousand Oaks, CA: Sage, 1995).

Japan's Freeters Turn the Psychological Contract Upside Down More than 2 million young Japanese have become "freeters": casual workers with an equally casual psychological contract that emphasizes personal freedom over loyalty. Generally they want employment that is short-term, transactional, and flexible—just the opposite of what their parents expected in an employment relationship. "Living as a freeter, I get more freedom and I like that," says Mika Onodera, a 28-year-old bakery employee in Tokyo (shown in this photo). Japan's struggling economy partially explains why an increasing number of young people are willing to accept temporary work; but recent surveys also suggest that freeters simply don't worry at all about long-term careers, and they think job-hopping is a badge of honor. The Japanese government is so concerned about the freeter trend that it provides financial aid to companies who hire freeters so they can "test-drive" a permanent job. It has also introduced a program in high schools to teach students the value of holding a full-time job.[71]

Relational contracts, on the other hand, are rather like marriages; they are long-term attachments that encompass a broad array of subjective mutual obligations. Employees with a relational psychological contract are more willing to contribute their time and effort without expecting the organization to pay back this debt in the short term. Relational contracts are also dynamic, meaning that the parties are more flexible regarding when they expect a payback for their contributions to the relationship. Not surprisingly, organizational citizenship behaviors are more likely to prevail under relational than transactional contracts. Permanent employees are more likely to believe they have a relational contract.

Psychological Contracts across Cultures and Generations

Psychological contracts are influenced by the social contexts in which the contracting process occurs.[72] In other words, they vary across cultures and groups of employees based on their unique cultures and cohort experiences. For instance, employees in the United States, United Kingdom, and several other countries expect some involvement in company decisions (that is, they have low power distance), whereas employees in Taiwan and Mexico are more willing to accept arbitrary orders from their supervisors (they have high power distance).

In Japan, employees traditionally expected lifetime employment in return for loyalty and hard work. However, this relational psychological contract shifted as a result of the country's extended recession in the 1990s. The emerging psychological contract among many young Japanese is a startling contrast to their parents. Specifically, Japan is experiencing a rising tide of "freeters" – young people who hop from one job to the next, usually with a distinctly transactional psychological contract. The psychological contract expectations of freeters has motivated the Japanese government to introduce various schemes intended to change their views on the employment relationship.

Psychological contracts also seem to vary across generations of employees. Older employees grew up with "organization man" expectations in which dedicated employees worked in secure jobs with steady promotions through the hierarchy. They often devoted their entire lives to the same company, put in regular hours, and rarely thought about changing employers.[73] The implicit contract was that if you are loyal to the company and perform your job reasonably well, the company will be loyal to you by providing job security and managing your career development. When the "new deal" of employability arrived, these older employees felt betrayed–their psychological contracts had been violated (see Chapter 1).[74]

However, some scholars suggest that job security has less value to Generation-X and Generation-Y employees than to baby boomers. Workforce newcomers have mainly experienced a psychological contract based on employability and are comfortable with weaker job security. "Employees are developing the view that their only job security in the future must be based on their ability and their competence," says Gary L. Howard, a Motorola vice president, "and not on keeping a job at some particular company."[75]

Psychological contracts are changing, as is the entire field of organizational behavior as it embraces new knowledge about emotions in the workplace. Emotional brain centers, emotional labor, emotional intelligence, and other topics in this chapter were unheard of 10 or 15 years ago. Now they are essential reading to improve our grasp of the complex dynamics of employee attitudes and behavior. You will see several references to emotions-related concepts throughout this book, including the next chapter about employee motivation.

Chapter Summary

Emotions are physiological, behavioral, and psychological episodes experienced toward an object, person, or event that create a state of readiness. Emotions are typically organized into a bipolar circle (circumplex) based on their pleasantness and activation. Emotions differ from attitudes, which represent the cluster of beliefs, feelings, and behavioral intentions toward a person, object, or event. Beliefs are a person's established perceptions about the attitude object. Feelings are positive or negative evaluations of the attitude object. Behavioral intentions represent a motivation to engage in a particular behavior with respect to the target.

Attitudes have traditionally been described as a process in which we logically calculate our feelings toward the attitude object based on an analysis of our beliefs. Thus beliefs predict feelings, which predict behavioral intentions, which predict behavior. But this traditional perspective overlooks the role of emotions, which have an important influence on attitudes and behavior. Emotions typically form before we think through situations, so they influence this rational attitude formation process. This dual process is apparent when we internally experience a conflict between what logically seems good or bad and what we emotionally feel is good or bad in a situation. Emotions also affect behavior directly.

Behavior sometimes influences our subsequent attitudes through cognitive dissonance. People also have personality traits that affect their emotions and attitudes.

Emotional labor is the effort, planning, and control needed to express organizationally desired emotions during interpersonal transactions. This is more common in jobs requiring a variety of emotions and more intense emotions, as well as where interaction with clients is frequent and for longer durations. The extent to which we are expected to hide or reveal our true emotions in public depends to some extent on the culture in which we live.

Emotional labor can be challenging for most of us because it is difficult to conceal true emotions and to display the emotions required by the job. It also creates emotional dissonance when required and true emotions are incompatible with each other. Deep acting can minimize this dissonance, as can the practice of hiring people with a natural tendency to display desired emotions.

Emotional intelligence is the ability to perceive and express emotion, assimilate emotion in thought, understand and reason with emotion, and regulate emotion in oneself and others. This concept includes four components arranged in a hierarchy: self-awareness, self-management, social awareness, and relationship management. Emotional intelligence can be learned to some extent, particularly through personal coaching.

Job satisfaction represents a person's evaluation of his or her job and work context. Although surveys indicate Americans are moderately or very satisfied with their jobs, these results may be somewhat inflated by the use of single-item questions and distorted by cultural differences. The exit–voice–loyalty–neglect model outlines four possible consequences of job dissatisfaction. Job satisfaction has a moderate relationship with job performance and with customer satisfaction. Job satisfaction is also a moral obligation in many societies.

Affective organizational commitment (loyalty) refers to the employee's emotional attachment to, identification with, and involvement in a particular organization. This contrasts with continuance commitment, which is a calculated bond with the organization. Affective commitment improves motivation and organizational citizenship and produces somewhat higher job performance, whereas continuance commitment is associated with lower performance and organizational citizenship. Companies build loyalty through justice and support, shared values, trust, organizational comprehension, and employee involvement.

The psychological contract refers to the individual's beliefs about the terms and conditions of a reciprocal exchange agreement between that person and another party. Transactional psychological contracts are primarily short-term economic exchanges, whereas relational contracts are long-term attachments that encompass a broad array of subjective mutual obligations. Psychological contracts seem to vary across cultures as well as across generations of employees.

Key Terms

attitudes, p. 106
cognitive dissonance, p. 110
continuance commitment, p. 119
emotional dissonance, p. 112
emotional intelligence (EI), p. 113
emotional labor, p. 110
emotions, p. 104
exit–voice–loyalty–neglect (EVLN) model, p. 116
job satisfaction, p. 115
organizational (affective) commitment, p. 119
psychological contract, p. 121
trust, p. 120

Critical Thinking Questions

1. After a few months on the job, Susan has experienced several emotional episodes ranging from frustration to joy about the work she has been assigned. Explain how these emotions affect Susan's level of job satisfaction with the work itself.
2. A recent study reported that college instructors are frequently required to engage in emotional labor. Identify the situations in which emotional labor is required for this job. In your opinion, is emotional labor more troublesome for college instructors or for telephone operators working at an emergency service?
3. "Emotional intelligence is more important than cognitive intelligence in influencing an individual's success." Do you agree or disagree with this statement? Support your perspective.
4. Describe a time when you effectively managed someone's emotions. What happened? What was the result?
5. The latest employee satisfaction survey in your organization indicates that employees are unhappy with some aspects of the organization. However, management tends to pay attention to the single-item question asking employees to indicate their overall satisfaction with the job. The results of this item indicate that 86 percent of staff members are very or somewhat satisfied, so management concludes that the other results refer to issues that are probably not important to employees. Explain why management's interpretation of these results may be inaccurate.
6. "Happy employees create happy customers." Explain why this statement might be true, and identify conditions in which it might not be true.
7. What factors influence an employee's organizational loyalty?
8. This chapter argues that psychological contracts vary across cultures and generations. Identify some of the psychological contract expectations around which younger and older employees differ in the country where you live.

Case Study 4.1 DIANA'S DISAPPOINTMENT: THE PROMOTION STUMBLING BLOCK

Rosemary Maellaro, University of Dallas

Diana Gillen had an uneasy feeling of apprehension as she arrived at the Cobb Street Grille corporate offices. Today she was meeting with her supervisor, Julie Spencer, and regional director, Tom Miner, to learn the outcome of her promotion interview for the district manager position. Diana had been employed by this casual dining restaurant chain for 12 years and had worked her way up from waitress to general manager. Based on her track record, she was the obvious choice for the promotion; and her friends assured her that the interview process was merely a formality. Diana was still anxious, though, and feared that the news might not be positive. She knew she was more than qualified for the job, but that didn't guarantee anything these days.

Nine months ago, when Diana interviewed for the last district manager opening, she thought her selection for the job was inevitable. She was shocked when that didn't happen. Diana was so upset about not getting promoted then that she initially decided not to apply for the current opening. She eventually changed her mind–after all, the company had just named her "restaurant manager of the year" and trusted her with managing their flagship location. Diana thought her chances had to be really good this time.

A multi-unit management position was a desirable move up for any general manager and was a goal to which Diana had aspired since she began working in the industry. When she had not been promoted the last time, Julie, her supervisor, explained that her people skills needed to improve. But Diana knew that explanation had little to do with why she hadn't gotten the job–the real reason was corporate politics. She heard that the person they hired was some superstar from the outside–a district manager from another restaurant company who supposedly had strong multi-unit management experience and a proven track record of developing restaurant managers. Despite what she was told, she was convinced that Tom, her regional manager, had been unduly pressured to hire this person, who had been referred by the CEO.

The decision to hire the outsider may have impressed the CEO, but it enraged Diana. With her successful track record as a store manager for the Cobb Street Grille, she was much more capable, in her opinion, of overseeing multiple units than someone who was new to the operation. Besides, district managers had always been promoted internally from among the store managers, and she was unofficially designated as the next one to move up to a district position. Tom had hired the outside candidate as a political maneuver to put himself in a good light with management, even though it meant overlooking a loyal employee like her in the process. Diana had no patience with people who made business decisions for the wrong reasons. She worked very hard to avoid politics–and it especially irritated her when the political actions of others negatively impacted her.

Diana was ready to be a district manager nine months ago, and she thought she was even more qualified today–provided the decision was based on performance. She ran a tight ship, managing her restaurant completely by the book. She meticulously adhered to policies and procedures and rigorously controlled expenses. Her sales were growing, in spite of new competition in the market, and she received relatively few customer complaints. The only number that was a little out of line was the higher turnover among her staff.

Diana was not too concerned about the increasing number of terminations, however; there was a perfectly logical explanation for this. It was because she had high standards for both herself and her employees. Any employee who delivered less than 110 percent at all times would be better off finding a job somewhere else. Diana didn't think she should bend the rules for anyone, for whatever reason. A few months ago, for example, she had to fire three otherwise good employees who decided to try a new customer service tactic–a so-called innovation they dreamed up–rather than complying with the established process. As the general manager, it was her responsibility to make sure that the restaurant was managed strictly in accordance with the operations manual, and she could not allow deviations. This by-the-book approach to managing had served her well for many years. It got her promoted in the past, and she was not about to jinx that now. Losing a few employees now and then–particularly those who had difficulty following the rules–was simply the cost of doing business.

During a recent store visit Julie suggested that Diana might try creating a friendlier work environment because she seemed aloof and interacted with employees somewhat mechanically. Julie even told her that she overheard employees refer to Diana as the "ice maiden" behind her back. Diana was surprised that Julie brought this up because her boss rarely criticized her. They had an unspoken agreement: Because Diana was so technically competent and always met her financial targets, Julie didn't need to give her much input. Diana was happy to be left alone to run her restaurant without needless advice.

At any rate, Diana rarely paid attention to what employees said about her. She wasn't about to let something as childish as a silly name cause her to modify a successful management strategy. What's more, even though she had recently lost more than the average number of employees due to "personality differences" or "miscommunications" over her directives, her superiors did not seem to mind when she consistently delivered strong bottom-line results every month.

As she waited in the conference room for the others, Diana worried that she was not going to get this promotion. Julie had sounded different in the voicemail message she left to inform her about this meeting, but Diana couldn't put her finger on exactly what it was. She would be very angry if she was passed over again and wondered what excuse they would have this time. Then her mind wandered to how her employees would respond to her if she did not get the promotion. They all knew how much she wanted the job, and she cringed at how embarrassed she would be if she didn't get it. Her eyes began to mist over at the sheer thought of having to face them if she was not promoted today.

Julie and Tom entered the room then, and the meeting started. They told Diana, as kindly as they could, that she would not be promoted at this time; one of her colleagues would become the new district manager. She was incredulous. The individual who got promoted had been with the company only three years–and Diana had trained her! She tried to comprehend how this happened, but it did not make sense. Before any further explanation could be offered, she burst into tears and left the room. As she tried in vain to regain her composure, Diana was overcome with crushing disappointment.

Discussion Questions

1. Within the framework of the emotional intelligence domains of self-awareness, self-management, social awareness, and relationship management, discuss the various factors that might have led to Diana's failure to be promoted.
2. What competencies does Diana need to develop to be promotable in the future? What can the company do to support her developmental efforts?

Case Study 4.2 TROUBLING EXITS AT MICROSOFT

BusinessWeek For most of its three decades, Microsoft has faced intense criticism, mostly from the outside world regarding its heavy-handed tactics. Now, the Redmond, Washington-based company is receiving its sharpest criticism from its own current and former employees. When superstar computer scientist Kai-Fu Lee bolted for Google, he called his former employer "incompetent." Around the same time, two current employees sent Microsoft chairman Bill Gates a memo saying that "everyone sees that a crisis is imminent." The 12-page document outlined "10 crazy ideas" to help Microsoft get out of its crisis.

This *BusinessWeek* case study describes several criticisms that Microsoft employees have complained about to their employer, and what some of them have done about the situation. The article examines some of the perks that Microsoft employees appreciate, as well as some of the current concerns they have working at the world's largest software company. Read the full text of this *BusinessWeek* article at www.mhhe.com/mcshane4e and prepare for the discussion questions below.

Discussion Questions

1. Use the exit-voice-loyalty-neglect model to describe some of the behaviors of Microsoft employees who seem dissatisfied with the software company.
2. What factors seem to dampen employee loyalty at Microsoft? Do you think continuance commitment is weak or strong here?

Source: J. Greene, "Troubling Exits at Microsoft," *BusinessWeek*, 26 September 2005, 98.

Class Exercise 4.3 STEM-AND-PROBE INTERVIEW ACTIVITY

PURPOSE To help you develop better awareness of others as well as to observe the effects of positive organizational behavior.

MATERIALS None.

INSTRUCTIONS This simple yet powerful exercise consists of students conducting and receiving a detailed stem-and-probe interview with other students in the class. Each student will have an opportunity to interview and be interviewed. However, to increase the variation and novelty of this experience, the student conducting the first interview should *not* be interviewed by the student who was just interviewed. Instead the instructor will either form groups of four students (two pairs) at the beginning of this exercise, or have two pairs of students swap after the first round. Each of the two sets of interviews should take 10 to 15 minutes and use a stem-and-probe interview method. The stem-and-probe method, as well as the topic of the interview, are described next.

STEM-AND-PROBE INTERVIEWING This interview method attempts to receive more detail from the interviewee than typically occurs in semistructured or structured interviews. The main interview question, called the "stem," is followed by a series of probing questions that encourages the interviewee to provide more details relating to a particular incident or situation. The stem question for this exercise is provided next. The interviewee can use several "probes" to elicit more detail; the best probe depends on the circumstances, such as what information has already been provided. Some common probe questions include these:

- "Tell me more about that."
- "What did you do next?"
- "Could you explain that further, please?"
- "What else can you remember about that event?"

Notice that these probes are open-ended questions, not closed-ended questions such as "Is there anything else you want to tell me?" in which a simple yes or no is possible. Stem-and-probe interviewing also improves when the interviewer engages in active listening and isn't afraid of silence–giving the interviewee time to think and motivating him or her to fill in the silence with new information.

INTERVIEW TOPIC In both sets of interviews, the "stem" question is this: "Describe two or three things you did this past week that made someone else feel better."

Throughout this interview process, the interviewer's task is to receive as much information as possible (that the interviewee is willing to divulge) about the details of these two or three things that the interviewee did over the past week.

Following the two sets of interviews (when each student has interviewed and been interviewed once), the class will discuss the emotional and attitudinal dynamics of this activity.

Team Exercise 4.4 RANKING JOBS BY THEIR EMOTIONAL LABOR

PURPOSE This exercise is designed to help you understand the jobs in which people tend to experience higher or lower degrees of emotional labor.

INSTRUCTIONS

1. Individually rank order the extent to which the jobs listed here require emotional labor. Assign a "1" to the job you believe requires the most effort, planning, and control to express organizationally desired emotions during interpersonal transactions. Assign a "10" to the job you believe requires the least amount of emotional labor. Mark your rankings in column 1.
2. The instructor will form teams of four or five members, and each team will rank order the items based on consensus (not simply averaging the individual rankings). These results should be placed in column 2.
3. The instructor will provide expert ranking information. This information should be written in column 3. Then you can calculate the differences in columns 4 and 5.
4. The class will compare the results and discuss the features of jobs with high emotional labor.

Occupational Emotional Labor Scoring Sheet

Occupation	(1) Individual Ranking	(2) Team Ranking	(3) Expert Ranking	(4) Absolute Difference of 1 and 3	(5) Absolute Difference of 2 and 3
Bartender					
Cashier					
Dental hygienist					
Insurance adjuster					
Lawyer					
Librarian					
Postal clerk					
Registered nurse					
Social worker					
Television announcer					
			TOTAL		
				Your score	Team score

(The lower the score, the better)

Self-Assessment 4.5

SCHOOL COMMITMENT SCALE

PURPOSE This self-assessment on page 130 is designed to help you understand the concept of organizational commitment and to assess your commitment to the college or university you are currently attending.

OVERVIEW The concept of commitment is as relevant to students enrolled in college or university courses as it is to employees working in various organizations. This self-assessment adapts a popular organizational commitment instrument, so it refers to your commitment as a student to the school you are attending.

INSTRUCTIONS Read each of the following statements and circle the response that best fits your personal belief. Then use the scoring key in Appendix B of this book to calculate your results. This self-assessment is completed alone so that you can rate yourself honestly without concerns of social comparison. However, class discussion will focus on the meaning of the different types of organizational commitment and how well this scale applies to the commitment of students toward the college or university they are attending.

Self-Assessment 4.6

DISPOSITIONAL MOOD SCALE (STUDENT OLC)

This self-assessment is designed to help you understand mood states or personality traits of emotions and to assess your own mood or emotion personality. This self-assessment consists of several words representing various emotions that you might have experienced. For each word presented, indicate the extent to which you have felt this way generally across all situations *over the past six months.* You need to be honest with yourself to receive a reasonable estimate of your mood state or personality trait on these scales. The results provide an estimate of your level on two emotional personality scales. This instrument is widely used in research, but it is only an estimate. You should not assume that the results are accurate without a more complete assessment by a trained professional.

School Commitment Scale

To what extent does each statement describe you? indicate your level of agreement by marking the appropriate response on the right	Strongly agree	Moderately agree	Slightly agree	Neutral	Slightly disagree	Moderately disagree	Strongly disagree
1. I would be very happy to complete the rest of my education at this school.	☐	☐	☐	☐	☐	☐	☐
2. One of the difficulties of leaving this school is that there are few alternatives.	☐	☐	☐	☐	☐	☐	☐
3. I really feel as if this school's problems are my own.	☐	☐	☐	☐	☐	☐	☐
4. Right now, staying enrolled at this school is a matter of necessity as much as desire.	☐	☐	☐	☐	☐	☐	☐
5. I do not feel a strong sense of belonging to this school.	☐	☐	☐	☐	☐	☐	☐
6. It would be very hard for me to leave this school right now even if I wanted to.	☐	☐	☐	☐	☐	☐	☐
7. I do not feel emotionally attached to this school.	☐	☐	☐	☐	☐	☐	☐
8. Too much of my life would be disrupted if I decided to move to a different school now.	☐	☐	☐	☐	☐	☐	☐
9. I do not feel like part of the "family" at this school.	☐	☐	☐	☐	☐	☐	☐
10. I feel that I have too few options to consider leaving this school.	☐	☐	☐	☐	☐	☐	☐
11. This school has a great deal of personal meaning for me.	☐	☐	☐	☐	☐	☐	☐
12. If I had not already put so much of myself into this school, I might consider completing my education elsewhere.	☐	☐	☐	☐	☐	☐	☐

Source: Adapted from: J.P. Meyer, N.J. Allen, and C.A. Smith, "Commitment to Organizations and Occupations: Extension and Test of a Three-Component Model," *Journal of Applied Psychology* 78 (1993), pp. 538–51.

After reading this chapter, if you need additional information, see **www.mhhe.com/mcshane4e** for more in-depth interactivities that correspond with this material.

David Gachuru lives by a motto that motivates employees more than money can buy: "If an employee's work calls for a thumbs-up, I will appreciate him or her as many times as possible." Translating this advice into practice is a daily event for the general manager of Panafric Hotel in Nairobi, Kenya. In addition to thanking staff personally and through e-mail messages, Gachuru holds bimonthly meetings where top-performing employees are congratulated and receive paid holidays with their family. Employee achievements are also celebrated in the hotel's newsletter, which is distributed to guests as well as employees.

Panafric Hotel in Nairobi, Kenya, motivates its employees through plenty of praise and recognition. "If an employee's work calls for a thumbs-up, I will appreciate him or her as many times as possible," says Panafric general manager David Gachuru, shown in this photo (left) presenting an award to employee of the month Matayo Moyale.

Panafric Hotel and other firms are returning to good old-fashioned praise and recognition to motivate staff. Share options can evaporate and incentive plans might backfire, but a few words of appreciation almost always create a warm glow of satisfaction and renewed energy. The challenge of recognition is to "catch" employees doing extraordinary things. Keyspan Corporation chairman Bob Catell resolves this by regularly asking managers for lists of "unsung heroes" at the New England gas utility. He calls an employee every week, often spending the first few minutes convincing the listener that the CEO really is calling. "They start by saying, 'Hey, you can't fool me, this isn't Catell!' But once they realize it is me, they are pleased that I would take the time to do this."

Along with recognition from managers, approximately one-third of large American firms rely on peer recognition as one way to motivate employees. Among them is Yum Brands Inc., the parent company of KFC, Taco Bell, and Pizza Hut. Yum's restaurants around the world use a recognition program in which employees reward colleagues with "Champs" cards, an acronym for KFC's values (cleanliness, hospitality, and so on). The Ritz Carlton Hotel in Kuala Lumpur, which is rated as one of the best places to work in Asia, applies a similar peer recognition process using First Class cards. Nancy Teoh, Ritz Carlton Kuala Lumpur's human resources manager, explains that "congratulatory messages or words of appreciation are written down by any member of the team to another and even as far as from the hotel and corporate senior leaders." Teoh adds, "This serves as a motivational aspect of the work environment."[1]

5

Motivation in the Workplace

LEARNING OBJECTIVES

After reading this chapter you should be able to

1. Explain why motivating employees has become more challenging in recent years.
2. Summarize Maslow's needs hierarchy and discuss its contribution and limitations to employee motivation.
3. Describe four-drive theory and explain how these drives influence motivation.
4. Summarize McClelland's learned needs theory, including the three needs he studied.
5. Discuss the practical implications of motivation theories relating to needs and drives.
6. Diagram the expectancy theory model and discuss its practical implications for motivating employees.
7. Describe the characteristics of effective goal setting and feedback.
8. Summarize the equity theory model, including how people try to reduce feelings of inequity.
9. Identify the factors that influence procedural justice, as well as the consequences of procedural justice.

Learning Objectives

After reading this section you should be able to

1. Explain why motivating employees has become more challenging in recent years.

Motivating Employees

motivation
The forces within a person that affect his or her direction, intensity, and persistence of voluntary behavior.

First Class cards at Ritz Carlton Hotel, Champs cards at Yum Brands, telephone calls from the CEO of Keyspan, and various celebrations for good performance at Panafric Hotel are designed to maintain and improve employee motivation. **Motivation** refers to the forces within a person that affect the direction, intensity, and persistence of voluntary behavior.[2] Motivated employees are willing to exert a particular level of effort (intensity) for a certain amount of time (persistence) toward a particular goal (direction). Motivation is one of the four essential drivers of individual behavior and performance (see the MARS model in Chapter 2) and, consequently, is an integral component of employee engagement. An engaged workforce is an important predictor of an organization's competitiveness, so it's easy to see why employee motivation is continuously on the minds of corporate leaders.

The quest for a motivated and engaged workforce has not been easy, however. Most employers–92 percent of them, according to one major survey–say that motivating employees has become more challenging. Three factors seem to be responsible for this increasing challenge. First, globalization, information technology, corporate restructuring, and other changes have dramatically altered the employment relationship. These changes potentially undermine the levels of trust and commitment necessary to energize employees beyond minimum standards.[3]

Second, in decades past, companies typically relied on armies of supervisors to closely monitor employee behavior and performance. Even if commitment and trust were low, employees performed their jobs with the boss watching them closely. But most companies thinned their supervisory ranks when they flattened organizational structure to reduce costs. Supervisors now have many more employees, so they can't possibly keep a watchful eye out for laggards. This is just as well because today's educated workforce resents the old command-and-control approach to performance management. Most people enjoy the feeling of being motivated, but this requires the right conditions; so employers need to search for more contemporary ways to motivate staff.

The third challenge is that a new generation of employees has brought different expectations to the workplace. A few years ago various writers disparaged Generation-X and Generation-Y employees as slackers, cynics, whiners, and malcontents. Now we know that the problem wasn't their lack of motivational potential; it was that employers didn't know how to motivate them! It seems that many companies still haven't figured this out: According to one report more than 40 percent of employees aged 25 to 34 sometimes or frequently feel demotivated, compared to 30 percent of 35- to 44-year-olds and just 18 percent of 45- to 54-year-olds.[4]

We begin the process of understanding and facilitating employee motivation by looking at the core theories of motivation in organizational settings. The chapter begins by describing Maslow's needs hierarchy theory and explaining the shortfalls of this incredibly popular theory as well as other needs hierarchy models. We then turn to four-drive theory and McClelland's learned needs theory, both of which offer more promise. Next this chapter introduces expectancy theory, which is a rational decision approach to employee motivation. The fourth section of this chapter covers the key elements of goal setting and feedback, including the topics of multisource feedback and executive coaching. In the final section we look at organizational justice, including the dimensions and dynamics of equity theory and procedural justice.

Learning Objectives

After reading this section you should be able to

2. **Summarize Maslow's needs hierarchy and discuss its contribution and limitations to employee motivation.**
3. **Describe four-drive theory and explain how these drives influence motivation.**
4. **Summarize McClelland's learned needs theory, including the three needs he studied.**
5. **Discuss the practical implications of motivation theories relating to needs and drives.**

Needs, Drives, and Employee Motivation

needs
Deficiencies that energize or trigger behaviors to satisfy those needs.

drives
Instinctive or innate tendencies to seek certain goals or maintain internal stability.

Motivation begins with individual needs and their underlying drives. In spite of some confusion in the literature regarding these terms, we will define **needs** as deficiencies that energize or trigger behaviors to satisfy those needs. Unfulfilled needs create a tension that makes us want to find ways to reduce or satisfy those needs. The stronger your needs, the more motivated you are to satisfy them. Conversely, a satisfied need does not motivate. **Drives** are instinctive or innate tendencies to seek certain goals or maintain internal stability. Drives are hardwired in the brain–everyone has the same drives–and they most likely exist to help the species survive.[5] Needs are typically produced by drives, but they may also be strengthened through learning (reinforcement) and social forces such as culture and childhood upbringing. We'll discuss needs and drives later in this section after describing Maslow and other needs hierarchy theories.

Maslow's Needs Hierarchy Theory

Maslow's needs hierarchy theory
Maslow's motivation theory of five instinctive needs arranged in a hierarchy, whereby people are motivated to fulfill a higher need as a lower one becomes gratified.

More people have probably heard about **Maslow's needs hierarchy theory** than any other concept in organizational behavior. Developed by psychologist Abraham Maslow in the 1940s, the model has been applied in almost every human pursuit, from marketing products to rehabilitating prison inmates. This incredible popularity is rather odd considering that most research has reported little or no support for the theory. According to his later journal entries, even Maslow was amazed that people had accepted his theory wholeheartedly with any critique. Normally a theory that fails to live up to its predictions is laid to rest. However, Maslow's model is described here because it significantly altered the way experts now think about and study motivation and behavior in the workplace.

self-actualization
The need for self-fulfillment—a sense that a person's potential has been realized.

Maslow's needs hierarchy theory condenses and integrates the long list of needs that had been studied previously into a hierarchy of five basic categories.[6] As Exhibit 5.1 illustrates, physiological needs (food, air, water, shelter, and the like) are at the bottom of the hierarchy. Next are safety needs–the need for a secure and stable environment and the absence of pain, threat, or illness. Belongingness includes the need for love, affection, and interaction with other people. Esteem includes self-esteem through personal achievement as well as social esteem through recognition and respect from others. At the top of the hierarchy is **self-actualization**, which represents

Exhibit 5.1
Maslow's Needs Hierarchy

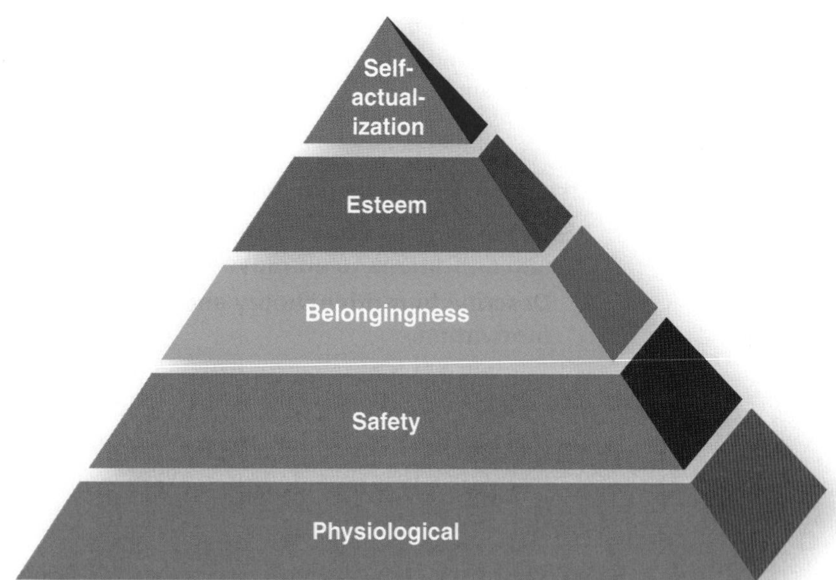

Source: Based on information in: A.H. Maslow, "A Theory of Human Motivation," *Psychological Review* 50 (1943), pp. 370–96.

the need for self-fulfillment–a sense that a person's potential has been realized. In addition to these five, Maslow describes the need to know and need for aesthetic beauty as two needs that do not fit within the hierarchy.

Maslow says that we are motivated simultaneously by several needs, but the strongest source is the lowest unsatisfied need at the time. As a person satisfies a lower-level need, the next higher need in the hierarchy becomes the primary motivator and remains so even if never satisfied. Physiological needs are initially the most important, and people are motivated to satisfy them first. As they become gratified, safety needs emerge as the strongest motivator. As safety needs are satisfied, belongingness needs become most important, and so forth. The exception to this need fulfillment process is self-actualization; as people experience self-actualization, they desire more rather than less of this need. Thus while the bottom four groups are *deficiency needs* because they become activated when unfulfilled, self-actualization is known as a *growth need* because it continues to develop even when fulfilled.

As was mentioned earlier, Maslow's needs hierarchy theory has not received much scientific support.[7] Researchers have found that needs do not cluster neatly around the hierarchy's five categories. Also, gratification of one need level does not necessarily lead to increased motivation to satisfy the next higher need level. Some people can be very hungry and yet strive to fulfill their social needs; others can self-actualize while working in a risky environment. The theory also assumes that need priorities shift over months or years, whereas the importance of a particular need likely changes more quickly with the situation.

Maslow's Contribution to Motivation Theories In spite of the flaws of needs hierarchy theory, Maslow's writing dramatically shifted the study of human motivation to one that is more holistic, humanistic, and positive. First, Maslow brought a more holistic perspective by introducing the notion that needs are related to each other and, consequently, should be studied together. Prior to his needs hierarchy model,

Belongingness Needs Top the Hierarchy for Some Employees These UBS Warburg employees in Chicago seem to be enjoying each other's company, suggesting that they are experiencing some fulfillment of their belongingness needs. But do they all have the same needs hierarchy? Not according to emerging research and writing on this subject. Contrary to Maslow's well-known theory, needs are not hardwired into a universal hierarchy. Instead a person's needs hierarchy seems to be strongly influenced by his or her value system, so needs hierarchies vary from one person to the next and possibly from one culture to the next. The UBS Warburg staff in this photo probably have somewhat different value systems, so their needs hierarchies would be different.

motivation experts had splintered needs and drives into dozens of categories, each studied in isolation using nontypical subjects (usually animals or people with severe psychological dysfunctions).[8] He argued that isolating narrowly defined needs and drives was inappropriate because human behavior is typically initiated by more than one of these needs or drives with varying degrees of influence on that behavior. Second, when most researchers focused on human instincts as direct drivers of employee motivation and behavior, Maslow argued that higher-order needs are influenced by social dynamics and culture, not just instincts. In other words, he explained how human thoughts play a role in motivation.

Maslow's third contribution was to introduce a more positive perspective of employee motivation. Previously scholars focused on drive "deprivation" (particularly hunger), whereas Maslow suggested that need "gratification" is just as important in motivating people. Indeed Maslow's most important contribution is his work on self-actualization, which he considered far more important than the needs hierarchy model.[9] Throughout his career Maslow emphasized that people are naturally motivated to reach their potential (once lower needs are fulfilled) and that organizations and societies need to be structured to help people continue and develop this motivation. Maslow called for more "enlightened management" to provide meaningful work and freedom, rather than tedious work with oppressive bureaucratic controls, so employees can experience self-actualization and fulfill their other needs.[10] This view of employee motivation, which was novel at the time, has become the foundation of **positive organizational behavior** (a variation of *positive psychology*), which focuses on building positive qualities and traits within individuals or institutions as

positive organizational behavior
Building positive qualities and traits within individuals or institutions as opposed to focusing on just trying to fix what might be wrong with them.

opposed to focusing on just trying to fix what might be wrong with them. In other words, this approach emphasizes building on strengths rather than trying to correct weaknesses.[11]

What's Wrong with Needs Hierarchy Models?

ERG theory
A needs hierarchy theory consisting of three instinctive needs—existence, relatedness, and growth.

Maslow's theory is not the only attempt to map employee needs onto a single hierarchy. The most comprehensive of the alternative models is **ERG theory**, which reorganizes Maslow's five groups into three–existence, relatedness, and growth.[12] Unlike Maslow's theory, which only explained how people progress up the hierarchy, ERG theory also describes how people regress down the hierarchy when they fail to fulfill higher needs. ERG theory seems to explain human motivation somewhat better than Maslow's needs hierarchy, but that's mainly because it is easier to cluster human needs around ERG's three categories than Maslow's five categories. Otherwise, the research findings are fairly clear that ERG theory only marginally improves our understanding of human needs.[13]

Why have Maslow's needs hierarchy, ERG theory, and other needs hierarchies largely failed to explain the dynamics of employee needs? The most glaring explanation is that people don't fit into a single universal needs hierarchy. Some people seem preoccupied with social status even though they haven't fulfilled their lower needs; others consider personal development and growth an ongoing priority over social relations or status. There is increasing evidence that needs hierarchies are unique, not universal, because needs are strongly influenced by each individual's personal values. If your most important values lean toward stimulation and self-direction, you probably pay more attention to self-actualization needs. If power and achievement are at the top of your value system, then status needs might be stronger most of the time. This connection between values and needs suggests that a needs hierarchy is unique to each person and can change over time, just as values change over a lifetime.[14]

Four-Drive Theory

Motivation experts have mostly abandoned needs hierarchy theories, but not the notion that needs and drives are relevant. On the contrary, recent discoveries about how the brain functions have prompted experts to consider a more coherent and integrated approach to innate drives. Building on recent research on neuroscience, emotions, anthropology, and emotional intelligence, Harvard Business School professors Paul Lawrence and Nitin Nohria have proposed **four-drive theory** to explain human motivation.[15] This model is both holistic (it pulls together the many drives and needs) and humanistic (it considers human thought and social influences rather than just instinct). These were two conditions that Maslow felt were essential for a solid theory of human motivation.

four-drive theory
A motivation theory based on the innate drives to acquire, bond, learn, and defend that incorporates both emotions and rationality.

Four Fundamental Drives

Four-drive theory organizes drives into four categories: the drives to acquire, bond, learn, and defend. These drives are innate and universal, meaning that they are hardwired in our brains through evolution and are found in everyone. They are also independent of each other, so one drive is neither dependent on nor inherently inferior or superior to another drive. Four-drive theory also states that these four drives are a complete set–no other fundamental drives are excluded from the model. Another key feature is that three of the four drives are "proactive," meaning that we regularly try to fulfill them. Thus any notion of fulfilling drives is temporary at best.

- *Drive to acquire.* This is the drive to seek, take, control, and retain objects and personal experiences. The drive to acquire extends beyond basic food and water; it includes the need for relative status and recognition in society. Thus it is the foundation of competition and the basis of our need for esteem. Four-drive theory states that the drive to acquire is insatiable because the purpose of human motivation is to achieve a higher position than others, not just to fulfill our physiological needs.
- *Drive to bond.* This is the drive to form social relationships and develop mutual caring commitments with others. It also explains why people form social identities by aligning their self-image with various social groups (see Chapter 3). Research indicates that people invest considerable time and effort forming and maintaining relationships without any special circumstances or ulterior motives. Indeed, recent evidence shows that people who lack social contact are more prone to serious health problems.[16] The drive to bond motivates people to cooperate and, consequently, is a fundamental ingredient in the success of organizations and the development of societies.
- *Drive to learn.* This is the drive to satisfy our curiosity, to know and understand ourselves and the environment around us. When observing something that is inconsistent with or beyond our current knowledge, we experience a tension that motivates us to close that information gap. In fact, studies in the 1950s revealed that people who are removed from any novel information will crave even boring information (outdated stock reports) to satisfy their drive to learn![17] The drive to learn is related to the higher-order needs of growth and self-actualization described earlier.
- *Drive to defend.* This is the drive to protect ourselves physically and socially. Probably the first drive to develop, it creates a "fight-or-flight" response in the face of personal danger. The drive to defend goes beyond protecting our physical selves. It includes defending our relationships, our acquisitions, and our belief systems. The drive to defend is always reactive–it is triggered by threat. In contrast, the other three drives are always proactive–we actively seek to improve our acquisitions, relationships, and knowledge.

How Drives Influence Employee Motivation To understand how these four drives translate into employee motivation, recall from previous chapters that our perceptions of the external world are influenced by our emotions. Every meaningful bit of information we receive is quickly and unconsciously tagged with emotional markers that subsequently shape our logical analysis of the situation. Our motivation to act is a result of rational thinking influenced by these emotional markers.[18]

The four drives fit into this tango of emotionality and rationality because they determine which emotional markers, if any, are attached to the perceived information. For example, suppose your department has just received a new computer program that you are curious to try out (triggered by your drive to learn). However, your boss says that you are not experienced enough to use the new system yet, which makes you somewhat angry (triggered by your drive to defend against the "inexperience" insult). Both the curiosity about the software program and your anger from the boss's beliefs about your experience demand your attention and energize you to act. The key point here is that the four innate drives determine which emotions are generated in each situation.

Four-drive theory further explains that this process is conscious (humanistic) rather than instinctive because these drives produce independent and often competing

Exhibit 5.2 Four-Drive Theory of Motivation

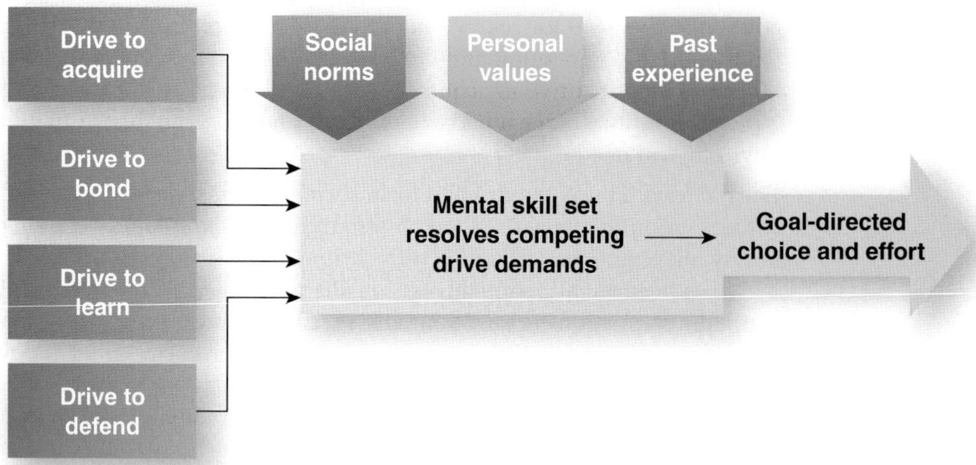

Source: Based on information in P.R. Lawrence and N. Nohria, *Driven: How Human Nature Shapes Our Choices* (San Francisco: Jossey-Bass, 2002).

signals that often require our attention.[19] As Exhibit 5.2 illustrates, we resolve these dilemmas through a built-in skill set that takes into account social norms, past experience, and personal values. The result is goal-directed decision making and effort that fit within the constraints of cultural and moral expectations. In other words, our conscious analysis of competing demands from the four drives generates needs that energize us to act in ways acceptable to society and our own moral compass.

Evaluating Four-Drive Theory Four-drive theory potentially offers a rich explanation for employee motivation. It avoids the assumption found in needs hierarchy theories that everyone has the same needs hierarchy. Instead it explains how our needs are based on innate drives, how emotions are generated from those drives in the context of a specific situation, and how personal experience and cultural values influence the intensity, persistence, and direction of effort. Four-drive theory also provides a much clearer understanding about the role of emotional intelligence in employee motivation and behavior. Employees with high emotional intelligence are more sensitive to competing demands from the four drives, are better able to avoid impulsive behavior from those drives, and can judge the best way to act to fulfill those drive demands in a social context.

Four-drive theory is based on some fairly solid evidence regarding (1) the existence and dynamics of the four innate drives and (2) the interaction of emotions and cognitions (logical thinking) in employee behavior. However, the overall model is quite new and requires much more work to clarify the role of skill sets in forming goal-directed choice and effort. The theory also ignores the fact that needs can be strengthened through learning. Four-drive theory likely accommodates the notion of learned needs, but it does not explain them. Fortunately other motivational researchers, notably David McClelland, have provided some clarification about learned needs, which we examine next.

Theory of Learned Needs

At the beginning of this chapter we learned that needs typically originate from drives. For instance, your need for belongingness is created out of the innate drive to bond. But needs can also be strengthened through reinforcement, including through childhood learning, parental styles, and social norms. Psychologist David McClelland popularized the idea of learned needs years ago through his research on three learned needs: achievement, power, and affiliation.

need for achievement (nAch)
A learned need in which people want to accomplish reasonably challenging goals, and desire unambiguous feedback and recognition for their success.

- *Need for achievement (nAch).* People with a strong **need for achievement (nAch)** want to accomplish reasonably challenging goals through their own effort. They prefer working alone rather than in teams, and they choose tasks with a moderate degree of risk (neither too easy nor impossible to complete). High nAch people also desire unambiguous feedback and recognition for their success. Money is a weak motivator, except when it provides feedback and recognition.[20] In contrast, employees with a low nAch perform their work better when money is used as an incentive. Successful entrepreneurs tend to have a high nAch, possibly because they establish challenging goals for themselves and thrive on competition.[21]

need for affiliation (nAff)
A learned need in which people seek approval from others, conform to their wishes and expectations, and avoid conflict and confrontation.

- *Need for affiliation (nAff).* **Need for affiliation (nAff)** refers to a desire to seek approval from others, conform to their wishes and expectations, and avoid conflict and confrontation. People with a strong nAff try to project a favorable image of themselves. They tend to actively support others and try to smooth out workplace conflicts. High nAff employees general work well in coordinating roles to mediate conflicts, and in sales positions where the main task is cultivating long-term relations. However, they tend to be less effective at allocating scarce resources and making other decisions that potentially generate conflict. People in decision-making positions must have a relatively low need for affiliation so that their choices and actions are not biased by a personal need for approval.[22]

need for power (nPow)
A learned need in which people want to control their environment, including people and material resources, to benefit either themselves (personalized power) or others (socialized power).

- *Need for power (nPow).* People with a high **need for power (nPow)** want to exercise control over others and are concerned about maintaining their leadership positions. They frequently rely on persuasive communication, make more suggestions in meetings, and tend to publicly evaluate situations more frequently. McClelland pointed out that there are two types of nPow. Those who enjoy their power for its own sake use it to advance personal interests, and wear their power as a status symbol have *personalized power.* Others mainly have a high need for *socialized power* because they desire power as a means to help others.[23] McClelland asserted that leaders are more effective when they have a high need for socialized rather than personalized power. They should have a high degree of altruism and social responsibility and must be concerned about the consequences of their own actions on others.

Learning Needs McClelland argued that achievement, affiliation, and power needs can be strengthened through learning, so he developed training programs for this purpose. In his achievement motivation program, trainees write achievement-oriented stories and practice achievement-oriented behaviors in business games. They also complete a detailed achievement plan for the next two years and form a reference group with other trainees to maintain their newfound achievement motive style.[24] These programs seem to work. Participants attending a need for achievement course in India subsequently started more new businesses, had greater community involvement, invested more in expanding their businesses, and employed twice as many people as nonparticipants. Research on similar achievement motive courses for American small business owners reported dramatic increases in the profitability of the participants' businesses.

Practical Implications of Needs/Drive-Based Theories

Needs- and drive-based theories, and particularly four-drive theory, offer some practical advice for motivating employees. The main recommendation that Lawrence and Nohria provide from four-drive theory is to ensure that individual jobs and workplaces provide balanced opportunities to fulfill the drives to acquire, bond, learn, and defend.[25] There are really two key recommendations here. The first one is that everyone in the workplace needs to regularly fulfill all four drives. This contrasts sharply with the ill-fated needs hierarchy theories, which suggested that employees are motivated mainly by one need at a time. Four-drive theory says that each of us continuously seeks fulfillment of our innate drives. Thus the best workplaces for motivation and morale provide sufficient rewards, learning opportunities, social interaction, and so forth for all employees.

The second recommendation from four-drive theory is that these four drives must be kept in "balance"; that is, organizations should avoid too much or too little opportunity to fulfill each drive. The reason for this advice is that the four drives counterbalance each other. Companies that help employees fulfill one drive but not the others will face long-term problems. An organization that energizes the drive to acquire without the drive to bond may eventually suffer from organizational politics and dysfunctional conflict. Change and novelty in the workplace will aid the drive to learn, but too much of it will trigger the drive to defend so that employees become territorial and resistant to change. Creating a workplace that supports the drive to bond can, at extreme levels, undermine the diversity and constructive debate required for effective decision making.

Another recommendation from the needs/drives-based theories is to offer employees a choice of rewards rather than giving everyone the same specific reward. Although we possess the same drives and require their ongoing fulfillment, people differ in their needs at any given time. Due to their unique value systems and experiences, some employees generally have a strong need to achieve, whereas others are motivated more by social factors. A narrow application of this recommendation is to let employees choose their own rewards. Farm Fresh Supermarkets accomplishes this by awarding points to employees for good customer service. These points are later redeemed for reward gifts from a catalog. "There are several hundred items in [the catalog], and they can get everything from a T-shirt to a toaster oven, coffee maker, and a vacuum

Sony Suffers from Lack of Four-Drive Balance According to four-drive theory, companies that help employees fulfill one drive much more than the others will face long-term problems. This seems to explain the current challenges facing Sony. The Japanese company, which led the electronics world a decade ago with its Walkman and Playstation innovations, is now struggling to keep up with competitors. One reason for the current difficulties is that Sony executives allowed a hypercompetitive culture to develop, where engineers were encouraged to outdo each other rather than work together. This competitive culture fed employees' drive to acquire, but the lack of balance with the drive to bond led to infighting and information hoarding. For instance, competitive rivalries within Sony delayed the company's launch of a digital music player and online music service to compete against Apple's iPod and iTunes music Web site.[26]

cleaner," explains Ron Dennis, president of the Virginia Beach, Virginia–based grocery chain.[27] At a broader level, employees need to have career choices and diverse opportunities to discover and experience their potential. One of the enduring recommendations from Maslow's work on self-actualization is that employees must have sufficient freedom to discover their potential. It cannot be assumed or dictated by management.

Learning Objectives

After reading this section you should be able to

6. Diagram the expectancy theory model and discuss its practical implications for motivating employees.

Expectancy Theory of Motivation

expectancy theory The motivation theory based on the idea that work effort is directed toward behaviors that people believe will lead to desired outcomes.

The theories described so far mainly explain what motivates employees. But how do these drives and needs translate into specific effort and behavior? One of the best theories to answer this question is expectancy theory of motivation. **Expectancy theory** is based on the idea that work effort is directed toward behaviors that people believe will lead to desired outcomes.[28] Through experience, we develop expectations about whether we can achieve various levels of job performance. We also develop expectations about whether job performance and work behaviors lead to particular outcomes. Finally, we naturally direct our effort toward outcomes that help us fulfill our needs.

Expectancy Theory Model

The expectancy theory model is presented in Exhibit 5.3. The key variable of interest in expectancy theory is *effort*–the individual's actual exertion of energy. An individual's effort level depends on three factors: effort-to-performance (E-to-P) expectancy, performance-to-outcome (P-to-O) expectancy, and outcome valences (V). Employee motivation is influenced by all three components of the expectancy theory model. If any component weakens, motivation weakens.

E-to-P Expectancy The *effort-to-performance (E-to-P) expectancy* is the individual's perception that his or her effort will result in a particular level of performance. Expectancy is defined as a probability and therefore ranges from 0.0 to 1.0. In some

Exhibit 5.3
Expectancy Theory of Motivation

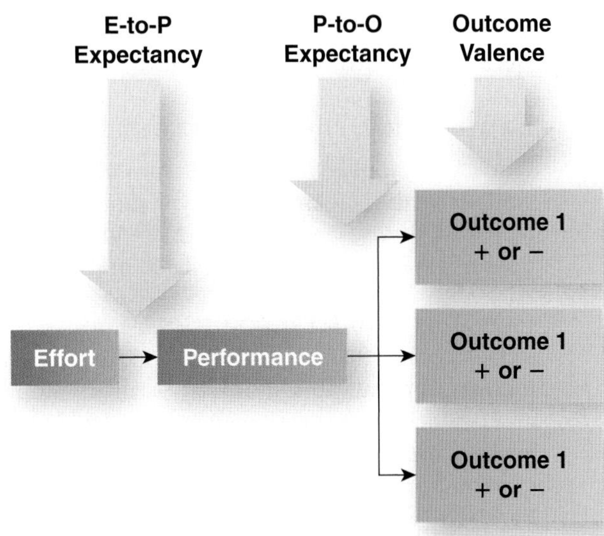

situations employees may believe that they can unquestionably accomplish the task (a probability of 1.0). In other situations they expect that even their highest level of effort will not result in the desired performance level (a probability of 0.0). For instance, unless you are an expert skier, you probably aren't motivated to try some of the black diamond ski runs at Vale. The reason is a very low E-to-P expectancy. Even your best effort won't get you down the hill on your feet! In most cases the E-to-P expectancy falls somewhere between these two extremes.

P-to-O Expectancy The *performance-to-outcome (P-to-O) expectancy* is the perceived probability that a specific behavior or performance level will lead to specific outcomes. This probability is developed from previous learning. For example, students learn from experience that skipping class either ruins their chance of a good grade or has no effect at all. In extreme cases employees may believe that accomplishing a particular task (performance) will definitely result in a particular outcome (a probability of 1.0), or they may believe that this outcome will have no effect on successful performance (a probability of 0.0). More often the P-to-O expectancy falls somewhere between 0.0 and 1.0.

One important issue in P-to-O expectancies is which outcomes we think about. We certainly don't evaluate the P-to-O expectancy for every possible outcome; there are too many of them. Instead we think only about outcomes of interest to us at the time. Sometimes your motivation to complete a task may be fueled mainly by the likelihood of getting off work early to meet friends. At other times your motivation to complete the same task may be based more on the P-to-O expectancy of a promotion or pay increase. The main point is that your motivation depends on the probability that a behavior or job performance level will result in outcomes that you think about.

valence
The anticipated satisfaction or dissatisfaction that an individual feels toward an outcome.

Outcome Valences The third element in expectancy theory is the **valence** of each outcome that you consider. Valence refers to the anticipated satisfaction or dissatisfaction that an individual feels toward an outcome. It ranges from negative to positive. (The actual range doesn't matter; it may be from −1 to +1 or from −100 to +100.) An outcome valence represents a person's anticipated satisfaction with the outcome.[29] Outcomes have a positive valence when they are consistent with our values and satisfy our needs; they have a negative valence when they oppose our values and inhibit need fulfillment. If you have a strong need for social interaction, for example, you would value group activities and other events that help to fulfill that need. Outcomes that move you further away from fulfilling your social need–such as working alone from home–will have a strong negative valence.

Expectancy Theory in Practice

One of the appealing characteristics of expectancy theory is that it provides clear guidelines for increasing employee motivation by altering the person's E-to-P expectancies, P-to-O expectancies, and/or outcome valences.[30] Several practical implications of expectancy theory are listed in Exhibit 5.4 and described next.

Increasing E-to-P Expectancies E-to-P expectancies are influenced by the individual's belief that he or she can successfully complete the task. Some companies increase this can-do attitude by assuring employees that they have the necessary competencies, clear role perceptions, and necessary resources to reach the desired levels of performance. Matching employees to jobs based on their abilities and clearly communicating the tasks required for the job is an important part of this process. Similarly, E-to-P expectancies are learned, so behavioral modeling and supportive

Exhibit 5.4 Practical Applications of Expectancy Theory

Expectancy theory component	Objective	Applications
E→P expectancies	To increase the belief that employees are capable of performing the job successfully.	• Select people with the required skills and knowledge. • Provide required training and clarify job requirements. • Provide sufficient time and resources. • Assign simpler or fewer tasks until employees can master them. • Provide examples of similar employees who have successfully performed the task. • Provide coaching to employees who lack self-confidence.
P→O expectancies	To increase the belief that good performance will result in particular (valued) outcomes.	• Measure job performance accurately. • Clearly describe the outcomes that will result from successful performance. • Describe how the employee's rewards were based on past performance. • Provide examples of other employees whose good performance has resulted in higher rewards.
Valences of outcomes	To increase the expected value of outcomes resulting from desired performance.	• Distribute rewards that employees value. • Individualize rewards. • Minimize the presence of countervalent outcomes.

feedback (positive reinforcement) typically strengthen the individual's belief that he or she is able to perform the task.[31]

Increasing P-to-O Expectancies The most obvious ways to improve P-to-O expectancies are to measure employee performance accurately and distribute more valued rewards to those with higher job performance. Unfortunately many organizations have difficulty putting this straightforward idea into practice. Some executives are reluctant to withhold rewards for poor performance because they don't want to experience conflict with employees. Others don't measure employee performance very well. For instance, fewer than half of the 6,000 employees surveyed in one study said they know how to increase their base pay or cash bonuses. In other words, most employees and managers have a generally low P-to-O expectancy regarding their paychecks.[32] Chapter 6 looks at reasons why rewards aren't connected to job performance.

P-to-O expectancies are perceptions, so employees should believe that higher performance will result in higher rewards. Having a performance-based reward system is important, but this fact must be communicated. When rewards are distributed, employees should understand how their rewards have been based on past performance. More generally, companies need to regularly communicate the existence of a performance-based reward system through examples, anecdotes, and public ceremonies.

Increasing Outcome Valences Performance outcomes influence work effort only when those outcomes are valued by employees. This brings us back to what we learned from the needs/drives-based theories of motivation–namely, that companies should develop more individualized reward systems so that employees who perform well are offered a choice of rewards. Expectancy theory also emphasizes the need to discover and neutralize countervalent outcomes. These are performance outcomes that have negative valences, thereby reducing the effectiveness of existing reward systems. For example, peer pressure may cause some employees to perform their jobs at the minimum standard even though formal rewards and the job itself would otherwise motivate them to perform at higher levels.

Does Expectancy Theory Fit Reality?

Expectancy theory remains one of the better theories for predicting work effort and motivation. In particular, it plays a valuable role by detailing a person's thinking process when translating the competing demands of the four drives into specific effort. Expectancy theory has been applied to a wide variety of studies, such as predicting student motivation to participate in teaching evaluations, using a decision support system, leaving the organization, and engaging in organizational citizenship behaviors.[33] Research also indicates that expectancy theory predicts employee motivation in different cultures.[34]

One limitation is that expectancy theory seems to ignore the central role of emotion in employee effort and behavior. As we learned earlier in this and previous chapters, emotions serve an adaptive function that demands our attention and energizes us to take action. The valence element of expectancy theory captures some of this emotional process, but only peripherally. Thus theorists probably need to redesign the expectancy theory model in light of new information about the importance of emotions in motivation and behavior.

Learning Objectives

After reading this section you should be able to

7. Describe the characteristics of effective goal setting and feedback.

Goal Setting and Feedback

Walk into almost any call center and you will notice that performance is judged on several metrics such as average pickup time (time to answer the call), length of time per call, and abandon rates (customers who hang up before the call is handled by a customer service representative). For example, one recent survey reported that the average pickup time for call centers in the United States is 35 seconds, the average talk time is 11 minutes for government and 6.5 minutes for private call centers, and the average time on hold is 33 seconds. Some call centers have large electronic boards showing how many customers are waiting and the average time they have been waiting. Employees sometimes receive feedback on their computers, such as the average length of time for each call at their workstation.[35] Associated with these numbers are specific goals, and supervisors conduct goal-setting sessions with each employee to help them understand and achieve those objectives.

goal setting
The process of motivating employees and clarifying their role perceptions by establishing performance objectives.

Call centers rely on goal setting and feedback to motivate employees and achieve superior performance.[36] **Goal setting** is the process of motivating employees and clarifying their role perceptions by establishing performance objectives. It potentially improves employee performance in two ways: (1) by stretching the intensity and persistence of effort and (2) by giving employees clearer role perceptions so that their effort is channeled toward behaviors that will improve work performance.

Stretch Goals Send Speedera Staff to the Beach Near the end of a recent financial quarter, Speedera Network's 120 employees in Bangalore, India, and Santa Clara, California, received an enticing challenge from founder and CEO Ajit Gupta: "If we pull together to achieve our business targets [for the next quarter], then we'll all be on a beach in May." Employees at the Internet applications company (now merged with Akamai) even voted on the preferred destination (a Hawaiian resort). Speedera would cover employee expenses as well as 50 percent of a spouse's or family member's expenses for four days. Everyone worked feverishly toward the company's goals, which included a hefty increase in revenue. Their motivation was further fueled with constant reminders of the Hawaiian trip. "The offices were transformed to look like tropical islands," says Gupta. Staff also received postcards and brochures with tempting images of the resort and its attractions. Much to everyone's delight, the company achieved its goals and Speedera staff from both countries had a memorable bonding experience on Hawaiian beaches.[37]

Characteristics of Effective Goals

Goal setting is more complex than simply telling someone to "do your best." Instead it requires six conditions to maximize task effort and performance: specific goals, relevant goals, challenging goals, goal commitment, participation in goal formation (sometimes), and goal feedback.[38]

- *Specific goals.* Employees put more effort into a task when they work toward specific goals rather than "do your best" targets.[39] Specific goals have measurable levels of change over a specific and relatively short time frame, such as "reduce scrap rate by 7 percent over the next six months." Specific goals communicate precise performance expectations so employees can direct their effort more efficiently and reliably.
- *Relevant goals.* Goals must also be relevant to the individual's job and within his or her control. For example, a goal to reduce waste materials would have little value if employees don't have much control over waste in the production process.
- *Challenging goals.* Challenging goals (rather than easy ones) cause people to raise the intensity and persistence of their work effort and to think through information more actively. They also fulfill a person's need for achievement or self-actualization needs when the goal is achieved. General Electric, Goldman Sachs, and many other organizations emphasize *stretch goals.* These goals don't just stretch your abilities and motivation; they are goals that you don't know how to reach, so you need to be creative to achieve them.[40]
- *Goal commitment.* Although goals should be challenging, employees also need to be committed to accomplishing goals. Thus we need to find an optimal level of goal difficulty where the goals are challenging, yet employees are still motivated to achieve them.[41] This is the same as the E-to-P expectancy that we learned about in the section about expectancy theory. The lower the E-to-P expectancy that the goal can been accomplished, the less committed (motivated) the employee is to the goal.
- *Goal participation* (sometimes). Goal setting is usually (but not always) more effective when employees participate in setting goals.[42] Employees identify more with goals

they are involved in setting than goals assigned by a supervisor. In fact, today's workforce increasingly expects to be involved in goal setting and other decisions that affect them. Participation may also improve goal quality because employees have valuable information and knowledge that may not be known to managers who develop these goals alone. Thus participation ensures that employees buy into the goals and have the competencies and resources necessary to accomplish them.

feedback
Any information that people receive about the consequences of their behavior.

- *Goal feedback.* Feedback is another necessary condition for effective goal setting.[43] **Feedback** is any information that people receive about the consequences of their behavior. Feedback lets us know whether we have achieved a goal or are properly directing our effort toward it. Feedback is also an essential ingredient in motivation because our growth needs can't be satisfied unless we receive information about goal accomplishment. Feedback is so central to goal setting that we will look more closely at it next.

Characteristics of Effective Feedback

Feedback is a key ingredient in goal setting and employee performance. It communicates what behaviors are appropriate or necessary in a particular situation (that is, it clarifies role perceptions) and improves ability by frequently providing information to correct performance problems. Information that identifies a gap between actual and ideal performance is known as *corrective feedback* because it raises awareness of performance errors and identifies ways to correct those errors.

Under some circumstances, feedback also motivates employees. This is particularly true when feedback is positive, such as the peer-to-peer recognition activities described in the opening vignette to this chapter. These recognition programs communicate feedback as rewards, so they have the double benefit of informing employees about their performance and fulfilling their needs. Constructive feedback can also be motivating when employees have a strong "can-do" attitude toward the task and a learning orientation. For these people, less-than-ideal performance feedback triggers the drive to learn (improve their performance), not their drive to defend.[44]

Many of the characteristics of effective goal setting also apply to effective feedback (see Exhibit 5.5). First, feedback should be *specific.* The information provided should be connected to the details of the goal, rather than subjective and general phrases such as "your sales are going well." Second, feedback must be *relevant*; it must relate to the individual's behavior rather than to conditions beyond the individual's control. This ensures that the feedback is not distorted by situational factors. Third, feedback should be *timely*; it should be available as soon as possible after the behavior or results. Timeliness helps employees see a clear association between their behavior and its consequences. The fourth characteristic of effective feedback is that it should be *credible.* Employees are more likely to accept feedback (particularly corrective feedback) from trustworthy and credible sources.

Finally, feedback should be *sufficiently frequent.* How frequent is "sufficiently"? The answer depends on at least two things. One consideration is the employee's knowledge and experience with the task. Feedback is a form of reinforcement, so employees working on new tasks should receive more frequent corrective feedback because they require more behavior guidance and reinforcement (see Chapter 3). Employees who are repeating familiar tasks can receive less frequent feedback. The second factor is how long it takes to complete the task. Feedback is necessarily less frequent in jobs with a long cycle time (executives and scientists) than in jobs with a short cycle time (grocery store cashiers).

Exhibit 5.5
Characteristics of Effective Feedback

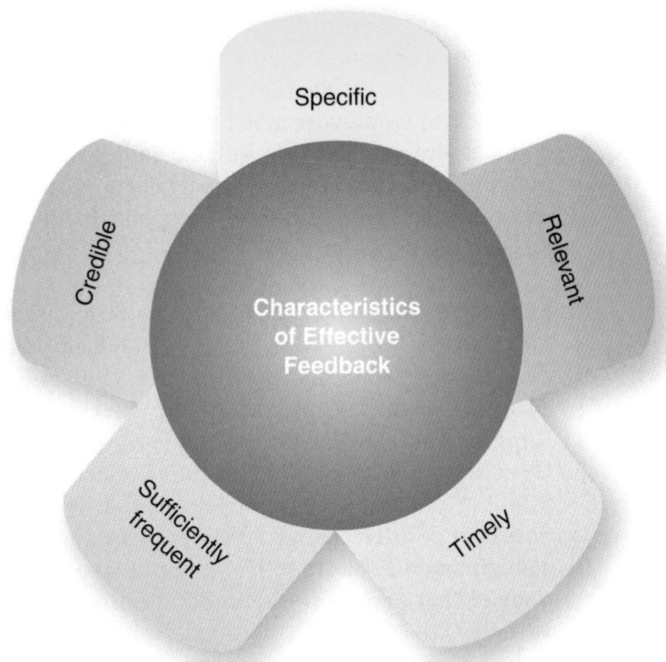

Sources of Feedback

Feedback can originate from nonsocial or social sources. Nonsocial sources provide feedback without someone communicating that information. The opening paragraph to this section mentioned that call centers have various forms of nonsocial feedback, such as electronic displays showing how many callers are waiting and the average time they have been waiting.[45] Some professionals have "executive dashboards" on their computer screens that display the latest measures of sales, inventory, and other indicators of corporate success. The job itself can be a nonsocial source of feedback. Many employees see the results of their work effort while making a product or providing a service where good and poor performance is fairly obvious.

Social sources of feedback include supervisors, clients, co-workers, and anyone else who communicates information about the employee's behavior or results. Supervisors in some call centers meet with each employee a few times each month to review monitored calls and discuss ways to improve those events. In most other organizations employees receive formal feedback maybe once or twice each year, but informal feedback occurs more often. Customer surveys have become a popular form of feedback for teams of employees, such as everyone who works at a bank branch.

Multisource (360-Degree) Feedback According to some estimates, managers at almost all *Fortune* 500 firms receive feedback about their job performance from a full circle of people, including direct reports, peers, bosses, vendors, customers, and partners.[46] Most plans (87 percent) also give employees complete freedom to choose who will rate them. This **multisource or 360-degree feedback** tends to provide more complete and accurate information than feedback from a supervisor alone. It is particularly useful when the supervisor is unable to observe the employee's behavior or performance throughout the year. Lower-level employees also feel a greater sense of fairness and open communication when they are able to provide upward feedback about their boss's performance.[47]

multisource (360-degree) feedback
Performance feedback received from a full circle of people around an employee.

However, multisource feedback also creates challenges. Having several people review so many co-workers can be expensive and time-consuming. With multiple opinions, the 360-degree process can also produce ambiguous and conflicting feedback, so employees may require guidance to interpret the results. A third concern is that peers may provide inflated rather than accurate feedback to avoid conflicts over the forthcoming year. A final concern is that critical feedback from many people can create stronger emotional reactions than if the critical judgment originates from just one person (your boss).[48]

Executive Coaching Soon after his promotion to a senior management position at P&O Nedlloyd (now Maersk Line), Bob Kemp hired an executive coach to help him discover and repair his vulnerabilities. He was particularly keen to shore up his self-awareness skills because, as the top executive, there was no one above him at the shipping and logistics firm to regularly monitor his interpersonal style as a leader. Over several sessions, the executive coach teased out Kemp's weak spots, such as listening skills and being approachable. Before long Kemp's colleagues and wife noticed a positive change. "Very early in the process, people started telling me I was changing and I started to feel more at ease in the new role," Kemp recalls. He also noticed that people were "walking out of my office with a slightly more positive attitude."[49]

executive coaching
A helping relationship using behavioral methods to assist clients in identifying and achieving goals for their professional performance and personal satisfaction.

Bob Kemp and numerous other executives have turned to **executive coaching**, which uses a variety of behavioral methods to help clients identify and achieve goals for their performance and well-being. Executive coaching is usually conducted by an external consultant and is essentially one-on-one "just-in-time" personal development using feedback and other techniques. Coaches do not provide answers to the employee's problems. Rather they are "thought partners" who offer more accurate feedback, open dialogue, and constructive encouragement to improve the client's performance and personal well-being.

The evidence so far is that executives who work with an executive coach perform better than those who do not. Coaching comes in many forms, so this positive result should be treated cautiously. Still, executive coaching has become a popular form of feedback and development for executives in many countries. For instance, a few years ago Alison Clark was burning out from overwork, and her business, Tickles Child Care Center in Te Puke, New Zealand, was suffering from high staff turnover. With the guidance of an executive coach, Clark discovered the leadership issues she needed to address and thereby improve the business and her personal life. The ongoing coaching had a demonstrable effect: Clark recently earned awards for her entrepreneurship and team development among businesses in New Zealand.[50]

Choosing Feedback Sources With so many sources of feedback–executive coaching, multisource feedback, executive dashboards, customer surveys, equipment gauges, nonverbal communication from your boss, and so on–which one works best under which conditions? The preferred feedback source depends on the purpose of the information. To learn about their progress toward goal accomplishment, employees usually prefer nonsocial feedback sources, such as computer printouts or feedback directly from the job. This is because information from nonsocial sources is considered more accurate than information from social sources. Corrective feedback from nonsocial sources is also less damaging to self-esteem. This is probably just as well because social sources tend to delay negative information, leave some of it out, and distort the bad news in a positive way.[51] When employees want to improve their

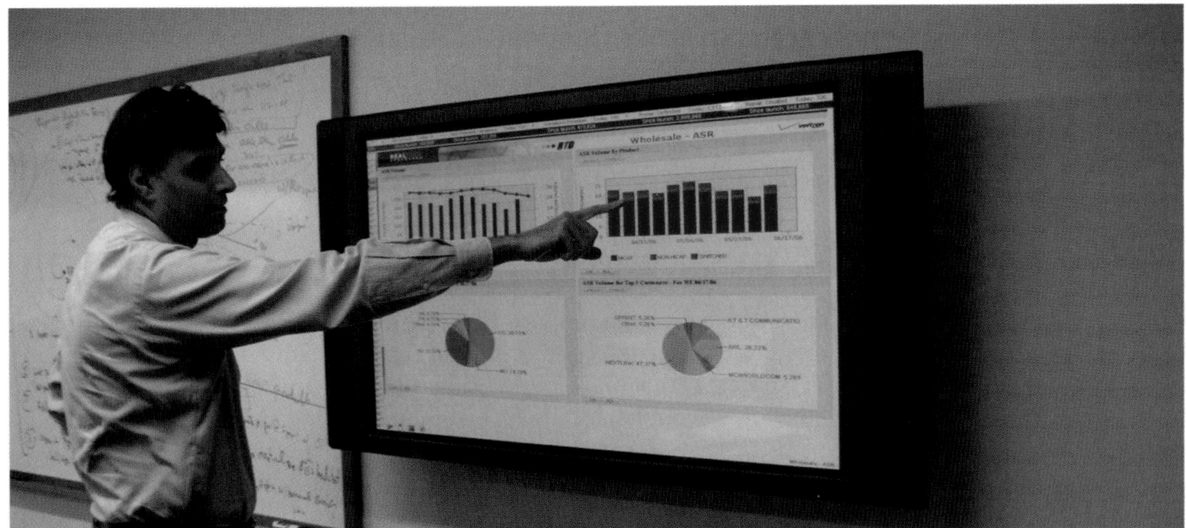

Executive Feedback Drives through the Dashboard Corporate intranets now allow many executives to receive feedback instantaneously on their computer, usually in the form of graphic output on an executive dashboard. Almost half of Microsoft employees use a dashboard to monitor project deadlines, sales, and other metrics. Microsoft CEO Steve Ballmer regularly reviews dashboard results in one-on-one meetings with his seven business leaders. "Every time I go to see Ballmer, it's an expectation that I bring my dashboard with me," says Jeff Raikes, who heads the Microsoft Office division. Verizon CIO Shaygan Kheradpir (shown in this photo) also appreciates the instant feedback provided by his dashboard, which is a huge plasma screen on the wall of his office. Called the "Wall of Shaygan," the screen displays the status of more than 100 network systems around the country in green, yellow, or red lights. Another part of the screen also shows sales, voice portal volumes, call center results, and other business metrics.[52]

self-image, they seek out positive feedback from social sources. It feels better to have co-workers say that you are performing the job well than to discover this from a computer printout.

Evaluating Goal Setting and Feedback

A recent survey of organizational behavior researchers recently identified goal setting as one of the top OB theories in terms of validity and usefulness.[53] This high score is not surprising given the impressive research support and wide application of this concept in a variety of settings. In partnership with goal setting, feedback also has an excellent reputation for improving employee motivation and performance.

Nevertheless, both goal setting and feedback have a few limitations.[54] One problem is that combining goals with monetary incentives motivates many employees to set up easy rather than difficult goals. In some cases employees have negotiated goals with their supervisor that have already been completed! Another limitation is that goal setting potentially focuses employees on a narrow subset of measurable performance indicators while ignoring aspects of job performance that are difficult to measure. The saying "What gets measured, gets done" applies here. A third problem is that setting performance goals is effective in established jobs, but it seems to interfere with the learning process in new, complex jobs. Thus we need to be careful not to apply goal setting where an intense learning process is occurring.

Learning Objectives

After reading this section you should be able to

8. **Summarize the equity theory model, including how people try to reduce feelings of inequity.**
9. **Identify the factors that influence procedural justice, as well as the consequences of procedural justice.**

Organizational Justice

Patti Anderson came from a family of Boeing engineers, so she was proud to also work as a manufacturing engineer at the aerospace company's commercial airplane division in Renton, Washington. But that pride evaporated when Anderson discovered that the men in her family earned more than her at Boeing for performing the same work. "My husband, brother, and dad also performed the same job as me, and each was paid more than me and consistently received higher raises than I did," said Anderson in a legal statement. "I know this because I saw their pay stubs."[55]

Most corporate leaders know that treating employees fairly is both morally correct and good for employee motivation, loyalty, and well-being. Yet the feelings of injustice that Patti Anderson describes are regular occurrences in a variety of situations. To minimize these incidents, we need to first understand that there are two forms of organizational justice: distributive justice and procedural justice.[56] **Distributive justice** refers to perceived fairness in the outcomes we receive relative to our contributions and the outcomes and contributions of others. **Procedural justice,** on the other hand, refers to fairness of the procedures used to decide the distribution of resources. Patti Anderson felt distributive injustice because male colleagues were paid significantly more than she was, even though their contribution to the organization was comparable. Andersen also experienced procedural injustice because of the way Boeing initially responded to her concerns.

distributive justice
The perceived fairness in outcomes we receive relative to our contributions and the outcomes and contributions of others.

procedural justice
The fairness of the procedures used to decide the distribution of resources.

Distributive Justice and Equity Theory

The first thing we usually think about and experience in situations of injustice is distributive injustice–the belief (and its emotional response) that the distribution of pay and other outcomes is unfair. What is considered "fair" varies with each person and situation. We apply an *equality principle* when we believe that everyone in the group should receive the same outcomes. Companies apply this principle when allocating some employee benefits and parking spaces, for example. The *need principle* is applied when we believe that those with the greatest need should receive more outcomes than others with less need. Patti Anderson applied the *equity principle* by inferring that people should be paid in proportion to their contribution. The equity principle is the most common distributive justice rule in organizational settings, so let's look at it in more detail.

Elements of Equity Theory To explain how the equity principle operates in our heads, OB scholars developed **equity theory,** which says that employees determine feelings of equity by comparing their own outcome/input ratio to the outcome/input ratio of some other person.[57] The outcome/input ratio is the value of the outcomes you receive divided by the value of inputs you provide in the exchange relationship. Anderson probably included her skills and level of responsibility as inputs. Other inputs might include experience, status, performance, personal reputation, and

equity theory
A theory that explains how people develop perceptions of fairness in the distribution and exchange of resources.

amount of time worked. Outcomes are the things employees receive from the organization in exchange for the inputs. For Anderson, the main outcomes are the paycheck and pay raises. Some other outcomes might be promotions, recognition, or an office with a window.

Equity theory states that we compare our outcome/input ratio with a comparison other.[58] In our earlier example, Anderson compared herself with her male family members and likely other men who worked in the same jobs at Boeing. However, the comparison other may be another person, group of people, or even yourself in the past. It may be someone in the same job, another job, or another organization. Chief executives have no direct comparison within the firm, so they tend to compare themselves with their counterparts in other organizations. Some research suggests that employees frequently collect information about several referents to form a "generalized" comparison other.[59] For the most part, however, the comparison other varies from one person to the next and is not easily identifiable.

Equity Evaluation We form an equity evaluation after determining our own outcome/input ratio and comparing this with the comparison other's ratio. Let's consider the experience of Patti Anderson again. Anderson feels *underreward* inequity because her male counterparts receive higher outcomes (pay) for inputs that are, at best, comparable to what she contributes at Boeing. This condition is illustrated in Exhibit 5.6(a).

In the equity condition Anderson would believe that her outcome/input ratio is similar to the ratio of male colleagues. Specifically, if she believes that she provides the same inputs as male family members and other men who work in the same jobs at Boeing, then she would feel equity if both men and women received the same pay and other outcomes (see Exhibit 5.6(b)). It is also possible that Anderson's male family members experience *overreward* inequity (Exhibit 5.6(c)). They would feel that their performance is similar to Anderson's performance, yet they earn more money. However, overreward inequity isn't as common as underreward inequity because people quickly change their perceptions to justify the higher outcomes.

Correcting Inequity Feelings We experience an emotional tension with perceived inequities; and when sufficiently strong, the tension motivates us to reduce the inequities. But what are we motivated to do to reduce this tension? Research has identified several reactions that people have to inequity. Some actions are reasonable, whereas others are dysfunctional; some are illegal, such as theft and sabotage. Here are the main ways that people correct inequity feelings when they are underrewarded compared to a co-worker (comparison other):[60]

Exhibit 5.6
Equity Theory Model

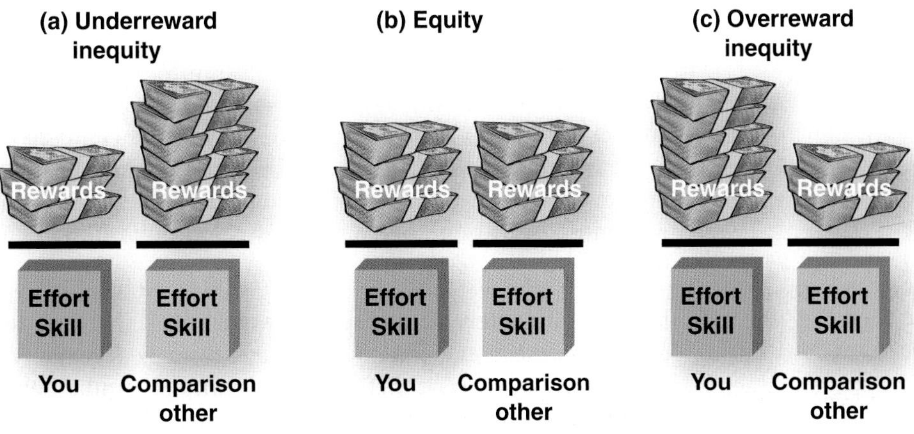

"O.K., if you can't see your way to giving me a pay raise, how about giving Parkerson a pay cut?"

- *Reduce our inputs.* Perform at a lower level, give fewer helpful suggestions, engage in less organizational citizenship behavior.
- *Increase our outcomes.* Ask for a pay increase, make unauthorized use of company resources.
- *Increase the comparison other's inputs.* Subtly ask the better-off co-worker to do a larger share of the work to justify his or her higher pay or other outcomes.
- *Reduce comparison other's outcomes.* Ask the boss to stop giving favorable treatment to the co-worker.
- *Change our perceptions.* Believe the co-worker really is doing more (such as working longer hours) or that the higher outcomes (perhaps a better office) he or she receives really aren't so much better than what we get.
- *Change the comparison other.* Compare ourselves to someone else closer to our situation (job duties, pay scale).
- *Leave the field.* Avoid thinking about the inequity by keeping away from the office where the co-worker is located, taking more sick leave, moving to another department, or quitting the job.

Although the categories remain the same, people who feel overreward inequity would, of course, act differently. For example, overrewarded employees don't usually correct this tension by working harder. Instead they might encourage the referent to work at a more leisurely pace or, more likely, change their perceptions to justify why they are given more favorable outcomes. As the author Pierre Burton once said, "I was underpaid for the first half of my life. I don't mind being overpaid for the second half."[61]

equity sensitivity
A person's outcome/input preferences and reaction to various outcome/input ratios.

Individual Differences: Equity Sensitivity Thus far we have described equity theory as though everyone has the same feelings of inequity in a particular situation. The reality, however, is that people vary in their **equity sensitivity**–that is, their outcome/input preferences and reactions to various outcome/input ratios.[62] At one end of

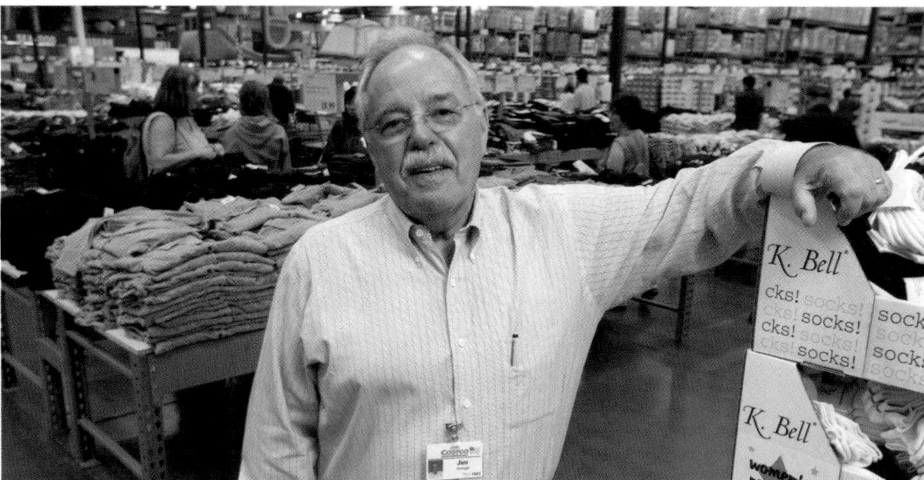

Costco Wholesale CEO Keeps Executive Pay Equitable John Pierpont Morgan, who in the 1800s founded the financial giant now called J.P. Morgan Chase, warned that no CEO should earn more than 20 times an average worker's pay. That advice didn't stop William B. Harrison Jr., the current CEO of J.P. Morgan Chase, from receiving $15–20 million in pay, bonuses, and stock options for each of the past few years. That's more than 700 times the pay of the average employee in the United States. Costco Wholesale chief executive Jim Sinegal (shown in this photo) thinks such a large wage gap is blatantly unfair and can lead to long-term employee motivation problems. "Having an individual who is making 100 or 200 or 300 times more than the average person working on the floor is wrong," says Sinegal, who cofounded the Issaquah, Washington, company. With annual salary and bonus of $550,000, Sinegal ranks as one of the lowest-paid executives even though Costco is one of the country's largest retailers and its employees among the highest paid in the industry.[63]

the equity sensitivity continuum are the "benevolents"–people who are tolerant of situations where they are underrewarded. They might still prefer equal outcome/input ratios, but they don't mind if others receive more than they do for the same inputs. In the middle are people who fit the standard equity theory model. These "equity sensitives" want their outcome/input ratio to be equal to the outcome/input ratio of the comparison other. Equity sensitives feel increasing inequity as the ratios become different. At the other end are the "entitleds." These people feel more comfortable in situations where they receive proportionately more than others. They might accept having the same outcome/input ratio as others, but they would prefer receiving more than others performing the same work.[64]

Evaluating Equity Theory Equity theory is widely studied and quite successful at predicting various situations involving feelings of workplace injustice, such as major baseball league salary disputes and remuneration of British CEOs.[65] Feelings of inequity are regular occurrences in every workplace. Some tensions are minor and temporary misunderstandings of the situation; others produce unpleasant emotions or worse, major theft and sabotage of company resources. Feelings of inequity are based on the moral principle of distributive justice (see Chapter 2), so companies that act unfairly toward their employees also face the charge of unethical conduct.

In spite of its research support, equity theory has a few limitations. One concern is that the theory isn't sufficiently specific to predict employee motivation and behavior. It doesn't indicate which inputs or outcomes are most valuable, and it doesn't identify the comparison other against which the outcome/input ratio is evaluated. These vague and highly flexible elements may explain why OB experts think equity theory is highly valid but only moderately useful.[66] A second problem is that equity theory incorrectly assumes people are individualistic, rational, and selfish. In reality, people are social creatures who define themselves as members of various groups (see the discussion of social identity theory in Chapter 3). They share goals with other members of these groups and commit themselves to the norms of their groups. A third limitation is that recent studies have found that equity theory accounts for only some of our feelings of fairness or justice in the workplace. Experts now say that procedural justice, which we look at next, is at least as important as distributive justice.

Procedural Justice

For many years OB scholars believed that distributive justice was more important than procedural justice in explaining employee motivation, attitudes, and behavior. This belief was based on the assumption that people are driven mainly by self-interest, so they try to maximize their personal outcomes. Today we know that people seek justice for its own sake, not just as a means to improve their paychecks. Thus procedural justice seems to be as important as (and some experts say more important than) distributive justice in explaining employee attitudes, motivation, and behavior.[67]

Structural Rules of Justice Procedural justice is influenced by both structural rules and social rules (see Exhibit 5.7).[68] Structural rules represent the policies and practices that decision makers should follow. The most frequently identified structural rule in procedural justice research is people's belief that they should have a "voice" in the decision process.[69] Voice allows employees to convey what they believe are relevant facts and views to the decision maker. Voice also provides a "value-expressive" function;

Exhibit 5.7 Components of Organizational Justice

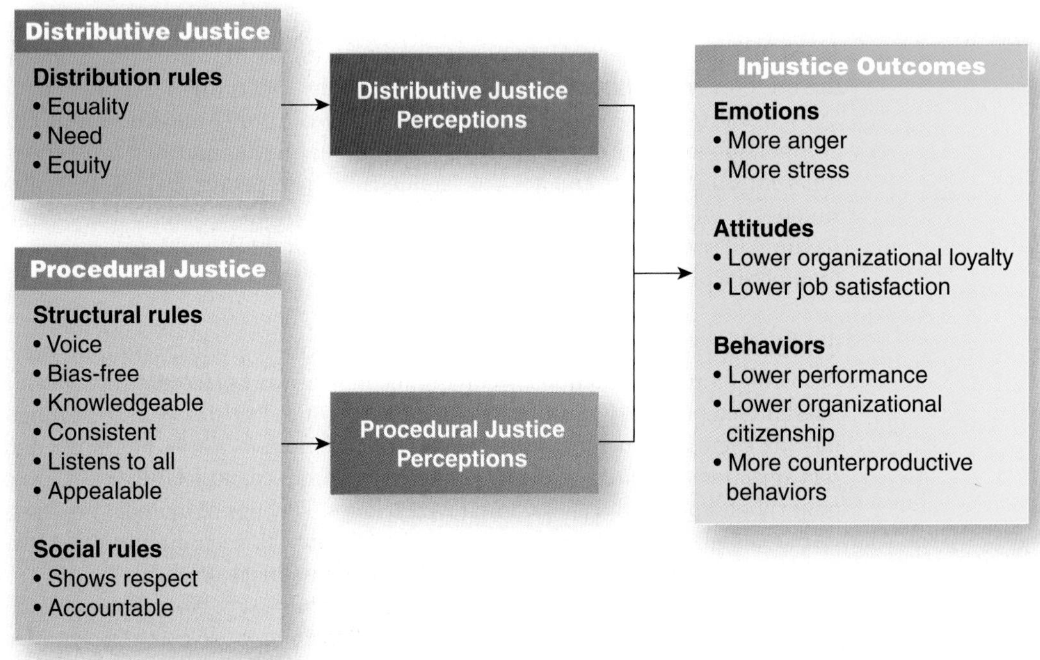

employees tend to feel better after having an opportunity to speak their minds. Other structural rules are that the decision maker is unbiased, relies on complete and accurate information, applies existing policies consistently, has listened to all sides of the dispute, and allows the decision to be appealed to a higher authority.[70]

Social Rules of Justice Along with structural rules, procedural justice is influenced by social rules–that is, how well the decision maker treats employees during the process. The two key social rules are respect and accountability. Employees feel greater procedural justice when they are treated with respect. For instance, one study found that nonwhite nurses who experienced racism tended to file grievances only after experiencing disrespectful treatment in their attempt to resolve the racist situation. Another study found that employees with repetitive strain injuries were more likely to file workers' compensation claims after experiencing disrespectful behavior from management. A third recent study noted that employees have stronger feelings of injustice when the manager has a reputation of treating people unfairly most of the time.[71]

The other social rule that has attracted attention is accountability. People believe that they are entitled to explanations about decisions, particularly when the results have potentially negative consequences for them. For instance, suppose a co-worker receives a better office than you do (distributive injustice). Chances are that you will feel less injustice after hearing the decision maker's explanation for that decision.

Consequences of Procedural Injustice Procedural justice strongly influences a person's emotions and motivation. Employees tend to experience anger toward the source of the injustice, which generates various response behaviors that scholars categorize as either withdrawal or aggression.[72] Notice how these response behaviors are similar to the fight-or-flight responses described earlier in the chapter regarding situations that activate our drive to defend. Withdrawal behaviors might include avoiding those who acted unjustly or being less willing to comply with their future requests. For instance, employees who believe their boss relies on an unfair decision process may be less likely to "walk the extra mile" in the future and might complete any assigned work only at a minimal standard.

Aggressive responses to procedural injustice include several counterproductive work behaviors, such as sabotage, theft, conflict, and acts of violence.[73] However, most employees who experience injustice respond with milder forms of retaliation, such as showing indignation and denouncing the decision maker's competence. Research suggests that being treated unfairly undermines our self-esteem and social status, particularly when others see that we have been unjustly treated. Consequently employees retaliate to restore their self-esteem and reinstate their status and power in the relationship with the perpetrator of the injustice. Employees also engage in these counterproductive behaviors to educate the decision maker, thereby minimizing the chance of future injustices.[74]

Organizational Justice in Practice

One of the clearest lessons from equity theory is that we need to continually treat people fairly in the distribution of organizational rewards. Unfortunately this is perhaps one of life's greatest challenges because most of us seem to have unique opinions about the value of inputs and outcomes. Decision makers need to carefully understand these dynamics along with the distribution rules–equity, equality, or need–that the organization wants to apply. From the procedural justice literature, we can see that justice also depends on whether employees believe the decision-making process follows a fair set of rules and whether they are personally treated fairly in that process.

In spite of the many challenges of creating justice in the workplace, managers can improve their procedural fairness through training programs. In one study, supervisors participated in role-play exercises to develop several procedural justice practices in the disciplinary process, such as maintaining the employee's privacy, giving employees some control over the process, avoiding arbitrariness, and exhibiting a supportive demeanor. Judges subsequently rated supervisors who received the procedural justice training as behaving more fairly than supervisors who did not receive the training. In another study, managers received procedural justice training through lectures, case studies, role-playing, and discussion. Three months later subordinates of the trained managers had significantly higher organizational citizenship behaviors than the subordinates of managers who did not receive procedural justice training.[75] Overall it seems that justice can be improved in the workplace.

Chapter Summary

Motivation refers to the forces within a person that affect his or her direction, intensity, and persistence of voluntary behavior in the workplace. Motivation has become more challenging because of an increasingly turbulent work environment, the removal of direct supervision as a motivational instrument, and the lack of understanding about what motivates the new generations of people entering the workforce.

Maslow's needs hierarchy groups needs into a hierarchy of five levels and states that the lowest needs are initially most important, but higher needs become more important as the lower ones are satisfied. Although very popular, the theory lacks research support–as does ERG theory, which attempted to overcome some of the limitations in Maslow's needs hierarchy. Both models assume that everyone has the same hierarchy, whereas emerging evidence suggests that needs hierarchies vary from one person to the next based on their personal values.

Four-drive theory states that everyone has four innate drives–the drives to acquire, bond, learn, and defend. These drives create emotional markers that motivate us. The drives generate competing emotions, however, so we consciously reconcile these competing impulses through a skill set that considers social norms, past experience, and personal values. Four-drive theory offers considerable potential for understanding employee motivation, but it still requires clarification and research to understand how people translate competing emotions into motivated behavior.

McClelland's learned needs theory argues that needs can be strengthened through learning. The three needs studied in this respect have been need for achievement, need for power, and need for affiliation.

The practical implication of needs/drives-based motivation theories is that corporate leaders must provide opportunities for everyone in the workplace to regularly fulfill all four drives; that organizations should avoid too much or too little opportunity to fulfill each drive; and that employees should be offered a choice of rewards rather than given the same reward as everyone else.

Expectancy theory states that work effort is determined by the perception that effort will result in a particular level of performance (E-to-P expectancy); the perception that a specific behavior or performance level will lead to specific outcomes (P-to-O expectancy); and the valences that the person feels for those outcomes. The E-to-P expectancy increases by improving the employee's ability and confidence to perform the job. The P-to-O expectancy increases by measuring performance accurately, distributing higher rewards to better performers, and showing employees that rewards are performance-based. Outcome valences increase by finding out what employees want and using these resources as rewards.

Goal setting is the process of motivating employees and clarifying their role perceptions by establishing performance objectives. Goals are more effective when they are specific, relevant, and challenging; have employee commitment; and are accompanied by meaningful feedback. Participative goal setting is important in some situations. Effective feedback is specific, relevant, timely, credible, and sufficiently frequent (which depends on the length of the task cycle and the employee's knowledge and experience with the task). Two increasingly popular forms of feedback are multisource (360-degree) assessment and executive coaching. Feedback from nonsocial sources is also beneficial.

Organizational justice consists of distributive justice (perceived fairness in the outcomes we receive relative to our contributions and the outcomes and contributions of others) and procedural justice (fairness of the procedures used to decide the distribution of resources). Equity theory, which considers the most common principle applied in distributive justice, has four elements: outcome/input ratio, comparison other, equity evaluation, and consequences of inequity. The theory also explains what people are motivated to do when they feel inequitably treated. Equity sensitivity is a personal characteristic that explains why people react differently to varying degrees of inequity.

Procedural justice is influenced by both structural rules and social rules. Structural rules represent the policies and practices that decision makers should follow; the most frequently identified is giving employees a voice in the decision process. Social rules refer to standards of interpersonal conduct between employees and decision makers; they are best observed by showing respect and providing accountability for decisions. Procedural justice is as important as distributive justice, and it influences organizational commitment, trust, and various withdrawal and aggression behaviors.

Key Terms

distributive justice, p. 152
drives, p. 135
equity sensitivity, p. 154
equity theory, p. 152
ERG theory, p. 138
executive coaching, p. 150
expectancy theory, p. 143
feedback, p. 148
four-drive theory, p. 138
goal setting, p. 146
Maslow's needs hierarchy, p. 135
motivation, p. 134
multisource (360-degree) feedback, p. 149
need for achievement (nAch), p. 141
need for affiliation (nAff), p. 141
need for power (nPow), p. 141
needs, p. 135
positive organizational behavior, p. 137
procedural justice, p. 152
self-actualization, p. 135
valence, p. 144

Critical Thinking Questions

1. This chapter begins by suggesting that motivating employees has become more challenging in recent years, partly because younger employees (Generation-X and Generation-Y) have different expectations than baby boomers. How do you think these younger and older generation groups differ in their expectations? Generally speaking, what would motivate a typical Generation-Y worker (under 25 years old) more than a typical baby boomer worker (over 45 years old)?
2. Four-drive theory is conceptually different from Maslow's needs hierarchy (as well as ERG theory) in several ways. Describe these differences. At the same time, needs are typically based on drives, so the four drives should parallel the seven needs that Maslow identified (five in the hierarchy and two additional needs). Map Maslow's needs to the four drives in four-drive theory.
3. Use all three components of expectancy theory to explain why some employees are motivated to show up for work during a severe storm whereas others make no effort to leave their homes.
4. What are the limitations of expectancy theory in predicting an individual's work effort and behavior?
5. Using your knowledge of the characteristics of effective goals, establish two meaningful goals related to your performance in this class.
6. When do employees prefer feedback from nonsocial rather than social sources? Explain why nonsocial sources are preferred under these conditions.
7. Several service representatives are upset that a newly hired representative with no previous experience will be paid $3,000 a year above the usual starting salary in the pay range. The department manager explained that the new hire would not accept the entry-level rate, so the company raised the offer by $3,000. All five reps currently earn salaries near the top of the scale ($15,000 higher than the new recruit), although they all started at the minimum starting salary a few years earlier. Use equity theory to explain why the five service representatives feel inequity in this situation.
8. Organizational injustice can occur in the classroom as well as in the workplace. Identify classroom situations in which you experienced feelings of injustice. What can instructors do to maintain an environment that fosters both distributive and procedural justice?

Case Study 5.1 BUDDY'S SNACK COMPANY

Russell Casey, Clayton State University, and Gloria Thompson, University of Phoenix

Buddy's Snack Company is a family-owned company located in the Rocky Mountains. Buddy Forest started the business in 1951 by selling homemade potato chips out of the back of his pickup truck. Nowadays Buddy's is a $36 million snack food company that is struggling to regain market share lost to Frito-Lay and other fierce competitors. In the early eighties Buddy passed the business to his son, Buddy Jr., who is currently grooming his son, Mark, to succeed himself as head of the company.

Six months ago Mark joined Buddy's Snacks as a salesperson, and after four months he was quickly promoted to sales manager. Mark recently graduated from a local university with an MBA in marketing, and Buddy Jr. was hoping that Mark would be able to implement strategies that could help turn the company around. One of Mark's initial strategies was to introduce a new sales performance management system. As part of this approach, any salesperson who receives a below-average performance rating would be required to attend a mandatory coaching session with his or her supervisor. Mark Forest is hoping that these coaching sessions will motivate employees to increase their sales. This case describes the reaction of three salespeople who have been required to attend a coaching session because of their low performance over the previous quarter.

Lynda Lewis

Lynda is a hard worker who takes pride in her work ethic. She has spent a lot of time reading the training material and learning selling techniques, viewing training videos on her own time, and accompanying top salespeople on their calls. Lynda has no problem asking for advice and doing whatever needs to be done to learn the business. Everyone agrees that Lynda has a cheery attitude and is a real "team player," giving the company 150 percent at all times. It has been a tough quarter for Lynda due to the downturn in the economy, but she is doing her best to make sales for the company. Lynda feels that failure to make quota during this past quarter is due not to lack of effort, but just bad luck in the economy. She is hopeful that things will turn around in the next quarter.

Lynda is upset with Mark about having to attend the coaching session because this is the first time in three years that her sales quota has not been met. Although Lynda is willing to do whatever it takes to be successful, she is concerned that the coaching sessions will be held on a Saturday. Doesn't Mark realize that Lynda has to raise three boys by herself and that weekends are an important time for her family? Because Lynda is a dedicated employee, she will somehow manage to rearrange the family's schedule.

Lynda is now very concerned about how her efforts are being perceived by Mark. After all, she exceeded the sales quota for the previous quarter, yet she did not receive thanks or congratulations for those efforts. The entire experience has left Lynda unmotivated and questioning her future with the company.

Michael Benjamin

Michael is happy to have his job at Buddy's Snack Company, although he really doesn't like sales work that much. Michael accepted this position because he felt that he wouldn't have to work hard and would have a lot of free time during the day. Michael was sent to coaching mainly because his customer satisfaction reports were low; in fact, they were the lowest in the company. Michael tends to give canned presentations and does not listen closely to the customer's needs. Consequently, Michael makes numerous errors in new sales orders, which delay shipments and lose business and goodwill for Buddy's Snack Company. Michael doesn't really care because most of his customers do not spend much money, and he doesn't think it is worth his while.

There has been a recent change in the company commission structure. Instead of selling to the warehouse stores and possibly earning a high commission, Michael is now forced to sell to lower-volume convenience stores. In other words, he will have to sell twice as much product to earn the same amount of money. Michael does not think this change in commission is fair, and he feels that the coaching session will be a waste of time. He believes that the other members of the sales team are getting all of the good leads, and that is why they are so successful. Michael doesn't socialize with others in the office and attributes others' success and promotions to "whom they know" in the company rather than the fact that they are hard workers. He thinks that no matter how much effort is put into the job, he will never be adequately rewarded.

Kyle Sherbo

For three of the last five years Kyle was the number one salesperson in the division and had hopes of being promoted to sales manager. When Mark joined the company, Kyle worked closely with Buddy Jr. to help Mark learn all facets of the business. Kyle thought this close relationship with Buddy Jr. would assure his upcoming promotion to the coveted position of sales manager, and he was devastated to learn that Mark received the promotion that he thought was his.

During the past quarter there was a noticeable change in Kyle's work habits. It has become commonplace for Kyle to be late for appointments or miss them entirely, not return phone calls, and not follow up on leads. His sales performance declined dramatically, which resulted in a drastic loss of income. Although Kyle had been dedicated and fiercely loyal to Buddy Jr. and the company for many years, he is now looking for other employment. Buddy's Snacks is located in a rural community, which leaves Kyle with limited job opportunities. He was, however, offered a position as a sales manager with a competing company in a larger town, but Kyle's wife refuses to leave the area because of her strong family ties. Kyle is bitter and resentful of his current situation and now faces a mandatory coaching session that will be conducted by Mark.

Discussion Questions

1. You have met three employees of Buddy's Snacks. Explain how each employee's situation relates to equity theory.
2. Explain the motivation of these three employees in terms of the expectancy theory of motivation.

Case Study 5.2 FAT MERGER PAYOUTS OF CEOs

Mergers have roared back in corporate America, and with them have come highly lucrative payouts for the executives who triggered or accepted the acquisitions. One example is Gillette CEO James M. Kilts, who received a whopping $165 million, including stock options and severance, for selling the razor maker to Procter & Gamble. Bruce L. Hammonds, CEO of MBNA Corp., was apparently promised $102 million in connection with the credit-card company's acquisition by Bank of America Corp. Further behind but still well ahead of the average employee's lifetime income is Toys 'R' Us Inc. CEO John H. Eyler, who will receive cash and benefits worth about $63 million when the struggling toy retailer is purchased by an investment group. But several observers say these special perks are blatantly unfair. Others point out that the bonuses perversely reward the people who made the company vulnerable to takeover.

This *BusinessWeek* case study examines the new "Gilded Age" of executive payouts from mergers and acquisitions. It considers the complaints hurled at these generous rewards and justifications that the beneficiaries give in response. Read the full text of this *BusinessWeek* article at www.mhhe.com/mcshane4e and prepare for the discussion questions below.

Discussion Questions

1. Use equity theory to explain some of the criticisms that are leveled against these large merger payouts.
2. The article states that some CEOs are quite persistent about negotiating their payouts. Use four-drive theory to explain why this is so.
3. What are these golden payouts supposed to motivate in these executives? What unintended behaviors might they also (or alternatively) motivate?

Source: E. Thornton, "Fat Merger Payouts of CEOs," *BusinessWeek*, 12 Decmeber 2005, 34.

Class Exercise 5.3 NEEDS PRIORITY EXERCISE

PURPOSE This class exercise is designed to help you understand the characteristics and contingencies of employee needs in the workplace.

INSTRUCTIONS

1. The accompanying table lists in alphabetical order 14 characteristics of the job or work environment. Working alone, use the far left column to rank order these characteristics in terms of how important they are to you personally. Write "1" beside the most important characteristic, "2" for the second most important, and so on through to "14" for the least important characteristic on this list.
2. In the second column, rank order these characteristics in the order that you think human resource managers believe they are important for their employees.
3. Your instructor will provide results of a recent large-scale survey of employees. When these results are presented, identify the reasons for any noticeable differences. Relate these differences to your understanding of the emerging view of employee needs and drives in work settings.

Importance to you	What HR managers believe are important to employees	
______	______	Autonomy and independence
______	______	Benefits (health care, dental, and so on)
______	______	Career development opportunities
______	______	Communication between employees and senior managers
______	______	Compensation/pay
______	______	Feeling safe in the work environment
______	______	Flexibility to balance work/life issues
______	______	Job security
______	______	Job specific training
______	______	Management recognition of employee job performance
______	______	Opportunities to use skills and abilities
______	______	Organization's commitment to professional development
______	______	Relationship with immediate supervisor
______	______	The work itself

Team Exercise 5.4 A QUESTION OF FEEDBACK

PURPOSE This exercise is designed to help you understand the importance of feedback, including problems that occur with imperfect communication in the feedback process.

MATERIALS The instructor will distribute a few pages of exhibits to one person on each team. The other students will need a pencil with an eraser and some blank paper. Movable chairs and tables in a large area are helpful.

INSTRUCTIONS

1. The class will be divided into pairs of students. Each pair is ideally located in a private area, away from other students and where one person can write. One student is given the pages of exhibits from the instructor. The other student in each pair is not allowed to see these exhibits.
2. The student holding the materials will describe each of the exhibits; the other student's task is to accurately replicate each exhibit. The pair of students can compare the replication with the original at the end of each drawing. They may also switch roles for each exhibit if they wish. If roles are switched, the instructor must distribute exhibits separately to each student so that they are not seen by the other person. Each exhibit has a different set of limitations, as described here:
   - *Exhibit 1.* The student describing the exhibit cannot look at the other student or at the student's drawing. The student drawing the exhibit cannot speak or otherwise communicate with the person describing the exhibit.
   - *Exhibit 2.* The student describing the exhibit may look at the other student's diagram. However, he or she may say only "yes" or "no" when the student drawing the diagram asks a specific question. In other words, the person presenting the information can use only these words for feedback and only when asked a question by the writer.
   - *Exhibit 3* (optional, if time permits). The student describing the exhibit may look at the other student's diagram and may provide any feedback at any time to the person replicating the exhibit.
3. The class will gather to discuss this exercise. This may include conversation about the importance of feedback and the characteristics of effective feedback for individual motivation and learning.

Self-Assessment 5.5

MEASURING YOUR EQUITY SENSITIVITY

PURPOSE This self-assessment is designed to help you estimate your level of equity sensitivity.

INSTRUCTIONS Read each of the following statements and circle the response that you believe best reflects your position regarding each statement. Then use the scoring key in Appendix B to calculate your results. You will complete this exercise alone so you can assess yourself honestly without concerns of social comparison. However, class discussion will focus on equity theory and the effect of equity sensitivity on perceptions of fairness in the workplace.

Equity Preference Questionnaire

To what extent do you agree or disagree that...	Strongly agree	Agree	Neutral	Disagree	Strongly disagree
1. I prefer to do as little as possible at work while getting as much as I can from my employer.	☐	☐	☐	☐	☐
2. I am most satisfied at work when I have to do as little as possible.	☐	☐	☐	☐	☐
3. When I am at my job, I think of ways to get out of work.	☐	☐	☐	☐	☐
4. If I could get away with it, I would try to work just a little bit more slowly than the boss expects.	☐	☐	☐	☐	☐
5. It is really satisfying to me when I can get something for nothing at work.	☐	☐	☐	☐	☐
6. It is the smart employee who gets as much as he or she can while giving as little as possible in return.	☐	☐	☐	☐	☐
7. Employees who are more concerned about what they can get from their employer rather than what they can give to their employer are the wisest.	☐	☐	☐	☐	☐
8. When I have completed my tasks for the day, I help out other employees who have yet to complete their tasks.	☐	☐	☐	☐	☐
9. Even if I receive low wages and poor benefits from my employer, I would still try to do my best at my job.	☐	☐	☐	☐	☐
10. If I had to work hard all day at my job, I would probably quit.	☐	☐	☐	☐	☐
11. I feel obligated to do more than I am paid to do at work.	☐	☐	☐	☐	☐
12. At work, my greatest concern is whether I am doing the best job I can.	☐	☐	☐	☐	☐
13. A job that requires me to be busy during the day is better than a job that allows me a lot of loafing.	☐	☐	☐	☐	☐
14. At work, I feel uneasy when there is little work for me to do.	☐	☐	☐	☐	☐
15. I would become very dissatisfied with my job if I had little or no work to do.	☐	☐	☐	☐	☐
16. All other things being equal, it is better to have a job with a lot of duties and responsibilities than one with few duties and responsibilities.	☐	☐	☐	☐	☐

Source: K.S. Sauleya and A.G. Bedeian, "Equity Sensitivity: Construction of a Measure and Examination of Its Psychometric Properties," *Journal of Management* 26 (September 2000), pp. 885–910.

Self-Assessment 5.6

MEASURING YOUR GROWTH NEED STRENGTH (STUDENT OLC)

Abraham Maslow's needs hierarchy theory distinguished between deficiency needs and growth needs. Deficiency needs become activated when unfulfilled, such as the need for food or belongingness. Growth needs, on the other hand, continue to develop even when temporarily fulfilled. Maslow identified self-actualization as the only category of growth needs. Research has found that Maslow's needs hierarchy theory overall doesn't fit reality, but specific elements such as the concept of growth needs have not been rejected. This self-assessment is designed to estimate your level of growth need strength. This instrument asks you to consider what about a job is most important to you. Please indicate which of the two jobs you personally would prefer if you had to make a choice between them. In answering each question, assume that everything else about the jobs is the same. Pay attention only to the characteristics actually listed.

After reading this chapter, if you need additional information, see www.mhhe.com/mcshane4e for more in-depth interactivities that correspond with this material.

Fifteen years ago Nucor was an upstart in an industry dominated by Bethlehem Steel, National Steel, and other megafirms. Today, battered by global competition, two-thirds of American steel companies have disappeared or are under bankruptcy protection. Nucor, on the other hand, has become the largest steel company in America and 10th largest in the world. And although it now employs 11,000 people, Nucor remains nimble, highly competitive, and profitable, handily beating most other companies in the Standard & Poor's 500 index in shareholder returns over the past five years.

Nucor has survived and thrived in the turbulent steel industry through the benefits of performance-based rewards, job design, and empowerment.

What's Nucor's secret to success? Aside from technological innovations and avoiding "legacy" payroll costs, the company relies on applied performance practices that create phenomenal levels of employee engagement. To begin with, it has an extreme performance reward system. The average Nucor steelworker earns more than $70,000 in a typical year, but only one-third of that is guaranteed. "We pay a real low base wage, but high bonuses on a weekly basis," explains Nucor human resources vice president Jim Coblin. "The bonuses are based on the quality and tons produced and shipped through a team. The average base pay is about $9 to $10 an hour, but they could get an additional $15 to $20 an hour for bonuses."

Nucor's team-based bonus system also includes penalties. If employees catch a bad batch of steel before it leaves the minimill, they lose their bonus for that shipment. But if a bad batch makes its way to the customer, the team loses three times its usual bonus. A profit-sharing bonus (recently more than $15,000) on top of the fixed and bonus pay further motivates Nucor employees to keep mills running and to discover ways to improve steel quality and output.

Along with rewarding performance, Nucor gives employees the freedom and job flexibility to make key decisions and adjust their work to fit demands. Most decisions are made at the plant level—in fact, the head office in North Carolina has only 65 people—and employees take the initiative without waiting for management approval.

Consider the recent incident in which the electrical grid failed at Nucor's minimill in Hickman, Arkansas, potentially shutting down the operation for an entire week. When three Nucor electricians in North Carolina and Alabama heard the news, they drove or flew to Hickman and within three days had the minimill back in business. Nucor management didn't tell them to go, and their heroism didn't come with any extra pay. Yet these three Nucor employees gave up their weekend because they knew their effort could make a huge difference to Nucor's success. While remarkable in most companies, this is just a routine example at Nucor. "It happens daily," says a Nucor executive.[1]

6

Applied Performance Practices

LEARNING OBJECTIVES

After reading this chapter you should be able to

1. **Discuss the advantages and disadvantages of the four reward objectives.**
2. **Identify several team- and organization-level performance-based rewards.**
3. **Describe five ways to improve reward effectiveness.**
4. **Discuss the advantages and disadvantages of job specialization.**
5. **Diagram the job characteristics model of job design.**
6. **Identify three strategies to improve employee motivation through job design.**
7. **Define *empowerment* and identify strategies to support empowerment.**
8. **Describe the five elements of self-leadership.**

Nucor's success is a testament to the potential value of rewards, job design, and empowerment. This chapter looks at each of these applied performance practices as well as a fourth practice, self-leadership, which is also evident in Nucor employees. The chapter begins with an overview of financial reward practices, including the different types of rewards and how to implement rewards effectively. Next we look at the dynamics of job design, including specific job design strategies to motivate employees. We then consider the elements of empowerment as well as conditions that support empowerment. The final part of this chapter explains how employees manage their own performance through self-leadership.

Learning Objectives

After reading this section you should be able to

1. **Discuss the advantages and disadvantages of the four reward objectives.**
2. **Identify several team- and organization-level performance-based rewards.**
3. **Describe five ways to improve reward effectiveness.**

Financial Reward Practices

Financial rewards is probably the oldest–and certainly the most fundamental–applied performance practice in organizational settings. At the most basic level, financial rewards represent a form of exchange; employees provide their labor, skill, and knowledge in return for money and benefits from the organization. From this perspective, money and related rewards align employee goals with organizational goals.

However, financial rewards do much more than pay employees back for their contributions to organizational objectives. They are a symbol of success, a reinforcer and motivator, a reflection of employees' performance, and a source of reduced anxiety. With so many different purposes, it is little wonder that people rank pay and benefits as two of the most important features in the employment relationship.[2]

The value and meaning of money also vary considerably from one person to the next. One large-scale survey revealed that men in almost all of the 43 countries studied attach more importance or value to money than do women. This result is consistent with public opinion polls reporting that money has a higher priority for men than for women, particularly as a symbol of power and status.[3] Cultural values also seem to influence the meaning and value of money. People in countries with high power distance (such as China and Japan) tend to have a high respect and priority for money, whereas people in countries with a strong egalitarian culture (such as Denmark, Austria, and Israel) are discouraged from openly talking about money or displaying their personal wealth.[4]

Financial rewards come in many forms, which can be organized into the four specific objectives identified in Exhibit 6.1: membership and seniority, job status, competencies, and performance.

Membership- and Seniority-Based Rewards

Membership- and seniority-based rewards (sometimes called "pay for pulse") represent the largest part of most paychecks. Some employee benefits, such as free or discounted meals in the company cafeteria, remain the same for everyone, whereas

Exhibit 6.1 Reward Objectives, Advantages, and Disadvantages

Reward objective	Sample rewards	Advantages	Disadvantages
Membership/seniority	• Fixed pay. • Most employee benefits. • Paid time off.	• May attract applicants. • Minimizes stress of insecurity. • Reduces turnover.	• Doesn't directly motivate performance. • May discourage poor performers from leaving. • Golden handcuffs may undermine performance.
Job status	• Promotion-based pay increase. • Status-based benefits.	• Tries to maintain internal equity. • Minimizes pay discrimination. • Motivates employees to compete for promotions.	• Encourages hierarchy, which may increase costs and reduce responsiveness. • Reinforces status differences. • Motivates job competition and exaggerated job worth.
Competencies	• Pay increase based on competency. • Skill-based pay.	• Improves workforce flexibility. • Tends to improve quality. • Consistent with employability.	• Subjective measurement of competencies. • Skill-based pay plans are expensive.
Task performance	• Commissions. • Merit pay. • Gainsharing. • Profit sharing. • Stock options.	• Motivates task performance. • Attracts performance-oriented applicants. • Organizational rewards create an ownership culture. • Pay variability may avoid layoffs during downturns.	• May weaken job content motivation. • May distance reward giver from receiver. • May discourage creativity. • Tends to address symptoms, not underlying causes of behavior.

others increase with seniority. For example, employees at the City of Pawtucket, Rhode Island, receive longevity bonuses of approximately $2,000 or more after completion of four years of service. Police officers in Petaluma, California, were recently awarded a 30 percent increase over three years to catch up to pay rates of officers in other Bay Area communities.[5] In many companies employees with greater seniority receive longer vacation time. Many Asian companies distribute a "13th month" bonus, which every employee expects to receive each year no matter how well the company performed over the previous year.

These membership- and seniority-based rewards potentially attract job applicants (particularly those who desire predictable income) and reduce turnover. However, they do not directly motivate job performance; on the contrary, they discourage poor performers from seeking work better suited to their abilities. Instead the good

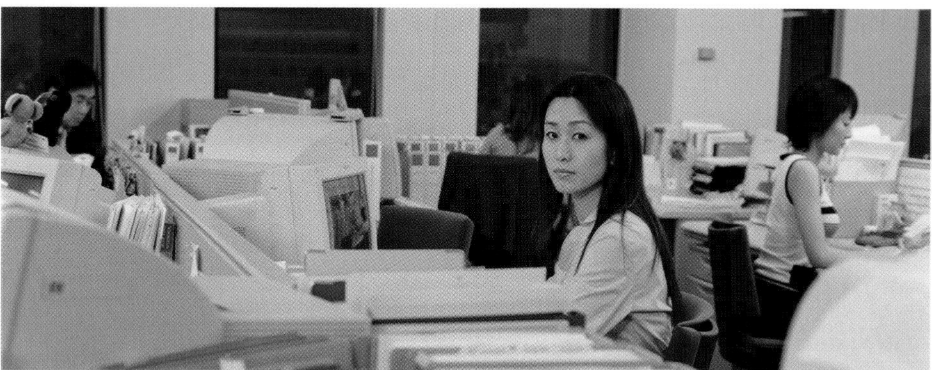

Japanese Firms Reward Age, Seniority, and Babies Since World War II employees in most large Japanese companies have received pay rates and increases determined entirely by their age or seniority, usually topping out around age 45. Not even the value of the specific jobs performed affected how much employees earned. Tough times in the 1990s forced many Japanese firms to introduce performance-based pay systems in which annual pay increases varied with employees' contributions. The shift toward pay for performance continues today, but labor groups still oppose such programs, and a few companies have not been happy with the results. Concerned that employees were becoming too stressed over their variable pay rates each year, Tokai Rubber Industries Ltd. recently reintroduced an age-based bonus pay system. "Even during that period [when they can't perform as well as expected], we raise salaries according to their age," says Tokai Rubber president Akira Fujii. Meanwhile Japanese firms are replacing monthly family allowances (where employees receive higher pay for the number of children they support) with a one-time lump sum childbirth bonus. For example, employees at Daiwa House Industry Co. in Osaka previously received an extra $45 per month for each child. Now the company pays a one-time lump sum of $9,000 for each childbirth.[6]

performers are lured to better-paying jobs. Some of these rewards are also golden handcuffs, which, as we learned in Chapter 4, can potentially weaken job performance by creating continuance commitment.

Job Status–Based Rewards

job evaluation
Systematically evaluating the worth of jobs within an organization by measuring their required skill, effort, responsibility, and working conditions.

Almost every organization rewards employees to some extent based on the status or worth of the jobs they occupy. **Job evaluation** is commonly used to rate the worth or status of each job, with higher pay rates going to jobs that require more skill and effort, have more responsibility, and have more difficult working conditions.[7] Aside from receiving higher pay, employees with more valued jobs sometimes receive larger offices, company-paid vehicles, and other perks.

Job status–based rewards maintain feelings of equity (people in higher-valued jobs should get higher pay) and motivate employees to compete for promotions. However, when companies are trying to be more cost efficient and responsive to the external environment, job status–based rewards potentially do the opposite by encouraging bureaucratic hierarchy. These rewards also reinforce a status mentality, whereas Generation-X and Generation-Y employees expect a more egalitarian workplace. Furthermore, status-based pay potentially motivates employees to compete with each other for higher-status jobs and to raise the value of their own jobs by exaggerating job duties and hoarding resources.[8]

Competency-Based Rewards

Many firms have shifted from job status to competency-based rewards. For instance, Syracuse University in upstate New York replaced its 20 pay-grade hierarchy with just 7 wider pay bands. Employees now receive pay increases within each pay band partly based on how well they have acquired new knowledge and skills.[9] *Skill-based pay* is a variation of competency-based rewards in which employees are rewarded for the number of skill modules mastered and consequently the number of jobs they can perform.

Competency-based rewards improve workforce flexibility by motivating employees to learn a variety of skills and thereby perform a variety of jobs. Product or service quality tends to improve because employees with multiple skills are more likely to understand the work process and know how to improve it. Competency-based rewards are also consistent with employability because they reward employees who continuously learn skills that will keep them employed. One potential problem is that measuring competencies can be subjective, particularly when described as personality traits or personal values. Skill-based pay systems measure specific skills, so they are usually more objective. However, they are expensive because employees spend more time learning new tasks.[10]

Performance-Based Rewards

Performance-based rewards have existed since Babylonian days in the 20th century BC, but their popularity has increased dramatically over the past couple of decades.[11] Here is an overview of some of the most popular individual, team, and organizational performance-based rewards.

Individual Rewards Many employees receive individual bonuses or awards for accomplishing a specific task or exceeding annual performance goals. Real estate agents and other salespeople typically earn *commissions*, in which their pay increases with sales volume. Piece rate systems reward employees based on the number of units produced. For example, lawn care staff at The Lawn Mowgul in Dallas, Texas, earn a form of piece rate (called "piecemeal") based on the number of yards cut; housekeeping staff in some British hotels earn a piece rate for each room they clean (about $3 per room).[12] At Pretoria Portland Cement in South Africa, employees individually receive financial rewards for suggestions that improve productivity. Hong Kong communications company PCCW rewards employees with up to one month's pay if they exceed their performance goals.[13]

Team Rewards Most brokerage firms on Wall Street, as well as other financial institutions, are shifting their focus from individuals to teams. Consequently, employees in these companies are finding a larger part of their total paycheck determined by team performance. One example is National City Bank in Cleveland, where brokers now earn bonuses based on the collective sales performance of their team. As was described at the beginning of this chapter, most of the paycheck that Nucor employees receive is determined by team performance. Specifically, employees at each minimill are organized into teams, and individuals earn bonuses based on the volume and quality of the team's output. A few years ago Home Depot introduced team-based rewards whereby employees earn a bonus based on how well their store meets or exceeds specific financial goals.[14]

gainsharing plan
A reward system in which team members earn bonuses for reducing costs and increasing labor efficiency in their work process.

Gainsharing plans are a form of team-based compensation that calculates bonuses from the work unit's cost savings and productivity improvement. At Whole Foods Market, for example, each department within a store is run by a team with a monthly payroll budget. If payroll money is unspent at the end of the month, the surplus is divided among members of that Whole Foods' team. Most gainsharing plans distribute some of the gains and return the rest to the company's coffers. The majority of mining companies in North America have a gainsharing bonus system, typically where mining teams share the cost savings of extracting more ore at lower cost. With considerable caution, American hospitals have introduced gainsharing programs in which surgeons and other medical staff are rewarded for cost reductions in surgery and patient care.[15] Gainsharing plans tend to improve team dynamics, knowledge sharing, and pay satisfaction. They also create a reasonably strong link between effort and performance because much of the cost reduction and labor efficiency is within the team's control.

employee stock ownership plans (ESOPs)
A reward system that encourages employees to buy stock in the company.

Organizational Rewards Along with individual-and team-based rewards, many firms rely on organization-level rewards to motivate employees. **Employee stock ownership plans (ESOPs)** encourage employees to buy shares of company stock, usually at a discounted price or with a no-interest loan. Employees are subsequently rewarded through dividends and market appreciation of those shares. Approximately 10 percent of the private sector U.S. workforce participates in an ESOP. Sears Roebuck and UPS were two of the earliest companies to distribute stocks to their employees. ESOPs are also gaining popularity in other countries. For example, Dairibord Zimbabwe employees own more than one-fifth of the outstanding shares of the Zimbabwe dairy products company. Most Dairibord workers who bought a few thousand shares a decade ago are now millionaires from the share appreciation and receive a sizable bonus from the annual dividend.[16]

stock options
A reward system that gives employees the right to purchase company stock at a future date at a predetermined price.

Whereas ESOPs involve actually purchasing company shares, **stock options** give employees the right to purchase shares from the company at a future date at a predetermined price up to a fixed expiration date. For example, an employer might offer employees the right to purchase 100 shares at $50 anywhere between two and six years from now. If the stock price is, say, $60 two years later, employees could earn $10 from these options or wait for up to six years for the stock price to rise further. If the stock never rises above $50 during that time, then employees are "out of the money" and would just let the options expire. The intention of stock options is to motivate employees to make the company more profitable, which should raise the company's stock price and thereby allow them to reap the value above the exercise price of the stock options.

profit sharing plans
A reward system that pays bonuses to employees based on the previous year's level of corporate profits.

Profit-sharing plans, a third organization-level reward system, calculate bonuses from the previous year's level of corporate profits. As was noted in the opening vignette to this chapter, Nucor employees earn a profit-sharing bonus on top of their fixed pay and team bonuses. Specifically, the steelmaker distributes 10 percent of its earnings before taxes to employees each year, which recently amounted to more than $17,000 per employee.[17]

balanced scorecard (BSC)
A reward system that pays bonuses for improved results on a composite of financial, customer, internal process, and employee factors.

A fourth organization-level reward strategy, called **balanced scorecard (BSC)**, is a goal-oriented performance measurement system that rewards people (typically executives) for improving performance on a composite of financial, customer, and internal processes, as well as employee factors. The better the measurement improvements across these dimensions, the larger the bonus awarded. Best Buy, Ingersoll-Rand, Crown Castle, and, according to some sources, almost 60 percent of major companies use some variation of BSC, usually to reward and direct the performance of management staff, although the system is also used to reward nonmanagement employees. For instance, KT (formerly Korea

Telecom) relied on BSC to transform the former government-owned telephone company into a more competitive business after privatization. "It guided our employees with clear direction and balanced perspectives," says Song Young-han, KT's executive senior vice president. "By gathering all the employees around BSC, we were able to concentrate our foundation for the performance-oriented organization culture."[18]

Evaluating Organization-Level Rewards How effective are organization-level rewards? ESOPs, stock options, and balanced scorecards tend to create an "ownership culture" in which employees feel aligned with the organization's success. Balanced scorecards have the added benefit of aligning rewards to several specific measures of organizational performance. However, BSC is potentially more subjective and requires a particular corporate culture for effective implementation. Profit sharing tends to create less ownership culture, but it has the advantage of automatically adjusting employee compensation with the firm's prosperity, thereby reducing the need for layoffs or negotiated pay reductions during recessions.[19]

The main problem with ESOPs, stock options, and profit sharing (less so with balanced scorecards) is that employees often perceive a weak connection between individual effort and corporate profits or the value of company shares. Even in small firms, the company's stock price or profitability is influenced by economic conditions, competition, and other factors beyond the employees' immediate control. This low individual performance-to-outcome expectancy weakens employee motivation. Another

Hugo Stays Boss with Balanced Scorecard In the highly competitive fashion industry, Hugo Boss Industries commands an impressive brand image and market share (30 percent for business suits in some markets). This success is due in part to a balanced scorecard that captures diverse performance measures across the Swiss company's various product groups. "You can't expect miracles, and no tool is going to do the job," concedes Werner Lackas, HBI's head of operations. "But the scorecard serves a very important purpose in focussing attention on the things that are being measured and where we are trying to go." Lackas explains that the scorecard gives HBI managers and employees "a pretty rigid skeleton" within which to be flexible and creative. The scorecard, which includes a range of hard (e.g., return on capital) and soft (e.g., staff development and satisfaction) objectives, is the foundation of performance bonuses received by all of HBI's 350 employees and managers.[20]

concern is that some companies in a few countries (including the United States) use ESOPs as a replacement for employee retirement plans. This is a risky strategy because company stock pension funds lack diversification. If the company goes bankrupt, employees lose both their jobs and a large portion of their retirement savings.[21]

Improving Reward Effectiveness

Performance-based rewards have come under attack over the years for discouraging creativity, distancing management from employees, distracting employees from the meaningfulness of the work itself, and being quick fixes that ignore the true causes of poor performance. Although these issues have kernels of truth under specific circumstances, they do not necessarily mean that we should abandon performance-based pay. On the contrary, the top-performing companies around the world are more likely to have performance-based rewards.[22] Reward systems do motivate most employees, but only under the right conditions. Here are some of the more important strategies to improve reward effectiveness.

Link Rewards to Performance Behavior modification theory (Chapter 3) and expectancy theory (Chapter 5) both recommend that employees with better performance should be rewarded more than those with poorer performance. Unfortunately this simple principle seems to be unusually difficult to apply. In one recent large-scale survey, fewer than half of Malaysian employees said they believe their company rewards high performance or deals appropriately with poor performers. A Gallup survey at an American telecommunications company revealed an equally devastating observation: Management's evaluation of 5,000 customer service employees was uncorrelated with the performance ratings that customers gave those employees. "Whatever behavior the managers were evaluating were irrelevant to the customers," concluded Gallup executives. "The managers might as well have been rating the employees' shoe sizes, for all the customers cared."[23]

How can companies improve the pay–performance linkage? Inconsistencies and bias can be minimized by introducing gainsharing, ESOPs, and other plans that use objective performance measures. Where subjective measures of performance are necessary, companies should rely on multiple sources of information, such as 360-degree feedback. Companies also need to apply rewards soon after the performance occurs, and in a large enough dose (such as a bonus rather than pay increase) so employees experience positive emotions when they receive the rewards.[24]

Ensure That Rewards Are Relevant Companies need to align rewards with performance within the employee's control. The more employees see a "line of sight" between their daily actions and a reward, the more they are motivated to improve performance. Wal-Mart applies this principle by rewarding bonuses to top executives based on the company's overall performance, whereas frontline employees earn bonuses based on the sales volume of the stores where they work. Reward systems also need to correct for situational factors. Salespeople in one region may have higher sales because the economy is stronger there than elsewhere, so sales bonuses need to be adjusted for these economic factors.

Use Team Rewards for Interdependent Jobs Team rewards should be used rather than individual rewards when employees work in highly interdependent jobs because it is difficult to measure individual performance in these situations. Nucor relies on team-based bonuses for this reason; steelmaking is a team effort, so employees earn bonuses based on team performance. Team rewards also encourage cooperation,

Connections 6.1

When Rewards Go Wrong

There is an old saying that "what gets rewarded, gets done." But what companies reward isn't always what they had intended for employees to do. Here are a few dramatic examples:

- Stock options are supposed to motivate executives to improve corporate performance. Instead they seem to motivate some leaders to inflate share values through dodgy accounting practices. Recent research estimates that for every 25 percent increase in stock options awarded to executives, the risk of fraud rises by 68 percent. The companies with the largest corporate fraud in recent years have, on average, eight times as many options as similar companies that did not experience fraud.
- Integrated steel companies often rewarded managers for increased labor efficiency. The fewer labor hours required to produce a ton of steel, the larger the manager's bonus. Unfortunately steel firms usually didn't count the work of outside contractors in the formula, so the reward system motivated managers to hire expensive contractors in the production process. By employing more contractors, managers actually increased the cost of production.
- Toyota rewards its dealerships based on customer satisfaction surveys, not just car sales. What Toyota discovered, however, is that this motivates dealers to increase satisfaction scores, not customer satisfaction. One Toyota dealership received high ratings because it offered free detailing to every customer who returned a "Very Satisfied" survey. The dealership even had a special copy of the survey showing clients which boxes to check. This increased customer ratings but not customer satisfaction.
- Donnelly Mirrors (now part of the Magna International empire) introduced a gainsharing plan that motivated employees to reduce labor but not material costs. Employees at the automobile parts manufacturer knew they worked faster with sharp grinding wheels, so they replaced the expensive diamond wheels more often. This action reduced labor costs, thereby giving employees the gainsharing bonus. However, the labor savings were offset by much higher costs for diamond grinding wheels.

Sources: F.F. Reichheld, *The Loyalty Effect* (Boston, MA: Harvard University Press, 1996), p. 236; D.R. Spitzer, "Power Rewards: Rewards That Really Motivate," *Management Review*, May 1996, pp. 45–50; J.A. Byrne, "How To Fix Corporate Governance," *Business Week*, 6 May 2002, p. 68; A. Holeck, "Griffith, Ind., Native Takes Over as Steel Plant Manager," *Northwest Indiana Times*, 25 May 2003; H. Connon, "Over-hyped, Overpaid, and Overextended," *The Observer* (London), 20 March 2005, p. 5.

which is more important when work is highly interdependent. A third benefit of team rewards is that they tend to support employee preferences for team-based work. One concern, however, is that employees (particularly the most productive employees) in the United States and many other low-collectivism cultures prefer rewards based on their individual performance rather than team performance.[25]

Ensure That Rewards Are Valued It seems obvious that rewards work best when they are valued. Yet companies sometimes make false assumptions about what employees want–with unfortunate consequences. The solution, of course, is to ask employees what they value. Campbell Soup did this a few years ago at its distribution centers in Canada. Executives thought the employees would ask for more money in a special team reward program. Instead, distribution staff said the most valued reward was a leather jacket with the Campbell Soup logo on the back. These leather jackets cost much less yet were worth much more than the financial bonus the company had otherwise intended to distribute.[26]

Watch Out for Unintended Consequences Performance-based reward systems sometimes have an unexpected–and undesirable–effect on employee behavior. Consider the pizza company that decided to reward its drivers for on-time delivery. The plan got more hot pizzas to customers on time, but it also increased the accident rates of its drivers because the incentive motivated them to drive recklessly.[27] Connections 6.1 describes a few other examples where reward systems had unintended consequences. The solution here is to carefully think through the consequences of rewards and, where possible, test incentives in a pilot project before applying them across the organization.

Financial rewards come in many forms and, as was mentioned at the outset of this section, influence employees in complex ways. But money isn't the only thing that motivates people to join an organization and perform effectively. "High performers don't go for the money," warns William Monahan, CEO of Oakdale, Minnesota-based Imation Corp. "Good people want to be in challenging jobs and see a future where they can get even more responsibilities and challenges." Rafik O. Loutfy, a Xerox research center director, agrees with this assessment. "Our top stars say they want to make an impact–that's the most important thing," he says. "Feeling they are contributing and making a difference is highly motivational for them."[28] In other words, Imation, Xerox, and other companies motivate employees mainly by designing interesting and challenging jobs, which we discuss next.

Learning Objectives

After reading this section you should be able to

4. Discuss the advantages and disadvantages of job specialization.

5. Diagram the job characteristics model of job design.

6. Identify three strategies to improve employee motivation through job design.

Job Design Practices

How do you build a better job? That question has challenged organizational behavior experts as well as psychologists, engineers, and economists for centuries. Some jobs have few tasks and usually require little skill. Other jobs are immensely complex and require years of experience and learning for mastery. From one extreme to the other, jobs have different effects on work efficiency and employee motivation. The challenge, at least from the organization's perspective, is to find the right combination so work is performed efficiently but employees are motivated and engaged.[29] This challenge requires careful **job design**–the process of assigning tasks to a job, including the interdependency of those tasks with other jobs. A job is a set of tasks performed by one person. To understand this issue more fully, let's begin by describing early job design efforts aimed at increasing work efficiency through job specialization.

job design
The process of assigning tasks to a job, including the interdependency of those tasks with other jobs.

Job Design and Work Efficiency

One production line at the Magna Steyr manufacturing plant in Graz, Austria, is responsible for assembling Chrysler's European minivan. On average, assembly workers on this line take three minutes to attach their assigned pieces to the chassis before repeating their work on the next vehicle. In North America, Chrysler employees assembling the same vehicle have an average job cycle time of 64.5 seconds. The difference isn't that Austrian employees are slower. Rather, Chrysler's North American employees are assigned fewer tasks in their work cycles. In other words they have somewhat more **job specialization**.[30]

job specialization
The result of division of labor in which each job includes a subset of the tasks required to complete the product or service.

Job specialization occurs when the work required to build an automobile–or any other product or service–is subdivided into separate jobs assigned to different people. Each resulting job includes a narrow subset of tasks, usually completed in a short cycle time. *Cycle time* is the time required to complete the task before starting over with a new work unit. Chrysler's minivan assemblers have an average cycle time of 64.5 seconds, which means they repeat the same set of tasks about 58 times each hour and probably about 230 times before they take a meal break.

Why would companies divide work into such tiny bits? The simple answer is that job specialization improves work efficiency. In fact, the economic benefits of dividing work into specialized jobs have been described and applied for at least two millennia. More than 2,300 years ago the Chinese philosopher Mencius and Greek philosopher Plato noted that division of labor improves work efficiency. In AD 1436 the waterways of Venice became an assembly line loading 10 galleons in just six hours. More than 200 years ago economist Adam Smith described a small factory where 10 pin makers collectively produced as many as 48,000 pins per day because they performed specialized tasks, such as straightening, cutting, sharpening, grinding, and whitening the pins. In contrast, Smith explained that if these 10 people worked alone producing complete pins, they would collectively manufacture no more than 200 pins per day.[31]

One reason why job specialization potentially increases work efficiency is that employees have fewer tasks to juggle and therefore spend less time changing activities. They also require fewer physical and mental skills to accomplish the assigned work, so less time and resources are needed for training. A third reason is that employees practice their tasks more frequently with shorter work cycles, so jobs are mastered quickly. A fourth reason why work efficiency increases is that employees with specific aptitudes or skills can be matched more precisely to the jobs for which they are best suited.[32]

scientific management
Involves systematically partitioning work into its smallest elements and standardizing tasks to achieve maximum efficiency.

Scientific Management One of the strongest advocates of job specialization was Frederick Winslow Taylor, an American industrial engineer who introduced the principles of **scientific management** in the early 1900s.[33] Scientific management consists of a toolkit of activities. Some of these interventions–training, goal setting, and work incentives–are common today but were rare until Taylor popularized them. However, scientific management is mainly associated with high levels of job specialization and standardization of tasks to achieve maximum efficiency.

According to Taylor, the most effective companies have detailed procedures and work practices developed by engineers, enforced by supervisors, and executed by employees. Even the supervisor's tasks should be divided: One person manages operational efficiency, another manages inspection, and another is the disciplinarian. Taylor and other industrial engineers demonstrated that scientific management significantly improves work efficiency. No doubt some of the increased productivity can be credited to the training, goal setting, and work incentives; but job specialization quickly became popular in its own right.

Frederick Taylor and his contemporaries focused on how job specialization reduces labor "waste" by improving the mechanical efficiency of work (matching skills, faster learning, less switchover time). Yet they didn't seem to notice how this extreme job specialization has an adverse effect on employee attitudes and motivation. Some jobs–such as assembling Chrysler minivans–are so specialized that they quickly become tedious, trivial, and socially isolating. Employee turnover and absenteeism tend to be higher in specialized jobs with very short time cycles. Companies sometimes have to pay higher wages to attract job applicants to this dissatisfying, narrowly defined work.[34]

Job specialization often reduces work quality because employees see only a small part of the process. As one observer of an automobile assembly line work reports, "Often [employees] did not know how their jobs related to the total picture. Not knowing, there was no incentive to strive for quality–what did quality even mean as it related to a bracket whose function you did not understand?"[35]

Equally important, Taylor's reliance on job specialization to improve employee performance ignores the motivational potential of jobs. As jobs become specialized, the work tends to become easier to perform but less motivating. As jobs become more complex, work motivation increases but the ability to master the job decreases. Maximum job performance occurs somewhere between these two extremes, where most people can eventually perform the job tasks efficiently, yet the work is interesting.

Job Design and Work Motivation

motivator–hygiene theory
Herzberg's theory stating that employees are primarily motivated by growth and esteem needs, not by lower-level needs.

job characteristics model
A job design model that relates the motivational properties of jobs to specific personal and organizational consequences of those properties.

Industrial engineers may have overlooked the motivational effect of job characteristics, but it is now the central focus of many job design changes. Organizational behavior scholar Frederick Herzberg is credited with shifting the spotlight when he introduced **motivator–hygiene theory** in the 1950s.[36] Motivator–hygiene theory proposes that employees experience job satisfaction when they fulfill growth and esteem needs (called *motivators*), and they experience dissatisfaction when they have poor working conditions, job security, and other factors categorized as lower-order needs (called *hygienes*). Herzberg argued that only characteristics of the job itself motivate employees, whereas the hygiene factors merely prevent dissatisfaction. It might seem obvious to us today that the job itself is a source of motivation, but it was radical thinking when Herzberg proposed the idea.

Motivator–hygiene theory didn't find much research support, but Herzberg's ideas generated new thinking about the motivational potential of the job itself.[37] Out of subsequent research emerged the **job characteristics model** shown in Exhibit 6.2.

Exhibit 6.2
The Job Characteristics Model

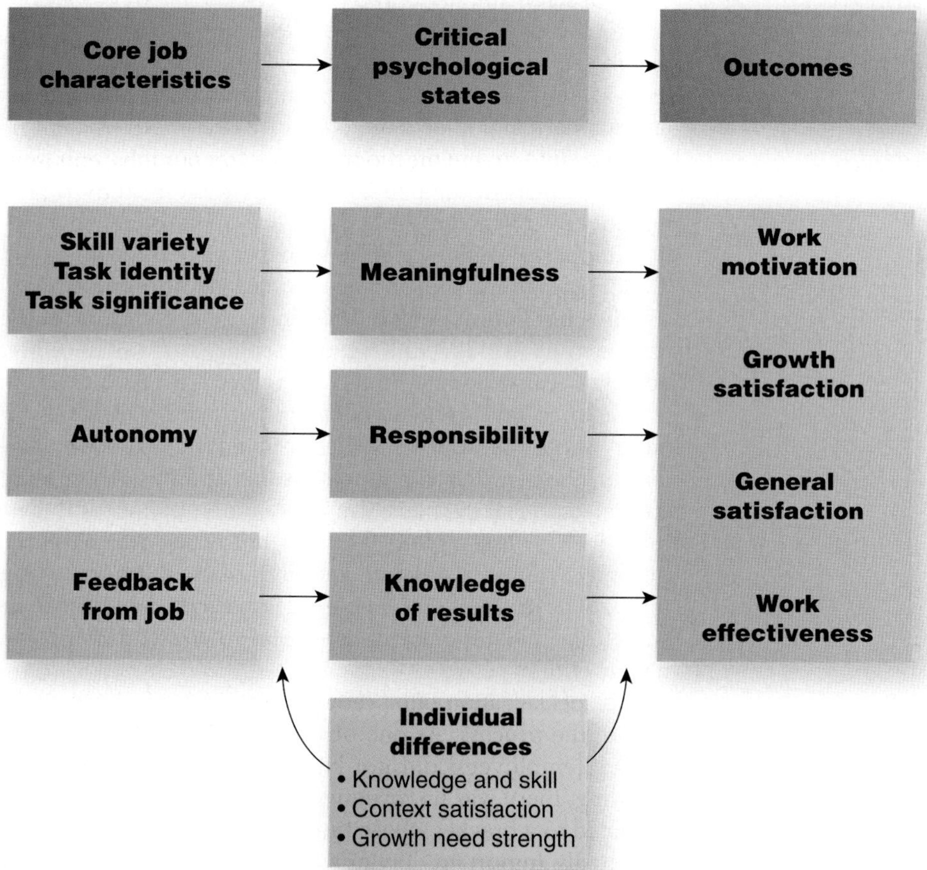

Source: J.R. Hackman and G. Oldham, *Work Redesign* (Reading, MA: Addison-Wesley, 1980), p. 90. Used with permission.

The job characteristics model identifies five core job dimensions that produce three psychological states. Employees who experience these psychological states tend to have higher levels of internal work motivation (motivation from the work itself), job satisfaction (particularly satisfaction with the work itself), and work effectiveness.[38]

Core Job Characteristics The job characteristics model identifies five core job characteristics. Under the right conditions, employees are more motivated and satisfied when jobs have higher levels of these characteristics:

skill variety
The extent to which employees must use different skills and talents to perform tasks within their job.

task identity
The degree to which a job requires completion of a whole or an identifiable piece of work.

task significance
The degree to which the job has a substantial impact on the organization and/or larger society.

autonomy
The degree to which a job gives employees the freedom, independence, and discretion to schedule their work and determine the procedures used in completing it.

- *Skill variety.* **Skill variety** refers to the use of different skills and talents to complete a variety of work activities. For example, sales clerks who normally only serve customers might be assigned the additional duties of stocking inventory and changing storefront displays.
- *Task identity.* **Task identity** is the degree to which a job requires completion of a whole or identifiable piece of work, such as assembling an entire broadband modem rather than just soldering in the circuitry.
- *Task significance.* **Task significance** is the degree to which the job affects the organization or society. For instance, many employees at Medtronic, the Minneapolis-based maker of pacemakers and other medical equipment, have high job specialization, yet 86 percent say their work has special meaning and 94 percent feel pride in what they accomplish. The reason for their high task significance is that they attend seminars that show how the products they manufacture save lives. "We have patients who come in who would be dead if it wasn't for us," says a Medtronic production supervisor.[39]
- *Autonomy.* Jobs with high levels of **autonomy** provide freedom, independence, and discretion in scheduling the work and determining the procedures to be used to complete the work. In autonomous jobs, employees make their own decisions rather than relying on detailed instructions from supervisors or procedure manuals.
- *Job feedback.* Job feedback is the degree to which employees can tell how well they are doing based on direct sensory information from the job itself. Airline pilots can tell how well they land their aircraft, and road crews can see how well they have prepared the roadbed and laid the asphalt.

Critical Psychological States The five core job characteristics affect employee motivation and satisfaction through three critical psychological states shown in Exhibit 6.2. One of these psychological states is *experienced meaningfulness*–the belief that one's work is worthwhile or important. Skill variety, task identity, and task significance directly contribute to the job's meaningfulness. If the job has high levels of all three characteristics, employees are likely to feel that their jobs are highly meaningful. Meaningfulness drops as a job loses one or more of these characteristics.

Work motivation and performance increase when employees feel personally accountable for the outcomes of their efforts. Autonomy directly contributes to this feeling of *experienced responsibility.* Employees must be assigned control of their work environment to feel responsible for their successes and failures. The third critical psychological state is *knowledge of results.* Employees want information about the consequences of their work effort. Knowledge of results can originate from co-workers, supervisors, or clients. However, job design focuses on knowledge of results from the work itself.

Individual Differences Job design doesn't increase work motivation for everyone in every situation. Employees must have the required skills and knowledge to master the more challenging work. Otherwise job design tends to increase stress and reduce job performance. The original model also suggests that increasing the motivational potential of jobs will not motivate employees who are dissatisfied with their work context (such as working conditions or job security) or who have a low growth need strength. However, research findings have been mixed, suggesting that employees might be motivated by job design no matter how they feel about their job context or how high or low they score on growth needs.[40]

Job Design Practices That Motivate

Three main strategies can increase the motivational potential of jobs: job rotation, job enlargement, and job enrichment. This section also identifies several ways to implement job enrichment.

job rotation
The practice of moving employees from one job to another.

Job Rotation At the beginning of this topic on job design, we mentioned that assembly line employees at Chrysler have a high degree of specialization. Chrysler executives are aware of the motivational and physiological problems that this repetitive work can create, so they have introduced a policy where employees work in teams and rotate to a different workstation within that team every few hours. **Job rotation** is the practice of moving employees from one job to another. "The whole idea of job rotation makes a big difference," says Chrysler executive vice president of manufacturing Frank Ewasyshyn. "The job naturally gets better, quality improves, throughput improves." The Jeep assembly plant in Toledo, Ohio, was Chrysler's first U.S. facility to switch to team assembly, and significant improvements in productivity and morale became apparent within the first year. Job rotation offers "important ergonomic benefits to workers, improvements in product quality, and higher employee satisfaction," says Tom Maxon, a senior Chrysler manager in Toledo.[41]

From the experience at Chrysler and many other companies, we can identify three potential benefits of job rotation. First, it minimizes health risks from repetitive strain and heavy lifting because employees use different muscles and physical positions in the various jobs. Second, it supports multiskilling (employees learn several jobs), which increases workforce flexibility in the production process and in finding replacements for those on vacation. A third benefit of job rotation is that it potentially reduces the boredom of highly repetitive jobs. However, organizational behavior experts continue to debate whether job rotation really is job redesign because each job is still highly specialized. Critics argue that job redesign requires changes within the job, such as job enlargement.

job enlargement
Increasing the number of tasks employees perform within their job.

Job Enlargement **Job enlargement** adds tasks to an existing job. This might involve combining two or more complete jobs into one, or just adding one or two more tasks to an existing job. Either way, skill variety increases because there are more tasks to perform. Video journalists represent a clear example of an enlarged job. As Exhibit 6.3 illustrates, a traditional news team consists of a camera operator, a sound and lighting specialist, and the journalist who writes and presents or narrates the story. One video journalist performs all of these tasks.

Job enlargement significantly improves work efficiency and flexibility. However, research suggests that simply giving employees more tasks won't affect motivation, performance, or job satisfaction. Instead these benefits result only when skill variety is combined with more autonomy and job knowledge.[42] In other words, employees

Exhibit 6.3
Job Enlargement of Video Journalists

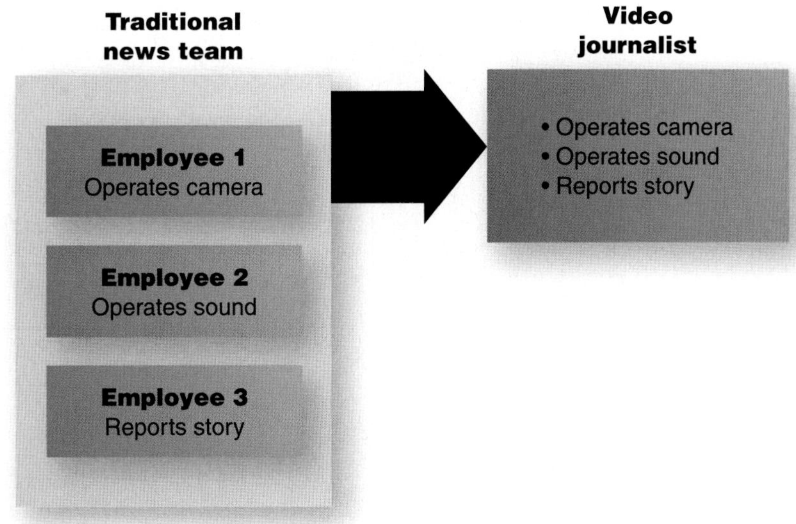

are motivated when they perform a variety of tasks *and* have the freedom and knowledge to structure their work to achieve the highest satisfaction and performance. These job characteristics are at the heart of job enrichment.

job enrichment
Giving employees more responsibility for scheduling, coordinating, and planning their own work.

Job Enrichment **Job enrichment** occurs when employees are given more responsibility for scheduling, coordinating, and planning their own work.[43] People in enriched jobs usually experience higher job satisfaction and work motivation, along with lower absenteeism and turnover. Productivity is also higher when task identity and job feedback are improved. Product and service quality tend to improve because job enrichment increases the jobholder's felt responsibility and sense of ownership over the product or service.[44]

One way to increase job enrichment is by combining highly interdependent tasks into one job. This *natural grouping* approach is reflected in the video journalist job. Video journalist was earlier described as an enlarged job, but it is also an example of job enrichment because it naturally groups tasks together to complete an entire product (a news clip). By forming natural work units, jobholders have stronger feelings of responsibility for an identifiable body of work. They feel a sense of ownership and therefore tend to increase job quality. Forming natural work units increases task identity and task significance because employees perform a complete product or service and can more readily see how their work affects others.

A second job enrichment strategy, called *establishing client relationships*, involves putting employees in direct contact with their clients rather than using the supervisor as a go-between. By being directly responsible for specific clients, employees have more information and can make decisions affecting those clients.[45] Establishing client relationships also increases task significance because employees see a line-of-sight connection between their work and consequences for customers. This was apparent among medical secretaries at a large regional hospital in Sweden after the hospital reduced its workforce by 10 percent and gave the secretaries expanded job duties. Although these employees experienced more stress from the higher workloads, some of them also felt more motivated and satisfied because they now had direct interaction with patients. "Before, I never saw a patient; now they have a face," says one medical secretary. "I feel satisfied and pleased with myself; you feel someone needs you."[46]

Video Journalists Get Enriched on the Job Traditionally up to four people have been required to shoot a video news clip: a reporter, camera operator, sound operator, and production editor. Now, thanks to technology and innovative thinking about job design in the newsroom, many TV networks are turning staff into video journalists (VJs) who perform all of these tasks in one job. Michael Rosenblum, who became one of the world's first VJs two decades ago, has transformed BBC, NYT-TV, Oxygen, and many other television companies into VJ shops. He also recently trained staff at KRON-TV in San Francisco, which is now making the transition. This photo shows one of KRON's VJs at work. "The VJ model will empower a new breed of broadcast journalist who will take a story from concept to finished segment," says Mark Antonitis, president and general manager of KRON-TV. "This sort of complete ownership will provide the station with stories that have a singular and unique voice."[47]

Forming natural task groups and establishing client relationships are common ways to enrich jobs, but the heart of the job enrichment philosophy is to give employees more autonomy over their work. This basic idea is at the core of one of the most widely mentioned–and often misunderstood–practices, known as empowerment.

Learning Objectives

After reading the next two sections you should be able to

7. Define empowerment and identify strategies to support empowerment.

8. Describe the five elements of self-leadership.

Empowerment Practices

A large American hotel had a policy that if a guest questioned a bill, front-desk staff were supposed to defend the bill no matter what. If the guest asked to speak with the manager, the manager would override the charge. The hotel manager thought that this "good cop, bad cop" approach was useful; but Rick Garlick, a consultant hired by the hotel, suggested that they immediately change the policy. Instead front-desk staff should have the autonomy to decide alone whether the complaint was justified. The result? Within a few months the hotel's guest satisfaction scores soared from near the bottom to near the top among hotels in the company's chain. "Empowering employees was one of a number of key improvements in manager–staff relations that ultimately resulted in much higher guest satisfaction," says Garlick.[48]

empowerment
A psychological concept in which people experience more self-determination, meaning, competence, and impact regarding their role in the organization.

Empowerment is a term that has been loosely tossed around in corporate circles and has been the subject of considerable debate among academics. However, the most widely accepted definition is that empowerment is a psychological concept represented by four dimensions: self-determination, meaning, competence, and impact of the individual's role in the organization. Empowerment consists of all four dimensions. If any dimension weakens, the employee's sense of empowerment will weaken.[49]

- *Self-determination.* Empowered employees feel that they have freedom, independence, and discretion over their work activities.
- *Meaning.* Employees who feel empowered care about their work and believe that what they do is important.
- *Competence.* Empowered people are confident about their ability to perform the work well and have a capacity to grow with new challenges.
- *Impact.* Empowered employees view themselves as active participants in the organization; that is, their decisions and actions have an influence on the company's success.

Supporting Empowerment

Chances are that you have heard corporate leaders say they are "empowering" the workforce. What these executives really mean is that they are changing the work environment to support empowerment.[50] Numerous individual, job design, and organizational or work context factors support empowerment. At the individual level, employees must possess the necessary competencies to be able to perform the work as well as handle the additional decision-making requirements. Although other individual factors have been proposed (such as locus of control), they do not seem to have any real effect on whether employees feel empowered.[51]

Job characteristics clearly influence the dynamics of empowerment.[52] To generate beliefs about self-determination, employees must work in jobs with a high degree of autonomy with minimal bureaucratic control. To maintain a sense of meaningfulness, jobs must have high levels of task identity and task significance. And to maintain a sense of self-confidence, jobs must provide sufficient feedback.

Several organizational and work context factors also influence empowerment. Employees experience more empowerment in organizations where information and other resources are easily accessible. Empowerment also requires a learning orientation culture. In other words, empowerment flourishes in organizations that appreciate the value of the employee learning and that accept reasonable mistakes as a natural part of the learning process. Furthermore, empowerment requires corporate leaders who trust employees and are willing to take the risks that empowerment creates. "Executives must give up control and trust the power of talent," advises Ricardo Semler, head of Semco Corporation in São Paulo, Brazil.[53]

With the right individuals, job characteristics, and organizational environment, empowerment can have a noticeable effect on motivation and performance. For instance, a study of bank employees concluded that empowerment improved customer service and tended to reduce conflict between employees and their supervisors. Other research links empowerment with higher trust in management, which ultimately influences job satisfaction, belief and acceptance of organizational goals

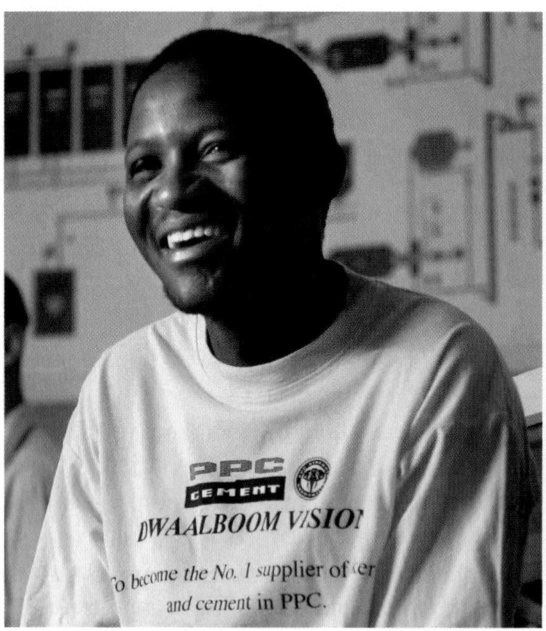

Kambuku Empowerment Kambuku is the name of one of the largest tusked elephants in Africa. It is also the symbolic title for a "people focused, value added" initiative that has transformed Pretoria Portland Cement (PPC) into a performance-oriented company and one of South Africa's best employers. The company had a long way to go to reach its goal. A few years ago PPC was a top-down, autocratic organization where managers gave "oodles of supervision and checking that people do the right things," recalls PPC chief executive John Gomersall. Now he says, "We have passed the ownership to the people." Departments and teams are given much more autonomy. Company leaders seek out employee ideas, offer continuous training, and reward teams and individuals for their performance. "We attribute our ongoing success and strength to the fact that every employee in the company has the opportunity to make a contribution and be recognized for their input to achieving success," says chief operating officer Orrie Fenn. "Empowered employees ensure a committed workforce, which eventually translates into sustainable business performance."[54]

and values, and organizational commitment. Empowerment also tends to increase personal initiative because employees identify with and assume more psychological ownership of their work.[55]

Self-Leadership Practices

What is the most important characteristic that companies look for in their employees? Leadership potential, ability to work in a team, and good communication skills are important, but a survey of 800 British employers concludes that they don't top the list. Instead the most important employee characteristic is self-motivation. The staff at Universal Insurance Services, Inc., can identify with those results. The Grand Rapids insurance company is one of Michigan's "cool places to work" because, according to its own Web site, "Our culture encourages self-management and total accountability." This isn't a blank statement. Universal's employees are expected to score their own performance and provide evidence of that score![56]

Most of the concepts introduced in this chapter and Chapter 5 have assumed that corporate leaders do things to motivate employees. Certainly these theories and practices are valuable; but they overlook the fact that the most successful employees ultimately motivate and manage themselves. In other words, they engage in self-leadership.

self-leadership
The process of influencing oneself to establish the self-direction and self-motivation needed to perform a task.

Self-leadership refers to the process of influencing oneself to establish the self-direction and self-motivation needed to perform a task.[57] This concept includes a toolkit of behavioral activities borrowed from social learning theory and goal setting. It also includes constructive thought processes that have been extensively studied in sports psychology. Overall, self-leadership takes the view that individuals mostly regulate their own actions through these behavioral and cognitive (thought) activities.

Exhibit 6.4 **Elements of Self-Leadership**

Although we are in the early stages of understanding the dynamics of self-leadership, Exhibit 6.4 identifies the five main elements of this process. These elements, which generally follow each other in a sequence, are personal goal setting, constructive thought patterns, designing natural rewards, self-monitoring, and self-reinforcement.[58]

Personal Goal Setting

The first step in self-leadership is to set goals for your own work effort. This applies the ideas learned in Chapter 5 about goal setting, such as identifying goals that are specific, relevant, and challenging. The main difference is that self-leadership involves setting goals alone rather than having them assigned by or jointly decided with a supervisor. Research suggests that employees are more focused and perform better when they set their own goals, particularly in combination with other self-leadership practices.[59]

Constructive Thought Patterns

Before beginning a task and while performing it, employees should engage in positive (constructive) thoughts about that work and its accomplishment. In particular, employees are more motivated and better prepared to accomplish a task after they have engaged in positive self-talk and mental imagery.

self-talk
Talking to ourselves about our own thoughts or actions for the purpose of increasing our self-confidence and navigating through decisions in a future event.

Positive Self-Talk

Do you ever talk to yourself? Most of us do, according to a major study of university students.[60] **Self-talk** refers to any situation in which we talk to ourselves about our own thoughts or actions. Some of this internal communication assists the decision-making process, such as weighing the advantages of a particular choice. Self-leadership is mostly interested in evaluative self-talk, in which you evaluate your capabilities and accomplishments.

The problem is that most evaluative self-talk is negative; we criticize much more than encourage or congratulate ourselves. Negative self-talk undermines our confidence and potential to perform a particular task. In contrast, positive self-talk creates a "can-do" belief and thereby increases motivation by raising our effort-to-performance expectancy. We often hear that professional athletes "psych" themselves up before an important event. They tell themselves that they can achieve their goal and that they have practiced enough to reach that goal. They are motivating themselves through positive self-talk.

mental imagery
Mentally practicing a task and visualizing its successful completion.

Mental Imagery

You've probably heard the phrase "I'll cross that bridge when I come to it!" Self-leadership takes the opposite view. It suggests that we need to mentally practice a task and imagine successfully performing it beforehand. This process, known as **mental imagery** has two parts. One part involves mentally practicing the task, anticipating obstacles to goal accomplishment, and working out solutions to those obstacles before they occur. By mentally walking through the activities required to accomplish the task, we begin to see problems that may occur. We can then imagine what responses would be best for each contingency.[61]

While one part of mental imagery helps us to anticipate things that could go wrong, the other part involves visualizing successful completion of the task. We imagine the experience of completing the task and the positive results that follow. Everyone daydreams and fantasizes about being in a successful situation. You might imagine yourself being promoted to your boss's job, receiving a prestigious award, or taking time off work. This visualization increases goal commitment and motivates us to complete the task effectively. This is the strategy that Tony Wang applies to motivate himself. "Since I am in sales, I think about the reward I get for closing new business–the commission check–and the things it will allow me to do that I really enjoy," explains Wang. "Or I think about the feeling I get when I am successful at something and how it makes me feel good, and use that to get me going."[62]

Designing Natural Rewards

Self-leadership recognizes that employees actively craft their jobs. To varying degrees, they can alter tasks and work relationships to make the work more motivating.[63] One way to build natural rewards into a job is to alter how a task is accomplished. People often have enough discretion in their jobs to make slight changes to suit their needs and preferences. For instance, you might try out a new software program to design an idea rather than sketching the image with pencil. By using the new software, you are adding challenge to a task that may have otherwise been mundane.

Self-Monitoring

Self-monitoring is the process of keeping track at regular intervals of one's progress toward a goal using naturally occurring feedback. Some people can receive feedback from the job itself, such as a road crew that can see how well they are laying the roadbed and asphalt. But many of us are unable to observe our work output so readily. Instead many people need to design feedback systems. Salespeople might arrange to receive monthly reports on sales levels in their territory. Production staff might have gauges or computer feedback systems installed so they can see how many errors are made on the production line. Research suggests that people who have control over the timing of performance feedback perform their tasks better than those with feedback assigned by others.[64]

Self-Reinforcement

Self-leadership includes the social learning theory concept of self-reinforcement. Self-reinforcement occurs whenever an employee has control over a reinforcer but doesn't "take" the reinforcer until completing a self-set goal.[65] A common example is taking a break after reaching a predetermined stage of your work. The work break is a self-induced form of positive reinforcement. Self-reinforcement also occurs when you decide to do a more enjoyable task after completing a task that you dislike. For example, after slogging through a difficult report, you might decide to spend time doing a more pleasant task, such as catching up on industry news by scanning Web sites.

Self-Leadership in Practice

Self-leadership is shaping up to be a valuable applied performance practice in organizational settings. A respectable body of research shows consistent support for most elements of self-leadership. Self-set goals and self-monitoring increased the frequency

eSilicon Corp. Flies with Employees Who Lead Themselves Jack Harding (top left in photo) has had his share of ups and downs over his career as an entrepreneur in Silicon Valley. Fortunately the company he founded in 2000, eSilicon Corp., has become the fastest-growing private company in Silicon Valley and is winning accolades throughout the industry for its design and manufacturing of custom chips for electronics companies. Looking back, Harding says that employee self-leadership played a key role in the company's growth. "You look for character and experience" when hiring new employees, Harding suggests. "They need to be smart, team players and self-motivated—and you can't instill that."[66]

of wearing safety equipment among employees in a mining operation. Airline employees who received constructive thought training experienced better mental performance, enthusiasm, and job satisfaction than co-workers who did not receive this training. Mental imagery helped supervisors and process engineers in a pulp and paper mill to transfer what they learned in an interpersonal communication skills class back to the job.[67] Studies also indicate that self-set goals and constructive thought processes improve individual performance in swimming, tennis, ice skating, soccer, and other sports. Indeed, studies show that almost all Olympic athletes rely on mental rehearsal and positive self-talk to achieve their performance goals.[68]

Self-leadership behaviors are more frequently found in people with specific personality characteristics, notably conscientiousness and extroversion.[69] However, one of the benefits of self-leadership is that it can be learned. Training programs have helped employees to improve their self-leadership skills. Organizations can also encourage self-leadership by providing sufficient autonomy and establishing rewards that reinforce self-leadership behaviors. Employees are also more likely to engage in self-monitoring in companies that emphasize continuous measurement of performance. Overall, self-leadership promises to be an important concept and practice for improving employee motivation and performance.

Self-leadership, job design, empowerment, and rewards are valuable approaches to improving employee performance. However, performance is also affected by work-related stress. As we learn in the next chapter, too much stress is causing numerous problems with employee performance and well-being, but there are also ways to combat this epidemic.

Chapter Summary

Money and other financial rewards are a fundamental part of the employment relationship, but their value and meaning vary from one person to the next. Organizations reward employees for their membership and seniority, job status, competencies, and performance. Membership-based rewards may attract job applicants and seniority-based rewards reduce turnover, but these reward objectives tend to discourage turnover among those with the lowest performance. Rewards based on job status try to maintain internal equity and motivate employees to compete for promotions. However, they tend to encourage bureaucratic hierarchy, support status differences, and motivate employees to compete and hoard resources. Competency-based rewards are becoming increasingly popular because they improve workforce flexibility and are consistent with the emerging idea of employability. However, they tend to be subjectively measured and can result in higher costs as employees spend more time learning new skills.

Awards and bonuses, commissions, and other individual performance–based rewards have existed for centuries and are widely used. Many companies are shifting to team-based rewards such as gainsharing plans and to organizational rewards such as employee stock ownership plans (ESOPs), stock options, profit sharing, and balanced scorecards. ESOPs and stock options create an ownership culture, but employees often perceive a weak connection between individual performance and organizational rewards.

Financial rewards have a number of limitations, but reward effectiveness can be improved in several ways. Organizational leaders should ensure that rewards are linked to work performance, rewards are aligned with performance within the employees' control, team rewards are used where jobs are interdependent, rewards are valued by employees, and rewards have no unintended consequences.

Job design refers to the process of assigning tasks to a job, including the interdependency of those tasks with other jobs. Job specialization subdivides work into separate jobs for different people. This increases work efficiency because employees master the tasks quickly, spend less time changing tasks, require less training, and can be matched more closely with the jobs best suited to their skills. However, job specialization may reduce work motivation, create mental and physical health problems, lower product or service quality, and increase costs through discontentment, absenteeism, and turnover.

Contemporary job design strategies reverse job specialization through job rotation, job enlargement, and job enrichment. The job characteristics model is a template for job redesign that specifies core job dimensions, psychological states, and individual differences. Organizations introduce job rotation to reduce job boredom, develop a more flexible workforce, and reduce the incidence of repetitive strain injuries. Two ways to enrich jobs are clustering tasks into natural groups and establishing client relationships.

Empowerment is a psychological concept represented by four dimensions: self-determination, meaning, competence, and impact regarding the individual's role in the organization. Individual characteristics seem to have a minor influence on empowerment. Job design is a major influence—particularly autonomy, task identity, task significance, and job feedback. Empowerment is also supported at the organizational level through a learning orientation culture, sufficient information and resources, and corporate leaders who trust employees.

Self-leadership is the process of influencing oneself to establish the self-direction and self-motivation needed to perform a task. This includes personal goal setting, constructive thought patterns, designing natural rewards, self-monitoring, and self-reinforcement. Constructive thought patterns include self-talk and mental imagery. Self-talk refers to any situation in which a person talks to himself or herself about his or her own thoughts or actions. Mental imagery involves mentally practicing a task and imagining successfully performing it beforehand.

Key Terms

autonomy, p. 179
balanced scorecard (BSC), p. 172
employee stock ownership plans (ESOP), p. 172
empowerment, p. 183
gainsharing plans, p. 171
job characteristics model, p. 178
job design, p. 176
job enlargement, p. 180
job enrichment, p. 181
job evaluation, p. 170
job rotation, p. 180
job specialization, p. 176
mental imagery, p. 185
motivator–hygiene theory, p. 178
profit-sharing plans, p. 172
scientific management, p. 177
self-leadership, p. 184
self-talk, p. 185
skill variety, p. 179
stock options, p. 172
task identity, p. 179
task significance, p. 179

Critical Thinking Questions

1. As a consultant, you have been asked to recommend either a gainsharing plan or a profit-sharing plan for employees who work in the four regional distribution and warehousing facilities of a large retail organization. Which reward system would you recommend? Explain your answer.
2. You are a member of a team responsible for developing performance measures for your college or university department or faculty unit based on the balanced scorecard approach. Identify one performance measurement for each of the following factors: financial, customer satisfaction, internal processes, and employee performance.
3. Numbat Tire Corp. redesigned its production facilities around a team-based system. However, the company president believes that employees will not be motivated unless they receive incentives based on their individual performance. Give three explanations why Numbat Tire should introduce team-based rather than individual rewards in this setting.
4. What can organizations do to increase the effectiveness of financial rewards?
5. Most of us have watched pizzas being made while waiting in a pizzeria. What level of job specialization do you usually notice in these operations? Why does this high or low level of specialization exist? If some pizzerias have different levels of specialization than others, identify the contingencies that might explain these differences.
6. Can a manager or supervisor "empower" an employee? Discuss this fully.
7. Describe a time when you practiced self-leadership to successfully perform a task. With reference to each step in the self-leadership process, describe what you did to achieve this success.
8. Can self-leadership replace formal leadership in an organizational setting?

Case Study 6.1 THE REGENCY GRAND HOTEL

Lisa Ho, Prada Singapore under the supervision of Steven L. McShane

The Regency Grand Hotel is a five-star hotel in Bangkok, Thailand. The hotel was established 15 years ago by a local consortium of investors and has been operated by a Thai general manager throughout this time. The hotel is one of Bangkok's most prestigious hotels, and its 700 employees enjoy the prestige of being associated with the hotel. The hotel provides good welfare benefits, above–market rate salary, and job security. In addition, a good year-end bonus amounting to four months' salary is rewarded to employees regardless of the hotel's overall performance during the year.

Recently the Regency was sold to a large American hotel chain that was very keen to expand its operations into Thailand. When the acquisition was announced, the general manager decided to take early retirement when the hotel changed ownership. The American hotel chain kept all of the Regency employees, although a few were transferred to other positions. John Becker, an American with 10 years of management experience with the hotel chain, was appointed as the new general manager of Regency Grand Hotel. Becker, was selected as the new general manager because of his previous successes in integrating newly acquired hotels in the United States. In most of the previous acquisitions Becker, took over operations with poor profitability and low morale.

Becker is a strong believer in empowerment. He expects employees to go beyond guidelines and standards to consider guest needs case by case. That is, employees must be guest-oriented at all times to provide excellent customer service. From his U.S. experience Becker has found that empowerment increases employee motivation, performance, and job satisfaction, all of which contribute to a hotel's profitability and customer service ratings. Soon after becoming general manager in Regency Grand, Becker introduced the practice of empowerment to replicate the successes that he had achieved back home.

The Regency Grand hotel has been very profitable since it opened 15 years ago. The employees have always worked according to management's instructions. Their responsibility was to ensure that the instructions from their managers were carried out diligently and conscientiously. Innovation and creativity were discouraged under the previous management. Indeed, employees were punished for their mistakes and discouraged from trying out ideas that had not been approved by management. As a result, employees were afraid to be innovative and to take risks.

Becker met with Regency's managers and department heads to explain that empowerment would be introduced in the hotel. He told them that employees must be empowered with decision-making authority so that they could begin to use their initiative, creativity, and judgment to satisfy guest needs or handle problems effectively and efficiently. However, he stressed that the more complex issues and decisions were to be referred to superiors, who were to coach and assist rather than provide direct orders. Furthermore, Becker stressed that although mistakes were allowed, the same mistakes could not be tolerated more than twice. He advised his managers and department heads not to discuss with him minor issues and problems and not to consult with him about minor decisions. Nevertheless, he told them that they were to discuss important and major issues and decisions with him. He concluded the meeting by asking for feedback. Several managers and department heads told him that they liked the idea and would support it, while others simply nodded their heads. Becker, pleased with the response, was eager to implement his plan.

In the past the Regency had emphasized administrative control, resulting in many bureaucratic procedures throughout the organization. For example, the front counter employees needed to seek approval from their manager before they could upgrade guests to another category of room. The front counter manager would then have to write and submit a report to the general manager justifying the upgrade. Soon after his meeting with managers, Becker reduced the number of bureaucratic rules at the Regency and allocated more decision-making authority to frontline employees. This action upset those who previously had decision-making power over these issues. As a result, several of these employees left the hotel.

Becker also began spending a large portion of his time observing and interacting with the employees at the front desk, lobby, restaurants, and various departments. This direct interaction with Becker helped many employees to understand what he wanted and expected of them. However, the employees had much difficulty trying to distinguish between major and minor issues and decisions. More often than not, supervisors would reverse employee decisions by stating that they were major issues requiring management approval. Employees who displayed initiative and made good decisions in satisfying the needs of the guests rarely received any positive feedback from their supervisors. Eventually most of these employees lost confidence in making decisions, reverting back to relying on their superiors for decision making.

Not long after the implementation of the practice of empowerment, Becker realized that his subordinates were consulting him more frequently than before. Most of them came to him with minor issues and decisions. He had to spend most of his time attending to his subordinates. Soon he began to feel frustrated and exhausted, and often he would tell his secretary that "unless the hotel is on fire, don't let anyone disturb me."

Becker thought that the practice of empowerment would benefit the overall performance of the hotel. However, contrary to his expectations, the business and overall performance of the hotel began to deteriorate. There had been an increasing number of guest complaints. In the past the hotel had minimal guest complaints. Now there were a significant number of formal written complaints every month. Many other guests voiced their dissatisfaction verbally to hotel employees. The number of mistakes made by employees had increased. Becker was very upset when he realized that two local newspapers and an overseas newspaper had published negative feedback about the hotel's service. He was most distressed when an international travel magazine voted the hotel as "one of Asia's nightmare hotels."

The stress levels of the employees were continuously mounting since the introduction of the practice of empowerment. Absenteeism due to illness was increasing at an alarming rate. In addition, the employee turnover rate had reached an all-time high. The good working relationships that were established under the old management had been severely strained. The employees were no longer united and supportive of each other. They were quick to point fingers at or to backstab one another when mistakes were made and when problems occurred.

Discussion Questions

1. Identify the symptoms indicating that problems exist in this case.
2. Diagnose the problems in this case using organizational behavior concepts.
3. Recommend solutions to overcome or minimize the problems and symptoms in this case.

Note: This case is based on true events, but the industry and names have been changed.

Case Study 6.2 THE BOTTOM LINE ON OPTIONS

Stock options became popular in the 1990s as a tool that was supposed to "align the interests" of shareholders and management–in other words, reward CEOs for concentrating on raising their stock price. The popularity of these options–more than 10 million employees received them at the height of the options boom in 2002–was partly due to accounting rules in which stock options cost nothing when handed out. Not any more. The new rules require U.S. companies to count stock options as an expense. The result is that companies are turning to other forms of financial rewards for top executives and, in many cases, curtailing financial rewards altogether for professional and lower management staff.

This *BusinessWeek* case study describes how several companies have responded to new accounting rules regarding stock options. It also looks at the motivational effect of stock options. Read the full text of this *BusinessWeek* article at www.mhhe.com/mcshane4e and prepare for the discussion questions below.

Discussion Questions

1. When are stock options effective for motivating and rewarding employees?
2. How have financial rewards for senior executives shifted since the new stock option accounting rules were introduced? In your opinion, will the new financial rewards motivate executives differently than did stock options?

Source: M. Gimein, "The Bottom Line on Options," *BusinessWeek*, 3 April 2006, 32.

Team Exercise 6.3 IS STUDENT WORK ENRICHED?

PURPOSE This exercise is designed to help you learn how to measure the motivational potential of jobs and to evaluate the extent to which jobs should be further enriched.

INSTRUCTIONS Being a student is like a job in several ways. You have tasks to perform, and someone (such as your instructor) oversees your work. Although few people want to be students most of their lives (the pay rate is too low!), it may be interesting to determine how enriched your job is as a student.

1. Students are placed into teams (preferably four or five people).
2. Working alone, students complete both measures in this exercise. Then, using the guidelines here, they individually calculate the score for the five core job characteristics as well as the overall motivating potential score for the job.
3. Members of each team compare their individual results. The group should identify differences of opinion about each core job characteristic. They should also note which core job characteristics

have the lowest scores and recommend how these scores could be increased.

4. The entire class meets to discuss the results of the exercise. The instructor may ask some teams to present their comparisons and recommendations for a particular core job characteristic.

Job Diagnostic Survey

Circle the number on the right that best describes student work.	Very little			Moderately			Very much
1. To what extent does student work permit you to decide on your own how to go about doing the work?	1	2	3	4	5	6	7
2. To what extent does student work involve doing a whole or identifiable piece of work, rather than a small portion of the overall work process?	1	2	3	4	5	6	7
3. To what extent does student work require you to do many different things, using a variety of your skills and talents?	1	2	3	4	5	6	7
4. To what extent are the results of your work as a student likely to significantly affect the lives and well-being of other people (within your school, your family, or society)?	1	2	3	4	5	6	7
5. To what extent does working on student activities provide information about your performance?	1	2	3	4	5	6	7

Circle the number on the right that best describes student work.	Very inaccurate			Uncertain			Very accurate
6. Being a student requires me to use a number of complex and high-level skills.	1	2	3	4	5	6	7
7. Student work is arranged so that I do NOT have the chance to do an entire piece of work from beginning to end.	7	6	5	4	3	2	1
8. Doing the work required of students provides many chances for me to figure out how well I am doing.	1	2	3	4	5	6	7
9. The work students must do is quite simple and repetitive.	7	6	5	4	3	2	1
10. The work of a student is one where a lot of other people can be affected by how well the work gets done.	1	2	3	4	5	6	7
11. Student work denies me any chance to use my personal initiative or judgment in carrying out the work.	7	6	5	4	3	2	1
12. Student work provides me the chance to completely finish the pieces of work I begin.	1	2	3	4	5	6	7
13. Doing student work by itself provides few clues about whether I am performing well.	7	6	5	4	3	2	1
14. As a student, I have considerable opportunity for independence and freedom in how I do the work.	1	2	3	4	5	6	7
15. The work I perform as a student is NOT very significant or important in the broader scheme of things.	7	6	5	4	3	2	1

Adapted from the Job Diagnostic Survey, developed by J.R. Hackman and G.R. Oldham. The authors have released any copyright ownership of this scale. See J.R. Hackman and G.R. Oldham, *Work Redesign* (Reading, MA: Addison-Wesley, 1980), p. 275.

CALCULATING THE MOTIVATING POTENTIAL SCORE

SCORING CORE JOB CHARACTERISTICS Use the following calculations to estimate the motivating potential score for the job of being a student. Use your answers from the Job Diagnostic Survey that you just completed.

Skill variety (SV) $\dfrac{\text{Questions } 3 + 6 + 9}{3} = \_\_\_\_$

Task identity (TI) $\dfrac{\text{Questions } 2 + 7 + 12}{3} = \_\_\_\_$

Task significance (TS) $\dfrac{\text{Questions } 4 + 10 + 15}{3} = \_\_\_\_$

Autonomy $\dfrac{\text{Questions } 1 + 11 + 14}{3} = \_\_\_\_$

Job feedback $\dfrac{\text{Questions } 5 + 8 + 13}{3} = \_\_\_\_$

CALCULATING MOTIVATING POTENTIAL SCORE (MPS) Use the following formula and the previous results to calculate the motivating potential score. Notice that skill variety, task identity, and task significance are averaged before being multiplied by the score for autonomy and job feedback.

$$\left(\frac{SV + TI + TS}{3}\right) \times \text{Autonomy} \times \text{Job feedback}$$

$$\left(\frac{\quad + \quad + \quad}{3}\right) + \_\_\_\_ + \_\_\_\_ = \_\_\_\_$$

Self-Assessment 6.4

WHAT IS YOUR ATTITUDE TOWARD MONEY?

PURPOSE This exercise is designed to help you understand the types of attitudes toward money and to assess your own attitude toward money.

INSTRUCTIONS Read each of the following statements and circle the response that you believe best reflects your position regarding each statement. Then use the scoring key in Appendix B to calculate your results. This exercise is completed alone so you can assess yourself honestly without concerns of social comparison. However, class discussion will focus on the meaning of money, including the dimensions measured here and other aspects of money that may influence behavior in the workplace.

Money Attitude Scale

To what extent do you agree or disagree that...	Strongly agree ▼	Agree ▼	Neutral ▼	Disagree ▼	Strongly disagree ▼
1. I sometimes purchase things because I know they will impress other people.	5	4	3	2	1
2. I regularly put money aside for the future.	5	4	3	2	1
3. I tend to get worried about decisions involving money.	5	4	3	2	1
4. I believe that financial wealth is one of the most important signs of a person's success.	5	4	3	2	1
5. I keep a close watch on how much money I have.	5	4	3	2	1
6. I feel nervous when I don't have enough money.	5	4	3	2	1
7. I tend to show more respect to people who are wealthier than I am.	5	4	3	2	1
8. I follow a careful financial budget.	5	4	3	2	1
9. I worry about being financially secure.	5	4	3	2	1
10. I sometimes boast about my financial wealth or how much money I make.	5	4	3	2	1
11. I keep track of my investments and financial wealth.	5	4	3	2	1
12. I usually say "I can't afford it" even when I can afford something.	5	4	3	2	1

Sources: Adapted from J.A. Roberts and C.J. Sepulveda, "Demographics and Money Attitudes: A Test of Yamauchi and Templer's (1982) Money Attitude Scale in Mexico," *Personality and Individual Differences* 27 (July 1999), pp. 19–35; K. Yamauchi and D. Templer, "The Development of a Money Attitudes Scale," *Journal of Personality Assessment* 46 (1982), pp. 522–28.

Self-Assessment 6.5

ASSESSING YOUR SELF-LEADERSHIP (STUDENT OLC)

This exercise is designed to help you understand self-leadership concepts and to assess your self-leadership tendencies. Self-leadership is the process of influencing yourself to establish the self-direction and self-motivation needed to perform a task. Please indicate the extent to which each statement in this instrument describes you very well or does not describe you at all. Complete each item honestly to get the best estimate of your score on each self-leadership dimension.

Self-Assessment 6.6

STUDENT EMPOWERMENT SCALE (STUDENT OLC)

Empowerment is a concept that applies to people in a variety of situations. This instrument is specifically adapted to your position as a student at this college or university. Indicate the extent to which you agree or disagree with each statement in this instrument. Then request the results, which provide an overall score as well as scores on each of the four dimensions of empowerment. Complete each item honestly to get the best estimate of your level of empowerment.

After reading this chapter, if you need additional information, see www.mhhe.com/mcshane4e for more in-depth interactivities that correspond with this material.

Joe Straitiff realized that his leisure life was in trouble when his boss hung a huge neon sign in the workplace with the words "Open 24 Hours." The former Electronic Arts (EA) software developer also received frequent e-mail messages from the boss to the team, saying that he would see them on the weekend. "You can't work that many hours and remain sane," says Straitiff, who no longer works at the Redwood City, California, electronic games company. "It's just too harsh."

Straitiff's complaints were not exaggerations. Two days after joining EA's Los Angeles operations, video programmer Leander Hasty was sucked into a "crunch" period of intense work on *Lord of the Rings: the Battle for Middle Earth*. Soon the entire team was working 13-hour days, seven days per week. Exasperated, Hasty's fiancée, Erin Hoffman, wrote a lengthy diatribe on the Internet describing the dire situation. "The love of my life comes home late at night complaining of a headache that will not go away and a chronically upset stomach," she wrote. Within two days she received more than 1,000 sympathetic messages from people at EA and other video game companies. This flashpoint sparked several lawsuits against EA for unpaid overtime.

Josh Holmes has fond memories of working at EA, but he admits that the long hours were stressful. "From the minute I joined the company (EA), I put every waking hour of my day into my work....It definitely took its toll," says Holmes. After 10 years at EA, Holmes was burned out, so he quit. "We had done a lot of really long grueling hours. I know I was thinking that there's got to be a way to do things a little differently."

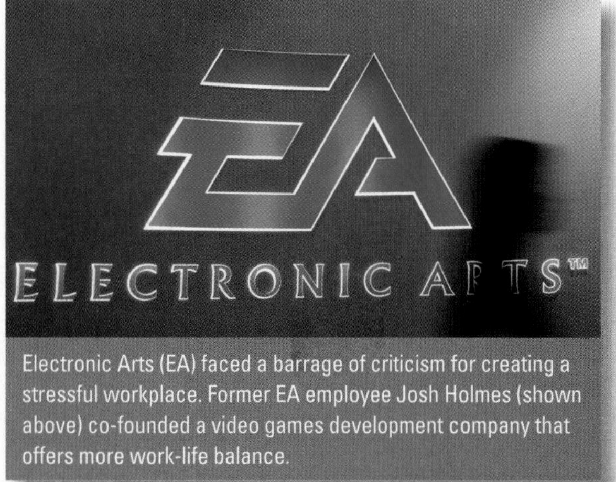

Electronic Arts (EA) faced a barrage of criticism for creating a stressful workplace. Former EA employee Josh Holmes (shown above) co-founded a video games development company that offers more work-life balance.

So in their quest for a less stressful electronic games company, Holmes and three other senior EA staff formed Propaganda Games (now part of Disney's video game division, Buena Vista Games) with the unique values of creativity, risk taking, and work–life balance. "Senior management knows what it's like to burn out on the job. They've been there," says Propaganda's Web site. "That's why they've set up the studio right from the start to reflect work–life balance. Normal working hours. Proper planning. And, above all, keeping things in perspective."[1]

7

Work-Related Stress and Stress Management

LEARNING OBJECTIVES

After reading this chapter you should be able to

1. Define *stress* and describe the stress experience.
2. Outline the stress process from stressors to consequences.
3. Identify the different types of stressors in the workplace.
4. Explain why a stressor might produce different stress levels in two people.
5. Discuss the physiological, psychological, and behavioral effects of stress.
6. Identify five work–life balance initiatives.
7. Describe the five strategies to manage workplace stress.

Working longer hours has been a serious concern among staff at EA and in many other video game development companies. But they are not alone in the rising tide of work-related stress. One survey reported that almost one-third of college-educated male adults in the United States regularly log 50 hours or more per week at work, up from 22 percent in 1980. A recent poll conducted by the New York–based Families and Work Institute revealed that 44 percent of Americans say they are often or very often overworked, with 26 percent of them experiencing this in the previous month. Another survey stated that 80 percent of Americans feel too much stress on the job; nearly half indicate that they need help coping with it.

Chronic work-related stress is not just an American affliction. Approximately one in every four employees in the United Kingdom feels "very or extremely stressed," and this condition has become the top cause of absenteeism there. A survey of 4,700 people across Asia reported that one-third were feeling more stress than in the recent past. People in Taiwan reported the highest stress; those in Thailand reported the lowest stress. More than half of Australian employees across all occupations feel under pressure a significant amount of the time; one in five say they feel exhausted on the job. The Japanese government, which tracks work-related stress every five years, has found that the percentage of Japanese employees who feel "strong worry, anxiety, or stress at work or in daily working life" has increased from 51 percent in 1982 to almost two-thirds of the population today.[2]

In this chapter we look at the dynamics of work-related stress and how to manage it. The chapter begins by describing the stress experience. Next the causes and consequences of stress are examined, along with the factors that cause some people to experience stress when others do not. The final section of this chapter looks at ways to manage work-related stress from either an organizational or individual perspective.

Learning Objectives

After reading the next two sections you should be able to

1. **Define *stress* and describe the stress experience.**
2. **Outline the stress process from stressors to consequences.**
3. **Identify the different types of stressors in the workplace.**

What Is Stress?

stress
An individual's adaptive response to a situation that is perceived as challenging or threatening to the person's well-being.

Stress is an adaptive response to a situation that is perceived as challenging or threatening to a person's well-being.[3] The stress response is a complex emotion that produces physiological changes to prepare us for "fight or flight"—to defend ourselves from the threat or flee from it. Specifically, our heart rates increase, muscles tighten, breathing speeds up, and perspiration increases. Our bodies also moves more blood to the brain, release adrenaline and other hormones, fuel the system by releasing more glucose and fatty acids, activate systems that sharpen our senses, and conserve resources by shutting down our immune systems.

We often hear about stress as a negative consequence of modern living. People are stressed from overwork, job insecurity, information overload, and the increasing pace of life. These events produce *distress*—the degree of physiological, psychological, and behavioral deviation from healthy functioning. There is also a positive side of stress, called *eustress*, which refers to the healthy, positive, constructive outcome of stressful events and the stress response. Eustress is the stress experience in moderation, enough to activate and motivate people so that they can achieve goals, change

Exhibit 7.1
Selye's General Adaptation Syndrome

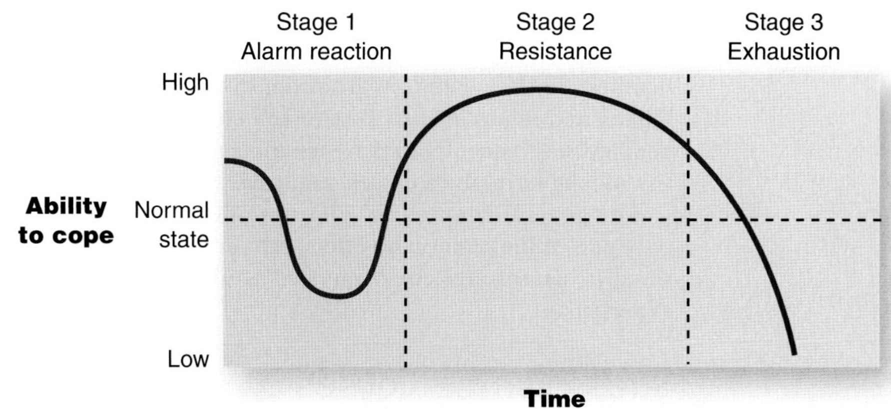

Source: Adapted from H. Selye, *The Stress of Life* (New York: McGraw-Hill, 1956).

their environments, and succeed in life's challenges. In other words, we need some stress to survive.[4] However, most research focuses on distress because it is a significant concern in organizational settings. Employees frequently experience enough stress to hurt their job performance and increase their risk of mental and physical health problems. Consequently our discussion will focus more on distress than on eustress.

General Adaptation Syndrome

general adaptation syndrome
A model of the stress experience, consisting of three stages: alarm, resistance, and exhaustion.

The stress experience was first documented 50 years ago by stress research pioneer Hans Selye.[5] Selye determined that people have a fairly consistent physiological response to stressful situations. This response, called the **general adaptation syndrome**, provides an automatic defense system to help us cope with environmental demands. Exhibit 7.1 illustrates the three stages of the general adaptation syndrome: alarm, resistance, and exhaustion. The line in this exhibit shows the individual's energy and ability to cope with the stressful situation.

Alarm Reaction The alarm reaction stage occurs when a threat or challenge activates the physiological stress responses that we noted earlier, such as increased respiration rate, blood pressure, heartbeat, and muscle tension. The individual's energy level and coping effectiveness decrease in response to the initial shock. In extreme situations this shock can result in incapacity or death because the body is unable to generate enough energy quickly enough. Most of the time the alarm reaction alerts the person to the environmental condition and prepares the body for the resistance stage.

Resistance The person's ability to cope with the environmental demand rises above the normal state during the resistance stage because the body activates various biochemical, psychological, and behavioral mechanisms. For example, we have higher-than-normal levels of adrenaline and glucose during this stage, which give us more energy to overcome or remove the source of stress. At the same time, the body shuts down the immune system to focus energy on the source of the stress. This explains why people are more likely to catch a cold or other illness when they experience prolonged stress.

Exhaustion People have a limited resistance capacity, and if the source of stress persists, they will eventually move into the exhaustion stage. In most work situations the general adaptation syndrome process ends long before total exhaustion. Employees resolve tense situations before the destructive consequences of stress become manifest, or they withdraw from the stressful situation, rebuild their survival capabilities, and return later to the stressful environment with renewed energy. However, people who frequently experience the general adaptation syndrome have increased risk of long-term physiological and psychological damage.[6]

The general adaptation syndrome describes the stress experience, but this is only part of the picture. To effectively manage work-related stress, we must understand its causes and consequences as well as individual differences in the stress experience.

Stressors: The Causes of Stress

stressors
The causes of stress, including any environmental conditions that place a physical or emotional demand on the person.

Stressors, the causes of stress, include any environmental conditions that place a physical or emotional demand on a person.[7] There are numerous stressors in organizational settings and other life activities. Exhibit 7.2 lists the four main types of work-related stressors: interpersonal, role-related, task control, and organizational and physical environment stressors.

Interpersonal Stressors

Among the four types of stressors, interpersonal stressors seem to be the most pervasive in the workplace. The trend toward teamwork generates interpersonal stressors because employees must interact more with co-workers. Organizational politics, which we'll discuss in Chapter 12, are another interpersonal stressor. Bad

Exhibit 7.2
Causes and Consequences of Stress

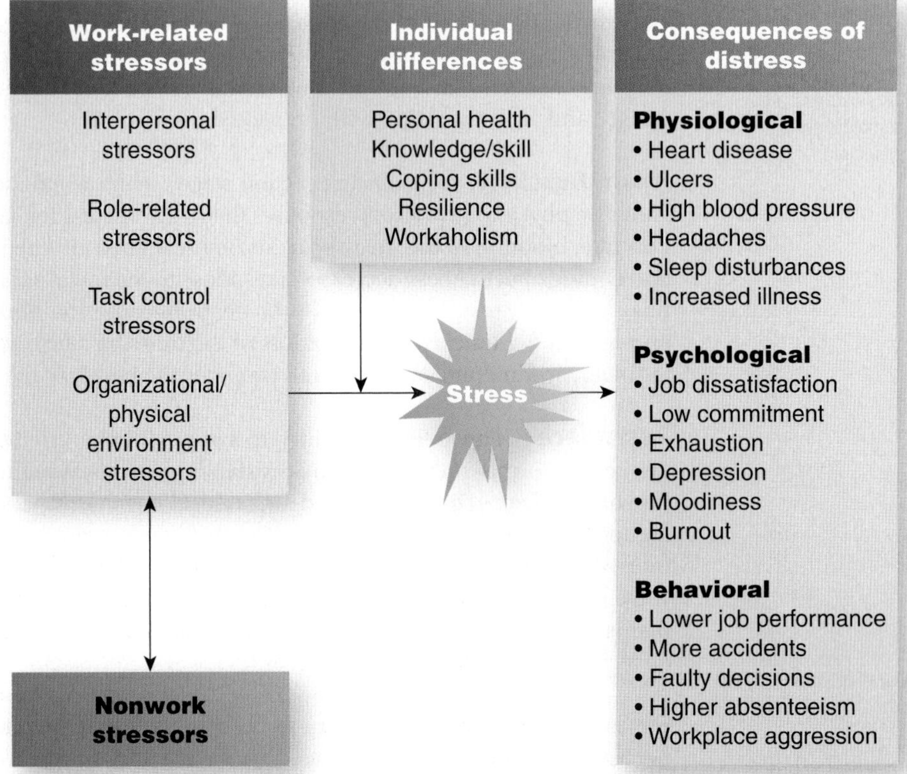

bosses can also be quite stressful. For instance, one study discovered that female health care assistants experienced much higher blood pressure when working with an ineffective rather than an effective supervisor. Over a sustained period this higher blood pressure would increase the risk of stroke by 38 percent![8] Two other interpersonal stressors are workplace violence and harassment, which are discussed next.

Workplace Violence Workplace violence is a serious interpersonal stressor. In the United States more than 600 employees are murdered on the job each year, and 2 million others experience lesser forms of physical violence. An International Labor Organization study reported that more than 60 percent of health care staff in Bulgaria, Australia, South Africa, and Portugal experienced at least one incident of physical or psychological violence in the previous year. A recent survey reported that more than a quarter of the 3,000 British nurses questioned had been physically attacked at work, half of those within the previous 12 months.[9]

Victims of workplace violence experience severe stress symptoms. Those who observe the violence also tend to experience stress. After a serious workplace incident, counselors assist many employees, not just the direct victims. Even employees who have not directly experienced or observed violence may show signs of stress if they work in jobs that expose them to a higher incidence of violence.

psychological harassment
Repeated and hostile or unwanted conduct, verbal comments, actions, or gestures that affect an employee's dignity or psychological or physical integrity and that result in a harmful work environment for the employee.

Psychological and Sexual Harassment One of the fastest-growing sources of workplace stress is **psychological harassment**. Psychological harassment includes repeated and hostile or unwanted conduct, verbal comments, actions, or gestures that affect an employee's dignity or psychological or physical integrity and that result in a harmful work environment for the employee. This covers a broad landscape of behaviors, from threats and bullying to subtle yet persistent forms of incivility.[10] Three large surveys reported strikingly similar results–namely that 70 percent or more Americans think people are less civil today than 20 years ago. In another U.S. poll 10 percent of respondents said they witness incivility daily in their workplaces and are targets of that abuse at least once each week.[11]

Psychological harassment also permeates workplaces in other countries. One global survey reported that almost 40 percent of German and Dutch finance and human resource professionals have experienced workplace bullying, compared with 33 percent in New Zealand, 25 percent in Australia and the United Kingdom, and only 9 percent in Italy. Other polls suggest that these figures might underestimate the actual levels of psychological harassment. A recent survey suggests that more than half of U.K. human resource managers have been bullied at work, mostly by their immediate supervisors. More than half of the 1,800 lawyers polled in the Australian state of New South Wales say they have been bullied or intimidated. When the province of Quebec, Canada, recently passed the first workplace antiharassment legislation in North America (modeled after similar laws in Sweden, France, and Belgium), nearly 5,000 complaints were received during the first two years![12]

sexual harassment
Unwelcome conduct of a sexual nature that detrimentally affects the work environment or leads to adverse job-related consequences for its victims.

Sexual harassment is a variation of harassment in which a person's employment or job appraisal is conditional on unwanted sexual relations (called *quid pro quo*) and/or the person experiences sexual conduct from others (such as posting pornographic material) that unreasonably interferes with work performance or creates an intimidating, hostile, or offensive working environment (called a *hostile work environment*). One study points out that men tend to have a narrower interpretation than do women over what constitutes a hostile work environment, so they sometimes engage in this

Five-Star Bullying in Posh London Hotels Working at a London five-star hotel has not been pleasant for Ahmet (not his real name). For the past six long months the Moroccan migrant worker has experienced racial harassment, as well as shouting and screaming from managers and customers who pointed their fingers at his head. At one point the harassment became so severe that Ahmet burst into tears, had to go on medication, and received counseling. Another five-star hotel, which welcomes migrant workers in its induction as a "home away from home," is apparently just as abusive. Workers there complain about the daily verbal attacks from managers, who hurl profanities and ridicule one ethnic group against another. "These are the top luxury hotels. Just imagine the rest of them," says Julio Haro, race equality officer of Britain's General Union, adding that these incidents are the norm, not the exception, in the hotel industry.[13]

form of sexual harassment without being aware of their transgressions.[14] Another issue is that sexual harassment sometimes escalates into psychological harassment after the alleged victim complains about the sexual wrongdoing. The good news, however, is that the number of charges alleging sexual harassment in the United States has declined steadily from 16,000 in 2000 to less than 13,000 in 2005. The Equal Employment Opportunity Commission attributes the improvement to better supervisor training and concerted management action to address harassment issues before they reach litigation.

Psychological and sexual harassment are stressful experiences that undermine employee well-being and performance. Past behavior is the best predictor of future behavior, so companies should carefully screen applicants for past incidents. Multisource feedback is another valuable tool to let employees know that co-workers and direct reports find their behavior intimidating or sexually inappropriate. Along with these practices, companies need to develop a grievance, mediation, or other conflict resolution process that employees trust when they become victims of workplace harassment.

Role-Related Stressors

role conflict
Incongruity or incompatibility of expectations associated with a person's role.

Role-related stressors include conditions in which employees have difficulty understanding, reconciling, or performing the various roles in their lives. Three types of role-related stressors are role conflict, role ambiguity, and work overload. **Role conflict** refers to the degree of incongruity or incompatibility of expectations associated with a person's role. Some people experience stress when they have two roles that conflict with each other. For example, various studies have recently reported this inter-role conflict among human service workers and health care providers, where workloads and bureaucratic procedures interfered with their ability to serve clients or patients.[15] Role conflict also occurs when an employee's personal values are incompatible with organizational values, a topic that was detailed in Chapter 2.

role ambiguity
A lack of clarity and predictability of the outcomes of a person's behavior.

Role ambiguity refers to the lack of clarity and predictability of the outcomes of a person's behavior. Role ambiguity produces unclear role perceptions, which directly affect job performance. It is also a source of stress in a variety of situations, such as joining an organization or working in a new joint venture, because people are uncertain about task and social expectations.[16]

Work Overload A half-century ago social scientists predicted that technology would allow employees to enjoy a 15-hour workweek at full pay by 2030.[17] So far it hasn't turned out that way. As the opening vignette to this chapter described, employees at Electronic Arts and many other companies in the video games industry are experiencing stress due to *work overload*–working more hours and more intensely during those hours than they can reasonably handle.

Why do employees work such long hours? One explanation is the combined effects of technology and globalization. "Everyone in this industry is working harder now because of e-mail, wireless access, and globalization," says Christopher Lochhead, chief marketing officer of Mercury Interactive, a California-based consultancy with offices in 35 countries. "You can't even get a rest on the weekend," he says. A second cause, according to a recent study, is that many people are caught up in consumerism; they want to buy more goods and services, which require more income

Asian Professionals Are Dying to Get Ahead Throughout Asia professionals are working long hours as a badge of honor. For some this is a short-lived honor. According to the Japanese government, employees who work more than 80 hours of overtime per month have a significantly higher risk of *karoshi*—death from overwork. Currently more than 20 percent of male Japanese employees exceed that level of overtime. Governments in South Korea—which has among the world's highest average work hours—and Taiwan are also paying closer attention to workplace casualties linked to long work hours. In China, the media are now using the term *guolaosi* (overwork death) to describe this disturbing trend. In one recent incident two young faculty members at China's top engineering school died suddenly, apparently from exhaustion and overwork. The Chinese media themselves seem to suffer from *guolaosi*. A study of journalists in China's major news outlets revealed that the average age of death was 46 years. Long hours and corresponding poor lifestyle were identified as factors in this shorter life expectancy.[18]

through longer work hours. A third reason, called the "ideal worker norm," is that professionals expect themselves and others to work longer work hours. For many people, toiling away far beyond the normal workweek is a badge of honor, a symbol of their superhuman capacity to perform above others.[19] This badge of honor is particularly pronounced in Japan, South Korea, Taiwan, China, and several other Asian countries, to the point where "death from overwork" is now part of the common language (*karoshi* in Japanese and *guolaosi* in Chinese).

Task Control Stressors

As a private driver for an executive in Jakarta, Eddy knows that traffic jams are a way of life in Indonesia's largest city. "Jakarta is traffic congestion," he complains. "All of the streets in the city are crowded with vehicles. It is impossible to avoid this distressing fact every day." Eddy's boss complains when traffic jams make him late for appointments, which makes matters even more stressful. "Even watching soccer on TV or talking to my wife doesn't get rid of my stress. It's driving me mad."[20] Eddy and many other people experience stress due to a lack of task control. Along with driving through congested traffic, low task control occurs where the employee's work is paced by a machine, the job involves monitoring equipment, or the work schedule is controlled by someone else. Computers, cell phones, and other technology also increase stress by limiting a person's control of time and privacy.[21]

The degree to which low task control is a stressor increases with the burden of responsibility the employee must carry. Assembly line workers have low task control, but their stress can be fairly low if their level of responsibility is also low. In contrast, sports coaches are under immense pressure to win games (high responsibility) yet have little control over what happens on the playing field (low task control). Similarly, Eddy (the Jakarta driver) is under pressure to get his employer to a particular destination on time (high responsibility), yet he has little control over traffic congestion (low task control).

Organizational and Physical Environment Stressors

Organizational and physical environment stressors come in many forms. Downsizing is stressful for those who lose their jobs. Even those who keep their jobs (called layoff survivors) experience stress because of the reduced job security, chaos of change, additional workloads, and guilt of having a job as others lose theirs. For example, one study reported that long-term sick leave doubled among surviving government employees in Finland after a major downsizing.[22] Physical work environment stressors include excessive noise and poor lighting. People working in dangerous environments also tend to experience higher stress levels.

Work–Nonwork Stressors

The stress model shown earlier in Exhibit 7.2 has a two-way arrow, indicating that stressors from work spill over into nonwork and vice versa.[23] There are three types of work–nonwork stressors: time-based, strain-based, and role-based conflict.

Time-Based Conflict *Time-based conflict* refers to the challenge of balancing the time demanded by work with family and other nonwork activities. Time-based conflict relates back to the work overload stressor described earlier. The problem of longer work hours that we discussed earlier (as well as more intensely during those hours) is

Blackberry Divorce Nick Salaysay (shown in this photo) admits that his work routinely gets mixed in with his personal time. "I have a BlackBerry, so I check my e-mail a lot when I'm supposed to be on vacation," says the corporate lawyer at Gowling Lafleur Henderson in Calgary, Canada. Salaysay also acknowledges that having work spill over into his time off "really annoys my girlfriend." Amy Schulman is another dedicated BlackBerry user. The New York–based partner with law firm DLA Piper Rudnick Gray Cary recalls that "the BlackBerry was at first a significant intrusion on family life," but she believes family members now understand that the device makes it easier for her to process several hundred e-mail messages each day. As a consolation, Schulman adds that "I don't generally look at my e-mail during mealtimes, and I try not to look at it in movie theaters." Nick Salaysay and Amy Schulman are comfortable using their BlackBerries during family time. But research indicates that when electronic devices spill work into home life, they increase the risk of strain-based stress and possibly result in the additional stress of relationship and marital problems.[24]

compounded by the fact that employees have little time or energy left for themselves and their family. Inflexible work schedules, business travel, and rotating shift schedules also take a heavy toll because they reduce the ability to effectively juggle work and nonwork.[25] Time-based conflict is usually more acute for women than for men because housework and child care continue to fall more on their shoulders as a "second shift" in most dual-career families.

Strain-Based Conflict *Strain-based conflict* occurs when stress from one domain spills over to the other. Relationship problems, financial difficulties, and loss of a loved one usually top the list of nonwork stressors. New responsibilities, such as marriage, birth of a child, and a mortgage, are also stressful to most of us. Stress at work spills over to an employee's personal life and often becomes the foundation of stressful relations with family and friends. Strain-based conflict may be increasing as technology allows work and nonwork activities to spread from one domain to the other. For instance, many professionals now routinely use their cell phones, pagers, and BlackBerry wireless devices for work-related tasks while at home and even on vacation. Similarly, many employees use technology at work to complete household obligations, such as online banking or purchases.[26]

Role Behavior Conflict A third work–nonwork stressor, called *role behavior conflict,* occurs when people are expected to act quite differently at work than in nonwork roles. For instance, people who act logically and impersonally at work have difficulty switching to a more compassionate behavioral style in their personal lives. Thus stress occurs in this adjustment from one role to the other.[27]

Exhibit 7.3 **Stressors in Occupations**

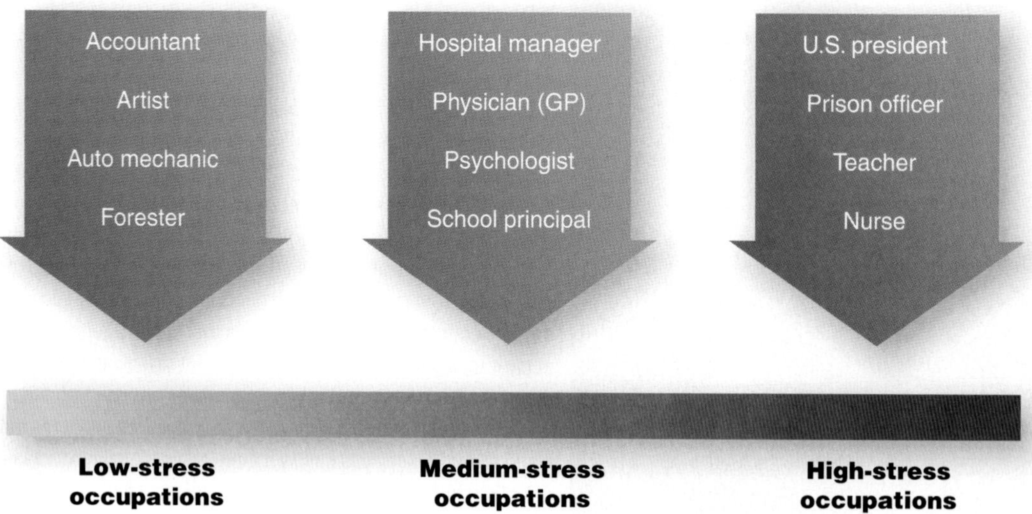

Stress and Occupations

Several studies have attempted to identify which jobs have more stressors than others.[28] These lists are not in complete agreement, but Exhibit 7.3 identifies a representative sample of jobs and their relative level of stressors. We need to view this information with some caution, however. One problem with rating occupations in terms of their stress levels is that a particular occupation may have considerably different tasks and job environments across organizations and societies. A nurse's job may be less stressful in a small-town medical clinic, for instance, than in the emergency room of a large city hospital.

Another important point to remember when looking at Exhibit 7.3 is that a major stressor to one person may be less significant to another. Thus not everyone in so-called high-stress occupations actually experiences more stress than people in other occupations. High-stress jobs have more stressors, but people don't experience more stress if they are carefully selected and trained for this type of work. The next section discusses individual differences in stress.

Learning Objectives

After reading the next two sections you should be able to

4. **Explain why a stressor might produce different stress levels in two people.**
5. **Discuss the physiological, psychological, and behavioral effects of stress.**

Individual Differences in Stress

Due to unique personal characteristics, people have different stress experiences when exposed to the same stressor. One reason is that they have different threshold levels of resistance to the stressor. Younger employees generally experience fewer and less severe stress symptoms than older employees because they have a larger store of energy to cope with high stress levels. Exercise and healthful lifestyles (including work-free holidays) are discussed later in this chapter as ways to manage stress because these activities rebuild this store of energy. A second reason for different stress outcomes is

Stress-Free at Finster Honey Farms Working around honeybees is a heart-thumping experience for most of us. But Hakija Pehlic (shown here) doesn't worry when he pushes his nose through a layer of European honeybees to determine the type of honey produced on a honeycomb frame. Pehlic, a beekeeper at Finster Honey Farms in Schuyler, New York, doesn't experience much stress in this situation because he is trained to know when it's safe to smell the honey and how to avoid getting stung. Most of the time, says Pehlic, honeybees are gentle insects that won't bother you. Maybe so, but you probably shouldn't try this at home.[29]

that people use different coping strategies, some of which are more effective than others. Research suggests that employees who try to ignore or deny the existence of a stressor suffer more in the long run than those who try to find ways to weaken the stressor and seek social support.[30]

The third reason why some people experience less stress than others in the same situation is that they have different beliefs about the threat and their ability to withstand it. This explanation really has two parts. The first part refers to the notion that people with more knowledge and skill usually feel more confident about successfully managing or overcoming the threat. Someone who flies a plane for the first time tends to experience much more stress than an experienced pilot, for instance. The second part refers to the idea that people who are optimistic, confident, and often experience positive emotions tend to feel less stress.[31] This characteristic extends beyond the person's knowledge and skill; it refers to an important emerging concept known as *resilience.*

Resilience and Stress

resilience The capability of individuals to cope successfully in the face of significant change, adversity, or risk.

Resilience is the capability of individuals to cope successfully in the face of significant change, adversity, or risk. Everyone has some resilience; it occurs every time we pull through stressful experiences. Although the word literally means to "leap back," resilience in this context refers mainly to withstanding adversity rather than recovering from it. Although everyone needs to recuperate to some extent following a stressful experience, people with high resilience are better able to maintain an equilibrium and consequently have lost little ground in the first place. In fact, some writers believe that resilience moves people to a higher plateau after the adversity.[32]

Experts have looked at the characteristics of resilience from different perspectives. One perspective is that resilient people have personality traits that generate more optimism, confidence, and positive emotions. These traits include high extroversion, low neuroticism, internal locus of control, high tolerance of change, and high self-esteem.[33]

A second perspective is that resilience involves specific competencies and behaviors to respond and adapt more effectively to stressors. Research indicates that resilient people have higher emotional intelligence and good problem-solving skills. They also apply productive coping strategies, such as analyzing the sources of stress and finding ways to neutralize these problems. In contrast, people with low resilience tend to avoid or deny the existence of stressors.[34]

The third perspective is that resilience is an inner force that motivates us to move forward. This emerging view is connected to the concept of self-actualization that psychologist Abraham Maslow popularized and made his life's work a half-century ago (see Chapter 5). It is also connected to recent OB writing on *workplace spirituality*, which investigates a person's inner strength and how it nurtures and is nurtured by the workplace. Resilience as an inner force has some empirical support. Research has found that resilience is stronger when people have a sense of purpose and are in touch with their personal values.[35]

Workaholism and Stress

While resilience helps people to withstand stress, another personal characteristic–workaholism–attracts more stressors and weakens the capacity to cope with them. The classic **workaholic** (also called *work addict*) is highly involved in work, feels compelled or driven to work because of inner pressures, and has a low enjoyment of work. He or she is compulsive and preoccupied with work, often to the exclusion and detriment of personal health, intimate relationships, and family. Work addicts are typically hard-driving, competitive individuals who tend to be impatient, lose their tempers, and interrupt others during conversations.[36] These latter characteristics are collectively known as the **Type A behavior pattern**.

workaholic
A person who is highly involved in work, feels compelled to work, and has a low enjoyment of work.

Type A behavior pattern
A behavior pattern associated with people having premature coronary heart disease; type As tend to be impatient, lose their temper, talk rapidly, and interrupt others.

According to a large-scale study at Israel's University of Haifa, 12.7 of Americans are traditional workaholics, followed by 9.3 percent of Japanese workers and 8.1 percent of Israeli workers. Further down the workaholism scale are employees in Belgium (6.8 percent) and the Netherlands (6.5 percent). Along with classic workaholics, the academic literature identifies two other workaholic types: *enthusiastic workaholics* and *work enthusiasts.* Enthusiastic workaholics have high levels of all three components–high work involvement, drive to succeed, and work enjoyment. Work enthusiasts have high work involvement and work enjoyment, but low drive to succeed.

Workaholism is relevant to this discussion of stress because classic work addicts are more prone to job stress and burnout. They also have significantly higher scores on depression, anxiety, and anger than do nonworkaholics, as well as lower job and career satisfaction. Furthermore, work addicts of both sexes report more health complaints.[37]

Consequences of Distress

The previous sections on workplace stressors and individual differences in stress have made some reference to the various outcomes of the stress experience. These stress consequences are typically grouped into physiological, psychological, and behavioral categories.

Physiological Consequences

Stress takes its toll on the human body.[38] The stress response shuts down the immune system, which makes us more vulnerable to viral and bacterial infection. Many people experience tension headaches due to stress. Others get muscle pain and related back problems. These physiological ailments are attributed to muscle contractions that occur when people are exposed to stressors.

Cardiovascular disease is one of the most disturbing effects of stress in modern society. Strokes and heart attacks were rare a century ago but are now among the leading causes of death among adults in the United States and other countries. Stress also influences hypertension (high blood pressure). In spite of better lifestyle and medical treatment, recent evidence suggests that hypertension continues to increase, particularly among older people and non-Hispanic blacks in the United States. Along with these health problems, a recent study of 60,000 people in Norway found that those with high scores on an anxiety test were 25 percent more likely to have premalignant tumors seven years later.[39]

Psychological Consequences

Stress produces various psychological consequences, including job dissatisfaction, moodiness, depression, and lower organizational commitment.[40] Emotional fatigue is another psychological consequence of stress and is related to job burnout.

job burnout
The process of emotional exhaustion, cynicism, and reduced efficacy (lower feelings of personal accomplishment) resulting from prolonged exposure to stress.

Job Burnout **Job burnout** refers to the process of emotional exhaustion, cynicism, and reduced feelings of personal accomplishment resulting from prolonged exposure to stress.[41] It is a complex process that includes the dynamics of stress, coping strategies, and stress consequences. Burnout is caused by excessive demands made on people who serve or frequently interact with others. In other words, burnout is due mainly to interpersonal and role-related stressors, and is most common in helping occupations (nurses, teachers, police officers).

Exhibit 7.4 diagrams the relationship among the three components of job burnout. *Emotional exhaustion*, the first stage, is characterized by a lack of energy, tiredness, and a feeling that one's emotional resources are depleted. Emotional exhaustion is sometimes called *compassion fatigue* because the employee no longer feels able to give as much support and care to clients.

Exhibit 7.4
The Job Burnout Process

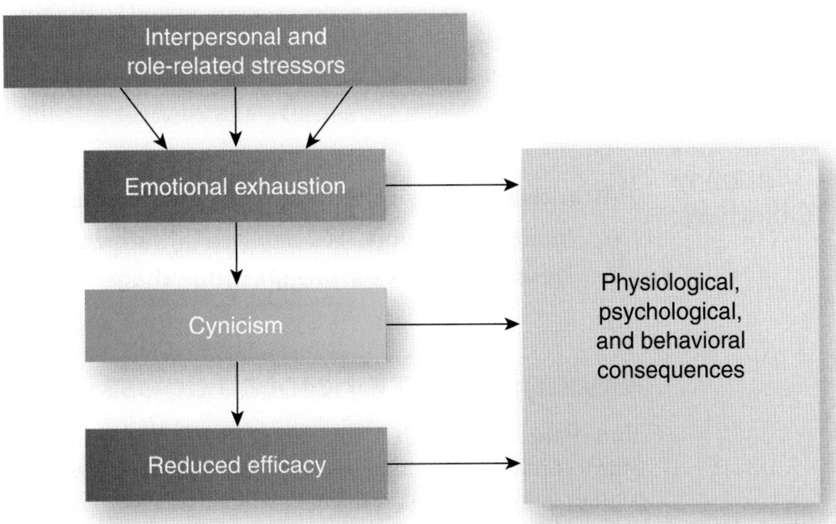

Cynicism (also called *depersonalization*) follows emotional exhaustion. It is identified by an indifferent attitude toward work and the treatment of others as objects rather than people. At this stage employees become emotionally detached from clients and cynical about the organization. This detachment is to the point of callousness–far beyond the normal level in helping occupations. Cynicism is also apparent when employees strictly follow rules and regulations rather than trying to understand the client's needs and searching for a mutually acceptable solution.

Reduced professional efficacy (also called *reduced personal accomplishment*), the final component of job burnout, refers to feelings of diminished confidence in one's ability to perform the job well. In these situations employees develop a sense of learned helplessness as they no longer believe that their efforts make a difference.

Behavioral Consequences

Moderate levels of stress focus our attention and concentrate resources where they are most needed. But when stress becomes distress, job performance falls, memory becomes impaired, workplace accidents are more frequent, and decisions are less effective.[42] You have probably experienced this in an exam or emergency work situation. You forget important information, make mistakes, and otherwise "draw a blank" under intense pressure.

Overstressed employees also tend to have higher levels of absenteeism. One reason is that stress makes people susceptible to viral and bacterial infections. The other reason is that absenteeism is a coping mechanism. At a basic level, we react to stress through "fight or flight." Absenteeism is a form of flight–temporarily withdrawing from the stressful situation so that we can reenergize. Companies may try to minimize absenteeism, but it sometimes helps employees avoid the exhaustion stage of the stress experience.[43]

Workplace Aggression Workplace aggression is more than the serious interpersonal stressor described earlier. It is also an increasingly worrisome behavioral consequence of stress. Aggression represents the fight (instead of flight) reaction to stress. In its mildest form, employees engage in verbal harassment. They "fly off the handle" and are less likely to empathize with co-workers. Like most forms of workplace behavior, co-worker aggression is caused by both the person and the situation. Although certain individuals are more likely to be aggressive, their behavior is also usually a consequence of extreme stress to some extent.[44] In particular, employees are more likely to engage in aggressive behavior if they believe they have been treated unfairly, experience other forms of frustration beyond their personal control, and work in physical environments that are stressful (such as being hot or noisy).

Learning Objectives

After reading this section you should be able to

6. Identify five work–life balance initiatives.

7. Describe the five strategies to manage workplace stress.

Managing Work-Related Stress

Tony Bates had a high-flying career as head of private banking at Macquarie Bank, but he preferred a shorter workweek with proportionately lower pay. When Bates tried to discuss his need for work–life balance with the three executives above him–all

Exhibit 7.5
Stress Management Strategies

baby boomers with no children–one replied, "If you work your guts out for 30 years, you'll retire at 55 and get [work–life] balance in the last 30 years."

That was enough for Bates, a Generation-Xer and father of three children. He started his own boutique financial planning business, spacing his work across four days per week. "I'm on about 60 percent of the money I used to make, and working fewer hours," says Bates. "Just knowing I can pick up the kids after school takes out the stress, so I'm happier at home and happier at work."

Tony Bates was fortunate. He was able to change his work habits before matters got worse. Unfortunately many of us deny the existence of our stress until it is too late. This avoidance strategy creates a vicious cycle because the failure to cope with stress becomes another stressor on top of the one that created the stress in the first place. The solution is for both employers and employees to discover the toolkit of effective stress management strategies identified in Exhibit 7.5 and to determine which ones are best for the situation.[45]

Remove the Stressor

From the categories in Exhibit 7.5, some writers argue that the only way companies can effectively manage stress is by removing the stressors that cause unnecessary strain and job burnout. Other stress management strategies may keep employees "stress-fit," but they don't solve the fundamental causes of stress.

Removing the stressor usually begins by identifying areas of high stress and determining its main causes. Ericsson conducts this diagnosis in its North American operations through an annual survey that includes a stress index. Executives at the telecommunications company use the index to identify departments where stress problems may be developing. "We look at those scores, and if there appears to be a problem in a particular group, we put in action plans to try and remedy and improve the work situation that may be causing the stress," explains an Ericsson executive.[46]

Monitoring stress is one of the first steps in a more comprehensive stress management strategy–changing the corporate culture to support a work–life balance rather than dysfunctional workaholism. Another strategy is to give employees more control over their work and work environment. Role-related stressors can be minimized by selecting and assigning employees to positions that match their competencies. Noise and safety risks are stressful, so improving these conditions would also go a long way to minimize stress in the workplace. Workplace harassment can be minimized by carefully selecting employees and having clear guidelines of behavior and feedback to people who violate those standards.[47]

Employees can also take an active role in removing stressors. If stress is caused by ambiguous role expectations, for example, employees might seek more information from others to clarify these expectations. If a particular piece of work is too challenging, they might break it into smaller sets of tasks so that the overall project is less threatening or wearing. To some extent employees can also minimize workplace harassment by learning to identify early warning signs of aggression in customers and co-workers and by developing interpersonal skills that dissipate aggression.

Work–Life Balance Initiatives In a variety of ways companies can help employees experience a better balance between their work and personal lives. Five of the most common work–life balance initiatives are flexible work time, job sharing, telecommuting, personal leave, and child care support.

- *Flexible work time.* Some firms are flexible on the hours, days, and amounts of time employees work. For instance, accounting firm Deloitte & Touche allows employees to work part-time as well as to take up to five years off for personal leave. Flexible and part-time work schedules have become so popular at PricewaterhouseCoopers that the accounting firm now has an online program for employees to schedule them.
- *Job sharing.* Job sharing splits a career position between two people so they experience less time-based stress between work and family. They typically work different parts of the week with some overlapping work time in the weekly schedule to coordinate activities. Although traditionally aimed at nonmanagement positions, job sharing is also starting to occur in executive jobs.[48]

Flexible Accounting Several years ago, Deloitte & Touche partners discovered that many promising female accountants were leaving because they wanted more flexibility in their work schedule. Today, the accounting giant is a leader in flexible work arrangements and other forms of work-life balance. Tricia Schetz, a senior manager for Deloitte's audit group in Grand Rapids, Michigan, is a case in point. Schetz works 16 to 20 hours a week so she can spend more time raising her two children. Cathy Levatino (shown in this photo with her two children), also works a reduced schedule at Deloitte & Touche to satisfy her work-balance needs. Even on this flexible schedule, Levatino was recently admitted to the partnership.[49]

- *Telecommuting.* Chapter 1 described how an increasing number of employees are telecommuting. This reduces the time and stress of commuting to work and makes it easier to fulfill family obligations, such as temporarily leaving the home office to pick the kids up from school. Research suggests that telecommuters experience a healthier work–life balance.[50] However, telecommuting may increase stress for those who crave social interaction and who lack the space and privacy necessary to work at home.
- *Personal leave.* Employers with strong work–life values offer extended maternity, paternity, and personal leave to care for a new family or take advantage of a personal experience. The U.S. Family and Medical Leave Act gives expecting mothers (and anyone considered to have an "illness") 12 weeks of unpaid, job-protected leave. However, almost every other developed nation requires employers to provide paid maternity leave. In Austria, for instance, both parents are entitled to paid parental leave of two years.[51]
- *Child care support.* According to one estimate, almost one-quarter of large American employers provide on-site or subsidized child care facilities. Child care support reduces stress because employees are less rushed to drop off children and less worried during the day about how well they are doing.[52]

Given the high levels of work–life conflict that we have read about, you would think that organizations are encouraging employees to apply these initiatives. The reality, according to some critics, is that while these practices are available, employees either feel guilty about using them or are discouraged from using them. To ensure that employees actually develop a work–life balance, the top 500 managers at accounting firm RSM McGladrey, Inc., receive annual 360-degree reviews in which peers, subordinates, and managers rate how well the executives respect and encourage "balance of work and personal life priorities" among employees.[53]

Withdraw from the Stressor

Removing the stressor may be the ideal solution, but it is often not feasible. An alternative strategy is to permanently or temporarily remove employees from the stressor. Permanent withdrawal occurs when employees are transferred to jobs that better fit their competencies and values.

Temporary Withdrawal Strategies Temporarily withdrawing from stressors is the most frequent way that employees manage stress. SAS Institute employees in Cary, North Carolina, enjoy live piano recitals at lunch. Consulting firms Segal Co. in New York and Vielife in London have nap rooms where staff can recover with a few winks of sleep. Admiral Insurance doesn't have sleep facilities yet, but the Welsh insurance company offers other ways for employees to take temporary breaks from work. "We have an Indian head-masseur who visits monthly, we have a number of chill-out rooms with sofas, TVs, and games consoles for all staff to use, and we are currently trialing a 'relaxation chair,' which reclines and massages the user while playing chilled-out music through headphones," says an Admiral Insurance spokesperson.[54]

Personal days off and vacations represent somewhat longer temporary withdrawals from stressful conditions. Oxygen Business solutions in Auckland, New Zealand, offers employees two "wellness" days per year "so people can call in and say they're too well to come to work today," says Oxygen chief executive Mike Smith. Sabbaticals represent an extended version of vacations, whereby employees take up to several months of paid leave after several years of service. Approximately 5 percent of U.S. companies offer paid sabbaticals to some employees. McDonald's Corp. has had paid sabbaticals for the past 40 years, offering employees eight weeks of paid time off after every 10 years of service.[55]

Change Stress Perceptions

Earlier we learned that employees often experience different levels of stress in the same situation because they have different levels of self-confidence and optimism. Consequently corporate leaders need to look at ways for employees to strengthen their confidence and self-esteem so that job challenges are not perceived as threatening. Self-leadership practices seem to help here. For example, positive self-talk can boost self-confidence. A study of newly hired accountants reported that personal goal setting and self-reinforcement can also reduce the stress that people experience when they enter new work settings.[56] Humor can also improve optimism and create positive emotions by taking some psychological weight off the situation.

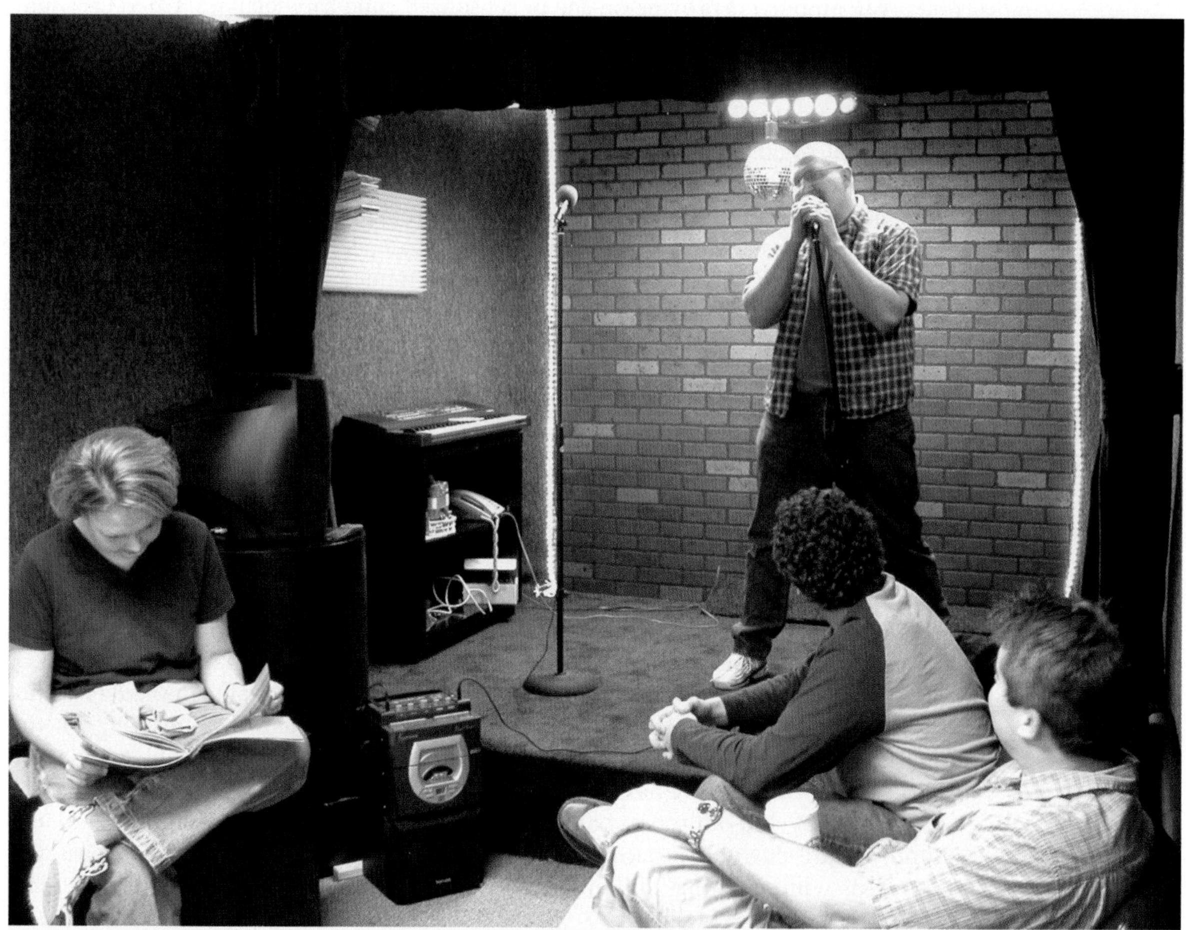

Singing the Stress Away When employees at Liggett-Stashower Inc. need a short break from the daily stresses of work, they retreat to one of three theme rooms specially designed for creativity and respite. Staff at the Cleveland advertising firm can enter the bowling room and knock down a few pins. Or they might try out the Zen room, which serves as a quiet, relaxing place to think. The third room features karaoke in which frustrated employees can belt out tunes. "The higher the stress level, the more singing there is going on," says Kristen Flynn, a Liggett art director.[57]

Control the Consequences of Stress

Coping with workplace stress also involves controlling its consequences. For this reason many companies have fitness centers where employees can keep in shape. Research indicates that physical exercise reduces the physiological consequences of stress by helping employees moderate their breathing and heart rates, muscle tension, and stomach acidity.[58] Another way to control the physiological consequences of stress is through relaxation and meditation. For instance, employees at Wilmington, Delaware–based pharmaceutical company AstraZeneca practice a form of meditation called Qi Gong during department meetings and coffee breaks. Research has found that Qi and other forms of meditation reduce anxiety, reduce blood pressure and muscle tension, and moderate breathing and heart rate.[59]

Along with fitness and relaxation/meditation, 81 percent of U.S. employers with at least 50 employees have wellness programs. These programs educate and support employees in better nutrition and fitness, regular sleep, and other good health habits. For example, employees at Pitney-Bowes receive up to $200 for completing online wellness surveys three times each year. More than 80 percent of Minitab Inc. employees in State College, Pennsylvania, participate in the software developer's wellness program, which includes annual on-site checkups and meditation classes.[60]

employee assistance programs (EAPs)
Counseling services that help employees overcome personal or organizational stressors and adopt more effective coping mechanisms.

Many large employers offer **employee assistance programs (EAPs)**—counseling services that help employees overcome personal or organizational stressors and adopt more effective coping mechanisms. Most EAPs are "broadbrush" programs that assist employees with any work or personal problems. Family problems often represent the largest percentage of EAP referrals, although this varies with industry and location. For instance, major banks provide posttrauma stress counseling for employees after a robbery. EAPs can be one of the most effective stress management interventions when the counseling helps employees to understand the stressors, acquire stress management skills, and practice those stress management skills.[61]

Receive Social Support

Social support from co-workers, supervisors, family members, friends, and others is generally regarded as one of the more effective stress management practices. However, this benefit occurs when the stressed individual reaches out for support, not when the support is imposed by others. *Social support* refers to the person's interpersonal transactions with others and involves providing either emotional or informational support to buffer the stress experience. Seeking social support is called a "tend and befriend" response to stress, and research suggests that women often follow this route rather than the "fight-or-flight" alternative that was mentioned earlier in this chapter.[62]

Social support reduces stress in at least three ways.[63] First, employees improve their perceptions that they are valued and worthy. This, in turn, increases resilience because they have higher self-esteem and confidence to cope with stressors. Second, social support provides information to help employees interpret, comprehend, and possibly remove stressors. For instance, social support might reduce a new employee's stress if co-workers describe ways to handle difficult customers. Finally, emotional support from others can directly help to buffer the stress experience. This last point reflects the idea that "misery loves company." People seek out and benefit from the emotional support of others when they face threatening situations.[64]

Social support is an important way to cope with stress that everyone can practice by maintaining friendships. This includes helping others when they need a little support from the stressors of life. Organizations can facilitate social support by providing opportunities for social interaction among employees as well as their families. People in leadership roles also need to practice a supportive leadership style when employees work under stressful conditions and need this social support. Mentoring relationships with more senior employees may help junior employees cope with organizational stressors.

Chapter Summary

Stress is an adaptive response to a situation that is perceived as challenging or threatening to a person's well-being. Distress represents high stress levels that have negative consequences, whereas eustress represents the moderately low stress levels needed to activate people. The stress experience, called the general adaptation syndrome, involves moving through three stages: alarm, resistance, and exhaustion. The stress model shows that stress is caused by stressors, but the effect of these stressors on stress is moderated by individual characteristics.

Stressors are the causes of stress and include any environmental conditions that place a physical or emotional demand on a person. Stressors are found in the physical work environment, employees' various life roles, interpersonal relations, and organizational activities and conditions. Conflicts between work and nonwork obligations are a frequent source of employee stress.

Two people exposed to the same stressor may experience different stress levels because they have different threshold levels of resistance to the stressor, use different coping strategies, or have different beliefs about the threat and their ability to withstand it. People experience less stress when they have high resilience–the capability of individuals to cope successfully in the face of significant change, adversity, or risk. Classic workaholics (work addicts)–those who are highly involved in work, feel compelled or driven to work because of inner pressures, and have a low enjoyment of work–tend to experience more stress.

Intense or prolonged stress can cause physiological symptoms such as cardiovascular disease, headaches, and muscle pain. Psychologically, stress reduces job satisfaction and organizational commitment and increases moodiness, depression, and job burnout. Job burnout refers to the process of emotional exhaustion, cynicism, and reduced efficacy resulting from prolonged exposure to stress. It is mainly due to interpersonal and role-related stressors and is most common in helping occupations. Behavioral symptoms of stress include lower job performance, poorer decisions, more workplace accidents, higher absenteeism, and more workplace aggression.

Many interventions are available to manage work-related stress. Some directly remove unnecessary stressors or remove employees from the stressful environment. Others help employees alter their interpretation of the environment so that it is not viewed as a serious stressor. Wellness programs encourage employees to build better physical defenses against stress experiences. Social support provides emotional, informational, and material resource support to buffer the stress experience.

Key Terms

employee assistance programs (EAPs), p. 215
general adaptation syndrome, p. 199
job burnout, p. 209
psychological harassment, p. 201
resilience, p. 207
role ambiguity, p. 203
role conflict, p. 202
sexual harassment, p. 201
stress, p. 198
stressors, p. 200
Type A behavior pattern, p. 208
workaholic, p. 208

Critical Thinking Questions

1. Several Web sites–including www.unitedmedia.com/comics/dilbert/ and www.cartoonbank.com–use humor to describe problems that people experience at work. Scan through these and other Web sites and determine what types of work-related stressors are depicted.

2. Is being a full-time college or university student a stressful role? Why or why not? Contrast your response with other students' perspectives.
3. Two recent college graduates join the same major newspaper as journalists. Both work long hours and have tight deadlines to complete their stories. They are under constant pressure to scout out new leads and be the first to report new controversies. One journalist is increasingly fatigued and despondent and has taken several days of sick leave. The other is getting the work done and seems to enjoy the challenges. Use your knowledge of stress to explain why these two journalists are reacting differently to their jobs.
4. Resilience is an individual characteristic that plays an important role in moderating the effect of stressors. Suppose you have been put in charge of a task force in a large government department to ensure that employees are highly resilient. What would you and your task force do to accomplish this objective?
5. If you were asked to identify people who are classic workaholics (work addicts), what would you look for?
6. A friend says that he is burned out by his job. What questions might you ask this friend to determine whether he is really experiencing job burnout?
7. What should organizations do to reduce employee stress? What is the responsibility of an employee to manage stress effectively? How might fitness programs help employees working in stressful situations?
8. A senior official of a labor union stated, "All stress management does is help people cope with poor management. [Employers] should really be into stress reduction." Discuss the accuracy of this statement.

Case Study 7.1 HOW DID I GET HERE?

Dr. Russell Casey, Clayton State University, and Marc Bacon, Fabgroups Technologies Inc.

Something was not right. John Breckenridge opened his eyes, saw the nurse's face, and closed them once more. Cobwebs slowly cleared from his brain as he woke up from the operation. He felt a hard tube in his nostril, and he tried to lift his hand to pull it out, but it was strapped down to the bed. John tried to speak but could make only a croaking sound. Nurse Thompson spoke soothingly, "Just try to relax, Mr. Breckenridge. You had a heart attack and emergency surgery, but you're going to be OK."

Heart attack? How did I get here? As the anesthesia wore off and the pain set in, John began to recall the events of the past year; and with the memories came another sort of pain–that of remembering a life where success was measured in hours worked and things accomplished, but which of late had not measured up.

John recalled his years in college, where getting good grades had been important, but not so much as his newly developing love for Karen, the girl with auburn hair who got her nursing degree the same year as he graduated with a degree in software engineering. They married the summer after graduation and moved from their sleepy university town in Indiana to Aspen, Colorado. There John got a job with a new software company while Karen worked evenings as a nurse. Although they didn't see much of each other during the week, weekends were a special time, and the surrounding mountains and nature provided a superb quality of life.

Life was good to the Breckenridges. Two years after they were married, Karen gave birth to Josh and two years later to Linda. Karen reduced her nursing to the minimum hours required to maintain her license, and concentrated on rearing the kids. John, on the other hand, was busy providing for the lifestyle they increasingly became used to, which included a house, car, SUV, ski trips, and all of the things a successful engineering career could bring. The company grew in leaps and bounds, and John was one of the main reasons it grew so fast. Work was fun. The company was growing, his responsibilities increased, and he and his team were real buddies. With Karen's help at home, he juggled work, travel, and evening classes that led to a master's degree. The master's degree brought another promotion–this time to vice president of technology at the young (for this company) age of 39.

The promotion had one drawback: It would require working out of the New York office. Karen sadly said goodbye to her friends, convinced the kids that the move would be good to them, and left the ranch house for another one, much more expensive and newer, but smaller and just across the river in New Jersey from the skyscraper where her husband worked. Newark was not much like Aspen, and the kids had a hard time making friends, especially Josh, who was now 16. He grew sullen and withdrawn and began hanging around with a crowd that Karen thought looked very tough. Linda, always the quiet one, stuck mostly to her room.

John's new job brought with it money and recognition, as well as added responsibilities. He now had to not only lead software development but also actively participate in steering the company in the right direction for the future, tailoring its offerings to market trends. Mergers and acquisitions were the big thing in the software business, and John found a special thrill in picking small companies with promising software, buying them out, and adding them to the corporate portfolio. Karen had everything a woman could want and went regularly to a health club. The family lacked for no material need.

At age 41 John felt he had the world by its tail. Sure, he was a bit overweight, but who wouldn't be with the amount of work and entertaining that he did? He drank some, a habit he had developed early in his career. Karen worried about that, but he reassured her by reminding her that he had been really drunk only twice and would never drink and drive. Josh's friends were a worry, but nothing had yet come of it.

Not all was well, however. John had been successful in Colorado because he thought fast on his feet, expressed his opinions, and got people to buy into his decisions. In the New York corporate office things were different. All of the top brass except the president and John had Ivy League, moneyed backgrounds. They spoke of strategy but would take only risks that would further their personal careers. He valued passion, integrity, and action, with little regard for personal advancement. They resented him, rightly surmising that the only reason he had been promoted was because he was more like the president than they were, and he was being groomed as heir apparent.

On November 2, 2004, John Breckenridge's world began to unravel. The company he worked for, the one he had given so much of his life to build, was acquired in a hostile takeover. The president who had been his friend and mentor was let go, and the backstabbing began in earnest. John found himself the odd man out in the office as the others jostled to build status in the new firm. Although his stellar record allowed him to survive the first round of job cuts, that survival only made him more of a pariah to those around him. Going to work was a chore now, and John had no friends like those he had left in Aspen.

Karen was little help. John had spent nearly two decades married more to his job than his wife, and he found she was more of a stranger than a comforter as he struggled in his new role. When he spoke about changing jobs, she blew up. "Why did I have to give up nursing for your career?" she said. "Why do we have to move again, just because you can't get along at work? Can't you see what the move did to our kids?"

Seeing the hurt and anger in Karen's eyes, John stopped sharing and turned to his bottle for comfort. In time that caused even more tension in the home, and it slowed him down at work when he really needed to excel. John would often drink himself into oblivion when on business trips rather than thinking about where his life and career were going. On his last trip he hadn't slept much and had worked far too hard. Midmorning he had been felled by a massive heart attack.

All of this history passed through John Breckenridge's mind as he awoke after the operation. It was time for a change.

Discussion Questions

1. Identify the stressors in John Breckenridge's life. Which ones could he have prevented?
2. What were the results of the stress? Would you consider these to be typical responses to stress situations and lifestyle choices John made, or was John Breckenridge unlucky?
3. Assume you are a career coach retained by John Breckenridge to guide him through his next decisions. How would you recommend that John modify his lifestyle and behavior to reduce stress? Should he change jobs? Do you believe he is capable of reducing his stress alone? If not, where should he seek help?

Case Study 7.2 THE REAL REASONS YOU'RE WORKING SO HARD

BusinessWeek

Do you feel overworked? If so, you are not alone. Surveys estimate that 31 percent of college-educated male workers are regularly logging 50 or more hours a week at work, up from 22 percent in 1980. About 40 percent of American adults get less than seven hours of sleep on weekdays, up from 34 percent in 2001. Almost 60 percent of meals are rushed, and 34 percent of lunches are choked down on the run.

This *BusinessWeek* case study investigates why more Americans are enduring long hours at the workplace. It also looks at ways that companies are trying to reduece unnecessary work hours. Read the full text of this *BusinessWeek* article at www.mhhe.com/mcshane4e and prepare for the discussion questions below.

Discussion Questions

1. What are the main reasons identified in this article as to why Americans are working long hours?
2. Describe ways that companies are trying to reduce these work hours.

Source: M. Mandel, "The Real Reasons You're Working So Hard... and what you can do about it," *Business Week*, 3 October 2005, 60.

Team Exercise 7.3 STAGE FRIGHT!

PURPOSE This exercise is designed to help you to diagnose a common stressful situation and determine how stress management practices apply to this situation.

BACKGROUND Stage fright–including the fear of public speaking–is one of the most stressful experiences many people have in everyday life. According to some estimates, nearly three-quarters of us frequently get stage fright, even when speaking or acting in front of a small audience. Stage fright is an excellent topic for this team activity on stress management because the psychological and physiological symptoms of stage fright are really symptoms of stress. In other words, stage fright is the stress experience in a specific context involving a public audience. Based on the personal experiences of team members, your team will be asked to identify the symptoms of stage fright and to determine specific stress management activities that effectively combat stage fright.

INSTRUCTIONS

1. Students are organized into teams of typically four to six students. Ideally each team should have one or more people who acknowledge that they have experienced stage fright.
2. Each team's first task is to identify the symptoms of stage fright. The best way to organize these symptoms is to look at the three categories of stress outcomes described in the textbook: physiological, psychological, and behavioral. The specific stage fright symptoms may be different from the stress outcomes described in the textbook, but the three broad categories are relevant. Teams should be prepared to identify several symptoms and to present one or two specific examples of stage fright symptoms based on personal experiences of team members. (Individual students are not required to describe their experiences to the entire class.)
3. Each team's second task is to identify specific strategies people could or have applied to minimize stage fright. The five categories of stress management presented in the textbook will likely provide a useful template in which to organize the specific stage fright management activities. Each team should document several strategies to minimize stage fright and be able to

present one or two specific examples to illustrate some of these strategies.

4. The class will congregate to hear each team's analysis of symptoms and solutions to stage fright. This information will then be compared to the stress experience and stress management practices, respectively.

Self-Assessment 7.4

CONNOR–DAVIDSON RESILIENCE SCALE (CD-RISC)

PURPOSE This self-assessment is designed to help you estimate your personal level of resilience.

INSTRUCTIONS See the assessment scale on page 221. Please check the box indicating the extent to which each statement has been true for you *over the past month.* Then use the scoring key in Appendix B of this book to calculate your results. There are no right or wrong answers to these questions. This self-assessment is completed alone so you can use this instrument honestly without concerns of social comparison. However, class discussion will focus on the meaning of resilience and how it relates to workplace stress.

Self-Assessment 7.5

WORK ADDICTION RISK TEST (STUDENT OLC)

This self-assessment is designed to help you identify the extent to which you are a workaholic. This instrument presents several statements and asks you to indicate the extent to which each statement is true of your work habits. You need to be honest with yourself to obtain a reasonable estimate of your level of workaholism.

Self-Assessment 7.6

PERCEIVED STRESS SCALE (STUDENT OLC)

This self-assessment is designed to help you estimate your perceived general level of stress. The items in this scale ask you about your feelings and thoughts during the last month. In each case, please indicate how often you felt or thought a certain way. You need to be honest with yourself to obtain a reasonable estimate of your general level of stress.

Connor-Davidson Resilience Scale (CD-RISC)

To what extent were these statements true about you over the past month?	Not at all true	Rarely true	Sometimes true	Often true	True nearly all of the time
1. I am able to adapt to change.					
2. I have close and secure relationships.					
3. I take pride in my achievements.					
4. I work to attain my goals.					
5. I feel in control of my life.					
6. I have a strong sense of purpose.					
7. I see the humorous side of things.					
8. Things happen for a reason.					
9. I have to act on a hunch.					
10. I can handle unpleasant feelings.					
11. Sometimes fate or God can help.					
12. I can deal with whatever comes my way.					
13. Past success gives me confidence for new challenges.					
14. Coping with stress strengthens me.					
15. I like challenges.					
16. I can make unpopular or difficult decisions.					
17. I think of myself as a strong person.					
18. When things look hopeless, I don't give up.					
19. I give my best effort, no matter what.					
20. I can achieve my goals.					
21. I am not easily discouraged by failure.					
22. I tend to bounce back after a hardship or illness.					
23. I know where to turn for help.					
24. Under pressure, I focus and think clearly.					
25. I prefer to take the lead in problem solving.					

Source: K.M. Connor and J.R.T. Davidson, "Development of a New Resilience Scale: The Connor–Davidson Resilience Scale (CD-RISC)," *Depression and Anxiety* 18, no. 2 (2003), pp. 76–82.

Self-Assessment 7.7

STRESS COPING PREFERENCE SCALE (STUDENT OLC)

This self-assessment is designed to help you identify the type of coping strategy you prefer to use in stressful situations. This scale lists a variety of things you might do when faced with a stressful situation. You are asked how often you tend to react in these ways. You need to be honest with yourself to obtain a reasonable estimate of your preferred coping strategy.

After reading this chapter, if you need additional information, see **www.mhhe.com/mcshane4e** for more in-depth interactivities that correspond with this material.

Part Three
Team Processes

What does a swarm of robot bees sound like? Cory Hawthorne tried to figure that out by listening to dozens of sounds and loops. Suddenly the sound effects specialist at Radical Entertainment found the right combination when he mixed his humming through a kazoo with the noise of operating an electric beard trimmer across the surface of his bathtub. The robot bees now had a menacing audio effect in the electronic game that Hawthorne was working on: *The Simpsons: Hit and Run.*

Radical Entertainment founder Ian Wilkinson (third from right) meets with employees every week to reinforce the Vancouver-based games developer's emphasis on creative decision making and employee involvement.

Radical depends on Cory Hawthorne and its other 230 employees to have plenty of such discovery moments to succeed in the competitive video game marketplace. "Hit games are made by people who have the freedom and support to put unconventional ideas in motion," explains Ian Wilkinson, founder and CEO of the Vancouver, Canada, company (now a division of Los Angeles–based Vivendi Universal Games). "So we give our employees the autonomy to drive real change, whatever their role in the company. No other game developer offers this level of creative freedom."

Danielle Michael, Radical's vice president of business development, echoes Wilkinson's view that the best decisions in this fast-paced industry come from employee involvement and autonomy: "People are hugely empowered to be creative, to go beyond the call of duty to come up with great ideas and to actually implement them," says Michael.

To help guide employee decision making, posters hung throughout Radical's headquarters state the company's succinct values, including this one: "Take risks, always learn." Wilkinson takes these values seriously. He lunches with a half dozen employees each week (as shown in this photo—Wilkinson is third from the right), encouraging them to apply the company's values in their everyday decisions.

Creative ideas are also cross-pollinated through Radical's monthly "game fair" day, in which teams show off their products and make presentations to other teams in the organization. "I don't want to be hearing what other companies are doing," Wilkinson advises staff. "I want to do innovative stuff and have some people say we're crazy."[1]

8

Decision Making and Creativity

LEARNING OBJECTIVES

After reading this chapter you should be able to

1. Describe the six stages in the rational choice decision process.
2. Explain why people have difficulty identifying problems and opportunities.
3. Explain why people do not follow the rational choice model when evaluating alternative choices.
4. Describe three ways in which emotions influence the selection of alternatives.
5. Outline how intuition operates.
6. Describe four causes of escalation of commitment.
7. Describe four benefits of employee involvement in decision making.
8. Identify four contingencies that affect the optimal level of employee involvement.
9. Outline the four steps in the creative process.
10. Describe the characteristics of employees and the workplace that support creativity.

decision making
A conscious process of making choices among one or more alternatives with the intention of moving toward some desired state of affairs.

Employees at Radical Entertainment are in the creativity business, but every organization depends on creativity to some extent in almost all decisions. **Decision making** is a conscious process of making choices among alternatives with the intention of moving toward some desired state of affairs.[2] This chapter begins by outlining the rational choice paradigm of decision making. Then we examine this perspective more critically by recognizing how people identify problems and opportunities, choose among alternatives, and evaluate the success of their decisions differently from the rational model. Bounded rationality, escalation of commitment, and intuition are three of the more prominent topics in this section. Next we explore the role of employee involvement in decision making, including the benefits of involvement and the factors that determine the optimal level of involvement. The final section of this chapter examines the factors that support creativity in decision making, including characteristics of creative people, work environments that support creativity, and creativity activities.

Learning Objectives

After reading the next two sections you should be able to

1. **Describe the six stages in the rational choice decision process.**
2. **Explain why people have difficulty identifying problems and opportunities.**

Rational Choice Paradigm of Decision Making

rational choice paradigm
A deeply held view that people should and do make decisions based on pure logic using all necessary information.

How do people make decisions in organizations? For most of written history, philosophers, economists, and scholars in Western societies have stated or assumed that people should–and typically do–make decisions based on pure logic or rationality. This **rational choice paradigm** began 2,500 years ago when Plato and his Greek contemporaries raised logical debate and reasoning to a fine art. A few centuries later Greek and Roman Stoics insisted that one should always "follow where reason leads" rather than fall victim to passion and emotions. About 500 years ago, several European philosophers emphasized that the ability to make logical decisions is one of the most important accomplishments of human beings. By the 1900s, social scientists and mathematicians had developed elegant rational choice models and formulas that are now embedded in operations research and other decision sciences.[3]

Exhibit 8.1 illustrates the rational choice process.[4] The first step is to identify the problem or recognize an opportunity. A problem is a deviation between the current and the desired situation–the gap between "what is" and "what ought to be." This deviation is a symptom of more fundamental root causes that need to be corrected.[5] An opportunity is a deviation between current expectations and a potentially better situation that was not previously expected. In other words, decision makers realize that some decisions may produce results beyond current goals or expectations.

The second step involves deciding how to process the decision.[6] One issue is whether the decision maker has enough information or needs to involve others in the process. Later in this chapter we'll examine whether and how much others should be involved in the decision. Another issue is whether the decision is programmed or nonprogrammed. *Programmed decisions* follow standard operating procedures; they have been resolved in the past, so the optimal solution has already been identified and documented. In contrast, *nonprogrammed decisions* require all steps in the decision model because the problems are new, complex, or ill-defined. The third step is to develop a list of possible solutions. This usually begins by searching for ready-made solutions, such as practices that have worked well on similar problems. If an acceptable solution cannot be found, then decision makers need to design a custom solution or modify an existing one.

Exhibit 8.1
Rational Choice Decision-Making Process

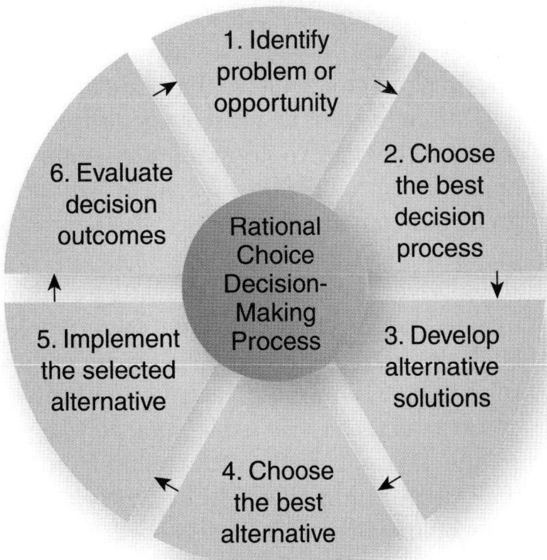

The fourth step is to choose from among the alternatives. The rational choice paradigm assumes that people naturally select the alternative with the highest *subjective expected utility*.[7] Subjective expected utility refers to how much the selected alternative benefits or satisfies the decision maker. Figuring out the alternative with the highest utility (total value or happiness) involves identifying all the outcomes that would occur if the alternative is selected and estimating the amount of satisfaction the person would feel from each of those outcomes. This is incredibly complex, but rational choice assumes that everyone does this calculation without any problem. The fifth step is to implement the selected alternative. This is followed by the sixth step, evaluating whether the gap has narrowed between "what is" and "what ought to be." Ideally this information should come from systematic benchmarks so that relevant feedback is objective and easily observed.

Problems with the Rational Choice Paradigm

The rational choice paradigm seems so logical, yet it is rarely practiced in reality. One reason is that the model assumes people are efficient and logical information-processing machines. But as the next few pages will reveal, people have difficulty recognizing problems; they cannot (or will not) simultaneously process the huge volume of information needed to identify the best solution; and they have difficulty recognizing when their choices have failed. The second reason why the rational model doesn't fit reality is that it focuses on logical thinking and completely ignores the fact that emotions also influence–perhaps even dominate–the decision-making process. As we will discover in this chapter, emotions both support and interfere with our quest to make better decisions.[8] With these points in mind, let's look again at each step of decision making, but with more detail about what really happens.

Identifying Problems and Opportunities

When Albert Einstein was asked how he would save the world in one hour, he replied that the first 55 minutes should be spent defining the problem and the last 5 minutes solving it.[9] Einstein's point was that problem identification is not just the first step in decision making; it is arguably the most important step. But problems and opportunities do not appear on our desks as well-labeled objects. Instead decision makers translate information into evidence that something is wrong or that an opportunity is available.

To some extent this discovery process occurs through conscious evaluation of the facts and persuasive arguments by other people. But what is becoming increasingly apparent is that a fair amount of problem recognition actually occurs during the mostly unconscious processes of perceptual selective attention and attitude formation (described in Chapter 3 and 4, respectively).[10] Specifically we evaluate information as soon as we perceive it by attaching emotional markers (anger, caution, delight,or the like) to that information. These automatic emotional responses, together with logical analysis and the emotions triggered by that analysis, determine whether you perceive something as a problem, as an opportunity, or as irrelevant.

Let's say that a worried-looking colleague tells you that the company's salesperson in Atlanta just quit. Your initial reaction (emotions generated upon hearing the news that the salesperson quit) might be worry and frustration. Meanwhile the rational part of your brain works through this information, recalling that the former salesperson's performance was mediocre and that an excellent salesperson at another company wants to join your firm in that state. What initially felt like a problem was really an opportunity based on your rational analysis of the situation. The initial emotions of worry or frustration might have been wrong in this situation, but sometimes your emotions provide a good indicator of problems or opportunities.

Problems with Problem Identification

The problem identification stage is itself filled with problems. Here are five of the most widely recognized concerns:[11]

1. *Stakeholder framing.* Employees, clients, and other stakeholders with vested interests try to "frame" the situation by persuading decision makers that the available information points to a problem or an opportunity or has no importance at all. This framing of facts tends to short-circuit the decision maker's full assessment of the situation.
2. *Perceptual defense.* People sometimes block out bad news as a coping mechanism. Their brains refuse to see information that threatens self-esteem. This phenomenon is not true for everyone. Some people inherently avoid negative information, whereas others are more sensitive to it. Recent studies also report that people are more likely to disregard danger signals when they have limited control over the situation.[12]
3. *Mental models.* Mental models (cognitive templates of the external world) are essential road maps that provide stability and predictability to guide a person's preferences and behaviors. Unfortunately mental models also produce assumptions and expectations that prevent people from seeing unique problems or opportunities. If an idea doesn't fit the existing mental model of how things should work, then the idea is dismissed as unworkable or undesirable. Connections 8.1 describes how narrow mental models are the source of several famous missed or nearly missed opportunities.

"My team has created a very innovative solution, but we're still looking for a problem to go with it."

Famous Missed Opportunities

Mental models create road maps that guide our decisions. Unfortunately these maps also potentially block our ability to see emerging problems and opportunities. Here are a few famous examples:

- The best television commercial in history (as rated by *Advertising Age*) almost never saw the light of day. The Apple Macintosh "Why 1984 won't be like 1984" clip features a female athlete hurling a sledgehammer at a giant TV screen of an Orwellian Big Brother, liberating thousands of subjugated followers. Apple initially rejected the ad agency's (Chiat-Day) now-memorable phrase in an Apple II newspaper ad, but agreed to use this theme to launch the Macintosh computer during the 1984 Superbowl. The Macintosh team and sales force were ecstatic with rough cuts of the ad, but every outside director on Apple's board despised it. One remarked that it was the worst commercial of all time; another insisted that Apple immediately change its ad agency. Based on the board's reaction, Apple CEO John Sculley asked Chiat-Day to cancel the Superbowl ad space. Fortunately the agency claimed it could sell off only some of the time, so Apple had to show the commercial. The single 60-second ad shown during the Superbowl had such a huge effect that it was featured on evening news programs over the next several days. A month later Apple's board members applauded the Macintosh team for a successful launch and apologized for their misjudgment of the 1984 commercial.
- Graphical user interfaces, mice, windows, pull-down menus, laser printing, distributed computing, and Ethernet technologies weren't invented by Apple, Microsoft, or IBM. These essential elements of contemporary personal computing originated in the 1970s from researchers at Xerox PARC. Unfortunately Xerox executives were so focused on their photocopier business that they didn't bother to patent most of these inventions. Xerox has successfully applied some of its laser technology, but the lost value of Xerox PARC's other computing discoveries is much larger than the entire photocopier industry today.
- Nia Vardalos wrote a comedy screenplay based on incidents involving her Greek Canadian family. Unfortunately none of Hollywood's literary agents were interested. "They all said it's not good; it's not funny," said Vardalos, who honed her writing and acting skills at the Second City comedy group. Undeterred, Vardalos turned the script into a successful one-woman show in Los Angeles. None of Hollywood's talent agents accepted her invitation to see the show, but when actors Rita Wilson and Tom Hanks watched her skits, they immediately supported her in making a movie. Even with Hanks on board, Hollywood studios rejected the script, but HBO agreed to provide a paltry $2.5 million "as a favor" to Hanks. With a budget of only $5 million, *My Big Fat Greek Wedding* became one of the highest-grossing independent films of all time. The screenplay that no one in Hollywood wanted was also nominated for an Oscar.
- When the World Wide Web burst onto the cyberspace scene in the early 1990s, Bill Gates wondered what all the fuss was about. Even as late as 1996, the Microsoft founder lampooned investors for their love-in with companies that made Internet products. However, Gates eventually realized the error in his mental model of computing. Making up for lost time, Microsoft bought Hotmail and other Web-savvy companies and added Internet support to its Windows operating system.

The best television commercial in history—the Apple Macintosh 1984 ad—almost never saw the light of day because it was so different from existing mental models of what a good TV ad should look like.

Sources: T. Abate, "Meet Bill Gates, Stand-Up Comic," *San Francisco Examiner*, 13 March 1996, p. D1; O. Port, "Xerox Won't Duplicate Past Errors," *Business Week*, 29 September 1997, p. 98; P. Nason, "A Big Fat Hollywood Success Story," *United Press International*, 12 December 2002; M. McCarthy, "Top 20 in 20 Years: Apple Computer—1984," *Adweek Online*, www.adweek.com/adweek/creative/top20_20years/index.jsp (accessed 16 January 2003); A. Hertzfeld, "1984," www.folklore.org (accessed 31 July 2005); G. James, "The Future That Never Was: Seven Products That Could Have Changed the Industry but Didn't," *Electronic Business* 31 (December 2005), p. 46.

4. *Decisive leadership.* Studies report that people view leaders as more effective when they are decisive decision makers.[13] Consequently, eager to appear effective, many decision makers zero in on a problem and its solution without sufficiently analyzing the facts.
5. *Solution-focused problems.* Various studies have found that decision makers often find a solution almost as soon as a problem is identified.[14] Indeed, you will sometimes hear people define problems in terms of their pet solutions, such as "The problem is that we need more control over our suppliers." This solution-focused identification of problems occurs because it provides comforting closure to the otherwise ambiguous and uncertain nature of problems. People with a strong need for cognitive closure (those who feel uncomfortable with ambiguity) are particularly prone to solution-focused problems. Some decision makers take this solution focus a step further by seeing all problems in terms of solutions that have worked well for them in the past, even though they were applied under different circumstances. Again, the familiarity of past solutions makes the current problem less ambiguous or uncertain.

Identifying Problems and Opportunities More Effectively

Recognizing problems and opportunities will always be a challenge, but the process can be improved through awareness of these perceptual and diagnostic limitations. By keeping in mind that mental models restrict a person's perspective of the world, decision makers are more motivated to consider other perspectives of reality. A second method of minimizing perceptual and diagnostic weaknesses is to discuss the situation with colleagues. Decision makers discover blind spots in problem identification by hearing how others perceive certain information and diagnose problems. Opportunities also become apparent when outsiders explore this information from their different mental models. Third, leaders require considerable willpower to resist appearing decisive when a more thoughtful examination of the situation should occur. Finally, successful decision makers experience "divine discontent": They are never satisfied with the status quo, and this aversion to complacency creates a mindset that more actively searches for problems and opportunities.[15]

Learning Objectives

After reading the next two sections you should be able to

3. **Explain why people do not follow the rational choice model when evaluating alternative choices.**
4. **Describe three ways in which emotions influence the selection of alternatives.**
5. **Outline how intuition operates.**
6. **Describe four causes of escalation of commitment.**

Evaluating and Choosing Alternatives

bounded rationality
Processing limited and imperfect information and satisficing rather than maximizing when choosing among alternatives.

According to the rational choice paradigm of decision making, people rely on logic to evaluate and choose alternatives. This paradigm assumes that decision makers have well-articulated and agreed-on organizational goals, that they efficiently and simultaneously process facts about all alternatives and the consequences of those alternatives, and that they choose the alternative with the highest payoff.

Nobel Prize–winning organizational scholar Herbert Simon questioned these assumptions half a century ago. He argued that people engage in **bounded rationality**

Exhibit 8.2 Rational Choice Assumptions versus Organizational Behavior Findings about Choosing Alternatives

Rational Choice Paradigm Assumptions	Observations from Organizational Behavior
Goals are clear, compatible, and agreed upon.	Goals are ambiguous, in conflict, and lack full support.
Decision makers can calculate all alternatives and their outcomes.	Decision makers have limited information processing abilities.
Decision makers evaluate all alternatives simultaneously.	Decision makers evaluate alternatives sequentially.
Decision makers use absolute standards to evaluate alternatives.	Decision makers evaluate alternatives against an implicit favorite.
Decision makers use factual information to choose alternatives.	Decision makers process perceptually distorted information.
Decision makers choose the alternative with the highest payoff.	Decision makers choose the alternative that is good enough (satisficing).

because they process limited and imperfect information and rarely select the best choice.[16] Simon and other OB experts demonstrated that how people evaluate and choose alternatives differs from the rational choice paradigm in several ways, as illustrated in Exhibit 8.2. These differences are so significant that even economists have shifted from rational choice to bounded rationality assumptions in their theories. Let's look at these differences in terms of goals, information processing, and maximization.

Problems with Goals

We need clear goals to choose the best solution. Goals identify "what ought to be" and therefore provide a standard against which each alternative is evaluated. The reality, however, is that organizational goals are often ambiguous or in conflict with each other. One survey found that 25 percent of managers and employees felt decisions are delayed because of difficulty agreeing on what they want the decision to achieve.[17]

Problems with Information Processing

People do not make perfectly rational decisions because they don't process information very well. One problem is that decision makers can't possibly think through all of the alternatives and the outcomes of those alternatives. Consequently, they look at only a few alternatives and only some of the main outcomes of those alternatives.[18] For example, there may be dozens of computer brands to choose from and dozens of features to consider, yet people typically evaluate only a few brands and a few features.

implicit favorite
The decision maker's preferred alternative against which all other choices are judged.

A related problem is that decision makers typically look at alternatives sequentially rather than all at the same time. As a new alternative comes along, it is immediately compared to an **implicit favorite**. An implicit favorite is an alternative that the decision maker prefers and uses as a comparison against which to judge other choices. The implicit favorite is formed early and usually unconsciously in the decision-making process, which means that it is not necessarily the best choice to compare against the others.[19]

Although the implicit favorite comparison process works well some of the time, it more often undermines effective decision making because people unconsciously distort information to favor their implicit favorite over the alternative choices. Specifically, they tend to forget limitations of the implicit favorite and advantages of the alternative. Decision makers also overweight factors where the implicit favorite is better and underweight areas where the alternative is superior.[20] This effect was observed in a study of auditing students who had to decide whether a company described in a case had significant financial problems. Those who decided that the company did have significant problems distorted the available information to make those problems appear worse. Students who felt the financial problems were not significant enough to report in a formal audit minimized any reference to the negative information in their case reports.[21]

Problems with Maximization

satisficing
Selecting a solution that is satisfactory, or "good enough" rather than optimal or "the best."

Decision makers tend to select the alternative that is acceptable or "good enough" rather than the one with the highest payoff (the highest subjective expected utility). In other words, they engage in **satisficing** rather than maximizing. Satisficing occurs because it isn't possible to identify every alternative, and information about available alternatives is imperfect or ambiguous. Satisficing also occurs because, as mentioned already, decision makers tend to evaluate alternatives sequentially, not all at the same time. They evaluate each alternative against the implicit favorite and eventually select an option that scores above a subjective minimum point considered to be good enough to satisfy their needs or preferences.[22]

Evaluating Opportunities

Opportunities are just as important as problems, but what happens when an opportunity is "discovered" is quite different from the process of problem solving. According to a recent study of decision failures, decision makers do not evaluate several alternatives when they find an opportunity; after all, the opportunity *is* the solution, so why look for others? An opportunity is usually experienced as an exciting and rare revelation, so decision makers tend to have an emotional attachment to the opportunity. Unfortunately this emotional preference motivates decision makers to apply the opportunity and short-circuit any detailed evaluation of it.[23]

Emotions and Making Choices

Herbert Simon and many other experts have presented considerable evidence that people do not evaluate alternatives nearly as well as is assumed by the rational choice paradigm. However, they neglected to mention another glaring weakness with rational choice: It completely ignores the effect of emotions in human decision making. Just as both the rational and emotional brain centers alert us to problems, they also influence our choice of alternatives.

Emotions affect the evaluation of alternatives in three ways. First, the emotional marker process described earlier in this chapter as well as in previous chapters (Chapters 3 through 5) determines our preferences for each alternative. Our brain quickly attaches specific emotions to information about each alternative, and our preferred alternative is strongly influenced by those initial emotional markers. Of course, logical analysis also influences which alternative we choose, but it requires strong logical evidence to change our initial preferences (initial emotional markers). But even logical analysis depends on emotions to sway our decision. Specifically, neuroscientific evidence says that information produced from logical analysis is also tagged with emotional markers, which then motivate us to choose or avoid a particular alternative. Ultimately emotions, not rational logic, energize us to make the preferred choice. (People with damaged emotional brain centers have difficulty making choices.)

Second, a considerable body of literature indicates that moods and specific emotions influence the *process* of evaluating alternatives. For instance, we pay more attention to details when in a negative mood, possibly because a negative mood signals that there is something wrong that requires attention. When in a positive mood, on the other hand, we pay less attention to details and rely on a more programmed decision routine. Regarding specific emotions, decision makers rely on stereotypes and other shortcuts to speed up the choice process when they experience anger. Anger also makes them more optimistic about the success of risky alternatives, whereas the emotion of fear tends to make them less optimistic.[24]

The third way that emotions influence the evaluation of alternatives is through a process called "emotions as information." Marketing experts have found that we listen in on our emotions to provide guidance when making choices.[25] Most emotional experiences remain below the radar screen of awareness, but sufficiently intense emotions are picked up consciously and figured into our decision. Suppose that you are in the process of choosing one of several advertising firms to work with your company. You would logically consider several factors, such as previous experience, the agency's resources, and so on. But you would probably also pay attention to your gut feeling about each agency. If you sense positive feelings about a particular advertising firm, those conscious assessments of your emotions tend to get weighted into the decision. Some people pay more attention to these gut feelings, and personality tests such as the Myers-Briggs Type Indicator (see Chapter 2) identify those who listen in on their emotions more than others.[26] But all of us use our emotions as information to some degree. This phenomenon ties directly into our next topic: intuition.

Intuition and Making Choices

Linda, a trainee nurse in the neonatal intensive care unit of a hospital, was responsible for Melissa, a premature baby with no problems other than needing support to grow out of her sensitive condition. One day Melissa was a little sleepier than normal and was a bit lethargic during feeding. A spot on her heel where a blood sample had been taken was bleeding slightly, but that might be due to a sloppy sample prick. Melissa's temperature had also dropped slightly over several checks, but was still within the normal range. None of these conditions would seem unusual to most people, including Linda, the trainee nurse. But when Darlene, an experienced nurse, happened to walk by, she immediately sensed that Melissa "just looked funny," as she put it. After reviewing Melissa's charts and asking Linda a few questions, Darlene rushed to call a physician with the details. The physician immediately prescribed antibiotics to correct what blood tests later confirmed was sepsis.[27]

intuition
The ability to know when a problem or opportunity exists and select the best course of action without conscious reasoning.

The gut instinct that helped Darlene save this baby's life is known as **intuition**–the ability to know when a problem or opportunity exists and to select the best course of action without conscious reasoning.[28] Intuition is both an emotional experience and a rapid unconscious analytic process. As was mentioned in the previous section, the gut feelings we experience are emotional signals that have enough intensity to make us consciously aware of them. These signals warn us of impending danger, such as a sick baby, or motivate us to take advantage of an opportunity. Some intuition also directs us to preferred choices relative to other alternatives in that situation.

All gut feelings are emotional signals, but not all emotional signals are intuition. The key distinction is that intuition involves rapidly comparing what we see or otherwise sense with deeply held patterns learned through experience.[29] These templates represent tacit knowledge that has been implicitly acquired over time. When a template fits or doesn't fit the current situation, emotions are produced that motivate us to act. Intuition also relies on mental models–internal representations of the external world that allow us to anticipate future events from current observations. Darlene's years of experience produced mental templates of unhealthy babies that matched what she saw on that fateful day. Studies have also found that chess masters receive emotional signals when they sense an opportunity through quick observation of a chessboard. They can't immediately explain why they see a favorable move on the chessboard; they just sense it.

As mentioned, some emotional signals (gut feelings) are not intuition because they are not based on well-grounded templates or mental models. Instead they occur when we compare the current situation to our templates and mental models of distant circumstances, which may or may not be relevant. Thus whether or not the emotions we experience in a situation represent intuition depends largely on our level of experience in that situation.

So far intuition has been described as an emotional experience (gut feeling) and a process of pattern matching in which we compare the current situation with well-established templates and mental models. Intuition also relies on *action scripts*–preprogrammed routines for responding to pattern matches or mismatches.[30] Action scripts are programmed decision routines; they provide instant road maps to follow without consciously evaluating the alternatives. These action scripts are generic, so we need to consciously adapt them to the specific situation; but they speed up the decision–action process.

Making Choices More Effectively

It is difficult to get around the human limitations of making choices, but a few strategies may help. One important discovery is that decisions tend to have a higher failure rate when leaders are decisive rather than contemplative about the available options. Of course problems also arise when decisions take too long, but research indicates that a lack of logical analysis is a greater concern. By systematically evaluating alternatives, decision makers minimize the implicit favorite and satisficing problems that occur when they rely on general subjective judgments. Intuition still figures into this analysis, but so does careful consideration of relevant information.[31]

Another issue is how to minimize the adverse effects of emotions on the decision process. The first recommendation here is that we need to be constantly aware that decisions are influenced by both rational and emotional processes. With this awareness, some decision makers deliberately revisit important issues so they look at the information in different moods and have allowed their initial emotions to subside.

scenario planning
A systematic process of thinking about alternative futures, and what the organization should do to anticipate and react to those environments.

Others practice **scenario planning**, in which they anticipate emergencies long before they occur, so that alternative courses of action are evaluated without the pressure and emotions that occur during real emergencies.[32]

Evaluating Decision Outcomes

postdecisional justification
Justifying choices by unconsciously inflating the quality of the selected option and deflating the quality of the discarded options.

Contrary to the rational choice paradigm, decision makers aren't completely honest with themselves when evaluating the effectiveness of their decisions. One concern is that after making a choice, decision makers tend to support their choice by forgetting or downplaying the negative features of the selected alternative and emphasizing its positive features. This perceptual distortion, known as **postdecisional justification**, results from the need to maintain our self-esteem.[33] Postdecisional justification gives people an excessively optimistic evaluation of their decisions, but only until they receive clear and undeniable information to the contrary. Unfortunately it also inflates the decision maker's initial evaluation of the decision, so reality often comes as a painful shock when objective feedback is finally received.

Escalation of Commitment

escalation of commitment
The tendency to repeat an apparently bad decision or allocate more resources to a failing course of action.

A second problem when evaluating decision outcomes is **escalation of commitment**—the tendency to repeat an apparently bad decision or allocate more resources to a failing course of action.[34] There are plenty of escalation examples around the world. Tokyo's Metropolitan Transport Bureau promised to build a 20-mile high-speed subway loop under the city in record time and at enormous profit. Instead the multi-

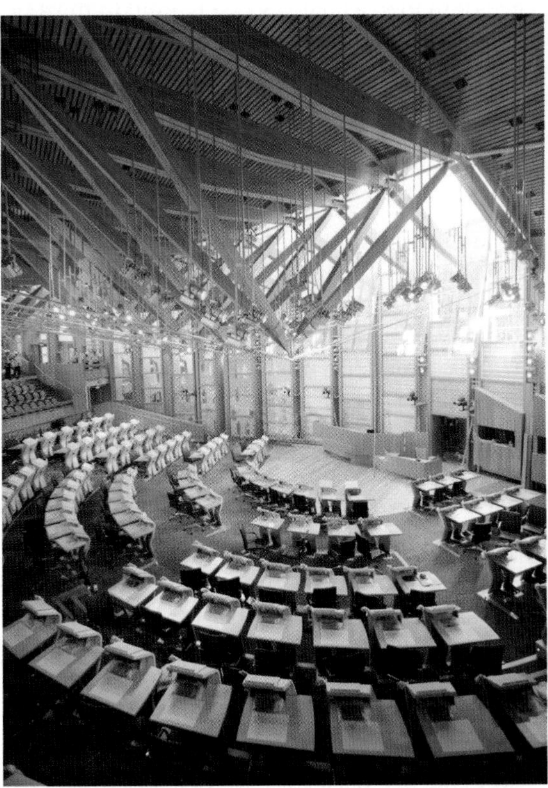

Scottish Parliament Escalates Sky High In 1997 the estimated cost of Scotland's new parliament was £50 million (US $80 million), and it was supposed to be built by 2001. Instead it cost £430 million and was finished three years later than planned. Some writers say that elected officials didn't want to lose face over building contracts they had signed before choosing a different site (Holyrood) and doubling the building size. In spite of warnings from critics, government leaders were also extremely overoptimistic that the many design changes would not escalate costs. The editor of Scottish architecture journal *ARCA* wrote, "The Parliament building will set an all-time world record for waste of money, incompetent management, and covering backsides and political reputations."[35]

billion-dollar project was seriously over budget, more than three years overdue, and won't be profitable until 2040, if ever. Denver's International Airport was supposed to include a state-of-the-art automated baggage handling system. Instead the project was eventually abandoned, causing the airport to open 16 months late and $2 billion over budget. Escalation also occurred years ago when the British government continued funding the Concorde supersonic jet long after its lack of commercial viability was apparent. To this day some fields of science refer to escalation of commitment as the "Concorde fallacy.[36]

Causes of Escalating Commitment Why are people led deeper and deeper into failing projects? There are several reasons, including self-justification, prospect theory effect, perceptual blinders, and closing costs.

- *Self-justification.* Individuals are motivated to maintain their course of action when they have a high need to justify their decision. This self-justification is particularly evident when decision makers are personally identified with the project and have staked their reputations to some extent on the project's success.[37] The Scottish parliament debacle seems to be partly caused by this factor. Elected officials signed contracts for a smaller building on a different site and were possibly worried that terminating those contracts would symbolize that they had made a mistake.
- *Prospect theory effect.* You would think that people dislike losing $50 just as much as they like receiving $50, but that isn't true for most of us. We actually dislike losing a particular amount more than we like gaining the same amount. We also take fewer risks to receive gains and take more risks to avoid losses. This effect, called **prospect theory**, is a second explanation for escalation of commitment. Stopping a project is a certain loss, which is more painful to most people than the uncertainty of success associated with continuing to fund the project. Given the choice, decision makers choose the less painful option.[38] The prospect theory effect might have been an influence in the escalation of commitment in the Holyrood parliament project. In spite of the numerous setbacks, elected officials in Scotland falsely believed that luck would be on their side in keeping costs low, even after allowing numerous design changes.

prospect theory
An effect in which losing a particular amount is more disliked than gaining the same amount.

- *Perceptual blinders.* Escalation of commitment sometimes occurs because decision makers do not see the problems soon enough. They unconsciously screen out or explain away negative information to protect self-esteem. Serious problems initially look like random errors along the trend line to success. Even when they see that something is wrong, the information is sufficiently ambiguous that it can be misinterpreted or justified.
- *Closing costs.* Even when a project's success is in doubt, decision makers will persist because the costs of ending the project are high or unknown. Terminating a major project may involve large financial penalties, a bad public image, or personal political costs.

These four conditions make escalation of commitment look irrational. Usually it is, but there are exceptions. Recent studies suggest that throwing more money into a failing project is sometimes a logical attempt to further understand an ambiguous situation. This strategy is essentially a variation of testing unknown waters. By adding more resources, the decision maker gains new information about the effectiveness of these funds, which provides more feedback about the project's future success. This strategy is particularly common where the project has high closing costs.[39]

Evaluating Decision Outcomes More Effectively

One of the most effective ways to minimize escalation of commitment and postdecisional justification is to separate decision choosers from decision evaluators. This minimizes the self-justification effect because the person responsible for evaluating the decision is not connected to the original decision. A second strategy is to publicly establish a preset level at which the decision will be abandoned or reevaluated. This is similar to a stop-loss order in the stock market, whereby the stock is sold if it falls below a certain price. The problem with this solution is that conditions are often so complex that it is difficult to identify an appropriate point at which to abandon a project.[40]

A third strategy is to find a source of systematic and clear feedback.[41] For example, elected officials in the Scottish parliament might have avoided some of the cost escalation if they had received less ambiguous and conflicting information about the true costs of the project during the first few years. (In fact, civil servants hid some of these costs from elected officials.) Finally, projects might have less risk of escalation if several people are involved. Co-workers continuously monitor each other and might notice problems sooner than someone working alone on a project. Employee involvement offers these and other benefits to the decision-making process, as we learn next.

Learning Objectives

After reading the next two sections you should be able to

7. Describe four benefits of employee involvement in decision making.

8. Identify four contingencies that affect the optimal level of employee involvement.

9. Outline the four steps in the creative process.

10. Describe the characteristics of employees and the workplace that support creativity.

Employee Involvement in Decision Making

Boeing Co. is finding that staying competitive requires the brainwork of every employee, so it is pushing decisions down to the level closest to the activity. At Boeing's subassembly plant in Macon, Georgia, for example, employees identify ways to improve work effectiveness and track their own goals and performance metrics. "We encourage employees to be proactive," says Macon site leader Obie Jones. "When they see a problem or have an idea about process improvements, they take the initiative to start the process improvements, they take the initiative to start the corrective action process or incorporate improvement ideas through the proper channels." Partly due to this high level of employee involvement, *Industry Week* magazine recently named Boeing's Macon facility as one of the 10 best manufacturing plants in the United States.[42]

In this world of rapid change and increasing complexity, leaders rarely have enough information to make the best decisions alone. Whether this information is about reducing costs or improving the customer experience, employee involvement can potentially solve problems or realize opportunities more effectively. **Employee involvement** (also called *participative management*) refers to the degree to which employees influence how their work is organized and carried out.[43] Every organization has some form and various levels of employee involvement. At the lowest level, participation involves asking employees for information. They do not make recommendations and might not even know what the problem is about. At a moderate level of involvement, employees are told about the problem and provide recommendations to the decision maker. At the highest level of involvement, the entire decision-making process is handed over to employees. They identify the problem, choose the best alternative, and implement their choice.

employee involvement The degree to which employees influence how their work is organized and carried out.

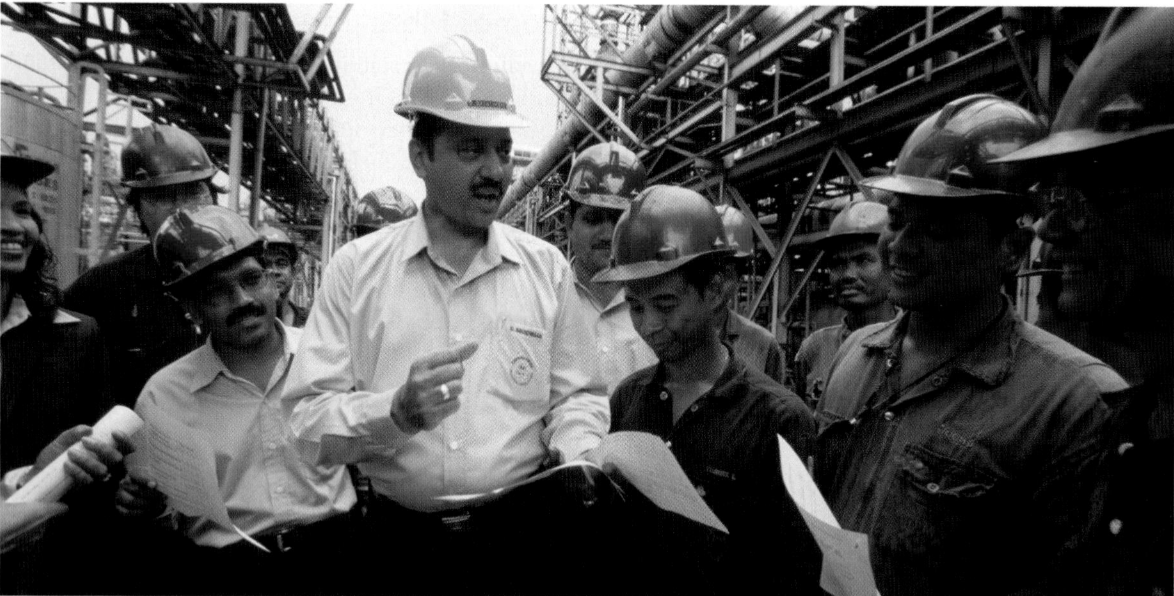

High Involvement Keeps Thai Carbon Black in the Black Thai Carbon Black, which makes the black coloring agent in tires, inks, and many other products, views all of its employees as problem solvers. "The 'can do' attitude of every employee is important," says Subburaman Srinivasan, president of the Thai–Indian joint venture. Each year staff members submit over 600 productivity improvement suggestions, placing their ideas in one of the little red boxes located around the site. Participatory management meetings are held every month, where employees are encouraged to come up with new ideas about ways to improve day-to-day operations. For instance, the company cut its transport costs by more than 10 percent after employees developed a special shipping bag allowing packers to stuff more product into the same volume. Thanks in part to this emphasis on employee involvement, Thai Carbon Black is one of the few companies outside Japan to receive the Deming Prize for total quality management. It has also received the Thailand Quality Class award, *Forbes* magazine's recognition as one of the best managed companies, and Hewitt Associates' ranking as one of the best employers in Asia and Thailand.[44]

Benefits of Employee Involvement

For the past half century organizational behavior scholars have advised that employee involvement potentially improves decision-making quality and commitment.[45] Involved employees can help improve decision quality by recognizing problems more quickly and defining them more accurately. Employees are, in many respects, the sensors of the organization's environment. When the organization's activities misalign with customer expectations, employees are usually the first to know. Employee involvement ensures that everyone in the organization is quickly alerted to these problems.[46]

Employee involvement can also potentially improve the number and quality of solutions generated. In a well-managed meeting, team members create synergy by pooling their knowledge to form new alternatives. In other words, several people working together can potentially generate more and better solutions than the same people working alone. A third benefit is that employee involvement often improves the likelihood of choosing the best alternative. This occurs because the decision is reviewed by people with diverse perspectives and a broader representation of values.[47]

Along with improving decision quality, employee involvement tends to strengthen employee commitment to the decision. Rather than viewing themselves as agents of someone else's decision, staff members feel personally responsible for its success. It also has positive effects on employee motivation, satisfaction, and turnover. A recent study reported that employee involvement also increases skill variety, feelings of autonomy, and task identity, all of which increase job enrichment and potentially employee motivation. Participation is also a critical practice in organizational change because employees are more motivated to implement the decision and less likely to resist changes resulting from the decision. As a respected OB expert concluded, "The new organizational realities are that top-down decision making is not sufficiently responsive to the dynamic organizational environment. Employees must be actively involved in decisions–or completely take over many decisions."[48]

Contingencies of Employee Involvement

If employee involvement is so wonderful, why don't leaders leave all decisions to employees? The answer is that the optimal level of employee involvement depends on the situation. The employee involvement model, shown in Exhibit 8.3, lists four contingencies: decision structure, source of decision knowledge, decision commitment, and risk of conflict in the decision process.

- *Decision structure.* At the beginning of this chapter we learned that some decisions are programmed, whereas others are nonprogrammed. Programmed decisions are less likely to need employee involvement because the solutions are already worked out from past experience. In other words, the benefits of employee involvement increase with the novelty and complexity of the problem or opportunity.
- *Source of decision knowledge.* Subordinates should be involved in some level of decision making when the leader lacks sufficient knowledge and subordinates have additional information to improve decision quality. In many cases employees are closer to customers and production activities, so they often know where the company can save money, improve product or service quality, and realize opportunities. This is particularly true for complex decisions where employees are more likely to possess relevant information.[49]

Exhibit 8.3
Model of Employee Involvement in Decision Making

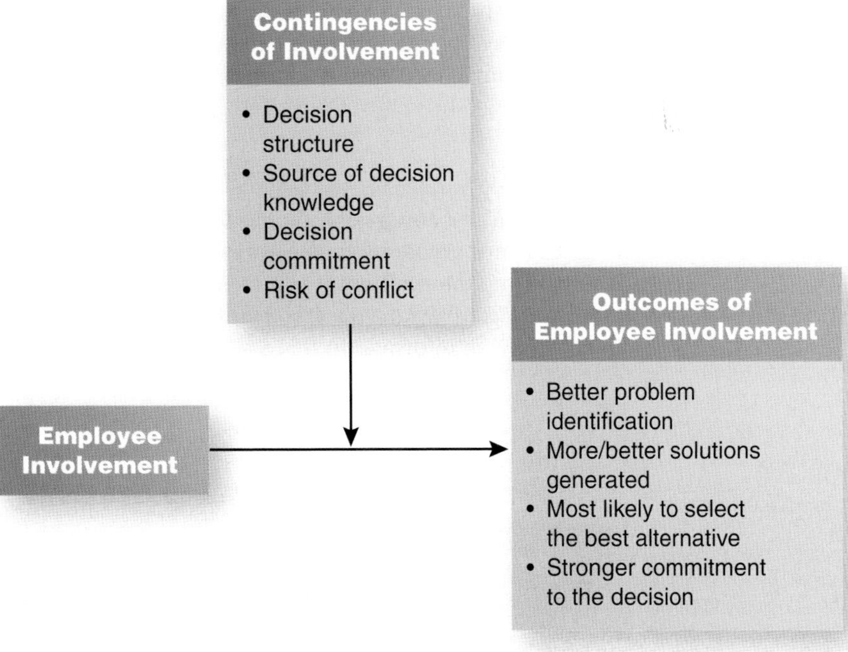

- *Decision commitment.* Participation tends to improve employee commitment to the decision. If employees are unlikely to accept a decision made without their involvement, then some level of participation is usually necessary.
- *Risk of conflict.* Two types of conflict undermine the benefits of employee involvement. First, if employee goals and norms conflict with the organization's goals, then only a low level of employee involvement is advisable. Second, the degree of involvement depends on whether employees will reach agreement on the preferred solution. If conflict is likely, then high involvement (where employees make the decision alone) would be difficult to achieve.

Employee involvement is an important component of the decision-making process. To make the best decisions, we need to involve people who have the most valuable information and who will increase commitment to implement the decision. Another important component of decision making is creativity, which we discuss next.

Creativity

Parcel delivery might seem like a routine business, but that's not how the folks at Yamato Transport Company see it. The Japanese company invented door-to-door next-day parcel delivery in Japan, and its name is now synonymous with the service. Yamato was also the first to offer "cool takkyubin" (delivering chilled or frozen items to any address) and to deliver customers' ski equipment to resorts and homes. To keep better track of shipments, customers receive the mobile telephone numbers of Yamato's delivery personnel, not just distribution centers. One local branch office is testing the use of lockers at train stations around Japan for pickup and delivery locations, notifying customers by e-mail of the delivery times.[50]

creativity
Developing an original product, service, or idea that makes a socially recognized contribution.

Yamato Transport is successful in Japan's fiercely competitive delivery service industry because it relies on creativity for innovative new services. **Creativity** is the development of original ideas that make a socially recognized contribution.[51] Although there are unique conditions for creativity that we discuss over the next few pages, it is really part of the decision-making process described earlier in the chapter. We rely on creativity to find problems, identify alternatives, and implement solutions. Creativity is not something saved for special occasions. It is an integral part of decision making.

The Creative Process Model

One of the earliest and most influential models of creativity is shown in Exhibit 8.4.[52] The first stage is preparation–the person's or group's effort to acquire knowledge and skills regarding the problem or opportunity. Preparation involves developing a clear understanding of what you are trying to achieve through a novel solution, then actively studying information that seems related to the topic.

Exhibit 8.4
The Creative Process Model

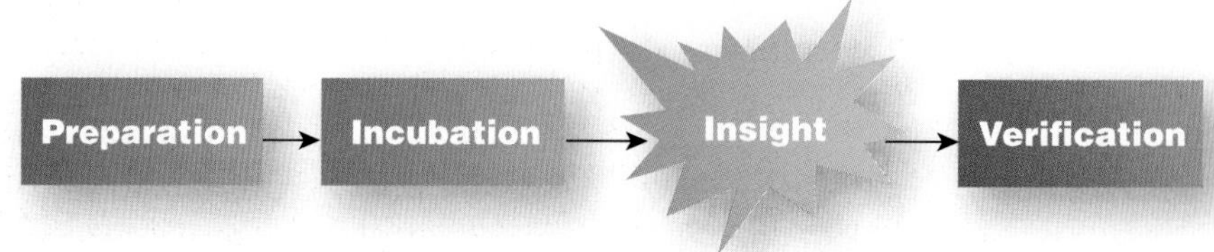

The second stage, called incubation, is the stage of reflective thought. We put the problem aside, but our mind is still working on it in the background.[53] The important condition here is to maintain a low-level awareness by frequently revisiting the problem. Incubation does not mean that you forget about the problem or issue. Incubation assists **divergent thinking**–reframing the problem in a unique way and generating different approaches to the issue. This contrasts with convergent thinking–calculating the conventionally accepted "right answer" to a logical problem. Divergent thinking breaks us away from existing mental models so we can apply concepts or processes from completely different areas of life. Consider the following classic example: Years ago the experimental bulbs in Thomas Edison's lab kept falling off their fixtures until a technician wondered whether the threaded caps that screwed down tightly on kerosene bottles would work on lightbulbs. They did, and the design remains to this day.[54]

divergent thinking
Reframing a problem in a unique way and generating different approaches to the issue.

Insight, the third stage of creativity, refers to the experience of suddenly becoming aware of a unique idea.[55] Insight is often visually depicted as a lightbulb, but a better image would be a brief flash of light or perhaps a flickering candle because these bits of inspiration are fleeting and can be quickly lost if not documented. For this reason many creative people keep a journal or notebook nearby at all times, so that they can jot down these ideas before they disappear. Also, these flickering ideas don't keep a particular schedule; they might come to you at any time of day or night. Insights are merely rough ideas. Their usefulness still requires verification through conscious evaluation and experimentation. Thus, although verification is labeled as the final stage of creativity, it is really the beginning of a long process of experimentation and further creativity.

Creative People and Work Environments

Radical Entertainment, which was introduced at the beginning of this chapter, has an impressive list of successful electronic games, including *The Simpsons: Road Rage, Crash Tag Team Racing,* and *The Incredible Hulk.* The company achieves this success by finding creative people and putting them in an environment that encourages creative ideas. In other words, Radical's executives know that creativity is a function of both the person and the situation.

Characteristics of Creative People Everyone is creative, but some people seem to be more creative than others. Four of the main features of creative people are intelligence, persistence, subject matter knowledge and experience, and inventive thinking style. First, creative people have above-average intelligence to synthesize information, analyze ideas, and apply their ideas.[56] Like the fictional sleuth Sherlock Holmes, creative people recognize the significance of small bits of information and are able to connect them in ways that no one else could imagine. Then they have the capacity to evaluate the potential usefulness of their ideas.

Persistence is the second feature of creative people. The fact is that innovations derive more from trial and error than from intelligence and experience. Persistence drives creative people to continue developing and testing after others have given up. In other words, people who develop more creative products and services are those who develop more ideas that don't work. Thomas Edison emphasized this point in his famous statement that genius is 1 percent inspiration and 99 percent perspiration. Edison and his staff discovered hundreds of ways not to build a lightbulb before they got it right! This persistence is based on a high need for achievement and a moderate or high degree of self-confidence.[57]

Persistence Becomes the Cure for Peptic Ulcers Barry Marshall (left) and Robin Warren (right) faced plenty of doubters when they first proposed that peptic ulcers are caused by specific bacteria. The prevailing belief was that these ulcers are caused by weak stomach linings, gastric acid, and unhealthful diets. Few believed that bacteria could survive, let alone thrive, in the highly acidic stomach environment. Marshall and Warren's initial research supported the bacteria theory, but their paper was rejected because none of the reviewers believed the findings! The paper was eventually published after a British researcher replicated the results in his lab. Bacteria experts soon embraced the theory, but most stomach ulcer experts remained skeptical. To further convince the doubters, Marshall ingested the bacteria into his healthy stomach and developed symptoms within a few days. "It took 10 years and there was a lot of opposition," recalls one expert. "[But Marshall] had this enormous self-belief that what he'd found was right." Marshall and Warren were recently awarded the Nobel Prize in medicine for their discovery. Fittingly, the Nobel committee acknowledged their "tenacity and a prepared mind challenging prevailing dogmas."[58]

A third feature of creative people is that they possess sufficient knowledge and experience in the subject.[59] Creativity experts explain that discovering new ideas requires knowledge of the fundamentals. For example, the 1960s rock group the Beatles produced most of their songs only after they had played together for several years. They developed extensive experience in singing and adapting the music of other people before their creative talents soared.

Although knowledge and experience may be important in one sense, they can also undermine creativity because people develop mental models that lead to "mindless behavior," whereby they stop questioning their assumptions.[60] This explains why some corporate leaders like to hire people from other industries and areas of expertise. For instance, Ballard Power Systems founder Geoffrey Ballard hired a chemist to develop a better battery. When the chemist protested that he didn't know anything about batteries, Ballard replied, "That's fine. I don't want someone who knows batteries. They know what won't work."[61] Ballard explained that he wanted to hire people who would question and investigate what experts stopped questioning.

The fourth characteristic of creative people is that they have an inventive thinking style. Creative types are divergent thinkers and risk takers. They are not bothered by making mistakes or working with ambiguous information. They take a broad view of problems, don't like to abide by rules or status, and are unconcerned about social approval of their actions.[62]

Organizational Conditions Supporting Creativity Hiring creative people is only part of the creativity equation. Corporate leaders also need to maintain a work environment that supports the creative process for everyone.[63] However, it is overly simplistic to identify one best environment in which creativity flourishes. Instead we need to recognize that it emerges through different combinations of processes, mechanisms, and structures.[64] With this caveat in mind, here are some of the conditions that seem to encourage creative thinking.

One of the most important conditions is that the organization has a learning orientation; that is, leaders recognize that employees make reasonable mistakes as part of the creative process. Motivation from the job itself is another important condition for creativity.[65] Employees tend to be more creative when they believe their work has a substantial impact on the organization and/or society (task significance) and when they have the freedom to pursue novel ideas without bureaucratic delays (autonomy). This emphasis on autonomy is apparent at Radical Entertainment, the Vancouver-based electronic games maker described at the beginning of this chapter. Creativity is about changing things, and change is possible only when employees have the authority to experiment. More generally, jobs encourage creativity when they are challenging and aligned with the employee's competencies.

Along with supporting a learning orientation and intrinsically motivating jobs, companies foster creativity through open communication and sufficient resources. They provide a reasonable level of job security, which explains why creativity suffers during times of downsizing and corporate restructuring.[66] To some degree creativity also improves with support from leaders and co-workers. One recent study reported that effective product champions provide enthusiastic support for new ideas. Other studies suggest that co-worker support can improve creativity in some situations, whereas competition among co-workers improves creativity in other situations.[67] Similarly, it isn't clear how much pressure should be exerted on employees to produce creative ideas. Extreme time pressures are well-known creativity inhibitors, but lack of pressure doesn't seem to produce the highest creativity, either.

Activities That Encourage Creativity

Along with hiring creative people and giving them a supportive work environment, organizations have introduced numerous activities that attempt to crank up the creative potential. One set of activities encourages employees to redefine the problem. This occurs when we revisit old projects that have been set aside. After a few months of neglect, these projects might be seen in new ways.[68] Another strategy involves asking people unfamiliar with the issue (preferably with different expertise) to explore the problem with you. You would state the objectives and give some facts, then let the other person ask questions to further understand the situation. By verbalizing the problem, listening to questions, and hearing what others think, you are more likely to form new perspectives on the issue.[69]

A second set of creativity activities, known as *associative play*, ranges from art classes to impromptu storytelling. Employees at pan-African cellular communications giant Vodacom and South African financial institution ABSA have used Lego blocks to build models that mapped out where they wanted their company to go in the future. These companies also engaged employees in impromptu storytelling, in which participants randomly contributed to the development of characters and storyline. OMD, the British media giant, gets creative juices flowing by sending employees to two-day retreats in the countryside where they play grapefruit croquet, chant like medieval monks, and pretend to be dog collars. "Being creative is a bit like an emotion–we need to be stimulated," explains Harriet Frost, one of OMD's specialists in building creativity. "The same is true for our imagination and its ability to come up with new ideas. You can't just sit in a room and devise hundreds of ideas."[70]

Another associative play activity, called *morphological analysis*, involves listing different dimensions of a system and the elements of each dimension, then looking at each combination. This encourages people to carefully examine combinations that initially seem nonsensical. Tyson Foods, the world's largest poultry producer, applied this activity to identify new ways to serve chicken for lunch. The marketing and research team assigned to this task focused on three categories: occasion, packaging, and taste. Next the team worked through numerous combinations of items in the three categories. This created unusual ideas, such as cheese chicken pasta (taste) in pizza boxes (packaging) for concessions at baseball games (occasion). Later the team looked more closely at the feasibility of these combinations and sent them to customer focus groups for further testing.[71]

A third set of activities that encourages creativity in organizations is known as *cross-pollination.*[72] Cross-pollination occurs when people from different areas of the organization exchange ideas. As described in the opening story to this chapter, Radical Entertainment practices cross-pollination through its monthly "game fair" day, in which teams show off their products and make presentations to other teams in the organization. IDEO, the California-based product design company, has a similar effect by mixing together employees from different past projects so they share new knowledge with each other.

Cross-pollination highlights the fact that creativity rarely occurs alone. Some creative people may be individualistic, but most creative ideas are generated through teams and informal social interaction. This probably explains why Jonathon Ive, the award-winning designer of Apple Computer products, always refers to his team's creativity rather than his own. "The only time you'll hear [Jonathan Ive] use the word 'I' is when he's naming some of the products he helped make famous: iMac, iBook, iPod," says one writer.[73] The next chapter introduces the main concepts in team effectiveness. Then in Chapter 10 we learn about high-performance teams, including ways to improve team decision making and creativity.

Chapter Summary

Decision making is a conscious process of making choices among one or more alternatives with the intention of moving toward some desired state of affairs. The rational choice paradigm of decision making includes identifying problems and opportunities, choosing the best decision style, developing alternative solutions, choosing the best solution, implementing the selected alternative, and evaluating decision outcomes.

Persuasion by stakeholders, perceptual biases, and poor diagnostic skills affect our ability to identify problems and opportunities. We can minimize these challenges by being aware of these human limitations and discussing the situation with colleagues.

Evaluating and choosing alternatives are often challenging because organizational goals are ambiguous or in conflict; human information processing is incomplete and subjective; and people tend to satisfice rather than maximize. Decision makers also short-circuit the evaluation process when faced with an opportunity rather than a problem. Emotions shape our preferences for alternatives and the process we follow to evaluate alternatives. We also listen to our emotions for guidance when making decisions. This latter activity relates to intuition–the ability to know when a problem or opportunity exists and to select the best course of action without conscious reasoning. Intuition is both an emotional experience and a rapid unconscious analytic process that involves both pattern matching and action scripts.

People generally make better choices by systematically evaluating alternatives. Scenario planning can help us make future decisions without the pressure and emotions that occur during real emergencies.

Postdecisional justification and escalation of commitment make it difficult to accurately evaluate decision outcomes. Escalation is mainly caused by self-justification, the prospect theory effect, perceptual blinders, and closing costs. These problems are minimized by separating decision choosers from decision evaluators, establishing a preset level at which the decision is abandoned or reevaluated, relying on more systematic and clear feedback about the project's success, and involving several people in decision making.

Employee involvement (or participation) refers to the degree that employees influence how their work is organized and carried out. The level of participation may range from an employee providing specific information to management without knowing the problem or issue, to complete involvement in all phases of the decision process. Employee involvement may lead to higher decision quality and commitment; but several contingencies need to be considered, including the decision structure, source of decision knowledge, decision commitment, and risk of conflict.

Creativity is the development of original ideas that make a socially recognized contribution. The four creativity stages are preparation, incubation, insight, and verification. Incubation assists divergent thinking, which involves reframing the problem in a unique way and generating different approaches to the issue.

Four of the main features of creative people are intelligence, subject matter knowledge and experience, persistence, and inventive thinking style. Creativity is also strengthened for everyone when the work environment supports a learning orientation, the job has high intrinsic motivation, the organization provides a reasonable level of job security, and project leaders provide appropriate goals, time pressure, and resources. Three types of activities that encourage creativity are redefining the problem, associative play, and cross-pollination.

Key Terms

bounded rationality, p. 230
creativity, p. 240
decision making, p. 226
divergent thinking, p. 241
employee involvement, p. 237
escalation of commitment, p. 235
implicit favorite, p. 232
intuition, p. 234
postdecisional justification, p. 235
prospect theory, p. 236
rational choice paradigm, p. 226
satisficing, p. 232
scenario planning, p. 235

Critical Thinking Questions

1. A management consultant is hired by a manufacturing firm to determine the best site for its next production facility. The consultant has had several meetings with the company's senior executives regarding the factors to consider when making the recommendation. Discuss the decision-making problems that might prevent the consultant from choosing the best site location.
2. You have been asked to personally recommend a new travel agency to handle all airfare, accommodation, and related travel needs for your organization of 500 staff. One of your colleagues, who is responsible for the company's economic planning, suggests that the best travel agent could be selected mathematically by inputting the relevant factors for each agency and the weight (importance) of each factor. What decision-making approach is your colleague recommending? Is this recommendation a good idea in this situation? Why or why not?
3. Intuition is both an emotional experience and an unconscious analytic process. One problem, however, is that not all emotions signaling that there is a problem or opportunity represent intuition. Explain how we would know if our "gut feelings" are intuition or not, and if not intuition, suggest what might be causing them.
4. A developer received financial backing for a new business financial center along a derelict section of the waterfront, a few miles from the current downtown area of a large European city. The idea was to build several high-rise structures, attract large tenants to those sites, and have the city extend transportation systems out to the new center. Over the next decade, the developer believed that others would build in the area, thereby attracting the regional or national offices of many financial institutions. Interest from potential tenants was much lower than initially predicted, and the city did not build transportation systems as quickly as expected. Still the builder proceeded with the original plans. Only after financial support was curtailed did the developer reconsider the project. Using your knowledge of escalation of commitment, discuss three possible reasons why the developer was motivated to continue with the project.
5. Ancient Book Company has a problem with new book projects. Even when others are aware that a book is far behind schedule and may engender little public interest, sponsoring editors are reluctant to terminate contracts with authors whom they have signed. The result is that editors invest more time with these projects than on more fruitful projects.

As a form of escalation of commitment, describe two methods that Ancient Book Company can use to minimize this problem.

6. Employee involvement applies just as well to the classroom as to the office or factory floor. Explain how student involvement in classroom decisions typically made by the instructor alone might improve decision quality. What potential problems may occur in this process?
7. Think of a time when you experienced the creative process. Maybe you woke up with a brilliant (but usually sketchy and incomplete) idea, or you solved a baffling problem while doing something else. Describe this incident to your class and explain how the experience followed the creative process.
8. Two characteristics of creative people are that they have relevant experience and are persistent in their quests. Does this mean that people with the most experience and the highest need for achievement are the most creative? Explain your answer.

Case Study 8.1 EMPLOYEE INVOLVEMENT CASES

Case 1: The Sugar Substitute Research Decision

You are the head of research and development (R&D) for a major beer company. While working on a new beer product, one of the scientists in your unit seems to have tentatively identified a new chemical compound that has few calories but tastes closer to sugar than current sugar substitutes. The company has no foreseeable need for this product, but it could be patented and licensed to manufacturers in the food industry.

The sugar substitute discovery is in its preliminary stages and would require considerable time and resources before it would be commercially viable. This means that it would necessarily take some resources away from other projects in the lab. The sugar substitute project is beyond your technical expertise, but some of the R&D lab researchers are familiar with that field of chemistry. As with most forms of research, it is difficult to determine the amount of research required to further identify and perfect the sugar substitute. You do not know how much demand is expected for this product. Your department has a decision process for funding projects that are behind schedule. However, there are no rules or precedents about funding projects that would be licensed but not used by the organization.

The company's R&D budget is limited, and other scientists in your work group have recently complained that they need more resources and financial support to get their projects completed. Some of these other R&D projects hold promise for future beer sales. You believe that most researchers in the R&D unit are committed to achieving the company's interests.

Case 2: Coast Guard Cutter Decision

You are the captain of a 200-foot Coast Guard cutter, with a crew of 16, including officers. Your mission is general at-sea search and rescue. At 2:00 a.m. this morning, while en route to your home port after a routine 28-day patrol, you received word from the nearest Coast Guard station that a small plane had crashed 60 miles offshore. You obtained all the available information concerning the location of the crash, informed your crew of the mission, and set a new course at maximum speed for the scene to search for survivors and wreckage.

You have now been searching for 20 hours. Your search operation has been increasingly impaired by rough seas, and there is evidence of a severe storm building. The atmospherics associated with the deteriorating weather have made communications with the Coast Guard station impossible. A decision must be made shortly about whether to abandon the search and place your vessel on a course that would ride out the storm (thereby protecting the vessel and your crew, but relegating any possible survivors to almost certain death from exposure) or to continue a potentially futile search and the risks it would entail.

Before losing communications, you received an update weather advisory concerning the severity and duration of the storm. Although your crew members are extremely conscientious about their responsibility, you believe that they would be divided on the decision of leaving or staying.

Discussion Questions (for Both Cases)

1. To what extent should your subordinates be involved in this decision? Select one of the following levels of involvement:
   - *No involvement.* You make the decision alone without any participation from subordinates.
   - *Low involvement.* You ask one or more subordinates for information relating to the problem, but you don't ask for their recommendations and might not mention the problem to them.
   - *Medium involvement.* You describe the problem to one or more subordinates (alone or in a meeting) and ask for any relevant information as well as their recommendations on the issue. However, you make the final decision, which might or might not reflect their advice.
   - *High involvement.* You describe the problem to subordinates. They discuss the matter, identify a solution without your involvement (unless they invite your ideas), and implement that solution. You have agreed to support their decision.
2. What factors led you to choose this level of employee involvement rather than the others?
3. What problems might occur if less or more involvement occurred in this case (where possible)?

Sources: The Sugar Substitute Research Decision is written by Steven L. McShane, ©2002. The Coast Guard cutter case is adapted from V.H. Vroom and A.G. Jago, *The New Leadership: Managing Participation in Organizations* (Englewood Cliffs, NJ: Prentice Hall, 1988), ©1987 V.H. Vroom and A.G. Jago. Used with permission of the authors.

Case Study 8.2 CHAMPIONS OF INNOVATION

BusinessWeek

In an era when Six Sigma controls no longer guarantee competitive advantage, when outsourcing to China and India is universal, when creeping commoditization of products, services, and information hammers prices, innovation is the new currency of competition. The most innovative companies rely on champions who are able to bring out more creative thinking in their employees. They know how to select creative types, give them a work environment that supports creativity, and find strategies that boost the creative juices.

This *BusinessWeek* case study describes the practices of five champions of innovation at Google, Old Navy, Procter & Gamble, HP, and Citigroup. The article examines how these champions find creativity in people, work environments, and creativity-enhancing activities. Read the full text of this *BusinessWeek* article at www.mhhe.com/mcshane4e and prepare for the discussion questions below.

Discussion Questions

1. In your opinion, which of these five companies pays the most attention to creativity as a characteristic of individuals?
2. Describe the work environments that these companies create to support creativity and innovation.
3. What special practices are noted in this article that help people to think more creatively?

Source: M. Conlin, "Champions of Innovation", *Business Week*, 19 June 2006, 18.

Class Exercise 8.3 FOR WHAT IT'S WORTH

PURPOSE This exercise is designed to help you understand issues with making perfectly rational decisions.

MATERIALS The instructor will either bring to class or show computer images of three products. Students will need their Social Security numbers (a driver's license or other piece of identity with several numbers can substitute).

INSTRUCTIONS

1. The instructor will show the three products (or images of the products) to the class and describe the features of each product so students are sufficiently informed about their features and functions. The instructor will *not* provide any information about the price paid or market value of these products.
2. Working alone, each student will write at the top of Exhibit 1 the last two digits of his or her identification number. Each student will also write in the left column of Exhibit 1 the name of each product shown by the instructor. Then each student will circle "yes" or "no" in Exhibit 1 for each product, indicating whether he or she would be willing to pay the dollar equivalent of the two-digit number for each product if seeking to purchase such a product.
3. In the right column of the Exhibit 1 each student (still working alone) will write the maximum dollar value he or she would be willing to pay for each product if seeking to purchase such a product.
4. After completing their calculations alone, students will be organized into four or five groups as specified by the instructor. Group size is unimportant, but the instructor's criterion for organizing teams is important and must be followed. Each team will calculate the average price that students within that group were willing to pay for each product. The team will also calculate the percentage of people within the group who indicated "yes" (willing to purchase at the stated price) for each product.
5. Each team will report its three average maximum willingness-to-pay prices as well as the percentage of students in the team who circled "yes" for each product. The instructor will outline a concept relevant to rational decision making and how that concept relates to this exercise.

Exhibit 1
For What It's Worth Calculation Sheet

Two-Digit Number: _______ _______

Product name (Write in product names below.)	**Willing to pay two-digit number price for this product?** (Circle your answer.)	**Maximum willingness to pay for this product**
____________________	No Yes	$ ____________: 00
____________________	No Yes	$ ____________: 00
____________________	No Yes	$ ____________: 00

Source: Based on information in D. Ariely, G. Loewenstein, and D. Prelec, "'Coherent Arbitrariness': Stable Demand Curves without Stable Preferences," *Quarterly Journal of Economics*, February 2003, pp. 73–105.

Team Exercise 8.4 WHERE IN THE WORLD ARE WE?

PURPOSE This exercise is designed to help you understand the potential advantages of involving others in decisions rather than making decisions alone.

MATERIALS Students require an unmarked copy of the map of the United States with grid marks (Exhibit 2). Students are not allowed to look at any other maps or use any other materials. The instructor will provide a list of communities located somewhere on Exhibit 2. The instructor will also provide copies of the answer sheet after students have individually and in teams estimated the locations of communities.

INSTRUCTIONS

1. Write in Exhibit 1 the list of communities identified by your instructor. Then, working alone, estimate the location in Exhibit 2 of these communities, all of which are in the United States. For example, mark a small "1" in Exhibit 2 on the spot where you believe the first community is located. Mark a small "2" where you think the second community is located, and so on. Please be sure to number each location clearly and with numbers small enough to fit within one grid space.
2. The instructor will organize students into roughly equal teams (typically five or six people per team). Working with your team members, reach a consensus on the location of each community listed in Exhibit 1. The instructor might provide teams with a separate copy of the map, or members can identify the team's numbers using a different color pen on the individual maps. The team's decision for each location should occur by consensus, not voting or averaging.
3. The instructor will provide an answer sheet showing the correct locations of the communities. Using this answer sheet, count the minimum number of grid squares between the location you individually marked and the true location of each community. Write the number of grid squares in the third column of Exhibit 1, then add up the total. Next, count the minimum number of grid squares between the location the team marked and the true location of each community. Write the number of grid squares in the fourth column of Exhibit 1, then add up the total.
4. The instructor will ask for information about the totals, and the class will discuss the implications of these results for employee involvement and decision making.

Exhibit 1
List of Selected Communicaties in the United States

Number	Communities	Individual distance in grid units from the true location	Team distance in grid units from the true location
1			
2			
3			
4			
5			
6			
7			
8			
		Total:	Total:

Exhibit 2 Map of the United States

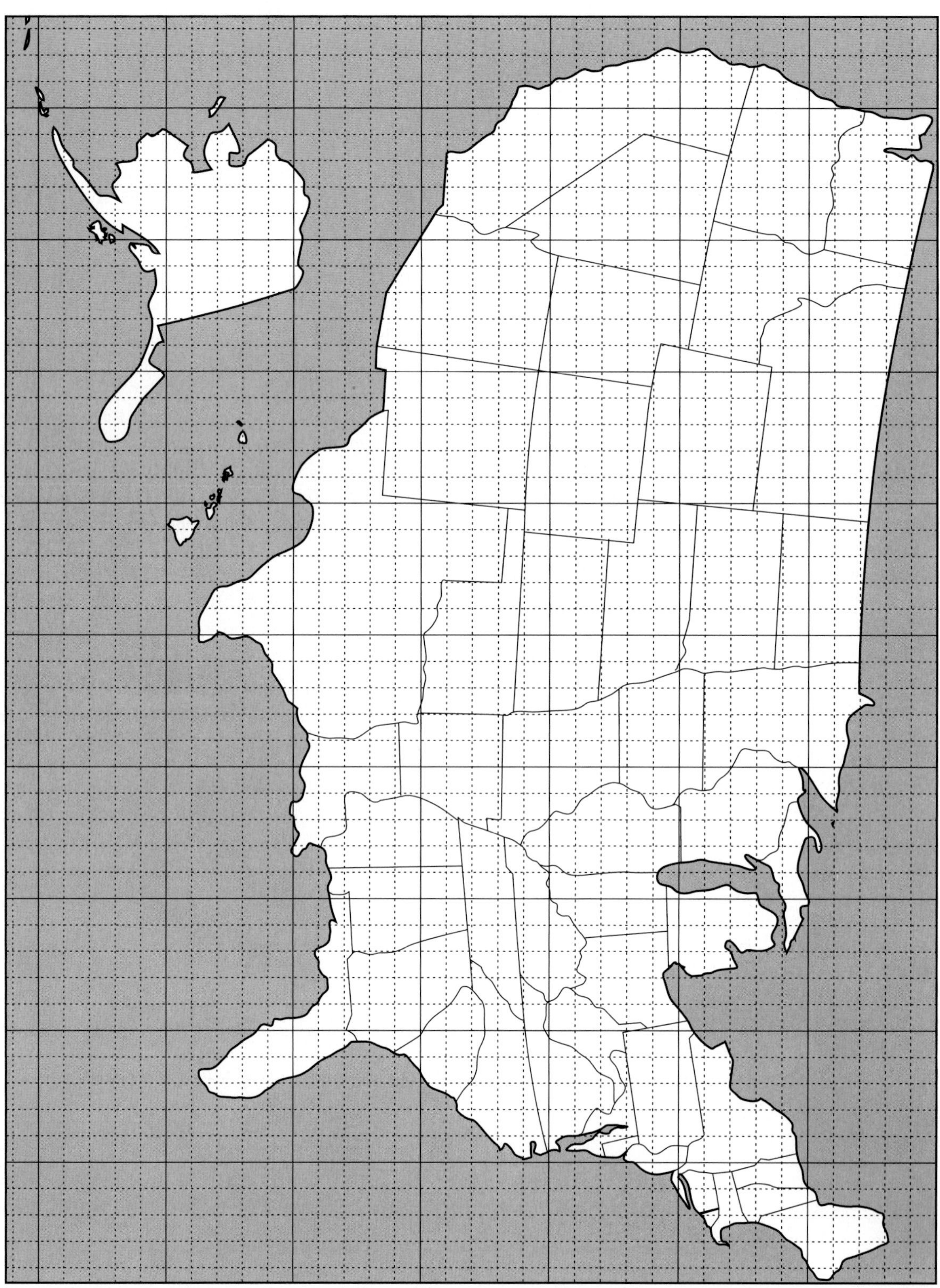

Team Exercise 8.5 WINTER SURVIVAL EXERCISE

PURPOSE This exercise is designed to help you understand the potential advantages of involving others in decisions rather than making decisions alone.

INSTRUCTIONS

1. Read the situation that follows. Then, working alone, rank order the 12 items shown in the accompanying chart according to their importance to your survival. In the "individual ranking" column indicate the most important item with "1" continuing to "12" for the least important. Keep in mind the reasons why each item is or is not important.
2. The instructor will divide the class into small teams (four to six people). Each team will rank order the items in the third column. Team rankings should be based on consensus, not simply averaging the individual rankings.
3. When the teams have completed their rankings, the instructor will provide an expert's ranking, which can be entered in the fourth column.
4. Each student will compute the absolute difference (ignore minus signs) between the individual ranking and the expert's ranking, record this information in column five, and sum the absolute values at the bottom of column five.
5. In column six record the absolute difference between the team's ranking and the expert's ranking, and sum these absolute scores at the bottom. A class discussion will follow regarding the implications of these results for employee involvement and decision making.

SITUATION

You have just crash-landed somewhere in the woods of southern Manitoba or possibly northern Minnesota. It is 11:32 a.m. in mid-January. The small plane in which you were traveling crashed on a small lake. The pilot and copilot were killed. Shortly after the crash, the plane sank completely into the lake with the pilot's

Winter survival tally sheet

Items	Step 1 Your individual ranking	Step 2 Your team's ranking	Step 3 Survival expert's ranking	Step 4 Difference between steps 1 and 3	Step 5 Difference between steps 2 and 3
Ball of steel wool					
Newspaper					
Compass					
Hand ax					
Cigarette lighter					
45-caliber pistol					
Section air map					
Canvas					
Shirt and pants					
Can of shortening					
Whiskey					
Chocolate bars					
			Total	Your score	Team score

(The lower the score, the better)

Source: Adapted from "Winter Survival" in D. Johnson and F. Johnson, *Joining Together,* 3rd ed. (Englewood Cliffs, NJ: Prentice Hall, 1984).

and copilot's bodies inside. Everyone else on the flight escaped to land dry and without serious injury.

The crash came suddenly before the pilot had time to radio for help or inform anyone of your position. Because your pilot was trying to avoid a storm, you know the plane was considerably off course. The pilot announced shortly before the crash that you were 45 miles northwest of a small town that is the nearest known habitation.

You are in a wilderness area made up of thick woods broken by many lakes and rivers. The snow depth varies from above the ankles in windswept areas to more than knee-deep where it has drifted. The last weather report indicated that the temperature would reach 5 degrees Fahrenheit in the daytime and minus 15 degrees at night. There are plenty of dead wood scraps and twigs in the area around the lake. You and the other surviving passengers are dressed in winter clothing appropriate for city wear–suits, pantsuits, street shoes, and overcoats. While escaping from the plane, your group salvaged the 12 items listed in the accompanying chart. You may assume that the number of survivors in the group is the same as the number in your class group and that you have agreed to stay together.

Class Exercise 8.6 THE HOPPING ORANGE

PURPOSE This exercise is designed to help you understand the dynamics of creativity and team problem solving.

INSTRUCTIONS

You will be placed in teams of six students. One student serves as the official timer for the team and must have a watch, preferably with a stopwatch timer. The instructor will give each team an orange (or similar object) with a specific task involving use of the orange. The objective is easily understood and nonthreatening and will be described by the instructor at the beginning of the exercise. Each team will have a few opportunities to achieve the objective more efficiently. To maximize the effectiveness of this exercise, no other information is provided here.

Class Exercise 8.7 CREATIVITY BRAINBUSTERS

PURPOSE This exercise is designed to help you understand the dynamics of creativity and team problem solving.

INSTRUCTIONS

This exercise may be completed alone or in teams of three or four people. If teams are formed, students who already know the solutions to one or more of these problems should identify themselves and serve as silent observers. When you have finished (or, more likely, when time is up), the instructor will review the solutions and discuss the implications of this exercise. In particular, be prepared to discuss what you needed to solve these puzzles and what may have prevented you from solving them more quickly (or at all).

1. *Double circle problem.* Draw two circles, one inside the other, with a single line and with neither circle touching the other (as shown here). In other words, you must draw both of these circles without lifting your pen.

2. *Nine dot problem.* Here are nine dots. Without lifting your pen, draw no more than four straight lines that pass through all nine dots.

3. *Nine dot problem revisited.* Referring to the same nine dot exhibit, describe how, without lifting your pen, you could draw a line through all the dots with three or fewer straight lines.

4. *Word search.* In the following line of letters, cross out five letters so that the remaining letters, without altering their sequence, spell a familiar English word.

CFRIVEELATETITEVRSE

5. *Burning ropes.* You have two pieces of rope of unequal lengths and a box of matches. In spite of their different lengths, each piece of rope takes one hour to burn; however, parts of each rope burn at unequal speeds. For example, the first half of one piece might burn in 10 minutes. Use these materials to accurately determine when 45 minutes have elapsed.

Self-Assessment 8.8

MEASURING YOUR CREATIVE PERSONALITY

PURPOSE This self-assessment is designed to help you measure the extent to which you have a creative personality.

INSTRUCTIONS

Listed on page 254 is an adjective checklist with 30 words that may or may not describe you. Put a mark in the box beside the words that you think accurately describe you. Please *do not* mark the boxes for words that do not describe you. When finished, you can score the test using the scoring key in Appendix B. This exercise is completed alone so you assess yourself without concerns of social comparison. However, class discussion will focus on how this scale might be applied in organizations, as well as the limitations of measuring creativity in work settings.

Self-Assessment 8.9

TESTING YOUR CREATIVE BENCH STRENGTH (STUDENT OLC)

This self-assessment takes the form of a self-scoring quiz. It consists of 12 questions that require divergent thinking to identify the correct answers. For each question, type your answer in the space provided. When finished, look at the correct answer for each question, along with the explanation for that answer.

Adjective Checklist					
Affected	☐	Honest	☐	Reflective	☐
Capable	☐	Humorous	☐	Resourceful	☐
Cautious	☐	Individualistic	☐	Self-confident	☐
Clever	☐	Informal	☐	Sexy	☐
Commonplace	☐	Insightful	☐	Sincere	☐
Confident	☐	Intelligent	☐	Snobbish	☐
Conservative	☐	Inventive	☐	Submissive	☐
Conventional	☐	Mannerly	☐	Suspicious	☐
Dissatisfied	☐	Narrow interests	☐	Unconventional	☐
Egotistical	☐	Original	☐	Wide interests	☐

Source: Adapted from and based on information in H.G. Gough and A.B. Heilbrun Jr., *The Adjective Check List Manual* (Palo Alto, CA: Consulting Psychologists Press, 1965).

Self-Assessment 8.10

DECISION MAKING STYLE INVENTORY (STUDENT OLC)

People have different styles of decision making that are reflected in how they identify problems or opportunities and make choices. This self-assessment estimates your decision-making style through a series of statements describing how individuals go about making important decisions. Please indicate whether you agree or disagree with each statement. Answer each item as truthfully as possible so that you get an accurate estimate of your decision-making style. This exercise is completed alone so you assess yourself honestly without concerns of social comparison. However, class discussion will focus on the decision-making styles that people prefer in organizational settings.

After reading this chapter, if you need additional information, see www.mhhe.com/mcshane4e for more in-depth interactivities that correspond with this material.

A decade ago Paul Tramontano was typical of most Wall Street brokers, single-handedly providing advice to hundreds of clients. Not any more. Today the director of wealth management at Citigroup's Smith Barney heads a 12-person team (called the Topeka Wealth Management Group) that provides expertise in a range of services 24 hours a day. The team includes technical specialists to complement his own focus on financial, estate planning, and advisory business. Tramontano and others at Smith Barney realized that clients needed a wider variety of services than any single person can deliver. "That's why I think the team approach is the model for what this industry will look like," says Tramontano.

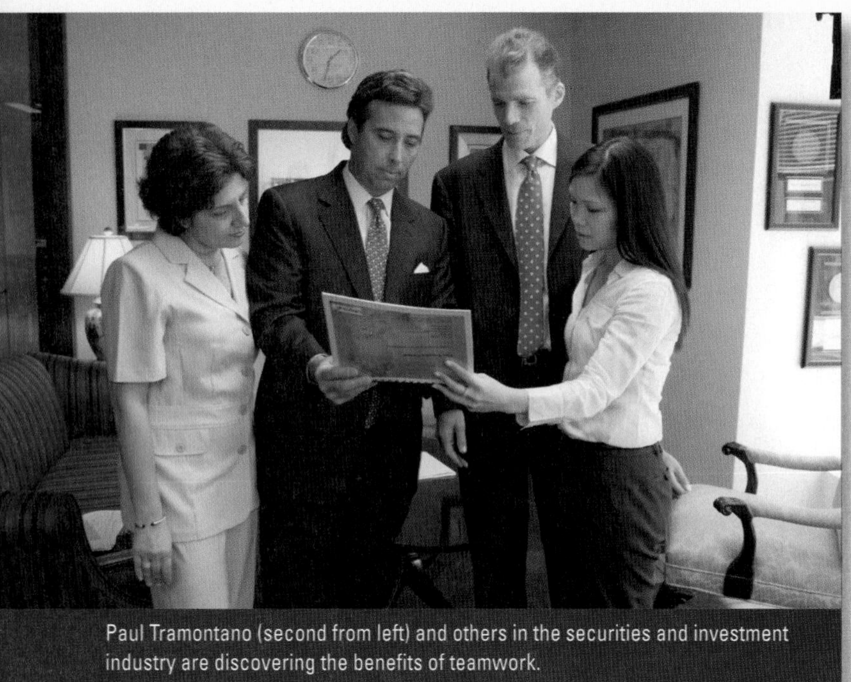
Paul Tramontano (second from left) and others in the securities and investment industry are discovering the benefits of teamwork.

Teamwork has become the mantra of success throughout the investment industry. Nearly 40 percent of Smith Barney advisers are now assigned to teams. Merrill Lynch has organized over half of its financial advisers into 3,000 teams. When Mark Mobius, head of the Templeton Emerging Markets Fund, was asked whether individual fund managers are the real "brands" for a mutual fund, Mobius quickly replied, "The funds are actually run by teams of people and do not depend on one person."

Goldman, Sachs & Co. is widely recognized for successfully combining competitive performance with cooperative teamwork. Goldman employees are evaluated annually by their bosses, peers, and subordinates on how well they perform as well as how well they work as team members. Teamwork even extends to leadership roles: Goldman Sachs departments are run by "co-heads"—two people in charge of each unit. "At Goldman's, you have an alpha organization made up of alpha individuals, working together; it's quite something," says Goldman Sachs vice chairwoman Suzanne Nora Johnson.

In spite of the hoopla, getting investment professionals to actually engage in teamwork has not been easy. Robert Fischer, a securities representative with Legg Mason in Richmond, Virginia, has had his share of frustrations, particularly the extra time required to maintain teams as new members are added. "There's a cost to that—the time, the planning element, the learning curve," warns Fischer. Fifth Third Securities also experienced teamwork problems, particularly in encouraging financial experts to share resources. One strategy that particularly helped Fifth Third Securities strengthen team dynamics was to literally move team members into the same room. "It took a lot of work collaborating and colocating these officers into teams," says a senior executive at the Cincinnati-based securities firm.[1]

Foundations of Team Dynamics

LEARNING OBJECTIVES

After reading this chapter you should be able to

1. Define *teams* and distinguish them from informal groups.
2. Discuss the potential benefits of teams in organizations.
3. Outline the model of team effectiveness.
4. Identify six organizational and team environmental elements that influence team effectiveness.
5. Explain how a team's task, size, and composition influence its effectiveness.
6. Summarize the team development process.
7. Discuss how team norms develop and are maintained and how they may be altered.
8. List six factors that influence team cohesiveness.
9. Discuss the limitations of teams.
10. Explain how companies minimize social loafing.

Organizations ultimately consist of individuals, but corporate leaders on Wall Street and throughout the securities industry are discovering that people working alone usually lack sufficient knowledge or capacity to achieve organizational objectives. Instead teams have become a source of competitive advantage. This focus on teamwork extends to most industries. At General Electric's (GE) Aircraft Engines division in Durham, North Carolina, employees are organized into over a dozen 16-member teams who receive feedback and rewards based partially on team performance. Ford Motor Company's legal department was recently identified as one of the best legal departments in the country, partly because almost everything the department does is achieved through project teams. C&S Wholesale Grocers, the second largest grocery wholesaler in the United States, created self-directed work teams throughout its warehouse operation, resulting in significantly higher productivity and lower absenteeism.[2]

This chapter introduces the concept of teams and provides a foundation to understand the complex conditions that make teams more or less effective in organizational settings. We begin by explaining why people join informal groups and why organizations rely on teams. Most of the chapter examines each part of this model, including team and organizational environment, team design, and the team processes of development, norms, roles, and cohesiveness.

Learning Objectives

After reading this section you should be able to

1. **Define *teams* and distinguish them from informal groups.**
2. **Discuss the potential benefits of teams in organizations.**

Teams and Groups

teams
Groups of two or more people who interact and influence each other, are mutually accountable for achieving common goals associated with organizational objectives, and perceive themselves as a social entity within an organization.

Teams are groups of two or more people who interact and influence each other, are mutually accountable for achieving common goals associated with organizational objectives, and perceive themselves as a social entity within an organization.[3] All teams exist to fulfill some purpose, such as assembling a product, providing a service, designing a new manufacturing facility, or making an important decision. Team members are held together by their interdependence and need for collaboration to achieve common goals. All teams require some form of communication so members can coordinate and share common objectives. Team members also influence each other, although some members are more influential than others regarding the team's goals and activities.

Exhibit 9.1 briefly describes various types of (usually) formal work teams in organizations. Notice that some teams are permanent, whereas others are temporary. Some are responsible for making products or providing services; others exist to make decisions or share knowledge. Each of these types of teams has been created deliberately to serve an organizational purpose. Some teams, such as skunkworks teams, are not initially sanctioned by management; yet they are called "teams" because members clearly work toward an organization objective.

groups
Two or more people with a unifying relationship.

All teams are **groups** because they consist of people with a unifying relationship. But not all groups are teams; some groups are just people assembled together without any necessary interdependence or organizationally focused objective. Along with formal work teams, organizations consist of *informal groups.* Informal groups are not initiated by the organization and usually do not perform organizational goals (thus they are "informal"). Instead they exist primarily for the

Exhibit 9.1 Several Types of Formal Teams in Organizations

Team Type	Description
Departmental teams	Employees have similar or complementary skills located in the same unit of a functional structure; usually minimal task interdependence because each person works with employees in other departments.
Production/service/leadership teams	Typically multiskilled (employees have diverse competencies), team members collectively produce a common product/service or make ongoing decisions; production/service teams typically have an assembly line type of interdependence, whereas leadership teams tend to have tight interactive (reciprocal) interdependence.
Self-directed work teams	Similar to production/service teams except (1) they produce an entire product or subassembly that has low interdependence with other work units, and (2) they have very high autonomy (this type of team has no supervisors and usually controls inputs, flow, and outputs).
Advisory teams	Entities that provide recommendations to decision makers, includes committees, advisory councils, work councils, and review panels; may be temporary, but often permanent, some with frequent rotation of members.
Task force (project) teams	Usually multiskilled, temporary entities whose assignment is to solve a problem, realize an opportunity, or develop a product or service.
Skunkworks	Multiskilled entities that are usually located away from the organization and are relatively free of its hierarchy; these teams are often initiated by an entrepreneurial team leader (*innovation champion*) who borrows people and resources (*bootlegging*) to create a product or develop a service.
Virtual teams	Formal teams whose members operate across space, time, and organizational boundaries and are linked through information technologies to achieve organizational tasks; may be a temporary task force or a permanent service team.
Communities of practice	May be formally designed, but are usually informal groups bound together by shared expertise and passion for a particular activity or interest; often similar to virtual teams in that many rely on information technologies as a main source of interaction, but the purpose is to share information, not make a product or provide a service.

benefit of their members. The groups you meet for lunch and chat with in the hallway are informal groups. In each case you associate with these groups for your own benefit.

Why Rely on Teams?

Goldman Sachs, Fifth Third Securities, C&S Wholesale Grocers, and many other organizations have put a lot of energy into reorganizing their companies around teams. In fact, one major survey of U.S. human resource professionals concluded, "Teams are now an integral part of workplace management." Why all the fuss about teams? The answer to this question has a long history, dating back to research on British coal mining in the 1940s and the Japanese economic miracle of the 1970s.[4] These early studies revealed that *under the right conditions,* teams make better decisions, develop better products and services, and create a more energized workforce compared with employees working alone. "One of the things I think people overlook is the quality of the team," says Rose Marie Bravo, the American executive who engineered the remarkable turnaround of Burberry, the London fashion house. "It isn't one person, and it isn't two people. It is a whole

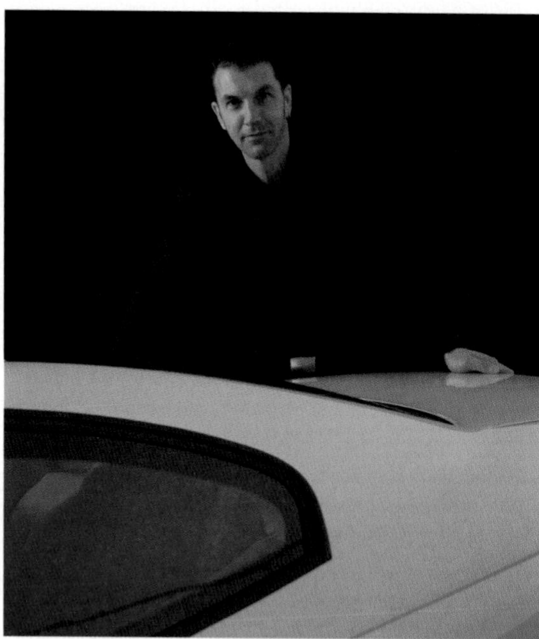

GM Holden's Secret Skunkworks In the late 1990s eight designers at General Motors' small development center in Australia secretly worked on a souped-up coupé, something that was missing from GM's lineup. "It had to stay quiet," recalls Michael Simcoe (shown in this photo), who led the clandestine skunkworks group. "It wasn't an official Holden (GM's Australian company) project, and management hadn't asked us to produce a coupé. It was all after-hours work; people stayed on at the office instead of going straight home at night, and they even came in on weekends to make it happen." The project was so secret that the family room wall at one team member's home was used to complete the first full-size line drawings. When GM Holden executives were notified, they excitedly supported the project, which eventually became the Monaro in Australia and the Pontiac GTO in North America. Members of the skunkworks team are now working with their American colleagues on a new version of the Camaro; Simcoe is now global head of new car design at General Motors' headquarters in Detroit.[5]

group of people—a team that works cohesively toward a goal—that makes something happen or not."[6]

As a form of employee involvement, teams are generally more successful than individuals working alone at identifying problems, developing alternatives, and choosing from those alternatives. For instance, Goldman Sachs teams consist of experts from various disciplines who collectively provide better expertise and service to clients than an individual working alone. Similarly, team members can quickly share information and coordinate tasks, whereas these processes are slower and prone to more errors in traditional departments led by supervisors. Teams typically provide superior customer service because they provide more breadth of knowledge and expertise to customers than individual "stars" can offer.

In many situations people are *potentially* more energized or engaged when working on teams than alone.[7] Employees have a drive to bond and are motivated to fulfill the goals of groups to which they belong. For instance, one study reported that individuals have a stronger sense of belongingness when they work in teams rather than alone. Another consideration is that people potentially have higher motivation in a team environment because they are more accountable to fellow team members, who monitor performance more closely than a traditional supervisor.

Why People Belong to Informal Groups

Employees are not required to join informal groups, yet they exist throughout organizations. One reason is that human beings are social animals. Experts suggest that our drive to bond is a hardwired evolutionary development, which includes the drive to belong to informal groups.[8] This is evidenced by the fact that people invest considerable time and effort in forming and maintaining social relationships without any special circumstances or ulterior motives. A second explanation is provided by social identity theory, which states that individuals define themselves by their group affiliations. Thus we join informal groups–particularly groups viewed favorably by others and that are similar to our existing values–because they shape and reinforce our self-images.[9]

A third reason why people join informal groups is to accomplish tasks that cannot be achieved by individuals working alone. For example, employees will sometimes form a group to oppose organizational changes because the group collectively has more power than individuals complaining alone. A fourth explanation for informal groups is that in stressful situations we are comforted by the mere presence of other people and are therefore motivated to be near them. When in danger, people congregate near each other even though it serves no apparent purpose. Similarly, employees tend to mingle more often when hearing rumors that the company might be sold.[10]

Learning Objectives

After reading the next three sections you should be able to

3. **Outline the model of team effectiveness.**
4. **Identify six organizational and team environmental elements that influence team effectiveness.**
5. **Explain how a team's task, size, and composition influence its effectiveness.**

A Model of Team Effectiveness

You might have noticed that we hedged our glorification of teams by saying that they are "potentially" better than individuals "under the right conditions." The reason for this cautious writing is that many organizations have introduced team structures that later became spectacular failures. Why are some teams effective while others fail? This question has challenged organizational researchers for some time, and as you might expect, numerous models of team effectiveness have been proposed over the years.[11]

team effectiveness
The extent to which a team achieves its objectives, achieves the needs and objectives of its members, and sustains itself over time.

Let's begin by clarifying the meaning of **team effectiveness.** Team effectiveness refers to how a team affects the organization, individual team members, and the team's existence.[12] First, most teams exist to serve some purpose relating to the organization or other system in which the group operates. Some informal groups also have task-oriented (although not organizationally mandated) goals, such as sharing information in an informal community of practice.

Second, team effectiveness relies on the satisfaction and well-being of its members. People join groups to fulfill their personal needs, so effectiveness is partly measured by this need fulfillment. Finally, team effectiveness includes the team's viability–its ability to survive. It must be able to maintain the commitment of its members, particularly during the turbulence of the team's development. Without this commitment, people leave and the team will fall apart. It must also secure sufficient resources and find a benevolent environment in which to operate.

Exhibit 9.2 presents the model of team effectiveness that we will examine closely throughout the rest of this chapter. We begin by looking at elements of the team's and organization's environment that influence team design, processes, and outcomes.

Exhibit 9.2
Model of Team Effectiveness

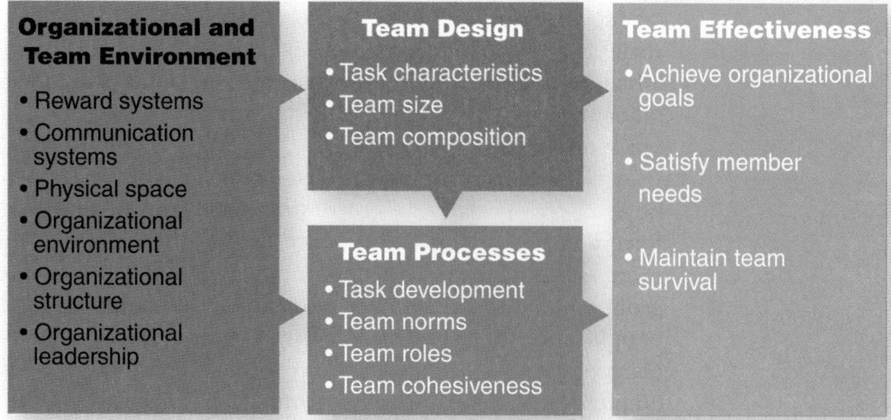

Organizational and Team Environment

The discussion of team effectiveness logically begins with the contextual factors that influence a team's design, processes, and outcomes.[13] Many elements in the organizational and team environment influence team effectiveness. Six of the most important elements are reward systems, communication systems, physical space, organizational environment, organizational structure, and organizational leadership.

- *Reward systems.* Team members tend to work together more effectively when they are at least partly rewarded for team performance.[14] For instance, a large portion of the paycheck earned by Nucor employees is performance pay determined by team results. This doesn't mean that everyone on the team should receive the same amount of pay based on the team's performance. On the contrary, research indicates that employees in the United States and other Western cultures work better on teams when their rewards are based on a combination of individual and team performance.
- *Communication systems.* A poorly designed communication system can starve a team of valuable information and feedback, or it may swamp it with information overload. As we will learn in the next chapter, communication systems are particularly important for geographically dispersed (virtual) teams.
- *Physical space.* The physical layout of an office or manufacturing facility improves team dynamics in at least two ways: (1) It improves communication among team members, and (2) it shapes employee perceptions about being together as a team. Medrad Inc. recently reorganized its production workspace so teams now work in U-shaped "cells" rather than along a straight assembly line. Toyota puts up to 30 people from engineering, design, production, marketing, and other areas in a large room (called an *obeya*) so they have a sense of being a team and can communicate more quickly and effectively. The *obeya* arrangement has cut Toyota's product development time and costs by 25 and 50 percent, respectively. "The reason *obeya* works so well is that it's all about immediate face-to-face human contact," explains the head of Toyota Motor Manufacturing North America."[15]
- *Organizational environment.* Team success depends on the company's external environment. If the organization cannot secure resources, for instance, the team cannot fulfill its performance targets. Similarly, high demand for the team's output creates feelings of success, which motivates team members to stay with the team. A competitive environment can motivate employees to work together more closely.

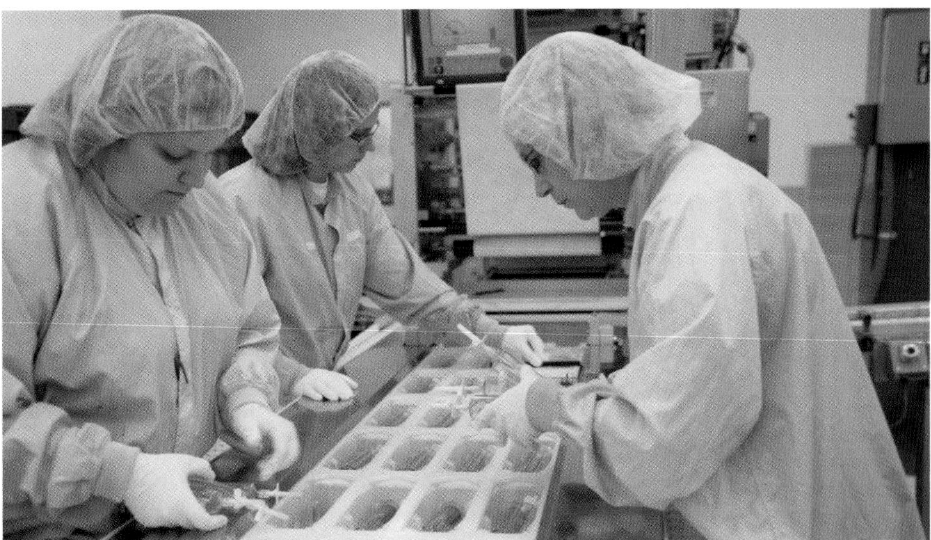

Medrad Sees the U in Team Medrad Inc. has become a team-based organization, particularly since it adopted the philosophy and practices of lean manufacturing. The Indianola, Pennsylvania, medical device manufacturer relies on cross-functional teams to track down wasted time, space, and distance in the work process. One team also redesigned the production process from a straight-line assembly to clustered structures in which members of each team now work more closely in U-shaped work cells. A successful trial confirmed that the U-shaped cell physical arrangement boosted team performance by improving the ability of team members to observe and assist each other.[16]

- *Organizational structure.* Many teams fail because the organizational structure does not support them. Teams work better when there are few layers of management and teams are given autonomy and responsibility for their work. This structure encourages interaction with team members rather than with supervisors. Teams also flourish when employees are organized around work processes rather than specialized skills. This structure increases interaction among team members.[17]
- *Organizational leadership.* Teams require ongoing support from senior executives to align rewards, organizational structure, communication systems, and other elements of team context. They also require team leaders or facilitators who provide coaching and support. Team leaders are also enablers, meaning that they ensure teams have the authority to solve their own problems and resources to accomplish their tasks.[18] Leaders also maintain a value system that supports team performance more than individual success.

Team Design Features

There are several elements to consider when designing an effective team. Three of the main design elements are task characteristics, team size, and team composition. As we saw in the team effectiveness model (Exhibit 9.2), these design features influence team effectiveness directly as well as indirectly through team processes, described later.

Task Characteristics

What type of work is best handled by teams rather than individuals working alone? OB experts are still figuring out the answer to this question.[19] Some research says that teams are more effective when their tasks are well-structured because the clear structure makes it easier to coordinate work among several people. At the same time, other studies indicate that teams flourish more on complex tasks because the complexity motivates them to work together as a team. The difficulty here is that while task structure and task complexity aren't opposites, it can be difficult to find complex work that is well structured.

task interdependence
The extent to which team members must share common inputs to their individual tasks, need to interact in the process of executing their work, or receive outcomes (such as rewards) that are partly determined by the performance of others.

Task Interdependence One task characteristic that is definitely important for teams is **task interdependence**–the extent to which team members must share common inputs to their individual tasks, need to interact in the process of executing their work, or receive outcomes (such as rewards) that are partly determined by the performance of others.[20] The general rule is that the higher the level of task interdependence, the greater the need for teams rather than individuals working alone.

Teams are well suited to highly interdependent tasks because people coordinate better when working together than separately. High task interdependence also tends to increase employee motivation and satisfaction for team members. In other words, high interdependence makes people want to be part of the team, and they feel good about being part of the team. However, this motivation and satisfaction occur only when team members have the same task goals, such as serving the same clients or collectively assembling the same product. In contrast, employees are more likely to experience frustration when each team member is assigned tasks with unique goals (such as serving different clients) but must depend on other team members (high task interdependence) to achieve those unique goals.[21] The bottom line, then, is to assign highly interdependent tasks to teams rather than individuals, but only when those tasks relate to the same goals. If tasks have unique goals, the advantages of teamwork will be less apparent.

Exhibit 9.3 illustrates three levels of task interdependence.[22] Pooled interdependence is the lowest level of interdependence (other than independence), in which

Exhibit 9.3
Levels of Task Interdependence

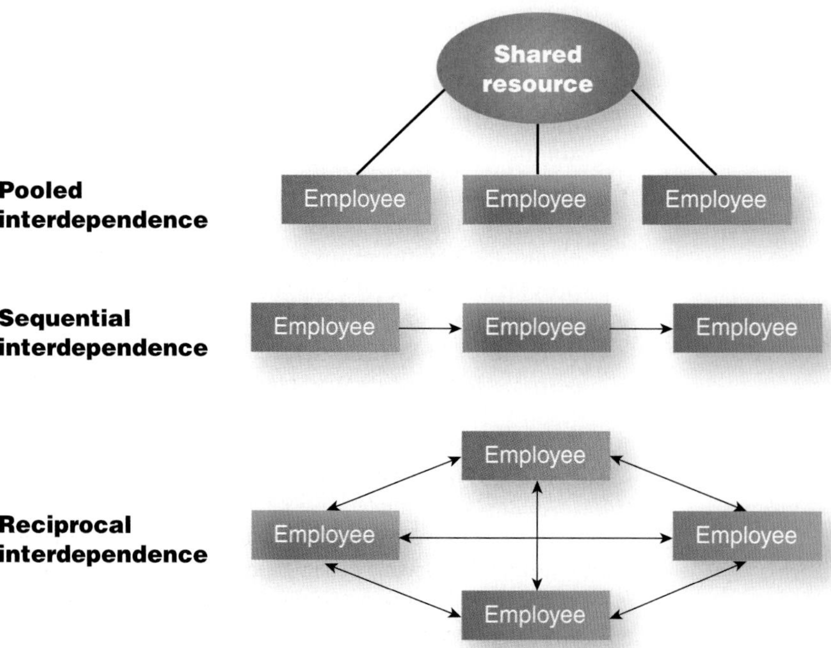

individuals operate independently except for reliance on a common resource or authority. Employees share a common payroll, cafeteria, and other organizational resources. In most cases they can work well alone rather than in teams if pooled interdependence is the highest relationship among them.

Sequential interdependence occurs where the output of one person becomes the direct input for another person or unit. This interdependent linkage is found in most assembly lines. Although employees in the production line process usually work alone, they are sufficiently interdependent that Toyota and other companies create teams around these processes. Reciprocal interdependence represents the highest level of interdependence, in which work output is exchanged back and forth among individuals. Employees with reciprocal interdependence should almost always be organized into teams to facilitate coordination in their interwoven relationship.

Team Size

Jim Hassell is a strong believer in teamwork, but the Sun Microsystems executive also recognizes that putting together the best team requires careful consideration of its optimal size. "[A] big challenge in building a team is getting the number of people in the team right. You need to have a balance between having enough people to do all the things that need to be done, while keeping the team small enough so that it is cohesive and can make decisions effectively and speedily."[23]

Team size is an important concern for Jim Hassell and other executives. Some writers claim that team size should be no more than 10 people; but optimal team size really depends on several factors, such as the number of people required to complete the work and the amount of coordination needed to work together. As Hassell described, the general rule is that teams should be large enough to provide the necessary competencies and perspectives to perform the work, yet small enough to maintain efficient coordination and meaningful involvement of each member.[24]

Larger teams are typically less effective because members consume more time and effort coordinating their roles and resolving differences. For instance, some of the continuous improvement process teams at Varian Australia suffered because they had more than a dozen members, making it difficult to reach agreement on ideas. In these larger teams, individuals have less opportunity to participate and consequently are less likely to feel that they are contributing to the team's success. Larger work units tend to break into informal subgroups around common interests and work activities, causing members to form stronger commitments to their subgroups than to the larger team.

Team Composition

When Hewlett-Packard (HP) hires new talent, it doesn't look for just technical skills and knowledge. The high-tech computer manufacturer looks for job applicants who fit into a team environment. "It's important for candidates to prove to us that they can work well with others," explains business development manager Bill Avey. "We're looking for people who value the different perspectives that each individual brings to a team." Avey describes how HP recruiters will ask applicants to recall a time they worked in a group to solve a problem. "Successful candidates tend to show how they got differences out in the open and reached a resolution as a team," says Avey.[25]

Hewlett-Packard has a strong team orientation, so it carefully selects people with the necessary motivation and competencies for teamwork. Royal/Dutch Shell also pays close attention to job applicants who can work effectively in teams. In fact, as Connections 9.1 describes, Shell has developed a unique five-day event, called the Shell Gourami Business Challenge, to help identify university students with both technical and team skills.

Team Diversity Challenges Students in Shell's Gourami Business Challenge

Royal Dutch/Shell (Shell) discovered long ago that a job interview isn't the best way to determine a job applicant's technical skills, nor how well he or she works in a team environment. That's why the global energy company launched the Shell Gourami Business Challenge, a five-day event involving four dozen engineering and business university students. Shell introduced the Gourami Business Challenge a decade ago in Europe and recently in the United States, Asia, and the Middle East.

Students are split into several teams representing different departments, including exploration and production, refining operations, manufacturing, human resources, finance, and sales and marketing. Teams initially develop business plans for their own departments; later they must merge the departmental plans into an organizationwide business strategy. On the final day, the multiteam's strategy is presented to Gourami's board of directors, which consists of senior executives from Shell. Shell leaders emphasize that the Gourami event is not a competition for limited jobs; everyone could be hired if they are qualified.

Throughout the five-day event, Shell assessors evaluate students on how effectively they work in diverse teams, not just on their technical skills. The need for strong social skills is quickly apparent to most participants. Maureen Valencia, a business student from the Philippines who attended the Asian Gourami exercise, admitted feeling some initial tension because the Australians were "more straightforward and tell you right away if you're doing something right or wrong."

Andrew Wang, a Singaporean business student who also attended the Asian Gourami event, says he was easy to get along with—the Filipino participants gave him the nickname *babaero,* which means sweet talker in Tagalog. Yet he admits to a few irritations, including one in which another team member kept interrupting. Eventually, says Wang "my teammate mediated because the atmosphere just got tense."

Team skills were also vital to help students work with people from different specializations. "Coming from a business background, it's most difficult to understand the engineering aspect of the oil industry," admitted Arpan Shah, a University of Texas finance student who attended the Gourami exercise in Rancho Mirage, California. "We have to work together so that both sides understand each other."

Claire Gould, who attended the European session, also noticed the challenges and learning when working with students from other disciplines. "Hard science students can be dismissive of what they see as 'fluffy' disciplines like human resources management and vice versa," admits Gould, a mechanical engineering undergraduate at Imperial College in London. "Dealing with the 'real-life' challenges of Gourami made us all aware of the value of other skills and aptitudes and the need to work as a team."

Sources: P. Wise, "How Shell Finds Student World's Brightest Sparks," *Financial Times* (London), 8 January 2004, p. 12; "Shell Oil Introduces Undergrads to Gourami Business Challenge," University of Texas at Austin news release, 15 August 2005; S. Ganesan, "Reality-Style Recruitment," *Malaysia Star,* 9 October 2005; Z. Nazeer, "You're Hired!" *The New Paper* (Singapore), 31 October 2005; J. Ng, "Shell Uses 'The Apprentice' Contest to Recruit Staff," *Straits Times* (Singapore), 3 October 2005.

Royal Dutch/Shell has found a better way to identify the team skills of prospective job applicants by observing business and engineering students in the Shell Gourami Business Challenge.

What do Royal Dutch/Shell, Hewlett-Packard, and other companies look for in effective team members? First, teams require members who are motivated to remain team members. In particular, they must be motivated to work together rather than alone, abide by the team's rules of conduct, and buy into the team's goals. Employees with a strong collectivist orientation–those who value group goals more than their own personal goals–tend to perform better in work teams.[26] Effective team members also possess valuable skills and knowledge for the team's objectives and can work well with others. Notably, research suggests that high-performing team members have strong social skills and emotional intelligence and generally demonstrate more cooperative behavior toward others.[27]

homogeneous teams
Teams that include members with common technical expertise, demographics (age, sex), ethnicity, experiences, or values.

heterogeneous teams
Teams that include members with diverse personal characteristics and backgrounds.

Team Diversity Another important dimension of team composition is the diversity of team members.[28] **Homogeneous teams** include members with common technical expertise, demographics (age, sex), ethnicity, experiences, or values, whereas **heterogeneous teams** have members with diverse personal characteristics and backgrounds. Some forms of diversity are apparent on the surface, such as differences in sex and race. *Deep-level diversity,* on the other hand, refers to differences in the personalities, values, attitudes, and other psychological characteristics of team members. *Surface-level diversity* is apparent as soon as the team forms, whereas deep-level diversity emerges over time as team members discover each other's values and beliefs.[29]

Should teams be homogeneous or heterogeneous? Both have advantages and disadvantages, and their relative effectiveness depends on the situation.[30] Heterogeneous teams experience more conflict and take longer to develop. They are susceptible to "faultlines"–hypothetical dividing lines that may split a team into subgroups along gender, ethnic, professional, or other dimensions. Teams with strong faultlines–such as where team members fall into two or more distinct demographic groups–have a higher risk of dysfunctional conflict and other behaviors that undermine team effectiveness. Under these circumstances, leaders need to restructure the work to minimize interaction among these subgroups.[31] In contrast, members of homogeneous teams experience higher satisfaction, less conflict, and better interpersonal relations. Consequently, homogeneous teams tend to be more effective for tasks requiring a high degree of cooperation and coordination, such as emergency response teams.

Although heterogeneous teams have these difficulties, they are generally more effective than homogeneous teams in executive groups and in other situations involving complex problems requiring innovative solutions. One reason is that people from different backgrounds see a problem or opportunity from different perspectives. A second reason is that they usually have a broader knowledge base. For example, Paul Tramontano's team of financial experts at Smith Barney (described in the opening story) is necessarily composed of a diverse group of people who have deep knowledge in several fields, ranging from estate planning to tax planning. Without these heterogeneous characteristics, the team would be much less effective in its assigned task.

A third reason why heterogeneous teams are generally more effective than homogeneous teams is that the diversity provides representation to the team's constituents, such as other departments or clients from similarly diverse backgrounds. When a team represents various professions or departments, those constituents are more likely to accept and support the team's decisions and actions.

Learning Objectives

After reading this section you should be able to

6. **Summarize the team development process.**
7. **Discuss how team norms develop and are maintained and how they may be altered.**
8. **List six factors that influence team cohesiveness.**

Team Processes

We've looked at two sets of elements in the team effectiveness model so far: (1) organizational and team environment and (2) team design. Over the next few pages we will learn about the third set of team effectiveness elements, collectively known as team processes. These processes–team development, norms, roles, and cohesiveness–are influenced by both team design and organizational and team environment factors.

Team Development

A few years ago the U.S. National Transportation Safety Board (NTSB) studied the circumstances under which airplane cockpit crews were most likely to have accidents and related problems. What they discovered was startling: 73 percent of all incidents took place on the crew's first day, and 44 percent occurred on the crew's very first flight together. This isn't an isolated example. NASA studied fatigue of pilots after returning from multiple-day trips. Fatigued pilots made more errors in the NASA flight simulator, as one would expect. But the NASA researchers didn't expect the discovery that fatigued crews who had previously worked together made fewer errors than did rested crews who had not yet flown together.[32]

The NTSB and NASA studies reveal that team members must resolve several issues and pass through several stages of development before emerging as an effective work unit. They must get to know each other, understand their respective roles, discover appropriate and inappropriate behaviors, and learn how to coordinate their work or social activities. The longer team members work together, the better they develop common mental models, mutual understanding, and effective performance routines to complete their work.

The five-stage model of team development, shown in Exhibit 9.4, provides a general outline of how teams evolve by forming, storming, norming, performing, and eventually adjourning.[33] The model shows teams progressing from one stage to the next in an orderly fashion, but the dashed lines illustrate that they might also fall back to an earlier stage of development as new members join or other conditions disrupt the team's maturity.

1. *Forming*–The first stage of team development is a period of testing and orientation in which members learn about each other and evaluate the benefits and costs of continued membership. People tend to be polite during this stage and will defer to the existing authority of a formal or informal leader who must provide an initial set of rules and structures for interaction. Members try to find out what is expected of them and how they will fit into the team.
2. *Storming*–The storming stage is marked by interpersonal conflict as members become more proactive and compete for various team roles. Coalitions may form to influence the team's goals and means of goal attainment. Members try to establish norms of appropriate behavior and performance standards. This is a

Exhibit 9.4
Stages of Team Development

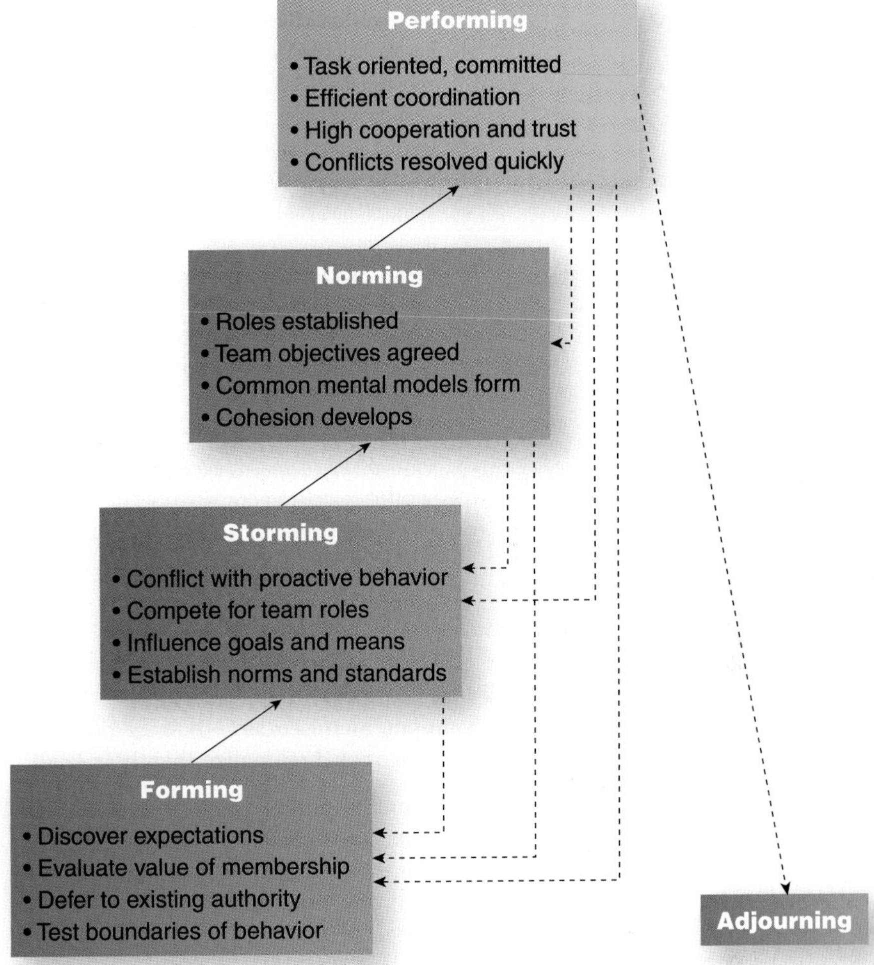

tenuous stage in the team's development, particularly when the leader is autocratic and lacks the necessary conflict management skills.

3. *Norming*–During the norming stage, the team develops its first real sense of cohesion as roles are established and a consensus forms around group objectives. Members have developed relatively similar mental models, so they have common expectations and assumptions about how the team's goals should be accomplished. They have developed a common team-based mental model that allows them to interact more efficiently so they can move into the next stage, performing.[34]
4. *Performing*–The team becomes more task-oriented in the performing stage. Team members have learned to coordinate and resolve conflicts more efficiently. Further coordination improvements must occasionally be addressed, but the greater emphasis is on task accomplishment. In high-performance teams members are highly cooperative, have a high level of trust in each other, are committed to group objectives, and identify with the team. There is a climate of mutual support in which team members feel comfortable about taking risks, making errors, or asking for help.[35]
5. *Adjourning*–Most work teams and informal groups eventually end. Task forces disband when their projects are completed. Informal work groups may reach this stage when several members leave the organization or are reassigned elsewhere.

Sky-High Team Development Reaching the "performing" stage of team development isn't just a goal for the Blue Angels; it's an absolute necessity to ensure that the U.S. Navy's aerial demonstration team completes its maneuvers with near-perfect timing. Although highly experienced before joining the squad, the pilots put in long hours of practice to reach the pinnacle of team development. The F/A-18A Hornets initially fly with large spaces between them, but the team gradually tightens up the formation over the 10-week training program until the fighter jets are at times only 18 inches apart. Lt. Cdr. John Saccomando, who flies the No. 2 position, explains that the training improves trust and common mental models about each maneuver. "I know exactly what [the lead] jet is going to do, and when," he says. "It takes a while to build that confidence." Team development is also sped up through candid debriefings after every practice. "We close the door, and there's no rank," says Saccomando, who is expected to offer frank feedback to commanding officer and flight leader Cdr. Stephen R. Foley. Foley points out that the safety and success of the Blue Angels depend on how well the team development process works. "The team concept is what makes [everything] here click," Foley emphasizes.[36]

Some teams adjourn as a result of layoffs or plant shutdowns. Whatever the cause of team adjournment, members shift their attention away from task orientation to a socioemotional focus as they realize that their relationship is ending.

The team development model is a useful framework for thinking about how teams develop. Indeed, a recent study suggests that it fits nicely with student recollections of their team development experiences.[37] Still, the model is not a perfect representation of the dynamics of team development. It does not explicitly show that some teams remain in a particular stage longer than others and that team development is a continuous process. As membership changes and new conditions emerge, teams cycle back to earlier stages in the developmental process to regain the equilibrium or balance lost by the changes (as shown by the dashed lines in Exhibit 9.4).

Team Norms

norms
The informal rules and shared expectations that groups establish to regulate the behavior of their members.

Have you ever noticed how employees in one branch office practically run for the exit door the minute the workday ends, whereas their counterparts in another office seem to be competing for who can stay at work the longest? These differences are partly due to **norms**–the informal rules and shared expectations that groups establish to regulate the behavior of their members. Norms apply only to behavior, not to private thoughts or feelings. Moreover, norms exist only for behaviors that are important to the team.[38] Norms guide how team members deal with clients, how they share resources, whether they are willing to work longer hours, and many other behaviors in organizational life. Some norms ensure that employees support organizational goals, whereas other norms might conflict with organizational objectives.

Conformity to Team Norms

Everyone has experienced peer pressure at one time or another. Co-workers grimace if we are late for a meeting or make sarcastic comments if we don't have our part of the project completed on time. In more extreme situations, team members may try to enforce norms by temporarily ostracizing deviant co-workers or threatening to terminate their membership. This heavy-handed peer pressure isn't as rare as you might think. One survey revealed that 20 percent of employees have been pressured by their colleagues to slack off at work. Half the time, the peer pressure occurred because colleagues didn't want to look like poor performers against their more productive co-workers.[39]

Norms are also directly reinforced through praise from high-status members, more access to valued resources, or other rewards available to the team. But team members often conform to prevailing norms without direct reinforcement or punishment because they identify with the group and want to align their behavior with the team's expectations. The more tightly the person's social identity is connected to the group, the more the individual is motivated to avoid negative sanctions from that group.[40] This effect is particularly strong in new members because they are uncertain of their status and want to demonstrate their membership in the team.

How Team Norms Develop Norms develop as soon as teams form because people need to anticipate or predict how others will act. Even subtle events during the team's formation, such as how team members initially greet each other and where they sit in the first meetings, can initiate norms that are later difficult to change. At first most norms are fuzzy, such as "team members should communicate frequently with each other." Over time norms tend to become more specific, such as "check and reply to your e-mail daily."[41]

Norms form as team members discover behaviors that help them function more effectively (such as the need to respond quickly to e-mail). In particular, a critical event in the team's history can trigger formation of a norm or sharpen a previously vague one. As an example, if a co-worker slipped on metal scraps and was seriously injured, team members might develop a strong norm to keep the work area clean. Along with the effect of initial experiences and critical events, a third influence on team norms is the past experiences and values that members bring to the team. If most people who join a new team value work–life balance, then norms are likely to develop that discourage long hours and work overload.[42]

Preventing and Changing Dysfunctional Team Norms Team norms often become deeply anchored, so the best way to avoid norms that undermine organizational success or employee well-being is to establish desirable norms when teams are first formed. As was just mentioned, norms form from the values that people bring to a team, so one strategy is to select people with appropriate values. If organizational leaders want their teams to have strong safety norms, they should hire people who already value safety.

Another strategy is to clearly state desirable norms as soon as a team is created. For instance, when Four Seasons Hotels & Resorts opens a new hotel, it forms a 35-person task force of respected staff from other Four Seasons hotels to get the new hotel up and running. Their mandate also includes helping to "Four Seasonize" the new staff by watching for behaviors and decisions that are inconsistent with the Four Seasons way of doing things. "The task force helps establish norms [in the new hotel]," explains a Four Seasons manager who has served on these task forces.[43]

Of course most teams are not just starting up, so how can norms change in older teams? One way is for the leader to explicitly discuss the counterproductive norm with team members using persuasive communication tactics. For example, the surgical team of one hospital had developed a norm of arriving late for operations. Patients and other hospital staff often waited 30 minutes or more for the team to arrive. The hospital CEO eventually spoke to the surgical team about their lateness and, through moral suasion, convinced team members to arrive for operating room procedures no more than five minutes late for their appointments.[44]

Team-based reward systems can sometimes weaken counterproductive norms. Unfortunately the pressure to conform to the counterproductive norm is sometimes stronger than the financial incentive. This problem occurred in the classic story of a pajama factory where employees were paid under a piece rate system. Some individuals in the group were able to process up to 100 units per hour and thereby earn more money, but they all chose to abide by the group norm of 50 units per hour. Only after the team was disbanded did the strong performers working alone increase their performance to 100 units per hour.[45]

Finally, a dysfunctional norm may be so deeply ingrained that the best strategy is to disband the group and replace it with people having more favorable norms. Organizational leaders should seize the opportunity to introduce performance-oriented norms when a new team is formed and select members who will bring desirable norms to the group.

Team Roles

role
A set of behaviors that people are expected to perform because they hold certain positions in a team and organization.

Every work team and informal group has various roles necessary to coordinate the team's task and maintain the team's functioning. A **role** is a set of behaviors that people are expected to perform because they hold certain positions in a team and organization.[46] Some roles help a team achieve its goals; other roles maintain relationships so the team survives and team members fulfill their needs. Some team roles are formally assigned to specific people. For example, team leaders are usually expected to initiate discussion, ensure that everyone has an opportunity to present her or his views, and help the team reach agreement on the issues discussed. But team members often take on various roles informally based on their personality, values, and expertise. These role preferences are usually worked out during the storming stage of team development. However, in a dynamic environment, team members often need to assume various roles temporarily as the need arises.[47]

Various team role theories have been proposed over the years, but Meredith Belbin's team role theory is the most popular.[48] The model identifies nine team roles (see Exhibit 9.5) that are related to specific personality characteristics. People have a natural preference for one role or another, although they can adjust to a secondary role. Belbin's model emphasizes that all nine roles must be engaged for optimal team performance. Moreover, certain team roles should dominate over others at various stages of the team's project or activities. For example, shapers and coordinators are key figures when the team is identifying its needs, whereas completers and implementers are most important during the follow-through stage of the team's project.

How accurate is Belbin's team roles model? The evidence is mixed.[49] Research agrees that teams require a balance of roles and that people tend to prefer one type of role. However, Belbin's nine roles typically boil down to six or seven roles in empirical studies. For example, the implementer and completer roles are the same or too similar to distinguish from each other. Scholars have also criticized how Belbin's roles are measured, which creates difficulty in determining the accuracy of the model. Overall, teams do have a variety of roles that must be fulfilled for team effectiveness, but we are still trying to figure out what these roles are and how to measure them.

Team Cohesiveness

team cohesiveness
The degree of attraction people feel toward the team and their motivation to remain members.

Team cohesiveness–the degree of attraction people feel toward the team and their motivation to remain members–is an important factor in a team's success.[50] Employees feel cohesiveness when they believe their team will help them achieve their personal goals, fulfill their need for affiliation or status, or provide social support during times of crisis or trouble. Cohesiveness is an emotional experience, not just

Exhibit 9.5
Belbin's Team Roles

Role Title	Contributions	Allowable Weaknesses
Plant PL	Creative, imaginative, unorthodox. Solves difficult problems.	Ignores details. Too preoccupied to communicate effectively.
Resource investigator RI	Extrovert, enthusiastic, communicative. Explores opportunities. Develops contacts.	Overoptimistic. Loses interest once initial enthusiasm has passed.
Coordinator CO	Mature, confident, a good chairperson. Clarifies goals, promotes decision making, delegates well.	Can be seen as manipulative. Delegates personal work.
Shaper SH	Challenging, dynamic, thrives on pressure. Has the drive and courage to overcome obstacles.	Can provoke others. Hurts people's feelings.
Monitor/ evaluator ME	Sober, strategic, discerning. Sees all options. Judges accurately.	Lacks drive and ability to inspire others. Overly critical.
Team worker TW	Cooperative, mild, perceptive, diplomatic. Listens, builds, averts friction, calms the waters.	Indecisive in crunch situations. Can be easily influenced.
Implementer IMP	Disciplined, reliable, conservative, efficient. Turns ideas into practical actions.	Somewhat inflexible. Slow to respond to new possibilities.
Completer/ Finisher CF	Painstacking, conscientious, anxious. Searches out errors and omissions. Delivers on time.	Inclined to worry unduly. Reluctant to delegate. Can be a nitpicker.
Specialist SP	Single-minded, self-starting, dedicated. Provides knowledge and skills in rare supply.	Contributes on only a narrow front. Dwells on technicalities. Overlooks the "big picture."

Sources: R.M. Belbin, *Team Roles at Work* (Oxford, UK: Butterworth-Heinemann, 1993); www.belbin.com.

a calculation of whether to stay or leave the team. It exists when team members make the team part of their social identity (see Chapter 3). Cohesiveness is the glue or *esprit de corps* that holds the group together and ensures that its members fulfill their obligations.

Influences on Team Cohesiveness Several factors influence team cohesiveness: member similarity, team size, member interaction, difficult entry, team success, and external competition or challenges. For the most part these factors reflect the individual's social identity with the group and beliefs about how team membership will fulfill personal needs.[51] Several of these factors are related to our earlier discussion about why people join informal groups and how teams develop. Specifically, teams become more cohesive as they reach higher stages of development and are more attractive to potential members.

- *Member similarity.* Earlier in this chapter we learned that highly diverse teams potentially create faultlines that can lead to factious subgroups and higher turnover among team members. Other research has found that people with similar values have a higher attraction to each other. Collectively these findings suggest that homogeneous teams are more cohesive than heterogeneous teams. However, not all forms of diversity reduce cohesion. For example, teams consisting of people from different job groups seem to gel together just as well as teams of people from the same job.[52]
- *Team size.* Smaller teams tend to be more cohesive than larger teams because it is easier for a few people to agree on goals and coordinate work activities. The smallest teams aren't always the most cohesive, however. Small teams are less cohesive when they lack enough members to perform the required tasks. Thus team cohesiveness is potentially greatest when teams are as small as possible, yet large enough to accomplish the required tasks.
- *Member interaction.* Teams tend to be more cohesive when team members interact with each other fairly regularly. This occurs when team members perform highly interdependent tasks and work in the same physical area.
- *Somewhat difficult entry.* Teams tend to be more cohesive when entry to the team is restricted. The more elite the team, the more prestige it confers on its members, and the more they tend to value their membership in the unit. Existing team members are also more willing to welcome and support new members after they have "passed the test," possibly because they have shared the same entry experience. This raises the issue of how difficult the initiation for entry into the team should be. Research suggests that severe initiations can potentially lead to humiliation and psychological distance from the group, even for those who successfully endure the initiation.[53]
- *Team success.* Cohesion is both emotional and instrumental, with the latter referring to the notion that people feel more cohesion to teams that fulfill their needs and goals. Consequently cohesion increases with the team's level of success.[54] Furthermore, individuals are more likely to attach their social identities to successful teams than to those with a string of failures. Team leaders can increase cohesiveness by regularly communicating and celebrating the team's successes. Notice that this can create a positive self-fulfilling prophecy effect. Successful teams are more cohesive, and under certain conditions higher cohesiveness increases a team's success.
- *External competition and challenges.* Team cohesiveness tends to increase when members face external competition or a valued objective that is challenging. This might include a threat from an external competitor or friendly competition from other teams. These conditions tend to increase cohesiveness because employees value the team's ability to overcome the threat or competition if they can't solve the problem individually. They also value their membership as a

A Tight-Knit Lighthouse The staff members at Lighthouse Publishing are a highly cohesive group that successfully keeps its much larger competitors off-guard. "Lighthouse staff members [have] kept us independent in the face of stiff competition and corporate takeovers," says Lynn Hennigar, president of the small publishing company in Bridgewater, Nova Scotia, Canada. Its weekly newspaper, the *Bridgewater Bulletin,* is judged as best in class for Atlantic Canada and one of the top five across Canada. In all, the company received more than two dozen awards over the past year. Lighthouse's mostly female staff often demonstrate their cohesion when faced with new challenges. For instance, the team performed above any reasonable expectations when the press broke down, which threatened to delay getting the paper out on time. On another occasion, when putting together an interactive CD-ROM promoting Nova Scotia tourism, Lighthouse staff displayed skills that Hennigar admits she didn't even know about. "Lighthouse succeeds because of its multitalented, highly dedicated team of employees," says Hennigar. "It's a team that embraces change."[55]

form of social support. We need to be careful about the degree of external threat, however. Evidence suggests that teams seem to be less effective when external threats are severe. Although cohesiveness tends to increase, external threats are stressful and cause teams to make less effective decisions.[56]

Consequences of Team Cohesiveness Every team must have some minimal level of cohesiveness to maintain its existence. People who belong to high-cohesion teams are motivated to maintain their membership and to help the team perform effectively. Compared to low-cohesion teams, high-cohesion team members spend more time together, share information more frequently, and are more satisfied with each other. They also provide each other with better social support in stressful situations.[57]

Members of high-cohesion teams are generally more sensitive to each other's needs and develop better interpersonal relationships, thereby reducing dysfunctional conflict. When conflict does arise, members tend to resolve these differences swiftly and effectively. With better cooperation and more conformity to norms, high-cohesion teams usually perform better than low-cohesion teams. However, the relationship is a little more complex. Exhibit 9.6 illustrates how the effect of cohesiveness on team performance depends on the extent to which team norms are consistent with organizational goals. Cohesive teams will likely have lower task performance when norms conflict with organizational objectives because cohesiveness motivates employees to perform at a level more consistent with group norms.[58]

Exhibit 9.6
Effect of Team Cohesiveness on Task Performance

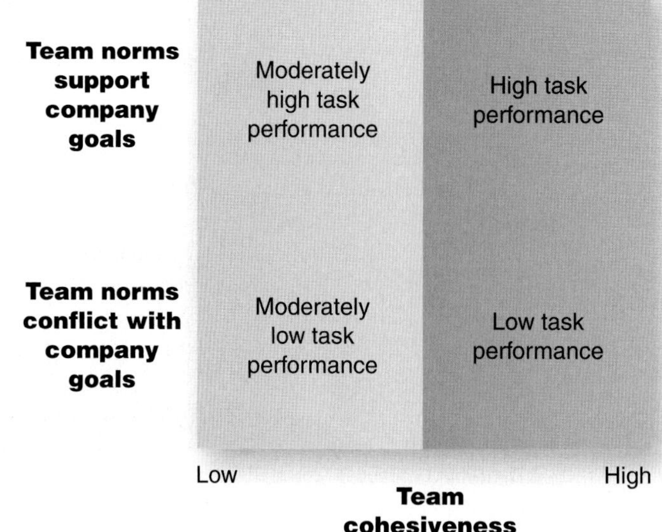

Learning Objectives

After reading this section you should be able to

9. Discuss the limitations of teams.

10. Explain how companies minimize social loafing.

The Trouble with Teams

As we explained near the beginning of this chapter, organizational leaders are placing a lot more emphasis on teams these days. Although this chapter has outlined the benefits of teams, the reality is that teams sometimes have more costs than benefits.[59] "The now fashionable team in which everybody works with everybody on everything from the beginning rapidly is becoming a disappointment," warned the late management guru Peter Drucker.[60]

For the reasons we outline next, some tasks are performed just as easily and effectively by one person as by a group. As was mentioned earlier, the best tasks for teams are complex (require multiple skill sets), highly interdependent, and have mutual goals. In contrast, tasks should be assigned to individuals when one person has the required skills and ability to perform the work. Similarly, tasks with low interdependence don't usually require a formal team because employees won't benefit from working closely (physically or psychologically) with other people.

Process Losses and Brooks's Law

process losses
Resources (including time and energy) expended toward team development and maintenance rather than the task.

The main problem with teams is that they have additional costs beyond those of individuals working alone. Experts refer to these hidden costs as **process losses**–resources (including time and energy) expended toward team development and maintenance rather than the task.[61] It is much more efficient for an individual to work out an issue alone than to resolve differences of opinion with other people. Teams need to sort out their differences, develop mutual understanding of issues and goals (known as forming a team mental model), and learn to coordinate with each other. The effort to accomplish these team development and maintenance activities is much higher than within one person. Researchers point out that the cost of process losses may be offset by the benefits of teams. Unfortunately few companies conduct a cost–benefit analysis of their team activities.[62]

The process loss problem is particularly apparent when adding new people to the team. The group has to recycle through the team development process to bring everyone up to speed. The software industry even has a name for this. "Brooks's law" (also called the "mythical man-month") says that adding more people to a late software project only makes it later. According to some sources, Apple Computer may have fallen into this trap in the recent development of its professional photography software program, called Aperture. When the project started to fall behind schedule, the manager in charge of the Aperture project increased the size of the team–some sources say it ballooned from 20 to almost 150 engineers and quality assurance staff within a few weeks. Unfortunately adding so many people further bogged down the project. The result? When Aperture was finally released, it was nine months late and considered one of Apple's buggier software offerings.[63]

Along with process loss costs, teams require the right environment to flourish. Many companies forget this point by putting people in teams without changing anything else. As we noted earlier, teams require appropriate rewards, communication systems, team leadership, and other conditions. Without these, the shift to a team structure could be a waste of time. At the same time critics suggest that changing these environmental conditions to improve teamwork could result in higher costs than benefits for the overall organization.[64]

Social Loafing

social loafing
A situation in which people exert less effort (and usually perform at a lower level) when working in groups than when working alone.

Perhaps the best-known limitation of teams is the risk of productivity loss due to **social loafing.** Social loafing occurs when people exert less effort (and usually perform at a lower level) when working in groups than when working alone.[65] A few scholars question whether social loafing is common, but students can certainly report many instances of this problem in their team projects!

Social loafing is most likely to occur in large teams where individual output is difficult to identify. This particularly includes situations in which team members work alone toward a common output pool (that is, they have low task interdependence). Under these conditions, employees aren't as worried that their performance will be noticed. Social loafing is less likely to occur when the task is interesting because individuals have a higher intrinsic motivation to perform their duties. It is less common when the group's objective is important, possibly because individuals experience more pressure from other team members to perform well. Finally, social loafing occurs less frequently among members with a strong collectivist value because they value group membership and believe in working toward group objectives.[66]

How to Minimize Social Loafing By understanding the causes of social loafing, we can identify ways to minimize this problem. Some of the strategies listed here reduce social loafing by making each member's performance more visible. Others increase each member's motivation to perform his or her tasks within the group:[67]

- *Form smaller teams.* Splitting a team into several smaller groups reduces social loafing because each person's performance becomes more noticeable and important for team performance. A smaller group also potentially increases cohesiveness, so would-be shirkers feel a greater obligation to perform fully for their team.

- *Specialize tasks.* Each person's contribution is easier to see when each team member performs a different work activity. For example, rather than pooling their effort for all incoming customer inquiries, each customer service representative might be assigned a particular type of client.
- *Measure individual performance.* Social loafing is minimized when each member's contribution is measured. Of course, individual performance is difficult to measure in some team activities, such as problem-solving projects in which the team's performance depends on one person discovering the best answer.
- *Increase job enrichment.* Social loafing is minimized when team members are assigned more motivating jobs, such as requiring more skill variety or having direct contact with clients. More generally, social loafing is less common among employees with high job satisfaction.
- *Select motivated employees.* Social loafing can be minimized by carefully selecting job applicants who are motivated by the task and have a collectivist value orientation. Those with a collectivist value are motivated to work harder for the team because they value their membership in the group.

This chapter has laid the foundation for our understanding of team dynamics. To build an effective team requires time, the right combination of team members, and the right environment. We will apply these ingredients of environment and team processes in the next chapter, which looks at high-performance teams, including self-directed teams and virtual teams.

Chapter Summary

Teams are groups of two or more people who interact and influence each other, are mutually accountable for achieving common objectives, and perceive themselves as a social entity within an organization. All teams are groups because they consist of people with a unifying relationship; not all groups are teams because some groups do not have purposive interaction.

Groups can be categorized in terms of their permanence (teams versus informal groups) and formality in the organization. Informal groups exist primarily for the benefit of their members rather than for the organization. Teams have become popular because they tend to make better decisions, support the knowledge management process, and provide superior customer service. In many situations employees are potentially more energized and engaged working in teams rather than alone.

Team effectiveness includes a group's ability to survive, achieve its system-based objectives, and fulfill the needs of its members. The model of team effectiveness considers the team and organizational environment, team design, and team processes. The team or organizational environment influences team effectiveness directly as well as through team design and team processes. Six elements in the organizational and team environment that influence team effectiveness are reward systems, communication systems, physical space, organizational environment, organizational structure, and organizational leadership.

Three team design elements are task characteristics, team size, and team composition. Teams tend to be more effective when they work on well-structured or complex tasks. The need for teamwork increases with task interdependence. Teams should be large enough to perform the work, yet small enough for efficient coordination and meaningful involvement. Effective teams are composed of people with the competencies and motivation to perform tasks in a team environment. Heterogeneous teams operate best on complex projects and problems requiring innovative solutions.

Teams develop through the stages of forming, storming, norming, performing, and eventually adjourning. Teams develop norms to regulate and guide member behavior. These norms may be influenced by initial experiences, critical events, and the values and experiences that team members bring to the group. Team members also have roles–a set of behaviors they are expected to perform because they hold certain positions in a team and organization.

Cohesiveness is the degree of attraction people feel toward a team and their motivation to remain members.

the afternoon shift packages even less product than the morning shift, so the backlog continues to build. The backlog adds to Treetop's inventory costs and increases the risk of damaged stock.

Treetop has added Saturday overtime shifts as well as extra hours before and after the regular shifts for the packaging department employees to process this backlog. Last month the packaging department employed 10 percent of the workforce but accounted for 85 percent of the overtime. This is frustrating to Treetop's management because time and motion studies recently confirmed that the packaging department is capable of processing all of the daily sawmill and planer production without overtime. Moreover, with employees earning one and a half or two times their regular pay on overtime, Treetop's cost competitiveness suffers.

Employees and supervisors at Treetop are aware that people in the packaging department tend to extend lunch by 10 minutes and coffee breaks by 5 minutes. They also typically leave work a few minutes before the end of shift. This abuse has worsened recently, particularly on the afternoon shift. Employees who are temporarily assigned to the packaging department also seem to participate in this time loss pattern after a few days. Although they are punctual and productive in other departments, these temporary employees soon adopt the packaging crew's informal schedule when assigned to that department.

Discussion Questions

1. Based on your knowledge of team dynamics, explain why the packaging department is less productive than other teams at Treetop.
2. How should Treetop change the nonproductive norms that exist in the packaging group?
3. What structural and other changes would you recommend that may improve this situation in the long term?

Case Study 9.2 MOSH PITS OF CREATIVITY

The Razr, Motorola's highly successful ultralight cell phone, was designed through a process that differed from the electronics company's traditional research and development center. Much of the critical work on the phone was done in an innovation lab where cross-functional teams of engineers, marketers, and others work together in funky open-space offices that foster information sharing. Mattel, Steelcase, Boeing, Wrigley, Procter & Gamble, and many other firms are also turning to cross-functional teams to creatively and efficiently design new products or solve perplexing problems. Some companies have also designed their workplace to improve informal group dynamics that support the creative process.

This *BusinessWeek* case study examines this trend toward collaborative cross-functional teamwork in product development. It describes the characteristics of these "mosh pits," including their separation from the normal corporate bureaucracy and how employees are rotated through these special centers for inspiration. Read the full text of this *BusinessWeek* article at www.mhhe.com/mcshane4e and prepare for the discussion questions below.

Discussion Questions

1. What elements of the team dynamics model are Motorola, Procter & Gamble, and other companies applying to make these product development teams successful?
2. Identify the potential team dynamics challenges these product development teams might face in the situations described in this case study.
3. How are these companies supporting informal groups, and how might these groups aid the creative process?

Source: J. Weber, "'Mosh Pits' of Creativity," *BusinessWeek*, 7 November 2005, 98.

Team Exercise 9.3 TEAM TOWER POWER

PURPOSE This exercise is designed to help you understand team roles, team development, and other issues in the development and maintenance of effective teams.

MATERIALS The instructor will provide enough Lego® pieces or similar materials for each team to complete the assigned task. All teams should have identical (or very similar) amounts and types of pieces. The instructor will need a measuring tape and stopwatch. Students may use writing materials during the design stage (Step 2). The instructor will distribute a Team Objectives Sheet and Tower Specifications Effectiveness Sheet to each team.

INSTRUCTIONS

1. The instructor will divide the class into teams. Depending on class size and space available, teams may have four to seven members, but all should be approximately equal size.
2. Each team is given 20 minutes to design a tower that uses only the materials provided, is freestanding, and provides an optimal return on investment. Team members may wish to draw their tower on paper or a flip chart to assist in the tower's design. Teams are free to practice building their towers during this stage. Preferably teams should be assigned to their own rooms so the designs can be created privately. During this stage each team will complete the Team Objectives Sheet distributed by the instructor. This sheet requires the Tower Specifications Effectiveness Sheet, also distributed by the instructor.
3. Each team will show the instructor that it has completed its Team Objectives Sheet. Then, with all teams in the same room, the instructor will announce the start of the construction phase. The time elapsed for construction will be closely monitored, and the instructor will occasionally call out time elapsed (particularly if there is no clock in the room).
4. Each team will notify the instructor as soon as it has completed its tower. The team will write down the time elapsed that the instructor has determined. It may be asked to help the instructor by counting the number of blocks used and height of the tower. This information is also written on the Team Objectives Sheet. Then the team calculates its profit.
5. After presenting the results, the class will discuss the team dynamics elements that contribute to team effectiveness. Team members will discuss their strategy, division of labor (team roles), expertise within the team, and other elements of team dynamics.

Source: Several published and online sources describe variations of this exercise, but there is no known origin of this activity.

Self-Assessment 9.4

TEAM ROLES PREFERENCES SCALE

PURPOSE This self-assessment is designed to help you identify your preferred roles in meetings and similar team activities.

INSTRUCTIONS Read each of the following statements and circle the response that you believe best reflects your position regarding each statement. Then use the scoring key in Appendix B to calculate your results for each team role. This exercise is completed alone so you can assess yourself honestly without concerns of social comparison. However, class discussion will focus on the roles that people assume in team settings. This scale assesses only a few team roles.

Team Roles Preferences Scale

Circle the number that best reflects your position regarding each of these statements	Does not describe me at all ▼	Does not describe me very well ▼	Describes me somewhat ▼	Describes me well ▼	Describes me very well ▼
1. I usually take responsibility for getting the team to agree on what the meeting should accomplish.	1	2	3	4	5
2. I tend to summarize to other team members what the team has accomplished so far.	1	2	3	4	5
3. I'm usually the person who helps other team members overcome their disagreements.	1	2	3	4	5
4. I try to ensure that everyone gets heard on issues.	1	2	3	4	5
5. I'm usually the person who helps the team determine how to organize the discussion.	1	2	3	4	5
6. I praise other team members for their ideas more than do others in the meetings.	1	2	3	4	5
7. People tend to rely on me to keep track of what has been said in meetings.	1	2	3	4	5
8. The team typically counts on me to prevent debates from getting out of hand.	1	2	3	4	5
9. I tend to say things that make the group feel optimistic about its accomplishments.	1	2	3	4	5
10. Team members usually count on me to give everyone a chance to speak.	1	2	3	4	5
11. In most meetings, I am less likely than others to criticize the ideas of teammates.	1	2	3	4	5
12. I actively help teammates to resolve their differences in meetings.	1	2	3	4	5
13. I actively encourage quiet team members to describe their ideas about each issue.	1	2	3	4	5
14. People tend to rely on me to clarify the purpose of the meeting.	1	2	2	4	5
15. I like to be the person who takes notes or minutes of the meeting.	1	2	3	4	5

Source: ©Copyright 2000 Steven L. McShane.

After reading this chapter, if you need additional information, see **www.mhhe.com/mcshane4e** for more in-depth interactivities that correspond with this material.

PricewaterhouseCoopers LLC (PwC) employs more than 200 training professionals in 70 offices across the United States. These professionals, along with many more consultants and academics who provide employee development services, routinely form virtual teams for new projects. "Virtual teaming is the norm for us," says Peter Nicolas, one of PwC's Learning Solutions manager in Florham Park, New Jersey.

PwC's training group supports these virtual teams by offering a variety of information technologies, including electronic calendars, shared databases, computer-based video meetings, virtual classrooms, and e-mail. But even the techno-savvy professionals in PwC's training group know that technology doesn't quite replace the unique ability of face-to-face interaction to bond people together. "I always try to do the kickoff meeting face-to-face," says Scott Patterson, one of PwC's Learning Solutions managers in Atlanta. "We also try to bring the group back together for major milestones in a project."

Peter Nicolas, a Learning Solutions manager for PricewaterhouseCoopers LLP, prepares for a virtual teaming meeting.

While PwC's learning and education department grapples with virtual teams across the United States, the accounting firm's transaction services group is finding ways to improve virtual teams whose members are scattered around the planet. Every 18 months the group brings together hundreds of employees for a dedicated team-building event. One such gathering was recently held at Disney's EPCOT World Showcase in Orlando. The 850 attendees (300 from outside the United States) were organized into 35 diverse teams and given a packet of background information about a fictitious client that required PwC's help. The teams spent one day visiting EPCOT's various pavilions to gather details before submitting their report on the client's acquisition opportunities as well as cultural issues that needed to be addressed.

PwC executives evaluated the 35 team reports, then invited the top 10 teams to join them for a private breakfast the next morning. After breakfast all PwC attendees watched the captains of the top 10 teams on stage explain their teams' analysis. The PwC executives then selected the top three team leaders, who were further interviewed on stage about the previous day's investigation. After watching a video of the previous day's events at EPCOT, PwC's Global Advisory Leader announced the winning team that had been hired by the fictitious client.

"We were overwhelmed with the results of this program," remarked Barbara Jean Cummins, the PwC manager who coordinated the team-building event with Disney Institute. "I've never seen borders come down so quickly, and everyone was completely engaged in the program."[1]

Developing High-Performance Teams

LEARNING OBJECTIVES

After reading this chapter you should be able to

1. Identify the characteristics of self-directed work teams (SDWTs).
2. Describe the four conditions in sociotechnical systems theory that support SDWTs.
3. Summarize three challenges to SDWTs.
4. Explain why organizations rely increasingly on virtual teams.
5. Describe the roles of communication systems, task structure, team size, and team composition in virtual team effectiveness.
6. Summarize the three foundations of trust in teams.
7. Identify five constraints on team decision making.
8. Describe five team structures that potentially improve creativity and decision making in team settings.
9. Discuss the potential benefits and limitations of brainstorming.
10. Outline the four types of team building.

PricewaterhouseCoopers is forging new directions in building high-performance virtual teams. This chapter extends our discussion of teams by focusing on high-performance teams, including self-directed work teams, virtual teams, effective decision making in teams, and team-building strategies. The first section introduces the features of self-directed work teams as well as the elements of sociotechnical systems theory, upon which these high-performance teams are based. Next we look at the increasing popularity of virtual teams and summarize current research about how to ensure that these virtual teams are effective. We also look at the important topic of trust in virtual teams and other groups. This chapter then focuses on effective decision making in teams, including challenges and strategies to minimize problems with effective team decision making. The last section of this chapter looks at various team-building strategies.

Learning Objectives

After reading this section you should be able to

1. **Identify the characteristics of self-directed work teams (SDWTs).**
2. **Describe the four conditions in sociotechnical systems theory that support SDWTs.**
3. **Summarize three challenges to SDWTs.**

Self-Directed Work Teams

Whole Foods Market isn't your typical grocery retailer. Yes, the company's products are more organic, but so is its approach to managing the business. Whereas some food chains still make most decisions at the top, Whole Foods hands over day-to-day responsibility to the teams in each store. "Whole Foods Market is organized into self-managing work teams," explains CEO John Mackey. Each store has about eight teams, such as the seafood team, prepared foods team, and cashier/front end team. Each team has authority to make decisions for its own part of the business, and the overall store works around its own profit-and-loss statement. "The [store] team is responsible for managing inventory, labor productivity, gross margins; and its members are responsible for many of the product placement decisions," explains Mackey.[2]

self-directed work teams (SDWTs)
Cross-functional work groups organized around work processes that complete an entire piece of work requiring several interdependent tasks, and that have substantial autonomy over the execution of those tasks.

Whole Foods Market and many other organizations have adopted a form of work structure that relies on **self-directed work teams (SDWTs).** Surveys estimate that approximately three-quarters of medium-sized and large organizations in the United States use SDWT structures for part of their operations.[3] SDWTs vary somewhat from one firm to the next, but they are generally defined by two distinctive features. First, they complete an entire piece of work requiring several interdependent tasks.[4] This high interdependence is important because the work clusters the team members together and minimizes their interdependence with employees outside the team. The result is a closely knit group that depends on each other to accomplish their individual tasks. For example, employees in the prepared foods team at a Whole Foods store would naturally work more closely with each other than with members of other teams.

Second, SDWTs have substantial autonomy over the execution of their tasks. In particular, these teams plan, organize, and control work activities with little or no direct involvement of a higher-status supervisor. They tend to control most work input, flow, and output, such as work directly with suppliers and customers. The team's autonomy extends to responsibility for correcting workflow problems as they occur.

With substantial autonomy and responsibility, SDWTs also receive plenty of team-level feedback and rewards. Whole Foods teams make decisions about incoming resources, including working with local suppliers. They also can rearrange the workplace as well as vote on permanently hiring new recruits.

You may have noticed from this description that members of SDWTs have enriched and enlarged jobs. The team's work includes all the tasks required to make an entire product or provide a service. The team is also mostly responsible for scheduling, coordinating, and planning these tasks.[5] Self-directed work teams were initially designed around production processes. However, they are also found in administrative and service activities (such as at Whole Foods), banking services, city government administration, and customer assistance teams in courier services.[6]

Sociotechnical Systems Theory and SDWTs

sociotechnical systems (STS) theory
A theory stating that effective work sites have joint optimization of their social and technological systems, and that teams should have sufficient autonomy to control key variances in the work process.

How do companies create successful self-directed work teams? To answer this question, we need to look at **sociotechnical systems (STS) theory,** which is the main source of current SDWT practices. STS theory was introduced during the 1940s at Britain's Tavistock Institute, where researchers had been studying the effects of technology on coal mining in the United Kingdom.[7]

The Tavistock researchers observed that the new coal mining technology (called the "long wall" method) led to lower, not higher, job performance. They analyzed the causes of this problem and established the idea that organizations need "joint optimization" between the social and technical systems of the work unit. In other words, they need to introduce technology in a way that creates the best structure for semi-autonomous work teams. Furthermore, the Tavistock group concluded that teams should be sufficiently autonomous so that they can control the main "variances" in the system. This means that the team must control the factors with the greatest impact on quality, quantity, and the cost of the product or service. From this overview of STS, we can identify four main conditions for high-performance SDWTs.[8]

Responsible for an Entire Work Process STS theory suggests that self-directed teams work best when they are responsible for making an entire product, providing a service, or otherwise completing an entire work process. By making an entire product or service, the team is sufficiently independent that it can make adjustments without interfering, or having interference from, other work units. At the same time the primary work unit ensures that employees perform interdependent subtasks within their team so they have a sense of cohesiveness by working toward a common goal.[9]

Sufficient Autonomy STS theory says that an SDWT must have sufficient autonomy to manage the work process. The team should be able to organize and coordinate work among its members to respond more quickly and effectively to its environment. This autonomy also motivates team members through feelings of empowerment.

Control Key Variances STS theory says that high-performance SDWTs have control over "key variances." These variances represent the disturbances or interruptions in the work process that affect the quality or performance of the product or service. For instance, the mixture of ingredients would be a key variance for employees in food processing because the mixture is within the team's control and influences the quality of the final product. In contrast, self-directed teams have fewer advantages when the primary causes of good or poor performance are mainly due to technology, supplies, or other factors beyond the team's control.

joint optimization
A key requirement in sociotechnical systems theory that a balance must be struck between social and technical systems to maximize an operation's effectiveness.

Operate under Joint Optimization Perhaps the most crucial feature of STS theory is **joint optimization**–the notion that the work process needs to balance the social and technical subsystems.[10] In particular, the technological system should be implemented in a way that encourages or facilitates team dynamics, job enrichment, and meaningful feedback. This idea of joint optimization was quite radical in the 1940s when many thought that technology dictated how employees should be organized. In many cases technology resulted in people working alone with little opportunity to directly coordinate their work or share knowledge and ideas. Sociotechnical systems theory, on the other hand, says that companies can and must introduce technology so that it supports a semi-autonomous, team-based structure.

Applying STS Theory and Self-Directed Work Teams

Numerous studies have found that with a few important caveats to consider, self-directed work teams make a difference. A decade ago Canon Inc. introduced self-directed teams at all 29 of its Japanese plants. The camera and copier company claims that a team of a half-dozen people can now produce as much as 30 people in the old assembly line system. One study found that car dealership service garages that organized employees into self-directed teams were significantly more profitable than service garages where employees worked without a team structure. Another reported that both short- and long-term measures of customer satisfaction increased after street cleaning employees in a German city were organized into SDWTs.[11] DaimlerChrysler improved productivity and quality at its Mexican operations by switching to SDWTs. As Connections 10.1 describes, the Chrysler group is now transforming its American plants to "smart manufacturing" with SDWTs.

STS theory provides some guidance for designing self-directed work teams, but it doesn't provide enough detail regarding the optimal alignment of the social and technical systems. Volvo's Uddevalla manufacturing plant in Sweden is an example.[12] Opened in 1988 as a model of sociotechnical design, the Uddevalla plant replaced the traditional assembly line with fixed workstations at which teams of approximately 20 employees assembled and installed components in an unfinished automobile chassis. The work structure created a strong team orientation, but productivity was among the lowest in the automobile industry. (Producing a car at Uddevalla took 50 hours versus 25 hours at a traditional Volvo plant and 13 hours at a Toyota plant.)

The Uddevalla plant was shut down in 1993 and reopened two years later. The plant still uses highly skilled teams, but they are organized around a more traditional assembly line process (similar to Toyota's production system). Some writers argue that organizational politics and poor market demand closed the Uddevalla experiment prematurely. However, Federal Signal recently had a similar experience in its truck assembly plant in the United States. It seems that both Volvo and Federal Signal failed to identify the best alignment of the social and technical subsystems.

Challenges to Self-Directed Work Teams

Along with determining the best combination of social and technical subsystems, corporate leaders need to recognize and overcome at least three potential barriers to self-directed work teams: cross-cultural issues, management resistance, and employee and labor union resistance.

Cross-Cultural Issues SDWTs are more difficult to implement in high power distance cultures.[13] Employees in these cultures are more comfortable when supervisors give them directions, whereas low power distance employees value their involvement in decisions. One study reported that SDWTs may be more difficult to introduce in

Connections 10.1

Chrysler's Lean Self-Directed Work Teams

Chrysler CEO Tom La Sorda is pushing the automaker into an era of "smart manufacturing" that relies more on self-directed work teams (SDWTs). This photo shows La Sorda meeting employees at the company's plant in Saltillo, Mexico, which has already introduced SDWTs.

The "Big Three" automakers—General Motors, Ford, and Chrysler—are under intense pressure to improve productivity and quality. Chrysler CEO Tom La Sorda believes one of the key ingredients to the company's future is "smart manufacturing," which includes introducing lean manufacturing in plants operated by self-directed work teams (SDWTs).

SDWTs were introduced a decade ago at Chrysler's operations in Mexico, where management and employees were determined to make the team-based process successful. The plant in Saltillo, Mexico, for instance, organizes employees into teams of a dozen people responsible for a specific set of integrated tasks, including maintenance, quality control, safety, and productivity in that work area. Team members operate a workstation within their team for a few hours before rotating to another workstation. This mandatory rotation process increases skill flexibility, minimizes repetitive strain, and creates a sense of team ownership over the tasks within their mandate. Saltillo's productivity has increased by almost 30 percent since the team-based structure was introduced.

Now Chrysler is introducing SDWTs in its U.S. plants, including the assembly plants in Toledo, Ohio, and Belvidere, Illinois, where union members voted in favor of more flexible work arrangements. "The people within Belvidere say we should have done this a long time ago," says United Auto Workers union vice president Nate Gooden. "The boredom and everything they have (had) on the job—it's a different culture. You don't have to come to work every day and do the same job over and over again."

To assist the culture change, team leaders completed 40 hours of training to understand their new role as service leaders—serving the teams rather than vice versa. The physical workspace was also rearranged to create a more intimate team environment. Even the lockers were relocated near the teams' work area to maximize efficiency and create a sense of common team space. "Since the plant went to teams, [the assembly area] feels smaller," says Le Etta Bush, a team member at the Belvidere assembly plant.

The transformation to SDWTs has already had a noticeable effect. Scott Dahle, a supervisor on a traditional assembly line, discovered the change when he was asked to cover one day for Margo Barr, a team leader of one of Belvidere's new SDWTs. "The day he filled in for Margo, his pager never went off, his phone never rang, and no one called him on his radio. He even checked the batteries to see if they were dead," recalls Belvidere plant manager Kurt Kavajecz. "This traditional first-line supervisor, who is used to putting out fires and reacting to crises, came into the new area and was amazed because the team members and the team leaders were running the area. They were taking care of business."

Sources: M. Connelly, "Chrysler Wants to Put Team Assembly in All Plants," *Automotive News*, 30 May 2005, p. 53; J.B. White, "LaSorda's Chrysler Challenge," *The Wall Street Journal*, 15 August 2005, p. B5; J. Leute, "Union, Management Work in Lockstep at Belvidere, Ill., Plant," *Janesville Gazette* (Illinois), 18 July 2005; J. Smith, "Building Cars, Building Teams," *Plant Engineering*, 1 December 2005; M. Connelly, "Chrysler Boosts Belvidere Flexibility," *Automotive News*, 13 February 2006, p. 44.

Mexico because employees in that country (which has a high power distance culture) expect managers to make decisions affecting their work. However, as Connections 10.1 described, Chrysler was able to introduce these teams at its Mexican operations almost a decade before they were introduced in the United States. One explanation may be that Chrysler's Mexican employees and managers were more motivated to improve productivity due to competitive threats from other low-wage countries. Also, Mexico has relatively high collectivism, so employees may feel more comfortable working in teams compared to their American counterparts. Overall, cultural values might be an impediment to SDWTs, but they are unlikely to completely prevent them in most countries.

Management Resistance Poet Robert Frost once wrote, "The brain is a wonderful organ; it starts working the moment you get up in the morning and does not stop until you get into the office." Frost's humor highlights the fact that many organizations expect employees to park their brains at the door. Consistent with this view, studies report that supervisors and higher-level managers are often the main source of resistance to the transition to self-directed work teams. Their main worry is losing power when employees gain power through empowered teams. Some are concerned that their jobs will lose value, whereas others believe that they will not have any jobs at all.[14]

Self-directed teams operate best when supervisors shift from "hands-on" controllers to "hands-off" facilitators, but many supervisors have difficulty changing their style. This was one of the biggest stumbling blocks to self directed work teams at a TRW auto parts plant. Many supervisors kept slipping back into their command-and-control supervisory style. As one TRW employee explains, "One of the toughest things for some of them was to shift from being a boss to a coach, moving from saying, 'I know what's good for you' to 'How can I help you?'" Research suggests that supervisors are less likely to resist self-directed work teams when they have personally worked in a high-involvement workplace and receive considerable training in their new facilitation role.[15]

Employee and Labor Union Resistance Employees sometimes oppose SDWTs because they require new skills or appear to require more work. Many feel uncomfortable as they explore their new roles, and they may be worried that they lack the

Learning to Lead Self-Directed Teams When Standard Motor Products (SMP) introduced self-directed work teams at its Edwardsville, Kansas, plant, supervisors had a tough challenge replacing their command-and-control management style with something closer to a mentor or facilitator. "It wasn't easy for managers who were raised in the top-down authority model," recalls Darrel Ray, the nationally recognized consultant who worked with the auto parts company during the transition. "It is far easier to be a tyrant than it is to be a psychologist or a teacher," explains distribution manager Don Wakefield. Steve Domann was one of the managers who had difficulty adjusting. "I thought about quitting when the changes were announced," says Domann, who now oversees plant work teams as a team developer. "Some of the old management team couldn't conform to the team, but I'm glad I did."[16]

skills to adapt to the new work requirements. For instance, professional surveyors at a Swedish company reported increased stress when their company introduced customer-focused self-directed teams.[17] Chrysler employees in Belvidere, Illinois, initially rejected the switch to self-directed work teams, possibly fearing increased workload due to job rotation and multiskilling requirements under the proposed flexible agreement.

Labor unions supported the early experiments in sociotechnical change in Europe and India, but some unions in other parts of the world have reservations about SDWTs.[18] One concern is that teams improve productivity at the price of higher stress levels among employees, which is sometimes true. Another worry is that SDWTs require more flexibility by reversing work rules and removing job categories that unions have negotiated over the years. Labor union leaders are therefore concerned that regaining these hard-fought union member rights will be a difficult battle.

In spite of these challenges, self-directed work teams offer enormous potential for organizations when they are implemented under the right conditions, as specified by sociotechnical systems theory. Meanwhile information technologies and knowledge work have enabled virtual teams to gain popularity. The next section examines this new breed of team, including strategies to create high-performance virtual teams.

Learning Objectives

After reading the next two sections you should be able to

4. **Explain why organizations rely increasingly on virtual teams.**
5. **Describe the roles of communication systems, task structure, team size, and team composition in virtual team effectiveness.**
6. **Summarize the three foundations of trust in teams.**

Virtual Teams

virtual teams
Teams whose members operate across space, time and organizational boundaries and who are linked through information technologies to achieve organizational goals.

As was described in the opening vignette to this chapter, PricewaterhouseCoopers relies on plenty of **virtual teams.** Virtual teams are teams whose members operate across space, time, and organizational boundaries and are linked through information technologies to achieve organizational tasks.[19] Virtual teams are similar to face-to-face teams in the sense that they consist of two or more people who interact and influence each other, are mutually accountable for achieving common goals associated with organizational objectives, and perceive themselves as a social entity within an organization. However, virtual teams differ from traditional teams in two ways: (1) they are not usually colocated (they do not work in the same physical area), and (2) due to their lack of colocation, members of virtual teams depend primarily on information technologies rather than face-to-face interaction to communicate and coordinate their work effort.

Virtual teams are one of the most significant developments in organizations over the past decade. One reason for their popularity is that the Internet, intranets, instant messaging, virtual whiteboards, and other products have made it easier to communicate with and coordinate people at a distance.[20] The shift from production-based to knowledge-based work has also made virtual teamwork feasible. Information technologies allow people to exchange knowledge work, such as software code, product development plans, and ideas for strategic decisions. In contrast, relying on virtual teams for production work, in which people develop physical objects, is less feasible.

Information technologies and knowledge-based work make virtual teams possible, but two other factors–globalization and knowledge management–make them increasingly necessary. As Chapter 1 described, companies are opening businesses overseas, forming tight alliances with companies located elsewhere, and serving customers who want global support. These global conditions require a correspondingly global response in the form of virtual teams that coordinate these operations. As one IBM manager stated, "IBM is a global company working in 170 countries in the world. Just that alone would dictate that we do work with people we've never met face-to-face and may never meet."[21]

Along with aiding global coordination, virtual teams support knowledge management by allowing and encouraging employees to share and use knowledge in distributed operations. This is one of the main drivers behind the popularity of virtual teams at PricewaterhouseCoopers. The global operations of PwC's transaction services group connects employees together because they need to share valuable information that resides throughout the organization.

Designing High-Performance Virtual Teams

As with all teams, high-performance virtual teams are influenced by the elements of the team effectiveness model in Chapter 9. Exhibit 10.1 outlines the key design issues for virtual teams that we discuss over the next couple of pages.

Virtual Team Environment Reward systems, communication systems, organizational environment, organizational structure, and leadership influence the effectiveness of all teams, including virtual teams. Communication systems are particularly important because, unlike conventional teams, virtual teams cannot rely on face-to-face meetings whenever they wish. As we will learn in the next chapter, face-to-face communication transfers the highest volume and complexity of information and offers the timeliest feedback. In contrast, e-mail, telephone, and other information technologies fall far behind in their ability to exchange information. "Having a four- to five-hour discussion is hard to do by phone, especially where you need to read body language," says an executive at accounting giant PricewaterhouseCoopers. Even videoconferencing, which seems similar to face-to-face meetings, actually communicates much less than we realize.[22]

Exhibit 10.1 Designing High-Performance Virtual Teams

Team design element	Special virtual team requirements
Team environment	• Virtual teams need several communication channels available to offset lack of face-to-face communication.
Team tasks	• Virtual teams operate better with structured rather than complex and ambiguous tasks.
Team size and composition	• Virtual teams usually require smaller team size than conventional teams. • Virtual team members must have skills in communicating through information technology and be able to process multiple threads of conversation. • Virtual team members are more likely than conventional team members to require cross-cultural awareness and knowledge.
Team processes	• Virtual team development and cohesiveness require some face-to-face interaction, particularly when the team forms.

Invensys Employees Are Virtually There Invensys PLC, the British-based process and control engineering company, relies on information technologies to make the best use of its far-reaching talent, often organizing employees into virtual teams at a moment's notice. "Our development projects operate in a virtual mode and [gather] people from multiple sites based on project needs," explains Joe Ayers, a manager at Invensys's process simulation unit in Lake Forest, California. "It is common for projects to utilize developers from three different time zones in a 'follow the sun' development mode." To assist the virtual teams that routinely develop out of this global business structure, Invensys provides a variety of communication tools, such as desktop sharing tools, voice over IP telephony, instant messaging, and video conferencing.[23]

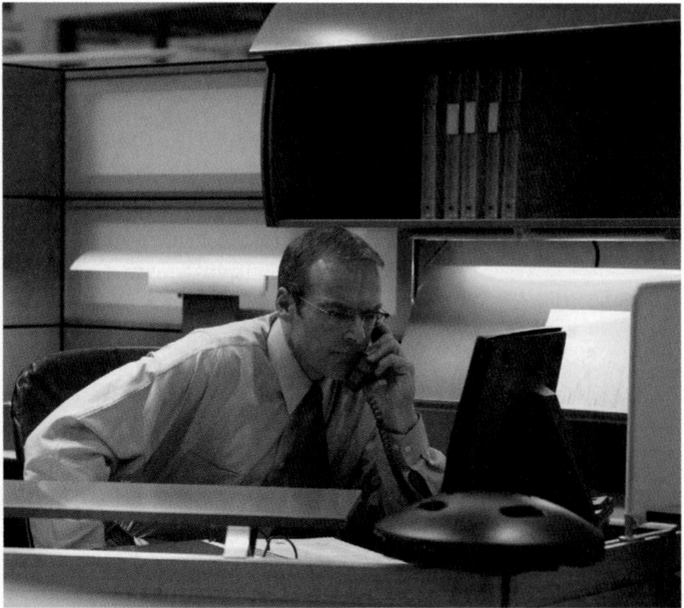

To support high-performance virtual teams, organizations need to provide a variety of communication media so that virtual team members have the freedom to creatively combine these media to match the task demands.[24] For instance, virtual team members might rely on e-mail to coordinate routine tasks but quickly switch to videoconferences and electronic whiteboards when emergencies arise. The lack of face-to-face communication isn't all bad news for virtual teams. Working through e-mail or intranet systems can minimize status differences. Team members whose first language is not English may be overwhelmed into silence in face-to-face meetings but have time to craft persuasive messages in cyberspace.

Virtual Team Tasks Experts suggest that virtual teams operate best with structured tasks requiring only moderate levels of task interdependence.[25] Consider the task structure of client service engineers at BakBone Software. Each day BakBone engineers in San Diego pick up customer support problems passed on from colleagues in Maryland and England. At the end of the workday they pass some of these projects on to BakBone co-workers in Tokyo. The assignments sent on to Tokyo must be stated clearly because overseas co-workers can't ask questions in the middle of San Diego's night.

BakBone's virtual team works well with these structured tasks, whereas the lack of colocation makes it difficult for them to consult and communicate about complex and ambiguous tasks. "You don't have the time for open-ended conversation [in a virtual team]," admits BakBone engineer Roger Rodriguez. "You can't informally brainstorm with someone."[26] Generally, complex and ambiguous tasks should be assigned to colocated teams. Similarly, virtual teams should work on tasks requiring moderate levels of interdependence among team members. High levels of interdependence require more intense communication, so they are better assigned to colocated teams.

Virtual Team Size and Composition The problems of team size described in the previous chapter are amplified in virtual teams due to the limits of information technologies. In other words, virtual teams need to be smaller than comparable co-located teams to develop as quickly and coordinate as effectively. The team composition issues covered in Chapter 9 also apply to virtual teams, with the added requirement that virtual team members need additional communication skills. They need to be sensitive to emotional reactions to e-mails and listen to more subtle non-verbal signals in teleconferences. "On a call, I use subtle listening," explains Procter & Gamble executive Karim Ladak, whose virtual team members live in six cities around the world. "I listen for a quiver or a pause. And even then I know that I can very quickly miss something."[27]

Virtual teams often span cultures, so team members must also be aware of cross-cultural issues. For example, one study reported that virtual teams of American and Belgian college students were easily confused by differing conventions in the use of commas versus decimal points in numbers (such as $2.953 million versus $2,953 million). They also experienced cultural differences in socializing. The American students were willing to engage in social communication after they completed the assignment, whereas the Belgian students were more interested in developing a relationship with their partners before beginning work on the project.[28]

Team Processes Team development and cohesiveness are particular concerns for virtual teams because they lack the face-to-face interaction that supports these processes. For example, one recent university study found that face-to-face teams communicate better than virtual teams during the early stages of a project; only after gaining experience did virtual teams share information as openly as face-to face teams. Other studies have reported that employees who work at a distance (such as through telecommuting) from other team members tend to feel less connected with their teams.[29]

Some companies try to ensure that virtual team members have good skills for communicating across distances. Others attempt to create virtual social events. For example, Grant Marshall, Australian country manager for California-based Agilent Technologies, strengthens the bonding process with his virtual team by scheduling a virtual "coffee pot chat" meeting once each month. "All the virtual team [members] call in via a conference line," explains Marshall, whose team members live throughout Asia. "There is no specific preplanned business agenda–the objective is to discuss general activities of what we have been doing." The casual meeting lasts 15 minutes to half an hour and includes such topics as "personal accomplishments, sporting activities, films, holidays, etc.–the type of discussion that you might have around the coffee station."[30]

Another solution, ironically, is to have virtual team members meet face-to-face once in a while. This is what leaders at PricewaterhouseCoopers discovered long ago. As the opening vignette described, PwC virtual teams in the training and development unit meet every few months, whereas global teams in PwC's transaction services group rendezvous every 18 months.

Team Trust

trust
A psychological state comprising the intention to accept vulnerability based on positive expectations of the intent or behavior of another person.

Any relationship–including the relationship among virtual team members–depends on a certain degree of trust between the parties.[31] **Trust** is a psychological state comprising the intention to accept vulnerability based on positive expectations of the intent or behavior of another person. A high level of trust occurs when others affect you in situations where you are at risk, but you believe they will not harm you.

Exhibit 10.2
Three Foundations of Trust in Teams

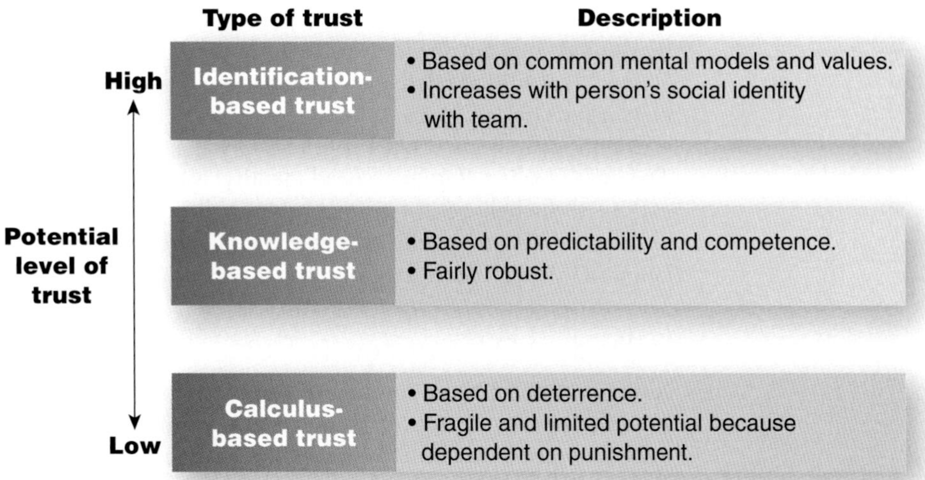

Trust has been discussed as both beliefs and conscious feelings about the relationship and other party. In other words, a person both logically evaluates the situation as trustworthy and feels that it is trustworthy.[32] Trust can also be understood in terms of the foundation of that trust. From this perspective, people trust others based on three foundations: calculus, knowledge, and identification (see Exhibit 10.2):

- *Calculus-based trust.* This minimal level of trust refers to an expected consistency of behavior based on deterrence. Each party believes that the other will deliver on its promises because punishments will be administered if they fail.[33] For example, most employees have at least calculus-based trust because co-workers could get fired if they attempt to undermine another employee's work effort.
- *Knowledge-based trust.* Knowledge-based trust is grounded on the other party's predictability. The more we understand others and can predict what they will do in the future, the more we trust them, up to a moderate level. For instance, employees are more willing to trust leaders who "walk the talk" because their actions are aligned with their words. Even if we don't agree with the leaders, this consistency generates some level of trust. Knowledge-based trust also relates to confidence in the other person's ability or competence. People trust others based on their known or perceived expertise, such as when they trust a physician.[34]
- *Identification-based trust.* This third foundation of trust is a mutual understanding and emotional bond between the parties. This identification occurs when one party thinks like, feels like, and responds like the other party. High-performance teams exhibit this level of trust because they share the same values and mental models. Identification-based trust is connected to the concept of social identity; the more you define yourself in terms of membership in the team, the more trust you have in that team.[35]

These three foundations of trust are arranged in a hierarchy. Calculus-based trust offers the lowest potential trust and is easily broken by a violation of expectations. Generally calculus-based trust alone cannot sustain a team's relationship because it relies on deterrence. Relationships don't become strong when based only on the threat of punishment if one party fails to deliver its promises. Knowledge-based trust offers a higher potential level of trust and is more stable because it develops over time. Suppose that another member of your virtual team submitted documentation to you on schedule in the past, but it arrived late this time. Knowledge-based trust might be dented, but not broken, in this incident. Through knowledge-based trust, you "know" that the late delivery is probably an exception because it deviates from the co-worker's past actions.

Identification-based trust is potentially the strongest and most robust of all three. The individual's self-image (social identity) is based partly on membership in the team, and he or she believes the team's values highly overlap; so any transgressions by other team members are quickly forgiven. People are more reluctant to acknowledge a violation of this high-level trust because it strikes at the heart of their self-image.

Individual Differences in Trust

Along with these three foundations of trust, the level of trust depends on a person's general *propensity to trust*.[36] Some people are inherently more willing than others to trust in a given situation. When joining a new work team, you might initially have very high trust in your new teammates, whereas another new team member might only feel a moderate level of trust. This difference is due to each individual's personality, values, and socialization experiences. Our willingness to trust others also varies with the emotions experienced at the moment. In particular, we trust people more when experiencing pleasant emotions than when angry, even if those emotions aren't connected with the other person.

Dynamics of Trust in Teams

A common misconception is that team members build trust from a low level when they first join the team. In truth, people typically join a virtual or conventional team with a moderate or high level–not a low level–of trust in their new co-workers. The main explanation for the initially high trust (called *swift trust*) in organizational settings is that people usually believe their teammates are reasonably competent (knowledge-based trust), and they tend to develop some degree of social identity with the team (identification-based trust). Even when working with strangers, most of us display some level of trust, if only because this supports our self-impression of being a nice person.[37]

However, trust is fragile in new relationships because it is based on assumptions rather than experience. Consequently, recent studies of virtual teams report that trust tends to decrease rather than increase over time. In other words, new team members experience trust violations, which pushes their trust to a lower level. Employees who join the team with identification-based trust tend to drop back to knowledge-based or perhaps calculus-based trust. Declining trust is particularly challenging in virtual teams because research identifies communication among team members as an important condition for sustaining trust. Equally important, employees become less forgiving and less cooperative toward others as their level of trust decreases, which undermines team and organizational effectiveness.[38]

Learning Objectives

After reading the next two sections you should be able to

7. Identify five constraints on team decision making.

8. Describe five team structures that potentially improve creativity and decision making in team settings.

9. Discuss the potential benefits and limitations of brainstorming.

10. Outline the four types of team building.

Team Decision Making

Self-directed work teams, virtual teams, and practically all other groups are involved to some degree in making decisions. Under certain conditions teams are more effective than individuals at identifying problems, choosing alternatives, and evaluating their decisions. To leverage these benefits, however, we first need to understand the constraints on effective team decision making. Then we look at specific team structures that try to overcome these constraints.

Constraints on Team Decision Making

Anyone who has spent enough time in a workplace can list several ways in which teams stumble in decision making. The five most common problems are time constraints, evaluation apprehension, pressure to conform, groupthink, and group polarization.

Time Constraints There's a saying that "committees keep minutes and waste hours." This reflects the fact that teams take longer than individuals to make decisions.[39] Unlike individuals, teams require extra time to organize, coordinate, and socialize. The larger the group, the more time required to make a decision. Team members need time to learn about each other and build rapport. They need to manage an imperfect communication process so that there is sufficient understanding of each other's ideas. They also need to coordinate roles and rules of order within the decision process.

Another time-related constraint found in most team structures is that only one person can speak at a time.[40] This problem, known as **production blocking,** undermines idea generation in several ways. First, team members need to listen to the conversation to find an opportune time to speak up, and this monitoring makes it difficult for them to concentrate on their own ideas. Second, ideas are fleeting, so the longer they wait to speak up, the more likely these flickering ideas will die out. Third, team members might remember their fleeting thoughts by concentrating on them, but this causes them to pay less attention to the conversation. By ignoring what others are saying, team members miss other potentially good ideas as well as the opportunity to convey their ideas to others in the group.

production blocking
A time constraint in team decision making due to the procedural requirement that only one person may speak at a time.

Evaluation Apprehension Individuals are reluctant to mention ideas that seem silly because they believe (often correctly) that other team members are silently evaluating them.[41] This **evaluation apprehension** is based on the individual's desire to create a favorable self-presentation and need to protect self-esteem. It is most common in meetings attended by people with different levels of status or expertise, or when members formally evaluate each other's performance throughout the year (as in 360-degree feedback). Creative ideas often sound bizarre or illogical when presented, so evaluation apprehension tends to discourage employees from mentioning them in front of co-workers.

evaluation apprehension
When individuals are reluctant to mention ideas that seem silly because they believe (often correctly) that other team members are silently evaluating them.

Pressure to Conform Recall from the previous chapter that cohesiveness leads individual members to conform to the team's norms. This control keeps the group organized around common goals, but it may also cause team members to suppress their dissenting opinions, particularly when a strong team norm is related to the issue. When someone does state a point of view that violates the majority opinion, other members might punish the violator or try to persuade him or her that the opinion is incorrect. Conformity can also be subtle. To some extent, we depend on the opinions that others hold to validate our own views. If co-workers don't agree with us, then we begin to question our own opinions even without overt peer pressure.

groupthink
The tendency of highly cohesive groups to value consensus at the price of decision quality.

Groupthink One team decision-making problem that most people have heard about is **groupthink**–the tendency of highly cohesive groups to value consensus at the price of decision quality.[42] Groupthink goes beyond the problem of conformity by focusing on how decisions go awry when team members try to maintain harmony. This desire for harmony exists as a group norm and is most apparent when team members have a strong social identity with the group. Along with a desire for harmony, groupthink supposedly occurs when the team is isolated from outsiders, the team leader is opinionated (rather than impartial), the team is under stress due to an external threat, the team has experienced recent failures or other decision-making problems, and the team lacks clear guidance from corporate policies or procedures.

Although the word *groupthink* is now part of everyday language, the concept is quickly losing favor among OB experts. The main problem is that groupthink includes the complex cluster of team characteristics. Recent studies have found that some of the groupthink characteristics just mentioned actually improve the team decision-making process in some situations.[43] However, a few elements of this concept do create problems in team decision making, so we need to be aware of them. One of these is team confidence. Studies consistently report that highly confident teams are less attentive in decision making than moderately confident teams. As a consequence, overly confident executive groups make sloppy decisions because they are complacent and have a false sense of invulnerability.[44]

group polarization
The tendency of teams to make more extreme decisions than individuals working alone.

Group Polarization **Group polarization** refers to the tendency of teams to make more extreme decisions than individuals working alone.[45] Suppose a group of people meets to decide the future of a new product. Individual team members might come to the meeting with various degrees of support or opposition to the product's future. Yet by the end of the meeting, chances are that the team will agree on a more extreme solution than the average person had when the meeting began.

There are three reasons why group polarization occurs (see Exhibit 10.3). First, team members become comfortable with more extreme positions when they realize that co-workers also generally support the same position. Second, persuasive arguments favoring the dominant position convince doubtful members and help form a consensus around the extreme option. Finally, individuals feel less personally responsible for the decision consequences because the decision is made by the team. Social

Exhibit 10.3
The Group Polarization Process

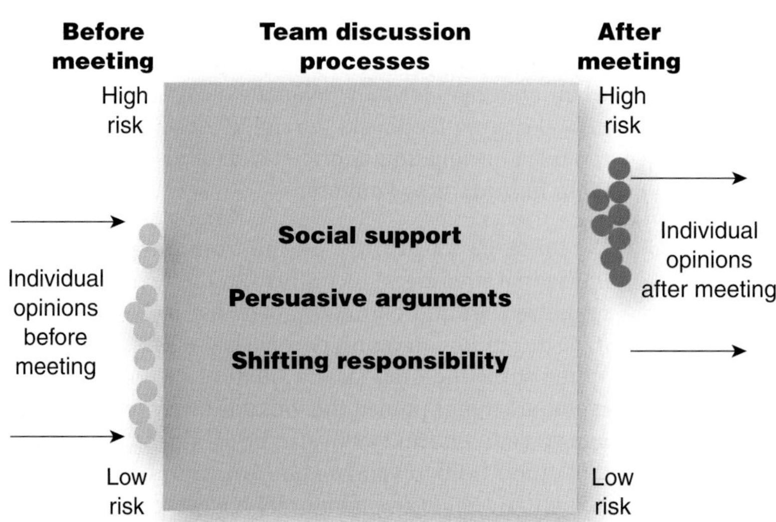

support, persuasion, and shifting responsibility explain why teams make extreme decisions, but they also make *riskier* decisions due to the natural tendency to take higher risks when facing certain losses. This higher risk preference is caused by the prospect theory effect described in Chapter 8—people try to avoid losses because they are more painful than the equivalent gain.[46]

Team Structures to Improve Creativity and Decision Making

The constraints on team decision making are potentially serious, but several solutions also emerge from these bad-news studies. Team members need to be confident in their decision making, but not so confident that they collectively feel invulnerable. This calls for team norms that encourage critical thinking as well as team membership that maintains sufficient diversity. Team leaders and other powerful members can sway the rest of the group, so checks and balances need to be in place to avoid the adverse effects of this power. Another practice is to maintain an optimal team size. The group should be large enough that members possess the collective knowledge to resolve the problem, yet small enough that the team doesn't consume too much time or restrict individual input.

Team structures also help to minimize the problems described over the previous few pages. Five team structures potentially improve creativity and decision making in team settings: constructive conflict, brainstorming, electronic brainstorming, Delphi method, and nominal group technique.

Constructive Conflict

Executives at Corning Inc. rely on several strategies to strengthen team decision making and creativity, but one of their favorites is to assign promising ideas to two-person teams, who spend up to four months analyzing the feasibility of their assigned idea. The unique feature about this process is that the team is deliberately designed so that one person is from marketing, while the other has technical expertise. This oil-and-water combination sometimes ruffles feathers, but it seems to generate better team decision making. "We find great constructive conflict this way," says Deborah Mills, who leads Corning's early-stage marketing team.[47]

constructive conflict
Occurs when team members debate their different perceptions about an issue in a way that keeps the conflict focused on the task rather than people.

Constructive conflict refers to conflict in which team members debate their different perceptions about an issue in a way that keeps the conflict focused on the task rather than people. This conflict is called "constructive" because participants pay attention to facts and logic and avoid statements that generate emotional conflict. The main advantage of this debate is that it presents different points of view, which encourages everyone to reexamine their assumptions and logic.

One problem with constructive conflict is that it is difficult to apply; healthy debate can slide into personal attacks. Also, the effect of constructive conflict on team decision making is inconsistent. Some research indicates that debate—even criticism—can be good for team decision making, whereas others say that all forms of conflict can be detrimental to teams. Constructive conflict will be discussed in more detail in Chapter 13, which also identifies specific strategies to minimize the emotional effects of conflict while maintaining a constructive debate.[48]

brainstorming
A free-wheeling, face-to-face meeting where team members aren't allowed to criticize, but are encouraged to speak freely, generate as many ideas as possible, and build on the ideas of others.

Brainstorming

In the 1950s, advertising executive Alex Osborn wanted to find a better way for teams to generate creative ideas.[49] Osborn's solution, called **brainstorming**, requires team members to abide by four rules. Osborn believed that these rules encourage divergent thinking while minimizing evaluation apprehension and other team dynamics problems:

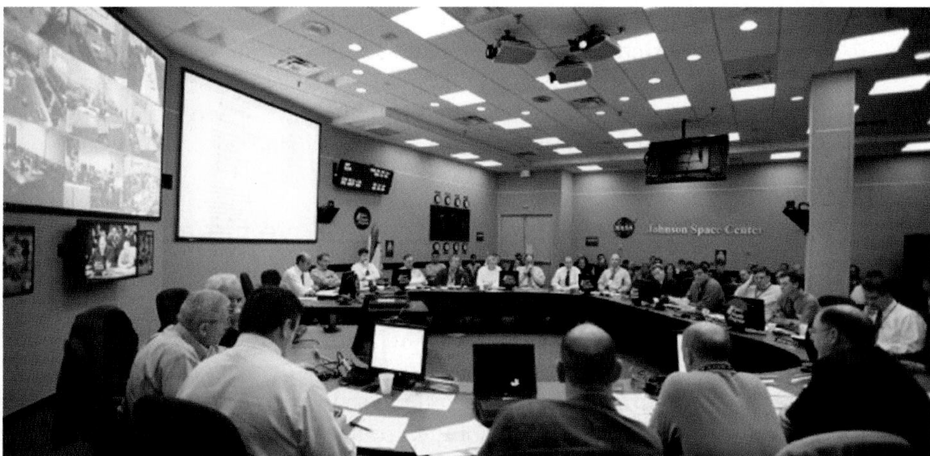

NASA's Constructive Conflict Room The ill-fated flight of the space shuttle *Columbia* was a wake-up call for how NASA's mission management team makes decisions. The *Columbia* accident investigation team concluded that concerns raised by engineers were either deflected or watered down because the mission management team appeared to be "immersed in a culture of invincibility" and hierarchical authority discouraged constructive debate. If top decision makers had more fully considered the extent of damage during takeoff, they might have been able to save *Columbia's* seven crew members. To foster more open communications and constructive debate, the mission management team's assigned seating rectangular table has been replaced by a C-shaped arrangement where people sit wherever they want (shown in photo). None of the 24 members stands out above the others in the new setup. Around the walls of the room are pearls of wisdom reminding everyone of the pitfalls of team decision making. "People in groups tend to agree on courses of action which, as individuals, they know are stupid," warns one poster.[50]

- *Speak freely.* Brainstorming welcomes wild and wacky ideas because these become the seeds of divergent thinking in the creative process. Crazy suggestions are sometimes crazy only because they break out of the mold set by existing mental models.
- *Don't criticize.* Team members are more likely to contribute wild ideas if no one tries to mock or criticize them. Thus a distinctive rule in brainstorming is that no one is allowed to criticize any ideas that are presented.
- *Provide as many ideas as possible.* Brainstorming is based on the idea that quantity breeds quality. In other words, teams generate better ideas when they generate many ideas. This relates to the belief that divergent thinking occurs after traditional ideas have been exhausted. Therefore the group should think of as many possible solutions as it can and go well beyond the traditional solutions to a problem.
- *Build on the ideas of others.* Team members are encouraged to "piggyback" or "hitchhike"–that is, combine and improve on the ideas already presented. Building on existing ideas encourages the synergy of employee involvement that was mentioned in Chapter 8.

Brainstorming is a well-known team structure for encouraging creative ideas. Yet for several years researchers concluded that this practice is ineffective. Lab studies found that brainstorming groups generate fewer ideas, largely because production blocking and evaluation apprehension still interfere with team dynamics. However, these conclusions contrast with more recent real-world evidence that highly creative firms such as IDEO, the Silicon Valley product design firm, thrive on brainstorming. "Brainstorming is the idea engine of IDEO's culture," says IDEO general manager Tom Kelley. "The more productive the group, the more it brainstorms regularly and effectively."[51]

There are a few explanations why the lab studies differ from real-world evidence.[52] First, the lab studies measured the number of ideas generated, whereas brainstorming seems to provide more creative ideas–which is the main reason why companies use brainstorming. Evaluation apprehension may be a problem for students brainstorming in lab experiments, but it is less of a problem in high-performing teams that trust each other and embrace a learning orientation culture. The lab studies also overlooked the fact that brainstorming participants interact and participate directly, thereby increasing decision acceptance and team cohesiveness.

Brainstorming sessions also provide valuable nonverbal communication that spreads enthusiasm, which in turn provides a more creative climate. Clients are sometimes involved in brainstorming sessions, so these positive emotions may produce higher customer satisfaction than if people are working alone on a product. Overall, although brainstorming might not always be the best team structure, it seems to be more valuable than some of the earlier research studies indicated.

electronic brainstorming
Using special computer software, participants share ideas while minimizing the team dynamics problems inherent in traditional brainstorming sessions.

Electronic Brainstorming

Electronic brainstorming tries to minimize many of the problems described above with face-to-face brainstorming by having people generate and share ideas through computers. A facilitator begins the process by posting a question. Participants then enter their answers or ideas on their computer terminal. Soon after, everyone's ideas are posted anonymously and randomly on the computer screens or at the front of the room. Participants eventually vote electronically on the ideas presented. Face-to-face discussion usually follows the electronic brainstorming process.

Research indicates that electronic brainstorming generates more ideas than traditional brainstorming and more creative ideas than traditionally interacting teams. Participants also tend to be more satisfied, motivated, and confident in the decision-making exercise than in other team structures.[53] One reason for these favorable outcomes is that electronic brainstorming significantly reduces production blocking. Participants are able to document their ideas as soon as they pop into their heads, rather than wait their turn to communicate.[54] The process also supports creative synergy because participants can easily develop new ideas from those generated by other people. Electronic brainstorming also minimizes the problem of evaluation apprehension because ideas are posted anonymously.

Despite these numerous advantages, electronic brainstorming is not widely used by corporate leaders. One possible reason is that it might be too structured and technology-bound for some executives. Furthermore, some decision makers may feel threatened by the honesty of statements generated through this process and by their limited ability to control the discussion. A third explanation is that electronic brainstorming may work best for certain types of decisions, but not for others. For example, electronic brainstorming may be less effective than face-to-face meetings where effective decision making is less important than social bonding and emotional interaction.[55] Overall, electronic brainstorming can significantly improve decision making under the right conditions, but more research is required to identify those conditions.

Delphi method
A structured team decision-making process of systematically pooling the collective knowledge of experts on a particular subject to make decisions, predict the future, or identify opposing views.

Delphi Method

The **Delphi method** was developed by the RAND think tank in the 1950s and has regained attention over the past decade. Delphi systematically pools the collective knowledge of experts on a particular subject to make decisions, predict the future, identify opposing views (called *dissensus*), or identify multiple causes of events.[56] One recent example is a Delphi analysis of the challenges facing agriculture in Finland. Another developed and prioritized a list of indicators that people use to evaluate ecotourism in Taiwan. A third study of 50 experts identified a range of causes of obesity in Australia, then in a second round rank ordered the importance of each cause, along with an explanation of their rankings. The results revealed a dissensus of opinion about why Australians are gaining weight.[57]

There are a few variations, but most Delphi groups have the following features. They do not meet face-to-face; in fact, participants are often located in different parts of the world and may not know each other's identity. As with electronic brainstorming, Delphi participants do not know who "owns" the ideas submitted. Typically Delphi group members submit possible solutions or comments regarding an issue to the central convener, although computer technology is turning this stage into an automatic compilation process. The compiled results are returned to the panel for a second round of comments. This process may be repeated a few more times until consensus or dissensus emerges.

nominal group technique A structured team decision-making process whereby team members independently write down ideas, describe and clarify them to the group, and then independently rank or vote on them.

Nominal Group Technique The **nominal group technique** is a variation of traditional brainstorming that tries to combine individual efficiencies with team dynamics.[58] The method is called nominal because participants form a group in name only during two stages of decision making. This process, shown in Exhibit 10.4, first involves the individual, then the group, and finally the individual again. After the problem is described, team members silently and independently write down as many solutions as they can. During the group stage, participants describe their solutions to the other team members, usually in a round-robin format. As with brainstorming, there is no criticism or debate, although members are encouraged to ask for clarification of the ideas presented. In the final stage, participants silently and independently rank order or vote on each proposed solution.

Nominal group technique tends to generate more and better-quality ideas compared with traditionally interacting and possibly brainstorming groups.[59] Due to its high degree of structure, nominal group technique usually maintains a high task orientation and relatively low potential for conflict within the team. However, team cohesiveness is generally lower in nominal decisions because the structure minimizes social interaction. Production blocking and evaluation apprehension still occur to some extent.

Exhibit 10.4 **Nominal Group Technique**

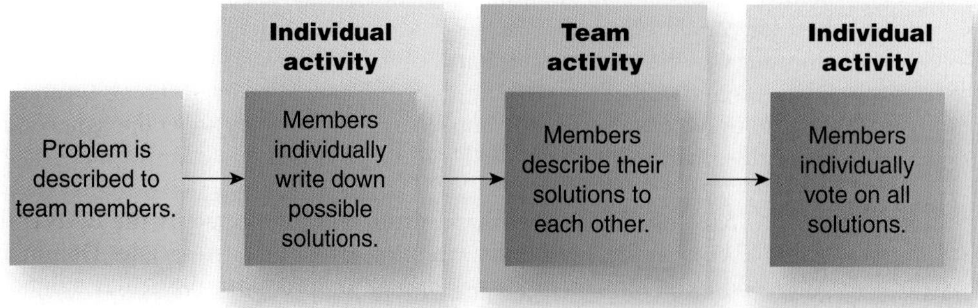
Problem is described to team members.
Individual activity
Members individually write down possible solutions.
Team activity
Members describe their solutions to each other.
Individual activity
Members individually vote on all solutions.

Team Building

HellermanTyton's 60 senior marketing executives recently gathered in what appeared to be the middle of a South American jungle. In reality the executives at the global maker of wire and cable products were participating in a team-building exercise located in a private wildlife reserve in Naples, Florida, complete with giraffes, leopards, chimpanzees, and alligators. "You would never think we were still in Naples, but we were," says Terry Tuttle, HellermannTyton's vice president of marketing. The safari-themed program tested the managers' teamwork, communication, and leadership skills in a realistic setting. One activity even put participants up close with a live Florida alligator. "Although many were skeptical at first, you could see the teams form and build with each exercise," says Tuttle. "By the end, everyone was pumped up. We established camaraderie as a group that is essential to getting business goals accomplished throughout the year."[60]

team building
Any formal activity intended to improve the development and functioning of a work team.

The executives at HellermannTyton rejuvenated team dynamics more quickly through **team building**–formal activities intended to improve the development and functioning of a work team.[61] Some team-building activities also reshape team norms

Volunteering Builds Better Teams When E.ON UK, the United Kingdom's largest integrated energy company, recently formed a social and corporate affairs team, it didn't rely on firewalking, camping in the woods, or the other usual forms of team building. Instead team members spent time creating pathways, tree guards, and fencing in parks operated by the National Trust. "We wanted to give something back to the local community, and as we were a new team we also wanted to bond," says team member Suzanne Doxey. "When we got back to the office we were more relaxed and had better relationships with each other." Community volunteering has become the latest trend in team building. Lockheed Martin employees, including the team shown in this photo helping with the New Orleans clean up following hurricune Katrina, have logged more than 2 million hours over the past three years, volunteering their services for environmental and community improvement projects while improving interpersonal relationships back at work. PricewaterhouseCoopers is another company that sees the dual benefits of volunteering. "It's a great opportunity for people to get to know each other in an environment where they're all doing exactly the same task so there's no hierarchy," says an executive at the global accounting firm. "It really does help people to understand each other and build teams."[62]

and strengthen cohesiveness. Team building is sometimes applied to newly established teams because team members are at the earliest stages of team development. However, it is more common among existing teams, such as at HellermannTyton, where employees need to reestablish camaraderie or where the team has regressed to earlier stages of team development. Team building is therefore most appropriate when the team experiences high membership turnover or members have lost focus on their respective roles and team objectives.

Types of Team Building

There are four main types of team building: goal setting, role definition, interpersonal processes, and problem solving.[63]

- *Goal setting.* Some team-building interventions clarify the team's performance goals, increase the team's motivation to accomplish these goals, and establish a mechanism for systematic feedback on the team's goal performance. This is very similar to individual goal setting described in Chapter 5, except that the goals are applied to teams.
- *Role definition.* Clarifying role definitions is often associated with goal-setting team building. Role definition team building involves clarifying and reconstructing members' perceptions of their roles as well as the role expectations they have of other team members. Various interventions may be applied, ranging from open discussion to structured analysis of the work process. Role definition encompasses the emerging concept of *team mental models.* Recall from Chapter 3 that mental models are internal representations of the external world. Research studies indicate that team processes and performance depend on how well teammates share common mental models about how they should work together.[64] Team-building activities help team members clarify and form a more unified perspective of their team mental models.
- *Interpersonal processes.* This category of team building covers a broad territory. Conflict management fits under this heading, both as a symptom to identify the team's underlying weaknesses and as an ongoing interpersonal process that team members learn to continuously manage constructively. Early team-building interventions relied on direct confrontation sessions to give the sources of conflict an airing. This can work with professional facilitation, but experts warn that open dialogue is not always the most effective way to solve team conflicts.[65] Another interpersonal process is building (or rebuilding) trust among team members. Popular interventions such as wilderness team activities, paintball wars, and obstacle course challenges are typically offered to build trust. "If two colleagues hold the rope for you while you're climbing 10 meters up, that is truly team-building," explains Jan Antwerpes, a partner in a German communications consulting firm.[66]
- *Problem solving.* This type of team building focuses on decision making, including the issues mentioned earlier in this chapter and the decision-making process described in Chapter 8. To improve their problem-solving skills, some teams participate in simulation games that require team decisions in hypothetical situations. PwC's adventure at Disney's EPCOT Center, which was described at the beginning of this chapter, is one such example of team building that improves problem-solving skills among team members.

Is Team Building Effective?

Are team-building interventions effective? Is the money well spent? So far the answer is an equivocal "maybe." Studies suggest that some team-building activities are successful, but just as many fail to build high-performance teams.[67] One problem is that corporate leaders assume team-building activities are general solutions to general team problems. No one bothers to diagnose the team's specific needs (such as problem solving or interpersonal processes) because the team-building intervention is assumed to be a broad-brush solution. A better approach is to begin with a sound diagnosis of the team's health, then select team-building interventions that address weaknesses.[68]

Another problem is that corporate leaders tend to view team building as a one-shot medical inoculation that every team should receive when it is formed. In truth, team building is an ongoing process, not a three-day jump start. Some experts suggest, for example, that wilderness experiences often fail because they rarely include follow-up consultation to ensure that team learning is transferred back to the workplace.[69]

Finally, we must remember that team building occurs on the job, not just on an obstacle course or in a national park. Organizations should encourage team members to reflect on their work experiences and to experiment with just-in-time learning for team development. This dialogue requires open communication, so employees can clarify expectations, coordinate work activities, and build common mental models of working together. The next chapter looks at the dynamics of communicating in teams and organizations.

Chapter Summary

Self-directed work teams (SDWTs) complete an entire piece of work requiring several interdependent tasks and have substantial autonomy over the execution of these tasks. Sociotechnical systems (STS) theory identifies four main conditions for high-performance SDWTs. SDWTs must be responsible for an entire work process have sufficient autonomy, have control over key variances, and operate under joint optimization. STS theory has been widely supported since its origins in the 1950s. However, it is not very helpful at identifying the optimal alignment of the social and technical system. SDWTs also face cross-cultural issues, management resistance, and labor union and employee resistance.

Virtual teams are teams whose members operate across space, time, and organizational boundaries and are linked through information technologies to achieve organizational tasks. Unlike conventional teams, virtual team members are not colocated, so they are more dependent on information technologies rather than face-to-face interaction. Virtual teams are becoming more popular because information technology and knowledge-based work makes it easier to collaborate from a distance. Virtual teams are becoming increasingly necessary because they represent a natural part of the knowledge management process. Moreover, as companies globalize, they must rely more on virtual teams than colocated teams to coordinate operations at distant sites.

Several elements in the team effectiveness model stand out as important issues for virtual teams. High-performance virtual teams require a variety of communication media, and virtual team members need to creatively combine these media to match the task demands. Virtual teams operate better with structured rather than complex and ambiguous tasks. They usually cannot maintain as large a team as is possible in conventional teams. Members of virtual teams require special skills in communication systems and should be aware of cross-cultural issues. Virtual team members should also meet face-to-face, particularly when the team forms, to assist team development and cohesiveness.

Trust is important in team dynamics, particularly in virtual teams. Trust is a psychological state comprising the intention to accept vulnerability based on positive expectations of the intent or behavior of another person. The minimal level of trust is calculus-based trust, which is based on deterrence. Teams cannot survive with this level of trust. Knowledge-based trust is a higher level of trust and is grounded on the other party's predictability. The highest level of trust, called identification-based trust, is based on mutual understanding and emotional bond between the parties. Most employees join a team with a fairly high level of trust, which tends to decline over time.

Team decisions are impeded by time constraints, evaluation apprehension, conformity to peer pressure, groupthink, and group polarization. Production blocking –where only one person typically speaks at a time–is a form of time constraint on teams. Evaluation apprehension occurs when employees believe that others are silently evaluating them, so they avoid stating seemingly silly ideas. Conformity keeps team members aligned with team goals, but it also tends to suppress dissenting opinions. Groupthink is the tendency of highly cohesive groups to value consensus at the price of decision quality. Group polarization refers to the tendency of teams to make more extreme decisions than individuals working alone.

To minimize decision-making problems, teams should be moderately (not highly) confident, ensure that the team leader does not dominate, maintain an optimal team size, and ensure that team norms support critical thinking. Five team structures that potentially improve team decision making are constructive conflict, brainstorming, electronic brainstorming, the Delphi method, and the nominal group technique. Constructive conflict occurs when team members debate their different perceptions about an issue in a way that keeps the conflict focused on the task rather than people. Brainstorming requires team members to speak freely, avoid criticism, provide as many ideas as possible, and build on the ideas of others. Electronic brainstorming uses computer software to share ideas while minimizing team dynamics problems. The Delphi method systematically pools the collective knowledge of experts on a particular subject without face-to-face meetings. In the nominal group technique participants write down ideas alone, describe these ideas in a group, then silently vote on these ideas.

Team building is any formal activity intended to improve the development and functioning of a work team. Four team-building strategies are goal setting, role definition, interpersonal processes, and problem solving. Some team-building events succeed, but companies often fail to consider the contingencies of team building.

Key Terms

brainstorming, p. 299
constructive conflict, p. 299
Delphi method, p. 301
electronic brainstorming, p. 301
evaluation apprehension, p. 297
group polarization, p. 298
groupthink, p. 298
joint optimization, p. 288
nominal group technique, p. 302
production blocking, p. 297
self-directed work teams (SDWTs), p. 286
sociotechnical systems (STS) theory, p. 287
team building, p. 303
trust, p. 294
virtual teams, p. 291

Critical Thinking Questions

1. How do self-directed work teams differ from conventional teams?
2. Advanced Telecom Inc. has successfully introduced self-directed work teams at its operations throughout the United States. The company now wants to introduce SDWTs at its plants in Thailand and Malaysia. What potential cross-cultural challenges might Advanced Telecom experience as it introduces SDWTs in these high power distance countries?
3. A chicken processing company wants to build a processing plant designed around sociotechnical systems principles. In a traditional chicken processing plant, employees work in separate departments–cleaning and cutting, cooking, packaging, and warehousing. The cooking and packaging processes are controlled by separate workstations in the traditional plant. How would the company change this operation according to sociotechnical systems design?
4. What can organizations do to reduce management resistance to self-directed work teams?
5. Suppose the instructor for this course assigned you to a project team consisting of three other students who are currently taking similar courses in Ireland, India, and Brazil. All students speak English and have similar expertise of the topic. Use your knowledge of virtual teams to discuss the problems that your team might face, compared with a team of local students who can meet face-to-face.

6. What can virtual teams do to sustain trust among team members?
7. Some firms in your region have turned to volunteering as a form of team building, whereby a group of employees spends a day working together on a community project, often outside their expertise. In what ways might volunteering be an effective team-building activity?
8. Bangalore Technologies wants to use brainstorming with its employees and customers to identify new uses for its technology. Advise Bangalore's president about the potential benefits of brainstorming, as well as its potential limitations.

Case Study 10.1 THE SHIPPING INDUSTRY ACCOUNTING TEAM

For the past five years I have been working at McKay, Sanderson, and Smith Associates, a midsized accounting firm in Boston that specializes in commercial accounting and audits. My particular specialty is accounting practices for shipping companies, ranging from small fishing fleets to a couple of the big firms with ships along the East Coast.

About 18 months ago McKay, Sanderson, and Smith Associates became part of a large merger involving two other accounting firms. These firms have offices in Miami, Seattle, Baton Rouge, and Los Angeles. Although the other two accounting firms were much larger than McKay, all three firms agreed to avoid centralizing the business around one office in Los Angeles. Instead the new firm–called Goldberg, Choo, and McKay Associates–would rely on teams across the country to "leverage the synergies of our collective knowledge" (an often-cited statement from the managing partner soon after the merger).

The merger affected me a year ago when my boss (a senior partner and vice president of the merger firm) announced that I would be working more closely with three people from the other two firms to become the firm's new shipping industry accounting team. The other team members were Elias in Miami, Susan in Seattle, and Brad in Los Angeles. I had met Elias briefly at a meeting in New York City during the merger but had never met Susan or Brad, although I knew that they were shipping accounting professionals at the other firms.

Initially the shipping team activities involved e-mailing each other about new contracts and prospective clients. Later we were asked to submit joint monthly reports on accounting statements and issues. Normally I submitted my own monthly reports to summarize activities involving my own clients. Coordinating the monthly report with three other people took much more time, particularly because different accounting documentation procedures across the three firms were still being resolved. It took numerous e-mail messages and a few telephone calls to work out a reasonable monthly report style.

During this aggravating process it became apparent–to me at least–that this team business was costing me more time than it was worth. Moreover, Brad in Los Angeles didn't have a clue about how to communicate with the rest of us. He rarely replied to e-mail. Instead he often used the telephone voice mail system, which resulted in lots of telephone tag. Brad arrived at work at 9:30 a.m. in Los Angeles (and was often late), which is early afternoon in Boston. I typically have a flexible work schedule from 7:30 a.m. to 3:30 p.m. so I can chauffeur my kids after school to sports and music lessons. So Brad and I have a window of less than three hours to share information.

The biggest nuisance with the shipping specialist accounting team started two weeks ago when the firm asked the four of us to develop a new strategy for attracting more shipping firm business. This new strategic plan is a messy business. Somehow we have to share our thoughts on various approaches, agree on a new plan, and write a unified submission to the managing partner. Already the project is taking most of my time just writing and responding to e-mail and talking in conference calls (which none of us did much before the team formed).

Susan and Brad have already had two or three misunderstandings via e-mail about their different perspectives on delicate matters in the strategic plan. The worst of these disagreements required a conference call with all of us to resolve. Except for the most basic matters, it seems that we can't understand each other, let alone agree on key issues. I have come to the conclusion that I would never want Brad to work in my Boston office (thank goodness he's on the other side of the country). Although Elias and I seem to agree on most points, the overall team can't form a common vision or strategy. I don't know how Elias, Susan, or Brad feel, but I would be quite happy to work somewhere that did not require any of these long-distance team headaches.

Discussion Questions

1. What type of team was formed here? Was it necessary, in your opinion?
2. Use the team effectiveness model in Chapter 9 and related information in this chapter to identify the strengths and weaknesses of this team's environment, design, and processes.
3. Assuming that these four people must continue to work as a team, recommend ways to improve the team's effectiveness.

Source: Copyright © 2004 Steven L. McShane.

Case Study 10.2 SEAGATE'S MORALE-ATHON

BusinessWeek

Team building activities come in many forms and are widely practiced, but few companies go as far as Seagate Technology. Each year, the giant American computer storage hardware manufacturer has been sending hundreds of employees from a dozen countries to a week-long team-building program called Eco-Seagate. CEO Bill Watkins championed the event to break down barriers, boost confidence, and make staffers better team players. "Some of you will learn about teamwork because you have a great team," Watson advises one group of participants. "Some of you will learn because your team is a disaster."

This *BusinessWeek* case study details the team-building events that "tribes" of employees participated in throughout a recent Eco-Seagate program in New Zealand. It describes how employees react to these activities, including the marathon race on the final day. Read the full text of this *BusinessWeek* article at www.mhhe.com/mcshane4e and prepare for the discussion questions below.

Discussion Questions

1. What type(s) of team building would you categorize the Eco-Seagate event? In your opinion, is this type of event effective for teambuilding? Why or why not?
2. What practices in the Eco-Seagate help team members to become more cohesive?

Source: S. Max, "Seagate's Morale-athon," *BusinessWeek,* 3 April 2006, 110

Team Exercise 10.3 EGG DROP EXERCISE

PURPOSE This exercise is designed to help you understand the dynamics of high-performance teams.

MATERIALS The instructor will provide various materials with which to complete this task. The instructor will also distribute a cost sheet to each team and will post the rules for managers and workers. Rule violations will attract penalties that increase the cost of production.

TEAM TASK The team's task is to design and build a protective device that will allow a raw egg (provided by the instructor) to be dropped from a great height without breaking. The team wins if its egg does not break using the lowest-priced device.

INSTRUCTIONS

1. The instructor will divide the class into teams of approximately six people. Team members will divide into groups of "managers" and "workers." The team can have as many people as it thinks is needed for managers and workers as long as all team members are assigned to one of these roles. Please note from the cost sheet that managers and workers represent a cost to your project's budget.
2. Within the time allotted by the instructor, each team's managers will design the device to protect the egg. Workers and managers will purchase supplies from the store, and workers will then build the egg protection device. Team members should read the rules carefully to avoid penalty costs.

Source: This exercise, which is widely available in many forms, does not seem to have any known origin.

Self-Assessment 10.4

THE TEAM PLAYER INVENTORY

Theresa Kline, University of Calgary

PURPOSE This exercise is designed to help you estimate the extent to which you are positively predisposed to working in teams.

INSTRUCTIONS Read each of the following statements and circle the response that you believe best indicates the extent to which you agree or disagree with that statement. Then use the scoring key in Appendix B to calculate your results for each scale. This exercise is completed alone so you can assess yourself honestly without concerns of social comparison. However, class discussion will focus on the characteristics of individuals who are more or less compatible with working in self-directed work teams.

The Team Player Inventory

To what extent do you agree or disagree that	Completely disagree	Disagree somewhat	Neither agree nor disagree	Agree somewhat	Completely agree
1. I enjoy working on team projects.	☐	☐	☐	☐	☐
2. Team project work easily allows others to "pull their weight."	☐	☐	☐	☐	☐
3. Work that is done as a team is better than work done individually.	☐	☐	☐	☐	☐
4. I do my best work alone rather than in a team.	☐	☐	☐	☐	☐
5. Team work is overrated in terms of the actual results produced.	☐	☐	☐	☐	☐
6. Working in a team gets me to think more creatively.	☐	☐	☐	☐	☐
7. Teams are used too often when individual work would be more effective.	☐	☐	☐	☐	☐
8. My own work is enhanced when I am in a team situation.	☐	☐	☐	☐	☐
9. My experiences working in team situations have been primarily negative.	☐	☐	☐	☐	☐
10. More solutions or ideas are generated when working in a team situation than when working alone.	☐	☐	☐	☐	☐

Source: T.J.B. Kline, "The Team Player Inventory: Reliability and Validity of a Measure of Predisposition toward Organizational Team Working Environments," *Journal for Specialists in Group Work* 24 (1999), pp. 102–12.

Self-Assessment 10.5

PROPENSITY TO TRUST SCALE (STUDENT OLC)

Trust is a psychological state comprising the intention to accept vulnerability based on positive expectations of the intent or behavior of another person. Although trust varies from one situation to the next, some people have a higher or lower propensity to trust. In other words, some people are highly trusting of others, even when first meeting them, whereas others have difficulty trusting anyone, even over a long time. This self-assessment provides an estimate of your propensity to trust. Indicate your preferred response to each statement, being honest with yourself for each item. This self-assessment is completed alone; class discussion will focus on the meaning of propensity to trust, why it varies from one person to the next, and how it affects teamwork.

After reading this chapter, if you need additional information, see www.mhhe.com/mcshane4e for more in-depth interactivities that correspond with this material.

How can corporate leaders conduct a casual conversation with 38,000 staff in dozens of countries? Sun Microsystems president Jonathan Schwartz handles the task through his own Weblog. Blogs (as Weblogs are commonly called) are online journals or diaries. Schwartz writes in his blog each week about a variety of topics, ranging from competition to new technology. Most viewers—up to 20,000 every day—are clients, suppliers, and curious Web surfers, but Schwartz also sees the value of his blogs for Sun's own workforce.

"There are 38,000 people at Sun," Schwartz explains. "I can't have an all-hands meeting. I'd love to put everybody in one room and say, 'Here's the strategy, here are the challenges, here are the obstacles, here's what you need to do to get around them.' I can't do that. But my blog gives me the best proxy for doing exactly that." Schwartz adds that blogging is better than writing memos or newsletters because it gives the information more of a personal touch. "There's an immediacy of interaction you can get with your audience through blogging that's hard to get any other way, except by face-to-face communication."

Sun Microsystems president Jonathan Schwartz says that blogs have a lot to offer as a communication medium in organizations.

Sun, IBM, Google, and a few other companies also provide resources for employees to create their own personal blogs. IBM has several outward-facing blogs for customers, but its inward-facing (restricted to IBM employees) BlogCentral hosts more than 3,000 personal blogs created by employees who want to share their thoughts and experiences with co-workers. Google's inward-facing blog has created a gigantic office water cooler effect. "We have seen a lot of different uses of blogs within the firewall," says Jason Goldman, Blogger product manager at Google. "People keeping track of meeting notes, sharing diagnostics information and sharing snippets of code, as well as more personal uses, like letting co-workers know what they're thinking about and what they're up to."

Meanwhile Children's Hospital and Regional Medical Center in Seattle is applying blogs in another way to improve employee communication. Rather than having professionals write employee newsletters or e-zines, the hospital keeps staff up-to-date through volunteer bloggers scattered throughout the organization. Dozens of Children's Hospital staff are authorized to post news and events in their departments to a central blog site that employees visit to learn what's happening. "The distributed authorship of people from different departments means the content is fresher" than the hospital's previous newsletter or e-zine, says Children's Hospital Web services manager Christian Watson.[1]

Communicating in Teams and Organizations

LEARNING OBJECTIVES

After reading this chapter you should be able to

1. Explain the importance of communication and diagram the communication process.
2. Describe problems with communicating through electronic mail.
3. Identify two ways in which nonverbal communication differs from verbal communication.
4. Identify two conditions requiring a channel with high media richness.
5. Identify four common communication barriers.
6. Discuss the degree to which men and women communicate differently.
7. Outline the key elements of active listening.
8. Summarize four communication strategies in organizational hierarchies.

Information technologies have transformed communication in organizations in recent years, yet we may still be at the beginning of this revolution. Wire cablegrams and telephones introduced a century ago are giving way to e-mail, instant messaging, Weblogs, and podcasting. Each of these inventions creates fascinating changes in how people interact with each other in the workplace. **Communication** refers to the process by which information is transmitted and *understood* between two or more people. We emphasize the word *understood* because transmitting the sender's intended meaning is the essence of good communication.

communication
The process by which information is transmitted and understood between two or more people.

Sun Microsystems, IBM, Google, and other large organizations require innovative strategies to keep communication pathways open. In fact, a communication audit of several large organizations reported that only 23 percent of employees agree that executives communicate well, and only 15 percent agree that the head office in general communicates effectively.[2] Smaller businesses may have fewer structural bottlenecks, but they too can suffer subtle communication problems.

Effective communication is vital to all organizations because it coordinates employees, fulfills employee needs, supports knowledge management, and improves decision making.[3] First, the ability to exchange information is an essential part of the coordination process, allowing employees to develop common mental models that synchronize their work. Second, communication is the glue that holds people together. It helps people satisfy their drive to bond and, as part of the dynamics of social support, eases work-related stress.

Communication is also a key driver in knowledge management. It brings knowledge into the organization and distributes it to employees who require that information. As such, it minimizes the "silos of knowledge" problem that undermines an organization's potential. Fourth, communication influences the quality of decision making. Individuals rarely have enough information alone to make decisions about the complex matters facing businesses today. Instead problem solvers require information from co-workers, subordinates, and anyone else with relevant knowledge.

This chapter begins by presenting a model of the communication process and discussing several communication barriers. Next, the different types of communication channels, including computer-mediated communication, are described, followed by factors to consider when choosing a communication medium. This chapter then examines cross-cultural and gender differences in communication and outlines strategies to improve interpersonal communication. The latter part of the chapter presents some options for communicating in organizational hierarchies and describes the pervasive organizational grapevine.

Learning Objectives

After reading this section you should be able to

1. **Explain the importance of communication and diagram the communication process.**
2. **Describe problems with communicating through electronic mail.**
3. **Identify two ways in which nonverbal communication differs from verbal communication.**

A Model of Communication

The communication model presented in Exhibit 11.1 provides a useful "conduit" metaphor for thinking about the communication process.[4] According to this model, communication flows through channels between the sender and receiver. The sender

Exhibit 11.1
The Communication Process Model

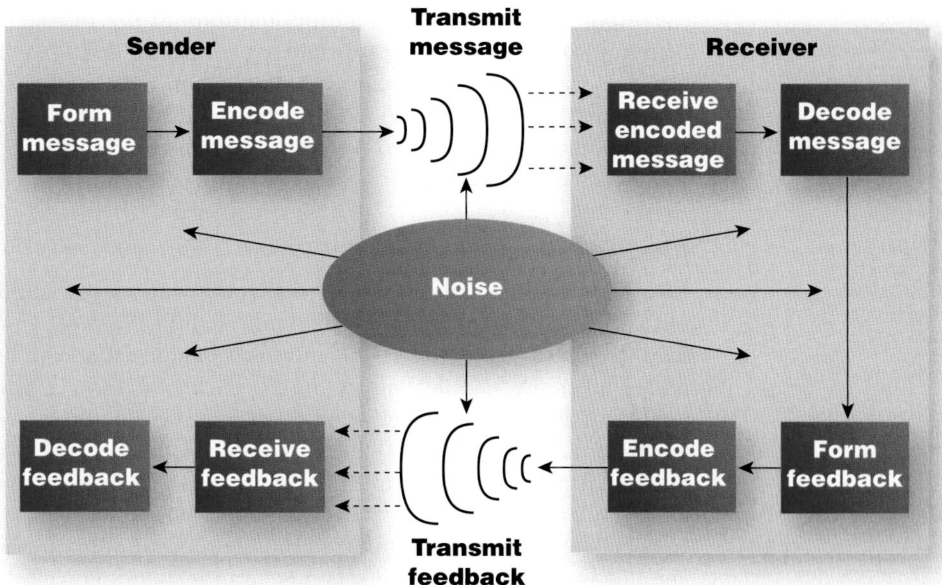

forms a message and encodes it into words, gestures, voice intonations, and other symbols or signs. Next the encoded message is transmitted to the intended receiver through one or more communication channels (media). The receiver senses the incoming message and decodes it into something meaningful. Ideally the decoded meaning is what the sender intended.

In most situations the sender looks for evidence that the other person received and understood the transmitted message. This feedback may be a formal acknowledgment, such as "Yes, I know what you mean," or indirect evidence from the receiver's subsequent actions. Notice that feedback repeats the communication process. Intended feedback is encoded, transmitted, received, and decoded from the receiver to the sender of the original message.

This model recognizes that communication is not a free-flowing conduit. Rather, the transmission of meaning from one person to another is hampered by noise–the psychological, social, and structural barriers that distort and obscure the sender's intended message. If any part of the communication process is distorted or broken, the sender and receiver will not have a common understanding of the message.

Communication Channels

A critical part of the communication model is the channel or medium through which information is transmitted. There are two main types of channels: verbal and nonverbal. Verbal communication includes any oral or written means of transmitting meaning through words. Nonverbal communication, which we discuss later, is any part of communication that does not use words.

Verbal Communication

Different forms of verbal communication should be used in different situations. Face-to-face interaction is usually better than written methods for transmitting emotions and persuading the receiver. This is because nonverbal cues accompany oral communications, such as voice intonation and facial expressions. Furthermore, face-to-face interaction provides the sender with immediate feedback from the receiver and the opportunity to adjust the emotional tone of the message accordingly. Written communication is more appropriate for recording and presenting technical details. This is because ideas are easier to follow when written down than when communicated aurally. Traditionally, written communication has been slow to develop and transmit, but electronic mail, Weblogs, and other computer-mediated communication channels have significantly improved written communication efficiency.

Electronic Communication

Electronic mail (e-mail) is revolutionizing the way we communicate in organizational settings. It has also become the medium of choice in most workplaces because messages are quickly formed, edited, and stored. Information can be appended and transmitted to many people with a simple click of a mouse. E-mail is asynchronous (messages are sent and received at different times), so there is no need to coordinate a communication session. This technology also allows fairly random access to information: You can select any message in any order, skip to different parts of a message, and search for any word in any message on your computer.

E-mail tends to be the preferred medium for coordinating work (such as confirming a co-worker's production schedule) and for sending well-defined information for decision making. It often increases the volume of communication and significantly alters the flow of information within groups and throughout the organization.[5] Specifically, it reduces some face-to-face and telephone communication but increases communication with people further up the hierarchy. Some social and organizational status differences still exist with e-mail, but they are less apparent than in face-to-face communication. E-mail also reduces many selective attention biases because it hides our age, race, weight, and other features that are observable in face-to-face meetings.

Problems with E-Mail In spite of the wonders of e-mail, anyone who has used this communication medium knows that it has limitations. One problem is that e-mail is an ineffective medium for communicating emotions. People rely on facial expressions and other nonverbal cues to interpret the emotional meaning of words, and e-mail lacks this parallel communication medium. E-mail aficionados try to clarify the emotional tone of their messages by inserting graphic faces called emoticons or "smileys."[6]

flaming
The act of sending an emotionally charged e-mail message to others.

A second problem with e-mail is that it seems to reduce our politeness and respect for others. This is mostly evident through the increased frequency of **flaming**–the act of sending an emotionally charged message to others. There are two explanations for this lack of diplomacy. First, people can quickly write and post e-mail messages before their emotions subside, whereas cooler thoughts might prevail before traditional memos or letters are sent. Second, e-mail is an impersonal medium, allowing employees to write things that they would never say verbally in face-to-face conversation. Fortunately, research has found that politeness and respect increase as team members get to know each other and when companies establish explicit norms and rules of communication.[7]

A third problem is that e-mail is an inefficient medium for communicating in ambiguous, complex, and novel situations. When two people lack mutual mental models, they need to transmit many e-mail messages to share enough information. Two-way face-to-face communication is a much more effective medium under these circumstances, but many employees are reluctant to break out of the e-mail dialogue. Realizing this, executives at St. Joseph's Regional Medical Center in Paterson, New Jersey, banned e-mail for one day in an attempt to "repersonalize the health care business." Similar bans have occurred at Liverpool City Council in the United Kingdom. John Caudwell become so fed up with e-mail that the CEO of British cell phone company

Flaming E-mail Executives at Admiral Insurance are concerned that the electronic communication medium is making staff at the Welsh company less polite to each other and to customers. "It is much easier to have a row by e-mail than it is face-to-face, and people are often ruder as a result," says Admiral spokesperson Justin Beddows. "Orders can be issued out and people can be quite abrupt because they feel protected by the distance the e-mail provides. But once an abusive e-mail is sent out, there is no getting it back and it can cause a rift that cannot be resolved easily." Along with reminding employees of e-mail's limitations as a communication medium, Admiral executives occasionally try to wean staff from e-mail dependence. "We hold 'no e-mail days' to encourage people to get off their backsides and visit people face-to-face," says Beddows.[8]

Phones 4U banned his 2,500 employees from e-mailing each other at all. Although the ban was short-lived, Caudwell claimed soon after the ban that "the quality and efficiency of communication have increased in one fell swoop."[9]

A fourth difficulty with e-mail is that it contributes to information overload, which we'll discuss in more detail later in this chapter. Many e-mail users are overwhelmed by hundreds of messages each week, many of which are either unnecessary or irrelevant to the receiver. This occurs because e-mail can be easily created and copied to thousands of people through group mailbox systems. E-mail overload may eventually decrease as people become more familiar with it, but this trend may take a while.

Other Computer-Mediated Communication Intranets, extranets, Blackberry wireless e-mailing, instant messaging, blogging, podcasting, and other forms of computer-mediated communication are fueling the hyperfast world of corporate information sharing. The opening story to this chapter described how blogs enable executives to more personally communicate with employees. Sun Microsystems and a few other firms support employee blogs because they empower staff to share information both internally and externally and let co-workers know more about each other. Blogs also allow firms to archive discussions, something that is less easily done in instant messaging. Podcasting may become another electronic communication medium that gains interest in organizations. Although primarily aimed at the public, podcasts–radiolike programs formatted for digital music players and computer music software–are starting to appear as messages from executives to employees and customers alike.[10]

Instant messaging (IM) is another emerging form of electronic communication that has gained popularity in some organizations. IM is more efficient than e-mail because messages are brief (usually just a sentence or two with acronyms and sound-alike letters for words) and appear on the receiver's screen as soon as they are sent. IM also creates real-time communities of practice as employees form clustered conversations around specific fields of expertise. Another advantage is that employees soon develop the capability of carrying on several IM conversations at the same time. "No matter how good you are on the phone, the best you can do is carry on two conversations at once," says one New York City broker. "With IM, I can have six going at once.... That allows me to get my job done and serve clients better."[11]

Nonverbal Communication

Nonverbal communication includes facial gestures, voice intonation, physical distance, and even silence. This communication channel is necessary where noise or physical distance prevents effective verbal exchanges and the need for immediate feedback precludes written communication. But even in quiet face-to-face meetings, most information is communicated nonverbally. Rather like a parallel conversation, nonverbal cues signal subtle information to both parties, such as reinforcing their interest in the verbal conversation or demonstrating their relative status in the relationship.[12]

Nonverbal communication differs from verbal communication in a couple of ways. First, it is less rule-bound than verbal communication. We receive a lot of formal training in how to understand spoken words but very little in understanding the nonverbal signals that accompany those words. Consequently nonverbal cues are generally more ambiguous and susceptible to misinterpretation. At the same time many facial expressions (such as smiling) are hardwired and universal, thereby providing the only reliable means of communicating across cultures. This point is powerfully illustrated in Connections 11.1. To overcome language and physical noise barriers, the quick-thinking leader of a coalition forces unit during the Iraq war relied on nonverbal communication to communicate its friendly intentions, thereby narrowly avoiding a potentially deadly incident.

The other difference between verbal and nonverbal communication is that the former is typically conscious, whereas most nonverbal communication is automatic and unconscious. We normally plan the words we say or write, but we rarely plan every blink, smile, or other gesture during a conversation. Indeed, as we just mentioned, many of these facial expressions communicate the same meaning across cultures because they are hardwired unconscious or preconscious responses to human emotions.[13] For example, pleasant emotions cause the brain center to widen the mouth, whereas negative emotions produce constricted facial expressions (squinting eyes, pursed lips, and the like).

emotional contagion
The automatic and unconscious tendency to mimic and synchronize one's own nonverbal behaviors with those of other people.

Emotional Contagion One of the most fascinating effects of emotions on nonverbal communication is the phenomenon called **emotional contagion,** which is the automatic process of "catching" or sharing another person's emotions by mimicking that person's facial expressions and other nonverbal behavior. Consider what happens when you see a co-worker accidentally bang his or her head against a filing cabinet. Chances are that you wince and put your hand on your own head as if you had hit the cabinet. Similarly, while listening to someone describe a positive event, you tend to smile and exhibit other emotional displays of happiness. While some of our nonverbal communication is planned, emotional contagion represents unconscious behavior–we automatically mimic and synchronize our nonverbal behaviors with other people.[14]

Emotional contagion serves three purposes. First, mimicry provides continuous feedback, communicating that we understand and empathize with the sender. To consider the significance of this, imagine employees remaining expressionless after watching a co-worker bang his or her head! The lack of parallel behavior conveys a lack of understanding or caring. Second, mimicking the nonverbal behaviors of other people seems to be a way of receiving emotional meaning from those people. If a

Connections 11.1

Nonverbal Gestures Help Crowd Control during Iraq War

The southern Iraqi city of Najaf is home to one of Islam's holiest sites, the Ali Mosque. The site is believed to be the final resting place of Ali, son-in-law of the prophet Mohammed. It is also home to Grand Ayatollah Ali Hussein Sistani, one of the most revered Shiites in the Muslim world and a potential supporter of U.S. efforts to introduce a more moderate government in Iraq.

One week before Saddam Hussein's regime was overthrown, Sistani sent word that he wanted to meet with senior officers of the American forces. Fearing assassination, he also asked for soldiers to secure his compound, located along the Golden Road near the mosque. But when 130 soldiers from the 101st Airborne's 2nd Battalion, 327th Infantry, and their gun trucks turned onto the Golden Road to provide security, hundreds of Iraqis in the area started to get angry. Clerics tried to explain to the crowd why the Americans were approaching, but they were drowned out. The crowd assumed the Americans would try to enter and possibly attack the sacred mosque.

The chanting got louder as the quickly growing crowd approached the soldiers. Anticipating a potentially deadly situation, Lieutenant Colonel Christopher Hughes, the battalion's commander, picked up a loudspeaker and called out the unit's nickname: "No Slack Soldiers!" Then he commanded, "All No Slack Soldiers, take a knee." According to journalists witnessing this incident, every soldier almost immediately knelt down on one knee. Hughes then called out, "All No Slack Soldiers, point your weapons at the ground." Again the soldiers complied.

With the crowd still chanting in anger, Hughes spoke through the loudspeaker a third time: "All No Slack Soldiers, smile," he commanded. "Smile guys, everybody smile." And in this intensely difficult situation, the kneeling troops showed the friendliest smiles they could muster toward the crowd.

Eyewitnesses say that these nonverbal gestures started to work; some people in the crowd smiled back at the Americans and stopped chanting. But insurgents in the crowd (apparently Hussein supporters planted to misinform the crowd) continued to yell. So Hughes spoke one more time: "All vehicles, all No Slack Soldiers, calmly stand up and withdraw from this situation," he said. "We'll go so the people understand we are not trying to hurt him. C'mon, Bravo, back off. Smile and wave and back off." And with that, the soldiers walked backward 100 yards, then turned around and returned to their compound.

Sources: W. Allison, "March to Mosque Provokes Worst Fears," *St. Petersburg Times* (Florida), 4 April 2003, p. 1A; "All Things Considered," National Public Radio (NPR), 4 April 2003; R. Chilcote, "Iraqis Mistakenly Believe Soldiers Have Their Sights on Sacred Landmark," CNN, 4 April 2003.

co-worker is angry with a client, your tendency to frown and show anger while listening helps you share that emotion more fully. In other words, we receive meaning by expressing the sender's emotions as well as by listening to the sender's words.

The third function of emotional contagion is to fulfill the drive to bond that was described in Chapter 5. Social solidarity is built out of each member's awareness of a collective sentiment. Through nonverbal expressions of emotional contagion, people see others share the same emotions that we feel. This strengthens team cohesiveness by providing evidence of member similarity.[15]

Learning Objectives

After reading the next three sections, you should be able to

4. **Identify two conditions requiring a channel with high media richness.**
5. **Identify four common communication barriers.**
6. **Discuss the degree to which men and women communicate differently.**

Choosing the Best Communication Channels

Employees perform better if they can quickly determine the best communication channels for a situation and are flexible enough to use different methods as the occasion requires. But which communication channels are most appropriate? We partly answered this question in our evaluation of the different communication channels. However, two additional contingencies worth noting are media richness and symbolic meaning.

Media Richness

media richness
The data-carrying capacity of a communication medium, including the volume and variety of information that can be transmitted during a specific time.

A critical factor to consider when selecting a communication channel is **media richness**. Media richness refers to the medium's data-carrying capacity–the volume and variety of information that can be transmitted during a specific time.[16] Exhibit 11.2 illustrates various communication channels arranged in a hierarchy of richness, with face-to-face interaction at the top and lean data-only reports at the bottom.

The media richness hierarchy is determined by three factors. First, rich media allow a person to simultaneously send messages in different ways. For instance, face-to-face communication scores high on media richness because it allows people to transmit their messages both verbally and nonverbally at the same. In contrast, financial reports have low media richness because the message is transmitted only one way (written). Second, rich media allow immediate feedback from receiver to sender, whereas feedback in lean media is delayed or nonexistent. Again this is apparent in face-to-face communication, in which the sender can quickly determine whether the receiver understood the message; in contrast, someone sending a financial report might never find out whether the message was received, let alone understood. Third, rich media allow the sender to customize the message to the receiver. People can

Exhibit 11.2 **Media Richness Hierarchy**

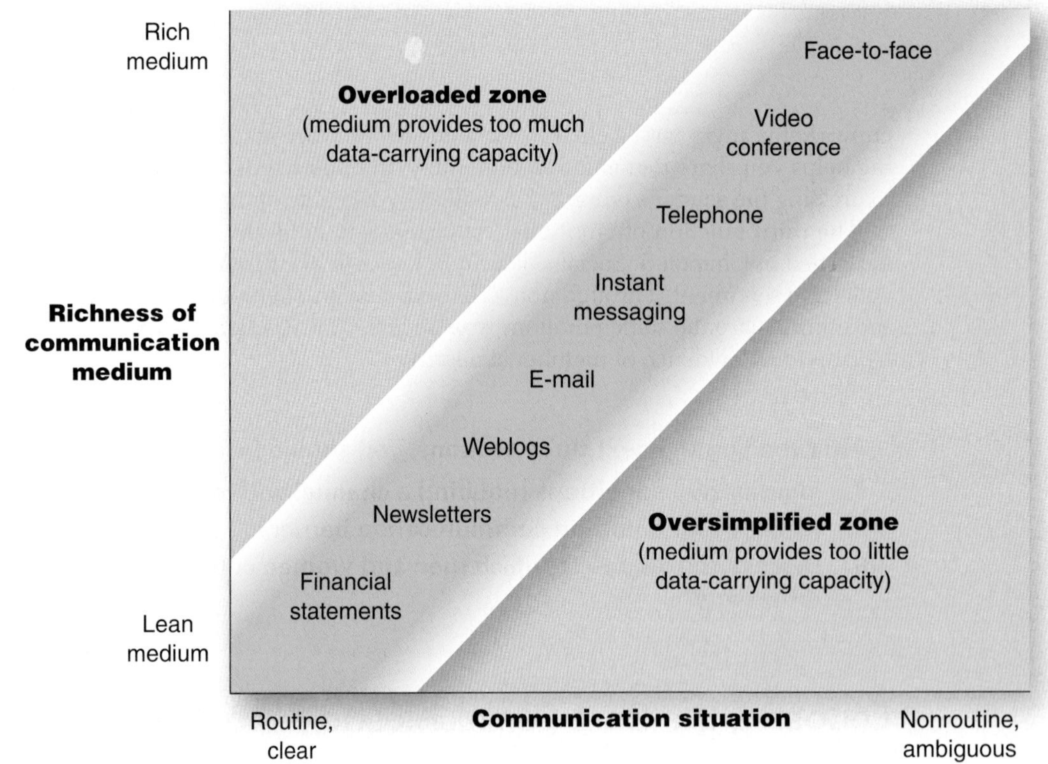

Source: Based on R. Lengel and R. Daft, "The Selection of Communication Media as an Executive Skill," *Academy of Management Executive* 2, no. 3 (August, 1988), p. 226; R.L. Daft and R.H. Lengel, "Information Richness: A New Approach to Managerial Behavior and Organization Design," *Research in Organizational Behavior*, 1984, p. 199.

quickly adjust their face-to-face conversations to suit the situation (such as the receiver's status or interest in the topic), whereas financial reports have low media richness because one size fits all—everyone gets the same information.

Exhibit 11.2 shows that rich media are better than lean media when the communication situation is nonroutine and ambiguous. In nonroutine situations (such as an unexpected and unusual emergency) the sender and receiver have little common experience, so they need to transmit a large volume of information with immediate feedback. Lean media work well in routine situations because the sender and receiver have common expectations through shared mental models. Ambiguous situations also require rich media because the parties must share large amounts of information with immediate feedback to resolve multiple and conflicting interpretations of their observations and experiences.[17]

What happens when we choose the wrong level of media richness for a situation? When the situation is routine or clear, using a rich medium—such as holding a special meeting—would seem like a waste of time. On the other hand, if a unique and ambiguous issue is handled through e-mail or another lean medium, then issues take longer to resolve and misunderstandings are more likely to occur.

Evaluating Media Richness Theory Research studying traditional channels (face-to-face communication, written memos, and so forth) generally supports the media richness proposition: Rich media are better than lean media when the situation is nonroutine or ambiguous. But the evidence is mixed when emerging information technologies are studied. One reason for this inconsistency is that we need to take into account the communicator's previous experience with e-mail, IM, and other means of communication that do not exist naturally. People who have plenty of experience with a particular communication medium can "push" the amount of media richness normally possible through that information channel. Experienced Blackberry users, for instance, can whip through messages in a flash, whereas new users struggle to type e-mail notes and organize incoming messages. Experience is less relevant with verbal conversation, report writing, and other traditional methods because they are learned early in life and, indeed, may be hardwired in our evolutionary development.[18]

A second factor to consider is the communicator's previous experience with the receiver. The more two or more people share common mental models, the less information exchange is required to communicate new meaning. People who know each other have similar "codebooks," so the sender can communicate with fewer words or other symbols and doesn't need to check as closely that the message has been understood. Without this common codebook, the sender needs to add in more redundancy (such as saying the same thing in two different ways) and requires more efficient feedback to ensure that the receiver understood the message.

Symbolic Meaning of the Medium

"The medium is the message."[19] This famous phrase by communications guru Marshall McLuhan means that the channel of communication has social consequences as much as (or perhaps more than) the content that passes through that medium. McLuhan was referring mainly to the influence of television and other "new media" on society; but this concept applies equally well to how the symbolic meaning of a communication medium influences our interpretation of the message and the relationship between sender and receiver.

The medium-as-message principle was apparent when KPMG gave layoff notices to hundreds of its British employees via e-mail. The public swiftly criticized the consulting firm—not because of the content of the message but because of the medium through which it was transmitted. Ironically KPMG delivered the bad news by e-mail because most employees had specifically asked for this method. Yet even the KPMG executives who sent the layoff notices were hesitant. "I was horrified about telling staff via e-mail as I knew it would make us look callous," admitted one executive.[20] The point here is that we need to be sensitive to the symbolic meaning of the communication medium to ensure that it amplifies rather than misinterprets the meaning found in the message content.

Communication Barriers (Noise)

In spite of the best intentions of sender and receiver to communicate, several barriers inhibit the effective exchange of information. As author George Bernard Shaw wrote, "The greatest problem with communication is the illusion that it has been accomplished." Four pervasive communication barriers (called "noise" earlier in Exhibit 11.1) are perceptions, filtering, language, and information overload. Later we will also investigate cross-cultural and gender communication barriers.

Perceptions

The perceptual process determines what messages we select or screen out, as well as how the selected information is organized and interpreted. This can be a significant source of noise in the communication process if the sender and receiver have different perceptual frames and mental models. For instance, corporate leaders are watched closely by employees, and the most inane words or gestures are interpreted with great meaning even though they often occur without intention.

Filtering

Some messages are filtered or stopped altogether on their way up or down the organizational hierarchy. Filtering may involve deleting or delaying negative information or using less harsh words so that events sound more favorable.[21] Employees and supervisors usually filter communication to create a good impression of themselves to superiors. Filtering is most common where the organization rewards employees who communicate mainly positive information and punishes those who convey bad news. John Stewart admits that reducing filtering isn't easy. "We have been trying hard to get people to be more open," says the chief executive of National Australia Bank. "To do that, you have to make sure your senior people are listening to staff when they bring problems to them, and not killing the messenger.... You have to do it–otherwise people will stop telling you and then nothing gets fixed."[22]

Language Barriers

Language problems can be a huge source of communication noise. Recall from Exhibit 11.1 that the sender encodes the message and the receiver decodes it. To make this process work, both parties need to have the same "codebook"; that is, they need to have a mutual understanding of what the words or other symbols being sent mean. Even when both people speak the same language, they might interpret words and phrases differently. If someone says "Would you like to check the figures again?" he or she may be politely *telling* you to double-check the figures or might be merely *asking* if you want to do this.

This language ambiguity isn't always dysfunctional noise.[23] Corporate leaders sometimes rely on metaphors and other vague language to describe ill-defined or complex ideas. Ambiguity is also used to avoid conveying or creating undesirable emotions. For example, one recent study reported that people rely on more ambiguous language when communicating with people who have different values and beliefs. In these situations ambiguity minimizes the risk of conflict.

jargon
The technical language and acronyms as well as recognized words with specialized meaning in specific organizations or social groups.

Along with ambiguity, people who generally speak the same language might not understand specific jargon within that language. **Jargon** consists of technical language and acronyms as well as recognized words with specialized meaning in specific organizations or social groups. Some jargon can improve communication efficiency when both sender and receiver understand this specialized language. But technical experts (including organizational behavior teachers!) sometimes use jargon without realizing that listeners don't have the codebook to translate those special words. In fact, one recent survey found that people react negatively to unnecessary jargon, which is probably contrary to the sender's intention to look "cool" using the latest buzzwords.[24]

Information Overload

Toni Ballard is busy enough with her music career in Massachusetts, but the continuous flow of 50 to 75 e-mail messages each day also takes a huge chunk of her time. To keep up, she will read through the high-priority items and move them into folders; but others might sit in Ballard's e-mail inbox for several days. "It's nice to be kept informed, but obviously, if you read it all the time, you'd never get anything done," says Ballard. In fact, some people *don't* get much else done beyond processing their e-mail! One estimate is that 22.3 trillion e-mail messages are now transmitted annually, up from just 1.1 trillion in 1998. A major U.S. survey recently revealed that professionals send and receive an average of 19,200 e-mail messages annually and spend an average of two hours per day processing e-mail.[25]

information overload
A condition in which the volume of information received exceeds a person's capacity to get through it.

E-mail is only one source of communication. Add in voice mail, cell phone text messages, Web site scanning, PDF file downloads, hard copy documents, and other sources of incoming information, and you have a perfect recipe for **information overload**.[26] Information overload occurs when the volume of information received exceeds a person's capacity to get through it. Employees have a certain *information processing capacity*–the amount of information that they are able to process in a fixed unit of time. At the same time, jobs have a varying *information load*–the amount of information to be processed per unit of time.[27] As Exhibit 11.3 illustrates, information overload occurs whenever a job's information load exceeds an individual's information processing capacity.

"That's my commendation for deciphering all the sales talk when we needed to upgrade the computer."

Information overload creates noise in the communication system because information gets overlooked or misinterpreted when people can't process it fast enough. It has also become a common cause of workplace stress. These problems can be minimized by increasing our information processing capacity, reducing the job's information load, or a combination of both. Information processing capacity increases when we learn to read faster, scan through documents more efficiently, and remove distractions that slow information processing speed. Time management also increases information processing capacity. When information overload is temporary, we can increase information processing capacity by working longer hours.

Exhibit 11.3
Dynamics of Information Overload

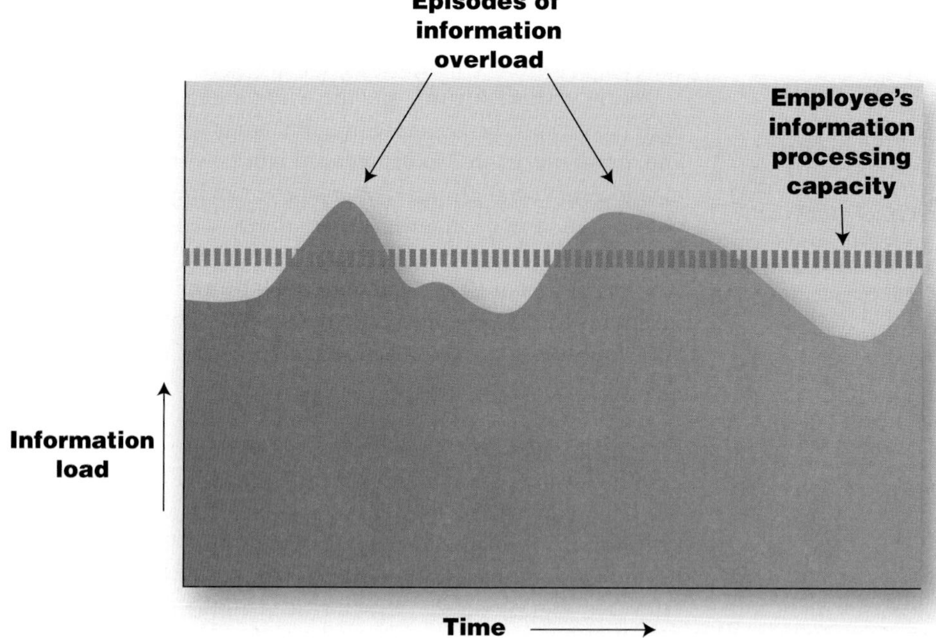

Three strategies help us to reduce information load: buffering, omitting, and summarizing.[28] Consider Microsoft chairman Bill Gates. Gates receives approximately 300 e-mail messages daily from Microsoft addresses that are outside a core group of people; these messages are buffered–routed to an assistant who reads each and sends Gates only the 30 or so messages considered essential. Gates also applies the omitting strategy by using software rules to redirect e-mail messages from distribution lists, nonessential sources, and junk mail (spam). These messages are dumped into preassigned folders to be read later, if ever. Gates likely also relies on the summarizing strategy by reading executive summaries rather than entire reports on some issues.

Perceptions, filtering, language barriers, and information overload are not the only sources of noise in the communication process; but they are probably the most common. Noise also occurs when we communicate across cultures or genders, both of which are discussed next.

Cross-Cultural and Cross-Gender Communication

In a world of increasing globalization and cultural diversity, organizations face new opportunities as well as communication challenges.[29] Language is the most obvious cross-cultural communication challenge. Words are easily misunderstood in verbal communication either because the receiver has a limited vocabulary or because the sender's accent distorts the usual sound of some words. The issue is further complicated in global organizations where employees from non-English countries often rely on English as the common business language. The problem discussed earlier of ambiguous language becomes amplified across cultures. For example, a French executive might call an event a "catastrophe" as a casual exaggeration, whereas someone in Germany usually interprets this word literally as an earth-shaking event.[30]

Mastering the same language improves one dimension of cross-cultural communication, but problems may still occur when interpreting voice intonation. Middle

Easterners tend to speak loudly to show sincerity and interest in the discussion, whereas Japanese people tend to speak softly to communicate politeness or humility. These different cultural norms regarding voice loudness may cause one person to misinterpret the other.

Nonverbal Differences

Nonverbal communication is more important in some cultures than in others. For example, people in Japan interpret more of a message's meaning from nonverbal cues. To avoid offending or embarrassing the receiver (particularly outsiders), Japanese people will often say what the other person wants to hear (called *tatemae*) but send more subtle nonverbal cues indicating the sender's true feelings (called *honne*). A Japanese colleague might politely reject your business proposal by saying "I will think about that" while sending nonverbal signals that he or she is not really interested. "In Japan, they have seven ways to say no; they never want to offend," advises Rick Davidson, global CIO at Manpower, Inc. "Sometimes they nod their head, and you think you have an agreement, but they're just saying, 'I hear you.' "[31]

Many unconscious or involuntary nonverbal cues (such as smiling) have the same meaning around the world, but deliberate gestures often have different interpretations. For example, most of us shake our head from side to side to say "No," but a variation of head shaking means "I understand" to many people in India. Filipinos raise their eyebrows to give an affirmative answer, yet Arabs interpret this expression (along with clicking one's tongue) as a negative response. Most Westerners are taught to maintain eye contact with the speaker to show interest and respect; yet Native Americans, Australian Aborigines, and others learn at an early age to show respect by looking down when an older or more senior person is talking to them.[32]

Even the common handshake communicates different meaning across cultures. Westerners tend to appreciate a firm handshake as a sign of strength and warmth in a friendship or business relationship. In contrast, many Asians and Middle Easterners favor a loose grip and regard a firm clench as aggressive. Germans prefer one good

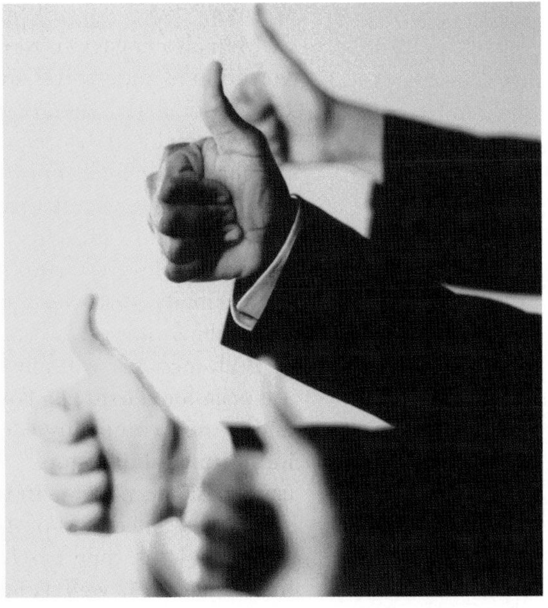

Thumbs-Up for Cross-Cultural (Mis)communication Patricia Oliveira made several cultural adjustments when she moved from Brazil to Australia. One of the more humorous incidents occurred in the Melbourne office where she works. A co-worker would stick his thumbs up when asked about something, signaling that everything was OK. But the gesture had a totally different meaning to Oliveira and other people from Brazil. "He asked me why I was laughing and I had to explain that in Brazil, that sign means something not very nice," recalls Oliveira. "After that, everyone started doing it to the boss. It was really funny."[33]

handshake stroke, whereas anything less than five or six strokes may symbolize a lack of trust in Spain. If this isn't confusing enough, people from some cultures view any touching in public–including handshakes–as a sign of rudeness.

Silence and Conversational Overlaps Communication includes silence, but its use and meaning varies from one culture to another.[34] A recent study estimated that silence and pauses represented 30 percent of conversation time between Japanese doctors and patients, compared to only 8 percent of the time between American doctors and patients. Why is there more silence in Japanese conversations? In Japan silence symbolizes respect and indicates that the listener is thoughtfully contemplating what has just been said.[35] Empathy is also important in Japan, and this shared understanding is demonstrated without using words. In contrast, most people in the United States and many other cultures view silence as a *lack* of communication and often interpret long breaks as a sign of disagreement.

Conversational overlaps also send different messages in different cultures. Japanese people usually stop talking when they are interrupted, whereas talking over the other person's speech is more common in Brazil and some other countries. The difference in communication behavior is again due to interpretations. Talking while someone is speaking to you is considered quite rude in Japan, whereas Brazilians are more likely to interpret this as a person's interest and involvement in the conversation.

Gender Differences in Communication

A number of popular books about gender differences in communication seem to conclude that men and women are completely different life forms from different planets.[36] In reality men and women have similar communication practices, but there are subtle distinctions that can occasionally lead to misunderstanding and conflict. One distinction is that men are more likely than women to view conversations as negotiations of relative status and power. They assert their power by directly giving advice to others ("You should do the following") and using combative language. There is also evidence that men dominate the talk time in conversations with women, as well as interrupt more, and adjust their speaking style less than women.[37]

Men also engage in more "report talk," in which the primary function of the conversation is impersonal and efficient information exchange. Women also use report talk, particularly when conversing with men; but conversations among women have a higher incidence of relationship building through "rapport talk." This emphasis on rapport rather than report talk is also apparent in studies of how women communicate in e-mail and other forms of online communication. Another gender distinction is that women use indirect requests such as "Have you considered... ?" Similarly, women apologize more often and seek advice from others more quickly than do men. Finally, research fairly consistently indicates that women are more sensitive than men to nonverbal cues in face-to-face meetings.[38]

Both men and women usually understand each other, but these subtle differences are occasional irritants. For instance, female scientists have complained that male scientists use a competitive debating style that makes it difficult for women to participate in meaningful dialogue.[39] Another irritant occurs when women seek empathy but receive male dominance in response. Specifically, women sometimes discuss their personal experiences and problems to develop closeness with the receiver. But when men hear problems, they quickly suggest solutions because this asserts their control over the situation. As well as frustrating a woman's need for common understanding, the advice actually says, "You and I are different; you have the problem and I have the answer." Meanwhile men become frustrated because they can't understand why women don't appreciate their advice.

Learning Objectives

After reading the next three sections, you should be able to

7. Outline the key elements of active listening.

8. Summarize four communication strategies in organizational hierarchies.

Improving Interpersonal Communication

Effective interpersonal communication depends on the sender's ability to get the message across and the receiver's performance as an active listener. In this section we outline these two essential features of effective interpersonal communication.

Getting Your Message Across

This chapter began with the statement that effective communication occurs when the other person receives and understands the message. To accomplish this difficult task the sender must learn to empathize with the receiver, repeat the message, choose an appropriate time for the conversation, and be descriptive rather than evaluative:

- *Empathize.* Recall from earlier chapters that empathy is a person's ability to understand and be sensitive to the feelings, thoughts, and situation of others. In conversations this involves putting yourself in the receiver's shoes when encoding the message. For instance, be sensitive to words that may be ambiguous or trigger the wrong emotional response.
- *Repeat the message.* Rephrase the key points a couple of times. The saying "Tell them what you're going to tell them; tell them; then tell them what you've told them" reflects this need for redundancy.
- *Use timing effectively.* Your message competes with other messages and noise, so find a time when the receiver is less likely to be distracted by these other matters.
- *Be descriptive.* Focus on the problem, not the person, if you have negative information to convey. People stop listening when the information attacks their self-esteem. Also, suggest things the listener can do to improve, rather than point to him or her as a problem.

Active Listening

"Nature gave people two ears but only one tongue, which is a gentle hint that they should listen more than they talk." Henry Schacht has followed this sage advice for most of his career. "The experience of doing nothing but being a very good listener for as long as you can stand it is the most important thing to do," advises the former CEO of Lucent Technologies in New Jersey.[40] To follow this advice, we need to recognize that listening is a process of actively sensing the sender's signals, evaluating them accurately, and responding appropriately. These three components of listening–sensing, evaluating, and responding–reflect the listener's side of the communication model described at the beginning of this chapter. Listeners receive the sender's signals, decode them as intended, and provide appropriate and timely feedback to the

Exhibit 11.4
Active Listening Process and Strategies

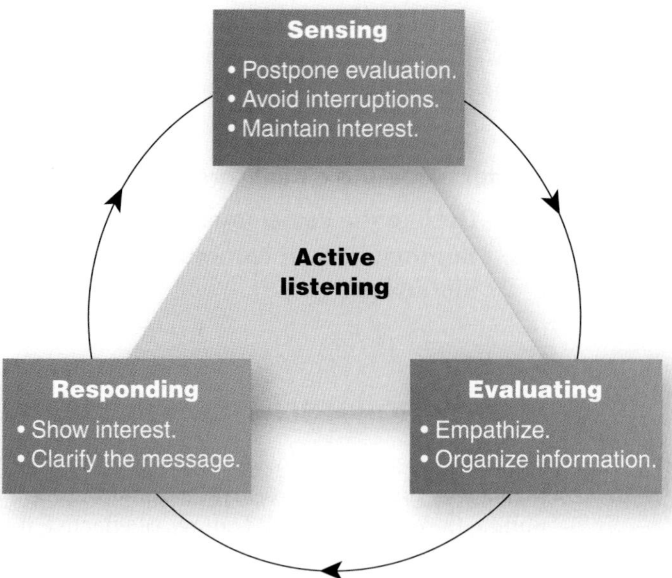

sender (see Exhibit 11.4). Active listeners constantly cycle through sensing, evaluating, and responding during the conversation and engage in various activities to improve these processes.[41]

Sensing Sensing is the process of receiving signals from the sender and paying attention to them. These signals include the words spoken, the nature of the sounds (speed of speech, tone of voice,and so on), and nonverbal cues. Active listeners improve sensing by postponing evaluation, avoiding interruptions, and maintaining interest:

- *Postpone evaluation.* Many listeners become victims of first impressions. They quickly form an opinion of the speaker's message and subsequently screen out important information. Active listeners, on the other hand, try to stay as open-minded as possible by delaying evaluation of the message until the speaker has finished.
- *Avoid interruptions.* Interrupting the speaker's conversation has two negative effects on the sensing process. First, it disrupts the speaker's idea, so the listener does not receive the entire message. Second, interruptions tend to second-guess what the speaker is trying to say, which contributes to the problem of evaluating the speaker's ideas too early.
- *Maintain interest.* As with any behavior, active listening requires motivation. Too often we close our minds soon after a conversation begins because the subject is boring. Instead active listeners maintain interest by taking the view–probably an accurate one–that there is always something of value in a conversation; it's just a matter of actively looking for it.

Evaluating This component of listening includes understanding the message meaning, evaluating the message, and remembering the message. To improve their evaluation of the conversation, active listeners empathize with the speaker and organize information received during the conversation:

- *Empathize.* Active listeners try to understand and be sensitive to the speaker's feelings, thoughts, and situation. Empathy is a critical skill in active listening because the verbal and nonverbal cues from the conversation are accurately interpreted from the other person's point of view.

- *Organize information.* Listeners process information three times faster than the average rate of speech (450 words per minute versus 125 words per minute), so they are easily distracted. Active listeners use this spare time to organize the information into key points. In fact, it's a good idea to imagine that you must summarize what people have said after they are finished speaking.

Responding Responding, the third component of listening, is feedback to the sender, which motivates and directs the speaker's communication. Active listeners do this by showing interest and clarifying the message:

- *Show interest.* Active listeners show interest by maintaining sufficient eye contact and sending back channel signals such as "Oh, really!" and "I see" during appropriate breaks in the conversation.
- *Clarify the message.* Active listeners provide feedback by rephrasing the speaker's ideas at appropriate breaks ("So you're saying that...?"). This further demonstrates interest in the conversation and helps the speaker determine whether you understand the message.

Communicating in Organizational Hierarchies

So far we have focused on "micro-level" issues in the communication process–namely the dynamics of sending and receiving information between two people in various situations. But in this era where knowledge is competitive advantage, corporate leaders also need to maintain an open flow of communication up, down, and across the organization. This section introduces four organizationwide communication strategies: workspace design, e-zines/blogs/wikis, employee surveys, and direct communication with top management.

Workspace Design

The ability and motivation to communicate is to some extent influenced by the physical space in which employees work. The location and design of hallways, offices, cubicles, and communal areas (cafeterias, elevators) all shape whom we speak to as

Pixar Building Animates Communication Communication was a top priority when Pixar Animation Studios designed its new campus in Emeryville, California, a few years ago. The animation company that brought us *The Incredibles, Finding Nemo,* and other blockbuster films created work areas that cluster team members and encourage ongoing informal communication. At the same time the campus is designed so that employees share knowledge through happenstance interactions with people on other teams. Pixar executives call this the "bathroom effect": Team members must leave their isolated pods to fetch their mail, have lunch, or visit the restroom. The building also invites staff to mingle in the central airy atrium. "It promotes that chance encounter," says Pixar creative director John Lasseter. "You run into people constantly. It worked from the minute we arrived. We just blossomed here."[42]

well as the frequency of that communication. Some companies try to encourage communication within the team by organizing employees into clusters. This cluster approach is used at product design firm IDEO. The physical space literally groups employees together so face-to-face communication within the team is easy, whereas interaction with people in other teams is minimized.

Another increasingly popular workspace strategy is to replace traditional offices with open space arrangements in which all employees (including management) work in the same open area. Anecdotal evidence suggests that people do communicate more often with fewer walls between them. However, research also suggests that open office design potentially increases employee stress due to the loss of privacy and personal space. According to an analysis of 13,000 employee surveys in 40 major organizations, the most important function of workspace is to provide a place to concentrate on work without distraction. The second most important function is to support informal communication with co-workers.[43] In other words, workspace needs to balance privacy with opportunities for social interaction.

E-Zines, Blogs, and Wikis

For decades, employees have received official company news through hard copy newsletters and magazines. Many firms still use these communication devices, but most have supplemented or replaced them completely with Web-based information sources. Web-based or PDF-only format newsletters, called *e-zines*, are inexpensive and allow companies to post new information quickly. However, information from e-zines tends to be brief because many employees have difficulty reading long articles on a computer screen.[44]

The opening story to this chapter described how *blogs* are entering the corporate world as another communication vehicle. One recent survey reported that while only 7 percent of CEOs engage in blogging, 59 percent believed that blogs are useful for communicating with employees.[45] Blogs written by senior executives offer direct communication to employees and, if written casually, have a personal touch that makes the information more credible than formal magazines. Executive blogs also allow employees to submit their comments, which isn't possible in e-zines or newsletters. In addition to executive blogs, Matsushita and a few other firms are turning to employee blogs in which people in a work unit post updates about events in their areas.

Wikis (Hawaiian for "fast") are a collaborative variation of blogs in which anyone in a group can write, edit, or remove material from the Web site. Wikipedia, the popular online encyclopedia, is a massive example of a wiki. Wikis are also slowly finding their way into traditional organizations. Employees at Aperture Technologies Inc. in Stamford, Connecticut, use wikis to write documentation, brainstorm ideas, and coordinate marketing projects. "Wikis allow this collaboration much better than anything else, so we get things done faster," says Aperture founder Nicholas Pisarro Jr.[46]

Employee Surveys

Almost all of the "best companies to work for," as well as the majority of large firms throughout the United States and several other countries, conduct employee surveys at least once each year. In fact, leaders in two-thirds of high-performing companies claim that surveying employees is one of their most effective ways to strengthen employee engagement levels. Surveys are useful upward communication devices for a variety of purposes. Tennessee Valley Authority surveys its employees annually using a 60-item "cultural health index" that the energy producer found predicts subsequent

Kowloon Shangri-La's "State of the Hotel" Meetings Communicating with employees can be a challenge when the organization is a large hotel that operates around the clock. But these conditions haven't prevented senior management at Kowloon Shangri-La from holding "state of the hotel" meetings with all 700 staff twice each year. Two sessions are held—one in the morning, the other in the afternoon—so all employees at the Hong Kong hotel can attend without leaving the hotel short-staffed. General manager Mark Heywood conducts no-holds-barred sessions in which employees are updated about the hotel's financial performance, upcoming events, and renovations. "It's a chance to communicate about the good, the bad, and the ugly," says Heywood. "We don't just share good news and positive things." He also outlines his vision for the hotel and reinforces its "one team-one way" culture.[47]

productivity in each work unit. Bell Canada surveys its 60,000 employees each year using 84 questions about several themes, including career mobility, job challenge, information sharing, and trust in the company's leadership. Canada's largest telephone company also has quarterly "pulse surveys" that measure attitudes about specific policies such as early retirement.[48]

Direct Communication with Top Management

"The best fertilizer in any field is that of the farmer's footsteps!" This old Chinese saying means that farms are most successful when the farmers spend time in the fields directly observing the crop's development. In an organizational context this means that to fully understand the issues, senior executives need to get out of the executive suite and meet directly with employees at all levels and on their turf. Nearly 40 years ago people at Hewlett-Packard coined a phrase for this communication strategy: **management by walking around (MBWA)**.[49] Greg Aasen, chief operating officer and cofounder of PMC-Sierra, does his MBWA by running with employees during lunch. "Even the senior guys I've worked with for 10 years, they tell you a lot more running out on the trails than they would in your office. It's less intimidating, I guess," says Aasen.[50]

management by walking around (MBWA)
A communication practice in which executives get out of their offices and learn from others in the organization through face-to-face dialogue.

Along with MBWA, executives are getting more direct communication with employees through "town hall meetings," where large groups of employees hear about a merger or other special news directly from the key decision makers. For example, soon after becoming chief executive of McDonald's in the UK, Peter Beresford instituted a monthly online town hall event where board members answer questions from any McDonald's staff.[51] Some executives also conduct employee roundtable forums to hear opinions from a small representation of staff about various issues. All of these direct communication strategies potentially minimize filtering because executives listen directly to employees. They also help executives acquire a deeper, quicker understanding of internal organizational problems. A third benefit of direct communication is that employees might have more empathy for decisions made further up the corporate hierarchy.

Communicating through the Grapevine

grapevine
An unstructured, informal network founded on social relationships rather than organizational charts or job descriptions.

No matter how much corporate leaders try to communicate through e-zines, blogs, wikis, surveys, MBWA, and other means, employees will still rely on the oldest communication channel: the corporate **grapevine**. The grapevine is an unstructured, informal network founded on social relationships rather than organizational charts or job descriptions. What do employees think about the grapevine? Surveys of employees in two U.S. firms–one in Florida, the other in California–provide the answer. Both surveys found that almost all employees use the grapevine, but very few of them prefer this source of information. The California survey also reported that only one-third of employees believe grapevine information is credible. In other words, employees turn to the grapevine when they have few other options.[52]

Grapevine Characteristics

Research conducted several decades ago reported that the grapevine transmits information very rapidly in all directions throughout the organization. The typical pattern is a cluster chain, whereby a few people actively transmit rumors to many others. The grapevine works through informal social networks, so it is more active where employees have similar backgrounds and can communicate easily. Many rumors seem to have at least a kernel of truth, possibly because they are transmitted through media-rich communication channels (face-to-face) and employees are motivated to communicate effectively. Nevertheless, the grapevine distorts information by deleting fine details and exaggerating key points of the story.[53]

Some of these characteristics might still be true, but other features of the grapevine have changed due to the dramatic effects of information technologies in the workplace. E-mail, instant messages, and even blogs have replaced the traditional water cooler as sources of gossip. Social networks have expanded as employees communicate with each other around the globe, not just around the next cubicle. Public blogs and Web forums have extended gossip to anyone–not just employees connected to social networks.

Grapevine Benefits and Limitations

Should the grapevine be encouraged, tolerated, or quashed? The difficulty in answering this question is that the grapevine has both benefits and limitations.[54] One benefit, as was mentioned earlier, is that employees rely on the grapevine when information is not available through formal channels. It is also the main conduit through which organizational stories and other symbols of the organization's culture are communicated. A third benefit of the grapevine is that this social interaction relieves anxiety. This explains why rumor mills are most active during times of uncertainty.[55] Finally, the grapevine is associated with the drive to bond. Being a recipient of gossip is a sign of inclusion, according to evolutionary psychologists. Trying to quash the grapevine is, in some respects, an attempt to undermine the natural human drive for social interaction.[56]

Although the grapevine offers these benefits, it is not the preferred communication medium. Grapevine information is sometimes so distorted that it escalates rather than reduces employee anxiety. Furthermore, employees develop more negative attitudes toward the organization when management is slower than the grapevine in communicating information. What should corporate leaders do with the grapevine? The best advice seems to be to listen to the grapevine as a signal of employee anxiety, then correct the cause of this anxiety. Some companies also listen to the grapevine and step in to correct blatant errors and fabrications. Most important, corporate leaders need to view the grapevine as a competitor–and eventually win the challenge to inform employees before they receive the news through the grapevine.

Chapter Summary

Communication refers to the process by which information is transmitted and understood between two or more people. Communication supports work coordination, employee well-being, knowledge management, and decision making. The communication process involves forming, encoding, and transmitting the intended message to a receiver, who then decodes the message and provides feedback to the sender. Effective communication occurs when the sender's thoughts are transmitted to and understood by the intended receiver.

Electronic mail (e-mail) is an increasingly popular way to communicate, and it has changed communication patterns in organizational settings. However, e-mail is an ineffective channel for communicating emotions; tends to reduce politeness and respect; is an inefficient medium for communicating in ambiguous, complex, and novel situations; and contributes to information overload. Instant messaging, blogs, and podcasts are also gaining popularity in organizations.

Nonverbal communication includes facial gestures, voice intonation, physical distance, and even silence. Unlike verbal communication, nonverbal communication is less rule-bound and is mostly automatic and unconscious. Emotional contagion refers to the automatic and unconscious tendency to mimic and synchronize our nonverbal behaviors with other people. The most appropriate communication medium depends on its data-carrying capacity (media richness) and its symbolic meaning to the receiver. Nonroutine and ambiguous situations require rich media.

Several barriers create noise in the communication process. People misinterpret messages because of perceptual biases. Some information is filtered out as it gets passed up the hierarchy. Jargon and ambiguous language are barriers when the sender and receiver have different interpretations of the words and symbols used. People also screen out or misinterpret messages due to information overload.

Globalization and workforce diversity have brought new communication challenges. Words are easily misunderstood in verbal communication if the receiver has a limited vocabulary or if the sender's accent distorts the usual sound of some words. Voice intonation, silence, and nonverbal cues have different meanings and importance in other cultures. There are also some communication differences between men and women, such as the tendency for men to exert status and engage in report talk in conversations, whereas women use more rapport talk and are more sensitive than are men to nonverbal cues.

To get a message across, the sender must learn to empathize with the receiver, repeat the message, choose an appropriate time for the conversation, and be descriptive rather than evaluative. Listening includes sensing, evaluating, and responding. Active listeners support these processes by postponing evaluation, avoiding interruptions, maintaining interest, empathizing, organizing information, showing interest, and clarifying the message.

Some companies try to encourage informal communication through workspace design, although open offices run the risk of increasing stress and reducing the ability to concentrate on work. Many larger organizations also rely on e-zines to communicate corporate news. Employee surveys are widely used to measure employee attitudes or involve employees in corporate decisions. Some executives also meet directly with employees, through either management by walking around or other arrangements, to facilitate communication across the organization.

In any organization employees rely on the grapevine, particularly during times of uncertainty. The grapevine is an unstructured, informal network founded on social relationships rather than organizational charts or job descriptions. Although early research identified several unique features of the grapevine, some of these features may be changing as the Internet plays an increasing role in grapevine communication.

Key Terms

communication, p. 314
emotional contagion, p. 318
flaming, p. 316
grapevine, p. 331
information overload, p. 323
jargon, p. 323
management by walking around (MBWA), p. 331
media richness, p. 319

Critical Thinking Questions

1. A company in a country that is just entering the information age intends to introduce electronic mail for office staff at its three buildings located throughout the city. Describe two benefits as well as two potential problems that employees will likely experience with this medium.
2. Corporate and employee blogs might become increasingly popular over the next few years. What

are the advantages and disadvantages of this communication medium?

3. Marshall McLuhan coined the popular phrase "The medium is the message." What does this phrase mean, and why should we be aware of it when communicating in organizations?
4. Why is emotional contagion important in organizations? What effect does the increasing reliance on e-mail have on this phenomenon?
5. Under what conditions, if any, do you think it is appropriate to use e-mail to notify an employee that he or she has been laid off or fired? Why is e-mail usually considered an inappropriate channel to convey such information?
6. Explain why men and women are sometimes frustrated with each other's communication behaviors.
7. In your opinion, has the introduction of e-mail and other information technologies increased or decreased the amount of information flowing through the corporate grapevine? Explain your answer.
8. Wikis are collaborative Web sites where anyone in a group can post, edit, or delete any information. Where might this communication technology be most useful in organizations?

Case Study 11.1 BRIDGING THE TWO WORLDS—THE ORGANIZATIONAL DILEMMA

William Todorovic, Purdue University

I had been hired by Aluminum Elements Corp. (AEC), and it was my first day of work. I was 26 years old, and I was now the manager of AEC's customer service group, which looked after customers, logistics, and some of the raw material purchasing. My superior, George, was the vice president of the company. AEC manufactured most of its products, a majority of which were destined for the construction industry, from aluminum.

As I walked around the shop floor, the employees appeared to be concentrating on their jobs, barely noticing me. Management held daily meetings in which various production issues were discussed. No one from the shop floor was invited to these meetings unless there was a specific problem. Later I also learned that management had separate washrooms and separate lunchrooms, as well as other perks that floor employees did not have. Most of the floor employees felt that management, although polite on the surface, did not really feel they had anything to learn from the floor employees.

John, who worked on the aluminum slitter, a crucial operation required before any other operations could commence, had suffered a number of unpleasant encounters with George. As a result George usually sent written memos to the floor to avoid a direct confrontation with John. Because the directions in the memos were complex, these memos were often more than two pages in length.

One morning as I was walking around, I noticed that John was very upset. Feeling that perhaps there was something I could do, I approached John and asked him if I could help. He indicated that everything was just fine. From the looks of the situation and John's body language, I felt that he was willing to talk, but John knew that this was not the way things were done at AEC. Tony, who worked at the machine next to John's, then cursed and said that the office guys cared only about schedules, not about the people down on the floor. I just looked at him, and then said that I began working here only last week, and I thought that I could address some of their issues. Tony gave me a strange look, shook his head, and went back to his machine. I could hear him still swearing as I left. Later I realized that most of the office staff were also offended by Tony's language.

On the way back to my office Lesley, a recently hired engineer from Russia, approached me and pointed out that the employees were not accustomed to managers talking to them. Managers only issued orders and made demands. As we discussed the different perceptions between office and floor staff, we were interrupted by a loud lunch bell, which startled me. I was happy to join Lesley for lunch, but she asked me why I was not eating in the office lunchroom. I replied that if I was going to understand how AEC worked, I had to get to know all the people better. In addition, I realized that this was not how things were done, and I wondered about the nature of this apparent division between the managers and the floor workers. In the lunchroom the other workers were amazed to see me there, commenting that I was just new and had not learned the ropes yet.

After lunch, when I asked George, my supervisor, about his recent confrontation with John, George was surprised that John got upset, and exclaimed, "I just wanted John to know that he did a great job, and as a result, we will be able to ship on time one large order to the West Coast. In fact, I thought I was complimenting him."

Earlier, Lesley had indicated that certain behavior was expected from managers and therefore from me. I reasoned that I do not think that this behavior works, and besides it is not what I believe or how I care to behave. For the next couple of months I simply walked around the floor and took every opportunity to talk to the shop floor employees. Often when the employees related specific information about their workplaces, I felt that it went over my head. Frequently I had to write down the information and revisit it later. I made a point of listening to them, identifying where they were coming from, and trying to understand them. I needed to keep my mind open to new ideas. Because the shop employees expected me to make requests and demands, I made a point of not doing any of that. Soon enough the employees became friendly and started to accept me as one of their own, or at least as a different type of management person.

During my third month of work the employees showed me how to improve the scheduling of jobs, especially those on the aluminum slitter. In fact, the greatest contribution was made by John, who demonstrated better ways to combine the most common slitting sizes and reduce waste by retaining some of the "common-sized" material for new orders. Seeing the opportunity, I programmed a spreadsheet to calculate and track inventory. This, in addition to better planning and forecasting, allowed us to reduce our new order turnarounds from four to five weeks to one or two days.

By the time I was employed for four months, I realized that members from other departments came to me and asked me to relay messages to the shop employees. When I asked why they were delegating this task to me, they stated that I spoke the same language as the shop employees. Increasingly I became the messenger for the office-to-floor shop communication.

One morning George called me into his office and complimented me on the levels of customer service and the improvements that had been achieved. As we talked, I mentioned that we could not have done it without John's help. "He really knows his stuff, and he is good," I said. I suggested that we consider him for some type of promotion. Also, I hoped that this would be a positive gesture that would improve the communication between the office and shop floor.

George turned and pulled a flyer out of his desk: "Here is a management skills seminar. Do you think we should send John to it?"

"That is a great idea," I exclaimed. "Perhaps it would be good if he were to receive the news from you directly, George." George agreed, and after discussing some other issues, we parted company.

That afternoon John came into my office, upset and ready to quit. "After all my effort and work, you guys are sending me for training seminars. So am I not good enough for you?"

Discussion Questions

1. What barriers to effective communication existed in Aluminum Elements Corp? How did the author deal with these? What would you do differently?
2. Identify and discuss why John was upset at the end of the case. What should the writer do at this time?

Case Study 11.2 INTO THE WILD BLOG YONDER

Defense contractors and aerospace companies aren't known for their openness, but Boeing Co. is embracing a level of transparency that would be unthinkable a few years ago. In some divisions of the Chicago-based company, executives are bearing their personal thoughts through internal Web logs (blogs) and sharing their public opinions through external blogs. James F. Albaugh, the chief executive of Boeing Integrated Defense Systems, uses an internal blog to get conversations going and allow employees to raise issues anonymously. Randy Baseler, vice president for marketing at Boeing Commercial Airplanes, got rapped when he started a Web log that wasn't personal enough, but has since "found his voice."

This *BusinessWeek* case study case study details the experiences of blogging at Boeing, including its potential benefits and problems. Read the full text of this *BusinessWeek* article at www.mhhe.com/mcshane4e and prepare for the discussion questions below.

Discussion Questions

1. Describe the main advantages that Boeing executives say that blogging offer the organization and its employees.
2. Some blogs work and some don't. Based on the information in this article, as well as your own opinions, what are the characteristics of successful blogs?

Source: S. Holmes, "Into the Wild Blog Yonder," *BusinessWeek*, 22 May 2006, 84.

Team Exercise 11.3 ANALYZING THE BLOGOSPHERE

PURPOSE This exercise is designed to help you understand the dynamics of corporate blogs as a way to communicate around organizations.

INSTRUCTIONS This activity is usually conducted between classes as a homework assignment. The instructor will divide the class into teams (although this exercise can also be conducted by individuals). Each team will identify a corporate blog (written by a company or government executive and aimed at customers, employees, or the wider community). The team will analyze content in the selected blog and answer the following questions for class (preferably with brief samples where applicable):

1. Who is the main intended audience of the selected blog?
2. To what extent do you think this blog attracts the interest of its intended audience? Please explain.
3. What are the main topics in recent postings about this organization? Are they mostly good or bad news? Why do you think this has occurred?

Team Exercise 11.4 ACTIVE LISTENING EXERCISE

Mary Gander, Winona State University

PURPOSE This exercise is designed to help you understand the dynamics of active listening in conversations and to develop active listening skills.

INSTRUCTIONS For each of the four vignettes presented here, student teams (or students working individually) will compose three statements that demonstrate active listening. Specifically, one statement will indicate that you show empathy for the situation; the second will ask for clarification and detail in a nonjudgmental way; and the third statement will provide nonevaluative feedback to the speaker. Here are details about each of these three types of responses:

> *Showing empathy: acknowledge feelings.* Sometimes it sounds like a speaker wants you to agree with him or her, but in reality the speaker mainly

wants you to understand how he or she feels. "Acknowledging feelings" involves taking in the speaker's statements while looking at the "whole message" including body language, tone of voice, and level of arousal, and trying to determine what emotion the speaker is conveying. Then you let the speaker know that you realize what he or she is feeling by acknowledging it in a sentence.

Asking for clarification and detail while withholding your judgment and own opinions. This conveys that you are trying to understand and not just trying to push your opinions onto the speaker. To formulate a relevant question in asking for more clarification, you will have to listen carefully to what the speaker says. Frame your question as someone trying to understand in more detail; often asking for a specific example is useful. This also helps the speaker evaluate his or her own opinions and perspective.

Providing nonevaluative feedback: feeding back the message you heard. This will allow the speaker to determine if he or she conveyed the message to you and will help prevent troublesome miscommunication. It will also help the speaker become more aware of how he or she is coming across to another person (self-evaluation). Just think about what the speaker is conveying; paraphrase it in your own words, and say it back to the speaker (without judging the correctness or merit of what was said), asking him or her if that is what was meant.

After teams (or individual students) have prepared the three statements for each vignette, the instructor will ask them to present their statements and explain how these statements satisfy the active listening criteria.

VIGNETTE #1 A colleague stops by your desk and says, "I am tired of the lack of leadership around here. The boss is so wishy-washy, he can't get tough with some of the slackers around here. They just keep milking the company, living off the rest of us. Why doesn't management do something about these guys? And *you* are always so supportive of the boss; he's not as good as you make him out to be."

Develop three statements that respond to the speaker in this vignette by (a) showing empathy, (b) seeking clarification, and (c) providing nonevaluative feedback.

VIGNETTE #2 Your co-worker stops by your cubicle; her voice and body language show stress, frustration, and even some fear. You know she has been working hard and has a strong need to get her work done on time and done well. You are trying to concentrate on some work and have had a number of interruptions already. She abruptly interrupts you and says, "This project is turning out to be a mess. Why can't the other three people on my team quit fighting with each other?"

Develop three statements that respond to the speaker in this vignette by (a) showing empathy, (b) seeking clarification, and (c) providing nonevaluative feedback.

VIGNETTE #3 One of your subordinates is working on an important project. He is an engineer who has good technical skills and knowledge and was selected for the project team because of that. He stops by your office and appears to be quite agitated: His voice is loud and strained, and his face has a look of bewilderment. He says, "I'm supposed to be working with four other people from four other departments on this new project, but they never listen to my ideas and seem to hardly know I'm at the meeting!"

Develop three statements that respond to the speaker in this vignette by (a) showing empathy, (b) seeking clarification, and (c) providing nonevaluative feedback.

VIGNETTE #4 Your subordinate comes into your office in a state of agitation, asking if she can talk to you. She is polite and sits down. She seems calm and does not have an angry look on her face. However, she says, "It seems like you consistently make up lousy schedules; you are unfair and unrealistic in the kinds of assignments you give certain people, me included. Everyone else is so intimidated they don't complain, but I think you need to know that this isn't right and it's got to change."

Develop three statements that respond to the speaker in this vignette by (a) showing empathy, (b) seeking clarification, and (c) providing nonevaluative feedback.

Team Exercise 11.5 CROSS-CULTURAL COMMUNICATION GAME

PURPOSE This exercise is designed to develop and test your knowledge of cross-cultural differences in communication and etiquette.

MATERIALS The instructor will provide one set of question-and-answer cards to each pair of teams.

INSTRUCTIONS

1. The class is divided into an even number of teams. Ideally each team would have three students. (Two- or four-student teams are possible if matched with an equal-sized team.) Each team is then paired with another team, and the paired teams (teams "A" and "B") are assigned a private space away from other matched teams.
2. The instructor will hand each pair of teams a stack of cards with the multiple-choice questions face down. These cards have questions and answers about cross-cultural differences in communication and etiquette. No books or other aids are allowed.
3. The exercise begins with a member of team A picking up one card from the top of the pile and posing the question on that card to members of team B. The information given to team B includes the question and all alternatives listed on the card. Team B has 30 seconds to give an answer after the question and alternatives have been read. Team B earns one point if the correct answer is given. If team B's answer is incorrect, however, team A earns that point. Correct answers to each question are indicated on the card and, of course, should not be revealed until the question is correctly answered or time is up. Whether or not team B answers correctly, it picks up the next card on the pile and asks its question to members of team A. In other words, cards are read alternately to each team. This procedure is repeated until all of the cards have been read or time has elapsed. The team receiving the most points wins.

Important note: The textbook provides little information pertaining to the questions in this exercise. Rather, you must rely on past learning, logic, and luck to win.

Source: ©2001 Steven L. McShane.

Self-Assessment 11.6

ACTIVE LISTENING SKILLS INVENTORY

PURPOSE This self-assessment is designed to help you estimate your strengths and weaknesses in various dimensions of active listening.

INSTRUCTIONS Think back to face-to-face conversations you have had with a co-worker or client in the office, hallway, factory floor, or other setting. Indicate the extent to which each item in the accompanying chart describes your behavior during those conversations. Answer each item as truthfully as possible to get an accurate estimate of where your active listening skills need improvement. Then use the scoring key in Appendix B to calculate your results for each scale. This exercise is completed alone so you can assess yourself honestly without concerns of social comparison. However, class discussion will focus on the important elements of active listening.

Active Listening Skills Inventory

Check the response to the right that best indicates the extent to which each statement describes you when listening to others.	Not at all	A little	Some-what	Very much
1. I keep an open mind about the speaker's point of view until he or she has finished talking.	☐	☐	☐	☐
2. While listening, I mentally sort out the speaker's ideas in a way that makes sense to me.	☐	☐	☐	☐
3. I stop the speaker and give my opinion when I disagree with something he or she has said.	☐	☐	☐	☐
4. People can often tell when I'm not concentrating on what they are saying.	☐	☐	☐	☐
5. I don't evaluate what a person is saying until he or she has finished talking.	☐	☐	☐	☐
6. When someone takes a long time to present a simple idea, I let my mind wander to other things.	☐	☐	☐	☐
7. I jump into conversations to present my views rather than wait and risk forgetting what I wanted to say.	☐	☐	☐	☐
8. I nod my head and make other gestures to show I'm interested in the conversation.	☐	☐	☐	☐
9. I can usually keep focused on what people are saying to me even when they don't sound interesting.	☐	☐	☐	☐
10. Rather than organizing the speaker's ideas, I usually expect the person to summarize them for me.	☐	☐	☐	☐
11. I always say things like "I see" or "uh-huh" so people know that I'm really listening to them.	☐	☐	☐	☐
12. While listening, I concentrate on what is being said and regularly organize the information.	☐	☐	☐	☐
13. While a speaker is talking, I quickly determine whether I like or dislike his or her ideas.	☐	☐	☐	☐
14. I pay close attention to what people are saying even when they are explaining something I already know.	☐	☐	☐	☐
15. I don't give my opinion until I'm sure the other person has finished talking.	☐	☐	☐	☐

After reading this chapter, if you need additional information, see **www.mhhe.com/mcshane4e** for more in-depth interactivities that correspond with this material.

For three long days junior trader Dennis Gentilin received the cold shoulder from his boss, Luke Duffy. Duffy, who ran National Australia Bank's (NAB) foreign currency options desk in Melbourne, had discovered that Gentilin complained to Duffy's boss, Gary Dillon, that Duffy was altering transaction records to "smooth" his group's profits. Smoothing (which includes carrying forward trading losses) was apparently common at one time, but traders had recently been warned to stop the practice.

National Australia Bank rogue trader Luke Duffy (shown here after sentencing) and his colleagues created losses of $350 million, thanks in part to Duffy's power and influence tactics.

On the fourth day, Duffy called Gentilin into a private meeting and, according to Gentilin, launched into a tirade: "I felt like ... killing someone the other day," Duffy said pointedly to Gentilin. "If you want to stay in the team, I demand loyalty and don't want you going to Dillon about what's happening in the team."

Duffy was apparently accustomed to getting his way. Gentilin explained that Duffy, Dillon, and a few other senior traders were "untouchables" who were given free rein at NAB due to their expertise. "They just created this power base where they were laws unto themselves," claims Gentilin.

Anyone who interfered with Duffy's plans was apparently mocked into submission. For example, Duffy taunted a co-worker in London who he thought was too skeptical and conservative. Duffy called him "the London stench boy" because he "was always making a stink about things whether they were going on, both good and bad, and you could smell the stink coming from London," Duffy admitted in court.

Soon after his private meeting with Duffy, Gentilin was transferred to NAB's London office, still working in the foreign exchange group. Duffy's unit in Melbourne continued to fudge the numbers so upper management wouldn't notice any problems with the trading results. But when the group bet the wrong way against a rising Australian dollar, the cover-ups escalated, including creation of fictitious trades to offset the losses. The idea was that they could recover the losses and receive their cherished bonuses by year-end.

Fatefully, Gentilin got wind from London of these subsequent trading problems, so he asked Vanessa McCallum, a junior NAB trader in Melbourne, to have other people look into Duffy's transactions. McCallum later acknowledged that she was terrified about asking for the audit. "My greatest fear was, if nothing is wrong I'm going to have to leave the desk because you had to be loyal to Luke [Duffy]," explained McCallum, who no longer works at the bank.

What senior NAB executives discovered shook the Australian bank to its core. Duffy and other senior traders had become a rogue team that amassed $350 million in losses in one year. Their unrestrained power and influence kept everyone (except Gentilin and McCallum) in line, resulting in countless transaction record irregularities and over 800 breaches of the bank's trading limits. Duffy and a few other traders were jailed for securities violations. Several executives, including both NAB's chief executive and chairman, lost their jobs.[1]

12

Power and Influence in the Workplace

LEARNING OBJECTIVES

After reading this chapter you should be able to

1. Define the meaning of *power* and *counterpower*.
2. Describe the five bases of power in organizations.
3. Explain how information relates to power in organizations.
4. Discuss the four contingencies of power.
5. Summarize the eight types of influence tactics.
6. Discuss three contingencies to consider when deciding which influence tactic to use.
7. Distinguish influence from organizational politics.
8. Describe the organizational conditions and personal characteristics that support organizational politics.
9. Identify ways to minimize organizational politics.

The National Australia Bank saga illustrates how power and influence can have profound consequences for employee behavior and the organization's success. Although this story has an unhappy ending, power and influence can equally influence ethical conduct and improve corporate performance. The reality is that no one escapes from organizational power and influence. They exist in every business and, according to some writers, in every decision and action.

This chapter unfolds as follows: First we define *power* and present a basic model depicting the dynamics of power in organizational settings. The chapter then discusses the five bases of power, as well as information as a power base. Next we look at the contingencies that amplify or weaken the potential of those sources of power. The latter part of this chapter examines the various types of influence in organizational settings as well as the contingencies of effective influence strategies. The final section of this chapter looks at situations in which influence becomes organizational politics, as well as ways of minimizing dysfunctional politics.

Learning Objectives

After reading the next three sections you should be able to

1. **Define the meaning of *power* and *counterpower*.**
2. **Describe the five bases of power in organizations.**
3. **Explain how information relates to power in organizations.**
4. **Discuss the four contingencies of power.**

The Meaning of Power

power
The capacity of a person, team, or organization to influence others.

Power is the capacity of a person, team, or organization to influence others.[2] Power is not the act of changing others' attitudes or behavior; it is only the potential to do so. People frequently have power they do not use; they might not even know they have power.

The most basic prerequisite of power is that one person or group believes it is dependent on another person or group for something of value.[3] This relationship is shown in Exhibit 12.1, where Person A has power over Person B by controlling something that Person B needs to achieve his or her goals. You might have power over others by controlling a desired job assignment, useful information, important resources, or even the privilege of being associated with you! In the opening story Luke Duffy wielded power because he controlled the job security and workplace resources of the NAB foreign exchange staff. To make matters more complex, power is ultimately a perception, so people might gain power simply by convincing others that they have something of value. Thus power exists when others believe that you control resources they want.[4]

Exhibit 12.1
Dependence in the Power Relationship

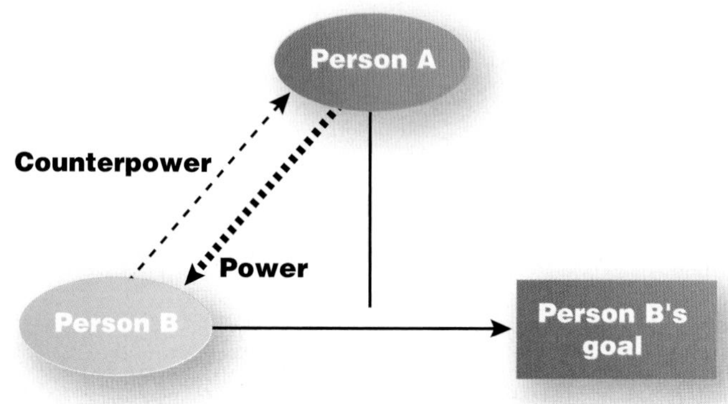

Exhibit 12.2
A Model of Power within Organizations

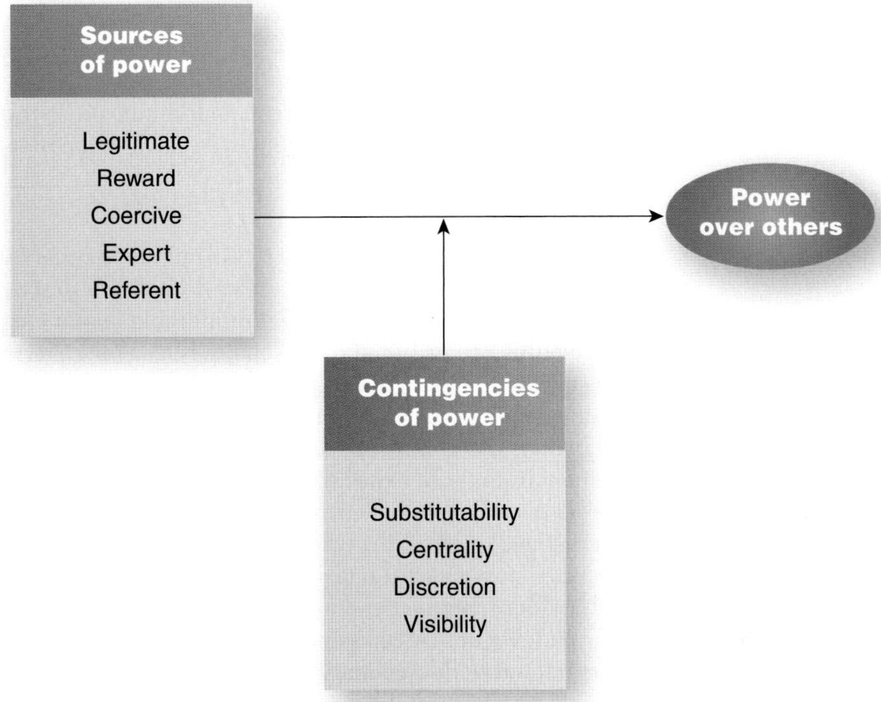

counterpower
The capacity to a person, team, or organization to keep a more powerful person or group in the exchange relationship.

Although power requires dependence, it is really more accurate to say that the parties are interdependent. One party may be more dependent than the other, but the relationship exists only when each party has something of value to the other. Exhibit 12.1 shows a dashed line to illustrate the weaker party's (Person B's) power over the dominant participant (Person A). This **counterpower**, as it is known, is strong enough to maintain Person A's participation in the exchange relationship. For example, executives have power over subordinates by controlling their job security and promotional opportunities. At the same time, employees have counterpower by controlling their ability to work productively and thereby creating a positive impression of the supervisor to his or her boss. Counterpower usually motivates executives to apply their power judiciously so that the relationship is not broken.

A Model of Power in Organizations

Power involves more than just dependence. As we see in Exhibit 12.2, the model of power includes both power sources and contingencies. It indicates that power is derived from five sources: legitimate, reward, coercive, expert, and referent. The model also shows that these sources yield power only under certain conditions. The four contingencies of power include the employee's or department's substitutability, centrality, discretion, and visibility. Finally, as we will discuss later, the type of power applied affects the type of influence the power holder has over the other person or work unit.

Sources of Power in Organizations

More than 40 years ago social scientists John French and Bertrand Raven listed five sources of power within organizations: legitimate, reward, coercive, expert, and referent. Many researchers have studied these five power bases and searched for others.

For the most part, French and Raven's list remains intact.[5] The first three power bases are derived from the power holder's position; that is, the person receives these power bases because of the specific authority or roles he or she is assigned in the organization. The latter two sources of power originate from the power holder's own characteristics. In other words, people bring these power bases to the organization.

Legitimate Power

legitimate power
The capacity to influence others through formal authority.

Legitimate power is the capacity to influence others through formal authority. This perceived right partly comes from formal job descriptions as well as informal rules of conduct. Executives have considerable legitimate power, but all employees also have this power based on company rules and government laws.[6] For example, an organization might give employees the right to request customer files if this information is required for their job.

Legitimate power depends on more than job descriptions. It also depends on mutual agreement from those expected to abide by this authority. Your boss's power to make you work overtime partly depends on your agreement to this power. Stories and movies about mutinies, such as *The Caine Mutiny* and *Crimson Tide*, illustrate this point; mutinies occur when bosses step too far outside the range of authority that employees deem acceptable. More frequently, employees question their bosses' right to make them stay late or perform unsafe tasks and other activities. Thus, legitimate power is a person's authority to make discretionary decisions as long as followers accept this discretion.[7]

People in high power distance cultures (that is, those who accept an unequal distribution of power) are more likely to comply with legitimate power than are people in low power distance cultures. Legitimate power is also stronger in some organizations than in others. A 3M scientist might continue to work on a project after being told by

Legitimate Power Meets a Mutiny *Crimson Tide* is a riveting novel and film about the limits of legitimate power. When radical Russian nationalists threaten World War III, the nuclear submarine *USS Alabama* is sent to prepare for retaliation with its own nuclear arsenal. The signal to launch does come in, but the message is incomplete before the submarine goes into silent mode. Alabama's commander, Captain Frank Ramsey (Gene Hackman, right in photo), is ready to have his crew push the button, whereas Lieutenant Commander Ron Hunter (Denzel Washington, left in photo), opposes this decision. What ensues is a mutiny that divides the loyalties of the *Alabama's* crew. The story illustrates how Captain Ramsey's decision and its consequences tested the limits of his legitimate power over his crew.

superiors to stop working on it because the 3M culture supports an entrepreneurial spirit, which includes ignoring your boss's authority from time to time. More generally, employees are becoming less tolerant of legitimate power. They increasingly expect to be involved in decisions rather than being told what to do.[8] Thus the command style of leadership that often guided employee behavior in the past must be replaced by other forms, particularly expert and referent power, which are described below.

Reward Power

Reward power is derived from a person's ability to control the allocation of rewards valued by others and to remove negative sanctions (negative reinforcement). Managers have formal authority that gives them power over the distribution of organizational rewards such as pay, promotions, time off, vacation schedules, and work assignments. Employees also have reward power over their bosses through the use of 360-degree feedback systems. Employee feedback affects supervisors' promotions and other rewards, so they tend to behave differently toward employees after 360-degree feedback is introduced.

Coercive Power

Coercive power is the ability to apply punishment. In the opening story to this chapter, Luke Duffy demonstrated his coercive power by reprimanding and threatening employees into submission. Employees also have coercive power, ranging from sarcasm to ostracism, to ensure that co-workers conform to team norms. Many firms also rely on the coercive power of team members to control co-worker behavior.

For instance, when asked how AirAsia maintained attendance and productivity when the Kuala Lumpur–based discount airline removed the time clocks, chief executive Tony Fernandes replied, "Simple. Peer pressure sees to that. The fellow employees, who are putting their shoulders to the wheel, will see to that." General Electric's Aircraft Engines division also relies on co-workers to guide employee behavior. "There is no better pressure than peer pressure," says GE's team plant manager in Durham, North Carolina.[9]

Expert Power

Legitimate, reward, and coercive power mainly originate from the individual's position in the organization. In contrast, expert power originates from within each person. It is an individual's or work unit's capacity to influence others by possessing knowledge or skills that they value. Luke Duffy and other "untouchables" mentioned in the opening story had expert power over more senior executives at National Australia Bank, apparently to the point that they performed much of their work with minimal checks and balances. Employees are also gaining expert power as our society moves from an industrial to a knowledge-based economy.[10] The reason is that employee knowledge becomes the means of production and is ultimately outside the control of those who own the company. And without this control over production, owners are more dependent on employees to achieve their corporate objectives.

Referent Power

referent power
The capacity to influence others based on the identification and respect they have for the power holder.

People have **referent power** when others identify with them, like them, or otherwise respect them. Like expert power, referent power comes from within a person. It is largely a function of the person's interpersonal skills and usually develops slowly. Referent power is usually associated with charismatic leadership. *Charisma* is often defined as a form of interpersonal attraction whereby followers develop respect for and trust in the charismatic individual.[11]

Information and Power

Information is power.[12] This phrase, which is increasingly relevant in a knowledge-based economy, exists in two forms. First, people gain information power when they control the flow of information to others. These information gatekeepers can alter perceptions of the situation and restrict information as a resource that others need to accomplish their work. For example, supervisors tend to have more information power in a centralized hierarchy where information flows through them to employees. But when information systems (such as intranets and corporate blogs) bypass supervisors, their information power declines.[13]

Second, information power is higher for those who seem to be able to cope with organizational uncertainties. Organizations value the ability to cope with environmental uncertainties because it allows them to more easily secure resources, introduce more efficient work processes, and estimate demand for their outputs. In other words, coping increases the organization's adaptability to its environment. Individuals and work units gain power by offering one or more of the following ways to cope with uncertainty, with the first being the most powerful:[14]

- *Prevention.* The most effective strategy is to prevent environmental changes from occurring. For example, financial experts acquire power by preventing the organization from experiencing a cash shortage or defaulting on loans.
- *Forecasting.* The next best strategy is to predict environmental changes or variations. In this respect, marketing specialists gain power by predicting changes in consumer preferences.
- *Absorption.* People and work units also gain power by absorbing or neutralizing the impact of environmental shifts as they occur. An example is the ability of maintenance crews to come to the rescue when machines break down and the production process stops.

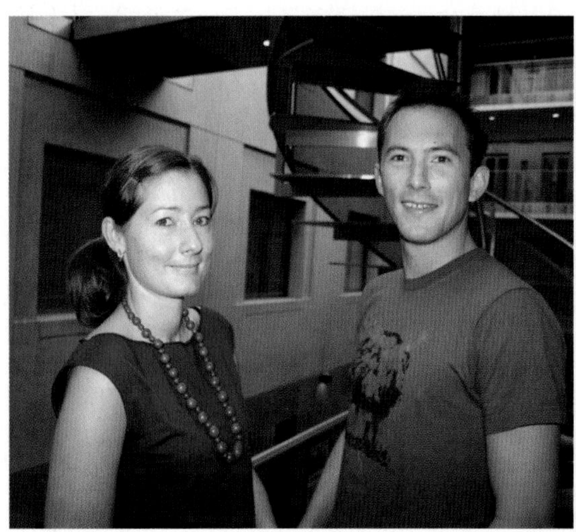

Trend Spotters Have Information Power People who can forecast the future are worth their weight in gold. The reason is this: Information about the future helps companies cope with environmental uncertainties. Corporate leaders can ramp up production to cash in on growing demand and can take corrective action to minimize damage from falling demand. "It's good to have advance-warning radar about what's happening among consumers," says London-based trend spotter Zoe Lazarus. Lazarus and Richard Welch in New York (both shown here) jointly lead a trend analysis unit for Lowe Worldwide, one of several ad agencies that have recently introduced trend analysis teams that peer into the future. Along with scanning offbeat magazines *(Sleazenation, Relax)*, Lazarus and Welch anticipate social changes by listening to more than 500 bartenders, photographers, disc jockeys, architects, journalists, designers, and other "influencers" in 52 cities across several countries. "[We're] looking for leading-edge trends that will eventually filter into the mainstream in one to two years' time, changing patterns in leisure behavior, holiday destinations, music choices, as well as fashion trends," Lazarus explains.[15]

Contingencies of Power

Let's say that you have expert power by virtue of your ability to forecast and possibly even prevent dramatic changes in the organization's environment. Does this expertise mean that you are influential? Not necessarily. As we saw earlier in Exhibit 12.2, power bases generate power only under certain conditions. The four conditions–called the *contingencies of power*–include substitutability, centrality, discretion, and visibility.[16] These are not sources of power; rather, they determine the extent to which people can leverage their power bases. You may have lots of expert power, but you won't be able to influence others with this power base if the contingency factors are not in place.

Substitutability

substitutability
The extent to which people dependent on a resource have alternatives.

Substitutability refers to the availability of alternatives. Power is strongest when someone has a monopoly over a valued resource. Conversely, power decreases as the number of alternative sources of the critical resource increases. If only you have expertise across the organization on an important issue, you would be more powerful than if several people in your company possessed this valued knowledge. Substitutability refers not only to other sources that offer the resource, but also to substitutions for the resource itself. For instance, labor unions are weakened when companies introduce technologies that replace the need for their union members. At one time a strike by telephone employees would have shut down operations, but computerized systems and other technological innovations now ensure that telephone operations continue during labor strikes and reduce the need for telephone operators during normal operations. Technology is a substitute for employees and consequently reduces union power.

How do people and work units increase their power through nonsubstitutability? There are several ways, although not all of them are ethical. We describe some of them here for your information–not necessarily for you to practice:

- *Controlling tasks.* Governments pass laws that give certain professions an exclusive right to perform particular tasks. As an example, most countries require publicly traded corporations to have their financial statements audited by a specific accounting group (certified public accountants, chartered accountants, or the like). The simmering conflict between medical doctors and nurse practitioners in some countries is also based on the exclusive rights of doctors to perform specific medical procedures that nurse practitioners want within their mandate.
- *Controlling knowledge.* Professions control access to the knowledge of their work domain, such as through restricted enrollment in educational programs. Knowledge is also restricted on the job. Several years ago maintenance workers in a French tobacco processing plant had become very powerful because they controlled the knowledge required to repair the tobacco machines.[17] The maintenance manuals had mysteriously disappeared, and the machines had been redesigned enough that only the maintenance staff knew how to fix them if they broke down (which they often did). Knowing the power of nonsubstitutability, maintenance staff carefully avoided documenting the repair procedures and didn't talk to production employees about their trade knowledge.
- *Controlling labor.* Aside from their knowledge resource, people gain power by controlling the availability of their labor. Labor unions attempt to organize as many people as possible within a particular trade or industry so that employers have no other source of labor supply. Unions have an easier time increasing wages when their members produce almost all of a particular product or service

in the industry. The union's power during a strike is significantly weakened when the employer can continue production through outside contractors or other nonunion facilities.

- *Differentiation.* Differentiation occurs when an individual or work unit claims to have a unique resource–such as raw materials or knowledge–that others would want. By definition, the uniqueness of this resource means no one else has it. The tactic here isn't so much the nonsubstitutability of the resource, but making others believe that the resource is unique. Some people claim that consultants use this tactic. They take skills and knowledge that many consulting firms can provide and wrap them into a package (with the latest buzzwords, of course) so that it looks like a service that no one else can offer.

Centrality

centrality
The degree and nature of interdependence between the power holder and others.

Centrality refers to the degree and nature of interdependence between the power holder and others.[18] Think about your own centrality for a moment: If you decided not to show up for work or school tomorrow, how many people would be affected, and how much time would pass before they were affected? If you have high centrality, most people in the organization would be adversely affected by your absence, and they would be affected quickly. This centrality was apparent when, as Connections 12.1 describes, New York City transit workers staged an illegal walkout. Within hours, commuters and businesses were affected. When it ended three days later, the strike had cost the city and its businesses more than $1 billion. Notice, however, that the power of centrality in the New York transit strike was partly offset by its substitutability–dedicated and sometimes ingenious New York commuters and business leaders found ways during the strike to reduce their dependence on the transit system.

Discretion

The freedom to exercise judgment–to make decisions without referring to a specific rule or receiving permission from someone else–is another important contingency of power in organizations. Consider the plight of first-line supervisors. It may seem that they have legitimate and reward power over employees, but this power is often curtailed by specific rules. This lack of discretion makes supervisors largely powerless even though they may have access to some of the power bases described earlier in this chapter. "Middle managers are very much 'piggy-in-the-middle,'" complains a middle manager at Britain's National Health System. "They have little power, only what senior managers are allowed to give them."[19]

Visibility

Several years ago as a junior copywriter at advertising agency Chiat/Day, Mimi Cook submitted an idea for a potential client to her boss, who then presented it to cofounder Jay Chiat. Chiat was thrilled with the concept, but Cook's boss "never mentioned the idea came from me," recalls Cook. Cook confronted her boss, who claimed the oversight was unintentional. But when a similar incident occurred a few months later, Cook left the agency for another firm.[20]

Mimi Cook, who has since progressed to associate creative director at another ad agency, knows that power does not flow to unknown people in the organization. Those who control valued resources or knowledge will yield power only when others are aware of these power bases–in other words, when it is visible. One way to increase visibility is to take people-oriented jobs and work on projects that require

Connections 12.1

New York Transit Strike Reveals Its Centrality, But Also Its Substitutability

New York City's 7 million commuters were recently on the receiving end of centrality of power when transit workers illegally walked off the job for three days (legislation bans transit strikes in New York). The strike's effect on commuters and businesses was immediate and widespread, amplified by the fact that the strike occurred during peak Christmas shopping and while the weather was cold and blustery. Roads were clogged just hours after the strike began, even though cars with fewer than four passengers were denied entry to the city center. Downtown department stores were noticeably quieter in spite of one-day sales to counter the strike's effect. Some businesses estimated that half of their employees did not arrive to work or were very late. Some public schools started two hours later than usual. New York's mayor estimated the three-day stoppage cost the city and its businesses more than $1 billion.

"[The Metropolitan Transit Authority] told us we got no power, but we got power," said striking transit worker Fausto Fienco. "We got the power to stop the city." The strike ended after three days because courts imposed heavy fines on the transit union and promised jail terms for its leaders.

Although some newspaper headlines claimed the strike "paralyzed" New York City, it did not cause mass chaos, largely because the union's centrality was offset by substitutability as determined commuters found alternative ways to get to work. New Jersey residents took the less well-known PATH transit system into New York City, tripling the usual number of riders on the first day. Some Wall Street securities firms arranged special busing for their staff. Television stations booked hotel rooms nearby so key staff could avoid the need for any commuting. Telecommuting at American Express and other firms shot up for the strike's three days.

For many others, the only alternative to an expensive taxi ride was to walk dozens of city blocks or bicycle even farther. "I live in Brooklyn and I walked all the way here," says Giovanni Magana, a security guard at Macy's downtown store. "It took me about three hours, and I'll have to walk back home tonight."

Seven million New York City commuters felt the effects of the transit union's centrality when its members walked off the job just before Christmas.

Sources: "N.Y. Transit Strike Sends TV, Film Biz Scrambling," *Reuters News,* 20 December 2005; J. Frankston, "PATH Ridership Spikes during Strike, Authority Chairman Pushes for New Service," *Associated Press,* 24 December 2005; S. D. Harrington and B. Ivry, "For Commuters, a Day to Adapt," *The Record* (Bergen, New Jersey), 21 December 2005, p. A01; S. McCarthy, "Transit Strike Cripples New York," *Globe & Mail* (Toronto), 21 December 2005, p. A17; R. Richmond, "During Strike, Some New Yorkers Go to Work Virtually," *Dow Jones Newswires,* 21 December 2005.

frequent interaction with senior executives. "You can take visibility in steps," advises an executive at a U.S. pharmaceutical firm. "You can start by making yourself visible in a small group, such as a staff meeting. Then when you're comfortable with that, seek out larger arenas."[21]

Employees also gain visibility by being, quite literally, visible. Some people strategically move into offices or cubicles where co-workers pass most often (such as closest to the elevator or office lunchroom). People often use public symbols as subtle (and not-so-subtle) cues to make their power sources known to others. Many professionals display their educational diplomas and awards on office walls to remind visitors of their expertise. Medical professionals wear white coats with a stethoscope around their necks to symbolize their legitimate and expert power in hospital settings. Other people play the game of "face time"–spending more time at work and showing that they are working productively. One engineer working on a color laser printer project made a habit of going to the office once each week at 2 a.m. after her boss once saw her working at that hour. "[A]fter the reaction I got from my manager I decided it was important to do that early morning work in the office," explains the engineer. "It is better to be seen here if you are going to work in the middle of the night."[22]

mentoring
The process of learning the ropes of organizational life from a senior person within the company.

Another way to increase visibility is through **mentoring**–the process of learning the ropes of organizational life from a senior person within the company. Mentors give protégés more visible and meaningful work opportunities and open doors for them to meet more senior people in the organization. Mentors also teach these newcomers influence tactics supported by the organization's senior decision makers.[23]

Networking and Power

networking
Cultivating social relationships with others to accomplish one's goals.

"It's not what you know, but whom you know that counts!" This often-heard statement reflects the reality that employees get ahead not just by developing their competencies, but by **networking**–cultivating social relationships with others to accomplish one's goals. Networking increases a person's power in three ways. First, networks represent a critical component of *social capital*–the knowledge and other resources available to people or social units (teams, organizations) due to a durable network that connects them to others. Networks consist of people who trust each other, which increases the flow of knowledge among those within the network. The more you network, the more likely you will receive valuable information that increases your expert power in the organization.[24]

Second, people tend to identify more with partners within their own networks, which increases referent power among people within each network. This network-based referent power may lead to more favorable decisions by others in the network. Finally, effective networkers are better known by others in the organization, so their talents are more readily recognized. This power increases when networkers place themselves in strategic positions in the network, thereby gaining centrality.[25] For example, these people might be regarded as the main person who distributes information in the network or who keeps the network connected through informal gatherings.

Networking is a natural part of the informal organization, yet it can create a formidable barrier to those who are not actively connected to it.[26] Women are often excluded from powerful networks because they do not participate in golf games and other male-dominated social events. That's what Deloitte and Touche executives discovered when they investigated why so many junior female employees left the accounting and consulting firm before reaching partnership level. Deloitte and Touche now relies on mentoring, formal women's network groups, and measurement of career progress to ensure that female staff members have the same career development opportunities as their male colleagues.[27]

Learning Objectives

After reading the next section you should be able to

5. **Summarize the eight types of influence tactics.**
6. **Discuss three contingencies to consider when deciding which influence tactic to use.**

Influencing Others

Up to this point we have focused on the sources and contingencies of power. But power is only the capacity to influence others. It represents the potential to change someone's attitudes and behavior. Influence, on the other hand, refers to any behavior that attempts to alter someone's attitudes or behavior.[28] Influence is power in motion. It applies one or more power bases to get people to alter their beliefs, feelings, and activities. Consequently our focus in the remainder of this chapter is on how people use power to influence others.

Influence tactics are woven throughout the social fabric of all organizations. This is because influence is an essential process through which people coordinate their effort and act in concert to achieve organizational objectives. Indeed, influence is central to the definition of leadership. Influence operates down, across, and up the corporate hierarchy. Executives ensure that subordinates complete required tasks. Employees influence co-workers to help them with their job assignments. Subordinates engage in upward influence tactics so corporate leaders make decisions compatible with subordinates' needs and expectations.

Types of Influence Tactics

Organizational behavior researchers have devoted considerable attention to the various types of influence tactics found in organizational settings. A groundbreaking study over 25 years ago identified several influence strategies, but recent evidence suggests that some of them overlap.[29] The original list also seems to have a Western bias that ignores influence tactics used in Asian and other cultures.[30] With these caveats in mind, we will focus on the following influence tactics identified in the current literature (see Exhibit 12.3): silent authority, assertiveness, information control, coalition formation, upward appeal, ingratiation and impression management, persuasion, and exchange. The first five are known as *hard influence tactics* because they force behavior change through position power (legitimate, reward, and coercion).

Exhibit 12.3
Types of Influence Tactics in Organizations

Influence Tactic	Description
Silent authority	Influencing behavior through legitimate power without explicitly referring to that power base.
Assertiveness	Actively applying legitimate and coercive power by applying pressure or threats.
Information control	Explicitly manipulating someone else's access to information for the purpose of changing their attitudes and/or behavior.
Coalition formation	Forming a group that attempts to influence others by pooling the resources and power of its members.
Upward appeal	Gaining support from one or more people with higher authority or expertise.
Ingratiation/impression management	Attempting to increase liking by, or perceived similarity to, some targeted person.
Persuasion	Using logical arguments, factual evidence, and emotional appeals to convince people of the value of a request.
Exchange	Promising benefits or resources in exchange for the target person's compliance.

The latter three–ingratiation and impression management, persuasion, and exchange–are called *soft tactics* because they rely more on personal sources of power (referent, expert) and appeal to the target person's attitudes and needs.

Silent Authority The silent application of authority occurs when someone complies with a request because of the requester's legitimate power as well as the target person's role expectations. We often refer to this condition as *deference to authority*.[31] This deference occurs when you comply with your boss's request to complete a particular task. If the task is within your job scope and your boss has the right to make this request, then this influence strategy operates without negotiation, threats, persuasion, or other tactics.

Silent authority is often overlooked as an influence strategy in the United States, but it is the most common form of influence in high power distance cultures. Employees comply with supervisor requests without question because they respect the supervisor's higher authority in the organization. Silent authority also occurs when leaders influence subordinates through role modeling. One study reported that Japanese managers typically influence subordinates by engaging in the behaviors that they want employees to mimic.[32]

Assertiveness In contrast to silent authority, assertiveness might be called *vocal authority* because it involves actively applying legitimate and coercive power to influence others. Assertiveness includes persistently reminding a target of his or her obligations, frequently checking the target's work, confronting the target, and using threats of sanctions to force compliance. Assertiveness typically applies or threatens to apply punishment if the target does not comply. Explicit or implicit threats range from job loss to losing face by letting down the team. Extreme forms of assertiveness include blackmailing colleagues, such as by threatening to reveal the other person's previously unknown failures unless he or she complies with your request. Associates claim that Luke Duffy influenced his staff at National Australia Bank largely through assertiveness, including threatening to fire them if they didn't keep quiet and follow his wishes.

Information Control Luke Duffy also used information control as an influence tactic. Specifically, the rogue National Australia Bank trader hid hundreds of illegal transactions from his boss and other executives to avoid their involvement in the unit's trading problems. Information control involves explicitly manipulating others' access to information for the purpose of changing their attitudes or behavior. With limited access to potentially valuable information, others are at a disadvantage. Although the NAB incident is more extreme than most, hiding information isn't unusual in organizations. Almost half of the employees in one major survey believe people keep their colleagues in the dark about work issues if it helps their own cause. Employees also influence executive decisions by screening out (filtering) information flowing up the hierarchy. Indeed, one recent study found that CEOs also influence their board of directors by selectively feeding information to board members.[33]

coalition
An informal group that attempts to influence people outside the group by pooling the resources and power of its members.

Coalition Formation When people lack sufficient power alone to influence others in the organization, they might form a **coalition** of people who support the proposed change. A coalition is influential in three ways.[34] First, it pools the power and resources of many people, so the coalition potentially has more influence than any number of people operating alone. Second, the coalition's mere existence can be a source of power by symbolizing the legitimacy of the issue. In other words, a coalition creates a sense that the issue deserves attention because it has broad support. Third, coalitions tap into the power of the social identity process introduced in Chapter 3. A coalition is essentially an informal group that advocates a new set of norms and behaviors. If the coalition has a broad-based membership (that is, if its members come from various parts of the organization), then other employees are more likely to identify with that group and consequently accept the ideas the coalition is proposing.

upward appeal
A type of coalition in which one or more members have higher authority or expertise.

Upward Appeal Have you ever had a disagreement with a colleague in which one of you eventually says, "I'm sure the boss (or teacher) will agree with me on this. Let's find out!" This tactic–called **upward appeal**–is a form of coalition in which at least one member is someone with higher authority or expertise. Upward appeal ranges from a formal alliance to the perception of informal support from someone with higher authority or expertise. Upward appeal also includes relying on the authority of the firm as an entity without approaching anyone further up the hierarchy. For instance, one study reported that Japanese managers influence employees by reminding them of their obligation to support the organization's objectives.[35] By reminding the target that your request is consistent with the organization's overarching goals, you are implying support from senior executives without formally involving anyone with higher authority in the situation.

ingratiation
Any attempt to increase liking by, or perceived similarity to, the targeted person.

Ingratiation and Impression Management Silent authority, assertiveness, information control, coalitions, and upward appeals are forceful ways to influence other people. At the opposite extreme is a "soft" influence tactic called **ingratiation**, which includes any attempt to increase liking by, or perceived similarity to, some targeted person.[36] Flattering your boss in front of others, helping co-workers with their work, exhibiting similar attitudes (such as agreeing with your boss's proposal to change company policies), and seeking the other person's counsel (perhaps asking for his or her "expert" advice) are all examples of ingratiation. Collectively, ingratiation behaviors are better than most other forms of influence at predicting career success (performance appraisal feedback, salaries, and promotions).[37]

Ingratiation is potentially influential because it increases the perceived similarity of the source of ingratiation to the target person, which causes the target person to form more favorable opinions of the ingratiator. However, people who are obvious in their ingratiation risk losing any influence because their behaviors are considered insincere and self-serving. The derogatory terms "apple polishing" and "brown-nosing" are applied to those who ingratiate to excess or in ways that suggest selfish motives for the ingratiation. Sure enough, research indicates that people who engage in high levels of ingratiation are less (not more) influential and are less likely to get promoted.[38]

impression management
The practice of actively shaping one's public image.

Ingratiation is part of a larger influence tactic known as **impression management**, which is the practice of actively shaping our public images.[39] These public images might be crafted as being important, vulnerable, threatening, or pleasant. For the most part employees routinely engage in pleasant impression management behaviors to satisfy the basic norms of social behavior, such as the way they dress and how they behave toward colleagues and customers. Impression management is a common strategy for people trying to get ahead in the workplace. For instance, almost all job applicants in a recent study relied on one or more types of impression management.

As with ingratiation, employees who use too much impression management tend to be less influential because their behaviors are viewed as insincere.[40] However, until they are caught, some people have successfully gained influence by exaggerating their credentials. Somewhere between 25 and 50 percent of application forms and résumés contain false information. Although most of these inaccuracies are minor, there are also many high-profile misrepresentations.[41] For example, a former CEO of Radio

Shack, an executive at NASA, a football coach at the University of Notre Dame, and a mayor of Rancho Mirage, California, embellished their educational credentials. Lucent Technologies discovered that a former executive had lied about having a PhD from Stanford University and hid his criminal past involving forgery and embezzlement. Ironically the executive was Lucent's director of recruiting!

One of the most elaborate misrepresentations occurred a few years ago when a Singaporean entrepreneur sent out news releases claiming to be a renowned artificial intelligence researcher, the author of several books, and the recipient of numerous awards from MIT and Stanford University (one of the awards was illustrated on his Web site). These falsehoods were so convincing that the entrepreneur almost received a real award, the "Internet Visionary of the Year" at the Internet World Asia Industry Awards.

persuasion
Using logical arguments, facts, and emotional appeals to encourage people to accept a request or message.

Persuasion Along with ingratiation, **persuasion** is one of the most effective influence strategies for career success. The ability to present facts, logical arguments, and emotional appeals to change another person's attitudes and behavior is not just an acceptable way to influence others; in many societies it is a noble art and a quality of effective leaders. The literature about influence strategies has typically described persuasion as the use of reason through factual evidence and logical arguments. However, recent studies have begun to adopt a "dual process" perspective in which persuasion is influenced by both the individual's emotional reaction and rational interpretation of incoming information.[42] Thus persuasion is an attempt to convince people by using emotional appeals as well as factual evidence and logical arguments.

The effectiveness of persuasion as an influence tactic depends on characteristics of the persuader, message content, communication medium, and the audience being persuaded.[43] What makes one person more persuasive than another? One factor is the person's perceived expertise. Persuasion attempts are more successful when listeners believe the speaker is knowledgeable about the topic. People are also more persuasive when they demonstrate credibility, such as when the persuader does not seem to profit from the persuasion attempt and states a few points against the position.[44]

Steve Jobs's Persuasiveness Creates a Reality Distortion Field Wearing his trademark black turtleneck and faded blue jeans, Apple Computer cofounder and CEO Steve Jobs is famous for stirring up crowds with evangelical fervor as he draws them into his "reality distortion field." A reality distortion field occurs when people are caught in Steve Jobs's visionary headlights. Apple Computer manager Bud Tribble borrowed the phrase from the TV series *Star Trek* to describe Jobs's overwhelming persuasiveness. "In his presence, reality is malleable," Tribble explained to newly hired Andy Hertzfeld in 1981. " He [Steve Jobs] can convince anyone of practically anything. It wears off when he's not around, but it makes it hard to have realistic schedules." As one journalist wrote, "Drift too close to Jobs in the grip of one of his manias and you can get sucked in, like a wayward asteroid straying into Jupiter's gravitational zone."[45]

Message content is more important than the messenger when the issue is important to the audience. Persuasive message content acknowledges several points of view so the audience does not feel cornered by the speaker. The message should also be limited to a few strong arguments, which are repeated a few times, but not too frequently. The message content should use emotional appeals (such as graphically showing the unfortunate consequences of a bad decision), but only in combination with logical arguments so the audience doesn't feel manipulated. Also, emotional appeals should always be accompanied with specific recommendations to overcome the threat. Finally, message content is more persuasive when the audience is warned about opposing arguments. This **inoculation effect** causes listeners to generate counterarguments to the anticipated persuasion attempts, which makes opponents' subsequent persuasion attempts less effective.[46]

inoculation effect
A persuasive communication strategy of warning listeners that others will try to influence them in the future and that they should be wary of the opponent's arguments.

Two other considerations when persuading people are the medium of communication and characteristics of the audience. Generally, persuasion works best in face-to-face conversations and through other media-rich communication channels. The personal nature of face-to-face communication increases the persuader's credibility, and the richness of this channel provides faster feedback about whether the influence strategy is working. With respect to audience characteristics, it is more difficult to persuade people who have high self-esteem and intelligence, as well as those whose targeted attitudes are strongly connected to their self-identities.[47]

Exchange Exchange activities involve the promise of benefits or resources in exchange for a target person's compliance with your request. This tactic also includes reminding the target of past benefits or favors with the expectation that the target will now make up for that debt. The norm of reciprocity is a central and explicit theme in exchange strategies. According to the *norm of reciprocity*, individuals are expected to help those who have helped them.[48] Negotiation, which we discuss more fully in Chapter 13, is also an integral part of exchange influence activities. For instance, you might negotiate with your boss for a day off in return for working a less desirable shift at a future date. Networking is another form of exchange as an influence strategy. Active networkers build up "exchange credits" by helping colleagues in the short term for reciprocal benefits in the long term.

Networking as an influence strategy is a deeply ingrained practice in several cultures. The Chinese term *guanxi* refers to special relationships and active interpersonal connectedness. It is based on traditional Confucian values of helping others without expecting future repayment. However, some writers suggest that the original interpretation and practice of guanxi has shifted to include implicit long-term reciprocity, which can slip into cronyism. As a result, some Asian governments are discouraging guanxi-based decisions, preferring more arms-length transactions in business and government decisions.[49] *Blat* is a Russian word that also refers to special relationships or connections. Unlike guanxi, however, blat was originally associated with survival during times of scarcity and continues to have a connotation of self-interest and possible illegality.[50]

Consequences and Contingencies of Influence Tactics

Now that the main influence strategies have been described, you are probably wondering which ones are best. The best way to answer this question is to identify the three ways in which people react when others try to influence them: resistance, compliance, or commitment.[51] *Resistance* occurs when people or work units oppose the behavior desired by the influencer and consequently refuse, argue, or delay engaging in the behavior. *Compliance* occurs when people are motivated to implement the influencer's request at a minimal level of effort and for purely instrumental reasons. Without external

Exhibit 12.4
Consequences of Hard and Soft Influence Tactics

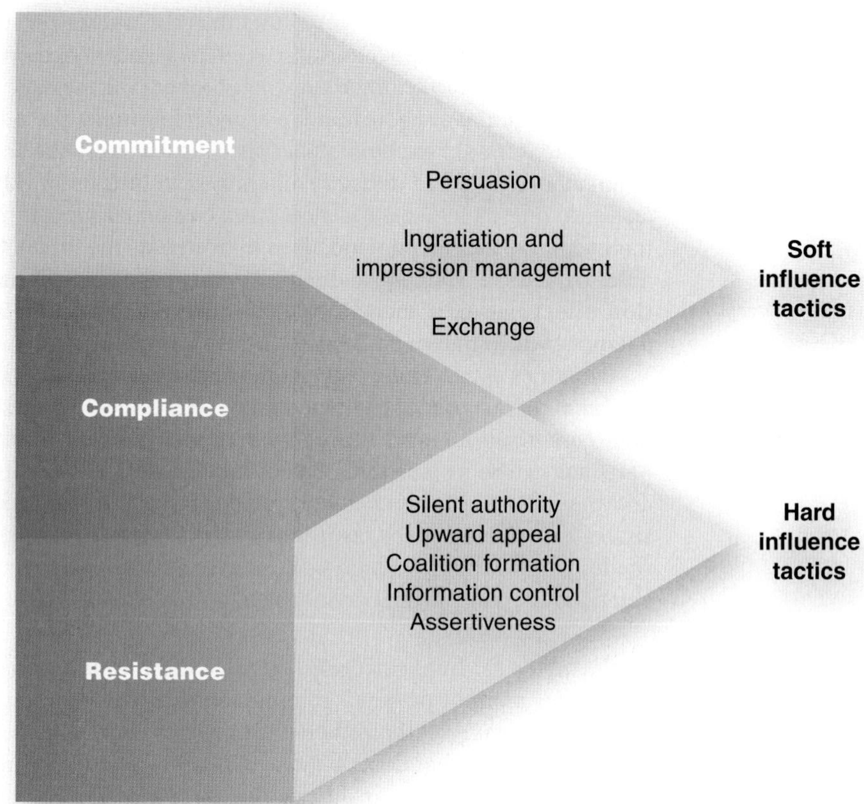

sources to prompt the desired behavior, it would not occur. *Commitment* is the strongest form of influence, whereby people identify with the influencer's request and are highly motivated to implement it even when extrinsic sources of motivation are no longer present.

Research has found that people generally react more favorably to "soft" tactics such as friendly persuasion and subtle ingratiation than to "hard" tactics such as upward appeal and assertiveness (see Exhibit 12.4). Soft tactics rely on personal power bases (expert and referent power), which tend to build commitment to the influencer's request. For example, co-workers tend to "buy in" to your ideas when you apply moderate levels of ingratiation and impression management tactics or use persuasion based on expertise. In contrast, hard influence tactics rely on position power (legitimate, reward, and coercion), so they tend to produce compliance or, worse, resistance. Hard tactics also tend to undermine trust, which can hurt future relationships. For example, the potential influence of coalitions is sometimes limited when the group's forcefulness is threatening to those being influenced.[52]

Upward, Downward, or Lateral Influence Aside from the general preference for soft rather than hard tactics, the most appropriate influence strategy depends on a few contingencies. One consideration is whether the person being influenced is higher, lower, or at the same level in the organization. Employees have some legitimate power over their boss, but they may face adverse career consequences by being too assertive with this power. Similarly, it may be more acceptable for supervisors to control information access than for employees to control what information they distribute to co-workers and people at higher levels in the organization.

The Influencer's Power Base A second contingency is the influencer's power base. Those with expertise tend to be more successful using persuasion, whereas those with a strong legitimate power base are usually more successful applying silent authority.[53]

Personal and Cultural Values Studies indicate that personal values guide our preference for some influence methods more than others.[54] The general trend in the United States and elsewhere is toward softer influence tactics because younger employees tend to have more egalitarian values compared with those near retirement. As such, silent authority and assertiveness are tolerated less than a few decades ago. Acceptance of influence tactics also varies across cultures. Research indicates that American managers and subordinates alike often rely on ingratiation because it minimizes conflict and supports a trusting relationship. In contrast, managers in Hong Kong and other high power distance cultures rely less on ingratiation, possibly because this tactic disrupts the more distant roles that managers and employees expect in these cultures. Instead, as we noted earlier, influence through exchange tends to be more common and accepted in Asian cultures because of the importance of interpersonal relationships (guanxi).

Gender Differences in Influence Tactics

Men and women seem to differ in their use of influence tactics. Some writers say that men are more likely than women to rely on direct impression management tactics. Specifically, men tend to advertise their achievements and take personal credit for successes of others reporting to them, whereas women are more reluctant to force the spotlight on themselves, preferring instead to share the credit with others. At the same time, women are more likely to apologize–personally take blame–even for problems not caused by them. Men are more likely to assign blame and less likely to assume it.[55]

Some research also suggests that women generally have difficulty exerting some forms of influence in organizations, and this has limited their promotional opportunities. In particular, women are viewed as less (not more) influential when they try to directly influence others by exerting their authority or expertise. In job interviews, for example, direct and assertive female job applicants were less likely to be hired than were male applicants using the same influence tactics. Similarly, women who directly disagreed in conversations were less influential than women who agreed with the speaker.[56] These findings suggest that women may face problems applying "hard" influence tactics such as assertiveness. Instead, until stereotypes change, women need to rely on softer and more indirect influence strategies, such as ingratiation.

Learning Objectives

After reading this section you should be able to

7. **Distinguish influence from organizational politics.**
8. **Describe the organizational conditions and personal characteristics that support organizational politics.**
9. **Identify ways to minimize organizational politics.**

Influence Tactics and Organizational Politics

You might have noticed that organizational politics has not been mentioned yet, even though some of the practices or examples described over the past few pages are usually considered political tactics. This phrase was carefully avoided because, for the most part, "organizational politics" is in the eye of the beholder. I might perceive your attempt to influence our boss as normal behavior, whereas someone else might perceive your tactic as brazen organizational politics. This is why experts mainly discuss influence tactics as behaviors and organizational politics as perceptions. The influence tactics described earlier are behaviors that might be considered organizational politics, or they might be considered normal behavior. It all depends on the observer's perception of the situation.[57] Of course, some tactics are so blatantly selfish that almost everyone views them as political. However, many incidents of using influence are viewed from different perspectives; some think the employee is helping the company whereas others think the employee is helping himself or herself. For these reasons organizational politics should be considered a perception.

organizational politics Behaviors that others perceive as self-serving tactics for personal gain at the expense of other people and possibly the organization.

When are influence tactics perceived as **organizational politics**? Increasingly OB researchers say that influence tactics are organizational politics when they seem to benefit the perpetrators at the expense of others and usually the entire organization or work unit. Organizational politics has a number of negative effects. Those who believe their organization is steeped in organizational politics have lower job satisfaction, organizational commitment, and organizational citizenship, as well as high levels of work-related stress. Employees affected by organizational politics also engage in more "neglect" behaviors, such as reducing work effort, paying less attention to quality, and increasing absenteeism and lateness.[58]

Some incidents involving organizational politics have devastating effects on the organization. The opening story to this chapter is one such example. Luke Duffy's political acts of hiding transactions and threatening or criticizing those who attempted to report the wrongdoing ultimately resulted in huge losses for the bank. Connections 12.2 describes an even more extreme example, whereby WorldCom executives used their assertiveness, information control, and other influence practices to protect their financial interests. Ultimately these actions led to the largest accounting fraud and bankruptcy in American history.

Conditions Supporting Organizational Politics

Organizational politics flourishes under the right conditions.[59] One of those conditions is scarce resources. When budgets are slashed, people rely on political tactics to safeguard their resources and maintain the status quo. Office politics also flourishes when resource allocation decisions are ambiguous, complex, or lack formal rules. This occurs because decision makers are given more discretion over resource allocation, so potential recipients of those resources use political tactics to influence the factors that should be considered in the decision. Organizational change encourages political behaviors for this reason. Change creates uncertainty and ambiguity as the company moves from an old set of rules and practices to a new set. During these times, employees apply political strategies to protect their valued resources, positions, and self-images.[60]

Organizational politics also becomes commonplace when it is tolerated and transparently supported by the organization.[61] Companies sometimes promote people who are the best politicians, not necessarily the best talent to run the company. If left unchecked, organizational politics can paralyze an organization as people focus more on protecting themselves than fulfilling their roles. Political activity becomes self-reinforcing unless the conditions supporting political behavior are altered.

Personal Characteristics Several personal characteristics affect a person's motivation to engage in organizational politics.[62] Some people have a strong need for personal as opposed to socialized power. They seek power for its own sake and use political tactics to acquire more power. People with an internal locus of control are more likely than those with an external locus of control to engage in political behaviors.

Politics at WorldCom Leads to Record-Breaking Accounting Fraud

Bernie Ebbers built WorldCom, Inc. (since acquired by Verizon Communications, Inc.), into one of the world's largest telecommunications firms. Yet he and chief financial officer (CFO) Scott Sullivan have become better known for creating a massive corporate accounting fraud that led to the largest bankruptcy in U.S. history. Two investigative reports and subsequent court cases concluded that WorldCom executives were responsible for billions in fraudulent or unsupported accounting entries. How did this mammoth accounting scandal occur without anyone raising the alarm? Evidence suggests that Ebbers and Sullivan held considerable power and influence that prevented accounting staff from complaining, or even knowing, about the fraud.

Ebbers's inner circle held tight control over the flow of all financial information. The geographically dispersed accounting groups were discouraged from sharing information. Ebbers's group also restricted distribution of company-level financial reports and prevented sensitive reports from being prepared at all. Accountants didn't even have access to the computer files where some of the largest fraudulent entries were made. As a result, employees had to rely on Ebbers's executive team to justify the accounting entries that were requested.

Another reason why employees complied with questionable accounting practices was that CFO Scott Sullivan wielded immense personal power. He was considered a "whiz kid" with impeccable integrity who had won the prestigious "CFO Excellence Award." Thus when Sullivan's office asked staff to make questionable entries, some accountants assumed Sullivan had found an innovative—and legal—accounting loophole. If Sullivan's expert power didn't work, other executives took a more coercive approach. Employees cited incidents where they were publicly berated for questioning headquarters' decisions and intimidated if they asked for more information. When one employee at a branch refused to alter an accounting entry, WorldCom's controller threatened to fly in from WorldCom's Mississippi headquarters to make the change himself. The employee changed the entry.

Ebbers wielded similar influence over WorldCom's board of directors. Sources indicate that his personal charisma and intolerance of dissension produced a passive board that rubber-stamped most of his recommendations. As one report concluded, "The Board of Directors appears to have embraced suggestions by Mr. Ebbers without question or dissent, even under circumstances where its members now readily acknowledge they had significant misgivings regarding his recommended course of action."

Sources: United States Bankruptcy Court, Southern District of New York. In Re: WorldCom, Inc., et al., Debtors. Chapter 11 Case No. 02-15533 (AJG) Jointly Administered Second Interim Report of Dick Thornburgh, Bankruptcy Court Examiner, June 9, 2003; Report of Investigation by the Special Investigative Committee of the Board of Directors of WorldCom, Inc. Dennis R. Beresford, Nicholas Deb. Katzenbach, C.B. Rogers, Jr., Counsel, Wilmer, Cutler & Pickering, Accounting Advisors, PricewaterhouseCoopers LLP, March 31, 2003. Also see T. Catan et al., "Before the Fall," *Financial Times* (London), 19 December 2002, p. 17; J. O'Donnell and A. Backover, "Ebbers's High-Risk Act Came Crashing Down on Him," *USA Today,* 12 December 2002, p. B1; C. Stern, "Ebbers Dominated Board, Report Says," *Washington Post,* 5 November 2002, p. E1; D.S. Hilzenrath, "How a Distinguished Roster of Board Members Failed to Detect Company's Problems," *Washington Post,* 16 June 2003, p. E1; S. Pulliam and A. Latour, "Lost Connection," *The Wall Street Journal,* 12 January 2005, p. A1; S. Rosenbush, "Five Lessons of the WorldCom Debacle," *Business Week Online,* 16 March 2005.

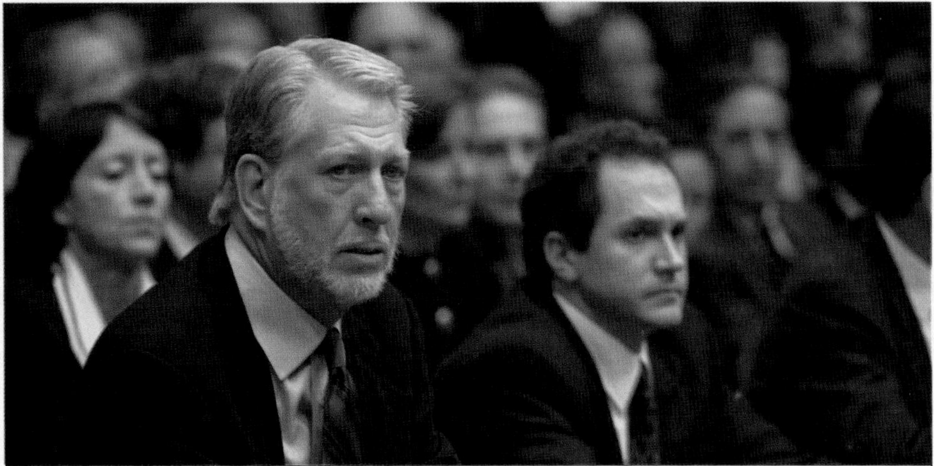

Former WorldCom CEO Bernard Ebbers (left), chief financial officer Scott Sullivan (right), and other executives perpetrated one of the largest cases of accounting fraud in history by using influence tactics for personal gain.

This does not mean that internals are naturally political; rather, they are more likely to use influence tactics when political conditions are present because, unlike externals, they feel very much in charge of their own destiny.

Some individuals have strong **Machiavellian values**. Machiavellianism is named after Niccolò Machiavelli, the 16th-century Italian philosopher who wrote *The Prince*, a famous treatise about political behavior. People with high Machiavellian values are comfortable with getting more than they deserve, and they believe that deceit is a natural and acceptable way to achieve this goal. They seldom trust co-workers and tend to use cruder influence tactics, such as bypassing their bosses or being assertive, to get their own way.[63] The opening vignette to this chapter suggests that National Australia Bank's rogue trader displayed Machiavellian characteristics, including rough assertiveness and controlling information.

Machiavellian values
The belief that deceit is a natural and acceptable way to influence others.

Minimizing Organizational Politics and its Consequences The conditions that fuel organizational politics also give us some clues about how to control dysfunctional political activities.[64] One strategy to keep organizational politics in check is to introduce clear rules and regulations to specify the use of scarce resources. Corporate leaders also need to actively support the all-channels communication structure described earlier in this chapter so that political employees do not misuse power through information control. As mentioned, organizational politics can become a problem during times of organizational change. Effective organizational change practices–particularly education and involvement–can minimize uncertainty and consequently politics during the change process.

Organizational politics is either supported or punished, depending on team norms and the organization's culture. Thus leaders need to actively manage group norms to curtail self-serving influence activities. They also need to support organizational values that oppose political tactics, such as altruism and customer focus. One of the most important strategies is for leaders to become role models of organizational citizenship rather than symbols of successful organizational politicians.

Along with minimizing organizational politics, companies can limit the adverse effects of political perceptions by giving employees more control over their work and keeping them informed about organizational events. Research has found that employees who know what is going on in the organization and who are involved in organizational decisions are less likely to experience stress, job dissatisfaction, and absenteeism as a result of organizational politics.

Chapter Summary

Power is the capacity to influence others. It exists when one party perceives that he or she is dependent on another for something of value. However, the dependent person must also have counterpower–some power over the dominant party–to maintain the relationship.

There are five power bases. Legitimate power is the capacity to influence others through formal authority, but only to the extent employees agree to this authority. Reward power is derived from the ability to control the allocation of rewards valued by others and to remove negative sanctions. Coercive power is the ability to apply punishment. Expert power is the capacity to influence others by possessing knowledge or skills that they value. People have referent power when others identify with them, like them, or otherwise respect them.

Information plays an important role in organizational power. Employees gain power by controlling the flow of information that others need and by being able to cope with uncertainties related to important organizational goals.

Four contingencies determine whether these power bases translate into real power. Individuals and work units are more powerful when they are nonsubstitutable–that is, there is a lack of alternatives. Employees, work units, and organizations reduce substitutability by controlling tasks, knowledge, and labor and by differentiating themselves from competitors. A second contingency is centrality. People have more power when they have high centrality: They affect many people quickly by their actions. Discretion, the third contingency of power, refers to the freedom to exercise judgment. Power increases when people are free to use it. The fourth contingency, visibility, refers to the idea that power increases to the extent that a person's or work unit's competencies are known to others.

Networking involves cultivating social relationships with others to accomplish one's goals. This activity increases an individual's expert and referent power as well as visibility and possibly centrality. However, networking can limit opportunities for people outside the network, as many women in senior management positions have discovered.

Influence refers to any behavior that attempts to alter someone's attitudes or behavior. The most widely studied influence tactics are silent authority, assertiveness, information control, coalition formation, upward appeal, ingratiation and impression management, persuasion, and exchange. "Soft" influence tactics such as friendly persuasion and subtle ingratiation are more acceptable than "hard" tactics such as upward appeal and assertiveness. However, the most appropriate influence tactic also depends on the influencer's power base; whether the person being influenced is higher, lower, or at the same level in the organization; and personal and cultural values regarding influence behavior.

Organizational politics refers to influence tactics that others perceive to be self-serving behaviors at the expense of others and sometimes contrary to the interests of the entire organization or work unit. Organizational politics is more prevalent when scarce resources are allocated using complex and ambiguous decisions and when the organization tolerates or rewards political behavior. Individuals with a high need for personal power, an internal locus of control, and strong Machiavellian values have a higher propensity to use political tactics.

Organizational politics can be minimized by providing clear rules for resource allocation, establishing a free flow of information, using education and involvement during organizational change, supporting team norms and a corporate culture that discourage dysfunctional politics, and having leaders who model organizational citizenship rather than political savvy.

Key Terms

centrality, p. 348
coalition, p. 352
counterpower, p. 343
impression management, p. 353
ingratiation, p. 353
inoculation effect, p. 355
legitimate power, p. 344
Machiavellian values, p. 360
mentoring, p. 350
networking, p. 350
organizational politics, p. 358
persuasion, p. 354
power, p. 342
referent power, p. 345
substitutability, p. 347
upward appeal, p. 353

Critical Thinking Questions

1. What role does counterpower play in the power relationship? Give an example of your own encounter with counterpower at school or work.
2. Several years ago the major league baseball players' association went on strike in September, just before the World Series started. The players' contract expired at the beginning of the season (May), but they held off the strike until September when they would lose only one-sixth of their salaries. In contrast, a September strike would hurt the owners financially because they earn a larger portion of their revenue during the playoffs. As one player explained, "If we strike next spring, there's nothing stopping [the club owners] from letting us go until next June or July because they don't have that much at stake." Use your knowledge of the sources and contingencies of power to explain why the baseball players' association had more power in negotiations by walking out in September rather than March.
3. You have just been hired as a brand manager of toothpaste for a large consumer products company. Your job mainly involves encouraging the advertising and production groups to promote and manufacture your product more effectively. These departments aren't under your direct authority, although company procedures indicate that they must complete certain tasks requested by brand managers. Describe the sources of power you can use to ensure that the advertising and production departments will help you make and sell toothpaste more effectively.

4. How does networking increase a person's power? What networking strategies could you initiate now to potentially enhance your future career success?
5. Discuss how the eight influence tactics described in this chapter are used by students to influence their university teachers. Which influence tactic is applied most often? Which is applied least often, in your opinion? To what extent is each influence tactic considered legitimate behavior or organizational politics?
6. How do cultural differences affect the following influence factors: (a) silent authority and (b) upward appeal?
7. A few years ago the CEO of Apple Computer invited Steve Jobs (who was not associated with the company at the time) to serve as a special adviser and raise morale among Apple employees and customers. While doing this, Jobs spent more time advising the CEO on how to cut costs, redraw the organization chart, and hire new people. Before long, most of the top people at Apple were Jobs's colleagues, who began to systematically evaluate and weed out teams of Apple employees. While publicly supporting Apple's CEO, Jobs privately criticized him and, in a show of nonconfidence, sold 1.5 million shares of Apple stock he had received. This action caught the attention of Apple's board of directors, who soon after decided to replace the CEO with Steve Jobs. The CEO claimed Jobs was a conniving backstabber who used political tactics to get his way. Others suggest that Apple would be out of business today if he hadn't taken over the company. In your opinion, were Steve Jobs's actions examples of organizational politics? Justify your answer.
8. This book frequently emphasizes that successful companies engage in knowledge management. How do political tactics interfere with knowledge management objectives?

Case Study 12.1 RHONDA CLARK: TAKING CHARGE AT THE SMITH FOUNDATION

Joseph C. Santora, Essex County College and TST, Inc.

Dr. Rhonda Clark was ecstatic as she hung up the telephone. Bennett Mitchell, chairperson of KLS Executive Search firm, had just informed her that she landed the coveted position of chief executive officer (CEO) at the Smith Foundation, a nonprofit organization whose mission was to fund public awareness campaigns and research programs about eye care. Clark knew that she had just pulled off a major coup. Her appointment to this new, challenging position would indeed be *the* high point in a long, arduous climb to the executive suite. As an organizational outsider–one with no work experience within the hiring organization–she assumed that her appointment as CEO signaled a strong desire by the board to shake up the organizational status quo. However, she heard from a reliable inside source that the same board that hired her and charged her with the responsibility of transforming the foundation was extremely fragmented. The often rambunctious board had forced the last five CEOs to resign after short tenures. Clark's feeling of exhilaration was rapidly being replaced by cautious optimism. As a new CEO, she pondered the rather thorny question of how she could take charge of the board of directors to ensure the mission of the organization would be accomplished.

Background

Charlie Smith, an industrialist and philanthropist, had founded the Smith Foundation 40 years ago with a multimillion-dollar endowment. Despite this generous financial start-up capital and additional income derived from several financial investments and major corporate donations, in recent years the foundation's endowment has been slowly dwindling as a result of significant funding awards to academics, community organizations, and smaller, less well-funded foundations. Board members had held some preliminary discussions about developing new innovative strategies to strengthen the balance sheet of the organization. Currently the foundation was operating on an annual budget of slightly less than $1,500,000 (USD).

In the last five years some foundation board members had begun to abandon many of their fiduciary responsibilities. Over the past few months several board meetings had been canceled because the meetings lacked a quorum. In general, this 13-member board seemed to drift aimlessly in one direction or another. The board had been operating at only 70 percent capacity for the past two years with nine active board members–five men and four women.

Challenges

Dr. Rhonda Clark believed she was the one who could lead the Smith Foundation. She had great academic credentials and management experience that would help her tackle her new position as the foundation head. In the last 30 years the 54-year-old Clark, who held a PhD in political science and policy analysis from a major U.S. West Coast university, had gained an enviable amount of managerial experience in the nonprofit and public sectors. Past professional experiences included a graduate school professorship, as well as being a director of research for a major statewide political office holder, the director of planning in a large metropolitan hospital, and the director of programs at a small foundation.

Immediately upon taking office, Clark was astounded to learn that a small but active and influential faction on the board had withdrawn its initial verbal promise to assist her in working closely with the corporate community. Essentially, she was informed that she was solely responsible for all external corporate relations. Clark thought to herself, "I wonder if they hired me because they thought they would get a 'do-nothing' female leader. These folks want me to either sink or swim on my own. Perhaps they set me up for failure by giving me a one-year appointment." She lamented, "I won't let this happen. I really need to learn about the key decision makers and stakeholders on the board and in the larger community, and fast."

At the last board meeting Clark detailed the major elements of her latest proposal. Yet several board members seemed totally unfazed by it. Soon she began to encounter stiff resistance from some male board members. Jim Jackson, in particular, told Clark, "We are disappointed that you failed to win a city contract to conduct a feasibility study to determine if we can erect a facility in another section of town. We're not certain if you have the right stuff to run this foundation, and we certainly won't help you to gain financial support for the foundation by using our personal, corporate, or political contacts." Jackson thought to himself, "We've removed CEOs before; we can remove Clark, too."

After hearing Jackson's comments, Clark decided to take another tack. She began to focus on making external and internal inroads that she believed could result in some modest gains for the foundation. For example, she identified and developed a close relationship with a few well-connected city agency executives, persuaded some supporters to nominate her for membership on two influential boards, and forged a relationship with two key foundation decision makers and political power brokers. She reconfigured the internal structure of the foundation to increase maximum productivity from the staff, and she tightened budgetary controls by changing some fiscal policies and procedures.

Clark also sought the support of Susan Frost, a board member who likely had been instrumental in Clark's appointment as CEO. Clark said to herself, "If I can develop a strong symbiotic relationship with some female board members, like Sue, to support my plan, then maybe I get some traction." To do this Clark held a number of late evening meetings with Sue and another female board member. They indicated their willingness to help her, but only if she would consider implementing a few of their ideas for the foundation as well as recommending their close friend for a current staff vacancy. Clark knew they were trying to exercise their political influence; yet she believed that everyone could benefit from this *quid quo pro* relationship. She said to herself, "I guess it's a matter of you scratch my back, and I scratch yours." She eagerly agreed to move their agenda along. In a matter of a few weeks, as promised, they began working on a couple of relatively sympathetic board members. One day Clark got a terse but crucial telephone call from Sue. "Several of us support you. Proceed!"

Once she heard this, Clark began to move at lightning speed. She formed a 15-member coalition of community, educational, and quasi-governmental agencies that would apply for a collaborative federal grant to create a public awareness campaign for children's eye health. Through the dissemination of various media, coalition members would help to inform the community about various eye diseases that afflict young children. Shortly afterward Clark received notification from a federal agency that this multi-agency project would be awarded a million-dollar grant. Clark would serve as the administrative and fiscal agent of the grant, and as a result, she would be able to earmark a considerable amount of the administrative oversight dollars for the foundation's budget. For her efforts in coordinating this project, Clark received high marks from coalition and community members alike.

Yet despite this important initial accomplishment, Clark had the unpleasant task of notifying the full board that due to some unforeseen problems and their lack of support on certain key initiatives, the foundation would still experience a financial deficit. She heard several rumors that her next employment contract would not be renewed by the executive committee of the board. At this point she thought about directly confronting the obstructionists on the board by telling them that they were unreasonable and in fact that they were why the foundation had not recovered during the past year ... but she hesitated: She had signed on to do a job, and she was unsure if this was the wisest action to take at this time.

Despite this latest conflict between herself and certain board members, she paused to reflect on what she believed to have been a tumultuous year as CEO.

Discussion Questions

1. Does Clark have any sources of power and any contingencies of power? If so, list and discuss them.
2. To what degree were Clark's methods of influencing board members the most effective possible under the circumstances presented in the case?
3. Do you think her methods of getting things done at the foundation were ethical? Why or why not?

Note: The names and some managerial actions in this case have been altered to preserve the integrity and anonymity of the organization. This case is intended to be used as a basis for class discussion rather than to illustrate either effective or ineffective handling of a management situation.

 Source: Joseph C. Santora, Essex County College and TST, Inc.

Case Study 12.2 SHAKING UP OXFORD

John Hood may be soft-spoken, but the New Zealand-born vice chancellor of Oxford University shows flashes of the steely determination that first convinced Oxford's search committee to hire him to give the place a top-to-bottom management overhaul. Hood's decisive actions have created few friends among the scholars, but he claims he is merely working in the university community's best interests. "I am here as the servant of the scholars," says Hood. "One has no power or authority in this job."

This *BusinessWeek* case study describes the changes that John Hood is making at Oxford and how academics at the British university are responding to those changes. The article looks at Hood's influence strategies, the methods used by Oxford's professors to resist those changes, and some of the politics of change that has occurred. Read the full text of this *BusinessWeek* article at www.mhhe.com/mcshane4e and prepare for the discussion questions below.

Discussion Questions

1. John Hood claims that he has no power or authority in his job. Is he correct? What other sources of power work for and against him during this change process?
2. What influence tactics has Hood used that are most apparent in this case study?
3. What influence tactics have professors and other stakeholders used to resist Hood's changes? Would you call any of these influence tactics "organizational politics"?

Source: S. Reed, "Shaking Up Oxford," *BusinessWeek*, 5 December 2005, 48.

Team Exercise 12.3 BUDGET DELIBERATIONS

Sharon Card

PURPOSE This exercise is designed to help you understand some of the power dynamics and influence tactics that occur across hierarchical levels in organizations.

MATERIALS This activity works best where one small room leads to a larger room, which leads to a larger area.

INSTRUCTIONS These exercise instructions are based on a class size of about 30 students. The instructor may adjust the size of the first two groups slightly for larger classes. The instructor will organize students as follows: A few (three or four) students are assigned the position of executives. They are preferably located in a secluded office or corner of a large classroom. Another six to eight students are assigned positions as middle managers. These people will ideally be located in an adjoining room or space, allowing privacy for the executives. The remaining students represent the nonmanagement employees in the organization. They are located in an open area outside the executive and management rooms.

RULES Members of the executive group are free to enter the space of either the middle management or nonmanagement groups and to communicate whatever they wish, whenever they wish. Members of the middle management group may enter the space of the nonmanagement group whenever they wish, but must request permission to enter the executive group's space. The executive group can refuse the middle management group's request. Members of the nonmanagement group are not allowed to disturb the top group in any way unless specifically invited by members of the executive group. The nonmanagement group does have the right to request permission to communicate with the middle management group. The middle management group can refuse the lower group's request.

TASK Your organization is in the process of preparing a budget. The challenge is to balance needs with financial resources. Of course the needs are greater than the resources. The instructor will distribute a budget sheet showing a list of budget requests and their costs. Each group has control over a portion of the budget and must decide how to spend the money over which they have control. Nonmanagement staff members have discretion over a relatively small portion, and the executive group has discretion over the greatest portion. The exercise is finished when the organization has negotiated a satisfactory budget, or when the instructor calls time out. The class will then debrief with the following questions and others the instructor might ask.

Discussion Questions

1. What can you learn from this exercise about power in organizational hierarchies?
2. How is this exercise similar to relations in real organizations?
3. How did students in each group feel about the amount of power they held?
4. How did they exercise their power in relations with the other groups?

Self-Assessment 12.4

UPWARD INFLUENCE SCALE

PURPOSE This exercise is designed to help you understand several ways of influencing people up the organizational hierarchy as well as estimate your preferred upward influence tactics.

INSTRUCTIONS Read each of the following statements and circle the response that you believe best indicates how often you engaged in that behavior over the past six months. Then use the scoring key in Appendix B to calculate your results. This exercise is completed alone so you can assess yourself honestly without concerns of social comparison. However, class discussion will focus on the types of influence in organizations and the conditions under which particular influence tactics are most and least appropriate.

Upward Influence Scale

How often in the past six months have you engaged in these behaviors?	Never ▼	Seldom ▼	Occasionally ▼	Frequently ▼	Amost always ▼
1. I obtain the support of my co-workers in persuading my manager to act on my request.	1	2	3	4	5
2. I offer an exchange in which I will do something that my manager wants if he or she will do what I want.	1	2	3	4	5
3. I act very humble and polite while making my request.	1	2	3	4	5
4. I appeal to higher management to put pressure on my manager.	1	2	3	4	5
5. I remind my manager of how I have helped him or her in the past and imply that now I expect compliance with my request.	1	2	3	4	5
6. I go out of my way to make my manager feel good about me before asking him or her to do what I want.	1	2	3	4	5
7. I use logical arguments to convince my manager.	1	2	3	4	5
8. I have a face-to-face confrontation with my manager in which I forcefully state what I want.	1	2	3	4	5
9. I act in a friendly manner toward my manager before making my request.	1	2	3	4	5
10. I present facts, figures, and other information to my manager in support of my position.	1	2	3	4	5
11. I obtain the support and cooperation of my subordinates to back up my request.	1	2	3	4	5
12. I obtain the informal support of higher management to back me.	1	2	3	4	5
13. I offer to make a personal sacrifice such as giving up my free time if my manager will do what I want.	1	2	3	4	5
14. I very carefully explain to my manager the reasons for my request.	1	2	3	4	5
15. I verbally express my anger to my manager in order to get what I want.	1	2	3	4	5
16. I use a forceful manner; I try such things as demands, the setting of deadlines, and the expression of strong emotion.	1	2	3	4	5
17. I rely on the chain of command—on people higher up in the organization who have power over my supervisor.	1	2	3	4	5
18. I mobilize other people in the organization to help me in influencing my supervisor.	1	2	3	4	5

Source: C. Schriesheim and T. Hinkin, "Influence Tactics Used by Subordinates: A Theoretical and Empirical Analysis and Refinement of the Kipnis, Schmidt, and Wilkinson Subscales," *Journal of Applied Psychology* 75 (1990), pp. 246–57.

Self-Assessment 12.5

GUANXI ORIENTATION SCALE (STUDENT OLC)

Guanxi, which is translated as interpersonal connections, is an important element of doing business in China and some other Asian countries with strong Confucian cultural values. Guanxi is based on traditional Confucian values of helping others without expecting future repayment. This instrument estimates your guanxi orientation–that is, the extent to which you accept and apply guanxi values. This self-assessment is completed alone so you can rate yourself honestly without concerns of social comparison. However, class discussion will focus on the meaning of guanxi and its relevance for organizational power and influence.

Self-Assessment 12.6

MACHIAVELLIANISM SCALE (STUDENT OLC)

Machiavellianism is named after Niccolò Machiavelli, the 16th-century Italian philosopher who wrote *The Prince,* a famous treatise about political behavior. Out of Machiavelli's work emerged this instrument that estimates the degree to which you have a Machiavellian personality. Indicate the extent to which you agree or disagree that each statement in this instrument describes you. Complete each item honestly to get the best estimate of your level of Machiavellianism.

Self-Assessment 12.7

PERCEPTIONS OF POLITICS SCALE (POPS) (STUDENT OLC)

Organizations have been called "political arenas"–environments where political tactics are common because decisions are ambiguous and resources are scarce. This instrument estimates the degree to which you believe the school where you attend classes has a politicized culture. This scale consists of several statements that might or might not describe the school where you are attending classes. These statements refer to the administration of the school, not the classroom. Please indicate the extent to which you agree or disagree with each statement.

After reading this chapter, if you need additional information, see **www.mhhe.com/mcshane4e** for more in-depth interactivities that correspond with this material.

By any measure, Microsoft Corp. is a monolithic money machine. Its $12 billion annual earnings exceed those of Cisco, Dell, Google, and Apple combined. And although most of these profits come from its computer operating system (Windows) and software (Office), Microsoft is reaching into new markets, such as Xbox for games and MSN for online portals.

Yet various sources conclude that Microsoft is riddled with dysfunctional conflict that could soon hamper its ability to remain competitive. One source of strife is between employees and management. "We have over 61,000 employees, only 8,000 of whom are developers," quips a computer science graduate who recently joined Microsoft. "Doesn't sound right, does it? Not to me anyway." Jeff B. Erwin, who left the company after five years, agrees. "Microsoft has some of the smartest people in the world, but they [managers] are just crushing them."

Various sources conclude that Microsoft is riddled with dysfunctional conflict that could soon hamper its ability to remain competitive.

The rift between management and employees may widen under a new reward system that pays management substantial bonuses while most staff continue to receive market rates. Even within project teams, a bell-curved performance system pits one employee against another. If the entire team performs well to get the product completed, the reward system still forces some team members into the low performance category. "It creates competition in the ranks, when people really want community," says a former Microsoft vice president.

But conflict between management and employees and within groups is subtle compared to the almost vicious infighting across product groups. The squabbling is amplified by top management's strategy of "integrated innovation"; in other words, the groups are expected to work more closely together than ever before. "Pretty much across the board people are saying that Microsoft is dysfunctional," concludes one industry analyst. "They are not cooperating across business groups."

For example, MSN delayed releasing search software to compete against Google Desktop because the Windows group, which has a similar search tool for its long-delayed Vista operating system, objected. The two groups negotiated for more than a month to reach a compromise. The MSN group also fought against the Office people over MSN's desire to connect their online calendar with the calendar in Office. The Office group balked because "then MSN could cannibalize Office," says an employee who recently left Microsoft. "Windows and Office would never let MSN have more budget or more control."[1]

Conflict and Negotiation in the Workplace

LEARNING OBJECTIVES

After reading this chapter you should be able to

1. Outline the conflict process.
2. Distinguish constructive from socioemotional conflict.
3. Discuss the advantages and disadvantages of conflict in organizations.
4. Identify six sources of organizational conflict.
5. Outline the five interpersonal styles of conflict management.
6. Summarize six structural approaches to managing conflict.
7. Outline four situational influences on negotiations.
8. Describe four behaviors that are characteristic of effective negotiators.
9. Compare and contrast the three types of third-party dispute resolution.

Most organizations experience some backbiting and infighting among employees and across business groups, but Microsoft's current situation illustrates the importance of understanding the causes and consequences of conflict before it becomes a dysfunctional disease that seeps into a company's cultural mindset. This chapter investigates the dynamics of conflict in organizational settings, beginning with a description of the conflict process. Next, this chapter discusses the consequences and sources of conflict in organizational settings. Five conflict management styles are then described, followed by a discussion of the structural approaches to conflict management. The last two sections of this chapter introduce two procedures for resolving conflict: negotiation and third-party resolution.

Learning Objectives

After reading this section you should be able to

1. **Outline the conflict process.**
2. **Distinguish constructive from socioemotional conflict.**
3. **Discuss the advantages and disadvantages of conflict in organizations.**

The Conflict Process

conflict
The process in which one party perceives that its interests are being opposed or negatively affected by another party.

Conflict is a process in which one party perceives that its interests are being opposed or negatively affected by another party.[2] Conflict was reported between Microsoft's MSN and Office groups, for example, because they viewed the other division's product development activities as a threat to their own interests. Similarly, frontline technical employees experience conflict with management's heavy-handed control systems that seem to further delay product development.

When describing an incident involving conflict, we are usually referring to the observable part of conflict–the angry words, shouting matches, and actions that symbolize opposition. But this manifest conflict is only a small part of the conflict process. As Exhibit 13.1 illustrates, the conflict process begins with the sources of conflict.[3] Incompatible goals, different values, and other conditions lead one or both parties to perceive that conflict exists. We will look closely at these sources of conflict later in this chapter because understanding and changing them is the key to effective conflict management.

Exhibit 13.1
The Conflict Process

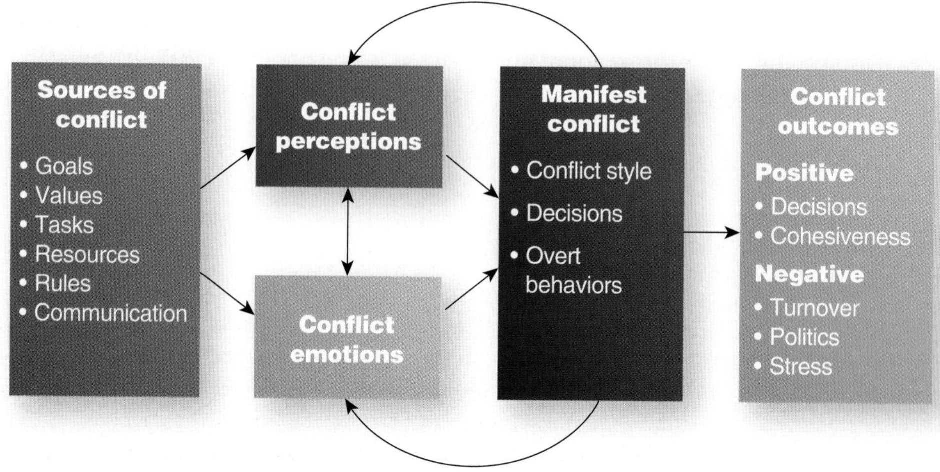

Conflict Perceptions and Emotions

At some point the sources of conflict lead one or both parties to perceive that conflict exists. They become aware that one party's statements and actions are incompatible with their own goals. These perceptions usually interact with emotions experienced about the conflict. Infighting at Microsoft is likely stoked with emotions, such as the anger employees experience when they work late completing monthly performance reports for management rather than spending more time meeting customers. "Instead of promoting the product to customers, I'd get stuck in the office until midnight preparing slides for my monthly product review," complains a frustrated Windows XP marketing employee.[4]

Manifest Conflict

Conflict perceptions and emotions usually manifest themselves in the decisions and overt behaviors of one party toward the other. These conflict episodes may range from subtle nonverbal behaviors to warlike aggression. Particularly when people experience high levels of conflict emotions, they have difficulty finding words and expressions that communicate effectively without further irritating the relationship.[5] Conflict is also manifested by the style each side uses to resolve the conflict. Some people tend to avoid the conflict, whereas others try to defeat those with opposing views. Conflict management styles will be described later in this chapter. At this point you should know that these styles influence the other party's perceptions and actions regarding the conflict, which then either defuse or further escalate the conflict.

Conflict Escalation Cycle The conflict process in Exhibit 13.1 shows arrows looping back from manifest conflict to conflict perceptions and emotions. These loops represent the fact that the conflict process is really a series of episodes that potentially link in an escalation cycle or spiral.[6] It doesn't take much to start this conflict cycle–just an inappropriate comment, a misunderstanding, or action that lacks diplomacy. These behaviors communicate to the other party in a way that creates a perception of conflict. If the first party did not intend to demonstrate conflict, the second party's response may create that perception.

If the conflict remains focused on perceptions, both parties can often resolve the conflict through logical analysis. However, the communication process has enough ambiguity that a wrong look or word may trigger strong emotions and set the stage for further conflict escalation. These distorted beliefs and emotions reduce each side's motivation to communicate, making it more difficult for them to discover common ground and ultimately resolve the conflict. The parties then rely more on stereotypes and emotions to reinforce their perceptions of the other party. Some structural conditions increase the likelihood of conflict escalation. Employees who are more confrontational and less diplomatic also tend to escalate conflict.[7]

Conflict Outcomes

Recent events at Microsoft illustrate some of the dysfunctional consequences of conflict: delayed product releases because one group obstructs another group's product launch; restricted flow of information across divisions; lower morale and higher turnover of key employees. Employees are often distracted from their work by internal feuds and, in some cases, engage in dysfunctional behaviors such as withholding valuable knowledge and other resources. Ongoing conflict also increases stress and turnover while reducing organizational commitment and job satisfaction. At the

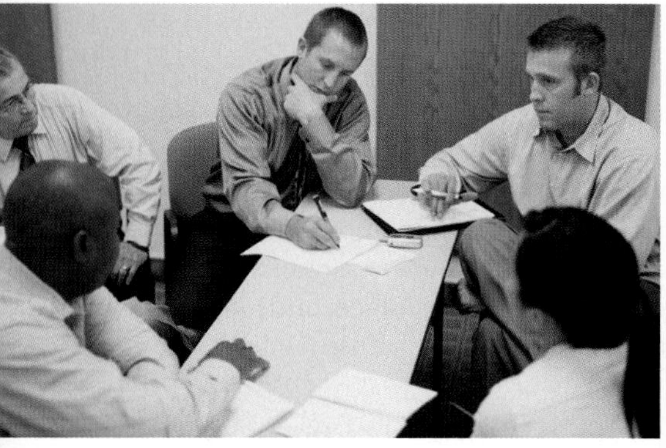

Constructive Confrontation Inside Intel Former Goldman Sachs president John Thornton has had his share of executive debates, but even he was surprised after joining the board of Intel Corp. regarding the "constructive confrontation" that permeates the chipmaker's culture. "It can be kind of shocking at first," says Thornton. "You realize quickly that [Intel managers] practice a form of honesty that borders on brutality." Intel cofounder and former chairman Andy Grove nurtured constructive confrontation many years ago when he noticed that meetings generate better ideas when staff actively debate rather than politely defer to ideas that others put forward. But Grove emphasizes that this conflict is constructive only under specific circumstances. "Constructive confrontation does not mean being loud, unpleasant, or rude, and it is not designed to affix blame," warns Grove. "The essence of it is to attack a problem by speaking up in a businesslike way." Intel also holds confrontation training seminars to help staff become more comfortable with the brutal honesty in its meetings.[8]

intergroup level, conflict with people outside the team may cause the team to become more insular–increasing their cohesiveness while distancing themselves from outsiders who are critical of the team's past decisions.[9]

conflict management Interventions that alter the level and form of conflict in ways that maximize its benefits and minimize its dysfunctional consequences.

Given these problems, it's not surprising that people normally associate **conflict management** with reducing or removing conflict. However, conflict management refers to interventions that alter the level and form of conflict in ways that maximize its benefits and minimize its dysfunctional consequences. This sometimes means increasing the level of **constructive conflict** (also known as *task-related conflict*).[10] Recall from Chapter 10 that constructive conflict occurs when team members debate their different perceptions about an issue in a way that keeps the conflict focused on the task rather than people. This form of conflict tests the logic of arguments and encourages participants to reexamine their basic assumptions about the problem and its possible solution.

constructive conflict Occurs when team members debate their different perceptions about an in issue in a way that keeps the conflict focused on the task rather than people.

To some extent Microsoft encourages constructive conflict. For instance, Microsoft employees can openly complain on their employee blogs, whereas Google has a reputation for firing employees who dissent in public. When Ray Ozzie, a renowned programmer who developed Lotus Notes and more recently Groove Networks, recently joined Microsoft's executive team, one of his first observations was Microsoft executives engaged in "vigorous disagreement" over business models. Microsoft has a history of encouraging this constructive conflict because senior management believes debate generates better decisions and ultimately better strategies and products.

socioemotional conflict A negative outcome that occurs when differences are viewed as personal attacks rather than attempts to resolve an issue.

The challenge is to engage in constructive conflict without having it escalate into **socioemotional conflict** (also known as *relationship conflict*). When socioemotional conflict dominates, differences are viewed as personal attacks rather than attempts to resolve an issue. The parties become defensive and competitive toward each other, which motivates them to reduce communication and information sharing.

Minimizing Socioemotional Conflict

The solution here seems obvious: Encourage constructive conflict for better decision making and minimize socioemotional conflict to avoid dysfunctional emotions and behaviors. This sounds good in theory, but recent evidence suggests that separating these two types of conflict isn't easy. Most of us experience some degree of socioemotional conflict during or after any constructive debate.[11] In other words, it is difficult to suppress defensive emotions when trying to resolve conflicts calmly and rationally. Fortunately conflict management experts have identified three strategies that might reduce the level of socioemotional conflict during constructive conflict episodes.[12]

- *Emotional intelligence.* Socioemotional conflict is less likely to occur, or is less likely to escalate, when team members have high levels of emotional intelligence. Emotionally intelligent employees are better able to regulate their emotions during debate, which reduces the risk of escalating perceptions of interpersonal hostility. People with high emotional intelligence are also more likely to view a co-worker's emotional reaction as valuable information about that person's needs and expectations, rather than as a personal attack.
- *Cohesive team.* Socioemotional conflict is suppressed when the conflict occurs within a highly cohesive team. The longer people work together, get to know each other, and develop mutual trust, the more latitude they give to each other to show emotions without being personally offended. Strong cohesion also allows each person to know about and anticipate the behaviors and emotions of teammates. Another benefit is that cohesion produces a stronger social identity with the group, so team members are motivated to avoid escalating socioemotional conflict during otherwise emotionally turbulent discussions.
- *Supportive team norms.* Various team norms can hold socioemotional conflict at bay during constructive debate. When team norms encourage openness, for instance, team members learn to appreciate honest dialogue without personally reacting to any emotional display during the disagreements. Other norms might discourage team members from displaying negative emotions toward co-workers. Team norms also encourage tactics that defuse socioemotional conflict when it first appears. For instance, research has found that teams with low socioemotional conflict use humor to maintain positive group emotions, which offsets negative feelings team members might develop toward some co-workers during debate.

Learning Objectives

After reading the next three sections you should be able to

4. Identify six sources of organizational conflict.
5. Outline the five interpersonal styles of conflict management.
6. Summarize six structural approaches to managing conflict.

Sources of Conflict in Organizations

Manifest conflict is really the tip of the proverbial iceberg. What we really need to understand are the sources of this conflict, which lie under the surface. The six main conditions that cause conflict in organizational settings are shown in Exhibit 13.2.

Incompatible Goals

A common source of conflict is goal incompatibility.[13] Goal incompatibility occurs when personal or work goals seem to interfere with another person's or department's goals. This source of conflict is apparent in the opening story. Managers in each Microsoft division are rewarded for the success of their products, so conflict results when other divisions threaten that success with similar products. Incompatible goals also explain conflict between employees and management. Microsoft managers are

Exhibit 13.2
Sources of Conflict in Organizations

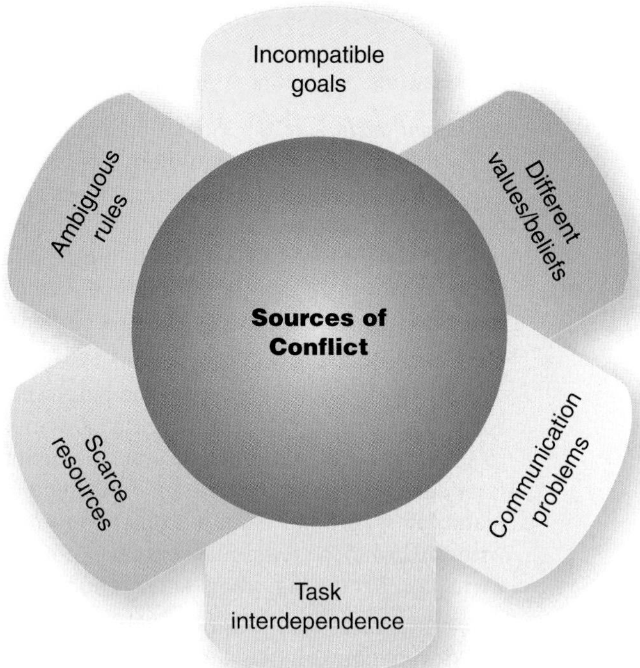

cutting costs and pushing for more accountability through performance management reports, yet employees believe these activities interfere with their own goals of developing or selling products and of taking home better paychecks.

Differentiation

Not long ago a British automotive company proposed a friendly buyout of an Italian firm. Executives at both companies were excited about the opportunities for sharing distribution channels and manufacturing technologies. But the grand vision of a merged company turned to a nightmare as executives began meeting over the details. Their backgrounds and experiences were so different that they were endlessly confused and constantly apologizing to the other side for oversights and misunderstandings. At one meeting–the last as it turned out–the president of the Italian firm stood up and, smiling sadly, said, "I believe we all know what is the problem here ... it seems your forward is our reverse; your down, our up; your right, our wrong. Let us finish now, before war is declared."[14]

These automobile executives discovered that conflict is often caused by different values and beliefs due to unique backgrounds, experiences, or training. Mergers often produce conflict because they bring together people with divergent corporate cultures. Employees fight over the "right way" to do things because of their unique experiences in the separate companies. The British and Italian automobile executives probably also experienced conflict due to different national cultures. Cultural diversity makes it difficult to understand or accept the beliefs and values that other people hold toward organizational decisions and events.

Along with conflict generated from cultural diversity, many companies are experiencing a rising incidence of cross-generational conflict.[15] Younger and older employees have different needs, different expectations, and somewhat different values, which sometimes produce conflicting preferences and actions. Generational gaps have always existed, but this source of conflict is more common today because employees across age groups work together more than ever before. Virtual teams represent a third area where conflict is amplified due to differentiation. Recent investigations indicate that virtual teams have a high incidence of conflict because, in addition to increased cultural diversity, they have more difficulty than face-to-face (colocated) teams in establishing common mental models, norms, and temporal rhythms.[16]

Task Interdependence

Conflict tends to increase with the level of task interdependence. Task interdependence exists when team members must share common inputs to their individual tasks, need to interact in the process of executing their work, or receive outcomes (such as rewards) that are partly determined by the performance of others. The higher the level of task interdependence, the greater the risk of conflict because there is a greater chance that each side will disrupt or interfere with the other side's goals.[17]

Other than complete independence, employees tend to have the lowest risk of conflict when working with others in a pooled interdependence relationship. Pooled interdependence occurs where individuals operate independently except for reliance on a common resource or authority (see Chapter 9). The potential for conflict is higher in sequential interdependence work relationships, such as an assembly line. The highest risk of conflict tends to occur in reciprocal interdependence situations. With reciprocal interdependence, employees are highly dependent on each other and consequently have a higher probability of interfering with each other's work and personal goals. This increased interdependence partly accounts for the escalating conflict at Microsoft. As top management expects divisions to work more closely together, they have moved from pooled to sequential and reciprocal interdependence, thereby increasing perceptions of interference from each other's goals.

Scarce Resources

Resource scarcity generates conflict because each person or unit that requires the same resource necessarily undermines others who also need that resource to fulfill their goals. Consider the feud among employees and divisional managers at Microsoft, described in the opening vignette to this chapter. Although the Redmond, Washington–based software company may dominate several markets, its staff members still fight over limited resources, including budgets, personnel, and customers. Some of this conflict escalated when Microsoft introduced cost-cutting measures within the past few years when its growth and profitability flattened out.

Ambiguous Rules

Ambiguous rules–or the complete lack of rules–breed conflict. This occurs because uncertainty increases the risk that one party intends to interfere with the other party's goals. Ambiguity also encourages political tactics, and in some cases employees enter a free-for-all battle to win decisions in their favor. This explains why conflict is more common during mergers and acquisitions. Employees from both companies have conflicting practices and values, and few rules have developed to minimize the maneuvering for power and resources.[18] When clear rules exist, on the other hand, employees know what to expect from each other and have agreed to abide by those rules. Connections 13.1 illustrates how ambiguity bred conflict at Arthur Andersen. The now defunct accounting and consulting firm lacked clear guidelines to determine

Ambiguous Fee Structure Creates Fractious Divisions at Arthur Andersen

To outsiders, Arthur Andersen's "One Firm" policy was solid. The Chicago-based accounting firm provided the same quality of work anywhere in the world by the same type of people trained the same way. But when Barbara Toffler joined Andersen as an ethics consultant in 1996, she discovered plenty of infighting. Arthur Andersen is now gone because of accounting fraud at its client Enron; but internal conflict may have contributed to the accounting firm's demise as well.

Much of the dysfunctional conflict was caused by Arthur Andersen's ambiguous fee structure, which generously rewarded one engagement partner (the person in charge of the overall project) at the expense of other partners who provided services to the client. To maximize fees, executives fought over who should be the project's engagement partner and played games that would minimize the fees going to other groups. "While I was at Arthur Andersen, the fight for fees defined my existence," recalls Toffler.

In one incident a partner demanded that he should be the engagement partner because he had made the initial connection with a client, even though the project relied mainly on expertise from Barbara Toffler's ethical practices group. The two argued all the way to the airport and in several subsequent "violent" phone arguments. In another client proposal Toffler flew to Japan, only to spend two days of her time there negotiating through a translator with Andersen's Japanese engagement partner over how to split fees.

In a third incident several Arthur Andersen partners met with a potential client, supposedly to discuss their services. Instead the partners openly criticized each other during the pitch so the client would spend more money on their particular specialization. A couple of partners also extended the length of their presentations so other partners would have less time to convince the client of their particular value in the project. "Eventually I learned to screw someone else before they screwed me," says Toffler. "The struggle to win fees for your office and your group—and not someone else's—came to define the firm."

Source: Adapted from B.L. Toffler, *Final Accounting: Ambition, Greed, and the Fall of Arthur Andersen* (New York: Broadway Books, 2003).

Although Arthur Andersen employees put up a united front during the firm's dying days (as this photo shows), its ambiguous fee structure generated internal conflict that undermined the accounting firm's performance.

who would be the engagement partner (the person who gets financial credit for soliciting a customer), so partners and associates battled and postured over who would get this coveted position.

Communication Problems

Conflict often occurs due to the lack of opportunity, ability, or motivation to communicate effectively. Let's look at each of these causes. First, when two parties lack the opportunity to communicate, they tend to use stereotypes to explain past behaviors and anticipate future actions. Unfortunately stereotypes are sufficiently subjective that emotions can negatively distort the meaning of an opponent's actions, thereby escalating perceptions of conflict. Furthermore, without direct interaction the two sides have less psychological empathy for each other. Second, some people lack the necessary skills to communicate in a diplomatic, nonconfrontational manner. When one party communicates its disagreement in an arrogant way, opponents are more likely to heighten their perception of the conflict. Arrogant behavior also sends a message that one side intends to be competitive rather than cooperative. This may lead the other party to reciprocate with a similar conflict management style.[19] Consequently, as we explained earlier, ineffective communication often escalates the conflict cycle.

Ineffective communication can also lead to a third problem: less motivation to communicate in the future. Socioemotional conflict is uncomfortable, so people avoid interacting with others in a conflicting relationship. Unfortunately less communication can further escalate conflict because there is less opportunity to empathize with the opponent's situation, and opponents are more likely to rely on distorted stereotypes of the other party. In fact, conflict tends to further distort these stereotypes through the process of social identity (see Chapter 3). We begin to see competitors less favorably so that our self-image remains strong during these uncertain times.[20]

The lack of motivation to communicate also explains (along with different values and beliefs, described earlier) why conflict is more common in cross-cultural relationships. People tend to feel uncomfortable or awkward interacting with co-workers from different cultures, so they are less motivated to engage in dialogue with them. With limited communication, people rely more on stereotypes to fill in missing information. They also tend to misunderstand each other's verbal and nonverbal signals, further escalating the conflict.[21]

Interpersonal Conflict Management Styles

win–win orientation
The belief that conflicting parties will find a mutually beneficial solution to their disagreement.

win–lose orientation
The belief that conflicting parties are drawing from a fixed pie, so the more one party receives, the less the other party will receive.

The six structural conditions just described set the stage for conflict. The conflict process identified in Exhibit 13.1 illustrates that these sources of conflict lead to perceptions and emotions. Some people enter a conflict with a **win–win orientation**. This is the perception that the parties will find a mutually beneficial solution to their disagreement. They believe that the resources at stake are expandable rather than fixed if the parties work together to find a creative solution. Other people enter a conflict with a **win–lose orientation**. They adopt the belief that the parties are drawing from a fixed pie, so the more one party receives, the less the other party will receive.

Conflict tends to escalate when the parties develop a win–lose orientation because they rely on power and politics to gain advantage. A win–lose orientation may occasionally be appropriate when the conflict really is over a fixed resource, but few organizational conflicts are due to perfectly opposing interests with fixed resources. Some degree of win–win orientation is usually advantageous–that is, believing that each side's goals are not perfectly opposing. One possibility is that each party needs different parts of the resource. Another possibility is that various parts of the shared resource have different levels of value to each side.

Consider the example of a supplier and customer resolving a disagreement over the price of a product. Initially this seems like a clear win–lose situation—the supplier wants to receive more money for the product, whereas the customer wants to pay less money for it. Yet further discussion may reveal that the customer would be willing to pay more if the product could be provided earlier than originally arranged. The vendor may actually value that earlier delivery because it saves inventory costs. By looking at the bigger picture, both parties can often discover common ground.[22]

Adopting a win–win or win–lose orientation influences our conflict management style—that is, how we act toward the other person. The five conflict resolution styles described next can be placed in a two-dimensional grid reflecting the person's degree of concern for his or her own interests and concern for the other party's interests (see Exhibit 13.3). Problem solving is the only style that represents a purely win–win orientation. The other four styles represent variations of the win–lose approach.

- *Problem solving.* Problem solving tries to find a mutually beneficial solution for both parties. Information sharing is an important feature of this style because parties collaborate to identify common ground and potential solutions that satisfy all of them.

Exhibit 13.3
Interpersonal Conflict Management Styles

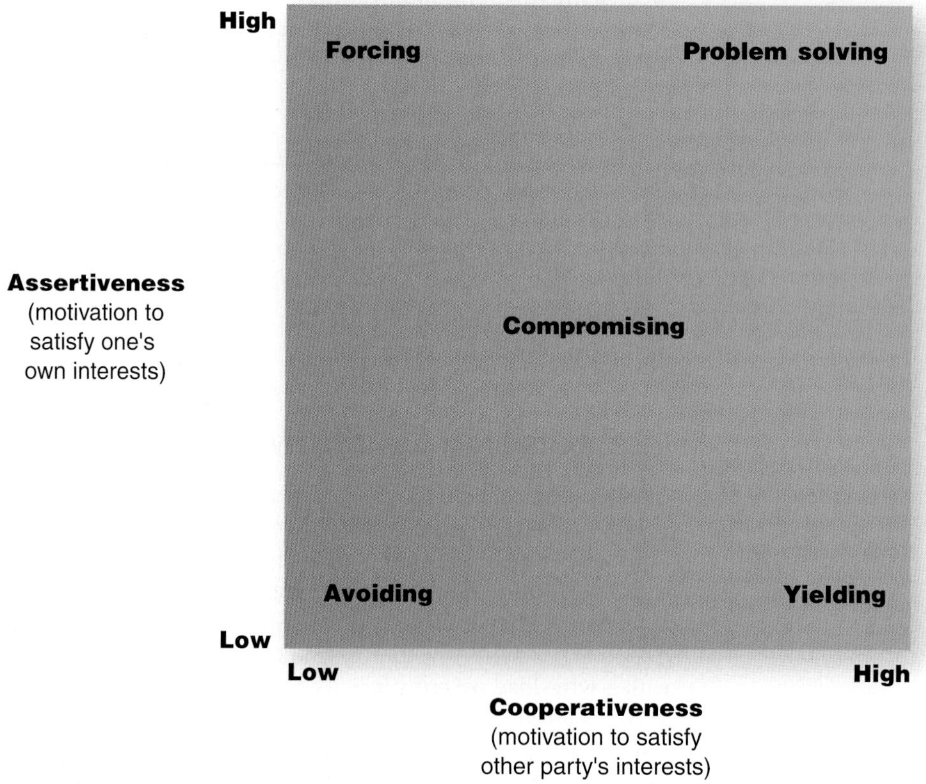

Source: C.K.W. de Dreu, A. Evers, B. Beersma, E.S. Kluwer, and A. Nauta, "A Theory-Based Measure of Conflict Management Strategies in the Workplace," *Journal of Organizational Behavior* 22 (2001), pp. 645–68. For earlier variations of this model, see T.L. Ruble and K. Thomas, "Support for a Two-Dimensional Model of Conflict Behavior," *Organizational Behavior and Human Performance* 16 (1976), p. 145.

NHLPA Shifts from Forcing to Problem Solving Bob Goodenow (left in photo) was called the Darth Vader of hockey. As the National Hockey League Players' Association (NHLPA) boss, his forcing style catapulted NHL player salaries from an average of $210,000 in the early 1990s to $1.3 million today. But while Goodenow's uncompromising approach rewarded players handsomely, critics say it also helped sink the public's image of NHL players, priced professional hockey out of smaller markets, and contributed to the cancellation of an entire season due to the recent player's strike. Goodenow stepped down when players agreed to the NHL owners' request to cap team salaries. Taking his place is Ted Saskin (right in photo), whose diplomatic problem-solving conflict resolution style couldn't be more different from Goodenow's. "We've got to be able to work more cooperatively (with the NHL) in the future," Saskin announced on the day he took over. NHL board of governors chairman Harley Hotchkiss thinks Saskin's approach to resolving differences is good for the sport's future. "I will say nothing bad about Bob Goodenow," insists Hotchkiss. "I just think that in any business you need a spirit of cooperation to move forward, and I think Ted Saskin will handle that well."[23]

- *Avoiding.* Avoiding tries to smooth over or avoid conflict situations altogether. It represents a low concern for both self and the other party; in other words, avoiders try to suppress thinking about the conflict. For example, some employees will rearrange their work area or tasks to minimize interaction with certain co-workers.[24]
- *Forcing.* Forcing tries to win the conflict at the other's expense. This style, which has the strongest win–lose orientation, relies on some of the "hard" influence tactics described in Chapter 12, particularly assertiveness, to get your own way.
- *Yielding.* Yielding involves giving in completely to the other side's wishes, or at least cooperating with little or no attention to your own interests. This style involves making unilateral concessions and unconditional promises, as well as offering help with no expectation of reciprocal help.
- *Compromising.* Compromising involves looking for a position in which your losses are offset by equally valued gains. It involves matching the other party's concessions, making conditional promises or threats, and actively searching for a middle ground between the interests of the two parties.[25]

Choosing the Best Conflict Management Style

Most of us have a preferred conflict management style, but the best style varies with the situation.[26] The problem-solving style is the preferred approach to resolving conflict in many situations because it is the only one that actively tries to optimize the value for both parties. However, this style works well only when the parties do not have perfectly opposing interests and when they have enough trust and openness to share information.

You might think that avoiding is an ineffective conflict management strategy, but it is actually the best approach where conflict has become socioemotional or where negotiating has a higher cost than the benefits of conflict resolution.[27] At the same time, conflict avoidance should not be a long-term solution where the conflict persists because it increases the other party's frustration. The forcing style of conflict resolution is usually inappropriate because organizational relationships rarely involve complete opposition. However, forcing may be necessary when you know you are correct and the dispute requires a quick solution. For example, a forcing style may be necessary when the other party engages in unethical conduct because any degree of unethical behavior is unacceptable. The forcing style may also be necessary where the other party would take advantage of more cooperative strategies.

The yielding style may be appropriate when the other party has substantially more power or the issue is not as important to you as to the other party. On the other hand, yielding behaviors may give the other side unrealistically high expectations, thereby motivating them to seek more from you in the future. In the long run, yielding may produce more conflict rather than resolve it. The compromising style may be best when there is little hope for mutual gain through problem solving, both parties have equal power, and both are under time pressure to settle their differences. However, compromise is rarely a final solution and may cause the parties to overlook options for mutual gain.

Cultural and Gender Differences in Conflict Management Styles

Cultural differences are more than just a source of conflict. Cultural background also affects the preferred conflict management style.[28] Some research suggests that people from collectivist cultures–where group goals are valued more than individual goals–are motivated to maintain harmonious relations and consequently are more likely than those from low collectivism cultures to manage disagreements through avoidance or problem solving. However, this view may be somewhat simplistic because people in some collectivist cultures are also more likely to publicly shame those whose actions conflict with expectations.[29]

Some writers suggest that men and women also tend to rely on different conflict management styles.[30] Generally speaking, women pay more attention than do men to the relationship between the parties. Consequently they tend to adopt a problem-solving style in business settings and are more willing to compromise to protect the relationship. Men tend to be more competitive and take a short-term orientation to the relationship. Of course we must be cautious about these observations because gender has a weak influence on conflict management style.

Structural Approaches to Conflict Management

Conflict management styles refer to how we approach the other party in a conflict situation. But conflict management also involves altering the underlying structural causes of potential conflict. The main structural approaches are identified in Exhibit 13.4. Although this section discusses ways to reduce conflict, we should keep in mind that conflict management sometimes calls for increasing conflict. This occurs mainly by reversing the strategies described over the next few pages.[31]

Emphasizing Superordinate Goals

A decade ago salespeople at Microchip Technology acted more like opponents than colleagues. As clients moved business to Asia, the U.S. and Asian sales reps would often compete for the same business, sometimes even undercutting each other's proposals. To minimize the dysfunctional conflict, the Mountain View, California, company made an unprecedented decision: It completely replaced sales commissions with stocks and bonuses based on the company's overall performance. Today sales staff are much more cooperative through mutual regard for the bigger picture–Microchip's long-term success.[32]

Exhibit 13.4
Structural Approaches to Conflict Management

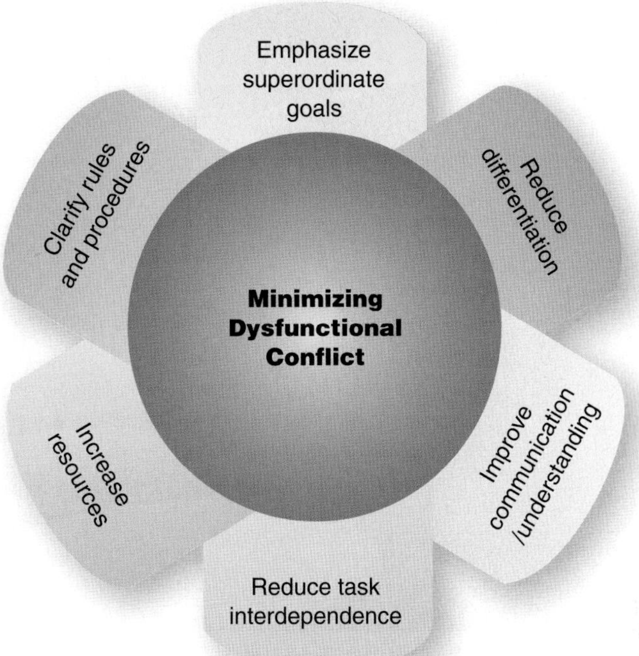

superordinate goals
Common objectives held by conflicting parties that are more important than their conflicting departmental or individual goals.

Microchip's executives minimized conflict among sales staff by getting them to focus on the company's superordinate goals rather than their conflicting subordinate goals. **Superordinate goals** are common objectives held by conflicting parties that are more important than the departmental or individual goals on which the conflict is based. By increasing commitment to corporatewide goals, employees place less emphasis on and therefore feel less conflict with co-workers over competing individual or departmental-level goals. They also potentially reduce the problem of differentiation by establishing a common frame of reference. For example, one study revealed that marketing managers in Hong Kong, China, Japan, and the United States were more likely to develop a collaborative conflict management style when executives aligned departmental goals with corporate objectives.[33]

Reducing Differentiation

Another way to minimize dysfunctional conflict is to reduce the differences that produce the conflict in the first place. The more employees think they have common backgrounds or experiences with co-workers, the more motivated they are to coordinate their activities and resolve conflict through constructive discussion with those co-workers.[34] One way to increase this commonality is by creating common experiences. The Manila Diamond Hotel in the Philippines accomplishes this by rotating staff across different departments. Hibernia Management and Development Company, which operates a large oil platform off the coast of Newfoundland, Canada, removed the "destructive differences" between hourly and salaried personnel by putting employees on salary rather than hourly wages. Multinational peacekeeping forces reduce differentiation among troops from the representative nations by providing opportunities for them to socialize and engage in common activities, including eating together.[35]

Toyota Drums Out Differences Employees at Toyota Motor Sales U.S.A. are drumming their way to a common bond and cooperation. Over the past three years, more than 3,000 Toyota employees have visited the automaker's training center (University of Toyota) in Torrance, California, to participate in drum circles. Typically in groups of 15 to 50 from one department, employees begin banging on one of the 150 percussion instruments available in the drum room. Few have played a percussion instrument before, so the first attempt rarely is worth recording. "At first it sounds pretty terrible, with everyone competing to be the loudest," admits Ron Johnson, Toyota's resident drum guru and a training center manager in Torrance. But most groups soon find a common beat without any guidance or conductor. Johnson recalls his first drum circle experience: "I'll never forget the spirit that came alive inside me. In a matter of moments, perfect strangers came together in synchronistic rhythm to share a common vision." By the end of the hourlong event most groups have formed a special bond that apparently increases their cooperation and sense of unity when they return to their jobs.[36]

Improving Communication and Understanding

A third way to resolve dysfunctional conflict is to give the conflicting parties more opportunities to communicate and understand each other. This recommendation relates back to the contact hypothesis described in Chapter 3. Specifically, the more meaningful interaction we have with someone, the less we rely on stereotypes to understand that person.[37] This positive effect is more pronounced when people work closely and frequently together on a shared goal in a meaningful task where they need to rely on each other (that is, cooperate rather than compete with each other). Another important ingredient is that the parties have equal status in that context.

There are two important caveats regarding the communication–understanding strategy. First, this strategy should be applied only *after* differentiation between the two sides has been reduced. If perceived differentiation remains high, attempts to manage conflict through dialogue might have the opposite effect because defense mechanisms are more likely to kick into action. These self-preservation forces increase stereotyping and tend to distort incoming sensory information. In other words, when forced to interact with people who we believe are quite different and in conflict with us, we tend to select information that reinforces that view.[38] Thus communication and understanding interventions are effective only when differentiation is sufficiently low.

Second, resolving differences through direct communication with the opposing party is a distinctly Western strategy that is not as comfortably applied in most parts of Asia and in other collectivist cultures.[39] As noted earlier, people in high collectivism cultures prefer an avoidance conflict management style because it is the most consistent with harmony and saving face. Direct communication is a high-risk strategy because it easily threatens the need to save face and maintain harmony.

Talking Circles Where avoidance is ineffective in the long run, some collectivist groups engage in structured forms of dialogue that enable communication with less risk of upsetting harmony. One such practice in Native American culture is the talking circle.[40] A talking circle is an ancient group process used to educate, make decisions, and repair group harmony due to conflict. Participants sit in a circle and often begin with song, prayer, shaking hands with the next person, or some other communal activity. Then they share their experiences, information, and stories relating to the issue.

A talking stick or other natural object (such as a rock or feather) is held by the person speaking, which minimizes interruptions and dysfunctional verbal reactions by others. Talking circles are not aimed at solving problems through negotiated discussion. In fact, talking circle norms usually discourage participants from responding to someone else's statements. Rather, the emphasis is on healing relationships and restoring harmony, typically through the circle's communal experience and improved understanding of each person's views. Talking circles are still rare in business organizations, but they have been applied in meetings between aboriginal people and government representatives in several countries.

Reducing Task Interdependence

Conflict increases with the level of interdependence, so minimizing dysfunctional conflict might involve reducing the level of interdependence between the parties. If cost-effective, this might occur by dividing the shared resource so that each party has exclusive use of part of it. Sequentially or reciprocally interdependent jobs might be combined to form a pooled interdependence. For example, rather than having one employee serve customers and another operate the cash register, each employee could handle both customer activities alone. Buffers also help to reduce task interdependence between people. Buffers include resources, such as adding more inventory between people who perform sequential tasks.

Organizations also use human buffers–people who serve as intermediaries between interdependent people or work units who do not get along through direct interaction. For instance, one business school dean worked effectively with corporate leaders but held little affection for faculty. To minimize potential conflict, the dean hired a faculty-friendly associate dean to fulfill the internal leadership role. The associate dean became an intermediary who minimized the amount of time during which the dean and faculty needed to directly interact with each other.

Increasing Resources

An obvious way to reduce conflict due to resource scarcity is to increase the amount of resources available. Corporate decision makers might quickly dismiss this solution because of the costs involved. However, they need to carefully compare these costs with the costs of dysfunctional conflict arising out of resource scarcity.

Clarifying Rules and Procedures

Conflicts that arise from ambiguous rules can be minimized by establishing rules and procedures. Armstrong World Industries Inc. applied this strategy when consultants and information systems employees clashed while working together on development of a client–server network. Information systems employees at the flooring and building materials company thought they should be in charge, whereas consultants believed they had the senior role. Also, the consultants wanted to work long hours and take Friday off to fly home, whereas Armstrong employees wanted to work regular hours. The company reduced these conflicts by having both parties agree on specific responsibilities and roles. The agreement also assigned two senior executives at the companies to establish rules if future disagreements arose.[41]

Rules establish changes to the terms of interdependence, such as an employee's hours of work or a supplier's fulfillment of an order. In most cases the parties affected by these rules are involved in the process of deciding these terms of interdependence. By redefining the terms of interdependence, the strategy of clarifying rules is part of the larger process of negotiation.

Learning Objectives

After reading the next two sections you should be able to

7. Outline four situational influences on negotiations.

8. Describe four behaviors that are characteristic of effective negotiators.

9. Compare and contrast the three types of third-party dispute resolution.

Resolving Conflict through Negotiation

Think back through yesterday's events. Maybe you had to work out an agreement with other students about what tasks to complete for a team project. Chances are that you shared transportation with someone, so you had to clarify the timing of the ride. Then perhaps there was the question of who made dinner. Each of these daily events created potential conflict, and they were resolved through negotiation. **Negotiation** occurs whenever two or more conflicting parties attempt to resolve their divergent goals by redefining the terms of their interdependence. In other words, people negotiate when they think that discussion can produce a more satisfactory arrangement (at least for them) in their exchange of goods or services.

negotiation
Two or more conflicting parties attempt to resolve their divergent goals by redefining the terms of their interdependence.

As you can see, negotiation is not an obscure practice reserved for labor and management bosses when hammering out a collective agreement. Everyone negotiates daily. Most of the time you don't even realize that you are in negotiations. Negotiation is particularly evident in the workplace because employees work interdependently with each other. They negotiate with their supervisors over next month's work assignments, with customers over the sale and delivery schedules of their product, and with co-workers over when to have lunch. And yes, they occasionally negotiate with each other in labor disputes and workplace agreements.

Some writers suggest that negotiations are more successful when the parties adopt a problem-solving style, whereas others caution that this conflict management style is sometimes costly.[42] We know that any win–lose style (forcing, yielding, or the like) is unlikely to produce the optimal solution because the parties have not shared information necessary to discover a mutually satisfactory solution. On the other hand, we must be careful about adopting an open problem-solving style until mutual trust has been established.

Exhibit 13.5 **Bargaining Zone Model of Negotiations**

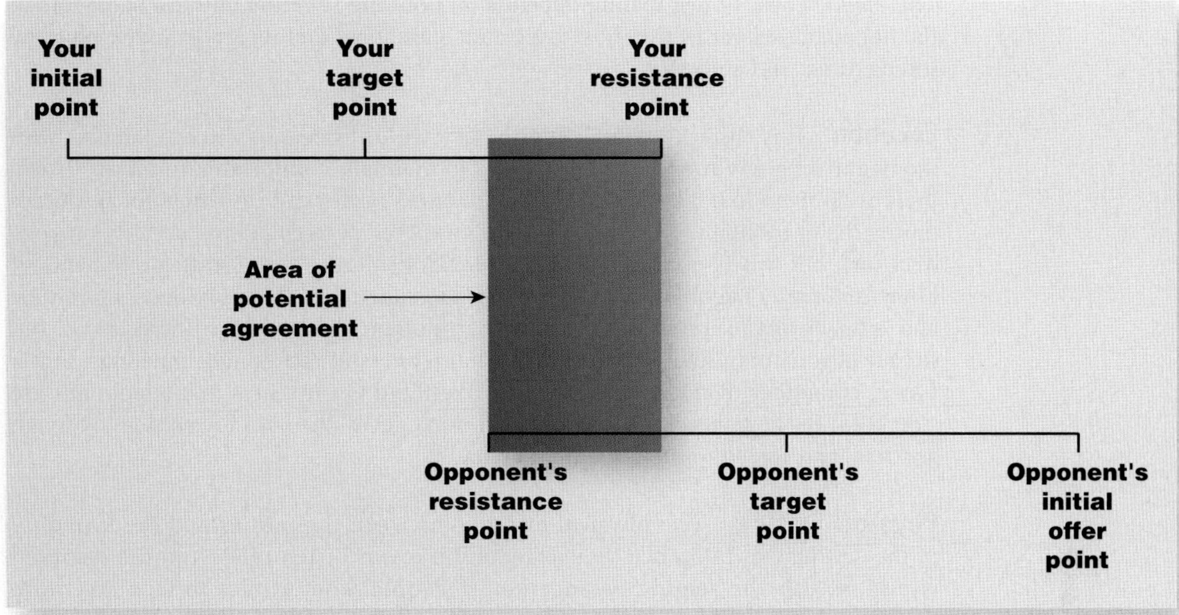

The concern with the problem-solving style is that information is power, so information sharing gives the other party more power to leverage a better deal if the opportunity occurs. Skilled negotiators often adopt a cautious problem-solving style at the outset by sharing information slowly and determining whether the other side will reciprocate. In this respect they try to establish trust with the other party.[43] They switch to one of the win–lose styles only when it becomes apparent that a win–win solution is not possible or the other party is unwilling to share information with a cooperative orientation.

Bargaining Zone Model of Negotiations

The negotiation process moves each party along a continuum with an area of potential overlap called the *bargaining zone*.[44] Exhibit 13.5 displays one possible bargaining zone situation. This linear diagram illustrates a purely win–lose situation–one side's gain will be the other's loss. However, the bargaining zone model can also be applied to situations in which both sides potentially gain from the negotiations. As this model illustrates, the parties typically establish three main negotiating points. The *initial offer point* is the team's opening offer to the other party. This may be its best expectation or a pie-in-the-sky starting point. The *target point* is the team's realistic goal or expectation for a final agreement. The *resistance point* is the point beyond which the team will make no further concessions.

The parties begin negotiations by describing their initial offer points for each item on the agenda. In most cases the participants know that this is only a starting point that will change as both sides offer concessions. In win–lose situations neither the target nor the resistance point is revealed to the other party. However, people try to discover the other side's resistance point because this knowledge helps them determine how much they can gain without breaking off negotiations. When the parties have a win-win orientation, on the other hand, the objective is to find a creative solution that keeps everyone close to their initial offer points. They hope to find an arrangement by which each side loses relatively little value on some issues and gains significantly more on other issues.

Situational Influences on Negotiations

The effectiveness of negotiating depends on both the situation and the behaviors of the negotiators. Four of the most important situational factors are location, physical setting, time, and audience.

Location It is easier to negotiate on your own turf because you are familiar with the negotiating environment and are able to maintain comfortable routines.[45] Also, there is no need to cope with travel-related stress or depend on others for resources during the negotiation. Of course you can't walk out of negotiations as easily on your own turf, but this is usually a minor issue. Considering these strategic benefits of home turf, many negotiators agree to neutral territory. Telephones, videoconferences, and other forms of information technology potentially avoid territorial issues, but skilled negotiators usually prefer the media richness of face-to-face meetings. Frank Lowy, cofounder of retail property giant Westfield Group, says that telephones are "too cold" for negotiating. "From a voice I don't get all the cues I need. I go by touch and feel, and I need to see the other person."[46]

Physical Setting The physical distance between the parties and the formality of the setting can influence their orientation toward each other and the disputed issues. So can the seating arrangements. People who sit face-to-face are more likely to develop a win–lose orientation toward the conflict situation. In contrast, some negotiation groups deliberately intersperse participants around the table to convey a win–win orientation. Others arrange the seating so that both parties face a white board, reflecting the notion that both parties face the same problem or issue.

Time Passage and Deadlines The more time people invest in negotiations, the stronger their commitment becomes to reaching an agreement. This increases the motivation to resolve the conflict, but it also fuels the escalation of commitment problems described in Chapter 8. For example, the more time put into negotiations, the stronger the tendency to make unwarranted concessions so that the negotiations do not fail.

Time deadlines may be useful to the extent that they motivate the parties to complete negotiations. However, time pressures are usually a liability in negotiations.[47] One problem is that time pressure inhibits a problem-solving conflict management style because the parties have less time to exchange information or present flexible offers. Negotiators under time pressure also process information less effectively, so they have less creative ability to discover a win–win solution to the conflict. There is also anecdotal evidence that negotiators make excessive concessions and soften their demands more rapidly as a deadline approaches.

Audience Characteristics Most negotiators have audiences–anyone with a vested interest in the negotiation outcomes, such as executives, other team members, or the general public. Negotiators tend to act differently when their audience observes the negotiation or has detailed information about the process, compared to situations in which the audience sees only the end results.[48] When the audience has direct surveillance over the proceedings, negotiators tend to be more competitive, less willing to make concessions, and more likely to engage in political tactics against the other party. This "hardline" behavior shows the audience that the negotiator is working for their interests. With their audience watching, negotiators also have more interest in saving face.

Negotiator Behaviors

Negotiator behaviors play an important role in resolving conflict. Four of the most important behaviors are setting goals, gathering information, communicating effectively, and making concessions.

- *Preparation and goal setting.* Research consistently reports that people have more favorable negotiation results when they prepare for the negotiation and set goals.[49] In particular, negotiators should carefully think through their initial offer, target, and resistance points. They need to consider alternative strategies in case the negotiation fails. Negotiators also need to check their underlying assumptions, as well as goals and values. Equally important is the need to research what the other party wants from the negotiation. "You have to be prepared every which way about the people, the subject, and your fallback position," advises former Bombardier CEO Tellier. "Before walking into the room for the actual negotiation, I ask my colleagues to throw some curve balls at me," he says.[50]
- *Gathering information.* "Seek to understand before you seek to be understood." This popular philosophy from management guru Stephen Covey applies to effective negotiations. It means that we should spend more time listening closely to the other party and asking for details.[51] One way to improve the information-gathering process is to have a team of people participate in negotiations. Asian companies tend to have large negotiation teams for this purpose.[52] With more information about the opponent's interests and needs, negotiators are better able to discover low-cost concessions or proposals that will satisfy the other side.
- *Communicating effectively.* Effective negotiators communicate in a way that maintains effective relationships between the parties. Specifically, they minimize socio-emotional conflict by focusing on issues rather than people. Effective negotiators also avoid irritating statements such as "I think you'll agree that this is a generous offer." Third, effective negotiators are masters of persuasion. They structure the content of their message so it is accepted by others, not merely understood.[53]
- *Making concessions.* Concessions are important because they (1) enable the parties to move toward the area of potential agreement, (2) symbolize each party's motivation to bargain in good faith, and (3) tell the other party the relative importance of the negotiating items.[54] How many concessions should you make? This varies with the other party's expectations and the level of trust between you. For instance, many Chinese negotiators are wary of people who change their position during the early stages of negotiations. Similarly, some writers warn that Russian negotiators tend to view concessions as a sign of weakness, rather than a sign of trust.[55] Generally the best strategy is to be moderately tough and give just enough concessions to communicate sincerity and motivation to resolve the conflict.[56] Being too tough can undermine relations between the parties; giving too many concessions implies weakness and encourages the other party to use power and resistance.

Third-Party Conflict Resolution

third-party conflict resolution
Any attempt by a relatively neutral person to help the parties resolve their differences.

Most of this chapter has focused on people directly involved in a conflict, yet many disputes in organizational settings are resolved with the assistance of a third party. **Third-party conflict resolution** is any attempt by a relatively neutral person to help the parties resolve their differences. There are generally three types of third-party dispute resolution activities: arbitration, inquisition, and mediation. These activities can be classified by their level of control over the process and control over the decision (see Exhibit 13.6).[57]

Exhibit 13.6
Types of Third-Party Intervention

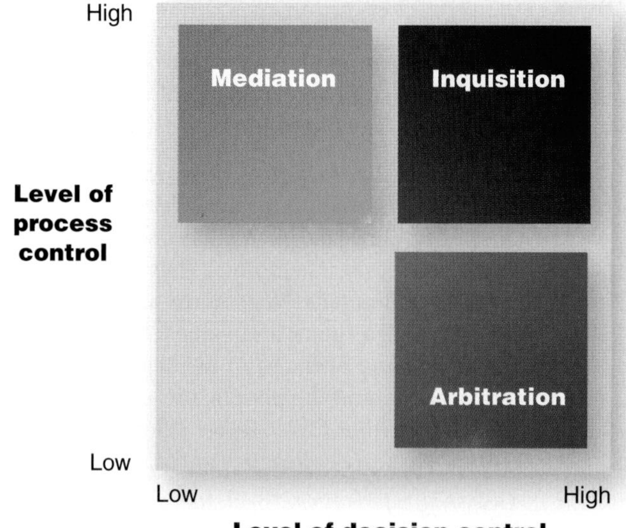

- *Arbitration.* Arbitrators have high control over the final decision but low control over the process. Executives engage in this strategy by following previously agreed rules of due process, listening to arguments from the disputing employees, and making a binding decision. Arbitration is applied as the final stage of grievances by unionized employees, but it is also becoming more common in nonunion conflicts.
- *Inquisition.* Inquisitors control all discussion about the conflict. Like arbitrators, they have high decision control because they choose the form of conflict resolution. However, they also have high process control because they choose which information to examine and how to examine it, and they generally decide how the conflict resolution process will be handled.
- *Mediation.* Mediators have high control over the intervention process. In fact, their main purpose is to manage the process and context of interaction between the disputing parties. However, the parties make the final decision about how to resolve their differences. Thus mediators have little or no control over the conflict resolution decision.

Choosing the Best Third-Party Intervention Strategy

Team leaders, executives, and co-workers regularly intervene in disputes between employees and departments. Sometimes they adopt a mediator role; other times they serve as arbitrators. However, research suggests that people in positions of authority (like managers) usually adopt an inquisitional approach whereby they dominate the intervention process as well as making a binding decision.[58] Managers like the inquisition approach because it is consistent with the decision-oriented nature of managerial jobs, gives them control over the conflict process and outcome, and tends to resolve disputes efficiently.

However, the inquisitional approach to third-party conflict resolution is usually the least effective in organizational settings.[59] One problem is that leaders who take an inquisitional role tend to collect limited information about the problem using this approach, so their imposed decision may produce an ineffective solution to the conflict. Also, employees often view inquisitional procedures and outcomes as unfair because they have little control over this approach.

Which third-party intervention is most appropriate in organizations? The answer partly depends on the situation, such as the type of dispute, the relationship between the manager and employees, and cultural values such as power distance.[60] But generally speaking, for everyday disputes between two employees, the mediation approach is usually best because this gives employees more responsibility for resolving their own disputes. The third-party representative merely establishes an appropriate context for conflict resolution. Although not as efficient as other strategies, mediation potentially offers the highest level of employee satisfaction with the conflict process and outcomes.[61] When employees cannot resolve their differences, arbitration seems to work best because the predetermined rules of evidence and other processes create a higher sense of procedural fairness. Moreover, arbitration is preferred where the organization's goals should take priority over individual goals.

Alternative Dispute Resolution After a two-year educational leave, Michael Kenney returned to Eastman Kodak Co. as a contractor, not the permanent position he previously held. A year later Kodak announced that Kenney's digitizing technician

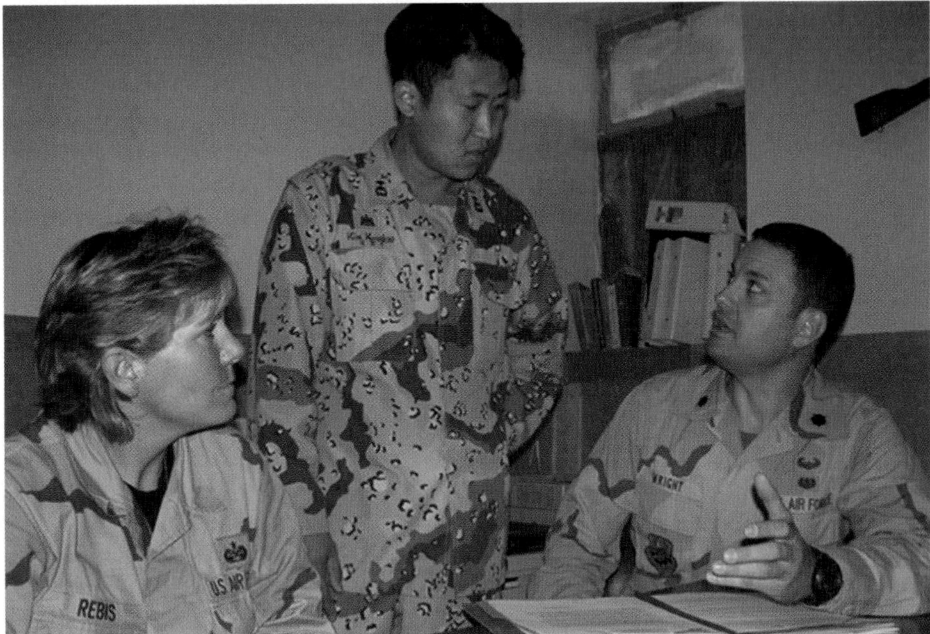

U.S. Air Force Staff Resolve Workplace Battles through ADR Rather than battle each other in court or external arbitration, the U.S. Air Force and its civilian staff have resolved most workplace conflicts quickly and with improved mutual understanding through alternative dispute resolution (ADR). "The parties, in essence, maintain control over the [ADR] process and its outcome," explains Air Mobility Command civilian programs branch chief Diana Hendrix. Some Air Force bases retain a mediator to identify issues and explore options with the parties without imposing a solution. Other bases use peer review panels consisting of four to six union and nonunion employees who examine facts, listen to the parties, and make a final binding decision. The U.S. Air Force's goal is to use ADR for at least half of its employee disputes. ADR currently processes most disputes in less than one month. But even with these formal third-party systems in place, Diana Hendrix explains that supervisors are the first line of defense in resolving workplace conflict. "Ultimately, it's about Air Force employees and supervisors resolving conflicts in an efficient and effective manner so they can continue performing the Air Force mission of supporting and defending the United States of America," she says.[62]

position would disappear and that he would soon be jobless. Kenney didn't think losing his permanent position status was fair, so he took his dispute to Kodak's Resolution Support Services program. The program gives trained employees and managers the right to hear both sides of the conflict and, if appropriate, overturn management's decision. A trained adjudicator listened to Kenney's side of the story and then, with Kenney excused, listened to the supervisor and other witnesses. The adjudicator decided that Kenney should have a permanent position because Kodak applied its educational leave policy inconsistently.[63]

alternative dispute resolution (ADR)
A third-party dispute resolution process that includes mediation, typically followed by arbitration.

Eastman Kodak has joined a long list of firms that have taken third-party resolution one step further through an **alternative dispute resolution (ADR)** process. ADR combines third-party dispute resolution in an orderly sequence. ADR typically begins with a meeting between the employee and employer to clarify and negotiate their differences. If this fails, a mediator is brought in to help the parties reach a mutually agreeable solution. If mediation fails, the parties submit their case to an arbitrator whose decision may be either binding or voluntarily accepted by the employer. Although most ADR systems rely on professional arbitrators, some firms, such as Eastman Kodak and some U.S. Air Force bases, prefer peer arbitrations, which include a panel of co-workers and managers who are not involved in the dispute.[64] Overall, ADR helps the parties solve their own problems and tends to be more conciliatory than courtroom battles.

Whether resolving conflict through third-party dispute resolution or direct negotiation, we need to recognize that many solutions come from the sources of conflict that were identified earlier in this chapter. This may seem obvious; but in the heat of conflict, people often focus on each other rather than the underlying causes. Recognizing these conflict sources is the role of effective leadership, which is discussed in the next chapter.

Chapter Summary

Conflict is the process in which one party perceives that its interests are being opposed or negatively affected by another party. The conflict process begins with the sources of conflict. These sources lead one or both sides to perceive a conflict and to experience conflict emotions. This, in turn, produces manifest conflict, such as behaviors toward the other side. The conflict process often escalates through a series of episodes.

Conflict management maximizes the benefits and minimizes the dysfunctional consequences of conflict. Constructive conflict, a possible benefit of conflict, occurs when team members debate their different perceptions about an issue in a way that keeps the conflict focused on the task rather than people. Socioemotional conflict, a negative outcome, occurs when differences are viewed as personal attacks rather than attempts to resolve an issue. Socioemotional conflict tends to emerge in most constructive conflict episodes, but it is less likely to dominate when the parties are emotionally intelligent, have a cohesive team, and have supportive team norms. The main problems with conflict are that it may lead to job stress, dissatisfaction, and turnover.

Conflict tends to increase when people have incompatible goals, differentiation (different values and beliefs), interdependent tasks, scarce resources, ambiguous rules, and problems communicating with each other. Conflict is more common in a multicultural workforce because of greater differentiation and communication problems among employees.

People with a win–win orientation believe the parties will find a mutually beneficial solution to their disagreement. Those with a win–lose orientation adopt the belief that the parties are drawing from a fixed pie. The latter tends to escalate conflict. Among the five interpersonal conflict management styles, only problem solving represents a purely win–win orientation. The four other styles–avoiding, forcing, yielding, and compromising–adopt some variation of a win–lose orientation. Women and people with high collectivism tend to use a problem-solving or avoidance style more than men and people with high individualism.

Structural approaches to conflict management include emphasizing superordinate goals, reducing differentiation, improving communication and understanding, reducing task interdependence, increasing resources, and clarifying rules and procedures. These elements can also be altered to stimulate conflict.

Negotiation occurs whenever two or more conflicting parties attempt to resolve their divergent goals by redefining the terms of their interdependence. Negotiations are influenced by several situational factors, including location, physical setting, time passage and deadlines, and audience. Important negotiator behaviors include preparation and goal setting, gathering information, communicating effectively, and making concessions.

Third-party conflict resolution is any attempt by a relatively neutral person to help the parties resolve their differences. The three main forms of third-party dispute resolution are mediation, arbitration, and inquisition. Managers tend to use an inquisition approach, although mediation and arbitration are more appropriate, depending on the situation. Alternative dispute resolution applies mediation but may also involve negotiation and eventually arbitration.

Key Terms

alternative dispute resolution (ADR), p. 390
conflict, p. 370
conflict management, p. 372
constructive conflict, p. 372
negotiation, p. 384
socioemotional conflict, p. 372
superordinate goals, p. 381
third-party conflict resolution, p. 387
win–lose orientation, p. 377
win–win orientation, p. 377

Critical Thinking Questions

1. Distinguish constructive conflict from socioemotional conflict and explain how to apply the former without having the latter become a problem.
2. The chief executive officer of Creative Toys Inc. has read about cooperation in Japanese companies and vows to bring this same philosophy to the company. The goal is to avoid all conflict so that employees will work cooperatively and be happier at Creative Toys. Discuss the merits and limitations of the CEO's policy.
3. Conflict among managers emerged soon after a French company acquired a Swedish firm. The Swedes perceived the French management as hierarchical and arrogant, whereas the French thought the Swedes were naive, cautious, and lacking in achievement orientation. Describe ways to reduce dysfunctional conflict in this situation.
4. This chapter describes three levels of task interdependence that exist in interpersonal and intergroup relationships. Identify examples of these three levels in your work or school activities. How do these three levels affect potential conflict for you?
5. Jane has just been appointed as purchasing manager of Tacoma Technologies Corp. The previous purchasing manager, who recently retired, was known for his "winner-take-all" approach to suppliers. He continually fought for more discounts and was skeptical about any special deals that suppliers would propose. A few suppliers refused to do business with Tacoma Technologies, but senior management was confident that the former purchasing manager's approach minimized the company's costs. Jane wants to try a more collaborative approach to working with suppliers. Will her approach work? How should she adopt a more collaborative approach in future negotiations with suppliers?
6. You are a special assistant to the commander-in-chief of a peacekeeping mission to a war-torn part of the world. The unit consists of a few thousand peacekeeping troops from the United States, France, India, and four other countries. The troops will work together for approximately one year. What strategies would you recommend to improve mutual understanding and minimize conflict among these troops?
7. Suppose you head one of five divisions in a multinational organization and are about to begin this year's budget deliberations at headquarters. What are the characteristics of your audience in these negotiations, and what effect might they have on your negotiation behavior?
8. Managers tend to use an inquisitional approach to resolving disputes between employees and departments. Describe the inquisitional approach and discuss its appropriateness in organizational settings.

Case Study 13.1 CONFLICT IN CLOSE QUARTERS

A team of psychologists at Moscow's Institute for Biomedical Problems (IBMP) wanted to learn more about the dynamics of long-term isolation in space. This knowledge would be applied to the International Space Station, a joint project of several countries that would send people into space for more than six months. It would eventually include a trip to Mars taking up to three years.

IBMP set up a replica of the *Mir* space station in Moscow. They then arranged for three international researchers from Japan, Canada, and Austria to spend 110 days isolated in a chamber the size of a train car. This chamber joined a smaller chamber where four Russian cosmonauts had already completed half of their 240 days of isolation. This was the first time an international crew was involved in the studies. None of the participants spoke English as their first language, yet they communicated throughout their stay in English at varying levels of proficiency.

Judith Lapierre, a French–Canadian, was the only female in the experiment. Along with obtaining a PhD in public health and social medicine, Lapierre had studied space sociology at the International Space University in France and conducted isolation research in the Antarctic. This was her fourth trip to Russia, where she had learned the language. The mission was supposed to have a second female participant from the Japanese space program, but she was not selected by IBMP.

The Japanese and Austrian participants viewed the participation of a woman as a favorable factor, says Lapierre. For example, to make the surroundings more comfortable, they rearranged the furniture, hung posters on the wall, and put a tablecloth on the kitchen table. "We adapted our environment, whereas the Russians just viewed it as something to be endured," she explains. "We decorated for Christmas because I'm the kind of person who likes to host people."

New Year's Eve Turmoil

Ironically, it was at one of those social events, the New Year's Eve party, that events took a turn for the worse. After drinking vodka (allowed by the Russian space agency), two of the Russian cosmonauts got into a fistfight that left blood splattered on the chamber walls. At one point a colleague hid the knives in the station's kitchen because of fears that the two Russians were about to stab each other. The two cosmonauts, who generally did not get along, had to be restrained by other men. Soon after that brawl, the Russian commander grabbed Lapierre, dragged her out of view of the television monitoring cameras, and kissed her aggressively–twice. Lapierre fought him off, but the message didn't register. He tried to kiss her again the next morning.

The next day the international crew complained to IBMP about the behavior of the Russian cosmonauts. The Russian institute apparently took no action against any of the aggressors. Instead the institute's psychologists replied that the incidents were part of the experiment. They wanted crew members to solve their personal problems with mature discussion without asking for outside help. "You have to understand that *Mir* is an autonomous object, far away from anything," Vadim Gushin, the IBMP psychologist in charge of project, explained after the experiment had ended in March. "If the crew can't solve problems among themselves, they can't work together."

Following IBMP's response, the international crew wrote a scathing letter to the Russian institute and the space agencies involved in the experiment. "We had never expected such events to take place in a highly controlled scientific experiment where individuals go through a multistep selection process," they wrote. "If we had known ... we would not have joined it as subjects." The letter also complained about IBMP's response to their concerns.

Informed about the New Year's Eve incident, the Japanese space program convened an emergency meeting on January 2 to address the incidents. Soon after the Japanese team member quit, apparently shocked by IBMP's inaction. He was replaced with a Russian researcher on the international team. Ten days after the fight–a little over a month after the international team began the mission–the doors between the Russian and international crews' chambers were barred at the request of the international research team. Lapierre later emphasized that this action was taken because of concerns about violence, not the incident involving her.

A Stolen Kiss or Sexual Harassment

By the end of the experiment in March, news of the fistfight between the cosmonauts and the commander's attempts to kiss Lapierre had reached the public. Russian scientists attempted to play down the kissing incident by saying that it was one fleeting kiss, a clash of cultures, and a female participant who was too emotional.

"In the West, some kinds of kissing are regarded as sexual harassment. In our culture it's nothing," said Russian scientist Vadim Gushin in one interview. In another interview he explained, "The problem of sexual harassment is given a lot of attention in North America but less in Europe. In Russia it is even less of an issue, not because we are more or less moral than the rest of the world; we just have different priorities."

Judith Lapierre says the kissing incident was tolerable compared to this reaction from the Russian scientists who conducted the experiment. "They don't get it at all," she complains. "They don't think anything is wrong. I'm more frustrated than ever. The worst thing is that they don't realize it was wrong."

Norbert Kraft, the Austrian scientist on the international team, also disagreed with the Russian interpretation of events. "They're trying to protect themselves," he says. "They're trying to put the fault on others. But this is not a cultural issue. If a woman doesn't want to be kissed, it is not acceptable."

Discussion Questions

1. Identify the different conflict episodes that exist in this case. Who was in conflict with whom?
2. What are the sources of conflict for these conflict incidents?
3. What conflict management style(s) did Lapierre, the international team, and Gushin use to resolve these conflicts? What style(s) would have worked best in these situations?
4. What conflict management interventions were applied here? Did they work? What alternative strategies would work best in this situation and in the future?

The facts of this case were pieced together by Steven L. McShane from the following sources: G. Sinclair Jr., "If You Scream in Space, Does Anyone Hear?" *Winnipeg Free Press*, 5 May 2000, p. A4; S. Martin, "Reining in the Space Cowboys," *Globe & Mail*, 19 April 2000, p. R1; M. Gray, "A Space Dream Sours," *Maclean's*, 17 April 2000, p. 26; E. Niiler, "In Search of the Perfect Astronaut," *Boston Globe*, 4 April 2000, p. E4; J. Tracy, "110-Day Isolation Ends in Sullen ... Isolation," *Moscow Times*, 30 March 2000, p. 1; M. Warren, "A Mir Kiss?" *Daily Telegraph* (London), 30 March 2000, p. 22; G. York, "Canadian's Harassment Complaint Scorned," *Globe & Mail*, 25 March 2000, p. A2; S. Nolen, "Lust in Space," *Globe & Mail*, 24 March 2000, p. A3.

Case Study 13.2 THE HOUSE OF PRITZKER

BusinessWeek

Just four years after the death of patriarch Jay Pritzker, one of America's wealthiest families is being torn apart by sibling rivalry and resentment. At the heart of the dispute is a rift over control of the family businesses and fortune, which include Hyatt Hotels, thousands of apartment units, industrial conglomerate Marmon Group, and stakes in Reliant Pharmaceuticals and First Health Group. Tom, the eldest son, was groomed to lead the family business and had demonstrated the ability to invest and negotiate. But even Tom could not prevent the escalating disputes among other Pritzker family members.

This *BusinessWeek* case study examines the feud in one of America's wealthiest families. It describes the tensions that have built up in recent years, and identifies the solutions that Jay Pritzker and his son, Tom, have tried to use to diffuse the conflict. Read through this *BusinessWeek* article at www.mhhe.com/mcshane4e and prepare for the discussion questions below.

Discussion Questions

1. Identify the sources of conflict that explain current relations in the Pritzker family.
2. What did Tom do to try to minimize the conflict among family members? Did any of it work? Why or why not?
3. What other organizational behavior concepts seem to be relevant to this story about rivalries in the Pritzker family and its businesses?

Source: J. Weber, "The House of Pritzker," *BusinessWeek*, 17 March 2003, 58.

Class Exercise 13.3 THE CONTINGENCIES OF CONFLICT HANDLING

Gerard A. Callanan and David F. Perri, West Chester University of Pennsylvania

PURPOSE This exercise is designed to help you understand the contingencies of applying conflict handling styles in organizational settings.

INSTRUCTIONS

1. Participants will read each of the five scenarios presented here and select the most appropriate response from among the five alternatives. Each scenario has a situationally correct response.
2. *(Optional)* The instructor may ask each student to complete the Dutch Test for conflict handling self-assessment in this chapter (Self-Assessment 13.5) or a similar instrument. This instrument will provide an estimate of your preferred conflict handling style.
3. As a class, participants will give their feedback on the responses to each of the scenarios, with the instructor guiding discussion on the contextual factors embodied in each scenario. For each scenario the class should identify the response selected by the majority. In addition, participants will discuss how they decided on the choices they made and the contextual factors they took into account in making their selections.
4. Students will compare their responses to the five scenarios with their results from the conflict handling self-assessment. Discussion will focus on the extent to which each person's preferred conflict handling style influenced his or her choices in this activity, as well as the implications of this style preference for managing conflict in organizations.

SCENARIO #1

SETTING You are a manager of a division in the accounting department of a large eastern U.S. bank. Nine exempt-level analysts and six nonexempt clerical staff report to you. Recently one of your analysts, Jane Wilson, has sought the bank's approval for tuition reimbursement for the cost of an evening MBA program specializing in organizational behavior. The bank normally encourages employees to seek advanced degrees on a part-time basis. Indeed, through your encouragement, nearly all members of your staff are pursuing additional schoolwork. You consult the bank's policy manual and discover that two approvals are necessary for reimbursement–yours and that of the manager of training and development, Kathy Gordon. Further, the manual states that approval for reimbursement will be granted only if the coursework is "reasonably job related." Based on your review of the matter, you decide to approve Jane's request for reimbursement. However, Kathy Gordon rejects it outright by claiming that coursework in organizational behavior is not related to an accounting analyst position. She states that the bank will reimburse the analyst only for a degree in either accounting or finance. In your opinion, however, the interpersonal skills and insights to be gained from a degree in organizational behavior are job related and can also benefit the employee in future assignments. The analyst job requires interaction with a variety of individuals at different levels in the organization, and it is important that interpersonal and communication skills be strong.

After further discussion it becomes clear that you and Kathy Gordon have opposite views of the matter. Because both of you are at the same organizational level and have equal status, it appears that you are at an impasse. Although the goal of reimbursement is important, you are faced with other pressing demands on your time. In addition, the conflict has diverted the attention of your work group away from its primary responsibilities. Because the school term is about to begin, it is essential that you and Kathy Gordon reach a timely agreement to enable Jane to pursue her coursework.

ACTION ALTERNATIVES FOR SCENARIO #1 Please indicate your first (1) and second (2) choices from among the following alternatives by writing the appropriate numbers in the space provided.

Action Alternative	Ranking (1st and 2nd)
1. You go along with Kathy Gordon's view and advise Jane Wilson to select either accounting or finance as a major for her MBA.	______
2. You decide to withdraw from the situation completely and tell Jane to work it out with Kathy Gordon on her own.	______
3. You decide to take the matter to those in higher management levels and argue forcefully for your point of view. You do everything in your power to ensure that a decision will be made in your favor.	______
4. You decide to meet Kathy Gordon halfway to reach an agreement. You advise Jane to pursue her MBA in accounting or finance, but also recommend that she minor in organizational behavior by taking electives in that field.	______
5. You decide to work more closely with Kathy Gordon by attempting to get a clear as well as flexible policy written that reflects both of your views. Of course this will require a significant amount of your time.	______

SCENARIO #2

SETTING You are the vice president of a relatively large division (300 employees) in a medium-sized consumer products company. Due to the recent turnover of minority staff, your division has fallen behind in meeting the company's goal for Equal Employment Opportunity (EEO) hiring. Because of a scarcity of qualified minority candidates, it appears that you may fall further behind in achieving the stated EEO goals.

Although you are aware of the problem, you believe that the low level of minority hiring is due to increased attrition in minority staff as well as the lack of viable replacement candidates. However, the EEO officer believes that your hiring criteria are too stringent, resulting in the rejection of minority candidates with the basic qualifications to do the job. You support the goals and principles of EEO; however, you are concerned that hiring less qualified candidates will weaken the performance of your division. The EEO officer believes that your failure to hire minority employees is damaging to the company in the short term because corporate goals will not be met, and in the long term because it will restrict the pool of minority candidates available for upward mobility. Both of you regard your concerns as important. Further, you recognize that both of you have the company's best interests in mind and that you have a mutual interest in resolving the conflict.

ACTION ALTERNATIVES FOR SCENARIO #2 Please indicate your first (1) and second (2) choices from among the following alternatives by writing the appropriate numbers in the space provided.

Action Alternative	Ranking (1st and 2nd)
1. You conclude that the whole problem is too complex an issue for you to handle right now. You put it on the "back burner" and decide to reconsider the problem at a later date.	______
2. You believe that your view outweighs the perspective of the EEO officer. You decide to argue your position more vigorously and hope that your stance will sway the EEO officer to agree with your view.	______
3. You decide to accept the EEO officer's view. You agree to use less stringent selection criteria and thereby hire more minority employees.	______
4. You give in to the EEO officer somewhat by agreeing to relax your standards a little bit. This would allow slightly more minority hiring (but not enough to satisfy the EEO goal) and could cause a small reduction in the overall performance of your division.	______
5. You try to reach a consensus that addresses each of your concerns. You agree to work harder at hiring more minority applicants and request that the EEO officer agree to help find the most qualified minority candidates available.	______

SCENARIO #3

SETTING You are the manager in charge of the financial reporting section of a large insurance company. It is the responsibility of your group to make periodic written and oral reports to senior management regarding the company's financial performance. The company's senior management has come to rely on your quick and accurate dissemination of financial data as a way to make vital, timely decisions. This has given you a relatively high degree of organizational influence. You rely on various operating departments to supply financial information according to a preestablished reporting schedule.

In two days you must make your quarterly presentation to the company's board of directors. However, the claims department has failed to supply several key pieces of information that are critical to your presentation. You check the reporting schedule and realize that you should have had the information two days ago. When you call Bill Jones, the claims department manager, he informs you that he cannot possibly get you the data within the next two days. He states that other pressing work has a higher priority. Although you explain the critical need for this data, he is unwilling to change his position. You believe that your presentation is vital to the company's welfare and explain this to Bill Jones. Although Bill has less status than you, he has been known to take advantage of individuals who are unwilling or unable to push their point of view. With your presentation less than two days away, it is critical that you receive information from the claims department within the next 24 hours.

ACTION ALTERNATIVES FOR SCENARIO #3
Please indicate your first (1) and second (2) choices from among the following alternatives by writing the appropriate numbers in the space provided.

Action Alternative	Ranking (1st and 2nd)
1. Accept the explanation from Bill Jones and try to get by without the figures by using your best judgment as to what they would be.	________
2. Tell Bill Jones that unless you have the data from his department on your desk by tomorrow morning, you will be forced to go over his head to compel him to give you the numbers.	________
3. Meet Bill Jones halfway by agreeing to receive part of the needed figures and using your own judgment on the others.	________
4. Try to get your presentation postponed until a later date, if possible.	________
5. Forget about the short-term need for information and try to achieve a longer-term solution, such as adjusting the reporting schedule to better accommodate your mutual needs.	________

SCENARIO #4

SETTING You are the production manager of a medium-sized building products company. You control a production line that runs on a three-shift basis. Recently Ted Smith, the materials handling manager, asked you to accept a different packaging of the raw materials for the production process than what has been customary. He states that new machinery he has installed makes it much easier to provide the material in 100-pound sacks instead of the 50-pound bags that you currently receive. Ted further explains that providing the material in the 50-pound bags would put an immense strain on his operation, and he therefore has a critical need for you to accept the change. You know that accepting materials in the new packaging will cause some minor disruption in your production process but should not cause long-term problems for any of the three shifts. However, you are a little annoyed by the proposed change because Ted did not consult with you before he installed the new equipment. In the past you and he have been open in your communication. You do not think that this failure to consult you represents a change in your relationship.

Because you work closely with Ted, it is essential that you maintain the harmonious and stable working relationship that you have built over the past few years. In addition, you may need some help from him in the future: You already know that your operation will have special material requirements in about two months. You also know that Ted has influence at higher levels of the organization.

ACTION ALTERNATIVES FOR SCENARIO #4
Please indicate your first (1) and second (2) choices from among the following alternatives by writing the appropriate numbers in the space provided.

Action Alternative	Ranking (1st and 2nd)
1. Agree to accept the raw material in the different format.	________
2. Refuse to accept the material in the new format because it would disrupt your operation.	________
3. Propose a solution in which you accept material in the new format during the first shift but not during the second and third.	________
4. Tell Ted Smith that you do not wish to deal with the issue at this time, but that you will consider his request and get back to him at a later date.	________
5. Tell Ted Smith about your concern regarding his failure to consult with you before installing new equipment. You inform him that you wish to find longer-term solutions to the conflict between you.	________

SCENARIO #5

SETTING You supervise the compensation and benefits section in the human resources department of a medium-sized pharmaceutical company. Your staff of three clerks is responsible for maintaining contacts with the various benefits providers and answering related questions from the company's employees. Your section shares secretarial, word processing, and copier resources with the training and development section of the department. Recently a disagreement has arisen between you and Beth Hanson, the training and development supervisor, over when the secretarial staff should take their lunch breaks. Beth would like the secretarial staff to take their breaks an hour later to coincide with the time most of her people go to lunch. You know that the secretaries do not want to change their lunchtimes. Further, the current time is more convenient for your staff.

At this time you are hard-pressed to deal with the situation. You have an important meeting with the provider of dental insurance in two days. It is critical that you are well prepared for this meeting, and these other tasks are a distraction.

ACTION ALTERNATIVES FOR SCENARIO #5 Please indicate your first (1) and second (2) choices from among the following alternatives by writing the appropriate numbers in the space provided.

Action Alternative	Ranking (1st and 2nd)
1. Take some time over the next day and propose a solution in which three days a week the secretaries take their lunch at the earlier time and two days at the later.	________
2. Tell Beth Hanson you will deal with the matter in a few days after you have addressed the more pressing issues.	________
3. Let Beth Hanson have her way by agreeing to a later lunch hour for the secretarial staff.	________
4. Tell Beth Hanson that you will not agree to a change in the secretaries' lunchtime.	________
5. Devote more time to the issue. Attempt to achieve a broad-based consensus with Beth Hanson that meets her needs as well as yours and those of the secretaries.	________

Source: G.A. Callanan and D.F. Perri, "Teaching Conflict Management Using a Scenario-Based Approach," *Journal of Education for Business* 81 (January/February 2006), pp. 131–39.

Team Exercise 13.4 UGLI ORANGE ROLE-PLAY

PURPOSE This exercise is designed to help you understand the dynamics of interpersonal and intergroup conflict as well as the effectiveness of negotiation strategies under specific conditions.

MATERIALS The instructor will distribute roles for Dr. Roland, Dr. Jones, and a few observers. Ideally each negotiation should occur in a private area away from other negotiations.

INSTRUCTIONS

1. The instructor will divide the class into an even number of teams of three people each, with one participant left over for each team formed (for example, there will be six observers if there are six teams). Half of the teams will take the role of Dr. Roland and the other half will be Dr. Jones. The instructor will distribute roles after these teams have been formed.
2. Members within each team are given 10 minutes (or another time limit stated by the instructor) to learn their roles and choose a negotiating strategy.
3. After reading their roles and discussing strategy, each Dr. Jones team is matched with a Dr. Roland team to conduct negotiations. Observers will receive observation forms from the instructor, and two observers will be assigned to watch the paired teams during prenegotiations and subsequent negotiations.
4. As soon as Roland and Jones reach agreement or at the end of the time allotted for the negotiation (whichever comes first), the Roland and Jones teams report to the instructor for further instruction.
5. At the end of the exercise the class will congregate to discuss the negotiations. Observers, negotiators, and the instructor will then discuss their observations and experiences and the implications for conflict management and negotiation.

Source: This exercise was developed by Robert J. House, Wharton Business School, University of Pennsylvania. A similar activity is also attributed to earlier writing by R.R. Blake and J.S. Mouton.

Self-Assessment 13.5

THE DUTCH TEST FOR CONFLICT HANDLING

PURPOSE This self-assessment is designed to help you identify your preferred conflict management style.

INSTRUCTIONS Read each of the following statements and circle the response that you believe best reflects your position regarding each statement. Then use the scoring key in Appendix B to calculate your results for each conflict management style. This exercise is completed alone so you can assess yourself honestly without concerns of social comparison. However, class discussion will focus on the different conflict management styles and the situations in which each is most appropriate.

Dutch Test for Conflict Handling

When I have a conflict at work, I do the following:	Not at all ▼				Very much ▼
1. I give in to the wishes of the other party.	1	2	3	4	5
2. I try to reach a middle-of-the-road solution.	1	2	3	4	5
3. I push my own point of view.	1	2	3	4	5
4. I examine issues until I find a solution that really satisfies me and the other party.	1	2	3	4	5
5. I avoid confrontation about our differences.	1	2	3	4	5
6. I concur with the other party.	1	2	3	4	5
7. I emphasize that we have to find a compromise solution.	1	2	3	4	5
8. I search for gains.	1	2	3	4	5
9. I stand for my own and the other's goals and interests.	1	2	3	4	5
10. I avoid differences of opinion as much as possible.	1	2	3	4	5
11. I try to accommodate the other party.	1	2	3	4	5
12. I insist that we both give in a little.	1	2	3	4	5
13. I fight for a good outcome for myself.	1	2	3	4	5
14. I examine ideas from both sides to find a mutually optimal solution.	1	2	3	4	5
15. I try to make differences loom less severe.	1	2	3	4	5
16. I adapt to the parties' goals and interests.	1	2	3	4	5
17. I strive whenever possible toward a 50–50 compromise.	1	2	3	4	5
18. I do everything to win.	1	2	3	4	5
19. I work out a solution that serves my own and the other's interests as well as possible.	1	2	3	4	5
20. I try to avoid a confrontation with the other.	1	2	3	4	5

Source: C.K.W. de Dreu, A. Evers, B. Beersma, E.S. Kluwer, and A. Nauta, "A Theory-Based Measure of Conflict Management Strategies in the Workplace," *Journal of Organizational Behavior* 22 (2001), pp. 645–68.

After reading this chapter, if you need additional information, see **www.mhhe.com/mcshane4e** for more in-depth interactivities that correspond with this material.

Infosys has grown into one of India's largest and most successful information technology companies, and chief executive Nandan Nilekani wants to maintain that momentum by focusing his attention on leadership development. "Given our pace of growth, transferring the values and beliefs, the DNA of the organization, to the next generations of leaders is one of my most important functions," says Nilekani, who is actively involved in the company's leadership development workshops and mentoring activities.

"In essence, leadership is about dreaming the impossible and helping followers achieve the same," says Nandan Nilekani, chief executive of Infosys, one of India's largest and most successful information technology companies.

Building a strong cadre of leaders required Nilekani and his executive team to carefully think about the meaning of effective leadership. "We believe our future leaders need to learn how to set direction, to create a shared vision, encourage execution excellence, embrace inclusive meritocracy," he says. Nilekani particularly emphasizes the importance of values and vision. "In essence, leadership is about dreaming the impossible and helping followers achieve the same. Moreover, the dream has to be built on sound and context-invariant values to sustain the enthusiasm and energy of people over a long time."

Nilekani's definition of leadership bears an uncanny resemblance to the one formed by Pacific Gas & Electric Company (PG&E) CEO Peter Darbee. "A leader needs to first be able to dream great dreams, and establish a vision," he says. Furthermore, great leaders translate that broad vision into more precise objectives, goals, and metrics, all of which are guided by strategy and supported by the organization's culture. Darbee also advises that "the glue that holds this all together is your values. You have to lead from your values."

Richard Brajer, CEO of Liposcience Inc., adds another view of leadership. He suggests that leadership isn't about being front-and-center, but nurturing an environment where everyone can achieve their potential. "I think the power and role of a leader are to release the potential of an organization," he says. "This means not to take my brain and replicate it in the brains of the people around me, but to release their potential to work toward an agreed-upon direction." Microsoft Australia chief executive Steve Vamos makes a similar observation. "It's not about having all the answers. The role of the leader is to create environments where others can do great work—and then to get out of the way."[1]

14

Leadership in Organizational Settings

LEARNING OBJECTIVES

After reading this chapter you should be able to

1. Define *leadership* and *shared leadership*.
2. List seven competencies of effective leaders.
3. Describe the people-oriented and task-oriented leadership styles.
4. Outline the path–goal theory of leadership.
5. Summarize leadership substitutes theory.
6. Distinguish transformational leadership from transactional and charismatic leadership.
7. Describe the four elements of transformational leadership.
8. Describe the implicit leadership perspective.
9. Discuss the influence of culture on perceptions of effective leaders.
10. Discuss similarities and differences in the leadership styles of women and men.

Learning Objectives

After reading the next three sections you should be able to

1. **Define *leadership* and *shared leadership*.**
2. **List seven competencies of effective leaders.**

What Is Leadership?

leadership
Influencing, motivating, and enabling others to contribute toward the effectiveness and success of the organizations of which they are members.

The world is changing, and so is our concept of leadership. Gone is yesteryear's image of the command-and-control boss. Also gone is the more recent view that leaders are front-and-center charismatic heroes. Instead, as Nandan Nilekani, Peter Darbee, Richard Brajer, and Steve Vamos stated in the opening vignette, leadership is about values, vision, enabling, and coaching. A few years ago 54 leadership experts from 38 countries reached a consensus that **leadership** is about influencing, motivating, and enabling others to contribute toward the effectiveness and success of the organizations of which they are members.[2] Leaders apply various forms of influence–from subtle persuasion to direct application of power–to ensure that followers have the motivation and role clarity to achieve specified goals. Leaders also arrange the work environment–such as allocating resources and altering communication patterns–so employees can achieve corporate objectives more easily.

Shared Leadership

shared leadership
The view that leadership is broadly distributed rather than assigned to one person, such that people within the team and organization lead each other.

Leadership isn't restricted to the executive suite. Anyone in the organization may be a leader in various ways and at various times.[3] This view is variously known as **shared leadership** or the leaderful organization. Effective self-directed work teams, for example, consist of members who share leadership responsibilities or otherwise allocate this role to a responsible coordinator. W.L. Gore & Associates is a case in point. The

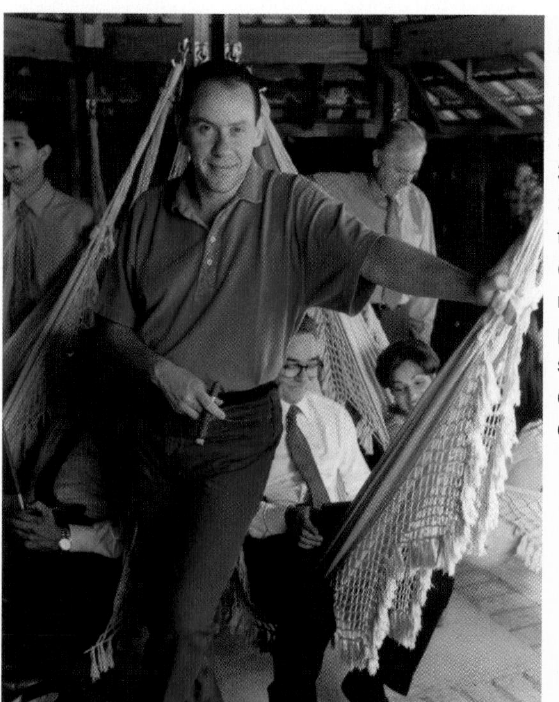

Shared Leadership at Semco If anyone can say they lead a company of leaders, it would be Ricardo Semler, CEO of Semco Corporation, SA. Headquartered in Sao Paulo, Brazil, the manufacturing and services conglomerate delegates almost total responsibility to its 3,000 employees. Organized into small groups of 6 to 10 people, Semco employees choose their objectives every six months, hire their co-workers, work out their budgets, set their own salaries, decide when to come to work, and even elect their own bosses. This may seem radical, but Semler says that the company is "only 50 or 60 percent where we'd like to be." Semler (shown here with head office staff) believes that replacing the head office with several satellite offices around Sao Paulo would give employees even more opportunity to lead themselves.[4]

company's 6,500 employees are organized around self-directed work teams and consequently have few formal leaders. Yet the company has no shortage of leaders. When asked in the company's annual survey "Are you a leader?" more than 50 percent of Gore employees answered "Yes."[5]

Shared leadership also extends to organizational clients, as was dramatically illustrated in the recent revival of St. Magloire. The small village in Quebec, Canada, near the Maine border, had suffered population decline as children grew up and moved to larger population centers. When the Quebec government threatened to close the only school, Julie Bercier and a handful of other citizens rallied to attract new residents. At first people were skeptical, suggesting that Bercier and her friends were dreaming to think that anyone could reverse the rural exodus. But persistence paid off as people eventually got involved in marketing and developing St. Magloire as a better lifestyle for city folks. Newspaper campaigns, a new resident welcoming program, and government support attracted 54 people within a year. The school remained open as enough children enrolled the following year. Although the village mayor and school leaders played important roles, Bercier and others became leaders by providing the passion and vision of what the small community could become with enough ingenuity and effort.[6]

Perspectives of Leadership

Leadership has been contemplated since the days of Greek philosophers, and it is one of the most popular research topics among organizational behavior scholars. This has resulted in an enormous volume of leadership literature, most of which can be organized into the five perspectives shown in Exhibit 14.1.[7] Although some of these perspectives are currently more popular than others, each helps us to more fully understand this complex issue.

Exhibit 14.1
Perspectives of Leadership

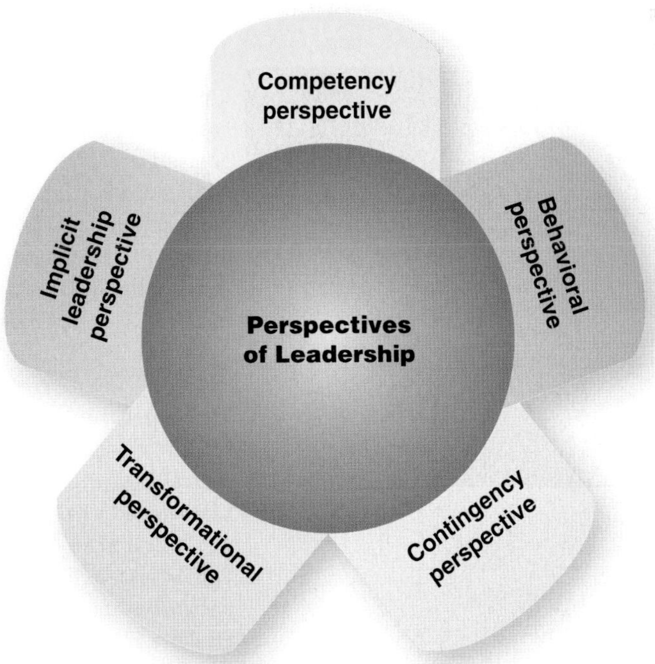

Some researchers examine leadership competencies, whereas others look at leadership behaviors. More recent studies have looked at leadership from a contingency approach by considering the appropriate leader behaviors in different settings. Currently the most popular perspective is that leaders transform organizations through their vision, communication, and ability to build commitment. Finally, an emerging perspective suggests that leadership is mainly a perceptual bias. We distort reality and attribute events to leaders because we feel more comfortable believing that a competent individual is at the organization's helm. This chapter explores each of these five perspectives of leadership. In the final section we also consider cross-cultural and gender issues in organizational leadership.

Competency Perspective of Leadership

When Helene Gayle was recently appointed president of CARE, the Atlanta-based global aid agency, numerous colleagues and observers were quick to point out several attributes that make her an excellent leader. She has a deep knowledge of global health issues, has drive and determination to bring about meaningful change, is highly trusted, and demonstrates a high level of emotional intelligence. These characteristics of Helene Gayle reflect the notion that people require specific competencies to fulfill leadership roles.

Since the beginning of recorded civilization, people have been interested in the personal characteristics that distinguish great leaders from the rest of us. A major review in the late 1940s concluded that no consistent list of traits could be distilled from the hundreds of studies conducted up to that time. A subsequent review suggested that a few traits are consistently associated with effective leaders, but most are unrelated to effective leadership.[8] These conclusions caused many scholars to give up their search for personal characteristics that distinguish effective leaders.

Over the past decade leadership researchers and consultants have returned to the notion that leadership requires specific personal characteristics. One recent study established that inherited personality characteristics significantly influence *leadership*

CAREing Leadership Competencies By all accounts Helene Gayle has the competencies of an effective leader. Recently appointed as president of CARE, the Atlanta-based global aid agency, Gayle brings a wealth of experience from her previous executive positions with the Bill & Melinda Gates Foundation and the Centers for Disease Control (CDC). "Her leadership, commitment, and talents are well demonstrated," says CARE board chairman Lincoln Chen. William Foege, who worked with Gayle when he was head of the CDC, also points to her incredible drive and motivation. "Helene has the capacity to go full-tilt day after day and week after week," he notes. "It's almost as if she doesn't know what fatigue is like." Others have commented on her high degree of integrity. "Helene Gayle may be the most trusted public health leader in the world," says David Satcher, who has served as CDC director and U.S. surgeon-general. Still others describe Gayle's high level of emotional intelligence. "Helene has a tremendous natural empathy," says Ashok Alexander, director of the Gates' Foundation AIDS program in India.[9]

Exhibit 14.2
Seven Competencies of Effective Leaders

Leadership trait	Description
Emotional intelligence	The leader's ability to monitor his or her own and others' emotions, discriminate among them, and use the information to guide his or her thoughts and actions.
Integrity	The leader's truthfulness and tendency to translate words into deeds.
Drive	The leader's inner motivation to pursue goals.
Leadership motivation	The leader's need for socialized power to accomplish team or organizational goals.
Self-confidence	The leader's belief in his or her own leadership skills and ability to achieve objectives.
Intelligence	The leader's above-average cognitive ability to process enormous amounts of information.
Knowledge of the business	The leader's tacit and explicit knowledge about the company's environment, enabling him or her to make more intuitive decisions.

emergence–the perception that someone is a leader in a leaderless situation.[10] More striking, however, is the resurgence in interest in discovering leadership *competencies* that enable companies to select and develop future leaders.[11] Competencies encompass a broad range of personal characteristics, including knowledge, skills, abilities, and values. The recent leadership literature identifies several leadership competencies, most of which can be grouped into the seven categories listed in Exhibit 14.2 and described next.[12]

- *Emotional intelligence.* Research points to emotional intelligence as an important attribute of effective leaders.[13] They have the ability to perceive and express emotion, assimilate emotion in thought, understand and reason with emotion, and regulate emotion in themselves and others (see Chapter 4). Helene Gayle and other leaders can empathize, build rapport, and network with others. The contingency leadership perspective described later in this chapter assumes that effective leaders have sufficient emotional intelligence to know when to adjust their behavior so it matches the situation.

- *Integrity.* Integrity refers to the leader's truthfulness and tendency to translate words into deeds. This characteristic is sometimes called *authentic leadership* because the individual acts with sincerity. He or she has a high moral capacity to judge dilemmas based on sound values and to act accordingly. Several large-scale studies have reported that integrity or honesty is the most important characteristic of effective leaders. Employees and other stakeholders want honest leaders whom they can trust.[14] Helene Gayle is known as a highly trustworthy leader because she engages in honest dialogue, demonstrates knowledge of the subject matter, and shows sincere interest in the needs of others. "I have been impressed with her ability–not just in Africa and Asia, but everywhere–to work with people from different cultures and to gain their trust. She has a way of relating to others," says former surgeon-general David Satcher. Unfortunately Gayle is in the minority regarding authentic leadership. Two recent surveys reported that only about a third of American employees believe top managers display integrity and morality. Another recent survey reported that fewer than a third of the 115,000 Asian workers polled are satisfied with their level of trust in management.[15]

- *Drive.* Helene Gayle and other successful leaders have a high need for achievement (see Chapter 5). This drive represents the inner motivation that leaders possess to pursue their goals and encourage others to move forward with theirs. Drive inspires inquisitiveness, an action orientation, and boldness to take the company into uncharted waters. A recent survey of 3,600 bosses identified a "drive for results" as one of the five most important competencies of effective middle managers. This evidence is backed up by Larry Bossidy's experience leading thousands of managers. "When assessing candidates, the first thing I looked for was energy and enthusiasm for execution," says the former CEO of Honeywell and Allied Signal. Bossidy says that this bias for action is so important that "if you have to choose between someone with a staggering IQ...and someone with a lower IQ who is absolutely determined to succeed, you'll always do better with the second person."[16]

- *Leadership motivation.* Leaders have a strong need for power because they want to influence others (see Chapter 5). However, they tend to have a need for "socialized power" because their motivation is constrained by a strong sense of altruism and social responsibility. In other words, effective leaders try to gain power so they can influence others to accomplish goals that benefit the team or organization.[17]
- *Self-confidence.* Leaders demonstrate confidence in their leadership skills and ability to achieve objectives. Effective leaders are typically extroverted–outgoing, sociable, talkative, and assertive–but they also remain humble.
- *Intelligence.* Leaders have above-average cognitive ability to process enormous amounts of information. Leaders aren't necessarily geniuses; rather, they have superior ability to analyze a variety of complex alternatives and opportunities.
- *Knowledge of the business.* Effective leaders possess tacit and explicit knowledge of the business environment in which they operate. Consider once again the characteristics of CARE president Helene Gayle. With a quarter century of experience at the Centers for Disease Control and the Bill & Melinda Gates Foundation, Gayle has gained tremendous knowledge and experience working with health foundations and political leaders around the world, particularly in the fight against AIDS. This knowledge and experience support Gayle's intuition to recognize opportunities and understand the organization's capacity to capture those opportunities.

Competency (Trait) Perspective Limitations and Practical Implications

Although the competency perspective is gaining popularity (again), it assumes that all leaders have the same personal characteristics and that all of these qualities are equally important in all situations. This is probably a false assumption; leadership is far too complex to have a universal list of traits that apply to every condition. Some competencies might not be important all the time. Another limitation is that alternative combinations of competencies may be equally successful. In other words, people with two different sets of competencies might be equally good leaders.[18]

As we discuss later in this chapter, several leadership researchers have also warned that some personal characteristics might only influence our perception that someone is a leader–not determine whether the individual really makes a difference to the organization's success. People who exhibit self-confidence, extroversion, and other traits are called leaders because they fit our stereotype of an effective leader. Or we might see a successful person, call that person a leader, and then attribute unobservable traits that we consider essential for great leaders.

Aside from these limitations, the competency perspective recognizes that some people possess personal characteristics that offer them a higher potential to be great leaders. The most obvious implication of this is that organizations are turning to competency-based methods to hire people with strong leadership potential. The competency perspective of leadership does not necessarily imply that leadership is something you are either born with or must live without. On the contrary, competencies indicate only leadership potential, not leadership performance. People with these characteristics become effective leaders only after they have developed and mastered the necessary leadership behaviors. People with somewhat lower leadership competencies may become effective leaders because they have leveraged their potential more fully.

Learning Objectives

After reading the next three sections you should be able to

3. Describe the people-oriented and task-oriented leadership styles.

4. Outline the path–goal theory of leadership.

Behavioral Perspective of Leadership

In the 1940s and 1950s leadership experts at several universities launched an intensive research investigation to answer the question "What behaviors make leaders effective?" Questionnaires were administered to subordinates, asking them to rate their supervisors on a large number of behaviors. These studies distilled two clusters of leadership behaviors from literally thousands of leadership behavior items.[19]

One cluster represented people-oriented behaviors. This included showing mutual trust and respect for subordinates, demonstrating a genuine concern for their needs, and having a desire to look out for their welfare. Leaders with a strong people-oriented style listen to employee suggestions, do personal favors for employees, support their interests when required, and treat employees as equals. The other cluster represented a task-oriented leadership style and included behaviors that define and structure work roles. Task-oriented leaders assign employees to specific tasks, clarify their work duties and procedures, ensure that they follow company rules, and push them to reach their performance capacity. They establish stretch goals and challenge employees to push beyond those high standards.

Choosing Task-Oriented versus People-Oriented Leadership

Should leaders be task-oriented or people-oriented? This is a difficult question to answer because each style has advantages and disadvantages. Recent evidence suggests that both styles are positively associated with leader effectiveness, but differences are often apparent only in very high or very low levels of each style. Absenteeism, grievances, turnover, and job dissatisfaction are higher among employees who work for supervisors with very low levels of people-oriented leadership. Job performance is lower among employees who work for supervisors with low levels of task-oriented leadership.[20] Research also suggests that university students value task-oriented instructors because they want clear objectives and well-prepared lectures that abide by the unit's objectives.[21]

One problem with the behavioral leadership perspective is that the two categories are broad generalizations that mask specific behaviors within each category. For instance, task-oriented leadership includes planning work activities, clarifying roles, and monitoring operations and performance. These clusters of activities are fairly distinct and likely have different effects on employee well-being and performance. A second concern is that the behavioral approach assumes that high levels of both styles are best in all situations. In reality the best leadership style depends on the situation.[22] On a positive note, the behavioral perspective lays the foundation for two of the main leadership styles–people-oriented and task-oriented–found in many contemporary leadership theories. These contemporary theories, which adopt a contingency perspective, are described next.

Contingency Perspective of Leadership

The contingency perspective of leadership is based on the idea that the most appropriate leadership style depends on the situation. Most (although not all) contingency leadership theories assume that effective leaders must be both insightful and flexible.[23] They must be able to adapt their behaviors and styles to the immediate situation. This isn't easy to do, however. Leaders typically have a preferred style. It takes considerable effort for leaders to learn when and how to alter their styles to match the situation. As we noted earlier, leaders must have high emotional intelligence so they can diagnose the circumstances and match their behaviors accordingly.

Path–Goal Theory of Leadership

path–goal leadership theory
A contingency theory of leadership based on expectancy theory of motivation that relates several leadership styles to specific employee and situational contingencies.

Several contingency theories have been proposed over the years, but **path–goal leadership theory** has withstood scientific critique better than most others. The theory has roots in the expectancy theory of motivation (see Chapter 5).[24] Early research incorporated expectancy theory into the study of how leader behaviors influence employee perceptions of expectancies (paths) between employee effort and performance (goals). Out of this early work was born path–goal theory as a contingency leadership model.

Using the language of expectancy theory, path–goal theory states that effective leaders strengthen the performance-to-outcome expectancy and valences of those outcomes, thereby ensuring that employees who perform their jobs well have a higher degree of need fulfillment than employees who perform poorly. Effective leaders also strengthen the effort-to-performance expectancy by providing the information, support, and other resources necessary to help employees complete their tasks.[25]

servant leadership
The belief that leaders serve followers by understanding their needs and facilitating their work performance.

In other words, path–goal theory advocates **servant leadership**.[26] Servant leaders do not view leadership as a position of power; rather they are coaches, stewards, and facilitators. Leadership is an obligation to understand employee needs and to facilitate their work performance. Servant leaders ask, "How can I help you?" rather than expecting employees to serve them. As Microsoft Australia chief executive Steve Vamos stated at the beginning of this chapter, "The role of the leader is to create environments where others can do great work–and then to get out of the way." Similarly, when Financial Planning Association president Jim Barnash was recently asked about his leadership style, he replied, "I try to live a servant leader's life, which means being more interested in your needs than my needs."[27]

Path–Goal Leadership Styles

Exhibit 14.3 presents the path–goal theory of leadership. This model specifically highlights four leadership styles and several contingency factors leading to three indicators of leader effectiveness. The four leadership styles are[28]

Exhibit 14.3
Path–Goal Leadership Theory

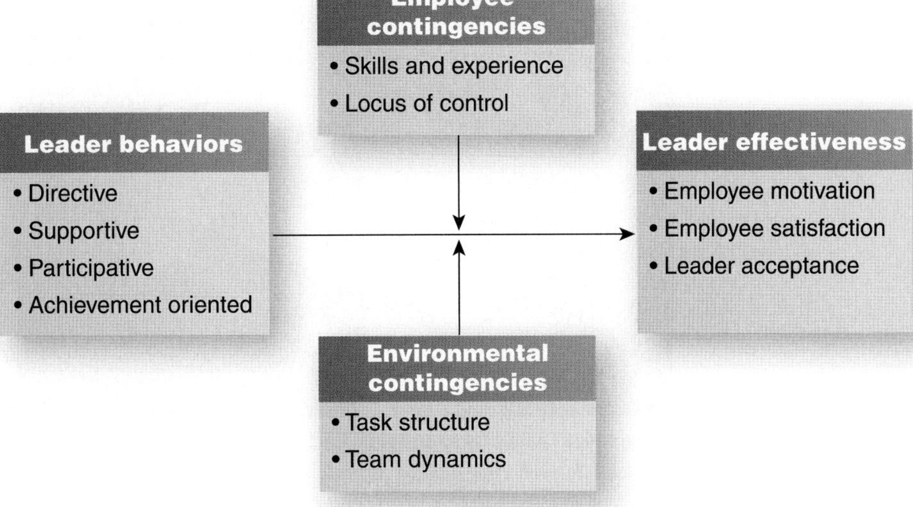

- *Directive.* These are clarifying behaviors that provide a psychological structure for subordinates. The leader clarifies performance goals, the means to reach those goals, and the standards against which performance will be judged. This style also includes judicious use of rewards and disciplinary actions. Directive leadership is the same as task-oriented leadership (described earlier) and echoes our discussion in Chapter 2 about the importance of clear role perceptions in employee performance.
- *Supportive.* These behaviors provide psychological support for subordinates. The leader is friendly and approachable; makes the work more pleasant; treats employees with equal respect; and shows concern for the status, needs, and well-being of employees. Supportive leadership is the same as people-oriented leadership (described earlier) and reflects the benefits of social support to help employees cope with stressful situations.
- *Participative.* These behaviors encourage and facilitate subordinate involvement in decisions beyond their normal work activities. The leader consults with employees, asks for their suggestions, and takes these ideas into serious consideration before making a decision. Participative leadership relates to involving employees in decisions (see Chapter 8).
- *Achievement-oriented.* These behaviors encourage employees to reach their peak performance. The leader sets challenging goals, expects employees to perform at their highest levels, continuously seeks improvement in employee performance, and shows a high degree of confidence that employees will assume responsibility and accomplish challenging goals. Achievement-oriented leadership applies goal-setting theory (Chapter 5) as well as positive expectations in self-fulfilling prophecy (Chapter 3).

The path–goal model contends that effective leaders are capable of selecting the most appropriate behavioral style (or styles) for a situation. Leaders might simultaneously use two or more styles. For example, they might be both supportive and participative in a specific situation.

Supportive Leader Takes Britain's Top Spot What does it take to be voted the best boss in Great Britain? You will likely find the answer by watching Bruce Draper at work. The managing director of Geotechnical Instruments was recently named Britain's best boss. According to personal assistant Hannah Delany, Draper provides plenty of supportive leadership to the company's 85 staff members. "Bruce cares about his staff and never takes them for granted," she says. "He appears friendly, approachable, and kind and makes sure everyone is content in their job." Fiona Cannon, head of equality and diversity at Lloyds TSB, the financial institution that cosponsored the award, says that supportive leadership is vital in organizations today. "Having a good boss can make a huge difference, not only to the success of a business but also to the happiness and well-being of those who work for them." She adds, "Bruce Draper particularly stood out from the crowd."[29]

Contingencies of Path–Goal Theory

As a contingency theory, path–goal theory states that each of these four leadership styles will be effective in some situations but not in others. The path–goal leadership model specifies two sets of situational variables that moderate the relationship between a leader's style and effectiveness: (1) employee characteristics and (2) characteristics of the employee's work environment. Several contingencies have already been studied within the path–goal framework, and the model is open for more variables in the future.[30] However, only four contingencies are reviewed here (see Exhibit 14.4).

Skill and Experience A combination of directive and supportive leadership is best for employees who are (or perceive themselves to be) inexperienced and unskilled.[31] Directive leadership gives subordinates information about how to accomplish the task, whereas supportive leadership helps them cope with the uncertainties of unfamiliar work situations. Directive leadership is detrimental when employees are skilled and experienced because it introduces too much supervisory control.

Locus of Control Recall from Chapter 2 that people with an internal locus of control believe that they have control over their work environment. Consequently these employees prefer participative and achievement-oriented leadership styles and may become frustrated with a directive style. In contrast, people with an external locus of control believe that their performance is due more to luck and fate, so they tend to be more satisfied with directive and supportive leadership.

Exhibit 14.4 Selected Contingencies of Path–Goal Theory

	Directive	Supportive	Participative	Achievement-oriented
Employee contingencies				
Skill, experience	Low	Low	High	High
Locus of control	External	External	Internal	Internal
Environmental contingencies				
Task structure	Nonroutine	Routine	Nonroutine	???
Team dynamics	Negative norms	Low cohesion	Positive norms	???

Task Structure Leaders should adopt the directive style when a task is nonroutine because this style minimizes the role ambiguity that tends to occur in these complex work situations (particularly for inexperienced employees).[32] The directive style is ineffective when employees have routine and simple tasks because the manager's guidance serves no purpose and may be viewed as unnecessarily close control. Employees in highly routine and simple jobs may require supportive leadership to help them cope with the tedious nature of the work and lack of control over the pace of work. Participative leadership is preferred for employees performing nonroutine tasks because the lack of rules and procedures gives them more discretion to achieve challenging goals. The participative style is ineffective for employees in routine tasks because they lack discretion over their work.

Team Dynamics Cohesive teams with performance-oriented norms act as a substitute for most leader interventions. High team cohesiveness substitutes for supportive leadership, whereas performance-oriented team norms substitute for directive and possibly achievement-oriented leadership. Thus when team cohesiveness is low, leaders should use the supportive style. Leaders should apply a directive style to counteract team norms that oppose the team's formal objectives. For example, the team leader may need to use legitimate power if team members have developed a norm to "take it easy" rather than get a project completed on time.

Practical Implications and Limitations of Path–Goal Theory

Path–goal theory has received more research support than other contingency leadership models, but the evidence is far from complete. A few contingencies (such as task structure) do not have a clear-cut association with any leadership style. Other contingencies and leadership styles in the path–goal leadership model haven't received research investigation at all, as indicated by the question marks in Exhibit 4.4.[33] The path–goal model was expanded a few years ago to include more leadership styles and contingencies, but these additions have received limited investigation.

Another concern is that as path–goal theory expands, the model may become too complex for practical use. Although the expanded model provides a closer representation of the complexity of leadership, it may become too cumbersome for training people in leadership styles. Few people would be able to remember all the contingencies and appropriate leadership styles for those contingencies. In spite of these limitations, path–goal theory remains a relatively robust contingency leadership theory.

Learning Objectives

After reading the next two sections you should be able to

5. Summarize leadership substitutes theory.

6. Distinguish transformational leadership from transactional and charismatic leadership.

7. Describe the four elements of transformational leadership.

Other Contingency Theories

At the beginning of this chapter we noted that numerous leadership theories have developed over the years. Most of them are found in the contingency perspective of leadership. Some overlap with the path–goal model in terms of leadership styles, but most use simpler and more abstract contingencies. We will briefly mention just two here because of their popularity and historical significance to the field.

Situational Leadership Theory

situational leadership theory (SLT)
Development by Hersey and Blanchard, this model suggests that effective leaders vary their styles with the "readiness" of followers.

One of the most popular contingency theories among practitioners is the **situational leadership theory (SLT)**, also called the life cycle theory of leadership, developed by Paul Hersey and Ken Blanchard.[34] SLT suggests that effective leaders vary their style with the "readiness" of followers. (An earlier version of the model called this "maturity.") Readiness refers to the employee's or work team's ability and willingness to accomplish a specific task. *Ability* refers to the extent to which the follower has the skills and knowledge to perform the task without the leader's guidance. *Willingness* refers to the follower's self-motivation and commitment to performing the assigned task. The model compresses these distinct concepts into a single situational condition.

The situational leadership model also identifies four leadership styles–telling, selling, participating, and delegating–that Hersey and Blanchard distinguish in terms of the amount of directive and supportive behavior provided. For example, "telling" has high task behavior and low supportive behavior. The situational leadership model has four quadrants, with each quadrant showing the leadership style that is most appropriate under different circumstances.

In spite of its popularity, several studies and at least three reviews have concluded that the situational leadership model lacks empirical support.[35] Only one part of the model apparently works–namely that leaders should use "telling" (that is, directive style) when employees lack motivation and ability. (Recall that this is also documented in path–goal theory.) The model's elegant simplicity is attractive and entertaining, but most parts don't represent reality well.

Fiedler's Contingency Model

Fiedler's contingency model
Development by Fred Fiedler, a model that suggests that leader effectiveness depends on whether the person's natural leadership style is appropriately matched to the situation.

Fiedler's contingency model, developed by Fred Fiedler and his associates, is the earliest contingency theory of leadership.[36] According to this model, leader effectiveness depends on whether the person's natural leadership style is appropriately matched to the situation. The theory examines two leadership styles that essentially correspond to the previously described people-oriented and task-oriented styles. Unfortunately Fiedler's model relies on a questionnaire that does not measure either leadership style well.

Fiedler's model suggests that the best leadership style depends on the level of *situational control*–that is, on the degree of power and influence the leader possesses in a particular situation. Situational control is affected by three factors in the following order of importance: leader–member relations, task structure, and position power.[37] *Leader–member relations* refers to how much employees trust and respect the leader and are willing to follow his or her guidance. *Task structure* refers to the clarity or ambiguity of operating procedures. *Position power* is the extent to which the leader possesses legitimate, reward, and coercive power over subordinates. These three contingencies form the eight possible combinations of *situation favorableness* from the leader's viewpoint. Good leader–member relations, high task structure, and strong position power create the most favorable situation for the leader because he or she has the most power and influence under these conditions.

Fiedler has gained considerable respect for pioneering the first contingency theory of leadership. However, his theory has fared less well. As mentioned, the leadership style scale used by Fiedler has been widely criticized. There is also no scientific justification for placing the three situational control factors in a hierarchy. Moreover, it seems that leader–member relations are actually an indicator of leader effectiveness (as in path–goal theory) rather than a situational factor. Finally, the theory considers only two leadership styles, whereas other models present a more complex and realistic array of behavior options. These concerns explain why the theory has limited empirical support.[38]

Changing the Situation to Match the Leader's Natural Style Fiedler's contingency model may have become a historical footnote, but it does make an important and lasting contribution by suggesting that leadership style is related to the individual's personality and consequently is relatively stable over time. Leaders might be able to alter their style temporarily, but they tend to use a preferred style in the long term. More recent scholars have also proposed that leadership styles are "hard-wired" more than most contingency leadership theories assume.[39]

If leadership style is influenced by personality, then organizations should engineer situations to fit the leader's dominant style, rather than expect leaders to change their style with situations. A directive leader might be assigned inexperienced employees who need direction rather than seasoned people who work less effectively under a directive style. Alternatively, companies might transfer supervisors to workplaces where their dominant styles fit best. For instance, directive leaders might be parachuted into work teams with counterproductive norms, whereas leaders who prefer a supportive style should be sent to departments in which employees face work pressures and other stressors.

Leadership Substitutes

leadership substitutes
A theory that identifies conditions that either limit a leader's ability to influence subordinates or make that particular leadership style unnecessary.

So far we have looked at theories that recommend using different leadership styles in various situations. But one theory, called **leadership substitutes**, identifies conditions that either limit a leader's ability to influence subordinates or make that particular leadership style unnecessary. The literature identifies several conditions that possibly substitute for task-oriented or people-oriented leadership. For example, performance-based reward systems keep employees directed toward organizational goals, so they might replace or reduce the need for task-oriented leadership. Task-oriented leadership is also less important when employees are skilled and experienced. Notice how these propositions are similar to path–goal leadership theory: Directive leadership is unnecessary–and may be detrimental–when employees are skilled or experienced.[40]

Some research suggests that effective leaders help team members learn to lead themselves through leadership substitutes; in other words, co-workers substitute for leadership in high involvement team structures.[41] Co-workers instruct new employees, thereby providing directive leadership. They also provide social support, which reduces stress among fellow employees. Teams with norms that support organizational goals may substitute for achievement-oriented leadership, because employees encourage (or pressure) co-workers to stretch their performance levels.[42]

Self-leadership–the process of influencing oneself to establish the self-direction and self-motivation needed to perform a task (see Chapter 6)–is another possible leadership substitute.[43] Employees with high self-leadership set their own goals, reinforce their own behavior, maintain positive thought processes, and monitor their own performance, thereby managing both personal motivation and abilities. As employees become more proficient in self-leadership, they presumably require less supervision to keep them energized and focused toward organizational objectives.

The leadership substitutes model has intuitive appeal, but the evidence so far is mixed. Some studies show that a few substitutes do replace the need for task- or people-oriented leadership, but others do not. The difficulties of statistically testing for leadership substitutes may account for some problems; however, a few writers contend that the limited support is evidence that leadership plays a critical role regardless of the situation.[44] At this point we can conclude that a few conditions such as self-directed work teams, self-leadership, and reward systems might reduce the importance of task- or people-oriented leadership, but they probably won't completely replace leaders in these roles.

Transformational Perspective of Leadership

In the opening vignette to this chapter, Infosys chief executive Nandan Nilekani stated that effective leaders create a shared vision and encourage excellent execution toward that vision. Leadership, he explains, is essentially "about dreaming the impossible and helping followers achieve the same." Nandan Nilekani is referring to **transformational leadership**. Transformational leaders are agents of change. They create, communicate, and model a shared vision for the team or organization, inspiring followers to strive for that vision.[45]

transformational leadership
A leadership perspective that explains how leaders change teams or organizations by creating, communicating, and modeling a vision for the organization or work unit and inspiring employees to strive for that vision.

Transformational versus Transactional Leadership

Transformational leadership differs from **transactional leadership**.[46] Transactional leadership is "managing"–helping organizations achieve their current objectives more efficiently, such as by linking job performance to valued rewards and ensuring that employees have the resources needed to get the job done. The contingency and behavioral theories described earlier adopt the transactional perspective because they focus on leader behaviors that improve employee performance and satisfaction. In contrast, transformational leadership is about "leading"–changing the organization's strategies and culture so they fit better with the surrounding environment.[47] Transformational leaders are change agents who energize and direct employees to a new set of corporate values and behaviors.

transactional leadership
Leadership that helps organizations achieve their current objectives more efficiently, such as linking job performances to valued rewards and ensuring that employees have the resources needed to get the job done.

Organizations require both transactional and transformational leadership.[48] Transactional leadership improves organizational efficiency, whereas transformational leadership steers companies into a better course of action. Transformational leadership is particularly important in organizations that require significant alignment with the external environment. Unfortunately too many leaders get trapped in the daily managerial activities that represent transactional leadership.[49] They lose touch with the transformational aspect of effective leadership. Without transformational leaders, organizations stagnate and eventually become seriously misaligned with their environments.

Transformational versus Charismatic Leadership

One topic that has generated some confusion and controversy is the distinction between transformational and charismatic leadership.[50] Many researchers either use the words interchangeably, as if they have the same meaning, or view charismatic leadership as an essential ingredient of transformational leadership. Others take this view further by suggesting that charismatic leadership is the highest degree of transformational leadership.

However, the emerging view, which this book adopts, comes from a third group of experts who contend that charisma is distinct from transformational leadership. These academics point out that charisma is a personal trait that provides referent power over followers, whereas transformational leadership is a set of behaviors that people use to lead the change process.[51] Charismatic leaders might be transformational leaders; indeed, their personal power through charisma is a tool to change the behavior of followers. However, some research points out that charismatic or "heroic" leaders easily build allegiance in followers, but they do not necessarily change the organization. Other research suggests that charismatic leaders produce dependent followers, whereas transformational leaders have the opposite effect–they support follower empowerment, which tends to reduce dependence on the leader.[52]

The distinction between charismatic and transformational leadership is illustrated in recent leadership dynamics at Procter & Gamble. The American household goods company lost market share and innovativeness under the previous charismatic leader. Yet as Connections 14.1 describes, it has experienced a dramatic turnaround under Alan G. Lafley, who is not known for being charismatic. Instead Lafley applies the classic elements of transformational leadership, which we describe next.

Elements of Transformational Leadership

There are several descriptions of transformational leadership, but most include the four elements illustrated in Exhibit 14.5. These elements include creating a strategic vision, communicating the vision, modeling the vision, and building commitment to the vision.

Creating a Strategic Vision Transformational leaders shape a strategic vision of a realistic and attractive future that bonds employees together and focuses their energy toward a superordinate organizational goal. A shared strategic vision represents the substance of transformational leadership. It reflects a future for the company or work unit that is ultimately accepted and valued by organizational members. Strategic vision creates a "higher purpose" or superordinate goal that energizes and unifies employees.[53] A strategic vision might originate with the leader, but it is just as likely to emerge from employees, clients, suppliers, or other constituents. A shared strategic vision plays an important role in organizational effectiveness.[54] Visions offer the motivational benefits of goal setting, but they are compelling future states that bond employees and motivate them to strive for those objectives. Visions are typically described in a way that distinguishes them from the current situation, yet makes the goal both appealing and achievable.

Communicating the Vision If vision is the substance of transformational leadership, then communicating that vision is the process. Transformational leaders communicate meaning and elevate the importance of the visionary goal to employees. They frame messages around a grand purpose with emotional appeal that captivates employees and other corporate stakeholders. Framing helps transformational leaders establish a common mental model so that the group or organization will act collectively toward the desirable goal.[55]

Procter & Gamble Trades Charisma for Transformational Substance

A.G. Lafley has turned around beleaguered Procter & Gamble through transformational leadership behaviors without being charismatic or heroic.

A few days after becoming CEO of Procter & Gamble (P&G), Alan George Lafley made an impression by walking unannounced into a dinner party of executives who had left P&G for other companies. This act was highly symbolic because the household goods giant famously promoted from within and treated anyone who left the company before retirement as outcasts. P&G was in trouble: It lacked new products, and its existing offerings were under siege from competitors. So Lafley's visit to P&G alumni (the first such visit by a P&G CEO) quickly signaled that the company would embrace ideas and people from outside the organization.

In addition to greeting former employees, Lafley incessantly communicates the mantra that "the consumer is boss" and that the company's future depends on creativity. Far from the heroic, charismatic style of P&G's previous CEO, who failed to turn the company around and was ousted in just 18 months, Lafley is distinctly "unassuming" with "a humble demeanor that belies his status." One industry observer is more blunt: "If there were 15 people sitting around the conference table, it wouldn't be obvious that he was the CEO."

Yet Lafley has transformed P&G where others could not. His calm self-assurance, consistent vision, and symbolic and strategic actions toward a more customer-friendly and innovative organization have provided the direction and clarity that the company lacked. Lafley also walks the talk—his behavior is closely aligned with the message that he conveys. He restructured the company, pruned costs, made significant acquisitions (Gillette and Clairol), and rekindled a spirit of innovation through special creativity teams. Lafley is also out in the field 10 to 15 days each year, meeting with customers and closely observing what they like and don't like about the company's and competitor's products.

To instill the creative spirit at the top, Lafley took P&G's entire 40-person leadership council to a one-day innovation workshop in San Francisco led by design firm IDEO. IDEO also built an innovation center (called "the Gym") where P&G staff learn brainstorming, prototyping, observation, and other ways to become more innovative. Lafley revamped the executive offices into an open-space plan that improves information sharing. He has also hired an army of creative types from other organizations and paired them with long-service P&G staff. The result: P&G has become the industry's hot spot for innovation, its market share and profitability have experienced sustained growth, and its stock price has soared.

Sources: K. Brooker and J. Schlosser, "The Un-CEO," *Fortune*, 16 September 2002, pp. 88–93; B. Nussbaum, "The Power of Design," *BusinessWeek*, 17 May 2004, p. 86; N. Buckley, "The Calm Reinventor," *Financial Times* (London), 29 January 2005, p. 11; S. Ellison, "Women's Touch Guides P&G Chief's Firm Hand in Company Turnaround," *The Wall Street Journal Europe*, 1 June 2005, p. A1; S. Hill Jr., "P&G's Turnaround Proves Listening to Customer Pays," *Manufacturing Business Technology*, July 2005, p. 64; J. Tylee, "Procter's Creative Gamble," *Campaign*, 18 March 2005, pp. 24–26.

Transformational leaders bring their visions to life through symbols, metaphors, stories, and other vehicles that transcend plain language. Metaphors borrow images of other experiences, thereby creating richer meaning of the vision that has not yet been experienced. As an example, McDonald's executive George Cohen was handed the difficult task of opening the fast-food company's first restaurants in Russia during the 1980s, when the Soviet Union had limited infrastructure and poor quality standards. To communicate a higher purpose of this challenging initiative, Cohen reminded staff that they were establishing "hamburger diplomacy."[56]

Modeling the Vision Transformational leaders not only talk about a vision; they enact it. They "walk the talk" by stepping outside the executive suite and doing things that symbolize the vision.[57] They are also reliable and persistent in their actions, thereby legitimizing the vision and providing further evidence that they can be trusted. For example, when Chick-fil-A opens a new store, many customers camp out the day before opening, hoping to be among the first 100 adults to receive a year's worth of free Chick-fil-A combo meal coupons. CEO Dan Cathy participates in the grand opening by bringing his own tent, mingling with the crowd throughout the night, and, when the store opens, putting on his customer service hat to greet customers entering the store. "I'll camp out this year about 40 times," says Cathy. "I like to model the practice I stand for."[58]

Leaders walk the talk through significant events such as camping out with customers, moving their offices closer to employees or customers, and holding ceremonies to destroy outdated policy manuals. However, they also alter mundane activities–meeting agendas, office locations, executive schedules–so they are more consistent with the vision and its underlying values. Modeling the vision is important because employees and other stakeholders are executive watchers who look for behaviors that symbolize values and expectations. The greater the consistency between the leader's words and actions, the more employees will believe and follow the leader. Walking the talk also builds employee trust because it is partly determined by the consistency of the person's actions.

"As an executive, you're always being watched by employees, and everything you say gets magnified–so you teach a lot by how you conduct yourself," advises Carl Bass, CEO of California software company Autodesk. Peter Farrell, founder and chief executive of San Diego–based ResMed, agrees. "There are lots of people who talk a good story, but very few deliver one," he warns. "You've got to mean what you say, say what you mean, and be consistent." Surveys suggest that some employees don't see this consistency in their leaders. In one global poll, only 48 percent of employees in Germany and the United Kingdom believed management decisions are consistent

Exhibit 14.5
Elements of Transformational Leadership

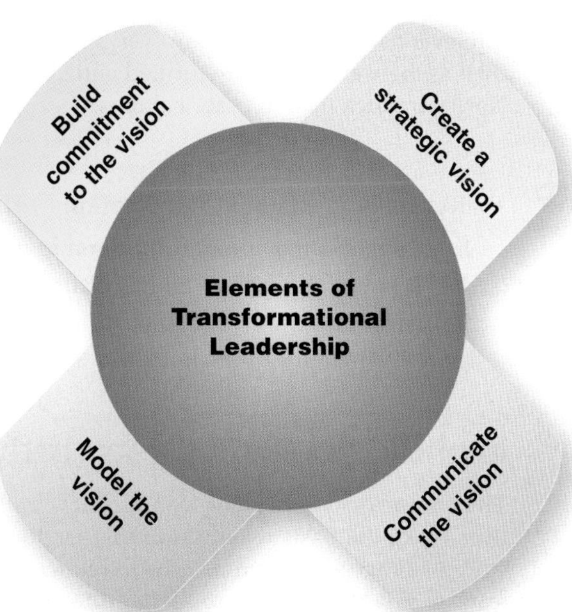

with the company's core values. This figure was higher in the United States (64 percent) and Canada (76 percent). Another recent survey estimated that only 28 percent of Taiwanese employees believe senior management behaves in accordance with the company's core values.[59]

Building Commitment to the Vision Transforming a vision into reality requires employee commitment. Transformational leaders build this commitment in several ways. Their words, symbols, and stories build a contagious enthusiasm that energizes people to adopt the vision as their own. Leaders demonstrate a "can do" attitude by enacting their vision and staying on course. Their persistence and consistency reflect an image of honesty, trust, and integrity. Finally, leaders build commitment by involving employees in the process of shaping the organization's vision.

Evaluating the Transformational Leadership Perspective

Transformational leaders do make a difference. Subordinates are more satisfied and have higher affective organizational commitment under transformational leaders. They also perform their jobs better, engage in more organizational citizenship behaviors, and make better or more creative decisions. One study of bank branches also reported that organizational commitment and financial performance seem to increase where the branch manager completed a transformational leadership training program.[60]

Transformational leadership is currently the most popular leadership perspective, but it faces a number of challenges. One problem is that some writers engage in circular logic by defining transformational leadership in terms of the leader's success.[61] They suggest that leaders are transformational when they successfully bring about change, rather than whether they engage in certain behaviors we call transformational. Another concern is that the transformational leadership model seems to be universal rather than contingency-oriented. Only very recently have writers begun to explore the idea that transformational leadership is more appropriate in some situations than others.[62] For instance, transformational leadership is probably more appropriate when organizations need to adapt than when environmental conditions are stable. Preliminary evidence suggests that the transformational leadership perspective is relevant across cultures. However, specific elements of transformational leadership, such as the way visions are formed and communicated, may be more appropriate in North America than in other cultures.

Learning Objectives

After reading the next two sections you should be able to

8. **Describe the implicit leadership perspective.**
9. **Discuss the influence of culture on perceptions of effective leaders.**
10. **Discuss similarities and differences in the leadership styles of women and men.**

Implicit Leadership Perspective

The competency, behavior, contingency, and transformational leadership perspectives make the basic assumption that leaders make a difference. Certainly there is evidence that senior executives influence organizational performance. However, leaders might have less influence than most of us would like to believe. Some leadership experts suggest that people inflate the importance of leadership in explaining organizational events. These processes, including stereotyping, attribution errors, and the need for situational control, are collectively called **implicit leadership theory**.[63]

implicit leadership theory
A theory hypothesizing that perceptual processes cause people to inflate the importance of leadership as the cause of organizational events.

Stereotyping Leadership

Implicit leadership theory states that everyone has preconceived notions about the features and behaviors of an effective leader. These perceptions are stereotypes or prototypes of idealized leadership that develop through socialization within the family and society.[64] Mental images of an ideal leader shape our expectations and acceptance of people as leaders, which in turn affect their ability to influence us as followers. We rely on leadership stereotypes partly because a leader's success might not be apparent for months or possibly years. Consequently employees depend on immediate information to decide whether a leader is effective. If the leader fits the mold, then employees are more confident that the leader is effective.[65]

Attributing Leadership

Implicit leadership is also influenced by attribution errors. Research has found that (at least in Western cultures) people tend to attribute organizational events to the leader, even when those events are largely caused by factors beyond the leader's control. This attribution is partly caused by fundamental attribution error (see Chapter 3) in which leaders are given credit or blame for the company's success or failure because employees do not readily see the external forces that also influence these events. Leaders reinforce this belief by taking credit for organizational successes.[66]

Need for Situational Control

A third perceptual distortion of leadership suggests that people want to believe leaders make a difference. There are two basic reasons for this belief.[67] First, leadership is a useful way for us to simplify life events. It is easier to explain organizational successes and failures in terms of the leader's ability than by analyzing a complex array of other forces. For example, there are usually many reasons why a company fails to change quickly enough in the marketplace, yet we tend to simplify this explanation down to the notion that the company president or some other corporate leader was ineffective.

Second, there is a strong tendency in the United States and other Western cultures to believe that life events are generated more from people than from uncontrollable natural forces.[68] This illusion of control is satisfied by believing that events result from the rational actions of leaders. In short, employees feel better believing that leaders make a difference, so they actively look for evidence that this is so.

The implicit leadership perspective questions the importance of leadership, but it also provides valuable advice to improve leadership acceptance. This approach highlights the fact that leadership is a perception of followers as much as the actual behaviors and characteristics of people calling themselves leaders. Potential leaders must be sensitive to this fact, understand what followers expect, and act accordingly. Individuals who do not make an effort to fit leadership prototypes will have more difficulty bringing about necessary organizational change.

Leading with *Ubuntu* Values in Africa Woven into the fabric of African society is the concept of *ubuntu,* a collection of values representing harmony, compassion, respect, human dignity, and collective unity. It is "that profound African sense that each of us is human through the humanity of other human beings," explains former South African president Nelson Mandela. *Ubuntu* is about connectedness, so leaders must be comfortable with the highly participative process of making decisions through consensus. It requires leaders to coach, facilitate, and possibly mediate as the group moves toward mutual agreement. *Ubuntu* also values a collective respect for everyone in the system, so leaders must view their role as someone who supports followers, not the other way around. The heroic leader who steps in front—and typically looks down from a higher plateau—is not consistent with *ubuntu.*[69]

Cross-Cultural and Gender Issues in Leadership

Along with the five perspectives of leadership presented throughout this chapter, we need to keep in mind that societal cultural values and practices affect what leaders do. Culture shapes the leader's values and norms, which influence his or her decisions and actions. These cultural values also shape the expectations that followers have of their leaders. This is apparent in Africa, where *ubuntu* values shape the preferred leadership behaviors and style. *Ubuntu* stands for harmony and connectedness, which is incompatible with the heroic leadership styles that are still common in some Western cultures.

An executive who acts inconsistently with cultural expectations is more likely to be perceived as an ineffective leader. Furthermore, leaders who deviate from those values may experience various forms of influence to get them to conform to the leadership norms and expectations of that society. In other words, implicit leadership theory (described in the previous section of this chapter) explains differences in leadership practices across cultures.

Over the past few years 150 researchers from dozens of countries have worked together on Project GLOBE (Global Leadership and Organizational Behavior Effectiveness) to identify the effects of cultural values on leadership.[70] The project organized countries into 10 regional clusters, of which the United States, Great Britain, and similar countries are grouped into the "Anglo" cluster. The results of this massive investigation are just beginning to appear, but preliminary work suggests that some features of leadership are universal and some differ across cultures.

Specifically the GLOBE project reports that "charismatic visionary" is a universally recognized concept, and that middle managers around the world believe that it is characteristic of effective leaders. Charismatic visionary represents a cluster of concepts including visionary, inspirational, performance orientation, integrity, and decisiveness.[71] In contrast, participative leadership is perceived as characteristic of effective leadership in low power distance cultures but less so in high power distance cultures. For instance, one study reported that Mexican employees expect managers to make decisions affecting their work. Mexico is a high power distance culture, so followers expect leaders to apply their authority rather than delegate their power most of the time.[72] In summary, there are similarities and differences in the concepts and preferred practices of leadership across cultures.

Gender Differences in Leadership

Do women lead differently than men? Several writers think so. They suggest that women have an interactive style that includes more people-oriented and participative leadership.[73] They also believe that women are more relationship-oriented, cooperative, nurturing, and emotional in their leadership roles. They further assert that these qualities make women particularly well suited to leadership roles when companies are adopting a stronger emphasis on teams and employee involvement. These arguments are consistent with sex role stereotypes–namely that men tend to be more task-oriented whereas women are more people-oriented.

Are these stereotypes true? Do women adopt more people-oriented and participative leadership styles? The answer is no and yes, respectively. Leadership studies outside university labs (that is, in real work settings) have generally found that male and female leaders do not differ in their levels of task-oriented or people-oriented leadership. The main explanation is that real-world jobs require similar behavior from male and female job incumbents.[74]

However, women do adopt a participative leadership style more readily than their male counterparts. One possible reason is that compared to boys, girls are often raised to be more egalitarian and less status-oriented, which is consistent with being participative. There is also some evidence that women have somewhat better interpersonal skills than men, and this translates into their relatively greater use of the participative leadership style. A third explanation is that subordinates expect female leaders to be more participative, based on their own sex stereotypes, so female leaders comply with follower expectations to some extent.

Several recent surveys report that women are rated higher than men on the emerging leadership qualities of coaching, teamwork, and empowering employees.[75] Yet research also suggests that women are evaluated negatively when they try to apply the full range of leadership styles, particularly more directive and autocratic approaches. Thus, ironically, women may be well suited to contemporary leadership roles, yet they often continue to face limitations of leadership through the gender stereotypes and prototypes of leaders held by followers.[76] Overall both male and female leaders must be sensitive to the fact that followers have expectations about how leaders should act, and negative evaluations may go to leaders who deviate from those expectations.

Chapter Summary

Leadership is a complex concept that is defined as the ability to influence, motivate, and enable others to contribute toward the effectiveness and success of the organizations of which they are members. Leaders use influence to motivate followers and arrange the work environment so that they can do the job more effectively. Leaders exist throughout the organization, not just in the executive suite.

The competency perspective tries to identify the characteristics of effective leaders. Recent writing suggests that leaders have emotional intelligence, integrity, drive, leadership motivation, self-confidence, above-average intelligence, and knowledge of the business. The behavioral perspective of leadership has identified two clusters of leader behavior–people-oriented and task-oriented. People-oriented behaviors include showing mutual trust and respect for subordinates, demonstrating a genuine concern for their needs, and having a desire to look out for their welfare. Task-oriented behaviors include assigning employees to specific tasks, clarifying their work duties and procedures, ensuring that they follow company rules, and pushing them to reach their performance capacity.

The contingency perspective of leadership takes the view that effective leaders diagnose the situation and adapt their style to fit that situation. The path–goal model is the prominent contingency theory that identifies four leadership styles–directive, supportive, participative, and achievement-oriented–and several contingencies relating to the characteristics of the employee and of the situation.

Two other contingency leadership theories include the situational leadership theory and Fiedler's contingency theory. Research support is quite weak for both theories. However, a lasting element of Fiedler's theory is the idea that leaders have natural styles and that companies consequently need to change leaders' environments to suit their style. Leadership substitutes theory identifies contingencies that either limit the leader's ability to influence subordinates or make a particular leadership style unnecessary.

Transformational leaders create a strategic vision, communicate that vision through framing and use of metaphors, model the vision by "walking the talk" and acting consistently, and build commitment to the vision. This contrasts with transactional leadership, which involves linking job performance to valued rewards and ensuring that employees have the resources needed to do their jobs. The contingency and behavioral perspectives adopt the transactional view of leadership.

According to the implicit leadership perspective, people inflate the importance of leadership through attribution, stereotyping, and fundamental needs for human control. Implicit leadership theory is evident across cultures because cultural values shape the behaviors that followers expect of their leaders.

Cultural values also influence the leader's personal values, which in turn influence his or her leadership practices. The GLOBE project data reveal that there are similarities and differences in the concepts and preferred practices of leadership across cultures. Women generally do not differ from men in the degree of people-oriented or task-oriented leadership. However, female leaders more often adopt a participative style. Research also suggests that people evaluate female leaders based on gender stereotypes, which may result in higher or lower ratings.

Key Terms

Fiedler's contingency model, p. 412
implicit leadership theory, p. 419
leadership, p. 402
leadership substitutes, p. 413
path–goal leadership theory, p. 408
servant leadership, p. 408
shared leadership, p. 402
situational leadership theory (SLT), p. 412
transactional leadership, p. 414
transformational leadership, p. 414

Critical Thinking Questions

1. Why is it important for top executives to value and support leadership demonstrated at all levels of the organization?
2. Find two newspaper ads for management or executive positions. What leadership competencies are mentioned in these ads? If you were on the selection panel, what methods would you use to identify these competencies in job applicants?
3. Consider your favorite teacher. What people-oriented and task-oriented leadership behaviors did he or she use effectively? In general, do you think students prefer an instructor who is more people-oriented or task-oriented? Explain your preference.
4. Your employees are skilled and experienced customer service representatives who perform nonroutine tasks, such as solving unique customer problems or special needs with the company's equipment. Use path–goal theory to identify the most appropriate leadership style(s) you should use in this situation. Be sure to fully explain your answer and discuss why other styles are inappropriate.
5. Transformational leadership is currently the most popular perspective of leadership. However, it is far from perfect. Discuss the limitations of transformational leadership.
6. This chapter emphasized that charismatic leadership is not the same as transformational leadership. Still, charisma is often mentioned in discussions of leadership. In your opinion, how does charisma relate to leadership?
7. Identify a current political leader (president, governor, mayor) and his or her recent accomplishments. Now, using the implicit leadership perspective, think of ways that these accomplishments of the leader may be overstated. In other words, explain why they may be due to factors other than the leader.
8. You hear two people debating the merits of women as leaders. One person claims that women make better leaders than do men because women are more sensitive to their employees' needs and involve them in organizational decisions. The other person counters that although these leadership styles may be increasingly important, most women have trouble gaining acceptance as leaders when they face tough situations in which a more autocratic style is required. Discuss the accuracy of the comments made in this discussion.

Case Study 14.1 A WINDOW ON LIFE

For Gilbert LaCrosse, there is nothing quite as beautiful as a handcrafted wood-framed window. LaCrosse's passion for windows goes back to his youth in Eau Claire, Wisconsin, where he learned from an elderly carpenter how to make residential windows. He learned about the characteristics of good wood, the best tools to use, and how to choose the best glass from local suppliers. LaCrosse apprenticed with the carpenter in his small workshop, and when the carpenter retired, he was given the opportunity to operate the business himself.

LaCrosse hired his own apprentice as he built up business in the local area. His small operation soon expanded as the quality of windows built by LaCrosse Industries Inc. became better known. Within eight years the company employed nearly 25 people, and the business had moved to larger facilities to accommodate the increased demand from Wisconsin. In these early years LaCrosse spent most of his time in the production shop, teaching new apprentices the unique skills that he had mastered and applauding the workers for their accomplishments. He would constantly repeat the point that LaCrosse products had to be of the highest quality because they gave families a "window on life."

After 15 years LaCrosse Industries employed over 200 people. A profit-sharing program was introduced to give employees a financial reward for their contribution to the organization's success. Due to the company's expansion, headquarters had to be moved to another area of the city; but the founder never lost touch with the workforce. Although new apprentices were now taught entirely by the master carpenters and other craftspeople, LaCrosse would still chat with plant and office employees several times each week.

When a second work shift was added, LaCrosse would show up during the evening break with coffee and boxes of doughnuts and discuss how the business was doing and how it became so successful through quality work. Production employees enjoyed the times when he would gather them together to announce new contracts with developers from Chicago and New York. After each announcement LaCrosse would thank everyone for making the business a success. They knew that LaCrosse quality had become a standard of excellence in window manufacturing across the eastern part of the country.

It seemed that almost every time he visited, LaCrosse would repeat the now well-known phrase that LaCrosse products had to be of the highest quality because they provided a window on life to so many families. Employees never grew tired of hearing this from the company founder. However, it gained extra meaning when LaCrosse began posting photos of families looking through LaCrosse windows. At first LaCrosse would personally visit developers and homeowners with a camera in hand. Later, as the "window on life" photos became known by developers and customers, people would send in photos of their own families looking through elegant front windows made by LaCrosse Industries. The company's marketing staff began using this idea, as well as LaCrosse's famous phrase, in their advertising. After one such marketing campaign, hundreds of photos were sent in by satisfied customers. Production and office employees took time after work to write personal letters of thanks to those who had submitted photos.

As the company's age reached the quarter-century mark, LaCrosse, now in his mid-fifties, realized that the organization's success and survival depended on expansion to other parts of the United States. After consulting with employees, LaCrosse made the difficult decision to sell a majority share to Build-All Products Inc., a conglomerate with international marketing expertise in building products. As part of the agreement, Build-All brought in a vice president to oversee production operations while LaCrosse spent more time meeting with developers. LaCrosse would return to the plant and office at every opportunity, but often this would be only once a month.

Rather than visiting the production plant, Jan Vlodoski, the new production vice president, would rarely leave his office in the company's downtown headquarters. Instead production orders were sent to supervisors by memorandum. Although product quality had been a priority throughout the company's history, less attention had been paid to inventory controls. Vlodoski introduced strict inventory guidelines and outlined procedures on using supplies for each shift. Goals were established for supervisors to meet specific inventory targets. Whereas employees previously could have tossed out several pieces of warped wood, they would now have to justify this action, usually in writing.

Vlodoski also announced new procedures for purchasing production supplies. LaCrosse Industries had highly trained purchasing staff who worked closely with senior craftspeople when selecting suppliers, but Vlodoski wanted to bring in Build-All's procedures. The new purchasing methods removed production leaders from the decision process and, in some cases, resulted in trade-offs that LaCrosse's employees would not have made earlier. A few employees quit during this time, saying that they did not feel comfortable about producing a window that would not stand the test of time. However, there were few jobs for carpenters, so most staff members remained with the company.

After one year inventory expenses decreased by approximately 10 percent, but the number of defective windows returned by developers and wholesalers had increased markedly. Plant employees knew that the number of defective windows would increase as they used somewhat lower-quality materials to reduce inventory costs. However, they heard almost no news about the seriousness of the problem until Vlodoski sent a memo to all production staff saying that quality must be maintained. During the latter part of the first year under Vlodoski, a few employees had the opportunity to personally ask LaCrosse about the changes and express their concerns. LaCrosse apologized, saying due to his travels to new regions, he had not heard about the problems, and he would look into the matter.

Exactly 18 months after Build-All had become majority shareholder of LaCrosse Industries, LaCrosse called together five of the original staff in the plant. The company founder looked pale and shaken as he said that Build-All's actions were inconsistent with his vision of the company, and for the first time in his career, he did not know what to do. Build-All was not pleased with the arrangement either. Although LaCrosse windows still enjoyed a healthy market share and were competitive for the value, the company did not quite provide the minimum 18 percent return on equity that the conglomerate expected. LaCrosse asked his long-time companions for advice.

Discussion Questions

1. Identify the symptoms indicating that problems exist at LaCrosse Industries Inc.
2. Use one or more leadership theories to analyze the underlying causes of the current problems at LaCrosse Industries. What other organizational behavior theories might also help to explain some of the problems?
3. What should Gilbert LaCrosse do in this situation?

Case Study 14.2 MACK ATTACK

John J. Mack, who had left Morgan Stanley four years earlier, was back as CEO, replacing Philip J. Purcell, who had resigned weeks earlier after mounting criticism that he was mismanaging the once-mighty investment bank. Whereas Purcell was a top-down strategist and tended to hole up in his office, Mack is drawing on his skills as a salesman and operator to make Morgan Stanley as nimble and dynamic as possible. He also hired key people to help him put the new culture in place.

This *BusinessWeek* case study examines the leadership of Morgan Stanley CEO John J. Mack. It describes his actions to change the investment bank's culture and to redirect decision making so it is more aggressive rather than timid. Read through this *BusinessWeek* article at www.mhhe.com/mcshane4e and prepare for the discussion questions below.

Discussion Questions

1. Based on the information in this case study, describe the competencies that seem strongest in John Mack.
2. To what extent has John Mack exhibited transformational leadership behaviors to shift Morgan Stanley's culture and decision making?

Source: E. Thornton, Mack Attack, *BusinessWeek*, 3 July 2006, 88.

Team Exercise 14.3 LEADERSHIP DIAGNOSTIC ANALYSIS

PURPOSE To help students learn about the different path–goal leadership styles and when to apply each style.

INSTRUCTIONS

1. Students should individually write down two incidents in which someone was an effective manager or leader over them. The leader and situation might be from work, a sports team, a student work group, or any other setting where leadership might emerge. For example, students might describe how their supervisor in a summer job pushed them to reach higher performance goals than they would have done otherwise. Each incident should state the actual behaviors that the leader used, not just general statements (for example, "My boss sat down with me and we agreed on specific targets and deadlines, then he said several times over the next few weeks that I was capable of reaching those goals"). Each incident only requires two or three sentences.
2. After everyone has written their incidents, the instructor will form small groups (typically four to five students). Each team will answer the following questions for each incident presented in that team:
   a. Which path–goal theory leadership style(s)–directive, supportive, participative, or achievement-oriented–did the leader apply in this incident?
   b. Ask the person who wrote the incident about the conditions that made this leadership style (or these styles, if more than one was used) appropriate in this situation. The team should list these contingency factors clearly and, where possible, connect them to the contingencies described in path–goal theory. (*Note:* The team might identify path–goal leadership contingencies that are not described in the book. These too should be noted and discussed.)
3. After the teams have diagnosed the incidents, each team will describe to the entire class the most interesting incidents as well as the team's diagnosis of that incident. Other teams will critique the diagnosis. Any leadership contingencies not mentioned in the textbook should also be presented and discussed.

Self-Assessment 14.4 LEADERSHIP DIMENSIONS INSTRUMENT

PURPOSE This assessment is designed to help you understand two important dimensions of leadership and identify which of these dimensions is more prominent in your supervisor, team leader, coach, or other person to whom you are accountable.

INSTRUCTIONS Read each of the following statements and circle the response that you believe best describes your supervisor. You may substitute for "supervisor" anyone else to whom you are accountable, such as a team leader, CEO, course instructor, or sports coach. Then use the scoring key in Appendix B to calculate the results for each leadership dimensions. After completing this assessment, be prepared to discuss in class the distinctions between these leadership dimensions.

Leadership Dimensions Instrument

	My Supervisor	Strongly agree ▼	Agree ▼	Neutral ▼	Disagree ▼	Strongly disagree ▼
1.	Focuses attention on irregularities, mistakes, exceptions, and deviations from what is expected of me.	5	4	3	2	1
2.	Engages in words and deeds that enhance his or her image of competence.	5	4	3	2	1
3.	Monitors performance for errors needing correction.	5	4	3	2	1
4.	Serves as a role model for me.	5	4	3	2	1
5.	Points out what I will receive if I do what is required.	5	4	3	2	1
6.	Instills pride in being associated with him or her.	5	4	3	2	1
7.	Keeps careful track of mistakes.	5	4	3	2	1
8.	Can be trusted to help me overcome any obstacle.	5	4	3	2	1
9.	Tells me what to do to be rewarded for my efforts.	5	4	3	2	1
10.	Makes me aware of strongly held values, ideals, and aspirations that are shared in common.	5	4	3	2	1
11.	Is alert for failure to meet standards.	5	4	3	2	1
12.	Mobilizes a collective sense of mission.	5	4	3	2	1
13.	Works out agreements with me on what I will receive if I do what needs to be done.	5	4	3	2	1
14.	Articulates a vision of future opportunities.	5	4	3	2	1
15.	Talks about special rewards for good work.	5	4	3	2	1
16.	Talks optimistically about the future.	5	4	3	2	1

Source: Items and dimensions are adapted from D.N. Den Hartog, J.J. Van Muijen, and P.L. Koopman, "Transactional versus Transformational Leadership: An Analysis of the MLQ," *Journal of Occupational & Organizational Psychology* 70 (March 1997), pp. 19–34. Den Hartog et al. label transactional leadership as "rational–objective leadership" and label transformational leadership as "inspirational leadership." Many of their items may have originated from B.M. Bass and B.J. Avolio, *Manual for the Multifactor Leadership Questionnaire* (Palo Alto, CA: Consulting Psychologists Press, 1989).

After reading this chapter, if you need additional information, see **www.mhhe.com/mcshane4e** for more in-depth interactivities that correspond with this material.

Part four
Organizational Processes

Globalization is playing havoc with the organizational structures of advertising agencies. Some multinational firms, such as Samsung, have centralized marketing decisions, requiring ad firms to also concentrate their expertise globally. Other companies, such as Coca-Cola and Procter & Gamble, have positioned their advertising decisions at the regional level, so agencies serving these clients need to offer both regional and global expertise. Meanwhile, believing that global advertising firms are too bureaucratic, several client companies are turning to boutique agencies for local expertise.

Boutique advertising firm Nitro relies on an organizational structure that keeps it nimble and responsive to customer needs.

Nitro may have found an organizational structure that satisfies this mishmash of client needs. Each local Nitro office has account service staff, but a global creative team is parachuted in as required. This micro-network structure began in Shanghai, China, and within three years had expanded to New York, London, Taipei, Hong Kong, Sydney, and Melbourne. Its global billings have already reached US $300 million, catapulting it to the 66th spot in the global ranking of ad agencies.

Nitro's balance of regional decentralization and global centralization gives clients direct access to the agency's top creatives, who move from one office to the next, solving client issues and contributing their specialized knowledge as needed. Founder Chris Clarke also intends to keep Nitro boutique-size by limiting the number of clients. "We want to remain small, as a certain size gives us the ability to be fast and nimble," he says. Wei Wei Chen, Nitro's head of operations for Greater China, says that the company's unique structure minimizes the bureaucracy of most global agencies. "The speed at which we can move gives us a competitive edge. We believe in erasing the lines between departments and between us and the client."

Nitro isn't alone in designing an organizational structure aligned with the need for global and regional balance. Lowe Worldwide recently introduced a "lighthouse structure" that reorganized its offices in 91 countries around a dozen "lighthouses" or centers of creativity in key markets. "The Lighthouse structure eliminates the bureaucratic system of regional management and pools resources, talent, and processes," explains one executive at the ad agency, which operates out of London and New York. Another adds, "[The Lighthouse structure] means access to top-flight talent around the world—talent that has access to local markets and the creativity and flexibility to execute."[1]

15

Organizational Structure

LEARNING OBJECTIVES

After reading this chapter you should be able to

1. Describe three types of coordination in organizational structures.
2. Justify the optimal span of control in a given situation.
3. Discuss the advantages and disadvantages of centralization and formalization.
4. Distinguish organic from mechanistic organizational structures.
5. Identify and evaluate five pure types of departmentalization.
6. Describe three variations of divisionalized structure and explain which one should be adopted in a particular situation.
7. Diagram the matrix structure for a project-based organization and a large global business.
8. Describe the features of team-based organizational structures.
9. Identify four characteristics of external environments and discuss the preferred organizational structure for each environment.
10. Summarize the influences of organizational size, technology, and strategy on organizational structure.

There is something of a revolution occurring in how organizations are structured. Nitro, Lowe Worldwide, and other companies are rethinking their organizational charts and trying out new designs that they hope will achieve organizational objectives more effectively. **Organizational structure** refers to the division of labor as well as the patterns of coordination, communication, workflow, and formal power that direct organizational activities. An organizational structure reflects the organization's culture and power relationships.[2]

organizational structure
The division of labor and the patterns of coordination, communication, work flow, and formal power that direct organizational activities.

Organizational structures are frequently used as tools for change because they establish new communication patterns and align employee behavior with the corporate vision.[3] For example, to steer Charles Schwab Co. out of its financial trouble, founder Charles Schwab held a two-day marathon session in which the company's top executives were asked to redraw the organization chart in a way that would make the company simpler, more decentralized, and refocused on the customer. Every executive in the room, including those whose jobs would be erased from the new structure, was asked for her or his input.[4]

We begin this chapter by considering the two fundamental processes in organizational structure: division of labor and coordination. This is followed by a detailed investigation of the four main elements of organizational structure: span of control, centralization, formalization, and departmentalization. The latter part of this chapter examines the contingencies of organizational design, including organizational size, technology, external environment, and strategy.

Learning Objectives

After reading the next two sections you should be able to

1. **Describe three types of coordination in organizational structures.**
2. **Justify the optimal span of control in a given situation.**
3. **Discuss the advantages and disadvantages of centralization and formalization.**
4. **Distinguish organic from mechanistic organizational structures.**

Division of Labor and Coordination

All organizational structures include two fundamental requirements: the division of labor into distinct tasks and the coordination of that labor so that employees can accomplish common goals.[5] Organizations are groups of people who work interdependently toward some purpose. To efficiently accomplish their goals, these groups typically divide the work into manageable chunks, particularly when there are many different tasks to perform. They also introduce various coordinating mechanisms to ensure that everyone is working effectively toward the same objectives.

Division of Labor

Division of labor refers to the subdivision of work into separate jobs assigned to different people. Subdivided work leads to job specialization because each job now includes a narrow subset of the tasks necessary to complete the product or service. Launching a space shuttle at NASA, for example, involves tens of thousands of specific tasks that are divided among thousands of people. Tasks are also divided vertically, such as having supervisors coordinate work while employees perform the work.

Work is divided into specialized jobs because this potentially increases work efficiency.[6] Job incumbents can master their tasks quickly because work cycles are very short. Less time is wasted changing from one task to another. Training costs are

Exhibit 15.1 Coordinating Mechanisms in Organizations

Form of coordination	Description	Subtypes
Informal communication	Sharing information about mutual tasks; forming common mental models to synchronize work activities.	• Direct communication. • Liaison roles. • Integrator roles.
Formal hierarchy	Assigning legitimate power to individuals, who then use this power to direct work processes and allocate resources.	• Direct supervision. • Corporate structure.
Standardization	Creating routine patterns of behavior or output.	• Standardized skills. • Standardized processes. • Standardized output.

Source: Based on information in J. Galbraith, *Designing Complex Organizations* (Reading, MA: Addison-Wesley, 1973), pp. 8–19; H. Mintzberg, *The Structuring of Organizations* (Englewood Cliffs, NJ: Prentice Hall, 1979), Chapter 1; D.A. Nadler and M.L. Tushman, *Competing by Design: The Power of Organizational Architecture* (New York: Oxford University Press, 1997), Chapter 6.

reduced because employees require fewer physical and mental skills to accomplish the assigned work. Finally, job specialization makes it easier to match people with specific aptitudes or skills to the jobs for which they are best suited.

Coordinating Work Activities

As soon as people divide work among themselves, coordinating mechanisms are needed to ensure that everyone works in concert. Every organization–from the two-person corner convenience store to the largest corporate entity–uses one or more of the following coordinating mechanisms:[7] informal communication, formal hierarchy, and standardization (see Exhibit 15.1).

Coordination through Informal Communication Informal communication is a coordinating mechanism in all organizations. This includes sharing information about mutual tasks as well as forming common mental models so that employees synchronize work activities using the same mental road map.[8] Informal communication is vital in nonroutine and ambiguous situations because employees can exchange a large volume of information through face-to-face communication and other media-rich channels.

Coordination through informal communication is easiest in small firms such as Nitro, although information technologies have further leveraged this coordinating mechanism in large organizations. Companies employing thousands of people, such as auto parts manufacturer Magna International, also support informal communication by keeping each production site small (usually fewer than 200 employees). Toyota and other automakers further support this coordinating mechanism by occasionally moving dozens of employees responsible for developing a new product into one large room.[9]

Larger organizations also encourage coordination through informal communication by creating *integrator roles.* These people are responsible for coordinating a work process by encouraging employees in each work unit to share information and informally coordinate work activities. Integrators do not have authority over the people involved in that process, so they must rely on persuasion and commitment. Brand managers at Procter & Gamble coordinate work among marketing, production, and design groups.[10]

Coordination through Formal Hierarchy Informal communication is the most flexible form of coordination, but it can be time-consuming. Consequently, as organizations grow, they develop a second coordinating mechanism: formal hierarchy. Hierarchy assigns legitimate power to individuals, who then use this power to direct work processes and allocate resources. In other words, work is coordinated through direct supervision. Any organization with a formal structure coordinates work to some extent through formal hierarchy. For instance, team leaders at computer chip maker Intel are responsible for ensuring that employees on their team remain on schedule and that their respective tasks are compatible with tasks completed by other team members.

Formal hierarchy also coordinates work among executives through the division of organizational activities. If the organization is divided into geographic areas, this structure gives regional group leaders legitimate power over executives responsible for production, customer service, and other activities in those areas. If the organization is divided into product groups, the heads of those groups have the right to coordinate work across regions.

Formal hierarchy has traditionally been applauded as the optimal coordinating mechanism for large organizations. A century ago administrative scholars argued that organizations are most effective where managers exercise their authority and employees receive orders from only one supervisor. Coordination should occur through the chain of command–that is, up the hierarchy and across to the other work units.[11]

Coordination through formal hierarchy may have been popular with classic organizational theorists, but it can be an inefficient coordinating mechanism. Without relying on other coordinating mechanisms, managers can supervise only a limited number of employees. As the business grows, the number of supervisors and layers of management must also increase, resulting in a costly bureaucracy. Also, communicating through the chain of command is rarely as fast or accurate as direct communication between employees. A third concern is that today's workforce is less tolerant of rigid structures. For instance, Wegmans Food Market is one of the best places to work partly because the Rochester, New York–based grocery chain minimizes formal hierarchy as a coordinating mechanism.

Coordination through Standardization Standardization, the third means of coordination, involves creating routine patterns of behavior or output. This coordinating mechanism takes three distinct forms:

- *Standardized processes.* Quality and consistency of a product or service can often be improved by standardizing work activities through job descriptions and procedures.[12] This coordinating mechanism is feasible when the work is routine (such as mass production) or simple (such as making pizzas) but is less effective in nonroutine and complex work such as product design.
- *Standardized outputs.* This form of standardization involves ensuring that individuals and work units have clearly defined goals and output measures (such as customer satisfaction and production efficiency). For instance, to coordinate the work of salespeople, companies assign sales targets rather than specific behaviors.
- *Standardized skills.* When work activities are too complex to standardize through processes or

"Shipwrecked or not, Bradley, we must maintain the chain of command."

goals, companies often coordinate work efforts by extensively training employees or hiring people who have learned precise role behaviors from educational programs. This form of coordination is used in hospital operating rooms. Surgeons, nurses, and other operating room professionals coordinate their work more through training than through goals or company rules.

Division of labor and coordination of work represent the two fundamental ingredients of all organizations. How work is divided, who makes decisions, which coordinating mechanisms are emphasized, and other issues are related to the four elements of organizational structure.

Elements of Organizational Structure

Every company is configured in terms of four basic elements of organizational structure. This section introduces three of them: span of control, centralization, and formalization. The fourth element–departmentalization–is presented in the next section.

Span of Control

span of control
The number of people directly reporting to the next level in the organizational hierarchy.

Span of control refers to the number of people directly reporting to the next level in the hierarchy. Almost 100 years ago French engineer and administrative theorist Henri Fayol strongly recommended formal hierarchy as the primary coordinating mechanism. Consequently he prescribed a relatively narrow span of control: typically no more than 20 employees per supervisor and 6 supervisors per manager. These prescriptions were based on the assumption that managers simply cannot monitor and control any more subordinates closely enough. Today we know better. The best-performing manufacturing plants currently have an average of 38 production employees per supervisor.[13]

What's the secret here? Did Fayol and others miscalculate the optimal span of control? The answer is that Fayol and many other scholars sympathetic to hierarchical control believed that employees should do the work, whereas supervisors and other management personnel should monitor employee behavior and make most of the decisions. In contrast, the best-performing manufacturing operations today rely on self-directed work teams, so direct supervision (formal hierarchy) is just a backup coordinating mechanism. The underlying principle is that the optimal span of control depends on the presence of other coordinating mechanisms. Self-directed work teams supplement direct supervision with informal communication and specialized knowledge.[14]

Along with the presence of other coordinating mechanisms, the best span of control depends on the nature of the task. A wider span of control is possible when employees perform routine tasks, whereas a narrower span of control is required when employees perform novel or complex tasks. Routine tasks have few exceptions, so there is less need for direction or advice from supervisors; in contrast, novel or complex tasks tend to require more supervisory decisions or coaching. This principle is illustrated in a survey of American property and casualty insurers. The average span of control in commercial policy processing departments is around 15 employees per supervisor, whereas the span of control is 6.1 in claims service and 5.5 in commercial underwriting. Staff members in the latter two departments perform more technical work, so they have more novel and complex tasks. Commercial policy processing, on the other hand, is production-like work where tasks are routine and have few exceptions.[15]

A third influence on span of control is the degree of interdependence among employees within the department or team. One recent study of airline flight departure crews reported that supervisors responsible for highly interdependent teams need to provide more feedback and coaching than where employees are less interdependent. When tasks are highly linked, employees lack unique performance indicators for their own work, so supervisory feedback must be introduced. This increased coaching and feedback means that supervisors need a narrower span of control when managing highly interdependent teams.[16]

Tall and Flat Structures A few years ago BASF's European Seal Sands plant organized employees into self-directed work teams and dramatically restructured the work process. These actions did much more than increase efficiency and lower costs at the bulk chemical plant. They also chopped out several layers of hierarchy. "Seven levels of management have been cut basically to two," says a BASF executive.[17]

BASF's European Seal Sands plant joins a long list of companies that are moving toward flatter organizational structures. This trend toward delaying–moving from a tall to flat structure–is partly in response to the recommendations of management gurus. Twenty years ago, for example, management guru Tom Peters challenged corporate leaders to cut the number of layers to three within a facility and to five within the entire organization.[18] The main reasons why BASF and other companies are moving toward flatter organizational structures is that it potentially cuts overhead costs and puts decision makers closer to front-line staff and information about customer needs. With fewer managers, employees might also experience more empowerment due to greater autonomy over their work roles.

However, some organizational experts warn that corporate leaders may be cutting out too much hierarchy. They argue that the much-maligned "middle managers" serve a valuable function by controlling work activities and managing corporate growth. Furthermore, companies will always need hierarchy because someone has to make quick decisions and represent a source of appeal over conflicts.[19] The conclusion here is that there is an optimal level of delayering in most organizations. Flatter structures offer several benefits, but cutting out too much management can offset these benefits.

One last point before leaving this topic: The size of an organization's hierarchy depends on both the average span of control and the number of people employed by the organization. Exhibit 15.2 illustrates this principle. A tall structure has many hierarchical levels, each with a relatively narrow span of control, whereas a flat structure has few levels, each with a wide span of control. Larger organizations that depend on hierarchy for coordination necessarily develop taller structures. For instance, HP is considered a high-involvement organization, yet it has 8 levels of corporate hierarchy (recently reduced from 11 levels) to coordinate its tens of thousands of employees.[20]

Centralization and Decentralization

centralization
The degree to which formal decision authority is held by a small group of people, typically those at the top of the organizational hierachy.

Centralization and decentralization represent a second element of organizational design. **Centralization** means that formal decision-making authority is held by a small group of people, typically those at the top of the organizational hierarchy. Most organizations begin with centralized structures because the founder makes most decisions and tries to direct the business toward his or her vision. But as organizations grow, they diversify and their environments become more complex. Senior executives aren't able to process all the decisions that significantly influence the business.

Consequently, larger organizations tend to *decentralize*; that is, they disperse decision authority and power throughout the organization. Barrick Gold Corp., the world's largest gold producer, is a case in point. "Barrick had always been run on this command-

Exhibit 15.2 Span of Control and Tall/Flat Structures

Tall structure/ Narrow span of control

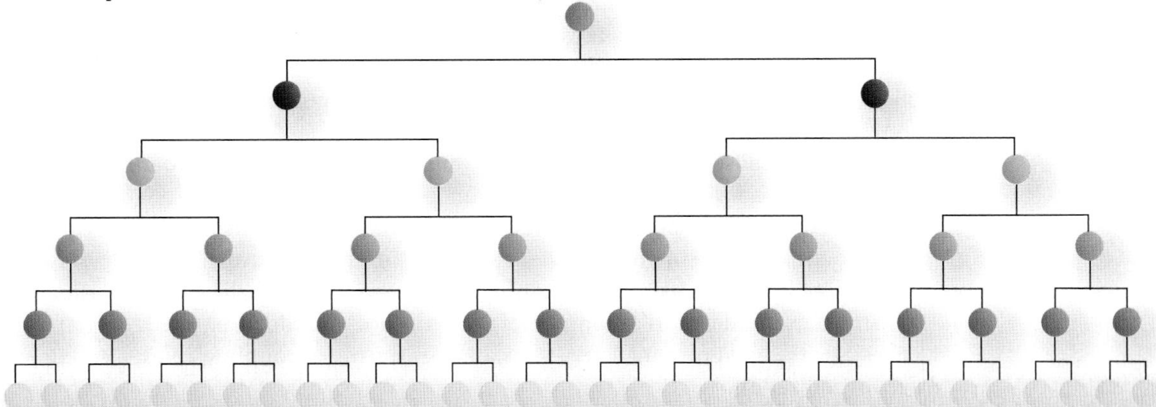

Flat structure/ Wide span of control

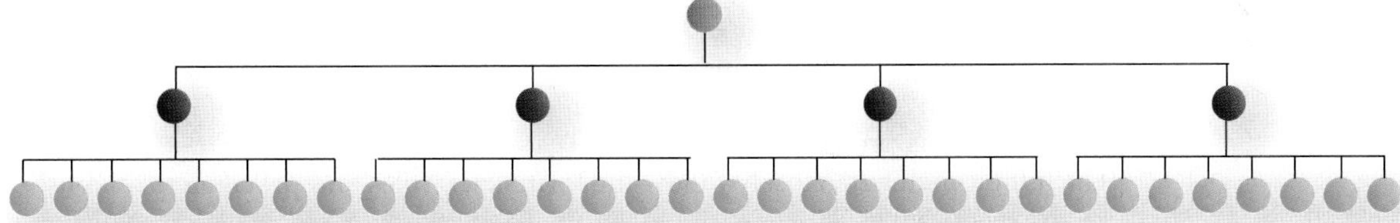

and-control model, a centrist approach that saw all the decision making made in Toronto," says CEO Greg Wilkins. "That worked while the company was small and operating only in North America. But all of a sudden we are in four continents and seven countries, and it becomes pretty clear that you just can't do it any more." The company has since decentralized its operations around three regions of the world.[21]

The optimal level of centralization or decentralization depends on several contingencies that we will examine later in this chapter. However, we also need to keep in mind that different degrees of decentralization can occur simultaneously in different parts of the organization. Nestlé has decentralized marketing decisions to remain responsive to local markets. At the same time the Swiss-based food company has centralized production, logistics, and supply chain management activities to improve cost efficiencies and avoid having too much complexity across the organization. "If you are too decentralized, you can become too complicated–you get too much complexity in your production system," explains Nestlé CEO Peter Brabeck.[22] Firms also tend to rapidly centralize during times of turbulence and organizational crisis. When the problems are over, the company should decentralize decisions again, although this reversal tends to occur slowly because leaders are reluctant to give up decision-making power.

formalization
The degree to which organizations standardize behavior through rules, procedures, formal training, and related mechanisms.

Formalization

Have you ever wondered why McDonald's hamburgers in Seattle look and taste the same as the McDonald's hamburgers in Singapore? The reason is that the fast-food company has engineered out all variation through formalization. **Formalization** is the degree to which organizations standardize behavior through rules, procedures, formal training, and related mechanisms.[23] In other words, formalization represents the establishment of standardization as a coordinating mechanism.

McDonald's restaurants have a formalized structure because they rely heavily on standardization of work processes as a coordinating mechanism. Employees have precisely defined roles, right down to how much mustard should be dispensed, how many pickles should be applied, and how long each hamburger should be cooked. In contrast, Nitro, described in the opening story to this chapter, has relatively little formalization because job descriptions and output expectations are broadly defined to accommodate varying tasks and responsibilities.

Older companies tend to become more formalized because work activities become routinized, making them easier to document into standardized practices. Larger companies formalize as a coordinating mechanism because direct supervision and informal communication among employees do not operate as easily. External influences, such as government safety legislation and strict accounting rules, also encourage formalization.

Problems with Formalization Formalization may increase efficiency and compliance, but it can also create problems. Rules and procedures reduce organizational flexibility, so employees follow prescribed behaviors even when the situation clearly calls for a customized response. Thus, high levels of formalization undermine a learning orientation required for knowledge management and creativity. Some work rules become so convoluted that organizational efficiency would decline if they were actually followed as prescribed. Labor unions sometimes invoke work-to-rule strikes in which their members closely follow the formalized rules and procedures established by an organization. This tactic is effective if the company's productivity falls when employees follow the rules that are supposed to guide their behavior.

Formalized structures are fine for employees who value a stable workplace, but many employees today feel disempowered–they lack feelings of self-determination, meaning, competence, and impact of their organizational role–when working in highly formalized organizations. Finally, rules and procedures have been known to take on a life of their own in some organizations. They become the focus of attention rather than the organization's ultimate objectives of producing a product or service and serving the dominant stakeholders.

Mechanistic versus Organic Structures

We have discussed span of control, centralization, and formalization together because they usually cluster into two forms: mechanistic and organic structures.[24] A **mechanistic structure** is characterized by a narrow span of control and high degree of formalization and centralization. Mechanistic structures have many rules and procedures, limited decision making at lower levels, tall hierarchies of people in specialized roles, and vertical rather than horizontal communication flows. Tasks, which are rigidly defined, are altered only when this is sanctioned by higher authorities.

mechanistic structure
An organizational structure with a narrow span of control and high degrees of formalization and centralization.

Companies with an **organic structure** have the opposite characteristics. Nitro, the boutique advertising firm described at the beginning of this chapter, is a clear example of an organic structure because it has a wide span of control, decentralized decision making, and little formalization. Tasks are fluid, adjusting to new situations and organizational needs. The organic structure supports knowledge management practices, particularly the view that information may be located anywhere in the organization rather than among senior executives. Thus, communication flows in all directions with little concern for formal hierarchy.

organic structure
An organizational structure with a wide span of control, with little formalization, and decentralized decision making.

Harbinger Partners is a "manager-free zone." That's because the business intelligence and creative services company has no bosses. All 20 employees (actually they're partners) own a piece of the company and are involved in making company decisions. Harbinger doesn't even have a formal headquarters—just a post office box number in St. Paul, Minnesota. The company's partners work either from their homes or in clients' offices. This arrangement might give some executives sleepless nights, but not Scott Grausnick (center), who founded Harbinger in 1999. Instead he deliberately created this highly organic structure so staff could cater more effectively to customer needs while satisfying their entrepreneurial spirit. The structure seems to work: Harbinger Partners weathered the downturn that affected other firms and receives very high satisfaction ratings from customers and staff alike.[25]

As a general rule, mechanistic structures operate better in stable environments because they rely on efficiency and routine behaviors, whereas organic structures work better in rapidly changing (dynamic) environments because they are more flexible and responsive to these changes. Organic structures are also more compatible with knowledge and quality management because they emphasize information sharing rather than hierarchy and status.[26] However, the benefits of organic structures in dynamic environments occur only when employees have developed well-established roles and expertise.[27] In other words, effective organic companies rely on employee expertise and team development. Without these conditions, employees are unable to coordinate effectively with each other, resulting in errors and gross inefficiencies.

Start-up companies, particularly those in new industries, often face this problem, known as the "liability of newness." Newness makes start-up firms more organic, but their employees often lack industry experience and their teams have not developed sufficiently for peak performance. As a result, the organic structures of new companies cannot compensate for the poorer coordination and significantly lower efficiencies caused by this lack of structure from past experience and team mental models. Nitro is an excellent counterexample because, although a new firm, the ad agency relies on a team of highly experienced industry creatives who swoop into a local office to assist the new operations with specific accounts. Thus, Nitro enjoys an organic structure yet has the foundations of well-established roles and expertise to deliver service.

Learning Objectives

After reading this section you should be able to

5. **Identify and evaluate five pure types of departmentalization.**
6. **Describe three variations of divisionalized structure and explain which one should be adopted in a particular situation.**
7. **Diagram the matrix structure for a project-based organization and a large global business.**
8. **Describe the features of team-based organizational structures.**

Forms of Departmentalization

Span of control, centralization, and formalization are important elements of organizational structure, but most people think about organizational charts when the discussion of organizational structure arises. The organizational chart represents the fourth element in the structuring of organizations, called *departmentalization*. Departmentalization specifies how employees and their activities are grouped together. It is a fundamental strategy for coordinating organizational activities because it influences organizational behavior in the following ways:[28]

- Departmentalization establishes the chain of command–the system of common supervision among positions and units within the organization. It frames the membership of formal work teams and typically determines which positions and units must share resources. Thus, departmentalization establishes interdependencies among employees and subunits.
- Departmentalization focuses people around common mental models or ways of thinking, such as serving clients, developing products, or supporting a particular skill set. This focus is typically anchored around the common budgets and measures of performance assigned to employees within each departmental unit.
- Departmentalization encourages coordination through informal communication among people and subunits. With common supervision and resources, members within each configuration typically work near each other, so they can use frequent and informal interaction to get the work done.

There are almost as many organizational charts as there are businesses, but we can identify five pure types of departmentalization: simple, functional, divisional, matrix, and team-based. In addition, this section describes the network structure, which extends beyond internal departments.

Simple Structure

Most companies begin with a *simple structure*.[29] They employ only a few people and typically offer only one distinct product or service. There is minimal hierarchy–usually just employees reporting to the owners. Employees are grouped into broadly defined roles because there are insufficient economies of scale to assign them to specialized roles. The simple structure is highly flexible and minimizes the walls that form between employees in other structures. However, the simple structure usually depends on the owner's direct supervision to coordinate work activities, so it is difficult to operate as the company grows and becomes more complex.

Functional Structure

functional structure
An organizational structure that organizes employees around specific knowledge or other resources.

Organizations that grow large enough use functional structures at some level of the hierarchy or at some time in their history. A **functional structure** organizes employees around specific knowledge or other resources. Employees with marketing expertise are grouped into a marketing unit; those with production skills are located in manufacturing; engineers are found in product development; and so on. Organizations with functional structures are typically centralized to coordinate their activities effectively. Standardization of work processes is the most common form of coordination used in a functional structure.

Evaluating the Functional Structure The functional structure encourages specialization and increases employees' identification with their profession. It permits greater specialization so that the organization has expertise in each area. Direct supervision is easier because managers have backgrounds in that functional area, and employees approach them with common problems and issues. Finally, the functional structure creates common pools of talent that typically serve everyone in the organization. This provides more economies of scale than if functional specialists are spread over different parts of the organization.[30]

The functional structure also has limitations.[31] Grouping employees around their skills tends to focus attention on those skills and related professional needs rather than on the company's product, service, and client needs. Unless people are transferred from one function to the next, they might not develop a broader understanding of the business. Compared with other structures, the functional structure usually produces higher dysfunctional conflict and poorer coordination in serving clients or developing products. These problems occur because employees need to work with co-workers in other departments to complete organizational tasks, yet they have different subgoals and mental models of ideal work. Together these problems require substantial formal controls and coordination when people are organized around functions.

Divisional Structure

divisional structure
An organizational structure that groups employees around geographic areas, clients, or outputs.

The **divisional structure** groups employees around geographic areas, outputs (products and services), or clients. This type of structure creates minibusinesses that may operate as subsidiaries rather than departments (sometimes called *strategic business units*); they are far more autonomous than functional departments. Exhibit 15.3 illustrates the three variations of divisional structure. The *geographic structure* organizes employees around distinct regions of the country or globe. Exhibit 15.3(a) illustrates a geographic divisionalized structure recently adopted by Barrick Gold Corp. The *product/service structure* organizes work around distinct outputs. Exhibit 15.3(b) illustrates this type of structure at Philips. The Dutch electronics company divides its workforce mainly into five product divisions, ranging from consumer electronics to semiconductors. The *client structure* represents the third form of divisional structure, in which employees are organized around specific customer groups. Exhibit 15.3(c) illustrates the customer-focused structure similar to one adopted by the U.S. Internal Revenue Service.[32]

Which form of divisionalization should large organizations adopt? The answer depends mainly on the primary source of environmental diversity or uncertainty.[33] Suppose an organization sells one type of product to people across the country. If customer needs vary across regions, or if state governments impose different regulations on the product, then a geographic structure would be best to be more vigilant of

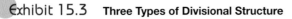

Exhibit 15.3 **Three Types of Divisional Structure**

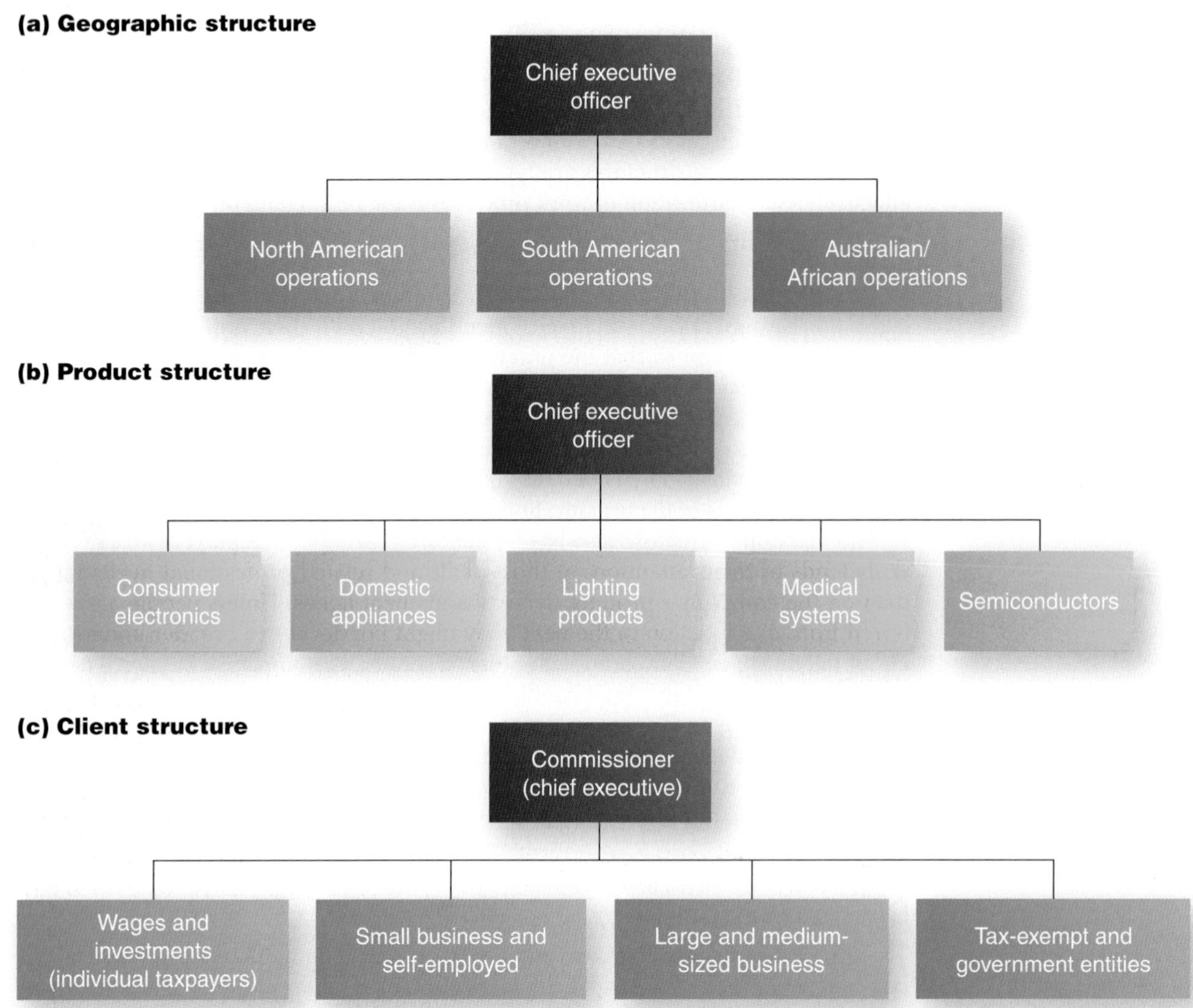

this diversity. On the other hand, if the company sells several types of products across the country and customer preferences and government regulations are similar everywhere, then a product structure would likely work best.

Coca-Cola, Nestlé, and many other food and beverage companies are organized mainly around geographic regions because consumer tastes and preferred marketing strategies vary considerably around the world. Even though McDonald's makes the same Big Mac around the planet, it has more fish products in Hong Kong and more vegetarian products in India in line with traditional diets in those countries. Philips, on the other hand, is organized around products because consumer preferences are similar within each group. Hospitals from Geneva, Switzerland, to Santiago, Chile, purchase similar medical equipment from Philips, whereas manufacturing and sales of these products are quite different from Philips' semiconductor business.

Many divisionalized companies are moving away from geographical structures.[34] One reason is that clients can purchase online and communicate with businesses from almost anywhere in the world, so local representation is less critical. Reduced geographic variation is another reason for the shift away from geographical structures; freer trade has reduced government intervention for many products, and consumer preferences for many products and services are becoming more similar (converging) around the world. The third reason is that large companies increasingly have global business customers who demand one global point of purchase, not one in every country or region.

Evaluating the Divisionalized Structure The divisional form is a building block structure in that it accommodates growth relatively easily. Related products or clients can be added to existing divisions with little need for additional learning. Different products, services, or clients can be accommodated by sprouting a new division. Organizations typically reorganize around divisional structures as they expand into distinct products, services, and domains of operation because coordinating functional units becomes too unwieldy with increasing diversity.[35]

These advantages are offset by a number of limitations. First, the divisionalized structure tends to duplicate resources, such as production equipment and engineering or information technology expertise. Also, unless the division is quite large, resources are not used as efficiently as in functional structures where resources are pooled across the entire organization. The divisionalized structure also creates silos of knowledge. Expertise is spread throughout the various business units, which reduces the ability and perhaps motivation of these people to share their knowledge with counterparts in other divisions. In contrast, a functional structure groups experts together, which supports knowledge sharing.

Finally, as was already explained, the preferred divisionalized structure depends on the company's primary source of environmental diversity or uncertainty. This principle seems to be applied easily enough at Coca-Cola, McDonald's, and Philips. But the decision of whether to choose a geographic, product, or client structure is really quite difficult because global organizations experience diversity and uncertainties in many ways. The decision also affects political dynamics in the organization. If corporate leaders switch from a geographic to product structure, people who led the geographical fiefdoms suddenly get demoted under the product chiefs. Consequently, global organizations revise their structures back and forth, with each transition usually resulting in one or more executives leaving the company.

Matrix Structure

Electronic games developer BioWare launched its business with a simple or team structure in which everyone worked together to create BioWare's first game, *Shattered Steel.* But when the company launched a second project, *Baldur's Gate,* founders Ray Muzyka and Greg Zeschuk had to decide on a new structure. One option would be to simply have two teams working independently; but this multiteam structure would duplicate resources, possibly undermine information sharing among people with the same expertise across teams, and weaken employee loyalty to the overall company.

Alternatively, the game developer could create departments around the various specializations, including art, programming, audio, quality assurance, and design. This would allow employees with similar technical expertise to share information and create new ideas within their specialization. However, employees would not have the same level of teamwork or commitment to the final product as they would in a team-based project structure.

matrix structure
A type of departmentalization that overlays two organizational forms in order to leverage the benefits of both.

To gain the benefits of both alternatives, BioWare adopted a **matrix structure** in which employees belonged to departments but were assigned to specific teams based on needs. A matrix structure overlays two organizational forms to leverage the benefits that each has to offer. BioWare's matrix structure, which is similar to the diagram

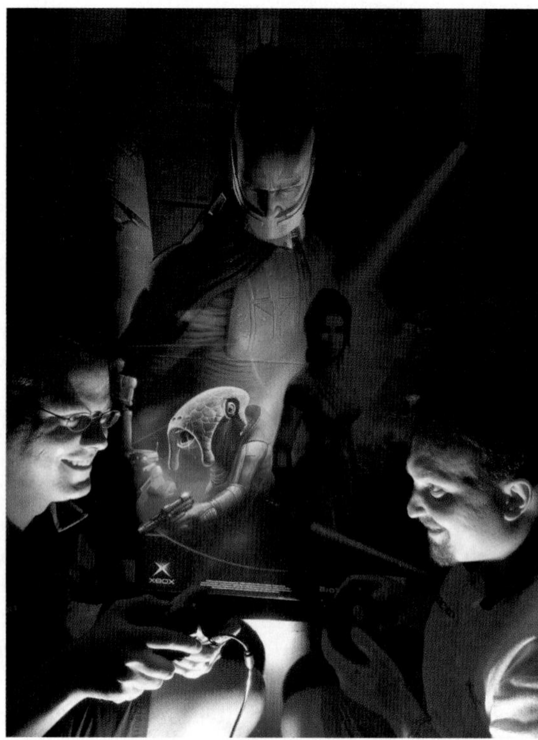

BioWare Enters the Matrix Executives at electronic games developer BioWare adopted a matrix organizational structure to gain the benefits of both a functional structure and a team or project-based structure. BioWare employees belong to departments but are assigned to specific projects for several months or longer. A matrix structure can be challenging, so BioWare holds "synchronization meetings" where functional and project leaders resolve conflicts. They also carefully select applicants who can work with the ambiguity of a matrix structure. The result is a company that has a much higher success rate than most companies in the competitive electronic games business. "They've been amazingly successful," the editor of one electronic games magazine recently applauded. "Anything that comes out of [BioWare] is on everyone's radar."[36]

in Exhibit 15.4, is organized around both functions (art, audio, programming, and so on) and products (games). Employees are assigned to a cross-functional team responsible for a specific game project, yet they also belong to a permanent functional unit from which they are redistributed when their work is completed on a particular project.[37] Muzyka and Zeschuk say the matrix structure encourages employees to think in terms of the final product, yet keeps them organized around their expertise to encourage knowledge sharing. "The matrix structure also supports our overall company culture where BioWare is the team, and everyone is always willing to help each other whether they are on the same project or not," explain Muzyka and Zeschuk.

BioWare's structure, in which project teams overlap with functional departments, is just one form of matrix structure. Another variation, which is common in large firms with global business, is to have geography on one dimension and products/services or client groups on the other. General Motors applies this global matrix structure in its information technology group.[38] One dimension consists of GM's five regional operations (North America, Europe, Asia, and so forth) led by chief information officers (CIOs) who provide IT support in their appointed regions. The other dimension consists of five business processes (services), including production, customer experience, supply chain, product development, and business services. Each process is led by a "process information officer" who is responsible for global IT support in that particular business activity. Thus, a manager who oversees supply chain information systems in Brazil would report to both the CIO for Latin America and the process information officer who heads the supply chain group.

Evaluating the Matrix Structure The matrix structure usually optimizes the use of resources and expertise, making it ideal for project-based organizations with fluctuating workloads. When properly managed, it improves communication efficiency, project flexibility, and innovation compared to purely functional or divisional designs.

Exhibit 15.4 Project-Based Matrix Structure (Similar to BioWare's Structure)

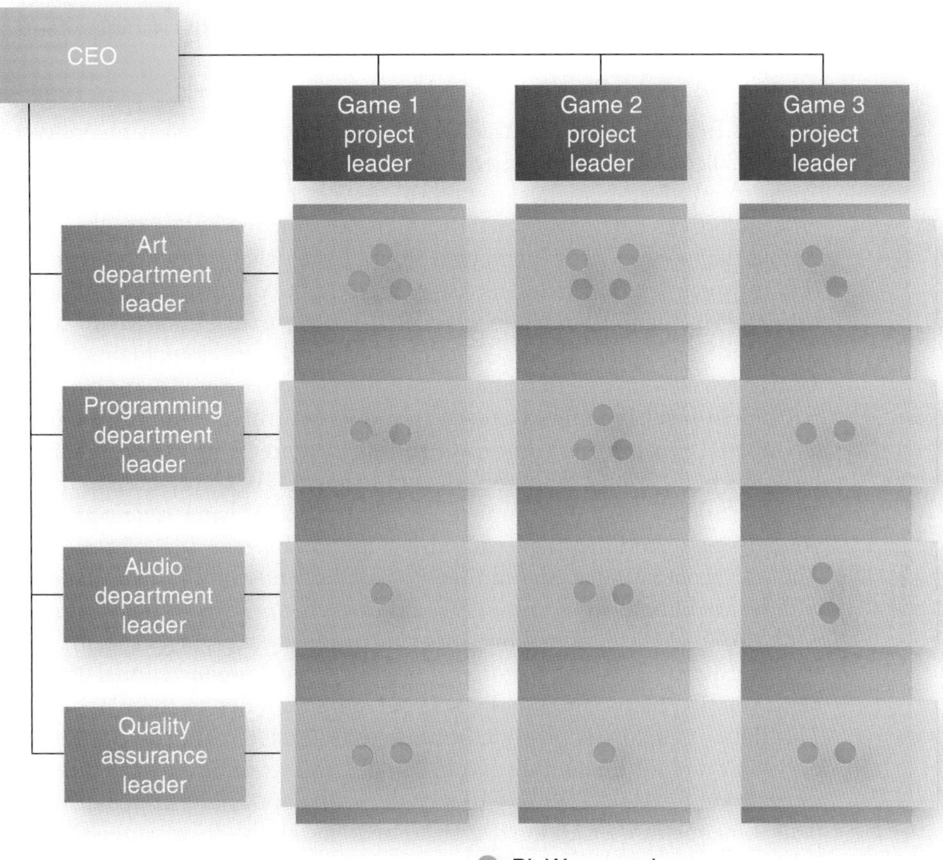

It focuses employees on serving clients or creating products, yet keeps expertise organized around their specialization so knowledge sharing improves and resources are used more efficiently. The matrix structure is also a logical choice when, as in the case of GM's IT group, two different dimensions (regions and processes) are equally important. Structures determine executive power and what is important; the matrix structure works when two different dimensions deserve equal attention.

In spite of these advantages, the matrix structure has several well-known problems.[39] One concern is that it increases goal conflict and ambiguity. Employees working at the matrix level have two bosses and, consequently, two sets of priorities that aren't always aligned with each other. Project leaders might squabble over specific employees who are assigned to other projects. They may also disagree with employee decisions, but the employee's functional leader has more say than the project leader about the individual's technical competence. Aware of these concerns, BioWare holds several "synchronization meetings" each year involving all department directors (art, design, audio, and so on), producers (game project leaders), and the human resources manager. These meetings sort out differences and ensure that staff members are properly assigned to each game project.

Another challenge is that the existence of two bosses can dilute accountability. In a functional or divisionalized structure, one manager is responsible for everything, even the most unexpected issues. But in a matrix structure the unusual problems don't get resolved because neither manager takes ownership for them.[40] The result of conflict and ambiguity in matrix structures is that some employees experience more stress, and some managers are less satisfied with their work arrangements.

Team-Based Structure

Medrad Inc. threw out the traditional assembly line when it recently consolidated some of its manufacturing operations into a new facility. For several years the Indianola, Pennsylvania, maker of medical devices has nurtured a team culture, and the new site provided an opportunity to add more structure to this emphasis on teamwork. Rather than a supervised long-line assembly, the new facility relies on clusters of work cells in which self-directed work teams manage the process with minimal involvement from management. Within two years of the changeover, productivity at Medrad's new facility increased by 30 percent compared to the previous plants, while employee satisfaction shot up due to higher autonomy and opportunities for cross-training.[41]

team-based structure
A type of departmentalization with a flat hierarchy and relatively little formalization, consisting of self-directed work teams responsible for various work processes.

Medrad Inc. has adopted a **team-based structure** in its production operations. The team-based structure has a few distinguishing features from other organizational forms. First, it is built around self-directed work teams (SDWTs) rather than traditional teams or departments. SDWTs complete an entire piece of work requiring several interdependent tasks, and they have substantial autonomy over the execution of their tasks. The teams operating at Medrad plan, organize, and control their own work activities without traditional supervision. Second, these teams are typically organized around work processes, such as making a specific product or serving a specific client group.

A third distinguishing feature of the team-based organizational structure is that it has a very flat hierarchy, usually with no more than two or three management levels. This flatter structure is possible because self-directed teams do not rely on direct supervision to coordinate their work. Finally, the team-based structure has very little formalization. Almost all day-to-day decisions are made by team members rather than someone further up the organizational hierarchy. Teams are given relatively few rules about how to organize their work. Instead the executive team typically assigns output goals to the team, such as the volume and quality of product or service, or productivity improvement targets for the work process. Teams are then encouraged to use available resources and their own initiative to achieve those objectives.

Team-based structures are usually found within the manufacturing operations of larger divisionalized structures. For example, automobile parts giant TRW Automotive has a team-based structure in many of its 200 plants, but these plants are linked together within the company's divisionalized structure. However, a few firms apply the team-based structure from top to bottom. Perhaps the most famous example of this is W. L. Gore & Associates, whose extreme team-based structure is described in Connections 15.1.

Evaluating the Team-Based Structure The team-based organization represents an increasingly popular structure because it is usually more responsive and flexible than traditional functional or divisionalized structures.[42] It tends to reduce costs because teams have less reliance on formal hierarchy (direct supervision). A cross-functional team structure improves communication and cooperation across traditional boundaries. With greater autonomy, this structure also allows quicker and more informed decision making.[43] For this reason, some hospitals have shifted from functional departments to cross-functional teams. Teams composed of nurses, radiologists, anesthesiologists, a pharmacology representative, and possibly social workers, a rehabilitation therapist, and other specialists communicate and coordinate more efficiently, therefore reducing delays and errors.[44]

Connections 15.1

The Extreme Team Structure of W. L. Gore & Associates Inc.

Diane Davidson admits that her first few months at W. L. Gore & Associates Inc. were a bit frustrating. "When I arrived at Gore, I didn't know who did what," recalls the apparel industry sales executive hired to market Gore-Tex fabrics to brand name designers. "I wondered how anything got done here. It was driving me crazy." Davidson kept asking her "starting sponsor" who her boss was, but the sponsor firmly replied, "Stop using the B-word." Gore must have managers, she thought, but they probably downplay their status. But there really aren't any bosses, not in the traditional sense. "Your team is your boss because you don't want to let them down," Davidson eventually learned. "Everyone's your boss, and no one's your boss."

From its beginnings in 1958, the Newark, Delaware-based manufacturer of fabrics (Gore-Tex), electronics, and industrial and medical products has adopted an organizational structure in which most employees (or "associates" as they are known) are organized around self-directed teams. The company has an incredibly flat hierarchy with a high degree of decentralized authority. Associates make day-to-day decisions within their expertise without approval from anyone higher up. Bigger issues, such as hiring and compensating staff, are decided by teams. "We make our own decisions and everything is discussed as well," explains Phyllis Tait, a medical business support leader at Gore's U.K. business unit.

The company has a divisional structure, organized around products and clients, such as fabrics, medical, electronics, and industrial. But most of Gore's 7,000 associates work at 45 self-sufficient manufacturing and sales offices around the world. Each facility is deliberately limited to about 200 people so they can coordinate more effectively through informal communication. Within those units, new projects are started through individual initiative and support from others. "There is no positional power," explains a Gore team leader. "You are a leader only if teams decide to respect and follow you."

As Diane Davidson discovered, Gore operates without job titles, job descriptions, or a formal chain of command. This ambiguous structure was established so associates can be creative and responsive by coordinating directly with people in other areas of the organization. "You go to whomever you need to get things done," says Gore sales veteran Tom Erickson (left in photo with colleague John Cusick). "If I want to talk to a person on the manufacturing line about a particular job, I just go out and talk to him. That's one thing that sets us apart. There's no fear of any person going over another's head."

W. L. Gore & Associates Inc. has an extreme team-based organizational structure that eliminates traditional hierarchy. "There's no fear of any person going over another's head," says Gore sales veteran Tom Erickson, shown here (left) with co-worker John Cusick in Gore's testing room.

Sources: "The Firm That Lets Staff Breathe," *Sunday Times* (London), 24 March 2002; A. Brown, "Satisfaction All in a Day's Work for Top 3," *Evening News* (Edinburgh, Scotland), 23 March 2002, p. 13; M. Weinreb, "Power to the People," *Sales & Marketing Management*, April 2003, pp. 30–35; L.D. Maloney, "Smiles in the Workplace," *Test & Measurement World*, March 2004, p. 5; A. Deutschman, "The Fabric of Creativity," *Fast Company*, December 2004, pp. 54–59; M.L. Diamond, "Change in Management for Medical Device Company," *Asbury Park Press* (New Jersey), 6 February 2006; P.J. Kiger, "Power of the Individual," *Workforce Management*, 27 February 2006, pp. 1–7.

Against these benefits, the team-based structure can be costly to maintain due to the need for ongoing interpersonal skills training. Teamwork potentially takes more time to coordinate than formal hierarchy during the early stages of team development. Employees may experience more stress due to increased ambiguity in their roles. Team leaders also experience more stress due to increased conflict, loss of functional power, and unclear career progression ladders.[45]

Network Structure

BMW isn't eager to let you know this, but some of its vehicles designed and constructed with Germanic precision are neither designed nor constructed by BMW or in Germany. The BMW X3, for example, was not only assembled by auto parts giant Magna International in Austria, but much of the vehicle's engineering was designed by Magna specialists. BMW is the hub organization that owns and markets the BMW brand, whereas Magna and other supplier firms are spokes around the hub that provide production, engineering, and other services that get BMW products to customers.[46]

network structure
An alliance of several organizations for the purpose of creating a product or serving a client.

BMW is moving toward a **network structure** as it creates an alliance of several organizations for the purpose of creating a product or serving a client.[47] Exhibit 15.5 illustrates how this collaborative structure typically consists of several satellite organizations beehived around a hub or core firm. The core firm orchestrates the network process and provides one or two other core competencies, such as marketing or product development. In our example, BMW is the hub that provides marketing and distribution, whereas other firms perform most other functions. The core firm might be the main contact with customers, but most of the product or service delivery and support activities are farmed out to satellite organizations located anywhere in the world. Extranets (Web-based networks with partners) and other technologies ensure that information flows easily and openly between the core firm and its array of satellites.[48]

One of the main forces pushing toward a network structure is the recognition that an organization has only a few *core competencies.* A core competency is a knowledge base that resides throughout the organization and provides a strategic advantage. As companies discover their core competency, they "unbundle" noncritical tasks to other organizations that have a core competency in performing those tasks.

Companies are also more likely to form network structures when technology is changing quickly and production processes are complex or varied.[49] Many firms cannot keep up with the hyperfast changes in information technology, so they have

Exhibit 15.5
A Network Structure

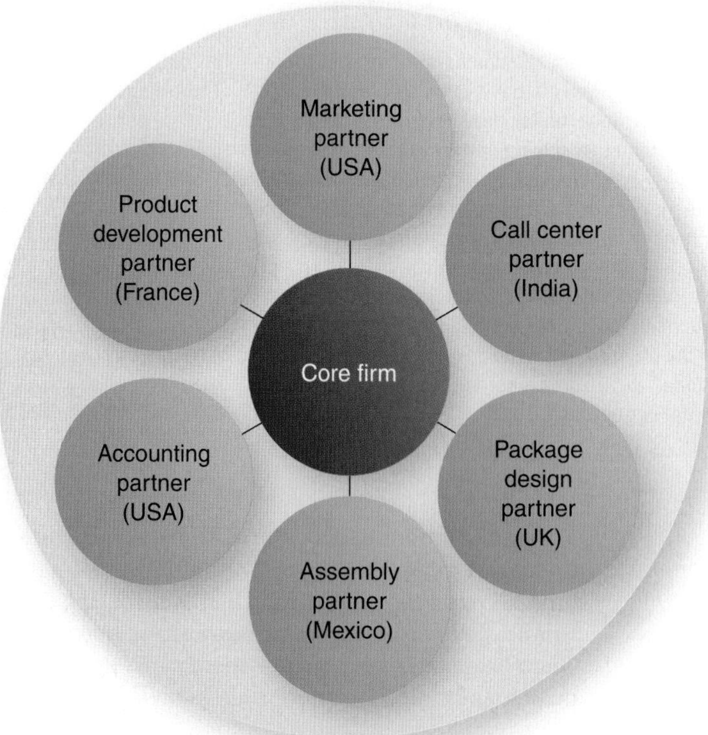

outsourced their entire information systems departments to IBM, EDS, and other firms that specialize in information systems services. Similarly, many high-technology firms form networks with Solectron, Celestica, and other electronics equipment manufacturers because they have expertise in diverse production processes.

virtual corporations Network structures representing several independent companies that form unique partnership teams to provide customized products or services, usually to specific clients, for a limited time.

Virtual Corporations

The network structure generally performs a patterned set of tasks for all clients. In contrast, some network structures–known as **virtual corporations**–represent several independent companies that form unique partnership teams to provide customized products or services, usually to specific clients, for a limited time.[50] A good example of this is host universal. The British advertising firm (which spells its name all lowercase) has no employees or clients. Instead it serves a specific project by forming a unique team of partners, who then disband when the project is finished. "At host we have no clients or employees, which enables us to pull the most effective teams together from our network without foisting redundant skills, fees, and hierarchy onto clients," explains one of host's founding partners.[51]

Virtual corporations exist temporarily and reshape themselves quickly to fit immediate needs. When an opportunity emerges, a unique combination of partners in the alliance forms a virtual corporation that works on the assignment until it is completed. Virtual corporations are self-organizing, meaning that they rearrange their own communication patterns and roles to fit the situation. The relationship among the partners is mutually determined rather than imposed by a core firm.

Evaluating the Network Structure

For several years organizational behavior theorists have argued that organizational leaders must develop a metaphor of organizations as plasma-like organisms rather than rigid machines.[52] Network structures come close to the organism metaphor because they offer the flexibility to realign their structures with changing environmental requirements. If customers demand a new product or service, the core firm forms new alliances with other firms offering the appropriate resources. For example, by working with Magna International, BMW was probably able to develop and launch the X3 vehicle much sooner than if it had performed these tasks on its own. When BMW needs a different type of manufacturing, it isn't saddled with nonessential facilities and resources. Network structures also offer efficiencies because the core firm becomes globally competitive as it shops worldwide for subcontractors with the best people and the best technology at the best price. Indeed, the pressures of global competition have made network structures more vital, and computer-based information technology has made them possible.[53]

A potential disadvantage of network structures is that they expose the core firm to market forces. Other companies may bid up the price for subcontractors, whereas the short-term cost would be lower if the company hired its own employees to provide this function. Another problem is that although information technology makes worldwide communication much easier, it will never replace the degree of control organizations have when manufacturing, marketing, and other functions are in-house. The core firm can use arm's-length incentives and contract provisions to maintain the subcontractor's quality, but these actions are relatively crude compared to those used to maintain performance of in-house employees.

Learning Objectives

After reading the next section you should be able to

9. **Identify four characteristics of external environments and discuss the preferred organizational structure for each environment.**
10. **Summarize the influences of organizational size, technology, and strategy on organizational structure.**

Contingencies of Organizational Design

Most organizational behavior theories and concepts have contingencies: Ideas that work well in one situation might not work as well in another situation. This contingency approach is certainly relevant when firms choose the most appropriate organizational structure.[54] In this section we introduce four contingencies of organizational design: external environment, size, technology, and strategy.

External Environment

The best structure for an organization depends on its external environment. The external environment includes anything outside the organization, including most stakeholders (clients, suppliers, government), resources (raw materials, human resources, information, finances), and competitors. Four characteristics of external environments influence the type of organizational structure best suited to a particular situation: dynamism, complexity, diversity, and hostility:[55]

- *Dynamic versus stable environments.* Dynamic environments have a high rate of change, leading to novel situations and a lack of identifiable patterns. Organic structures, including the team-based structure at Nitro, are better suited to this type of environment so that the organization can adapt more quickly to changes, but only if employees are experienced and coordinate well in teamwork.[56] In contrast, stable environments are characterized by regular cycles of activity and steady changes in supply and demand for inputs and outputs. Events are more predictable, enabling the firm to apply rules and procedures. Mechanistic structures are more efficient when the environment is predictable, so they tend to work better than organic structures under these conditions.
- *Complex versus simple environments.* Complex environments have many elements, whereas simple environments have few things to monitor. As an example, a major university library operates in a more complex environment than a small town public library. The university library's clients require several types of services–book borrowing, online full-text databases, research centers, course reserve collections, and so on. A small town public library experiences fewer of these demands. The more complex the environment, the more decentralized the organization should become. Decentralization is a logical response to complexity because decisions are pushed down to people and subunits with the necessary information to make informed choices.
- *Diverse versus integrated environments.* Organizations located in diverse environments have a greater variety of products or services, clients, and regions. In contrast, an integrated environment has only one client, product, and geographic area. The more diversified the environment, the more a firm needs to use a divisionalized form aligned with that diversity. If it sells a single product around the world, a geographic divisionalized structure would align best with the firm's geographic diversity, for example.
- *Hostile versus munificent environments.* Firms located in a hostile environment face resource scarcity and more competition in the marketplace. Hostile environments are typically dynamic ones because they reduce the predictability of access to resources and demand for outputs. Organic structures tend to be best in hostile environments. However, when the environment is extremely hostile–such as a severe shortage of supplies or lower market share–organizations tend to temporarily centralize so that decisions can be made more

7-Eleven's Centralized–Decentralized Structure 7-Eleven tries to leverage the buying power and efficiencies of its 25,000 stores in 19 countries by centralizing decisions about information technology and supplier purchasing. At the same time, the convenience store chain's customers have diverse preferences from Australia to Japan to North America. This diversity exists even within countries. For example, weather and special events can be dramatically different from one city to the next, which means that product demand will also vary. To thrive in this diverse and complex environment, 7-Eleven's business in the United States has what it calls a "centrally decentralized" structure in which store managers make local inventory decisions using a centralized inventory management system. Along with ongoing product training and guidance from regional consultants, store managers have the best information about their customers and can respond quickly to local market needs. "We could never predict a busload of football players on a Friday night, but the store manager can," explains 7-Eleven president and CEO Jim Keyes, shown in this photo with a 7-Eleven employee.[57]

quickly and executives feel more comfortable being in control.[58] Ironically, centralization may result in lower-quality decisions during organizational crises because top management has less information, particularly when the environment is complex.

Organization Size

Larger organizations should have different structures from smaller organizations.[59] As the number of employees increases, job specialization increases due to a greater division of labor. This greater division of labor requires more elaborate coordinating mechanisms. Thus larger firms make greater use of standardization (particularly work processes and outcomes) to coordinate work activities. These coordinating mechanisms create an administrative hierarchy and greater formalization. Historically, larger organizations have made less use of informal communication as a coordinating mechanism. However, emerging information technologies and increased emphasis on empowerment have caused informal communication to regain its importance in large firms.[60]

Larger organizations also tend to be more decentralized. Executives have neither sufficient time nor expertise to process all the decisions that significantly influence the business as it grows. Therefore, decision-making authority is pushed down to lower levels, where incumbents can cope with the narrower range of issues under their control.

Technology

Technology is another factor to consider when designing the best organizational structure for the situation.[61] *Technology* refers to the mechanisms or processes by which an organization turns out its products or services. One technological contingency is its *variability*–the number of exceptions to standard procedure that tend to occur. In work processes with low variability, jobs are routine and follow standard operating procedures. Another contingency is *analyzability*–the predictability or difficulty of the required work. The less analyzable the work, the more it requires experts with sufficient discretion to address the work challenges.

Assembly line technology has low variability and high analyzability; the jobs are routine and highly predictable. This type of technology works best with a structure consisting of high formalization and centralization. When employees perform tasks with high variety and low analyzability, they apply their skills to unique situations with little opportunity for repetition. Research project teams operate under these conditions. These situations call for an organic structure with low formalization, highly decentralized decision-making authority, and coordination mainly through informal communication among team members.

High-variety and high-analyzability tasks have many exceptions to routines, but these exceptions can usually be resolved through standard procedures. Maintenance groups and engineering design teams experience these conditions. Work units that fall into this category should use an organic structure, but it is possible to have somewhat greater formalization and centralization due to the analyzability of problems. Skilled trades people tend to work in situations with low variety and low analyzability. Their tasks involve few exceptions, but the problems that arise are difficult to resolve. This situation allows more centralization and formalization than in a purely organic structure, but coordination must include informal communication among the skilled employees so that unique problems can be resolved.

Organizational Strategy

organizational strategy The way an organization positions itself in its setting in relation to its stakeholders, given the organization's resources, capabilities, and mission.

Organizational strategy refers to the way an organization positions itself in its setting in relation to its stakeholders, given the organization's resources, capabilities, and mission.[62] In other words, strategy represents the decisions and actions applied to achieve the organization's goals. Although size, technology, and environment influence the optimal organizational structure, these contingencies do not necessarily determine structure. Instead corporate leaders formulate and implement strategies that shape both the characteristics of these contingencies as well as the organization's resulting structure.

This concept is summed up with the simple phrase "Structure follows strategy."[63] Organizational leaders decide how large to grow and which technologies to use. They take steps to define and manipulate their environments rather than letting the organization's fate be entirely determined by external influences. Furthermore, organizational structures don't evolve as a natural response to these contingencies. Instead they result from organizational decisions. Thus organizational strategy influences both the contingencies of structure and the structure itself.

The structure follows strategy thesis that has become the dominant perspective of business policy and strategic management. An important aspect of this view is that organizations can choose the environments in which they want to operate. Some businesses adopt a *differentiation strategy* by bringing unique products to the market or attracting clients who want customized goods and services. They try to distinguish their outputs from those provided by other firms through marketing, providing special services, and innovation. Others adopt a *cost leadership strategy* in which they maximize productivity and are thereby able to offer popular products or services at a competitive price.[64]

The type of organizational strategy selected leads to the best organizational structure to adopt.[65] Organizations with a cost leadership strategy should adopt a mechanistic, functional structure with high levels of job specialization and standardized work processes. This is similar to the routine technology category described earlier because this approach maximizes production and service efficiency. A differentiation strategy, on the other hand, requires more customized relations with clients. A matrix or team-based structure with less centralization and formalization is most appropriate here so that technical specialists can coordinate their work activities more closely with clients' needs. Overall, it is now apparent that organizational structure is influenced by size, technology, and environment, but the organization's strategy may reshape these elements and loosen their connection to organizational structure.

Chapter Summary

Organizational structure refers to the division of labor as well as the patterns of coordination, communication, workflow, and formal power that direct organizational activities. All organizational structures divide labor into distinct tasks and coordinate that labor to accomplish common goals. The primary means of coordination are informal communication, formal hierarchy, and standardization.

The four basic elements of organizational structure include span of control, centralization, formalization, and departmentalization. At one time scholars suggested that firms should have a tall hierarchy with a narrow span of control. However, span of control can be much wider when other coordinating mechanisms are present. Span of control should be narrower when employees perform novel or complex tasks and where their work is highly interdependent with co-workers.

Centralization occurs when formal decision authority is held by a small group of people, typically senior executives. Many companies decentralize as they become larger and more complex because senior executives lack the necessary time and expertise to process all the decisions that significantly influence the business. Formalization is the degree to which organizations standardize behavior through rules, procedures, formal training, and related mechanisms. Companies become more formalized as they grow older and larger.

Span of control, centralization, and formalization cluster into mechanistic and organic structures. Mechanistic structures are characterized by a narrow span of control and high degree of formalization and centralization. Companies with an organic structure have the opposite characteristics.

Departmentalization specifies how employees and their activities are grouped together. It establishes the chain of command, focuses people around common mental models, and encourages coordination through informal communication among people and subunits. A functional structure organizes employees around specific knowledge or other resources. This fosters greater specialization, improves direct supervision, but increases conflict in serving clients or developing products. It also focuses employee attention on functional skills rather than on the company's product/service or client needs.

A divisional structure groups employees around geographic areas, clients, or outputs. This structure accommodates growth and focuses employee attention on products or customers rather than on tasks. However, this structure creates silos of knowledge and duplication of resources.

The matrix structure combines two structures to leverage the benefits of both types of structure. However, this approach requires more coordination than functional or pure divisional structures, may dilute accountability, and increases conflict.

Team-based structures are very flat with low formalization and organize self-directed teams around work processes rather than functional specialties. A network structure is an alliance of several organizations for the purpose of creating a product or serving a client. Virtual corporations are network structures that can quickly reorganize themselves to suit the client's requirements.

The best organizational structure depends on the firm's external environment, size, technology, and strategy. The optimal structure depends on whether the environment is dynamic or stable, complex or simple, diverse or integrated, and hostile or munificent. As organizations increase in size, they become more decentralized and more formalized, with greater job specialization and more elaborate coordinating mechanisms. The work unit's technology–including variety of work and analyzability of problems–influences whether to adopt an organic or mechanistic structure. These contingencies influence but do not necessarily determine structure. Instead corporate leaders formulate and implement strategies that shape both the characteristics of these contingencies as well as the organization's resulting structure.

Key Terms

centralization, p. 434
divisional structure, p. 439
formalization, p. 435
functional structure, p. 439
matrix structure, p. 441
mechanistic structure, p. 436
network structure, p. 446
organic structure, p. 436
organizational strategy, p. 450
organizational structure, p. 450
span of control, p. 433
team-based structure, p. 444
virtual corporations, p. 447

Critical Thinking Questions

1. Boutique advertising agency Nitro has an organic, team-based structure. What coordinating mechanism dominates in this type of organizational structure? Describe the extent and form in which the other two forms of coordination might be apparent at Nitro.
2. Think about the business school or other organizational unit whose classes you are currently attending. What is the dominant coordinating mechanism used to guide or control the instructor? Why is this coordinating mechanism used the most here?
3. Administrative theorists concluded many decades ago that the most effective organizations have a narrow span of control. Yet today's top-performing manufacturing firms have a wide span of control. Why is this possible? Under what circumstances, if any, should manufacturing firms have a narrow span of control?
4. If we could identify trends in organizational structure, one of them would be decentralization. Why is decentralization becoming more common in contemporary organizations? What should companies consider when determining their degree of decentralization?
5. Diversified Technologies LLC (DTL) makes four types of products, each type to be sold to different types of clients. For example, one product is sold exclusively to automobile repair shops, whereas another is used mainly in hospitals. Customer expectations and needs are surprisingly similar throughout the world. However, the company has separate marketing, product design, and manufacturing facilities in Asia, North America, Europe, and South America because, until recently, each jurisdiction had unique regulations governing the production and sales of these products. Now several governments have begun the process of deregulating the products that DTL designs and manufactures, and trade agreements have opened several markets to foreign-made products. Which form of departmentalization might be best for DTL if deregulation and trade agreements occur?
6. Why are many organizations moving away from geographic divisional structures?
7. From an employee perspective, what are the advantages and disadvantages of working in a matrix structure?
8. Suppose that you have been hired as a consultant to diagnose the environmental characteristics of your college or university. How would you describe the school's external environment? Is the school's existing structure appropriate for this environment?

Case Study 15.1 FTCA—REGIONAL AND HEADQUARTERS RELATIONS

Swee C. Goh, University of Ottawa

The FTCA is a government agency that provides services to the public but also serves an enforcement role. It employs over 20,000 people who are located at headquarters and in many regional offices across the country. Most staff members are involved with direct counter-type services for both individuals and businesses. These services include collections, inquiries, payments, and audits. The agency also has large centers in various parts of the country to process forms and payments submitted by individuals and businesses.

FTCA is a typical federal government agency; many employees are unionized and have experienced numerous changes over the years. Because of the increasing complexity of regulations and the need to be more cost-effective in service delivery, FTCA has evolved into an organization that uses technology to a great extent. The agency's leaders increasingly emphasize the need for easier and faster service and turnaround in dealing with clients. They also expect staff to depend more on electronic means of communication for interaction with the public.

As the population has grown over the years, the regional offices of this government organization have expanded. Each regional office is headed by an assistant director (AD) who has a budget and an increasing number of staff for the various functional activities related to the region, such as a manager for information systems. Every region also has offices located in the major cities. The managers of these city center offices report directly to the regional AD. The regional ADs report to the director who is the overall head of the agency.

FTCA has a strong emphasis on centralized control, particularly in the functional units. This emphasis occurs because of legal requirements as well as the fact that the agency has extensive direct interaction with the public. For example, one functional unit at headquarters (HQ) is responsible for collections and enforcement. If a regional manager has the same functional activity, FTCA executives believe that person should be accountable to the HQ functional AD. However, as mentioned earlier, the regional manager also reports directly to the regional AD; and the budget for the agency comes from the regional budget allocations, not from the HQ functional group.

This arrangement produces a dual reporting relationship for regional functional managers. Regional managers complain that this situation is awkward. Who is the real boss under the circumstances: the regional AD or the functional HQ AD for these managers? Also, who should be responsible for evaluating the work performance of these dual-reporting regional managers? And if a regional manager makes a serious error, which of the two supervisors of that manager is ultimately accountable?

The potential for confusion about responsibility and accountability has made the roles and reporting relationships of the senior managers vague. This has also increased conflict between regional managers and HQ managers.

To address this growing problem, a consultant was brought in to do an independent evaluation of the current organization structure of FTCA. The consultant asked for an organization chart of FTCA, which is shown here. The consultant became aware of the concerns just described by conducting interviews with various staff members throughout the agency. Other information such as budgets and financial allocations, some earlier organizational studies, the mandate of the agency, and the like were also provided to the consultant.

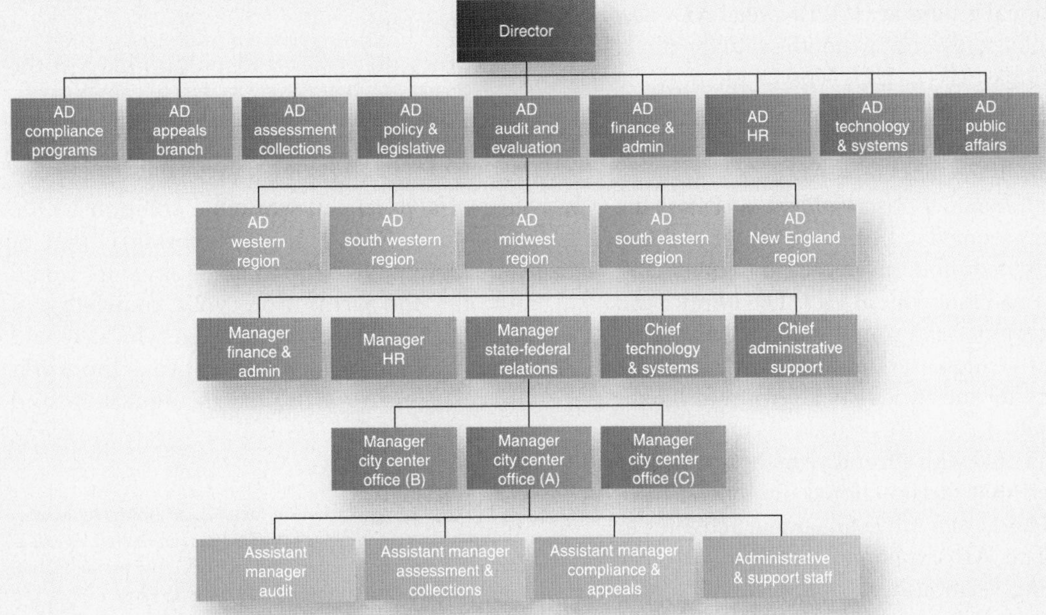

The discussions with staff members were interesting. Some viewed this issue as a people problem and not a structural one. That is, if regional and HQ managers learned how to cooperate and work with each other, this would not be an issue at all: They should take a shared responsibility approach and try to work together. But the view of the HQ functional groups was quite different. They argued that FTCA is a functional organization, so these functional unit leaders should have authority and power over regional managers performing the same function. In effect, these regional managers should report to the functional unit ADs or at least be accountable to HQ policies and objectives.

To compound the problem, the regional managers saw this problem completely differently. They argued that the functional HQ managers should have a policy development function. On an annual basis they should develop broad objectives and targets in consultation with regional managers. Once these were approved, it should be the responsibility of the regional managers to carry them out in light of the environment and constraints they face. The functional unit ADs opposed the regional managers' position, pointing out that if the regional managers did not achieve their objectives, the functional ADs would suffer the consequences.

After hearing these views, the consultant formed the opinion that this was an intractable and complex problem that could be related to both people and structure. The consultant also noted that the regional budgets were huge, sometimes larger than the budgets for functional groups at HQ. Regional ADs also met infrequently–only once a month–with the director and functional ADs at HQ. Most of the time the regions seemed to operate fairly autonomously, whereas the director seemed to have ongoing involvement with the functional ADs.

An HQ staff member observed that over time the regional offices seemed to be getting bigger and had become fairly autonomous with functional staff mirroring the staff functions at HQ. The implication was that the regional staff would soon view the functional units at headquarters as a distant group that only set policy for the regions to interpret or ignore as they pleased.

A functional AD with several years of seniority at FTCA warned that the functional units must have some control audit and other functional activities in the region. The AD explained that without clear roles, reporting relationships, and accountabilities between the regions and HQ, FTCA could not provide citizens with transparent and fair treatment in the services under its mandate.

The regional ADs, however, saw their responsibilities as facilitating horizontal coordination within the regions to ensure that actions and decisions were consistent and reflected the legislative responsibility of the agency.

After a month of study and discussions with FTCA staff, the consultant realized that this was not going to be an easy problem to resolve. There were also rumblings as the project progressed that some regional ADs did not like the idea of restructuring FTCA to deal with these issues. They seemed to have considerable clout and power in the organization as a group and would resist any change to the status quo.

As the consultant sat down to write the report, a number of critical questions became apparent: Was FTCA a purely functional organization? Could the accountability issues be resolved through an acceptable organizational process and people training without the need for restructuring? What about power, politics, and conflict in this situation? Finally, would resistance to change become a problem as well?

Discussion Questions

1. Describe the current organization structure of FTCA. What is it? What are the strengths and weaknesses of such a structure?
2. Can FTCA operate effectively as a purely functional structure?
3. What roles do power and politics play in the current situation?
4. What kind of conflict is FTCA experiencing between HQ and regional managers?
5. Suggest a practical, workable solution to the problem at FTCA. If restructuring is part of your solution, describe what the structure would look like and justify from your knowledge of organization theory and design why it would work–that is, how it would improve the working relationship between headquarters and regional staff.

Materials in this case are based on factual and nonfactual information about a government agency. This case is written for classroom discussion and not to demonstrate effective or ineffective management of an organization.

Case Study 15.2 BALLMER'S MICROSOFT

It didn't take long after Bill Gates handed over Microsoft's top job to his buddy Steve Ballmer that Ballmer realized things had to change. In particular, Microsoft had become a very large organization that was not moving as quickly as it should in the marketplace. To make Microsoft more responsive, Ballmer restructured the organization and introduced practices to ensure those structural changes worked well.

This *BusinessWeek* case study looks at the changes that Steve Ballmer is making at Microsoft. It describes specific adjustments to the company's organizational structure, as well as coordination mechanisms to support that structure. Read through this *BusinessWeek* article at www.mhhe.com/mcshane4e and prepare for the discussion questions below.

Discussion Questions

1. What symptoms or conditions suggested that Microsoft's current organizational structure wasn't sufficiently effective?
2. What changes did Steve Ballmer ultimately make to Microsoft's departmentalization? What problems occurred with the initial changes in departmentalization?
3. Along with changing the organizational chart, what other organizational structure changes did Steve Ballmer make at Microsoft? Do these changes seem reasonable under the circumstances?

Source: J. Greene, S. Hamm, and J. Kerstetter, "Ballmer's Microsoft," *BusinessWeek,* 17 June 2002, 66–72.

Team Exercise 15.3 THE CLUB ED EXERCISE

Cheryl Harvey and Kim Morouney, Wilfred Laurier University

PURPOSE This exercise is designed to help you understand the issues to consider when designing organizations at various stages of growth.

MATERIALS Each student team should have enough overhead transparencies or flip chart sheets to display several organizational charts.

INSTRUCTIONS Each team discusses the scenario presented. The first scenario is presented next. The instructor will facilitate discussion and notify teams when to begin the next step. The exercise and debriefing require approximately 90 minutes, although fewer scenarios can reduce the time somewhat.

1. Students are placed in teams (typically four or five people).
2. After reading Scenario #1 presented here, each team will design an organizational chart (departmentalization) that is most appropriate for this situation. Students should be able to describe the type of structure drawn and explain why it is appropriate. The structure should be drawn on an overhead transparency or flip chart for others to see during later class discussion. The instructor will set a fixed time (perhaps 15 minutes) to complete this task.

   Scenario #1 Determined never to shovel snow again, you are establishing a new resort business on a small Caribbean island. The resort is under construction and is scheduled to open one year from now. You decide it is time to draw up an organizational chart for this new venture, called Club Ed.
3. At the end of the time allowed, the instructor will present Scenario #2 and each team will be asked to draw another organizational chart to suit that situation. Again, students should be able to describe the type of structure drawn and explain why it is appropriate.

4. At the end of the time allowed, the instructor will present Scenario #3 and each team will be asked to draw another organizational chart to suit that situation.
5. Depending on the time available, the instructor might present a fourth scenario. The class will gather to present their designs for each scenario. During each presentation, teams should describe the type of structure drawn and explain why it is appropriate.

Source: Adapted from C. Harvey and K. Morouney, *Journal of Management Education* 22 (June 1998), pp. 425–29. Used with permission of the authors.

Self-Assessment 15.4

IDENTIFYING YOUR PREFERRED ORGANIZATIONAL STRUCTURE

PURPOSE This exercise is designed to help you understand how an organization's structure influences the personal needs and values of people working in that structure.

INSTRUCTIONS Personal values influence how comfortable you are working in different organizational structures. You might prefer an organization with clearly defined rules or no rules at all. You might prefer a firm where almost any employee can make important decisions, or where important decisions are screened by senior executives. Read the following statements and indicate the extent to which you would like to work in an organization with that characteristic. When finished, use the scoring key in Appendix B to calculate your results. This self-assessment is completed alone so you can complete it honestly without concerns of social comparison. However, class discussion will focus on the elements of organizational design and their relationship to personal needs and values.

Organizational Structure Preference Scale

I would like to work in an organization where...	Not at all	A little	Some-what	Very much	Score
1. A person's career ladder has several steps toward higher status and responsibility.	☐	☐	☐	☐	___
2. Employees perform their work with few rules to limit their discretion.	☐	☐	☐	☐	___
3. Responsibility is pushed down to employees who perform the work.	☐	☐	☐	☐	___
4. Supervisors have few employees, so they work closely with each person.	☐	☐	☐	☐	___
5. Senior executives make most decisions to ensure that the company is consistent in its actions.	☐	☐	☐	☐	___
6. Jobs are clearly defined so there is no confusion over who is responsible for various tasks.	☐	☐	☐	☐	___
7. Employees have their say on issues, but senior executives make most of the decisions.	☐	☐	☐	☐	___
8. Job descriptions are broadly stated or nonexistent.	☐	☐	☐	☐	___
9. Everyone's work is tightly synchronized around top management operating plans.	☐	☐	☐	☐	___
10. Most work is performed in teams without close supervision.	☐	☐	☐	☐	___
11. Work gets done through informal discussion with co-workers rather than through formal rules.	☐	☐	☐	☐	___
12. Supervisors have so many employees that they can't watch anyone very closely.	☐	☐	☐	☐	___
13. Everyone has clearly understood goals, expectations, and job duties.	☐	☐	☐	☐	___
14. Senior executives assign overall goals but leave daily decisions to trontline teams.	☐	☐	☐	☐	___
15. Even in a large company, the CEO is only three or four levels above the lowest position.	☐	☐	☐	☐	___

After reading this chapter, if you need additional information, see **www.mhhe.com/mcshane4e** for more in-depth interactivities that correspond with this material.

During the peak of the dot-com boom, Charles Schwab & Co. then-CEO David Pottruck was convinced that as investors grew wealthier they would migrate from the San Francisco—based discount broker to full-service firms that offered more personalized service. So Schwab paid top dollar to acquire U.S. Trust, a high-brow New York–based private bank that served only clients with at least $10 million to invest. Schwab customers who became wealthy would be shunted over to U.S. Trust for more personalized service.

Executives at Charles Schwab & Co. underestimated the influence of organizational culture on behavior when they acquired U.S. Trust.

The strategy backfired—partly because Schwab's customers still wanted cheap trades as they grew wealthier, and partly because Schwab ignored the acquisition's cultural dynamics. Schwab's employees valued rapid change, cost-cutting frugality, process efficiency, and egalitarianism. In contrast, U.S. Trust was an exclusive club that was slow to adopt technology and preferred to admit new clients through referrals from existing clients. Clients were pampered by "wealth advisers" who earned huge bonuses and worked in an environment that reeked of luxury.

While negotiating the takeover, U.S. Trust executives expressed concern about these cultural differences, so Schwab agreed to leave the firm as a separate entity. This separation strategy didn't last long. Schwab cut U.S. Trust employees' lucrative bonuses and tied their annual rewards to Schwab's financial performance. U.S. Trust executives were pushed to cut costs and set more aggressive goals. Schwab even tried to acculturate several hundred U.S. Trust employees with a board game that used a giant mat showing hills, streams, and a mountain with founder Charles Schwab's face carved into the side. U.S. Trust staff complained that the game was demeaning, particularly wearing smocks as they played the role of investors.

In meetings immediately following the acquisition, U.S. Trust executives winced when Schwab frequently used the term *customers*. They reminded Schwab's staff that U.S. Trust has *clients*, which implies much more of a long-term relationship. U.S. Trust advisers also resisted Schwab's referrals of newly minted millionaires in blue jeans. "We were flabbergasted," said one Schwab board member of the cultural clash. "Some of the U.S. Trust officers simply refused to accept our referrals."

When the depth of cultural intransigence became apparent, Pottruck replaced U.S. Trust's CEO with Schwab executive Alan Weber. Weber later insisted that "there is no culture clash" because Schwab "never tried to change the nature of the organization." Meanwhile, sources say that more than 300 U.S. Trust wealth advisers have defected to competitors since the acquisition, taking many valued clients with them. Pottruck lost his job as Schwab CEO, in part because the U.S. Trust acquisition stumbled. The acquisition is now worth less than half of its purchase price.

"Here are two first-class companies, but structural and cultural problems keep the combination from the kind of success they expected," explains a financial adviser in Florida.[1]

16

Organizational Culture

LEARNING OBJECTIVES

After reading this chapter you should be able to

1. Describe the elements of organizational culture.
2. Discuss the importance of organizational subcultures.
3. List four categories of artifacts through which corporate culture is deciphered.
4. Identify three functions of organizational culture.
5. Discuss the conditions under which cultural strength improves corporate performance.
6. Compare and contrast four strategies for merging organizational cultures.
7. Identify four strategies to strengthen an organization's culture.
8. Describe the stages of organizational socialization.
9. Explain how realistic job previews assist the socialization process.

organizational culture
The basic pattern of shared values and assumptions governing the way employees within an organization think about and act on problems and opportunities.

Schwab's acquisition of U.S. Trust is a classic tale of the perils of ignoring organizational culture. **Organizational culture** consists of the values and assumptions shared within an organization.[2] It defines what is important and unimportant in the company and consequently directs everyone in the organization toward the "right way" of doing things. You might think of it as the organization's DNA–invisible to the naked eye, yet a powerful template that shapes what happens in the workplace.[3]

This chapter begins by examining the elements of organizational culture and how culture is deciphered through artifacts. This is followed by a discussion of the relationship between organizational culture and corporate performance, including the effects of cultural strength, fit, and adaptability. Then we turn to the issue of mergers and corporate culture, followed by specific strategies for maintaining a strong organizational culture. The last section of this chapter zooms in on employee socialization, which is identified as one of the more important ways to strengthen organizational culture.

Learning Objectives

After reading the next two sections you should be able to

1. **Describe the elements of organizational culture.**
2. **Discuss the importance of organizational subcultures.**
3. **List four categories of artifacts through which corporate culture is deciphered.**

Elements of Organizational Culture

Exhibit 16.1 illustrates how the shared values and assumptions of an organization's culture relate to each other and are associated with artifacts, which are discussed later in this chapter. *Values*, which we introduced in Chapter 1, are stable, evaluative beliefs that guide our preferences for outcomes or courses of action in a variety of situations.[4] They are conscious perceptions about what is good or bad, right or wrong. Values exist as a component of organizational culture in the form of *shared values.* Shared values are values that people within the organization or work unit have in common and place near the top of their hierarchy of values.[5] At Charles Schwab & Co., employees place a high priority on rapid change, cost-cutting frugality, process efficiency, and egalitarianism.

It has become trendy for leaders to determine and publicly announce their company's shared values. Yahoo, the online portal company, is no exception. Its Web site proudly says that six values represent "what makes it tick": excellence, innovation, customer fixation, teamwork, community, and fun. Do these values really represent the content of Yahoo's culture? Maybe, but what companies say they value–their *espoused values*–isn't necessarily what they actually value (called *enacted values*). Values are socially desirable, so people create a positive public image by claiming to believe in values that others expect them to embrace (see Chapter 2).

For instance, one large international corporation hung signs around its headquarters proclaiming that its culture embraced "trust"; yet the same company required all employees to be searched whenever they entered or exited the building. Even if an organization's dozen or so top executives embrace the stated values, they are not necessarily the values held by most people throughout the organization. *Enacted values*, on the other hand, represent the values that people actually rely on to guide their decisions and actions. These values-in-use are apparent by watching people in action. An organization's culture consists of these enacted values, not espoused values.[6]

Exhibit 16.1
Organizational Culture Assumptions, Values, and Artifacts

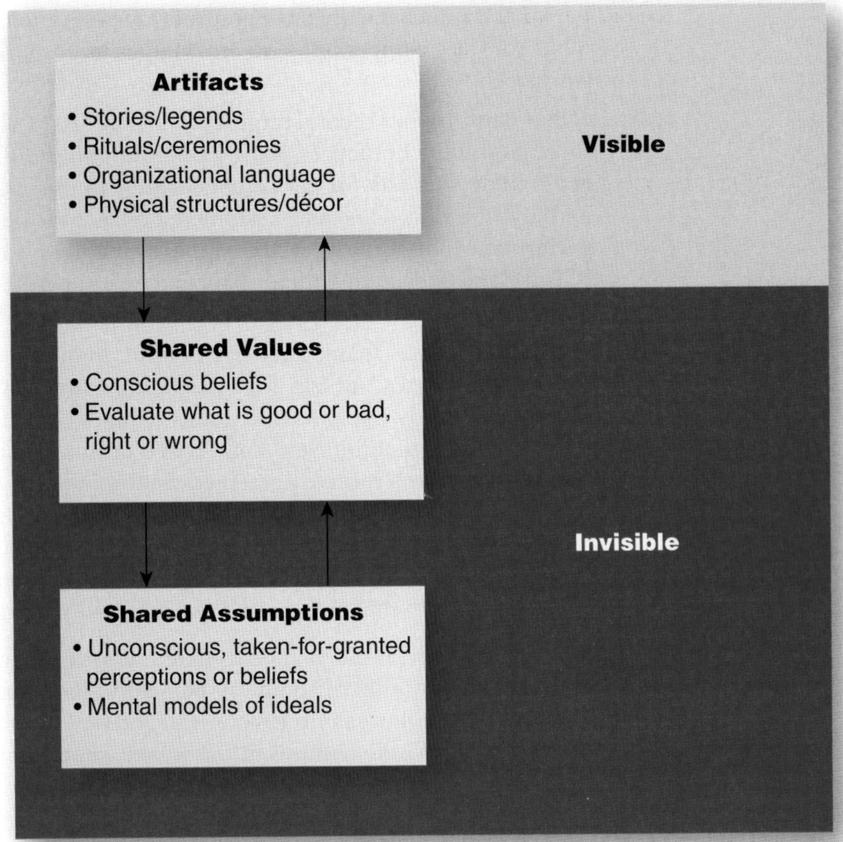

Source: Based on information in E.H. Schein, *Organizational Culture and Leadership: A Dynamic View* (San Francisco: Jossey-Bass, 1985).

Along with shared values, corporate culture consists of a deeper element–some experts believe it is really the essence of culture–called *shared assumptions.* These are unconscious taken-for-granted perceptions or beliefs that have worked so well in the past that they are considered the correct way to think and act toward problems and opportunities. Shared assumptions are so deeply ingrained that you probably wouldn't discover them by surveying employees. Only by observing employees, analyzing their decisions, and debriefing them about their actions would these assumptions rise to the surface.

Content of Organizational Culture

Organizations differ in their cultural content–that is, the relative ordering of values and assumptions. The culture of Charles Schwab & Co. values rapid change, cost-cutting frugality, process efficiency, and egalitarianism. At U.S. Trust employees embrace stability, dedicated service, and reputation. Here are a few more companies and their apparent dominant cultures:

- *SAS Institute.* Spend some time at SAS Institute and you will soon discover that the world's largest privately held software company has one of the most employee-friendly cultures on the planet. Located on a 200-acre campus in Cary, North Carolina, SAS supports employee well-being with free on-site medical care, unlimited sick days, heavily subsidized day care, ski trips, personal trainers, inexpensive gourmet cafeterias, and tai chi classes. Unlike other software companies, SAS encourages its employees to stick to a 35-hour workweek.[7]

- *ICICI Bank.* India's second largest bank exudes a performance-oriented culture. Its organizational practices place a premium on training, career development, goal setting, and pay for performance, all with the intent of maximizing employee performance and customer service. "We believe in defining clear performance for employees and empowering them to achieve their goals," says ICICI Bank executive director Kalpana Morparia. "This has helped to create a culture of high performance across the organization."[8]
- *JetBlue.* JetBlue has soared higher and faster than other new airlines because its culture "humanizes" air travel by providing comfort and service at low prices. As JetBlue quickly expands operations, Founder and CEO David Neeleman wants to ensure that the New York–based airline maintains this culture, so all new staff members receive a deep education in JetBlue's shared values. "The cultural aspects of our training programs are at least as important as the technical aspects," says Mike Barger, vice president of JetBlue University. "The People Department will find the right people, and we will inculcate the culture into them and nurture that culture until we release them out into the operation."[9]

Employee-friendly. Performance-oriented. Customer-focused. How many corporate cultural values are there? Some writers and consultants have attempted to classify organizational cultures into several categories. One of these models claims that there are seven corporate cultures in the world: attention to detail, outcome orientation, people orientation, team orientation, aggressiveness, stability, and innovation and risk taking. Another organizational culture model identifies eight cultures organized around a circle, indicating that some cultures are opposite to each other. A rules-oriented culture is opposite to an innovation culture; an internally focused culture is opposed to an externally focused culture; a controlling culture is opposite to a flexible culture; and a goal-oriented culture is opposite to a supportive culture.[10]

These organizational culture models may help to sort out organizational values to some extent, but unfortunately they also oversimplify the diversity of cultural values in organizations. The fact is, there are dozens of individual values, so there are likely

Cirque du Soleil's High-Wire Risk Culture Cirque du Soleil, the entertainment company that combines circus with theater, thrives on a culture of risk and creativity. This culture is apparent in the size and grandeur of its performances. Its most recent production, Ka, is a $150 million extravaganza representing the largest entertainment gamble ever made in Las Vegas. Cirque du Soleil also has a permanent show at Disney World in Florida and five traveling events around the world. Cirque du Soleil also took risks when it opened its first Las Vegas show, Mystère, which was dark and moody—a sharp contrast to the upbeat style of Las Vegas entertainment. Mystère had sellout crowds soon after its opening night. "(We stop growing) if we start being afraid of taking risks and if we start diminishing our creative pertinence," says Guy Laliberté, who founded Cirque du Soleil in 1984.[11]

as many organizational values. Thus we need to be wary of models that reduce the variety of organizational cultures into a few simple categories with catchy labels. They would certainly reflect the values of many organizations, but they may also distort rather than clarify our attempts to diagnose corporate culture.

Organizational Subcultures

When discussing organizational culture, we are actually referring to the *dominant culture*–that is, the themes shared most widely by the organization's members. However, organizations are also comprised of *subcultures* located throughout their various divisions, geographic regions, and occupational groups.[12] Some subcultures enhance the dominant culture by espousing parallel assumptions, values, and beliefs; others are called *countercultures* because they directly oppose the organization's core values.

Subcultures, particularly countercultures, potentially create conflict and dissension among employees, but they also serve two important functions.[13] First, they maintain the organization's standards of performance and ethical behavior. Employees who hold countercultural values are an important source of surveillance and critique over the dominant order. They encourage constructive conflict and more creative thinking about how the organization should interact with its environment. Subcultures prevent employees from blindly following one set of values and thereby help the organization to abide by society's ethical values.

The second function of subcultures is that they are the spawning grounds for emerging values that keep the firm aligned with the needs of customers, suppliers, society, and other stakeholders. Companies eventually need to replace their dominant values with ones that are more appropriate for the changing environment. If subcultures are suppressed, the organization may take longer to discover and adopt values aligned with the emerging environment.

Deciphering Organizational Culture through Artifacts

artifacts
The observable symbols and signs of an organization's culture.

We can't directly see an organization's cultural assumptions and values. Instead, as Exhibit 16.1 illustrated earlier, we decipher organizational culture indirectly through **artifacts**. Artifacts are the observable symbols and signs of an organization's culture, such as the way visitors are greeted, the organization's physical layout, and how employees are rewarded.[14] Some experts suggest that these artifacts are the essence of organizational culture, whereas others view artifacts as symbols or indicators of culture. Either way, artifacts are important because, as we will learn later, they reinforce and potentially support changes to an organization's culture.

Artifacts are also important because they offer the best evidence about a company's culture. Discovering an organization's culture isn't accomplished just by surveying its executives or employees. Instead, to accurately understand the company's dominant values and assumptions, we need to observe workplace behavior, listen to everyday conversations among staff and with customers, study written documents and e-mails, and interview staff about corporate stories. In other words, we need to conduct an anthropological investigation of the company. [15]

The Mayo Clinic recently took this approach to learning about its corporate culture. The Rochester, Minnesota, clinic brought in an anthropologist, who interviewed managers, shadowed employees on duty, joined physicians on patient visits, and posed as a patient to observe what happens in waiting rooms. So, understanding a company's culture involves sampling information from the broad range of organizational artifacts. In this section, we review the four broad categories of artifacts: organizational stories and legends, rituals and ceremonies, language, and physical structures and symbols.

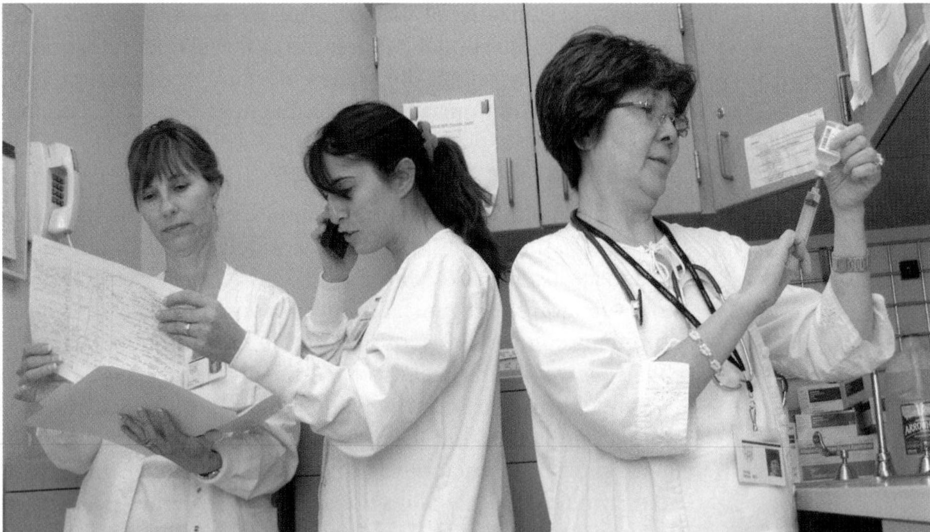

Mayo Clinic's Cultural Expedition The Mayo Clinic has a well-established culture at its original clinic in Rochester, Minnesota; but maintaining that culture in its expanding operations in Florida and Arizona has been challenging. "We were struggling with growing pains; we didn't want to lose the culture, and we were looking at how to keep the heritage alive," explains Matt McElrath, Mayo Clinic human resources director in Arizona. The Mayo Clinic retained anthropologist Linda Catlin to decipher Mayo's culture and identify ways to reinforce it at the two newer sites. Catlin shadowed employees and posed as a patient to observe what happens in waiting rooms. "She did countless interviews, joined physicians on patient visits, and even spent time in the operating room," says McElrath. At the end of her six-week cultural expedition, Catlin submitted a report outlining Mayo's culture and how its satellite operations varied from that culture. The Mayo Clinic adopted all of Catlin's 11 recommendations, such as requiring all new physicians at the three sites to attend an orientation in Rochester where they learn about Mayo's history and values.[16]

Organizational Stories and Legends

Stories permeate strong organizational cultures. Some tales recount heroic deeds by employees; others ridicule past events that deviated from the firm's core values. These stories and legends serve as powerful social prescriptions of the way things should (or should not) be done. They provide human realism to corporate expectations, individual performance standards, and the criteria for getting fired. These stories also create emotions in listeners, which tends to improve their memory of the lessons within the stories. Stories have the greatest effect at communicating corporate culture when they describe real people, are assumed to be true, and are known by employees throughout the organization.[17]

Rituals and Ceremonies

rituals
The programmed routines of daily organizational life that dramatize the organization's culture.

Rituals are the programmed routines of daily organizational life that dramatize an organization's culture. They include how visitors are greeted, how often senior executives visit subordinates, how people communicate with each other, how much time employees take for lunch, and so on. For instance, BMW's fast-paced culture is quite literally apparent in the way employees walk around the German carmaker's offices. "When you move through the corridors and hallways of other companies' buildings, people kind of crawl; they walk slowly," says BMW board of management chairman Helmut Panke. "But BMW people tend to move faster."[18] **Ceremonies** are more formal artifacts than rituals. Ceremonies are planned activities conducted specifically for the benefit of an audience. This would include publicly rewarding (or punishing) employees or celebrating the launch of a new product or newly won contract.

ceremonies
Planned and usually dramatic displays of organizational culture, conducted specifically for the benefit of an audience.

Organizational Language

The language of the workplace speaks volumes about the company's culture. How employees address co-workers, describe customers, express anger, and greet stakeholders are all verbal symbols of cultural values. Employees at The Container Store compliment each other about "being Gumby," meaning that they are being as flexible as the once-popular green toy–going outside their regular jobs to help a customer or another employee. (A human-sized Gumby is displayed at the retailer's headquarters.)[19] Language as a cultural artifact is also apparent in the opening story to this chapter. U.S. Trust executives insisted on using the term *clients* rather than *customers*, the term Schwab executives used freely. This language reflects the long–term, deep relationships that U.S. Trust staff members have with their clients, compared with the more impersonal connections between Schwab's staff members and their customers.

Language also highlights values held by organizational subcultures. For instance, consultants working at Whirlpool kept hearing employees talk about the appliance company's "PowerPoint culture." This phrase, which names Microsoft's presentation software, is a critique of Whirlpool's hierarchical culture in which communication is one-way (from executives to employees.).[20]

Physical Structures and Symbols

Winston Churchill once said, "We shape our buildings; thereafter, they shape us."[21] The former British prime minister was reminding us that buildings both reflect and influence an organization's culture. The size, shape, location, and age of buildings might suggest a company's emphasis on teamwork, environmental friendliness, flexibility, or any other set of values. An extreme example is the "interplanetary headquarters" of Oakley, Inc. The ultrahip eyewear and clothing company built a vaultlike structure in Foothills Ranch, California, complete with towering metallic walls studded with oversize bolts, to represent its secretive and protective culture. "We've always had a fortress mentality," says an Oakley executive. "What we make is gold, and people will do anything to get it, so we protect it."[22]

Even if the building doesn't make much of a statement, there is a treasure trove of physical artifacts inside. Desks, chairs, office space, and wall hangings (or lack of them) are just a few of the items that might convey cultural meaning. Stroll through Wal-Mart's headquarters in Bentonville, Arkansas, and you will find a workplace that almost screams frugality and efficiency. The world's largest retailer has a spartan waiting room for suppliers, rather like government office waiting areas. Visitors pay for their own soft drinks and coffee. In each of the building's inexpensive cubicles, employees sit at inexpensive desks finding ways to squeeze more efficiencies and lower costs out of suppliers as well as their own work processes.[23] Each of these artifacts alone might not say much, but put enough of them together and the company's cultural values become easier to decipher.

Learning Objectives

After reading the next two sections you should be able to

4. Identify three functions of organizational culture.

5. Discuss the conditions under which cultural strength improves corporate performance.

6. Compare and contrast four strategies for merging organizational cultures.

Is Organizational Culture Important?

Why do executives at the Mayo Clinic, the Container Store, Oakley, BMW, and other companies pay so much attention to organizational culture? The answer is that they believe a strong culture is a competitive advantage. "Culture is one of the most precious things a company has, so you must work harder on it than anything else," says Herb Kelleher, founder of Southwest Airlines. Does corporate culture really make a difference? The answer is yes ... potentially. Various studies indicate that companies with strong cultures are more likely to be successful, but only under a particular set of conditions.[24] The explanation of how organizational culture influences corporate prosperity and employee well-being has a few twists and turns, which we walk through in this section.

To begin, the effect of organizational culture depends partly on its strength. Corporate culture *strength* refers to how widely and deeply employees hold the company's dominant values and assumptions. In a strong organizational culture, most employees across all subunits hold the dominant values. These values are also institutionalized through well-established artifacts, thereby making it difficult for those values to change. Furthermore, strong cultures tend to be long-lasting; some can be traced back to the company founder's values and assumptions. In contrast, companies have weak cultures when the dominant values are short-lived and held mainly by a few people at the top of the organization. A strong corporate culture potentially increases a company's success by serving three important functions:

1. *Control system.* Organizational culture is a deeply embedded form of social control that influences employee decisions and behavior.[25] Culture is pervasive and operates unconsciously. You might think of it as an automatic pilot, directing employees in ways that are consistent with organizational expectations.
2. *Social glue.* Organizational culture is the "social glue" that bonds people together and makes them feel part of the organizational experience.[26] Employees are motivated to internalize the organization's dominant culture because this helps fulfill their need for social identity. This social glue is increasingly important as a way to attract new staff and retain top performers.
3. *Sense-making.* Organizational culture assists the sense-making process.[27] It helps employees understand what goes on and why things happen in the company. Corporate culture also makes it easier for them to understand what is expected of them and to interact with other employees who know the culture and believe in it.

Contingencies of Organizational Culture and Performance

Strong cultures are *potentially* good for business, as we just explained, but studies have found only a modestly positive relationship between culture strength and success.[28] Why the weak relationship? One reason is that a strong culture increases organizational performance only when the cultural content is appropriate for the organization's environment (see Exhibit 16.2). Recall from a few pages back that culture *content*

Exhibit 16.2
Organizational Culture and Performance

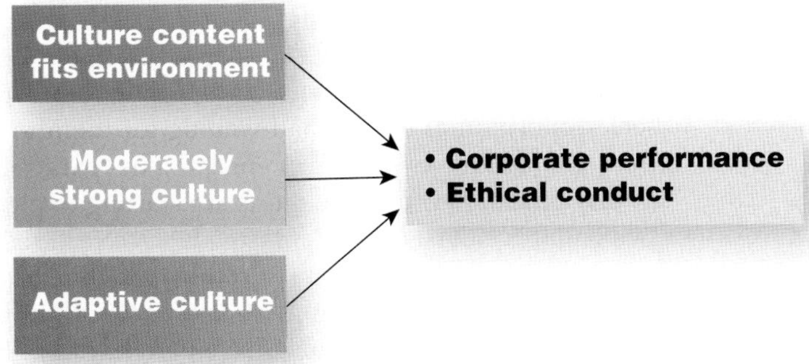

refers to the relative ordering of values and assumptions. Trouble occurs when the relative ordering of cultural values is misaligned with its environment. This lack of fit causes employees to make decisions and engage in behaviors that are inconsistent with the company's best interests. Strong cultures create a greater risk than weak cultures when values are misaligned because culture strength indicates that a greater number of employees will be guided by those values and assumptions.

Consider the problems described at the beginning of this chapter regarding Charles Schwab & Co.'s acquisition of U.S. Trust. Schwab's frugal and egalitarian culture helped it to succeed as a discount broker. But when this culture was imposed on U.S. Trust, top-performing brokers defected with their clients. U.S. Trust's existing culture was not perfectly adapted to the times (it lagged competitors with new financial products and was fined for poor record keeping), but Schwab's culture would have been an even worse fit for U.S. Trust's competitive space.

A second reason why companies with strong cultures aren't necessarily more effective is that strong cultures lock decision makers into mental models that blind them to new opportunities and unique problems. Thus strong cultures might cause decision makers to overlook or incorrectly define subtle misalignments between the organization's activities and the changing environment. Several bankrupt steel manufacturers apparently suffered from this problem. "It was 100 years of integrated culture," recalls Mittal Steel vice president John Mang III, who worked at one of the now-bankrupt firms for three decades. "People in the organization are inbreds, including myself. You grew up in the culture; you didn't see anything else. You didn't typically see people even at very high levels in the steel organization coming in from the outside–even financial, executive, or management. It is a culture from within, so you have these rose-colored glasses that everything's fine."[29]

A third consideration is that very strong cultures tend to suppress dissenting subcultural values. As we noted earlier, subcultures encourage constructive conflict, which improves creative thinking and offers some level of ethical vigilance over the dominant culture. In the long run the subculture's nascent values could become important dominant values as the environment changes. Strong cultures suppress subcultures, thereby undermining these benefits.

adaptive culture
An organizational culture in which employees focus on the changing needs of customers and other stakeholders, and support initiatives to keep pace with those changes.

Adaptive Cultures

So far we have learned that strong cultures are more effective when the cultural values are aligned with the organization's environment. Also, no corporate culture should be so strong that it blinds employees to alternative viewpoints or completely suppresses dissenting subcultures. One last point to add to this discussion is that organizations are more likely to succeed when they have an adaptive culture.[30] An **adaptive culture** exists when employees focus on the changing needs of customers and other stakeholders, supporting initiatives to keep pace with these changes. Adaptive cultures have an external focus, and employees assume responsibility for the organization's performance. As a result, they are proactive and quick. Employees seek opportunities rather than waiting for them to arrive. They act quickly to learn through discovery rather than engaging in "paralysis by analysis."

Organizational culture experts are starting to piece together the elements of adaptive cultures.[31] First and foremost, adaptive cultures have an external focus. Employees hold a common mental model that the organization's success depends on continuous change to support stakeholders. Nortel Networks has shifted from telephones to Internet gear. Nokia has moved from toilet paper and rubber boots to cellular telephones. Both of these firms have maintained an adaptive culture because employees believe that change is both necessary and inevitable to keep pace with a changing external environment.

Second, employees in adaptive cultures pay as much attention to organizational processes as they do to organizational goals. They engage in continuous improvement of internal processes (production, customer service, and the like) to serve external stakeholders. Third, employees in adaptive cultures have a strong sense of ownership. They assume responsibility for the organization's performance. In other words, they believe "it's our job" rather than "it's not my job."

Organizational Culture and Business Ethics

Along with other forms of performance, an organization's culture can potentially influence ethical conduct. In fact, in one recent survey executives identified organizational culture as one of the three main influences on ethical conduct at work. (The other two were executive leadership and personal commitment to ethical principles.)[32] This makes sense because, as we learned in Chapter 2, good behavior is driven by ethical values. An organization can guide the conduct of its employees by embedding ethical values in its dominant culture.

Citibank's Culture Pushes Ethical Boundaries Citibank Japan director Koichiro Kitade thrived in Citigroup's intensely bottom-line corporate culture. Each year his group handily exceeded the ever-increasing targets set by Citigroup's top executives in New York. Over six years Citibank Japan increased its clientele tenfold and delivered profits that outscored all other private banks in the company's huge network. Unfortunately the Japanese government's financial watchdog recently concluded that Citibank's culture also encouraged Kitade to push aside ethical and financial compliance rules. Japan's regulator accused Citibank of constructing "a law-evading sales system," citing infractions ranging from grossly overcharging clients to helping them to falsify profit and manipulate stock. With 83 infractions, Citigroup was told to close some of its Japanese operations. "It's our fault, because all we talk about is delivering the numbers. We've done this forever," admits Citigroup chief executive Charles Prince. This photo shows Prince (right) with a colleague bowing at a Tokyo news conference in apology for the violations. Prince fired several top executives in Tokyo and New York and is now on a mission to change Citibank's culture. He has a major challenge ahead of him. Dow Jones news service reports that Citigroup has an "established reputation for pushing the limits of acceptable banking behavior."[34]

Organizational culture is also potentially a source of ethical problems when it applies excessive control over employees. All organizations require some values congruence. As explained in Chapter 2, this congruence ensures that employees make decisions that are compatible with organizational objectives. Congruence also improves employee satisfaction, loyalty, and longevity (that is, it helps create low turnover). But a few organizations imprint their cultural values so strongly on employees that they risk becoming corporate cults. They take over employees' lives and rob people's individualism.

This cultlike phenomenon was apparently one of the factors that led to the downfall of Arthur Andersen. The accounting firm's uniting principle, called "One Firm," emphasized consistent service throughout the world by developing Andersen employees the same way. Andersen carefully selected university graduates with compatible values, then subjected these "green beans" to a powerful indoctrination process to further imprint Andersen's culture. This production of Andersen think-alikes, called "Androids," improved service consistency, but it also undermined the ethics of individualism.[33] Thus an organization's culture should be consistent with society's ethical values, and the culture should not be so strong that it undermines individual freedom.

Merging Organizational Cultures

4C Corporate Culture Clash and Chemistry is a company with an unusual name and mandate. The Dutch consulting firm helps clients determine whether their culture is aligned ("chemistry") or incompatible with ("clash") a potential acquisition or merger partner. The firm also analyzes the company's culture with its strategy. There should be plenty of demand for 4C's expertise. According to various studies, the majority of corporate mergers and acquisitions fail, mostly because corporate leaders are so focused on the financial or marketing logistics of a merger that they fail to conduct due diligence audits on their respective corporate cultures.[35]

Schwab's acquisition of U.S. Trust, described at the beginning of this chapter, is one example. The marriage of AOL Time Warner is another. AOL's culture valued youthful, high-flying, quick deal making, whereas Time Warner had a buttoned-down, hierarchical, and systematic culture.[36] For both Schwab and AOL, the culture clash undermined job performance, increased dysfunctional conflict, and resulted in lost talent.

IBM's acquisition of PricewaterhouseCooper's (PwC) consulting business has recently turned into yet another well-publicized culture clash. IBM employees tend to be cost conscious and flexible, whereas PwC staff are accustomed to flying business class and having large personal offices (IBM workers tend to share office space, called "hot desking"). PwC staff are also much more conservative than their IBM counterparts. At one event in Australia, a senior IBM executive was dressed as American tennis star Andre Agassi. "The IBMers went mad that time–nuts, standing and cheering. They loved it," recalls one onlooker. "The PwC folk were stunned. Silent." Less than two years after IBM had acquired PwC's consulting business, up to a quarter of PwC's partners had apparently quit.[37]

bicultural audit
A diagnosis of cultural relations between companies prior to a merger and a determination of the extent to which cultural clashes are likely to occur.

Bicultural Audit

Organizational leaders can minimize these cultural collisions and fulfill their duty of due diligence by conducting a bicultural audit. A **bicultural audit** diagnoses cultural relations between companies and determines the extent to which cultural clashes will likely occur.[38] The bicultural audit process begins by identifying cultural differences between the merging companies. Next the bicultural audit data are analyzed to determine which differences between the two firms will result in conflict and which cultural values provide common ground on which to build a cultural foundation in the merged organization. The final stage involves identifying strategies and preparing action plans to bridge the two organizations' cultures.

A few years ago pulp and paper conglomerate Abitibi-Price applied a bicultural audit before it agreed to merge with rival Stone Consolidated. Specifically, Abitibi developed the Merging Cultures Evaluation Index (MCEI), an evaluation system that helped Abitibi executives compare its culture with other companies in the industry. The MCEI analyzed several dimensions of corporate culture, such as concentration of power versus diffusion of power, innovation versus tradition, wide versus narrow flow of information, and consensus versus authoritative decision making. Abitibi and Stone executives completed the questionnaire to assess their own culture, then compared the results. The MCEI results, along with financial and infrastructural information, served as the basis for Abitibi-Price to merge with Stone Consolidated to become Abitibi-Consolidated, the world's largest pulp and paper firm.[39]

Strategies to Merge Different Organizational Cultures

In some cases a bicultural audit results in a decision to end merger talks because the two cultures are too different to merge effectively. However, even with substantially different cultures, two companies may form a workable union if they apply the appropriate merger strategy. The four main strategies for merging different corporate cultures are assimilation, deculturation, integration, and separation (see Exhibit 16.3).[40]

Assimilation Assimilation occurs when employees at the acquired company willingly embrace the cultural values of the acquiring organization. Typically this strategy works best when the acquired company has a weak, dysfunctional culture, whereas the acquiring company's culture is strong and aligned with the external environment. Cultural clashes are less common with assimilation because the acquired firm's culture is weak and employees are looking for better cultural alternatives. Research in Motion (RIM), the Canadian company that makes Blackberry wireless devices, applies the assimilation strategy by

Exhibit 16.3 Strategies for Merging Different Organizational Cultures

Merger strategy	Description	Works best when:
Assimilation	Acquired company embraces acquiring firm's culture.	Acquired firm has a weak culture.
Deculturation	Acquiring firm imposes its culture on unwilling acquired firm.	Rarely works—may be necessary only when acquired firm's culture doesn't work but employees don't realize it.
Integration	Combining the two or more cultures into a new composite culture.	Existing cultures can be improved.
Separation	Merging companies remain distinct entities with minimal exchange of culture or organizational practices.	Firms operate successfully in different businesses, requiring different cultures.

Source: Based on ideas in A.R. Malekazedeh and A. Nahavandi, "Making Mergers Work by Managing Cultures," *Journal of Business Strategy,* May/June 1990, pp. 55–57; K.W. Smith, "A Brand-New Culture for the Merged Firm," *Mergers and Acquisitions* 35 (June 2000), pp. 45–50.

deliberately acquiring only small start-up firms. "Small companies...don't have cultural issues," says RIM co-CEO Jim Balsillie, adding that they are typically absorbed into RIM's culture with little fuss or attention.[41]

Deculturation Assimilation is rare. Employees usually resist organizational change, particularly when they are asked to throw away personal and cultural values. Under these conditions some acquiring companies apply a *deculturation* strategy by imposing their culture and business practices on the acquired organization. The acquiring firm strips away artifacts and reward systems that support the old culture. People who cannot adopt the acquiring company's culture are often terminated.

Deculturation may be necessary when the acquired firm's culture doesn't work but employees aren't convinced of this. However, this strategy is difficult to apply effectively because the acquired firm's employees resist the cultural intrusions from the buying firm, thereby delaying or undermining the merger process. These problems were apparent at U.S. Trust after it was acquired by Charles Schwab & Co.

Integration A third strategy is to combine the cultures into a new composite culture that preserves the best features of the previous ones. Integration is slow and potentially risky because many forces preserve the existing cultures. Still, this strategy should be considered when the companies have relatively weak cultures or when their cultures include several overlapping values. Integration also works best when people realize that their existing cultures are ineffective and are therefore motivated to adopt a new set of dominant values.

Separation A separation strategy occurs if the merging companies agree to remain distinct entities with minimal exchange of culture or organizational practices. This strategy is most appropriate when the two merging companies are in unrelated industries or operate in different countries: The most appropriate cultural values tend to differ by industry and national culture. Charles Schwab & Co. tried to apply a separation strategy with U.S. Trust. However, in many companies that attempt this approach, executives in the acquiring firm have difficulty keeping their hands off the acquired firm. It's not surprising, therefore, that only 15 percent of acquisitions leave the purchased organization as a stand-alone unit.[42]

A Marriage of Cultural Separation Cisco Systems, the California-based Internet equipment maker, has acquired approximately 90 companies over the past two decades, most of them small, privately held start-up firms with technical expertise in high-growth niches compatible with Cisco's own products. Cisco typically assimilates the smaller firm into its own culture. Linksys, the home wireless network company was an exception. Linksys employs 400 people and was just a few years younger than Cisco. Furthermore, unlike Cisco, Linksys had developed a low-cost business with mass-market retail channels. To avoid disrupting its success, Cisco made sure that Linksys kept its own culture. Cisco executives were so concerned about this that a "filtering team" was formed to prevent Cisco's culture or its leaders from taking over the smaller enterprise. So far the strategy has worked. Linksys continues to thrive in a competitive low-cost market even though it is wholly owned by Cisco, which focuses on high-end networks.[43]

Learning Objectives

After reading the next two sections you should be able to

7. Identify four strategies to strengthen an organization's culture.

8. Describe the stages of organizational socialization.

9. Explain how realistic job previews assist the socialization process.

Changing and Strengthening Organizational Culture

Is it possible to change an organization's culture? Yes, but it isn't easy, it rarely occurs quickly, and often the culture ends up changing (or replacing) corporate leaders. Consider the plight of Hewlett-Packard. As Connections 16.1 describes, board members hired outsider Carly Fiorina with specific instructions to change the high-technology firm's famous "HP way" culture. The strategy backfired according to several observers. Why? Because corporate culture is deeply embedded in the collective mindset. Employees don't even question why they believe certain values are appropriate and corresponding behaviors are the right thing to do. Indeed, when outsiders critique those culturally congruent decisions and actions, employees often respond with disbelief that anyone would doubt such logical courses of action. Artifacts further reinforce this cultural mindset.

The lesson here is that changing an organization's culture can be a leader's greatest challenge. At the same time, as we noted earlier, organizational culture can be a powerful influence on a company's success. So how do some people successfully change and strengthen organizational culture? Over the next few pages we highlight four strategies that have had some success. This list, outlined in Exhibit 16.4, is not exhaustive; but each activity seems to work well under the right circumstances.

Exhibit 16.4 Strategies to Change and Strengthen Organizational Culture

Changing and Strengthening Organizational Culture

Actions of founders and leaders
- Symbolize the new culture (or need for one) through memorable events.
- Model the new culture through subtle decisions and actions.

Culturally consistent rewards
- Reward employees for culturally consistent behaviors.
- Reward managers who help employees understand the culture.

Selecting and socializing employees
- Hire people whose values are consistent with the culture.
- Inform and indoctrinate new staff about what the culture means.

Aligning artifacts
- Share stories supporting the culture.
- Celebrate goals/milestones to support the culture.
- Inhabit buildings that reflect the culture.

Connections 16.1

Defeated by the HP Way

Many executives have been driven out of organizations because they tried to change the organization's culture. Carly Fiorina, the former CEO of Hewlett-Packard (HP), was one such casualty. The California-based technology company's legendary culture, known as the "HP Way," revered innovation, employee well-being, and collegial teamwork. It was a role model for cultures in other Silicon Valley companies. But Hewlett-Packard started to lose ground to Dell, Compaq, and other competitors who were responding with more agility and efficiency to customer demands. Furthermore, an internal assessment revealed that Hewlett-Packard's culture had shifted. "The HP Way has been misinterpreted and twisted as a gentle bureaucracy of entitlement instead of a performance-based meritocracy," said Fiorina soon after becoming Hewlett-Packard's CEO.

As Hewlett-Packard's first CEO hired from outside the company, Fiorina's task was to alter the HP Way so the company would become more competitive. She launched "The Rules of the Garage," a set of cultural values with symbolic reference to the Palo Alto garage where founders William Hewlett and David Packard started the company in 1939. Fiorina reinforced these performance-focused values with a customer-driven bonus system and organizational structure. Her biggest initiative was acquiring Compaq, a fast-paced and aggressive competitor from Texas. The merger was intended to inject "a little of Compaq's DNA into the HP Way, especially speed and agility," said a Compaq executive who later took an executive position at Hewlett-Packard.

Hewlett-Packard's acquisition of Compaq seems to have had some effect on Hewlett-Packard's culture—but at a cost. Both board members from the founding families (Hewlett and Packard) quit over the changed culture; Hewlett-Packard lost its status as one of the top 10 best places to work in America (it isn't even on the top 100 today); and Fiorina was ousted as CEO. On the surface, Hewlett-Packard's board lost confidence in Fiorina because she failed to raise the company's profitability and achieve related targets. But sources say that Fiorina also tried to change more of the HP Way than was necessary, which battered employee loyalty, productivity, and ultimately profitability. "A little of the HP Way would probably work pretty well right now," says Quantum CEO and former Hewlett-Packard executive Richard E. Belluzzo soon after Fiorina was fired. "The strength of HP has always been its culture and its people."

Sources: B. Pimentel, "Losing Their Way?" *San Francisco Chronicle*, 6 September 2001; P. Burrows, *Backfire: Carly Fiorina's High-Stakes Battle for the Soul of Hewlett-Packard* (New York: John Wiley & Sons, 2003); C. Swett, "HP Seems to Have Digested Compaq," *Sacramento Bee* (California), 13 May 2003, p. D1; P. Burrows, "The HP Way out of a Morass," *BusinessWeek Online*, 14 February 2005; D. Gillmor, "Getting Back the HP Way," *Computerworld*, 7 March 2005, pp. 24–25.

Actions of Founders and Leaders

An organization's culture begins with its founders and leaders.[44] You can see this at Charles Schwab & Co., where founder Charles Schwab has established a culture that is frugal, egalitarian, and fast-paced. Founders set the tone and develop compatible systems and structures, emphasizing what is most important and what should receive a lower priority. They are often visionaries who provide a powerful role model for others to follow. Experts suggest that a company's culture sometimes reflects the founder's personality, and that this cultural imprint often remains with the organization for decades.

Founders establish an organization's culture, but they and subsequent CEOs can sometimes reshape that culture if they apply the transformational leadership concepts that were described in Chapter 14 and organizational change practices described in Chapter 17. Transformational leaders alter and strengthen organizational culture by communicating and enacting their vision of the future.[45]

Introducing Culturally Consistent Rewards

Reward systems strengthen corporate culture when they are consistent with cultural values. If Carly Fiorina had any success at infusing a performance-oriented culture at Hewlett-Packard, it was in large part because she introduced reward systems that reinforced employee performance. John Deere took a similar approach. When the farm implement manufacturer was reorganized into a team-based structure a few years ago, it replaced its individual-oriented incentive plan with a team-based continuous improvement plan. The team bonus helped to shift John Deere's cultural values so that employees now think in terms of team dynamics and work flow efficiencies.[46]

Aligning Artifacts

Artifacts represent more than just the visible indicators of a company's culture. They are also mechanisms that keep the culture in place. Thus by altering artifacts–or creating new ones–leaders can potentially adjust organizational culture. Consider how Louis Gerstner began the long journey of transforming IBM's culture in the 1990s. Gerstner showed up on the first day wearing a blue shirt. What's so symbolic about the incoming CEO wearing a blue shirt? Quite a lot at IBM, where every male employee wore a neatly starched white shirt. (Several decades earlier, IBM founder Thomas Watson had disapproved of anyone wearing shirts that weren't white.) Gerstner's blue shirt attire wasn't accidental. It was a deliberate signal that he intended to break the technology firm's culture of following mindless rules. He also made the point to everyone that IBM employees are not evaluated by the color of their shirts. Instead they should wear attire appropriate for the occasion, and they are rewarded for their performance.[47]

Buildings and décor are artifacts of an organization's culture, but some leaders are moving into offices that reflect what they want the company's culture to become. National Australia Bank's (NAB) National@Docklands, a low-rise campuslike building in Melbourne's docklands area, is a case in point. The building's open design and colorful décor symbolize a more open, egalitarian, and creative culture, compared to the closed hierarchical culture that NAB executives are trying to shed. The docklands building project was initiated when executives realized that MLC, a financial services firm that NAB had acquired a few years earlier, was able to change its culture after moving into its funky headquarters in Sydney. "There's no doubt that MLC has moved its culture over the last few years to a more open and transparent style which is a good example for the rest of the group to follow," admits a NAB executive.[48]

Corporate cultures are also altered and strengthened through the artifacts of stories and behaviors. According to Max De Pree, former CEO of furniture manufacturer Herman Miller Inc., every organization needs "tribal storytellers" to keep the organization's history and culture alive.[49] Leaders play a role by creating memorable events that symbolize the cultural values they want to develop or maintain. At Wall Street investment firm Goldman Sachs, this leadership function is so important that such people are called "culture carriers." Goldman's senior executives live and breathe the company's culture so much that they can effectively transmit and reinforce that culture.[50] Companies also strengthen culture in new operations by transferring current employees who abide by the culture.

Selecting and Socializing Employees

People at Bristol-Myers noticed that executives hired from the outside weren't as successful as those promoted from within. Within a year, many quit or were fired. When managers looked closely at the problem, they arrived at the following conclusion: "What came through was, those who left were uncomfortable in our culture or violated some core area of our value system," says a Bristol-Myers executive. From this discovery, Bristol-Myers assessed its culture–it's team-oriented, consistent with the firm's research and development roots. Now applicants are carefully screened to ensure that they have compatible values.[51]

Bristol-Myers and a flock of other organizations strengthen and sometimes reshape their corporate cultures by hiring people with beliefs, values, and assumptions similar to those cultures. They realize that a good fit of personal and organizational values makes it easier for employees to adopt the corporate culture. A good person–organization fit also improves job satisfaction and organizational loyalty because new hires with values compatible to the corporate culture adjust more quickly to the organization.[52]

Job applicants also pay attention to corporate culture during the hiring process. They realize that as employees, they must feel comfortable with the company's values, not just the job duties and hours of work. Thus job applicants tend to look at corporate culture artifacts when deciding whether to join a particular organization. By diagnosing the company's dominant culture, they are more likely to determine whether its values are compatible to their own.

organizational socialization
The process by which individuals learn the values, expected behaviors, and social knowledge necessary to assume their roles in the organization.

Along with selecting people with compatible values, companies maintain strong cultures through the process of organizational socialization. **Organizational socialization** refers to the process by which individuals learn the values, expected behaviors, and social knowledge necessary to assume their roles in the organization.[53] If a company's dominant values are clearly communicated, job candidates and new hires are more likely to internalize these values quickly and deeply. Socialization is an important process for absorbing corporate culture as well as helping newcomers to adjust to co-workers, work procedures, and other corporate realities. Thus the final section of this chapter looks more closely at the organizational socialization process.

Whole Foods Spreads Its Culture like Yogurt How do companies maintain their corporate culture when expanding operations? At Whole Foods Market the solution is yogurt. "One of our secrets is what I refer to as our 'yogurt culture,'" explains Whole Foods cofounder John McKey. This strategy involves transferring employees who carry Whole Foods' unique culture to new stores so recently hired employees learn and embrace that cultural milieu quickly. "For example, in our Columbus Circle store in New York, about 25 percent of the team members transferred from existing stores," McKey recalls. "They were the starting culture for the fermentation that turned Columbus Circle into a true Whole Foods store." Some employees even took lesser titles just to help Columbus Circle adopt Whole Foods' cultural values. For example, the store's two associate store team leaders previously operated their own stores in Georgetown, Maryland, and Albuquerque, New Mexico, before coming to New York.[54]

Organizational Socialization

Nadia Ramos had plenty of job opportunities after she graduated from business school, but Bank of Nova Scotia won the contest hands down. Ramos was impressed by the panel interview with senior commercial banking managers and by the many opportunities to work overseas. But it was the little things that really won Ramos over to the Canadian financial institution. Rather than seeing only the company boardroom and company recruiters, Ramos toured the offices where she would actually work and met with fellow international banking associates, who immediately welcomed her to the team and offered advice for apartment hunting in Toronto. ScotiaBank also assigned a buddy to help Ramos adjust to the workplace over the first two years. "We have to make sure, once they are in the door, that they start having a great experience as an employee–and that we haven't overpromised," says Sylvia Chrominska, ScotiaBank's executive vice president of human resources.[55]

ScotiaBank successfully brings employees into the organization by going beyond selecting applicants with the right competencies. It relies on several organizational socialization practices to help newcomers learn about and adjust to the company's culture, physical layout, procedures, and so on. Research indicates that when employees are effectively socialized into an organization, they tend to perform better and have higher job satisfaction.[56]

Organizational socialization is a process of both learning and adjustment. It is a learning process because newcomers try to make sense of the company's physical workplace, social dynamics, and strategic and cultural environment. They learn about the organization's performance expectations, power dynamics, corporate culture, company history, and jargon. Organizational socialization is also a process of adjustment because individuals need to adapt to their new work environment. They develop new work roles that reconfigure their social identity, adopt new team norms, and practice new behaviors. Research reports that the adjustment process is fairly rapid for many people–usually within a few months. However, newcomers with diverse work experience seem to adjust better than those with limited previous experience, possibly because diverse work experience provides a larger toolkit of knowledge and skills to make the adjustment easier.[57]

Newcomers absorb the organization's dominant culture to varying degrees. Some people deeply internalize the company's culture; a few others rebel against these attempts to change their mental models and values. Ideally newcomers adopt a level of "creative individualism" in which they accept the essential elements of the organization's culture and team norms, yet maintain a healthy individualism that challenges the allegedly dysfunctional elements of organizational life.

Stages of Socialization

Socialization is a continuous process, beginning long before the first day of employment and continuing throughout a person's career within the company. However, it is most intense when people move across organizational boundaries, such as when they first join a company or get transferred to an international assignment. Each of these transitions is a process that can be divided into three stages. Our focus here is on the socialization of new employees, so the three stages are called preemployment socialization, encounter, and role management (see Exhibit 16.5). These stages parallel the individual's transition from outsider to newcomer and then to insider.[58]

Exhibit 16.5 Stages of Organizational Socialization

Preemployment socialization (outsider)	Encounter (newcomer)	Role management (insider)	Socialization outcomes
• Learn about the organization and job. • Form employment relationship expectations.	• Test expectations against perceived realities.	• Strengthen work relationships. • Practice new role behaviors. • Resolve work–nonwork conflicts.	• Higher motivation. • Higher loyalty. • Higher satisfaction. • Lower stress. • Lower turnover.

Stage 1: Preemployment Socialization Think back to the months and weeks before you began working in a new job (or attending a new school). You actively searched for information about the company, formed expectations about working there, and felt some anticipation about fitting into that environment. The preemployment socialization stage encompasses all of the learning and adjustment that occurs prior to the first day of work in a new position. In fact, a large part of the socialization adjustment process occurs before the first day of work.[59]

The main problem with preemployment socialization is that individuals are outsiders, so they must rely on friends, employment interviews, recruiting literature, and other indirect information to form expectations about what it is like to work in the organization. Furthermore, the information exchange between applicants and employers is usually less than perfectly honest.[60] Job applicants might distort their résumés, whereas employers hide their blemishes by presenting overly positive images of organizational life. Job applicants avoid asking sensitive questions–such as pay increases and faster promotions–to maintain a good image to recruiters.

To make matters worse, job applicants tend to engage in postdecisional justification during preemployment socialization. Before the first day of work they tend to increase the importance of favorable elements of the job and justify or completely forget about some negative elements. At the same time they reduce the perceived quality of job offers that they turned down. Employers often distort their expectations of new hires in the same way. The result is that both parties develop higher expectations of each other than they will actually experience during the encounter stage.

Stage 2: Encounter The first day on the job typically marks the beginning of the encounter stage of organizational socialization. This is the stage in which newcomers test their prior expectations with the perceived realities. Many companies fail the test because newcomers often believe that their employers are not delivering the promised employment experience. To varying degrees these people have experienced **reality shock**–the stress that results when employees perceive discrepancies between their preemployment expectations and on-the-job reality.[61] The larger the gap, the stronger the reality shock. Reality shock doesn't necessarily occur on the first day; it might develop over several weeks or even months as newcomers form a better understanding of their new work environment. Along with experiencing unmet expectations,

reality shock
Perceived discrepancies between preemployment expectations and on-the-job reality.

reality shock occurs when newcomers are overwhelmed by the experience of sudden entry into a new work environment. In other words, reality shock also includes the stress of information overload and the challenges of adjusting quickly to new roles.

Stage 3: Role Management During the role management stage in the socialization process, employees settle in as they make the transition from newcomers to insiders. They strengthen relationships with co-workers and supervisors, practice new role behaviors, and adopt attitudes and values consistent with their new positions and organizations. Role management also involves resolving the conflicts between work and nonwork activities. In particular, employees must redistribute their time and energy between work and family, reschedule recreational activities, and deal with changing perceptions and values in the context of other life roles. They must address any discrepancies between their existing values and those emphasized by the organizational culture. New self-identities are formed that are more compatible with the work environment.

Improving the Socialization Process

Before hiring people for its new computer assembly plant in Winston-Salem, North Carolina, Dell Inc. invites applicants to understand the company and the jobs better. "We will discuss the soul of Dell, give them a realistic job preview, and give them the opportunity to complete a job application," explains Ann Artzer, Dell's human resource manager for the plant. "It will be a chance to determine the mutual interest between the candidates and Dell."[62]

realistic job preview (RJP)
The process of giving job applicants a balance of positive and negative information about the job and work context.

Dell improves the socialization process by providing a **realistic job preview (RJP)**—a balance of positive and negative information about the job and work context.[63] As described at the beginning of this section on organizational socialization, the ScotiaBank human resource executive also tries to make sure that the financial institution hasn't overpromised to job applicants. Unfortunately many companies do overpromise. They often exaggerate positive features of a job and neglect to mention undesirable elements, hoping that the best applicants will get "stuck" on the organization. In contrast, an RJP helps job applicants decide for themselves whether their skills, needs, and values are compatible with a job and organization.

Although RJPs scare away some applicants, they tend to reduce turnover and increase job performance.[64] This occurs because RJPs help applicants develop more accurate preemployment expectations, which in turn minimize reality shock. RJPs represent a type of vaccination by preparing employees for the more challenging and troublesome aspects of work life. There is also some evidence that RJPs increase organizational loyalty. A possible explanation for this is that companies providing candid information are easier to trust. They also show respect for the psychological contract and concern for employee welfare.[65]

Socialization Agents Nadia Ramos received plenty of support to help her adjust to a career at ScotiaBank. As was mentioned at the beginning of this section, Ramos's future co-workers welcomed her to the team and offered advice on finding an apartment. ScotiaBank also assigned an experienced employee (a buddy) to offer Ramos special assistance and guidance. ScotiaBank leaders seem to be aware that a lot of organizational socialization occurs informally through socialization agents, including co-workers, bosses, and friends who work for the company.

Supervisors tend to provide technical information, performance feedback, and information about job duties. They also improve the socialization process by giving newcomers reasonably challenging first assignments, buffering them from excessive demands, and helping them to form social ties with co-workers.[66] Co-workers are particularly important socialization agents because they are easily accessible, can answer questions when problems arise, and serve as role models for appropriate behavior. New employees tend to receive this information and support when co-workers integrate them into the work team. Co-workers also aid the socialization process by being flexible and tolerant in their interactions with these new hires. Newcomers who quickly form social relations with co-workers tend to have a less traumatic socialization experience and are less likely to quit their jobs within the first year of employment.[67] However, co-workers sometimes engage in hazing–the practice of fooling or intimidating newcomers as a practical joke or initiation ritual.

The challenge is for organizations to ensure that co-workers offer the necessary support. ScotiaBank and many other organizations rely on a "buddy system" whereby newcomers are assigned to co-workers as sources of information and social support. Progressive Inc., the Mayfield, Ohio–based insurance firm, relies on current employees to recruit and socialize job applicants. "I think candidates can trust and respect people who already work here," says Jennifer Cohen, Progressive's national employment director. "They get a lot of honest information about the company." ExtendMedia also has a formal buddy system, but equally valuable is the box of doughnuts put on every newcomer's desk on the first day of work. "The [doughnuts] are there to break the ice so that other people come and talk to them. We are introducing people through their stomachs," explains an executive at the interactive media company.[68]

Chapter Summary

Organizational culture is the basic pattern of shared assumptions and values that governs behavior within a particular organization. Assumptions are the shared mental models or theories-in-use on which people rely to guide their perceptions and behaviors. Values are more stable, long-lasting beliefs about what is important. They help us define what is right or wrong, or good or bad, in the world. Culture content refers to the relative ordering of shared values and assumptions.

Organizations have subcultures as well as dominant cultures. Subcultures maintain the organization's standards of performance and ethical behavior. They are also the source of emerging values that replace aging core values.

Artifacts are the observable symbols and signs of an organization's culture. Four broad categories of artifacts include organizational stories and legends, rituals and ceremonies, language, and physical structures and symbols. Understanding an organization's culture requires assessment of many artifacts because they are subtle and often ambiguous.

Organizational culture has three main functions. It is a deeply embedded form of social control. It is also the "social glue" that bonds people together and makes them feel part of the organizational experience. Third, corporate culture helps employees make sense of the workplace.

Companies with strong cultures generally perform better than those with weak cultures, but only when the cultural content is appropriate for the organization's environment. Also, the culture should not be so strong that it drives out dissenting values, which may form emerging values for the future. Organizations should have adaptive cultures so that employees focus on the need for change and support initiatives and leadership that keep pace with these changes.

Mergers should include a bicultural audit to diagnose the compatibility of the organizational cultures. The four main strategies for merging different corporate cultures are integration, deculturation, assimilation, and separation.

Organizational culture may be altered and strengthened through the actions of founders and leaders, the introduction of culturally-consistent rewards, the alignment of artifacts, and the selection and socialization of employees.

Organizational socialization is the process by which individuals learn the values, expected behaviors, and social knowledge necessary to assume their roles in the organization. It is a process of both learning about the work context and adjusting to new work roles, team norms, and behaviors. Employees typically pass through three socialization stages: preemployment, encounter, and role management. To improve the socialization process, organizations should introduce realistic job previews (RJPs) and recognize the value of socialization agents in the process.

Key Terms

adaptive culture, p. 467
artifacts, p. 463
bicultural audit, p. 469
ceremonies, p. 465
organizational culture, p. 460
organizational socialization, p. 475
realistic job preview (RJP), p. 478
reality shock, p. 477
rituals, p. 464

Critical Thinking Questions

1. The Superb Consultants company has submitted a proposal to analyze the cultural values of your organization. The proposal states that Superb has developed a revolutionary new survey to tap a company's true culture. The survey takes just 10 minutes to complete, and the consultants say results can be based on a small sample of employees. Discuss the merits and limitations of this proposal.
2. Some people suggest that the most effective organizations have the strongest cultures. What do we mean by the "strength" of organizational culture, and what possible problems are there with a strong organizational culture?
3. The CEO of a manufacturing firm wants everyone to support the organization's dominant culture of lean efficiency and hard work. The CEO has introduced a new reward system to reinforce this culture and personally interviews all professional and managerial applicants to ensure that they bring similar values to the organization. Some employees who criticized these values had their careers sidelined until they left. Two midlevel managers were fired for supporting contrary values, such as work–life balance. Based on your knowledge of organizational subcultures, what potential problems is the CEO creating?
4. Identify at least two artifacts you have observed in your department or school from each of the four broad categories: (a) organizational stories and legends; (b) rituals and ceremonies; (c) language; and (d) physical structures and symbols.
5. "Organizations are more likely to succeed when they have an adaptive culture." What can an organization do to foster an adaptive culture?
6. Acme Corp. is planning to acquire Beta Corp., which operates in a different industry. Acme's culture is entrepreneurial and fast-paced, whereas Beta employees value slow, deliberate decision making by consensus. Which merger strategy would you recommend to minimize culture shock when Acme acquires Beta? Explain your answer.
7. Suppose you are asked by senior officers of a city government to identify ways to reinforce a new culture of teamwork and collaboration. The senior executive group clearly supports these values, but it wants everyone in the organization to embrace them. Identify four types of activities that would strengthen these cultural values.
8. Progressive, Inc., ExtendMedia, and other organizations rely on current employees to socialize new recruits. What are the advantages of relying on this type of socialization agent? What problems can you foresee (or you have personally experienced) with co-worker socialization practices?

Case Study 16.1 HILLTON'S TRANSFORMATION

Twenty years ago Hillton was a small city (about 70,000 residents) that served as an outer suburb to a large Midwest metropolitan area. The city treated employees like family and gave them a great deal of autonomy in their work. Everyone in the organization (including the two labor unions representing employees) implicitly agreed that the leaders and supervisors of the organization should rise through the ranks based on their experience. Few people were ever hired from the outside into middle or senior positions. The rule of employment at Hillton was to learn the job skills, maintain a reasonably good work record, and wait your turn for promotion.

Hillton has grown rapidly since the mid-1970s. As the population grew, so did the municipality's workforce to keep pace with the increasing demand for municipal services. This meant that employees were promoted fairly quickly and were almost guaranteed employment. In fact, until recently Hillton had never laid off any employee. The organization's culture could be described as one of entitlement and comfort. Neither the elected city council members nor the city manager bothered the department managers about their work. There were few cost controls because rapid growth forced emphasis on keeping up with the population expansion. The public became somewhat more critical of the city's poor service, including road construction at inconvenient times and the apparent lack of respect some employees showed toward taxpayers.

During these expansion years Hillton put most of its money into "outside" (also called "hard") municipal services such as road building, utility construction and maintenance, fire and police protection, recreational facilities, and land use control. This emphasis occurred because an expanding population demanded more of these services, and most of Hillton's senior people came from the outside services group. For example, Hillton's city manager for many years was a road development engineer. The "inside" workers (taxation, community services, and the like) tended to have less seniority, and their departments were given less priority.

As commuter and road systems developed, Hillton attracted more upwardly mobile professionals to the community. Some infrastructure demands continued, but now these suburban dwellers wanted more "soft" services, such as libraries, social activities, and community services. They also began complaining about how the municipality was being run. The population had more than doubled between the 1970s and 1990s, and it was increasingly apparent that the city organization needed more corporate planning, information systems, organization development, and cost control systems. Residents voiced their concerns in various ways that the municipality was not providing the quality of management that they would expect from a city of its size.

In 1996 a new mayor and council replaced most of the previous incumbents, mainly on the platform of improving the municipality's management structure. The new council gave the city manager, along with two other senior managers, an early retirement buyout package. Rather than promoting from the lower ranks, council decided to fill all three positions with qualified candidates from large municipal corporations in the region. The following year several long-term managers left Hillton, and at least half of those positions were filled by people from outside the organization.

In less than two years Hillton had eight senior or departmental managers hired from other municipalities who played a key role in changing the organization's value system. These eight managers became known (often with negative connotations) as the "professionals." They worked closely with each other to change the way middle and lower-level managers had operated for many years. They brought in a new computer system and emphasized cost controls where managers previously had complete autonomy. Promotions were increasingly based more on merit than seniority.

These managers frequently announced in meetings and newsletters that municipal employees must provide superlative customer service, and that Hillton would become one of the most customer-friendly places for citizens and those doing business with the municipality. To this end these managers were quick to support the public's increasing demand for more soft services, including expanded library services and recreational activities. And when population growth flattened for a few years, the city manager and the other professionals gained council support to lay off a few outside workers due to lack of demand for hard services.

One of the most significant changes was that the outside departments no longer held dominant positions in city management. Most of the professional managers had worked exclusively in administrative and related inside jobs. Two had Master of Business Administration degrees. This led to some tension between the professional managers and the older outside managers.

Even before the layoffs, managers of outside departments resisted the changes more than others. These managers complained that their employees with the highest seniority were turned down for promotions. They argued for more budget and warned that infrastructure problems would cause liability problems. Informally these outside managers were supported by the labor union representing outside workers. The union leaders tried to bargain for more job guarantees, whereas the union representing inside workers focused more on improving wages and benefits. Leaders of the outside union made several statements in the local media that the city had "lost its heart" and that the public would suffer from the actions of the new professionals.

DISCUSSION QUESTIONS

1. Contrast Hillton's earlier corporate culture with the emerging set of cultural values.
2. Considering the difficulty in changing organizational culture, why did Hillton's management seem to be successful at this transformation?
3. Identify two other strategies that the city might consider to reinforce the new set of corporate values.

Case Study 16.2 IKEA: SWEDISH FOR CORPORATE CULTURE

Ikea is the quintessential global cult brand. The furniture retailer has more than 200 stores in several countries, but is just beginning to grow in the United States (where it had only one store in 2000, 25 stores by 2005, and an expected 50 stores by 2010). But Ikea is also a role model of how to nurture an effective corporate culture. Its chief cheerleader is founder Ingvar Kamprad. Although officially retired, Kamprad remains a vital link to the company's culture. For instance, Ikea is still run by managers who were trained and groomed by Kamprad himself.

This *BusinessWeek* case study describes the success of Ikea and provides some insight into its organizational culture. Read through this *BusinessWeek* article at www.mhhe.com/mcshane4e and prepare for the discussion questions below.

Discussion Questions

1. What are the values that dominate Ikea's culture?
2. How does Ikea seem to maintain a strong organizational culture?
3. Ikea is accelerating store rollouts around the world. In this context, how can Ikea maintain its cultural values and ensure that they are embedded in the newly opened stores?

Source: K. Capell, "Ikea: How the Swedish Retailer became a Global Cult Brand," *BusinessWeek,* 14 November 2005, 96

Web Exercise 16.3 DIAGNOSING CORPORATE CULTURE PROCLAMATIONS

PURPOSE To understand the importance and context in which corporate culture is identified and discussed in organizations.

INSTRUCTIONS This exercise is a take-home activity, although it can be completed in classes with computers and Internet connections. The instructor will divide the class into small teams (typically four to five people per team). Each team is assigned a specific industry such as energy, biotechnology, or computer hardware.

The team's task is to search Web sites of several companies in the selected industry for company statements about corporate culture. Use company

Web site search engines (if they exist) to find documents with key phrases such as "corporate culture" or "company values."

DISCUSSION QUESTIONS

1. What values seem to dominate the corporate cultures of the companies you searched? Are these values similar or diverse across companies in the industry?
2. What was the broader content of the Web pages where these companies described or mentioned their corporate cultures?
3. Do companies in this industry refer to their corporate cultures on their Web sites more or less than companies in other industries searched by teams in this class?

Team Exercise 16.4 TRUTH IN ADVERTISING

PURPOSE This team activity is designed to help you diagnose the degree to which recruitment advertisements and brochures provide realistic previews of jobs and organizations.

MATERIALS The instructor will bring to class either recruiting brochures or newspaper advertisements.

INSTRUCTIONS The instructor will place students into teams and give them copies of recruiting brochures and/or advertisements. The instructor might assign one lengthy brochure; alternatively several newspaper advertisements may be assigned. All teams should receive the same materials so that everyone is familiar with the items and results can be compared. Teams will evaluate the recruiting material(s) and answer the following questions for each item.

DISCUSSION QUESTIONS

1. What information in the text of this brochure or advertisement identifies conditions or activities in this organization or job that some applicants may not like?
2. If there are photographs or images of people at work, do they show only positive conditions, or do any show conditions or events that some applicants may not like?
3. After reading this item, would you say that it provides a realistic preview of the job and/or organization?

Self-Assessment 16.5

CORPORATE CULTURE PREFERENCE SCALE

PURPOSE This self-assessment is designed to help you identify a corporate culture that fits most closely with your personal values and assumptions.

INSTRUCTIONS Read each pair of the statements in the Corporate Culture Preference Scale and circle the statement that describes the organization you would prefer to work in. Then use the scoring key in Appendix B to calculate your results for each subscale. The scale does not attempt to measure your preference for every corporate culture–just a few of the more common varieties. Also keep in mind that none of these corporate cultures is inherently good or bad. The focus here is on how well you fit within each of them. This exercise is completed alone so you can assess yourself honestly without concerns of social comparison. However, class discussion will focus on the importance of matching job applicants to the organization's dominant values.

Corporate Culture Preference Scale

I would prefer to work in an organization:				
1a.	Where employees work well together in teams.	*or*	1b.	That produces highly respected products or services.
2a.	Where top management maintains a sense of order in the workplace.	*or*	2b.	Where the organization listens to customers and responds quickly to their needs.
3a.	Where employees are treated fairly.	*or*	3b.	Where employees continuously search for ways to work more efficiently.
4a.	Where employees adapt quickly to new work requirements.	*or*	4b.	Where corporate leaders work hard to keep employees happy.
5a.	Where senior executives receive special benefits not available to other employees.	*or*	5b.	Where employees are proud when the organization achieves its performance goals.
6a.	Where employees who perform the best get paid the most.	*or*	6b.	Where senior executives are respected.
7a.	Where everyone gets their jobs done like clockwork.	*or*	7b.	That is on top of innovations in the industry.
8a.	Where employees receive assistance to overcome any personal problems.	*or*	8b.	Where employees abide by company rules.
9a.	That is always experimenting with new ideas in the marketplace.	*or*	9b.	That expects everyone to put in 110 percent for peak performance.
10a.	That quickly benefits from market opportunities.	*or*	10b.	Where employees are always kept informed about what's happening in the organization.
11a.	That can quickly respond to competitive threats.	*or*	11b.	Where most decisions are made by the top executives.
12a.	Where management keeps everything under control.	*or*	12b.	Where employees care for each other.

After reading this chapter, if you need additional information, see **www.mhhe.com/mcshane4e** for more in-depth interactivities that correspond with this material.

A half-dozen years ago, district and store managers at Home Depot made their own decisions, routinely ignored directives from the head office, and opposed anything that looked like bureaucracy or hierarchy. "Whether it was an aisle, department, or store, you were truly in charge of it," recalls a former store operations manager. This decentralized, freewheeling culture likely fueled Home Depot's phenomenal growth, but it turned into a liability when Lowe's and Wal-Mart brought more intense competition to the marketplace. Home Depot needed more structure and efficiency, so the board of directors plucked Robert Nardelli from General Electric (GE) to become the new CEO and chief architect for change. His objective, not surprisingly, was to "GE-ize" Home Depot, turning it into a much more regimented, centralized, and measurement-focused organization.

Home Depot CEO Robert Nardelli has dramatically changed the big box retailer's culture by introducing systems that reinforce the new values.

Nardelli took a structural approach to change by introducing precise measures of corporate performance and drilling managers with weekly performance objectives around those metrics. The previous hodge-podge of subjective performance reviews was replaced with one centralized fact-based system to evaluate store managers and weed out poor performers. Nardelli instituted quarterly business review meetings in which objective measures of revenue, margins, inventory turns, cash flow, and other key indicators were analyzed across stores and regions. A two-hour weekly conference call became a ritual in which Home Depot's top executives were held accountable for the previous week's goals.

These changes occurred with lightning speed. "The rate of change internally has to be greater than the rate of change externally or else you're pedaling backward," advises Nardelli. For example, Dennis Donovan, one of several GE alumni Nardelli hired into key management posts, was given 90 days to develop a centralized purchasing system that would leverage more buying power than the existing decentralized process. "In the game of change, velocity is your friend," says Donovan, adding that Nardelli works by a stopwatch, not a time clock.

These rapid structural change interventions have helped Home Depot increase operating efficiency and double sales and profits over Nardelli's first five years. Employee engagement scores initially suffered, but they have now risen above the industry average. However, critics point out that these changes resulted in the departure of almost all of Home Depot's top management as well as ongoing turnover rates well above those at Lowe's. "[Nardelli's] lost so much good talent out of that place," observes one former executive. "The guys I still talk to there say they're waiting for the next shoe to drop."

Equally troubling is that Home Depot's customer service levels have sunk to new lows (one survey ranks Home Depot dead last among major U.S. retailers). "[Nardelli's] made Home Depot much more profitable and more streamlined, but messed up everything that has to do with serving the customer," complains one retail consultant. Wall Street isn't impressed, either; Home Depot's share price hasn't budged since Nardelli arrived.[1]

17

Organizational Change

LEARNING OBJECTIVES

After reading this chapter you should be able to

1. Describe the elements of Lewin's force field analysis model.
2. Outline six reasons why people resist organizational change.
3. Discuss six strategies to minimize resistance to change.
4. Outline the conditions for effectively diffusing change from a pilot project.
5. Describe the action research approach to organizational change.
6. Outline the "Four-D" model of appreciative inquiry and explain how this approach differs from action research.
7. Explain how parallel learning structures assist the change process.
8. Discuss four ethical issues in organizational change.

Robert Nardelli's extraordinary effort to transform Home Depot into a more performance-oriented and fact-based organization illustrates several practices, as well as the risks and complexities, of managing organizational change. Nardelli's relative success is due in part to his clear vision and careful realignment of information and reward systems to match the desired future state. At the same time, the change process was punctuated with various forms of resistance–only some of which Nardelli's parachuted team of former GE executives was able to offset.

This chapter investigates the dynamics of change and how to actively manage the change process in organizational settings. It begins by introducing Lewin's model of change and its component parts, including sources of resistance to change, ways to minimize this resistance, and ways to stabilize desired behaviors. Next, this chapter examines three approaches to organizational change: action research, appreciative inquiry, and parallel learning structures. The last section of this chapter considers both cross-cultural and ethical issues in organizational change.

Learning Objectives

After reading this section you should be able to

1. **Describe the elements of Lewin's force field analysis model.**
2. **Outline six reasons why people resist organizational change.**

Lewin's Force Field Analysis Model

Social psychologist Kurt Lewin developed the force field analysis model to help us understand how the change process works (see Exhibit 17.1).[2] Although developed more than 50 years ago, Lewin's **force field analysis** model remains the preeminent way of viewing this process.

force field analysis
Lewin's model of system-wide change that helps change agents diagnose the forces that drive and restrain proposed organizational change.

One side of the force field model represents the *driving forces* that push organizations toward a new state of affairs. Chapter 1 described some of the driving forces in the external environment, including globalization, virtual work, and a changing workforce. Along with these external forces, corporate leaders create driving forces within the organization so the organization anticipates the external forces. These

Exhibit 17.1
Lewin's Force Field Analysis Model

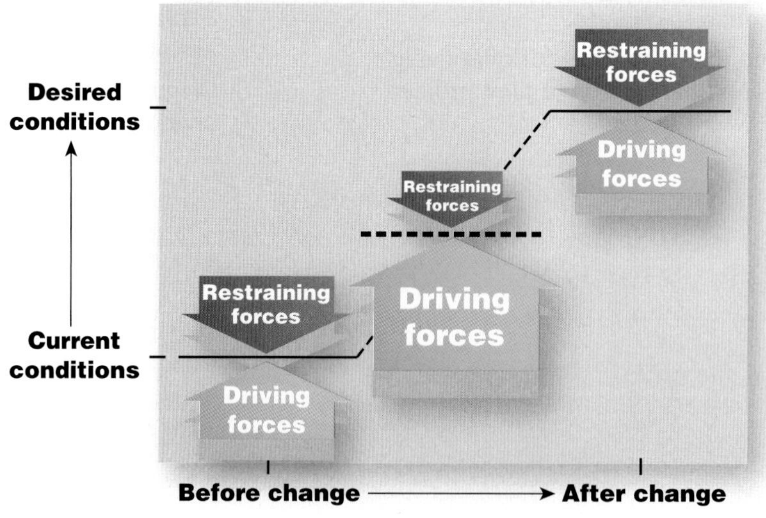

internally originated forces are difficult to apply because they lack external justifications, so effective transformational leadership as well as structural change mechanisms are necessary to legitimate and support internal driving forces.

The other side of Lewin's model represents the *restraining forces* that maintain the status quo. These restraining forces are commonly called "resistance to change" because they appear as employee behaviors that block the change process. Stability occurs when the driving and restraining forces are roughly in equilibrium–that is, when they are of approximately equal strength in opposite directions.

unfreezing
The first part of the change process whereby the change agent produces disequilibrium between the driving and restraining forces.

refreezing
The latter part of the change process in which systems and conditions are introduced that reinforce and maintain the desired behaviors.

Lewin's force field model emphasizes that effective change occurs by **unfreezing** the current situation, moving to a desired condition, and then **refreezing** the system so that it remains in this desired state. Unfreezing involves producing disequilibrium between the driving and restraining forces. As we describe later, this may occur by increasing the driving forces, reducing the restraining forces, or having a combination of both. Refreezing occurs when the organization's systems and structures are aligned with the desired behaviors. They must support and reinforce the new role patterns and prevent the organization from slipping back into the old ways of doing things. Over the next few pages we use Lewin's model to understand why change is blocked and how the process can evolve more smoothly.

Restraining Forces

Economist John Kenneth Galbraith once quipped that when faced with the prospect of changing or proving why change isn't needed, most people get busy on the proof! Jacques Nasser, the former CEO of Ford Motor Company, would likely attest to the

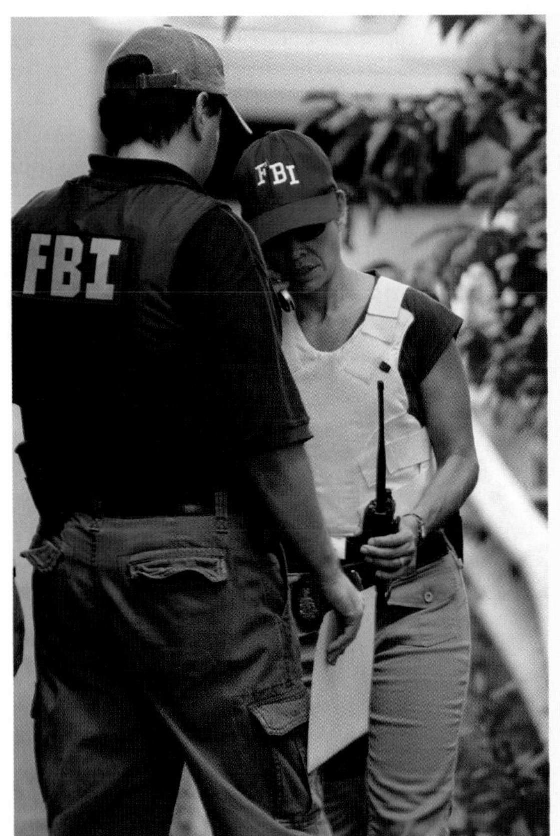

FBI Meets Its Own Resistance In 1993, following the first terrorist attacks on the World Trade Center, the U.S. Federal Bureau of Investigation (FBI) promised to refocus itself from a reactive law enforcement agency (solving crimes) to a proactive domestic intelligence agency (preventing terrorism). Yet two government reports recently concluded that resistance from FBI staff has hampered this change process. One report even stated that the FBI (as well as CIA) "seem to be working harder and harder just to maintain a status quo that is increasingly irrelevant to the new challenges." The reports claim that FBI employees and managers are unable or unwilling to change because solving crimes (rather than intelligence gathering) is burned into their mindset, routines, career paths, and decentralized structure. Most FBI field managers were trained in law enforcement, so they continue to give preferential treatment and resources to enforcement rather than to terrorist prevention initiatives. An information access barrier called "the wall" further isolates FBI intelligence officers from the mainstream criminal investigation staff. Historical turf wars with the CIA have also undermined FBI respect for the bureau's intelligence-gathering initiative. "One of the most difficult things one has to do is to bring an entity through the development of a change of business practices," FBI director Robert Mueller recently admitted.[3]

accuracy of that statement. Over two tumultuous years Nasser tried to shift the automaker from engineering prowess to "cyber-savviness," from quality to efficiency, and from an old boys' club to a performance-focused competitor. In one year he rammed through a performance review system that took General Electric nearly a decade to implement. The changes were too much for many Ford employees. Some engineers grumbled that quality had declined; employees stung by the performance system launched age discrimination lawsuits. "When you induce change, you get a reaction," explained a senior Ford executive. "I have letters from employees congratulating us. I have letters from employees doing the opposite." In the latter group was the Ford family, who eventually replaced Nasser with William Clay Ford as CEO.[4]

Of course Ford Motor Company employees aren't the only ones to engage in resistance to change. According to various surveys, more than 40 percent of executives identify employee resistance as the most important barrier to corporate restructuring or improved performance. This is consistent with a recent survey in which most employees admitted they don't follow through with organizational changes because they "like to keep things the way they are" or the changes seem to be too complicated or time-wasting.[5] Robert Nardelli experienced this and other forms of resistance when changing Home Depot's culture and practices. Disenchanted staff began calling the company "Home Despot" because the changes took away their autonomy. Others named it "Home GEpot," a cutting reference to the many former GE executives Nardelli hired into top positions.

Employee resistance takes many forms, including passive noncompliance, complaints, absenteeism, turnover, and collective action (such as strikes and walkouts). In extreme cases of resistance, the chief change agent eventually leaves or is pushed out. This resistance is a symptom of deeper problems in the change process; so rather than directly correcting incidents of passive noncompliance, change agents need to understand why employees are not changing their behavior in the desired ways.[6] In some situations employees may be worried about the *consequences* of change, such as how the new conditions will take away their power and status. In other situations employees show resistance because of concerns about the *process* of change itself, such as the effort required to break old habits and learn new skills. The main reasons why people resist change are shown in Exhibit 17.2 and described on the next page.[7]

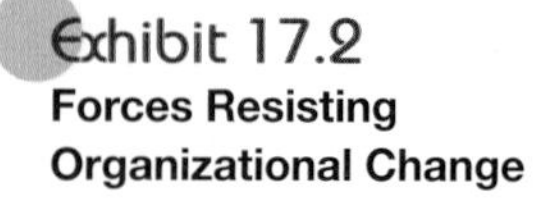

Forces Resisting Organizational Change

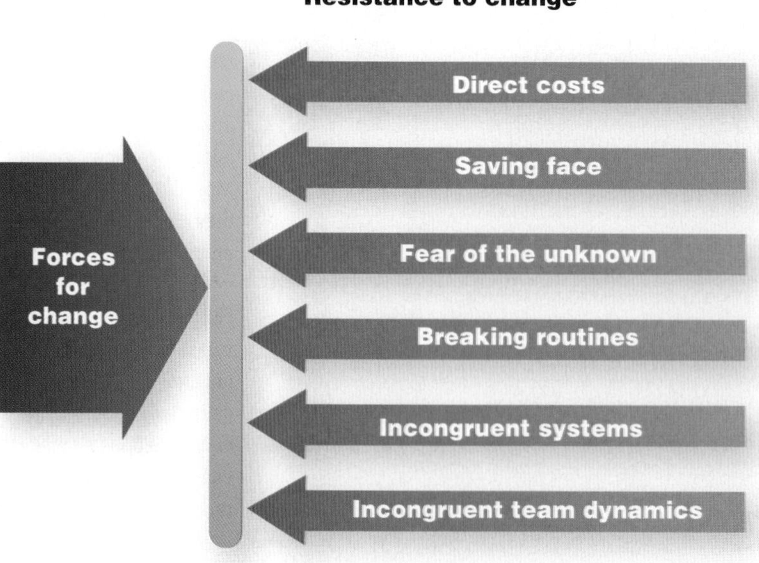

- *Direct costs.* People tend to block actions that result in higher direct costs or lower benefits than the existing situation. Many Home Depot employees resisted the change that CEO Robert Nardelli was pushing through because it threatened their autonomy, job security, and career opportunities.
- *Saving face.* Some people resist change as a political strategy to "prove" that the decision is wrong or that the person encouraging change is incompetent. This occurred when senior executives in a manufacturing firm bought a computer other than the system recommended by the information systems department. Soon after the system was in place, several information systems employees let minor implementation problems escalate to demonstrate that senior management had made a poor decision.
- *Fear of the unknown.* People resist change out of worry that they cannot adjust to the new work requirements. This fear of the unknown increases the risk of personal loss. For example, one company owner wanted sales staff to telephone rather than personally visit prospective customers. With no experience in telephone sales, they complained about the changes. Some even avoided the training program that taught them how to make telephone sales.[8]
- *Breaking routines.* Chapter 1 described how organizations need to unlearn, not just learn. This means employees need to abandon behavioral routines that are no longer appropriate. Unfortunately people are creatures of habit. They like to stay within comfort zones by continuing routine role patterns that make life predictable. Consequently many people resist organizational changes that force them out of their comfort zones and require investing time and energy learning new role patterns.
- *Incongruent organizational systems.* Rewards, selection, training, and other control systems ensure that employees maintain desired role patterns. Yet the organizational systems that maintain stability also discourage employees from adopting new ways. The implication, of course, is to do what Nardelli did at Home Depot–alter organizational systems to fit the desired future state. Unfortunately control systems can be difficult to change, particularly when they have supported role patterns that worked well in the past.[9]
- *Incongruent team dynamics.* Teams develop and enforce conformity to a set of norms that guide behavior. However, conformity to existing team norms may discourage employees from accepting organizational change. Team norms that conflict with the desired changes need to be altered.

Learning Objectives

After reading the next two sections you should be able to

3. Discuss six strategies to minimize resistance to change.

4. Outline the conditions for effectively diffusing change from a pilot project.

Unfreezing, Changing, and Refreezing

According to Lewin's force field analysis model, effective change occurs by unfreezing the current situation, moving to a desired condition, and then refreezing the system so it remains in this desired state. Unfreezing occurs when the driving forces are stronger than the restraining forces. This happens by making the driving forces stronger, weakening or removing the restraining forces, or a combination of both.

With respect to the first option, driving forces must increase enough to motivate change. Change rarely occurs by increasing driving forces alone, however, because the restraining forces often adjust to counterbalance the driving forces. This is rather like the coils of a spring. The harder corporate leaders push for change, the more strongly the restraining forces push back. This antagonism threatens the change effort by producing tension and conflict within the organization. The change effort at Home Depot was likely hampered to some extent by Nardelli's strategy of forcefully pushing the change through without sufficiently addressing the sources of resistance to that change. Only a year or two later, when resistance was still apparent, did Home Depot's executive team address some of the sources of resistance, as will be described later. The preferred option is to both increase the driving forces and reduce or remove the restraining forces. Increasing the driving forces creates an urgency for change, whereas reducing the restraining forces minimizes resistance to change.

Creating an Urgency for Change

It is by now cliché to say that organizations today operate in more dynamic, fast-paced environments than they did a few decades ago. These environmental pressures represent the driving forces that push employees out of their comfort zones. They energize people to face the risks that change creates. In many organizations, however, corporate leaders buffer employees from the external environment to such an extent that these driving forces are hardly felt by anyone below the top executive level. The result is that employees don't understand why they need to change, and leaders are surprised when their change initiatives do not have much effect. Thus the change process must begin by ensuring that employees feel an urgency to change; this typically occurs by informing them about competitors, changing consumer trends, impending government regulations, and other driving forces.[10]

DaimlerChrysler took this approach after its initial attempt to create a team-based organizational structure met with resistance at its Belvidere, Illinois, assembly plant. "There is a need to change," says Belvidere plant manager Kurt Kavajecz. The problem, he explains, is that employees didn't see the need for change. They knew that "we build cars pretty well...So why do we have to change?" To develop a stronger urgency to change, Kavajecz told employees about the challenges the company faced. "If you show them what's going on in the industry, if you give them the information, the data on why we are changing, at the end of the presentation, they get it. They see that plants are closing and jobs are going away. We talk very openly about those things, and they understand why we're changing." The Belvidere plant eventually introduced team-based work.[11]

Customer-Driven Change Another way to fuel the urgency to change is by putting employees in direct contact with customers. Dissatisfied customers represent a compelling driving force for change because of the adverse consequences for the organization's survival and success. Customers also provide a human element that further energizes employees to change current behavior patterns.[12]

Executives at Shell Europe applied customer-driven change when they discovered that middle managers seemed blissfully unaware that Shell was neither achieving its financial goals nor satisfying customer needs. So to create an urgency for change, the European managers were loaded onto buses and taken out to talk with customers and employees who worked with customers every day. "We called these 'bus rides.' The idea was to encourage people to think back from the customer's perspective rather than from the head office," explains Shell Europe's vice president of retailing. "The

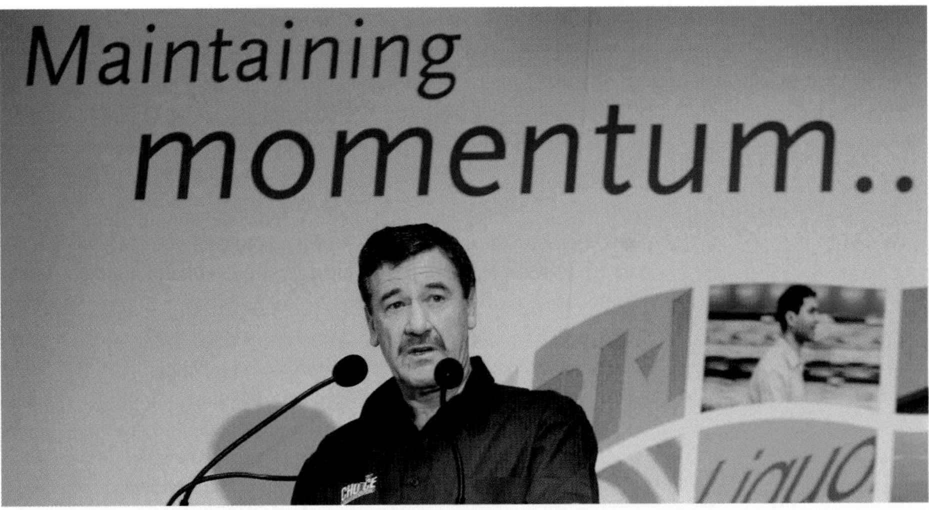

Coles Myer Chief Maintains the Momentum for Change Coles Myer chief executive John Fletcher has led the challenging task of transforming Australia's second largest retailer into a more nimble and customer-focused organization. The change process is starting to show positive results, including a more engaged workforce and better customer service. But Fletcher points out that as the company becomes more successful, his role as a change agent becomes even more difficult. "The thing now is to maintain momentum; it's critical in change programs when things start to look good," Fletcher advises. "Change programs are easier when things are bad. When things improve, people relax and think, we're there."[13]

bus rides were difficult for a lot of people who, in their work history, had hardly ever had to talk to a customer and find out what was good and not so good about Shell from the customer's standpoint."[14]

Urging Change without External Forces Exposing employees to external forces can strengthen the urgency for change, but leaders often need to begin the change process before problems come knocking at the company's door. "You want to create a burning platform for change even when there isn't a need for one," says Steve Bennett, CEO of financial software company Intuit.[15] Creating an urgency for change when the organization is riding high requires a lot of persuasive influence that helps employees visualize future competitive threats and environmental shifts.

For instance, Apple Computer's iPod dominates the digital music market, but Steve Jobs wants the company to be its own toughest competitor. Just when sales of the iPod Mini were soaring, Jobs challenged a gathering of 100 top executives and engineers to develop a better product to replace it. "Playing it safe is the most dangerous thing we can do," Jobs warned. Nine months later, the company launched the iPod Nano, which replaced the still-popular iPod Mini before competitors could offer a better alternative.[16]

Reducing the Restraining Forces

Effective change requires more than making employees aware of the driving forces. It also involves reducing or removing the restraining forces. Exhibit 17.3 summarizes six ways to overcome employee resistance. Communication, learning, employee

Exhibit 17.3 Strategies to Minimize Resistance to Change

Strategy	Example	When Used	Problem
Communication	Customer complaint letters are shown to employees.	When employees don't feel an urgency for change, or don't know how the change will affect them.	Time-consuming and potentially costly.
Learning	Employees learn how to work in teams as company adopts a team-based structure.	When employees need to break old routines and adopt new role patterns.	Time-consuming and potentially costly.
Employee involvement	Company forms a task force to recommend new customer service practices.	When the change effort needs more employee commitment, some employees need to save face, or employee ideas would improve decisions about the change strategy.	Very time-consuming. Might also lead to conflict and poor decisions if employees' interests are incompatible with organizational needs.
Stress management	Employees attend sessions to discuss their worries about the change.	When communication, training, and involvement do not sufficiently ease employee worries.	Time-consuming and potentially expensive. Some methods may not reduce stress for all employees.
Negotiation	Employees agree to replace strict job categories with multiskilling in return for increased job security.	When employees will clearly lose something of value from the change and would not otherwise support the new conditions. Also necessary when the company must change quickly.	May be expensive, particularly if other employees want to negotiate their support. Also tends to produce compliance but not commitment to the change.
Coercion	Company president tells managers to "get on board" the change or leave.	When other strategies are ineffective and the company needs to change quickly.	Can lead to more subtle forms of resistance, as well as long-term antagonism with the change agent.

Sources: Adapted from J.P. Kotter and L.A. Schlesinger, "Choosing Strategies for Change," *Harvard Business Review* 57 (1979), pp. 106–14; P.R. Lawrence, "How to Deal With Resistance to Change," *Harvard Business Review,* May–June 1954, pp. 49–57.

involvement, and stress management try to reduce the restraining forces and, if feasible, should be attempted first.[17] However, negotiation and coercion are necessary for people who will clearly lose something from the change and when the speed of change is critical.

Communication Honest and frequent communication is the highest priority and first strategy required for any organizational change.[18] Communication improves the change process in at least two ways. First, as was mentioned earlier, leaders develop an urgency to change by candidly telling employees about the driving forces for change. Whether through town hall meetings with senior management or by directly meeting with disgruntled customers, employees become energized to change. Second, communication can potentially reduce fear of the unknown. The more corporate leaders communicate their images of the future, the more easily employees can visualize their own role in that future. This effort may also begin the process of adjusting team norms to be more consistent with the new reality.

Learning Learning is an important process in most change initiatives because employees need new knowledge and skills to fit the organization's evolving requirements. When a company introduces a new sales database, for instance, representatives must learn how to adapt their previous behavior patterns to benefit from the new system. Action learning, which was described in Chapter 3, is another potentially powerful learning process for organizational change because it develops management skills while discovering ways to improve the organization.[19] Coaching is yet another form of learning that provides more personalized feedback and direction during the learning process. Coaching and other forms of learning are time-consuming, but they help employees break routines by learning new role patterns.

Employee Involvement Except in times of extreme urgency or where employee interests are highly incompatible with the organization's needs, employee involvement is almost an essential part of the change process. Rather than viewing themselves as agents of someone else's decision, employees prefer to feel personally responsible for the success of the change effort.[20] Involvement also minimizes problems of saving face and fear of the unknown. Furthermore, the complexity of today's work environment demands that more people provide ideas regarding the best direction of the change effort.

Employee involvement was not part of Robert Nardelli's game plan for change when he first arrived at Home Depot (see the opening vignette to this chapter). But after 18 months of resistance from store and district managers, Home Depot's senior management team held several five-day "learning forums" that tried to make these managers feel more involved in the change process. In particular, the sessions challenged staff members to think through how they would change the home improvement retailer. "Large-scale organizational change is not a spectator sport, and it's easy to be a cynic when you're in the stands," says Dennis Donovan, the Home Depot executive who led the learning forums.

The problem with Home Depot's "learning forum" strategy is that the sessions began long after Nardelli had launched many of the changes, thereby making it difficult for managers to feel that they were part of the change initiative. In contrast, Carlos Ghosn relied on employee involvement from the outset of an important change process at Nissan Motor Company. As Connections 17.1 describes, Ghosn formed a dozen cross-functional management teams and gave them three months to identify ways to save the company from possible bankruptcy.

Minimizing resistance to change through employee involvement is also possible in large organizations through **future search** events. Future search conferences "put the entire system in the room," meaning that they try to involve as many employees and other stakeholders as possible associated with the organizational system. These multiday events ask participants to identify trends or issues and establish strategic solutions for those conditions.[21]

future search
Systemwide group sessions, usually lasting a few days, in which participants identify trends and identify ways to adapt to those changes.

In the corporate world, Microsoft, the U.S. Forest Service, and Peco Energy have used future search conferences to assist the change process. Every five years Whole Foods Market gathers together several hundred employees, shoppers, and shareholders for a future search meeting to help identify new directions for the food retailer. Search conferences have been more widely used as a form of community involvement. The State of Washington Department of Corrections recently held a future search event in which a representative 75 employees and managers reached a consensus about the department's future direction. Specific executives in the department were then assigned specific recommendations to ensure that the conference results were put into place.[22]

Connections 17.1

Carlos Ghosn Relies on High Involvement to Transform Nissan

Nissan Motor Company was on the brink of bankruptcy when French automaker Renault purchased a controlling interest and installed Carlos Ghosn as the effective head of the Japanese automaker. Along with Nissan's known problems of high debt and plummeting market share, Ghosn (pronounced "gone") saw that Nissan managers had no apparent sense of urgency for change. "Even though the evidence is against them, they sit down and they watch the problem a little bit longer," says Ghosn.

Ghosn's challenge was to act quickly, yet minimize the inevitable resistance that arises when an outsider tries to change traditional Japanese business practices. "I was non-Nissan, non-Japanese," he says. "I knew that if I tried to dictate changes from above, the effort would backfire, undermining morale and productivity. But if I was too passive, the company would simply continue its downward spiral."

To resolve this dilemma, Ghosn formed nine cross-functional teams of 10 middle managers each, giving them the mandate to identify innovative proposals for a specific area (marketing, manufacturing, and so on) within three months. Each team could form subteams with additional people to analyze issues in more detail. In all, over 500 middle managers and other employees were involved in the so-called "Nissan Revival Plan."

After a slow start—Nissan managers weren't accustomed to such authority or working with colleagues across functions or cultures—ideas began to flow as Ghosn stuck to his deadline, reminded team members of the automaker's desperate situation, and encouraged teams to break traditions. Three months later the nine teams submitted a bold plan to close three assembly plants, eliminate thousands of jobs, cut the number of suppliers by half, reduce purchasing costs by 20 percent, return to profitability, cut the company's debt by half, and introduce 22 new models within the next two years.

Although risky, Ghosn accepted all of the proposals. Moreover, when revealing the plan publicly on the eve of the annual Tokyo Motor Show, Ghosn added his own commitment to the plan: "If you ask people to go through a difficult period of time, they have to trust that you're sharing it with them," Ghosn explains. "So I said that if we did not fulfill our commitments, I would resign."

Ghosn's strategy for organizational change and the Nissan Revival Plan worked. Within 12 months the automaker had increased sales and market share and posted its first profit in seven years. The company has introduced innovative models and expanded operations. Ghosn has received high praise throughout Japan and abroad and has since become head of Renault.

Sources: C. Lebner, "Nissan Motor Co.," *Fast Company,* July 2002, p. 80; C. Dawson, "On Your Marks," *Business Week,* 17 March 2003, p. 52; D. Magee, *Turn Around: How Carlos Ghosn Rescued Nissan* (New York: HarperCollins, 2003); C. Ghosn and P. Riès, *Shift: Inside Nissan's Historic Revival* (New York: Currency Doubleday, 2005).

Carlos Ghosn launched a turnaround at Nissan Motor Company that saved the Japanese automaker and relied on change management practices rarely seen in Japan.

Future search meetings potentially minimize resistance to change and assist the quality of the change process, but they also have limitations.[23] One problem is that involving so many people invariably limits the opportunity to contribute and increases the risk that a few people will dominate the process. Another concern is that these events generate high expectations about an ideal future state that is difficult to satisfy in practice. Furthermore, some executives forget that future search conferences and other forms of employee involvement require follow-up action. If employees do not see meaningful decisions and actions resulting from these meetings, they begin to question the credibility of the process and are more cynical of similar subsequent change management activities.[24]

Stress Management Organizational change is a stressful experience for many people because it threatens self-esteem and creates uncertainty about the future. Communication, learning, and employee involvement can reduce some of these stressors. However, research indicates that companies also need to introduce stress management practices to help employees cope with the changes.[25] In particular, stress management minimizes resistance by removing some of the direct costs and fear of the unknown of the change process. Stress also saps energy, so minimizing stress potentially increases employee motivation to support the change process.

Wachovia Corp. was aware of the need for stress management when it merged with First Union Corp. The Charlotte, North Carolina–based financial institution set up a toll-free telephone number that employees and other stakeholders could call for updates on the merger process. It also dispatched 400 middle and upper-level managers called "ambassadors" to keep everyone informed. Wachovia offered special sessions to help employees cope with change and stress. Shortly after the merger was announced, the company sent out a memo reminding people about the company's employee assistance counseling service.[26]

Negotiation As long as people resist change, organizational change strategies will require some influence tactics. Negotiation is a form of influence that involves the promise of benefits or resources in exchange for the target person's compliance with the influencer's request. This strategy potentially activates those who would otherwise lose out from the change. However, it tends to merely gain compliance rather than commitment to the change effort, so it might not be effective in the long term.

Coercion If all else fails, leaders can use coercion to change organizations. Coercion can include persistently reminding people of their obligations, frequently monitoring behavior to ensure compliance, confronting people who do not change, and using threats of sanctions to force compliance. Replacing people who will not support the change is an extreme step, but this is fairly common in senior management ranks. The opening story to this chapter described how almost all of Home Depot's top management team departed within one year after Robert Nardelli arrived. Many of these people did not leave voluntarily.

Replacing staff is a radical form of organizational "unlearning" (see Chapter 1) because replacing executives removes knowledge of the organization's past routines. This potentially opens up opportunities for new practices to take hold.[27] At the same time, coercion is a risky strategy because survivors (employees who are not fired) may have less trust in corporate leaders and engage in more political tactics to protect their own job security. Forcing people to leave isn't always necessary, even during times of radical change. One of the notable features of the turnaround at Nissan Motor Company, described earlier in Connections 17.1, was that few executives were replaced. More generally, various forms of coercion may change behavior through compliance, but they won't develop commitment to the change effort (see Chapter 12).

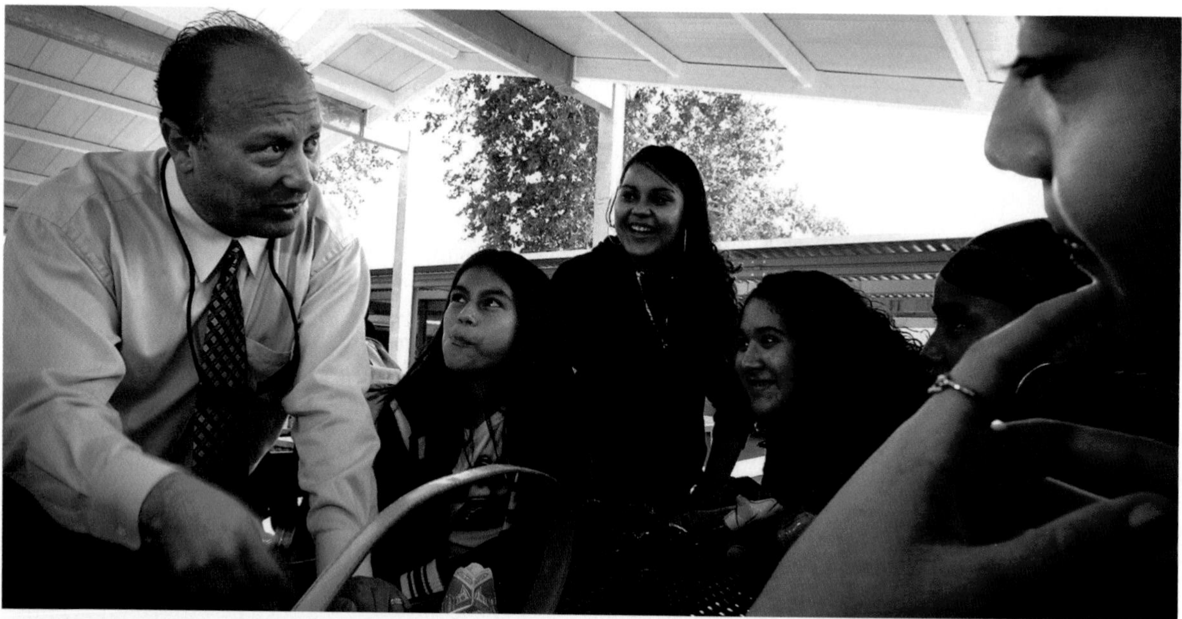

Change the School by Changing the Principal A few years ago, test results at Sun Valley Middle School were so low that the San Fernando Valley, California, school was put on a U S. federal government watch list for closer scrutiny. The Los Angeles unified school district tried to help the principal and staff to improve, but to no avail. When a state audit reported that the school suffered from poor management, unsanitary conditions, and uneven classroom instruction, the school district applied a more radical change strategy: It replaced Sun Valley's principal and four assistant principals with new leaders. Sun Valley's new principal, Jeff Davis (shown with students in this photo), introduced extra English language instruction, reorganized class locations, and launched team teaching to foster a more collegial atmosphere among staff. Sun Valley still has a long way to go, but student test scores in math and English have tripled over the past three years. "That school is absolutely headed in the right direction," says Sue Shannon, superintendent of schools in the eastern San Fernando Valley.[28]

Refreezing the Desired Conditions

Unfreezing and changing behavior patterns won't result in lasting change. People are creatures of habit, so they easily slip back into past patterns. Therefore leaders need to refreeze the new behaviors by realigning organizational systems and team dynamics with the desired changes.[29] This is the main change strategy that helped Robert Nardelli transform Home Depot. The former GE executive introduced new information systems and realigned the reward system to support the desired future state. Feedback, organizational structures, and physical layout of buildings are among the other tools used to refreeze desired behaviors.

Strategic Visions, Change Agents, and Diffusing Change

Kurt Lewin's force field analysis model is a useful template to explain the dynamics of organizational change. But it overlooks three other ingredients in effective change processes: strategic visions, change agents, and diffusing change. Every successful change requires a well-articulated and appealing vision of the desired future state.[30] We can see this critical element in the opening vignette. Robert Nardelli had a clear vision of what he wanted Home Depot to become. Similarly, A.G. Lafley was able to revive Procter & Gamble's flagging sales by describing and finding ways to support a much more creative and customer-focused culture. Generally the leader's vision provides a sense of direction and establishes the critical success factors against which the real changes are evaluated. It also minimizes employee fear of the unknown and provides a better understanding of what behaviors employees must learn for the future state.

Change Agents

change agent
Anyone who possesses enough knowledge and power to guide and facilitate the organizational change effort.

Every organizational change, whether large or small, requires one or more change agents. A **change agent** is anyone who possesses enough knowledge and power to guide and facilitate the change effort. Change agents come in different forms, and more than one person is often required to serve in these different roles. Transformational leaders such as Robert Nardelli and A.G. Lafley are the primary agents of change because they form a vision of the desired future state, communicate that vision in ways that are meaningful to others, behave in ways that are consistent with the vision, and build commitment to the vision.[31] Transformational leaders are the architects who shape the overall direction for the change effort and motivate employees to achieve that objective.

Organizational change also requires transactional leaders who implement the change by aligning the daily behavior of individual employees with the organization's new goals.[32] If a company wants to provide better customer service, then supervisors and other transactional leaders need to arrange rewards, resources, feedback, and other conditions that support better customer service behaviors in employees. Consultants from either inside or outside the organization represent a third change agent role. Consultants typically bring unique expertise to the change process through a toolkit of change processes, some of which we introduce later in this chapter. Finally, just as employees are encouraged to become leaders anytime and anywhere, they also can assist the change process as role models for others to follow.

Diffusion of Change

Change agents often test the transformation process with a pilot project, and then diffuse what has been learned from this experience to other parts of the organization. Unlike centralized, systemwide changes, pilot projects are more flexible and less risky.[33] The pilot project approach also makes it easier to select organizational groups that are most ready for change, which increases the pilot project's success.

But how do we ensure that the change process started in the pilot project is adopted by other segments of the organization? The MARS model introduced in Chapter 2 offers a useful template to organize the answer to this question. First, employees are more likely to adopt the practices of a pilot project when they are motivated to do so.[34] This occurs when they see that the pilot project is successful and people in the pilot project receive recognition and rewards for changing their previous work practices. Diffusion also requires supervisor support and reinforcement of the desired behaviors. More generally, change agents need to minimize the sources of resistance to change that we discussed earlier in this chapter.

Second, employees must have the ability–the required skills and knowledge–to adopt the practices introduced in the pilot project. According to innovation diffusion studies, people adopt ideas more readily when they have an opportunity to interact and learn from others who have already applied the new practices.[35] Thus pilot projects get diffused when employees in the original pilot are dispersed to other work units as role models and knowledge sources.

Third, pilot projects get diffused when employees have clear role perceptions; that is, they understand how the practices in a pilot project apply to them even though the change is applied in a completely different functional area. For instance, accounting department employees won't easily recognize how they can adopt quality improvement practices developed by employees in the production department. The challenge here is for change agents to provide guidance that is neither too specific (because it might not seem relevant to other areas of the organization) nor too abstract (because this makes the instructions too vague). Finally, employees require supportive situational factors, including the resources and time necessary to adopt the practices demonstrated in the pilot project.

Learning Objectives

After reading the next two sections you should be able to

5. **Describe the action research approach to organizational change.**
6. **Outline the "Four-D" model of appreciative inquiry and explain how this approach differs from action research.**
7. **Explain how parallel learning structures assist the change process.**
8. **Discuss four ethical issues in organizational change.**

Three Approaches to Organizational Change

So far this chapter has examined the dynamics of change that occur every day in organizations. However, organizational change agents and consultants also apply various approaches to organizational change. This section introduces three of the leading approaches to organizational change: action research, appreciative inquiry, and parallel learning structures.

Action Research Approach

action research
A data-based, problem-oriented process that diagnoses the need for change, introduces the intervention, and then evaluates and stabilizes the desired changes.

Along with introducing the force field model, Kurt Lewin recommended an **action research** approach to the change process. Action research takes the view that meaningful change is a combination of action orientation (changing attitudes and behavior) and research orientation (testing theory).[36] On one hand, the change process needs to be action-oriented because the ultimate goal is to bring about change. An action orientation involves diagnosing current problems and applying interventions that resolve those problems. On the other hand, the change process is a research study because change agents apply a conceptual framework (such as team dynamics or organizational culture) to a real situation. As with any good research, the change process involves collecting data to diagnose problems more effectively and to systematically evaluate how well the theory works in practice. In other words, action research embraces the notion of organizational learning and knowledge management (see Chapter 1).[37]

Within this dual framework of action and research, the action research approach adopts an open systems view. It recognizes that organizations have many interdependent parts, so change agents need to anticipate both the intended and unintended consequences of their interventions. Action research is also a highly participative process because open systems change requires both the knowledge and commitment of members within that system. Indeed, employees are essentially co-researchers as well as participants in the intervention. Overall, action research is a data-based, problem-oriented process that diagnoses the need for change, introduces the intervention, and then evaluates and stabilizes the desired changes (see Exhibit 17.4).[38]

Exhibit 17.4 The Action Research Process

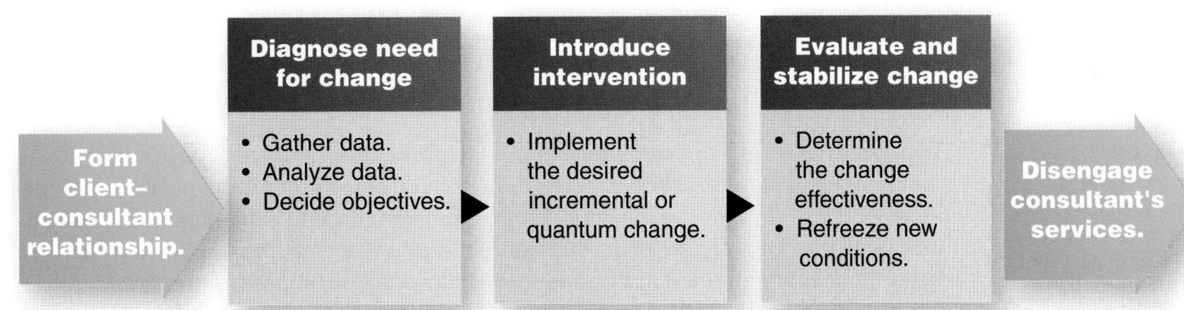

1. *Form client–consultant relationship*–Action research usually assumes that the change agent originates outside the system (as does a consultant), so the process begins by forming the client–consultant relationship. Consultants need to determine the client's readiness for change, including whether people are motivated to participate in the process, are open to meaningful change, and possess the abilities to complete the process.
2. *Diagnose the need for change*–Action research is a problem-oriented activity that carefully diagnoses the problem through systematic analysis of the situation. Organizational diagnosis identifies the appropriate direction for the change effort by gathering and analyzing data about an ongoing system, such as through interviews and surveys of employees and other stakeholders. Organizational diagnosis also includes employee involvement in agreeing on the appropriate change method, the schedule for these actions, and the expected standards of successful change.
3. *Introduce intervention*–This stage in the action research model applies one or more actions to correct the problem. It may include any of the prescriptions mentioned in this textbook, such as building more effective teams, managing conflict, building a better organizational structure, or changing the corporate culture. An important issue is how quickly the changes should occur.[39] Some experts recommend *incremental change* in which the organization fine-tunes the system and takes small steps toward a desired state. Others claim that *quantum change* is often required, in which the system is overhauled decisively and quickly. Quantum change is usually traumatic to employees and offers little opportunity for correction. But incremental change is also risky when the organization is seriously misaligned with its environment, thereby threatening its survival.
4. *Evaluate and stabilize change*–Action research recommends evaluating the effectiveness of the intervention against the standards established in the diagnostic stage. Unfortunately, even when these standards are clearly stated, the effectiveness of an intervention might not be apparent for several years or might be difficult to separate from other factors. If the activity has the desired effect, the change agent and participants need to stabilize the new conditions. This refers to the refreezing process that was described earlier. Rewards, information systems, team norms, and other conditions are redesigned to support the new values and behaviors.

The action research approach has dominated organizational change thinking since it was introduced in the 1940s. However, some experts complain that the problem-oriented nature of action research–in which something is wrong that must be fixed–focuses on the negative dynamics of a group or system rather than its positive opportunities and potential. This concern with action research has led to the development of a more positive approach to organizational change called *appreciative inquiry*.[40]

Appreciative Inquiry Approach

appreciative inquiry An organizational change process that directs attention away from the group's own problems and focuses participant's on the group's potential and positive elements.

Appreciative inquiry tries to break out of the problem-solving mentality of traditional change management practices by reframing relationships around the positive and the possible. It searches for organizational (or team) strengths and capabilities, then adapts or applies that knowledge for further success and well-being. Appreciative inquiry is therefore deeply grounded in the emerging philosophy of *positive organizational behavior* (a variation of *positive psychology*), which focuses on building positive qualities and traits within individuals or institutions as opposed to focusing just on trying to fix what might be wrong with them. In other words, this approach emphasizes building on strengths rather than trying to correct weaknesses.[41]

Appreciative inquiry typically directs its inquiry toward successful events and successful organizations or work units. This external focus becomes a form of behavioral modeling, but it also increases open dialogue by redirecting the group's attention away from its own problems. Appreciative inquiry is especially useful when participants are aware of their "problems" or already suffer from negativity in their relationships. The positive orientation of appreciative inquiry enables groups to overcome these negative tensions and build a more hopeful perspective of their future by focusing on what is possible.[42]

The "Four-D" model of appreciative inquiry (named after its four stages) shown in Exhibit 17.5 begins with *discovery*–identifying the positive elements of the observed events or organization.[43] This might involve documenting positive customer experiences elsewhere in the organization. Or it might include interviewing members of another organization to discover its fundamental strengths. As participants discuss their findings, they shift into the *dreaming* stage by envisioning what might be possible in an ideal organization. By directing their attention to a theoretically ideal

Canadian Tire's Appreciative Journey After effectively battling the American juggernauts Wal-Mart and Home Depot over the past decade, Canadian Tire's executive team wanted to hear from employees and store owners about what made the Canadian hardware and auto parts retailer so successful, then rebuild its core values around those positive experiences. Appreciative inquiry played an important role in this re-envisioning process. Internal consultants conducted detailed interviews with 377 staff members across the organization, asking each to describe occasions where they felt Canadian Tire was working at its best and what they valued most about the company. Some people described the excitement of holiday season where products were flying out the door. Others recalled the teamwork of employees volunteering to work late to clean up a store after a major delivery. These appreciative incidents were organized around six team values (owners, driven, accountable, and so on), which the executive team discussed and affirmed. Canadian Tire then held a one-day conference in which middle and senior managers developed a common understanding of these values. Next, store managers discussed the six team values with their staff members and participated in an appreciative exercise in which employees visualized a good news story about Canadian Tire's success.[44]

Exhibit 17.5 **The "Four-D" Model of Appreciative Inquiry**

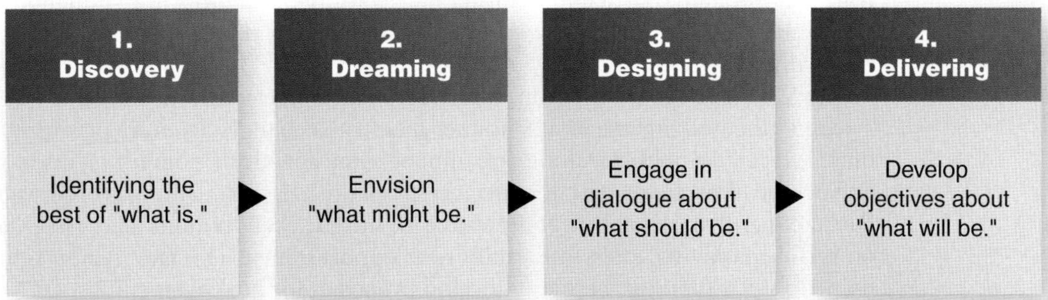
1.
Discovery
Identifying the best of "what is."
2.
Dreaming
Envision "what might be."
3.
Designing
Engage in dialogue about "what should be."
4.
Delivering
Develop objectives about "what will be."

Source: Based on F.J. Barrett and D.L. Cooperrider, "Generative Metaphor Intervention: A New Approach for Working with Systems Divided by Conflict and Caught in Defensive Perception," *Journal of Applied Behavioral Science* 26 (1990), p. 229; D. Whitney and C. Schau, "Appreciative Inquiry: An Innovative Process for Organization Change," *Employment Relations Today* 25 (Spring 1998), pp.11–21; J. M. Watkins and B.J. Mohr, *Appreciative Inquiry: Change at the Speed of Imagination* (San Francisco: Jossey-Bass, 2001), pp. 25, 42–45.

organization or situation, participants feel safer revealing their hopes and aspirations than if they were discussing their own organization or predicament.

As participants make their private thoughts public to the group, the process shifts into the third stage, called *designing*. Designing involves dialogue in which participants listen with selfless receptivity to each other's models and assumptions and eventually form a collective model for thinking within the team. In effect, they create a common image of what should be. As this model takes shape, group members shift the focus back to their own situation. In the final stage of appreciative inquiry, called *delivering*, participants establish specific objectives and direction for their own organization based on their model of what will be.

Appreciative inquiry was developed 20 years ago, but it really gained popularity only within the past few years, partly due to success stories at the U.S. Environmental Protection Agency, AVON Mexico, American Express, Green Mountain Coffee Roasters, and Hunter Douglas, among others.[45] At AVON Mexico, for example, a team of employees and consultants interviewed people for their stories illustrating best practices in gender equality. These stories were presented at two-day sessions, and participants built on these best practices to discover how AVON could extend these experiences. Over the next few years the company won the Catalyst award for gender equality; its profits increased dramatically (attributed partly to the appreciative inquiry process); and women found their way into more senior positions at AVON Mexico.

Although appreciative inquiry shows promise as an approach to organizational change, experts warn that it requires a particular mindset among participants in which they are willing to let go of the problem-oriented approach and in which leaders are willing to accept appreciative inquiry's less structured process.[46] Another concern is that research has not yet examined the contingencies of this approach.[47] Specifically, we don't yet know under what conditions appreciative inquiry is the best approach to organizational change or under what conditions it is less effective. Overall, appreciative inquiry has much to offer the organizational change process, but we are just beginning to understand its potential and limitations.

parallel learning structures
Highly participative groups constructed alongside (i.e., parallel to) the formal organization with the purpose of increasing the organization's learning and producing meaningful organizational change.

Parallel Learning Structure Approach

Parallel learning structures are highly participative arrangements composed of people from most levels of the organization who follow the action research model to produce meaningful organizational change. They are social structures developed alongside the formal hierarchy with the purpose of increasing the organization's learning.[48] Ideally participants in parallel learning structures are sufficiently free from the constraints of the larger organization so they can effectively solve organizational issues.

Royal Dutch/Shell relied on a parallel learning structure to introduce a more customer-focused organization.[49] Rather than try to change the entire organization at once, executives held weeklong "retail boot camps" with six country teams of front-line people (such as gas station managers, truck drivers, and marketing professionals). Participants learned about competitive trends in their regions and were taught powerful marketing tools to identify new opportunities. The teams then returned home to study their markets and develop proposals for improvement.

Four months later, boot camp teams returned for a second workshop in which each proposal was critiqued by Royal/Dutch Shell executives. Each team had 60 days to put its ideas into action, then return for a third workshop to analyze what worked and what didn't. This parallel learning process did much more than introduce new marketing ideas. It created enthusiasm in participants that spread contagiously to their co-workers, including managers above them, when they returned to their home countries.

Cross-Cultural and Ethical Issues in Organizational Change

One significant concern with some organizational change interventions is that they originate in the United States and other Western countries and may conflict with cultural values in some other countries.[50] A few experts point out that this Western perspective of change is linear, as is Lewin's force field model shown earlier. It also assumes that the change process is punctuated by tension and overt conflict. Indeed, some organizational change practices encourage open display of conflict.

But change as a linear and conflict-ridden process is incompatible with cultures that view change as a natural cyclical process with harmony and equilibrium as the objectives.[51] For instance, people in many Asian countries try to minimize conflict in order to respect others and save face.[52] These concerns do not mean that Western-style change interventions are necessarily ineffective elsewhere. Rather, it suggests that we need to develop a more contingency-oriented perspective with respect to the cultural values of participants.

Ethical Issues with Organizational Change Some organizational change practices also face ethical issues.[53] One ethical concern is threats to the privacy rights of individuals. The action research model is built on the idea of collecting information from organizational members, yet this requires employees to provide personal information and emotions that they may not want to divulge.[54] A second ethical concern is that some change activities potentially increase management's power by inducing compliance and conformity in organizational members. This power shift occurs because change creates uncertainty and may reestablish management's position in directing the organization. For instance, action research is a systemwide activity that requires employee participation rather than allowing individuals to get involved voluntarily.

A third concern is that some organizational change interventions undermine the individual's self-esteem. The unfreezing process requires participants to disconfirm their existing beliefs, sometimes including their own competence at certain tasks or interpersonal relations. Some specific change practices involve direct exposure to personal critique by co-workers as well as public disclosure of one's personal limitations and faults. A fourth ethical concern is the change management consultant's role in the change process. Ideally consultants should occupy "marginal" positions with the clients they are serving. This means that they must be sufficiently detached from the organization to maintain objectivity and avoid having the client become too dependent on them. However, some consultants tend to increase, rather than decrease, clients' dependence for financial gain. Others have difficulty maintaining neutrality because they often come to the situation with their own biases and agendas.

Organizational change is a complex process with a variety of approaches and issues. Many corporate leaders have promised more change than they were able to deliver because they underestimated the time and challenges involved with this process. Yet the dilemma is that most organizations operate in hyperfast environments that demand continuous and rapid adaptation. As Home Depot CEO Robert Nardelli stated in the opening story to this chapter, "The rate of change internally has to be greater than the rate of change externally or else you're pedaling backward." Organizations survive and gain competitive advantage by mastering the complex dynamics of moving people through the continuous process of change faster than the external environment is changing.

Personal Change for the Road Ahead

In this last section of this textbook we thought it would be a good idea to shift attention from organizational change to a few practical ideas about personal change and development in organizations. Whether you are just starting your career or are already well along the trail, the following principles should help you improve both your prospects and your long-term career satisfaction. These points do not cover everything you need to remember about developing your career. Instead they highlight some key strategies that will help you along the road ahead.

Understand Your Needs and Values

The first piece of advice regarding personal growth and development is to understand your needs and values. How do you know what path is most fulfilling for you? This involves doing self-assessments of your vocational interests and recounting experiences you have enjoyed. Holland's occupational choice model presented in Chapter 2 helps to align your personality and interests with the work environment. It may also be useful to get feedback from others regarding activities that they notice you like or dislike, or that they see you excelling at. This applies the Johari Window model described in Chapter 3, whereby you learn more about yourself through information presented by close associates.

Understand Your Competencies

Knowing yourself also involves knowing what you are capable of doing.[55] Although you might visualize your future as an Albert Einstein, the head of a *Fortune* 500 company, or the political leader of your country, you need to take your potential abilities into account. The more closely the work you perform is aligned with your personal competencies, the more you will develop feelings of satisfaction and empowerment. Self-assessments, performance results, and constructive feedback from friends can help identify your capabilities. Also keep in mind that competencies extend beyond technical skills: Employers also look for generic competencies, such as communication, problem solving, and emotional intelligence.

Set Career Goals

Goal setting is a powerful way to motivate and achieve results, and this applies as much to careers as to any other activity. Career goals are benchmarks against which we evaluate our progress and identify strategies to develop our competencies. Career consultant Barbara Moses emphasizes that career goal setting is a fundamental element in becoming a "career activist." It involves writing your own script rather than waiting for someone to write it for you, being vigilant by identifying and preparing for opportunities, and becoming an independent agent by separating your self-identity from your job title, your organization, or what other people think you should be.[56]

Maintain Networks

Networking makes a difference in personal career growth. This observation is supported by several research studies and from evidence in executive placement firms. One large placement firm reported that 64 percent of the 7,435 clients in its executive career transition program found new employment through networking. As one successful job hunter advises, "Be prepared, know your story, and network, network, network."[57] Some networks are more effective than others, however. Specifically, job seekers tend to be more successful with large nonredundant networks. Networks that extend beyond your current sphere of work are also critical. Careers change much more today than in the past, so you need to establish connections to other fields where you may someday find yourself.[58]

Get a Mentor

Thus far our discussion has emphasized self-leadership in personal development. We need to set our own goals, motivate ourselves for career advancement, and visualize where we want to go. But personal development in organizational settings also benefits from the help of others. Mentoring is the process of learning the ropes of organizational life from a senior person within the company. Mentors give protégés more visible and meaningful work opportunities, and they also provide ongoing career guidance. You might think of them as career coaches because they provide ongoing advice and feedback.[59]

Organizational Behavior: The Journey Continues

Nearly 100 years ago American industrialist Andrew Carnegie said, "Take away my people, but leave my factories, and soon grass will grow on the factory floors. Take away my factories, but leave my people, and soon we will have a new and better factory." Carnegie's statement reflects the message woven throughout this textbook that organizations are not buildings, machinery, or financial assets. Rather they are the people in them. Organizations are human entities–full of life, sometimes fragile, always exciting.

Chapter Summary

Lewin's force field analysis model states that all systems have driving and restraining forces. Change occurs through the process of unfreezing, changing, and refreezing. Unfreezing produces disequilibrium between the driving and restraining forces. Refreezing realigns the organization's systems and structures with the desired behaviors.

Restraining forces are manifested as employee resistance to change. The main reasons why people resist change are direct costs, saving face, fear of the unknown, breaking routines, incongruent organizational systems, and incongruent team dynamics. Resistance to change may be minimized by keeping employees informed about what to expect from the change effort (communicating); teaching employees valuable skills for the desired future (learning); involving them in the change process; helping employees cope with the stress of change; negotiating trade-offs with those who will clearly lose from the change effort; and using coercion (sparingly and as a last resort).

Organizational change also requires driving forces. This means employees need to feel an urgency for change by becoming aware of the environmental conditions that demand change in the organization. The change process also requires refreezing the new behaviors by realigning organizational systems and team dynamics with the desired changes.

Every successful change requires a clear, well-articulated vision of the desired future state. Change agents rely on transformational leadership to develop a vision, communicate that vision, and build commitment to the vision of a desirable future state. The change process also often applies a diffusion process in which change begins as a pilot project and eventually spreads to other areas of the organization.

Action research is a highly participative, open-systems approach to change management that combines action orientation (changing attitudes and behavior) with research orientation (testing theory). It is a data-based, problem-oriented process that diagnoses the need for change, introduces the intervention, and then evaluates and stabilizes the desired changes.

Appreciative inquiry embraces the positive organizational behavior philosophy by focusing participants on the positive and possible. It tries to break out of the problem-solving mentality that dominates organizational change through the action research model. The four stages of appreciative inquiry include discovery, dreaming, designing, and delivering. A third approach, parallel learning structures, relies on social structures developed alongside the formal hierarchy with the purpose of increasing the organization's learning. These are highly participative arrangements, composed of people from most levels of the organization who follow the action research model to produce meaningful organizational change.

One significant concern is that organizational change theories developed with a Western cultural orientation potentially conflict with cultural values in some other countries. Also, organizational change practices can raise ethical concerns, including increasing management's power over employees, threatening individual privacy rights, undermining individual self-esteem, and making clients dependent on the change consultant.

Five strategies that assist personal development in organizational settings are understanding your needs and values, understanding your competencies, setting career goals, maintaining networks, and getting a mentor.

Key Terms

action research, p. 500
appreciative inquiry, p. 502
change agent, p. 499
force field analysis, p. 488
future search, p. 495
parallel learning structure, p. 503
refreezing, p. 489
unfreezing, p. 489

Critical Thinking Questions

1. Chances are that the school you attend is currently undergoing some sort of change to adapt more closely with its environment. Discuss the external forces that are driving these changes. What internal drivers for change also exist?
2. Use Lewin's force field analysis to describe the dynamics of organizational change at Nissan Motor Company (Connections 17.1).
3. Employee resistance is a *symptom*, not a *problem*, in the change process. What are some of the real problems that may underlie employee resistance?
4. Senior managers of a large multinational corporation are planning to restructure the organization. Currently the organization is decentralized around geographical areas so that the executive responsible for each area has considerable autonomy over manufacturing and

sales. The new structure will transfer power to the executives responsible for different product groups; the executives responsible for each geographic area will no longer be responsible for manufacturing in their areas but will retain control over sales activities. Describe two types of resistance senior managers might encounter from this organizational change.

5. Web Circuits is a Malaysia-based custom manufacturer for high-technology companies. Senior managers want to introduce lean management practices to reduce production costs and remain competitive. A consultant has recommended that the company start with a pilot project in one department and, when successful, diffuse these practices to other areas of the organization. Discuss the advantages of this recommendation and identify three ways (other than the pilot project's success) to make diffusion of the change effort more successful.
6. Suppose you are vice president of branch services at the Bank of East Lansing. You notice that several branches have consistently low customer service ratings even though there are no apparent differences in resources or staff characteristics. Describe an appreciative inquiry process in one of these branches that might help to overcome these problems.
7. This chapter suggests that some organizational change activities create ethical concerns. Yet several consultants actively use these processes because they believe they benefit the organization and do less damage to employees than it seems on the surface. For example, some activities try to open up the employees' hidden areas (see the discussion of the Johari Window in Chapter 3) so there is better mutual understanding with co-workers. Discuss this argument and identify where you think organizational change interventions should limit this process.
8. Career activism is a concept that is gaining interest because it emphasizes managing your own development in organizations. What concepts introduced throughout this book are compatible with the career activist concept? In what ways might a person be a career activist?

Case Study 17.1 THE EXCELLENT EMPLOYEE

Mary Gander, Winona State University

Emily, who had the reputation of being an excellent worker, was a machine operator in a furniture manufacturing plant that had been growing at a rate of between 15 percent and 20 percent each year for the past decade. New additions were built onto the plant, new plants opened in the region, workers hired, new product lines developed–lots of expansion–but with no significant change in overall approaches to operations, plant layout, ways of managing workers, or design processes. Plant operations as well as organizational culture were rooted in traditional Western management practices and logic, based largely on the notion of mass production and economies of scale. Over the past four years the company had grown in number and variety of products and in market penetration; however, profitability was flattening and showing signs of decline. As a result, managers were beginning to focus on production operations (internal focus) rather than mainly focusing on new market strategies, new products, and new market segments (external focus) in developing their strategic plans. They hoped to reduce manufacturing costs, improving consistency of quality and ability to meet delivery times better while decreasing inventory and increasing flexibility.

One of several new programs initiated by managers in this effort to improve flexibility and lower costs was to get workers cross-trained. However, when a representative from Human Resources explained this program to Emily's supervisor, Jim, he reluctantly agreed to cross-train most of his workers, but *not* Emily.

Jim explained to the Human Resources person that Emily worked on a machine that was very complex and not easy to effectively operate. She had to "babysit" it much of the time. He had tried to train many workers on it, but Emily was the only person who could consistently get products through the machine that were within specifications and still meet production schedules. When anyone else tried to operate the machine, which performed a key function in the manufacturing process, it ended up either being a big bottleneck or producing excessive waste, which created a lot of trouble for Jim.

Jim went on to explain that Emily knew this sophisticated and complicated machine inside and out; she had been running it for five years. She liked the challenge, and she said it made the day go by faster, too. She was meticulous in her work–a skilled employee who really cared about the quality of her work. Jim told the HR person that he wished all of his workers were like Emily. In spite of the difficulty of running this machine, Emily could run it so well that product piled up at the next workstation in the production process, which couldn't keep up with her!

Jim was adamant about keeping Emily on this machine and not cross-training her. The HR person was frustrated. He could see Jim's point, but he had to follow executive orders: "Get these people cross-trained."

Around the same time a university student was doing a field study in the section of the plant where Emily worked, and Emily was one of the workers he interviewed. Emily told the student that in spite of the fact that the plant had some problems with employee morale and excessive employee turnover, she really liked working there. She liked the piece-rate pay system and hoped she did not have to participate in the recent "program of the month," which was having operators learn each other's jobs. She told the student that it would just create more waste if they tried to have other employees run her machine. She told him that other employees had tried to learn how to operate her machine but couldn't do it as well as she could.

Emily seemed to like the student and began to open up to him. She told him that her machine really didn't need to be so difficult and touchy to operate: With a couple of minor design changes in the machine and better maintenance, virtually anyone could run it. She had tried to explain this to her supervisor a couple of years ago, but he just told her to "do her work and leave operations to the manufacturing engineers." She also said that if workers upstream in the process would spend a little more time and care to keep the raw material in slightly tighter specifications, it would go through her machine much more easily; but they were too focused on speed and making more piece-rate pay. She expressed a lack of respect for the managers who couldn't see this and even joked about how "managers didn't know anything."

Discussion Questions

1. Identify the sources of resistance to change in this case.
2. Discuss whether this resistance is justified or could be overcome.
3. Recommend ways to minimize resistance to change in this incident or in future incidents.

Source: Copyright 2001 Mary J. Gander. This case is based on actual events, but names have been changed to maintain anonymity.

Case Study 17.2 INSIDE INTEL

For years, Intel thrived on a business model that co-founder Andy Grove perfected and reinforced under his leadership and the leadership of his successor, Craig Barrett. But Intel's latest CEO, Paul Otellini has different plans. Rather than continuing to build faster chips just for PC computers, Otellini sees bigger opportunities in new "platforms." Otellini also wants to raise the profile of marketing, rather than let engineers determine what products are developed. Even the famous Intel logo (with a lowered "e") is being ditched for a more contemporary design.

This *BusinessWeek* case study reviews the changes that Paul Otellini is introducing at Intel and explains how he is building momentum toward these changes. The article also describes how employees are responding to these changes. Read through this *BusinessWeek* article at www.mhhe.com/mcshane4e and prepare for the discussion questions below.

Discussion Questions

1. What change management strategies has Paul Otellini used to help introduce the various changes at Intel?
2. Discuss evidence that some employees are resisting these changes? What, if anything, can Otellini do to minimize this resistance?

Source: C. Edwards, "Inside Intel," *BusinessWeek*, 9 January 2006, 46.

Team Exercise 17.3 STRATEGIC CHANGE INCIDENTS

PURPOSE This exercise is designed to help you identify strategies to facilitate organizational change in various situations.

INSTRUCTIONS

1. The instructor will place students into teams, and each team will be assigned one of the scenarios presented here.
2. Each team will diagnose its assigned scenario to determine the most appropriate set of change management practices. Where appropriate, these practices should (a) create an urgency to change, (b) minimize resistance to change, and (c) refreeze the situation to support the change initiative. Each of these scenarios is based on real events.
3. Each team will present and defend its change management strategy. Class discussion of the appropriateness and feasibility of each strategy will occur after all teams assigned the same scenario have presented their recommendations. The instructor will then describe what the organizations actually did in these situations.

SCENARIO 1: GREENER TELCO

The board of directors at a large telephone company wants its executives to make the organization more environmentally friendly by encouraging employees to reduce waste in the workplace. There are also expectations by government and other stakeholders for the company to take this action and be publicly successful. Consequently, the managing director wants to significantly reduce the use of paper, as well as refuse and other waste throughout the company's many widespread offices. Unfortunately, a survey indicates that employees do not value environmental objectives and do not know how to "reduce, reuse, recycle." As the executive responsible for this change, you have been asked to develop a strategy that might bring about meaningful behavioral change toward these environmental goals. What would you do?

SCENARIO 2: GO FORWARD AIRLINE

A major airline has experienced a decade of rough turbulence, including two bouts of bankruptcy protection, 10 chief executives, and morale so low that employees have ripped company logos off their uniforms out of embarrassment. Service is terrible, and the airplanes rarely arrive or leave the terminal on time. This is costing the airline significant amounts of money in passenger layovers. Managers are paralyzed by anxiety, and many have been with the firm so long that they don't know how to set strategic goals that work. One-fifth of all flights lose money, and the company overall is near financial collapse (just three months to defaulting on payroll obligations). The newly hired CEO and you must get employees to quickly improve operational efficiency and customer service. What actions would you take to bring about these changes in time?

Self-Assessment 17.4

TOLERANCE OF CHANGE SCALE

PURPOSE This exercise is designed to help you understand how people differ in their tolerance for change.

INSTRUCTIONS Read each of the following statements and circle the response that best fits your personal beliefs. Then use the scoring key in Appendix B of this book to calculate your results. This self-assessment is completed alone so you can rate yourself honestly without concerns of social comparison. Class discussion will focus on the meaning of the concept measured by this scale and its implications for managing change in organizational settings.

After reading this chapter, if you feel that you need additional information, see www.mhhe.com/mcshane4e for more in-depth interactivities that correspond to this material.

Tolerance of Change

To what extent does each statement describe you? indicate your level of agreement by marking the appropriate response on the right	Strongly agree	Moderately agree	Slightly agree	Neutral	Slightly disagree	Moderately disagree	Strongly disagree
1. An expert who doesn't come up with a definite answer probably doesn't know too much.	☐	☐	☐	☐	☐	☐	☐
2. I would like to live in a foreign country for a while.	☐	☐	☐	☐	☐	☐	☐
3. There is really no such thing as a problem that can't be solved.	☐	☐	☐	☐	☐	☐	☐
4. People who fit their lives into a schedule probably miss most of the joy of living.	☐	☐	☐	☐	☐	☐	☐
5. A good job is one where it is always clear what is to be done and how it is to be done.	☐	☐	☐	☐	☐	☐	☐
6. It is more fun to tackle a complicated problem than to solve a simple one.	☐	☐	☐	☐	☐	☐	☐
7. In the long run, it is possible to get more done by tackling small, simple problems rather than large, complicated ones.	☐	☐	☐	☐	☐	☐	☐
8. Often the most interesting and stimulating people are those who don't mind being different and original.	☐	☐	☐	☐	☐	☐	☐
9. What we are used to is always preferable to what is unfamiliar.	☐	☐	☐	☐	☐	☐	☐
10. People who insist on a yes or no answer just don't know how complicated things really are.	☐	☐	☐	☐	☐	☐	☐
11. A person who leads an even, regular life in which few surprises or unexpected happenings arise really has a lot to be grateful for.	☐	☐	☐	☐	☐	☐	☐
12. Many of our most important decisions are based on insufficient information.	☐	☐	☐	☐	☐	☐	☐
13. I like parties where I know most of the people more than ones where all or most of the people are complete strangers.	☐	☐	☐	☐	☐	☐	☐
14. Teachers or supervisors who hand out vague assignments give people a chance to show initiative and originality.	☐	☐	☐	☐	☐	☐	☐
15. The sooner everyone acquires similar values and ideals, the better.	☐	☐	☐	☐	☐	☐	☐
16. A good teacher is one who makes you wonder about your way of looking at things.	☐	☐	☐	☐	☐	☐	☐

Source: Adapted from S. Budner, "Intolerance of Ambiguity as a Personality Variable," Journal of Personality 30 (1962), pp. 29–50.

additional cases

Case 1: ARCTIC MINING CONSULTANTS

Tom Parker enjoyed working outdoors. At various times in the past he had worked as a ranch hand, high steel rigger, headstone installer, prospector, and geological field technician. Now 43, Parker was a geological field technician and field coordinator with Arctic Mining Consultants. He had specialized knowledge and experience in all nontechnical aspects of mineral exploration, including claim staking, line cutting and grid installation, soil sampling, prospecting, and trenching. He was responsible for hiring, training, and supervising field assistants for all of Arctic Mining Consultants' programs. Field assistants were paid a fairly low daily wage (no matter how long they worked, which might be up to 12 hours or more) and were provided meals and accommodation. Many of the programs were operated by a project manager who reported to Parker.

Parker sometimes acted as a project manager, as he did on a job that involved staking 15 claims near Eagle Lake, Alaska. He selected John Talbot, Greg Boyce, and Brian Millar, all of whom had previously worked with Parker, as the field assistants. To stake a claim, the project team marked a line with flagging tape and blazes along the perimeter of the claim, cutting a claim post every 500 yards (called a "length"). The 15 claims would require almost 60 miles of line in total. Parker had budgeted seven days (plus mobilization and demobilization) to complete the job. This meant that each of the four stakers (Parker, Talbot, Boyce, and Millar) would have to complete a little over seven "lengths" each day. The following is a chronology of the project.

Day 1

The Arctic Mining Consultants crew assembled in the morning and drove to Eagle Lake, from where they were flown by helicopter to the claim site. On arrival they set up tents at the edge of the area to be staked and agreed on a schedule for cooking duties. After supper they pulled out the maps and discussed the job–how long it would take, the order in which the areas were to be staked, possible helicopter landing spots, and areas that might be more difficult to stake.

Parker pointed out that with only a week to complete the job, everyone would have to average seven and a half lengths per day. "I know that is a lot," he said, "but you've all staked claims before, and I'm confident that each of you is capable of it. And it's only for a week. If we get the job done in time, there's a $300 bonus for each man." Two hours later Parker and his crew members had developed what seemed to be a workable plan.

Day 2

Millar completed six lengths, Boyce six lengths, Talbot eight, and Parker eight. Parker was not pleased with Millar's or Boyce's production. However, he didn't make an issue of it, thinking they would develop their rhythm quickly.

Day 3

Millar completed five and a half lengths, Boyce four, and Talbot seven. Parker, who was nearly twice as old as the other three, completed eight lengths. He also had enough time remaining to walk over and check the quality of stakes that Millar and Boyce had completed, then walk back to his own area for helicopter pickup back to the tent site.

That night Parker exploded with anger. "I thought I told you that I wanted seven and a half lengths a day!" he shouted at Boyce and Millar. Boyce said that he was slowed down by unusually thick underbrush in his assigned area. Millar said that he had done his best and would try to pick up the pace. Parker did not mention that he had inspected their work. He explained that as far as he was concerned, the field assistants were supposed to finish their assigned area for the day, no matter what.

Talbot, who was sharing a tent with Parker, talked to him later. "I think that you're being a bit hard on them, you know. I know that it has been more by luck than anything else that I've been able to do my quota. Yesterday I had only five lengths done after the first seven hours and there was only an hour before I was supposed to be picked up. Then I hit a patch of really open bush and was able to do three lengths in 70 minutes. Why don't I take Millar's area tomorrow and he can have mine? Maybe that will help."

"Conditions are the same in all of the areas," replied Parker, rejecting Talbot's suggestion. "Millar just has to try harder."

Day 4

Millar did seven lengths and Boyce completed six and a half. When they reported their production that evening, Parker grunted uncommunicatively. Parker and Talbot did eight lengths each.

Day 5

Millar completed six lengths, Boyce six, Talbot seven and a half, and Parker eight. Once again Parker blew up, but he concentrated his diatribe on Millar. "Why don't you do what you say you are going to do? You know that you have to do seven and a half lengths a day. We went over that when we first got here, so why don't you do it? If you aren't willing to do the job, you never should have taken it in the first place!"

Millar replied by saying that he was doing his best, that he hadn't even stopped for lunch, and that he didn't know how he could possibly do any better. Parker launched into him again: "You have got to work harder! If you put enough effort into it, you will get the area done!"

Later Millar commented to Boyce, "I hate getting dumped on all the time! I'd quit if it didn't mean that I'd have to walk 50 miles to the highway. And besides, I need the bonus money. Why doesn't he pick on you? You don't get any more done than me; in fact, you usually get less. Maybe if you did a bit more he wouldn't be so bothered about me."

"I work only as hard as I have to," Boyce replied.

Day 6

Millar raced through breakfast, was the first one to be dropped off by the helicopter, and arranged to be the last one picked up. That evening the production figures were Millar eight and a quarter lengths, Boyce seven, and Talbot and Parker eight each. Parker remained silent when the field assistants reported their performance for the day.

Day 7

Millar was again the first out and last in. That night he collapsed in an exhausted heap at the table, too tired to eat. After a few moments he announced in an abject tone, "Six lengths. I worked like a dog all day and I got only a lousy six lengths!" Boyce completed five lengths, Talbot seven, and Parker seven and a quarter.

Parker was furious. "That means we have to do a total of 34 lengths tomorrow if we are to finish this job on time!" With his eyes directed at Millar, he added, "Why is it that you never finish the job? Don't you realize that you are part of a team, and that you are letting the rest of the team down? I've been checking your lines and you're doing too much blazing and wasting too much time making picture-perfect claim posts! If you worked smarter, you'd get a lot more done!"

Day 8

Parker cooked breakfast in the dark. The helicopter dropoffs began as soon as morning light appeared on the horizon. Parker instructed each assistant to complete eight lengths and, if they finished early, to help the others. Parker said that he would finish the other ten lengths. Helicopter pickups were arranged for one hour before dark.

By noon, after working as hard as he could, Millar had completed only three lengths. "Why bother," he thought to himself, "I'll never be able to do another five lengths before the helicopter comes, and I'll catch the same amount of abuse from Parker for doing six lengths as for seven and a half." So he sat down and had lunch and a rest. "Boyce won't finish his eight lengths either, so even if I did finish mine, I still wouldn't get the bonus. At least I'll get one more day's pay this way."

That night Parker was livid when Millar reported that he had completed five and a half lengths. Parker had done ten and a quarter lengths, and Talbot had completed eight. Boyce proudly announced that he finished seven and a half lengths, but he sheepishly added that Talbot had helped him with some of it. All that remained were the two and a half lengths that Millar had not completed.

The job was finished the next morning, and the crew demobilized. Millar has never worked for Arctic Mining Consultants again, despite being offered work several times by Parker. Boyce sometimes does staking for Arctic, and Talbot works full-time with the company.

Case 2: BIG SCREEN'S BIG FAILURE

Fiona McQuarrie, University College of the Fraser Valley

Bill Brosnan stared at the financial statements in front of him and shook his head. The losses from *Conquistadors,* the movie that was supposed to establish Big Screen Studios as a major Hollywood power, were worse than anyone had predicted. In fact, the losses were so huge that Brosnan's predecessor, Buck Knox, had been fired as a result of this colossal failure. Brosnan had wanted to be the head of a big movie production company for as long as he could remember, and he was thrilled to have been chosen by the board of directors to be the new president. But he had never expected that the first task in his dream job would be to deal with the fallout from one of the most unsuccessful movies ever.

The driving force behind *Conquistadors* was its director, Mark Frazier. Frazier had made several profitable movies for other studios and had a reputation as being a maverick with a "vision." He was a director with clearly formulated ideas of what his movies should look like, and he also had no hesitation about being forceful with producers, studios, actors, and technical staff to ensure that his ideas came to life as he envisioned them. For several years, while Frazier had been busy on other projects, he had also been working on a script about two Spanish aristocrats in the 16th century who set out for America to find riches and gold, encountering many amazing adventures on their travels. Frazier was something of an amateur historian, which led to his interest in the real-life stories of the Spanish conquistadors and bringing those stories to life for a 21st-century audience. But he also felt that creating an epic tale like this would establish him as a serious writer and filmmaker in the eyes of Hollywood, some of whose major powers had dismissed his past work as unimaginative or hackneyed.

When Big Screen Studios approached Frazier to see if he would be interested in working for them, the company was going through something of a rough spot. Through several years of hard work and mostly successful productions, Buck Knox, the president of Big Screen, had established Big Screen as a studio that produced cost-efficient and profitable films. The studio also had a good reputation for supporting the creative side of filmmaking; actors, writers, directors, and producers generally felt that Big Screen trusted them enough to give them autonomy in making decisions appropriate for their productions. (Other studios had reputations for keeping an overly tight rein on production budgets and for dictating choices based on cost rather than artistic considerations.) However, in the last two years Big Screen had invested in several major productions–a musical, a horror film, and the sequel to a wildly successful film adaptation of a comic book–that for various reasons had all performed well below expectations. Knox had also heard through the grapevine that several of the studio's board members were prepared to join together to force him out of the presidency if Big Screen did not come up with a hit soon.

Knox knew that Frazier was being wooed by several other studios for his next project, and he decided to contact Frazier to see if he was interested in directing any of the productions Big Screen was considering in the next year or so. After hearing Knox's descriptions of the upcoming productions, Frazier said, "What I'd really be interested in doing is directing this script I've been writing." He described the plot of *Conquistadors* to Knox, and Knox was enchanted by the possibilities–two strong male lead characters, a beautiful woman the men encountered in South America whose affections they fought over, battles, sea journeys, and challenging journeys over mountains and through jungles. However, Knox could also see that this movie might be extremely expensive to produce. He expressed this concern to Frazier, and Frazier replied, "Yes, but it will be an investment that will pay off. I know this movie will work. And I've mentioned it to two other studios and they are interested in it. I would prefer to make it with Big Screen, but if I have to, I will go somewhere else to get it made. That is how strongly I believe in it. However, any studio I work with has to trust me. I won't make the film without adequate financial commitment from the studio, I want final approval over casting, and I won't make the film if I don't get final cut." ("Final cut" means the director, not the studio, edits the version of the movie that is released to theaters, and the studio cannot release a version of the movie that the director does not approve.)

Knox told Frazier that he would get back to him later that week, and he asked Frazier not to commit to any other project until then. He spent several days mulling over the possibilities. Like Frazier, he believed that *Conquistadors* could be a huge success. It certainly sounded like it had more potential than anything else Big Screen had in development. However, Knox was still concerned about the potential cost and the amount of control over the project that Frazier was demanding. Frazier's reputation as a maverick meant that he likely would not compromise on his demands. Knox was also concerned about his own vulnerability if the movie failed. But on the other hand, Big Screen needed a big hit soon. Big Screen would look bad if it turned down *Conquistadors* and the movie became a gigantic hit for some other studio. Frazier had a respectable track record of producing moneymakers, so even if he might be difficult to work with, the end product usually was successful. At the end of the week Knox phoned Frazier and told him that Big Screen was willing to produce *Conquistadors.* Frazier thanked Knox, adding, "This film is going to redeem me, and it's going to redeem Big Screen as well."

Preproduction on the film started almost immediately after Frazier and the studio negotiated a budget of $50 million. This was slightly higher than Knox had anticipated, but he believed this was not an excessive amount to permit Frazier to realize the grand vision he had described. Knox further reassured himself by assigning John Connor, one of his trusted vice presidents, to act as the studio's liaison with Frazier and to be executive producer on the film. Connor was a veteran of many years in the movie production industry and was experienced in working with directors and budgets. Knox trusted Connor to make Frazier contain the costs of the production within the agreed limits.

The first major problem the film encountered involved casting. The studio gave Frazier final approval over casting as he had requested. Frazier's first signing was Cole Rogan, a famous action star, to be one of the male leads. The studio did not object to this choice; in fact, Knox and Connor felt that Rogan was an asset because he had a reputation as a star that could "open" a film (in other words, audiences would come to a movie just because he was in it). However, Frazier then decided to cast Frank Monaco as the other male lead. Monaco had made only a few films to date, and those were fluffy romantic comedies. Frazier said that Monaco would bring important qualities of vulnerability and innocence to the role, which would be a strong contrast to Rogan's rugged machismo. However, Connor told Knox that he saw two major problems with Monaco's casting: Monaco had never proven himself in an epic adventure role, and he was an accomplished enough actor that he would make the rather wooden Rogan look bad. Knox told Connor to suggest to Frazier that Rogan's role be recast. Unfortunately Frazier had signed Rogan to a "pay or play" deal, meaning that if the studio released Rogan from the project, the studio would have to pay him a considerable sum of money. Knox was somewhat bothered that Frazier had made this deal with Rogan without consulting either him or Connor. But he told Connor to instruct Frazier to release Rogan and recast the role, and the studio would just accept the payment to Rogan as part of the production costs. Although Frazier complained, he did as the studio asked and chose as a replacement Marty Jones, who had had some success in films but mostly in supporting roles. However, Jones was thrilled to be cast in a major role, and Connor felt that he would be capable of convincingly playing the part.

A few weeks after casting was completed, Connor called Knox and asked to see him immediately. "Buck," he told him once he arrived at Knox's office, "we have a really big problem." Connor said Frazier was insisting that the majority of the production be filmed in the jungles of South America, where most of the action took place, rather than on a studio soundstage or in a more accessible location that resembled the South American locale. Not only that, but Frazier was also insisting that he needed to bring along most of the crew that had worked on his previous films, rather than staffing the production locally. "Why does he want that? That's going to cost a hell of a lot," Knox said. "I know," Connor said, "but he says it's the only way the film is going to work. He says it just won't be the same if the actors are in a studio or in some swamp in the southern United States. According to him, the actors and the crew need to be in the real location to truly understand what the conquistadors went through, and audiences won't believe it's a real South American jungle if the film isn't made in one."

Knox told Connor that Frazier had to provide an amended budget to reflect the increased costs before he would approve the location filming. Connor took the request to Frazier, who complained that the studio was weakening its promise to support the film adequately, and added that he might be tempted to take the film to another studio if he was not allowed to film on location in South America. After a few weeks he produced an amended budget of $75 million. Knox was horrified that the budget for *Conquistadors* had grown by half in a few weeks. He told Connor that he would accept the amended budget only under two conditions: First, Connor would go on the location shoot to ensure that costs stayed within the amended budget, and second, if the costs exceeded Frazier's estimates, he would have to pay any excess himself. Frazier again complained that the studio was attempting to compromise his vision, but he grudgingly accepted the modified terms.

Frazier, Connor, and the cast and crew then headed off to the South American jungles for a scheduled two-month shoot. Immediately it became apparent that there was more trouble. Connor, who reported daily to Knox, told him after two weeks that Frazier was shooting scenes several times over—not because the actors or the crew were making mistakes or because there was something wrong with the scene, but because the output just didn't meet his artistic standards. This attention to detail meant that the filming schedule was nearly a week behind after only the first week's work. Also, because the filming locations were so remote, the cast and crew were spending nearly four hours of a scheduled seven-hour workday traveling to and from location, leaving only three hours in which they could work at regular pay rates. Work beyond those hours meant they had to be paid overtime; and because Frazier's demanding vision required shooting 10 or 12 hours each day, the production was incurring huge overtime costs. As if that wasn't bad enough, the "rushes" (the finished film produced each day) showed that Monaco and Jones didn't have any chemistry as a pair; and Gia Norman, the European actress Frazier had cast as the love interest, had such a heavy accent that most of her lines couldn't be understood.

Knox told Connor that he was coming to the location right away to meet with Frazier. After several days of arduous travel, Knox, Connor, and Frazier met in the canvas tent that served as the director's office in the middle of the jungle. Knox didn't waste any time with pleasantries. "Mark," he told Frazier, "there is no way you can bring this film in for the budget you have promised or within the deadline you agreed to. John has told me how this production is being managed, and it's just not acceptable. I've done some calculations, and at the rate you are going, this picture is going to cost $85 million and have a running time of four and a half hours. Big Screen is not prepared to support that. We need a film that's a commercially viable length, and we need it at a reasonable cost."

"It needs to be as long as it is," replied Frazier, "because the story has to be told. And if it has to cost this much, it has to cost this much. Otherwise it will look like crap and no one will buy a ticket to see it."

"Mark," replied Knox, "we are prepared to put $5 million more into this picture, and that is it. You have the choice of proceeding under those terms and keeping John fully aware of the costs so he can help you stay within the budget. If you don't agree to that, you can leave the production, and we will hire another director and sue you for breach of contract."

Frazier looked as though he was ready to walk into the jungle and head back to California that very minute, but the thought of losing his dream project was too much for him. He muttered, "OK, I'll finish it."

Knox returned to California, nursing several nasty mosquito bites, and Connor stayed in the jungle and reported to him regularly. Unfortunately it didn't seem like Frazier was paying much attention to the studio's demands. Connor estimated that the shoot would run three months rather than two, and that the total cost of the shoot would be $70 million. This left only $10 million of the budget for postproduction, distribution, and marketing, which was almost nothing for an epic adventure. To add to Knox's problems, he got a phone call from Richard Garrison, the chairman of Big Screen's board of directors. Garrison had heard gossip about what was going on with *Conquistadors* in the jungles of South America, and he wanted to know what Knox was going to do to curb Frazier's excesses. Knox told Garrison that Frazier was operating under clearly understood requirements, and that Connor was on the set to monitor the costs. Unfortunately, Knox thought, Connor was doing a good job of reporting, but he didn't seem to be doing much to correct the problems he was observing.

Frazier eventually came back to California after three and a half months of shooting, and he started editing the several hundred hours of film he had produced. Knox requested that Frazier permit Connor or himself to participate in the editing, but Frazier retorted that permitting that would infringe on his right to "final cut"; he refused to allow anyone associated with the studio to be in the editing room. Knox scheduled a release date for the film in six months' time and asked the studio's publicity department to start working on an ad campaign for the film; but not much could be done on either of these tasks without at least a rough cut of the finished product.

Three weeks into the editing, Connor called Knox. "I heard from Mark today," he said. "He wants to do some reshoots." "Is that a problem?" Knox asked. "No," said Connor, "most of it is interior stuff that we can do here. But he wants to add a prologue. He says that the story doesn't make sense without more development of how the two lead characters sailed from Spain to South America. He wants to hire a ship."

"He wants to WHAT?" exclaimed Knox.

"He wants to hire a sailing ship, like the conquistadors traveled on. There's a couple of tall ships that would do, but the one he wants is in drydock in Mexico and would cost at least a million to make seaworthy and sail up to Southern California. And that's on top of the cost of bringing the actors and crew back for a minimum of a week. I suggested to him that we try some special effects or a computerized animation for the scenes of the ship on the ocean, and shoot the shipboard scenes in the studio, but he says that won't be the same and it needs to be authentic."

At this point Knox was ready to drive over to the editing studios and take care of Frazier himself. Instead he called Garrison and explained the situation. "I won't commit any more money to this without the board's approval. But we've already invested $80 million into this already, so is a few more million that much of a deal if it gets the damn thing finished and gets Frazier out of our hair? If we tell him no, we'll have to basically start all over again, or just dump the whole thing and kiss $80 million goodbye." At the other end of the line, Garrison sighed, and said, "Do whatever you have to do to get it done."

Knox told Connor to authorize the reshoots, with a schedule of two months and the expectation that Frazier would have a rough cut of the film ready for the studio executives to view in three months. However, because of the time Frazier had already spent in editing, Knox had to change the release date, which meant changing the publicity campaign as well–and releasing the film at the same time that one of Big Screen's major competitors was releasing another epic adventure that was considered a surefire hit. However, Knox felt he had no choice. If he didn't enforce some deadline, Frazier might sit in the editing room and tinker with his dream forever.

Connor supervised the reshoots and reported that they went as well as could be expected. The major problem was that Gia Norman had had plastic surgery on her nose after the first shoot was completed, and she looked considerably different than she had in the jungles of South America. However, creative lighting, makeup, and costuming managed to minimize the change in her appearance. By all accounts the (very expensive) sailing ship looked spectacular in the rushes, and Frazier was satisfied that his vision had been sufficiently dramatized.

Amazingly, Frazier delivered the rough cut of the film at the agreed time. Knox, Connor, Garrison, and the rest of the studio's executives crowded into the screening room to view the realization of Frazier's dream. Five and a half hours later, they were in shock. No one could deny that the movie looked fantastic and that it was an epic on a grand scale. But there was no way the studio could commercially release a film that was over five hours long–plus Frazier had agreed to produce a movie that was at most two and a half hours long. Knox was at his wits' end. He cornered Garrison in the hallway outside the screening room. "Will you talk to Mark? He won't listen to me, he won't listen to John. But we can't release this. It won't work." Garrison agreed, contacting Frazier the next day. He reported back to Knox that Frazier, amazingly, had agreed to cut the film to two hours and fifteen minutes. Knox, heartened by this news, proceeded with the previously set release date, which by now was a month away, and got the publicity campaign going.

Two days before the scheduled release date, Frazier provided an advance copy of his shortened version of *Conquistadors* for a studio screening. Knox had asked him to provide a copy sooner, but Frazier said he could not produce anything that quickly. As a consequence, the version of the film that the studio executives were seeing for the first time was the version that already had thousands of copies duplicated for distribution to movie theaters all across North America. In fact, those copies were on their way by courier to the theaters as the screening started.

At the end of the screening, the studio executives were stunned. The movie was shorter, but now it made no sense. Characters appeared and disappeared randomly, the plot was impossible to follow, and the dialogue did not make sense at several key points in the small parts of plot that were discernible. The film was a disaster. Several of the executives present voiced the suspicion that Frazier had deliberately edited the movie this way to get revenge on the studio for not respecting his vision and forcing him to reduce the film's length. Others suggested that Frazier was simply a lunatic who never should have been given so much autonomy in the first place.

Knox, Garrison, and Connor held a hastily called meeting the next morning. What could the studio do? Recall the film and force Frazier to produce a more coherent shorter version? Recall the film and release the five-and-a-half-hour version? Or let the shorter version be released as scheduled and hope that it wouldn't be too badly received? Knox argued that the film should be recalled and Frazier should be forced to produce the product he agreed to produce. Connor said that he thought Frazier had been doing his best to do what the studio wanted, based on what Connor saw on the set, and that making Frazier cut the movie so short compromised the vision that Frazier wanted to achieve. He said the studio should release the long version and present it as a "special cinematic event." Garrison, as chairman of the board, listened to both sides, and after figuring out the costs of recalling and/or reediting the film–not to mention the less tangible costs of further worsening the film's reputation–said, "Gentlemen, we really don't have any choice. *Conquistadors* will be released tomorrow."

Knox immediately canceled the critics' screenings of *Conquistadors* scheduled for that afternoon so that bad reviews would not appear on the day of the film's release. Despite that preemptive step and an extensive advertising campaign, *Conquistadors* was a complete and utter flop. On a total outlay of $90 million, the studio recouped less than $9 million. The reviews of the film were terrible, and audiences just didn't arrive. The only place *Conquistadors* was even close to successful was in some parts of Europe, where film critics called the edited version an example of American studios' crass obsession with making money by compromising the work of a genius. The studio attempted to capitalize on this note of hope by releasing the five-and-a-half-hour version of *Conquistadors* for screening at some overseas film festivals and cinema appreciation societies; but the revenues from these screenings were so small that they made no difference to the overall financial results.

Three months after *Conquistadors* was released, Garrison called Knox in and told him he was fired. Garrison told Knox the board appreciated what a difficult production *Conquistadors* had been to manage, but that the costs of the production had been unchecked to a degree that the board no longer had confidence in Knox's ability to operate Big Screen Studios efficiently. Connor was offered a generous early retirement package, and he accepted it. The board then hired Bill Brosnan, a vice president at another studio, as Knox's replacement.

After reviewing *Conquistadors'* financial records and the notes that Knox had kept throughout the production, Brosnan was determined that a disaster like this would not undermine his career as it had Knox's. But what could he do to ensure this would not happen?

Case 3: HIGH NOON AT ALPHA MILLS

Arif Hassan and Thivagar Velayutham, International Islamic University Malaysia

Alpha Plantations was an oil palm plantation located in Malaysia. It consisted of an oil palm estate and one palm oil mill. It was a wholly owned subsidiary of a British multinational company and was founded with the purpose of supplying crude palm oil for its parent company's detergent manufacturing business. Since its formation, most of the managers had been recruited from the United Kingdom, with many British ex-soldiers and police officers joining up. Ang Siow Lee first joined Alpha Mill in 1965 at the age of 15 as a laborer, rising through the ranks to become the most senior nonmanagerial staff member in Alpha. Ang was now the senior production supervisor in Alpha's palm oil mill. His immediate superior was the mill manager, and he had two junior supervisors to assist him. The mill operated on a three-shift cycle of 25 operators each, and each supervisor (including Ang) was in charge of one shift.

Ang was responsible for the smooth daily palm oil processing operations. He coordinated the activities of all three shifts with the two supervisors, prepared the daily production reports, addressed short-term human resource planning issues and minor discipline issues, and set and evaluated short-term performance targets for the three shifts. In addition, he acted as the "gatekeeper": Any mill workers who wished to see the mill manager had to first see Ang, who tried to solve the problem, which could be anything from house repairs to a request for an advance on wages. Only in rare cases when Ang could not resolve the issue was the matter brought up to the mill manager. Ang ran a tight ship, and he never let anyone forget it. His superb technical competency helped him keep the mill in top shape. He was accustomed to receiving the highest appraisal ratings from the mill manager, who appreciated his firm, methodical, and almost militarily efficient way of running the mill.

The palm oil industry in Malaysia faced many challenges in 1999. World oil prices plunged due to oversupply; palm oil prices hit a 15-year low. This cut the profit margins of all palm oil producers and caused Alpha Mill to post losses regularly.

Captain Chubb, the 54-year-old ex–Royal Engineer and mill manager, had no idea how to improve performance. "We are doing nothing wrong, and have met all our efficiency targets. It's this market that is killing us!" he exasperatedly explained during the annual year-end visit of the directors from London. Soon Captain Chubb was given his marching orders. In early 2000 a new mill manager was appointed who was different from his predecessors. Ian Davison, a 32-year-old from Edinburgh, Scotland, was not a career plantation engineer and had never managed an agricultural product processing mill before. He was actually an electronics engineer with an Ivy League MBA on the fast track to a top management position. His previous appointment was as factory manager of a detergent factory in Egypt, where he managed to streamline and modernize operations and increase financial performance drastically. Headquarters in London hoped he would be able to do the same with Alpha Mill and return it to profitability. His first action was to analyze operations at Alpha Mill and look for ways to reduce production costs and increase profits. He arrived at the following conclusions:

- Current performance standards allowed too much machine breakdown and changeover time. Better standards were achievable with the latest technology.
- Waste could be reduced and yield improved drastically by installing machinery based on new technology.
- Personnel numbers were too high–they could be reduced with technology and multitasking and unleashing the full potential of workers.

- Personnel were just "cruising along"; they were not fully committed to achieving better performance.
- Hygiene needs were not being met.
- The old colonial, hierarchical company culture was not conducive to performance improvement.
- Information was not shared across the mill. Operators knew about only their own little areas in the mill and almost nothing about the company as a whole.

Davison proposed to remedy the situation with the following initiatives:

- Empower operators by reorganizing the shifts into self-directed production teams where the supervisors would now play the role of "facilitators," thereby gaining commitment.
- Install new technology and automation.
- Adopt more stringent performance measures.

Davison implemented and executed these initiatives by first organizing an excursion to a local picnic spot for the entire factory. After the icebreakers, games, and lunch, he held a briefing session on the beach, where he explained the situation Alpha Mill was in and the need to make changes. He then unveiled his plan. The response was enthusiastic, although some operators privately confessed to not understanding some of the terminology Davison used. At the end of the excursion, when there was some time allocated for feedback, Ang expressed his full support for Davison's plan. "We in Alpha Mill have full confidence in you, our new leader, and we assure you of our 110 percent support to make your plan a success!" he said at the end of his speech.

When the new machinery had been installed and each shift had been reorganized into self-directed work teams, the plan was put into motion. Whenever the team faced a problem during processing and tried to find a solution using the techniques that had been taught, Ang would step in after some time, issue instructions, and take over the process. "This is a simple problem, no need to waste time over it. Just do it . . ." His instructions were always followed, and the immediate problem was always solved. However, the production team reverted to the old ways of working, and none of the expected benefits of teaming were realized. Given the new tighter performance standards and reduced staffing levels, the teams consistently underperformed. Team meetings were one-way affairs where Ang would tell everyone else what had gone wrong.

Ang's response was to push himself harder. He was always the first to arrive and the last to leave. He would spend a lot of time troubleshooting process problems. He pushed his operators even harder, but he felt that he had less control over his operators now that they had direct access to the mill manager and most of their minor needs were taken care of by him. Sometimes he became annoyed at his operators' mistakes and would resort to shouting and cursing, which had the immediate effect of moving people in the direction he wanted. This was in contrast to the mere glare that would have sufficed previously.

The continued poor performance of Alpha Mill affected Ang's midyear appraisal rating, which fell from excellent to merely adequate. During the appraisal interview, an annoyed Davison bluntly told Ang that he needed to understand clearly what the initiatives were all about, and that he had to let the team take some responsibility, make mistakes, and learn from them. "With your knowledge of this mill, you should be able to provide them with all the technical input they need," he said. Davison also added, "It might help if you treated our people with a little more respect. We aren't living in the 1940s anymore, you know." Ang was thunderstruck by the appraisal but did not raise any objections on the spot. He silently deferred to Davison's judgment and promised to do better. He also reiterated his utmost support for Davison and his plan.

After the midyear appraisal there was a noticeable change in Ang's demeanor. He became very quiet and began to take a less active role in the daily running of the mill. He was superficially polite to the operators and answered most requests for help with "Get the team together and discuss it among yourselves. Show the boss that you can solve it for yourselves." At first the teams were at a loss and mill performance suffered badly, but within two weeks the teams had found their feet and performance began to improve. One of Ang's junior supervisors, Mr. Raman, was able to coordinate between production teams to ensure that the performance gains were maintained. The effect on Ang was devastating. He became withdrawn and began to drink more than usual. His presence at team meetings became a mere formality and he contributed next to nothing, taking a back seat to other team members. He spoke little to mill personnel and became a mere shadow of his former self.

Davison was aware of the changes taking place on the mill floor. He decided that it was time to remove Ang from his position. He began to plan for a reshuffling of Alpha Mill's organization chart where Ang would be promoted to the new position of mill executive, a staff position with a small pay raise. His responsibility would be to advise the mill manager on technical, quality, and efficiency problems faced by the mill. He would be assigned to carry out minor improvement projects and performance audits from time to time. Raman would be promoted to supervisor and would report directly to the mill manager. Ang would no longer have any line authority over the production team. This reorganization was quickly approved by the head office, and Davison proceeded to lay the groundwork for the announcements and the necessary paperwork. Little did he foresee what was to follow.

Ang was in the head office one morning when the personnel executive's clerk congratulated him on his imminent promotion. A surprised Ang inquired further and learned of the plans that Davison had in store for him. It was the final straw. He rushed back to Alpha Mill just as Davison was about to conduct his noon mill inspection. The confrontation was loud, acrimonious, and public. It ended with Ang being terminated for insubordination and gross misconduct.

After Ang had left, Davison felt that the obstacle to better commitment and morale was gone and that performance would improve greatly. He was wrong. Team performance began to deteriorate, and no amount of pep talks could improve it. He began to wonder what had gone wrong.

Case 4: KEEPING SUZANNE CHALMERS

Thomas Chan hung up the telephone and sighed. The vice president of software engineering at Advanced Photonics Inc. (API) had just spoken to Suzanne Chalmers, who had called to arrange a meeting with Chan later that day. She didn't say what the meeting was about, but Chan almost instinctively knew that Suzanne was going to quit after working at API for the past four years. Chalmers was a software engineer in Internet Protocol (IP), the software that directed fiber optic light through API's routers. It was very specialized work, and Suzanne was one of API's top talents in that area.

Thomas Chan had been through this before. A valued employee would arrange a private meeting. The meeting would begin with a few pleasantries; then the employee would announce that he or she wanted to quit. Some employees said they were leaving because of the long hours and stressful deadlines. They said they needed to decompress, get to know the kids again, or whatever. But that was not usually the real reason. Almost every organization in this industry was scrambling to keep up with technological advances and the competition. They would just leave one stressful job for another one.

Also, many of the people who left API joined a start-up company a few months later. These start-up firms could be pressure cookers where everyone worked 16 hours each day and had to perform a variety of tasks. For example, engineers in these small firms might have to meet customers or work on venture capital proposals rather than focus on specialized tasks related to their knowledge. API had over 1,000 employees, so it was easier to assign people to work matching their technical competencies.

No, the problem wasn't the stress or long hours, Chan thought. The problem was money—too much money. Most of the people who left were millionaires. Suzanne Chalmers was one of them. Thanks to generous stock options that had skyrocketed on the NASDAQ stock market, many employees at API had more money than they could use. Most were under 40 years old, so they were too young to retire. But their financial independence gave them less reason to remain with API.

The Meeting

The meeting with Suzanne Chalmers took place a few hours after the telephone call. It began like the others, with the initial pleasantries and brief discussion about progress on the latest fiber optic router project. Then Suzanne made her well-rehearsed statement: "Thomas, I've really enjoyed working here, but I'm going to leave Advanced Photonics." Suzanne took a breath, then looked at Chan. When he didn't reply after a few seconds, she continued, "I need to take time off. You know, get away to recharge my batteries. The project's nearly done and the team can complete it without me. Well, anyway, I'm thinking of leaving."

Chan spoke in a calm voice. He suggested that Suzanne take an unpaid leave for two or maybe three months, complete with paid benefits, then return refreshed. Suzanne politely rejected that offer, saying that she needed to get away from work for a while. Thomas then asked Suzanne whether she was unhappy with her work environment—whether she was getting the latest computer technology to do her work and whether there were problems with co-workers. The workplace was fine, Susanne replied. The job was getting a bit routine at times, but she had a comfortable workplace with excellent co-workers.

Chan then apologized for the cramped work space, due mainly to the rapid increase in the number of people hired over the past year. He suggested that if Suzanne took a couple of months off, API would have a larger work space with a better view of the park behind the campuslike building when she returned. She politely thanked Chan for that offer, but it wasn't what she needed. Besides, it wouldn't be fair to have a large work space when other team members worked in smaller quarters.

Chan was running out of tactics, so he tried his last hope: money. He asked whether Suzanne had higher offers. Suzanne replied that she regularly received calls from other companies, and some of them offered more money. Most were start-up firms that offered a lower salary but higher potential gains in stock options. Chan knew from market surveys that Suzanne was already paid well in the industry. He also knew that API couldn't compete on stock option potential. Employees working in start-up firms sometimes saw their shares increase by 5 or 10 times their initial value, whereas shares at API and other large firms increased more slowly. However, Chan promised Suzanne that he would recommend that she receive a significant raise—maybe 25 percent—and more stock options. Chan added that Chalmers was one of API's most valuable employees and that the company would suffer if she left the firm.

The meeting ended with Chalmers promising to consider Chan's offer of higher pay and stock options. Two days later Chan received her resignation in writing. Five months later Chan learned that after a few months of travel with her husband, Chalmers joined a start-up software firm in the area.

Case 5: MAGIC CABLE

Joseph Kavanaugh, Henry S. Maddux III, and Harry Gene Redden, Sam Houston State University

"I think I've found what I'm looking for," Gary Roberts said.

"Oh yeah, what is that?" Jim Handley asked, as he handed Roberts a pair of vise-grip pliers.

"I'm thinking I might have found a way out of this dump. No more tile dust, no more 40-mile-an-hour winds blowing through the plant, and no more Al Wright for me," Roberts replied.

Wright, the plant manager, and Roberts, maintenance mechanic for Tile-Elite, had been at odds for years. Roberts had been hired during a manufacturing plant expansion at Tile-Elite, and Wright had promised Roberts a production supervisor's job upon its completion. However, when the expansion was completed and the last production line was ready, Wright told Roberts to forget the supervisor's job because he was more valuable to the company as a maintenance mechanic.

"I know what I said, Gary, but I think you're going to be a mechanic here even if you stay 20 years," Wright had stated at the time.

After that encounter almost five years ago, Wright and Roberts had mixed like oil and water. Roberts had to admit that he was probably more valuable to the company as a maintenance mechanic in the short run, but he had been looking at the long run. He wanted to be more involved in the production process. He had just turned 40, was recently divorced, and had been involved in maintenance of some type since his military service in Vietnam 20 years earlier. While working full-time at his previous job, Roberts had completed his bachelor's degree in business. His major had been management, and it had taken him six long years to graduate. He had then wanted a position where he could use his management education. The company for which he was working while going to school had promised him a supervisor's position when he graduated, but that promise had evaporated when the company went bankrupt during the oil recession of the 1980s.

During his years with Tile-Elite Roberts had searched for another company that would give him a chance as a supervisor, but it seemed no one wanted a man his age with minimal management experience. The oil recession had left the employment market flooded with unemployed managers with significant supervisory experience. Consequently Roberts decided he would stick with what he knew best, maintenance, because jobs were more plentiful and the pay was reasonably good.

"Magic Cable in Fresno is looking for a maintenance mechanic. I've got an interview tomorrow morning," Roberts said to Handley.

"I've seen their plant over on Cook Street, behind the county barn, but I've never been in it. What do they build there?" Handley asked.

"Shoot, I don't know and I don't really care. All machines are alike. Just some are bigger than other ones, so my job will be basically the same. What I want is better working conditions and a chance for advancement. I'd even take a slight cut in pay to get out of here," Roberts answered.

"I understand where you're coming from, but don't tell Magic Cable that! Well, good luck tomorrow, Gair. I hope you get that job," Handley said as he closed his toolbox and started moving toward the time clock.

Roberts hated it when Handley called him "Gair". It sounded so trite. The only reason he hadn't said something was because Jim was such a good friend and he had taught him a lot.

Magic Cable was just two miles farther from Roberts's home than Tile-Elite. The facility was considerably smaller, but the grounds were kept neatly trimmed, and Roberts considered that a good sign. The parking was also directly in front of the plant, which would be good during bad weather.

"I've got a good feeling about this place," Roberts muttered to himself as he drove through the gate.

After parking in a vacant visitor parking space, Roberts gathered his resume and the completed employment application, took a couple of deep breaths, and headed toward the door labeled "Personnel." Once inside, all he saw was a doorbell mounted on a wall, a door with a peephole and mail slot, and a poster that displayed a picture of the building and a narrative describing the company's history. The poster was on the outside wall opposite the bell. Above the doorbell was a small sign: "Ring for Personnel." There was also a sign below the button that read, "We are NOT accepting applications." The word "not" was hanging loosely so it could be removed if needed. "Lucky I've got an appointment," Roberts thought.

After pushing the button produced no sound, Roberts said out loud to himself, "Just my luck. The stupid thing is broken and no one even knows I'm here."

Almost immediately the door opened partially and a neatly dressed young woman stuck her head out and asked, "Gary Roberts?" Roberts nodded his head in reply. "Bill Lindsey, the manufacturing engineer, will be right with you," she added before shutting the door again.

"Great, more waiting," Roberts thought. After looking around the sparsely furnished lobby for a minute, Roberts occupied himself by reading the narrative written on the poster. It said Magic Cable had been started in a small warehouse in Oakland in 1977 by a group of friends with a good idea. They started manufacturing throttle and drive cables for outdoor equipment. The business grew very fast, and in 1979 the plant was moved to Fresno. Now they were producing push–pull cables for cars and aircraft with a workforce consisting of about 300 employees.

Just as Roberts finished reading the poster, the inside door swung open a second time and a tall gray-haired man in an open-collared shirt emerged.

"Hi, I'm Bill Lindsey, the manufacturing engineer. You must be Gary Roberts. Come in here." As Roberts edged through the door, Lindsey added, "We need to go up and meet Bob Walters. He's our manufacturing manager. We'll both be interviewing you." And with that Lindsey turned to go up the set of stairs to his right. "Have you ever met Bob Walters?"

Roberts remembered seeing Bob Walters's name on the list of people who started Magic Cable. "No, sir, I haven't," he answered.

"He's kind of rough around the edges, so don't let him run you off," Lindsey said with a wry smile. Roberts smiled back and said that he wouldn't.

Lindsey and Roberts went up one flight of stairs and proceeded down the hall. One wall of the corridor was glass, and Roberts could see the entire production floor. The floor was organized into small production cells. Each group of operators in a work cell was busy at their machines doing their individual tasks. He noticed that many of the workers were female and of various minorities.

"They really look overworked, don't they?" Lindsey asked while showing a slight sarcastic smile. Roberts noticed that Lindsey walked with a slight limp. He had to make a conscious effort to walk slowly and not pass him. "He must be disabled somehow," Roberts thought to himself. Magic Cable appeared to be a lot different than the ceramic tile plant with all of its dust, heat, noisy conveyors, and frantic production pace. Gary Roberts had his second good feeling about Magic Cable.

As the pair approached the third office, Gary noticed the expression on Bill Lindsey's face change. It became somber, almost showing agony. Lindsey turned and knocked on the door facing the hall. Roberts maintained his position behind Lindsey while they both stood quietly and waited to be acknowledged.

"Bill, ya'll come on in," the man inside the office said. As Lindsey and Roberts entered the office, Bob Walters rose so he could shake Roberts's hand. "This is Gary Roberts, Bob. He's here to interview for the mechanic position."

"Great, have a seat, Gary," said Walters, gesturing to an empty office chair across from his desk. He was a good bit taller than Roberts and appeared to be in his middle fifties. He was dressed in Western style and had an air of arrogance in his manner and speech, which gave Gary an uneasy feeling.

"First, Gary, tell me why you want to leave Tile-Elite," Walters said. In reply Roberts described the working conditions at Tile-Elite, explaining that there was no overtime and little chance for advancement. He purposely omitted his feeling about Al Wright, the plant manager. Walters sat almost motionless and listened.

"What about the people you work for?" Walters asked, expecting Roberts to add to his explanation. So Roberts related that he and management had had some differences, but said that he preferred not to expound upon them. Walters seemed satisfied with that explanation. He knew Gary's present boss personally and understood the problems. He also knew that if Gary had said there were no problems, he would have been lying, and there was no room at Magic Cable for a liar.

Walters began to explain what Magic Cable had to offer a plant employee. He compared Magic Cable to the tile plant. Magic Cable's working conditions were fairly pleasant. He described how the building was air-conditioned, clean, and reasonably quiet. Maintenance staff members always got overtime because they were required to work six shifts of 10 hours each per week, with no exceptions. If the production floor was not working, maintenance people could always find something to do. The hourly pay was not quite up to Tile-Elite's level, but Walters explained that Roberts could expect to catch up in salary after a 90-day probationary period. Magic Cable paid an incentive bonus every three months, and the maintenance department was included in that program.

"I've got one final question," Walters added. "How do you feel working with women? We have around 150 women on first shift and about 100 on second shift, so if there's going to be a problem in that area, I need to know it now."

"It's not a problem for me. I don't believe in dating anyone where I work," Roberts replied.

"Great, as far as I'm concerned you've got the job if you want it. What do you think, Bill?" Walters said, after turning to face Lindsey.

"Sounds great to me. Gary, you ready for work?" Lindsey asked.

"Let me give Tile-Elite a week's notice and I'll be here with bells on," Roberts answered, smiling broadly.

Roberts loved his new job. When people asked him what he did at Magic Cable, he would reply that he was semiretired. The work was easy, the machines were simple, and the 60 hours a week did wonders for his bank account. On the sixth day, Saturday, most of his time was spent in the machine shop teaching himself to run the machines. He had some small conflicts with the way things were run, but nothing serious. The most significant problem was that he wanted to be given formal training relating to the new electronics being integrated into production processes. However, Magic Cable had shown no interest in providing that training. Roberts hoped that attitude would change. He knew he had to have patience.

As the months passed, the machine repair procedures became routine. As a result the days became boring, and the sixth 10-hour shift of every week felt more like 20 hours. Roberts suggested to his maintenance supervisor that the mechanics could take turns being off on Saturday. That would give everyone some recreational time and save Magic Cable some money.

When the supervisor voiced the proposal to Walters, he went ballistic. He did not bother relaying his reply through the supervisor; he came to the floor himself to find Roberts. As the manager quickly strode through the maintenance shop gate with the supervisor right behind him, Roberts thought to himself, "Uh-oh!"

Walters stopped in front of the workbench where Roberts was putting seals in a gearbox. He pointed his finger at the mechanic and said tensely, "When you came to work here you agreed to work six 10-hour shifts a week, and that is what you are going to work. The choice is not yours. If you do not want to live up to your agreement, you need to load up your toolbox and move on."

Roberts had no reply other than a rather weak "Yes, sir." With that response, Walters turned and left the maintenance shop without speaking another word.

For the next two years Roberts and the other members of the maintenance department worked within the work schedule guidelines set by Walters. Although some weekends off would have been nice, the steady overtime pay enabled them to have a higher standard of living. One mechanic purchased a newer, larger home, and Roberts purchased the new sports car he had been wishing for.

Then one Monday morning a new production supervisor, Dale Wood, met Roberts at the time clock just inside the plant door. He appeared to be a different type of person than Walters. Wood handed Roberts a white sheet of paper folded in half so that the print was covered. As he did this, he said, "This memo outlines the new policy covering the work schedule of the maintenance department and machine shop. Rick Tanal is over the maintenance department and the machine shop from now on. He broke the news to me this morning and told me to pass it on to you and the other guys."

Tanal was the plant manager. He was a retired major from the military and had a terrible attitude toward the guys, but he was sweet as sugar to the girls. One indicator of his personality was that he would shoot armadillos and rabbits while hunting on the company deer lease with his .458 magnum rifle (elephant gun) and then brag to everyone about how many pieces they were blown into. Roberts disliked him immensely and did not try to hide it. His "big me, little you" attitude had caused more than a few problems and clashes with male employees. His favorite reply, when asked about something the company had promised but had not delivered, was "You got that in writing?" The hourly personnel had not signed a contract, so their answer was always no. His typical comment was that if the promise was not in writing it was not binding.

Roberts opened the folded sheet and read the memo. It stated that as of the previous Friday evening the maintenance department and the machine shop were not part of engineering anymore; they were now a part of the production department. The memo also stated that the personnel in those two departments would be limited to 40 hours of work per week for an indefinite period. As he read the memo, Roberts's temperature skyrocketed. He yelled, almost screamed, several vulgar words and made derogatory statements concerning Tanal and his parentage as he headed for the production office.

When Roberts got to Tanal's office he did not even knock on the door. He rushed in through the doorway, causing the plant manager to abruptly stop a telephone conversation in midsentence.

Holding the memo up in Tanal's face, he asked, "What the hell is this crap?"

"New orders from the front office," Tanal replied, smiling slightly. Tanal told the party on the other end of the phone line goodbye and hung up the phone.

"This is not what I agreed on when I went to work here. Bob Walters said that overtime was a requirement of the job. When I tried to get him to cut the hours back, he threatened to fire me," Roberts almost yelled.

"That is in the past and has nothing to do with what is required at this time," Tanal answered. "You and the rest of the department need to learn how to live on 40 hours a week," he continued. "If you had been doing that all along, you would not be hurt by the cutback in working hours."

"I don't know who the hell you think you are, but don't tell me how to live. I spend as I see fit, whether I make my money here. . . or somewhere else." Roberts paused, and then added, "I'll tell you what, I'll give you a week, unless you don't want it, then I'm out of here."

"Are you saying that you quit?" Tanal asked.

"That's what I'm saying. I don't want to work for a thief, and I consider you a thief," Gary stated.

"A thief. How do you get that?" Tanal asked.

"Whenever you take something away you promised without discussing it, you're stealing–and that's what you did. As far as I'm concerned, you stole my overtime hours from me, which amounts to about half of my check, " Roberts returned.

Tanal did not have a chance to reply to this conjecture because Roberts turned abruptly and exited the office.

Roberts worked his last week grudgingly. He did not want to stay at Magic Cable, but he said he would, so he did. By the end of the week he had secured a job as a line mechanic for a local bottling plant, loaded his toolboxes in his truck, and moved on.

Case 6: MEXFABRICS

*Martha Burkle, Monterrey Institute of Technology**

Juan Diego Martinez watched the sunset over the city of Guadalajara. It was not only the heat that made the human resources manager at MexFabrics sweat during the day. Production orders from headquarters in Mexico City were far more a problem for him. After the Easter holidays another seven workers had quit work without a particular reason. High turnover of MexFabrics' production employees, most of whom were women, had been a constant problem since Martinez started his job two years ago. Now the problem had turned into a serious matter threatening the company's reputation. How could he finish orders on time and also maintain high standards of quality without the experienced people he needed? The work was highly dependent on handwork because automation was almost nonexistent in most of the small manufacturing plants in Mexico; and MexFabrics' most important competitive advantage was the high quality of its products.

People at the head office in Mexico City expected excellent results this year, and Martinez knew that this could not be achieved until he solved the problem of the high staff turnover. He thought that this was especially difficult looking at the personal situations of many of his female workers and the specific context in Mexico. A strategy had to be developed whereby the situation was radically improved and a stable, well-trained, experienced workforce established.

MexFabrics: The Company

The company had started its operation in 1938 by importing fine Italian, French, and Spanish ties under the names of several recognized brands. Years after that the MexFabrics group decided to manufacture high-quality ties in Mexico. By the 1970s the company's production became an addition to the already large clothes manufacturing industry in Mexico, which had begun in 1966 with the purpose of promoting foreign investment and technology transfer in the country. Manufacturing industries in Mexico had enjoyed a large growth spurt during the 1990s, supported by the implementation of NAFTA, foreign investment from other countries (particularly the United States, Canada, and Japan), and cheap hand labor. Currently there were over 4,500 garment manufacturing plants employing over 2 million people in Mexico. So MexFabrics had entered an already large industry sector. Over the years compatible products were added to the line of ties: fine shirts, trousers, cuff links, belts, and scarves.

Now MexFabrics was one of the largest and best-known manufacturers of fine clothes in Mexico. The company manufactured and marketed 30 different high-quality products for men. In total, the company employed 1,000 people in Mexico, of which almost 400 manufactured 80 percent of the products in Guadalajara. The operations were divided between formal and casual wear, which were then further divided into several subgroups. In both fields shirts and ties were among the most important products. Last year MexFabrics had sold around a million articles with a sales volume of more than 300 million Mexican pesos (30 million US dollars). Shirts represented 35 percent of sales, followed by ties with 30 percent and trousers with 15 percent. MexFabrics was the number one supplier to the two largest mall chains in Mexico in relation to sales and prestige.

The work performed at MexFabrics could appear easy and repetitive; employees simply received raw materials, and after sewing and cutting, a final piece of work was produced. But nothing was further from the truth. In fact, being an employee at MexFabrics was a challenging task. The manufacture of quality clothing demands high levels of employee skills and special abilities supported by regular training to be able to produce a high-quality piece quickly.

Operations and Human Resources Challenges for Group MexFabrics

In 1991 the first shirt factory of the group was built in Guadalajara in response to the company's need to offer better service to the group and to improve quality control standards. In 1994 the leather and ties factory was transferred from Mexico City to Guadalajara, and in 1997 the plant for casual shirts and trousers began operations. Daily production in these plants consisted of approximately 1,300 shirts, 1,200 ties, 300 trousers, and 950 leather products such as belts and wallets.

The production process started with the production order, which documented the specifications and quantities, and the receipt of the raw material, which was imported from Italy, France, or Spain and received at the general warehouse in Mexico City. After the first quality inspection, the raw materials were sent to production, where the forms were designed and the product fabricated. Product quality was maintained by frequently inspecting random samples throughout the production process.

After packing, products were sent to the distribution center in Guadalajara and then shipped to the different outlets around Mexico.

MexFabrics had recently experienced a number of challenges and opportunities regarding employees. The high turnover among personnel (up to 20 percent per month by the end of 2004) threatened product quality as inexperienced employees filled jobs vacated by expert staff. The problem of fulfilling the planned production output, together with the time required for recruiting new personnel, was also putting a great deal of pressure on plant managers and on the human resources manager.

MexFabrics received many job applicants, but selecting the appropriate personnel for the demanding production process was a difficult task. Out of every 100 applications, the human resources department in Guadalajara selected about 50 for individual interviews and chose about 10 people for employment in the plants. There they received specific training in manufacturing MexFabrics' different products, from shirts to trousers. After about two weeks of this training, the new recruits began working in assigned production jobs, receiving advice and instruction for several more weeks. It took about six months for a typical worker to be fully trained.

All workers received salary increases based on the number of weeks they had worked for the company. These increases were proportional to the country's general inflation rate. To give an example, during the first semester last year, inflation had been 0.8 percent. So after 8 weeks the salary increased 0.5 percent, and this increase reached 1 percent after 48 weeks. After that the salary increase policy was replaced by a bonus policy that encouraged employees' loyalty to the company over a period of 18 months. Employees also received bonuses for punctuality and attendance. Moreover, there was an incentive for the different operation units, trousers or belts for example, in which workers earned more money by improving productivity (total pieces produced per person-hour). However, employees seldom received these productivity bonuses because high turnover kept productivity too low.

MexFabrics' Organizational Culture

Buses operated on specific routes every morning to facilitate workers' transportation to the plant. For those who lived far from the bus routes, a certain amount of money was designated to pay for public transportation. Because women represented a large percentage of the workforce, MexFabrics had a child care center, which was offered to workers who had been employed for at least five years in the company and had a good work record. This strategy created satisfaction among the women who could enjoy the benefit but was not well seen by those who were still new to the company. Moreover, to reduce the turnover of workers during the first weeks while they were still in training, MexFabrics paid a special bonus for those who learned their jobs quickly.

An internal magazine promoted MexFabrics' organizational culture. Boards across the plant also stated the company's values and mission: to be a flexible, dynamic, and efficient company that responded to market needs. Distributed information also promoted employee loyalty to the company.

However, promoting loyalty was a difficult task for the HR department. Low literacy skills and lack of responsibility seemed to be a constant characteristic among many manufacturing employees in developing countries. Coming from poor families, many employees just wanted to survive day-to-day and had no vision of the possibilities that working in the sector could give them, such as skills development and economic stability.

Personal problems among the workers or social problems within their households were seen as the main reasons for the high turnover, resulting in a shortage of experienced personnel. Many employees lacked the necessary education to perform the work, whereas others lacked commitment to the company. Often without any reason people would fail to show up for work for a day or would suddenly quit. There was an urgent need to analyze and overcome these problems.

Martinez, MexFabrics' human resources manager, was not too keen to go to bed that night; he knew the problem of chronic employee turnover would not let him sleep well. At a meeting scheduled on Monday morning, MexFabrics' directors expected Martinez to outline a decisive strategy to significantly reduce turnover. He would certainly present some things that he thought were crucial. But within the context of the firm, the economic and social climate of Mexican industry, and the day-to-day personal and social challenges experienced by the mainly female workers, things were not always so easy to realize.

*Jaschar Saedi of the Otto Beisheim Graduate School of Management, Germany, assisted in developing this case study.

Case 7: NIRVANA ART GALLERY

Christine Ho, University of Adelaide

It was an irony not lost on many of the employees of Nirvana Art Gallery. This gallery was far from being a place of harmony and joy. In fact, some of the employees preferred to refer to management using the acronym "NAG" in a derogatory manner.

Nirvana was regarded as one of the leading art museums in Australia. The collection of Australian art was one of the oldest and best known in the country. This museum also housed an enviable aboriginal collection and an international collection of considerable breadth and depth.

Rod was the assistant curator for the curatorial unit. Despite his job title, his time was divided between the curatorial and research units because there was not enough work in the former to keep him occupied from week to week. It was agreed between the managers of the two units that he work Mondays through Wednesdays at curatorial and then the remaining days at research. Although Rod would have preferred to work solely for curatorial because that was where his interests lay, he was in no position to argue with either manager. He hoped that when he finished his PhD in art history he would be employed full-time in curatorial, where he could fully use his specialized knowledge and meet his aspiration to be a curator.

Rod did not particularly enjoy coming to work on Thursdays. The research he was asked to do was okay. It was not that stimulating, but he convinced himself that it was useful to understand the functions of the different units in the gallery and not restrict himself to purely curatorial issues. The research unit was quite small, and the staff were very serious. Because they were located within close proximity to each other, he tried initially to be friendly to them while they worked.

When he kept getting frowns and annoyed looks from his colleagues, it became obvious that they did not like being interrupted. Further, they assumed he did not have enough work to do, so they kept giving him more tasks. Rod found himself falling behind and having to ask for permission to stay late to finish his work. Because the gallery housed expensive art works, security was tight. All staff members were expected to leave by 5 p.m. and not return until the following morning after 8 a.m. Managers were strict about granting this special permission because security had to be notified so that alarm systems could be adjusted and monitored accordingly. Because the research manager, Nelly, often stayed late she did not mind granting Rod permission as well.

On Friday morning Rod met with Nelly to give her the report he had written about business plans.

"Thanks Rod, it looks good," said Nelly, as she flipped through the document. "You're still working on that draft document on the current spending and budget allocation for this year, aren't you? Andrew can help you with this."

Rod hesitated. "Oh, I think I have all the necessary information, and I'm sure Andrew is busy anyway. If I stay late tonight, I might be able to give it to you before I leave work."

"What's wrong?" asked Nelly.

"It's nothing. I just always get the impression that I'm disturbing everyone in research. They seem really busy all the time and don't seem to have time for anything else. I'm more of a sociable and friendly person, and I like to talk with others while I work."

Nelly gave him a look that Rod did not know how to decipher. I hope she does not think I am complaining about my job or my colleagues, Rod thought to himself as he walked out of her office. He liked the fact that no one was breathing down his neck all the time. And the last thing he needed was to create animosity between himself and the rest of research. It was bad enough that they always went out for lunch together and never invited him. But at least they could say hello whenever he was there.

The following Thursday, when Nelly came into the research area to talk to one of the researchers, she came by his desk to say that she had read both his reports that he finished last week, thanked him for his hard work, and asked how his work was going. He appreciated the attention. Over the following weeks when he was in research, she would come by and talk to him. This sometimes included complimenting him on his appearance. How his shirt color emphasized his eyes, or his new stylish haircut made him look more handsome. At least someone was talking to me, thought Rod. He did not think her comments were appropriate, but he accepted them graciously with a smile, making sure he kept his comments professional. He also tried to minimize how often he had to stay late at work so as not to give the wrong impression. But usually that was not possible given his workload.

It was not long before the other researchers noticed the attention she gave him. He started noticing the surreptitious looks and frowns he received whenever she spoke to him. Rod thought he was being paranoid. A couple of times when he had walked into the research area, some of the researchers were talking in low voices, but they would stop when they noticed him.

Rod wondered what was going on. It was not like he was not pulling his own weight around here. He got the projects done on time even though he worked only two days each week in research, and Nelly had told him numerous times that he was doing a good job. Rod put his thoughts aside and focused on his day's tasks. He went home that weekend pleased for once that he did not have to work late.

He arrived at work on Monday in good spirits. He had studied all weekend and nearly completed his final draft of his PhD thesis. He always enjoyed working in the curatorial unit. He found his work preparing upcoming exhibitions interesting. Further, he liked the curatorial team. His manager, Sarah, was approachable; and despite his being the most junior team member, his colleagues regularly asked for his input during the weekly Monday meetings. The team was friendly, and he found he had a lot in common with many of them. Sometimes he would be invited to lunch when he was there on one of his curatorial days. Working in curatorial also meant that he was not in research. He would not have to put up with Nelly's comments, which were beginning to really make him feel uncomfortable, and he did not have to put up with the whispers or silent stares he got from his research colleagues. Rod was looking forward to working on a catalog for an aboriginal exhibition the gallery was to host next month when Nelly walked in.

"Rod, you're looking sexy today. Andrew is away sick. Can you come and work in research today?" she asked.

"Um, I can't, Nelly. I'm supposed to work in curatorial today, and it's really busy at the moment. We've got this exhibition coming up and we're behind. Claire is on maternity leave, and two others in curatorial are sick as well with that flu that's going around at the moment. Sorry, but I can't."

Nelly frowned and left without a backward glance. I'll be at research soon enough on Thursday anyway, thought Rod.

Later that day Rod received an e-mail message from Nelly:

Rod,

There has been a change in your work arrangement to start this week. The assistant director and I have decided that instead of working in curatorial three days and research two days, you will now work in curatorial only two days, and then on Wednesday switch over to research for the rest of the week.

Nelly.

Rod began to feel panicky. The whole point of this job was to gain curatorial experience, which was why he had changed his PhD status to part-time. He went to see Sarah to see if she could get his work days changed back. Unfortunately Sarah just confirmed the arrangement.

"There's nothing I can do about this, Rod. I wish I could, but Nelly helped me get this job. You're a valuable member of curatorial, and we both know everyone on the team is flat out with the others away sick or on leave. Nelly has more authority than me and is good friends with the assistant director."

When Rod arrived in research on Wednesday, Nelly told him that the desk arrangements were to be changed around. His desk was now visible from her office at all times. Other things began to change in research as well. Nelly rarely spoke to him except to pass on job assignments. And because he was there an extra day each week, he was able to complete his tasks without having to stay after hours. Rod was pleased about that. However, as the weeks passed, there were not enough tasks to keep him occupied, and he was told to find something to do. He felt as if he was wasting his time, especially because curatorial continued to be short-staffed and research was now brimming with staff and limited work. Rod hated that sometimes he had to pretend to be busy.

To make matters worse, when he would arrive at work Nelly had started to remark, "So *now* you've decided to turn up to work" or "Getting your beauty sleep, were we?" His fellow researchers began to chime in with similar snide remarks, like "While you've been having your coffee, we've been at work since 8 a.m."

It was getting unbearable in research for Rod. Even though his colleagues were talking to him now, he much preferred it when they were not.

Rod was unhappy. He was at lunch with some of the curatorial staff and told them about the e-mail message.

"You'll just have to do the time with research and hope that you get back on the good side of Nelly. She may eventually change things back so that you can work more in curatorial. She's a NAG who likes to use her power over others. It's happened before."

Case 8: WOODLAND COMMUNITY CENTER CORPORATION

Joseph C. Santora, Essex County College & TST, Inc.

Fred Chambers, the recently appointed executive director of the Woodland Community Center Corporation (WCCC), leaned back in his overstuffed executive chair and contemplated his new job. At 60 years old, he felt young and fit. His career as a nonprofit executive director had spanned more than 25 years at five diverse nonprofit organizations. Once he believed his job was done at an organization, he moved on to accept the challenges of a new executive position. Most of all, Chambers resisted complacency, and he wanted to avoid getting stale in the saddle.

After retiring about four years ago, Chambers heard the trumpet's call to lead once again, so he sought short-term or interim leadership positions in nonprofit organizations. He enjoyed the challenges of the unique organizational niche he had carved out for himself. His last three interim executive director appointments had lasted six months, two years, and one year respectively and served both him and the hiring boards of directors well. By hiring Chambers on an interim basis, boards of directors, many of whom lacked the foresight to prepare an executive succession plan, could conduct a more thorough executive search for a permanent replacement rather than hastily appointing someone who did not fit the organization.

Once appointed, Chambers was given carte blanche by the boards to make the necessary internal organizational changes; and despite some initial rocky starts, things had worked out well for both him and the nonprofits he led. Chambers got an opportunity to travel to different locations throughout the country, met some interesting people, received a lucrative compensation package, and enjoyed a fixed-term contract agreement; on the other hand, the boards got the opportunity to hire an outsider–someone with diversified senior administrative experiences–to develop and implement a strategy for organizational change. The overall assessment of

Chambers as a "gun for hire" by his various board employers was quite respectable.

But unlike past situations, Chambers felt uneasy about this new executive appointment. This time, against his wife's advice, he had taken a full-time permanent executive director position as a replacement for Alain Yates, the articulate, charismatic, long-term executive director at the WCCC. From time to time, the community center board had heard some internal rumblings about the organizational culture at the agency, but it failed to act because Yates held considerable power over the board as a result of his longevity in office and the constant turnover of board members. Chambers's appointment as executive director signaled the community center board's earnest desire to change the organizational culture at the agency. As Chambers conducted his fact-finding mission, he uncovered what the board in general seemed to know about the organizational culture: Yates had encouraged policies of "double standards" that demotivated some long-term and industrious agency employees. Perhaps Chambers should have heeded his wife's warning about taking a full-time position. After assessing his situation, he now thought, "Be careful what you wish for–you just might get it."

Gail Katz, a social worker, had founded the Woodland Community Center Corporation (WCCC) in 1926 to deliver a variety of social and human services to the indigent population of Woodland, an East Coast seaport city. Over time the organization had a series of executive directors. Alain Yates had been the longest-reigning executive director and had led the WCCC for the past 25 years. Yates assumed the leadership of the agency after a tumultuous internal struggle almost caused the agency to cease operations. He gained support for the position from several powerful administrative and staff members in the agency. This internal groundswell forced the board of directors to appoint Yates as the executive director of the agency. Once the board approved his three-year contract as executive director, Yates immediately began repaying the political debts he owed these in-group members for their support. He simultaneously initiated a number of bold steps to clean up the agency, and through his adroitness the local media turned Yates into a savior figure; yet some agency employees began to say quietly that Yates was just an ordinary leader who now began to display a new attitude toward employees. One employee who was especially critical of Yates's leadership stated, "Yates *believes* his own newspaper clippings."

Alain Yates, more so than any previous WCCC executive director, had shaped the organizational culture of the agency. For him seniority was sacrosanct, and neither creativity nor hard work replaced it. Many employees enjoyed a secure work environment, and few employees were fired for a poor work ethic. The key to employee survival and its attendant rewards was loyalty, not competency. Furthermore, loyalty was the sole way to advance in the agency or to receive a pay increase for the agency's over 100 employees. However, not all employees felt comfortable with Yates's leadership style. For example, some employees were upset with Yates's decision to give certain employees reserved parking spaces while they had to walk a considerable distance to the agency–a policy that irked them particularly during inclement weather. In addition, other employees became vexed after Yates denied their requests to attend a local off-site management seminar; he often quipped, "We really don't have enough money in the budget" or "Do you really need to attend this seminar? Nothing in management has changed that much." One employee was so outraged when she discovered that Yates had on the same day approved a request for an in-group employee to attend a high-priced, out-of-state conference that she announced to some colleagues, "I'll do my job, but nothing more as long as Yates is here."

This two-tiered structure created a further wedge between the agency's so-called "haves and have nots." Yates's actions resulted in a small but noticeable agency fissure that led to a growing rift between employees who sought to excel and those who just got by on their loyalty. One long-time employee opined, "I simply do not believe in just getting by, but . . ."

Despite this, many employees decided not to leave the agency because, as a result of Yates's external political contacts and connections with philanthropic funding agencies, employee salaries were superior to those in similar organizations. Moreover, members of the out-group–employees not part of the agency in-group elite whom Yates constantly rewarded–decided to remain at the agency because as one employee succinctly put it, "We are committed to working for the betterment of the agency and its clients, and we will stay despite *his* preferential treatment of 'pet' employees." But over time, as employees retired or slowly trickled out of the agency because they could no longer tolerate what one employee called "employment injustices," they were replaced by new employees who were connected to agency in-group members or financial contributors to the agency. Both, regardless of how they arrived at the agency, had one characteristic in common: They swore undying loyalty to Yates. The agency was becoming more incestuous and a breeding ground for a groupthink mentality. At this month's staff meeting Yates had informed staff about some serious agency problems. However, no one dared mention that these problems and their negative organizational impact were a result of several major strategic leadership blunders Yates had made. One astute observer sitting in the last row of the cavernous room where staff meetings were held whispered in a muffled voice, "I guess I am the only one who noticed that the emperor has no clothes."

Yates also informed managers and staff that he was retiring as the executive director of the agency. But prior to announcing his retirement plans after his 25th year in office, Yates had recommended to the board of directors a successor from among his most trusted managers to continue his legacy. Agency managers and employees prepared several lavish retirement celebrations for Yates–they held a formal retirement dinner, hosted several large parties, and even etched Yates's name in gold leaf on the glass entrance doors to the agency.

Despite all the hoopla and festive mood, the board of directors dealt Yates a major blow when it announced that Fred Chambers would succeed him. Board members had been quietly working behind the scenes, waiting for the right opportunity to create an environment for changing the organizational culture. Board members believed that their change to Chambers would do this. They had already exerted strong pressure on him to reduce costs, to begin downsizing the nonessential politically connected staff, and to restore a new sense of professionalism to the agency. Chambers knew that he was a good leader, knew he had the confidence of the board, and most important, knew he had to change the organizational culture that had existed in the organization for last quarter of a century. He thought to himself, "My legacy won't be etched on any glass doors." But first he had to begin the process of changing the organizational culture that was so deeply embedded in the WCCC.

Note: The names and some managerial actions in this case have been altered to preserve the integrity and anonymity of the organization. This case is intended to be used as a basis for class discussion rather than to illustrate either effective or ineffective handling of a management situation.

Source: ©Joseph C. Santora.

VIDEO CASES FOR PART ONE

TROUBLES AT GENERAL MOTORS

General Motors Corporation isn't bankrupt, but the once-great automaker is on the rocks, laying off employees and recently losing $4 billion. Its market share, which was almost 50 percent a few decades ago, has dropped to 25 percent. While part of this problem may be due to poor strategy, a major burden is GM's legacy costs. The company spends $5.2 billion annually on health care for its 145,000 workers and more than 1 million retirees. That equates to a cost disadvantage of $1,500 for every car that GM makes. This video program describes GM's current woes and how it got there.

Discussion Questions

1. Describe General Motors' current problems in terms of the demands from its various stakeholders.
2. Rather than laying off redundant workers, GM has a jobs bank in which employees can transfer to other jobs or remain fully paid while serving the community until a job becomes available. Discuss this practice in terms of corporate social responsibility.

NEW BELGIUM BREWERY

This video program outlines the various ways in which New Belgium Brewery in Fort Collins, Colorado, tries to operate an environmentally sustainable business. The company accomplishes impressive environmental standards through new technology, alternative forms of energy, and waste minimization. The program reveals these environmentally sustainable strategies and describes how employees buy into this model of doing business.

Discussion Questions

1. Describe the various ways that New Belgium Brewery supports environmental sustainability.
2. How did New Belgium Brewery's founders gain employee support for environmental sustainability?

VIDEO CASES FOR PART TWO

GOOD BUSINESS DEEDS

You might not expect to see British American Tobacco, McDonald's, and Microsoft at a meeting on corporate social responsibility, but in their own way these firms are taking steps to become better employers and citizens in the community. This video program describes how these and other firms are embracing values and corporate social responsibility. It particularly highlights a few firms that serve as role models in this regard. One of these is Greyston Bakery, a multimillion dollar gourmet operation that takes people who need help and turns them into contributing members of the organization and society. Another is Eileen Fisher Company, which promotes good labor practices both at home and overseas, and helps customers meet their needs. In each case, the company's values are aligned more closely with employee values than at your typical organization.

Discussion Questions

1. Employees at Greyston Bakery, Eileen Fisher Company, Feed the Children, Green@Work, and other organizations described in this video program seem to have a strong congruence of their personal values with the organization's values. What are the apparent benefits of this values congruence?
2. Discuss the implications of corporate social responsibility in terms of employer branding. What companies come to mind whose employer brand is "doing good" for the community?

WORKPLACE BIAS

Wal-Mart is known for its low prices, but many former and current female employees claim the company also has discriminatory low pay and promotional opportunities for women. This video program presents the views of several women who have joined in one of the largest class action sex discrimination lawsuits in history. They claim that qualified women at Wal-Mart receive fewer promotions than their male counterparts. Others say they were fired for launching a sexual harassment complaint. The program describes statistics showing that male district managers earn significantly more than their female counterparts.

Discussion Questions

1. Use your knowledge of social identity theory, stereotyping, and prejudice to explain how sex discrimination might exist at Wal-Mart and in other large retail organizations. Be sure to note any evidence described in this program to support your explanation.
2. If you were a senior manager at Wal-Mart and believed that some of these complaints are due to stereotyping and other biases among middle managers, what interventions would you recommend to correct these biases?

MONEY & ETHICS

Is business ethics an oxymoron? Although stock manipulation and other forms of business fraud have occurred for hundreds of years, Barbara Toffler, an ethics professor and former ethics consultant at Arthur Andersen, believes that business can be more ethical. Still, she acknowledges that being ethical isn't easy. Most executives know right from wrong, yet they make unethical decisions when the financial rewards and pressure to perform are high enough. This video case study documents Toffler's experience at Arthur Andersen, where greed overwhelmed ethical values. It also tells the story of grocer Stew Leonard, Sr., who was jailed for tax fraud just two years after being featured in an ethics video.

Discussion Questions

1. Identify the various strategies described in this video program to encourage ethical conduct and discourage or punish wrongdoing. Explain why each of these practices is, or is not, effective.
2. Use the expectancy theory of motivation, discussed in Chapter 5, to explain why people engage in unethical behavior even though they know it is wrong.

NOW WHO'S BOSS?

Jonathan Tisch, CEO of Loews Hotels, had plenty of opportunity to empathize with staff when he spent five days performing a variety of frontline jobs. Although Tisch began his career working on the front desk, times have changed. Tisch discovered the complexities of computer technology as well as the challenges of greeting irritable guests, making beds, and working in sweaty polyester outfits. In this video program Tisch recalls his five-day experience.

Discussion Questions

1. Relate the frontline experience that Tisch went through to the Johari Window model.
2. Is working on the frontlines an effective way for executives to understand the business? Why or why not?

PIKE PLACE FISH MARKET

Fifteen years ago, Pike Place Fish Market in Seattle had unhappy employees and was in financial trouble. Rather than close shop, owner John Yokoyama sought help from consultant Jim Bergquist to improve his leadership and energize the workforce. Rather than rule as a tyrant, Yokoyama learned how to actively involve employees in the business. Soon, staff felt more empowered and gained more enjoyment from their work. They also began to actively have fun at work, including setting goals as a game, throwing fish to each other as sport, and pretending they are "world famous". Today, thanks to these and other strategies described in this video case, Pike Place is world famous. The little shop has become a tourist attraction and customers from California to New York call in orders.

Discussion Questions

1. Based on the model of emotions and attitudes in Chapter 4, explain how the changes at Pike Place Fish Market improved job satisfaction and reduced turnover. How did these attitude changes affect customer satisfaction?
2. Goal setting is discussed as an important activity at Pike Place. Evaluate the effectiveness of this goal setting process in the context of the characteristics of effective goals described in Chapter 5 of this textbook.
3. How is coaching applied at Pike Place, and how does this coaching influence employee performance?

STRESS IN JAPAN

Stress from overwork has become an epidemic in Japan. This video program consists of two segments that illustrate the degree to which some Japanese employees are overworked, as well as the consequences of their overwork. The first segment follows a typical day of a Japanese manager, from his two-hour morning commute to his late night working hours. The program also shows how he is under constant pressure to improve efficiency, and experiences a heavy burden and responsibility to do better. The second segment describes how karoshi–death from overwork–took the life of 23-year-old Yoshika. It reconstructs Yoshiko's work life as a graphic artist up to the time when she died suddenly on the job due to a brain hemorrhage.

Discussion Questions

1. Identify the various sources of stress (i.e. stressors) that the Japanese manager in the first segment likely experiences each day. Does he do anything to try to manage his stress?
2. What conditions led up to the karoshi death of Yoshika? Are these conditions commonly found in the country where you live?

AMERICA: AN OVERWORKED NATION (WORKING SMART)

Americans are working more hours, even when not at the office (thanks to technology). E-mails alone consume up to one full day each week. In this video program, you'll hear from people on the street about their long work days. The program cites surveys on how many hours people work, how much of their vacation they use, and what are the consequences of overwork. The program closes by recommending several steps to reduce work overload.

Discussion Questions

1. What seems to be the main causes of work overload? Which jobs would likely have these conditions more than others?
2. This program identifies several strategies to minimize work overload. Organize these recommendations into the various stress management categories described in Chapter 7. Does this program overlook any of the stress management categories in its recommendations? If so, what recommendations can you generate from those overlooked categories regarding overwork?

VIDEO CASES FOR PART THREE

BULLY BROADS

Women executives in Silicon Valley who seem to be over-aggressive are sent to (or voluntarily join) a reform program called the Bully Broads Program. The program provides executive coaching as well as group activities to curb the impulse to influence others through too much assertiveness. But while the program tries to change women, its founder and participants also believe there is a double standard; aggressive male executives aren't sent to similar programs, whereas women are expected to act more genteel.

Discussion Questions

1. Use your knowledge of leadership theories to explain why aggressive women are told to be less aggressive whereas this behavior is acceptable in men.
2. Are there situations where employees are more likely to accept aggressive female leaders?

CELEBRITY CEO CHARISMA

Does the cult of CEO charisma really make a difference to company profits? This NBC program takes a brief look at chief executives who acted like superheroes but failed to deliver, as well as a few low-key executives who really made a difference. The program hears from Harvard business school professor Rakesh Khurana, author of "Searching for a Corporate Savior", a book warning that charismatic leaders are not necessarily effective leaders.

Discussion Questions

1. Why do company boards tend to hire charismatic CEOs?
2. What can corporate boards do to minimize the charisma effect when filling chief executive officer and other senior executive positions?

SOUTHWEST CEO: GET TO KNOW GARY KELLY

Southwest Airlines remains one of the most successful airlines in the United States. Its secret to success? Treat customers as kings and queens, and treat employees even better. This video program shows how Southwest Airlines CEO Gary Kelly keeps in touch with day-to-day activities at the airline. It also describes some of the challenges that Kelly and his executive team have ahead of them.

Discussion Questions

1. Discuss the transactional and transformational leadership of Gary Kelly.
2. How does Gary Kelly's leadership reinforce Southwest Airlines' organizational culture?

VIDEO CASE FOR PART FOUR

JETBLUE AIRWAYS

JetBlue Airways is one of America's great aviation success stories. In just a few short years after its startup, the New York-based discount airline has become both profitable and highly popular among customers. Founder David Neeleman claims that the notion of a "JetBlue experience" emerged from customer feedback about their travels on JetBlue. This unique experience is based on the company's customer-focused culture and the many decisions focused on giving customers the best possible encounters.

Discussion Questions

1. Identify the activities or conditions that have developed and maintained JetBlue's customer service culture.
2. How has JetBlue's culture and explicit values influenced its decision making?

appendix A

Theory Building and Systematic Research Methods

People need to make sense of their world, so they form theories about how the world operates. A **theory** is a general set of propositions that describes interrelationships among several concepts. We form theories for the purpose of predicting and explaining the world around us.[1] What does a good theory look like? First, it should be stated as clearly and simply as possible so that the concepts can be measured and there is no ambiguity regarding the theory's propositions. Second, the elements of the theory must be logically consistent with each other because we cannot test anything that doesn't make sense. Finally, a good theory provides value to society; it helps people understand their world better than without the theory.[2]

Theory building is a continuous process that typically includes the inductive and deductive stages shown in Exhibit A.1.[3] The inductive stage draws on personal experience to form a preliminary theory, whereas the deductive stage uses the scientific method to test the theory.

The inductive stage of theory building involves observing the world around us, identifying a pattern of relationships, and then forming a theory from these personal observations. For example, you might casually notice that new employees want their supervisor to give direction, whereas this leadership style irritates long-service employees. From these observations you form a theory about the effectiveness of directive leadership. (See Chapter 14 for a discussion of this leadership style.)

Positivism versus Interpretivism

Research requires an interpretation of reality, and researchers tend to perceive reality in one of two ways. A common view, called **positivism**, is that reality exists independent of people. It is "out there" to be discovered and tested. Positivism is the foundation for most quantitative research (statistical analysis). It assumes that we can measure variables and that those variables have fixed relationships with other variables. For example, the positivist perspective says that we could study whether a supportive style of leadership reduces stress. If we find evidence of this, then someone else studying leadership and stress would "discover" the same relationship.

Interpretivism takes a different view of reality. It suggests that reality comes from shared meaning among people in that environment. For example, supportive leadership is a personal interpretation of

Exhibit A.1 **Theory Building and Theory Testing**

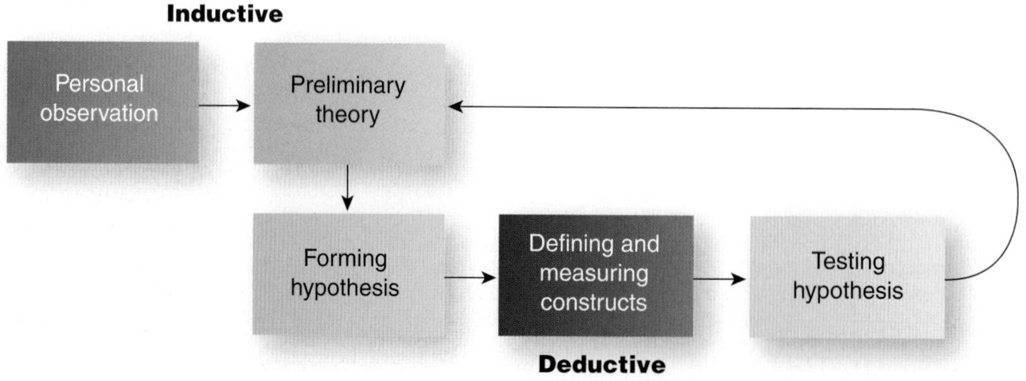

reality, not something that can be measured across time and people. Interpretivists rely mainly on qualitative data, such as observation and nondirective interviews. They particularly listen to the language people use to understand the common meaning that people have toward various events or phenomena. For example, they might argue that you need to experience and observe supportive leadership to effectively study it. Moreover, you can't really predict relationships because the specific situation shapes reality.[4]

Most OB scholars identify themselves somewhere between the extreme views of positivism and interpretivism. Many believe that inductive research should begin with an interpretivist angle. We should enter a new topic with an open mind and search for the shared meaning of people in that situation. In other words, researchers should let the participants define reality rather than let the researcher's preconceived notions shape that reality. This process involves gathering qualitative information and letting this information shape the theory.[5] After the theory emerges, researchers shift to the positivist perspective by quantitatively testing relationships in that theory.

Theory Testing: The Deductive Process

Once a theory has been formed, we shift into the deductive stage of theory building. This process includes forming hypotheses, defining and measuring constructs, and testing hypotheses (see Exhibit A.1). **Hypotheses** make empirically testable declarations that certain variables and their corresponding measures are related in a specific way proposed by the theory. For instance, to find support for the directive leadership theory described earlier, we need to form and then test a specific hypothesis from that theory. One such hypothesis might be this: "New employees are more satisfied with supervisors who exhibit a directive rather than a nondirective leadership style." Hypotheses are indispensable tools of scientific research because they provide the vital link between theory and empirical verification.

Defining and Measuring Constructs Hypotheses are testable only if we can define and then form measurable indicators of the concepts stated in those hypotheses. Consider the hypothesis in the previous paragraph about new employees and directive leadership. To test this hypothesis, we first need to define the concepts, such as *new employees, directive leadership,* and *supervisor.* These are known as **constructs** because they are abstract ideas constructed by the researcher that can be linked to observable information. Organizational behavior researchers developed the construct called *directive leadership* to help them understand the different effects that leaders have over followers. We can't directly see, taste, or smell directive leadership; instead we rely on indirect indicators that it exists, such as observing someone giving directions, maintaining clear performance standards, and ensuring that procedures and practices are followed.

As you can see, defining constructs well is important: These definitions become the foundation for finding or developing acceptable measures of those constructs. We can't measure directive leadership if we have only a vague idea about what this concept means. The better a construct is defined, the better our chances of finding or developing a good measure of that construct. However, even with a good definition, constructs can be difficult to measure because the empirical representation must capture several elements in the definition. A measure of directive leadership must be able to identify not only people who give directions, but also those who maintain performance standards and ensure that procedures are followed.

Testing Hypotheses The third step in the deductive process is to collect data for the empirical measures of the variables. Following our directive leadership example, we might conduct a formal survey in which new employees indicate the behavior of their supervisors and their attitudes toward their supervisors. Alternatively, we might design an experiment in which people work with someone who applies either a directive or nondirective leadership style. When the data have been collected, we can use various procedures to statistically test our hypotheses.

A major concern in theory building is that some researchers might inadvertently find support for their theory simply because they use the same information used to form the theory during the inductive stage. Consequently, the deductive stage must collect new data that are completely independent of the data used during the inductive stage. For instance, you might decide to test your theory of directive leadership by studying employees in another organization. Moreover, the inductive process may have relied mainly on personal observation, whereas the deductive process might use survey questionnaires. By studying different samples and using different measurement tools, we minimize the risk of conducting circular research.

Using the Scientific Method

Earlier we said that the deductive stage of theory building follows the scientific method. The **scientific method** is systematic, controlled, empirical, and critical investigation of hypothetical propositions about the presumed relationships among natural phenomena.[6] There are several elements to this definition, so let's look at each one. First, scientific research is *systematic* and *controlled* because researchers want to rule out all but one explanation for a set of interrelated events. To rule out alternative explanations, we need to control them in some way, such as by keeping them constant or removing them entirely from the environment.

Second, we say that scientific research is *empirical* because researchers need to use objective reality–or as close as we can get to it–to test theory. They measure observable elements of the environment, such as what a person says or does, rather than relying on their own subjective opinions to draw conclusions. Moreover, scientific research analyzes these data using accepted principles of mathematics and logic.

Finally, scientific research involves *critical investigation*. This means that the study's hypotheses, data, methods, and results are openly described so that other experts in the field can properly evaluate the research. It also means that scholars are encouraged to critique and build on previous research. Eventually the scientific method encourages the refinement and eventually the replacement of a particular theory with one that better suits our understanding of the world.

Grounded Theory: An Alternative Approach

The scientific method dominates the quantitative approach to systematic research; but another approach, called **grounded theory**, dominates research using qualitative methods.[7] Grounded theory is a process of developing knowledge through the constant interplay of data collection, analysis, and theory development. It relies mainly on qualitative methods to form categories and variables, analyze relationships among these concepts, and form a model based on the observations and analysis. Grounded theory combines the inductive stages of theory development by cycling back and forth between data collection and analysis to converge on a robust explanatory model. This ongoing reciprocal process results in theory that is grounded in the data (thus the name *grounded theory*).

Like the scientific method, grounded theory is a systematic and rigorous process of data collection and analysis. It requires specific steps and documentation and adopts a positivist view by assuming that the results are generalizable to other settings. However, grounded theory also takes an interpretivist view by building categories and variables from the perceived realities of the subjects rather than from an assumed universal truth.[8] It also recognizes that personal biases are not easily removed from the research process.

Selected Issues in Organizational Behavior Research

There are many issues to consider in theory building, particularly when we use the deductive process to test hypotheses. Some of the more important issues are sampling, causation, and ethical practices in organizational research.

Sampling in Organizational Research When finding out why things happen in organizations, we typically gather information from a few sources and then draw conclusions about the larger population. If we survey several employees and determine that older employees are more loyal to their company, then we would like to generalize this statement to all older employees in our population, not just those whom we surveyed. Scientific inquiry generally requires researchers to engage in **representative sampling**–that is, sampling a population in such a way that we can extrapolate the results of that sample to the larger population.

One factor that influences representativeness is whether the sample is selected in an unbiased way from the larger population. Let's suppose you want to study organizational commitment among employees in your organization. A casual procedure might result in sampling too few employees from the head office and too many located elsewhere in the country. If head office employees actually have higher loyalty than employees located elsewhere, then the biased sampling would cause the results to underestimate the true level of loyalty among employees in the company. If you repeat the process again next year but somehow overweight employees from the head office, the results might wrongly suggest that employees have increased their organizational commitment over the past year. In reality, the only change may be the direction of sampling bias.

How do we minimize sampling bias? The answer is to randomly select the sample. A randomly drawn sample gives each member of the population an equal probability of being chosen, so there is less likelihood that a subgroup within that population dominates the study's results.

The same principle applies to random assignment of subjects to groups in experimental designs. If we want to test the effects of a team development training program, we need to randomly place some employees in the training group and randomly place others in a group that does not receive training. Without this random selection, each group might have different types of employees, so we wouldn't know whether the training explained the differences between the two groups. Moreover, if employees were to respond differently to the training program, we couldn't be sure that the training program results were representative of the larger population. Of course random sampling does not necessarily produce a perfectly representative sample; but we do know that this is the best approach to ensure unbiased selection.

The other factor that influences representativeness is sample size. Whenever we select a portion of the population, there will be some error in our estimate of the population values. The larger the sample, the less error will occur in our estimate. Let's suppose you want to find out how employees in a 500-person firm feel about smoking in the workplace. If you asked 400 of those employees, the information would provide a very good estimate of how the entire workforce in that organization feels. If you survey only 100 employees, the estimate might deviate more from the true population. If you ask only 10 people, the estimate could be quite different from what all 500 employees feel.

Notice that sample size goes hand-in-hand with random selection. You must have a sufficiently large sample size for the principle of randomization to work effectively. In our example of attitudes toward smoking, we would do a poor job of random selection if our sample consisted of only 10 employees from the 500-person organization. The reason is that these 10 people probably wouldn't capture the diversity of employees throughout the organization. In fact, the more diverse the population, the larger the sample size should be to provide adequate representation through random selection.

Causation in Organizational Research Theories present notions about relationships among constructs. Often these propositions suggest a causal relationship—namely, that one variable has an effect on another variable. When discussing causation, we refer to variables as being independent or dependent. *Independent* variables are the presumed causes of *dependent* variables, which are the presumed effects. In our earlier example of directive leadership, the main independent variable (there might be others) would be the supervisor's directive or nondirective leadership style because we presume that it causes the dependent variable (satisfaction with supervision).

In laboratory experiments (described later), the independent variable is always manipulated by the experimenter. In our research on directive leadership, we might have subjects (new employees) work with supervisors who exhibit directive or nondirective leadership behaviors. If subjects are more satisfied under the directive leaders, then we would be able to infer an association between the independent and dependent variables.

Researchers must satisfy three conditions to provide sufficient evidence of causality between two variables.[9] The first condition of causality is that the variables are empirically associated with each other. An association exists whenever one measure of a variable changes systematically with a measure of another variable. This condition of causality is the easiest to satisfy because there are several well-known statistical measures of association. A research study might find, for instance, that heterogeneous groups (in which members come from diverse backgrounds) produce more creative solutions to problems. This might be apparent because the measure of creativity (such as number of creative solutions produced within a fixed time) is higher for teams that have a high score on the measure of group heterogeneity. They are statistically associated or correlated with each other.

The second condition of causality is that the independent variable precedes the dependent variable in time. Sometimes this condition is satisfied through simple logic. In our group heterogeneity example, it doesn't make sense to say that the number of creative solutions caused the group's heterogeneity because the group's heterogeneity existed before it produced the creative solutions. In other situations, however, the temporal relationship among variables is less clear. One example is the ongoing debate about job satisfaction and organizational commitment. Do companies develop more loyal employees by increasing their job satisfaction, or do changes in organizational loyalty cause changes in job satisfaction?

Simple logic does not answer these questions; instead researchers must use sophisticated longitudinal studies to build up evidence of a temporal relationship between these two variables.

The third requirement for evidence of a causal relationship is that the statistical association between two variables cannot be explained by a third variable. There are many associations that we quickly dismiss as being causally related. For example, perhaps there is a statistical association between the number of storks in an area and the birthrate in that area. We know that storks don't bring babies, so something else must cause the association between these two variables. The real explanation is that both storks and births have a higher incidence in rural areas.

In other studies, the third variable effect is less apparent. Many years ago, before polio vaccines were available, a study in the United States reported a surprisingly strong association between consumption of a certain soft drink and the incidence of polio. Was polio caused by drinking this pop, or did people with polio have an unusual craving for this beverage? Neither. Both polio and consumption of the soft drink were caused by a third variable: climate. There was a higher incidence of polio in the summer months and in warmer climates, and people drink more liquids in these climates.[10] As you can see from this example, researchers have a difficult time supporting causal inferences because third variable effects are sometimes difficult to detect.

Ethics in Organizational Research Organizational behavior researchers need to abide by the ethical standards of the society in which the research is conducted. One of the most important ethical considerations is the individual subjects' freedom to participate in the study. For example, it is inappropriate to force employees to fill out a questionnaire or attend an experimental intervention for research purposes only. Moreover, researchers have an obligation to tell potential subjects about any potential risks inherent in the study so that participants can make an informed choice about whether to be involved.

Finally, researchers must be careful to protect the privacy of those who participate in the study. This usually includes letting people know when they are being studied as well as guaranteeing that their individual information will remain confidential (unless publication of identities is otherwise granted). Researchers maintain anonymity through careful security of data. The research results usually aggregate data in numbers large enough that they do not reveal the opinions or characteristics of any specific individual. For example, we would report the average absenteeism of employees in a department rather than state the absence rates of each person. When sharing data with other researchers, it is usually necessary to specially code each case so that individual identities are not known.

Research Design Strategies

So far we have described how to build a theory, including the specific elements of empirically testing that theory within the standards of scientific inquiry. But what are the different ways to design a research study so that we get the data necessary to achieve our research objectives? There are many strategies, but they mainly fall under three headings: laboratory experiments, field surveys, and observational research.

Laboratory Experiments A **laboratory experiment** is any research study in which independent variables and variables outside the researcher's main focus of inquiry can be controlled to some extent. Laboratory experiments are usually located outside the everyday work environment, such as in a classroom, simulation lab, or any other artificial setting in which the researcher can manipulate the environment. Organizational behavior researchers sometimes conduct experiments in the workplace (called *field experiments*) in which the independent variable is manipulated. However, the researcher has less control over the effects of extraneous factors in field experiments than in laboratory situations.

Advantages of Laboratory Experiments Laboratory experiments have many advantages. By definition this research method offers a high degree of control over extraneous variables that would otherwise confound the relationships being studied. Suppose we wanted to test the effects of directive leadership on the satisfaction of new employees. One concern might be that employees are influenced by how much leadership is provided, not just the type of leadership style. An experimental design would allow us to control how often the supervisor exhibited this style so that this extraneous variable does not confound the results.

A second advantage of lab studies is that the independent and dependent variables can be developed more precisely than in a field setting. For example, the researcher can ensure that supervisors in a lab study apply specific directive or nondirective behaviors, whereas real-life supervisors would use a more complex mixture of leadership behaviors. By using more precise measures, we can be more certain that we are measuring the intended construct. Thus if new employees are more satisfied with supervisors in the directive leadership condition, we are more confident that the independent variable was directive leadership rather than some other leadership style.

A third benefit of laboratory experiments is that the independent variable can be distributed more evenly among participants. In our directive leadership study, we can ensure that approximately half of the subjects have a directive supervisor, whereas the other half have a nondirective supervisor. In natural settings we might have trouble finding people who have worked with a nondirective leader, and consequently we couldn't determine the effects of this condition.

Disadvantages of Laboratory Experiments With these powerful advantages, you might wonder why laboratory experiments are the least appreciated form of organizational behavior research.[11] One obvious limitation of this research method is that it lacks realism, so the results might differ in the real world. Another argument is that laboratory experiment subjects are less involved than their counterparts in an actual work situation. This is sometimes true, although many lab studies have highly motivated participants. An additional criticism is that the extraneous variables controlled in the lab setting might produce a different effect of the independent variable on the dependent variables. This might also be true, but remember that the experimental design controls variables in accordance with the theory and its hypotheses. Consequently this concern is really a critique of the theory, not the lab study.

Finally, there is the well-known problem that participants are aware they are being studied, and this causes them to act differently than they normally would. Some participants try to figure out how the researcher wants them to behave and then deliberately try to act that way. Other participants try to upset the experiment by doing just the opposite of what they believe the researcher expects. Still others might act unnaturally simply because they know they are being observed. Fortunately experimenters are well aware of these potential problems and are usually (although not always) successful at disguising the study's true intent.

Field Surveys **Field surveys** collect and analyze information in a natural environment–an office, factory, or other existing location. The researcher takes a snapshot of reality and tries to determine whether elements of that situation (including the attitudes and behaviors of people in that situation) are associated with each other as hypothesized. Everyone does some sort of field research. You might think that people from some states are better drivers than others, so you "test" your theory by looking at how people with out-of-state license plates drive. Although your methods of data collection might not satisfy scientific standards, this is a form of field research because it takes information from a naturally occurring situation.

Advantages and Disadvantages of Field Surveys One advantage of field surveys is that the variables often have a more powerful effect than they would in a laboratory experiment. Consider the effect of peer pressure on the behavior of members within the team. In a natural environment, team members would form strong cohesive bonds over time, whereas a researcher would have difficulty replicating this level of cohesiveness and corresponding peer pressure in a lab setting.

Another advantage of field surveys is that the researcher can study many variables simultaneously, thereby permitting a fuller test of more complex theories. Ironically this is also a disadvantage of field surveys; it is difficult for the researcher to contain his or her scientific inquiry. There is a tendency to shift from deductive hypothesis testing to more inductive exploratory browsing through the data. If these two activities become mixed together, the researcher can lose sight of the strict covenants of scientific inquiry.

The main weakness with field surveys is that it is difficult to satisfy the conditions for causal conclusions. One reason is that the data are usually collected at one point in time, so the researcher must rely on logic to decide whether the independent variable really preceded the dependent variable. Contrast this with the lab study, in which the researcher can usually be confident that the independent variable was applied before the dependent variable occurred. Increasingly organizational behavior studies use longitudinal research to provide a better indicator of temporal relations among variables; but this is still not as precise as the lab setting. Another reason why causal analysis is difficult in field surveys is that extraneous variables are not controlled as they are in lab studies. Without this control, there is a higher chance that a third variable might explain the relationship between the hypothesized independent and dependent variables.

Observational Research

In their study of brainstorming and creativity, Robert Sutton and Andrew Hargadon observed 24 brainstorming sessions at IDEO, a product design firm in Palo Alto, California. They also attended a dozen "Monday morning meetings," conducted 60 semistructured interviews with IDEO executives and designers, held hundreds of informal discussions with these people, and read through several dozen magazine articles about the company.[12]

Sutton and Hargadon's use of observational research and other qualitative methods was quite appropriate for their research objectives, which were to reexamine the effectiveness of brainstorming beyond the number of ideas generated. Observational research generates a wealth of descriptive accounts about the drama of human existence in organizations. It is a useful vehicle for learning about the complex dynamics of people and their activities, such as brainstorming. (The results of Sutton and Hargadon's study are discussed in Chapter 10.)

Participant observation takes the observation method one step further by having the observer take part in the organization's activities. This experience gives the researcher a fuller understanding of the activities compared to just watching others participate in those activities.

Disadvantages of Observational Research In spite of its intuitive appeal, observational research has a number of weaknesses. The main problem is that the observer is subject to the perceptual screening and organizing biases that we discuss in Chapter 3 of this textbook. There is a tendency to overlook the routine aspects of organizational life, even though they may prove to be the most important data for research purposes. Instead observers tend to focus on unusual information, such as activities that deviate from what the observer expects. Because observational research usually records only what the observer notices, valuable information is often lost.

Another concern with the observation method is that the researcher's presence and involvement may influence the people whom he or she is studying. This can be a problem in short-term observations, but in the long term people tend to return to their usual behavior patterns. With ongoing observations, such as Sutton and Hargadon's study of brainstorming sessions at IDEO, employees eventually forget that they are being studied.

Finally, observation is usually a qualitative process, so it is more difficult to empirically test hypotheses with the data. Instead observational research provides rich information for the inductive stages of theory building. It helps us form ideas about how things work in organizations. We begin to see relationships that lay the foundation for new perspectives and theory. We must not confuse this inductive process of theory building with the deductive process of theory testing.

Notes

[1]F.N. Kerlinger, *Foundations of Behavioral Research* (New York: Holt, Rinehart, & Winston, 1964), p. 11.

[2]J.B. Miner, *Theories of Organizational Behavior* (Hinsdale, IL: Dryden, 1980), pp. 7–9.

[3]Miner, *Theories of Organizational Behavior,* pp. 6–7.

[4]J. Mason, *Qualitative Researching* (London: Sage, 1996).

[5]A. Strauss and J. Corbin (eds.), *Grounded Theory in Practice* (London: Sage, 1997); B.G. Glaser and A. Strauss, *The Discovery of Grounded Theory: Strategies for Qualitative Research* (Chicago: Aldine, 1967).

[6]Kerlinger, *Foundations of Behavioral Research,* p. 13.

[7]Strauss and Corbin (eds.), *Grounded Theory in Practice*; Glaser and Strauss, *The Discovery of Grounded Theory.*

[8]W.A. Hall and P. Callery, "Enhancing the Rigor of Grounded Theory: Incorporating Reflexivity and Relationality," *Qualitative Health Research* 11 (March 2001), pp. 257–72.

[9]P. Lazarsfeld, *Survey Design and Analysis* (New York: The Free Press, 1955).

[10]This example is cited in D.W. Organ and T.S. Bateman, *Organizational Behavior,* 4th ed. (Homewood, IL: Irwin, 1991), p. 42.

[11]Organ and Bateman, *Organizational Behavior,* p. 45

[12]R.I. Sutton and A. Hargadon, "Brainstorming Groups in Context: Effectiveness in a Product Design Firm," *Administrative Science Quarterly* 41 (1996), pp. 685–718.

appendix B

Scoring Keys for Self-Assessment Activities

The following pages provide scoring keys for self-assessments that are presented in this textbook. Most (although not all) of these self-assessments, as well as the self-assessments that are summarized in this book, are scored on the student Online Learning Center.

Chapter 2

Scoring Key for Self-Monitoring Scale

Scoring Instructions: Use the following table to assign numbers to each box you checked. Insert the number for each statement on the appropriate line after the table. For example, if you checked "somewhat false" for statement #1 ("In social situations, I have the ability..."), you would write a "2" on the line with "(1)" underneath it. After assigning numbers for all 13 statements, add up your scores to estimate your self-monitoring personality.

For statement items 1, 2, 3, 4, 5, 6, 7, 8, 10, 11, 13	For statement items 9, 12
Very true = 6	Very true = 1
Somewhat true = 5	Somewhat true = 2
Slightly more true than false = 4	Slightly more true than false = 3
Slightly more false than true = 3	Slightly more false than true = 4
Somewhat false = 2	Somewhat false = 5
Very false = 1	Very false = 6

Sensitive to expressive behavior of others

___ + ___ + ___ + ___ + ___ + ___ = ___
(2) (4) (5) (6) (8) (11) (A)

Ability to modify self-presentation

___ + ___ + ___ + ___ + ___ + ___ +
(1) (3) (7) (9) (10) (12)

___ = ___
(13) (B)

Self-monitoring total score

___ + ___ = ___
(A) (B) Total

Interpreting Your Score: Self-monitoring consists of two dimensions: (a) sensitivity to expressive behavior of others and (b) ability to modify self-presentation. These two dimensions as well as the total score are defined in the following table, along with the range of scores for high, medium, and low levels of each scale:

Self-monitoring dimension and definition	Score interpretation
Sensitive to expressive behavior of others: This scale indicates the extent to which you are aware of the feelings and perceptions of others, as expressed by their facial expressions, subtle statements, and other behaviors.	High: 25 to 36 Medium: 18 to 24 Low: Below 18
Ability to modify self-presentation: This scale indicates the extent to which you are adept at modifying your behavior in a way that is most appropriate for a situation or social relationship.	High: 30 to 42 Medium: 21 to 29 Low: Below 21
Self-monitoring total: Self-monitoring refers to an individual's level of sensitivity to the expressive behavior of others and ability to adapt appropriately to these situational cues.	High: 55 to 78 Medium: 39 to 54 Low: Below 39

Chapter 3

Scoring Key for Assessing Your Personal Need for Structure

Scoring Instructions: Use the following table to assign numbers to each box you checked. For example, if you checked "moderately disagree" for statement #3 ("I enjoy being spontaneous."), you would assign a "5" to that statement. After assigning numbers for all 12 statements, add up your scores to estimate your personal need for structure.

For statement items 1, 5, 6, 7, 8, 9, 10, 12	For statement items 2, 3, 4, 11
Strongly agree = 6	Strongly agree = 1
Moderately agree = 5	Moderately agree = 2
Slightly agree = 4	Slightly agree = 3
Slightly disagree = 3	Slightly disagree = 4
Moderately disagree = 2	Moderately disagree = 5
Strongly disagree = 1	Strongly disagree = 6

Interpreting Your Score: Some people need to "make sense" of things around them more quickly or completely than do other people. This personal need for perceptual structure relates to selective attention as well as perceptual organization and interpretation. For instance, people with a strong personal need for closure might form first impressions, fill in missing pieces, and rely on stereotyping more quickly than people who don't mind incomplete perceptual situations.

This scale, called the personal need for structure (PNS) scale, assesses the degree to which people are motivated to structure their world in a simple and unambiguous way. Scores range from 12 to 72, with higher scores indicating a high personal need for structure. PNS norms vary from one group to the next. For instance, a study of Finnish nurses reported a mean PNS score of 34, whereas a study of 236 male and 303 female undergraduate psychology students in the United States had a mean score of 42. The norms in the following table are based on scores from these undergraduate students:

Personal need for structure score	Interpretation
58 to 72	High need for personal structure.
47 to 57	Above-average need for personal structure.
38 to 46	Average need for personal structure.
27 to 37	Below- average need for personal structure.
12 to 26	Low need for personal structure.

Chapter 4

Scoring Key for School Commitment Scale

Scoring Instructions: Use the following table to assign numbers to each box you checked. Insert the number for each statement on the appropriate line after the table. For example, if you checked "moderately disagree" for statement #1 ("I would be very happy…"), you would write a "2" on the line with "(1)" underneath it. After assigning numbers for all 12 statements, add up your scores to estimate your affective and continuance school commitment.

For statement items 1, 2, 3, 4, 6, 8, 10, 11, 12	For statement items 5, 7, 9
Strongly agree = 7	Strongly agree = 1
Moderately agree = 6	Moderately agree = 2
Slightly agree = 5	Slightly agree = 3
Neutral = 4	Neutral = 4
Slightly disagree = 3	Slightly disagree = 5
Moderately disagree = 2	Moderately disagree = 6
Strongly disagree = 1	Strongly disagree = 7

Affective commitment

___ + ___ + ___ + ___ + ___ + ___ = ___
(1) (3) (5) (7) (9) (11)

Continuance commitment

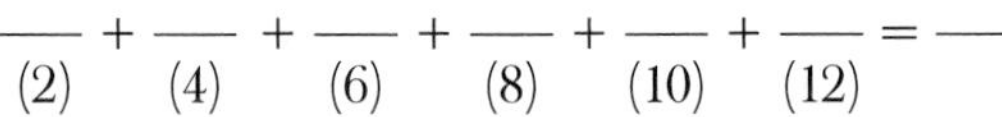

___ + ___ + ___ + ___ + ___ + ___ = ___
(2) (4) (6) (8) (10) (12)

Interpreting Your Affective Commitment Score: This scale measures both affective commitment and continuance commitment. *Affective commitment* refers to a person's emotional attachment to, identification with, and involvement in a particular organization. In this scale, the organization is the school you are attending. How high or low is your affective commitment? The ideal would be to compare your score with the collective results of other students in your class. You can also compare your score with the following results, which are based on a sample of employees:

Affective commitment score	Interpretation
Above 36	High level of affective commitment.
32 to 36	Above-average level of affective commitment.
28 to 31	Average level of affective commitment.
20 to 27	Below-average level of affective commitment.
Below 20	Low level of affective commitment.

Interpreting Your Continuance Commitment Score: *Continuance commitment* occurs when people believe it is in their own personal interest to remain with an organization. People with a high continuance commitment have a strong calculative bond with the organization. In this scale, the organization is the school you are attending. How high or low is your continuance commitment? The ideal would be to compare your score with the collective results of other students in your class. You can also compare your score with the following results, which are based on a sample of employees:

Continuance commitment score	Interpretation
Above 31	High level of continuance commitment.
26 to 31	Above-average level of continuance commitment.
21 to 25	Average level of continuance commitment.
13 to 20	Below-average level of continuance commitment.
Below 13	Low level of continuance commitment.

Chapter 5

Scoring Key for Equity Sensitivity

Scoring Instructions: To score this scale, called the equity preference questionnaire (EPQ), complete these three steps:

1. Write your circled numbers for the following items and add them up:

   ___ + ___ + ___ + ___ + ___ + ___ + ___ +
   (1) (2) (3) (4) (5) (6) (7)

   ___ = __________
   (10) Subtotal A

2. The remaining items in the equity preference questionnaire need to be reverse-scored. To calculate a reverse score, subtract the direct score from 6. For example, if you circled 4 in one of these items, the reverse score would be 2 (i.e., $6 - 4 = 2$). If you circled 1, the reverse score would be 5 (i.e., $6 - 1 = 5$). Calculate the reverse score for each of the following items and write them in the spaces provided. Then calculate Subtotal B by adding up these reverse scores:

   ___ + ___ + ___ + ___ + ___ + ___ + ___ +
   (8) (9) (11) (12) (13) (14) (15)

   ___ = __________
   (16) Subtotal B

3. Calculate the total score by summing Subtotal A and Subtotal B:

   __________ + __________ = __________
   (Subtotal A) (Subtotal B) TOTAL

Interpreting Your Score: The equity preference questionnaire measures the extent to which you are a "benevolent," "equity sensitive," or "entitled." Generally, people who score as follows fall into one of these categories:

EPQ score	Equity preference category
59 to 80	Benevolents—are tolerant of situations where they are underrewarded.
38 to 58	Equity sensitives—want an outcome–input ratio equal to the ratio of the comparison other.
16 to 37	Entitleds—want to receive proportionally more than others (like to be overrewarded).

Chapter 6

Scoring Key for the Money Attitude Scale

Scoring Instructions: This instrument presents three dimensions with a smaller set of items than the original money attitude scale. To calculate your score on each dimension, write the number you circled in the scale above the corresponding item number in the scoring key at the top of the next page. For example, write the number you circled for the scale's first statement ("I sometimes purchase things...") on the line above "Item 1." Then add up the numbers for that dimension. The money attitude total score is calculated by adding up all scores and all dimensions.

Money attitude dimension	Calculation	Your score
Money as power/prestige	_____ _____ _____ _____ Item 1 + Item 4 + Item 7 + Item 10 =	_____
Retention time	_____ _____ _____ _____ Item 2 + Item 5 + Item 8 + Item 11 =	_____
Money anxiety	_____ _____ _____ _____ Item 3 + Item 6 + Item 9 + Item 12 =	_____
Money attitude total	Add up all dimension scores =	_____

Interpreting Your Score: The three money attitude scale dimensions measured here, as well as the total score, are defined as follows:

Money as power/prestige: People with higher scores on this dimension tend to use money to influence and impress others.

Retention time: People with higher scores on this dimension tend to be careful financial planners.

Money anxiety: People with higher scores on this dimension tend to view money as a source of anxiety.

Money attitude total: This is a general estimate of how much respect and attention you give to money.

The following table shows how a sample of MBA students scored on the money attitude scale. The table shows percentiles, that is, the percentage of people with the same or lower scores. For example, the table indicates that a score of 12 on the retention scale is quite low because only 20 percent of students would have scored at this level or lower (80 percent scored higher). However, a score of 12 on the prestige scale is quite high because 80 percent of students scored at or below this number (only 20 percent scored higher).

Chapter 7

Scoring Key for the Connor–Davidson Resilience Scale

Scoring Instructions: Use the following values to assign numbers to each box you checked in the Connor–Davidson resilience scale; then add up the scores for all 25 items:

0 = Not at all true
1 = Rarely true
2 = Sometimes true
3 = Often true
4 = True nearly all of the time

Interpreting Your Score: Resilience is the capability of individuals to cope successfully in the face of significant change, adversity, or risk. Everyone has some resilience; it occurs every time we pull through

Percentile (% with scores at or below this number)	Prestige score	Retention score	Anxiety score	Total money score
Average score	9.89	14.98	12.78	37.64
Highest score	17	20	18	53
90	13	18	16	44
80	12	17	15	42
70	11	17	14	40
60	10	16	14	39
50	10	15	13	38
40	9	14	12	36
30	8	14	11	34
20	7	12	10	32
10	7	11	8	29
Lowest score	4	8	6	23

stressful experiences. Although everyone needs to recuperate to some extent following a stressful experience, people with high resilience are better able to maintain equilibrium and, consequently, have lost little ground in the first place. The Connor–Davidson resilience scale was recently developed to estimate levels of resilience. Scores range from 0 to 100. Preliminary studies indicate that people with post-traumatic stress disorder score much lower (average score of 48) than primary health care outpatients (average score of 72), who score lower than the general population (average score of 80). The following table allows you to compare your score against the results of 577 people in the general U.S. population:

Resilience score	Interpretation
92 to 100	Top 20th percentile (very high resilience).
86 to 91	21st—40th percentile.
77 to 85	41st—60th percentile (middle of the pack).
65 to 76	61st—80th percentile.
0 to 64	81st—100th percentile (low resilience in general population).

Chapter 8

Scoring Key for Assessing Your Creative Personality

Scoring Instructions: Assign one positive (+1) point to the following words if you put a check mark beside them: *capable, clever, confident, egotistical, humorous, individualistic, informal, insightful, intelligent, inventive, original, reflective, resourceful, self-confident, sexy, snobbish, unconventional, wide interests.*

Assign one negative (–1) point to the following words if you put a check mark beside them: *affected, cautious, commonplace, conservative, conventional, dissatisfied, honest, mannerly, narrow interests, sincere, submissive, suspicious.* Words without check marks receive zero points. Add up the total score, which will range from –12 to +18.

Interpreting Your Score: This instrument estimates your creative potential as a personal characteristic. The scale recognizes that creative people are intelligent, persistent, and possess an inventive thinking style. Creative personality varies somewhat from one occupational group to the next. The following table provides norms based on undergraduate and graduate university students:

Creative disposition score	Interpretation
Above +9	You have a high creative personality.
+1 to +9	You have an average creative personality.
Below +1	You have a low creative personality.

Chapter 9

Scoring Key for the Team Roles Preferences Scale

Scoring Instructions: Write the scores circled for each item on the appropriate lines here (statement numbers are in parentheses); then add up each scale.

Encourager	___ (6)	+ ___ (9)	+ ___ (11)	= ___
Gatekeeper	___ (4)	+ ___ (10)	+ ___ (13)	= ___
Harmonizer	___ (3)	+ ___ (8)	+ ___ (12)	= ___
Initiator	___ (1)	+ ___ (5)	+ ___ (14)	= ___
Summarizer	___ (2)	+ ___ (7)	+ ___ (15)	= ___

Interpreting Your Score: The five team roles measured here are different from Belbin's roles described in the textbook. However, these roles are also based on academic writing. These five roles are defined as follows, along with the range of scores for high, medium, and low levels of each role. These norms are based on results from a sample of MBA students:

Team role and definition	Interpretation
Encourager: People who score high on this dimension have a strong tendency to praise and support the ideas of other team members, thereby showing warmth and solidarity to the group.	High: 12 and above Medium: 9 to 11 Low: 8 and below

Team role and definition	Interpretation
Gatekeeper: People who score high on this dimension have a strong tendency to encourage all team members to participate in a discussion.	High: 12 and above Medium: 9 to 11 Low: 8 and below
Harmonizer: People who score high on this dimension have a strong tendency to mediate intragroup conflicts and reduce tension.	High: 11 and above Medium: 9 to 10 Low: 8 and below
Initiator: People who score high on this dimension have a strong tendency to identify goals for a meeting, including ways to work on those goals.	High: 12 and above Medium: 9 to 11 Low: 8 and below
Summarizer: People who score high on this dimension have a strong tendency to keep track of what was said in a meeting (that is, act as the team's memory).	High: 10 and above Medium: 8 to 9 Low: 7 and below

Chapter 10

Scoring Key for the Team Player Inventory

Scoring Instructions: To calculate your score on the team player inventory, use the following table to assign numbers to each box that you checked. Then add up the numbers to determine your total score.

For statement items 1, 3, 6, 8, 10	For statement items 2, 4, 5, 7, 9
Completely agree = 5	Completely agree = 1
Agree somewhat = 4	Agree somewhat = 2
Neither agree nor disagree = 3	Neither agree nor disagree =3
Disagree somewhat = 2	Disagree somewhat = 4
Completely disagree = 1	Completely disagree = 5

Interpreting Your Score: The team player inventory estimates the extent to which you are positively predisposed to working on teams. The higher your score, the more you enjoy working in teams and believe that teamwork is beneficial. The following table allows you to compare your team player inventory score against the norms for this scale. These norms are derived from undergraduate psychology students:

Team player inventory score	Interpretation
40 to 50	You have a strong predisposition or preference for working in teams.
21 to 39	You are generally ambivalent about working in teams.
10 to 20	You have a low predisposition or preference for working in teams.

Chapter 11

Scoring Key for the Active Listening Skills Inventory

Scoring Instructions: Use the following table to score the response you checked for each statement. Write the score for each item on the appropriate line below the table (statement numbers are in parentheses), and add up each subscale. For example, if you checked "A little" for statement #1 ("I keep an open mind…"), you would write a "1" on the line with "(1)" underneath it. Then calculate the overall active listening inventory score by summing all subscales.

For statement items 3, 4, 6, 7, 10, 13	For statement items 1, 2, 5, 8, 9, 11, 12, 14, 15
Not at all = 3	Not at all = 0
A little = 2	A little = 1
Somewhat = 1	Somewhat = 2
Very much = 0	Very much = 3

Avoiding interruption(AI)	___ (3)	+	___ (7)	+	___ (15)	=	___
Maintaining interest(MI)	___ (6)	+	___ (9)	+	___ (14)	=	___
Postponing evaluation(PE)	___ (1)	+	___ (5)	+	___ (13)	=	___
Organizing information(OI)	___ (2)	+	___ (10)	+	___ (12)	=	___
Showing interest(SI)	___ (4)	+	___ (8)	+	___ (11)	=	___

Active listening (total score): ___

Interpreting Your Score: The five active listening dimensions and the overall active listening scale measured here are defined in the following table, along with the range of scores for high, medium, and low levels of each dimension based on a sample of MBA students:

Active listening dimension and definition	Score interpretation
Avoiding interruption: People with high scores on this dimension have a strong tendency to let a speaker finish his or her statements before responding.	High: 8 to 9 Medium: 5 to 7 Low: Below 5
Maintaining interest: People with high scores on this dimension have a strong tendency to remain focused and concentrate on what a speaker is saying even when the conversation is boring or the information is well known.	High: 6 to 9 Medium: 3 to 5 Low: Below 3
Postponing evaluation: People with high scores on this dimension have a strong tendency to keep an open mind and avoid evaluating what a speaker is saying until the speaker has finished.	High: 7 to 9 Medium: 4 to 6 Low: Below 4
Organizing information: People with high scores on this dimension have a strong tendency to actively organize a speaker's ideas into meaningful categories.	High: 8 to 9 Medium: 5 to 7 Low: Below 5
Showing interest: People with high scores on this dimension have a strong tendency to use nonverbal gestures or brief verbal acknowledgments to demonstrate that they are paying attention to the speaker.	High: 7 to 9 Medium: 5 to 6 Low: Below 5
Active listening (total): People with high scores on this total active listening scale have a strong tendency to actively sense a sender's signals, evaluate them accurately, and respond appropriately.	High: Above 31 Medium: 26 to 31 Low: Below 26

Note: The active listening inventory does not explicitly measure two other dimensions of active listening, namely, empathizing and providing feedback. Empathizing is difficult to measure with behaviors; providing feedback involves similar behaviors as showing interest.

Chapter 12

Scoring Key for the Upward Influence Scale

Scoring Instructions: To calculate your scores on the upward influence scale, write the number circled for each statement on the appropriate line here (statement numbers are in parentheses), and add up each scale.

Scale							
Assertiveness	___ (8)	+	___ (15)	+	___ (16)	=	___
Exchange	___ (2)	+	___ (5)	+	___ (13)	=	___
Coalition formation	___ (1)	+	___ (11)	+	___ (18)	=	___
Upward appeal	___ (4)	+	___ (12)	+	___ (17)	=	___
Ingratiation	___ (3)	+	___ (6)	+	___ (9)	=	___
Persuasion	___ (7)	+	___ (10)	+	___ (14)	=	___

Interpreting Your Score: *Influence* refers to any behavior that attempts to alter someone else's attitudes or behavior. There are several types of influence, including the following six measured by this instrument: assertiveness, exchange, coalition formation, upward appeal, ingratiation, and persuasion. This instrument assesses your preference for using each type of influence on your boss or other people at higher levels in the organization. Each scale has a potential score ranging from 3 to 15 points. Higher scores indicate that a person has a greater preference for that particular tactic. The six upward influence dimensions measured are defined here, along with the range of scores for high, medium, and low levels of each tactic:

Influence tactic and definition	Score interpretation
Assertiveness: Assertiveness involves actively applying legitimate and coercive power to influence others. This tactic includes persistently reminding others of their obligations, frequently checking their work, confronting them, and using threats of sanctions to force compliance.	High: 8 to 15 Medium: 5 to 7 Low: 3 to 4
Exchange: Exchange involves the promise of benefits or resources in exchange for the target person's compliance with your request. This tactic also includes reminding the target of past benefits or favors with the expectation that the target will now make up for that debt. Negotiation is also part of the exchange strategy.	High: 10 to 15 Medium: 6 to 9 Low: 3 to 5

Influence tactic and definition	Score interpretation
Coalition formation: Coalition formation occurs when a group of people with common interests band together to influence others. This tactic pools the power and resources of many people, so the coalition potentially has more influence than if each person operated alone.	High: 11 to 15 Medium: 7 to 10 Low: 3 to 6
Upward appeal: Upward appeal occurs when you rely on support from a higher-level person to influence others. In effect, this is a form of coalition in which one or more members are people with higher authority or expertise.	High: 9 to 15 Medium: 6 to 8 Low: 3 to 5
Ingratiation: Flattering your boss in front of others, helping your boss with his or her work, agreeing with your boss's ideas, and asking for your boss's advice are all examples of ingratiation. This tactic increases the perceived similarity of the source of ingratiation to the target person.	High: 13 to 15 Medium: 9 to 12 Low: 3 to 8
Persuasion: Persuasion refers to using logical and emotional appeals to change others' attitudes. According to several studies, it is also the most common upward influence strategy.	High: 13 to 15 Medium: 9 to 12 Low: 3 to 8

Chapter 13

Scoring Key for the Dutch Test for Conflict Handling

Scoring Instructions: Write the number circled for each item on the appropriate line here (the statement number is under the line), and add up each subscale:

Interpreting Your Score: The five conflict handling dimensions are defined here, along with the range of scores for high, medium, and low levels of each dimension:

Conflict handling dimension and definition	Score interpretation
Yielding: Yielding involves giving in completely to the other side's wishes, or at least cooperating with little or no attention to your own interests. This style involves making unilateral concessions, and unconditional promises, as well as offering help with no expectation of reciprocal help.	High: 14 to 20 Medium: 9 to 13 Low: 4 to 8
Compromising: Compromising involves looking for a position in which your losses are offset by equally valued gains. It involves matching the other party's concessions, making conditional promises or threats, and actively searching for a middle ground between the interests of the two parties.	High: 17 to 20 Medium: 11 to 16 Low: 4 to 10
Forcing: Forcing involves trying to win the conflict at the other's expense. It includes "hard" influence tactics, particularly assertiveness, to get your own way.	High: 15 to 20 Medium: 9 to 14 Low: 4 to 8
Problem solving: Problem solving tries to find a mutually beneficial solution for all parties. Information sharing is an important feature of this style because the parties need to identify common ground and potential solutions that satisfy all of them.	High: 17 to 20 Medium: 11 to 16 Low: 4 to 10
Avoiding: Avoiding tries to smooth over or avoid conflict situations altogether. It represents a low concern for both self and the other party. In other words, avoiders try to suppress thinking about the conflict.	High: 13 to 20 Medium: 8 to 12 Low: 4 to 7

Conflict handling dimension	Calculation	Your score
Yielding	_____ _____ _____ _____ Item 1 + Item 6 + Item 11 + Item 16 =	_____
Compromising	_____ _____ _____ _____ Item 2 + Item 7 + Item 12 + Item 17 =	_____
Forcing	_____ _____ _____ _____ Item 3 + Item 8 + Item 13 + Item 18 =	_____
Problem solving	_____ _____ _____ _____ Item 4 + Item 9 + Item 14 + Item 19 =	_____
Avoiding	_____ _____ _____ _____ Item 5 + Item 10 + Item 15 + Item 20 =	_____

Chapter 14

Scoring Key for Leadership Dimensions Instrument: Transactional Leadership

Scoring Instructions: Add up the scores for the odd-numbered items. The maximum score here is 40.

Interpreting Your Score: Transactional leadership is "managing"–helping organizations to achieve their current objectives more efficiently, such as by linking job performance to valued rewards and ensuring that employees have the resources needed to do their jobs. The following table shows the range of scores for high, medium, and low levels of transactional leadership:

Transactional leadership score	Interpretation
32 to 40	The person you evaluated seems to be a highly transactional leader.
25 to 31	The person you evaluated seems to be a moderately transactional leader.
Below 25	The person you evaluated seems to display few characteristics of a transactional leader.

Scoring Key for Leadership Dimensions Instrument: Transformational Leadership

Scoring Instructions: Add up the scores for the even numbered items. The maximum score here is 40. Higher scores indicate that your supervisor has a strong inclination toward transformational leadership.

Interpreting Your Score: Transformational leadership involves changing teams or organizations by creating, communicating, and modelling a vision for the organization or work unit, and inspiring employees to strive for that vision. The following table shows the range of scores for high, medium, and low levels of transformational leadership:

Transformational leadership score	Interpretation
32 to 40	The person you evaluated seems to be a highly transformational leader.
25 to 31	The person you evaluated seems to be a moderately transformational leader.
Below 25	The person you evaluated seems to display few characteristics of a transformational leader.

Chapter 15

Scoring Key for the Organizational Structure Preference Scale

Scoring Instructions: Use the following table to assign numbers to each response you checked. Insert the number for each statement on the appropriate line after the table. For example, if you checked "Not at all" for item #1 ("A person's career ladder..."), you would write a "0" on the line with "(1)" underneath it. After assigning numbers for all 15 statements, add up the scores to estimate your degree of preference for a tall hierarchy, formalization, and centralization. Then calculate your overall score by summing all scales.

For statement items 2, 3, 8, 10, 11, 12, 14, 15	For statement items 1, 4, 5, 6, 7, 9, 13
Not at all = 3	Not at all = 0
A little = 2	A little = 1
Somewhat = 1	Somewhat = 2
Very much = 0	Very much = 3

Tall hierarchy ___ + ___ + ___ = ___ + ___ = ___
(H) (1) (4) (10) (12) (15) (H)

Formalization ___ + ___ + ___ = ___ + ___ = ___
(F) (2) (6) (8) (11) (13) (F)

Centralization ___ + ___ + ___ = ___ + ___ = ___
(C) (3) (5) (7) (9) (14) (C)

Total score ___ + ___ + ___ = ___
(mechanistic) (H) (F) (C) Total

Interpreting Your Score: The three organizational structure dimensions and the overall score are defined here, along with the range of scores for high, medium, and low levels of each dimension based on a sample of MBA students:

Organizational structure dimension and definition	Interpretation
Tall hierarchy: People with high scores on this dimension prefer to work in organizations with several levels of hierarchy and a narrow span of control (few employees per supervisor).	High: 11 to 15 Medium: 6 to 10 Low: Below 6
Formalization: People with high scores on this dimension prefer to work in organizations where jobs are clearly defined with limited discretion.	High: 12 to 15 Medium: 9 to 11 Low: Below 9
Centralization: People with high scores on this dimension prefer to work in organizations where decision making occurs mainly among top management rather than being spread out to lower-level staff.	High: 10 to 15 Medium: 7 to 9 Low: Below 7
Total score (mechanistic): People with high scores on this dimension prefer to work in mechanistic organizations, whereas those with low scores prefer to work in organic organizational structures. Mechanistic structures are characterized by a narrow span of control and a high degree of formalization and centralization. Organic structures have a wide span of control, little formalization, and decentralized decision making.	High: 30 to 45 Medium: 22 to 29 Low: Below 22

Chapter 16

Scoring Key for the Corporate Culture Preference Scale

Scoring Instructions: In each space here, write in a "1" if you circled the statement and a "0" if you did not. Then add up your scores for each subscale.

Interpreting Your Score: These corporate cultures may be found in many organizations, but they represent only four of many possible organizational cultures. Also, keep in mind that none of these subscales is inherently good or bad. Each is effective in different situations. The four corporate cultures are defined here, along with the range of scores for high, medium, and low levels of each dimension based on a sample of MBA students:

Corporate culture dimension and definition	Score interpretation
Control culture: This culture values the role of senior executives to lead the organization. The goal is to keep everyone aligned and under control.	High: 3 to 6 Medium: 1 to 2 Low: 0
Performance culture: This culture values individual and organizational performance and strives for effectiveness and efficiency.	High: 5 to 6 Medium: 3 to 4 Low: 0 to 2
Relationship culture: This culture values nurturing and well-being. It considers open communication, fairness, teamwork, and sharing a vital part of organizational life.	High: 6 Medium: 4 to 5 Low: 0 to 3
Responsive culture: This culture values its ability to keep in tune with the external environment, including being competitive and realizing new opportunities.	High: 6 Medium: 4 to 5 Low: 0 to 3

Culture													
Control culture	___ (2a)	+	___ (5a)	+	___ (6b)	=	___ (8b)	+	___ (11b)	+	___ (12a)	=	___
Performance culture	___ (1b)	+	___ (3b)	+	___ (5b)	=	___ (6a)	+	___ (7a)	+	___ (9b)	=	___
Relationship culture	___ (1a)	+	___ (3a)	+	___ (4b)	=	___ (8a)	+	___ (10b)	+	___ (12b)	=	___
Responsive culture	___ (2b)	+	___ (4a)	+	___ (7b)	+	___ (9a)	+	___ (10a)	+	___ (11a)	=	___

Chapter 17

Scoring Key for the Tolerance of Change Scale

Scoring Instructions: Use the following table to assign numbers to each box you checked. For example, if you checked "Moderately disagree" for statement #1 ("An expert who doesn't come up ..."), you would write a "2" beside that statement. After assigning numbers for all 16 statements, add up your scores to estimate your tolerance for change.

For statement items 2, 4, 6, 8, 10, 12, 14, 16	For statement items 1, 3, 5, 7, 9, 11, 13, 15
Strongly agree = 7	Strongly agree = 1
Moderately agree = 6	Moderately agree = 2
Slightly agree = 5	Slightly agree = 3
Neutral = 4	Neutral = 4
Slightly disagree = 3	Slightly disagree = 5
Moderately disagree = 2	Moderately disagree = 6
Strongly disagree = 1	Strongly disagree = 7

Interpreting Your Score: This measurement instrument is formally known as the "tolerance of ambiguity" scale. Although it was developed over 40 years ago, the instrument is still used today in research. People with a high tolerance for ambiguity are comfortable with uncertainty, sudden change, and new situations. These are characteristics of the hyperfast changes occurring in many organizations today. The following table indicates the range of scores for high, medium, and low tolerance for change. These norms are based on results for MBA students:

Tolerance for change score	Interpretation
81 to 112	You seem to have a high tolerance for change.
63 to 80	You seem to have a moderate level of tolerance for change.
Below 63	You seem to have a low degree of tolerance for change. Instead, you prefer stable work environments.

glossary

The number(s) in parentheses indicates the chapter(s) where the term is formally defined. See the subject index for other places in the textbook where the term is discussed.

A

ability Both the natural aptitudes and learned capabilities required to successfully complete a task. (2)

absorptive capacity The ability to recognize the value of new information, assimilate it, and apply it to commercial ends. (1)

achievement–nurturing orientation A competitive versus cooperative view of relations with other people. (2)

action learning A variety of experiential learning activities in which employees are involved in a "real, complex, and stressful problem," usually in teams, with immediate relevance to the company. (3)

action research A data-based, problem-oriented process that diagnoses the need for change, introduces the intervention, and then evaluates and stabilizes the desired changes. (17)

adaptive culture An organizational culture in which employees focus on the changing needs of customers and other stakeholders, and support initiatives to keep pace with those changes. (16)

alternative dispute resolution (ADR) A third-party dispute resolution process that includes mediation, typically followed by arbitration. (13)

appreciative inquiry An organizational change process that directs attention away from the group's own problems and focuses participant's on the group's potential and positive elements. (17)

artifacts The observable symbols and signs of an organization's culture. (16)

attitudes The cluster of beliefs, assessed feelings, and behavioral intentions toward an object. (4)

attribution process The perceptual process of deciding whether an observed behavior or event is caused largely by internal or by external factors. (3)

autonomy The degree to which a job gives employees the freedom, independence, and discretion to schedule their work and determine the procedures used in completing it. (6)

B

balanced scorecard (BSC) A reward system that pays bonuses for improved results on a composite of financial, customer, internal process, and employee factors. (6)

behavior modification A theory that explains learning in terms of the antecedents and consequences of behavior. (3)

bicultural audit A diagnosis of cultural relations between companies prior to a merger and a determination of the extent to which cultural clashes are likely to occur. (16)

"Big Five" personality dimensions The five abstract dimensions representing most personality traits: conscientiousness, agreeableness, neuroticism, openness to experience, and extroversion (CANOE). (2)

bounded rationality Processing limited and imperfect information and satisficing rather than maximizing when choosing among alternatives. (8)

brainstorming A free-wheeling, face-to-face meeting where team members aren't allowed to criticize, but are encouraged to speak freely, generate as many ideas as possible, and build on the ideas of others. (10)

C

categorical thinking The mostly unconscious process of organizing people and objects into preconceived categories that are stored in our long-term memory. (3)

centrality The degree and nature of interdependence between the power holder and others. (12)

centralization The degree to which formal decision authority is held by a small group of people, typically those at the top of the organizational hierachy. (15)

ceremonies Planned and usually dramatic displays of organizational culture, conducted specifically for the benefit of an audience. (16)

change agent Anyone who possesses enough knowledge and power to guide and facilitate the organizational change effort. (17)

coalition An informal group that attempts to influence people outside the group by pooling the resources and power of its members. (12)

cognitive dissonance A psychological tension that occurs when people perceive an inconsistency between their beliefs, feelings, and behavior. (4)

collectivism The extent to which people value duty to groups to which they belong, and to group harmony. (2)

communication The process by which information is transmitted and understood between two or more people. (11)

communities of practice Informal groups bound together by shared expertise and passion for a particular activity or intrest. (1)

competencies Skills, knowledge, aptitudes, and other characteristics of people that lead to superior performance. (2)

conflict The process in which one party perceives that its interests are being opposed or negatively affected by another party. (13)

conflict management Interventions that alter the level and form of conflict in ways that maximize its benefits and minimize its dysfunctional consequences. (13)

constructive conflict Occurs when team members debate their different perceptions about an issue in a way that keeps the conflict focused on the task rather than people. (10) (13)

contact hypothesis A theory stating that the more we interact with someone, the less we rely on stereotypes to understand that person. (3)

contingency approach The idea that a particular action may have different consequences in different situations. (1)

contingent work Any job in which the individual does not have an explicit or implicit contract for long-term employment, or one in which the minimum hours of work can vary in a nonsystematic way. (1)

continuance commitment A calculative decision to remain with an organization because quitting would be costly. (4)

corporate social responsibility (CSR) An organization's moral obligation towards its stakeholders. (1)

counterpower The capacity to a person, team, or organization to keep a more powerful person or group in the exchange relationship. (12)

counterproductive work behaviors (CWBs) Voluntary behaviors that are potentially harmful to the organization's effectiveness. (2)

creativity Developing an original product, service, or idea that makes a socially recognized contribution. (8)

D

decision making A conscious process of making choices among one or more alternatives with the intention of moving toward some desired state of affairs. (8)

deep-level diversity The differences in the psychological characteristics of employees, including personalities, beliefs, values, and attitudes. (1)

Delphi method A structured team decision-making process of systematically pooling the collective knowledge of experts on a particular subject to make decisions, predict the future, or identify opposing views. (10)

distributive justice The perceived fairness in outcomes we receive relative to our contributions and the outcomes and contributions of others. (5)

divergent thinking Reframing a problem in a unique way and generating different approaches to the issue. (8)

divisional structure An organizational structure that groups employees around geographic areas, clients, or outputs. (15)

drives Instinctive or innate tendencies to seek certain goals or maintain internal stability. (5)

E

electronic brainstorming Using special computer software, participants share ideas while minimizing the team dynamics problems inherent in traditional brainstorming sessions. (10)

emotional contagion The automatic and unconscious tendency to mimic and synchronize one's own nonverbal behaviors with those of other people. (11)

emotional dissonance A conflict between a person's required and true emotions. (4)

emotional intelligence (EI) The ability to perceive and express emotion, assimilate emotion in thought, understand and reason with emotion, and regulate emotion in oneself and others. (4)

emotional labor The effort, planning, and control needed to express organizationally desired emotions during interpersonal transactions. (4)

emotions Psychological, behavioral, and physiological episodes experienced toward an object, person, or event that create a state of readiness. (4)

empathy A person's understanding and sensitivity to the feelings, thoughts, and situation of others. (3)

employability An employment relationship in which people perform a variety of work activities rather than hold specific jobs, and are expected to continuously learn skills that will keep them employed. (1)

employee assistance programs (EAPs) Counseling services that help employees overcome personal or organizational stressors and adopt more effective coping mechanisms. (7)

employee engagement Employees' emotional and cognitive (rational) motivation, their ability to perform their jobs, their possessing a clear understanding of the organization's vision and their specific roles in that vision, and a belief that they have been given the resources to get their jobs done. (2)

employee involvement The degree to which employees influence how their work is organized and carried out. (8)

employee stock ownership plans (ESOPs) A reward system that encourages employees to buy stock in the company. (6)

empowerment A psychological concept in which people experience more self-determination, meaning, competence, and impact regarding their role in the organization. (6)

equity sensitivity A person's outcome/input preferences and reaction to various outcome/input ratios. (5)

equity theory A theory that explains how people develop perceptions of fairness in the distribution and exchange of resources. (5)

ERG theory A needs hierarchy theory consisting of three instinctive needs–existence, relatedness, and growth. (5)

escalation of commitment The tendency to repeat an apparently bad decision or allocate more resources to a failing course of action. (8)

ethical sensitivity A personal characteristic that enables people to recognize the presence and determine the relative importance of an ethical issue. (2)

ethics The study of moral principles or values that determine whether actions are right or wrong and outcomes are good or bad. (1) (2)

evaluation apprehension When individuals are reluctant to mention ideas that seem silly because they believe (often correctly) that other team members are silently evaluating them. (10)

executive coaching A helping relationship using behavioral methods to assist clients in identifying and achieving goals for their professional performance and personal satisfaction. (5)

exit-voice-loyalty-neglect (EVLN) model The four ways, as indicated in the name, employees respond to job dissatisfaction. (4)

expectancy theory The motivation theory based on the idea that work effort is directed toward behaviors that people believe will lead to desired outcomes. (5)

extinction Occurs when the target behavior decreases because no consequence follows it. (3)

extroversion A "Big Five" personality dimension that characterizes people who are outgoing, talkative, sociable, and assertive. (2)

F

feedback Any information that people receive about the consequences of their behavior. (5)

Fiedler's contingency model Development by Fred Fiedler, a model that suggests that leader effectiveness depends on whether the person's natural leadership style is appropriately matched to the situation. (14)

flaming The act of sending an emotionally charged e-mail message to others. (11)

force field analysis Lewin's model of systemwide change that helps change agents diagnose the forces that drive and restrain proposed organizational change. (17)

formalization The degree to which organizations standardize behavior through rules, procedures, formal training, and related mechanisms. (15)

four-drive theory A motivation theory based on the innate drives to acquire, bond, learn, and defend that incorporates both emotions and rationality. (5)

functional structure An organizational structure that organizes employees around specific knowledge or other resources. (15)

fundamental attribution error The tendency to attribute the behavior of other people more to internal than to external factors. (3)

future search Systemwide group sessions, usually lasting a few days, in which participants identify trends and identify ways to adapt to those changes. (17)

G

gainsharing plan A reward system in which team members earn bonuses for reducing costs and increasing labor efficiency in their work process. (6)

general adaptation syndrome A model of the stress experience, consisting of three stages: alarm, resistance, and exhaustion. (7)

globalization Economic, social, and cultural connectivity (and interdependence) with people in other parts of the world. (1)

goal setting The process of motivating employees and clarifying their role perceptions by establishing performance objectives. (5)

grapevine An unstructured, informal network founded on social relationships rather than organizational charts or job descriptions. (11)

grounded theory A process of developing theory through the constant interplay between data gathering and the development of theoretical concepts. (1)

group polarization The tendency of teams to make more extreme decisions than individuals working alone. (10)

groups Two or more people with a unifying relationship. (9)

groupthink The tendency of highly cohesive groups to value consensus at the price of decision quality. (10)

H

halo effect A perceptual error whereby our general impression of a person, usually based on one prominent characteristic, colors the perception of other characteristics of that person. (3)

heterogeneous teams Teams that include members with diverse personal characteristics and backgrounds. (9)

homogeneous teams Teams that include members with common technical expertise, demographics (age, sex), ethnicity, experiences, or values. (9)

I

implicit favorite The decision maker's preferred alternative against which all other choices are judged. (8)

implicit leadership theory A theory hypothesizing that perceptual processes cause people to inflate the importance of leadership as the cause of organizational events. (14)

impression management The practice of actively shaping one's public image. (12)

individualism The extent to which a person values independence and personal uniqueness. (2)

information overload A condition in which the volume of information received exceeds a person's capacity to get through it. (11)

ingratiation Any attempt to increase liking by, or perceived similarity to, the targeted person. (12)

inoculation effect A persuasive communication strategy of warning listeners that others will try to influence them in the future and that they should be wary of the opponent's arguments. (12)

intellectual capital The sum of an organization's human capital, structural capital, and relationship capital. (1)

introversion A "Big Five" personality dimension that characterizes people who are quiet, shy, and cautious. (2)

intuition The ability to know when a problem or opportunity exists and select the best course of action without conscious reasoning. (8)

J

jargon The technical language and acronyms as well as recognized words with specialized meaning in specific organizations or social groups. (11)

job burnout The process of emotional exhaustion, cynicism, and reduced efficacy (lower feelings of personal accomplishment) resulting from prolonged exposure to stress. (7)

job characteristics model A job design model that relates the motivational properties of jobs to specific personal and organizational consequences of those properties. (6)

job design The process of assigning tasks to a job, including the interdependency of those tasks with other jobs. (6)

job enlargement Increasing the number of tasks employees perform within their job. (6)

job enrichment Giving employees more responsibility for scheduling, coordinating, and planning their own work. (6)

job evaluation Systematically evaluating the worth of jobs within an organization by measuring their required skill, effort, responsibility, and working conditions. (6)

job rotation The practice of moving employees from one job to another. (6)

job satisfaction A person's evaluation of his or her job and work context. (2) (4)

job specialization The result of division of labor in which each job includes a subset of the tasks required to complete the product or service. (6)

Johari Window The model of personal and interpersonal understanding that encourages disclosure and feedback to increase the open area and reduce the blind, hidden, and unknown areas of oneself. (3)

joint optimization A key requirement in sociotechnical systems theory that a balance must be struck between social and technical systems to maximize an operation's effectiveness. (10)

K

knowledge management Any structured activity that improves an organization's capacity to acquire, share, and use knowledge in ways that improve its survival and success. (1)

L

leadership Influencing, motivating, and enabling others to contribute toward the effectiveness and success of the organizations of which they are members. (14)

leadership substitutes A theory that identifies conditions that either limit a leader's ability to influence subordinates or make that particular leadership style unnecessary. (14)

learning A relatively permanent change in behavior (or behavior tendency) that occurs as a result of a person's interaction with the environment. (3)

learning orientation The extent that an organization or individual supports knowledge management, particularly opportunities to acquire knowledge through experience and experimentation. (3)

legitimate power The capacity to influence others through formal authority. (12)

locus of control A personality trait referring to the extent to which people believe events are within their control. (2)

M

Machiavellian values The belief that deceit is a natural and acceptable way to influence others. (12)

management by walking around (MBWA) A communication practice in which executives get out of their offices and learn from others in the organization through face-to-face dialogue. (11)

Maslow's needs hierarchy theory Maslow's motivation theory of five instinctive needs arranged in a hierarchy, whereby people are motivated to fulfill a higher need as a lower one becomes gratified. (5)

matrix structure A type of departmentalization that overlays two organizational forms in order to leverage the benefits of both. (15)

mechanistic structure A organizational structure with a narrow span of control and high degrees of formalization and centralization. (15)

media richness The data-carrying capacity of a communication medium, including the volume and variety of information that can be transmitted during a specific time. (11)

mental imagery Mentally practicing a task and visualizing its successful completion. (6)

mental models The broad worldviews or "theories in-use" that people rely on to guide their perceptions and behaviors. (3)

mentoring The process of learning the ropes of organizational life from a senior person within the company. (12)

moral intensity The degree to which an issue demands the application of ethical principles. (2)

motivation The forces within a person that affect his or her direction, intensity, and persistence of voluntary behavior. (2) (5)

motivator–hygiene theory Herzberg's theory stating that employees are primarily motivated by growth and esteem needs, not by lower-level needs. (6)

multisource (360-degree) feedback Performance feedback received from a full circle of people around an employee. (5)

Myers-Briggs Type Indicator (MBTI) A personality inventory designed to identify individuals' basic preferences for perceiving and processing information. (2)

N

need for achievement (nAch) A learned need in which people want to accomplish reasonably challenging goals, and desire unambiguous feedback and recognition for their success. (5)

need for affiliation (nAff) A learned need in which people seek approval from others, conform to their wishes and expectations, and avoid conflict and confrontation. (5)

need for power (nPow) A learned need in which people want to control their environment, including people and material resources, to benefit either themselves (personalized power) or others (socialized power). (5)

needs Deficiencies that energize or trigger behaviors to satisfy those needs. (5)

negative reinforcement Occurs when the removal or avoidance of a consequence increases or maintains the frequency or future probability of a behavior. (3)

negotiation Two or more conflicting parties attempt to resolve their divergent goals by redefining the terms of their interdependence. (13)

networking Cultivating social relationships with others to accomplish one's goals. (12)

network structure An alliance of several organizations for the purpose of creating a product or serving a client. (15)

nominal group technique A structured team decision-making process whereby team members independently write down ideas, describe and clarify them to the group, and then independently rank or vote on them. (10)

norms The informal rules and shared expectations that groups establish to regulate the behavior of their members. (9)

O

open systems Organizations that take their sustenance from the environment and, in turn, affect that environment through their output. (1)

organic structure An organizational structure with a wide span of control, with little formalization and decentralized decision making. (15)

organizational behavior (OB) The study of what people think, feel, and do in and around organizations. (1)

organizational citizenship Behaviors that extend beyond the employee's normal job duties. (2)

organizational commitment The employee's emotional attachment to, identification with, and involvement in a particular organization. (4)

organizational culture The basic pattern of shared assumptions, values, and beliefs governing the way employees within an organization think about and act on problems and opportunities. (16)

organizational politics Behaviors that others perceive as self-serving tactics for personal gain at the expense of other people and possibly the organization. (12)

organizational socialization The process by which individuals learn the values, expected behaviors, and social knowledge necessary to assume their roles in the organization. (16)

organizational strategy The way an organization positions itself in its setting in relation to its stakeholders, given the organization's resources, capabilities, and mission. (15)

organizational structure The division of labor and the patterns of coordinations, communications, work flow, and formal power that direct organizational activities. (15)

organizations Groups of people who work interdependently toward some purpose. (1)

P

parallel learning structures Highly participative groups constructed alongside (i.e., parallel to) the formal organization with the purpose of increasing the organization's learning and producing meaningful organizational change. (17)

path–goal leadership theory A contingency theory of leadership based on expectancy theory of motivation that relates several leadership styles to specific employee and situational contingencies. (14)

perception The process of receiving information about and making sense of the world around us. (3)

personality The relatively stable pattern of behaviors and consistent internal states that explain a person's behavioral tendencies. (2)

persuasion Using logical arguments, facts, and emotional appeals to encourage people to accept a request or message. (12)

positive organizational behavior An emerging philosophy that focuses on building positive qualities and traits within individuals or institutions as opposed to focusing on just trying to fix what might be wrong with them. (3) (5)

positive reinforcement Occurs when the introduction of a consequence increases or maintains the frequency or future probability of a behavior. (3)

postdecisional justification Justifying choices by unconsciously inflating the quality of the selected option and deflating the quality of the discarded options. (8)

power The capacity of a person, team, or organization to influence others. (12)

power distance The extent to which people accept unequal distribution of power in a society. (2)

prejudice The unfounded negative emotions and attitudes toward people belonging to a particular stereotyped group. (3)

primacy effect A perceptual error in which we quickly form an opinion of people based on the first information we receive about them. (3)

procedural justice The fairness of the procedures used to decide the distribution of resources. (5)

process losses Resources (including time and energy) expended toward team development and maintenance rather than the task. (9)

production blocking A time constraint in team decision making due to the procedural requirement that only one person may speak at a time. (10)

profit sharing plans A reward system that pays bonuses to employees based on the previous year's level of corporate profits. (6)

projection bias A perceptual error in which we believe that other people have the same beliefs and behaviors that we do. (3)

prospect theory An effect in which losing a particular amount is more disliked than gaining the same amount. (8)

psychological contract The individual's beliefs about the terms and conditions of a reciprocal exchange agreement between that person and another party. (4)

psychological harassment Repeated and hostile or unwanted conduct, verbal comments, actions, or gestures that affect an employee's dignity or psychological or physical integrity and that result in a harmful work environment for the employee. (7)

punishment Occurs when a consequence decreases the frequency or future probability of a behavior. (3)

R

rational choice paradigm A deeply held view that people should and do make decisions based on pure logic using all necessary information. (8)

realistic job preview (RJP) The process of giving job applicants a balance of positive and negative information about the job and work context. (16)

reality shock Perceived discrepancies between preemployment expectations and on the job reality. (16)

recency effect A perceptual error in which the most recent information dominates one's perception of others. (3)

referent power The capacity to influence others based on the identification and respect they have for the power holder. (12)

refreezing The latter part of the change to the process in which systems and conditions are introduced that reinforce and maintain the desired behaviors. (17)

resilience The capability of individuals to cope successfully in the face of significant change, adversity, or risk. (7)

rituals The programmed routines of daily organizational life that dramatize the organization's culture. (16)

role A set of behaviors that people are expected to perform because they hold certain positions in a team and organization. (9)

role ambiguity A lack of clarity and predictability of the outcomes of a person's behavior. (7)

role conflict Incongruity or incompatibility of expectations associated with a person's role. (7)

S

satisficing Selecting a solution that is satisfactory, or "good enough" rather than optimal or "the best." (8)

scenario planning A systematic process of thinking about alternative futures, and what the organization should do to anticipate and react to those environments. (8)

scientific management Involves systematically partitioning work into its smallest elements and standardizing tasks to achieve maximum efficiency. (6)

scientific method A set principles and procedures that help researchers to systematically understand previously unexplained events and conditions. (1)

selective attention The process of filtering information received by our senses. (3)

self-actualization The need for self-fulfillment–a sense that a person's potential has been realized. (5)

self-directed work teams (SDWTs) Cross-functional work groups organized around work processes that complete an entire piece of work requiring several interdependent tasks, and that have substantial autonomy over the execution of those tasks. (10)

self-fulfilling prophecy Occurs when our expectations about another person cause that person to act in a way that is consistent with those expectations. (3)

self-leadership The process of influencing oneself to establish the self-direction and self-motivation needed to perform a task. (6)

self-monitoring A personality trait referring to an individual's level of sensitivity behavior of others and the ability to adapt appropriately to these situational cues. (2)

self-reinforcement Occurs whenever someone has control over a reinforcer but delays it until a self-set goal has been completed. (3)

self-serving bias A perceptual error whereby people tend to attribute their favorable outcomes to internal factors and their failures to external factors. (3)

self-talk Talking to ourselves about our own thoughts or actions for the purpose of increasing our self-confidence and navigating through decisions in a future event. (6)

servant leadership The belief that leaders serve followers by understanding their needs and facilitating their work performance. (14)

sexual harassment Unwelcome conduct of a sexual nature that detrimentally affects the work environment or leads to adverse job-related consequences for its victims. (7)

shared leadership The view that leadership is broadly distributed rather than assigned to one person, such that people within the team and organization lead each other. (14)

situational leadership theory (SLT) Development by Hersey and Blanchard, this model suggests that effective leaders vary their styles with the "readiness" of followers. (14)

skill variety The extent to which employees must use different skills and talents to perform tasks within their job. (6)

social identity theory A conceptual framework based on the idea that how we perceive the world depends on how we define ourselves in terms of our membership in various social groups. (3)

social learning theory A theory stating that much learning occurs by observing others and then modeling the behaviors that lead to favorable outcomes and avoiding the behaviors that lead to punishing consequences. (3)

social loafing A situation in which people exert less effort (and usually perform at a lower level) when working in groups than when working alone. (9)

socioemotional conflict A negative outcome that occurs when differences are viewed as personal attacks rather than attempts to resolve an issue. (13)

sociotechnical systems (STS) theory A theory stating that effective work sites have joint optimization of their social and technological systems, and that teams should have sufficient autonomy to control key variances in the work process. (10)

span of control The number of people directly reporting to the next level in the organizational hierarchy. (15)

stakeholders Shareholders, customers, suppliers, governments, and any other groups with a vested interest in the organization. (1)

stereotyping The process of assigning traits to people based on their membership in a social category. (3)

stock options A reward system that gives employees the right to purchase company stock at a future date at a predetermined price. (6)

stress An individual's adaptive response to a situation that is perceived as challenging or threatening to the person's well-being. (7)

stressors The causes of stress, including any environmental conditions that place a physical or emotional demand on the person. (7)

substitutability The extent to which people dependent on a resource have alternatives. (12)

superordinate goals Common objectives held by conflicting parties that are more important than their conflicting departmental or individual goals. (13)

surface-level diversity Observable demographic or physiological differences in people, such as their race, ethnicity, gender, age, and physical disabilities. (1)

T

tacit knowledge Knowledge embedded in our actions and ways of thinking, and transmitted only through observation and experience. (3)

task identity The degree to which a job requires completion of a whole or an identifiable piece of work. (6)

task interdependence The extent to which team members must share common inputs to their individual tasks, need to interact in the process of executing their work, or receive outcomes (such as rewards) that are partly determined by the performance of others. (9)

task significance The degree to which the job has a substantial impact on the organization and/or larger society. (6)

team-based structure A type of departmentalization with a flat hierarchy and relatively little formalization, consisting of self-directed work teams responsible for various work processes. (15)

team building Any formal activity intended to improve the development and functioning of a work team. (10)

team cohesiveness The degree of attraction people feel toward the team and their motivation to remain members. (9)

team effectiveness The extent to which a team achieves its objectives, achieves the needs and objectives of its members, and sustains itself over time. (9)

teams Groups of two or more people who interact and influence each other, are mutually accountable for achieving common goals associated with organizational objectives, and perceive themselves as a social entity within an organization. (9)

third-party conflict resolution Any attempt by a relatively neutral person to help the parties resolve their differences. (13)

transactional leadership Leadership that helps organizations achieve their current objectives more efficiently, such as linking job performances to valued rewards and ensuring that employees have the resources needed to get the job done. (14)

transformational leadership A leadership perspective that explains how leaders change teams or organizations by creating, communicating, and modeling a vision for the organization or work unit and inspiring employees to strive for that vision. (14)

trust A person's positive expectations toward another person in situations involving risk. (4) (10)

Type A behavior pattern A behavior pattern associated with people having premature coronary heart disease; Type As tend to be impatient, lose their temper, talk rapidly, and interrupt others. (7)

U

uncertainty avoidance The degree to which people tolerate ambiguity or feel threatened by ambiguity and uncertainty. (2)

unfreezing The first part of the change process whereby the change agent produces disequilibrium between the driving and restraining forces. (17)

upward appeal A type of coalition in which one or more members have higher authority or expertise. (12)

V

valence The anticipated satisfaction or dissatisfaction that an individual feels toward an outcome. (5)

values Stable, long-lasting beliefs about what is important in a variety of situations, that guide our decisions and actions. (1) (2)

values congruence A situation wherein two or more entities have similar value systems. (2)

virtual corporations Network structures representing several independent companies that form unique partnership teams to provide customized products or services, usually to specific clients, for a limited time. (15)

virtual teams Teams whose members operate across space, time, and organizational boundaries and who are linked through information technologies to achieve organizational goals. (10)

virtual work Work practices whereby employees use information technology to perform their jobs away from the traditional physical workplace. (1)

W

win–lose orientation The belief that conflicting parties are drawing from a fixed pie, so the more one party receives, the less the other party will receive. (13)

win–win orientation The belief that conflicting parties will find a mutually beneficial solution to their disagreement. (13)

work–life balance Minimizing conflict between work and nonwork demands. (1)

workaholic A person who is highly involved in work, feels compelled to work, and has a low enjoyment of work. (7)

references

CHAPTER 1

1. J. McHugh, "Google vs. Evil," *Wired,* January 2003; A. Hermida, "Google Looks to See Off Rivals," *BBC News Online,* 30 March 2004; M. Liedtke, "Google vs. Yahoo: Heavyweights Attack from Different Angles," *Associated Press Newswires,* 18 December 2004; F. Vogelstein, "Google @ $165," *Fortune,* 13 December 2004, pp. 98–104; R. Basch, "Doing Well by Doing Good," *Searcher Magazine,* January 2005, pp. 18–28; K. Coughlin, "Goooood Move," *Star-Ledger (Newark, NJ),* 5 June 2005, p. 1; A. Ignatius and L.A. Locke, "In Search of the Real Google," *Time,* 20 February 2006, p. 36.

2. M. Warner, "Organizational Behavior Revisited," *Human Relations* 47 (October 1994), pp. 1151–66; R. Westwood and S. Clegg, "The Discourse of Organization Studies: Dissensus, Politics, and Peradigms," in *Debating Organization: Point–Counterpoint in Organization Studies,* ed. R. Westwood and S. Clegg (Malden, MA: Blackwood, 2003), pp. 1–42. Some of the historical bases of OB mentioned in this paragraph are described in J.A. Conger, "Max Weber's Conceptualization of Charismatic Authority: Its Influence on Organizational Research," *The Leadership Quarterly* 4, no. 3–4 (1993), pp. 277–88; R. Kanigel, *The One Best Way: Frederick Winslow Taylor and the Enigma of Efficiency* (New York: Viking, 1997); J.H. Smith, "The Enduring Legacy of Elton Mayo," *Human Relations* 51, no. 3 (1998), pp. 221–49; T. Takala, "Plato on Leadership," *Journal of Business Ethics* 17 (May 1998), 785–98; and J.A. Fernandez, "The Gentleman's Code of Confucius: Leadership by Values," *Organizational Dynamics* 33, no. 1 (February 2004), pp. 21–31.

3. J. Micklethwait and A. Wooldridge, *The Company: A Short History of a Revolutionary Idea* (New York: Random House, 2003).

4. B. Schlender, "The Three Faces of Steve," *Fortune,* 9 November 1998, pp. 96–101.

5. D.K. Katz, R.L., *The Social Psychology of Organizations* (New York: Wiley, 1966), Chapter 2; R.N. Stern and S.R. Barley, "Organizations as Social Systems: Organization Theory's Neglected Mandate," *Administrative Science Quarterly* 41 (1996), pp. 146–62.

6. N. Hooper, "Call Me Irresistible," *Australian Financial Review,* 5 December 2003, p. 38.

7. J. Pfeffer, *New Directions for Organization Theory* (New York: Oxford University Press, 1997), pp. 7–9.

8. P.R. Lawrence and N. Nohria, *Driven: How Human Nature Shapes Our Choices* (San Francisco: Jossey-Bass, 2002), Chapter 6.

9. P.R. Lawrence "Historical Development of Organizational Behavior," in *Handbook of Organizational Behavior,* ed. L.W. Lorsch (Englewood Cliffs, NJ: Prentice Hall, 1987), pp. 1–9; S.A. Mohrman, C.B. Gibson, and A.M. Mohrman Jr., "Doing Research That Is Useful to Practice: A Model and Empirical Exploration," *Academy of Management Journal* 44 (April 2001), pp. 357–75. For a contrary view, see A.P. Brief and J.M. Dukerich, "Theory in Organizational Behavior: Can It Be Useful?" *Research in Organizational Behavior* 13 (1991), pp. 327–52.

10. M.S. Myers, *Every Employee a Manager* (New York: McGraw-Hill, 1970).

11. D. Yankelovich, "Got to Give to Get," *Mother Jones* 22 (July 1997), pp. 60–63; D. MacDonald, "Good Managers Key to Buffett's Acquisitions," *Montreal Gazette,* 16 November 2001. The two studies on OB and financial performance are B.N. Pfau and I.T. Kay, *The Human Capital Edge* (New York: McGraw-Hill, 2002); and I.S. Fulmer, B. Gerhart, and K.S. Scott, "Are the 100 Best Better? An Empirical Investigation of the Relationship between Being a 'Great Place to Work' and Firm Performance," *Personnel Psychology* 56, no. 4 (Winter 2003), pp. 965–93.

12. V. Kopytoff, "Google Making Its Mark Worldwide," *San Francisco Chronicle,* 20 September 2004, p. H1.

13. J. Guyon, "David Whitwam (CEOs on Managing Globally)," *Fortune,* 26 July 2004, p. 174; P. Loewe and J. Rufat-Latre, "The Changing Face of Global Business," *Optimize* (June 2004), pp. 32–37; L. Uchitelle, "Globalization: It's Not Just Wages," *New York Times,* 17 June 2005, pp. C1, C4.

14. S. Fischer, "Globalization and Its Challenges," *American Economic Review* (May 2003), pp. 1–29. For discussion of the diverse meanings of *globalization,* see M.F. Guillén, "Is Globalization Civilizing, Destructive or Feeble? A Critique of Five Key Debates in the Social Science Literature," *Annual Review of Sociology* 27 (2001), pp. 235–60.

15. The ongoing debate regarding the advantages and disadvantages of globalization is discussed in Guillén, "Is Globalization Civilizing, Destructive or Feeble?"; D. Doane, "Can Globalization Be Fixed?" *Business Strategy Review* 13, no. 2 (2002), pp. 51–58; J. Bhagwati, *In Defense of Globalization* (New York: Oxford University Press, 2004); and M. Wolf, *Why Globalization Works* (New Haven, CT: Yale University Press, 2004).

16. C.L. Cooper and R. J. Burke, *The New World of Work: Challenges and Opportunities* (Oxford: Blackwell, 2002); C. Higgins and L. Duxbury, *The 2001 National Work–Life Conflict Study: Report One, Final Report* (Ottawa: Health Canada, March 2002).

17. K. Ohmae, *The Next Global Stage* (Philadelphia: Wharton School Publishing, 2005).

18. R. House, M. Javidan, and P. Dorfman, "Project Globe: An Introduction," *Applied Psychology: An International Journal* 50 (2001), pp. 489–505; M.A. Von Glinow, E.A. Drost, and M.B. Teagarden, "Converging on IHRM Best Practices: Lessons Learned from a Globally Distributed Consortium on Theory and Practice," *Human Resource Management* 41, no. 1 (April 2002), pp. 123–40; M.M. Javidan et al., "In the Eye of the Beholder: Cross-Cultural Lessons in Leadership from Project Globe," *Academy of Management Perspectives* 20, no. 1 (February 2006), pp. 67–90.

19. Verizon, *Making Connections: Verizon Corporate Responsibility Report 2004* (New York: Verizon, December 2004); J. Carlton, "Dig In: At Google, a Global Workforce Translates into a Global Cafeteria Menu," *The Wall Street Journal,* 14 November 2005, p. R9; P. Goffney, "Champions of Diversity: The Path to Corporate Enlightenment," *Essence,* May 2005, pp. 149–57.

20. M.F. Riche, "America's Diversity and Growth: Signposts for the 21st Century," *Population Bulletin* (June 2000), pp. 3–43; U.S. Census Bureau, *Statistical Abstract of the United States: 2004–2005* (Washington: U.S. Census Bureau, May 2005).

21. Association of American Medical Colleges, "Table 1: Women Applicants, Enrollees–Selected Years 1949–1950 through 2002–2003" (14 July 2003), http://www.aamc.org/members/wim/statistics/stats03/start.htm (accessed 20 June 2005); U.S. Census Bureau, *Statistical Abstract of the United States: 2004–2005,* (Table no. 570, p. 371).

22. D.A. Harrison et al., "Time, Teams, and Task Performance: Changing Effects of Surface- and Deep-Level Diversity on Group Functioning," *Academy of Management Journal* 45, no. 5 (2002), pp. 1029–46.

23. R. Zemke, C. Raines, and B. Filipczak, *Generations at Work: Managing the Clash of Veterans, Boomers, Xers, and Nexters in Your Workplace* (New York: Amacom, 2000); M.R. Muetzel, *They're Not Aloof, Just Generation X* (Shreveport, LA: Steel Bay, 2003); S.H. Applebaum, M. Serena, and B.T. Shapiro, "Generation X and the Boomers: Organizational Myths and Literary Realities," *Management Research News* 27, no. 11/12 (2004), pp. 1–28.

24. O.C. Richard, "Racial Diversity, Business Strategy, and Firm Performance: A Resource-Based View," *Academy of Management Journal* 43 (2000), pp. 164–77; D.D. Frink et al., "Gender Demography and Organization Performance: A Two-Study Investigation with Convergence," *Group & Organization Management* 28 (March 2003), pp. 127–47; T. Kochan et al., "The Effects of Diversity on Business Performance: Report of the Diversity Research Network," *Human Resource Management* 42 (2003), pp. 3–21.

25. C. Hymowitz, "The New Diversity," *The Wall Street Journal,* 14 November 2005, p. R1; Sempra Energy, "Case History: Putting Diversity to Work," (San Diego, CA: Sempra Energy, 2005), www.sempra.com/diversity.htm (accessed 21 June 2005).

26. R.J. Ely and D.A. Thomas, "Cultural Diversity at Work: The Effects of Diversity Perspectives on Work Group Processes and Outcomes," *Administrative Science Quarterly* 46 (June 2001), pp. 229–73; T. Kochan et al., "The Effects of Diversity on Business Performance: Report of the Diversity Research Network," *Human Resource Management* 42, no. 1 (2003), pp. 3–21; D. van Knippenberg and S.A. Haslam, "Realizing the Diversity Dividend: Exploring the Subtle Interplay between Identity, Ideology and Reality," in *Social Identity at Work: Developing Theory for Organizational Practice,* ed. S.A. Haslam et al. (New York: Taylor and Francis, 2003), pp. 61–80; D. van Knippenberg, C.K. W. De Dreu, and A.C. Homan, "Work Group Diversity and Group Performance: An Integrative Model and Research Agenda," *Journal of Applied Psychology* 89, no. 6 (2004), pp. 1008–22; E. Molleman, "Diversity in Demographic Characteristics, Abilities, and Personality Traits: Do Faultlines Affect Team Functioning?" *Group Decision and Negotiation* 14, no. 3 (2005), pp. 173–93.

27. A. Birritteri, "Workplace Diversity: Realizing the Benefits of an All-Inclusive Employee Base," *New Jersey Business,* November 2005, p. 36.

28. S.-A. Chia and E. Toh, "Give Employees a Break," *Straits Times (Singapore),* 23 July 2005.

29. W.G. Bennis and R.J. Thomas, *Geeks and Geezers* (Boston: Harvard Business School Press, 2002), pp. 74–79; E.D.Y. Greenblatt, "Work–Life Balance: Wisdom or Whining," *Organizational Dynamics* 31, no. 2 (2002), pp. 177–93.

30. Basch, "Doing Well by Doing Good"; Coughlin, "Goooood Move."

31. M.V. Roehling et al., "The Nature of the New Employment Relationship(s): A Content Analysis of the Practitioner and Academic Literatures," *Human Resource Management* 39 (2000), pp. 305–20; W.R. Boswell et al., "Responsibilities in the 'New Employment Relationship': An Empirical Test of an Assumed Phenomenon," *Journal of Managerial Issues* 13 (Fall 2001), 307–27; M. Fugate, A.J. Kinicki, and B.E. Ashforth, "Employability: A Psycho-Social Construct, Its Dimensions, and Applications," *Journal of Vocational Behavior* 65, no. 1 (2004), pp. 14–38.

32. M. Jenkins, "Yours for the Taking," *Boeing Frontiers,* June 2004, http://www.boeing.com/news/frontiers/index.html.

33. A.E. Polivka, "Contingent and Alternative Work Arrangements, Defined," *Monthly Labor Review* 119 (October 1996), pp. 3–10; D.H. Pink, *Free Agent Nation* (New York: Time Warner, 2002); C.E. Connelly and D.G. Gallagher, "Emerging Trends in Contingent Work Research," *Journal of Management* 30, no. 6 (2004), pp. 959–83.

34. B.A. Lautsch, "Uncovering and Explaining Variance in the Features and Outcomes of Contingent Work," *Industrial & Labor Relations Review* 56 (October 2002), pp. 23–43; S. Ang, L. Van Dyne, and T.M. Begley, "The Employment Relationships of Foreign Workers versus Local Employees: A Field Study of Organizational Justice, Job Satisfaction, Performance, and OCB," *Journal of Organizational Behavior* 24 (2003), pp. 561–83; A.L. Kalleberg, "Flexible Firms and Labor Market Segmentation," Work and Occupations 30, no. 2 (May 2003), pp. 154–75; B.A. Lautsch, "The Influence of Regular Work Systems on Compensation for Contingent Workers," *Industrial Relations* 42, no. 4 (October 2003), pp. 565–88; Connelly and Gallagher, "Emerging Trends in Contingent Work Research"; B. Pocock, J. Buchanan, and I. Campbell, "Meeting the Challenge of Casual Work in Australia: Evidence, Past Treatment and Future Policy," *Australian Bulletin of Labour* 30, no. 1 (March 2004), pp. 16–32.

35. S. de Castro and Y.-C. Tham, "Home Work," *Digital Life,* 8 February 2005.

36. Australian Telework Advisory Committee (ATAC), *Telework–International Developments (Paper III)* (Canberra: Commonwealth of Australia, March 2005); M. Conlin, "The Easiest Commute of All," *Business Week,* 12 December 2005, p. 78.

37. "AT&T Telecommute Survey Indicates Productivity Is Up," AT&T News release, (New York: 6 August 2002); L. Duxbury and C. Higgins, "Telecommute: A Primer for the Millennium Introduction," in *The New World of Work: Challenges and Opportunities,* ed. C.L. Cooper and R.J. Burke (Oxford: Blackwell, 2002), pp. 157–99; V. Illegems and A. Verbeke, "Telework: What Does It Mean for Management?" *Long Range Planning* 37 (2004), pp. 319–34; S. Raghuram and B. Wiesenfeld, "Work–Nonwork Conflict and Job Stress among Virtual Workers," *Human Resource Management* 43, no. 2/3 (Summer/Fall 2004), pp. 259–77.

38. D.E. Bailey and N.B. Kurland, "A Review of Telework Research: Findings, New Directions, and Lessons for the Study of Modern Work," *Journal of Organizational Behavior* 23 (2002), pp. 383–400; D.W. McCloskey and M. Igbaria, "Does 'Out of Sight' Mean 'Out of Mind'? An Empirical Investigation of the Career Advancement Prospects of Telecommuters," *Information Resources Management Journal* 16 (April–June 2003), pp. 19–34; Sensis, *Sensis® Insights Report: Teleworking,* (Melbourne: Sensis, June 2005).

39. J. Lipnack and J. Stamps, *Virtual Teams: People Working across Boundaries with Technology* (New York: John Wiley & Sons, 2001); L.L. Martins, L.L. Gilson, and

M.T. Maynard, "Virtual Teams: What Do We Know and Where Do We Go from Here?" *Journal of Management* 30, no. 6 (2004), pp. 805–35; G. Hertel, S. Geister, and U. Konradt, "Managing Virtual Teams: A Review of Current Empirical Research," *Human Resource Management Review* 15, no. 1 (2005), pp. 69–95.

40. C. Kelly et al., *Deriving Value from Corporate Values* (The Aspen Institute and Booz Allen Hamilton Inc., February 2005).

41. B.M. Meglino and E.C. Ravlin, "Individual Values in Organizations: Concepts, Controversies, and Research," *Journal of Management* 24, no. 3 (1998), pp. 351–89; B.R. Agle and C.B. Caldwell, "Understanding Research on Values in Business," *Business and Society* 38, no. 3 (September 1999), pp. 326–87; S. Hitlin and J.A. Pilavin, "Values: Reviving a Dormant Concept," *Annual Review of Sociology* 30 (2004), pp. 359–93.

42. Some of the popular books that emphasize the importance of values include J.C. Collins and J.I. Porras, *Built to Last: Successful Habits of Visionary Companies* (London: Century, 1995); C.A. O'Reilly III and J.Pfeffer, *Hidden Value* (Cambridge, MA: Harvard Business School Press, 2000); J.M. Kouzes and B.Z. Posner, *The Leadership Challenge,* 3rd ed. (San Francisco: Jossey-Bass, 2002).

43. The role of values as a control system is discussed in T.M. Begley and D.P. Boyd, "Articulating Corporate Values through Human Resource Policies," *Business Horizons* 43, no. 4 (July 2000), pp. 8–12; and M.G. Murphy and K.M. Davey, "Ambiguity, Ambivalence and Indifference in Organizational Values," *Human Resource Management Journal* 12 (2002), pp. 17–32.

44. Middle East Company News, "Accountability, Teamwork, and Continuous Improvement Define Core Operating Values at DED," Middle East Company News News release (Dubai: 4 January 2005).

45. "Believe It," *BC Business,* July 2004, p. 130; "Multi-Year Study Finds 21% Increase in Americans Who Say Corporate Support of Social Issues Is Important in Building Trust," *Business Wire,* 9 December 2004; J. Milne, "Do the Right Thing," *MIS UK,* 1 December 2005, p. 20.

46. M. van Marrewijk, "Concepts and Definitions of CSR and Corporate Sustainability: Between Agency and Communion," *Journal of Business Ethics* 44 (May 2003), pp. 95–105.

47. S. Zadek, *The Civil Corporation: The New Economy of Corporate Citizenship* (London: Earthscan, 2001), Chapter 9; The Warehouse, *This Way Forward: Society and Environment Report* 2005 (2005); S. Zambon and A. Del Bello, "Toward a Stakeholder Responsible Approach: The Constructive Role of Reporting," *Corporate Governance* 5, no. 2 (2005), pp. 130–42.

48. "Wal-Mart to Cut Ties with Bangladesh Factories Using Child Labour," *CBC News (Toronto),* 30 November 2005; P. Foster, "Heaven Can Wait," *National Post,* 2 July 2005, p. FP17.

49. A. Brown, "Trust Makes the Difference," *Evolution–The Business and Technology Magazine from SKF,* 25 May 2004; J. Reingold, "Walking the Talk," *Fast Company,* November 2005, pp. 80–85.

50. M.N. Zald, "More Fragmentation? Unfinished Business in Linking the Social Sciences and the Humanities," *Administrative Science Quarterly* 41 (1996), pp. 251–61. Concerns about the "trade deficit" in OB are raised in C. Heath and S.B. Sitkin, "Big-B versus Big-O: What Is Organizational about Organizational Behavior?" *Journal of Organizational Behavior* 22 (2001), pp. 43–58.

51. N. Nicholson, "Evolutionary Psychology: Toward a New View of Human Nature and Organizational Society," *Human Relations* 50 (September 1997), pp. 1053–78; B.D. Pierce and R. White, "The Evolution of Social Structure: Why Biology Matters," *Academy of Management Review* 24 (October 1999), pp. 843–53; Lawrence and Nohria, *Driven: How Human Nature Shapes Our Choices.*

52. A.C. Strauss, J., *Grounded Theory in Practice* (London: Sage Publications, 1997). For an overview of the importance of qualitative methods in organizational behavior, see R.P. Gephart Jr., "Qualitative Research and the *Academy of Management Journal,"* *Academy of Management Journal* 47 (2004), pp. 454–62.

53. C.M. Christensen and M.E. Raynor, "Why Hard-Nosed Executives Should Care about Management Theory," *Harvard Business Review* (September 2003), pp. 66–74. For an excellent critique of the "one best way" approach in early management scholarship, see P.F. Drucker, "Management's New Paradigms," *Forbes* (5 October 1998), pp. 152–77.

54. H.L. Tosi and J.W. Slocum Jr., "Contingency Theory: Some Suggested Directions," *Journal of Management* 10 (1984), pp. 9–26.

55. D.M.H. Rousseau, "Meso Organizational Behavior: Avoiding Three Fundamental Biases," in *Trends in Organizational Behavior,* ed. C.L. Cooper and D.M. Rousseau (Chichester, UK: John Wiley & Sons, 1994), pp. 13–30.

56. E. Zore, "When We Grow Together, We Grow Stronger," *Executive Speeches,* October 2005, p. 20.

57. F.E. Kast and J.E. Rosenweig, "General Systems Theory: Applications for Organization and Management," *Academy of Management Journal* (1972), pp. 447–65; P.M. Senge, *The Fifth Discipline: The Art and Practice of the Learning Organization* (New York: Doubleday Currency, 1990); A. De Geus, *The Living Company* (Boston: Harvard Business School Press, 1997); R.T. Pascale, M. Millemann, and L. Gioja, *Surfing on the Edge of Chaos* (London: Texere, 2000).

58. V.P. Rindova and S. Kotha, "Continuous 'Morphing': Competing through Dynamic Capabilities, Form, and Function," *Academy of Management Journal* 44 (2001), pp. 1263–80; J. McCann, "Organizational Effectiveness: Changing Concepts for Changing Environments," *Human Resource Planning* 27, no. 1 (2004), pp. 42–50.

59. R. Martin, "The Virtue Matrix: Calculating the Return on Corporate Responsibility," *Harvard Business Review* 80 (March 2002), pp. 68–85.

60. M.L. Tushman, M.B. Nadler, and D.A. Nadler, *Competing by Design: The Power of Organizational Architecture* (New York: Oxford University Press, 1997).

61. G. Huber, "Organizational Learning: The Contributing Processes and Literature," *Organizational Science* 2 (1991), pp. 88–115; E.C. Nevis, A.J. DiBella, and J.M. Gould, "Understanding Organizations as Learning Systems," *Sloan Management Review* 36 (1995), pp. 73–85; G. Miles et al., "Some Conceptual and Research Barriers to the Utilization of Knowledge," *California Management Review* 40 (Spring 1998), pp. 281–88; D.A. Garvin, *Learning in Action: A Guide to Putting the Learning Organization to Work* (Boston: Harvard Business School Press, 2000).

62. T.A. Stewart, *Intellectual Capital: The New Wealth of Organizations* (New York:

Currency/Doubleday, 1997); H. Saint-Onge and D. Wallace, *Leveraging Communities of Practice for Strategic Advantage* (Boston: Butterworth-Heinemann, 2003), pp. 9–10; J.-A. Johannessen, B. Olsen, and J. Olaisen, "Intellectual Capital as a Holistic Management Philosophy: A Theoretical Perspective," *International Journal of Information Management* 25, no. 2 (2005), pp. 151–71.

63. There is no complete agreement on the meaning of *organizational learning* (or *learning organization*), and the relationship between organizational learning and knowledge management is still somewhat ambiguous. For example, see S.C. Goh, "The Learning Organization: An Empirical Test of a Normative Perspective," *International Journal of Organization Theory & Behavior* 4, no. 3/4 (August 2001), pp. 329–55; and B.R. McElyea, "Knowledge Management, Intellectual Capital, and Learning Organizations: A Triad of Future Management Integration," *Futurics* 26 (2002), pp. 59–65.

64. C.W. Wick and L.S. Leon, "From Ideas to Actions: Creating a Learning Organization," *Human Resource Management* 34 (Summer 1995), pp. 299–311; L. Falkenberg et al., "Knowledge Acquisition Processes for Technology Decisions," in *Proceedings of the Academy of Management 2002 Annual Conference* (2002), pp. J1–J6; S. Lloyd, "Smarter Spending Habits," *Business Review Weekly,* 10 November 2005, p. 130.

65. W. Cohen and D. Levinthal, "Absorptive Capacity: A New Perspective on Learning and Innovation," *Administrative Science Quarterly* 35 (1990), pp. 128–52; J.L. Johnson, R.S. Sohi, and R. Grewal, "The Role of Relational Knowledge Stores in Interfirm Partnering," *Journal of Marketing* 68 (July 2004), pp. 21–36; M. Rogers, "Absorptive Capacity and Economic Growth: How Do Countries Catch Up?" *Cambridge Journal of Economics* 28, no. 4 (July 2004), pp. 577–96.

66. G.S. Richards and S.C. Goh, "Implementing Organizational Learning: Toward a Systematic Approach," *The Journal of Public Sector Management* (Autumn 1995), pp. 25–31; C. O'Dell and C.J. Grayson, "If Only We Knew What We Know: Identification and Transfer of Internal Best Practices," *California Management Review* 40 (Spring 1998), pp. 154–74; R. Ruggles, "The State of the Notion: Knowledge Management in Practice," *California Management Review* 40 (Spring 1998), pp. 80–89.

67. R. Garud and A. Kumaraswamy, "Vicious and Virtuous Circles in the Management of Knowledge: The Case of Infosys Technologies," *MIS Quarterly* 29, no. 1 (March 2005), pp. 9–33.

68. E.C. Wenger and W.M. Snyder, "Communities of Practice: The Organizational Frontier," *Harvard Business Review* 78 (January–February 2002), pp. 139–45; Saint-Onge and Wallace, *Leveraging Communities of Practice for Strategic Advantage;* M. Thompson, "Structural and Epistemic Parameters in Communities of Practice," *Organization Science* 16, no. 2 (March–April 2005), pp. 151–64.

69. Saint-Onge and Wallace, *Leveraging Communities of Practice for Strategic Advantage,* Chapter 5.

70. B.P. Sunoo, "The Sydney Challenge," *Workforce,* September 2000, pp. 70–73; N. Bita and J. Lehmann, "Five-Ring Circuit for Olympic Organisers," *The Australian,* 12 September 2005, p. 27; E. Semertzaki, "A Brief but Intense Job," *Information Outlook,* May 2005, pp. 29–35.

71. H. Beazley, J. Boenisch, and D. Harden, "Knowledge Continuity: The New Management Function," *Journal of Organizational Excellence* 22 (2003), pp. 65–81.

72. D. Cline, "On a Roll," *Augusta Chronicle,* 2 February 2003, p. D1.

73. M.E. McGill and J.W. Slocum Jr., "Unlearn the Organization," *Organizational Dynamics* 22, no. 2 (1993), pp. 67–79; D. Lei, J.W. Slocum, and R.A. Pitts, "Designing Organizations for Competitive Advantage: The Power of Unlearning and Learning," *Organizational Dynamics* 27 (Winter 1999), pp. 24–38.

CHAPTER 2

1. "Owens Corning Makes Smart Investments in Employee Training," *The Resource (Newsletter of Jackson State's Division of Economic and Community Development),* Fall 2004, p. 1; M. Millar, "Getting the Measure of Its People," *Personnel Today,* 14 December 2004, p. 6; J. Robison, "ASB Bank: Good Isn't Good Enough," *Gallup Management Journal,* 12 August 2004; V. Ratanjee, "Wake-up Call for Thailand, Inc.," *Gallup Management Journal,* 12 May 2005; T.J. Tschida, "Creating an Employee-Centric Call Center," *Gallup Management Journal,* 13 October 2005; "Employee Engagement Levels Are Focus of Global Towers Perrin Study," *Towers Perrin Monitor (Online),* January 2006, www.towersperrin.com; "Gallup Study: Feeling Good Matters in the Workplace," *Gallup Management Journal,* 12 January 2006.

2. Thanks to senior officers in the Singapore Armed Forces for discovering the handy "MARS" acronym. Thanks also to Chris Perryer at the University of Western Australia for pointing out that the full model should be called the "MARS BAR" because the outcomes are "behavior and results"! The MARS model is a variation of earlier models and writing by several sources, including E.E. Lawler III and L.W. Porter, "Antecedent Attitudes of Effective Managerial Performance," *Organizational Behavior and Human Performance* 2, no. 2 (1967), pp. 122–42; and K.F. Kane, "Special Issue: Situational Constraints and Work Performance," *Human Resource Management Review* 3 (Summer 1993), pp. 83–175.

3. T.A. Judge and R. Illies, "Relationship of Personality to Performance Motivation: A Meta-Analytic Review," *Journal of Applied Psychology* 87, no. 4 (2002), pp. 797–807; S. Roccas et al., "The Big Five Personality Factors and Personal Values," *Personality and Social Psychology* 28 (June 2002), pp. 789–801.

4. C.C. Pinder, *Work Motivation in Organizational Behavior* (Upper Saddle River, NJ: Prentice-Hall, 1998); G.P. Latham and C.C. Pinder, "Work Motivation Theory and Research at the Dawn of the Twenty-First Century," *Annual Review of Psychology* 56 (2005), pp. 485–516.

5. K. Brown, "Putting Leadership Rubber to the Manager Road," *Human Resources Magazine (Australia),* 15 June 2005.

6. R. Jacobs, "Using Human Resource Functions to Enhance Emotional Intelligence," in *The Emotionally Intelligent Workplace,* ed. C. Cherniss and D. Goleman (San Francisco: Jossey-Bass, 2001), pp. 159–81.

7. "New Euro 16m Centre to Train 1,000 Toyota Staff a Year," *Just-Auto,* 24 March 2006; Y. Kageyama, "Toyota Workers Learn Knack of Auto Production in New Global Push," *Associated Press Newswires,* 17 April 2006.

8. S. Brady, "Deep in the Heart of AT&T Dallas," *Cable World,* 7 October 2002, p. 37.

9. J. Waresh, "750 Workers Log 16-Hour Days to Restore Power," *Palm Beach Post (Florida),* 9 November 2005, p. 1.

10. Kane, "Special Issue: Situational Constraints and Work Performance"; S.B. Bacharach and P. Bamberger, "Beyond Situational Constraints: Job Resources

Inadequacy and Individual Performance at Work," *Human Resource Management Review* 5, no. 2 (1995), pp. 79–102; G. Johns, "Commentary: In Praise of Context," *Journal of Organizational Behavior* 22 (2001), pp. 31–42.

11. J.P. Campbell, "The Definition and Measurement of Performance in the New Age," in *The Changing Nature of Performance: Implications for Staffing, Motivation, and Development,* ed. D.R. Ilgen and E.D. Pulakos (San Francisco: Jossey-Bass, 1999), pp. 399–429; R.D. Hackett, "Understanding and Predicting Work Performance in the Canadian Military," *Canadian Journal of Behavioural Science* 34, no. 2 (2002), pp. 131–40.

12. D.W. Organ, "Organizational Citizenship Behavior: It's Construct Clean-up Time," *Human Performance* 10 (1997), pp. 85–97; J.A. LePine, A. Erez, and D.E. Johnson, "The Nature and Dimensionality of Organizational Citizenship Behavior: A Critical Review and Meta-Analysis," *Journal of Applied Psychology* 87 (February 2002), pp. 52–65; B. Erickson, "Nature Times Nurture: How Organizations Can Optimize Their People's Contributions," *Journal of Organizational Excellence* 24, no. 1 (Winter 2004), pp. 21–30; M.A. Vey and J.P. Campbell, "In-Role or Extra-Role Organizational Citizenship Behavior: Which Are We Measuring?" *Human Performance* 17, no. 1 (2004), pp. 119–35.

13. M. Rotundo and P. Sackett, "The Relative Importance of Task, Citizenship, and Counterproductive Performance to Global Ratings of Job Performance: A Policy-Capturing Approach," *Journal of Applied Psychology* 87 (February 2002), pp. 66–80; P. D. Dunlop and K. Lee, "Workplace Deviance, Organizational Citizenship Behaviour, and Business Unit Performance: The Bad Apples Do Spoil the Whole Barrel," *Journal of Organizational Behavior* 25 (2004), pp. 67–80.

14. B. Carey, "Truckload's New Recruiting Routes," *Traffic World,* 22 August 2005; D. Simanoff, "Hotels Plagued by Staff Vacancies," *Tampa Tribune,* 30 January 2006, p. 1.

15. Watson Wyatt, "U.S. Workers City Hypocrisy and Favoritism–Rather Than Financial Misdeeds–as Biggest Ethical Lapses at Work," Watson Wyatt News release (Washington, DC: 12 January 2005); Watson Wyatt, *WorkCanada 2004/2005–Pursuing Productive Engagement* (Toronto: Watson Wyatt, January 2005).

16. T.R. Mitchell, B.C. Holtom, and T.W. Lee, "How to Keep Your Best Employees: Developing an Effective Retention Policy," *Academy of Management Executive* 15 (November 2001), pp. 96–108.

17. D.A. Harrison and J.J. Martocchio, "Time for Absenteeism: A 20-Year Review of Origins, Offshoots, and Outcomes," *Journal of Management* 24 (Spring 1998), pp. 305–50; C.M. Mason and M.A. Griffin, "Group Absenteeism and Positive Affective Tone: A Longitudinal Study," *Journal of Organizational Behavior* 24, no. 6 (2003), pp. 667–87; A. Vaananen et al., "Job Characteristics, Physical and Psychological Symptoms, and Social Support as Antecedents of Sickness Absence among Men and Women in the Private Industrial Sector," *Social Science & Medicine* 57, no. 5 (2003), pp. 807–24.

18. J. Miller, "Tom's of Maine Co-Founder, in Portsmouth, Relates His Philosophy," *Union-Leader (Manchester, NH),* 22 May 2003, p. D8.

19. Some of the more popular books that encourage executives to develop values statements include J.C. Collins and J.I. Porras, *Built to Last: Successful Habits of Visionary Companies* (London: Century, 1995); C. A. O'Reilly III and J. Pfeffer, *Hidden Value* (Cambridge, MA: Harvard Business School Press, 2000); and J.M. Kouzes and B.Z. Posner, *The Leadership Challenge,* 3rd ed. (San Francisco: Jossey-Bass, 2002).

20. B.M. Meglino and E.C. Ravlin, "Individual Values in Organizations: Concepts, Controversies, and Research," *Journal of Management* 24, no. 3 (1998), pp. 351–89; B.R. Agle and C.B. Caldwell, "Understanding Research on Values in Business," *Business and Society* 38, no. 3 (September 1999), pp. 326–87; S. Hitlin and J.A. Pilavin, "Values: Reviving a Dormant Concept," *Annual Review of Sociology* 30 (2004), pp. 359–93.

21. D. Lubinski, D.B. Schmidt, and C.P. Benbow, "A 20-Year Stability Analysis of the Study of Values for Intellectually Gifted Individuals from Adolescence to Adulthood," *Journal of Applied Psychology* 81 (1996), pp. 443–51.

22. B. Kabanoff and J. Daly, "Espoused Values in Organizations," *Australian Journal of Management* 27, Special issue (2002), pp. 89–104.

23. S.H. Schwartz, "Universals in the Content and Structure of Values: Theoretical Advances and Empirical Tests in 20 Countries," *Advances in Experimental Social Psychology* 25 (1992), pp. 1–65; S.H. Schwartz, "Are There Universal Aspects in the Structure and Contents of Human Values?" *Journal of Social Issues* 50 (1994), pp. 19–45; M. Schwartz, "The Nature of the Relationship between Corporate Codes of Ethics and Behavior," *Journal of Business Ethics* 32, no. 3 (2001), p. 247; D. Spini, "Measurement Equivalence of 10 Value Types from the Schwartz Value Survey across 21 Countries," *Journal of Cross-Cultural Psychology* 34, no. 1 (January 2003), pp. 3–23; S.H. Schwartz and K. Boehnke, "Evaluating the Structure of Human Values with Confirmatory Factor Analysis," *Journal of Research in Personality* 38, no. 3 (2004), pp. 230–55.

24. "Building a Solid Foundation on Value-Driven Principles," *Business Leader* 14 (June 2003), p. 6.

25. G.R. Maio and J.M. Olson, "Values as Truisms: Evidence and Implications," *Journal of Personality and Social Psychology* 74, no. 2 (1998), pp. 294–311; G.R. Maio et al., "Addressing Discrepancies between Values and Behavior: The Motivating Effect of Reasons," *Journal of Experimental Social Psychology* 37, no. 2 (2001), pp. 104–17; B. Verplanken and R.W. Holland, "Motivated Decision Making: Effects of Activation and Self-Centrality of Values on Choices and Behavior," *Journal of Personality and Social Psychology* 82, no. 3 (2002), pp. 434–47; A. Bardi and S.H. Schwartz, "Values and Behavior: Strength and Structure of Relations," *Personality and Social Psychology Bulletin* 29, no. 10 (October 2003), pp. 1207–20; M.M. Bernard and G.R. Maio, "Effects of Introspection about Reasons for Values: Extending Research on Values-as-Truisms," *Social Cognition* 21, no. 1 (2003), pp. 1–25.

26. M.L.A. Hayward, V.P. Rindova, and T.G. Pollock, "Believing One's Own Press: The Causes and Consequences of CEO Celebrity," *Strategic Management Journal* 25, no. 7 (July 2004), pp. 637–53.

27. K.F. Alam, "Business Ethics in New Zealand Organizations: Views from the Middle and Lower Level Managers," *Journal of Business Ethics* 22 (November 1999), pp. 145–53; S.R. Chatterjee and C.A.L. Pearson, "Indian Managers in Transition: Orientations, Work Goals, Values and Ethics," *Management International Review* (January 2000), pp. 81–95.

28. A.L. Kristof, "Person–Organization Fit: An Integrative Review of Its Conceptualizations, Measurement, and Implications," *Personnel Psychology* 49, no. 1 (Spring 1996), pp. 1–49; M.L. Verquer, T.A. Beehr, and

S.H. Wagner, "A Meta-Analysis of Relations between Person–Organization Fit and Work Attitudes," *Journal of Vocational Behavior* 63 (2003), pp. 473–89; J.W. Westerman and L.A. Cyr, "An Integrative Analysis of Person–Organization Fit Theories," *International Journal of Selection and Assessment* 12, no. 3 (September 2004), pp. 252–61; D. Bouckenooghe et al., "The Prediction of Stress by Values and Value Conflict," *Journal of Psychology* 139, no. 4 (2005), pp. 369–82.

29. K.M. Eisenhardt, J.L. Kahwajy, and L. J. Bourgeois III, "Conflict and Strategic Choice: How Top Management Teams Disagree," *California Management Review* 39 (Winter 1997), pp. 42–62; D. Arnott, *Corporate Cults* (New York: AMACOM, 1999).

30. Coles Myer Ltd., *Corporate Social Responsibility Report 2005* (Tooronga, Victoria: Coles Myer, July 2005); F. Smith et al., "25 True Leaders," *Australian Financial Review,* 12 August 2005, p. 62.

31. T. Simons, "Behavioral Integrity: The Perceived Alignment between Managers' Words and Deeds as a Research Focus," *Organization Science* 13, no. 1 (January–February 2002), pp. 18–35. Values at Meyners & Co. are described in K.A. McDonald, "Meyners Does a Reality Check," *Journal of Accountancy* 201, no. 2 (2006), p. 51.

32. T.A. Joiner, "The Influence of National Culture and Organizational Culture Alignment on Job Stress and Performance: Evidence from Greece," *Journal of Managerial Psychology* 16 (2001), pp. 229–42; Z. Aycan, R.N. Kanungo, and J.B.P. Sinha, "Organizational Culture and Human Resource Management Practices: The Model of Culture Fit," *Journal of Cross-Cultural Psychology* 30 (July 1999), pp. 501–26.

33. W. Sekiguchi, "Managing Means People, Visions," *Nikkei Weekly (Japan),* 12 December 2005.

34. D. Oyserman, H.M. Coon, and M. Kemmelmeier, "Rethinking Individualism and Collectivism: Evaluation of Theoretical Assumptions and Meta-Analyses," *Psychological Bulletin* 128 (2002), pp. 3–72; C.P. Earley and C.B. Gibson, "Taking Stock in Our Progress on Individualism–Collectivism: 100 Years of Solidarity and Community," *Journal of Management* 24 (May 1998), pp. 265–304; F.S. Niles, "Individualism–Collectivism Revisited," *Cross-Cultural Research* 32 (November 1998), pp. 315–41.

35. Oyserman, Coon, and Kemmelmeier, "Rethinking Individualism and Collectivism: Evaluation of Theoretical Assumptions and Meta-Analyses." The relationship between individualism and collectivism is still being debated. Some researchers suggest that there are different types of individualism and collectivism, and some of these types may be opposites. Others say the lack of association is due to the way we measure these concepts. See E.G.T. Green, J.-C. Deschamps, and D. Paez, "Variation of Individualism and Collectivism within and between 20 Countries," *Journal of Cross-Cultural Psychology* 36, no. 3 (May 2005), pp. 321–39; S. Oishi et al., "The Measurement of Values across Cultures: A Pairwise Comparison Approach," *Journal of Research in Personality* 39, no. 2 (2005), pp. 299–305.

36. M.H. Bond, "Reclaiming the Individual from Hofstede's Ecological Analysis–A 20-Year Odyssey," *Psychological Bulletin* 128 (2002), pp. 73–77; M. Voronov and J.A. Singer, "The Myth of Individualism–Collectivism: A Critical Review," *Journal of Social Psychology* 142 (August 2002), pp. 461–80.

37. J. Chao, "Culture Clash Looms as Lenovo Gobbles IBM Unit," *Palm Beach Post,* 19 December 2004, p. 3F; D. Roberts and L. Lee, "East Meets West, Big Time," *BusinessWeek,* 9 May 2005, p. 74.

38. H. Trinca, "It's about Soul, but Don't Get Too Soft," *Australian Financial Review,* 12 August 2005, p. 56.

39. G. Hofstede, *Culture's Consequences: Comparing Values, Behaviors, Institutions, and Organizations across Nations,* 2nd ed. (Thousand Oaks, CA: Sage, 2001).

40. G. Hofstede, *Cultures and Organizations: Software of the Mind* (New York: McGraw-Hill, 1991). Hofstede used the terms *masculinity* and *femininity* for achievement and nurturing orientation, respectively. We have adopted the latter terms to minimize the sexist perspective of these concepts.

41. J.S. Osland et al., "Beyond Sophisticated Stereotyping: Cultural Sensemaking in Context," *Academy of Management Executive* 14 (February 2000), pp. 65–79; S.S. Sarwono and R.W. Armstrong, "Microcultural Differences and Perceived Ethical Problems: An International Business Perspective," *Journal of Business Ethics* 30 (March 2001), pp. 41–56; Voronov and Singer, "The Myth of Individualism–Collectivism: A Critical Review"; N. Jacob, "Cross-Cultural Investigations: Emerging Concepts," *Journal of Organizational Change Management* 18, no. 5 (2005), pp. 514–28.

42. C. Savoye, "Workers Say Honesty Is Best Company Policy," *Christian Science Monitor,* 15 June 2000; Kouzes and Posner, *The Leadership Challenge;* J. Schettler, "Leadership in Corporate America," *Training & Development,* September 2002, pp. 66–73.

43. J. Moir, "Dishing the Dirt on China's Corporate Criminals," *South China Morning Post (Hong Kong),* 20 August 2005, p. 1; M. Wilkinson and D. Snow, "Going against the Grain," *Sydney Morning Herald,* 5 November 2005, p. 28; J. Spencer and K. Scannell, "Gemstar Ex-CEO Is Ordered to Pay $22.3 Million," *The Wall Street Journal,* 9 May 2006, p. A3.

44. P.L. Schumann, "A Moral Principles Framework for Human Resource Management Ethics," *Human Resource Management Review* 11 (Spring–Summer 2001), pp. 93–111; J. Boss, *Analyzing Moral Issues,* 3rd ed. (New York: McGraw-Hill, 2005), Chapter 1; M.G. Velasquez, *Business Ethics: Concepts and Cases,* 6th ed. (Upper Saddle River, NJ: Prentice-Hall, 2006), Chapter 2.

45. T.J. Jones, "Ethical Decision Making by Individuals in Organizations: An Issue Contingent Model," *Academy of Management Review* 16 (1991), pp. 366–95; B.H. Frey, "The Impact of Moral Intensity on Decision Making in a Business Context," *Journal of Business Ethics* 26 (August 2000), pp. 181–95; D.R. May and K.P. Pauli, "The Role of Moral Intensity in Ethical Decision Making," *Business and Society* 41 (March 2002), pp. 84–117.

46. J.R. Sparks and S.D. Hunt, "Marketing Researcher Ethical Sensitivity: Conceptualization, Measurement, and Exploratory Investigation," *Journal of Marketing* 62 (April 1998), pp. 92–109.

47. Alam, "Business Ethics in New Zealand Organizations: Views from the Middle and Lower Level Managers"; K. Blotnicky, "Is Business in Moral Decay?," *Chronicle-Herald (Halifax),* 11 June 2000; B. Stoneman and K.K. Holliday, "Pressure Cooker," *Banking Strategies,* January–February 2001, p. 13.

48. S. Greengard, "Golden Values," *Workforce Management,* March 2005, pp. 52–53.

49. B. Farrell, D.M. Cobbin, and H.M. Farrell, "Codes of Ethics: Their Evolution, Development and Other Controversies," *Journal of Management Development* 21,

no. 2 (2002), pp. 152–63; G. Wood and M. Rimmer, "Codes of Ethics: What Are They Really and What Should They Be?" *International Journal of Value-Based Management* 16, no. 2 (2003), p. 181.

50. P. J. Gnazzo and G.R. Wratney, "Are You Serious about Ethics?" *Across the Board* 40 (July/August 2003), p. 46ff; T.F. Lindeman, "A Matter of Choice," *Pittsburgh Post-Gazette,* 30 March 2004; B. Schultz, "Ethics under Investigation," *Network World,* 26 April 2004; K. Tyler, "Do the Right Thing," *HRMagazine* 50, no. 2 (February 2005), pp. 99–103.

51. E. Aronson, "Integrating Leadership Styles and Ethical Perspectives," *Canadian Journal of Administrative Sciences* 18 (December 2001), pp. 266–76; D.R. May et al., "Developing the Moral Component of Authentic Leadership," *Organizational Dynamics* 32 (2003), pp. 247–60. The Vodafone director quotation is from R. Van Lee, L. Fabish, and N. McGaw, "The Value of Corporate Values," *Strategy+Business* (Summer 2005), pp. 1–13.

52. Roccas et al., "The Big Five Personality Factors and Personal Values,"

53. H.C. Triandis and E.M. Suh, "Cultural Influences on Personality," *Annual Review of Psychology* 53 (2002), pp. 133–60.

54. B. Reynolds and K. Karraker, "A Big Five Model of Disposition and Situation Interaction: Why a 'Helpful' Person May Not Always Behave Helpfully," *New Ideas in Psychology* 21 (April 2003), pp. 1–13; W. Mischel, "Toward an Integrative Science of the Person," *Annual Review of Psychology* 55 (2004), pp. 1–22.

55. W. Immen, "Prospective Hires Put to the Test," *Globe & Mail,* 26 January 2005, p. C1.

56. R.M. Guion and R.F. Gottier, "Validity of Personnel Measures in Personnel Selection," *Personnel Psychology* 18 (1965), pp. 135–64; N. Schmitt et al., "Meta-Analyses of Validity Studies Published between 1964 and 1982 and the Investigation of Study Characteristics," *Personnel Psychology* 37 (1984), pp. 407–22.

57. P.G. Irving, "On the Use of Personality Measures in Personnel Selection," *Canadian Psychology* 34 (April 1993), pp. 208–14.

58. K.M. DeNeve and H. Cooper, "The Happy Personality: A Meta-Analysis of 137 Personality Traits and Subjective Well-Being," *Psychological Bulletin* 124 (September 1998), pp. 197–229; T.A. Judge et al., "Personality and Leadership: A Qualitative and Quantitative Review," *Journal of Applied Psychology* 87, no. 4 (2002), pp. 765–80; R. Ilies, M.W. Gerhardt, and H. Le, "Individual Differences in Leadership Emergence: Integrating Meta-Analytic Findings and Behavioral Genetics Estimates," *International Journal of Selection and Assessment* 12, no. 3 (September 2004), pp. 207–19.

59. This historical review, and the trait descriptions in this section, are discussed in J.M. Digman, "Personality Structure: Emergence of the Five-Factor Model," *Annual Review of Psychology* 41 (1990), pp. 417–40; M.K. Mount and M.R. Barrick, "The Big Five Personality Dimensions: Implications for Research and Practice in Human Resources Management," *Research in Personnel and Human Resources Management* 13 (1995), pp. 153–200; R.J. Schneider and L.M. Hough, "Personality and Industrial/Organizational Psychology," *International Review of Industrial and Organizational Psychology* 10 (1995), pp. 75–129.

60. T.A. Judge and R. Ilies, "Relationship of Personality to Performance Motivation: A Meta-Analytic Review," *Journal of Applied Psychology* 87, no. 4 (2002), pp. 797–807; A. Witt, L.A. Burke, and M.R. Barrick, "The Interactive Effects of Conscientiousness and Agreeableness on Job Performance," *Journal of Applied Psychology* 87 (February 2002), pp. 164–69.

61. C.G. Jung, *Psychological Types,* trans. H.G. Baynes (Princeton, NJ: Princeton University Press, 1971); I.B. Myers, *The Myers-Briggs Type Indicator* (Palo Alto, CA: Consulting Psychologists Press, 1987).

62. M. Gladwell, "Personality Plus," *New Yorker,* 20 September 2004, pp. 42–48; R.B. Kennedy and D.A. Kennedy, "Using the Myers-Briggs Type Indicator in Career Counseling," *Journal of Employment Counseling* 41, no. 1 (March 2004), pp. 38–44. The Portsmouth City and Dell Computer examples are found in E. Ross, "Enough Chiefs," *BRW,* 6 October 2005, p. 66; M. Hoyer, "The Quiet Man of Portsmouth: City Manager James Oliver," *Public Management,* April 2006, p. 28.

63. W.L. Johnson et al., "A Higher-Order Analysis of the Factor Structure of the Myers-Briggs Type Indicator," *Measurement and Evaluation in Counseling and Development* 34 (July 2001), pp. 96–108; R.M. Capraro and M.M. Capraro, "Myers-Briggs Type Indicator Score Reliability across Studies: A Meta-Analytic Reliability Generalization Study," *Educational and Psychological Measurement* 62 (August 2002), pp. 590–602; J. Michael, "Using the Myers-Briggs Type Indicator as a Tool for Leadership Development? Apply with Caution," *Journal of Leadership & Organizational Studies* 10 (Summer 2003), pp. 68–81.

64. P.E. Spector, "Behavior in Organizations as a Function of Employees' Locus of Control," *Psychological Bulletin* 91 (1982), pp. 482–97; J.M. Howell and B.J. Avolio, "Transformational Leadership, Transactional Leadership, Locus of Control, and Support for Innovation: Key Predictors of Consolidated-Business-Unit Performance," *Journal of Applied Psychology* 78 (1993), pp. 891–902; P.E. Spector et al., "Do National Levels of Individualism and Internal Locus of Control Relate to Well-Being: An Ecological Level International Study," *Journal of Organizational Behavior* 22 (2001), pp. 815–32.

65. M. Snyder, *Public Appearances/Private Realities: The Psychology of Self-Monitoring* (New York: W. H. Freeman, 1987).

66. R.J. Ellis and S.E. Cronshaw, "Self-Monitoring and Leader Emergence: A Test of Moderator Effects," *Small Group Research* 23 (1992), pp. 113–29; M. Kilduff and D.V. Day, "Do Chameleons Get Ahead? The Effects of Self-Monitoring on Managerial Careers," *Academy of Management Journal* 37 (1994), pp. 1047–60; M.A. Warech et al., "Self-Monitoring and 360-Degree Ratings," *Leadership Quarterly* 9 (Winter 1998), pp. 449–73; A. Mehra, M. Kilduff, and D.J. Brass, "The Social Networks of High and Low Self-Monitors: Implications for Workplace Performance," *Administrative Science Quarterly* 46 (March 2001), pp. 121–46.

67. J.L. Holland, *Making Vocational Choices: A Theory of Careers* (Englewood Cliffs, NJ: Prentice Hall, 1973).

68. G.D. Gottfredson and J.L. Holland, "A Longitudinal Test of the Influence of Congruence: Job Satisfaction, Competency Utilization, and Counterproductive Behavior," *Journal of Counseling Psychology* 37 (1990), pp. 389–98; A. Furnham, "Vocational Preference and P-O Fit: Reflections on Holland's Theory of Vocational Choice," *Applied Psychology: An International Review* 50 (2001), pp. 5–29.

69. J. Tupponce, "Listening to Those Inner Voices," *Richmond Times-Dispatch,* 11 May 2003, p. S3.

70. Furnham, "Vocational Preference and P-O Fit: Reflections on Holland's Theory of Vocational Choice"; R.P. Tett and D.D. Burnett, "A Personality Trait-Based Interactionist Model of Job Performance," *Journal of Applied Psychology* 88, no. 3 (2003),

pp. 500–517; W. Yang, G.S. Stokes, and C.H. Hui, "Cross-Cultural Validation of Holland's Interest Structure in Chinese Population," *Journal of Vocational Behavior* (2005), In Press.

71. G.D. Gottfredson, "John L. Holland's Contributions to Vocational Psychology: A Review and Evaluation," *Journal of Vocational Behavior* 55, no. 1 (1999), pp. 15–40.

CHAPTER 3

1. J. Lynch and M. Dagostino, "Man in Motion," *People Magazine,* 26 August 2002, p. 89; N. Hooper, "Call Me Irresistible," *Australian Financial Review,* 5 December 2003, p. 38; D. Knight, "Hands-on CEO Gets IPL Back on Track," *Indianapolis Star,* 21 November 2004; K. Capell, "Ikea; How the Swedish Retailer Became a Global Cult Brand," *BusinessWeek,* 14 November 2005, p. 96; W. Frey, "Rubbish Boy Doing Well as Junk Man," *Metro-Vancouver,* 25 April 2005, p. 11; L. Morrell, "Taking the Floor," *Retail Week,* 18 November 2005.

2. Plato, *The Republic,* trans. D. Lee (Harmondsworth, England: Penguin, 1955).

3. R.H. Fazio, DR. Roskos-Ewoldsen, and M.C. Powell, "Attitudes, Perception, and Attention," in *The Heart's Eye: Emotional Influences in Perception and Attention,* ed. P.M. Niedenthal and S. Kitayama (San Diego,CA: Academic Press, 1994), pp. 197–216.

4. The effect of the target in selective attention is known as "bottom-up selection"; the effect of the perceiver's psychodynamics on this process is known as "top-down selection." C.E. Connor, H.E. Egeth, and S. Yantis, "Visual Attention: Bottom-Up Versus Top-Down," *Current Biology* 14, no. 19 (2004), pp. R850–R852.

5. A. Mack et al., "Perceptual Organization and Attention," *Cognitive Psychology* 24, no. 4 (1992), pp. 475–501; A.R. Damasio, *Descartes' Error: Emotion, Reason, and the Human Brain* (New York: Putnam Sons, 1994).

6. R. Henry, "Police Departments Scale Back 'Always Armed' Policies," *Associated Press,* 26 November 2005.

7. C.N. Macrae et al., "Tales of the Unexpected: Executive Function and Person Perception," *Journal of Personality and Social Psychology* 76 (1999), pp. 200–13; C. Frith, "A Framework for Studying the Neural Basis of Attention," *Neuropsychologia* 39, no. 12 (2001), pp. 1367–71; N. Lavie, "Distracted and Confused? Selective Attention under Load," *Trends in Cognitive Sciences* 9, no. 2 (2005), pp. 75–82.

8. E. Byron, "To Master the Art of Solving Crimes, Cops Study Vermeer," *The Wall Street Journal,* 27 July 2005, p. A1; D.J. Hall, "The Justice System Isn't Always Just," *Capital Times & Wisconsin State Journal,* 27 November 2005, p. D1.

9. C.N. Macrae and G.V. Bodenhausen, "Social Cognition: Thinking Categorically about Others," *Annual Review of Psychology* 51 (2000), pp. 93–120. For literature on the automaticity of the perceptual organization and interpretation process, see J.A. Bargh, "The Cognitive Monster: The Case against the Controllability of Automatic Stereotype Effects," in *Dual Process Theories in Social Psychology,* ed. S. Chaiken and Y. Trope (New York: Guilford, 1999), pp. 361–82; J.A. Bargh and M.J. Ferguson, "Beyond Behaviorism: On the Automaticity of Higher Mental Processes," *Psychological Bulletin* 126, no. 6 (2000), pp. 925–45; and M. Gladwell, *Blink: The Power of Thinking without Thinking* (New York: Little, Brown, 2005).

10. E.M. Altmann and B.D. Burns, "Streak Biases in Decision Making: Data and a Memory Model," *Cognitive Systems Research* 6, no. 1 (2005), pp. 5–16. For discussion of cognitive closure and perception, see A.W. Kruglanski and D.M. Webster, "Motivated Closing of the Mind: 'Seizing' and 'Freezing,'" *Psychological Review* 103, no. 2 (1996), pp. 263–83.

11. N. Ambady and R. Rosenthal, "Half a Minute: Predicting Teacher Evaluations from Thin Slices of Nonverbal Behavior and Physical Attractiveness," *Journal of Personality and Social Psychology* 64, no. 3 (March 1993), pp. 431–41. For other research on thin slices, see N. Ambady and R. Rosenthal, "Thin Slices of Expressive Behavior as Predictors of Interpersonal Consequences: A Meta-Analysis," *Psychological Bulletin* 111, no. 2 (1992), pp. 256–74; and N. Ambady et al., "Surgeons' Tone of Voice: A Clue to Malpractice History," *Surgery* 132, no. 1 (July 2002), pp. 5–9.

12. P.M. Senge, *The Fifth Discipline: The Art and Practice of the Learning Organization* (New York: Doubleday Currency, 1990), Chapter 10; P.N. Johnson-Laird, "Mental Models and Deduction," *Trends in Cognitive Sciences* 5, no. 10 (2001), pp. 434–42; A.B. Markman and D. Gentner, "Thinking," *Annual Review of Psychology* 52 (2001), pp. 223–47; T.J. Chermack, "Mental Models in Decision Making and Implications for Human Resource Development," *Advances in Developing Human Resources* 5, no. 4 (2003), pp. 408–22.

13. H. Tajfel, *Social Identity and Intergroup Relations* (Cambridge: Cambridge University Press, 1982); B.E. Ashforth and F. Mael, "Social Identity Theory and the Organization," *Academy of Management Review* 14 (1989), pp. 20–39; M.A. Hogg and D.J. Terry, "Social Identity and Self-Categorization Processes in Organizational Contexts," *Academy of Management Review* 25 (January 2000), pp. 121–40; S.A. Haslam, R.A. Eggins, and K.J. Reynolds, "The Aspire Model: Actualizing Social and Personal Identity Resources to Enhance Organizational Outcomes," *Journal of Occupational and Organizational Psychology* 76 (2003), pp. 83–113. Although this topic is labeled *social identity theory,* it also incorporates an extension of social identity theory, called *self-categorization theory.*

14. J.E. Dutton, J.M. Dukerich, and C.V. Harquail, "Organizational Images and Member Identification," *Administrative Science Quarterly* 39 (June 1994), pp. 239–63; B. Simon and C. Hastedt, "Self-Aspects as Social Categories: The Role of Personal Importance and Valence," *European Journal of Social Psychology* 29 (1999), pp. 479–87.

15. M.A. Hogg et al., "The Social Identity Perspective: Intergroup Relations, Self-Conception, and Small Groups," *Small Group Research* 35, no. 3 (June 2004), pp. 246–76; J. Jetten, R. Spears, and T. Postmes, "Intergroup Distinctiveness and Differentiation: A Meta-Analytic Integration," *Journal of Personality and Social Psychology* 86, no. 6 (2004), pp. 862–79.

16. J.W. Jackson and E.R. Smith, "Conceptualizing Social Identity: A New Framework and Evidence for the Impact of Different Dimensions," *Personality & Social Psychology Bulletin* 25 (January 1999), pp. 120–35.

17. L. Falkenberg, "Improving the Accuracy of Stereotypes within the Workplace," *Journal of Management* 16 (1990), pp. 107–18; S.T. Fiske, "Stereotyping, Prejudice, and Discrimination," in *Handbook of Social Psychology,* ed. D.T. Gilbert, S.T. Fiske, and G. Lindzey, 4th ed. (New York: McGraw-Hill, 1998), pp. 357–411; Macrae and Bodenhausen, "Social Cognition: Thinking Categorically about Others."

18. C.N. Macrae, A.B. Milne, and G.V. Bodenhausen, "Stereotypes as Energy-

Saving Devices: A Peek inside the Cognitive Toolbox," *Journal of Personality and Social Psychology* 66 (1994), pp. 37–47; J.W. Sherman et al., "Stereotype Efficiency Reconsidered: Encoding Flexibility under Cognitive Load," *Journal of Personality and Social Psychology* 75 (1998), pp. 589–606; Macrae and Bodenhausen, "Social Cognition: Thinking Categorically about Others."

19. L. Sinclair and Z. Kunda, "Motivated Stereotyping of Women: She's Fine If She Praised Me but Incompetent If She Criticized Me," *Personality and Social Psychology Bulletin* 26 (November 2000), pp. 1329–42; J.C. Turner and S.A. Haslam, "Social Identity, Organizations, and Leadership," in *Groups at Work: Theory and Research,* ed. M.E. Turner (Mahwah, NJ: Lawrence Erlbaum Associates, 2001), pp. 25–65.

20. Y. Lee, L.J. Jussim, and C.R. McCauley, *Stereotype Accuracy: Toward Appreciating Group Differences* (Washington, DC: American Psychological Association, 1996); S. Madonet al., "The Accuracy and Power of Sex, Social Class, and Ethnic Stereotypes: A Naturalistic Study in Person Perception," *Personality & Social Psychology Bulletin* 24 (December 1998), pp. 1304–18; F.T. McAndrew, "A Multicultural Study of Stereotyping in English-Speaking Countries," *Journal of Social Psychology* (August 2000), pp. 487–502.

21. A.L. Friedman and S.R. Lyne, "The Beancounter Stereotype: Towards a General Model of Stereotype Generation," *Critical Perspectives on Accounting* 12, no. 4 (2001): 423–451

22. "Employers Face New Danger: Accidental Age Bias," *Omaha World-Herald,* 10 October 2005, p. D1; "Tiptoeing through the Employment Minefield of Race, Sex, and Religion? Here's Another One," *North West Business Insider (Manchester, UK),* February 2006.

23. S.O. Gaines and E.S. Reed, "Prejudice: From Allport to Dubois," *American Psychologist* 50 (February 1995), pp. 96–103; Fiske, "Stereotyping, Prejudice, and Discrimination"; M. Billig, "Henri Tajfel's 'Cognitive Aspects of Prejudice' and the Psychology of Bigotry," *British Journal of Social Psychology* 41 (2002), pp. 171–88; M Hewstone, M. Rubin, and H. Willis, "Intergroup Bias," *Annual Review of Psychology* 53 (2002), pp. 575–604.

24. J. Sinclair, "Breaking Down the Barriers," *The Age (Melbourne),* 30 January 2002, p. 14; L. Giovanelli, "Gender Divide," *Winston-Salem Journal,* 3 July 2005, p. 1; V. Reitman, "Caltech to Harvard: Redo the Math," *Los Angeles Times,* 20 June 2005.

25. "Army Chief's Warning KKK Photo May Lead to Officers' Dismissals," *Townsville Bulletin,* 25 June 2005, p. 7; M. Patriquin, "Quebec Farm Segregated Black Workers," *Globe & Mail,* 30 April 2005, p. A1; C. Spivak and D. Bice, "Looks Like Some to Face Bias Up North," *Milwaukee Journal Sentinel,* 16 October 2005, p. A2; J.W. Anderson, "French Firm Tests Colorblind Hiring," *Washington Post,* 29 January 2006, p. A20.

26. J.A. Bargh and T.L. Chartrand, "The Unbearable Automaticity of Being," *American Psychologist* 54, no. 7 (July 1999), pp. 462–79; S.T. Fiske, "What We Know Now About Bias and Intergroup Conflict, the Problem of the Century," *Current Directions in Psychological Science* 11, no. 4 (August 2002), pp. 123–28. For recent evidence that shows that intensive training can minimize stereotype activation, see K. Kawakami et al., "Just Say No (to Stereotyping): Effects of Training in the Negation of Stereotypic Associations on Stereotype Activation," *Journal of Personality and Social Psychology* 78, no. 5 (2000), pp. 871–88; and E.A. Plant, B.M. Peruche, and D.A. Butz, "Eliminating Automatic Racial Bias: Making Race Non-Diagnostic for Responses to Criminal Suspects," *Journal of Experimental Social Psychology* 41, no. 2 (2005), pp. 141–56.

27. M. Bendick, M.L. Egan, and S.M. Lofhjelm, "Workforce Diversity Training: From Anti-Discrimination Compliance to Organizational Development HR," *Human Resource Planning* 24 (2001), pp. 10–25; L. Roberson, C.T. Kulik, and M.B. Pepper, "Using Needs Assessment to Resolve Controversies in Diversity Training Design," *Group & Organization Management* 28, no. 1 (March 2003), pp. 148–74; D.E. Hogan and M. Mallott, "Changing Racial Prejudice through Diversity Education," *Journal of College Student Development* 46, no. 2 (March/April 2005), pp. 115–25.

28. P. Babcock, "Detecting Hidden Bias," *HRMagazine,* February 2006, p. 50.

29. T.F. Pettigrew, "Intergroup Contact Theory," *Annual Review of Psychology* 49 (1998), pp. 65–85; S. Brickson, "The Impact of Identity Orientation on Individual and Organizational Outcomes in Demographically Diverse Settings," *Academy of Management Review* 25 (January 2000), pp. 82–101; J. Dixon and K. Durrheim, "Contact and the Ecology of Racial Division: Some Varieties of Informal Segregation," *British Journal of Social Psychology* 42 (March 2003), pp. 1–23.

30. B.F. Reskin, "The Proximate Causes of Employment Discrimination," *Contemporary Sociology* 29 (March 2000), pp. 319–28.

31. T. Phillips, "UPS Sends Executives on Diversity Sabbaticals," *Indianapolis Business Journal,* November 2004, p. 10; S. Teicher, "Corner-Office Volunteers," *Christian Science Monitor,* 19 July 2004, pp. 14–15; "Walking in Their Shoes," *Training,* June 2005, p. 19; C. Darden, "Pursuing Excellence–Constructive Dissatisfaction," *Executive Speeches,* February 2005, p. 1.

32. H.H. Kelley, *Attribution in Social Interaction* (Morristown, NJ: General Learning Press, 1971).

33. J.M. Feldman, "Beyond Attribution Theory: Cognitive Processes in Performance Appraisal," *Journal of Applied Psychology* 66 (1981), pp. 127–48.

34. J.M. Crant and T.S. Bateman, "Assignment of Credit and Blame for Performance Outcomes," *Academy of Management Journal* 36 (1993), pp. 7–27; B. Weiner, "Intrapersonal and Interpersonal Theories of Motivation from an Attributional Perspective," *Educational Psychology Review* 12 (2000), pp. 1–14; N. Bacon and P. Blyton, "Worker Responses to Teamworking: Exploring Employee Attributions of Managerial Motives," *International Journal of Human Resource Management* 16, no. 2 (February 2005), pp. 238–55.

35. Fundamental attribution error is part of a larger phenomenon known as correspondence bias. See D.T. Gilbert and P.S. Malone, "The Correspondence Bias," *Psychological Bulletin* 117, no. 1 (1995), pp. 21–38.

36. I. Choi, R.E. Nisbett, and A. Norenzayan, "Causal Attribution across Cultures: Variation and Universality," *Psychological Bulletin* 125, no. 1 (1999), pp. 47–63; D.S. Krull et al., "The Fundamental Attribution Error: Correspondence Bias in Individualist and Collectivist Cultures," *Personality and Social Psychology Bulletin* 25, no. 10 (October 1999), pp. 1208–19; R.E. Nisbett, *The Geography of Thought: How Asians and Westerners Think Differently–and Why* (New York: Free Press, 2003), Chapter 5.

37. F. Lee and L.Z. Tiedens, "Who's Being Served? 'Self-Serving' Attributions in Social Hierarchies," *Organizational Behavior and Human Decision Processes* 84, no. 2 (2001), pp. 254–87; E.W.K. Tsang, "Self-

Serving Attributions in Corporate Annual Reports: A Replicated Study," *Journal of Management Studies* 39, no. 1 (January 2002), pp. 51–65.

38. Similar models are presented in D. Eden, "Self-Fulfilling Prophecy as a Management Tool: Harnessing Pygmalion," *Academy of Management Review* 9 (1984), pp. 64–73; R.H.G. Field and D.A. Van Seters, "Management by Expectations (MBE): The Power of Positive Prophecy," *Journal of General Management* 14 (Winter 1988), pp. 19–33; D.O. Trouilloud et al., "The Influence of Teacher Expectations on Student Achievement in Physical Education Classes: Pygmalion Revisited," *European Journal of Social Psychology* 32 (2002), pp. 591–607.

39. D. Eden, "Interpersonal Expectations in Organizations," in *Interpersonal Expectations: Theory, Research, and Applications* (Cambridge, UK: Cambridge University Press, 1993), pp. 154–78.

40. D. Eden, "Pygmalion Goes to Boot Camp: Expectancy, Leadership, and Trainee Performance," *Journal of Applied Psychology* 67 (1982), pp. 194–99; R.P. Brown and E.C. Pinel, "Stigma on My Mind: Individual Differences in the Experience of Stereotype Threat," *Journal of Experimental Social Psychology* 39, no. 6 (2003), pp. 626–33.

41. S. Madon et al., "Self-Fulfilling Prophecies: The Synergistic Accumulative Effect of Parents' Beliefs on Children's Drinking Behavior," *Psychological Science* 15, no. 12 (2005), pp. 837–45 A.E. Smith, L. Jussim, and J. Eccles, "Do Self-Fulfilling Prophecies Accumulate, Dissipate, or Remain Stable over Time?" *Journal of Personality and Social Psychology* 77, no. 3 (1999), pp. 548–65.

42. S. Madon, L. Jussim, and J. Eccles, "In Search of the Powerful Self-Fulfilling Prophecy," *Journal of Personality and Social Psychology* 72, no. 4 (April 1997), pp. 791–809.

43. A.R. Remo, "Nurture the Good to Create an Asset," *Philippine Daily Inquirer,* 6 December 2004.

44. D. Eden et al., "Implanting Pygmalion Leadership Style through Workshop Training: Seven Field Experiments," *Leadership Quarterly* 11 (2000), pp. 171–210; S.S. White and E.A. Locke, "Problems with the Pygmalion Effect and Some Proposed Solutions," *Leadership Quarterly* 11 (Autumn 2000), pp. 389–415; H.A. Wilkinson, "Hope, False Hope, and Self-Fulfilling Prophecy," *Surgical Neurology* 63, no. 1 (2005), pp. 84–86. For literature on positive organizational behavior, see K. Cameron, J.E. Dutton, and R.E. Quinn, *Positive Organizational Scholarship: Foundations of a New Discipline* (San Francisco: Berrett Koehler, 2003).

45. C.L. Kleinke, *First Impressions: The Psychology of Encountering Others* (Englewood Cliffs, NJ: Prentice Hall, 1975); E.A. Lind, L. Kray, and L. Thompson, "Primacy Effects in Justice Judgments: Testing Predictions from Fairness Heuristic Theory," *Organizational Behavior and Human Decision Processes* 85 (July 2001), pp. 189–210; O. Ybarra, "When First Impressions Don't Last: The Role of Isolation and Adaptation Processes in the Revision of Evaluative Impressions," *Social Cognition* 19 (October 2001), pp. 491–520.

46. D.D. Steiner and J.S. Rain, "Immediate and Delayed Primacy and Recency Effects in Performance Evaluation," *Journal of Applied Psychology* 74 (1989), pp. 136–42; K.T. Trotman, "Order Effects and Recency: Where Do We Go from Here?" *Accounting & Finance* 40 (2000), pp. 169–82; W. Green, "Impact of the Timing of an Inherited Explanation on Auditors' Analytical Procedures Judgments," *Accounting and Finance* 44 (2004), pp. 369–92.

47. W.H. Cooper, "Ubiquitous Halo," *Psychological Bulletin* 90 (1981), pp. 218–44; K.R. Murphy, R.A. Jako, and R.L. Anhalt, "Nature and Consequences of Halo Error: A Critical Analysis," *Journal of Applied Psychology* 78 (1993), pp. 218–25; T.H. Feeley, "Comment on Halo Effects in Rating and Evaluation Research," *Human Communication Research* 28, no. 4 (October 2002), pp. 578–86.

48. G.G. Sherwood, "Self-Serving Biases in Person Perception: A Re-Examination of Projection as a Mechanism of Defense," *Psychological Bulletin* 90 (1981), pp. 445–59; R.L. Gross and S.E. Brodt, "How Assumptions of Consensus Undermine Decision Making," *Sloan Management Review* (January 2001), pp. 86–94.

49. C. Duan and C.E. Hill, "The Current State of Empathy Research," *Journal of Counseling Psychology* 43 (1996), pp. 261–74; W.G. Stephen and K.A. Finlay, "The Role of Empathy in Improving Intergroup Relations," *Journal of Social Issues* 55 (Winter 1999), pp. 729–43; S.K. Parker and C.M. Axtell, "Seeing Another Viewpoint: Antecedents and Outcomes of Employee Perspective Taking," *Academy of Management Journal* 44 (December 2001), pp. 1085–1100; G.J. Vreeke and I.L. van der Mark, "Empathy, an Integrative Model," *New Ideas in Psychology* 21, no. 3 (2003), pp. 177–207.

50. D. Goleman, R. Boyatzis, and A. McKee, *The New Leaders* (London: Little, Brown, 2002).

51. T.W. Costello and S.S. Zalkind, *Psychology in Administration: A Research Orientation* (Englewood Cliffs, NJ: Prentice Hall, 1963), pp. 45–46; J.M. Kouzes and B.Z. Posner, *The Leadership Challenge,* 3rd ed. (San Francisco: Jossey-Bass, 2002), Chapter 3.

52. J. Luft, *Group Processes* (Palo Alto, CA: Mayfield Publishing, 1984). For a variation of this model, see J. Hall, "Communication Revisited," *California Management Review* 15 (Spring 1973), pp. 56–67.

53. L.C. Miller and D.A. Kenny, "Reciprocity of Self-Disclosure at the Individual and Dyadic Levels: A Social Relations Analysis," *Journal of Personality and Social Psychology* 50 (1986), pp. 713–19.

54. "Wipro: Leadership in the Midst of Rapid Growth," *Knowledge@Wharton,* February 2005.

55. I. Nonaka and H. Takeuchi, *The Knowledge-Creating Company* (New York: Oxford University Press, 1995); E.N. Brockmann and W.P. Anthony, "Tacit Knowledge and Strategic Decision Making," *Group & Organization Management* 27 (December 2002), pp. 436–55; P. Duguid, "'The Art of Knowing': Social and Tacit Dimensions of Knowledge and the Limits of the Community of Practice," *The Information Society* 21 (2005), pp. 109–18.

56. B.F. Skinner, *About Behaviorism* (New York: Alfred A. Knopf, 1974); J. Komaki, T. Coombs, and S. Schepman, "Motivational Implications of Reinforcement Theory," in *Motivation and Leadership at Work,* ed. R.M. Steers, L.W. Porter, and G.A. Bigley (New York: McGraw-Hill, 1996), pp. 34–52; R.G. Miltenberger, *Behavior Modification: Principles and Procedures* (Pacific Grove, CA: Brooks/Cole, 1997).

57. T. K. Connellan, *How to Improve Human Performance* (New York: Harper & Row, 1978), pp. 48–57; F. Luthans and R. Kreitner, *Organizational Behavior Modification and Beyond* (Glenview, Ill.: Scott, Foresman, 1985), pp. 85–88

58. Miltenberger, *Behavior Modification: Principles and Procedures,* Chapters 4–6.

59. Punishment can also include removing a pleasant consequence, such as when

employees must switch from business to economy class flying when their sales fall below the threshold for top-tier sales "stars."

60. T.R. Hinkin and C.A. Schriesheim, "'If You Don't Hear from Me You Know You Are Doing Fine,'" *Cornell Hotel & Restaurant Administration Quarterly* 45, no. 4 (November 2004), pp. 362–72.

61. L.K. Trevino, "The Social Effects of Punishment in Organizations: A Justice Perspective," *Academy of Management Review* 17 (1992), pp. 647–76; L.E. Atwater et al., "Recipient and Observer Reactions to Discipline: Are Managers Experiencing Wishful Thinking?" *Journal of Organizational Behavior* 22, no. 3 (May 2001), pp. 249–70.

62. G.P. Latham and V.L. Huber, "Schedules of Reinforcement: Lessons from the Past and Issues for the Future," *Journal of Organizational Behavior Management* 13 (1992), pp. 125–49; B.A. Williams, "Challenges to Timing-Based Theories of Operant Behavior," *Behavioural Processes* 62 (April 2003), pp. 115–23.

63. S. Overman, "Many Offer Basic Wellness Initiatives, Few Track Results," *Employee Benefit News,* 15 April 2006; H. Wecsler, "Sick Day Incentive Plan Favored by NLR Board," *Arkansas Democrat Gazette,* 17 February 2006, p. 14.

64. T.C. Mawhinney, "Philosophical and Ethical Aspects of Organizational Behavior Management: Some Evaluative Feedback," *Journal of Organizational Behavior Management* 6 (Spring 1984), pp. 5–13; G.A. Merwin, J.A. Thomason, and E.E. Sandford, "A Methodological and Content Review of Organizational Behavior Management in the Private Sector: 1978–1986," *Journal of Organizational Behavior Management* 10 (1989), pp. 39–57; "New Warnings on the Fine Points of Safety Incentives," *Pay for Performance Report,* September 2002.

65. Bargh and Ferguson, "Beyond Behaviorism: On the Automaticity of Higher Mental Processes." Some writers argue that behaviorists long ago accepted the relevance of cognitive processes in behavior modification. See I. Kirsch et al., "The Role of Cognition in Classical and Operant Conditioning," *Journal of Clinical Psychology* 60, no. 4 (April 2004), pp. 369–92.

66. ExxonMobil, *UK and Ireland Corporate Citizenship* (ExxonMobil, August 2004); "ExxonMobil Recognizes Employees, Contractors for Outstanding," *Bernama Daily Malaysian News,* 27 June 2005.

67. A. Bandura, *Social Foundations of Thought and Action: A Social Cognitive Theory* (Englewood Cliffs, NJ: Prentice Hall, 1986).

68. A. Pescuric and W.C. Byham, "The New Look of Behavior Modeling," *Training & Development* 50 (July 1996), pp. 24–30.

69. M.E. Schnake, "Vicarious Punishment in a Work Setting," *Journal of Applied Psychology* 71 (1986), pp. 343–45; Trevino, "The Social Effects of Punishment in Organizations: A Justice Perspective"; J.B. DeConinck, "The Effect of Punishment on Sales Managers' Outcome Expectancies and Responses to Unethical Sales Force Behavior," *American Business Review* 21, no. 2 (June 2003), pp. 135–40.

70. A. Bandura, "Self-Reinforcement: Theoretical and Methodological Considerations," *Behaviorism* 4 (1976), pp. 135–55; C.A. Frayne and J.M. Geringer, "Self-Management Training for Improving Job Performance: A Field Experiment Involving Salespeople," *Journal of Applied Psychology* 85, no. 3 (June 2000), pp. 361–72; J.B. Vancouver and D.V. Day, "Industrial and Organisation Research on Self-Regulation: From Constructs to Applications," *Applied Psychology* 54, no. 2 (April 2005), pp. 155–85.

71. D. Woodruff, "Putting Talent to the Test," *The Wall Street Journal Europe,* November 14 2000, p. 25. The simulation events described here were experienced by the author of this article, but we reasonably assume that Mandy Chooi, who also completed the simulation, experienced similar scenarios.

72. D.A. Kolb, *Experiential Learning* (Englewood Cliffs, NJ: Prentice-Hall, 1984); S. Gherardi, D. Nicolini, and F. Odella, "Toward a Social Understanding of How People Learn in Organizations," *Management Learning* 29 (September 1998), pp. 273–97; D.A. Kolb, R.E. Boyatzis, and C. Mainemelis, "Experiential Learning Theory: Previous Research and New Directions," in *Perspectives on Thinking, Learning, and Cognitive Styles,* ed. R.J. Sternberg and L.F. Zhang (Mahwah, NJ: Lawrence Erlbaum, 2001), pp. 227–48.

73. J. Jusko, "Always Lessons to Learn," *Industry Week* (15 February 1999), p. 23; R. Farson and R. Keyes, "The Failure-Tolerant Leader," *Harvard Business Review* 80 (August 2002), pp. 64–71.

74. I. Teotonio, "Rescuers Pull 'Victims' from Rubble," *Toronto Star,* 8 April 2005, pp. B01, B03.

75. R.W. Revans, *The Origin and Growth of Action Learning* (London: Chartwell Bratt, 1982), pp. 626–27; M.J. Marquardt, *Optimizing the Power of Action Learning: Solving Problems and Building Leaders in Real Time* (Palo Alto, CA: Davies-Black, 2004).

76. J.A. Conger and K. Xin, "Executive Education in the 21st Century," *Journal of Management Education* (February 2000), pp. 73–101; R.M. Fulmer, P. Gibbs, and M. Goldsmith, "Developing Leaders: How Winning Companies Keep on Winning," *Sloan Management Review* (October 2000), pp. 49–59; "Strategies Needed to Nurture Top Talent," *South China Morning Post (Hong Kong),* 7 August 2004, p. 4; M.J. Marquardt, "Harnessing the Power of Action Learning," *T+D,* June 2004, pp. 26–32.

CHAPTER 4

1. F. Bilovsky, "Wegmans Is Named America's No. 1 Employer," *Democrat & Chronicle* (Rochester,New York), 11 January 2005; M. Boyle, "The Wegmans Way," *Fortune,* 24 January 2005, 62; B. Niedt, "Wegmans Reaches No. 1 on List of Workplaces," *Post Standard* (Syracuse), 11 January 2005, p. A1; M. Sommer and J.F. Bonfatti, "Wegmans Employees Feel Challenged, Valued," *Buffalo News,* 16 January 2005, p. B7.

2. The centrality of emotions in marketing, economics, and sociology is discussed in G. Loewenstein, "Emotions in Economic Theory and Economic Behavior," *American Economic Review* 90, no. 2 (May 2000), pp. 426–32; D.S. Massey, "A Brief History of Human Society: The Origin and Role of Emotion in Social Life," *American Sociological Review* 67 (February 2002), pp. 1–29; and J. O'Shaughnessy and N.J. OShaughnessy, *The Marketing Power of Emotion* (New York: Oxford University Press, 2003).

3. The definition presented here is constructed from information in the following sources: N.M. Ashkanasy, W.J. Zerbe, and C.E.J. Hartel, "Introduction: Managing Emotions in a Changing Workplace," in *Managing Emotions in the Workplace,* ed. N.M. Ashkanasy, W.J. Zerbe, and C.E.J. Hartel (Armonk, NY: M.E. Sharpe, 2002), pp. 3–18; H.M. Weiss, "Conceptual and Empirical Foundations for the Study of Affect at Work," in *Emotions in the Workplace,* ed. R.G. Lord, R.J. Klimoski, and R. Kanfer (San Francisco: Jossey-Bass, 2002), pp. 20–63. However, the

meaning of emotions is still being debated. See, for example, M. Cabanac, "What Is Emotion?" *Behavioural Processes* 60 (2002), pp. 69–83.

4. R. Kanfer and R.J. Klimoski, "Affect and Work: Looking Back to the Future," in *Emotions in the Workplace*, ed. R.G. Lord, R.J. Klimoski, and R. Kanfer (San Francisco: Jossey-Bass, 2002), pp. 473–90; J.A. Russell, "Core Affect and the Psychological Construction of Emotion," *Psychological Review* 110, no. 1 (2003), pp. 145–72.

5. R.B. Zajonc, "Emotions," in *Handbook of Social Psychology*, ed. D.T. Gilbert, S.T. Fiske, and L. Gardner (New York: Oxford University press, 1998), pp. 591–634.

6. N.A. Remington, L.R. Fabrigar, and P.S. Visser, "Reexamining the Circumplex Model of Affect," *Journal of Personality and Social Psychology* 79, no. 2 (2000), pp. 286–300; R.J. Larson, E. Diener, and R.E. Lucas, "Emotion: Models, Measures, and Differences," in *Emotions in the Workplace*, ed. R.G. Lord, R.J. Klimoski, and R. Kanfer (San Francisco: Jossey- Bass, 2002), pp. 64–113.

7. A.H. Eagly and S. Chaiken, *The Psychology of Attitudes* (Orlando, FL: Harcourt Brace Jovanovich, 1993); A.P. Brief, *Attitudes in and around Organizations* (Thousand Oaks, CA: Sage, 1998). There is ongoing debate about whether attitudes represent only feelings or all three components described here. However, those who adopt the single-factor perspective still refer to beliefs as the cognitive *component* of attitudes. For example, see I. Ajzen, "Nature and Operation of Attitudes," *Annual Review of Psychology* 52 (2001), pp. 27–58.

8. S.D. Farley and M.F. Stasson, "Relative Influences of Affect and Cognition on Behavior: Are Feelings or Beliefs More Related to Blood Donation Intentions?" *Experimental Psychology* 50, no. 1 (2003), pp. 55–62.

9. C.D. Fisher, "Mood and Emotions While Working: Missing Pieces of Job Satisfaction?" *Journal of Organizational Behavior* 21 (2000), pp. 185–202; M. Pergini and R.P. Bagozzi, "The Role of Desires and Anticipated Emotions in Goal-Directed Behaviors: Broadening and Deepening the Theory of Planned Behavior," *British Journal of Social Psychology* 40 (March 2001), pp. 79-; J.D. Morris et al., "The Power of Affect: Predicting Intention," *Journal of Advertising Research* 42 (May-June 2002), pp. 7–17. For a review of the predictability of the traditional attitude model, see C.J. Armitage and M. Conner, "Efficacy of the Theory of Planned Behavior: A Meta-Analytic Review," *British Journal of Social Psychology* 40 (2001), pp. 471–99.

10. This explanation refers to a singular "cognitive (logical reasoning) center" and "emotional center." Although many scholars refer to a single location for most emotional transactions, an emerging view is that both the emotional and rational "centers" are distributed throughout the brain. J. Schulkin, B.L. Thompson, and J. B. Rosen, "Demythologizing the Emotions: Adaptation, Cognition, and Visceral Representations of Emotion in the Nervous System," *Brain and Cognition* (*Affective Neuroscience*) 52 (June 2003), pp. 15–23.

11. J.A. Bargh and M.J. Ferguson, "Beyond Behaviorism: On the Automaticity of Higher Mental Processes," *Psychological Bulletin* 126, no. 6 (2000), pp. 925–45; R. H. Fazio, "On the Automatic Activation of Associated Evaluations: An Overview," *Cognition and Emotion* 15, no. 2 (2001), pp. 115–41; M. Gladwell, *Blink: The Power of Thinking without Thinking* (New York: Little, Brown, 2005).

12. A.R. Damasio, *Descartes' Error: Emotion, Reason, and the Human Brain* (New York: Putnam Sons, 1994); A. Damasio, *The Feeling of What Happens* (New York: Harcourt Brace and Co., 1999); P. Ekman, "Basic Emotions," in *Handbook of Cognition and Emotion*, ed. T. Dalgleish and M. Power (San Francisco: Jossey-Bass, 1999), pp. 45–60; J.E. LeDoux, "Emotion Circuits in the Brain," *Annual Review of Neuroscience* 23 (2000), pp. 155–84; R.J. Dolan, "Emotion, Cognition, and Behavior," *Science* 298, no. 5596 (8 November 2002), pp. 1191–94.

13. H.M. Weiss and R. Cropanzano, "Affective Events Theory: A Theoretical Discussion of the Structure, Causes, and Consequences of Affective Experiences at Work," *Research in Organizational Behavior* 18 (1996), pp. 1–74.

14. N. Schwarz, "Emotion, Cognition, and Decision Making," *Cognition and Emotion* 14, no. 4 (2000), pp. 433–40; M.T. Pham, "The Logic of Feeling," *Journal of Consumer Psychology* 14, no. 4 (2004), pp. 360–69.

15. G.R. Maio, V.M. Esses, and D.W. Bell, "Examining Conflict between Components of Attitudes: Ambivalence and Inconsistency Are Distinct Constructs," *Canadian Journal of Behavioural Science* 32, no. 2 (2000), pp. 71–83.

16. P.C. Nutt, *Why Decisions Fail* (San Francisco: Berrett-Koehler, 2002); S. Finkelstein, *Why Smart Executives Fail* (New York: Viking, 2003); P.C. Nutt, "Search during Decision Making," *European Journal of Operational Research* 160 (2005), pp. 851–76.

17. Weiss and Cropanzano, "Affective Events Theory."

18. L. Festinger, *A Theory of Cognitive Dissonance* (Evanston, IL: Row, Peterson, 1957); G.R. Salancik, "Commitment and the Control of Organizational Behavior and Belief," in *New Directions in Organizational Behavior*, ed. B.M. Staw and G.R. Salancik (Chicago: St. Clair, 1977), pp. 1–54; A.D. Galinsky, J. Stone, and J. Cooper, "The Reinstatement of Dissonance and Psychological Discomfort Following Failed Affirmation," *European Journal of Social Psychology* 30, no. 1 (2000), pp. 123–47.

19. T.A. Judge, E.A. Locke, and C.C. Durham, "The Dispositional Causes of Job Satisfaction: A Core Evaluations Approach," *Research in Organizational Behavior* 19 (1997), pp. 151–88; A.P. Brief and H.M. Weiss, "Organizational Behavior: Affect in the Workplace," *Annual Review of Psychology* 53 (2002), pp. 279–307.

20. C.M. Brotheridge and A.A. Grandey, "Emotional Labor and Burnout: Comparing Two Perspectives of 'People Work,'" *Journal of Vocational Behavior* 60 (2002), pp. 17–39; P.G. Irving, D.F. Coleman, and D.R. Bobocel, "The Moderating Effect of Negative Affectivity in the Procedural Justice-Job Satisfaction Relation," *Canadian Journal of Behavioural Science* 37, no. 1 (January 2005), pp. 20–32.

21. J. Schaubroeck, D.C. Ganster, and B. Kemmerer, "Does Trait Affect Promote Job Attitude Stability?" *Journal of Organizational Behavior* 17 (1996), pp. 191–96; C. Dormann and D. Zapf, "Job Satisfaction: A Meta-Analysis of Stabilities," *Journal of Organizational Behavior* 22 (2001), pp. 483–504.

22. R. Corelli, "Dishing Out Rudeness," *Maclean's*, 11 January 1999, pp. 44–47; D. Matheson, "A Vancouver Cafe Where Rudeness Is Welcomed," *Canada AM, CTV Television* (11 January 2000).

23. B.E. Ashforth and R.H. Humphrey, "Emotional Labor in Service Roles: The Influence of Identity," *Academy of Management Review* 18 (1993), pp. 88–115. For a recent review of the emotional labor concept, see T.M. Glomb and M.J. Tews,

"Emotional Labor: A Conceptualization and Scale Development," *Journal of Vocational Behavior* 64, no. 1 (2004), pp. 1–23.

24. R. Strauss, "Seminar on Smiling Brightens the Shore," *The New York Times*, 28 August 2005, p. 8.

25. J.A. Morris and D.C. Feldman, "The Dimensions, Antecedents, and Consequences of Emotional Labor," *Academy of Management Review* 21 (1996), pp. 986–1010; D. Zapf, "Emotion Work and Psychological Well-Being: A Review of the Literature and Some Conceptual Considerations," *Human Resource Management Review* 12 (2002), pp. 237–68.

26. E. Forman, "'Diversity Concerns Grow as Companies Head Overseas,' Consultant Says," *Sun-Sentinel (Fort Lauderdale, Florida)*, 26 June 1995. Cultural differences in emotional expression are discussed in F. Trompenaars, "Resolving International Conflict: Culture and Business Strategy," *Business Strategy Review* 7, no. 3 (Autumn 1996), pp. 51–68; F. Trompenaars and C. Hampden-Turner, *Riding the Waves of Culture*, 2nd ed. (New York: McGraw-Hill, 1998), Chapter 6.

27. R. Hallowell, D. Bowen, and C. I. Knoop, "Four Seasons Goes to Paris," *Academy of Management Executive* 16, no. 4 (November 2002), pp. 7–24.

28. This relates to the automaticity of emotion, which is summarized in P. Winkielman and K.C. Berridge, "Unconscious Emotion," *Current Directions in Psychological Science* 13, no. 3 (2004), pp. 120–23; K.N. Ochsner and J.J. Gross, "The Cognitive Control of Emotions," *TRENDS in Cognitive Sciences* 9, no. 5 (May 2005), pp. 242–49.

29. W.J. Zerbe, "Emotional Dissonance and Employee Well-Being," in *Managing Emotions in the Workplace*, ed. N.M. Ashkanasy, W.J. Zerbe, and C.E.J. Hartel (Armonk, NY: M.E. Sharpe, 2002), pp. 189–214; R. Cropanzano, H.M. Weiss, and S.M. Elias, "The Impact of Display Rules and Emotional Labor on Psychological Well-Being at Work," *Research in Occupational Stress and Well Being* 3 (2003), pp. 45–89.

30. A. Schwitzerlette, "Cici's Pizza Coming to Beckley," *Register-Herald* (Beckley, West Virginia), 24 August 2003.

31. Brotheridge and Grandey, "Emotional Labor and Burnout: Comparing Two Perspectives of 'People Work"; Zapf, "Emotion Work and Psychological Well-Being"; J.M. Diefendorff, M.H. Croyle, and R.H. Gosserand, "The Dimensionality and Antecedents of Emotional Labor Strategies," *Journal of Vocational Behavior* 66, no. 2 (2005), pp. 339–57.

32. C. Fox, "Shifting Gears," *Australian Financial Review*, 13 August 2004, p. 28; J. Thomson, "True Team Spirit," *Business Review Weekly*, 18 March 2004, p. 92.

33. J.D. Mayer, P. Salovey, and D.R. Caruso, "Models of Emotional Intelligence," in *Handbook of Human Intelligence*, ed. R.J. Sternberg, 2nd ed. (New York: Cambridge University Press, 2000), pp. 396–420. This definition is also recognized in C. Cherniss, "Emotional Intelligence and Organizational Effectiveness," in *The Emotionally Intelligent Workplace*, ed. C. Cherniss and D. Goleman (San Francisco: Jossey-Bass, 2001), pp. 3–12; and M. Zeidner, G. Matthews, and R.D. Roberts, "Emotional Intelligence in the Workplace: A Critical Review," *Applied Psychology: An International Review* 53, no. 3 (2004), pp. 371–99.

34. These four dimensions of emotional intelligence are discussed in detail in D. Goleman, R. Boyatzis, and A. McKee, *Primal Leadership* (Boston: Harvard Business School Press, 2002), Chapter 3. Slight variations of this model are presented in R. Boyatzis, D. Goleman, and K.S. Rhee, "Clustering Competence in Emotional Intelligence," in *The Handbook of Emotional Intelligence*, ed. R. Bar-On and J.D.A. Parker (San Francisco: Jossey-Bass, 2000), pp. 343–62; and D. Goleman, "An EI-Based Theory of Performance," in *The Emotionally Intelligent Workplace*, ed. C. Cherniss and D. Goleman (San Francisco: Jossey-Bass, 2001), pp. 27–44.

35. H.A. Elfenbein and N. Ambady, "Predicting Workplace Outcomes from the Ability to Eavesdrop on Feelings," *Journal of Applied Psychology* 87, no. 5 (2002), pp. 963–71.

36. The hierarchical nature of the four EI dimensions is discussed by Goleman but is more explicit in the Salovey and Mayer model. See D.R. Caruso and P. Salovey, *The Emotionally Intelligent Manager* (San Francisco: Jossey-Bass, 2004).

37. P.J. Jordan et al., "Workgroup Emotional Intelligence: Scale Development and Relationship to Team Process Effectiveness and Goal Focus," *Human Resource Management Review* 12 (2002), pp. 195–214; H. Nel, W.S. De Villiers, and A.S. Engelbrecht, "The Influence of Emotional Intelligence on Performance in a Call Centre Environment," in *First International Conference on Contemporary Management*, ed. A. Travaglione et al. (Adelaide, Australia, 1–2 September 2003), pp. 81–90; P.N. Lopes et al., "Emotional Intelligence and Social Interaction," *Personality and Social Psychology Bulletin* 30, no. 8 (August 2004), pp. 1018–34; C.S. Daus and N.M. Ashkanasy, "The Case for the Ability-Based Model of Emotional Intelligence in Organizational Behavior," *Journal of Organizational Behavior* 26 (2005), pp. 453–66. Not all studies have found that EI predicts job performance. See S. Newsome, A.L. Day, and V.M. Catano, "Assessing the Predictive Validity of Emotional Intelligence," *Personality and Individual Differences*, no. 29 (December 2000), pp. 1005–16; A.L. Day and S.A. Carroll, "Using an Ability-Based Measure of Emotional Intelligence to Predict Individual Performance, Group Performance, and Group Citizenship Behaviours," *Personality and Individual Differences* 36 (2004), pp. 1443–58.

38. S.C. Clark, R. Callister, and R. Wallace, "Undergraduate Management Skills Courses and Students' Emotional Intelligence," *Journal of Management Education* 27, no. 1 (February 2003), pp. 3–23; B. Carey, "Measuring Emotions," *Journal Gazette* (Fort Wayne, Indiana), 20 April 2004, p. 8B.

39. E.A. Locke, "The Nature and Causes of Job Satisfaction," in *Handbook of Industrial and Organizational Psychology*, ed. M. Dunnette (Chicago: Rand McNally, 1976), pp. 1297–1350; H.M. Weiss, "Deconstructing Job Satisfaction: Separating Evaluations, Beliefs, and Affective Experiences," *Human Resource Management Review* no. 12 (2002), pp. 173–94. Some definitions still include emotion as an element of job satisfaction, whereas the definition presented in this book views emotion as a cause of job satisfaction. Also, this definition views job satisfaction as a "collection of attitudes," not several "facets" of job satisfaction.

40. Ipsos-Reid, "Ipsos-Reid Global Poll Finds Major Differences in Employee Satisfaction around the World," news release (Toronto: 8 January 2001); International Survey Research, *Employee Satisfaction in the World's 10 Largest Economies: Globalization or Diversity?* (Chicago: International Survey Research, 2002); Watson Wyatt Worldwide, "Asia-Pacific Workers Satisfied with Jobs Despite Some Misgivings with Management and Pay," Watson Wyatt news release (Singapore: 16 November

2004); "Most U.S. Workers Satisfied with Their Jobs: Study," *Reuters News*, 31 August 2005.

41. "Hudson Employment Index Data Suggest Suggests U.S. Workers Will Jump Ship," *PR Newswire* (New York), 7 January 2004; Watson Wyatt Worldwide, "Malaysian Workers More Satisfied with Their Jobs Than Their Companies' Leadership and Supervision Practices," Watson Wyatt Worldwide news release, (Kuala Lumpur), 30 November 2004; K. Keis, "HR Needs Happy Staff to Show Its Success," *Canadian HR Reporter*, 14 February 2005, p. 14.

42. The problems with measuring attitudes and values across cultures are discussed in G. Law, "If You're Happy & You Know It, Tick the Box," *Management-Auckland* 45 (March 1998), pp. 34–37; P.E. Spector et al., "Do National Levels of Individualism and Internal Locus of Control Relate to Well-Being? An Ecological Level International Study," *Journal of Organizational Behavior* 22 (2001), pp. 815–32; L. Saari and T.A. Judge, "Employee Attitudes and Job Satisfaction," *Human Resource Management* 43, no. 4 (Winter 2004), pp. 395–407.

43. M.J. Withey and W.H. Cooper, "Predicting Exit, Voice, Loyalty, and Neglect," *Administrative Science Quarterly* 34 (1989), pp. 521–39; W.H. Turnley and D.C. Feldman, "The Impact of Psychological Contract Violations on Exit, Voice, Loyalty, and Neglect," *Human Relations* 52 (July 1999), pp. 895–922.

44. T.R. Mitchell, B.C. Holtom, and T.W. Lee, "How to Keep Your Best Employees: Developing an Effective Retention Policy," *Academy of Management Executive* 15 (November 2001), pp. 96–108; C.P. Maertz and M.A. Campion, "Profiles of Quitting: Integrating Process and Content Turnover Theory," *Academy of Management Journal* 47, no. 4 (2004), pp. 566–82.

45. A.A. Luchak, "What Kind of Voice Do Loyal Employees Use?" *British Journal of Industrial Relations* 41 (March 2003), pp. 115–34.

46. J.D. Hibbard, N. Kumar, and L.W. Stern, "Examining the Impact of Destructive Acts in Marketing Channel Relationships," *Journal of Marketing Research* 38 (February 2001), pp. 45–61; J. Zhou and J.M. George, "When Job Dissatisfaction Leads to Creativity: Encouraging the Expression of Voice," *Academy of Management Journal* 44 (August 2001), pp. 682–96.

47. M.J. Withey and I.R. Gellatly, "Situational and Dispositional Determinants of Exit, Voice, Loyalty, and Neglect," *Proceedings of the Administrative Sciences Association of Canada, Organizational Behaviour Division* (June 1998); M.J. Withey and I. R. Gellatly, "Exit, Voice, Loyalty and Neglect: Assessing the Influence of Prior Effectiveness and Personality," *Proceedings of the Administrative Sciences Association of Canada, Organizational Behaviour Division* 20 (1999), pp. 110–19.

48. D.P. Schwab and L.L. Cummings, "Theories of Performance and Satisfaction: A Review," *Industrial Relations* 9 (1970), pp. 408-30; M.T. Iaffaldano and P. M. Muchinsky, "Job Satisfaction and Job Performance: A Meta-Analysis," *Psychological Bulletin* 97 (1985), pp. 251–73.

49. T.A. Judge et al., "The Job Satisfaction-Job Performance Relationship: A Qualitative and Quantitative Review," *Psychological Bulletin* 127 (2001), pp. 376–407; Saari and Judge, "Employee Attitudes and Job Satisfaction."

50. Judge et al., "The Job Satisfaction–Job Performance Relationship: A Qualitative and Quantitative Review."

51. "The Greatest Briton in Management and Leadership," *Personnel Today* (18 February 2003), p. 20. The Wegmans motto is mentioned in R. Levering and M. Moskowitz, "The Best 100 Companies to Work For," *Fortune*, 24 January 2005, pp. 90–96.

52. J.I. Heskett, W.E. Sasser, and L.A. Schlesinger, *The Service Profit Chain* (New York: Free Press, 1997); D.J. Koys, "The Effects of Employee Satisfaction, Organizational Citizenship Behavior, and Turnover on Organizational Effectiveness: A Unit-Level, Longitudinal Study," *Personnel Psychology* 54 (April 2001), pp. 101–14; W.-C. Tsai and Y.-M. Huang, "Mechanisms Linking Employee Affective Delivery and Customer Behavioral Intentions," *Journal of Applied Psychology* 87, no. 5 (2002), pp. 1001–8; T. DeCotiis et al., "How Outback Steakhouse Created a Great Place to Work, Have Fun, and Make Money," *Journal of Organizational Excellence* 23, no. 4 (Autumn 2004), pp. 23–33; G.A. Gelade and S. Young, "Test of a Service Profit Chain Model in the Retail Banking Sector," *Journal of Occupational & Organizational Psychology* 78 (2005), pp. 1–22. However, some studies have found only a weak relationship between employee attitudes and sales outcomes.

53. P. Guenzi and O. Pelloni, "The Impact of Interpersonal Relationships on Customer Satisfaction and Loyalty to the Service Provider," *International Journal of Service Industry Management* 15, no. 3–4 (2004), pp. 365–84; S.J. Bell, S. Auh, and K. Smalley, "Customer Relationship Dynamics: Service Quality and Customer Loyalty in the Context of Varying Levels of Customer Expertise and Switching Costs," *Journal of the Academy of Marketing Science* 33, no. 2 (Spring 2005), pp. 169–83.

54. DeCotiis et al., "How Outback Steakhouse Created a Great Place to Work, Have Fun, and Make Money."

55. R.T. Mowday, L.W. Porter, and R.M. Steers, *Employee Organization Linkages: The Psychology of Commitment, Absenteeism, and Turnover* (New York: Academic Press, 1982).

56. J.P. Meyer, "Organizational Commitment," *International Review of Industrial and Organizational Psychology* 12 (1997), pp. 175–228. Along with affective and continuance commitment, Meyer identifies *normative commitment*, which refers to employee feelings of obligation to remain with the organization. This commitment has been excluded here so that students focus on the two most common perspectives of commitment.

57. R.D. Hackett, P. Bycio, and P.A. Hausdorf, "Further Assessments of Meyer and Allen's (1991) Three-Component Model of Organizational Commitment," *Journal of Applied Psychology* 79 (1994), pp. 15–23.

58. F.F. Reichheld, *The Loyalty Effect* (Boston: Harvard Business School Press, 1996), Chapter 4; J.P. Meyer et al., "Affective, Continuance, and Normative Commitment to the Organization: A Meta-Analysis of Antecedents, Correlates, and Consequences," *Journal of Vocational Behavior* 61 (2002), pp. 20–52; M. Riketta, "Attitudinal Organizational Commitment and Job Performance: A Meta-Analysis," *Journal of Organizational Behavior* 23 (2002), pp. 257–66.

59. B.L. Toffler, *Final Accounting: Ambition, Greed, and the Fall of Arthur Andersen* (New York: Broadway Books, 2003).

60. J. Churchill, "To the Bitter End," *Registered Rep*, March 2006, p. 59.

61. J.P. Meyer et al., "Organizational Commitment and Job Performance: It's the Nature of the Commitment That Counts," *Journal of Applied Psychology* 74 (1989), pp. 152–56; A.A. Luchak and I.R. Gellatly, "What Kind of Commitment Does a Final-Earnings Pension Plan Elicit?" *Relations Industrielles* 56 (Spring 2001), pp. 394–417; Z.X. Chen and A.M.

Francesco, "The Relationship between the Three Components of Commitment and Employee Performance in China," *Journal of Vocational Behavior* 62, no. 3 (2003), pp. 490–510; D.M. Powell and J.P. Meyer, "Side-Bet Theory and the Three-Component Model of Organizational Commitment," *Journal of Vocational Behavior* 65, no. 1 (2004), pp. 157–77.

62. E.W. Morrison and S.L. Robinson, "When Employees Feel Betrayed: A Model of How Psychological Contract Violation Develops," *Academy of Management Review* 22 (1997), pp. 226–56; J.E. Finegan, "The Impact of Person and Organizational Values on Organizational Commitment," *Journal of Occupational and Organizational Psychology* 73 (June 2000), pp. 149–69.

63. D.M. Cable and T.A. Judge, "Person-Organization Fit, Job Choice Decisions, and Organizational Entry," *Organizational Behavior and Human Decision Processes* 67, no. 3 (1996), pp. 294–311; T.J. Kalliath, A.C. Bluedorn, and M.J. Strube, "A Test of Value Congruence Effects," *Journal of Organizational Behavior* 20, no. 7 (1999), pp. 1175–98; J.W. Westerman and L.A. Cyr, "An Integrative Analysis of Person-Organization Fit Theories," *International Journal of Selection and Assessment* 12, no. 3 (September 2004), pp. 252–61.

64. D.M. Rousseau et al., "Not So Different after All: A Cross-Discipline View of Trust," *Academy of Management Review* 23 (1998), pp. 393–404.

65. S. Ashford, C. Lee, and P. Bobko, "Content, Causes, and Consequences of Job Insecurity: A Theory-Based Measure and Substantive Test," *Academy of Management Journal* 32 (1989), pp. 803–29; C. Hendry, Chris, and R. Jenkins, "Psychological Contracts and New Deals," *Human Resource Management Journal* 7 (1997), pp. 38–44.

66. T.S. Heffner and J.R. Rentsch, "Organizational Commitment and Social Interaction: A Multiple Constituencies Approach," *Journal of Vocational Behavior* 59 (2001), pp. 471–90.

67. E. White, "Know Your Duties, the Firm to Reduce New-Job Surprises," *The Wall Street Journal*, 27 December 2005, p. A16.

68. P. Kruger, "Betrayed by Work," *Fast Company*, November 1999, p. 182.

69. S.L. Robinson, M.S. Kraatz, and D.M. Rousseau, "Changing Obligations and the Psychological Contract: A Longitudinal Study," *Academy of Management Journal* 37 (1994), pp. 137–52; Morrison and Robinson, "When Employees Feel Betrayed: A Model of How Psychological Contract Violation Develops."

70. D.M. Rousseau, *Psychological Contracts in Organizations* (Thousand Oaks, CA: Sage, 1995); M. Janssens, L. Sels, and I. Van den Brande, "Multiple Types of Psychological Contracts: A Six-Cluster Solution," *Human Relations* 56, no. 11 (2003), pp. 1349–78.

71. "Officials Worry as Younger Japanese Embrace 'Freeting,'" *Taipei Times* (Korea), 4 June 2003, p. 12; "Ministry Scheme Lets You Test-Drive a Job," *Yomiuri Shimbun* (Tokyo), 22 April 2005; C. Fujioka, "Idle Young Adults Threaten Japan's Workforce," *Reuters News*, 28 February 2005; "40% of Students Accept Becoming 'Freeters' to Realize Dreams: Survey," *Kyodo News* (Tokyo), 2 May 2006.

72. P.R. Sparrow, "Reappraising Psychological Contracting: Lessons for the Field of Human Resource Development from Cross-Cultural and Occupational Psychology Research," *International Studies of Management & Organization* 28 (March 1998), pp. 30–63; D.C. Thomas, K. Au, and E.C. Ravlin, "Cultural Variation and the Psychological Contract," *Journal of Organizational Behavior* 24 (2003), pp. 451–71.

73. W.H. Whyte, *Organization Man* (New York: Simon & Schuster, 1956), p. 129; C. Hendry and R. Jenkins, "Psychological Contracts and New Deals," *Human Resource Management Journal* 7 (1997), pp. 38–44.

74. R.J. Burke, "Organizational Transitions," in *The New World of Work: Challenges and Opportunities,* ed. C.L. Cooper and R.J. Burke (Oxford: Blackwell, 2002), pp. 3–28; F. Patterson, "Developments in Work Psychology: Emerging Issues and Future Trends," *Journal of Occupational and Organizational Psychology* 74 (November 2001), pp. 381–90.

75. L. Uchitelle, "As Job Cuts Spread, Tears Replace Anger," *The New York Times*, 5 August 2001. Psychological contract expectations of young employees are discussed in P. Herriot and C. Pemberton, "Facilitating New Deals," *Human Resource Management Journal* 7 (1997), pp. 45–56; and P.R. Sparrow, "Transitions in the Psychological Contract: Some Evidence from the Banking Sector," *Human Resource Management Journal* 6 (1996), pp. 75–92.

CHAPTER 5

1. D. Creelman, "Interview: Bob Catell & Kenny Moore," *HR.com*, February 2005; W.L. Lee, "Net Value: That Loving Feeling," *The Edge Financial Daily* (Malaysia), 25 April 2005; N. Mwaura, "Honour Staff for Good Work," *Daily Nation* (Nairobi, Kenya), 27 September 2005; E. White, "Praise from Peers Goes a Long Way," *The Wall Street Journal*, 19 December 2005, p. B3.

2. C.C. Pinder, *Work Motivation in Organizational Behavior* (Upper Saddle River, NJ: Prentice-Hall, 1998); R.M. Steers, R.T. Mowday, and D.L. Shapiro, "The Future of Work Motivation Theory," *Academy of Management Review* 29 (2004), pp. 379–87.

3. "Towers Perrin Study Finds, Despite Layoffs and Slow Economy, a New, More Complex Power Game Is Emerging between Employers and Employees," *Business Wire* news release, (New York: 30 August 2001); K.V. Rondeau and T.H. Wagar, "Downsizing and Organizational Restructuring: What Is the Impact on Hospital Performance?" International Journal of Public Administration 26 (2003), pp. 1647–68.

4. C. Lachnit, "The Young and the Dispirited," *Workforce* 81 (August 2002), p. 18; S.H. Applebaum, M. Serena, and B.T. Shapiro, "Generation X and the Boomers: Organizational Myths and Literary Realities," *Management Research News* 27, no. 11/12 (2004), pp. 1–28. Motivation and needs across generations are also discussed in R. Zemke and B. Filipczak, *Generations at Work: Managing the Clash of Veterans, Boomers, Xers, and Nexters in Your Workplace* (New York: AMACOM, 2000).

5. T.V. Sewards and M.A. Sewards, "Fear and Power-Dominance Drive Motivation: Neural Representations and Pathways Mediating Sensory and Mnemonic Inputs, and Outputs to Premotor Structures," *Neuroscience and Biobehavioral Reviews* 26 (2002), pp. 553–79; K.C. Berridge, "Motivation Concepts in Behavioral Neuroscience," *Physiology & Behavior* 81, no. 2 (2004), pp. 179-209.

6. A.H. Maslow, "A Theory of Human Motivation," *Psychological Review* 50 (1943), pp. 370–96; A.H. Maslow, *Motivation and Personality* (New York: Harper & Row, 1954).

7. D.T. Hall and K.E. Nougaim, "An Examination of Maslow's Need Hierarchy in an Organizational Setting," *Organizational Behavior and Human Performance* 3, no. 1

(1968), p. 12; M.A. Wahba and L.G. Bridwell, "Maslow Reconsidered: A Review of Research on the Need Hierarchy Theory," *Organizational Behavior and Human Performance* 15 (1976), pp. 212–40; E. L. Betz, "Two Tests of Maslow's Theory of Need Fulfillment," *Journal of Vocational Behavior* 24, no. 2 (1984), pp. 204–20; P.A. Corning, "Biological Adaptation in Human Societies: A 'Basic Needs' Approach," *Journal of Bioeconomics* 2, no. 1 (2000), pp. 41–86.

8. A.H. Maslow, "A Preface to Motivation Theory," Psychsomatic Medicine 5 (1943), pp. 85-92.

9. K. Dye, A.J. Mills, and T.G. Weatherbee, "Maslow: Man Interrupted–Reading Management Theory in Context," February 2005, Wolfville, Nova Scotia. As Maslow acknowledged, self-actualization was introduced with a broader meaning by fellow psychologist Kurt Goldstein.

10. A.H. Maslow, *Maslow on Management* (New York: John Wiley & Sons, 1998).

11. F.F. Luthans, "Positive Organizational Behavior: Developing and Managing Psychological Strengths," *The Academy of Management* Executive 16, no. 1 (2002), pp. 57–72; S.L. Gable and J. Haidt, "What (and Why) Is Positive Psychology?" *Review of General Psychology* 9, no. 2 (2005), pp. 103–10; M.E.P. Seligman et al., "Positive Psychology Progress: Empirical Validation of Interventions," *American Psychologist* 60, no. 5 (2005), pp. 410–21.

12. C.P. Alderfer, *Existence, Relatedness, and Growth* (New York: Free Press, 1972).

13. J. Rauschenberger, N. Schmitt, and J.E. Hunter, "A Test of the Need Hierarchy Concept by a Markov Model of Change in Need Strength," *Administrative Science Quarterly* 25, no. 4 (December 1980), pp. 654–70; J.P. Wanous and A.A. Zwany, "A Cross-Sectional Test of Need Hierarchy Theory," *Organizational Behavior and Human Performance* 18 (1977), pp. 78–97.

14. B.A. Agle and C.B. Caldwell, "Understanding Research on Values in Business," *Business and Society* 38 (September 1999), pp. 326–87; B. Verplanken and R.W. Holland, "Motivated Decision Making: Effects of Activation and Self-Centrality of Values on Choices and Behavior," *Journal of Personality and Social Psychology* 82, no. 3 (2002), pp. 434–47; S. Hitlin and J.A. Pilavin, "Values: Reviving a Dormant Concept," *Annual Review of Sociology* 30 (2004), pp. 359–93.

15. P.R. Lawrence and N. Nohria, Driven: *How Human Nature Shapes Our Choices* (San Francisco: Jossey-Bass, 2002).

16. R.E. Baumeister and M.R. Leary, "The Need to Belong: Desire for Interpersonal Attachments as a Fundamental Human Motivation," *Psychological Bulletin* 117 (1995), pp. 497–529; S. Kirkey, "Being Shy, Unsociable Is Bad for Your Health, Study Finds," *Ottawa Citizen*, 21 November 2005, p. A1.

17. W.H. Bexton, W. Heron, and T.H. Scott, "Effects of Decreased Variation in the Sensory Environment," *Canadian Journal of Psychology* 8 (1954), pp. 70–76; G. Loewenstein, "The Psychology of Curiosity: A Review and Reinterpretation," *Psychological Bulletin* 116, no. 1 (1994), pp. 75–98.

18. A.R. Damasio, *Descartes' Error: Emotion, Reason, and the Human Brain* (New York: Putnam Sons, 1994); J.E. LeDoux, "Emotion Circuits in the Brain," *Annual Review of Neuroscience* 23 (2000), pp. 155–84; P. Winkielman and K.C. Berridge, "Unconscious Emotion," *Current Directions in Psychological Science* 13, no. 3 (2004), pp. 120–23.

19. Lawrence and Nohria, *Driven: How Human Nature Shapes Our Choices*, pp. 145–47.

20. D.C. McClelland, *The Achieving Society* (New York: Van Nostrand Reinhold, 1961).

21. S. Shane, E.A. Locke, and C.J. Collins, "Entrepreneurial Motivation," *Human Resource Management Review* 13, no. 2 (2003), pp. 257–79.

22. D.C. McClelland and D.H. Burnham, "Power Is the Great Motivator," *Harvard Business Review* 73 (January–February 1995), pp. 126–39; J.L. Thomas, M.W. Dickson, and P.D. Bliese, "Values Predicting Leader Performance in the U.S. Army Reserve Officer Training Corps Assessment Center: Evidence for a Personality-Mediated Model," *The Leadership Quarterly* 12, no. 2 (2001), pp. 181–96.

23. D. Vredenburgh and Y. Brender, "The Hierarchical Abuse of Power in Work Organizations," *Journal of Business Ethics* 17 (September 1998), pp. 1337–47.

24. D. Miron and D.C. McClelland, "The Impact of Achievement Motivation Training on Small Business," *California Management Review* 21 (1979), pp. 13–28.

25. Lawrence and Nohria, *Driven: How Human Nature Shapes Our Choices*, Chapter 11.

26. P. Dvorak, "Out of Tune," *The Wall Street Journal*, 29 June 2005, p. A1.

27. R. Turcsik, "The Prince of Tidewater," *Progressive Grocer*, 15 April 2003.

28. Expectancy theory of motivation in work settings originated in V.H. Vroom, *Work and Motivation* (New York: Wiley, 1964). The version of expectancy theory presented here was developed by Edward Lawler. Lawler's model provides a clearer presentation of the model's three components. P-to-O expectancy is similar to "instrumentality" in Vroom's original expectancy theory model. The difference is that instrumentality is a correlation, whereas P-to-O expectancy is a probability. See J.P. Campbell et al., *Managerial Behavior, Performance, and Effectiveness* (New York: McGraw-Hill, 1970); E.E. Lawler III, *Motivation in Work Organizations* (Monterey, CA: Brooks-Cole, 1973); and D.A. Nadler and E.E. Lawler, "Motivation: A Diagnostic Approach," in *Perspectives on Behavior in Organizations*, 2nd edition, ed. J.R. Hackman, E.E. Lawler III, and L.W. Porter (New York: McGraw-Hill, 1983), pp. 67–78.

29. M. Zeelenberg et al., "Emotional Reactions to the Outcomes of Decisions: The Role of Counterfactual Thought in the Experience of Regret and Disappointment," *Organizational Behavior and Human Decision Processes* 75, no. 2 (1998), pp. 117–41; B.A. Mellers, "Choice and the Relative *Pleasure of Consequences*," Psychological Bulletin 126, no. 6 (November 2000), pp. 910–24; R.P. Bagozzi, U.M. Dholakia, and S. Basuroy, "How Effortful Decisions Get Enacted: The Motivating Role of Decision Processes, Desires, and Anticipated Emotions," *Journal of Behavioral Decision Making* 16, no. 4 (October 2003), pp. 273–95.

30. Nadler and Lawler, "Motivation: A Diagnostic Approach."

31. T. Janz, "Manipulating Subjective Expectancy through Feedback: A Laboratory Study of the Expectancy-Performance Relationship," *Journal of Applied Psychology* 67 (1982), p. 480–85; K.A. Karl, A.M. O' Leary-Kelly, and J.J. Martocchio, "The Impact of Feedback and Self-Efficacy on Performance in Training," *Journal of Organizational Behavior* 14 (1993), pp. 379–94; R.G. Lord, P.J. Hanges, and E.G. Godfrey, "Integrating Neural Networks into Decision-Making and Motivational Theory: Rethinking Vie Theory," *Canadian Psychology* 44, no. 1 (2003), pp. 21–38.

32. P.W. Mulvey et al., *The Knowledge of Pay Study: E-Mails from the Frontline* (Scottsdale, Arizona: WorldatWork, 2002).

33. M.L. Ambrose and C.T. Kulik, "Old Friends, New Faces: Motivation Research in the 1990s," *Journal of Management* 25 (May 1999), pp. 231–92; C.L. Haworth and P.E. Levy, "The Importance of Instrumentality Beliefs in the Prediction of Organizational Citizenship Behaviors," *Journal of Vocational Behavior* 59 (August 2001), pp. 64–75; Y. Chen, A. Gupta, and L. Hoshower, "Marketing Students' Perceptions of Teaching Evaluations: An Application of Expectancy Theory," *Marketing Education Review* 14, no. 2 (Summer 2004), pp. 23–36.

34. T. Matsui and I. Terai, "A Cross-Cultural Study of the Validity of the Expectancy Theory of Motivation," *Journal of Applied Psychology* 60 (1979), pp. 263–65; D.H.B. Welsh, F. Luthans, and S.M. Sommer, "Managing Russian Factory Workers: The Impact of U.S.-Based Behavioral and Participative Techniques," *Academy of Management Journal* 36 (1993), pp. 58–79.

35. L. Hollman, "Seeing the Writing on the Wall," *Call Center* (August 2002), p. 37; S. Zeller, "Good Calls," *Government Executive*, 15 May 2005.

36. K.H. Doerr and T.R. Mitchell, "Impact of Material Flow Policies and Goals on Job Outcomes," *Journal of Applied Psychology* 81 (1996), pp. 142–52; L.A. Wilk and W.K. Redmon, "The Effects of Feedback and Goal Setting on the Productivity and Satisfaction of University Admissions Staff," *Journal of Organizational Behavior Management* 18 (1998), pp. 45–68.

37. A. Prayag, "All Work...and More Play," *Business Line (The Hindu)*, 13 June 2005, p. 4; S. Rajagopalan, "Bangalore to Hawaii, an All-Paid Holiday," *Hindustan Times*, 7 May 2005; J.A. Singh, "Hola for Success!" *Business Standard* (India), 4 June 2005.

38. G.P. Latham, "Goal Setting: A Five-Step Approach to Behavior Change," *Organizational Dynamics* 32, no. 3 (2003), pp. 309–18; E.A. Locke and G.P. Latham, *A Theory of Goal Setting and Task Performance* (Englewood Cliffs, NJ: Prentice Hall, 1990). Some practitioners rely on the acronym "SMART" goals, referring to goals that are specific, measurable, acceptable, relevant, and timely. However, this list overlaps key elements (for example, specific goals are measurable *and* timely) and overlooks the key elements of being challenging and feedback-related.

39. K. Tasa, T. Brown, and G.H. Seijts, "The Effects of Proximal, Outcome, and Learning Goals on Information Seeking and Complex Task Performance," *Proceedings of the Annual Conference of the Administrative Sciences Association of Canada, Organizational Behavior Division* 23, no. 5 (2002), pp. 11–20.

40. K.R. Thompson, W.A. Hochwarter, and N.J. Mathys, "Stretch Targets: What Makes Them Effective?" *Academy of Management Executive* 11 (August 1997), pp. 48–60; S. Kerr and S. Landauer, "Using Stretch Goals to Promote Organizational Effectiveness and Personal Growth: General Electric and Goldman Sachs," *Academy of Management Executive* 18, no. 4 (2004), pp. 134–38.

41. A. Li and A.B. Butler, "The Effects of Participation in Goal Setting and Goal Rationales on Goal Commitment: An Exploration of Justice Mediators," Journal of Business and Psychology 19, no. 1 (Fall 2004), pp. 37-51.

42. Locke and Latham, *A Theory of Goal Setting and Task Performance*, Chapters 6 and 7; J. Wegge, "Participation in Group Goal Setting: Some Novel Findings and a Comprehensive Model as a New Ending to an Old Story," *Applied Psychology: An International Review* 49 (2000), pp. 498–516.

43. M. London, E.M. Mone, and J.C. Scott, "Performance Management and Assessment: Methods for Improved Rater Accuracy and Employee Goal Setting," *Human Resource Management* 43, no. 4 (Winter 2004), pp. 319–36; G.P. Latham and C.C. Pinder, "Work Motivation Theory and Research at the Dawn of the Twenty-First Century," *Annual Review of Psychology* 56 (2005), pp. 485–516.

44. S.P. Brown, S. Ganesan, and G. Challagalla, "Self-Efficacy as a Moderator of Information-Seeking Effectiveness," *Journal of Applied Psychology* 86, no. 5 (2001), pp. 1043–51; P.A. Heslin and G.P. Latham, "The Effect of Upward Feedback on Managerial Behaviour," *Applied Psychology: An International Review* 53, no. 1 (2004), pp. 23–37; D. Van-Dijk and A.N. Kluger, "Feedback Sign Effect on Motivation: Is It Moderated by Regulatory Focus?" Applied Psychology: *An International Review* 53, no. 1 (2004), pp. 113–35; J.E. Bono and A.E. Colbert, "Understanding Responses to Multi-Source Feedback: The Role of Core Self-Evaluations," *Personnel Psychology* 58, no. 1 (Spring 2005), pp. 171–203.

45. Hollman, "Seeing the Writing on the Wall."

46. C. Mabey, "Closing the Circle: Participant Views of a 360-Degree Feedback Programme," *Human Resource Management Journal* 11 (2001), pp. 41–53. However, one recent study reported that fewer than half of the 55 human resource executives surveyed (most from *Fortune* 500 companies) use 360-degree feedback. See E.E. Lawler III and M. McDermott, "Current Performance Management Practices," *WorldatWork Journal* 12 (Second Quarter 2003), pp. 49–60.

47. W.W. Tornow and M. London, *Maximizing the Value of 360-Degree Feedback: A Process for Successful Individual and Organizational Development* (San Francisco: Jossey-Bass, 1998); L.E. Atwater, D.A. Waldman, and J.F. Brett, "Understanding and Optimizing Multisource Feedback," *Human Resource Management Journal* 41 (Summer 2002), pp. 193–208; J.W. Smither, M. London, and R.R. Reilly, "Does Performance Improve Following Multisource Feedback? A Theoretical Model, Meta-Analysis, and Review of Empirical Findings," *Personnel Psychology* 58, no. 1 (2005), pp. 33–66.

48. A.S. DeNisi and A.N. Kluger, "Feedback Effectiveness: Can 360-Degree Appraisals Be Improved?" *Academy of Management Executive* 14 (February 2000), pp. 129–39; M.A. Peiperl, "Getting 360-Degree Feedback Right," *Harvard Business Review* 79 (January 2001), pp. 142–47; "Perils & Payoffs of Multi-Rater Feedback Programs," *Pay for Performance Report* (May 2003), p. 1; M.-G. Seo, L.F. Barrett, and J.M. Bartunek, "The Role of Affective Experience in Work Motivation," *Academy of Management Review* 29 (2004), pp. 423–49.

49. E. Ross, "Know Yourself," *Business Review Weekly*, 17 March 2005, p. 86.

50. J.W. Smither et al., "Can Working with an Executive Coach Improve Multisource Feedback Ratings over Time? A Quasi-Experimental Field Study," *Personnel Psychology* 56 (Spring 2003), pp. 23–44; C. Udy, "Coaching a Winner," *Bay of Pleny Times* (New Zealand), 23 November 2005, p. P01.

51. S.J. Ashford and G.B. Northcraft, "Conveying More (or Less) Than We Realize: The Role of Impression Management in Feedback Seeking," *Organizational Behavior and Human Decision Processes* 53 (1992), pp. 310–34; M. London, "Giving Feedback: Source-Centered Antecedents

and Consequences of Constructive and Destructive Feedback," *Human Resource Management Review* 5 (1995), pp. 159–88; J.R. Williams et al., "Increasing Feedback Seeking in Public Contexts: It Takes Two (or More) to Tango," *Journal of Applied Psychology* 84 (December 1999), pp. 969–76.

52. A. Dragoon, "Sleepless in Manhattan," CIO, April 2005, p. 1; S.E. Ante, "Giving the Boss the Big Picture," *Business Week*, 13 February 2006, p. 48.

53. J.B. Miner, "The Rated Importance, Scientific Validity, and Practical Usefulness of Organizational Behavior Theories: A Quantitative Review," *Academy of Management Learning and Education* 2, no. 3 (2003), pp. 250–68. Also see C.C. Pinder, *Work Motivation in Organizational Behavior* (Upper Saddle River, NJ: Prentice-Hall, 1997), p. 384.

54. P.M. Wright, "Goal Setting and Monetary Incentives: Motivational Tools That Can Work Too Well," *Compensation and Benefits Review* 26 (May–June 1994), pp. 41–49; E.A. Locke and G.P. Latham, "Building a Practically Useful Theory of Goal Setting and Task Motivation: A 35-Year Odyssey," *American Psychologist* 57, no. 9 (2002), pp. 705–17.

55. "Boeing Settles Sex Discrimination Suit for up to $73m," *Puget Sound Business Journal*, 16 July 2004; S. Holmes, "A New Black Eye for Boeing?" *BusinessWeek*, 26 April 2004, p. 90; S. Holt, "Boeing Gender-Bias Lawsuit Brings Women's Buried Stories to Surface," *Knight Ridder/Tribune Business News*, 6 July 2004; S. Holt and D. Bowermaster, "Rare Trial Nears: 28,000 Women Accuse Boeing of Gender Bias," *The Seattle Times*, 14 May 2004, p. A1.

56. J. Greenberg and E.A. Lind, "The Pursuit of Organizational Justice: From Conceptualization to Implication to Application," in *Industrial and Organizational Psychology: Linking Theory with Practice*, ed. C.L. Cooper and E.A. Locke (London: Blackwell, 2000), pp. 72–108; R. Cropanzano and M. Schminke, "Using Social Justice to Build Effective Work Groups," in *Groups at Work: Theory and Research*, ed. M.E. Turner (Mahwah, NJ: Lawrence Erlbaum Associates, 2001), pp. 143–71; D.T. Miller, "Disrespect and the Experience of Injustice," *Annual Review of Psychology* 52 (2001), pp. 527–53.

57. Adams, "Toward an Understanding of Inequity"; Mowday, "Equity Theory Predictions of Behavior in Organizations"; Cropanzano, "Progress in Organizational Justice: Tunneling through the Maze"; Powell, "Justice Judgments as Complex Psychocultural Constructions: An Equity-Based Heuristic for Mapping Two- and Three-Dimensional Fairness Representations in Perceptual Space."

58. C.T. Kulik and M.L. Ambrose, "Personal and Situational Determinants of Referent Choice," *Academy of Management Review* 17 (1992), pp. 212–37; G. Blau, "Testing the Effect of Level and Importance of Pay Referents on Pay Level Satisfaction," *Human Relations* 47 (1994), pp. 1251–68.

59. T.P. Summers and A.S. DeNisi, "In Search of Adams' Other: Reexamination of Referents Used in the Evaluation of Pay," *Human Relations* 43 (1990), pp. 497–511.

60. Y. Cohen-Charash and P.E. Spector, "The Role of Justice in Organizations: A Meta-Analysis," *Organizational Behavior and Human Decision Processes* 86 (November 2001), pp. 278–321.

61. Canadian Press, "Pierre Berton, Canadian Cultural Icon, Enjoyed Long and Colourful Career," *Times Colonist* (Victoria, B.C.), 30 November 2004.

62. K.S. Sauleya and A.G. Bedeian, "Equity Sensitivity: Construction of a Measure and Examination of Its Psychometric Properties," *Journal of Management* 26 (September 2000), pp. 885–910.

63. B. Murphy, "Rising Fortunes," *Milwaukee Journal Sentinel*, 10 October 2004, p. 1; S. Greenhouse, "How Costco Became the Anti-Wal-Mart," *The New York Times*, 17 July 2005, p. BU1.

64. The meaning of these three groups has evolved over the years. These definitions are based on W.C. King Jr. and E.W. Miles, "The Measurement of Equity Sensitivity," *Journal of Occupational and Organizational Psychology* 67 (1994), pp. 133–42.

65. M. Ezzamel and R. Watson, "Pay Comparability across and within UK Boards: An Empirical Analysis of the Cash Pay Awards to CEOs and Other Board Members," *Journal of Management Studies* 39, no. 2 (March 2002), pp. 207–32; J. Fizel, A.C. Krautman, and L. Hadley, "Equity and Arbitration in Major League Baseball," *Managerial and Decision Economics* 23, no. 7 (October–November 2002), pp. 427–35.

66. Miner, "The Rated Importance, Scientific Validity, and Practical Usefulness of Organizational Behavior Theories: A Quantitative Review."

67. Cohen-Charash and Spector, "The Role of Justice in Organizations: A Meta-Analysis"; J.A. Colquitt et al., "Justice at the Millennium: A Meta-Analytic Review of 25 Years of Organizational Justice Research," *Journal of Applied Psychology* 86 (2001), pp. 425–45.

68. Several types of justice have been identified, and there is some debate over whether they represent forms of procedural justice or are distinct from procedural and distributive justice. The discussion here adopts the former view, which seems to dominate the literature. See C. Viswesvaran and D.S. Ones, "Examining the Construct of Organizational Justice: A Meta-Analytic Evaluation of Relations with Work Attitudes and Behaviors," *Journal of Business Ethics* 38 (July 2002), 193.

69. Greenberg and Lind, "The Pursuit of Organizational Justice: From Conceptualization to Implication to Application." For a recent study of voice and injustice, see J. B. Olson-Buchanan and W.R. Boswell, "The Role of Employee Loyalty and Formality in Voicing Discontent," *Journal of Applied Psychology* 87, no. 6 (2002), pp. 1167–74.

70. R. Folger and J. Greenberg, "Procedural Justice: An Interpretive Analysis of Personnel Systems," *Research in Personnel and Human Resources Management* 3 (1985), pp. 141–83; L.B. Bingham, "Mediating Employment Disputes: Perceptions of Redress at the United States Postal Service," *Review of Public Personnel Administration* 17 (Spring 1997), pp. 20–30.

71. R. Hagey et al., "Immigrant Nurses' Experience of Racism," *Journal of Nursing Scholarship* 33 (Fourth Quarter 2001), pp. 389–95; K. Roberts and K.S. Markel, "Claiming in the Name of Fairness: Organizational Justice and the Decision to File for Workplace Injury Compensation," *Journal of Occupational Health Psychology* 6 (October 2001), pp. 332–47; D.A. Jones and D.P. Skarlicki, "The Effects of Overhearing Peers Discuss an Authority's Fairness Reputation on Reactions to Subsequent Treatment," *Journal of Applied Psychology* 90, no. 2 (2005), pp. 363–72.

72. Miller, "Disrespect and the Experience of Injustice."

73. S. Fox, P.E. Spector, and E.W. Miles, "Counterproductive Work Behavior (CWB) in Response to Job Stressors and Organizational Justice: Some Mediator and Moderator Tests for Autonomy and Emotions," *Journal of Vocational Behavior* 59 (2001), pp. 291–309; I.M. Jawahar, "A Model of Organizational Justice and

Workplace Aggression," *Journal of Management* 28, no. 6 (2002), pp. 811–34; M.M. LeBlanc and J. Barling, "Workplace Aggression," *Current Directions in Psychological Science* 13, no. 1 (2004), pp. 9–12.

74. M.L. Ambrose, M.A. Seabright, and M. Schminke, "Sabotage in the Workplace: The Role of Organizational Injustice," *Organizational Behavior and Human Decision Processes* 89, no. 1 (2002), pp. 947–65.

75. N.D. Cole and G.P. Latham, "Effects of Training in Procedural Justice on Perceptions of Disciplinary Fairness by Unionized Employees and Disciplinary Subject Matter Experts," *Journal of Applied Psychology* 82 (1997), pp. 699–705 D.P. Skarlicki and G.P. Latham, "Increasing Citizenship Behavior within a Labor Union: A Test of Organizational Justice Theory," *Journal of Applied Psychology* 81 (1996), pp. 161–69.

CHAPTER 6

1. V.L. Parker, "Org Charts Turn around with Teams," *News & Observer* (Raleigh, North Carolina), 21 July 2005, p. D1; N. Byrnes and M. Arndt, "The Art of Motivation," *BusinessWeek*, 1 May 2006, p. 56.

2. H. Das, "The Four Faces of Pay: An Investigation into How Canadian Managers View Pay," *International Journal of Commerce & Management* 12 (2002), pp. 18–40. For recent ratings of the importance of pay and benefits, see P. Babcock, "Find What Workers Want," *HRMagazine*, April 2005, pp. 50–56.

3. R. Lynn, *The Secret of the Miracle Economy* (London: SAE, 1991), cited in A. Furnham and R. Okamura, "Your Money or Your Life: Behavioral and Emotional Predictors of Money Pathology," *Human Relations* 52 (September 1999), pp. 1157–77. The opinion polls are summarized in J. O'Rourke, "Show Boys the Money and Tell Girls You Care," *Sun-Herald* (Sydney, Australia), 10 December 2000, p. 43; M. Steen, "Study Looks at What Good Employees Want from a Company," *San Jose Mercury*, 19 December 2000.

4. A. Furnham, B.D. Kirkcaldy, and R. Lynn, "National Attitudes to Competitiveness, Money, and Work among Young People: First, Second, and Third World Differences," *Human Relations* 47 (January 1994), pp. 119–32; V.K.G. Lim, "Money Matters: An Empirical Investigation of Money, Face, and the Confucian Work Ethic," *Personality and Individual Differences* 35 (2003), pp. 953–70; T.L.-P. Tang, A. Furnham, and G.M.-T. Davis, "A Cross-Cultural Comparison of the Money Ethic, the Protestant Work Ethic, and Job Satisfaction: Taiwan, the USA, and the UK," *International Journal of Organization Theory and Behavior* 6, no. 2 (Summer 2003), pp. 175–94.

5. J.L. Sanchez Jr., "City OKs Police Pay Hikes," *Press Democrat* (Santa Rosa, California), 18 October 2005, p. B1; J. Castellucci, "Longevity Bonus Now a Bone of Contention," *Providence Journal*, 31 January 2006, p. C01.

6. "Seniority Pay System Seeing Revival," *Kyodo News* (Tokyo), 29 March 2004; "More Firms Offering Childbirth Allowances," *Daily Yomiuri* (Tokyo), 29 September 2005, p. 4.

7. D.M. Figart, "Equal Pay for Equal Work: The Role of Job Evaluation in an Evolving Social Norm," *Journal of Economic Issues* 34 (March 2000), pp. 1–19; G.T. Milkovich, J.M. Newman, and C. Milkovich, *Compensation* (Burr Ridge, IL: McGraw-Hill/Irwin, 2002).

8. E.E. Lawler III, *Rewarding Excellence: Pay Strategies for the New Economy* (San Francisco: Jossey-Bass, 2000), pp. 30–35, 109–19; R. McNabb and K. Whitfield, "Job Evaluation and High Performance Work Practices: Compatible or Conflictual?" *Journal of Management Studies* 38 (March 2001), pp. 293–312.

9. "Syracuse's Restructured Flexible Pay Plan Makes Managing Employees Easier," *HR On Campus*, 5 December 2002. For discussion of why companies are shifting to competency-based pay, see R.L. Heneman, G.E. Ledford Jr., and M.T. Gresham, "The Changing Nature of Work and Its Effects on Compensation Design and Delivery," in *Compensation in Organizations: Current Research and Practice*, ed. S. Rynes and B. Gerhart (San Francisco: Jossey-Bass, 2000), pp. 195–240.

10. E.E. Lawler III, "From Job-Based to Competency-Based Organizations," *Journal of Organizational Behavior* 15 (1994), pp. 3–15; B. Murray and B. Gerhart, "Skill-Based Pay and Skill Seeking," *Human Resource Management Review* 10 (August 2000), pp. 271–87; J.D. Shaw et al., "Success and Survival of Skill-Based Pay Plans," *Journal of Management* 31, no. 1 (February 2005), pp. 28–49.

11. E.B. Peach and D.A. Wren, "Pay for Performance from Antiquity to the 1950s," *Journal of Organizational Behavior Management* (1992), pp. 5–26.

12. L. Spiers, "Piece by Piecemeal," *Lawn & Landscape Magazine*, 5 August 2003; H.-H. Pai, "'Our Eyes Have Been Opened to the Abuse,'" *The Guardian* (London), 29 April 2006, p. 2.

13. C. Petrie, "PCCW Puts the Focus on Rewarding Staff," *South China Morning Post* (Hong Kong), 17 July 2004, p. 4.

14. H. Stock Jr. "At National City, Reps Are Judged on a Whole Lot More Than Their Production," *Bank Investment Consultant*, 1 December 2004, p. 26; K. Whitehouse, "More Employers Link Pay to Performance," *Dow Jones Commodities Service*, 7 December 2005.

15. J.M. Welch, "Gainsharing Returns: Hospitals and Physicians Join to Reduce Costs," *Journals of Health Care Compliance* 7, no. 3 (May/June 2005), pp. 39–42; D. Jacobson, "Best-Kept Secrets of the World's Best Companies: Gainsharing," *Business 2.0*, April 2006, p. 82. For evaluations of gainsharing programs, see L.R. Gomez-Mejia, T.M. Welbourne, and R.M. Wiseman, "The Role of Risk Sharing and Risk Taking under Gainsharing," *Academy of Management Review* 25 (July 2000), pp. 492–507; and K.M. Bartol and A. Srivastava, "Encouraging Knowledge Sharing: The Role of Organizational Reward System," *Journal of Leadership & Organizational Studies* 9 (Summer 2002), pp. 64–76.

16. C. Rukuni, "Employee Share Schemes Change Workers' Fortunes," *LiquidAfrica*, 9 October 2004.

17. "Nucor Pays $200m in Bonuses to Employees," *Steel Business Briefing*, 16 December 2005.

18. "KT Seeks New Growth Engines," *Korea Herald*, 2 March 2004.

19. J. Chelius and R.S. Smith, "Profit Sharing and Employment Stability," *Industrial and Labor Relations Review* 43 (1990), pp. 256s–273s; S.H. Wagner, C.P. Parkers, and N.D. Christiansen, "Employees That Think and Act Like Owners: Effects of Ownership Beliefs and Behaviors on Organizational Effectiveness," *Personnel Psychology* 56, no. 4 (Winter 2003), pp. 847–71; G. Ledford, M. Lucy, and P. Leblanc, "The Effects of Stock Ownership on Employee Attitudes and Behavior: Evidence from the Rewards at Work Studies," *Perspectives (Sibson)*, January 2004; P. Andon, J. Baxter, and H. Mahama, "The Balanced Scorecard: Slogans, Seduction, and State of Play,"

Australian Accounting Review 15, no. 1 (March 2005), pp. 29–38.

20. T. Lester, "Performance at Hugo Boss," *Executive Briefing (Economist Intelligence Unit)*, 4 May 2006, 1

21. A.J. Maggs, "Enron, ESOPs, and Fiduciary Duty," *Benefits Law Journal* 16, no. 3 (Autumn 2003), pp. 42–52; C. Brodzinski, "ESOP's Fables Can Make Coverage Risky," *National Underwriter P & C*, 13 June 2005, pp. 16–17.

22. J. Pfeffer, *The Human Equation* (Boston: Harvard Business School Press, 1998); B.N. Pfau and I.T. Kay, *The Human Capital Edge* (New York: McGraw-Hill, 2002). The problems with performance-based pay are discussed in W.C. Hammer, "How to Ruin Motivation with Pay," *Compensation Review* 7, no. 3 (1975), pp. 17–27; A. Kohn, Punished by *Rewards* (Boston: Houghton Mifflin, 1993); M. O'Donnell and J. O' Brian, "Performance-Based Pay in the Australian Public Service," *Review of Public Personnel Administration* 20 (Spring 2000), pp. 20–34; and M. Beer and M.D. Cannon, "Promise and Peril of Implementing Pay-for-Performance," *Human Resource Management* 43, no. 1 (Spring 2004), pp. 3–48.

23. M. Buckingham and D.O. Clifton, *Now, Discover Your Strengths* (New York: Free Press, 2001); Watson Wyatt, *WorkMalaysia* (Kuala Lumpur: Watson Wyatt, 2004), http://www.watsonwyatt.com/asia-pacific/research/workasia/workmy_key-findings.asp (accessed 2 December 2005).

24. S. Kerr, "Organization Rewards: Practical, Cost-Neutral Alternatives That You May Know, but Don't Practice," *Organizational Dynamics* 28 (Summer 1999), pp. 61–70.

25. J.S. DeMatteo, L.T. Eby, and E. Sundstrom, "Team-Based Rewards: Current Empirical Evidence and Directions for Future Research," *Research in Organizational Behavior* 20 (1998), pp. 141–83; S. Rynes, B. Gerhart, and L. Parks, "Personnel Psychology: Performance Evaluation and Pay for Performance," *Annual Review of Psychology* 56 (2005), pp. 571–600.

26. "Dream Teams," *Human Resources Professional*, November 1994, pp. 17–19.

27. D.R. Spitzer, "Power Rewards: Rewards That Really Motivate," *Management Review* May 1996, pp. 45–50. For a classic discussion of the unintended consequences of pay, see S. Kerr, "On the Folly of Rewarding A, While Hoping for B," *Academy of Management Journal* 18 (1975), pp. 769–83.

28. "Strong Leaders Make Great Workplaces," *CityBusiness*, 28 August 2000; P.M. Perry, "Holding Your Top Talent," *Research Technology Management* 44 (May 2001), pp. 26–30.

29. J.R. Edwards, J.A. Scully, and M.D. Brtek, "The Nature and Outcomes of Work: A Replication and Extension of Interdisciplinary Work-Design Research," *Journal of Applied Psychology* 85, no. 6 (2000), pp. 860–68; F.P. Morgeson and M.A. Campion, "Minimizing Trade-offs When Redesigning Work: Evidence from a Longitudinal Quasi-Experiment," *Personnel Psychology* 55, no. 3 (Autumn 2002), pp. 589–612.

30. P. Siekman, "This Is Not a BMW Plant," *Fortune*, 18 April 2005, p. 208.

31. Accel-Team, "Scientific Management: Lessons from Ancient History through the Industrial Revolution," www.accel-team.com; A. Smith, *The Wealth of Nations* (London: Dent, 1910).

32. H. Fayol, *General and Industrial Management*, trans. C. Storrs (London: Pitman, 1949); E.E. Lawler III, *Motivation in Work Organizations* (Monterey,CA: Brooks/Cole, 1973), Chapter 7; M.A. Campion, "Ability Requirement Implications of Job Design: An Interdisciplinary Perspective," *Personnel Psychology* 42 (1989), pp. 1–24.

33. F.W. Taylor, *The Principles of Scientific Management* (New York: Harper & Row, 1911); R. Kanigel, *The One Best Way: Frederick Winslow Taylor and the Enigma of Efficiency* (New York: Viking, 1997).

34. C.R. Walker and R.H. Guest, *The Man on the Assembly Line* (Cambridge, MA: Harvard University Press, 1952); W.F. Dowling, "Job Redesign on the Assembly Line: Farewell to Blue-Collar Blues?" *Organizational Dynamics* (Autumn 1973), pp. 51–67; E.E. Lawler III, *High-Involvement Management* (San Francisco: Jossey-Bass, 1986).

35. M. Keller, *Rude Awakening* (New York: Harper Perennial, 1989), p. 128.

36. F. Herzberg, B. Mausner, and B.B. Snyderman, *The Motivation to Work* (New York: Wiley, 1959).

37. S.K. Parker, T.D. Wall, and J.L. Cordery, "Future Work Design Research and Practice: Toward an Elaborated Model of Work Design," *Journal of Occupational and Organizational Psychology* 74 (November 2001), pp. 413–40. For a decisive critique of motivator–hygiene theory, see N. King, "Clarification and Evaluation of the Two Factor Theory of Job Satisfaction," *Psychological Bulletin* 74 (1970), pp. 18–31.

38. J.R. Hackman and G. Oldham, *Work Redesign* (Reading, MA: Addison-Wesley, 1980).

39. D. Whitford, "A Human Place to Work," *Fortune*, 8 January 2001, pp. 108–19.

40. J.E. Champoux, "A Multivariate Test of the Job Characteristics Theory of Work Motivation," *Journal of Organizational Behavior* 12, no. 5 (September 1991), pp. 431–46; R.B. Tiegs, L.E. Tetrick, and Y. Fried, "Growth Need Strength and Context Satisfactions as Moderators of the Relations of the Job Characteristics Model," *Journal of Management* 18, no. 3 (September 1992), pp. 575–93.

41. "Region Positioned among DCX Leaders in Advanced Manufacturing," *Toledo Business Journal*, August 2004, p. 1; M. Connelly, "Chrysler Wants to Put Team Assembly in All Plants," *Automotive News*, 20 May 2005, p. 53.

42. M.A. Campion and C.L. McClelland, "Follow-up and Extension of the Interdisciplinary Costs and Benefits of Enlarged Jobs," *Journal of Applied Psychology* 78 (1993), pp. 339–51; N.G. Dodd and D.C. Ganster, "The Interactive Effects of Variety, Autonomy, and Feedback on Attitudes and Performance," *Journal of Organizational Behavior* 17 (1996), pp. 329–47.

43. J.R. Hackman et al., "A New Strategy for Job Enrichment," *California Management Review* 17, no. 4 (1975), pp. 57–71; R.W. Griffin, *Task Design: An Integrative Approach* (Glenview, IL: Scott Foresman, 1982).

44. P.E. Spector and S.M. Jex, "Relations of Job Characteristics from Multiple Data Sources with Employee Affect, Absence, Turnover Intentions, and Health," *Journal of Applied Psychology* 76 (1991), pp. 46–53; P. Osterman, "How Common Is Workplace Transformation and Who Adopts It?" *Industrial and Labor Relations Review* 47 (1994). pp. 173–88; R. Saavedra and S.K. Kwun, "Affective States in Job Characteristics Theory," *Journal of Organizational Behavior* 21 (2000), pp. 131–46.

45. Hackman and Oldham, *Work Redesign*, pp. 137–38.

46. A. Hertting et al., "Personnel Reductions and Structural Changes in Health Care: Work–Life Experiences of Medical Secretaries," *Journal of Psychosomatic Research* 54 (February 2003), pp. 161–70.

47. Business Wire, "WKRN-TV and KRON-TV to Become First U.S. Broadcast Stations to Utilize Video Journalism Model to Maximize News Gathering Capabilities and Branding," *Business Wire* news release (San Francisco: 29 June 2005); DV Dojo, "Michael Rosenblum" (2005), http://www.dvdojo.com/who.php (accessed 27 July 2005).

48. K. Tyler, "The Boss Makes the Weather," *HRMagazine*, May 2004, pp. 93–96.

49. This definition is based mostly on G.M. Spreitzer and R.E. Quinn, "*A Company of Leaders: Five Disciplines for Unleashing the Power in Your Workforce* " (2001). However, most elements of this definition appear in other discussions of empowerment. See, for example, R. Forrester, "Empowerment: Rejuvenating a Potent Idea," *Academy of Management Executive* 14 (August 2000), pp. 67–80; W.A. Randolph, "Re-Thinking Empowerment: Why Is It So Hard to Achieve?" *Organizational Dynamics* 29 (November 2000), pp. 94–107; and S.T. Menon, "Employee Empowerment: An Integrative Psychological Approach," *Applied Psychology: An International Review* 50 (2001), pp. 153–80.

50. The positive relationship between these structural empowerment conditions and psychological empowerment is reported in H.K.S. Laschinger et al., "A Longitudinal Analysis of the Impact of Workplace Empowerment on Work Satisfaction," *Journal of Organizational Behavior* 25, no. 4 (June 2004), pp. 527–45.

51. C. S. Koberg et al., "Antecedents and Outcomes of Empowerment," *Group and Organization Management* 24 (1999), pp. 71–91; Y. Melhem, "The Antecedents of Customer-Contact Employees' Empowerment," *Employee Relations* 26, no. 1/2 (2004), pp. 72–93.

52. B.J. Niehoff et al., "The Influence of Empowerment and Job Enrichment on Employee Loyalty in a Downsizing Environment," *Group and Organization Management* 26 (March 2001), pp. 93–113; J. Yoon, "The Role of Structure and Motivation for Workplace Empowerment: The Case of Korean Employees," Social *Psychology Quarterly* 64 (June 2001), pp. 195–206; T.D. Wall, J.L. Cordery, and C.W. Clegg, "Empowerment, Performance, and Operational Uncertainty: A Theoretical Integration," *Applied Psychology: An International Review* 51 (2002), pp. 146–69.

53. R. Semler, *The Seven-Day Weekend* (London: Century, 2003), p. 61. The organizational factors affecting empowerment are discussed in G.M. Spreitzer, "Social Structural Characteristics of Psychological Empowerment," *Academy of Management Journal* 39 (April 1996), pp. 483–504; J. Godard, "High Performance and the Transformation of Work? The Implications of Alternative Work Practices for the Experience and Outcomes of Work," *Industrial & Labor Relations Review* 54 (July 2001), pp. 776–805; and P.A. Miller, P. Goddard, and H.K. Spence Laschinger, "Evaluating Physical Therapists' Perception of Empowerment Using Kanter's Theory of Structural Power in Organizations," *Physical Therapy* 81 (December 2001), pp. 1880–88.

54. D. Furlonger, "Best Company to Work For," *Financial Mail* (South Africa), 30 September 2005, p. 20; A. Hogg, "John Gomersall: CEO, PPC" (South Africa, 26 October 2005), http://www.moneyweb.co.za/specials/corp_gov/509689.htm (accessed 4 January 2006); Pretoria Portland Cement, "PPC Wins Best Company to Work for 2005," *Meropa Communications* news release (Sandton, South Africa: 29 September 2005). Information was also collected from the 2003, 2004, and 2005 annual reports of Pretoria Portland Cement.

55. J.-C. Chebat and P. Kollias, "The Impact of Empowerment on Customer Contact Employees' Role in Service Organizations," *Journal of Service Research* 3 (August 2000), pp. 66–81; H.K.S. Laschinger, J. Finegan, and J. Shamian, "The Impact of Workplace Empowerment, Organizational Trust on Staff Nurses' Work Satisfaction and Organizational Commitment," *Health Care Management Review* 26 (Summer 2001), pp. 7–23.

56. D. Czurak, "Cool Places to Work... Universal Insurance: Where You Rate Yourself," *Grand Rapids Business Journal*, 29 August 2005, p. E8; "Bosses Love Team Workers," *Lancashire Evening Post* (U.K.), 25 May 2006.

57. C.P. Neck and C.C. Manz, "Thought Self-Leadership: The Impact of Mental Strategies Training on Employee Cognition, Behavior, and Affect," *Journal of Organizational Behavior* 17 (1996), pp. 445–67.

58. C.C. Manz, "Self-Leadership: Toward an Expanded Theory of Self-Influence Processes in Organizations," *Academy of Management Review* 11 (1986), pp. 585–600; C.C. Manz and C. Neck, *Mastering Self-Leadership*, 3rd ed. (Upper Saddle River, NJ: Prentice Hall, 2004).

59. O.J. Strickland and M. Galimba, "Managing Time: The Effects of Personal Goal Setting on Resource Allocation Strategy and Task Performance," *Journal of Psychology* 135 (July 2001), pp. 357–67.

60. R.M. Duncan and J.A. Cheyne, "Incidence and Functions of Self-Reported Private Speech in Young Adults: A Self-Verbalization Questionnaire," *Canadian Journal of Behavioral Science* 31 (April 1999), pp. 133–36.

61. J.E. Driscoll, C. Copper, and A. Moran, "Does Mental Practice Enhance Performance?" *Journal of Applied Psychology* 79 (1994), pp. 481–92; C.P. Neck, G.L. Stewart, and C.C. Manz, "Thought Self-Leadership as a Framework for Enhancing the Performance of Performance Appraisers," *Journal of Applied Behavioral Science* 31 (September 1995), pp. 278–302. Some research separates mental imagery from mental practice, whereas most studies combine both into one concept.

62. A. Joyce, "Office Parks: Re-Energize to Get through the Blahs," *Washington Post*, 28 August 2005, p. F05.

63. A. Wrzesniewski and J.E. Dutton, "Crafting a Job: Revisioning Employees as Active Crafters of Their Work," *Academy of Management Review* 26 (April 2001). pp. 179–201.

64. M.I. Bopp, S.J. Glynn, and R.A. Henning, *Self-Management of Performance Feedback during Computer-Based Work by Individuals and Two-Person Work Teams.* Paper presented at the APA-NIOSH conference (March 1999).

65. A.W. Logue, *Self-Control: Waiting until Tomorrow for What You Want Today* (Englewood Cliffs, NJ: Prentice-Hall, 1995).

66. P. Mannion, "Never Lose Focus," *Electronic Engineering Times*, 30 May 2005, p. 1.

67. Neck and Manz, "Thought Self-Leadership: The Impact of Mental Strategies Training on Employee Cognition, Behavior, and Affect"; A.M. Saks and B.E. Ashforth, "Proactive Socialization and Behavioral Self-Management," *Journal of Vocational Behavior* 48 (1996), pp. 301–23; L. Morin and G. Latham, "The Effect of Mental Practice and Goal Setting as a Transfer of Training Intervention on Supervisors' Self-Efficacy and Communication Skills: An Exploratory Study," *Applied Psychology: An International Review* 49 (July 2000), pp. 566–78; J.S. Hickman and E.S. Geller, "A Safety Self-Management Intervention

for Mining Operations," *Journal of Safety Research* 34 (2003), pp. 299–308.

68. S. Ming and G.L. Martin, "Single-Subject Evaluation of a Self-Talk Package for Improving Figure Skating Performance," *Sport Psychologist* 10 (1996), pp. 227–38; D. Landin and E.P. Hebert, "The Influence of Self-Talk on the Performance of Skilled Female Tennis Players," *Journal of Applied Sport Psychology* 11 (September 1999), pp. 263–82; K.E. Thiese and S. Huddleston, "The Use of Psychological Skills by Female Collegiate Swimmers," *Journal of Sport Behavior* (December 1999), pp. 602–10; J. Bauman, "The Gold Medal Mind," *Psychology Today* 33 (May 2000), pp. 62–69; A. Papaioannou et al., "Combined Effect of Goal Setting and Self-Talk in Performance of a Soccer-Shooting Task," *Perceptual and Motor Skills* 98, no. 1 (February 2004), pp. 89–99.

69. J. Houghton, D. et al., "The Relationship between Self-Leadership and Personality: A Comparison of Hierarchical Factor Structures," *Journal of Managerial Psychology* 19, no. 4 (2004), pp. 427–41. For discussion of constructive thought patterns in the context of organizations, see J. Godwin, C.P. Neck, and J. Houghton, "The Impact of Thought Self-Leadership on Individual Goal Performance: A Cognitive Perspective," *Journal of Management Development* 18 (1999), pp. 153–69.

CHAPTER 7

1. E. Frauenheim, "For Developers, It's Not All Fun and Games," *CNET News.com*, 18 November 2004; A. Pham, "Video Game Programmers Get Little Time to Play," *Houston Chronicle*, 21 November 2004, p. 6; N. Davidson, "Vancouver Developer Looks to Make Video Games without Burning Out Staff," *Canadian Press*, 21 February 2006; N. Wong, "Exclusive: Nicole Wong Reveals Identity of EA Spouse," *Mercury News* (San Jose), 25 April 2006.

2. T. Haratani, "Job Stress Trends in Japan," in *Job Stress Trends in East Asia (Proceedings of the First East Asia Job Stress Meeting)*, ed. A. Tsutsumi (Tokyo: Waseda University, 8 January 2000), pp. 4–10; "New Survey: Americans Stressed More Than Ever," *PR Newswire*, 26 June 2003; "Hong Kong People Still Most Stressed in Asia–Survey," *Reuters News*, 2 November 2004; E. Galinsky et al., *Overwork in America: When the Way We Work Becomes Too Much* (New York: Families and Work Institute, March 2005); M. Mandel, "The Real Reasons You're Working So Hard . . . And What You Can Do about It," *BusinessWeek*, 3 October 2005, p. 60; Mind, *Stress and Mental Health in the Workplace* (London: Mind, May 2005); D. Passmore, "We're All Sick of Work," *Sunday Mail* (Brisbane), 27 November 2005, p. 45.

3. J.C. Quick et al., *Preventive Stress Management in Organizations* (Washington, DC: American Psychological Association, 1997), pp. 3–4; R.S. DeFrank and J.M. Ivancevich, "Stress on the Job: An Executive Update," *Academy of Management Executive* 12 (August 1998), pp. 55–66.

4. Quick et al., *Preventive Stress Management in Organizations*, pp. 5–6; B.L. Simmons and D.L. Nelson, "Eustress at Work: The Relationship between Hope and Health in Hospital Nurses," *Health Care Management Review* 26, no. 4 (October 2001), p. 7ff.

5. H. Selye, *Stress without Distress* (Philadelphia: J.B. Lippincott, 1974).

6. S.E. Taylor, R.L. Repetti, and T. Seeman, "Health Psychology: What Is an Unhealthy Environment and How Does It Get under the Skin?" *Annual Review of Psychology* 48 (1997), pp. 411–47.

7. K. Danna and R.W. Griffin, "Health and Well-Being in the Workplace: A Review and Synthesis of the Literature," *Journal of Management* (Spring 1999), pp. 357–84.

8. N. Wager, G. Fieldman, and T. Hussey, "The Effect on Ambulatory Blood Pressure of Working under Favourably and Unfavourably Perceived Supervisors," *Occupational and Environmental Medicine* 60, no. 7 (1 July 2003), pp. 468–74. For further details on the stressful effects of bad bosses, see E.K. Kelloway et al., "Poor Leadership," in *Handbook of Workplace Stress*, ed. J. Barling, E.K. Kelloway, and M. Frone (Thousand Oaks, CA: Sage, 2005), pp. 89–112.

9. Bureau of Labor Statistics, "National Census of Fatal Occupational Injuries in 2004," U.S. Department of Labor news release (Washington, DC: 25 August 2005); N. Paton, "Nurses on the Verge of Breakdown," *Occupational Health*, April 2006, p. 4.

10. This is a slight variation of the definition in the Quebec antiharassment legislation. See www.cnt.gouv.qc.ca. For related definitions and discussion of workplace incivility, see H. Cowiea et al., "Measuring Workplace Bullying," *Aggression and Violent Behavior* 7 (2002), pp. 33–51; C.M. Pearson and C.L. Porath, "On the Nature, Consequences, and Remedies of Workplace Incivility: No Time for 'Nice'? Think Again," *Academy of Management Executive* 19, no. 1 (February 2005), pp. 7–18.

11. Pearson and Porath, "On the Nature, Consequences, and Remedies of Workplace Incivility"; J. Przybys, "How Rude!" *Las Vegas Review-Journal*, 25 April 2006, p. 1E.

12. "HR Bullied Just as Much as Anyone Else," *Personnel Today*, November 2005, p. 3; T. Goldenberg, "Thousands of Workers Intimidated on Job: Study," *Montreal Gazette*, 11 June 2005, p. A9; S. Toomey, "Bullying Alive and Kicking," *The Australian*, 16 July 2005, p. 9; V. Raman, "One Worker in Three Has Experienced Bullying," *National Business Review* (New Zealand), 10 March 2006.

13. H.-H. Pai, "'Our Eyes Have Been Opened by the Abuse'" *The Guardian* (London), 29 April 2006, p. 2.

14. V. Schultz, "Reconceptualizing Sexual Harassment," *Yale Law Journal* 107 (April 1998), pp. 1683–1805; M. Rotundo, D.-H. Nguyen, and P.R. Sackett, "A Meta-Analytic Review of Gender Differences in Perceptions of Sexual Harassment," *Journal of Applied Psychology* 86 (October 2001), pp. 914–922.

15. E.K. Kelloway and J. Barling, "Job Characteristics, Role Stress, and Mental Health," *Journal of Occupational Psychology* 64 (1991), pp. 291–304; M. Siegall and L.L. Cummings, "Stress and Organizational Role Conflict," *Genetic, Social, and General Psychology Monographs* 12 (1995), pp. 65–95; J. Lait and J.E. Wallace, "Stress at Work: A Study of Organizational-Professional Conflict and Unmet Expectations," *Relations Industrielles* 57, no. 3 (Summer 2002), pp. 463–87; E. Grunfeld et al., "Job Stress and Job Satisfaction of Cancer Care Workers," *Psycho-Oncology* 14, no. 1 (May 2005), pp. 61–69.

16. A.M. Saks and B.E. Ashforth, "Proactive Socialization and Behavioral Self-Management," *Journal of Vocational Behavior* 48 (1996), pp. 301–23; A. Nygaard and R. Dahlstrom, "Role Stress and Effectiveness in Horizontal Alliances," *Journal of Marketing* 66 (April 2002), pp. 61–82.

17. Past predictions of future work hours are described in B.K. Hunnicutt, *Kellogg's Six-Hour Day* (Philadelphia: Temple University Press, 1996).

18. C.B. Meek, "The Dark Side of Japanese Management in the 1990s: Karoshi

and Ijime in the Japanese Workplace," *Journal of Managerial Psychology* 19, no. 3 (2004), pp. 312–31; J. Shi, "Beijing's High Flyers Dying to Get Ahead," *South China Morning Post* (Hong Kong), 8 October 2005, p. 8; N. You, "Mantra: Work for Life, Rather Than Live to Work," *China Daily*, 26 March 2005.

19. R. Drago, D. Black, and M. Wooden, *The Persistence of Long Work Hours*, Melbourne Institute Working Paper Series (Melbourne: Melbourne Institute of Applied Economic and Social Research, University of Melbourne, August 2005).

20. L. Wahyudi S., "'Traffic Congestion Makes Me Crazy," *Jakarta Post*, 18 March 2003. Traffic congestion is linked to stress in G.W. Evans, R.E. Wener, and D. Phillips, "The Morning Rush Hour: Predictability and Commuter Stress," *Environment and Behavior* 34 (July 2002), pp. 521–30.

21. F. Kittell et al., "Job Conditions and Fibrinogen in 14,226 Belgian Workers: The Belstress Study," *European Heart Journal* 23 (2002), pp. 1841–48; S.K. Parker, "Longitudinal Effects of Lean Production on Employee Outcomes and the Mediating Role of Work Characteristics," *Journal of Applied Psychology* 88, no. 4 (2003), pp. 620–34.

22. R.J. Burke and C.L. Cooper, *The Organization in Crisis: Downsizing, Restructuring, and Privatization* (Oxford, UK: Blackwell, 2000); M. Kivimaki et al., "Factors Underlying the Effect of Organizational Downsizing on Health of Employees: Longitudinal Cohort Study," *British Medical Journal* 320 (8 April 2000), pp. 971–75; M. Sverke, J. Hellgren, and K. N"swall, "No Security: A Meta-Analysis and Review of Job Insecurity and Its Consequences," *Journal of Occupational Health Psychology* 7 (July 2002), pp. 242–64; R.J. Burke, "Correlates of Nursing Staff Survivor Responses to Hospital Restructuring and Downsizing," *Health Care Manager* 24, no. 2 (2005), pp. 141–49.

23. L.T. Eby et al., "Work and Family Research in IO/OB: Content Analysis and Review of the Literature (1980–2002)," *Journal of Vocational Behavior* 66, no. 1 (2005), pp. 124–97.

24. N. Chesley, "Blurring Boundaries? Linking Technology Use, Spillover, Individual Distress, and Family Satisfaction," *Journal of Marriage and Family* 67, no. 5 (2005), pp. 1237–48; T. Taylor, "Hard-Working Canadians Find It Tough to Disconnect," *Calgary Herald*, 18 May 2005, p. A10; R. Parloff, "Secrets of Greatness-How I Work: Amy W. Schulman," *Fortune*, 20 March 2006, p. 66.

25. C. Higgins and L. Duxbury, *The 2001 National Work-Life Conflict Study: Report One, Final Report* (Ottawa: Health Canada, March 2002); M. Shields, "Shift Work and Health," *Health Reports (Statistics Canada)* 13 (Spring 2002), pp. 11–34.

26. E.K. Kelloway, B.H. Gottlieb, and L. Barham, "The Source, Nature, and Direction of Work and Family Conflict: A Longitudinal Investigation," *Journal of Occupational Health Psychology* 4 (October 1999), pp. 337–46; C.M. Brotheridge and R.T. Lee, "Impact of Work-Family Interference on General Well-Being: A Replication and Extension," *International Journal of Stress Management* 12, no. 3 (2005), pp. 203-21.

27. A.S. Wharton and R.J. Erickson, "Managing Emotions on the Job and at Home: Understanding the Consequences of Multiple Emotional Roles," *Academy of Management Review* (1993), pp. 457–86.

28. B. Keil, "The 10 Most Stressful Jobs in NYC," New York Post, 6 April 1999, p. 50; A. Smith et al., *The Scale of Occupational Stress: A Further Analysis of the Impact of Demographic Factors and Type of Job* (Sudbury, Suffolk: United Kingdom, Health & Safety Executive, 2000).

29. J.L. Hernandez, "What's the Buzz in Schuyler? Just Ask Beekeeper Finster," *Observer-Dispatch* (Utica, New York), 23 June 2003.

30. S.J. Havlovic and J.P. Keenen, "Coping with Work Stress: The Influence of Individual Differences; Handbook on Job Stress [Special Issue]," *Journal of Social Behavior and Personality* 6 (1991), pp. 199–212.

31. S.C. Segerstrom et al., "Optimism Is Associated with Mood, Coping, and Immune Change in Response to Stress," *Journal of Personality & Social Psychology* 74 (June 1998), pp. 1646–55; S.M. Jex et al., "The Impact of Self-Efficacy on Stressor-Strain Relations: Coping Style as an Explanatory Mechanism," *Journal of Applied Psychology* 86 (2001), pp. 401–9.

32. S.S. Luthar, D. Cicchetti, and B. Becker, "The Construct of Resilience: A Critical Evaluation and Guidelines for Future Work," *Child Development* 71, no. 3 (May–June 2000), pp. 543–62; F. Luthans, "The Need for and Meaning of Positive Organizational Behavior," *Journal of Organizational Behavior* 23 (2002), pp. 695–706; G.A. Bonanno, "Loss, Trauma, and Human Resilience: Have We Underestimated the Human Capacity to Thrive after Extremely Aversive Events?" *American Psychologist* 59, no. 1 (2004), pp. 20–28.

33. K.M. Connor and J.R.T. Davidson, "Development of a New Resilience Scale: The Connor–Davidson Resilience Scale (CD-RISC)," *Depression and Anxiety* 18, no. 2 (2003), pp. 76–82; M.M. Tugade, B.L. Fredrickson, and L. Feldman Barrett, "Psychological Resilience and Positive Emotional Granularity: Examining the Benefits of Positive Emotions on Coping and Health," *Journal of Personality* 72, no. 6 (2004), pp. 1161-90; L. Campbell-Sills, S.L. Cohan, and M.B. Stein, "Relationship of Resilience to Personality, Coping, and Psychiatric Symptoms in Young Adults," *Behaviour Research and Therapy*, in press (2006).

34. M. Beasley, T. Thompson, and J. Davidson, "Resilience in Response to Life Stress: The Effects of Coping Style and Cognitive Hardiness," *Personality and Individual Differences* 34, no. 1 (2003), pp. 77–95; I. Tsaousis and I. Nikolaou, "Exploring the Relationship of Emotional Intelligence with Physical and Psychological Health Functioning," *Stress and Health* 21, no. 2 (2005), pp. 77–86.

35. Y. Kim and L. Seidlitz, "Spirituality Moderates the Effect of Stress on Emotional and Physical Adjustment," *Personality and Individual Differences* 32, no. 8 (June 2002), pp. 1377–90; G.E. Richardson, "The Metatheory of Resilience and Resiliency," *Journal of Clinical Psychology* 58, no. 3 (2002), pp. 307–21.

36. J.T. Spence, and A.S. Robbins, "Workaholism: Definition, Measurement, and Preliminary Results," *Journal of Personality Assessment* 58 (1992), pp. 160–78; R.J. Burke, "Workaholism in Organizations: Psychological and Physical Well-Being Consequences," *Stress Medicine* 16, no. 1 (2000), pp. 11–16; I. Harpaz and R. Snir, "Workaholism: Its Definition and Nature," *Human Relations* 56 (2003), pp. 291–319; R.J. Burke, A.M. Richardson, and M. Martinussen, "Workaholism among Norwegian Senior Managers: New Research Directions," *International Journal of Management* 21, no. 4 (December 2004), pp. 415–26.

37. R.J. Burke and G. MacDermid, "Are Workaholics Job Satisfied and Successful in Their Careers?" *Career Development I nternational* 4 (1999), pp. 277–82; R.J. Burke and S. Matthiesen, "Short Communication: Workaholism among Norwegian

Journalists: Antecedents and Consequences," *Stress and Health* 20, no. 5 (2004), pp. 301–8.

38. D. Ganster, M. Fox, and D. Dwyer, "Explaining Employees' Health Care Costs: A Prospective Examination of Stressful Job Demands, Personal Control, and Physiological Reactivity," *Journal of Applied Psychology* 86 (May 2001), pp. 954–64.

39. M. Kivimaki et al., "Work Stress and Risk of Cardiovascular Mortality: Prospective Cohort Study of Industrial Employees," *British Medical Journal* 325 (19 October 2002), pp. 857–60; "Banishing the Blues Could Cut the Chances of Cancer," *The Scotsman* (23 June 2003); I. Hajjar and T.A. Kotchen, "Trends in Prevalence, Awareness, Treatment, and Control of Hypertension in the United States, 1988–2000," *JAMA: Journal of the American Medical Association* 290 (9 July 2003), pp. 199–206; A. Rosengren et al., "Association of Psychosocial Risk Factors with Risk of Acute Myocardial Infarction in 11,119 Cases and 13,648 Controls from 52 Countries (the Interheart Study): Case-Control Study," *The Lancet* 364, no. 9438 (11 September 2004), pp. 953–62; S. Yusuf et al., "Effect of Potentially Modifiable Risk Factors Associated with Myocardial Infarction in 52 Countries (the Interheart Study): Case–Control Study," *The Lancet* 364, no. 9438 (11 September 2004), pp. 937–52.

40. R.C. Kessler, "The Effects of Stressful Life Events on Depression," *Annual Review of Psychology* 48 (1997), pp. 191–214; M. Jamal and V.V. Baba, "Job Stress and Burnout among Canadian Managers and Nurses: An Empirical Examination," *Canadian Journal of Public Health* 91, no. 6 (November-December 2000). pp. 454–58.

41. C. Maslach, W.B. Schaufeli, and M.P. Leiter, "Job Burnout," *Annual Review of Psychology* 52 (2001), pp. 397–422; J.R.B. Halbesleben and M.R. Buckley, "Burnout in Organizational Life," *Journal of Management* 30, no. 6 (2004), pp. 859–79.

42. M. Jamal, "Job Stress and Job Performance Controversy: An Empirical Assessment," *Organizational Behavior and Human Performance* 33 (1984), pp. 1–21; G. Keinan, "Decision Making under Stress: Scanning of Alternatives under Controllable and Uncontrollable Threats," *Journal of Personality and Social Psychology* 52 (1987), pp. 638–44. The positive effects of moderate stress are reported in L. Van Dyne, K.A. Jehn, and A. Cummings, "Differential Effects of Strain on Two Forms of Work Performance: Individual Employee Sales and Creativity," *Journal of Organizational Behavior* 23, no. 1 (2002), pp. 57–74; E. Chajut and D. Algom, "Selective Attention Improves under Stress: Implications for Theories of Social Cognition," *Journal of Personality and Social Psychology* 85, no. 2 (2003), pp. 231–48.

43. R.D. Hackett and P. Bycio, "An Evaluation of Employee Absenteeism as a Coping Mechanism among Hospital Nurses," *Journal of Occupational & Organizational Psychology* 69 (December 1996), pp. 327–38; A. Vaananen et al., "Job Characteristics, Physical and Psychological Symptoms, and Social Support as Antecedents of Sickness Absence among Men and Women in the Private Industrial Sector," *Social Science & Medicine* 57, no. 5 (September 2003), pp. 807–24; L. Tourigny, V.V. Baba, and T.R. Lituchy, "Job Burnout among Airline Employees in Japan: A Study of the Buffering Effects of Absence and Supervisory Support," *International Journal of Cross Cultural Management* 5, no. 1 (April 2005), pp. 67–85.

44. L. Greenburg and J. Barling, "Predicting Employee Aggression against Coworkers, Subordinates, and Supervisors: The Roles of Person Behaviors and Perceived Workplace Factors," *Journal of Organizational Behavior* 20 (1999), pp. 897–913; H. Steensma, "Violence in the Workplace: The Explanatory Strength of Social (In)Justice Theories," in *The Justice Motive in Everyday Life*, ed. M. Ross and D.T. Miller (New York: Cambridge University Press, 2002), pp. 149–67; J.D. Leck, "Violence in the Canadian Workplace," *Journal of the American Academy of Business* 7, no. 2 (September 2005), pp. 308–15.

45. Siegall and Cummings, "Stress and Organizational Role Conflict."

46. "Employee Wellness," *Canadian HR Reporter*, 23 February 2004, pp. 9–12.

47. J.L. Howard, "Workplace Violence in Organizations: An Exploratory Study of Organizational Prevention Techniques," *Employee Responsibilities and Rights Journal* 13 (June 2001), pp. 57–75.

48. C.R. Cunningham and S.S. Murray, "Two Executives, One Career," *Harvard Business Review* 83, no. 2 (February 2005), pp. 125–31.

49. C. Reister, "Schedule Flexing," *Grand Rapids Press* (Michigan), 11 September 2005, p. H1; K. Rives, "Deloitte Offers up to 5 Years Away," *News & Observer* (Raleigh, North Carolina), 10 July 2005, p. E1.

50. S.R. Madsen, "The Effects of Home-Based Teleworking on Work-Family Conflict," *Human Resource Development Quarterly* 14, no. 1 (2003), pp. 35–58.

51. B. Pettit and J. Hook, "The Structure of Women's Employment in Comparative Perspective," *Social Forces* 84, no. 2 (December 2005), pp. 779–801.

52. M. Secret, "Parenting in the Workplace: Child Care Options for Consideration," *The Journal of Applied Behavioral Science* 41, no. 3 (September 2005), pp. 326–47.

53. M. Blair-Loy and A.S. Wharton, "Employees' Use of Work-Family Policies and the Workplace Social Context," *Social Forces* 80 (March 2002), pp. 813–45; M. Jackson, "Managers Measured by Charges' Work-Life Accountability Programs Let Firms Calculate Progress," *Boston Globe*, 2 February 2003, p. G1.

54. "Office Stress? Just Sleep on It," *Western Mail* (Cardiff, Wales), 2 November 2004, p. 12; K. Redford, "Is It Time to Get Bossy?" *Employee Benefits* (U.K.), 7 December 2005, p. S25; J. Saranow, "Anybody Want to Take a Nap?" *The Wall Street Journal*, 24 January 2005, p. R5.

55. S. Overman, "Sabbaticals Benefit Companies as Well as Employees," *Employee Benefit News*, 15 April 2006.

56. M. Waung, "The Effects of Self-Regulatory Coping Orientation on Newcomer Adjustment and Job Survival," *Personnel Psychology* 48 (1995), pp. 633–50; Saks and Ashforth, "Proactive Socialization and Behavioral Self-Management."

57. S. Moreland, "Strike Up Creativity," *Crain's Cleveland Business*, 14 April 2003. p. 3.

58. W.M. Ensel and N. Lin, "Physical Fitness and the Stress Process," *Journal of Community Psychology* 32, no. 1 (January 2004), pp. 81–101.

59. S. Armour, "Rising Job Stress Could Affect Bottom Line," *USA Today*, 29 July 2003; V.A. Barnes, F.A. Treiber, and M.H. Johnson, "Impact of Transcendental Meditation on Ambulatory Blood Pressure in African-American Adolescents," *American Journal of Hypertension* 17, no. 4 (2004), pp. 366–69; M.S. Lee et al., "Effects of Qi-Training on Anxiety and Plasma Concentrations of Cortisol, Acth, and Aldosterone: A Randomized Placebo-Controlled Pilot Study," *Stress and Health* 20, no. 5 (2004), pp. 243–48; P. Manikonda

et al., "Influence of Non-Pharmacological Treatment (Contemplative Meditation and Breathing Technique) on Stress Induced Hypertension–A Randomized Controlled Study," *American Journal of Hypertension* 18, no. 5, Supplement 1 (2005), pp. A89–A90.

60. L. Chordes, "Here's to Your Health," *Best's Review*, April 2006, pp. 52–55; D. Gill, "Get Healthy . . . Or Else," *Inc.*, April 2006, pp. 35–38; J. Wojcik, "Pitney Bowes Tool Encourages Workers to Live Healthier," *Business Insurance*, 3 April 2006, p. 4.

61. T. Rotarius, A. Liberman, and J.S. Liberman, "Employee Assistance Programs: A Prevention and Treatment Prescription for Problems in Health Care Organizations," *Health Care Manager* 19 (September 2000), pp. 24–31; J.J.L. van der Klink et al., "The Benefits of Interventions for Work-Related Stress," *American Journal of Public Health* 91 (February 2001), pp. 270–76.

62. S.E. Taylor et al., "Biobehavioral Responses to Stress in Females: Tend-and-Befriend, Not Fight-or-Flight," *Psychological Review* 107, no. 3 (July 2000), pp. 411–29; R. Eisler and D.S. Levine, "Nurture, Nature, and Caring: We Are Not Prisoners of Our Genes," *Brain and Mind* 3 (2002), pp. 9–52; J.T. Deelstra et al., "Receiving Instrumental Support at Work: When Help Is Not Welcome," *Journal of Applied Psychology* 88, no. 2 (2003), pp. 324–31.

63. J.S. House, *Work Stress and Social Support* (Reading, MA: Addison-Wesley, 1981).

64. S. Schachter, *The Psychology of Affiliation* (Stanford, CA: Stanford University Press, 1959).

CHAPTER 8

1. P. Withers, "Few Rules Rule," *B.C. Business*, January 2002, p. 24; G. Huston, I. Wilkinson, and D. Kellogg, "Dare to Be Great," *B.C. Business*, May 2004, pp. 28–29; P. Withers and L. Kloet, "The Best Companies to Work for in B.C.," *B C. Business*, December 2004, pp. 37–53; M. Andrews, "How to Make Robot Bees, and Other Sound Secrets," *National Post*, 5 March 2005, p. TO32; P. Wilson, "Radical Entertainment to Hire Staff, Expand Studio," *Vancouver Sun*, 6 May 2005, p. C3.

2. F.A. Shull Jr., A.L. Delbecq, and L.L. Cummings, *Organizational Decision Making* (New York: McGraw-Hill, 1970), p. 31.

3. R.E. Nisbett, *The Geography of Thought: How Asians and Westerners Think Differently–and Why* (New York: Free Press, 2003); D. Baltzly, "Stoicism" (Stanford Encyclopedia of Philosophy, 2004), http://plato.stanford.edu/entries/stoicism/ (accessed 8 March 2005); R. Hanna, "Kant's Theory of Judgment" (Stanford Encyclopedia of Philosophy, 2004), http://plato.stanford.edu/entries/kant-judgment/ (accessed 12 March 2005).

4. This model is adapted from several sources, including H.A. Simon, *The New Science of Management Decision* (New York: Harper & Row, 1960); H. Mintzberg, D. Raisinghani, and A. Théorêt, "The Structure of 'Unstructured' Decision Processes," *Administrative Science Quarterly* 21 (1976), pp. 246–75; W.C. Wedley and R. H.G. Field, "A Predecision Support System," *Academy of Management Review* 9 (1984), pp. 696–703.

5. P.F. Drucker, *The Practice of Management* (New York: Harper & Brothers, 1954), pp. 353–57; B.M. Bass, *Organizational Decision Making* (Homewood, IL: Irwin, 1983), Chapter 3.

6. L.R. Beach and T.R. Mitchell, "A Contingency Model for the Selection of Decision Strategies," *Academy of Management Review* 3 (1978), pp. 439–49; I.L. Janis, *Crucial Decisions* (New York: The Free Press, 1989), pp. 35–37; W. Zhongtuo, "Meta-Decision Making: Concepts and Paradigm," *Systematic Practice and Action Research* 13, no. 1 (February 2000), pp. 111–15.

7. J.G. March and H.A. Simon, *Organizations* (New York: John Wiley & Sons, 1958).

8. N. Schwarz, "Social Judgment and Attitudes: Warmer, More Social, and Less Conscious," *European Journal of Social Psychology* 30 (2000), pp. 149–76; N.M. Ashkanasy and C.E.J. Hartel, "Managing Emotions in Decision Making," in *Managing Emotions in the Workplace*, ed. N.M. Ashkanasy, W.J. Zerbe, and C.E.J. Hartel (Armonk, NY: M.E. Sharpe, 2002); S. Maitlis and H. Ozcelik, "Toxic Decision Processes: A Study of Emotion and Organizational Decision Making," *Organization Science* 15, no. 4 (July–August 2004), pp. 375–93.

9. A. Howard, "Opinion," *Computing* (8 July 1999), p. 18.

10. A.R. Damasio, *Descartes' Error: Emotion, Reason, and the Human Brain* (New York: Putnam Sons, 1994); P. Winkielman and K.C. Berridge, "Unconscious Emotion," *Current Directions in Psychological Science* 13, no. 3 (2004), pp. 120–23; A. Bechara and A.R. Damasio, "The Somatic Marker Hypothesis: A Neural Theory of Economic Decision," *Games and Economic Behavior* 52, no. 2 (2005), pp. 336–72.

11. T.K. Das and B.S. Teng, "Cognitive Biases and Strategic Decision Processes: An Integrative Perspective," *Journal of Management Studies* 36, no. 6 (November 1999), pp. 757–78; P. Bijttebier, H. Vertommen, and G.V. Steene, "Assessment of Cognitive Coping Styles: A Closer Look at Situation-Response Inventories," *Clinical Psychology Review* 21, no. 1 (2001), pp. 85–104; P.C. Nutt, "Expanding the Search for Alternatives during Strategic Decision Making," *Academy of Management Executive* 18, no. 4 (November 2004), pp. 13–28.

12. J. Brandtstadter, A. Voss, and K. Rothermund, "Perception of Danger Signals: The Role of Control," *Experimental Psychology* 51, no. 1 (2004), pp. 24–32; M. Hock and H.W. Krohne, "Coping with Threat and Memory for Ambiguous Information: Testing the Repressive Discontinuity Hypothesis," *Emotion* 4, no. 1 (2004), pp. 65–86.

13. P.C. Nutt, *Why Decisions Fail* (San Francisco: Berrett-Koehler, 2002); S. Finkelstein, *Why Smart Executives Fail* (New York: Viking, 2003).

14. E. Witte, "Field Research on Complex Decision-Making Processes–the Phase Theorum," *International Studies of Management and Organization* (1972), pp. 156–82; J.A. Bargh and T.L. Chartrand, "The Unbearable Automaticity of Being," *American Psychologist* 54, no. 7 (July 1999), pp. 462–79.

15. R. Rothenberg, "Ram Charan: The Thought Leader Interview," *strategy + business* (Fall 2004).

16. H.A. Simon, *Administrative Behavior*, 2nd ed. (New York: The Free Press, 1957); H.A. Simon, "Rational Decision Making in Business Organizations," *American Economic Review* 69, no. 4 (September 1979), pp. 493–513.

17. D. Sandahl and C. Hewes, "Decision Making at Digital Speed," *Pharmaceutical Executive* 21 (August 2001), p. 62.

18. Simon, Administrative *Behavior*, pp. xxv, 80–84.

19. P.O. Soelberg, "Unprogrammed Decision Making," *Industrial Management Review* 8 (1967), pp. 19–29; J.E. Russo, V. H. Medvec, and M.G. Meloy, "The Distortion of Information during Decisions," *Organizational Behavior & Human Decision Processes* 66 (1996), pp. 102–10.

20. A.L. Brownstein, "Biased Predecision Processing," *Psychological Bulletin 129, no.* 4 (2003), pp. 545–68.

21. F. Phillips, "The Distortion of Criteria after Decision Making," *Organizational Behavior and Human Decision Processes* 88 (2002), pp. 769–84.

22. H.A. Simon, "Rational Choice and the Structure of Environments," *Psychological Review* 63 (1956), pp. 129–38; H. Schwartz, "Herbert Simon and Behavioral Economics," *Journal of Socio-Economics* 31 (2002), pp. 181–89.

23. P.C. Nutt, "Search during Decision Making," *European Journal of Operational Research* 160 (2005), pp. 851–76.

24. J.P. Forgas, "Affective Intelligence: Toward Understanding the Role of Affect in Social Thinking and Behavior," in *Emotional Intelligence in Everyday Life*, ed. J.V. Ciarrochi, J.P. Forgas, and J.D. Mayer (New York: Psychology Press, 2001), pp. 46–65; J.P. Forgas and J.M. George, "Affective Influences on Judgments and Behavior in Organizations: An Information Processing Perspective," *Organizational Behavior and Human Decision Processes* 86 (September 2001), pp. 3–34; G. Loewenstein and J.S. Lerner, "The Role of Affect in Decision Making," in *Handbook of Affective Sciences*, ed. R.J. Davidson, K.R. Scherer, and H.H. Goldsmith (New York: Oxford University Press, 2003), pp. 619–42; J.S. Lerner, D. A. Small, and G. Loewenstein, "Heart Strings and Purse Strings: Carryover Effects of Emotions on Economic Decisions," *Psychological Science* 15, no. 5 (2004), pp. 337–41.

25. M.T. Pham, "The Logic of Feeling," *Journal of Consumer Psychology* 14 (September 2004), pp. 360-69; N. Schwarz, "Metacognitive Experiences in Consumer Judgment and Decision Making," *Journal of Consumer Psychology* 14 (September 2004), pp. 332–49.

26. L. Sjöberg, "Intuitive vs. Analytical Decision Making: Which Is Preferred?" *Scandinavian Journal of Management* 19 (2003), pp. 17–29.

27. G. Klein, *Intuition at Work* (New York: Currency/Doubleday, 2003), pp. 3–7.

28. W.H. Agor, "The Logic of Intuition," *Organizational Dynamics* (Winter 1986), pp. 5–18; H.A. Simon, "Making Management Decisions: The Role of Intuition and Emotion," *Academy of Management Executive* (February 1987), pp. 57–64; O. Behling and N.L. Eckel, "Making Sense out of Intuition," *Academy of Management Executive* 5 (February 1991), pp. 46–54.

29. M.D. Lieberman, "Intuition: A Social Cognitive Neuroscience Approach," *Psychological Bulletin* 126 (2000), pp. 109–37; Klein, *Intuition at Work*; E. Dane and M.G. Pratt, "Intuition: Its Boundaries and Role in Organizational Decision Making," in *Academy of Management Best Papers Proceedings* (New Orleans, 2004), pp. A1–A6.

30. Klein, *Intuition at Work*, pp. 12–13, 16–17.

31. Y. Ganzach, A.H. Kluger, and N. Klayman, "Making Decisions from an Interview: Expert Measurement and Mechanical Combination," *Personnel Psychology* 53 (Spring 2000), pp. 1–20; A. M. Hayashi, "When to Trust Your Gut," *Harvard Business Review* 79 (February 2001), pp. 59–65. Evidence of high failure rates from quick decisions is reported in Nutt, *Why Decisions Fail*; and Nutt, "Search during Decision Making."

32. P. Goodwin and G. Wright, "Enhancing Strategy Evaluation in Scenario Planning: A Role for Decision Analysis," *Journal of Management Studies* 38 (January 2001), pp. 1–16; R. Bradfield et al., "The Origins and Evolution of Scenario Techniques in Long-Range Business Planning," *Futures* 37, no. 8 (2005), pp. 795–812.

33. R.N. Taylor, *Behavioral Decision Making* (Glenview,IL: Scott, Foresman, 1984), pp. 163–66.

34. G. Whyte, "Escalating Commitment to a Course of Action: A Reinterpretation," *Academy of Management Review* 11 (1986), pp. 311–21; J. Brockner, "The Escalation of Commitment to a Failing Course of Action: Toward Theoretical Progress," *Academy of Management Review* 17, no. 1 (January 1992), pp. 39–61.

35. I. Macwhirter, "Let's Build a Parliament," *The Scotsman* (17 July 1997), p. 19; "Macdome," *Mail on Sunday* (16 December 2001); P. Gallagher, "New Bid to Rein in Rising Costs of Scots Parliament," *Aberdeen Press and Journal* (Scotland), 11 June 2003, p. 1; I. Swanson, "Holyrood Firms Face Grilling over Costs," *Evening News* (Edinburgh), 6 June 2003, p. 2.

36. P. Ayton and H. Arkes, "Call It Quits," *New Scientist* (20 June 1998); M. Fackler, "Tokyo's Newest Subway Line a Saga of Hubris, Humiliation," *Associated Press Newswires* (20 July 1999).

37. F.D. Schoorman and P.J. Holahan, "Psychological Antecedents of Escalation Behavior: Effects of Choice, Responsibility, and Decision Consequences," *Journal of Applied Psychology* 81 (1996), pp. 786–93.

38. G. Whyte, "Escalating Commitment in Individual and Group Decision Making: A Prospect Theory Approach," *Organizational Behavior and Human Decision Processes* 54 (1993), pp. 430–55; D.J. Sharp and S.B. Salter, "Project Escalation and Sunk Costs: A Test of the International Generalizability of Agency and Prospect Theories," *Journal of International Business Studies* 28, no. 1 (1997), pp. 101–21.

39. J.D. Bragger et al., "When Success Breeds Failure: History, Hysteresis, and Delayed Exit Decisions," *Journal of Applied Psychology* 88, no. 1 (2003), pp. 6–14. A second logical reason for escalation, called the martingale strategy, is described in J.A. Aloysius, "Rational Escalation of Costs by Playing a Sequence of Unfavorable Gambles: The Martingale," *Journal of Economic Behavior & Organization* 51 (2003), pp. 111–29.

40. I. Simonson and B.M. Staw, "Deescalation Strategies: A Comparison of Techniques for Reducing Commitment to Losing Courses of Action," *Journal of Applied Psychology* 77 (1992), pp. 419–26; W. Boulding, R. Morgan, and R. Staelin, "Pulling the Plug to Stop the New Product Drain," *Journal of Marketing Research* 34 (1997), pp. 164–76; B.M. Staw, K.W. Koput, and S.G. Barsade, "Escalation at the Credit Window: A Longitudinal Study of Bank Executives' Recognition and Write-Off of Problem Loans," *Journal of Applied Psychology* 82 (1997), pp. 130–42; M. Keil and D. Robey, "Turning around Troubled Software Projects: An Exploratory Study of the Deescalation of Commitment to Failing Courses of Action," *Journal of Management Information Systems* 15 (Spring 1999), pp. 63–87.

41. D. Ghosh, "Deescalation Strategies: Some Experimental Evidence," *Behavioral Research in Accounting* 9 (1997), pp. 88–112.

42. M. Bruno, "Macon: Big Acclaim for a Small Facility," *Boeing Frontiers Online*, June 2005.

43. M. Fenton-O'Creevy, "Employee Involvement and the Middle Manager: Saboteur or Scapegoat?" *Human Resource Management Journal* 11 (2001), pp. 24–40. Also see V.H. Vroom and A.G. Jago, *The New Leadership: Managing Participation in Organizations* (Englewood Cliffs, NJ: Prentice Hill, 1988).

44. S.W. Crispin, "Workers' Paradise," *Far Eastern Economic Review*, 17 April 2003, pp. 40–41; "Thai Carbon Black: Worker-Driven Focus Key to Firm's Success," *The Nation* (Thailand), 3 June 2004.

45. Some of the early OB writing on employee involvement includes C. Argyris, *Personality and Organization* (New York: Harper & Row, 1957); D. McGregor, *The Human Side of Enterprise* (New York: McGraw-Hill, 1960); and R. Likert, *New Patterns of Management* (New York: McGraw-Hill, 1961).

46. A.G. Robinson and D.M. Schroeder, *Ideas Are Free* (San Francisco: Berrett-Koehler, 2004).

47. A. Kleingeld, H. Van Tuijl, and J.A. Algera, "Participation in the Design of Performance Management Systems: A Quasi-Experimental Field Study," *Journal of Organizational Behavior* 25, no. 7 (2004), pp. 831–51.

48. K.T. Dirks, L.L. Cummings, and J.L. Pierce, "Psychological Ownership in Organizations: Conditions under Which Individuals Promote and Resist Change," *Research in Organizational Change and Development* 9 (1996), pp. 1–23; J.P. Walsh and S.-F. Tseng, "The Effects of Job Characteristics on Active Effort at Work," *Work & Occupations* 25 (February 1998), pp. 74–96; B. Scott-Ladd and V. Marshall, "Participation in Decision Making: A Matter of Context?" *Leadership & Organization Development Journal* 25, no. 8 (2004), pp. 646–62. The quotation is from E.E. Lawler III, *Rewarding Excellence: Pay Strategies for the New Economy* (San Francisco: Jossey-Bass, 2000), pp. 23–24.

49. G.P. Latham, D.C. Winters, and E.A. Locke, "Cognitive and Motivational Effects of Participation: A Mediator Study," *Journal of Organizational Behavior* 15 (1994), pp. 49–63; J.A. Wagner III et al., "Cognitive and Motivational Frameworks in U.S. Research on Participation: A Meta-Analysis of Primary Effects," *Journal of Organizational Behavior* 18 (1997), pp. 49–65.

50. Y. Utsunomiya, "Yamato Continues to Deliver New Ideas," *Japan Times*, 8 July 2003; "Yamato Transport Co., Ltd.–SWOT Analysis," *Datamonitor Company Profiles*, 7 July 2004.

51. J. Zhou and C.E. Shalley, "Research on Employee Creativity: A Critical Review and Directions for Future Research," *Research in Personnel and Human Resources Management* 22 (2003), pp. 165–217; M.A. Runco, "Creativity," *Annual Review of Psychology* 55 (2004), pp. 657–87.

52. B. Kabanoff and J.R. Rossiter, "Recent Developments in Applied Creativity," *International Review of Industrial and Organizational Psychology* 9 (1994), pp. 283–24.

53. R.S. Nickerson, "Enhancing Creativity," in *Handbook of Creativity*, ed. R.J. Sternberg (New York: Cambridge University Press, 1999), pp. 392–430.

54. R.I. Sutton, *Weird Ideas That Work* (New York: Free Press, 2002), p. 26.

55. For a thorough discussion of insight, see R.J. Sternberg and J.E. Davidson, *The Nature of Insight* (Cambridge, MA: MIT Press, 1995).

56. R.J. Sternberg and L.A. O' Hara, "Creativity and Intelligence," in *Handbook of Creativity*, ed. R.J. Sternberg (New York: Cambridge University Press, 1999), pp. 251–72; S. Taggar, "Individual Creativity and Group Ability to Utilize Individual Creative Resources: A Multilevel Model," *Academy of Management Journal* 45 (April 2002), pp. 315–30.

57. G.J. Feist, "The Influence of Personality on Artistic and Scientific Creativity," in *Handbook of Creativity*, ed. R.J. Sternberg (New York: Cambridge University Press, 1999), pp. 273–96; Sutton, *Weird Ideas That Work*, pp. 8–9, Chapter 10.

58. V. Laurie, "Gut Instinct," *The Australian Magazine*, 10 December 2005, p. 1; J. Robotham, "Of Guts and Glory," *Sydney Morning Herald*, 5 October 2005, p. 16; M. Irving, "Nobel Deeds, Words of Praise," *West Australian* (Perth), 14 January 2006, p. 4. Some facts are also found in Robin Warren's 2005 Nobel lecture. See J. Robin Warren, "Nobel Lecture: The Ease and Difficulty of a New Discovery," RealVideo presentation at http://nobelprize.org/medicine/laureates/2005/warren-lecture.html.

59. R.W. Weisberg, "Creativity and Knowledge: A Challenge to Theories," in *Handbook of Creativity*, ed. R.J. Sternberg (New York: Cambridge University Press, 1999), pp. 226–50.

60. Sutton, *Weird Ideas That Work*, pp. 121, 153–54; C. Andriopoulos, "Six Paradoxes in Managing Creativity: An Embracing Act," *Long Range Planning* 36 (2003), pp. 375–88.

61. T. Koppell, *Powering the Future* (New York: Wiley, 1999), p. 15.

62. D.K. Simonton, "Creativity: Cognitive, Personal, Developmental, and Social Aspects," *American Psychologist* 55 (January 2000), pp. 151–58.

63. M.D. Mumford, "Managing Creative People: Strategies and Tactics for Innovation," *Human Resource Management Review* 10 (Autumn 2000), pp. 313–51; T.M. Amabile et al., "Leader Behaviors and the Work Environment for Creativity: Perceived Leader Support," *The Leadership Quarterly* 15, no. 1 (2004), pp. 5–32; C.E. Shalley, J. Zhou, and G.R. Oldham, "The Effects of Personal and Contextual Characteristics on Creativity: Where Should We Go from Here?" *Journal of Management* 30, no. 6 (2004), pp. 933–58.

64. R. Westwood and D.R. Low, "The Multicultural Muse: Culture, Creativity and Innovation," *International Journal of Cross Cultural Management* 3, no. 2 (2003), pp. 235–59.

65. T.M. Amabile, "Motivating Creativity in Organizations: On Doing What You Love and Loving What You Do," *California Management Review* 40 (Fall 1997), pp. 39–58; A. Cummings and G.R. Oldham, "Enhancing Creativity: Managing Work Contexts for the High-Potential Employee," *California Management Review* 40 (Fall 1997), pp. 22–38.

66. T.M. Amabile, "Changes in the Work Environment for Creativity during Downsizing," *Academy of Management Journal* 42 (December 1999), pp. 630–40.

67. J.M. Howell and K. Boies, "Champions of Technological Innovation: The Influence of Contextual Knowledge, Role Orientation, Idea Generation, and Idea Promotion on Champion Emergence," *The Leadership Quarterly* 15, no. 1 (2004), pp. 123–43; Shalley, Zhou, and Oldham, "The Effects of Personal and Contextual Characteristics on Creativity."

68. A. Hiam, "Obstacles to Creativity–and How You Can Remove Them," *Futurist* 32 (October 1998), pp. 30–34.

69. M.A. West, *Developing Creativity in Organizations* (Leicester, UK: BPS Books, 1997), pp. 33–35.

70. S. Hemsley, "Seeking the Source of Innovation," *Media Week*, 16 August 2005, p. 22; S. Planting, "When You Need to Get Serious, Get Playful," *Financial Mail* (South Africa), 4 February 2005, p. 14.

71. J. Neff, "At Eureka Ranch, Execs Doff Wing Tips, Fire up Ideas," *Advertising Age*, 9 March 1998, pp. 28–29.

72. A. Hargadon and R.I. Sutton, "Building an Innovation Factory," *Harvard Business Review* 78 (May–June 2000), pp. 157–66; T. Kelley, *The Art of Innovation* (New York: Currency Doubleday, 2001), pp. 158–62.

73. K.S. Brown, "The Apple of Jonathan Ive's Eye," *Investor's Business Daily*, 19 September 2003.

CHAPTER 9

1. S. Konig, "The Challenge of Teams," *On Wall Street*, August 2003; D. Jamieson, "8 Most Common Myths about Teams," *On Wall Street*, May 2005; H.J. Stock, "A 'Cheat Sheet' to Cross Sell," *Bank Investment Consultant*, April 2005, p. 28; L. Wei, "Brokers Increasingly Use Teamwork," *The Wall Street Journal*, 23 February 2005; V. Knight, "Wealth Managers Sell Their Clients Safety, Security," *The Wall Street Journal*, 3 May 2006, p. B3E; M. Santoli, "The Goldman Sachs Way: Minting Money," *Barron's*, 10 April 2006, p. 22; R. Wachman, "Wall Street's Alpha Female Wants to Smash Glass Ceilings," *The Observer* (London), 15 January 2006, p. 7.

2. V.L. Parker, "Org Charts Turn Around with Teams," *News & Observer* (Raleigh, North Carolina), 21 July 2005, p. D1; J. Springer, "Eyes on the Prize," *Supermarket News*, 1 August 2005, p. 12; D. Hechler, "Teamwork Is Job One at Ford," *Fulton County Daily Report* (Atlanta), 16 May 2006, p. 16.

3. This definition and very similar variations are found in M.E. Shaw, *Group Dynamics*, 3rd ed. (New York: McGraw-Hill, 1981), p. 8; S.A. Mohrman, S.G. Cohen, and A.M. Mohrman Jr., *Designing Team-Based Organizations: New Forms for Knowledge Work* (San Francisco: Jossey-Bass, 1995), pp. 39–40; M.A. West, "Preface: Introducing Work Group Psychology," in *Handbook of Work Group Psychology*, ed. M.A. West (Chichester, UK: Wiley, 1996), p. xxvi; S.G. Cohen and D.E. Bailey, "What Makes Teams Work: Group Effectiveness Research from the Shop Floor to the Executive Suite," *Journal of Management* 23 (May 1997), pp. 239–90; and E. Sundstrom, "The Challenges of Supporting Work Team Effectiveness," in *Supporting Work Team Effectiveness*, ed. E. Sundstrom and Associates (San Francisco: Jossey-Bass, 1999), pp. 6-9.

4. M. Moldaschl and W. Weber, "The 'Three Waves' of Industrial Group Work: Historical Reflections on Current Research on Group Work," *Human Relations* 51 (March 1998), pp. 347–88. The survey quotation is found in J.N. Choi, "External Activities and Team Effectiveness: Review and Theoretical Development," *Small Group Research* 33 (April 2002), pp. 181–208. Several popular books in the 1980s encouraged teamwork, based on the Japanese economic miracle. These books included W. Ouchi, *Theory Z: How American Management Can Meet the Japanese Challenge* (Reading,MA: Addison-Wesley, 1981); and R.T. Pascale and A.G. Athos, *Art of Japanese Management* (New York: Simon and Schuster, 1982).

5. A. Doak, "New-Age Style, Old-Fashioned Grunt, but How Will It Look with Fluffy Dice?" *The Age* (Melbourne), 16 October 1998, p. 4; W. Webster, "How a Star Was Born," *Daily Telegraph* (Sydney), 17 October 1998, p. 11; R. Edgar, "Designers Front up to World Stage," *The Age* (Melbourne), 11 February 2004, p. 6; P. Gover, "The Camaro Commandos," *Herald-Sun* (Melbourne), 7 April 2006, p. G07.

6. S. Beatty, "Bass Talk: Plotting Plaid's Future," *The Wall Street Journal*, 9 September 2004, p. B1

7. J. Godard, "High Performance and the Transformation of Work? The Implications of Alternative Work Practices for the Experience and Outcomes of Work" *Industrial & Labor Relations Review* 54 (July 2001), pp. 776–805; J. Pfeffer, "Putting People First," *Stanford Social Innovation Review* 3, no. 1 (Spring 2005), pp. 26–33.

8. B.D. Pierce and R. White, "The Evolution of Social Structure: Why Biology Matters," *Academy of Management Review* 24 (October 1999), pp. 843–53; P.R. Lawrence and N. Nohria, *Driven: How Human Nature Shapes Our Choices* (San Francisco: Jossey-Bass, 2002); J.R. Spoor and J.R. Kelly, "The Evolutionary Significance of Affect in Groups: Communication and Group Bonding," *Group Processes & Intergroup Relations* 7, no. 4 (2004), pp. 398–412.

9. M.A. Hogg et al., "The Social Identity Perspective: Intergroup Relations, Self-Conception, and Small Groups," *Small Group Research* 35, no. 3 (June 2004), pp. 246–76; N. Michinov, E. Michinov, and M.-C. Toczek-Capelle, "Social Identity, Group Orocesses, and Performance in Synchronous Computer-Mediated Communication," *Group Dynamics: Theory, Research, and Practice* 8, no. 1 (2004), pp. 27–39; M. Van Vugt and C.M. Hart, "Social Identity as Social Glue: The Origins of Group Loyalty," *Journal of Personality and Social Psychology* 86, no. 4 (2004), pp. 585–98.

10. S. Schacter, *The Psychology of Affiliation* (Stanford, CA: Stanford University Press, 1959), pp. 12–19; R. Eisler and D.S. Levine, "Nurture, Nature, and Caring: We Are Not Prisoners of Our Genes," *Brain and Mind* 3 (2002), pp. 9–52; A.C. DeVries, E.R. Glasper, and C.E. Detillion, "Social Modulation of Stress Responses," *Physiology & Behavior* 79, no. 3 (August 2003), pp. 399–407.

11. M.A. West, C.S. Borrill, and K.L. Unsworth, "Team Effectiveness in Organizations," *International Review of Industrial and Organizational Psychology* 13 (1998), pp. 1–48; R. Forrester and A.B. Drexler, "A Model for Team-Based Organization Performance," *Academy of Management Executive* 13 (August 1999), pp. 36–49; J.E. McGrath, H. Arrow, and J.L. Berdahl, "*The Study of Groups: Past, Present, and Future*," *Personality & Social Psychology Review* 4, no. 1 (2000), pp. 95–105; M.A. Marks, J.E. Mathieu, and S.J. Zaccaro, "A Temporally Based Framework and Taxonomy of Team Processes," *Academy of Management Review* 26, no. 3 (July 2001), pp. 356-76.

12. G.P. Shea and R.A. Guzzo, "Group Effectiveness: What Really Matters?" *Sloan Management Review* 27 (1987), pp. 33–46; J.R. Hackman et al., "Team Effectiveness in Theory and in Practice," in *Industrial and Organizational Psychology: Linking Theory with Practice*, ed. C.L. Cooper and E.A. Locke (Oxford, UK: Blackwell, 2000), pp. 109–29.

13. Choi, "External Activities and Team Effectiveness: Review and Theoretical Development"; T.L. Doolen, M.E. Hacker, and E.M. Van Aken, "The Impact of Organizational Context on Work Team Effectiveness: A Study of Production Teams," *IEEE Transactions on Engineering Management* 50, no. 3 (August 2003), pp. 285–96.

14. J.S. DeMatteo, L.T. Eby, and E. Sundstrom, "Team-Based Rewards: Current Empirical Evidence and Directions for Future Research," *Research in Organizational Behavior* 20 (1998), pp. 141–83; E.E. Lawler III, *Rewarding Excellence: Pay Strategies for the New Economy* (San Francisco: Jossey-Bass, 2000), pp. 207–14; G. Hertel, S. Geister, and U. Konradt, "Managing Virtual Teams: A Review of Current Em-

pirical Research," *Human Resource Management Review* 15 (2005), pp. 69–95.

15. A. Niimi, "The Slow and Steady Climb toward True North," Toyota Motor Manufacturing North America news release, 7 August 2003; B. Andrews, "Room with Many Views," *Business Review Weekly*, 15 January 2004, p. 68; L. Chappell, "Toyota Trims Development Time," *Automotive News*, 4 August 2005, p. 14.

16. L. Adams, "Medrad Works and Wins as a Team," *Quality Magazine*, October 2004, p. 42; "Lean Manufacturing Increases Productivity, Decreases Cycle Time," *Industrial Equipment News*, October 2005.

17. R. Wageman, "Case Study: Critical Success Factors for Creating Superb Self-Managing Teams at Xerox," *Compensation and Benefits Review* 29 (September–October 1997), pp. 31–41; G. Gard, K. Lindström, and M. Dallner, "Toward a Learning Organization: The Introduction of a Client-Centered Team-Based Organization in Administrative Surveying Work," *Applied Ergonomics* 34 (2003), pp. 97–105.

18. S.D. Dionne et al., "Transformational Leadership and Team Performance," *Journal of Organizational Change Management* 17, no. 2 (2004), pp. 177–93.

19. M.A. Campion, E.M. Papper, and G.J. Medsker, "Relations between Work Team Characteristics and Effectiveness: A Replication and Extension," *Personnel Psychology* 49 (1996), pp. 429–52; D.C. Man and S.S.K. Lam, "The Effects of Job Complexity and Autonomy on Cohesiveness in Collectivistic and Individualistic Work Groups: A Cross-Cultural Analysis," *Journal of Organizational Behavior* 24 (2003), pp. 979–1001.

20. R. Wageman, "The Meaning of Interdependence," in *Groups at Work: Theory and Research*, ed. M.E. Turner (Mahwah, N J: Lawrence Erlbaum Associates, 2001), pp. 197–217.

21. R. Wageman, "Interdependence and Group Effectiveness," *Administrative Science Quarterly* 40 (1995), pp. 145–80; G.S. Van der Vegt, J.M. Emans, and E. Van de Vliert, "Patterns of Interdependence in Work Teams: A Two-Level Investigation of the Relations with Job and Team Satisfaction," *Personnel Psychology* 54 (Spring 2001), pp. 51–69; S.M. Gully et al., "A Meta-Analysis of Team-Efficacy, Potency, and Performance: Interdependence and Level of Analysis as Moderators of Observed Relationships," *Journal Of Applied Psychology* 87, no. 5 (October 2002), pp. 819–32.

22. J.D. Thompson, *Organizations in Action* (New York: McGraw-Hill, 1967), pp. 54–56. One concern with Thompson's typology is that it isn't clear how much more interdependence is created by each of these three forms. See G. Van der Vegt and E. Van de Vliert, "Intragroup Interdependence and Effectiveness: Review and Proposed Directions for Theory and Practice," *Journal of Managerial Psychology* 17, no. 1/2 (2002), pp. 50–67.

23. J. O'Toole and D. Tessmann-Keys, "The Power of Many: Building a High-Performance Management Team," *ceoforum.com.au*, March 2003.

24. G. Stasser, "Pooling of Unshared Information during Group Discussion," in *Group Process and Productivity*, ed. S. Worchel, W. Wood, and J.A. Simpson (Newbury Park, CA: Sage, 1992); J.R. Katzenbach and D.K. Smith, *The Wisdom of Teams: Creating the High-Performance Organization* (Boston: Harvard University Press, 1993), pp. 45–47.

25. S.E. Nedleman, "Recruiters Reveal Their Top Interview Questions," *Financial News Online*, 16 February 2005.

26. P.C. Earley, "East Meets West Meets Mideast: Further Explorations of Collectivistic and Individualistic Work Groups," *Academy of Management Journal* 36 (1993), pp. 319–48; L.T. Eby and G.H. Dobbins, "Collectivist Orientation in Teams: An Individual and Group-Level Analysis," *Journal of Organizational Behavior* 18 (1997), pp. 275–95; S.B. Alavi and J. McCormick, "Theoretical and Measurement Issues for Studies of Collective Orientation in Team Contexts," *Small Group Research* 35, no. 2 (April 2004), pp. 111–27.

27. M.R. Barrick et al., "Relating Member Ability and Personality to Work-Team Processes and Team Effectiveness," *Journal of Applied Psychology* 83 (1998), pp. 377–91; S. Sonnentag, "Excellent Performance: The Role of Communication and Cooperation Processes," *Applied Psychology: An International Review* 49 (2000), pp. 483–97; F.P. Morgenson, M.H. Reider, and M.A. Campion, "Selecting Individuals in Team Settings: The Importance of Social Skills, Personality Characteristics, and Teamwork Knowledge," *Personnel Psychology* 58, no. 3 (2005), pp. 583–611.

28. S.E. Jackson and A. Joshi, "Diversity in Social Context: A Multi-Attribute, Multilevel Analysis of Team Diversity and Sales Performance," *Journal of Organizational Behavior* 25 (2004), pp. 675–702; D. van Knippenberg, C.K. W. De Dreu, and A.C. Homan, "Work Group Diversity and Group Performance: An Integrative Model and Research Agenda," *Journal of Applied Psychology* 89, no. 6 (2004), pp. 1008–22.

29. D.A. Harrison et al., "Time, Teams, and Task Performance: Changing Effects of Surface- and Deep-Level Diversity on Group Functioning," *Academy of Management Journal* 45 (October 2002), pp. 1029–45.

30. K.Y.O.R. Williams, C.A., "Demography and Diversity in Organizations: A Review of 40 Years of Research," in *Research in Organizational Behavior*, ed. B.M. Staw and L.L. Cummings (Greenwich, CT: JAI, 1998), pp. 77–140; C.M. Riodan, "Relational Demography within Groups: Past Developments, Contradictions, and New Directions," in *Research in Personnel and Human Resources Management*, ed. G.R. Ferris (Greenwich, CT: JAI, 2000), pp. 131–73.

31. D.C. Lau and J.K. Murnighan, "Interactions within Groups and Subgroups: The Effects of Demographic Faultlines," *Academy of Management Journal* 48, no. 4 (August 2005), pp. 645–59.

32. The NTSB and NASA studies are summarized in J.R. Hackman, "New Rules for Team Building," *Optimize*, July 2002, pp. 50–62.

33. B.W. Tuckman and M.A.C. Jensen, "Stages of Small-Group Development Revisited," *Group and Organization Studies* 2 (1977), pp. 419–42.

34. J.E. Mathieu and G.F. Goodwin, "The Influence of Shared Mental Models on Team Process and Performance," *Journal of Applied Psychology* 85 (April 2000), pp. 273–84.

35. A. Edmondson, "Psychological Safety and Learning Behavior in Work Teams," *Administrative Science Quarterly* 44 (1999), pp. 350–83.

36. W.B. Scott, "Blue Angels," *Aviation Week & Space Technology*, 21 March 2005, pp. 50–57.

37. D.L. Miller, "The Stages of Group Development: A Retrospective Study of Dynamic Team Processes," *Canadian Journal of Administrative Sciences* 20, no. 2 (2003), pp. 121–34. For other models of team development, see J.G. Gersick, "Time and Transition in Work Teams: Toward a New Model of Group Development," *Academy of Management Journal* 31 (March 1988), pp. 9–41; J.E. Jones and W.L. Bearley, "Facilitating Team Development: A View

from the Field," *Group Facilitation* 3 (Spring 2001), pp. 56–65; and H. Arrow et al., "Time, Change, and Development: The Temporal Perspective on Groups," *Small Group Research* 35, no. 1 (February 2004), pp. 73–105.

38. D.C. Feldman, "The Development and Enforcement of Group Norms," *Academy of Management Review* 9 (1984), pp. 47-53; E. Fehr and U. Fischbacher, "Social Norms and Human Cooperation," *Trends in Cognitive Sciences* 8, no. 4 (2004), pp. 185-90.

39. "Employees Terrorized by Peer Pressure in the Workplace," Morgan & Banks news release, September 2000. For further discussion of sanctions applied to people who outperform others in the group, see J.J. Exline and M. Lobel, "The Perils of Outperformance: Sensitivity about Being the Target of a Threatening Upward Comparison," *Psychological Bulletin* 125, no. 3 (1999), pp. 307–37.

40. N. Ellemers and F. Rink, "Identity in Work Groups: The Beneficial and Detrimental Consequences of Multiple Identities and Group Norms for Collaboration and Group Performance," *Advances in Group Processes* 22 (2005), pp. 1–41.

41. C.R. Graham, "A Model of Norm Development for Computer-Mediated Teamwork," *Small Group Research* 34, no. 3 (June 2003), pp. 322–52.

42. J.J. Dose and R.J. Klimoski, "The Diversity of Diversity: Work Values Effects on Formative Team Processes," *Human Resource Management Review* 9, no. 1 (Spring 1999), pp. 83–108.

43. R. Hallowell, D. Bowen, and C.-I. Knoop, "Four Seasons Goes to Paris," *Academy of Management Executive* 16, no. 4 (November 2002), pp. 7–24.

44. L.Y. Chan and B.E. Lynn, "Operating in Turbulent Times: How Ontario's Hospitals Are Meeting the Current Funding Crisis," *Health Care Management Review* 23, no. 3 (1998), pp. 7–18.

45. L. Coch and J. French Jr., "Overcoming Resistance to Change," *Human Relations* 1 (1948), pp. 512–32.

46. A.P. Hare, "Types of Roles in Small Groups: A Bit of History and a Current Perspective," *Small Group Research* 25 (1994), pp. 443–48.

47. S.H.N. Leung, J.W.K. Chan, and W.B. Lee, "The Dynamic Team Role Behavior: The Approaches of Investigation," *Team Performance Management* 9 (2003), pp. 84–90.

48. R.M. Belbin, *Team Roles at Work* (Oxford, UK: Butterworth-Heinemann, 1993).

49. W.G. Broucek and G. Randell, "An Assessment of the Construct Validity of the Belbin Self-Perception Inventory and Observer's Assessment from the Perspective of the Five-Factor Model," *Journal of Occupational and Organizational Psychology* 69 (December 1996), pp. 389–40; S.G. Fisher, T.A. Hunter, and W.D.K. Macrosson, "The Structure of Belbin's Team Roles," *Journal of Occupational and Organizational Psychology* 71 (September 1998), pp. 283–88; J.S. Prichard and N.A. Stanton, "Testing Belbin's Team Role Theory of Effective Groups," *Journal of Management Development* 18 (1999), pp. 652–65; G. Fisher, T.A. Hunter, and W.D.K. Macrosson, "Belbin's Team Role Theory: For Non-Managers Also?" *Journal of Managerial Psychology* 17 (2002), pp. 14–20.

50. C.R. Evans and K.L. Dion, "Group Cohesion and Performance: A Meta-Analysis," *Small Group Research* 22 (1991), pp. 175–86; B. Mullen and C. Copper, "The Relation between Group Cohesiveness and Performance: An Integration," *Psychological Bulletin* 115 (1994), pp. 210–27; A.V. Carron et al., "Cohesion and Performance in Sport: A Meta-Analysis," *Journal of Sport and Exercise Psychology* 24 (2002), pp. 168–88; D.J. Beal et al., "Cohesion and Performance in Groups: A Meta-Analytic Clarification of Construct Relations," *Journal of Applied Psychology* 88, no. 6 (2003), pp. 989–1004.

51. N. Ellemers, R. Spears, and B. Doosie, "Self and Social Identity," *Annual Review of Psychology* 53 (2002), pp. 161–86; K.M. Sheldon and B.A. Bettencourt, "Psychological Need Satisfaction and Subjective Well-Being within Social Groups," *British Journal of Social Psychology* 41 (2002), pp. 25-38.

52. K.A. Jehn, G.B. Northcraft, and M.A. Neale, "Why Differences Make a Difference: A Field Study of Diversity, Conflict, and Performance in Workgroups," *Administrative Science Quarterly* 44, no. 4 (1999), pp. 741–63; van Knippenberg, De Dreu, and Homan, "Work Group Diversity and Group Performance: An Integrative Model and Research Agenda." For evidence that diversity/similarity does not always influence cohesion, see S.S. Webber and L.M. Donahue, "Impact of Highly and Less Job-Related Diversity on Work Group Cohesion and Performance: A Meta-Analysis," *Journal of Management* 27, no. 2 (2001), pp. 141–62.

53. E. Aronson and J. Mills, "The Effects of Severity of Initiation on Liking for a Group," *Journal of Abnormal and Social Psychology* 59 (1959), pp. 177–81; J.E. Hautaluoma and R.S. Enge, "Early Socialization into a Work Group: Severity of Initiations Revisited," *Journal of Social Behavior & Personality* 6 (1991), pp. 725–48.

54. Mullen and Copper, "The Relation between Group Cohesiveness and Performance: An Integration."

55. F. Piccolo, "Brownie Points," *Atlantic Business*, October/November 2004, p. 22.

56. M. Rempel and R.J. Fisher, "Perceived Threat, Cohesion, and Group Problem Solving in Intergroup Conflict," *International Journal of Conflict Management* 8 (1997), pp. 216-34; M.E. Turner and T. Horvitz, "The Dilemma of Threat: Group Effectiveness and Ineffectiveness under Adversity," in *Groups at Work: Theory and Research*, ed. M.E. Turner (Mahwah, NJ: Lawrence Erlbaum Associates, 2001), pp. 445–70.

57. W. Piper et al., "Cohesion as a Basic Bond in Groups," *Human Relations* 36 (1983), pp. 93-108; C.A. O'Reilly, D.E. Caldwell, and W.P. Barnett, "Work Group Demography, Social Integration, and Turnover," *Administrative Science Quarterly* 34 (1989), pp. 21–37.

58. C. Langfred, "Is Group Cohesiveness a Double-Edged Sword? An Investigation of the Effects of Cohesiveness on Performance," *Small Group Research* 29 (1998), pp. 124-43; K.L. Gammage, A.V. Carron, and P.A. Estabrooks, "Team Cohesion and Individual Productivity: The Influence of the Norm for Productivity and the Identifiability of Individual Effort," *Small Group Research* 32 (February 2001), pp. 3–18.

59. "The Trouble with Teams," *Economist*, 14 January 1995, p. 6; H. Robbins and M. Finley, *Why Teams Don't Work* (Princeton, NJ: Peterson's/Pacesetters, 1995), Chapter 20; E.A. Locke et al., "The Importance of the Individual in an Age of Groupism," in *Groups at Work: Theory and Research*, ed. M.E. Turner (Mahwah, NJ: Lawrence Erbaum Associates, 2001), pp. 501–28; N.J. Allen and T.D. Hecht, "The 'Romance of Teams': Toward an Understanding of Its Psychological Underpinnings and Implications," *Journal of Occupational and Organizational Psychology* 77 (2004), pp. 439–61.

60. P. Panchak, "The Future Manufacturing," *Industry Week* 247 (September 21 1998), pp. 96–105.

61. I.D. Steiner, *Group Process and Productivity* (New York: Academic Press, 1972); N.L. Kerr and S.R. Tindale, "Group Performance and Decision Making," *Annual Review of Psychology* 55 (2004), pp. 623–55.

62. D. Dunphy and B. Bryant, "Teams: Panaceas or Prescriptions for Improved Performance?" *Human Relations* 49 (1996), pp. 677–99. For discussion of Brooks's Law, see F.P. Brooks, ed., *The Mythical Man-Month: Essays on Software Engineering*, 2nd ed. (Reading, MA: Addison-Wesley, 1995).

63. J. Gruber, "More Aperture Dirt" (Daring Fireball, 4 May 2006), http://daringfireball.net/2006/05/more_aperture_dirt (accessed 7 June 2006); J. Gruber, "Aperture Dirt" (Daring Fireball, 28 April 2006), http://daringfireball.net/2006/04/aperture_dirt (accessed 30 April 2006).

64. R. Cross, "Looking before You Leap: Assessing the Jump to Teams in Knowledge-Based Work," *Business Horizons* (September 2000); Q.R. Skrabec Jr., "The Myth of Teams," *Industrial Management* (September–October 2002), pp. 25-27.

65. S.J. Karau and K.D. Williams, "Social Loafing: A Meta-Analytic Review and Theoretical Integration," *Journal of Personality and Social Psychology* 65 (1993), pp. 681–706; R.C. Liden et al., "Social Loafing: A Field Investigation," *Journal of Management* 30 (2004), pp. 285–304.

66. M. Erez and A. Somech, "Is Group Productivity Loss the Rule or the Exception? Effects of Culture and Group-Based Motivation," *Academy of Management Journal* 39 (1996), pp. 1513–37; Kerr and Tindale, "Group Performance and Decision Making."

67. E. Kidwell and N. Bennett, "Employee Propensity to Withhold Effort: A Conceptual Model to Intersect Three Avenues of Research," *Academy of Management Review* 19 (1993), pp. 429–56; J.M. George, "Asymmetrical Effects of Rewards and Punishments: The Case of Social Loafing," *Journal of Occupational and Organizational Psychology* 68 (1995), pp. 327–38; T. A. Judge and T.D. Chandler, "Individual-Level Determinants of Employee Shirking," *Relations Industrielles* 51 (1996), pp. 468–86.

CHAPTER 10

1. J. Gordon, "Do Your Virtual Teams Deliver Only Virtual Performance?" *Training*, June 2005, pp. 20–24; A. Graham, "Teambuilding Reveals Its Serious Side," *Corporate Meetings & Incentives*, May 2005, pp. S6–S11.

2. C. Fishman, "The Anarchist's Cookbook," *Fast Company*, July 2004, p. 70; J. Mackey, "Open Book Company," *Newsweek*, 28 November 2005, p. 42.

3. S.G. Cohen, J. Ledford, G.E., and G.M. Spreitzer, "A Predictive Model of Self-Managing Work Team Effectiveness," *Human Relations* 49 (1996), pp. 643–76; E.E. Lawler, *Organizing for High Performance* (San Francisco: Jossey-Bass, 2001); V.U. Druskat and J.V. Wheeler, "How to Lead a Self-Managing Team," *MIT Sloan Management Review* 45, no. 4 (Summer 2004), pp. 65–71.

4. S.A. Mohrman, S.G. Cohen, and J. Mohrman, A.M., *Designing Team-Based Organizations: New Forms for Knowledge Work* (San Francisco: Jossey-Bass, 1995); B.L. Kirkman and D.L. Shapiro, "The Impact of Cultural Values on Employee Resistance to Teams: Toward a Model of Globalized Self-Managing Work Team Effectiveness," *Academy of Management Review* 22 (July 1997), pp. 730–57; D.E. Yeatts and C. Hyten, *High-Performing Self-Managed Work Teams: A Comparison of Theory and Practice* (Thousand Oaks, CA: Sage, 1998).

5. P.S. Goodman, R. Devadas, and T.L.G. Hughson, "Groups and Productivity: Analyzing the Effectiveness of Self-Managing Teams," in *Productivity in Organizations*, ed. J.P. Campbell, R.J. Campbell, and associates (San Francisco: Jossey-Bass, 1988), pp. 295–327.

6. D. Tjosvold, *Teamwork for Customers* (San Francisco: Jossey-Bass, 1993); J. Childs, "Five Years and Counting: The Path to Self-Directed Work Teams," *Hospital Materiel Management Quarterly* 18 (May 1997), pp. 34–43; A. de Jong and K. de Ruyter, "Adaptive versus Proactive Behavior in Service Recovery: The Role of Self-Managing Teams," *Decision Sciences* 35, no. 3 (2004), pp. 457–91.

7. E.L. Trist et al., *Organizational Choice* (London: Tavistock, 1963); N. Adler and P. Docherty, "Bringing Business into Sociotechnical Theory and Practice," *Human Relations* 51, no. 3 (1998), pp. 319–45; R.J. Torraco, "Work Design Theory: A Review and Critique with Implications for Human Resource Development," *Human Resource Development Quarterly* 16, no. 1 (Spring 2005), pp. 85–109.

8. The main components of sociotechnical systems are discussed in M. Moldaschl and W. G. Weber, "The 'Three Waves' of Industrial Group Work: Historical Reflections on Current Research on Group Work," *Human Relations* 51 (March 1998), pp. 259–87; and W. Niepce and E. Molleman, "Work Design Issues in Lean Production from Sociotechnical System Perspective: Neo-Taylorism or the Next Step in Sociotechnical Design?" *Human Relations* 51, no. 3 (March 1998), pp. 259–87.

9. E. Ulich and W.G. Weber, "Dimensions, Criteria, and Evaluation of Work Group Autonomy," in *Handbook of Work Group Psychology*, ed. M.A. West (Chichester, UK: John Wiley and Sons, 1996), pp. 247–82.

10. K.P. Carson and G.L. Stewart, "Job Analysis and the Sociotechnical Approach to Quality: A Critical Examination," *Journal of Quality Management* 1 (1996), pp. 49–65; C.C. Manz and G.L. Stewart, "Attaining Flexible Stability by Integrating Total Quality Management and Socio-Technical Systems Theory," *Organization Science* 8 (1997), pp. 59–70.

11. C.R. Emery and L.D. Fredendall, "The Effect of Teams on Firm Profitability and Customer Satisfaction," *Journal of Service Research* 4 (February 2002), pp. 217–29; I.M. Kunii, "He Put the Flash Back in Canon," *Business Week* (16 September 2002), p. 40; A. Krause and H. Dunckel, "Work Design and Customer Satisfaction: Effects of the Implementation of Semi-Autonomous Group Work on Customer Satisfaction Considering Employee Satisfaction and Group Performance (Translated Abstract)," *Zeitschrift fur Arbeits-und Organisationspsychologie* 47, no. 4 (2003), pp. 182–93.

12. J.P. Womack, D.T. Jones, and D. Roos, *The Machine That Changed the World* (New York: MacMIllan, 1990); P.S. Adler and R.E. Cole, "Designed for Learning: A Tale of Two Auto Plants," *Sloan Management Review* 34 (Spring 1993), pp. 85–94; C. Berggren, "Volvo Uddevalla: A Dead Horse or a Car Dealer's Dream?" in *Actes du GERPISA* (May 1993), pp. 129–43; J. Å. Granath, "Torslanda to Uddevalla Via Kalmar: A Journey in Production Practice in Volvo," Paper presented at Seminário Internacional Reestruturação Produtiva, Flexibilidade do Trabalho e Novas Competências Profissionais COPPE/UFRJ, Rio de Janeiro, Brasil, 24–25 August 1998; Emery and Fredendall, "The Effect of Teams on Firm Profitability and Customer Satisfaction" ; J. Boudreau et al., "On the Interface between Operations and Human Resources Management," *Manufacturing & Service Operations Management* 5, no. 3 (Summer 2003), pp. 179–202.

13. C.E. Nicholls, H.W. Lane, and M.B. Brechu, "Taking Self-Managed Teams to Mexico," *Academy of Management Executive* 13 (August 1999), pp. 15–25; B.L. Kirkman and D.L. Shapiro, "The Impact of Cultural Values on Job Satisfaction and Organizational Commitment in Self-Managing Work Teams: The Mediating Role of Employee Resistance," *Academy of Management Journal* 44 (June 2001), pp. 557–69.

14. C.C. Manz, D.E. Keating, and A. Donnellon, "Preparing for an Organizational Change to Employee Self-Management: The Managerial Transition," *Organizational Dynamics* 19 (Autumn 1990), pp. 15–26; J.D. Orsburn and L. Moran, *The New Self-Directed Work Teams: Mastering the Challenge* (New York: McGraw-Hill, 2000), Chapter 11. The Robert Frost quotation is found at www.quoteland.com.

15. M. Fenton-O'Creevy, "Employee Involvement and the Middle Manager: Saboteur or Scapegoat?" *Human Resource Management Journal* 11 (2001), pp.24–40; R. Wageman, "How Leaders Foster Self-Managing Team Effectiveness," *Organization Science* 12, no. 5 (September–October 2001), pp. 559–77; C. Douglas and W. L. Gardner, "Transition to Self-Directed Work Teams: Implications of Transition Time and Self-Monitoring for Managers' Use of Influence Tactics," *Journal of Organizational Behavior* 25 (2004), pp. 47–65. The TRW quotation is found in J. Jusko, "Always Lessons to Learn," Industry Week (15February 1999), pp. 23–30.

16. D. Stafford, "Sharing the Driver's Seat," *Kansas City Star*, 11 June 2002, p. D1.

17. G. Garda, K. Lindstrom, and M. Dallnera, "Toward a Learning Organization: The Introduction of a Client-Centered Team-Based Organization in Administrative Surveying Work," *Applied Ergonomics* 34 (2003), pp. 97–105.

18. R. Hodson, "Dignity in the Workplace under Participative Management: Alienation and Freedom Revisited," *American Sociological Review* 61 (1996), pp. 719–38; R. Yonatan and H. Lam, "Union Responses to Quality Improvement Initiatives: Factors Shaping Support and Resistance," *Journal of Labor Research* 20 (Winter 1999), pp. 111–31.

19. J. Lipnack and J. Stamps, *Virtual Teams: People Working across Boundaries with Technology* (New York: John Wiley and Sons, 2001); B.S. Bell and W.J. Kozlowski, "A Typology of Virtual Teams: Implications for Effective Leadership," *Group & Organization Management* 27 (March 2002), pp. 14–49; G. Hertel, S. Geister, and U. Konradt, "Managing Virtual Teams: A Review of Current Empirical Research," *Human Resource Management Review* 15 (2005), pp. 69–95.

20. G. Gilder, *Telecosm: How Infinite Bandwidth Will Revolutionize Our World* (New York: Free Press, 2001); L.L. Martins, L.L. Gilson, and M.T. Maynard, "Virtual Teams: What Do We Know and Where Do We Go Form Here?" *Journal of Management* 30, no. 6 (2004), pp. 805–35. The Novartis quotation is from S. Murray, "Pros and Cons of Technology: The Corporate Agenda: Managing Virtual Teams," *Financial Times (London)*, 27 May 2002, p. 6.

21. J.S. Lureya and M.S. Raisinghani, "An Empirical Study of Best Practices in Virtual Teams," *Information & Management* 38 (2001), pp. 523–44; Y.L. Doz, J.F.P. Santos, and P.J. Williamson, "The Metanational Advantage," *Optimize* (May 2002), p. 45ff; K. Marron, "Close Encounters of the Faceless Kind," *Globe & Mail*, 9 February 2005, p. C1.

22. Martins, Gilson, and Maynard, "Virtual Teams." The quotation is found in S. Gasper, "Virtual Teams, Real Benefits," *Network World*, 24 September 2001, p. 45.

23. D. Robb, "Global Workgroups," *Computerworld*, 15 August 2005, pp. 37–38.

24. D. Robey, H.M. Khoo, and C. Powers, "Situated Learning in Cross-Functional Virtual Teams," *Technical Communication* (February 2000), pp. 51–66.

25. Lureya and Raisinghani, "An Empirical Study of Best Practices in Virtual Teams."

26. S. Alexander, "Virtual Teams Going Global," *InfoWorld* (13 November 2000), pp. 55–56.

27. S. Prashad, "Building Trust Tricky for 'Virtual' Teams," *Toronto Star*, 23 October 2003, p. K06.

28. S. Van Ryssen and S.H. Godar, "Going International without Going International: Multinational Virtual Teams," *Journal of International Management* 6 (2000), pp. 49–60.

29. B.J. Alge, C. Wiethoff, and H.J. Klein, "When Does the Medium Matter? Knowledge-Building Experiences and Opportunities in Decision-Making Teams," *Organizational Behavior and Human Decision Processes* 91, no. 1 (2003), pp. 26–37; D. Robey, K.S. Schwaig, and L. Jin, "Intertwining Material and Virtual Work," *Information & Organization* 13 (2003), pp. 111–29; U. Bernard, R. Gfrörer, and B. Staffelbach, "Der Einfluss Von Telearbeit Auf Das Team: Empirisch Analysiert Am Beispiel Eines Versicherungsunternehmens (translated abstract)," *Zeitschrift für Personalforschung* 19, no. 2 (2005), pp. 120–38.

30. "Leading a Virtual Team: Agilent's Grant Marshall," ceoforum.com.au, March 2005; "Supporting Australian Innovation," *Electronics News*, 11 January 2005; M. Conlin, "The Easiest Commute of All," *Business Week*, 12 December 2005, p. 78.

31. S.L. Robinson, "Trust and Breach of the Psychological Contract," Administrative Science Quarterly 41 (1996), pp. 574–99; D.M. Rousseau et al., "Not So Different After All: A Cross-Discipline View of Trust," *Academy of Management Review* 23 (1998), pp. 393–404; D.L. Duarte and N. T. Snyder, *Mastering Virtual Teams: Strategies, Tools, and Techniques That Succeed*, 2nd ed. (San Francisco, CA: Jossey-Bass, 2000), pp. 139–55; A.C. Costa, "Work Team Trust and Effectiveness," *Personnel Review* 32, no. 5 (2003), pp. 605–24; S. Kiffin-Petersen, "Trust: A Neglected Variable in Team Effectiveness Research," *Journal of the Australian and New Zealand Academy of Management* 10, no. 1 (2004), pp. 38–53.

32. D.J. McAllister, "Affect- and Cognition-Based Trust as Foundations for Interpersonal Cooperation in Organizations," *Academy of Management Journal* 38, no. 1 (February 1995), pp. 24–59; M. Williams, "In Whom We Trust: Group Membership as an Affective Context for Trust Development," *Academy of Management Review* 26, no. 3 (July 2001), pp. 377–96.

33. O.E. Williamson, "Calculativeness, Trust, and Economic Organization," *Journal of Law and Economics* 36, no. 1 (1993), pp. 453–86.

34. E.M. Whitener et al., "Managers as Initiators of Trust: An Exchange Relationship Framework for Understanding Managerial Trustworthy Behavior," *Academy of Management Review* 23 (July 1998), pp. 513–30; J.M. Kouzes and B.Z. Posner, *The Leadership Challenge*, 3rd ed. (San Francisco: Jossey-Bass, 2002), Chapter 2; T. Simons, "Behavioral Integrity: The Perceived Alignment between Managers' Words and Deeds as a Research Focus," *Organization Science* 13, no. 1 (January–February 2002), pp. 18–35.

35. M.A. Hogg et al., "The Social Identity Perspective: Intergroup Relations, Self-Conception, and Small Groups," *Small Group Research* 35, no. 3 (June 2004), pp. 246–76.

36. J.R. Dunn and M.E. Schweitzer, "Feeling and Believing: The Influence of Emotion on Trust," *Journal of Personality and Social Psychology* 88, no. 5 (May 2005), pp. 736–48;

H. Gill et al., "Antecedents of Trust: Establishing a Boundary Condition for the Relation between Propensity to Trust and Intention to Trust," *Journal of Business and Psychology* 19, no. 3 (Spring 2005), pp. 287–302.

37. T.K. Das and B. Teng, "Between Trust and Control: Developing Confidence in Partner Cooperation in Alliances," *Academy of Management Review* 23 (1998), pp. 491–512; S.L. Jarvenpaa and D.E. Leidner, "Communication and Trust in Global Virtual Teams," *Organization Science* 10 (1999), pp. 791–815; J.K. Murnighan, J.M. Oesch, and M. Pillutla, "Player Types and Self-Impression Management in Dictatorship Games: Two Experiments," *Games and Economic Behavior* 37, no. 2 (2001), pp. 388–414; M.M. Pillutla, D. Malhotra, and J. Keith Murnighan, "Attributions of Trust and the Calculus of Reciprocity," *Journal of Experimental Social Psychology* 39, no. 5 (2003), pp. 448–55.

38. K.T. Dirks and D.L. Ferrin, "The Role of Trust in Organizations," *Organization Science* 12, no. 4 (July-August 2004), pp. 450–67.

39. V.H. Vroom and A.G. Jago, *The New Leadership* (Englewood Cliffs, NJ: Prentice-Hall, 1988), pp. 28–29.

40. M. Diehl and W. Stroebe, "Productivity Loss in Idea-Generating Groups: Tracking Down the Blocking Effects," *Journal of Personality and Social Psychology* 61 (1991), pp. 392–403; R.B. Gallupe et al., "Blocking Electronic Brainstorms," *Journal of Applied Psychology* 79 (1994), pp. 77–86; B.A. Nijstad, W. Stroebe, and H.F.M. Lodewijkx, "Production Blocking and Idea Generation: Does Blocking Interfere with Cognitive Processes?" *Journal of Experimental Social Psychology* 39, no. 6 (November 2003), pp. 531–48.

41. B.E. Irmer, P. Bordia, and D. Abusah, "Evaluation Apprehension and Perceived Benefits in Interpersonal and Database Knowledge Sharing," *Academy of Management Proceedings* (2002), pp. B1–B6.

42. I.L. Janis, *Groupthink: Psychological Studies of Policy Decisions and Fiascoes*, 2nd ed. (Boston: Houghton Mifflin, 1982); J.K. Esser, "Alive and Well after 25 Years: A Review of Groupthink Research," *Organizational Behavior and Human Decision Processes* 73, no. 2–3 (1998), pp. 116–41.

43. J.N. Choi and M.U. Kim, "The Organizational Application of Groupthink and Its Limitations in Organizations," *Journal of Applied Psychology* 84, no. 2 (April 1999), pp. 297–306; N.L. Kerr and S.R. Tindale, "Group Performance and Decision Making," *Annual Review of Psychology* 55 (2004), pp. 623–55.

44. D. Miller, *The Icarus Paradox: How Exceptional Companies Bring About Their Own Downfall* (New York: HarperBusiness, 1990); S. Finkelstein, *Why Smart Executives Fail* (New York: Viking, 2003); K. Tasa and G. Whyte, "Collective Efficacy and Vigilant Problem Solving in Group Decision Making: A Non-Linear Model," *Organizational Behavior and Human Decision Processes* 96, no. 2 (March 2005), pp. 119–29.

45. D. Isenberg, "Group Polarization: A Critical Review and Meta-Analysis," *Journal of Personality and Social Psychology* 50 (1986), pp. 1141–51; C. McGarty et al., "Group Polarization as Conformity to the Prototypical Group Member," *British Journal of Social Psychology* 31 (1992), pp. 1–20; C.R. Sunstein, "Deliberative Trouble? Why Groups Go to Extremes," *Yale Law Journal* 110, no. 1 (October 2000), pp. 71–119.

46. D. Friedman, "Monty Hall's Three Doors: Construction and Deconstruction of a Choice Anomaly," *American Economic Review* 88 (September 1998), pp. 933–46; D. Kahneman, "Maps of Bounded Rationality: Psychology for Behavioral Economics," *American Economic Review* 93, no. 5 (December 2003), pp. 1449–75.

47. H. Collingwood, "Best-Kept Secrets of the World's Best Companies: Outside-in R&D," *Business* 2.0, April 2006, p. 82.

48. K.M. Eisenhardt, J.L. Kahwajy, and L. J. Bourgeois III, "Conflict and Strategic Choice: How Top Management Teams Disagree," *California Management Review* 39 (1997), pp. 42–62; R. Sutton, *Weird Ideas That Work* (New York: Free Press, 2002); C. J. Nemeth et al., "The Liberating Role of Conflict in Group Creativity: A Study in Two Countries," *European Journal of Social Psychology* 34, no. 4 (2004), pp. 365–74. For discussion on how all conflict is potentially detrimental to teams, see C.K.W. De Dreu and L.R. Weingart, "Task Versus Relationship Conflict, Team Performance, and Team Member Satisfaction: A Meta-Analysis," *Journal of Applied Psychology* 88 (August 2003), pp. 587–604; P. Hinds and D.E. Bailey, "Out of Sight, Out of Sync: Understanding Conflict in Distributed Teams," *Organization Science* 14, no. 6 (2003), pp. 615–32.

49. A.F. Osborn, *Applied Imagination* (New York: Scribner, 1957).

50. K. Darce, "Ground Control: NASA Attempts a Cultural Shift," *The Seattle Times*, 24 April 2005, p. A3; R. Shelton, "NASA Attempts to Change Mindset in Wake of Columbia Tragedy," *Macon Telegraph* (Macon, GA), 7 July 2005.

51. C. Stewart, "Six Degrees of Innovation," *Orange County Register* (California), 22 March 2006. The problems with brainstorming are described in B. Mullen, C. Johnson, and E. Salas, "Productivity Loss in Brainstorming Groups: A Meta-Analytic Integration," *Basic and Applied Psychology* 12 (1991), pp. 2–23. For recent evidence that group brainstorming is beneficial, see V.R. Brown and P.B. Paulus, "Making Group Brainstorming More Effective: Recommendations from an Associative Memory Perspective," *Current Directions in Psychological Science* 11, no. 6 (2002), pp. 208–12; K. Leggett Dugosh and P.B. Paulus, "Cognitive and Social Comparison Processes in Brainstorming," *Journal of Experimental Social Psychology* 41, no. 3 (2005), pp. 313–20.

52. R.I. Sutton and A. Hargadon, "Brainstorming Groups in Context: Effectiveness in a Product Design Firm," *Administrative Science Quarterly* 41 (1996), pp. 685–718; T. Kelley, *The Art of Innovation* (New York: Currency Doubleday, 2001), Chapter 4.

53. R.B. Gallupe, L.M. Bastianutti, and W.H. Cooper, "Unblocking Brainstorms," *Journal of Applied Psychology* 76 (1991), pp. 137–42; W.H. Cooper et al., "Some Liberating Effects of Anonymous Electronic Brainstorming," *Small Group Research* 29, no. 2 (April 1998), pp. 147–78; A.R. Dennis, B.H. Wixom, and R.J. Vandenberg, "Understanding Fit and Appropriation Effects in Group Support Systems via Meta-Analysis," *MIS Quarterly* 25, no. 2 (June 2001), pp. 167–93; D.S. Kerr and U.S. Murthy, "Divergent and Convergent Idea Generation in Teams: A Comparison of Computer-Mediated and Face-to-Face Communication," *Group Decision and Negotiation* 13, no. 4 (July 2004), pp. 381–99.

54. P. Bordia, "Face-to-Face versus Computer-Mediated Communication: A Synthesis of the Experimental Literature," *Journal of Business Communication* 34 (1997), pp. 99–120; P.B. Paulus and H.-C. Yang, "Idea Generation in Groups: A Basis for Creativity in Organizations," *Organizational Behavior and Human Decision Processes* 82, no. 1 (2000), pp. 76–87; R.R.E. Potter, "The Role of Individual Memory and Attention Processes during Electronic Brainstorming," *MIS Quarterly* 28, no. 4 (December 2004), pp. 621–43.

55. B. Kabanoff and J.R. Rossiter, "Recent Developments in Applied Creativity," *International Review of Industrial and Organizational Psychology* 9 (1994), pp. 283–324; A. Pinsoneault et al., "Electronic Brainstorming: The Illusion of Productivity," *Information Systems Research* 10 (1999), pp. 110–33.

56. H.A. Linstone and M. Turoff, *The Delphi Method: Techniques and Applications* (Reading, MA: Addison-Wesley, 1975); P. M. Mullen, "Delphi: Myths and Reality," *Journal of Health Organization and Management* 17, no. 1 (2003), pp. 37–51; J. Landeta, "Current Validity of the Delphi Method in Social Sciences," *Technological Forecasting and Social Change* 73, no. 5 (June 2006), pp. 467–82.

57. C. Banwell et al., "Reflections on Expert Consensus: A Case Study of the Social Trends Contributing to Obesity," *The European Journal of Public Health* 15, no. 6 (December 2005), pp. 564–68; P. Rikkonen, J. Aakkula, and J. Kaivo-oja, "How Can Future Long-Term Changes in Finnish Agriculture and Agricultural Policy Be Faced? Defining Strategic Agendas on the Basis of a Delphi Study," *European Planning Studies* 14, no. 2 (February 2006), pp. 147–68; S.-H. Tsaur, Y.-C. Lin, and J.-H. Lin, "Evaluating Ecotourism Sustainability from the Integrated Perspective of Resource, Community and Tourism," *Tourism Management* 27, no. 4 (2006), pp. 640–53.

58. A.L. Delbecq, A.H. Van de Ven, and D.H. Gustafson, *Group Techniques for Program Planning: A Guide to Nominal Group and Delphi Processes* (Middleton, WI: Green Briar Press, 1986).

59. S. Frankel, "NGT + MDS: An Adaptation of the Nominal Group Technique for Ill-Structured Problems," *Journal of Applied Behavioral Science* 23 (1987), pp. 543–51; H. Barki and A. Pinsonneault, "Small Group Brainstorming and Idea Quality: Is Electronic Brainstorming the Most Effective Approach?" *Small Group Research* 32, no. 2 (April 2001), pp. 158–205.

60. Graham, "Teambuilding Reveals Its Serious Side."

61. W.G. Dyer, *Team Building: Current Issues and New Alternatives*, 3rd ed. (Reading, MA: Addison-Wesley, 1995); C.A. Beatty and B.A. Barker, *Building Smart Teams: Roadmap to High Performance* (Thousand Oaks, CA: Sage Publications, 2004).

62. J. Murray, "Office Hours," *The Guardian* (London), 5 September 2005, p. 4; S. Williams, "Thanks, but No Thanks," *Australian Financial Review*, 20 August 2005, p. 32; "Lockheed Volunteers Get Bush Nod," *Los Angeles Daily News*, 9 May 2006, p. AV2.

63. M. Beer, *Organizational Change and Development: A Systems View* (Santa Monica, CA: Goodyear, 1980), pp. 143–46; E. Sundstrom, K.P. De Meuse, and D. Futrell, "Work Teams: Applications and Effectiveness," *American Psychologist* 45 (1990), pp. 120–33.

64. J. Langan-Fox and J. Anglim, "Mental Models, Team Mental Models, and Performance: Process, Development, and Future Directions," *Human Factors and Ergonomics in Manufacturing* 14, no. 4 (2004), pp. 331–52; J.E. Mathieu et al., "Scaling the Quality of Teammates' Mental Models: Equifinality and Normative Comparisons," *Journal of Organizational Behavior* 26 (2005), pp. 37–56.

65. R. Beckhard, "The Confrontation Meeting," *Harvard Business Review* 45, no. 4 (1967), pp. 159–65; H.D. Glover, "Organizational Change and Development: The Consequences of Misuse," *Leadership & Organization Development Journal* 13, no. 1 (1992), pp. 9–16. For recent discussion about problems with confrontation in teams, see M.A. Von Glinow, D.L. Shapiro, and J.M. Brett, "Can We *Talk*, and Should We? Managing Emotional Conflict in Multinational Teams," *Academy of Management Review* 29, no. 4 (2004), pp. 578–92.

66. "German Businesswoman Demands End to Fun at Work," *Reuters* (9 July 2003).

67. R.W. Woodman and J.J. Sherwood, "The Role of Team Development in Organizational Effectiveness: A Critical Review," *Psychological Bulletin* 88 (1980), pp. 166–86.

68. L. Mealiea and R. Baltazar, "A Strategic Guide for Building Effective Teams," *Personnel Management* 34, no. 2 (Summer 2005), pp. 141–60.

69. G.E. Huszczo, "Training for Team Building," *Training and Development Journal* 44 (February 1990), pp. 37–43; P. McGraw, "Back from the Mountain: Outdoor Management Development Programs and How to Ensure the Transfer of Skills to the Workplace," *Asia Pacific Journal of Human Resources* 31 (Spring 1993), pp. 52–61.

CHAPTER 11

1. J.C. Perez, "Google Sees Benefits in Corporate Blogging," *Network World*, 29 November 2004, p. 28; E. Cone, "Rise of the Blog," *CIO Insight*, April 2005, p. 54; M. Delio, "The Enterprise Blogosphere," *InfoWorld*, 28 March 2005, pp. 42–47; S. Stern, "Word on the Blog Says Sun King Rules," *Daily Telegraph* (London), 5 January 2006, p. 3.

2. R. Gray, "Finding the Right Direction," *Communication World*, November–December 2004, pp. 26-32.

3. I. Nonaka and H. Takeuchi, *The Knowledge–Creating Company* (New York: Oxford University Press, 1995); R.T. Barker and M.R. Camarata, "The Role of Communication in Creating and Maintaining a Learning Organization: Preconditions, Indicators, and Disciplines," *Journal of Business Communication* 35 (October 1998), pp. 443-67; D. Te'eni, "A Cognitive–Affective Model of Organizational Communication for Designing It," *MIS Quarterly* 25 (June 2001), pp. 251–312.

4. C.E. Shannon and W. Weaver, *The Mathematical Theory of Communication* (Urbana, IL: University of Illinois Press, 1949); K.J. Krone, F.M. Jablin, and L.L. Putnam, "Communication Theory and Organizational Communication: Multiple Perspectives," in *Handbook of Organizational Communication: An Interdisciplinary Perspective*, ed. F.M. Jablin et al. (Newbury Park, CA: Sage, 1987), pp. 18–40.

5. W. Lucas, "Effects of E-Mail on the Organization," *European Management Journal* 16, no. 1 (February 1998), pp. 18–30; D. A. Owens, M.A. Neale, and R.I. Sutton, "Technologies of Status Management Status Dynamics in E-Mail Communications," *Research on Managing Groups and Teams* 3 (2000), pp. 205–30; N. Ducheneaut and L.A. Watts, "In Search of Coherence: A Review of E-Mail Research," *Human–Computer Interaction* 20, no. 1–2 (2005), pp. 11–48.

6. J.B. Walther, "Language and Communication Technology: Introduction to the Special Issue," *Journal of Language and Social Psychology* 23, no. 4 (December 2004), pp. 384-96; J.B. Walther, T. Loh, and L. Granka, "Let Me Count the Ways: The Interchange of Verbal and Nonverbal Cues in Computer–Mediated and Face-to-Face Affinity," *Journal of Language and Social Psychology* 24, no. 1 (March 2005), pp. 36–65.

7. G. Hertel, S. Geister, and U. Konradt, "Managing Virtual Teams: A Review of Current Empirical Research," *Human Resource Management Review* 15 (2005), pp. 69–95; H. Lee, "Behavioral Strategies

for Dealing with Flaming in an Online Forum," *The Sociological Quarterly* 46, no. 2 (2005), pp. 385–403.

8. S. Williams, "Apologies and Rows by E-mail Are a New Sin for Hi-Tech Cowards," *Western Mail* (Cardiff, Wales), 1 April 2006, p. 11.

9. "A Day without E-Mail?" *Modern Healthcare*, 30 June 2003, p. 36; M. Greenwood, "I Have Banned E-mails: They Are a Cancer of Modern Business," *The Mirror* (London), 19 September 2003, p. 11.

10. K. Restivo, "Coming to an iPod near You," *National Post*, 16 July 2005, p. FP4.

11. D. Robb, "Ready or Not...Instant Messaging Has Arrived as a Financial Planning Tool," *Journal of Financial Planning* (July 2001), pp. 12–14; J. Black, "Why Offices Are Now Open Secrets," *Business Week*, 17 September 2003; A.F. Cameron and J. Webster, "Unintended Consequences of Emerging Communication Technologies: Instant Messaging in the Workplace," *Computers in Human Behavior* 21, no. 1 (2005), pp. 85–103.

12. L.Z. Tiedens and A.R. Fragale, "Power Moves: Complementarity in Dominant and Submissive Nonverbal Behavior," *Journal of Personality and Social Psychology* 84, no. 3 (2003), pp. 558–68.

13. P. Ekman and E. Rosenberg, *What the Face Reveals: Basic and Applied Studies of Spontaneous Expression Using the Facial Action Coding System* (Oxford, England: Oxford University Press, 1997); P. Winkielman and K.C. Berridge, "Unconscious Emotion," *Current Directions in Psychological Science* 13, no. 3 (2004), pp. 120–23.

14. E. Hatfield, J.T. Cacioppo, and R.L. Rapson, *Emotional Contagion* (Cambridge, England: Cambridge University Press, 1993); S.G. Barsade, "The Ripple Effect: Emotional Contagion and Its Influence on Group Behavior," *Administrative Science Quarterly* 47 (December 2002), pp. 644–75; M. Sonnby-Borgstrom, P. Jonsson, and O. Svensson, "Emotional Empathy as Related to Mimicry Reactions at Different Levels of Information Processing," *Journal of Nonverbal Behavior* 27 (Spring 2003), pp. 3–23.

15. J.R. Kelly and S.G. Barsade, "Mood and Emotions in Small Groups and Work Teams," *Organizational Behavior and Human Decision Processes* 86 (September 2001), pp. 99–130.

16. R.L. Daft and R.H. Lengel, "Information Richness: A New Approach to Managerial Behavior and Organization Design," *Research in Organizational Behavior* 6 (1984), pp. 191–233; R.H. Lengel and R.L. Daft, "The Selection of Communication Media as an Executive Skill," *Academy of Management Executive* 2 (1988), pp. 225–32.

17. R.E. Rice, "Task Analyzability, Use of New Media, and Effectiveness: A Multi-Site Exploration of Media Richness," *Organization Science* 3 (1992), pp. 475–500.

18. J.R. Carlson and R.W. Zmud, "Channel Expansion Theory and the Experiential Nature of Media Richness Perceptions," *Academy of Management Journal* 42 (April 1999), pp. 153–170; N. Kock, "Media Richness or Media Naturalness? The Evolution of Our Biological Communication Apparatus and Its Influence on Our Behavior toward E-Communication Tools," *IEEE Transactions on Professional Communication* 48, no. 2 (June 2005), pp. 117–30.

19. M. McLuhan, *Understanding Media: The Extensions of Man* (New York: McGraw-Hill, 1964).

20. K. Griffiths, "KPMG Sacks 670 Employees by E-Mail," *The Independent* (London), 5 November 2002, p. 19; P. Nelson, "Work Practices," *Personnel Today*, 12 November 2002, p. 2.

21. D. Goleman, R. Boyatzis, and A. McKee, *Primal Leaders* (Boston: Harvard Business School Press, 2002), pp. 92–95.

22. J. Kavanaugh, "National Emergency," *Business Review Weekly*, 3 November 2005, p. 32.

23. L.L. Putnam, N. Phillips, and P. Chapman, "Metaphors of Communication and Organization," in *Handbook of Organization Studies*, ed. S.R. Clegg, C. Hardy, and W.R. Nord (London: Sage, 1996), pp. 373–408; G. Morgan, *Images of Organization*, 2nd ed. (Thousand Oaks, CA: Sage, 1997); M. Rubini and H. Sigall, "Taking the Edge Off of Disagreement: Linguistic Abstractness and Self-Presentation to a Heterogeneous Audience," *European Journal of Social Psychology* 32 (2002), pp. 343–51.

24. K.M. Jackson, "Buzzword Backlash Looks to Purge Jibba-Jabba from Corporate-Speak," *Boston Globe*, 17 April 2005, p. G1.

25. L. Eckelbecker, "Click Tricks: Taming the E-mail Monster," *Worcester Telegram & Gazette*, 3 March 2006, p. A1; K. Hilpern, "Office Hours: Cc Me in on That," *The Guardian* (London), 9 January 2006, p. 3; "New Survey Reveals: Enterprises and Employees Continue to Struggle with Growing E-mail Overload Burden," *PR Newswire* (Richmond, Virginia), 7 December.

26. T. Koski, "Reflections on Information Glut and Other Issues in Knowledge Productivity," *Futures* 33 (August 2001), pp. 483–95; D.D. Dawley and W.P. Anthony, "User Perceptions of E-Mail at Work," *Journal of Business and Technical Communication* 17, no. 2 (April 2003), pp. 170–200; "E-mail Brings Costs and Fatigue," *Western News* (University of Western Ontario, London, Ontario), 9 July 2004.

27. A.G. Schick, L.A. Gordon, and S. Haka, "Information Overload: A Temporal Approach," *Accounting, Organizations & Society* 15 (1990), pp. 199–220; A. Edmunds and A. Morris, "The Problem of Information Overload in Business Organizations: A Review of the Literature," *International Journal of Information Management* 20 (2000), pp. 17–28.

28. D. Kirkpatrick, "Gates and Ozzie: How to Escape E-Mail Hell," *Fortune*, 27 June 2005, pp. 169–71.

29. D.C. Thomas and K. Inkson, *Cultural Intelligence: People Skills for Global Business* (San Francisco: Berrett-Koehler, 2004), Chapter 6; D. Welch, L. Welch, and R. Piekkari, "Speaking in Tongues," *International Studies of Management & Organization* 35, no. 1 (Spring 2005), pp. 10–27.

30. D. Woodruff, "Crossing Culture Divide Early Clears Merger Paths," *The Asian Wall Street Journal*, 28 May 2001, p. 9.

31. M. Brandel, "Global CIO," *Computerworld*, 21 November 2005, pp. 39–41. *Tatamae* and *hone* are discussed in H. Yamada, *American and Japanese Business Discourse: A Comparison of Interaction Styles* (Norwood, NJ: Ablex, 1992), p. 34; and R.M. March, *Reading the Japanese Mind* (Tokyo: Kodansha International, 1996), Chapter 1.

32. P. Harris and R. Moran, *Managing Cultural Differences* (Houston: Gulf, 1987); H. Blagg, "A Just Measure of Shame?" *British Journal of Criminology* 37 (Autumn 1997), pp. 481–501; R.E. Axtell, *Gestures: The Do's and Taboos of Body Language around the World*, revised ed. (New York: Wiley, 1998).

33. M. Griffin, "The Office, Australian Style," *Sunday Age*, 22 June 2003, p. 6.

34. S. Ohtaki, T. Ohtaki, and M.D. Fetters, "Doctor–Patient Communication:

A Comparison of the USA and Japan," *Family Practice* 20 (June 2003), pp. 276–82; M. Fujio, "Silence during Intercultural Communication: A Case Study," *Corporate Communications* 9, no. 4 (2004), pp. 331–39.

35. D.C. Barnlund, *Communication Styles of Japanese and Americans: Images and Realities* (Belmont,CA: Wadsworth, 1988); Yamada, *American and Japanese Business Discourse: A Comparison of Interaction Styles*, Chapter 2; H. Yamada, *Different Games, Different Rules* (New York: Oxford University Press, 1997), pp. 76–79.

36. This stereotypical notion is prevalent throughout J. Gray, *Men Are from Mars, Women Are from Venus* (New York: Harper Collins, 1992). For a critique of this view see J.T. Wood, "A Critical Response to John Gray's Mars and Venus Portrayals of Men and Women," *Southern Communication Journal* 67 (Winter 2002), pp. 201–10.

37. D. Tannen, *You Just Don't Understand: Men and Women in Conversation* (New York: Ballentine Books, 1990); D. Tannen, *Talking from 9 to 5* (New York: Avon, 1994); M. Crawford, *Talking Difference: On Gender and Language* (Thousand Oaks, CA: Sage, 1995), pp. 41–44; L.L. Namy, L.C. Nygaard, and D. Sauerteig, "Gender Differences in Vocal Accommodation: The Role of Perception," *Journal of Language and Social Psychology* 21, no. 4 (December 2002), pp. 422–32.

38. A. Mulac et al., "'Uh-Huh. What's That All About?' Differing Interpretations of Conversational Backchannels and Questions as Sources of Miscommunication across Gender Boundaries," *Communication Research* 25 (December 1998), pp. 641–68; N.M. Sussman and D.H. Tyson, "Sex and Power: Gender Differences in Computer-Mediated Interactions," *Computers in Human Behavior* 16 (2000), pp. 381–94; D.R. Caruso and P. Salovey, *The Emotionally Intelligent Manager* (San Francisco: Jossey-Bass, 2004), p. 23; D. Fallows, *How Women and Men Use the Internet* (Washington, DC: Pew Internet and American Life Project, 28 December 2005).

39. P. Tripp-Knowles, "A Review of the Literature on Barriers Encountered by Women in Science Academia," *Resources for Feminist Research* 24 (Spring/Summer 1995), pp. 28–34.

40. The opening quotation is cited in K. Davis and J.W. Newstrom, *Human Behavior at Work: Organizational Behavior*, 7th ed. (New York: McGraw-Hill, 1985), p. 438. Henry Schacht's quotation is found in T. Neff and J. Citrin, "You're in Charge. Now What?" *Fortune*, 24 January 2005, pp. 109–15.

41. The three components of listening discussed here are based on several recent studies in the field of marketing, including S.B. Castleberry, C.D. Shepherd, and R. Ridnour, "Effective Interpersonal Listening in the Personal Selling Environment: Conceptualization, Measurement, and Nomological Validity," *Journal of Marketing Theory and Practice* 7 (Winter 1999), pp. 30–38; L.B. Comer and T. Drollinger, "Active Empathetic Listening and Selling Success: A Conceptual Framework," *Journal of Personal Selling & Sales Management* 19 (Winter 1999), pp. 15–29; and K. de Ruyter and M.G.M. Wetzels, "The Impact of Perceived Listening Behavior in Voice-to-Voice Service Encounters," *Journal of Service Research* 2 (February 2000), pp. 276–84.

42. S.P. Means, "Playing at Pixar," *Salt Lake Tribune* (Utah), 30 May 2003, p. D1; G. Whipp, "Swimming against the Tide," *Daily News of Los Angeles*, 30 May 2003, p. U6.

43. G. Evans and D. Johnson, "Stress and Open-Office Noise," *Journal of Applied Psychology* 85 (2000), pp. 779–83; F. Russo, "My Kingdom for a Door," *Time Magazine*, 23 October 2000, p. B1.

44. B. Sosnin, "Digital Newsletters 'E-Volutionize' Employee Communications," *HRMagazine*, May 2001, pp. 99–107.

45. E. Booker, "Rethinking the Blogosphere," *B to B*, 14 November 2005, p. 10.

46. R.D. Hof, "Something Wiki Comes This Way," *BusinessWeek*, 7 June 2004, p. 128; K. Swisher, "Boomtown: 'Wiki' May Alter How Employees Work Together," *The Wall Street Journal*, 29 July 2004, p. B1; Delio, "The Enterprise Blogosphere."

47. S. Greengard, "Employee Surveys: Ask the Right Questions, Probe the Answers for Insight," *Workforce Management*, December 2004, p. 76; A. Kover, "And the Survey Says…" *Industry Week*, September 2005, pp. 49–52.

48. R. Rodwell, "Regular Staff Meetings Help Build Morale," *South China Morning Post* (Hong Kong), 27 August 2005, p. 4.

49. The original term is "management by *wandering* around," but this has been replaced with "walking" over the years. See W. Ouchi, *Theory Z* (New York: Avon Books, 1981), pp. 176–77; T. Peters and R. Waterman, *In Search of Excellence* (New York: Harper and Row, 1982), p. 122.

50. D. Penner, "Putting the Boss Out Front," *Vancouver Sun*, 7 June 2002.

51. D. Thomas, "HR Challenges…I'm Lovin' It," *Personnel Today*, 6 September 2005, p. 11.

52. R. Rousos, "Trust in Leaders Lacking at Utility," *The Ledger* (Lakeland, Florida), 29 July 2003, p. B1; B. Whitworth and B. Riccomini, "Management Communication: Unlocking Higher Employee Performance," *Communication World*, March–April 2005, pp. 18–21.

53. K. Davis, "Management Communication and the Grapevine," *Harvard Business Review* 31 (September-October 1953), pp. 43–49; W.L. Davis and J.R. O'Connor, "Serial Transmission of Information: A Study of the Grapevine," *Journal of Applied Communication Research* 5 (1977), pp. 61–72.

54. H. Mintzberg, *The Structuring of Organizations* (Englewood Cliffs, NJ: Prentice Hall, 1979), pp. 46–53; D. Krackhardt and J.R. Hanson, "Informal Networks: The Company Behind the Chart," *Harvard Business Review* 71 (July-August 1993), pp. 104–11.

55. C.J. Walker and C.A. Beckerle, "The Effect of State Anxiety on Rumor Transmission," *Journal of Social Behaviour & Personality* 2 (August 1987), pp. 353–60; R.L. Rosnow, "Inside Rumor: A Personal Journey," *American Psychologist* 46 (May 1991), pp. 484–96; M. Noon and R. Delbridge, "News from Behind My Hand: Gossip in Organizations," *Organization Studies* 14 (1993), pp. 23–36.

56. N. Nicholson, "Evolutionary Psychology: Toward a New View of Human Nature and Organizational Society," *Human Relations* 50 (September 1997), pp. 1053–78.

CHAPTER 12

1. R. Gluyas, "Fear and Loathing in NAB's Forex Fiasco," *The Australian*, 6 August 2005, p. 35; E. Johnston, "'Anything Goes,' Ex-Trader Says," *Australian Financial Review*, 2 August 2005, p. 3; E. Johnston, "Expletives and Stench in Hothouse of NAB Dealers," *Australian Financial Review*, 6 August 2005, p. 3.

2. For a discussion of the definition of power, see H. Mintzberg, *Power in and around Organizations* (Englewood Cliffs,

NJ: Prentice Hall, 1983), Chapter 1; J. Pfeffer, *Managing with Power* (Boston: Harvard Business University Press, 1992), pp. 17, 30; J. Pfeffer, *New Directions in Organizational Theory* (New York: Oxford University Press, 1997), Chapter 6; J.M. Whitmeyer, "Power through Appointment," *Social Science Research* 29 (2000), pp. 535–55.

3. R.A. Dahl, "The Concept of Power," *Behavioral Science* 2 (1957), pp. 201–18; R.M. Emerson, "Power-Dependence Relations," *American Sociological Review* 27 (1962), pp. 31-41; A.M. Pettigrew, *The Politics of Organizational Decision-Making* (London: Tavistock, 1973).

4. K.M. Bartol and D.C. Martin, "When Politics Pays: Factors Influencing Managerial Compensation Decisions," *Personnel Psychology* 43 (1990), pp. 599–614; D.J. Brass and M.E. Burkhardt, "Potential Power and Power Use: An Investigation of Structure and Behavior," *Academy of Management Journal* 36 (1993), pp. 441–70.

5. J.R.P. French and B. Raven, "The Bases of Social Power," in *Studies in Social Power*, ed. D. Cartwright (Ann Arbor, MI: University of Michigan Press, 1959), pp. 150-67; P. Podsakoff and C. Schreisheim, "Field Studies of French and Raven's Bases of Power: Critique, Analysis, and Suggestions for Future Research," *Psychological Bulletin* 97 (1985), pp. 387–411; S. Finkelstein, "Power in Top Management Teams: Dimensions, Measurement, and Validation," *Academy of Management Journal* 35 (1992), pp. 505–38; P.P. Carson and K.D. Carson, "Social Power Bases: A Meta-Analytic Examination of Interrelationships and Outcomes," *Journal of Applied Social Psychology* 23 (1993), pp. 1150–69.

6. B.H. Raven, "The Bases of Power: Origins and Recent Developments," *Journal of Social Issues* 49 (1993), pp. 227–51; G.A. Yukl, *Leadership in Organizations*, 3rd ed. (Englewood Cliffs, NJ: Prentice Hall, 1994), p. 13.

7. C. Barnard, *The Function of the Executive* (Cambridge, MA: Harvard University Press, 1938); C. Hardy and S.R. Clegg, "Some Dare Call It Power," in *Handbook of Organization Studies*, ed. S.R. Clegg, C. Hardy, and W.R. Nord (London: Sage, 1996), pp. 622–41.

8. L.A. Conger, *Winning 'Em Over: A New Model for Managing in the Age of Persuasion* (New York: Simon & Schuster, 1998), Appendix A.

9. V.L. Parker, "Org Charts Turn Around with Teams," *News & Observer* (Raleigh, North Carolina), 21 July 2005, p. D1; L.S. Sya, "Flying to Greater Heights," *New Sunday Times* (Kuala Lumpur), 31 July 2005, p. 14.

10. P.F. Drucker, "The New Workforce," *The Economist*, 3 November 2001, pp. 8–12.

11. J.D. Kudisch and M.L. Poteet, "Expert Power, Referent Power, and Charisma: Toward the Resolution of a Theoretical Debate," *Journal of Business & Psychology* 10 (Winter 1995), pp. 177–95; H.L. Tosi et al., "CEO Charisma, Compensation, and Firm Performance," *Leadership Quarterly* 15, no. 3 (2004), pp. 405–20.

12. G. Yukl and C.M. Falbe, "Importance of Different Power Sources in Downward and Lateral Relations," *Journal of Applied Psychology* 76 (1991), pp. 416-23; B.H. Raven, "Kurt Lewin Address: Influence, Power, Religion, and the Mechanisms of Social Control," *Journal of Social Issues* 55 (Spring 1999), pp. 161–86.

13. P.L. Dawes, D.Y. Lee, and G.R. Dowling, "Information Control and Influence in Emergent Buying Centers," *Journal of Marketing* 62, no. 3 (July 1998), pp. 55-68; D.J. Brass et al., "Taking Stock of Networks and Organizations: A Multilevel Perspective," *Academy of Management Journal* 47, no. 6 (December 2004), pp. 795–817.

14. C.R. Hinings et al., "Structural Conditions of Intraorganizational Power," *Administrative Science Quarterly* 19 (1974), pp. 22–44. Also see C.S. Saunders, "The Strategic Contingency Theory of Power: Multiple Perspectives," *The Journal of Management Studies* 27 (1990), pp. 1–21.

15. S. Elliott, "Hunting for the Next Cool in Advertising," *The New York Times*, 1 December 2003, p. C19; S. Delaney, "Predicting the Birth of the Cool," *The Independent* (London), 5 September 2005, p. 15; A. McMains, "Trend-Spotting Division Adds to Lowe's Evolution," *Adweek*, 11 April 2005, p. 11.

16. D.J. Hickson et al., "A Strategic Contingencies' Theory of Intraorganizational Power," *Administrative Science Quarterly* 16 (1971), pp. 216-27; Hinings et al., "Structural Conditions of Intraorganizational Power"; R.M. Kanter, "Power Failure in Management Circuits," *Harvard Business Review* (July-August 1979), pp. 65–75.

17. M. Crozier, *The Bureaucratic Phenomenon* (London: Tavistock, 1964).

18. Hickson et al., "A Strategic Contingencies' Theory of Intraorganizational Power"; J.D. Hackman, "Power and Centrality in the Allocation of Resources in Colleges and Universities," *Administrative Science Quarterly* 30 (1985), pp. 61–77; Brass and Burkhardt, "Potential Power and Power Use: An Investigation of Structure and Behavior."

19. Kanter, "Power Failure in Management Circuits"; B.E. Ashforth, "The Experience of Powerlessness in Organizations," *Organizational Behavior and Human Decision Processes* 43 (1989), pp. 207–42; L. Holden, "European Managers: HRM and an Evolving Role," *European Business Review* 12 (2000).

20. J. Voight, "When Credit Is Not Due," *Adweek*, 1 March 2004, p. 24.

21. R. Madell, "Ground Floor," *Pharmaceutical Executive (Women in Pharma Supplement)*, June 2000, pp. 24–31.

22. L.A. Perlow, "The Time Famine: Toward a Sociology of Work Time," *Administrative Science Quarterly* 44 (March 1999), pp. 5–31.

23. B.R. Ragins, "Diversified Mentoring Relationships in Organizations: A Power Perspective," *Academy of Management Review* 22 (1997), pp. 482–521; M.C. Higgins and K.E. Kram, "Reconceptualizing Mentoring at Work: A Developmental Network Perspective," *Academy of Management Review* 26 (April 2001), pp. 264–88.

24. D. Krackhardt and J.R. Hanson, "Informal Networks: The Company behind the Chart," *Harvard Business Review* 71 (July-August 1993), pp. 104–11; P.S. Adler and S.-W. Kwon, "Social Capital: Prospects for a New Concept," *Academy of Management Review* 27, no. 1 (2002), pp. 17–40.

25. A. Mehra, M. Kilduff, and D.J. Brass, "The Social Networks of High and Low Self-Monitors: Implications for Workplace Performance," *Administrative Science Quarterly* 46 (March 2001), pp. 121–46.

26. B.R. Ragins and E. Sundstrom, "Gender and Power in Organizations: A Longitudinal Perspective," *Psychological Bulletin* 105 (1989), pp. 51–88; M. Linehan, "Barriers to Women's Participation in International Management," *European Business Review* 13 (2001).

27. D.M. McCracken, "Winning the Talent War for Women: Sometimes It Takes a Revolution," *Harvard Business Review* (November–December 2000), pp. 159–67; D.L. Nelson and R.J. Burke, "Women

Executives: Health, Stress, and Success," *Academy of Management Executive* 14 (May 2000), pp. 107–21.

28. K. Atuahene-Gima and H. Li, "Marketing's Influence Tactics in New Product Development: A Study of High Technology Firms in China," *Journal of Product Innovation Management* 17 (2000), pp. 451–70; A. Somech and A. Drach-Zahavy, "Relative Power and Influence Strategy: The Effects of Agent/Target Organizational Power on Superiors' Choices of Influence Strategies," *Journal of Organizational Behavior* 23 (2002), pp. 167–79.

29. D. Kipnis, S.M. Schmidt, and I. Wilkinson, "Intraorganizational Influence Tactics: Explorations in Getting One's Way," *Journal of Applied Psychology* 65 (1980), pp. 440–52. Also see C. Schriesheim and T. Hinkin, "Influence Tactics Used by Subordinates: A Theoretical and Empirical Analysis and Refinement of the Kipnis, Schmidt, and Wilkinson Subscales," *Journal of Applied Psychology* 75 (1990), pp. 246–57; W.A. Hochwarter et al., "A Reexamination of Schriesheim and Hinkin's (1990) Measure of Upward Influence," *Educational and Psychological Measurement* 60 (October 2000), pp. 755–71.

30. Some of the more thorough lists of influence tactics are presented in A. Rao and K. Hashimoto, "Universal and Culturally Specific Aspects of Managerial Influence: A Study of Japanese Managers," *Leadership Quarterly* 8 (1997), pp. 295–312; L.A. McFarland, A.M. Ryan, and S.D. Kriska, "Field Study Investigation of Applicant Use of Influence Tactics in a Selection Interview," *Journal of Psychology* 136 (July 2002), pp. 383–98.

31. R.B. Cialdini and N.J. Goldstein, "Social Influence: Compliance and Conformity," *Annual Review of Psychology* 55 (2004), pp. 591–621.

32. Rao and Hashimoto, "Universal and Culturally Specific Aspects of Managerial Influence." Silent authority as an influence tactic in non-Western cultures is also discussed in S.F. Pasa, "Leadership Influence in a High Power Distance and Collectivist Culture," *Leadership & Organization Development Journal* 21 (2000), pp. 414–26.

33. "Be Part of the Team If You Want to Catch the Eye," *Birmingham Post* (U.K.), 31 August 2000, p. 14; S. Maitlis, "Taking It from the Top: How CEOs Influence (and Fail to Influence) Their Boards," *Organization Studies* 25, no. 8 (2004), pp. 1275–1311.

34. A.T. Cobb, "Toward the Study of Organizational Coalitions: Participant Concerns and Activities in a Simulated Organizational Setting," *Human Relations* 44 (1991), pp. 1057–79; E.A. Mannix, "Organizations as Resource Dilemmas: The Effects of Power Balance on Coalition Formation in Small Groups," *Organizational Behavior and Human Decision Processes* 55 (1993), pp. 1–22; D.J. Terry, M.A. Hogg, and K.M. White, "The Theory of Planned Behavior: Self-Identity, Social Identity, and Group Norms," *British Journal of Social Psychology* 38 (September 1999), pp. 225–44.

35. Rao and Hashimoto, "Universal and Culturally Specific Aspects of Managerial Influence."

36. D. Strutton and L.E. Pelton, "Effects of Ingratiation on Lateral Relationship Quality within Sales Team Settings," *Journal of Business Research* 43 (1998), pp. 1–12; R. Vonk, "Self-Serving Interpretations of Flattery: Why Ingratiation Works," *Journal of Personality and Social Psychology* 82 (2002), pp. 515–26.

37. C.A. Higgins, T.A. Judge, and G.R. Ferris, "Influence Tactics and Work Outcomes: A Meta-Analysis," *Journal of Organizational Behavior* 24 (2003), pp. 90–106.

38. D. Strutton, L.E. Pelton, and J. Tanner Jr., "Shall We Gather in the Garden? The Effect of Ingratiatory Behaviors on Buyer Trust in Salespeople," *Industrial Marketing Management* 25 (1996), pp. 151–62; J. O' Neil, "An Investigation of the Sources of Influence of Corporate Public Relations Practitioners," *Public Relations Review* 29 (June 2003), pp. 159–69.

39. A. Rao and S.M. Schmidt, "Upward Impression Management: Goals, Influence Strategies, and Consequences," *Human Relations* 48 (1995), pp. 147–67.

40. A.P.J. Ellis et al., "The Use of Impression Management Tactics in Structured Interviews: A Function of Question Type?" *Journal of Applied Psychology* 87 (December 2002), pp. 1200–8; M.C. Bolino and W.H. Tunley, "More Than One Way to Make an Impression: Exploring Profiles of Impression Management," *Journal of Management* 29 (2003), pp. 141–60.

41. S.L. McShane, "Applicant Misrepresentations in Résumés and Interviews in Canada," *Labor Law Journal*, January 1994, pp. 15–24; J. Jaucius, "Internet Guru's Credentials a True Work of Fiction," *Ottawa Citizen*, 12 June 2001; S. Romero and M. Richtel, "Second Chance," *The New York Times*, 5 March 2001, p. C1; "Up to 40 Percent of U.S. Workers Pad Their Résumés," *Agence France Presse* (Washington, D.C.), 22 February 2006; P. Sabatini, "Fibs on Résumés Commonplace," *Pittsburgh Post-Gazette*, 24 February 2006.

42. J. Dillard and E. Peck, "Persuasion and the Structure of Affect: Dual Systems and Discrete Emotions as Complementary Models," *Human Communication Research* 27 (2000), pp. 38–68; S. Fox and Y. Amichai-Hamburger, "The Power of Emotional Appeals in Promoting Organizational Change Programs," *Academy of Management Executive* 15 (November 2001), pp. 84–94; E.H.H.J. Das, J.B.F. de Wit, and W. Stroebe, "Fear Appeals Motivate Acceptance of Action Recommendations: Evidence for a Positive Bias in the Processing of Persuasive Messages," *Personality and Social Psychology Bulletin* 29 (May 2003), pp. 650–64; R. Buck et al., "Emotion and Reason in Persuasion: Applying the ARI Model and the CASC Scale," *Journal of Business Research* 57, no. 6 (2004), pp. 647–56.

43. A.P. Brief, *Attitudes in and Around Organizations* (Thousand Oaks, CA: Sage, 1998), pp. 69–84; D.J. O'Keefe, *Persuasion: Theory and Research* (Thousand Oaks, CA: Sage Publications, 2002).

44. Conger, *Winning 'Em Over: A New Model for Managing in the Age of Persuasion*; J.J. Jiang, G. Klein, and R.G. Vedder, "Persuasive Expert Systems: The Influence of Confidence and Discrepancy," *Computers in Human Behavior* 16 (March 2000), pp. 99–109.

45. S. Gilmor, "Ahead of the Curve," *Infoworld*, 13 January 2003, p. 58; M. Hiltzik, "Apple CEO's Visions Don't Guarantee Sustained Gains," *Los Angeles Times*, 14 April 2003, p. C1. The origin of the term *reality distortion field* is described at www.folklore.org.

46. These and other features of message content in persuasion are detailed in R. Petty and J. Cacioppo, *Attitudes and Persuasion: Classic and Contemporary Approaches* (Dubuque, IA: W.C. Brown, 1981); D.G. Linz and S. Penrod, "Increasing Attorney Persuasiveness in the Courtroom," *Law and Psychology Review* 8 (1984), pp. 1–47; M. Pfau, E.A. Szabo, and J. Anderson, "The Role and Impact

of Affect in the Process of Resistance to Persuasion," *Human Communication Research* 27 (April 2001), pp. 216–52; O'Keefe, *Persuasion: Theory and Research,* Chapter 9.

47. N. Rhodes and W. Wood, "Self-Esteem and Intelligence Affect Influenceability: The Mediating Role of Message Reception," *Psychological Bulletin* 111, no. 1 (1992), pp. 156–71.

48. A.W. Gouldner, "The Norm of Reciprocity: A Preliminary Statement," *American Sociological Review* 25 (1960), pp. 161–78.

49. Y. Fan, "Questioning Guanxi: Definition, Classification, and Implications," *International Business Review* 11 (2002), pp. 543–61; D. Tan and R.S. Snell, "The Third Eye: Exploring Guanxi and Relational Morality in the Workplace," *Journal of Business Ethics* 41 (December 2002), pp. 361–84; W.R. Vanhonacker, "When Good Guanxi Turns Bad," *Harvard Business Review* 82, no. 4 (April 2004), pp. 18–19.

50. A. Ledeneva, *Russia's Economy of Favors: Blat, Networking and Informal Exchange* (New York: Cambridge University Press, 1998); S. Michailova and V. Worm, "Personal Networking in Russia and China: Blat and Guanxi," *European Management Journal* 21 (2003), pp. 509–19.

51. C.M. Falbe and G. Yukl, "Consequences for Managers of Using Single Influence Tactics and Combinations of Tactics," *Academy of Management Journal* 35 (1992), pp. 638–52.

52. Falbe and Yukl, "Consequences for Managers of Using Single Influence Tactics and Combinations of Tactics"; Atuahene-Gima and Li, "Marketing's Influence Tactics in New Product Development."

53. R.C. Ringer and R.W. Boss, "Hospital Professionals' Use of Upward Influence Tactics," *Journal of Managerial Issues* 12 (2000), pp. 92–108.

54. G. Blickle, "Do Work Values Predict the Use of Intraorganizational Influence Strategies?" *Journal of Applied Social Psychology* 30, no. 1 (January 2000), pp. 196–205; P.P. Fu et al., "The Impact of Societal Cultural Values and Individual Social Beliefs on the Perceived Effectiveness of Managerial Influence Strategies: A Meso Approach," *Journal of International Business Studies* 35, no. 4 (July 2004), pp. 284–305.

55. D. Tannen, *Talking from 9 to 5* (New York: Avon, 1994), Chapter 2; M. Crawford, *Talking Difference: On Gender and Language* (Thousand Oaks, CA: Sage, 1995), pp. 41–44.

56. S. Mann, "Politics and Power in Organizations: Why Women Lose Out," *Leadership & Organization Development Journal* 16 (1995), pp. 9–15; E.H. Buttner and M. McEnally, "The Interactive Effect of Influence Tactic, Applicant Gender, and Type of Job on Hiring Recommendations," Sex Roles 34 (1996), pp. 581–91; L.L. Carli, "Gender, Interpersonal Power, and Social Influence," *Journal of Social Issues* 55 (Spring 1999), pp. 81–99.

57. This definition of organizational politics has become the dominant perspective over the past 15 years. See G.R. Ferris and K.M. Kacmar, "Perceptions of Organizational Politics," *Journal of Management* 18 (1992), pp. 93–116; R. Cropanzano et al., "The Relationship of Organizational Politics and Support to Work Behaviors, Attitudes, and Stress," *Journal of Organizational Behavior* 18 (1997), pp. 159–80; E. Vigoda and A. Cohen, "Influence Tactics and Perceptions of Organizational Politics: A Longitudinal Study," *Journal of Business Research* 55 (2002), pp. 311–24. However, organizational politics was previously viewed as influence tactics outside the formal role that could be either selfish or altruistic. This older definition is less common today, possibly because it is incongruent with popular views of politics and because it overlaps too much with the concept of influence. For the older perspective of organizational politics, see J. Pfeffer, *Power in Organizations* (Boston: Pitman, 1981); Mintzberg, *Power in and around Organizations.*

58. K.M. Kacmar and R.A. Baron, "Organizational Politics: The State of the Field, Links to Related Processes, and an Agenda for Future Research," in *Research in Personnel and Human Resources Management,* ed. G.R. Ferris (Greenwich, CT: JAI Press, 1999), pp. 1–39; L.A. Witt, T.F. Hilton, and W.A. Hochwarter, "Addressing Politics in Matrix Teams," *Group & Organization Management* 26 (June 2001), pp. 230–47; E. Vigoda, "Stress-Related Aftermaths to Workplace Politics: The Relationships among Politics, Job Distress, and Aggressive Behavior in Organizations," *Journal of Organizational Behavior* 23 (2002), pp. 571–91.

59. C. Hardy, *Strategies for Retrenchment and Turnaround: The Politics of Survival* (Berlin: Walter de Gruyter, 1990), Chapter 14; M.C. Andrews and K.M. Kacmar, "Discriminating among Organizational Politics, Justice, and Support," *Journal of Organizational Behavior* 22 (2001), pp. 347–66.

60. S. Blazejewski and W. Dorow, "Managing Organizational Politics for Radical Change: The Case of Beiersdorf–Lechia S.A., Poznan," *Journal of World Business* 38 (August 2003), pp. 204–23.

61. H. Mitzberg, "The Organization as Political Arena," *Journal of Management Studies* 22 (1985), pp. 133–54; G.R. Ferris, G.S. Russ, and P.M. Fandt, "Politics in Organizations," in *Impression Management in the Organization,* ed. R.A. Giacalone and P. Rosenfeld (Hillsdale, NJ: Erlbaum, 1989), pp. 143–70.

62. L.W. Porter, R.W. Allen, and H.L. Angle, "The Politics of Upward Influence in Organizations," *Research in Organizational Behavior* 3 (1981), pp. 120–22; R.J. House, "Power and Personality in Complex Organizations," *Research in Organizational Behavior* 10 (1988), pp. 305–57.

63. R. Christie and F. Geis, *Studies in Machiavellianism* (New York: Academic Press, 1970); S.M. Farmer et al., "Putting Upward Influence Strategies in Context," *Journal of Organizational Behavior* 18 (1997), pp. 17–42; K.S. Sauleya and A.G. Bedeian, "Equity Sensitivity: Construction of a Measure and Examination of Its Psychometric Properties," *Journal of Management* 26 (September 2000), pp. 885–910.

64. G.R. Ferris et al., "Perceptions of Organizational Politics: Prediction, Stress-Related Implications, and Outcomes," *Human Relations* 49 (1996), pp. 233–63.

CHAPTER 13

1. B. Dudley, "Bring Back the Dazzle," *The Seattle Times,* 23 September 2005; J. Greene, "Troubling Exits at Microsoft," *BusinessWeek,* 26 September 2005, p. 98; A. Linn, "Microsoft Reorganizes to Compete Better with Google, Yahoo," *Associated Press Newswires,* 21 September 2005; V. Murphy, "Microsoft's Midlife Crisis," *Forbes,* 3 October 2005, p. 88; L. Vaas, "Microsoft Expands Bureaucracy, Crowns MSN King," *eWeek,* 20 September 2005; J.L. Yang, "Microsoft's New Brain," *Fortune,* 1 May 2006, p. 56.

2. J.A. Wall and R.R. Callister, "Conflict and Its Management," *Journal of Management,* 21 (1995), pp. 515–58; M.A. Rahim, "Toward a Theory of Managing Organizational Conflict," *International Journal of Conflict Management* 13, no. 3 (2002), pp. 206–35.

3. L. Pondy, "Organizational Conflict: Concepts and Models," *Administrative Science Quarterly* 2 (1967), pp. 296–320; K.W. Thomas, "Conflict and Negotiation Processes in Organizations," in *Handbook of Industrial and Organizational Psychology*, ed. M.D. Dunnette and L.M. Hough, 2nd ed. (Palo Alto, CA: Consulting Psychologists Press, 1992), pp. 651–718.

4. Murphy, "Microsoft's Midlife Crisis."

5. M.A. Von Glinow, D.L. Shapiro, and J.M. Brett, "Can We Talk, and Should We? Managing Emotional Conflict in Multicultural Teams," *Academy of Management Review* 29, no. 4 (2004), pp. 578–92.

6. G.E. Martin and T.J. Bergman, "The Dynamics of Behavioral Response to Conflict in the Workplace," *Journal of Occupational & Organizational Psychology* 69 (December 1996), pp. 377–87; J.M. Brett, D.L. Shapiro, and A.L. Lytle, "Breaking the Bonds of Reciprocity in Negotiations," *Academy of Management Journal* 41 (August 1998), pp. 410–24.

7. H. Witteman, "Analyzing Interpersonal Conflict: Nature of Awareness, Type of Initiating Event, Situational Perceptions, and Management Styles," *Western Journal of Communications* 56 (1992), pp. 248–80; Wall and Callister, "Conflict and Its Management."

8. A. Grove, "How to Make Confrontation Work for You," in *The Book of Management Wisdom*, ed. P. Krass (New York: John Wiley & Sons, 2000), pp. 83–89; B. Schlender, "Inside Andy Grove's Latest Crusade," *Fortune*, 23 August 2004, p. 68.

9. M. Rempel and R.J. Fisher, "Perceived Threat, Cohesion, and Group Problem Solving in Intergroup Conflict," *International Journal of Conflict Management* 8 (1997), pp. 216–34.

10. D. Tjosvold, *The Conflict-Positive Organization* (Reading, MA: Addison-Wesley, 1991); K.M. Eisenhardt, J.L. Kahwajy, and L.J. Bourgeois III, "Conflict and Strategic Choice: How Top Management Teams Disagree," *California Management Review* 39 (Winter 1997), pp. 42–62; L.H. Pelled, K.M. Eisenhardt, and K.R. Xin, "Exploring the Black Box: An Analysis of Work Group Diversity, Conflict, and Performance," *Administrative Science Quarterly* 44 (March 1999), pp. 1–28; S. Schulz-Hardt, M. Jochims, and D. Frey, "Productive Conflict in Group Decision Making: Genuine and Contrived Dissent as Strategies to Counteract Biased Information Seeking," *Organizational Behavior and Human Decision Processes* 88 (2002), pp. 563–86.

11. C.K.W. De Dreu and L.R. Weingart, "Task versus Relationship Conflict, Team Performance, and Team Member Satisfaction: A Meta-Analysis," *Journal of Applied Psychology* 88 (August 2003), pp. 587–604.

12. J. Yang and K.W. Mossholder, "Decoupling Task and Relationship Conflict: The Role of Intergroup Emotional Processing," *Journal of Organizational Behavior* 25 (2004), pp. 589–605.

13. R.E. Walton and J.M. Dutton, "The Management of Conflict: A Model and Review," *Administrative Science Quarterly* 14 (1969), pp. 73–84.

14. D.M. Brock, D. Barry, and D.C. Thomas, "'Your Forward Is Our Reverse, Your Right, Our Wrong': Rethinking Multinational Planning Processes in Light of National Culture," *International Business Review* 9 (2000), pp. 687–701.

15. R. Zemke and B. Filipczak, *Generations at Work: Managing the Clash of Veterans, Boomers, Xers, and Nexters in Your Workplace* (New York: Amacom, 1999); P. Harris, "Boomers vs. Echo Boomer: The Work War," *T+D*, May 2005, pp. 44–49.

16. P. Hinds and D.E. Bailey, "Out of Sight, Out of Sync: Understanding Conflict in Distributed Teams," *Organization Science* 14, no. 6 (2003), pp. 615–32; P. Hinds and M. Mortensen, "Understanding Conflict in Geographically Distributed Teams: The Moderating Effects of Shared Identity, Shared Context, and Spontaneous Communication," *Organization Science* 16, no. 3 (May–June 2005), pp. 290–307.

17. P.C. Earley and G.B. Northcraft, "Goal Setting, Resource Interdependence, and Conflict Management," in *Managing Conflict: An Interdisciplinary Approach*, ed. M.A. Rahim (New York: Praeger, 1989), pp. 161–70; K. Jelin, "A Multimethod Examination of the Benefits and Detriments of Intragroup Conflict," *Administrative Science Quarterly* 40 (1995), pp. 245–82.

18. A. Risberg, "Employee Experiences of Acquisition Processes," *Journal of World Business* 36 (March 2001), pp. 58–84.

19. K.A. Jehn and C. Bendersky, "Intragroup Conflict in Organizations: A Contingency Perspective on the Conflict–Outcome Relationship," *Research in Organizational Behavior* 25 (2003), pp. 187–242.

20. J. Jetten, R. Spears, and T. Postmes, "Intergroup Distinctiveness and Differentiation: A Meta-Analytic Integration," *Journal of Personality and Social Psychology* 86, no. 6 (2004), pp. 862–79.

21. Von Glinow, Shapiro, and Brett, "Can We Talk, and Should We?"

22. J.M. Brett, *Negotiating Globally: How to Negotiate Deals, Resolve Disputes, and Make Decisions across Cultural Boundaries* (San Francisco: Jossey-Bass, 2001); R.J. Lewicki et al., *Negotiation*, 4th ed. (Burr Ridge, IL: McGraw-Hill/Irwin, 2003), Chapter 4.

23. D. Cox, "Goodenow's Downfall," *Toronto Star*, 29 July 2005, p. A1; A. Maki, "NHLPA's New Leader Is a Peacemaker, Not Warrior," *Globe & Mail*, 29 July 2005, p. S1; M. Spector, "Players: He Is Your Father," *National Post*, 29 July 2005, p. B8.

24. Jelin, "A Multimethod Examination of the Benefits and Detriments of Intragroup Conflict."

25. C.K.W. De Dreu et al., "A Theory-Based Measure of Conflict Management Strategies in the Workplace," *Journal of Organizational Behavior* 22 (2001), pp. 645–68.

26. D.W. Johnson et al., "Effects of Cooperative, Competitive, and Individualistic Goal Structures on Achievement: A Meta-Analysis," *Psychological Bulletin* 89 (1981), pp. 47–62; D. Tjosvold, *Working Together to Get Things Done* (Lexington,MA: Lexington, 1986); C.K.W. De Dreu, E. Giebels, and E. Van de Vliert, "Social Motives and Trust in Integrative Negotiation: The Disruptive Effects of Punitive Capability," *Journal of Applied Psychology* 83, no. 3 (June 1998), pp. 408–22; G.A. Callanan and D.F. Perri, "Teaching Conflict Management Using a Scenario-Based Approach," *Journal of Education for Business* 81, no. 3 (2006), pp. 131–39.

27. C.K.W. De Dreu and A.E.M. Van Vianen, "Managing Relationship Conflict and the Effectiveness of Organizational Teams," *Journal of Organizational Behavior* 22 (2001), pp. 309–28; Lewicki et al., *Negotiation*, pp. 35–36.

28. M.W. Morris and H.-Y. Fu, "How Does Culture Influence Conflict Resolution? Dynamic Constructivist Analysis," *Social Cognition* 19 (June 2001), pp. 324–49; S. Ting-Toomey, J.G. Oetzel, and K. Yee-Jung, "Self-Construal Types and Conflict Management Styles," *Communication Reports* 14 (Summer 2001), pp. 87–104; C.H. Tinsley, "How Negotiators Get to Yes: Predicting the Constellation of Strategies Used across Cultures to Negotiate Conflict," *Journal of Applied Psychology* 86, no. 4 (2001), pp. 583–93.

29. C.H. Tinsley and E. Weldon, "Responses to a Normative Conflict among American and Chinese Managers,"

International Journal of Conflict Management 3, no. 2 (2003), pp. 183–94. Also see D.A. Cai and E.L. Fink, "Conflict Style Differences between Individualists and Collectivists," *Communication Monographs* 69 (March 2002), pp. 67–87.

30. N. Brewer, P. Mitchell, and N. Weber, "Gender Role, Organizational Status, and Conflict Management Styles," *International Journal of Conflict Management* 13 (2002), pp. 78–95; N.B. Florea et al., "Negotiating from Mars to Venus: Gender in Simulated International Negotiations," *Simulation & Gaming* 34 (June 2003), pp. 226–48.

31. E. Van de Vliert, "Escalative Intervention in Small Group Conflicts," *Journal of Applied Behavioral Science* 21 (Winter 1985), pp. 19–36.

32. M. Alva, "Teamwork Means Getting All Hands Ready for a Touchdown," *Investor's Business Daily*, 12 June 2006, p. A07.

33. M. Sherif, "Superordinate Goals in the Reduction of Intergroup Conflict," *American Journal of Sociology* 68 (1958), pp. 349–58; K.M. Eisenhardt, J.L. Kahwajy, and L.J. Bourgeois III, "How Management Teams Can Have a Good Fight," *Harvard Business Review*, July–August 1997, pp. 77–85; X.M. Song, J. Xile, and B. Dyer, "Antecedents and Consequences of Marketing Managers' Conflict-Handling Behaviors," *Journal of Marketing* 64 (January 2000), pp. 50–66.

34. H.C. Triandis, "The Future of Workforce Diversity in International Organizations: A Commentary," *Applied Psychology: An International Journal* 52, no. 3 (2003), pp. 486–95.

35. E. Elron, B. Shamir, and E. Bem-Ari, "Why Don't They Fight Each Other? Cultural Diversity and Operational Unity in Multinational Forces," *Armed Forces & Society* 26 (October 1999), pp. 73–97; "How Hibernia Helped Its Hourly Employees Make a Leap to PFP," *Pay for Performance Report*, January 2000, p. 2; "Teamwork Polishes This Diamond," *Philippine Daily Inquirer*, 4 October 2000, p. 10.

36. K.R. Lewis, "(Drum) Beatings Build Corporate Spirit," *Star Tribune* (Minneapolis), 3 June 2003, p. 3E; "Oh What a Feeling!" *Music Trades*, May 2004, pp. 94–95; D. Cole, "Joining the Tom-Tom Club," *U.S. News & World Report*, 22 March 2004, p. D12.

37. T.F. Pettigrew, "Intergroup Contact Theory," *Annual Review of Psychology* 49 (1998), pp. 65–85; S. Brickson, "The Impact of Identity Orientation on Individual and Organizational Outcomes in Demographically Diverse Settings," *Academy of Management Review* 25 (January 2000), pp. 82–101; J. Dixon and K. Durrheim, "Contact and the Ecology of Racial Division: Some Varieties of Informal Segregation," *British Journal of Social Psychology* 42 (March 2003), pp. 1–23.

38. Triandis, "The Future of Workforce Diversity in International Organizations."

39. Von Glinow, Shapiro, and Brett, "Can We Talk, and Should We?"

40. P.O. Walker, "Decolonizing Conflict Resolution: Addressing the Ontological Violence of Westernization," *American Indian Quarterly* 28, no. 3/4 (July 2004), pp. 527–49; Native Dispute Resolution Network, "Glossary of Terms" (Tucson, Arizona, 2005), http://nativenetwork.ecr.gov (accessed 15 September 2005).

41. E. Horwitt, "Knowledge, Knowledge, Who's Got the Knowledge," *Computerworld*, 8 April 1996, pp. 80, 81, 84.

42. For a critical view of the problem-solving style in negotiation, see J.M. Brett, "Managing Organizational Conflict," *Professional Psychology: Research and Practice* 15 (1984), pp. 664–78.

43. R.E. Fells, "Developing Trust in Negotiation," *Employee Relations* 15 (1993), pp. 33–45; R.E. Fells, "Overcoming the Dilemmas in Walton and McKersie's Mixed Bargaining Strategy," *Industrial Relations* (Laval) 53 (March 1998), pp. 300–25.

44. R. Stagner and H. Rosen, *Psychology of Union–Management Relations* (Belmont, CA: Wadsworth, 1965), pp. 95–96, 108–10; R.E. Walton and R.B. McKersie, *A Behavioral Theory of Labor Negotiations: An Analysis of a Social Interaction System* (New York: McGraw-Hill, 1965), pp. 41–46; L. Thompson, *The Mind and Heart of the Negotiator* (Upper Saddle River, NJ: Prentice-Hall, 1998), Chapter 2.

45. J.W. Salacuse and J.Z. Rubin, "Your Place or Mine? Site Location and Negotiation," *Negotiation Journal* 6 (January 1990), pp. 5–10; J. Mayfield et al., "How Location Impacts International Business Negotiations," *Review of Business* 19 (December 1998), pp. 21–24.

46. J. Margo, "The Persuaders," *Boss Magazine*, 29 December 2000, p. 38. For a full discussion of the advantages and disadvantages of face-to-face and alternative negotiations situations, see M.H. Bazerman et al., "Negotiation," *Annual Review of Psychology* 51 (2000), pp. 279–314.

47. A.F. Stuhlmacher, T.L. Gillespie, and M.V. Champagne, "The Impact of Time Pressure in Negotiation: A Meta-Analysis," *International Journal of Conflict Management* 9, no. 2 (April 1998), pp. 97–116; C.K.W. De Dreu, "Time Pressure and Closing of the Mind in Negotiation," *Organizational Behavior and Human Decision Processes* 91 (July 2003), pp. 280–95. However, one recent study reported that speeding up these concessions leads to better negotiated outcomes. See D.A. Moore, "Myopic Prediction, Self-Destructive Secrecy, and the Unexpected Benefits of Revealing Final Deadlines in Negotiation," *Organizational Behavior and Human Decision Processes* 94, no. 2 (2004), pp. 125–39.

48. Lewicki et al., *Negotiation*, pp. 298–322.

49. S. Doctoroff, "Reengineering Negotiations," *Sloan Management Review* 39 (March 1998), pp. 63–71; D.C. Zetik and A.F. Stuhlmacher, "Goal Setting and Negotiation Performance: A Meta-Analysis," *Group Processes & Intergroup Relations* 5 (January 2002), pp. 35–52.

50. B. McRae, *The Seven Strategies of Master Negotiators* (Toronto: McGraw-Hill Ryerson, 2002), pp. 7–11.

51. L.L. Thompson, "Information Exchange in Negotiation," *Journal of Experimental Social Psychology* 27 (1991), pp. 161–79.

52. L. Thompson, E. Peterson, and S.E. Brodt, "Team Negotiation: An Examination of Integrative and Distributive Bargaining," *Journal of Personality and Social Psychology* 70 (1996), pp. 66–78; Y. Paik and R.L. Tung, "Negotiating with East Asians: How to Attain "Win-Win" Outcomes," *Management International Review* 39 (1999), pp. 103–22.

53. D.J. O'Keefe, *Persuasion: Theory and Research* (Thousand Oaks, CA: Sage Publications, 2002).

54. Lewicki et al., *Negotiation*, pp. 90–96; S. Kwon and L.R. Weingart, "Unilateral Concessions from the Other Party: Concession Behavior, Attributions, and Negotiation Judgments," *Journal of Applied Psychology* 89, no. 2 (2004), pp. 263–78.

55. J.J. Zhao, "The Chinese Approach to International Business Negotiation," *Journal of Business Communication*, July 2000, pp. 209–37; N. Crundwell, "U.S.–Russian Negotiating Strategies," *BISNIS Bulletin*, October 2003, pp. 5–6.

56. J.Z. Rubin and B.R. Brown, *The Social Psychology of Bargaining and Negotiation* (New York: Academic Press, 1976), Chapter 9.

57. L.L. Putnam, "Beyond Third Party Role: Disputes and Managerial

Intervention," *Employee Responsibilities and Rights Journal* 7 (1994), pp. 23–36; A.R. Elangovan, "The Manager as the Third Party: Deciding How to Intervene in Employee Disputes," in *Negotiation: Readings, Exercises, and Cases*, ed. R.J. Lewicki, J.A. Litterer, and D. Saunders, 3rd ed. (New York: McGraw-Hill, 1999), pp. 458–69. For a somewhat different taxonomy of managerial conflict intervention, see P.G. Irving and J.P. Meyer, "A Multidimensional Scaling Analysis of Managerial Third-Party Conflict Intervention Strategies," *Canadian Journal of Behavioural Science* 29, no. 1 (January 1997), pp. 7–18.

58. B.H. Sheppard, "Managers as Inquisitors: Lessons from the Law," in *Bargaining inside Organizations*, ed. M.H. Bazerman and R.J. Lewicki (Beverly Hills, CA: Sage, 1983); N.H. Kim, D.W. Sohn, and J.A. Wall, "Korean Leaders' (and Subordinates') Conflict Management," *International Journal of Conflict Management* 10, no. 2 (April 1999), pp. 130–53.

59. R. Karambayya and J.M. Brett, "Managers Handling Disputes: Third Party Roles and Perceptions of Fairness," *Academy of Management Journal* 32 (1989), pp. 687–704; R. Cropanzano et al., "Disputant Reactions to Managerial Conflict Resolution Tactics," *Group & Organization Management* 24 (June 1999), pp. 124–53.

60. A.R. Elangovan, "Managerial Intervention in Organizational Disputes: Testing a Prescriptive Model of Strategy Selection," *International Journal of Conflict Management* 4 (1998), pp. 301–35; P.S. Nugent, "Managing Conflict: Third-Party Interventions for Managers," *Academy of Management Executive* 16, no. 1 (February 2002), pp. 139–54.

61. J.P. Meyer, J.M. Gemmell, and P.G. Irving, "Evaluating the Management of Interpersonal Conflict in Organizations: A Factor-Analytic Study of Outcome Criteria," *Canadian Journal of Administrative Sciences* 14 (1997), pp. 1–13.

62. "AMC Uses Alternative Dispute Resolution to Solve Workplace Conflicts," Department of Defense, U.S. Air Force news release (Scott Air Force Base, IL), 13 July 2005.

63. K. Downey, "With Its Dispute Resolution Process, Kodak Joins a Trend," *Washington Post*, 21 September 2003, p. F1.

64. C. Hirschman, "Order in the Hearing," *HRMagazine* 46 (July 2001), p. 58; D. Hechler, "No Longer a Novelty: ADR Winning Corporate Acceptance," *Fulton County Daily Report*, 29 June 2001; S.L. Hayford, "Alternative Dispute Resolution," *Business Horizons* 43 (January–February 2000), pp. 2–4.

CHAPTER 14

1. "Building a Solid Foundation on Value-Driven Principles," *Business Leader*, June 2003, p. 6; N. Nilekani, "How Do I Develop Next Generation Leaders?" *Economic Times* (India), 25 November 2005; D. Tarrant, "The Leading Edge," *The Bulletin*, 15 November 2005; R. Stavros, "The Ultimate CEOs," *Public Utilities Fortnightly*, 1 June 2006, p. 40.

2. R. House, M. Javidan, and P. Dorfman, "Project Globe: An Introduction," *Applied Psychology: An International Review* 50 (2001), pp. 489–505; R. House et al., "Understanding Cultures and Implicit Leadership Theories across the Globe: An Introduction to Project Globe," *Journal of World Business* 37 (2002), pp. 3–10.

3. R.G. Issac, W.J. Zerbe, and D.C. Pitt, "Leadership and Motivation: The Effective Application of Expectancy Theory," *Journal of Managerial Issues* 13 (Summer 2001), pp. 212–26; C.L. Pearce and J.A. Conger, eds., *Shared Leadership: Reframing the Hows and Whys of Leadership* (Thousand Oaks, CA: Sage, 2003); J.S. Nielson, *The Myth of Leadership* (Palo Alto, CA: Davies-Black, 2004).

4. S. Caulkin, "Who's in Charge Here?" *The Observer* (London), 27 April 2003, p. 9; D. Gardner, "A Boss Who's Crazy about His Workers," *Sunday Herald* (Glasgow, Scotland), 13 April 2003, p. 6; S. Moss, "Portrait: 'Idleness Is Good,'" *The Guardian* (London), 17 April 2003, p. 8; R. Semler, *The Seven-Day Weekend* (London: Century, 2003); "Ricardo Semler Set Them Free," *CIO Insight*, April 2004, p. 30.

5. J. Raelin, "Preparing for Leaderful Practice," *T&D*, March 2004, p. 64.

6. L. Gyulai, "It Takes Children to Raise a Village," *Montreal Gazette*, 30 July 2005, p. A14.

7. Many of these perspectives are summarized in R.N. Kanungo, "Leadership in Organizations: Looking Ahead to the 21st Century," *Canadian Psychology* 39 (Spring 1998), pp. 71–82; G.A. Yukl, *Leadership in Organizations*, 6th ed. (Upper Saddle River, NJ: Pearson Education, 2006).

8. R.M. Stogdill, *Handbook of Leadership* (New York: The Free Press, 1974), Chapter 5.

9. "Care Board Names Dr. Helene Gayle as New President/CEO," CARE news release, (Atlanta), 2 December 2005; M. Bixler, "Chief's Global View to Influence Goals," *Atlanta Journal-Constitution*, 12 April 2006, p. F1; P. Bock, "In Every Way, Helene Gayle Cares in All Capital Letters," *Washington Post*, 1 January 2006, p. D01.

10. R. Ilies, M.W. Gerhardt, and H. Le, "Individual Differences in Leadership Emergence: Integrating Meta-Analytic Findings and Behavioral Genetics Estimates," *International Journal of Selection and Assessment* 12, no. 3 (September 2004), pp. 207–19.

11. J. Intagliata, D. Ulrich, and N. Smallwood, "Leveraging Leadership Competencies to Produce Leadership Brand: Creating Distinctiveness by Focusing on Strategy and Results," *Human Resources Planning* 23, no. 4 (2000), pp. 12–23; J.A. Conger and D.A. Ready, "Rethinking Leadership Competencies," *Leader to Leader*, Spring 2004, pp. 41–47; S.J. Zaccaro, C. Kemp, and P. Bader, "Leader Traits and Attributes," in *The Nature of Leadership*, ed. J. Antonakis, A.T. Cianciolo, and R.J. Sternberg (Thousand Oaks, CA: Sage, 2004), pp. 101–24.

12. This list is based on S.A. Kirkpatrick and E.A. Locke, "Leadership: Do Traits Matter?" *Academy of Management Executive* 5 (May 1991), pp. 48–60; R.M. Aditya, R.J. House, and S. Kerr, "Theory and Practice of Leadership: Into the New Millennium," in *Industrial and Organizational Psychology: Linking Theory with Practice*, ed. C.L. Cooper and E.A. Locke (Oxford, UK: Blackwell, 2000), pp. 130–65; D. Goleman, R. Boyatzis, and A. McKee, *Primal Leaders* (Boston: Harvard Business School Press, 2002); T.A. Judge et al., "Personality and Leadership: A Qualitative and Quantitative Review," *Journal of Applied Psychology* 87, no. 4 (August 2002), pp. 765–80; T.A. Judge, A.E. Colbert, and R. Ilies, "Intelligence and Leadership: A Quantitative Review and Test of Theoretical Propositions," *Journal of Applied Psychology* 89, no. 3 (June 2004), pp. 542–52; Zaccaro, Kemp, and Bader, "Leader Traits and Attributes."

13. J. George, "Emotions and Leadership: The Role of Emotional Intelligence," *Human Relations* 53 (August 2000), pp. 1027–55; Goleman, Boyatzis, and McKee, *Primal Leaders*; R.G. Lord and R.J. Hall, "Identity, Deep Structure, and the Development of Leadership Skill,"

Leadership Quarterly 16, no. 4 (August 2005), pp. 591–615; C. Skinner and P. Spurgeon, "Valuing Empathy and Emotional Intelligence in Health Leadership: A Study of Empathy, Leadership Behavior, and Outcome Effectiveness," *Health Services Management Research* 18, no. 1 (February 2005), pp. 1–12.

14. D.R. May et al., "The Moral Component of Authentic Leadership," *Organizational Dynamics* 32 (August 2003), pp. 247–60. The large-scale studies are reported in C. Savoye, "Workers Say Honesty Is Best Company Policy," *Christian Science Monitor*, 15 June 2000; J.M. Kouzes and B.Z. Posner, *The Leadership Challenge*, 3rd ed. (San Francisco: Jossey-Bass, 2002), Chapter 2; J. Schettler, "Leadership in Corporate America," *Training & Development*, September 2002, pp. 66–73.

15. Watson Wyatt Worldwide, "Asia-Pacific Workers Satisfied with Jobs Despite Some Misgivings with Management and Pay," Watson Wyatt Worldwide news release, (Singapore), 16 November 2004; J. Cremer, "Asian Workers Give Low Marks to Leaders," *South China Morning Post* (Hong Kong), 30 July 2005, p. 8; D. Jones, "Optimism Puts Rose-Colored Tint in Glasses of Top Execs," *USA Today*, 16 December 2005, p. B1; E. Pondel, "Friends & Bosses?" *Seattle Post-Intelligencer*, 10 April 2006, p. C1.

16. R. Charan, C. Burke, and L. Bossidy, *Execution: The Discipline of Getting Things Done* (New York: Crown Business, 2002). The survey of managerial competencies is reported in D. Nilsen, B. Kowske, and A. Kshanika, "Managing Globally," *HRMagazine*, August 2005, pp. 111–15.

17. R.J. House and R.N. Aditya, "The Social Scientific Study of Leadership: Quo Vadis?" *Journal of Management* 23 (1997), pp. 409–73.

18 R. Jacobs, "Using Human Resource Functions to Enhance Emotional Intelligence," in *The Emotionally Intelligent Workplace*, ed. C. Cherniss and D. Goleman (San Francisco: Jossey-Bass, 2001), pp. 161–63; Conger and Ready, "Rethinking Leadership Competencies."

19. P.G. Northouse, *Leadership: Theory and Practice*, 3rd ed. (Thousand Oaks, CA: Sage, 2004), Chapter 4; Yukl, *Leadership in Organizations*, Chapter 3.

20. A.K. Korman, "Consideration, Initiating Structure, and Organizational Criteria-A Review," *Personnel Psychology* 19 (1966), pp. 349–62; E.A. Fleishman, "Twenty Years of Consideration and Structure," in *Current Developments in the Study of Leadership*, ed. E.A. Fleishman and J.C. Hunt (Carbondale, IL: Southern Illinois University Press, 1973), pp. 1–40; T.A. Judge, R.F. Piccolo, and R. Ilies, "The Forgotten Ones? The Validity of Consideration and Initiating Structure in Leadership Research," *Journal of Applied Psychology* 89, no. 1 (2004), pp. 36–51; Yukl, *Leadership in Organizations*, pp. 62–75.

21. V.V. Baba, "Serendipity in Leadership: Initiating Structure and Consideration in the Classroom," *Human Relations* 42 (1989), pp. 509–25.

22. S. Kerr et al., "Toward a Contingency Theory of Leadership Based upon the Consideration and Initiating Structure Literature," *Organizational Behavior and Human Performance* 12 (1974), pp. 62–82; L.L. Larson, J.G. Hunt, and R.N. Osbom, "The Great Hi-Hi Leader Behavior Myth: A Lesson from Occam's Razor," *Academy of Management Journal* 19 (1976), pp. 628–41.

23. R. Tannenbaum and W.H. Schmidt, "How to Choose a Leadership Pattern," *Harvard Business Review*, May-June 1973, pp. 162–80.

24. For a thorough study of how expectancy theory of motivation relates to leadership, see R.G. Isaac, W.J. Zerbe, and D. C. Pitt, "Leadership and Motivation: The Effective Application of Expectancy Theory," *Journal of Managerial Issues* 13 (Summer 2001), pp. 212–26.

25. R.J. House, "A Path-Goal Theory of Leader Effectiveness," *Administrative Science Quarterly* 16 (1971), pp. 321–38; M.G. Evans, "Extensions of a Path-Goal Theory of Motivation," *Journal of Applied Psychology* 59 (1974), pp. 172–78; R.J. House and T.R. Mitchell, "Path-Goal Theory of Leadership," *Journal of Contemporary Business*, Autumn 1974, pp. 81–97; M.G. Evans, "Path-Goal Theory of Leadership," in *Leadership*, ed. L.L. Neider and C.A. Schriesheim (Greenwich, CT: Information Age Publishing, 2002), pp. 115–38.

26. Various thoughts about servant leadership are presented in L.C. Spears and M. Lawrence, eds., *Focus on Leadership: Servant Leadership* (New York: John Wiley & Sons, 2002).

27. "2006 Movers & Shakers," *Financial Planning*, January 2006, p. 1.

28. R.J. House, "Path-Goal Theory of Leadership: Lessons, Legacy, and a Reformulated Theory," *Leadership Quarterly* 7 (1996), pp. 323–52.

29. "Why Geotechnical Instruments Boss Draper Is One in a Million," *Birmingham Post* (United Kingdom), 2 June 2006, p. 26; N. Whitten, "Best Boss Sets Examples to Staff," *Evening Chronicle* (Newcastle, U.K.), 15 June 2006, p. 24.

30. J. Indvik, "Path-Goal Theory of Leadership: A Meta-Analysis," *Academy of Management Proceedings*, 1986, pp. 189–92; J.C. Wofford and L.Z. Liska, "Path-Goal Theories of Leadership: A Meta-Analysis," *Journal of Management* 19 (1993), pp. 857–76.

31. J.D. Houghton and S.K. Yoho, "Toward a Contingency Model of Leadership and Psychological Empowerment: When Should Self-Leadership Be Encouraged?" *Journal of Leadership & Organizational Studies* 11, no. 4 (2005), pp. 65–83.

32. R.T. Keller, "A Test of the Path-Goal Theory of Leadership with Need for Clarity as a Moderator in Research and Development Organizations," *Journal of Applied Psychology* 74 (1989), pp. 208–12.

33. C.A. Schriesheim and L.L. Neider, "Path-Goal Leadership Theory: The Long and Winding Road," *Leadership Quarterly* 7 (1996), pp. 317–21.

34. P. Hersey and K.H. Blanchard, *Management of Organizational Behavior: Utilizing Human Resources*, 5th ed. (Englewood Cliffs, NJ: Prentice Hall, 1988).

35. R.P. Vecchio, "Situational Leadership Theory: An Examination of a Prescriptive Theory," *Journal of Applied Psychology* 72 (1987), pp. 444–51; W. Blank, J.R. Weitzel, and S.G. Green, "A Test of the Situational Leadership Theory," *Personnel Psychology* 43 (1990), pp. 579–97; C.L. Graeff, "Evolution of Situational Leadership Theory: A Critical Review," *Leadership Quarterly* 8 (1997), pp. 153–70.

36. F.E. Fiedler, *A Theory of Leadership Effectiveness* (New York: McGraw-Hill, 1967); F.E. Fiedler and M.M. Chemers, *Leadership and Effective Management* (Glenview, IL: Scott, Foresman, 1974).

37. F.E. Fiedler, "Engineer the Job to Fit the Manager," *Harvard Business Review* 43, no. 5 (1965), pp. 115–22.

38. For a summary of criticisms, see Yukl, *Leadership in Organizations*, pp. 217–18.

39. N. Nicholson, *Executive Instinct* (New York: Crown, 2000).

40. This observation has also been made by C.A. Schriesheim, "Substitutes-for-

Leadership Theory: Development and Basic Concepts," *Leadership Quarterly* 8 (1997), pp. 103–8.

41. D.F. Elloy and A. Randolph, "The Effect of Superleader Behavior on Autonomous Work Groups in a Government Operated Railway Service," *Public Personnel Management* 26 (Summer 1997), pp. 257–72; C.C. Manz and H. Sims Jr., *The New SuperLeadership: Leading Others to Lead Themselves* (San Francisco: Berrett-Koehler, 2001).

42. M.L. Loughry, "Co-workers Are Watching: Performance Implications of Peer Monitoring," *Academy of Management Proceedings* (2002), pp. O1–O6.

43. C.C. Manz and C. Neck, *Mastering Self-Leadership*, 3rd ed. (Upper Saddle River, NJ: Prentice Hall, 2004).

44. P.M. Podsakoff and S.B. MacKenzie, "Kerr and Jermier's Substitutes for Leadership Model: Background, Empirical Assessment, and Suggestions for Future Research," *Leadership Quarterly* 8 (1997), pp. 117–32; S.D. Dionne et al., "Neutralizing Substitutes for Leadership Theory: Leadership Effects and Common-Source Bias," *Journal of Applied Psychology* 87, no. 3 (June 2002), pp. 454–64; J.R. Villa et al., "Problems with Detecting Moderators in Leadership Research Using Moderated Multiple Regression," *Leadership Quarterly* 14, no. 1 (February 2003), pp. 3–23; S.D. Dionne et al., "Substitutes for Leadership, or Not," *The Leadership Quarterly* 16, no. 1 (2005), pp. 169–93.

45. J.M. Burns, *Leadership* (New York: Harper & Row, 1978); B.M. Bass, *Transformational Leadership: Industrial, Military, and Educational Impact* (Hillsdale, NJ: Erlbaum, 1998); S.B. Proctor-Thomson and K.W. Parry, "What the Best Leaders Look Like," in *Leadership in the Antipodes: Findings, Implications, and a Leader Profile*, ed. K.W. Parry (Wellington, N.Z.: Institute of Policy Studies and Centre for the Study of Leadership, 2001), pp. 166–91; B.J. Avolio and F.J. Yammarino, eds., *Transformational and Charismatic Leadership: The Road Ahead* (Greenwich, CT: JAI Press, 2002).

46. V.L. Goodwin, J.C. Wofford, and J.L. Whittington, "A Theoretical and Empirical Extension to the Transformational Leadership Construct," *Journal of Organizational Behavior* 22 (November 2001), pp. 759–74.

47. A. Zaleznik, "Managers and Leaders: Are They Different?" *Harvard Business Review* 55, no. 5 (1977), pp. 67–78; W. Bennis and B. Nanus, *Leaders: The Strategies for Taking Charge* (New York: Harper & Row, 1985). For a recent discussion regarding managing versus leading, see G. Yukl and R. Lepsinger, "Why Integrating the Leading and Managing Roles Is Essential for Organizational Effectiveness," *Organizational Dynamics* 34, no. 4 (2005), pp. 361–75.

48. Both transformational and transactional leadership improve work unit performance. See B.M. Bass et al., "Predicting Unit Performance by Assessing Transformational and Transactional Leadership," *Journal of Applied Psychology* 88 (April 2003), pp. 207–18. This point is also argued in Yukl and Lepsinger, "Why Integrating the Leading and Managing Roles Is Essential for Organizational Effectiveness."

49. For discussion of the tendency to slide from transformational to transactional leadership, see W. Bennis, *An Invented Life: Reflections on Leadership and Change* (Reading, MA: Addison-Wesley, 1993).

50. R.J. House, "A 1976 Theory of Charismatic Leadership," in *Leadership: The Cutting Edge*, ed. J.G. Hunt and L.L. Larson (Carbondale, IL.: Southern Illinois University Press, 1977), pp. 189–207; J.A. Conger, "Charismatic and Transformational Leadership in Organizations: An Insider's Perspective on These Developing Streams of Research," *Leadership Quarterly* 10 (Summer 1999), pp. 145–79.

51. J. Barbuto, J.E., "Taking the Charisma out of Transformational Leadership," *Journal of Social Behavior & Personality* 12 (September 1997), p. 689–97; Y.A. Nur, "Charisma and Managerial Leadership: The Gift That Never Was," *Business Horizons* 41 (July 1998), pp. 19–26; M.D. Mumford and J.R. Van Doorn, "The Leadership of Pragmatism-Reconsidering Franklin in the Age of Charisma," *Leadership Quarterly* 12, no. 3 (Fall 2001), pp. 279–309.

52. R.E. De Vries, R.A. Roe, and T.C.B. Taillieu, "On Charisma and Need for Leadership," *European Journal of Work and Organizational Psychology* 8 (1999), pp. 109–33; R. Khurana, *Searching for a Corporate Savior: The Irrational Quest for Charismatic CEOs* (Princeton, NJ: Princeton University Press, 2002).

53. Bennis and Nanus, *Leaders*, pp. 27–33, 89; I.M. Levin, "Vision Revisited," *Journal of Applied Behavioral Science* 36 (March 2000), pp. 91–107; J.R. Sparks and J.A. Schenk, "Explaining the Effects of Transformational Leadership: An Investigation of the Effects of Higher-Order Motives in Multilevel Marketing Organizations," *Journal of Organizational Behavior* 22 (2001), pp. 849–69; D. Christenson and D.H.T. Walker, "Understanding the Role of 'Vision' in Project Success," *Project Management Journal* 35, no. 3 (September 2004), pp. 39–52; R.E. Quinn, *Building the Bridge as You Walk on It: A Guide for Leading Change* (San Francisco: Jossey-Bass, 2004), Chapter 11.

54. J.R. Baum, E.A. Locke, and S.A. Kirkpatrick, "A Longitudinal Study of the Relation of Vision and Vision Communication to Venture Growth in Entrepreneurial Firms," *Journal of Applied Psychology* 83 (1998), pp. 43–54; S.L. Hoe and S.L. McShane, "Leadership Antecedents of Informal Knowledge Acquisition and Dissemination," *International Journal of Organisational Behaviour* 5 (2002), pp. 282–91.

55. J.A. Conger, "Inspiring Others: The Language of Leadership," *Academy of Management Executive* 5 (February 1991), pp. 31–45; G.T. Fairhurst and R.A. Sarr, *The Art of Framing: Managing the Language of Leadership* (San Francisco: Jossey-Bass, 1996); A.E. Rafferty and M.A. Griffin, "Dimensions of Transformational Leadership: Conceptual and Empirical Extensions," *Leadership Quarterly* 15, no. 3 (2004), pp. 329–54.

56. L. Black, "Hamburger Diplomacy," *Report on Business Magazine*, August 1988, pp. 30–36.

57. D.E. Berlew, "Leadership and Organizational Excitement," *California Management Review* 17, no. 2 (Winter 1974), pp. 21–30; Bennis and Nanus, *Leaders*, pp. 43–55; T. Simons, "Behavioral Integrity: The Perceived Alignment between Managers' Words and Deeds as a Research Focus," *Organization Science* 13, no. 1 (January-February 2002), pp. 18–35.

58 C. Salter, "Customer-Centered Leader Chick-fil-A," *Fast Company*, October 2004, pp. 83–84; L. Cannon, "2005 Golden Chain: Dan T. Cathy," *Nation's Restaurant News*, 19 September 2005; H. Jett, "Businesses Use Grand Openings to Attract Audience, Establish Roots," *Free Lance-Star* (Fredericksburg, Virginia), 24 March 2005.

59. M. Webb, "Executive Profile: Peter C. Farrell," *San Diego Business Journal*, 24 March 2003, p. 32; P. Benesh, "He Likes Them Breathing Easy," *Investor's Business*

Daily, 13 September 2005, p. A04; C. Hymowitz, "Today's Bosses Find Mentoring Isn't Worth the Time and Risks," *The Wall Street Journal*, 13 March 2006, p. B1. The two surveys are reported in ISR, "Driving an Innovative Culture: Insights from Global Research and Implications for Businesses in Hong Kong" (ISR, 2004), www.isrsurveys.com.au/pdf/insight/IHRM%20Show-18Nov04.pdf (accessed 22 December 2005); Watson Wyatt Worldwide, "Worktaiwan: Key Findings" (Singapore: Watson Wyatt Worldwide, 2004), www.watsonwyatt.com/asia-pacific/research/workasia/worktw_keyfindings.asp (accessed 2 December 2005).

60. J. Barling, T. Weber, and E.K. Kelloway, "Effects of Transformational Leadership Training on Attitudinal and Financial Outcomes: A Field Experiment," *Journal of Applied Psychology* 81 (1996), pp. 827–32.

61. A. Bryman, "Leadership in Organizations," in *Handbook of Organization Studies*, ed. S.R. Clegg, C. Hardy, and W.R. Nord (Thousand Oaks, CA: Sage, 1996), pp. 276–92.

62. B.S. Pawar and K.K. Eastman, "The Nature and Implications of Contextual Influences on Transformational Leadership: A Conceptual Examination," *Academy of Management Review* 22 (1997), pp. 80–109; C.P. Egri and S. Herman, "Leadership in the North American Environmental Sector: Values, Leadership Styles, and Contexts of Environmental Leaders and Their Organizations," *Academy of Management Journal* 43, no. 4 (2000), pp. 571–604.

63. J.R. Meindl, "On Leadership: An Alternative to the Conventional Wisdom," *Research in Organizational Behavior* 12 (1990), pp. 159–203; L.R. Offermann, J. J.K. Kennedy, and P.W. Wirtz, "Implicit Leadership Theories: Content, Structure, and Generalizability," *Leadership Quarterly* 5, no. 1 (1994), pp. 43–58; R.J. Hall and R.G. Lord, "Multi-Level Information Processing Explanations of Followers' Leadership Perceptions," *Leadership Quarterly* 6 (1995), pp. 265–87; O. Epitropaki and R. Martin, "Implicit Leadership Theories in Applied Settings: Factor Structure, Generalizability, and Stability over Time," *Journal of Applied Psychology* 89, no. 2 (2004), pp. 293–310.

64. L.M.A. Chong and D.C. Thomas, "Leadership Perceptions in Cross-Cultural Context: Pakeha and Pacific Islanders in New Zealand," *Leadership Quarterly* 8 (1997), pp. 275–93; R.G. Lord et al., "Contextual Constraints on Prototype Generation and Their Multilevel Consequences for Leadership Perceptions," *The Leadership Quarterly* 12, no. 3 (2001), p. 311–38; T. Keller, "Parental Images as a Guide to Leadership Sensemaking: An Attachment Perspective on Implicit Leadership Theories," *Leadership Quarterly* 14 (2003), pp. 141–60.

65. S.F. Cronshaw and R.G. Lord, "Effects of Categorization, Attribution, and Encoding Processes on Leadership Perceptions," *Journal of Applied Psychology* 72 (1987), pp. 97–106; J.L. Nye and D.R. Forsyth, "The Effects of Prototype-Based Biases on Leadership Appraisals: A Test of Leadership Categorization Theory," *Small Group Research* 22 (1991), pp. 360–79.

66. R. Weber et al., "The Illusion of Leadership: Misattribution of Cause in Coordination Games," *Organization Science* 12, no. 5 (2001), pp. 582–98; N. Ensari and S.E. Murphy, "Cross-Cultural Variations in Leadership Perceptions and Attribution of Charisma to the Leader," *Organizational Behavior and Human Decision Processes* 92 (2003), pp. 52–66; M.L.A. Hayward, V.P. Rindova, and T.G. Pollock, "Believing One's Own Press: The Causes and Consequences of CEO Celebrity," *Strategic Management Journal* 25, no. 7 (July 2004), pp. 637–53.

67. Meindl, "On Leadership: An Alternative to the Conventional Wisdom," p. 163.

68. J. Pfeffer, "The Ambiguity of Leadership," *Academy of Management Review* 2 (1977), pp. 102–12.

69. M.P. Mangaliso, "Building Competitive Advantage from *Ubuntu*: Management Lessons from South Africa," *Academy of Management Executive* 15 (August 2001), pp. 23–43; L. van der Colff, "Leadership Lessons from the African Tree," *Management Decision* 41 (2003), pp. 257–61; L.L. Karsten and H. Illa, "*Ubuntu* as a Key African Management Concept: Contextual Background and Practical Insights for Knowledge Application," *Journal of Managerial Psychology* 20, no. 7 (July 2005), pp. 607–20. Speech by President Nelson Mandela at his 80th birthday party, Kruger National Park, 16 July 1998.

70. Six of the Project GLOBE clusters are described in a special issue of the *Journal of World Business* 37 (2000). For an overview of Project GLOBE, see House, Javidan, and Dorfman, "Project Globe: An Introduction"; House et al., "Understanding Cultures and Implicit Leadership Theories across the Globe: An Introduction to Project Globe."

71. J.C. Jesiuno, "Latin Europe Cluster: From South to North," *Journal of World Business* 37 (2002), p. 88. Another GLOBE study of Iranian managers also reported that charismatic visionary stands out as a primary leadership dimension. See A. Dastmalchian, M. Javidan, and K. Alam, "Effective Leadership and Culture in Iran: An Empirical Study," *Applied Psychology: An International Review* 50 (2001), pp. 532–58.

72. D.N. Den Hartog et al., "Culture Specific and Cross-Cultural Generalizable Implicit Leadership Theories: Are Attributes of Charismatic/Transformational Leadership Universally Endorsed?" *Leadership Quarterly* 10 (1999), pp. 219–56; F.C. Brodbeck et al., "Cultural Variation of Leadership Prototypes across 22 European Countries," *Journal of Occupational and Organizational Psychology* 73 (2000), pp. 1–29; E. Szabo et al., "The Europe Cluster: Where Employees Have a Voice," *Journal of World Business* 37 (2002), pp. 55–68. The Mexican study is reported in C.E. Nicholls, H.W. Lane, and M.B. Brechu, "Taking Self-Managed Teams to Mexico," *Academy of Management Executive* 13 (August 1999), pp. 15–25.

73. J.B. Rosener, "Ways Women Lead," *Harvard Business Review* 68 (November-December 1990), pp. 119–25; S.H. Appelbaum and B.T. Shaprio, "Why Can't Men Lead Like Women?" *Leadership and Organization Development Journal* 14 (1993), pp. 28–34; N. Wood, "Venus Rules," *Incentive* 172 (February 1998), pp. 22–27.

74. G.N. Powell, "One More Time: Do Female and Male Managers Differ?" *Academy of Management Executive* 4 (1990), pp. 68–75; M.L. van Engen and T.M. Willemsen, "Sex and Leadership Styles: A Meta-Analysis of Research Published in the 1990s," *Psychological Reports* 94, no. 1 (February 2004), pp. 3–18.

75. R. Sharpe, "As Leaders, Women Rule," *BusinessWeek*, 20 November 2000, p. 74; M. Sappenfield, "Women, It Seems, Are Better Bosses," *Christian Science Monitor*, 16 January 2001; A.H. Eagly and L.L. Carli, "The Female Leadership Advantage: An Evaluation of the Evidence," *The Leadership Quarterly* 14, no. 6 (December 2003), pp. 807–34; A.H. Eagly, M.C. Johannesen-Schmidt, and M.L. van Engen, "Transformational, Transactional,

and Laissez-Faire Leadership Styles: A Meta-Analysis Comparing Women and Men," *Psychological Bulletin* 129 (July 2003), pp. 569–91.

76. A.H. Eagly, S.J. Karau, and M.G. Makhijani, "Gender and the Effectiveness of Leaders: A Meta-Analysis," *Psychological Bulletin* 117 (1995), pp. 125–45; J.G. Oakley, "Gender-Based Barriers to Senior Management Positions: Understanding the Scarcity of Female CEOs," *Journal of Business Ethics* 27 (2000), pp. 821–34; N.Z. Stelter, "Gender Differences in Leadership: Current Social Issues and Future Organizational Implications," *Journal of Leadership Studies* 8 (2002), pp. 88–99; M. E. Heilman et al., "Penalties for Success: Reactions to Women Who Succeed at Male Gender-Typed Tasks," *Journal of Applied Psychology* 89, no. 3 (2004), pp. 416–27; A.H. Eagly, "Achieving Relational Authenticity in Leadership: Does Gender Matter?" *The Leadership Quarterly* 16, no. 3 (June 2005), pp. 459–74.

CHAPTER 15

1. L. Sinclair, "Morris Vows to Aid and Abet Nitro," *The Australian*, 30 September 2004, p. 21; "Nimble Nitro Steals a March on the Big Networks," *Marketing Week*, 9 June 2005, p. 13; P. Chatterjee, "'India Vital Part of Our Jigsaw,'" *Business Line* (The Hindu, India), 17 November 2005, p. 1; S. Elliott, "Watch Out, Giant Agencies. Boutique Shops Like Nitro Are Winning Some Big Clients," *The New York Times*, 4 April 2005, p. 6; E. Hall, "Nitro Takes 'Substantial' Chunk of UK's Soul," *Advertising Age*, 18 April 2005, p. 22; A. Hargrave-Silk, "Chen Named Chairman for Nitro Greater China," *Media*, 6 May 2005; N. Shatrujeet, "The Light at Lowe," *Economic Times* (India), 29 June 2005. Also see www.nitro-group.com.

2. S. Ranson, R. Hinings, and R. Greenwood, "The Structuring of Organizational Structure," *Administrative Science Quarterly* 25 (1980), pp. 1–14.

3. J.-E. Johanson, "Intraorganizational Influence," *Management Communication Quarterly* 13 (February 2000), pp. 393–435.

4. B. Morris, "Charles Schwab's Big Challenge," *Fortune*, 30 May 2005, p. 88.

5. H. Mintzberg, *The Structuring of Organizations* (Englewood Cliffs, NJ: Prentice Hall, 1979), pp. 2–3.

6. E.E. Lawler III, *Motivation in Work Organizations* (Monterey,CA: Brooks/Cole, 1973); M.A. Campion, "Ability Requirement Implications of Job Design: An Interdisciplinary Perspective," *Personnel Psychology* 42 (1989), pp. 1–24.

7. Mintzberg, *The Structuring of Organizations*, pp. 2–8; D.A. Nadler and M.L. Tushman, *Competing by Design: The Power of Organizational Architecture* (New York: Oxford University Press, 1997), Chapter 6.

8. C. Downs, P. Clampitt, and A.L. Pfeiffer, "Communication and Organizational Outcomes," in *Handbook of Organizational Communication*, ed. G. Goldhaber and G. Barnett (Norwood, NJ: Ablex, 1988), pp. 171–211; I. Nonaka and H. Takeuchi, *The Knowledge-Creating Company* (New York: Oxford University Press, 1995).

9. A.L. Patti, J.P. Gilbert, and S. Hartman, "Physical Co-Location and the Success of New Product Development Projects," *Engineering Management Journal* 9 (September 1997), pp. 31–37; M. Hoque, M. Akter, and Y. Monden, "Concurrent Engineering: A Compromise Approach to Develop a Feasible and Customer-Pleasing Product," *International Journal of Production Research* 43, no. 8 (15 April 2005), pp. 1607–24.

10. For a discussion of the role of brand manager at Procter & Gamble, see C. Peale, "Branded for Success," *Cincinnati Enquirer* (20 May 2001), p. A1. Details about how to design integrator roles in organizational structures are presented in J.R. Galbraith, *Designing Organizations* (San Francisco: Jossey-Bass, 2002), pp. 66–72.

11. Fayol's work is summarized in J.B. Miner, *Theories of Organizational Structure and Process* (Chicago: Dryden, 1982), pp. 358–66.

12. Y.-M. Hsieh and A. Tien-Hsieh, "Enhancement of Service Quality with Job Standardisation," *Service Industries Journal* 21 (July 2001), pp. 147–66.

13. D. Drickhamer, "Lessons from the Leading Edge," *Industry Week*, 21 February 2000, pp. 23–26.

14. D.D. Van Fleet and B.A.G., "A History of the Span of Management," *Academy of Management Review* 2 (1977), pp. 356–72; Mintzberg, *The Structuring of Organizations*, Chapter 8.

15. J. Greenwald, "Ward Compares the Best with the Rest," *Business Insurance*, 26 August 2002, p. 16.

16. J.H. Gittell, "Supervisory Span, Relational Coordination, and Flight Departure Performance: A Reassessment of Postbureaucracy Theory," *Organization Science* 12, no. 4 (July–August 2001), pp. 468–83.

17. "BASF Culling Saves (GBP) 4M," *Personnel Today* (19 February 2002), p. 3.

18. T. Peters, *Thriving on Chaos* (New York: Knopf, 1987), p. 359.

19. Q.N. Huy, "In Praise of Middle Managers," *Harvard Business Review* 79 (September 2001), pp. 72–79; H.J. Leavitt, *Top Down: Why Hierarchies Are Here to Stay and How to Manage Them More Effectively* (Cambridge: Harvard Business School Press, 2005).

20. A. Lashinsky, "The Hurd Way," *Fortune*, 17 April 2006, p. 92.

21. W. Stueck, "Revamped Barrick Keeps Eyes on the Hunt for the Golden Prize," *Globe & Mail*, 17 September 2005, p. B4.

22. P. Brabeck, "The Business Case against Revolution: An Interview with Nestle's Peter Brabeck," *Harvard Business Review* 79 (February 2001), p. 112; H.A. Richardson et al., "Does Decentralization Make a Difference for the Organization? An Examination of the Boundary Conditions Circumscribing Decentralized Decision Making and Organizational Financial Performance," *Journal of Management* 28, no. 2 (2002), pp. 217–44; G. Masado, "To Centralize or Decentralize?" *Optimize*, May 2005, p. 58.

23. Mintzberg, *The Structuring of Organizations*, Chapter 5.

24. T. Burns and G. Stalker, *The Management of Innovation* (London: Tavistock, 1961).

25. D. Youngblood, "Computer Consultants Win Business with Creative Strategies," *Star Tribune* (Minneapolis, MN), 15 July 2001; S. Brouillard, "Right at Home," *Minneapolis-St. Paul Business Journal*, 23 August 2002; J. Fure, "Staying Connected," *Minneapolis-St. Paul Business Journal*, 20 August 2004.

26. J. Tata, S. Prasad, and R. Thom, "The Influence of Organizational Structure on the Effectiveness of TQM Programs," *Journal of Managerial Issues* 11, no. 4 (Winter 1999), pp. 440–53; A. Lam, "Tacit Knowledge, Organizational Learning and Societal Institutions: An Integrated Framework," *Organization Studies* 21 (May 2000), pp. 487–513.

27. W.D. Sine, H. Mitsuhashi, and D.A. Kirsch, "2006," *Academy of Management Journal* 49, no. 1, pp. 121–32.

28. Mintzberg, *The Structuring of Organizations*, p. 106.

29. Mintzberg, *The Structuring of Organizations*, Chapter 17.

30. Galbraith, *Designing Organizations*, pp. 23–25.

31. E.E. Lawler III, *Rewarding Excellence: Pay Strategies for the New Economy* (San Francisco: Jossey-Bass, 2000), pp. 31–34.

32. These structures were identified from corporate Web sites and annual reports. These companies include a mixture of other structures, so the charts shown are adapted for learning purposes.

33. M. Goold and A. Campbell, "Do You Have a Well-Designed Organization?" *Harvard Business Review* 80 (March 2002), pp. 117–24.

34. J.R. Galbraith, "Structuring Global Organizations," in *Tomorrow's Organization*, ed. S.A. Mohrman et al. (San Francisco: Jossey-Bass, 1998), pp. 103–29; C. Homburg, J.P. Workman Jr., and O. Jensen, "Fundamental Changes in Marketing Organization: The Movement toward a Customer-focused Organizational Structure," *Academy of Marketing Science. Journal* 28 (Fall 2000), pp. 459–78; T. H. Davenport, J.G. Harris, and A.K. Kohli, "How Do They Know Their Customers So Well?" *Sloan Management Review* 42 (Winter 2001), pp. 63–73; J.R. Galbraith, "Organizing to Deliver Solutions," *Organizational Dynamics* 31 (2002), pp. 194–207.

35. D. Robey, *Designing Organizations*, 3rd ed. (Homewood, IL: Irwin, 1991), pp. 191–97.

36. R. Muzyka and G. Zeschuk, "Managing Multiple Projects," *Game Developer*, March 2003, pp. 34–42; M. Saltzman, "The Ex-Doctors Are In," *National Post*, 24 March 2004, p. AL4; R. McConnell, "For Edmonton's Bioware, Today's the Big Day," *Edmonton Journal*, 14 April 2005, p. C1.

37. R.C. Ford and W.A. Randolph, "Cross-Functional Structures: A Review and Integration of Matrix Organization and Project Management," *Journal of Management* 18 (1992), pp. 267–94.

38. J. Teresko, "Transforming GM," *Industry Week*, December/January 2002, pp. 34–38; E. Prewitt, "GM's Matrix Reloads," *CIO Magazine*, 1 September 2003.

39. G. Calabrese, "Communication and Cooperation in Product Development: A Case Study of a European Car Producer," *R & D Management* 27 (July 1997), pp. 239–52; T. Sy and L.S. D'Annunzio, "Challenges and Strategies of Matrix Organizations: Top-Level and Mid-Level Managers' Perspectives," *Human Resource Planning* 28, no. 1 (2005), pp. 39–48.

40. Nadler and Tushman, *Competing by Design*, Chapter 6; M. Goold and A. Campbell, "Structured Networks: Toward the Well-Designed Matrix," *Long Range Planning* 36, no. 5 (October 2003), pp. 427–39.

41. "Lean Manufacturing Increases Productivity, Decreases Cycle Time," *Industrial Equipment News*, October 2005.

42. J.R. Galbraith, E.E. Lawler III, and Associates, *Organizing for the Future: The New Logic for Managing Complex Organizations* (San Francisco, CA: Jossey-Bass, 1993); R. Bettis and M. Hitt, "The New Competitive Landscape," *Strategic Management Journal* 16 (1995), pp. 7–19.

43. P.C. Ensign, "Interdependence, Coordination, and Structure in Complex Organizations: Implications for Organization Design," *Mid-Atlantic Journal of Business* 34 (March 1998), pp. 5–22.

44. M.M. Fanning, "A Circular Organization Chart Promotes a Hospital-Wide Focus on Teams," *Hospital & Health Services Administration* 42 (June 1997), pp. 243–54; L.Y. Chan and B.E. Lynn, "Operating in Turbulent Times: How Ontario's Hospitals Are Meeting the Current Funding Crisis," *Health Care Management Review* 23 (June 1998), pp. 7–18.

45. R. Cross, "Looking before You Leap: Assessing the Jump to Teams in Knowledge-Based Work," *Business Horizons* (September 2000); M. Fenton-O'Creevy, "Employee Involvement and the Middle Manager: Saboteur or Scapegoat?" *Human Resource Management Journal* 11 (2001), pp. 24–40; G. Garda, K. Lindstrom, and M. Dallnera, "Toward a Learning Organization: The Introduction of a Client-Centered Team-Based Organization in Administrative Surveying Work," *Applied Ergonomics* 34 (2003), pp. 97–105; C. Douglas and W.L. Gardner, "Transition to Self-Directed Work Teams: Implications of Transition Time and Self-Monitoring for Managers' Use of Influence Tactics," *Journal of Organizational Behavior* 25 (2004), pp. 47–65.

46. P. Siekman, "This Is Not a BMW Plant," *Fortune*, 18 April 2005, p. 208.

47. R.F. Miles and C.C. Snow, "The New Network Firm: A Spherical Structure Built on a Human Investment Philosophy," *Organizational Dynamics* 23, no. 4 (1995), pp. 5–18; C. Baldwin and K. Clark, "Managing in an Age of Modularity," *Harvard Business Review* 75 (September–October 1997), pp. 84–93.

48. J. Hagel III and M. Singer, "Unbundling the Corporation," *Harvard Business Review* 77 (March–April 1999), pp. 133–41; R. Hacki and J. Lighton, "The Future of the Networked Company," *McKinsey Quarterly* 3 (2001), pp. 26–39.

49. M.A. Schilling and H.K. Steensma, "The Use of Modular Organizational Forms: An Industry-Level Analysis," *Academy of Management Journal* 44 (December 2001), pp. 1149–68.

50. W.H. Davidow and T.W. Malone, *The Virtual Corporation* (New York: Harper Business, 1992); L. Fried, *Managing Information Technology in Turbulent Times* (New York: John Wiley and Sons, 1995).

51. C. Taylor, "Agency Teams Balancing in an Ever-Changing Media World," *Media Week* (1 June 2001), p. 20.

52. G. Morgan, *Images of Organization*, 2nd ed. (Newbury Park, CA: Sage, 1996); G. Morgan, *Imagin-I-Zation: New Mindsets for Seeing, Organizing, and Managing* (Thousand Oaks, CA: Sage, 1997).

53. H. Chesbrough and D.J. Teece, "When Is Virtual Virtuous? Organizing for Innovation," *Harvard Business Review* (January–February 1996), pp. 65–73; P.M.J. Christie and R. Levary, "Virtual Corporations: Recipe for Success," *Industrial Management* 40 (July 1998), pp. 7–11.

54. L. Donaldson, *The Contingency Theory of Organizations* (Thousand Oaks, CA: Sage, 2001); J. Birkenshaw, R. Nobel, and J. Ridderstrâle, "Knowledge as a Contingency Variable: Do the Characteristics of Knowledge Predict Organizational Structure?" *Organization Science* 13, no. 3 (May–June 2002), pp. 274–89.

55. P.R. Lawrence and J.W. Lorsch, *Organization and Environment* (Homewood, IL: Irwin, 1967); Mintzberg, *The Structuring of Organizations*, Chapter 15.

56. Burns and Stalker, *The Management of Innovation*; Lawrence and Lorsch, Organization and Environment.

57. J.G. Kelley, "Slurpees and Sausages: 7-Eleven Holds School," *Richmond (Virginia) Times-Dispatch*, 12 March 2004, p. C1; S. Marling, "The 24-Hour Supply Chain," *InformationWeek*, 26 January 2004, p. 43.

58. Mintzberg, *The Structuring of Organizations*, p. 282.

59. D.S. Pugh and C.R. Hinings, *Organizational Structure: Extensions and Replications* (Farnborough, England: Lexington Books, 1976); Mintzberg, *The Structuring of Organizations*, Chapter 13.

60. G. Hertel, S. Geister, and U. Konradt, "Managing Virtual Teams: A Review of Current Empirical Research," *Human Resource Management Review* 15 (2005), pp. 69–95.

61. C. Perrow, "A Framework for the Comparative Analysis of Organizations," *American Sociological Review* 32 (1967), pp. 194–208; D. Gerwin, "The Comparative Analysis of Structure and Technology: A Critical Appraisal," *Academy of Management Review* 4, no. 1 (1979), pp. 41–51; C.C. Miller et al., "Understanding Technology–Structure Relationships: Theory Development and Meta-Analytic Theory Testing," *Academy of Management Journal* 34, no. 2 (1991), pp. 370–99.

62. R.H. Kilmann, *Beyond the Quick Fix* (San Francisco: Jossey-Bass, 1984), p. 38.

63. A.D. Chandler, *Strategy and Structure* (Cambridge, MA: MIT Press, 1962).

64. A.M. Porter, *Competitive Strategy* (New York: The Free Press, 1980).

65. D. Miller, "Configurations of Strategy and Structure," *Strategic Management Journal* 7 (1986), pp. 233–49.

CHAPTER 16

1. F. Vogelstein and E. Florian, "Can Schwab Get Its Mojo Back?" *Fortune*, 17 September 2001, p. 93; B. Morris, "When Bad Things Happen to Good Companies," *Fortune*, 8 December 2003, p. 78; S. Craig and K. Brown, "Schwab Ousts Pottruck as CEO," *The Wall Street Journal*, 21 July 2004, p. A1; R. Frank, "U.S. Trust Feels Effects of Switch," *The Wall Street Journal*, 21 July 2004, p. A8; R. Frank and S. Craig, "White-Shoe Shuffle," *The Wall Street Journal*, 15 September 2004, p. A1; C. Harrington, "Made in Heaven? Watching the Watchovia–Tanager Union," *Accounting Today*, 20 December 2004, p. 18; J. Kador, "Cultures in Conflict," *Registered Rep.*, October 2004, p. 43.

2. A. Williams, P. Dobson, and M. Walters, *Changing Culture: New Organizational Approaches* (London: Institute of Personnel Management, 1989); E.H. Schein, "What Is Culture?" in *Reframing Organizational Culture*, ed. P.J. Frost et al. (Beverly Hills, CA: Sage, 1991), pp. 243–53.

3. Williams, Dobson, and Walters, *Changing Culture: New Organizational Approaches*; Schein, "What Is Culture?"

4. B.M. Meglino and E.C. Ravlin, "Individual Values in Organizations: Concepts, Controversies, and Research," *Journal of Management* 24, no. 3 (1998), pp. 351–89; B.R. Agle and C.B. Caldwell, "Understanding Research on Values in Business," *Business and Society* 38, no. 3 (September 1999), pp. 326–87; S. Hitlin and J.A. Pilavin, "Values: Reviving a Dormant Concept," *Annual Review of Sociology* 30 (2004), pp. 359–93.

5. N.M. Ashkanasy, "The Case for Culture," in *Debating Organization*, ed. R. Westwood and S. Clegg (Malden, MA: Blackwell, 2003), pp. 300–10.

6. Edgar Schein's original model suggested that organizational culture consists of espoused values; but others have subsequently pointed out that enacted values are a more logical part of culture because enacted values are consistent with other elements of the model, namely shared assumptions on one side and artifacts on the other. See D. Denison, "Organizational Culture: Can It Be a Key Lever for Driving Organizational Change?" in *International Handbook of Culture and Climate*, ed. C. Cooper, S. Cartwright, and P.C. Earley (New York: John Wiley & Sons, 2000).

7. M. Fan, "Cary, N.C., Software Firm Posts Steady Growth without IPO," *San Jose Mercury News*, 29 July 2001; B. Darrow, "James Goodnight, Founder and CEO, SAS Institute," *Computer Reseller News*, 12 December 2005, p. 23.

8. "New-Age Banks Bet on Variable Pay Plan," *Business Line* (India), 22 September 2003; "Golden Handshake, the ICICI Bank Way," *Financial Express* (India), 6 July 2003.

9. S. Huettel, "Soaring Ahead," *St. Petersburg Times* (Florida), 24 October 2005, p. 1D; E P. Lima, "Winning Cultures," *Air Transport World*, 1 February 2006, p. 54.

10. J.J. van Muijen, "Organizational Culture," in *A Handbook of Work and Organizational Psychology: Organizational Psychology*, ed. P.J.D. Drenth, H. Thierry, and C.J. de Wolff, 2nd ed. (East Sussex, UK: Psychology Press, 1998), pp. 113–32.

11. M. Miller, "The Acrobat," *Forbes*, 15 March 2004, pp. 100n3; R. Ouzounian, "Cirque's Dream Factory," *Toronto Star*, 1 August 2004; "Cirque Du Soleil's Creator Goes from a Busker to a Billionaire," *Knight Ridder Tribune Business News*, 9 January 2005, p. 1; P. Donnelly, "Grandiose at the Grand," *The Gazette* (Montreal), 29 January 2005, p. D1; L. Tischler, "Join the Circus," *Fast Company*, July 2005, pp. 52–58.

12. J.S. Ott, *The Organizational Culture Perspective* (Pacific Grove, CA: Brooks/Cole, 1989), pp. 45–47; S. Sackmann, "Culture and Subcultures: An Analysis of Organizational Knowledge," *Administrative Science Quarterly* 37 (1992), pp. 140–61.

13. A. Sinclair, "Approaches to Organizational Culture and Ethics," *Journal of Business Ethics* 12 (1993); A. Boisnier and J. Chatman, "The Role of Subcultures in Agile Organizations," in *Leading and Managing People in Dynamic Organizations*, ed. R. Petersen and E. Mannix (Mahwah, NJ: Lawrence Erlbaum Associates, 2003), pp. 87–112.

14. Ott, *The Organizational Culture Perspective*, Chapter 2; J.S. Pederson and J.S. Sorensen, *Organizational Cultures in Theory and Practice* (Aldershot, England: Gower, 1989), pp. 27–29; M.O. Jones, *Studying Organizational Symbolism: What, How, Why?* (Thousand Oaks, CA: Sage, 1996).

15. E.H. Schein, "Organizational Culture," *American Psychologist*, February 1990, pp. 109–19; A. Furnham and B. Gunter, "Corporate Culture: Definition, Diagnosis, and Change," *International Review of Industrial and Organizational Psychology* 8 (1993), pp. 233–61; E.H. Schein, *The Corporate Culture Survival Guide* (San Francisco: Jossey-Bass, 1999), Chapter 4.

16. M. Doehrman, "Anthropologists–Deep in the Corporate Bush," *Daily Record* (Kansas City, MO), 19 July 2005, p. 1.

17. A.L. Wilkins, "Organizational Stories as Symbols Which Control the Organization," in *Organizational Symbolism*, ed. L.R. Pondy et al. (Greenwich, CT: JAI Press, 1984), pp. 81–92; R. Zemke, "Storytelling: Back to a Basic," *Training* 27 (March 1990), pp. 44–50; J.C. Meyer, "Tell Me a Story: Eliciting Organizational Values from Narratives," *Communication Quarterly* 43 (1995), pp. 210–24; W. Swap et al., "Using Mentoring and Storytelling to Transfer Knowledge in the Workplace," *Journal of Management Information Systems* 18 (Summer 2001), pp. 95–114.

18. "The Ultimate Chairman," *Business Times Singapore*, 3 September 2005.

19. D. Roth, "My Job at the Container Store," *Fortune*, 10 January 2000, pp. 74–78.

20. R.E. Quinn and N.T. Snyder, "Advance Change Theory: Culture Change at Whirlpool Corporation," in *The Leader's Change Handbook*, ed. J.A. Conger, G.M. Spreitzer, and E.E. Lawler III (San Francisco: Jossey-Bass, 1999), pp. 162–93.

21. Churchill apparently made this statement on October 28, 1943, in the British House of Commons, when London, damaged by bombings in World War II, was about to be rebuilt.

22. P. Roberts, "The Empire Strikes Back," *Fast Company* 22 (February–March 1999), pp. 122-31. Some details are also found at www.oakley.com and americahurrah.com/Oakley/Entry.htm.

23. A. D'Innocenzio, "Wal-Mart's Town Becomes New Address for Corporate America," *Associated Press*, 19 September 2003; J. Useem, "One Nation under Wal-Mart," *Fortune*, 3 March 2003, pp. 65–78.

24. T.E. Deal and A.A. Kennedy, *Corporate Cultures* (Reading, MA: Addison-Wesley, 1982); J.B. Barney, "Organizational Culture: Can It Be a Source of Sustained Competitive Advantage?" *Academy of Management Review* 11 (1986), pp. 656–65; C. Siehl and J. Martin, "Organizational Culture: A Key to Financial Performance?" in *Organizational Climate and Culture*, ed. B. Schneider (San Francisco: Jossey-Bass, 1990), pp. 241–81; C.P.M. Wilderom, U. Glunk, and R. Maslowski, "Organizational Culture as a Predictor of Organizational Performance," in *Handbook of Organizational Culture and Climate*, ed. N.M. Ashkanasy, C.P.M. Wilderom, and M.F. Peterson (Thousand Oaks, CA: Sage, 2000), pp. 193–210; C.F. Fey and D.R. Denison, "Organizational Culture and Effectiveness: Can American Theory Be Applied to Russia?" *Organization Science* 14, no. 6 (2003), pp. 686–706; A. Carmeli and A. Tishler, "The Relationships between Intangible Organizational Elements and Organizational Performance," *Strategic Management Journal* 25 (2004), pp. 1257–78.

25. C.A. O'Reilly and J.A. Chatman, "Culture as Social Control: Corporations, Cults, and Commitment," *Research in Organizational Behavior* 18 (1996), pp. 157–200; J.C. Helms Mills and A.J. Mills, "Rules, Sensemaking, Formative Contexts, and Discourse in the Gendering of Organizational Culture," in *International Handbook of Organizational Climate and Culture*, ed. N. Ashkanasy, C. Wilderom, and M. Peterson (Thousand Oaks, CA: Sage, 2000), pp. 55–70; J.A. Chatman and S.E. Cha, "Leading by Leveraging Culture," *California Management Review* 45 (Summer 2003), pp. 20–34.

26. B. Ashforth and F. Mael, "Social Identity Theory and the Organization," *Academy of Management Review* 14 (1989), pp. 20–39.

27. M.R. Louis, "Surprise and Sensemaking: What Newcomers Experience in Entering Unfamiliar Organizational Settings," *Administrative Science Quarterly* 25 (1980), pp. 226–51; S.G. Harris, "Organizational Culture and Individual Sensemaking: A Schema-Based Perspective," *Organization Science* 5 (1994), pp. 309–21.

28. D.R. Denison, *Corporate Culture and Organizational Effectiveness* (New York: Wiley, 1990); G.G. Gordon and N. DiTomasco, "Predicting Corporate Performance from Organizational Culture," *Journal of Management Studies* 29 (1992), pp. 783–98; J.P. Kotter and J.L. Heskett, *Corporate Culture and Performance* (New York: Free Press, 1992).

29. A. Holeck, "Griffith, Ind., Native Takes over as Steel Plant Manager," *The Times* (Munster, Ind.), 24 May 2003.

30. Kotter and Heskett, *Corporate Culture and Performance*; J.P. Kotter, "Cultures and Coalitions," *Executive Excellence* 15 (March 1998), pp. 14–15.

31. The features of adaptive cultures are described in W.F. Joyce, *MegaChange: How Today's Leading Companies Have Transformed Their Workforces* (New York: Free Press, 1999), pp. 44–47.

32. M. Acharya, "A Matter of Business Ethics," *Kitchener-Waterloo Record*, 23 March 1999, p. C2.

33. D. Griesing, "'Boot Camp' Failed to Teach All They Could Be," *Chicago Tribune*, 21 April 2002, p. C1; B.L. Toffler, *Final Accounting: Ambition, Greed, and the Fall of Arthur Andersen* (New York: Broadway Books, 2003).

34. "Japanese Officials Order Citibank to Halt Some Operations," *Dow Jones Business News*, 17 September 2004; "Citigroup CEO Prince Holds Press Conference in Japan," *Business Wire* (Tokyo), 25 October 2004; A. Morse, "Citigroup Extends Apology to Japan," *The Wall Street Journal*, 26 October 2004, p. A3; M. Pacelle, M. Fackler, and A. Morse, "Mission Control," *The Wall Street Journal*, 22 December 2004, p. A1.

35. M.L. Marks, "Adding Cultural Fit to Your Diligence Checklist," *Mergers & Acquisitions* 34, no. 3 (November–December 1999), pp. 14–20; Schein, *The Corporate Culture Survival Guide*, Chapter 8; M.L. Marks, "Mixed Signals," *Across the Board*, May 2000, pp. 21–26; J.P. Daly, R. W. Pouder, and B. Kabanoff, "The Effects of Initial Differences in Firms' Espoused Values on Their Postmerger Performance," *Journal of Applied Behavioral Science* 40, no. 3 (September 2004), pp. 323–43.

36. A. Klein, "A Merger Taken AO-Ill," *Washington Post*, 21 October 2002, p. E1; A. Klein, *Stealing Time: Steve Case, Jerry Levin, and the Collapse of AOL Time Warner* (New York: Simon & Shuster, 2003).

37. E. Connors, "Not Drowning, Dancing," *Australian Financial Review*, 12 November 2004, p. 22.

38. S. Greengard, "Due Diligence: The Devil in the Details," *Workforce*, October 1999, p. 68; Marks, "Adding Cultural Fit to Your Diligence Checklist."

39. Greengard, "Due Diligence: The Devil in the Details"; Marks, "Adding Cultural Fit to Your Diligence Checklist."

40. A.R. Malekazedeh and A. Nahavandi, "Making Mergers Work by Managing Cultures," *Journal of Business Strategy*, May–June 1990, pp. 55–57; K.W. Smith, "A Brand-New Culture for the Merged Firm," *Mergers and Acquisitions* 35 (June 2000), pp. 45–50.

41. T. Hamilton, "RIM on a Roll," *Toronto Star*, 22 February 2004, p. C01.

42. Hewitt Associates, "Mergers and Acquisitions May Be Driven by Business Strategy–But Often Stumble over People and Culture Issues," *PR Newswire news release*, (Lincolnshire, Illinois), 3 August 1998.

43. I. Mount, "Be Fast Be Frugal Be Right," *Inc* 26, no. 1 (January 2004), pp. 64–70; S. Anthony and C. Christensen, "Mind over Merger," *Optimize*, February 2005, pp. 22–27.

44. E.H. Schein, "The Role of the Founder in Creating Organizational Culture," *Organizational Dynamics* 12, no. 1 (Summer 1983), pp. 13–28; R. House, M. Javidan, and P. Dorfman, "Project Globe: An Introduction," *Applied Psychology: An International Review* 50 (2001), pp. 489–505; R. House et al., "Understanding Cultures and Implicit Leadership Theories across the Globe: An Introduction to Project Globe," *Journal of World Business* 37 (2002), pp. 3–10.

45. T.J. Peters, "Symbols, Patterns, and Settings: An Optimistic Case for Getting

Things Done," *Organizational Dynamics* 7, no. 2 (Autumn 1978), pp. 2–23; E.H. Schein, *Organizational Culture and Leadership* (San Francisco: Jossey-Bass, 1985), Chapter 10.

46. J. Kerr and J. W. Slocum Jr., "Managing Corporate Culture through Reward Systems," *Academy of Management Executive* 1 (May 1987), pp. 99–107; K.R. Thompson and F. Luthans, "Organizational Culture: A Behavioral Perspective," in *Organizational Climate and Culture*, ed. B. Schneider (San Francisco: Jossey-Bass, 1990), pp. 319–44. John Deere's reward system is described in G.B. Sprinkle and M.G. Williamson, "The Evolution from Taylorism to Employee Gainsharing: A Case Study Examining John Deere's Continuous Improvement Pay Plan," *Issues in Accounting Education* 19, no. 4 (November 2004), pp. 487–503.

47. "Big Blue Is Finally Living up to Its Name," *Charleston Daily Mail*, 9 February 1995, p. 5H.

48. J. Hewett, "Office Politics," *Australian Financial Review*, 27 September 2003, p. 29.

49. M. De Pree, *Leadership Is an Art* (East Lansing, MI: Michigan State University Press, 1987).

50. B. McLean, "Inside the Money Machine," *Fortune*, 6 September 2004, p. 84.

51. C. Daniels, "Does This Man Need a Shrink?" *Fortune*, 5 February 2001, pp. 205–8.

52. Chatman and Cha, "Leading by Leveraging Culture"; A.E.M. Van Vianen, "Person–Organization Fit: The Match between Newcomers' and Recruiters' Preferences for Organizational Cultures," *Personnel Psychology* 53 (Spring 2000), pp. 113–49; C.A. O'Reilly III, J. Chatman, and D.F. Caldwell, "People and Organizational Culture: A Profile Comparison Approach to Assessing Person–Organization Fit," *Academy of Management Journal* 34 (1991), pp. 487–516.

53. J. Van Maanen, "Breaking In: Socialization to Work," in *Handbook of Work, Organization, and Society*, ed. R. Dubin (Chicago: Rand McNally, 1976).

54. C. Fishman, "The Anarchist's Cookbook," *Fast Company*, July 2004, p. 70; "World's Finest Food Retailers: Whole Foods, Not Holy Food," *The Grocer*, 12 November 2005, p. 32.

55. V. Galt, "Kid-Glove Approach Woos New Grads," *Globe & Mail*, 9 March 2005, p. C1.

56. C.L. Adkins, "Previous Work Experience and Organizational Socialization: A Longitudinal Examination," *Academy of Management Journal* 38 (1995), pp. 839–62; J.D. Kammeyer-Mueller and C.R. Wanberg, "Unwrapping the Organizational Entry Process: Disentangling Multiple Antecedents and Their Pathways to Adjustment," *Journal of Applied Psychology* 88, no. 5 (2003), pp. 779–94.

57. J.M. Beyer and D.R. Hannah, "Building on the Past: Enacting Established Personal Identities in a New Work Setting," *Organization Science* 13 (November/December 2002), pp. 636–52; H.D.C. Thomas and N. Anderson, "Newcomer Adjustment: The Relationship between Organizational Socialization Tactics, Information Acquisition and Attitudes," *Journal of Occupational and Organizational Psychology* 75 (December 2002), pp. 423–37.

58. L.W. Porter, E.E. Lawler III, and J.R. Hackman, *Behavior in Organizations* (New York: McGraw-Hill, 1975), pp. 163–67; Van Maanen, "Breaking In: Socialization to Work"; D.C. Feldman, "The Multiple Socialization of Organization Members," *Academy of Management Review* 6 (1981), pp. 309–18.

59. B.E. Ashforth and A.M. Saks, "Socialization Tactics: Longitudinal Effects on Newcomer Adjustment," *Academy of Management Journal* 39 (1996), pp. 149–78; Kammeyer-Mueller and Wanberg, "Unwrapping the Organizational Entry Process."

60. Porter, Lawler, and Hackman, *Behavior in Organizations*, Chapter 5.

61. Louis, "Surprise and Sensemaking: What Newcomers Experience in Entering Unfamiliar Organizational Settings."

62. R. Craver, "Dell Thinning out List of Job Candidates," *Winston-Salem Journal*, 23 April 2005.

63. J.A. Breaugh, *Recruitment: Science and Practice* (Boston: PWS-Kent, 1992); J.P. Wanous, *Organizational Entry* (Reading, MA: Addison-Wesley, 1992).

64. J.M. Phillips, "Effects of Realistic Job Previews on Multiple Organizational Outcomes: A Meta-Analysis," *Academy of Management Journal* 41 (December 1998), pp. 673–90.

65. Y. Ganzach et al., "Social Exchange and Organizational Commitment: Decision-Making Training for Job Choice as an Alternative to the Realistic Job Preview," *Personnel Psychology* 55 (Autumn 2002), pp. 613–37.

66. C. Ostroff and S.W.J. Koslowski, "Organizational Socialization as a Learning Process: The Role of Information Acquisition," *Personnel Psychology* 45 (1992), pp. 849–74; E.W. Morrison, "Newcomer Information Seeking: Exploring Types, Modes, Sources, and Outcomes," *Academy of Management Journal* 36 (1993). pp. 557–89; U. Anakwe and J.H. Greenhaus, "Effective Socialization of Employees: Socialization Content Perspective," *Journal of Managerial Issues* 11, no. 3 (Fall 1999), pp. 315–29.

67. S.L. McShane, *Effect of Socialization Agents on the Organizational Adjustment of New Employees* (Big Sky, MT: Annual Conference of the Western Academy of Management, March 1988).

68. D. Francis, "Work Is a Warm Puppy," *National Post*, 27 May 2000, p. W20; C. Goforth, "Still Recruiting Staff," *Akron Beacon Journal*, 15 July 2001.

CHAPTER 17

1. D. Howell, "Nardelli Nears Five-Year Mark with Riveting Record," *DSN Retailing Today*, 9 May 2005, pp. 1, 38; R. Charan, "Home Depot's Blueprint for Culture Change," *Harvard Business Review*, April 2006, pp. 61–70; R. DeGross, "Five Years of Change: Home Depot's Results Mixed under Nardelli," *Atlanta Journal-Constitution*, 1 January 2006, p. F1; B. Grow, D. Brady, and M. Arndt, "Renovating Home Depot," *BusinessWeek*, 6 March 2006, pp. 50–57.

2. K. Lewin, *Field Theory in Social Science* (New York: Harper & Row, 1951)

3. "The Wrong People Doing the Right Job: Reforming the FBI," *The Economist*, 17 April 2004, p. 371; National Commission on Terrorist Attacks upon the United States, *The 9/11 Commission Report* (Washington, DC: U.S. Government Printing Office, July 2004); D. Eggen, "FBI Fails to Transform Itself, Panel Says," *Washington Post*, 7 June 2005, p. A04; C. Ragavan and C.S. Hook, "Fixing the FBI," *U.S. News & World Report*, 28 March 2005, pp. 18–24, 26, 29–30; The Commission on the Intelligence Capabilities of the United States Regarding Weapons of Mass Destruction, *Report to the President of the United States* (Washington, DC: 31 March 2005).

4. M. Riley, "High-Revving Nasser Undone by a Blind Spot," *Sydney Morning Herald*, 3 November 2001; J. McCracken, "Nasser Out; Ford In," *Detroit Free Press*, 30 October 2001; M. Truby, "Can Ford Chief

Ride Out Storm?" *Detroit News*, 24 June 2001; M. Truby, "Ford Revolution Spawns Turmoil," *Detroit News*, 29 April 2001.
5. C.O. Longenecker, D.J. Dwyer, and T.C. Stansfield, "Barriers and Gateways to Workforce Productivity," *Industrial Management*, March-April 1998, pp. 21–28; J. Seifman, "Middle Managers-the Meat in the Corporate Sandwich," *China Staff*, June 2002, p. 7; *Bosses Want Change but Workers Want More of the Same!* (Sydney: Talent2, 29 June 2005).
6. E.B. Dent and S.G. Goldberg, "Challenging 'Resistance to Change,'" *Journal of Applied Behavioral Science* 35 (March 1999), pp. 25–41; D.B. Fedor, S. Caldwell, and D.M. Herold, "The Effects of Organizational Changes on Employee Commitment: A Multilevel Investigation," *Personnel Psychology* 59, no. 1 (2006), pp. 1–29.
7. D.A. Nadler, "The Effective Management of Organizational Change," in *Handbook of Organizational Behavior*, ed. J.W. Lorsch (Englewood Cliffs, NJ: Prentice Hall, 1987), pp. 358–69; R. Maurer, *Beyond the Wall of Resistance: Unconventional Strategies to Build Support for Change* (Austin, TX: Bard Books, 1996); P. Strebel, "Why Do Employees Resist Change?" *Harvard Business Review*, May-June 1996, pp. 86–92; D.A. Nadler, *Champions of Change* (San Francisco: Jossey-Bass, 1998).
8. "Making Change Work for You-Not against You," *Agency Sales Magazine* 28 (June 1998), pp. 24–27.
9. D. Miller, "What Happens after Success: The Perils of Excellence," *Journal of Management Studies* 31 (1994), pp. 325–58.
10. T.G. Cummings, "The Role and Limits of Change Leadership," in *The Leader's Change Handbook*, ed. J.A. Conger, G.M. Spreitzer, and E.E. Lawler III (San Francisco: Jossey-Bass, 1999), pp. 301–20; J.P. Kotter and D.S. Cohen, *The Heart of Change* (Boston: Harvard Business School Press, 2002), pp. 15–36.
11. J. Smith, "Building Cars, Building Teams," *Plant Engineering*, December 2005, pp. 41–50.
12. L.D. Goodstein and H.R. Butz, "Customer Value: The Linchpin of Organizational Change," *Organizational Dynamics* 27 (June 1998), pp. 21–35.
13. F. Smith et al., "25 True Leaders," *Australian Financial Review*, 12 August 2005, p. 62.
14. I.J. Bozon and P.N. Child, "Refining Shell's Position in Europe," *McKinsey Quarterly*, no. 2 (2003), pp. 42–51.
15. D. Darlin, "Growing Tomorrow," *Business 2.0*, May 2005, p. 126.
16. L. Grossman and S. Song, "Stevie's Little Wonder," *Time*, 19 September 2005, p. 63; S. Levy, "Honey, I Shrunk the iPod. A Lot," *Newsweek*, 19 September 2005, p. 58.
17. J.P. Kotter and L.A. Schlesinger, "Choosing Strategies for Change," *Harvard Business Review*, March-April 1979, pp. 106–14.
18. B. Nanus and S.M. Dobbs, *Leaders Who Make a Difference* (San Francisco: Jossey-Bass, 1999); Kotter and Cohen, *The Heart of Change*, pp. 83–98.
19. M.J. Marquardt, *Optimizing the Power of Action Learning: Solving Problems and Building Leaders in Real Time* (Palo Alto, CA: Davies-Black, 2004).
20. K.T. Dirks, L.L. Cummings, and J.L. Pierce, "Psychological Ownership in Organizations: Conditions under Which Individuals Promote and Resist Change," *Research in Organizational Change and Development* 9 (1996), pp. 1–23.
21. B.B. Bunker and B.T. Alban, *Large Group Interventions: Engaging the Whole System for Rapid Change* (San Francisco: Jossey-Bass, 1996); M. Weisbord and S. Janoff, *Future Search: An Action Guide to Finding Common Ground in Organizations and Communities* (San Francisco: Berrett-Koehler, 2000). For a description of the first future search conference, see M.R. Weisbord, "Inventing the Search Conference: Bristol Siddeley Aircraft Engines, 1960," in *Discovering Common Ground*, ed. M.R. Weisbord (San Francisco: Berret-Koehler, 1992), pp. 19–33.
22. W. Kaschub, "Peco Energy Redesigns HR," *HR Focus* 74 (March 1997), p. 3; R. Larson, "Forester Defends 'Feel-Good' Meeting," *Washington Times*, 28 November 1997, p. A9; R.E. Purser and S. Cabana, *The Self-Managing Organization* (New York: Free Press, 1998); T. Shapley, "Trying to Fix What Everyone Else Has Broken," *Seattle Post-Intelligencer*, 16 November 2005, p. B8.
23. For criticism of a recent search conference for lacking innovative or realistic ideas, see A. Oels, "Investigating the Emotional Roller-Coaster Ride: A Case Study-Based Assessment of the Future Search Conference Design," *Systems Research and Behavioral Science* 19 (July-August 2002), pp. 347–55; M.F.D. Polanyi, "Communicative Action in Practice: Future Search and the Pursuit of an Open, Critical and Non-Coercive Large-Group Process," *Systems Research and Behavioral Science* 19 (July 2002), pp. 357–66.
24. S.M. Weber, "the Dangers of Success: Diffusion and Transition of Large Group Interventions in German-Speaking Countries," *Journal of Applied Behavioral Science*, 41 (March 2005), 111–121.
25. M. McHugh, "The Stress Factor: Another Item for the Change Management Agenda?" *Journal of Organizational Change Management* 10 (1997), pp. 345–62; D. Buchanan, T. Claydon, and M. Doyle, "Organisation Development and Change: The Legacy of the Nineties," *Human Resource Management Journal* 9 (1999), pp. 20–37.
26. T. Joyner, "Merger Toil Replaced Fun in Sun," *Atlanta Journal and Constitution*, 5 August 2001, p. A1.
27. D. Nicolini and M.B. Meznar, "The Social Construction of Organizational Learning: Conceptual and Practical Issues in the Field," *Human Relations* 48 (1995), pp. 727–46.
28. D. Helfand, "School Is Down but Looking Up," *Los Angeles Times*, 14 October 2004, p. B1; "Mrs. Bush Remarks on Helping America's Youth in Sun Valley, California," The White House news release (Sun Valley, CA: 27 April 2005), http://www.whitehouse.gov/news/releases/2005/04/20050427-5.html.
29. R.H. Miles, "Leading Corporate Transformation: Are You up to the Task?" in *The Leader's Change Handbook*, ed. J.A. Conger, G.M. Spreitzer, and E.E. Lawler III (San Francisco: Jossey-Bass, 1999), pp. 221–67; E.E. Lawler III, "Pay Can Be a Change Agent," *Compensation & Benefits Management* 16 (Summer 2000), pp. 23–26; Kotter and Cohen, *The Heart of Change*, pp. 161–77.
30. R.E. Quinn, *Building the Bridge as You Walk on It: A Guide for Leading Change* (San Francisco: Jossey-Bass, 2004), Chapter 11.
31. J.P. Kotter, "Leading Change: Why Transformation Efforts Fail," *Harvard Business Review*, March-April 1995, pp. 59–67; J.P. Kotter, "Leading Change: The Eight Steps to Transformation," in *The Leader's Change Handbook*, ed. J.A. Conger, G.M. Spreitzer, and E.E. Lawler III (San Francisco: Jossey-Bass, 1999), pp.221–67.
32. R. Caldwell, "Models of Change Agency: A Fourfold Classification," *British Journal of Management* 14 (June 2003), pp. 131–42.
33. M. Beer, R.A. Eisenstat, and B. Spector, *The Critical Path to Corporate Renewal* (Boston, MA: Harvard Business School Press, 1990).

34. R.E. Walton, "Successful Strategies for Diffusing Work Innovations," *Journal of Contemporary Business*, Spring 1977, pp. 1–22; R.E. Walton, *Innovating to Compete: Lessons for Diffusing and Managing Change in the Workplace* (San Francisco: Jossey-Bass, 1987); Beer, Eisenstat, and Spector, *The Critical Path to Corporate Renewal*, Chapter 5.
35. E.M. Rogers, *Diffusion of Innovations*, 4th ed. (New York: Free Pree, 1995).
36. P. Reason and H. Bradbury, *Handbook of Action Research* (London: Sage, 2001); D. Coghlan and T. Brannick, "Kurt Lewin: The 'Practical Theorist' for the 21st Century," *Irish Journal of Management* 24, no. 2 (2003), pp. 31-37; C. Huxham and S. Vangen, "Researching Organizational Practice through Action Research: Case Studies and Design Choices," *Organizational Research Methods* 6 (July 2003), pp. 383–403.
37. V.J. Marsick and M.A. Gephart, "Action Research: Building the Capacity for Learning and Change," *Human Resource Planning* 26 (2003), pp. 14–18.
38. L. Dickens and K. Watkins, "Action Research: Rethinking Lewin," *Management Learning* 30 (June 1999), pp. 127–40; J. Heron and P. Reason, "The Practice of Cooperative Inquiry: Research 'with' Rather Than 'on' People," in *Handbook of Action Research*, ed. P. Reason and H. Bradbury (Thousand Oaks, CA: Sage, 2001), pp. 179–88.
39. D.A. Nadler, "Organizational Frame Bending: Types of Change in the Complex Organization," in *Corporate Transformation: Revitalizing Organizations for a Competitive World*, ed. R.H. Kilmann, T.J. Covin, and Associates (San Francisco: Jossey-Bass, 1988), pp. 66–83; K.E. Weick and R.E. Quinn, "Organizational Change and Development," *Annual Review of Psychology*, 1999, pp. 361–86.
40. T.M. Egan and C.M. Lancaster, "Comparing Appreciative Inquiry to Action Research: OD Practitioner Perspectives," *Organization Development Journal* 23, no. 2 (Summer 2005), pp. 29–49.
41. F.F. Luthans, "Positive Organizational Behavior: Developing and Managing Psychological Strengths," *The Academy of Management Executive* 16, no. 1 (2002), pp. 57–72; N. Turner, J. Barling, and A. Zacharatos, "Positive Psychology at Work," in *Handbook of Positive Psychology*, ed. C.R. Snyder and S. Lopez (Oxford, UK: Oxford University Press, 2002), pp. 715–30; K. Cameron, J.E. Dutton, and R.E. Quinn, eds., *Positive Organizational Scholarship: Foundation of a New Discipline* (San Francisco: Berrett Koehler Publishers, 2003); J.I. Krueger and D.C. Funder, "Toward a Balanced Social Psychology: Causes, Consequences, and Cures for the Problem-Seeking Approach to Social Behavior and Cognition," *Behavioral and Brain Sciences* 27, no. 3 (June 2004), pp. 313–27; S.L. Gable and J. Haidt, "What (and Why) Is Positive Psychology?" *Review of General Psychology* 9, no. 2 (2005), pp. 103–10; M.E.P. Seligman et al., "Positive Psychology Progress: Empirical Validation of Interventions," *American Psychologist* 60, no. 5 (2005), pp. 410–21.
42. D. Whitney and D.L. Cooperrider, "The Appreciative Inquiry Summit: Overview and Applications," *Employment Relations Today* 25 (Summer 1998), pp. 17–28; J.M. Watkins and B.J. Mohr, *Appreciative Inquiry: Change at the Speed of Imagination* (San Francisco: Jossey-Bass, 2001).
43. F.J. Barrett and D.L. Cooperrider, "Generative Metaphor Intervention: A New Approach for Working with Systems Divided by Conflict and Caught in Defensive Perception," *Journal of Applied Behavioral Science* 26 (1990), pp. 219–39; Whitney and Cooperrider, "The Appreciative Inquiry Summit: Overview and Applications"; Watkins and Mohr, *Appreciative Inquiry: Change at the Speed of Imagination*, pp. 15–21.
44. Canadian Tire, *Team Values Development Process*, Powerpoint File (Toronto: Canadian Tire, 24 September 2001); Canadian Tire, *Leadership Guide* (Toronto: Canadian Tire, 2002).
45. M. Schiller, "Case Study: Avon Mexico," in *Appreciative Inquiry: Change at the Speed of Imagination*, ed. J.M. Watkins and B.J. Mohr (San Francisco: Jossey-Bass, 2001), pp. 123–26; D. Whitney and A. Trosten-Bloom, *The Power of Appreciative Inquiry: A Practical Guide to Positive Change* (San Francisco: Berrett-Koehler Publishers, 2003); P. Babcock, "Seeing a Brighter Future," *HRMagazine* 50, no. 9 (September 2005), p. 48; D.S. Bright, D.L. Cooperrider, and W.B. Galloway, "Appreciative Inquiry in the Office of Research and Development: Improving the Collaborative Capacity of Organization," *Public Performance & Management Review* 29, no. 3 (2006), p. 285.
46. T.F. Yaeger, P.F. Sorensen, and U. Bengtsson, "Assessment of the State of Appreciative Inquiry: Past, Present, and Future," *Research in Organizational Change and Development* 15 (2004), pp. 297–319; G.R. Bushe and A.F. Kassam, "When Is Appreciative Inquiry Transformational? A Meta-Case Analysis," *Journal of Applied Behavioral Science* 41, no. 2 (June 2005), pp. 161–81.
47. G.R. Bushe, "Five Theories of Change Embedded in Appreciative Inquiry," in *18th Annual World Congress of Organization Development* (Dublin, Ireland: July 14–18, 1998).
48. G.R. Bushe and A.B. Shani, *Parallel Learning Structures* (Reading, MA: Addison-Wesley, 1991); E.M. Van Aken, D.J. Monetta, and S.D. Sink. "Affinity Groups: The Missing Link in Employee Involvement," *Organization Dynamics* 22 (Spring 1994), pp. 38–54.
49. D.J. Knight, "Strategy in Practice: Making It Happen," *Strategy & Leadership* 26 (July-August 1998), pp. 29–33; R.T. Pascale, "Grassroots Leadership-Royal Dutch/Shell," *Fast Company* 14 (April-May 1998), pp. 110–20; R.T. Pascale, "Leading from a Different Place," in *The Leader's Change Handbook*, ed. J A. Conger, G.M. Spreitzer, and E.E. Lawler III (San Francisco: Jossey-Bass, 1999), pp. 301–20; R. Pascale, M. Millemann, and L. Gioja, *Surfing on the Edge of Chaos* (London: Texere, 2000).
50. C.M. Lau, "A Culture-Based Perspective of Organization Development Implementation," *Research in Organizational Change and Development* 9 (1996), pp. 49–79.
51. T.C. Head and P.F. Sorenson, "Cultural Values and Organizational Development: A Seven-Country Study," *Leadership and Organization Development Journal* 14 (1993), pp. 3–7; R.J. Marshak, "Lewin Meets Confucius: A Review of the OD Model of Change," *Journal of Applied Behavioral Science* 29 (1993), pp. 395–415; C.M. Lau and H.Y. Ngo, "Organization Development and Firm Performance: A Comparison of Multinational and Local Firms," *Journal of International Business Studies* 32, no. 1 (2001), pp. 95–114.
52. For an excellent discussion of conflict management and Asia values, see several articles in K. Leung and D. Tjosvold, eds., *Conflict Management in the Asian Pacific: Assumptions and Approaches in Diverse Cultures* (Singapore: John Wiley & Sons, 1998).
53. M. McKendall, "The Tyranny of Change: Organizational Development Revisited," *Journal of Business Ethics* 12 (February 1993), pp. 93–104; C.M.D. Deaner, "A Model of Organization Development Ethics," *Public Administration Quarterly* 17 (1994), pp. 435–46.
54. G.A. Walter, "Organization Development and Individual Rights," *Journal*

of Applied Behavioral Science 20 (1984), pp. 423–39.

55. B. Moses, "Give People Belief in the Future," *Workforce*, June 2000, pp. 134–41.

56. B. Moses, "Career Activists Take Command," *Globe & Mail*, 20 March 2000, p. B6.

57. Drake Beam Morin, *1999 DBM Career Transition Study* (Drake Beam Morin, November 2000); F.T. McCarthy, "Career Evolution," *The Economist*, 29 January 2000.

58. B. Moses, *The Good News about Careers: How You'll Be Working in the Next Decade* (San Francisco: Jossey-Bass, 1999); S.E. Sullivan, "The Changing Nature of Careers: A Review and Research Agenda," *Journal of Management* 25 (May 1999), pp. 457–84.

59. S.C. Van Collie, "Moving up through Mentoring," *Workforce*, March 1998, pp. 36–40; N. Beech and A. Brockbank, "Power/Knowledge and Psychosocial Dynamics in Mentoring," *Management Learning* 30 (March 1999), pp. 7–24.

photo credits

CHAPTER 1

page 2: AP/Wide World Photos

page 7: © Hans Rudolf Oeser/The New York Times

page 14: Department of Economic Development, Government of Dubai

page 16: © John Gillooly, Professional Event Images, Inc.

page 23: © The Augusta Chronicle

CHAPTER 2

page 32: Reprinted with permission of Owens Corning. All Rights Reserved.

page 36: AP/Wide World Photos

page 40: © Norbert von der Groeben/ The Image Works

page 44: © PARRAMATTA/Newspix

page 47: © Cancan Chu/Getty Images

page 50: Courtesy of Molson Coors

page 55: © C. Blanchard, Richmond Times-Dispatch

CHAPTER 3

page 66: © Bob Finlayson/Newspix

page 70: AP/Wide World Photos

page 74: © Mel Melcon, 2005, Los AngelesTimes; Reprinted with permission.

page 77: © Melanie Stetson Freeman/ The Christian Science Monitor/Getty Images

page 81: Courtesy of Cocoplans

page 88: Courtesy of Exxon Mobil

page 91: © Michael Stuparyk, Toronto Star

CHAPTER 4

page 102: Courtesy of Wegmans

page 104: Copyright © Ted Goff, 2001 www.tedgoff.com. Used with permission.

page 109: Courtesy of CXtec

page 112: Courtesy of Four Seasons Hotels and Resorts

page 117: Photo Courtesy of Outback Steakhouse

page 122: © Yuriko Nakao/Reuters/ Landov

CHAPTER 5

page 132: Courtesy of Sarova Panafric Hotel

page 137: © Ed Wheeler Photography, Inc.

page 142: AP/Wide World Photos

page 147: Photo courtesy of Akamai

page 151: Courtesy of Verizon

page 154: © The New Yorker Collection 2001 Barbara Smaller from cartoonbank. com. All rights reserved.

page 155: © Peter Yates/The New York Times

CHAPTER 6

page 166: © Will Crockett, Shoot Smarter

page 170: © Jason Dewey/Getty Images

page 173: Wolfgang von Brauchitsch/ Bloomberg News/Landov

page 182: Photo by Kevin Adler, Kron 4

page 184: Courtesy of Pretoria Portland Cement Company

page 187: Courtesy of eSilicon Corporation

CHAPTER 7

page 196 (top): Courtesy of Buena Vista Games

page 196 (bottom): Munshi Ahmed/Bloomberg News/Landov

page 202: © Wolfgang Schmidt/Peter Arnold, Inc.

page 203: © Larry Dale Gordon/Getty Images

page 205: Photo by Mikael Kjellstrom/ Calgary Herald, May 18, 2005

page 207: © Observer-Dispatch

page 212: Image courtesy of Deloitte

page 214: Photo courtesy of Liggett Stashower

CHAPTER 8

page 224: Ron Sangha Photography

page 228: Copyright © Randy Glasbergen. Reprinted with special permission from www.glasbergen.com.

page 229: © Apple Computer, Inc. Use with permission. All rights reserved. Apple® and the Apple logo are registered trademarks of Apple Computer, Inc.

page 235: © Scottish Parliamentary Corporate Body – 2006

page 238: © Yvan Cohen/OnAsia Images Pte. Ltd.

page 242: AP/Wide World Photos

CHAPTER 9

page 256: Courtesy of Paul Tramontano, Smith Barney

page 260: Car Design News Ltd.

page 263: MEDRAD INC.

page 266: Photo courtesy of Shell International Ltd.

page 270: U.S. Navy photo by Photographer's Mate 1st Class Casey Akins

page 275: Courtesy of Lighthouse Publishing Limited, Robert Hirtle, photographer

CHAPTER 10

page 284: Photo Courtesy of PricewaterhouseCoopers LLP. Visit us on the Web at www.pwc.com/us.

page 289: AP/Wide World Photos

page 290: Photo Courtesy of Standard Motor Company

page 293: © Royalty Free/Corbis

page 300: Johnson Space Center/ NASA

page 303: Courtesy of Lockheed Martin Corporation

CHAPTER 11

page 312: Photo Courtesy of Sun Microsystems, Inc.

page 317: Photo courtesy of Admiral Insurance

page 323: © Ted Goff

page 325: © Mark M. Lawrence/ Corbis

page 329: Photo courtesy of www.aintitcool.com

page 331: Courtesy of Shangri-La Hotels & Resorts

CHAPTER 12

page 340: Craig Abraham/Fairfax Photos

page 344: ©Topham/The Image Works

page 346: Photo courtesy of Lowe Worldwide

page 349: © Scott Sendrow, Bridge and Tunnel Club

page 354: AP/Wide World Photos

page 359: © Martin H. Simon/Corbis

CHAPTER 13

page 368: © Reuters/Corbis

page 372: © Reza Estakhrian/Getty Images

page 376: AP/Wide World Photos

page 379: AP/Wide World Photos

page 382: Edward Carreon/Newhouse News Service

page 389: U.S. Air Force photo by Tech. Sgt. Bob Oldham

CHAPTER 14

page 400: AP/Wide World Photos

page 402: Photo courtesy of Semco

page 404: AP/Wide World Photos

page 410: © Empics

page 415: AP/Wide World Photos

page 420: © ADREES LATIF/Reuters/Corbis

CHAPTER 15

page 428: Photo courtesy of Nitro Group

page 432: Edward Smith/Artizans.com. Reprinted with permission.

page 437: The Minnesota Business Journal/Used with permission by Harbinger Partners Inc.

page 442: © The Edmonton Journal

page 445: © Bill Cramer

page 449: Photo courtesy of 7-Eleven, Inc.

CHAPTER 16

page 458: AP/Wide World Photos

page 462: © Munson, John/Star Ledger/Corbis

page 464: Courtesy of Mayo Clinic

page 469: Yuriko Nakao/Reuters

page 471: Noah Berger/Bloomberg News/Landov

page 475: AP/Wide World Photos

CHAPTER 17

page 486: © Najlah Feanny/Corbis

page 489: AP/Wide World Photos

page 493: William West/AFP/Getty Images

page 496: © Eriko Sugita/Reuters/Corbis

page 498: © Brian Vander Brug, 2004, Los Angeles Times. Reprinted with permission.

page 502: Norm Betts/Bloomberg News/Landov

organization index

name index

A

B

C

H

I

N

T

subject index

D

E

F

G

H

P

S

W

Y

url index